FILM REVIEW ANNUAL

1995

Films of 1994

FILM REVIEW ANNUAL

1995

Films of 1994

Film Review Publications
JEROME S. OZER, PUBLISHER

Editor: Jerome S. Ozer
Associate Editor: Richard Zlotowitz
Assistant Editor: Genant B. Sheridan

ISBN 0-89198-148-9
ISSN 0737-9080

Manufactured in the United States of America

Jerome S. Ozer, Publisher
340 Tenafly Road
Englewood, NJ 07631

TABLE OF CONTENTS

PREFACE

PREFACE

The FILM REVIEW ANNUAL provides, in a convenient format, a single reference volume covering important reviews—*in their entirety*—of full-length films released in major markets in the United States during the course of the year.

The format of the FILM REVIEW ANNUAL has been kept as clear and simple as possible. Films are reviewed in alphabetical order by title. Following each film title, we provide production information, cast and crew listings, the running time, and the MPAA rating. The reviews for each film are arranged alphabetically by publication. Each review is identified by the name of the publication, the date of the review, the page number, and the name of the reviewer. After the last review of a film, there is an *Also reviewed* section which lists other publications in which the film was reviewed. Because of restrictions in obtaining permission, we were unable to include reviews from certain publications. However, we felt that users of the FILM REVIEW ANNUAL should have help in gaining access to those reviews. Therefore, we included the *Also reviewed* section.

At the end of the FILM REVIEW ANNUAL, we provided full listings of the major film awards, including the nominees as well as the winners.

There are eight Indexes in the FILM REVIEW ANNUAL: Cast, Producers, Directors, Screenwriters, Cinematographers, Editors, Music, and Production Crew.

We have not attempted to force a single editorial style upon the reviews for the sake of achieving consistency. The reader will readily recognize that some reviews were written under deadline pressure and that others were prepared in a more leisurely and reflective style. Some reviews were written to help the moviegoer determine whether or not to see the film. Other reviews assumed the reader had already seen the film and was interested in getting another point of view. We believe this diversity of purposes and styles is one of the major strengths of the FILM REVIEW ANNUAL.

Because of our respect for the integrity of the writers' styles, we made changes from the original only where absolutely necessary. These changes were confined to typographical errors in the original review and errors in the spelling of names. When the reviewer made a reference to another film, we inserted the name of that film. Otherwise the reviews remain as written. British spelling used in English publications has been kept.

We have tried to make the FILM REVIEW ANNUAL pleasurable to read as well as useful for scholars and students of film, communications, social and cultural history, sociology, and also for film enthusiasts. We, the editors, would appreciate your suggestions about how we might make subsequent editions of the FILM REVIEW ANNUAL even more useful.

FILM REVIEWS

A LA MODE

A Miramax Films release of a Lilli Productions/France2 Cinema coproduction in association with Soficas Investimage 4/Sofinergie 3 and the participation of Centre National de la Cinematographie/Canal Plus. *Producers:* Joël Faulon and Daniel Daujon. *Director:* Rémy Duchemin. *Screenplay (French with English subtitles):* Richard Morgiève and Rémy Duchemin. *Based on the novel "Fausto" by:* Richard Morgiève. *Director of Photography:* Yves Lafaye. *Editor:* Maryline Monthieux. *Music:* Denis Barbier. *Sound:* Michel Kharat and Thierry Delor. *Casting:* Pierre Amzallag. *Art Director:* Gilbert Druart. *Set Dresser:* Dominique Beucamps and Marie Gandois. *Costumes:* Annie Perier. *Costumes (Fausto):* Philippe Guillotel. *Make-up:* Odile Fourquino. *Stunt Coordinator:* Daniel Vérité. *Running time:* 77 minutes. *MPAA Rating:* R.

CAST: Jean Yanne (Mietek Breslauer); Ken Higelin (Fausto Barbarïco); François Hautesserre (Raymond); Florence Darel (Tonie); Maurice Benichou (Lucien); Bruce Meyers (Roger); Marianne Groves (Myriam); Maité Nahyr (Rivka); François Chattot (Director); Frédérique Leyes (Max's Girlfriend); Alfred Cohen (Boss); Renaud Ménager (Le Rouquin); Arnaud Churin (Rouge Gorge); Georges de Cannes (TV Journalist) Sir Ali (Voice).

LOS ANGELES TIMES, 8/12/94, Calendar/p. 10, Kevin Thomas

"A la Mode," which marks a winning feature debut for French writer-director Rémy Duchemin, is a warm, funny and inspired coming-of-age comedy set in an old Jewish quarter of Paris during the '60s. Our hero, bright, skinny 17-year-old Fausto (Ken Higelin), lives in a vast old orphanage, but his prospects are about to brighten considerably.

That's because it's time for Fausto to learn a trade, and he has the good fortune to be apprenticed to Mietek Breslauer (Jean Yanne), a stocky, apparently widowed Jewish tailor who takes great pride in his craft (and in driving a hard deal). Breslauer is a stern taskmaster but even more, he's a loving father figure. Consequently, when Fausto declares that he'd rather design dresses for women, Breslauer is prepared to go along with him. "A la Mode" is especially effective in capturing the exhilaration of Fausto's self-discovery; he really has the talent and skill to make it as a *couturier*, and his imagination coincides perfectly with, the Mod styles of the '60s.

Undeniably, "A la Mode" is sentimental, but it's so affectionate, so overflowing with good cheer that its sunny spirit is endearing. Fausto and his burly best pal Raymond (Francois Hautesserre), who's a regular *Le Petomane* engage in many teen-age shenanigans, and Fausto begins to discover true love in the form of the nearby mechanic's daughter Tonie (Florence Darel), who's as self-confident as she is beautiful, an ideal model for his creations.

Duchemin, a veteran assistant director, and his co-writer Richard Morgieve eschew the usual sizable obstacles along Fausto's path to success and happiness. They're able to get away with this in part because they've dared to open the film on a dire note that has the effect of getting life's unavoidable losses out of the way right at the start; its effect is to leave us with the feeling that Fausto is thereafter *entitled* to as smooth a path as possible.

Duchemin would seem really to care for actors, for they certainly glow under his direction. His young people couldn't be more ingratiating, but for the longtime fan of French films, "A la Mode's" key pleasure is in seeing the veteran Yanne get a change of pace. Having first come to the attention of American audiences in the title role of Claude Chabrol's "This Man Must Die" (1969) and more recently seen as the world-weary, sinister police chief of Saigon in "Indochine," Yanne is cast invariably in serious or malevolent roles. The proud, amusing Mietek allows Yanne to reveal that he's as skilled at being comical as he is in playing heavies.

NEW YORK POST, 8/12/94, p. 46, Thelma Adams

The frothy French fantasy "A la Mode" is sweet to watch and instantly melts from memory.

First-time director Remy Duchemin treads lightly over well-trod coming-of-age territory. Elfin 17-year-old Fausto (Ken Higelin) goes from being an adored only child to an orphan in a fatal tractor accident.

Orphanage life is ugly until Fausto forms a makeshift family with Raymond (Francois Hautesserre), a portly lad with a talent for musical flatulence.

The resourceful Fausto becomes a tailor's apprentice and finds himself "adopted" by Mietek. Jean Yanne, the actor who wooed Catherine Deneuve in "Indochine," plays the childless Jewish tailor with relish.

Gray-bearded, well-fed Mietek teaches Fausto the trade, its traditions, and his theories about the human body and the tyranny of the stomach.

The balance of power shifts when Fausto discovers his love for cloth and becomes a flamboyant, virtuoso couturier. It all begins when the "young sex fiend," as Mietek calls Fausto, designs a suit made from grass.

Mietek scoffs, calling the garment "the ideal suit for garden parties," but a local hipster purchases four grass suits at an exorbitant price.

Mietek and Fausto become partners, surrogate father and son, and the business takes off at a dizzying pace. Exit somber flannels, enter red checks and tie-dye—and cash!

"A la Mode" wouldn't be a coming-of-age story if Fausto didn't lose his virginity. He falls for Tonie (Florence Darel) a forward red-haired Jewess and they fall into bed.

Quicker than you can say gestation, Tonie's pregnant. But since this is whimsy, not tragedy, all's well that ends well. The movie's central fantasy is the gentile boy's easy acceptance into Paris' insular Jewish community circa 1964.

As the big-eyed, pointy-eared Fausto, Higelin has the gangly good looks of the young Matt Dillon. The supporting cast, well-directed by Duchemin, provides a chorus of good feeling.

Fausto's fanciful fashions (designed by Philippe Guillotel) can't make up for the episodic script, but the final wedding scene in which the young tailor riffs on yarmulkes and prayer shawls to the music of a Hasidic band ends the movie on the right joyous note.

To paraphrase Mietek on Fausto's grass suit, for a first try, it's well-made; so is "A la Mode."

NEWSDAY, 8/12/94, Part II/p. B7, Jonathan Mandell

Fausto comes by his career choice by accident ... literally: His parents are killed on the road. Just 17 years old, he is sent to live in a Parisian orphanage, which in due time (after a few standard scenes of orphanage abuse and orphan bonding) dispatches him to a Jewish tailor named Mietek in hopes the man will accept the boy as his apprentice.

Mietek is dubious about Fausto Barbarico's potential because the teenager is of Italian heritage. Fausto bristles at this, but Mietek tells him he knows all about Italian tailors; just look at the Pope: "Is it normal to dress a man like a pregnant woman?"

Thus begins the odd-couple pairing that is among the most rewarding parts of "A la Mode," which is translated as "in fashion" rather than "topped with ice cream," though this French comedy is certainly sweet—at times smotheringly so.

For all his bluster, Mietek (Jean Yanne) takes a chance on Fausto (Ken Higelin), who, it turns out, has a flair not just for tailoring but for fashion. The young man listens intently as Mietek discourses on the secrets of the trade, all decidedly idiosyncratic: The magic word of men's fashion is ... stomach; women are harder to dress because they have four stomachs (including their breasts and their rear end); needles are human beings that a good tailor must woo, tame and, finally, love. Fausto quickly learns Mietek's sartorial catechism, and soon finds his own magic word: publicity.

As the surrogate father-son relationship deepens, Fausto also shares dreams and fantasies with his best orphan-buddy, the fat, farting Raymond, and falls in love with the local mechanic's daughter, the beautiful Tonie, pursuing her as he sketches his designs in the dusty windshields of her father's shop.

And so we are set up for a sweeping comic tale of Fausto's life and loves and rags-to-rag-trade success. We are even informed that it is 1964, a sure promise that we will see both Fausto and the House of Barbarico mature over the decades.

But "A la Mode" stays small and in the present (which is to say the past) tense. The low budget starts to take a toll, with the film feeling increasingly claustrophobic and the plot advancing by rote. Perhaps the lack of moment and sweep would be less of a letdown if the first half had not been so promising, with good actors portraying likable characters. Maybe it would have worked better if Fausto's fashion designs—his outfits, created by designer Philippe Guillotel, include suits made of real grass and vests of real money—were as charming and inventive and outrageous in execution as they are clearly meant to be in conception.

First-time director Remy Duchemin has fashioned something familiar and comfortable, if a bit tight, from some appealing material and a suitable, albeit well-worn, pattern. True, the seams show, and it's nowhere near big enough. But there's enough in "A la Mode" to leave you, at least much of the time, in stitches.

SIGHT AND SOUND, 7/94, p. 40, Martin Bright

Paris, 1965. 17-year-old Fausto Barbarico, the son of Italian immigrants, has recently lost both his parents. He goes to an orphanage where he is bullied, but is befriended by the obese Raymond, whose speciality is playing fart tunes. Fausto is taken on by Mietek, a tailor in the Jewish quarter, who teaches him his trade. He explains that everything in tailoring centres on a good presentation of the stomach, and advises Fausto to steal ends of cloth when he is not looking. Fausto deicdes he wants to be a famous woman's couturier.

Obsessed with women, Fausto and Raymond make hundreds of elaborate paper flowers and send them with passionate love letters to the women of the quarter. The women are flattered and Fausto becomes something of a local celebrity. While he is strolling through the quarter, a beautiful girl on a balcony catches his eye.

On the way to buy fabric, Mietek's car breaks down. He and Fausto take it to a mechanic, whose daughter, Tonie, turns out to be the beautiful girl. Fausto strikes a deal whereby Mietek gets his car repaired in return for making the mechanic a suit and his daughter a dress. While being measured, Tonie lets Fausto touch her breasts.

One night, Fausto stays late in the workshop and makes himself a suit out of grass. He wears it around town to advertise for Mietek's shop. A local spiv, Max the Cat, offers Mietek 5000 francs for grass suits, for a pop group he manages. Meanwhile, Raymond is offered an apprenticeship by Mietek's friend, a kosher butcher. He too develops an advertising gimmick—a costume consisting of a cow's head on a table. But while wearing it, he gets over-excited and is knocked down by a passing car. In hospital, Raymond lies in a coma. Fausto makes a pact with God to give up smoking if Raymond opens his eyes. Raymond wakes and is released from hospital a few days later.

Mietek and the butcher decide to adopt the two orphans and give them their own room. Fausto gets his name on the door of the tailor's shop, as Mietek's partner. In a search for '*le style Barbarico*', Fausto makes Tonie into a junk sculpture in her father's garage. They make love. From now on, Raymond is forced to sleep outside the boys' room. The Barbarico style of large patchwork designs soon becomes the talk of the town. Max the Cat advises Fausto to learn to love money and advises him to eat a banknote a day. This gives him the idea of making clothes out of money. When he and Tonie wear the money-clothes at the opening night of a concert, they are a great success. Tonie is pregnant and Fausto asks her to marry him.

A peculiar quirk of the French film industry is that there are enormous subsidies available for people to make first films. *Fausto*, the debut feature by advert director Rémy Duchemin, is a typical product of this system: a mildly appealing film school idea stretched to feature length.

There are some rather charming setpieces, but even these would have shown up to better advantage in a *court-métrage*. For example, when Fausto visits Raymond in hospital to tell him that he has lost his virginity, the nurses and doctors break into a rendition of Beethoven's Fifth. In a shorter film, this would have been quite amusing, but by the time this scene is reached, the sexual adventures of the pimply twosome have already become tiresome beyond belief. Most of the rest of the film is padded with stock Parisian clichés straight from advertising: a rooftop scene with a dark blue night sky backdrop; a hustling, bustling all-life-is-there bridge scene; and a couple of scenes in the Lutèce Arena in the Latin Quarter. This last setting is so improbably cinegenic that you can't help thinking it has been used in desperation to rescue an otherwise unwatchable film.

According to the publicity, the film is supposed to be "a fairy tale for the twentieth century." At the beginning of the film, Fausto even appears have magical powers. When he first arrives at the orphanage, he is bullied by his room-mates and with sheer force of will persuades them that he has poisoned them. This is quite promising, but then Duchemin, who is also the scriptwriter, simply seems to have forgotten that he has given Fausto any such powers. The only time we see

Fausto use them again is when he wishes Raymond would open his eyes after his accident. Even here it is unclear whether there is any causal link, or whether Fausto is just doing what any kid would do if his best friend were lying in a coma. It is probably wise to credit the director with enough intelligence to have intended this scene as the resurrection scene that links Fausto to his namesake, but it is by no means certain.

But the worst of the film's many faults is its cloying nostalgia. No-one expects this kind of light comedy to be an accurate portrayal of period, but there are real liberties taken here. During this period, Italians were a badly-paid underclass in France, much as North Africans are today. The idea that life in the 60s was a riot for Italian orphans and their Jewish employers just does not wash.

The French film industry produces so many films that every now and again it throws up something of genuine interest. The trouble is that for every *Les Nuits fauves*, there are a hundred *Faustos*. And *Fausto* is like one of its hero's technicolour-dreamcoat designs—motley.

VILLAGE VOICE, 8/23/94, p. 58, Randy Gener

Clothes can make a comedy, and Rémy Duchemin's first effort, *A la Mode*, is dressed to be silly. This airy piffle about an orphaned teenager who becomes a Jewish tailor's apprentice tries to strike a tone of off-the-cuff whimsicality, but it's a tepid coming-of-age fantasy about surviving loss and picking oneself up by the bootstraps. Gangly, mischievous Fausto Barbarico (Ken Higelin) is a sponge and quick study. The blustery tailor—a loquacious father figure who later adopts him—imparts the fundamentals of sewing, its philosophy, and body algebra (a man's tummy = brain + heart). From his overweight best bud Raymond he makes the connection that cutting fabric in 1960s Christian DiorLand tears a far from seamless path to fashion notoriety and girls' lacy undies.

Miramax's rechristening of *A la Mode* from its fest-circuit title *Fausto* points up the movie's lack of focus; it feels like a male buddy flick, switches to family-values sitcom, then slums briefly in sex farce. Mostly, it ambles for serendipity and paces awkwardly, picking up stray pieces of plot and patching together something that, like Higelin's cutely angular face, flirts with charming. Once the nuptial-cum-fashion show comes along—as a designer, Fausto graduates from woven-grass jackets to coin-slotted, knitted-paper-bill extravaganzas—the movie has really just taken a confident stride toward waggish flamboyance. But then it's over.

Had Duchemin gone for John Waters camp-kitsch, *A la Mode* could've been *Multiple Stitches*. If he had a feeling for nostalgia, it might've been *400 Buttons*, or, if he topped it with a scoop of hang-dog enchantment, a *Fausto Scissorhands*. Raymond's tubalike farts, though, have more gusto than anything else in *A la Mode*. It's a bright, makeshift fairy tale that, like a piece of mismatched jewelry, is at odds with its budding artiste hero, never quite finding its own style.

Also reviewed in:
CHICAGO TRIBUNE, 8/19/94, Friday, p. H. Johanna Steinmetz
NEW YORK TIMES, 8/12/94, p. C3, Janet Maslin
VARIETY, 5/24/93, p. 48, Lisa Nesselson
WASHINGTON POST, 8/27/94, p. B3, Rita Kempley

ABOVE THE RIM

A New Line Pictures release. *Executive Producer:* James D. Brubaker. *Producer:* Jeff Pollack and Benny Medina. *Director:* Jeff Pollack. *Screenplay:* Barry Michael Cooper and Jeff Pollack. *Story:* Jeff Pollack and Benny Medina. *Director of Photography:* Tom Priestley, Jr. *Editor:* Michael Ripps and James Mitchell. *Music:* Marcus Miller. *Music Editor:* Earl Ghaffari. *Sound:* Michael Barosky. *Sound Editor:* Craig Berkey. *Casting:* Marie E. Nelson and Ellyn Long Marshall. *Production Designer:* Ina Mayhew. *Set Decorator:* Paul Weathered. *Set Dresser:* Anthony Baldasare, Douglas Fecht, Stephen Finkin, Mitch Towse and Suzanne E. Cestare. *Costumes:* Karen Perry. *Make-up:* Ellie Winslow. *Stunt Coordinator:* Jeff Ward. *Running time:* 96 minutes. *MPAA Rating:* R.

CAST: Duane Martin (Kyle-Lee Watson); Leon (Shep); Tupac Shakur (Birdie); David Bailey (Rollins); Tonya Pinkins (Mailika Williams); Marlon Wayans (Bugaloo); Bernie Mac (Flip Johnson); Byron Minns (Monroe); Sherwin David Harris (Motaw); Shawn Michael Howard (Bobby); Henry Simmons II (Starnes); Iris Little Thomas (Waitress); Michael Rispoli (Richie); Eric Nies (Montrose); Mill Raftery (Himself); James Williams (Speedy); Richard Ray Kirkland (Phil Redd); Tyrone Batista (Tyrone); Cinnamon Paige (Young Woman); Debra Rubins (Hostess); Frank Martin (Will); Jesse Williams and Robert Harvey (Officials); Cuffee and Anthony Hargraves (Referees); Darien Berry (Younger Player).

LOS ANGELES TIMES, 3/23/94, Calendar/p. 6, Peter Rainer

Kyle (Duane Martin) is a high school basketball phenom in Harlem who wants to be a college whiz and an NBA all-star. Irked that the big college recruiters have yet to sign him, he showboats on the court in the closing games of his final season. It's bad teamwork but great to watch: Kyle is totally fulfilled as he soars through the air.

"Above the Rim" would have been better had it stuck with Kyle's love for the game and depended less on a mess of tired melodrama about his involvement with a brutal drug dealer, Birdie (Tupac Shakur), and his estranged brother Shep (Leon), who had been a great neighborhood basketball star before he skipped town. It's not that this material is inappropriate to Kyle's story; it's just that it never comes to life in the way the basketball scenes do. That's the problem with sports movies: If the ball-playing footage is any good, the rest of thc action tends to look like filler.

Director Jeff Pollack, who co-created NBC's "Fresh Prince of Bel Air," shoots the basketball scenes with vigor and understanding. (Some sports movies look as if they were directed by couch potatoes.) But he isn't aided by Barry Michael Cooper's script, which has Kyle rebounding among confrontations with his mother (Tonya Pinkins), his coach (David Bailey), Shep, Birdie and just about everybody else. He's supposed to be an Angry Young Man pulled between crime and ethics, but he doesn't seem to be all that angry. His fights have a trumped-up-for-high-drama feeling.

The film is much better when it drops the arch theatrics and just moves along to the great rap soundtrack. The hang-loose scenes between Kyle and his dotty friend Bugaloo (Marlon Wayans) are the best not only because they seem the most realistic but also because they don't make a big fuss about how socially conscious they are.

They make you want to shoot a few hoops.

NEW YORK POST, 3/23/94, p. 35, Michael Medved

"Above the Rim" is an ordinary film that features a collection of extraordinary performances—a slick team of engaged and gifted actors struggling to make something compelling out of a silly, cliché-ridden script.

The plot centers on a confused high school basketball star in Harlem, impeccably played by former NYU and New York Knicks point guard Duane Martin.

He's desperately trying to attract the attention of college scouts, but in the process he hogs the ball during games and undermines his team.

Meanwhile, he falls under the influence of a smooth, seductive neighborhood drug lord (Tupac Shakur), who wants to recruit Martin for his team in the fiercely contested "Shoot Out" basketball tournament that takes place each year at a local playground.

This association greatly displeases the boy's iron-willed single mother (the formidable Tonya Pinkins) who tries to keep him on the straight and narrow.

She's aided by the new man in her life (Leon), a security guard at the local high school who's haunted by a shadowy past. It turns out that this brooding mystery man is not only the long-lost brother (!) of the ruthless drug dealer, but he's also a former basketball great who gave up his promising career after an accident with his best friend.

Amazingly enough, the cast manages to bring life to each of these clumsy, thinly-written characters.

Last year, Leon showed his impressive range by playing both a lovable Jamaican bobsledder in "Cool Runnings" and a sadistic killer in "Cliffhanger," but his smoldering performance here marks him more clearly than ever before as one of the industry's more versatile rising stars. Controversial rapper Tupac Shakur is similarly effective as the "evil twin" gang leader, who offers a radical contrast to the nice-guy letter carrier he played as the only birth spot in the dreadful "Poetic Justice."

Shakur's kinetic screen presence and his effortless assurance at handling even the stupidest scenes show what a shame it would be if his well-publicized problems with the law and his self-destructive off-screen behavior prematurely terminated his movie career.

Debuting director Jeff Pollack (co-creator of NBC's hit series "Fresh Prince of Bel Air") earns credit for bringing out the best in all his performers, but also deserves blame for collaborating on the clunky script (with Barry Michael Copper, who previously wrote "Sugar Hill" and "New Jack City").

Pollack's basketball scenes provide plenty of punch and sizzle, but his Harlem locations never convey an authentic, atmospheric sense of place. Though he filmed much of the action at Rucker's Playground, a celebrated basketball mecca at 155th Street and Eighth Avenue, the images on screen look so generic that he might as well have shot in Toronto.

There's also a resort to the dumbest of all dumb sports movie conventions: a climactic, big-game grudge match that's supposed to settle all sorts of issues that no mere game could possibly resolve.

Other basketball movies of recent months ("Blue Chips," "The Air Up There," and "White Men Can't Jump") focused on white coaches or players finding their niche in what has increasingly become an African-American game.

If nothing else, "Above the Rim" scores a few points for finally placing black characters at center stage, but these world-class performers deserve to play together on some future team with a more developed and sophisticated game plan.

NEWSDAY, 3/30/94, Part II/p. B9, Ira Robbins

In the cineplex sports standings, basketball long lagged behind baseball, football and boxing as a popular realm for feature films. But ever since hip-hop soundtracks and rappers-turned-actors made African-American urban youth culture a viable Hollywood commodity, it was inevitable that movies would finally take serious note of the inner-city participation sport of choice: playground hoops.

"Above the Rim," the first film directed by TV mogul Jeff Pollack—one of the brains behind the deracinated rap style of "Fresh Prince of Bel Air"—has real locations and all those words you can't say on television, but otherwise comes straight out of the committee-run sitcom fantasy school.

As predictable as a Kareem Abdul-Jabbar hook shot, "Above the Rim" sets its hero, Monarch H.S. basketball star Kyle-Lee Watson (Duane Martin) racing back and forth between the evil clutches of drug lord Birdie (Tupac Shakur) and the collective good graces of his widowed mom (Tonya Pinkins), devoted coach (David Bailey, in the film's token white role) and Shep (Leon), a somber security guard with a traumatic ball-related past.

The story plods toward the obligatory big showdown for neighborhood bragging rights (how many drug dealers *actually* sponsor amateur sports teams?) through a familiar thicket of conflicts: college recruitment, Kyle-Lee's ambivalent loyalties to his best friend and his coach, the romance between Shep and Kyle-Lee's mom, a row with a quixotic bum and so on. Even the occasional court scenes, though spirited, can't energize the tired formula action.

The soap opera plot twists are duly melodramatic, but there's only one truly explosive moment, when Kyle-Lee and his friend Bug witness a burst of brutality (which elicits one of the film's clever rejoinders: "You need a role model or a hug or somethin' "). Otherwise, the only real thrill here is watching Shakur and Leon battle the flat script, ineffectual direction and, gently, each other for domination in the film's charisma stakes.

Sporting an impressive facial scar, bandanas and a diamond nose stud, Shakur seems muzzled in his depiction of a temperamental killer with a winning smile. For his part, Leon relies on a soulful, anguished stare that has all the silent reserve of a young Clint Eastwood. Martin is fine, with impressive emotional range, but—like many such essentially passive roles in films that favor action—his performance is almost incidental to the men who are competing for his allegiance.

To the filmmakers' credit, "Above the Rim" holds violence to a minimum, leaves sex offscreen and portrays its positive characters as genuinely good people who aren't punished for their beneficence. But lacking imagination and style, the film has the dramatic slack and facile morality of an after-school special.

If not as out of touch as the worst blaxploitation flicks of the '70s—a genre it specifically acknowledges—"Above the Rim" never nails the realism it intends. Even the soundtrack, an all-star collection of hard-hitting cool cuts, seems haphazardly and arrhythmically attached to the action, as if making the connection of rap and basketball is all the effort needed. It isn't. They shoot, they miss.

SIGHT AND SOUND, 12/94, p. 40, Nick Hasted

Kyle is his Harlem high school's star basketball player. Desperately waiting for a sports scholarship to college, he is the despair of coach Rollins, because he won't play for the team. After a game, Kyle meets his old friend Bugaloo, just out of jail, who introduces him to local gangster Birdie. Birdie gives Kyle money, and shows interest in his playing. The next morning, as Kyle and Bugaloo are playing basketball, local tramp Flip challenges Kyle to a game. They get into a fight, and Kyle is pulled off by Shep, the school security guard, whom Flip treats with awe. Unknown to Kyle, Shep was once the school's star player, but ran away when his best friend fell to his death from a roof as they played—an accident caused by Shep's arrogance, and which he dreams of constantly.

The next day, Rollins asks Shep to replace him as coach, but Shep refuses. Kyle tells Rollins that at the upcoming neighbourhood Shoot-Out, he'll play for Birdie's team, not the school's. In a graveyard, Birdie finds Shep, standing by his mother's tombstone; they are brothers. That night, Kyle, Bugaloo and Birdie go out on the street. As they drive, Kyle sees Shep, who is replaying the game which killed his friend, and is surprised at his skill. Birdie happens upon two drug-dealing cronies, and beats them up. Shep meets Kyle's mother, Mailika, for a movie. When Kyle finds out, he is appalled. Later, with Birdie, he is told by Flip that Shep and Birdie are brothers. That night, as Kyle plays for his school, watched by Shep and Mailika, Birdie slices Flip to death. At the game, Kyle's play disintegrates and he is taken off. In the locker room, he tells Shep to stay away from Mailika. Shep visits Mailika to tell her he is leaving town, and she dismisses him for walking out on Kyle. Shep finds Kyle, tells him that Birdie killed Flip, and beats him at a game.

On the day of the Shoot-Out, Kyle gives Birdie back Bugaloo's money, and announces that he'll be playing for Rollins. Birdie says that if Kyle doesn't throw the game, the college recruiters will find out about his help. Rollins tells Kyle that his scholarship has been granted. As Rollins' team struggle, Shep appears, and offers to play. Between them, Shep and Kyle win the game. Birdie orders Kyle to be shot, but Shep leaps in front of Kyle to take the bullet. Later, Bugaloo shoots Birdie dead. Later still, Mailika, Rollins and a recovered Shep watch Kyle play for his college on TV.

If you thought it was no longer possible for a character to appear in the final reel of a sports movie and say "Put *me* in, coach!" and go on to win a game in the final second, you were wrong. Jeff Pollack's directing and co-scripting debut is full of such scenes. It's as if he'd been told that a sports movie must be a set of clichés, and was worried he might miss one. Above the Rim is comprehensively unsurprising, full of aspirations and expectations fulfilled. In small doses, or with the nerve for an avalanche of sentiment on the level of Barry Levinson's *The Natural*, this might still be rousing. But Pollack simply pushes so many worn down buttons, in such a perfunctory manner—just another shift on the American dream—that the emotional connection is nil. Feeble as a sports movie, *Above the Rim* is pulled back from the brink only by its gangsta background, and even here it has problems.

These scenes can safely be credited to co-writer Barry Michael Cooper, as they expand on the flaws of his previous films *New Jack City* and, especially, *Sugar Hill.* Cooper seems to believe that any scenario involving black people in New York will involve gangsta temptation, and that all New York gangstas will have a brother trying to make good. This is not far from the essence of much current black American art, specifically rap music and thrillers, both of which are informed by the intersection of crime with everyday black urban life. Cooper's problem is that he can't raise the stakes of his dramas with enough conviction to make either aspect count. His good brothers are too saintly to be breathing, let alone to justify the moral triumphs he allows them, and which he seems to engineer—as with Shep's healed bullethole—by the miracle of narrative conformity. The perceived need for social comment in black thrillers just confuses him. In a film about a low-level gangster corrupting low-level sport, each element drags down the other, till the winning of a basketball game—and the fact that it can trigger two gangland hits—seem equally dumb. The missing link is suggested when Shep takes Mailika to a revival of *Shaft*. It's that film's air of unselfconscious energy which made *New Jack City*, flawed and clumsy as it often was, so enjoyable, and which even *Sugar Hill* took a few guilty hits from. *New Jack City*, too, delivered its moral pieties with a smirk. *Above the Rim*'s social conscience is dutifully inept. As slice-of-life and gangsta pic and sports film, it fumbles the ball.

Its details are better. Some of the dialogue is unusually free-flowing, some actors hit the script's strange edges (Leon blank, Tonya Pinkins distracted). Marcus Miller's score, too, is especially effective. The soundtrack is also stuffed with rap and swingbeat, but this only uncovers more failings. For all the film's welcome use of rap's noise, it neither matches nor successfully exploits the music's narrative economy and openness. Unlike Abel Ferrara's use of Schooly D, for instance, this is music plastered on more in hope than understanding. Warren G's 'Regulate', played over the credits, has more soul, bloodshed and sadness in three minutes than this movie in a hundred.

Somewhere in the muddle is a simpler, rougher film. Pollack says he was inspired by Harlem's street basketball, played at a high level by people unlikely to make it as pros. If he'd decided to follow that through, the unforced conviction of Steven Zaillian's *Innocent Moves*—which worked with street *chess*!—might have been his.

VILLAGE VOICE, 3/29/94, p. 60, Selwyn Seyfu Hinds

It is still the season for tales of little black boys. Thus far we've had little black boys and their drugs, little black boys and their drugs and guns. Now it's little black boys and their drugs, guns, and balls. There's no question that films that attempt to speak to and for young black men are extremely important, but by the time the distilled versions arrive on the screen more often than not they are pathetically predictable and poorly executed. Personally, if you're going to tell my story badly, I'd rather you shut the fuck up.

Above the Rim tries. But somewhere in the transitions between morality play-crime drama-basketball flick it gets lost. Kyle-Lee Watson (Duane Martin) is a high school basketball star trying to play for Georgetown. On his way there he must contend with the seductive influence of Birdie, the neighborhood hood (Tupac Shakur), who offers Kyle money and women in an effort to make him run with Birdie's squad for an upcoming playground tournament. Kyle's drift into Birdie's web threatens to eliminate his chances of getting into the NCAA. Only by reaching within himself and looking to Shep (Leon) can he maintain.

Tom Shepard is a former high school star struggling to reconcile his role in the death of a close friend. During the course of the film he becomes involved with Kyle's strong-willed mother (Tonya Pinkins), a relationship that causes frustration and rage in her son and pushes him even further off the path to play. Resolution for both men can and does happen when each faces his responsibilities to himself and those close to him.

Above the Rim's attempt to develop and present two central stories (Kyle's and Shep's) produces a meandering effect throughout the entire film—from the plot to the actors. Duane Martin drifts between irritating and nauseating. Shakur as requisite bad seed makes some attempt to recapture the neurotic, off-the-wall promise exhibited in *Juice*. But it's a half-hearted thing, as if Birdie himself knows that Bishop would punk him out with the quickness. Leon manages to provide some saving grace with a quietly intense performance, that is whenever the script doesn't place him in ridiculously hackneyed situations. It takes a certain generosity to watch Shep turn up at *the* most crucial moment of *the* most crucial game and say, "Coach, put me in," without falling out.

For all its effort, *Above the Rim* never quite makes its shots. The film has a difficult time finding focus. Its characters and relationships are never fully explored and narrative richness is only hinted at. This is a movie that stutters along without finding a groove ... Well, all right, the soundtrack is phat, the basketball scenes are great, and all the extras look "real"; nevertheless, half-assed storytelling gets no points in my book.

Also reviewed in:
NEW YORK TIMES, 3/23/94, p. C17, Janet Maslin
VARIETY, 3/21-27/94, p. 57, Brian Lowry
WASHINGTON POST, 3/23/94, p. B4, Desson Howe

ACE VENTURA: PET DETECTIVE

A Warner Bros. release of a Morgan Creek production. *Executive Producer:* Gary Barber. *Producer:* James G. Robinson. *Director:* Tom Shadyac. *Screenplay:* Jack Bernstein, Tom Shadyac and Jim Carrey. *Story:* Jack Bernstein. *Director of Photography:* Julio Macat. *Editor:* Don Zimmerman. *Music:* Ira Newborn. *Music Editor:* Jeff Carson. *Sound:* Russell C. Fager and (music) Tim Boyle and Raymond Blair. *Sound Editor:* Michael Hilkene. *Casting:* Mary Jo Slater. *Production Designer:* William Elliott. *Art Director:* Alan E. Muraoka. *Set Designer:* Rich Fojo. *Set Decorator:* Scott Jacobson. *Set Dresser:* Frederick W. Schwendel, Michael Calabrese and Stuart Wein. *Special Effects:* Michael N. Arbogast. *Costumes:* Bobbie Read. *Make-up:* Sheryl Ptak. *Stunt Coordinator:* Artie Malesci. *Running time:* 85 minutes. *MPAA Rating:* PG-13.

CAST: Jim Carrey (Ace Ventura); Courteney Cox (Melissa); Sean Young (Einhorn); Tone Loc (Emilio); Dan Marino (Himself); Noble Willingham (Riddle); Troy Evans (Podacter); Raynor Scheine (Woodstock); Udo Kier (Camp); Frank Adonis (Vinnie); Tiny Ron (Roc); David Margulies (Doctor); John Capodice (Aguado); Judy Clayton (Martha); Bill Zuckert (Mr. Finkle); Alice Drummond (Mrs. Finkle); Rebecca Ferratti (Sexy Woman); Mark Margolis (Shickadance); Antoni Corone (Reporter #1); Margo Peace (Reporter #2); Randall "Tex" Cobb (Gruff Man); Henry Landivar (Burnout); Florence Mistrot (Neighbor); Robert Ferrell (Carlson); Will Knickerbocker (Manager); Gary Munch (Director); Terry Miller (Assistant Director); John Archie (Reporter #3); Cristina Karman (Reporter #4); Tom Wahl (Reporter #5); Herbert Goldstein (Crazy Guy); Manuel L. Garcia (Dolphin Trainer); Chaz Mena (Another Cop); Robert Short and Douglas S. Turner (Puppeteers).

LOS ANGELES TIMES, 2/4/94, Calendar/p. 6, Chris Willman

Let's talk elasticity: When Jim Carrey goes on a crying jag, his enormous mouth turns into such a gaping canyon that your mind might wander to wondering just how many whole grapefruits could be stuffed into it. When he deigns to close those choppers, he doesn't so much smile as he clinches every muscle within a six-inch radius of his overbite into a maniacal grin that makes him look like a handsomely dimpled gerbil.

Here, you think, is a guy who may have spent too much time working out at the facial-tic gym. The term *rubber-mugged* hardly begins to suffice, when even Carrey's tiniest expressions of physicality are so broadly exaggerated he makes Jim Varney look like Charles Bronson by comparison.

A movie with such a relentlessly manic guy at its constant center sounds as if it would probably be irritating as hell. And to a lot of people, it will be. But "Ace Ventura: Pet Detective," uneven as its farcical pleasures may be, proves perfectly capable of inducing the most unexpected giggle fits. Carrey's refusal to be anything less than utterly inhuman on screen is heroic on its own brave, nutty, pretty funny terms. He's so over-energized from the start you keep thinking he'll wear out his welcome pronto; an hour and a half later, his lunacy is still hard to take your eyes off.

Carrey, best known as a stand-up comic and TV sketch artist (of "In Living Color" fame), plays a celebrated "pet dick," or finder of missing mammals. A lot of his work involves recovering cats and dogs in disputed divorce cases. ("Make any good collars lately?" mock the police. "Or were they leashes?") But he stumbles across bigger fish to fry when he's called in to look for the missing aquatic mascot of Miami's pro football franchise, which has been dolphin-napped just before a Super Bowl.

Along the way he gets romantically involved with a team rep (Courteney Cox, not having much to do but look comely in the Priscilla Presley role) and crosses swords with an adversarial police lieutenant (Sean Young, enjoying yet another self-parodying part in which she gets to be called "psycho-woman").

Puerility does sometimes reach its limits here. And the movie is necessarily limited by Carrey's never getting to evolve beyond cartoon-character status; he's like Roger Rabbit or Howard the Duck, so far adrift is his two-dimensional lunacy from the "straight" world. But as live-action cartoons go, he's a fairly inspired one.

Ace winds up wildly patronizing virtually everyone he comes across, in that popular post-modern way. But lest the picture bog down completely in the ironic comedy of condescension (a la, say, Chevy Chase's singularly smug "Fletch" sleuth), the hero is also afforded a childlike bond with the mutts, fish and fowl of the world.

Director Tom Shadyac (who co-wrote with Jack Bernstein and Carrey) just barely holds back from overplaying the Dr. Doolittle angle. But it's nice that for almost every wicked put-down Ace Ventura dishes out, he also gets to enjoy an innocent moment of purely animalistic *joie de vivre*, like the way he sticks his head out the car window every time he drives.

Who among us—possibly excepting pro-vivisection radicals or the severely Jerry Lewis phobic—is prepared to resist a hero so liberated he lives his entire life doggy style?

NEW YORK POST, 2/4/94, p. 37, Michael Medved

When a movie's most convincing and entertaining performances comes from all-pro quarterback Dan Marino playing himself, then you know you're not exactly dealing with a candidate for the film festival circuit.

Unfortunately, "Ace Ventura: Pet Detective" fails not only on all artistic terms, but even flops in its attempts to deliver dumb, diverting, outrageous comedy.

Star Jim Carrey (best known for his often amusing sketches on "In Living Color") told the press that, "If you want to see something that's, completely out of its mind and over the top, then this is the movie to see." He's wrong, since the biggest problem with this film isn't just that it's brain-dead, but that it's shockingly bland.

Carrey plays Ace Ventura, an impoverished Florida sleuth who specializes in tracking missing pets. The Miami Dolphins call for his help when their popular mascot, a bottlenose dolphin named Snowflake, is stolen from his tank on the eve of their appearance (dream on!) in the Super Bowl.

The situation for the Florida team soon goes from bad to worse when the mysterious bad guys kidnap an even more valuable mammal: quarterback Dan Marino.

Could the two disappearances be connected? And how are they related to a notorious missed field goal from a Super Bowl 10 years ago?

While answering these questions, Ace takes time for a torrid affair with the Dolphins' marketing director, played by the gorgeous Courteney Cox.

The problem with Ace is that the script shows that he really is a brilliant detective (and a formidable love machine), so that even after all his shameless mugging we can't laugh at him as just a lovable jerk.

Jim Carrey's natural good looks and undeniable charm actually work against all his rubber-faced contortions and childish slapstick, in a boring bomberino (shaped by a first-time director and former comedian named Tom Shadyac) that will appeal only to the highly specialized audience that finds Jim Varney's "Ernest" movies too challenging and sophisticated.

NEWSDAY, 2/4/94, Part II/p. 65, Terry Kelleher

If the main purpose of a movie is to showcase its star, but the movie leaves you wishing it had starred someone else, what do you call that movie?

Bad?

Not necessarily. Warner Bros. calls it "Ace Ventura, Pet Detective," though the title should have been "Jim Carrey Unchained." The publicity material says the comedian, popular from the Fox series "In Living Color," agreed to do "Ace Ventura" on the condition that the lead character be refashioned in his TV image. "The people who watch me on 'In Living Color' expect something really crazed," Carrey explains.

So Carrey and first-time director Tom Shadyac took co-writer Jack Bernstein's amusing premise—scuffling private eye specializes in locating missing or stolen pets—and converted it into a jungle gym for a young star with a ridiculous amount of excess energy. Carrey mugs, leaps, bounds, gyrates, semi-moonwalks. If it wouldn't weigh him down, he'd probably wear a sign that screamed, "Look at Me! I'm Really, *Really* Crazed!!!"

Shadyac describes Carrey as "Robin Williams meets Jerry Lewis." Like Williams, he has a weakness for gratuitous impressions (heaven only knows why Ace suddenly starts mimicking the "Star Trek" crew). Like Lewis in his heyday, he resembles a hyperactive child in an adult's body. However, Carrey's tendency to bare his mouthful of gleaming teeth in extreme closeup invites comparison with another, less celebrated farceur—Jim ("Ernest Scared Stupid") Varney.

Carrey's talent is undeniable, but the movie suffers from his apparent compulsion to demonstrate all of it in every scene. "Ace Ventura" would be funnier as well as easier to take, if the gumshoe went about his goofy business with a Leslie Nielsen-like deadpan. The filmmakers have come up with a few clever sight gags; we'd be more inclined to sit back and enjoy them if the star weren't working so hard to clown us into submission.

Football fans will chuckle at the plot, which concerns the pre-Super Bowl kidnaping of the Miami Dolphins' mascot by an embittered ex-placekicker. The very fact of Coach Don Shula's wordless cameo figures to bring a smile, but quarterback Dan Marino is actually called upon to deliver lines and simulate distress. Let's just say he's no Joe Namath.

The detective's love interest (Courteney Cox) is inexplicably charmed by his moronic behavior, and it seems even a beautiful police lieutenant (Sean Young) can't help groping him. But the cop turns out to have a tasteless joke up her sleeve, or somewhere on her person.

SIGHT AND SOUND, 5/94, p. 38, Richard Skinner

Ace Ventura, unconventional but savvy, is an expert at reclaiming lost or stolen pets. When the mascot for the Miami Dolphins football team, a dolphin called Snowflake, is mysteriously abducted a week before the Superbowl, he is called in on the case by two board members—the coach, Roger, and Melissa, a secretary. Searching the empty tank where Snowflake was kept, Ace finds a small gemstone.

At first, Ace suspects a local billionaire businessman after discovering that he has recently purchased inordinate amounts of tackle and is an ardent collector of fish. As chance would have it, Melissa has been invited to the billionaire's drinks party that evening. Ace accompanies her in order to snoop around. He stumbles upon a huge tank in an outhouse, only to discover a very large shark but no Snowflake. When leaving the party, Ace notices a ring the billionaire is wearing and this provides him with his first real lead: the gemstone comes from an AFC Superbowl Championship ring.

Ace and Melissa go through photos of the Miami Superbowl team of 1984 but are interrupted by the news of Roger's apparent suicide. At the scene, Ace confounds the suicide theory and pronounces it murder, much to the chagrin of long-suffering Lieutenant Einhorn. Later, by a variety of means, Ace checks out the rings worn by members of the Superbowl squad but finds nothing.

Seemingly back at square one, Melissa shows Ace another photo taken slightly later than the rest. There is one person in this photo not present in the others—Ray Finkle, field goal kicker and the player who lost the Superbowl for the Dolphins by missing a field goal in the dying seconds of the game. Ace locates Ray's parents and discovers evidence of Finkle's dementia towards the Dolphins in general and their quarterback Dan Marino in particular. At the sanatorium where Ray was admitted, Ace finds out that Finkle has had a sex-change and has become none other than Lieutenant Einhorn.

Meanwhile, aware of Ace's progress, Einhorn has kidnapped Dan Marino and taken him to where Snowflake is being kept; but she is hotly pursued by Ace. Einhorn plans to set Ace up as the abductor but after being exposed by Ace, Einhorn is stopped and the Superbowl takes place with Snowflake waving a dorsal at the crowd.

Hot on the heels (tails?) of last year's US hit *Free Willy* comes *Ace Ventura*, which has already made more money in the States than they know what to do with. And it's easy to see why—this has sure-thing hit written all over it with its winning combo of goofiness and genre send-ups. The opening scene is the funniest—our hero holds a cardboard box marked "FRAGILE" and proceeds to bash it into every shape geometry knows. (It's a ploy to nick a fussy little dog from a nasty big man in order to return it to a very appreciative owner.)

By turns screwball comedy, *Naked Gun*-style spoof and all-American feel-good movie, the film motors along frantically from implausible fortuity to impossible plot twist. But this is a film whose plot drives the set pieces, rather than vice versa. Character-wise, it's predictably thin; the female characters hardly get a look in here, dominated as the film is by Jim Carrey's performance. Courteney Cox is the gal-to-be-got while Sean Young once again disrobes, this time to be revealed as a transsexual baddie (to the strains of "The Crying Game").

As a vehicle for TV comic Jim Carrey, the movie shows him to be very much in control of a potential runaway disaster. His Ace—impressively expansive and very silly—is a sort of cross between a rockabilly (complete with blow-dried quiff) and a Jerry Lewis nerd. He manages to include just about every genre tic imaginable—hanging off the side of a skyscraper while actually standing on the ground, and entering rooms, police-style, using his hand as a gun. The heart of the humour lies in the thin line Carrey treads between belly-laughs and toe-curls, between realism and biff-bang-pow expressionism. Its generic cousins are films such as *Action Hero*, and in common with it *Ace Ventura* is rather like summer in Britain: bright, breezy and instantly forgettable.

Also reviewed in:
CHICAGO TRIBUNE, 2/4/94, Friday/p. F, Mark Caro
NEW YORK TIMES, 2/4/94, p. C8, Stephen Holden
VARIETY, 2/7-13/94, p. 40, Steve Gaydos
WASHINGTON POST, 2/4/94, p. C1, Rita Kempley
WASHINGTON POST, 2/4/94, Weekend/p. 43, Desson Howe

ADVENTURES OF PRISCILLA, QUEEN OF THE DESERT, THE

A Gramercy Pictures release of a Polygram Filmed Entertainment presentation in association with the Australian Finance Corporation of a Latent Image/Specific Films production. *Executive Producer:* Rebel Pen-fold-Russell. *Producer:* Al Clark and Michael Hamlyn. *Director:* Stephan Elliott. *Screenplay:* Stephan Elliott. *Director of Photography:* Brian J. Breheny. *Editor:* Sue Blainey. *Music:* Guy Gross. *Choreographer:* Mark White. *Sound:* Guntis Sics and (music) Phil Judd. *Production Designer:* Owen Paterson. *Art Director:* Colin Gibson. *Costumes:* Lizzy Gardiner and Tim Chappel. *Make-up:* Cassie Hanlon. *Stunt Coordinator:* Robert Simper. *Running time:* 102 minutes. *MPAA Rating:* R.

CAST: Terence Stamp (Bernadette); Hugo Weaving (Tick/Mitzi); Guy Pearce (Adam/Felicia); Bill Hunter (Bob); Sarah Chadwick (Marion); Mark Holmes (Benji); Julia Cortez (Cynthia); Ken Radley (Frank); Alan Dargin (Aboriginal Man); Rebel Russell (Logowoman); June Marie Bennett (Shirley); John Casey (Bartender); Murray Davies (Miner); Frank Cornelius (Piano Player); Bob Boyce (Petrol Station Attendant); Leighton Picken (Young Adam); Maria Kmet (Ma); Joseph Kmet (Pa); Daniel Kellie (Young Ralph); Hannah Corbett (Ralph's Sister); Trevor Barrie (Ralph's Father).

FILMS IN REVIEW, 11-12/94, p. 61, Harry Pearson, Jr.

The Adventures of Priscilla, Queen of the Desert is, in its purest form, an updating of an expansion upon a uniquely American institution, the "road" movie. Road movies are a genre the Europeans have never quite been comfortable with even in the best examples (vide, Bertrand Blier). Perhaps you simply have to live in a big country, with a considerable emptiness to explore, to get the "feel" of the road movie right. Wide open spaces are diminishing these days in the U.S. of A. but they are undiminished in Australia, where the Aussies have given the road movie an unique and futuristic twist (vide the *Mad Max* movies). As the Australians go into the wilderness—which is their past—they seem to be seeing our future.

Do not doubt for a second that *Priscilla* is devoid of its own take on the future. Even if it be only the near future. I, for one, cannot imagine a transsexual, a bi-sexual and a gay man—drag queens three and dressed to the gilt—on the loose and actually surviving among redneck macho outbackers in anytime soon to come, but the makers of the film can and do for our benefit. In any archetypal journey, there are the mythic moments. So there are here, and oh so clearly played as such, as our three "heroes" mount the high redrock peaks, in billowing regalia, to sing the sun to sleep.

There are the darker moments as well, as the three encounter and aggravate a virulent and dangerous homophobia (thus providing an all too believable core for this futuristic fantasy), which they manage to overcome with pluck, a fisticuff or two, or the quick bon mot. Is it not singularly appropriate that they do a version of "I Will Survive," by starlight, for an appreciate Aborigine audience in the film's most uproarious (and somehow sad) single sequence?

Thus the movie manages to transcend genre and become an experience that is both liberated (no holds barred here, not verbally anyway) and the liberating (it says that being different doesn't make you any the less human, but perhaps more). The essentially straight audiences in the two theaters where I caught it had a ball, once they caught on to the picture's rhythms.

The movie starts slowly and, at first, the three leads aren't sympathetic. There is an alien quality about them. And it alienates us. The actors don't play for our sympathy, and yet, by picture's end, those qualities that were at first irritating have become endearing. We accept their grittiness because we accept our own. By film's end, we have come to see the three individually, even when they are playing upon and against the stereotyped regard in which they are held by the average bloke.

Much of the credit for achieving this sense of humanity belongs to the lead actor, Terence Stamp (in private life, a roaring heterosexual, as, so go the tales, are the other two actors, Hugo Weaving playing the bisexual and Guy Pearce who gives an impersonation of a kind of near-screaming queen that is as good, if not more impressive, than that you'd find in life). Stamp's performance is a marvel of control, dignity and subtlety. He also gets some of the most caustic and scalding (not to mention truly vulgar) lines and delivers them with the timing of a "real" queen. You won't much care for Stamp's character at first, and then, as events unfold, you get the measure of his (her) mettle. Stamp brings so many illuminating touches to his role that it's not possible to single out the best, but, for starters, watch what he does just after he defends Pearce from a vicious bigot. It's a small gesture, but it has floored every woman (I've talked with). Multiply these small details many times over and fold them into a living personality and you'll see why this is an award worthy performance.

The plot of *Priscilla* is simple enough. Stamp, the transsexual, has just lost a "husband" and Weaving convinces this retired drag queen to come out of mourning and do a performance in Alice Springs, at the center of the continent. Weaving and Pearce have engineered a two-week stand at a hotel there, run by Weaving's ex-wife. (The others don't know he was married.) Pearce's mom, who helps him select the outfits he wears, gives the three an old bus (the eponymous Priscilla). Soon enough, they are on the road with Priscilla. It's not too long before they take a short cut through the desert and the bus breaks down. And they are on their own, exotic birds, one and all. I see no purpose in spoiling the fun by telling you their adventures.

There is, however, one measure of the film's fearlessness. A little boy who turns up toward the end, and he is obviously deeply impressed with the drag queens and their act. I doubt there would be any equivalent (and approving) child in the Spielberg-produced American version that will descend upon us next year; indeed, it will be interesting to compare the two in terms of how much the U.S. version softens its hard edges for mid-American consumption. In this movie, the little boy and his admiration are presented with a kind of tacit approval that takes for granted that no one is being corrupted, that love is love, no matter who's doing it.

And, besides, *Priscilla* is a fall-down funny, joyous comedy that affirms the quirky and irregular in human affairs and shows us that these can be seen, in conjunction with a loving heart, as a measure of our worth.

LOS ANGELES TIMES, 8/10/94, Calendar/p. 1, Kenneth Turan

"Drag is the Drug," the posters at Cannes promoting "The Adventures of Priscilla, Queen of the Desert" announced, not without reason. The comic pizazz and bawdy dazzle of this film's vision of gaudy drag performers trekking across the Australian outback certainly has a boisterous, addictive way about it.

But like any self-respecting drug, "Priscilla" comes with its own built-in hangover. Sharing screen space with the film's raunchy humor and outrageous musical numbers is a strain of conventional sentimentality that would not be inappropriate on the Disney Channel. It doesn't ruin the fun, but it certainly takes the edge off it.

One of the reasons writer-director Stephan Elliott has given for making "Priscilla" was a desire to bring back the vintage Hollywood musical, and, like the old MGM classics, this film is definitely at its best when its trio of performers are out there with a lip-synced song in their hearts.

Whether it's Mitzi (Hugo Weaving) opening the movie with a torchy rendition of "I've Been to Paradise but I've Never Been to Me" or Felicia (Guy Pearce) belting out a Verdi aria in a silver lamé gown on top of a moving bus, or the two of them plus Bernadette (Terence Stamp) going into synchronized versions of "I Will Survive," "Shake Your Groove Thing" and almost anything by ABBA, all in outfits that beggar description, the musical numbers are sure-fire and irresistible.

While Mitzi and Felicia are more conventional (if that is the right word) drag queens who also answer to the names Tick and Adam, respectively, Bernadette is a hormone-ingesting transsexual who goes ballistic whenever her former given name of Ralph crosses anyone's lips.

Despite having made a career out of being what Elliott calls "a heterosexual icon," Stamp is the movie's major surprise, gracefully convincing as Bernadette, a woman no longer trapped in a man's body. Elegant and dignified with enough hauteur for an entire royal family, the resilient Bernadette is a creature of haunted and exquisite gestures, and Stamp doesn't allow you to feel that even the smallest of them is false.

Though this performance is "Priscilla's" most fully realized, the other two leads are also expertly done, partly because Elliott has written them with a well-adjusted liveliness and specificity that gives the actors a good deal to work with.

Tick is the most solid and stable of the three, an established performer and the catalyst for the trip as well. (Weaving, incidentally, was memorable in a completely different role as the angry blind photographer in Jocelyn Moorehouse's "Proof.")

Unknown to his pals, Tick was married before he became a fixture of Sydney's gay scene, and out of nowhere he gets a phone call from his ex, who manages a resort in middle-of-nowhere Alice Springs and is desperate for entertainers. Can he make the trip and, more important, dare he tell his friends who asked him to perform?

Bernadette, grieving for a recently dead husband, is persuaded to come along for a change of scene. Adam, an amusingly malicious party animal, is always up for something new and even produces the money for the group's bus, christened Priscilla. Besides, he confesses, he's always wanted to travel to the outback and "climb Kings Canyon as a queen," decked out in a Gautier gown, heels and a tiara.

The trio's alcohol-drenched trip through the desert (which caused French critics to call the film "Florence d'Arabie") takes up most of "Priscilla." The best part of that is the ribald interaction among the three performers, all of whom, especially "cesspool mouth" Adam, have rude and dangerous tongues that can flay the flesh off the unwary.

Less unsettling, in fact regrettably predictable, are most of the adventures that these three run into on their pilgrimage. Not surprisingly, their appearance completely flummoxes the uncomprehending and often angry straight people at each of their stops, and the homophobic scrapes that result have a tendency to feel contrived.

And with the exception of auto mechanic Bob (veteran all-purpose Australian actor Bill Hunter), those met on the road who are not hostile, like Tick's wife, are as unconvincingly cheerful and saccharine as Adam is blistering. Their glibness and compassion make an odd contrast with the bitchy talk on the bus, but, to its credit, whenever things get too treacly, "Priscilla" knows enough to break out those frocks and get the show in gear. That is entertainment for sure.

NEW YORK, 8/29/94, p. 112, David Denby

In *The Adventures of Priscilla, Queen of the Desert,* two Australian drag queens—one young and butch (Guy Pearce), one burdened and regretful (Hugo Weaving)—and one old, distinguished, and lonely transsexual (Terence Stamp) tour the Outback in a ravaged bus and perform for cowboys and desert rats. Stephan Elliott, the writer-director doesn't so much make a movie as package it; Priscilla is a slick, shrewdly ingratiating entertainment that jumps from highlight to highlight and lives on sparkle—not just the three men in heels, feathers, and huge headdresses, like Carmen Miranda without bananas, but also Guy Pearce standing on the roof of the old bus with a huge silk pennant trailing gaudily in the wind. *Whee!* Terence Stamp, his hands clasped together, his noble prow of a face composed in a formidable mask, gets off some viciously funny lines—Stamp might be a Roman senator's wife whose toga has slipped a little. In between quips, the movie, of course, makes a profound contribution to philosophy. It suggests that there is no difference between extreme artifice and raw nature. The boys hobnob with Gila monsters and display themselves on canyon cliffs, their glitter and turbans facing the barbaric natural splendor. If you've got it, flaunt it, whether you're a drag queen or a rock.

NEW YORK POST, 8/10/94, p. 35, Thelma Adams

"Take the short cut."

In a road movie, these are famous last words. No sooner does Bernadette (Terence Stamp) say them than she and drag queens Mitzi (Hugo Weaving) and Felicia (Guy Pearce) find themselves lip-synching to Abba for an astonished Gila monster in the Australian outback.

Plump up your falsies and straighten your garters, it's going to be a bumpy ride.

"The Adventures of Priscilla. Queen of the Desert" is the kitschy, kooky, campy tale of three Australian showgirls—two males and a transsexual—who leave the relative safety of Sydney for a gig in the interior.

"Priscilla," like most road movies, is character-driven. Stone-faced Stamp ("Wall Street") plays his aging transsexual as a weathered Faye Dunaway, more inclined toward tasteful pantsuits and French manicures than sequins and glitz in his off-hours.

Pearce is the hyperactive hunk who gets off on planting bees in his fellow travelers' oversized bonnets. Done up in diva gear, Pearce is a gutsy beauty with body-builder biceps.

The wide-eyed, elastic-faced Weaving, known to art-house audiences for his starring role as the blind photographer in "Proof," is the movie's spiritual center.

When it comes to drag, Weaving's Mitzi is an artist. He's a whiz at makeup, costumes and choreography and a crowd-pleasing performer. But, of the three, Mitzi is the most sexually ambivalent. His efforts to come to terms with his identity fuel the plot, such as it is.

And who's Priscilla? She's the pink, painted lady of a bus that takes the girls on their journey of discovery.

The laughs—and there are many—come from the trio's catty banter, the lavishly costumed musical numbers, and the fish-out-of-water comedy of three urban queens beached in the sticks.

There are the predictable dramatic twists: a bar brawl where the queens win over the locals with two-fisted fighting and drinking; a scene of homophobic violence; and a roadside romance that turns serious.

Like its namesake, "Priscilla's" problem is that the gears keep grinding and something is wrong with the fuel line. The movie jerks from humorous bit to bit, and lurches toward sentimental moments, making for an uneven ride.

Much will be made of ice-blue-eyed, he-man Terence Stamp in a frock. As long as he is sitting still. Stamp lends depth and dignity to his character.

Stamp, an excellent dramatic actor, stumbles during the dance numbers, making his role as an aging Les Girls star implausible. He dances like a stereotypical straight white male: elbow's tensed, lips twisted in a grimace of concentration, and forehead wrinkled with the thought of where to place his feet next.

NEWSDAY, 8/10/94, Part II/p. B9, John Anderson

Overdressed but staunchly pro-urban, "The Adventures of Priscilla, Queen of the Desert"—wherein three drag queens make their way across the Australian desert to the sound of ABBA—puts a half-twist on road movies, buddy pictures, gay films and bad musicals, and ends up a bit of a paradox: In trying to be both funny and moving, is it exploiting the very thing that makes its three tart-tongued tarts so funny and moving? It's probably an unanswerable question, which itself says a lot about the problematic "Priscilla." Any moviegoer predisposed to the idea that cross-dressing cabaret performers are intrinsically ridiculous won't have his or her mind changed much. On the other hand, those inclined to sympathize with or admire the brass of our lip-synching, bra-stuffing trio may find "Priscilla" to be just their cup of Gump.

Preconceived notions aside—including those about British actors playing in drag—few will remain unaffected by Terence Stamp, who as Bernadette, a dignified, jaded transsexual veteran of the drag circuit, is the comedic center and moral compass of the movie. As they make their way across the parched wasteland of central Australia and toward a much-needed gig in glorious Alice Springs, Bernie will clash constantly with the honey-bunned, preening and much-younger Felicia/Adam (Guy Pearce) and offer the kind of sardonic observations that can only make their high-strung organizer, Mitzi/Tick (Hugo Weaving of "Proof"), more nervous. She's a bitch, as well as adulterated Tennessee Williams; Stamp refines resolve and regret into the kind of fractured, faded class that Vivien Leigh gave Blanche Dubois, although without Bernie's double shot of self-awareness. There were moments when I was so caught up in Stamp's performance, or, maybe just confused, that I started thinking: Bernadette was a woman impersonating a man.

Priscilla, by the way, is something of a character in Stephan Elliott's often audacious comedy, but she's also as big as a bus. In fact she is a bus, one that the three struggling dancers-lip-synchers use to get from Sydney— where they're known and appreciated and where gay men aren't E.T.—to the resort, owned by Mitzi's ex-wife. Yes, he was married once, and it's a source of torture for him now. As is the frontier: The trio's various encounters with rural intelligence make "Priscilla" a fist in the air for the liberating anonymity of city life.

That the rest of "Priscilla" isn't quite up to Stamp—thereby making Bernadette all the more touching doesn't mean it isn't funny, although it is a bit, well, broad. The three travelers hit a small town, where Bernie drinks a hard-as-nails lesbian under the table and where some vicious AIDS-related graffiti is sprayed on Priscilla. With a new coat of lavender paint, they head for Alice Springs, their trip replete with some spectacular shots by cinematographer Brian J. Breheny: of Mitzi atop the moving bus—adorned with brilliant, streaming fabrics that trail like flames—and of the equally gaudy wildlife around them. In another town, they hook up with Bob (Bill Hunter), a mechanic married to Cynthia (Julia Cortez), a clearly insane ex-stripper who treats the locals to an exhibition involving Ping-Pong balls.

Bob and Bernie will warm up to each other, there's some violence, the trio makes it to their gig and "Priscilla," a trip to a Lavender City in an alternative Oz, ends up telling us there's no place like home.

SIGHT AND SOUND, 11/94, p. 38, Lizzie Francke

Sydney. Bernadette, a middle-aged transsexual showgirl, is mourning the recent death of her lover. In order to help her get over her loss, her drag queen friend Tick, aka Mitzi, invites her to accompany him on a month's cabaret engagement in Alice Springs. Tick also recruits Adam/Felicia and the threesome set off to their desert location in a violently-painted school bus which they name Priscilla.

It transpires that the resort hotel which they are going to is run by Tick's wife. Bernadette and Felicia are upset that Tick has been so secretive about his past. When they stop off in a small outback town, they are greeted with derision by the locals until they start joking around, and then everyone accepts them. However, the following morning their bus is covered with homophobic graffiti. Later, they break down in the middle of nowhere. Eventually an Aboriginal man turns up and takes them to his settlement, where the trio do their routine. Then a truck arrives driven by Bob, who offers to help. He takes them back to his place and reveals that he was a big fan of Bernadette's old act.

Bob persuades the girls to do their show at the local pub, but they are upstaged by his wife Cynthia, who, much to Bob's embarrassment, has a fascinating act of her own. The following day, Bob drives them back to repair their bus, and ends up travelling with them. They stop off at an underground mining town. Visiting the local bar on his own, Adam is mistaken for a woman, but is beaten up when the truth is revealed. Bob comes to his rescue. He stays on the road with the group, and an attraction seems to be developing between him and Bernadette.

Finally they arrive at Alice Springs. Tick's wife Marion is happy to see them all and they find that Tick has a young son, Benji, whom Marion would like Tick to look after for a while. Tick, anxious about his son finding out about his new career, tries to act very straight around him. But Benji knows all about his dad and demands to see a much talked-about Abba floor show. Tick takes Benji back to Sydney, leaving Bernadette and Bob behind at the hotel. In Sydney, Benji is in heaven as his dad and Felicia go through their Abba routine.

As Bernadette, Mitzi and Felicia get into their purple-painted wagon, Bernadette says that she wants their conversation to be about more than "penis sizes, wigs, bust sizes and Abba." In the end the road-bound chat fulfils all her worst expectations. But she—and the audience —are meant to love it. This camping holiday movie is a post-Queer, post-'Supermodel' *La Cage aux Folles*. It plays to a mainstream appetite for men in spangles and feathers strutting their stuff to Gloria Gaynor, Village People (heavens, even Wayne and Garth danced to 'YMCA' this year), or doing a darn fine pass for the Abba girls in white satin thigh boots, crocheted berets and lashings of blue eyeliner.

With all this comes the expected salty banter, although in this case it's hardly lewd enough for the average self-disrespecting drag artiste. But then *The Adventures of Priscilla Queen of the Desert* is an outing for all the family (boasting *Neighbours* and *Home and Away* star Guy Pearce). In this respect, it is similar to *La Cage aux Folles*, which demonstrated to a 70s audience that 'queers' were people you could take home to meet your auntie, who fall in love and have feelings like everyone else. They just know how to have a better time about it. But although in *Priscilla*, Auntie may now swop blusher tips with Mitzi (who sells a line in heavy duty cosmetics for "the woman in us all"), she is not expected to be that finely tuned to the differences between a drag queen and a transsexual. Writer and director Stephan Elliott easily conflates the two—as if, after all, they're all just men in fabulous frocks.

The outfits, extravagant confections of satin and lace, galvanise the film. Dressed up to the nines, the threesome shimmer like tropical fish beached in the desert. The movie's prime joke is for its three suburban sirens to find that it's rough in the outback; in the first town they visit, the women prove more macho than they are, although Bernadette, elegant in twin-set and pearls, is able to drink one liquor-swilling Sheila under the table. The desert also has its charms, as when the Aboriginal man takes them back to his settlement. But from his oblique passing comment ("Nice night for it"), this sequence becomes a little too cute, as the trio belt out 'I Will Survive' for a captive audience. In keeping with the rest of the film, it just pays lip-glossed service to a more complex politics.

VILLAGE VOICE, 8/16/94, p. 48, Georgia Brown

Some movies—*Stranger Than Paradise* and *Easy Rider* are examples—have no plot to speak of; they're occasions for scenery, mood, tunes, and two large scoops of attitude. Such is Stephan Elliott's *The Adventures of Priscilla Queen Of the Desert*: musical, road movie, ice cream cone, and a series of wistful, defiant postcards from down under.

Priscilla starts off with an almost incidental funeral. Dead is the 25-year-old Trumpet, to be defined by his lover as "just the last kid who had a thing for transsexuals." The transsexual who loved him (sort of), Bernadette (Terence Stamp, yes, Terence Stamp), can now be persuaded to take a bus journey to Alice Springs, in the center of Australia, in order to do a gig. Already on the bus and in the group are two transvestite performers, Tick (Hugo Weaving, last seen in *Proof*) and Adam (Guy Pearce), a/k/a Mitzi and Felicia. They've christened the bus Priscilla.

Felicia declares she just wants to climb a well-known mountain in her sequined gown. "Just what this country needs," observes Bernadette, "a cock in a frock on a rock."

It is what every country needs, you come to understand, but this one is exceptionally suited to play backdrop to flashy boas, wedding cake wigs, and kilometers of bright tulle. Central Australia here looks like a cross between the American West, the moon, and the volcanic terrain of *Teorema*.

Besides, this is the land of the Walkabout. In Bruce Chatwin's *The Songlines* we learned that these days Aboriginals follow their dreamtimes by train or car. I'm sure buses will do, too.

Filmmaker Elliott says the inspiration for *Priscilla* came while walking down a Sydney street after the annual Gay and Lesbian Mardi Gras and seeing a bright plume that had been blown by the breeze into a drab, forlorn area. What would it be like to take this show on the road?

As I said, not that much happens. Some yokels along the way are shocked. Someone paints AIDS FUCKERS GO HOME on Priscilla's flank. Priscilla breaks down in the desert (gas tank sabotage) and Felicia uses the free time to paint the old girl pink. Aboriginals appreciate their act; some participate. Felicia and Bernadette bitch and bicker (Felicia calls Bernadette Ralph) while Tick keeps the peace. Tick reveals that the entertainment coordinator of the hotel in Alice Springs is his wife. A gentle mechanic named Bob (Bill Hunter) comes aboard, his patient eye on Bernadette. New towns, new gowns. We discover that Felicia is an ABBA freak whose father was a pedophile (this last, to my mind, is the film's one sour note).

Felicia is nearly mauled by a vicious mob until Bernadette kicks butt. And Tick, it turns out, has a son as well as a wife, and the child may be waiting at the end of the line.

One road sign reads "Kangaroo: Next 25 miles," but we never see any. You do see a woman—Bob's ornery mail-order bride—spit Ping-Pong balls out her snatch. This too may be Australia.

With his silver-blond locks and discreet dewlap, the handsome Stamp has such regalness and dignity. Bernadette never smiles: She's seen too much. Yet she bestows great class on this shimmering enterprise. Once again, Stamp leaves his stamp.

Also reviewed in:
CHICAGO TRIBUNE, 8/26/94, Friday/p. M, Clifford Terry
NEW YORK TIMES, 3/10/94, p. C9, Janet Maslin
VARIETY, 5/9-15/94, p. 76, David Stratton
WASHINGTON POST, 8/26/94, p. D7, Rita Kempley
WASHINGTON POST, 8/26/94, Weekend/p. 43, Desson Howe

ADVOCATE, THE

A Miramax Films release of a BBC/CiBy 2000 production with the participation of British Screen Finance/The European Co-production Fund. *Executive Producer:* Michael Wearing and Claudine Sainderichin. *Producer:* David M. Thompson. *Director:* Leslie Megahey. *Screenplay:* Leslie Megahey. *Director of Photography:* John Hooper. *Editor:* Isabelle Dedieu. *Music:* Alexandre Desplat. *Choreographer:* Jane Gibson and Deborah Pope. *Sound:* Daniel Brisseau and (music) Ted Swanscott, John Timperley and Gérard Chiron. *Sound Editor:* Joe Walker. *Casting:* Joyce Nettles. *Production Designer:* Bruce Macadie. *Art Director:* Jane Broomfield, Jacques Mollon and Jane Shepherd. *Special Effects:* Stuart Brisdon. *Costumes:* Anna Buruma. *Make-up:* Jan Sewell. *Stunt Coordinator:* Mario Luraschi. *Running time:* 101 minutes. *MPAA Rating:* R.

CAST: Colin Firth (Richard Courtois); Ian Holm (Albertus); Donald Pleasence (Pincheon); Amina Annabi (Samira); Nicol Williamson (Seigneur Jehan d'Auferre); Michael Gough (Magistrate Boniface); Harriet Walter (Jeannine); Jim Carter (Mathieu); Lysette Anthony (Filette d'Auferre); Justin Chadwick (Gérard d'Auferre); Sophie Dix (Maria); Michael Cronin (Dark Stranger); Elizabeth Spriggs (Madame Langlois); Emil Wolk (Print Seller); Vincent Grass (Bailiff Labatier); Raoul Delfosse (Blind Georges); Jean-Pierre Stewart (Sheriff); Dave Atkins (Vallière); François Lalande (Builder); Vernon Dobtcheff (Apothecary); Sami Bouajila (Mahmoud); Joanna Dunham (Lady Catherine d'Auferre); Peter Hudson (Sheriff's Officer).

Charles Dale and Gordon Langford Rowe (Witnesses); Judy Pascoe, Roy Evans and Robert Putt (Traveling Players); Ralph Nossek (Poiccard); Melissa Wilks (Young GIrl); David Larkin (Young Boy); Patricia Psaltopoulos (Peasant Woman); Alain Blazquez (Cuckolded Man); Isabelle Marcoz and Marie-Pierre Charliot (Roger Landrier).

LOS ANGELES TIMES, 8/24/94, Calendar/p. 8, Peter Rainer

Richard Courtois (Colin Firth), the Parisian lawyer in "The Advocate," is a medieval post-yuppie. Forsaking the big bad city for the villagey environs of Abbeville, he looks forward to defending the grateful peasantry and getting all idyllic.

But lawyer-haters will be glad to know that lawyers had it bad back then too. It turns out that Courtois underestimates how grody these villages (and villagers) can be. Abbeville is ruled by the Seigneur (Nicol Williamson), a merchant who specializes in pinched smiles and glazed gazes. He purchased his title—it's kind of like buying a black belt in karate—and the rule of law along with it. His prosecutor, Pincheon (Donald Pleasence), has that groggy, on-the-payroll look. When he squares off with Courtois in court, it's a tossup to see if he'll nod off before Courtois storms off.

What is it about Middle Ages movies that almost always provoke giggles? Maybe it's the way all that clanking and posturing clashes with modern acting styles. Maybe it's because Monty Python has made it just about impossible to look at the 15th Century on film without expecting John Cleese to totter about in armor. "The Advocate," written and directed by Leslie Megahey, makes the mistake of taking itself seriously—but not quite seriously enough. It makes a fuss about the conflict between civil and religious law, it tries for a You Were There quality. It keeps flashing title cards, for that Important Movie effect.

But it also seems as campy as those old Roger Corman Edgar Allan Poe pictures, with Williamson in the Vincent Price role. Courtois just happens to be boarding in what turns out to be a sort of hostel-brothel, which provides the opportunity for some explicit medieval nookie. Cleavage was big back then. There's also the requisite banquet eating scenes, with platters of cooked game and a sultry (is there any other kind?) Gypsy girl doing a dance of veils. You half expect Victor Mature and Anita Ekberg to show up. When Courtois and the Gypsy (Amina Annabi) have one of those it-can-never-be-I-am-not-of-your-world romances, we wait for the inevitable A Part of Me Stays With You parting.

The underpinnings of the plot concern the fact that, under medieval law, everything created by God was subject to his laws. So we're subjected to scenes in which Courtois calls rats to testify in a murder trial, but not the Jewish surgeon, without rights in this world, who discovered the body.

(You half expect him to bemoan, "Hath not a Jew whiskers?")

It's not always clear if Megahey is aware of how risible this stuff is—if he was, why didn't he just turn it into a comedy? The actors do their best to keep their faces uncracked, but Williamson has a high old time acting parched and smarmy, Pleasence is ingratiatingly rheumy, and Firth holds the screen even when there's nothing to hold (which is often).

Ian Holm plays a priest who unofficially disbelieves the village's superstitions, and he's good enough to make you wish he was in something more amenable to his talents—like Shakespeare. Lysette Anthony, who was Sydney Pollack's airheaded squeeze in Woody Allen's "Husbands and Wives," is lively, with a bright, quacking laugh, in her role as the Seigneur's unmarriageable daughter.

You may have noticed that the ads for "The Advocate" are dredging up that old "don't tell the secret" chestnut from "Crying Game" fame. (Miramax released both.) Audiences and critics are supposed to keep quiet about who the Courtois' chief client is. Miramax would be wiser encouraging audiences and critics to refrain from revealing how mediocre the film is.

Since the identity of the client would appear to be the film's biggest—only—selling point, the marketing ploy seems particularly dunderheaded. And since, in any event, the identity is signaled from the opening credits, and revealed not long after, this "secret" business seems like a not terribly subtle way of coercing the press into pumping up the film's wanna-see quotient.

But we'll play along anyway. We just wanted to you to know that this ham-fisted attempt to squelch squealers is not strictly kosher.

NEW YORK POST, 8/24/94, p. 35, Thelma Adams

Salt of the earth or scum of the earth?

When sophisticated lawyer Courtois (Colin Firth) flees Paris for Abbeville's simple country pleasures, ca. 1400, he's in for a surprise among the provincial natives.

In this twist on the country cousin, "The Advocate" discovers that he has traded urban power struggles for a nest of intrigue and superstition in the sticks.

Where the lawyer expected to plead the people's case in simple land disputes and domestic squabbles, Courtois discovers a full docket of bestiality, rape, and a serial murder with a cover-up conspiracy worthy of Oliver Stone.

The simple country folk turn out to be not so simple.

British character stalwarts Nicol Williamson, Donald Pleasence and Ian Holm have a field day as, respectively, a crafty Seigneur who has bought his title and lords over the district, the dry prosecutor he has in his pocket, and the randy priest who has the power to stand up to the noble but resists defecating in his own backyard.

Writer-director Leslie Megahey uses an actual case in which a French pig was tried for murder in order to explore the conflicts between medieval superstition and modern reason, church and state and the individuals caught in the middle, good and evil, youthful zeal and mature conservatism.

Megahey's approach is humanistic without being preachy, humorous without being ahistorical.

The notorious sex scenes between Colin Firth and serving wench Sophie Dix which originally brought "The Advocate" an NC-17 rating have been chipped away until they push the envelope of R. They are no more bawdy than Chaucer's "Canterbury Tales."

The difference is that, thanks to the wonders of modern tech, the naked romps are in color and little is left to the imagination. The scenes serve to show a pre-Puritanical period in history when sex was considered as natural as sleep, and the divisions between public and private life were much less strict.

And, thankfully, unlike such recent Hollywood borderline porn like "Color of Night," the cavorting characters in "The Advocate" actually seem to be enjoying themselves.

In contrast to the Merchant Ivory Productions which have become the gold standard of historical film fiction. "The Advocate" is pretty without being precious; the costumes and coiffures never overwhelm the drama's human scale.

Firth, who played the title role in Milos Forman's "Valmont." finds the right balance of intelligence, humor and naivete as the self-assured hero who quickly finds himself over his head.

Director Megahey is on surer ground building characters and atmosphere than in constructing a totally satisfying thriller. The unraveling of the murder plot becomes increasingly messy. Dream sequences that delve into Courtois' unconscious solving of the crime could easily be tossed out of court without losing anything.

But these lapses don't detract from making "The Advocate" one of the summer's wisest and sexiest movies.

NEWSDAY, 8/24/94, Part II/p. B7, Jonathan Mandell

A man is about to be hanged, convicted of crimes against nature. Next to him stands his mule, also about to be hanged for the same crime. Suddenly a priest rushes to the rescue, waving testimony attesting to the good character ... of the mule.

The mule is spared, the man is hanged, and we are introduced to the odd world of "The Advocate," a medieval French village where the line between man and animal is often indistinct. Barnyard beasts are prosecuted for crimes, and a corrupt human society is "gripped by ignorance and superstition," according to the written prologue that rolls up the screen at graduate-level speed.

That prologue also includes what may be the most arresting—even redeeming—aspect of this alternately dark and droll feature: "Unbelievable as it may seem, all cases in this film are based on historical fact." It is 1452, the time of the Black Plague, and Parisian Richard Courtois (Colin Firth) has moved to the countryside to get away from the complications of city life. He is a modern man for the 15th Century, idealistic and educated, and when he gallops onto the scene of a band of innocent gypsies who are being menaced by the sheriff and his men, he fends them off using the only weapon he has mastered: the law. The gypsies have not violated any statutes, tells the ruffians primly. Our hero is a lawyer.

How's that for an original concept?

Courtois has arrived in the village to become its new public defender, expecting a bucolic life of peace and simplicity. Instead, he must handle a society as absurd as it is evil. At first, Courtois remains confident that his skills as an advocate will win out.

But his decency is overwhelmed by the power and corruption of the church and state—represented by the feudal Seigneur (Nicol Williamson), a nouveau riche merchant who has purchased his title and with it his absolute power.

"The Advocate" was one of the two films for which Miramax publicly announced the hiring of its own advocate, William Kunstler, to fight the original NC-17 rating; it has since quietly snipped off a few seconds to get the R. Marketing strategy, not idealism, thus seems to have guided them, and this continues with the packaging of "The Advocate" as a "courtroom thriller" and the request that the identity of the client in Courtois' major case not be revealed. This is ridiculous. "The Advocate" is no "Crying Game," no John Grisham thriller. It is more a period piece heavy in atmosphere and historical details. The client is a pig, accused of murdering a Jewish child. This revelation will not ruin the movie for anybody; it was actually called "The Hour of the Pig" in Europe.

Miramax may be resorting to these gimmicks because it understands how difficult some audiences will find the real movie, which is rarely pretty, confused in tone and focus and—most to the point—an adult film. This does not mean steamy. It means complex, requiring patience and provoking thought.

SIGHT AND SOUND, 2/94, p. 53, Phillip Strick

Abbeville, a rural town in the Ponthieu region of medieval France. Idealistic young lawyer Richard Courtois arrives from Paris with his clerk Mathieu to serve as defence attorney in cases brought by the local prosecutor Pincheon. He finds a community riddled with prejudice and superstition, cynically exploited by the priest Albertus and the powerful landowner Seigneur Jehan d'Auferre. Successfully negotiating the acquittal of a peasant accused of murder, Courtois finds his next case more complex: he rescues Jeannine, a woman accused of witchcraft, from all civil charges only to see her condemned to death by local Church ordinance against which he has no authority. To his fury, he is then required to defend a pig against a murder charge; a Jewish boy has been killed, and it is obvious to Courtois that the animal has been accused in order to protect the real culprit. He refuses to take on such an absurd assignment.

The pig belongs to gypsies who have settled nearby despite fears among the townsfolk that they are heathens and plague-carriers. Samira, a beautiful gypsy girl, offers Courtois every inducement to protect the pig, their only valuable possession. Although he is enjoying an affair with Maria, a servant girl at the inn where he is staying until a house has been constructed for him, he finds Samira difficult, to refuse. He is also under pressure from d'Auferre, who has him in mind as a permanent replacement to Pincheon, at an astronomical salary; d'Auferre is similarly keen to get the pig case settled quickly. Courtois is introduced to d'Auferre's son Gérard, a precocious youth with a passion for hunting, and to d'Auferre's daughter Filette, who is available for matrimony, complete with substantial dowry. Courtois finds that wherever he goes he is under surveillance from an unknown man he assumes to be in d'Auferre's employment. Failing to persuade Samira to accept enough money to buy two replacement pigs, Courtois attempts to have the case dismissed, but Pincheon and the local magistrate Boniface insist that the trial goes ahead.

Exercising his *droit de seigneur*, d'Auferre appoints himself as judge to the proceedings. Although it is clear to Courtois that the witnesses have been well rehearsed, while the discovery of another child's remains indicates the pig's unarguable innocence, a verdict against the animal is only postponed by the bells of Advent. During the recess, Courtois rescues a stable-boy from attack by an unknown horseman, who turns on him but is driven away by the watching stranger, later identified as a spy for the Inquisition. Prompted by hints from Albertus who, through confessional, knows the truth, Courtois confronts d'Auferre, who admits that Gérard is the miscreant and has now been sent to England for treatment. The pig, however, must still die to protect the family name from scandal. Accepting the charade for Samira's sake, Courtois produces a new pig in court, with witnesses swearing to its guilt, and Samira's pig is exonerated.

Determined to return to Paris, Courtois is unable to persuade Samira to go with him. Mathieu also stays behind to work with Pincheon. As Courtois leaves by wagon, a knight in shining armour arrives at Abbeville, as predicted by Jeannine on the scaffold, his body bearing the plague-sores of the Black Death.

Part whodunnit, part rustic comedy and part historical pageant, *The Hour of the Pig* embraces its opportunities with an enthusiastic but precarious grasp, seemingly reluctant to decide on a main argument. Opening with the enjoyably bizarre spectacle of a last-minute reprieve for a donkey on a scaffold, released "without a stain to her character" as her quaking owner is briskly hanged, the film seems prepared for a series of macabre amusements based on the premise that animals were often brought to judgement in the Middle Ages. In belated reinforcement of this theme, an end title records that more than 90 such trials occurred in France between 1403 and 1596 (although Geoffrey Cush's play *The Criminal Prosecution and Capital Punishment of Animals*, recently staged in London, shows a continuation of the custom well into the 1790s). But there have been too many diversions by this point for the film to provide a convincingly typical instance. Instead, the pig itself—while a handsome enough example of reportedly Iron Age pedigree—has been largely obscured by the intervening intrigues, seductions and power struggles, as well as being abruptly marginalised by a more significant agenda, the arrival of the Black Death. Despite its claims, the one thing the film does not do is explain how animals were for centuries seriously subjected to legal constraints (notoriously, a swarm of locusts was once tried in absentia) when none of the participants on this occasion, including the bribed witnesses, regard the proceedings as anything but an elaborate farce.

Since the pig's innocence is not an issue, the plot turns on the identity of glaringly obvious culprit in emerald blue, with an unhealthy interest in butcher-birds and an inherited taste for the hunting of human prey, his unmasking is delayed by a number of contrivances, notably the sinister if mostly irrelevant presence of a spy for the Inquisition. Lurking among the shadows, the so-called Dark Stranger might more suitably observe the misbehaviour of the local priest than prowl around the indiscretions of the young lawyer, but at least he is available to scare off the opposition when most needed. Less useful is the obscure Cathar sect, much given to hoods and masonic ceremonies, through which the Seigneur maintains his grip on the whole neighbourhood. But hints of Hellfire Club depravity are soon dispelled by the revelation that the brotherhood's chief concern is the control of grain prices. Glumly perplexed by such distractions, the lawyer's sleuthing does little to uncover what seems an open secret until—by extreme coincidence—he intervenes in the killer's latest abduction. Even then, he has to be all but told the man's name by the priest who, much like the rest of us, has known it all along.

Adding to the muddle of events, the film is cluttered with disconnected moments and interludes, as when the disembodied voice of the Seigneur suddenly invites the lawyer to a party, or when there is an unresolved discussion about a possible reference to a servant-girl's anatomy. In one sequence, as the lawyer and the gypsy stroll by the river, unknown silhouettes watch them from the bushes while a sword is drawn and a youth scrambles in terror among the trees—hotly pursued by the camera but not, apparently, by anybody else. In occasional bursts of luridly entertaining fantasy, we share the lawyer's dreams, where naked couples are chased by horsemen, blood sprinkles his pillow, and half the cast wanders waist-high in water. Another meaningless omen is provided by the falling candle which sets light to the papers on his desk, the resulting blaze promptly extinguished by a toppling mug of wine; as well he might, the lawyer studies this apparently supernatural vandalism with a dull inscrutability.

Magnificently served by his production designers, Leslie Megahey can be forgiven for allowing his debut feature script to stray, with intricate humour, along such vivid but ill-defined pathways. The fun of *The Hour of the Pig* is mostly to be had from the contrast between its plausible costumes and settings and the inescapable anachronism of its performers, wonderfully familiar as they are—the furtive glances of Ian Holm, the eye-rolling sardonicism of Donald Pleasence, the lofty drawl of Michael Gough. Effortlessly dominant is the welcome, if slightly battered, Nicol Williamson, shamelessly mugging his despair over an appalling daughter and exerting, with icy gaze and rat-trap mouth, an unequivocal authority over the entire drama. Settling for broad comedy, despite the potentialities of the text, the players seem to have decided on a *Carry On Canterbury Tales* approach, encouraged by Megahey's Greenaway-like inclination to fill the screen with nudes and lewds at every turn. The result is a tangle of ribaldry and half-told tales, promising more than it can deliver, a not inexcusable waste of a colourful panoply of talents.

Also reviewed in:
CHICAGO TRIBUNE, 2/2/94, Friday/p. D, John Petrakis
NEW YORK TIMES, 8/24/94, p. C11, Janet Maslin
VARIETY, 10/25/93, p. 82, Lisa Nesselson
WASHINGTON POST, 9/2/94, p. D1, Hal Hinson
WASHINGTON POST, 9/2/94, Weekend/p. 38, Desson Howe

AILEEN WUORNOS: THE SELLING OF A SERIAL KILLER

A Strand Releasing release of a Lafayette Film production. *Executive Producer:* Peter Moore. *Producer:* Nick Broomfield and Rieta Oord. *Director:* Nick Broomfield. *Screenplay:* Nick Broomfield. *Director of Photography:* Barry Ackroyd. *Editor:* Richard M. Lewis and Rick Vick. *Music:* David Bergeaud. *Sound:* Nick Broomfield. *Running time:* 87 minutes. *MPAA Rating:* Not Rated.

LOS ANGELES TIMES, 3/31/94, Calendar/p. 11, Peter Rainer

Aileen "Lee" Wuornos, the subject of Nick Broomfield's documentary "Aileen Wuornos: The Selling of a Serial Killer." has the hard-bitten look of someone whose life has been hell and who has made a hell of the lives of others. Commentators have often noted how shockingly *normal* serial killers like Jeffrey Dahmer or Ted Bundy look; Wuornos doesn't inspire the same befuddlement.

But one of the points of Broomfield's movie is that perhaps Wuornos is not in the strictest definition, a serial killer at all. Between 1989 and 1990, while working as a prostitute on a Florida interstate highway, Wuornos shot and killed seven men. While admitting the killings, she repeatedly characterized them during her trial as acts of self-defense, a charge she reiterates during the interview she gives Broomfield at the end of the film.

When we hear Wuornos in the courtroom go into painstaking detail about how her first murder victim sexually tortured her and planned to kill her, she appears to be reliving the horror. It's almost unbearable to listen to and watch.

If her murders had been confined to that one alone, she probably would have escaped death row. (She's still there, pending appeal.) But her claims of self-defense in the other six don't jog the same vehement feminist fury. Wuornos is a jangle of mixed motives: She claims to accept her guilt and wants to be put to death but when she is sentenced she screams at the judge, "May your wife and kids get raped."

Wuornos' plea of no contest to one of the murders, which led to her sentencing, was engineered by her attorney Steven Glazer and Arlene Pralle, a born-again Christian and horse farmer who adopted Wuornos just before the murder trial because she claims "Lee" had a "heart of gold."

Broomfield seems manifestly concerned with how the Wuornos murders have turned into a commercial enterprise. He draws out a Florida policeman, Brian Jarvis, who claims that police officers conspired to sell the rights to the Wuornos case before she had been arrested, and that Wuornos' estranged female lover Tyria Moore, who some believe was a co-conspirator, was in on the deal in exchange for her freedom.

Broomfield's tack is to highlight the commercialization of the case and, in the process, to encourage the view that Wuornos has been sacrificed. When she finally relents to be interviewed by him at the end of the film, and underscores her position as a victim of abuse who murdered in self-defense, his interrogation is not very probing.

Unremarked, or glossed over in this film, is the fact that Wuornos had already been arrested and jailed for armed robbery in 1982, that she had married a 70-year-old man in 1976 and that the marriage broke up on battery charges (each accused the other), that she had a baby at 13 that was taken from her, that she had tried to kill herself. Also glossed over or unexamined is the weight of evidence against her, charges of self-defense: the fact that all the men she murdered were white men between the ages of 40 and 60 and drove fairly expensive vehicles; that space had been rented by her to store the spoils; that in all the murders she was careful enough to leave behind only one fingerprint; that she was not above trying to cut her own deals.

"The Selling of a Serial Killer" is properly cynical of the commercial motives behind the case but it isn't skeptical enough about Wuornos, who, despite her entreaties to Broomfield at the end to investigate police corruption, remains remorseless about the murders. The film finally becomes an extension of thc current vogue in courtroom special pleading: Wuornos is martyred because of her abusive childhood and her degradation as a prostitute. The film presents her as the first documented female serial killer but what you come away with is something else: Wuornos is the first politically correct serial killer.

NEW YORK, 2/7/94, p. 65, John Powers

Three years ago, Aileen "Lee" Wuornos was arrested in Daytona Beach and charged with multiple murder. Although she claimed to have acted in self-defense each time—killing only men who had threatened her, or worse—she was soon being marketed by the media as America's first female serial killer. Nick Broomfield's gripping documentary *Aileen Wuronos: The Selling of a Serial Killer* shows how this 35-year-old lesbian and occasional prostitute became congealed in such a misogynist caricature. Like *The Executioner's Song*, it's a tale crawling with buffoonish hustlers: Florida cops who allegedly dickered with Hollywood for rights to Wuornos's story even before she was caught; her born-again adoptive mother, who thinks Aileen lucky to have gotten a death sentence because now she can meet her Maker; her fat, furry-headed lawyer, who urges a "no contest" plea and then tells her Woody Allen jokes about the electric chair. From her perfidious lover, Tyria, to the white-trash politicians who want to fry her at election time, all of Wuornos's many interpreters drip with self-interest, often demanding money for doing interviews. When Broomfield finally meets Lee in prison and she's able to speak for herself, she seems saner than most of those who claim to be defending her interests or explaining her behavior. Abused as a child, unloved as an adult, and mad as hell about both, Lee Wuornos is no serial killer or she-devil. She's an open wound wrapped in the black-comic pages of tabloid America.

NEW YORK POST, 2/5/94, p. 16, Thelma Adams

Mass murder is big media business. Before the bodies are buried, networks are sniffing around for sensational stories to rush to movie-of-the-week spots, and hucksters hover around the cops and criminals for crumbs.

Before Nick Broomfield's slap-dash documentary, "Aileen Wuornos: The Selling of a Serial Killer," opened yesterday at the Cinema Village, TV audiences were already offered "Overkill," starring Jean ("Designing Women") Smart as the woman dubbed "America's first female serial killer."

(For those lacking serial killer bubble-gum cards, three years ago hitchhiking hooker Aileen Wuornos killed seven men on Florida highways. She claimed she acted in self-defense.)

Tyria Moore, Wuornos' lesbian !over, cooperated with the police. Moore distanced herself from Wuornos and tried to sell her story to Hollywood.

Did Wuornos' lover and local police conspire to suppress evidence and cash in on a movie deal? It's a conspiracy theory befitting Oliver Stone, but Broomfield fails to mount conclusive evidence.

The director subscribes to the iffy school of camera-thrusting in which an absent subject incriminates himself by silence. The fact that Broomfield had no access to Moore and the allegedly corrupt cops, makes them easy prey to the director's guilty-in-absentia methodology.

Far from objective, he becomes part of a bidding war to gain access to Wuornos, who sits on Florida's death row.

The director's chief contacts are two enterprising stepchildren of the '60s. Wuornos' lawyer, Steven Glazer, is a roly-poly, pot-smoking, former folk singer who once opened for Leon Redbone.

Glazer moonlights as an agent for Aileen's "mother," Arlene Pralle, a new-age rancher only 6 years older than the killer. With her hand resolutely out, Pralle claims she adopted Aileen in the name of Christian love.

Which image of the 35-year-old Wuornos sells best? Was she a man-hating lesbian betrayed by the woman she loved? Or was she a prostitute who was raped by her Johns and fought back?

Broomfield tilts toward a vision of Wuornos as a victim—of men, women, her lawyer, her adoptive mother, the police, a justice system that looks away when prostitutes are raped or murdered.

Certainly, with the Menendez and Bobbitt cases, the victim defense is in vogue.

But after 87 minutes of Broomfield huffing and puffing, making the local Floridians look as if they were all first cousins, Wuornos remains elusive. Interviewed once by Broomfield, Wuornos appears as the oddly sane center in concentric circles of deceit. Seen in court, she is an angry, vicious, defiant woman in chains.

Wuornos killed seven men and claimed self-defense. If you buy that, you might as well believe Broomfield, too.

NEWSDAY, 2/4/94, Part II/p. 66, Jack Mathews

If English filmmaker Nick Broomfield had brought along a second cameraman, he could have made both"Aileen Wuornos: The Selling of a Serial Killer" and "Nick Broomfield: The Selling of the Selling of a Serial Killer."

The first film would have been what it is, a sleazy documentary about the commercial parasites who attached themselves to a mentally unbalanced woman accused of multiple murders in Florida, and the second an equally sleazy look at Broomfield's own opportunism.

"The Selling of A Serial Killer" is tabloid filmmaking fobbing itself off as gonzo journalism. Given the useless footage included in the movie—Broomfield having doors slammed in his face, people turning their backs on him—it might have made more sense to screen it for the IRS and take his write-off.

Yet, the film, which depends heavily on the news archives of local TV stations, slogs on, as if Broomfield were carefully rooting out some pestilence everyone else was afraid to touch.

If you accept Broomfield's speculative conclusion, that Wuronos, a prostitute facing the death penalty for one of her seven confessed killings of roadside pickups, was railroaded by avaricious redneck cops, you can see him as the hero of the story. Certainly, the film's other central figures are lower than the pond scum at the bottom of the Okaloacoochee Slough.

Among them:

● Wuornos' lawyer, a pot-smoking ambulance chaser who admits, after having talked Wuornos into pleading guilty, that he wouldn't know how to conduct a criminal defense.

● Wuornos' lesbian lover, Tyria Moore, who shed suspicion that she was an accomplice to some of the killings by talking Wuornos into a solo confession, then allegedly participating with Sheriff's officials in hawking the story of America's "first woman serial killer" to TV producers.

● Arlene Pralle, a local farmer who wormed her way into Wuornos' confidence by claiming to have been psychically alerted to her innocence, then, after legally adopting the woman, offered to sell what she wheedled out of her to the media's highest bidder.

Yes, the stench is thick her, but Broomfield's work doesn't do much to clear the air. Frankly, it's a hard call as to which gives off a worse odor, people who offer to sell ill-gotten information or those who agree to buy it.

As for Wuornos, the real tragedy is that she didn't have proper representation in court. She was a drug addict and vagrant, and her claim that she killed all those men in self-defense after they began beating her during sex seems a mighty stretch.

But if it weren't for the tabloid rush to label her a serial killer, thus attracting the parasites, a public defender might at least have got the court to examine her for what she os obviously is, a mental case.

NEWSWEEK, 3/7/94, p. 65, David Ansen

Aileen Wuornos, a hitchhiking prostitute who murdered seven men in Florida in 1989 and 1990 and is now in prison facing the electric chair, is no one's idea of a heroine. Tough, foulmouthed and unglamorous, she throws the finger at the judge who sentences her to death and curses her enemies: "May your wife and kids get raped ..." Yet one of the several astonishing things about Nick Broomfield's documentary *Aileen Wuornos: The Selling of a Serial Killer* is that this self-confessed killer is the most sympathetic figure in it. At the New York Film Festival, where the film was shown last fall, audiences actually cheered her.

Broomfield went to Florida not so much to pursue her personal story as to investigate the media feeding frenzy that surrounded the case, a big-bucks circus that led to a TV movie ("Overkill"), book contracts and myriad tabloid TV and magazine stories. He discovers a jaw-dropping carnival of greed, betrayal and bad faith. At the center of the story is Arlene Pralle, a perky horse breeder and born-again Christian who legally adopted Wuornos—six years her junior—after she was arrested. She claims that she can "read people's eyes" and knew Wuornos couldn't have done the things she was accused of. Pralle asks the filmmaker for $25,000 for the story—later reduced to 10 grand. Her cohort/agent is a rotund, bearded, guitar-strumming lawyer, Steve Glazer (his TV ads urge you to "Dial Dr. Legal"). He startles the legal world when he convinces Wuornos (with Pralle's consent) to enter a no-contest plea to four other murder charges, resulting in more death sentences for his client. "Why not go for it? She could be home with Jesus," the bright-eyed Pralle coos, while the viewer is left with the clear impression that her "daughter" is worth more to her and Glazer dead than alive.

Allegations emerge that local cops were negotiating to sell movie rights to the story even before Wuornos was arrested—and the one cop pursuing this trail is harassed and demoted. It's to everyone's financial benefit that Wuornos be seen as a man-hating serial killer—it's a narrative that sells—though she repeatedly claims that she was acting in self-defense. (Her graphic account at her trial of her rape by her first victim is hair-raising.) There is also reason to suspect a second woman was involved—Wuornos's lover Tyria Moore, who betrays Wuornos by persuading her to confess, and is never charged with any crime herself.

Not exempting himself from the charge of checkbook journalism, Broomfield participates in the cavalcade of sleaze with open eyes and mounting frustration: he has an angry confrontation with Pralle when she throws him off her farm after collecting money from him. Much of what we see evokes grim laughter. But the portrait that emerges of Wuornos, a brutalized woman victimized at every turn of her life, is sad and haunting. The movie doesn't exonerate her, but it does shed appalling light on how she came to kill, and raises troubling questions about the conduct of her case. Wuornos's blunt, enraged honesty makes her the most human figure on the screen.

"Aileen Wuornos" is raw, fascinating and less than ideally organized. But as a portrait of a world obsessed with cashing in on tragedy, it couldn't be more timely. Though he shot it well before the travails of Michael, Tonya and the Bobbitts, Broomfield has stumbled on the perfect metaphor for these trial-by-media times. And just as with those other stories, you can't turn your eyes away.

VILLAGE VOICE, 2/8/94, p. 58, Georgia Brown

For a woman to become notorious, Just let her dramatically harm a man. Or men. Over an 11-month period, a Florida prostitute named Aileen Wuornos killed seven of her johns and found herself billed as "the first female serial killer." (And what do you call those little old ladies who did in their lodgers?) Wuornos is no Lorena Yes-Ma'am Bobbitt. She's a big, broad, tough-mouthed dyke who, when sentenced to the chair, gave the judge the finger and muttered, "may your wife and kids get raped in the ass." Forced anal sex, Wuornos had claimed in court, motivated her first murder. (After the rape, the perpetrator shot rubbing alcohol into her rectum.)

News stories about Wuornos would never have made me as sympathetic to her as does seeing her directly in Nick Broomfield's fascinating documentary, *Aileen Wuornos: The Selling of a Serial Killer*. Next to the truly venal slugs denying her rights and cashing in on her story, she gains enormous credibility. Betrayed all around—by her longtime lover, her lawyer, her new adoptive mother, and perhaps even by law-enforcement agents who arrested her—Wuornos comes off as uncompromisingly honest. "All I want to do," she says at one point, "is get off this planet." No wonder. She's been closeted with such trash.

Hardly inspiring confidence as a reporter, Broomfield seems to have a congenital aversion to clarity. Nor does he want to entertain the eye. His preferred shot seems to be from the front seat of an automobile, staring down heat-baked Florida highways. Almost haphazardly, he joins footage from TV newscasts, Wuornos's two trials, and the police video of Wuornos's confession, as well as his own scattered interviews with other principals, such as two spectacularly obtuse book authors. For a Brit, Broomfield is surprisingly inarticulate. Finally gaining access to Wuornos herself, the boy is at a loss for words.

If Errol Morris's *The Thin Blue Line*—an investigation into another botched conviction—was elegant, artful, and overwhelmingly persuasive, *Aileen Wuornos* is clumsy, artless, and exasperating. If Broomfield wants his material to dominate his method, it does.

Testifying at her trial for the first murder, Wuornos seems to make a solid case for self-defense. But the judge (there was no jury) appears biased and her court-appointed attorney inadequate. (These are impressions, since Broomfield hardly presents a coherent picture of the proceedings.) Then, somewhere along the line (chronology is not this picture's strong point), Wuornos becomes a hot story for the tabloid media. The most dramatic, perhaps fatal, consequence is that she's taken up by a pair of local nutcases.

These two dubious characters are the movie's centerpiece. The first, Arlene Pralle, is a batty horse (and wolf) breeder, who decides to adopt Aileen, six years her Junior. A newspaper photo of Wuornos, Pralle says, sent a wave of love through her body, miraculously healing an accident injury. The second protagonist, Pralle's associate, is a jolly, bearded lawyer, Steve Glazer, who becomes Wuornos's attorney, agent, and spiritual adviser. Glazer's intention is not to represent her in a trial but to enter her guilty plea. "I'm sure that she wants to die," he says. To help, he's assured her he'll "sit there with her when they strap her in." (In the privacy of his four-wheel drive, however, Glazer jokes that he ought to advise her à la Woody Allen: "When you get to the chair, don't sit down.") Broomfield includes extensive footage of Glazer singing and accompanying himself.

Initially Pralle and Glazer want $25,000 from Broomfield, but later they settle for $10,000. What Broomfield gets for his cash (we see it changing hands) is Pralle's dotty ramblings: "I read people's eyes and I decided she was not capable of being a serial killer." Soon after offering her revelations, Pralle orders Broomfield off her horse farm.

Subtitling his film "The Selling of a Serial Killer," Broomfield makes it clear that the economics of the sensational is his prime story. Sitting on death row, Wuornos, he lets us see, nearly gets lost in the fun house. Her fate—poignant as well as urgent—deserves someone's undivided attention.

Also reviewed in:
CHICAGO TRIBUNE, 3/25/94, Friday/p. G, John Petrakis
NEW YORK TIMES, 2/4/94, p. C15, Vincent Canby
VARIETY, 12/7/92, p. 73, Derek Elley

AIR UP THERE, THE

A Buena Vista Pictures release of a Hollywood Pictures presentation of an Interscope Communications/Polygram Filmed Entertainment production. *Executive Producer:* Lance Hool and Scott Kroopf. *Producer:* Ted Field, Rosalie Swedlin and Robert W. Cort. *Director:* Paul M. Glaser. *Screenplay:* Max Apple. *Director of Photography:* Dick Pope. *Editor:* Michael E. Polakow. *Music:* David Newman. *Music Editor:* Lise Richardson. *Sound:* David Lee and (music) Tim Boyle. *Sound Editor:* Michael D. Wilhoit. *Casting:* Mali Finn and Donn Finn. *Production Designer:* Roger Hall. *Art Director:* Leith Ridley, Hans van der Zanden and Alicia Keywan. *Set Decorator:* Karen Mary Brookes, Marianne Kaplan and Steve Shewchuk. *Set Dresser:* Shane Bunce and Lulu Archer. *Special Effects:* Martin Malivoire and W.A. Andrew Sculthorp. *Costumes:* Hope Hanafin. *Make-up:* Gabriella Molnar. *Stunt Coordinator:* Gary Jensen and Craig Ginsberg. *Running time:* 108 minutes. *MPAA Rating PG.*

CAST: Kevin Bacon (Jimmy Dolan); Charles Gitonga Maina (Saleh); Yolanda Vazquez (Sister Susan); Winston Ntshona (Urudu); Mabutho "Kid" Sithole (Nyaga); Sean McCann (Ray Fox); Dennis Patrick (Father O'Hara); Ilo Mutombo (Mifumdo); Nigel Miguel (Halawi); Eric

Menyuk (Mark Collins); Keith Gibbs (Buddy Wilson); Miriam Owiti (Beisa); Douglas Leboyare (Ikedo); Francis Mutei (St. George); Gibson Gathu Mbugua (Harimbo); Vusi Kunene (Ntzuko); Connie Chiume (Mrs. Urudu); John Matshikiza (Mingori Mining Company Clerk); Ken Gampu (Itumbo); Fanyana H. Sidumo (Lilo); Peter Khubeke (Mimo); Salathial Maake (Dahwi); Jomo Lewarani (The Bodyguard); John Lesley (Banquet Emcee); Wendell Brereton (St. Joseph's Player #1); Falconer Abraham (St. Joseph's Player #2); Dennis Orina (Ruwala); Danstan Ojoo (Sololo); Peter Kigadi (Opozo 1); Benson Rateng (Opozo 2); Bright Tjatji (Winabi Boy); Ramolao Makhene (Pawn Broker); Frans Matome Matloga (Referee); Lincoln M. Letsoalo (Referee); Michael Cartwright, Nigel Dunkley and Paul Evry (Climbers).

LOS ANGELES TIMES, 1/7/94, Calendar/p. 4, Kevin Thomas

The story of an American college coach's attempt to recruit a taller-than-tall African basketball player, "The Air Up There" may be the first movie to be high concept both literally and metaphorically. But that doesn't mean it's going to make anybody happy.

A feeble and simplistic attempt at an adventure comedy, "Air" is a movie that never should have been let out of development hell. In truth, it probably snuck out, because nothing about it is as well-developed as Charles Gitonga Maina, the 6-foot-10 Kenyan who stars as Saleh, the object of that coach's attention.

The coach is Jimmy Dolan (Kevin Bacon), a hard-driving assistant at mythical St. Joseph's. Once known as "the mouth that scored," Dolan is a former hot-shot college player considered too self-centered to be head coaching material. If you think all that is about to change, you're way ahead of this game.

Determined to work his way out of the doghouse, Dolan gets the cracked idea of going to Kenya to sign up a tower of power "with the hang time of a hot-air balloon" he glimpses in the background of a video about missionaries.

That turns out to be Saleh, an affable young man (pleasantly played by Maina) who would like nothing better than matriculating in the states. However, his father (veteran South African actor Winston Ntshona) has other plans for him at home, and Dolan's slick recruiter's attitude is so obnoxious even a saintly nun (Yolanda Vazquez) breaks down and calls him "a sports pimp." Will the coach have to go home empty-handed? Guess again.

The inspiration, if that is the right word, for "The Air Up There" is the careers of such transplanted-to-the-NBA stars as Nigeria's Hakeem Olajuwon and the Sudan's Manute Bol. Novelist Max Apple got the idea and is credited with the screenplay, though its high percentage of bathroom jokes leads one to suspect that a committee of 10-year-old boys really did the work,

If Apple was the screenwriter, he must have come up with the plot after holing up for the weekend with a gross of videos, for "The Air" (blandly directed by Paul M. Glaser) is jammed with as many narrative clichés as its hour and 46 minutes will allow.

And though the production went to the trouble of shooting in Africa and using Kenya's Samburu tribe as the inspiration for the film's fictional Winabi, its treatment of Africans is so cartoonish it might as well have been shot on some back lot. And of course the real purpose of having Africans in this film at all is to enable a pale face to mature and shine. Some things never do seem to change.

NEW YORK POST, 1/7/94, p. 39, Michael Medved

The only surprise in "The Air Up There" is the movie's stubborn refusal to develop its own premise: the story of a 6-foot-10 African tribesman who's recruited from a remote village to play basketball for an American college.

You keep expecting to see this towering phenom cutting a swath through the NCAA or adjusting to challenges of campus life, but you never do. They must be saving that material for a sequel.

The plot plays itself out almost entirely in Africa where the only real question is whether a determined assistant coach (Kevin Bacon) can persuade the young giant to sign up for an athletic scholarship.

It's hardly the sort of tension that will lead to a dangerous elevation of your heart rate, so screenwriter Max Apple (best known as a novelist and journalist) throws in additional dangers to keep the proceedings mildly diverting.

It turns out that the basketball prospect is no ordinary kid: He is (surprise!) the son of a chief and the future of his people depends on him. That future is menaced by greedy capitalists from a nearby city who want to drive the (fictional) Winabi tribe from its ancient lands in order to mine copper from their hills.

Ultimately, the only way to resolve the dispute is a showdown basketball game, in which the visiting American agrees to coach the barefoot tribesmen in their underdog struggle against the well-drilled bullies from the big town.

As if all this weren't hokey enough there's a soppy subplot about lost soul Kevin Bacon finding himself. He's a former college star with a damaged knee who has never been able to live down his brief moment of glory as a member of a national championship team.

Needless to say, he ultimately overcomes his arrogance and self-pity to discover timeless wisdom in the mystic initiation rites of the Winabi tribe. In other words, he finds true happiness as a Winabi wannabe.

Bacon who has built his entire career out of easygoing competence, displays surprising depth and emotion in this dumb part. He transcends the script and makes us believe in the edgy, embittered, utterly single-minded Jimmy Dolan.

His co-star, Charles Gitonga Maina is a 19-year-old Kenyan who has never acted before but projects the sort of effortless charisma and likability that disarms criticism.

The only aspect of the huge young man's performance that seems to fall (ahem) short is his display of basketball skill.

Along the same lines, the movie's climactic basketball duel offers lots of color and quirkiness, but little of the athletic grace you'd expect from the movie's big set piece.

NEWSDAY, 1/7/94, Part II/p. 62, Jack Mathews

A sportswriter I once worked with at a small newspaper in Southern California nearly lost his job after writing an April Fool's Day column about a 7-foot-4 Eskimo basketball phenom who he said was about to enroll at the local college. The writer forgot to say "April fool!" at the end of his story, and for 24 hours, the town was abuzz with talk of a national championship.

You can't kid around with basketball fans. They take rumors of slam-dunking giants in far-off lands very seriously, especially with such towering African imports as Manute Bol and Hakeem Olajuwon now patrolling the boards in the NBA.

It is that fantasy that inspired 5-foot-4 Rice University professor and basketball superfan Max Apple to write "The Air Up There," a tall tale about a hot-shot college coach who travels into the African bush to recruit a willowy native he saw doing a mid-air ballet in the background of a missionary film shown at a faculty dinner.

Directed by Paul M. Glaser ("The Cutting Edge"), and starring the reliably uninteresting Kevin Bacon, "The Air Up There" is something like a bad April fool's joke itself. Apple's script, the first for the novelist and essayist, is an endless string of movie and basketball clichés, some of them borderline racist.

Watching the film, you'd get the impression that every tribe in Africa (except Pygmies, of course) has a basketball hoop in the middle of its village, and that when the warriors aren't getting painted for some mutilation ritual, they're choosing up sides for a game of half-court.

Charles Gitonga Maina, the 6-10 Kenyan who plays the coveted recruit Saleh, grew up in Nairobi, where basketball is indeed a popular sport and where the success of players like Bol and Olajuwon is celebrated. Maina is obviously a talented player, the product of years of stiff competition. But among the fictional Winabi, who live in a village so remote a bus hasn't been there in 20 years, the message seems to be that if you put a round ball in the hands of a tall black man, he'll jam it.

Still, Maina, whose most natural gift may be his dazzling smile, is the only compelling figure in the movie. Maina, 19, was recruited by the filmmakers for his basketball ability, but there is a calmness to his personality that is genuinely engaging, and a welcome relief to the shrill overacting of Bacon and Yolanda Vazquez, the contentious nun trying to save Saleh from Dolan's corrupting influence.

Saleh doesn't need much help. The purity of his innocence soon smoothes over Dolan's cynical edges, and the question becomes not whether Saleh will return to the United States to save

Dolan's bacon, but whether Dolan, bad knee and all, can help the Winabi five defeat the neighboring Mingori in the pickup game of the century.

The predictability of all this might even be OK if the court sequences were well done. No sport outside gymnastics and figure skating has the fluid beauty of basketball. But Glaser, a former action TV star ("Starsky and Hutch") didn't create a single eloquent image. The game action, with Saleh, Dolan and the Winabi bench making a miraculous fourth quarter rally, is so feebly shot and edited, there is neither grace nor suspense.

Sports movies timed to the seasons have been popular in Hollywood ever since Ron Shelton's baseball hit "Bull Durham." We had two football movies last fall, and this season's second basketball picture, the William Friedkin-directed, Ron Shelton-written "Blue Chip," starring Nick Nolte and real-life pro Shaquille O'Neal as his star, opens next month.

Better director, better writer, better stars. Better wait.

SIGHT AND SOUND, 7/94, p. 35, Louise Gray

Jimmy Dolan's job as assistant basketball coach at St Joseph's College is in the balance after he fails to sign Buddy Wilson to the team. At an alumni dinner, chief coach Ray Fox announces his imminent retirement; Dolan has two weeks to capture some new star players. If he fails, the coaching job will go to Mark Collins. Watching a film of Father O'Hara's missionary work with the Winabi tribe in Kenya, Dolan spots Saleh playing on a makeshift basketball court. Dolan sets out to the remote Winabi district; on the way, he meets Nyaga, owner of the Mingori copper mine, which has its own well-drilled ball team and star player, Mifundo. Halawi, Saleh's elder brother, works for Nyaga as driver and factotum.

On reaching the Winabi, Dolan tries to persuade Saleh's father, Chief Urudu, to allow his son to join St Joe's. Sister Susan, O'Hara's assistant, disapproves of Dolan's mission. Saleh is tempted by Dolan's offer of a basketball scholarship, but he has duties to his tribe as his father's heir. Saleh explains that Nyaga is stealing the Winabi cattle and forcing them off their land; he tells him how Halawi had gone to the mine owner to reason for his tribe and had been subsequently disowned by Urudu. At the wedding of Saleh's sister Beisa, Nyaga's men attack and burn the Winabi village. Urudu visits Nyaga in the town and proposes a bet: a ball game between the Winabi and Mingori. If Nyaga's town wins, he will get the Winabi land. If the Winabi win, Nyaga will leave the tribe in peace.

Dolan begins training a Winabi team, but when point guard St George is injured, Urudu insists that Dolan himself play. He must first undergo Winabi initiation rites. Dolan agrees and the match day arrives. When Dolan is injured by Mifundo, Halawi steps in. The Winabi win within seconds of the final whistle. Back in the US, Saleh steps onto the St Joseph's court for the first game, followed by Dolan, now chief coach.

Although the fictional Winabi territory is a long way from the OK Corral, *The Air Up There* has at heart the structure of a Western. Dolan is the stranger who orchestrates the survival of the Winabi tribe, and although the final shoot-out is held on a basketball court, the goodies and baddies seem clearly delineated.

The Air Up There was written by Max Apple, who as a professor at Rice University presumably has first-hand knowledge of the pressure that colleges face to succeed in the stadium, in addition to recognising that sport provides the United States with their most prevalent cultural ritual. To become the consummate hero, Dolan has to shed the hustling persona of the college coach and recognise that life can be more important than a ball game. However, it is the underlying meaning of ritual that provides Apple's script with a dynamic as gripping as the film's overt action. The real voyage that Dolan makes is not his literal journey to Africa, but his transition from an individual player to a member of a tribe where his actions take place in a larger social context.

His key moment comes near the end of a gruelling initiation ritual which involves physical hardship and skill. Standing on top of a mountain, he throws his championship ring—previously a prized item, not for sale at any price—into the wilderness below. It is an action which acknowledges the cultural consequences that greed—be it his own player-harvesting or Nyaga's expanding commercial operation—can have. The game's prize becomes the survival of Dolan's adopted tribe.

The relationship between sports and race was recently studied in *White Men Can't Jump*, which explored racial stereotypes surrounding basketball. *In The Air Up There*, Western commerce is portrayed as a corrupting influence: Glaser's film does not shirk the disturbing similarity between the way sportsmen and cattle are bought and sold. In his pursuit of profit and worldly success, Nyaga shares characteristics with the unreconstructed Dolan, and it is only the peaceful Winabi who remain untainted. The main thrust of the film lies in its equation between individual and collective duty where team and tribe share the same positions. This is something pertinent to several of the key actors—Zairean Ilo Mutombo and US-born Nigel Miguel (Halawi) were basketball stars at US colleges, while Charles Gitonga Maina holds the Nairobi slam-dunk title, and hopes to follow hundreds of other Africans to the US on a sports scholarship.

In keeping with the knowledge that Western commerce can be seriously disruptive to tribal life, Glaser's film is sensitively made. It was filmed on location primarily in Kenya and South Africa, the semi-nomadic Samburu tribe providing both model and actors for the story's Winabi. Two Samburus (Douglas Leboyare and Jomo Lewarani) gained key roles as Saleh's warrior companions, while elsewhere Glaser utilised Samburu craftsmen and shepherds to complete his portrayal of Winabi culture. The results are arresting, some of the best scenes being those where tribal chanting is intercut with the action of the final basketball game. Added to a first-class soundtrack which includes a healthy dose of African jive and high-life music, *The Air Up There* is a fast and exciting film.

Kevin Bacon fills out Dolan's role well; his transition from the fast-talking hustle of assistant coach is believably managed and his entrance into Winabi society achieved without sentimentality. Well-established actors Winston Ntshona and Mabutho 'Kid' Sithole lend their characters gravity and menace respectively; Maina handles his first acting role with elegance and poise; and Yolanda Vazquez has a strong presence as Sister Susan, the nun who functions as Dolan's challenger.

The Air Up There deserves a wider success than it has so far received at the us box office. Whether or not its secondary effect will be a tribe of starstruck Samburu is an imponderable issue. However, Glaser's handling seems co-operative rather than exploitative, and, if Apple's script produces a greater awareness of the cultural economy of sporting competition, then a process will begin that only starts with this film.

VILLAGE VOICE, 1/18/94, p. 55, Julie Lang

Professor and screenwriter Max Apple says he's "a great basketball fan." He further explains, "I'm 5-4 and white ... I always wanted to be 6-10 and black. The only way to accomplish that is "to dream." In *The Air Up There*, that dream remains a fantasy, a cultural illusion, since all blacks in his film are either mysterious and primal or conniving and opportunistic. Sure, he wants to become one of the brothers, but never completely. After all, if you're black, you'd better stick with basketball (or perhaps bobsledding), and if you're Apple, you can always change your dream.

The Air Up There begins with college basketball assistant coach Jimmy Dolan's (Kevin Bacon) quest to recruit "tower of power" Winabi warrior Saleh (Charles Gitonga Maina), and evolves into a tribal war between the seminomadic Winabis and the beer-drinkin', land-lootin' Mingoris. Of course, there's a twist: Instead of the war being waged on land, it's fought on the basketball court. If the Winabis win, they keep their land and cattle, and Saleh returns with Dolan to the St. Joseph Bulls in the States. If not, the Western-tainted Mingoris get everything.

Because of an injury to the sole Winabi point guard, the only chance for the Winabi team to win is to recruit Dolan (finally, Apple can live out his dream). To become one of them, he must paint his face fierce, wrap red fringes around his legs, slash his stomach, climb cliffs, pummel through thick Kenyan jungle, and sleep in the rain, which makes Dolan cry. (Think "Iron John.")

In this tale of sports bonding, there are the requisite two female characters. One, Sister Susan (Yolanda Vazques), eventually throws off her habit and falls for Dolan. The other, Winabi Beisa (Miriam Owiti), is the basketball player (we're told three times) "with tits." She doesn't speak, but fouls out and is thrown from the rest of the movie because she chucks a basketball into a Mingori's crotch after he cops a feel during the game. Say goodbye to the most interesting character in the film.

In the midst of this Disney fare, Dick Pope's cinematography is stunning. The great blue African sky hangs over and across a thick land alive and pure of anything we know to really be there. Forget CNN's Somalia, Burundi, Rwanda, even Kenya. The audience certainly did, yelpin' and stompin' its approval. Still, sitting in *The Air Up There*, you can forget that hail is pouring into the New York gray air, that the next day the concrete will smear into a brown slush, and that in the winter it is almost impossible to notice anyone's skin color or sex.

Also reviewed in:
CHICAGO TRIBUNE, 1/7/94, Friday/p. I, Mark Caro
NEW YORK TIMES, 1/7/94, p. C16, Janet Maslin
VARIETY, 1/10-16/94, p. 58, Brian Lowry
WASHINGTON POST, 1/7/94, p. B1, David Mills
WASHINGTON POST, 1/7/94, Weekend/p. 34, Desson Howe

AIRHEADS

A Twentieth Century Fox release of an Island World/Robert Simonds production. *Executive Producer:* Todd Baker. *Producer:* Robert Simonds and Mark Burg. *Director:* Michael Lehmann. *Screenplay:* Rich Wilkes. *Director of Photography:* John Schwartzman. *Editor:* Stephen Semel. *Music:* Carter Burwell. *Music Editor:* Michael T. Ryan, Adam Smalley and Steve McCroskey. *Sound:* Douglas Axtell, Russell C. Fager, and (music) Mike Farrow and Scott Ansel. *Sound Editor:* Jerry Ross and Hamilton Sterling. *Casting:* Billy Hopkins and Suzanne Smith. *Production Designer:* David Nichols. *Art Director:* Edward McAvoy. *Set Designer:* Larry Hubbs and Robert Fechtman. *Set Decorator:* Jan Bergstrom and Jerie Kelter. *Set Dresser:* Michael Vojvoda, Glenn "Spanky" Roberts, John Ceniceros, Quent Schierenberg, and Dwain Wilson. *Special Effects:* Dave Kelsey. *Costumes:* Bridget Kelly. *Make-up:* Deborah LaMia Denevar. *Stunt Coordinator:* Ernie Orsatti. *Running time:* 81 minutes. *MPAA Rating:* PG-13.

CAST: Brendan Fraser (Chazz); Steve Buscemi (Rex); Adam Sandler (Pip); Chris Farley (Wilson); Michael McKean (Milo); Judd Nelson (Jimmie Wing); Ernie Hudson (O'Malley); Amy Locane (Kayla); Nina Siemaszko (Suzzi); Marshall Bell (Carl Mace); Reginald E. Cathey (Marcus); David Arquette (Carter); Michael Richards (Doug Beech); Joe Mantegna (Ian); Michelle Hurst (Yvonne); Allen Covert (Cop); Sarah Reinhardt (Secretary); Lexie Bigham and Lydell M. Cheshier (Security Guards); Sam Whipple (Personal Manager); Uri Ryder (Teen); Dana Jackson (Receptionist); Ryan Holihan (Kid); Kurt Loder (Himself); Tiiu Leek (Newswoman); Kurek Ashley and Pablo Alvear (Psycho Rockers); Alejando Quezada (Rocker); Harold Ramis (Chris Moore); China Kantner and Rebecca Donner (Rockers); Vinnie DeRamus (D & D Rocker); Lemmy Von Motorhead (School Newspaper Rocker); Rich Wilkes (Corduroy Rocker); "Stuttering" John Melendez (Masturbating Rocker); John Zarchen and Rennie Laurence (Cops); Zander Lehmann (Tyke); Mike Judge (Radio Voice of Beavis and Butt Head).

LOS ANGELES TIMES, 8/5/94, Calendar/p. 8, Peter Rainer

The L.A. rock 'n' roll scene is ripe for a great comedy. "Airheads," directed by Michael Lehmann and scripted by Rich Wilkes, is far from great. But it sure is ripe. It's bursting with bad ideas, half-good ideas, good and bad actors yelling and mugging. Like a lot of youth comedies, it's frenetic where it should be inspired.

The rock group the Lone Rangers can't get anybody to listen to their demo tape. When Chazz (Brendan Fraser), the group's leader, sneaks into and then gets booted out of the office of a bigshot record producer (Judd Nelson), he cooks up a desperate scheme to invade rebel radio station KPPX and get their demo aired. The Lone Rangers, turning realistic-looking water rifles on the staff, end up taking them hostage. Because the drama is being aired live, the group becomes folk heroes to the kids massed outside the station. Celebrity beckons—so does prison.

The only reason to endure their antics is for the occasional funny cameo performance. Joe Mantegna plays the station's dyspeptic dee-jay, and he's hilarious. He has the haggard, aggravated look of someone who spends his life yowling at total strangers through a microphone. As the program manager, Michael McKean is good enough to remind you of his role as the British rocker in the great mock rockumentary "This Is Spinal Tap" (which he also co-wrote). Chris

Farley, as a cop on the scene, keeps threatening to be funny, but the role doesn't often allow for his explosive talents. (He does have one memorable moment when he intimidates a male rocker by plucking his nipple ring.)

The three Rangers aren't particularly convincing as anything but actors trying to play rock 'n' rollers. Besides Fraser, who is stuck with the "sincere" role—he doesn't want a record contract if it's only based on the group's notoriety—there's Steve Buscemi's Rex, whose ranting wears thin fast, and Adam Sandler's Pip, who seems to be sharing a joke we're not in on. As the plot escalates and turns into a mishmashed comment on how the media turn criminals into celebrities, the whole thing begins to look like "Dog Day Afternoon" for—well—airheads.

Now if only the Lone Rangers had been played by Beavis and Butt-head.

NEW YORK POST, 8/5/94, p. 43, Thelma Adams

"Airheads" is a rock 'n' roll comedy about three unsung musicians with wind between their ears who capture a radio station to get airplay for their demo reel.

Chazz (Brendan Fraser), Rex (Steve Buscemi) and Pip (Adam Sandler) are three stooges in search of the American dream: a chicken in every pot and a rock star in every garage.

The Lone Rangers—it's a running gag that if there are three rangers, they can't be lone—are willing to go to extreme lengths to achieve instant stardom and a chance to be heard by the masses (and score with Heather Locklear).

But there's a catch. In the central Generation X joke, their ambition outstrips their talent. These lovable losers want to be heard, but they haven't a clue what to say.

Rebel Radio's captive deejay, Ian (a loud and tired Joe Mantegna swilling Budweiser and Pepto-Bismol), stumps Chazz when he asks him what he would say to a stadium crowd. "Rock 'n' roll!" the lead singer finally yells, right hand raised in a fist.

The Lone Rangers make Elvis look like Aristotle.

While director Michael Lehmann's "Airheads" doesn't surpass his black comedy "Heathers," it bops from gag to gag, getting laughs without parodying its three stars. Working from first-timer Rick Wilkes' script, Lehmann captures characters from the Hollywood music scene like bugs in a zapper.

Clearly drawn, Fraser ("Encino Man"), Buscemi ("Reservoir Dogs"), and Sandler ("Saturday Night Live"'s Opera Man) are a delightfully silly mix of idealism and vanity, arrested development and a child's capacity for joy, and a stubborn idiocy that bears impossible fruit.

The supporting cast includes comic turns by physical comedian Michael Richards ("Seinfeld"'s Kramer), multi-chinned Chris Farley ("Saturday Night Live"), brat-packer-turned-weasel Judd Nelson, and Michael McKean, co-star and co-writer of that classic rocker comedy "This is Spinal Tap!"

The irony of "Airheads" is that Rebel Radio doesn't welcome rebels. Behind the screaming guitars, the ticking of adding machine tape can be heard.

The hard-rock station the Lone Rangers hijack is a day away from being turned into an EZ listening station where the tag line will be "relax to the mellow sound of the rain."

While the last 20 minutes of "Airheads" winds down from the anarchic highs of the first hour, few comedies this summer have offered such guitar-driven escape and genuine laughs.

NEWSDAY, 8/5/94, Part II/p. B2, John Anderson

There's stupid, and then there's Stooopid; both are dumb, one is art. "Airheads" knows this, and tries very hard, but's really just generic imbecility.

Irresponsible, too. Hey kids! Let's take over a radio station at gunpoint!

Then they'll play our records! And give us a contract so we can join the thoroughly corrupt and tasteless major music industry! Good idea. It works for The Lone Rangers—hunky Chazz (Brendan Fraser), hairy-angry Rex (Steve Buscemi) and dumber-than-a-bag-of-rocks Pip (Adam Sandler)—who throughout the hostage situation they've created with a plastic Uzi full of hot pepper sauce keep talking about what they want from the cops on the outside. When they asked for a football helmet full of cottage cheese, I thought the movie had a chance. But didn't they ever see "Dog Day Afternoon"? Or even "Pump Up the Volume"?

Somebody did. When Chazz starts chanting "Rodney King! Rodney King!" to the crowd outside the besieged station, it's Al Pacino all over again (why was he chanting about Attica, anyway?). And the benevolent spirit of Christian Slater hovers over the scene as the unifying, we-are-the-world power of free airwaves brings the people together in an orgy of good vibrations (whoops, wrong California band).

The Lone Rangers (an oxymoronic joke) have tried using the system, and have been thrown out of every record company and radio station in town. So in a desperate ploy to get veteran rock-jock Ian (Joe Mantegna) to play their tape, they break in and are mistaken for musical terrorists. While the cops and the crowd multiply outside, inside the Rangers clash with the sleazy station manager, Milo (Michael McKean), whose brand of so-called "rebel radio" precludes any good music (translation: anything the Rangers like) from making the airwaves. "If they're so hot, why aren't they burning up the charts?" he asks about one group, to which Rex responds, "Because you won't play them."

Meanwhile, the station's accountant, Doug Beech (Michael Richards, "Seinfeld's" Kramer), has slipped away and spends the movie crawling through the air ducts communicating via cellular phone with a SWAT team commander (Allen Covert) who wants to invade the building while Sgt. O'Malley (Ernie Hudson) tries to keep things calm.

Buscemi (to us, he'll always be Mr. Pink in "Reservoir Dogs") has some inspired moments of lunacy as the volatile bass-playing Rex, but it's that kind of ornery sidekick role. Conversely, Fraser ("With Honors," "School Ties") has to walk the fine line between idol and idiot, no mean feat—not like "SNL's" Sandler, who gets not only the easy moron role, and the good lines, but the girl (Nina Siemaszko).

To its credit, "Airheads" makes some very valid points: that the record industry is run by lawyers and suits with no criteria but the bottom line who force feed the public whatever they want, make their girlfriends into pop stars and bury whatever music doesn't fit their agenda; that radio stations play what the record companies give them, in part so they can have tickets—tickets ordinary fans can't buy—to give away on the air; and that classic rock is a constipated fraud. On the other hand, this is a fairly big-budget movie made by a studio owned by one of the biggest union-busting media magnates in the world, so who's kidding whom?

SIGHT AND SOUND, 11/94, p. 39, Caren Myers

The Lone Rangers, an unsigned Los Angles rock band, are desperate for a record deal. Lead singer Chazz routinely sneaks into the offices of Palatine Records to try to interest music executives in their demo tape, but he is always summarily ejected. When his girlfriend Kayla kicks him out of her apartment, Chazz moves in with Rex, the band's excitable bass player, and his younger brother Pip, the drummer. Then inspiration strikes: they will hold up their favourite radio station, KPPX, and demand that their demo be played over the air.

Armed with realistic-looking water pistols, the intrepid trio break into the station and descend upon Ian, KPPX's star DJ. Ian tries to humour them, but they are interrupted by Milo, the slimy studio head, and their tape is destroyed in a freak accident. Left with no tape and half a dozen hostages, the band begins negotiating with the police. While the law looks for Kayla, who has the only other copy of the tape, The Lone Rangers make friends with their prisoners, unaware that one of the station employees, Beech, is conducting a one-man rescue operation through the air vents. As news of the hostage situation spreads, an enthusiastic crowd gathers outside, and record company executives start making offers.

The police find Kayla and retrieve the tape, but she has a fight with Chazz and smashes the circuit board. Beech ambushes them just as their plastic guns are discovered, inadvertently provoking Chazz with a real gun. When an executive from Palatine infiltrates the station, The Lone Rangers finally sign their contract. Shortly afterwards, their video 'Live and In Prison' is on heavy rotation on MTV. The Lone Rangers start touring in six months—three if they behave.

With his transcendentally vicious debut, *Heathers*, Michael Lehmann barrelled onto the film scene as if he were the hipster progeny of John Waters and Edward Albee. *Heathers* wasn't saying anything—the film had no more emotional depth than an episode of *Beverly Hills 90210*—but the baroque bitching of its teenage characters achieved an usually vivid portrait of emptiness. Then he got sidetracked. If *Meet The Applegates*, in which alien insects impersonate a suburban family, was a puzzling follow-up, the Bruce Willis vehicle *Hudson Hawk* was a flop of near-*Ishtar* proportions. By rights, *Airheads* should have been Lehmann's comeback, but it has fared poorly at the US box office after being shrugged off by the critics. The fact that it is being released after a rather tiring wave of dumb rock-'n'-roller movies can't have helped. Neither can the fact that it sports, in Brendan Fraser, a leading man best known for the unedifying *Encino Man* (*California Man* in the UK).

It's too bad, because *Airheads* is an enjoyable, sweet-natured farce. Lehmann's flair for black comedy may be muzzled here, but at least the film doesn't coast by on pointless parodies of other films. First-time screenwriter Rich Wilkes has a proper grasp of the rock milieu: The Lone Rangers are not very smart, but they have a dim sense of the greater glory of rock which gives their absurd quest internal logic and ultimately a kind of grace. Like hundreds of real bands before them, they honestly believe that playing loud, generic rock music and wearing bandanas constitutes an Important Statement. It's a measure of the believability of the film that when Chazz finally gets his big moment on air, all he has to say is "Rock 'n' Roll!" Wilkes also has an ear for a rock band's self-importance: when Ian asks The Lone Rangers what kind of music they play, they all get defensive about being pigeonholed.

The action, admittedly, is not terribly dynamic. Once our heroes get comfortably ensconced at the radio station, there's really nowhere else for them (or the picture) to go. There are overly theatrical scenes between Chazz and his girlfriend, and a sloppy sub-plot about a militaristic cop, that simply evaporates. But the characters are funny and likeable and the acting is fine—for the double act of rodent-like Steve Buscemi and dazed babe magnet Adam Sandler alone, you don't mind being cooped up with them.

VILLAGE VOICE, 8/9/94, p. 50, Natasha Stovall

When a scheme to get their band's demo tape played on the radio goes haywire, *Airheads*'s upwardly mobile metalheads (Brendan Fraser, Steve Buscemi, and Adam Sandler) take the station hostage—ditching the cheesy playlist to talk shit and play Soundgarden. Great idea—corporate radio sucks—but these guerilla broadcasters are so moronic that when the LAPD arrives on the scene, all the 'heads want to know is, "How did the police know we were here?"

Like, duh. *Airheads* tries to squeeze some laughs out of youth culture quirks and the generation gap, but it all boils down to stupid people doing stupid things in the name of slapstick and rock 'n' roll. Fraser, Buscemi, and Sandler are supposed to be populist counter-culture heroes, I guess, since they continually stick it to the Man and draw a crowd of their *Headbangers Ball* peers to cheer them on. (The Man in *Airheads* is represented by a cornucopia of actors seminal to all media-saturated twentysomethings; *The Breakfast Club*'s Judd Nelson, MTV's Kurt Loder, *Laverne and Shirley* and *Spinal Tap*'s Michael McKean, and two of the four Ghostbusters. Seems that coming of age in the '90s means watching childhood icons reincarnated as authority figures.)

Youth solidarity be damned—the Airheads are so asinine you don't want them as your heroes, or anyone else's. Fraser—in fake tattoos and a wig down to his ass—is particularly irritating, but Rich Wilkes's script is so stuffed with baby boomer clichés and mindlessly rebellious "kids these days," there's no room for a good performance, even if somebody was motivated to give one. Wilkes's take on youth culture is clearly inspired by his couch and his remote control; toilet humor comes in a close third. When offered a record contract as ransom in the 11th hour, Fraser thinks for a second, then wipes his ass with it. Huh-huh, huh-huh, huh-huh. Sucks.

Also reviewed in:
CHICAGO TRIBUNE, 8/5/94, Friday/p. F, Michael Wilmington
NEW YORK TIMES, 8/5/94, p. C10, Janet Maslin
NEW YORKER, 8/22 & 29/94, p. 115, Anthony Lane
VARIETY, 8/1-7/94, p. 44, Leonard Klady
WASHINGTON POST, 8/5/94, p. C5, Richard Harrington
WASHINGTON POST, 8/5/94, Weekend/p. 36, Kevin McManus

ALMA'S RAINBOW

A Paradise Plum presentation of a Crossgrain Pictures/Rhincerous Productions film in association with Channel 4. *Producer:* Ayoka Chenzira, Howard Brickner, and Charles Lane. *Director:* Ayoka Chenzira. *Screenplay:* Ayoka Chenzira. *Editor:* Lillian Benson. *Director of Photography:* Ronald K. Gray. *Music:* Jean-Paul Bourelly. *Choreographer:* Thomas Osha Pinnock. *Casting:* Thomas Osha Pinnock. *Set Designer:* Peggy Dillard Toone. *Costumes:* Sidney Kai Innis. *Running time:* 85 minutes. *MPAA Rating:* Not Rated.

CAST: Kim Weston-Moran (Alma Gold); Victoria Gabriella Platt (Rainbow Gold); Mizan Nunes (Ruby Gold); Lee Dobson (Blue); Isiah Washington IV (Miles); Jennifer Copeland (Babs); Keyonn Sheppard (Pepper); Roger Pickering (Sea Breeze).

NEWSDAY, 6/23/94, Part II/p. B9, John Anderson

Alma Gold (Kim Weston-Moran), smart, attractive and terminally prim, runs a neighborhood beauty shop out of her rambling Brooklyn brownstone, a place adorned with kitschy souvenirs, ancient furniture and undusted memories. It's the kind of home that reflects its owner: Both are caught in a time warp.

Alma's daughter, Rainbow (Victoria Gabriella Platt), on the other hand, is about ready to bust out of her Catholic school uniform. Under a constant maternal barrage of "don'ts"— about boys and sex and pregnancy and boys—she spends her free time developing a hip-hop act with two male friends (one of whom constantly teases her about her lack of physical development) and her early mornings binding her breasts so her mother won't realize just how womanly she is.

Their extraordinary complex relationship sets the arc of "Alma's Rainbow," a low-budget but highly ambitious feature by Ayoka Chenzira that asks whether motherhood means the end of a woman's life. ("Did you stop having fun when you were my age, or older?" Rainbow asks Alma.) And it starts off doing what it should: We don't know anything about Alma and what made her what she is, but we want to. And we will. And we'll see what happens to their troubled relationship when Ruby (Mizan Nunes), Alma's haughty, free-spirited sister, brings her Josephine Baker-inspired self back to Brooklyn and gives her niece the inspiration she needs.

Chenzira, unfortunately, has less than full control of her material. Stylistically, "Alma's Rainbow" is goulash. Psychologically, it's shallow: The mother-daughter dynamic, which has some pretty deep-seated problems, isn't probed satisfactorily. And the director shoots herself in the foot toward the end of the film, with two clumsy sex scenes that are supposed to be epiphanies, but which are, instead, wildly incongruous to the movie's tone and as such seem crude and gratuitous.

The acting, however, is fine. Weston-Moran generates both sympathy and infuriation as a woman whose preoccupation with keeping her daughter "safe" doesn't extend to disease, just pregnancy (as I said, she's a little retro). Platt, who looks like a young Billie Holiday, is too old for the part—her very embarrassing, very public encounter with her first monthly cycle is almost impossible to buy—but she's an accomplished actress. And Nunes provides the saucy complement this household needs.

The men, predictably perhaps, are either goofy or a nuisance. Blue (Lee Dobson), for instance, the handyman with whom Alma will shed clothing, has a wardrobe that could inspire blindness, and his ostentatious gold tooth drives her crazy. But men are superfluous to what "Alma's Rainbow" is about, which is sisterhood, in all its twisted and occasionally destructive permutations. The film may be flawed, but it does have something to say. And it may even know what it's talking about.

VILLAGE VOICE, 8/16/94, p. 50, Ororonke Iodowu

The John Hughes bayou of teen-age films dried up once he abandoned adolescents for the younger audiences of *Home Alone* and *Baby's Day Out*. Flowing in its place, though, are wonderfully diverse tales of how African Americans come of age in America. If you visited the

Boyz N the Hood, or spent a nostalgic summer at *The Inkwell*, then you're ready for *Alma's Rainbow*, the long-missing young black woman's perspective on growing up.

Rainbow Gold (Victoria Gabriella Platt), the tomboyish daughter of Alma (Kim Weston-Moran), is struggling through the angst of puberty. The wall of tension between straightlaced mother and sprightly daughter is colorfully chiseled away by Rainbow's drama queen aunt Ruby (Mizan Nunes), a sexy exotic in the tradition of Josephine Baker. Ruby acts as both a living souvenir of fun for Alma and a catalyst to the blossoming confidence of Rainbow, who we first meet shrouding her breasts in a mummy-like wrap. Instead of a suburban mall, director Ayoka Chenzira's middle-class Harlem canvas has a city park as a focal point—Rainbow and her pals rehearse new dance steps there, and it's where she's introduced to her menses. And in this matriarchal household, our heroine doesn't need a Prince Charming to affirm her sense of loveliness and self-worth. It is Rainbow's eccentric aunt and practical mom who remind her she is beautifully a little of each of them.

Also reviewed in:
NEW YORK TIMES, 6/23/94, p. C5, Stephen Holden
VARIETY, 4/11/94, p. 38, Deborah Young

AMATEUR

A Sony Pictures Classics release of an UGC-Zenith and True Fiction Pictures production in association with Channel Four Films/ American Playhouse Theatrical Films/La Sept Cinéma. *Executive Producer:* Jerome Brownstein, Lindsay Law, Scott Meek, and Yves Marmion. *Producer:* Ted Hope and Hal Hartley. *Director:* Hal Hartley. *Screenplay:* Hal Harley. *Director of Photography:* Michael Spiller. *Editor:* Steven Hamilton. *Music:* Jeff Taylor and Ned Rifle. *Sound:* Jeff Pullman. *Casting:* Billy Hopkins and Suzanne Smith. *Production Designer:* Steve Rosenzweig. *Art Director:* Ginger Tougas. *Set Decorator:* Jennifer Baime and Amy Tapper. *Special Effects:* Drew Jiritano. *Costumes:* Alexandra Welker. *Make-up:* Judy Chin and Marjorie Durand. *Stunt Coordinator:* Phil Neilson. *Running time:* 105 minutes. *MPAA Rating:* R.

CAST: Isabelle Huppert (Isabelle); Martin Donovan (Thomas); Elina Lowensohn (Sofia); Damian Young (Edward); Chuck Montgomery (Jan); David Simonds (Kurt); Pamela Stewart (The Policewoman); Erica Gimpel (The Angry Woman); Jan Leslie Harding (The Waitress); Terry Alexander (Frank, the Cook); Holt McCallany (Usher); Hugh Palmer (Warren); Michael Imperioli (Doorman at Club); Angel Caban (Detective); Emmanuel Xureb (Bartender); Lennie Loftin (Taxi Driver); David Greenspan (George, the Photographer); Adria Tennor (Kid Reading "The Odyssey"); Parker Posey (Girl Squatter); Currie Graham (Video Store Clerk); Jamie Harrold (Pizza Guy); Patricia Scanlon (Young Irate Mother); James McCauley and Benny Nieves (Policemen); David Troup (Guard); Tim Blake Nelson (Young Detective); Marissa Copeland (Sister at Door); Dael Orlandersmith (Mother Superior); Michael Gaston (Sharpshooter); Paul Schulze (Cop Who Shoots Thomas).

LOS ANGELES TIMES, 5/19/95, Calendar/p. 8, Peter Rainer

In "Amateur," writer-director Hal Hartley's usual minimalism edges toward the maximal. The director of such wiggy art-house mood pieces as "The Unbelievable Truth" and "Trust" is trying for an action movie—or, to be more precise, an inaction action movie. But it's still Hartley land on the screen: lots of stranded, blankish characters in desolate decor. Hartley hasn't really changed his stripes, just his tempo.

Hartley has always drawn from a lot of disparate pop influences, from Godard to film noir, but never more so than in "Amateur." Although the film is ostensibly about "redemption" and "exploitation"—this according to the director in interviews—what it's really about is moviemaking as personal style. Hartley turns what might have been a lurid pulp thriller into a freeze-dried art thing. He squeezes all the juice out of pulp.

Martin Donovan, a Hartley regular, plays Thomas, an amnesia victim trying to recover his past, which almost certainly involves sordid cruelties involving Sofia (Elina Lowensohn), a porno actress and prostitute who in turn is hooked up to corporate assassins (Chuck Montgomery and David Simonds). And then there's Thomas' blitzed-out former partner Edward (Damian Young) and Isabelle Huppert's Isabelle, an ex-nun who writes short stories for porno magazines and believes the Virgin Mary has singled her out to redeem Sofia. (She describes herself as a nymphomaniac virgin.)

Hired assassins, drug dealers, shootouts in Grand Central Station, Catholic iconography—Hartley stirs it all up but there's little resonance. The actors are energetically enigmatic and Hartley doesn't encourage them to drop their cool. Everything fits together as a mosaic of freeze-dried pop. And because so much pop these days is overheated, Hartley's restraint at least is bracing. It's just isn't all that wonderful.

NEW YORK POST, 9/29/94, p. 42, Larry Worth

Catholicism takes a beating, much like the sad-sack protagonists of director/writer Hal Hartley's "Amateur," at the New York Film Festival. But the angels still smiled on his new foray into surreal cinema leaving Hartley with his most inspired effort.

The Rubik's Cube plot concerns four losers whose paths are destined to cross over a few days in New York. The quirky quartet is comprised of a nun-turned-pornographer (Isabelle Huppert), a handsome amnesiac (Hartley regular Martin Donovan), a triple-X-rated actress (Elina Lowensohn) and an accountant (Damian Young) who's in for the shock of his life.

The script—part thriller, part comedy, all offbeat—is filled with great dialogue, polished to perfection by actors who deliver it in wonderfully deadpan style. Isabelle Huppert is a particular standout, subtly transforming herself from the Virgin Mary to Mary Magdalene.

Granted, a few running jokes go stale and the finale could be trimmed. But those are minor setbacks to this slick, savvy production. In fact, the only amateurish element is the title.

NEW YORK POST, 4/7/95, p. 44, Thelma Adams

Assumed, switched, confused or missing identities; being the wrong man in the right place, the right man wronged: These dilemmas are the modeling clay of American mysteries and European existential cinema.

Writer/director Hal Hartley combines both in "Amateur," an original comedy about redemption which its star, Isabelle ("Entre Nous") Huppert, describes as a "metaphysical thriller."

In Hartley's Manhattan of empty lofts, cobblestoned back alleys, diners and vast public spaces like Grand Central Terminal, family ties are severed and adults in a child-free world reinvent themselves.

Porn star Sofia (played by Hartley regular Elina Lowensohn with a fallen countess beauty) wants to change her life. She pushes her pornographer husband Thomas (Martin Donovan, star of Hartley's "Trust") out a window and launches a chain of events that confirms the old adage, "Be careful what you wish for, you might just get it.

The brutal Thomas awakes with amnesia. With high cheekbones and big features that don't quite match, Donovan is leading-man material of the Harrison Ford/Kurt Russell school.

Thomas wanders into a diner. In one of many chance encounters, Isabelle (the riveting Huppert) ministers to his head wound and takes him in. Isabelle is in the middle of radical reconstructive surgery on her own life.

A former nun turned porn writer, she camps in the diner, chain-smoking and churning out poetic, non-commercial smut.

With the foresight of a film noir voiceover, she bangs the following phrase into her computer just before Thomas's arrival: "And this man will die ..., and there is nothing any of us can do about it."

Isabelle calls herself a nymphomaniac but confesses to Thomas that she's a virgin. He comments on the irony of this statement and she responds in Hartleys characteristic deadpan humor, "I'm choosey."

The delicate ex-nun in her plain green dress and droopy cardigan and the amnesiac sharpie, reborn as a good guy, are drawn to each other like strangers on Hitchcock's train with an exquisite, unconsummated sexual tension.

Meanwhile, Sofia, believing she has killed Thomas, makes matters worse by trying to blackmail his ex-boss, a European businessman with shady sidelines. She brings a pair of corporate assassins down around their heads.

Thus a story that begins with an attempted murder adds guns, late-model cars, inventive tortures, shootouts, chase scenes and showdowns with the cops—the stuff of pulp—into an intimate tragi-comedy about shedding one's old skin and growing a new one.

Quirky supporting players surround Huppert, Donovan and Lowensohn. Officer Melville (Pamela Stewart) is a cop on the verge of a nervous breakdown as she deals with lost-identity cases.

Dressed-for-success MBA assassins Jan (Chuck Montgomery) and Kurt (David Simonds) bitch about their cellular phones while contemplating the torture of wild-haired, emu-like Edward (Damian Young).

"We were accountants together," Edward pleads to Jan. "You were a good accountant." Starlet Parker Posey (the coming "Party Girl") steals a scene as a squatter who discovers Edward's body and, unfazed, jumps up to catch a curtain fluttering in the breeze with a Holly Golightly brightness.

Hartleys intelligent, modern characters lack families but they have goals. They want to be movers and shakers. "My aspiration was defamatory journalism," says the editor of "Pillow Talk," a porn glossy. "Things happen. We drift away from our vocation."

We are all amateurs in creating ourselves; we lack the experience of past lives (except for Shirley MacLaine). We have to get it right in this life, even if that means reinventing ourselves and believing in the potential of redemption, of change.

As a filmmaker, Hartley gets it right. He's no "Amateur."

NEWSDAY, 4/7/95, Part II/p. 85, John Anderson

Naivete has always been a sophisticated gag for Hal Hartley. In his earlier features—"The Unbelievable Truth," "Trust," "Simple Men"—no one was ever quite what he or she appeared to be, and certainly never as innocent.

But the babes in the woods who populate "Amateur"—Hartley's "action" film and his most broadly funny are precisely what we think they are. They're just not what *they* think they are. Which raises the question of what we think Hartley is.

The filmmaker has long been accused of making European films in America. In "Amateur," he moves the action from his old hometown of Lindenhurst to Manhattan, renders the city all but unrecognizable and populates it with Europeans. You think Hartley's been playing Godard? OK, here's Godard in your eye.

Hartley wants to both celebrate and spoof whatever "European" is supposed to be. So he starts in a café (all right, a downtown diner). We find Isabelle (the marvelous French actress Isabelle Huppert) composing, out loud, one of the stories she writes for porn magazines. In the Paris of the cinema, one can sit, write and declaim all day without buying anything; in New York, employees and patrons start screaming at her. "But I bought a muffin this morning," she protests.

Into this group wanders Thomas (Hartley stalwart Martin Donovan), who's clearly disturbed and bleeding from a head wound. He has no memory of who he is; Isabelle adopts him.

What we learn about them amounts to one joke about moral purity coupling with another, and delivered in Hartley's typical deadpan. Isabelle, an ex-nun, thinks she's a nymphomaniac. (Thomas: "Have you ever had sex?" Isabelle: "No." Thomas: "How can you be a nymphomaniac and never had sex?" Isabelle: "I'm very choosy.") Thomas, the wounded saint, turns out to have a past that's extremely ugly. His *wife* turns out to be Sofia (Elina Lowensohn), the "world's most notorious porn actress," who, in trying to change her life, pushed Thomas out a window.

"Amateur" somersaults New Wave veneration (of Hollywood) with American emulation (of Godard, among others), while deflating both. Sofia, Thomas and Isabelle become embroiled in a blackmail scheme that backfires, and are pursued by the vicious Jan (Chuck Montgomery) on behalf of the unseen Mr. Jacques (are these guys mobsters or beauticians?), while Hartley turns everybody inside out: Isabelle, the supposed innocent, is the model of jaded ennui; Sofia, whom

Thomas turned into a prostitute at age 12, is naive and guileless. Thomas, given a wonderful portrayal by Donovan, has been transformed by his head wound from a brute into a noble, if confused, innocent. Redemption through blood? That the whole thing ends in a convent is a pretty broad stroke. And yet, amid all the burlesque, the same old Hartley sneaks through: in the deadpan non sequiturs, the *nouvelle vague* rhythms and the process of astonished discovery. "I don't know what I'm sorry for, but I'm sorry," Thomas says. "That's gotta mean something, right?" It means, in "Amateur," that to be innocent you seek redemption even when you don't need it.

SIGHT AND SOUND, 1/95, p. 42, Philip Kemp

A man, Thomas, lies in a New York alley, apparently dead. A dark-haired young woman peers at the body, then runs away. Thomas revives and staggers into a coffee shop where he meets Isabelle, an ex-nun trying to make a living writing pornography. Since Thomas is suffering from amnesia, Isabelle takes him home and looks after him. Talking in his sleep, he threatens someone called Sofia.

Sofia, the dark-haired woman, contacts Edward, a shady accountant, and tells him she has killed Thomas. He was her husband, a vicious crook who forced her into prostitution and porno films, and was trying to blackmail Jacques, the powerful Dutch businessman running Thomas's gang. Edward suggests she take refuge in an empty house he knows of in Porchester, upstate New York. But Sofia unwisely phones Jacques, who sends two heavies, Jan and Kurt, after her. She evades them, but they capture Edward and torture him.

Deducing that Sofia is Sofia Ludens, international porn-movie queen, Thomas and Isabelle find her apartment, where Isabelle dresses in Sofia's clothes. They are about to make love when Jan and Kurt show up and they hide. Sofia arrives and is tied up by the hitmen; while Jan goes to phone Jacques, Kurt prepares to torture her. Thomas and Isabelle emerge, force Kurt out of the window to his death, and escape with Sofia in Jan's car, making for Porchester.

Edward, deranged by torture, tries desperately to contact Sofia. His violent behaviour gets him arrested, but he shoots a cop and steals a police car. At Porchester, Sofia, still mistrustful of Thomas, refuses to tell him who she is. Edward arrives; a stand-off between him and Thomas is interrupted by the arrival of Jan, who shoots Sofia. Edward kills Jan, and they drive the wounded Sofia to Isabelle's old convent which is nearby. There, Sofia tells Isabelle about Thomas's past, but Isabelle is undeterred. The police, trailing Edward, arrive and surround the convent, and when Thomas opens the gates they shoot him dead.

A recent piece in *Film Comment* described *Amateur* as an "underwhelmer". It's not clear how far this was meant as a putdown, since underwhelming is Hal Hartley's preferred mode. The melodramatic content of his plots is constantly undercut by deadpan playing, coolly distanced photography and dialogue with its inverted-commas quizzically raised. His own summary of the film as "an action thriller ... with one flat tyre" catches the mood; we're a million miles from the hi-tech multiple pile-ups that pass for action movies these days. *Amateur*, with its fated, philosophising characters, evokes a subtler style of thriller altogether, the post-war French school of doomy existentialist gangster-*mélos* such as *Le Doulos* or *Touchez pas au grisbi* — or even, given its ironic, half-mocking slant on its noirish trappings, Truffaut's *Tirez sur le pianiste*.

Derivations apart, though, the relatively dense plotting gives *Amateur* an edge over Hartley's last feature, *Simple Men*, which ran out of plot halfway through and thereafter bogged down in its own whimsical talkiness. The present film uses dialogue to salt the action, not as a substitute for it—with the paradoxical result that we get closer to the characters, whereas those of *Simple Men* tended to retreat from us behind a fog of verbiage. At the climax, with Thomas gunned down on the brink of accepting his new, gentler persona and Isabelle's love, there's even a hint of genuine tragic feeling—something of a fresh departure in Hartley's work.

Not that fans of his trademark quirky cameos and off-the-wall dialogue need feel short-changed. "Jan, we go way back," pleads Edward as the heavies prepare to torture him, "we were accountants together." As always with Hartley, aspirations and career choices furnish some of his best lines: the pornographer for whom Isabelle works muses, "I never intended this. My ambition was defamatory journalism." Indeed it's a running gag in the film that most of the people seem hopelessly unsuited to what they do, from Isabelle Huppert's inept porno-writer to the soft-hearted cop (an appealingly tremulous performance from Pamela Stewart) disastrously determined to find good in everyone.

Hence, no doubt, the title—although Hartley disarmingly claims it also refers to the way he feels as a filmmaker. But in fact *Amateur* is his most assured performance so far, skilfully hijacking the conventions of a main-stream genre to explore his personal angles and preoccupations. His characters always have a tentative, fingertip attitude, as though testing out reality to see if it will bear their weight—a quality for which Huppert's withdrawn, ethereal air is ideally suited, blending seamlessly in alongside Hartley regulars like Martin Donovan and Elina Lowensohn. *Simple Men* aroused fears that the freshness of *Trust* and *The Unbelievable Truth* might be turning into a reflex action, offbeat-by-numbers. But this, it seems, was only a temporary hiatus: *Amateur* finds Hartley transporting his idiosyncratic vision unimpaired into a whole new field.

Also reviewed in:
CHICAGO TRIBUNE, 4/28/95, Friday/p. L, Michael Wilmington
NEW REPUBLIC, 4/24/95, p. 31, Stanley Kauffmann
NEW YORK TIMES, 4/7/95, p. C21, Caryn James
NEW YORKER, 4/17/95, p. 110, Terrence Rafferty
VARIETY, 5/23-29/94, p. 56, Todd McCarthy

ANCHORESS

An International Film Circuit release in association with Upstate Films of a British Film Institue/Corsan Productions coproduction in association with the Ministry of the Flemish Community/BRTN/ASLK-CGER/National Loterij/Channel Four Television. *Executive Producer:* Angela Topping. *Producer:* Paul Breuls and Ben Gibson. *Director:* Chris Newby. *Screenplay:* Judith Stanley-Smith and Christine Watkins. *Director of Photography:* Michel Baudour. *Editor:* Brand Thumin. *Sound:* Andre Patrouillie. *Sound Editor*: Martin Evans. *Production Designer:* Niek Kortekaas. *Set Dresser:* Marsha Roddy and Mai Gulbrandsen. *Special Effects:* Harry Wiessenhaan and Rob Wiessenhaan. *Costumes:* Annie Symons. *Running time:* 108 minutes. *MPAA Rating:* Not Rated.

CAST: Natalie Morse (Christine Carpenter); Eugene Bervoets (The Reeve); Toyah Willcox (Pauline Carpenter); Christopher Eccleston (Priest); Peter Postlethwaite (William Carpenter); Michael Pas (Drover); Brenda Bertin (Meg Carpenter); Annette Badland (Mary); Veronica Quilligan (Daisy); Julie T. Wallace (Bertha); Ann Way (Alice); François Beukelaers (Bishop); Jan Decleir (Mason); David Boyce (Ragged Martin); Micke de Groote (Ragged Martin's Wife); Erik Konstantyn (Carter); Guy Pion (Innkeeper); Peter van Ashbroeck (Dyer); Grant Oatley (Oswald); Timothy Barlow (Old Pilgrim); Hugo Harold Harrison (Priest/s Boy); Corinne Michel and Nancy Michel (Pilgrims).

NEWSDAY, 11/9/94, Part II/p. B9, John Anderson

Like exorcists and Torquemada, the anchorite tradition is something the Catholic church has tended to bury for the last few centuries. Small wonder: Walled off, or "enclosed" for a lifetime of devotion, the medieval anchorite was as clear a renunciation of a church-run world as he was a manifestation of religious passion. When the entombed was a female or "anchoress," the ambiguity was deeper. Burdened with second-class sexuality, the anchoress, far from within her tiny sepulcher, achieved a social status almost equal to that of a man.

Status did not equal posterity, of course. The only reason we know about Christine Carpenter (played by Natalie Morse), the fact-based subject of Chris Newby's exhilarating and highly speculative debut feature, "Anchoress," is that she was a renegade. According to letters written in the 1320s by the bishop of Winchester—and discovered by screenwriter Judith Stanley-Smith on the walls of a church in Shere, England—Carpenter, who was probably illiterate, bolted from her cell and caused the clerics no end of irritation. Her incorrigibility made her immortal.

The daughter of a midwife and general-purpose earth mother (Toyah Willcox), Christine is a visionary of uncertain inspiration. Her devotion to Mary leads her to steal the apples of the reeve of the manor (Eugene Bervoets) and arrange them in radiating patterns at the foot of the Virgin's new statue. The reeve is incensed, but the priest (Christopher Eccleston) sees in her devotion an opportunity for personal advantage and control—an anchoress, after all, was not only a link to heaven, but a tourist attraction as well. He convinces her to be walled into a small room attached to the church. Knowing that both men covet her, and that each is unscrupulous, Christine opts for enclosure.

There she becomes a local oracle, dispensing cryptic advice, and pursues her own muse. She discovers the pleasures of her own body. She embroiders, not picture stories of the Virgin, but a history of local women. She revels in the Earth. "The Virgin's house," she says, "is in the ground."

The precocious Newby knows that to recreate the 14th Century, one doesn't adorn, one strips away. His sets are open fens and rampaging skies and the iconic faces of people mired in dung and dust. Like the medieval conceits of Bergman or Herzog, the visual power of "Anchoress" lies in the stark cruelty of the physical world Newby creates, and the fear it provokes. Because the characters have less than us, they are our superiors; the nothingness of their world, and the primitive nature of their spirituality, heightens their physicality. And, they make us doubt how far we've really come.

In taking on the church, especially the 14th Century edition, Newby and his screenwriters—Stanley-Smith and Christine Watkins—are shooting fish in a barrel. Their joke, if we can call it that, is about how little actually separates man-made church teaching from female-centered animism, how the priest can use the terror of the supernatural to enforce his will and how redemption may be relative. But given that the church was a barometer of European intellectual life, and its male-centrism, they might have made the priest and reeve less stock villains and more agents of alienation—of man from God, of man from the earth.

But this is why Newby says more with the camera than he does with the script. Shot in stunning black and white, "Anchoress" is always inspiring rapture in nature, and finding the miraculous in the ordinary. "Anchoress" is less effective as a polemic than as a celebration of earthly glory. And in seeking out the source of that glory, is coincidentally religious.

SIGHT AND SOUND, 10/93, p. 38, Geoffrey Macnab

England, the fourteenth century. Christine, a young peasant woman, finds herself increasingly drawn to a new statue of the Virgin Mary recently installed in the village church. Along with her younger sister, she gathers apples to lay at the statue's feet, and spends every spare moment worshipping at the Virgin's shrine. The two dominant figures in the village are both interested in her: the priest, a rigorous, self-satisfied theologian, wants her as a mistress, while the reeve, responsible for administering the Manor's affairs, is keen to marry her. One day, while Christine is out in the fields, the reeve proposes, but she turns him down, much to her mother's displeasure.

The villagers frown on Christine's obsession with the Virgin, and don't believe her when she claims to have had visions of the Our Lady. But the priest, won over by the intensity of her belief, suggests she should immure herself in the church walls and become an anchoress, to live side by side with the statue she adores. Despite her family's disapproval, Christine agrees and is walled up in a small dark cell. After several months, she is established within the community as a religious woman; members of the village visit her, speaking to her through a chink in the wall, and asking for her advice and blessing. She is under constant supervision from the priest, but her own fervent visions of the Virgin often conflict with his beliefs.

Christine's mother Pauline—the village herbalist and doctor—has scant respect for the priest, whom she holds directly responsible for her daughter's incarceration. When she delivers the priest's lover of a still-born child, he decides to get even with her. First, he manages to persuade Pauline's dim-witted husband that she "lay" with a goat. Then he whips the villagers into a frenzy, accusing her of being a witch. Pursued by a lynch mob, Pauline hides in a well, but when she falls into the water, the priest refuses to allow anybody to help her, saying that as a sorceress she will surely float; Pauline drowns. Meanwhile, Christine has managed to dig herself out of her cell, and sneaks off with her childhood friend, the drover, to hide in the countryside.

Hearing of her escape, the priest demands she be put back in her hermitage. But the reeve, now married to Christine's younger sister, insists she be executed. Christine, disguised, heads off to town to seek the Bishop's blessing for her return to the outside world. The reeve and the priest, whose rivalry threatens to spill into bloodshed, also visit the Cathedral. While they await an audience, Christine rushes the Bishop's dais and begs to be exempted from her vows. The Bishop is apoplectic with rage, and his men try to recapture the escaped anchoress. Christine manages to escape through a trap door in the floor of the cathedral into the bowels of the earth. She wanders away through a succession of beautiful caves with a rapt expression on her face.

A low-budget British-Belgian co-production, *Anchoress* at least manages the delicate feat of depicting medieval England without resorting to 'olde worlde' heritage cliché or succumbing to codpiece comedy. Like Tarkovsky's *Andrei Rublev*—by now, surely the touchstone for films set in the Middle Ages—it is shot in austere black and white, with a constant emphasis on rain, wind and mud which lends its landscapes a raw, elemental aspect. Costumes are appropriately grey and rumpled; apparently they were churned around in a cement mixer until they had just the right, crinkled feel. Even the production design verges on the rancid: soured buttermilk was used to give the buildings a suitable air of pale decrepitude.

This is a rigorous little fable, based on true accounts of the so-called Anchoress of Shere, a fourteenth-century carpenter's daughter who had visions of the Virgin Mary while working out in the fields and decided, as contemporary records put it, "to vow herself solemnly to continence and perpetual chastity and to let herself be shut up in a narrow place in the Parish Church."

There wouldn't appear to be much mileage in a film which confines its leading character to a tiny cell, but as Bresson showed in *A Man Escaped*, it is perfectly possible to dramatize solitude. Anyway, writers Christine Watkins and Judith Stanley-Smith have broadened the scope of the story. *Anchoress* may be an introspective meditation on religious faith, but it is also concerned with the dynamics of medieval village life, and in particular with the stranglehold exercised by the twin patriarchal institutions of Church and Manor. Christine's decision to immure herself from the world is political as well as spiritual. As the production notes observe, "the celibate anchoress was endowed with considerable status and was judged to be almost as valuable as a man." She was given a smattering of religious education and a right to self-expression. Had she stayed working in the fields, all she could have looked forward to was marriage and child-rearing.

If only in terms of its actors' physiognomies, the film is shrewdly cast. Among the denizens of the village are a mad zealot priest, with pudding-bowl haircut and blazing stare, a dead ringer for the similarly obsessive Antonin Artaud in Dreyer's *Joan of Arc*; a bald-headed reeve who dresses always in black; the Anchoress herself, a beautiful, lustrous-eyed virgin visionary; and various hoaded, craggy-featured peasants who could have stumbled out of a Breughel painting. Striking though these figures are, it's hard to avoid the suspicion *Anchoress* would have worked better as a silent movie, where their faces could have been scrutinized in rapt, leisurely close-up.

Unfortunately, director Chris Newby's eye for images is infinitely sharper than his ear for dialogue. He seems beholden to his cinematographer. Shots are held for too long, and narrative momentum is often lost. If characters speak, it almost seems to violate the stark mood created by the virtuoso camera work. Sound editing is on the eccentric side: whenever it rains, the noise is deafening. The minutest little reverberation is amplified. Given that he has a story to tell, Newby's fondness for poetic symbolism is only fitfully effective. In one misconceived scene, as the angry villagers hunt the anchoress's mother down, believing her to be a witch, the camera focuses for an inordinately long time on a bucket of water balanced precariously on a footbridge. When the villagers cross the bridge, the water ripples and the bucket threatens to topple. What might have seemed an exciting, Tarkovsky-like flourish is so ponderously handled and so self-conscious it merely grates.

Even if its formal elements don't quite coalesce, there is much in the film to savour. Just as the anchoress reacts to the ennui of imprisonment by sewing dramatic embroideries which represent her visions , the film-makers overcome the constrictions placed on them by such an intractable tale by reaching for as many startling images as possible. Whether it be a trapped pigeon fluttering its wings as a motif for Christine's imprisonment; or the scene where she digs herself out of her cell and her fingers sprout from the ground like tiny tendrils; or the ludicrously comic moment where her mother seems about to make love to a goat; or the final sequence, where

Christine escapes into a vast, glistening catacomb, the picture remains arresting to look at, however frequently it runs into a narrative cul-de-sac.

VILLAGE VOICE, 11/15/94, p. 67, Amy Taubin

Based on a true story (or at least an elliptical exchange of letters), Chris Newby's *Anchoress* is about a 14th-century ecstatic visionary who becomes (in the film, if not in real life) an underground outlaw.

The most attractive girl in her English village, Christine Carpenter is a pawn in the struggle between the patriarchal powers of church and state. The sadistic Reeve (the village steward) desires her for a wife; the corrupt village priest wants to make use of her religious leanings for his own greater glory. Christine has had visions of the Virgin Mary. The priest encourages her to become an anchoress—to be walled up forever in a tiny stone cell within the chapel of Our Lady.

With seeming effortlessness, *Anchoress* suggests modern psychological readings of motives and desires. The adolescent Christine, in rebellion against her coarse, cynical mother, is attracted to the Virgin because she is everything her mother is not. The Virgin is her refuge not only from her mother but also the sexual advances of the Reeve. As for Christine's mother: because she understands the misogyny on which patriarchal power is based, she can't keep her anger at the priest, the Reeve, and her idiot husband under wraps. And in turn, because she sees through them, the men seek to destroy her.

At first, Christine's life is richer walled in her cell than when she was free. Through A tiny window she can contemplate the statue of her beloved virgin. Another window opens onto the outside world. Supplicants stream to the window to offer gifts and ask advice. The priest, however, who believes that women are easy prey for the devil (which doesn't stop him from fucking around with the village women), chastises Christine when he finds her spontaneously touching the people who come to her window. But not only does Christine refuse to keep the outside world at arm's length, she insists that the Virgin wear red robes, and embroiders altar cloths with the faces of the village women rather than scenes from the lives of the saints. In revenge, the priest denounces her mother as a witch.

Shot in tinted black and white, Anchoress focuses on the glorious intricacy of the natural world, suggesting that Christine's vision is more pantheistic than Catholic. Natalie Morse is luminous as Christine; she avoids the narcissist trap into which actors portraying religious mystics invariably—and perhaps correctly—fall. If Anchoress is less than fully satisfying, it's because it falls between the cracks—it's neither a fully ecstatic vision nor a thorough secular analysis. Nevertheless, the modern implication of the film is quite clear: Misogyny is so deeply woven into the foundation of the church as to make it beyond repair.

Also reviewed in:
CHICAGO TRIBUNE, 5/12/95, Friday/p. L, Michael Wilmington
NEW YORK TIMES, 11/9/94, p. C12, Caryn James
VARIETY, 5/17/93, p. 96, Lisa Nesselson
WASHINGTON POST, 4/14/95, p. D6, Hal Hinson

... AND GOD SPOKE

A Live Entertainment release of a Brookwood Entertainment production. *Producer:* Mark Rothman and Richard Raddon. *Director:* Arthur Borman. *Screenplay:* Gregory S. Malins and Michael Curtis. *Based on a story by:* Arthur Borman and Mark Borman. *Director of Photography:* Lee Daniel. *Editor:* Wendy Stanzler. *Music:* John Masarri. *Sound:* Brian Tracy. *Art Director:* Joe Tintfass. *Running time:* 83 minutes. *MPAA Rating:* R.

CAST: R. C. Bates (God); Anna B. Choi (Claudia); Andy Dick (Abel); Lou Ferrigno (Cain); Fred Kaz (Noah); Eve Plumb (Mrs. Noah); Stephen Rappaport (Marvin Handelman); Michael Riley (Clive Walton); Soupy Sales (Moses) and Daniel Tisman (Chip Greenfield).

LOS ANGELES TIMES, 9/23/94, Calendar/p. 15, Kevin Thomas

A hilarious "mockumentary" in the tradition of "This is Spinal Tap," "... And God Spoke" follows a pair of Hollywood schlockmeisters every trouble-plagued step of the way in their attempt to film the Bible, no less, on a low budget. Don't they remember when John Huston tried to do it?

Anyway, Michael Riley's director Clive Walton and Stephen Rappaport's producer Marvin Handleman have managed, as a team, to turn out 11 pictures in 15 years, including such unforgettable gems as "Dial S for Sex" and "Nude Ninjas," all of which are glimpsed in delicious clips. Somehow they've gotten a studio to give them enough money to spark their delusions of grandeur, and now, basking in the constant attention of a documentarian's camera, they've become a pair of comically pretentious auteurs, explaining how they managed to insert social significance even into "Nude Ninjas."

Not surprisingly, Brando turns down the role of God, but Clive and Marvin take every setback with the determined optimism of an Ed Wood. The only trouble is that there seems to be nothing but setbacks—a Noah's Ark too wide to go through a sound stage door, an Eve who never let on about that tattoo until the cameras roll and, finally, in the name of product placement, a Moses who carries a six-pack of Coke along with the Ten Commandments.

A prize-winning UCLA cinema alumnus and a production assistant on several major studio films, Borman, making his feature debut, clearly knows the ins and outs of how movies are made, which makes all the more convincing his depiction of all the wrong ways of going about it. This aura of authenticity serves only to fuel the laughter: Satire this film may be, but its exaggerations, as outrageous as they may seem, are really not that far from reality. After all, the late screenwriter Paddy Chayefsky insisted that everything in "Network" was inspired by actual incidents: surely, everything that happens in "... And God Spoke" has occurred at one time or another.

In the large and marvelous cast up pops three good-humored guest stars: Lou Ferrigno as Cain (to skinny Andy Dick's kvetching Abel), Eve Plumb as Mrs. Noah and, best of all, Soupy Sales as Moses. Sales' moments on screen have got to be among the funniest of the year. As dumb and foolish as Clive and Marvin seem to be, Riley and Rappaport make you root for them as the odds keep escalating against their chances for success. Indeed, you start wondering just how Borman and his co-writers are going to wrap up "... And God Spoke," only to discover they've saved their best joke for last.

NEW YORK POST, 9/23/94, p. 46, Thelma Adams

Brando isn't biting, so the casting agent selects an aging acid rocker for the central role of God. Eve has a serpent tattooed from her neck to her navel, Adam is a nudist, Jesus has a messiah complex, Noah dislikes animals, and Cain (played by incredible hulk Lou Ferrigno) squashes Abel like a bug.

In Arthur Borman's silly mockumentary about the making of a biblical epic, " ... And God Spoke," the fictional producer (Stephen Rappaport) spiels: " ... If you're going to do a movie based on a book, that's the book to do." The Bible's a best seller with a built-in audience in the billions—who cares if he never read it himself.

"God wrote it through me," the screenwriter says of the script. Of course, it's hard to cram the book of books into a feature, so a few things have been dropped—like Revelation, Deuteronomy and Job. Jesus walks on water but, when the production goes over budget, the messiah is cut to a bit part.

Eve Plumb, who played middle daughter Jan in "The Brady Bunch" has a walk-on in the thankless role of Noah's wife. The Post's own Michael Medved turns up to plant his seal of disapproval, describing the finished product as "scraping the bottom of the barrel."

Borman, working with his brother Mark Borman and Richard Raddon, has fashioned a funny, production-assistant's-eye-view of the perils and pleasures of moviemaking. If it's not as consistently funny as it could have been, it does have one priceless bit.

Zany TV dino Soupy Sales—who claims he has been popped in the face by more than 19,000 pies in his 40-year career—hits the set to play the Charlton Heston role, Moses.

Spouting shaggy one-liners and sporting an even shaggier beard Sales is the movie's best entertainer, a feat that's nothing short of miraculous.

NEWSDAY, 9/23/94, Part II/p. B7, John Anderson

Eight apostles lurch into a rowboat for the big walking-on-water scene and the director is beside himself. Eight apostles?!! That's not right. Is it? Wasn't it 10 apostles. Let's roll ...

The making of "... And God Spoke"—"the greatest nondenominational Bible story ever told" and the world's worst movie—is the fictional subject of " ... And God Spoke," a ragged, frequently esoteric but consistently witty comedy by Arthur Borman, in which nothing is ever left alone, no one knows what they're doing and the creative process is a hideous thing to behold.

It's one of the delicious depravities of the movie business when "making of" movies turn out better than their subjects. And the "mockumentary"—such as this year's "Fear of a Black Hat," or its own progenitor, "This is Spinal Tap"—takes the whole process a step beyond.

The movie-within-a-movie premise of " ... And God Spoke" takes it farther still: a fictional documentary wrapped around a fictional epic being made by the most ill-equipped filmmaking team in the history of motion pictures. There's incompetent director Clive Walton (Michael Riley) and oleaginous producer Marvin Handleman (Stephen Rappaport), whose filmography already includes "Nude Ninja," "Alpha Deatha-Dekappa" and "The Airport" (not to be confused with that other movie). They set out to make a movie based on the Bible—"one of the most beautiful of all the religious books," as Clive explains solemnly. And, of course, they don't have to buy rights to the story, and get an automatic target audience of 4 billion.

The unseen, unnamed "documentary maker" goes about his business with a cold eye, gathering bizarre interviews with the screenwriter ("God wrote through me," he says), the cast and the crew: the caterer who likes to serve theme food—rabbit, for instance, on the set of "Fatal Attraction." The obtuse cinematographer (Michael Saad) who proudly shows us the light meter he got from Sven Nykvist ("When he saw my film, he told me, 'You need this more than I do'"). Elsewhere, God (R.C, Bates) pontificates about Led Zeppelin; Adam is an exhibitionist; Eve has a full-body tattoo. The money boys are nervous. And Clive and Marvin keep talking about passion and vision.

Riley and Rappaport play Clive and Marvin just right, as talentless con men who've been faking it so long they've forgotten they're pulling a scam. Hence, the cameo appearances—Soupy Sales as Moses (who, in keeping with the movie's tone, plugs his real-life sons' music career), onetime "Hulk" Lou Ferrigno, former "Brady Bunch" star Eve Plumb and movie critic Michael Medved—become send-ups within a send-up. One is never sure who is and isn't aware of what's going on, or whether they know they're being ridiculed. It's cruel, but it's funny. And it lifts " ... And God Spoke" out of the realm of mere satire and into a post-modern category all its own.

VILLAGE VOICE, 9/27/94, p. 66, Natasha Stovall

"Art! Art! Art!" shrieks the director, defending his cinematic vision against the crass commercialism of his producer—who screams back "Money! Money! Money!" to explain why Moses is carrying a six-pack of Coca-Cola along with the Ten Commandments. In mockumentary fashion, *...And God Spoke* follows the archetypical Hollywood duo—fast-talking, cheap-suited producer Marv (Stephen Rappaport) and napkin-twisting, visionary director Clive (Michael Riley)—as they film a mishap-ridden Bible epic. The disasters pile up—dead animals on Noah's Ark, no money, a fireproof burning bush—and Clive and Marv gradually lose faith, eventually pinning all their art and commerce hopes on Moses, played by Soupy Sales.

Irreverent caricatures, dexterous one-liners, and bizarrely blasphemous juxtapositions make up *... And God Spoke*'s sharpest moments, and between Hollywood and the Bible, director Arthur Borman should have enough material for a *Nashville*-size epic. Casting God is a bucket of chuckles: an improbably coiffed agent reels off the possibilities, "Brando, Philip Michael Thomas, Potsy from *Happy Days*," but Marv and Clive end up with R. C. Bates, a bearded hippie-papa who waxes psychedelic over Led Zeppelin memories and proudly displays his Betty Page tattoos. Alas, *... And God Spoke* doesn't have the speedball momentum that splits sides wide open in the wickedest parodies, but it does have the power of hilarious heresy on its side. So rarely seen at the multiplex, blasphemy is its own reward.

Also reviewed in:
NEW YORK TIMES, 9/23/94, p. C10, Caryn James
VARIETY, 10/11/93, p. 72, Emanuel Levy

ANDRE

A Paramount Pictures release of a Kushner-Locke production. *Executive Producer:* Peter Locke and Donald Kushner. *Producer:* Annette Handley and Adam Shapiro. *Director:* George Miller. *Screenplay:* Dana Baratta. *Based on the book "A Seal Called Andre" by:* Harry Goodridge and Lew Dietz. *Director of Photography:* Thomas Burstyn. *Editor:* Harry Hitner and Patrick Kennedy. *Music:* Bruce Rowland. *Music Editor:* Stan Jones, Carl Zittrer and Mark Heyes. *Sound:* Michael McGee and (music) Robin Grey. *Sound Editor:* G. Michael Graham. *Casting:* Annette Benson and Lindsay Walker. *Production Designer:* William Elliot. *Art Director:* Sheila Haley. *Set Decorator:* Barry Kemp. *Set Dresser:* Chuck Robinson and Gordon A. Clapp. *Special Effects:* Bill Orr. *Costumes:* Maya Mani. *Make-up:* Jacky Wilkinson, Beverly Benjamin, and Donna Spahn. *Stunt Coordinator:* Danny Virtue. *Running time:* 94 minutes. *MPAA Rating:* PG.

CAST: Keith Carradine (Harry Whitney); Tina Majorino (Toni Whitney); Chelsea Field (Thalice Whitney); Aidan Pendleton (Paula Whitney); Shane Meier (Steve Whitney); Keith Szarabajka (Billy Baker); Joshua Jackson (Mark Baker); Shirley Broderick (Mrs. McCann); Andrea Libman (Mary May); Jay Brazeau (Griff Armstrong); Bill Dow (Ellwyn); Joy Coghill (Betsy); Stephen Dimpoulos (Dan Snow); Frank C. Turner (John Miller); Kristian Ayre (Gerald); Gregory Smith (Bobby); Ric Reid (Henry White); Duncan Fraser (Jack Adams); Gary Jones (Lance Tindall); Teryl Rothery (Jennifer File); Douglas Newell (Lou).

LOS ANGELES TIMES, 8/17/94, Calendar/p. 1, Kevin Thomas

"Andre" is as irresistible as the adorable baby seal from which it takes its title—and could prove a worthy successor to "Free Willy." It is the quintessential family film: appealing to all ages, insulting to the intelligence of none, and going out of its way to avoid an aura of contrivance. Like all good straightforward movies, everything that happens grows out of the characters and nature of the people involved. What's more, these people seem unusually real for the genre—even the good guys aren't perfect. That "Andre," which begins in the summer of 1962, is based on a real story surely has to help.

When Harry Whitney (Keith Carradine), harbor master for picturesque Rockport, Me., and his younger daughter, Toni (Tina Majorino), encounter a freshly orphaned baby seal with great big dark eyes and a perplexed, scared expression, what can they do but try to nurse it back to health? Through trial and error they succeed. In no time Andre, as he is named by Toni, becomes part of the family. But the father and daughter's relationship with Andre does not stop there, for Andre becomes a performer of remarkable intelligence and skill, and finally such a tourist attraction, he's invited to appear on "The Ed Sullivan Show."

Andre's vibrant, larger-than-life presence has to have an impact on the Whitneys in particular and Rockport in general, and that's the heart of the matter. Adapted by Dana Baratta from a book by Lew Dietz and the late Harry Goodridge—the Goodridges are the real-life family who took in the actual Andre—the film counterpoints Andre's eerily anthropomorphic high jinks with a serious consideration of the possibilities and limitations of relationships between humans and animals.

On an everyday level, the Whitneys discover that if Andre brings joy, he has plenty of potential for generating grief as well. One suspects that Baratta has dabbled in a bit of dramatic license, but if so, it's all to the good, for the film's moments of adventure and danger develop from credible situations.

Right away the family dog is put off by Andre, who exerts his territorial imperative with as much ease as he wins most hearts. Harry's older, teen-age daughter, Paula (Aidan Pendleton), probably already chafing at the close bond between Toni and their father, eventually comes to feel, not without some justification, that he cares more for the seal than for her.

Because Harry's a laid-back guy to start with, his growing fascination with studying Andre's intellectual capacity not only jeopardizes his family life but finally his job. In particular, Harry incites the rapidly escalating enmity of Billy (Keith Szarabajka), a hard-drinking, struggling fisherman and a single father barely able to provide for his son (Joshua Jackson), who is fast becoming Paula's boyfriend. An honest Yankee, Billy admits forthrightly that he envies Harry for his decent-paying job; his inviting, mellow old home; his attractive wife (Chelsea Field), as strong as she is good-humored, and, to top it off, the newfound celebrity Andre has brought Harry.

Animals and children, especially one as beguiling as 9-year-old Majorino, are notorious scene-stealers, but Carradine really does hold his own. That's thanks to George Miller's astute direction (he's the "Man From Snowy River" Miller, not the "Mad Max" one, though both are Australian), Carradine's own charisma and talent, and a very well-written role. Indeed, the linchpin of the entire film is Harry's rock-solid marriage with Field's Thalice, whose capacity for understanding is matched by her forthrightness with her husband and children, which include Shane Meier as her lively son Steve.

Tory, a 10-year-old sea lion that performs at a California theme park, and his trainer Suzanne Fortier, deserve no end of credit for making Andre such a charmer. Although the film ends on a note of finality, it's hard to believe that we've seen the last of Andre.

NEW YORK POST, 8/17/94, p. 37, Michael Medved

The big problem with "Andre" is that the entire project falls flat whenever its charismatic star waddles off camera.

This dominating talent, a 10-year-old sea lion named Tory, even demonstrates his dramatic range by successfully impersonating a member of another species; the title character is a harbor seal who lived off the coast of Maine, but the animal actor is a California sea lion—easier to train, and with greater land-based mobility on his lower end.

In any event, this cunning critter is a joy to watch—expressive, intelligent, adorable and amazingly responsive to his human co-stars. Unfortunately, those co-stars are such drab performers in such contrived situations that the long sequences in which the animal fails to appear make us miss him even more than they do.

The movie is based on the true story of an orphaned newborn seal who's picked up by a kindly harbor master (Keith Carradine) in 1962, Daddy and his youngest daughter (played by 9-year-old Tina Marjorino, who's so sensationally good in "Corrina, Corrina") nurse the bruised beast back to health, name him Andre, raise him as a member of the family and teach him amusing tricks that make him a celebrity in the town of Rockport.

Nevertheless, the frozen waters at wintertime represent enough of a danger that his adopted family places him in a Boston aquarium. The plan is that he'll be turned loose in the spring to join other seals in the wild, but Andre confounds the experts and swims several hundred miles to return to his family in Maine.

It's a touching little tale, but to stretch it into a full-length feature film the movie makers introduce all sorts of unconvincing subplots.

The dumbest of these involves an angry fisherman (Keith Szabarajka) so consumed by jealousy of Carradine's job as harbor master that he repeatedly tries to slaughter the seal.

Casting is also a problem. Carradine looks decidedly uncomfortable in the father-knows-best role. And Chelsea Field, who plays his long-suffering spouse, is dreadfully wrong as a rural New England housewife in 1962.

The settings are similarly unauthentic: synthetic-looking reconstructions placed on the Pacific coast near Vancouver and bearing little resemblance to small towns in Maine.

None of this will keep little ones from enjoying the picture, or prevent parents from relishing those too brief moments when Tory the Sea Lion turns up on screen. But "Andre" remains the sort of manipulative project that gives family filmmaking a bad name. It's not that it's sticky-sweet, but it feels insincere, and hardly merits a seal of approval.

NEWSDAY, 8/17/94, Part II/p. B7, John Anderson

If Andre were a kid, he'd be sent to his room. He defies authority, watches too much television, and responds to any command with rude noises. He's a brat. But he's also a seal, so he gets away with it.

And because he does, kids will probably like "Andre," the story of a Rockport, Maine, family and the seal who came to dinner.

Parents may find the whole thing predictable and manipulative—"Free Willy" with whiskers—but there's nothing here that will either send them screaming into the lobby, or cause hyperglycemia. But there's also little to recommend it, other than the performance by Tina Majorino, the bright little actress who plays Toni Whitney, the human centerpiece of this decidedly aquatic adventure. Toni, though very sweet, is kind of a reject; kids at school set her up for cruel gags, and she spends a lot of time alone. She needs a friend. And when Andre comes along, she has one.

This is well-traveled territory, of course: The slightly askew child, finding a sense of self-worth through an animal. It's the Lassie story, the Flicka story; when the animal turns the family around, it's "Beethoven" redux. When the community becomes involved, the film draws on everything from "Gentle Ben" to Jack London's "White Fang." Add to this the inevitable question of returning Andre to the wild, and the references are endless.

"Andre," which is based on the popular book "A Seal Called Andre," recalls all these in some way, and wraps them up in quilted domestic warmth. Toni's dad, Harry (Keith Carradine, with more than a touch of Will Rogers), is more concerned with animals than in his job of harbormaster—in a community of fishermen, who by nature abhor seals. Her mom, Thalice (Chelsea Field), is a good-natured New England wife in Capri pants and mohair who indulges her husband's and daughter's fascination with animals; their household includes ducks and goats as well as a sister, Paula (Aidan Pendleton), and a brother, Steve (Shane Meier). Andre is the catalyst for everyone's personal crises, and then teaches everyone a lesson.

He also teaches the town of Rockport, whose resident grump is Billy Baker (Keith Szarabajka), a bitter, foul-tempered widower who's really more envious of Harry's life than he is angered by the presence of the seal. But he gets his young son, Mark (Joshua Jackson), who's romancing Paula, involved in his vendetta, and this leads to the climactic crisis, and a general catharsis.

Director George Miller ("The Man From Snowy River," "The Neverending Story II") keeps things moving too quickly for the characters to properly develop, or for many of their actions to make sense. But it's probably a good technique for keeping younger children interested. For adults, there's the question of time, place and plot to ponder: An unwanted black orphan arrives in a lily-white New England town in 1961, and turns everything upside down. Is "Andre" a big, wet metaphor? I don't think so. Not with a sound track that includes Shelley Fabares singing "Johnny Angel."

SIGHT AND SOUND, 3/95, p. 34, Jo Comino

Rockport Maine 1962. Seven-year-old Toni Whitney lives with her parents, her teenage sister and brother, and an assortment of stray animals in an old weatherboard house overlooking the sea. Toni is a loner, the butt of practical jokes at school. Her father Harry is harbour master of the small fishing town but he devotes more attention to his menagerie. Local fishermen (especially Billy Baker) attribute their poor catches to his negligence.

Harry finds an orphaned seal pup and, with Toni's assistance, nurses it back to health. As he grows up, the seal, named Andre, shares boisterously in Toni's activities, boosting her popularity at school. Harry encourages Andre to swim but the sight of a dead seal floating out at sea dissuades him from returning the pup to the wild. Blaming seals for the damage to his nets, a drunken Billy attacks Andre. By intervening, Harry misses the Liberty Pageant in which his older daughter, Paula, has a starring role. Thus she too begins to resent Andre.

As winter sets in, it is time for Andre to migrate south, but Harry fears the seal will not be able to fend for himself and so builds him an indoor bath. Andre pines in confinement, escaping only to return, a little the worse for wear, in the spring. His fame spreads and tourists flock to Rockport. Paula and Mark, Billy's son, decide to get rid of him. They take him out to sea but Paula prevents Mark from shooting him. Toni sees them and gives chase in her dinghy. As a ferocious storm brews, Harry and Billy put aside their differences and set off to rescue Toni. She is about to founder on rocks when Andre tows her to safety.

Andre is then taken away by the Marine Mammal Protection Agency while Toni is consoled by his new keeper. Harry lands a job with the agency and Billy takes his place as harbour master. In spring, Toni travels to Boston to release Andre into the sea. As reports of sightings come in, the inhabitants of Rockport gather to welcome Andre after an astounding 250-mile journey home. A pattern is established whereby Andre winters in the aquarium and swims back to his adoptive family for the summer.

A canny blend of ingredients ensures that this animal feature should appeal to a broad audience. For small children there's the spectacle of wild animals made accessible, and enough anthropomorphism for gags (Andre posing in Aloha shirt and sunglasses, Andre interacting with Lassie on the television screen), Sentimentality is kept at bay by Andre's blowing raspberries. For older kids there's the hint of a teen romance between Toni's sister Paula and Billy Baker's son Mark. In Billy Baker the story has a boorish, bearded villain who can be requisitioned for male bonding. Finally, for the benefit of adults, the film supplies a healthy dollop of early 60s retro by including some of the more exuberant golden oldies of the era.

Predictably enough for a film of this nature, the human family looms large and comes clean cut. Toni, who narrates the story, wields an uncomplicated androgynous charm that is hard to resist. It is perhaps significant that when we first see her she is attempting to perform a marriage ceremony for two fully costumed pigeons, confusing male with female. As far as gender specifics and adolescent traumas are concerned, it is the teenagers who must redress the balance. Thalice, the highly attractive mother, comes across as a domestic paragon who finds time for knocking out her own work on a typewriter. As a superior being, she's probably just too busy to intervene. Harry, the father, is implicitly caring but flawed; too preoccupied with his animal charges to take heed of what's going on. Billy Baker is the perfect foil, a snarling single parent with the spectres of divorce, drink and domestic violence hanging round him, yet somehow in tune. It is he who castigates Harry for his ideal family and home, thus building self-criticism like a safety valve into the body of the film.

Andre is based on a true story. Given that it strives successfully to please, it seems ironic that matters of authenticity have run the production into controversy. Apparently Andre is not played by a seal but by a sea-lion—a Californian one at that. Nevertheless there is little disharmony in the fictional balance between nature and civilization. On the one hand, there is the mysterious world of seals; on the other, the ties that bind Andre to the Whitney family and Rockport—a latter-day Garden of Eden set apart in time and location from the ravages of commercialism. This is a film which does not baulk at hedging its bets.

Also reviewed in:
NEW YORK TIMES, 8/17/94, p. C9, Janet Maslin
VARIETY, 8/15-21/94, p. 44, Steven Gaydos
WASHINGTON POST, 8/17/94, p. B1, Hal Hinson
WASHINGTON POST, 8/19/94, Weekend/p. 42, Desson Howe

ANGELS IN THE OUTFIELD

A Walt Disney Pictures release in association with Caravan Pictures. *Executive Producer:* Mary Stutman. *Producer:* Irby Smith, Joe Roth, and Roger Birnbaum. *Director:* William Dear. *Screenplay (based on the 1951 film "Angels in the Outfield):* Dorothy Kingsley, George Wells, and Holly Goldberg Sloan. *Director of Photography:* Matthew F. Leonetti. *Editor:* Bruce Green. *Music:* Randy Edelman. *Music Editor:* Joanie Diener. *Sound:* Willie Burton and (music) Dennis Sands. *Sound Editor:* John A. Larsen. *Casting:* Pam Dixon Mickelson. *Production Designer:* Dennis Washington. *Art Director:* Thomas T. Targownik. *Set Decorator:* John Anderson. *Set Dresser:* Don Watson. *Special Effects:* Frank W. Tarantino and Jan H. Aaris. *Costumes:* Rosanna Norton. *Make-up:* Scott H. Eddo and Diane Hammond. *Stunt Coordinator:* Rocky Capella. *Running time:* 105 min utes. *MPAA Rating:* PG.

CAST: Danny Glover (George Knox); Brenda Fricker (Maggie Nelson); Tony Danza (Mel Clark); Christopher Lloyd (Al the Angel); Ben Johnson (Hank Murphy); Jay O. Sanders (Ranch Wilder); Joseph Gordon-Levitt (Roger); Milton Davis, Jr. (J.P.); Taylor Negron (David Montagne); Tony Longo (Triscuitt Messmer); Neal McDonough (Whitt Bass); Stoney Jackson (Ray Mitchell); Adrien Brody (Danny Hemmerling); Tim Conlon (Wally); Matthew McConaughey (Ben Williams); Israel Juarbe (Jose Martinez); Albert Alexander Garcia (Pablo Garcia); Dermot Mulroney (Roger's Father); Robert Clohessy (Frank Gates); Connie Craig (Carolyn); Jonathan Proby (Miguel); Michael Halton (Hairy Man); Mark Conlon (Photographer); Danny Walcoff (Marvin); James C. King (Home Plate Umpire); Tony Reitano (Singing Umpire); Diane Amos (Woman Next to J. P.); Christopher Leon DiBiase (Teenager); Robert Stuart Reed (Guard); Ruth Beckford (Judge); Victoria Skerritt (Social Worker); Devon Dear (National Anthem Singer); O. B. Babbs (Angles Player/Mapel); Mitchell Page (Angels Player/Abascal); Mark Cole (Angels Player/Norton); Chuck Dorsett (Usher); Carney Lansford (Kesey); Pamela West (Ms. Ange); Oliver Dear (Rookie Angel); Lionel Douglass (Brother Angel); Bundy Chanock (Umpire); John Howard Swain (First Base Umpire); Marc Magdaleno (Home Plate Umpire #2); Ron Roggé (Angels Coach); Steven Meredith (Toronto Player); Bill Dear (Toronto Manager).

LOS ANGELES TIMES, 7/15/94, Calendar/p. 7, Peter Rainer

The premise of "Angels in the Outfield" is that children—because they are children—tell the truth. Unlike their elders, kids walk among us as the pure-in-heart. When they tell you they see angels, you better believe it.

Motherless angel-gazer Roger (Joseph Gordon-Levitt) is a ward of the state. His father (Dermot Mulroney), leather-jacketed and grubby-looking, tells his boy at the start of the film that "we'll be a family again when the Angels win the pennant," and zooms off on his motorcycle, It's a kiss-off—the California Angels are in dead-last place.

But then Roger is visited by Al the Angel (Christopher Lloyd) in the ballpark during a typically bumbling Angels performance and before long, the team is rising to first place under the stewardship of a bevy of grinning, winged guardians. But only Roger can see them.

J.P., Roger's best buddy, can't. (He's played by that little charmer Milton Davis Jr., who stared down Shaquille O'Neal in a Pepsi commercial.) But J.P. believes his friend—he, too, is orphaned. The film is about how the Angels gruff, obscenity-spewing manager, George Knox (Danny Glover), also comes to believe. He's purified by his bond with the boys.

The sap in this movie rises almost as high as the Angels. It's a special kind of kiddie sentimentality: fantastical and self-congratulatory. Children are allowed the ability to see the magical in the everyday and then work their wisdom on the unbelieving adults in their world, And they do it all in the name of love. Roger's special vision, after all, comes from his prayers for a family.

Baseball movies have been getting preachier and more peewee-like in recent years: consider "The Sandlot," "Rookie of the Year," and, just a few weeks ago, "Little Big League." "Angels in the Outfield," loosely remade from a 1951 GM film where the angels were all off-screen, is the drippiest (and the goofiest) of the bunch. It's a Disney-fied morality play complete with corn and sniffles. Roger may be able to see angels, but he's not particularly wowed by his gift. He's too blandly virtuous to get really excited about anything.

The real kids in this film are the adults—the players, managers and sportscasters. They're the ones who show some temper, some spirit. Just about all the funny bits in the movie involve their antics on and off the field: The catcher (Tony Longo) gorges on junk food and looks and sounds like Curly from the Three Stooges; one of the pitchers (Neal McDonough) is a bundle of tics and feints, the teams PR director (Taylor Negron) is continually squirted with mustard and glopped with nacho cheese by the two tykes in his charge. (Of course, the goody-goodies Roger and J.P. don't do it on purpose.) Ranch Wilder (Jay O. Sanders), who was once George's nemesis on the playing field, is the big-jawed cartoon meanie who announces the Angels radio broadcasts. He breaks the potentially embarrassing story that George's winning streak is angel-inspired. (The press conference scene in which George and his teammates stand up for the right to believe in miracles isn't exactly up there with the Scopes trial from "Inherit the Wind," although it's played just about as straight.)

Director William Dear and screenwriters Dorothy Kingsley, George Wells and Holly Goldberg Sloan muster most of their energies for the funny, nutball jaunts on the playing field. As the kids' ward, Brenda Fricker, doing her best to squelch her Irish accent, is fine in a serious mode, and so is Tony Danza as an over-the-hill hurler. But, for the most part, "Angels in the Outfield" is tolerable when it's at its loopiest.

The quick, zoomy shots of the slapstick angels dipping their big bright golden wings are funny in an original way. These moments are probably what the adults in the audience will take away from the film. And it's probably what kids will take away from it too—along with the squirted mustard and the baseline tantrums. They'll blot out the soppy moralizing. After all, kids know they don't always tell the truth, even if Hollywood doesn't.

NEW YORK POST, 7/15/94, p. 39, Michael Medved

A sad-eyed 11-year-old baseball fanatic (Joseph Gordon-Levitt), who's been dumped by his widower father in a foster home with some other hard-luck kids, offers a bedtime prayer to the Great Cosmic Umpire in the sky.

"I'd really like a family," he sighs. "But my dad says that won't happen until the Angels win the pennant. So maybe you could help them win a little?"

If this setup strikes you as so insufferably sticky-sweet that it presents a serious risk of tooth decay, then you'd better steer clear of "Angels in the Outfield."

If, on the other hand, you're soft-hearted (or soft-headed) enough to fall for such industrial strength sentimentality, then you can join in enjoying this endearing, uplifting combination of bathos and baseball.

One of the reasons this picture works as well as it does is the persuasive and heartfelt starring performance by Danny Glover as the embittered, short-tempered manager of the California Angels.

He gradually comes to recognize a supernatural dimension in the miraculous transformation of his team of ill-assorted losers, and he learns to rely on the little boy who's the only one who can see the winged seraphs in glittering white robes (commanded by an appropriately odd, other-worldly Christopher Lloyd) who make timely ballpark appearances to assist the more prosaic-clad Angels of the American League West.

Though it's co-produced by a baseball specialist (Irby Smith) who previously brought "Major League" and "Rookie of the Year" to the screen this new contender lacks the big-game authenticity of other recent offerings like "Little Big League."

Obviously, realism isn't your top priority when you're showing radiant angels lifting outfielders high into the air to make impossible catches, or adding English to feeble pitches from an over-the-hill hurler making a desperate comeback attempt (Tony Danza in a surprisingly affecting performance).

Nevertheless, there's no excuse for some of the film's more obvious errors, like focusing on the down-to-the-wire battle for the division championship between the California Angels and the Chicago White Sox—even though the two teams no longer play in the same division.

Meanwhile, the Heavenly Division angels create additional problems: In the original (and delightful) 1951 version of the story the audience never saw them, leaving some doubt as to the true nature of the supernatural visions that the kid (a little girl 40 years ago) insisted she saw.

In one of the few false moves in this otherwise capable remake, director William Dear (who previously created the similarly charming "Harry and the Hendersons") felt the need to take advantage of whiz-bang, up-to-date special effects, thereby giving his film an unnecessary literalism.

For the most part, however, Dear's warmth and wit keep the whole enterprise flying, without a trace of campiness or condescension even in all the constructive messages the film sends to kids in the audience—anti-cursing (the heavenly messengers can't stand it), anti-lying, anti-smoking, anti-racism, anti-cynicism.

The underlying theme ("You gotta believe!") relates to the incontrovertible truth that it's always easier to acknowledge a just and benign God when your favorite team happens to be winning.

This profound maxim might also help to explain the fact that several of the more memorable recent baseball movies ("The Natural," "Field of Dreams") feature such prominent supernatural and religious elements.

"Angels in the Outfield" may not be in their league, but it's still a high-flying crowdpleaser that provides more than enough fun (and faith) to take wing at the mid-summer box office.

NEWSDAY, 7/15/94, Part II/p. B7, John Anderson

As Tom Hanks once said, there is no crying in baseball. *No crying in baseball.* Baseball movies, however, are a whole other ballgame. From "Pride of the Yankees" through "Field of Dreams" and sliding right into "A League of Their Own," a liberal use of wet sentiment has usually made the baseball film the moral equivalent of a spitball.

"Angels in the Outfield" is not exactly a remake of the 1951 Clarence Brown fantasy—in which angels were summoned by a young fan to help her struggling big-league team—but it more than upholds the tradition. Swinging for the emotional seats, director William Dear and his screenwriters take few chances. In the original, you never saw the angels; this time you do, and sometimes wish you didn't (the special-effects department needed a leash). And the girl of the original has transmutated into a boy named Roger (Joseph Gordon-Levitt). But otherwise things are pretty predictable, and predictably sentimental.

The fix was in, of course. Baseball as a film metaphor is always about familial bonds (unlike its cousin, the western, which is primarily about individuality). And the yearnings it portrays—for father, for family, for a pennant—are universal and easily manipulated.

Roger, who would be even more of a tool for tears if young Gordon-Levitt could act, has already lost his mother and is being dumped by his tattooed, chain-smoking, biker father (Dermot Mulroney) at a foster home run by the kindly Maggie Nelson (Brenda Fricker). "When will we be a family again?" Roger asks plaintively, as Dad guns the Harley. "When the Angels win the pennant," he's told.

Dad's no dope: The team in question has been in the basement longer than the pipes. The California Angels slip, slide, collide and never fail to embarrass their manager, the cranky but lovable George Knox (Danny Glover), while maintaining their status as the '90s version of the Senators, a la "Damn Yankees." Knox, who's come over from the successful Reds to lead this gang of incompetents owned by Gene Autry-clone Hank Murphy (played by western vet Ben Johnson), is thoroughly frustrated, to the point where he fights with one of his pitchers—on the mound, during a game. His status is shaky, his temper is short, and he's desperate enough to believe Roger when he says angels are helping his team.

Led by the supercilious Al (Christopher Lloyd), who materializes in a bubble, a drink cup or anywhere else the oppressive special-effects team wants to put him, the angels don't just help the team swing the bat or pitch: If a long ball is questionable, Lloyd moves the foul pole. Opposing players are sent stumbling across the diamond in such ridiculous fashion that one Angel is able to accomplish the seldom-seen infield home run. Divine intervention has seldom been so blatant, nor the suspension of disbelief so abused.

The film does have the talents of Fricker and Glover to shore it up. Affecting an American accent, Flicker is delightfully warm; Glover, for all his bluster, can put his arm around a kid without making you wince. They're assisted by Tony Danza, who does a kind of Norman Desmond as the washed-up former Reds pitcher Mel Clark ("I know you. You used to be Mel Clark.") who takes the mound for that decisive game, with the Angels one game out of first place, and the inevitable question pending: Can they do it on their own? Mel gets into trouble early. He loses his stuff. The team falls behind, the Angels respond with a couple of brilliant, semi-miraculous plays. A hit. A bunt. A slide, and it comes down to one pitch ... and ... and ...

Somewhere in this favored land, the sun is shining bright. The band is playing somewhere; somewhere hearts are light. That place, of course, is the wonderful world of Disney, where they're already counting the money from this one—which, after the fat lady has sung and gone, is basically a .200 hitter in a league that's having a bad season.

SIGHT AND SOUND, 7/95, p. 38, Amy Friedman

Baseball fans Roger and J.P. live in Maggie Nelson's short-term foster home and support the last place team, the Angels. Roger's father announces he is going to make Roger a ward of court, telling Roger sarcastically that they'll be a family again when the Angels win the division pennant.

Angels' manager George Knox watches his team lose their 14th consecutive game, brawls with his own pitcher, and slugs a reporter. Roger prays for God to help the Angels win.

At the next game, angels assist with miraculous plays. One of them, Al, explains to Roger that only he can see them. The Angels win. Shy J.P. wins a photo with George, but Roger stands in, telling George that angels are helping the team now. George delivers Roger's picture and questions Roger about the angels. He explains that he prayed for them. George seats Roger and J.P. by the dugout the next day. They agree Roger will flap his arms to signal if he sees angels. The angels return and the Angels win again. George decides Roger and J.P. will attend all home games and confer on the phone when they play away.

Roger sees an angel with injured pitcher Mel Clark, so George takes him off the reserve list. Mel pitches a no-hit game. To reward Roger and J.P., George plays baseball with them and their friends. The winning Angels are now two games from a division title. On the day of the first playoff game, Roger and Maggie have to attend family court. Roger is made a ward of court and his father says goodbye to him in the courtroom. Roger misses the game and the Angels lose. J.P. inadvertently tells radio commentator Ranch Wilder about the angels. Maggie explains to Roger that now he can be adopted permanently by a family. The newspaper carries a front page story about Roger and the angels. Owner Hank Murphy threatens to fire George if he doesn't renounce his belief in the angels at a press conference. George speaks instead of the importance of faith and Hank reinstates him as manager.

At the final playoffs, Al explains to Roger that the angels aren't coming because championships have to be won alone. In the last inning the Angels lead by one run. Roger gives the signal for an angel, although he doesn't really see one. J.P. the team, and finally the entire stadium stand and flap their arms. Mel pitches, the batter hits, and Mel catches the ball for an out. The Angels win the pennant. Back at Maggie's, George tells Roger and J.P. he has applied to adopt them both.

The dazzling sun breaking through clouds in a cobalt sky over a baseball diamond: it's the perfect American scene, the vista James Earl Jones evokes as Terence Mann in *Field of Dreams* when he speaks of the people who will come to the game, "Innocent as children... to sit in their shirt sleeves on a perfect afternoon". It's the perfect backdrop for the titles of this Disney baseball fantasy which chews over the same conflation of baseball, pan-spiritual faith and the afterlife. "Roger," asks J. P. as they cycle past the stadium, "Do you believe in heaven?" You could cut seamlessly to the long-dead John Kinsella cosmically reunited with his son for a final, reconciling game of catch, answering, "It's the place dreams come true."

In this remake of Clarence Brown's 1951 film *Angels in the Outfield*, Roger's world is simplified by a basic Manichaean aesthetic. His dissolute biker father is first glimpsed through a haze of cigarette smoke, wearing black leather and a dark spiky goatee. Al the Angel, a gurning, grinning Christopher Lloyd, wears white and beams incessantly, speaking in parental epigrams: "Keep your nose clean and your eyes open!" The California Angels are a goofy cartoon team; the credits list a number of baseball advisers, and we get to see a lot of quirky comic playing both bad and good, but these players are all rubbery gestures and irreverence, cheeks bulging with gum or mouths spitting huge streams of tobacco. The zooming camera exaggerates their appeal as likeable misfits.

Danny Glover's George Knox initially fills the screen in bug-eyed, flush-faced fits of rage; as the angels release his team from defeat, the cartoon angles gradually ease up as well. The 1951 Knox was a tyrant; the put-upon Glover has more dignity, less spurious torment. A running gag has Roger and J.P surrounded by a widening sea of Angels baseball merchandise. Considering that J.P. is played by seven-year-old Milton Davis Jnr, who achieved international fame telling basketball superstar Shaquille O'Neal not to even think about stealing his cola, the film seems sure of its critique of the commodification of sport. But when the sell-out crowd pours into the stadium for the payoff game wearing wings and silver halos that light up and spin, the film loses sight of its own marketing.

Once the heavenly angels arrive there's never much doubt that the last place Angels will soon rise up the league. But the faith required to see these desperate losers succeed remains a convenient, all-inclusive humanitarianism. Baseball movies have developed their own mystic tradition which, how ever non-denominational, offers miracles to winners and little solace to losers. When Roger addresses his prayer to a God who could be male or female, concluding

"Amen, a woman too" he is thus applying the same baggy faith the aggressive, hard Knox professes at the press conference: "I do believe there are times in life when something stronger, higher or maybe spiritual is with you." Stronger, higher, *and* able to splinter a baseball bat to smithereens when smashing a home run for the chosen few.

TIME, 8/1/94, p. 58, Richard Shickel

[*Angels in the Outfield* was reviewed jointly with *The Client*; see Schickel's review of that film.]

VILLAGE VOICE, 8/2/94, p. 50, Tom Kertes

Disney's reasons for remaking the 1951 *Angels in the Outfield*—no more than a pleasant little time-passer anyway—remain shrouded in heavenly mystery. After all, mush should at least be *original* mush. As it is, even the usually can't-miss combination of well-shot baseball scenes, super-cute kids, and some exceptional acting—by Danny Glover and Tony Danza (!)—can't make this oh-so-sticky concoction quite fly.

Eleven-year-old California Angels fan Roger is ditched by his deadbeat Dad. Worse, when prior to the final ditchery he pitifully inquires, "Dad, when do you think we might be a family again?" he gets a nasty "When the Angels win the pennant!"

Good luck. These reel-life Angels suck even worse than the real-life California losers. (The magic of the movies, I suppose.) However, as Roger's (carefully nondenominational) prayers get answered by some heavenly intervention, the buffoons become world-beaters in no time. Their gruff manager, played by Glover, gets humanized in the process and—guess what?— ends up adopting cute Roger.

It's a well-known Hollywood adage that whimsy is done best with a "less is more" attitude—but director William Dear, with his Louisville Slugger style, obviously disdains subtlety. The sticky messages (faith solves all, prayers do get answered, you gotta believe) and the syrupy metaphors (children equal love, baseball equals family) ooze throughout. And have we yet mentioned the film's antilying, anticursing, anticynicism, and yes, even antismoking propagandizing?

Amidst all this mush making, some major comic talents get totally wasted. Christopher Lloyd is reduced to idiotic mugging as Al the Head Angel. And why would Taylor Negron, who showed such vicious satirical sensibility in *Easy Money*, take a barely stock "comic bad guy" role? Easy money?

Glover, though, somehow manages to come across as a real person even in this hopelessly hammy romp. Still, Danza dominates the action as a rag-armed, nicotine-addicted pitcher on his very last hurrah; you simply can't take your eyes off him. *Tony Danza*? He had to be helped by angels.

Also reviewed in:
CHICAGO TRIBUNE, 7/15/94, Friday/p. F, John Petrakis
NEW YORK TIMES, 7/15/94, p. C10, Stephen Holden
VARIETY, 7/18-24/94, p. 38, Brian Lowry
WASHINGTON POST, 7/15/94, p. B6, Hal Hinson
WASHINGTON POST, 7/15/94, Weekend/p. 38, Desson Howe

ANGIE

A Buena Vista Pictures release of a Hollywood Pictures presentation in association with Caravan Pictures of a Morra-Brezner-Steinberg-Tenenbaum production. *Executive Producer:* Joe Roth and Roger Birnbaum. *Producer:* Larry Brezner and Patrick McCormick. *Director:* Martha Coolidge. *Screenplay:* Todd Graff. *Based on the book "Angie, I Says" by:* Avra Wing. *Director of Photography:* Johnny E. Jensen. *Editor:* Steven Cohen. *Music:* Jerry Goldsmith. *Music Editor:* Ken Hall and Darrell Hall. *Choreographer:* Michael Smuin. *Sound:* Ed Novick and (music) Bruce Botnick. *Sound Editor:* Kim B. Christensen. *Casting:* Juliet Taylor. *Production Designer:* Mel Bourne. *Art Director:* Gae S. Buckley. *Set Decorator:* Etta Leff. *Special Effects:*

Al DiSarro and Damon Allison. *Costumes:* Jane Robinson. *Make-up:* Richard Dean. *Stunt Coordinator:* Michael G. Russo. *Running time:* 108 minutes. *MPAA Rating:* R.

CAST: Geena Davis (Angie); Stephen Rea (Noel); James Gandolfini (Vinnie); Aida Turturro (Tina); Philip Bosco (Frank); Jenny O'Hara (Kathy); Michael Rispoli (Jerry); Betty Miller (Joanne); Susan Jaffe (Ballerina); Jeremy Collins (Lover); Robert Conn (Death); Ray Xifo (Dr. Gould); Rosemary DeAngelis (Aunt Vicky); Rae Allen (Aunt Violetta); Ida Bernardini (Aunt Louisa); Frank Pellegrino (Uncle Marty); Michael Laskin (Surgeon); Jean Marie Barnwell (Young Angie); Elaine Kagan (Aunt Jean); Olga Merediz (Roz); Mary Louise Burke (Fern); Mike Jefferson (Tony); Marin Hinkle (Young Joanne); Nancy Giles (Bedside Nurse); Antoinette Peragine (Circulating Nurse); Charlayne Woodard (Floor Nurse); Adam LeFevre (Museum Guard); Michael Goldfinger (Director); Joanne Baron (ICU Nurse #1); April Grace (ICU Nurse #2); Vernee Watson-Johnson (ICU Desk Nurse); Bibi Osterwald (Dr. Gould's Nurse); Robbie Wenger (Boy in Park); Matt Hofherr (Coffee Shop Waiter); Louis Gigante (Priest); Joanna Sanchez (Admissions Nurse #1); Margaret Cho (Admissions Nurse #2); Anthony Baracco (Tina's Son #1); Leonard Spinelli (Tina's Son #2); John Toles-Bey (Hospital Guard); Eileen Davis (Cranky Labor Nurse); Roseanne Tucci (Bernadette); Maria Venusio (Denise); Marie Coluccio (Nicole); Lauren Cona (Donna); Marya Delia Javier (Alba); Diane DiLascio (Lori); Marc Lewis (Man in Wheelchair); Dawn Hudson (Woman on Bus); James Plair (Bus Driver); Simone Study (Woman at Bar); Ron Michaels (Mechanic #1); Tony Ray Rossi (Mechanic #2); Sharon Claveau (Woman in Window).

LOS ANGELES TIMES, 3/4/94, Calendar/p. 1, Kenneth Turan

Stardom is a ladder with many rungs, and "Angie" is at the top. An unapologetic star vehicle whose every moment is crafted to showcase her various abilities, this is as much a coronation as a motion picture, a trumpet call to the world insisting that attention be paid.

It's not that Davis, always a fluid, engaging actress has lacked for attention up to now. "The Accidental Tourist" won her an Oscar, "Thelma & Louise" earned a second nomination and "A League of Their Own" was a considerable hit. But while those were roles the actress took hold of and made her own, "Angie" is a part specificality tailored to demonstrate what she can do.

And as Ms. Scacciapensieri, a feisty Italian American resident of the Bensonhurst section of Brooklyn whose unexpected pregnancy brings on the usual journey of self-discovery, Davis gets to do a lot. She laughs and cries, talks dirty and acts sexy, lashes out in anger and whispers in repentance. Plus she wears big earrings and participates in an unusually hectic delivery room scene that is the film's comic centerpiece.

Judged as a vehicle to display Davis' talent, "Angie" can't be faulted, and neither can the actress's pumped-up performance as a woman in the process of harnessing her emotional strength. Brash and irresistible, Davis is as assured as she's ever been, displaying a believable Brooklyn accent and taking every advantage of the scenes laid on for her specific pleasure.

When "Angie" is considered apart from its lead performance, however, the results are much more mixed. As directed by Martha Coolidge ("Rambling Rose") and written by Todd Graff from a novel by Avra Wing, "Angie" is too much the standard women's picture, over-loaded with a laundry list of uninspired soap-opera dilemmas.

Abandoned at age 3 by a free-spirited mother she's never heard from or forgotten, Angie, in her early 30s, is a Brooklyn working woman whose life has settled into a not unpleasant routine. She and best friend Tina (the feisty Aida Turturro) spend their days working in Manhattan. At night Angie goes to movies like "Cliffhanger" with the good-hearted Vinnie (James Gandolfini), a plumber who's been her boyfriend since ninth grade.

But when Angie finds herself pregnant, very little stays the same. Vinnie, a stand-up guy, is ecstatic and eager for an immediate wedding, but Angie is not sure she wants to get married at all. Her pregnancy has brought to the surface a raft of discontents—submerged dissatisfactions with her father (Philip Bosco), her meddling stepmother (Jenny O'Hara), even poor dare-to-be-average Vinnie.

Like any fairy-tale heroine, Angie is destined for other things. And another man. During a daring day-light visit to the Metropolitan Museum of Art, she attracts the notice of Noel ("The

Crying Game's" Stephen Rea), a smooth Irishman who knows lots about art and ballet and isn't above sharing his knowledge with the forthright Angie.

Though Noel turns out to have a few wrinkles of his own, he is symptomatic of where "Angie" misfires. Even as fine an actor as Rea can't make something involving out of his stock character, the fantasy boyfriend, is-he-too-good-to-be-true division. And just about every situation Angie finds herself in is similarly schematic.

Whether it's worrying about commitment and the demands of motherhood or making jokes about vibrators and gynecological exams, all of Angie's actions seem to come off some grand checklist of required female-friendly plot elements, there because they have to be, not because they fit.

And though the performances of Davis and Turturro and the writing behind their characters' wit go a ways to keep things lively, "Angie" ends up feeling like "Cliffhanger" in drag, a mechanical piece of work set in motion to push the buttons in women the way that the over-amped Sly Stallone vehicle tries to do for men.

NEW YORK POST, 3/4/94, p. 29, Michael Medved

If "Angie" had been released last December as originally planned, then Geena Davis would be attending the coming Oscar ceremonies as one of the top contenders for best actress.

As is, she can only hope that Academy voters will display the good sense—and long memories—to keep her in mind for next year's awards.

Her feisty, funny, earthy and intensely emotional performance certainly merits that consideration. She plays Angela Scacciapensieri (whose unpronounceable last name causes consternation for many characters in the film).

She's a bright, sassy butcher's daughter from Bensonhurst who works at a clerical job in the city and feels an unfocused itch for a more exciting life beyond the cozy confines of her neighborhood.

Her mother, a notorious free spirit who once caused a minor scandal by dancing for joy in her nightgown in the snow, ran off when Angie was still a little girl; the daughter seems to have inherited some of this rebel's restless spirit. She's genuinely fond of Vinnie (James Gandolfini), a good-hearted plumber and her boyfriend since childhood, but when she discovers she's pregnant with his baby she refuses to marry him.

Instead, she stumbles into a whirlwind affair with a witty, wealthy leprechaun of an Irish Manhattan lawyer (played by Stephen Rea of "The Crying Game") despite the fact that she's pregnant with another man's child.

Above all, Angie wants to avoid the fate of her uncomplaining, salt-of-the-earth best friend (vividly portrayed by Aida Turturro) who is already raising two kids while married to a loutish, verbally abusive guy from the neighborhood.

As she tries to sort out her priorities, Angie encounters several huge shocks—which no critic should even dream of giving away. In their own way, these surprises produce an even stronger impact than the famous revelation in "The Crying Game," precisely because they feel like life, rather than a movie gimmick.

Director Martha Coolidge handles this challenging material with astonishing grace, shaping a draining, dizzying roller coaster of a movie that turns on a dime, lurching from humor to horror, from romantic tenderness to searing pain without once going off the track.

Her secret—as in her previous triumph "Rambling Rose"—is the tremendous warmth and affection she brings to even the most minor characters in a large, distinguished cast.

In contrast to the squawking caricatures in screenwriter Todd Graff's previous effort "Used People," none of these New Yorkers comes across as primitive, exotic, or self-consciously "colorful"; they are real people, full of dignity and decency.

Philip Bosco is especially treasurable as Angie's compassionate father, and Geena Davis herself performs the rarest sort of acting alchemy: you quickly forget you're watching a popular movie star and focus instead on a fresh, hugely appealing character you've never seen before.

Typically endearing is the scene in which Angie, 8 months pregnant, dresses as Santa Claus at an office party and does a little dance that's both provocative and hilarious.

"Everybody's got something. Something broken," Angie says, and the movie evokes the deepest sympathy for this universe of wounds and malfunctions. At the same time, there's nothing broken about the film itself, where all the moving parts work together like a charm.

NEWSDAY, 3/4/94, Part II/p. B6, Jack Mathews

Somewhere beneath the uneven surface of Martha Coolidge's "Angie," a very good book seems to be trying to break out. There is an internal voice inside Geena Davis' confused character champing at the bit to describe Angie's feelings, and her revelations about her life, but never quite expressing them.

I haven't read that book, Avra Wing's "Angie, I Says," but I'm sure those who have know Angie Scacciapensieri in a way the film's viewers cannot possibly, and that they followed her journey of self-discovery with an intimacy the movie can only suggest.

Reduced to a plot description, "Angie" doesn't sound very promising. It's the story of a pregnant working class Bensonhurst woman who breaks up with her plumber fiancé , has an affair with a glib Irish lawyer, then abandons her new baby while setting out on a cross-country search for the mother who, 25 years earlier, had abandoned her.

"Angie" is not quite a road movie, but it is a head trip, with all the emotional adventures duly noted, and Angie emerges with a radically altered view of her world. But as easy as it is to understand how events change her attitudes, it remains a cool, unaffecting experience.

Geena Davis is much too winsome a personality to make Angie totally unsympathetic, but without quite knowing what's going on in her mind, Angie isn't very appealing, either. She is self-absorbed, deluded, a little ditzy, at times even cruel.

She's also, at times, very funny. The script, by Todd Graff ("Used People"), goes to great efforts to capture the particular personality of the Italian-Americans of Bensonhurst, the aggressive verbal and body language, and Angie is the most expressive of them all. The delivery room scene, where Angie is screaming expletives while the doctor, nurse and her best friend are singing Marvin Hamlisch show tunes, almost makes the whole film worthwhile.

However, that same scene demonstrates the problems Coolidge and Graff had in translating Wing's novel. Elements of comedy and tragedy, pain and pleasure overlap here, as they often do in life, but for audiences laughing themselves silly one moment and being urged to weep the next the shifts are far too abrupt.

After establishing a convincing working class environment, and Angie's relationships with her best friend Tina (Aida Turturro), her good-natured boyfriend Vinnie (James Gandolfini), her father (Philip Bosco) and stepmother (Jenny O'Hara), "Angie" suddenly takes on the exaggerated rhythms of episodic soap opera.

Angie's first encounter with the Irish lawyer Noel (Stephen Rea) in the Metropolitan Museum is such a meet-cute cliché it makes you squirm, and though their affair causes Angie to avoid a life with Vinnie she knows she doesn't want, and to eventually set out in search of her mother, there is nothing about it that seems remotely honest to us.

Rea, making his inevitable major studio debut after the independent hit "The Crying Game," has an amiable presence, but he seems more a fantasy figure than a real person, and when he vanishes only Angie could possibly miss him.

The best performances are those in the movie's margins. Gandolfini and Turturro (John Turturro's cousin) are absolutely right as working class stiffs absorbing the punishment, and the pleasure, of life as it comes to them. Bosco is also very solid as Angie's tortured father, an ordinary man trying to protect his daughter from a past he doesn't understand.

In the end, we feel we know more about these characters than we do about Angie herself. We see what she does, how she reacts, where she ends up. To understand what really happens to her, we'll have to read the book.

SIGHT AND SOUND, 7/94, p. 36, Lizzie Francke

Angie has lived in Brooklyn all her life. She and her childhood friend Tina both work on a computer magazine in Manhattan. Angie's biggest regret is that she has lost contact with her natural mother, who walked out when she was a kid. When Angie discovers that she is pregnant, her longtime boyfriend Vinnie, father Frank and step-mother Kathy are overjoyed and plans are made for the wedding. Angie, however, has reservations. One day she visits the Metropolitan Museum, where she is chatted up by a stranger who introduces himself as Noel and gives her his number. They start an affair and it transpires that Noel is a successful lawyer. Angie tells Vinnie their relationship is over. Subsequently she tells Noel that she is pregnant. He does not seem to mind and they continue to see one another on a casual basis. Her parents are not happy about the new situation, and it is Tina who supports Angie through the pregnancy. Angie goes into labour at Christmas at the office party. She is rushed to hospital and gives birth to a boy, but it turns out that he has a club hand and may face major surgery. To compound Angie's distress, the baby will not let her nurse him.

Angie and the baby go to stay with her parents. A few days later, she visits Noel, who has not been in touch since the night of the birth. He finishes their relationship. Angie receives this news calmly, but back home she feels increasingly alienated from her son. Once she goes to him when he cries to find her step-mother nursing him. Distraught, Angie decides to leave for Texas where her mother is reputed to be living. She tells Tina, who catches a train and meets her at her destination. They make their way to the roadhouse where her mother is supposedly working. The bar owner tells them that Angie's mother left 11 years ago. Tina tries to persuade Angie to return to Brooklyn, but Angie refuses and Tina leaves without her. When the bar closes, Angie follows the owner to a nearby bungalow where she confronts her, guessing that the woman is her aunt. It transpires that her mother, who is schizophrenic, does live there. With all the family secrets out in the open, Angie rings home, only to hear that her son has been rushed to hospital. She returns to Brooklyn, and at the hospital patches up her differences with her step-mother and father and attends to her son. He pulls through and she is finally able to nurse him.

Adapted from Avra Wing's novel, *Angie, I Says*, Martha Coolidge's film begins with an engagingly droll monologue from its eponymous heroine, who is played with great gusto by Geena Davis. Apparently following in the footsteps of *Thelma & Louise*, this is a woman's film about two working-class, Italian-American friends, Angie and Tina (Aida Turturro swelling the ranks of brilliant and under-used American actresses). Angie herself is just another girl on the IRT. She has big hair, loud earrings, Brooklyn twang ("very De Niro" as the Irish Noel says) and a boyfriend in a shiny suit called Vinnie. The opening credit sequence of a busy station at night with New York City glittering alluringly in the distance suggests that there are journeys Angie must make. But she does not take recklessly to the road. Nor is this the story of a working girl's passage from typing pool to executive suite. It is about the everyday excursions that seem to get you nowhere.

The movie opens with the 11-year-old Angie playing with other girls in the street and asking the perennial question: "What will it be like when we grow up?" Just then, the adult Angie and Tina pass by, and Angie, her face smudged with eye make-up in a desperate bid to leave girlhood behind, looks longingly at her younger self. This fragment is shot in slow motion, an evocative moment announcing Angie's intention of dealing with what growing up might mean for its female protagonist.

The film's strength is that it recognises the messiness of life, whether in relationships with family, friends and men, or in aspirations that are never quite fulfilled. Unusually for a Hollywood studio film, *Angie* is also matter-of-fact about the other kinds of mess women have to deal with, such as the blood, sweat and milk of pregnancy and mothering. Angie's girl friends graphically describe their labour-day experiences, while Angie's own session in the delivery room is a comic *tour de force*. She grimaces, groans and shouts expletives while holding Tina's hand in a vice-like grip.

Coolidge gives the physical agony a hysterical twist: Angie's gynaecologist recommends singing a Marvin Hamlisch show-stopper while following Lamaze breathing techniques. Cue an outburst of "One Singular Sensation", with Angie forced to join in through gritted teeth.

One wishes that Coolidge and screenwriter Todd Graff had adopted this irreverent approach at other moments too. The film falters towards the end as Angie tries to come to terms with the fact that not only has she just become a mother, but that her son has a deformed arm. She takes flight, and there is a melancholy about her search for her mother and the discovery of her schizophrenia. But this chaos of emotions is dealt with too tidily in a neatly sewn-up finale, in which Angie is reconciled with everyone around her and happy in her grown-up role.

VILLAGE VOICE, 3/8/94, p. 60, Amy Taubin

Starring Geena Davis in a role originally developed for the pre-*Sex* Madonna, *Angie* is set in a Bensonhurst that, aside from dentalized consonants and glottal stops, is just like any other Disney theme park. Madonna might have seemed more to the manor (six rooms, stucco, very low taxes) born, but Davis at least gives the picture some reason for being. *Angie* was once called *Angie, I Says*—a title that would have nailed its condescending tone while adding to the overall narrative confusion, since no one except Angie is on screen long enough to merit the first person singular.

"I guess I'll just have to let my story tell itself," says Angie, offering a transparent excuse for a script that goes—generically and literally—all over the map without breaking custom or cliché. Pushing 30, Angie has lived in Bensonhurst all her life. She has an inchoate desire for cultcha, but her boyfriend Vinnie (James Gandolfini) is phobic about bridges and tunnels. When Angie gets pregnant, she feels the walls closing in. Not wanting to end up like her best friend Tina (Aida Turturro)—the sole supporter of an abusive husband and two cowed kids—she flees to the Metropolitan Museum of Art, where she meets Noel (Stephen Rea), a romantically stoop-shouldered Dublin bohemian living in Soho and practicing international law in Midtown. Angie dumps Vinnie, but not exactly for Noel, who doesn't mind her being pregnant, but isn't committed to fatherhood either.

Angie begins as a screwball but falls into postpartum bathos when Angie discovers that motherhood isn't what it's like in the movies or, at least, in movies that start off like this one. Martha Coolidge, who once directed an ebullient, underrated coming-of-age pic called *Real Genius* but is better known for the nostalgic *Rambling Rose*, shows her talent for comedy in a few of the early scenes; no one could do much with the rest. *Angie* is only notable for the physical and emotional spectacle that is Geena Davis and the fact that none of the men that surround her—father, boyfriends, gynecologist—are up to her size.

Also reviewed in:
CHICAGO TRIBUNE 3/4/94, Friday/p. C, Michael Wilmington
NEW YORK TIMES, 3/4/94, p. C6, Janet Maslin
VARIETY, 3/7-13/94, p. 59, Todd McCarthy
WASHINGTON POST, 3/4/94, p. C9, Richard Harrington

BABY'S DAY OUT

A Twentieth Century Fox release. *Executive Producer:* William Ryan. *Producer:* John Hughes and Richard Vane. *Director:* Patrick Read Johnson. *Screenplay:* John Hughes. *Director of Photography:* Thomas E. Ackerman. *Editor:* David Rawlins. *Music:* Bruce Broughton. *Music Editor:* Patricia Carlin. *Sound:* Ronald Judkins and (music) Armin Steiner. *Sound Editor:* Richard Hymns. *Casting:* Janet Hirshenson and Jane Jenkins. *Production Designer:* Doug Kraner. *Art Director:* Joseph Lucky. *Set Designer:* Henry Alberti, Richard Fernandez, Robert Goldstein, Masako Masuda, Eric Orbom, and Randy Wilkins. *Set Decorator:* Beth Rubino. *Set Dresser*: Troy Borisy. *Special Effects:* Michael Wood. *Visual Effects*: Michael Fink and John Knoll. *Costumes:* Lisa Jensen. *Make-up:* Linda Melazzo. *Special Effects Make-up:* Ken Myers. *Stunt Coordinator:* Freddie Hice. *Running time:* 90 minutes. *MPAA Rating:* PG.

CAST: Joe Mantegna (Eddie); Lara Flynn Boyle (Laraine); Joe Pantoliano (Norby); Brian Haley (Veeko); Cynthia Nixon (Gilbertine); Fred Dalton Thompson (FBI Agent Grissom); John Neville (Mr. Andrews); Matthew Glave (Bennington); Adam Robert Worton (Baby Bink); Jacob Joseph Worton (Baby Bink); Brigid Duffy (Sally); Guy Hadley (FBI Agent); Eddie Bracken (Old Timer); Kenneth L. Jordahl (Old Soldier #1); Raymond Henders (Old Soldier #2); Jim Foley (Old Soldier #3); Jack Baird (Old Soldier #4); Oscar Carr (Old Soldier #5); Dan Frick (Bus Driver); Robin Baber (Big Woman); John Drury (Male Anchor); Jennifer Say Gan (Ronnie Lee); Dawn Maxey (Teenage Girl); Megan Haffey (Baby Girl); Roslyn

Alexander (Woman in Cab); Manny Sosa (Taxi Cab Driver); Anna Thomson (Mrs. McCray); Jenna Pozzi (McCray Child); Erika Leigh Blackwell (School Teacher); Neil Flynn (Cop #1); William Holmes (Cop #2); Don Rimgale (Hard Hat #1); Warren Rice (Hard Hat #2); Tim Schueneman (UPS Man); Sandra O. Rogers (Woman in Apartment); Kirsten Nelson (Woman in Park); John Alexander (Gorilla); Jurgen Heimann (Puppeteer #1); Tom Hester (Puppeteer #2); Mark Setrakian (Puppeteer #3); Marc L. Tyler (Puppeteer #4).

LOS ANGELES TIMES, 7/1/94, Calendar/p. 6, Peter Rainer

"Baby's Day Out" is one of those frenetic John Hughes ideas that manages to seem uproarious and cruel at the same time. It's another entry in his kiddie specialty—clobber comedies featuring people without nervous systems. He's making animated features without the animation.

Nine-month-old Baby Bink (played alternately by identical twins Adam Robert and Jacob Joseph Worton) has been whisked from his well-to-do parents (Lara Flynn Boyle and Matthew Glave) by a trio of bumbling kidnapers (Joe Mantegna, Joe Pantoliano, Brian Haley) who proceed to lose the baby in the middle of Chicago's hubbub.

If you were upset by the scene in the Coen brothers' "Raising Arizona" where the kidnaped baby is left unattended in the middle of a highway, you'll positively blanch at "Baby's Day Out," where Baby Bink is allowed to crawl through and under traffic, get whisked through revolving doors, waddle across a think plank hundreds of feet in the air, swing out on a steel girder, nestle with a caged gorilla—for starters.

Hughes, whose script was directed by Patrick Read Johnson, buys off the queasiness one may feel at all this unsupervised mayhem by making Baby Bink obliviously happy. Bink is delighted to be on this daylong outing—it's like a full-scale re-enactment of one of his nursery book jaunts.

Either you buy into this slapstick bliss or you reject the movie altogether. It's the same choice we were offered by "Home Alone," where an accidentally abandoned child is terrorized by a pair of scurvy housebreakers. Hughes and Johnson are so adept at turning this peewee and his tormentors into comic cut-ups that the maliciousness at the movie's center never really takes hold.

What registers instead are the occasional heart tugs. Hughes' movies would be better if they were even nastier: They lack the courage of their own heartlessness. As Bink's mother, Lara Flynn Boyles plays a high-society matron who initially regards her baby as a kind of cuddly ornament; she wants his picture taken for the newspaper society pages. It's the baby's nanny (Cynthia Nixon) who instinctively knows where the lost baby is heading. That's because she's untainted by riches. (The movie plays up her maternal gifts only to give her short shrift at the end.) Baby Bink himself is a snuggly-wuggly cherub without a yowling moment. He's much too good for his parents. (His experience, of course, teaches them to be better parents.)

The filmmakers are clever at concocting ways for Baby Bink to get fed and diaper-changed while paddling about the city on all fours. They manage to anticipate most of our literal-minded objections—which helps to ground the plot's outlandishness. As the kidnapers, Mantegna, Pantoliano and Haley are adept clobber comics, and they fit right into the cartoonish landscapes. Chicago—courtesy of visual effects supervisor Mike Fink—is transformed into an anything-goes wonder world where giggly babies atop skyscrapers can swing out over the city with aplomb.

When this sort of stuff works, as it does a fair amount of the time in "Baby's Day Out," it points up how much can be done with state-of-the-art special effects. "Baby's Day Out" could not have been made nearly as well even five years ago. (Whether it *should* be made is another story.) Nowadays just about anything that once was visualized as animation can be duplicated as live-action. And for an in-your-face comedy master blaster like Hughes, the live-action mode is the best way to pin us to the wall. If the Three Stooges were alive today, not to mention Baby Leroy, he's have them waddling and bludgeoning in eye-popping hyperspace.

NEW YORK POST, 7/1/94, p. 43, Michael Medved

As I left screening of "Baby's Day Out," I pulled my slouch hat over one eye, hunched my shoulders, and skulked toward the exit, hoping that no one would recognize me.

Frankly, I felt profoundly embarrassed over the fact that for the last 90 minutes I'd been laughing so hard.

Baby's Day Out" is a stupid, one-joke movie, filled with gross, sadistic slapstick—but it is also undeniably, irresistibly, irrationally funny.

The premise, from the peripatetic writer-producer John Hughes, is pure baby formula: warm, sweet and easy to digest.

Lara Flynn Boyle and Matthew Glave play wealthy Chicago socialites who dote on their 9-month-old heir, Bennington Cotwell Jr., familiarly known as "Baby Bink."

Unfortunately, the child (played by the photogenic and endearing Worton twins of Newark, Del.) is kidnapped while posing for formal photographs and the three crooks who snatch him demand a huge ransom.

While the desperate mother and father meet with the FBI (led by the formidable Fred Dalton Thompson), Baby Bink takes matters into his own hands (and knees)—crawling away from the kidnappers and thereafter leading the bumbling baddies on a merry chase through Chicago.

The clever twist in this silliness involves the step-by-step sequence of his adventures, as he follows the pattern in his favorite picture book, "Baby's Day Out," which has been read to him countless times by his kindly British nanny (Cynthia Nixon).

Like Sweetpea in the old "Popeye" cartoons, Baby Bink happily crawls from one terrifying situation to another, gurgling cheerfully all the while, totally untouched by fear or risk.

There's also a cartoon quality to the klutzy kidnappers, played by Joe Mantegna, Joe Pantoliano and Brian Haley; the only difference between these villains and the slapstick thieves in Hughes' "Home Alone" pictures is that this time there are three instead of two.

Director Johnson (whose only previous credit is the forgettable "Spaced Invaders") brings a handsome, burnished, once-upon-a-time glow to each sequence of the movie, suggesting he may be an even better John Hughes director than Hughes himself.

Bruce Broughton's lush, hummable, gorgeously orchestrated musical score also helps give the movie heart and sentiment to go along with the gags. All in all, it's an attractive package that kids will love, while parents needn't feel too ashamed of their own enjoyment.

NEWSDAY, 7/1/94, Part II/p. B7, John Anderson

I remember reading once about a medieval European pastime called "tossing the tot"—the hurling of swaddled babes for distance and, only coincidentally, accuracy. Clearly, they didn't call 'em the Dark Ages for nothing, but the point was that the cherishing of children, like romantic love, is a relatively recent phenomenon, that the sentimental gloss we apply to childhood shines not only with ardor but with fresh paint.

Oh yes, despite a litany of modern crimes against children, we're far more enlightened than those mead-swigging tot-tossers who were deaf to biological clocks and disinterested in diapers. And yet, enlightenment exacts an awful price. "Baby's Day Out," a shamelessly violent comedy in which writer-producer John Hughes ("Home Alone," "Curly Sue," "She's Having a Baby") exploits infant-worship in a way that may have you longing for the days of black death.

The basic premise guarantees a cheaply visceral response: The pretty, pampered Baby Bink (twins Adam Robert and Jacob Joseph Worton), having crawled away from his inept kidnapers, travels a seemingly blessed path through the perilous streets of Chicago.

The implied contract between filmmakers and audiences guarantees he'll never get hurt. But Hughes and his accomplice, first-time director Patrick Read Johnson, compensate by committing gruesome bits of mayhem against kidnapers Eddie, Norby and Veeko (Joe Mantegna, Joe Pantoliano and Brian Haley), who suffer each time Bink escapes.

"Baby's Day Out" also suffers, from a basic contradiction: Babies are portrayed as glorious—and, in this case, white, blond and privileged—products.

The raw materials, however, are under constant attack. I counted six separate. male-groin-injury gags, including an extended one in which Eddie's pelvic region is twisted, tortured and finally set on fire. Like the gratuitous nudity—a shot of Bink's bottom being powdered—it's the kind of thing that will keep kids in the audience hysterical.

If hard-core slapstick were his only crime, Hughes wouldn't be quite as offensive as he is when installing the parents at the helm of this careening pram of pap. Bink's doting, status-conscious mother, Laraine (Lara Flynn Boyle), is desperate to get Bink's picture in the paper (Do papers run baby pictures anymore? A Hughes' trademark is inventing such plot conveniences). Eddie (an over-the-top Mantegna), disguised as the photographer, exploits her eagerness to make off with the baby.

To the film's credit, it knows that parental obsession is often about self-worship—adoration of one's own divine miniature. But the sequences involving Laraine's are so awash in unctuous sentiment they make Hughes' earlier work seem like social realism.

In a summer when the live-action reproduction of cartoons (and virtual cartoons) seems to be Hollywood's highest aspiration—"The Flintstones," or "Speed"—"Baby's Day Out" at least sets its aim higher, borrowing boldly from Max Fleischer's original "Popeye." When Swee'pea did what Bink does, though, it somehow seemed more compelling. And a lot shorter.

NEWSWEEK, 7/11/94, p. 50, David Ansen

From the teenagers of "The Breakfast Club" to the prepubescent Kevin of "Home Alone" to 9-month-old Baby Bink the hero of this live-action cartoon, John Hughes's subjects have become increasingly puerile. So, alas have his movies.

The adorable tot gets kidnapped by three stooges Joe Mantegna, Joe Pantoliano and Brian Haley), then leads them on a wild chase around Chicago, subjecting his hapless captors to one sadistic punishment after another. Director Patrick Read Johnson follows writer/producer Hughes's familiar formula with crass fidelity: four doses of slapstick humiliation to one dose of unadulterated sentimentality. Shaken, not stirred. Kids in the audience when I saw it couldn't get enough of the crotch-stomping fun. Parents may want to wait in the lobby.

SIGHT AND SOUND, 9/94, p. 36, Geoffrey Macnab

A summer morning in the countryside outside Chicago. Baby Bink Cotwell is preparing for the day ahead. His nanny reads him his favourite story, 'Baby's Day Out', his father goes off to work and his mother Laraine gets him ready for a newspaper photo shoot. Eddie Mauser, Norby LeBlaw and Veeko Riley, three small-time hoodlums, turn up at the house pretending to be the photographers. Eddie hoodwinks Laraine into leaving him alone with Bink and then promptly kidnaps the toddler, making his exit through the window. The three men and the stolen baby hide out in an apartment, demanding a ransom of $5 million. However, when Norby falls asleep, Baby Bink climbs out onto the fire escape and crawls toward the roof. The three give chase, but Bink eludes their grasp. For the rest of the day, Bink, recreating the events from 'Baby's Day Out', hitches rides in shopping baskets, on buses and in taxis. He leads the hoodlums on a chaotic chase which takes them from department store to zoo before ending up on a busy construction site.

Meanwhile, Bink's parents have joined forces with local FBI agent Grissom and are searching the city for clues. They get nowhere, but the Nanny hears reports of various sightings of babies all over Chicago and realises that the locations correspond to those in 'Baby's Day Out'. She deduces that Bink's next port of call, if he goes by the book, will be the Old Soldiers' Home. Sure enough, Bink has crawled his way in to meet the elderly veterans. He is reunited with his parents. As he is being driven home, he makes gurgling noises and points out of the window. Grissom realises he is trying to reveal the whereabouts of his kidnappers. Following Bink's lead, they cordon off the street, surround the building and flush the hoodlums out. Back in his cot, Baby Bink looks at a new book, 'Baby's Trip To China'.

In a sense, *Baby's Day Out* is the picture that John Hughes has been building down to all his career. It was almost inevitable that after his long march backward through adolescence (the brat-pack movies) and prepubescent childhood (*Home Alone*) he would turn his attention to toddlers.

Polymorphously perverse and gleefully anarchic, babies make ideal leading characters in cartoons. One thinks, for instance, of Fleischer brothers yarns where Popeye has all sorts of unfortunate, and very violent, adventures in babysitting, or of the cigar-smoking, gun-toting gangster in the pram who bawls his way into various Bugs Bunny stories. What these cartoons acknowledge is the babies' potential for disruption: the tots may seem powerless and vulnerable, but given a chance, they'll turn into rampaging agents of destruction. Hughes and director Patrick Read Johnson set out to harness this infantile energy. In the course of the film, the three hapless kidnappers holding Baby Bink to ransom are spat upon, bludgeoned, walloped, set on fire, covered in cement and generally made to endure every sort of indignity a cartoon villain might be exposed to.

But the meshing of animation and live-action techniques is always difficult. There is a strong vein of sentimentality here which seems incongruous amid all the choreographed carnage. The villains are flesh and blood characters: it's more jarring than funny to see them at the receiving end of so much wanton violence. There is also a disturbing sense that they're being punished on account of their background. As blue-collar, working-class Americans, they're treated throughout as objects of ridicule whose habits and stupidity can be lampooned, and whose bodies can be battered. By contrast, Baby Bink's preppy, affluent parents are handled with kid gloves. Hughes' script celebrates consumption: Bink's palatial nursery, the country house where he lives, and Chicago's most exclusive department store are lovingly filmed: the city is reduced to an extended adventure playground for privileged toddlers.

This makes it all the more tempting to sympathise with the dispossessed hoodlums. The actors, at least, deserve our pity: Eddie Bracken, Preston Sturges' conquering hero, is made to play a doddering, senile army veteran who pulls faces for Bink's benefit; John Neville is condemned to that purgatorial role as English butler which seems to be foisted on all distinguished Shakespearian actors who go to Hollywood. Joe Mantegna, usually to be found snapping out David Mamet's elliptical dialogue, is reduced to mimicry and groans. He is even ritually emasculated: Baby Bink sets fire to the crotch of his trousers.

The premise of *Baby's Day Out* must have seemed a little risky—baby-snatching is not the most tasteful of themes. As usual, though, Hughes gives the material a sugary, bland coating. The movie broaches questions of class, snobbery and parenting without answering any of them. Ironically, it also paints a picture of domestic dysfunction: Bink's mother seems more concerned with getting his picture in the paper than with his well-being. His father is so preoccupied with work that he scarcely notices the toddler. Mom, pop and kid are all reunited in the final scenes, but any notions of happy families have to be treated with scepticism. As the film ends, Bink, back in his old, familiar crib, is already contemplating another adventure, leafing through a new book—'Baby's Trip to China'. Whether or not this presages a sequel, it implies he is none too happy with life at home.

VILLAGE VOICE, 7/12/94, p. 48, Gary Dauphin

As children's movies go, *Baby's Day Out* is good fast food, the kind of "if-you-don't-take-me-now-you're-a-really-bad-parent"rest stop kids tend to demand on even the shortest summer drive. Disney's *Lion King* will probably capture the bulk of the tykes' attention, but if you don't get them this damned Happy Meal you'll never hear the end of it. The third installment in writer-producer John Hughes's chain of *Home Alone* franchises, *Baby's Day Out* concerns nine-month-old ransom bait Baby Bink (played by identical twins Adam and Jacob Worton) and his drooly adventures in the big city, After crawling away from a trio of inept babynappers, Bink all-fours it across rooftops, through traffic, into a construction site and so on, while the three idiots chasing him pratfall Wiley Coyote-like from insane heights. (Bink wanders into the movie's various jungle-gym locales in a preliterate attempt to recreate scenes from his favorite storybook, but *Baby's Day Out* is better understood as a live-action adaptation of those Popeye cartoons where Sweet Pea gets into mischief.)

Cute and blond as a mass-produced button, Bink is too busy sliding blissfully down high steel girders to learn any lessons while he's away from mommy (played with momentum-killing sincerity by Lara Flynn Boyle), but the pre-adolescents who are this film's target audience will pick up plenty. Besides little discoveries about the dire stupidity of grown-ups or the roachlike ability of infants to wander around unnoticed underfoot, there's the little-known fact that adult testicles will make this great crunching sound when struck properly, like a bag full of marbles being hit with a ballpeen hammer. The violence in this flick has a strictly cartoon quality, but the kidnappers (especially Joe Mantegna) suffer so much groin area trauma that I spent a number of scenes hiding behind my legal pad. Bink comes through all this smelling like a diaper-scented rose, of course, making the Industrial Light & Magic team who did the baby-in-danger effects the real stars of *Baby's Day Out*. So much so that when one of the grownups consoles Bink's mom with the words "someone somewhere watches over all the babies" you can't help but think they're talking about George Lucas.

Also reviewed in:
CHICAGO TRIBUNE, 7/1/94, Friday/p. L, Johanna Steinmetz
NEW YORK TIMES, 7/1/94, p. C3, Stephen Holden
VARIETY, 6/20-26/94, p. 41, Leonard Klady
WASHINGTON POST, 7/1/94, p. D1, Hal Hinson

BABYFEVER

A Rainbow Film Company release of a Jagtoria production. *Producer:* Judith Wolinsky. *Director:* Henry Jaglom. *Screenplay:* Henry Jaglom and Victoria Foyt. *Director of Photography:* Hanania Baer. *Editor:* Henry Jaglom. *Sound:* Sunny Meyer. *Running time:* 110 minutes. *MPAA Rating:* Not Rated.

CAST: Victoria Foyt (Gena); Matt Salinger (James); Dinah Lenney (Roz); Eric Roberts (Anthony); Frances Fisher (Rosie); Elaine Kagan (Millie); Zack Norman (Mark).

LOS ANGELES TIMES, 4/13/94, Calendar/p. 10, Chris Willman

It's been awhile now since jokesters regarded Alan Alda as the poster boy—or whipping boy—for extreme male sensitivity. Though director Henry Jaglom probably isn't mainstream enough to ever rate a "Tonight Show" gag, he seems to have taken up the Alda memorial mantle, releasing movies you could justifiably call "women's pictures," albeit not the kind Douglas Sirk used to make.

Given his apparent desire to surround himself with actresses and actresses alone, and spill their innermost hopes and fears, you figure Jaglom's either extraordinarily attuned to the estrogen cycle of the Zeitgeist or just afflicted with Venus envy.

Having eavesdropped already on one of the two great gender-specific fixations of our time, the thinness obsession, here he gets around to the other, the desire to be with child. "Babyfever" does for delayed procreation what his earlier art-house success, "Eating," did for food-related frustrations. This movie, too, is amazingly unwavering in single-minded devotion to its subject, and after almost two hours of baby chat served up with Jaglom's usual deliberate technical crudity, childless women won't be the only ones feeling their clocks ticking. But when it comes to being a compleatist, he does deliver.

The movie is principally a very long, very philosophic Malibu baby shower, which some inevitably feel ambivalent about attending, not having realized their own dreams of motherhood. Chief among the reluctant is Victoria Foyt, established in a brief setup as expectant of being expectant; she's supposed to get her results back by the end of the afternoon, which lends the laconic party a little suspense.

Gorgeous and driven, Foyt has no fewer than two guys who say they'd like to sire her children, but the one who may have impregnated her is an overly safe, responsible "suit" type (Matt Salinger), and the one she feels some real passion for is, of course, a fly-by-night rapscallion (Eric Roberts). Few of her contemporaries are blessed with even that considerable a choice of sperm donors. Among the other showerers who show up sans child, there's much bitterness over childlessness, and commitment-phobic men come in for a lot of lashing in this extended ladies' room.

Make no mistake, this *is* the date movie from hell.

But for viewers less immediately inclined toward conception anxiety, "Babyfever" begets a definite fascination, remarkable in its comprehensive documentary aspects, at least. (He's created a great time capsule, if not necessarily a great time.) Jaglom is, as always, big on *vérité* and improvisation; with such a large cast milling about the airy, oceanside house, he's managed to cover just about every conceivable baby base, with sentiments ranging from banal self-interest to self-conscious belly laughs, and a lot of very real, undeniably affecting poignancy in-between.

But Jaglom's success as an unofficial documentarian here undercuts his intentions as a dramatist. For much of the movie's mid-section, Foyt's concerns get set aside while Jaglom crams in as many dozens of different talking heads as possible; even Foyt's fairly involving character seems to come out of a Jaglom-esque void where women aren't given any outside social context that doesn't relate directly to the matter at hand—i.e., this time, their uteruses.

Despite her character's shortshrift, Foyt (credited with co-writing the scripted part of the film with Jaglom, and making her starring debut here) is flat-out terrific.

It wouldn't be giving too much away to suggest that Jaglom finds a noncommittal way to have his cake and eat it too at the end, first with a slightly downbeat yet exultantly liberated climax, then an absurdly cheerful, non sequitur coda in which Foyt has found an unnamed, unseen great guy (presumably Jaglom, her real -life husband) and blown up like a balloon.

NEW YORK POST, 5/4/94, p. 33, Michael Medved

One of Hollywood's persistent problems involves the appalling inequality in opportunities for male and female performers. According to a landmark study by the Screen Actors Guild, 71 percent of all roles in recent films went to men.

Filmmaker Henry Jaglom seems single-handedly determined to redress that balance. His new film, "Babyfever," like his 1991 art-house hit, "Eating," is a wise and witty investigation of one of the most significant issues in the lives of contemporary women; it features a cast comprised of several dozen altogether extraordinary actresses.

Jaglom's previous film focused on the complex love-hate relationship between women and food. "Babyfever" explores an even more fundamental question: In the face of demanding careers and chronically unreliable relationships, how should today's women respond to the primal urge to have babies?

Victoria Foyt plays a capable professional who works in the office of a real estate developer and who thinks she might be pregnant by her dull, doting yuppie boyfriend (played by the endearing and accomplished Matt Salinger).

Before she goes to the doctor to confirm that she's expecting, she meets up with an old flame (an irresponsible but exciting TV actor played by Eric Roberts). He wants to renew their relationship.

Thoroughly confused, she attends a baby shower for one of her best friends and plans to call the doctor's office at the end of the day to hear the results of her pregnancy test.

The bulk of the movie takes place at the baby shower, where a dazzling variety of guests speak with heart-breaking candor about their feelings regarding children.

These commentators range from a loving lesbian couple making plans for conception to a gorgeous African-American who's an articulate, self-confident evangelical Christian and who knows that God will bring her to the right decision.

Jaglom presents each of these women with unmistakable affection, preserving the spontaneous quality of their comments even though some of the lines seem too good to be ad-libbed.

"I thing having a baby is the female equivalent of men joining the Marines," says one guest. "And I'm sorry I haven't been man enough to do it."

In her first starring role in feature films, Victoria Foyt (Jaglom's real-life wife) makes a formidable leading lady—a woman of sharp edges and substance rather than some simple-minded sweetie pie. She also collaborated with Jaglom on the script, which contains more of a plot than is customary in his films. Off-screen, she is currently expecting their second child.

"Babyfever" is one of those rare films so engaging and so insightful that many moviegoers will want to see it more than once. Jaglom's longtime fans will love every minute of it, while it should win many new admirers for America's most personal and provocative filmmaker.

NEWSDAY, 5/4/94, Part II/p. B9, John Anderson

Besides seeming longer than a pregnancy, Henry Jaglom's "Baby Fever" never bothers to acknowledge, much less answer, the very question it raises: What's love got to do with it?

Amid all the whining and wailing of the women (actresses) whom Jaglom interviews (directs), and the dramatic subplot involving Gena (Victoria Foyt) and her ovarian crisis, we hear a lot about biological clocks, the unfairness of time, the relentlessness of menopause, and trade-offs made—career for children or vice versa. But seldom do we hear a reference to men that isn't derisive, or a mention of the oh-so-longed-for child that includes a motive other than simply having it all.

If these were actual women, talking from the heart, it would be one thing. But it's Jaglom's baby, so to speak; he's created the context and the content. As such, he's like a voyeur peeking in the windows of his own house.

In "Eating," he dealt with women and their relationship to food. Here, he uses a similar structure to explore the fact that fertility isn't forever. Personifying this not-quite-revelatory concept is Gena (Foyt is Jaglom's wife and the mother of his child), a professional woman caught between choosing the security of marriage to James (Matt Salinger), with whom she might be pregnant, and the erotic lure of Anthony (Eric Roberts), an actor who once dumped her but who's suddenly come back talking bassinets and bottle-warmers.

With Gena wrestling her two demons and awaiting the results of her pregnancy test, we follow her to a baby shower at the home of Millie (Elaine Kagan), whose husband (Zack Norman) is busy selling the house out from under her, Millie's trying to dissuade her sister Roz (Dinah Lenney) from pursuing the singing career she abandoned to have children.

Meanwhile, a woman hired to videotape the party interviews its guests—thus setting up the intrusive, Jaglom-esque interrogations—and gets a variety of viewpoints about childbearing. Some involve feminism's legacy and the cost of self-actualization; it's one of the film's few intriguing aspects that the youngest women at the party, unpressured by time, have the sanest views about men and pregnancy. Two guests at the party, the only black women there, downplay the whole issue: One never wants kids, for purely selfish reasons; the other, a fundamentalist Christian, figures if the biblical Sarah could have children at 90, so can she. To Jaglom's shame, only one of the women (Deborah Skelly) protests just how absurd this whole interview process is. And personally, I couldn't get enough of her.

VILLAGE VOICE, 5/17/94, p. 58, Anne Glusker

The latest from Henry Jaglom, the Man Who (Thinks He) Knows Women, investigates reproductive yearning, with a cast of thirty-whatever women, worrying about their eggs getting too old and tired to do them any good. Jaglom has all the self-conscious pretentiousness of someone firmly embedded in the mainstream who sees himself as avant-garde, but you can say one thing for him: he's got a direct linkup to the zeitgeist. Whether it's love and commitment or women's disordered relationship to food (*Someone to Love, Always, Eating*), Jaglom's eternally ready to weigh in with an almost right, slightly non-narrative look at the moment's topic, complete with some faux-documentary close-ups and plenty of extemporaneous-sounding dialogue.

None of this ever goes very deep, however, and in *Babyfever* it gets quite tiresome. Jaglom starts off with a fairly interesting conceit: bright. perky career girl Gena (Victoria Foyt, Jaglom's wife and the film's cowriter) has a too-nice, hunky boyfriend, James (Matt Salinger), who wants to marry her and make babies. Somehow, all James's proffered architectural plans just don't appeal to Gena. Along comes dangerous bad-boy ex-flame Anthony (played to pouty perfection by Eric Roberts) who definitely does appeal—and is as wrong now as when he broke Gena's heart a few years earlier. He too wants to procreate. What's a girl with ever wizening eggs to do?

The answer could have made an intriguing two hours. But instead Jaglom meanders through Gena's visit to a haute Beverly Hills baby shower: pearls are present in abundance, and the waterfall that swoops down from the edge of the house is truly something else again. Jaglom uses the shower as a clunky device to present the core of his film: cinema verité-style perorations from each of the shower guests on having babies, not having babies, being a lesbian mom, counting on God to provide man and baby, and the "ethics" of tricking a man into reproducing.

The film clearly comes down on the she's-gotta-have-one side of the baby question ("I will feel completely robbed if I don't have a child," says one shower guest), although the unconverted certainly get their say ("I feel like people who have children abdicate their lives," says another). The film's downfall lies in its failure to explore why exactly this is such a hot subject in this particular culture at this particular time, and why, obvious time-clock reasons notwithstanding, it's a lightning rod for women only. After all, when was the last time you heard a man asked how he felt about the presence or absence of babies in his life?

Also reviewed in:
CHICAGO TRIBUNE, 5/6/94, Friday/p. D, Michael Wilmington
NEW YORK TIMES, 5/4/94, p. C16, Janet Maslin
VARIETY, 4/18-24/94, p. 63, Emanuel Levy
WASHINGTON POST, 6/6/94, p. D7, Rita Kempley

BACKBEAT

A Gramercy Pictures release of a Polygram Filmed Entertainment and Scala Productions presentation in association with Channel Four Films of a Scala/Woolley/Powell/Dwyer and Fortcoming production. *Executive Producer:* Nik Powell and Hanno Huth. *Producer:* Finola Dwyer and Stephen Woolley. *Director:* Iain Softley. *Screenplay:* Iain Softley, Michael Thomas, and Stephen Ward. *Director of Photography:* Ian Wilson. *Editor:* Martin Walsh. *Music:* Don Was. *Sound:* Chris Munro and (music) Rik Pekkonen. *Sound Editor:* Glenn Freemantle. *Casting:* John Hubbard, Ros Hubbard, Diane Crittenden and Vicky Hinrichs. *Production Designer:* Joseph Bennett. *Art Director:* Michael Carlin and Joseph Plagge. *Costumes:* Sheena Napier. *Make-up:* Pat Hay. *Running time:* 100 minutes. *MPAA Rating:* R.

CAST: Sheryl Lee (Astric Kirchherr); Stephen Dorff (Stuart Sutcliffe); Ian Hart (John Lennon); Gary Bakewell (Paul McCartney); Chris O'Neill (George Harrison); Scot Williams (Pete Best); Kai Wiesinger (Klaus Voormann); Jennifer Ehle (Cynthia Powell); Marcelle Duprey (Singer); John White, Bernard Merrick, and Nicholas Tennant (Sailors); Finola Geraghty (Model); Rob Spendlove (Arthur Ballard); Charlie Caine (Lord Woodbine); Frieda Kelly (Mrs. Harrison); Paul Humpoletz (Bruno); Christiana Uriarte, Abigail Wrapson, and Galit Hershkovitz (Groupies); Gertan Klauber (Pimp); Stephen Grothgar (Barman); Lynn Lowton (Hooker); Manuel Harlan (Johannes); Britta Gartner and Dirk Winkler (Exis); Wolf Kahler (Bert Kaempfert); James Doherty (Tony Sheridan); Paul Duckworth (Ringo); Joerg Stabler (Policeman); Alexei Jawdokimov (Napoleon); Albert Welling (Doctor).

CHRISTIAN SCIENCE MONITOR, 4/15/94, p. 13, David Sterritt

A definitive movie about the Beatles has yet to be made, but the early years of the all-time-greatest rock group have drawn the attention of more than one filmmaker. "Backbeat," directed by newcomer Iain Softley, comes soon after "The Hours and Times," in which Christopher Münch explored the complex relationship between John Lennon and Brian Epstein, the band's first manager.

"Backbeat" is more conventional and commercial than Münch's offbeat character study, but it follows some of the same patterns. Again the story focuses mainly on Lennon, playing down the dynamics of the Beatles as a group. And again the film's intention is to study Lennon's personality as revealed encounters with a colleague who's at once a friend, a rival, and something of an enigma to everyone around him.

The colleague in "Backbeat" is Stuart Sutcliffe, who became the first bass guitarist of the Beatles despite a total lack of the extraordinary talent that exploded from Paul McCartney and George Harrison as well as Lennon himself. Sutcliffe's place in the group is further complicated by his indecision over what career to follow—painting, which he's loved all his life or music, which he finds more exciting, sociable, and just plain fun.

His overdose of career ambivalence and underdose of musical skill drives the other Beatles crazy. But his friendship with Lennon guarantees him a berth in the band as long as he cares to stay, and he enjoys many aspects of the rock-and-roll life.

This includes the chance to meet adoring fans, such as an intelligent young photographer named Astrid Kirchherr, who takes a strong liking to the Beatles in general and to Sutcliffe in particular. Their acquaintance blossoms into romance, adding new uncertainty to Sutcliffe's future and new tension to his relationship with Lennon, who greets the love affair with a mixture of acceptance, jealousy, and resentment. This emotional ambivalence persists when Sutcliffe starts encountering the health problems that led to his untimely death in 1962.

"Backbeat" is more worldly than the best bio-pics to emerge from the rock-and-roll scene over the years, such as "The Buddy Holly Story" and "La Bamba," which reflected the fresh-faced 1950s as accurately as this film reflects the sensation-hungry '60s. The sexual escapades of the Beatles get plenty of on-screen attention, some of it quite explicit, and even the story's calmer interludes are interspersed with scenes of drinking, carousing, and brash behavior.

At its core, however, the movie seems serious in its fascination with the Beatles and sincere in its curiosity about what made the group tick during its early and most formative years. While no great insights emerge, the film paints a credible portrait no only of the band's superstar members (the final constituent, Ringo Starr, eventually arrives to replace Pete Best, the group's original drummer), but also of a likable guy (Sutcliffe), who *almost* had a shot at superstardom, but passed it up for reasons that will be discussed and debated as long as rock history endures.

Ian Hart and Stephen Dorff give solid performances as Lennon and Sutcliffe, respectively, although they're such similar types that it is sometimes hard to remember which actor is playing which part. Sheryl Lee is just right as Kirchherr and German actor Kai Weisinger is well cast as Klaus Voorman, an intellectual boyfriend of Kirchherr, who became an early Beatles supporter.

Directing the action from a screenplay he wrote with Michael Thomas and Stephen Ward, filmmaker Softley keeps the pace reasonably quick and the images reasonably absorbing. Ian Wilson did the cinematography, which combines quiet professionalism with the rough-and-ready atmosphere of the story's time and place.

LOS ANGELES TIMES, 4/15/94, Calendar/p. 1, Peter Rainer

Before the Beatles were Fab or Yellow Submarined or Maharishied, they were a scrounging group just like other mortal rockers. "Backbeat" deals with the pre-Ringo years of 1960 to mid-1962, when Pete Best was the drummer and Stu Sutcliffe, on and off, played bass guitar.

Focusing primarily on Sutcliffe, played by Stephen Dorff, and his knockabout friendship with Ian Hart's John Lennon, "Backbeat" keeps fuzzing our memories of the Beatles with lots of unfamiliar shenanigans. The effect is both alienating and humanizing: They don't seem to be *our* Beatles, and yet these early struggles bring them closer to us. They were people before they were pop icons.

Would "Backbeat" have the same resonance if it were about a fictitious rock band? It's doubtful. The film plays off our knowledge—and ignorance—of the Beatles. It doesn't go into any particular depth about the relationships between Sutcliffe and Lennon and the other Beatles; it gives a once-over-lightly view of the Liverpool and Hamburg concert scene in the early '60s, where most of the action takes place. Director and co-writer Iain Softley is mostly interested in getting across the lurching, frenetic atmosphere of those days, when rockers were trying out their Elvis and James Dean poses and Pop was just around the corner.

Despite its flash and bite, "Backbeat" is also a fairly conventional view of celebrity heartbreak. The goading, teasing subtext to this film is: Just imagine! Sutcliffe could have been a Beatle! Softley tries to have it both ways. He shows us how Sutcliffe, who died from a brain hemorrhage in 1962 after he had already fallen out with the Beatles, was actually a talented painter who found fulfillment with Astrid Kirchherr (Sheryl Lee), the Hamburg photographer whose photographs of the group helped fix their "look." (The haircuts were her idea.)

But Softley also plays up the sad sack side of Sutcliffe's story. He coulda been a contenda. The doom and gloom doesn't really jibe with what we're shown of his life with the Beatles (or, even more, with what's been documented about that period). After all, Sutcliffe, as the film shows, could hardly play the bass or sing; he joined the group as a lark, and, as he tranced into the Hamburg underground of unisex pop poseurs, he lost interest in taking the stage. Even if Sutcliffe hadn't lost interest, Paul McCartney (played in the film by Gary Bakewell) wanted him gone, and even Lennon, who threatened to leave if Stu were dropped, finally backed down. The heartbreak scenario that Softley twangs in "Backbeat" is misguided. If Sutcliffe had stayed with the Beatles, they would not have been the Beatles.

The film also takes Sutcliffe a bit too mythically. Dorff has the right bantamweight James Dean look—it's the look that smote Astrid at first sight—but he doesn't get behind the look. Sutcliffe was a paradox: He tried on rebellions as a pose—he rebelled against his middle-class home, his art training, his rock career. And yet, as a painter, he was the real thing, even though the movie conveys his artistry in the standard bio-pic way. He attacks his canvases with a Van Gogh-like ravenousness.

Sutcliffe is the film's center but he's a centerless character. He takes on the colorations of the surrounding scenery. When Astrid, along with her long-term friend and lover Klaus Voormann (Kai Weisinger), dresses him up in modish existential duds, he seems most alive. He strikes attitudes, and that's probably part of what attracted Lennon to him; Lennon was trying on attitudes too in those days (and later too).

The unspoken sexual tension between Sutcliffe and Lennon is also lightly underlined in "Backbeat." It's supposed to be the mirror image of Sutcliffe's love affair with Astrid but it has more passion than anything going on with his *fraulein*. Ian Hart, who also played Lennon in "The Hours and the Times," is phenomenal in the role: he almost makes Lennon's grasping, desperate, overbearing relationship with Sutcliffe come alive.

Hart's Lennon is so volatile and self-hating and self-infatuated that he seems to be having a wild carnal affair with himself. It's a lot more exciting than the confabs between Sutcliffe and Astrid, which should be creepier than they appear here. Astrid, in her photos, was a zonked pixie, and she merged her look with Sutcliffe's as they grew closer together. Their love had the element of a twinship fantasy.

Most movies about rock are such dithery jobs that "Backbeat" may seem more impressive than it really is. It's lively and full of good music and it plays around with a fascinating subject—the Fifth Beatle and his one true love. But it doesn't really illuminate that subject or those years or that music. It's a Pop treatment of Pop.

NEW YORK, 4/25/94, p. 88, David Denby

What if Beethoven had a musical soul mate who rented a skiff on the Rhine, fell in love with trout fishing, and never composed a note? And what if Picasso's sketching buddy in Barcelona decided to spend his life hanging out with bullfighters? What a loss to art!

I intend no mockery of Stu Sutcliffe, the early member of the Beatles who withdrew and then died at the age of 22 of a brain hemorrhage, but I don't quite get the point of centering a movie on his life. The very pleasant but rather vacuous *Backbeat* returns to Hamburg, in 1960 and 1961. Back there in the dank, damp, beer-stinking cellar clubs of the Reeperbahn, John, Paul, George, and Pete Best (Ringo replaced him in 1962) find an audience and something of a release from the stifling provincialities of Liverpool. Handsome, soulful Stu Sutcliffe (Stephen Dorff, John Lennon's art-school pal, is also a member of the Beatles, hanging on for the girls and the fun, but his heart isn't in it. Onstage, Stu, hiding behind dark glasses, stands around pretending he's a musician. John wants him in the group, but Stu wants to paint, and he falls in love with a German photographer and Hamburg aesthete, Astrid Kirchherr (Sheryl Lee), who pulls him away.

As *Backbeat* tells it Astrid is a kind of prescient earth mother who not only loves Stu but senses that the Beatles have to face into the future without him to encounter their greatness. She takes pictures of the boys, giving them some sense of who they are. She gives Stu the haircut that becomes *the* haircut. Then, by taking Stu off, she frees John Lennon to become John Lennon; she consciously creates the Beatles.

Well, I don't know. *Maybe*. The movie, directed by Iain Softley and written by Softley, Michael Thomas, and Stephen Ward, has the slightly dismal feeling of a late-night bull session (Brian Epstein really created the Beatles. No, Astrid did it). Miss Kirchherr, still living in Hamburg, cooperated with the filmmakers and appears to have exercised some control over the production. I suspect that her role has been exaggerated, that she's grabbing on to a place in history. This is understandable enough, and anyway, few of us serve even as handmaidens to greatness. But it sends the movie askew: We keep expecting some revelation that never comes. Stu Sutcliffe's contribution to the Beatles was minimal, and his career as a painter was tragically cut off. In *Backbeat*, you don't get that ache of "Oh, this might have been." It's more a case of never was. As Stu, pretty little Stephen Dorff (an American) suffers nicely from headaches, and Sheryl Lee (another one, from *Twin Peaks*) smiles a great deal with womanly wisdom, bares her breasts joyously, and manages to give Astrid a thin glaze of European cultivation.

What held Lennon and Sutcliffe together? The filmmakers hint at a homoerotic attachment on John's part. For some reason, people keep trying to push John Lennon into hitherto unsuspected closets. (This is easier when the subject cannot hire a lawyer.) A 1992 film, *The Hours and the Times*, wove a pattern of supposition around a vacation Lennon took with Brian Epstein, who was certainly gay. Ian Hart, the Liverpudlian who played Lennon in that film, plays him again here, and Hart is the best thing in the movie. Fast, witty, saturnine, this voluble young lout has an edge of ambition and aggression that makes him different. Yet the filmmakers have delivered themselves into a trap. At times, the movie suggests (rightly, I think) that John's working-class energy and roughness was the true path to art, at least the true path to rock and roll, and that Astrid's Euro aestheticism—weird, slinky nightclubs serving blue drinks—was a crock of shite. But in that case, what did Astrid give the Beatles? A haircut?

What created the Beatles as a mass art phenomenon was the idiosyncratic blend of Paul's romantic tenderness and John's intellectual stringency and bite. That and the boys' sense of play, a surge of pure oxygen that burst onto the kitsch-clouded pop scene of the early sixties like a ray of light in a murky cave. At its occasional best, *Backbeat* captures some of the fun—the cheekiness of John, the happy grunge of the cellar-club life, the boys' progress from cover versions of sturdy Chuck Berry songs to their own music. Much of the movie is relaxed and joshing, in the early rambunctious style of the Beatles themselves. Yet the higher spirituality of the Stu-John relationship escapes me. From this movie, you might get the impression that Paul McCartney was a mere petulant boor. Something is askew; the central story of the early Beatles still hasn't been told on film.

NEW YORK POST, 4/15/94, p. 31, Michael Medved

In June of 1961, a talented 21-year-old with aspirations as both a painter and a rock musician made one of the least timely career moves in the history of western civilization.

After more than a year of playing bass guitar with a struggling Liverpool band he had helped to name "The Beatles," Stuart Sutcliffe abandoned the group to pursue his studies at a Hamburg art school and to continue an affair with a chic German photographer.

Some 16 months later, his former mates released their first single ("Love Me Do") and began their rapid climb to unequalled heights of worldwide popularity.

Unfortunately, Sutcliffe never lived to witness their success; he died of a brain hemorrhage in 1962, shortly before his 22nd birthday. An account of his brief career makes for a poignant footnote in rock 'n' roll history, but offers only a flimsy basis for a motion picture.

"Backbeat" despite the integrity and artistry with which it's been made, remains a drab, unsatisfying cinematic experience.

Inevitably, this well-intentioned film feels like a mournful little prelude to the real story of the Beatles, which is only just getting started when the picture ends as abruptly and awkwardly as Sutcliffe's short life.

Part of the problem is that the two lead performers fail to reproduce any sense of the potent charisma that their characters displayed in real life. The actual Sutcliffe bore a striking resemblance to James Dean and exerted such a powerful influence on his art school chum John Lennon, that Lennon insisted he stay with the band despite a lack of visible musical ability.

By contrast, actor Stephen Dorff (who previously starred as a South African boxer in "The Power of One") is such a fatally bland screen presence, giving such an understated performance, that his friendship with the kinetic Lennon (Ian Hart) is impossible to understand.

By the same token, American actress Sheryl Lee comes across as ordinary and earthbound playing the ethereal, irresistible photographer Astrid Kirchherr. She and Dorff generate no chemistry in their love scenes together.

The "grand passion" that led Stuart to leave the Beatles thus makes no sense, leaving the film with a hollow center and some painfully pedestrian dialogue. "I do love him, John!" Astrid tells Lennon, to which Stuart's best friend portentously replies: "So do we all!"

Playing Lennon, Liverpudlian Ian Hart (who bears scant physical resemblance to the late musician) gives by far the film's best performance, conveying a moving sense of the insecurity and rage that lay below his character's cutting, ironic edge.

First-time director Iain Softley does a good job portraying the sad, seedy atmosphere in the Hamburg seaport dives in which the Beatles played a long series of exhausting gigs in their early days. He also puts together a fine sound-alike band that re-creates the raw, infectious sound that the boys reportedly produced before they became world famous.

Anyone who cares about the Beatles' music can certainly enjoy the lively, authentic-looking scenes of them performing songs like "Money" and "Twist and Shout." But whenever the music stops and the talk begins, energy drains from this sad little picture like the air from a punctured balloon.

NEWSDAY, 4/15/94, Part II/p. B3, Jack Mathews

For a brief moment in the opening scene of Iain Softley's "Backbeat," when we see a young John Lennon and another member of the Beatles mocking a group of hooligans in a Liverpool nightclub, it looks as if we might be in for another of those worshipful paens to the wisecracking wonder boys of "A Hard Day's Night."

But the scene turns quickly ugly, as the hooligans chase the two musicians into an alley and beat one of them, Stuart Sutcliffe, nearly senseless. From then on, nothing about "Backbeat" is like anything done about the Beatles before.

The gang attack in 1959, and its probable role in Sutcliffe's death from a brain hemorrhage in April, 1962, frame a marvelously compelling story of friendship, sexual ambiguity, love and tragedy among European youths both on the cusp of a social revolution and, in the case of the Beatles, about to play a key role in it.

"Backbeat," to writer-director Softley's enormous credit, doesn't allow the aura of the Beatles' legend anywhere near it. The story ends six months before their first hit, and though there is plenty of music, recorded by a studio band, the sound is that of raw, classic rock and roll.

All five of the original Beatles are here—Lennon, Sutcliffe, Paul McCartney, George Harrison, drummer Pete Best—but Softley's focus is so specifically on the relationship between best friends Lennon (Ian Hart) and Sutcliffe (Stephen Dorff), and Sutcliffe's romance with German photographer Astrid Kirchherr (Sheryl Lee), that the others barely register.

The story covers the last 2½ years of Sutcliffe's life but is concentrated on the Beatles' Hamburg period. It was there, in the sleazy clubs of the city's notorious red-light district, that the Beatles got their first steady gig and developed their technique.

It was also where sex, drugs and rock and roll were just being joined, and where the young Beatles could experiment in excess. "Backbeat" suggests the seaminess of their lifestyle there, the easy sex and the amphetamines that kept them going night after night. But when we leave the club, it is always to follow Lennon and Sutcliffe, whose relationship, the movie hints, had its own sexual undercurrent.

Sutcliffe, often called the Fifth Beatle, was the one girls seemed to like most, and Astrid Kirchherr, a free spirit at the center of Hamburg's existential art community, was no exception. The movie verges on cliché when Astrid shows up at the club and locks eyes with Sutcliffe. Once that connection is made, however, and Lennon begins a losing battle with his jealousy, "Backbeat" hits its emotional stride.

These are terrific performances from Hart and Dorff, who develop a chemistry that charges every scene they share. Hart uses Lennon's famous anger as dramatic kindling and builds a furious fire at times and Dorff, playing a tragic figure who could easily be overdrawn, makes Sutcliffe the most human character in the story.

Softley, a Cambridge graduate making his feature debut after directing commercials, music videos and plays, shows amazing restraint with his subject. Pop stars, like most famous historical figures, often seem too aware of their destiny in biographical pictures. Filmmakers can't resist dropping in little hints of what's to come.

The only echoes from the future in "Backbeat" are Astrid's contributions to the group (she gave the Beatles their mop-tops, and her photographs are said to have inspired the style of "A Hard Day's Night") and the cool relationship between Lennon and McCartney.

John and Paul (played by McCartney dead ringer Gary Bakewell) were the co-leaders of the group but never close friends. Their professional relationship, we're shown here, was strained almost to breaking by McCartney's insistence that Sutcliffe's weakness as a guitarist was holding them back.

Sutcliffe solved the conflict by dropping out himself. His real passion was for art, and for Astrid, and he was relishing both before his paralyzing headaches gave way to violent fits and, finally, to death.

NEWSWEEK, 4/18/94, p. 60, David Ansen

For a while "Backbeat" is lively, unpretentious fun, a glimpse into the early days of the Beatles when Pete Best was still the drummer, their ducktails hadn't turned mop top and they were doing covers of American R&B in seedy Hamburg clubs. The focus is on the little-known Beatle, Stuart Sutcliffe (Stephen Dorff), John Lennon's best mate, a promising painter and lackluster bass player who cut a cool figure on stage but never sought musical success. Lennon is played by Ian Hart (who did him in Christopher Munch's brilliant film "The Hours and Times"); as long as "Backbeat" stays with him, Sutcliffe and the rousing music, director Iain Softley's movie maintains a funky charm. But when "existential" German photographer Astrid Kirchherr (Sheryl Lee) slinks into the story to fall in love with Sutcliffe, the movie turns solemn and silly. Kirchherr seems an irritating poseur; her tragic affair with Sutcliffe strikes tinny, overwrought emotions. Get back, get back to where you once belonged, you want to shout. But the movie is stuck in the wrong groove.

NEW STATESMAN & SOCIETY, 4/8/94, p. 35, Jonathan Romney

The key sequence in *Backbeat* comes when the Beatles are in a Hamburg studio, recording backing for Tony Sheridan's version of "My Bonnie". One of them isn't there, though. Their bass player Stu Sutcliffe is doing something infinitely more important. He's taking a short cut to rock'n'roll immortality: having his photo taken—or, better, being *styled*—by his girlfriend Astrid Kirchherr.

If the Beatles were a 1990s band, the whole premise of *Backbeat* would be academic. It wouldn't matter that Sutcliffe was a deadbeat at his instrument; in fact, he wouldn't need to play at all. He could just waggle silent maracas, or better still, just *be* there, modelling a pout, turning up for the odd interview. He wouldn't have to say anything, just punctuate John Lennon's pithy repartee with a beautiful, model-boy sneer.

As a 1990s film, *Backbeat* looks with bemused nostalgia on an unthinkable pre-sampling age when bands had to play their instruments. There's more than a note of regret for the notion of hard-won success, rock'n'roll as graft, the rigour of the road. But that Luddite mythology is cast in an ironic light, since the moment at which the Beatles win their spurs is the moment when the simple act of playing music begins to be supplanted by the more complex notion of *being a band.*

Of course, the Beatles got there by slogging the Chuck Berry repertoire for all it was worth, all night and every night, in a variety of Hamburg strip joints, and *Backbeat* considers that notion with due awe. But their first real exposure to the art of being a band came when Kirchherr roped them into those moody photo sessions on docks and railway bridges. And no one could stand side-on sneering with quite the glacial grace of Sutcliffe.

Iain Softley's film, in its cheap and cheerful way—and, disparaging as those epithets sound, they do sum up its sarky, slightly tacky brio—constitutes an extended tract on glamour. It's about how some are born glamorous (Sutcliffe), some achieve glamour (John Lennon), others have glamour thrust on them (the other lads in the band).

The catch is that Sutcliffe's glamour isn't terribly interesting. Everyone loves a footnote, and Sutcliffe is one of the best: he got out before the going was good, then died. He was the first figure in British pop whose claim to star status resided entirely in his ability to wear dark glasses. A classic pouter in the James Dean style, his musical prowess was so-so, and in the film his brief, strangled attempt at singing "Love Me Tender" almost changes history, scaring away a record company man. Twenty years later, he could have worn a swastika and sung "My Way".

Backbeat has all the appeal of those parallel-world sci-fi stories—there's the "what if?" factor, a sense that things could have been different. The best retrospective irony hangs on John Lennon. He is shown evolving as a guru of pithy absurdism precisely because he's way out of kilter with the art-school cool Sutcliffe represented, and to which Lennon desperately aspires. Out of his depth in a young existentialists' dive (*La Dolce Vita* out of *Absolute Beginners*), he throws a fit, bellowing, "It's all dick!" Of course, it's just that: he can't handle the sexual ambiguity of the scene, because it's there in his relationship with Sutcliffe.

The homoerotic slant is nicely played up by casting Ian Hart as Lennon, reprising his role in Christopher Münch's remarkable *The Hours and Times*, in which Lennon had Brian Epstein as an implied sexual sparring partner. Here, the sense of Lennon's rage is no less clear—a not-quite-straight working-class boy's impatience with sexually more adventurous would-be aristos of style.

Backbeat is about the choice between two paths to rock'n'roll nirvana—one, via cheek-bone-and-photo-shoot cool, the other through sheer expenditure of nerd libido. And Hart is an inspired nerd, a perfect incarnation of Lennon's oddly pithy wit that wasn't quite wit, more a refusal to cooperate: "Liverpool!" he announces, "home of ... Liverpudlians". Stephen Dorff's Sutcliffe just can't compete, but then he's not meant to: he's just a neat pair of jeans and a cowlick, and he's adequate for that. But Sheryl Lee's casting as Kirchherr is a disaster. This woman had the Nordic mysterioso of Nico and Marianne Faithfull rolled into one, but Lee plays her as a jolly, flirty hamster.

As the title suggests, *Backbeat* is wilfully revisionist, but it does remind us, just when we'd forgotten, why anyone might have wanted to stay up night after night, fuelled by tarts' Preludin, playing old Little Richard songs in the first place. The pre-Lennon/McCartney repertoire is bashed out here by a wildly improbable tribute band composed of members of Sonic Youth, REM, Nirvana *et al*, and it's a dream—note-for-note accuracy, but so vigorously bile-enhanced you can see why people might have wanted to rip out cinema seats to Bill Haley.

It's the film's commitment to the enduring crud of rock'n'roll that allows it to flirt with sentimentality and the sloppiness of legend. After Sutcliffe's death, Lennon devotes a song "for absent friends". The band begins a maudlin "Love Me Tender" then, after a couple of bars, starts blasting out "Twist and Shout". That's what counts: the rest is "all dick". Burn your *Sergeant Pepper* CD and see this.

SIGHT AND SOUND, 4/94, p. 35, Robert Yates

Liverpool, 1960. Art school friends John Lennon and Stuart Sutcliffe fail to escape from a group of men they have insulted in a club; Sutcliffe is beaten, receiving a heavy blow to the head. Soon afterwards, despite Sutcliffe's misgivings about abandoning his painting, the two leave for Hamburg where their band, the Beatles, is booked to play. There, performing nightly, the Beatles begin to gain a following, and Sutcliffe and Lennon take to the life of drink, drugs and easy sex. They also meet Klaus Voormann, a local artist, and his girlfriend, photographer Astrid Kirchherr, who invite the Beatles to the Bar Enfer, home to Hamburg's Existentialist scene. Lennon, who has noticed that Kirchherr and Sutcliffe are drawn to each other, explodes, dismissing the Enfer crowd as hypocrites. However, Kirchherr persuades him and the rest of the band to let her photograph them.

Sutcliffe begins to court Kirchherr. At one show he takes the microphone and sings to her, abysmally. A record company scout in the audience is frightened away, causing band member Paul McCartney, seeing an opportunity lost, to attack Sutcliffe as a liability and a mediocre musician who is carried by the rest of the band; Lennon defends his friend. Sutcliffe overhears the argument and leaves the club for Astrid's home. On the way, his thoughts become scrambled, the first signs of the brain haemorrhage that will kill him. He misses a show and the band's first recording session to be with Astrid, confiding in her that he is anxious to start painting again. The two sleep together, Kirchherr leaves Voormann and Sutcliffe moves in with her.

The Beatles' success is checked by a forced return to Liverpool when George Harrison is discovered to be too young to work legally, but they go back to Hamburg straight after Harrison's eighteenth birthday. Sutcliffe now spends most of his time with Astrid and is painting feverishly. A fight with Lennon over his commitment signals his break from the band and he is delighted to win a place in Hamburg art school, although his health is still a concern after he suffers a blackout. When the Beatles return to England, Sutcliffe stays behind, and becomes engaged to Kirchherr, but not before his instability is emphasised by a violent, unprovoked attack on Voormann. He continues to paint with a passion, hearing of the Beatles' growing reputation, until he is seized by a convulsion and dies. April 1962. The Beatles are due to return to Hamburg to play. Kirchherr tells Lennon of Sutcliffe's death, and later watches their performance at the Star Club.

The recent slice of history on which *Backbeat*'s script is based might have been invented by Steve Wooley and Nik Powell as exemplary raw material for a British feature. The first film from the pair's Scala production company, it tells a British story which boasts British characters as loud and ambitious as young Americans. What's more, among its principals are the Beatles, peerless exponents in music of what Woolley and Powell have repeatedly trumpeted as their design in film: pop art.

As with Woolley and Powell's Palace productions, the film has been thought through as a clever package. The mostly British cast is led by two American semi-stars, which should help it travel, while the songs were recorded for the film's soundtrack by a band of left-field pop luminaries, which should stir the interests of young music fans. Both decisions are fine: the Americans, Dorff and Lee, do all that is required of them, while the film only benefits from the superband's take on the punky, pre-fame Beatles.

However, making a script from a package is a trickier feat, resulting, as occasionally happens here, in events and behaviour which jar as crudely emblematic. "It's all about the origins of Pop Art," first-time director Iain Softley has said of *Backbeat*. Raw English musicians, imbued with America, meet and are influenced by German aesthetes. Identifying the different currents at work are some pretty predictable markers. For bedtime reading to Sutcliffe, Kirchherr chooses Rimbaud, confirming the belief that it is only characters in films or plays—those the writers need to flag as arty—who still read Rimbaud.

Yet the film's strengths are also the product of its broad strokes. The rock 'n' roll life is rendered in a knockabout cartoon fashion. In an image that flirts, as the film half-heartedly does, with Lennon's possible bisexuality, Lennon, having sex with a groupie on his lower bunk bed, calls up to Sutcliffe, entangled with another groupie on the upper bunk, and asks, "Are you glad you came?" They sustain their antics by popping pills, and play on a Reeperbahn whose seediness has been treated to a saucy postcard makeover, more slap-and-tickle than sordid. More vivid still are the costumes, haunts and posturing of Astrid's crowd who really did call themselves, it seems, the Existentialists. *Backbeat*'s design team evidently enjoyed turning them into bohemians as styled by Tony Hancock.

Fleshing out this engaging cartoon is an excellent performance by Ian Hart as Lennon (his second stab at him, the first being in Christopher Münch's *The Hours and Times*). Hart sometimes seems to be working from his own script, so favoured is he with the best lines. This is Lennon as the clever anti-intellectual, the champion of rude, low art. Van Gogh, he tells Sutcliffe, would be in a blues band if he were alive in the 60s (could the scriptwriters not have thought of a painter with two good ears?). His routine response when faced with what he views as the pretensions of Astrid's crowd is, "It's all dick." Hart's portrayal suggests vulnerability behind the swagger and acclaims nervy wit as a creative defense mechanism.

Of course, the film's focus is meant to be on Sutcliffe. But the character does not really hang together, riven as it is by the types it is asked to play. He is both cool rocker (he is rock 'n' roll attitude, cries Lennon) and fevered artist; beautiful object (on stage he is almost motionless, a statue in dark glasses) turned into driven subject. Sutcliffe threatens to stand exposed as a mere peg to hang the film on. Alternatively—to credit the film with more subtlety than it perhaps deserves—we may prefer to view Sutcliffe as a character trying to assemble himself. He has a go at being James Dean, plays at *Cabaret* and finally attempts garret power-painting. *Backbeat* is certainly effective—mostly because of Hart—as a picture of young men learning, and learning how to bluff. Research carried out for the film suggests that the 'real' Sutcliffe was chancing his arm as preposterously as the standard over-reaching 20-year-old: "I have shrivelled like a sucked grape," and "In a piss-pot sits my soul," he wrote in letters from Hamburg.

Tempting as it might be to forget all references to 'real' people, *Backbeat* will be scrutinised for its spin on the Beatles story. However, Lennon apart, there's only a sketchy, mean-spirited McCartney to step out of the shadows and trouble Mop-top spotters (although period detail fiends will gasp at the glaring anachronism of the huge "Welcome to Merseyside" sign at Liverpool Airport—the metropolitan council was not established until 1974). The film does, though, have an angle on the Beatles story, which is to underline the lessons learned in Hamburg from Kirchherr and Voormann (who later designed the *Revolver* album sleeve) on the value of projecting an image, which these days is a new band's first lesson. However, *Backbeat* does not encourage the viewer to sympathise with the Hamburg sophisticates—probably because it is most at ease as a restive pop romp—and invites us instead to echo Lennon, and cry out, "It's all dick."

TIME, 5/2/94, p. 74, Richard Corliss

The most pungent cultural spillage from the early death of any rock star—of Buddy Holly or Ritchie Valens, Jim Morrison or Sid Vicious—may be the movie made from his life. Producers paw through old press clippings, take a quick snort of the current zeitgeist, tack on a note of mythical tragedy and voilà!, a tale for our time with a hit sound track guaranteed.

This is a low business, exploiting a musician's notoriety and an audience's star lust. It has reached a nadir of sorts with *Backbeat*, a homoerotic paean to Stuart Sutcliffe (Stephen Dorff), the fifth Beatle. Or maybe the sixth, if you count pre-Ringo drummer Pete Best and leave out George Martin and Murray the K.

Stu, a budding painter and middling bassist, may seem a long shot for rock immortality. He died at 22, months before the group, which he had earlier quit, cut its first record. But according to *Backbeat*, Stu was the dreamboat heart of the combo and John Lennon (Ian Hart) was its soul. Paul McCartney (Gary Bakewell) and George Harrison (Chris O'Neill) only whined and purred, respectively, while Lennon and Sutcliffe did the heavy lifting. John, you see, was Liverpool's own angry young man and the sole creator of this proto-punk, *ur*-grunge band (don't you love revisionism?). And Stu, preening moodily, was John's closet love god—before a brain tumor drove Stu mad and killed him, thus establishing his credentials as a rock Rimbaud.

Backbeat has an attractive cast and a passionate rock-'n'-roll score (played by some top young musicians). But with its attention to the posturings of Lennon and the untalented Stu, the movie succumbs to the post-Madonna notion that pop success is all a matter of attitude. That's so misguided. If you have any doubt, listen to the songs.

VILLAGE VOICE, 4/19/94, p. 54, Georgia Brown

A couple of years ago, with his 60-minute *The Hours and Times*, Christopher Münch pulled off something amazingly delicate. Münch's lovingly shot, black-and-white film took off from an actual four-day visit to Barcelona made by John Lennon and Brian Epstein in 1963, right after Lennon's son Julian was born. (The new dad visited the hospital once, a week after the birth, and then took off for Barcelona.)

Told mostly in dialogue, the film evolves into a rich psychodrama about friendship and longing and isolation. The gay, erudite Epstein suffers valiantly while Lennon plays subtly on, to, and "around Epstein's vulnerability—now sadistically, now tactfully—deliberating whether to relinquish his position of power. Here was inspired use of pop icons—their humanity given the full benefit of the doubt.

The Hours and Times had only a limited release (in New York it debuted at New Directors and had a couple of short runs). Not many saw it. Though surely Britain's Iain Softley must have seen it somewhere, because his *Backbeat* seems to owe it an enormous debt. Many more viewers will see Softley's new musical melodrama—somewhat in the same new-band-in-town vein as *The Commitments*, but not as charming—which handles Lennon's relation to Stuart Sutcliffe, an art school mate, as obliquely as would any male buddy picture. The same superb actor, Ian Hart, plays Lennon in both films.

Backbeat opens in 1960 and centers on John and Stu (Stephen Dorff), who puts his painting on hold to join John's band. The group is leaving Liverpool for Hamburg and some gigs in a sleaze pit—they'll perform between strippers. Stu comes along mostly for the kicks and the girls. One of the movie's refrains has Paul (Gary Bakewell) griping about both Stu ("He just stands there") and drummer Pete Best (Scot Williams). John keeps challenging Paul, saying if Stu goes he goes. Guess who goes?

Enter Astrid (Laura Palmer ... uh, Sheryl Lee), a cool blond Hamburg photographer, girlfriend of the baby-faced Klaus (Kai Wiesinger), who's discovered the Beatles in their dive. Members of Hamburg's black-velvet underground, both Astrid and Klaus are innocuously androgynous-looking. While the Liverpudlians are still in pompadours, the Germans sport mod helmet cuts. Who'd have suspected Beatle style came out of the Teutonic demimonde? (Astrid claims the haircut came from French films.) Stu and Astrid lock eyes across the crowded club, and Stu all but falls off the stage. Astrid, pronounces John, has "je ne sais fucking quoi."

Although Astrid eventually takes Stu from the Beatles, she seals the homoerotic bond between John and Stu, since John loves her, too. (And Klaus loves all the Beatles and Astrid.) Later, the dowdy Cynthia (Jennifer Ehle) makes a brief visit and is almost treated as a person (I won't go so far as to say an equal). Cynthia wants babies, it's said. Astrid, on the other hand, suggests a proto-Yoko, foreign-born artist and mother-authority figure. Professionally, she anticipates Richard Lester, capturing the band frolicking for the camera.

The frisson the movie wants to offer is seeing the lads just at the start, before they've composed a Beatles song, as if the outcome is in doubt. Except that Softley can't resist telegraphing the inevitable, belaboring the obvious. As in John's: "We're going to be too big for Hamburg; we're going to be too big for Liverpool; we're going to be too big for the fucking world." Or this, also from John: "They'll say, there goes Stu Sutcliffe. He could have been one of the Beatles."

As it should be in musicals, the best part of *Backbeat* is the exuberant numbers. Don Was has put together a sophisticated band—including Soul Asylum's Dave Pirner, Nirvana's Dave Grohl, and Sonic Youth's Thurston Moore—capable of sounding both spontaneous and youthfully enthusiastic. The movie's most touching scene is its next to last, when John launches into a few soulful bars of "Love Me Tender" (to Stu, of course) and then veers into "Twist and Shout" and the joint goes wild. But Softley goes and ruins his ending, tacking on a really corny beach romp in silhouette. If only he knew how to let it be.

Also reviewed in:
CHICAGO TRIBUNE, 4/22/94, Friday/p. A, Michael Wilmington
NATION, 5/2/94, p. 606, Stuart Klawans
NEW REPUBLIC, 5/9/94, p. 26, Stanley Kauffmann
NEW YORK TIMES, 4/15/94, p. C15, Janet Maslin
VARIETY, 1/31-2/6/94, p. 66, Todd McCarthy
WASHINGTON POST, 4/22/94, p. C1, Richard Harrington
WASHINGTON POST, 4/22/94, Weekend/p. 44, John F. Kelly

BAD GIRLS, (Kollek, director)

A Castle Hill Productions Inc. release. *Producer:* Julian Schlossberg. *Director:* Amos Kollek. *Screenplay:* Amos Kollek. *Director of Photography:* Ed Talavera. *Editor:* Dana Congdon. *Costumes:* Catherin Pierson. *Running time:* 85 minutes. *MPAA Rating:* Not Rated.

CAST: Amos Kollek (Jack); Marla Sucharetza (Lori); Mari Nelson (Mary Lou); Gilbert Giles (Vernon); Jessica Sager (Susan); Alicia Miller (Tina); Erin McMurtry (Lisa); Robert Kerbeck (Bob); Phil Parolisi (Tony); David Kener (Nicko); Nancy McPherson, Pat "Delightful" Kelly, Sylvia Hill, Stacy Goodwin, Abelard "Chino" Coimbre, and Kathy White (Themselves).

NEW YORK POST, 1/28/94, p. 45, Thelma Adams

The director of "Bad Girls" has been a very bad boy—and should be spanked!

Israeli writer-director-actor Amos ("Forever Lulu") Kollek went slumming in Hell's Kitchen. His mission? To satisfy his curiosity about prostitution. (There aren't whores in Haifa?)

Kollek, a.k.a. Jack, moves into a Manhattan drugs-and-sluts hotel ostensibly to write a book about streetwalking. Blurring fact and fiction the son of Jerusalem's former mayor creates a voyeuristic docudrama about our girls in high heels.

Nursing wounds from his broken marriage, Jack becomes involved with two hookers, Lori (Marla Sucharetza) and Mary Lou (Mari Nelson). Kollek weaves their fictionalized encounters into actual interviews with streetwalkers and a pimp.

The line between fact and fiction is not the only one Kollek blurs. With its drabbly lit shots of live sex shows, al fresco fellatio, and bare-breasted prostitutes, is "Bad Girls" porn or about porn? Does the director exploit his access to the joygirls to touch their skin or get under it?

A bit of both, I suspect.

Kollek's portrait of the girls-who-grope is titillating and oddly moving. They emerge, for the most part as drug-abusing, aimless women from the West often sexually abused as children.

The prostitutes are angry, manipulative, tribal and bored. Most are mothers. Some enjoy sex with men, some with women, some don't like it at all. But, damn them, they have hearts of gold.

What redeems Kollek's movie is his "self-portrait" as a schlepper without a cause. A good-humored unattractive, hairy-armed man widening into middle-age, he's more a listener than a lover. He idolizes Hemingway and Jack London; he's closer to Walter Mitty.

If exile to the isle of hookers is his therapy for a life lived without passion, the whores of Hell's Kitchen aren't going to take it lying down.

An angry Lori yells at him, "You're a miserable person looking for someone more miserable."

She's right. Kollek's willingness to skewer himself, to examine and misunderstand his own motives, to give the hookers the best lines, elevates "Bad Girls" from porn, but doesn't quite make it art.

NEWSDAY, 1/28/94, Part II/p. 63, Jack Mathews

"I always wanted to be a great writer, like Hemingway or Jack London," says the narrator in the opening moments of "Bad Girls," a docudrama about a man researching a book on the lives of street hookers in midtown Manhattan. "I don't know why, but somehow I never got to write the books I really wanted to write."

The flat, dramatically dead voice belongs to Amos Kollek who is also the star, writer and director of the movie, and if you have seen his earlier films, you know he is speaking from the heart. Kollek may have always wanted to be a great filmmaker, like Cassavetes or Costa-Gavras, but somehow never had the talent.

"Bad Girls" is the work of an earnest amateur, and oddly, that is its best quality. Kollek spent two months in mid-1991 interviewing working girls on the streets of Hell's Kitchen, near Port Authority, and though we have seen and heard these titillating bits many times before, their raw, unrehearsed footage provides some relief from Kollek's melodramatic writing and stony performance.

For a while, there seems the possibility that "Bad Girls" is meant as satire, a '90s version of "42nd Street." It opens with Toni Tennille singing "You Must Have Been a Beautiful Baby" over a montage of hard, emaciated prostitutes walking their beat, and later, after getting a little too interested in a hooker named Mary Lou, Kollek croaks out a few hilarious bars of Buddy Holly's "Hello, Mary Lou."

But no, this is a sincere dramatic exploration of the hows and whys of whoredom, with Kollek stunned to learn that most of the working girls are the products of broken homes and sexual abuse, that they sell their bodies in order to maintain drug habits, and that they are often brutalized by both pimps and tricks.

Several of the prostitutes who appear in interviews also play themselves in speaking parts, but the two main hooker roles—Mary Lou (Mari Nelson) and Lori (Marla Sucharetza)—a willowy blond with the hard beauty of Ellen Barkin, actually managed to make a real character out of Lori, the fallen woman Kollek's Jack is determined to prop up.

Kollek saved the central role for himself, of course, and though we are told through his narration that he undergoes a radical personality change, from aloof journalistic observer to caring friend and white knight, you could chart the actual arc of his performance with a straight edge.

Better known in his native Israel as the son of the former mayor of Jerusalem than he is for his movies, Kollek made his acting debut opposite Julie Hagerty in his 1985 "Goodbye, New York." Since then, he has managed to write and fill the role of a balding, unattractive middle-aged man in "Forever Lulu," which co-starred Hanna Schygulla and Alec Baldwin, and "Double Edge," with Faye Dunaway.

Filmmaking is a hard craft to learn, even when you start at the top.

VILLAGE VOICE, 2/1/94, p. 59, Devon Jackson

Three summers ago, Israeli writer and filmmaker Amos Kollek (son of Jerusalem's ex-mayor Teddy Kollek) camped out in mid Manhattan and interviewed the area's street prostitutes—with the somewhat pedestrian idea that he'd make a film, an oral history project, so to speak. Instead he made a fiction film, *Bad Girls*. Oddly enough it works: it raises questions. What does it mean that the women playing the prostitutes are practically indistinguishable from the film's real-life prostitutes?

Kollek bravely casts himself in the role of Jack the writer—another Hemingway-infected, moralizing patriarch. In a word, a dickbag, in two, James Toback. Paying to listen to their stories, Jack soon becomes enamored of two women: the dirty blond, sassy Lori (Marla Sucharetza, who inhabits her role as convincingly as River Phoenix did his in *My Own Private Idaho*), and the demure, candy-apple blond Mary Lou (Mari Nelson). Jack tries to civilize, romance, and reform them both. Into this potential ménage, however, enters a jilted ex-john of Lori's, and then the film begins to unravel. An ugly rape-snuff scene leads to Jack wreaking vengeance Travis Bickle-style on the johns.

Similar in its quotidian drone to Lizzie Borden's *Working Girls*, to *Christiane F.*'s grittiness, to the Q&A format of *sex, lies and videotape*, and Jaglomesque in nature, it leaves one wondering how much more powerful the film would've been had Kollek enlisted the camera and perspective of someone like Borden to follow him around as he made *Bad Girls*: Imagine a documentary questioning Kollek's reasons for making a pseudodocumentary about prostitutes. As it is, Jack/Amos only partially exposes and indicts himself as a male. Kollek's is gutsier than most other films that explore/exploit prostitution, but by how much?

Also reviewed in:
NEW YORK TIMES, 1/28/94, p. C8, Stephen Holden

BAD GIRLS (Kaplan, director)

A Twentieth Century Fox release of a Ruddy Morgan production. *Executive Producer:* Lynda Obst. *Producer:* Albert S. Ruddy, Andre E. Morgan, and Charles Finch. *Director:* Jonathan Kaplan. *Screenplay:* Ken Friedman and Yolande Finch. *Story:* Albert S. Ruddy, Charles Finch, and Gray Frederickson. *Director of Photography:* Ralf Bode. *Editor:* Jane Kurson. *Music*: Jerry Goldsmith. *Sound:* Jose Antonio Garcia. *Sound Editor:* Scott Hecker, Elliott Koretz, Bruce Lacey, Larry Mann, Marvin Walowitz, and Susan Dudeck. *Casting:* Mike Fenton, Julie Ashton, and Julie Selzer. *Production Designer:* Guy Barnes. *Art Director:* M. Nord Haggerty. *Set Decorator:* Michael Taylor. *Set Dresser:* Loren Patrick Lyons. *Special Effects:* John C. Hartigan. *Costumes:* Susie DeSanto. *Make-up:* Patty York. *Make-up Effects:* Tony Gardner. *Stunt Coordinator:* Walter Scott. *Running time:* 97 minutes. MPAA Rating: R.

CAST: Madeleine Stowe (Cody Zamora); Mary Stuart Masterson (Anita Crown); Andie MacDowell (Eileen Spenser); Drew Barrymore (Lilly Laronette); James Russo (Kid Jarrett); James LeGros (William Tucker); Robert Loggia (Frank Jarrett); Dermot Mulroney (Josh McCoy); Jim Beaver (Detective Graves); Nick Chinlund (Detective O'Brady); Neil Summers (Ned); Daniel O'Haco (Roberto); Richard E. Reyes (Rico); Alex Kubik (Yuma); Will MacMillan (Colonel Clayborne); Harry Northup (Preacher); Don Hood (Echo City Sheriff); Donald L. Montoya (Station Master); Zoaunne LeRoy (Widow Clayborne); Jimmy Lewis, Jr. (Surrey Driver); Millie Weddles (Widow's Maid); Vince Davis (Apparel Clerk); Blue Deckert (Rich Citizen); Rodger Boyce (Bank Manager); Nik Hagler (Aqua Dulce Marshal); Mark Feltch (Teller); Max Bode (Boy in Bank); Cooper Huckabee (Deputy Earl); Richard Robbins (Posse Member); Beulah Quo (Chinese Herbalist); Rick Lundin (Wagon Driver Jack); Mark Carlton (Lawyer Lurie); Amber Leigh (Laughing Woman); Chuck Bennett (Covered Wagon Driver); R.C. Bates (Tector).

LOS ANGELES TIMES, 4/22/94, Calendar/p. 1, Peter Rainer

They swear and carouse and kick up dust. They charge across the crimson horizon on their trusty steeds. They blast grown men right out of their skivvies with their pistols. They wear color-coordinated outfits. They're the Bad Girls of "Bad Girls" but they're really Good Girls, or at least Good Bad Girls. Whatever righteous wrath they expend, however smudged their cheeks, they always manage to look as stylish as a fashion catalogue layout for Hot Nights in the Old West.

The timing for this film is right: This is the movie era for women with guns and an attitude. "Bad Girls" combines the renascence of the Western with post-"Thelma & Louise" syndrome. It displays four of our busiest and most popular actresses—Madeleine Stowe, Andie MacDowell, Mary Stuart Masterson and Drew Barrymore—in a vehicle as form-fittingly tailored for them as "The Magnificent Seven" was for its actors. The high concept is preposterously low-slung and amusing—even more so because director Jonathan Kaplan plays the material straight. He's trying to be John Ford in designer jeans.

Audiences may not enjoy this movie in quite the way it was intended—as some kind of revisionist feminist spree—but that's all right. Sometimes movies are enjoyable for all the wrong reasons. What's ticklish about "Bad Girls" is how it shoe-horns feminist anger into a plot that amply provides for stylish sashaying.

The Bad Girls begin the movie as prostitutes in a Bible-Belted Colorado town, which they flee after their leader, Cody Zamora (Stowe), plugs an unruly customer. Chased by two Pinkerton detectives into Texas, the girls set their sights on a sawmill that Anita (Masterson) thinks could be turned into a thriving business. She had planned to purchase the homestead with her husband before he died of cholera and she became a prostitute.

The sawmill idea meets with surprisingly little resistance. "We sold our bodies says one of the girls. "Why can't we sell some wood?" This is the spirit that made the West. (A friend referred to this part of the film as "Fried Green Tamales.") But en route to the mill complications ensue. Cody's grubstake gets swiped by the scurvy, stubbly *bandido* (James Russo) she used to run around with. (He flourishes a whip and, in a modest skinny-dip scene, we see the lash marks on her back.) Eileen (MacDowell) gets captured and jailed but makes googly eyes at her jailer, William Tucker (James LeGros), and escapes into the night.

A handsome stranger (Dermot Mulroney) keeps popping up for Cody at the most opportune moments, helping to treat her back wounds and heartaches. He's quite possibly the most Liberated Guy in Western movie history—a Shane with sensitivity training. He could care less that Cody is characterized on the reward posters as the Honky Tonk Harlot.

It helps, of course, that, with the exception of Tucker, all the other men in this movie, most notably Robert Loggia's Frank Jarrett, seem to be out of a Sam Peckinpah road company. This reinforces the film's feminist point: Times were tough for single women on the range. As a breed, men were sadistic scamps. The Bad Girls bring them into line with pistol and Gatling gun.

One reason you can't take the revisionism in this movie all that seriously—besides the have-your-cake-and-eat-it-too fashion prancing—is because Kaplan keeps hauling up buckets of hoary Western clichés. If you're going to rework a genre, a good place to start is with the dialogue, and there are far too many lines in this movie like the one where Cody looks longingly at her old lover and says, "We had some times, didn't we?" (At least we're spared seeing those times in flashback.) The film could use more scenes like the dirty-nasty one where the girls skin snakes for dinner and Cody says, "Can't tell one meat from another—just like men." Screenwriters Ken Friedman and Yolande Finch may have had more interesting ideas than the ones that ended up in "Bad Girls." The scenario seems hemmed in by the usual Hollywood honcho fears that the women might actually show some rough edges, some rage—might actually be (gasp) *unsympathetic*.

Despite the life-is-tough stuff, all the Bad Girls, save Cody, seem oddly untouched by the mayhem. MacDowell's beatific smiles are the same ones she's been proffering in movie after movie—she's starting to seem more than a bit ga-ga. Barrymore could be posing for a new perfume—Hellcat, perhaps?

Stowe, however, invests so much passion in her role that she single-handedly keeps the film honest—at least whenever she's on screen. Her rage in this film is the real thing. It's an extraordinary performance, but then Stowe is often extraordinary. When will she get a starring role in a movie that really challenges her. She has the ability to transcend pulp even as she exposes it. It's a great gift to have in a cruddy movie era but putting Stowe behind a Gatling gun is not, to put it gently, the best use of her talents.

NEW YORK, 5/9/94, p. 70, David Denby

Bad Girls, a western with four heroines, is the kind of thing Andy Warhol might have done 25 years ago with $50,000 and a few "superstars" summoned from Max's Kansas City (with maybe a gorgeous blond boy or two thrown in). The movie would have been languidly, deliberately absurd—entertaining low camp with lots of skin. But Jonathan Kaplan's *Bad Girls*, shot in the wide-horizons style of Sergio Leone, is nothing if not serious, and skin is something hinted at but not shown. Kaplan (*The Accused*) has gone out of his way to avoid anything farcical or exploitative. This is a solemn feminist Western about honor. The four women—Madeleine Stowe, Andie MacDowell, Mary Stuart Masterson, and Drew Barrymore—ride, shoot, and tumble, and though we can see the stuntpersons filling in here and there, and the occasional faked or trick-edited sequence, we're meant to take all of it straight.

Forced into prostitution, the four women run away from a whorehouse/saloon and remain loyal to one another, riding tall in the saddle like any other group of Western outlaws. The strongest and toughest of them, Madeleine Stowe, is also vulnerable to men, and Stowe, falling in and out of love, gives the defiant performance that she now gives better than anyone else—husky voice, flamelike strength, and a gun pointed straight at your heart. I wish the filmmakers had started all over with Stowe in a gun belt and thrown out the rest of the movie. What these Hollywood folk are most serious about, I'm afraid, is not restoring women to their rightful place in the old West but putting them into creaky old Westerns. The filmmakers wheel out the ritual clichés of the genre—the rescue by buckboard of someone about to be hanged, a shoot-out, a final stand-and-draw duel between good and evil. *Bad Girls* is not a travesty, but it's not interesting either.

NEW YORK POST, 4/22/94, p. 41, Thelma Adams

Welcome to Marlboro Country—where the women are smoking!

"Bad Girls"—a gals in garters 'n' guns western—isn't so much bad as silly.

Madeleine Stowe leads the game cast as a sexy, sharp-shooting, steely hooker. Her fellow working girls include: the cupid-lipped, baby-chinned boy toy Drew Barrymore (tattoos hidden); the coyly seductive Andie MacDowell; and the scrubbed, girl-next-door Mary Stuart Masterson.

All four are playfully delicious—even if they are in a constant state of gorgeousness. These women might be angels with dirty faces riding unhappy trails, but their hair is fabulous, lipstick perfect, eye shadow a naughty shade in the naturals.

Whoa, horsies! Circle the hairdressers' wagons.

The characters wear their profession like a badge of courage. Epithets are hurled against them like racial slurs: jezebel, scarlet temptress, honky-tonk harlot, and heartless whore. A preacher even says to Stowe, "You have a scorpion between your legs."

Masterson tells a (male) lawyer at one point. "I was worthless before I married. Now I'm worthless as a widow ... If your laws don't apply to me, than to hell with them." At least, as a whore, she had a value.

These good old girls might seem to be riding tall in the saddle on the feminist frontier, but what's new about a western where all the women are playing whores? Sounds like the same old quicksand to me, sidewinder.

The girls do get a chance to defend themselves without waiting for Clint Eastwood to rescue them.

But the committee of screenwriters (Ken Friedman and Yolande Finch wrote the screenplay from a story by Albert Ruddy, Charles Finch and Gray Frederickson) have no shortage of women-in-peril plot twists. At various points one or another of the women are threatened, gang raped and bull-whipped.

Director Jonathan Kaplan ("The Accused" and "Unlawful Entry") doesn't crack the whip over the plot. Events meander like the Rio Grande as the uneven director herds his plucky stars towards the inevitable gunfight at the chauvinist pig corral.

As Stowe and her pistol-packin' mamas ride into the sunset, a yellow haze mixing with red dust, the music swelled and I could almost make out a faraway cry: Shoot the screenwriters! Spare the hairdressers!

NEWSDAY, 4/22/94, Part II/p. B3, Jack Mathews

Deep in the cinematic trash bins of my mind, there is the faded recollection of a Western movie once made with an all-midget cast. With time and luck, the memory of Jonathan Kaplan's "Bad Girls," the adventures of four "parlor girls" in 19th-Century Texas, may get lost in there, too.

In the meantime, the images are painfully sharp. There's Drew Barrymore in chaps with a cigarette dangling from her lips. Andie MacDowell and Mary Stuart Masterson sitting tall in the saddle. Madeleine Stowe glaring at a whiskey-soaked cowboy, daring him to go for his gun and "die like a man."

"Bad Girls," a sort of "Wild Bunch" with pantaloons, is about the silliest thing a Hollywood studio has done in a while. The movie combines two commercial trends—the revived Western and the women-on-the-run outlaw film (a la "Thelma & Louise")—and could put an end to both of them right here.

This might have worked as a comedy, a "Blazing Saddles" parody of the mythic Westerns of Sam Peckinpah, John Ford and Sergio Leone. But Kaplan, who took over for Tamra Davis and gets sole blame, is in dead earnest. Not necessarily to match the feminist statement of his unflinchingly honest "The Accused"a few years back, though the abuse of women is a central theme, but at least to make a conventional Western.

"Bad Girls" has every cliché known to the genre. Backlit silhouettes on the range, runaway wagons, jail breaks, blistering shoot-outs, sweeping orchestral accompaniment. The only difference is that the heroes are heroines, honky-tonk whores who take no guff from no man, and who can ride and shoot with the best of them.

The script, by Ken Friedman and Yolande Finch, tells what happens to the four women after Cody Zamara (Stowe) kills a drunk roughing up Anita Crown (Masterson) in their Colorado saloon brothel, and all four ride out of town with a posse and a pair of Pinkerton detectives on their trail.

That night, over a meal of barbecued rattlesnake, they decide to throw in together and start a new life. They'll go to Texas to pick up the money Cody has been saving in a bank there, then to Oregon to build a sawmill on land left to Anita by her late husband.

"We sold our bodies," Anita says. "We might as well sell some wood."

But while drawing out her money in that Texas bank Cody runs into homicidal outlaw Kid Jarrett (James Russo), a bitter ex-lover, and it is soon her gang against his. Bet on the babes.

Stowe, despite having some of the worst lines in the movie, plays Cody with admirable sincerity, and is responsible for what few interesting moments there are. It takes courage for a woman to imitate John Wayne and Clint Eastwood simultaneously, and Stowe is up to it. Barrymore, her hair a golden blond, acts as if she were playing charades at a party in Malibu (dress: Western casual), and MacDowell, playing a phony New Orleans belle hiding a mundane past, looks as if she'd like to find a place to hide herself.

The men, not surprisingly, come off even worse. Russo is standard-issue Western villain, a cold-blooded killer aching for a painful end. James LeGros, the shy rancher smitten with MacDowell, and Dermot Mulroney, the mysterious stranger smitten with Stowe, barely stand out from the sagebrush.

Maybe I should give that all-midget Western another chance.

SIGHT AND SOUND, 7/94, p. 37, Leslie Felperin Sharman

1890. Echo City, Colorado. Cody, Anita, Eileen and Lilly all work as prostitutes in the local saloon. When a client starts to get rough with Anita, Cody shoots him dead. The town tries to hang her, but her three friends rescue her from the noose in the nick of time and together they go on the run, with Pinkerton detectives on their trail. Anita, whose husband died of cholera, still has a claim to some land in the Oregon Territory. The four women decide to go there, but first they must go to a bank in Texas and withdraw Cody's life savings.

En route they meet Josh McCoy, a young prospector on his way to the Klondike, who warns them that there are posters of Cody advertising a reward for her return. In Aqua Dulce, Texas, Cody attempts to withdraw her savings, only to be apprehended by the Pinkertons. The arrest is aborted when the bank is robbed by Kid Jarrett, an old flame of Cody's, who frees her but steals her money. Cody, Lilly and Anita get away, but Eileen is captured by the sheriff. William, a local farmer, is deputised to guard her and is soon seduced by her charms.

Cody rides to Kid's hideout, where plans are being laid to hijack an army train for gold and a Gatling gun. Cody tries to get her money back but is whipped and possibly raped by Kid. Josh, who has been tracking the Jarrett Gang, finds her and takes her to a Chinese woman for treatment. Anita and Lilly get Eileen out of jail and join up with Cody and Josh. Josh joins forces with the women, explaining that he wants revenge on Frank Jarrett, Kid's father, for killing his own father and raping his mother.

The four women and Josh go to hide out at William's ranch. Romance blossoms between Cody and Josh, and Eileen and William. All six ambush Kid's gang and hijack the booty from the train. Kid's gang catches Lilly, but the women capture Kid's father, Frank, and hope to do a prisoner swap with the guns. Lilly is raped by Kid. Meanwhile, Anita learns that her land claim is useless without her husband. Frank taunts Josh about his mother, so Josh kills him. To make up for scotching their chances of a prisoner swap, Josh springs Lilly from the hideout but is caught in the process. The women ride to Kid's with the Gatling gun to trade for Josh; but once the swap is made, Kid shoots Josh anyway, and he dies in Cody's arms. After a huge gunfight, the women emerge victorious, having wiped out the whole gang. Eileen decides to stay on at the ranch with William, while Cody, Anita, and Lilly ride off for the Klondike, with the Pinkertons still on their trail.

Classical Hollywood Westerns tended to be the most reactionary of the major genres, depicting a West where men were men and women were at home and made the corn fritters. Moreover, the men were generally white men unless they were evil Indians or shifty Mexicans. The liberationist politics of the 60s undermined the values of the Western, and the genre fell into neglect. Now, for whatever strange matrix of reasons, the Western is back on the horse again but this time round star-billing in the saddle are all those oppressed minorities who never got a chance to hold the reins when the old guard was in power. Thus we've had Afro-American Westerns (*Posse*), faintly feminist Westerns (*The Ballad of Little Jo*), Native American Westerns (*Dances With Wolves*) and even Senior Citizen Westerns (*Unforgiven*).

Bad Girls is more or less in this revisionist strain, featuring as it does four wronged women fighting against a patriarchal society which does not recognise a woman's right to own land or shoot a man in self-defence. Or so it seems on the surface. In actual fact, *Bad Girls* is about as politically correct as a L'Oreal hair mousse commercial, which it resembles far more than *The Searchers* or even *Johnny Guitar*.

By all accounts, *Bad Girls* had a rough ride to the screen. Originally to be directed by Tamra Davis, with Cynda Williams co-starring, its street cred halved when its budget doubled. The woman director and black actress were dropped in favour of Jonathan Kaplan and an all white-bread-fed cast. One wonders what remnants of the original script remain. Possibly, bonding above and beyond the ordinary realms of female friendship and starting a small logging business might have been on the agenda. That would explain the strangely foregrounded kiss Eileen plants on the lips of Lilly early on, and the latter's testy jealousy when Eileen stays behind with a man. Sadly, these are only the faintest tinges of anything remotely sapphic in this resolutely straight-acting, straight-shooting, drearily straight-faced farce. The Western's substantial following of gays and lesbians will have to wait for Gus Van Sant's *Even Cowgirls Get the Blues*, if it ever gets released in Britain, to satisfy their appetite for cowpoke camp. In the meantime, *Bad Girls* will hardly satisfy them or anyone else, though it has to be said that Madeleine Stowe looks fetchingly butch for most of the film, despite her excessive quantities of hair.

By far the most unsatisfying thing about *Bad Girls* is that they aren't nearly bad enough. At regularly timed points throughout, each one is allowed a little monologue to explain how she was forced into prostitution by circumstances. Two of them have to be raped before they seriously think about getting some revenge (Kaplan also directed *The Accused*). Cody has such a ridiculously developed sense of fairness that she even tosses Kid Jarrett a bullet so that he has an chance in a draw to the death; "Pick it up, put it in and die like a man," she snarls. The Office of Fair Trading should be notified about the title, which ought to be *Victimised Girls Who Are Quite Nice Really.*

VILLAGE VOICE, 5/3/94, p. 49, J. Hoberman

The much vaunted Year of the Bad Girl promised by the media absorption of Tonya Harding, the New Museum's two-part, bicoastal "Bad Girls" show, and the appointment of Karen Durbin to run *The Village Voice* comes up a bit short with Jonathan Kaplan's new western—actually the season's second release to appropriate the name.

It's not that Kaplan's *Bad Girls* lacks a measure of self-awareness. The crudely wistful opening has the most straitlaced of cowtown hookers (Mary Stuart Masterson) pensively reading about the adventures of stunt-journalist Nellie Bly as some hot-to-trot client pounds on her door, bellowing for his birthday kiss. Minutes later this potbellied army colonel is beating on Masterson herself and, soon after, shooting up the downstairs saloon—an infraction for which he's plugged dead by the lissome bartender (Madeleine Stowe).

Thus, Iron Jane meets Calamity John: Stowe's summary justice more or less sets *Bad Girls* in motion. Dragged to an instant lynching party presided over by a blatantly Moral Majority preacher who hallucinates a scorpion between her legs, Stowe is rescued by Masterson and two other bordello colleagues, played by Andie MacDowell and Drew Barrymore. Once safely out in the sagebrush, the movie grinds to a halt, stuck in a morass of unlikely dialogue as the bad girls try to figure out just what's next. How about starting a sawmill in Oregon? "We sold our bodies, why can't we sell some wood?"

Although each of the four has a past (and the cosmetic bruises to show for it), Stowe—who demonstrated she could play period in *The Last of the Mohicans*—is clearly the designated star with MacDowell, the first actress to cover her entire personality with lip gloss, running a close second. We know this because they are the only bad girls to become emotionally involved with the cast's male cuties: James LeGros and Dermot Mulroney. Masterson remains in petulant thrall to her dead husband, while confused dumpling Drew Barrymore is still referred to as daddy's girl.

Pursued by a pair of Pinkertons hired by the harridan widow of the late colonel, the girls head down to Texas to collect Stowe's nest egg. While withdrawing her funds, however, Stowe is swept up in a group of bankrobbers led by an erstwhile admirer, James Russo. Left behind, MacDowell captivates a dim-witted rancher (LeGros) with her bogus Southern charm. Stowe follows Russo into his outlaw den of adobe entropy and must be rescued by saddle tramp Mulroney. Then, everyone temporarily out of harm's way, it's back to the LeGros spread 'til morning.

Not always so unpromising, *Bad Girls* was originally a project for Tamra Davis, who began shooting last summer only to lose, first, her cinematographer Lisa Rinzler (who worked with Davis on *Guncrazy*), and, soon afterward, her job. Production shut down. The script was rewritten and a number of actors fired, including Cynda Williams (whose turn in *One False Move* rivaled Barrymore's in *Guncrazy* as the B-movie moll of the '90s). Davis was replaced by Kaplan, whose credentials as a two-fisted woman's director—the femme race-car meller *Heart Like a Wheel* and Jodie Foster's mature Oscar vehicle *The Accused*—may have been less important than his having directed Stowe in *Unlawful Entry*.

Davis's conception was evidently low-budget and gritty and, as with much popular art, revenge was the motor. According to an interview in the current *US*, she wanted to show the women pushed into violence and responding in their own particular way: "There was one scene where a prostitute bites a bad guy's dick. It was funny but from the beginning the men insisted I cut it out." There's no such vengeful Bobbittry in the current *Bad Girls*—although one can detect remnants of antipatriarchal didacticism as well as evidence of an excised lesbian relationship between MacDowell and Barrymore. But despite the occasional sense of giddy sorority, *Bad Girls* alternates between an exercise in cross-dressing bravado and *Designing Women on the Range*—it's forever ripping open its own bodice.

Thanks to Kaplan's professionalism, *Bad Girls* has a full measure of western hokum, although his many nods to *The Wild Bunch* (everything from the credit-scene temperance march to the Gatling gun finale and *mucho más* in between, including the deathless invitation to "kiss my sister's black cat's ass") are so relentlessly robotic as to ultimately seem less like ritual genuflections than the self-administered jolts of a particularly desperate form of shock therapy.

After a while the movie is just rowdy by rote. For all the endlessly intersecting stories of revenge and justice and the continual rescue of some male or female damsel in distress, there's not much tension here. In fact, the proceedings seem pretty slack, allowing characters ample time to hide out, ride into town to consult lawyers and check claims, rob trains and stockpile dynamite, and still be back for breakfast.

Bad Girls is more a blazing mediocrity than a flaming failure but, given an ending of total sappiness, it's scarcely surprising that glum Barrymore would exit blubbering. She's not exactly miscast as a trick rider gone to turning tricks, but her lackadaisical performance suggests that even bad girls get the blahs.

Also reviewed in:
CHICAGO TRIBUNE, 4/22/94, Friday/p. C, Michael Wilmington
NEW YORK TIMES, 4/22/94, p. C8, Janet Maslin
VARIETY, 4/25-5/1/94, p. 30, Todd McCarthy
WASHINGTON POST, 4/22/94, p. C5, Rita Kempley
WASHINGTON POST, 4/22/94, Weekend/p. 44, Eve Zibart

BARCELONA

A Castle Rock Entertainment and Fine Line Features release. *Producer:* Whit Stillman. *Director:* Whit Stillman. *Screenplay:* Whit Stillman. *Director of Photography:* John Thomas. *Editor:* Christopher Tellefsen. *Music:* Marc Suozzo. *Sound:* Ted Spencer. *Sound Editor:* Catherine Benedek. *Casting:* Billy Hopkins and Simone Reynolds. *Production Designer:* José Mareía Botines. *Set Dresser:* Margalida Obrador. *Special Effects:* Reyes Abades. *Costumes:* Edi Giguere. *Make-up:* Chass Llach. *Running time:* 101 minutes. *MPAA Rating:* PG-13.

CAST: Taylor Nichols (Ted); Chris Eigeman (Fred); Tushka Bergen (Montserrat); Mira Sorvino (Marta); Pep Munné (Ramon); Nuria Badia (Aurora); Hellena Schmied (Greta); Francis Creighton (Frank); Thomas Gibson (Dickie); Jack Gilpin (Consul); Pere Ponce (Young Doctor); Laura Lopez (Ted's Assistant); Edmon Roch (Javier); Andrea Montero (Trade Fair Girl); Paca Barrera (Plain Princess); Nico Baixas (Hangar Trumpeter); Gerardo Seeliger (Weekending Doctor); Merce Puy and Rosa Grifell (Hospital Nurses); Francesco X. Canals (Marta's Other Guy); Juan Martinez-Lage (Terrorist Gunman); Isabel Ruiz de Villa and Montserat Zubiria (Sevillanas Dancers); Debbon Ayer (Betty); George H. Beane (Professor Thompson); Jonni Bassiner (Catalan Businessman); Gavin Kovaks (Young Ted at Lake); Wayne Carney (Jack of IHSMOCO).

CHRISTIAN SCIENCE MONITOR, 7/29/94, p. 11, David Sterritt

Four years ago, filmmaker Whit Stillman made a smashing debut with "Metropolitan," a smart and often hilarious comedy about the younger members of New York's social elite.

Its characters were precocious preppies, debutantes, and hangers-on trying desperately to enjoy their coddled live's despite occasional suspicions that their privileges are undeserved. Wry, talkative, and deliberately undramatic, the film achieved wide popularity while avoiding the temptations of today's money-driven movie marketplace.

Stillman's new movie, "Barcelona," serves the same delightful dish with an international flavor. Set in the colorful Spanish city during the last years of the cold war, it follows the adventures of two American men—a bookish sales representative and his cousin, a pushy Navy officer—as they wrestle with professional problems, romantic entanglements, and their own uneasy relationship.

At moments, Stillman goes beyond his previous work by injecting notes of high emotion and even melodrama into the tale. This reflects certain tensions that existed in Barcelona during its early days of post-Franco freedom, when years of repression gave way to new explorations of heedless and even hedonistic living. Yet the film's primary interest remains fixed on the itchy inner lives rather than the fleeting outer experiences of its superbly written characters.

Here as in "Metropolitan," what distinguishes the best of these characters is their poignant blend of self-assertion and self-doubt , expressed through finely tuned dialogue and also through details of body language. It's always rewarding to watch how Stillman's performers stand, sit, and position themselves in relation to others, even during scenes that do little to advance the story. Few filmmakers have such insight into the tumultuous innards of apparently placid personalities, and even fewer are bold enough to anchor whole movies on such subtleties.

Acting is naturally a key ingredient of Stillman's films, and "Barcelona" is only a tad less ingenious than "Metropolitan" in this regard. The main characters are played by "Metropolitan" alumni, Taylor Nichols and Chris Eigeman, who have mastered the demands of Stillman's approach. Other key members of the cast, including Tushka Bergen and Mira Sorvino as the women who attract our heroes, slide into the Stillman wavelength with equal dexterity. Jack Gilpin and Hellena Schmied are among the expertly chosen performers in smaller roles.

In the technical department, a special nod goes to John Thomas for his exquisite camera work. He also worked on "Metropolitan."

The setting and story of "Barcelona" present different visual challenges, and Thomas has triumphantly met them, capturing the continual color and intermittent chaos of his subject without lapsing into mere prettiness.

Like everyone else involved, he deserves applause for a thoughtfully made and refreshingly literate film that also packs an assortment of ironic laughs. Three cheers.

FILMS IN REVIEW, 11-12/94, p. 59, Eva Kissin

This is a small film about a big subject—Americans abroad and their romances there. However, Henry James can rest easy. There's nothing to worry about.

The scene is Barcelona in the late 80s. Spain is in an interesting stage, just catching up to the sexual revolution in the rest of the world. Our heroes, two young Americans, are feeling their way at the beginning of their careers abroad. Ted, recovering from a sexually charged failed affair, represents ISHMO (the Illinois High Speed Motor Corporation), and his cousin Fred, a glowing American patriot, Lieutenant J.G,, is an advance man for the American 6th Fleet. Ted, seriously bruised by his recent affair, has determined to go out with only plain girls, to free romance from beauty, to find a girl with her soul in her eyes, and marry her. Ambitious and idealistic re his new career in salesmanship and his marital plans, he soaks up Ben Franklin and Dale Carnegie, frequently attempting to apply the rules of the game to his love affairs.

Ted has been leading a quiet life until cousin Fred bursts in wearing his navy uniform in full glory and irritating the Spanish with his "American imperialism.," Because instinct almost always triumphs over politics, the young men get involved with the beautiful English-speaking local girls at the Trade Fair. The girls' sexual freedom surprises the two young men. Perhaps the best line in a fairly flat script occurs when one Spanish girl seriously states that she will no longer sleep with someone merely for sex. She has to be attracted to him.

The careers and romances wax and wane against a background of anti-Americanism that is reflected in terrorist bombing and angry Spanish behavior toward the ostentatious navy man. The film points up the contrast between world events and the limited lives of the two anti-heroes. In the long run, the affairs sort themselves out and the girls appear later at an American picnic happily munching that much hated symbol of Yankee innocence abroad, the hamburger.

While the film does manage to catch the trial and error quality of early careers and concomitant romance against the golden magic of Barcelona, it's a rather small film nevertheless. Whit Stillman (the talented director of *Metropolitan*) does recreate the mood of the city at a specific moment in time, and Taylor Nichols and Chris Eigman as the cousins, suggest an air of youthful authenticity. However, that's just not enough steam to move this somewhat sophomoric vehicle.

LOS ANGELES TIMES, 8/5/94, Calendar/p. 1, Kenneth Turan

"Barcelona" is only Whit Stillman's second feature, but he has already staked out a territory and a sensibility quite his own. Arch, eccentric romantic comedies that manage to be delicately off-balance without ever falling, Stillman's films are as unmistakable as his buttoned-down Brooks Brothers name.

Stillman's first film as a writer-director, "Metropolitan," was that rare $300,000 movie that was admired enough to be nominated for an Oscar (for best original screenplay). A knowing look into the improbable universe of New York's youthful socialites, it revealed how well Stillman knows his people and how cleverly he can reproduce their line of chat, gifts that "Barcelona" more than confirms.

Once again, Stillman is back in WASP World, where "I don't care for your tone" is considered a killing retort and it's obvious, without even looking, that people are wearing wingtips or Weejuns. This time around his characters grew up in the Midwest, not Manhattan, and they're far from home in Barcelona, but the way they talk is still unmistakable.

And it is Stillman's ear for their kind of glib, slightly exaggerated conversation, for articulate upper-crust dialogue that is withering and ironic by turns, that marks him as that rarity among filmmakers, someone with a voice to call his own.

It is characteristic of Stillman's quirky sensibility that he claims that the original notion for "Barcelona" came to him when, after seeing the Richard Gere-Debra Winger film "An Officer and a Gentleman," he decided to make a film about two people, one an officer and the other a gentleman.

It is the gentleman, Ted Boynton (Taylor Nicols), who narrates "Barcelona," in an engagingly querulous voice-over. The local representative for a Chicago-based manufacturing company, Ted is a bit priggish, with a passionate Dale Carnegie-inspired belief in the culture of sales. Likely, if left alone, to spend his evenings simultaneously reading the Old Testament and shuffling around his apartment to the sounds of Glenn Miller's "Pennsylvania 6-5000," Ted has to be considered an unlikely protagonist.

Attached though he is to his quiet life, Ted finds it permanently disrupted when his cousin Fred, a Naval officer on special assignment from the Sixth Fleet and the kind of guest who, as Ted says, begins to stink on the first day, comes to town and moves in.

Fred, energetically played by Chris Eigeman, is one of those impossible people who are just amusing enough to prevent their friends from killing them., A self-absorbed freeloader who has never considered that he might be wrong or someone else might be right, Fred is the kind of arrogant individual who thinks changing the "No" to "Si" on anti-American graffiti is making an important socio-political statement.

The graffiti are around because "Barcelona" is carefully set "in the last decade of the cold war," when anti-Americanism was pervasive enough to lead to political violence. It was also a time when the sexual revolution, almost out of fashion in America, had become a way of life in Spain, causing one young woman to seriously say, "I don't want to go to bed with just anyone anymore. I have to be attracted to them sexually."

Aside from driving Ted crazy by starting rumors that he wears painful leather straps on his underwear, Fred does have a positive effect on his cousin's social life. Though Ted has just about taken a vow to date nothing but "plain or rather homely girls" as a protest against the cult of attractiveness, he is soon going out with the glamorous Montserrat (Tushka Bergen) while Fred escorts the equally attractive Marta (Mira Sorvino).

Well-mannered and well-brought-up, Ted and Fred think they know what they're about, both in terms of the sensibilities of the city and the psyches of women. But it is one of the themes of "Barcelona" that in reality they are over their heads on all counts, more the "big, unsophisticated children" the Spaniards consider them to be than they'd ever like to admit.

As veterans of "Metropolitan," both Nichols and Eigeman handle Stillman's quirky dialogue exceptionally well, and Bergen and Sorvino are so adept it's a surprise to realize neither one is Spanish. As for the director, his personal connections to Barcelona, a city he lived in for years, gives the film a special integrity. Stillman simply sees the world differently than anyone else, and "Barcelona" underlines that that's what originality is all about.

NEW YORK, 8/15/94, p. 55, David Denby

Like many other people, I was charmed by the Park Avenue teen socialites in Whit Stillman's chiffon-smooth first movie, *Metropolitan*. The articulate patter devoted to transcendental angst as well as small matters of behavior finally ripened into an expression of manners. The movie actually made one think there was something worthwhile in the old Peter Duchin standards of taste; something like firmness. But the two men of *Barcelona*, a Navy officer abroad (Chris Eigeman) and a sales rep for an American company (Taylor Nichols), have reached their mid- or late twenties, and they are still dithering on like kids. They now seem like prissy second-raters—twits. Why any of the beautiful young Spanish women in the movie should be attracted to them is a mystery. In any case, the men seem more interested in each other than in the women, who are moved around like pieces on a chessboard. Stillman introduces ideas about the Cold War and anti-Americanism and Madrid leftists and then tosses them away like so many crunched-up pieces of paper. The city of Barcelona looks beautiful, but everything in the movie is negligent, underdeveloped, unfelt.

NEW YORK POST, 7/29/94, p. 42, Michael Medved

I's true the sexual revolution is over," declares the gorgeous, free-spirited Marta (Mira Sorvino) in a disco conversation in Whit Stillman's "Barcelona" "Now I don't go to bed with just anyone. I have to be strongly attracted to him first."

Moviegoers, meanwhile, should be strongly attracted to this superb little picture—an unmitigated delight that specializes in dialogue that's both witty and believable.

Writer-director Stillman (who won a well-deserved Oscar nomination for his screenplay for 1990's wistful, ironic "Metropolitan") delivers more than his share of laughs in "Barcelona," but his main achievement lies in creating some of the richest, quirkiest, most engaging characters to turn up anywhere in recent films.

Chief among them is Ted (Taylor Nichols), a thoughtful, insecure young American who runs the Barcelona sales office for an Illinois manufacturer of industrial equipment.

At the beginning of the picture (which takes place in "the last decade of the Cold War") he's just recovering from the latest in a series of disastrous relationships. "I've got a real romantic illusion problem," he says. "I've resolved to go out only with really plain or even homely girls."

This resolution quickly collapses when he meets the absurdly beautiful trade show translator, Montserrat (well-played by British-born actress Tushka Bergen), who is, unfortunately, living with the caddish, left-wing Spanish journalist Ramon (Pep Munne).

As if this situation weren't enough to confuse poor Ted he gets a most unwelcome visit from his cousin Fred (Chris Eigeman), now a lieutenant in the U.S. Navy who has been assigned to report on the anti-American tensions in the city before the arrival of the Sixth Fleet.

It turns out that Fred is a cocksure slickster who borrows Ted's money without telling him—"to avoid the acrimony," he says—but always leaves careful IOUs. Ted, on the other hand, is the dreamy sort who spends his free time reading the Book of Ecclesiastes (hidden inside a current issue of The Economist) while dancing to the strains of "Pennsylvania 6-5000."

Much of the humor of "Barcelona" stems from the way that these two WASPy, odd-duck Americans run with a crowd of hip, bohemian Barcelona radicals—leather-jacketedsophisticates who solemnly preach about the evil conspiracy headed by the sham, U.S. union "the AFL-CIA."

Near the end of the movie, Stillman provides some surprising plot twists that show that this unthinking mid-1980s anti-Americanism was, in the final analysis, no laughing matter.

All of the acting in "Barcelona" is superb with Nichols and Eigeman (both featured in the wonderful ensemble cast of "Metropolitan") utterly convincing as two bickering relatives who both hate and need one another. In fact, it's hard to understand why the big studios haven't snapped up both of these charismatic and accomplished leading men.

Visually, the film is above average, with affectionate views of beautiful Barcelona (the hometown of director Stillman's wife, and his current residence), but the emphasis remains firmly fixed on talk and character, rather than glossy images.

This movie is richly romantic, but never in the least bit schmaltzy; it tickles the palate like a chilled glass of the finest dry white wine, and leaves you with a distinct craving for more.

NEWSDAY, 7/29/94, Part II/p. B9, John Anderson

With a body of work that now consist of two films, it can safely be said that no one makes movies like Whit Stillman: dry-as-dust humor; walking, talking superegos disguised as characters, who mount half-hearted defenses of fossilizing mores and dying social traditions, and imagery that includes an American, alone in his Barcelona apartment, dancing with a Bible to Glenn Miller's "Pennsylvania 6-5000."

The American is Ted, a sales representative employed by a Chicago-based motor company, an obsessive theorist about the cult of sales who's been disillusioned at love. Ted, as played by Taylor Nichols, is almost identical to Charlie in Stillman's widely praised 1990 debut "Metropolitan," who was also played by Taylor Nichols.

As the film opens—some merry music is followed by a terrorist bombing—Ted is paid an unannounced visit by his cousin, Fred, a naval officer and advance man for the Sixth Fleet. As played by Chris Eigeman, Fred is a lot like Eigeman's smarmy, caustic Nick in "Metropolitan."

Has Stillman made the same movie? "Metropolitan" was about Upper East Side preppies at Christmas; "Barcelona" is about the romantic entanglements and political hostility experiences by two Americans "in the last decade of the Cold War." So the answer is: sort of.

There's an enlightening little exchange, however, between Fred and Ted about literary criticism, in which Fred sarcastically asks, "What do they call what's right above the subtext?" Ted says "The text." The problem with Stillman is distinguishing one from the other. And there isn't that much subtext, really. Despite the raft of anti-American, anti-NATO rhetoric that comes their way, Ted and Fred aren't right-wing ideologues, or imperialist symbols. Like almost everyone they encounter, they're emotional opportunists: When they find their mores colliding with those of the more sexually liberal Barcelonans—the deceitful Marta (Mira Sorvino), with whom Fred reconnoiters, or Montserrat (Tushka Bergen), with whom Ted falls in love—they adjust. When Montserrat's strident (ex-?) boyfriend Ramon (Pep Munne) discourses on the evils of the "AFL-CIA," Ted and Fred get indignant, but they're just as ill-informed.

Stillman may appear to take wealthy people more seriously than anyone since F. Scott Fitzgerald—and he was an outsider—but Stillman is less interested in specifics of class or politics than in certain themes: how we hang on to obsolete ideas for security, for instance, or defend the indefensible because it's ours. Self-indulgence is the chief issue, and Stillman has chosen his kinds of characters because they're essentially anachronisms, know they're anachronisms, and who nevertheless take umbrage at any assault on the worldview that makes them anachronisms.

"Barcelona" has a comically cool tone, and a pronounced sense of distance—when Fred is shot by a drive-by terrorist, there's barely a burp in the pace or feel of the film. Ted, of course, despite being driven crazy by his cousin, sees him through. The overall effect is one of wonder, childlike almost. You might even say that "Barcelona," and "Metropolitan," are like Charles Schulz' "Peanuts." The existence of adults is acknowledged, but we never see any.

NEWSWEEK, 8/15/94, p. 64, David Ansen

Sales reps and Navy men may be common in real life, but they are rarely the subjects of American movies, much less American independent movies. Whit Stillman announced with his first feature, the 1990 "Metropolitan," that he marched to a different drummer. That droll social comedy about the WASPy world of New York debutantes is now followed up by "Barcelona", an equally singular comedy about the amorous adventures of two American cousins—WASPs to the core—in Spain in "the last decade of the cold war." Ted (Taylor Nichols) is the Barcelona sales rep for an American company, so obsessed with the physical beauty of women (and so upset by the breakup of his last relationship) that he vows to date only homely girls. His orderly life (he's a devotee of the philosophy of Dale Carnegie) is seriously upset by the arrival of his gratingly callow cousin Fred (Chris Eigeman), an advance man for the Sixth Fleet who moves into his flat, stirs up trouble and refuses to leave. Libidinous but straight arrowed, these two America-firsters cut odd figures in swinging, disco-driven post-Franco Barcelona, where terrorist bombings and anti-American sentiments accost them at every turn. As do beautiful women. Fred takes up with sultry Marta (Mira Sorvino); Ted, in spite of his vows, is smitten with the comely blonde Montserrat (Tushka Bergen), only to discover that she's still living with a leftist journalist who is writing stories declaring Fred a CIA agent.

"Barcelona" comes replete with explosions and assassination attempts, but its pleasures, like those of "Metropolitan," have little to do with plot and everything to do with its highly chatty and trickily ironic tone. Though the director remains at wry arm's length from Ted and Fred, it's clear that he subscribes both to their America-centric world view and their beauty-fixated view of women. Just why all these gorgeous señoritas fall for these two puritanical gringos remains an unsolved mystery. Stillman, whose wife is from Barcelona, isn't much interested in what lies behind the eyeball-pleasing surface of his female characters; he's an ogler, albeit a courtly one.

Nonetheless, Stillman remains a deftly funny portrait painter of the young, willfully self-involved Anglo-Saxon male. The primly hangdog Nichols and the spectacularly annoying Eigeman, both veterans of "Metropolitan," are perfect vessels for the filmmakers arch comic sensibility. You may not be able to bring yourself to love them—Fred may be the only man in the U.S.A. who identified with Katharine Ross's jilted blond groom at the end of "The Graduate"—but you will surely be amused. The prickly, conservative, jacket-and-tie iconoclasm of "Barcelona" is like nothing else around.

SIGHT AND SOUND, 2/95, p. 41, Nick James

American sales executive Ted Boynton lives a reclusive life in Barcelona on the rebound from a failed relationship. His US Navy cousin Fred arrives, assuming he can stay while he prepares the path for the forthcoming visit of the US Sixth Fleet. On a nighttime drive, Ted explains his decision to date only plain women in future while Fred gets irritated by some anti-American graffiti.

A car pulls up and Marta, a trade fair translator, invites them to a fancy dress party. The cousins are introduced to Aurora, who seems to fit Ted's dating criteria. Aurora invites Ted to a jazz concert but another more attractive trade fair girl, Montserrat, turns up in her place. Later, on the disco floor, they finally strike a rapport. A few weeks into their affair, Montserrat reveals that she is still living with a journalist, Ramon, in an open relationship.

A USO office is bombed, killing an American sailor who is shipped home after a short service attended by the cousins. On the celebratory Night of San Juan, Fred parades his uniform at parties and organises a samba dancing session that falls flat. Ted and Montserrat berate him but later Ted himself loses his cool when he overhears Ramon claim that the Americans probably did the bombing themselves.

Ted asks Fred to move out as Montserrat is about to move in. A country outing with Montserrat and her friends ends badly when Fred's petulant crushing of some ants is thought typical of Americans. Montserrat leaves with Ramon, ostensibly to pick up her things for the move. However, she does not return, and days later, asks to see him for a "serious talk". He responds with silence, a selling strategy known as Manouevre X. Montserrat moves to Paris. Ted learns that Dickie Taylor has been put in charge of sales at his head office. He assumes he is going to be fired.

Meanwhile Fred is convinced he is being followed; his paranoia increases when a newspaper article by Ramon appears, naming Fred as a likely CIA agent. Fred is shot by a motorcycle pillion rider, and hospitalised. Convinced there is a conspiracy of negligence at the hospital, Ted arranges the best possible care and a constant vigil of friends to be in attendance. Among them is the angelic Greta. Montserrat visits and explains her disappearance. Ted meets Dickie and discovers that he is in fact being promoted. He and the recovered Fred reconcile their differences on Ted's wedding day, and Fred receives an apology from Ramon. Ted marries Greta in Barcelona's gothic cathedral.

Whit Stillman's second film is, if anything, more ambitious in scope than his impressive debut *Metropolitan*. Although set in the mid-80s heyday of post-Franco hedonistic abandon in the Catalan capital, it reaches for the complexity of theme and character of a nineteenth-century novel. The uneasy social relations incumbent on Stillman's two foreign residents, Ted and Fred, are compounded with political tensions around the US military presence in the Mediterranean. The cousins may be scions of American WASPdom, but they're anything but the 'Masters of the Universe' evoked by Tom Wolfe in *The Bonfire of the Vanities*. Their almost Victorian mixture of arrogance, awkwardness and naivety makes them more like scared young subalterns of Kipling's Raj, and they have something of the political pawns' bewilderment that Tom Stoppard gave to Rosencrantz and Guildernstern. But Catalonia is hardly Elsinore or the North-West Frontier and their paranoid bleating is puzzling until it proves to be justified by the shooting of Fred.

As with *Metropolitan*, the point of view is that of the American patrician class. Thus, although alien enough for Ted and Fred, the Barcelona we see is very much restricted to its chic districts. For example, the notorious ancient red-light district of abject poverty, the Barrio Chino (where the crew of a US aircraft carrier was notoriously fleeced in the early 80s) is hardly glimpsed. Instead we get the fashionable midtown of Gaudi and Bofill, of Art Nouveau facades and minimalist dancefloors. There's no way that these American cousins are interested in slumming. They are busy representing the American conscience on an international stage and therefore a certain decorum must be preserved, even in the disco.

Stillman pokes affectionate fun at these prissy, curious stiffs. Ted's attempt to maintain a moral stance, through sexual abstinence and dancing with his bible, is besieged from all sides—as much by Fred's constant cash borrowing as by the easy-going sexuality of Spanish girlfriends. His bringing Dale Carnegie-style business philosophies to bear on his relationship with Montserrat ought to be contemptible, but instead it serves to underline his uneasiness about his own neurotic identity in the presence of her vivacity. Similarly, Fred's paranoid self-loathing wills the attempted assassination on himself, making him temporarily absent at the point where the plot needs to focus on Ted, and then vulnerable enough to gain some arguably unwarranted sympathy at the end. Such characterisation is Stillman's boldest stroke. He is unafraid to hang his carefully thought-out panorama on the shoulders of two pathetic characters, who are very hard to like or respect.

However, the cousins' lack of charm has an unfortunate impact on Stillman's overall scheme. In the generous party atmosphere that pervades the film and invades the Americans' consciousness, there is an evident desire to give a proper representation to the Spanish characters, yet it is never quite realised. We never know why the women at the trade fair, who seem an adroit and cosmopolitan crew, would want to marry any of these young Americans, beyond the fact that they are young Americans. The film comforts male angst with such assumptions. But then Stillman's world is one where there is always a thick quality overcoat ready for drooping shoulders and where quiet reasoned conversation is always the palliative for difficult twists of fate. It makes a unique and beguiling contrast to the cinema of his current American peers and if it is a shade over-ambitious, there is always the sense that, given further opportunities, he might just surpass all expectations.

TIME, 9/12/94, p. 86, Richard Corliss

[*Barcelona* was reviewed jointly with *Clerks*; see Corliss' review of that film.]

VILLAGE VOICE, 8/2/94, p. 43, J. Hoberman

Andrew Bergman's *It Could Happen to You* may be a tabloid fairytale [see Hoberman's review] and Whit Stillman's *Barcelona* a pre-Tina *New Yorker* short story, but these two romantic comedies convey a similarly poignant yearning for a lost destiny—the imaginary days when the U.S. was good cop and global Santa in one.

I don't want to force the comparison—even if both flicks do fetishize the pop music of the '40s. After all, *It Could Happen to You* is a briskly cute Hollywood movie that wants to be all heart and addresses itself to the domestic sphere, while *Barcelona* is a languorously wry indie, sentimental but cerebral, that concerns itself with foreign affairs. One may be Clinton Democrat, the other Bush Republican, but, populist or preppie, both feature lovably sincere, straight-arrow authority figures who rise above the machinations of *muchachas* and the media to prevail upon an uncertain world.

Barcelona, the more curious of the pair, is Stillman's follow-up to his well-regarded *Metropolitan*. Like that droll examination of upper-crust ingenuos, *Barcelona* surveys a scene of languid, loquacious, privileged young people—only here there are none outside the clique offering another perspective. The decorous Ted (Taylor Nichols), who represents a Chicago-based motor manufacturer in Barcelona, entertains a not altogether welcome visit from his abrasive cousin Fred (Chris Eigeman), an advance man for the Sixth Fleet. Together and separately each embarks on a tortuous affair of the heart.

Fred's first night in town, the cousins wind up at a costume party—Fred's uniform having been mistaken for a costume. Although this is but the first of numerous insults to America's honor, Fred does have a salutary effect on his uptight cousin's social life—he can't resist regaling Ted's female associates, mainly translators at the trade fair, with lurid tales of the sales rep's hidden

Sadean proclivities. In reality, Ted is a puritanical disciple of Dale Carnegie who, in one memorable bit of business, consults the Old Testament while gyrating to Glenn Miller, thus prompting Fred to label him "a pathetic Bible-dancing goody-goody."

The latter scene represents *Barcelona* at its most delirious. For all the late-'70s disco, the movie's sober, insipid theme constantly verges on Pachelbel's Canon. Indeed, there are neither Gaudí buildings nor much Gothic quarter in Stillman's Barcelona, which, although invitingly presented, is mainly a generically ungrateful, enigmatic, and hedonistic Old World populated by disgruntled leftists and foxy young women distinguished by their sexual availability and quaint elocutions: "Are you proposing that we shake up together?" (Malapropisms not-withstanding, the banter can be heavy—some scenes suggesting the deployment of unwieldy, inherited furniture.)

The two cousins may be borderline eccentrics but their corn-fed innocence seems increasingly moral as the movie's plot thickens. Continually offended by anti-Americanism, even as he provokes it, foolhardy Fred assumes a more heroic stature after the terrorist bombing of a USO club; indeed, the movie briefly takes on a thriller aspect once he is fingered by a jealous left-wing reporter as a CIA op. In its way, *Barcelona* seems designed to defend the notion of America in the world—as purveyor of universally admired lifestyle and defender of universally accepted rights.

While *Barcelona*'s opening title places action during "the last decade of the Cold War," the movie really compresses the last 40 years. Although it's set amid controversies over Pershing missiles and nuclear freeze, Fred is still defending American involvement in Vietnam. Smarting over being called a *facha* (militarist), he insists that the U.S. saved Europe from fascism in World War II, perversely unaware that NATO supported the fascist Franco for 30 years thereafter. Such comic denial is hardly odd in a movie that, for all its drawling soap operatics, seems bent on justifying American insularity.

Stillman (whose father served various Democratic administrations) has said that the idea for making *Barcelona*'s representative Americans a soldier and a sales rep came from the title *An Officer and a Gentleman*. The connection is more than fortuitous—that 1982 success, another late Cold War relic, was a key Reaganite text for its recuperative, post-Vietnam celebration of the U.S. military as vehicle for patriarchal character-molding.

According to Stillman, he and his wife much enjoyed *An Officer and a Gentleman* and were incredulous to discover that, having grown up under precisely that system which the film glorifies, their Spanish friends regarded it as distastefully *facha*. We should be less surprised. *Barcelona*, after all, is a movie where the natives speak accented English even to each other.

Also reviewed in:
CHICAGO TRIBUNE, 8/5/94, Friday/p. J, Michael Wilmington
NEW REPUBLIC, 8/15/94, p. 30, Stanley Kauffmann
NEW YORK TIMES, 7/29/94, p. C3, Janet Maslin
NEW YORKER, 8/15/94, p. 77, Terrence Rafferty
VARIETY, 6/13-19/94, p. 54, Todd McCarthy
WASHINGTON POST, 8/12/94, p. F7, Hal Hinson
WASHINGTON POST, 8/12/94, Weekend/p. 37, Desson Howe

BEANS OF EGYPT, MAINE, THE

A Live Entertainment release of an American Playhouse Theatrical Films/I.R.S. Media production. *Executive Producers:* Lindsay Law, Miles Copeland III, and Paul Colichman. *Producer:* Rosilyn Heller. *Director:* Jennifer Warren. *Screenplay:* Bill Phillips. *Based on the book by:* Carolyn Chute. *Director of Photography:* Stevan Larner. *Editor:* Paul Dixon. *Music:* Peter Manning Robinson. *Sound:* Mark Weingarten. *Casting:* Donald Paul Pemrick, Judi Rothfield, and Katie Ryan. *Production Designer:* Rondi Tucker. *Costumes:* Candace Clements. *Running time:* 99 minutes. *MPAA Rating:* R.

CAST: Martha Plimpton (Earlene Pomerleau); Kelly Lynch (Roberta Bean); Rutger Hauer (Rueben Bean); Patrick McGaw (Beal Bean); Richard Sanders (Lee Pomerleau).

LOS ANGELES TIMES, 11/23/94, Caleandar/p. 6, Peter Rainer

"The Beans of Egypt, Maine" is full of family and place. Adapted from Carolyn Chute's 1984 debut novel, it showcases a shambling cast of characters and enough backwoodsy local color to double as a documentary. The film, like the book, has an almost messianic mission: It wants to give poor rural white people their due after generations of caricature.

It doesn't really succeed in vaulting cartoonishness, though a few of the performers score personal triumphs.

Directed by Jennifer Warren and scripted by Bill Phillips, the film works up a woodsy Romeo and Juliet-style atmosphere. Earlene Pomerleau (Martha Plimpton) lives with her family next door to the rowdy Beans, a clan of shaggy varmints and ne'er-do-wells including patriarch Reuben (Rutger Hauer) and his mate, Roberta (Kelly Lynch), and Beal (Patrick McGaw), who likes to chop wood with his shirt off. Earlene, despite her father's almost biblical distaste for the Beans, gets pregnant by Beal—and pulled into the clan.

It's more than she bargained for but, as the years wind on, she becomes one of them, and it's not so bad. She finds in the Beans the coziness of family, a sense of belonging. Her long-term scrapes with Beal, and her growing attachment to Roberta, who has her own brood by Beal, keep her rooted.

Rootedness is real big in "Beans." But the film does a better job by the roots than the plants. The Beans, with the exception of Roberta, never seem like full-bodied people. They don't shed their shaggy, scary trappings the more we get to know them. Salt-of-the-earth types often come across as stunted in the movies, and the Beans are more stunted than most. By comparison, the Joads in "Grapes of Wrath" seem like a gaggle of Ph.Ds.

But some of the family-feeling stuff comes through anyway because of the performances of Plimpton and Lynch. Jennifer Warren is also a veteran actress, and her work with these women is exemplary. Plimpton goes from a randy, hormone-driven girl to a caring, full-grown woman. She's worldly in her world.

Lynch is even better: She's great at conveying how Roberta's lust for Beal is cross-wired with her exasperation with him. When Roberta emerges as a "respectable" wife, we don't see her transformation as a victory for the middle-class over the dirt-poor. It's just a change in circumstance for Roberta, and she's as gracious and intuitive in wealth as in poverty. "Beans" is a long haul but Plimpton and Lynch pull you through it.

NEW YORK POST, 11/23/94, p. 50, Thelma Adams

There's a dividing line between people who view life through a picture window and those who take action. In "The Beans of Egypt, Maine," there's a further division between those who eat squirrel and those who don't.

Earlene Pomerleau (Martha Plimpton)—a sheltered middle-class girl—pines to roll in the mud with the, tacky trailer trash next door. All the soap her God-fearing father pours into her mouth cannot keep her from the downward spiral—and spiritual redemption—of mixing with the Beans.

Carolyn Chute's novel about rural life among the working poor in the Pine Tree State has been given the American Playhouse treatment by actress Jennifer Warren in her feature-length directorial debut. Well-intentioned and cautious, it suffers from the "It's a Small World" syndrome. From the folksy score to the flannel shirts, the details are right, but the sting is gone.

Plimpton's Earlene has a bluesy, beaten-down, waifish charm, but all the voice-over narration in the world can't make her as compelling as the in-depth exploration of her interior life which remains the novel's domain.

Rock-solid Rutger Hauer plays the Bean patriarch, a role unfortunately curtailed by an incarceration that spans the movie's choppy middle. His few scenes have the weight and intensity that inspire emotional response. He returns from jail saying, "Believe me, I am no longer a pr--k. I am reformed." But Papa Bean is as cranked and charismatic as ever, a dangerous and irresistible man.

Sexy additions to the cast include Kelly Lynch as Papa Bean's fertile common-law wife and the frequently shirtless Patrick McGaw as Beal Bean, the boy who seduces Earlene away from her comfy but cloistered life.

Bill Phillips' screenplay falls into the literary-adaptations trap. He riffles through the book, highlighting key scenes, but the sinews that build dramatic tension are chopped away. The director's desperate use of slow motion during the climactic violent scenes can't compensate for a script with all the raw emotional power of Cliff Notes.

NEWSDAY, 11/23/94, Part II/p. B13, John Anderson

In her picturesque 1985 novel, "The Beans of Egypt, Maine," Carolyn Chute endowed the dirt-poor white trash of her native New England with a kind of nobility—not by softsoaping the festering boil of their existence, or making them heroes, but through her idiosyncratic use of language, a crazy music punctuated by rude violence, rutting sex and economic strangulation.

Whether that music can be transferred to film remains an open question, I suppose. What's clear, however, is that in the version adapted by screenwriter Bill Phillips and directed by onetime actress Jennifer Warren, "The Beans of Egypt, Maine" has become discordant and abrasive, less a failure than a pathology. What happens when filmmakers are too enamored of their source material? When they take too long to get that material on screen? When they've been at it so long they can no longer step back and see what they've cooked up? In "The Beans," it's an inedible mess.

First rule of film adaptations: You shouldn't have had to read the book: To anyone who hasn't, however, the story of Earlene Pomerleau (Martha Plimpton)—who with her father (Richard Sanders) grows up a few yards and one link up the food chain from the dark and incestuous Bean clan—won't make a lot of sense. Nor is there much here to inspire an audience to bother bridging the information gap.

Although the hardscrabble environment of the financially and dentally challenged Beans is kept raw and dirty—with the exception of Kelly Lynch as Roberta, who looks like she just stepped out of a tooth-polish ad—the editing is sloppy and the direction is weak. Martha Plimpton as Earlene and Patrick McGaw as her main Bean, Beal, are adequate but uninspiring. The most memorable cast member is Rutger Hauer as the reprobate Reuben Bean, who appears, disappears, reappears and does a credible impersonation of psychic road kill.

"The Beans," which recounts Earlene's crush on, seduction by, marriage to and childbearing with the ill-fated Beal—whom she knows has always had a thing for his aunt, Roberta—is a well-intentioned misfire: Warren devoted nine years to realizing this project, which is only partially realized.

Pieces of dialogue are lifted from the book but don't make sense within the whole of the film; characters are included in the movie only because they appear in the book, not because their presence on screen makes sense. The plot, as it were, falters when unsupported by Chute's pungent style. The bittersweetness is replaced by an atmosphere of what the novelist carefully avoided, condescension. "Beans," in short, is full of beans.

TIME, 12/5/94, p. 92, Richard Schickel

The Beans are no-accounts too numerous to count. They are the one-family inner city of dismal little Egypt, Maine. They do odd jobs. They hunt deer out of season and do stupid, self-destructive things in all seasons. They seem to have never heard of contraception. They have heard of welfare, but they are too ornery to accept it.

Growing up in a prim, God-fearing little house across the road from their slatternly encampment, Earlene Pomerleau (Martha Plimpton) watches the Beans' messy comings and goings through her picture window, paying particular attention to hunky Beal Bean (Patrick McGay), who is not paying much attention to her. He's sleeping with his father's common-law wife, Roberta (Kelly Lynch), while the old man (Rutger Hauer) does time in jail for beating a game warden half to death. This drama is, as Earlene says, better than watching television: it is live, and it is X-rated.

And *The Beans of Egypt, Maine*, adapted by Bill Phillips from the novel by Carolyn Chute, has this advantage over just about any other movie one is likely to encounter these days: it takes marginal American lives seriously. It does not patronize them. It does not invest them with tragic significance. It does not turn them into case studies. The film has a style that might be called sympathetic objectivity. Under Jennifer Warren's clear-eyed direction, it simply, almost uninflectedly recounts what happens to Earlene when she finally crosses the road to share Beal with Roberta. This new life takes the chill out of her bones. But it also contains relentless poverty, intermittent abuse, the constant threat of self-destruction. These people can never escape whatever desperate moment they are caught in, never know the luxury of foresight. It is hard watching fate enfold them. But it is also a bracing experience not easily shaken off.

VILLAGE VOICE, 12/6/94, p. 66, Francine Russo

The Beans of Egypt, Maine has an attitude problem. Though it's based on Carolyn Chute's gritty, unsparing look at the hearty, nose-picking white trash of rural Maine, the film delivers the novel's Hollywood mirror-image. It patronizes and trivializes its characters, whose scraggy-necked selves are played by beautiful people. And its rollicking *Beverly Hillbilly* music camps up the story's essential brutality.

The story follows many years in the life of Earlene (Martha Plimpton), whose family is one step above the Beans, an unruly clan who inhabit a broken-down trailer next door. As a growing girl, Earlene watches the clan noisily enact their lusty, bloody lives. The patriarch Ruby (Rutger Hauer) is hauled away to jail after smashing a game warden with a rifle butt. His woman, Roberta (Kelly Lynch), takes up with her "nephew" Beal (Patrick McGaw), whom Earlene lusts after and eventually marries. There's coupling galore, babies out of wedlock, and Earlene and Roberta forge a sisterly bond through hardship.

As the film flashes over the years, all these relationships seem sketchy, as if we've missed part of the movie. Moreover, from the trash-strewn trailer yard to the dead lamb flung on the kitchen table, everything looks fake, and the characters' feelings seem least authentic of all. The camera leers at the assorted pantings and gropings of the gorgeous as if the film were one long dirty joke.

What's an actor to do? Rutger Hauer plays Ruby as a dumber-than-life rube and Patrick McGaw looks slackjawed and clueless most of the time. Kelly Lynch's fertility-goddess Roberta is at least womanly and winning, and Martha Plimpton's performance gathers weight as the film darkens.

As the married couple Earlene and Beal spiral downward, the film looks close-up at physical anguish and tragedy—and the screen shimmers briefly. But then *Beans* retreats to its prevailing attitude, Television America's condescension to people even tackier than themselves.

Also reviewed in:
NEW YORK TIMES, 11/23/94, p. C13, Stephen Holden
VARIETY, 5/30-6/5/94, p. 51, Leonard Klady
WASHINGTON POST, 12/2/94, p. F7, Hal Hinson
WASHINGTON POST, 12/2/94, Weekend/p. 54, Desson Howe

BEING HUMAN

A Warner Bros. release of an Enigma production. *Producer:* Robert F. Colesberry and David Puttnam. *Director:* Bill Forsyth. *Screenplay:* Bill Forsyth. *Director of Photography:* Michael Coulter. *Editor:* Michael Ellis. *Music:* Michael Gibbs. *Music Editor:* Andrew Glen and Robin Clarke. *Sound:* Louis Kramer and (music) Gary Thomas. *Sound Editor:* Leslie Hodgson and Ian Fuller. *Casting:* Susie Figgis and Sharon Howard Field. *Production Designer:* Norman Garwood. *Art Director:* Keith Pain. *Set Dresser:* Maggie Gray. *Special Effects:* Peter Hutchinson. *Costumes:* Sandy Powell. *Make-up:* Linda Armstrong, Meg Speirs, and Danny Parker. *Stunt Coordinator:* Marc Boyle. *Running time:* 118 minutes. *MPAA Rating:* PG-13.

CAST: Robin Williams (Hector); Kelly Hunter (Deirdre); Maudie Johnson (Girl Child); Max Johnson (Boy Child); Robert Carlyle (Priest); Eoin McCarthy (Leader); John Turturro (Lucinnius); Grace Mahlaba (Thalia); Danny Kanaber (Gallus); Bill Nighy (Julian); Jim

Hooper and Robin Hooper (Julian's Slaves); Simon McBurney (Hermas); Vivienne Ritchie (Dalmia); David Morrissey and Andrew Tiernan (Cyprian's Men); Laurance Rudic (Solus); Mark Long (Slave); Rouchdi Mohamed and Hassan Mekkiat (Men at Cyprian's); Simon Clark (Man in Bathhouse); Sam Guttman (Sailor); Anna Galiena (Beatrice); Vincent D'Onofrio (Priest); Winnie Watts (Nun); Gemma Frances (Girl on Wagon); Finlay Welsh (Pedlar); Andrew Charleson (Wagon Driver); Matteo Mazzetti Di Pietralata (Beatrice's Son); Maria Mazzetti Di Pietralata (Beatrice's Daughter); Elena Salvoni (Beatrice's Mother); Paul Higgins (Soldier); John Surman (Soldier); Conrad Asquith (Officer); Zoot Lynman (Boy Squire); George Dillon (Peter); Jonathan Hyde (Francisco); Lizzy McInnerny (Ursula); Hector Elizondo (Dom Paulo); Gregor Henderson-Beggs (Nuno); Ken Stott (Gasper Dias); Steve Shill (Luis); Peter Kelly (Father Diogo); Don Sumpter (Salgado); Tobie Cronjé (Dario); Bhasker (Andre); Ewan McGregor (Alvarez); Gavin Richards (Da Cunha); Nicholas Hewetson and Tim McMullan (Deserters); Stefan Weclawek (Dom Paulo's Son); Willie Jonah (Slave); Luke Hardy (Sailor); Helen Miller (Betsy); Charles Miller (Tom); Lindsay Crouse (Janet); Lorraine Bracco (Anna); John X. Heart (Donald); William H. Macy (Boris); Rafiu Omidiiji Bello (Cab Driver); Jeanne Reynolds and Andrew Dolan (Reporters); Karen L. Thorson (News Sound); Louis Landman (NY Policeman #1); John Finn (Detective Cobb); Jose Perez (Santiago); Adam Bryant and Diane Gnagnarelli (Neighbors); Nina Lektorsky (Mrs. Philippopilis); David Proval (George); Danny Kovacs (NY Policeman #2); Rob Brezny (TV Man/Psychic); Robert F. Keefe (Tony); Theresa Russell (The Storyteller).

LOS ANGELES TIMES, 5/6/94, Calendar/p. 4, Kenneth Turan

With a film like "Being Human," there is no point belaboring the obvious. Misconceived, misguided and a completely miserable viewing experience, this is one to avoid at all costs and for all time.

Given that it stars Robin Williams, was produced by David Puttnam and directed by Bill Forsyth, the fact that "Being Human" appeared in theaters with little advance warning or publicity was not the best of signs. Still, no one could have predicted what a colossus of tedium it turned out to be.

Williams stars as a character named Hector, an Everyman type who is shown trying to muddle through life as best he can in five different epochs in history. There is a modern story, one set in the Bronze Age, one involving a Roman slave, another showing a soldier returning from the Crusades and a final episode about a Portuguese nobleman shipwrecked in Africa.

It is difficult to convey how unconvincing in every respect each of these tales are, how ineptly they relate to one another and how little they add up to. In fact, apart from the vague notion that human beings are fond of love and emotional connection, it is hard to tell exactly what this film is trying to convey.

Writer-director Forsyth, so adept when dealing with his native Scotland in films like "Gregory's Girl" and "Local Hero," has fearfully overreached himself in attempting to portray 2,000 years of human history. None of the cast, not even John Turturro, can survive its pathetic qualities, and poor Robin Williams can do no more than look increasingly worried as the film goes on and on.

Perhaps the single most irritating aspect of "Being Human" is its nauseating, insufferably coy voice-over narration, read by Theresa Russell sounding like Cybill Shepherd. Devoid of energy and wit, the only purpose this film serves is making every other failed film you've seen this year look much better by comparison.

NEW YORK, 5/23/94, p. 72, David Denby

Bill Forsyth's *Being Human* has the formal attributes of art but little of the drive or excitement of art. In five separate stories, set in the Bronze Age, the Roman epoch, the Middle Ages, the sixteenth century, and the present, Robin Williams plays a father cut off from his family and longing to get home—a man trying to belong. The character, however, is not fierce and resourceful like Odysseus but a mild fellow enslaved to one thing or another—a Roman master, a terrible job, love itself. In other words, the character is a schlump (a boring man multiplied by five), and though Williams has lovely moments, he can't break out of a concept that allows him no more than harassed, ordinary-man decency. Forsyth might have subtitled the picture "Five Studies in Abjection."

One episode is very fine—the one set in a distant, dusty outpost of the Roman Empire. John Turturro (in a toga) is at his most inspired as a stupid, hysterically nervous merchant who decides to commit suicide and expects his slave (Williams) to die with him. The looks of mute expostulation that Williams gives Turturro are almost Chaplinesque. And the sequence looks great—even the stage-set Roman villa is wonderful. Forsyth has a lovely feeling for light (remember the glowing air in his masterpiece, *Local Hero*?), for the hushed magic of man alone in nature, at the ocean's edge, held in expectation.

Forsyth has loaded the stories with recurring symbols and visual motifs and even a figure that turns up each time and watches warily from the sidelines. Is it God? The storyteller? Unfortunately, Forsyth dispels whatever sense of mystery he has built up by pasting a self-conscious narration (poorly read by Theresa Russell) over the stories. In truth, recurring visual portents look academic in a movie if they aren't used to charge up the atmosphere with a little menace. Here, one just notices the recurrences—oh dear, there's another crucifix. Forsyth has established a huge, overarticulated structure to say commonplace things.

NEW YORK POST, 5/16/94, p. 36, Thelma Adams

VOICEOVER: ... *And the review said to itself how do I begin?*

In horror movies, when the heroine opens the door you know she's in danger.

Lately, when I hear a voiceover—a disembodied voice takng over the sound track—nine out of 10 times it's a signal that the movie's in danger.

Bill Forsyth's "Being Human" reeks with voiceover. It raised the hair on the back of my neck.

The director of the wonderful "Local Hero" has cast Robin Williams as a cosmic schlemiel. Hector roams through history like a Shirley MacLaine autobiography, riffling through the Bronze Age, the Roman Empire, the Middle Ages, the Age of Discovery, modern times—all with a sort of middle-aged, mid-lifey, sodden humanism.

... *well, said the reviewer to herself,* for years, I've been wishing Robin Williams (the screen actor, not the comic) would mellow out. Beware your wishes, they might come true!

We get to see the many haircuts of Williams—the greasy before-the-dawn-of-shampoo look, the bowl cut, the medieval shag, the slicked-back modern weasel—but the face remains the same.

Hector falls into the same category of Williams' hapless Peter Pan in "Hook" and the ineffectual daddy dearest of "Mrs. Doubtfire." It's Williams, the Juilliard-trained executive's son, clean and sober and plagued by self-doubt.

Absent is the comic inventiveness and pathos of Williams' homeless man in "The Fisher King," the comic riffs that carried a flawed plot in "Good Morning, Vietnam."

And "Being Human" is a movie that cries out to be carried by Williams—or begs for a Monty Python rewrite.

Hector, an Everyman damned by inaction must live five lives before he gets the hang of it.

Once upon a time, long, long ago and far, far and a short nap away, the circular story has the neolithic Hector hanging back while his wife and children are stolen by a strange tribe. Wandering Medieval Hector sacrifices the love of a perfumed woman to seek out his own children in a distant land.

Modern divorced daddy Hector finds the secrets of the universe unlocked when he reconciles with his estranged children.

And what is this great humanistic secret that it has taken us since the dawn of man to discover?

"Everything is going to be OK," says Hector.

"This is it ..." replies his daughter, "enjoy it."

Isn't every story all the one story, every review all the one review? No. Some reviews are good and some are bad.

NEWSDAY, 5/6/94, Part II/p. B3, Jack Mathews

Robin Williams and Scottish director Bill Forsyth would seem to form an irresistibly agreeable alliance in these troubled times, especially with a movie exploring man's inherent needs for comfort, contact and rootedness in life. There is a gentleness always lurking beneath Williams' manic riffs, and Forsyth's films, "Local Hero" and "Housekeeping" among them, have been warm baths for the soul.

So, why is "Being Human" such an interminable bore? The answer, ironically, is that in writing his episodic script, Forsyth didn't take the hints of his own muse.

The movie, which is five slices of life cut from the Bronze to the Computer Ages of human history, each about a man separated from his home or family, offers us no comfort, little contact, and only the longing for stability.

It also fails our two greatest expectations. Though he is in virtually every scene, Williams is script-bound and almost and almost entirely humorless, and while Forsyth's films have all used eccentric characters to illuminate the human condition, their themes have previously enjoyed the company of a good tale.

The lessons in the five vignettes of "Being Human" are footprints in wet mud, momentarily distinct, then gone. At the end, you feel like you've watched a two-hour movie inspired by a wall plaque, "Home is where the heart is"

With the exception of the last piece , about a divorced man trying to reconnect with his two children during a weekend at a New Jersey beach house, the "Being Human" segments—one about a cave dweller set upon by marauders, one about a confused slave in Roman times, another about a war-weary traveler in medieval Europe, and the fourth about a 16th-Century Portuguese nobleman shipwrecked with his ex-lover and her boyfriend—don't even end the stories they begin.

What links the five vignettes, other than the characters' name (always Hector), is the range of needs and emotions consistent throughout human history. The needs for spiritual guidance, ethics, love, family, shelter. The emotions of joy, anguish, passion, grief. Life, in other words, as we all experience it. Forsyth acknowledges the lack of dramatic context in his opening narration (read by an unseen Theresa Russell), which attempts to give the stories their own human qualities, and therefore excuse their weaknesses. It is an engaging device, like God instructing Clarence at the opening of "It's a Wonderful Life," but then the stories begin, and with them, the gradual realization that life lessons is all they are.

The goodwill mentioned earlier does make "Being Human" more tolerable than it might be. A kinder, gentler movie about kidnaping, suicide, adultery, hangings, starvation and divorce you will not see. But a little tension would have done wonders for it.

Williams doesn't give a bad performance, so much as he gives no performance at all. Even though he plays a subservient slave in one segment and a master in another, it's hard to see a difference between them. All of his Hectors seem caught in a brooding melancholy, more on the verge of surrendering to life than learning to manage it.

What makes Williams so effective in films like "Mrs. Doubtfire," "Good Morning, Vietnam" and "The Fisher King" is that he is able to intimate complex characters beneath his improvisational wizardry. Forsyth has turned him inside-out, forcing him to carry his emotional burdens like a yoked ox, not even allowing us a glimpse of the clown we know is trapped inside.

Forsyth hasn't made many mistakes in his career, largely because he hasn't been afraid to season his quirky tales with a pinch of magic. But here, trying to catch the emotional highlights of the human odyssey, and with one of the most likable figures on Earth as his guide, he has committed an inexcusable error. He forgot to let the genie out of the bottle.

VILLAGE VOICE, 5/17/94, p. 54, Georgia Brown

It takes a long time to grow up. A single lifetime flames out like a struck match. In *Being Human*, Scottish writer-director Bill Forsyth gives his modest hero thousands of years and still he doesn't get things right. Playing five men named Hector (after *The Iliad's* father-husband?) at different stages of history—we won't say evolution—Robin Williams is always essentially the same "small" melancholy figure, forever evading commitment, losing wives, letting children down. "Don't forget the children," warns the movie's voiceover conscience. But everyone does.

A Time Bandits for grown-ups, the magical *Being Human* may not work entirely—and will no doubt suffer commercially for its wonderfully subtle perversities—but it contains more hidden depth and sweet mystery and more superbly understated acting than anything this reviewer has seen in a long time. Forsyth's eccentric narrative makes you realize once again how increasingly stultified and formulaic most movies are and how it's more and more difficult for audiences to adapt to deviations from the usual 1-2-3-The End. (And why do I get the feeling that even the putative parent, Warner Bros., which released this movie with only two last-minute screenings, doesn't appreciate it?)

"This is a story of a story," begins the female voiceover. She's not even a character in the action but something of an omniscient, though not entirely disinterested, narrator. She might have said that this is a story in search of a story, which is what it feels like for a while. Forsyth requires you to suspend more than disbelief here; you have to forget about continuity entirely. Not one of the five episodes makes an obvious point, until perhaps when you come to the present, you may see all roads leading to a few overwhelming questions. If you come to think of it' you may understand why the voiceover is a woman's.

It doesn't help that the film's first episode—the caveman one—is the weakest and most off-putting, the section with few of the riches found in those to follow. Here Hector is the father in a nuclear neolithic family, a little band of four with no apparent support group. When a raiding party shows up, the home team is no match and after token resistance the mild-mannered strangers row off with his wife and kids.

In episode two, set in some outpost of the Roman Empire, Hector is a captive slave, and the family shown this time belongs to his master, Lucinnius (John Turturro). Being close to a family but not of it presumably instills in Hector desire for one of his own. Lucinnius's closest relationship, on the other hand, is not to his wife and son but to Hector, who will betray him in the end. Betrayal is a common theme, and it's usually Hector doing the honors. But summary doesn't do justice to any of these episodes because their considerable pleasures lie in Forsyth's trademark details and gentle off-center jokes—and in the tantalizing mysteries of what is being left out. Forsyth manages to communicate a strong impression that what we are seeing truly is some ingenious *slice* into time.

In the Middle Ages, Hector takes up with a lovely widow (the strikingly vivid Anna Galiena from *The Hairdresser's Husband*). Neither understands the other's language, but she brings him home, dresses him in her husband's clothes (Hector is forever stepping into the shoes of another man), and introduces her two children. The sweet radiance of her son trying to win this new man is simply heartbreaking. (Each of the episodes, by the way, has a fatherless boy.) When Hector tells the widow he's leaving, her grief-stricken face illuminates the screen. Forsyth seems to me a genius with actors. For starters, he holds Williams's manic side in absolute check.

The movie's quirky understatement is increasingly delightful. It seems that Forsyth would sooner chop off his hand than hit you on the head with anything. In the Middle Ages section, for example, there's a scene with a dead boy (turned to stone for spying?) that could haunt you forever.

When we arrive in the present (episode five), Hector is a divorced New York father trying, in one weekend, to get to know the two kids he'd deserted a few years earlier. But even now Forsyth approaches the point obliquely. (The section begins with a Queens woman who's fallen through the floor while sitting on the toilet.) If the whole weight of past lives comes to rest, or roost, during the weekend with these two remarkable children, it doesn't do so in any way we've seen onscreen before.

What a daring project! Never repeating himself or rubbing in a message, Forsyth merely requires patience and openness. In the end *Being Human* strikes its chord, not with any grand sentimental flourish, but ever so softly. What's the sound of petals falling?

Also reviewed in:
CHICAGO TRIBUNE, 5/6/94, Friday/p. A, Michael Wilmington
NEW REPUBLIC, 6/6/94, p. 26, Stanley Kauffmann
NEW YORK TIMES, 5/6/94, p. C10, Janet Maslin
VARIETY, 5/9-15/94, p. 68, Todd McCarthy
WASHINGTON POST, 5/6/94, p. B7, Rita Kempley
WASHINGTON POST, 5/6/94, Weekend/p. 48, Joe Brown

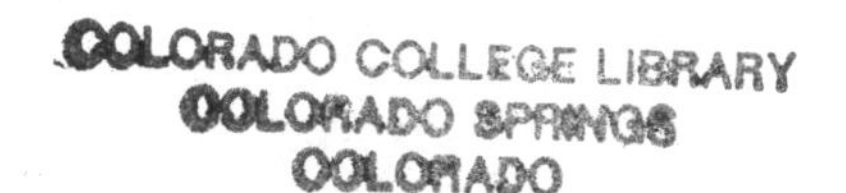

BELLE EPOQUE

A Sony Pictures Classics release of a Fernando Trueba Film Production film in collaboration with Lola Films/Animatografo/French Production with the cooperation of Sogepaq/Eurimages. *Executive Producer:* Andrés Vicente Gómez. *Producer:* Cristina Huete. *Director:* Fernando Trueba. *Screenplay (Spanish with English subtitles):* Rafael Azcona. *Story:* Rafael Azcona, José Luis Garcia Sanchez, and Fernando Trueba. *Director of Photography:* José Luis Alcaine. *Editor:* Carmen Frías. *Music:* Antoine Duhamel. *Sound:* Georges Prat and (music) Enrique Rielo. *Art Director*: Juan Botella. *Special Effects:* Filipe Cardoso. *Costumes:* Lala Huete. *Make-up:* Ana Lorena. *Running time:* 108 minutes. *MPAA Rating:* R.

CAST: Fernando Fernán Gómez (Manolo); Jorge Sanz (Fernando); Maribel Verdú (Rocío); Ariadna Gil (Violeta); Miriam Díaz-Aroca (Clara); Penélope Cruz (Luz); Mary Carmen Ramírez (Amalia, Manolo's Wife); Michel Galabru (Danglard, Amalia's Manager); Gabino Diego (Juanito, Rocío's Suitor); Chus Lampreave (Doña Asun, Juanito's Mother); Agustín González (Don Luis, The Priest); Juan José Otegui (First Soldier/Father-in-Law); Jesús Bonilla (Second Soldier); María Galiana (Polonia, the Madam); Juan Potau (Paco); Félix Cubero (Palomo); Marciano De La Fuente (The Mayor); José Antonio Sacristán (Rorro); Manuel Huete (Villager); Luis Zagalo (Cañán); Adelina Andrade (La Encarna); João Salaviza Silva (Jesusin).

FILMS IN REVIEW, 5-6/94, p. 58, Eva H. Kissin

Arco, a small town in Spain, is the semi-tropical setting of this Spanish romp in the sunshine. Here, pale green willows dip seductively into silent reflecting pools—and spring is apparently the season.

The time is 1931—the period between the end of the monarchy and the birth of the short lived Spanish republic. It is obviously a period of change—of new freedoms in a formerly rigid Catholic society.

A deserter from the King's army, a handsome young Republican, Fernando is befriended by another Republican, aging Manolo, who needs a companion who can cook in his large empty house until his four daughters arrive for their annual spring airing. Fernando, who is supposed to leave on their arrival, changes his mind as four nubile swaying bodies descend from the train. He is convinced that all of the fun is not where the republic is being conceived.

The young women are equally taken with the striking ex-soldier whose face is such a splendid combination of lust and innocence that it brings out their erotic and maternal instincts simultaneously.

A carnival provides a humorous moment for disguises and Fernando is reluctantly dressed as a girl. He is pursued in complete macho Spanish style by one of the daughters who turns out to be a lesbian. If this fast affair proves disappointing, he is not let down for long because the other three daughters are more than willing and the film is alive with charming scenes of seduction and family jealousy. Increased competition with a rich ardent neighbor piles on the conflicts. However, like all good comedies, the right couples marry in the end and go off to be fruitful.

The film is fun with its Renoir-like setting and flushed willing young women who are all anxious to produce Manolo's first grandson.

Nevertheless, the darker side of Spanish life is also felt in a meaningless murder and the subsequent suicide of the two Civilian Guards who had captured the young deserter before he was befriended by Manolo. The darkness is also evident in the local church where the happy couples have come to cement their relationships. A second suicide is hanging from the rafters.

Like the dried blood never removed from the matador's clothing in every exhibition case in Spain, the triumph of joy is never completely distant from the tragic. However, in this Academy Award film, spring and new life appear forever rather than merely perennial. Director Fernando Trueba has produced an interesting and sensitive work, and Jorge Sanz is a delicious young deserter.

LOS ANGELES TIMES, 3/2/94, Calendar/p. 3, Kevin Thomas

Fernando Trueba's sexy, bittersweet and contemplative comedy, "Belle Epoque," takes us back in time and place to an uncertain but hopeful moment of calm before the storm.

It's February, 1931, somewhere in Spain. The previous December, there was an uprising in Madrid against King Alfonso XIII, who would soon leave the country, paving the way for the Republicans to gain control of the government by the end of the year.

Trueba and his co-writers imagine a magical interlude in a sunny idyllic setting, where freedom and passion reign. He views the workings of the human comedy with the wisdom and detached compassion of Jean Renoir, to whom the Oscar-nominated "Belle Epoque," could stand as a homage.

Fleeing Madrid for the countryside and dreaming vaguely of emigrating to America, Fernando (Jorge Sanz), a handsome young army deserter, lands in a charming rural community after a darkly comic—and ultimately prophetic—encounter with a pair of Civil Guards. In the parlor of the local brothel, where the leaders of tiny Arcos, including the priest, regularly play cards, Fernando is taken under the wing of the leading member of the landed gentry, the aging but vital Don Manolo (the great veteran character star Fernando Fernán Gómez).

Don Manolo lives alone in his fine old manor house, and takes a paternal interest in Fernando. Several days later, Fernando has said his farewells, when suddenly the Don's four attractive daughters descend upon their father. The bowled-over Fernando, not surprisingly, manages to miss his train.

In good time he manages to have his way with them—and vice versa. There's Clara (Miriam Díaz-Aroca), a man-hungry recent widow; the gorgeous Rocío (Maribel Verdú), clumsily, presumptuously pursued by a rich nerd (Gabino Diego) and his titanically overbearing mother (veteran comedian Chus Lampreave); the pig-tailed, virginal Luz (Penélope Cruz) and Violeta (Ariadna Gil), a lesbian who finds herself attracted to Fernando once she's got herself in a military uniform and him dressed as a maid, costumed for a carnival celebration.

Trueba looks beyond these lusty, comic and uninhibited couplings to envision a world where reigns a pagan freedom of spirit, epitomized by the open-minded, uninhibited Don Manolo, grateful for the hugely theatrical arrival of his opera-singer wife (Mary Carmen Ramírez), accompanied by her rich, devoted manager/lover (France's peerless comedian Michel Galabru).

Trueba casts us into a ribald "You Can't Take It With You," but subtly reminds us that like life, liberty itself can be fleeting. Trueba's people, meanwhile, are too joyously partaking of life, speaking as freely as they make love, to realize how special this interlude is in which for once life pretty much proceeds the way it ought to.

Even though Spanish audiences are unquestionably at an advantage in regard to the film's political context and its literary allusions, "Belle Epoque" surely possesses a warm, universal appeal.

NEW YORK POST, 2/25/94, p. 37, Michael Medved

The only surprise about the new Spanish movie "Belle Epoque" is the Oscar nomination it received two weeks ago as Best Foreign Language Film. This is a pleasant piffle, a nostalgic, fluffy fantasy that may look more important than it is due to its subtitles and historic overtones.

The "Belle Epoque" (or "Beautiful Era") of the title refers to personal memories of these fictional characters, but also evokes that brief period in modern Spanish history between the collapse of the monarchy (1931) and the beginning of the horrendously bloody Civil War (1936)

The main character (Jorge Sanz) is an agnostic former seminarian and an unwilling soldier who deserts from his barracks amid the chaos in Madrid and makes his way toward the sunny south.

He survives a surprisingly dark and violent encounter with two country cops who try to apprehend him and eventually moves in with an elderly, eccentric artist (Fernando Fernan Gomez) in his sprawling farm house.

He decides to stay longer than he had planned when the old man's four unattached and irresistible daughters arrive from Madrid for a visit.

The bulk of the film plays out like a classic adolescent male fantasy, as our shy hero enjoys sex with all four of these very different daughters in sequence.

The most memorable of these encounters involves the boyish sister who dresses in mens clothes and has previously shown no interest whatever in the opposite sex: She basically rapes the protagonist when he's dressed as a woman, and she's dressed as a mustachioed soldier, for a costume celebration in the village square.

The most fanciful element in these amatory adventures involves the failure of any of the four sisters to feel even the slightest pangs of jealousy. They pass Sanz from one to the other like a cuddly new puppy, and the only real tension in the plot involves which one of the willful women is going to keep him.

There's an aspect of female fantasy as well in the way the hero is presented: He's earnest, handsome, gentle, eager to please, none too bright and a fabulous cook.

All the performances are likable and fetching, but the only actor who portrays a character with any deeper feeling as a fully realized human being is Fernando Fernan Gomez as the crusty old artist.

Director Fernando Trueba seems intent on keeping the tone light and breezy, without touching any messy or complicated questions of life and love, and the sun-drenched rustic locations make for a most appealing surface.

The many references to Spanish politics of the 1930s, and the bitter division between Monarchists and Republicans, seems an almost arbitrary intrusion—as if the picture were straining for some social significance it hardly deserves.

In that regard, it resembles the 1991 Italian film "Mediterraneo" waiting out World War II on a remote, tranquil Greek Island—as another slow, stately exploration of an escapist idyll in the midst of turbulent times.

Though hardly a big ambitious statement movie, "Mediterraneo" generated enough easygoing charm to win an unexpected Academy Award as Best Foreign Language Film,

"Belle Epoque," though definitely an underdog contender, hopes to work the same sort of summery magic on this year's Oscar voters.

NEWSDAY, 2/25/94, Part II/p. 62, Jack Mathews

The title of Spanish director Fernando Trueba's "Belle Epoque" refers not to historical period but to the delirious luck of a young army deserter who befriends a painter with four beautiful and eager daughters and comes to stay with them. But since he is as much the seducee as the seducer of the tale, a pretty good time is had by all.

The winner of nine Goyas, the Spanish equivalent of the Oscars,"Belle Epoque" is a sunny, bawdy burlesque that retells some of the best of the Italian Comedies of a generation ago, and it is the perfect dessert for those who didn't get their fill of romantic fantasy with the Mexican film "Like Water for Chocolate."

"Belle Epoque," like "Like Water for Chocolate," occurs during a period of political turmoil. It is 1931, just as the Spanish people are about to evict Alfonso XIII from the throne, and the idealistic Fernando (Jorge Sanz) is one of many deserters from the king's army.

Trueba, and screenwriter Rafael Azcona, don't have a thing to say about the mini-revolution, and the related rebellion against the Catholic Church, though they keep coming back to them as reference. In fact, those events seem a far distance from the country villa where Fernando settles in with the spirited old painter Manolo (Fernando Fernan Gomez) and the quartet of daughters—three single, one widowed—visiting from Madrid.

The sisters are Rocio (Maribel Verdu), a voluptuous flirt who drives both Fernando and local suitor Juanito (Gabino Diego) wild; Clara (Miriam Diaz-Aroca), whose husband died and left her with an appetite for paella and sex; Violeta (Ariadna Gil), a brooding cross-dresser with a Marlene Dietrich glare; and Luz (Penelope Cruz), the baby of the family hurriedly trying to grow up.

For the virginal Fernando, who is unable to distinguish lust from love, the prospects are daunting. He looks at the women and sees four potential brides. Three of them look at him and see a sex object. Every time he gets seduced, he proposes, and is rejected. Whether he can run the erotic and emotional gauntlet and have enough innocence left for true romance is the noble challenge, and the great fun, of the movie.

Everyone involved in "Belle Epoque," from Trueba to the most minor member of the cast, is perfectly in tune with its buoyant, farcical tone, and some of the performances are wonderfully overdrawn. Sanz gives Fernando a sincere, wide-eyed innocence, then sort of gets out of the way of the others. He becomes a prop, in more ways than one, for the women, particularly Verdu, a terrific comic actress, and Gil, who is a revelation as the aggressively single-minded Violeta.

There is a hilarious sequence in which Violeta takes Fernando to a costume party—she's dressed as a man, he as a woman—and plays out their role reversal for the entire evening, from the dance floor to the hayloft, leaving him at the end deflowered and befuddled.

It is instructive that "Belle Epoque" was nominated for the Academy Award for best foreign-language film. An American picture with such slight intentions, and with such a zestful appetite for sexual humor, wouldn't stand a chance in the main competition. It's as if Hollywood can only condone this sort of behavior when it comes from another culture.

As it is, it has little chance of winning over "Farewell My Concubine" or "The Wedding Banquet," but as a movie that, as Trueba, says, won't remind anyone of how miserable life is, it's nice to see it on the ballot.

SIGHT AND SOUND, 4/94, p. 38, Paul Julian Smith

Spain, 1931. On the eve of the declaration of the Republic, Fernando, a young deserter from the King's army in Madrid, is captured by two Civil Guards. When both of them are killed in a quarrel, the lucky Fernando takes refuge in a brothel. There he meets the elderly libertine and artist Manolo, who invites him back to his large country house in which he lives, separated from his wife. Fernando resolves to return to Madrid incognito, but remains in the village when he catches sight of Manolo's four beautiful daughters as they arrive at the station: the recently widowed Clara, the masculine-identified Violeta, the seductive Rocío, engaged to a local Royalist, and the virginal Luz.

Fernando sleeps with three of them in turn. He is seduced by Violeta when both are cross-dressed at the local carnival; by Rocío when she seeks consolation after an argument with her fiancé; and by Clara, after she has pushed him into the lake where her husband drowned. Meanwhile, Manolo's wife Amalia, an aging diva of the Spanish operetta, pays an unexpected visit to husband and daughters. The reunion is ecstatic, even though she brings her stage-manager/lover, who reveals that Amalia's career is by no means as successful as she claims. After his amorous experiments, Fernando has finally come to believe that it is the youngest daughter, Luz, who is his true love. They become engaged and Luz visits him in bed on the morning before their wedding. Finally, the three elder sisters leave the station for Madrid, while Fernando and Luz set out for a new life in America, leaving Manolo alone once more.

In the prologue to *Belle Epoque*, the fortunate Fernando is let off free after the Civil Guards who arrest him as a deserter conveniently kill each other off. In the narrative of transparent wish-fulfilment which follows, director Fernando Trueba seems to be hoping that his audience will be similarly indulgent and will absolve him of the charges of aestheticism and sexism aroused by his film, with its period art design and its multiple seduction plot, with each daughter surrendering herself in turn to the puppy-eyed Jorge Sanz.

As the story develops *Belle Epoque* nonetheless offers many pleasures. The picturesque decor (filmed in Portugal not Spain) is beautifully shot by Almodóvar regular José Luis Alcaine, who manfully resists the temptation of soft focus, which ruined so many Spanish period films of the 80s; and the four young women offer splendidly assured performances. Miriam Diaz-Aroca essays a demure modesty far from the petulant sensuality she lent Almodóvar's *High Heels*; Ariadna Gil does her best to stop Violeta turning into a straight fantasy of a lipstick lesbian; Maribel Verdú (from Vicente Aranda's *Amantes* and currently Spain's hottest young actress) brings intelligence to her customary passion; and Penelope Cruz (from Bigas Luna's *Jamón, Jamón*) pouts prettily as the neglected virgin.

While it comes as no surprise to learn that this lazy plot was cooked up by Trueba and his male collaborators over a series of long lunches, the film's heterosexual wish-fulfilment is partially mitigated by the fact that the passive male is invariably humiliated by the active females before they offer themselves to him. Fernando is pushed into a lake by Clara, and dressed as a maid for the carnival by Violeta, revealing in the process an unnerving likeness to Tony Curtis in *Some Like It Hot*. This episode, in which Gil, cross-dressed, straddles the nonplussed Sanz while quite literally blowing his trumpet, is perhaps the film's most successfully comic and erotic moment.

One suspects, however, that the many awards garnered by Gil from the role derive from her perceived courage in Spain in playing a lesbian at all.

More pervasive problems crystallise around Fernando Fernán Gómez's patriarch. The most ubiquitous actor in Spanish cinema, he has been perfecting his crusty old man act for at least 20 years. Here he replays it as an unlikely provincial libertine, freely accepting the lesbianism of one daughter and the lost virginity of the others. The problem is that—as with the film's profane priest or its parodic treatment of political conservatives—*Belle Epoque*'s sunny good humour simply conjures away the real conflicts of Spanish history, encouraging the contemporary audience to adopt the comforting, ironic distance of its anachronistically permissive family.

While domestic audiences clearly appreciated the absence of that po-faced seriousness with which much state-sponsored cinema of the 80s addressed the Civil War (making this one of the biggest-grossing Spanish films of all time), *Belle Epoque*'s attitude to the past is one of anaesthetic amnesia. Where Merchant/Ivory's films offer a gilded image of a British social order now definitively lost, Trueba's equally aestheticized period piece holds up a mirror to that tolerant, and sometimes indifferent, libertarianism on which Spain came to pride itself after the death of Franco. At a time when that achievement is threatened by mass unemployment and the rise of the Right, the escapist attractions of such rewriting of Spanish history are all too obvious.

The film ends with a moment of closure and of evasion: Fernando marries the youngest daughter and emigrates with her to America. The chastening of Fernando echoes the domestication of Trueba and his collaborators: one would hardly guess that scriptwriter Rafael Azcona was responsible for some of the most grotesque and bizarre Spanish features of the Franco era, when he worked with directors such as Luis Berlanga and Marco Ferreri. The significance of the extraordinary popular and critical success of *Belle Epoque* is surely in its rejection of that vein of corrosive humour and perverse violence that was once so characteristic of Spanish film. It is Trueba's achievement to have shown that a Spaniard can direct a period picture as polished and inoffensive as any in European art cinema.

TIME, 3/21/94, p. 71, Richard Schickel

It begins with two policemen falling into a comic argument over whether to let their prisoner, an army deserter, escape. The quarrel leads to one of them killing the other and then committing suicide. It climaxes with a priest—a worldly and genial man—hanging himself in his church. He has fallen into despair after too profound an exposure to the antireligious writings of the poet-philosopher Miguel de Unamuno.

Between these two events, the young deserter, Fernando (the wide-eyed Jorge Sanz), having been given shelter by a retired painter and full-time ironist (superbly played by Fernando Fernán Gómez), seduces, or is seduced by, all four of the old man's lovely daughters.

In short, *Belle Epoque*, an Oscar nominee for Best Foreign Film, is a very funny movie. Yes, really. For there's a little bit of Luis Buñuel nestled in the heart of every Spaniard, something at once black and farcical, and director Fernando Trueba is no exception. He also loves the sun-splashed romanticism of Jean Renoir; the film's cheerful look, its air of bemused wonder at the things people do when the time is right for frolic, is a homage to that most civilized of directors.

And the time is indeed right. For the title refers to that brief moment in 1931 when the Spanish Republic was proclaimed, ending the long night of decadent monarchy and preceding the still darker night of civil war and Francoism. It was a historical nanosecond when everyone felt frisky intellectually and emotionally, and this surprising film, which wears its complexities so lightly, pays sweet tribute to that spirit. It is rendered the more poignant by our knowledge—not, of course, shared by the characters—of how brief and repressible their irrepressibility would prove to be.

VILLAGE VOICE, 3/1/94, p. 50, Georgia Brown

Setting a Spanish film in 1931 as Fernando Trueba does with *Belle Epoque*, seems to invite political, even allegorical, readings. Yet Trueba insists—vehemently to WNYC's Leonard Lopate—that his film should be taken simply as a vision of paradise, a fantasy version of things as they once were, and, if God were just, ought to be. Trueba cites Renoir, Sturges, Truffaut, and Billy Wilder as his models. Also, his older countryman Berlanga. (The film is written by Berlanga's longtime collaborator, Rafael Azcona.)

As a brisk erotic farce, *Belle Epoque* is something of a young man's wet dream. Maybe an old man's as well. The docile, child-like hero, a willing prisoner in the house of love, is played by Jorge Sanz, who embodied a more sinister version of the same pliable character in Vicente Aranda's *Lovers*. (As a real child, incidentally, Sanz was the young Arnold Schwarzenegger in *Conan the Barbarian*.) Here he's Fernando, like the filmmaker. An ex-seminary student and army deserter—fed up apparently with both church and state—he's rescued providentially by a retired man of the world, Manolo (Fernando Fernan Gomez). Although his villa has many bedrooms, Manolo invites Fernando to share his bed: "This house is like an icebox." "Are you queer?" Fernando asks. Manolo reassures the boy by asking him to read him to sleep from Ecclesiastes.

The rub is that Manolo's four daughters are due the next day for their annual summer holiday. And once Fernando spies the prancing beauties, he offers to stay on as a cook since none of the women seems at home in the kitchen. Ideally, Manolo would like to remain friends with the young man—a relationship he senses will change once the girls arrive. "Gain a son-in-law, lose a friend" is one of the old man's mottos. The only real question, of course, is which sister will Fernando choose? More accurately, which will choose him?

The eldest, Clara (Miriam Diaz-Aroca), is a lonesome widow, mourning a husband who whipped up a delicious paella shortly before drowning (he didn't wait long enough to go in the water). Fernando's paella Clara pronounces even more scrumptious than her husband's. The second sister, Rocio (Marabel Verdú, also from *Lovers*), is a ripe, rather undiscriminatingpeach. She's also being courted by a rich, foolish local boy, a teacher in thrall to his religious mother (Chus Lampreave). The third sister, Violeta (Ariadna Gil), is a lesbian ("Mama wanted a boy") who wants to *be* a man, not to *have* one. But on carnival night, with Fernando in wig and skirt and herself as a mustachioed soldier, she suddenly finds him irresistible.

Since this is a fairy tale, naturally the prince will marry the youngest, the virgin. Luz (Penelope Cruz, the sultry dish from *Jamon Jamon*) must wait, though, until he's tasted her three sisters, "I want you to do with me what you did with them," Luz murmurs when the two finally bed down. (It isn't so much that he has rejected the other three; two find him wanting.)

In the meantime, Mama (Mary Carmen Ramírez) stops by the house for a visit. A singer of arias, Mama is on a world tour, accompanied by her manager-sponsor-lover—anarrangement that can't make Manolo happy, especially since he's impotent with anyone other than his wife ("Here I am a rebel, an infidel, and a libertine by nature, living life like a scared old bourgeois"). Manolo is a patriarch of patience, tolerance, and mature resignation. And like every other male here, he seems content for women to exercise their sovereign wills.

Jealousy, as you see, has no place in paradise. Nor has suffering. All longings exist to be satisfied. There are no villains here—not even the fiancé's fanatically conservative mother. No one is disciplined or expelled. Oh, a priest hangs himself. Not from disgust at the anticlerical climate or prevalent licentiousness. He's been reading Unamuno.

In the interests of full disclosure, farce is not my favorite genre, and *Belle Epoque*, while pleasant enough, didn't convert me. What I find intriguing though is that this, Spain's most popular film last year, should find paradise in such unequal relations between the sexes. What pleasure can women find in these wimps? To be sure, men preside over the intellectual realm, but a pretty empty one it is, leading to endless card games and, eventually perhaps, suicide. This particular view of gender roles, I might add, conforms to one reinforced in Spanish films historically: At its extreme, there was the devouring mother, the infantilized, castrated male.

So it's fitting that Ariadna Gil won Spain's Goya for Best Actress over her more frilly sisters. *Belle Epoque*'s highpoint is Violeta's suave quasi-rape of our hero dressed as a serving maid.

Also reviewed in:
CHICAGO TRIBUNE, 4/15/94, Friday/p. B, Johanna Steinmetz
NEW REPUBLIC, 2/21/94, p. 28, Stanley Kauffmann
NEW YORK TIMES, 2/25/94, p. C10, Janet Maslin
VARIETY, 12/21/92, p. 62, Peter Besas
WASHINGTON POST, 3/25/94, p. D1, Rita Kempley
WASHINGTON POST, 3/25/94, Weekend/p. 45, Desson Howe

BERENICE ABBOTT: A VIEW OF THE 20TH CENTURY

An Ishtar Films release. *Producer:* Martha Wheelock and Kay Weaver. *Director:* Martha Wheelock and Kay Weaver. *Editor:* Martha Wheelock and Kay Weaver. *Director of Photography:* Martha Wheelock. *Running time:* 57 minutes. *MPAA Rating:* Not Rated.

WITH: Berenice Abbott (Herself) and with commentary by: Hilton Kramer, Daniel Walkowitz, Dr. Michael Sundell, Dr. Philip Morrison, Julia Van Haaften, Maria Morris Hamburg.

NEW YORK POST, 12/7/94, p. 37, Larry Worth

"The last thing the world wants is an independent woman."

Well, that's debatable, but 92-year-old photographer Berenice Abbott voiced the sentiment when reflecting on her wildly diverse career. What's not debatable: The world of cinema is considerably richer for the new documentary "Berenice Abbott: A View of the 20th Century."

Co-directors Kay Weaver and Martha Wheelock have comprised a striking combination of the nonagenarian's incisive comments, great period footage and copious examples of the pictures which earned her renown.

Logically, the film begins with Abbott's early years of capturing the avant-garde in Paris of the '20s. A decade later, she became "smitten" with New York and brilliantly shot the skyscrapers' rise. Finally, Abbott illustrated physics phenomena at MIT while recording Route l's path from Fort Kent, Maine, to Key West, Fla.

Though the filmmakers skimp on Abbott's personal life, proof that they've effectively covered their subject comes when viewers hear of Abbott's death at age 93. An air of melancholy suddenly proves overpowering, assuaged only by the body of work she left behind.

Among those immortalized in Abbott's lens: Margaret Anderson, who—not so coincidentally—is the subject of a 30-minute co-feature, "Beyond Imagining: Margaret Anderson & The Little Review."

Wendy Weisberg's Academy Award-nominated short opens with Anderson's mantra—"I will become something beautiful." Anderson made good on her claim in 1914 by editing the Little Review, a magazine that complemented her socialist sympathies while luring writers such as e.e. cummings, Ezra Pound and Gertrude Stein.

Together, "A Look at the 20th Century" and "Beyond Imagining" emerge as two remarkable films about two remarkable women who suffered for being ahead of their time and gloriously independent.

Also reviewed in:
NEW YORK TIMES, 12/7/94, p. C15, Stephen Holden

BEST OF THE INTERNATIONAL TOURNEE OF ANIMATION, THE

Seventeen animated shorts. *Running time:* 85 minutes. *MPAA Rating:* Not Rated.

NEW YORK POST, 8/5/94, p. 43, Bill Hoffmann

Animation festivals are usually a hit-or-miss proposition, with the misses often outweighing the hits.

That's why it's a pleasure to report that "The Best of the International Tournee of Animation" is a big winner and perfect entertainment for the dog days of August.

There certainly aren't any dogs here. Instead, you have the cream of the crop from 25 years of animation festivals.

Among the standouts are:

■Nick Park's "Creature Comforts," in which zoo animals with British accents talk about the pros and cons of living behind bars. Satirical and smart, this short certainly deserved the 1990 Oscar for animated short.

■"Ode to G.I. Joe," the bizarre story of how a dozen G.I. Joe dolls take over their young owner's room to practice maneuvers and party.

■The psychedelic "Sunbeam," in which a daring flying ace paints a vivid world of color and motion. It's a delightful throwback to the '60s in the "Yellow Submarine" vein.

■"The Cat Came Back," in which a cantankerous old man goes to extraordinary lengths to rid himself of a pesky kitten and fails every time. Hysterical.

■The computer-generated "Tin Toy," featuring the title character desperately trying to stay out of the way of a frisky baby.

■"Technological Threat," the laugh-out-loud tale of one worker's battle against automation taking over his office.

Above all, these 17 shorts show why animation, while it has always been under-rated, is one of the most innovative forms of filmmaking. See it!

NEWSDAY, 8/5/94, Part II/p. B7, Gene Seymour

Oh, how I've missed "The Cat Came Back" ever since I first saw it at the 1988 edition of the International Tournee of Animation. What I've missed most about Canadian animator Cordell Barker's outrageous take on that hoary old nonsense dirge is that totally blank expression on the teeny yellow cat's face as it blithely murders various pieces of furniture.

It's a too-perfect contrast to the baroque variations of hysteria registered on Old Man Johnson's face as he desperately tries to ditch the little beast in the woods, under the sea, down a mine shaft.

I've also missed, from that same year, "Tin Toy," an affecting saga of a mechanical drummer's hazardous relationship with a baby. Historians may yet say—if they haven't already—that this five-minute classic by John Lasseter and William Reeves marked the point when computer-generated animation found its soul.

It was good seeing them again in this greatest-hits compilation. Those who haven't been at any of the previous toon fests should enjoy this one because they'll know, going in, that there's little chance of tripping over a short subject that bores like the Whitewater hearings and gobbles like a turkey.

And speaking of animals, Nick Park's 1990 Oscar winner, "Creature Comforts," is back. As with other classic cartoons, this oft-screened short of animated clay animals sounding off about their lives in the zoo gets funnier with age. This time around, I especially appreciated the rambling puma who declares to his unseen interviewers his need for ... "*Space*! You know? ... I need SPACE!"

Gregory P. Grant's "Ode to G.I. Joe" delivers similar jolts of hilarity as it depicts a contingent of those classic 12-inch-tall soldier dolls turning a small boy's room into their own rest-and-recreation spa to the tune of the Staple Singers' "I'll Take You There."

And for those who doubt that these "Tournees" have any impact on global culture, this "Best of" show climaxes with 1990's "Big House Blues," which stars a then-obscure chihuahua named Ren Hoek and a lumpy cat named Stimpy. You know what became of them. what you may wonder is how their inspired creator, John Kricfalusi, was ever allowed to leave them in other animators' hands.

Other highlights:

• "Second Class Mail" (1984), by British animators Alison Snowden and David Fine, is an exemplar of minimalist character study as it tracks a lonely woman's star-crossed relationship with an inflated man.

• "Sunbeam" (1985) is an exercise in pure technique that could charm the splinters off a board. British animator Paul Vester uses the 1941 pop ditty "What's at the Top of a Sunbeam?" as a departure point for a series of bright, juicy slices of surrealism.

• "The Fly" (1980), by Hungarian director Ferenc Rofusz, follows the last minutes in the life of a pest with deft authority.

Also reviewed in:
WASHINGTON POST, 7/29/94, p. D6, Richard Harrington

BETWEEN THE TEETH

A Todo Mundo Ltd. release. *Producer:* Joel D. Hinman. *Director:* David Byrne and David Wild. *Director of Photography:* Roger Tonry. *Editor:* David Wild and Lou Angelo. *Music:* 10 Car Pile-Up, Bobby Allende, Jonathan Best, Angel Fernandez, Ite Jerez, Lewis Kahn, George Porter, Jr., Hector Rosado, Steve Sacks, and Oscar Salas. *Running time:* 71 minutes. *MPAA Rating:* Not Rated.

LOS ANGELES TIMES, 3/10/94, Calendar/p. 2, Chris Willman

David Byrne and salsa music make classic star-crossed lovers. His yelpy, existential New York nervousness and the Latin music's tightly played, jubilantly felt release are unlikely enough suitors that only in irony the twain shall really meet, but there's a good amount of fun in the attempt. "Between the Teeth," an unadorned movie rendering of Byrne's 1992 tour, effectively documents the multicultural mirth.

Of course, it pales within the large shadow cast by 1984's "Stop Making Sense," arguably the best concert movie ever, filmed before Byrne made the bad career move of breaking up Talking Heads. Lately he's been less a rock force to be reckoned with than a commercially negligible pop anthropologist, rendering the solo album this tour was promoting, "Uh-Oh," a sales stiff. And Byrnes own co-direction of this filmic follow-up (with David Wild) follows the model Jonathan Demme set down with "Sense"—keep it simple, while shooting each song with a different philosophy of lighting, camera movement and editing—without really expanding on it.

But if diminished expectations are the order of the day, "Teeth" still has a pretty sharp sonic bite to it. Byrne's nine-piece backup band—including such heroes of world-beat as Cuban percussionist Oscar Salas and ex-Meters bassist George Porter Jr., plus a very busy horn section—cooks up a swell funk, equally percussive but more Brazil-based than "Sense's" African-dominated polyrhythms. For more xenophobic fans, there's a fair amount of Talking Heads traditionalism in the song choices and overall sound, too.

The best visual moments take in the scope of the big band on stage. But for variety, presumably, some songs leave the camera lingering tightly on the middle two-thirds of Byrne's sweat-beaded face, leaving lots of time to ponder whether he really does have anything caught between his teeth or not. For most fans the best bet may be to wait for the video or laser disc to come out and make an audiotape copy for the car. In lieu of dancing, the Byrne band's hyperdrive makes better music to motor to than to sit placidly through.

NEWSDAY, 2/2/94, Part II/p. 59, Ira Robbins

If concert movies were reliably good, no one would need ever attend big rock shows; in terms of ticket price, safety, visibility, comfort and convenience, there's no comparison. Now that onstage spontaneity is largely a thing of the past, so is the primary reason for actually witnessing concerts in real time.

Film adds so many dimensions to its subject, however, pointing a camera and shooting is never enough. Between the attempt to expand a routine stage performance into something grander than a static view of what a fan would see, and the need to somehow convey the visceral charge of live music, concert film-making has bedeviled musicians and directors for decades.

As an instrumental figure in "Stop Making Sense," Jonathan Demme's acclaimed 1984 Talking Heads concert film, David Byrne helped considerably to raise the form's ante.

Nearly a decade later, with precious few films reaching such rarefied standards, the multi-cultural singer and guitarist—who has been a solo artist since the Heads ceased to exist—took his own challenge, with this documentary of a Halloween 1992 concert at the Count Basie Theater in Red Bank, N.J.

In "Between the Teeth," Byrne and co-director David Wild initially find a subtle way to carry the music from the stage to the screen. For three songs, Byrne stands alone with an acoustic guitar, performing in silhouette, half-caught in side lighting. It's no big deal, but the framed drama amplifies and sharpens Byrne's unadorned delivery.

But then Byrne, joined by 10 Car Pile-Up, a superlative Latin/American 10-piece with horns, percussion and keyboards, sings selections from his recent "Uh-Oh" album and Talking Heads' 1988 swan song, "Naked." Although performed with typical passion and precision and shot with crisp onstage efficiency, the film offers nothing more than an excellent vantage point.

"Between the Teeth" finally hits on something with the Heads' familiar "Life During Wartime." Shot and edited into a relentless frenzy of strobe lights and blurry, hand-held shots weaving wildly among the musicians, it's an enthralling segment with all the instant excitement of a frantic news report. But it's a premature climax, and everything that follows—the cool jazz riffs and blue lights of "Women vs. Men," the harsh white fluorescents of "Hanging Upside Down" and the extreme close-ups of faces and hands in "Lie to Me"—looks weak in its wake. While certainly a treat for fans, "Between the Teeth" will not send them home humming the scenery.

NEW YORK POST, 2/2/94, p. 29, Larry Worth

If David Byrne was ever on the road to where, you couldn't tell from his cinematic resume.

He highlighted the Talking Heads concert film "Stop Making Sense," directed the comically bizarre "True Stories" and won an Oscar for scoring "The Last Emperor."

Now, Byrne's returned to the silver screen with perhaps his most unique adventure, "Between the Teeth."

It could have been a basic documenting of the superstar's 1992 "Uh-Oh Tour." But not with Byrne and David Wild behind the camera. Their intent was to lens each song in a different style.

Well, to say that *every* tune has its own mood is wishful thinking on the part of both Davids. But there's still lots of variety among the 15 selections.

As the show opens Byrne's alone on stage, illuminated only by a swinging lantern. After a couple choruses, his nine-man band 10 Car Pile-Up, appears. That's when—figuratively and literally—everything comes to light.

Dark, intimate motifs segue into the silhouetting of performers against a skyblue scrim, just before each is showered in a butter-yellow glow. A number later, dramatic shadows become more prominent than those casting them. And in "Life During Wartime," a strobe's eerie flashes make the stage pulsate with menace.

The camerawork is even wilder. It goes from blistering close-ups of Byrne's features to dizzying jump cuts to a hand-held dance around the slickly attired celeb.

But as evidenced before, Byrne's presence is the ultimate drawing card. Who can resist watching him move his head like a chicken while prancing across stage, whipping his sweat-soaked hair back and forth with clock-work timing?

Though some of his individuality has dissolved over the years, making him at times seem like a hipper James Taylor, he remains the master showman. Never resorting to special effects, he generates charisma to spare, while ensuring that listeners' feet are always tapping.

Speaking of the beat, selections range from standards "And She Was" and "Blind" to Brazilian-inspired "Rei Momo" offerings and the unprecedented likes of "Buck Naked." It's a smooth mix all the way.

"Between the Teeth" is shown with an amusing three-minute short—which Byrne and Wild also co-directed—"April 19, 1989." It zaps between 22 individuals shuffling in front of pull-down screens of beaches, office settings, whatever. They appear to be waiting—uncomfortably—for something to happen.

Thankfully, those watching Byrne's latest efforts won't be able to relate.

VILLAGE VOICE, 2/28/94, p. 65, Amy Taubin

When it comes to music, I feel the weight of my years. I remember the Velvets at the Dom on St. Marks Place in '65, Television at CBGB in '72, and Talking Heads at the Kitchen in '76 or so. (Gus Van Sant remembers Talking Heads at RISD when he was a preppie and they were New Wavers. He went to a party where they played and felt totally out of place. What made it worse was that you couldn't dance to their music.) I also think *Stop Making Sense* is a great concert movie, second only to a black-and-white camcorder video of James Chance at Max's (which by now is probably a sticky, magnetized mess in the archives of the Kitchen, so don't go bothering them about it).

So maybe it's because I'm jaded that I didn't stomp and cheer at the end of *Between The Teeth,* the concert film of David Byrne and his band 10 Car Pile-Up at the Count Basie Theater in Red Bank, New Jersey, on Halloween 1992. Byrne is at the top of his form (manic but looser than I've ever seen him, more vocally expressive and musically assured, and still teasing the mike with the best diction in rock and roll); every sideman in 10 Car Pile-Up plays with wild accomplishment (in close-up they look like refugees from a Michael Caine movie); and dancing is no longer a problem (sitting still in your movie theater seat is).

Codirectors Byrne and David Wild take a straightforward but elegant approach. The camera movement is fluid, the lighting sharply angular, the sound everything you'd expect. "Life During Wartime" is the one tour-de-force camera-editing bit, with zip pans and attack-dog zooms, cut so fast that it superimposes in your eye.

Next to the old songs, some of Byrne's new ones sound a bit pale and pop. He does inspired covers of his former self in "Mr. Jones" and "Nothing but Flowers." Somewhere in the middle of "And She Was," however, I started thinking something ain't right. As a matter of fact, it was downright weird to hear so many "she's" and "girls, girls, girls, girls, girls" without one in sight. I miss Tina, never thought I would. Is this Byrne's first band without a woman, or just a boy's night out?

Also reviewed in:
CHICAGO TRIBUNE, 4/1/94, Friday/p. M, John Petrakis
NEW YORK TIMES, 2/2/94, p. C15, Jon Pareles
WASHINGTON POST, 3/4/94, p. C9, Richard Harrington

BEVERLY HILLS COP III

A Paramount Pictures release of a Mace Neufeld and Robert Rehme production in association with Eddie Murphy Productions. *Executive Producer:* Mark Lipsky. *Producer:* Mace Neufield and Robert Rehme. *Director:* John Landis. *Screenplay:* Steve E. de Souza. *Based on characters created by:* Danilo Bach, and Daniel Petrie, Jr. *Director of Photography:* Mac Ahlberg. *Editor:* Dale Belden. *Music:* Nile Rodgers. *Music Editor:* Jeff Carson. *Choreographer:* Smith Wordes. *Sound:* Joseph Geisinger. *Sound Editor:* Rick Franklin and Doug Jackson. *Casting:* Jackie Burch. *Production Designer:* Michael Seymour. *Art Director:* Thomas P. Wilkins. *Set Decorator:* Marvin March. *Set Dresser:* Tamara Clinard. *Special Effects:* Jon G. Belyeu. *Costumes:* Catherine Adair. *Make-up:* Marietta Carter. *Stunt Coordinator:* Rick Avèry. *Running time:* 103 minutes. *MPAA Rating:* R.

CAST: Eddie Murphy (Axel Foley); Judge Reinhold (Billy Rosewood); Hector Elizondo (Jon Flint); Jon Tenney (Levine); Joey Travolta (Giolito); Eugene Collier (Leppert); Jimmy Ortega (Rondell); Ousaun Elam (Pederson); Ray Lykins (Nixon); Tim Gilbert (McKee); Rick Avery (Cline); Gil Hill (Todd); Dick Purtan (Detroit Disc Jockey); Fred Asparagus (Bobby); Louis Lombardi (Snake); Lindsey Ginter (Holloway); Timothy Carhart (Ellis DeWald); Michael Bowen (Fletch); David Parry (Taddeo); Stephen McHattie (Steve Fulbright); Al Green (Minister); Hattie Winston (Mrs. Todd); Tracy Lindsey (Ticket Booth Girl); Gregory McKinney (Kimbrough); Forry Smith (Rondy); Theresa Randle (Janice); Dan Martin (Cooper); Steven Banks (Spider Ride Operator); George Lucas (Disappointed Man); Christina Venuti (Disappointed Girl); Jonathan Hernandez (Scared Boy); Christy Alvarez (Scared Girl); Yareli Arizmendi (Scared Kids' Mom); John Saxon (Orrin Sanderson); Aileen Acain (Waitress); Alan Young (Uncle Dave Thornton); Martha Coolidge (Security Woman); Bronson Pinchot (Serge); Symba Smith, Julie Strain, and Heather Parkhurst (Annihilator Girls); George Schaefer (Mike); Joe Dante (Jailer); Curtis Williams (Little Kid); Helen Martin (Grandma);

Theodore Borders (Big Kid); Albie Selznick and Charles Chun (Technicians); Roger Reid (Man on Phone); Royce Reid (Feisty Kid); Hector Correa (Man with Video Camera); Elaine Kagan (Sanderson's Secretary); Tino Insana (Burly Cop); John Rubinow (Doctor); Hank McGill (Paramedic); Cherily Shea (Girl at Corner); Peter Medak (Man at Corner); Arthur Hiller, Ray Harryhausen, and Robert Sherman (Bar Patrons); Gene Elman (Bartender); Jerry Dunphy (Newscaster); Barbet Schroeder (Man in Porsche); Philip Levien (Serge's Assistant); John Singleton (Fireman); Lisa Allen and Julie Dolan (Prescott Pig); Christian Heath and Pat Quinn (Oki-Doki); Sean Spence and James Makinnon (Rufus Rabbit); Jennifer Cobb and Lynn Walsh (Meyer Lion); Susan Gayle and Devin McRae (Kopy Kat); Wendy Harpenau and Felicia Wong (Liddle Bear); Marlene Hoffman and Felicia Wong (Big Bear); Liz Macawili and Robin Navlyt (Floyd Fox); Dave Myers and Matt Myers (Tippy Turtle); Nick Hermz and Tim Shuster (Tadross Gorilla).

FILMS IN REVIEW 7-8/94, p. 57, Keith Edwards

Beverly Hills Cop III is an Eddie Murphy Production starring none other than Mr. Murphy himself. For the record, the associate producer is one Ray Murphy, Jr.

This is a live action cartoon whose main function is to showcase the star and provide mindless summer diversion along with the string of bomb movies that have invaded the marketplace. Its appeal rests solely on how you respond to the Murphy persona that he has carefully packaged and promoted over the years. If you find him charismatic and do not object to the excessive employment of firearms, this film might engage you. However, the enormous arsenal ranges from hand pistols to mammoth bazookas which are in constant use and central to the plot. There should be a violence disclaimer at the finish, as they make a case for weapons as glamorous and heroic, and I find this offensive, since the star is a probable role model for impressionable youngsters.

Also back and offensive is Bronson Pinchot as the popular lisping limp-wristed homosexual parody that Mr. Murphy clearly endorses. Mr. Pinchot is a talented performer who deserves better material and one hopes he'll pass on Beverly IV.

LOS ANGELES TIMES, 5/25/94, Calendar/p. 1, Peter Rainer

There was a memorable moment in "Beverly Hills Cop" when Eddie Murphy's Axel Foley jammed a banana in a parked police car's tailpipe.

Walking out of "Beverly Hills Cop III," you may be moved to ask. "Anybody have a banana for this movie."

The existence of this film is a testament to star power—or, to be more precise, recycling power. We're supposed to be so grateful to once again see Eddie Murphy as Axel that we can overlook how crude and shopworn this picture really is. It's one of the most cynically engineered sequels ever.

The kicky appeal of the "Cop" series—at least potentially—has always been the idea of a street-smart black cop from Detroit who outmaneuvers the (mostly) white Beverly Hills honchos who underestimate him. It's a neat racial joke that provided a few chuckles in "Beverly Hills Cop" and virtually none in its hyperpowered Stallone-ish sequel.

Stallone, in fact, was originally supposed to star in "Beverly Hills Cop," and the series has never gotten very far from his over-muscled shadow. For most of the way in "Beverly Hills Cop III" we might as well be watching any old standard-issue action hunk dodging bullets and lobbing grenades (and, in a masterstroke, saving children in peril). But Murphy gives us less than those action hunks do; he's playing out his own fantasy image of a righteous avenger, and the fantasy is essentially humorless. There's little trace of his gift for con-man mimicry. It's as if he set out to trash his own franchise.

Once again Axel wearing his Detroit Lions jacket is brought back to Beverly Hills from Detroit to track down the killers of a close associate. And once again he gets propelled into shootouts and car chases with a clan of murderous nasties, headed by John Saxon and Timothy Carhart. Their base of operations is a theme park called WonderWorld, which—how'd you guess?—features a dinosaur ride. "Jurassic Cop," anyone?

The Beverly Hills police force retains series' regular Judge Reinhold, who now has his own office and his own SWAT team. Bronson Pinchot also turns up again as the oddly accented Serge.

He has graduated from an art gallery to a boutique selling personalized luxury weapons, which is a fair way of gauging how far the inspiration in the series has dropped.

At a time when police detective shows on television are better than they ever have been, what excuse is there for the slovenliness of "Beverly Hills Cop III"? Director John Landis and screenwriter Steven E. de Souza (who worked on "48 HRS." and the "Die Hard" films) are strictly smash-and-grab guys. Like the other films in the series, this one has no muscle tone, it wobbles opportunistically between wan slapstick and routine bang bang, with lots of gratuitous cheesecake for scenery.

It's not easy to make audiences laugh at a comedy where characters are actually shot on camera. And, in the post-Rodney G. King era, a racialty tinged film involving cops and violence in L.A. carries a lot of unwanted baggage.

Taken simply as pure action, the mayhem in this movie may be routine but, in the context of a knockabout comedy it's deeply offensive. The film begins with a bunch of workmen in a Detroit auto shop shimmying to a record by the Supremes. The scene is played for broad, dumb laughs: then, in a scene that's not played for laughs, they get bloodily ventilated.

But it's near the end, when the assorted good guys wobble and collapse into frame with their wounds, that the corruption of this enterprise sinks in.

There's a fundamental lack of human feeling in "Beverly Hills Cop III" that makes you want to avert your eyes from the people around you when the lights come up. Attending this movie makes you feel like an accomplice to the corruption.

NEW YORK, 6/6/94, p. 53, David Denby

In the dreadful *Beverly Hills Cop III*, there's one hilarious sequence. Bronson Pinchot returns in the tiny role of Serge, who has left the art gallery that he inhabited in the original *Beverly Hills Cop*. Serge has opened the Survival Boutique, a salon for people seeking luxury self-defense items, including, of course, the Annihilator 2000—a machine gun "for home and travel" that comes with a built-in compact-disc player. Ducking coyly behind his big nose, his long hair cloaking his neck and ears like chain mail, Pinchot compliments people on their looks and sells them on "colonics," a method of retrieving intestinal wastes. I don't know what is more satisfying—Pinchot's piquantly garbled English or the desperate sweetness of Serge, an attentive, bustling man who wants only to serve the rich.

As Pinchot talks, there is nothing Eddie Murphy can do but stand and watch a comic at work. Certainly Murphy himself no longer believes in comedy. The original idea of the Axel Foley character—that he was a street-smart guy from Detroit who could talk his way in and out of posh situations in Beverly Hills—has been completely lost. Now he's just a summer-season action hero, dodging bullets, crashing through sets, and taking part in wild car chases. (Gee, ever seen one of those before?) John Landis's direction offers all the variety of a pinball machine—bullets bounce off everything and lights flash on and off—and while watching the movie, I felt myself float away. Except for Pinchot, there are no characters, no human qualities in it. Is an audience really out there ready to believe that *Beverly Hills Cop III* is a movie?

NEW YORK POST, 5/25/94, p. 32, Michael Medved

"Beverly Hills Cop III" tries hard to provide the cinematic equivalent of a theme park thrill ride but succeeds only in producing motion sickness.

The story begins in Detroit with police detective Axel Foley (Eddie Murphy) supervising a routine bust of a stolen car chop shop. When the operation goes wrong and results in the death of his long-suffering superior officer (Gil Hill), Foley tracks the killers to (you guessed it!) Beverly Hills.

There he connects with his old pal, officer Billy Rosewood (a very tired-looking Judge Reinhold), and even makes a new friend, Detective Jon Flint (Hector Elizondo, who, in effect, replaces John Ashton from previous films).

Together, they follow clues to WonderWorld, an internationally celebrated theme park that ties a facade of innocence to mask a sinister conspiracy.

During his very first visit to the park, the Man from Motown instantly finds his friend's killer—thereby ending the movie's main mystery after just 15 minutes.

The rest of this bloated, tedious picture leaves time for our hero to rescue two frightened kids from a malfunctioning daredevil ride. That wretchedly edited sequence—with closeups of a worried-looking Murphy awkwardly interspersed with footage of leaping stuntmen—highlights the main problem with the movie.

Foley is no longer a street-wise, smart-mouthed underdog who uses wit and sass as his primary weapons; this time he's just another invincible action hero with superhuman powers.

This is the sort of muscle-bound muscle-headed role more suited to Sylvester Stallone than to the talented Murphy (ironically, the original "Beverly Hills Cop" was first written for Stallone).

Director John Landis previously worked with Murphy on two of his biggest hits ("Trading Places" and "Coming to America"), but the laughs that characterized these prior collaborations are missing in action here.

In fact, "BHC III" seems to have undergone a humor-ectomy. Landis concentrates nearly all his attention on lavish, overproduced reproductions of WonderWorld's tacky rides, and then delights in wantonly destroying them.

Watching a screen version of a theme park is only entertaining if the attractions are more dazzling than what you can get at a real-life fantasy land: But here, the papier-mache offerings are so clearly sub-par that they would surely have been smashed by hordes of angry kids long before Axel Foley ever got to them.

The diabolical plot that Foley ultimately uncovers makes no sense at all, since the stunningly pedestrian operation of the brain-dead criminal "masterminds" hardly needs the cover of a big theme park.

At the surprisingly bloody climax to this nonsense, Hector Elizondo asks our hero, "Any chance you can explain any of this to me?" Though Axel Foley never gets to speak the line, the answer is obviously no.

NEWSDAY, 5/25/94, Part II/p. B3, John Anderson

Eddie Murphy has been telling interviewers, in no uncertain terms, that "Beverly Hills Cop III" is not his comeback film. And he's right.

A strictly paint-by-numbers action/adventure yarn, with little sense of humor and even less sense of purpose, "Beverly Hills Cop III" effectively nullifies Murphy's main asset—comedy—in favor of making him another Sylvester Stallone. Which is not something we desperately needed.

At the same time, it defuses the whole dramatic premise behind the first two "Beverly Hills Cop" movies (the first of which was vastly superior to the others), which was Axel Foley as bureaucratic victim—a streetwise Detroit detective, a cop out of water, defying the uptight, rulebook-bound Beverly Hills police to fight the good fight. He was smarter than your average underdog. Now, he just seems rude.

When Axel gets to Beverly Hills this time around, he's chasing a gang of cop killers who eluded him in Detroit after an opening shootout that's a good example of both false advertising—the action's never this hot again—and director John Landis' debauched way with movie violence. Bullets and blood are sprayed with equal abandon, cars and humans are liberally riddled, and each slug ends its trajectory target with a fat, soft thud. Much like the jokes. The Secret Service doesn't want the gang caught; they're up to uncovering something much bigger, apparently, than the killing of Detroit cops. Axel is unmoved. "________ the federal government," he says, not caring who or what he demolishes en route to getting what he wants. He's like a cop with a multi-picture deal. The pursuit takes him to WonderWorld, a Disneyland knockoff inspired by the Walt-like Uncle Dave (Alan Young) and under the de facto control of Ellis DeWald (Timothy Carhart), the ruthless killer Foley is chasing. That this one deliciously perverse aspect of "BHC III" is not exploited for anything close to its subversive potential is symptomatic of the movie's failings. Disney-fascists vs. the state. It could have been great.

But "Beverly Hills Cop III" lumbers on its way to a predictable, and predictably violent, conclusion, with Axel's BH buddy Billy Rosewood (Judge Reinhold) consistently befuddled, Det. Flint (Hector Elizondo) trying to protect his post-retirement job at WonderWorld, Bronson Pinchot reprising the unpronounceable Serge, who's now in the personal security business, and some shamelessly cheesy action sequences. Theresa Randle, as the WonderWorld worker sympathetic to Axel's cause, is really the sole cast member worth watching.

Whether "BHC III" signifies anything in terms of Murphy's career is moot; the actor hasn't had anywhere to come back from, not if you're talking box office. Even when he's turned out incendiary devices such as "Harlem Nights" or "Boomerang" he's made money. Artistically, of course, it's another story. He hasn't really fulfilled his comedic potential since ... well, maybe the original "Beverly Hills Cop." But it clearly doesn't bother him. If Eddie Murphy felt he had anything to prove, he wouldn't have done Part III of a movie series that had already run out of gas, wouldn't have hooked up with as lame a director as Landis, and certainly would have read Stephen de Souza's script (you don't think he actually read this script ... ?)

SIGHT AND SOUND, 7/94, p. 38, Ben Thompson

When his boss is killed during a raid on a crooked auto yard Detroit cop Axel Foley is determined to find the culprits. He traces their stolen van to LA's WonderWorld theme park and returns to Beverly Hills, where he meets up with his newly promoted friend Billy Rosewood and Billy's colleague Jon Flint, who is nearing retirement. Snooping around at WonderWorld, Foley is shot at by security guards. Having saved two children from disaster on a malfunctioning ride, he is frog-marched into the presence of Ellis DeWald, the park's head of security. DeWald turns out to be the man who killed Foley's boss, but he is an upstanding citizen and no-one takes Foley's accusations seriously.

At his hotel, Foley is visited by WonderWorld's owner, Uncle Dave, who shows him a mysterious note the park's designer sent him just before he disappeared. At a dinner where DeWald is receiving an award, Foley gets into a fight with him and is ordered by Fulbright, who is leading a federal investigation into the auto yard gang, to leave town. But in the meantime, Rosewood's men have tracked down the stolen van and inside it Foley discovers the remains of currency paper. Back at WonderWorld, with the help of Uncle Dave's trusty employee Janice, he finds a secret room where DeWald and his cronies are printing counterfeit money. But by the time Fulbright responds to Foley's call, the presses have been changed to WonderWorld promotional material.

Foley realises that Uncle Dave's note was written on currency paper, but before they can take the evidence to police headquarters, DeWald traps them and shoots the old man. Foley escapes and drives the ailing Dave to hospital, but he is suspected of doing the shooting. Dewald holds Janice hostage to force Foley to return to WonderWorld. With the help of Rosewood, Flint and the Annihilator 2000—an extraordinary weapon picked up from his old friend Serge, who has forsaken the art world for personal survival consultancy—Foley saves Janice and foils the counterfeiters' plot. In a final shoot-out, Foley kills both DeWald and Fulbright, who, it transpires, was part of the conspiracy. Rosewood, Flint and Foley all sustain serious gunshot wounds, but recover enough to watch the revived Uncle Dave open a new ride—the Axel Fox.

If the drop in quality between *Beverly Hills Cop* and its sequel had been repeated in this third episode of the Axel Foley saga, we would have had a real stinker on our hands. As it is, director John Landis and star Eddie Murphy have succeeded in making a rousing old-fashioned swashbuckler which almost achieves classic action movie status. In the intervening years between episodes two and three, Eddie Murphy has all but lost and—thanks mainly to *Boomerang*—partially regained his star lustre. The early signs in this movie are not promising. There is a depressingly formulaic quality to the extreme violence of the opening sequence, and it is not until our hero is back in Beverly Hills, on fish-out-of-water territory, that matters pick up.

The theme park setting is not exactly an original idea, but WonderWorld itself is imaginatively used. It provides the backdrop to some highly effective action sequences—Foley's mid-air rescue of two children on a disintegrating hi-tech ferris wheel, for example—while also serving to highlight the ambivalent nature of Foley himself, as he flits in and out of sight in an environment of blatant but strangely innocent commercial exploitation. The movie's gung-ho celebration of excess firepower and law enforcement is mediated by a healthy measure of satire—as with the character of Serge, the art world stooge from *Beverly Hills Cop*, who now deals in outlandish designer weapons for "urban survivalists who want to survive with style". No longer simply the weapons he supplies—with microwave and fax attached—parody the consumer sadism that plays such a large part in the series' success.

If the movie does not exactly break genre conventions, it certainly has fun with them. Detective Flint's revelation that he is just a few weeks away from retirement should mark him out for certain death, yet he survives. And Landis has been relatively restrained with cameo appearances—with the exception of Al Green as a singing vicar, they are all directors (Joe Dante, Barbet Schroeder, John Singleton) whom even the most eagle-eyed buff would be hard put to recognise.

TIME, 6/6/94, p. 66, Richard Schickel

Eddie Murphy needs to shoot off his mouth. It's his best weapon, and the one that's unique to his arsenal. When a movie mostly requires him to shoot off a gun he becomes just another action star, and another talent wasted in lazily miscalculated material.

It has been almost a decade since Murphy appeared in a movie that correctly balanced cheekiness and car chases. As it happened, that was *Beverly Hills Cop*. Ever since, the comedian has been a loose cannon, rolling aimlessly around on ships variously listing and listless. *Beverly Hills Cop II*, Murphy's first reprise of Axel Foley, the street-smart Detroit plainclothesman set down in Rodeo Drive and environs, was frantic and noisy. *Beverly Hills Cop III* is possibly a little less frazzling, but it's also a movie that's just going through the motions, without comic conviction, surprises or suspense. *Hey, it's Eddie in his best part*, the studio must have been thinking. *No sweat, can't miss*.

But of course, it can. This time Axel is investigating a gang of counterfeiters operating out of an L.A. theme park meant to suggest Disneyland. The mystery is minimal, just an excuse to get everybody on the rides. Steven E. de Souza's script is not so much written as constructed—boom boom here, bang bang there. John Landis' direction consists mostly of just running the camera.

It's a measure of this dreadful movie's stupidity that it brings back Bronson Pinchot, the funny, madly accented art dealer of the first film, has him owning a security boutique, and then forces him to go on well past the point of the joke. *Beverly Hills Cop III* just might mark the point of no return in Eddie Murphy's career.

VILLAGE VOICE, 6/7/94, p. 60, Evette Porter

Hyped as Eddie Murphy's comeback, *Beverly Hills Cop III* isn't so much a Murphy movie as it is a testament to a certain kind of Hollywood filmmaking. But the packaged talent and proven story line Paramount is banking on are what *Cop III* suffers from most.

It's easy to forget the original, wiseass Axel Foley, especially when much of Murphy's work since, like *Boomerang* and *The Distinguished Gentleman*, has been about moving beyond the usual black comic shtick. Those movies' modest success must have made another blockbuster *Cop* sound good.

Like déjà vu, *Cop III* opens in Detroit with a shoot-out and high-speed chase after which Foley finds himself headed back to L.A. This time he's not the naive dick discovering the wonders of Lalaland, but a more cynical hero executing staccato comedy routines, a bit like *Coming To America*. Almost immediately, Foley finds his old buddy Billy Rosewood (Judge Reinhold), who's been promoted to some inane desk job. Rosewood and his sidekick Jon Flint (Hector Elizondo) reluctantly agree to help Foley, which takes them to a fantasy theme park called WonderWorld. In what's certainly the corniest line of the movie, Foley proclaims, "I'm going to WonderWorld!"

At the amusement park, Foley uncovers a counterfeiting ring and the killer who's behind it. With the help of a park employee (Theresa Randle) and the kindly old Walt Disney-like founder (Alan Young), Foley manages to break up the operation, but not before destroying most of WonderWorld itself. Besides the stock crash-and-burn sequences, there are cameos by George Lucas and John Singleton, and the return of Serge, the Bronson Pinchot character from the first *Cop*.

The formula has stayed the same, but Murphy isn't the Foley of 10 years ago. The only thing that remains is his patented Chiclet grin.

Also reviewed in:
NEW YORK TIMES, 5/25/94, p. C16, Caryn James
VARIETY, 5/30-6/5/94, p. 42, Richard Natale
WASHINGTON POST, 5/25/94, p. C12, Desson Howe
WASHINGTON POST, 5/29/94, Weekend/p. 42, Joe Brown

BEYOND IMAGINING

A Women Make Movies release. *Producer:* Wendy L. Weinberg; *Director:* Wendy L. Weinberg; *Screenplay:* Wendy L. Weinberg; *Editor:* Wendy L. Weinberg; *Director of Photography:* Wendy L. Weinberg; *Music:* Michael Aharon. *Running time:* 30 minutes. *MPAA Rating:* Not Rated.

WITH: Marcia Saunders (Voice of Margaret Anderson).

NEW YORK POST, 17/7/94, p. 37, Larry Worth

[*Beyond Imagining* was reviewed jointly with *Bernice Abbott: A View of the 20th Century*. See Worth's review of that film.]

Also reviewed in:
NEW YORK TIMES, 12/7/94, p. C15, Stephen Holden

BHAJI ON THE BEACH

A First Look Pictures release of an UMBI Films production in association with Channel Four. *Producer:* Nadine Marsh-Edwards. *Director:* Gurinder Chadha. *Screenplay:* Meera Syal. *Based on a story by:* Meera Syal and Gurinder Chadha. *Director of Photography:* John Kenway. *Editor:* Oral Norrie Ottley. *Music:* Craig Pruess and John Altman. *Sound:* Ronald Bailey. *Sound Editor:* Glen Freemantle. *Casting:* Suzanne Crawley. *Production Designer:* Derek Brown. *Art Director:* Helen Raynor. *Costumes:* Annie Symons. *Make-up:* Julie Van Praag. *Running time:* 100 minutes. *MPAA Rating:* Not Rated.

CAST: Kim Vithana (Ginder); Jimmi Harkishin (Ranjit); Sarita Khajuria (Hashida); Mo Sesay (Oliver); Lalita Ahmed (Asha); Shaheen Khan (Simi); Zohra Segal (Pushpa); Amer Chadha-Patel (Amrik); Nisha Nayar (Ladhu); Renu Kochar (Madhu); Surendra Kochar (Bina); Souad Faress (Rekha); Tanveer Ghani (Balbir); Akbar Kurtha (Manjit); Peter Cellier (Ambrose Waddington); Rudolph Walker (Leonard Baptiste); Fraser James (Joe); Dean Gatiss (Paul); Martin Greenwood (Ray); Shireen Shah (Hashida's Mother); Gurdial Sira (Hashida's Father); Adlyn Ross (Ranjit's Mother); Moti Makan (Ranjit's Father); Baddi Uzzaman (Uncle); Bharti Patel (Refuge Woman); Hugo Speer (Andy/White Youth); Judith David (Café Owner); Karen Montero (Balli); Ash Verez (Prem); Shad Ali (Raman); N.J. Willow (Leena); Neera Sharma (Madhu and Ladhu's Mother); David Tse (Chan); Phil Croft (Steve); Raymond Wallbank (Organ Player); Jonathan Cohen, Steve Burgland, and Mark Mayhem (Nightclub Dancers); Chila Burman (Prithi); Matt Young (Karaoke Man); Becky Marling (Waitress).

CHRISTIAN SCIENCE MONITOR, 3/28/94, p. 14, David Sterritt

"Bhaji on the Beach" takes its title from a snack food often served by Indian restaurants in England, where the movie takes place. The main characters are British-Asian women who go on a pleasure trip to a seaside town. This turns into great fun for some of the participants, but brings difficulty to others when they find that their domestic problems won't stay neatly behind until the excursion is over.

Although the story begins on an overfamiliar note, with fantasy sequences and household squabbles that have little new to say, "Bhaji on the Beach" picks up surprising momentum once its heroines board the bus to Blackpool, taking with them such troubles as an unwanted pregnancy and anxieties over an estranged husband. The climax and conclusion of the story are especially effective , with powerful acting and offbeat cinematic work.

Directed by Gurinder Chadha, a native Kenyan who has lived in Britain most of her life, the movie is due for a mid-April theatrical debut thanks to First Look Pictures.

CINEASTE, Vol. XX, No. 4, 1994, p. 48, Leonard Quart

Gurinder Chadha's first feature film, *Bhaji on the Beach*, is a work of social realism suffused in charm and a deft sense of comedy. Chadha speaks about owing an artistic debt to the English realist director Ken Loach (*Riff-Raff*), but she has made a more carefully shaped, winsome, crowd-pleasing film than anything he has ever done. *Bhaji* is also a feminist film which makes its political points more through seductive humor than through polemics.

Her narrative is built around a day trip that three generations of lower-middle- and middle-class Asian women (in England defined as women from India, Pakistan, and Bangladesh) take from Birmingham to the working-class, seaside resort of Blackpool. The film abounds in subplots, chance encounters, and angry confrontations, but its most striking aspect is its complex, ironic view of how Asian women live in England today. The cast of women characters includes three "aunties"—traditional, moralizing older women wearing saris; Ginder (Kim Vithana), who has fled with her five-year-old son from her handsome, abusive husband and his claustrophobic, controlling family; Hashida (Sarita Khajuria), one of the community's shining hopes with a place in medical school, but pregnant by her West Indian boy friend, Oliver (Mo Sesay), a relationship she's kept secret from her parents; two giggly teenage sisters carrying a boom box and obsessed with English boys; Rekha (Souad Faress), a chic, moneyed visitor from Bombay, who is dressed in fashionable Western clothes; and Simi (Shaheen Khan), the trip's organizer, a passionate feminist, wearing a leather jacket over a sari, who is deeply linked to the Asian community while being critical of many of its values.

There are too many characters for Chadha to do much more than sketch them with a few salient personality traits or problems, although none of them are reduced to a social type. Still, the film's prime interest does not lie in illuminating the women's internal states or psyches, but in providing a nuanced perspective on their feelings about ethnicity and gender. Simi is a tense, sharp-tongued, and politically committed community worker who can preach political jargon to the group of women about "the double yoke of racism and sexism," be aware of how absurd the words sound, and then tell them to go off for the day and have a "female fun time." Ginder is no feminist heroine—she is ready to go back to her spinelessly brutal husband if he is willing to leave his oppressive family. Asha (Lalita Ahmed), the most appealing and least rigid of the three older women, suffers from headaches and escapes from her life into soft-focused, garishly-colored fantasies which Chadha has constructed as sly parodies of traditional Bombay film melodramas. (In one of Asha's fantasies, for example, Hashida turns into a blond-wigged, miniskirted slattern wantonly dancing in a Hindu temple—a lampoon of a Bombay movie, *Purab Aur Pachim*, which carries a harsh commentary on growing up in the West.) Though college-educated, Asha is committed to duty and sacrifice, but we sense an undercurrent of dissatisfaction with a life consumed by serving her family and working in her husband's newsstand and video shop.

Chadha never sentimentalizes Asian immigrant culture. She clearly has no use for its racism. Hashida's dishonor is compounded by the fact that her boyfriend is black, and mixed race relationships are taboo in the Asian community. In a revelatory scene in a Blackpool working-class cafe, Chadha captures the racism and parochialism of both the English and Asians when the proprietress indulges in a racist harangue against Pushpa (Zhora Segal), the most narrow-minded of the older Asian women, for bringing their own food into the cafe. Pushpa simultaneously rages against Hashida, calling her a "whore," and laments that England "has cost us our children." In *Bhaji* neither the English nor the Asians have a premium on insularity and intolerance. Chadha is unwilling to facilely divide the world up into oppressors and victims. Though the Asian women have less power in the society than the English or Asian men, they still have the capacity to abuse and tyrannize each other.

What disturbs Chadha more than Asian racism is the authoritarian nature of marriage in the Asian community. The older women adhere to the notion that women must obey their husbands, to in effect become their property. The Asian men in the film—Ginder's husband Ranjit (Jimmi Harkishin) and his crude, macho older brother—operate in just that manner, viewing Ginder as a possession that must be returned to its proper place. What is primary is not a woman's needs or desires, but the preservation of traditional roles and power relations. If there is a glimmer of hope for Asian men, it comes from Ranjit's younger, more sensitive brother Manjit (Akbar Kurtha), who ultimately recoils and rebels against his brother's oppressive sexism.

Chadha's few, basically peripheral English characters are less sympathetically depicted than her Asian ones. Besides the racist cafe owner, there are a group of drunken louts whose rude, bigoted advances at a rest stop are answered in kind by the Asian women. There are also two silly, red-haired English boys who pursue the teenage sisters, and a florid actor in a straw boater, Ambrose (Peter Cellier), who attempts to court Asha. He's well-meaning and harmless, a melancholy relic from another time, who likes "exotic women" and whose saccharine idea of India was formed by *Gunga Din* and other Hollywood fabrications.

Ambrose is a regular on the streets of Blackpool, a resort whose tacky ambience Chadha's camera successfully captures. Her camera tracks along the streets, peering at souvenir shops, bed and breakfasts, penny arcades, bingo parlors, snake charmers, and ultimately enters a bar featuring male strippers. Chadha also both seamlessly cross-cuts between the various subplots, never losing the thread of narrative, and, in a buoyant manner, uses *bhangra* music on the soundtrack (dance hall music which is a hybrid of English and Indian pop songs).

Bhangra music's ability to fuse cultures (e.g., in *Bhaji on the Beach* Chadha takes Cliff Richard's "Summer Holiday" and rewrites the lyrics in Punjabi, and then has a *bhangra* band remix the music) is a perfect reinforcement of the film's commitment to the idea that Asians must create a new identity in England. It's not assimilation or, obviously, traditional immigrant culture that Chadha holds out as an answer, but a fluid, open, bilingual identity that represents for her the new England. For Chadha, "difference is celebratory," but not exclusive. She has little use for characters like Oliver's black friend who closes off identity by seeing the world in purely racial terms.

For a first-time feature director, Chadha's direction is generally smooth and self-assured. It's a directorial style that suits *Bhaji on the Beach*, a film that is lighter and more sanguine about life in England than works by other contemporary English directors like Hanif Kureishi, Derek Jarman, and Isaac Julian, whose much darker, less commercial films have centered on the lives of racial, ethnic, and sexual minorities. There are times, however, when the film seems given to soap-operatic narrative devices—Hashida's pregnancy and reconciliation with Oliver, and Ranjit's failed abduction of his child, with Asha coming to Ginder's defense.

It also can be too calculating. Pushpa can't be allowed to remain unsympathetic throughout the film. Consequently, she's humanized by having her laugh and be titillated when she dances with the male English strippers in a tedious strip club sequence. And the final scene brings the film to a predictable, though moving conclusion. The van carrying the women home passes through Blackpool's nighttime-illuminations, with the women (including Pushpa) forgetting all their value differences and expressing a strong sense of female solidarity.

The word *Bhaji* from the film's title means snack food, and, on the surface, *Bhaji* is just that. But the film's captivating, pleasurable tone succinctly and perceptively captures the entire gamut of values that Asian women choose in response to English and Asian immigrant society and culture. It's a subject that was touched on in Frears-Kureishi s *My Beautiful Laundrette*, but *Bhaji* takes it much further. The film conveys what it means to be an Asian woman in a society where the English often either patronize or insult you, and Asian men treat you as domestic possessions. Chadha has made an adroit film whose commercial contrivances don't detract from the striking image it projects of women who have begun to wrestle with the reality of a society built, in Simi's jargon, on "patriarchy" and "racism."

LOS ANGELES TIMES, 6/22/94, Calendar/p. 1, Kenneth Turan

"Bhaji on the Beach" is one of those small but remarkable pictures that smiles at the supposed difficulties of movie-making. Warm and charming while sacrificing neither its integrity nor its point of view, it covers considerable personal and political territory without overreaching or condescending. And it never forgets to have fun.

The debut film of director and co-story writer Gurinder Chadha, apparently the first Indian woman living in Britain to direct a film in that country, "Bhaji" is further evidence that Britain's supposedly moribund film industry is turning into cinema's most celebrated invalid. Though economic difficulties have seriously curtailed output, those British films that do get made are invariably models of strength and compassion.

The seriocomic story of a day trip to the seaside resort of Blackpool by several generations of women, "Bhaji" has points in common with other socially conscious British directors, particularly the pioneering Ken Loach, who Chadha views as a mentor, and Mike Leigh, whose ideas of extensive rehearsals to define character she has made her own use of.

Yet as indicated by the *bhaji* of the title, an only-in-England snack derived from a traditional Indian dish, this is very much its own film, flavored by the distinctive sensibility of the Indian community that it depicts.

For while "Bhaji's" key protagonists may sound just like the English they live among, they are separated from them not only by skin color but also by the difficulties of being a transitional generation, with one foot in the clannish, fearful society of their immigrant parents and the other in the modern Western world their futures will take place in.

"Bhaji" begins in Birmingham, an industrial city in the Midlands, and its almost too-rapid introduction of characters gives audiences a sense of the crowded, hectic conditions of the Indian community there, with married children still living with their parents, and the whole business overseen by a network of vaguely related, invariably censorious older women known collectively (as they were in the similarly themed "The Joy Luck Club") as aunties.

But by the time a bus holding a cross-section of women sets out for a day of "female fun" at Blackpool under the tutelage of feminist Simi (Shaheen Khan), two of the passengers, each with her own romantic crisis, have come into focus as the film's parallel protagonists.

Ginder (Kim Vithana) has precipitated a crisis in the close-knit community by leaving her husband, Ranjit (Jimmi Harkishin), and moving into a women's shelter with her young son. And Hashida (Sarita Khajuria), a college graduate about to enter medical school, knows she will cause even more of a sensation if word gets out that a) she is pregnant though unmarried and b) the father is a young black man of Caribbean descent named Oliver (Mo Sesay).

When the bus arrives at Blackpool, the city itself, with its gaudy, Coney Islandish air of down-at-the-heels frivolity, becomes a character in the film. A place like this by definition encourages a loosening of bonds, allowing everyone from teen-age sisters Ladhu and Madhu to decorous Auntie Asha (Lalita Ahmed) to engage in amusing flirtations. And with both Ranjit and Oliver headed toward Blackpool to try to resolve their difficulties, more serious events are likely as well.

It is this ability to move with grace and ease between comedy and drama that is "Bhaji's" particular accomplishment. For though Meera Syal's script deals with provocative issues from racism to the place of women and the often injurious power of custom and tradition, both she and director Chadha employ a fluid touch that allows points to be made with welcome subtlety.

Critical to this accomplishment is the fondness and empathy for its characters that marks the film's every scene. The chance to put situations close to their own experience onto the screen must have meant a great deal to everyone involved, and the sense of vivid life that results has made "Bhaji on the Beach" into a film that manages to be as pleasant as it is pointed.

NEW YORK, 7/18/94, p. 58, David Ansen

In the lively, bighearted *Bhaji on the Beach* a busload of Indian women sets off from Birmingham, England, on an "Asian ladies" outing to the Blackpool seaside. Hardly a homogeneous group, they range from the feminist tour guide, Simi, who invokes them to throw off "the yoke of racism and sexism" to the sari-clad elders, Pushpa and Asha, who cling to traditional ways, to two teenagers looking for romance. The beautiful Ginder is fleeing an abusive husband who tracks her down in Blackpool: Premed student Hashida, apple of her family's eyes, is a wreck: she's just discovered she's pregnant by her black boyfriend, and the gossips on the bus are about to find out. Director Gurinder Chadha and writer Meera Syal have a gift for drawing complex characters in quick, seriocomic strokes. By the end of this delightful outing, a fresh corner of contemporary England has been vibrantly revealed.

NEW YORK POST, 5/18/94, p. 31, Thelma Adams

The freshest movie to emerge from this spring's New Directors/New Films series at the Museum of Modern Art was "Bhaji on the Beach."

The British film, the first fiction outing by documentarian Gurinder Chadha, is that rare delight— a feminist comedy rooted in character and contradiction.

Chadha, working from Meera Syal's script, employs a deceptively simple plot. A group of Anglo-Asian women takes a bus trip to Blackpool, a tacky seaside resort akin to Coney Island.

"You've struggled under the double yoke of racism and sexism," trip organizer Simi (Shaheen Khan) tells the assembled women before the bus leaves Birmingham. When they respond with silence, Simi follows up with the more warmly received, "This is your day. Have a female fun time."

Chadha serves up more than a dozen characters with the self-assurance of a Robert Altman ("Nashville," "Short Cuts").

From traditional housewife Asha (Lalita Ahmed) and prune-faced auntie Pushpa (Zohra Segal) to pregnant pre-med Hashida (Sarita Khajuria) and single mom Ginder (Kim Vithana), Chadha creates rounded, realistic characters who are neither victims nor role models.

The women within the close-knit community struggle with traditional values of duty, honor and sacrifice in a changing world. Ginder offers a modern perspective, "You'll never please everyone—so you might as well please yourself," but even she can't accept her own advice.

Whether Chadha's painting the canvas of Anglo-Asian female culture or tromping through the Blackpuddlian streets, the director has a documentary filmmaker's eye for the telling detail. She doesn't stint on local color, getting comic relief from a married couple dressed in shark costumes and a dapper local thespian (Peter Cellier) who notes "careful you don't get harpooned."

The movie is at its most contrived when Ginder's handsome husband Ranjit (Jimmi Harkishin) and Hashida's black boyfriend, Oliver (Mo Sesay), come chasing after their women to complicate the plot.

In both subplots, the climaxes are overblown. The weakest scene is an awkwardly staged, rain-soaked fistfight under the boardwalk where all the carefully planted contradictions seem to wash away, leaving in their wake the suds of soap opera.

The true climax comes earlier, when Hashida encounters Pushpa in a tea shop. Pushpa slams Hashida for being a whore, wailing "this country has cost us our children." At the same, the white proprietor curses Pushpa for bringing Indian food into the shop. Hashida turns the tables on them both.

In the tea shop, Chadha exposes the gap between generations and races, while demonstrating the universality of prejudice. The director isn't interested in entering the victim sweepstakes.

My favorite moments in this comedy shot through with dark threads come when the director sets aside the social realist vein and enters Asha's fantasy world. Chadha lampoons the Hollywood (Hollywood by way of Bombay) extravaganzas she grew up watching.

I couldn't resist the tightly wrapped, middle-aged Asha's romantic fantasy. As coy and cunning as any dewy Bombay starlet in a white saree, Asha runs through a celluloid Eden. Her pursuer? The aging Blackpool thespian, his brown hair dye running in the gentle spring rain.

NEWSDAY, 5/18/94, Part II/p. B7, John Anderson

A day at the beach is no day at the beach, not for the women of the Saheli Asian women's center. In trying to find a little peace, they find themselves instead, figuratively and literally, with their backs to the sea.

In "Bhaji on the Beach," Gurinder Chadha's frank, multi-character, multi-crisis film, assimilation is a black hole, and the promised land, so to speak, is Blackpool, the slightly seedy seaside resort of Britain's working class. Here, amid a day trip of touring, shopping, psychodramatics and wading in the surf, a group of women with very little in common except their subcontinental heritage will find out that India, the idea of India, is also the great divisive force in their lives.

Taking cues from fellow Brits and blue-collar celebrants Mike Leigh and Ken Loach—and, in a converse fashion, from the India-centric cinema of "Hollywood"—Chadha doles out her masala of modern concerns among a variety of women, from the elderly, racist and tradition-bound

Pushpa (Zohra Segal), to the abused young mother Ginder (Kim Vithana) to the distraught, doctor-and single-mother-to-be Hashida (Sarita Khajuria) to the boy-struck sisters Lahdu and Mahdu (Nisha Nayar and Renu Kochar).

Somewhere in their spiritual midst is Asha (Lalita Ahmed), a middle-aged, sari-wearing merchant who runs a newsstand back in Birmingham ("They Curried My Budgie!!" screams one headline) and who is visited by stormy electric visions of the backlit Lord Rama, profane women and fantastic symbols of cultural confusion. She's torn between self-actualization and preserving the ideas of "home." "How long has it been since you've *been* home?!" asks the fashionable, liberated Rekha (Souad Faress), fresh from Bombay. "Your idea of home is 20 years old!" Asha's epiphanies will be the most profound on a day when female consciousness is busting out all over.

Men, of course, are the quandary, but Chadha is reasonably democratic. She knows that Ginder's husband Ranjit (Jimmi Harkishin), who comes looking to drag her and their son back to his parents' home, are products of a culture that's preserved as much by women like Pushpa as it is by men. But like Simi (Shaheen Khan), the women's leader and bus driver, she also sees through the male smokescreen: Ranjit only seems civilized because you can't see Ginder's injuries.

His brothers are less ambiguous: Balbir (Tanveer Ghani) is a bully who flirts with blondes while threatening the white boys who approach Ladhu and Madhu; the younger Manjit (Akbar Kurtha) really wants to leave Ginder in peace. And Hashida's lover, Oliver (Mo Sesay, of Isaac Julien's "Young Soul Rebels"), struggles with the ramifications not only of her unplanned pregnancy, but that he's black and she's of a family that says things like "You can't trust the dark ones." And without a bit of irony.

Oliver and Hashida will reconcile. Chadha, and perhaps you, will prefer they didn't, because the trap seems set. Ginder will redefine herself, Asha, and even Pushpa, will redefine "duty" and almost everyone will see the light, and the fact that England, and the concept of assimilation, contain many mirages.

SIGHT AND SOUND, 2/94, p. 47, Farrah Anwar

Birmingham. The Saheli Women's Centre, run by Simi, organises a trip to Blackpool. Among the day-trippers are Ginder, a young mother who has taken sanctuary in Simi's shelter after being physically abused by her husband Ranjit; her six-year-old son Amrik; Hashida, a student about to start medical school, who has discovered she is pregnant; Asha, a middle-aged newsagent with a university degree, who feels neglected by her husband and children and frustrated by unfulfilled personal aspirations; Ladhu and Madhu, a pair of sexually inexperienced teenagers; Pushpa, an elderly Indian housewife and grocer; Rekha, a glamorous visitor from Bombay who has time to spare during her husband's business trips to London; and Bina, a shop assistant in Marks and Spencer.

Urged on by his parents, Ranjit sets off in pursuit of the Saheli minibus. He is accompanied by his two brothers, the aggressively macho Balbir (who procures Ginder's whereabouts by physically intimidating the other young wives at the Centre), and the more compassionate Manjit. Also chasing the minibus is Oliver, a West Indian art student, who has had a secret sexual relationship with Hashida. Having originally rejected Hashida's pregnant plight, he has been urged on by his father and personal remorse to try and help her through the crisis. Meanwhile Asha continues to be troubled by visions, often of a religious nature, during which she loses track of time and place. After a racist verbal attack at a motorway service station, the women arrive safely in Blackpool. However, when Hashida's pregnancy becomes an open secret, she abruptly separates from the group. Unable to contact Oliver, she visits an abortion advice centre.

Ginder begins to relax, but her anxieties are reawakened when Amrik goes missing. Although she finds him relatively easily, unknown to her, Ranjit has caught up with them and is planning to confront her later in the day. During one of her trances, Asha walks into the sea and is rescued by a charming Blackpool thespian, Ambrose Waddington, who takes Asha on a tour of the town, culminating in a visit to a vacant theatre. Ladhu and Madhu have a fling with a couple of burger-sellers, and the whole group (minus Hashida, who is reunited with Oliver) rendezvous at a nightclub where they find themselves part of the audience participation act of three male strippers. When one of them accidentally undresses Ginder and reveals her bruises, the women leave hastily, only to be confronted by Ranjit and his brothers. Failing to dissuade Ginder verbally, he is reduced to using physical force to abduct Amrik. When Manjit refuses to open the door of the get-away car, Ranjit is forced away by the women and Asha chastises him for his behaviour. When Balbir tries to intervene, Manjit floors him with a punch. Driving out of a nocturnally illuminated Blackpool, the women comfort Ginder and Amrik.

In 1992, Gurinder Chadha directed a film about a group of elderly Asians who shoot and edit their own home-movie/documentary, *Acting Our Age*. Structured as a series of interviews with English (white) authority figures, it wittily juxtaposed various MPs, policemen and community liaison officers with the gaping holes in their explanations (or denials) pertaining to racism. The programme was rounded off by some genuinely moving accounts of personal hardship and strife by those making the film.

The finished product (shown on BBC2) was not only redolent of great respect for the elderly immigrant (*buzurgh*) experience, but offered some trenchant observations about prevalent prejudices and what the younger, British-born generation of Asians had to offer. In *Bhaji on the Beach*, her feature film debut, Chadha has tried to adhere to this code of *buzurgh* loyalty (the age span of the participants ranges from six to late 60s), while trying to encompass the more awkward and raw elements thrown up by contemporary Asian women's lives: arranged marriages, miscegenation, intra-community racism, patriarchal sexism within a matriarchal society and the restrictions on feminine sexuality within these dual values.

As Simi bluntly announces at one point, "it's not often that we women get away from the patriarchal demands made on us in our daily lives, struggling between the double yoke of racism and sexism." However, this yoke proves too much for the film to carry. In an ensemble piece like this, with a cast which is eventually destined for the road, either the journey or the protagonists have to take centre stage. The problem is that having taken the time to introduce the characters, *Bhaji* then makes the pay-off of the film more dependent on issues rather than the people. Each person in the cast carries her own emotional baggage—an unwanted pregnancy, menopausal angst, physical abuse—but then has to deal with it through a cultural barrier: parental disapproval of a career outside medicine (Hashida), familial frowning on love-marriage brides (Ginder), and the casual dismissal of female academic achievements within Asian society (Asha). Significantly, the women unfettered by any worries (Rekha and Bina) are rendered narratively redundant the moment they board the bus.

The men in *Bhaji* fare no better. As scripted by Meera Syal, they have only two polarities to occupy: weak-kneed ineffectuality (Manjit, the older husbands) or macho aggression (Ranjit, Balbir), with the Afro-Caribbean Oliver (literally) left holding the baby between the two. Syal clearly has an axe to grind about Asian men—ideally against their testicles. But to balance such an exercise in castration, the film needed a more convincing foil than Jimmi Harkishin's Method-suffering husband and father and less cypherish support from the disparately aged Saheli women.

Whereas on paper the premise of such a wide-ranging age group must have been appealing, in practice their presence dilutes some of the frissons between the 'sisters' because they are of the more familiar generational-gap variety. It also leads, paradoxically, to a less collectively cohesive response to male aggression. The fact that Ranjit will eventually catch up with Ginder is never in doubt, so it is the resolution to their estrangement which is set up as *Bhaji*'s climax. And here, the older women, although unequivocally against the violence, are less convincing in their acceptance of the choices open to Ginder. It's difficult to believe that Pushpa or Asha have turned their backs on such rigidly established institutions like Asian marriages or the role of women within it. The former's shrug of "What can you do?" is much harder to believe in.

Not surprisingly, the freshest and most successful characters in *Bhaji* are those who are allowed to be themselves: Ladhu and Madhu, two teenagers looking to Blackpool to fulfil frustrated desires for (limited) sex and romance, and Balbir, ferociously combining the worst excesses of Indian patriarchy with British boot-boy thuggery (Tanveer Ghani, easily the best of the male cast, creates British cinema's first authentic vindaloo and lager lout).

When not hampered by the script's more heavy-handed moments, Gurinder Chadha's direction is reassuringly light and evocative. Among the film's highlights are a Punjabi rendition of 'Summer Holiday' and a magical take on Blackpool lighting up in the dark. The director's political commitment is clearly important, because at least the Asian community can recognise itself in her work, by comparison with the recent TV adaptation of Hanif Kureishi's *The Buddha of Suburbia*. Unfortunately, in trying to explore all of these commitments in one work, *Bhaji* topples over well before the end.

VILLAGE VOICE, 5/24/94, Film Special/p. 26, Georgia Brown

Once I saw *Do the Right Thing* in Paris and it looked different from when I'd seen it in the States. Any difficulties I had with Mookie and Radio Raheem dropped away, and all I saw was Brooklyn, American talent, beautiful color, and home. I imagined all the Frenchies around me envying our glorious melting pot.

This is the way I feel about Gurinder Chadha's teeming *Bhaji on the Beach*. Seeing it from abroad I can only be deeply touched by England, by all these first- and second-generation Birmingham Asians (which is what Brits call Indians, Pakistanis, and Bangladeshis) taking a day trip to Blackpool. They're so bloody English! Even the aunties in their saris and with their crimson third eyes and carrying—along with chili powder for the chips—their closed minds and horrid prejudices. What a vital, spicy crew!

But Chadha—Britain's first female Asian director—has some thing more local and political in mind, and I can appreciate that too. She's said she took writer Meera Syal's idea for a women's trip to the seaside and threw in "the two most taboo subjects within the Asian community": divorce and miscegenation. She didn't want "just a comedy." Instead, *Bhaji* (the word is short for the Indian dish *bhujia*) is the best kind of soap opera; it's neither gentrified nor excessively formulaic. Not surprisingly, Chadha says her favorite filmmaker is Ken Loach.

The Blackpool escapade is organized by the resourceful Simi (Shaheen Khan), a hip social worker at the Saheli Women's Centre, Simi wears a sari and a black leather jacket and makes a loaded speech to the ladies at the outset to the effect that "it's not often we women get away from the demands of patriarchy ... struggling as we do between the double yoke of racism and sexism." She ends the speech, "Have a female fun time!" The latter is greeted with more comprehension than the former, at least by the sari-wrapped elders like the prudish Pushpa (Zohra Segal) or dreamy Asha (Lalita Ahmed).

But at least two of the travelers have a clear idea of what Simi means by patriarchy and sexism. One is Hashida (Sarita Khajuria), who, just before starting med school, has discovered she's pregnant by her West Indian boyfriend, Oliver (Mo Sesay from *Young Soul Rebels*); the whole relationship has been kept secret from her tradition-minded parents. Then there's the pretty Ginder (Kim Vithana) and her six-year-old son, who've been staying at the center since Ginder left husband Ranjit (Jimmi Harkishin), a wife beater with qualms. Mindful of the shame—of divorce, not wife beating—Ranjit's family urges him to bring her, or at least the child, back by any means possible. Thus Ranjit, his thuggish brother Balbir (Tanveer Ghani), and milder brother Manjit, start out for Blackpool in their Mercedes. Separately but with kinder motives, Hashida's Oliver sets off on his motorcycle. This view of men as the uninvited trying to crash the tea party is not the whole of the film's attitude.

These several characters are just the tip of Chadha's ensemble iceberg. On the bus, there are also two giggly teenage sisters, Ladhu and Madhu; another older working woman, Bina; and Rekha, a well-heeled visitor from Bombay and the only one of the over-40 set to be dressed completely in Western clothes. (When Pushpa and Bina first spot her fuchsia miniskirt and spike heels, they roll their eyes.) At one point, fed up with these women's smug allusions to India as the authoritative and retrograde homeland, Rekha blurts out, "Home! How long since you've been home? Look at your clothes!" It's Rekha who, on first spying the carnival lights of Blackpool's main drag, exclaims with awe, "*Bombay!*"

Except for a couple of rude encounters with some white boy bigots, the outgoing trip is taken up with defining Hashida's anxiety over her pregnancy and Ginder's over her separation. Both situations generate rigid responses from their elders, making the younger women all the more miserable. There's a kind of ageism operating here in that the older women are almost entirely obstructionist while the younger ones are presented from the inside, as if their problems take moral precedence. Even Asha—potentially the movie's most interesting character—doesn't really get a full hearing.

For outsiders, the most compelling conflicts may revolve around family issues. Ginder has left the babied and baby-faced Ranjit because he won't stand up to his parents who think a wife's place is pampering her husband and bossing her sons. (Or is it the other way round?) They also think wives should be bought and sold, not chosen out of some Western notion of "love." Higher education, or meaningful work, is out of the question. Even Hashida, who looks wholly emancipated, is following her parents' dictum that the only respectable profession for a woman is medicine; she really wants to study art. In Blackpool, Oliver finds her because he spots a poster for a Mervyn Peake exhibit at the local museum.

By these standards, even Asha has a shady past: a university degree. Now she works in her husband's newsstand and video store—a mindless routine that leaves her hibernating in private fantasies based on India's pop cinema. During the Blackpool idyll, Asha comes to the attention of a local lothario in ascot and straw boater, Ambrose Waddington (Peter Cellier). A former thespian, Ambrose has a weakness for "exotic" women, though what his ultimate designs are unfortunately isn't clarified. (A little bondage and weewee perhaps?)

The charm of Bhaji—an attention-getter in New Directors and on the international festival circuit—is that it packs in so much and does it so rudely. It hardly matters that some small portions are unintelligible to those for whom Punjabi isn't a second language. (The highlight of the film's bouncy *bhangra* score is Chadha's recasting Cliff Richard's "Summer Holiday" into Punjabi.) There's no question, however, that *Bhaji*'s language will be picked up immediately by women everywhere. This bus ride is more than a female fun time but it's that too.

Also reviewed in:
NEW YORK TIMES, 8/18/94, p. C20, Janet Maslin
VARIETY, 10/11/93, p. 73, Deborah Young
WASHINGTON POST, 7/8/94, Weekend/p. 38, Desson Howe
WASHINGTON POST, 7/9/94, p. C3, Hal Hinson

BITTER MOON

A Fine Line Features release of an R.P. Productions/Timothy Burrill Productions film with the participation of Les Films Alain Sarde/Canal+. *Executive Producer:* Robert Benmussa, Alain Sarde, and Timothy Burrill. *Producer:* Roman Polanski. *Director:* Roman Polanski. *Screenplay:* Roman Polanski, Gérard Brach, and John Brownjohn. *Based on the book "Lunes de fiel" by:* Pascal Bruckner. *Director of Photography:* Tonino Delli Colli. *Editor:* Hervé de Luze. *Music:* Vangelis. *Choreographer:* Redha. *Sound:* Daniel Brisseau. *Casting:* Bonnie Timmerman, Mary Selway, and Françoise Menidrey. *Production Designer:* Willy Holt. *Set Dresser:* Philippe Turlure. *Special Effects:* Jean-Louis Trinquier. *Costumes:* Jackie Budin. *Make-up:* Didier Lavergne. *Stunt Coordinator:* Jean-Louis Ainola. *Running time:* 135 minutes. *MPAA Rating:* R.

CAST: Hugh Grant (Nigel); Kristin Scott Thomas (Fiona); Emmanuelle Seigner (Mimi); Peter Coyote (Oscar); Victor Bannerjee (Mr. Singh); Sophie Patel (Amrita); Stockard Channing (Beverly); Patrick Albenque (Steward); Smilja Mihailovitch and Leo Eckmann (Bridge Players); Luca Vellani (Dado); Richard Dieux (Partygoer); Danny Garcy (Bandleader); Daniel Dhubert (Bus Inspector); Nathalie Galan (Girl in Boutique); Eric Gonzales (Cook); Jim-Adhi Limas (Thai MD); Boris Bergman (Oscar's Friend); Olivia Brunaux (Cindy); Heavon Grant (Basil); Charlene (Hooker); Geoffrey Carey (Neighbour with Dog); Robert Benmussa (Flight Dispatcher); Claire Lopez (Model); Shannon Finnegan (Housewife); Frédérique Lopez (Brunette); Yse Marguerite Tran (Eurasian Girl); Claude Bonnet (Mayor).

LOS ANGELES TIMES, 3/18/94, Calendar/p. 1, Peter Rainer

This much can be said for Roman Polanski's carnal hoot-fest "Bitter Moon"—it keeps you wondering from scene to scene if the director has gone bonkers. No doubt a lot of the lunacy is intentional, but it's still lunacy.

And not terribly enjoyable lunacy either. The film plays like a dirty joke that somehow got lost in the translation. Polanski, with his screenwriters Gerard Brach and John Brownjohn, must have figured that an obsessive sadomasochistic love triangle (or is it a love parallelogram?) would work better if the whole thing was tarted up and fatuous—equal parts put-down and put-on. They try for a rollicking, aghast tone to mimic the mood-swings of sexual compulsion. And, to be sure, "Bitter Moon" holds your attention. How could it not when we're allowed into a world where our hero-heel, Peter Coyote's Oscar, indulges in sex crimes disguised as a giant oinker?

The film begins with a suggestively slow zoom in and out of a luxury cruise ship's portal—a sly hint of subtleties to come. Nigel (Hugh Grant) and Fiona (Kristin Scott-Thomas) are a tight-lipped British couple Bombay-bound for their second honeymoon when they encounter Mimi (Emmanuelle Seigner), a seriously smashed *jeune fille* throwing up in the ladies' room. (It's meet-cute time in Polanski World.) Nigel, a (yawn) Eurobond trader, is drawn to this messy-mouthed bundle of curves in spite of himself. That evening he wanders over to the bar and spots Mimi's little impromptu hoochie-coochie rumba numba and gets turned on by being brushed off. (He says "blimey" a lot, just in case we failed to recognize what a repressed twit he is.) She leaves the porthole of opportunity slight ajar though. This woman could smell a masochist five fathoms deep.

Oscar, her husband, can too. Wolfish and wheelchair-bound, he encourages Nigel's itch. He dragoons the chap into a series of monologues about his marriage that have a heady, "Arabian Nights" effect on the poor man. Nigel keeps harrumphing and then coming back for more. Oscar, crazed and cackling about what a sick joke his life has become, regales Nigel with tales of how he fell desperately in love with Mimi and how that love eventually became sour and twisted.

The flashbacks, mostly set in a distinctly untouristy, twilit Paris, come complete with Oscar's florid voice-over narration. Example: He describes his first communion with Mimi by saying, "I might have been Adam with the taste of apple fresh in my mouth." Oscar is supposed to be a failed American expatriate novelist—a Henry Miller with the glands but not the talent.

Mimi, a shy dancer who responds swoonily to Oscar's oo-la-la entrancements, first shows her mettle when she accidentally nicks him shaving. The blood tastes warm. Later she sort of accidentally spills a carton of milk on her breasts whereupon Oscar develops a powerful thirst. Even when she evolves into a dominatrix and uses Oscar for a privy or roots him out in his pig-man mode she's still his adoring co-conspirator. But Oscar becomes bored suiting up for decadence and his passion turns sadistic. He troops other women around his cramped, book-lined pad and turns Mimi into a frumpy clown. She's pathetic until you realize—perhaps before Mimi does-that she's biding her time for some pay-back.

"Bitter Moon" can be taken as a cockeyed allegory for what happens when love runs dry but lust doesn't (or maybe it's the other way around). It's a movie about the jollies of sexual degradation made by a martinet. Polanski, who is married to Seigner, is probably working out some sort of married-man crisis in this film. That's one of the advantages of being a movie director—you get to really work out your crises with the camera.

But what's disappointing about the shocks are how conventional they are. Polanski the expressionist libertine heads straight for the most bourgeois transgressions: Mimi's crowning insult to Oscar is to (gasp) get it on with a *black* man. Her final insult to Nigel is a naughty whopper that plays like a racier kicker to a "Love Boat" episode. The point of all thc parading seems to be to reconcile Nigel and his wife in a there-but-for-the-grace-of-God rapprochement. Polanski ascends to the pulpit.

He is at least a more interesting scourge than, say, the Louis Malle who made "Damage." The sexual obsession in that film was as heavy as a 10-ton shroud. By comparison, the Zalman King huff-a-thons, like "9½ Weeks" and "Wild Orchid," are trashier and campier and more fun—maybe because the women in them lose their marbles about as often as the men. But Polanski, like Malle, seems fixated on showing us how sex can turn men into dumbos—or porkies. It's a deranged kind of alternate-universe feminism: It's OK for women to drive men nuts because men are pigs. Life is a wallow.

Could "Bitter Moon" be the movie that brings the Bobbitts back together again?

NEW STATESMAN & SOCIETY, 10/2/92, p. 36, Anne Billson

This has not been a good year for relationships. The newspapers have been full of the celebrity schisms of Chas and Di, Andy and Fergie, Woody and Mia. And most of us know of at least two or three other, non-celebrity couples who have auto-combusted after years of close-knit comfort.

I blame it on Hollywood—not on those immoral lifestyles they supposedly lead, but on the diet of romantic movies on which most of us have been weaned. Without realising it, we have assimilated an unrealistic and totally impractical blueprint for life, which involves two people getting married and living happily ever after.

It's an idealised formula that might once have been a convenient way of keeping the plebs parcelled up into smooth-running units, but it's hopelessly out of synch with the way people live now. It would be so much easier, as Gore Vidal suggested in NSS a few weeks ago, if people stuck to partners of the same gender. Or if they were at least to set out with an awareness that the twin peaks of sex and romance are not in themselves enough to sustain a lifetime of mutual devotion.

Anyway, I have always found films that scupper the notion of true romance far more affecting than the starry-eyed variety. *Vertigo*, for example, is one of the great romantic films of all time, because it deals in delusion—the very stuff from which romance is fabricated.

So I reckon Roman Polanski's *Bitter Moon* is the ideal movie for dating couples. Take your partner! See what he or she thinks! Bicker about it afterwards! And there will be plenty to bicker about.

Bitter Moon, like the same director's *Knife in the Water*, is set at sea but in 30 years Polanski has replaced the crisp economy of his debut with a sort of cynicism so baroque that it's no longer possible to tell where his funnybone stops and starts.

Hugh Grant and Kristin Scott-Thomas play characters who are celebrating their seventh wedding anniversary—a traditionally itchy point in any long-running relationship. These two behave like a couple from some frightfully British E M Forster adaptation who have strayed into an overripe continental sex farce starring Peter Coyote as a ranting paraplegic, and Emmanuelle Seigner (aka Mrs Polanski) as his blowsy wife.

Like *The Comfort of Strangers*, this is the tale of innocence lured down the dark alleyway of corruption, but—oddly, and against the grain of the story—it also seems to be Polanski's most optimistic film in years, in that innocence goes hand in hand with delusion, and corruption may be able to teach us a thing or two.

Grant, looking like Prince Andrew and playing up his "I say, steady on" Englishness for all it's worth, is intrigued by Seigner, and duly has his ears bent by the wheelchair-bound Coyote, a failed American writer in Paris who unleashes a torrent of intimate but embarrassingly clichéd reminiscence about his marriage. "Nothing ever surpassed the rapture of that first awakening," he blathers.

In a series of flashbacks, we follow the course of their true lurve from initial infatuation and the winning-of-the-fluffy-toy-at-the-funfair, via erotic shimmying and milk-dribbling, dressing up in PVC macs and Pig masks, to cruelty, degradation and despair—an entire relationship stripped down to its extremes.

Discerning film-goers will think cool Scott-Thomas is a hundred times sexier than Seigner. The point is, though, that Seigner is *precisely* the sort of pouting sexpuss that movie directors and third-rate writers would like to have as their willing sex slave.

Bitter Moon is male fantasy, but not entirely bogus in its claim that women collude in the fashioning of their own bonds. If you ever doubted it, here's Mrs Polanski herself acting it out before our very eyes.

This may well be the most controversial movie of the year, though not for its sado-masochistic sex, nor even for its cynicism. *Bitter Moon* is controversial because no one can agree as to whether or not it was *intended* as a comedy. The nervous tittering at the preview I attended indicated the audience had decided that the laughs were unintentional.

But the words "Polanski and "humour" have never sat cosily together, particularly when taking what we know of his private life into account. I have yet to meet anyone who finds the so-called comedy *Dance of the Vampire* hilarious, though parts of it have given me the heebie-jeebies more effectively than anything in, say, *Repulsion*.

Conversely, there are moments in *Rosemary's Baby* that are far more rib-tickling than *Pirates*, which is not the rollicking laff-riot its director fancied it to be, but a deeply disturbing meditation on fate and big toe abuse.

We are talking here about a director whose unfunny films are often funnier than his funny ones. Try deciding to which of these categories *Bitter Moon* belongs, and you've got problems. But why should it matter? We're so used to films laying it on the line in black and white that it's refreshing to be confronted by a few grey areas, even if the ambiguities are as much in the tone as in the material. So bicker on.

NEW YORK, 3/28/94, p. 96, John Powers

"It's such a fine line between stupid and clever," says one of the dim rockers in *This is Spinal Tap*. He could well have been referring to Roman Polanski's latest swan dive into the murky depths of eroticism. Queasy and absurd, *Bitter Moon* is the most mesmerizing movie I've seen this year. It's also a mishmash—a romantic potboiler so sublimely misconceived that it becomes a small triumph of camp.

Nigel and Fiona are a prim English couple taking a boat to India, looking for "inner serenity, that kind of stuff." This banal fantasy is shattered when they get involved with a moody French sexpot, Mimi (Emmanuelle Seigner), and her wheelchair-bound husband, Oscar (Peter Coyote), a failed American novelist who spent years chasing the shadows of Hemingway and Miller in Paris. Oscar insists on telling Nigel the story of their relationship before he was crippled, dangling the lure of an amorous night with Mimi in return. Nigel's more than willing to hear all about it. And so, savoring his words, Oscar recounts his affair with Mimi from their first meeting on a bus through various sexual crescendos (latex, urine) to the moment when their love curdles and he starts trying to dump her. Listening raptly, the dull, decent Nigel sips his whiskey, tut-tuts prudishly at the dirty parts, and periodically rushes off to see the neglected Fiona—before scurrying back for the next installment.

"Every relationship," Oscar tells him, "contains the seeds of farce or tragedy." *Bitter Moon* contains bushels of knock-about farce (Oscar nearly throttling his poodle in ecstasy as he's being fellated by a hooker), most of its comedy rising from the head-on collision of stereotypes. As played by Hugh Grant and Kristin Scott-Thomas, Nigel and Fiona are standard-issue movie Brits—proper and repressed but innately kinky—who must learn about life's dark side from decadent Continentals. Mimi is a pure male fantasy of the Parisienne, a vulva with legs and a two-figure IQ; she squeezes herself into dresses so tight you could take her blood pressure, and gulps milk from the bottle until it runs down her face and onto her breasts. It's licked up by Oscar, who, riding the crest of Peter Coyote's hammy performance, becomes a parody of the middle-aged swinger who thinks himself an artist—he slinks through Paris like the world's lankiest weasel.

Oscar dominates the movie with his malignant chortle, rotting brown teeth, and endless supply of overheated metaphors. It's hard not to howl when he compares Mimi's vagina to "a carnivorous flower, a baby's mouth greedily sucking my fingers," but eventually this laughter starts feeling strained and facetious. Polanski may be having a ball sending up these stick figures, but to what good purpose? He's blasting away at stereotypes that have already crumbled from old age.

Kenneth Tynan once noted that Polanski's great subject is *imposition,* the shifting psychological landscape as one person attempts to force his vision of the world on another. *Bitter Moon* suddenly starts cutting to the bone when Oscar and Mimi's love goes sour, and Polanski captures the awful arc of the innumerable love affairs that begin in shared ecstasy and wind up in ritualized games of domination. At first, Oscar is in control, cheating on Mimi, mocking her appearance in public, and despising her all the more for accepting such humiliations. Once he's crippled, though, Mimi becomes the pitiless alter ego of the goo-goo-eyed sex toy she had earlier been, dancing erotically with another guy in front of the unmanned Oscar.

Polanski obviously gets off on the comedy of this mutual torture—it's not for nothing that he played the hood who slices Jack Nicholson's nose in *Chinatown*. But he marinates these scenes in such a palpably dank sense of sin and disgust that you can tell this material makes his bowels clutch. Vicious and unsettling, the lovers' tit-for-tat cruelty has a nasty authenticity, and I kept wondering why Polanski would cast Seigner, his real-life wife, in such an unsavory role (he did the same in *Frantic*). He brings total conviction to such absurd moments as Oscar crawling around in a G-string and a pig mask while Mimi chases him with a riding crop. Polanski's never been one to feel superior to other people's perversity.

But he is one to feel superior to other people's decency. Just as the prospect of having Mimi keeps Nigel listening to Oscar's tale, so this movie draws us in with its promise of ever more titillation. Polanski takes pleasure in rubbing the dirt in our faces, as if it were his calling to teach the world that life is unclean. In *Knife in Water, Cul-de-Sac*, and *Chinatown*, he had enough sly, sharp, sinister wit to keep from being oppressive—those movies drew blood like a stiletto. Nothing is at risk in *Bitter Moon*, a dull-edged broadsword whose most uproarious bits probably weren't supposed to be funny and whose fiercest emotions melt away long before the bloody climax on New Year's Eve. By the end you may find that your laughter has been replaced by regret. Consciously or not (and he seems to half know it), Polanski's become depressingly like Oscar—a jaded, bullying storyteller who manages to make male-female relationships look even worse than they actually are. Expecting wisdom about sexual love from Roman Polanski is like asking a barracuda about manners.

NEW YORK POST, 3/18/94, p. 36, Michael Medved

In recent interviews Roman Polanski insists that his controversial film "Bitter Moon" was actually intended as dark comedy. It's too bad that he did so little to let the audience in on the joke.

Part of the problem is the elaborate structure of the film, which tells its story through flashbacks, extensively narrated in pretentious, purple prose by the movie's main character, a failed novelist played by Peter Coyote. Inevitably, Coyote's voice becomes the voice of the film.

The story begins with an elegant but repressed British couple (played by the capable Kristin Scott-Thomas and Hugh Grant, who also appear together in the superb "Four Weddings and a Funeral") taking an Adriatic cruise in the hopes of restoring some spark to their fading marriage.

On board ship, they meet Coyote, an American expatriate living in Paris who is confined to a wheelchair, and his much-younger French wife (played by Polanski's own, much-younger wife, Emmanuelle Seigner).

Grant is instantly attracted to Seigner (who has been deliberately gowned and groomed to resemble cartoon temptress Jessica Rabbit) and Coyote uses that interest in his wife to force Grant to listen to the story of their romance in appallingly intimate detail.

The point of that story is that obsessive love will ultimately turn to obsessive cruelty, but the two lovers are both so lacking in smarts and self-awareness that their tale seems merely sick and pathetic, never tragic.

In the 1981 Pascal Bruckner novel that inspired the film, the characters are apparently far more intelligent and perceptive concerning their own self-destructive tendencies.

In the film version it's difficult to feel much compassion for people who express affection at the peak of their affair by playing a CD of barnyard animals, while Coyote dons a pig's mask and is whipped as "naughty beast" by his leather-clad mistress.

We see plenty of such "daring" sex scenes, but they seem silly rather than erotic, partly because Seigner is completely miscast. She comes across as a big, healthy, likable, unsophisticated and altogether unremarkable young woman. And despite all the provocative costumes in which her director-husband dresses her, never conveys the slightest hint of a dangerous, demonic femme fatale.

Coyote, on the other hand, makes the most of his impossible part: He leaves a vivid and disturbing impression as both the reckless rake in the flashback sequences, and the crippled cynic who narrates that tale.

In telling this story, Polanski deploys all of his old visual virtuosity, seducing the eye with rich, lurid colors and a vague atmosphere of festering decay, which is intensified by Vangelis' haunting film score.

"What gives you the idea that I enjoy being used as a rubbish dump for your unsavory reminiscences?" Hugh Grant demands of Coyote during, one of their endless conversations, summarizing the likely reaction of most moviegoers to this meandering muddle.

Despite , its artful elements, Polanski's "Moon" isn't just bitter it's rancid.

NEWSDAY, 3/18/94, Part II/p. 69, Jack Mathews

Cruel irony is a staple of horror films and Roman Polanski serves it up in heaping helpings in "Bitter Moon," a perversely comic mix of sexual obsession, temptation, betrayal and humiliation, most of it told by a writer whose purple prose would embarrass a Victorian pornographer.

Sound good so far? Read on. "Bitter Moon" is "Love Boat" meets "Last Tango in Paris," a feverishly goofy psychodrama about a proper British couple who, while aboard a cruise ship, meet a strange, wheel-chair-bound writer and his exotic French wife and take a side trip on the wild side.

The writer is Oscar (Peter Coyote), an American expatriate attempting to relive the hedonist literary life of Henry Miller in Paris, but succeeding only at being the most self-indulgent failure and the biggest sexual bully on the Left Bank.

Mimi (Emmanuelle Seigner) is the waitress who becomes the object of Oscar's obsession, his lover, his burden, his enemy and his partner in a series of increasingly bizarre sex games. She's the one in the black stockings with the whip, he's the one in the pig's mask making oinking sounds behind the dresser.

But I'm getting behind in the story. We don't see Oscar and Mimi performing these feats until Oscar has lured tweedy Nigel (Hugh Grant) into his cabin aboard ship and, with language heavily laced with floral-genital metaphors, recalls the sordid details of their relationship.

The story, shown in flashbacks that drag "Bitter Moon" out for two hours and 19 minutes, is a doozy, filled with sexual adventures and violent retribution, and before it's over, Nigel will understand why Oscar is in a wheelchair and Mimi is being mistaken for Shanghai Lily.

A person with any sense hearing Oscar's story would leap overboard and try to swim to shore. But Nigel, his protests growing fainter by the anecdote, is aroused by Oscar's colorful imagery and is soon champing at the bit to have a go at Mimi himself.

This would all be a lot more fun if Polanski weren't taking so much of it so seriously. A scene where Mimi, drinking from a carton, slops milk all over her breasts and has Oscar lap it up could be a howl, even sexy, if the characters appeared to be remotely in on the joke. But Oscar finds the cleanup detail more erotic than the pigs 'n' whips game, and as they slip into ecstasy, you may feel like slipping under your seat.

Coyote is one of those third-tier actors who seems to relish playing prattling, self-indulgent boors like Oscar, and though his performance is pretty much destroyed by his unbearably campy dialogue ("We were inseparable by day, insatiable by night"), he succeeds in giving us the creeps.

Seigner, who is Polanski's wife, could sue for divorce on grounds of professional abuse. Mimi is a horrible fictional invention, a character who is either pathetically dependent or homicidally vindictive, never believable, rarely sympathetic and often shot from unflattering angles, naked.

Grant, in an almost totally reactive role, gives the film's best performance. His shocked expressions and double-takes, and his attempts to suppress his sexual excitement, are priceless. Kristin Scott-Thomas' Fiona spends most of the trip sulking in her cabin, but when she finally emerges, with a surprise of her own, she steals the remnants of the show.

"Bitter Moon" marks a return of sorts to Polanski's pre-fugitive career, to the absurdist nightmares of "The Tenant" and "Rosemary's Baby," and though it is a far drop in quality from those films, its tone at least, reminds us of what we have been missing.

NEWSWEEK, 3/28/94, p. 58, David Ansen

Roman Polanski has never played it safe. Not in life, and certainly not in his wild corrosive, smuttily funny "Bitter Moon." Recklessly perched on the edged of the ludicrous, this examination of a destructive erotic passion unfolds with an unsettling mixture of steam and mordant irony. Audiences conditioned on the tonal simplicities of Hollywood may feel the need to ward it off with derisive laughter. Big, if understandable, mistake. "Bitter Moon's" unpredictable laughs are quite intentional, the bitter cackle of a romantic bottoming out on his blasted illusions.

We are on a luxury liner bound for Istanbul. En route, a failed American novelist in a wheelchair, Oscar (Peter Coyote) accompanied by his lusciously seductive Parisian wife, Mimi (Emmanuelle Seigner, Polanski's wife), decides to tell the twisted history of their relationship to a very proper, uptight young Brit named Nigel (Hugh Grant). Though Nigel is accompanied by his equally well-bred wife, Fiona (Kristin Scott-Thomas), he can't keep his mind off Mimi.

Oscar's overcooked verbiage ("Eternity for me began one fall day in Paris ...") takes us back to the beginnings of his romantic obsession with Mimi and spares no detail in describing to the horrified Nigel the most graphic details of their love life.

Like Nigel, we are bewitched, appalled and unable to turn away from Oscar's gleefully masochistic candor. For what begins with florid American-in-Paris romanticism and progresses through athletic (and hilarious) bouts of experimental sex turns darker and kinkier as the relationship becomes increasingly hermetic. Sated, Oscar's obsession turns into boredom, love turns into hate, and the S&M games are played for emotional keeps. As the flashbacks get more nastily melodramatic, back on shipboard, the two repressed Brits are ensnared in Oscar and Mimi's erotic games, with startling results.

Coyote's broken, bitter Oscar, with his bad teeth and sickly pallor, is a sadistic Scheherazade, perversely compelled to spin out his lurid tale. It's a sly performance and Grant, squirming with rattled propriety, makes a wickedly funny sounding board. Seigner has little technique as an actress, but her awkwardness adds to her poignancy. She's as sensually overripe as Oscar's prose.

In perfect contrast, the deft Scott-Thomas is all sharp, precise angles.

It's hard to watch the dead-end decadence of Oscar and Mimi without thinking of Polanski's own famously extreme life, and realizing that for all its subversive naughtiness, "Bitter Moon" is actually a a rather conservative cautionary tale. Oscar and Mimi have tested the limits of romantic obsession, and their relationship, having nothing to feed off but itself, turns to poison. But Polanski, bless him, will never be a conventional moralist. This sea cruise may be headed for hell, but he'll always reserve his right to giggle his way through the horror.

SIGHT AND SOUND, 10/92, p. 54, Julian Graffy

Nigel Dobson, a British Eurobond dealer, and Fiona, his wife of seven years, are sailing to Istanbul en route for India. They encounter a beautiful French woman, Mimi, and that night Nigel meets her again, as she dances alone in the ship's bar; later, her crippled American husband, Oscar, takes Nigel to his cabin and begins to tell him their story... After living in Paris for several years, trying to be a writer, he becomes obsessed by a young woman with whom he has a chance encounter on a bus. Tracking her down, he finds her working as a waitress (though her ambition is to be a dancer); they begin a rapturous love affair, and soon Oscar is "enslaved body and soul"...

Next day, Oscar joins Nigel and Fiona at lunch and borrows Nigel to continue his narrative... Over time, his relationship with Mimi had dulled, needing to be spiced up with doses of perversity and sado-masochism, and was further distorted by jealousy... Later that day, Mimi insists on talking to Nigel, who is tricked into betraying his growing attraction to her. Oscar tells of a dinner with a New York literary editor, Beverly, being sabotaged by the jealous Mimi. During a violent argument he throws her to the floor and concusses her. Chastened, he takes her back to the funfair of their early love, but then throws her out. After a night drinking in a bar, he finds her lying outside his flat. He takes her back but treats her with calculated callousness; when she tells him that she is pregnant, he talks her into an abortion, and then tricks her into flying off alone to Martinique...

Nigel's increasingly long absences and evident fascination with the story of Oscar and Mimi provoke Fiona into bitter recriminations about their marriage and her childlessness. Oscar continues his story... Two years pass and Mimi becomes a distant memory. He stops pretending to be a writer, concentrating on his hedonistic night life. Then, early one morning, he is knocked down by a car and breaks his leg. The only person to visit him in hospital is—Mimi. She pushes him out of bed, causing injuries that paralyse him from the waist down. After this, she becomes his taunting, sadistic nurse. For his birthday, she gives him a gun. Then she marries him; they are "survivors of a catastrophe"...

New Year is celebrated with a party on board ship. Nigel dances with Mimi and confesses he has fallen in love with her. She replies, "I'm just a fantasy, it's just a game". Later Mimi dances alone; Fiona joins her and they kiss. A violent storm breaks up the party and Nigel retires alone to the deck. Then, looking for Fiona, he returns to Mimi's cabin, where Oscar is watching the "two nymphs" lying together in bed. Nigel tries to strangle Oscar; Oscar shoots Mimi and then himself.

In Roman Polanski's first feature, *Knife in the Water*, middle-aged couple pick up a young hitch-hiker and take him on their sailing trip, during which the husband involves him in an increasingly sinister power game. In Ian McEwan's novella, *The Comfort of Strangers*, filmed by Paul Schrader, a young English couple in Venice are drawn into the corrupt web of an Italian and his crippled Canadian wife. In *Bitter Moon*, Polanski seems to blend these two prototypes (the actual source is a novel by Pascal Bruckner), but somehow manages to jettison both the meticulous detail and emotional precision of *Knife in the Water* and the cool rigour and taut prose of McEwan.

The clash between its two couples, between the prim propriety of the English and the reckless blatancy of the Parisians, is central to the meaning of *Bitter Moon*. But the film fundamentally miscalculates which couple's story might be the more interesting, and grossly overestimates the audience's fascination with Oscar and Mimi's *danse macabre*. After a promising start, Oscar's story soon lapses into a succession of flaccid clichés, from Notre Dame by night to rides at the funfair, to bars and girls and whisky and the lower depths. The relentless vapidity of his first-person narration ("the rapture of that first awakening", "our mad love was a sacrament") makes it amply clear why Oscar has failed to emulate his mentors Hemingway, Miller and Scott Fitzgerald, and Beverly the literary editor is surely right that Paris, this Paris, is "vieux jeu".

The script of *Bitter Moon* is a lazy male fantasy in which a beautiful, compliant young woman (Emmanuelle Seigner, again cast by Polanski, as she was in *Frantic*, as a wild girl getting involved with an American in Paris) remains besotted with a middle-aged man no matter how badly he treats her. It is shot through with a nasty, prurient misogyny, which first subjects her to any number of cruel humiliations and then presents her intricate revenge as merely a variation of emotional thralldom, requiring us to believe that Mimi will trade working as a dancer in Martinique for a place between the handles of Oscar's wheelchair. In one of the film's few genuinely powerful scenes, Mimi, her sculpted black dress and lustrous hair recalling another icon of decadence, Anita Ekberg in *La Dolce Vita*, is joined on the dance floor by Fiona in sardonically complicitous rebellion against masculine inadequacy. But her escape is short-lived, and the script's final misogynistic trump is for Oscar to choose the timing of her death.

Potentially much more interesting is the film's Forsterian strain, the English journey abroad in search of emotional awakening. Both Oscar and Mimi suggest on occasion (though these hints of parodic intent seem a lamely self-defensive device on the writers' part) that their story may not be true, that it may be a fantasy designed to trigger a response in Nigel and Fiona. Hugh Grant gives a finely nuanced performance as dull, decent Nigel, repeatedly at a loss for words, a hilariously clumsy dancer, powerless in the face of emotional aggression, and Kristin Scott-Thomas (who, like Grant, has played this kind of part before) brings a haunting sadness to brittle, frustrated Fiona.

Their parts are underwritten, however, and their emotional turmoil disdained, though it is through their encounters with the dignified widower Mr Singh (Victor Bannerjee) and his grave and quiet daughter that the film finds its fragile moments of insight. Asked by Mr Singh why they are going to Bombay, Nigel suggests that "India's got so much to teach the West. Inner serenity, that kind of stuff...". Mr Singh replies that India is the noisiest place on earth. At the film's close, the couple stand huddled together on deck, their Passage to India no longer necessary.

VILLAGE VOICE, 3/22/94, p. 43, J. Hoberman

By now, the survivors of the '60s' various cinematic New Waves have themselves reached their sixties. Few however are better entitled to sing "My Way" than multiple comeback artists Jean Luc Godard and Roman Polanski.

Polanski's *Bitter Moon* and Godard's *Hélas Pour Moi*, both opening here Friday, are evidence of a self-consuming passion that is not yet spent. As their acrid titles suggest, these movies are knowingly pathological and utterly self-willed—two masterful exercises in technique so personal that they beg to be misunderstood.

The more commercial of the two, *Bitter Moon* is also the more nakedly self-reflexive. Although adapted from a French bestseller, the premise echoes that of Polanski's internationally acclaimed first feature, *Knife in the Water* (1962). There, a successful middle-aged big shot with his hot young wife pick up a student hitchhiker and bring him aboard their sailboat for a series of escalating sex and power games. Here, the priggish British couple Nigel and Fiona (Hugh Grant and Kristin Scott-Thomas), embarked on a cruise to India, strike up a morbid shipboard relationship with a lush femme fatale, Mimi (Emmanuelle Seigner, the current Mrs. Polanski), and Oscar, her irascible, wheelchair-bound husband (Peter Coyote).

Nigel is hypnotized by Mimi (whom he spots entertaining the ship's bar by a writhing solo to "Fever") but captured by Oscar ("good of you to take pity on an obnoxious cripple"), who tells him their story in a series of lengthy flashbacks. The narrative is embroidered of rich purple and studded with massive clichés: "Eternity began for me one fall day in Paris ..." Oscar is an American-in-Paris writer manqué; Mimi, whom he meets on a bus, is the eternal gamine. At first, they live on "love and stale croissants," augmented by Mimi's exotic dancing and Oscar's licking breakfast off her silky bosom.

As devoted to Seigner as the camera is, one can't help thinking that Polanski is pimping his wife just as Oscar uses Mimi as the bait for Nigel's attention. The tale's first installment ends (back in the Now) with Oscar hilariously regaling the mortified Nigel with the details of his wife's sexual apparatus; the second installment begins (also in the Now), with Oscar treating his listener to a description of an orgasmic golden shower. "For God's sake, man!" Nigel feebly protests as the tale of Oscar and Mimi grows increasingly pornographic, both steamy and absurd, to climax in a failed *maîtresse*-and-pig scenario complete with taped sound effects. "The spell was broken at last," Oscar muses. ("Jolly good thing," Nigel can't help but add.)

But the story has only just begun. We've yet to discover just how the teller landed in the wheelchair he at one point offers his listener. *Bitter Moon* is one long (too long), convoluted, and fabulously nasty jape, As the garrulous and jaded narrator, Coyote gives the best movie performance of his career, a yellow-toothed, avidly babbling cadaver whose self-mocking mock-Scheherazade narrative hilariously transgresses the bounds of polite discourse. Nigel is paralyzed by this display of poor taste—as are we all.

Part of the joke is considering whether the images Polanski provides are how the repressed Nigel imagines Oscar's tale as it spirals ever deeper into sadomasochism. Before long, two marriages are approaching critical mass. If nothing else, *Bitter Moon* provides unexpected compensation for anyone who's suffered through *Four Weddings and a Funeral*. The casting of Hugh Grant and Kristin Scott-Thomas in both creates a perfect parallel. One only has to make the reasonable assumption that Grant's character is dumped by Andie MacDowell's to transform the Polanski film into *Four Wedding's* monstrous punch line.

The current *Film Comment* has hailed *Bitter Moo*n as Polanski's best effort in the 20 years since *Chinatown*. (Of course, the only other candidate is his underappreciated 1976 psychodrama, *The Tenant*.) If *Bitter Moon* crosses over into self-parody, it does give full reign to Polanski's cruel and tactile mixture of black humor, bleak surrealism, and sexual Grand Guignol. Events come to a head with the almost medieval frenzy of the ship's New Year's Eve costume party—Nigel attempting to dance with Mimi while Oscar, grotesquely raffish in a red fez, leeringly flashes him the thumbs up, then tonelessly screams "Nearer My God to Thee" when the ship hits a swell.

Is *Bitter Moon* meant to be funny? In a recent Arts and Leisure profile, Hugh Grant confessed that he couldn't figure it out. Although an uproarious screening at the last Toronto Film Festival, where Fine Line acquired the movie nearly a year after its European release, positioned *Bitter Moon* as a comedy, that wasn't always the case. "It's a serious film," Polanski had told the *Los Angeles Times* during production, back when the emphasis was on the explicit sexuality and publicists were predicting a new *Last Tango in Paris*

Since then, Polanski has pragmatically changed his tack. He's quoted in *Film Comment* explaining that "unfortunately, some people, like the critics here in Europe, don't dare to laugh at a Polanski film. But the public does laugh. When I saw [*Bitter Moon*] in a cinema I was really thrilled, because every bit we intended to be funny came out the way we wanted."

Still, clumsy is not always funny. Clearly, the timorous British couple are designed to provide a comic foil to the grand obsession of their Franco-American shipmates. Indeed, one suspects that, for Polanski, the movie is not the story of one particular relationship but all relationships—evoked in a shifting balance of power, the adhesive force of shared history and the bond of mutual shame.

Certainly no filmmaker has known humiliation more intimately than Polanski. It's a condition that, well before the better-known tabloid horrors of his Hollywood tenure, he experienced as a

Jewish child in Nazi-occupied Poland. Laughter in his films is a further refinement of pain. *Bitter Moon* revels in degradation without precisely making light of it.

Also reviewed in:
CHICAGO TRIBUNE, 4/8/94, Friday/p. A, Michael Wilmington
NATION, 3/21/94, p. 391, Stuart Klawans
NEW REPUBLIC, 4/4/94, p. 24, Stanley Kauffmann
NEW YORK TIMES, 3/18/94, p. C8, Janet Maslin
NEW YORKER, 4/11/94, p. 98, Terrence Rafferty
VARIETY, 8/31/92, p. 60, Derek Elley
WASHINGTON POST, 4/15/94, p. D1, Desson Howe
WASHINGTON POST, 4/15/94, Weekend/p. 45, Joe Brown

BLACK BEAUTY

A Warner Bros. release. *Producer:* Robert Shapiro and Peter Macgregor-Scott. *Director:* Caroline Thompson. *Screenplay:* Caroline Thompson. *Based on the book by:* Anna Sewell. *Director of Photography:* Alex Thomson. *Editor:* Claire Simpson. *Music:* Danny Elfman. *Music Editor:* Bob Badami. *Sound:* Simon Kaye and (music) Shawn Murphy. *Sound Editor:* Richard E. Yawn. *Casting:* Mary Selway. *Production Designer:* John Box. *Art Director:* Les Thomkins. *Set Decorator:* Eddie Fowlie. *Special Effects:* Joss Williams. *Costumes:* Jenny Beavan. *Make-up:* Magdalen Gaffney and Yvonne Coppard. *Stunt Coordinator:* Vic Armstrong. *Running time:* 87 minutes. *MPAA Rating:* G.

CAST: Sean Bean (Farmer Grey); David Thewlis (Jerry Barker); Jim Carter (John Manly); Peter Davison (Squire Gordon); Alun Armstrong (Reuben Smith); John McEnery (Mr. York); Eleanor Bron (Lady Wexmire); Peter Cook (Lord Wexmire); Andrew Knott (Joe Green); Alan Cumming (Voice of Black Beauty); Adrian Ross-Magenty (Lord George); Lyndon Davies (Head Groom); Georgina Armstrong (Jessica Gordon); Gemma Paternoster (Molly Gordon); Anthony Walters (Alfred Gordon); Rosalind Ayres (Mistress Gordon); Vic Armstrong (Job Horse Boss); Sean Baker (Ostler); Bill Stewart (Coachman); Bronco McLouglin (Vicar); Angus Barnett (Ned Burnham); David Ryall (Carriagemaker); Philip Taylor (Carriagemaker's Assistant); Robert Demeger (Horse Market Buyer); Vincent Regan (Sleazy Horse Dealer); Matthew Scurfield (Horse Dealer); Sean Blowers (Hard-faced Man); Emma Richler (Polly Barker); Keeley Flanders (Dolly Barker); Freddie White (Harry Barker); Conrad Asquith (Guv'nor Crenshaw); Dido Miles (Dinah); Rupert Penry Jones (Wild-looking Young Man); John Quarmby (Butler); Julian Maud (Drunken Gentleman); Bronco McLouglin (Granary Cart Drive); Bill McCabe (First Driver); Niall O'Brien (Farmer Thoroughgood); Jonathan Hirst (Willie Thoroughgood); Ian Kelsey (Older Joe Green).

FILMS IN REVIEW, 9-10/94, p. 60, Andy Pawelczak

Black Beauty, Anna Sewell's classic children's novel, is a Dickensian story of sorrow and oppression with a horse instead of an orphan at the mercy of the free market and other malign forces. Caroline Thompson's film version is full of late Victorian period detail—teeming, cobblestoned London streets, a carnival with bearded lady and fire-eater, stately houses of landed gentry and aristocrats—but it never loses its focus on the dolorous equine drama at its center. The horses are the stars here, with humans demoted to supporting players.

Narrated by the eponymous hero himself, the picture tells his story from birth to retirement. The opening scenes, in which Black Beauty cavorts with his mother, are shot in a sumptuous, pictorial style with close-ups of flowers, colorful insects and small animals. Young children might respond to this evocation of Edenic mother/child symbiosis, heightened by Danny Elfman's rhapsodic, folkish music which makes these scenes, and some that come later, into equestrian ballets.

Black Beauty's first foray into the real world is at the home of a kindly county squire where he falls in love with another horse, heroically saves his groom from drowning, and establishes a lifelong attachment to the groom's nephew. Things go downhill when the squire's wife—she's one of those frail, perhaps neurasthenic Victorian gentlewomen—has to move south for her health, and Black Beauty is sold to a cruel aristocrat, where he is mistreated and finally sold to a horse rental agency, once he is unfit for service as a showpiece in the fashionable world. Eventually, he's saved by a gentle London cab driver, played by David Thewlis, and his life, though hard, is filled with affection once again. Thewlis stands out from the human cast, all uniformly good, because his role is such a radical departure from his award winning performance as a violent, angry young prole in last year's *Naked.* As Jerry the cabdriver, he's an almost saintly man, with reservoirs of concern and sympathy for humans and animals alike. In one of the film's sadder moments, discreetly told from the horse's point of view, Jerry comes down with lung disease and has to sell Black Beauty to a grain dealer. Thompson doesn't belabor the point, but it's clear that Victorian life was brutal for horses and working class folk too.

Black Beauty inevitably has some anthropomorphic sentimentality, but it doesn't slop over the edges, and though it's a children's movie—when I saw it I was the only adult unaccompanied by a pre-teen child—anyone with a soft spot for horses can enjoy it. The shots of horses cantering, gamboling, trotting, galloping and just standing in statuesque repose are often stirring, and make you understand why artists have lavished so much paint and attention on horses.

LOS ANGELES TIMES, 7/29/94, Calendar/p. 1, Kenneth Turan

"I am writing the life of a horse," Anna Sewell modestly confided to her journal in what proved to be quite an understatement. Her 1877 novel, "Black Beauty," described as being "translated from the original equine," became the horse story of all time, reaching worldwide sales of 20 million by 1935 and gaining a permanent place in the fantasies of children.

Sewell's first and only novel (she died shortly after it was published) has been brought to the screen several times, but screenwriter Caroline Thompson ("Edward Scissorhands," "Homeward Bound," "The Secret Garden") was happy with none of the attempts. She wanted to stick closer to the original, and, as a lifelong horse lover, felt the only way to guarantee that was to make the film her directing debut as well.

Created, as the novel was, from the heart, this latest version of "Black Beauty" is as simple and straightforward as its source. Though not especially inspired, it uses integrity to make up for that lack, and its unaffected "just the oats, ma'am" approach makes it a fine film for younger viewers.

While she has made some small changes in the plot, Thompson has retained the book's straight-from-the-horse's-mouth conceit. Introduced happily grazing by a limpid stream, Black Beauty is quick to tell us (in a voiceover read, sometimes too enthusiastically, by Alan Cumming), that things weren't always so cushy. "Mine is a story of trust and betrayal and learning to trust again," the horse informs us. "And I remember everything."

"Everything" includes the act of being born (something Sewell wouldn't have dreamed of describing) into a pleasant farm in that storybook England where the gentry ruled and servants knew their place. Between kindly Farmer Grey (Sean Bean) and Beauty's wise mother, he learns all he can before reality takes over. "We don't get to choose the people in our lives," Beauty astutely points out. "For us, it's all chance."

The first family Beauty lands with is a good one, and the horse is put under the wise care of the aptly named John Manly (Jim Carter) and his good-hearted but initially clueless assistant Joe ("Secret Garden's" Andrew Knott).

But even performing heroic deeds and risking his life can't save Beauty from being sold into the stables of unfeeling aristocrats Lord and Lady Wexmire (Peter Cook and Eleanor Bron), where all horses must be slaves to fashion though they be treated cruelly in the process.

One of the reasons Sewell, an animal-rights activist before her time, wrote "Black Beauty" was to forcefully protest the several ways horses were mistreated, and to Thompson's credit this aspect of the book is given its due and the philosophy that "kind treatment makes good horses" enthusiastically supported.

Conversely, perhaps the most curious change from the book, and one whose silliness will be apparent even to those who haven't read it, is the decision to jump-start the relationship between Beauty and Ginger, the high-strung mare who is his sometime stablemate.

While in the best Victorian tradition of the original, the two horses told the press they were just good friends, the film has Beauty fall giddily and rather preposterously in love with Ginger, to the point of exclaiming at one point, "She likes me, she really likes me." Perhaps Thompson felt the staid original needed a bit more juice, but this solution is not a workable one.

Though the energetic American quarter horse who plays Beauty is deservedly the film's center of attention, the picture comes most alive in its second half, when David Thewlis enters as Jerry Barker, the kindly London cabbie who shows the horse what it's like to live and work in the big city.

While this simple part is literally a drive through the park for Thewlis after his agonizing starring role in Mike Leigh's "Naked," his ability to bring a level of emotional connection to the portrayal makes his scenes stand out as the most believable around.

Thompson also gets good marks for resisting the temptation to over-sentimentalize "Beauty's" story. But, more workmanlike than dazzling as a director, she is unable to bring the kind of excitement or magic to the project that animated a classic horse movie like Carroll Ballard's "The Black Stallion." This picture is not that kind of thoroughbred, but it is solid and dependable, and those qualities are no doubt rarer in films than they are in horses.

NEW YORK POST, 7/29/94, p. 42, Michael Medved

We've all heard the expression "It's a dog's life," but when you think about it for a moment, you'll realize that horses generally have a far worse time of it than canines.

The handsome new movie version of "Black Beauty" makes the basic point about the hard life of a horse again and again—and again. It's a serious, sensitive, visually stunning film, but it's hardly the feel-good family treasure that all the ads and promos seem to suggest.

First-time director Caroline Thompson (who previously wrote the screenplays for everything from "The Addams Family" to "The Secret Garden" to "Edward Scissorhands") follows the 1877 novel of "Black Beauty" more faithfully than either of the two previous movie versions of this tale, but that's not necessarily a good thing.

Anna Sewell's book emphasized the cruelties endured by a once proud stallion who ends up as a broken, dispirited nag after he's passed from master to master in Victorian England, and the novel became so popular that it led to some significant improvements in that era's treatment of horses.

The movie is unlikely to have any comparable impact—or resonance—since so few members of its audiences, in contrast to 19th-century readers, have ever enjoyed significant contact with horses.

Another problem involves the narration (read by Alan Cummings) that is supposed to represent Black Beauty's recollections of his troubled life, from his idyllic days as a carefree colt with Farmer Grey (Sean Bean), to his years as a pampered young horse with Squire Gordon (Peter Davison), to dreary times pulling a coach for a poor but kindly London cabbie (David Thewlis).

The narration fills nearly every scene in the film, and any time you hear an actor expressing the thoughts of a horse whose impassive face is featured onscreen then it means that Mr. Ed rears his silly head—despite the solemn tone of the movie.

To make matters worse, Justin, the equine star who plays the title character, proves himself an actor of distinctly limited range. This 6-year-old American quarter horse manages to wiggle his neck and shake his head, and then occasionally rears upon his impressive hind legs, but that's about it. Other members of his species, in the recent Australian film "The Silver Stallion," for instance, have demonstrated far more capacity to convey emotion.

Oddly enough, the other horses that Beauty encounters never speak as he does, so their relationships seem especially unbalanced. We're also left with the same ambiguity with which the book, in its Victorian modesty, treated the mane character's connection to the lovely mare, Ginger. When they are forced to separate, Beauty declares "Goodbye, my sweet one," but we never even catch a hint as to whether they are merely good friends and stable mates, or more significantly involved.

These reservations aside, "Black Beauty" is an honorable, often touching piece of work that features an out-of-left-field happy ending (straight from the book) and valuable messages about the importance of kindness and consideration—to people as well as animals.

Parents will enjoy the lush visions of English country estates and lively re-creations of last century's London and older kids (particularly girls) will relish the shots of Beauty in his glory days running with the wind.

With the very young, however, be prepared for some serious talks about a film that remains, like the book that inspired it, inescapably sad.

NEWSDAY, 7/29/94, Part II/p. B9, John Anderson

For the second week in a row, we have a major motion picture about an animal, and the differences couldn't be more pronounced. Last week "Lassie" attempted to update a classic story by adorning it with obnoxious children, and failed to be either contemporary or meaningful. This week "Black Beauty," Caroline Thompson's lush and lovely version of the 1877 Anna Sewell book, tells the story straight from the horse's mouth, and makes its moral points as well as anyone ever has.

It remains a children's story, especially since Thompson has returned the story to its original form—Sewell subtitled her book "The Autobiography of a Horse," and here it really is. Adults might find the narrative style a bit jarring: Black Beauty (the voice of Alan Cumming) relates most of this story in past tense, except when urgency requires otherwise ("Come back, Joe!!"). But the film loves its horses, and cinematographer Alex Thomson ("Cliffhanger") takes full advantage of the bucolic English landscapes they travel.

The fabled jet-black colt with the white star on his head is born in the barn of Farmer Grey (Sean Bean, of "Patriot Games") and remembers every detail. ("It was cold ... and much too bright!"). From there, his story becomes one of good owner/bad owner/good owner/bad owner. Along the way, he meets Ginger, a red mare, Merrylegs the pony, and the boy Joe (Andrew Knott), who'll save him in the end.

Black Beauty will be grossly mistreated by the cruel Countess of Wexmire (Eleanor Bron) and treated with kindness by the likes of cab driver Jerry Barker (the marvelous David Thewlis). Hearing the horse's thoughts will take children inside his head and may give them a profound respect for animals and the thoughtless way they're often treated. It's not an entirely happy story—Beauty's treatment is occasionally harsh, and he suffers. But Thompson handles the material sensitively, and the lessons to be learned would certainly seem to outweigh whatever passing discomfort a young moviegoer might feel.

SIGHT AND SOUND, 2/95, p. 42, Geoffrey Macnab

The late nineteenth century. An elderly stallion, at rest in a field in the English countryside, reminisces about his eventful life. Born in a lantern-lit stable on Farmer Grey's estate, he grows up into a handsome horse and is sold to Squire Gordon. The Squire's wife names him Black Beauty on account of his bright black coat. He befriends Merrylegs, a little pony, and Ginger, a red mare who was treated cruelly by a previous owner and has developed a ferocious temper.

Beauty saves the head coachman, John Manly, from drowning, but almost dies himself when stableboy Joe Green forgets to wrap him up in his rug. Joe later makes amends, rescuing Beauty and Ginger from a huge fire. The Squire leaves England, hoping his wife's health will improve in warmer climes. Black Beauty and Ginger are sold to Lady Wexmire. She is not interested in their well-being, but merely wants them to look well turned out. Beauty has a horrific accident when a drunken stableman fails to notice that he is not properly shod. His knees are so disfigured that the Wexmires no longer want him in their stables. He is sold again. He works briefly as a job horse, available for hire. Then he is bought by Jerry Barker, a kindly London cabbie. As he pounds the streets, he spots his old friend Ginger, who is also pulling a cab. She is in a pitiful state and he sees her corpse being dragged past a day or two later.

Jerry Barker is too sick to carry on his business. Beauty is taken over by a corn dealer, who makes him work till he drops. Ragged and broken, he looks certain to end up in the knacker's yard. However Joe Green buys him and sets him out to pasture. Gradually, his health and spirits return. Joe promises that he will never be sold again.

"The attraction of all stories for me is the metaphor," Caroline Thompson told *Sight and Sound* last year when asked what led her to adapt Frances Hodgson Burnett's *The Secret Garden* for the screen. Before digging out the metaphor, though, she first needed to attend to the surface details:

to capture the nuances of class, costume and behaviour in turn-of-the-century England. But this was the problem: the posh little kids in frocks and waistcoats were posh little kids in frocks and waistcoats, however well she wrote about them.

With her debut as director, Thompson makes a second foray into Victorian children's fiction. This time, she has found more tractable material. For a start, horses and cinema go way back. Anna Sewell's novel was published in 1877, only a year before Eadweard Muyrbridge's famous attempt to capture a photographic record of a stallion in motion with a dozen still cameras. Then there's the story itself, a pathos-saturated tale not so very different from her own most famous script: like *Edward Scissorhands, Black Beauty* is an estranged hero, adopted, loved and abused by humans.

The narrative doesn't exactly rattle along. In the early scenes in particular, affairs move at a leisurely, pastoral pace: horses gambol up and down the fields, the camera picks out butterflies, snails and other assorted wildlife. These idyllic moments are interspersed with various night-time set-pieces in which the film-making style suddenly darkens and quickens, with Thompson moving into Gothic groove: a bridge collapses in a flood, there is a spectacular fire in the stables and a delirious, drunken ride through the woods.

Thompson's attitude toward the horses themselves is not always clear. On the one hand, she fetishises them, showing Black Beauty and Ginger rising on their hind legs like wild stallions and galloping at vast speed across the verdant pastures. To look at, they're powerful, primitive animals who slightly scare the humans they come into contact with. (In this respect, *Black Beauty* echoes Carroll Ballard's equally pagan *The Black Stallion.*) On the other hand, anthropomorphism holds sway. Beauty recounts his own story in flashback, Nan Cumming's childlike voice making him sound like an excitable schoolboy on an outing to the seaside.

Sewell's novel was written "to induce kindness, sympathy and an understanding treatment of horses," and was distributed by animal rights campaigners as well as booksellers. Forget the fact that Black Beauty is a horse, and it reads like a variation of David Copperfield or Oliver Twist. It's full of Dickensian archetypes: the stableboy, the cab-driver, the squire and the haughty, affected aristocrat. This world has been evoked again and again by the movies. There's nothing especially original in this vision of nineteenth century England, but costumes and production design are handsome enough, and there are enjoyable character turns from Jim Carter, Alun Armstrong and David Thewlis.

Perhaps Thompson's adaptation is a little staid; it keeps close to the original, with no Tim Burton-like flights of fancy to leaven matters. Still, she preserves the ingenuous, wide-eyed innocence which made Sewell's story so effective in the first place. The sentiment may be cloying, but it's hard not to admire the film-making.

VILLAGE VOICE, 8/9/94, p. 48, Amy Taubin

At an afternoon press screening of *Black Beauty*, 20 children ages six to 10, most of them girls, sat raptly attentive from beginning to end. "I almost cried three times" confided one girl to another, thus confirming my suspicion that the film works even better for children than for adults. Although I shed tears, there were also moments when I was more interested in watching the young audience than the screen.

A remarkably faithful adaptation of Anna Sewell's 19th-century children's novel, the film, which was written and directed by Caroline Thompson, is narrated in the first person by Black Beauty, an intelligent, obedient, and hard-working horse who always tries to do the right thing even in the worst circumstances. Full of honest horse sense and practical information about horse and human interaction, the film, for me, is as prosaic as the book, much to my surprise, seemed on a recent reading. Children, on the other hand, are likely to find the film as magical as I once did the novel. Personally, however, I missed the lyricism of *The Secret Garden* or *Edward Scissorhands* (two films scripted though not directed by Thompson).

Unlike previous adaptations, this version of *Black Beauty* views the humans (narratively if not visually) from an equine point of view. The horse's subjectivity, in so far as it can be humanly understood and expressed, is primary. This technique may be makeshift but it's extremely useful in encouraging children to love and respect animals.

Brought up by a sensitive owner who sells him to an equally caring family, Black Beauty then experiences much brutality at the hands of ignorant or sadistic handlers, only to be saved from death by a former stable boy who loved him as a colt. The story is told in flashback (the first and last image is of a contented Black Beauty lying in his beloved meadow), thus sparing young audiences anxiety about the horse's fate. That said, the film doesn't cosmeticize Black Beauty's life or that of his far less lucky friend Ginger.

"A horse never knows who may buy him or who may drive him. It's all chance for us," Black Beauty's mother explains to her son. Children identify with the horse's vulnerability to the powerful humans who control his life (*Black Beauty* abounds with child-abuse metaphors), but they also desire the horse for his physical strength and latent freedom of movement. Like the best horse stories, Thompson's *Black Beauty* allows us to mix identification with desire to our own measure.

Also reviewed in:
CHICAGO TRIBUNE, 7/29/94, Friday/p. D, Johanna Steinmetz
NEW YORK TIMES, 7/29/94, p. C19, Janet Maslin
VARIETY, 7/25-31/94, p. 57, Todd McCarthy
WASHINGTON POST, 7/29/94, p. B6, Hal Hinson

BLANK CHECK

A Buena Vista Pictures release of a Walt Disney Pictures presentation. *Executive Producer:* Hilary Wayne and Blake Snyder. *Producer:* Craig Baumgarten and Gary Adelson. *Director:* Rupert Wainwright. *Screenplay:* Blake Snyder and Colby Carr. *Director of Photography:* Bill Pope. *Editor:* Hubert de La Bouillerie and Jill Savitt. *Music:* Nicholas Pike. *Music Editor:* Michael Connell. *Sound:* David Kirschner. *Sound Editor:* John A. Larsen. *Casting:* Reuben Cannon. *Production Designer:* Nelson Coates. *Art Director:* Burton Rencher. *Set Decorator:* Cecilia Rodarte. *Special Effects:* Randy E. Moore. *Costumes:* Deborah Everton. *Make-up:* Katharina Hirsch-Smith. *Stunt Coordinator:* Patrick Romano. *Running time:* 90 minutes. *MPAA Rating:* PG.

CAST: Brian Bonsall (Preston Waters); Karen Duffy (Shay Stanley); James Rebhorn (Fred Waters); Jayne Atkinson (Sandra Waters); Michael Faustino (Ralph Waters); Chris Demetral (Damian Waters); Miguel Ferrer (Quigley); Michael Lerner (Biderman); Tone Loc (Juice); Rick Ducommun (Henry); Alex Zuckerman (Butch); Alex Allen Morris (Riggs); Debbie Allen (Yvonne); Michael Polk (Yvonne's Assistant); Lu Leonard (Udowitz); Mary Chris Wall (Betty Jay); Bernie Engel (Mr. Appleton); Dorothy Layne (Mrs. Appleton); Angee Hughes (Lady in Parking Lot); Mike Fairchild (Police Officer in Bank); Terry G. Mross and Eric Glenn (Truck Drivers); Gil Glasgow (Van Driver); Jason Tirado (Delivery Guy); Randy Moore (Maitre d'); Greg Dial (Hired Guard at Party); Colom L. Keating (Cop at Party); Steve Shearer (Chauffeur at Party); Turk Pipkin (Magician); Richard Dillard (Guest #1); Diane Perella (Guest #2); Joe Stevens (First Neighbor); John Edson (Second Neighbor); Amanda Baumgarten (Girl at Amusement Park); Seth Corr (Boy at Water Park); Roger Fields (Bystander).

LOS ANGELES TIMES, 2/11/94, Calendar/p. 8, Peter Rainer

Eleven-year-old Preston Waters (Brian Bonsall) finds himself the recipient of a blank check in "Blank Check" and proceeds to cash it for a million bucks and shower himself with toys and gizmos. It's a child's fantasy that's also an adult fantasy—particularly in Hollywood. For its producers, the fantasy, of course, is that the movie will shower them with millions.

It's also clear from the get-go that this movie also wants to practice Good Values—it wants to demonstrate that money isn't everything. It's a standard Hollywood two-step: Indulge but Moralize.

Preston is supposed to be a nerdy kid whose father (James Rebhorn) is a taskmaster and skinflint. Actually, Preston seems pretty spunky. His creepy rep with his classmates is undeserved. Have our filmmakers even forgotten how to convincingly characterize a nerd? Was "Revenge of the Nerds" all for naught?

A movie about a kid who goes gaga buying toys and gizmos is a natural for product placements, there is so much brand-name merchandise highlighted in this film that watching it is like riffling though a mail-order catalogue.

For the children in the audience, all those gizmos may turn out to be overkill. What's missing from this film is any trace of the joy in simple pleasures. Preston isn't a very imaginative child; he's a goodies gatherer.

The supporting cast tries hard to inject some spunk into the proceedings. As the bad guy whose blank check sets the plot in motion, Miguel Ferrer does a junior-league variation on his even worse guy in "RoboCop." Tone Loc shows up as Ferrer's assistant, and he's so out of place in this fantasy that he seems weirdly *in* place. Best is Rick Ducommun as Preston's chauffeur; his scenes with the boy have a goofy charm. They both have a weakness for tubs of ice cream. Miraculously, the ice cream is not identified by brand.

NEW YORK POST, 2/11/94, p. 37, Thelma Adams

Some things are worse than gratuitous sex and violence. "Blank Check," a second-rate Disney family comedy, is morally bankrupt.

Writers Blake Snyder and Colby Carr drew a blank in the idea department. They've cobbled together a "Home Alone" clone about Preston (Brian Bonsall), a lonely 11-year-old pre-yuppie who cashes a blank check to the tune of $1 million. He outfoxes criminals and G-men alike, but blows the. bucks in six days.

Setting aside the unbelievable premise, I was put off by the rampant materialism. It opens with criminal Quigley (Miguel Ferrer) kissing greenbacks. When Preston scores, he obscenely lolls in a bed of cash.

I squirmed during two upbeat montages of getting and spending and playing with ludicrously expensive toy's to the tunes "Money (That's what I Want)" and "I Want Candy,"

This is a kid who sits in an upscale dining room and whines to his pinch-penny father: "If we're not poverty-stricken, there must be some other reason I'm so depressed."

I feel sorry—not!

"Blank Check" suffers from "Home Alone" syndrome: a smug kids-know-best, parents-are-self-involved, adults-can't-be-trusted attitude. It adds to the mix a degree of sexism that is as surprising in a kiddie comedy as it is unnecessary.

Mom (Jayne Atkinson) is a complete non-entity. Debbie Allen, in a small role as a party planner, is a big-haired runaway shrew. And, during a farcical bank routine, a woman's curvy butt provides the distraction.

And what about that "Summer of '42" romance between prepubescent Preston and Shay (Karen "Duff" Duffy) Stanley, G-woman, sex bomb, love interest?

First-time director Rupert Wainwright shoots Shay sex-object-style from the moment she steps on screen in high heels and mini. MTV veejay Duff carries it off with more good nature than the movie deserves, but when Shay dines with the pre-teen, she behaves like it's the best date she's ever had. Right!

After a playful postprandial dip in a fountain, the wet couple relax together in the back of a limo. Her skimpy dress plastered to her curves, Shay is all cleavage and crossed-legs shot from below—the picture of sexual availability. And for what?

I've seen full frontal nudity that was less obscene. Like the queasy Lolita-and-father sexual tension in Disney's current "My Father, the Hero," this preteen's near-conquest of an older woman is somebody's fantasy. But whose?

In the end, "Blank Check" slaps its own hand with morals about money, family, and friends—but all the fun is in the getting and spending. It's the kind of movie-by-committee that will inspire gales of kiddie laughter during slapstick moments, but is instantly forgettable.

NEWSDAY, 2/11/94, Part II/p. 79, John Anderson

A deadlier screen presence than the dull-eyed Brian Bonsall is hard to imagine in a major motion picture comedy, although "Blank Check" is not a major motion picture comedy. Imagine it instead as a therapeutic exercise for residents of the Home for Wayward Reagan Appointees, who pine for the glory days when greed was good and cupidity was in flower.

It's avarice that propels this gaudy show of a movie, and avarice that provides its few moments of entertainment. Let's face it: As Lotto proves each week, unearned wealth is the American dream, and everyone wants to be the kid in the candy shop. Whether they want to be this kid—or want their kids to be this kid—is another question.

As 11-year-old Preston Waters, Bonsall—who played Michael J. Fox's little brother in the long-running sitcom "Family Ties"—is one of those creatures who exist solely in bad movies. He's a kind of human substitute, whose character is determined by the plot, whose personality mutates and transmogrifies in whatever way the screenwriters find convenient, whose circumstances are artificial and whose motivation is absurd. As a study in abnormal psychology, such a person might be fascinating. As a subject of drama or even alleged comedy, he's a horror show.

And it's Preston who's supposed to be the brains in this family. The child of cartoonishly insensitive Midwestern parents (James Rebhorn and Jayne Atkinson) and the brother of cretins (Michael Faustino and Chris Demetral), it's Preston who is the computer whiz, who intellectually outraces everyone around him. But it's also Preston who whines about his privileged lot in life, and who, when presented with a blank check—which he gets accidentally after Quigley the mobster (Miguel Ferrer) runs over his bike—fills in $1 million, goes on a stupendous shopping spree and then loses track of how much he has till it's gone.

Want more? There are racial and ethnic caricatures provided by Tone Loc as Quigley's cohort Juice; Debbie Allen, in a shameless performance as Preston's party planner; Michael Lerner as the corrupt banker Biderman (what's he doing running a Midwest bank?) who helps Quigley try to get his money back, and Karen Duffy, as an FBI agent who's lovely but defies logic. Rick Ducommun, as Preston's chauffeur Henry, injects some humanity into this otherwise dreary enterprise, but the script often leaves him abandoned on the side of the road.

SIGHT AND SOUND, 9/94, p. 37, Andrew Pulver

Eleven-year-old computer freak Preston Waters is bullied by his older brothers and kept short of pocket money by his work-ethic parents. Preston's feelings of deprivation, intensified by a no-money humiliation at a schoolkids' party in a local theme park, turn into a plan of action to raise a million dollars and buy his own house. He tries to open a bank account with his savings of 11 dollars, but is turned away kindly by bank clerk Shay. On his way out, his bicycle is flattened by a car belong to ex-con Quigley, who has been visiting bank manager Biderman in order to forcibly organise a money-laundering operation. Quigley is anxious to get rid of Preston, and hurriedly gives him a blank cheque to pay for the damaged bike.

Preston can't resist the temptation to fill in the cheque for a million dollars, and takes it back to the bank to cash. He arrives minutes before Quigley's sidekick Juice arrives to collect his laundered cash, and Biderman hands the money over in a case of mistaken identity. Realizing the error, the three set out to search for Preston. Meanwhile, Preston starts spending, inventing the alias Mr Mackintosh to help him buy a house and hire a limo. His chauffeur proves an unexpectedly helpful companion, and joins in the games spree that commences.

Shay, meanwhile, turns out to be an undercover FBI agent, and when Preston shyly asks her for a date on the pretence of arranging a meeting with the mysterious Mr Mackintosh, she accepts. Preston next decides to hold a birthday party for Mr Mackintosh, but realises in the middle of the celebrations that the money has run out, and everybody leaves. Quigley and his gang finally track the boy down, and while they are interrogating him, the FBI burst in. Quigley claims he is Mackintosh to cover his identity, and is promptly arrested for handling stolen money. Preston finally returns home.

Although it purports to be a parable warning kids of the dangers of materialism and to "be careful what you wish for," *Blank Cheque* is as blatant a celebration of excess consumption as you're likely to encounter. The plot—mind-numbingly simple yet at the same time bizarrely complex—is an updating of *Risky Business*-style oh-to-be-an-adult fantasy, with a bit of *Indecent Proposal* moral philosophising chucked into the mix. The result, though, becomes increasingly peculiar as Preston Waters—the clued-up kid at the centre of things—indulges in his dreamed-of financial independence.

After, predictably enough, accumulating every toy, video game, and virtual reality machine available in America, Preston emerges from his buying spree attired like some overdressed party tot—in the sort of clothes that any sensible kid would give almost anything to avoid. Even weirder, he develops the hots for a comely bank clerk (who turns out to be an undercover Fed) and a 'date', arranged on behalf of Preston's adult alias, turns into a grotesquely inappropriate spectacle—not only does she turn up wearing the kind of gown normally reserved for perfume commercials, but the two end up waltzing sensuously among erupting fountains in a staggeringly overt piece of symbolism.

Whatever the deficiencies of the narrative, there is at least a clutch of decent performances that forestalls the film's descent into abject failure. Best of the lot, as the heavy, is Tone Loc who has clearly built up his role from a scripter's cipher into one of considerable comic impact. On the other hand, Rick Ducommun, who plays Preston's genial chauffeur chum, gamely tries and fails to emulate John Candy's boyish demeanour. You can't help but admire Brian Bonsall's spirit in the lead role, but the movie itself is such an awkward construction of spare parts that the energy he cooks up seems, inevitably, to go nowhere.

Also reviewed in:
CHICAGO TRIBUNE, 2/11/94, Friday/p. M, Johanna Steinmetz
NEW YORK TIMES, 2/11/94, p. C12, Stephen Holden
VARIETY, 2/14-20/94, p. 41, Joe Leydon
WASHINGTON POST, 2/12/94, p. G12, Richard Harrington

BLANKMAN

A Coumbia Pictures release of a Wife N' Kids production. *Executive Producer:* Damon Wayans. *Producer:* Eric L. Gold and C.O. Erickson. *Director:* Mike Binder. *Screenplay:* Damon Wayans and J.F. Lawton. *Story:* Damon Wayans. *Director of Photography:* Tom Sigel. *Editor:* Adam Weiss. *Music:* Miles Goodman. *Music Editor:* Nancy Fogarty. *Sound:* Curt Frisk and (music): Joel Moss. *Sound Editor:* Tom McCarthy and Roxanne Jones. *Production Designer:* James Spencer. *Art Director:* Keith Burns. *Set Designer:* Stephanie J. Gordon. *Set Decorator:* Michael C. Claypool. *Special Effects:* Richard O. Helmer. *Costumes:* Michelle Cole. *Make-up:* Cindy Reece Thorne. *Stunt Coordinator:* William H. Washington. *Running time:* 91 minutes. *MPAA Rating:* PG-13.

CAST: Damon Wayans (Darryl Walker); David Alan Grier (Kevin Walker); Robin Givens (Kimberly Jonz); Christopher Lawford (Mayor Marvin Harris); Lynne Thigpen (Grandma Walker); Jon Polito (Michael "The Suit" Minelli); Nicky Corello (Sammy The Blade); Jason Alexander (Mr. Stone); Harris Peet (Commissioner Gains); Joe Vassallo (Tony the Match); Michael Wayans (Young Darryl); Damon Wayans (Young Kevin); John Moschitta, Jr. (Mr. Crudd); Frazer Smith (Ned Beadie); Mark Schiff (Bus Driver); Robert Schimmel (Officer); Mike Binder (Dr. Victor Norris); Simone Brooks (Crying Girl); June Christopher (Pregnant Woman); Brad LaFave (The Reporter); Cara Mia Wayans (Little Girl); Christopher James Williams (Production Manager); Mark Burton (Harris' Assistant); Greg Kinnear (Talk Show Host); Tony Cox (Midgetman); Kevin West (Gay Man); Yvette Wilson (Fat Girl); Gwen E. Davis (Lady); Benjamin Gates, Jr. (TV Broadcaster); Christopher Spencer (Stevens); Dwayne L. Barnes (McDonald's Customer); Mary Schiff (Liquor Store Owner); Conroy Gedeon (New Mayor); Campion Murphy and Michael Ramirez (Policemen); Shuko Akune (Campaign Worker); Gordon McClure (Man of God); Biff Manard (Biff); Andy Flaster and Tatiana Saunders (Onlookers); Richard Bonner (Harris' Assistant); Jesse Felsot (Concerned Teenager); Theodore S. Maier (Bank Guard); Michael Marloe (Scuzzy Bum); Arsenio Hall (Himself); Leonard Willis (Street Kid).

LOS ANGELES TIMES, 8/22/94, Calendar/p. 3, Peter Rainer

"Coming to Save Your Butt!" blare the ads for "Blankman." Whose butt are we talking about here? Not *my* butt.

Damon Wayans plays Darryl, a cretinous would-be super-hero—a cross between Jerry Lewis in "The Nutty Professor" and Spike Lee's Mars Blackmon from "She's Gotta Have It"—who rescues his city from the stranglehold of crime.

Darryl has no superpowers but he's a great inventor: He concocts Rube Goldberg crime-fighting contraptions. Clunky but game, he goes up against the local mob boss (Jon Polito) and saves the day.

This terrible little movie—directed by Mike Binder and co-written by Wayans and J. F. Lawton—does have a teensy fascination. As with Robert Townsend's "Meteor Man" last summer, "Blankman" posits a cartoony bumbling super-hero as the way out of inner-city misery. That misery, even in a gooffball nothing of a movie like this, is so much more harrowing than the loopy attempts to fight it that the effect is almost poignant.

David Alan Grier, playing Darryl's brother, has a few fine low-comic moments, and Robin Givens, as a TV newscaster, keeps flashing a smile that could shatter the Hope diamond. But the all-too-aptly-named Blankman probably won't make it as a sequelized movie hero.

Wayans may intend him as a sweet-souled avenger, but he comes across less child-like than imbecilic. He's a fey geek. Can this be what the filmmakers had in mind?

NEW YORK POST, 8/22/94, p. 27, Michael Medved

When a movie studio tries to hide one of its major releases from the critics forbidding advance screenings so that reviews will appear only after the film's opening weekend, then it's a good indication that they know they haven't exactly got an Oscar contender on their hands.

That's certainly the case with "Blankman" a dumb, clumsy comedy that only occasionally rises to the level of plodding mediocrity.

The film's main asset is the seemingly indestructible likability of its two stars Damon Wayans and David Alan Grier, both best known for their work on TV's "In Living Color."

Wayans goes over the top playing a terminally immature nerd with taped-together glasses who spends his time tinkering with eccentric inventions fashioned from pieces of discarded junk; Grier is his protective, hard-working big brother.

When their grandmother (Lynne Thigpen) is murdered by a ruthless all-powerful mob boss (Jon Poiito), the Wayans character, a boyhood devotee of the campy old "Batman" TV series transforms himself into a crusading superhero to rid the city of crime and corruption.

Donning red pajamas, with his grandmother's housecoat as a cape, be becomes "Blankman" and uses his oddball gadgets to battle the bad guys. His heroics soon attract the attention of a glamorous reporter played by Robin Given who brings an energizing charisma and glamour to every scene in which she appears.

She's fascinated with the mysterious masked marvel after interviewing him at his "Blankstation" headquarters at an abandoned subway stop, where he explains, "That's what Blankman stands for. Every man who looks out his window and sees wrong and wants to do something about it."

The movie's attempts at inspiration as well as its prevailing humor, remain stuck at the level of giggly pre-adolescent boys. There is consistent emphasis on gross bodily functions as when Blankman proudly tells his brother that he has invented "stink bombs made from concentrated flatulence. I collected it while you were sleeping."

Wayans has no one to blame but himself for such lines since in addition to starring in the film, he also co-wrote it and served as executive producer. The fatally slack direction, however, is provided by Mike Binder, who displays the same pacing and structure problems that characterized his meandering autobiographical projects "Crossing the Bridge" and "Indian Summer."

The pokey tempo and the failed gags can't entirely obscure a strange subtext in the film's vision of urban blight: Every one of the dozens of criminals who play on the populace, including street-corner muggers, happens to be white.

Of course, the real tragedy of today's inner cities is black-on-black crime, which claims the overwhelming majority of African-American victims. It would be altogether unreasonable to expect this silly little comedy to address that crisis seriously (or responsibly). But the odd distortions only contribute to an atmosphere that is forced, phony and relentlessly unfunny.

Also reviewed by:
NEW YORK TIMES, 8/20/94, p. 13, Stephen Holden
VARIETY, 8/22-28/94, p. 55, Emanuel Levy
WASHINGTON POST, 8/20/94, p. B2, Rita Kempley

BLINK

A New Line Cinema release. *Executive Producer:* Robert Shaye and Sara Risher. *Producer:* David Blocker. *Director:* Michael Apted. *Screenplay:* Dana Stevens. *Director of Photography:* Dante Spinotti. *Editor:* Rick Shaine. *Music:* Brad Fiedel. *Music Editor:* Allan K. Rosen. *Sound:* Chris Newman, D. Webster Hill, Jeff Ward and (music) Tim Boyle. *Sound Editor:* Lucy Coldsnow-Smith and John A. Larsen. *Casting:* Linda Lowy. *Production Designer:* Dan Bishop. *Art Director:* Jefferson Sage. *Set Designer:* Amy J. Smith. *Set Decorator:* Dianna Freas. *Set Dresser:* Roger G. Anderson. *Special Effects:* Sam Barkan. *Visual Effects:* Art Durinski. *Costumes:* Susan Lyall. *Make-up:* Jeff Goodwin. *Stunt Coordinator:* Tim A. Davison. *Animal Trainer:* Steve McAuliff. *Running time:* 106 minutes. *MPAA Rating:* R.

CAST: Madeleine Stowe (Emma Brody); Aidan Quinn (Detective John Hallstrom); James Remar (Thomas Ridgely); Peter Friedman (Dr. Ryan Pierce); Bruce A. Young (Lt. Mitchell); Laurie Metcalf (Candice); Matt Roth (Crowe); Paul Dillon (Neal Booker); Michael P. Byrne (Barry); Anthony Cannata (Ned); Greg Noonan (Frank); Heather Schwartz (Young Emma); Marily Dodds Frank (Emma's Mother); Michael Stuart Kirkpatrick (Michael); Sean C. Cleland (Sean); Craig Winston Damon (Winston); David Callahan (David); Jackie Moran (Jackie); Mary Ann Thebus (Mrs. Davison); Joy E. Gregory (Valerie Wheaton); Lucy Childs (Margaret Tattersall); Blake Whealy (Mark Tattersall); Tim Monsion (Mr. Tattersall); Shirley Spiegler Jacobs (Grandmother); Don Forston (Priest); Debra Dusay (Female Detective); Lia D. Mortensen (Reporter); Mario Tanzi (Cuchetto); Kate Buddeke (Mrs. Whitney); Adele Robbins (Davison Doctor); Rick Lefevour (Driver); Darryl Rocky Davis (Forensics); Sam Sanders (Bobby); Dallas J. Crawford (Kid); Mark Nagel (Parking Guard); Les Podewell (Old Man); Lucina Paquet (Mrs. Goldman); Glendon Gabbard (Mr. Goldman); Gene Janson (Mr. Getz); Renee Lockett-Lawson (Admitting Nurse); Mary Seibel (Records Nurse); Valerie Spencer (Children's Nurse); Kathryn Miller (Children's Nurse); Donna Alexander (Veterinarian); Jackie Samuel (Woman Conductor); Kevin B. Swerdlow (Receiving Cop); Kevin Matthews (Man on Train); Ted Gilbert (Ted); Chantal Wentworth (Backup Singer); Joe McConnell and Bob Lanier (Basketball Announcers); Ray Clay (Stadium Announcer).

FILMS IN REVIEW, 5-6/94, p. 58, Andy Pawelczak

The neurologist Oliver Sacks recently wrote an article about a man whose sight was restored after years of blindness. Sacks' main point was that the man had to learn to see once the physiological impairment was removed, that organizing the fluid, chaotic field of vision, giving names to the things that mysteriously swim into it, is a learned skill. In Michael Apted's new thriller, *Blink*, Emma Brody (Madeleine Stowe) gets a cornea transplant after twenty years of blindness, and at first we think the film will dramatize her moral and intellectual triumph in learning to see again. But unhappily Apted barely touches that theme and instead gives us a standard, rather sluggish thriller without much psychological depth, though it's still worth seeing for Stowe's intelligent, seductive performance.

We first see Emma on the bandstand as she plays the violin with a Chicago based traditional Irish band. She's rapt with the music, closed off, separated from the audience by her blindness and the inviolability of the stage. John Hallstrom (Aidan Quinn), a cop out with his drinking buddies, tries to breach that distance by performing a drunken, vulgar strip tease in front of the stage, but of course the blind Emma doesn't respond. Once Emma gets a transplant and becomes the only witness who can identify the killer of her upstairs neighbor, she and Hallstrom begin a contentious, on again, off again romance as he protects her from the stalking killer. The rest of the movie has all the familiar trappings of this kind of thriller: ritual murders, chases through a subway and a parking garage, and a psychotic killer whose motivation is more preposterous than usual. But the movie is really about bringing Emma/Stowe closer to us as it enters her charmed circle and humanizes the remote goddess without divesting her of aura and radiance.

Madeleine Stowe has been in several movies—most notably *The Last of the Mohicans* and *Short Cuts*—but it's only with this low grade thriller that she emerges as a star. As Emma she's both a virginal Renaissance princess locked in a tower—Chicago's Flatiron Building—and a tough, bawdy working class woman who knows how to take care of herself. In a film that's at least nominally about a woman learning to see, Apted celebrates what feminists have called the male gaze—his camera unabashedly revels in Stowe's hugely photogenic beauty.

As Hallstrom, Aidan Quinn is miscast and hobbled by a cliché ridden script. Hallstrom is a standard issue tough talking womanizer determined not to get involved in a serious relationship, but his resistance to the radiant Emma strikes us as blind and foolish—he's the one who has to learn to see. In the movie's most effective scene, Emma tells him—when he thinks she's interested in another man—that her eyes are filled with him, and Stowe with her serious, clairvoyantly blue eyes captures a deeply romantic feeling, while Quinn is just boyishly avid.

As Robert Mitchum once said about Steve McQueen, Michael Apted, a British director perhaps best known for his series of documentaries beginning with *7 Up*, doesn't bring much to the party. Outside of a few evocatively noirish shots of Chicago, his direction follows well trodden paths and depends too much on electronic gimmickry with shots from Emma's point of view of shape shifting forms in a visual miasma. But at those moments when he's in touch with Stowe's special poise and charisma, he really does make us see—it's too bad that such privileged moments tend to get lost in the banalities of the movie's plot.

LOS ANGELES TIMES, 1/26/94, Calendar/p. 4, Peter Rainer

The scenario for "Blink" is so convoluted that even Hitchcock might have gotten tangled up in it.

Emma Brody (Madeleine Stowe) is a country-rock musician, a violinist, who lost her sight as a child when her mother rammed her head into a mirror. A corneal transplant operation has restored Emma's sight—sort of. She sees things as a blur and, in some cases, she retains images that only become clear a day or two later. (Her optometrist calls this phenomenon "ocular flashback.") When she responds to a scuffle in her apartment one night, the next day offers up the image of the murderer.

But will the cops believe her as an eyewitness?

Full of severe shadows and jagged shock effects, "Blink" is compelling without, being very pleasurable. It has an acrid, cruel undercurrent that disguises an essential hollowness. (The Faye Dunaway-Tommy Lee Jones shocker "Eyes of Laura Mars," which influenced "Blink," was much stronger.)

Without the visual trickeries of director Michael Apted, "Blink" might just seem like a muddled thriller. It sort of seems that way anyway, but it does have at least one thing to recommend it: Madeleine Stowe's performance.

Stowe has been cast primarily for her extraordinary beauty in films like "Revenge," "Unlawful Entry" and "The Last of the Mohicans" but, as she demonstrated in Robert Altman's "Short Cuts." she's also an extraordinary actress. The shorn lyricism of her beauty in "Blink" gives her a scary frailty; she's entirely convincing as a woman whose damaged eyes are her only way into the world. Stowe doesn't play Emma as a forlorn helpless maiden though; there's a frazzled gutsiness in the way she maneuvers against the serial killer who stalks her.

As the detective in charge of tracking down the killer, Aidan Quinn seems to be posturing for another movie altogether—a more enjoyable one. He's always fun to watch but he doesn't connect with Stowe's hyperventilating vim; their romance seems scripted rather than felt. He acts like he's prepping to star in a TV cop series. ("Columbo's Nephew," maybe?)

"Blink," which was scripted by Dana Stevens, does keep you guessing about the killer's identity. That's not intended as compliment, exactly. The guessing is just a way for us to stay in the movie. If you don't bother to sort out the clues and red herrings, what reason is there to stay put?

NEW YORK, 1/31/94, p. 64, John Powers

Ever since Charlie Chaplin exalted the poor flower girl in *City Lights*, Hollywood has had a thing for beautiful blind women, believing that their vulnerability makes them all the more alluringly feminine. For its first half-hour, the new thriller *Blink* has some good, trashy fun standing this cliché on its head. Its heroine, Emma Brody, a blind violinist for a Chicago bar band, doesn't merely talk as tough and dirty as a man—she acts that way, too. After getting corneal transplants, she sees a serial killer fleeing a murder and must convince the skeptical cops that despite her hallucinations and still-spotty vision, she's the witness they need to solve the crime.

Hot-blooded and fidgety, Emma initially seems to be a plum role for Madeleine Stowe, the ambitious young actress who is turning out to be the closest thing Hollywood has to a brunette Michelle Pfeiffer. Although Stowe's magnetism is sparked by the gap between her delicate, winsome beauty and her prickly intelligence—L.A. novelist Steve Erickson calls her "the thinking man's sex symbol"—many of her directors haven't seen beyond her looks. There was always a whiff of aggravation to her work in movies like *Revenge* or *Unlawful Entry*, her lips pulling down irritably as if she couldn't believe that an actress so exquisitely sharp was being asked to play the trophy in a duel between pugs like Kurt Russell and Ray Liotta. All that pent-up anger found a stunning release in *Short Cuts*, where, as Tim Robbins's much cheated-on wife, she was a classic study in rue and bitchy laughter—the angriest doe in the world. Wavy tresses flowing and cheeks flushed with desire, Stowe starts out wonderfully in *Blink*, barking at the cops and making randy jokes with her girlfriend, even as she fights the temptation to retreat into the familiar safety of blindness.

Stowe's edgy glamour carries the opening scenes, but director Michael Apted, who started out making documentaries for English TV, including the *7 Up* series, is much too square to find the irresponsible fun in a formula thriller; he likes his comic books down-to-earth. Here, he has Aidan Quinn play Chicago cop John Hallstrom as a crass, arrogant jerk in the Bobby Knight vein: His idea of wit is to moon a whole barroom. Now, it's intriguing to have a handsome leading man who's so convincingly charmless—intriguing, but disastrous when you realize that Emma's supposed to find him winning. Your heart sinks when she provokes him into one of those glossy, passionless, bare-breasts-and-buns love scenes that don't even have the conviction to be pornographic. Orson Welles once remarked that there were two things he couldn't believe in the movies: people making love and people praying. Watching Stowe and Quinn roll around, I didn't believe they were making love, but you may well believe they're praying for this embarrassing scene to end.

Once Emma and the cop start coupling, there's nothing left to *Blink* but stale formula. Apted directs the action like a deli owner scraping mold from a cheese, and Stowe is again devoured by an ill-written role. To keep the plot going, Emma must suddenly start behaving as idiotically as the doomed-to-die high-school slut in a *Friday the 13th* picture. If you were half-blind and being stalked by a serial killer, would you sneak off from your police bodyguard to go fight with your boyfriend? Only if a script made you. This one does, tossing away everything fresh in its idea for the sake of a climax filched from a hundred other thrillers. I'm told that preview audiences cheer when the psycho killer gets it, but I can't imagine that even those who bay like hounds really think the movie's any good. *Blink* starts out subverting one of the hoariest Hollywood clichés and winds up reinforcing the newest: Putting the pistol in the woman's hand has become Hollywood's idea of feminism.

NEW YORK POST, 1/26/94, p. 35, Michael Medved

"Blink" offers a dazzling demonstration of the way sheer star power can transform even the most shopworn material.

Madeleine Stowe and Aidan Quinn are such charismatic leads, and they generate so many sparks in their memorable scenes together, that they manage to redeem two of the dumbest plot devices in the book: hard-boiled cop falling in love with his only witness, and blind girl in jeopardy.

Stowe plays the vision-impaired heroine, but her situation contains a surprising twist: Near the beginning of the film her character undergoes corneal transplant surgery which helps to restore her sight.

Nevertheless, her vision remains so blurry and uncertain that she can provide the police with little help when it comes to identifying the suspect she saw leaving her Chicago apartment building after the brutal murder of her upstairs neighbor.

To make her experience even more confusing, she suffers from an aftereffect of her surgery known as "retroactive vision," in which her mind doesn't register key images she sees until a day later.

Skeptical doctors may scoff at this notion, but first-time screen writer Dana Stevens insists that she found references to the phenomenon in the medical literature, and what's more important is that the movie makes you believe it.

Director Michael Apted deploys some artful special effects to render the main character's point of view and Stowe's performance is so fierce and so fine that you can't help feel both convinced and captivated by every move she makes.

In each of her previous starring roles ("Stakeout," "Revenge," "Closet Land" "The Last of the Mohicans," and "Unlawful Entry") Stowe has played some variety of damsel-in-distress—a hapless victim alternately menaced and rescued by powerful men around her.

In "Blink," for the first time, she plays a tough independent, tart-tongued, immensely capable woman who refuses to become an object of pity, even when she is blind. Her character, Emma is a fiddler with a struggling Irish folk band (Played by the sensational real-life ensemble, the Drovers) and even her violin playing looks just right.

This strong role suits Stowe far better than any of the parts she's had before (with the possible exception of her brief but breathless turn in "Short Cuts") and if there are any male moviegoers who haven't yet fallen in love with this stunning beauty, "Blink" is the movie that should do the trick.

British director Apted has always done his best work with movies centered on powerful women ("Coal Miner's Daughter," "Gorillas in the Mist") but he also gives his due to Aidan Quinn as the arrogant cop who needs Emma to crack his case.

The part is nicely written: He's a brooding detective with a wild sense of humor who listens to Vivaldi as well as Pearl Jam; he memorizes poetry but would never confess it to his hard-drinking macho buddies. Quinn does a marvelous job with both his character's superficial swagger and his underlying vulnerability, and that combination helps to create rare electricity in his intimate scenes with his co-star.

As the murder mystery unfolds, it provides a few shocks and a conclusion that follows its own bizarre logic; this is one thriller that manages to avoid an "Aw, c'mon!" climax that strains all credibility.

James Remar (as Quinn's partner) and Laurie Metcalf (as Stowe's best friend from the band) are top-flight in supporting roles, but it's the lavishly romantic relationship between the two stars that gives the audience its money's worth.

NEWSDAY, 1/26/94, Part II/p. 59, Jack Mathews

Subscriptions to medical journals and access to the psychology stacks of libraries ought to be denied to Hollywood screenwriters. Just look at the mischief they've done with reports on multiple personality disorder, amnesia and post traumatic stress syndrome.

Or take the case of "Blink," a wildly improbable suspense thriller that grew from a tiny seed planted in the mind of screenwriter Dana Stevens. While researching the literature on recovered eyesight, Stevens found that in rare instances, people who have their vision restored after long periods of blindness experience a delay between the moment they look at something and when their mind actually registers it.

Stevens called this phenomenon "retroactive hallucination," and for Michael Apted's "Blink," gave a case of it to Emma Brody (Madeleine Stowe), a saucy Chicago folk musician who, soon after having a double-corneal transplant, gets a good look at the man who just murdered her upstairs neighbor, goes back to bed, then wakes up in the morning and ... sees him!

The local homicide detectives, a pair of apparent screw-ups named Hallstrom (Aidan Quinn) and Ridgely (James Remar), don't take Emma very seriously, until they find themselves in her building later that day, examining her neighbor's murdered body.

From that moment on, "Blink" follows the formula of "Wait Until Dark," "Jennifer 8" and every other suspense thriller in which a single woman, blind or in some other way handicapped, is being stalked by a madman, from whom she is sure to be rescued before the final credits by the cop she loves.

Beyond its gimmick about retroactive vision, which evolves into something closer to psychic phenomena, Stevens' script is a compendium of genre clichés and red herrings, and if the ending isn't exactly expected, neither is it very satisfying.

Despite all that, there is something stubbornly compelling about "Blink," this idea of someone walking through life with an entirely different sense of perception. The devices Apted and cinematographer Dante Spinotti came up with to show us Emma's distorted vision give it a cheap horror film look, as if we're seeing through the eyes of a fly, but we identify with her circumstances nonetheless.

There is also something very appealing about the match-up of Stowe, a strong actress playing Emma as anything but a helpless victim, and Quinn, who turns what might have been a caricature of a film noir cop into someone charmingly ambivalent. Speaking of time warps, they are a '90s couple trapped in a '40s potboiler.

Stowe has been down this road before, as a suburban woman pursued by an obsessive cop in "Unlawful Entry," but like Quinn, director Apted ("Coal Miner's Daughter") is trying his hand at suspense for the first time. He managed a couple of genuine scary moments in the early going, but he was much more successful developing the relationship between Hallstrom and Emma, and in building sexual tension between them.

Fortunately, for them, for us, and for the movie, they get it worked out.

NEWSWEEK, 1/31/94, p. 58, David Ansen

The bargain you make with a thriller is simple. If it succeeds in scaring you, you're willing to forgive a whole lot of hokum. If the claptrap quotient gets too high, however, the goose bumps won't blossom. Michael Apted's "Blink" walks a fine line, but if you're willing to accept it on its frankly formulaic terms, it delivers some good jolts.

Madeleine Stowe stars as a '90s-style damsel in distress. Her character, Emma Brody, plays the fiddle in the Chicago Irish band The Drovers. She's strong, foul-mouthed, gorgeous and sexy. She is also blind, but about to get a corneal transplant which will allow her to see for the first time since she was blinded at the age of 8 by her violent mother. Just her Irish luck, her upstairs neighbor is soon after murdered by a necrophiliac serial killer, and Emma witnesses the killer in the hallway. Sort of. Because of her unreliable new eyesight, she's subject to "retroactive vision": it isn't until the next day that she actually sees the image in front of her the night before. This poses an obvious problem for the detective on the case (Aidan Quinn), who can't be sure his witness isn't hallucinating. He believes her—because he's falling in love with her—but his hardheaded colleagues are predictably contemptuous of Emma's tale.

Dana Stevens's screenplay has both clever turns and creaky contrivances. The banter ranges from the witty to the unconvincingly hard-nosed. When these two good-looking lovers quarrel, their fights seem dictated by a screenwriting textbook demanding conflict, not by any inner necessity. In spite of all this, "Blink's" central conceit (it's a vision thing) provides a good opportunity for Apted to show his finesse as a suspense director. Working with cinematographer Dante Spinotti, he contrives some creepily effective point-of-view distortions to hurl us into the disoriented perspective of his heroine. (For real insight into the perils of regaining vision, read Dr. Oliver Sacks.) "Blink" has another big asset in the formidable Stowe, a wonderfully sensual performer who gets to cook on all burners in this tough-cookie role. She and Quinn are a mighty hot couple. But the secret ingredient of this adrenaline-pumper is the sound mix, supervised by Chris Newman, who also happened to work on "The Exorcist." "The French Connection" and "The Silence of the Lambs," tense movies all. We're rarely conscious of it, but what really frightens us in movies is often not what we see but what we hear. Not the guy with the knife but the man at the dials, splicing in an electronic "boo!"

SIGHT AND SOUND, 6/94, p. 42, Leslie Felperin Sharman

Emma Brody, blind ever since she was attacked by her mother as a child, is a violinist with a band called The Drovers. When a pair of suitable corneas from an organ donor becomes available, she has her sight restored. At first, not only is her sight cloudy, but she also suffers from 'retroactive vision', a kind of visual echo, whereby she 'sees' things only a day or two after first perceiving them.

One night, when Emma is getting drunk alone in her apartment, the young woman upstairs is murdered. Emma sees the murderer descending the stairs but, because of her poor vision, mistakes him for the building's janitor. The next day she has a 'retroactive vision' of the murderer's face. She tries to report the incident to the police, who have been investigating a serial killer who leaves distinctive clues, but Detective John Hallstrom is sceptical of Emma's story. When they find the body, he believes her, but Emma is unable to identify the mug shots because of her poor sight. The murderer stalks Emma, and hits and injures her dog with a car. Hallstrom has Emma placed under police protection. Gradually, he and Emma become romantically involved.

Soon another murder takes place. The only traceable clue which unites all the victims is the fact that each received organs from a dead girl in transplant operations before being killed. The killer is a hospital orderly who knew the dead donor; because of a mistaken address the murderer killed the girl upstairs instead of Emma. He lures Emma to an abandoned garage. In the struggle in the dark, Emma manages to shoot and kill her attacker. At the end, Emma, Hallstrom and her dog are all reunited.

Like the organs of the dissected corpse that is the main mechanism of its plot, the donated elements from other films have been grafted into the body of *Blink*. Most of its vitals have been transplanted from good stock, such as *The Silence of the Lambs* (serial killer, climactic scramble-in-the-dark scene) and *Wait Until Dark* (visually-impaired waify heroine). The combination of the victim-cop love affair and weird optical visions recalls the ultra-silly Faye Dunaway and Tommy Lee Jones film, *The Eyes of Laura Mars*. The morphing of a killer's face into that of the policeman-lover's even hints that the latter might be the real murderer, as in the climactic denouement of *Laura Mars*. But *Blink* is not even that interesting, just a plodding reworking of the bog-standard rhythms of menace, chase, escape, menace, sex, chase, escape, cycled over and over, assembled from a generic donor bank of thriller tropes. Its only missing organ is a brain.

Ever since *Peeping Tom*, thrillers have often gleefully dwelt on the sadistic side of scopophilia. Paralleling the omniscient viewpoint of the camera or the audience, the killer always has the best views. Victims are punished for their inability to see, sometimes literally as in the case of *Wait Until Dark*. By this token, blind or sight-impaired characters make the best victims in movies. It is as if, in some twisted pseudo-Freudian way, they are being punished for their inability to appreciate films fully.

Bang on genre convention, *Blink* plumbs all the depths of these metaphoric permutations on primal scene anxiety. By focalizing through Emma's distorted vision, *Blink* might be seen as an attempt to restore the balance of viewpoints, even though she is to some extent punished by the film for 'daring to look'. Psychoanalytic readings such as this are positively invited by the film, which helpfully supplies a *Marnie*-ish flashback to Emma's childhood when she was blinded by her mother for wearing make-up. Later on, the moment when, at Hallstrom's insistence, she keeps her eyes open when they make love symbolises her acceptance of the visual economy and transition to sexual and emotional maturity. On the other hand, it might be a pathetic attempt at 'sensitivity' in an otherwise typically lecherous sex scene.

To render the blurry harsh world Emma sees, cinematographer Dante Spinotti and special effects expert Art Durinski use a combination of special lenses, filters and computer imaging. The effect is mildly interesting, like a demonstration at an electronics trade show. More than anything else, 'Emmavision' is reminiscent of the images generated by the device in Wenders' *Until the End of the World* that could record visual perceptions for the blind. Like the Jeanne Moreau character in that film, who dies of despair after finally seeing the world, Emma, surrounded by a grey, seedy-looking Chicago, is unsurprisingly saddened by the gift of sight. The best a friend can offer her after she asks to see something beautiful is Michael Jordan playing basketball—admittedly a thing of beauty, but hardly compensation for years of blindness.

Overall, *Blink* is so numbingly banal and predictable it might as well have been called *Wink*, of which you need 40 to get through it. Even Madeleine Stowe and Aidan Quinn as the leads seem to be sleepwalking, exchanging gestures of tough vulnerability and vulnerable toughness respectively.

Director Michael Apted sloshes it all together with perfunctory anonymity, halfheartedly tossing in the obligatory nods to Hitchcock and Powell. The diegetic soundtrack, by the frighteningly 'real' band The Drovers, is a twee sub-Levellers folk-pop which spoils the pleasure of pretending you are blind for the film's entirety.

TIME, 1/24/94, p. 64, Richard Schickel

The suspense is not as tightly wound as it might be. The mystery is not as deep or, when unraveled, as stunning as it could be. The detective (Aidan Quinn) is a little more crudely macho than he needs to be.

But all that is unimportant, for *Blink* has two terrific things going for it. One is director Michael Apted's gritty use of Chicago as a setting. He makes you feel the wind in your bones, and he puts its blue-collar toughness in your face all the time. The other is Madeleine Stowe.

Her intensity was visible but somewhat shaded in *Short Cuts* and *The Last of the Mohicans*. In *Blink* she lets it rip. Emma Brody, blinded in early childhood, plays the violin in an Irish rock band, and onstage she looks ethereal. Offstage her anger is like an exposed nail; it catches and tears at everyone who brushes against it. As the result of an operation, Emma begins to recover her sight, and curiously that renders her vulnerable. A world of blurs and shadows is scarier to her than the darkness she has known. One of these developing shadows, as it happens, is that of the man who murdered her upstairs neighbor. This means, of course, that he is going to stalk her.

She covers her fear with ferocity and blistering outrage at the ineptitude of the cops on the case. When she becomes romantically involved with Quinn, their love scenes have the scratch-and-bite fury that people generate when they are not at all sure they're doing the right thing. Whatever she's doing, however, Stowe transforms an ordinary sort of movie into something extraordinary.

VILLAGE VOICE, 2/1/94, p. 51, J. Hoberman

In its way, Michael Apted's *Blink* offers an alternative history of the movies. The film's protagonist (Madeleine Stowe) is a blind woman who gets corneal transplant surgery and gradually regains her sight. What she sees is first represented as prismatic white light and unfocused smears, later as a haze of warped street scenes and astigmatic faces. Quickly losing its visual innocence, however, *Blink* devolves from a Stan Brakhage movie into a woman-in-danger thriller. The payoff is Stowe's hot romance with a charming, if diffident, police detective (Aidan Quinn).

Similarly, the introduction of a serial killer (however uniquely motivated) serves to banalize Dana Stevens's script, which, initially at least, suggests a '40s experimental psychodrama with a sordid, neurotic edge. The heroine was blinded as a child when her mother smashed her face into a mirror, and although she recovers her sight, she still lacks self-image. Unhappy with her reflection (despite its resemblance to Madeleine Stowe), she's convinced that she looks like her mother, telling the detective (an unsatisfactory stand-in for a shrink) that "the last time I looked, I was a little girl."

Thus, *Blink* quickly normalizes itself although, sumptuously shot by Dante Spinotti in a series of desolate neighborhoods, it offers a dankly glamorous vision of Chicago. The special effects were designed by computer animator Art Durinski, the impersonal direction might have been designed by one of his computers.

Also reviewed in:
NEW YORK TIMES, 1/26/94, p. C15, Janet Maslin
NEW YORKER, 2/14/95, p. 95, Anthony Lane
VARIETY, 1/17-23/93, p. 104, Leonard Klady
WASHINGTON POST, 1/26/94, p. D1, Rita Kempley
WASHINGTON POST, 1/28/94, Weekend/p. 38, Desson Howe

BLOWN AWAY

A Metro-Goldwyn-Mayer release of a Trilogy Entertainment Group production. *Executive Producer:* Lloyd Segan. *Producer:* John Watson, Richard Lewis, and Pen Densham. *Director:* Stephen Hopkins. *Screenplay:* Joe Batteer and John Rice. *Story:* John Rice, Joe Batteer, and M. Jay Roach. *Director of Photography:* Peter Levy. *Editor:* Timothy Wellburn. *Music:* Alan Silvestri. *Music Editor:* Ken Karmen. *Choreographer:* Liam Harney. *Sound:* Thomas Causey and (music) Dennis Sands. *Sound Editor:* Bob Newlan. *Casting:* Michael Fenton and Allison Cowitt. *Production Designer:* John Graysmark. *Art Director:* Steve Cooper and Lawrence A. Hubbs. *Set Designer:* Robert Fechtman. *Set Decorator:* Peg Cummings. *Set Dresser:* Melissa Levander. *Special Effects:* William D. Harrison. *Costumes:* Joe I. Tompkins. *Make-up:* Edouard Henriques. *Stunt Coordinator:* Vince Deadrick, Jr. *Running time:* 120 minutes. *MPAA Rating:* R.

CAST: Jeff Bridges (Jimmy Dove); Tommy Lee Jones (Ryan Gaerity); Suzy Amis (Kate); Lloyd Bridges (Max); Forest Whitaker (AnthonyFranklin); Stephi Lineburg (Lizzy); John Finn (Captain Roarke); Caitlin Clarke (Rita); Chris De Oni (Cortez); Loyd Catlett (Bama); Ruben Santiago-Hudson (Blanket); Lucinda Weist (Nancy); Brenda Burns (Kevin); Patricia A. Heine (Connie); Josh McLaglen (Prison Guard #1); Ken Kerman (Prison Guard #2); David Hodges (Prisoner); Robert "Bobby Z" Zajonc (Helicopter Pilot #1); Alan Purwin (Helicopter Pilot #2); David Nowel (Helicopter News Cameraman); Dee Nelson (Mother); Judd Daniel King (Justin); Chris O'Neil (Boyle); Whitney Cline (Babysitter); Michael Macklin (TV Reporter #1); Sara Edwards (TV Reporter #2); Evelyn Lee-Jones (Gospel Singer); Mark Berry (Motorcycle Cop); Faleena Hopkins (Irish Girl).

FILMS IN REVIEW, 9-10/94, p. 58, Andy Pawelczak

The makers of *Blown Away*, a mechanical pastiche of summer thrillers past and present, must have felt they needed to jump-start their movie with a little nitroglycerine. In the movie's first five minutes, Tommy Lee Jones, decked out in what looks like Halloween makeup with shoulder length hair, blasts his way out of a Northern Ireland prison and escapes to Boston. After this there are some bigger and better explosions, but in between the pyrotechnics there's nothing much to occupy your time except a pallid domestic drama and some stenographic gestures towards the interracial cop buddy movie.

Jones is Ryan Gaerity, a mad bomber loosely associated with the IRA. In Boston, he plots vengeance on an old comrade who betrayed him and now works as a cop on the bomb disposal unit, Jimmy Dove (Jeff Bridges) learned everything he knows about bombs from Gaerity—who is his demonic alter ego, get it?—and now pursues his dangerous vocation as a form of penance for the past. Jimmy does a lot of agonizing as Gaerity picks off his colleagues in the bomb disposal unit and threatens his wife and daughter. In one of the movie's big set pieces, we're led to believe that Gaerity has planted a bomb somewhere in Jimmy's house. As Jimmy's daughter turns on the stove, the camera goes inside for a close-up of the flame going whoosh. Does the bomb go off? I'll leave it to those who are interested to find out. At any rate, the filmmakers, knowing a good thing when they see one, repeat the whole idea of common household appliances as infernal devices a short while later, this time with Jimmy's partner Anthony (Forest Whitaker as the victim.

As Jimmy, Jeff Bridges, a very good actor who made being down look good in *The Fabulous Baker Boys*, is marooned with such lines as, "How can I fight him if I can't find him?" Jones doesn't fare much better as he blathers on about the country of chaos and the government of anarchy, but at least he gets the chance to mug wildly and gyrate to U2 singing "With Or Without You," a great song that, even in this context, was a pleasure to hear. Jones is supposed to be some kind of wacko mystic obsessed with the martyred St. Sebastian and the big bang theory of the origin of the universe, but he comes across as an eyeball rolling, ham villain in a nineteenth century melodrama. Forest Whitaker indulges in such an assortment of distracting tics and mannerisms that you're never quite sure what he's supposed to be.

Stephen Hopkins' direction doesn't bring any elan or style to the tired plot and empty, clichéd characterizations. Even on a sultry summer day when I would have been grateful for the most minimal escapist entertainment, I just sat there and wondered at the conspicuous waste of talent and blown up cars and trucks. This is the way the world ends, not with a bang, but a whimper.

LOS ANGELES TIMES, 7/1/94, Calendar/p. 1, Peter Rainer

Babies are often content to be entertained by things that go boom. Adults may require a bit more with their boom—like a story that makes a smidgen of sense, characters that we can connect with, a few good jokes maybe, a few thrills.

"Blown Away" is graced with none of these attributes. It's a baby-go-boom movie with an attitude. Jeff Bridges plays Jimmy Dove, the star of Boston's Bomb Squad, who, 20 years before when his name was Liam, fled the Irish Republican Army after sabotaging an explosion that would have killed innocent bystanders. Now the mastermind of that thwarted attack, Tommy Lee Jones' Ryan Gaerity, has broken out of a Northern Ireland prison and set his sights on dismembering Liam/Jimmy—but not before systematically exploding his Bomb Squad buddies and violinist girlfriend (Suzy Amis) and her daughter.

It makes sense that a movie with this many explosions would be stylistically over the top. Everyone in it seems pitched for destruction; even a child's back-yard birthday party is turned into a hyperkinetic frenzy, just to get our juices flowing. The action, and the acting, are so hyperbolic and overscaled that at times "Blown Away" seems on the verge of becoming an opera—not an opera anybody would want to watch.

There's so much talent connected with this film—from the cast, which also includes Forest Whitaker and Lloyd Bridges, to director Stephen Hopkins—that its bludgeoning badness is like a sick joke. "Blown Away" is a lesson in how a movie cooked up with sure-fire commercial elements can self-destruct as messily as one of Gaerity's bombs. The reason it's so rank is because it exists only to make lucre and kaboom. And although movie audiences seem more than willing to turn terrible movies into hits, the arrant cynicism of "Blown Away" will probably turn off far more people than it turns on.

Besides, there's a much better film out there right now that manages to do most of what "Blown Away" attempts—"Speed." That movie isn't much more than a whiz-bang mechanical job laced with outlandish heroics, but it has an awareness of its own preposterousness that makes it fun to watch, and its heroes are winning—superhuman ordinary people.

But in "Blown Away," Jimmy Dove is such a high-tension-wire jitterbug and Gaerity such a Gaelic meanie that they seem to be competing for this year's Most Implausible Character award. (When he isn't singing "Pop Goes the Weasel," Gaerity is grooving to tapes of the Irish rock group U2.)

Bridges and Jones flail about in a purgatory of bad acting, which is particularly upsetting since they're two of the best actors in the business. They're probably much worse in these roles than routine actors would be because they're reaching for something raw. Couldn't they see how overcooked their roles already were? On the undercooked side, you've got one of the screen's finest actresses, Suzy Amis, loitering in one of those Jimmy-I-Don't-Even-Know-Who-You-Are-Anymore roles and then there's Lloyd Bridges brogueing about like a superannuated leprechaun.

Since Jimmy learned his bomb expertise from Gaerity, we look forward to a game of wits between these two. But the screenwriters, Joe Batteer and John Rice, must think we'll be bored with all that cat-and-mouse business. As the film lurches along from explosion to explosion, there's less of the entertaining Should-I-Cut-the-Red-Wire-or-the-White-Wire stuff and more yelling and throttling. The work of a modern-day bomb squad in the era of micro-technology is a terrific movie subject. It deserves more than the firestorms of "Blown Away."

Here's something more punishing to contemplate than anything in the movie. What if some malevolent theater owner decides to double-bill "Blown Away" with "Backdraft"?

NEW YORK, 7/18/94, p. 51, David Denby

In *Blown Away*, which has something to do with Ireland, Boston, and bombs, the men all talk with harsh, grinding voices, as if Irishness were an affliction of the larynx. The men also roar and grab at one another, and there's much barging and lunging and many scenes of anguish. Jeff

Bridges, in a rare terrible performance, screws up his face into a mask of torment and, at one point, shoots a revolver into a hot tub. Director Stephen Hopkins seems to be a bit of a hysteric. Hopkins can't stage anything clearly, and he throws the dialogue, including crucial bits of exposition, into the corners of the scenes, as if he were trying to lose it. Myself, I lost the struggle just to see and hear the movie: The generally greenish-brown color scheme, the muck and clutter, may be right for a story about obscure hatreds and unfathomable fanaticisms, but still, *Blown Away* is remarkably ugly to look at. Even Tommy Lee Jones looks foolish—as the madman, he talks in funny voices and wears more hats and masks than Jim Carrey.

NEW YORK POST, 7/1/94, p. 43, Michael Medved

The biggest problem with "Blown Away" is that it simply can't get up to "Speed."

This ambitious thriller arrives in theaters just one month after the debut of the most popular action film so far this summer, and the similarities between the two projects are too obvious to ignore.

Once again, a mad bomber is on the loose, battling a soft-spoken, fearless cop. There's even a chase scene near the climax of "Blown Away" in which a which a car's been rigged with bombs set to go off the moment the driver touches the brake, so the vehicle careens wildly through the streets of Boston.

Like everything else in the picture, the sequence is well-staged and beautifully shot. So why does the movie fail to generate the thrills you get from similar situations in "Speed"?

The answer is that the tone here is all wrong: "Blown Away" takes itself much too seriously. Rather than a straight-ahead, unpretentious, edge-of-your-seat dazzler, this is a somber, ham-handed melodrama with incoherent political overtones.

Jeff Bridges plays the ace of the Boston bomb squad, who marries Suzy Amis and agrees to her pleas to leave his dangerous line of work and to accept a more routine police assignment.

Before he can settle into that peaceful life, however, a master terrorist (Tommy Lee Jones) literally blasts his way out of prison in Northern Ireland and makes his way to Massachusetts.

It turns out that Bridges has been harboring dark secrets about his past, and that he'd known this evil killer in a well-concealed previous life.

Now Jones has his black heart set on revenge and he begins planting diabolically deadly bombs near all the people who mean most to Bridges—including a salt-of-the-earth former cop (played with admirable gusto by Lloyd Bridges, the star's real-life father) and the hero's cool, arrogant new partner (Forest Whitaker).

Watching Jeff Bridges patiently and meticulously defuse intricate explosives is at first utterly absorbing, but the pattern is repeated so often that it becomes dull and predictable.

Even more annoying is the alternate routine in which Bridges fails to reach a bomb in time to prevent its explosion. This movie seems uncomfortably crammed with scenes in which the hero hollers out "Noooooo!!!" in slow motion agony while one or another of his friends or relatives is obliterated in an impressive-looking fireball.

Normally, one of the most reliable and versatile of all motion picture performers, Jeff Bridges is clearly off his game with this woozy, furrowed-brow performance that does nothing to make his character's double-identity comprehensive or believable.

Tommy Lee Jones fares better. As usual, the psychotic villain can let himself go and overact with impunity.

Australian director Stephen Hopkins has a penchant for imposing dark, brooding atmosphere on his slick action scenes, as previously demonstrated in "Judgment Night" and "Predator 2." But in this movie, the air of grim foreboding seems painfully overdone.

The movie is still too solid and professional to qualify as an out-and-out bomb. But in view of the acting talent involved, "Blown Away" does constitute a blown opportunity.

NEWSDAY, 7/1/94, Part II/p. B3, Jack Mathews

Apropos its Fourth of July weekend opening, there are bombs going off throughout Stephen Hopkins' "Blown Away," a deliriously noisy action thriller about a mad bomber loose in Boston. But the movie itself doesn't explode until the relatively quiet scene where Jeff Bridges' legendary bomb squad expert Jimmy Dove tries to explain to his wife who the killer is and what he wants.

Seems that Jimmy and Tommy Lee Jones' Ryan Gaerity were subversives together back in Ireland 20 years earlier, and that Jimmy, in fact, had learned the bomb business from Gaerity before realizing, duh, that innocent people can get hurt in explosions, and that Jimmy did something that sent him off to find a new identity in the United States and Gaerity off to stew in an Irish prison.

Now, Gaerity is out, he's in Boston, he's mad, and he intends to blow away everybody and everything Jimmy holds dear, including his cocky bomb squad buddy Anthony (Forest Whitaker), his feisty dad (Lloyd Bridges), his new wife (Suzy Amis) and her daughter.

The soulful bluntness with which Jeff Bridges delivers this ludicrous speech, and the dumbfounded look on Amis' face, are priceless, and it's hard to take anything about the story seriously afterward.

For Jeff Bridges, "Blown Away" may have seemed like an opportunity for that mainstream hit that has always eluded him. But he is not, essentially, a physical actor, and in trying to make Jimmy more than he was written to be, he makes himself look silly. There's a scene where Jimmy is roused from a drunken stupor in a hot tub that is one of the worst bits of acting Jeff Bridges has done.

Keanu Reeves took the opposite tack in "Speed," the summer's other mad-bomber movie, and emptying his police hero of all psychological baggage at least allowed the film to play out as an action cartoon.

Tommy Lee Jones certainly didn't see Gaerity as anything other than a cartoon figure. The character is vaguely political and gleefully homicidal. In the opening scene, we find him reading next to the makeshift library in his cell and assume he is a thinking man's felon. But the next minute, he kills his cellmate, turns his porcelain toilet into a bomb and blows an escape route through the prison wall.

From then on, Jones' over-the-top performance makes Gaerity seem like a villain in a Batman movie, setting up bombs and cheerfully daring Jimmy to find and defuse them before they and the loved ones to whom they are attached go boom, which they occasionally do.

The real attractions in the film, of course, are the spectacular explosions, all set up and executed before multiple cameras in various blocked-off Boston locales, including the shoreline of the harbor and the familiar band shell where Kate plays violin with the Boston Pops.

As well staged as most of the explosions and action sequences are, the suspense actually decreases as the story wears on. Director Hopkins, whose only previous action film was the mindless "Predator 2," gets so cute with the red herrings, teasing us about when and in which household appliance bombs may be about to go off, that we quit playing the game. If these scenes are just there, like so many cats leaping out of the dark, they defuse themselves.

In the end, "Blown Away" is a spectacle no more frightening than the colorful fireworks about to light up over Boston and the rest of the United States. And many times less entertaining.

NEWSWEEK, 7/11/94, p. 50, Jack Kroll

If you liked the toilet-bomb scene in "Lethal Weapon 2," you'll love "Blown Away," in which explosives are planted in computers, stereo speakers, auto brakes, children's toys, boats and other beloved American artifacts. The mad bomber, Gaerity (Tommy Lee Jones), is an Irish terrorist who "can make a bomb out of Bisquick," quotes T. S. Eliot and aims to blow away Dove (Jeff Bridges), the star of the Boston Bomb Squad. Oscar winner Jones is a master wacko, and Bridges gives texture to a guy who has some bombs in his own belfry. But the stars of Stephen Hopkins's ("Predator 2") movie are those ticking, clicking, KA-POWING critters. This flick isn't dynamite, but it's no bomb.

SIGHT AND SOUND, 9/94, p. 38, Ben Thompson

Psychotic terrorist Ryan Gaerity escapes from prison in Northern Ireland and escapes to Boston. There he sees news on TV of the heroic exploits of city bomb disposal officer Jimmy Dove. Gaerity knows that Dove's real name is Liam McGinley; 20 years earlier McGinley was involved in Irish terrorist bombing, until his conscience caused him to bungle a mission, causing the death of his sweetheart, Gaerity's sister. Gaerity is bent on revenge; meanwhile Dove, increasingly disturbed by his memories, has decided to move from active duty to a teaching post, to marry his violinist girlfriend Kate and be a father to her child Lizzy.

Halfway through their wedding party, the bomb squad members present are called out to deal with an explosive device, which in a supposedly controlled detonation kills one of their number. Finding out that it had been planted with this purpose in mind, Dove wants to return to work until the bomber is found. Another bomb kills two more disposal experts, and in the midst of the carnage, Gaerity phones Dove from Kate's house. Dove rushes round to find his dog killed, and sends Kate and Lizzy into hiding on Cape Cod. He reveals the bomber's identity to his colleagues, but lies about how he knows. A bomb is planted in the stereo headphones of Anthony Franklin, Dove's bumptious replacement in the squad, but Dove manages to defuse it. Gaerity sends the squad a message hinting at Dove's secret, and Franklin begins to suspect.

Dove and Franklin are tracking Gaerity to his hideout on a derelict freighter, when Dove's uncle Max calls him from a pub, having used his Irish republican contacts to track down Gaerity. But Gaerity captures Max and wires him up to an explosive mechanism, which Max detonates himself, rather than have Dove risk his life trying to save him. Gaerity hunts down Dove's family to Cape Cod and plants a bomb in their jeep. Kate returns to find Dove in despair, and spurs him into action. He returns to Gaerity's hideout and struggles with him for control of the bomb in Kate's jeep, while she plays in an Independence Day concert. Franklin arrives in time to save Dove, and Gaerity is killed as the ship blows up. Dove rushes back to save Kate and Lizzy, and disarms the bomb in the speeding car. Franklin promises not to reveal the truth about his past if he will allow him to take the credit for foiling Gaerity.

The summer of 1994 will live long in the memory of all fans of the distinctive "the red wire... no, the blue wire" thrill of the Big Bomb movie. With the Keanu Reeves vehicle *Speed* revving up in the wings, this superficially very similar but actually very different film will whet the appetites of pyromaniacs and stress-fiends alike, as well as confounding anyone who ever doubted that international terrorism can be fun.

Blown Away is a bizarre mixture of laughable American-Irishisms, ham-fisted direction, bad clothes and unrepentant sadism, which after a dull start eventually becomes compulsively entertaining. The three-minute Bomb-Imminent tension-building period about a third of the way through, in which the camera sets up camp inside a succession of domestic appliances in order to mislead us that one of them contains a bomb, is one of the best of its kind in screen history.

Up to that point, the whole thing is rather disappointing. The totally excessive opening prison escape scene (does Northern Ireland's prison population really live in a cute big old castle?) sets an overwrought tone which the story and the dialogue take a while to live up to. Jeff Bridges' good guy—basically Mel Gibson in *Lethal Weapon* with a side order of Catholic guilt—is chronically underwritten, and Tommy Lee Jones as a demonic terrorist takes a while to warm to the job in hand ("I've come here to create a new country called chaos and a new government called anarchy"). But when he warms, he really warms. Not as natural as, say Dennis Hopper might have been, Jones nonetheless attains two or three moments of true greatness here: not least a virtuoso drunken bomb-making scene to the sound of U2's 'I Still Haven't Found What I'm Looking For'.

Among the supporting cast, a terrible 'top-o'-the-morning' turn by Jeff's dad Lloyd is out-faced by some great work from the perennially undervalued Forest Whitaker. Two scenes contend, however, for the film's real high point: the moment in Boston's genuine Irish bar where an order for Guinness is met with what look like two glasses of Safeways Beaujolais, and the following exchange between Jeff Bridges and his long-suffering wife—"Was it... the IRA?"—"No, he was too crazy for that."

VILLAGE VOICE, 7/12/94, p. 50, Amy Taubin

Everything that's right about *Speed* is wrong in *Blown Away*, the second major-studio, mad-bomber movie of the summer. *Blown Away*'s script is as sloppy as its images are muddy. The pyrotechnics—the picture's sole raison d'être—are stunningly inert. Every explosion is predictable; the resultant fires light up the screen long enough to demonstrate how totally under the control of the special effects department they are. *Blown Away* exploits the trouble in Ireland for a hackneyed plot device, wrapping it in crucifixion imagery and crummy liturgical-sounding music, as if pretense and cliché were the equivalent of meaning, politics, empathy. And it's a sin what it does to its actors: Jeff Bridges, Tommy Lee Jones, Suzy Amis, Forest Whitaker, all of whom turn in the worst performances of their careers. There are actors' directors and then there is Stephen (*Judgment Night*) Hopkins. Hopkins guides his performers straight into their weaknesses (for Bridges, it's his earnestness; for Jones, his cynicism) and leaves them there to twist in the wind.

Bridges plays Dove, a Boston bomb squad expert whose overdue retirement is short-circuited by the arrival of Gaerity (Jones), an Irish extremist who was "too crazy for the IRA" and who "can make bombs out of Bisquick." In the opening scene, Gaerity blasts his way out of an Irish prison with a device made of mattress stuffing and the fresh warm blood of his cellmate. Gaerity comes to Boston to take revenge on Dove by killing his nearests and dearests starting with his dog. It seems that Dove had once been a member of Gaerity's underground cell but had refused to go along with a plot to blow up a busy market square. As a result of his betrayal, the other members of the cell are killed and Gaerity is sent up for life. Dove escapes to America where he takes on a new identity and joins the bomb squad to expiate his sins. Whenever he dismantles a bomb he sees black-and-white flashback images of his former comrades' scattered body parts.

One wonders at what point in production did Bridges, a giant among American film actors, realize he was in trouble. Perhaps as early as his restaurant tête-à-tête with Amis where he seems to be trying to swallow his words along with his pasta. "You think you know me but you don't," he chides between chews, and then slips an engagement ring on her finger. Amis has little to do except look nervous and gullible enough to be taken in by Gaerity's charming eccentricities. One also wonders when the powers behind this debacle realized that they had been preempted by *Speed*. "Whatever you do, don't put your foot on the brake," yells Bridges to Amis as he leaps from his racing motorcycle onto the roof of her booby-trapped car. How's that for déjà vu? But it's not because *Speed* was first out of the gate that it wins by a mile. It's because Jan De Bont's inspired vehicle for a common L.A. bus has everything *Blown Away* lacks: style, formal smarts, a stout heart, a witty millennial metaphor, and enormous pleasure in the ride.

Also reviewed in:
CHICAGO TRIBUNE, 7/1/94, Friday/p. C, Michael Wilmington
NATION, 7/25-8/1/94, p. 139, Stuart Klawans
NEW YORK TIMES, 7/1/94, p. C3, Caryn James
VARIETY, 6/27-7/3/94, p. 85, Leonard Klady
WASHINGTON POST, 7/1/94, p. D6, Hal Hinson
WASHINGTON POST, 7/1/94, Weekend/p. 34, Desson Howe

BLUE CHIPS

A Paramount Pictures release. *Executive Producer:* Ron Shelton and Wolfgang Glattes. *Producer:* Michele Rappaport. *Director:* William Friedkin. *Screenplay:* Ron Shelton. *Director of Photography:* Tom Priestley, Jr. *Editor:* Robert K. Lambert and David Rosenbloom. *Music:* Nile Rodgers, Jeff Beck, and Jed Leiber. *Music Editor:* Allan K. Rosen. *Sound:* Kirk Francis. *Sound Editor:* J. Paul Huntsman. *Casting:* Louis Di Giaimo. *Production Designer:* James Bissell. *Art Director:* Ed Verreaux. *Set Designer:* John H.M. Berger and Lauren Polizzi. *Set Decorator:* Thomas L. Roysden. *Set Dresser:* Francis Hendrick, Jr. and Michael E. Hendrick. *Costumes:* Bernie Pollack. *Make-up:* Ben Nye, Jr. *Make-up (Nick Nolte):* Robert Ryan. *Running time:* 108 minutes. *MPAA Rating:* PG-13.

CAST: Nick Nolte (Pete Bell); Mary McDonnell (Jenny); J.T. Walsh (Happy); Ed O'Neill (Ed); Alfre Woodard (Lavada McRae); Bob Cousy (Vic); Shaquille O'Neal (Neon Bodeaux); Anfernee "Penny" Hardaway (Butch); Matt Nover (Ricky); Cylk Cozart (Slick); Anthony C. Hall (Tony); Kevin Benton (Jack); Bill Cross (Freddie); Marques Johnson (Mel); Robert Wuhl (Marty); Sam Armato (Lecturer); Jim Beaver (Ricky's Father); Debbie Young

(Ricky's Mother); Tony Gonzalez (Dolphin Mascot); Frank Anthony Rossi (Charlie); Qiana Petty, Alicia N. Jones, and Britney Mitchell (McRae Daughters); Dorothy McCann (Grandmother); Allan Malamud (Reporter); Wayne K. LeBeaux (Equipment Manager); Eric Harmon (Referee); James Jackson (Man with Lexus); Michael Johnson (Cash Man); Mark Murray and Andre L. Jones (Restaurant Sports Fans); Gary Vitti (Trainer); Larry Bird, Jim Boeheim, Dick Baker, Marty Blake, Lou Campanelli, Todd Donoho, Bobby Knight, Richard Pitino, George Raveling, Siv Svendsen, Jerry Tarkanian, and Dick Vitale (Themselves).

LOS ANGELES TIMES, 2/18/94, Calendar/p. 6, Peter Rainer

Sports movies don't always have to be great to be fun. The ritualistic confrontations, the banter, the job of physical release can keep you watching even when the characters are stock and the plot predictable.

"Blue Chips" starts Nick Nolte as Pete Bell, the basketball coach of Western U., on the verge of his first losing season after winning two championships and eight conference titles. The film is about how the valiant, by-the-book Pete, in an effort to recruit three blue-chip high school phenoms to save his job, crosses the line into corruption.

At its best, though, "Blue Chips" is really about the wiggy, muscle-twitch world of high-pressure college athletics. The movie is best around the edges, when it's jamming and anecdotal and not taking itself so heroically seriously. Corruption in college athletics is not quite the eye-opener this movie makes it out to be, it may be a measure of our cynicism that we can't take a story like this straight anymore. Outrage is certainly called for but too often "Blue Chips" assumes we were born, if not yesterday, the day before.

It helps that Nolte is such a heroic presence that his waverings and capitulations seem immensely poignant. He doesn't go in for a lot of heavy-browed agonizing; without making a big deal of it he shows us how small Pete feels when he looks the other way. Pete's love of the game is bound up with his love of winning. By the end of the film he learns to recognize that the two cannot always co-exist.

Co-existence is also a problem with the shaggy, catch-all wit of screenwriter Ron Shelton and the head-pounding style of director William ("The French Connection) Friedkin. "Blue Chips" is set up to be looser and funnier than it turns out to be.

Shelton, who wrote and directed "Bull Durham" and "White Men Can't Jump," the two best sports-themed films of the past 10 years, understands how athletic release can loosen you up all over. Sports becomes a way of jazzing your life, of giving it a rhythm you can carry in your head like a tune.

The congregation of characters in Shelton's movies are spangled, combative, intuitive, with a line of rap that's an extension of their sports playing. Though some of the characters and situations in "Blue Chips" are, for Shelton, sub-par—he wrote the script 12 years ago—the film might still have taken off if he had directed it. His best ideas—like the rival scouts who dog Pete's trail and who resemble a Preston Sturges troupe—require a more glancing touch.

And so do the basketball sequences. Friedkin shows us amazing ball handlers like Shaquille O'Neill, Anfernee "Penny" Hardaway and Matt Nover (as the three recruits) and then films their skirmishes in a crunch-and-thud style more appropriate to professional wrestling or stock car racing. What's missing is the poetry of the sport—the poetry that must have attracted not only Pete to the game but the players too. If we had seen more of the beauty of basketball, the corruptions of the three phenoms would have carried a more ambiguous force. (Their sellouts might have seemed tragic, like Pete's.)

The subplot involving Pete and his former wife (Mary McDonnell) is a bit too undeveloped and touchy-feely, and the only thing missing from the scenes with J.T. Walsh as a wicked alumni organization head are rattlesnakes on the soundtrack. A few sequences, including the ones at the very end, seem truncated, and superb actors like Robert Wuhl and Lou Gossett pop up for teensy cameos.

There are still fine moments, like the way Alfre Woodard, as the mother of one of the blue chips, cuts to the quick in her conversation with Pete. (She wants a new home and an expensive office.) Boston Celtic legend Bob Cousy, as Western U.'s athletic director, has a wonderful, bemused openness; he has a terrific scene where he converses with Pete while sinking a seemingly endless succession of baskets.

Shaquille O'Neal doesn't really try to act but he's so upfront about what he's doing that his amateurishness is kind of endearing. And he can stand next to Nolte and make him seem puny—no small feat.

"Blue Chips" should be better than it is—a movie about standing up to corruption shouldn't be this eager to go for the commercial jugular. But in flashes it makes you realize why you like sports—and sports movies—in the first place.

NEW YORK, 3/7/94, p. 65, John Powers

Enjoyable but preachy, *Blue Chips* stars Nick Nolte as Pete Bell, a squeaky-clean basketball coach devoted to the game he considers the purest thing in life. But shell-shocked by his first losing season, he hits the road and discovers the real world of modern college athletics: the tough ghetto mom (Alfre Woodard) who demands a house and a job in exchange for her son's letter of commitment; the pious Christian farmer who expects, but won't ask for, a tractor in exchange for his son's letter; the slippery-sympathetic athletic director (Bob Cousy) who calmly sinks free throws as he tries not to hear what's really going on in his coach's recruiting wars. Seduced by the talent within his grasp, Bell does what it takes to land his three top prospects, including a giant played by the ubiquitous Shaquille O'Neal (who might have been better advised to spend his time developing a go-to move).

In the year of Tonya Harding, there's nothing new about *Blue Chips*'s lament that amateur sports have been corrupted by money. Luckily, the movie's screenplay was written by Ron Shelton, who wrote and directed *Bull Durham* and *White Men Can't Jump*, and who may be the most splendidly American artist in Hollywood. All Shelton's work celebrates our country s best possibilities—honor, racial tolerance, sexual pleasure, the athletic Tao, the boundless joys of banter—without ever becoming full of itself. And in the hulking Nolte, who suddenly looks like Michael J. Fox whenever he stands next to Shaq, the movie has a quintessentially American actor to put these values across. Never one for showy performances, Nolte effortlessly makes us think of Bobby Knight (who has an amusing, beet-faced cameo) but exudes a sweetness missing from the Indiana coach: Nolte's Pete Bell has the strange, missionary boyishness that can make a man love a game more than his own wife. Too bad, then, that William Friedkin is the Bill Laimbeer of directors, elbowing his way through comic byplay that should be delicate and giving the basketball sequences all the grace of a rugby match at Leeds. Even when a scene should be fraught with melancholy, he makes every slam dunk sound like a nuclear blast.

NEW YORK POST, 2/18/94, p. 48, Michael Medved

Friedkin's "Blue Chips" opens with 10 minutes of the most ferociously effective moviemaking you are ever likely to see.

A college basketball team on a losing streak gathers in their glum locker room before a big game as enraged head coach Nick Nolte storms onto the scene and proceeds to curse them out, slamming doors and smashing water coolers with explosive fury. Even from the safety of your theater seat, you will tremble from the shock waves of his wrath.

Like many other moments of this picture, the sequence is simultaneously funny and frightening: You can't imagine how the unfortunate team members could even stand up after the abuse they've received from their "inspirational" coach, let alone go out and play a game.

But somehow, they do run out to the wild cheers of the huge home crowd, facing their confident opponents in game footage so exhilarating, brilliantly edited and altogether authentic that you can almost taste the sweat.

For most of us "Blue Chips" is as close as we'll ever come to actually playing big-time basketball and unlike other sports movies, the dramatized play is even more fun to watch than actual games on the tube.

The plot centers on coach Nolte's desperate desire to rebuild his team at L.A.'s fictional Western University so he can save his job and return to the glory days of 10 years earlier when he won a pair of national championships.

The only way to achieve this dream is to travel the country to recruit high school superstars—the "blue chip" players who can instantly turn it all around.

The problem is that in today's competitive environment, these canny kids expect all kinds of rewards for signing up for Nolte's school. That includes a home and job for a struggling mother (Alfre Woodard), a gleaming new tractor for daddy's farm, even a gym bag stuffed with thousands in unmarked bills.

Nolte has always run a "clean" program that refused to make such compromises. But if he wants these players badly enough, then unscrupulous alumni booster J.T. Walsh will quietly do whatever it takes to get them.

Meanwhile, the coach's schoolteacher ex-wife (the always luminous Mary McDonnell) remains his best friend and serves as the stubborn voice of his conscience.

When it comes to recruitment coups, director Friedkin scored a triumph by casting three basketball standouts (Shaquille O'Neal and Anfernee Hardaway of the NBA, and Indiana University star Matt Nover) who can act nearly as well as they play.

The 7-foot-tall O'Neal, playing a tough-but-tender street kid from New Orleans, turns out to be as powerful, graceful and dominating in front of a camera as he is on the court, and his dazzling smile can single-handedly light an arena.

Screenwriter Ron Shelton (who previously wrote and directed "Bull Durham" and "White Men Cant Jump") provides a limp conclusion so preachy and pathetic that it undermines the fine work that's come before—like blowing a brilliant game in the fourth quarter.

Part of the problem is that the Walsh character is a one-dimensional cartoon as the devilish temper from the alumni association. Had he been more sympathetic and believable, Nolte's situation would have come across as more comprehensible and compelling.

Still, "Blue Chips" is never less than watchable and exciting, focusing at all times on its superbly played protagonist's unshakable love of the game of basketball.

It's a passion clearly, shared by director Friedkin ("The French Connection" "To Live and Die in L.A."), who after a few stumbles, detours, and disappointments, here returns to championship form.

NEWSDAY, 2/18/94, Part II/p. 74, Jack Mathews

As a former college basketball fanatic, I find William Friedkin's "Blue Chips" both a joy and a pain to watch. A joy because the quality of basketball depicted is as good as it gets in movies. A pain because the recruiting violations, alumni interference and academic hypocrisies at the heart of the story are the chief reasons I no longer care much about the game.

Those and the fact that my alma mater, UCLA, whose colors are worn by the film's fictional Western University, hasn't won a national championship in 20 years.

You don't have to be a sports fan to be aware of the corrupting influences on modern college athletics. Television money has turned the highest-profile games—basketball and football—into major profit centers for the schools that play them best, and the cheating that evolves out of the pressure to win ends up grabbing as many headlines as the personal and team achievements.

"Blue Chips," written by sports-savvy Ron Shelton ("Bull Durham"), dramatizes that pressure in a story about Pete Bell (Nick Nolte), a beleaguered college basketball coach who, desperate to return struggling Western to its former glory agrees to let scurrilous alumni "buy" a trio of prospects who might otherwise go elsewhere.

For Ricky Roe (Matt Nover), a 6-foot-8 forward with a precision outside shot, there is a satchel full of $20 bills, and a brand-new John Deere tractor for dad back on the farm in Indiana.

For Butch McRae (Anfernee Hardaway), the balletic point guard from St. Joseph's High in Chicago, there is a job for mom (Alfre Woodard) and a new home for her and the family near the university's Los Angeles campus.

For Neon Bodeaux (Shaquille O'Neal), the 7-4 giant discovered playing pickup games in a bayou town in Louisiana, there is a new car, a tutor to help him with tests and a pipeline to the pros. Sure enough, the three players turn Western into an overnight powerhouse. But can the school get away with such flagrant violations, what with that investigative sports reporter (Ed O'Neill) snooping around, and can coach Bell live with himself even if he doesn't get caught?

Shelton spares us the subtleties of the debate. This is a dramatized commentary, with every point slam-dunked. There is great evil out there, and it's name is alumni. Specifically, it is Happy (J. T. Walsh), an alumnus who, in another life, must have run a children's slave trade in Cairo. Happy isn't happy just helping athletes financially; he wants to control their performance on the court so he can safely bet the point spread.

Besides the alumni, and his own greed, Bell has to deal with a passive athletic director (former NBA star Bob Cousy), a hostile media, and a suffering wife (Mary McDonnell) who refuses to continue a marriage being played like a full-court press.

As melodramatic as the story is, the basketball is sound. Friedkin wisely filled the players' roles with current professional and college stars. They give the game footage a verisimilitude you almost never see in sports movies, and a couple gave surprisingly credible off-court performances.

Shaquille O'Neal doesn't fool anybody. You know you're watching a jock read his lines, but he's perfectly pleasant company, and Hardaway, O'Neal's real-life teammate with the Orlando Magic, holds his own in a couple of dramatic scenes with Nolte.

Some people may think Nolte's performance is wildly over the top, but the truth is you can't exaggerate the courtside behavior of a college basketball coach. You watch Nolte screaming at referees, berating his players, throwing and kicking inanimate objects, getting so red in the face he seems about to explode, and you see ... Bobby Knight!

Knight, the Hun who coaches perennial power Indiana, actually makes a couple of appearances, directing the efforts of Western's toughest opponent. He is one of several major college coaches whose vanity apparently prodded them into contributing to this indictment of their sport. Among the others: Syracuse's Jim Boeheim, Kentucky's Rick Pitino, and Jerry Tarkanian, the former Las Vegas coach whose resume could be mistaken for a rap sheet.

There are moments throughout "Blue Chips" where art and life seem to merge, and that's not necessarily a compliment.

NEWSWEEK, 2/28/94, p. 63, David Ansen

Any sports movie that isn't a knockoff of "Rocky" is already ahead of the game. "Blue Chips," directed by William Friedkin from a 12-year-old script by Ron ("Bull Durham") Shelton, examines the corruption of college basketball by filthy lucre. The dilemma facing coach Pete Bell (Nick Nolte), whose once great program at Western U has fallen on bad times, is that the only way to win (and keep his job) is to recruit the best high-school players in the land, and the only way to get them is by breaking the rules. The players expect cash, cars, homes for their moms. The alumni demand a winning team (it's worth big bucks to the school) and they assure Coach their money-laundering techniques are untraceable. The hotheaded Bell is an old-fashioned guy: he's always prided himself on running a clean program. But faced with the temptation of three NBA-class recruits, played by Shaquille O'Neal (a surprisingly ingratiating actor), Matt Nover and Anfernee (Penny) Hardaway ... well, maybe just this once ...

Stocked with basketball legends like Bob Cousy (as the school's athletic director), Bobby Knight and Larry Bird, directed with frenetic realism and peppered with Shelton's wit, "Blue Chips" is a fast-break, PG-13 entertainment that makes up in energy what it lacks in subtlety. Succumbing to last-minute sermonizing, Shelton gets coach Bell out of his jam as abruptly as he gets him into it (plotting is not Shelton's forte). The cliché villain, a rich alumnus (J.T. Walsh), would twirl his mustache if he had one. But the film's passion for the game—and Nolte's rabid commitment—are contagious. Anyone sick of the Go-for-It "Rocky" philosophy will warm to a tale that suggests winning isn't all it's cracked up to be.

Also reviewed in:

CHICAGO TRIBUNE, 2/18/94, Friday/p. H, Mark Caro
NEW YORK TIMES, 2/18/94, p. C17, Janet Maslin
VARIETY, 2/21-27/94, p. 36, Todd McCarthy
WASHINGTON POST, 2/18/94, Weekend/p. 55, Desson Howe
WASHINGTON POST, 2/19/94, p. G9, Hal Hinson

BLUE SKY

An Orion Pictures release. *Producer:* Robert H. Solo. *Director:* Tony Richardson. *Screenplay:* Rama Laurie Stagner, Arlene Sarner, and Jerry Leichtling. *Story:* Rama Laurie Stagner. *Director of Photography:* Steve Yaconelli. *Editor:* Robert K. Lambert. *Music:* Jack Nitzsche. *Music Editor:* Richard Whitfield. *Choreographer:* Greg Rosatti. *Sound:* Jacob Goldstein, Susumu Tokunow and (music) Dean Drabin. *Sound Editor:* Bruce Richardson. *Casting:* Lynn Stalmaster. *Production Designer:* Timian Alsaker. *Art Director:* Gary John Constable. *Set Decorator:* Leslie Rollins. *Set Dresser:* Matt A. Marich, Kimberly Lannaghan, Lloyd R. Whittaker, and Robin Solo. *Special Effects:* Cliff Wenger, and Mack Chapman. *Costumes:* Jane Robinson. *Make-up:* Bob Arrollo. *Make-up (Jessica Lange):* Dorothy Pearl. *Stunt Coordinator:* Don Pike. *Running time:* 101 minutes. *MPAA Rating:* PG-13.

CAST: Jessica Lange (Carly Marshall); Tommy Lee Jones (Hank Marshall); Powers Boothe (Vince Johnson); Carrie Snodgress (Vera Johnson); Amy Locane (Alex Marshall); Chris O'Donnell (Glenn Johnson); Mitchell Ryan (Ray Stevens); Dale Dye (Colonel Mike Anwalt); Tim Scott (Ned Owens); Annie Ross (Lydia); Anna Klemp (Becky Marshall); Anthony Rene Jones (Helicopter Pilot); Jay H. Seidl (Soldier on Island); David Bradford (Soldier #1); Matt Battaglia (NATO Soldier); John J. Fedak (Adjutant); Michael McClendon (Lt. Colonel Jennings); Harriet Courtney Sumner and Shannon Laramore (Salesladys); Ray Sergeant (Administrative 1st Sergeant); Merlin Marston (Lt. Colonel George Land); Billy Lawson (Band Leader); Joseph Wilkins (Soldier at Bar); Carl C. Morgan, III (Attention Sergeant); Dion Anderson (General Derrick); Richard Jones (Jimmy); Art Wheeler (Piano Player); Sharlene Ross (Nurse); David Lee Lane (Stockade Guard); Ed Lee Corbin (Stockade MP); Gary Bullock (Doctor Vankday); Angela Paton (Dottie Owens); Babs George, Rod Masterson, and Sean McGraw (Reporters); David Dwyer (Newscaster); Geoff McKnight (Engineer); Whitt Brantley (Desk Clerk).

LOS ANGELES TIMES, 9/16/94, Calendar/p. 6, Kenneth Turan

"Blue Sky" is a confounding film, simultaneously silk purse and sow's ear. What begins as a compelling and beautifully acted portrait of a complex adult relationship ends with a B-picture finale about military secrecy, a turn of events as baffling as it sounds.

The last picture of Tony Richardson's career, completed almost simultaneously with his death in 1991 but not released until now, "Blue Sky" is a throwback to the emotional intensity of the director's early British work (strong films like "Look Back in Anger" and "The Loneliness of the Long Distance Runner") with the added advantage of a lifetime's accumulated filmmaking skill.

Richardson also had the benefit of Jessica Lange and Tommy Lee Jones as Carly and Maj. Hank Marshall, a military couple enmeshed in a still-passionate but agonizing 18-year marriage. Though Lange and Jones are Oscar winners who have not lacked for strong parts, the combination of their ease with each other and their obvious trust in Richardson has resulted in intense, volatile performances that have to be considered among the strongest in both their careers.

Rama Laurie Stagner, whose story "Blue Sky" is taken from (and who wrote the script with Arlene Sarner & Jerry Leichtling), based the work on her parents' relationship, and much of that verisimilitude clings to this project.

Its depiction of a family fighting for life, of two people whose ragged frailties make them all the more sympathetic, is enough to make most of "Blue Sky" play like a textbook on how to convey emotional truth on screen.

It's Carly who's seen first, and as the film's passion flower opening image blends into a credit sequence of a red-nail-polished hand turning the pages of glamorous movie magazines the type of woman she is seems clear.

But Southern-bred Carly, as is shown in the scene of her exuberantly sunbathing topless on a beach in Hawaii while her husband and some of the men in his command helicopter pass, is too tempestuous to be just a type. A full-bore exhibitionist and tale-spinner who finds reality much too confining, she has a hunger for experience the more controlling major admires even though there are hints it has led her astray.

"Blue Sky" is set in 1962, and Maj. Marshall, a military scientist involved in detecting radiation from U.S. nuclear testing, has a habit of speaking his mind to his superiors in a way that is not always appreciated. One result is a transfer for the Marshalls and their daughters from the paradise of Hawaii to the dismal backwater of Ft. Matthews, Ala.

As the drabness of their new surroundings sinks in, the other side of Carly emerges. A true manic-depressive, Carly has a fragility as acute as her bravado, and her capacity for self-destruction is awesome. Lange's highly emotional yet controlled performance as a woman in agony determined, in her husband's words, to "take everything right over the edge" perfectly captures the pitch of this difficult character.

And as the partner who holds the family together, Jones is more sensitive and emotionally vulnerable than he's allowed himself to be before. Love, he tells their daughters, is "an exchange of energy over time," and just as water remains water even when it turns to vapor or even ice, he and their mother are determined to care for each other no matter what form their passions take.

But when Carly becomes a magnet for the major's formidable commanding officer, Col. Vince Johnson (Powers Boothe), as well as a good friend to the colonel's wife (Carrie Snodgress), the pain in Hank's eyes deepens, and Jones' performance carefully conveys how much being in love with an unchartable whirlwind like Carly has cost him.

"Blue Sky" handles this emotional material so well it is a shock when, with no warning to speak of, the film at the last minute abandons what it does best and concentrates its energies on an indifferent scenario involving official suppression of test data, a subplot that was probably intended to be socially relevant but isn't.

Though at first having Maj. Marshall involved with nuclear radiation makes an interesting counterpoint to the volatility of his marital relationship, "Blue Sky's" infatuation with melodrama pushes the least original and successful parts of the movie to the forefront and squanders hard-won believability.

Still, the acting here is so exceptional, extending down to Amy Locane and Anna Klemp as the two Marshall daughters and Chris O'Donnell as the former's new boyfriend (and the colonel's son), that it hurts to have to mention the down side. While "Blue Sky's" vibrancy points up how rare that quality has become, the way everything finally falls to earth underlines the difficulty even promising projects have in staying on track all the way to the end.

NEW YORK, 9/26/94, p. 98, David Denby

Blue Sky, the last movie directed by Tony Richardson, is like Tennessee Williams without poetry, imagination, or sense. In the early sixties, an American military wife, Carly (Jessica Lange)—too much woman, too big for her restricted role—is going crazy with boredom. She longs for glamour and dreams of Ava, Marilyn, Liz, and Brigitte. Carly is good-hearted and would never intentionally hurt anyone, but she's also promiscuous and slightly crazy, and she keeps making scenes, humiliating her patient and loving army-major husband (Tommy Lee Jones) over and over. The movie has an aura of dumb fatality about it: You wait for Carly to fall apart and make a mess and then for the loving hubby to forgive her. The actors are both strong, and Richardson brings some heat to the material, but the script is too lame to sustain serious interest.

NEW YORK POST, 9/16/94, p. 44, Thelma Adams

Few recent American movies touch the raw nerve at the core of every marriage like Tony Richardson's "Blue Sky. The pairing of Tommy Lee Jones and Jessica Lange as a stoic miliary scientist and his oversexed, manic-depressive wife is electrifying.

Set in 1962,"Blue Sky" begins with the Marshall family's transfer from Hawaii to Alabama after Carly (Lange), reinventing herself as Brigitte Bardot, bathes topless. This delights the enlisted men, but her husband's superiors are not amused—neither with Carly's antics nor Hank's criticism of nuclear testing practices.

The Marshalls' arrival at desolate digs in Alabama launches Carly—now looking like Marilyn Monroe—into a curtain-ripping, wall-banging tantrum so true it hurts. The camera cuts to her two daughters, Alex and Becky (well-played by Amy Locane and Anna Klemp) curved around each other on a twin bed. They've been through these rages before—but the repetition is shattering.

Carly lights out in the family car with Hank (Jones) in hot pursuit. She flees into a yardage store, alarming the locals. When Hank catches up with her, he coaxes his angry wife back into his arms like a fireman rescuing a cat from a tree.

When the couple returns home, Hank puts Carly to bed, rubbing her feet with a familiar tenderness that says as much about their relationship as the lovemaking that follows. They are the F. Scott and Zelda Fitzgerald of the military set.

This sequence early in the film anchors Carly and Hank's push-pull relationship. It lays bare the twisted threads of trust, need, passion, understanding and destruction that tie the pair together—and shows their impact on the girls.

As Alex says the next day, "He's blind and she's crazy."

"They're perfect for each other," her sister responds.

Jones, the comforting calm of his voice the iron bar the family clings to, demonstrates a range and control only hinted at in his three summer movies, "The Client," "Natural Born Killers," and "Blown Away." The actor's power here is in the quiet moments, rather than the over-the-top rages and exhibitionistic bits that showcase Lange.

British director Richardson pulls off this delicate balancing act triumphantly. Richardson, whose films range from "Look Back in Anger" (1958) and "Tom Jones" (1963) to "The Hotel New Hampshire" (1984), made this film shortly before he died in 1991. Orion Pictures' money woes have left it sitting on the shelf ever since.

What interests Richardson is the relationship between Carly and Hank. "Blue Sky" offers a rare mature take on marital love and the way couples curve around each other emotionally.

The director appears less interested—and the movie is less interesting—in the treatment of the military's handling of underground nuclear testing and the cover-up in which Hank becomes entangled. Co-screenwriter Rama Laurie Stagner's semi-autobiographical script (written with Arlene Sarner and Jerry Leichtling) unravels when it steps away from the domestic drama and into army intrigue.

Though flawed, the impact of "Blue Sky" lies in the underground explosion of a nuclear family—and the explosive performances of Lange and Jones.

NEWSDAY, 9/16/94, Part II/p. B5, Jack Mathews

It would be nice to report that "Blue Sky," the film the late British director tony Richardson completed just before his death in 1991, is in a class with "Look Back in Anger," "The Long Distance Runner" and "Tom Jones," the classics of his early career.

Unfortunately, about the only connection "Blue Sky" can claim with those movies is that it is set in 1962, when Richardson reigned as the leader of the "Angry Young Men" movement in England.

Like most other great directors of his time, Richardson's literary tastes and sensibilities became arcane values to a film business bent on feeding the appetites of children and young adults in the '80s, and what few assignments he had in his final years were with generally mundane subjects.

"Blue Sky," a domestic drama about the pressures on a military family at the height of the Cold War, may be the most mundane of them all. Or so it becomes. The film starts out promising a potent psychological drama, in the mode of Tennessee Williams, then veers away and becomes a colossally silly adventure.

"Blue Sky," whose release was delayed by its distributor's financial problems, drops in on the lives of Major Hank Marshall (Tommy Lee Jones), a military scientist charged with measuring the data from U.S. A-bomb tests; his restlessly sultry wife, Carly (Jessica Lange), a bombshell in her own right, and their two teenage daughters.

The major, a strong-willed fellow with a troubled conscience (about The Bomb), and Carly, a weak-willed manic-depressive with a troubled conscience (about her philandering), make a fascinating couple, deeply in love and just as deeply in trouble. There is a desperation in their determination to stay together, as if each would truly self-destruct without the other.

As long as the film, supposedly based on the memories of the Army brat who cowrote the script, stays focused on the fragile relationship between the couple, and on the effects Carly's explosive outbursts have on the children, "Blue Sky" is compelling drama. And the performances by Jones and Lange are among the best of their careers. Lange playing Carly as a blend of Marilyn Monroe, Maggie the Cat and Blanche du Bois, has never been more relaxed or as physically expansive in a role.

But when the story shifts its focus to its subplot about Hank's and then Carly's attempts to expose a military coverup of radiation leaks in the Nevada desert, "Blue Sky" sinks to the level of a Chuck Norris movie. Unfortunately, for both the actors and the reputation of their director, it is the film's wretched last act that audiences are likeliest to remember.

SIGHT AND SOUND, 6/95, p. 56, Leslie Felperin

Paradise Island, 1962. Hank Marshall is an Army scientist studying the effects of nuclear fallout who lives on the army base with his wife, Carly, and their two daughters, Alex and Becky. When Carly scandalises the local military community with her nude-sunbathing and kittenish Brigitte Bardot impersonations, the family is transferred to Anniston Alabama. Upon arriving at the dilapidated house assigned to them, Carly, who has a history of mental instability and marital infidelity (and is now modelling her dress and hair on Marilyn Monroe), becomes hysterical and goes into a depressive state.

Hank copes with the domestic chores until she rallies. She joins the officers' wives' dramatic society, while Alex becomes friendly with Glenn, the son of Hank's commanding officer, Vince Johnson. At a dance, Carly grinds and bumps with Vince provocatively in clear view of everyone, not least Hank. With a lecherous eye on Carly, Vince has Hank transferred to the Blue Sky project in Nevada, where they are pioneering the underground detonation of nuclear weapons. Two cowboys inadvertently wander into the range during a test and are irradiated, but no one will heed Hank's calls for stricter precautions and compensation for these indifferent victims of fallout.

Back in Anniston, lonely for Hank, Carly has sex with Vince. Alex and Glenn stumble upon them and the news spreads throughout the base. The officers' wives silently snub Carly, and Alex insists that she call Hank in Nevada and confess her betrayal. He returns to Anniston, and an argument with Vince about the Blue Sky project results in Hank punching him in the face. The Army persuades Carly to have Hank committed to a psychiatric hospital "for his own good", but really in order to shut him up about the Blue Sky project. When she sees him heavily drugged and with his spirit broken, Carly decides that the only way to secure his release is by exposing the Blue Sky project to media attention.

She goes to Nevada, rides into the test site on horseback, and is promptly arrested, drawing the attention of reporters. Carly negotiates with the army to remain silent if they give Hank a discharge. Finally reunited, the family are last seen bound for Berkeley, California, where Hank is to take up a teaching post where he can freely express his now firm anti-nuclear philosophy. Carly has had a makeover and now looks like Elizabeth Taylor.

Most feature films have a few subplots that intersect or overlap with the main one, but *Blue Sky* seems more like two separate films loosely stitched together. One is about a marriage on the edge of a nervous breakdown. Carly's sporadic mental instability continually threatening to implode the fragile domestic bubble.The other film concerns the explosive fallout (literally and figuratively) of a military coverup during the early 60s atomic research programme. To bring these two films together, *Blue Sky* pivots its plot around the quantum mechanics of a nuclear family.

Despite being partly based on the childhood of one of the producers, Rama Laurie Stagner, the cold fusion of these two plots feels more like something thrown up by a screenwriters' brainstorming session, an exercise in stretching metaphor rather than an integrated realist narrative. The weakness of the bonding becomes clearly apparent at the most critical points: instead of attacking Vernon for fucking his wife, Hank confronts him about the management of the *Blue Sky* project. Alright, so he's meant to be in denial, but this is pushing it a little too far in the light of what we've already learned about him. Similarly Carly's final act of heroism, which all too neatly exculpates her guilt, seems unfeasibly resourceful for a woman whose character has been established as so feckless. More than anything, the latter plot twist seems fashioned to allow Lange and the film-makers to pay hommage to Marilyn Monroe in *The Misfits*, whose final act of heroism also served to erase the stain of her character's sexuality. *Blue Sky* won't allow itself to be as dark as this earlier film, a pity because a tragic ending, with Carly fried in the fission blast or Hank lobotomised (as he seems to be at one point) would have endowed the film with more emotional gravity. Instead we get a happily reconstituted molecule of domestic bliss poised to catalyse the 60s with a proto-hippy philosophy of peace and disarmament.

What carries the movie in the end, and, despite its fundamental flaws, makes it compulsively watchable, are the lead actors' finely grained performances. Jessica Lange has already been lavishly praised and duly rewarded with an academy award for her turn as Carly, which although very good is perhaps just a trifle overwrought. Good hysterics are like a pavlovian bell to critics and academy members, setting off droolings of praise. More impressive are her quieter moments. As the family drives to their new house, the street becoming progressively seedier, optimism and resolve slackens from her face by tiny degrees beautifully rendered. Equally, Tommy Lee Jones in the more subtle but possibly more challenging role of Hank, reaffirms what a fine actor he is. By the most delicate of gestures and expressions he conveys both the rigidity and the sexual obsessiveness so crucial to the character and so unexplained and avoided by the dialogue.

This was Tony Richardson's last film and it seems appropriate that for a director so much associated with the 50s and 60s (even though he made several fine films in subsequent decades) he should have concluded his career with a period piece about the kind of instinctive rebel who eventually made things swing. This film also demonstrates both his greatest strengths and his blind spots as a film-maker. It illustrates how he could draw out better performances from accomplished thespians than they offered as a matter of routine, a point proved with Laurence Olivier in *The Entertainer* and Albert Finney in *Tom Jones*, and even coax remarkable tonal variations from more limited performers such as Rita Tushingham and Jack Nicholson. (Nicholson's unsympathetic character's sacrifice in *The Border* bears some similarity to Carly's.) But here, as in some of Tony Richardson's weaker films such as *The Hotel New Hampshire*, he exhibits a tendency to cram too much in and to overindulge a promising but fractious screenplay. Still, for all its faults, *Blue Sky* remains a worthy send-off for one of Britain's more mercurial and intriguing directors, one that really deserves better than its limited theatrical release in this country.

VILLAGE VOICE, 9/20/94, p. 64, Ella Taylor

Bored army wife (Jessica Lange) with monster libido raises hell at early-'60s Alabama test-site base. Drives devoted nuclear-scientist hubbie (Tommy Lee Jones) and teenage daughter (Amy Locane) to desperate acts. Heals self and family by exposing military cover-up of top-secret nuclear testing. Thus liberated, turns brunette and heads for California, home of free spirits.

Based on the early life of screenwriter Rama Laurie Stagner, Tony Richardson's posthumously released last film—he died of AIDS in 1991—has a lumbering plot and a ho-hum script ("What we call love is really the exchange of energy over time"), But who cares? *Blue Sky* is a wildly sexy bodice-ripper, with Lange letting rip those generous hips as a Bardot-Monroe bad seed with Blanche Dubois diction, Jones beautifully buttoned up as the besotted stick of a husband who tries to contain her, and Powers Boothe enchantingly sleazoid as the base commander who undresses Lange approximately every 20 minutes. As a piece of left-liberation theology the movie has all the subtlety of an A-bomb, but it's a fitting final salvo for sexual freedom from the director of *Tom Jones* and *A Taste of Honey*.

Also reviewed in:
NEW REPUBLIC, 10/24/94, p. 31, Stanley Kauffmann
NEW YORK TIMES, 9/16/94, p. C8, Caryn James
VARIETY, 9/12-18/94, p. 41, Todd McCarthy
WASHINGTON POST, 9/16/94, p. F7, Rita Kempley
WASHINGTON POST, 9/16/94, Weekend/p. 49, Kevin McManus

BODY SNATCHERS

A Warner Bros. release. *Producer:* Robert Solo. *Director:* Abel Ferrara. *Screenplay:* Stuart Gordon, Dennis Paoli and Nicholas St. John. *From the story by:* Raymond Cistheri and Larry Cohen. *Based on the book "The Body Snatchers" by:* Jack Finney. *Director of Photography:* Bojan Bazelli. *Editor:* Anthony Redman. *Music:* Joe Delia. *Sound:* Michael Barosky. *Casting:* Ferne Cassel. *Production Designer:* Peter Jamison. *Art Director:* John Huke. *Set Decorator:* Linda Spheeris. *Special Effects:* Phil Cory. *Special Make-up Effects:* Tom Burman and Bari Dreiband-Burman. *Costumes:* Margaret Mohr. *Stunt Coordinator:* Phil Neilson. *Running time:* 87 minutes. *MPAA Rating:* R.

CAST: Gabrielle Anwar (Marti Malone); Terry Kinney (Steve Malone); Billy Wirth (Tim); Meg Tilly (Carol Malone); Forest Whitaker (Major Collins); Christine Elise (Jenn Platt); R. Lee Ermey (General Platt); Reilly Murphy (Andy Malone); G. Elvis Phillips (Pete); Kathleen Doyle (Mrs. Platt).

LOS ANGELES TIMES, 2/4/94, Calendar/p. 1, Kenneth Turan

"They're out there, they're everywhere. They get you while you sleep." And now they're back. Again.

For "Body Snatchers" is at least the third version of Jack Finney's classic pulp science-fiction tale of sinister pods from outer space who take over unsuspecting humans and turn them into unfeeling automatons. Director Don Siegel did the original "Invasion of the Body Snatchers" in 1956, and given that Phil Kaufman didn't even come close to improving on it in 1978, Abel Ferrara may seem foolhardy to try it again today.

But Ferrara hasn't merely remade "Body Snatchers", he has reimagined and reinvigorated it, using the best of special-effects talent and cool directorial skill to turn out a splendidly creepy and unsettling piece of genre filmmaking that knows how to scare you and isn't afraid to try.

The people "Body Snatchers" have scared the most, apparently, are the executives at Warner Bros., who have been sitting on this disturbing chiller for at least a year, and are only now giving it the kind of limited release (one puny theater, the Festival in Westwood) usually associated with delicate tea-bag dramas, not brazen epics of paranoia.

For one of the things that Ferrara and his five credited screenwriters (screenplay by Stuart Gordon & Dennis Paoli and Nicholas St. John, story by Raymond Cistheri and Larry Cohen) have done is change the emphasis from the protest against conformity that characterized the Siegel version to a look at the more modern terror of paranoia, of not knowing who is going to turn on you or when the betrayal will take place.

To restrict himself within the limits of the remake of a classic may seem like an odd choice for as visceral director as Ferrara, a man with a reputation for doing out-there outlaw cinema ranging from his early "Ms. 45" to the more recent "Bad Lieutenant."

But these restrictions don't negate Ferrara's abilities, they merely focus them. And because "Body Snatchers'" story is so familiar to so many filmgoers, the film benefits considerably from his ability to energize a situation, to keep, audiences fixed on the screen though they know what's going to happen.

Clocking in at a lean 90 minutes, "Body Snatchers" also has the advantage of wasting no time getting into the story, shrewdly set this time at an Army base in the South where people are so habitually obedient it is doubly difficult to determine who is a soulless pod and who is just following orders.

New at the base are the Malone family, father Steve (Terry Kinney) being a visiting scientist from the Environmental Protection Agency assigned to investigate hazardous waste. With him are his second wife, Carol (Meg Tilly), their 5-year-old son Andy (Reilly Murphy) and heroine Marti (Gabrielle Anwar), Steve's rebellious daughter from his first marriage.

While Steve pokes around the base and commiserates with Maj. Collins (an edgy Forest Whitaker), the head of medical care who has a slew of patients "exhibiting paranoia about other people's identities," Marti is hanging out with Jenn (Christine Elise), the commander's wayward daughter, and a handsome helicopter pilot named Tim (Billy Wirth). But these young people barely have time to get acquainted before the pods take over with a vengeance and pandemonium breaks out all over.

Taking advantage of the latest in movie magic technology, special makeup artists Tom Burman and Bari Dreiband-Burman have endowed this version of "Body Snatchers" with the most graphic version yet of how the pods go about their nefarious business. Definitely not for the squeamish, the film's ghoulish transformation scenes are both beautiful and repellent, filmed with awe and with a touch of mystery.

Horrific as all this is, "Body Snatchers" has more than technology going for it. Both composer Joe Delia, who wrote a classically disturbing score, and cinematographer Bojan Bazelli, whose searchlight-lit scene of the pods being harvested is completely chilling, are major forces in helping Ferrara create the film's palpable sense of unease and uncertainty.

From these big concerns to small but unforgettable moments like the pods' hair-raising warning signal, director Ferrara has envisioned this movie whole from beginning to end. The world does not quite look the same when "Body Snatchers" is over, and there is little more you can ask of a science-fiction/horror film than that.

NEW YORK, 2/21/94, p. 48, John Powers

For a pop song to become a standard, it must have enough "give" that many different kinds of singers can make it their own. Perhaps the only movie to approach such resiliency is *The Invasion of the Body Snatchers*, Don Siegel's 1956 sci-fi masterpiece about a small town taken over by emotionless "pod people." The perfect pulp allegory for whatever form of thought control is around at the time, it was remade in 1978 by Philip Kaufman, who set the story in San Francisco and satirized the human-potential movement, whose endless prattle about personal growth actually meant turning people into vegetables. Now comes *Body Snatchers*, a creepy, knockabout remake set on an Alabama military base. Tough-guy director Abel Ferrara obviously has no fondness for the wised-up slickness of Kaufman's version (though he cheerfully steals its famous closing scream) and returns the story to the original's B-movie roots. The movie is fast, funny, and a little bit cheesy—everything happens in shorthand.

Gabrielle Anwar plays Marti Malone, an alienated teenager whose family moves to a military base so that her EPA-man dad can check the area for toxins. They haven't even reached the camp when a crazy-eyed soldier looms from the dark, moaning, "They get you when you sleep!" Marti doesn't know what he means, but we know—and Ferrara knows that we know. *Body Snatchers* doesn't expect us to be startled when people turn into zombies overnight. It expects us to revel in *how* this familiar story is unfolding.

Ferrara wants us to appreciate the sinister wit of setting scene after scene at dusk, when shapes lose their definition and the enemy, sleep, is just around the corner. He wants us to cackle and shudder at the nifty special effects: collapsing heads, alien corpses shrinking to the texture of strawberry crepes, space pods shooting wormy tendrils up their victims' noses. Ferrara's camera is tireless, stalking each new victim with baleful delight and trailing away from Marti's story to show us alien skulduggery through the underbrush. In a movie where everyone has a soulless double waiting in the wings, the director composes his shots so that characters are constantly accompanied by their own ominous shadows.

And Ferrara draws the characters with rapid pen strokes—they're ideograms, not people. There's Marti's boyfriend, Tim (Billy Wirth), the honest chopper pilot; there's the base commander's punk daughter, Jenn (Christine Elise), whose booze-and-bonking rebelliousness means she's sure to be podded; there's the camp psychiatrist, Major Collins (Forest Whitaker), whose hysterics would be right at home in Samuel Fuller's *Shock Corridor*. Even the talented Anwar can't keep Marti from being simply another teenage girl jealous of her dad's new wife, played by Meg Tilly, and hot for the cute guy she just met. *Body Snatchers* isn't much shallower than the original film, but it has none of the emotional resonance, possibly because it's been made for a far younger audience. Its real subject is adolescent angst, the terror that the adult world will turn one's youthful uniqueness into a dull, quiescent middle-aged conformity.

It's a fear shared by Ferrara, who has always played the outlaw, loudly refusing to make the safe, conformist pictures of the Hollywood careerist. He would rather be ridiculous than mediocre, and he often is: *Bad Lieutenant* was the best movie I saw last year, except for the parts that were laughable. Taut but tinny, *Body Snatchers* marks a temporary departure from the sleaze, psychodrama, and festering sense of sin that fueled *King of New York, Bad Lieutenant,* and *Dangerous Game.* But you can still hear Ferrara's rebel yell in the movie's fiery coda, when Marti and Tim begin attacking the military base in search of vengeance. The aliens win, but Ferrara makes damn sure his heroes do some damage.

NEW YORK POST, 2/4/94, p. 37, Thelma Adams

If director Abel Ferrara wanted to reduce Don Siegel's 1956 classic, "Invasion of the Body Snatchers," to pulp sci-fi, then his "Body Snatchers" is a roaring success.

Both are based on Jack Finney's novel, "The Body Snatchers." In 1978, Philip Kaufman remade the movie with Donald Sutherland.

In Siegel's chilling political allegory about alien pods turning common citizen into automatons, the director set McCarthy era paranoia against the smalltown U.S.A of sweater girls and Studebakers.

Ferrara holds onto the paranoia, but loses middle America, then he updates the story to the MTV era. His hero is not the wise, vaguely smart-ass, small-town M.D. (Kevin McCarthy) but an airhead of the new generation, a nubile high schooler (Gabrielle Anwar) with a daddy complex.

Anwar has the presence of dead meat in a "Friday the 13th" serial. She is joined by forgettable performances from Terry Kinney and Billy Wirth. As a military doctor, Forest Whitaker has no place to run. Only Meg Tilly holds her own; for her, playing a zombie is typecasting.

Ferrara and his pack of screenwriters (five are credited) exploit latent anti-military hostility by setting "Body Snatchers" on a military base. This allows them to put the stilted speechifying in the mouth of an already-suspect cartoon general.

"Abandon yourself and join us," says the glassy-eyed leader. "It's the race that's important, not the individual."

Did someone have an acid flashback while watching a "be all that you can be" Army promo on TV? What makes Siegel's movie so smart and ferocious is that the townies begin as trusted neighbors and become enemies—they don't start out that way.

Making use of modern effects, "Body Snatchers" is more graphic—though less imaginative, and less scary—than the original. The pods are seen in action sending out slurpy worms to suck the life from their victims.

Ferrara's leaden remake adds gratuitous breast-baring to the mix; ironically, it's less sexy than the original, which raised temperatures with witty repartee and a few well-timed kisses between major characters.

In fact, the original actually had characters! Ferrara has alienation, a theme he picked at in "Bad Lieutenant" and the recent Madonna bomb "Dangerous Game."

Ferrara and company sum up what little they have to say in the movie's last line, droned in voiceover: "There's no one like you left."

So what? In the case of pretentious directors, sometimes one is more than enough.

NEWSDAY, 2/4/94, Part II/p. 67, Jack Mathews

Don Siegel's classic 1956 "Invasion of the Body Snatchers," a science-fiction film tailored to the paranoia gripping cold war America, was so much a product of its time it would have seemed pointless for anyone else to attempt to remake, update or expand on it.

Yet, it has happened twice, in 1978, as an homage to Siegel by Philip Kaufman, and now, for reasons that are not apparent onscreen, by Abel Ferrara, whose tough urban dramas are very much a product of *his* time.

In the '50s the story about aliens attempting to take over the world by replicating, then destroying their human models, played to two of Americans' great dreads: the idea that there might be intelligent and hostile life in outer space, and, of more immediate concern, that our neighborhoods were being infested with communist spies. Red hysteria was still alive when Kaufman's remake appeared, but no one took it for more than a really classy horror film, Siegel's movie redone in color, with a big budget and state-of-the-art special effects. It made up in suspense and visual shocks what was missing in psychological and political underpinnings.

Ferrara's version, under the shortened title "Body Snatchers," springs full-blown from the loins of nothing. It's got a lot of gooey special effects, the aliens' slimy tendrils snaking like mad spaghetti into the orifices of its human victims, but these scenes are nothing next to the eerily repellent pod births in the first two versions, and it doesn't have even an echo of their underlying terror.

"Body Snatchers," written by the "Re-Animator" team of Stuart Gordon and Dennis Paoli with the credited help of long-time Ferrara collaborator Nicholas St. John, resets the story (originally based on the 1950 novel by Jack Finney) in Selma, Ala., next to a military base where the aliens have set up shop.

The main character in this tale is Marti Malone (Gabrielle Anwar, Al Pacino's dance partner in "Scent of a Woman"), the rebellious teenage daughter of a government scientist (Terry Kinney) sent to oversee a toxic waste clean-up operation at the base. Soon after the Malones, whose members include Marti's stepmother (Meg Tilley) and her 5-year-old half-brother (Reilly Murphy), move into their base home, people begin showing up with dead eyes and monotonal voices.

Half the fun of the "Invasion" movies is trying to figure out which of the protagonists' friends—and, in this case, family—have been taken over, and Ferrara plays that to the hilt. When the ratio of aliens-to-humans has shifted and the base community is overrun with the monsters, any mortal detected among them sets off a voice alarm shrill enough to drown out an air raid siren.

To his credit, Ferrara didn't take the outdated story's original themes too seriously. He was given an opportunity to wallow in B movie genre and does it with an unapologetic reverence for sci-fi horror clichés. If you watch it strictly on that level, it can be great fun.

But the only viewers likely to feel the paranoid horror of the earlier movies are those fathers, like me, who tend to see aliens lurking wherever their teenage daughters go.

TIME, 2/14/94, p. 68, Richard Corliss

Marti Malone (Gabrielle Anwar) stops at a gas station near the Army base where her family is to spend the next month. In the restroom she is surprised by a large man who stifles her cries and whispers the warning "They get you when you sleep!" His words are like a bedtime story's ultimate threat: Keep listening to this tale, my child. If you nod off before the end, you could die.

Sleep is supposed to be the kingdom of our own monsters—that nightscape where the id, unshackled by scruple, runs wild and plays out every dreamer's scenarios of fear fulfillment. But in his 1954 science-fiction novel *The Body Snatchers*, Jack Finney had an even spookier idea: that sleep is when the sentry of common sense nods off and allows our enemies, not ourselves, to invade and conquer. Pod seeds fall from outer space and rob sleeping humans of their emotions, their very selves. It was Us vs. Them, cold-war style—and in this cunning parable of persecution, Them could be communism or McCarthyism. It could be any ism bent on robbing the U. S. (Us) of its ragged individualism.

Finney's fable has passed the time test (40 years is forever in pop culture), having been filmed twice as *Invasion of the Body Snatchers*, by Don Siegel in 1956 and Philip Kaufman in 1978. The first movie, punctuating California's small-town sunniness with the thunder of deadpan mobocracy, became a cult classic. Both pictures met the horror-movie challenge: they kept moviegoers up all night, ashiver with apprehension.

And now, just when you thought it was safe to take a nap, comes a third version. *Body Snatchers*, as the story is called this time, is smart and spooky. It cleverly twists the plot so the lonely hero battling the pods is now a plucky, skeptical teenage girl. And it expands on the theme of emotional isolation until it embraces, and then nearly annihilates, the whole postnuclear family.

Long before the pods start wrapping their tendrils around sleeping bodies, Marti and her family are plenty estranged. The girl is annoyed with her father (Terry Kinney), resentful of her stepmother (Meg Tilly) and jealous of the woman's attentions to her own small son (Reilly Murphy). Why, Marti might almost believe—as so many teens do of their own families—that her broody brood is a pack of soulless zombies from another planet. But paranoia is merely another word for self-preservation; and Marti, who never hides her raw feelings, is just the person to detect the wholesale poddifying of her family. By the end, and for the noblest cause—saving the earth—she will need to see them all killed.

This handsomely crafted studio production, unaccountably left to languish for a year in the Warner Bros. vault, comes from an unlikely auteur: poverty-row director Abel Ferrara, whose earlier work, from *Ms. 45* to *Bad Lieutenant*, is a gallery of Grunge Guignol. Somehow, flanked by five scripters (including his regular collaborator Nicholas St. John), he managed to stoke his tale with the eerie subtlety of the best old B movies.

He also coaxed top performances from his cast, especially the lead actresses. Tilly, with her otherworldly glamour, is a New Age evil stepmother; in her sleepytime voice, pod threats have the thrill of seduction. And Anwar (Al Pacino's dance partner in *Scent of a Woman*) plays Marti as honest, balky, easily bruised; already she has the edgy assurance of a pro slated for stardom. Her soft lashes and wary eyes, which make her look as if she has just been prodded awake into a nightmare, key this haunting film's message: that life has to be faced with eyes wide open. Otherwise ... to sleep, perchance to scream.

VILLAGE VOICE, 2/15/94, p. 51, J. Hoberman

As the second remake of the most famous B-movie allegory of the 1950s, Abel Ferrara's *Body Snatchers* isn't freighted with a sense of cultural guilt. Thanks to Philip Kaufman's elaborate 1978 update, the original *Invasion of the Body Snatchers*, directed by Don Siegel and released in early 1956, has already been snatched.

As much as it was anything, Siegel's *Body Snatchers* was a source of outrageous simile. The familiar Cold War fantasy of extraterrestrial invasion was here given an additionally paranoid twist. Drifting down from the sky, seedpods from outer space replicated human beings and replaced them (while they slept) with perfect, if emotionless, doubles—thus successfully colonizing earth with the asexual Organization Men of a harmoniously insectlike mass society.

If *High Noon* (1952) provided metaphoric justification for American foreign policy, *Invasion of the Body Snatchers* was an all-purpose allegory of the nation's domestic life. Like *High Noon*, similarly set in a nondescript Western town, *Invasion of the Body Snatchers* lent itself to both right- and left-wing readings—alternatively a drama of communist subversion or suburban conformity, unfolding in a hilariously bland atmosphere of extreme hypervigilance. The transformation of ordinary Americans into soullessly Sovietized Babbitts was a pop *1984* complete with the notion of subversive sex crime.

Given its maximally lurid title, *Invasion of the Body Snatchers* was all the more enjoyable for the podlike quality of its impassive performances and cheap *noir* naturalism. Nor was this the only source of deadpan humor. Psychology was identified with brainwashing, adjustment synonymous with coercion. Looking back on the Cold War from the post-McCarthy period, Siegel not only naturalized the Red Scare but imbued it with Darwinian angst—the fear that communism might actually be a higher stage on the evolutionary ladder.

While the Siegel movie opened on the bottom half of a double bill and was evidently deemed too disreputable to warrant a *New York Times* review, the Kaufman remake was released for Christmas and hailed by *The New Yorker* as "the American movie of the year—a new classic." Still, the original *Invasion of the Body Snatchers* is so intrinsically '50s that Kaufman felt compelled to link his remake to the epic revival that began around the time of Nixon's reelection (and continued through the middle of Reagan's second term): "We were all asleep in a lot of ways in the fifties ... Now we've gone back to sleep again." To sleep, of course, is to be podified—although Kaufman's intermittently rhapsodic remake was less concerned with subversion and conformity than with fighting psychobabble and protecting the environment, his aging hippie protagonists employed by San Francisco's Department of Health.

Ferrara's *Body Snatchers*, by contrast, is fast-paced, impersonal, and completely imagistic—the rolling and tumbling visuals serve to buff the leaden dialogue. This new *Body Snatchers* appropriates several aspects of the Kaufman version (both were produced by Robert H. Solo) but only to elaborate on Kaufman's more sensational special effects. The transformation from human to pod—invisible in Siegel—is here even more visceral, with tendrils descending upon sleeping humans and snaking into their various orifices. Ferrara further expands the capacity for pod-people to transform themselves into banshee alarm systems.

Although a more expensive production than Kaufman's, Ferrara's returns the material to its B-movie roots—reimagining it as a tough-talking action flick set not in northern California but on an Alabama military base. One unmistakable Ferrara touch: When a military pod wants to check the status of a passing-for-pod, he tells him, "Just so you know, I fucked your girlfriend." Another is the brash bit of slapstick that has a half-formed pod-body come crashing through the roof as an unsuspecting pod-to-be dozes in her bath.

So familiar has the *Body Snatchers* metaphor become that it's worth noting that back in 1956 *Variety* found the original sometimes "difficult to follow due to the strangeness of its scientific premise." As Noel Carroll pointed out some years ago in the *Soho Weekly News*, however, the movie offers a near textbook illustration of the condition called Capgras syndrome—the delusional belief that close relatives or associates (sometimes including oneself) have been replaced by sinister doubles.

In a setting of heightened suspicion, the spouses or parents of Capgras sufferers are rejected as imposters. *I Married a Monster From Outer Space* (1958) and the original *Invaders From Mars* (1953) are related examples of Capgrasoid sci-fi, and a study of the syndrome's case histories shows that imagined communist conspiracies were scarcely unknown during the Cold War. Capgras syndrome has been variously analyzed as a paranoid projection (a familiar person no longer elicits the same affective response; the person must have changed, not the subject's feelings) or as the denial of certain traits in one with whom the subject has strong emotional ties. It makes sense then that the original *Invasion of the Body Snatchers* would appear immediately after the 1948-53 period of maximum mobilization—after it was safe to dramatize the recent hysteria and meditate on the Pod That Failed.

But Capgras syndrome has also been theorized as a defensive maneuver allowing the subject to handle erotic or aggressive feelings toward a parental figure, and it is in this sense that Ferrara's *Body Snatchers* is most vivid. Almost completely devoid of children, the 1978 *Body Snatchers* focuses exclusively on mature heterosexual relationships. Seen today, the movie seems enacted by the cast of *Seinfeld.* The current version, though, concerns the nuclear family. The protagonist Marti Malone (Gabrielle Anwar) is an alienated teenage stepdaughter—for her, mother has long since been replaced by the soulless pod of the second Mrs. Malone (Meg Tilly). The big chill here is an on-base daycare center where "the children produce identical finger paintings; the key sequence has Mrs. Malone disintegrate in her sleep, then reappear stark naked and impassively witchy before her five-year-old son ("That isn't my mommy!"), who is subsequently trapped between zombie day-care and imposter mom.

The movie feeds on the tension between father and daughter, pitting Marti and her off-limits soldier boyfriend (Billy Wirth) against the rest of the family. That Mr. Malone (Terry Kinney) works for the EPA is basically a red herring—although, unlike both previous *Body Snatchers* Ferrara's makes the resident shrink (Forest Whitaker) a heroic pod-fighter. As the last individual fighting to stay awake, Whitaker is a torrent of human emotion—shouting, drooling, sweating, crying, and all but deliquescing on screen.

The army base where this latest *Body Snatchers* is set is at once an updated suburbia, a prison camp, and a toxic waste dump. Ferrara turns the Capgras syndrome into a universal principle: Given the demands of military discipline, how can you tell when a soldier is a pod? The Klaxon blare of the base's full-alert only amplifies the individual's need to protect their ego by remaining awake. As the troubled Malone family is a transplant from *Rebel Without a Cause*, so the base commander is played by R. Lee Ermey, promoted from his tour of duty as marine drill sergeant in *Full Metal Jacket*. Explicitly post-Desert Storm (the war commanded by the most severely pod of U.S. presidents), featuring a complete panoply of firefights, choppers, and bombing raids, as well as a story of adolescent sexual acting out, the movie collapses all Boomer history, from the Cold War through Vietnam to the New World Order, into a single slick package.

Ferrara and his writers further manage to evoke Oliver Stone—the pod subversion is envisioned as a military coup. And yet, if this latest *Body Snatchers* leaves less of a residue than did Kaufman's, the fault is less Ferrara's than history's. The original *Invasion of the Body Snatchers* provided an imaginative visualization of the national security state and reckoned its psychic cost to America's self-image. At this point—and this may be the point—we no longer even have that identity left to lose.

Also reviewed in:
CHICAGO TRIBUNE, 2/25/94, Friday/p. C, Michael Wilmington
NEW YORK TIMES, 2/4/94, p. C6, Caryn James
VARIETY, 5/3/93, p. 39, Lawrence Cohn
WASHINGTON POST, 2/18/94, p. G7, Richard Harrington

BOSNA!

A Zeitgeist Films release of a Bosnia-Herzegovina Radio Television and France 2 Cinéma with Canal+ and the Centre National de la Cinématographie production. *Director:* Bernard-Henri Lévy and Alain Ferrari. *Screenplay (French with English subtitles):* Bernard-Henri Lévy and Giles Herzog. *Director of Photography:* Pierre Boffety. *Editor:* Yann Kassile and Frédéric Lossignol. *Music:* Denis Barbier. *Production Designer:* Dominique Charitat. *Running time:* 117 minutes. *MPAA Rating:* Not Rated.

NARRATOR: Bernard-Henri Lévy.

NEW YORK, 10/24/94, p. 62, David Denby

Two brilliant, and utterly dissimilar, French documentaries about the siege of Sarajevo and the West's near-abandonment of Bosnia should be seen by much larger audiences than they are now reaching—Marcel Ophuls's *The Troubles We've Seen*, which has no American distributor at this moment (PBS, are you listening?), and Bernard-Henri Lévy's *Bosna!*, which is playing through October 25 at Film Forum. The films share a similar point of view: The truth of Serbian aggression and atrocities has been known almost from the beginning of the war, but the West, not wanting to get involved, has insisted on the baffling moral complexities of a war that was never all that hard to understand.

Ophuls focuses on thc moral ambiguities of wartime journalism, the play of courage, vanity, self-seeking, and selflessness that makes war correspondents the most fascinating of reporters. In Sarajevo, such people as John F. Burns, the *Times* correspondent, have played an exemplary role in getting the word out to the willingly deaf Western capitals. Ophuls himself is far from unambiguous about his own role, and the movie is saturated in irony, media history, movie lore, as if Ophuls could establish his right to make a movie about Sarajevo only by airing over and over the impossibility of his making it. Ophuls's playfulness masks his despair. The West's acceptance of "ethnic cleansing" not only negates thc lesson of World War II, it negates the lessons of such Ophuls works as *The Sorrow and the Pity*. Lévy, on the other hand, is too angry for self-scrutiny. Lévy's movie is offered without irony. Lévy, a Paris philosophe, works in a tradition of impassioned moral analysis—stern, proclamatory, yet lyrical and witty-stretching from Voltaire to Malraux. This is a thrilling piece of cinematic and literary rhetoric—propaganda, perhaps, but at a very high intellectual level. *Bosna!* is a fighting film. Lévy wants to remove the Bosnians once and for all from the condescension of Western charity. These are not victims but an embattled people deserving of our support. Thc movie is scorchingly lucid.

NEW YORK POST, 10/12/94, p. 36, Larry Worth

Watching reports on the evening news, you need a scorecard to separate the Serbs from the Bosnians, never mind the Croatians. Who's fighting who and how did the former Yugoslavia turn into a war zone about to implode?

In "Bosna!" a sobering, thought-provoking documentary co-directed by French philosopher Bernard-Henri Levy and Alain Ferrari, the answers become painfully clear.

Divided into five related segments, Levy and Ferrari's amazing footage qualifies as the ultimate horror story. It's the history of a world gone mad, with an ethnic-cleansing subject matter drawing inevitable Holocaust comparisons.

At one point, the narrator assesses the world's sentiments after Auschwitz: "We didn't know"; 50 years later on Sarajevo: "We don't understand."

Suffice to say no one witnessing "Bosna" will leave uninformed or neutral. Making no pretense at objectivity, the filmmakers state that Bosnia's move for independence was answered with Serbian bullets turning Sarajevo into a permanent firing range, Dubrovnic into a shell. Then Croatia entered the fray against Bosnia and still no help from the West.

Dripping with sarcasm, the narrator states: Bosnia, unlike Kuwait, made the mistake of having no oil.

But even if the film qualifies as a polemic, one can't deny the unbelievable scenes of carnage: Bodies frozen in the snow, others charred to a crisp, a child screaming over the gaping hole in his stomach, a man getting his arm amputated with a hacksaw, a pile of bloody torsos—and the nearby severed heads.

That's counterpointed with a Serbian soldier's recollections of instructions to slit his victims' throats, an act that made him "feel nothing." He then admits to raping several women and arbitrarily killing two of them.

The barrage of powerhouse images stops only with the end credits. And therein lies the film's chief flaw. There's too much to absorb in one sitting. Levy also tries to gild the lily by integrating newsreels of World War II food drops and making analogies to the Spanish Civil War.

But those are minor flaws. The bulk of the production commands full attention, making viewers feel as if they're dodging behind sandbags along with the besieged Bosnians.

As an unforgettable tribute to a defiant people, "Bosna!" is appropriately chilling, wrenching and disturbing. And for those interested in humanity's future, it's required viewing.

VILLAGE VOICE, 10/18/94, p. 61, Leslie Camhi

For those who missed Marcel Ophüls's *The Troubles I've Seen*, a brilliant documentary on war correspondents stationed in Sarajevo (which screened just once at the NYFF), *Bosna!* offers an opportunity to catch up on the panorama of human valor and evil currently at work in ex-Yugoslavia. French philosopher and enfant-truly-terrible Bernard-Henri Lévy codirected this documentary, which lionizes the Bosnian resistance while providing a scathing indictment of Western democracies' indifference to this ongoing genocide.

A political, moral, and human disaster of such monstrosity might inspire humility in a foreign witness, but self-effacement has never been Lévy's strong point, nor is it his intention. *Bosna!* suffers from his non-stop voiceover, a ponderous sense of historical self-importance and less-than-skillful editing. It's in part a paean to the Bosnian army, yet I can't help wondering if in long-besieged Sarajevo, military machismo is of any use against a sniper.

Nevertheless, *Bosna!* is illuminated by a heartfelt moral passion; it's most adept at depicting the international betrayal that transformed a question of law into one of "humanitarian" charity. From the opening shots of the post-apocalyptic lunar landscape in the hills above Sarajevo to the horrifyingly familiar scenes of concentration camps, its images are indelible. So, too, are the voices of the players in this tragedy: Serbian General Mladic's radio messages ordering his snipers to shoot at "antlike" civilians; the chilling testimony of a Serb prisoner sentenced to death for his part in a rape and killing; the tragic guardian of Sarajevo's morgue, who daily notes the dead in a register that includes his son's name. Together they raise a powerful cry of *j'accuse!*, issuing directly from an open wound in contemporary Europe.

Also reviewed in:
NEW YORK TIMES, 10/12/94, p. C13, Stephen Holden
VARIETY, 5/23-29/94, p. 57, Emanuel Levy

BOYS LIFE

A Strand Releasing release of a compilation of three shorts. *Running time:* 90 minutes. *MPAA Rating:* Not Rated.

POOL DAYS—*Executive Producer:* Robert Miller. *Producer:* Brian Sloan. *Director:* Brian Sloan. *Screenplay:* Brian Sloan. *Director of Photography:* Jonathan Schell. *Editor:* Brian Sloan. *Music:* Hundred Pound Head. *Sound:* Francois Keraudren, Myra Paci, and Katie Fleischer.

WITH: Josh Weinstein (Justin); Nick Poletti (Russell); Kimberly Flynn (Vicky); Richard Salamanca.

A FRIEND OF DOROTHY—*Producer:* Raoul O'Connell. *Director:* Raoul O'Connell. *Screenplay:* Raoul O'Connell. *Director of Photography:* W. Mott Hupfel III. *Editor:* Chris Hougton. *Music:* Tom Judson. *Set Designer:* Adrian Davey and Kevin Donaldson. *Sound:* Chris Drozdowski.

WITH: Raoul O'Connell (Winston); Anne Zupa (Anne); Kevin McClatchy (Tom); Greg Lauren (Matt).

THE DISCO YEARS—*Producer:* Robert Lee King, John Peter James, and Richard Hoffman. *Director:* Robert Lee King. *Screenplay:* Robert Lee King. *Director of Photography:* Greg Gardiner. *Editor:* Paul McCudden. *Music:* Wendall J. Yuponce. *Production Designer:* Greg Gardiner. *Costumes:* Neal San Teguns. *Running time:* 90 minutes. *MPAA Rating:* Not Rated.

WITH: Matt Nolan (Tom); Gwen Welles (Melissa); Dennis Christopher (Mr. Reese); Russell Scott Lewis (Matt).

NEW YORK POST, 12/2/94, p. 51, Thelma Adams

Coming out of the closet while coming of age is the theme of three short films about gay life by promising young directors opening today at the Quad Cinema.

In New York University film school grad Brian Sloan's "Pool Days" an attractive young teen (Josh Weinstein) gets a summer job as a lifeguard at a suburban pool. The short, which played at New Directors at the Museum of Modern Art last spring, uses a light touch to detail the high schooler's discovery that he is more attracted to a buff male swimmer than an aggressive female aerobics instructor.

Another NYU grad, Raoul O'Connell, uses an equally light touch in "A Friend of Dorothy." (The title refers to a code phrase for gay men who appreciate Judy Garland.) O'Connell cast himself in the lead as an amiable NYU sophomore who has a crush on his roommate and confides in his chubby, upbeat gal pal.

Robert Lee King's "The Disco Years" is the least slick of the three, and the most ready to address conflict. Tom (Matt Nolan) falls for golden boy Matt (Russell Scott Lewis), his high school tennis teammate.

They have a one-night stand. Tom takes the liaison seriously, but Matt rejects Tom, gets a girlfriend and starts gay bashing. When Matt and his clique harass a gay English teacher (Dennis Christopher), Tom must decide whether to take a stand. This leads Tom to a confrontation with his mother (Gwen Welles), who cannot accept her son's homosexuality.

While all three directors demonstrate a film-school polish, they approach their subject with the tameness of an after-school special. Coming out is no doubt wrenching, but the filmmakers couch the process in a cliched coming-of-age format with three of the most middle-class, fresh-faced and attractive leads to roam outside of 90210.

NEWSDAY, 12/2/94, Part II/p. B7, Frank DeCaro

As rites of passage go, gay coming-of-age is often fraught with frustration; a time of jangled nerves, bruised egos, and emotional skittishness. But while this time is 70 percent hell, 29 percent Clearasil and 1 percent condoms, it's also incredibly exciting—the mighty real beginnings of gay adulthood.

"Boys Life," a trio of hopeful, upbeat short films, sensitively explores this turning point in the lives of three gay teenagers. All just happen to be nice, cute, masculine and well-built—gay made easy! But the films are imbued with enough flashes of genuine humanity to vault these shorts out of realm of the superficial.

In "Pool Days" by Brian Sloan, high school senior Justin (Josh Weinstein) takes a summer job as a lifeguard at a health club and discovers his sexuality when he meets Russell (Nick Poletti), an older massage therapist. Their first date is touching, but it scares the bejesus out of Justin, who runs into the arms of Vicky (Kimberly Flynn), an aerobics teacher. Justin can run but he can 't hide.

Raoul O'Connell's "A Friend of Dorothy" is the best of the lot. O'Connell wrote, directed, produced and starred in this film about a Streisand fanatic and Madonna worshipper named Winston, who comes to NYU and promptly falls in love with his sexy dorm-mate Tom (Kevin McClatchy). But he can never score, despite coaching from his best friend, Anne (Ann Zupa), a sexy, chubby gayboy gal pal. He'll try anything, though, in the pursuit of homo-happiness.

Spoofing "The Wonder Years," Robert Lee King's touching "The Disco Years" remembers the pre-AIDS era of the late 1970s and deals most explicitly with the homophobia gay teens face. Tom (Matt Nolan) falls for his tennis team buddy, Matt (Russell Scott Lewis). They play (and play around), but it means nothing to Matt. For Tom, whose gay feelings are no phase, it's devastating. But these events, like many coming-out experiences, lead to self-acceptance and ultimately happiness.

Also reviewed in:
CHICAGO TRIBUNE, 2/17/95, Friday/p. K, John Petrakis
NEW YORK TIMES, 12/2/94, p. C16, Stephen Holden
VARIETY, 1/9-15/95, p. 72, Godfrey Cheshire
WASHINGTON POST, 2/3/95, p. D6, Hal Hinson

BOYS OF ST. VINCENT, THE

An Alliance Communications release of A Les Productions Tele-Action/National Film Board of Canada coproduction in association with the Canadian Broadcasting Corporation with the participation of Telefilm Canada. *Executive Producer:* Claudio Luca and Colin Neale. *Producers:* Sam Grana and Claudio Luca. *Director:* John N. Smith. *Screenplay:* Des Walsh, John N. Smith, and Sam Grana. *Director of Photography:* Pierre Letarte. *Editor:* Werner Nold and Andre Corriveau. *Music:* Neil Smolar. *Sound:* Serge Beauchemin. *Casting*: Nadia Rona and Rosina Bucci. *Production Designer:* Real Ouellette. *Set Decorator:* Claire Alary and Annie McLeod. *Costumes:* Denis Sperdouklis. *Running time:* 93 minutes (each part). *MPAA Rating:* Not Rated.

CAST: Henry Czerny (Peter Lavin); Johnny Morina (Kevin Reevey, age 10); Sebastian Spence (Kevin Reevey, age 25); Brian Dodd (Steven Lunny, age 10); David Hewlett (Steven Lunny, age 25); Jonathan Lewis (Eddie Linnane); Jeremy Keefe (Mike Sproule); Phillip Dinn (Mike Finn); Brian Dooley (Detective Noseworthy); Greg Thomey (Brother Glackin); Michael Wade (Brother MacLaverty); Lise Roy (Chantal Lavin); Kristine Demers (Sheilah); Timothy Webber (Brian Lunny, age 30); Ashley Billard (Brian Lunny, age 16); Alain Goulem (Brother Glynn); Ed Martin (Tomy Kennedy); Sam Grana (Monsignor); Maurice Podbrey (Archbishop); Pierre Gauthier (Lavin's Psychiatrist).

NEW YORK, 6/13/94, p. 83, David Denby

The sexual abuse of children, which is perhaps the hardest of the perversions to comprehend, is also (if the newspapers and daytime talk shows are to be believed) the most common. Yet how can it be treated in a movie without exploitation or evasion? Well, a miracle has happened: The two-part Canadian drama *The Boys of St. Vincent*, now playing at Film Forum, is a great piece of work—explicit but unsensational, psychologically complex, fully engaged with its excruciating subject. The director, John N. Smith, and his screenwriting collaborators, Des Walsh and Sam Grana, have made a heroic attempt to understand vice without relinquishing judgment of it. From start to finish, they stay focused on their prepossessing villain, Brother Peter Lavin, a strong, handsome, intelligent young man who bears, in the person of actor Henry Czerny, a rather startling resemblance to Tyrone Power. Lavin is the director of a Newfoundland orphanage run by the All Saints Brothers—and a pederast. The steely-voiced Czerny offers a classic portrait in repression, hypocrisy, and rage.

The filmmakers have the courage to get inside Lavin's obsession. In the orphanage, we see the young boys as the lustful Lavin sees them—in the shower, their backs to the camera, graceful shapes gleaming with water and soap. One boy in particular, the beautiful, wary 10-year-old orphan Kevin, becomes Lavin's special victim, forced to enter his office at night. For a while, the movie is built on gothic suggestion—a lonely, frightened boy, say, wandering down a corridor. Only slowly do we realize, to our horror, that many of the other Brothers in the orphanage are indulging the same obsessions, and that the boys are frozen in terror, afraid to open their mouths lest they be thrown into the street. They can only submit.

The Boys of St. Vincent is a fictionalized version of an actual case. Part One, set in 1975, is essentially a rescue story: The orphanage's illiterate janitor realizes what's going on and in tandem with an honest policeman forces an investigation, with the result that the Church quietly transfers Lavin and a few of the more flagrant violators. Yet this section of the movie ends with a chilling tableau worthy of *The Godfather*. After Church and government officials have swept the scandal under the rug, we see a smug ceremony in which government funding passes to the orphanage, and the plump elders of the Church smile in satisfaction while the boys look tight and fearful. Their nightmare will continue.

Part Two picks up the story fifteen years later. Lavin, having quit his Holy Order, is now a married man with an admirably tough-minded wife and two young sons, while his former charges, in their mid-twenties, struggle to come to terms with feelings of guilt and loathing. The government reopens the case, and the cover-up unravels. Some of the dramatic issues—whether to testify and risk succumbing to the terrors of memory—we've seen in other works, but the movie shrewdly, and freshly, brings into the picture the women who suffer from the men's obsessions, the women who must break into the memories or get shut out. And *Boys* stays fastened to Lavin, a desolate man who believes, in the convolutions of his self-justifying wrath, that he was protecting his boys. In movies, evil is usually something caricatured. But Lavin receives realistic treatment, and as the full range of his wretchedness becomes clear, he seems more and more dangerous.

Is *Boys* anti-Catholic? No, but it certainly suggests that the traditions of celibacy and secrecy within the Church make the sexual abuse of children a regular temptation. Though irreproachably made, *The Boys of St. Vincent* will always be controversial. In Canada, the government kept it off the air for a while, and in America the only network that will touch it is A&E (which has scheduled it for cablecast next January). One would almost think the crimes—with their attendant shame and secrecy—were still being covered up.

NEW YORK POST, 6/1/94, p. 31, Bill Hoffmann

Pedophilia is not an easy subject to think about, let alone film.

And yet the makers of "The Boys of St. Vincent" have done it with great skill and a no-nonsense approach that makes this production a haunting, riveting experience for adventurous, mature filmgoers.

It's a two-part horror show with demons scarier than in any slasher movie you're likely to see.

The place is St. Vincent's, a dark and creepy Catholic-run orphanage for Canadian boys, where it looks as if there's a gremlin in every crack and crevice.

It is strictly run by a smug, humorless brother named Peter Lavin, around whom all of the boys are visibly uncomfortable.

We soon discover Lavin is the head child molester in a nest of pedophiles who've been quietly abusing the kids for years while evoking the name of God. To keep them quiet, the brothers threaten them with hell, beatings and worse.

Lavin is obsessed with a 10-year-old named Kevin, whom he regularly excuses from class for "counseling sessions." Behind closed doors the terrified boy is forced to call him "mother" and submit to his lewd sexual demands.

Eventually, one boy spills the beans, leading to a police probe that's ultimately covered up by the church and government. Fifteen years later, the investigation is reopened with Lavin, now married with two kids, and others being arrested and tried.

The performances of Henry Czerny as the completely evil Lavin and Johnny Morina as Kevin are remarkable and so realistic it's like being there. To director John Smith's great credit, their extraordinary sex scenes are disturbing without being explicit or exploitive.

But no sensation is needed in a story this explosive. It's all so horrific, that the jolts and screams come, just like in a big Hollywood thriller.

You'll actually find yourself cowering when the bad guys are on screen and rooting for the boys as they try to escape their abusers.

"The Boy's of St. Vincent" was inspired by a true story, shot for Canadian TV, and later banned from broadcast.

It packs a big wallop and should be seen by anyone with compassion for the terrible problem it probes with such force.

NEWSDAY, 6/1/94, Part II/p. B7, John Anderson

When people wax nostalgic about times having been more "civilized," what they usually mean is more discreet: Certain things simply were not discussed, and therefore did not happen.

They happen in "The Boys of St. Vincent," though, and in a way that makes this two-part Canadian Broadcasting Corp. film—about sexual abuse in a Catholic orphanage—as potently indiscreet as a film can be.

The film's broadcast history has been one of controversy, injunctions, blackouts and scandal: Closely paralleling Newfoundland's infamous Mount Cashel case, the fictional film was kept off the air by lawyers defending four former Christian Brothers accused of having molested their young charges, on the grounds it was prejudicial to their case (they were probably right).

The archbishop who had denied director John N. Smith access to Catholic facilities when the film was being shot was later indicted on charges of covering up the crimes of his subordinates. When help lines were set up in Toronto after the film finally aired nationwide last December (having been completed in mid-'92), the phones were flooded with calls from those claiming to be victims of abuse. "The Boys of St. Vincent" is not just a film, at this point, but an important part of its own story. The story itself is a Dickensian tale of horror, of trust betrayed, of political hackery, and of evil. And there is never any doubt where the villainy lies: Brother Peter Lavin (Henry Czerny), head of the St. Vincent's orphanage for boys in St. John's, Newfoundland, a megalomaniacal martinet, volatile and violent, whose indulgence of his own sexually aberrant impulses sets the tone for the home he's supposed to be supervising. Boys are fondled in their beds, beatings are delivered with erotic pleasure. And no one will say a word.

Lavin's own favorite, however, is young Kevin Reevey (Johnny Morina), who runs away to escape "Bro's" attentions. But the police bring Kevin back—the authorities continually aid and abet the abuse of the boys—and in a scene of skin-crawling sexual terror, Kevin is nuzzled and undressed by Lavin. "Mamma loves you," Lavin murmurs. "You're not my mother," Kevin finally says, at which point Lavin beats him nearly to death.

From here, the cloak of silence hanging over St. Vincent's begins to unravel. The school's kindly janitor, Mike Finn (Phillip Dinn), takes Kevin to a doctor, whose suspicions are aroused, and then seeks the help of a detective named Noseworthy (Brian Dooley), who will see the case resolved 15 years later, in the second part of the film (requiring a separate admission).

Although there are certain qualities in "*The Boys of St. Vincent*" that betray its television origins—there's simply too much here for it all to be fully realized—it's a special film regardless.

There are no easy denouements. Finn, fired by Lavin, disappears forever; Noseworthy engages the wrath of his Catholic superiors and the stonewalling of the church hierarchy and has to break a promise to get Kevin out. The ease with which either the church or the state sacrifices children to save political skin is devastating. And the complex performance of Henry Czerny—in the film's second and much less gothic half he almost makes Lavin sympathetic—is literally breathtaking.

"The Boys of St. Vincent" is unstinting in its portrayal of what can happen to children who are the victims of sexual abuse, and of the hypocrisy with which society treats such crimes: Stephen Lunny (David Hewlett), testifying as to what happened to him as a boy, is pilloried for being an adult drug addict, petty criminal and prostitute. No one ever lays Stephen's ruined adult life at the feet of St. Vincent's, except John N. Smith, who is laudably unafraid to lay blame where it belongs.

VILLAGE VOICE, 6/7/94, p. 49, J. Hoberman

The Boys of St. Vincent is part topical muckraker, part eternal Gothic—an effective piece of work by any standard, and perhaps the most sensational rabble-rouser ever produced by normally circumspect Canadian TV. Dealing with pederasty and sadism in a hyper-Catholic environment, this two-part docudrama is programmed to offend. (Film Forum, where it opens a three-week run today, should prepare for picket, as well as ticket, lines.) I've never seen a more compelling movie on the tyranny of adults and the exploitation of children—or one more poised to intervene.

Directed by CBC veteran John N. Smith, *The Boys of St. Vincent* is a fictionalized amalgam of several incidents, drawing mainly on a late-'80s investigation into the sexual abuse of inmates at a Church-administered orphanage in Newfoundland. Originally scheduled to be televised in December 1992, the movie was successfully enjoined by lawyers for four ex-brothers charged with similar crimes; as a result, the telecast was blacked out in Ontario and parts of Quebec (Canada's two most populous provinces). For all the buzz occasioned by its inclusion in a subsequent Toronto Film Festival, it was still not nationally broadcast until this past December—and only then after withstanding a second legal challenge.

The movie follows a nocturnal, morning-after structure. The first of two 93-minute parts, set mainly in the orphanage, is posh and gloomy. St. Vincent's dark, empty corridors are populated by sinister shadows and typically shot from the low-angle viewpoint of a 10-year-old kid. The action is oblique and eerily suffused with liturgical music—namely the inmates' sweetly piping, prepubescent voices. St. Vincent is a place of long nights and mysterious doings. Every activity seems regulated, yet power reigns unchecked. Smith gives the movie the brooding, polished mahogany look of *The Godfather*—particularly in the surprisingly frequent scenes of church leaders eating, drinking, and otherwise hobnobbing with secular politicians.

A respected local institution, the orphanage is administered by the young, Byronically handsome Brother Lavin (Henry Czerny). Driven and ambitious, striding through the narrative with a crazy glint and a crucifix tucked like a dagger in his belt, Lavin not only hisses scary bedtime stories to teach his charges the virtues of submission but practices what he preaches—lavishing unwanted affection, as well as no small amount of punishment, on his "boy," Kevin. As the charismatic commandant of a psychic concentration camp, Lavin would seem a prime candidate for villain of the year. (Czerny, who plays him with a full panoply of symptoms, is due this summer in the new Harrison Ford vehicle, *Clear and Present Danger*. His director, meanwhile, has been rewarded—for his skill directing children?—with a Disney contract.)

Although *The Boys of St. Vincent* is mainly positioned at the child's perspective, the film doesn't shy from an adult sense of pedophilic temptation. The images of the innocent boys' soapy little butts are as flagrant as the high school shower scene that opens *Carrie*. The movie can be disturbingly explicit—as much for what is said as for what is done. "Mama loves you," Lavin croons over a half-naked Kevin between kisses and fondling—then goes ballistic when the boy points out that "you're not my mother." (A bloody Jesus watches as Kevin is beaten, the snow swirling outside.) Lust at St. Vincent is not an abstract principle, although it is a matter of dispute where it originates. As Lavin tells the cops who return a runaway boy, "One thing these youngsters have in common is an insatiable need for attention."

That the outside world is demonstrably colder than St. Vincent is part of the movie's strategy. Smith doesn't downplay the orphanage comraderie or the atmosphere of roughhouse fun. Nor is every brother a mini-Lavin. But the emphasis is on entrapment. The short-lived freedom of Kevin's hopeless escape is scarcely noted except to establish the freezing void into which he flees. Far more emphasized are the specifics of his capture and return. Struggle is demonstrably futile. Once the orphanage's illiterate salt-of-the-earth janitor stumbles upon the mad doings and attempts to file a police report, Lavin's reign of terror escalates. Warning against the spread of "evil lies from hell," he threatens the boys with the wrath of God and worse. The scandal is smothered in purges, broken promises, and official cover-ups—a hypocritical performance consecrating an unholy alliance between church and state.

Although *The Boys of St. Vincent*'s first part ends with a venerable horror-movie twist, the defeated monster abruptly replaced with an even grimmer-looking version, the sequel never returns to the orphanage. Its subject is the orphans. "We all carry scars of one kind or another," the old cardinal muses at the close of Part One; by focusing on the reopening of the case 15 years later, Part Two serves to reinforce his point. The first scene establishes a typical two-kid family and a comfortable home in Montreal presided over by ...Brother Lavin. The shock is compounded five seconds later when the children answer a knock at the door, and, in a tumult of Kafka-esque domestic terror, police barge in to arrest their father.

The introduction of this "new" Lavin not only deranges one's sympathies but reinforces the existential point that the captured criminal who stands accused before the law can never be the same individual who freely committed the crime. Brought back to Newfoundland, the once omnipotent Lavin suggests a better-looking Nixon at the center of his own private Watergate. The investigation unfolds, orchestrating various narratives and courtroom melodramatics against an increasingly strident talk-radio chorus. Most crucial are Lavin's psychiatric sessions—the closest he will ever come to making a confession during the course of which it is revealed that he too was an orphan and a foster child. (The shrink is played by Dr. Pierre Gauthier, the psychotherapist attached to the production.)

Given these scenes, one wishes that the analysis had been richer. While the cast of characters achieves the homely familiarity of a hit TV series, the characterizations border on schematic. When two orphan brothers are reunited after 15 years, one is a repressed hetero householder and the other a flaming homo junkie hustler; meanwhile, the tormented Kevin has matured into as hunky a youth as he was adorable a child. Driving toward the climactic spectacle of Lavin's day in court, the movie ultimately turns away from the roots of Lavin's pathology (including his relationship with his "normal" family) and barely touches on the grown Kevin's agonized realization that, for an otherwise abandoned child, "love" is love.

As a director, Smith isn't up to the dream sequences he employs to explore Kevin's trauma, although the prosaic quality of the movie's second part only makes the first seem all the more nightmarish. Still, *The Boys of St. Vincent* declines to provide the catharsis of an exorcism. For all his increasingly frantic prayers, the monster (last glimpsed squinting in the light of public disclosure), falls back into evil—defined here in secular humanist terms as an arid egotism, the inability to imaginatively put oneself in another's place. Leaving its antihero a figure of pity as well as horror, it is *The Boys of St. Vincent*'s signal accomplishment to render that lack of identification almost impossible.

Film Forum is treating the two halves of *The Boys of St. Vincent* as two movies, each with a separate admission charge. For some, the spectacle may be too painful to watch; for others, it will prove so absorbing, they'll want to see both parts at a single sitting. *The Boys of St. Vincent* may not be a masterpiece, but it's surely more than an experience.

Also reviewed in:
CHICAGO TRIBUNE, 11/11/94, Friday/p. K, Michael Wilmington
NEW REPUBLIC, 7/4/94, p. 26, Stanley Kauffmann
NEW YORK TIMES, 6/1/94, p. C11, Janet Maslin
NEW YORKER, 6/6/94, p. 90, Terrence Rafferty
VARIETY, 9/27/93, p. 37, Todd McCarthy

BRAINSCAN

A Triumph Releasing Corporation release of a Coral Productions film. *Executive Producer:* Esther Freifeld, Earl Berman, Andrew Martin and Bob Hayward. *Producer:* Michel Roy. *Director:* John Flynn. *Screenplay:* Andrew Kevin Walker. *Story:* Brian Owens. *Director of Photography:* François Protat. *Editor:* Jay Cassidy. *Music:* George S. Clinton. *Music Editor:* Phil Linson. *Sound:* Don Cohen. *Sound Editor:* Dave Hankins. *Casting:* Joy Todd, Vera Miller, and Nadia Rona. *Production Designer:* Paola Ridolfi. *Set Dresser:* Josianne Noreau, Alain Clouatre, and John Fredericks. *Special Visual Effects:* René Daalder. *Costumes:* Gaudeline Sauriol. *Make-up:* Marie-Angèle Breitner Protat. *Make-up Effects:* Steve Johnson. *Stunt Coordinator:* Dave McKeown. *Running time:* 96 minutes. *MPAA Rating:* R.

CAST: Edward Furlong (Michael); Frank Langella (Detective Hayden); T. Ryder Smith (The Trickster); Amy Hargreaves (Kimberly); Jamie Marsh (Kyle); Victor Ertmanis (Martin); David Hemblen (Dr. Fromberg); Vlasta Vrans (Frank); Dom Fiore (Ken); Claire Riley (News Anchor); Tod Fennel (Young Michael); Michele-Barbara Pelletier (Stacie); Dean Hagopian (Mr. Keller); Donna Bacalla (Mrs. Keller); Jerome Thiberghian (Mr. Tebb); Don Jordan (Cop #1); Greg Calpaki (Jock); Pete White (Dog Owner); Peter Colvey (John); Paul Stewart (Bob); Richard Zeman (Police Officer).

LOS ANGELES TIMES, 4/22/94, Calendar/p. 15, Kevin Thomas

"Brainscan" skillfully takes us into the mind of a bright, likable but diffident 16-year-old (Edward Furlong, always a fine actor). Several years earlier his mother was killed in a car accident that left him with a slight limp, and his father is often away on business, leaving him alone much of the time in an expensive suburban home. Somewhat shy and something of an outsider, he spends most of his spare time in his spacious attic quarters, which are equipped with an array of electronic goodies—and also a telescope with which to peep at the pretty girl (Amy Hargreaves) who lives nearby.

Furlong's Michael is already an ardent horror picture fan when he's introduced to a new CD-ROM interactive virtual reality game called "Brainscan." He slips in a disc one evening and swiftly finds himself entering the back yard of a house in his neighborhood, breaking in and brutally killing a man asleep in his bed. It's as if Michael has been asleep himself, awakening with a jolt, elated at having experienced an ultimate trip.

There's a hitch, however, for the cops, led by a tough-talking Frank Langella, are soon swarming the area, searching for the killer of that sleeping man.

Director John Flynn and writer Andrew Kevin Walker set up "Brainscan" expertly, and their film certainly does supply its own jolt. Although it's more ambitious and intelligent than most teen horror flicks, it doesn't live up to its potential and could use a lighter, more humorous touch.

Kids will probably go for the Trickster (T. Ryder Smith), whom Smith aptly describes as a "psychic Frankenstein, a kind of child of Iggy Pop and Keith Richards." However, as the game's mastermind and physical embodiment, the Trickster is too literal, a highly theatrical cadaverous guy with a Mohawk haircut who materializes and disintegrates at will to tempt and taunt poor Michael. The filmmakers might better have left the Trickster as a hologram, as he was originally conceived.

As the picture progresses, you suspect there's going to be trouble in coming up with a satisfactory ending, yet with its razzle-dazzle special effects, hard-driving score, and sufficient quantity of blood and guts it will probably score with teen audiences. It's been often said that horror pictures that have been specifically made for teens provide a catharsis for their anxieties over sex and romance, and that seems especially true of "Brainscan." For those any younger, however, "Brainscan" will only give them nightmares.

NEW YORK POST, 4/22/94, p. 40, Michael Medved

"Brainscan" is a diabolically disturbing horror fantasy about an ingenious video game that gives a whole new meaning to the phrase "cutting edge"; in fact, it's so outrageously brutal that it makes Mortal Kombat look like Ms. Pac-Man.

Naturally, this shocking new form of electronic entertainment appeals to the 16-year-old protagonist, Michael, a shy, lonely techie with an absent, workaholic father and a dead mother.

As played by Edward Furlong, of "Terminator 2," the troubled suburban kid loves low-budget exploitation flicks (like this one) so he eagerly awaits the new CD-ROM interactive virtual reality game called "Brainscan." It promises to put players into the shoes of a savage serial killer.

With startling vividness, it invites you to slip into a sleeping home, creep up the stairs, enter the bedroom, then murder and mutilate the head of the household.

The object is to accomplish the deed and to erase all evidence within the allotted time. Furlong is thrilled with the challenge.

The only problem is that the morning after he initially plays the game. police (led by a brooding detective played by Frank Langella) discover a murder in a neighbor's house that closely resembles the killing the boy enacted on his video screen.

Has electronic fantasy crossed the line into the real world?

It's an intriguing premise, given eerie life by some cunning special effects and the captivating character of "The Trickster," host and embodiment of the Brainscan game.

Played by Shakespearean stage actor T. Ryder Smith in a riveting big-screen debut, The Trickster comes across like a witty, charismatic combination of Freddy Krueger and Keith Richards.

Journeyman director John Flynn has been doing competent work since 1968 on films that no one usually notices ("The Outfit," "Rolling Thunder," "Best Seller," "Lock Up" and others), but "Brainscan" should finally put him on the map.

It's handsomely shot (near Montreal) and crisply edited, with a haunting soundtrack featuring alternative music bands like White Zombie, Dandelion and Mudhoney.

The movie ultimately suffers from a much-too-easy, groan-inducing, cop-out ending, and features an embarrassingly gratuitous sex scene with the girl-next-door (Amy Hargreaves). But it also displays an unfailing sense of humor about its own limitations.

When Michaels' high school principal declares, "Don't you see! Senseless violence is not entertainment!," the young man smugly responds, "What is it, then?"

By the same token, the makers of "Brainscan" understand that their picture is another example of this senseless violence. But they've made it perversely entertaining nonetheless.

NEWSDAY, 4/22/94, Part II/p. B7, John Anderson

For Michael (Edward Furlong), the high school techie-cum mass murderer of "Brainscan," cocooning with one's computer is about control. And he's made it an art: When he plays the voyeur with the girl next door, he not only videotapes her, he watches the playback on his console, buried inside his attic room, even before she's put on her clothes and disappeared from view.

No, there can never be too much control, too many degrees of separation, too many layers of media between a boy and his loved ones. His father, who travels, is just a voice on the phone. His mother, the stuff of flashbacks, died in the same car wreck that left Michael's right leg crippled and, presumably, contributed to his antisocial attitude and death obsession. Except for running his high school's soon-to-be-outlawed Horror Club—where they watch such primal works as "Death, Death, Death, Part II"—his only human contacts are his soon-to-be-slacker buddy Kyle (Jamie Marsh) and that nubile neighbor Kim (Amy Hargraves). Who, by the way, knows he's watching.

Turning Michael's reclusive, insular little electronic world inside out is Brainscan—"the ultimate experience in interactive terror"— which transports Michael into virtual reality, and into a neighbor's house, where he slaughter's the homeowner in his sleep. "It was sick," Michael says, when he thinks it's a game. And then he sees the news broadcast.

At this point, "Brainscan" is less stock horror than satire—HAL as a CD-ROM, "The Eyes of Laura Mars" on a color monitor and you can't help getting a little satisfaction in watching the ennui-ridden Michael being shaken to his shoes. But when he resists the second step on the Brainscan menu, the Trickster (T. Ryder Smith) appears, a 3-dimensional grotesquerie who threatens and cajoles Michael into playing all four stages of the murderous game. And the film becomes more of a generic blood bath.

Furlong ("Terminator 2") exudes a totally inconsequential physical presence, which helps make Michael's general disenchantment believable. It also adds an ominous aspect to his confrontations with Detective Hayden, played by the hulking Frank Langella, whose animal quality terrifies the cerebral Michael, and makes their cat-and-mouse game all the more tense.

There's cleverness in Andrew Kevin Walker's script—when Michael calls the Brainscan number and gets a live voice, he's both appalled and apologetic: "Sorry," he says. "I thought you were a machine." And both Marsh and Hargreave are refreshingly real. But given T. Ryder Smith's over-the-top Trickster, the incongruous elements of teen romance/angst and gratuitous gore, what might have been a tart little sendup of modern obsessions becomes an unpalatable soup.

SIGHT AND SOUND, 11/94, p. 40, Kim Newman

Sixteen-year old Michael Brower left with a limp after the death of his mother in a car accident, is the introverted school misfit, obsessed with horror films and computer games. With his father away on business for weeks, Michael stays at home peeping into the bedroom of Kimberly, the girl next door. Fromberg, the school principal, bans Michael's horror club and insists any film or game to be shown be viewed by him first.

Kyle, Michael's only friend, passes on word about Brainscan, supposedly a cutting-edge computer game that delivers genuine fear. Michael telephones the company, who send him the first in a series of four discs. Playing, Michael is put in the position of committing a murder, sawing off the victim's foot as a trophy. When he comes round after the game, a real foot is in his fridge and local Detective Hayden is investigating an equivalent murder. The Trickster, malevolent spirit of the game, materialises and tells Michael he must play the other three discs to prevent himself being caught. When he plays the second disc, Michael finds he has murdered Kyle, and the third, which he plays in order to clear evidence, leads to the deaths of Fromberg and a policeman. The Trickster tells him his last victim, with the fourth disc, must be Kimberly, but in the girl's bedroom she reveals that she too has watched Michael and taken photographs of him.

Michael rebels against the Trickster, but Hayden turns up and shoots the suspected murderer. Michael, who has all the while been in the world of the first disc, wakes up annoyed at the serious trauma the game has put him through. He asks Kimberly to go out with him and she non-committally turns him down, letting him see she really has photographed him from a distance. Michael gives the Brainscan disc to Fromberg, and the Trickster appears in the principal's office.

Like such unassuming quickies as *Trick or Treat* and *976-Evil*, with which it shares its high school Faust theme, *Brainscan* has the markings of a pre-planned franchise, hooking into the horror subculture with a plot device that hinges on an advert in *Fangoria* magazine and littering its running time with heavy metal and teen in-group talk. The Trickster character is an obvious attempt to devise the sort of continuing monster (complete with cool clothes and cynical wisecracks) that have made successes of the *Elm Street* and *Hellraiser* series. However, this cackling and mysterious games master actually does very little to get worked up about, outside of some body-meld morphing which is remarkably close to effects seen in the latest instalments of those series, as the Trickster swallows Michael's head whole or intertwines with him in a Siamese-twin merger.

After the first murder, a hackneyed bit of subjective camera stalk-and-slash, the film loses interest in straight horror and omits much of its plot in favour of an escalating series of disorienting incidents. Edward Furlong, given a limp and semi-orphan status because he is way too cute to be the geek the script would have him, orders his voice-activated telephone around with proper teenage arrogance, and generally does better than expected as the much-abused hero. There is even one amusingly-handled bit of comic horror as Furlong tries to bury the incriminating severed foot in the woods, only to turn around and find that a large friendly dog has the frozen extremity clamped in his jaws.

Oddly, the most distinctive aspect of *Brainscan* is its ending, at once a variation on the ancient it-was-a dream copout and a genuinely surprising extension of the concept that *Total Recall*, for one, couldn't bear to play out to its logical conclusion. Michael's reaction to a game which really has delivered on its promise to put him through untold fear is entirely credible, as he trashes his high-tech room. The way his fantasies have shaped his cyberspace adventure is neatly demonstrated by the contrast between the game's climax, with Kimberly tearfully declaring love for him, and the real-world resolution as the girl instinctively, but not definitively, refuses to go out with him.

Also reviewed in:
NEW YORK TIMES, 4/22/94, p. C12, Janet Maslin
VARIETY, 4/25-5/1/94, p. 30, Joe Leydon
WASHINGTON POST, 4/22/94, p. C6, Desson Howe
WASHINGTON POST, 4/22/94, Weekend/p. 44, Joe Brown

BROWNING VERSION, THE

A Paramount Pictures release of a Percy Main production. *Producer:* Ridley Scott and Mimi Polk. *Director:* Mike Figgis. *Screenplay:* Ronald Harwood. *Based on the play by:* Terence Rattigan. *Director of Photography:* Jean-François Robin. *Editor:* Hervé Schneid. *Music:* Mark Isham. *Music Editor:* Robin Clarke. *Sound:* Chris Munro. *Sound Editor:* Martin Evans. *Casting:* Susie Figgis. *Production Designer:* John Beard. *Art Director:* Lucy Richardson. *Set Decorator:* Crispian Allis. *Costumes:* Fotini Dimou. *Make-up:* Lesley Rouvray, Tricia Cameron, and Heather Jones. *Running time:* 97 minutes. *MPAA Rating:* R.

CAST: Albert Finney (Andrew Crocker-Harris); Greta Sacchi (Laura Crocker-Harris); Matthew Modine (Frank Hunter); Julian Sands (Tom Gilbert); Michael Gambon (Dr. Frobisher); Ben Silverstone (Taplow); James Sturgess (Bryant); Joe Beattie (Wilson); Mark Boltham (Grantham); Tom Havelock (Laughton); Walter Micklethwait (Buller); Jotham Annan (Prince Abakendi); David Lever (David Fletcher); Bruce Myers (Dr. Rafferty); Maryann d'Abo (Diana Rafferty); Heathcote Williams (Dr. Lake); Oliver Milburn (Trubshaw); Jeff Nutall (Lord Baxter); Dinah Stabb (Jane Frobisher); Belinda Low (Rowena Baxter); Stephen Mitchelson (Newton); David Pullan (Trimmer); George Harris (Adakendi Senior); Mark Long (Foster).

CHRISTIAN SCIENCE MONITOR, 9/8/94, p. 14, David Sterritt

A movie given mixed notices by most critics at Montreal [World Film Festival] is *The Browning Version*, adapted by Ronald Harwood from Terence Rattigan's respected stage drama. As in the original play and the first film version with Michael Redgrave, the protagonist is an aging English schoolteacher who's becoming painfully aware of the emptiness and loneliness he's accumulated during a lifetime of rigid pedantry.

Just about everyone who's seen the new "Browning Version" agrees that Albert Finney, one of Britain's most brilliant actors, is at the top of his form in a demanding and sometimes daunting role. Greta Scacchi and Matthew Modine are also strong as the main character's unfaithful wife and her secret lover. Less impressive is Mike Figgis's film-making, which is visually unimaginative and relies far too much on Mark Isham's overbearing music.

FILMS IN REVIEW, 11-12/94, p. 55, Maria Garcia

In Anthony Asquith's 1951 film, *The Browning Version*, the aging Mr. Crocker-Harris (Michael Redgrave) confronts the failures of his lifetime, as a teacher, as a husband, and as a man. A classics professor in an English boys' school, he is known to the student body as "The Croc" and the "Himmler of the lower fifth," a humorless man whose passion seems buried in his neurotic obsessions for discipline and punctuality. In Michael Figgis' remake, Crocker-Harris (Albert Finney) takes on heroic proportions; instead of assuming the demeanor of a defeated man, and a cuckolded husband, Crocker-Harris becomes one of the last of a breed of ruling patriarchs. He's King Lear, exchanging his princely robes for the clothes of a man, beginning that painful, introspective journey which, in the lives of great men and women, often precedes old age.

The film opens with Crocker-Harris sitting alone on a bench, the walls of the time-honored Abbey School behind him, and it closes with his triumphant departure in which he actually removes his academic robes, shedding the raiment that ties him to the decaying conventions of the patriarchate. (Unfortunately, the impact of this final shot is diminished by the closing titles.) Crocker-Harris immersed himself in Western civilization's most profound stories, yet he remained tragically unaware of their psychological and emotional implications. When as a young man he translated "perhaps the greatest play ever written," Aeschylus' *Agamemnon*, into rhyming couplets, he unknowingly wrote his own epithet. Like Agamemnon, who is betrayed and vanquished by Clytemnestra, the wife he abandoned, Crocker-Harris is emasculated by Laura (Greta Scacchi), the wife he deserted, emotionally and sexually.

Laura has more of Clytemnestra's power, however, a flaw in the film's narrative structure. Sadly, this pivotal character has not changed since the Asquith version, in which Mrs. Crocker-Harris (Jean Kent) was a totally unsympathetic character, a brittle, caustic woman. Lacking its full realization, Laura's character appears to have sprung from the womb an emasculator. Actually, she is the bitterly disappointed wife of a man of weak character. In the absence of her disappointment and her unrelenting bitchiness, Crocker-Harris might never have confronted his emotional detachment; pushed to the edge of endurance by Laura, he experiences that heroic transformation which allows him to begin living in a more authentic way. Although Scacchi's performance is good, had her character possessed the depth and proportion of Crocker-Harris', the film might have had a stronger narrative structure and it would have reflected the modern sensibilities—as well as the classic dilemmas—it so clearly wishes to portray.

The Browning Version (which refers to Robert Browning's translation of *Agamemnon*) represents a departure for the director, Mike Figgis, whose previous films include *Internal Affairs* (1990) and *Stormy Monday* (1988), strongly atmospheric thrillers with flimsy scripts. In this film, the screenplay (Ronald Harwood from a play by Terence Rattigan) is better, and Figgis' direction is good, mostly because he has a great talent for establishing intimacy. He achieves that intimacy with intense close ups of Finney's leonine features which compel us to empathize with the character's pain and humiliation, as well as his remarkable transformation. Finney's brilliant performance, and Figgis' ability to showcase it, are most evident at a stunning moment of catharsis, shot close up, in which Crocker-Harris cries after a student, Taplow (Ben Silverstone), gives him a parting gift—Browning's translation. Figgis also gets good performances from unproven actors like Scacchi and Matthew Modine (who plays her lover, as well as novices like Silverstone.

In the interior shots of the school, and of the Crocker-Harris' home, Figgis displays his talent for creating an atmosphere that illustrates, cinematically, the characters' dilemmas. One can almost feel the dust of centuries in those rooms, a weight which seems to have fallen heavily upon the professor and his wife. Figgis' skill is most apparent in the closing scene where Crocker-Harris stands below the seal of England on a red carpet that runs the length of the school's darkly paneled Anglican church. The church and the seal are imbued with incredible mass and consequence so that we may recognize the heroic effort involved in turning away from them, which is what Crocker-Harris is about to do. Realizing that he failed to understand and communicate the majestic promises inherent in those powerful symbols, the teacher delivers a dramatic and heartfelt apology to his students.

During his parting remarks, we experience that peculiar sense of transcendence which characterizes the great tragedies of Aeschylus. That triumph is represented by the hero who confronts The Furies and reconciles himself (or herself) with the world: Crocker-Harris may be a broken man, but he is transformed into one who will live a more conscious life. The Western society he represents must also be transformed and one hopes, as it reconciles itself to modernity, it will not indiscriminately dispose of such heroes.

LOS ANGELES TIMES, 10/12/94, Calendar/p. 3, Peter Rainer

Adapted from the celebrated Terence Rattigan play, "The Browning Version" is a high-class tear-jerker, but Albert Finney's performance is considerably more than that. As Andrew Crocker-Harris, the classics professor for more than two decades at a posh British boys' school, Finney is remarkably good at conveying the rumblings of emotion in this musty, disappointed man. Finney doesn't slobber us with sentiment. His restraint really shines.

Rattigan's warhorse, which he expanded for the screen in the famous 1951 film starring Michael Redgrave, is the kind of material where every emotion is calibrated, every nuance signaled. Screenwriter Ronald Harwood has done an intelligent job updating the material, and Mike Figgis has directed with enormous tact, but, excepting Finney's performance, the film doesn't really work up a sweat. It's no "Dead Poets Society" jamboree (thankfully). "The Browning Version" keeps its cool even though it's mostly about people in misery, and maybe that's a clue to its high-browish appeal. It presents a way of dealing with suffering that allows art-house audiences the opportunity to sniffle stoically. Its pathos won't run your makeup.

Crocker-Harris is married to a considerably younger woman, Laura (Greta Scacchi), who is having an affair with the chemistry professor, Frank (Matthew Modine), an American teaching in England through an exchange program. The love went out of their marriage long ago; what's left is mostly spite and recrimination.

For most of the movie she picks away at her mate, as he recoils and disapproves. It's like a stuffed-shirt rendering of a Strindberg marriage, and Harwood hasn't softened very much Rattigan's borderline cruelty toward Laura. She's the villain of the piece—her lover is merely deluded by her rapacious wiles. We can't quite see in Laura the young woman who would have been entranced by the brainy classics scholar. Scacchi doesn't provide the soundings of character that might humanize her.

The core relationship in "The Browning Version" is really between Crocker-Harris and Taplow (Ben Silverstone), a student who—realizing what a hated reputation his teacher has with his classmates—warms up to him anyway. Taplow doesn't entirely fit in with the other students; he still retains a fresh-faced idealism that has already been drummed out of his mates. He's not a terribly swift student but he's open to experience, and so he's open to what Crocker-Harris can teach him—not only about Aeschylus but about life. It takes a while for Crocker-Harris to perceive the boy's innate decency, but when he does—when Taplow gifts him with a second-hand copy of Robert Browning's translation of the "Agamemnon"— he's deeply, unspeakably moved.

Finney plays this scene, and the subsequent scene when he believes he has been taken for a fool, with the utmost artistry. When Crocker-Harris' brittle, settled reserve shatters it's almost unbearable to watch. He has assumed so many layers of protection that his rawness has a tragic, unseemly power.

As Michael Redgrave played him, Crocker-Harris was a parched sufferer who looked primped as if by an undertaker; it was a great performance, but Finney's, more bullish and hefty, is equally amazing. Finney gives us a man whose correspondence with the classics is a key to his faraway glaze.

In his sessions with his students he must play the bemused tyrant to make them learn, and that degrades his life. What's why he's so replenished when Taplow makes a gesture of friendship: The boy inscribes a Greek quotation in the Browning gift, and it's as if Crocker-Harris had received a holy book. In moments like these, "The Browning Version" is great. A flash of human decency burns into high drama.

NEW YORK POST, 10/12/94, p. 34, Michael Medved

"The Remains of the Day' meets "Goodbye, Mr. Chips."

That's the stodgy setup for "The Browning Version." It's one of those high-gloss British imports that uses gorgeous scenery, impressive acting and largely irrelevant literary references to try to hide the fact that it's dramatically static and empty.

Like Anthony Hopkins in "Remains," Albert Finney plays a pathetic soul who's wasted his entire life on corrupt, upper-crust institutions that in no way deserve his loyalty; both characters are tragically incapable of breaking through their exaggerated British reserve to express the love they feel for the one woman who's touched their hearts.

And like "Mr. Chips" (in either screen version of James Hilton's sentimental novel), Finney's supposed to be a stuffy, dedicated schoolmaster, mocked by pupils and disregarded by colleagues, who only upon his retirement realize how deeply he's touched the generations of students who passed through his class.

In "The Browning Version," this retirement is particularly painful because the schoolmaster's spirited young wife (Greta Scacchi) is in the midst of an affair with one of his colleagues, an American chemistry teacher nicely played by Matthew Modine.

After extended scenes of stoic suffering and humiliation Finney finally feels that his life might be worthwhile after all when one of his students (14-year-old Ben Silverstone) presents him with a precious gift retrieved from a used book stall—a rare translation ("The Browning Version") of "The Agamemnon" by Aeschylus.

The source material for this film isn't quite as old as Aeschylus, but it's certainly musty enough; it's based on a 1939 one-act play by Sir Terence Rattigan (who also wrote the screenplay for the 1969 "Mr. Chips").

Even as adapted by veteran screenwriter Ronald Harwood ("The Dresser"), this new "Browning Version" shows all the classic limitations of any one-act; it's a sensitive sketch that feels artificially extended on screen, playing itself out in a single mood with no notable plot structure.

The film's strengths and weaknesses are actually quite similar to a 1951 black-and-white version of the material, though the lovely locations (at historic Sherbourne school, in Dorset) and luminous cinematography this time around make the story feel all the more hollow in contrast to the understated intimacy of the original.

Finney, like Michael Redgrave in the earlier film, makes the most of his part, effectively communicating his character's agony and panic behind the stiff-upper-lip exterior. Greta Scacchi is even more effective; no actress in films today does a better job combining smoldering sexuality and fierce intelligence, making it easy to understand why her husband would be intimidated by her.

Director Mike Figgis, previously best known for his gritty, brutal cops-and-gangsters melodramas "Stormy Monday" and "Internal Affairs," here seems to make a conscious effort to hold himself back in order to win a new genteel respectability.

The result is a handsome, admirable, monochromatic tableaux without energy or edge, by a filmmaker who unfortunately seems as constipated and constrained as his main character.

NEWSDAY, 10/19/94, Part II/p. B7, John Anderson

Anglophilia certainly helped make the innocuous but English-accented "Four Weddings and a Funeral" a hit. It keeps the BBC-infatuated PBS in contributions. It drove people to buy—perchance to read—Maggie Thatcher's autobiography.

And it may help "The Browning Version"—Terence Rattigan's 1939 play, a 1951 film with Michael Redgrave, and now a fresh and thoughtful remake directed by the unlikely Mike Figgis ("Internal Affairs," "Stormy Monday"). To call it an update would be to miss the point: Reality be damned, the sylvan, tradition-bound England of film and TV never changes, which is what makes it attractive.

What's different here, though, is that, like Fergie and Diana, "The Browning Version" spins on the downside of England as the precious stone set in the silver sea, the royal throne of kings, the demi-paradise, etc. It's about rigidity and mortification rather than burnished history.

The not-so-happy breed of men Rattigan wrote about are the teachers of the too rich/too thick population of a prestigious boys public (in the British sense) academy, the Abbey School. Chief among its victims is Andrew Crocker-Harris (Albert Finney), a classics scholar getting ready to retire after 18 years to "teach English to foreigners," as his visibly dissatisfied wife, Laura (Greta Scacchi), puts it.

The school has denied his pension, his health is bad, and Laura is having an affair with the American teacher Frank Hunter (Matthew Modine)—something Andrew knows, but propriety forbids him to acknowledge.

The academic traditions, the resistance to those traditions, the emotional outrages perpetrated by those traditions and the school's blatant hypocrisy all combine to make Crocker-Harris what he is: A man who has been drained of color. Laura is angry and unhappy, not only with Andrew but with losing her status in the village. A natural flirt, she's the stuff of schoolboy anxiety, but Frank is no schoolboy and he's done with her.

In a Tarantino movie, Laura and Andrew would have gone for each other's throats, but the maliciousness here finds more refined outlets: When Andrew is given a gift—the Robert Browning translation of Aeschylus' "Agamemnon," from a young student named Taplow (Ben Silverstone)—Laura cruelly deprives her husband of this one moment of joy, and brings both their marital woes and Andrew's professional crisis to a restrained boil.

Much of the satisfaction in "The Browning Version" comes from watching Finney internalize Andrew's sense of failure. The most moving moments are unspoken, delivered in the disappointed faces of Andrew and Laura (Scacchi, a brunette for this role, looks a bit like Frida Kahlo).

Andrew's one moment of unbridled passion—reading "Agamemnon" aloud to a class, and drawing an implied parallel between Laura and Clytemnestra—is accompanied by such swelling music it almost loses its tartness.

Besides Scacchi and Modine—who as the informal American provides comic relief—the film also features Julian Sands as Andrew's replacement, an almost invisible role. Which contrasts nicely with Andrew's almost-invisible man, to whom Finney applies flesh and bone and makes distinct, and not a bit too sympathetic.

SIGHT AND SOUND, 11/94, p. 41, Geoffrey Macnab

The Abbey School, shortly before the end of term. Andrew Crocker-Harris, the long-serving classics teacher, is standing down because of poor health. He is approached by Taplow, a boy in the Lower Fifth who wants permission to switch from classics to science. Crocker-Harris replies to his request obliquely, but reminds him to turn up in the afternoon for his extra Greek lesson. Crocker-Harris' replacement, Tom Gilbert, sits in on the last class of the 'Croc' or the 'Hitler of the Lower Fifth'—a stern disciplinarian who makes no attempt to be liked.

Later in the day, Taplow turns up at Crocker-Harris' cottage for extra tuition. Here, he runs into science teacher Frank Hunter, who wants to ask about the next term's timetable. As they wait for Crocker-Harris to arrive, Taplow mimics the 'Croc'. Crocker-Harris and Taplow retire to the garden for their lesson. At first, Taplow's fanciful translation of Aeschylus exasperates Crocker-Harris, but the teacher softens as he is reminded of his own teenage years as a brilliant classical scholar.

The headmaster, Dr. Frobisher, tells Crocker-Harris that the governors have decided against awarding him a pension. When Crocker-Harris' wife Laura is informed of this, she bitterly attacks her husband. The next morning, she visits Frank Hunter, her lover, and entreats her to spend some of the summer with her; Hunter, guilty in the relationship, reacts coldly.

Sports Day. Dr. Frobisher asks Crocker-Harris to forfeit his right as the senior departing teacher to speak last during prize giving. Crocker-Harris meekly agrees to make way for the more charismatic Mr. Fletcher. He is approached by Taplow, who presents him with a book—Aeschylus in Robert Browning's translation. He is immensely moved by the gift, but Laura spites him by saying it was merely a bribe. However, Hunter consoles him, insisting that Taplow genuinely cares about him, and also confessing to his affair with Laura. Crocker-Harris tells his wife their marriage is over. The next day, during the prize ceremony, he insists on speaking last. His moving address, acknowledging that he has failed as a teacher, earns the sympathetic applause of teachers, pupils and governors alike.

In conventional histories of post-war British theatre, Albert Finney and Terence Rattigan exist on opposite sides of a great divide. Indeed, one could go further and say that the reason Rattigan languished in obscurity for so long was precisely because of Finney, Osborne, Richardson and co: in the post-Suez Britain of the 50s and early 60s, the days of the Royal Court and Free Cinema, Rattigan was regarded as a quaint old war-horse of the stage—class-bound, affected, too metropolitan for contemporary tastes.

The divisions have long since become blurred. These days, Rattigan is no more and no less ripe for revival than Wesker or Osborne, and Finney, as senior statesman of stage and screen, doesn't seem so very different from the actor-knights who went before him. It still comes as a surprise, though, to see the star of *Saturday Night, Sunday Morning* cast as Crocker-Harris in *The Browning Version*: it's a bit like seeing Marlon Brando play drawing-room comedy.

Finney makes a doleful, sonorous classics teacher, but, for all the pathos he squeezes out of the part he is too sturdy and monolithic a figure to seem especially tortured by his plight. He lacks the febrile, anguished quality that Michael Redgrave brought to the role in the 1951 Anthony Asquith screen adaptation. Writing about that film, the critic Jeffrey Richards observed that it derived "much of its force from Rattigan's exploration of emotional repression, of the world of incompatibility, deceit and loathing that was all a part of his own experience in the homosexual demi-monde of fashionable and theatrical London." This isn't a world that Finney manages, or even tries, to hint at. As his frustrated wife, Laura, Greta Scacchi offers infinitely the more dynamic performance, combining bitterness, lust and sadness in equal measure.

In terms of recent British cinema, this latest version can perhaps best be seen as the third part of a triptych. The story of a repressed, middle-aged Englishman thawing out his long-frozen emotions, it follows the same trajectory as *The Remains of the Day* and *Shadowlands*. It is an exercise in mannered restraint, not least for the filmmakers themselves. Producer Ridley Scott and director Mike Figgis eschew their usual visual flamboyance. Here, they're beholden to script and locations. The picture, shot at Sherborne in Dorset, boasts its fair quota of cobbled streets, ancient abbeys, musty classrooms and thatched cottages.

Its most jarring and confusing aspect is the way it welds past and present together. Although ostensibly updated to the present day, there's little in the look of the film that would be out of place in the 50s or even earlier. Teachers may mention computers, but there is no sign of them. The preferred means of transport is the bicycle. The English cricket team is referred to as the MCC, and the cult of the gentleman amateur, judging from Fletcher—the nice-but-dim teacher who bats with improbable, Lara-like flair in the end-of-term match—is alive and well. The myths and rituals of the English public school are celebrated rather than debunked. Education is still a matter of cricket, classics and ragging in the dorm. Furthermore, it's a boys only affair.

Ronald Harwood's adaptation tweaks events here and there, and skilfully opens out what was originally a one-act, one-set play. It adds an irrelevant sub-plot about the strained relations between the Sixth Form and the Lower Fifth ("I hear your mother is a really good fuck," bullying prefect Trubshaw taunts Taplow in the showers—hardly dialogue you could imagine Rattigan writing). And, like the Asquith version, it depicts Crocker-Harris' prize-giving speech instead of simply referring to it, thereby buying itself a big emotional climax. This is a perfectly sturdy piece of work, but it lacks any discernible attitude toward the material. Harwood fails to communicate what makes *The Browning Version* relevant to 1994, or to chart any of the social or political changes since it was first performed in 1948.

Rather than pondering the reasons behind this remake, it is probably best to sit back and enjoy the character performances. From Robert Donat and Will Hay onward, British actors have always had a knack for playing school masters: Michael Gambon's venial head and Julian Sands' ingenuous new language teacher follow in the tradition. Matthew Modine is brisk and sympathetic as the American science teacher with whom Laura has an affair, and the child actors are also proficient. In the end, though, these consolations are scarcely enough. One can't help returning to the question of why the film was made if neither director, scriptwriter nor star had anything new to add to the innumerable *Browning Versions* that have gone before it.

VILLAGE VOICE, 10/18/94, p. 61, Kevin Maynard

Why bother with a remake of *The Browning Version*? Anthony Asquith's 1951 version of the Terence Rattigan play is still perfectly English, in that reserved, seemingly right as rain *Remains of the Day* kind of way. With great grace and skill, Michael Redgrave gave an understated performance as the pathetic Greek and Latin schoolmaster, Andrew Crocker-Harris. Jean Kent is still gloriously nasty as his fed-up wife, a scheming Clytemnestra who wounds with words her woeful Agamemnon.

Mike Figgis's retelling stays close to the original, with some contemporary bits thrown in for good measure. Crocker-Harris still stands for the classical canon at the school, but he is now threatened by the new professor's (Julian Sands) multicultural curriculum. This pseudo-p.c. sensibility is shown by throwing one black boy, a child of Nigerian dignitaries, into the mix of moppets. Also, Mrs. Crocker-Harris's lover is now a strapping American academic played by

Matthew Modine like a J. Crew model late for the shoot. As for the Mrs. herself, I'll take Kent's sly succubus any day over Greta Scacchi's bitchy but tender deep down inside.

Of course, Albert Finney is an accomplished actor with a paunchy bulldog build that's ideal for tragedy, but this film doesn't let him give a real performance. Ronald Harwood's script keeps feeding Finney cue after cue for Big Oscar Moments. By the time he gives his farewell speech to the entire school for the big climax, Mark Isham's score swelling with sentiment in the background, Crocker-Harris has been thoroughly redeemed by his peers and pupils—and Finney has all but given his thank-you speech to the Academy.

Also reviewed in:
NEW REPUBLIC, 10/31/94, p. 38, Stanley Kauffmann
NEW YORK TIMES, 10/12/94, p. C17, Caryn James
NEW YORKER, 10/31/94, p. 106, Terrence Rafferty
VARIETY, 5/23-29/94, p. 54, Leonard Klady
WASHINGTON POST, 10/14/94, Weekend/p. 48, Desson Howe
WASHINGTON POST, 10/17/94, p. B4, Hal Hinson

BRUCE BROWN'S THE ENDLESS SUMMER II

A New Line Cinema release. *Executive Producer:* Michael Harpster. *Producer:* Ron Moler and Roger Riddell. *Director:* Bruce Brown. *Screenplay:* Bruce Brown and Dana Brown. *Director of Photography:* Mike Hoover. *Editor:* Bruce Brown and Dana Brown. *Music:* Gary Hoey and Phil Marshall. *Music Editor:* Phil Marshall. *Sound:* Beverly Johnson and (music) Tim Jaquette. *Sound Editor:* Marc D. Fishman. *Stunt Coordinator:* Corey Rossal. *Running time:* 100 minutes. *MPAA Rating:* PG.

CAST: Robert "Wingnut" Weaver, Patrick O'Connell, Robert August, J. T. Barron, Jeff Booth, Tom Carroll, Tom Curren, Mike Diffenderfer, Darrick Doerner, Eulie, Sunny Garcia, Johnny Boy Gomes, Craig D. Green, Laird John Hamilton, Derek Ho, Michael Ho, Buzzy Kerbox, Gerry Lopez, Made' and Risal, Liam McNamara, Francois-Xavier Maurin, Tom Morey, Walter Ngcobo, Marco Pacheco, Rusty Pedersen, Kelly Slater, Mike Stewart, Rell Sunn, Shaun Tomson, Beau Young, Robert Nat Young, and John Whitmore.

LOS ANGELES TIMES, 6/3/94, Calendar/p. 12, Kevin Thomas

In "The Endless Summer II," creator-narrator Bruce Brown takes pains to tell us how much has changed since he began filming his definitive surfing movie, "The Endless Summer," 30 years ago. He takes pride in the international popularity of the sport he helped popularize and ticks off its various innovations. He does not shy away from showing how crowded some Hawaiian beaches now are or how the once-deserted beach at a still-choice surfing spot near Capetown, South Africa, is now covered with expensive condos and tract houses. To his credit, he makes a passing acknowledgment of polluted waters.

What Brown is really doing, however, is shrewdly getting such matters out of the way in order to celebrate all that mercifully hasn't yet changed: fabulous beaches that attract world-class surfers to ride the most spectacular waves. Brown's conceit is that a couple of likable young surfer pals, Robert (Wingnut) Weaver—he has the dark hair—and the blond Patrick O'Connell, are such fans of the original "Endless Summer" that they dip into some surfing prize money to finance a globe-girdling retracing, more or less, of their surfing counterparts in the first film, Robert August and Mike Hynson, who were in search of the perfect wave.

While it's anybody's guess if Brown's mix of awesome surfing sequences interspersed with travelogue material and good-natured cornball antics will play as well as it did decades ago, this "Endless Summer" is no less endearing than the original. That this sequel is as fresh as it is is probably in large part due to the fact that Brown deliberately backed off from further surfer movies after making the first "Endless Summer" (which was part of an entire cycle of surfer epics, all the others lesser efforts).

Working with far more sophisticated equipment this time out, Brown, backed by a large crew, once again displays a sense of the visual that's in key with the ebb and flow of the waves. Indeed, what makes both films work is that in their friendly, unpretentious way they celebrate man coming into harmony with nature in truly beautiful images.

Wingnut and Pat's journey takes them from Southern California to Costa Rica (which Brown intercuts with side trips to Alaska and Hawaii not involving his stars), to France, South Africa, Fiji, Australia, Bali and Java, which from the looks of it just might be the most glorious, unspoiled place to surf on the face of the globe.

Along the way Wingnut and Pat meet champion surfers like Tom Curren (in Biarritz) and Laird Hamilton and Gerry Lopez (in Java). They also meet several men from the first film, hearty rugged types like Capetown's John Whitmore and Brisbane's Nat Young, a veritable Crocodile Dundee, who takes Wingnut and Pat riding the rapids in a rubber raft.

Accompanied by Gary Hoey and Phil Marshall's driving score, "The Endless Summer II" is such a pleasure to watch, so effective in its ability to take you away and into the healthy, carefree world of surfing, at once exciting and uncomplicated, that you're actually sorry when it's over.

NEW YORK POST, 6/3/94, p. 41, Michael Medved

Cowabunga, surf dudes!

Thirty years after the original "Endless Summer" became a surprise box-office smash and made a mighty contribution to the explosion of international interest in the sport of surfing, filmmaker Bruce Brown is back with another impressive paean to fun, sun and gnarly waves.

"Endless Summer II" makes the same basic point as the original film: that if you're willing to trek to remote corners of the earth you can erase all seasonal distinctions and find a sunny beach on any day of the year.

Like the first movie, the sequel follows two young surfers (in this case, 28-year-old Robert "Wingnut" Weaver and 22-year-old Pat O'Connell) in a globe-girding pursuit of the perfect waves.

After three decades, Brown's youthful exuberance remains firmly intact, as does the adolescent sense of humor he brings to the narration of his waterlogged travelogue.

The camerawork, however, is vastly improved; in place of the single 14-pound, 16mm camera Brown used in the first film, he here employs 3,000 pounds of 35mm equipment and a crew of 12. The results are altogether spectacular—especially the breath-taking slow-motion scenes o£ the movie's protagonists "tubed" or "shooting the curl"—gliding along sideways inside a breaking wave that gradually arcs over their heads—and over the camera. On several dozen occasions, I found myself slapping my forehead in astonishment and trying to figure out how, in heaven's name, they ever managed to get these shots.

Beyond the lyrical surfing footage that comprises heart and soul of his film, Brown also provides amusing background accounts on the adventures of his protagonists on their way to the beaches of Costa Rica, France, South Africa, Australia, Fiji and Indonesia.

We meet kangaroos, crocodiles, and lions, as well as a remarkably accomplished surfing dog, and Hawaii's top 5-year-old human waverider. Brown additionally introduces us to older, legendary surfers on five continents including Robert August who starred in the original film. (His co-star, Mike Hynson was unavailable for the sequel due to a previous commitment to the Vista, Calif., jail where he was serving time for drug-related offenses).

Unfortunately, we never learn much about the personalities of the two new stars—it seems that the only significant difference between them is that "Wingnut" specializes in the traditional long board, while Pat prefers the new-fangled short board. The music is also a drawback—a tinny and tacky pastiche that's seldom equal to the powerful poetry of the visual images.

Nevertheless, "Endless Summer II" remains one of those rare films that's potentially relaxing, but never boring in the least. It's nearly as much fun as a day at the beach and you don't even have to worry about getting sunburned.

NEWSDAY, 6/3/94, Part II/p. B7, John Anderson

Way back in the '60s, before drugs and Nixon defined the era, the counterculture included surfing: guys wearing their baggies and bushy blond hairdos, listening to the Ventures, catching a wave, wiping out. It was subversive, vicariously transcendent, predominantly male and even people who'd never surfed—like four-fifths of the Beach Boys—celebrated it.

Surfing had water, sand, music, and with Bruce Brown's 1964 "Endless Summer," it had cinema. Chronicling the travels of surfers Mike Hynson and Robert August as they avoided winter, it gave the sport to the world, and paid homage to hedonism.

Partly for historical purposes, partly for self-celebration, Brown flashes back to the original during his sequel, "Endless Summer II," and that moment when Hynson and August crossed the South African sand and encountered their perfect waves in the Indian Ocean. When he returns to the present and his new duo—Robert (Wingnut) Weaver and Patrick O'Connell— what they find there is a vista obscured by luxury housing, and an altered ocean: To keep the sand from disturbing the residents, grass has been planted on the dunes, which keeps the sand from blowing into the water and filling in the sea floor, changing the waves and making them distinctly imperfect.

And what does Brown do with this startling bit of ecological mayhem? Not a thing. "Endless Summer II" is strictly sun, sand and surfs up! and as such is perfect and innocuous: The beaches, particularly in Indonesia, are stunning; the photography is flawless, and the action, while repetitious, is humbling. But if you were expecting political or environmental insight, or any ironic awareness about the film's own sense of self-indulgence, forget it.

The two main dudes in "Endless Summer II"—which includes appearances by such international surfing stars as Gerry Lopez, Shaun Tomson, Laird Hamilton and even a 48-year-old August—are cute and tan but their laughter seems forced. The film's humor in general has a strained feel to it, and as such evokes the '60s in a rather inadvertent way: Brown stages his comedic bits—O'Connell "accidentally" ordering snails in a French restaurant, for instance—unashamedly, but it's the kind of thing documentarians haven't done in 30 years. Even then, it was mostly Disney doing it.

O'Connell and Weaver get to visit Costa Rica, France, Africa, Fiji, Java and Brisbane. We also get to see Alaskan grizzlies and Oahu. And hear words like "pumped," "stoked" and "gnarly" used with utter sincerity.

VILLAGE VOICE, 6/7/94, p. 60, Natasha Stovall

"Our journey began one night in Southern California ... " Figures. *Endless Summer II*—sequel to surf obsessive-director Bruce Brown's 1966 *Endless Summer*—slicks up the original around-the-world-on-a-surfboard adventure in a docu-comedy that combines *NatureMax* photography with the acrobatics of *Wide World of Sports*, and the gags of *America's Funniest Home Videos*.

Endless II's cornball narrative sends contemporary surfer dudes Pat O'Connell and Robert "Wingnut" Weaver to comb the global village in search of the perfect wave—after catching a rerun of the original flick on the late movie. First stop, Costa Rica, where the duo join *Endless Summer I* wavemeister Robert August to enjoy "hideous" curls and equatorial Bettys. (Though Brown's narration points out that women surf, too, *Endless II*'s females are strictly jigglers.) Surf culture imperialists, Pat and Wingnut are stoked to hang 10 in Fiji, Indonesia, and a strangely deracinated South Africa, goofing on *weeeird* native customs and spreading surfing's spiritual Word. While the "plot" sputters early on, Mike Hoover's cinematography redeems *Endless* with visual treasures: underwater shots of sparkling sea and quasi-erotic scenes of graceful boys gliding on sun-drenched surf raise the question of why you're watching an endless summer in a darkened theater and not soaking it up in the flesh.

Endless Summer II is both a paean to the pleasures of ripping a gnarly wave, and a criticism of development and overcrowding. Pat and Wingnut rush over the dunes at Cape Frances, South Africa—anticipating the bootylicious "perfect wave" found there in the first Endless Summer—only to see 1000 luxury homes with grassy lawns that have destroyed the wave break they crossed the globe to ride. *Quel bummer*, dude. But Brown, Pat, and Wingnut, like most people who live to shred and are unconstrained by slackerish monetary concerns, are optimists;

surfing paradise is always just around the corner. Their motto: no matter where you go, there you are—just a short hop from the perfect wave.

Also reviewed in:
CHICAGO TRIBUNE, 6/3/94, Friday/p. F, Michael Wilmington
NEW YORK TIMES, 6/3/94, p. C12, Stephen Holden
VARIETY, 6/6-12/94, p. 44, Brian Lowry
WASHINGTON POST, 6/3/94, p. C7, Hal Hinson
WASHINGTON POST, 6/3/94, Weekend/p. 44, Joe Brown

BUDDHA OF SUBURBIA, THE

A BBC Enterprises Ltd. release. *Executive Producer:* Michael Wearing. *Producer:* Kevin Loader. *Director:* Roger Michell. *Screenplay:* Hanif Kureishi and Roger Michell. *From the novel by:* Hanif Kureishi. *Director of Photography:* John McGlashan. *Editor:* Kate Evans. *Music:* David Bowie. *Production Designer:* Roger Camp. *Costumes:* Alexandra Byrne. *Make-up:* Marilyn MacDonald. *Running time:* 220 minutes. *MPAA Rating:* Not Rated.

CAST: Roshan Seth (Haroon Amir); Naveen Andrews (Karim Amir); Susan Fleetwood (Eva Kay); Steven Mackintosh (Charlie Kay); Brenda Blethyn (Margaret Amir); John McEnery (Uncle Ted); Janet Dale (Auntie Jean); Nisha Nayar (Jamila); Badi Uzzaman (Anwar); David Bamber (Shadwell); Harish Patel (Changez); Donald Sumpter (Matthew Pyke); Jemma Redgrave (Eleanor).

NEW YORK POST, 12/9/94, p. 48, Larry Worth

Controversy has overwhelmed "The Buddha of Suburbia" since its telecast on British television last year. London tabs screamed "Shame on the BBC" for depictions of group sex, incest and bisexuality.

The bottom line: The hoopla pretty much KO'd the adaptation of Hanif Kureishi's novel from a PBS showing in the United States. And that's where the Public Theater comes in.

"Buddha" was chosen to conclude the Public's extensive series of BBC dramas; it will be screened through Dec. 27, broken into two 110-minute segments.

But can any film live up to such advance billing? Fortunately, "Buddha" holds its own. Better still, the bared skin isn't what makes it interesting.

To maintain viewers' attention over nearly four hours, director Roger Michell fashions an absorbing mosaic of political and social tensions in London of the '70s, with a country of Anglo-Saxons pitted against an ever-increasing number of Indian immigrants.

Kureishi, who co-wrote the script with Michell, focuses on the handsome, slightly androgynous Karim, a young man torn between his Indian-born father and WASP mother.

Karim's dad, Haroon, only fuels the chaos. Deemed to be a wise dirman from his spiritual teachings, he's earning fame in the lily-white suburbs as the grooviest of gurus, meanwhile having a torrid affair with one of his pupils—a lonely housewife.

The ever-confused Karim soon finds himself drawn to both the hunky son of his father's mistress and a gorgeous cousin being forced into an arranged marriage.

Still following? Well, that's just the beginning as the hapless hero is initiated into the worlds of sex, drugs and rock 'n' roll. And racism, adultery, obsession, hypocrisy and compromise.

The results are rarely pretty, but as in his Oscar-nominated screenplay for "My Beautiful Laundrette," Kureishi builds a powerful portrait of a culture about to explode.

Elevating the script is its evenhanded treatment of the clash, with ugliness emanating from both sides. Indeed, each is populated by three-dimensional characters that—refreshingly—can't qualify as either heroes or villains.

Kureishi also incorporates much subtly handled humor, off-set by surprise twists, an evocative period setting and a great score (highlighted by David Bowie's title tune). And for all its bed-swapping, Kereishi sidesteps the soap opera cliches.

The fine cast is led by Naveen Andrews, best known as the star of "Wild West" and "Mississippi Masala." With his soulful eyes and Jaye Davidson-like looks, Andrews' Karim is a wonderfully-nuanced modern-day Candide, perfectly complemented by Roshan Seth's brilliant turn as his perplexed father.

On the down side, the pace occasionally slows, and the production could lose a half hour without missing a beat.

But nobody ever said the show was perfect. And for those who thought they'd never get to see it, "Buddha"—flaws and all—will seem positively divine.

VILLAGE VOICE, 12/13/94, p. 63, J. Hoberman

Hanif Kureishi's 1990 novel *The Buddha of Suburbia* has been translated into 23 languages but the jargon of television may be the most apt. The most enjoyable TV miniseries garnish their multigenerational family sagas with pop-history factoids and light them up with lurid glamour; as adapted by Kureishi and director Roger Michell, the four hour-long episodes of *The Buddha of Suburbia* more than do the mode proud.

Too spicy for timid American broadcasters, *The Buddha of Suburbia*, which is having its local premiere as the culmination of the Public Theater's current BBC series, is near-perfect intellectual junk food, a multiculti, one-dimensionally Dickensian mélange of comic types and ridiculous situations—not to mention sex, drugs, and rock 'n' roll.

Karim, the youthful hero, is, like his creator, the product of an English working-class woman, a Pakistani professional father and a bourgeois South London suburb, graduating from school into a 1970s sufficiently nebulous to encompass the dotage of Swinging London and the birth pangs of Punk, (Wittily, David Bowie, the age's key transitional figure, was commissioned to provide the score.) What the miniseries loses by dropping the novel's sardonic, first-person narration, it gains in deadpan pseudo-objectivity. Albeit more wide-eyed and pliant looking, Naveen Andrews, last seen here in *Wild West* as an Anglo-Pakistani Garth Brooks wannabe, has a marked physical resemblance to Kureishi. As much as it's about anything, *The Buddha of Suburbia* is about the author's own climb to fashionable media-stardom.

Karim has grown up brown but British; the first jolt to his compound identity comes when his hitherto staid father Haroon (the redoubtable, spaniel-eyed Roshan Seth) decides to personify a stereotyped Asian-ness by passing himself off as Buddhist sage, lecturing to comfortably upholstered living rooms hazy with incense and credulous Brits in flowing robes. "They know more about India than you do," Karim hisses, having accompanied Haroon on one such gig. Karim soon learns the guru's doctrine is not purely spiritual—his father is carrying on an affair with his devotee Eva, even as Karim lusts after her son, the would-be rock 'n' roller, Charlie.

Alternately wry and madcap, *The Buddha of Suburbia* takes the tradition of lower-middle-class domestic comedy—tumultuous doings squeezed through a series of narrow row houses—and combines it with a far more freewheeling satire of British social mores. The best scenes crackle like the exploding seeds in one of Charlie's badly rolled joints. As in Kureishi's earlier scripts, *My Beautiful Laundrette* and *Sammy and Rosie Get Laid* (which was originally intended to be a kind of epic miniseries), the emphasis is largely on coupling the presumably uncoupleable.

Even as Karim's father moves in with Eva, Karim pursues one of Haroon's younger, more impressionable female followers. (In a memorably failed attempt to make contact, he's dissed by her racist dad, then humped by the family dog.) Meanwhile, on the other side of the color line, Haroon's childhood friend—the beleaguered grocer Anwar—goes on a Gandhi-esque hunger strike to force his daughter Jamila, a militant feminist and advocate of Black Power, to embark upon an arranged marriage. That the imported bridegroom, played with grotesque effervescence by Indian comedian Harish Patel, is tubby and deformed, considerable raises the comic cruelty quotient.

Karim, by contrast, is sad but seductive, bemused yet opportunistic. Andrews plays him as a kind of Candide on the make, more innocent than need be as he wanders from scene to scene, motivated by both a desire to please and an ambition to get ahead, and usually leaving a small mess in his wake. If Karim is fascinated by the young blondies he encounters, they are also taken with him—albeit in unpredictable ways. (His nickname "Creamy" is laced with multiple ironies.) Two-episodes end with the hero in flagrante—most spectacularly at an intimate dinner party hosted by a left-wing theater director and his horny wife. (The scene, in which a pair of unhappily swapped couples fuck in tandem, has intimations of a hardcore *I Love Lucy* with the two women, both actresses, competing in orgasmic histrionics.)

Omnisexual, as well as Anglo-Indian, Kureishi's deterritorialized alter-ego navigates several worlds. The issue of identity becomes paramount midway through when everyone moves to London. There, as arrogant Charlie stumbles upon the nascent punk scene and, having seen the no future, reinvents himself as an ersatz Johnny Rotten, Karim takes up acting, which, in the context of the British theatrical avant-garde, means learning to portray a culturally determined version of himself. For his first role, Karim is compelled to adopt a Bengali accent in order to play Mowgli in a hilariously pretentious production of *The Jungle Book*; later he's recruited by a Peter Brook-type for a series of workshop improvisations that will "stage our postcolonial world." Karim's first impulse is to satirize the grocer Anwar, for which he is attacked as self-hating by the company's other member of color (and then, of course, by the rest of the group).

By telefilm's end, however, the Kureishi hero has successfully attained the status of professional (or representative) Asian. Unlike the novel, the miniseries links this to the ascension of Margaret Thatcher. The juxtaposition of Thatcher's victory with Karim's provides the show's most complicated joke—it's a coupling that effectively places quotation marks around the very concepts of marginality and alienation that seem intrinsic to the Kureishi worldview.

Also reviewed in:
NEW YORK TIMES, 12/9/94, p. C8, Caryn James
VARIETY, 5/9-15/94, p. 78, Dennis Harvey

BULLETS OVER BROADWAY

A Miramax Films release of a Sweetland Films presentation of a Jean Doumanian Productions film. *Executive Producer:* Jean Doumanian and J. E. Beaucaire. *Producer:* Robert Greenhut. *Director:* Woody Allen. *Screenplay:* Woody Allen and Douglas McGrath. *Director of Photography:* Carlo Di Palma. *Editor:* Susan E. Morse. *Music:* Dick Hyman. *Choreographer:* Graciela Daniele. *Sound:* James Sabat. *Sound Editor:* Bob Hein. *Casting:* Juliet Taylor. *Production Designer:* Santo Loquasto. *Art Director:* Tom Warren. *Set Decorator:* Susan Bode and Amy Marshall. *Set Dresser:* Dave Weinman. *Costumes:* Jeffrey Kurland. *Make-up:* Joe Campayno and Frances Kolar. *Running time:* 99 minutes. *MPAA Rating:* PG.

CAST: John Cusack (David Shayne); Jack Warden (Julian Marx); Chazz Palminteri (Cheech); Joe Viterelli (Nick Valenti); Jennifer Tilly (Olive Neal); Rob Reiner (Sheldon Flender); Mary-Louise Parker (Ellen); Dianne Wiest (Helen Sinclair); Harvey Fierstein (Sid Loomis); Jim Broadbent (Warner Purcell); Tracey Ullman (Eden Brent); Paul Herman (Maitre'd); James Reno (Sal); Tony Sirico (Rocco); Stacey Nelkin (Rita); Margaret Sophie Stein (Lili); Charles Cragin (Rifkin); Gerald E. Dolezar (Café Waiter); Nina Sonya Peterson (Josette); Shannon Laumeister and Fran McGee (Movie Theater Victims); Annie-Joe Edwards (Venus); Brian McConnachie (Mitch Sabine); Edie Falco (Lorna); Kernan Bell (Speakeasy Waiter); Hope W. Sacharoff (Hilda Marx); Debi Mazar (Vi); Nick Iacovino and Frank Aquilino (Hoods); Sam Ardeshir and Molly Regan (Helen's Party Guests); Phil Stein (Stagehand); John Doumanian and Dayle Haddon (Backstage Wellwishers); Tony Darrow (Aldo); Jennifer Van Dyck (Olive's Understudy); Peter McRobbie (Man at Theatre); Howard Erskine, Benay Venuta, and Ken Roberts (Theater Wellwishers).

CHRISTIAN SCIENCE MONITOR, 12/13/94, p. 12, David Sterritt

At a key moment in Woody Allen's new movie, "Bullets Over Broadway," the main character—a Roaring '20s playwright trying to pull off his first major production—decides he's not the artist he thought he was, but rather an entertainer who's better at pleasing the public than expressing the depths of his soul.

With all the public and private travails Allen has been through, it wouldn't be surprising if he wanted to give up personal expression in his own career, cranking out popular entertainments and lowering his profile as an intrepid explorer of the contemporary psyche. It's also undeniable that his more frivolous recent films, such as the much-praised "Manhattan Murder Mystery," have drawn better responses than such heavy pictures as "September" and "Another Woman," full of angst and gloom.

Add this together, and it's tempting to think the "Bullets Over Broadway" hero is acting out Allen's wish to chuck the high-seriousness game in favor of crowd-pleasing fluff. But the situation isn't that simple. For one thing, such above-average Allen films as "Crimes and Misdemeanors" and "Hannah and Her Sisters" resist labeling as either straight drama *or* light comedy, since they blend elements of both.

For another, "Bullets Over Broadway" itself has a notably serious side—suggesting that wholesome activities, like putting on Broadway plays, might call for unwholesome compromises, like accepting help from wealthy crooks.

For all its boisterous laughs, crazy characters, and loony situations, the movie is laced with interesting thoughts about the American way of art, business, and crime. If silliness seems to have displace sobriety in most of the story, it's because Allen the thinker is holding Allen the clown in front of him like a ventriloquist's dummy.

As if bearing out the movie's hope to be taken seriously, the US premiere of "Bullets Over Broadway" marked Allen's first showing at the New York Film Festival.

The protagonist of the picture is David Shayne, a would-be dramatist who's determined to direct his latest play on the New York stage. Funding is elusive until his agent talks to a powerful mobster with (a) lots of money and (b) a girlfriend who's dying to move from chorus-line kicking to Broadway acting. The crook will finance the show if a key female role—a brainy psychiatrist—goes to Olive, his nearly illiterate lover.

David makes the fateful compromise and starts up rehearsals, whereupon two new shocks come his way. One is that the new actress's bodyguard, a murderous thug named Cheech, must oversee every step of the production to make sure his employer is well served.

The other is that Cheech has a talent for narrative, dialogue, and psychology that puts the playwright himself in the shade. David is embarrassed by this at first, but the play's success is what matters most, so before long he's eagerly accepting Cheech's rewrites—and wondering what solutions his brutish collaborator might have for other problems dogging the show, including the rotten performances Olive gives night after night.

The serious aspects of "Bullets Over Broadway" are anchored partly in David's dubious partnership with crime in the name of art, and partly in his conversations with a radical friend who thinks any attempt at artistic success is a shameful sellout to capitalist commercialism. Allen's interest in these matters is commendable, as is his willingness to explore them in what's otherwise an amusing farce.

The presence of Allen the thinker doesn't automatically mean his thoughts will be deep or profound, however, and it can't be said that "Bullets Over Broadway" delves very far into the issues it raises. At heart it's a lively little comedy that suffers from the same narrowness of vision found in most of Allen's earlier pictures.

For one example of this narrowness, after some 25 films he still seems only dimly aware of how social and economic factors help determine the development of people's lives; this allows him to resurrect that galling racial stereotype, the wisecracking black servant, to be a "colorful" background figure in "Bullets Over Broadway" as in "The Purple Rose of Cairo" a few years ago. Such second-rate nostalgia is no major sin in itself, but it indicates how limited Allen's artistry has remained in some respects.

In filmmaking terms, "Bullets Over Broadway." is crafted with Allen's usual finesse. John Cusack plays David with a whiny tone that effectively recalls Allen's own acting style. Jennifer Tilly gives the dreadful Olive a brassy charm that recalls such predecessors as Jean Hagen and Judy Holliday in various Hollywood classics.

Dianne Wiest and Tracey Ullman stand out as performers in the play-within-the-film. Chazz Palminteri is ideal as Cheech, and Rob Reiner is perfect as David's radical friend. Jack Warden, Joe Viterelli, Mary-Louise Parker, Harvey Fierstein, and Jim Broadbent round out the superbly chosen cast. Allen regulars carried out the key technical tasks—including cinematographer Carlo Di Palma and designer Santo Loquasto—and Allen wrote the screenplay with Douglas McGrath.

FILMS IN REVIEW, 11-12/94, p. 57, Kevin Lewis

The Broadway and gangster sagas of the Golden Age of Hollywood are among the most fondly remembered of movies. Woody Allen's newest movie recaptures much of the fun of those movies of the late 1920s and early 1930s and even turns the form on its ear.

Bullets Over Broadway recreates the Manhattan of the post-World War I period when the hayseeds with intellectual pretensions invaded New York and reinvented themselves as Broadway sophisticates. They contributed to the era of "wonderful nonsense" and helped American drama and art grow up and achieve maturity. Allen, the quintessential New Yorker, lovingly pokes fun at these nouveau salon types in this tale of a Freudian play financed by a gangster as a showcase for his hard and talentless nightclub dancer moll.

As always in an Allen movie, a myriad of characters masks the lack of viable ideas. All the actors are superb, including John Cusack as the Ben Hecht-type playwright, Dianne Wiest as the monstrous Broadway grande dame, Tracey Ullman as the flapper sidekick of the star, Jennifer Tilly as the ignorant but ambitious moll, Chazz Palminteri as the moll's bodyguard with a talent for dramatic construction, Rob Reiner as the obnoxious and arrogant Greenwich Village unpublished "genius," Jack Warden as the producer who doesn't care where his financing comes from, Joe Viterelli as the gangster, Mary Louise Parker the faithful girlfriend of the playwright, and Jim Broadbent as the ham actor.

When the movie satirizes the intellectual pretensions of the emerging American theater, it is superb. The audience never knows what the original drama is about, except that it is a turgid Eugene O'Neil-type of psychological drama. The joke is that the playwright from Pittsburgh can be so easily seduced by the overblown dramatics of the Broadway star Helen Sinclair (Dianne Wiest) and threatened by the gangster's moll. Allen's resolution of this dilemma is a reworking of *Amadeus*, wherein the playwright is forced into accepting the script changes provided by the killer/bodyguard. The killer, it turns out, is a brilliant writer, a whiz at dramatic construction. There is much discussion by Cusack and Palminteri about how a trained writer cannot be a talented writer but an amoral killer can be an artist. This is coupled with another feeble subplot wherein the playwright is troubled by the thought that the woman he is in love with, his Pittsburgh sweetheart, loves him only because he is an artist rather than a man. The ending is particularly sentimental and begs the question. Allen's misogyny, or his lack of comprehension of female psychology, is clearly revealed in the film.

The set decoration of Santo Loquasto deserves an Oscar. The bygone Manhattan is accurately depicted down to the smallest details, including the reproduction of the original *Strange Interlude* poster as the poster for the Broadway show in the film.

Wiest gives the best performance in the movie; she captures the world-weary pose of the 1920s star a la Florence Reed, Katharine Cornell or Judith Anderson. If she evokes Geraldine Page in *Sweet Bird of Youth*, that is to her credit because Page was portraying the same sort of self-absorbed character. As the moll, Jennifer Tilly is shrill without the fun of a Jean Hagen or Barbara Pepper would have brought to the part.

Nevertheless, *Bullets Over Broadway* is a hilarious movie despite its weaknesses.

LOS ANGELES TIMES, 10/21/94, Calendar/p. 1, Peter Rainer

The life of the theater has lots of life in Woody Allen's "Bullets Over Broadway." Set in the Prohibition '20s, it's a theatrical satire crossed with a gangster satire, and the joke is in how close the two realms really are. The onstage prima donnas and posturers and leches are as conniving and strong-arming as gangsters—they just use barbs instead of bullets.

This collision of worlds comes about when the only backer for the Broadway production of a work by promising young playwright David Shayne (John Cusack) is mobster Nick Valenti (Joe Viterelli). The condition for the backing is that Nick's flouncy, aggressively untalented showgirl mistress, Olive (Jennifer Tilly), must be given a starring role. She ends up getting—and mangling—the role of the psychiatrist. (Allen is perhaps the world's best-known analysand. Is he dissing the profession here?)

David has perfected the somewhat emaciated Greenwich Village look of the "true" artist. (He also, as played by Cusack, acts and sounds suspiciously close to Woody Allen.) David quarrels with his producer (Jack Warden) about the indignity of casting Olive in order to rescue his show (which he also ends up directing).

When the dread decision is made, he wakes up screaming in the middle of the night and screams out the window, "I'm a whore." David is inflamed by compromise; he turns his selling out into high flamboyant drama. It's his worst—and finest—hour. David is a schnook with standards—a blood-brother to the Coen brothers' Barton Fink, who also primped his principles (while also selling out).

David's girlfriend Ellen (Mary-Louise Parker) is bemused by his tortuousness. When the aging, Norma Desmond-like star Helen Sinclair (Dianne Wiest) is cast as the lead in his play, David's flailing about becomes ever more foolish. Helen plays on his vanity; he falls in love with her. She knows his play is a stinker, but she figures he can at least expand her role if she name-drops his heroes—"Max Anderson, Gene O'Neill"—often enough.

But there's a wild card here. Olive's bodyguard, Cheech (very well played by Chazz Palminteri), sent by Nick to keep an eye on her during rehearsals, turns out to save better ideas on how to fix the play than the playwright. Without making a big fancy deal about it, "Bullets Over Broadway," co-written by Douglas McGrath, turns into a riff on the nature of artistry. David, with his haunted look and high-flown common-man sentiments, is the popular image of the Greenwich Village-style artist. But he's the artist as poseur. Cheech, the hit man who *really* comes from the streets, is the artist we don't recognize—don't *want* to recognize.

Allen knows how shopworn satire of the theater can be, but he has come up with a dandy crew of scene-stealers. There's Tracey Ullman, as a superannuated ingenue hugging her Chihuahua, Jim Broadbent as the voluminous ex-matinee idol whose waistline expands in direct proportion to his anxieties, Tilly as the swacked showgirl—she may be a bimbo, but, with her woozy wiles, and her nasally voice as loud as an air-raid siren, she's a bimbo of genius. All of these performers are "too much," but that's not a criticism. The only way they can play their roles is to overplay them—that's the nature of high theatrical satire.

Wiest is so gloriously over the top that she turns Helen into a sacred monster. She's the soul of theater—she's Mistress Thespian. Whether she's cocooned in furs or glazed in makeup, Helen is a powerhouse of intimidation. David doesn't stand a chance with her; he's a speck on the windshield of her ego. Wiest doesn't try for pathos—she's having too much fun for that. Every time you think she has gone too far in "Bullets Over Broadway," she redeems the foolery with her sozzled, spirited timing. She understands the royal pettiness, and the smarts, behind Helen's Great Lady act. Helen may be a big blur of narcissism, but she's great at sizing up weakness, including her own. That's why she goes after David so strenuously. Despite her self-proclaimed "legendary" status, she knows she needs a hit.

David, of course, is the most self-deluded character in the movie. By its end, he has his eyes opened. One of his cronies—an obnoxious, unproduced playwright played by Rob Reiner—tells him at one point that "an artist creates his own moral universe." The movie ends up being a kind of riposte to that gangsterish sentiment. (It's possible—though not very productive—to interpret the movie as Allen's apologia for his above-it-all public stance during the early stages of his famous troubles.)

Yet, Allen surely regards himself as an artist. He wants us to know that artistry isn't all it's cracked up to be—that it's better to be a decent human being and know your limitations and live a good life. But he also wants us to know he's enough of an artist to be able to humble himself in that way and still make a movie as good as "Bullets Over Broadway." So he has it both ways.

It's a neat hat trick.

NEW YORK, 10/17/94, p. 70, David Denby

Woody allen's *Bullets Over Broadway* is a beautiful-looking comedy set in a fantasy New York of white-on-white Deco apartments, gangsters in tuxedos, and slender women splendidly swathed, turbaned, and bejeweled. Some of it is very funny—Dianne Wiest gives a classic comic performance. Yet *Bullets Over Broadway* is not a satisfying movie. In fact, it's something of a bummer. There's too much contempt in it, contempt joined strangely with self-exculpation. And despite the beauty, the secondhandedness of the production becomes depressing. Woody Allen's familiar 1920s of flappers, gangsters, and Broadway actors and producers conveys less about the decade than about caricatures of the decade. Can experience ever be made fresh again? Is anyone even willing to try? Ouentin Tarantino put a perverse spin on pulp conventions in *Pulp Fiction*, but his originality may be unique. In movies now, almost every image is a new version of some earlier representation, every mood and emotion a polished, "ironic" cliché.

Bullets Over Broadway, which Douglas McGrath wrote with Allen, demonstrates that satire itself can be recycled. Woody Allen's theater people—extravagant, pretentious poseurs—might be escapees from such earlier ribbings of the stage as the famous 1934 Howard Hawks movie *Twentieth Century*. But the Hawks movie was all of a piece. In *Bullets*, the teasing is so broad and opportunistic that the movie seems in conflict with itself: The handsome, fully saturated color cinematography by Carlo Di Palma—the high style of the movie's visual scheme—completely outclasses the too easily composed farcical dialogue. The dark, burnished color promises depths that the movie has no intention of delivering. *Bullets Over Broadway* is far more entertaining than Allen's *Shadows and Fog*, but it has similar qualities of pastiche and meaninglessness.

What's fatally missing is any love for the way of life that's being mocked. In *Bullets Over Broadway*, the Broadway theater people, with their talk of "Max" Anderson and "Gene" O'Neill, are just phonies putting on ridiculous plays. And the "bohemians," sitting in their Village cafes, are even worse—fake intellectuals proud of their unproducible works, stoking their vanity with gush. All these deluded people misuse words, a sin not easily forgiven by Woody Allen. The snatches of stage dialogue we hear are routinely awful, the situations enacted onstage—we catch just a glimpse—the most pathetic rubbish.

I'm no lover of the theater, but I thought it unfair that Woody Allen hardly lets us see the actors working. Dianne Wiest, thrusting back her shoulders and turning her face into a mask of vanity, has great fun playing Helen Sinclair, a boozy, aging Broadway diva full of dominating little affectations. But is Helen also a fake on-stage? Or does she communicate something to the audience? Normally, I wouldn't raise such a question (satire has its prerogatives, one of which is that it shouldn't be taken literally), but the question of talent—who has it and who doesn't—is central to the movie. It seems not to have occurred to Allen that in the theater, extravagant temperament and absurd affectations may sometimes be inseparable from genius. His view is coldly ungenerous : These people have no taste, period.

John Cusack, the nominal hero—an eager young playwright with a tin ear—is a sellout from the first. He accepts, as a supporting actress in his play, the shrill-voiced mistress of a gangster, in order to get the gangster's backing. And he's quickly overwhelmed by his star, Helen, and rewrites her part to make it more glamorous. Why care about this guy? Nothing is at stake in his life. Yet the pathos of the untalented is not an impossible theme. George Segal played a failed writer in *The Owl and the Pussycat* and made something touching out of the man's grouchiness and hurt. John Cusack, with his earnest voice and slightly callow good looks, would seem to be perfectly cast, but he gives a hysterical and unattractive performance, throwing fits and shrieking "I'm a whore!" out the window. Even in his disillusion, he's a theater phony, and Allen shies away from him, hardly giving him a close-up. When the playwright finds redemption, the moment feels completely unconvincing.

Allen is much more successful with Dianne Wiest. A melodramatic lush, Wiest's Helen Sinclair enters the rehearsal stage, hands upheld, shaping the air. "This old theater, this church," she begins, carving the vapor, and she salutes the ghosts of all the great parts she has played there. In the past, her eyes crinkling adorably, Wiest has often seemed kittenish, fragile, almost too nice to draw a deep breath—a mistress of tentative emotions. She's had some lovely moments in movies, but she's never quite commanded the screen. Now she does: Playing this leather-voiced bitch, she seems a greater, stronger actress than before. Her manipulation of Cusack's young playwright—"Don't speak!" she commands, shutting his mouth with her hands, as if her emotions were too delicate for words—yields some classic, giddy moments.

There are other good spots. Tracey Ullman shows up with a tiny yapping dog. Annie-Joe Edwards's black maid, weighty and impervious as a truck, glides through the apartment of the gangster's mistress, an homage to such studio-era maids as Hattie McDaniel and a reminder that the racist conventions in old movies and plays at least had some comic use (the black maid in old movies often told off her mistress, as Edwards does here). Many of the casual details of *Bullets Over Broadway* are wonderful. But Allen has something to get off his chest.

It seems that not everyone is a phony. When the gangster's mistress (Jennifer Tilly) goes into the play, the gangster assigns his henchman Cheech (Chazz Palminteri) to look after her. A gravel-voiced thug, Cheech sits silently through rehearsals until he has an idea for improving the plot. Which he offers. And then an idea for some better dialogue. Which he also offers. The thug, it seems, is the true playwright, the true artist. Of course, you have to take this on faith—Cheech's great ideas, when we hear them, seem hardly less banal than what's already in the play. Yet if Cheech's artistry is no more than a comic conceit, the conceit has a didactic side. For Cheech is also a cold-blooded murderer, and a man who becomes increasingly ruthless in protecting the newly rewritten work. So it seems that Woody Allen is defying critics of his behavior: The artist, he's telling us, doesn't live by the same rules as everyone else; he does whatever is required to express himself and to protect his art, even murder someone. Taunting his pursuers and interpreters, Woody Allen may be indulging his own version of theatrical guff. If we believe what he's saying, any kind of stupid behavior can be justified as necessary in the service of art. What can't be justified, however—not even by Woody's sleight of hand—is bad art. *Bullets Over Broadway* has a distant, almost dissociated feeling to it. If Woody Allen is going to speak for the singular rights of the artist, he'd better do it from a stronger platform.

NEW YORK POST, 9/30/94, p. 47, Thelma Adams

Woody Allen isn't shooting blanks in "Bullets Over Broadway." It's a roaring good comedy set in the Runyonesque '20s when gunmen rub out rivals without splattering blood and directors bed their leading ladies without a hint of nudity.

In this ensemble acting spree bohemian writer/director John Cusack makes a Faustian deal with mobster Nick Valenti. He casts the bootlegger/s moll Jennifer Tilly in his tortured drama in exchange for financial backing.

Dianne Wiest swoops in as a fading diva who seduces Cusack away from his sweetheart, Mary-Louise Parker. In the art-imitates-life column, the philandering playwright must choose between an older actress and a younger waif.

West steals the show, biting off the movie's best lines. She enters the theater to rehearse and delivers a rapid-fire run-through of the great roles from Clytemnestra to Cordelia. "Each performance a birth, each curtain a death," she says.

Tilly, with her squeaky little-girl voice raised to a roar, has her best role yet. It's an underrated talent to play a bad actress well.

The twist is that Tilly's roughneck bodyguard, Chazz Palminteri, ends up fixing Cusack's arid, intellectual play, injecting it with truth and passion.

Artists, according to Allen, are born not made. In this meditation on art and commerce, creativity and compromise, Palminteri emerges as the real thing—willing to kill for his art rather than compromise—while Cusack is more fool than hero.

"Bullets Over Broadway," for all its jaunty humor, is an emotionally defensive movie. The biggest—and unintentional—laugh comes when the uncompromised and unproduced playwright Rob Reiner says, "Guilt is petty bourgeois crap. An artist creates his own universe ... You've gotta do what you've gotta do."

While it would be cruel to take this straight, it plays as an apologia for Allen's personal life.

It seems odd that Allen who has long been criticized for not casting minorities in major roles, would have the sole black character be a shuffling, smart-ass maid named Venus. But, then again an artist never compromises his vision to the whims of his critics.

NEWSDAY, 10/21/94, Part II/p. B5, Jack Mathews

One thing that can be said of the post-Mia/Soon Yi scandal phase of Woody Allen's career, demonstrated in his engaging new comedy "Bullets Over Broadway," the little scoundrel hasn't lost his sense of humor.

Co-written by Allen and New Republic magazine humorist Doug McGrath, "Bullets Over Broadway" is a mere air bubble in the Allen oeuvre, a little laughing gas to help him work out those spectacular new kinks in his public image. But it's as flat-out funny a movie as Allen has made since he last aligned the mob with the Great White Way in the 1984 "Broadway Danny Rose."

Allen, who sat this one out as an actor, takes us a little farther back into New York's entertainment past with "Bullets," a gorgeously designed and photographed backstage comedy set in the midst of the Prohibition era. It was a time when the mob had the franchise on America's favorite form of entertainment—hootch—and a potential role in almost every enterprise in need of both capital investment and upscale consumers.

Such is the status of "God of Our Fathers," a play written by a spunky, over-confident novice named David Shayne (John Cusack) and underwritten, against Shayne's better judgment, by a crime boss (Joe Viterelli) determined to get his nagging, untalented mistress (Jennifer Tilly) a role in a Broadway play. This is a pretty tired twist on the Faustian theme, but what Allen does with it is inspired. Just as the show seems locked on a predictable course, with the adenoidal Olive Neal (Tilly) about to destroy the morale of the cast and crew, her thug bodyguard Cheech (Chazz Palminteri) steps up with a suggestion or two about the play, and its author's ego and ethics begin to erode in ways he'd never considered.

"You don't write the way people talk," Cheech says, and after a few of his lines are quietly inserted into the manuscript, to the rave reviews of the cast and preview audiences in Boston, he becomes Shayne's eager and over-bearing ghostwriter, Cyrano de Corleone, and the author has to accept an ugly truth. Even uneducated killers are more in touch with the common man than he and the pseudo-intellectual, art-lit thumbsuckers he hangs out with down in Greenwich Village.

That's about all the heavy lifting Allen attempts in "Bullets," and that's fine. This is a gag-laden burlesque, filled with an assortment of oddball characters. Not all the gags and characters are well thought-out. Tracey Ullman makes a hilarious entrance, as an actress and little-dog pamperer cast in Shayne's play, then fades into the background like a stage prop. And Tilly's Judy Holliday impression gets old quick.

But what works, really works. Dianne Wiest leaves no scenery uneaten as Helen Sinclair, the vain theater legend who still knows how to seduce a punk playwright and get her role beefed up. Jim Broadbent's deadpan performance as the overeating matinee idol Warner Purcell is a scream. And Rob Reiner, speaking of big eaters, steals his scenes as an existential windbag holding court with the Greenwich Village groupies.

The real fun, however, is provided by Palminteri, who's doing a comic riff on the neighborhood crime boss he played in Robert De Niro's "A Bronx Tale." In the beginning, Cheech appears to be just another slicked-back mob henchman, a gofer in a sharkskin suit. But when he discovers his muse while standing guard during rehearsals for "God of Our Fathers," he takes over both the play and the movie.

Shayne, a fidgetey, neurotic whiner, is a youthful version of the character Allen usually plays, and it may mark a turn in the director's work. As long as he's writing roles for himself, they are limited to his approximate age, which limits his subject range, as well. With "Bullets," he and Cusack prove that he can reshape his own personality for other actors, and be just as effective. For people who can't bear to look at Allen anymore, that's crucial.

NEWSWEEK, 10/24/94, p. 75, David Ansen

"I'm an artist!" yelps earnest playwright David Shayne (John Cusack), refusing to change a word of his new play. These are the first words we hear in woody Allen's delicious *Bullets Over Broadway,* and they will come back to haunt David many times over by the time his Eugene O'Neillish melodrama has made its perilous progress to a Broadway opening night. Set in the roaring '20s, populated with tommy-gun-shooting gangsters, dumb chorus girls and theatrical grande dames, "Bullets Over Broadway," co-written by Douglas McGrath, itself uses a classical theatrical structure to explore the conflicting—and sometimes even deadly—demands of art and morality. The joy of this bouncy, brainy Allen outing is how effortlessly he meshes his serious, clearly personal conundrums with the giddy formulas of backstage farce.

David will change more than a word to get his play mounted: his entire notion of what it takes to be an artist will undergo a rude transformation. His first compromise comes when backing is supplied by mobster Nick Valenti (Joe Viterelli), on the condition that his singularly untalented, shriekingly nasal girlfriend Olive (Jennifer Tilly) gets cast in the play. She does—as a psychiatrist. As his leading lady David lands the legendary Helen Sinclair (Dianne Wiest), an alcoholic diva who wraps the narcissistic young playwright around her fingers and seduces him into giving her character a bit more "color." Then there's affable Warner Purcell (Jim Broadbent), an aging British stage idol with an unfortunate tendency, under stress, to overeat—and a dangerous yen for the mobster's moll. Add to the mix the highstrung Eden Brent (Tracey Ullman), forever accompanied by her lap dog, and Allen has equipped himself with a volatile menagerie of Old Broadway stereotypes he can ignite to maximum comic effect.

Lurking in the back of the theater at rehearsals is the movie's surprising trump card—a hood named Cheech (Chazz Palminteri), sent by Valenti to keep an eye on the flighty Olive. A coldblooded killer, he proves to David's most astute critic, and an artistic collaborator in possession of a native genius that the pretentious, well-schooled David could never hope to emulate. It would spoil too much of the fun of Allen's tale to reveal more of Cheech's role. Let's just say the movie's most resonant and startling moments come out of Cheech and David's artistic shotgun wedding.

"An artist creates his own moral universe," says the unproduced Marxist playwright Flender (Rob Reiner), who is busy seducing David's girlfriend (Mary-Louise Parker) while the success-obsessed writer is busy betraying her. "Bullets Over Broadway" takes this self-serving dictum to its ultimate black-comic conclusion, with results that are both hilarious and haunting. But whether one chooses to grasp on to the story's darker undertones or float along its bright, snappy surface, no recent Woody Allen movie has been so devoted to pleasuring its audience. The relish with which Wiest, Tilly, Broadbent, Palminteri, Ullman and Cusack feast upon their roles is contagious. This is ham cured and roasted to farcical perfection.

TIME, 10/17/94, p. 74, Richard Schickel

"An artist creates his own moral universe." The desire to remind David (John Cusack) of such a burden is irresistible—he's so young, so serious, so ambitious, so innocent. The trouble is that the universe he actually inhabits is the Broadway of the 1920s, where, as in all show-biz societies, morality is entirely ego driven and provisional.

Director-screenwriter Woody Allen and co-writer Douglas McGrath have comically and affectionately reimagined the archetypes of backstage dramas from the days when the New York theater was a robust and glamorous institution. They're all here, doing their best to bring David's neo-O'Neillian work to life: the wise, temporizing, desperately undercapitalized producer (Jack Warden); the aging ingenue (Tracey Ullman), complete with ill-tempered lapdog; the agreeably self-destructive leading man (Jim Broadbent); above all, the Great Lady of the Theater ("I don't play frumps or virgins"), portrayed by Dianne Wiest in a boldly swooping performance.

The wild card at their rehearsal table is Olive Neal (Jennifer Tilly), chorine, ineptly aspiring thespian and gangster's moll. Nick, her mobster lover (Joe Viterelli), is backing the show, in which, nasal accent and all, she is supposed to play a psychiatrist. Nick supplies Olive with a bodyguard. Try to cut one of her lines and you have a hood named Cheech (playwright-actor Chazz Palminteri) to deal with.

Nobody has to advise Cheech to create his own moral universe. His instinct for truth and falsehood has been honed by his profession, and his hot-wired street smarts make him far more acute on the subject of human behavior than any playwright. Slumped in a back row of the theater, keeping an eye on Olive, he is bored and offended by the pretentious twaddle emanating from the stage. Beginning with a few suggestions for line changes, Cheech is soon proposing structural alterations, then secretly joining David in a pool hall to rewrite the play, Among the young playwright's problems is that he lacks any real talent, but Cheech is good—maybe great—and he is quite literally (and hilariously) willing to kill to protect his vision.

Is there a deft little lesson here in how to distinguish raw genius from cautiously tutored craft? You bet there is. But Allen and McGrath also recognize how rude, disturbing and inconvenient greatness can be. And they grant gracious absolution to pretentious mediocrity, once it learns its place. Allen bathes his fable in a seductive, rosy light, grants everyone in the wonderful ensemble cast a comic high point, and gives us a film that combines impeccable craftsmanship and a basic exuberance that's been missing from his work for years.

SIGHT AND SOUND, 5/95, p. 40, Jonathan Romney

New York, the 20s. David Shayne, an aspiring, idealistic young playwright, is determined to direct his new play himself. Unexpectedly, producer Julian Marx tells him that he has backing—from mobster Nick Valenti, whose volatile and talentless girlfriend Olive Neal has ambitions to be an actress; the only condition is that Olive must play a lead. David and Marx approach grandiose, heavy-drinking Broadway star Helen Sinclair for a role. Rehearsals start: among the cast are dapper English leading man Warner Purcell, a compulsive eater, and irrepressibly chirpy actress Eden Brent. Olive is accompanied by Cheech, whom Valenti has assigned as her bodyguard, and who makes his threatening presence felt from the stalls.

David increasingly spends time with Helen, who captivates him with her flamboyant thespian glamour. Cheech begins to offer his own suggestions for the play, to David's dismay and the cast's general approval. While Cheech's back is turned, Olive and Warner begin a furtive affair. At a speakeasy, David runs into Cheech; the two make peace and Cheech begins to take even more of a hand, effectively becoming David's mentor and suggesting further changes, which David now eagerly incorporates. David embarks on a full-blown affair with Helen. Cheech tells Warner to keep away from Olive and the actor responds by going on an eating binge.

As the play gets under way, prior to its New York run, Cheech, increasingly possessive of 'his' work, becomes enraged by Olive's hopeless acting; at one performance she is replaced by an understudy and the play improves. Valenti demands more lines for Olive; furious, Cheech takes her away and shoots her dead. David confronts him, but Cheech will brook no debate. David's girlfriend Ellen, who by now suspects his affair with Helen, reveals she has become involved with their bohemian friend Sheldon Flender—formerly David's guru. Valenti, suspecting Cheech of Olive's murder, has his men follow him to the play's Broadway opening; Cheech is killed, and the critics assume that the gunshots are a brilliant dramatic touch. David has showdown with Ellen and Flender; he tells her he knows he is no artist. She agrees to return to Pittsburgh and marry him.

The last two lines of *Bullets Over Broadway* are a *reductio ad absurdum* of the eternal happy ending. The hero walks with his true love into a presumably duller but happier future: "Will you marry me?"—"Yes". However cynical we might expect Woody Allen to be about connubial bliss, this gentle up-turn seems unequivocal. Allen here seems to be celebrating his own reconciliation with the well-made play. Allen's lightest work for some time, *Bullets Over Broadway* is an unabashed entertainment with few of those troubling speculations on mortality that marked even such gentle exercises as *The Purple Rose of Cairo* and *A Midsummer Night's Sex Comedy*. Fresher and funnier than *Manhattan Murder Mystery*, the film might not provide that much grist for Allen's auteurist constituency, but it's enormously winning.

As a spectacle this is something like a scaled-down version of *The Cotton Club*, with a touch of *Some Like It Hot* in its flipness about gangland. As a backstage comedy, *Bullets* is all about putting on a show. Where recent Allen films have been self-consciously concerned with the textures of film—the expressionist pastiche of *Shadows and Fog*, the *cinema vérité* wobble of *Husbands and Wives*—*Bullets* largely takes cinema for granted, concentrating instead on stagecraft. Allen seems to be thinking theatrically these days: he recently directed a television version of his 1966 stage play *Don't Drink the Water*—an unsuccessful venture, by all accounts—as well as contributing a one-acter to a portmanteau off-Broadway show with David Mamet and Elaine May. But here we see a different kind of stagecraft. His cast is required not to underplay, but to let rip with fruity caricature. *Bullets* is peopled with comic ready-mades: Jim Broadbent's old-school British thesp, his gallantry hiding a core of bulimic hysteria; Tracey Ullman's frantically nice fusspot; and Jennifer Tilly's witless flapper, a role she makes work by turning up the screeching volume. It's a telling role, though, demonstrating how radically Allen's approach to acting is at odds with his hero's; Olive ruins the play by being intractably bigger-than-life, Tilly adds to the film overdoing it.

Acting the part versus being it is the film's central opposition. Pittsburgh boy David yearns to be a New York playwright, but he's not sure what role suits him best. He is as much a fish out of water amid the uptown swank of Helen's world as he is in the boho circle where his mentor Sheldon pontificates about the artist making "his own moral universe". That the film is primarily about performance is exemplified by Dianne Wiest's wildly histrionic turn as the diva who saves her highest ham for offstage, constantly swooning with Sarah Bernhardt hauteur. Her refrain "No! Don't speak!", gets funnier with further over-use.

There are some more traditional Allen obsessions at work too. *Bullets* is an inversion of *The Purple Rose of Cairo* in which fiction stepped off the screen and into the real; here the real takes a hand and rewrites imagination. It's a fresh take also on *Amadeus*: an idealistic slogger who believes passionately in his calling is ignominiously upstaged by a hugely talented newcomer who couldn't give a toss for 'art', but can't help being himself.

In presenting Cheech's argument that artists should just "be themselves", Allen is acting out his own attempt to balance the requirements of working in genre against the imperative to be himself. David writes what he thinks is a Broadway play, something stilted and impersonal; Cheech proves that a work should thrive on the idiosyncratic rhythms that an artist can't help producing. Hence, at the end, the film ditches the Broadway stereotypes to round off with a consummate Allen moment—a showdown between thinking lovers, which suddenly sends us straight back to the twitchy, mock-learned disputations of *Shadows and Fog*.

Bullets Over Broadway therefore engages in a commercial debate about what film should be doing, and whom it should be trying to please. David starts off trying to please the producers, then ends up having to do justice to the demands of art, even if it's someone else's. Cheech may be Mozart to his Salieri, but he's a killer, and becomes most fully evil the minute he becomes inspired by, and possessive of, his own writing. Sheldon, meanwhile, is a man of such integrity that none of his work ever gets produced; his posing is simply a pretext for moral slobbishness, but he's a sorry shadow of Cheech, who horrifically fulfills Sheldon's prescription for the artist forging his own ethical code.

Yet it's tempting to think that once David admits at last, "I'm not an artist", then he may yet get to be a playwright. There is, after all, more ambivalence in Allen's 'happily ever after' than is immediately apparent; this gentle farce may even be softening us up for stronger philosophical fare yet to come.

VILLAGE VOICE, 10/18/94, p. 54, Georgia Brown

Only two years ago lawyer-pundit Raoul Felder recommended Woody Allen "put his career in an envelope and mail it to Roman Polanski." *Time* announced: "Allen's life and eminence seem permanently branded." As we used to say, it just shows to go you. This summer Woody and Soon-Yi strolled Bleecker Street without being stoned. He looked so miserable, even I felt a pang: a 58-year-old having to spend Sunday afternoon parading the Village. I knew he wanted to be on Madison. (Later I wondered if strolling with Soon-Yi wasn't part of his campaign.)

Even so, Allen hasn't missed a beat in his filmmaking schedule, and here he is, not only rehabilitated—with that special NYFF niche for *Bullets Over Broadway*—but absolved by the powers that be. In last year's New Yorker profile, Adam Gopnik blamed for the fall not Allen but a "voyeuristic," "humorless" "culture of cruelty." "The stoical dignity of Bogart on the tarmac or, for that matter, Meursault in the courtroom" is no longer fashionable, Gopnik mourned. We demand that celebs confess and grovel and beg forgiveness. Then we relent.

Oh, yeah? Oh, prescient Mr. Gopnik, look at your Woody on the tarmac now. Or Michael Jackson. Not one grovel. The truth may be that if we want them back, they can do anything. And pretending nothing happened is best.

Early *Bullets* reviews treat the fall as if it never happened. Janet Maslin's rave—which starts out ratifying Woody not only as a great artist but one appreciated in his time—even suggests that bad behavior is justified by artistic results: "One way or another, Mr. Allen has been well served by recent experience." Andrew Sarris sees *Bullets* as Allen's mea (mia?) culpa, "as close as he'll ever get to saying 'I'm sorry.'" Allen has now wrested poetry from "pain and guilt ... regret and remorse."

Guilt, regret, remorse? But Woody insisted he felt none. That was the Bogart on the tarmac part. I guess if they don't display it, we can supply it for them.

I'm not saying Allen deserves living out his days in the doghouse. He isn't alleged to have slit Mia's throat. But it's odd that critics call *Bullets* a cri de coeur and artistic advance when it's very much like what he's done before (set circa 1928, it's in the *Radio Days, Broadway Danny Rose* vein), with the same obsessions (betrayal, irritating women, God, etc.), the same mock ethical dilemmas. It's also not very good. I guess the funnier, darker *Manhattan Murder Mystery* wouldn't have made a good comeback film. I mean, a husband killing his wife so he can run away with a much younger woman? (Here you just have an artist killing someone—OK, she's a woman—standing in the way of his success.)

The high ethical dilemmas of *Bullets*: Is a major artist justified in committing major criminal acts, and is a lesser artist justified in lesser immoral behavior—infidelity, for example? Which is more important, art or a life? As one of the movie's many buffoons, playwright Sheldon Flender (Rob Reiner) frames it: Fleeing a burning building, which should you save, the last extant copy of Shakespeare's plays or a real live person? (The answer is that if there's only one copy, the plays aren't worth saving. Sheldon, of course, is thinking of his building, his own precious manuscripts.)

Besides Sheldon, there are two other artists in *Bullets*: a pretentious, mediocre playwright, David Shayne (John Cusack), and an untutored gunsel called Cheech (Chazz Palminteri, author of *A Bronx Tale*). Cheech is a true, instinctive artist and Palminteri is also about as close as you'll get to a true Bogie type. As the movie's most (only?) sympathetic character, Cheech brings Allen's farce to life just as he brings David's play to life. Unfortunately, this doesn't happen until the movie's half over.

The first half of *Bullets* is a shrill, chattering mess moving between David, his inventive agent (Jack Warden), his mopey live-in girlfriend (Mary-Louise Parker), and several actors in David's play, called (what else?) "Gods of Our Fathers." The lead, Helen Sinclair (Dianne Wiest), is a grande dame who flirts madly with David, charming him with her posings in order to get more lines for herself and, if at all possible, an improved play. Two cheerful troupers more satisfied with their lot are the terminally nervous Eden Brent (Tracey Ullman), who announces that she breast-feeds her Chihuahua ("Just kidding!"), and the seemingly reliable Warner Purcell (Jim Broadbent, unrecognizable from his role as the father in *Life is Sweet*). Warner has a teensy flaw: He's a furtive glutton who bloats alarmingly as rehearsals go along. Finally, there's the squeaky-voiced floozy named Olive (Jennifer Tilly's grating shtick seems modeled on Mia Farrow's much dearer one in *Broadway Danny Rose*).

It's through Olive that bullets come to Broadway. She's been cast in David's play on the orders of its chief backer, her mobster boyfriend, Nick Valenti (Joe Viterelli). Valenti assigns his ace hit man, Cheech, to accompany Olive to rehearsals. Initially, Cheech can hardly bear listening to the play's inane dialogue; he'd rather be rubbing somebody out. Gradually, however, he succumbs to the inexplicable lure of the theater and begins to see ways to improve not merely the lines, but the plot. Helen adores the revisions: "It *reeks* with pubic sexuality!"

The surly, sad-eyed Cheech is so likable who wouldn't be on his side when he takes drastic action? (And after that tedious first half, we're ready to rub out a few of these cockroach actors ourselves.) David, who's merely mundanely cheating on his girlfriend, mounts his moral high horse, mouths some speeches and announces his own reform. He's given the movie's last words in a sappy, unconvincing conversion scene (which Sarris takes as Woody's "Chekhovian epiphany").

But David-the-petty-moralizer is the impostor Woody. Regret and remorse, what are they to the real artist or he to them? Paraphrasing pompous Sheldon Flender, "A great artist's gotta do what a great artist's gotta do." Quoting Flender: "Guilt is a lot of petit bourgeois crap." Meursault couldn't have put it better.

I just have one question. If he's such a great artist, why's he want to win back a public anyway?

Also reviewed in:
CHICAGO TRIBUNE, 10/28/94, Friday/p. C, Michael Wilmington
NATION, 11/14/94, p. 592, Stuart Klawans
NEW REPUBLIC, 10/31/94, p. 38, Stanley Kauffmann
NEW YORK TIMES, 9/30/94, p. C1, Janet Maslin
NEW YORKER, 10/24/94, p. 103, Anthony Lane
VARIETY, 9/12-18/94, p. 40, Todd McCarthy
WASHINGTON POST, 10/28/94, p. F1, Hal Hinson
WASHINGTON POST, 10/28/94, Weekend/p. 44, Desson Howe

CABIN BOY

A Buena Vista Pictures release of a Touchstone Pictures presentation. *Executive Producer:* Steve White and Barry Bernardi. *Producer:* Denise Di Novi and Tim Burton. *Director:* Adam Resnick. *Screenplay:* Adam Resnick. *Story:* Chris Elliott and Adam Resnick. *Director of Photography:* Steve Yaconelli. *Editor:* Jon Poll. *Music:* Steve Bartek. *Music Editor:* Alex Gibson. *Sound:* Edward Tise and (music) Bob Fernandez. *Sound Editor:* C.T. Welch. *Casting:* Rik Pagano, Sharon Bialy, and Debi Manwiller. *Production Designer:* Steven Legler. *Art Director:* Nanci B. Roberts and Daniel A. Lomino. *Set Designer:* Stephen Alesch. *Set Decorator:* Roberta J. Holinko. *Set Dresser:* D.C. "Gustav" Gustafson. *Special Effects:* Robert Knott. *Visual Effects:* Michael Lessa. *Costumes:* Colleen Atwood. *Make-up:* Mindy Hall. *Stunt Coordinator:* Ben Scott. *Running time:* 81 minutes. *MPAA Rating:* PG-13.

CAST: Chris Elliott (Nathanial Mayweather); Ritch Brinkley (Captain Greybar); James Gammon (Paps); Brian-Doyle Murray (Skunk); Brion James (Big Teddy); Melora Walters (Trina); Ann Magnuson (Calli); Russ Tamblyn (Chocki); Ricki Lake (Figurehead); Mike Starr (Mulligan); Andy Richter (Kenny); I.M. Hobson (Headmaster Timmons); Alex Nevil (Thomas); David Sterry (Lance); Bob Elliott (William Mayweather); Edward Flotard (Limo Driver); Jim Cummings (Cupcake); Earl Hofert (Old Salt in Fishing Village).

LOS ANGELES TIMES, 1/7/94, Calendar/p. 6, Chris Willman

From three-minute bits on "Late Night" to half-hours of "Get a Life" to—now—the big screen, Chris Elliott has developed a pretty singular, if slippery, comic persona. He's always inviting you to laugh *with* him and then *at* him, taking down the high and mighty while deserving a good tackle himself, alternately a provider and object of extreme condescension in almost the same beat. This fey, unctuous dolt deserves—and probably could carry—a good deliriously perverse movie farce.

"Cabin Boy" isn't it, not by a nautical mile. It's another cross-demographic picture that seems destined to bypass all demographics. There's a lot of juvenalia already built into Elliott's character, for sure, but his grown-up ironic sense gets dumbed down a little too much in the effort to make the movie a palatable kid-flick. In this climate you might appreciate the pains the film takes to avoid the profane, but Elliott's a master of black comedy, and this film desperately needs a little soot on its soul.

Elliott and writer-director Adam Resnick do at least generate enough good will with the bemusement of their concept to set sail for a while. Their farce is designed as a cross between vintage boy-at-sea adventures like "Captains Courageous" and the stop-motion fantasy of Ray Harryhausen's "Sinbad" and "Jason" pictures.

The "boy" coming of age here is Elliott, as spoiled-rotten Nathanial Mayweather, who sets off from a continental finishing school to rejoin daddy in the States. The ship he mistakenly steps onto isn't the Queen Elizabeth, of course, but rather the Filthy Whore, a fishing vessel full of gruff character actors. At first they're ready to pull a Jonah on this pampered stowaway, but all must band together when they run into adversaries like a fearsome iceberg and an island giant with a pocket protector.

The vividly colorful, set-bound set design (by Stephen Alesch) and art direction (Nanci B. Roberts, Daniel A. Lomino) cleverly establish "Cabin Boy" as parody, for those who care to recognize it. And at least the screenplay doesn't resort to references to other movies for its laughs. The problem is that it doesn't find a lot of laughs in much of anything, referential or otherwise. Resnick's script plays like a first draft rushed into production before most of the gags got penned in, or before anyone decided who they should be targeted at.

Elliott does have some very amusing bits of ridiculousness—literally licking the deck clean, or doing a quadruple-take underwater. Current Conan O'Brien sidekick Andy Richter gets washed overboard before too long, but in the early going enjoys a few amiably imbecilic moments as a doofus involved in Elliott's shipside misfortune.

But it's another "Late Night"-er who steals the movie. David Letterman pops up for a couple of unbilled minutes as a denizen of the dockside village Elliott visits pre-voyage, and he cackles his way through the entire scene, patronizing the befuddled star as hilariously as he used to in the NBC days of yore. This marks the first screen work Disney has gotten out of the talk-show host since making that multimillion-dollar movie deal with him some years back, he so lights up the screen in his brief time he makes you hope they talk him into a Letterman-and-Elliott feature, though breath-holding isn't advised.

NEW YORK POST, 1/7/94, p. 39, Michael Medved

When a performer earns a reputation as a "cult comedian" it usually means he has attracted devoted fans who laugh hysterically at every nervous tic and passing belch, while the rest of the world feels as if it hasn't been let in on the joke.

The bizarre comedy "Cabin Boy" will doubtless provoke the same divided response, thanks to the cult status of its star, Chris Elliott.

In his first starring role in a feature film, Elliott plays the same sort of "overconfident idiot" made famous by his Fox network TV series, "Get a Life," combining arrogance and naivete to a maddening degree.

This time, however, his character is a spoiled rich kid who graduated from an exclusive "finishing school for men" and plans a first-class cruise to Hawaii to meet his billionaire father (played on screen as in the TV series, by Elliott's real-life dad, Bob Elliott, of Bob and Ray fame).

Through a series of mishaps, the younger Elliott fails to board the luxury liner and winds up instead on the good ship "Filthy Whore," a squalid fishing boat with a crew comprised entirely of veteran character actors (James Gammon, Brion James, Brian Doyle-Murray and others) impersonating drunken, sadistic old salts.

As if this weren't bad enough for our prissy hero, he and his shipmates sail through a mysterious stretch of ocean known as "Hell's Bucket," where they encounter a creature who's half man and half shark (played by Russ Tamblyn), a walking iceberg, a blue seductress with six arms and lots of nail polish (Ann Magnuson), and a 50-foot-tall shoe salesman (Mike Starr),

This oddball assemblage has been written and directed by Elliott's long-time partner, Adam Resnick, a fellow alumnus of David Letterman's writing staff who boast that his new movie combines elements of "Captains Courageous" and "The Seven Voyages of Sinbad."

It turns out, however, that his work actually bears a closer resemblance to a more memorable masterpiece: "Pee-wee's Big Adventure."

The similarity is no accident, since Tim ("Batman") Burton, the director of Pee-wee Herman's screen debut, is listed as co-producer of this off-center effort. It's too bad that Burton didn't become more directly involved because "Cabin Boy" desperately needs his intensity, pacing and flair.

Some of the material is funny, but nearly all of it fizzles on screen because first-time director Resnick gives it no shape or punch.

A sad example involves an uncredited surprise appearance by a TV celebrity that might have been hilarious—except for the fact that Resnick keeps the Big Star on screen much longer than necessary and gives him nothing to do other than mug for the camera and chomp his cigar:

There are many other potentially funny scenes in which members of the cast stand around looking uneasy, seeming to wait for the cameras to shut down. A prime casualty of this confusion is the appealing Melora Walters who made such a strong impression as the sexy stripper in "Twenty Bucks," but is wasted here as a round-the-world swimmer and convenient love interest.

The special effects are another problem: They're supposed to recall the marvelous mid-1950s efforts of Ray Harryhausen, but their clumsy campiness hardly makes for an affectionate tribute. These creatures aren't silly enough to be funny, or slick enough to be genuinely impressive.

As one of the veteran sailors comments, "The ship was just hit with purple lightning. That's always a bad sign." This might serve as a summary for the entire project: a leaky vessel destined for a quick trip to Davey Jones' locker.

NEWSDAY, 1/7/94, Part II/p. 67, Terry Kelleher

Before he can receive his sexual education at the hands of the siren with six arms, the overgrown cabin boy in "Cabin Boy" must solve a series of riddles. His answers to her entrance exam are quite stupid and, truth to tell, not too funny, yet she offers him advanced placement.

"Oh, come over here, honey," the siren (Ann Magnuson) says with a shrug. "You've managed to charm me with your moronic innocence."

That cabin boy is Chris Elliott, and if you've caught his television act (on David Letterman's shows or the departed Fox series "Get a Life"), you know he's the kind of performer who eventually wears down your resistance and gets you giggling—provided you're broad-minded enough to use "charm" and "moronic" in the same sentence.

Rather than Elliott's first big-screen starring vehicle, "Cabin Boy" should have been one of those short films he does for Letterman. Did you see the recent one about the hitchhiking poetaster who annoys the hell out of a rough-edged truck driver? This is sort of the seagoing version: Pampered "fancy lad" fresh from a finishing school finds himself toiling on a foul fishing vessel called the Filthy Whore, where he annoys the hell out of the coarse, malodorous crew.

Even at 80 minutes, the quasi-legal minimum for a feature, "Cabin Boy" has trouble staying afloat. Writer-director Adam Resnick, Elliott's creative partner on "Get a Life," gets some nautical mileage out of the basic "Captains Courageous" parody, complemented by overripe color and baldly artificial sets. Although one gag is a treasure—Elliott dancing gawkily to the perennially annoying "Alley Cat Song," while his Filthy confreres amuse themselves by hurling beer cans at his head—too many others dredge up memories of "Yellowbeard" and other such spoofs that went down with all hands. Letterman contributes an enjoyable cameo, but you can see him on CBS and save the seven bucks.

When the film strays far off course to pick up a love interest (Melora Waters) for Elliott, only his most devoted fans won't feel an impulse to head over the side. Not a moment too soon, however, "Cabin Boy" begins to tickle us by indulging a fondness for silly fantasy—an iceberg that walks like a man, a jealous husband 50 feet tall. The effects are funny without being distractingly expensive.

By the time the star water-skis into the sunset on his girlfriend's back, Elliott-inclined viewers will be looking on the bright side. Sure, Andy Richter (Conan O'Brien's sidekick) was in the movie, but at least his character was swept overboard in a raging storm.

Those who were inclined to dismiss the star may end up conceding the possibility that Elliott, like seawater, could be a mind-altering new taste.

VILLAGE VOICE, 1/18/94, p. 54, Devon Jackson

Alas, if only Pasolini were alive, he'd know how to handle this Chris Elliott character. Despite Elliott and director-cowriter Adam Resnick's intentions, this is not *Captains Courageous* meets Monty Python, and it ain't *Sinbad* as deconstructed à la Andy Kaufman either. Drawing its inspiration from the Spencer Tracy classic in which Tracy and his crew turn a sheltered young boy into a man, Elliott comfortably takes on the role of Nathanial Mayweather, a pompous aristocrat and effeminate cad who mistakenly boards the *Filthy Whore* fishing boat. Asea at the mercy of the ship's beery, belching, raspy-voiced fishermen, Elliott, sporting a haughty, helium-squealing British accent and a vapid Jerry Lewis body language, gladly assumes the position: the first morning he wakes up in the arms of the captain; he's forced to swab the deck on all fours with his soapy tongue ("Oddly enough," he says, "it tastes like marzipan") as the salty dogs chuckle behind him; he gives one seaman a good shampooing in a tub; he's rescued by a mermaidish sharkman; and he has to dance for the harassing, entertainment-starved crew. But *Cabin Boy* never goes the whole 10 yards (as Frank Gifford might say) with its wonderfully set up male sex-slave fantasy: a girly-man alone on a boat with four sweaty men. The filmmakers squash the *Blueboy* angle under a forced female love interest (nearly reversing the flick's surprisingly nonhomophobic tone), and then Elliott loses his virginity to a six-armed enchantress (which is what really turns the effete Cabin Boy into just another repressed homosexual Cabin Man).

For a star vehicle, this film sure gives short shrift to its lead (Elliott inexplicably gets only one close-up), and as a spoof (attempts at cheesy pirate sets, obvious soundstage worlds, and the corny emulation of Ray Harryhausen's special effects) the film falls flat. The only amusing bits are Elliott's snide remarks, his loose-limbed dance scene, a cameo by David Letterman, and the wonderful non-sequitur hallucination of a cupcake spitting tobacco at a delirious Elliott (shades of *Life of Brian*). Yo, fellas, next time out, fuck narrative structure! (think Terry Gilliam, David Lynch), and if you ever tackle another male-dominated genre again, trash the chicks altogether and let the hairy apes pop the boy's cherry.

Also reviewed in:
NEW YORK TIMES, 1/7/94, p. C12, Caryn James
VARIETY, 1/10-16/94, p. 58, Brian Lowry
WASHINGTON POST, 1/8/94, p. G1, David Mills

CAFÉ AU LAIT

A New Yorker Films release of a Les Productions Lazennec/SFP Cinema-Nomad Films coproduction with the participation of Canal Plus and the CNC. *Executive Producer:* Christophe Rossignon. *Producer:* Adeline Lecallier and Alain Rocca. *Director:* Mathieu Kassovitz. *Screenplay (French with English subtitles):* Mathieu Kassovitz. *Director of Photography:* Pierre Aim and Georges Diane. *Editor:* Colette Farrugia and Jean-Pierre Segal. *Music:* Marie Daulne and Jean-Louis Daulne. *Sound:* Thomas Gauder. *Sound Editor:* Claude Ronzeau. *Set Designer:* Pierre André Roussotte *Casting:* Florence Dugowson. *Costumes:* Lydie Bonnaire. *Make-up:* Reine Marie Montemont. *Running time:* 94 minutes. *MPAA Rating:* Not Rated.

CAST: Julie Mauduech (Lola); Hubert Kounde (Jamal); Mathieu Kassovitz (Felix); Vincent Cassel (Max, Felix's Brother); Tadek Lokcinski (Felix's Grandfather); Jany Holt (Felix's Grandmother); Rywka Wajsbrot (Felix's Aunt); Eloise Rauth (Sarah, Felix's Sister); Berthe Bagoe (Lola's Grandmother); Marc Berman (Maurice, Felix's Boss); Andrée Damant (Maurice's Mother); Jean-Pierre Cassel (The Gynecologist); Félicité Wouassi (Maternity Nurse); Brigitte Bemol (Julie, Jamal's Girlfriend); Lydia Ewande (Marilyne, Jamal's Maid); Batrice Zeitoun (Lola's Friend at the Gym); Camille Japy (Felix's Friend at the Club); Peter Kassovitz (Professor); Freddy Provost (1st Taxi Driver); Christophe Rossignon (2nd Taxi Driver); Eric Pujol and Pierre Aim (Policemen).

LOS ANGELES TIMES, 8/25/95, Calendar/p. 5, Kevin Thomas

Mathieu Kassovitz's "Café au Lait" is an amusing, up-to-the-minute romantic comedy involving a Woody Allenish young messenger (Kassovitz), his beautiful girlfriend (Julie Mauduech), daughter of a white father and black mother, and her other boyfriend (Hubert Kounde), the rich, athletic son of an ambassador from an African nation. The plot turns upon the the girlfriend announcing her pregnancy—and her inability to say which lover is the father of her unborn child. The way the film resolves itself is fresh and encouraging—and, of course, very French.

NEW YORK POST, 8/19/94, p. 48, Thelma Adams

Is the world ready for a white, Jewish, French Spike Lee?

Ready or not, here comes Mathieu Kassovitz.

The 25-year-old writer-director of "Cafe au Lait" stars as Felix, a hostile, homely bike messenger with tape on his glasses who lives with his family, a raucous band of meddling Yiddishkeit.

An hour into the romantic comedy, Jamal (Hubert Kounde), Felix's rival for the ravishing Lola (Julie Mauduech), yells at the nebbish: "Stop talking like in a movie. You're not Spike Lee."

Maybe not, but Kassovitz pedals furiously through "She's Gotta Have It" territory—Lee's 1986 breakout hit about a free-spirited woman and her three lovers, Spike included.

In "Cafe au Lait," Kassovitz injects a "manic, street-wise energy into a love triangle between the mulatto Lola, the handsome African buppie Jamal, and the downwardly mobile Felix. They're an odd mix; the original title was "Metisse," or blended.

When Lola becomes pregnant. the ante gets upped but the comedy reverts to the obvious conflicts of "My Two Dads."

With her Pepsodent smile and buoyant energy, Lola is warmly played by first-timer Mauduech. She and Jamal are given a chance to be a real couple, and sexual sparks fly even when they spar.

At one point, Jamal pleads his case to Lola, a door chain separating them:"Our grandparents were slaves."

"Your grandparents were diplomats," Lola retorts.

Kassovitz hits the right notes in this repartee digging beneath the surface of racial tensions with comic tools, allowing his characters to speak and reveal themselves.

Lola and Jamal share moments of sexual intimacy that are denied to Felix's character. The romantic element never gets between the light-skinned beauty from Martinique and the pale Parisian nerd.

The unanswered question in this skewed triangle is what does Lola see in Felix.

Perhaps, like Spike Lee, Kassovitz's ego got in the way and he assumed we would see a sexual attraction that just isn't on the screen.

"Cafe au Lait" comes across as reheated.

NEWSDAY, 8/19/94, Part II/p. B7, Jack Mathews

There has reportedly been a tremendous buzz among New York talent agents over Mathieu Kassovitz' "Café au Lait," and it's easy to see why. There is a lot of young talent on display in this energetic French comedy beginning with the direction and writing of the 25-year-old Kassovitz, who, with lesser success, also plays one of three lead roles.

"Café au Lait," which in French can refer to either coffee with milk or a light-skinned black person, tells the deceptively simple story of a cafe au lait West Indian woman (Julie Mauduech) who's in love with two men, one black, one white, and one of whom (only she knows which) is the father of the baby she's carrying.

The men—Felix (Kassovitz), a testy bicycle messenger, and Jamal (Hubert Kounde), a wealthy foreign diplomat's son—meet one day at Lola's apartment door, learn that they have been having an affair with the same woman, and begin an endless ritual of macho posturing, while she tries to decide which, if either, she wants to live with.

As the birth of the mystery baby nears, Felix and Jamal strike a tentative truce, determined to see Lola through to the end, and the three finally set up housekeeping together.

Underpinning the often raucous comedy produced by the tenuous ménage à trois are some deft observations about racial politics in the supposedly open-minded air of Paris life. The three characters stand in for entire cultural and class divisions in the city—Felix is from a family of orthodox, financially stressed Jews, Jamal is a wealthy African Muslim, Lola a Christian—and their prejudices percolate to the surface whenever emotions heat up.

"Café au Lait" is a sharply assured first film, clipping along with the momentum of Felix' bike and the hip-hop music blaring through his Walkman earphones into the soundtrack. And in Mauduech, who has a relaxed confidence to match her wide-screen smile, Kassovitz has discovered a potential star.

The film's greatest problem is Kassovitz' performance as Felix, a character so juvenile and obnoxious, he nearly destroys *Lola's* credibility. Felix deals drugs, starts fights, bullies his kid sister, picks his nose in public, while Jamal is smart, sincere, dignified and devoted. Hey, Lola, why all the indecision?

It is to Kassovitz' credit as a director that we're able to overcome his own character's wretchedness. In fact, as the rough edges are sanded down in the sentimental trimester of the story, Felix becomes almost likable. Talent, indeed.

VILLAGE VOICE, 8/23/94, p. 49, J. Hoberman

In its relentless drive over the top toward oblivion, *Killing Zoe*'s characteristic movement is a slow-motion swan dive leading to a brain-jarring thud. [See Hoberman's review.] For *Café au Lait*, it's the frantic handheld camera maneuvering crowded spaces.

However strenuously deterritorialized, *Café au Lait*—known in France as *Métisse* (slang for racially mixed) is basically a fractious *Jules and Jim.* Lola (Julie Mauduech), the enigmatic, 18-

year-old apex of the ménage à trois, is a West Indian mulatta with a face like a Gauguin model, who has been impregnated by either of two lovers. Jamal (Hubert Koundé), a law student at the Sorbonne, is the wealthy and properly bourgeois son of an African ambassador; Félix is a Jewish bicycle messenger played, in a blatant homage to Mars Blackmon in *She's Gotta Have It*, by Mathieu Kassovitz, the film's appropriately fiery and diminutive, bespectacled auteur.

Although neither man was aware of the other and neither knows who the real father is, both agree to assume prenatal responsibilities. The ensuing highly volatile design for living is powered by a world music sound mix, basically rap-driven but sufficiently global to encompass a little Yiddish song and dance. As *Killing Zoe* riffs on the idea of the left-bank intellectuals, so *Café au Lait* stages a slugfest in Burger Bar.

Café au Lait is nothing if not self-conscious. ("Stop talking like in a movie—you're not Spike Lee," exclaims the exasperated Jamal to Félix at one point.) Kassovitz doesn't supply much of a plot, although *Café au Lait* does generate a fair amount of bogus excitement from the nonissue of whether Lola's baby will be black or white. Despite a key scene, which has the squabbling Félix and Jamal detained and interrogated by the Paris cops, the frequent race-baiting is glib and the various subcultures somewhat synthetic: Chez Félix features an older brother with a Star of David tattoo as well as a clamorous mélange of eccentric grandparents, simultaneously eating and talking, one with a Yiddish accent so heavy he requires French subtitles.

"I hope grandma's got batteries in her pacemaker," kid sister riffs when Félix brings Lola and Jamal home for Shabbat. She needn't fear. *Café au Lait* is enjoyably frantic, but it's not so utterly contempo there's no place in it for a *bubbe*'s wisdom.

Also reviewed in:
NEW REPUBLIC, 9/19 & 26/94, p. 38, Stanley Kauffmann
NEW YORK TIMES, 8/19/94, p. C1, Janet Maslin
NEW YORKER, 9/12/94, p. 96, Anthony Lane
VARIETY, 10/4/93, p. 45, Lisa Nesselson
WASHINGTON POST, 9/30/94, p. F7, Hal Hinson

CALENDAR

A Zeitgeist Films release of an Ego Film Arts and ZDF production. *Producer:* Arsinée Khanjian. *Director:* Atom Egoyan. *Screenplay:* Atom Egoyan. *Director of Photography:* Norayr Kasper. *Editor:* Atom Egoyan. *Sound:* Steven Munro. *Running time:* 75 minutes. *MPAA Rating:* Not Rated.

CAST: Arsinée Khanjian (Translator); Ashot Adamian (Driver); Atom Egoyan (Photographer).

CHRISTIAN SCIENCE MONITOR, 3/1/94, p. 14, David Sterritt

"Calendar," the new movie by Canadian director Atom Egoyan, is an offbeat film with an unusual history.

A filmmaker of great talent and spirit, Egoyan earned respect in the cinema community with such early works as "Speaking Parts" and "Family Viewing," which signal their interest in reflexivity— filmmaking that reflects on its own procedures and preoccupations—right from their titles.

His career received an important boost when "The Adjuster," a surrealistic fable about an insurance agent who gets involved in the lives of his clients, drew enthusiastic applause at the Cannes and New York film festivals.

That picture also thrilled judges at the Moscow Film Festival, where it won a major prize carrying a cash award—and a good deal of confusion, as Egoyan explained during a New York visit a few months ago.

The money was awarded to help finance his next movie, on the condition that it be shot within the Soviet Union's borders. Egoyan was happy to comply with this stipulation, since he was eager to make a film in Armenia, the land of his ancestors. No sooner did he begin planning his Armenian project, however, than the Soviet Union fell apart and Armenia became an independent nation.

This brought obvious complications to the geographical aspect of Egoyan's prize, and indeed, it threw a substantial shadow over the likelihood that he'd receive his million-ruble check in the first place—awarded to him, after all, by a government that no longer existed.

While a less adventurous artist might have written off the situation as a lost cause at this point, Egoyan was determined to proceed with his movie. He switched from a 35mm production setup—standard for feature films, but expensive—to a cheaper and more flexible 16mm operation. He also decided to limit his story to three major characters, and to play one of them himself, even though his cinematic skills lie in writing and directing rather than acting.

Forging ahead on this low-budget basis, he completed "Calendar" despite the odds, making up in talent and tenacity what he lacked in money and resources. On top of this, he has now succeeded in finding a commercial release for what might have seemed a specialized art movie destined for festivals and museums rather than conventional theaters. He and his distributor, Zeitgeist Films, deserve congratulations for their faith in this small-scale but captivating movie, which merits as wide an audience as any of the Hollywood pictures on the current scene.

The story of "Calendar" centers on a young Canadian photographer, played by Egoyan, who's visiting Armenia to take pictures of historic church buildings for a calendar manufacturer. Accompanying him is his wife, who documents the trip with a video camera, and a local guide who seems as interested in his employer's spouse as in the interminable series of churches on their itinerary.

The movie alternates footage of their journey, seen through photos and videotapes made along the way, with later scenes in which the photographer tries to understand what's gone wrong with his marriage, his project, and a whole portion of his life.

"Calendar" is as quirky as Egoyan's earlier films, joining a basically conventional story (a love triangle, pure and simple) with a deliberately unconventional structure and an ironic atmosphere. The combination fails to work at times, especially in a subplot involving the photographer's relationships with women after his Armenian excursion has ended.

Still, most of "Calendar" is engaging and ingratiating, telling a poignantly amusing tale through images of unusual clarity, economy, and loveliness. A million rubles couldn't have made it more lively or entertaining.

LOS ANGELES TIMES, 3/9/95, Calendar/p. 4, Kevin Thomas

Canadian filmmaker Atom Egoyan's "Calendar," a study of nationality, the filmmaking process and a troubled romance, is so personal as to be elusive, although it clearly involves Egoyan's usual concern with dealing with emotions while, as a filmmaker, being removed from them directly. Segments of him, off-camera, filming his lover, Arsinée Khanjian, translating into English the remarks of guide Ashot Adamian on a magnificent 13th-Century church in Armenia are intercut with the filmmaker entertaining in his apartment a series of beautiful women who all ask to use his phone to speak passionately in a foreign language , presumably to another man. Egoyan has explained what all this means, but that's no help to the moviegoer with no access to his film's press kit.

NEW YORK POST, 3/11/94, p. 42, Thelma Adams

"Calendar" is a movie one respects more than one loves.

Director Atom Egoyan, an international film festival fave for such off-beat films as "Family Viewing" and "Speaking Parts," casts himself as an uptight photographer.

Like Egoyan, the photographer is of Armenian descent and raised in Canada. An abrasive, self-involved wienie, he gets an assignment to photograph Armenian churches for a calendar. His

Armenian-speaking wife (Arsinee Khanjian) accompanies him; a local man (Ashot Adamian) drives.

Told in flashback month-by-month as the pages of the now finished calendar turn the film raised in Canada charts the shifting allegiance of the wife from the photographer to the driver.

The trio are a study in contrasts; the virile Armenian driver is as rooted in his culture as the churches themselves; the wife, raised in Beirut's Armenian community, retains strong ties to the language and tradition; and the assimilated photographer is cut off from the historic and spiritual value of the churches he shoots.

Not only is he separated from his roots; the photographer uses his camera as a barrier from the world around him. Egoyan who also wrote and edited "Calendar," uses a variety of visual techniques, wedding film, video and still photography, to underscore this distancing.

As the photographer frames the churches—and chases his wife and the driver out of the picture and into each other's arms—the director manipulates the story from behind his lens. This self-conscious strategy is nothing new, but Egoyan treats it with freshness, passion and wry wit.

The movie's juiciest element is not the visual tricks, but the charismatic performance of the cork-screw-curled Khanjian. In one raw video, she is shown chasing sheep, ungainly and charming, pale and zaftig.

The wife's love for her husband, trapped behind the video camera, flows from her dark eyes. "Hold me," she says, facing him and folding her arms and hugging herself. His hands stay on the camera.

For all Egoyan's careful framing, his ability to take a picture post-card snapshot, his weaving of different visual elements, the non-linear structure of the movie is as static and predictable as that of a calendar.

The incidents the director dramatizes aren't as ripe as the ideas behind them or as astonishing as the turreted, crumbling Armenian churches in the background. Other than the engaging Khanjian, the characters are never made flesh, the conflicts are set up but rarely pay off.

The challenge in a movie about boredom is to remain interesting. The challenge in "Calendar," a movie about separation, is to keep viewers engaged with the characters. The photographer might be alienated, but the audience must be moved by his experience.

Egoyan's passion for his subject does not translate into a passionate movie, but "Calendar" remains an interesting exercise by a fluent young filmmaker.

NEWSDAY, 3/11/94, Part II/p. 85, John Anderson

"Art Eats Man" might have been the title of Canadian filmmaker Atom Egoyan's intriguing fifth feature, "Calendar," in which memory is a movie, and love can't be articulated.

The plot, as it were, doesn't unfold chronologically. But, essentially, a Canadian photographer (Egoyan) has traveled to Armenia to shoot a series of venerable churches for an art calendar. During the trip, he's lost his translator/wife (Arsinee Khanjian) to their Armenian guide (Ashot Adamian).

It's not the romantic crisis as much as the way words have become anachronisms that concerns Egoyan ("The Adjuster," "Speaking Parts"). In the photographer's flashbacks, in his wife's unanswered messages on his phone machine, in the letters he tries to write her, we see that language is beyond his grasp. When we watch the wife on the film that runs through his mind's eye, the pictures are full of love. His mouth, however, is full of mush.

Egoyan wants to deconstruct language there are no subtitles, though much of the dialogue is in Armenian—and what it means: English-speakers may not understand the Armenian spoken by the guide, but there's obvious passion, which is what wins the wife over. When the photographer and his wife speak, we know the words, but there's nothing said.

There are several initially confusing sequences that recur, and then coalesce: A series of dinners at the photographer's home, for instance, each attended by a different woman, who after the wine is poured gets up to make a phone call in Armenian. This seems silly at first, until we realize that these are escorts hired to re-enact an event—presumably a call from the wife to the guide—which the photographer hopes will free his tongue, his pen and his petrified heart.

"Don't you feel the need to come closer, to touch, to feel?" the guide asks the photographer, via the translator/wife, about the churches they visit. The answer, of course, is yes I can't.

SIGHT AND SOUND, 2/94, p. 49, Farrah Anwar

A Canadian photographer of Armenian ancestry is visiting Armenia to take 12 photographs for a calendar. He takes along his wife to interpret, and hires a native guide to drive them around. By the end of the assignment, the photographer has twelve Armenian church photographs but has lost his wife to the driver.

Canada. Now alone at home, the photographer has the calendar on his wall, recording the places he and his wife visited. He has a series of monthly dinner dates at home with foreign women. While each of them gets up from the table to make an erotically-charged phone call to someone else, each in a different language, he writes to his wife and recalls the events in Armenia, seen in both film and video form. By May, his wife is leaving phone messages to him, and he sits masturbating to a video tape of her. In August, he writes to his adopted Armenian daughter, and asks if his wife has visited her and whether she was accompanied by another man. When his November date begins to talk erotically down the phone, the photographer stops her. She returns to the dinner table and they discuss her Armenian background. In December, a barely discernable phone message from his wife informs the photographer that when the car was driving through a herd of sheep, she and the driver had held hands; she wonders whether, while gripping his camera, the photographer had suspected anything.

"In conceiving *Calendar*," Atom Egoyan says in his Director's Statement, "I wanted to find a story that would deal with three levels of Armenian consciousness: Nationalist, Diasporan, and Assimilationist. Thus the guide, like Ashot Adamian [who plays him], is an Armenian who was born and raised in Armenia. The translator, like Arsinée Khanjian, is an Armenian raised in a large Armenian community outside of Armenia. And the photographer, like Atom Egoyan, is an Armenian completely assimilated into another culture."

Remarkably, for his sixth (and perhaps best) feature, Atom Egoyan has managed to extend his obsessions with the technology of imagery and communication well beyond artistic expectations. In *Calendar*, shot on 16mm and video, Egoyan has manoeuvred what to date have often proved to be distancing, and arguably de-humanising devices—the photograph (*The Adjuster*), video tape (*Family Viewing, Speaking Parts, The Adjuster*), and in *Calendar*, the telephone answering machine—to emphasise a very personalised sense of loss and social isolation.

Despite his above declaration, the predominant defining process in *Calendar* is neither the act of photographing national monuments (always visually resplendent in the background) nor the pithy, nationalist observations of the driver/guide/lover ("I think if you had children you would bring them to grow up here"), but the shift of emotional allegiances which takes place between the photographer and his wife. Egoyan has often been accused of being preoccupied with the aesthetic at the expense of his characters. In *Calendar* there seems to be a deliberate ploy to undermine the photographer's (and by proxy, the director's) need to remain in control. So while he chastises his wife for wasting batteries, or feels unable to participate in any Armenian social intercourse in case he misses the right shade of lighting or contrast, Egoyan's character is constantly drawn into watching and recording seemingly trivial details (the flock of sheep, the wife's careless laughter with the driver or her massaging of her tired limbs), which are clearly intruding into his consciousness but which he finds unable to process. His senses are only engaged via the camera or camcorder, without a concomitant cerebral response.

This sense of perceptual disturbance is heightened by *Calendar*'s refusal to follow the surface formality of the film's time structure. Although punctuated by the arrival (or departure) of each calendar month, the temporal relationships between people and events are constantly being distorted and replayed. Episodes are evoked by memory, sometimes spontaneously, at other times deliberately (the ritualistic dating); tapes are played back at normal and fast-forward speeds; and phone messages, whether banal (the escort bureau) or intensely emotive (the wife's messages from Armenia), are held in limbo until acknowledged by the absent photographer.

Behind the cameras, the photographer remains an ethereal presence, unseen and untouched, whereas in front of the churches, the driver is a physically strong, charismatic spirit, equally at home with a serenading guitar or an anecdote about architectural origins. Only the diasporan wife is able to engage and empathise with this sense of freedom, and all the photographer can do, as he points out, is to passively "watch whilst the two of you leave me and disappear into a landscape I'm about to photograph."

However, to share this nationalist freedom, a return to home terrain is not enough. There are several indications in the film that the photographer is absent in spirit in Canada as well. Phone messages constantly apologise for the fact that he's confined to his dark room "all day". And it takes more than just the departure of his wife to jolt him back to light. For months he remains on pause, unable to respond to his wife's letters and messages. Denial gives way to sadness and finally rationalisation, via Egoyan's well-worn metaphor for alienation—solitary masturbation in front of the video screen. But in *Calendar*, the ejaculate isn't semen but sentiment. Literally so, because the photographer breaks off a wank to start writing ("Yes, I received all your messages and your calls, and now feel ready to write back").

Intriguingly, as the artist lets down his emotional guard (that is, becomes less concerned with the aesthetic), the assimilationist's self-awareness becomes more obvious. The dirty foreign phone call becomes an incidental prop to the carefully constructed scenarios, dismissed as a delaying irritant by November. And significantly the photographs begin to blend and blur as their sequential progression with calendar months begins to falter. The photographer has been freed from his assimilation assignment, but at what cost? Given the self-referential and revisionist subtext of the film, this open-ended question evokes a sense of genuine anticipatory excitement for Egoyan's next venture.

VILLAGE VOICE, 3/15/94, p. 48, Georgia Brown

Besides the early (the good) De Palma, it's hard to think of a contemporary director so focused on voyeurism—the obsession, its mechanisms and technology—as Atom Egoyan. But if De Palma's peeper is stimulated into some gory primal acts, Egoyan's cool spectator is capable of thoroughly sublimating feeling in sight games. Neither, of course, sees women.

Usually I have trouble with Egoyan. While I admire the films' ingenuity and intricate strategies, their coldness and morbidity put me off. But *Calendar* is different. A haunting portrait of the artist, the film shines a light on the coldness. The artist, in this case, is the comic butt of the story.

A prissy photographer (played by Egoyan) goes to Armenia on assignment: He's shooting ancient churches for a calendar. His lively Armenian-born wife (played by Egoyan's wife of Armenian descent, actress Arsinée Khanjian) comes along as translator. He's hired a local guide (Ashot Adamian)—a gaunt, rather dour intellectual—to take them around. The wife and the guide get along, talk raptly, until, at the end of the shoot, she announces she's staying behind to discover her roots, perhaps with the guide's help.

The film's present tense takes place after the above events, with the photographer back in his tidy Canadian apartment, searching through videotapes of the journey—his 12 stages of loss—as if he could determine what went awry. (It's perfectly obvious to the viewer what's wrong.) As a further stimulus to memory, he hires a succession of foreign-born women—stand-ins for his wife—to perform a bizarre ritual. They come to his place for a sparse meal, a glass of Mouton Cadet, and then ask to use the phone. Standing next to his calendar, they pretend to talk to a lover in a foreign language. (One tribute to Egoyan is how he convinces you to accept some truly absurd situations.) Meanwhile, his wife, on a static-y transatlantic line, leaves concerned messages on his answering machine.

So, as the technology of memory proliferates—cinema, stills, video, sound recording—memory itself grows more elusive. Of course Egoyan makes use of as many technologies as possible, constructing his portrait of the artist as a frozen eye. "What I really feel like doing," he says to his wife, who asks him to walk with her in a golden field, "is standing here and watching while the two of you leave me and disappear into a landscape that I'm about to photograph."

Although *Calendar* seems complex—with its alternating media, overlapping sound, and the unfolding exotic/mundane mystery of the hired girls—it isn't, especially compared to Egoyan films like *Speaking Parts* or *Family Viewing*. What it contains, however, that these other films lack, are intimations of life outside all those hermetic systems—including the calendar itself—in which Egoyan's characters are always trapped. Here, the glorious 16mm images have a power of their own: The churches nestled into or astride their sites, the dun-colored ruins, the majestic foreign landscape all function as signs of potential clarity. Next to this, the color-bleached video—often fast-forwarded—is a sort of obsessive meditation. It stars his open, frank, and very appealing wife and her lurking potential lover. The home video is about subjective viewing: the photographer's closed mind, the origins of jealousy, his demise.

The guide reproves him for not coming closer to "touch and feel" the stone. To understand the buildings, he says, one must understand the builders' impulse—grasp the magic of the particular site. Both subject and context obviously are lost on the photographer. When his wife approaches the camcorder, her arms out, mouthing "Hold me," he doesn't: Her arms close around herself. Flash forward to the present and he's sitting naked on the couch, masturbating to her image. Egoyan doesn't deviate from his light, ironic tone: His artist is a stone; he can't even feel the ache.

Also reviewed in:
CHICAGO TRIBUNE, 8/19/94, Friday/p. M, Michael Wilmington
NATION, 3/21/94, p. 391, Stuart Klawans
NEW YORK TIMES, 3/11/94, p. C14, Stephen Holden
VARIETY, 3/1/93, p. 58, Derek Elley
WASHINGTON POST, 5/27/94, p. D7, Rita Kempley

CAMILLA

A Miramax Films release of a Shaftesbury Films/Skreba Creon production with the participation of Telefilm Canada, Ontario Film Development Corporation Foundation Fund to Underwrite New Drama for Pay Television, British Screen. *Executive Producer:* Jonathan Barker. *Producer:* Christina Jennings and Simon Relph. *Director:* Deepa Mehta. *Screenplay:* Paul Quarrington. *Based on an original story by:* Ali Jennings. *Director of Photography:* Guy Dufaux. *Editor:* Barry Farrell. *Music:* Daniel Lanois and John Altman. *Music Editor:* Bruce Fowler. *Sound:* Glen Gauthier. *Sound Editor:* Bruce Nyznik. *Casting:* Deirdre Bowen *Production Designer:* Sandra Kybartas. *Art Director:* Armando Sgrignuoli. *Set Decorator:* Carol Lavoie. *Set Dresser:* Dan Wladyka. *Special Effects:* David Lemmen. *Costumes:* Milena Canonero and Elisabetta Beraldo. *Make-up:* Patricia Green and Lizbeth Williamson. *Running time:* 90 minutes. *MPAA Rating:* PG-13.

CAST: Jessica Tandy (Camilla Cara); Bridget Fonda (Freda Lopez); Elias Koteas (Vincent Lopez); Maury Chaykin (Harold Cara); Graham Greene (Hunt Weller); Hume Cronyn (Ewald); Ranjit Chowdhry (Kapur); George Harris (Jerry); Sandi Ross (Border Guard); Gerry Quigley (Border Official); Atom Egoyan (Director); Devyani Saltzman and Camille Spence (Girls); Martha Cronyn (Coat Check Woman); Sheilanne Lindsay (Lauron Tinscheff); Don McKellar (Security Guard).

LOS ANGELES TIMES, 12/16/94, Calendar/p. 10, Kevin Thomas

"Camilla" affords the late Jessica Tandy with a delightful final starring role and also a final teaming with her husband, Hume Cronyn. Although the film has considerable charm, the Cronyns and Tandy's co-star Bridget Fonda are much better than it is.

Beautiful and elegant in the title role, Tandy and Fonda's Freda meet while the younger woman and her husband Vince (Elias Koteas), who live in Toronto, are vacationing on Peabo Island along Georgia's coast. Camilla, a former Toronto resident, is a violinist given to harmless exaggerations about professional triumphs and romantic conquests while Freda is a struggling composer whose husband dismisses her efforts as merely a hobby. A woman of spirit and imagination, Camilla is exactly the kind of person Freda needs to encourage her; Camilla in turn warms to Freda's friendship.

So far so good, especially since Vince, a commercial artist, quickly lands an advertising/promotion assignment with Camilla's son Harold (Maury Chaykin), an Atlanta-based soft-porn film producer. Meanwhile, the women are beginning to think how much fun it would be to take off for Toronto, where, according to Camilla, she experienced her greatest triumph at the landmark Elgin/Winter Garden Theaters.

Writer Paul Quarrington unfortunately makes a major mistake at this point. Instead of simply informing Vince and Harold of their plans, the women just take off. This not only has the effect of making them seem callous and irresponsible but also means that every time Tandy and Fonda are working up a lively scene, director Deepa Mehta has to cut away to show Vince and Harold becoming increasingly and understandably distraught over the women's disappearances.

Structurally, "Camilla" is a mess, but Tandy and Fonda are wonderful together as a fast friendship between Camilla and Freda develops. The reunion between Camilla and the Niagara Falls violin maker (Cronyn) who was her true love is inevitably poignant.

The chance to experience America's greatest acting team since the Lunts for one final time, plus the appealing Fonda, does in fact tempt you to forgive "Camilla" its various shortcomings.

NEW YORK POST, 12/16/94, p. 65, Thelma Adams

This will be remembered as the year Katharine Hepburn said the "F" word in "Love Affair" and the late Jessica Tandy skinny-dipped in "Camilla."

Canadian director Deepa Mehta's character-driven road movie features Tandy in the title role as a capricious former concert violinist who bonds with Bridget Fonda's aspiring musician, Freda.

On the lam from the loutish men in their lives—Camilla's overbearing son Harold (Maury Chaykin) and Freda's insensitive spouse Vince (Elias Koteas)—the two women leave Camilla's Georgia coast home bound for Toronto's Winter Garden Theater, the site of the violinist's past glory.

Released by some optimistic (or cynical) soul on a one-week run for Academy Award consideration in yet another year of slack competition in the Best Actress category, "Camilla" showcases Tandy in one of those chewing-the-kudzu roles where, in the grand manner, she offers up nostalgic monologues that begin with such dreck as "I remember barbecues ... " Hampered by Paul Quarrington's terminally whimsical script, Fonda doesn't fare any better despite hoisting her trademark tentative-yet-winning smile. As the part is written, she is supposed to be a talented but insecure composer. But Fonda is an honest actress more than an imaginative one and she can't sing or strum to save her life.

Hubby Vince is supposed to come across as a pig when he suggests that music is just Freda's hobby but, given her talent, he seems credible. It's Freda who seems ridiculous when she tells Vince, "You used to paint me playing the guitar naked singing a song about you painting me ... remember?" Ouch!

(I'm often asked if I look away from the screen during ultra-violent scenes; in fact, I watched certain scenes in "Camilla" through my fingers, overwhelmed by feelings of embarrassment for these two talented actresses).

(In a moment of nervous release, I whispered to the man sitting next to me in the theater, "Now I know why Tandy died." Without missing a beat, he replied "Shame.")

During the final 15 minutes, as the epiphanies begin to appear like attacks of the Hong Kong flu, Tandy's real-life husband, Hume Cronyn, arrives. In their seventh and final film together, Cronyn plays Camilla's elfin long-lost lover, Ewald. The couple's few scenes together have a spark and connection made all the more poignant by Tandy's recent death.

Fortunately, Tandy's last movie is one of the best of 1994 but it's not "Camilla." She'll be remembered for her role opposite Paul Newman in Robert Benton's sleeper, "Nobody's Fool," which opens Christmas Day.

NEWSDAY, 12/16/94, Part II/p. B7, John Anderson

The late Jessica Tandy used age the way she used almost all her personal qualities—as an acting tool. And while she had many tools, she didn't have a bulldozer, which is what she would have needed to get the leaden mass "Camilla" off her neck.

In what is presumably her last screen appearance (you never know about these things), Tandy is impish, wise, classy and charming as Camilla Cara, reclusive resident of the Georgia coast and a former virtuoso who was courted by the greats (or so she says) made a brilliant debut playing the Brahms Violin Concerto in Toronto (or so she says), and whose talent knew no bounds (you get the picture) She has a hostile relationship with her unsavory son Harold (Maury Chaykin), who rents their adjoining bungalow to vacationing Canadians Vince and Freda Lopez (Elias Koteas and Bridget Fonda). She's a guitarist, he's a frustrated artist, their relationship is rocky, and when Freda and Camilla become confidantes it sets the stage for a mutual escape.

Camilla finds in Freda a sympathetic soul, although Freda's career is stillborn. She has done most of her playing in the attic of her Toronto home, making great plans that will never be realized. Her future is as amorphous as Camilla's past; they hit it off immediately. And their instant camaraderie is distinctly unbelievable.

When Harold offers Vince a job, and he wants to head back to Toronto, Freda lets him go. He's thwarting her dream, she says. At this point we ask: Is director Deepa Mehta's point the self-delusion of the failed artist? No, it's not that deep. We're to accept that Freda's gifted, on faith—Mehta isn't interested in making fingers correspond to notes any more than she's interested in making notes add up to wonderful music. Camilla is an easier sell—even if Tandy can't hold a violin, the music we hear is as believable as Tandy's acting. Fonda, on the other hand, is suffering from a double handicap.

The film becomes a road/buddy picture when Freda and Camilla head off for Toronto, to hear a performance of the Brahms that Camilla played so long ago. Along the way there are episodes and antics that are meant to establish tone and character—an amusing one features Graham Greene as an audacious con man—but which serve only to delay the inevitable: Camilla's reunion in Toronto with her violin maker and almost-lover, Ewald (Hume Cronyn), and her realization of at least one thwarted dream.

There are lovely moments between Tandy and Cronyn, moments the couple apparently requested be included in the film when Tandy knew she was dying. They're sweet, but can't salvage the rest of this lifeless romp, which features what we presume to be the one and only Jessica Tandy nude scene (filmed from behind). This may not be how most of us want to remember this dignified actress.

SIGHT AND SOUND, 3/95, p. 35, Ben Thompson

Freda and Vince Lopez are a handsome Canadian couple, not all that happily married. He was once an artist, but gave up painting for the easier financial rewards of advertising; she has remained true to her ideals of becoming a musician and a songwriter, but lacks the self-confidence to realise these ambitions. They head down to the coast of the Deep South for a holiday. Once there, relations between Harold, the hard-headed producer of pornographic films who owns their holiday cottage, and his sprightly ex-concert violinist mother Camilla, who believes he owes her money, turn out to be similarly fraught, and the destinies of the two households become entangled. Harold offers Vince a job—which he jumps at—promoting soft porn films. Camilla's tales of artistic derring-do entrance Freda, whose attempts to win over local bar audiences are unsuccessful. She refuses to go back with Vince and Harold and, finding out that the Winter Gardens theatre in Toronto was the scene of one of Camilla's greatest triumphs, she persuades the older woman to come north to hear a favourite Brahms concerto.

They set off without telling the men where they're headed. While crossing a Georgia river, Freda's car rolls off the ferry. While Harold and Vince are struggling to track them down, the two women stop over in a deserted hotel on an idyllic holiday island. They play music together to an admiring audience of hotel staff and then hitch a ride with Hunt Weller. He claims to be a famous record producer but turns out to be a conman, and robs them. Camilla leaves a message with Harold pretending they have been kidnapped, ordering him to comply with certain instructions. On the way there, Camilla forces Freda to divert to Niagara Falls, where she is reunited with Ewald, the violin maker who was her long lost love. Despite knowing that Camilla's past was not as glorious as she had maintained, Freda is inspired by her example to make a success of her marriage and her career.

"Miss Fonda's guitar coach"—if ever there was a credit to strike a chill into film going hearts, it is that one. How many more sensitive and gifted individuals whose talents a cruel cold world refuses to recognise will Fonda have to play before we out there in the cold, cruel world get the message? Think of a number and treble it.

On the other hand, the considerable presence of Elias Koteas in the male lead (and fellow Atom Egoyan regular Maury Chaykin as Harry, and indeed Egoyan himself, fleetingly typecast as a director of salacious movies) leads one to expect this film to be more complex and sophisticated than it is, but then Koteas' presence raised the same hope for *Teenage Mutant Ninja Turtles*. In the end, the very simplicity of this almost disconcertingly straightforward work turns out to be its strength.

The sure knowledge that Fonda's terminally drippy singer-songwriter is going to be taught a valuable lesson in life by Jessica Tandy's game old violinist, and that Fonda's husband is going to learn a new respect for her as an artist and a woman, does not detract from the pleasure of the story's unfolding. In its early stages, this screenplay is so absurdly biased against its male characters and in favour of Freda's dewy-eyed fantasies of creativity ("Remember how you used to paint me naked, playing the guitar, writing a song about you painting me?") that much fun is to be had from siding with the former. Go on Elias, take the silver coins from Harold the sleazy pornographer, that's the way for you to really find yourself.

It is much to the film-makers' credit that audience sympathies are a great deal better balanced by the close. True, shifty Vince solidifies into a pillar of strength, and cheap sweaty Harold acquires unexpected emotional depths, but Freda and Camilla's relationship becomes less rather than more nauseating the longer it progresses. Tandy's performance is as bright-eyed and bushy tailed as could be wished. She starts out with the feistiness dial turned up well beyond eleven, but employs great subtlety in developing a sense of her character's vulnerability.

This lightness of touch is complemented by some sensitive direction from Deepa Mehta, who manages to convey a real sense of momentum without lapsing into road movie shorthand. The scene where a roomful of smiling black Southerners marvel at Camilla's and Freda's instinctive command of the boogie though is still a bit much.

Also reviewed in:
CHICAGO TRIBUNE, 3/24/95, Part I/p. 30, Michael Wilmington
NEW REPUBLIC, 1/23/95, p. 31, Stanley Kauffmann
NEW YORK TIMES, 12/16/94, p. C16, Janet Maslin
VARIETY, 11/28-12/4/94, p. 94, Brendan Kelly
WASHINGTON POST, 3/25/95, p. D6, Rita Kempley

CAMP NOWHERE

A Hollywood Pictures release. *Executive Producer:* Andrew Kurtzman and Eliot Wald. *Producer:* Michael Peyser. *Director:* Jonathan Prince. *Screenplay:* Andrew Kurtzman and Eliot Wald. *Director of Photography:* Sandi Sissel. *Editor:* Jon Poll. *Music:* David Lawrence. *Music Editor:* Charles Martin Inouye. *Sound:* David Kelson and (music) Rick Riccio. *Sound Editor:* Robert L. Sephton. *Casting:* Amy Lippens. *Production Designer:* Rusty Smith. *Art Director:* Keith Neely. *Set Designer:* Christopher S. Nushawg. *Set Decorator:* James I. Samson. *Set Dresser:* Stacy Doran. *Special Effects:* Frank Ceglia. *Costumes:* Sherry Thomnpsonn. *Make-up:* Kenny Meyers and Geri B. Oppenheim. *Stunt Coordinator:* Bobby M. Porter. *Running time:* 96 minutes. *MPAA Rating:* PG.

CAST: John Putch (Neil Garbus); Peter Scolari (Donald Himmel); Romy Walthall (Nancy Himmel); Jonathan Jackson (Morris "Mud" Himmel); Joshua G. Mayweather (Walter Welton); Andrew Keegan (Zack Dell); Devin Oatway (Tim); Kellen McLaughlin (J.D.); Brian Wagner (Lenny); Marne Patterson (Trish Prescott); Melody Kay (Gaby Nowicki); Christopher Lloyd (Dennis Van Welker); M. Emmet Walsh (T.R. Polk); Ray Baker (Norris Prescott); Kate Mulgrew (Rachel Prescott); Maryedith Burrell (Gwen Nowicki); Peter Onorati (Karl Dell); Burgess Meredith (Feln); Hillary Tuck (Betty Stoller); Paigé Andreé (Jill); Leah Theresa Hanner (Debbie); Mooky Arizona (Arnold); Kazz Wingate IV (Pete); Nathan Cavaleri (Steve); Heather DeLoach (Eileen); Nicolas Friedman (Ricky); Alyssa Poblador (Nicole); Allison Mack (Heather); Jessica Marie Alba (Gail); Tiffany Mataras (Ashley); Krystle Mataras (Amber); Ian Christopher Scott (Warren); Joe Scott (Delivery Guy); Tom Wilson (Lt. Eliot Hendricks); Wendy Makkena (Dr. Celeste Dunbar); Patrick LaBrecque

(Grocery Checker); Kevin Scannell (Manager, Country Store); Michael Zorek (Chez Cheez Guy); Kyra Stempel (Chez Cheez Clerk); Jonathan Prince (Mr. Burkey); Ron Fassler (Drama Dad); Bobette Buster (Drama Mom); Donzaleigh Avis Abernathy (Walter's Mom); William John Murphy (Trooper).

LOS ANGELES TIMES, 8/26/94, Calendar/p. 18, Kevin Thomas

The ingenious and amusing "Camp Nowhere" fulfills every summer camp veteran's dream of escaping all those killjoy rules, while spotlighting the antic talents of Christopher Lloyd.

Lloyd, the eccentric Doc of the "Back to the Future" trilogy and Uncle Fester in "The Addams Family" movies, plays anarchic Dennis Van Welker, an exuberant former junior high drama teacher relieved of his duties after he thought it would be a good idea to attempt a musical version of "Silence of the Lambs."

He's living in a ramshackle trailer when he's recruited by Morris "Mud" Himmel (Jonathan Jackson), a bright adolescent who's come up with a grand scheme to set up an alternative summer camp so that he and his classmates can escape those dreaded places their parents have in mind.

The idea is that Van Welker will impersonate a computer nerd camp director to impress Mud's rigid father (Peter Scolari), who wants to send his son off to Camp Microchippewa. He will then impersonate directors of military, diet and theater summer camps so that Mud's closest friends—and virtually all his classmates—will likewise be free of such regulated summers.

Van Welker does so well that Mud is able to collect sufficient parental funds to rent the run-down Camp Nowhere, where he and his pals will be able to enjoy a summer of fun without adult regulations.

The kids soon discover that there aren't any good times without responsibility—somebody has to be a leader, everybody has to pitch in for KP duties.

This provides the background for Lloyd to carry on gleefully as Van Welker, whom writers/executive producers Andrew Kurtzman and Eliot Wald deftly bring back into the action after the youngsters have had a chance to experience the exhilaration of total freedom.

Although Van Welker is always an eager participant in the kids' evasions from all representatives of authority, he's not as irresponsible as he seems, keeping an eye on the campers while stimulating their imaginations. Under feature debuting director Jonathan Prince, the film proceeds jauntily to its inspired climax, involving a complicated series of Parents' Day hoaxes.

A painstaking, well-crafted effort, "Camp Nowhere" showcases Lloyd's winning, offbeat presence to maximum advantage while providing an opportunity for a raft of young people to shine.

No less impressive than the highly focused Jackson are Andrew Keegan, as a rebel more sensitive and intelligent than he likes to acknowledge, Marne Patterson, as a pretty, ultra-popular girl whose mother (Kate Mulgrew) is pushing her hard into an acting career; and Melody Kay, whose perfectly normal amount of baby fat sets her mother (Maryedith Burrell) into diet frenzy.

Other adult roles are capably played by, among others, Wendy Makkena as an attractive and delightful physician who attracts Lloyd, M. Emmet Walsh as a comically intrepid repo man and Burgess Meredith as the laid-back owner of Camp Nowhere.

NEW YORK POST, 8/26/94, p. 45, Thelma Adams

For every "Lion King," Disney produces half a dozen forgettable live-action features—including "Camp Nowhere."

In this formulaic comedy, a gaggle of suburban teens too short for the "Beverly Hills 90210" cast create their own summer camp with the help of wayward drama teacher Dennis Van Welker (Christopher Lloyd).

The teens' mild rebellion against parents who insist on structuring their kids' summer to maximize their potential—Camp Slenderella, Camp Micro Chippewa—has a surface charm.

Screenwriters Andrew Kurtzman and Eliot Wald pack the zingers about acne, the mall and the burdens of being the children of self-absorbed, upwardly mobile parents (the lost Woodstock generation).

Straight from TV's "Blossom," Jonathan Prince's sitcom direction keeps the story hopping from set piece to set piece until the inevitable parents' day fiasco.

Young Jonathan Jackson plays the prepubescent hero, Morris "Mud" Himmel, with comic earnestness. The blue-eyed, clear-skinned Mud is a self-described "poster child for the adopted dork foundation."

As the only adult worth watching, Christopher Lloyd seems less like an actor than a trick pony. The irrepressible Lloyd ("Back to the Future") dutifully performs one rote comic routine after another with the occasional awkward pause for a sincere tete-a-tete. Who's choosing his material?

Also wandering through the script with less impact than a sitcom walk-on are M. Emmet Walsh as a repo man and Peter Scolari as Mud's father. Don't blink or you'll miss Burgess Meredith picking up a paycheck for three hours' work as a curmudgeon.

Underneath the canned laughter is the same mall materialism that soured Disney's spring offering, "Blank Check." The obligatory spending-spree scene is repeated. As the trucks roll into Camp Nowhere with large-screen televisions and cases of super-soakers, it's supposed to play as a kid's toy store fantasy.

It sets my teeth on edge.

What these gimme-gimme children of privilege are crabbing about is not that they have no camp to attend, but that their parents are wasting $3,000 on camps they don't like. We should all have such problems—or such parents.

When Lloyd wisecracks, "back in the '60s, when we said we wanted to change society, maybe we should have been more specific," he's right on the money.

Unfortunately, in the latest spate of Disney kiddie comedics ("Angels in the Outfield" excepted), money not only makes the world go round, it has become a childhood obsession.

NEWSDAY, 8/26/94, Part II/p. B6, Jack Mathews

If a good performance can prop up a lame idea, Christopher Lloyd does it in Jonathan Prince's "Camp Nowhere."

The Disney/Hollywood Pictures comedy is a sort of "Home Alone" at summer camp, the story of a group of adolescents who con their parents into sending them to a camp of their own invention, where they can indulge every fantasy of kids liberated from adult supervision.

Lloyd plays Dennis Van Welker, an unemployed high-school drama teacher and unreconstructed '60s dropout whom the kids blackmail into fronting the camp and selling it to their parents, and who then looks the other way while they blow the camp fees on truckloads of large-screen TVs, jet skis, junk food and party favors, and otherwise wallow in anarchy. It's "Lord of the Flies" on a sugar high.

Van Welker is a role tailor-made for Lloyd's campy comedy style, and the actor chews the scenery with a relaxed abandon that, if anything, is more energetic than the kids' high jinks. He has a better summer vacation than any of them.

The setup here is that each of the four principal teenagers are rebelling against another summer at Camp Boredom, specialty camps chosen to match their parents' interests in computers, military training, diet regimen and theater. Van Welker, in various guises, has to convince the parents to entrust their kids to him; then he reprises those roles when they show up for an unscheduled Parents Day.

"Camp Nowhere" politely avoids the sexual experimentation that would likely dominant the activity schedule at an unsupervised camp for 13- and 14-year-olds. A couple of romances bloom—between Morris (Jonathan Jackson), the brains behind the ramp scam, and Gaby (Melody Kay), and between brawny Zack (Andrew Keegan) and precociously voluptuous Trish (Marne Patterson)—but Prince and writers Andrew Kurtzman and Eliot Wald don't let sentiment or anything approaching a real-life issue dilute the farce.

They did make a mistake in creating a romantic subplot between Van Welker and the local doctor (Wendy Makkena) who forces him to behave like an adult, but they didn't have much choice. "Camp Nowhere" really has nowhere to go—it's less a story than a notion; call it Camp Lloyd—and they had to have some device for ending it.

VILLAGE VOICE, 9/13/94, p. 70, Jeff Salamon

What sort of movie about summer camp doesn't have any lanyard jokes? Or bug juice shtick? Or communal shower scenes? A film like *Camp Nowhere*, which actually celebrates its abundance of lack: "No Parents. No Counselors. No Rules!" reads the print ad. Like this is some sort of come-on: Though the "No Parents" part is right, the very fascination of summer camp is the structures that fall into place in the absence of the great providers—the little cruelties counselors visit upon their charges (and the way campers quickly learn to ape them amongst each other), the way the harsh, arbitrary rules of athletics get recreated in the harsh, arbitrary rules of bunk life. Summer camp's as loaded (and as repressedly homoerotic) a venue as the military or the British public school system, but every July and August we're treated to crappy kids films that squander the genre's potential in the name of fart humor or gore. (Though I'll admit I was thrilled that *Friday the 13th, Part 2* was shot at the sadistic jock factory I got sent to as an adolescent.) *Camp Nowhere* fits right into this trap; it's about a couple dozen kids who trick their folks into sending them to a nonexistent camp where they proceed to eat like pigs, blast music, and dodge the local authorities—under the glazed eye of nominal adult Christopher Lloyd. The result is *Home Alone* amidst the pines. What *Nowhere* does have, instead of macramé, color war, and tetherball, is a few good jokes and a kindly spirit. Neither of which is enough to rescue it from the half-assed, slapdash quality that seems to be the norm in Hollywood today (in one scene, the kids run inside to watch *Beavis and Butthead*; a few minutes later another kid complains that their TV doesn't get cable). Maybe next summer.

Also reviewed in:
NEW YORK TIMES, 8/26/94, p. C3, Janet Maslin
VARIETY, 8/29-9/4/94, p. 42, Steven Gaydos
WASHINGTON POST, 8/27/94, p. B3, Hal Hinson

CAR 54, WHERE ARE YOU?

An Orion Pictures release. *Producer:* Robert H. Solo. *Director:* Bill Fishman. *Screenplay:* Erik Tarloff, Ebbe Roe Smith, Peter McCarthy, and Peter Crabbe. *Story:* Erik Tarloff. *Based on the T.V. series created by:* Nat Hiken. *Director of Photography:* Rodney Charters. *Editor:* Alan Balsam and Earl Watson. *Music:* Pray for Rain and Bernie Worrell. *Choreographer:* April Ortiz. *Sound:* Peter Shewchuk. *Casting:* Eliza Simons. *Production Designer:* Catherine Hardwicke. *Art Director:* Gregory P. Keen. *Set Dresser:* Dan Wladyka. *Special Effects:* David Lemmen. *Costumes:* Margaret M. Mohr. *Make-up:* Suzanne Benoit. *Stunt Coordinator:* Shane Cardwell. *Running time:* 89 minutes. *MPAA Rating:* PG-13.

CAST: David Johansen (Gunther Toody); John C. McGinley (Francis Muldoon); Fran Drescher (Velma Velour); Nipsey Russell (Captain Dave Anderson); Rosie O'Donnell (Lucille Toody); Daniel Baldwin (Don Motti); Jeremy Piven (Herbert Hortz); Bobby Collins (Carlo); Louis Di Bianco (Nicco); Al Lewis (Leo Schnauzer); Barbara Hamilton (Mrs. Muldoon); Eliza Garrett (Boys in Blue Director); Rik Colitti (Sergeant Abrams); Penn & Teller (Luthers); Tone Loc (Hackman); Coati Mundi (Mambo Singer); Ellen Ray Hennessy (Arlene); Sally Cahill (Brandy); Jackie Richardson (Madam); Daniel Dion (Officer Brown); Michael Ricupero (Officer Nicholson); Arlene Duncan (Officer Kagan); Jason Scott (Officer Simons); Santino Buda (Officer Rodriquez); Peter Keleghan (DA #1); Conrad Coates (DA #2); Terry Howson (Henchman #1); Eli Gabay (Henchman #2); Joanna Bacalso (Beautiful Young Woman); Gina Darling (Nurse); Matt Robinson (Homeboy); Claude Salvas (Animal Rights Activist); Brian Chambers (Delivery Boy); Elena Kudaba (Mrs. Pirogi); Von Flores (Mr. Kim); Gina Vasic (Mrs. Manicotti); Khan Agha Soroor (Khan); Benjamin Barrett (Kid with Beanie); Faye Wayne (Spitting Lady); Dan Gallagher (E.D.N.A. Technician); Maria Diaz (Voice of E.D.N.A.); Floyd Flex and Devon Martin (Rap Fellows); Mojo Nixon (Sidewalk Preacher); Peter Silverman (Newscaster); Jack Anthony (Proprietor at Shooting Gallery); Doug Innis (Tunnel of Love Attendant); Rummy Bishop (Hotel Clerk); Jerry Joseph Hewitt (Boy at Coney Island); Michelyn Emelle (Mrs. Robb); Sani Stahlbrand (Office Executive); Tex Konig (Construction Worker); Jackie Harris (Woman in Slip); Phil Jarrett (FBI Plain Clothes); Lee

Arenberg (Ivan the Architect); Mark Beaver and Steve Camber (Moto Men); Diane Fabian (Pie Lady); Alan Markfield (Producer).

LOS ANGELES TIMES, 1/31/94, Calendar/p. 5, Kevin Thomas

"Car 54, Where Are You?," based on the popular Joe E. Ross and Fred Gwynne TV series of the '60s, bombs on the big screen in the '90s. Thanks to a relentlessly terrible script by many hands, it's a dumb movie about dumb cops that should have remained on the shelf, where it's been sitting for over two years.

Gravel-voiced David Johansen stars as Gunther Toody, not exactly Brooklyn's finest, who gets a new partner in John C. McGinley's uptight, by-the-book Francis Muldoon after Leo Schnauzer (Al Lewis, from the original series) at last retires. Amid uninspired non-stop shenanigans—many loaded with heavy-handed sexual innuendo—there's a nominal plot concerning the nailing of a Mafia kingpin, played by Daniel Baldwin as a Robert De Niro impression. (In case we don't get this, Baldwin is actually required to refer to De Niro). Cop groupie Velma Velour (Fran Drescher) vamps the virginal Muldoon while Toody endures shrewish wife Lucille (Rosie O'Donnell).

These and others—including Nipsey Rusell, also from the TV series, as the precinct's none-too-swift captain—are game under Bill Fishman's energetic direction, but one and all are done in by the dire, dated material. To give credit where credit is due, the film, a seamless blend of Toronto and Brooklyn locales, has colorful settings, but their authenticity serves only to underline the production's synthetic quality. Wonderfully seedy Coney Island is too good a backdrop to waste on the film's frenzied finish.

NEW YORK POST, 1/28/94, p. 45, Thelma Adams

"Car 54, Where Are You?" stinks.

Nothing shows Hollywood's idea vacuum like recycling old TV shows into movies. This remake of the '60s cop comedy starring Fred Gwynne is the most desperate effort to cash in on the tube.

Made in 1990, "Car 54" was held in dry-dock by Orion Pictures' money problems. This creaky comedy now shifts from the category of unreleased movies into those which should never have been released.

It would have been better off for the careers of all concerned if "Car 54, Where Are You?" had remained in limbo. With Rosie O'Donnell, Fran Drescher, and David Johansen, the cast has comic potential. Also on board are TV series regulars Al Lewis and Nipsey Russell.

But, as directed by Bill ("Tapeheads") Fishman, they come off like a high school company of "Grease." David Johansen, a.k.a. the lounge lizard Buster Poindexter, takes the lead as Officer Toody played in the series by Joe E. Ross.

Johansen did a memorable turn as a cab driver in "Scrooged." But in this central role, he grates big time. Whenever he opened his mouth, I winced. Johansen merits a scholarship to overactors anonymous.

Billed as Rosie O'Donnell's screen debut, the actress has since had far better parts in "A League of Their Own" and "Sleepless in Seattle." Here, she plays Toody's shrill, jealous wife, waddling around in pink capri pants.

This is a movie where the biggest laugh comes when octogenarian Al Lewis suffers a severe penis injury! By the time it reached its antic conclusion on the Cyclone at Coney Island, I just wanted to get off the crass roller coaster.

"Car 54, Where Are You?" may be recycled, but it's still rubbish.

NEWSDAY, 1/29/94, Part II/p. 25, Terry Kelleher

My, how "Car 54, Where Are You?" has changed. The '60s have given way to the '90s. the 53rd Precinct has moved from the Bronx to Brooklyn. Officer Toody still says, "Ooo! Ooo!"—only now it means he's having an orgasm.

The new-model "Car 54" is a movie that will make you long to travel back in time—if not all the way to 1961-63, when the original series was on NBC, then at least to the summer of 1990, when this misbegotten revival went before the cameras. Maybe that "Quantum Leap" guy could have nipped disaster in the bud.

Belatedly emerging from limbo after Orion Pictures' bankruptcy, "Car 54" has no significant assets and a crushing load of liabilities. The combined efforts of director Bill Fishman and four writers have produced a laughless mishmash that lacks even the virtue of genuine affection for the source material. Sure, they promote Nipsey Russell's character to captain and bring back Al Lewis as Leo Schnauzer. But they slap Schnauzer in the hospital and squeeze a cheap laugh out of his catheterization.

In this version, Gunther Toody (David Johansen, adding a touch of Joe E. Ross to his usual croak) is a happy-go-lucky party animal who makes whoopie with the wife (Rosie O'Donnell) whenever she's feeling jealous. Three decades ago, Toody never could have panted, "Let's do the wild thing, Lucille." Man, that's progress.

Toody's partner, Francis Muldoon (John C. McGinley, inheriting from Fred Gwynne) has become The Anal-Retentive Policeman, who overcomes severe sexual repression under the influence of hot-for-cops Velma Velour (Fran Drescher). "I lost the mob witness," Toody tells Muldoon. "I lost my virginity," Muldoon tells Toody. So file a report.

Fishman mostly tries to get by on obvious gags and loud music. One sequence bids for "Naked Gun" absurdism—an exotic beauty keeps changing costume as she leads Toody to a mob boss—but the whole business ends with him pointing out a "big booger" in her nose. Car 54, over and out.

Also reviewed in:
NEW YORK TIMES, 1/31/94, p. C16, Janet Maslin
VARIETY, 1/31-2/6/94, p. 66, Brian Lowry
WASHINGTON POST, 1/29/94, p. G2, David Mills

CARO DIARIO

A Fine line Features release of a Sacher Film/Banfilm/Le Sept Cinéma/Studio Canal+ production in association with RAI Uno and Canal+. *Producer:* Angelo Barbagallo, Nanni Moretti, and Nella Banfi. *Director:* Nanni Moretti. *Screenplay (Italian with English subtitles):* Nanni Moretti. *Director of Photography:* Giuseppe Lanci. *Editor:* Micro Garrone. *Music:* Nicola Piovani. *Sound:* Franco Borni and (music) Danilo Moroni. *Running time:* 96 minutes. *MPAA Rating:* Not Rated.

CAST: Nanni Moretti (Himself); Giovanna Bozzolo, Sebastiano Nardone, and Antonio Petrocelli (Actors in Italian Film); Giulio Base (Car Driver); Italo Spinelli (On the Wall at Spinaceto); Carlo Mazzacurati (Film Critic); Jennifer Beals (Herself); Alexandre Rockwell (Himself); Renato Carpentieri (Gerardo); Raffaella Lebboroni and Marco Paolini (First Salina Couple); Claudia Della Seta and Lorenzo Alessandri (Second Salina Couple); Antonio Neiwiller (Mayor of Stromboli); Conchita Airoldi (Inhabitant of Panarea); Moni Ovadia (Lucio); Valerio Magrelli, Sergio Lambiase, and Roberto Nobile (Dermatologists); Gianni Ferraretto (Assistant to the Prince); Pino Gentile (Allergist); Marlo Schiano (Prince of Dermatologists); Serena Nono (Reflexologist); Yu Ming Lun and Tou Yui Chang Pio (Chinese Doctors); Umberto Contarello (Assistant to the Chinese Doctors).

LOS ANGELES TIMES, 10/7/94, Calendar/p. 6, Kevin Thomas

Nanni Moretti's "Caro Diario" (Dear Diary) introduces the quirky Italian filmmaker whose eight films over the last 18 years have established him as a cult figure in his own country.

Although Moretti has an off-the-wall comic sensibililty wlth an anti-Establishment attitude and a graceful style, he is not likely to enjoy the same success in America as many other Italian filmmakers.

The man is funny, sometimes provocative, but he also seems parochial, his purported metaphysical concerns elusive—and he's not a little self-indulgent and long-winded.

Unfolding in three episodes, the film, his first to receive a U.S. release, is literally a visual diary. The first episode, "On My Vespa," is the strongest, in which Moretti, a trim, bearded man of 40, takes us on a highly personal motorcycle tour of Rome and its outskirts that is loaded with amusing encounters, including a meeting with none other than Jennifer Beals, the woman of his dreams ever since "Flashdance," a watershed experience for Moretti, a frustrated dancer.

There's a hilarious sequence that has him confronting an ailing critic (Carlo Mazzacurati) with his thuddingly pretentious review of "Henry: Portrait of a Serial Killer," which we glimpse dubbed into Italian. The episode concludes with Moretti paying a respectful visit to the site where controversial director Pier Paolo Pasolini was murdered. Throughout the "Caro Diario," Moretti is immensely aided by Nicola Piovani's vibrant, mood-establishing score.

In the second episode, "The Islands," Moretti and a friend, Gerardo (Renato Carpentieri), who's obsessed with both deciphering James Joyce's "Ulysses" and the medium of television, and supposed to be working on a script but embark on a tour of a series of idyllic island communities, where in one place they discover all the children love to give callers, eager to speak to their parents, a hard time on the phone.

If "The Islands" starts wearing thin, "Doctors," the final episode, wears even thinner as Moretti visits a raft of specialists, each with a different diagnosis and treatment, in search of a cure for his bad, widespread bodily itch. This single joke rapidly gets pretty tired, you soon wish you could tell Moretti to try slapping on some calamine lotion—and getting on with his life. But stringing us along—with varying effectiveness—*is* his life.

NEW YORK, 10/10/94, p. 73, David Denby

Perhaps too many years have gone by since I've been to Italy—or seen a good Italian film—but at the beginning of Nanni Moretti's *Caro Diario (Dear Diary)*, as the director himself tools around Rome on his Vespa early one summer morning, I was nearly overwhelmed by the desire to walk on Italian streets. Moretti wanders through residential neighborhoods, past handsome golden and ocher buildings; the surrounding trees and bushes spill over stone walls and balconies, softening and darkening everything. In the heat, the buildings and greenery seem to buckle slightly. Hot, maybe, but ravishing. Later, Moretti visits such islands as Lipari and Stromboli. This deeply funny little movie, a personal "diary" film, can be viewed, I suppose, as a kind of sophisticated travelogue—Italy as seen through the satirical but loving eyes of a brilliant native son.

The director, who is a considerable figure at home (this is his eighth film), appears to us in his own person, a slender, bearded fellow, fortyish, unencumbered, an artist-intellectual who gains almost palpable pleasure from simply moving about, observing and musing. He speaks to us confidentially, like Woody Allen at the beginning of *Annie Hall*, and his presence, like Allen's, is deceptively mild. Moretti makes jokes—some sweet-natured, some not—and airs his pet peeves. Pursuing his obsessions, he "interviews" various people with mock formality and then addresses us again, with complaints and raptures. He appears, by turns, whimsical, rude, and gravely serious.

The movie is deliberately slight—a rebuke, perhaps, to such overblown diary films as *Felini's Roma*. Yet despite the modest scale, the generally deflationary and anti-imperial tone, Moretti as a director and personality is anything but diffident. Part of the pleasure of *Caro Diario* lies in the outrageous arbitrariness of Moretti's wit. In the Rome section, he halts his wanderings to view an absurdly pretentious Italian movie, with breast-beating characters droning on—as good a demonstration as any of why Hollywood movies dominate the theaters of so many older cultures. Later, he goes to a theater and takes in an American movie, the independently made "art" horror film *Henry: Portrait of a Serial Killer*. Moretti sits in his seat squirming and suffering through the ghoulish violence; later, he reads to himself, with increasing disbelief, the nonsense written about the movie by a local intellectual critic. "Don't these critics ever feel remorse?" he demands, and he cuts to a scene in which he reads a whole selection of such reviews to the critic dying in his bed, who tearfully begs to be forgiven. Few revenge scenes are as satisfying. Moretti is himself composing criticism—of other movies, of lies and absurdities, of bad words and images.

The idea of turning the tables on a critic is funny not because of the way it's staged or acted but because Moretti actually went through with his fantasy of putting it onscreen. He shares Woody Allen's willfulness—the determination of an observant, indignant, unprepossessing man to speak his mind. In the second section of *Caro Diario*, the director, accompanied by a friend, makes his island tour, a kind of anti-Odyssey through banality, each island exhibiting an Italian idiosyncrasy that drives Moretti nuts. In the past, the director has made films with political themes, but what seems to exercise him now is cant and pretension in all its forms. The last section chronicles his travails with the medical profession, a sequence filled with an almost Kafkaesque anxiety and humiliation. Moretti, tormented by a powerful—and unceasing body itch, visits various owlish authorities who issue infuriatingly calm and invariably incorrect diagnoses. Drugs and bizarre treatments fill Moretti's days, but still the itch continues. This sequence could have gone even further into despair than it does, but it's still unsettling and extremely funny. Moretti's patience, his solemn methodicalness, almost resembles Buster Keaton's deadpan fortitude before catastrophe.

There's no cumulative story in *Caro Diario*. It's a true diary film—if you love it, as I do, you are drawn to Moretti as a personality and you prize everything he does. He puts a heavenly Italian quizzical wit back on the screen.

NEW YORK POST, 9/30/94, p. 46, Thelma Adams

Want to know the cheapest tour of Rome going? Jump on the back of Italian director Nanni Moretti's Vespa scooter and tool around his favorite neighborhoods in Rome without leaving your theater seat.

As the helmet-wearing hero prattles over his shoulder about his disgust with contemporary Italian movies, his love of "Flashdance," and takes you to the bedside of a movie reviewer who Moretti forces to listen to his published critiques until the critic cries into his pillow, you will share the euphoria of life as it's lived on a warm, sunny day spent with a good and entertaining friend.

Italian cinema's best kept secret, Moretti was named Best Director at this year's Cannes Film Festival. He has zipped onto American shores with his eighth film. "Caro Diario"—Italian for dear diary.

This seemingly spontaneous autobiographical tryptich is Moretti's first movie to get an American theatrical release. (A retrospective of his earlier films is now at the Public Theater in the East Village.).

Boats are the mode of transportation in the second vignette, "Islands." Moretti travels with a TV-obsessed academic while seeking a safe haven in which to work on a film project.

Like Goldilocks, Moretti finds that there's too much solitude on one island, too much socializing on another, and too much hostility on a third.

The most hilarious spot in this metaphor for adult lifestyle choices is an island populated only by children and their parents.

The fathers and mothers are obsessed with their kids (toilet training is a big topic); the kids dominate their parents. With the children holding the phones hostage, communication between adults is dead.

While the second section has the biggest laughs, it's also the most uneven. Moretti's offbeat sensibility can be both endearing and grating. Like a visit from a hyperactive favorite cousin who has gotten too wound up, sometimes the charm of his company wears thin.

The third section is an extended anecdote called "Doctors." Moretti reenacts his year-long battle with cancer and with the doctors who repeatedly misdiagnosed his symptoms—primarily a profound itch—as either the result of stress, dry skin, or food allergies.

The last section never achieves the effortless poignancy of the final moment of the first part, "On My Vespa."

Moretti visits the site where famed Italian director and poet Pier Paolo Pasolini was murdered—and cuts the scene without comment.

Most diaries are only sporadically interesting; why else would we search for the juicy bits among the daily trials they record? "Caro Diario" is more amusing than most, but it opens with a four-star chapter that the succeeding parts never quite match.

NEWSDAY, 9/30/94, Part II/p. B7, Jack Mathews

Nanni Moretti, an Italian director whose eighth feature, "Caro Diario," is the first to get a commercial U.S. release, has an engaging, ironically reflective world view. and it's a good thing, because he is also as self-indulgent a filmmaker as you are likely to see at work.

Moretti writes, directs and stars (as himself) in his movies, which are essentially cinematic expressions of his politics and his personality, both a little extreme, and if you can't enjoy him, you can't enjoy his films.

"Caro Diario" ("Dear Diary") is a three-piece journal—three vignettes in which the bearded filmmaker talks and acts his way through his feelings about current and past events in his life, as he reaches the 40 mark.

"On My Vespa" is pretty much as advertised: a day spent driving through the suburbs and beachside communities of Rome on his motorbike. It's summer—a Sunday, judging by the light traffic—and as we follow him through the streets, his voiced-over diary entries give us his views on subjects as wide-ranging as the decline and fall of modern Rome, the wimping out of Italian intellectuals, the sad status of movies, and Moretti's secret desire to be a dancer.

"'Flashdance' was the movie that changed my life," he says, moments before pulling over to have a talk with "Flashdance" star Jennifer Beals, who just happens to be walking down the street with a friend.

That's not the only Woody Allen trick in Moretti's bag. He occasionally stops to speak his thoughts directly to bemused passersby, and takes out his rage at critics who liked the movie "Henry: Portrait of a Serial Killer" by cornering one and forcing him to hear his own pompous reviews read back to him.

The second vignette, "Islands," is a laconic shaggy-dog story about Moretti's and a friend's attempt to get away from the city for a working holiday in the Lipari Islands. As tranquil as the islands appear to us, neither man can concentrate. Moretti is appalled by the bourgeois complacency of his once politically committed friends who live there, and Gerardo (Renato Carpentieri) discovers he cannot survive without daily infusions of TV soap operas.

The mood shifts dramatically in part three, "Doctors," in which Moretti re-enacts what was apparently an actual year-long medical odyssey that began with an itch and ended up with a diagnosis of cancer. It's the least successful of the three pieces, because Moretti is his least candid with his diary.

He begins it with an announcement that he has cancer, and that he has decided to film himself being treated for it. Then he recalls in sardonic detail the series of misdiagnoses and useless remedies prescribed for him. The vignette has funny moments—his bran bath is a hoot—but in the end it seems more self-exploitive than insightful.

"Caro Diario," which earned Moretti the Best Director award at this year's Cannes Film Festival, adds up to a patchwork of personal musings—some intellectual, some pure folly—and is a serviceable primer to the career of a filmmaker who is both his own inspiration and his own material.

NEWSWEEK, 10/24/94, p. 76, David Ansen

Most movies unfold like illustrated novels, but as Nanni Moretti delightfully shows us in *Caro Diario*, there are other forms an adventurous filmmaker can employ. Moretti, an actor-writer-director who's been called the Italian Woody Allen, is a household name in Italy, but this wickedly funny, unfailingly intelligent movie is the first of his films to be widely released in America. In it, Moretti forgoes plot to go one on one with the audience, constructing a film that's as personal as a diary, as smart and discursive as an essay.

Moretti leads us on a three-part tour of contemporary Italy— and the inside of his quirky, sardonic head. In "On My Vespa," he tools around summertime Rome, where he bumps into his "Flashdance" idol Jennifer Beals, offers a hilarious sendup of film critics and pays homage to the late film director Pasolini. In "Islands," he and his intellectual pal Gerardo—a TV hater who becomes addicted to soap operas—travel from island to island in search of a good place to work. They are woefully unsuccessful, but the trip yields wonderful satirical treasures, such as the island of doting parents where the indulged children have taken complete control. The comic odysseys of the first two parts are cast in a new, graver light in "Doctors," a mordant critique of the medical profession, in which Moretti's search for a cure for his itch leads to an encounter with his mortality. The winner of the best-director award at Cannes, the droll and wise "Dear Diary" suggests, in its unassuming, conversational way, a whole new way to make a movie.

NEW STATESMAN & SOCIETY, 11/25/94, p. 33, Jonathan Romney

How to sum up the uniquely skewed sensibility of Italian director-star Nanni Moretti? Actress Jennifer Beals tries to get it right ln *Dear Diary* when she and her husband encounter an excitable Moretti ln the street (Moretti's life, it seems, was changed by seeing her dancing in *Flashdance*). "Off-crazy but not quite...Whimsical—almost dumb. *Off* is about right for the director whose film *Palombella Rossa* contemplated the fate of the Italian Communist Party in the form of a game of water polo. And *Dear Diary* is the most uniquely off film I've seen for sometime. "Off" is what Moretti's humour and persona are—not eye-rolling manic like his fellow Italian director-comics Roberto Benigni and Maurizio Nichetti, but oblique, pensive, and not a little discomforting.

Dear Diary presents itself as three slices of the life of "Nanni Moretti". That is, the man in the film is and isn't Moretti—he undergoes the same medical treatment as Moretti did a couple of years ago, and Moretti produces documentary evidence in the form of his chemotherapy footage and reams of prescriptions made out in his name. But Moretti has stretched the self-portrait somewhat; he's sworn in interviews that he never wanted to dance like Jennifer Beals.

Dear Diary presents thorny problems for analysts of autobiographical cinema, but we are never less than convinced that this is a genuine *mis en scéne* of Moretti's inner life. The minute we see him write the rather child-like words "Dear Diary", we accept that the film is going to be a sort of magic slate on which Moretti sketches a version of his life and times. Not the definite self-portrait, though, but a provisional sketch in the loose and vaguely related fly-sheets.

From the first shot of Moretti on his Vespa swaying through the streets of Rome to a song by Angélique Kidjo, *Dear Diary* comes across as a beautifully casual film. It's a *flâneur*'s movie, restless, distracted, but apt at moments to let its mind go perfectly blank. In Part One, Moretti rides around deserted Roman streets, visits the duller parts of town, wonders why there's nothing on at the cinema except bad Italian films and *Henry: Portrait of a Serial Killer* (which he hates). He goes to berate the critic who recommended *Henry*, dances a bit of salsa, and finally, in a sequence of elegiac beauty, rides out to see the spot where Pasolini died.

In Part Two, he and an island-dwelling Joyce scholar head out across the sea in search of a quiet place to work, only to encounter manic social organisers, anguished majors, one-child families and anchorites. They finally give up the quest, because Moretti's friend contracts an addiction to American soap operas. And in Part Three, Moretti soberly recounts his long illness, which led him through an endless series of doctors and ointments; after being operated on for a lymphoma, he finally declares his faith in a glass of water taken every day with breakfast. That's the last shot of the film, and it's astounding that anything so simple (and apparently bathetic) can have such a joyous resonance.

That's what makes *Dear Diary* so surprising— the way that simple things gain the most extraordinary power because Moretti persuades us that his entire being is invested in them, *Dear Diary* is all those things associated with the canon of "great films": serious-minded, philosophical, humanist, rooted in a particular place and sensibility, but it often seems irredeemably trivial and self-regarding. This makes it an utterly radical film: It's about nothing except its own thought processes and rhythms.

The first segment is extraordinary in its distraction. Where *8½* was about a man trying to make a film, Moretti starts by day-dreaming about the films he might make. The scene where he reduces a critic to tears by reading him his own excruciating eulogies of David Cronenberg is overstated; but you accept lt, feeling this complaint came into Moretti's head on the spur of the moment and thus has a legitimate place in the film.

Certain other things jar; like the laborious gags about TV soaps and only children in Part Two. But they are offset by the fact that Moretti evidently isn't working too hard: he's just letting his mind sway the way his bike does in the long steadicam shots of Part One. On one island, he starts bobbing absent-mindedly to the rhythms of a Silvana Mangano film on TV, then muses about what a strange film it was. Later, in a beautiful *trompe l'oeil* shot, an ocean liner drifts languidly across a football field, and we just watch, letting our minds go as appreciatively blank as

Moretti's, who's observing it. No single section would mean quite the same if not for the other two, and it's the no-nonsense lucidity of the third section, "Doctors", that gives the film a completely different impetus, The film ends on a note that could seem utterly glib—that doctors know how to talk but not how to listen, and a glass of water is good for you—but doesn't, because it's utterly touching that Moretti has taken the trouble to document the pettifogging quotidian hell of prescription forms, and has the heart to shrug it off in a moment's closing gesture. *Dear Diary* casually pulls off, in the spirit of whimsy, what was once the grand project of cinema's avant-garde—to make films that were portraits of the thought process. *Dear Diary*, with all its narcissism, its flippancy, its off-ness, is just this. We may be tempted to think, so what, it's just cinema; Moretti makes us think it's also just life.

SIGHT AND SOUND, 12/94, p. 42, Peter Aspden

Nanni Moretti decides to film his own diary, in three chapters. In the first, 'On my Vespa', Moretti rides his scooter through Rome during the deserted month of August. He narrates his off-screen reflections about his childhood and the decay of Rome. He sees an Italian film in which all the characters reflect on their moral and spiritual decline since they were young, which depresses him. Stopping at a traffic light, he tells a passing motorist that he never feels at home with what the majority of people think. He continues driving, looking at houses, even inspecting them, pretending he is conducting location research for a musical.

Moretti muses that seeing the film *Flashdance* changed his life, and that he would love to dance like Jennifer Beals. Coming across a band playing *merengue* music in the middle of the day while young couples dance, he watches and joins in the singing. Returning from a drive to a housing estate, he encounters Jennifer Beals walking with her husband, film director Alexandre Rockwell. He goes to see *Henry: Portrait of a Serial Killer*; immensely depressed, he seeks out the reviewer who wrote a favourable piece on the film, making him weep with shame at his pretentious reviews. He rides out to the site of Pasolini's murder.

Chapter Two: 'Islands', Moretti travels to Lipari to visit Gerardo, a friend who has lived there for 11 years studying Joyce's *Ulysses*, and hasn't watched television for 30 years. Moretti is trying to write a new film, but there is too much traffic and noise, and the two of them travel to Salina for peace and quiet. During the trip, Gerardo watches television and is entranced. Salina is dominated by only children, to whom all parents defer. A couple boast that their son has never had a babysitter, because they have always stayed in with him. As a result, they have read most of the classics of literature and philosophy. Moretti and Gerardo leave for Stromboli, where the mayor reveals to them his plans to modernise the island. On the crater of the volcano, Gerardo sends Moretti to ask a group of Americans for the latest news of a soap opera, *The Bold and the Beautiful*. They travel to Panarea, where they are met by a woman who organises cocktail parties and business dinners; they instantly depart for Alicudi, the most remote island. Learning there is no television, Gerardo runs away, screaming.

Chapter Three: 'Doctors', Moretti films the last session of his own chemotherapy. He tells the story of how he arrived there. He starts to itch one day, and visits the dermatologist, who prescribes a series of drugs, which prove ineffective. He sees more specialists and accumulates many different drugs, but none works. He sees a reflexologist, and attends acupuncture sessions. He gets worse. Finally, after a CAT scan, which the hospital radiologist wrongly interprets as indicating an untreatable tumour, he finds he has Hodgkin's disease, which is treated. From now on, he will drink a glass of water every day before breakfast.

Nanni Moretti is a film-maker of immense charm; not the sentimental cuteness beloved of British audiences who made such a huge success of *Cinema Paradiso*, but the real thing: a gentle irony and effortless control of character which enables him to say the simplest things with maximum effect. His previous work has always contained autobiographical undertones, but this time he has gone all the way. His message in *Dear Diary* could be interpreted as a trite one—it is essentially a feel-good movie, with a few wry asides on modern society thrown in along the way—but the unravelling of his visual diary is so skilfully paced that one is left feeling something profound has taken place.

Not that the film is entirely convincing: the central section, as Moretti explores a handful of islands with his Joyce scholar-turned-telly addict friend Gerardo, is a little too obvious in it targets and drags a little. But even this episode contains delightful touches of wit (Gerardo, the great high-culture intellectual, finally succumbs to soap opera mania while reading a book in a ferry called the *Giovanni Bellini*) and lightly-applied satirical brushstrokes; the *bambini*-dominated parents of Salina in particular could have been much more harshly portrayed by a crueller commentator than Moretti.

The film's greatest moments are in the first and third chapters. In the first, Moretti roams the sun-soaked streets of Rome, but manages to avoid banality by ignoring virtually all of the city's historic sights; he prefers instead to wander round the suburbs and housing projects, finding something positive to say in each case. It is a shamelessly romantic view (has Rome ever been portrayed with so little traffic?), which dovetails perfectly with the director's disdain for those who wish to bring depression, violence and take-away pizzas to his beloved city. Why, he asks, should anyone who lives in such a vibrant, bracing milieu want to see films such as *Henry: Portrait of a Serial Killer*? The chapter's final episode, in which Moretti visits the site of Pasolini's brutal murder, has a haunting quality as the soundtrack (from Keith Jarrett's piano solo *The Köln Concert*) is allowed to run uninterruptedly alongside the director's lengthy tracking shots (Moretti's use of music throughout is superbly conceived, drawing on an ethnically eclectic mix of styles which includes Beninoise singer Angélique Kidjo and Algeria's Cheb Khaled).

Much darker in tone is Moretti's final chapter, in which he tells of the series of mistaken and careless diagnoses which he experienced while all the time suffering from Hodgkin's disease. The episode's jolting opening, using a real-life film of Moretti's final chemotherapy session, is followed by a succession of encounters with the medical profession, which resonate with frustration and bitterness. The tone is understated throughout; when Moretti sits in a bran bath, on the recommendation of a reflexologist, the camera lingers on his face just long enough to register the humiliation and deep sense of thwarted anger which is so familiar to anyone who has suffered a mysterious illness. Although there is humour throughout the chapter, it is intensely uncomfortable to watch, and Moretti has the good taste not to dwell on the terminal verdict mistakenly delivered by the hospital specialist to the director's friends. The whole affair is doubly moving for its unassuming narration; when Moretti smiles to camera at the end of his ordeal and downs his daily glass of water, life is being affirmed in the most modest, and effective, of ways.

TIME, 10/24/94, p. 77, Richard Corliss

Let's take a look at the fall fashions in movie directors' egos. Quentin Tarantino shows up in his own film, *Pulp Fiction*, and has everybody talk like him—which is fine, since he's a great talker. Wes Craven, director of *A Nightmare on Elm Street*, takes himself very seriously now, so he calls his new picture *Wes Craven's New Nightmare*, and it is the ultimate in self-reverential cinema.

Then there's Nanni Moretti, who displays a more genial egotism. Though the Italian actor-writer-director is in every scene of *Caro Diario* (Dear Diary)—an episodic film that is the equivalent of an artist's sketchbook—his is a skeptical, almost modest form of auteur hubris.

Join Nanni on his Vespa motoring through Rome, savoring the barren landscape, stopping at the spot where Pasolini was murdered, singing along with an outdoor band and looking—in his beard, dark glasses and black shirt—like an anarchist who has joined the Ricky Ricardo Orchestra. Visit the Italian islands with Nanni and his bookish friend (Renato Carpentieri) as they see their friends utterly dominated by bratty kids. Get lost in the labyrinth of Italian medicine as Nanni consults dozens of doctors to discover the source of a skin rash only to learn troubling truths about his body and their expertise.

This concluding vignette ends his vacation-like jaunt with a crash against the brick wall of immortality. But that still can't shake Moretti's take-it-as-it-comes philosophy. For this engaging artist, in life as on a scooter, the journey is the adventure.

VILLAGE VOICE, 10/4/94, p. 54, Georgia Brown

These are reasons Nanni Moretti is often compared to Woody Allen: Both are comics (at least I *think* Moretti qualifies) who write, direct, and star in their films; both play a fairly consistent persona—a worrier, a crank, a guy who has trouble with girls; both are obsessives; both suffer from anhedonia; both have created a cinema of complaint.

Now, here are some ways Moretti and Allen are totally different: (1) Moretti's complaints are deeper. (2) He's not a gagster. (3) He's political. (4) And Italian. (5) He doesn't cast himself as the romantic lead. (6) He doesn't follow existing genres. (7) His shtick is rude and tough and he makes no pretense of fitting in. (8) He would never call on Sven Nykvist.

More like Tati, and sharing Tati's stubborn compulsion to *rectify*, Moretti is an acquired taste. (It certainly took me more than one film to acquire it.) For Americans, the taste is hard enough to acquire simply because his films almost never come here. This is why the Public's retrospective is so welcome. Except for some beginning Super-8 work, the series, "Nanni X 7," presents the entire oeuvre: six features and a 1990 documentary on the fall-of-the-East-Bloccrisis in Italy's Communist Party.

Having said this, *Caro Diario*—opening after its appearance in the NYFF—provides a good starting place for a Nanni-chaperoned journey. Made after the 41-year-old director's recent bout with cancer (he's now in remission), this recent film is gentler and far more accessible. It's the closest Moretti has come to being endearing (whereas Woody has "Love Me" written in script on his forehead).

Like Gaul and *Pulp Fiction*, *Caro Diario (Dear Diary)* is divided into three parts. The first, "On My Vespa," follows Nanni through Roman neighborhoods commenting on architecture, movies, time, and change. He loves *Flashdance* and "coincidentally" runs into Jennifer Beals and Alexandre Rockwell on the street; he hates *Henry, Portrait of a Serial Killer* and rouses a critic from his bed, forcing him to submit to a reading of his effusions. (Don't try this at my home.) Finally, with Keith Jarrett on the soundtrack, he takes off for the spot where Pasolini was murdered, implicitly linking himself to that outlaw spirit.

In Part Two, trying to find a quiet place to work, Moretti and a friend (played by Renato Carpentieri) find themselves at odds with the lifestyles of the local Aeolean Islanders (the invisible presence on Stromboli being Rossellini). In Part Three, the allergy-racked Moretti seeks relief from an overwhelming *itch*. In point of fact, *Caro Diario* is probably the only Moretti film that won't make your skin creep a little.

You might describe Moretti's cinematic alter ego, Michele, as a congenital allergic. It's a syndrome that invariably casts outsiders as aggressors and puts him in the posture of "fending off." He's allergic to just about everyone but his mother. In the abrasive (scratchy) 1978 *Ecce Bombo*, Michele is a wretched refugee from the politics of the '60s, a twenty-something lout living at home, tormenting his parents and sister, hanging out with the *ragazzi*, lamenting the loss of a cause. With no apparent aesthetic pretensions, this film defined Italian slackers of the time (to themselves), and Moretti was on his way to becoming the cult hero he is today.

The disturbing 1981 *Sogni D'Oro (Sweet Dreams)* is often cited as Moretti's *8½*. You could also call it his *Stardust Memories*. A marginal young film director harassed by hecklers ("I doubt if a farmhand, a shepherd, or a housewife could relate to this film"), Michele is making a movie about Freud and Freud's mother while living at home with *his* mother. This is where Michele's and Moretti's oedipal fixations first get articulated—a theme that dominates ever after.

It's with the truly perverse *Bianca* (1984) that Moretti really blazes into his own. Here Michele is a math teacher at the progressive Scuola Marilyn Monroe, and he's even stranger than the school. The new French teacher, Bianca (Laura Morante, a Charlotte Rampling type), tells him, "I can't make out if you're being nice or mean." Two things are clear: Michele's obsession with couples and families and his aversion to contact. (The first thing he does in his new apartment is sterilize the bathroom, igniting toilet, bidet, sink, and tub in a blue flame.) The film turns into a variation on *Rear Window*: Michele spies on the neighbors, lectures and interrogates them, and ultimately invades their lives. Dreading love's loss, he pushes away the devoted Bianca. This story of a hypersensitive man exudes torment.

The pain continues. In the splendidly off-the-wall *La Messa E Finita (The Mass Is Over)*, Michele is a priest who leaves his island monastery to conduct his mission in the real world. (He literally takes the plunge—diving into the sea and swimming to the opposite shore.) As a priest, Moretti's moralism comes to full flower. Of course, the world lets him down. The previous priest is married. His unmarried sister is planning an abortion. His father walks out on his mother for a friend of his sister. (What would he say about Woody and Soon Yi?) His mother commits suicide. Perhaps the most moving passage in all of Moretti's work—so naked, so plaintive—is

Michele's lament over his mother's corpse: "I was happy with you ... Who'll love me now?" Flashbacks show a boy with a red ball. Already the little communist.

Moretti is consumed with childhood. Michele is always frantic to kick a soccer ball with some kids. Like someone still close to the ground, he's obsessed with the shoes people wear (he maintains a special prejudice against slippers and clogs). He loves sweets. Actually, he devours sweets constantly. (In real life, Moretti named his film company Sacher after the torte; his Rome movie house is the Nuovo Sacher and each year he bestows Sacher awards on deserving filmmakers.) He's turned Proust's dainty madeleine into a veritable Mont Blanc.

A kicking and screaming Proust, Michele doesn't just want to remember things past, he really wants them back. He's always throwing tantrums over time's irreversibility, fantasizing returns to some mother-son bliss. In the wonderful, outrageous *Palombella Rossa* (1989)—a movie I kick myself for not appreciating when I blurbed it in our 1989 NYFF coverage—Michele drives along making faces with children in the car in front of him and then runs off the road. The adult's subsequent amnesia—and specifically the amnesia of a contemporary Communist—sparks a regression. The movie—much of which takes place during a water polo match (!)—is all about dreams of light (*sogni d'oro*), dreams of a simpler past, dreams of a better tomorrow via a vital, viable Communist Party. More than his sweets, Michele craves a second chance. He wants desperately to be able to *turn around*, change his mind, do the shot over.

Choices, choices: the penalty of growing up. Meanwhile, at the concession stand, *Doctor Zhivago* plays on TV and Michele keeps returning to see whether this time Julie Christie will turn around to discover Omar Sharif staggering after her. Once again, he's crushed.

Perhaps nothing in the above sounds particularly funny. It's not as if I'm splitting my gut—though tears could run down my face. What's funny, and sad, is how blunt and outrageous Moretti is. How like a child unashamedly showing what a beastly, contradictory little tyrant he is. Like a child, he still expects a perfect world, a place where people are happy, behave intelligently, and have the sense to wear the right shoes.

Also reviewed in:
CHICAGO TRIBUNE, 11/25/94, Friday/p. L, Michael Wilmington
NATION, 10/17/94, p. 434, Stuart Klawans
NEW REPUBLIC, 10/7/94, p. 38, Stanley Kauffmann
NEW YORK TIMES, 9/26/94, p. C11, Janet Maslin
VARIETY, 12/6/93, p. 39, Deborah Young
WASHINGTON POST, 10/4/94, Weekend/p. 48, Desson Howe
WASHINGTON POST, 10/21/94, p. C7, Hal Hinson

CEMENT GARDEN, THE

An October Films release of a Constantin Film production in association with Torii Productions/Sylvia Montalti/Laurentic Film Productions. Made with the participation of the European Co-production Fund Ltd./Bayerische Landesanstadt fur Aufbaufinanzierung/ZDF/Canal Plus. *Executive Producer:* Bernd Eichinger and Martin Moszkowicz. *Producer:* Bee Gilbert and Ene Vanaveski. *Director:* Andrew Birkin. *Screenplay:* Andrew Birkin. *Based on the book by:* Ian McEwan. *Director of Photography:* Stephen Blackman. *Editor:* Toby Tremlett. *Music:* Edward Shearmur. *Sound:* Guillaume Sciama and (music) Peter Fuchs. *Sound Editor:* Andy Kennedy. *Production Designer:* Bernd Lepel. *Art Director:* Amanda Grenville. *Set Dresser:* Amanda Grenville. *Special Effects:* Bob Smoke. *Costumes:* Bernd Lepel. *Running time:* 101 minutes. *MPAA Rating:* Not Rated.

CAST: Andrew Robertson (Jack); Charlotte Gainsbourg (Julie); Alice Coulthard (Sue); Ned Birkin (Tom); Sinead Cusack (Mother); Hanns Zischler (Father); Jochen Horst (Derek); Gareth Brown (Willaim); William Hootkins (Commander Hunt's Voice); Dick Flockhart (Truck Driver); Mike Clark (Driver's Mate).

FILM QUARTERLY, Fall 1994, p. 32, William Johnson

At the time of its release, *The Cement Garden* gained notoriety as a film about teen incest, a misconception that put it in double jeopardy with critics and the public. The film does indeed involve teen incest, but anyone who goes to it in hopes of kinky sex will be disgruntled. On the other hand, *Garden* is certainly not a clinical case study. The distributor's press kit included an unintentionally hilarious commentary by incest authority Judith Alpert, who "wonders what went on off-screen" and detects sexual abuse in every corner. No doubt the distributors wanted to shield themselves against the Jesse Helmses on one side and feminist/child protection groups on the other by having Dr. Alpert endow the film with documentary values. But *The Cement Garden* is no more concerned with instruction than with titillation. It is fiction, and remarkable fiction at that.

While focusing on the everyday and not-so-everyday activities of a family in crisis, *Garden* explores the moral implications of individualism and collectivism, holding an even finer balance between realism and allegory than the novel on which it's based. I am using the term "allegory" here not in the traditional sense of a symbolic level that is easily distinguished from and bears a clear relationship to the ostensive level (as in Bunyan's *Pilgrim's Progress*) but in the looser modern sense that applies to such novels as Kafka's *The Trial* and *The Castle*, Golding's *Lord of the Flies*, and C. S. Lewis's *Perelandra* trilogy, in all of which the two levels frequently emerge.[1] It is at least theoretically possible to read such novels—or to see the film versions of *The Trial* and *Lord of the Flies*—without being conscious of their allegorical level. While Welles' *The Trial* rejects realism throughout and could be enjoyed as an expressionist fantasy, most films with an allegorical bent, including Westerns such as *High Noon* and science fiction such as *Invasion of the Body Snatchers*, in addition to *Lord of the Flies*, begin realistically and reveal their symbolic level with care. *The Cement Garden* takes a different approach: it begins unrealistically and then becomes more realistic as its allegory emerges.

Birkin prepares us for allegory at the outset with details of Father's obsessively neat garden and then a long shot of the house, a rectangular box that might well be made of cement, standing by itself in a wasteland that extends to high rises and cranes on the horizon. This recalls Tati country: everything appears real enough (the location is London's dockland), but the views are stylized, detached. Father, with his pipe and his determination to cover the entire yard with cement, also recalls Tati, though with a darker and far more constricted individualism.

Almost at once Father (who, like Mother, remains nameless) dies of a heart attack while working on the yard. Now the style and, for a time at least, the incidents shift to realism. The four children—Julie (about 17), Jack (16), Susie (12), and Tom (7)—variously squabble, brood, complain, or try to be helpful. Mother keeps busy looking after the household and trying to give the children moral support. But more and more she takes to her bed with a mysterious ailment, until she too dies.

The children decide not to report Mother's death to the authorities for fear they'll be split up among foster homes. Julie and Jack place Mother's body in a large metal locker in the basement and cover it with cement. Unlike the novel, the film doesn't try to explain why no one ever visits the family or inquires about Mother's absence. The stylized opening, along with intermittent shots of the house and its surrounding wasteland, establishes the family's isolation as a nonrealistic given. Also unlike the novel, the children's only interaction with other people away from the house consists of a few brief scenes at the school entrance. These differences could be due at least partly to budget constraints and to necessary changes in duration between written word and image plus sound. Nevertheless, they help to support the film's allegorical implications—the formation of an us-against-the-world group—amid the impact of its visual and aural realism.

After Mother's "burial," Julie acquires a boyfriend, a man named Derek, and it becomes clear that he wants to be accepted as part of the family group. It's also clear that Jack is jealous. Derek notices an odd smell in the house (Julie says it comes from Jack, who hasn't bathed since Mother died) and, in a scene that makes its allegorical point through suspense and believable reactions from all concerned, confronts the children: Isn't there a body under the cement in the basement? The children close ranks against him, and shortly afterward Julie seals his exclusion by going to bed with Jack.

The balance between realism and allegory rests largely on Birkin's skillful use of point of view. The novel is written in the first person with Jack as the narrator. Birkin preserves this focus without any heavy-handed use of subjective techniques. The only voiceovers come from a science-fiction novel that Jack reads, and they're spoken in the American-accented voice of its space-captain hero. The only conspicuous subjective camera views are parallel scenes of Father and Derek at the dining-room table. Birkin's primary strategy is to structure the film on scenes where Jack is present.

However, this strategy isn't applied rigidly. When Father dies, Jack has taken a short bathroom break from helping cement the yard, and the fatal collapse is intercut with his reaching a masturbatory climax. The scene where Derek interrogates the children about the smell in the basement begins shortly before Jack arrives. Such minor exceptions maintain fluidity and an element of surprise without blurring the focus on Jack.

At first he is a completely self-absorbed adolescent, lazy, messy, resentful of criticism and requests, and continually taking the short cut to gratifying his hormones—as his absence from Father's death ironically emphasizes. We, of course, are forced to live with this character, and although we may start out with a little sympathy—in the first subjective shot Father irritatingly nags Jack/us—we may also hope for change. The latitude of Birkin's focus reflects Jack's occasional signs of interest outside himself. He gazes at Mother as she sits lost in thought at the kitchen table with its breakfast debris. He shows an erotic interest in Julie. He even goes out of his way to threaten a bully who persecutes Tom at school.

There are also glimmers of a mind at work: Jack's fascination with the science-fiction novel, flashback memories of the family at the beach, and a striking juxtaposition of quasi-subjective images—bedridden Mother with Julie, Susie, and Tom sitting beside her, followed by a dilapidated bed against a cracked wall in a partly demolished house. This is a superb filmic equivalent of the scene in the novel where Jack explores a demolished house and sees a mattress: "I thought of my own bedroom, of Julie's, my mother's, all rooms that would one day collapse."

Jack begins to "emerge" after Mother's death. Though he can't quite bring himself to drag the body down to the basement (Julie does it), he willingly helps mix cement and cover the body in the locker. The turning point comes after he hears Julie attribute the basement smell to his body. That night Jack wakes to a storm and runs outside to dance naked in the rain. He now keeps himself clean; confronts Derek in the basement; helps Tom get back to sleep when he wakes at night crying; and finally is taken to bed by Julie.

Although these post-storm events are presented as realistically as ever—indeed, the lengthy continuous scene between first-time performers Andrew Robertson as Jack and Birkin's son Ned as Tom is a tour de force of easy naturalism[2]—Jack's behavior now appears in a much stronger allegorical light than before. There are no specific motives for the new Jack, any more than there are for Julie's readiness to have sex with him. Julie has existed more on the allegorical plane from the start, since the focus on Jack leaves her behavior mysterious. So now, at the end, the clearest explanation for their incest appears to be the allegorical one: Julie and Jack choose the solidarity of their group over outsiders.

It seems only natural that the ostensive level and the symbolic level of an allegory should work hand in hand and lead to the same conclusion. In *The Cement Garden*, however, they do not: the film leaves the viewer with a provocative crisscross of reactions. In the final sequence alone, the incest taboo is pitted against the happy tenderness of Julie and Jack, which in turn is pitted against the imminent threat of outsiders—the sound of Derek hammering at the cement in the basement and the flashing lamp of a police car. But the whole film has been quietly accumulating evidence on various sides of the incest/solidarity issue.

Father's death is a reminder that the family is now less stable, more vulnerable to outside forces. When Mother takes to her bed, the children tend to gravitate to her room: even Jack joins in when his 16th birthday party is held there. Planning to go into hospital, Mother tells Jack that he and Julie will have to be "father and mother." After her death, the children's desire for "family" becomes an obsession.

Seen as part of a narrative rather than a case study, the sexual elements that now emerge present a more varied picture than Dr. Alpert's preconceptions allow. Whereas Jack's staring at Julie's crotch belongs to the genital role of "father and mother," his brushing cement from her face after the basement burial implies affection and companionship. Later, when Julie and Susie dress Tom up as a girl, Jack is almost as shocked as Dr. Alpert; but Julie points out that it's okay for a girl to wear pants and a boy's shirt, implying that the converse is stigmatized not by sexual perversion but by sexism. When Jack climbs into Tom's bed to talk him to sleep he is naked, but there's no sign of any sexual inclination toward his kid brother. Narratively, all of these incidents mark the children's increasing physical and mental closeness that culminates in incest. There is a double irony here. Physical closeness blinds Jack and Julie to the imminent threat from Derek and the police; and Jack's progress from self-centered individual to group member has now spiraled around to bring him the gratification he always wanted.

Films rarely focus on the complex tension between individualism and solidarity. In most cases, either the two forces are blended in mutual loyalty (all for one and one for all) or any conflict between them is resolved in the triumph of one or the other. *The Cement Garden* begins by having viewers identify with an unappealing individualist and ends by confronting them with the equation, group solidarity = incest. Thus the question of when and to what extent individualism/solidarity is good in any group (familial, ethnic, political, national, etc.) vibrates through the entire fabric of the film. Not that *The Cement Garden* can be reduced to its allegory—the realistic details are too vivid and distinct for that. But the provocative question it leaves open at the end accounts for much of the film's power.

NOTES

1. In the *Encyclopedia of Poetry and Poetics* (ed. Alex Preminger, Princeton University Press, 1965), Northrop Frye writes: "We have allegory when the events of a narrative obviously and continuously refer to another simultaneous structure of events or ideas, whether historical events, moral or philosophical ideas, or natural phenomena." Many other definitions exist, and the borders between allegory, symbolism, fable, myth, etc., are in continual dispute.
2. All four children's roles are performed superbly, As Julie, Charlotte Gainsbourg (Birkin's French niece via his sister Jane) is the only one with previous film experience. Alice Coulthard as Susie was actually younger than her screen character. In addition, Sinead Cusack is effective as Mother, and two bilingual actors, Hanns Zischler and Jochen Horst, are more than adequate as Father and Derek (the film had German financing). Interestingly, the family group is represented by four different nationalities.

LOS ANGELES TIMES, 2/24/94, Calendar/p. 4, Peter Rainer

Most movies are so bland that occasionally the sheer *differentness* of a plot, an idea, a character can count for a lot. But sometimes a cigar is just a cigar and sometimes weirdness is just weirdness. "The Cement Garden," adapted from the 1978 Ian McEwan novel, certainly gets points for being different, but is it good?

The film opens with the kind of ghastly dysfunctional family dinner scene that immediately deposits us in Weirdsville. Jack (Andrew Robertson) is a surly, languid, pimply 15-year-old. His eldest sister Julie (Charlotte Gainsbourg) is combative. Their younger sister and brother, Sue (Alice Coultard) and Tom (Ned Birkin), seem normal until the plot kicks in. (Tom, for example, enjoys dressing up as a girl and wearing wigs to dinner.)

Their parents, played by Hanns Zischler and Sinead Cusack, are a classic mismatch: He's a martinet, she's an earth-mother realist. They live in a block-like building in the middle of nowhere on the rubbishy outskirts of London. When Father wants to cement over their garden, Jack discovers the joys of masturbation. His climax coincides with Father's collapse from a heart attack.

And so it goes.

McEwan's novel was celebrated for its matter-of-fact surrealism and the film, written and directed by Andrew Birkin, manages to capture McEwan's air of nightmare plausibility. But it's a coy, drab, chuckling nightmare. When the four kids also lose their mother, they contrive a cement coffin in the cellar and proceed to play out their oddest tendencies. Jack, who is priapic toward Julie in a dreamy, disconnected way, spends most of his time circling around her seductions. (She snipes at him, then asks him to rub her back with suntan lotion.) When she takes up with a rich, sporty twit (Jochen Horst), Jack's distress becomes painfully comic. Jealousy makes him industrious.

Birkin at least has the good sense to let this material play itself out without winking at the audience. He understands the demented complacency at the heart of McEwan's particular madness. A few of the performances, notably from Cusack and Gainsbourg (whose French accent, amazingly, is nowhere to be heard), are inspired.

But the direction isn't. Too often the matter-of-fact nuttiness is just blah. Cocteau and Polanski and Bunuel worked with similar material and managed to make their movies hair-raising without losing their cool. With Birkin, cool is just about all there is. His straight face is encased in cement.

NEW YORK, 2/14/94, p. 106, John Powers

Andrew Birkin's *The Cement Garden* is a slow, queasy adaptation of Ian McEwan's brisk, queasy novel of the same title. Set amid the urban wasteland of the London docklands, it shows how four siblings reconstitute a new kind of family after the death of their parents: It begins with a hormone-racked teenager masturbating as his father has a heart attack, and ends with a brother going to bed with his sister. Although the young actors are terrific, the movie doesn't yield its meanings easily. It hints at many themes—the origin of gender roles, the triumph of nature over culture, the future of England itself—but preserves the hermetic density of a parable. Or so I thought until I opened the film's press kit and found a commentary by one Judith Alpert, an NYU expert in sexual abuse who knows exactly what the movie is about: sibling incest. "One wonders what went on off-screen in this family which would lead to such breaking of boundaries and taboos," she writes. "This is a film of deeply troubled individuals. It shows the type of family structure which can lead to this perverted behavior."

Is anything more antithetical to art than the therapy worldview? The fact is, *The Cement Garden* isn't really a film about sibling incest, not does it depict the kids as engaging in "perverted behavior." On the contrary, the movie suggests that there is something grand and life-affirming about the moment the brother and sister finally lie together naked in bed. Now, many viewers will find this revolting or even reprehensible, but it's better that they be furious at Birkin and McEwan than be cowed by Alpert's expertise into thinking this movie is somehow supposed to be good for them.

NEW YORK POST, 2/11/94, p. 36, Michael Medved

"The Cement Garden" focuses on a British clan so hopelessly dysfunctional and lavishly weird that it makes the Addams family look like the Cleavers.

Father (Hanns Zischler) spends most of his energy covering their desolate back yard with concrete (hence the title) and in the midst of these exertions he drops dead.

At the precise moment of his demise, his teen-aged son (Andrew Robertson) is involved in one of his endless bouts of masturbation.

Shortly thereafter, Mother (Sinead Cusack) dies of a handy mysterious disease and her four fun-loving kids entomb her body in a cement-filled locker in the basement.

With both parents gone, the kids separate themselves from the outside world and make their grim home into an eccentric island in a sort of urban, co-educational version of "Lord of the Flies."

The 7-year-old boy (Ned Birkin) puts on his mother's wigs and begins dressing like a girl in order to play "house" with a macho little pal. The sophisticated and self-assured 17-year-old daughter (Charlotte Gainsbourg) endlessly tempts and teases her 15-year-old brother, despite the fact that he smells awful due to his refusal to bathe for weeks at a time.

She overcomes this barrier and initiates ecstatic, romantic, and lavishly detailed inter-sibling sex.

As this peculiar plot suggests, "The Cement Garden" is intended for what might politely be described as a "select audience." But those who are intrigued by the subject matter will find much to admire in this unusually artful, thoroughly disturbing film.

All the young actors deliver extraordinary performances and they interact as if they actually grew up together. This may in part reflect the fact that female lead Gainsbourg is the niece of writer/director Andrew Birkin, while the cross-dressing 7-year-old is played by his own son, Ned.

Gainsbourg, an accomplished French star at age 22, makes a particularly strong impression. She and co-star Andrew Robertson (making his movie debut at age 17), emit an unmistakably androgynous quality.

Despite obvious skill with his actors, director Birkin gets carried away with desolate lunar landscape visions of London's Dockland district, in a vain attempt to lend deeper significance to the story.

In an even more embarrassing effort to provide an aura of importance to this incestuous adventure, the producers gave the press copies of comments on the film by a psychology professor.

When filmmakers rely on academic speculation to explain what seems inexplicable on screen, you know they have a problem. For all its strengths, "The Cement Garden" remains a murky muddle—more a curiosity than an accomplishment.

NEWSDAY, 2/11/94, Part II/p. 79, John Anderson

Imagine a sexual "Lord of the Flies" set in a squalid Never Never Land, populated by Oedipal wrecks and equipped with a stern Warning for Parents: Don't drop dead, because your offspring will be indulging their basest instincts before the bodies are cold.

Such is Andrew Birkin's "The Cement Garden," based on Ian McEwan's respected novel, about four orphaned siblings who find themselves cast adrift in a world without boundaries and create their own moral universe. That was what the book was about, at least. Screenwriter-director Birkin is interested more in the incest, onanism and squalor that decorated McEwan's book than with the spiritual dereliction that was at its base. But if his aim was merely to evoke disgust, he's overshot the mark.

Long before the compulsively self-abusive Jack (Andrew Robertson) and his nubile older sister, Julie (Charlotte Gainsbourg), turn this into a real family affair, the gaminess is afoot, The home of their unhappy, unnamed group is a grimy cement box set in an English wasteland of gas tanks and garbage, trash-strewn lots and bombed-out houses. Jack's father (Hanns Zischler), a dictatorial pipe-smoker with a nasty hack, enlists Jack's help in the task of cementing over their grubby backyard, but Jack would rather steal off to the attic to pleasure himself. Dad, in the meantime, has a fatal heart attack.

That they suffer their climactic moments simultaneously is just the first linking of sex and death, and it's not the last; Jack and Julie's eventual coupling is treated like a liberating, existential suicide. But at least at the beginning Birkin gives us quick cuts and startling little bursts of noise and lights—which makes you wonder whether he indeed has something up his sleeve. If he does, it's still there.

Like Mom (Sinead Cusack), "The Cement Garden," suffers a slow death; unlike Mom, the film is not then entombed in the basement in a locker full of cement. It pursues the disintegration of the children, who keep their mother's death secret for fear of being institutionalized, and does so while evoking absolutely no sympathy for them.

Jack and Julie circle, sniff and skirt each other's territory, while the house accrues a patina of filth, food rots, and Jack refuses to bathe. The younger children suffer their own regressive symptoms. The intrusion of reality is Julie's wealthy and much older boyfriend, Derek (Jochen Horst), who must be a dim bulb considering how long it take's him to figure things out. But then again, I sat through this entire movie.

SIGHT AND SOUND, 11/93, p. 38, Christopher Bray

Jack is an unhappy and unkempt adolescent who has an uneasy relationship with his family. His resentment of his father is the focus for his adolescent frustrations. One day, while pouring cement over his weed-infested garden, Jack's father collapses and dies. Soon after, Jack's mother dies and, together with his older sister Julie, he decides to 'bury' his mother in a filing cabinet full of cement in the cellar. Fearful of being taken into care and separated, Jack and Julie take over the running of the house including taking care of their younger siblings, Sue and Tom. Soon Jack is shrinking away from responsibility, refusing to shop, clean or even wash himself. Julie begins a relationship with a property developer, Derek, whose intrusion into the house threatens Jack with the reinstatement of normal values. Derek is shocked to find Tom wearing a wig and a dress and becomes suspicious of the odour in the cellar. Returning unbidden one night he finds Jack and Julie making love and calls the police.

The auteurist critic does not have to look very far to find the thematic core of Andrew Birkin's work. Birkin is interested in youth. He wrote *The Lost Boys* for television and adapted *Peter Pan* for NBC. Now he has written and directed an adaptation of Ian McEwan's first novel, *The Cement Garden*. Being about teenage incest, *The Cement Garden* has taken a long time to get to the big screen; British television was unwilling to finance the film because of its risky subject. Maybe the subject is a risky one, but Birkin is no fast-buck sensationalist. This is a restrained and dignified film, "sensitive to its subject matter, generous in its instincts, emotionally wise and moving", in the words of Ian McEwan himself. All McEwan missed out was the bit about faithful to its source. Aside from a few minor changes in dialogue and the never quite explained transformation of Julie's boyfriend Derek from snooker-playing no-good to Thatcherite property developer, the film is a virtual facsimile of the novel.

Birkin is as interested in the disgusting detail as is McEwan. Early on, we are treated to a close-up of a gob of spittle douching a wall before a cigarette is lazily doused in it. Andrew Robertson, the spitter in question, has a face as pure as Perrier, but the camera likes to linger on the spots it develops when he stops washing.

It lingers on broken bricks and shattered glass too. The film is set in a run-down place, and while watching it I thought it had been made in Germany (it is part German financed). Certainly the house—which Birkin contrives to make look more like a child's drawing of home, with four windows and a door always seen flat on—seems not to be of this country. Birkin isolates it so well that it doesn't feel to be a part of any country; yet the film was shot in the no-man's land of London's Docklands. More properly, we are in no-adults' land. With both parents dead, the children inhabit a world where taboos can be broken.

Just as his characters eschew social norms, McEwan eschewed generic conventions in order to prevent his novel from sliding into the Gothic. Indeed, all the Gothic elements are there—the abandoned house, the overbearing patriarch, the dead mother in the cellar. But McEwan's lucid detachment ensured the genre's thematic baggage takes a back seat. The novel may well be an examination of the social construction of gender, but before it is that it is a beautifully written story. Birkin, however, is not so subtle. He makes Julie's speech about repressive dress codes the pivot of the film, clumsily shooting it in a succession of close-ups just to make sure we get the point.

Unlike McEwan, Birkin is too conscious of style to remain an onlooker. There is a lot of wide- and low-angle work here, designed to reinforce the weirdness of what we are watching. Exterior shots are heavily filtered with nacreous pinks and yellows. The interior of the house, all claustrophobic darkness and slats of light, is like something out of a *film noir*. The dust in the air isn't there just to tell us that the kids don't look after the place; Birkin is in love with the way the dust looks. As with camerawork, so with editing: Birkin pointedly cross-cuts between Jack wanking in the bathroom and his father's grubby death in a mound of wet cement. With its rhythms and rhymes of movement, the sequence looks good, but there is no thematic justification for this montage.

An obsession with form at the expense of content is the mark of a tyro director. Birkin is not a great director yet, but he does have his virtues. The film's closing shot of Jack and Julie in bed together, their bodies gradually suffused with the blue strobe of the police lights, has a quiet dignity. And Birkin clearly has a way with actors. In a film without a bad performance, it seems unfair to single out any one player, but the diffidently surly newcomer Andrew Robertson is a revelation. Blase and self-conscious, his Jack is so accurate a gangly adolescent that he can't even lean arrogantly against a wall without doubting himself. The film's best moment is when Jack, after his mother's death, lazily wipes a piece of toast across a slab of butter. It is a devastating detail all the better for not being lingered upon. In it one senses the seeds of a film-maker not in thrall to stylistics.

VILLAGE VOICE, 2/8/94, p. 64, Alyssa Katz

When The *Cement Garden* holds back on its sibling lovers. refusing to offer anything more to gawk at than what's offered in its raunchy trailer—BUT JU-LEE. HE"S YOR

BRUTHARR!—it's tempting to read the move as a clever tease, frustrating our own lurid desires for incestuous consummation. If the film were as creepily unassuming as the 1978 Ian McEwan novel it's based on, it could go far on the suggestion that the thrill of incest lies less in the act itself than in the rewriting of everyday encounters as self-centered fantasies, imaginary routes from familial alienation to absolute belonging. But trashy fun like this—relishing every omen of transgression while feigning to eat the cake of high art, too—doesn't have the luxury of restraint. The payoff is decidedly wimpy.

Pimply and pasty behind a mop of burnout hair, Jack (Andrew Robertson), as his name might suggest, is a slave to Onan and Narcissus both, masturbating in front of mirrors and in nests he's made around the posturban wasteland that surrounds his family's bunkerlike home—belatedly answering his father's call for help in the arid titular backyard, he sheepishly explains, "I came as quick as I could." Jack's portentous encounters with his big sister, Julie (Charlotte Gainsbourg, director Birkin's niece) would seem merely loopy if they weren't so gleefully deliberate. They and their two younger siblings squabble at breakfast; milk splashes on Julie's cheek. She wipes it away languorously while dreamily locking eyes with her brother, her knees akimbo under schoolgirl pleats. At Jack's 15th birthday party, Julie executes a flawless spread-legged handstand, prompting him to sing ."Greensleeves" in a cracking falsetto.

Their encounters get played for titillation, not opprobrium. an approach rendered feasible by the casting of actors who look not at all like sister and brother. The boyishly winsome Gainsbourg—who came of age as a performer singing "Lemon Incest," a hit duet with her father, Serge, the late Leonard Cohen of France—and the perfectly unpleasant Robertson don't project sexual engagement as much as they do the seductiveness of teen androgyny. *The Cement Garden* gets that point right, at least, and it doesn't entirely fail to penetrate the half-baked mind space of children faithfully aping the fecklessness of adults. But who wants to see it for *that?*

Also reviewed in:
CHICAGO TRIBUNE, 3/4/94, Friday/p. J, Michael Wilmington
NEW YORK TIMES, 2/11/94, p. C24, Caryn James
VARIETY, 3/8/93, p. 61, Derek Elley
WASHINGTON POST, 4/1/94, p. D6, Rita Kempley

CHANTONS SOUS L'OCCUPATION

An Argos Films release produced by Argos Films, Les Films Armorial and the Institut National de l'Audiovisuel. *Director:* André Halimi. *Commentary (French with English subtitles):* André Halimi. *Director of Photography:* Jean Rouch. *Editor:* Henri Colpi and Michel Valio. *Running time:* 95 minutes. *MPAA Rating:* Not Rated.

NARRATOR: Pascal Mazzzoti

NEW YORK POST, 11/25/94, p. 44, Larry Worth

Everyone remembers Maurice Chevalier for immortalizing "Thank Heaven for Little Girls." But did the heart of a collaborator fuel his Gallic charm?

And what of Edith Piaf? Was "the little sparrow" guilty of supporting the Third Reich since she continued to perform during its reign in the City of Light?

The conduct of Frenchmen and women under the Nazi occupation of Paris is one of those subjects doomed to endless moralizing and second-guessing. But director Andre Halimi tackles new ground by examining the culpability of entertainers during France's darkest hours.

Though getting off to a meandering start, "Chantons Sous L'Occupation" ("Singing Through the Occupation") mixes compelling modern-day interviews with French and German newsreel footage, producing fascinating, thought-provoking results.

According to Halimi, the gaiety never stopped, despite troopers marching through the Arc de Triomphe. Photos of the citizenry at amusement parks, the races or attending plays infer that many coped by sticking their heads in the sand.

And as the likes of Piaf and Chevalier continued to appear in clubs frequented by German officers or were heard on Radio Paris, the question arises; Were they merely boosting Frenchmen's morale—as they claimed—or supporting the Nazis' agenda?

There's plenty of arguments from both sides, with many who lived through the horror branding the troupers as traitors. Then again, they also castigate milliners who used fabric from a German patent.

Others say that at least the Germans were gentlemen, unlike the first American troops. One woman recalls the seductiveness of an SS man's smile, to which even the actress Arletty succumbed. She gained fame not only as the beautiful centerpiece of Marcel Carne's masterpiece, "Children of Paradise," but for her justification of a love affair with a German officer: "My heart is French, but my ass is international."

Where do you draw the line? Halimi seems unsure. Does Jean-Paul Sartre's continuing to produce plays in Paris earn the same condemnation as celebs who made anti-Semitic films or drank pre-war champagne at a German ambassador's party?

Initially, the director leaves it for viewers to draw their own conclusions, which seems the best way to go. But the film's last third gets far too heavy-handed with footage of Holocaust victims being bulldozed into mass graves. Did renowned author Colette's attendance at a Parisian art opening really send them to their deaths?

Another equally silly leap in logic comes when an interview subject states that gay men were drawn in by Germans' power, virility and military uniforms. Are we to assume that no homosexuals could resist the Aryans' siren call? Didn't thousands upon thousands agonizingly perish in concentration camps?

The issues of blame and collusion have been raised on screen before—and with greater success in documentaries such as "The Sorrow and the Pity" and this year's "The Wonderful, Horrible Life of Leni Riefenstahl."

But in "Chantons Sous L'Occupation," one needn't agree with all Halimi's points to applaud his production. And, without exception, each of those points is well worth debating.

NEWSDAY, 11/25/94, Part II/p. B7, John Anderson

For anyone whose image of World War II was formed strictly by Hollywood—Victor Laszlo leading "La Marseillaise" in "Casablanca," for instance—the French during the Occupation were strictly *résistance*, a population of millions devoted to a free France, not a free lunch.

It's an image exploded by Andre Halimi's 1976 documentary "Chantons Sous L'Occupation," or "Singing Through the Occupation," although not without casting lingering doubts about the filmmaker's techniques and intent.

According to Halimi, during the war the nation of France—Paris in particular—remained a place devoted to pleasure, where artists and entertainers amused the conquerors as well as the conquered. In some cases, the entertainers were war profiteers of a sort: As Halimi implies—as faces of the familiar and not so familiar artists fly by—the Nazis certainly provided an opportunity for second-raters who were willing to work when more conscience-stricken artist wouldn't. Who was who, however, is often left up to the viewer.

As a historical document, "Chantons Sous L'Occupation" provides interesting and sometimes disturbing footage, some from newsreels, some from post-war interviews, some from Alain Resnais' "Night and Fog." And while it will never replace "The Sorrow and the Pity" as an indictment of French complicity in its own humiliation, it shines some light in corners: A brothel owner, for instance, recalling the Germans as men who were "generous, paid well and acted the gentlemen." And who made the unheard of request for health tests.

But "Chantons Sous L'Occupation" also possesses a self-righteousness that's disturbing, unpleasant and a director who seems interested chiefly in castigating people for surviving. It's also irresponsible. Halimi runs clip after clip of singers and comedians and "variety artists"—among them Charles Trenet, Maurice Chevalier, Fernandel, Edith Piaf and Sacha Guitry—and the effect is to brand each one equally as a collaborator.

But there's no context: The footage is undated, uncredited and in some instances might even have been made by the Nazis, who were more than astute about the propaganda power of film. Were we to accept the Nazi pages of the Warsaw ghetto, for example—which is the only surviving film footage—it would alter historical perception. Halimi wants simply to place blame where he feels it belongs, of course, but it's too easy to juxtapose nightclub scenes with mass graves to get a visceral reaction. Halimi is too strident, and undermines his own purpose.

VILLAGE VOICE, 11/29/94, p. 73, Leslie Camhi

France as whore is the primary image that emerges from *Chantons Sous L'Occupation (Singing Through the Occupation)*, a provocative documentary on the French entertainment industry's collaboration with Nazi occupiers. Journalist André Halimi's 1976 film opens with an elderly madame explaining that she was sorry when the gentlemanly German soldiers, so careful about hygiene, were replaced by rude Americans. Halimi combines fascinating archival and newsreel footage with interviews he conducted in the '70s to show that occupied Paris was still, as Hitler intended, an International Capital of Pleasure.

Theater and nightlife thrived; Maxime's was hopping. Movie stars like Danielle Darrieux were exported to German film studios, while at home, Cocteau and company entertained visiting German celebrities, Bonnard attended the opening of an exhibit by official Reich sculptor Arno Breker, and Sartre's *Les Mouches* played to a theater full of German soldiers.

Motivated by ambition, enthusiasm, indifference, the hope of using collaboration for secret sub-version, or simply a need for the limelight under any circumstances, prominent French artists (at least the non-Jews among them) conducted business as usual. Did those who sang for a living need to keep working, just like butchers and bakers? Surely Maurice Chevalier didn't have to sound so cheery as his neighbors marched off to Auschwitz; surely he and Edith Piaf might have taken their golden voices elsewhere, though she at least seems sad as she sings hymns to *amour* in the occupied streets. This film, so obsessed with morality, offers the utterly perverse pleasure of hearing all those wonderful forties songs about love, hope, and Paris—though one wonders, as their freedom and fellow citizens lay dead how the performers felt.

Also reviewed in:
NEW YORK TIMES, 11/25/94, p. C12, Janet Maslin
VARIETY, 4/14/75, p. 24

CHASE, THE

A Twentieth Century Fox Films release of a Capitol Films presentation of an Elwes/Wyman production. *Executive Producer:* Eduard Sarlui and Charlie Sheen. *Producer:* Brad Wyman and Cassian Elwes. *Director:* Adam Rifkin. *Screenplay:* Adam Rifkin. *Director of Photography:* Alan Jones. *Editor:* Peter Schink. *Music:* Richard Gibbs. *Music Editor:* Will Kaplan. *Sound:* Tim Himes and (music) Gabriel Veltri and Daniel Buchanan. *Sound Editor:* Hari Ryatt and Gregory King. *Casting:* Jakki Fink. *Production Designer:* Sherman Williams. *Art Director:* Jack Cloud. *Set Decorator:* Craig Loper. *Special Effects:* Bill Purcell. *Costumes:* Yvette Correa. *Make-up:* Vivian Baker. *Make-up (Charlie Sheen):* David Anderson. *Make-up (Kristy Swanson):* Tyger Tate. *Stunt Coordinator:* Buddy Joe Hooker. *Running time:* 87 minutes. *MPAA Rating:* PG-13.

CAST: Charlie Sheen (Jack Hammond); Kristy Swanson (Natalie Voss); Henry Rollins (Officer Dobbs); Josh Mostel (Officer Figus); Wayne Grace (Chief Boyle); Rocky Carroll (Byron Wilder); Miles Dougal (Liam Segal); Ray Wise (Dalton Voss); Marshall Bell (Ari Josephson); Joe Segal (Sgt. Hodges); Claudia Christian (Yvonne Voss); Alex Allen Morris (Cop #1); Marco Perella (Cop #2); Wirt Cain (Bill Cromwell); Bree Walker (Wendy Sorenson); Brian Chessney (Officer Robinson); Joe Berryman (Officer Kraus); Natalija Nogulich (Frances Voss); David Harrod (Troy); John S. Davies (Corey Steinhoff); Chamblee Ferguson (Convenience Store Clerk); Larry Clifton (Ned Rice); Paul Dandridge (Himself); Hibbs (Windshield Corpse); Flea (Dale); Anthony Kiedis (Will); Sean McGraw (Tom Capone); Melissa Zoelle (Paige Grunion); Ron Hyatt (Channel 3 Cameraman); R. Bruce Elliot (Frank Smuntz); Cary Elwes (Steve Horsegroovy); Gabriella Lamiel (Lolly Juniper); Deborah Oliver Artis (Police Dispatcher); Windlind Smith (News Director); Steve Smith

(Finale Cop 1); James Black (Finale Cop 2); Eric Glenn (Finale Cop 3); Werner Richmond (Finale Cop 4); Cassian Elwes (The Producer); Brett Schramm (Bleeding Criminal); James Thomas and Michael Allan (Swat Persons).

LOS ANGELES TIMES, 3/14/94, Calendar/p. 14, Peter Rainer

"The Chase" is a no-brainer with the emphasis on the *no*. Charlie Sheen plays a wrongfully convicted bank robber running away from prison who inadvertently kidnaps an heiress (Kristy Swanson) and spends most of the movie speeding away from the police in her bright-red BMW.

Will a movie about a high-speed L.A. freeway chase satisfy an audience's fantasies for flight at a time when the freeways are cracked? Inquiring minds want to know.

The writer-director Adam Rifkin attempts to work some deep-think about tabloid media manipulation into this rollicking piece of movie road kill, but the film seems to be part of what it is attacking. It would take a more—uh—sophisticated touch to make the car flips and flame-outs in this film seem as hilarious as they are meant to be. Maybe Robert Altman, in his media-circus "Nashville" mode, could have done it. On the other hand, he would not have wanted to.

Sheen and Swanson go in for a lot of high-octane mugging but Josh Mostel, as one of the cops in pursuit, is fun, and there's a good bit involving cadavers.

That figures.

NEW YORK POST, 3/4/94, p. 34, Thelma Adams

Writer/director Adam Rifkin cuts to "The Chase"—and that's all there is to this stalled Charlie Sheen vehicle.

Jack Hammond (Sheen), convicted of a crime he didn't commit, escapes en route to prison. Cornered in a convenience store by two cops, Hammond grabs a hostage Natalie Voss (Kristy Swanson), and wisecracks to Mexico in her BMW.

It could happen!

While the police follow in hot pursuit, Sheen ("Wall Street") cruises along with his charm in low gear. Will these aging brat-packers look like boys until they're collecting Social Security?

Blonde-and-busty co-star Kristy Swanson starts out shrill and turns steely, showing some of the Valley Girl spunk that made her "Buffy the Vampire Slayer" so much fun.

"You can't kidnap somebody and expect them to be cute," Natalie tells Jack although she is. The duo rev the sex appeal—but they're all charged up with no place to go but an obligatory sex scene by the stick shift.

Newscaster Bree Walker, actor Cary Elwes, and Red Hot Chili Peppers' Flea toss off cameos between the puke-crotch-and-cadaver humor the script runs over like speed bumps.

"The Chase" is likely to park itself in mall cineplexes where it will play to the acne-set for whom it was aimed.

There was a time when moviegoers complained that car chases had taken over action flicks. Now along comes a movie that's all chase and no action.

NEWSDAY, 3/4/94, Part II/p. 81, Terry Kelleher

From the trailer you'd think "The Chase" was nothing but burning rubber, overturned vehicles and dangerous foreplay in the front seat of a speeding BMW.

In fact, that's only 75 percent of the movie (or about 74 percent too much). The rest is a well-targeted, if crudely executed, satire on the insatiable appetite of TV news for sensation "breaking stories." Unfortunately, by the time "The Chase" runs its course, the good stuff has faded in the rearview mirror.

Charlie Sheen, who really should have outgrown these parts by now, stars as Jack Hammond, a scruffy but decent Californian who decides to bolt for Mexico rather than do hard time for an armed robbery he honestly and truly did not commit. He stops at a convenience store for a Butterfinger and some butts, and wouldn't you know it? A couple of cops spot his stolen car. So Jack grabs a handy young female, commandeers her luxury import and tromps on the accelerator, promising to let her out at the earliest opportunity.

Problem No. 1: The hostage, Natalie Voss (Kristy Swanson), turns out to be the daughter of Dalton Voss (Ray Wise), whom the script describes as "the Donald Trump of California, one of the richest men in America." Suddenly, catching Jack has become area law enforcement's top priority.

Problem No. 2: Natalie, though pretty, is a spoiled, whiny nuisance.

Problem No. 3: Jack's flight is an instant media event. In one of the numerous police cars pursuing him, the officers are accompanied by a crew from a TV "reality" show called "The Fuzz." Also on Jack's tail are a traffic copter and several vans representing desperately competing local news operations.

Problem No. 1 is handled predictably, The police chief (Wayne Grace) is an idiot. The West Coast Trump is a flaming idiot. Jack can outwit them and their minions with one wit tied behind his back.

Problem No. 2 is handled even more predictably. Jack disarms Natalie with perceptive questions like: "So why do you hate your stepmom?" Natalie starts falling in love with her captor and reciting clichés like: "I don't know why, but I believe you, Jack."

Problem No. 3 is not a problem, as far as comedy is concerned. The TV news teams all have pseudo-authoritative anchors and hot-doggy slogans ("Channel 17 Hard-Core News"). The traffic reporter (Rocky Carroll) does an "unbelievable!" play-by-play worthy of ESPN's Dick Vitale.

But writer-director Adam Rifkin, who showed a taste for the disgusting in "The Dark Backward," feels compelled to counterbalance the actual humor with corpses tumbling onto the freeway and Natalie's flying vomit drenching a police car's windshield. In a shocking lapse of manners for an heiress, Natalie forgets to pop a breath-freshening mint before she and Jack draw "kissing close" at 90 mph.

SIGHT AND SOUND, 7/94, p. 39, Nick James

A dust-covered Mercedes draws into a Californian service station and out steps a nervous young man, Jack Hammond. A patrol car pulls up, and two policemen stroll in. Their radio reports a runaway prisoner who has stolen a Mercedes. Confronted by them, Jack kidnaps a young woman bystander, and drives off with her in her red BMW.

Local squad cars are soon in pursuit. Officers Dobbs and Figus have a documentary video team in the back when they get the call. They are directly on Jack's tail as he hits the freeway heading towards Mexico. Jack discovers that his hostage is Natalie Voss, daughter of powerful magnate Dalton Voss. The police assume that Jack deliberately kidnapped Natalie, and Voss' arrival at police headquarters prompts an all-out effort. Soon the news networks are broadcasting the high-speed chase from helicopters. Jack, who has long protested his innocence of the crime he was jailed for, calls his lawyer from the car. Voss calls and tries to bully and bribe him; seeing how unimpressed Jack is by her father's power, Natalie becomes more sympathetic.

An armed pursuit car attempts to box Jack in. He shoots out the tyres and the car tumbles off the road. A second attempt to stop Jack, engineered by two redneck 'road warriors' ends in their colliding with a truck, but they live on to be interviewed for a news report. As the BMW nears the Mexican border, where a roadblock awaits, Jack and Natalie make love. At the border, Jack pulls off the freeway and comes to a halt. He makes Natalie walk to safety with the gun in her bag. He then gets out, and is shot.

However, this proves to be an imagined scene. Instead, Jack comes out slowly and submits to being cuffed and abused by the cops, and then punched by Voss. But Natalie, holding documentary director Byron Wilder at gunpoint, makes the cops uncuff Jack and then hijacks her father's helicopter and convinces the pilot to fly them to freedom.

Taking a linear car chase from A to B as the basis for a film leads one to expect one of two things. We are likely to get either a technical exercise in dynamic visual thrills and spills which puts the viewer in the driver's seat, or a soulful road movie genre piece which tips its hat to the Badlands tradition. Being a typically unambitious post-modern hybrid, Adam Rifkin's film aims for a dash of both flavours. But he is no more able to dream up a new one than he is to take the tongue out of his cheek.

Certainly this half-witted, half-engaging semi-spoof jumps between its various image-gathering sources with skill and aplomb, thereby energising the chase once it has hit the straight and narrow of the freeway. Clearly, the home video boom has brought the jumpy camera style beloved of independent film-makers back into the mainstream as a routine signifier of energy. Clearly too, it acts as a translator when television images are co-opted for feature film, as they are here in abundance; *The Chase* makes liberal use of TV material in the currently prevalent hand-held video-diaries style.

However, hard as he tries, Rifkin fails to find a successful equivalent interplay in the dramatic material. The overall effect is of cleverness for its own sake, of reaching only as far as the next Californian in-joke—whether it be in the earnest and thoughtful cop routines of Henry Rollins and Josh Mostel (a standard trope of US cop shows such as *NYPD Blue*); the use of famous Californian newscasters; Charlie Sheen's 'which spoof is it this week?' eyebrow fencing; or the casting against type of hardcore punk ranter Rollins as a monomaniacal cop. Rifkin aims for the kind of satire that informs Altman's *The Player*, substituting the news-gathering industry for Hollywood, but he lets the fun and frolics blunt his edge.

VILLAGE VOICE, 3/22/94, p. 54, Devon Jackson

No, Roger and Gene, this isn't a poorer remake of Spielberg's lugubrious *Sugarland Express*, it's a parody of that film and a zillion other Hollywood car-chase scenes and flicks—all crammed in under the hood of a Charlie Sheen vehicle. Charlie Sheen. Name means? "Over the top"? The Jimmy Woods Jr. who was parodying himself since way back but didn't realize it until just a couple movies ago?

With a plot as pathetic as any other big-budget spectacle (Sheen's a wrongfully convicted nobleguy on the lam who kidnaps rich girl Kristy Swanson in a gas/food store, leading the cops and the media on an extended high-speed chase to Tijuana), writer-director Adam Rifkin has made a cartoon as stupidly entertaining as *Lethal Weapon 2*. Only here the tone lies somewhere between the corniness of *Airplane*! and the wired insanity of *Killer Klowns From Outer Space*: While being hotly pursued, Sheen and Swanson make goofy front-seat love against a ridiculously fake up-in-the-Kodak-clouds backdrop; earlier, corpses spill out onto the highway and into oncoming traffic.

At first, Rifkin's hyperkinetic camera style (imagine *NYPD Blue* on speed) feels empty and strangely slow, but for once, the casting of hipsters—Henry Rollins (who overacts beautifully as a gung-ho cop), Buster Poindexter, porn star Ron Jeremy, and Chili Peppers Flea and Anthony Kiedis—pays off. They add some zip.

Best of all, though, is Rifkin's dead-on burlesquing (*The Dark Backward* ring any love-hate bells?) of TV news—here, it's *Hardcore*—and its anchorpeople. It seems so easy to do, yet until now only *RoboCop* and *Bob Roberts* portrayed this medium for the maddeningly vacuous beast it's turned into. And the scene of Sheen and Swanson singing along to "Macho Man" will become a rewind treasure.

Also reviewed in:
CHICAGO TRIBUNE, 3/4/94, Friday/p. B, John Petrakis
NEW YORK TIMES, 3/4/94, p. C14, Stephen Holden
VARIETY, 3/7-13/94, p. 60, Brian Lowry
WASHINGTON POST, 3/4/94, p. C9, Hal Hinson

CHASERS

A Warner Bros. release of a Morgan Creek production. *Executive Producer:* Gary Barber. *Producer:* James G. Robinson. *Director:* Dennis Hopper. *Screenplay:* Joe Batteer, John Rice and Dan Gilroy. *Story:* Joe Batteer and John Rice. *Director of Photography:* Ueli Steiger. *Editor:* Christian A. Wagner. *Music:* Dwight Yoakam and Peter Anderson. *Music Editor:* Jim Henrikson. *Sound:* Roger Pietschmann. *Sound Editor:* Gregg Baxter and Wylie Stateman. *Casting:* Mary Jo Slater. *Production Designer:* Robert Pearson. *Art Director:* Natalie Wilson. *Set Decorator:* Kate Sullivan. *Set Dresser:* Drew Sywanyk. *Special Effects:* Michael Schorr. *Costumes:* Michael Boyd. *Make-up:* Allan Apone and Dean Jones. *Stunt Coordinator:* Eddy Donno. *Running time:* 112 minutes. *MPAA Rating:* R.

CAST: Tom Berenger (Rock Reilly); William McNamara (Eddie Devane); Erika Eleniak (Toni Johnson); Crispin Glover (Howard Finster); Matthew Glave (Rory Blanes); Grand L. Bush (Vance Dooly); Dean Stockwell (Salesman Stig); Bitty Schram (Flo); Gary Busey (Sgt. Vince Banger); Seymour Cassel (Master Chief Bogg); Frederic Forrest (Duane); Marilu Henner (Katie); Dennis Hopper (Doggie); Scott Marlowe (Fast Food Clown); Jim Grimshaw (Chief Yarboro); Mick McGovern (State Trooper); Charles Page (Guard Box Marine); Richard Pelzman (Redneck Guy); Laura Cathey (Checkout Girl); Jim Bath (Salvage Yard Guy); Michael Flippo (Biker Bartender); Rick Warner (Master Chief); Robert Priester (Seaman #1); Gene Dann (Wino); Jon Rodgers (Seaman #2); Michael Martin (Elderly Man); Matthew Sullivan (Seaman #3); Victori Duffy (Female Sailor #1); Michael O'Brien (Lieutenant); Elizabeth Hawkins (Female Sailor #2); Tony Donno (Ball Retriever); Wallace Wilkinson (Preacher); Robert Pentz (Street Tough #1); Jackson Pinckney III (Street Tough #2); Jimmy Lee Sessoms (Street Tough #3); Melissa Detwiler (Person #1 on Bridge); Ted Detwiler (Person #2 on Bridge); Bob Dorough (Piano Player/Singer); John Christopher Stuart (Flag Raiser); Toni Prima (Tour Guide).

LOS ANGELES TIMES, 4/25/94, Calendar/p. 2, Kevin Thomas

"Chasers" combines raucous humor and unflagging zest with considerable wit and sophistication as Yeoman Second-Class Eddie Devane (William McNamara), at the Charleston, S.C., naval base, finds himself assigned to Chief Petty Officer Rock Reilly (Tom Berenger) to drive to the marine brig at Camp Lejeune, N.C., and transport a prisoner back to Charleston. Tough-guy, by-the-book Reilly, as gravel-voiced as George C. Scott's Gen. Patton, sizes up the cocky Eddie as a "poster boy for petty crime"—little does he know just how well Devane has done for himself in the Navy Supply and Inventory Control. As mismatched as they are, they're both floored when their prisoner, a seaman second-class, turns out to be beautiful and sexy Toni Johnson (Erika Eleniak). The return trip turns out to be a rip-roaring comic adventure. Director Dennis Hopper has the anarchic spirit to make "Chasers" pay off, and writers Joe Batteer, John Rice and Dan Gilroy have provided him with a smart script, a deft mix of slapstick, sharp repartee and sentiment. What's shrewdest about the picture is that it waits till we get involved with this trio thoroughly before Toni's explanation of the inevitable extenuating circumstances of her arrest. The stars are really winning—even McNamara's Eddie, crook that he is—and Hopper has lined up Gary Busey, Crispin Glover, Dean Stockwell, Frederic Forrest and Marilu Henner plus himself for nifty cameos. There's a lot of screwball humor in "Chasers"' classically amoral plot, yet adding to the film's freshness is that visually it's an affectionate running commentary on the amusing tackiness of roadside Americana.

NEW YORK POST, 4/23/94, p. 18, Bill Hoffmann

All good directors are allowed one major turkey and for screen rebel Dennis Hopper, it's "Chasers"—a contrived and tiresome military comedy that will leave you stupified.

Watching this, you can almost forget that Hopper is the man responsible for "Easy Rider," "Colors" and other memorable efforts.

Here his skills are purely pedestrian—"Chasers" might as well be the work of some TV sitcom hack.

Reworking a theme so well done in "The Last Detail," "Chasers" is the story of two Navy men Rock Reilly and Eddie Devane (Tom Berenger and William McNamara) who are assigned to transport a female prisoner (Erika Eleniak) to the brig in what should be a routine six-hour ride through the Carolinas.

Soon she's escaping from the pair by dressing up as a waitress, clogging the gas tank with tampons, stealing the car of a horny motorist, climbing out of a mine shaft and other fun things.

She escapes, they capture her, she escapes, they capture her. You get the idea.

For rough-and-tough Rock, each incident is an outrage; for handsome young softie Eddie, it's a pleasure, as he finds himself falling head-over-heels for their sexy blonde jailbird.

But it's all so predictable and cliched that nothing clicks.

Not even the enjoyable country tunes that invade the sound track every 10 minutes to try to energize the worn antics can help.

A few gags do work. Gary Busey is a panic as the Army sergeant who hates the two Navy men and doesn't let them forget it. And Hopper steals the show as the sexed-up driver with a blow-up doll.

Still, even die-hard Hopper fans are going to be sorely disappointed.

This is definitely Hopper-Lite. Pray the full-strength Hopper returns soon.

NEWSDAY, 4/23/94, Part II/p. B5, John Anderson

Certain directors have created lasting associations with certain physical marvels. For John Ford, there was Monument Valley. For Hitchcock, Mt. Rushmore. For Merian C. Cooper ("King Kong"), the Empire State Building. And, for Dennis Hooper, there's Erika Eleniak.

The amply proportioned actress is certainly the most visually imposing of the three stooges who inhabit "Chasers," an alleged comedy about two sailors assigned to escort a pretty young seawoman to naval prison. And she may also have been the lone cast member who was the first choice for her role.

As the slickly charmless Eddie, who gets stuck with the detail on his penultimate day in the service—and just as he's about to clinch his biggest ripoff yet—William McNamara is clearly doing the Tom Cruise strut, complete with pout. As his reluctant partner, the gruff, tough veteran Rock Reilly (really), Tom Berenger inhabits a dimension somewhere between Jack Nicholson and Victor McLaglen.

The Nicholson lift is appropriate, given that the film is basically a '90s-ization of "The Last Detail" (1974) in which Nicholson and Otis Young took Randy Quaid to prison. Like Quaid's character, Toni (Eleniak) has gotten a raw deal: Denied leave to visit her dying brother, she went AWOL and then assaulted the arresting officer. Now, she faces seven-to-10, and isn't going without a fight.

Which makes Eddie and Rock's duty into a living hell, tempered only by the presence of Toni's voluptuousness, which Rock ogles and Eddie ... well, it's all a prelude to one of her myriad escape attempts, which go on and on with merciless predictability.

Tiresome doesn't begin to describe the plotline, with its predictable car crashes, near-escapes, "colorful" characters and shameless happy ending. Smug, however, would describe McNamara, and woeful might sum up Berenger. Eleniak? She shouldn't wait for silent movies to come back.

Hopper, who has directed infinitely better films than this, should have stayed in one driver's seat at a time: As the lecherous haberdasher who picks up the fleeing Toni in his convertible, Hopper is hysterical. But at the same time, his cameo emphasizes just what a unseaworthy barge the rest of this movie is.

SIGHT AND SOUND, 1/95, p. 43, Nick Hasted

Charleston, South Carolina. On his lat day in the Navy, cocky young con-man 'Fast' Eddie Devane is about to travel cross-country to pick up an illicit Porsche but is assigned to 'chaser' duty, helping the Shore Patrol transport a prisoner back to base. He and his partner, gruff Navy veteran Rock Reilly, discover that due to a clerical error they have been sent to escort a woman, Toni Johnson. Tricked into accepting the prisoner, they set out on their journey. At a diner, Johnson disguises herself as a waitress and escapes, only to have her getaway foiled by bad driving. Next, she causes the van to break down on a disused road. Now on foot, the three fall down a mining shaft. Johnson convinces the men to let her stand on their shoulders and get out; about to escape, she changes her mind and saves them.

The three begin to soften to each other, and exchange family details. Johnson reveals that she was jailed for striking an officer when refused emergency leave to visit her brother, as he lay dying of an overdose. That night, while Reilly sleeps, Johnson overhears Eddie as he discovers his Porsche has been taken in his absence. Later, drunk and depressed, Eddie releases Johnson to have sex. She escapes again, stealing a car, but is again recaptured. Losing their tempers as they lock her up, Reilly and Eddie fight each other to a standstill. Finally, they reach their destination and hand Johnson to the Navy.

The next morning, Reilly, whose sympathy for Johnson has grown, organises her escape, with Eddie's help. A year later, Eddie and Johnson are living in Mexico. They call up Reilly, who is retired and living with a waitress.

The second decline of Dennis Hopper's directing career has gone almost unnoticed, perhaps even by himself. Since the promising fresh start of *Colors*, the man who transformed Hollywood with his debut *Easy Rider*—then found himself thrown to the wolves for a decade after his folly *The Last Movie*—has become something very close to a hack. In recent interviews, Hopper has suggested that he is making films like *Chasers*, and its predecessors *The Hot Spot* and *Catchfire*, almost as a form of politeness—a demonstration of professionalism as a prelude to some new bout of wildness, by which time the studios will be on his side at last. It's a peculiarly ingenuous strategy, and a game only Hollywood can win. Hopper has gambled his creativity on a reward he may never touch, a future made more certain with each small-scale flop. *Chasers* is simply another bad dice-roll. That it's Hopper's worst film seems almost secondary.

In a sense, *Chasers*' faults are a product of one of the several chain reactions that *Easy Rider* sparked. Its script follows the bland youth-fascist assumptions which the briefly radicalised teen movie was reduced to by the onset of the 80s. Tom Berenger's Reilly can ooze character all he likes, but it's the kids that count. This could be stomached if William McNamara were not so vacuous. A Tom Cruise lookalike, communicating all that actor's superficial, sulky smugness, minus the saving hint that he might be acting, McNamara is a hole, permitted to kick Berenger to a standstill because he's young and therefore right. The use of veteran *Baywatch* babe Erika Eleniak, a better actor, is also dumb. Her stripping to her underwear to escape a mineshaft is a prelude to a sex scene designed to uncover her breasts. For all its pretensions to more, *Chasers* is at heart a film for frat-boys.

Surely aware of this weakness, Hopper has stuffed his cast with personal friends and canny improvisors, giving his film a fringe of eccentric naturalism (Dean Stockwell playing with toy cars, Gary Busey muttering about fish, Hopper himself howling, "It's the doggiest day!"). Like the cast of the studio-botched *Catchfire*, which ranged from Vincent Price to Bob Dylan, these friendly faces are a kind of insulation for Hopper's talent from the mess around him.

This sense of an artist not dead but resting is encouraged by *Chasers*' visual aspect. The film in fact achieves a peripheral vision of America which at times approaches profundity, astonishing in the context of such a minor film. Taking images which should be clichés, the familiar neon detritus of roadside signs which litter America, Hopper picks and focuses with such care that an extreme exoticism shows through. Roadside encounters which might otherwise be grotesque — such as Berenger's chasing of a pig-costumed burger waiter, or a fight amid a hail of crazy golf balls — are here funny without a hint of condescension. Seeing America from the typical vantage point of a moving car window, Hopper's eye is working with a clarity superior to *Easy Rider*, and again expressing one of that film's desires—for a wild nation ready to welcome freaks.

However, such attention to the poetry of detail when the big picture stinks is the province not of major directors, but of B-movie craftsmen—and that is the level at which Hopper is now stuck. *Chasers* is clearly the film of a talented man marking time.

Also reviewed in:
NEW YORK TIMES, 4/23/94, p. 15, Janet Maslin
VARIETY, 5/2-8/94, p. 90, Todd McCarthy

CHICKEN HAWK: MEN WHO LOVE BOYS

A Stranger Than Fiction Films release of a Side Man production. *Executive Producer:* Sam Sideman and Peter Smith. *Producer:* Adi Sideman. *Director:* Adi Sideman. *Director of Photography:* Nadav Harel. *Editor:* Nadav Harel. *Running time:* 55 minutes. *MPAA Rating:* Not Rated.

NARRATORS: Barbara Adler and Mimi Turner.

LOS ANGELES TIMES, 8/19/94, Calendar/p. 22, Kevin Thomas

In a calm, straightforward fashion, documentarian Adi Sideman, in "Chicken Hawk: Men Who Love Boys," invites several members of NAMBLA, the 1,500-member North American Man/Boy Love Assn. (which counts poet Allen Ginsberg among its members), to speak for themselves.

They explain that the organization is a support group and does not arrange meetings between men and boys. They all deplore being designated as child molesters, insisting that all forms of intimacy be strictly consensual. Some say they live—or try to live—sexually repressed lives in a society so hostile to them, but others are candid, even defiant, about their determination to have sexual and/or romantic relationships with underage youths.

Sideman also reports on the angry gay community reaction to known boy-lovers, and he examines the thorny challenge it presents to gay-rights leaders, who worry that groups like NAMBLA play into conservatives' fears that adult gays would like to "recruit" young children.

Although it is not possible for Sideman to begin to suggest answers to the emotionally charged issues his subject raises, he fails to deal with a substantial range of questions. We get the impression that none of these otherwise fairly ordinary men are attracted to pre-adolescents, but what age of consent would they pick if they had the choice? A number of them talk about the flirtatiousness of some of the boys with whom they have become involved. They point out that American society, with its puritanical roots, denies how early sexuality occurs in humans.

But what of the whole question of *responsibility* adults have to children, especially in regard to sexual and emotional situations? The irony is that Sideman, in not coming to terms with key implications in his explosive subject, makes himself vulnerable to hate-mongers' accusations that he has merely given NAMBLA a forum to espouse its cause.

"Chicken Hawk" will be preceded by the 25-year-old educational short "Meeting Strangers: Red Light, Green Light," which warns small children against strangers, counseling them to seek out the safety of parents, teachers and police. The film serves as a reminder that nowadays we are more willing to admit that, when it comes to children, no group of adults is automatically "safe."

NEW YORK POST, 7/8/94, p. 42, Larry Worth

It's the most unnerving film since "Psycho."

But "Chicken Hawk" deserves to be seen as it depicts the North American Man Boy Love Association (NAMBLA), for better or for worse. To his credit, director/producer Ari Sideman lets viewers draw their own conclusions: Is it an informative examination of a little-known subculture, or a cautionary peek at pedophiles? Are these ordinary-looking men just misunderstood outcasts, or unconscionable monsters?

One minute, viewers are watching NAMBLA members explain their impulses; the next, horrified parents of young children express their rage at such sentiments.

Among the most haunting scenes is that of a grade school teacher who was suspended for joining NAMBLA, even though he says he never touched a pupil. Gazing out on a playground full of boys, he laments feeling "like Moses overlooking the promised land but unable to enter."

Ditto for another NAMBLA member who talks about how 12- and 13-year-old boys "flirt" with him, which he finds "beautiful."

Those who don't share his feelings are well represented, too, including gays who vociferously denounce NAMBLA. They contend that members' actions contribute to a negative stereotype for all homosexuals.

Sideman competently bounces back and forth between the alternating ideologies, leaving viewers of every persuasion with plenty to think about. But thanks to the 55-minute running time, they're also left with plenty of questions.

Too many situations are presented without the necessary history, making viewers feel like they've walked in on the middle of a story. In addition, NAMBLA's most famous member, poet Allen Ginsberg, is shown addressing a meeting for 20 seconds. But his comments on being part of such a controversial assemblage go begging.

Sideman is far more informative with his look at NAMBLA's support group (featuring men who "try to avoid boys, but can't") or in tracing the history of man-boy relationships to Emperor Nero and Greek heroes from Sparta and Thebes.

Comic relief comes via a 20-minute short, "Meeting Strangers: Green Light, Red Light." Made as an educational film in the '60s, it's like "Reefer Madness" resculpted to address the dangers of child molesters. Most amusingly, it assumes that boys only have to worry about suspiciously friendly men while little girls should beware lonely lesbians. The director seems unaware that pedophiles come in all flavors and aren't necessarily gay.

Ultimately, the teaming of "Chicken Hawk" and "Meeting Strangers," proves auspicious. The package can stand with "Death in Venice," "The Boys of St. Vincent," "The Conviction" and "Lolita" as yet another eye-opening aspect of a subject most prefer to ignore.

NEWSDAY, 7/8/94, Part II/p. B7, John Anderson

Leland Stevenson, who spent several years in prison for the distribution of child pornography, is probably the scariest of the pedophiles who populate Adi Sideman's "Chicken Hawk." Smiling beatifically, wheedling his way into children's confidence as he cruises the strip malls, he recalls his sexual encounters with a joy that's unconfined, and thoroughly monstrous.

For all their quiet-civilized and seemingly rational defense of what is probably society's most loathed aberration, the members of the North American Man-Boy Love Association, or NAMBLA, never deal with the fact that they're interested in children, because they're children. An artist named Chuck Dodson makes fatuous declarations about kids exercising their sexual rights; Stevenson constantly perceives young boys "flirting" with him. But even if any of it were true, it wouldn't matter, because NAMBLA's prey shouldn't be obligated to fend off adult advances while determining their own sexual orientation.

To say Sideman has taken a hands-off position is a horrific pun, but it's also true, and wise. It would have been too easy to become strident, had he set out to make an agitprop piece about the evils of pedophilia. So he lets NAMBLA bury itself. And the organization obliges.

There's a certain grudging respect one gives these men for agreeing to appear onscreen and defend the indefensible. Renato Corazza, a teacher of Italian who claims he never engaged in physical pedophilia attempts to explain the esthetics of boy love, with creepy intelligence. The poet Allen Ginsberg, whose appearance here comes as something of a shock, reads a graphic ode to youth. Peter Melzer, the Bronx High School of Science teacher whose membership in NAMBLA gave WNBC/4's John Miller such a good ride, seems besieged.

The standard, unsubstantiated, arguments in favor of pedophilia are made: that victims often visit their molesters in prison; that boys call NAMBLA constantly in search of partners (and if anyone mentions the ancient Greeks again, I'm burning my Mary Renault books). Their pariah status makes them almost pitiful: At the 1993 gay march on Washington, NAMBLA's members are rightfully reviled for trying to hitch their wagon to a legitimate civil rights movement. And the venom of their antagonists almost makes NAMBLA seem like victims: In one particularly vile phone message left on the group's machine, the speaker's litany of vulgarities includes "kike,"which indicates that perhaps there's something else going on in his head.

But Sideman's most important accomplishment is this: If an adult can be swayed even a little by the case of child molesters, then imagine how easy it might be to seduce a child.

"Chicken Hawk" will be shown with "Red Light, Green Light," a mid-'60s educational film about avoiding "deviants." Obvious and antique, it includes a multi-racial cast of children and a crew of "bad People" who are almost all 30-ish, male, well-dressed and good looking—unlike the members of NAMBLA all of whom fit the stereotype of dirty old men.

VILLAGE VOICE, 7/12/94, p. 50, Gary Indiana

Pedophilia is, not surprisingly, a supercharged topic in America. One could even call it a peculiarly American obsession. Childhood, here, is held to be the condition of asexual innocence to which all Americans aspire. That it is something else was widely known long before Freud, and in many if not most countries in the world, the sexual curiosity of children isn't met with the same horror and puritanical outrage that it is here.

Certainly the bizarre insistence that "children," as an undifferentiated group, be protected from any knowledge about sex until some arbitrary age decided by the state, or by parents, contradicts the realities of the human species. We are the only mammals who compulsively hide our sexual organs, and no doubt the habitual frustration of our natural interest in same produces exactly the kinds of adult pathology depicted in *Chicken Hawk*. In societies where sexual development is openly acknowledged and discussed among parents and children, young people aren't such easy targets for disturbed older people, of whom there are, statistically, far fewer.

In *Chicken Hawk* you have several men, mostly middle-aged, many of them highly educated, who are, to the point of obsessiveness, interested in having "relationships" with extremely young men, apparently in the age range between 10 and 15. Some have served prison terms for various indiscretions. Like all good Americans, they belong to a "support group," namely the North American Man-Boy Love Association, or NAMBLA.

Some of NAMBLA's goals seem reasonable enough: lowering the age of consent to 16, for example. For legal reasons, the NAMBLA newsletter's contents are limited to political argument, suggestive prose, drawings, and merely evocative, nonnude photos of the extremely young males NAMBLA's members pine for while claiming that they avoid any contact with boys for fear of arrest. As an organization, NAMBLA does nothing illicit. However, in individual interviews, these men articulate their desires with such intoxicated specificity that one naturally imagines what they do when they can get away with it, and indeed the creepiest member of the group, one Leland Stevenson, recounts a "camping trip" with a little friend that culminated in anal intercourse. This episode was so natural and joyous that "no lubrication was required." While *Chicken Hawk* conveys no overt parti pris, the juxtaposition of Leland's overheated reveries with the outraged comments of his rural neighbors and the shrugging remark of one of his teen idols that "we knew he was kind of weird" exposes a predatory delusional system operating in high gear. Leland and his NAMBLA friends believe that virtually any youth they happen to fancy is "flirting" with them "in a very wonderful way." This may, of course, be true, but it's also likely that these kids have no idea where flirting might lead with someone like Leland. We see the stout, beaming pederast striking up a conversation with some teens outside a convenience store; into this innocuous brief encounter, he reads a ridiculously elaborate sexual subtext. What we have here is the absurd stuff of obsessive love, and, more alarmingly, the deluded raison d'etre of the stalker.

The other NAMBLA members in *Chicken Hawk* exhibit, to one degree or another, the same longings, but several have a better grip on themselves, including Peter Melzer, the Bronx High School of Science teacher removed from the classroom merely because he belongs to NAMBLA, and Renato Corazza, an Italian teacher whose East Village neighbors have papered the streets with WANTED posters, left obscene messages on his answering machine, and demonstrated outside his apartment building. Neither of these men has ever been arrested; as one of Melzer's students tells the camera, "He didn't do anything. He's not an active pedophile, as far as we know." The flip side of the issue is the gross pathology of NAMBLA's persecutors, who think the mere discussion of pedophilia is equivalent to child molestation. One of Corazza's neighbors, a Buttafuoco-like oaf named Tom McDonough, manfully declares that if he ever caught these people flagrante he would "take no prisoners." Later a voice is heard on Corazza's answering machine, spewing such gems of reasoned argument as "you baby-raping motherfucking cunt-licking kike," reflecting if anything a much richer ensemble of mental problems than Corazza's own. One of McDonough's confederates philosophizes that the gay movement needs NAMBLA because "they're all dying of AIDS, and they don't reproduce, so NAMBLA has to break in new recruits."

The film briefly touches on the nervousness and hostility NAMBLA excites among conventional gay groups, interviewing people at the 1993 Gay and Lesbian March on Washington. The range of opinions here interestingly mirrors that of the straight parents shown elsewhere in the film. Probably the most sensible line in *Chicken Hawk* comes from a woman receiving a pedophile leaflet outside Rockefeller Center: "Grownups should leave kids alone and let them grow up and then decide."

NAMBLA has few friends, and its aims are obviously far outside the mainstream of gay politics. On the other hand, *Chicken Hawk* suggests a lot of pertinent questions about the sexual education of children, about sex between adolescents, and, somewhat distantly, about self-image among homosexuals. While pedophilia is a distinct kind of warp, it can also be viewed as an exaggerated version of the youth worship rampant within the nominal gay community; even today, the sexual viability of male homosexuals over 35 is largely contingent on the possession of money, power, and/or fame, and Fran Lebowitz's classic "Notes on Trick" remains as true today as it was 20 years ago. I think NAMBLA will be around as long as middle-aged gays are too self-revulsed to sleep with each other.

Also reviewed in:
CHICAGO TRIBUNE, 11/4/94, Friday/p. K, John Petrakis
NEW YORK TIMES, 7/8/94, p. C8, Stephen Holden
VARIETY, 6/20-26/94, p. 43, Dennis Harvey

CHINA MOON

An Orion Pictures release of a Tig production. *Producer:* Barrie M. Osborne. *Director:* John Bailey. *Screenplay:* Roy Carlson. *Director of Photography:* Willy Kurant. *Editor:* Carol Littleton and Jill Savitt. *Music:* George Fenton. *Music Editor:* Sally Boldt. *Sound:* Jim Webb. *Sound Editor:* Bill Phillips. *Casting:* Elizabeth Leustig. *Production Designer:* Conrad E. Angone. *Art Director:* Robert W. Henderson. *Set Dresser:* William A. Cimino, Henry Dando, and Rick Recio. *Special Effects:* Lawrence J. Cavanaugh. *Costumes:* Elizabeth McBride. *Make-up:* Carl Fullerton. *Stunt Coordinator:* Artie Malesci. *Running time:* 99 minutes. *MPAA Rating:* R.

CAST: Charles Dance (Rupert Munro); Patricia Healy (Adele); Benicio Del Toro (Lamar Dickey); Ed Harris (Kyle Bodine); Tim Powell (Fraker); Larry Shuler (Patrolman at Turner's); Robb Edward Morris (Pinola); Paul Darby (CSU Photographer); Theresa Bean (Felicity Turner); Pruitt Taylor Vince (Daryl Jeeters); Allen Prince (Assistant M.E.); Madeleine Stowe (Rachel Munro); Gregory Avellone (JJ's Bartender); Sandy Martin (Gun Saleswoman); Joseph E. Louden (Detective); Janis Benson (Rupert's Secretary); Peggy O'Neal (Miami Desk Clerk); Buddy Dolan (Sergeant); Special "K" McCray (Bunny); Robert Koch (Miami Waiter); Roger Aaron Brown (Police Captain); Robert Burgos (Harlan James); Steve Zurk (Patrolman at Hq.); Terrie Jameson (Patrolwoman); Clifton Jones (Dr. Ocampo); Marc Macaulay (CSU Technician); Ralph Wilcox (Ballistic Technician); Michael McDougal (Sheriff).

LOS ANGELES TIMES, 3/4/94, Calendar/p. 8, Peter Rainer

It's been a while since we've had a murder mystery where the lead character talks about the strange things people do under a full moon.

"China Moon," starring Ed Harris as a homicide detective who becomes involved in a crime of passion with a sulky, abused millionaire's wife in Central Florida, played by Madeleine Stowe, is full of portentous mumbo-jumbo.

It's also full of hard-boiled attitudes out of James M. Cain and Raymond Chandler. The combo doesn't quite gel: when Harris' Kyle Bodine announces that he's an "orphan of destiny," you begin to long for Fred MacMurray's Walter Neff to step in and set him straight.

John Bailey, the celebrated cinematographer ("American Gigolo," "Ordinary People") making his directorial debut, doesn't try to shoot the works. His direction is a lot less florid than Ron Carlson's script. (Carlson, according to the press notes,"wroto counterintelligence manuals for the defense industry and the federal government before turning to screenplays.") Bailey's straight-ahead craftsmanship is an honest approach to all the crime-thriller shenanigans and switcheroos; he hews to the characters and this pays off when the surprises come. (When the big plot twist finally kicked in, a woman at the preview screening shouted, "*Now* we have a movie.)

The characters don't have much depth—just enough to elevate them from cardboard to poster board. Without the presence of Harris and Stowe, "China Moon" might have been ridiculous, but they both seem entranced by each other's moody, fixated stares. (On the heels of "Blink," Stowe seem to be making a specialty of ravaged, neurasthenic waifs.)

Perhaps they are playing out an actor's fantasy of enveloping oneself in film-noir fatalism. This may be the fantasy of the filmmakers too, which is why "China Moon" never quite seems real. It's a play-act thriller that retraces all the familiar paces without a wink of wit or irony.

Charles Dance, as the rich rotter of a husband, fits into the scummy pageant with a vengeance, and so does Kyle's partner, Lamar, played with a slippery strangeness by the highly gifted Benicio Del Toro, (He played Rosie Perez's husband in "Fearless.") They all deserve to be in a richer and twistier thriller, but at least "China Moon" keeps you guessing.

NEW YORK POST, 3/4/94, p. 37, Michael Medved

John Bailey is best known as the gifted cinematographer for a series of films by director Lawrence Kasdan, including "The Big Chill," "Silverado" and "The Accidental Tourist." But for his own directorial debut, Bailey chose to rip off another project by his mentor and collaborator.

That would be "Body Heat," and similarities between the now classic William Hurt-Kathleen Turner thriller and Bailey's "China Moon" are not only painfully obvious but entirely unflattering to the current project.

In both movies, a glamorous but lonely socialite seduces an unassuming everyman in small-town Florida and makes use of the poor guy in a complicated plot to bump off her wealthy husband. Since "Body Heat" itself deliberately evoked the "film noir" melodramas of the 1940s, "China Moon" seems doubly derivative; a pale, shadowy, smudged reflection of a reflection with little energy or conviction of its own.

Here, the reliable Ed Harris plays Kyle Bodine, chief homicide detective for the police department of the fictional town of Brayton, Fla.

He lives alone in a tidy trailer and takes great pride in the efficiency and integrity of his work. But one night at a bar, mopping up a few brews with his loyal but seemingly dim-witted partner (Benicio Del Toro), he spots a sulky sexpot played by Madeleine Stowe.

She's the badly abused wife of the town's top banker (played by Englishman Charles Dance, with a nasty sneer and molasses-dripping Southern accent). She soon commences a torrid affair with Harris.

"My grandmother used to say that when the moon is like a big old plate of china strange things happen" Harris declares, explaining the movie's enigmatic title just before he joins his new-found sweetie in a session of skinny-dipping in the waters of a local lake.

Before long, they've graduated to considerably less innocent pastimes, like discussing plans for liberating Stowe from her no-account husband without losing touch with his millions.

One of the movie's strong points is the painstakingly persuasive way it portrays the hero's seduction. Thanks to the sure-footed, sympathetic performance by Harris, you can see why this decent cop gradually abandons the code of honor that's given his whole life meaning.

Stowe, meanwhile, isn't as edgily effective as she was in the recent thriller "Blink" But since she's playing a blank, inscrutable character, her blank, inscrutable performance makes some sense.

She also happens to be so appallingly beautiful that acting seems almost irrelevant. She's arrayed in a collection of jaw-dropping outfits that demand attention even from those who rarely notice clothes in movies.

The problem is that all this style is deployed in behalf of a plot that falls apart completely in the movie's final half-hour. "China Moon" delivers some big surprises, all right, but at the expense of any shred of logic, credibility or coherence.

Director Bailey gives a handsome sheen to his first film, with some nighttime scenes that shimmer with especially evocative atmosphere. But the tired and empty screenplay means that this movie remains nothing more than a good-looking body—that generates no heat.

NEWSDAY, 3/4/94, Part II/p. 81, Gene Seymour

At this late date, it's hard to imagine what could be done with the tale of the poor schnook who lets a beautiful, sinister temptress draw him into the proverbial web of murder and betrayal.

James M. Cain all but purchased the patent on this format in the '30s with "Double Indemnity" and "The Postman Always Rings Twice." It's proven durable enough to withstand any number of variations, imitations and near-misses. But really now, how many surprises does this old sub-genre offer?

Not much, but "China Moon" makes a good try. Given the two years of trouble preceding its release (the most recent being some public trashing of the project by co-star Madeleine Stowe), it's amazing the film isn't more of a mess. In fact, director John Bailey and writer Roy Carlson, despite the attendant turmoil, have managed to serve up a decently paced and, at times, evocative example of neo-*noir*.

Florida is the setting. (It would have been California 40, 50 years ago.) The protagonist-victim is a shrewder-than-average homicide cop (Ed Harris), who prides himself on his keen powers of observation. At a bar one night, he observes a beautiful woman (Stowe) dressed in white who engages him in eye-contact tango. It turns out she's married to a philandering banker (Charles Dance). And she's looking for a way out of the marriage—without losing all the goodies that go with it.

The cop falls hard for the woman and ... well, you're probably connecting dots already. But don't connect them too quickly. Carlson's script is strewn with deep-fried, subtly-spiced red herrings. Concealed beneath the standard bends and turns of this Cain-like tale are tiny, well-timed surprises that keep you on your toes for much of the film's running time.

To say more than this would be to ruin the plot which is far leaner and, believe it or don't more clever than "Body Heat," another Florida-based neo-*noir* flick to which this is already being compared. But Bailey, a veteran cinematographer, forges his film with a finer calibration of grit and gauze than was evident in "Heat." Harris, a front-running candidate in the World's Most Underappreciated Leading Man sweepstakes, turns in his customary solid performance.

Stowe's not wrong about her ill-conceived role. But she pulls it off nonetheless. A less-intelligent actor would have gotten tangled up by the ambiguity. Stowe's smarts and sensuality fill in the blanks. Whether she likes it or not, her rapidly growing stardom will be enhanced by her work here.

VILLAGE VOICE, 3/8/94, p. 54, Georgia Brown

In the middle of the first sequence of *China Moon* I thought, Ah, John Bailey is making a cameraman's picture. There's a Peeping Tom setup, with the hidden voyeur snapping shots of a passionate (obviously illicit) pair tumbling into a motel. There's even a photographer in the next scene—a cop taking pictures of a nude corpse. A leading cinematographer (*American Gigolo* to *Groundhog Day*), Bailey debuts here as director. And for maybe one half of this noir, he does fine. The blue and red lights on the slick pavement, the ticky-tacky dives, the tidy little trailer—it all looks convincing without being too-too. But then the plot kicks in.

Steamy is the adjective you're meant to think of. The setting is Florida's Tampa area. Summertime. Ed Harris plays Bodine a veteran detective who falls fast and hard for a cool but sultry cookie named Rachel (Madeline Stowe). The cookie is married to a haughty cad, a mean banker named Rupert (Charles Dance). Rupert is the adulterer in the opening. Every time Rupert is present he says something rude and sniffy. Everyone wants Rupert to get his. But when he does Bodine is implicated and all we know for sure is that whatever sneaky tricks are being played, and whoever is playing them, poor, harried Bodine is being set up.

What writer Roy Carlson must have been thinking is *Body Heat*. Kasdan's neonoir neatly exploited the stock elements of the great '40s pictures (*Double Indemnity, The Postman Always Rings Twice*), but it was always ersatz. While it has the same sort of plot twists as *Body Heat*, *China Moon* is neither so slick nor tasteful. But then you start wishing it were. A little coherence would be nice. In the end, so many assaults are made on the brain, you exit feeling like Rupert's battered wife.

Also reviewed in:
CHICAGO TRIBUNE, 3/4/94, Friday/p. F, Michael Wilmington
NEW YORK TIMES, 3/4/94, p. C6, Caryn James
VARIETY, 1/17-23/94, p. 105, Emanuel Levy
WASHINGTON POST, 3/4/94, p. C1, Hal Hinson

CIAO, PROFESSORE!

A Miramax Films release of a Mario and Vittorio Cecchi Gori, Silvio Berlusconi Communications presentation of a Eurolux Produzione/Cecchi Gori Group/Tiger Cinematografica/Penta Film production. *Executive Producer:* Silvio Berlusconi. *Director:* Lina Wertmüller. *Screenplay (Italian with English subtitles):* Lina Wertmüller, Leo Benvenuti, Piero De Bernardi, Alessandro Bencivenni, and Domenico Saverni. *Based on the book "Io Speriamo Che Me Lo Cavo" by:* Marcello D'Orta. *Director of Photograhy:* Gianni Tafani. *Editor:* Pierluigi Leonardi. *Music:* D'Angio Greco. *Set Designer:* Enrico Job. *Costumes:* Gino Persico. *Running time:* 91 minutes. *MPAA Rating:* R.

CAST: Paolo Villaggio (Primary School Teacher, Mr. Sperelli); Isa Danieli (Principal); Gigio Morra (Custodian); Sergio Solli (Cardboard Dealer); Esterina Carloni (Esterina); Paolo Bonacelli (Ludovico); Marco Troncone (Giustino); Pier Francesco Borruto (Peppiniello); Adriano Pantaleo (Vincenzino); Ciro Esposito (Raffaele); Luigi L'Astorina (Toto); Ivano Salazoro (Giovanni); Antonio Scotto di Frega (Mimmuccio); Mario Bianco (Nicola); Salvatore Terracciano (Salvatore); Ilaria Troncone (Flora); Carmela Pecoraro (Tommasina); Maria Esposito (Rosiella); Annarita D'Auria (Lucietta); Dario Esposito (Gennarino); Alessandra De Tora (Angeluccia); Roberta Galli (Toto's Sister); Paolo Bonacelli (Ludovico Mazzullo); Anna De Magistris (Brigida); Filomena Lieto (Checchina); Consalvo Dell'Arti (Father Gabriele); Guiliano Amatucci (Mezzarecchia); Mario Porfito (Mayor); Pietro Bontempo (Toto's Father); Lucia Oreto (Gennarino's Mother); Eduard Criscuolo (Doctor Arnone); Salvatore Emilio (Tommasina's Father); Pietro Bertone (Doctor Nicolella); Fulvia Carotenuto (Raffaele's Mother); Enrichetta D'orta (Rosinella's Mother); Lilli Cecere (Caretaker's Wife); Marina Confalone (Nunziata Aiello).

LOS ANGELES TIMES, 7/22/94, Calendar/p. 12, Peter Rainer

Lina Wertmuller's "Ciao, Professore!" is a welcome, modest change from the blustery, slam-bang productions that made her reputation. "Swept Away" or "Seven Beauties" it is not. Her approach to drama is still exhaustingly knockabout but, because she's not working a political/sexual agenda in her new film, it doesn't seem as punishing.

The film is about what happens when a primary school teacher from northern Italy, Marco Sperelli (Paolo Villaggio), gets mistakenly transferred to a school in the southern village of Corzano. Marco doesn't want to be in this hothouse community of tiny truants, and for a long time his teaching job consists of rounding up his students in the streets and plunking them down in his classroom. Marco isn't a martinet—he tries to reach his students by appealing to their best instincts—but it's only after he slaps one of them that he gains their respect. (He regrets both the slap and the respect it earns him.) Because he cares about the children he becomes a hero to them.

Wertmuller and her team of five screenwriters don't spend much time involving us in Marco's classroom teaching. For a movie that centers on education there's very little learning going on. The lessons are all *outside* the classroom.

This is not exactly a novel approach—just about every classroom film from "To Sir, With Love" to "Renaissance Man" tried the same thing. And there's something dubious about a movie about the relationship between a teacher and his students that neglects the reasons for the learning in the first place. Still, the streets of Corzano are so bursting with life that you don't regret Wertmuller's decision to bring the film outdoors. There's lots to learn there too.

The children, many of them unprofessionals, are charmers, and Wertmuller indulges them—she practically pinches their cheeks for us. Hers is mostly an idealized view of childhood, but Italians have always had a special feeling for childhood revelry (and heartbreak too, as in many of De Sica's greatest films). The one bad seed in the bunch, the punkish Raffaele (Ciro Esposito), is in the movie to be redeemed.

But he doesn't go entirely flabby on us. When Marco, in a fit of pique, punches a nun, Raffaele reacts with awe. So do we.

NEW YORK POST, 7/15/94, p. 40, Thelma Adams

If you aren't amused by foul-mouthed kids, you won't like "Ciao, Professore!" The least salty expression used by cheeky third-graders in Lina Wertmuller's comedy is: Stop "crushing my cantaloupes."

In this "To Sir, With Love," Italian-style, a middle-aged Northern Italian elementary school teacher, Marco Sperelli (Paolo Villaggioo), is mistakenly assigned to the rough-and-tumble Southern town of Corzano.

When Sperelli arrives, he finds a school held hostage by a bossy custodian who sells toilet paper to the students, and neglected by a pregnant principal more concerned with her growing brood than with the young truants in her charge.

How foreign does this sound, given our metropolitan school system? Wertmuller develops a universal theme of hope-through-education as the lonely, uptight professor (his wife ran off with a dentist) rounds up a dozen of the cutest delinquents-in-training in all of Naples.

The professor teaches the kids how to write. They teach him how to cope with chaos—and clear away the cobwebs in his heart.

A junior mobster, a drunk's son, a sharp soda jerk, a round-cheeked madonna who has assumed her mother's place as head-of-household—Wertmuller creates an endearing group of foul-mouthed, high-spirited kids that are cute without being corny.

Loosely based on Marcello D'Orta's book, "Me, Let's Hope I Make It," an anthology of student essays written by Neapolitan street kids, the movie plays best scene-by-scene and offers few of the surprises of Wertmuller's early films.

In the '70s, Wertmuller was the bad girl of Italian cinema who reaped international fame with her ballsy exploration of the war between the sexes and classes, "Swept Away" (1974).

With "Seven Beauties" (1976), a dark exploration of a lady's man in World War II, Wertmuller became the first woman to be nominated for a Best Director Oscar. It wasn't until this year that "The Piano"'s Jane Campion joined Wertmuller, becoming the second woman to receive the nomination. Both women lost.

Originally an assistant to Fellini, Wertmuller's reputation has shrunk in recent years with a string of long-titled, forgettable movies: "The End of the World in our Usual Bed in a Night Full of Rain" (1978) and "Summer Night with Greek Profile, Almond Eyes and Scent of Basil" (1987).

"Ciao, Professore!" is Wertmuller-lite, a mainstream Italian comedy that floats on charming performances and ribald humor. The director might have lost the power to shock, but she still delights with a spicy mix of social critique and passion for the Italian people, North and South.

NEWSDAY, 7/15/94, Part II/p. B7, John Anderson

While that oh-so-whimsical exclamation point at the end of "Ciao, Professore!" seems calculated to evoke a kind of frothy romantic comedy,'60s-style, the name of its director—Lina Wertmuller—remains linked to the erotic politics of her '70s films, "Swept Away" and "Seven Beauties." The story itself? Imagine "To Sir With Love" or "Goodbye Mr. Chips" set in the squalid slums of southern Italy.

These are all red herrings, however, in adequately assessing Wertmuller's latest picture, probably her best in years, a gentle, accessible portrait of stunted slum life that marries low comedy to high hopes.

As Marco Sperelli, the teacher mistakenly assigned to a school in Corzano—he was supposed to go to *Corsano*, but the computer glitched—Paolo Villaggio is a round mound of sound wisdom, erudition and gentility that leaves him unprepared for what he finds: rampant truancy and a town grounded in Neapolitan fatalism.

Many children are out working, basically because they have to: As Wertmuller explains, through visual devices as well as narrative, child labor destroys adult jobs, thus forcing the young to keep theirs. Marco perceives his new neighbors with a northern bias—that they're shiftless idler's allergic to work. But when he goes out and drags his missing pupils back to the class, the parents applaud. Caught in a cycle of poverty, alcoholism and petty crime, they desperately want their children to break out.

Inevitably there's one young tough who refuses to respond to Masco's educational charms: Raffaelle (Ciro Esposito), an aspiring Mafioso who so enrages Marco he bloodies the child's nose. Wanting to apologize to the boy's mother, he's told instead that he's the woman's last hope to keep her son from following in his father's bloody footsteps.

Raffaele will come around, as do the rest of the kids, a spectacularly vulgar group whose profanity and skewed view of politics and history mirror the adult population they're in danger of becoming. And it's the adults whom Wertmuller vilifies, and whose corruption deprives the children. The janitor Mimi (Gigio Morra), who could be the patron saint of New York city school custodians, never works and sells the building's supplies—chalk to the teachers, toilet paper to the children.

The principal (Isa Danieli), on the other hand, is much too busy, and not with administration. Mother of six, she's a pregnant obstruction to education and embodies Wertmuller's bureaucratic nightmare. "Try to fit in," she tells Marco. He won't, of course, but he knows her kind is everywhere.

There are small bits of mute political commentary—an incongruous Mercedes, for instance, almost running down Marco and a student—and a marvelous group of students with gamin faces and hilariously filthy mouths. That they're virtually adults, of course, is what gives Wertmuller's film the sad leg it needs to rise above its inherent banality, and which also provides the director with her parting shot: Marco has to leave Corzano loving the children and knowing he can't really help them.

VILLAGE VOICE, 7/26/94, p. 50, Georgia Brown

Ciao, Professore! has screen play problems, too, but it has virtues *The Client* never dreamed of. [See Brown's review of *The Client*.] Directed by Lina Wertmüller, and written by committee (the Italians don't mind attaching multiple names to a script whereas we like to pretend there are only one or two writers), this cutesy, muckraking comedy is meant to instruct, indict, and persuade.

The film is based on Marcello D'Orta's bestseller, *Me, Let's Hope I Make It*, a collection of essays and stories written by Naples school children. Some compositions seem to be reproduced in the film (notably, one little girl's witty elucidation of the differences between Switzerland and Italy), but what the filmmakers attempt to do is create a fiction on which to hang the story of several students. This fiction is egregiously underwritten, however, so that instead of characters what we get are foils with adorable faces.

A third grade teacher, Marco Sperelli (the avuncular Paolo Villaggio), is victim of a computer error: Seeking an assignment in his hometown of Corsano in Italy's north, he's sent instead to Corzano, an impoverished port city near Naples. He arrives driving his classic VW bug, listening to Louis Armstrong, and immediately is struck by a quaint/disturbing mix of beauty and ugliness, health and disease. Education is viewed as an annoyance. His pint-size students are already working the family trade: One waits his table when he stops for an espresso, another peddles black market cigarettes, another is a budding mafioso. The school itself, a lead-paint nightmare, is hostage to a janitor who sells the only toilet paper and chalk. Almost immediately, *il professore* puts in for a transfer.

The best part is the kids—chosen for merry eyes, missing teeth, and abilities to curse colorfully ("fart jockey" and "fuck your ancestors" being favorite phrases). Clearly, the movie would be even more fun if you knew the dialect, but watching little hands wave and chop the air in familiar gestures is a hoot. The film falters badly when the teacher engages in action—as when he decides to help a kid steal a car to race his mother to the hospital.

What will strike people everywhere is how familiar this North-South split is: *We* deposit litter in receptacles; *they* foul their own nests; in the North corruption is sedate, in the South they kill senators. In the North we raise our kids right; in the South even tykes wear earrings and smoke cigarettes. It's easy to ridicule *Ciao, Professore!*'s sappiness, but as soft-edged social satire—as a painless teaching parable—it does lodge in the mind.

Also reviewed in:
CHICAGO TRIBUNE, 7/29/94, Friday/p. K, John Petrakis
NEW YORK TIMES, 7/15/94, p. C17, Caryn James
VARIETY, 12/20/93, p. 33, David Rooney
WASHINGTON POST, 7/29/94, p. B6, Hal Hinson

CITY SLICKERS II: THE LEGEND OF CURLY'S GOLD

A Castle Rock Entertainment and Columbia Pictures release of a Face production. *Executive Producer:* Peter Schindler. *Producer:* Billy Crystal. *Director:* Paul Weiland. *Screenplay:* Billy Crystal, Lowell Ganz, and Babaloo Mandel. *Director of Photography:* Adrian Biddle and Craig Haagensen. *Editor:* William Anderson and Armen Minasian. *Music:* Marc Shaiman. *Music Editor:* Michael Linn. *Sound:* Jeff Wexler, Don Coufal, Gary Holland and (music): Shawn Murphy. *Sound Editor:* David E. Stone. *Casting:* Naomi Yoelin and Amy Gerber. *Production Designer:* Stephen J. Lineweaver. *Art Director:* Philip Toolin. *Set Designer:* Richard McKenzie and Nancy Patton. *Set Decorator:* Clay A. Griffith. *Set Dresser:* Bruce Bellamy, Wayne Shepherd, Greg Wilkinson, John Garrett, Christopher Griffis, John Hartman, and Alan Kaneshiro. *Special Effects:* Steve Galich. *Costumes:* Llandys Williams. *Make-up:* Todd McIntosh and Peter Montagna. *Stunt Coordinator:* Mickey Gilbert. *Running time:* 116 minutes. *MPAA Rating:* PG-13.

CAST: Billy Crystal (Mitch Robbins); Daniel Stern (Phil Berquist); Jon Lovitz (Glen Robbins); Jack Palance (Duke/Curly Washburn); Patricia Wettig (Barbara Robbins); Pruitt Taylor Vince (Bud); Bill McKinney (Matt); Lindsay Crystal (Holly Robbins); Beth Grant (Lois); Noble Willingham (Clay Stone); David Paymer (Ira Shalowitz); Jayne Meadows (Mitch's Mother); Alan Charof (Mitch's Father); Kenneth S. Allen (Annoyed Man); Jennifer Crystal and Irmise Brown (Joggers); Molly McClure (Millie Stone); Helen Siff (Shushing Lady); Bill McIntosh and Mario Roberts (Clay's Sons).

LOS ANGELES TIMES, 6/10/94, Calendar/p. 1, Peter Rainer

In "City Slickers," Billy Crystal's Mitch Robbins was instructed by his wife to join a cattle drive and "go and find your smile." Mitch did more than that: He bonded with everything in sight and delivered a calf.

So you have to wonder—what could "City Slickers II: The Legend of Curly's Gold" do to top that earlier film's huggy buddy-buddy bathos? Will Mitch deliver twins this time? Will the film go sci-fi and have Jack Palance's Curly return from the dead to be delivered of a mewling infant?

Nothing so baroque, alas. With several years to ponder a way to honorably recycle "City Slickers," the filmmakers responsible for the sequel—director Paul Weiland and scripters Crystal, Lowell Ganz and Babaloo Mandel—have come up with a buried-treasure plot that would barely pass muster as an old Republic Pictures Western. The only things missing are the singing cowboys.

Mitch, having located his smile, sets out to locate a cache of hidden gold outlined in an old treasure map he accidentally uncovers in the brim of Curly's hat. (He's been keeping the hat as a keepsake of his cattle-driver chum; he's also held onto the calf he delivered, now a full-grown steer.) Accompanying Mitch into the valleys and buttes are his depresso buddy Phil (Daniel Stern), a repeat offender from the first film, and his loafing black-sheep-of -the-family brother, Glen (Jon Lovitz), who, at the drop of a Stetson, mimes scenes from "Godfather II." (Now *there* was a sequel.) Curly, inconveniently dead, is resurrected—sort of—in the person of his twin brother Duke (Palance), who is also on the gold trail.

The real gold chasers are the filmmakers, who keep pilfering moments from the first film to garland the sequel in order to repeat their success. There's something a bit unseemly about the way "City Slickers II" keeps fluffing our memories of "City Slickers," as if that film was some great classic worth recaping. It was far less than a classic—a sitcom on the range with a heavy helping of midlife-crisis sensitivity jags. It turns out that all that bonding/birthing stuff, more than the jokes, was probably what made the film a smash. It played out the audience's desire to chuck their boring jobs and get up on a horse and yell, "*Yee-Ha.*"

"City Slickers II" has its own variation on that film's squishiness. Mitch and his brother rediscover their love for each other, although Crystal in his "sincere" mode is enough to spook the cattle, and Lovitz on the level resembles nothing so much as his "Saturday Night Live" character The Liar. As if this weren't enough, Mitch and Phil rediscover their friendship, which is put to the test when Mitch is required to suck rattlesnake venom from Phil's posterior butte.

Most of the comedy is on this level, which makes you long—well, almost—for a few more midlife mouthings from the first film. With most of the film taken up with these city dudes, "City Slicker's II" has a skimpy, arid feeling, despite the Utah vistas. Only Palance returns with a flourish. He's as gnarled and critter-like as ever, and he gives his dumbest lines an orotund looniness that makes them hang in the air. Palance would be great playing Long John Silver in a newfangled "Treasure Island." He's a tall tale in motion.

What "City Slickers II" is really all about is movie stars play-acting cowboys. It's a boy's fantasy we're asked not so much to applaud as anoint. The first film roused a few laughs by showing how inept its city boys were on the range, but narcissism seems to have kicked in for the sequel. Crystal, who also produced the film, likes the way he looks on a horse. He likes the way he gazes steely-eyed at the horizon. He can be a highly inventive comic actor but, as long as he's being bathetic and legendary, is it OK if we don't come out to play?

NEW YORK POST, 6/10/94, p. 43, Michael Medved

You know a film's in trouble when it trots out not one, but two "long lost brother" plot twists.

In "City Slickers II: The Legend of Curly's Gold" one of these uncannily convenient siblings is supposed to be the tough-as-leather twin of the tough-as-leather trail boss who died in the first film—a dumb device allowing Jack Palance to make a return appearance in essentially the same role that won him a Best Supporting Actor Oscar in 1991.

The other brother is at least intermittently amusing—with Jon Lovitz as the black sheep of Billy Crystal's family, an unemployable deadbeat who cadges money, raids refrigerators, and quotes long stretches of dialogue from "The Godfather" films.

Lovitz arrives just in time to join brother Mitch Robbins (Crystal), now manager of a New York radio station and Mitch's best friend Daniel Stern, in heading west to search for a cache of long-buried outlaw gold.

They've become obsessed with the treasure map that Crystal discovered inside the lining of a cowboy hat that once belonged to poor dead Curly. Little do they know that Curly's twin, Duke, (Palance) is also looking for the loot, and they'll have to learn to cooperate in their quest.

This flimsy plot gives Crystal and company the chance for lots of funny lines and knowing references to "The Treasure of the Sierra Madre," but there's a joyless, rehearsed, mechanical quality to too much of the humor.

Crystal grins and mugs as if on cue; you can almost hear some inner voice commanding him, "OK, Billy, now it's time to act lovable!" The problem is that the sentimentally-sketched mid-life crisis that made his character so endearing in the first film can't be plausibly repeated for the sequel; instead of going west to find himself, this time Mitch is only trying to find gold.

Unfortunately, Crystal (who also produced the film and co-wrote the screenplay with Lowell Ganz and Babaloo Mandel) tries to fill the emptiness at the heart of this sequel with all sorts of graphic sexual references that are out of place in a film that's pitched at family audiences.

Would anyone have missed the detailed description of Crystal's elderly parents having sex on their kitchen table? Then there's a painfully prolonged gag about sucking rattlesnake venom out of Daniel Stern's rear-end—a comic inspiration that's no more funny here than it was in Paul Hogan's lamentable "Lightning Jack" earlier this year.

Director Paul Weiland (replacing Ron Underwood from the first film) is a British advertising specialist who can't be blamed for this movie's disappointments. He creates glowing vistas of Utah's Monument Valley (John Ford country) and handles his action scenes (including an impressive wild mustang stampede) with professionalism and aplomb.

The pretty surfaces, however, only contribute to the underlying sense that these "Slickers" are too slick—and shallow—to recommend with much enthusiasm.

NEWSDAY, 6/10/94, Part II/p. B7, John Anderson

When they make "City Slickers III"—and they will—they should bring back Bruno Kirby, who lent a nice acerbic edge to the original. And keep Jon Lovitz, who's the best thing about "City Slickers II." And considering how much depends on Phil, the all-purpose schlemiel, they'll have to retain the services of Daniel Stern as well.

Which means, sad to say, that Billy Crystal will simply have to go; four guys on the range would simply undo the delicate chemistry upon which a film like "City Slickers II: The Legend of Curly's Gold" is built. The only other way, as I see it, would be to kill off Crystal's character, Mitch Robbins, during the opening credits, milk every last drop of sentiment out of his passing (cloying sentimentality being the glue of this series) and then bring him back as his own twin brother.

Farfetched, you say? Don't tell Jack Palance, who was Curly, Mitch's bete noire in "City Slickers," and is Duke, the late Curly's sea-going twin brother, in "CSII." The result is the same basic character, the same basic jokes, with greed replacing fear-of-aging as the characters' major motivation.

Yes, Mitch is about to celebrate his 40th birthday, but now he's fairly content with what he's got: nice kids, a loving wife, Barbara (Patricia Wettig), a job running a growing radio station and a birthday night Barbara promises will be a carnal extravaganza. And then two things happen.

One, his black sheep brother Glen (Lovitz) comes to visit, bringing with him a sketchy employment record and penchants for borrowing money and reciting scenes from "The Godfather II." That the makers of "City Slickers II" would presume to rub their muzzles up against the best sequel ever made is shameless, but Lovitz' routine is deadpanned hilarity. Crystal counters by doing the Walter Huston dance from "The Treasure of the Sierra Madre"—several times—but Lovitz has it all over his co-star. But then, Lovitz isn't being asked to carry most of this movie around on his back like an old couch.

The story's second gear engages when a map falls out of Curly's hat—which Mitch inherited—on his big birthday evening. Why the cowboy hat in the boudoir? Never mind. But it shows the way to a long-buried cache of gold stolen by Curly's father. Mitch, who had been planning to attend a radio convention in Las Vegas, instead takes Phil, Glen and a detour to Utah—thus evoking not just Bogart and Pacino but the Johns, Wayne and Ford—and tries to find the treasure. Enter Duke.

"City Slickers II," like its predecessor, presumes a kind of macho pecking order, ruled by men like Duke—volatile, homophobic, immune to reason—who barely tolerate the co-existence of suburban bottom dwellers like Mitch, Glen and Phil. There's never a victory of mind over muscle in the "CS" movies. Quite the contrary: Mitch is grateful that Duke, like Curly, eventually recognizes his existence. It's an easy structure in which to build jokes about male anatomy and sexual security, but it's ultimately demeanng.

Directed by noted commercial maker Paul Weiland, the film is predictably formulaic, but no one is going to muck around with as winning a formula as this. Even if it eventually forces the demise of Billy Crystal.

NEWSWEEK, 6/27/94, p. 54, David Ansen

There have been and will be worse sequels that *City Slickers II: The Legend of Curly's Gold*, but there are few that seem so unnecessary. Now that Mitch Robbins (Billy Crystal) has recovered from his midlife crisis and is riding tall in the saddle, what uplifting life lessons does he need to learn from another exposure to the Wild West? Just that every overgrown boy needs a jolt of adventure every now and then to find his smile again. This message does not seem to inspire Crystal and fellow screenwriters Babaloo Mandel and Lowell Ganz to great heights of invention. They've dug into their bag of old movie archetypes, grabbed for "The Treasure of the Sierra Madre" and figured, "Why the hell not?" With a treasure map he's found in the late Curly's hat, Mitch—still inexplicably eager to escape his wife, though he was spiritually reborn in the original—sets off in quest of buried treasure. He's accompanied by his two stooges, the lonely-guy nerd Phil (Daniel Stern) and his albatross of a brother Glen (Jon Lovitz), a middle-aged slacker fond of quoting speeches from "Godfather II." Jack Palance's inconvenient demise in the original proves no problem: he returns as his own identical twin brother, which may give you some idea of the bold originality at play here. Crystal was more appealing in the first go-round; now that he's a born-again cowboy, a hint of smugness takes some of the fun out of him. "Slickers II," directed by Paul Weiland, is so harmless it's numbing: a little male bonding, some sagebrush slapstick, a couple of decent quips and a gift-wrapped moral. I kept wondering haw the filmmakers mustered up the energy to go to work every morning.

SIGHT AND SOUND, 10/94, p. 35, Farrah Anwar

Troubled by a recurrent nightmare about dead trail boss Curly, Mitch Robbins prepares to celebrate his fortieth birthday with his wife. But their intimate soiree is interrupted by the unexpected arrival of brother Glen and uninvited friend Phil Berquist. That night, Mitch accidentally finds a map marking a possible burial site for gold coins stolen from the railroad by one L. Washburn—a discovery coupled with yet another vision of Curly. Convinced that these two events are not coincidental, Mitch investigates further and confirms that Washburn (a dead ringer for Curly) did commit a robbery; although he was caught, the authorities never discovered where the money was hidden. Instead of firing Phil, Mitch inveigles him into a plan to use an upcoming business trip to Las Vegas as an excuse to hit the cowboy trail again in search of gold.

When Glen overhears the plan, he emotionally blackmails Mitch into letting him join in. Although insisting on secrecy, Phil manages to tell a couple of sinister store-keepers about the treasure; as a result, the trio is ambushed by them, only to rescued by Curly's 'ghost' (in fact, his twin brother Duke). Meaner than his brother, Duke initially tries to leave all three behind without the map. But when Mitch persuades him that he was a friend of Curly's, Duke allows them to ride alongside. After many diversions, including a stallion stampede, the quartet arrive at a warren of caves, one of which houses the loot. When Mitch stumbles onto the treasure chest, they are ambushed again by two men, and Glen intercepts a bullet intended for Mitch. Although Duke arrives in time to disarm the attackers, the whole incident is revealed to be part of an adventure holiday which the Stones (the ranchers who employed Curly) now run, including a fake treasure trail and a surprise ambush with blanks.

Disappointed, Mitch returns to Las Vegas, and is expecting his wife when Duke gatecrashes. He informs Mitch that he really did find the treasure in the cave, and that although he originally intended to double-cross his friends, he remembered that the one thing which was always so important to Curly was loyalty.

The original *City Slickers* had enough horse sense to keep most of its soft-core satirical swipes for the thirtysomething generation rather than the Westerns which they obviously grew up with and held in such affection. This was a feeling no doubt shared by scriptwriters Ganz and Mandel (joined in the sequel by Billy Crystal), who never lost sight of the fact that *City Slickers* had to deliver punchlines, pretty scenery and character development to complement the indulgence of something as little box-office-friendly as a cattle drive.

City Slickers II shares most of the original's cast, including a momentarily resurrected twin Jack Palance, although Bruno Kirby is here replaced by the gonzo-like Jon Lovitz. But this time the self-indulgence factor is very much to the fore, with the plot neatly encapsulated within the inverted commas of the subtitle. The sense of suburban inertia that urges Mitch, Phil and Glen to roam free on the range is now simply a creative vacuum sucking in as many movie references and borrowed comic devices as the running time requires. Starting with the *Carrie* dream sequence (does anybody visit a grave in Hollywood without being grabbed by a hand of the undead?), the film allows Crystal a free run. Literally so, in the case of the jogging sequence with Norman, the calf from the first film, now a fully uddered cow and possibly the only character in the film showing any signs of maturity; and metaphorically so, as he does a Walter Huston jig to acknowledge the shadow (and the Max Steiner score) of *The Treasure of the Sierra Madre*.

Thus Mitch is revealed as still harbouring a saddle-yearning itch on his fortieth birthday (wife Barbara continues to be the paradigm of a perfectly passive partner), while Phil can only aspire to carnal and emotional fulfilment on radio phone-ins. The only change is the arrival of Mitch's brother Glen (Lovitz), who sublimates his sibling rivalry by assuming the *Godfather* character Fredo Corleone (and who delivers the film's funniest turn). In fact, all three treasure hunters are so steeped in movie lore that the only surprising moment is when they fail to recognise Bill

McKinney and Pruitt Taylor Vince as the villainous holiday poopers from *Deliverance* (Vince being an almost exact body double for McKinney's original cohort, Herbert 'Cowboy' Coward).

All this might have been forgivable if the film had ended on the note of irony it briefly threatens to leave us with: the treasure map turns out to be a tourist ruse and Mitch is left empty-handed and alone in a Vegas hotel room, with the prospect of having to explain to his wife why he blew a lucrative business deal on a treasure hunt. It's a denouement framed almost as cruelly as the original *Sierra Madre*. Unfortunately, instead of saying something meaningful about grown men's inability to distinguish between film fantasy and everyday reality, *City Slickers II* compounds matters by having Duke discover (and then share) the treasure with his friends. It is a jarring moment, not just because of its sentimentality but also because it betrays the original film's own contribution to movie mythology—Palance's Oscar-winning turn as Duke's late twin.

TIME, 6/13/94, p. 74, Richard Schickel

City Slickers had a nice little concept going for it: urban tenderfeet learn to feel at home on the range and become better men for the experience. The problem for *II* is that having achieved that state of grace, there's no compelling reason for Mitch Robbins (Billy Crystal, who co-wrote the script with Lowell Ganz and Babaloo Mandel) and Phil Berquist (Daniel Stern) to head West again. Especially since Jack Palance's Curly, their comically tough mentor, was killed off three years ago. The film resorts to a *faux* ghost routine and a twin-brother conceit to get Palance up and snarling again. Instead of the Bruno Kirby sidekick we have a whiney Jon Lovitz playing a ne'er-do-well brother, so at least somebody can be seen to be growing up, getting better out there in the Big Country.

VILLAGE VOICE, 6/21/94, p. 50, Georgia Brown

In the 1991 *City Slickers*—a mellow sitcom that I quite enjoyed—middle-aged men also went in search of the "one thing" as Curly the trail boss (Jack Palance) called it. In *City Slickers II*, wouldn't you know, they go in search of the loot. *The Legend of Curly's Gold* is the movie's subtitle. Sound like a Hardy Boys adventure? *That*, buckaroos, would be an improvement.

You thought the three amigos learned a thing or two about love and life and priorities by acting out boyhood fantasies and bringing in the steers? A year later, Daniel Stern's Phil has reverted to the sexual and professional basket case he was. Billy Crystal's Mitch may no longer be morose, but he's still joking about his potency and avoiding his wife (Patricia Wettig). Only Bruno Kirby—the one who seemed a bit embarrassed at the cowhand bit—learned enough to stay away from sequels. Kirby is replaced here by chubby Jon Lovitz playing Mitch's half-wit brother, Glen.

The central difference between *I* and *II* is that the original had some narrative propulsion: The jokes hung on *something*; there was urgency to the cattle drive, some concern that the buddies would shape up. This time the plot—a meandering treasure hunt joined at one point by Curly's twin, Duke—is all fluff. Stern should've taken his cue from Kirby because his dopey character is barely addressed here. Lovitz is a jelly roll on a buckboard. Billy Crystal hosts rather than acts, so that the movie comes off as a stand-up gig.

One Crystal gag, mocking a radio call-in therapist's credentials, seems apt to cite in closing. "Last year," Mitch sneers, "he was doing traffic reports from a helicopter, and if this doesn't work out he'll be our new movie critic." If there's anywhere to go from there, let me know.

Also reviewed in:
CHICAGO TRIBUNE, 6/10/94, Friday/p. C, Michael Wilmington
NEW YORK TIMES, 6/10/94, p. C19, Janet Maslin
VARIETY, 6/6-12/94, p. 33, Leonard Klady
WASHINGTON POST, 6/10/94, p. D1, Rita Kempley
WASHINGTON POST, 6/10/94, Weekend/p. 42, Desson Howe

CLEAN SLATE

A Metro-Goldwyn-Mayer release of a Zanuck Company production. *Producer:* Richard D. Zanuck and Lili Fini Zanuck. *Director:* Mick Jackson. *Screenplay:* Robert King. *Director of Photography:* Andrew Dunn. *Editor:* Priscilla Nedd-Friendly. *Music:* Alan Silvestri. *Music Editor:* Jacqueline Tager. *Sound:* Willie Burton and (music) Dennis Sands. *Sound Editor:* Bruce Stambler. *Casting:* Mindy Marin. *Production Designer:* Norman Reynolds. *Art Director:* William Hiney. *Set Designer:* James Tocci and Harold Furhrman. *Set Decorator:* Anne Kuljian. *Set Dresser:* Brett Smith. *Special Effects:* Burt Dalton. *Costumes:* Ruth Myers. *Make-up:* Daniel Striepeke. *Stunt Coordinator:* Ted Grossman. *Running time:* 106 minutes. *MPAA Rating:* PG-13.

CAST: Dana Carvey (Pogue); Valeria Golino (Sarah/Beth); James Earl Jones (Dolby); Kevin Pollak (Rosenheim); Michael Gambon (Cornell); Michael Murphy (Dr. Doover); Jayne Brook (Paula); Vyto Ruginis (Hendrix); Olivia D'Abo (Judy); Angela Paton (Shirley Pogue); Mark Bringelson (Bodyguard #1); Christopher Meloni (Bodyguard #2); Tim Scott (Stanley); Gailard Sartain (Judge Block); Robert Wisdom (Mort); Phil Leeds (Landlord); Michael Monks (Lt. Willis); Peter Crook (Kipper); Reg E. Cathey (1st Cop); Mike Jolly (2nd Cop); Brad Blaisdell (Alley Cop); Ken Kerman and Bob Odenkirk (Cops); Ian Abercrombie (Leader); Myra Turley (Nurse); Jean Adams (Wrong Mom); Brian Reddy (Young Man); Brian Haley (Patient); Bryan Cranston (Club Official); Gary Bullock (Bailiff); D.H. Lewis (Stenographer); Jeff King (Journalist); Kevin West (Store Clerk); Blanche Brill (Elderly Customer); Sandra Jordan (Meter Maid); Steven Maines (Backstage Dresser); Fred Spencer, Don Lewis, and Mich'l Rios (Puppeteers); Barkley (Baby).

LOS ANGELES TIMES, 5/6/94, Calendar/p. 4, Peter Rainer

"Clean Slate" might seem even funnier if its premise wasn't so good. As it is, you keep comparing what it is with what it could have been.

It's about an L.A. cop-turned-gumshoe, Maurice Pogue (Dana Carvey), who suffers from a rare form of amnesia that wipes out his memory every time he falls asleep. He wakes up with no idea who he is or what happened the day before. Worse, he's about to appear as the key witness against a mobster in a murder case—but he can't remember the mobster or the murder.

The film begins with Pogue's terrier scooting across his porch and butting head first into a wall. The dog, you see, has a depth perception problem. (He wears an eye-patch.)

For a while, it looks as if "Clean Slate" is going to be one of those movies where the dog steals the show, particularly since no one else in the film seems to be performing up to the dog's level. (His real name is Barkley and, according to the press kit, he's "equally adept at comedy and drama.")

Things perk up a bit when the plot finally kicks in. The premise takes too long to establish, though. It's as if director Mick Jackson and screenwriter Robert King suffered from a form of amnesia themselves; they keep recapping stuff they've already established. They also milk jokes that weren't all that funny to begin with, like the mural artist who keeps effacing his rendition of "Mona Lisa" because Pogue doesn't recognize it.

Carvey would seem to be well-cast in the role of a man without an identity of his own. After all, Carvey's specialty on "Saturday Night Live" was impersonations. But gifted mimics, when they're called upon to create something closer to themselves, often blank out. (There's no there there.) Carvey is much better here than he was in his last leading man outing, "Opportunity Knocks," but he still seems weightless and wan. He's best when he plays around with his own wispiness instead of just being wispy. Some of his deadpan befuddlements are right on the mark. He has the look of a man who is patiently, dedicatedly trying to rejigger his memory bank.

The excellent supporting cast have a few inspired moments. Michael Gambon's mobster is a gelatinous dandy who regards Pogue as an annoying riddle. Michael Murphy, as Pogue's doctor, seems to enjoy his patient's quandaries: he's like a sadistic Oliver Sacks. Valeria Golina, playing Pogue's girlfriend (sort of), has a cushy comic sense. Rumbly-voiced James Earl Jones plays a district attorney named, appropriately, Dolby. Kevin Pollak is Pogue's assistant D.A. best friend who can't assimilate the hilariously obvious evidence that Pogue is having an affair with his fiancee. Pollak and Carvey get a real comic tempo ticking in some of their scenes: Pollak is like a revue-sketch Othello to Carvey's Stan Laurel-ish Iago.

Jackson attempts to jack up the high jinks with lots of quick cutting and swervy camera moves. Some of it works, some of it just seems like desperation. He works in doodly little references to "Groundhog Day" as well as "The 39 Steps," "The Big Sleep" and many other mystery thrillers: there's even what appears to be a plug for "That's Entertainment! Ill"—also an MGM production. (A bodyguard watches clips from it on TV while Pogue sweats it out in a locked sauna.)

"Clean Slate" is the kind of movie where just about everybody involved seems to be working below their best level. But glints of their best stuff comes through anyway, which makes this comedy about amnesia almost worth remembering.

NEW YORK POST, 5/6/94, p. 36, Michael Medved

Los Angeles private eye Maurice Pogue (Dana Carvey) wakes up each morning to face a perplexing array of mysteries.

He suffers from a rare form of amnesia that totally wipes out his memory when he falls asleep at night. So every day he must grapple anew with the most fundamental questions—like trying to remember his own name, or who shared his bed the night before, or where he stashed the dog food for his hungry roommate—a devoted Jack Russell terrier with an eye-patch and perceptual problems.

Pogue's only guide through this confusion is a pocket tape recorder on which he tapes instructions to himself each night before he goes to bed.

At the beginning of the picture, these observations inform him (and us) that the hero must hide his affliction and pretend that his memory is normal until he's given crucial courtroom testimony that will put a vicious crime boss (Michael Gambon) behind bars.

It's an inventive concept, and a clever script (by first-timer Robert King), encouraging Carvey to emphasize the inherent humor and pathos in the situation, rather than turning the hero into a slapstick caricature in the style of "Ace Ventura."

Unfortunately, this decision may disappoint Carvey's fans, since one of America's most versatile, outrageous comedians here brings a surprisingly bland, understated quality to his performance; he's playing the part for sympathy and likability, rather than laughs.

As a result, "Clean Slate" comes across as amusing and watchable rather than hilarious, helped considerably by a first-rate supporting cast.

Valeria Golino is captivating as the femme fatale claiming to be Carvey's one-time lover who was thought to have died in a car bombing; we have no more idea than he does whether she's telling the truth.

James Earl Jones turns up briefly as a gruff district attorney while Kevin Pollak is his nervous assistant—and Pogue's best friend, desperate to find out who's been secretly sleeping with his sensationally sexy fiance (Oliva D'Abo); it seems as if Carvey himself might well be the cad, but he doesn't remember.

British director Mick Jackson avoids any trace of the hamhanded solemnity he brought to "The Bodyguard," treating this silly material with a gentle, almost wistful touch. As he did in Steve Martin's "L.A. Stories," Jackson portrays a , range of colorful California locations—he deserves a citation from the Chamber of Commerce for making the L.A. areas look far more flavorful and fun than they actually are.

Unlike "I Married an Axe Murderer," the annoying, ill-fated solo venture by Carvey's "Wayne's World" partner Mike Myers, "Clean Slate" is no disaster. It's a pleasant piffle that can help pass an evening. But you'll remember nothing when you wake up the next morning.

NEWSDAY, 5/6/94, Part II/p. B7, Jack Mathews

It took just about a year for someone to do a knock-off of the early 1993 comedy hit "Groundhog Day," and like most knock-offs, it would have been better left undone.

Mick Jackson's "Clean Slate," starring Dana Carvey as a private eye who awakens every day to discover his memory has been erased, merely reverses the comic premise of "Groundhog Day." Where Bill Murray's weatherman replayed the same day over and over, accumulating detail and an encyclopedic knowledge of the town and people unknowingly reliving the day with him, Carvey's Maurice Pogue has to start each day from scratch with only his tape-recorded diary to explain what he'd been learning about himself in the preceding days.

It seems that Maurice had survived a car bomb blast, which left him with a rare form of amnesia. He can't even remember the woman who left a thank-you note next to a set of handcuffs on his bed the night before, or the name of his fabulously funny one-eyed dog, or how his apartment above the boardwalk at L. A.'s Venice Beach got riddled with bullets.

When we check in with Maurice, he's listening to his tape-recorded messages to himself on a Monday morning, four days before he is to testify in a murder trial. Before the day is over, he will have been visited by a mysterious client (Valeria Golino), a mob boss and two hitmen, and been feted at a surprise birthday party by a warehouse full of cops, none of which makes enough sense to be memorable to him or us.

The beauty of "Groundhog Day"—the beauty of any successful fantasy—is that it establishes its own reality. You have to suspend your disbelief to get into that world, but once inside, the events and behavior proceed logically.

There is almost no logic to Maurice Pogue's reactions to his dilemma. Instead of trying to find out who he is and what happened to him, he caroms from one encounter to another trying to fake recognition and familiarity, as if his only goal were to make it through the day without embarrassing himself.

At that, Maurice has more success than Carvey. Although the comedian has some funny moments, and a lot of charming ones, much of his performance is physical farce that doesn't work on any level. "Clean Slate" plays like a "Naked Gun" movie with the best sight gags removed!

Valeria Golino, who played the romantic straight woman to goofy comic leads in "Pee-wee's Big Adventure" and the two "Hot Shots!" movies, does a serviceable job, but the talents of James Earl Jones, Kevin Pollak and Michael Murphy are wasted in underdeveloped supporting roles.

The only exceptional performance in the film was delivered by Barkley, the amazing Jack Russell terrier who plays Maurice's accident-prone pooch. Barkley is a veteran character actor, having appeared in four movies and numerous TV commercials, and while miming a depth perception problem that has him perpetually 10 degrees to the left of where he wants to be, he is hilarious here.

To Carvey's genuine embarrassment, "Clean Slate" could become the break-out movie for a dog!

VILLAGE VOICE, 5/24/94, Film Special/p. 27, Laurie Stone

Dana Carvey walks around naked in his second starring vehicle—oh, he's wearing clothes, but he's stripped of a character, and it's not a pretty sight. His eyes search anxiously for George Bush, or Garth, or the Church Lady. Among *SNL* alums, Steve Martin and Bill Murray have fared best on the big screen, partly because they never really played characters but rather lent their comedy personas—Martin the suave idiot and Murray the confessional weasel—to different shtick. Since Carvey only comes alive inside some exaggerated cartoon, he's muted and flailing playing a real guy.

Even the premise of this flick is a weak echo of Murray's fugue on the theme of repetition, *Groundhog Day*. Carvey plays Pogue, a low-rent gumshoe who, due to a trauma, loses his memory every time he goes to sleep. Each day he has to relearn the story of his life and sort out friends from foes. Hitchcock turned this sort of ruptured identity tale into the brilliant comic nightmare *North by Northwest*, but instead of Cary Grant saving his skin with imaginative fast talk, we get Carvey, in scene after scene, sputtering emptily.

Clean Slate can't find a tone. It begs for laughs by sending a small, one-eyed dog smashing face first into walls. The bad guys have murdered a woman with a car bomb, but it's unclear whether they are dangerous or bumbling. Part of the problem is that Michael Gambon, of *Singing Detective* fame, infuses his villain with a complexity that's left hanging. And what stressed-out male ego first had the brainstorm of pitching heavy-breathing women at men who project zero eroticism? Are we expected not to notice that the love object, in this case Carvey, is a lox?

In the final half hour, when the movie elects for slapstick, it gets funny, including one daffy scene in which the dog terrorizes the bullies with a Ninja leap. Carvey does a Leslie Nielsen turn, affecting deadpan seriousness while uttering nonsense, and he's charming, as he always is when ensconced in a full-blown clown. Trouble is, it's late in the game by then and Nielsen waltzes more gracefully in those floppy shoes.

Also reviewed in:
NEW YORK TIMES, 5/6/94, p. C10, Caryn James
VARIETY, 5/9-15/94, p. 72, Brian Lowry
WASHINGTON POST, 5/6/94, p. B1, Rita Kempley
WASHINGTON POST, 5/6/94, Weekend/p. 47, Joe Brown

CLEAR AND PRESENT DANGER

A Paramount Pictures release. *Producer:* Mace Neufeld and Robert Rehme. *Director:* Phillip Noyce. *Screenplay:* Donald Stewart, Steven Zaillian, and John Milius. *Based on the novel by:* Tom Clancy. *Director of Photography:* Donald M. McAlpine. *Editor:* Neil Travis. *Music:* James Horner. *Music Editor:* Jim Henrikson. *Sound:* Arthur Rochester and (music) Shawn Murphy. *Sound Editor:* Bruce Stambler and John Leveque. *Casting:* Mindy Marin. *Production Designer:* Terence Marsh. *Art Director:* William Cruise. *Set Designer:* Dawn Snyder. *Set Decorator:* Mickey S. Michaels and Jay R. Hart. *Set Dresser:* Bob Camron, Jim Husbands, and John Schacht. *Special Effects:* Robert G. Willard. *Costumes:* Bernie Pollack. *Make-up:* Peter Robb-King and Pat Gerhardt. *Stunt Coordinator:* Dick Ziker. *Running time:* 142 minutes. *MPAA Rating:* PG-13.

CAST: Harrison Ford (Jack Ryan); Willem Dafoe (Clark); Anne Archer (Cathy Ryan); Joaquim de Almeida (Felix Cortez); Henry Czerny (Robert Ritter); Harris Yulin (James Cutter); Donald Moffat (President Bennett); Miguel Sandoval (Ernesto Escobedo); Benjamin Bratt (Captain Ramirez); Raymond Cruz (Chavez); Dean Jones (Judge Moore); Thora Birch (Sally Ryan); Ann Magnuson (Moira Wolfson); Hope Lange (Senator Mayo); Tom Tammi (Emile Jacobs); Tim Grimm (Dan Murray); Belita Moreno (Jean Fowler); James Earl Jones (Admiral Greer); Jaime Gomez (Sergeant Oso); Jorge Luke (Sipo); Jared Chandler (Insertion Team Radioman); Greg Germann (Petey); Ellen Geer (Rose); Ted Raimi (Satellite Analyst); Vondie Curtis-Hall (Voice-Print Analyst); John Lafayette and Beau Lotterman (CIA Analysts); Rex Linn (Washington Detective); Peter Weireter (FBI Director's Bodyguard); Victor Palmieri (Ambassador Ferris); Trip Hamilton (White House Guard); Ken Howard (Committee Chairman); Alexander Lester (John Ryan, Jr.); Reg E. Cathey (Sergeant Major); Clark Gregg (Staff Sergeant); Chris Conrad (Sniper Sergeant); Vaughn Armstrong (Blackhawk Pilot); John Putch (Blackhawk Co-Pilot); Colleen Flynn (Coast Guard Captain); Reed Diamond (Coast Guard Chief); Cam Brainard, Brendan Ford, and Michael Jace (Coast Guardsmen); Cameron Thor (DEA Surveillance Agent); Harley Venton and Miguel Perez (DEA Agent); Patrick Bauchau (Enrique Rojas); Juan Carlos Colombo (Cortez's Bodyguard); Blanca Guerra (Escobedo's Wife); Rufino Echegoyen (Escobedo's Driver); Honorato Magaloni (Mining Company Manager); Mario Ivan Martinez (Chemist); Eduardo Andrade (Eduardo); Hector Teller (Hector); Alejandro Bracho (Fernandez); Robert Arratia and Eliot Ferrer (Colombian Hitmen); David J. Negron, Jr. (Cartel Accountant); Michael A. Mendez (Cartel Gunman); Sebastian Silva (Cartel Member); Diana Sowle (Cartel Maid); Kamala Dawson (Venezuelan Telephonist); Guillermo Rios (Gate House Guard); Alejandro De Hoyos (Spanish Reporter); Leo Garcia (CNN Reporter); Barbara Harrison (TV Reporter); Mark Bailey and Elizabeth Dennehy (Reporter); Patricia Belcher (INS Officer); Aaron Lustig (Dr. Polk); Tom Isbell (Restaurant Doctor); Kim Flowers (Restaurant Hostess); Claudia Lobo (Ritter's Wife); Al Verdun (Ritter's Secretary); Lynne Marie Stewart (Greer's Secretary); Catherine MacNeal (Greer's Nurse); Denice Kumagai (Nurse); Christine J. Moore (Greer's Widow); Marjorie Lovett (President's Secretary); Lee Bear (Cutter's Bodyguard); Jeffrey King (Jefferson);

Glenn E. Coats (Hotel Clerk); Kevin Cooney (CIA Counsel); Elisabeth Kern (Horse Trainer); Thomas Luskey (Homicide Detective); John Rixey Moore (Spook).

CHRISTIAN SCIENCE MONITOR, 8/4/94, p. 11, David Sterritt

It has been widely reported that President Clinton is taking more criticism, from more people, on more positions along the political spectrum, than any president in a long time. With this national mood, it's not surprising that the TV promos for Harrison Ford's new movie, "Clear and Present Danger," show a fictional United States president who's just been "barked at" by our hero. There comes a time, the ads suggest, when bashing the chief executive is every patriot's duty. See the movie, and join the fun.

Interestingly, the President Bennett we meet in "Clear and Present Danger" turns out to resemble Ronald Reagan during the Iran-contra scandal more than Clinton during his current challenges. He's up to his neck in international adventures, and deniability has become his watchword.

Bennett wants direct violent action against the Colombian drug cartel that has recruited, corrupted, and murdered one of his old friends. He can't order a secret war without consulting Congress, and they'd never have the gumption to approve.

But his national security adviser knows what the boss's heart desires, and without the president having to say a direct word, the Colombian hills are soon crawling with American commandos, led by a former US agent who'd never cancel a bombing run just because children were spotted in the impact zone.

It's a nasty business, and it would be nastier still if Jack Ryan weren't on the scene. Fresh from various Tom Clancy novels and Hollywood films he's a dashing but unlikely good guy—generally softspoken, frequently nervous and so squeaky clean that his CIA buddies find him something of a wimp.

When his high-ranking supervisor becomes ill, he finds himself promoted from lowly analyst to powerful deputy director of intelligence, a privileged but dangerous position. Scorning his "Boy Scout" mentality, the national security adviser and his conspiratorial colleagues leave Ryan ignorant of their presidential escapade south of the equator. But we know he'll discover it and that sparks will immediately fly.

The previous Jack Ryan movies, "The Hunt for Red October" and "Patriot Games," struck me as dry, mechanical entertainments that went through their paces with little zest or imagination. "Clear and Present Danger" is more involving, largely because it raises a handful of issues too provocative for the picture's big-budget action scenes to submerge completely. Should the war on drugs really be a *war*? Is oversight by Congress a needed check on executive power, or a bothersome hindrance to getting things done? Are the US military and intelligence machines proud instruments of the American way, or unfortunate necessities capable of great destructiveness if steered by the wrong hands?

The movie doesn't delve very deeply into these questions. But at least it brings them up and lets them resonate behind the derring-do of the main story, providing food for thought when the heroics start to sag or lapse into pure contrivance—which happens regrettably often, especially when Ryan finds himself in some impossibly hazardous position that only a major dose of plot-manipulation can resolve.

For an example, check the rocket-attack-on-motorcade scene, where you can almost see the director's hand reach down and shield our hero from the certain death that wipes out his companions. It's as hokey as action sequences get—but then, lots of explosions are a must for this summer's movies, and this episode puts the picture well over its quota.

Ford does a credible job in his second go-round as Jack Ryan, following the dreary "Patriot Games," and James Earl Jones is equally persuasive in his third appearance (and last, since the character dies this time) as Ryan's dignified CIA boss. A sun-tanned Willem Dafoe is smartly sinister as the renegade CIA operative in Colombia, and Donald Moffat gives the president a suitable mixture of pride, pragmatism, and pretentiousness. Harris Yulin and Henry Czerny are just right as self-righteous government villains.

Unfortunately, only two women have a significant presence in this mostly male adventure, and neither fares very well with her underwritten part: Anne Archer as Ryan's wife, a successful physician whose tiny role says more about Hollywood tokenism than female professionalism, and

Ann Magnuson as a government secretary who enters the plot only to die in its nastiest, most gratuitous murder.

Donald Stewart, Steven Zaillian, and John Milius did the adaptation of Clancy's bestseller—an interesting combination of screenwriters, since Stewart and Zaillian have previously done well with somewhat progressive pictures (the excellent "Missing" and "Schindler's List," respectively) while Milius has crafted such macho musclefests as "Red Dawn" and "Conan the Barbarian" during his checkered career.

The vivid cinematography is by Donald M. McAlpine, and James Horner composed the reasonably effective score. The director is Australian filmmaker Phillip Noyce, who had nowhere to go but up after "Sliver," and has neatly resuscitated his reputation.

FILMS IN REVIEW, 9-10/94, p. 57, Andy Pawelczak

Clear and Present Danger is the third film featuring Jack Ryan, a very low keyed, anti-James Bond C.I.A. agent who first appeared in *The Hunt for Red October*. Based on all-but-unreadable novels by the military-dazzled and mega-successful Tom Clancy, the films jettison Clancy's neanderthal right-wing subtext and go for straight generic thrills. *Clear And Present Danger* has a plot twisty enough to keep you on your toes through most of the film and a smart, self-effacing performance by Harrison Ford as Ryan.

In these post-cold war days, the clear and present danger referred to in the title is the Cali drug cartels. At the beginning of the film, a close friend of the President of the United States is murdered by Colombian drug barons, and it soon turns out that this respectable member of the establishment was laundering drug money. The President, partly motivated by a desire for vengeance, authorizes a secret, illegal military action against the cartel, a plot that only the National Security Advisor (Harris Yulin) and a highly placed C.I.A. officer (Henry Czerny) are privy to. Once Ryan, who is Acting Director of Intelligence, finds out that there is, in fact, a military operation in Colombia, he's caught between the drug dealers and the dirty tricksters in his own agency, and before the film ends there are several double crosses and a sinister attempt at cover up in the highest reaches of government, as they say.

Jack Ryan is the perfect hero for the Nineties. He's a non-drinking, non-smoking, professorial family man who is comfortable around computers and is naively thrilled when the President actually takes his advice.

Hitchcock once said that a film actor is an expert at doing nothing, and Harrison Ford would have made a great Hitchcock leading man. As Ryan, he's a modest, tentative hero unencumbered by preening machismo—he looks convincingly frightened and vulnerable whenever somebody waves a gun in his direction. The film's swashbuckler is played by Willem Dafoe as a free-lance American agent who leads the military operation in Colombia. Apparently, soldiers of fortune these days must have as much panache with a computer as their old fashioned counterparts had with a blonde and a martini, and Dafoe is as adept as Ford at playing opposite a machine. Computers in this film take the place of the fantastic gadgetry in the James Bond movies, and one of the film's big set pieces involves a tense computer duel between Ryan and a rogue C.I.A. officer.

Clear and Present Danger's supporting cast adds a lot to the picture's realistic ambience of Beltway conspiracy and malfeasance. As the President, Donald Moffat captures the right combination of democratic bonhomie and imperial, above-the-law willfulness, and Harris Yulin and Henry Czerny (who starred in the recent Canadian film, *The Boys of St. Vincent*) are very good as his ambitious minions. The film gives the sense that this is the way government really works: a few ambiguous words and meaningful glances exchanged among these sworn upholders of the Constitution, and a conflagration is lit 3000 miles away. Joaquim de Almeida as Ryan's opposite number in the drug cartel is smoothly handsome and conscienceless, and Miguel Sandoval as the cartel boss is a loving family man with too much testosterone and a tendency to use a baseball bat on those who displease him. Anne Archer, making her second appearance as Ryan's wife, is a cloying deaccelerant of the picture's momentum.

Phillip Noyce, the movie's director, is equally skilled with dramatic confrontations and big action scenes, and an ambush in Bogota is scary and convincing. In the editing, Noyce goes for entertaining pop ironies. In one sequence, he crosscuts the President delivering a funeral oration in praise of a C.I.A. officer's integrity with the slaughter of a U.S. military unit which has been betrayed and abandoned by the government.

Clear and Present Danger is a smart renovation of the espionage thriller with a welcome political patina—the governmental conspiracy has overtones of Iran-contragate, which I'm happy to see somebody still remembers—but it did make me think of possible variations on the formula. How about a film in which the C.I.A. teams up with the K.G.B. to battle the Russian mafia which is smuggling nuclear weapons to Columbian drug cartels and Iranian terrorists? Ford could be the buttoned down American operative and Tommy Lee Jones the flamboyant, hard drinking Russian with Bruce Dern as a Carlos-like terrorist in the employ of a shadowy, corporate fifth column pursuing its own sinister and profitable ends. I'm waiting for a call from Hollywood on this one.

LOS ANGELES TIMES, 8/3/94, Calendar/p. 1, Kenneth Turan

"Clear and Present Danger" does more than provide the summer's most satisfying movie experience—which may sound like damning with faint praise, but shouldn't. It reaffirms, if reaffirmation is necessary, Harrison Ford's position as the most thankfully reliable action star around.

With those other big-ticket, big-muscle performers (you know who they are), it's not known until it's too late whether they've made a feast or a fiasco. Ford, by contrast, in searching for an emotional connection even in the brawniest of projects, has become as earnestly dependable as the characters he plays.

In fact, since "The Empire Strikes Back" in 1980, the actor has been the equivalent of a Good Housekeeping seal for the adventure genre, his presence guaranteeing an enviable level of professionalism, excitement and involvement in the thrillers, from "Witness" to "The Fugitive," that he has appeared in.

"Clear and Present Danger" is the third Tom Clancy novel about CIA analyst Jack Ryan to be adapted to the screen, and the second time Ford, director Phillip Noyce, cinematographer Donald M. McAlpine and other key members of the cast and crew have been involved, and the practice has been good for everyone. This is easily the best and most tightly wound of the Clancy films, notable for the intricacy of its plot and the nuances its actors bring to characterization.

Initial credit for this must go to "Danger's" jerry-built but effective script. Three very different writers—Clancy adaptation veteran Donald Stewart, character-sensitive Steven Zaillian ("Schindler's List") and action aficionado John Milius—share screen credit, and against all expectation the intelligent result is much closer to synergy than chaos.

If "Danger" does have a problem, it is that it starts too slowly. Partially this is a situation endemic to sequels, where all the familiar subsidiary faces, here including Anne Archer as Ryan's wife, Cathy, and James Earl Jones as his boss, Adm. James Greer, have to be laboriously reintroduced to a perhaps forgetful audience.

The plot too begins tentatively with a pair of almost simultaneous actions. Ryan is unexpectedly thrust into a more active role in the intelligence bureaucracy, with new responsibilities that include testifying before Congress and even briefing the President. And the first situation he has to deal with is the murder at sea of a lifelong friend and political supporter of the chief executive.

When Ryan traces the murders to the infamous Cali Colombia drug cartel, President Edward Bennett (Donald Moffat) is incensed. "Drugs pouring into the country and the drug dealers think we're powerless," he fumes to National Security Adviser James Cutter (Harris Yulin). Isn't it likely, he goes on, that the cartel represents "a clear and present danger to the national security of the United States," a situation that allows for the commitment of American military power?

Though the expected thing for "Danger" to do at this point is break down into a U.S. versus the drug lords scenario, what happens is more subtle. There turns out to be not one Colombian adversary but several, not necessarily on good terms with each other. And far from a single monolithic American presence, there are various power centers with different perspectives and antithetical agendas.

What results is a pleasantly complex story line in which these numerous strands, both in Washington and Colombia, twist and turn as they combine and recombine in unexpected ways. This classic wheels-within-wheels situation makes each succeeding scene in the film just a little bit more tense than the one that came before.

Keeping this complexity involving and fast-moving is director Noyce, assisted by the adroit cross cutting of editor Neil Travis, who also handles the rapid shifting of scenes between numerous South American locations (all apparently photographed in Mexico). The action-set pieces are crackerjack as well, especially a complex ambush filmed on a two-football-fields-long set nicknamed "The Kill Zone" that required eight full weeks of preparation.

What is rarer than good action is plausible dialogue and acting, and this is "Danger's" key strength. Especially convincing, and especially timely, is the film"s depiction of how covert operations go down in Washington, how ambitious men operate in a world of suggestion and innuendo, and how an ambiguous "the course of action I'd suggest is a course of action I can't suggest" can set all sorts of mayhem into motion.

Not only are the key subsidiary characters written in a subtle way, "Danger" has cast the parts with unusually capable actors. In this country, Donald Moffat makes a most convincing President, alternately affable and arrogant, and Henry Czerny and Harris Yulin are equally good as White House apparatchiks.

In Colombia, Willem Dafoe is an appropriately cool CIA field operative, and Portuguese actor Joaquim de Almeida makes a clever and devious opponent. Even smaller roles, such as Ann Magnuson as an FBI secretary and veteran Hope Lange as a suspicious senator, are perfectly carried out.

And once again, as in so many films in the past, Harrison Ford and his combination of intensity and integrity hold it all together. Capable of bringing to life and sympathy a character derided as "a damn Boy Scout" by his more cynical adversaries, Ford is an actor who believes his word to the audience is a bond guaranteeing the best he has to give. Would there were more like him around.

NEW YORK, 8/15/94, p. 54, David Denby

I settled into *Clear and Present Danger*, the latest thriller based on a Tom Clancy novel, like a hungry cow moving into a patch of soft, thick grass. Moo. There's no question of art here, or of risks taken or boundaries pushed back—for that, you may have to wait until Quentin Tarantino's *Pulp Fiction* opens in the fall. *Clear and Present Danger* is about as square as a thriller can be. Patriotic, stentorian, reliable. You know the kind of film: There is a solemn Arlington funeral, and a flag is folded, trumpets are sounded; American boys are rescued from the clutches of Third World monsters. And so on. But what a job of Hollywood craftsmanship.

In the last Jack Ryan thriller, *Patriot Games*, the ace CIA agent was called on to defend his house and family against a rump faction of fanatics, and the picture was so predictable in its procession of thriller gestures that it felt like an exercise. Well, this movie is the payoff. Most of the same team put it together—director Phillip Noyce, star Harrison Ford, cinematographer Don McAlpine, editor Neil Travis, producers Mace Neufeld and Robert Rehme. But this time, three screenwriters—Donald Stewart (who worked on the earlier Jack Ryan movies), Steven Zaillian, and the old rabble-rouser John Milius—have turned Clancy's laborious hugger-mugger into a swiftly moving tale of many layers. A U.S. president wages a private war against the Colombian drug lords, and the movie takes us to the outer edges of the American colossus, where corruptly intelligent men service our needs. The movie perfectly captures the country's ambivalence—the addictive hungers and physical strength, the mixture of violence and compunction.

Some of the casting is wonderfully malicious—Donald Moffat as the president, for instance. Moffat's waxy, painted-looking ruddiness, the hearty, massively dim manner, as of a blimp inching through fog, are all an obvious reminder of Ronald Reagan. And the scenes in which this president authorizes a secret war, without actually *saying* anything, will do fine as an imagined reconstruction of the way Iran-*contra* got started. The darkly intense Canadian actor Henry Czerny, as an Oliver North-Elliot Abrams zealot, winces and draws in his mouth with paranoid fury; Harris Yulin's heavy-browed lugubriousness has been properly used at last, in the role of the president's national-security adviser (Scowcroft in manner, Poindexter in deed).

Rather than burn a lot of metal for no particular purpose, *Clear and Present Danger* has the wit to convert the technology of violence itself into a character. We live, after all, in an age of simultaneity—someone in Washington can order an air strike on a cluster of houses in Libya.

Since movie editing manipulates time and space effortlessly, film, even more than the novel, is the snazziest medium for the international techno-thriller. *Danger* cuts back and forth between two geographical centers of intrigue: In Colombia, a squad of specially trained irregulars pushes through the jungle, blowing up coca-processing sites and calling in smart-bomb raids on the houses of drug lords. There are fascinating glimpses of the manners of the Medellin hacienda, which, for all I know, may be accurately portrayed in their grand-seigneurial largess. In Washington, Jack Ryan, sensing that something unauthorized and possibly unconstitutional is going on, swings into action. So we get both combat and sleuthing (largely by computer), all perfectly timed for suspense and blissfully free of Tom Clancy's tedious armament worship. The two narratives come together in a stunning, physically anguishing scene in which the FBI director and Ryan are ambushed in a narrow Bogota street.

Even though the operation against the drug lords is illegal—initiated without congressional authorization—I found myself rooting for it to be successful. The way it's staged, we *have* to root for it. So the movie, reproducing Clancy's little trick, gives us the double pleasure of seeing the cartels punished and then of watching Jack Ryan's indignation when he realizes what has been going on. I don't think this is a case of simple hypocrisy. One wants evil eradicated, but by constitutional means. It would have been better, however, if the movie had asked whether the drug lords *could* be attacked any way but secretly—whether public authorization would not have tipped off the cartels and set insuperable problems for the Colombian government. But the movie doesn't do that. Manfully, it pursues the righteous constitutional issue. The title is double-edged. There are two cases of clear and present danger. One is the importation of drugs; the other is American authorities who flout the Constitution.

NEW YORK POST, 8/3/94, p. 33, Michael Medved

"Clear and Present Danger" delivers everything you'd expect from a top-drawer action thriller, along with a surprising bonus: the rare and crucial element of believability.

Most recent films about conspiratorial shenanigans in the White House, from the slick comedy "Dave" to the overwrought melodrama "The Pelican Brief," come across as far-fetched and out of focus; "Clear and Present Danger," by contrast conveys all the chilling realism of Oval Office videotapes shot by hidden camera.

We see the president and his advisers wrestling with an all-too plausible sense of impotence at their inability to deliver victories in the "War on Drugs"—a feeling of frustration that's painfully intensified when one of the chief executive's close friends and longtime supporters is brutally murdered by a Colombian cocaine cartel.

The president (played with depth and nuance by Donald Moffatt) then drops broad hints to his brooding national security adviser (the suitably intense Harris Yulin) that the drug lords represent a "clear and present danger to the national security of the United States," thereby justifying a covert military operation in Colombia.

CIA field contractor Willem Dafoe organizes that operation with ruthless efficiency, and ultimately uses some high-tech "smart bomb" wizardry to blow up a hacienda hosting a cartel summit conference. The problem is that the cocaine merchants manage to strike back viciously at U.S. officials, and the entire secret war takes its gruesome toll without the knowledge of Congress, the Pentagon or, most seriously, our hero, Harrison Ford.

Ford once again plays Jack Ryan, the CIA analyst created by novelist Tom Clancy and previously featured in the films "Patriot Games" and "The Hunt for Red October" (where Alec Baldwin played the role). This time, Ryan has been promoted to deputy director of intelligence at "the Company" due to the critical illness of his heroic boss, Admiral James Greer (James Earl Jones).

For most of the movie, Ryan remains peripheral to the action since he knows nothing about the U.S. role in the bloody business in Colombia, but the film is so well-stocked with fascinating supporting characters (superbly placed by Henry Czerny, Joaquim de Alemeida, Ann Magnuson, Miguel Sandoval and others) that not even Ford's biggest fan will mind his temporary absence from center stage.

Australian Phillip Noyce, who previously directed "Patriot Games" as well as the stylish seagoing chiller "Dead Calm," wisely concentrates on human interaction rather than on wizardly gizmos or big action scenes—and that means that the explosions of masterfully shot, brilliantly edited violence, that do periodically punctuate the tension, strike with far more terrifying impact than in lesser thrillers.

It's only in its concluding scenes, with an over-the-top firefight and rescue followed by preachy moralizing by the hero (which closely follows the book), that the movie loses the realism and moral ambiguity that made it so fascinating to watch.

The unusually smart script, jointly credited to the titanic trio of Steven ("Schindler's List") Zaillian, Donald ("Patriot Games") Stewart, John ("Apocalypse Now") Milius, makes every character in this piece unmistakably human, with complex and compelling motivations.

It's too bad that in attempting a rousing, rah-rah conclusion the filmmakers undermined their own fundamental point that in the murky, dangerous, post Cold War world, clear black-and-white has given way to perplexing shades of gray.

NEWSDAY, 8/3/94, Part II/p. B2, Jack Mathews

Almost a year to the day after Harrison Ford came charging onto the late summer screens in "The Fugitive," he returns in the espionage thriller "Clear and Present Danger," and once again shows that if you're looking for rock solid reliability in an action vehicle, shop Ford.

The third and best adaptation of Tom Clancy's Jack Ryan novels, the second pairing Ford with director Phillip Noyce, is far the class of the summer's action films. Where "Speed" was all thrills and no context, "The Client" all character and no credibility, and "True Lies" all comedy and no suspense, "Clear and Present Danger" has it all.

It is a meticulously well-developed tale of political deception, abuse of power, and self-righteous international crime, laced with rich characterizations, taut suspense and eye-popping action sequences. And, at its center, an action star who actually seems to think.

Harrison Ford has been combining his intelligence and athleticism in film roles for a long time, and at 52, he's showing few signs of wear. If anything, those deepening age lines seems to accentuate the reflectiveness behind that rugged face. As Jack Ryan, the seasoned CIA agent disparagingly referred to by internal rivals as the "boy scout," Ford and his role mesh perfectly.

Having previously defended America from nuclear threat ("The Hunt For Red October") and an influx of IRA terrorists ("Patriot Games"), Ryan this time is caught in the middle of an illegal covert drug war, set in motion from the White House and conducted in the cocaine fields and factories of Colombia. Eventually, he will have to confront his own president and put his conscience before his career.

Oliver North may think it's a comedy.

"Clear and Present Danger," a phrase used to justify war, is invoked by President Bennett (Donald Moffatt) after learning that a close friend and his family have been murdered aboard their yacht by a Colombian drug cartel. Before Jack Ryan can investigate and report that the president's friend was, in fact, laundering money for the cartel, and killed for siphoning off $650 million for himself, the president's national security adviser (Harris Yulin) has ordered a reciprocal assault on foreign ground.

As the CIA's acting deputy director of intelligence, Ryan is kept in the dark about the clandestine militia operation, and unknowingly gives false testimony to the congressional committee overseeing its funding. When he discovers how he has been duped, and who the players are on both sides of the drug war, hell will be paid from Colombia to Pennsylvania Avenue.

Noyce, returning to form after the misstep of "Sliver," is equally at ease with suspense and action. The film can match explosions and chase scenes with its noisiest competitors, but it is in the relatively quiet conflicts—the cross-cut sequences of Ryan and another agent chasing evidence in a computer, and Ryan and a member of the drug cartel simultaneously discovering the presence of American troops in Colombia—that raise goosebumps.

"Clear and Present Danger," being an exercise in high-tech machismo, doesn't give its women much to do. Anne Archer, as Ryan's physician wife, gets to answer a phone now and then and appear either concerned or relieved, and Ann Magnuson is around just long enough, as a government secretary, to be seduced, used and terminated by her mysterious Latin lover.

But, hey, this is summer and they can't all be date movies. Besides, as evil as his character is, women may like Joaquim de Almeida, the striking Portuguese actor who plays Felix Cortez, a drug ring lieutenant scheming to unseat his boss (Miguel Sandoval) and take over the lucrative U. S. coke franchise.

Noyce also got strong performances from Willem Dafoe, playing the leather-hard South American CIA operative who leads the U. S. guerrilla troops into battle, and Canadian newcomer Henry Czerny, the agent illegally carrying out White House orders.

Donald McAlpine's luscious photography (the Colombian scenes were all shot in tropical Mexico) and Terence Marsh's elaborately complex sets, including White House, CIA and FBI interiors, as well as a two-block replica of a busy downtown Bogota street used in the film's action centerpiece, help round out the summer's only first-rate thriller.

Better late than never.

NEWSWEEK, 8/8/94, p. 54, Katrine Ames

In Hollywood, practice sometimes actually can make perfect. Harrison Ford has made a career of playing the same guys, but giving them a variety of textures. In the "Star Wars" and "Indiana Jones" trilogies, his Han Solo and Indy had a slightly different warp and woof every time. Ford took on CIA superhero Jack Ryan in "Patriot Games" (1992); in "Clear and Present Danger," he recuts Ryan's suit, and his elegant tailoring saves the movie.

When James Greer (James Earl Jones), the CIA's deputy director of intelligence, gets sick, Ryan must fill in. It's a role that makes him physically and ethically uncomfortable. An American businessman and his family are killed on a yacht in the Caribbean, and the slaughter smells of a drug-cartel hit. Since the man was a pal of the president (Donald Moffat), and the president got elected on an anti-drug platform, Ryan had better crack the case, fast. Armed with little more than his smarts and Greer's laconic advice ("Watch your back, Jack"), that's exactly what he does, dodging missiles, bombs and bullets, and—more to the point—muddying waters the weaselly prez wants to leave clear. For the enemy isn't just a Colombian drug lord and his minions, but (surprise!) men in the U.S. government, especially a steely CIA madman, Robert Ritter (Henry Czerny).

"Danger" moves predictably, and it's a little too complicated and slow for the genre, but director Phillip Noyce tightens key scenes, especially a taut computer battle between Ryan and Ritter. Despite some cardboard characters, the script, based on Tom Clancy's best seller, is unusually literate. It's the work of three master adapters: John Milius (Apocalypse Now") and Oscar winners Steven Zaillian ("Schindler's List") and Donald Stewart ("Missing"). Ford makes the most of it. When everything is falling apart, he says, with a hesitant shrug and a self-deprecating smile, "I hate this job." It's the kind of moment that eases the pain of paying $8 for a ticket.

SIGHT AND SOUND, 10/94, p. 36, Tom Tunney

A close friend of the US President is found murdered on his boat; it turns out he was implicated in Ernesto Escobedo's Colombian drugs cartel. At CIA HQ Admiral Greer assigns Jack Ryan to investigate the case; suffering from terminal cancer, Greer also asks Ryan to take over his duties as Deputy Director of Intelligence. The President gives his security advisor Cutter permission to devise a covert response. Cutter and his colleague Ritter keep their 'Operation Reciprocity' plan secret from Ryan because of his values of loyalty and honesty. In Panama, Ritter meets ex-CIA field operative Clark, who asks for a special forces team to be sent into the Colombian jungle.

Before leaving for Colombia, Ryan gives evidence to a Congressional hearing, and is asked to guarantee that no troops will be deployed. Meanwhile, the US troops are dropped in the Colombian jungle, where they destroy a drugs-laden aircraft and an underground drugs lab. Escobedo's intelligence chief Felix Cortez has an unwitting source of information on US strategy—Moira Wolfson, secretary of FBI chief Jacobs. Wolfson arranges a romantic assignation with Cortez, during which he strangles her. Ryan and the US Ambassador meet Jacobs and his delegation at Bogota Airport, but en route to the Embassy, they are attacked with grenade launchers by Escobedo's assassins; Ryan is one of the few survivors. A USN jet bombs a mansion, where a cartel meeting is taking place ; however, Escobedo survives.

Cortez makes a deal with Cutter, pledging to halve cocaine shipments to the US and provide regular arrests in exchange for details on the location of the US commando team. Ryan gains access to the Reciprocity computer files just as Ritter is deleting them. Clark loses contact with his men, who are subsequently ambushed by the cartel; meanwhile, the President gives a graveside elegy at Greer's funeral. Ryan arrives in Bogota to save the troops, but is kidnapped by the outraged Clark, who had been told that Ryan ordered the operation shutdown. Ryan and Clark search the jungle and find one survivor, US Army sniper Chavez. Ryan walks into Escobedo's mansion and gives him proof that Cortez is plotting against Escobedo. Ryan and Escobedo confront Cortez at his coffee factory HQ; Escobedo is shot. As the group escape by helicopter, Chavez shoots Cortez dead. Back in the US, the President tells Ryan the country can't afford another scandal; Ryan replies that he won't lie. He later gives evidence at a Congressional hearing on the affair.

After *The Hunt for Red October* and *Patriot Games*, this is the third Tom Clancy novel to be filmed, and the second to star Harrison Ford as Jack Ryan. Excepting some of the dialogue, the book is in every way superior to the movie, largely because of the film-makers' ham-fisted attempt to reshape Clancy's complex storyline into a straightforward star vehicle for Ford.

In both novel and film, Ryan is the moral centre, but the film jettisons the book's range of supporting characters whose differing values help define his position. It turns most of those who remain into caricature villains, and Ryan himself into a standard-issue action hero. In the book, however, Chavez and Clark each get roughly the same amount of space as Ryan and handle almost all the action scenes. By virtually eliminating Chavez from the screenplay and downgrading Clark to a supporting player, the screenwriters make more space for Ryan, but lose the moral perspective on him that these two provide.

Ford offers his best lump-in-throat queasy look—as perfected in *Presumed Innocent*—but, for most of the film, his tenuous position within the storyline is more reminiscent of an Alan J. Pakula movie than a conventional action thriller. For Clancy to put Ryan on the outside of things allowed him to maintain Ryan's integrity while at the same time developing an ironic scenario in which justice and the law are repeatedly seen to be at cross purposes. The screenplay, however, ignores this crucial theme, consistently leaving out those episodes in the novel which flesh it out. Instead, the President, Cutter and Ritter are made to be simply wrong and Ryan simply right. Clancy doesn't offer any easy solutions to the moral conundrum he creates for Ryan: should he get with the programme or go public? The film suppresses that problem and makes it easier for both Ryan and the audience to choose sides. Taking a very murky story, it transforms Ryan into a clear and present action hero.

Ryan's guarantee to the Senate hearing that he knows nothing of US covert involvement in Colombia is another screenplay invention to further foreground his integrity. But what are we to make of the intercutting between Greer's funeral and the ambush of the US troops? Do the troops represent a violation of the patriotic principles which defined Greer's life, or do they embody that spirit? This is both the most impressive and the most ambiguous sequence of the film, and the only sequence which approaches the book's involved level of moral debate. Clancy ends with Ryan agreeing to a cover-up of the operation. Given a suitably sarcastic slant, that ending would almost be worthy of a 70s conspiracy thriller, but it certainly wouldn't wash in what aims to be a feel-good blockbuster.

Hence the film's substitution of an industrial strength dose of heroic integrity for Ryan. Here, the rescue mission is a straightforward way for him to right wrongs and put the corrupt political past behind him. His actions in rescuing the survivors and in testifying before the House Committee will consign the President, Ritter and, by implication, every US foreign policy disaster from Vietnam to Somalia, to the dustbin of history.

By casting the elderly Donald Moffat as the President, and giving him some cynical new dialogue, the film-makers explicitly signal that he belongs to the past, to the Reagan-Bush era. Casting a younger, Clintonesque character actor would have been far more courageous because it would have suggested that the abuse of executive power was an on-going danger on Capitol Hill. As it is, Ryan is complacently presented as the first sweep of a new broom on a corrupt old era. "Truth needs a soldier," the limp publicity tag puts it—which is about as accurate a summing-up of Clancy's novel as "Truth needs a sailor" would be of *Moby Dick*.

TIME, 8/15/94, p. 61, Richard Schickel

What do Jack Ryan, a spectacularly energetic CIA operative, and a spectacularly sedentary movie reviewer have in common? In the end, both of them have to make an audience of clueless innocents, understand the incredibly complex series of events related in *Clear and Present Danger*—and keep them alert in the process.

As Jack, played by Harrison Ford, will ultimately testify before a Senate committee, it all starts with a President and his men deciding to insert a small guerrilla force into Colombia to hit one of the cocaine cartels. This is done in deep secrecy, and among those left out of the loop is Jack. After escaping an ambush, he learns that the men in suits are selling out the troops in the field and even trying to do a deal with one of the drug lords.

That's the main line. A whole lot of other interesting stuff feeds smoothly into it: the fight against cancer by Jack's shrewd old mentor (James Earl Jones); an FBI secretary seduced by the oiliest drug runner; the field operatives led by Willem Dafoe who do spectacular damage to the cartel's operations; amusing glimpses of the life-style of its rich and infamous boss. What's truly appealing about the film is that it plays fair with all this material and the audience. Unlike the typical action movie, which is always trampling over narrative logic in order to rush on to the next explosion, this movie had writers (John Milius, Donald Stewart, Steven Zaillian; the film is based on a Tom Clancy novel) who take the time to keep us in the picture. You may not remember all of it later, but as the plot unfolds, its logic is, you might say, clear and present.

The movie has two other qualities you don't always find in films of this kind: a sense of humor and a sense of character. At a particularly desperate moment when Jack must confront the drug boss, he simply walks up to the boss's gate and blandly presents a CIA business card to the menacing guards. It's a much smarter, more amusing choice than blasting his way in.

This is the third movie with Jack as its hero, so he is a known quantity—a humanist spook with an overdeveloped moral sense—but Ford, playing the part for the second time, knows how to keep his earnestness fresh. Meanwhile, Donald Moffat's President is tough and unctuous, his National Security Adviser (Harris Yulin) is tough and tense, and his chief aide (Henry Czerny) is tough and tough.

Director Phillip Noyce deserves credit for the easy confidence of his pace, his quick way with the telling detail. In this movie, unlike some others one might name, the lies ring true, and, at least for the length of its running time, absorb you in a conscientiously constructed fictional world.

VILLAGE VOICE, 8/23/94, p. 58, Lisa Kennedy

In these days of sullied hope, when the Whitewater hearings are just one more confirmation of how few of even the Beltway's "good guys" can resist dancing "the Potomac two-step," as the two-stepping prez of *Clear and Present Danger* says, it's nice to imagine someone like Jack Ryan. More than nice, it's increasingly necessary. As movie heroes go, Harrison Ford's Ryan has some of Messrs. Deeds and Smith in him. This being Clancy not Capra, however, Ryan does not go to Washington as a sheep to slaughter but is by, for, and of the town. And, more to the point, the ideals upon which it was founded. Amen.

Head and shoulders above *Patriot Games* (also directed by Phillip Noyce), *Clear and Present Danger* begins with a swirling ocean, a Coast Guard runner captained by a young woman, and a yacht in the possession of a couple of Colombian nationals who've swabbed it with the blood of an American businessman and his family. We quickly find out the dead entrepreneur is an old friend of the president. The president (Don Moffat) quickly finds out that his buddy was also a launderer for a Cali cartel, but not before he's mumbled something to his national security adviser (Harris Yulin) about these drug cartels representing a "clear and present danger" to national security; the adviser in turn insinuates in no uncertain terms to a CIA deputy director of operations that the chief wants something done, now. In other words, See ya, Congress, we're going in. Welcome to "discretionary warfare."

Clear and Present Danger is one of those tight, conspiracy-driven movies (I haven't told you the half of it) that can rev your entertainment motor even as they remind you the ethical sky is falling, and would collapse, if not for a few good men like CIA intelligence officer Ryan, and his mentor, Admiral James Greer. Here Greer, played by James Earl Jones, the booming voice of integrity for two previous Clancy forays, is dying of pancreatic cancer, And Ryan must step in. Indeed, the scenes of Greer growing weaker and grayer with disease are the stuff that makes this one of the best studio films of the summer (after *Speed* and *Lion King*).

I pause now to reflect on the nasty side of this otherwise uplifting ride. You know, of course, what I'm going to say, but say I must: *brrrrr*. Even with the nuanced work of writers Donald Stewart, Steven Zaillian, and John Milius, Clancy's Cold War jones is clear and present, what with the twinning of our Jack Ryan—a man of ideals—with theirs, a Latin smoothie formerly on Castro's payroll now trying to bumrush the coke-is-it trade. Still, with Ford working that lovely lived-in face, one can be seduced into believing that this is a movie about integrity not ideology, that Ryan's hope is our own.

Also reviewed in:
NEW REPUBLIC, 9/19 & 26/94, p. 38, Stanley Kauffmann
NEW YORK TIMES, 8/3/94, p. C11, Janet Maslin
NEW YORKER, 8/15/94, p. 75, Terrence Rafferty
VARIETY, 8/1-7/94, p. 44, Todd McCarthy
WASHINGTON POST, 8/3/94, p. BI, Rita Kempley
WASHINGTON POST, 8/5/94, Weekend/p. 36, Desson Howe

CLERKS

A Miramax Films release of a View Askew Productions film. *Producer:* Kevin Smith and Scott Mosier. *Director:* Kevin Smith. *Screenplay:* Kevin Smith. *Director of Photography:* David Klein. *Editor:* Scott Mosier and Kevin Smith. *Music:* Scott Angley. *Sound:* James von Buelow. *Sound Editor:* Scott Mosier and James von Buelow. *Make-up:* Leslie Hope. *Running time:* 91 minutes. *MPAA Rating:* Not Rated.

CAST: Brian O'Halloran (Dante Hicks); Jeff Anderson (Randal); Marilyn Ghigliotti (Veronica); Lisa Spoonauer (Caitlin); Jason Mewes (Jay); Kevin Smith (Silent Bob); Scott Mosier (William the Idiot Manchild/Angry Hockey Playing Customer/Angry Mourner); Scott Schiaffo (Chewlie's Rep); Al Berkowitz (Old Man); Walt Flanagan (Wooden Cap Smoker/Egg Man/Offended Customer/Cat Admiring Bitter Customer/Angry Mourner); Ed Hapstak (Sanford); Lee Bendick (#812 Wynarski); David Klein (Hunting Cap Smoking Boy/Low IQ Video Customer/Hub Cap Search Customer/Angry Mourner); Pattijean Csik (Coroner); Ken Clark (Administer of Fine); Donna Jeanne (Indecisive Video Customer); Virginia Smith (Caged Animal Masturbator); Betsy Broussard (Dental School Video Customer); Ernest O'Donnell (Trainer); Kimberly Loughran (Alyssa's Sister Heather); Gary Stern (Tabloid Reading Customer); Joe Bagnole (Cat Shit Watching Customer); John Henry Westhead (Olaf the Russian Metalhead); Chuck Dickel (Stock in Chips Can); Leslie Hope (Jay's Lady Friend); Connie O'Connor ('Happy Scrappy' Mom); Vincent Pereira (Hockey Goalie/Engagement Savvy Customer); Ashley Pereira ('Happy Scrappy' Kid); Erix Infante (Bed Wetting Dad/Cold Coffee Lover); Melissa Crawford (Video Confessor/Candy Confession Customer); Thomas Burke (Blue Collar Man); Dan Hapstak (Door Tugging Customer); Mitch Cohen (Man Leaning Against Wall); Matthew Banta (Burner Looking For Wood); Rajiv Thapar (Cut-off Customer); Ken Clark (Orderly); Mike Belicose (Customer with Diapers); Jane Kuritz (Customer with Vaseline and Rubber Gloves); Grace Smith (Milk Maid); Frances Cresci (Little Smoking Girl); Brian Drinkwater, Bob Fisler, and Derek Jaccodine (Hockey Players).

LOS ANGELES TIMES, 10/19/94, Calendar/p. 1, Kenneth Turan

Lenny Bruce would have loved "Clerks." Rude, boisterous, obscene and irreverently funny, it has all the crude energy and delight in life's profane chaos that the celebrated comedian found so irresistible.

One of the discoveries of last year's Sundance Film Festival (where it shared the Filmmakers Trophy) and later a prizewinner at the International Critics Week at Cannes, "Clerks" is also an example of what is best and most hopeful about the American independent-film scene.

Made in grainy black and white on a skimpy budget of $27,575, "Clerks" is the inspiration of 23-year-old Kevin Smith, who wrote, directed, co-edited, co-produced and even found time to play a cameo as the laconic Silent Bob.

Sporadically employed himself as a convenience-storeclerk, Smith did more than write a script based on his own cool and crazy life behind the counter; he actually filmed it in the Quick Stop in Leonardo, N.J., that hired him, shooting after it closed each night at 10:30 till the small hours of the morning.

But "Clerks" is not just a case of poor movie makes good. For Smith, a film-school dropout who used part of his tuition to finance his debut, has an anarchic gift for sketch humor and the raunchy banter of guys just hanging out. Though the politically incorrect language is tough enough to have earned "Clerks" an initial NC-17 rating (re-rated R on appeal), its exuberance gives it an alive and kicking feeling that is welcome and rare.

Simply structured as a day in the life of clerk Dante Hicks (Brian O'Halloran), Dante's saga begins unexpectedly with an early morning call from his boss telling him he'll have to open the store even though it's Saturday, his nominal day off.

Conscientious to a fault, Dante is unknowingly embarking on a spell of nonstop harassment and humiliation that leaves him understandably muttering, "bunch of savages n this town."

On the professional side, the Quick Stop's obstreperous customers subject Dante to a flood of eccentric behavior, from pelting him with cigarettes to scrutinizing every egg in the case to wanting the simultaneous use of the employees' bathroom and a choice porno magazine.

Paralleling this are Dante's romantic problems. His stand-up girlfriend Veronica (Marilyn Ghigliotti) brings him homemade lasagna for lunch, but outrages Dante with revelations about her past sexual habits that lead to one of the film's funniest colloquies.

And Dante can't get his mind off his ex, the glamorous Caitlin (Lisa Spoonauer), even though they broke up years ago and she cheated on him 8½ times while they were together. What was the half? A drunken tryst with Dante in a darkened room when she thought he was someone else.

Providing an ironic Greek chorus to all these woes is Dante's best friend, Randal (Jeff Anderson), the clerk at an adjoining video store whose stock is so feeble Randal himself rents elsewhere. A prankster and instigator, Randal believes in abusing his customers whenever possible and encourages Dante to be more aggressive in his dealings with the public.

Though Randal and Dante are the center of "Clerks," Smith has a profligate eye for odd and curious characters, and appearances by a manic drug dealer, a smug personal trainer and an intense Russian named Olaf who is desperate to play metal, are among the film's zany highlights.

Cast with either non-professionals or actors with no more than local experience, "Clerks" is unapologetically rough and even ragged at times. But its lack of circumspection turns out to be its charm. Unabashed and unashamed, "Clerks" is always itself, and that is something of an accomplishment.

NEW STATESMAN & SOCIETY, 5/5/95, p. 40, Jonathan Romney

According to a recent article in *Variety*, there's a simple explanation for the return of dialogue in American cinema. the new generation of directors is not emerging from the film schools as Scorsese and his Movie Brat contemporaries did; instead, they learned everything they know about cinema from working in video stores. The trouble with being a video clerk, though, is that you don't get to stand and watch movies all day; you have to turn your attention away from the screen every now and then to serve the occasional customer. But with a trained ear, you can still catch all the dialogue while you're looking elsewhere. Hence a generation of young cineasts who haven't entirely evolved a visual aesthetic all their own; but, boy, can they remember the best lines from their favourite movies.

As loopily reductive theories of film-making go this is inspired, but not entirely convincing. One of the article's subjects, Quentin Tarantino, can hardily have been a model assistant, because he somehow seems to have absorbed plenty about dialogue and visuals (mind you, he probably knew every tape's serial number by heart, too); while his colleague Roger Avary, judging from his film *Killing Joe*, must have been too busy with customers altogether, except when the shootouts came on. Kevin Smith's *Clerks* does seem to bear out the theory pretty well, with highly wrought dialogue and a devout visual minimalism. And yet, the character in the film who actually is a video store assistant doesn't seem inclined to pay attention to either customer of tapes, preferring to spend his time hanging out in the drugstore across the road. Make of that what you will.

Since the terms "slacker" and "Generation X" have come to denote a certain film genre—ie anything made since 1992 in which white kids wear their caps backwards—then, yes, *Clerks* is a slacker movie. It contains a lot of rancid thrash metal music, its characters sit around doing nothing but whingeing for much of the time , and its director and producer are likely to end up being, oh, at least as rich and famous as slacker-pic doyen Richard Linklater. Linklater is currently enjoying mainstream success with *Before Sunrise*, which sees him taking a rather suspect turn for the literal and Europhilic; he'll be ditching the Aerosmith T-shirt yet and making Jane Austen adaptations, just you wait.

I can't quite see Kevin Smith doing that, somehow, if only because none of Austen's novels provides opportunities for impromptu hockey games or litanies of hard-pom video titles. But as far as the language goes, Smith's scriptwriting is already as poised and lapidary as Whit Stillman's, or Eric Rohmer's might be if he hung around the quieter parts of New Jersey. This rather belies the widely touted impression that *Clerks* is a sort of live-action Beavis and Butt-head. It may be coarse and infantile, packed with jokes about beer and cigarettes and blowjobs, and it may climax with the most unbelievably black sex-and-death joke ever told on film, but the comparison ends there.

In fact, the much discussed New Dumbness in American cinema doesn't come into it. Smith's lead character—hapless shop assistants holding their own against a hostile and cigarette-hungry world—may act dumb, but it's only because they're smart enough to know when to face the world with the blankness it deserves. When idiot customers are in the shop, pelting them with cigarettes, testing each egg for perfection, asking for ice in their coffee, they react with all the fatigued peevishness they can muster; as soon as they can get a quiet moment, they're plumbing the mysteries of life, death and the role of roofing contractors in *The Empire Strikes Back*, with exemplary rigour.

The leads—Brian O'Halloran as harassed Dante, Jeff Anderson as his joyously malevolent video-store buddy Randal—rise to the occasion, rattling off their shamelessly over written lines with glee and some apparent discomfort, at top speed, as if they knew it was the only chance they'd get. At the time, it probably was: *Clerks* was shot on a paltry $27,000 which Smith and producer Scott Mosier raised themselves, largely from credit cards and Smith's comics collection. They shot the film on overnight sessions in the New Jersey store where Smith was working at the time (hence Smith's own weary demeanour as a silent loiterer hanging around with Russian heavy metal singers and other manic lowlifes). The film features the most succinct example ever of a low-budget film turning the structures of its making to good advantage. Because of the night shoot, the store shutters had to be permanently down; hence a running gag about how they have been jammed with chewing gum, the first of Dante's infernal ordeals of the day.

Structured as a series of madcap, excruciating vignettes, *Clerks* is like the best, densest sitcom you've ever seen, but without any of the sentimental pauses that US sitcoms routinely feature by way of lipservice to "real life"—this despite some tender but pithy play between Dante and his girlfriend Veronica (Marilyn Ghigliotti), who plies him with lasagna and sexual revelations. In fact, the comedy it most resembles is the surreal, claustrophobic British night-watchmen show *Nightingales*, but with more of a naturalistic take. By the time the guys lock up for the night, leaving a trail of breakage, scandal and obscenity behind them, you feel you've been through the day's rigours with them; you're just aching to get away from the cigarette counter. In fact, Smith clearly felt the same, since he breaks the closure twice—with a rooftop hockey game and a disastrous rush to a funeral parlour. So it flouts the unities—what did you expect, Racine?

NEW YORK, 11/7/94, p. 98, David Denby

For New Yorkers, *Clerks* is a taste of the forbidden, an immersion in that bizarre and scandalous land of anti-creation—New Jersey (i.e., the rest of the country, but frighteningly near). In Kevin Smith and Scott Mosier's defiantly and at times hilariously low-rent Jersey comedy, two hyperarticulate guys waste their days at a convenience store. The guys are guys and nothing but guys. They play roller hockey and curse a lot, and they talk coarsely of women, whom they nevertheless desperately need. A series of blackout comedy sketches, shot mainly from the customers' point of view, *Clerks* is naggingly funny, a kind of talented-slacker demo tape. What comes next?

NEW YORK POST, 10/19/94, p. 36, Thelma Adams

In high school, I worked in men's underwear—a clerk at a Montgomery Wards. We've all worked deadly, minimum wage jobs, but not everyone can turn that experience into a feature-length movie.

With "Clerks." guerrilla filmmaker Kevin Smith shares the humor and claustrophobia of being a register jockey at a Quick Stop convenience store and the adjacent video outlet.

In the past year, "Clerks" has become a festival darling, winning the 1994 Sundance Film Festival Filmmakers Trophy Award and screening at the Cannes Film Festival International Critics Week.

Inspired by "Slackers," newcomer Smith's low-low-budget comedy carves out a day in the life of two Jersey boys, Dante (Brian O'Halloran) and Randal (Jeff Anderson). They're a couple of white guys sittin' around venting and popping junk food, Beavis and Butthead in black and white.

The 22-year-old slackers serve the public with two very different attitudes. Randal has perfected the art of being rude to customers, at one pointing spitting water across the counter at a shopper. "This job would be great if it weren't for the f**king customers," he says.

Dante takes his job too seriously, but is barely more responsible. Over a single day, Dante comes across two corpses and tangles with two girlfriends. He sells countless packs of smokes while deciding whether to rekindle a relationship with his ex and contemplating the meaninglessness of his existence—("Have you ever noticed that all the prices end in 9?").

The dialogue crackles. The encounters are well-written and engagingly acted, with vignettes sandwiched between such ironic titles as "Syntax," "Harbinger," and "Catharsis." The characters are affectionately drawn, particularly Dante's devoted girlfriend Veronica (Marilyn Ghigliotti).

Early in the movie, there's a lovely intimacy between Dante and Veronica as they huddle together on the floor behind the counter. Dante polishes Veronica's nails as they talk—a great touch.

Veronica's struggles to better their lives through education are frustrated by Dante's inertia and refusal to trade in the clerking life for college.

The blue-collar couple's relationship seems fresh and real, but Smith goes for the cheap jokes. The discussion turns to cataloguing past sexual partners and the movie's primary comic motif—fellatio.

What is funny once or twice becomes dreadfully boring. Even Howard Stern at his dirtiest has a whole closet of subjects on which he riffs.

NEWSDAY, 10/19/94, Part II/p. B9, John Anderson

The hype on "Clerks" has accumulated like empties at a slacker sleepover. Yes, writer-director Kevin Smith really worked behind a convenience store counter. He and producer Scott Mosier put their film together for less than $30,000. They were discovered by Amy Taubin in the Village Voice, lauded in Sundance, feted in Cannes, adopted by Miramax and villified by Jack Valenti. Their original NC-17 rating—which only accelerated their publicity juggernaut while confirming the irrationality of the ratings board—was reduced to an R, thus channeling them into the mainstream. It just doesn't get any better than this.

And it doesn't get much funnier than "Clerks," which is astoundingly vulgar, howlingly irreverent and indicates a distinct gift on Smith's part for visual comedy. It isn't much of a cinematic achievement; it's low, low budget, grainy, itchy and scratchy. But so are its subjects, which makes for a very healthy marriage of subject and medium.

Set in a Quick Stop somewhere in New Jersey (in Leonardo, actually, where the director worked and filmed, mostly at night), "Clerks" is a day in the life of Dante Hicks (Brian O'Halloran), a long-suffering, Leo Bloomish kind of slacker, who lacks the requisite ennui to be representative of the species: His is an unaffected aimlessness, less like alienation than paralysis. He's 22, he's been at the store since he was 19, his girlfriend Veronica (Marilyn Ghigliotti) goes to college, and he doesn't. But he's also somehow devoid of culpability, an innocent passerby in his own life.

Despite his Generation X-terior, however, he has a strong sense of duty: Awakened on a groggy weekend morning, after having closed the store the night before, he's told to go back and work till noon when the boss will relieve him. Although he has a hockey game scheduled for the afternoon, he agrees to go back, and no one but Dante thinks he'll be leaving on time.

What happens at the store is supposed to be typical, which is part of the joke—a parade of whacked-out customers, drug dealers, Muscovite metalheads, guidance counselors having nervous breakdowns. He gets visitors—Veronica, who reveals more about her sex history than Dante wanted to know, and Caitlin (Lisa Spoonauer), his ex, who's been reactivating their relationship and then turns out to be engaged. And he participates in a daylong dialogue with Randal (Jeff Anderson), who runs the video store adjacent to the Quick Stop and provides the irritant that keeps Dante in a constant state of actual and philosophical flux.

The entire cast of newcomers is fresh and funny—Smith appears as Silent Bob, aide-de-camp to the coke-dealing Jay (Jason Mewes); Mosier plays several minor characters, two of whom are seen yelling at each other during Dante's rooftop hockey game. O'Halloran is particularly engaging. But Anderson is the secret weapon, an anarchist retailer who serves as Dante's conscience. Insulting customers, ignoring his job—indulging a taste for hermaphrodite videos during working hours—he constantly probes Dante's unfocused sense of virtue and morality, making him face up to the many unresolved issues in his life. Which is not to say "Clerks" should be taken as anything but a comedy—one that pushes the envelope of taste and decency, whatever they are. But Smith is also wise enough to know that truth is funnier than fiction. And there's more truth in "Clerks" than Dante, for instance, would want to admit.

NEWSWEEK, 10/31/94, p. 68, David Ansen

It's a bad day for Dante Hicks (Brian O'Halloran), the 22-year-old cash-register jockey at the Quick Stop convenience store in Leonardo, N.J. He was supposed to have a day off, to play hockey with his pals. Instead, he's stuck at work, fending off irate and pushy customers. He is fighting with his girlfriend, Veronica (Marilyn Ghigliotti), who stuns him with revelations of her past adventures in oral sex, and he's reeling from the news that his ex-girlfriend is about to marry "an Asian design major." Before the day is over, a customer will die on him, he'll be fined for selling cigarettes to a 4-year-old and his old flame will have sex with a corpse. Next door at the video store, his irritating best friend, Randal (Jeff Anderson), is busy insulting his customers and provoking Dante into deep trouble.

Clerks, which received an R rating after its NC-17 was successfully challenged, is a grungy, profane and often uproarious comedy of twenty something frustration. It's the work of 23-year-old Kevin Smith, a former employee of this very same Quick Stop. Inspired by such no-budget cult movies as "Stranger Than Paradise" and "Slacker" he mounted, this funky, black-and-white opus for a mere $27,575. A smash at the Sundance Film Festival, Smith's chatty, affectionate salute to brainy guys in brainless jobs exhibits a deadpan mastery of verbal comedy timing any veteran director might envy. Smith, who appears as Silent Bob, the sidekick of an obnoxious dope dealer, has a fine ear for his characters' needling small talk, lovers' snits, smutty harangues and whiny obsessions. Overhype won't do this modest film any favors, let's just say it's a hard film not to like.

SIGHT AND SOUND, 5/95, p. 42, Lizzie Francke

Dante works at his local convenience store. On his day off, his boss calls him and asks if he will do an extra shift. Dante reluctantly agrees, foregoing a lie-in as well as hockey practice. Veronica, his girlfriend, comes by and reveals in conversation that she has performed fellatio on 37 guys in the past. A horrified Dante discusses the matter with Randal, his best friend who works at the adjacent video store and is further upset by Randal's news that Dante's high-school sweetheart, Caitlin, is getting married.

Veronica returns and Randal teases her. Dante finds out that his boss has gone to Vermont and that he will have to miss his hockey game. Furious about this, Dante rearranges the match so that it takes place on the store's roof, although the game is abandoned when the ball disappears down the drain. Back at the store, an old man asks to use the bathroom, then he asks if he can borrow a porn mag. Dante and Randal hear that one of their old school friends has died. They go to the wake but leave quickly, Randal having knocked the casket over.

A fitness trainer turns up at the store. Dante learns that he used to go out with Caitlin at the same time as she was dating him. Later a trading inspector fines Dante for selling cigarettes to minors. Dante begins to feel persecuted. Things come to head when Caitlin turns up. She announces that she has broken off her engagement and wants to go out with him again.

She goes to the bathroom and returns to compliment Dante on his sexual performance in the dark. He doesn't understand. It transpires that she has just had sex with the corpse of the old man who went to the bathroom. Caitlin goes into shock and is taken off to hospital. Dante is appalled. He is also berated for not caring enough about Veronica. Meanwhile Randal has told Veronica about Caitlin which naturally upsets her. When Randal returns to the store, Dante picks a fight with him. Later they patch up their friendship as they set about closing the store.

As the put-upon Dante's day spirals increasingly out of control, there is pathos in his exasperation: "The real tragedy is that I'm not even meant to be her today." *Clerks* would seem to be the slacker's existentialist crisis movie. It's not that *nothing* happens; it's more that *everything* that does, however trivial, sets his life off-kilter. Yet there's a sense that there will always be an overnight stock check and that everything will be put back in place the following day to be disrupted once again by the assortment of odd-ball customers, with their bizarre habits and dumb questions acting as counterpoint to the fanciful digressions of the two clerks concerned. In this respect *Clerks* is a circumspect comedy about the mundane and profane, with Dante and Randal as stooges waiting for their daily punchline. (Here the incident involving Caitlin and the old guy in the bathroom is the gross-out comic climax).

The film is structured into 18 episodes with debut writer/director Kevin Smith granting Dante a jokey poetics through segments entitled "Vilification", "Syntax", "Vagary", "Malaise", "Harbinger", "Perspicacity", "Paradigm", "Whimsy", "Lamentation", "Juxtaposition" and "Catharsis". This is tragi-comedy New Jersey style. At the age of 23, Kevin Smith has made an auspicious start to his career. With the film made for around $27,000, he and his producer Scott Mosier demonstrate the kind of ingenuity that would make Roger Corman beam. Moonlighting at the Leonardo QuickStop store where Smith was working as a check-out clerk, the crew shot the film at night over a three week period. Thus the reason why the window shutters are down must be quickly established (they are jammed), and it becomes a running joke throughout the film.

Following the maxim "the budget is the aesthetic", whatever might have been wanting in the film is made up for in the script and the performances. The young cast have a gift with timing that is essential to the film's comic patois, with Brian O'Halloran perfecting a suitably wearied glare as the put-upon Dante ably matched by the deadpan iconoclastics of Jeff Anderson's Randal. As talk is cheap, it comes lean and fast here, all the time on the edge of absurdity. Smith is very much in the new generation of talk-heavy film-makers that includes Quentin Tarantino, Whit Stillman and Richard Linklater. His script is packed with observational but inconsequential set-piece riffs on such subjects as fellatio, friendship, semen snowballs and semantics. There is also the obligatory pop culture spiel—a debate on the ending of *Return of the Jedi* which segues into a discussion on home improvements and the moral universe of a roofing contractor.

The re-occurring preoccupations, however, are with people's basic habits from defecating to sex to smoking to those strange customers who insist on checking eggs to find the perfect dozen (allowing for the great riposte—"its not like you laid the eggs yourself"). If there is a binding concern to this film, then it is the peculiar predilections of those living in or passing through a small patch of New Jersey. This grass-roots catalogue of the weird and wondrous is contrasted with the more obvious oddities that make wacky headlines in *The National Inquirer* and which are commented upon in the film. The antics of Dante's customers and friends are rendered as fascinating, funny and compelling as anything in the newspaper this side of Elvis on the moon.

TIME, 9/12/94, p. 86, Richard Corliss

The Hollywood line is that this has been a summer of adult movies. But *Forrest Gump, Wolf* and *Clear and Present Danger* are not primarily for adults—that is, for grownups in search of films a bit more demanding than those in the standard coming-of-age, horror and thriller genres. Somebody has to wonder: Can there be other kinds of pictures? And if they exist, can they connect with a sufficient number of appreciative viewers?

The answers, right now, are yes and yes. American independent films—pictures made on low budgets and released by smaller distributors—are shouldering their way into the Top 20 chart of weekly box-office winners. How low is low-budget? Kevin Smith's *Clerks*, a wonderful day-in-the-life comedy set in a New Jersey convenience store, arrives next month. The total budget was $27,575. If Smith were given, say, the $100 million that *True Lies* is reputed to have cost, he could make 3,626 movies.

But forget the money. Almost by definition, independent films are acts of love, not commerce. They are informed by the moviemaker's passion to put a vision on screen, and the process usually takes torturous years. That may be one reason so many of these films seem on the sour side. When getting a picture made means hocking your car, borrowing on your inheritance and panhandling your friends, the art that results can look pretty desperate. All the new films discussed below, even the comedies, play like cries from the heart—want ads from the abused and the absurd.

White male, early 20s, just wants to get through the day.

Dante (Brian O'Halloran) has the night shift at the Quick Stop convenience store in Leonardo, New Jersey. Bright, dour and put-upon, he wastes or redeems his time by fretting about life—about everything but his place in it, which he accepts with a readiness that annoys his friend Randal (Jeff Anderson). *Clerks* is a nothing-much-happens-and-ain't-that-the-big-truth? movie that gets considerable mileage from a couple of white guys, and their friends and customers, sitting around talking.

The film looks no more expensive than it was; some of the acting (by local nonprofessionals) is spectacularly amateurish; the story is a series of anecdotes about hockey, shopping and loving the one you're with. But it's worth loitering in this shop. You never know what headline will show up on the cover of a tabloid (SPACE ALIEN REVEALED AS HEAD OF TIME WARNER—REPORT STOCK INCREASE).

Yes, the film has its share of scabrous banter—recombinant four-letter words galore—but the conceit of *Clerks* is that foul-mouthed Jersey louts have elaborate vocabularies and pensive personalities. When Randal isn't shocking the frail with a list of porn-movie titles, he is offering such bartender wisdom to Dante as this: "That seems to be the leitmotiv of your life, ever backing down." Insults cascade into insights; obscenity snowballs into philosophy. Keeping the mind alert and the tongue sharp—for the eloquent jerks in *Clerks*, that's more than a defense mechanism. It's a vocation.

White male, late teens, desires to be left alone, preferably in the bathroom.

Raymond (Jeremy Davies) is the ideal student, the ideal son. So when his bullying, philandering dad tells the boy to give up a prestigious summer job to care for his mother (Alberta Watson), he does so. Mom, who has broken her leg, is a dish, and David O. Russell's *Spanking the Monkey* soon reveals itself as *The Graduate* with one more taboo dropped. Instead of being seduced by his girlfriend's mother, Raymond eliminates the middle-woman and emulates Oedipus. The tone here is so dry that many viewers refuse to see this smart-looking film as a comedy. It is—a comedy of desperation, about a kid who really doesn't want to have sex with anyone but himself. The movie is finally predictable, but it has connected with a generation that believes it has been saddled with the thankless job of raising its own parents.

Hispanic females, late teens and already older than Eve, seek communal sisterhood. Motherhood we had forced upon us years ago.

In the Echo Park section of Los Angeles, it's hard for a man to survive. And it's almost harder for a woman to survive when her man is gunned down, sent to jail or on the lam from his responsibilities. From this sorority of the damned, writer-director Allison Anders (*Gas Food Lodging*) highlights four young women in the episodic *Mi Vida Loca/My Crazy Life*. For them, romantic yearning is like an image of lovers on a drive-in movie screen: huge and fleeting. The film has too many slow spots, and its message is laid on with a trowel, but it has a kind of perverse Hollywood glamour. When the camera holds on the gorgeous, thoughtful faces of Marlo Marron and Salma Hayek, beauty becomes truth—the repository of hope and despair.

Black male, 12, wishes to play chess and, somehow, stop the ghetto madness.

We've seen it all before—if not in movies, then on the local news. A boy still in grade school peddles cocaine for drug lords; he seems set for a short, brutal sentence in the prison of the inner city. But we have not seen that story *Fresh*, from the perspective of young Michael (Sean Nelson), who has a lively brain and a vengeful spirit to ensure his success on the streets. Nor have we seen the tale through the acute camera eye of writer-director Boaz Yakin.

With its forays into Manhattan's Washington Square Park for lessons in chess from a sympathetic father figure (here it's the always authoritative Samuel L. Jackson), the movie might aim to be a *Searching for Bobby Fischer in the Hood*. But *Fresh* is so much more: a really good film, for a start, made with a subtle precision that suggests a Vermeer landscape of the ninth circle of hell. *Fresh* alchemizes the terrifying clichés of urban melodrama into annihilating poetry. A guarantee: the film's last shot—just a boy's face, in ruins—will break your heart.

White male, late 20s, wants to visit Paris, pull off a bank heist with a psychotic old friend, and just maybe survive.

All right, just because a film is small, that doesn't guarantee it's good. Like Kevin Smith and Quentin Tarantino, Roger Avary is a graduate of clerking in video stores—the new film school. But Avary, who worked with Tarantino on *True Romance* and *Pulp Fiction*, has not yet found his voice, at least to judge from *Killing Zoe*, a noisy heist film with Eric Stoltz as the blasé American in Paris.

The movie is a replay of Tarantino's *Reservoir Dogs*, a bloody study of macho alienation and Method posturing. Jean-Hugues Anglade, the French star of *Betty Blue, La Femme Nikita* and the forth-coming *Queen Margot*, bites off huge chunks of scenery as the nutty gang leader; his performance is a great geyser of bad acting.

White female, fun-loving, 20s, want to meet some hot babes.

Go Fish, written by Guinevere Turner (who is also a charmer in the lead role of Max) and Rose Troche, and directed by Troche, offers a radical take on lesbians: they're human beings. Imagine! They can be funny and horny. They look for love and, when they're not looking, fall in it. Max, "a carefree Sappho lesbo" hooks up with gawky Ely (V.S. Brodie), who finds it hard to commit to anything, even a haircut. And just like real people—oh, yes—lesbians can be long-winded, tortured and smug.

The movie makes an asset of its minimal budget by interpolating abstract footage and a few surreal "trial" sequences that both tease and pay homage to gay feminism. For the uninitiated, there are a few comic "inside" glimpses, as when Max and her clan gossip about lesbians in history, from k. d. lang all the way back to Eve. At heart, though, *Go Fish* is a chummy date movie about the mundane, urgent business of finding a lover. Max could be any teen on the Friday-night prowl, but with a nice bending of Hollywood theology: girl meets girl, girl gets girl, nobody goes berserk.

Very white males, 20s, wish the world would accept them for what they are; American yuppies, and isn't that enough?

Whit Stillman always stands out in the grungy group portrait of American independents: he's the one in the navy-blue blazer and old school tie. In *Metropolitan*, released in 1990 he created an engaging circle of Manhattan debs and preppies enthralled by their own obsolescence. In *Barcelona*, on a larger canvas, Stillman paints a sympathetic portrait of two Americans—Ted (Taylor Nichols), a genteel businessman, and his snarkier cousin, Fred (Chris Eigeman), a naval officer—adrift in Spain during what the film, with beguiling pomposity, calls "the last decade of the cold war."

Two movies into what deserves to be a long and unfettered career, Stillman has fashioned a subspecies of civilized male that is as well defined as a Fitzgerald beau or a Cheever suburbanite. They are the young, Reagan-bred Republicans who astounded their parents by turning out exactly like them, but with a coating of Lettermanesque irony. They see *The Graduate* from the viewpoint of the spurned, stuffy groom. They believe that being a salesman is "not just a job but a culture." They read the Bible while dancing alone to Glenn Miller's *PEnnsylvania 6-5000*. And when they encounter sensuous señoritas who declare, "I don't go to bed with just anyone anymore—I have to be attracted to him sexually," these paragons of starched Waspness engage in prime Whit Stillman cross talk:

Ted: Spanish girls are very promiscuous.

Fred: You're such a prig.

Ted: I wasn't using *promiscuous* pejoratively.

Fred: I wasn't using *prig* pejoratively.

Barcelona has been scorned in some corners for wearing its conservatism on its tailored sleeve. But no film, especially an independent film, should hew to a company line of political rectitude. Besides, a Stillman movie delights because it shows its men-about-town to be just as estranged as any deli clerk or Harlem youth. And how eager they all are for love—as eager as any downtown lesbians. *Barcelona* is just that kind of post-modern romance: a *G.O.P. Fish*.

VILLAGE VOICE, 10/25/94, p. 51, J. Hoberman

Coolly outrageous or outrageously cool? Kevin Smith's *Clerks* has dodged the ratings bullet and, by winning reclassification on appeal, spared Miramax (and its corporate parent, Disney) the embarrassment of an NC-17. Still, as provocatively crass, cruddy, and lowbrow as *Clerks* is, Smith's exercise in verbal slapstick will never be mistaken for *Bullets Over Broadway*. A movie of considerable talk, but offscreen action only, *Clerks* is as déclassé as the rankest Mack Sennett two-reeler.

Produced for $27,575 in grainy black-and-white16mm, *Clerks* makes its sincere crudeness part of the joke. A slapdash succession of long takes and static two-shots, each vignette set off with a high-falutin title like "Syntax" or "Malaise," the movie recounts a singularly frustrating day in the life of a New Jersey convenience store clerk, Dante Hicks (Brian O'Halloran). The raw, avid performances are on the level of early John Waters. The constant gabfest gives the dialogue every opportunity to turn rancid, although the often amateurish line readings are sweetened with a garage band score (Soul Asylum, Bad Religion, Love Among Freaks). As with Waters, there's a backbeat of psychodrama. Director-writer-coproducer Smith (who appears as the aptly named dope dealer, Silent Bob) was actually employed behind the counter of the bunkerlike 7-Elevenoid where the movie unfolds.

Clerks opens one early Saturday morning, with the evocatively named Dante, 22 (same age as Smith when he began filming) and still living at home, called in for emergency duty at the Quick Stop Grocery. It ends, after a dozen or so hours in low-rent hell, at closing time, having afforded the droll spectacle of Dante coping (or not) with crises that range from a chewing-gum-jammed padlock and a rabble-rousing gum salesman posing as an antismoking activist to the announced engagement of his high school girlfriend Caitlin and the posthumous misadventures of two frisky corpses.

Much of the comedy is beyond broad. Smith's idea of a sight gag is a close-up of a dog's anus or the cat box that periodically materializes on Dante's counter. *Clerks* is obsessed with stroke books and blowjobs. (As Manny Farber once wrote of some George Kuchar opus, it's a movie in love with its own body odor.) But it's nothing if not self-aware. The Quick Stop magazine rack features *The Independent* and the movie is dedicated to indie gods Hal Hartley, Jim Jarmusch, Spike Lee, and Richard Linklater. Smith has called *Slacker*, which he says that he saw on his 21st birthday, "an epiphany." *Clerks*, however, is less celestial, more concerned with low-grade drudgery than high-concept goofing off. The depressed Dante is basically a spectator in his life; his recurring wail is "I'm not even supposed to be here today."

Reading of Caitlin's announced wedding to the never-seen character usually referred to as "an Asian design major" (or, by one dumbo, as "an Asian drum major"), Dante—who is constantly discovering and obsessing over his girlfriends' sexual peccadillos—clingsto the pathetic hope that the notice is a "typographical error." Similarly, *Clerks* manages to be both quotidian and hyperbolic—a saga of petty triumphs amid ongoing defeats. Stuck in the store, resourceful Dante arranges a rooftop hockey game that breaks up after a few minutes when an irate customer swats the lone puck down a sewer. All he needs to do is ask "Jesus Christ, what next?" in order to be hit with an excessive and unfair fine for selling cigarettes to a minor.

Like an extended vaudeville routine, the movie is a succession of one-on-ones—Dante variously contending with his volatile current girlfriend Veronica (Marilyn Ghigliotti), the mysterious Caitlin (Lisa Spoonauer), and his anarchic buddy Randal (Jeff Anderson), the man behind the counter at the video store next door. The two clerks have radically different styles. Whereas dutiful Dante, who is far more the victim of his customers than vice versa, gets stuck helping a guy with a can of Pringles wedged to his arm or wondering why every price seems to end in nine, the coolly swaggering Randal, unburdened by superego, specializes in provoking and insulting the public—heedlessly driving a young mother and child out of his store in the course of placing a lengthy order to his pornographic video distributor or, while visiting the Quick Stop, spitting water at a particularly garrulous patron.

In the movie's least-strained repartee (thanks in part to Anderson's facility as a natural born jerk), the two clerks trade tales of insane or "unruly" customers, regale each other with accounts of extravagant oral sex acts, engage in a prolonged discussion of the hypothetical role played by independent building contractors in the construction of the Death Star in *The Empire Strikes Back* and *Return of the Jedi* (this interrupted by a roofer who recounts his own experience with the local gangster class), and argue whether or not Dante is capable of changing his life.

It's a moot point. The version of *Clerks* shown at Sundance last January ended with a stickup wherein Dante got shot. The current ending is far more appropriately existential.

Also reviewed in:
CHICAGO TRIBUNE, 11/4/94, Friday/p. H, Michael Wilmington
NEW YORK TIMES, 10/19/94, p. C17, Janet Maslin
VARIETY, 1/31-2/6/94, p. 67, Todd McCarthy
WASHINGTON POST, 11/4/94, Weekend/p. 44, Desson Howe
WASHINGTON POST, 11/5/94, p. D5, Hal Hinson

CLIENT, THE

A Warner Bros. release in association with Regency Enterprises and Alcor Films. *Producer:* Arnon Milchan and Steven Reuther. *Director:* Joel Schumacher. *Screenplay:* Akiva Goldsman and Robert Getchell. *Based on the book "The Client" by:* John Grisham. *Director of Photography:* Tony Pierce-Roberts. *Editor:* Robert Brown. *Music:* Howard Shore. *Music Editor:* Ellen Segal. *Sound:* Petur Hliddal and (music) John Richards. *Sound Editor:* Charles L. Campbell and Donald J. Malouf. *Casting:* Mali Finn. *Production Designer:* Bruno Rubeo. *Art Director:* P. Michael Johnston. *Set Designer:* Marco Rubeo and Kevin Cross. *Set Decorator:* Anne D. McCulley. *Set Dresser:* Joseph Timothy Conway, Tom Gilbert, and David Weathers. *Special Effects:* Larry Fioritto. *Costumes:* Ingrid Ferrin. *Make-up:* David Craig Forrest. *Special Make-up Effects:* Randy Westgate. *Stunt Coordinator:* Glory Fioramonti and Rick Barker. *Running time:* 124 minutes. *MPAA Rating:* PG-13.

CAST: Susan Sarandon (Reggie Love); Tommy Lee Jones (Roy Foltrigg); Mary-Louise Parker (Dianne Sway); Anthony LaPaglia (Barry Muldano); J.T. Walsh (McThune); Anthony Edwards (Clint Von Hooser); Brad Renfro (Mark Sway); Will Patton (Sgt. Hardy); Bradley Whitford (Thomas Fink); Anthony Heald (Trumann); Kim Coates (Paul Gronke); Kimberly Scott (Doreen); David Speck (Ricky Sway); William H. Macy (Dr. Greenway); Ossie Davis (Harry Roosevelt); Micole Mercurio (Momma Love); William Sanderson (Wally Boxx); Walter Olkewicz (Romey); Amy Hathaway (Karen); Jo Harvey Allen (Claudette); Ron Dean (Johnny Sulari); William Richert (Harry Bono); Will Zahrn (Gill Beale); Mark Cabus (Detective Nassar); Dan Castellaneta (Slick Moeller); John Diehl (Jack Nance); Tom Kagy (Patient in Wheelchair); Alex Coleman, Linn Beck Sitler, Stephanie Weaver, and Todd Demers (Newscasters); Ashtyn Tyler (Amber); Ruby Wilson (Receptionist); Andy Stahl (Agent Scherff); Ronnie Landry (Waiter at Antoine's); Jeffry Ford (Bailiff); Macon McCalman (Ballatine); Michael Detroit (Jail Medic); John Fink (Lieutenant); Mimmye Goode (Night Nurse); Robert Hatchett (Paramedic); Connye Florance (Telda); Sandra Bray, Yvonne Sanders, Norm Woodel, and Karen Walker (Reporters); Rebecca Jernigan (Emergency Nurse); Tommy Cresswell (Third FBI Agent); Nat Robinson (Special Agent Boch); Mary McCusker (Pretty

Girl); Bettina Rose (Woman at Desire); Joey Hadley and Michael Sanders (Officers); Angelo R. Sales (Orderly); Christopher Gray and Jesse L. Dunlap (Security Guards); Joe Kent (Elvis Impersonator); Robbie Billings (Ballatine's Wife); John Mason, Robert H. Williams and Darrell D. Johnson (Musicians); Mark Pyles (Helicopter Pilot); Clay Lacy (Jet Pilot); Gerry Loew and Anthony C. Hall (Pizza Men); George Klein (Announcer).

CHRISTIAN SCIENCE MONITOR, 7/21/94, p. 12, David Sterritt

Just when it appeared the entire summer would be a parade of mad bombers and evil terrorists bent on blowing away the last remaining traces of Hollywood civility, along comes a warm-weather thriller with a reasonable degree of respect for its characters, its subject, and the intelligence of its audience.

That's not to say "The Client" is a thinking person's movie, or that its straight-out suspense scenes work as well as its more humanly scaled episodes. Just the opposite, in fact, since the moments that work hardest to put you on the edge of your seat are the ones most likely to set your mind wandering.

Generally speaking, though, "The Client" is the most cleverly conceived and skillfully made melodrama to emerge from a major studio in months. All of which comes as quite a surprise to me, since I was dreading the combination of filmmaker Joel Schumacher—whose "Falling Down" and "Dying Young" set new lows in pop-culture pretension—and the repetition of John Grisham's big, boring bestseller. The awfulness of the last movie based on a Grisham novel, "The Pelican Brief," didn't reassure me, either.

The screenplay of "The Client," by Akiva Goldsman and Robert Getchell, closely follows Grisham's plot, It focuses on young Mark Sway, a bright 11-year-old who stumbles on an adventure he never wanted—becoming sole witness to the drunken confession and bloody suicide of a mob lawyer, who knows where the body of a murdered senator is buried.

Fearing the exposure of their deadly secret, the mob would like to rub Mark out, or at least terrorize him into permanent silence. The police should be his friends under these circumstances, but Mark is far from certain they'd protect him from the retribution that would surely come if he cooperated. His only confidante is a lawyer he finds almost by accident, and while she's full of good intentions, she's far less experienced than the hard-boiled cops and unscrupulous crooks relentlessly dogging her client's trail.

What brings "The Client" more alive on the wide screen than on the printed page is a combination of well-chosen ingredients, starting with first-rate acting by two seasoned pros and one delightful newcomer.

The finest of the pros is Tommy Lee Jones, who seems to be everywhere this summer—he almost brings off a carelessly written role in the violent "Blown Away," and next month he'll arrive in "Natural Born Killers," where he plays a prison warden with an over-the-top energy that would be comfortably at home in a Three Stooges movie. His portrayal of a self-centered prosecutor in "The Client" ranks with his snappiest work in ages, perfectly timed and generously spiced with satirical humor.

Susan Sarandon gives a smart and energetic performance as Reggie, the lawyer with a troubled past and a challenging present. First-time actor Brad Renfro makes a sensational debut as her unusual young client. The supporting cast is exceptionally solid, with a long list of respected talents including Mary-Louise Parker as Mark's hard-pressed mother, J.T. Walsh as an ambitious cop, Anthony Edwards as Reggie's solicitous assistant, the magnetic Will Patton as a sly police officer, and the great Ossie Davis as a judge with limited patience for scoundrels.

Another key contributor to the film's success is Tony Pierce-Roberts, who did the extraordinarily good-looking camera work. The movie doesn't have a naturalistic appearance to mirror the novel's plodding realism; instead, it takes off in visual directions of its own, filling the screen with unexpected colors and patterns. Pierce-Roberts's credits include some of James Ivory's most eye-dazzling pictures, such as "Howards End" and "A Room With a View," both of which earned Oscar nominations for the cinematographer. Praise also goes to Robert Brown for editing Pierce-Roberts's shots with expressive precision.

Finally, even a non-Schumacher fan like me has to acknowledge his directorial competence in pulling together the movie's performances, cinematography, and editing so they work together in smooth, enjoyable harmony. It turns out that the auteur of "Flatliners" and "The Lost Boys" has a good movie in him after all—and here's hoping it's the first of many.

LOS ANGELES TIMES, 7/20/94, Calendar/p. 1, Kenneth Turan

John Grisham's novels are like flypaper: insubstantial but entangling. Not noted for characterization or style, their shark-like sense of unstoppable narrative drive practically forces the reader to keep turning those pages. That is a nice talent to have in a nation that does much of its reading on airplanes.

Because the originals are so insubstantial, the film versions of Grisham's books are more porous than most adaptations, prone to absorbing the aesthetic coloration of the people who direct them. "The Firm" was better for the care Sydney Pollack took with acting and characterization: "The Pelican Brief" got bogged down in Alan Pakula's oblique moroseness, and now "The Client" comes to us with the mark of Joel Schumacher on it.

Though his name is not yet on the short list for AFI's Life Achievement Award, Schumacher is in many ways a good match for Grisham material. The director of "Falling Down," "Dying Young" and "Flatliners," Schumacher is an unapologetically commercial filmmaker (as his next assignment on studio franchise "Batman III" underlines) and he is excited about the material in a way a more ethereal type wouldn't be.

The combination of Schumacher's on-the-nose eye for mass public appeal with Grisham's best-selling sensibility has produced a film that is probably truer to the spirit of the original novels than were its predecessors. Not particularly nuanced or fine-tuned, "The Client," like its source material, is both gimmicky and involving, a fast-moving comic-book version of a comic-book novel.

And while Schumacher has not been known as an actor's director, "The Client" is beefed up by a pair of satisfying star performances. Both on their own and in their scenes together, Susan Sarandon and Tommy Lee Jones are often more convincing than the film's story line, and the energy of their acting helps "The Client's" plot over a variety of rough spots.

Initially, however, neither Sarandon nor Jones are anywhere in sight. Instead, on a hot Memphis afternoon, two boys, 11-year-old Mark Sway (Brad Renfro) and his 8-year-old brother, Ricky (David Speck), go on the lam from their low-rent trailer-park home with a cigarette they've stolen from their working mother (a believable Mary-Louise Parker).

All kids have secret spots they favor, places they go to savor their triumphs, but on this particular day Mark and Ricky have their space in the woods invaded by a large, late-model car. Inside is a distraught Mafia lawyer from New Orleans named Romey Clifford (Walter Olkewicz), suicidal and prone to talking too much. Before long, Romey has told Mark things it could be worth his life to know.

And, not surprisingly, it doesn't take much time for interested parties both good and bad to focus in on little Mark. On the dark side, Barry "The Blade" Muldano (Anthony LaPaglia) and his cohorts would like to ensure the boy's silence, while ambitious, milk-drinking federal prosecutor Roy Foltrigg (Jones), called Reverend because he "knows Scripture better than the Lord," would scruple at nothing to get him to talk.

Though Mark is feisty to the point of obnoxiousness, even he knows he's overmatched. And since this is one of those movies where emotionally troubled, bargain-basement lawyers just happen to be the equal of the best legal talent anywhere, Mark manages to stumble on just such a diamond-in-the-rough in Reggie Love.

As played by Sarandon (and helped by the dialogue in the Akiva Goldsman and Robert Getchell script), Reggie is the emotional center of "The Client," a protective tornado who wants to do the best for bratty Mark for both personal and professional reasons. Her interchanges with the Reverend Roy, as cool as she is hot and expertly played by Jones, are the best "The Client" has to offer.

Though it never bores and creditably moves through all its paces, "The Client" on film plays like a series of predictable set-ups painted with too broad a brush. Yet such is the power of Grisham's narrative that even though much of what is seen isn't particularly convincing, it doesn't stop us from caring how it all turns out. Let other films worry about the fine points; "The Client" just wants to keep you turning the page.

NEW YORK, 8/1/94, p. 52, David Denby

What American has not uttered a curse in his heart against lawyers? We have created them in numbers beyond reason, and allowed them into every corner of our lives. Like priests in the Middle Ages, they hover over the essential rites of our civilization, talking, talking, talking. Humbly, we receive their blessing as they add suspicion and unnatural caution to all our relationships, whether personal or professional. They have altered intellectual life and public discourse as well. At times, legal reasoning begins to supplant reason itself, and the triumphs and defeats of lawyers replace justice. The result of our general surrender is clear enough. Lawyers have gained an imperial sense of their own importance. They are everywhere, safe in the knowledge that they are *needed*. Do yourself a favor: Snub a lawyer today.

Such irritable thoughts, and a great many more, passed through my head as I watched a peculiar new thriller, *The Client*, which is the third movie to be adapted from the works of John Grisham. Mr. Grisham, who has so profitably taken up fiction, is both a lawyer and a lawyer chauvinist, and *The Client*, whatever else it is—and some of it is extremely well made—is a classic case of legal-profession vanity. Unless you share the belief that everything that lawyers do is unspeakably important, you may feel, along with me, that the movie is off the wall.

The client in question, an 11-year-old boy, Mark (Brad Renfro), has a secret. A New Orleans Mafia lawyer, before committing suicide, has confided to Mark the whereabouts of a dead body—a United States senator murdered by the mob. A variety of policemen and prosecutors, led by Roy Foltrigg (Tommy Lee Jones), an ambitious U.S. Attorney from New Orleans, very much wants the information that Mark has. But instead of telling them and helping them put the mob killers away, the boy falls into the hands of a Memphis defense attorney, Reggie Love (Susan Sarandon), who tries to protect him.

The mob, stalking and terrorizing the kid, is obviously the main danger here, yet instead, Reggie exercises her legal skill to protect Mark from Foltrigg. The movie sets up an adversary relationship between her and the prosecutor. But why? Foltrigg is trying to catch a killer; he is presented as opportunistic and manipulative, but not as a fake. A power-hungry pol, eager for the governorship, Foltrigg is a mover who uses charm and intimidation to get what he wants. As in *The Fugitive*, Tommy Lee Jones radiates energy and will and appears to be enjoying himself immensely. He gives Foltrigg his legendary quickness, his alertness and speed. Expensively dressed, moving through the world like a svelte express train, his Foltrigg is a rascally southern showman who uses biblical quotations to drive home a point. But up close, he's quiet and deadly. When he threatens Reggie, there's an almost sexual intimacy in his voice.

As in so many of her recent pictures, Sarandon puts a real woman on the screen. She's gutsy and candid, but she adds a touch of vulnerability this time, a slight awkwardness, a kind of intellectual stutter. Reggie has made mistakes, and she can be hurt. A reformed boozer, Reggie lost custody of her children after a nasty divorce, and that's one reason she's drawn to little Mark. She's meant to be a good lawyer, too, but what in the world is she doing? As Foltrigg tries to get the information out of the kid, she blocks him with legal maneuvering, entangling him in procedure. He thrusts, she parries; he charges, she countercharges. Tommy Lee grins and fumes, and Sarandon opens her eyes wider and wider and sticks to her guns. The structure of the movie—an underdog against a suave bully—is geared to make us root for her.

But as all this was going on, I stared at the screen in amazement. Have the screenwriters, Akiva Goldsman and Robert Getchell, and the director, Joel Schumacher, lost their minds? Mob killers, deadly and clever, are moving in on the boy, we're terrified that he's going to be knifed, and meanwhile the filmmakers are asking us to be impressed by Reggie's great lawyering. Crazy. If I am not mistaking the responses around me, the audience wanted Mark to cooperate with the authorities and accept their protection: *Tell* them, and find some safe place to hide. That's certainly how I felt. The terrific legal expertise is all beside the point—lawyering for the sake of lawyering. Nothing but the strange American mystique of the lawyer could account for filmmakers making so naïve a miscalculation.

It's too bad, because there are some good things in the movie. Joel Schumacher, as always, is more excitable than intelligent; he's not a convincing director. Yet Schumacher (*St. Elmo's Fire, Falling Down*) definitely has some talent. He directs his actors shrewdly here (with the exception of Brad Renfro). Tommy Lee Jones and Susan Sarandon are electric together, and the talented Mary-Louise Parker, as Mark's poor-white-trash mother, is so hurt, confused, and hostile that she seems to have stepped out of a welfare center. Pale and abashed, her mouth and body slack, Parker goes all the way with her small role; she makes us regret the legal shenanigans even more because she seems the kind of defenseless person so often hurt by lawyers. And Anthony LaPaglia, bearded and greasy, like a ferret with a shark's skin, is thoroughly frightening as the despicable show-off Mafia killer Barry "The Blade" Muldano.

The movie, shot in Grisham territory—Memphis—has pace and atmosphere. If only it weren't so screwed up. From the beginning, Mark is much too tough and reckless; he seems scarcely credible as an 11-year-old boy. He shows little fear and listens to no one. Cocky young Brad Renfro, who has never acted before, seems to be on a defiance kick—he's tougher than the whole world. Schumacher fell down here: He should have taken Renfro in hand and rounded out his responses a little. Sarandon's Reggie is a bereft mother, but the scenes between her and Mark don't tug at our hearts—this kid doesn't need anyone. The story is infuriating: An endangered little boy runs around doing risky, unlikely things—poking into the Mafia's business—and the only purpose of his acts is to keep the plot going.

In the end, Reggie achieves something that she could have achieved right at the beginning, without all the brilliant legal maneuvering. We feel like we've been put through the wringer for nothing—for a display of lawyer's technique, lawyer's heroism. Unintentionally, the movie turns into an example of the pretentious wheel-spinning that we lawyer-phobes fear is the very essence of legal work.

NEW YORK POST, 7/20/94, p. 31, Michael Medved

What is it about movie versions of John Grisham novels?

The leaps in logic and the gaps in common sense never seem to cause trouble on the printed page, but they suddenly look ludicrous and inane when blown up on the big screen.

That's certainly a problem with "The Client," the disappointing new thriller that spins a yarn even more far-fetched than the contrived and implausible plots of "The Pelican Brief" and "The Firm."

This time we're asked to believe that a suicidal Mafia lawyer (Walter Olkewicz) confides in an 11-year-old stranger just moments before blowing his brains out, telling the unsuspecting kid exactly where the mob has buried the body of a murdered U.S. senator.

The plucky lad (Brad Renfro), a tough cookie who lives with his redneck single mother (Mary-Louise Parker) and kid brother in a trailer park, spends the rest of the movie running away from both gangsters and federal authorities who want to see how much he knows.

The boy's only friend in this ordeal is a tough-but-compassionate rookie lawyer (Susan Sarandon) he has found by chance, and who's willing to duel a politically ambitious, Bible-quoting federal prosecutor (Tommy Lee Jones) to protect her young client.

The story loses its few remaining shreds of credibility when Sarandon helps the kid escape from protective custody and agrees to join him in an utterly illogical expedition to dig up the dead senator's moldering remains—a task which this dynamite duo approaches in the same gee-whiz spirits as the Hardy boys going after buried treasure.

Not even skilled veterans like director Joel Schumacher ("Falling Down," "Flatliners") and cameraman Tony Pierce-Roberts ("A Room With a View," "The Remains of the Day") can make this goofiness work as a suspense thriller, and the interminable, formulaic chase scenes generate less excitement than a well-written legal brief.

Fortunately, the characters emerge with more conviction and clarity than the muddled plot. Sarandon in particular, makes the most of her role as a recovering alcoholic who has been deprived of her own kids by a bitter divorce, and so gives heart and soul to the young boy who seeks her help.

Eleven-year-old Brad Renfro, a first-time actor from Knoxville, Tenn., selected from 5,000 applicants for his role, plays that boy with impressive assurance and surprising sensitivity, easily holding his own against the old pros surrounding him.

Tommy Lee Jones is perfectly cast in his role, projecting appropriate levels of charisma and cunning, but his potentially fascinating character never gets the screen time or attention he deserves. The great Ossie Davis, meanwhile, makes a satisfying feast of his brief but juicy part as a wise old judge who deftly interposes himself between the various battling barristers.

It's only a shame that these intriguing performances can't altogether escape the lethargy and clumsiness of the lead-footed plot. When it's released on videocassette, viewers will want to fast-forward through all of "The Client's" intended scenes of excitement and danger and concentrate on the quiet and often touching moments of human interaction that turn up in between.

NEWSDAY, 7/20/94, Part II/p. B2, Jack Mathews

Novelist John Grisham has said that of the first two of his best-sellers adapted into movies, he preferred Alan J. Pakula's "The Pelican Brief" over Sydney Pollack's "The Firm," because Pakula and his writers stuck closer to the book.

Grisham, and fans who agree that his stories can't be improved upon, are going to love what Joel Schumacher did with "The Client." It *is* the book, an almost scene-for-scene realization, with its same prepubescent hero, his $1 lawyer, swarms of smarmy FBI agents and mob hitmen and (it wouldn't be a Grisham story without it) its tangle of legal hooey.

Having read all three novels and seen all three movies, I wish we could go back and assign Schumacher to direct "The Firm." It was by far the best of the three stories, and the only one that rated a respectful adaptation. Pollack is too fussy a literary intellect for the material, and he squandered Grisham's deftly satisfying ending by trying to make it, of all things, logical.

No such effort went into "The Client." Schumacher, a journeyman commercial Hollywood filmmaker ("Falling Down," "Flatliners"), seemed to figure that if millions of readers would swallow a story about a kid outrunning and outfoxing both the FBI and the Mafia, who was he to question it? He merely took a script mirroring the novel and cast the adult roles with the most interesting actors he could find, notably Susan Sarandon as the recovering alcoholic lawyer Reggie Love and Tommy Lee Jones, everybody's favorite villain these days, as the self-adoring federal prosecutor Roy Foltrigg.

Sarandon and Jones are marvelous adversaries, clashing constantly over the welfare of young Mark Sway (Brad Renfro), an 11-year-old boy holding the key to an investigation into the assassination of a U.S. Senator in New Orleans. Through a chance encounter with a suicidal mob lawyer in the film's taut opening sequence, Mark learns not only who killed the senator, but where his body is buried.

The rest of the movie is consumed by Foltrigg's attempts to pry the secret from Mark and make a quick, headline-grabbing arrest, by the mob's attempts to shut Mark up, and by Reggie Love's attempts to keep the child safe from both. If you're familiar with "The Firm" or "The Pelican Brief," and realize that Grisham is merely repeating the same story, you know it will be up to Mark to figure out how to beat the feds and the killers, and to cut a deal guaranteeing him and his loved ones a secure future in a sunny clime.

Schumacher has matched Grisham's eerie ability to propel us through the story, even while making us leap plot holes the size of the Shoemaker-Levy 9 dents on Jupiter. What he wasn't able to do was fill out the novel's sketchy characters. Mark and Reggie, whom he hires for the wrinkled buck in his pocket, have endless chats about Mark's abusive former stepfather and Reggie's abusive ex-husband, but we never really feel the sentiment implied.

The main problem is the boy, both the role and the performance. Rather than coming off as resilient and resourceful, Mark is more often just plain obnoxious, and that Reggie would let him make the big decisions, like the two of them going to New Orleans to see whether the senator's corpse is really buried there, makes you wonder if her fee wasn't a little high.

Renfro, a sixth grader recruited from Knoxville, Tenn., has the proper southern drawl, but neither the experience nor the talent to carry an entire movie, and the sharp supporting cast—which also includes Mary-Louise Parker as Mark's struggling mother and Anthony LaPaglia as the mob's dumb-as-a-tick hitman—doesn't have enough screen time.

If Grisham hopes to continue his lucrative book-to-screen parlays, he's going to have to remember not to invent any more heroes who can can't be played by Tom Cruise or Julia Roberts.

NEWSWEEK, 7/25/94, p. 53, David Ansen

Of the three filmed John Grisham thrillers, "The Client" is tightest the most consistently exciting. "The Firm" stays in the mind primarily for its great supporting cast—Gene Hackman,

Holly Hunter, David Strathairn, Gary Busey. But both Sydney Pollack and Alan J. Pakula, the director of the glum "The Pelican Brief," tried to inflate Grisham's potboilers with a portent they couldn't support. Joel Schumacher ("Falling Down," "Flatliners") doesn't make that mistake. He and his screenwriters, Akiva Goldsman and Robert Getchell, take Grisham at pulp face value. And they deliver the goods: "The Client" gets its hooks in you right off the bat and zips along so crisply that even when the plot starts to degenerate, as Grisham plots tend to do, the annoyance is minor.

The opening is smashing. The 11-year-old hero, Mark Sway (Brad Renfro), ventures out into the Memphis woods for a smoke with his little brother when he stumbles upon a fat Mafia lawyer in the midst of a suicide attempt. Before the lawyer bloodily succeeds, he has told the boy far too much about the death of a certain senator. Hereafter, the kid is in high jeopardy. The mob wants him, and an ambitious, vain, Bile-quoting federal prosecutor, "The Reverend" Roy Foltrigg (Tommy Lee Jones) wants to know what he knows. His little brother is in a coma from shock after the encounter in the woods, the life of his "trailer trash" mom (Mary-Louise Parker is threatened and his own days are numbered. So he looks for his own counsel and finds Reggie Love (Susan Sarandon), a neophyte lawyer struggling with her own demons from the past.

The thrills are efficiently dispatched, and only a few crowd-pleasing moments feel patently false. What gives "The Client" an extra claim on our emotions is the chemistry between the tough, suspicious boy and the tenacious but insecure attorney, a recovering alcoholic who's lost her own children in divorce. She has to win his trust, no easy task. The extraordinary Renfro, a real find, and the accomplished Sarandon make the gradually deepening bond between these two palpable and touching. This 11-year-old Tennessee boy, who'd never acted before, was chosen from thousands of kids to play the role. His tough, precocious bravado never feels strained; there's none of the forced charm of professional child actors. His Mark is a kid who's been forced to grow up fast. Wary, frightened but wise beyond his years, his instinctive heroism is utterly believable. Sarandon feels right as his surrogate mother. She's an actress who's not afraid of showing the mileage on her face. We don't really need the back story about how her own kids were taken away to feel the urgency of her connection to Mark: it's implicit in her volatile performance. Even when we roll our eyes at the foolish Hardy Boys risk they take late in the story, we never doubt the feelings the two actors generate. Add another sly, punchy Jones performance (when's on screen, it's hard to watch anyone else), a solid supporting cast and Howard Shore's gripping score, and the upshot is Schumacher's most satisfying entertainment, smartly balanced between lurid melodrama and real life.

SIGHT AND SOUND, 11/94, p. 42, Chris Darke

Memphis. In the woods, 11-year-old Mark Sway and his younger brother Ricky surprise a man who is attempting suicide by piping in his car exhaust. The man traps Mark in his car and explains that he is Romey Clifford, defence attorney of Mafia hitman Barry Muldano, who is accused of killing a senator; Clifford fears a slower more painful death because he knows the body's whereabouts. Mark escapes with Ricky and watches from his hiding place as Clifford shoots himself in the head. Meanwhile, Muldano searches for the attorney.

The police discover Clifford's body. Ricky is hospitalised with shock. A police officer questions Mark, who denies knowing why Clifford killed himself. Federal attorney Roy Foltrigg arrives to investigate, and arranges to question Mark the following day. A mob heavy, masquerading as a bereaved father, tries to elicit information from Mark. Realising that he is in danger, Mark finds the address of a law firm where he locates female attorney Reggie Love. Initially suspicious of her, Mark agrees to hire Reggie. Foltrigg's team pretend their meeting with Mark is informal and fail to advise him of his rights. However, Love has wired Mark and threatens to make her tape public to reveal Foltrigg's underhand tactics. Love offers the Sway family refuge under the Witness Protection Scheme. The Mafia despatch another heavy to threaten the family.

Desperate to get Mark onto the stand, Foltrigg and his team visit Reggie. Foltrigg reveals that he knows of Love's previous alcoholism and questions her competence. Love accuses Foltrigg of using the case to further his political ambitions and threatens to use the tape against him. Mark agrees to hide in Love's house. Meanwhile, the Mob have torched the Sway family's mobile home.

Foltrigg's team subpoena Mark to appear in court. Under pressure from Foltrigg's cross-examination, Mark takes the Fifth Amendment. Returned to custody, he feigns a heart condition and is admitted to hospital, then escapes, managing to shake off another mob heavy. Mark takes Reggie to the boathouse where Clifford claimed the body was hidden. There they encounter Muldano, who tries to kill Reggie; but they are fired on by the landowner on whose grounds they have trespassed. Muldano escapes, to be punished by his 'uncle' for his incompetence. Reggie does a deal with Foltrigg; in exchange for rehousing the Sways, he will get the glory for the case. As a plane waits to transport the reunited family, Reggie and Mark bid each other farewell.

In the wake of *The Firm* and *The Pelican Brief*, the vogue for adapting John Grisham's novels to the screen takes a particular turn with the arrival of *The Client*. According to the production notes, the novel was already optioned while still in galleys and the film was in pre-production six weeks before the book hit the shelves.

Once again, the machinations of the American legal system are the backdrop of the film's action, although to a lesser extent than in its predecessors. But *The Client*'s most notable, and more successful avatar, is Peter Weir's *Witness*, with its similar kid-who-knows-too-much scenario. The strength of *Witness* lay in the compression of its thriller elements within the claustrophobic locale of an Amish community; rather than simply remaining an abstract potential of the genre, the threat of discovery became the tangible physical prospect of the community's enclosed world being invaded. In *The Client*, the thriller element fares less well partly because its young hero is not so strictly confined, but also because the film's lack of conviction as a thriller is overtaken—although not compensated for—by its aspirations to be a film about a family under duress, a young boy's getting of wisdom and mother-son bonding.

A chief element of the suspense here is the deployment of Mafia heavies, but sadly, these are more than stereotypical Italianate thugs. It is as if the filmmakers conceive villainy as projections of Mark's adolescent imagination, one presumably nourished on a diet of too many TV movies and too little Coppola and Scorsese. These incompetently scampering cartoon figures remain too thinly characterised to be threatening; their pursuit of Mark delivers only some perfunctory chase sequences and Muldano's climactic confrontation with Reggie Love is simply ridiculous.

Tommy Lee Jones' Federal Attorney, 'Reverend' Roy—so called because of his habit of quoting the scriptures in court—further lowers the tension. Jones plays him in alternating registers of preening, media-hungry vanity and a sleek intimidation that only takes off in a confrontation with Sarandon: 'Miss a step,' he whispers, his face pressed up against hers, 'and I'll eat you alive.' But one can't avoid the feeling of an actor coasting on a minimal deployment of his considerable skills. This becomes especially evident during Roy and Mark's first meeting; Jones generates the most interest by playing on the contrast between his physical presence, with all its bull-necked menace, and his delicate manipulation of a dainty little carton of milk. Equally, Jones has fun with his character's vanity, checking out his best side for the TV crews, making sure he has the right pancake for the lights, and, wouldn't you know it, almost turning into a real softie for Mark's final leave-taking scene. However, there is a nice touch here: when Sarandon straightens Jones' tie before he meets the press, he looks both alarmed and surprised; a woman has recognised his essential narcissism but with a certain mocking tenderness.

If Jones' performance is marked by its extended cameo qualities, Sarandon comes across as more committed to her character. Reggie Love and Mark are the focus of the film to such an extent that Mark's brother's coma appears less the horrifying after-effect of misadventure than a narrative convenience. Equally, Mark's mother is sidelined, occasionally being pulled out from the margins either to unleash a screaming fit or simply to reinforce the good mother/bad mother opposition that the film sets up between her and Love.

Smoking and single parenthood, loaded items in the American PC agenda, get treated in *The Client* with a curious legerdemain, a sense of lesser and greater 'evils' being juggled—Love the divorced, ex-alcoholic mother and Mark, the surrogate son, bond over a shared cigarette—and it is a pity the film did not restrict itself to just these two rich subjects. But in having to contend with the film's uninspired thriller elements, they succeed only in delivering a climax that revels in sentimentality rather than in emotions that have really been earned.

TIME, 8/1/94, p. 58, Richard Schickel

In *The Client*, an 11-year-old boy named Mark Sway (Brad Renfro) must get out of dire straits on his own because his father is long gone and his mother is slatternly and foolish. In *Angels in the Outfield*, an 11-year-old boy named Roger (Joseph Gordon-Levitt) is left in a foster home by his feckless father and requires the intervention of a heavenly host to help him. In *North*, an 11-year-old boy named North (Elijah Wood) becomes so disaffected from his parents that he chooses "free agency" and spends the rest of the picture trying to get other grownups to pick up his contract.

What's going on here? A lost-boy trend? A commercial coincidence based on such earlier successes with this theme as the *Home Alone* pictures, *Terminator 2* and most of Steven Spielberg's oeuvre? An attempt by sly Hollywood to suggest that the family values it has but recently renewed its oath to uphold and defend are actually missing in much of America? Or—worst-case-scenario—an effort to subvert those values right in the middle of movies that are marketed and rated as family entertainment?

Possibly none of the above. Or some unlikely combination of them all. In generalizing about movies, it's always best to assume that business is being conducted as usual—that is to say, with a certain casualness about the moral implications of the products. Hey, got enough worries thinking about the weekend grosses.

On that score, the producers can probably relax about *The Client*. Of the boys of this summer, Mark Sway is the most interesting. He's a sort of updated Huck Finn. Mark is smart, self-reliant and deeply suspicious of grownups—with good reason, as it turns out. Out in the woods, smoking cigarettes stolen from Mom, he encounters a man in the process of committing suicide. Trying (and failing) to prevent it—the sequence is good and scary—Mark learns where a certain very interesting body is buried.

Talk about Huck! This lad is soon up the creek without raft or paddle. The Mafia wants to prevent him from talking about the stiff, and an ambitious, media-mad federal prosecutor (Tommy Lee Jones at his smarmy best) is equally determined to get his testimony. Mark's only ally is a nice lady lawyer (Susan Sarandon), shaky-brave and, since she's lost her own children in an ugly divorce, ready to do a little surrogate mothering.

Director Joel Schumacher has made the most successful movie yet of a John Grisham novel. Its acting is the best, its paranoia and its plotting are fairly plausible and, despite its obligations to thriller conventions, it says something pretty truthful about what it's like to be young and neglected these days. Finally, in Brad Renfro the filmmakers have a real find—a tough, appealing kid whose instinct is not to beg for sympathy but to let it accrue to him naturally.

This is wisdom not vouchsafed to the creators of *Angels in the Outfield*, a remake of a dryer, less hungrily sentimental 1952 movie of the same title. A moment before he is abandoned, young Roger asks his father when they might become a family again. "When the Angels win the pennant" the father says. He is talking about the more hopeless of the Los Angeles baseball teams. That night Roger offers up prayers, and seraphim respond. With their help, the Angels start winning. Only Roger can see the small-*a* angels, and so he is needed to tell the perpetually riled-up manager (Danny Glover) what moves to make when they're present. Thus man and boy are forced to bond. Will the Angels win the pennant? Will the skipper keep his cool? Will Roger find the father figure he needs? If you're asking those questions, you're just the sucker this movie is looking for.

North too is in touch with the supernatural. Wherever he goes, a nameless figure played by Bruce Willis turns up in various guises to help him. Director Rob Reiner strives hard for the tones of a fable, but the result is far from fabulous. There is something smug about North, and about the entire movie. All the substitute parents he interviews are as selfish as North's folks are, and the movie posits a mass movement in which other kids, all spoiled rotten, attempt to emulate North. At least the lost boys in the other movies have authentic problems and they don't suggest, as *North* does, that American loathsomeness has reached universal proportions.

Good or bad, realistic or fantastic in tone, all these movies reflect a profound unease with the present state of our domestic arrangements. At the end of all of them, their resourceful little heroes are safely clasped to loving bosoms, but in every case the piety seems perfunctory, nowhere near as affecting as the troubles the boys have seen.

VILLAGE VOICE, 7/26/94, p. 50, Georgia Brown

Last Saturday night, because the press screening wasn't until the following week, I took in a sneak preview of *The Client*. When I last went to the movies they were showing coming attractions. Now, I discover, there's all this education going on. To eat up the time for those who arrive early enough to get a place to sit, something called On-Screen Entertainment keeps throwing Movie Terms up on the screen. They even show you one of the FBI's most-wanted in case he turns around and asks you to keep your feet off his seat. A "B" Movie," we learned, is "The name for a modest budget film with second tier actors." Too bad, I must've been woolgathering, but my companion said they also defined "A Cliffhanger."

Those who were paying attention might think *The Client* a B movie. Even if Tommy Lee Jones and Susan Sarandon are first tier to you and me, they are not Tom Cruise. Moreover *The Client*'s real star is a child who's never been in a movie before. And given that nobody in *The Client* pilots a vehicle wired with explosives, people might even mistake this for a modest budget film. Should I write to On-Screen Entertainment and suggest they clear up some ambiguities?

Well, getting on to *The Client*, the film is directed by Joel Schumacher, who also directed such screen gems as *Dying Young* and *Falling Down*. (This is known as a "Track Record.") A director, in case you're wondering, is the person the studio head calls and asks to handle a property the studio has bought. The director replies, Oh boy, I love that idea or that book—if, as in this case, it is a book—and then he takes charge of what's left to take charge of, like hiring a personal assistant. *The Client*, as everyone in the theater but me probably knew, was a first-tier novel by John Grisham.

In the beginning of *The Client*, a boy named Mark (Brad Renfro), living in a trailer with his young mom (Mary-Louise Parker), takes his little brother down by the river for a smoke. We ail know people are smoking in movies more than ever, but is this going too far? Anyway, while down by the river the boys interrupt a fat man trying to commit suicide. Before finally succeeding, the fat man tells Mark about the murder of a state senator and where the body is hidden. We know this is the South because of the way people talk and the way they kill senators.

Then everyone is after Mark to find out what the boys saw. But Mark's afraid for his brother, who lies in the hospital sucking his thumb (post-traumatic stress, says the doctor), and for his mom who's soon zonked on Valium (doctor's orders). Poor Mark, only 11 and the family's grown-up. That's why he needs a surrogate parent like the lawyer Reggie Love. (That's a Southern name.) Just as Mark's alcoholic father deserted his family, so Reggie (Sarandon) is a former alcoholic who lost custody of her kids. How's that for a neat match?

People trying to get Mark are the law—local cops, FBI, and a loud federal prosecutor (Jones)—and the crooks who did away with the senator. Sometimes it's hard to tell who is who, but soon you learn to tell one bad guy by a mole between his eyes and another by barbed-wire tattoos on his hands. Jones's "Reverend" Roy Foltrigg is supposed to be pompous grandstander, a real camera hound, and is always working those deep facial creases. Though he and Reggie trade insults in a semi-flirtatious way, it turns out Roy is too full of himself to pay her real mind.

So, in the genre of child-who-new-too-much movies, this is no *Witness*. And despite the title and the Grisham imprint, there's just the tiniest bit of courtroom drama. What *The Client* has is a lot of chasing. On foot. Besides having to dodge cops and crooks, Mark is always losing faith in the world and running off by himself so Reggie has to coax him back and regain his trust. And when Mark is really stressed, Reggie lets him take a drag on her cigarette. And she never mentions his earring.

Frankly, I think there's something seriously wrong with *The Client*'s blueprint, er, screenplay. Maybe the book is really not too smart either. This or the director doesn't know how to make a suspenseful movie because this should have been a cliffhanger. Better yet, it might've made a great B movie. Too bad the budget wasn't more modest.

Also reviewed in:
NEW REPUBLIC, 8/22 & 29/94, p. 35, Stanley Kauffmann
NEW YORK TIMES, 7/20/94, p. C11, Janet Maslin
NEW YORKER, 8/1/94, p. 76, Terrence Rafferty
VARIETY, 6/13-19/94, p. 54, Todd McCarthy

WASHINGTON POST, 7/22/94, p. B1, Hal Hinson
WASHINGTON POST, 7/22/94, Weekend/p. 41, Desson Howe

CLIFFORD

An Orion Pictures release of a Morra, Brezner, Steinberg & Tenenbaum Entertainment, Inc. production. *Producer:* Larry Brezner and Pieter Jan Brugge. *Director:* Paul Flaherty. *Screenplay:* Jay Dee Rock and Bobby Von Hayes. *Director of Photography:* John A. Alonzo. *Editor:* Pembroke Herring and Timothy Board. *Music:* Richard Gibbs. *Music Editor:* Bob Badami. *Choreographer:* Russell Clark. *Sound:* Jeff Wexler and (music) Armin Steiner. *Sound Editor:* Larry Kemp and Lon Bender. *Casting:* Lynn Stalmaster. *Production Designer:* Russell Christian. *Art Director:* Bernie Cutler. *Set Designer:* Stephen M. Berger. *Set Decorator:* Catherine Mann. *Set Dresser:* Paul Myerberg, Michael E. Humburger, and Elijah Bryant. *Special Effects:* Dale Martin. *Costumes:* Robert de Mora. *Make-up:* John M. Elliot, Jr. *Stunt Coordinator:* Joe Dunne. *Running time:* 90 minutes. *MPAA Rating:* PG.

CAST: Martin Short (Clifford); Charles Grodin (Martin Daniels); Mary Steenburgen (Sarah Davis); Dabney Coleman (Gerald Ellis); Richard Kind (Julien Daniels); Jennifer Savidge (Theodora Daniels); Brandis Kemp (Woman on Plane); Ben Savage (Roger); Don Galloway (Captain); Tim Lane (Navigator); Susan Varon (Woman Passer-By); Josh Seal and Kevin Mockrin (Kevin); Timothy Stack (Kevin's Father); Marianne Muellerleile (Kevin's Mother); Kirsten Holmquist (Debi); Megan Kloner, Jessee Stock, and Creighton Douglas II (Daycare Center Children); Jennifer Nash (Wendy); Linda Hoffman (Stewardess #2); Shelley DeSai (Mini-mart Clerk); G.D. Spradlin (Parker Davis); Anne Jeffreys (Annabelle Davis); Channing Chase (Julia); Christopher Murray (Bartender); David Byrd (Senator); Gary Byron (Matthew); Anthony S. Johnson (Servant #1); R. Leo Schreiber (Servant #2); Greg Blanchard (Man at Party); Anabel Schofield (Woman at Party); Natalie Core (Older Woman at Party); Sonia Jackson (May Ella); Kathy Fitzgerald (Connie); Bergen Williams (Female Security Agent); Akuyoe (Airport Claims Clerk); Richard Fancy (Detective #1); Al Pugliese (Detective #2); Gregory "Mars" Martin (Brian); Patricia Bell and Jane Sullivan (Train Passengers); James "Gypsy" Haake (Transvestite); Sherlynn Hicks (Female Photographer); Barry Dennen (Terry the Pterodactyl); James Cary Flynn (Mitchell the Gate Guard); Alicia Gilbert and Kelly Shane Rivers (Teens at Party); Seth Binzer (Victor).

LOS ANGELES TIMES, 4/1/94, Calendar/p. 4, Peter Rainer

Is it bad form for a film critic to send readers to a lousy movie just because it has a few screamingly funny moments? On the other hand, who doesn't want to laugh out loud at the movies?

"Clifford," starring Martin Short as a precociously nasty 10-year-old, is not a good movie. It's not even good/bad. But Short has a few of those laugh-out-loud moments, like the scene where his uncle Martin (Charles Grodin) asks him if he could at least *try* to look normal and Clifford, making his best effort, scrunches his face into the look of a demented kiwi.

Short, at 42, is the ideal actor to play a 10-year-old because, at his best, he always seems to carry around inside him the animus of a wacked-out imp. Therapists who extol getting in touch with the child within should take a long hard look at Martin Short and reconsider.

Short never gets gooey in "Clifford." From his first scene as a boy, when, on a plane trip with his parents en route to Hawaii, he forces a landing in Los Angeles so he can visit Dinosaurworld, Short keeps Clifford intensely, almost passionately weird. There have been a lot of movies about adults as children, or vice versa, but Short is beholden to none of them. He's bopping to his own syncopation here—he's a peewee pain with an unaccountably lewd undercurrent. (It's the lewdness that lifts his impersonation out of the kiddie comic category.)

Most of the movie is taken up with Clifford's sojourn with his bachelor uncle and his girlfriend, Sarah (Mary Steenburgen). Ditched by his parents and longing for a day at the Jurassic

Park-like Dinosaurworld, Clifford at first comes on all adorable—and Short playing adorable is not a pretty sight. When Uncle Marty reneges on his plans to take the tyke to the theme park, Clifford turns Bad Seed. The funniest moments in the movie are the goony duets between Short and Grodin. Their comic styles couldn't be further apart: Short's nattery verve is a universe apart from Grodin's down tempo spaciness. If their scenes were better written (by Jay Dee Rock and Bobby Von Hayes) and directed (by Paul Flaherty), these two actors might have come up with some classic bits together. They come close a few times anyway, particularly when Uncle Martin grows homicidal toward his little charge and Clifford responds by tootling on his flute like a Pan gone crackers.

The filmmakers pull off the illusion of making Short seem convincingly, well, short. Cinematographer John Alonzo, production designer Russell Christian and costume designer Robert de Mora conspire to make Short the low center of gravity in his scenes. But the success of the illusion is often more inventive than anything going on inside it.

Still, you could do worse than to check out a movie where a foreshortened Short frugs on the dance floor beneath a forest of towering co-eds. Or a movie where Short impales Grodin with a bagel. If the producers of "Clifford" are smart, they'll release it on video as a trailer of its best scenes. If they were smarter, they would have released it into the theaters the same way.

NEW YORK POST, 4/1/94, p. 31, Michael Medved

In the hands of ordinary actors, the new comedy "Clifford" might have been a tedious and sadistic exercise, but Martin Short and Charles Grodin are no ordinary actors.

Their comic brilliance and uncanny rapport with one another transform this thin material into a wildly original romp that delivers uproarious laughs along with stinging insights about the uneasy interface between adults and kids.

The title character is a diabolically clever 10-year-old boy with an all-consuming obsession; he yearns to visit a heavily hyped California theme park called Dinosaurworld.

Clifford believes he's achieved his cherished goal when his weary parents leave him for a few weeks with his Los Angeles uncle (Charles Grodin), who agrees to care for the lad as a means of impressing his fiancee (Mary Steenburgen) with his natural affinity for children.

The problem is that Grodin's smarmy boss (Dabney Coleman) makes work demands that interfere with a planned visit to Dinosaurworld, and the enraged Clifford spends the rest of the movie seeking revenge on his hapless uncle. His ingenious schemes ultimately succeed in poisoning Grodin's relationships with his fiancee, his boss, and most of the rest of the world.

Casting 42-year-old Martin Short as the 10-year-old Clifford obviously represents this movie's biggest risk—and pays its biggest dividends. Short is so devastatingly good that at times you can almost believe he's a small boy—with the aid of effective makeup and costumes, plus the 6-inch platforms beneath his co-stars designed to make Short look shorter.

In the final analysis, the purpose of his astonishing performance isn't to make you believe that he's really a child any more than the aim of his long-ago SCTV impersonations of Katharine Hepburn was to make you believe he really was that legendary star.

Short's Clifford is a triumph of observation, subtlety and wit; an unforgettable meld of the charming exterior of Little Lord Fauntleroy with the twisted soul of The Bad Seed.

Since Clifford is supposed to be a brilliant, sophisticated kid who merely pretends to be childish and vulnerable ("Gee, Uncle Martin! You're the bestest uncle in the whole wide world"), it works especially well to see him played by a middle-aged man impeccably impersonating a squirmy, devious kid.

Grodin is of course, Hollywood's master straight man. Anyone who can hold his own as the long-suffering victim of a drooling St. Bernard ("Beethoven") and a snarling Robert De Niro ("Midnight Run") is the perfect foil for Clifford.

Director Paul Flaherty—a SCTV writing alumnus whose previous film credits include the ho-hum comedies "18 Again!" and "Who's Harry Crumb?"—handles the Short-Grodin interchanges with the spark and crackle of high voltage electricity.

Flaherty also brings energy and flair to the nightmarish, after-hours climax at Dinosaurworld; he re-creates an ambitious theme park that is both outrageously tacky and utterly captivating.

An awkward framing device, in which the movie both begins and ends with Clifford as a kindly and elderly priest, recalling his own childhood indiscretion, takes some of the edge off the story's undeniable nastiness.

Those moviegoers who happen to be "childless by choice" will view "Clifford" as confirmation of their good judgment while doting parents will recognize fleeting characteristics of even our most angelic offspring in the hero's manic manipulations.

NEWSDAY, 4/1/94, Part II/p. B7, Jack Mathews

The new Martin Short comedy "Clifford" is actually an old Martin Short comedy. It was finished in 1991, scheduled for Christmas release that year, then shelved when Orion Pictures plunged into a deep financial crisis.

Short might be wishing it had remained on the shelf. "Clifford," in which the comedy actor is disastrously cast as a 10-year-old bad seed terrorizing the uncle he comes to live with, is merely going to earn in 1994 what it would have earned in 1991, the onus of being one of the year's worst movies.

Setting aside the bad jokes and surface parallels to "Problem Child," which was a bad movie in its own right, "Clifford" seemed doomed by the concept. Having Martin Short, just because he is short, play a child in Little Lord Fauntleroy outfits might have been a good idea for a quick "Saturday Night Live" sketch, but it goes nowhere in a feature-length movie.

The story, told in flashback by an aging monk (Short) at a wayward boys home in the mid-21st Century, takes place in Los Angeles, after Clifford, a pre-"Jurassic Park" dinosaur fanatic, sabotages the plane carrying him and his parents to Hawaii, and finagles a layover with Uncle Martin (Charles Grodin).

The relationship is based on mutual exploitation. Clifford wants to use his uncle to get a day at a theme park called Dinosaur World, and Martin plans to use Short to convince his fiancée (Mary Steenburgen) she doesn't hate children as much as she thinks, even though he does. But Clifford is no ordinary child; he is a sadistic prankster who takes the satanic advice of a dinosaur doll, and he is soon destroying Uncle Marty's life.

Grodin, my choice for all-time underused comedy actor, actually does some funny things in the midst of this ludicrous tale. He has the best dead-pan expression of any actor in the business, and even when nothing else is funny, that look is.

Short had no chance with his character. Clifford is a monster to begin with, and no matter how cute people may think Short is as a man, he makes for one ugly, unbearable kid. From the moment you first see him, gleefully tormenting his parents and passengers on the plane, you feel like shoving him out the door.

Director Paul Flaherty ("Who's Harry Crumb?") didn't seem to know what to do with the concept, either. Half the time, he demonstrates Clifford's size by keeping Short's head and shoulders in the bottom of the frame, and the actor looking up, as if at Mt. Rushmore, at the co-stars soaring above him.

Whether Short was walking in trenches, or slumping in his seat, the illusion doesn't work. He is a little guy, but to be as little as he appears in some of these proportionally out-of-whack scenes, his legs would have to be about 6 inches long.

The best news is that the film is short, too, just 90 minutes. Critics have to be prepared to take their pleasure where they can.

VILLAGE VOICE, 4/19/94, p. 58, Laurie Stone

Swallowed by Orion's bankruptcy, *Clifford* has now been coughed up, and an odd puff of wind it turns out to be. Is this the fourth movie in recent years showing a mature man as a child? Martin Short is 10-year-old Clifford, a felon in dweeb's shortpants, a sadist savant with a trunk of tortures. He slyly replaces the contents of a Bloody Mary with Tabasco sauce and, after fiddling with an airplane's controls, precipitates an emergency landing. He has declared war on adults, and here the film displays some originality depicting children, who often have to plead for decency, and adults who feel burdened by the role of protester, as members of warring classes.

Clifford is one of those young-old kids, at once too smart and too dumb, clever but emotionally arrested. Jerry Lewis forged a movie career by playing the type—embodying sexual terror as a wobbly-kneed limp dick. He was easily wounded and, it was fancied, charming to women because unthreatening. Short's trademark Lewis impersonation at once teases Lewis for his unconsciousness and cheers him for exposing himself, but this sense of doubleness doesn't inform Short's performance here. Short plays Clifford the way Lewis would have; he isn't funny. And instead of satirizing the painfulness of childhood, writers Jay Dee Rock and Bobby Von Hayes resort to the tactics of a *Road Runner* cartoon.

Telling an anecdote the other night on Letterman, Short portrayed Tony Randall as pompous and intrusive for advising Short not to squander his talent in stupid movies. Fatuous Randall may be, but he was right. In *Clifford*, only Charles Grodin, as the young monster's uncle and the chief target of his animosity, generates a few laughs, by remaining steadfastly unsentimental about the brutalities of human relations and the indignities of acting in crap.

Also reviewed in:
CHICAGO TRIBUNE, 4/1/94, Friday/p. C, Michael Wilmington
NEW YORK TIMES, 4/1/94, p. C8, Caryn James
VARIETY, 4/4-10/94, p. 35, Brian Lowry
WASHINGTON POST, 4/1/94, p. D6, Desson Howe

COBB

A Warner Bros. release in association with Regency Enterprises and Alcor Films. *Executive Producer:* Arnon Milchan. *Producer:* David Lester. *Director:* Ron Shelton. *Screenplay:* Ron Shelton. *Based on the book "Cobb: A Biography" by*: Al Stump. *Director of Photography:* Russell Boyd. *Editor:* Paul Seydor and Kimberly Ray. *Music:* Elliot Goldenthal. *Music Editor:* Daniel Allen Carlin. *Sound:* Kirk Francis and (music) Joel Iwataki. *Sound Editor:* Bruce Fortune. *Casting:* Victoria Thomas. *Production Designer:* Armin Ganz and Scott Ritenour. *Art Director:* Troy Sizemore and Charles Butcher. *Set Decorator:* Claire Jenora Bowin. *Set Dresser:* Dwain Wilson. *Special Effects:* Jim Fredburg. *Costumes:* Ruth E. Carter. *Make-up:* Ve Neill and John Blake. *Stunt Coordinator:* Jerry J. Gatlin. *Running time:* 130 minutes. *MPAA Rating:* R.

CAST: Tommy Lee Jones (Ty Cobb); Robert Wuhl (Al Stump); Lolita Davidovich (Ramona); Lou Myers (Willie); Stephen Mendillo (Mickey Cochrane); William Utay (Jameson); J. Kenneth Campbell (Prof. Cobb); Rhoda Griffis (Ty's Mother); Allan Malamud (Mud); Ned Bellamy (Ray); Scott Burkholder (Jimmy); Bill Caplan (Bill); Jeff Fellenzer and Doug Krikorian (Sportswriters); Gavin Smith (Sportsman's Lounge Bartender); Gary Morris (Baptist Minister); Tyler Logan Cobb (Young Ty); Jerry J. Gatlin (Train Engineer); Harold Herthum and Jay Chevalier (Gamblers); Roger Clemens (Opposing Pitcher); George Rafferty and Jay Tibbs (Teammates); Rodney Max (Umpire); Gary D. Talbert (Opposing Catcher); Fred Lewis and David Hodges (Philly Fans); Joy Michiel (Last Chance Hotel Clerk); Michael "Mitch" Hrushowy (Harrah's Club Manager); Eloy Casados (Louis Prima); Paula Rudy (Keely Smith); Artie Butler (Harrah's Bartender); Robert Earl Berhigler (Croupier); George P. Wilbur (Casino Security Man); Steven Brown (Husband at Motel); Dana Y. Hill (Wife at Motel); Tony L. McCollum (Texas Motel Manager); Bobby Holcombe (Texas Motel Security Guard); Tom Todoroff (Hall of Fame Announcer); Ernie Harwell (Hall of Fame MC); Reid Cruickshanks (Pie Traynor); Rath Shelton (Paul Waner); Jim Shelton (Lloyd Waner); Stacy Keach Sr. (Jimmie Foxx); Clive Rosengren (Hall of Fame Director); Lawrence "Crash" Davis (Sam Crawford); Tommy Bush (Rogers Hornsby); Tracy Keehn-Dashnaw (Cobb's Wife); Jimmy Buffett (Heckler); Michael Moss (Lover); Janice Certain (Cobb's Daughter); Bradley Whitford (Process Server); Jeanne McCarthy and Patricia Forte (Nurses); Toni Prima (Hospital Receptionist); Michael Chieffo (Young Doctor); Don Hood (Older Doctor); Jennifer Decker (Sportsman's Lounge

Waitress); Bill Wittman (Newsreel Narrator); Brian Mulligan (Charlie Chaplin); Jerry Hauck (Handicapper).

CHRISTIAN SCIENCE MONITOR, 12/2/94, p. 14, David Sterritt

Movie biographies, known as "biopics" in the trade, are a tricky business. Many is the real-life figure whose undramatic experiences become compelling when embellished by studio experts. Equally numerous are the people whose fascinating careers become painfully dull when filmmakers miss the point or view things from the wrong perspective.

Be this as it may, the biopic genre keeps plugging away no matter how fashions change over the years. The latest examples, "Cobb" and "Tom & Viv," focus on subjects who have little in common except their freshly acquired status as the centerpieces of mediocre new movies.

The producers of "Cobb" had the good sense to fill their leading role with Tommy Lee Jones, an appealing actor whose success in "The Fugitive" has sent his star-power skyrocketing. He plays Ty Cobb, a legendary athlete if ever there was one—setting records for career runs scored (2,245) and lifetime batting average (.367) that endure to this day, 66 years since he retired.

Cobb's accomplishments on the ball field would make for an absorbing documentary, but it's the passions and pitfalls of his private life that dominate Ron Shelton's melodramatic film. In his later years, according to the movie, Cobb became obsessed with documenting his former greatness in a self-serving autobiography and he drafted sports reporter Al Stump to write the book for him. Shelton's screenplay probes the strained relationship between the odd couple—one an irascible celebrity, the other an earnest professional—and uses it to spark flashbacks that explore Cobb's history in sometimes grim detail.

"Cobb" would be a more persuasive picture if the filmmakers had a clearer idea of their intentions. The early scenes treat Cobb as a larger-than-life curmudgeon so explosively self-absorbed that he's almost a comical figure, overflowing with infantile demands and brandishing an ever-present pistol as readily as he shoots off his hyperactive mouth. Yet many of his excesses are the opposite of funny—bouts of misogyny, racism, and anti-Semitism are among them—and while Shelton's screenplay clearly doesn't approve of these evils, it has trouble reconciling them with its portrait of Cobb as a troublesome but picturesque old clown.

The film eventually takes on a seriousness appropriate to the issues it dredges up, increasing its dramatic power, especially when Cobb belatedly faces the abuses buried in his past. But this happens perilously late in the game, making us wonder why Shelton and company took so long to find the tone their story should have had all along.

Jones tackles the title role with his usual energy, but as his similarly overheated work in "Natural Born Killers" should have taught him, sheer forcefulness is no match for a bad script. It's hard to watch his exertions without remembering Paul Newman in "Blaze," another Shelton picture that confronted a good actor with impossible demands.

Robert Wuhl plays Stump with more sincerity than imagination, and Lolita Davidovich makes a brief appearance as an object of Cobb's lustful attentions. In all, this is the weakest of Shelton's sports-minded movies, making "Bull Durham" and "White Men Can't Jump" seem clever.

The title characters of "Tom & Viv" are poet T. S. Eliot and his first wife, Vivienne, an ill-starred couple whose marriage was destroyed by numerous factors, including Vivienne's chronic illness and what appears to have been an outrageous shortage of compassion on her husband's part. The movie chronicles their troubled life, climaxing with Eliot's acquiescence in a plan to institutionalize his spouse and write her out of his life.

As a lifelong admirer of Eliot's inexhaustibly brilliant poetry, I looked forward to seeing "Tom & Viv" at the Montreal World Film Festival, where it recently had its North American premiere.

The trouble with the movie is that it's not about T.S. Eliot the *poet*, but rather T.S. Eliot the *husband*, and this turns out to be a sadly uninteresting topic as the writer trudges predictably to fame while grappling with occasional fits of conscience. Vivienne is a far more engaging figure, but she's pushed into a second-banana position that's as unfair to her memory as Eliot's callousness was to her life.

Willem Dafoe and Natasha Richardson play the central roles as skillfully as one would expect, but they can't surmount the built-in deficiencies of the screenplay by Michael Hastings and Adrian Hodges, based on Hastings's original play. Brian Gilbert directed the disappointing drama.

LOS ANGELES TIMES, 12/2/94, Calendar/p. 1, Kenneth Turan

In his lifetime and after, as a player and a personality, Ty Cobb both astonished an horrified. A consensus pick, says biographer Al Stump, as "the most feared, castigated and acclaimed figure" in baseball history, Tyrus Raymond Cobb was too much for the world while he lived. Now, decades past his death, his memory alone has overmatched Ron Shelton.

Shelton, the gifted writer-director whose best work ("Bull Durham," "White Men Can't Jump") involves sports, has used Stump's agonizing relationship with his subject as the framework for "Cobb," an ambitious but uneven and finally unsatisfying look at a man succinctly summarized as "hell in spikes."

Viewed simply as a player, Cobb was arguably the greatest who ever lived. The first man elected to baseball's Hall of Fame, a competitor whose fire turned Gen. Douglas MacArthur into a tongue-tied acolyte, Cobb set 123 records during a career that lasted from 1905 to 1928, and his .367 lifetime batting average is one of several marks that no one is close to challenging even today.

Known for pioneering an aggressive approach to the game, Cobb was a terror during his off-hours. He was harsh, bigoted and probably psychotic, the kind of man who sent opponents to the hospital, took a blacksnake whip to his own son and proudly claimed to have pistol-whipped a street thug to death.

As shrewd as he was nasty, Cobb made millions in the stock market, secretly supported some of his old opponents and handsomely endowed the Cobb Scholarship Fund for students who couldn't afford college. But as he neared the end of his life in 1960, nearly crippled by numerous illnesses and convinced that no one had ever properly appreciated him, he formed an unlikely friendship with Stump.

A sportswriter hired to collaborate on the great one's autobiography, Stump became an alter ego who "drew his bath, got drunk with him, and knelt with him in prayer on black nights when he knew death was near."

Their book, "My Life in Baseball," did not, on Cobb's insistence, contain any of that life's less savory aspects. Shortly after the man's death, Stump wrote a celebrated magazine piece that did, called "Ty Cobb's Wild 10-Month Fight to Live," and has just published his second book on the subject, "Cobb: A Biography," a thorough and chilling look at the athlete seen whole.

Clearly, this is fascinating business and a film that concentrates more on the Cobb-Stump relationship than the former's playing career, as this one does, couldn't help but be of some interest. But like its subject, "Cobb" the movie invariably gets out of hand, its lack of sharp dramatic focus exacerbating problems in both casting and structure that prove difficult to overcome.

"Cobb's" initial trouble is that, to no great surprise, its namesake is much easier to take in print than on screen. Cobb's debilitating physical ailments, his propensity for shooting off his Luger as well as his mouth, the perpetual abuse he rains on anyone within reach, all inevitably become wearisome.

In theory, having the ferocious and talented Tommy Lee Jones play Cobb would lessen the pain, but it does not. Perhaps the actor is finally too tailor-made for the role, or maybe he and the director simply behaved as if he were. But the result, whether Cobb is wailing about greatness or ruminating about the dark circumstances around his father's death, is a performance too operatic and out of control.

Equally problematical is the way Stump is portrayed by actor Robert Wuhl. Shelton, who has used Wuhl in two of his earlier films and is clearly fond of him, wrote the role with the actor in mind, a major miscalculation.

Though the idea was apparently to portray Stump as sweet and vulnerable, in Wuhl's hands he comes off as the whiny, sniveling and servile half of a "The Champ and the Chump" double bill. As the harried man who watches over Cobb as he travels from the night life of Reno to an old-timer's banquet at Cooperstown, N.Y., to a trip to his Georgia roots, Stump is the main audience surrogate and it is fatal to have an irritating presence in that role.

Without anyone to care about, "Cobb's" script problems become increasingly intractable. Confronted by Cobb's volcanic personality, the film is completely nonplussed, unable to decide if it should be amused, piteous, reluctantly admiring or just plain disgusted.

A similar sense of uncertainty pervades all creative choices, from opening with an awkward fake newsreel detailing Cobb's baseball exploits to dealing with minor characters like an ill-used Reno cigarette girl (Lolita Davidovich) or even coming up with a plausible reason why Stump stuck around through all the abuse.

"You don't have a point of view, Stumpy, you're not worth killing," Cobb says, laying down his weapon in one of his quasi-sane moments, and it is a point well taken. Without a coherent aesthetic vision, this film and its ponderous emphasis on the cost of greatness is not what it might be either.

NEW YORK POST, 12/2/94, p. 51, Michael Medved

Ty Cobb was, by all accounts, a miserable human being, whose only redeeming characteristic involved an uncanny ability to hit a ball and run bases. Unfortunately, these athletic talents receive scant reference in "Cobb," which focuses instead on its protagonist as a lonely, viciously racist, alcoholic, cancer-ridden and altogether insufferable old man.

When the 74-year-old baseball legend (brilliantly played by Tommy Lee Jones) tells his horrified biographer (Robert Wuhl), "This is the closest you're ever gonna get to greatness, son," it's obviously meant ironically: What's so great about this pathetic specimen?

By the end of the picture, however, writer-director Ron Shelton ("Bull Durham," "White Men Can't Jump") suggests that Cobb may have been right after all—that the same implacable ferocity and single-minded selfishness that made him so obnoxious in his last years also made possible his epic achievements on the diamond.

It's an intriguing notion but it's not enough to carry the audience through two wearying hours with the most hateful character they're likely to meet in films this year.

The movie tells its story through the eyes of likable, long-suffering Al Stump, the sportswriter selected by the Great Man shortly before his death in 1961 to ghost-write his autobiography.

The story describes Stump's horror at the monster who takes over his life, as Cobb brandishes (and occasionally fires) a loaded Luger to get his way, drives at breakneck speed down snowy mountain roads, heads off to Reno to prove his virility, then abuses and humiliates a kind-hearted cigarette girl (Lolita Davidovich) who the shy Stump also fancied.

The relationship between the two men never develops much depth or emotion due in large part to the monochromatic performance by Robert Wuhl. He's a gifted comedian who's done wonderful work elsewhere (in the little-seen "Mistress," for instance) but here his character is predictably amazed or appalled in every scene. Wuhl makes it too easy to understand why Cobb would dismiss Stump as a lightweight.

Jones, on the other hand, is at the top of his game: As in many of his other most memorable parts ("The Fugitive," or TVs "Lonesome Dove," for instance) he displays a special gift for creating characters with a fanatical focus on some goal or other.

The problem is that you hardly get to see his character applying that fierceness as a young man: a splendid three-minute segment showing Cobb as a player, intimidating opponents, teammates, and even fans in the stands leaves you yearning for more, but you never get it. You also miss substantive flashbacks about his two nightmarish marriages, or his troubled relationships with his children.

There is, in short, far too much of the dying, cantankerous Cobb, and not nearly enough of the young firecracker who set the world on its ear and gave us some reason to care about that impossible oldster. In short, for a film that's all about focus and single-mindedness "Cobb" takes a swing at redefining greatness but fails to keep its eye on the ball.

NEWSDAY, 12/2/94, Part II/p. B2, Jack Mathews

If he had been born a dog, Ty Cobb's realm would have been the junkyard. No one would have dared come within 100 feet of him, and the day he lost a step, his owner would have taken him behind the shed and shot him. Too mean to keep around.

But he was a man, some say the best baseball player who ever lived, and when he was too old to lead the league in hits and too slow to threaten opposing infielders with his flying spikes, he had another 30 years in which to snarl, bite and lift his leg on the world. Tyrus Raymond Cobb, the "Georgia Peach," was an SOB.

Ron Shelton, the former minor leaguer who made such an amiable tribute to baseball with "Bull Durham," does nothing to soften the legend's off-field image in "Cobb," and Tommy Lee Jones, who is no peach himself, plays him with such uncontrolled fury, he seems about to leap off the screen, and attack members of the audience. The question for anybody who does not believe baseball is life, and that its legends are to be worshipped, whether they were decent human beings or not, is why should you subject yourself to this abuse? What was the appeal for Shelton? "He knows greatness," says Al Stump (Robert Wuhl), the sportswriter who traveled with Cobb during the last year of his life and whose love-hate relationship with him provides the focus of Shelton's biography. "I want to know about greatness."

What Stump learns about is not greatness, it's mean-spirited, pathological egomania. In the film's most repugnant sequence, the impotent, 73-year-old Cobb kidnaps a Reno cigar girl (Lolita Davidovich) at gunpoint, makes her disrobe, mentally rapes her, then offers her $1,000 to tell people she'd gotten the best sex of her life from the great Ty Cobb.

Cobb was obviously a gifted athlete—he retired in 1928 with a career batting average of .367—and he proved a wise investor of his earnings (the movie contains only a few seconds of baseball footage, to establish his record and his ruthlessness). But he was otherwise a mere thug, a little thing, a hateful racist who started fights on and off the field, and menaced people with the German Luger he had with him when he died in 1961.

It would be interesting to know what made Cobb meaner than a junkyard dog, but while making a big deal of the shotgun death of his father when Cobb was a teenager, Shelton makes it clear he was as vicious before as after. That event, portrayed as a mystery melodrama in recurring flashbacks, is grotesque, but not very illuminating.

Any honest biography of Cobb would be a sour affair. Unlike George Patton, and other unlovable historical subjects, Cobb's life had no moral vision or purpose. "Cobb" makes him less appealing by focusing on the pathetic last days of his life, when his body was ravaged by illness and his rage was exacerbated by pain, drugs, booze, self-pity and some apparent dementia. And also because Shelton chose to depict him as a sort of cartoonish lout, throwing bullet-spraying tantrums that would be the envy of Yosemite Sam.

Shelton made a similar mistake with "Blaze," having the normally restrained Paul Newman portray colorful Louisiana Governor Earl Long with an embarrassingly unrealistic gusto. Jones and Cobb are a better match, but the comic tone laid over many of his scenes (the first half-hour, in which Cobb takes Stump for a madcap ride down an icy mountain road, may be the most graceless introduction in the history of film biography) exaggerate a personality that was impossibly large to begin with.

"Cobb" makes much of the dilemma facing Stump, an honest journalist asked to ghostwrite a dishonest biography, and finally agreeing to protect the legend, and the sanctity of baseball. Shelton had a similar conflict both drawn to and repelled by Cobb, and managing finally to perpetuate his legend through the very act of destroying it.

Late in life, Cobb reportedly told someone that if he had his life to live over, he would have more friends. He had more than he knew.

NEWSWEEK, 12/12/94, p. 72, David Ansen

There are many folks who would say that Ty Cobb—who still holds the record for the highest lifetime batting average—was the greatest baseball player of all time. There are even a few people—some of the old ballplayers he anonymously supported with his considerable fortune—who'd say he was a great guy. But just about everybody else who ever crossed the path of this raging, bullheaded bigot and misanthrope would likely call him the meanest sonofabitch in the business. "I was the most hated man in baseball," says the 73-year-old Cobb (Tommy Lee Jones) in Ron Shelton's movie. It's a boast.

Cobb does not flinch from depicting this all-American bully in all his foul glory. Shelton's not interested in making a conventional biopic—mercifully, this is not "The Babe." It's not really a sports movie at all, but an investigation into the nature of our need to create heroic myths. That it arrives while the nation is grappling with the image/reality conundrum of O. J. Simpson adds bitter provocation.

"Cobb's" vantage point comes from sportswriter Al Stump, the author of two books on the man called the Georgia Peach.

Stump (Robert Wuhl) is summoned in 1960 to the ailing superstar's Nevada mountain lodge. Cobb wants him to write his life story—a glorious tale of baseball triumphs and record-breaking feats. Stump is turned on by the idea of encountering greatness—and appalled by the alcoholic, hate-filled egotist he encounters. Cobb beats up and nearly rapes a Reno cigarette girl (the excellent Lolita Davidovich), and when he takes the stage at Harrah's, launches into a racist diatribe against blacks and Jews. As Cobb's traveling companion in the last year of his life, Stump traps himself in a morally untenable position. Should he betray Cobb and write the truth about him, or should he betray his sense of truth and publish the official myth?

Shelton obviously has a love-hate thing for cantankerous, intransigent old goats: his first fact-based movie, "Blaze," was about Earl Long. "Cobb" is more satisfying because it has some of the ribald, manic spirit of his looser fictional films, "Bull Durham" and "White Men Can't Jump." There's a ghastly dark humor in the spectacle of Cobb's don't-give-a-damn rages. Jones may not look old enough for the part, but in every other way he's belligerently perfect, a wild boar in winter, a tragicomic King Leer. Wuhl, best known as a comic second banana, is competent, but somewhat overpowered. The one failing of Shelton's smart, uncompromising script is that too many of the Stump-Cobb scenes fall into a repetitious pattern: there's only so much drama you can get out of Stump's wrestling match with his conscience. But "Cobb" is a refreshingly spiky antidote to all the Hollywood paeans to the glory of the game. Ty Cobb approached baseball as he approached life: take no prisoners and leave scorched earth behind you. His greatness and his monstrosity can't be untangled. "Cobb" allows us to honor his achievements, but with no false illusions. It puts the ball in our hands: if this is an American hero, we need to figure out why.

SIGHT AND SOUND, 7/95, p. 42, Leslie Felperin

A newsreel explains the baseball career of Ty Cobb, one of the greatest and most ruthlessly aggressive players the game has ever known.

1960. Al Stump, a semi-famous sportswriter is invited to ghostwrite Cobb's autobiography. Meeting Cobb at his home in Tahoe, Stump discovers a vicious-tempered, racist, and very sick old man who wants "A prince and a good man has fallen here today" written on his tombstone. Finding Cobb unbearable company, with editorial control over what he writes, Stump tries to get out of the deal only to find that his hands are tied.

Cobb, who has been impotent for many years, insists he wants to visit Reno to get laid and Stump comes along. Stump meets Ramona, a cigarette-seller, and is about to go to bed with her when Cobb barges in and drags Ramona off to his room. He seems poised to rape her when his impotence asserts itself and he lets her go, giving her a $1,000 and instructions to tell everyone that he was the greatest lover she ever had. Stump decides to write two books: the first a hagiographic tribute, while the second, written on hidden scraps of paper, will be an honest portrait of Cobb's brutal personality and include material on how he beat a mugger to death, battered his wife, and how his father was killed by his mother when Cobb was a youth, all of which are revealed in flashbacks.

Cobb grows increasingly dependent on Stump and reveals more about his life as the two men start to become rancorous friends. They make their way across country to the Baseball Hall of Fame where a ceremony to induct Cobb and several other players onto the roster of the great is about to take place. It is revealed that Cobb, a canny stock market investor and a wealthy man, has been financially supporting an old teammate for years. At the ceremony, the newsreel shown at the beginning of the film rolls again, but this time Cobb hallucinates that the voiceover and images are revealing all his dark personal secrets.

The two men drive to Royston, Georgia, where Cobb was born. There, Cobb's daughter refuses to speak with him. Cobb reveals that his father was 'really' murdered by his wife's lover. Cobb discovers Stump's notes for the second book, but his rage is cut short when he starts coughing up blood, so he checks into a hospital. As Cobb dies, Stump finishes the book the way Cobb would have wanted it. When his friends ask him later what Cobb was really like, he replies, "a prince and a good man has fallen here today."

Cobb opens with newsreel film, contains contradictory flashbacks, and has a complex and legendary figure at its centre about whom a reporter is trying to find out the elusive truth. Possibly only the fear of it being mistaken for a film on corn harvesting prevented the studio from calling the film *Citizen Cobb*. To its deserved credit, however, this soft pastiche of *Citizen Kane* enhances the film's true colours which are surprisingly richer than those of the average biopic.

In some ways it goes one better than Welles' film. As writer-director Ron Shelton's best film. *Cobb* is akin to a pigeon standing on the statuesque shoulders of Welles' prototypical examination of a great-man-of-history: but it leaves tactical droppings on the very notion of mythmaking. After telling Stump the story of his father's murder for the first time, Cobb mocks his biographer's seizure of this fact as "the missing piece". Rather than allow this to be misread as a Rosebudian revelation, Cobb insists that he "was a prick before it happened, and a prick after it happened and you can stick that up your Sigmund Freud ass." By the time the ambiguous conclusion rolls around, the very need for heroes has been, if not completely dissected, then at least gutted and spread out on the table.

Baseball in general and baseball biopics in particular share a portion of the blame for forging modern American ideals of heroism, masculinity, and fatherhood in America. It seems appropriate then that Shelton should use the genre to deconstruct all of the above while still being able to convey the glamour and allure of the game. His powerful slow-motion, sepia-toned flashbacks skirt but never descend into cliché. In *Bull Durham* and *White Men Can't Jump*, Shelton displayed a sure touch for rendering the sporting life. Here, there's less playtime on screen, but what is there buttresses the narrative. Thus, if there's something missing from Cobb's character exposition, it's amply expressed in the way we see him steal bases and land a kick in the catcher's face as he flies home. If *Field of Dreams* movingly recuperated the myths of baseball, *Cobb* mangles them afresh, and cuttingly historicises them, albeit taking justifiable liberties with the facts. (Stump actually met Cobb on several occasions rather than just the one road-bound bonding session that we see here, for example.)

Having made a career out of playing good ol' boys with nasty streaks, Tommy Lee Jones nails the type down forever. Only an actor with precise comic timing could measure out such tragic moments as when, coughing up blood, he starts to say the Lord's Prayer and gives up the faded hope of redemption with a clipped "fuck it". Robert Wuhl is equally excellent playing catch with the smart dialogue and being a likable sort of blokey *mensch* as Al Stump. A collection of real life sportswriters put in cameos as Stump's bar-buddies, their crumpled mugs recalling similar cabals of *kvetches* in *Broadway Danny Rose* and *Diner*. Amongst all this foetid masculinity, Lolita Davidovich is the lone female in the locker room, but her little bit of screen time makes an indelible mark with a near-rape scene that lingers in the mind and keeps Cobb's character in focus.

Baseball movies, unless they star Kevin Costner, seldom go down well with British audiences, so it's unlikely that this one will wow them in Woking. It would be a pity if *Cobb* sunk unnoticed, however, because it's about much more than the life story of the man with the greatest ever lifetime batting average (.367). At the very least, it provokes the question why no one here has ever attempted to tell in cinematic terms the story of, say, George Best, a sporting hero of the same proportions as Ty Cobb.

TIME, 12/5/94, p. 92, Richard Schickel

Toward the end of *Cobb*, the hero suddenly starts coughing up blood. Death, which until now has been a second baseman to be charged, spiked and upended, is not going to drop the ball this time. It is a new experience for Ty Cobb. He has never encountered anything his psychopathic aggressiveness couldn't overwhelm. Tommy Lee Jones's utterly incautious performance—he's pure attack dog—permits his character a moment of naked panic. Then he looks in the mirror and accepts his fate, and calmly calls the hospital.

No one will ever confuse writer-director Ron Shelton's new film with *The Pride of the Yankees*. It is not really a baseball movie or a biopic at all. It is a meditation on the nature of genius, which is not a word we usually apply to ballplayers, even great ones. But that's how Ty Cobb saw himself, and that's how he wanted to be remembered. To that end, in the last year of his life, he hired a sportswriter named Al Stump to help him write his autobiography. Cobb's orders were to ignore anything in his life that did not directly relate to his career. A few flashbacks aside, Shelton's film records the battle of wills between this mad old man and an amanuensis (a wonderfully befuddled Robert Wuhl), whose motives (he needs the money but wants to write the truth) and emotions toward his subject are exquisitely mixed.

Cobb once held some 40 major-league hitting and base-running records, and his lifetime batting average (.367) remains unsurpassed. Aside from that, he had everything to hide: unquestionably a womanizer, a wife beater and a venomous racist, he was possibly a murderer and a fixer of ball games. But if he did not want all that written down for posterity, he did not otherwise deny who and what he was. He flaunted his nature in the same way he flaunted his talent on the playing field—with vicious abandon. His only virtue was his total lack of hypocrisy. His isolation when the cheering stopped was the price he proudly paid for greatness, and he would mouth no pieties to assuage his loneliness.

In this, perhaps, he had no choice. The man either had a genetic screw loose or was irreparably damaged by the fact that his mother (or maybe her lover) killed his revered father with a shotgun when he was 17. In telling this story, Shelton (creator as well of quite a different baseball tale, (*Bull Durham*) had no choice either. To cop some psychological plea for Cobb, to sentimentalize him would have been impossible. You have to allow him his monstrousness, and hope that honest people will find something of their worst selves in his manic cynicism and endless misanthropy.

Many won't be able to. They can justify their fastidiousness by observing that this is a messy movie, sometimes repetitive, sometimes too compressed and allusive. But that's like saying Ty Cobb was not a very good sport—irrelevant in comparison to the horrific fascination of his story.

VILLAGE VOICE, 12/6/94, p. 53, J. Hoberman

America's *dominant* baseball player from the heyday of Theodore Roosevelt through that of Warren G. Harding, Ty Cobb was the national pastime's supreme angry man—pathological, pugnacious, and like fellow Georgian Newt Gingrich, a skilled practitioner of "chimpanzee politics." The so-called Georgia Peach bobbed up as little more than colorful flotsam in the rolling eternity of Ken Burn's *Baseball* (which did note that fans were both attracted and repelled by the "cruelty" of Cobb's bullying, blustering Will to Power), but writer-director Ron Shelton, whose previous movies have celebrated the canny truculence of pols and athletes alike, rises to the bait.

Shelton, a onetime minor league prospect who, in *Bull Durham* and *White Men Can't Jump*, wrote and directed the two liveliest, least moralizing sports comedies of the past half-dozen years, would seem perfectly positioned to celebrate his subject's cosmic orneriness—he appreciates a whopper. For, in addition to the highest lifetime batting average in major-league history, Cobb boasts an unbeatable reputation for competitive aggro, racial invective, and off-field violence—reducing his spiritual descendant Pete Rose (who, in 1985, broke Cobb's record for lifetime base hits) to the status of a harmless Dudley Do-Right. Shelton doesn't flinch, but seeking to justify his subject, he goes enthusiastically schizoid: *Cobb* alternates between unpleasantness and sentimentality and, whenever confused, pours on the Americana.

Opening with a field holler cum Copland-esque fanfare worthy of Burns, *Cobb* is a priori nostalgic—set some 30-odd years after Cobb retired from baseball. Somewhere in Santa Barbara, a gaggle of smug sportswriters is arguing over who was the best when Al Stump (Robert Wuhl, the pitching coach in *Bull Durham*) receives the summons, from on high: the 72-year-old Cobb, is ready for his Boswell. Despite the Peach's reputation of being "difficult at best, psychotic at worst," Stumpy skids up to his Lake Tahoe lair where, even before he can ring the doorbell, he's bowled over by the comic exit of a fast-talking black man seemingly on his way back to the "feet do your duty" days of the 1930s. Welcome to Cobb World. The master himself, lying in bed listening to a recording of violinist Fritz Kreisler, shoots out the lights by way of a greeting.

As overembodied by Tommy Lee Jones, Cobb is an abusive, irascible, trigger-happy megalomaniac who slugs milk and bourbon for breakfast and, for a nightcap, injects his gut with insulin to pass out in your face. By building a movie around so monstrous a creature, Shelton optimistically follows the trail blazed by *Raging Bull*, although, as garrulous as his subject is, *Cobb* would give that title a whole new meaning. Jones is almost always on-screen, and his wheezing, choking, makeup-caked, Halloween-mask performance takes no more than a nanosecond to wear sufficiently thin for the actor to jab his elbow through the screen. Trying to steal his second Oscar, Jones hurls himself at the viewer the way Cobb did at enemy second basemen—Shelton couldn't possibly move the camera back far enough.

Endlessly harangued, Stumpy spends the movie chauffeuring Cobb around—driving down to Reno mid-blizzard so the Peach can pretend to get laid, heading back East to the Baseball Hall of Fame at Cooperstown for a star--studded testimonial dinner, proceeding down South to drop in on the daughter he hasn't seen in 15 years. When not regarding his subject with avid, red-faced, beady-eyed envy (eventually he does get to demonstrate the lessons of the master), smirky Stumpy is writing two books—an "official" one, *Ty Cobb's My Life in Baseball: The True Record*, which appeared in 1961, and a second secret tell-all, the just-published *Cobb: A Biography*. Shelton's *Cobb* draws on both. Watching the newsreel the Hall of Fame has pulled together in his honor, Cobb hallucinates his own version of *Citizen Kane*. His triumphs on the field are interspersed with scenes of his own drunken violence and carousing.

As *Bull Durham* demonstrated, Shelton is a gifted choreographer of baseball action, and *Cobb*'s few related moments are the gauzy flashbacks to Cobb's playing days. The forerunner of today's trash-talking hoop stars, Cobb is pelted by rambunctious fans and precipitates a brawl at every base. (One game ends with a bench-clearing rhubarb.) "I was the most hated man in baseball," he tells Stumpy with satisfaction. But, one too-brief ballgame aside, Shelton's most impressive stunt is presenting the candy-colored Reno casino where a simulated Louis Prima and Keely Smith wink and twitch their way through "That Old Black Magic" like a pair of auto-animatronic Disney robots. Once celebrity Cobb is brought up to the microphone, he empties the room with a diatribe directed against niggers, dagos, and kikes; Lolita Davidovich, imported for sex interest as a bewigged cigarette girl, is less lucky. The spectacle of Cobb preparing to rape her character is exceeded in repulsiveness only by the later image of him hacking up a sink full of bloody phlegm.

Where *White Men Can't Jump* was energized by the flux of stereotypes and counterstereotypes into the most entertaining of recent male bonding flicks, *Cobb* is gratingly monotonous. The trip from Reno to Cooperstown to Georgia is rip-snortingly glacial—the Peach waving his gun and ranting into a tape recorder even as Stumpy changes a flat. "With a friend like you I could go on forever," an exultant Cobb tells Stump at one point, suggesting nothing so much as the nightmarish father in Kafka's "The Judgement" who rises from his sick bed to sentence his grown son to death. Considering how little time has transpired and how long the movie feels, it's hard not to take the threat personally.

Early in *Cobb*, a pseudo newsreel with an overly sophisticated narrator hails the Georgia Peach as "the first celebrity athlete in American history." True or not (Cobb Played a nice-guy version of himself in the six-reel 1916 feature, *Somewhere in Georgia*), *Cobb* is a movie about the nature of celebrity worship: As the great man puts it, "The children of America need heroes."

Like *Mrs. Parker and the Vicious Circle* (reviewed here this week by Georgia Brown), *Cobb* uses a highly concentrated, self-consciously mannerist star turn to contemporize the notion of its half-forgotten, alcoholic subject as a vanguard Personality, marooned in the past. As *Mrs. Parker's* Dorothy Parker is, pace Elizabeth Wurtzel, something like Madonna with the ego of Sylvia Plath, so Cobb is the real Charles Barkley ... or worse. There is the suggestion that, among other things, professional athletics provides a socially sanctioned outlet for serious hostility. *Cobb* rewards those who stick with it to the end by reprising footage of its anti-hero kicking an opposing player in the nuts and bounding into a chest-thumping gorilla leap of triumph.

Shelton may be contemptuous of the parasitic sportswriters who presume to pass judgment on Greatness (the gargoyles he assembled as Stumpy's chorus are doubtless his surrogate for movie critics), but *Cobb* is smart enough to suggest that its subject's appeal may not be Greatness per se, so much as the license it grants to act without constraint. "I don't accommodate anybody," Cobb brags. "The desire for glory" may not be a "sin," per the Peach's favorite aphorism, but it certainly covers a multitude of them.

Glory is as glory does. The inevitable O.J connection notwithstanding, *Cobb* is already relevant. The movie is unlikely to be a blockbuster, but *Variety*'s postelection report, "Beltway's Right Turn," prominently featured a pull quote by Clinton aide turned phone-industry lobbyist Roy Neel: "National politics is now a sport played by the Ty Cobbs, not the Forrest Gumps." There's no guarantee that both roles will be nominated, but certainly by Oscar night we'll know if it's true.

Also reviewed in:
CHICAGO TRIBUNE, 12/2/94, Friday/p. C, Michael Wilmington
NEW YORK TIMES, 12/2/94, p. C8, Janet Maslin
NEW YORKER, 12/5/94, p. 130, Terrence Rafferty
VARIETY, 11/28-12/4/94, p. 94, Leonard Klady
WASHINGTON POST, 1/6/95, p C1, Hal Hinson
WASHINGTON POST, 1/6/95, Weekend/p. 37, Desson Howe

COLONEL CHABERT

An October Films release of a Film par film production in association with D.D. Films/TF1 Films/Orly Films. *Executive Producer:* Bernard Marescot. *Producer:* Jean-Louis Livi. *Director:* Yves Angelo. *Screenplay (French with English subtitles):* Jean Cosmos, Veronique Lagrange, and Yves Angelo. *Based on the book by:* Honor de Balzac. *Director of Photography:* Bernard Lutic. *Editor:* Thierry Derocles. *Sound:* Pierre Gamet. *Casting:* Alberte Garo. *Art Director:* Bernard Vezat. *Set Designer:* Bernard Vezat. *Costumes:* Franca Squarciapino. *Make-up:* Thi-Loan Nguyen. *Running time:* 110 minutes. *MPAA Rating:* Not Rated.

CAST: Gérard Depardieu (Chabert); Fanny Ardant (Countess Ferraud); Fabrice Luchini (Derville); André Dussollier (Count Ferraud); Daniel Prevost (Boucard); Olivier Saladin (Huré); Maxime Leroux (Godeschal); Eric Elmosnino (Desroches); Guillaume Romain (Simonnin); Patrick Bordier (Boutin); Claude Rich (Chamblin); Jean Cosmos (Costaz); Jacky Nercessian (Delbacq); Albert Delpy (Notary); Marc Maidenberg (Servant); Romane Bohringer (Sophie); Valerie Bettencourt (Julie); Florence Guerfy (Client); Julie Depardieu (Maid); Isabelle Wolfe (Nun).

LOS ANGELES TIMES, 12/23/94, Calendar/p. 10, Kenneth Turan

When cinematographers direct their first films, arresting imagery is to be expected. But even by those standards, what Yves Angelo has accomplished in "Colonel Chabert" is especially impressive.

Working here with director of photography Bernard Lutic, Angelo reveals the same gift for glowing visuals both intimate and panoramic he displayed in shooting "Tout Les Matins du Monde," "Un Coeur en Hiver," "The Accompanist" and "Germinal."

Set in the early 19th Century, "Colonel Chabert's" visual centerpiece is its re-creation of 1807's Battle of Eylau, one of Napoleon's costliest triumphs. The scenes of the French cavalry charge, the subsequent hand-to-hand combat, and especially the wrenching but beautiful sequence depicting the collection of swords, helmets, coats and the like from the bodies of the dead that opens the film all make up the best treatment of this kind of material since Orson Welles's benchmark "Falstaff."

But—and this is unusual for a former cinematographer—Angelo is as interested in the interior life of his people as in their appearance. Working here with co-screenwriter Jean Cosmos, Angelo was not surprisingly drawn to the Balzac story that "Colonel Chabert" is based on. For no writer has a greater zest for psychological acuity, for characters as revealed in melodramatic crisis, than the great French novelist.

"Chabert" proper begins 10 years after Eylau, in the busy (and beautifully mounted) Paris office of Derville (Fabrice Luchini), a wizardly lawyer who neither sleeps nor loses cases. A strange and distant man (Gérard Depardieu) has been showing up at all hours, insisting on a private audience. When it is finally arranged, the man tells the astonished Derville that he is Col. Chabert, one of Napoleon's favorites, thought killed at Eylau but now returned to a semblance of life. "I'd like not to be me," he says somberly, "but here I am."

What Chabert wants is to recover his property from his formidable former wife (Fanny Ardant), now the Countess Ferraud. Believing him dead, she increased the fortune she inherited from him and married the upwardly mobile Count Ferraud (André Dussollier) after the post-Napoleonic restoration of the monarchy.

Derville, who is also the Countess' attorney, is intrigued by this tale despite himself. Is this man truly Chabert or a deluded impostor? And what effect will his reappearance have on the Countess' marriage; potentially shaky because her Napoleonic past is getting in the way of her husband's ambitions?

Director Angelo has brought an elegant and precise style to the working out of this dramatic situation that nicely counterpoints the great passions involved. He has paid attention to everything, including the beauty of the spoken French and the creation of handsome physical settings for characters who worship wealth and possessions.

A former classical pianist, Angelo has also chosen the film's musical selections from Beethoven, Mozart, Scarlatti, Schumann and Schubert with more than usual care, and gotten seamless performances from his fine actors and even seen to it that his narrative has a subtle and haunting finale. If there's any more a debut film could accomplish, it's hard to think what it might be.

NEW YORK POST, 12/23/94, p. 554, Thelma Adams

"I have been buried under the dead; but now I am buried under the the living, under papers, under facts, under the whole of society, which wants to shove me underground again!"

This is Colonel Chabert's lament to the lawyer Derville in the slim novel by Honore de Balzac which inspired Yves Angelo's tragedy "Colonel Chabert."

Chabert (Gerard Depardieu) had the misfortune of being buried alive after distinguishing himself in Napoleon's army at the battle of Eylau. Ten years later, in 1817, the war hero has finally crawled back to Paris—gnarled, scarred, impoverished, unrecognizable—to reclaim wife and fortune.

All is not resolved in a simple "honey, I'm home." Chabert's wife, Countess Ferraud (Fanny Ardant), has remarried, using the Colonel's fortune to climb the social ladder. But the mother of two young children has her own problems: Count Ferraud (Andre Dussollier) has political ambitions and his low-born, wealthy wife has become an obstacle to his advancement.

Add to this that the true-blue Chabert still loves his wife, the Countess loves the Count, and the Count adores himself, and you have a triangle of the first order. The ambitious lawyer Derville (Fabrice Luchini) sorts out the situation—but to whose advantage?

Balzac endures because his novels are timeless, his insight into human nature profound. He looks clear-eyed into the heart of darkness and neither flinches, revels or moans. "Colonel Chabert" gives rein to two favorite Balzac themes: the virtuous are prey to the self-interested; and, if you follow the money, you will discover the true natures of those involved in any transaction.

Yves Angelo is not the clear-eyed thinker Balzac was. Making the leap from top-flight cinematographer ("Germinal") to director, he offers a stylish, ambiguous reworking of the minor classic. Out of universal material, he has created a period piece.

Angelo opens with scenes of Eylau: gauzy fog, rosy snow, blue corpses thrown into a pit, dark ponies tossed onto bonfires. All handsome, all poetically horrific and all superfluous to the story, despite Angelo's resurrection of these images throughout the movie as if they bore some inherent moral weight. The cinematographer can't resist, but the director should have known better.

Depardieu (the French answer to Tommy Lee Jones—he's in everything) chose the material, but he makes an odd Chabert. He hangs his head and hunches his shoulders beneath a greasy coat, but he never attains the broken-down, walking cadaver, repulsiveness of a soldier whose skull was cleaved from nape of neck to widow's peak.

Depardieu looks as if, with a little dusting off and a new hat, he would return to his old vigor—and easily win the Countess Ferraud. Ardant, who co-starred with Depardieu in Francois Truffaut's "The Woman Next Door"), gazes at the camera with worried bovine eyes. Is she concerned that she'll appear unsympathetic?

Ambiguity is everywhere, the beautiful hard edges of Balzac softened. In a winning performance, Luchini's Derville manipulates the situation with an oiled smoothness—but what exactly has he done? An unexplained leap in the storyline before the final scene leaves the audience aware that Chabert has fallen, but unsettled as to how precisely it happened and, therefore, what "Colonel Chabert" means.

NEWSDAY, 12/23/94, Part II/p. B7, John Anderson

The gorgeous and grisly opening scenes of "Colonel Chabert," Yves Angelo's adaptation of Balzac's novel, take place at Eylau, where Napoleon lost 10,000 men—or maybe 9,999. It is an exaltation of death: The palette is blue steel and wet crimson, the landscape is an ethereal plain worthy of David Lean, the atmosphere is repellent and seductive, beautiful and final. It's heaven and it's hell.

And it's been a home of sorts to Colonel Chabert (Gerard Depardieu), who was "killed" there—wounded, thrown in a mass grave—after leading his troops into battle. Returning to Paris after a decade of penniless suffering, he wants his wife, his fortune and, most of all, he wants to be alive again.

Spouses have been coming back from the dead at least since Irene Dunne in "My Favorite Wife" and as recently as "Sommersby," which was based on "The Return of Martin Guerre," which also starred Depardieu, who now has the record for resurrections—and who, despite making consistently silly English language movies, continues to be an amazing actor in his native tongue. As Colonel Chabert, he is weird and fascinating. The handsome Fanny Ardant as his wife, who has remarried and become the Countess Ferraud and sees Chabert's return as a threat to her station, is both a predator and victim of the Napoleonic code. Together they make one believe that "Colonel Chabert" is even more than it appears to be.

Part psychological mystery, part drawing-room drama, Yves Angelo's film is not entirely satisfying, perhaps because the tension and psychological substance we've been given along the way feel like they should add up to more. And while Chabert's true identity is supposed to be part of the mystery it's defused by the flashbacks to Eylau, which are Chabert's—which means, according to every rule of flashbacks, that he is who he says he is. But there are several startling scenes—Chabert's retelling of his "death," bookended by the Countess' plea for her social survival—that override the plot problems, and make for a riveting film.

It's a classic tale in the end, with the hostile parties becoming the victims, and the politicians and lawyers—Fabrice Luchini as the attorney Derville is a bilious little barrister—picking over the bones. And Depardieu again proves himself an actor of dynamic power who, despite Hollywood's best efforts, continues to come back from the dead.

SIGHT AND SOUND, 5/95, p. 43, Keith Reader

Paris 1817, two years after the restoration of the Bourbon monarchy. A shabby-looking individual attempts to see the lawyer Derville in his chambers; returning at one in the morning (the only time Derville is free), he explains that he is Colonel Chabert, a much-decorated Napoleonic soldier believed killed at the battle of Eylau ten years before. In fact he had remained alive beneath a pile of corpses. He has spent the intervening years penuriously making his way back to Paris and trying to establish his identity; it is for this purpose, and to return to his wife (now Countess Ferraud), that he enlists Derville's help.

Count Ferraud, meanwhile, is being advised by his friends at a worldly *soirée* that his ambition to become a peer will not be fulfilled unless he abandons his wife, who is compromised by her former life as a prostitute and by the fact that her fortune (once Chabert's) is of Napoleonic origin. Derville's clerk uncovers evidence which suggests that Chabert is telling the truth. Although committed to defending Countess Ferraud's interests, Derville takes pity on Chabert when he sees the appallingly squalid surroundings in which he is forced to live. He tries to resolve his compromised position by bringing Chabert and his 'ex-wife' together, initially keeping them out of sight of each other while he reads out the document he has drawn up. After a fraught confrontation he takes Chabert off to the Countess' country estate, where he progressively browbeats him into accepting an iniquitous financial settlement. When Chabert discovers that he will be required to disavow his newly re-established identity, he refuses even this.

In a coda, Count Ferraud has taken his friend's advice and abandoned the Countess for a match that is about to bring him the coveted peerage. Chabert is eking out his days in a hospice run by nuns, rejecting the name he has striven so hard to regain and electing henceforth to be known only by first name and number.

Given the expatriation of Luc Besson and (putatively) Léos Carax, and the restricted availability of films by what is left of the *nouvelle vague*, the heritage film genre inaugurated by Claude Berri's *Jean de Florette* and *Manon des Source* seems now to dominate the British view of French cinema to a degree that would have been unthinkable a decade ago. Yves Angelo's directorial debut (he was the cinematographer on Alain Corneau's *Tous les matins du monde* and Claude Sautet's *Un Coeur en hiver*) takes its place on a British distribution conveyor belt behind Patrice Chéreau's *La Reine Margot* and just ahead of Bertrand Tavernier's *La Fille de D'Artagnan*, to open in the summer.

Le Colonel Chabert exemplifies this genre in a number of ways, most obviously through lavish production values. Angelo expressly set out to "pay much attention to the physical trappings of wealth." Those of poverty and desolation are also expansively evoked in the harrowing montage of the aftermath of battle with which the film opens and in the odorous city farm where Chabert lives. Two other heritage hallmarks are also present and correct: a literary source (here canonical as with Berri's *Germinal* rather than popular as with the Pagnol and Dumas adaptations) and perhaps most importantly what might be called a permutational use of performance. Films are increasingly sold in France on the basis of their combination of stars, the most striking recent example being Huppert and Auteuil together for the first time in Christian Vincent's *La Séparation*. The recipe of *Le Colonel Chabert* is a predictable one: take France's megastar of megastars, juxtapose him with old friends rediscovered (Fanny Ardant from François Truffaut's *La Femme d'à côté*, Fabrice Luchini from Berri's *Uranus*) or new sparring partners (André Dussollier), and throw in an up-and-coming name cast against type (Romane Bohringer as the calmest and most compliant of ladies' maids).

The problem with this approach is that it can lead, as in *Le Colonel Chabert*, to a lazy, flabby form of intertextuality, cumbersomely underscored by visual or verbal reference. Sometimes this works, as with Derville's clear identification with the young Balzac—suggested in the novella by his monstrous appetite for toil and society, reinforced in the film by Luchini's appearance. Sometimes, however, it acts as a needlessly sharp elbow in the ribs, as when Derville proclaims that if Chabert is an impostor, "I shall have seen the most skilful actor of our time" (Depardieu—geddit?). Luchini and Depardieu deliver performances of high calibre, but little is asked of Ardant or Bohringer other than to look good in period costume. The sub-plot leading up to Ferraud's eventual desertion of the Countess is an addition to the novella, presumably by way of a history lesson, as is much of the dialogue. This need not have mattered, but Chabert's twice-uttered allusion to the colours of death as "first red, then blue" adds an incongruously poetico-philosophical element to the character.

Le Colonel Chabert may make one of Balzac's greatest and most neglected texts more widely known (it is still not available in paperback translation in this country) but it scarcely goes beyond what one would expect of a decent television serialisation. The catch-all range of music used—including the slow movement from Schubert's Piano Sonata in A, used to shattering effect in Robert Bresson's *Au Hasard Balthazar*—suggests an eagerness to market a CD package more than anything else. Before becoming an actor, Fabrice Luchini was a student in Roland Barthes' graduate seminar in Paris—the seminar that in its earlier days brought forth, in *S/Z*, a re-reading that revolutionised the study of Balzac. It is fittingly ironic then that his performance should be the best thing about this otherwise predictable and uninspiring film.

VILLAGE VOICE, 12/27/94, p. 74, Georgia Brown

In wars, the French seem to lose many things that eventually come back to haunt them. Perhaps this explains their cinema's minor obsession with soldiers missing in action who return many years later to reclaim their former lives. Many of you will recall Daniel Vigne's 1982 art-house hit *The Return of Martin Guerre*. Now Yves Angelo has unearthed a Balzac novel with a very similar theme, and darned if he doesn't choose *Martin Guerre*'s lead, Gérard Depardieu, to play the resurrected officer.

The year is 1817 and the bulky, slovenly Colonel Chabert, dressed in a fusty black suit fit for the tomb, returns not to his wife (Fanny Ardant)—now remarried and become the Countess

Ferraud—but to the district's cleverest lawyer, the canny Derville (Fabrice Luchini). Chabert claims not to want his wife back, but merely a partial settlement for his lost property. The Countess claims not to know him. The wily lawyer, focused always on his clients' vulnerabilities, recognizes that her former husband's reappearance would endanger the Countess's present marriage—i.e., she has much to lose.

Initially, a mystery surrounds a Chabert's real intentions, the Countess's, as well as the lawyer's. But such expectations may be a holdover from Vigne's film, where mysteries abound. From both the trembly Ardant and the volcanic Depardieu, we may also expect an upsurge of passion—but perhaps this too is a holdover from their volatile proximity in Truffaut's *The Woman Next Door*. I won't tell you this film's outcome, but will say that the other two were more intensely satisfying.

A former cinematographer (he shot both lovely classical-music: hits, *Tous les matins du monde* and *Un Coeur en hiver*), Angelo isn't afraid to avoid drama. The real drama—Chabert's struggle to return to the world of the living—seems to have taken place offscreen, in the 10-year interim since the fatal Battle of Eylau where Napoleon lost 10,000 men. Now, as the old soldier attempts to make his way in a world with new rules , new alliances, Depardieu has to restrain himself. Yet it's him nonetheless: frighteningly eccentric, fixing people in that mad, piercing gaze.

Also reviewed in:
CHICAGO TRIBUNE, 6/9/95, Friday/p. F, Michael Wilmington
NEW REPUBLIC, 12/26/94, p. 26, Stanley Kauffmann
NEW YORK TIMES, 12/23/94, p. C8, Janet Maslin
VARIETY, 9/19-25/94, p. 78, Joe Leydon
WASHINGTON POST, 2/17/95, p. F7, Rita Kempley
WASHINGTON POST, 2/17/95, Weekend/p. 42, Desson Howe

COLOR OF NIGHT

A Hollywood Pictures release of a Cinergi Pictures Entertainment production. *Executive Producer:* Andrew G. Vajna. *Producer:* Buzz Feitshans and David Matalon. *Director:* Richard Rush. *Screenplay:* Matthew Chapman and Billy Ray. *Story:* Billy Ray. *Director of Photography:* Dietrich Lohmann. *Editor:* Jack Hofstra. *Music:* Dominic Frontiere. *Music Editor:* Robin Katz. *Sound:* David Kelson. *Sound Editor:* Mark P. Stoeckinger and Trevor Jolly. *Casting:* Wendy Kurtzman. *Production Designer:* James L. Schoppe. *Art Director:* Gary A. Lee. *Set Designer:* Sydney Z. Litwack. *Set Decorator:* Cynthia McCormac. *Set Dresser:* Vito San Filippo, Ken Abraham, Joanne Gilliam, Max Brehme, and Taylor Black. *Special Effects:* Terry King. *Costumes:* Jacki Arthur. *Make-up:* Michele Burke and John Blake. *Make-up (Bruce Willis):* Mike Mills. *Make-up (Lesley Ann Warren):* Carrie Angland. *Running time:* 120 minutes. *MPAA Rating:* R.

CAST: Bruce Willis (Bill Capa); Jane March (Rose); Ruben Blades (Martinez); Lesley Ann Warren (Sondra); Scott Bakula (Bob Moore); Brad Dourif (Clark); Lance Henriksen (Buck); Kevin J. O'Connor (Casey); Andrew Lowery (Dale); Eriq La Salle (Anderson); Jeff Corey (Ashland); Kathleen Wilhoite (Michelle); Shirley Knight (Edith Niedelmeyer); John T. Bower (Medical Examiner); Avi Korein (Bouncer); Steven R. Barnett (Cop #1); Roberta Storm (Receptionist).

LOS ANGELES TIMES, 8/19/94, Calendar/p. 1, Kenneth Turan

It is sad, truly sad, to have to report that "Color of Night" is a disappointment in almost every respect.

Richard Rush, its director, is not only warmly remembered for having made "The Stunt Man," one of the most original American films of the past 20 years, but that 1980 success was followed by the kind of miserable luck that never seems to afflict the untalented.

For a variety of reasons, Rush has not had a film to call his own from that time to this. And while he was embroiled with "Night's" producer over final cut of this film, the director had to be hospitalized with a heart attack.

"Night's" star, Bruce Willis, has certainly proved his ability to please audiences when he's right for a project. But though Willis is in earnest about his role here, the idea of using him as a troubled and introspective New York psychiatrist is in its own way as dubious a piece of casting as was having Al Pacino play a sophisticated international Grand Prix driver in "Bobby Deerfield."

The same is true for Jane March, hardly a veteran actress but one who displayed an effective erotic presence in "The Lover." Her role as the mysterious romantic temptress in "Night" is so convoluted as to be just about unplayable, and it is no fun to see March drown in a storm not of her own making.

As for writers Matthew Chapman (credited with such previous illogical features as "Strangers Kiss" and "Consenting Adults") and Billy Ray, they have turned out a tepid pastiche that refers to so many Hitchcock films it's easy to lose count. Perhaps they should put their VCRs in the closet for a while.

The result of the collaboration between all these parties is an unconvincing movie that is simultaneously predictable and far-fetched, not a fortunate combination. Very little makes any kind of sense here, and very few people will care.

Willis plays Dr. Bill Capa, a Manhattan psychoanalyst, one of whose patients opts out of therapy in a rather violent and disturbing way. Though he knows you can't hide from your troubles, Dr. Bill decides to take a break and visit an old college pal and fellow mental-help professional Bob Moore (Scott Bakula) out in sunny Los Angeles.

The city may be sunny, but the therapy group Moore runs, which Dr. Bill sits in on, is not. Included among its members are an oversexed divorcée, a spoiled, rich-kid artist, an obsessive compulsive lawyer, a sexually confused teen-ager and a surly man wracked with unspecific guilt. It has a kind of over-the-top giddiness usually associated with skits on "Saturday Night Live."

But when Moore gets murdered, and a quirky police investigator (Ruben Blades) thinks someone in the group did it, both the sessions and the movie attempt to get more serious. Because of his way with phrases such as "Is there anything else you'd like to tell us?," Dr. Bill is asked to take over the group, and when he's not helping those fragile egos he's trying to solve his friend's murder.

As if there wasn't enough on his plate, Dr. Bill quite literally has a run-in with the mysterious Rose (Jane March) when her car clumsily bangs into his. Fascinated by her perky charm and the way she has of running out the door without leaving so much as a phone number after exhausting bouts of torrid sex, Dr. Bill wonders if this could be love.

Though Rush's trademark bemusement—his fascination with what is reality and what isn't—should in theory add another level to a conventional thriller, in practice its presence turns out to be a distraction, diluting what impact the film's menace can manage.

More troublesome is that darned script, which gets increasingly overloaded with twists both preposterous and obvious. By the time the solution dawns on Dr. Bill and the light of understanding bathes his face, everyone else in the theater (if there is anyone else in the theater) will have already figured it out.

NEW YORK POST, 8/19/94, p. 49, Michael Medved

They don't call mid-August the dog days of summer for nothing.

At this time of year, Hollywood studios unleash their cinematic bowsers, trotting out troubled projects at a point when Americans are more interested in beaches, barbecues or vacations than they are in movies.

And when it comes to alternate activities, even sun-bathing in Secaucus would be preferable to sitting through an unlovable mutt like "The Color of Night."

It might have been unintentionally funny, a high camp classic in the tradition of "Mommie Dearest," except for the fact that it's so insistently ugly. Bodies fall from 40 stories and make a noisy splat on the pavement, while a vicious nail gun punctures hands, arms, or foreheads of four different characters.

Amid all the guts and gore it's hard to enjoy lines like, "I cannot feel the pain I know I'm supposed to be feeling now" or "You're a pretty good therapist. How long does a man like you take to fix something that's broken?"

The therapist in question (played by an overly earnest Bruce Willis) is a Manhattan psychologist who flees to California after the suicide of one of his patients.

On the coast, he reconnects with old school chum an fellow shrink (Scott Bakula) just a few days before his pal is brutally murdered.

Willis and the police (led by the shamelessly scene-stealing Ruben Blades) are certain that the killer is a member of the dead doctor's therapy group—a coffee klatch that Willis agrees to take over when its members plead with him for guidance. This therapy group is obviously intended to make old-time New Yorker Willis feel right at home since it is Chock Full O'Nuts.

There's an anal-retentive lawyer with a morbid fear of germs (Brad Dourif), a nervous nymphomaniac (Lesley Ann Warren) and other assorted loonies. Director Richard Rush ("The Stunt Man") tries to show sympathy for these raving, twitching types, but the inane musical score (by Dominic Frontiere) always undermines him.

Whenever the group gets together, the sound track provides "hee-hee-hee" sitcom music reminiscent of "The Addams Family," as if psychosis and mutilation murder are as much fun as a barrel of Freudians.

The hard-working actors actually deserve better, especially glamorous and competent Jane March, who made such a splash in "The Lover," and who turns up here as yet another suspect.

She plays a flaky aspiring actress who seduces Willis and joins him for a couple of heavy-breathing sex scenes. (One of the sex scenes had to be trimmed to give it a rating of R rather than NC-17.)

Though these sequences are indeed reasonably steamy, die-hard fans who have been led to believe that they might catch a glimpse of Willis' penis will be disappointed; it's been snipped in order to slip the movie in under the "R" rating.

In its final 10 minutes, "The Color of Night" plummets from the merely pathetic to the jaw-droppingly awful, as the story coughs up an evil twin/multiple personality payoff that may stand as the most inane plot twist of the decade.

Other recent troubled shrink murder mysteries ("Final Analysis," "Whispers in the Dark") have boasted idiotic story elements, but they seem like models of common sense compared to this howler.

Sorry, Dr. Willis—a Prozac cocktail wouldn't be enough to get us to swallow this cinematic and psychological swill; acceptance here would actually require a lobotomy.

NEWSDAY, 8/19/94, Part II/p. B2, Jack Mathews

The prospect of seeing Bruce Willis play a psychologist is sort of a mind-blower in itself. Mr. Sensitive, right? just the guy to help you overcome, say, an ego problem. His wisecracks and smug self-love would send his patients screaming into the corridors, or, as it actually happens in the opening scene of "Color of Night," out the window of his high-rise Manhattan office.

Actually, the casting of Willis as Bill Capa, PhD, is the least of the film's problems. This is one of the star's most relaxed performances, and though you never quite feel the pain his tear-flooded cheeks suggest, he's about as sympathetic as he's going to get.

The story, written by Matthew Chapman (who wrote Walt Disney Studios' previous worst thriller, "Consenting Adults") and Billy Ray, is such a colossal whopper, however, that "Color of Night" is apt to sweep Willis and everyone else up in the embarrassment. The script reads like the winner of an amateur "Basic Instinct" lookalike contest and director Richard Rush—absent since his critically acclaimed 1980 "The Stunt Man"—may go another 14 years without a job.

"Color of Night" is a psychological thriller with more personality disorders than the Ted Bundy Fan Club. It's the story of a New York psychologist who takes over a murdered Los Angeles colleague's bickering therapy group, knowing that the killer may be in the group and that he could be the next victim.

The group includes Sondra (Leslie Ann Warren), a divorcee with a double mania (klepto- and nympho-); Clark (the perennially scary Brad Dourif) an unemployed attorney who is severely anal retentive (no lawyer jokes, please); Casey (Kevin J. O'Connor), a bitter artist whose work shows a flare for the kinky, and Buck (Lance Henriksen), a temperamental ex-cop depressed over the murders of his wife and daughter.

Capa isn't in much better shape himself. His guilt over a patient's suicide has left him professionally insecure and partially color-blind (he can't see blood red), and he's begun an obsessive love affair with a mysterious young woman (Jane March) who sounds eerily like the new young woman in each of his group members' lives. To cap it all, the flamboyant homicide detective (Ruben Blades) investigating Capa's friend's murder, suspects him of being the killer.

Can Capa find himself, solve the murders, cure his patients, see red and get the girl? Things were never this complex in "Die Hard."

Actually, if you can forgive "Color of Night" its spectacularly ridiculous ending, it has some modestly entertaining moments. The group sessions, which fluctuate wildly between torrential weeping and aggressive "you're crazier than I am" assaults, are often hilarious. And what remains of the Willis/March sex scenes that earned the original cut an NC17 rating have the body beautiful, soft-porn allure of Zalman King's "Red Shoes Diaries."

March, the young model who made her acting debut in Jean-Jacques Annoud's "The Lover" (also about an obsessive sexual relationship), has an easy, unselfconscious grace to go with her stunning looks, and Willis, who is on record as being resentful that his penis was edited out of the movie, has to be the best built shrink in Beverly Hills.

Voyeurs, call for group discounts.

SIGHT AND SOUND, 10/94, p. 38, Kim Newman

Struck with traumatic colour blindness after the suicide of a patient, New York psychologist Bill Capa visits his friend Bob Moore, also an analyst, in Los Angeles. Bob introduces Bill to his Monday night therapy group: promiscuous rich Sondra, obsessive lawyer Clark, grief-stricken ex-cop Buck, masochistic artist Casey and gender-confused teenager Richie. Bob, who has been receiving death threats and thinks one of the group is responsible, is stabbed to death. Bill is asked by Martinez, the cop on the case, to continue with the Monday group, which he reluctantly does.

Through a car accident, Bill meets Rose, a mysterious young woman with whom he begins a passionate affair. Bill is warned off by Dale, Richie's protective elder brother. A red car tries to force Bill off the road. Rose, who is Sondra's best friend in another identity, is interrupted in her seduction of Sondra by Bill's arrival, and has to escape before he realises her personality split. Casey is murdered in his studio and his paintings of a model he has talked about in therapy are mutilated. Bill discovers the body and retrieves a face from the fire, recognising Rose. Sondra, Clark and Buck all recognise a picture of Rose, who was also Bob's girlfriend, as 'Bonnie', a woman who has come into each of their lives with a personality that exactly fulfils their fantasies.

Looking up the widow of Richie's former therapist, Bill learns the dead man molested the boy and that Richie committed suicide. Bill goes to Dale's foundry and finds 'Richie' (actually Rose) nailed to a chair. Rose, who has a compulsion to be what people want her to be, took on her brother's personality to please Dale, who has committed the murders to keep Rose's Richie personality in place. Dale attacks Bill with a nailgun. Martinez intervenes and is stapled to a wall. Dale is killed by Rose, whom Bill talks out of suicide.

An entry in the currently-developing 'erotic thriller' stakes, *Color of Night* might, with a few more murders, have done as a scenario for one of the imitation Dario Argento *giali* of the early 70s (*Black Belly of the Tarantula, Seven Dead in the Cat's Eye*). Yet its mangling of psychology and sleaze harks back to the deliriously silly post-*Psycho* thrillers made by William Castle in the early 60s. There are precedents for the multiple role Jane March plays here, but the film-makers should have noted how few were successful (Castle's *Homicidal* comes close).

Terrible as the toothy March is in any of her incarnations, it is hard to think of anyone who could have got away with the part. However, Bruce Willis, screwing up his eyes to simulate the colour blindness that never becomes relevant to the plot, has no excuse. In his latest bizarre career choice, Willis gamely goes along with every fresh absurdity, traipsing between head-scratching confrontation of a mystery everyone will penetrate as soon as they see Richie's false teeth, and explicit but ridiculous sex scenes (*someone's* willy bobs underwater, but it's more likely to belong to a body double).

Almost as if the film-makers wanted to set off a ratings controversy, the script checks off as much 'offensive' matter as possible, from the saxophone-scored sex, degrees steamier than *Basic Instinct*, to the extensive use of a nailgun in the finale, complete with close-ups of Ruben Blades' hands being pinned to the wall. It's sad that the erratic and unprolific Richard Rush, who hasn't made a film since *The Stunt Man* in 1980 (although he did all the pre-production on *Air America*), should commit his undeniable talents to such an obviously dodgy project. Nevertheless, Rush's psycho-baroque touches and a sterling supporting cast manage to make the whole mass consistently gigglesome, and it might be charitable to assume that Willis and March are also sending themselves up.

The suspects are so well-cast that the mystery angle is blown out altogether: even if you don't recognise March as Richie, you wonder why the part isn't played by as high-profile a character maniac as the rest of the Monday group. Lesley Ann Warren is an alluringly brittle nymphomaniac; Brad Dourif is the compleat anal obsessive (his obsession with numbers conveniently doesn't extend to memorising the car number-plate which would have solved the case); and Lance Henriksen is the brooding animal, cringing at every thundercrash. Even such bit-part nutcases as Kathleen Wilhoite whose first-reel suicide sets off Willis traumas, and Shirley Knight, as the abusive shrink's hysterical widow limn their specific neuroses with high style. A sure bet for many Worst of the Year lists, this wholly terrible movie is far more enjoyable and astonishing than many halfway good ones.

VILLAGE VOICE, 8/30/94, p. 48, Amy Taubin

As if you cared, Bruce Willis's penis, once rumored to have put in a lengthy appearance in *Color of Night*, is nowhere in evidence in the version released last Friday. Perhaps it was inadvertently cut by a desperate editor, along with anything that would have given the plot logic or the characters consistency. If I had a penis, I wouldn't want it to make its debut in a film that makes people laugh when they're not supposed to. Willis should thank the powers-that-be at Disney for saving his willy for better things, instead of complaining on the talk shows about how pissed he is that it's been removed. And please, Bruce, don't throw it away on some pretentious director's-cut video.

Actually, I'm an admirer of Willis's talents as exhibited in *Moonlighting, Die Hard*, and the upcoming *Pulp Fiction*. But, as a psychoanalyst-cum-action hero ("I got my Ph.D. at NYU but I'm not a medical doctor") he's missing a certain je ne sais quoi. There's the problem of his smirk, which could drive a patient to suicide and, in fact, does, causing Bruce to go color-blind (he's repressing the sight of the blood), give up his practice, and move to L.A., where he is forced to pinch-hit as a therapy group leader when his college buddy, now a bestselling self-help book author, is murdered by one of his patients.

One day, out driving, Bruce is rear-ended by Jane March and soon they're having hot sex, or as hot as they can manage, given that Jane has to keep rearranging her body parts to hide Bruce's penis from the camera. Jane, who looked 12 years old in *The Lover*, seems about 15 here, which doesn't bother Bruce, although you'd think the psychoanalyst in him might be tempted to make one teeny-weeny comment about the disparity between their ages.

I solved the murder within the first hour and you will too if you remember to keep your eye on the collagen. Richard Rush, who 14 years ago made *The Stunt Man*, directs as if he's never seen a movie but is game to try out some things he once read in an interview with Brian De Palma. I'm telling all my friends to see *Color of Night* because it made me laugh more than I've laughed all summer. Unfortunately, it lacks the zeitgeist element that gives a cult film staying power. It's probably shriveled up and died already.

Also reviewed in:
NEW YORK TIMES, 8/19/94, p. C6, Janet Maslin
NEW YORKER, 9/5/94, p. 107, Terrence Rafferty
VARIETY, 8/22-28/94, p. 55, Todd McCarthy
WASHINGTON POST, 8/19/94, p. G1, Rita Kempley
WASHINGTON POST, 8/19/94, Weekend/p. 42, Desson Howe

COMING OUT UNDER FIRE

A Zeitgeist Films release of a Deep Focus production. *Producer:* Arthur Dong. *Director:* Arthur Dong. *Screenplay:* Allan Bérubé and Arthur Dong. *Based on the book by:* Allan Bérubé. *Director of Photography:* Stephen Lighthill. *Editor:* Veronica Selver. *Music:* Mark Adler. *Sound:* Lauretta Molitor. *Running time:* 71 minutes. *MPAA Rating:* Not Rated.

NARRATOR: Salome Jens.

LOS ANGELES TIMES, 7/19/94, Calendar/p. 6, Kevin Thomas

Arthur Dong's informative consciousness-raising "Coming out Under Fire" documents the experiences of nine gay and lesbian World War II veterans amid a plethora of archival footage and framed within the context of the recent and ongoing debate over gays in the military.

All the men and women state that they had no problems getting along with straights, many of whom assumed their sexual orientation and were not upset by it, but that they lived in constant fear of being denounced and subjected to the Draconian anti-gay regulations established early in the war.

Most left the service with well-earned honorable discharges, but several were not so fortunate, bearing scars from those experiences to this day. Yet if a gay male didn't lie to get into the service, the alternative was to be sent home bearing the stigma of "sexual pervert."

Dong, who based his film on Allan Bérubé's 1990 book of the same name, makes clear that World War II was the first time gays and lesbians were brought together in large numbers; this breaking down of isolation laid the foundation for the eventual gay liberation movement.

Since Dong's film is only 71 minutes long, he might well have interviewed straight World War II veterans as to their attitudes toward gays and lesbians in the ranks and also underlined the fact that ongoing discriminatory policies in the military provide impetus for other kinds of anti-gay legislation.

NEW YORK POST, 7/8/94, p. 42, Michael Medved

No matter how you happen to feel about the hot-button issue of gays in the military, this deeply moving documentary deserves respect and attention.

"Coming Out Under Fire" helps to rescue a lost chapter in American history, focusing on homosexual men and women who served their country in World War II—and 9,000 of whom suffered the life-shattering humiliation of military persecution and dishonorable discharge.

For decent people of any political persuasion, it's impossible not to feel outraged at these stories of gay GI's sentenced to a year's hard labor in brutal "queer stockades," or incarcerated in "Section 8" wards alongside dangerous psychopaths.

One former member of the Army Air Corps recalls in chilling detail his commitment to a psychiatric hospital after a military censor happened to read one of his private letters in which he jokingly addressed a male friend as "darling."

These personal details represent the movie's greatest strength, as its focus shifts among nine eloquent men and women who share their recollections with the camera.

Each of these people emerges as a distinct, sympathetic individual, and their highly-charged memories are brought to life through skillful editing (by Veronica Selver) of 50-year-old still photographs, and archive footage showing GIs in training, or undergoing medical examinations, psychiatric sessions, and even court-martials.

One especially haunting sequence shows a group of marines dressed in drag and performing a campy, high-stepping review for the entertainment of their colleagues.

Director, producer and co-writer Arthur Dong (who previously focused on the harsh treatment of Asian immigrants in the Oscar-nominated "Sewing Women") wisely elected to shoot his interviews in black-and-white to allow smoother transitions between the recollections of the principal characters and the perfectly chosen historical material.

A sensitive and elegiac musical score by Mark Adler further helps to elate this sad material to the level of tragedy.

Unfortunately, the movie conveys the misleading impression that the exceptionally articulate and charismatic men and women featured on screen are representative of all the thousands of gay people who served in the war.

This is obviously not the case, since the population of homosexual servicemen doubtless included the same percentage of losers as the rest of the armed forces—and the rest of humanity.

Moreover, the reminiscences presented here offer few accounts of combat experience; the people in this movie served as clerks, storekeepers, radio technicians, "psychological assistants," and typists, rather than front line battlefield troops.

Filmmaker Dong thereby ignores the familiar argument that the presence of openly gay servicemen might create special tensions in combat situations.

In fact, Dong never explores in any serious way the basis for the Armed Forces' fanatical World War II rules against homosexuals in the ranks. He might have added a richer dimension to his film had he interviewed some straight officers who anguished over the gratuitously cruel treatment of gay people, but still supported the general principle of their exclusion.

The only voice supporting that principle comes at the very end of the film, with embarrassing footage of Virginia Senator John Warner, trying to hector a witness during last year's Congressional hearings on gays in the military.

Using the bumbling, bone-headed Warner as the one real representative of the other side is a cheap shot, and a bow to a propagandistic purpose that's unworthy of all the riveting and significant personal accounts that preceded it.

NEWSDAY, 7/8/94, Part II/p. B7, John Anderson

Dr. Herbert Greenspan was one of the Navy's "90-day wonders" a physician trained in rudimentary psychiatry to process recruits during World War II. "It was very, very difficult for me to ever decide if somebody was a homosexual, regardless of his manner," the doctor said. "I mainly concerned myself with people who were trying to get out of the service, and there were many more people who weren't effeminate ... who were trying to get out."

Of course, Greenspan adds, "we weren't really psychiatrists." And that was OK. Because the people he was concerned with ferreting out weren't really considered Americans.

The disenfranchisement of the nation's homosexual community has seldom been better portrayed than by "Coming Out Under Fire," Arthur Dong's angry and ambitious documentary about gays in the military during World War II in which Greenspan appears.

The gay veterans who testify in Dong's film—most notably perhaps, Marvin Liebman, known today as a founder of the modern conservative movement and a veteran of the Army Air Corps—all thought they were part of a crusade to rid the world of fascism. "I think all young men like to fight, even gay guys," says one witness; "Believe it or not, I was a red-blooded American boy," says another. They and their lesbian counterparts entered the war effort like everyone else, knowing the peril they faced—Bruce Lee, an intelligence clerk, for instance, faced the dilemma of being gay and black. And then they had their worst fears confirmed.

The film, shot in a uniform black and white begins with deceptively bright view of gay military life—the barracks camaraderie, the drag revues, the bitchy newsletter circulated among gay soldiers—then turns decidedly darker. As the war wound down and the likelihood of victory grew, the Army could devote more time to weeding out the "psychos" and "deviants" in their ranks, and given the preoccupation of the military with its members' sex lives, it's a wonder we had time to win the war. But the most painful thing is how homosexuals were dealt with once they were found out. Not as badly as the Nazis might have treated them, of course. But at least as badly as we treated Japanese-Americans, or prisoners of war. And judging by the film's political bookends—Bill Clinton's soon-to-be-abandoned stance on lifting the gay ban, which begins the film, and Republican nitwit John Warner's insulting "give up your gayness" drivel closes it out—the war is still going on.

VILLAGE VOICE, 7/12/94, p. 50, Gary Indiana

Coming Out Under Fire, Arthur Dong's adaptation of Allan Bérubé's book, is a series of interviews with gay World War II veterans, interspersed with archive footage. As one lesbian tells us, World War II was "a much more patriotic war" than any subsequent ones the country has fought; all fit Americans were, at the time, highly motivated to serve. Moreover, for conscripts, the choice between joining up and lying about one's sexual preference or being stigmatized as a sexual deviant was not much of a choice.

Large psychiatric casualties in World War I prompted the military to screen out the mentally ill, which included "grotesque and pathological liars, vagabonds, petty offenders, swindlers, kleptomaniacs, pyromaniacs, alcoholic persons, and homosexual persons." As a gay army psychologist testifies, much of the screening process was pseudopsychology, and thousands of gays were drafted or joined up. Far from harming "morale," many served with distinction. When troop strength reached 10 million in 1943, the services began actively ferreting out and discharging homosexuals, accusing them of sodomy. Since female service personnel were physically incapable of committing sodomy, the criterion was broadened to exclude anyone thought to be homosexual. These purges became more virulent after the war.

The interviewees in this film are in late middle age or elderly. All are extremely likable, humorous, articulate, wry, intelligent, and humane. It comes as a very bad shock to learn that most of these good people were given "blue" discharges ("other than honorable"), therefore stripped of veteran's benefits and pensions, for no better reason than the fact that the country they fought for no longer required their services.

Coming Out Under Fire makes the undeniable point that gay and lesbian soldiers should not have been treated this way, and that the military's policy should have changed. It should still change. Personally, though, I think gay people who wish to serve in the current military, especially after the myriad ghastly deployments of the past 30 years, are infinitely less sympathetic figures than the veterans in this movie. The film does not address what war, and America, have become since Hiroshima, and how thoroughly mindless nationalism has been co-opted for corporate use in the New World Order.

Also reviewed in:
NATION, 7/25-8/1/94, p. 137, Stuart Klawans
NEW YORK TIMES, 7/8/94, p. C8, Stephen Holden
VARIETY, 2/7-13/94, p. 40, Emanuel Levy
WASHINGTON POST, 7/8/94, p. B6, Hal Hinson

CONFORMIST, THE

A Paramount Pictures re-release of a Mars Film/Marianne/Maran production. *Producer:* Maurice Lodi-Fè. *Director:* Bernardo Bertolucci. *Screenplay (Italian with English subtitles):* Bernardo Bertolucci. *Based on the book by:* Alberto Moravia. *Director of Photography:* Vittorio Storaro. *Editor:* Franco Arcalli. *Music:* Georges Delerue. *Production Designer:* Ferdinado Scarfcotti. *Art Director:* Nedon Azzini. *Costumes:* Gitt Magrini. *Running time:* 115 minutes. *MPAA Rating:* R.

CAST: Jean-Louis Trintignant (Marcello Clerici); Stefania Sandrelli (Giulia); Gastone Moschin (Manganiello); Enzo Taroscio (Luca Quadri); Pierre Clémenti (Lino Seminara); Dominique Sanda (Anna Quadri); Christian Alegny (Raoul); José Quaglio (Italo); Milly (Marcello's Mother); Giuseppe Addobbati (Marcello's Father); Yvonne Sanson (Giulia's Mother); Fosco Giachetti (Colonel); Benedetto Benedetti (Minister); Antonio Maestri (Confessor); Alessandro Haber (Drunk Blind Man); Pierangelo Civera (Franz); Pasquale Fortunato (Marcello as a boy).

NEW YORK POST, 7/1/94, p. 42, Thelma Adams

While "Last Tango in Paris" is Bernardo Bertolucci's most famous movie in America, "The Conformist" is his masterpiece.

Anyone confused, disappointed or annoyed by "Little Buddha," can see the movie that established the Italian director's reputation, starting today at the Film Forum, in a new 35mm print.

What makes this screening an event, rather than a revival, is the restoration of the five-minute "Dance of the Blind" sequence. Bertolucci cut this vibrant scene in response to a 1970 request by Paramount Pictures to shorten the movie for American audiences.

A rich period drama freely adapted from Alberto Moravia's novel, "The Conformist" develops a parallel between the rise-and-fall of fascism in Italy in the 30s and a young intellectual's search for identity.

Brilliantly underplayed by Jean-Louis Trintignant, Marcello, a latent homosexual, strives, in his own words, "to gain the impression of normality." Without love, he marries Giulia (Stefania Sandrelli), a middle-class woman who is "all bed and kitchen."

A coward rather than an idealist, he joins the fascist political police. He combines his Parisian honeymoon with his first assignment: to keep tabs on his former philosophy professor, the exiled Quadri (Enzo Tarascio), and his beautiful young wife, Anna (Dominique Sanda).

The movie seamlessly unfolds as a series of memories that occur to Marcello, framed by a single day of reckoning: Marcello pursues Quadri and his wife into the snowy French countryside in order to assassinate him, but is too cowardly to carry out the assignment.

The director's fluid handling of narrative time is a masterly achievement of poetry and architecture. The dialogue, written by Bertolucci, is sharp and taut, and the visual imagery astounds.

Assisted by Oscar-winning cinematographer Vittorio Storaro, Bertolucci goes for broke in every shot. But his virtuosity is always in the service of his metaphors, which often function as a counterpoint for his characters' confessions.

One of the most striking scenes is set in a Parisian dance hall. Anna leads a tipsy Giulia onto the floor where they perform a steamy tango (not Bertolucci's last tango in Paris, but perhaps his best).

The ecstatic newlywed Giulia then leads the gaily dressed dancers in an extended line dance. Shot from on high, the revelers spiral around Marcello, who stands alone in the middle, a small gray-suited figure, arms folded defensively across his chest.

For all Marcello's protests about wanting to conform, he can't join in. He can't abandon his thoughts and embrace the joyous body.

Literally the man-in-the-middle, squeezed tighter within this mass of humanity, the conformist is separated by his knowledge that he has already betrayed his wife and the Quadris and is no closer to discovering himself.

Dances are among Bertolucci's cinematic signatures and this visual set-piece is essential to the drama.

The restored "Dance of the Blind" scene—set at a colorful party hosted by Marcello's blind fascist friend—sheds light on the theme of blindness and sight. Marcello, who adopts blinders in order to conform, is the only sighted man in the room. It is the one moment in the film where he can see.

If Bertolucci had to trim something, he was wise to chose this scene which, though vivid, is not crucial to the narrative. But if its inclusion in the restored version lures moviegoers into the theater to see "The Conformist," it will have served an excellent purpose.

SIGHT AND SOUND, 4/94, p. 53, Chris Wagstaff

1938. Marcello Clerici is driven by an Italian political police agent, Manganiello, to supervise the assassination of his former philosophy professor, Luca Quadri, who directs anti-fascist missions from Paris. The journey is punctuated by flashbacks ... Marcello is in a radio studio, discussing his impending marriage to Giulia with Italo, his blind, gay friend who broadcasts fascist sermons. Marcello offers to spy on Quadri for the political police while on his honeymoon in Paris. He visits Giulia to discuss the wedding, and then his mother, who takes drugs procured for her by her Japanese chauffeur, who is also her lover. On the way to his mother's house he is accosted by Manganiello, who informs him that they must contact another agent in Ventimiglia for further orders. Marcello has Manganiello beat up the chauffeur and order him to leave. He goes with his mother to see his father, who is in a lunatic asylum. When Marcello asks his father about his fascist past, the old man demands to be put in a straitjacket. Before the wedding, Marcello goes to confession, and remembers his boyhood seduction by a chauffeur, Lino, after which the latter was shot by Marcello, who believes he killed him. Next, Marcello is at a pre-nuptial party thrown for him by Italo and his blind friends. The two discuss the way fascism offers people an antidote to the anxiety of feeling 'different'.

On the way to Paris by train, Giulia recounts to Marcello her seduction at the age of 16 by an elderly family lawyer, and he makes love to her. In Ventimiglia, Marcello is told that Quadri is to be killed. In Paris, he visits Quadri and his wife Anna. He falls for the latter, but she is contemptuous of him. Marcello goes to see Anna at the ballet school where she teaches and learns that she knows he is in Paris to kill her husband. He returns to his hotel room to find Anna seducing Giulia. The Clericis and the Quadris go dancing at Joinville, followed by Manganiello. Anna and Quadri plan to spend the weekend in Savoy, and when Anna decides to stay behind in Paris with the Clericis, Marcello tells Manganiello Quadri's route, so that the assassination can take place during the journey without harming Anna. The next morning, Marcello receives a telephone call from Manganiello to say that Anna has left with her husband after all. He follows them with Manganiello, hoping to save Anna, They catch up with the Quadris' car, whereupon the assassins, emerging from the trees, stab Quadri and chase Anna, shooting her.

September 1943. Mussolini is deposed, and Marcello goes into the streets of Rome with Italo, where he encounters Lino picking up a male prostitute. Marcello denounces Lino as the murderer of Quadri and his wife in 1938. A crowd of anti-fascist revellers sweeps Italo away, and Marcello is left looking at the male prostitute.

Few people can resist consider *Il conformista,* Bertolucci's masterpiece. He has constructed from Alberto Moravia's novel an Oedipal story of enormous complexity, both thematically and stylistically, reordering a chronological narrative into a dream, in which Marcello's psyche is gradually penetrated as though in a psychotherapy session during the cocooned car journey to Savoy. Marcello is driven by anxiety about his sexuality, by his sense of having been betrayed by his 'fathers' and by a fruitless search for a position of 'normality' in the social order. Quadri is an idealist living a hedonistic life in Paris while the struggle against fascism in Italy is the material one of the class struggle. A young man in 1970, Bertolucci questioned the credentials of middle-class anti-fascism, and killed his own father figures. The address and phone number at Quadri's apartment were in fact those of Jean-Luc Godard, and Quadri's account of Plato's myth of the cave can be understood as an expression of Godardian cinematic asceticism, in which images must be unmasked as purely images. Bertolucci opened on a sign advertising Renoir's *La vie est à nous* to manifest the need to make films that were accessible to a wide cinema-going public. To hide behind an austere idealism was to fail to engage with the real cinema audience. In the figure of Quadri, generational, political and cinematic issues are fused.

How well has *Il conformista* achieved its task of communication? The sheer mastery of the telling, the beauty of the images and of the camerawork, the control of the soundtrack, and the intensity with which the characters convey powerful psychic energies have all mesmerised audiences. Though much admired it remains slightly obscure. The title offers an interpretation: conformism. Marcello is an example of conformity, and the destruction it wreaks; fascism is conformism. The extent to which the film develops much more subtle themes than that can be overlooked. At the Berlin film festival in 1970, Bertolucci was persuaded to remove a four-minute episode, that of the pre-nuptial party, and the film has hitherto been distributed without this sequence. In this scene, Italo, blind and gay, says that he and Marcello share a sense of being 'different' from others. Normality is to enjoy the sight of a woman's behind. People need to feel part of a group. Marcello butts in: "Like a true fascist". This scene has now been restored. It may confirm viewers in the 'conformist' interpretation. But Marcello says "Like a true fascist" with an expression of disdain, and then removes himself from Italo's reach; the scene is shot with a basement window in the background, through which we see the legs of female prostitutes soliciting outside. Every time Marcello is confronted with reality, it turns out to be other than the 'normality' he seeks: the minister is a philanderer, Giulia the mistress of an old man, his mother a junkie, Anna a lesbian, the secret police a collection of neurotic bunglers, anti-fascism a bourgeois confidence trick ... The way in which the film depicts fascist ideology as just a prolongation of bourgeois idealist fantasising is only comprehensible when you conceive of a materialist, Marxist alternative to that middle-class ideology. Communists in 1970 could call upon a whole culture, for example that mixture of Freud and Marx that we find in Marcuse and the Frankfurt school, that would offer a devastating critique of Quadri's complicity in an ideology he shared in part with fascism. So is it the repressed, conformist Marcello wiping out the relaxed, freedom-loving Quadri? Is this how today's post-communist audiences will view the film? Will the restoration of the pre-nuptial party scene clarify matters, or will it reassure viewers in a banal interpretation of a film whose ambiguity previously forced them to work for a less simple interpretation?

Thematically, the scene offers plenty: blind people dancing and arguing about politics. The whole film plays on seeing what is not there, not seeing what is there, looking for what you want to see, having to see what you don't want to look at, looking at your own desire, trying not to see your own desire, screens, windows and objects that obstruct one's vision ... And the dialogue between Marcello and Italo with the prostitutes behind them is visually powerful and full of suggestion. But the dialogue itself clumsily brings out into rational discourse, and therefore reduces, what is elsewhere expressed by movement, sound, gesture and suggestion. Part of the scene is cluttered in a way that no other scene is; and it appears in the film without the subtle threads of transition—words, puns, sounds, images—which so effectively weld together the mosaic-like fragments of which the rest is constructed. Perhaps they were not so misguided at the 1970 Berlin film festival.

Also reviewed in:
CHICAGO TRIBUNE, 11/18/94, Friday/p. M, Michael Wilmington
NEW YORK TIMES, 9/19/70, p. 32, Vincent Canby
WASHINGTON POST, 11/25/94, p. B7, Hal Hinson
WASHINGTON POST, 11/25/94, Weekend/p. 60, Desson Howe
VARIETY, 7/8/70, p. 18

CONJUGAL BED, THE

A Leisure Time Features release of an Alpha Films International production. *Producer:* Oltea Munteanu. *Director:* Mircea Daneliuc. *Screenplay (Romanian with English subtitles):* Mircea Daneliuc. *Director of Photography:* Vivi Dragan Vasile. *Editor:* Melania Oproiu. *Sound:* Anusavan Salamanian. *Production Designer:* Mircea Ribinschi. *Running time:* 102 minutes. *MPAA Rating:* Not Rated

WITH: Gheorghe Dinica (Vasile); Coca Bloos (Carolina); Valentin Teodosiu (Misu); Lia Bugnar (Stela); Geo Costiniu (Eugen); Valentin Uritescu (The Actor); and Jana Gorea; Flavius Constantinescu; Nicolae Praida; Paul Chiributa; Cristian Motriue.

LOS ANGELES TIMES, 3/27/95, Calendar/p. 13, Kevin Thomas

Mircea Daneliuc's exceedingly dark comedy "The Conjugal Bed" (1993) suggests that life in Romania continues to be plenty tough, with paranoia, poverty and corruption rampant. Gheorghe Dinica stars as a virile, middle-aged manager of a derelict theater showing American movies whose life starts unraveling when his worn-looking wife becomes pregnant with a third child they cannot afford—but they can't afford an abortion either.

NEW YORK POST, 7/15/94, p. 40, Larry Worth

A shot of clapping hands opens and closes "The Conjugal Bed." And it's likely to be the only applause this production garners.

Director Mircea Daneliuc tries to mine black comedy out of Romania's state of turmoil after the bloody deposition of Nicolae Ceausescu. But what he gets is a chaotic fiasco.

Not that his world-gone-mad idea didn't have potential. The concept of attempting to survive a post-totalitarian atmosphere of duplicity and growing paranoia could have been whipped into a dark stew, a la Martin Scorsese's "After Hours."

Actually, Daneliuc's screenplay about a middle-aged man's disasters on the work front, and with family and mistress, begins auspiciously. Set in a gray universe of squalid apartments and barren offices, the guy's job of running a movie theater gets iffy after a body is found in the building.

Worse, his unhappy wife is trying to either miscarry or sell their unborn third child while his lover reaches sexual fulfillment only by staring at a Schwarzenegger poster. So far, so good.

Then Daneliuc takes a decided wrong turn. He force-feeds Ionescu-style absurdity into the proceedings, to the point that the premise drowns in a sea of symbolism. Further, the graphically violent ending hardly qualifies as bloody good fun.

And that's not even mentioning an extended epilogue. It's as if Daneliuc thought he could redeem the effort—or at least find a point to the ugliness—by throwing in a heavy-handed coda. Melodramatic music functions as yet another straw.

If the film has any redeeming feature, it's the acting. Gheorghe Dinica gives the anti-hero a shot of much-needed credibility while Coca Bloos nicely conveys pathetic entrapment as his wife. Though Lia Bugnar's mistress doesn't fare as well, that reflects more on the script than her abilities.

But despite its umpteen attempts to shock, the biggest stunner is the movie's submission as Romania's entry for 1993's foreign language film Oscar. Apparently, the country's problems aren't restricted to the likes of Ceausescu.

NEWSDAY, 7/15/94, Part II/p. B10, John Anderson

Black comedy doesn't come any blacker than "The Conjugal Bed," a bitterly sardonic romp through post-Ceausescu Romania where sex is money, money is sex, money is money and totalitarianism is a fond memory.

Seen through the slapstick, slaphappily twisted experiences of Vasile (Gheorghe Dinica), his pregnant/desperate wife Carolina (Coca Bloos) and his whore-to-be girlfriend Stela (Lia Bugnar), Romania's unqualified embrace of materialism is portrayed by writer/director Mircea Daneliuc as an insidious disease. Dollars are everything, and the country has nothing. Unable to support the children he has, Vasile tries to induce an abortion in Carolina—making her take hot baths, lift furniture or jump off a table. Carolina, on the other hand decides she wants to have the child and sell it, after Vasile, who thinks he's being set up, finds a huge wad of money in his desk.

The same desk plays host to the film's most pointed and hilarious merger of east-west decadence (Daneliuc is equally disgusted by crypto-monarchists who would bring back a dictator), when Vasile and Stela use it to have almost-fully-clothed sex. The phone rings, and while Vasile sucks up to some superior on the other end of the line, Stela achieves orgasm by staring at the Arnold Schwarzenegger and Jean-Claude Van Damme posters on the wall.

In keeping with a Romania with no moral order, Daneliuc plays fast and loose with convention, allowing Vasile to break through the fourth wall to comment on his life's absurdities. There are plenty. He loves Stela, whose husband pimps for her. His young son wants to emigrate. The government is making threatening noises. Someone hangs himself in the theater he manages. He tries to make love with Stela everywhere and is always frustrated. He tries to kill himself, suffers a breakdown, is institutionalized, and gets out to find that Carolina has rented out their home for a porno film. He tries to kill her, comes close, and asks her where his clean shirts are.

The film ends the way it began: with a 14-year-old named Decebalus making love to an old prostitute named Stela, in Romania circa 2006. That things tend to run in cycles, it seems, is what worries Daneliuc the most.

VILLAGE VOICE, 7/19/94, p. 47, J. Hoberman

True Lies isn't the lone Schwarzeneggerfest opening this week. The star, or rather his two-dimensional image, turns up throughout *The Conjugal Bed.* Rich, powerful, imaginary, Arnold presides over this brutal Romanian farce as the successful strong man, something like Hollywood's answer to Nicolae Ceauşescu.

Coming attractions for an ancient Arnold vehicle are projected, along with Kodak ads and newsreels of Ceauşescu's unsuccessful escape, in the drab movie house managed by Vasile, *The*

Conjugal Bed's middle-aged protagonist. Der Arnold's pinup also dominates the shabby office where Vasile has his daily tryst, all but fully clothed, on the desk with Stela, the theater's lissome ticket taker. (When Vasile is distracted, mid-fuck, by a phone call, Stela excites herself to orgasm just by craning her neck to gaze upon the implacable Schwarzenegger scowl.) The same pinup graces the cramped bedroom of Vasile's young son—in Romania, Arnold is an equal opportunity icon.

Costing somewhat less than *True Lies* purported $120 million and directed by 51-year-old Mircea Daneliuc, who heads one of Romania's five film studios, *The Conjugal Bed* is a cruel, purposefully ugly sitcom. (A recurring image is the close-up of cigarette butts flushed down the movie-theater toilet.) The action is situated in a landscape that seems half built and long abandoned; the atmosphere is thick with the vapors of half-understood conspiracies and half-baked schemes. *The Conjugal Bed*, however, pushes into new territory. It trafficks in all manner of previously taboo matters of sex, splatter, and social disgust.

Jacob, the only other Daneliuc opus to play here (it was included in the 1988 New York Film Festival), was a brooding thundercloud of a movie in which a sturdy Romanian miner was driven mad by life in a remote village. *The Conjugal Bed* provides another sort of prole apocalypse. There's no need for expressionist foreboding—the crack-up is already here. The volatile Vasile (Gheorghe Dinica), whose noble profile belies a haplessly primitive nature, divides his time between chasing Stela (Lia Bugnar), who graduates from ticket taker to tour guide cum currency whore, and raising capital to fund an abortion for his wife Carolina (Coca Bloos).

To fully appreciate this latter complication, one has to know that Ceauşescu's Romania was, perhaps, the most "prolife" regime on the planet: Not only were all forms of contraception unavailable, women had to submit to monthly examinations and, under penalty of law, carry all pregnancies to term. (The corollary to this, of course, was a fantastically high rate of infant mortality.) Because Vasile and Carolina have hardly amassed sufficient dollars to pay for the necessary operation—"It's my child and I want a sterile abortion!" the husband cries—Vasile runs through a grotesque repertoire of folk methods. He attempts to induce miscarriage by making the already haggard Carolina lift heavy furniture, by immersing her in scalding water, by persuading her to jump off a table. When these fail, the couple considers other tacks: Vasile figures that if the child is born in Belgium they can all emigrate; Carolina decides that it's best to have the baby and sell it.

Everything is reckoned in dollars, and money in this movie is represented by wads of the filthiest, most worn-looking bills imaginable. No scam is too low. Vasile keeps trying to peddle an old copy of Ceauşescu's *The Future of Romania* as a collector's item. Once he's arrested, having wandered into someone else's scheme, and committed to a mental hospital (where the inmates, not surprisingly, are obsessed with Ceauşescu), Carolina more profitably rents out their house as the studio for a political porn flick starring Stela and produced, naturally, for export to France.

Like the film within the film, *The Conjugal Bed* is concerned more with mise-en-scène than narrative flow. Vasile periodically steps out of character to comment on the action and prepare us for the awful crime that the movie dictates he commit: "What a scenario!" (The film itself starts to jump in the gate and dissolve after he's arrested.) Romania too is a series of breakdowns and deceptions. Schoolchildren are on strike—so are the unemployed, although they abandon their picket line and elbow each other aside in a mad race for a grocery store when someone thinks they've spotted a bargain. Former secret policemen change dollars on the street; miners disguise themselves as cops. The wreckage of Ceauşescu's helicopter has become a sacred shrine. Elderly women light candles, others just sit before it and stare. (Throughout the movie, helicopters hover like divine emissaries.) The new Party of the Original Democracy—that is, the Communists—are renting Vasile's theater for their mass meetings. Their symbol is an abstract helicopter blade.

Vasile is ultimately driven to solve the problem of Carolina's pregnancy in the most horrific manner possible and once again, fails. In its ghoulish way, *The Conjugal Bed* celebrates the life force. That unwanted baby is going to be born. Amazingly enough, Romania's has been the most artistically productive of post-Communist film industries and, as outrageously raunchy and absurd as it is, *The Conjugal Bed* offers a model for a new East European cinema. You might even think it optimistic: As terminal as the situation appears, a suitably tacky sci-fi epilogue is willing to envision "Romania 2006."

Also reviewed in:
NEW YORK TIMES, 7/15/94, p. C18, Stephen Holden
VARIETY, 3/8/93, p. 63, David Stratton
WASHINGTON POST, 1/6/95, p. C7, Hal Hinson

CONVICTION, THE

An International Film Circuit release. *Producer:* Pietro Valsecchi. *Director:* Marco Bellocchio. *Screenplay (Italian with English subtitles):* Massimo Fagioli and Marco Bellocchio. *Director of Photography:* Giuseppe Lanci. *Editor:* Mirco Garrone. *Music:* Carlo Crivelli. *Production Designer:* Giantito Burchiellaro. *Running time:* 92 minutes. *MPAA Rating:* Not Rated.

CAST: Vittorio Mezzogiorno (Lorenzo Colajanni); Claire Nebout (Sandra Celestini); Andrzej Seweryn (Giovanni Malatesta); Grazyna Szapolowska (Monica).

NEW YORK POST, 5/13/94, p. 38, Larry Worth

Marco Bellocchio's talent may be debatable. But you can't fault his timing.

Ever a master of controversy (his last film, "Devil in the Flesh," raised hackles for its graphic depiction of fellatio), Bellocchio is now tackling sexual harassment and the definition of rape.

No, Bill Clinton and Paula Jones aren't players. Neither are William Kennedy Smith and Patricia Bowman. Rather, "The Conviction" concerns a man and woman locked in a museum overnight. After three couplings, the two part—and the tale abruptly switches to a courtroom.

The protagonist is now wearing shackles, and charged with raping the young woman. The focus then shifts to the prosecuting attorney, who's having problems with his wife. She's siding with the accused, and on the verge of leaving her husband.

Unfortunately, Bellocchio and Massimo Fagioli's screenplay uses the quartet's emotional quagmire as a segue to yet more developments. Therein lies the problem.

Any of the subjects Bellocchio addresses could fill a movie, and then some. But he's barely presented one conundrum before it's compounded with another.

Long before the end credits, viewers are left reeling with sensory overload, having weathered equal doses of fascination and frustration.

With the likes of Anita Hill and Clarence Thomas still fanning the flames, the material succeeds as a launching pad for debate on what constitutes rape, the boundary between seduction and emotional manipulation, and culpability for the battle of the sexes. Such ideas depicted four decades ago in Akira Kurosawa's "Rashomon," certainly merit exploration in the '90s.

But there's no excuse for the torrent of speeches and imagery which comprise the last half-hour. It's as if Bellocchio couldn't decide on an ending, so he kept adding codas, losing credibility—and audience interest—in the process.

The principal combatants, Vittorio Mezzogiorno and Claire Nebout, do their best to bring dimension to their enigmatic characters, as do Andrzej Seweryn's lawyer and Grazyna Szapolowska's confused spouse.

But they can't overcome the film's chief flaw: excess. Ultimately, "The Conviction" makes a striking case for the adage that less is more.

NEWSDAY, 5/13/94, Part II/p. B7, John Anderson

Strictly as film, "The Conviction," which relies os heavily on the subtleties of language that it might have been a radio play, should probably be judged a failure. As an *agent provocateur* in the war between the sexes, however, it's wildly successful.

Where does seduction end and rape begin? Do women, deep down prefer force over foreplay? Or are men just glandular idiots? Good questions, as any devotee of Sigmund or Sally Jessy could tell you. By opening his film with Canova's sculpture of Apollo and Daphne—who, according to myth, was changed into a laurel tree to escape Apollo's advances—director Marco Bellocchio is defining the argument as timeless. What's not quite so clear is Bellocchio's position. Certainly, becoming botanical is a rather definite way of saying no. But the "rape" as depicted in Bellocchio's film is far from a vicious assault.

So what is it? When "The Conviction" won the Silver Bear at the 1991 Berlin Film Festival, there was an outcry from those who said the film portrayed women as wanting to be raped. That's not quite it. "The Conviction" separates the concept of power—which is what rape is always about—from the idea of force— which it's not about, necessarily.

When Sandra (Claire Nebout) gets lost in a museum one night she finds herself locked in with an architect named Lorenzo (Vittorio Mezzogiorno). Their sexual dance is prolonged and somewhat silly—like Brando in "Last Tango," Lorenzo never drops his drawers—but Sandra is complicit in what happens, enjoys it, and her orgasm seems induced as much by what Lorenzo says as what he does.

When Sandra subsequently charges him with rape, she isn't motivated by the act but by the circumstance: Lorenzo had the keys to the museum all the time, and Sandra, having been deprived of her free will, feels violated. Lorenzo, brought into court, offers Sandra's orgasm as proof no rape occurred. "I forced her," he says. "I didn't rape her." To Sandra it's the other way around. "He had a force of character which drives a woman to sexuality even if she doesn't want it," she says; the fact that Lorenzo controlled her mobility constituted rape.

Add to the crazy puzzle the fact that the prosecutor Giovanni (Andrzej Seweryn), is having his own sexual problems. He finds Lorenzo so compelling—as does his wife, Monica (Grazyna Szapolowska)—that he seeks Lorenzo's advice in prison.

Yes, Bellocchio goes a bit haywire, but he insults each sex equally, at least until the final sequence: A group of farmhands pursue a lone woman in a field, every indication saying she's going to be gang raped. But when Giovanni "saves" her, she laughs in his face.

"What was it?!" he cries, stupified by crossed sexual signals. "The Conviction" may be fascinating, but audiences will be asking the same question.

VILLAGE VOICE, 5/17/94, p. 55, Georgia Brown

Lord knows, the all-she-needs-is-a-good-fuck theory of relationship, like the great man theory of female progress, has been around since neolithic times. Most decent romantic movies still manage to make a good case for it. It's hard to imagine. however a more pretentious version than Marco Bellocchio's sub-Lawrentian *The Conviction*. (In the current *Film Comment*, Harlan Kennedy recommends a second viewing to soak up nuances, but frankly I'd rather have root canal.)

The first part is the most entertaining. This is where the pert Sandra (Claire Nebout) stalks the Castello Farnese museum like the shade of Monica Vitti: She pauses first before a sculpture of Daphne and Apollo, then takes in a Leonardo *Madonna e bambino* in the castle's "echo room," following the guide's suggestion, she goes into a corner, giggles, but can't think of a thing to whisper. (She's inhibited, you see.) Come closing time, she suddenly misses her keys, runs back to find them, and gets locked in.

As Bellocchio films her—vaguely possessed—Sandra half wants to get locked in. So it's more assignation than accident when she's joined in the night by the cocksure Lorenzo (Vittorio Mezzogiorno), an architect who lectures her on art, beauty, and genius before making a move. She runs, he follows; he sticks her standing up and then from behind. Suddenly, he abandons her mid-act. Why? she asks, hurt. "See that statue?" he asks. "It's cold, like you." Rising to his dare, Sandra strips to Naked-Maja mode and lets herself go.

Next thing we know Lorenzo is being tried for rape. He'd predicted Sandra would turn on him—the way a child betrays the one who gave birth to it, he says. His duty as genius is to take the consequences. "I obliged her," he tells the court, citing her orgasm as proof.

Testifying, Sandra admits the violence wasn't physical: "He has a force of character that drives a woman to make love. He knew I couldn't choose lucidly." Call it smugness as tool.

Abruptly, focus now shifts from Lorenzo and Sandra to the wimpy prosecutor, Giovanni (Andrzej Seweryn), who can't give his cranky wife Monica (Grazyna Szapolowska) an orgasm. Scorning her husband, Monica joins Lorenzo's adoring groupies. Poor Giovanni doesn't get it and through the movie's tedious second half, this sap gets mocked by the whole fecund world. Bellocchio wrote this daft tract with a psychiatrist, Massimo Fagioli, who, according to production notes, was "expelled from the Italian Psychoanalytic Society because of his controversial theories." Oh, so it's the work of two cranks, not one.

Also reviewed in:
NEW YORK TIMES, 5/13/94, p. C10, Caryn James

COPS AND ROBBERSONS

A TriStar Pictures release of a Channel production. *Producer:* Ned Tanen, Nancy Graham Tanen, and Ronal L. Schwary. *Director:* Michael Ritchie. *Screenplay:* Bernie Somers. *Director of Photography:* Gerry Fisher. *Editor:* Stephen A. Rotter and William S. Scharf. *Music:* William Ross. *Music Editor:* Jim Harrison. *Sound:* Kim H. Ornitz. *Sound Editor:* Don Hall. *Casting:* Rick Pagano, Sharon Bialy, and Debi Manwiller. *Production Designer:* Stephen J. Lineweaver. *Art Director:* Philip Toolin. *Set Decorator:* Gary P. Fettis. *Special Effects:* Clifford P. Wenger. *Costumes:* Wayne Finkelman. *Costumes (Chevy Chase):* Steve Ellsworth. *Make-up:* John M. Elliott, Jr. *Stunt Coordinator:* Chuck Waters. *Running time:* 95 minutes. *MPAA Rating:* PG.

CAST: Chevy Chase (Norman Robberson); Jack Palance (Jake Stone); Dianne Wiest (Helen Robberson); Robert Davi (Osborn); David Barry Gray (Tony Moore); Jason James Richter (Kevin Robberson); Fay Masterson (Cindy Robberson); Miko Hughes (Billy Robberson); Richard Romanus (Fred Lutz); Sal Landi (Jerry Callahan); Ronald L. Schwary (Producer); Jack Kehler (Caniff); Amy Powell (Marva Prescott); Dawn Landon (Video Clerk); Jim Holmes (Phil); Charlie O'Donnell (Newscaster); Patrick Patchen (Policeman); Nelly Bly (Girl in Police Station); Gus Savales (Cook); Preston Hanson (T-Men Announcer).

LOS ANGELES TIMES, 4/15/94, Calendar/p. 8, Kevin Thomas

On the surface "Cops and Robbersons" is the broad-appeal family comedy it presents itself to be, but its subtext is gratifyingly another matter. Its setting is a tract of unrelenting snug blandness, and a husband and father, Norman Robberson (Chevy Chase), who owns one of the homes, works at an office of equal uniformity. No one seems very happy or connected in the Robberson household, but its dominant figure, Norman's wife, Helen (Dianne Wiest), declares with finality that "Everything is fine!"

Seemingly, things are soon to get spectacularly better when Jack Palance's crusty veteran cop Jake Stone uses the Robberson house to stake out their new next-door neighbor (Robert Davi), an especially lethal double-crosser dealing in counterfeit money. Palance's rookie partner Tony (David Barry Gray) finds the attraction between him and the Robbersons' high school student daughter (Fay Masterson) mutual, and the two young Robberson sons (Jason James Richter, Miko Hughes) are as in awe of Jake as their parents are.

It so happens that Norman has always wanted to be a cop, at least in his fantasies, and is such a TV cop show fanatic that when he returns a "Police Woman" tape to a video store he feels compelled to point out that 11 seconds are missing.

Naturally, Norman feels that his opportunity to be a hero has arrived at last, but he's such a naive klutz that he very nearly destroys Jake's operation at the start. (Never mind that he actually uncovered some pertinent information.) In essence, what writer Bernie Somers, in an exceptional first-produced screenplay, reveals is that the arrival of Jake not only underlines Norman's lack of respect within his own family, but also worsens it. With his satirical eye for the absurdities of American middle-class life and his special awareness of competition, so much a part of the American character, director Michael Ritchie is just the man to bring out the darkest side of Somers' script with much compassionate humor.

Best of all, Ritchie has erased from Chase that easy superciliousness that can drive you crazy if you're not one of Chase's die-hard fans. Chase consistently underplays, and gains immeasurably from doing so. His Norman longs for recognition but never grovels for it, although he may pursue it recklessly. He is a nice, decent guy who deserves better from his family, who loves him but doesn't pay much attention to him, especially his children. He's an office worker who has consciously or otherwise deferred running the family and home to his wife. Well-meaning, she has taken on the role with missionary, perfectionist zeal. Helen can be a nit-picker, but Wiest shows us that she's really a good woman who's fundamentally devoted to her husband as well as her children.

So often cast as the villain throughout his long career, Palance has emerged in recent years as a hilarious comedian, starting with "Bagdad Cafe" and his Oscar-winning turn in "City Slickers." Jake may have a heart of gold lurking behind his tough-guy stance, but Palance plays his predicament in holding the Robberson family at bay while doing his job of surveillance with a comic gruffness that forestalls undue sentimentality. Jake is a showy, funny role and Palance really runs with it. So does Davi with his bad guy, who can be amusingly, disarmingly likable. The film's young actors provide winning support for the film's top-lined veterans.

Cameraman Gerry Fisher has brought to "Cops and Robbersons" a deceptively bright, shiny look that's just right to set off the film's darker undercurrents. The great thing is that the film doesn't cop out at the finish: It's Helen, after all, who keeps her cool in a crisis, and when finally Norman wins his family's attention and concern, it's a display of compassion and congratulations for heroics attempted rather than accomplished. There's a tinge of sadness amid the laughter in this surprisingly subversive family comedy.

NEW YORK POST, 4/15/94, p. 38, Michael Medved

Following his ill-fated foray into the world of late night television talk shows, Chevy Chase here returns to doing what he does best: playing a bumbling but good-hearted suburban dad who combines persistent delusions of wisdom and competence with hopeless ineptitude.

Fans of the three "National Lampoon's Vacation" movies will instantly recognize the character, who here appears without the cynical edge of those films and adds an intriguing new twist: an all-consuming obsession with TV cop shows.

Norman Robberson (Chase) gets to indulge his Walter Mitty fantasies when a murderous counterfeiter (the formidable Robert Davi) moves into the house next door in their peaceful tract neighborhood of "Pleasant Valley."

The police downtown want to place the bad guy under surveillance, and so send two undercover cops to live temporarily with the Robbersons.

One of them is a baby-faced rookie (David Barry Gray) who develops instant rapport with the Robbersons' pretty teen-aged daughter (Fay Masterson). The other is a grizzled veteran (Jack Palance) who becomes a hero to the two boys in the family (Jason James Richter of "Free Willy" and the adorable Miko Hughes of "Jack the Bear") as well as their father.

Palance seems to be having great fun with his role, performing essentially the same function he did with his Oscar-winning part in "City Slickers": He's a representative of a bygone era of primitive, heroic manliness who helps a nervous, middle-class guy discover new inner resources of machismo.

He even dares to defy the domineering super-mom of the household (the very sympathetic Dianne Wiest), who tries to stop him from indulging two of his favorite pastimes: smoking and swearing.

Early in his career, director Michael Ritchie made a number of challenging, individualistic films like "Smile," "The Candidate" and "Downhill Racer." More recently, he's settled into churning out competent but undistinguished action-comedies like "Diggstown" and the two "Fletch" films with Chevy Chase.

"Cops and Robbersons" definitely falls into the latter tradition. It's never inspired, but it is consistently amusing. Chase helps his own cause with a number of diverting slapstick bits—struggling with unwanted cream cheese on a bagel, or borrowing Palance's gun to make faces in the mirror.

Some parents might complain that a movie aimed at kids contains so much gunplay and violence, but the mayhem in "Robbersons" is no more intense than what most children watch on TV.

NEWSDAY, 4/15/94, Part II/p. B7, John Anderson

Given how insipid and artificial the new Chevy Chase comedy "Cops and Robberson" is, we assumed that the name Robberson was made up, too. But no. According to this newspaper's crack researchers, it is a real name, found occasionally in New England, but much more often in such states as Texas, Missouri and Arkansas.

Isn't, this fascinating? Believe me, it's more interesting than the movie. Although we're not sure of its ethnic origin or etymology, the name Robberson—a derivation of Robertson, or Robinson, perhaps?—enjoys its greatest popularity in the Mid- and Southwest. Maybe the following jokes will, too:

"You can't arrest people for rudeness," pungent detective Jake Stone (Jack Palance) tells moronic homeowner Norman Robberson (Chevy Chase).If you could, half of New York City would be on death row."

Or:

"Now I gotta whack a nice white middle-class suburban family," one gangster tells another, while holding the Robbersons hostage. "People are gonna notice this."

The implications are rude and frightening. But so is the movie, in which Norman, a Walter Mitty-esque accountant, plays host to Jake, the world's crustiest cop, as he stakes out the killer next door (Robert Davi). For Palance it's another chance to parody his own image; for Chase, another opportunity to act the buffoon.

For Norman, though, it should be a dream come true: obsessed with "Barnaby Jones" and every other hyperbolic TV police drama currently in reruns, he has the opportunity to watch two real detectives—Jake and his rookie partner, Tony (David Barry Gray)—without leaving the Barcalounger. But Norman soon injects himself, with very predictable results, into the investigation. And Jake quickly displaces Norman in the embrace of the Robberson family, indicating just how desperate they are for a father figure. Jake, after all, is the moral/esthetic equivalent of an overloaded ashtray.

On structural grounds, the film doesn't work. Norman's TV obsession, which is the film's Big Joke, is never pursued. There's certainly not enough made of his wife, Helen (played by the wonderful Dianne Wiest), her obsessively efficient homemaking or her violent reaction to the suggestion that something may be askew in the collective Robberson consciousness; their youngest child, (Miko Hughes) for instance, dresses like Eddie Munster and sleeps in a toy chest. And Jake's misanthropy—which, of course, is remedied by the affection of the family—is never given a cause either. All aspects of character are, à la sitcom, presented fully formed and rootless.

Which would be all right if any of the jokes contained an iota of wit or originality. But "Cops and Robbersons" is standard-issue Chase, with the once-sardonic comedian playing yet another dim bulb lost in a megawatt world. Look for it next week, on this weekend's list of top-grossing films.

Also reviewed in:
CHICAGO TRIBUNE, 4/15/94, Friday/p. M, John Petrakis
NEW YORK TIMES, 4/15/94, p. C23, Janet Maslin
VARIETY, 4/18-24/94, p. 63, Leonard Klady
WASHINGTON POST, 4/15/94, p. D6, Richard Harrington

CORIOLIS EFFECT, THE

A Seventh Art Releasing release. *Producer:* Kathryn Arnold. *Director:* Louis Venosta. *Screenplay:* Louis Venosta. *Director of Photography:* Paul Holohan. *Editor:* Luis Colina. *Music:* Hal Lindes. *Sound:* Lance Brown. *Production Designer:* Michael Hartog and Bjarne Slettland. *Running time:* 30 minutes. *MPAA Rating:* Not Rated.

CAST: Dana Ashbrook (Ray); Corinne Bohrer (Suzy); James Wilder (Stanley); David Patch (Supervisor); Jennifer Rubin (Ruby); Quentin Tarantino (Panhandle Slim).

LOS ANGELES TIMES, 10/21/94, Calendar/p. 10, Kevin Thomas

[*The Coriolis Effect* was reviewed jointly with *Makin' Up*; see Thomas' review of that film.]

NEW YORK POST, 9/16/94, p. 45, Larry Worth

[*The Coriolis Effect* was reviewed jointly with *Makin' Up*; see Worth's review of that film.]

NEWSDAY, 9/16/94, Part II/p. B5, John Anderson

[*The Coriolis Effect* was reviewed jointly with *Makin' Up*; see Anderson's review of that film.]

VILLAGE VOICE, 9/27/94, p. 66, Amey Taubin

[*The Coriolis Effect* was reviewed jointly with *Makin' Up*; see Taubin's review of that film.

Also reviewed in:
NEW YORK TIMES, 9/16/94, p. C8, Janet Maslin

CORRINA, CORRINA

A New Line Cinema release of a Steve Tisch production. *Executive Producer:* Ruth Vitale and Bernie Goldmann. *Producer:* Paula Mazur, Steve Tisch, and Jessie Nelson. *Director:* Jessie Nelson. *Screenplay:* Jessie Nelson. *Director of Photography:* Bruce Surtees. *Editor:* Lee Percy. *Music:* Bonnie Greenberg. *Music Editor:* Will Kaplan. *Sound:* David Kelson and (music) Tom Winslow *Sound Editor:* Steve Richardson. *Casting:* Mary Gail Artz and Barbara Cohen. *Production Designer:* Jeannine Claudia Oppewall. *Art Director:* Dina Lipton. *Set Designer:* Louisa Bonnie. *Set Decorator:* Lauren M. Gabor. *Set Dresser:* Mike Malone, Henry "Bud" Fanton, W.C. Nearhood, Don Elliot, Marc Duncan, Mike Thurman, Robert Young, Daniel Goldsmith, and John Quittner. *Special Effects:* Lou Carlucci. *Costumes:* Francine Jamison-Tanchuck. *Costumes (Whoopi Goldberg):* John Hayles. *Make-up:* Mike Germain. *Stunt Coordinator:* Ben Scott and Kym Washington. *Running time:* 115 minutes. *MPAA Rating:* PG.

CAST: Noreen Hennessey (High Heals); Lucy Webb (Shirl); Don Ameche (Grandpa Harry); Tina Majorino (Molly Singer); Erica Yohn (Grandma Eva); Ray Liotta (Manny Singer); Larry Miller (Sid); June C. Ellis (Miss O'Herlihy); Mimi Lieber (Rita Lang); Karen Leigh Hopkins (Liala Sheffield); Lin Shaye (Repeat Nanny); Pearl Huang (Mrs. Wang); Marcus Toji (Tommy); Louis Mustillo (Joe Allechinetti); Joan Cusack (Jonesy); Whoopi Goldberg (Corrina Washington); Patrika Darbo (Wilma); Don Pugsley (Delivery Man #1); Lynette Walden (Annie); Brent Spiner (Brent Witherspoon); Bryan Gordon (Business Associate); Jevetta Steele (Club Singer); Yonda Davis (Woman in Audience); Curtis Williams (Percy); Briahnna Odom (Lizzie); Ashley Taylor Walls (Mavis); Jenifer Lewis (Jevina); Harold Sylvester (Frank); Wendy Crewson (Jenny Davis); Steven Williams (Anthony T. Williams); Asher Metchik (Lewis); Courtland Mead (Howard); Sue Carlton (Mrs. Werner); Tommy Bertelsen (Bratty Boy); Kyle Orsi (Gregory); Maud Winchester (Mrs. Rodgers); K.T. Stevens (Mrs. Morgan); Chris Chisholm (John Brennan); Bryan A. Robinson (Chubby Boy); Roz Witt (Mrs. Murphy); Sean Moran (2nd Delivery Man).

LOS ANGELES TIMES, 8/12/94, Calendar/p. 1, Peter Rainer

In "Corrina, Corrina," 7-year-old Molly Singer (Tina Majorino) reacts to the death of her mother by becoming mute. Her father, Manny (Ray Liotta), has to hold down a job writing jingles for an ad agency so he interviews for a housekeeper and, after the usual comic mishaps, ends up with the distinctly overqualified Corrina Washington (Whoopi Goldberg). It's a foregone conclusion that Corrina will get the girl to speak again, just as it's inevitable that Manny and Corrina will become attracted to each other.

In fact, just about everything in this heartfelt plodder is predictable. First-time writer-director Jessie Nelson serves up vintage clichés in a '50s setting—the dullness seems to be part of the period decor.

It's a welcome moment early on when Molly begins talking again—partly because her protracted muteness becomes rapidly annoying—but you kind of wish some of the other characters would shut up. As Manny's mother, Erica Yohn really overdoes the *yenta* stuff. (The late Don Ameche, in his last, brief appearance, plays her husband. He's mute too.) A Prospective mate of Manny's (Wendy Crewson) is broadly caricatured as an on-the-make huntress. Corrina's sister, Jevina (Jenifer Lewis), is forever going on about how Corrina should settle down with the nice suitor across the street (Steven Williams) and forget about getting close to her white boss. But we know better. When Corrina—who has a college degree in musicology—helps Manny out of a rut on a jingle for Jell-O, their soulmate status is secured.

At the heart of the heartfeltness is Molly's wish for Corrina and her father to pair up. She's a pint-sized matchmaker who sees nothing odd in the pairing. (Her child's wisdom is supposed to shame our misgivings.) But even though Nelson takes a very "understanding" view of the interracial involvements, she points up the disparities between black and white so often that she never lets you forget them.

She cross-cuts between life at the Singer household and life with Jevina's large family, where Corrina also lives. The cross-referencing serves to keep these worlds apart rather than bring them together. And there's an embarrassing, misguided scene when Molly wings with Jevina's kids in the church choir, and they trade racial barbs without comprehending the force of what they're saying. (The scene is misguided because it's treated as a lickety-split learning experience; there's no pain in it.)

Even though the '50s period flavor is constantly reinforced, Corrina is more like a figure from the '90s. She makes no attempt to "fit into" the white world, and her standard-bearer stance seems a bit too self-righteous. Corrina comes across as archetypal anomaly; she's in the movie to bring Manny, the grieving atheist, to his senses and get him to talk to God.

But Goldberg is at her best when she's not being noble and edifying. She's been excellent in the movies for years, ranging from "The Long Walk Home," in which she also played a maid, to "Soapdish" and "The Player." Her comic timing was the only reason to check out "Made in America" and "Sister Act 2." In "Corrina, Corrina" she's best in the brief scenes in which she's dilly-dallying with Molly—when she's not trying to massage our social consciousness. In the scenes with Ray Liotta, who seems gamefully miscast, all we get is massage.

The two liveliest actors in the movie are not the leads. As the dingbat housekeeper who has a brief run with the Singers, Joan Cusack is marvelous, as usual. (Why isn't she getting bigger roles?) And, as Percy, one of Jevina's kids, little Curtis Williams steals every scene he's in. You get the feeling he could steal from the best.

NEW YORK POST, 8/12/94, p. 46, Michael Medved

Jessie Nelson, the veteran stage actress who's the writer-producer of "Corrina, Corrina," lost her mother in the late 1950s when she was only 7.

Her father, a hard-working composer of advertising jingles, went through 30 nannies before he found one that could comfort the little girl and help her deal with her grief.

This new addition to the family happened to be 70 years old and black, but young Jessie nevertheless nursed the secret wish that her 35-year-old father would find a way to marry her.

Nelson's recollections of the childhood fantasies provide the basis for her profoundly impressive feature film debut though she's changed one essential element in the story: Corrina, the warm-hearted domestic in the movie version is played by Whoopi Goldberg, who's supposed to be the same age as the father, powerfully portrayed by Ray Liotta.

This means that the romance between widower and caretaker is no longer just a childish whimsy, and in fact becomes the focus of the plot's second half.

That's a shame, because the love affair never feels entirely persuasive. Nelson makes all the predictable references to the prejudice of 1959, as both Goldberg's black family and Liotta's white Jewish clan (including the great Don Ameche in his last performance) oppose the developing intimacy between the maid and her boss.

Liotta's stereotypical Yiddish momma (Erica Yohn) even trots out the old line: "A fish and a bird can fall in love. But where will they build their nest?

Director Nelson shows such remarkable skill with actors and images (the look of the '50s is eerily accurate and uncannily evocative) that she can make even clumsily written scenes pay off on screen.

Nevertheless, there's a striking difference between the contrived attraction between the two principals and the heartbreaking intensity of the sequences focusing on a little girl's attempt to adjust to her mother's death.

Nine-year-old Tina Majorino, who made such a winning impression as the older daughter in "When a Man Loves a Woman," gives a stunning performance in which you can see her character change and grow before your eyes—an astonishing achievement for a performer of any age.

Nelson also introduces religious themes with rare assurance, as Corrina's unwavering faith repeatedly challenges Liotta's stubborn atheism.

When the father discovers that the new nanny has told the child that her mother is in heaven, he insists to the girl that "heaven, the angels and all of that is just something that people make up so they won't feel sad anymore," to which his daughter sensibly replies, "What's wrong with that?"

The movie is filled with such moments of insight, and it boasts Whoopi Goldberg's finest dramatic performance since "The Color Purple."

It's the third time she's played a maid, but unlike her prior roles as a domestic (in the overly-earnest "Clara's Heart" and "The Long Walk Home") she demanded that this character be given some formidable intellectual credentials.

Corrina is a graduate of Fisk University and an expert on jazz, who dreams of one day writing liner notes for record albums. Goldberg invests this character with such enormous wit and dignity that you fall in love with her despite her flaw's—in much the same way that it's easy to love this flawed but beautiful movie.

NEWSDAY, 8/12/94, Part II/p. B2, Jack Mathews

With apologies to Yogi Berra, I had déjà vu all over again watching Whoopi Goldberg in "Corrina, Corrina." I was sure I'd seen her play the super nanny once before, a woman of perfect spiritual balance who enters a troubled household and calms its occupants.

In fact, Goldberg's Corrina Washington is sort of a composite of the sassy Jamaican nanny she played in "Clara's Heart" and her resilient, headstrong southern maid in "The Long Walk Home." In any event, she's played the domestic a couple of times too many for someone anxious to eliminate racial stereotypes in Hollywood, and her tired performance suggests she didn't have her heart in it, either.

"Corrina, Corrina," written, directed and produced by former actress Jessie Nelson, takes us into the home of ad executive Manny Singer (Ray Liotta) and his 9-year-old daughter, Molly (Tina Majorino), whose lives in 1959 Southern California have been profoundly unsettled by the sudden death of his wife, her mother. Manny is unable to finish that Jell-O jingle he's been writing, and Molly has retreated into a mute silence, where she keeps her mother alive.

After interviewing a host of outrageously inappropriate housekeepers, and enduring one disastrous hire (a hilarious turn by a Mrs. Doubtfire-sized Joan Cusack), Manny settles on Corrina, whose playful manner makes a vague connection with Molly, and the wheels on this predictable sentimental journey are set in motion.

Goldberg says in the production notes that "Corrina" is "not a maid comes, maid fixes it, maid goes away tale," but it really is. The twist is that the maid and her employer become romantically involved, stir racist resentment among friends and relatives, and have to resolve whether she'll go away. But the middle hour of the movie is precisely a maid-comes-and-maid-fixes-it tale. With an irresistible blend of humor, intelligence, spiritual wisdom and common sense, Corrina puts Manny and Molly on the mend.

Nelson, an Obie Award-winning actress with New York's experimental Mabou Mines theater company, reportedly based her story on her own childhood. Her mother died when she was quite young and she became so emotionally attached to their 70-year-old housekeeper that she dreamed of her father and the housekeeper marrying.

That those honest childhood feelings became the basis for a contrived interracial love story says reams about the nature of Hollywood and star power. Nelson's script was nine years old when Goldberg signed on, and without her it might have languished forever.

The best moments of "Corrina, Corrina," and there are plenty, deal with Corrina's relationship with Molly, and with the child's mother-replacement fantasy. That part of Nelson's story, the idea of a stranger with the right chemistry assuming the emotional role of a lost loved one, is worth telling, and for a while that appears to be where the story is taking us.

Corrina becomes both a surrogate mother for Molly and—with their shared knowledge and appreciation for music—an amiable companion for Manny. Her presence is an analgesic for phantom pain.

If Nelson had stuck to those psychological dynamics, she'd have had something truly fresh, and enough grist to keep the daily talk-show mill grinding for a week. But "Corrina" drops that subtext and becomes a relatively conventional love story, with only its interracial and class conflicts setting it apart.

Even that is done halfheartedly. A busybody neighbor gets her dander up after seeing Manny and Corrina embrace, and Manny gets *his* dander up when some bozo in a restaurant mistakes Corrina for a waitress. But Nelson is too inexperienced a director to make these scenes crackle with any real tension, and though Liotta and Goldberg make the case that Manny and Corrina could be lifelong friends, maybe even writing partners in the jingle business, their romance is without a hint of passion.

After all these years, and all those rewrites, "Corrina, Corrina" remains the author's childhood fantasy.

SIGHT AND SOUND, 12/94, p. 43, Joanna Berry

Los Angeles, 1959. At her mother's funeral, seven-year-old Molly Singer sits under a table listening as people express their sympathies to her father Manny. Molly hasn't spoken a word since her mother died, and Manny is left with the task of finding a suitable housekeeper to look after his daughter so that he can return to his job as a jingle writer. After seeing a series of unsuitable candidates, Manny interviews Corrina for the job. She has a college degree and is clearly overqualified, but when he sees how she handles Molly, Manny hires her.

A few days later, Molly speaks to Corrina for the first time. Manny is elated when he comes home and learns his daughter can talk and, realising Corrina is responsible, he invites her to dinner. Molly begins school, but hates her first day. She begs Corrina to let her stay home, so Corrina takes her along on cleaning jobs. At home in the evening Manny cooks for his housekeeper and his daughter, and Molly happily believes that the three of them have become a family.

Meanwhile, Manny's boss is trying to pair him off with Jenny, an eligible divorcee. When Jenny arrives unexpectedly to visit Manny, she treats Corrina as a servant, causing her to leave. Disturbed that this woman may come between her father and Corrina, Molly successfully sabotages their evening. The next day, Corrina hands in her notice. Manny begs her to stay and she agrees. He kisses her—surprising both of them and a neighbour watching nearby. The neighbour tells Manny's parents, and Manny is sickened by everyone's attitude, insisting Corrina is the best thing for Molly. Manny and Corrina become closer than ever and kiss one evening in the park, noticing that Molly is watching.

When Manny discovers Corrina has been keeping Molly away from school, he sacks her for betraying him. Molly retreats into silence and is further disturbed when Manny's father dies. After the funeral, Manny goes to see Corrina to apologise. At first she rebukes him, but touched by his awkwardness, she embraces him. She takes him inside so he can meet her own family. The pair then return to Molly, who is comforting her grandmother with a gospel song Corrina has taught her. Molly smiles and stops singing when she sees Manny and Corrina walk up the path hand in hand.

Inter-racial relationships have been the backdrop for a series of recent mainstream movies, including *The Bodyguard* (which ignored the subject altogether) and *Made in America*—the "oops! wrong sperm" comedy which used the idea of a white man being the father of a black girl as a trigger for a few weak laughs. *Corrina, Corrina* does neither of these things, but instead uses the relationship between Ray Liotta's Manny and Whoopi Goldberg's Corrina as part of a larger story, and in doing so effectively and subtly depicts much more about such an affair.

Corrina, Corrina focuses on the relationship between a distraught child and the housekeeper who looks after her. It is the directorial debut of writer-director-producer Jessie Nelson, and is loosely based on the director's own experiences of the 35 nannies who came and went in her household after her mother died. Both the relationship between Corrina and the child Molly—played superbly by young actress Tina Majorino— and Molly's coming to terms with her bereavement are believable and understated, and there are surprisingly few of the mandatory sugar-sweet scenes.

VILLAGE VOICE, 8/16/94, p. 50, Beth Coleman

Corrina, Corrina, based on director-producer-writer Jessie Nelson's childhood experience as a girl who falls in love with her nanny and wants dad to marry the surrogate mom, provides the next opportunity for Whoopi Goldberg to play comic-romantic lead opposite a white guy who couldn't survive without her. From Jonathan Price to Ted Danson and Patrick Swayze, even Captain Picard and Data, they've gotta have her—her soul, her humor, her good wisdom.

It's Los Angeles, 1959, where nouveau art deco rules in the hose and the cars are spiffy with chrome. Manny Singer (Ray Liotta) and his young daughter Molly (Tina Marjorino) are widowed at an early age. They don't know how to talk to each other—Molly won't talk at all—or feed each other, or get on with their lives. So everyone pretends when Corrina (Whoopi Goldberg) shows up (as if from heaven, but actually off a bus from the poor side of town) that her saucy therapy is for the kid, not the man. She's the right color for a mammy, except that Corrina smokes (sign of cool), and Corrina has a degree in musicology (a sign of trouble). Unable to make a proper meal, she's just the woman to help Manny with his Mr. Potato Head jingle.

The child and the woman get along like conspirators from day one, yet the movie takes a good hour establishing that love nest and avoiding the other. Using the period and the mourning as camouflage, *Corrina* drags its tale getting to the good stuff, the adult romance. Because, frankly, what else are we here for? To see Whoopi finally get laid, *sans doute*. Don't hold your breath.

Corrina and Manny bond on cigarettes and music. They hum, light up, and talk through records, until Corrina is sitting at the table instead of serving, until Manny has someone to talk to with a better sense of humor than his late wife. "Have you ever been blocked?" he asks Corrina while he sits at the piano. "Yes, all my life," she says. And there you have it. Manny has the momentary pause, where Corrina has hit ceiling with rejection letters and buckets of soapsuds for other people's staircases.

We can see why he needs her. What is it, pray tell, about Manny that sends Corrina? His ability to rhyme words with "puddin'"? Is proximity to his whiteness reward enough for her thwarted career as a music critic, her million and one frustrations that help hone that sharp tongue? But he is, after all, the wounded romantic lead. Before anyone gets a chance to look around, they're an intimate household—she's a velvety backdrop (*Ghost Dad* meets ghost mom) for the Singers' delicately drawn recovery. What's missing in this transference drama is Corrina's side of the wherefore and how-much-was-it on the road to love.

The biggest surprises are in the casting. Both Liotta and Goldberg are rarely seen in this kind of low-key project—although Liotta has given subtle performances in films such as *Nicky and Gino* and *Field of Dreams*—and the director has successfully reined in their personalities so that the child is not overwhelmed by the more experienced actors. Goldberg, who usually whirls across the screen in a comic frenzy, still manages to crack a few jokes but is remarkably restrained as the nanny-with-the-heart-of-gold.

There are comic moments to be had, courtesy of Joan Cusack as Jonesy, a demented interviewee for the housekeeping position who tells Manny that, since she does everything a wife does around the house, she should get everything a wife gets. In fact, Manny's prospective employees are such a diverse bunch—one thinks she's Sophia Loren in *Houseboat*, while the male candidate for the position considers himself a "kid-magnet"—it makes one wonder just what Manny said in his advert for the job.

While the comedy is often light and effective, the relationship between father and child as they grieve could sustain the film on its own. Director Nelson adds the element of a black housekeeper to the mix, using her appearance as a tool to look at the way attitudes back in 1959 were not that different from those of today. Manny's parents and neighbours disapprove of his growing friendship with a black woman, and her struggle to rise above her "position" despite having a college degree is depicted without the audience being subjected to a lecture on rights issues. Yes, Corrina is humiliated in a restaurant when another diner assumes she is a waitress, and yes, she cannot get her written work about black singers published in mainstream journals, but the dogged Corrina sees this as how life is, and believes that no matter how much she wants to change things, this will not happen overnight.

In less than two hours, the audience not only learns something about Manny, Corrina and Molly, it learns something from them—and that is what makes *Corrina, Corrina* worthwhile.

Also reviewed in:
CHICAGO TRIBUNE, 8/19/94, Friday/p. C. Michael Wilmington
NEW YORK TIMES, 8/12/94, p. C3, Janet Maslin
VARIETY, 8/1-7/94, p. 45, Emanuel Levy
WASHINGTON POST, 8/26/94, p. D1, Rita Kempley
WASHINGTON POST, 8/26/94, Weekend/p. 42, Desson Howe

COWBOY WAY, THE

A Universal Pictures release of an Imagine Entertainment presentation. *Executive Producer:* G. Mac Brown, Karen Kehela, and Bill Wittliff. *Producer:* Brian Grazer. *Director:* Gregg Champion. *Screenplay:* Bill Wittliff. *Story:* Rob Thompson and Bill Wittliff. *Director of Photography:* Dean Semler. *Editor:* Michael Tronick. *Music:* David Newman. *Music Editor:* Carlton Kaller and Tom Villano. *Choreographer:* Patricia Birch. *Sound:* Tom Brandau and (music) Kim Boyle and Dennis Sands. *Sound Editor:* J. Paul Huntsman. *Casting:* Billy Hopkins, Suzanne Smith, and Kerry Barden. *Production Designer:* John Jay Moore. *Art Director:* William Barclay. *Set Decorator:* Leslie Pope. *Set Dresser:* Denis Zack, Bruce Swanson, Anne Wenniger, and Laura West. *Special Effects:* Steve Kirshoff. *Costumes:* Aude Bronson-Howard. *Make-up:* Bernadette Mazur. *Make-up (Woody Harrelson):* Ben Nye, Jr. *Stunt Coordinator:* Conrad E. Palmisano. *Running time:* 102 minutes. *MPAA Rating:* PG-13.

CAST: Woody Harrelson (Pepper); Kiefer Sutherland (Sonny); Dylan McDermott (Stark); Ernie Hudson (Officer Sam Shaw); Cara Buono (Teresa); Marg Helgenberger (Margarette); Tomas Milian (Huerta); Luis Guzman (Chango); Angel Caban (Boca); Matthew Cowles (Pop Fly); Joaquin Martinez (Nacho); Kristin Baer (Melba); Christian Aubert (Jacques); Emmanuel Xuereb (Gaston); Francie Hawks Swift (Desk Clerk); Christopher Durang (Waiter); Laura Ekstrand (Cello Player); Graciela Lecube (Pawn Shop Woman); Jose Zuniga (Carlos); Travis Tritt (Cowboy); Dan Spoon (Cowboy); John David Garfield (Cowboy); Duke Jackson (Cowboy); Larry Pennington (Rodeo Announcer); Frank Girardeau (Chief Barnes); Harsh Nayyar (Coroner); Allison Janney (Lady Cop); Karina Arroyave (Rosa); Ira Newborn (Taxi Driver); Victor Argo (Business Associate); Ken Simmons (Teddy); John J. Ventimiglia (Uniformed Cop); Jaime Tirelli (Monitor); Joe Mosso (Mounted Policeman); Esteban Fernandez (La Habanita Bartender); Robert Moran (Bartender at Party); Gabriel Marantz (Boy on Train); Rance Howard (Old Gentleman); Ahmed Ben Larby (Foreign Cab Driver); Doug Barron (Doorman); Randy Pearlstein (Hat Check Boy); Tim Williams (Mimic); Christopher

Murray (Water Cop); Leonard Thomas (Train Conductor); Leslie Ann Stefanson (Girl at Party); Travis Tritt (Himself).

LOS ANGELES TIMES, 6/3/94, Calendar/p. 1, Kenneth Turan

Woody Harrelson is the only reason to subject yourself to "The Cowboy Way," but to be a straight-shooter about things, he is not reason enough. Instead of enhancing his surroundings, Harrelson's breezy, amusing performance simply underlines everything the rest of the film is not.

Based on yet another idea from the cornucopian mind of producer Brian Grazer who, if the press notes are to be believed, came up with this gem "while horseback riding in his native California," "Cowboy" will be recognized by film buffs as a reworking of the tip-top "Coogan's Bluff," directed by Don Siegel and starring an especially laconic Clint Eastwood as an Arizona lawman out of his element on the steamy pavements of New York.

It is perhaps a sign of cinematic inflation that this time around "The Cowboy Way" is forced to send not one but two stand-up Western gentlemen into the wilds of Manhattan to right a wrong and see that justice is done.

New Mexico cowboys Pepper Lewis (Harrelson) and Sonny Gilstrap (Kiefer Sutherland) are a formidable team-roping combination and best pals since they were toddlers. But, in one of the film's many bogus plot contrivances, Sonny has been giving his partner "the Eskimo treatment" since Pepper was a mysterious no-show at the finals of a key tournament.

"There we were, one steer away from the national championship," grouses Sonny in one of the many pieces of presumably authentic Bill Wittliff dialogue. Pepper, you may be sure, had his reasons for staying away, but once revealed they, like much else here, turn out to be as tame as an overworked plowhorse.

Sonny and Pepper's best pal is a wise old Latino named Nacho (Joaquin Martinez) who accuses cranky Sonny of having "the heart of a tiny raisin." But before he can explain where he got such a gift for metaphor, Nacho is called to New York to try to rescue his daughter Teresa (Cara Buono).

She, illogically enough, is a dewy illegal just off the boat from Cuba who is in the unfortunate clutches of a bunch of slimeballs ramrodded by the nefarious Stark (Dylan McDermott). Forced to work in a sweatshop while Stark practically drools over her needlework, Teresa is clearly in need of the kind of help only two hopelessly naive cowboys in Manhattan can provide.

As directed by Gregg Champion, whose only previous theatrical feature was the forgotten "Short Time," "The Cowboy Way" has a tendency to milk every bumpkin-in-the-big-town situation it can think of. As a result, elements of "Midnight Cowboy" (Pepper catching the lascivious eye of effete fashion folk) awkwardly joust for position with cartoony violent echoes of "Home Alone."

Getting bruised in the melee are some usually reliable actors, including Ernie Hudson as a mounted policeman who loves the West. Especially lost is Sutherland, whose thankless role as the straight-arrow, censorious Sonny mostly calls on him to frown and say, "I've had it with you," to the irrepressible Pepper.

Losing patience with Pepper is always understandable. A macho pain in the neck who never stops talking and preening, he could exasperate a saint. But thanks to Harrelson's casual flair and his considerable comic energy, Pepper grows on you so much that his rare absences from the screen bring the picture to a dead halt.

While this is not a performance that wins awards, it does demonstrate the kind of star presence that the movies can never have too much of. What "The Cowboy Way" does best is underline how much more there is to Woody Harrelson than how he looks in his underwear or with a hat over his private parts.

NEW YORK POST, 6/3/94, p. 40, Michael Medved

"The Cowboy Way" is a braindead bomb from high-concept hell.

A week before the release of "City Slickers II," it offers us a sort of City Stinkers in reverse. In place of three neurotic New Yorkers galloping through the Wild West, this movie focuses on a pair of Wild Westerners who gallop through neurotic New York.

Kiefer Sutherland and Woody Harrelson play New Mexico rodeo riders who once worked as bull-roping partners but now can't stand each other.

Before you can say "bickering buddy movie" they are forced to work together again: a mutual friend (Joaquin Martinez) has disappeared in the big, bad city where he's gone to meet his beautiful daughter (Cara Buono) who's just illegally entered the USA from Cuba.

It turns out that this poor girl is just one of thousands of undocumented immigrants smuggled into the country by psychotic gangster Dylan McDermott, who then ruthlessly enslaves them in one of his sweatshops.

The only New Yorker willing to help the visiting saddle bums in battling this overacting bad guy is a mounted police officer with his own dreams of cowboy glory, played by Ernie Hudson in the film's most likable performance.

Harrelson, meanwhile, seems well-cast in the lovable lunkhead role. He generates a few laughs with some of his sincerely delivered malapropisms ("I wouldn't throw a bucket of water on your ass if you was drownin'!") but fails to develop any chemistry at all with his co-star.

Sutherland, for his part, appears to be appropriately embarrassed by the entire project. He offers a phoned-in perfunctory, send-the-check performance while trying to hide behind a big brush moustache.

Nothing about "The Cowboy Way" feels even momentarily convincing with the picture clumsily evoking innumerable fish-out-of-water cliches from "Crocodile Dundee" and even "Midnight Cowboy," as Harrelson turns up at a decadent party where the glitterati of the high-fashion world drool over his tight jeans and bow-legged swagger.

Unfortunately, director Gregg Champion (son of dancers Marge and Gower Champion) approaches his first big-budget assignment with a heavy-breathing, heavy-handed "significant statement" intensity altogether inappropriate for such silly material.

Some of the movie's sadistic and gory violence seems particularly out of place—especially since the characters are miraculously cured of even the most grievous and graphic wounds in the very next scene in which they appear.

Champion does display some hints of talent in the elaborate chase scene that concludes the movie, with our horseback heroes chasing a train across the Manhattan Bridge: Despite the fact that it makes no sense this sequence is capably staged and, for the most part, crisply edited.

It comes much too late, however, to save this inept and exploitative exercise, since many moviegoers will have to be hog-tied to their seat to stick with this cow-flop to the bitter end.

NEWSDAY, 6/3/94, Part II/p. B7, Jack Mathews

Woody Harrelson is standing on a bed, naked except for the Stetson on his head, the warpaint on his face and the purple bandana diaper-tied around his loins. He is also wearing a grin as dumb as a cork and speaking the broken English of movie Indians, as he directs a giggly playmate to turn "Big Chief" into "Happy Chief" by beating on his tom-tom.

If this isn't one of the most embarrassing scenes a major star has been asked to do in a movie, it's only because Harrelson is not a major star. Or apt to become one, after answering the call for Gregg Champion's "The Cowboy Way."

Harrelson has other opportunities to embarrass himself in this witless action-comedy about a New Mexico rodeo-riding team trying to break up a gang of slave traders in modern New York City, and he doesn't let a single one slip by. Reverting to the persona of the affable idiot he played on TV's "Cheers," Harrelson's Pepper Lewis clops through the New York scenes like the Encino Man dressed by Levi Strauss.

Costar Kiefer Sutherland comes off marginally better, but only because the contemplative personality of his character, Sonny Gilstrap, was written to contrast with Pepper's ill-bred impetuousness. They are the odd couple on the range, a loner and a loser united by their passion for—and skills at—ridin', ropin', and calf-wrestlin'.

When we meet them, Sonny and Pepper are estranged. The unreliable Pepper had failed to show up for a national event whose prize money Sonny was counting on using to buy a ranch. But when their mutual friend Nacho (Joaquin Martinez) heads east to meet a daughter he paid to have smuggled in from Cuba, Sonny and Pepper reteam and follow his trail right into a nest of human rattlers in midtown Manhattan.

Led by a sadist named Stark (Dylan McDermott), the gang uses relatives' money to bring immigrants into the city, then turns them over to sweat shop bosses. Using the "cowboy way," which proves to be the same as the bull-in-the-china-shop way, Sonny and Pepper set out to rescue Nacho's daughter.

But first, the hayseeds have to learn the big city ropes, and go through an array of painfully contrived culture clash scenes. They rankle a snooty waiter at the Waldorf-Astoria, build a campfire in Central Park, become sex objects for slumming socialites, befriend a horseback cop (Ernie Hudson) who's nursing his own cowboy fantasy.

Eventually, "The Cowboy Way" settles into conventional urban action, the sole difference being that in the big chase sequence, Sonny and Pepper are on horseback and the bad guys are on a Brooklyn-bound subway train. You'll get more realism in a Roadrunner cartoon.

When a movie misfires this badly, you can usually trace it to the moment of inspiration, and sure enough, the production notes reveal that gee-whiz producer Brian Grazer (Ron Howard's impetuous partner) came up with the idea of modern-day cowboys in New York while horseback riding in California.

Just think, Woody, had it rained that day, we might have all been spared.

TIME, 6/13/94, p. 74, Richard Schickel

Send a couple of rodeo riders to New York City and you have what everyone must have hoped was the perfect reverse spin on *City Slickers*. In *The Cowboy Way*, the two rubes have many stupid misadventures as they try to save a young woman from white slavery. The sheer laziness of the writing, direction and especially the playing by Woody Harrelson and Kiefer Sutherland is stunning. The stars seem to be improvising much of the time and winking to the audience, "Hey, folks, we're having a lot of fun!" Hey, guys, we're not.

VILLAGE VOICE, 6/21/94, p. 52, Mike Rubin

Both a clumsy attempt to cash in on country music's sales supernova and the foulest stench in the western wind that *Unforgiven* blew in, *The Cowboy Way* is one dead horse. Unlike Luke Perry's recent rodeo-driven *8 Seconds*, bronco-bustingprovides only a cursory background sketch for *Cowboy*'s cartoon characters: Sonny (Kiefer Sutherland) and Pepper (Woody Harrelson) , lasso-tossing former best friends now estranged—because of a championship competition that Pepper failed to show up for. (The film would have been infinitely more interesting if the protagonists were Sonny and Cher or Salt-N-Pepa.) This disagreeable duo travel from New Mexico to New York, where they take the law into their own hands to help save their Cuban farmhand's daughter from the clutches of Golden Venture-style slave-labor traders; along the way, of course, they encounter everything one expects dudes with big hats in the Big City would face: turbaned taxi drivers, snooty waiters, lusty society women, and queer fashion designers, plus Ernie Hudson—currently the Hardest Working Man in Show Business—seemingly typecast this summer as a policeman with a heart of gold.

The cowboy cop in Manhattan shtick is old hat, and this *McCloud* has no silver lining. *The Cowboy Way* borrows freely from other entries in the 10-gallon galoot genre: scenes of simpleton stud Harrelson wandering the streets of Midtown in his Stetson hearken back to *Midnight Cowboy*—there's even a rehash of that film's debauched party sequence—while *Urban Cowboy*'s mechanical bull has been replaced by the B train. Between in-jokes about his Calvin Klein underwear ads, Harrelson levels the dialogue to mulch with his thick Dustbowl drawl, while Sutherland just sounds, well, Canadian. The film's funniest moments actually come from its bumbling use of NYC geography—one chase scene starts in Williamsburg and 10 seconds later ends up in Midtown traffic—but it's hardly worth riding herd on continuity mishaps. Better to just put this bum steer out to pasture.

Also reviewed in:
CHICAGO TRIBUNE, 6/3/94, Friday/p. F, Michael Wilmington
NEW REPUBLIC, 6/20/94, p. 27, Stanley Kauffmann
NEW YORK TIMES, 6/3/94, p. C21, Caryn James

VARIETY, 6/6-12/94, p. 44, Brian Lowry
WASHINGTON POST, 6/3/94, p. C7, Rita Kempley
WASHINGTON POST, 6/3/94, Weekend/p. 44, Joe Brown

COWS

A Sogetel production with the collaboration of ICAA of the Spanish Ministry of Culture/The Culture Department of the Basque Government. *Executive Producer:* Jose Luis Olaizola and Fernando de Garcillán. *Director:* Julio Medem. *Screenplay (Spanish with English subtitles):* Julio Medem and Michel Gaztambide. *Based on an original story by:* Julio Medem. *Director of Photography:* Carles Gusi. *Editor:* Maria Elena Sainz de Rozas. *Music:* Alberto Iglesias. *Sound:* Julio Recuero. *Production Designer:* Rafale Palmero. *Special Effects:* Reyes Abades. *Costumes:* Maria José Iglesias. *Make-up:* Goyo Meoiri. *Running time:* 96 minutes. *MPAA Rating:* Not Rated.

CAST: Emma Suárez (Cristina); Carmelo Gómez (Peru); Ana Torrent (Catalina); Karra Elejalde (Ilegorri/Lucas); Klara Badiola (Clara); Txema Blasco (Manuel); Kándido Uranga (Juan/Carmelo); Pilar Barden (Paulina); Miguel Angel Garcia (Peru as a child); Ane Sánchez (Christina as a child); Magdalena Mikolajczyk (Daughter); Enara Azkue (Daughter as a child); Ortzi Balda (Ilegorri as a child/Lucas as a child); Elisabeth Ruiz (Daughter/old); Ramón Barea (Juez); Aitor Mazo and Xavier Aldanondo (Soldiers); Carlos Zabala (Official); Antxon Echeverria, Alberto Arizaga, and Niko Lizeaga (Carlist Soldiers); Patxi Santamaría and José Ramón Soroiz (Journalists).

NEW YORK POST, 6/1/94, p. 31, Larry Worth

In his film debut, director Julio Medem proves himself a master of mesmerizing camerawork and indelible imagery.

Now, all he has to do is connect with a story worth telling. "Vacas" (Cows) never came close.

The script, co-written by Medem with Michel Gaztambide, is a series of bizarre scenes linking two neighboring families in Spain's Basque countryside over 60 years, with all the goings-on observed by three generations of cows.

Divided into four episodes, the first 10 minutes set the tone with a nauseatingly graphic look at the horrors of war. As the ever-squabbling clan patriarchs fight the Carlist War of 1875, one is fatally shot in the neck. The other covers himself in blood from the gaping, pulsating wound to also appear dead.

When a trundle filled with soldiers' naked corpses rolls over his leg, the man can't even cry out for fear of discovery. The charade works well enough that the enemy throws him—along with his now-dangling appendage—onto the body pile, which he wriggles out from when the coast is clear. The only witness: a fly-ridden heifer.

Then it's on to depictions of incest, animal mutilation and unmitigated doom, which is all well and fine if there's a method to the madness, a point to be made.

Unfortunately, that's not the case, which keeps Medem from following in the footsteps of offbeat auteurs like David Lynch or Luis Buñuel.

The closest Medem comes to hooking viewers occurs in the second vignette: a look at the Romeo and Juliet of the ax-wielding set, as both families engage in a fierce log-chopping contest despite the lovebirds' protests. Even then, Medem wanders into metaphorical forays about black holes, the meaning behind shadows and whatever other irrelevancies apparently came to mind.

Meanwhile, the actors—all unknowns—play different roles as the epic progresses, with fair to forgettable results. By default, the cows steal the show.

Then again, who wants to watch an artfully framed shot of a bovine defecating? With such a lack of focus for Medem's talents, "Vacas" proves as off-putting as the cow chips.

NEWSDAY, 6/1/94, Part II/p. B9, John Anderson

It's 1875, and to escape the warfare raging all around him, Manuel (Carmelo Gomez), a champion woodchopper and coward, smears himself with blood and hides among the naked corpses of his fellow Basque soldiers. Slipping off a wagon en route to the grave, he lets it run over his leg rather than give himself away. Manuel wants to live.

His instinct for survival is just one of the ineluctable human impulses—the others being mating, warring and self-abasement—that propel "Vacas" ("Cows"), Julio Medem's strange, dizzying debut film in which survival, like everything else, has its price. Take Manuel: The only witness to his moment of total humiliation is the stolid, unwavering eye of a cow, a great black void into which Manuel—or at least his sanity—is swallowed up. He, lives, but becomes an aged painter (played by Txema Blasco), creating strange pictures of cows that mirror the tortured goings on both inside his head, and all around him.

He inhabits a crazy, mixed-up, incestuous world, chronicling two families' rivalries and love affairs, embellished by Manuel's madness and his belief that he's crossed into a world between life and death.

Bookended by wars—the Second Carlist War begins the film, the Spanish Civil war ends it—"Cows" places humankind on a inescapable cycle of intrigue and misery, kept spinning by its own flaws.

Using the same actors to portray different generations of the families it chronicles—who trace eerie parallels of the preceding generation's foibles—"Cows" is about the circular quality of existence, and the ultimate futility of all those ineluctable human instincts.

SIGHT AND SOUND, 7/93, p. 54, Robert Yates

Four interrelated stories, set in the Basque Country in Spain, center on the Irigibel and Mendiluze families. 'The Coward Aizkolari': 1875. In the trenches during the Second Carlist War, under enemy attack, Carmelo Mendiluze attempts to steady the nerves of Manuel Irigibel, his neighbour and a local hero as an *aizkolari*, a practitioner of the 'sport of the axe'. Helping Irigibel, Mendiluze is shot dead and as he lies dying, Irigibel smears blood from Mendiluze's wound on himself, thus feigning death. He keeps up the pretence even when his leg is run over and shattered by the cart that disposes of the dead bodies; crawling away later, he encounters a cow, and stares into its eyes. 'The Axes': 1905. Manuel Irigibel, now old and still lame, is home in the Guipuzcoan Valley, where he lives with his son Ignacio and Ignacio's wife and daughters. He spends his time painting cows and appears to be deranged, although his young granddaughter, the six-year old Cristina, seems to understand him. His son Ignacio and neighbour Juan—the son of Carmelo Mendiluze—are great rivals in the sport of the axe, part of a family rivalry born of old Manuel's cowardice in the war. A log-chopping match is organised, which Ignacio wins, the start of a successful career. From one victory, he returns home with the prize of a cow, named Pupille by old Manuel. Juan's hatred of his rival is compounded by the love affair between Ignacio and his sister, Catalina Mendiluze.

'The Lit Hole': 1915. Peru, the illegitimate son of Catalina and Ignacio, now ten, lives with his mother and unmarried uncle, Juan, but is welcome at the Irigibels: There, he and the now 16-year-old Cristina—their friendship hinting at sexual attraction—spend their time with grandfather Manuel. Meanwhile, Ignacio's successes with the axe are such that he returns home with a prize motor car, followed by reporters and photographers. His affair with Catalina continues while Juan, becoming increasingly imbalanced, attempts in vain to persuade his sister to sleep with him. Having stolen a camera, old Manuel and his two grandchildren develop an interest in photography until lovers Ignacio and Catalina take off together for America, later sending for Peru. Peru and Cristina keep in touch via letters and photographs; some time later, Peru tells her he has married and become a photographer. 'War In The Forest': 1936. Peru returns to the valley as a photographer covering the Civil War for an American newspaper, and meets Cristina. Their grandfather has died and together they look through his paintings, which had become increasingly sinister as he approached the end of his life. The Mendiluze house is empty, and Peru's uncle Juan has apparently joined up with the nationalists. A warning that soldiers are drawing near sends the village men out into the woods. Most of the men are killed, and Peru is captured and lined up to face a firing squad. There he faces Juan, who spares him. He finds Cristina and the two leave on horseback for France.

Vacas deals with what is commonly regarded as the typical stuff of Spanish drama. Codes of honour, deep-seated family rivalries, passion suppressed in a stagnant community, and passion unleashed—the stuff of Andalusian romance. *Vacas* is in fact directed by a Basque (a former film critic and feature debutant) and made in the Basque country, but the two regions are recognised as having affinities in their folklore. However, the typical is not necessarily brought into focus. For instance, Ignacio's wife Madalen—who is left at home while her husband seduces the neighbour, and who is eventually abandoned—might herself have been at the centre of a tragedy. But here she remains a shadowy figure, part of the backdrop.

What *Vacas* does draw on is a strong stylistic tendency in Spanish creativity, recognisable too in Spanish-American magic realism, in which the unexpected and the fantastical intrude on the realistic. It is an intrusion which film is particularly well suited to catch. Within a generally naturalistic style which at times has a graphic, documentary quality—a blood-encased calf is pulled with a rope from its mother's womb—the camera may sweep or tilt, or suddenly change viewpoint, so that we may be asked to view the world through the eyes of a cow. Or else it will transform a routine gesture, the throwing of an axe for instance, into a fantastic one: the rotating axe flying across fields.

This style collaborates with the episodic structure to suggest a fairy tale in which we accept that the extraordinary just happens. Two pairs of lovers—Ignacio and Catalina, Peru and Cristina—escape the mournful reality, the second couple after years apart and fleeing on a charger. It follows that *Vacas* also has the thinness of fairy tale in character and in motivation: Medem shows no interest in presenting psychologically complex individuals.

Fairy tales can also be brutal. Happiness in them is located elsewhere. Within the valley, this elsewhere is the woods, a favourite place of escape in children's fiction, while for old Manuel it is into his own fantasy world and his 'art: By contrast, 'reality' in the film is unremittingly dark. Action is bounded by bloody war, by two civil wars at that, neighbour killing neighbour; two of the characters are mad; one act of incest is attempted, and another is achieved. The fantasy, Medem suggests, grows out of this bleak world. Like Manuel's art, it is perhaps a strategy to cope with it. Medem's sure direction has the stylistic flexibility to accomodate these contrasting tones.

Cutting across the dialectic fantasy and reality dialectic is the interplay between observing and being observed, between possessing and being possessed. Manuel's obsession with cows—of which there are several, although they function as the same one—begins when he gazes into the eyes of one after feigning death, and imagines a look of accusation. Cows are particularly well suited as a screen for our projections because of the inscrutable expression they wear. Manuel's paintings—always of cows—become his means of observing in turn, his way of taking control. When he sees a camera for the first time, he seizes it less for its ability to produce another type of artefact, more because it allows him to get behind the lens, to occupy what he imagines to be the cow's position—observing and powerful.

Cows are also firmly embedded in the valley's economic realities: they are a source of income, valuable commodities (Ignacio is given one as a prize). There is no suggestion, however, that they have a value beyond this economic one (they are not, for instance, the religious icons that Hinduism makes of them) except, that is, for Manuel, whose imagination transforms the everyday, raising the messy animals to omnipotent status. As Medem's camera spins us through the eyes of a cow, taking us deep into its head—as a sci-fi TV programme might have taken us down a vortex—he alerts us to the comic absurdity of Manuel's musings.

VILLAGE VOICE, 6/7/94, p. 50, Leslie Camhi

A neighborly feud is the subject of *Cows*, Julio Medem's ambitious historical epic tracing war, adultery, incest, and madness through two Basque families over three generations: In the trenches of a Carlist uprising in the 1870's, Carmelo is shot, while his cowardly neighbor Manuel (Carmelo Gómez) survives by faking death, smearing his face with the blood of his not-quite-deceased rival. Crawling naked from a cart full of military corpses, he looks too closely at the dark eye of a wandering cow, and from that moment retains a special feeling for the species.

Thirty years later, he's a mad, retired peasant, painting folkloric, bovine, surrealist pictures. His son Ignacio is the rival of Juan, his dead rival's son; both are played by actors miraculously resurrected from the preceding generation. Their houses are separated by a fecund little wood, with the "pit," a sinister omphalos, at its center. The married Ignacio triumphs over the unstable Juan in the sport of log chopping and through the longing, adulterous looks of his neighbor's sister. In another 30 years their illegitimate son (Gómez again) returns from America as a newspaper photographer covering the Spanish Civil War, and falls in love with his own half sister.

Urban dwellers may appreciate some striking pastoral visuals: a single, sublime haystack, some grazing-level shots and slow pans across the vast continental expanse of a heifer's body; or the special moment when Ignacio, elbow-deep in a pregnant cow, pulls out her calf with the help of the whole family. And it's a pleasure to watch the fetching Gómez revived, progressively younger, through the ages.

But what is the relation of the bovine subplot to the larger historical drama? I came to think, unfortunately, that the cows had something to do with feminine sexuality. Manic men chop logs, make war, and covet their own or their neighbor's sister; the cows, less competitive, stay home and chew their cud with placid, domestic insanity. Hats off to Medem for originality.

Also reviewed in:
NEW YORK TIMES, 6/1/94, p. C16, Stephen Holden
VARIETY, 3/9/92, p. 57, David Stratton

CRIME BROKER

An A-Pix Entertainment release. *Producer:* Chris Brown, John Sexton, and Hiroyuki Ikeda. *Director:* Ian Barry. *Screenplay:* Tony Morphett. *Director of Photography:* Dan Burstall. *Editor:* Nicholas Beauman. *Music*: Roger Mason. *Running time:* 93 minutes. *MPAA Rating:* R.

CAST: Jacqueline Bisset (Holly McPhee); Masaya Kato (Dr. Jin Okazaki).

NEW YORK POST, 9/16/94, p. 41, Bill Hoffmann

"Crime Broker" isn't much of a movie, but it is a cinematic milestone of a sort.

This Australian-made entry proves without a doubt, that, at age 50, Jacqueline Bisset remains one of the most beautiful women in the world.

The ravages of time have been kind to this sexy, slim-bodied actress and she easily steals every bit of screen time she is given.

The bad news is that "Crime Broker" is an embarrassment for Bisset.

At its most distasteful, the script forces her to make love to a skinny, goateed Japanese psychopath and look like she's enjoying it.

"Crime Broker" tells the story of Holly McPhee (Bisset), a judge who deals out punishment to Australia's most common criminals—i.e. cat burglars, drunk drivers.

What nobody knows is that McPhee is a very uncommon criminal herself, laying out detailed plans for bank robberies and other heists and farming them out to a crime syndicate which gives her a quarter of the take.

Enter Dr. Jin Okazaki, a renowned Tokyo criminal psychologist who comes to study the Australian justice system.

Okazaki, for reasons we learn later, is actually a master criminal himself and soon finds out about McPhee's dastardly operation.

After confronting her, he forces her to join him in pulling a series of heists with him so they can split the loot 50-50.

The story doesn't sound bad, but the script is so weak that the characters don't always seem to know what their motivations are.

The dialogue doesn't help. It's often laughable.
Oh, Jackie, you deserve so much better!

Also reviewed in:
NEW YORK TIMES, 9/16/94, p. C14, Stephen Holden

CRONOS

An October Films release of a October Films/Consejo Nacional para la Cultura y las Artes/Instituto Mexicano de Cinematografia/Grupo del Toro/Guillermo Springall Carum/Arturo Whaley Martinez/ServicosFilmicos Atlc/Larson Sound Center/STPC de la RM presents an Iguana production in association with Ventana Films Fondo de Formento a la Calidad Cinematográfica with financial assistance from Universidad de Guadalajara. *Producer:* Bertha Navarro and Arthur H. Gorson. *Director:* Guillermo del Toro. *Screenplay (Spanish with English subtitles):* Guillermo del Toro. *Director of Photography:* Guillermo Navarro. *Editor:* Raul Davalos.*Music:* Javier Alverez. *Music Editor:* Kevin Kern. *Choreographer:* Esther Soler. *Sound:* Fernando Camara. *Sound Editor:* Burton M. Weinstein. *Production Designer:* Tolita Figueroa. *Art Director:* Brigitte Broch. *Special Effects:* Laurencio Cordero. *Costumes:* Genoveva Petitpierre. *Make-up:* M. Carrajal and Julieta Napoles. *Stunt Coordinator:* Gerardo Moreno. *Running time:* 92 minutes. *MPAA Rating:* Not Rated.

CAST: Federico Luppi (Jesús Gris); Ron Perlman (Angel de la Guardia); Claudio Brook (Dieter de la Guardia); Margarita Isabel (Mercedes Gris); Tamara Shanath (Aurora Gris); Damiel Giménez Cacho (Tito); Mario Iván Martínez (Alchemist); Juan Carlos Columbo (Funeral Director); Farnesio de Bernal (Manuelito); Luis Rodríguez (Buyer); Javier Alvárez (Bleeding Man); Gerardo Moscoso (Drunk); Eugenio Lobo (Stoned Man); Francisco Sánchez (Mimo); Laurencio Cordero (Watchman); Jorge Martínez de Hoya (Narrator).

LOS ANGELES TIMES, 4/22/94, Calendar/p. 1, Kenneth Turan

Bela Lugosi may have made it look easy, but being one of the undead, "Cronos" insists, is hardly a simple thing. It can be a lonely state, painful but also crazily comic in a charming if grotesque way. It's all on view in this pleasant and spooky film that gives surprising new life, so to speak, to a genre that won't die.

The first feature by 29-year-old Mexican writer-director Guillermo del Toro, "Cronos" exemplifies the good things that can happen when adventurous filmmakers choose to investigate traditional forms. Winner of both the Critics Week competition at Cannes and nine Ariels; Mexico's Academy Awards, "Cronos" surprises with its sophisticated and spirited look at a tale straight from the crypt.

"Cronos" opens with a prologue, detailing the strange history of an alchemist who fled the Spanish Inquisition to Veracruz in 1536 in order to continue working on his plans for a machine that granted eternal life, a machine he called the Cronos Device. Four hundred years later, the alchemist dies in a freak accident and though his mansion and its contents are sold, the portentous narrator informs, no mention was ever made of this device and "as far as anyone knew, it never existed."

Existing as well without any knowledge of all this is Jesus Gris (Frederico Luppi), a gray-haired antiques dealer in today's Veracruz who lives perhaps too quietly with his wife (Margarita Isabel) and his mostly silent granddaughter Aurora (Tamara Shanath).

One day, his attention drawn to a figure of an archangel in his shop, Jesus discovers a wondrous mechanical gold egg inside, an impressively elaborate mechanism that makes a fine, creaky sound when it's wound up and also does strange and insidious things to its owner once it is fully operational.

Before he can figure out quite how it works, Jesus and the device attract the attention of the sinister De la Guardias. Though concerned, in one of the film's many oddball touches, with a forthcoming nose job, nephew Angel (Ron Perlman) is basically the muscle, following the orders of his obsessed uncle Dieter (Claudio Brook).

A Howard Hughes type, Dieter lives in a germ-free environment, listening to opera and dreaming of life eternal. Forty years earlier, Dieter found the Cronos Device's instruction manual and now he wants the item itself, which he warns Jesus, should never be used without proper guidance. But Jesus already addicted to the machine's frightening, hypnotic actions, cannot turn back.

With this as the buildup, "Cronos" goes on to tell the story of how Jesus deals both with the De la Guardias and the device, which, we gradually and deliciously come to understand, is turning him into a vampire.

It is a mark of what makes this old-fashioned story so clever that this realization does manage to sneak up on us. Director Del Toro takes pleasure in turning the familiar horror story inside out, dispensing with the evil vampire of legend and concentrating on how an understandable desire for youth leads an average citizen into decidedly irregular paths.

One of "Cronos'" most characteristic features is its fondness for over-the-top Grand Guignol scenes that both graphically and comically illustrate the wear and tear of vampiredom, how bad it is for the complexion, for instance, how grueling and tiring it can be not to die even when circumstances make you wish for it.

Though veteran Latin American star Luppi gives a poignant amusing performance as a man trapped by his obsession, the real centerpiece of this film is writer-director Del Toro, who's made a exploitation material. Edgar Allan Poe with a sense of humor, Del Toro not only has fun mixing genres, he knows how to convey his enjoyment and make the result distinctly his own. With any luck he'll have a creative life as long as any vampire's.

NEW STATESMAN & SOCIETY, 12/2/94, p. 34, Jonathan Romney

Cronos is a vampire story with a difference—you couldn't by any stretch of the imagination call it a horror film. In spite of director Guillermo del Toro's stint as special effects man in Mexican TV horror, *Cronos* doesn't go for shock effects—it's the gentlest damnation comedy imaginable, nearly an undead feel-good movie.

It certainly has the most charming vampire seen in a while—not one of those suavely predatory Conde Draculas beloved of Mexican movie vampirology, but an amiable old cove, Jesús Gris (Federico Luppi), who runs a Mexico City antique shop. Unknowingly, he has in his possession the statue of an angel containing the Cronos Device—a satanic timepiece designed by a 16th-century Spanish alchemist in search of eternal life. When Jesús discovers the gizmo, it sprouts a fearsome set of gold claws, then sinks a blood-sucking mandible into his flesh—it's like something that Faberge might have thought of but rejected as too baroque.

Hoping to get his own claws on the device is Dieter de la Guardia (Claudio Brook), a moribund Howard Hughes figure who keeps his discarded body parts pickled for posterity. He sends his whimsically sinister nephew Angel (the exorbitantly craggy-faced Ron Perlman) in search of the device, which is what alerts Jesús to its existence—the best shock scene comes early on, when a cavalcade of cockroaches comes tumbling out of the angel's eye socket.

The effect on Jesús is instant, and rather benevolent. He may suffer agonising pangs by night, sending him to the fridge to contemplate a chunk of raw meat, but he also shaves off his moustache, and starts looking young and more dapper, to the delight of his tango-instructor wife. Here the film looks like taking a turn for the sexual dynamics that Jack Nicholson's lycanthropic outing *Wolf* so lamely aspired to. But del Toro has declared himself completely uninterested in the erotic approach to vampirism ("I have this theory that all vampires are sexually dead"). Hence the nice twist when Jesús and his wife go to a New Year Ball. Just when you think they're about to take a libidinal spin on the dance floor, he sneaks off to the toilet, wolfishly eyeing up a man with a nosebleed. Despite its sexual undertones, the following scene manages in a quite novel way to be entertainingly repulsive.

Del Toro is more concerned to play up his theme's religious aspects: the hero's path is patterned on Christ's death and resurrection. Explaining the insect-fuelled power of the device, old de la Guardia has the film's best line: "Jesus walked on water. So does a mosquito." But the religious symbolism would be rather more interesting if was less obvious. The vampire is called Jesús, angels are everywhere, the villain Angel de la Guardia is in a peculiar way Jesús' own guardian angel, directly responsible for his transformation. Del Toro give us all these clues, but never convinces us that they're worth playing with.

What's more interesting is what he leaves out. It's actually the sexual theme disclaimed by del Toro that provides the most intriguing undercurrent. However the story may be desexualised, there remains that unmistakably cruisy tone to the men's room scene, while Jesús' marital relationship is repressed to an almost excessive degree. The film's most disturbing figure is Jesús' virtually silent 8-year-old granddaughter Aurora (Tamara Shanath) who guards the device for him. When Jesús rises again and tries to contact his wife, Aurora keeps them apart; it's as if the child is entrusted with the narrative task of keeping sex out of the story, but in fact the sexual contact is strangely displaced onto her relationship with her grandfather. Explicitly, their relationship is no more sexual than the one between Peter Pan and Tinkerbell, but there's certainly an intense suggestion of jealousy in the way she scowls silently while the two adults flirt at their New Year's night out. You can see why del Toro has called *Cronos* "a sick but very tender love story."

The other absence in the film is Mexico itself. It has been argued that the film is an allegory of Mexico's relations to the US and to Europe. Mexico has been "invaded" by a bug (literally) from the Old World, while the vampire is stalked by powerful industrial predators who are presumably American. In fact, English-speaking Ron Perlman is the only actor who has an American accent, and even then comes across more like a generic stateless dubbed villain, no more American than Klaus Kinski, in all those spaghetti Westerns, was German.

It's hard to buy this internationalist reading, though, since the film doesn't do much to activate it. Despite the tango music that runs throughout, there's little sense of *Cronos* really being set in Mexico City. Despite this clearly not being a Hollywood-style movie, del Toro has simply made a vaguely cosmopolitan film that's calculated to appeal internationally without jarring as an overtly Mexican film and therefore hard to sell.

Cronos is simply too confused, too much a brain-storming film, full of inspired touches and one-off conceits that never quite gel into the myth that del Toro seems to aim at. There are some impressive flourishes here, but the overall construction is a little too elaborate, rather like the Cronos device itself—some lovely curlicues but can it actually tell the time?

NEW YORK POST, 3/30/94, p. 34, Thelma Adams

I have walked with a zombie. I have suffered the mummy's curse. But when it comes to horror movies, my heart (and the blood pulsing through) belongs to vampires.

I will watch almost, any vampire movie, from Bela Lugosi's "Dracula" and its Spanish-language twin through the Roger Corman cheapies of the '60s, from "Nosferatu" to Gary Oldman's fanged chameleon in "Bram Stoker's Dracula."

Growing up, I slept with the covers over my head to protect my neck and prayed that my Star of David would protect me (I lacked a cross.) I share my love for horror with newcomer Guillermo del Toro, the director of "Cronos." Among the Mexican director's first memories was being scared out of his diapers by an "Outer Limits" episode.

Like the syndicated TV show "Friday the 13th," which was set in an antique shop where each week some new demonic curio (a pen, a watch, a mirror) would send the proprietors into a labyrinth of fear and a struggle between good and evil, "Cronos" refers to an antique device that offers immortality for a soul-stealing price.

In the thrall of the golden Cronos, a peaceable Mexico City antiques dealer, Jesus Gris (Federico Luppi) reclaims his youthful vigor but suddenly craves human blood

A dying industrialist Dieter de la Guardla (Claudio Brook), wants the timepiece to prolong his life. He dispatches his bullying nephew, Angel (Ron Perlman from TVs "Beauty and the Beast"), to claim it.

The three actors have fun with their roles but are upstaged by the darling Tamara Shanath. As Aurora Gris, her love for her grandfather remains constant even as Jesus is transformed from a kindly Mister Rogers to a pathetic, patched-together, living corpse.

The first five minutes before the credits, which set up the story of the Cronos device are vividly accomplished and suggest a great talent. Peak moments follow. When the elegant self-possessed Gris kneels on a bathroom floor to lap up a drop of blood it's economical horror at its wittiest.

Black humor takes over at a funeral parlor where a virtuoso embalmer gleefully staple-guns Gris' forehead then throws an artistic hissy fit when he discovers that his prize corpse is to be cremated. Later, when Angel wants to inspect the body, the embalmer asks "medium rare or well-done?"

"Cronos" loses steam after the first hour. Despite the visual pleasures, black humor, and the actors' relish for their campy roles, del Toro doesn't quite stretch the familiar plot. Our delight in the details isn't enough to cover for our sagging attentions during the final free-for-all.

"Cronos" is an assured and self-conscious "Outer Limits" teased into a stylish full-length feature. That it won nine Ariels (the Mexican Oscars) might say something about the competition but del Toro's debut promises future horrors and sleepless nights for those of us who try but cant quite believe that vampires don't stalk the earth—especially in a dark theater.

NEWSDAY, 3/30/94, Part II/p. B11, John Anderson

Guillermo Del Toro genuflects at the altar of David Cronenberg. And Sam Raimi. And even Roger Corman. And especially Alejandro Jodorowsky. He's paying tribute as fast as he can.

The result of all this adoration is "Cronos, "an almost absurdly reverential homage to the great gore fetishists, who leave a trail of blood over the director's prostrate body. And yet, Del Toro shows with "Cronos," his first feature, that he's already capable of taking the horror genre certain places it's never been.

His is a far more stylish film than most of the work that seems to have influenced him, and one whose characters are more than just vehicles, or vessels, for supernatural hijinks. The mischievously named Jesus Gris (Federico Luppi), for instance, is an unassuming antiques dealer with a wife (Margarita Isabel) and a granddaughter (Tamara Shanath) and a generally uneventful existence, a man who, we can easily believe, has gotten caught up in something beyond his control—the Cronos Device, the creation of an alchemist who fled the Inquisition four centuries earlier, a kind of gilded cockroach whose mechanical bite delivers the stuff of eternal life.

It's an item Dieter de la Guarda (Claudio Brook), an industrialist obsessed with immortality, has been seeking ever since he came into possession of the alchemist's diary four decades earlier. With his sadistic nephew Angel (Ron Perlman), he pursues Jesus amid a pageant of violence and dark questions about eternal salvation.

One of the things that makes horror films so attractive to so many is, of course, retribution. The bad guys may win elsewhere, but never here; even the good guys must do penance for impure thoughts. Jesus begins by reveling in his newfound immortality, and ends by reviling life itself. It's all very reassuring.

Del Toro certainly overdoes what he does; there are moments when the pain is visceral, the visual horror alarmingly indulgent. But seldom does the director lose control of the tone of the film, which is somehow tongue-in-cheek and sentimental at the same time. And though "Cronos" may aspire to something greater than itself, its reach doesn't obscure its grasp.

SIGHT AND SOUND, 10/94, p. 38, John Kraniauskas

An alchemist escapes from late medieval Europe for colonial New Spain, where he becomes watchmaker to the Viceroy. He invents a timepiece, the 'Cronos device'. In the 1930s his dead body is found buried under the rubble of his basement, following an earthquake that shook Mexico City. In his mansion a body hangs bleeding, producing the food necessary to feed the alchemist's hunger in exchange for time and youth.

Present-day Mexico City: the device is found inside one of many statuettes of angels bought and sold by the antique dealer Jesús Gris. On being held by Jesús, the jewelled golden case articulates mechanical insect-like legs and digs them into his hand. Meanwhile, Dieter, a dying industrialist in possession of the alchemist's diaries, is searching for the device for his own ends. His agents have bought him news of the antique dealer's collection of statuettes and he sends his nephew Angel de la Guardia to investigate.

Jesús has developed an itchy wound on his hand, inflicted by the device, and an unending thirst. The device winds itself up on his blood, feeding a living organism that inhabits it. He hides it inside his grand-daughter Aurora's teddy-bear. The next morning Jesús shaves off his moustache, feeling massively rejuvenated. But the shop has been broken into by Angel de la

Guardia in his unsuccessful search for the device. Jesús follows him back to the industrialist's vault. Dieter shows Jesùs the alchemist's diaries and warns him of the dangers of the device.

De la Guardia eventually catches up with Jesús, now hungering for human blood. The antique dealer refuses to tell him the whereabouts of the device so he pushes Jesús over a cliff inside a car. Jesús dies, but resurrects in the mortuary where his body is being patched up for the funeral service. Now undead, he escapes and wanders the city streets. He returns to the vault with Aurora, where he peels off his grey skin; underneath he is white. To add colour to his complexion he will need human blood, the industrialist informs him before he dies in the ensuing struggle. Jesús drinks the industrialist's blood but realises that he wants his grand-daughter's too. He throws himself from a rooftop with Angel de la Guardia, who dies in the fall. With the assistance of the Cronos device, Jesús survives, but smashes it and back at home with his wife and grandchild, he sacrifices himself by giving himself up to the light.

Turning away from the erotics of vampiric desire, *Cronos* rather surveys need, a banal thirst for blood which reaches its extraordinary climax with Jesús licking up blood from the floor of a men's toilet on New Year's Eve. "I am Jesús Gris," he announces. The names have to be translated for this film to really work for an English-speaking public: "I am Grey Jesús." Cronos tells the story of how the main character comes to embody his name, and die (so that she—Jesús's grand-daughter Aurora—may live). It is a film about the ruin of Jesús's body.

The young Mexican director Guillermo del Toro has insisted on how important Catholicism is to his story of ordinary vampirism (addiction). Thus, rather than merely falling into sentimentalism, the end of *Cronos* arguably remains faithful to the structure of the plot on which it is modelled—the death and resurrection of Christ—revealing the melodramatic dimension of the central story of Christian religion. The twist in the tale is that the symbolically cannibalistic relationship to Christ practised in Catholic liturgy is here pressed into the service of del Toro's film about a now vampiric Jesús (is vampirism to cannibalism what soup is to the main meal?). In this sense, del Toro's 'copy' interestingly transforms our relationship to the 'original'.

The connections between cinema and religion are well-known, but rarely have they been presented so pointedly in film—although this has always been an important dimension of the vampire genre, most recently in Coppola's version of *Bram Stoker's Dracula*. This is where the character of the young Aurora becomes so important, and not merely as a symbol of future hope or the object of Jesús' desire. Aurora is an onlooker: she stands by, witnessing the action of the film and the transformation of her grandfather. More than anything else, Aurora looks on, mesmerised and hardly comprehending what she sees. From this point of view, she stands in for the viewer, infantilising his or her gaze. And as a potential 'blood donor', she also represents the colour—red—that Jesús's white body lacks: when he finally dies, and gives himself up to the light, his white skin is confused with the screen with which the film ends. If Jesús represents religion, Aurora might represent the cinema—and its most important colour, as both Godard and Polanski know very well. From the point of view of *Cronos*, and vampire films in general, film is essentially red and white, not black and white. It is this aspect of the cinematic experience—childish and religious—that cultural critics like Adorno warned against (and which film-makers like Spielberg market).

As is evident, like many contemporary films, *Cronos* is a film about film. It also, however, tells a movingly simple story about ageing, the yearning for more time, the fragility of the body and addiction. It quotes Cronenberg's Study of addiction, *Videodrome*—as Jesús inserts his hand under his grey skin before peeling it off—but its slightly lighter, humorous tone for some reason recalls another film about obsession, Patrice Leconte's *The Hairdresser's Husband*. The film's simple story line and slowed-down pace already distance it from the production values of conventional genre movies: it feels like an art-house film. More important, however, is the melancholic humour which Federico Luppi, who plays Jesús, displays towards this obsession with youth. In *Cronos*, however, this humour is eventually pushed to macabre extremes as the now resurrected Jesús, dressed up for his funeral, wanders the city streets with his black suit, white shirt and tie on back-to-front—as if his head had been twisted around (perhaps by Aurora) one hundred and eighty degrees: Jesús, un-dead and fragile, becomes a scruffy doll.

In this sense, *Cronos* remains a genre film, and like most vampire and horror movies from the American continent, it exhibits both the concerns of a post-colonial present unreconciled with the past (has the Cronos device been made from Aztec gold melted down by the Conquistadors? Is it Aztec sacrifice rather than Catholic ritual that makes its claim on Jesús?) and the perceived fragility of the body in a technologically changing world in which the machine-human interface is seen as increasingly blurred. The Cronos device is some kind of pre-industrial cyborg experiment gone horribly wrong.

VILLAGE VOICE, 4/5/94, p. 66, Georgia Brown

A flashy, ghoulish, but not very scary horror flick, *Cronos* is the prizewinning first feature by 29-year-old Guillermo del Toro from Guadalajara. The film swept the 1993 Ariels (Mexico's Oscars), was featured at Sundance and New Directors, and won the Grand Prize in Critics Week at Cannes last year, although I can't recall anyone mentioning it there.

In the 16th century, so the story goes, an alchemist fleeing from the Inquisition invented something called the Cronos Device, an elaborate gold scarab-shaped windup toy (it fits in the palm) with properties to overcome death. (Some living creature can be seen pulsing away inside.) Through an unlucky accident, however, the alchemist dies and the device gets mislaid. Then, in the latter part of the 20th century, it turns up, hidden inside a wooden angel, in the cluttered antique shop of the kindly, white-haired Jesús Gris (Federico Luppi).

Del Toro seems more interested in mood, or kinky bloodletting, than in psychology. His story's hero, Jesús, grandfather of the solemn Aurora (Tamara Shanath), is basically a cipher. Almost immediately "bitten" by the device, he becomes dependent on the pain/pleasure he experiences. He shaves his white mustache and indeed looks younger. The bug drives a hard bargain, however. One nasty side effect: He begins craving blood and is reduced to lapping another man's nosebleed off a restroom floor.

Meanwhile, an American, one of the ugly kinds—and one of the few named Dieter (Buñuel's actor, Claudio Brook)—is frantically seeking the device and quickly discovers where it is. Desperate to outwit his cancer, Dieter sends his thuggish nephew-henchman, Angel (Ron Perlman), to Jesús's shop. Following the wont of movie henchmen, Angel batters Jesús—well, he actually kills him, but Jesús, aided by the bug, doesn't die. Instead, he roams the alleys as a grisly cadaver until rescued by the fearless Aurora. Their relationship, the story's tender core, ought to be more touching than it is.

Del Toro seems less than gripped by his own story. There's no overriding logic to events and his characterizations tend to be campy set pieces. Angel and Dieter go through their villainous paces in slow motion. (You can predict every turn of the screw.) Angel's preoccupation with the nose job he'll get once his uncle kicks the bucket is the sort of quirk that comes out of any number of Hollywood noirs. The real creepiness of *Cronos* isn't where it ought to be—in the tale itself—but in the extraordinary bloodless detachment the film exudes.

Also reviewed in:
NEW YORK TIMES, 3/24/94, p. C16, Janet Maslin
VARIETY, 5/3/93, p. 41, Paul Lenti

CROOKLYN

A Universal Pictures release of a 40 Acres and a Mule production in association with Child Hoods Productions. *Executive Producer:* Jon Kilik. *Producer:* Spike Lee. *Director:* Spike Lee. *Screenplay:* Joie Susannah Lee, Cinqué Lee, and Spike Lee. *Story:* Joie Susannah Lee *Director of Photography:* Arthur Jafa. *Editor:* Barry Alexander Brown. *Music:* Terence Blanchard. *Music Editor:* James Flatto. *Sound:* Rolf Pardula and (music) James Nichols and Richard Clarke. *Casting:* Robi Reed. *Production Designer:* Wynn Thomas. *Art Director:* Chris Shriver. *Set Decorator:* Ted Glass. *Set Dresser:* Gary Aharoni, Anthony J. DiMeo, Philip Canfield, Deborah A. Dreyer, John W. Farraday, Robert Feltman, Howard Goldstein, Steve Krieger, Jeffrey Rollins, and James P. Sherman. *Special Effects:* Steve Kirshoff. *Costumes:* Ruth E. Carter. *Make-up:* Alvechia Ewing and Diane Hammond. *Stunt Coordinator:* Jeff Ward. *Running time:* 115 minutes. *MPAA Rating:* PG-13.

CAST: Alfre Woodard (Carolyn Carmichael); Delroy Lindo (Woody Carmichael); David Patrick Kelly (Tony Eyes); Zelda Harris (Troy); Carlton Williams (Clinton); Sharif Rashed (Wendell); Tse-Mach Washington (Joseph); Christopher Knowings (Nate); José Zuniga (Tommy La La); Isiah Washington (Vic); Ivelka Reyes (Jessica); Spike Lee (Snuffy); N. Jeremi Duru (Right Hand Man); Frances Foster (Aunt Song); Norman Matlock (Clem); Patriece Nelson (Viola); Joie Susannah Lee (Aunt Maxine); Vondie Curtis-Hall (Uncle Brown); Tiasha Reyes (Minnie); Raymond Reliford (Possom "George"); Harvey Williams (Possom "Tracey"); Peewee Love (Possom "Greg"); Bokeem Woodbine (Richard); Mildred Clinton (Mrs. Columbo); Emelise Aleandri (Florence); Omar Scroggins (Quentin); Danielle K. Thomas (Diane); Asia Gilyard (Cathy); Carmen Tillery (Brenda); Taneal Royal (Poochie); Kendell Freeman (Ronald); Kewanna Bonaparte (Peanut); Gary Perez (Juan); Arthur French (West Indian Store Manager); Manny Perez (Hector); RuPaul (Bodega Woman); Yolande Morris (Sheila); Dan Grimaldi (Con Ed Man); Susan Jacks (Tammy); David Patrick Kelly (Jim); Christopher Wynkoop (TV Evangelist); René Ojeda (Louie); Tracy Vilar (Monica); Keith Johnson (Cornell); Michele Shay (Drunk Woman); Hector M. Ricci, Jr. (Tito); Nadijah Abdul-Khalia (Vicki); Bruce Hawkins (Funeral Mourner); Richard Whiten and Michell Rosario (Neighbors); Maurie A. Chandler (Judy); Monet A. Chandler (Jody); Zay Smith (Boy in Street); Derrick Peart, Ulysses Terrero, Johnette Cook, and Desirée Murray (Supermarket Customers).

CHRISTIAN SCIENCE MONITOR, 5/16/94, p. 12, David Sterritt

Some artists feel a constant obligation to top themselves, making each enterprise more ambitious than the last. But others take a more sensible approach. As he was finishing the epic "Malcolm X" a couple of years ago, Spike Lee let it be known that his next picture would have a very different tone. It would be smaller and more intimate, he said—a personal project with a close-to-home feel.

He kept his word. "Crooklyn" is the warmest, most engaging movie of Lee's ever-fascinating career, exploring the rewards and challenges of family life with a good-humored casualness he's never shown before. It's not his best movie—a label still reserved for "Do the Right Thing," his 1989 masterpiece—but it's certainly the most lovable, revealing unexpected new depths in Lee's artistic personality.

The story focuses on the Carmichaels, an African-American family doing its best to live a contented life in a modest Brooklyn brownstone during the 1970s. Carolyn is the hard-pressed mother with five energetic children to handle. Woody is the out-of-work father, a musician whose artistic ideals get in the way of practical matters such as earning a living for his household.

Among the kids, the most irresistible is 10-year-old Troy, who uses her status as the only girl to coax as much special treatment as possible from her sometimes exasperated parents. She's clearly the princess of this little kingdom, and while the movie starts as a tale about all the Carmichaels, it soon makes Troy the central character of its loosely knit narrative—showing her to be as imperfect as she is adorable, prone to such unprincess-like behavior as fighting, nagging, and even shoplifting just for the naughty thrill.

Although most of "Crooklyn" is an affectionate look at the Carmichaels in their everyday Brooklyn surroundings, the centerpiece of the movie is a visit to a Southern branch of the family, which takes Troy in when financial hardships break her household apart. Here she copes with a strait-laced aunt and a feisty cousin, learning new lessons about life and growing up a little in the process. In the film's last portion she needs every speck of maturity she's acquired, as her return to Brooklyn coincides with the serious illness of her mother. The end of the story is both bitter and sweet, yet as life-affirming as everything that's come before.

On one level, "Crooklyn" works as a colorful chronicle of city life, depicting things as diverse as street-side games, weirded-out neighbors, and the ways children amuse themselves when stoops and sidewalks are their only playgrounds. Avoiding stereotyped visions of inner-city strife, Lee takes special pleasure in such details as the junk foods that provide the Carmichael kids with between-meals sustenance, and the lily-white programs that dominate TV screens in their mostly black neighborhood.

On another level, the movie is an engrossing comedy-drama with uncommon degrees of insight and empathy. These qualities are embedded in the ambling screenplay written by Lee with his sister and brother, Joie Susannah Lee and Cinque Lee, who based the story on their own memories of growing up. Also commendable are the superb performances by Alfre Woodard as Mom, Delroy Lindo as Dad, Zelda Harris as Troy, and an excellent supporting cast.

On yet another level, "Crooklyn" is Lee's most inventively *cinematic* film in years, with a camera that tracks, travels, swoops, and glides into every nook of its Brooklyn surroundings and every cranny of its characters' lives. The most daring visual coup happens during the Southern portion of the story, filmed with a distorting (anamorphic) lens that's deliberately "wrong" from a technical standpoint but hilariously right in its ability to convey the cramped, uncomfortable feelings that settle on Troy until she sets foot in Brooklyn again. This is sure to be among the year's most controversial filmmaking maneuvers but in my view it's a bold and bodacious success.

"Crooklyn" is a small-scale movie even when not measured against the massive "Malcolm X" that preceded it. Unfolding its characters' experiences through a slender story with a meandering structure, it's best watched in a quiet mood geared to small revelations and subtle surprises. On its own intimate terms, it's one of the most winning films on family life to reach the screen in ages.

LOS ANGELES TIMES 5/13/94, Calendar/p. 1, Kenneth Turan

Not everyone can tell a story, and not even good storytellers can't tell all stories equally well. And the most personal stories are often the hardest to convey to an audience that lacks the teller's intimate connection to the material. And so it is with writer-director Spike Lee's latest film, "Crooklyn."

Officially Lee, who co-wrote "Crooklyn" with his sister Joie and his brother Cinqué, will say only that the writers "drew some of their inspiration from their own lives." But interviews have indicated that this 1970s story of four brothers and a sister growing up in the Ft. Greene section of Brooklyn has more than a glancing resemblance to the details of the Lee family's situation.

For a director like Spike Lee, an adept cinematic polemicist whose best work, from "Do the Right Thing" to "Malcolm X," has never strayed far from film's hardest edges, this turn to the fuzzy, non-controversial areas of warm memory and nostalgia is a noticeable departure.

And there is something refreshing about seeing a studio film involved with a group like the Carmichaels, a feisty African American family with concerned and loving parents trying to do the best for their rambunctious kids. And having strong actors like Alfre Woodard and Delroy Lindo playing teacher Carolyn Carmichael and her jazz musician husband, Woody, can only add power to the mix.

But though this is a situation with potential, not to mention one that the director has a personal stake in, it does not play to Lee's strengths. Partly as a result, "Crooklyn" has turned out not particularly involving, an undernourished, aimless film that despite occasional moments of emotional connection never gets up a noticeable head of steam.

For one thing, "Crooklyn" does without much of a plot line. Set almost exclusively on the Brooklyn block where the Carmichaels have a brownstone, it is an episodic piece of work, with an unfocused script that adds incident to incident without much connective tissue to tie all of it together.

That block looks to have been a lively and multicultural one, with Italians and Latinos as well as black people getting on one another's nerves, a chaotic place but one with a heart. The setting is in its own way an age of innocence, when shoplifting was the worst crime and glue-sniffers (one of whom is played by Lee himself) the most dangerous characters.

What the Lee siblings' script places in this background are situations of the "remember when" variety, like "Remember when the electricity got turned off? or "Remember when Mom woke us up at 4 a.m. to do the dishes?" While some incidents, like the time oldest son Clinton (Carlton Williams) goes to an NBA championship game instead of his father's concert, are admittedly based on real incidents, they lack the consistently empathetic touch that would provide the emotional weight and meaning for an audience these situations have for the filmmakers.

Most noticeable in this respect is the interlude when daughter Troy (Zelda Harris) goes to visit a stuffy aunt in Maryland, a situation similar to the one at the center of "The Inkwell." The entire sequence is filmed with a distorting anamorphic lens, theoretically to emphasize how off-kilter the visit looked to Troy. What it feels like is a concerted attack on the aunt's bourgeois sensibility that plays more merciless and hostile than perhaps Lee intended.

Where "Crooklyn" is most successful and most involving is in the drawing of individual characters. Woodard is luminous as always as the mother who worries that her family is getting out of control, and Lindo is her match as the father determined to march to no one's music but his own. Also a pleasure is young Zelda Harris, who brings a fiery spirit to the role of Troy. With characters this alive, it's a pity that no one was able to build a more convincing film around them, instead of leaving everyone more or less out there on their own.

NEW YORK, 5/16/94, p. 88, David Denby

In Spike Lee's movies, everyone talks at once, and egos slam into one another like moths in a jar. Lee doesn't tell stories; he assembles charged-up vignettes, and at times, the frazzled audience, overstimulated by color and language, may be wondering, Why are we looking at this? In *Jungle Fever*, for instance, the central love story between a black man and a white woman got lost in the welter of huffy opinions everyone had about the affair. The relationship turned into a public event without ever quite becoming a private one. Spike Lee may have been saying that an interracial couple in New York can't *find* privacy, but if so, it was a self-defeating point. A love affair missing the dangers and pleasures of intimacy seemed like no love affair at all.

Inside the vignettes, Lee usually gets as many discordant notes and contradictory opinions going as possible. He's neither a frightened nor a simpleminded man, and his candor can be very exciting. He has never hesitated to show, for example, the weaknesses as well as the strengths of his black characters. His movies are about individual souls. Since he has superb judgment about actors, he has created one memorable character after another.

There are many reasons to be disappointed in *Crooklyn*—Lee's semi-autobiographical portrait of family life in Brooklyn during the seventies—but one of the main ones is that the two central characters never become grand enough. Woody (Delroy Lindo), the father, an unsuccessful jazz musician stranded at his piano, is a dignified but self-absorbed man. Delroy Lindo ("West Indian Archie" in *Malcolm X*) has a heavy, creased presence—one of the great lived-in faces and voices in current movies—and we wait for Woody to emerge as someone strong. Terrifically reassuring with his five children, Woody nevertheless brings no money into the house, and he casts an unfair burden onto his wife. But how should we take him? As a good musician who's been overlooked or as a narcissist deluded about his own talent? Spike Lee's actual father, Bill Lee, is also a jazz musician, and working with autobiographical material may have inhibited him (as well as his sister, Joie, and brother Cinqué, who worked on the screenplay).

Woody's wife, Carolyn (Alfre Woodard), teaches school and takes care of the five children and the family's beautiful old brownstone. There are endless scenes at the table, in the kitchen, in the TV room, and Carolyn is often in a rage—angry not so much at the children as at her unwanted fate as the drill sergeant who has to whip everyone into shape. Alfre Woodard has a few soft moments in which she's very lovely, but the screenplay doesn't give her enough to work with, and she's not particularly convincing as a work-horse mom. Her Carolyn seems a finer woman than the household drudge she's become—but finer for what purpose? What are the spiritual opportunities she's missing? If Lee is going to make something of the black family theme (and I appreciate that he wants to show sides of life normally ignored in movies), then he's got to go much deeper than this.

Lee gathers the vignettes together—there's plenty of life and Lee's flashing red and blues—but he doesn't build them into anything. (What happens between Woody and Carolyn is a relationship but not a story.) Most of the film is a celebration of Brooklyn as it once was, or as Spike Lee dreams it once was. Playing on the street, the kids enjoy a rowdy but innocent neighborhood life whose greatest danger is the pair of glue-sniffers who occasionally swoop down and try to stuff an innocent face into their fume-filled paper bag. (Are these the crooks of the baffling title?) There are neighborhood eccentrics—a screechy white man, effulgent Puerto Ricans with luscious hair. People get mad and sometimes even throw a punch, but that's the extent of the violence.

Despite the vociferous activity of many characters, the movie has a tentative, almost unformulated quality, perhaps because the Lees were torn between trying to tell the truth and trying to create a workable fiction (my unsolicited advice: Always choose fiction). Woody and

Carolyn's 10-year-old daughter, Troy (Zelda Harris), the only girl, takes over the last third of the movie, which turns out to be a strategic mistake. Zelda Harris is a beautiful and expressive child (she's 8), but her Troy is too young for dramatic experience. When she's sent off to a prissy, genteel aunt, Lee is reduced to using a distorting lens to give the scenes some spice. Troy feels a growing identification with her overburdened mother, but that's the kind of material—the growth of sensibility and character—that Lee's pinwheel-vignette style can't handle.

Spike Lee gets the music and the clothes right but forgets to ask what the period details are for. In a word, *Crooklyn* is boring. Spike Lee made this movie because he had the power to make it, not because he had something he wanted to say. He needs desperately to work with a good screenwriter. Over and over, he's trying to pull entire movies out of himself, and his "self" is a whirl of contradictions. At this point, no amount of high-flown talk about how central "collage" is to black culture can disguise the evidence of a talented director flying to pieces.

NEW YORK POST, 5/13/94, p. 38, Michael Medved

The best thing about "Crooklyn" is that, for most of its running time, it doesn't even feel like a Spike Lee movie.

In this warm and winning memory film, the characters and story seem to come first, not the director with his annoying habit of calling attention to himself.

The screenplay, on which Lee collaborated with his sister and brother, is an obviously autobiographical account of the struggles of a black family inhabiting a comfortable Brooklyn brownstone in the early '70s.

Like the real-life Lees, the movie's Carmichael clan includes an iron-willed school teacher mother (Alfre Woodward), a dreamy, often-unemployed jazz musician father (Delroy Lindo), four active boys and one sensitive girl (splendid newcomer Zelda Harris).

The film tells its story through her sad, serious eyes, as the family battles financial setbacks, separation of the parents and tragic illness.

The Lees do a remarkable job of recapturing the alternately loving and sadistic details of their childhood interaction with one another; anyone who grew up in a home with several siblings will instantly recognize this special brand of madness.

Alfre Woodard, one of today's most consistently superb performers, once again does Oscar-caliber work as the heroic mother, fighting single-handedly to hold back the tide of chaos that constantly threatens to engulf her family.

Her battles are occasionally painfully funny: When she accusingly yells upstairs, "Are you watching TV?" the five kids respond in emphatic unison "No"—even while they're all glued to "The Partridge Family."

Ironically, given Spike Lee's very public estrangement from his real-life father, jazz musician Bill Lee, the tender father in the movie comes across even more sympathetically than his long-suffering wife.

Delroy Lindo, who played West Indian Archie in "Malcolm X," does such a magnificent job of projecting his character's fierce love for wife and kids that the role should make him a major star.

The chief weakness in "Crooklyn" (aside from the title, which makes no sense for a film about a family that isn't crooked in the least) is an occasional sense of incoherence and loose ends—as if what we're seeing is a severely edited version of what once amounted to a much longer film.

If this is true, one can hope that Lee will someday release an expanded edition of "Crooklyn." These enormously endearing characters could certainly hold our attention for a more extended running time.

Only once near the end of this fine film does Lee's trademark self-indulgence reassert itself: During an extended sequence showing the little girl's visit to an aunt down South, the director suddenly shifts to an anamorphic lens, creating a funhouse effect that inexplicably alters the way the characters fit into the frame.

Despite this annoying interlude, Lee for the most part, lets the story tell itself, showing us what an interesting and effective filmmaker he can be when he deigns to take his foot off our chest and get his hot director's breath out of our faces.

NEWSDAY, 5/13/94, Part II/p. B3, Jack Mathews

The news was good that Spike Lee was setting aside his anger for a while, in order to make a sensitive comedy-drama about life for a family very much like his own in early '70s Brooklyn. Lee is an important filmmaker, the agitator general of the New Wave in African-American cinema, but his recent movies have been so bereft of humor and everyday humanity, it's been like watching a raw nerve flailing on the screen.

"Crooklyn," co-written by Lee with his brother Cinqué and "sister Joie Susannah Lee, has wit, humanity and tenderness to spare, and, with the performances of the always-good Alfre Woodard as matriarch of the Carmichael clan, and marvelous Delroy Lindo as her immature husband, it features two of his best-developed and most sympathetic characters.

What it doesn't have is a lick of narrative coherence. It's three very different movies in one, the first a jumble of childhood impressions, the second an ill-conceived farce, the third—and best— a bittersweet personal reminiscence.

A story does get told, from the point of view of 10-year-old Troy (Zelda Harris), about a family stretched to the breaking point by financial woes and emotionally strengthened through tragedy. But Lee's quirky choices and frequently clumsy execution make it more work than it should be to enjoy.

The best hour of "Crooklyn" is a noisy collision of ideas, characters, jokes, fights and feuds, pop symbolism, and random incidents, all intended to draw us into the chaotic whirl of daily life in the Carmichaels' brownstone, and in their ethnically mixed neighborhood but driving us away instead.

Lee's choppy, episodic style worked well in "Do the Right Thing," where he effectively got his audience to feel the racial tension building in his story. But family tension is a different matter altogether, and despite his attempts to show the underlying love among the Carmichaels, theirs remains a very uninviting household.

Through all the snap, crackle and pop of Lee's images, a family portrait does emerge. Of four boys, a girl, a proud, unemployed jazz musician dad, and an exhausted working mother. Of siblings squabbling over the television set (what's it going to be, "The Partridge Family," the Knicks game, or "Soul Train"?), and parents screaming at each other over unpaid bills.

That "Crooklyn" is Troy's story isn't clear until an hour into the movie, when her separated and financially strapped parents pack her off to live with a cartoonishly snooty aunt, her browbeaten husband and their over-protected daughter in a suburb in Maryland.

In a numbingly wrong-headed decision, Lee shot every scene at the relatives' house with an uncorrected wide lens, distorting everything and everybody like images in a funhouse mirror. The silliness that occurs in this tediously long segment, which edifies Troy's homesickness and Lee's disdain for the 'burbs, isn't worth the effort or the eyestrain.

Lee shows up himself in the film's other misguided comic invention, playing Snuffy, a neighborhood glue-sniffer who has a tendency to foam at the mouth and float upside-down when he gets high.

Snuffy is one of a host of non-sequiturs populating the carnival-like neighborhood. There's the fussy androgyne downstairs with the Coke-bottle glasses and the smelly dogs, the twitchy Vietnam vet boarding with the Carmichaels, a couple of grouchy women guarding their stoop. Career cross-dresser RuPaul even shows up, sexually taunting a horny Latino shopkeeper, a grotesque scene no more meaningless than any of the others occurring in view of the Carmichaels.

The real strength, the *only* strength, of "Crooklyn," is the warmth of the relationships between Troy and each of her parents, which is made possible by the indelibly fine work of Woodard and Lindo (West Indian Archie in Lee's "Malcolm X"). Zelda Harris is only 8, and never very convincing as the 10-year-old she's playing, but in the last 20 minutes, when a tragic illness shakes the movie loose of its trivial beginnings and gives shape to the lives of at least these three characters, "Crooklyn" becomes irresistibly tender.

Lee doesn't quite pull the rabbit out of the hat in these final moments, but he does show that he can handle sentiment with some finesse. The irony of his career so far is that while he hasn't flinched at expressing his anger and his intellectual outrage, his personal sensitivity has been a tenaciously guarded secret.

If he ever manages to balance his politics and humanity, something great might happen.

NEWSWEEK, 5/23/94, p. 60, David Ansen

In "Crooklyn," a memory film about growing up in Brooklyn in the '70s, Spike Lee abandons the Big Issues that generate his movies, and seems at a loss. Using 9-year-old Troy (the charming Zelda Harris) as his prism, Lee presents the Carmichael family, struggling to make ends meet, Father (Delroy Lindo) is a purist jazz composer who can't get work in a rock era. Mother (Alfre Woodard), a teacher, does the worrying and the screaming, riding herd on her five rowdy, TV-obsessed kids. Intended to be a tough-love saint, she comes across as a nag. "Crooklyn" is a family affair—Lee co-wrote it with his sister Joie Susannah and brother Cinqué—but the semiautobiographical script never shapes reminiscence into art. It's not the lack of story that makes it Lee's dullest movie, but its refusal to dig beneath the skin of its characters. Lee seems to confuse noise with drama: the bickering Carmichaels create quite a racket, but we're seldom moved by their plight. In his most desperate moment, Lee shoots a long sequence through a distorted lens. This is meant to show how disoriented Troy is, but most people will just think the projectionist screwed up.

NEW STATESMAN & SOCIETY, 3/31/95, p. 33, Jonathan Romney

When a major director makes a film that you can't get to see, it's always tempting to think it must be too exotic for public consumption. Sometimes it halfway is. The current Barry Levinson video-only release, *Jimmy Hollywood*, is head and shoulders above his hit *Disclosure*; but it bombed in the US, presumably by virtue of being too downbeat about the Tinseltown myth.

The latest *film maudit* to be rescued in Britain is Spike Lee's *Crooklyn*. After distributors UIP decided not to release it here, it was picked up by independent black distributor Electric Avenue. But *Crooklyn* is disappointing. Not disappointing as in: not as good as *Do the Right Thing*, but disappointing as in: what was he thinking of? The idea was good: a largely non-narrative evocation of Lee's early 1970s Brooklyn childhood. At just under two hours, *Crooklyn* is like an extended sitcom with sprawling, anarchic energies. Hitching most of its short scenes to classic soul numbers, it's mainly set in the brownstone inhabited by the Carmichael family. Father Woody (Delroy Lindo) is an idealistic jazz musician failing to make ends meet, while mother Carolyn (Alfre Woodard) is a teacher who earns the crust, balances the books and polices their five boys and one girl—10-year-old Troy (Zelda Harris), who acts as our guide to the Carmichael world.

Crooklyn scores its best shot in the credit sequence. Lee and cinematographer Arthur Jafa give us soaring crane moves and a selection of close-ups taking in a vista of street life, *Play School* style: kids playing clapping games, spinning tops and skipping ropes, all set to a breezy Stylistics number. Lee, who has stated his weariness with the current rut of rap-driven urban drama, effectively presents this hive of activity as a counterweight to the now-clichéd street panoramas of black American cinema—the tense homeboys-in-hell scenario of the *Boyz N The Hood* school. Instead, he gives us a largely untainted Eden, a safe adventure playground. "The worst thing that could happen", Lee has reminisced, "was that somebody might take your lunch money. Nobody was pulling an Uzi and spraying bullets." Because we're so used to seeing that violence, *Crooklyn* comes across as a film specifically about its absence: this whole sequence seems to be saying, if only kids could play stoopball again, no one would need to make films about drive-by shootings any more.

Lee co-wrote and co-produced the film with his brother and sister Cinqué and Joie, and it's because *Crooklyn* is seen through the optic of sibling togetherness that it never quite focuses, either as an idyll or as a tougher-edged reminiscence of the "We were poor but happy" variety. There is a harshness to this world, but the children's constant uproar drowns it out. The soundtrack keeps up a barrage of flip backchat, street noise, TV racket and chart hits, which simply seems to obscure any real drama: as if the film were afraid of silence.

The choice of period hits, fabulous though they are, to drive the action tends to obscure it, either with bludgeoning obviousness or by being too powerful. When Woody and Carolyn argue, Lee feels compelled to set us straight about their relationship with The Persuaders' "Thin Line Between Love and Hate"; when Carolyn kicks Woody out, the poignancy is lost because our attention is distracted by The Staples Singers. In one scene, Carolyn rouses the kids from bed with astounding vehemence; we know this is a comedy sequence because of the vigorous camera work and the briskness of Stevie Wonder's "Signed, Sealed, Delivered". Otherwise, we might easily think we were seeing a dysfunctional family at boiling point: when Carolyn yells at a kid, "You're gonna be crazy when I beat the brains out of your head," it's asking us to take a lot on trust to believe that this is anything other than horrifying. There's an alarming misjudgment in what's perceived as comic: zanier pranks include swinging a cat by its tail, and a dog getting crushed in a fold-out bed. They're jaw-droppingly mishandled: but then maybe they're Lee-family in-jokes.

The problem is this sense of whatever is part of the Carmichael family universe is basically good, while the rest of the world can stuff it. The kids shunt garbage into the yard of nerdy white neighbour Tony Eyes, and we're asked to take it on trust that he deserves it because his apartment smells awful. Likewise, a local glue sniffer Snuffy (Lee himself) receives a horrific blow on the head from Troy: the film just wants us to applaud her precocious feistiness.

The film doesn't even try to communicate. In the family scenes, there's a rare sense of kids just being kids, which must have been hard to achieve; but it makes it impossible to figure out who's saying what. After its first third, *Crooklyn* risks losing us completely: a sequence down south is inexplicably shot with a Scope lens, so that everything's suddenly stretched, and in a cursory final section, Carolyn dies and everything takes a turn for the lachrymose.

The one scene where Lee seems to be onto something genuinely strange is when Troy is confronted by the miraculous sight of a swaying, seven-foot drag queen (the much-feted Ru Paul). It's uncomfortable to be making a plea for the flagrantly bizarre, but at moments like this, and in the weird figure of Tony Eyes, you're suddenly aware of the strangeness of childhood, its frights and anxieties. Because she's so caught up in the family world, nothing outside it really seems to faze Troy. Childhood is a time of much darker perceptions than *Crooklyn* suggests, but the drive here seems to be to minimise the strangeness of the outside world. There's one contemporary hit that surprisingly isn't on the soundtrack, but then this is already too much of a "Family Affair".

TIME, 5/16/94, p. 81, Richard Schickel

Spike Lee is better at setting agendas than he is at making movies. The laudable intention behind *Crooklyn* is, he says, to move beyond "the hip-hop, drug, gangsta-rap, urban-inner-city movies," which he claims constitute "a rut" into which black filmmakers have fallen. He has a point, though some of his competitors' work (for example, *The Inkwell* has shown more range than he cares to admit. What he does not have here is a movie that attractively accomplishes his goal.

The Carmichaels are a middle-class black family living in Brooklyn in the early '70s. The father, Woody (Delroy Lindo), is a jazz musician who doesn't get much work because he only wants to play music he respects. He is easygoing and indulgent of his children, four boys and a girl, Troy (played by the adorable and spirited Zelda Harris in her first major role). The mother, Carolyn (Alfre Woodard), is hardworking and hard-nosed. She loves the kids but believes in discipline and denial.

This story may be in part autobiographical (Lee wrote it with his sister Joie Susannah and his brother Cinque), but the characters and their situation also owe something to 1945's *A Tree Grows in Brooklyn*, in which an immigrant family offered similar characters, though not so large a family, facing the same basic problems: clinging to their respectability and trying to make certain the kids grow up smart, honest and able to claim a surer place for themselves in the world.

These are good issues to make a movie about; most American families have faced them in one form or another. They transcend race and locale, and are rendered more poignant when you remember that the Carmichael kids are going to have to face prejudice too.

But our natural sympathy for the Carmichaels is sabotaged by crude and careless moviemaking. The first half of the film is a jumble of pointless anecdotes that fail to pull into a compelling narrative scheme or establish characters of any dimension. The boys squabble endlessly, humorlessly, inconsequentially, and Lindo and Woodard, both fine actors, are given only one note apiece to sound, respectively patience and impatience. In a middle passage, little Troy is sent to visit relatives in the South for no particular reason, except possibly to register Lee's disdain of smug bourgeois ways, and to contrast this with the fractiousness of her siblings and the liveliness of city street life. In the end, as if to make up for missed dramatic opportunities, Carolyn Carmichael is suddenly stricken with an undefined terminal illness. But fear, grief, loss—the powerful emotions bound to be loosed by this sudden realization of childhood's most terrifying fantasy—are avoided by Lee. Carolyn dies quietly offscreen. Her children, and the movie, are denied emotional release.

It is curious how often Lee's movies evade confrontation with the emotions or the controversial ideas they raise. Lee is a great self-promoter. After all his press releases and all his interviews, we are given films that are sketchy, unfelt and distancing—incidents in Lee's career, the only drama that really interests him.

SIGHT AND SOUND, 12/94, p. 44, Manohla Dargis

Brooklyn, the early 70s. The young Carmichael family—mother, father, four boys, one girl—live in a brownstone building that they own, renting out the top floor to a Vietnam veteran. The patriarch of the clan is Woody, a jazz musician who's seen better professional days; his wife Carolyn has recently returned to teaching. The cacophony of the street outside is matched by that of the dinner table, where Carolyn keeps order. When not arguing among themselves, the Carmichaels are plagued by their next door neighbour Tony Eyes, a would-be composer and small-dog owner. Although Tony is white and the Carmichaels are black, their racial difference is less at issue than the condition of Tony's foul-smelling apartment.

More pressing yet are Carolyn's attempts to discipline her five rowdy kids. In a quiet moment, however, Carolyn tells her daughter Troy she will be sent down south to spend a few weeks with relatives. Later, Woody interferes with another of Carolyn's attempts to control the children. Instead of siding with her, Woody takes the kids' side, infuriating her. Carolyn consequently asks him to leave, which he does for a few days. When Woody returns, he disappoints again because he has failed to pay the electric bill, causing the power to be cut.

Shortly after, Troy is sent south. There she befriends her cousin Viola, but remains less than fond of her aunt Song. A bible-thumper who dotes on her Pekinese, the aunt undoes Troy's braids and takes a hot comb to her hair. Troy pines for home and soon returns. At the airport in New York, she's met by another aunt and uncle who drive her to the hospital where the terminally ill Carolyn lies in wait. Soon afterwards, Carolyn dies.

Initially reluctant to attend her mother's funeral, Troy is convinced to go by her father. After the services, Clinton, the eldest Carmichael son, reaches out to his sister and takes her hand. Troy dreams that her mother is still alive, only to break down weeping in her mother's arms. Later, she imagines that Carolyn visits her. When the youngest son, Jimmy, asks Troy if he can play around outside, she consents. Troy follows him out, smiles, and gazes on a Brooklyn street full of children.

For a number of years now, Spike Lee has made more of a name for himself as an ideologue and entrepreneur than as a film-maker. Although he's one of the busiest of directors—six features, in addition to TV commercials, music videos, a production company, a record business, retail stores—his off-screen words and deeds have often commanded as much if not more attention than his work in film. Whatever the personal gain, Lee's extra-curricular activities have cost him dearly. Acclaimed by the black community (at least publicly), patronised, condemned and fetishised by the white media, the artist has been swamped by his own creation, a phenomenon otherwise known as Spike Lee.

Crooklyn is Lee's most personal work since his startling debut eight years ago with *She's Gotta Have It*, and decidedly his best to date. The semi-autobiographical film, which Lee co-wrote with his sister Joie and younger brother Cinqué, traces the emotional arc of the fictional Carmichael family over a few crucial months during the early 70s, a sentimental interlude that closes in tragedy. Amy Taubin has called the film "operatic", and it's not for nothing that in one scene the clan's patriarch and resident tortured artist Woody proclaims that he's writing a folk opera. Some 20 years after the fact, Lee has done just that.

Woody is a purist under siege. A composer and jazz musician, he's pressured by his wife Carolyn to compromise his art to put food on the table. Although clearly adoring, Carolyn is weary of playing the heavy for both her kids and husband. When Woody complains about her lack of support (he's just bounced his fifth cheque of the month), she reacts with fury, storming,

"I can't even take a piss without six people hanging off my tits," and pointedly counting him into the equation.

Bristling with passion, Carolyn is by turns nurturing and punishing, a woman whose frustrations with her family are tempered by overwhelming love. She's also Lee's most complicated female character since his first feature, and her eventual departure goes a long way toward explaining the general failings of his other cinematic women. While Woody sneaks the kids sweets and spins out promises, Carolyn is the one who rises at dawn, conjures the meals, and does time from nine to five. Tougher than Woody, and demonstrably less sympathetic, she's the only parent who's keeping it together.

For all that *Crooklyn* is a family melodrama, nearly as much time is devoted to the outside action as that rolling about inside the Carmichael brownstone. Lee launches his film with one of his characteristic flourishes, the camera sweeping over a riot of sounds and images, rushing to keep pace with all the children running, jumping and hurtling through these less than mean streets. This is Brooklyn as it use to be, a place where gossiping neigbours outnumber jiving glue sniffers, and racial unease simmers but rarely burns. More to the point, this is Brooklyn as remembered by its children.

One of the remarkable things about this remarkable film is that much of it is seen though the eyes of a nine-year-old African American girl. Troy is both the film's conduit and its wellspring, the one for whom the world slows down to a sensuous crawl, or squeezes together for a surreal kink. Devoted to her mother, enamoured with her daddy, Troy's gender makes her an outsider within the litter as well as, the script suggests, a keener witness to the family romance. For all that the boys of the Carmichael Five struggle to rock their world, it's Troy who signifies the loudest.

Shaped more by sensation than by narrative thrust, *Crooklyn* unfolds through a succession of shifting scenes, some little more than shots. With one striking exception (Troy's trip south, a sequence lasting roughly 20 minutes and related entirely through the use of an anamorphic lens), the mood is familiar, intimate, soulful. Arthur Jafa's camera keeps close to characters but doesn't crowd them, while the extraordinary soundtrack, as lush as that in *GoodFellas*, eases everyone on their way.

The original definition of melodrama is drama with music, and there's scarcely a moment in *Crooklyn* that isn't punctuated by either Terence Blanchard's plangent score or the wild style of over three dozen hot licks, pop hits, ballads, lamentations and sundry witless ditties. As much as the dialogue or lighting, it's music that shapes the film, filling in texture and building density. From Curtis Mayfield to the Partridge Family, the Carmichael awash in music, a fact that has as much to do with Woody's calling as with the cultural moment in which the director himself came of age. Long before he found his voice in film, Lee had discovered the pulse and pleasures of Brooklyn, New York.

VILLAGE VOICE, 5/17/94, p. 49, J. Hoberman

Deft or clumsy, Spike Lee is one of the most visceral of American filmmakers, directing each of his movies as though it were a campaign, if not a life or death struggle. Lee may have been liberated by the labor of *Malcolm X*, but he's not a man to take anything lightly. The iridescent poster of *Crooklyn*'s happy, house-proud family has blossomed like a summer bouquet on the city's subway platforms, but the movie it advertises is as clamorous and compelling as the scene around it.

If *Crooklyn* has been positioned as a nostalgic urban pastoral, it's still typically stressful. The joint is jumping. Lee treats the spectacle of a 10-year-old girl's coming of age in the early 1970s with a kind of frantic innocence. As the title suggests, *Crooklyn* is more state of being than narrative. For much of the movie, there's no particular plot. Set in and around the Carmichael family's comfortably cluttered Brooklyn brownstone, it's a flow of situations—the bits of business ricochet out like a spaldeen off a stoop, whizzing by your ear too quick to catch.

Crooklyn's dense, anecdotal script was written by siblings Spike, Joie, and Cinqué Lee; like their parents, the Carmichaels have four boys and a girl. Dad is a struggling jazz musician and mom an acerbic schoolteacher, both distinguished more by bohemian-nationalist attire than middle-class attitude. Professional parents, lots of kids, big old Brooklyn house: There's a sense in which *Crooklyn* reimagines the reigning family sitcom of the Reagan era, infusing Cosby's idealized rationality with the grittier specifics of the Lee family drama. Given the arguments over family finances or the kids' TV time, the Carmichael parents are a lot less relaxed than the Huxtables. Woody (Delroy Lindo) is alternately feckless and indulgent; fiery, practical Carolyn (Alfre Woodard) can be tender, although she's more often two steps from full-blown rage: "I can't even take a piss without six people hanging off my tits." Perhaps it was inevitable that Lee would become a show business maestro. In a family of five children, everything has to be performed for an audience (even if it's only eating Trix and watching some televised Hanna-Barberity). Everybody's face is in everyone else's—the Carmichael house is a world of continual self-assertion. The family is introduced fighting, as families will, over food, with Carolyn's maternal admonition to "put the salt down before I pull your head off" segueing to a shot of five kids watching a war movie on TV. (Naturalistically, the television is virtually a third parent, beaming out the comical cross-reference of *The Partridge Family* as well as basketball, cartoons, and ads for Afro-Sheen.)

The child star of Lee's last anti-sitcom, *Jungle Fever*, was a paradigm of cuteness so pert that she registered the sound of her parents' lovemaking with the knowing chuckle of a precocious Dr. Ruth. In *Crooklyn*, however, the kids' ensemble is never cloying and impressively self-absorbed. In addition to the protagonist Troy (Zelda Harris), one sib stands out—the eldest, Clinton (Carlton Williams). Setting the evening tele-agenda, boldly slugging Redi-Whip from the aerosol can, Clinton is the family prince. A pan around his fetish-ridden room is introduced to the mock preening opening of Jean Knight's "Mr. Big Stuff." That he is also young Spike may be deduced from his glasses and baggy Knicks uniform—it's an affectionately deflationary caricature.

Indeed, Snagglepuss is scarcely the movie's lone cartoon. Crazy neighbor Tony Eyes, one of the residual Italians in the Carmichaels' "changing," mainly black and Latino neighborhood, raises poodles in his living room and rains garbage on the Carmichael yard. A pair of glue-sniffing lay-abouts (one of them played by the director) haunt the street and Troy's dreams like some comic-evil spirits of the bush—in one of the movie's playful stunts, the camera spins over as they get high and lets them walk, upside down, through the workaday world. There's a sort of black Rambo living upstairs in perpetual post-Vietnam stress, and no less a figure than RuPaul shows up in blond wig and pink hot pants, tantalizing a bodega employee half her size by grinding a slow Watusi buttshake to Joe Cuba.

Not just another stage, the bodega is an important site for Troy, who is busted there for trying to steal a 10-cent bag of potato chips. Troy is the Carmichael child most interactive with the world: As irate and volatile as her mother, she appropriates Clinton's collection of Indian-head nickels to buy her friends ice cream and boosts a steak from the supermarket because she's mortified to be shopping with food stamps. Troy gradually comes to inhabit the center of the movie, finally taking over its consciousness. Two-thirds of the way through, she goes to stay with relatives in a Virginia suburb, Lee switching to an anamorphic lens and shooting the entire sequence so that everything is squeezed thin for the maximum alienated Giacometti look.

After this, there's no denying that *Crooklyn* is an art film. In his way, Lee is as much a showboat as Brian De Palma, with his own brand of jangling expression and a kindred love for the overhead spiral-in. Despite the pyrotechnics of Arthur Jafa (cinematographer on *Daughters of the Dust*), Lee's most aggressive format busting is aural. Throughout *Crooklyn*, a wall-to-wall mix of late-'60s, early-'70s soul works with and against the mellow harmonics of Terence Blanchard's neotraditional jazz. To call the score obtrusive is to miss the point. The soundtrack is one more assertive character, commenting on the action or, less often, being disrupted by it. (The Carmichael kids are watching *Soul Train* and dancing along, when Woody breaks in to deliver the news that Carolyn has cancer.)

Childhood, *Crooklyn* reminds us, is inherently overstimulating. The movie thrives on a pattern of emotional overlay and rhythmic disjunction made most apparent in the end credits combining vintage *Soul Train* with the rap title song. It's in every sense a raucous film—often so furious and unmodulated that the structural model might have been Sun Ra's organized chaos or Archie Shepp's strident "new thing." Certainly, life in the 'burbs has almost the same frenetic quality as life in the 'hood, even though the only two kids are Troy and her cousin and the lone permitted TV seems to be a white, Christian variety show.

To call *Crooklyn* the richest Hollywood movie released this year isn't much of a compliment. (The only competition is *That's Entertainment III.*) Still, when *Jungle Fever* opened here three years back, total strangers phoned me at home to complain because I made the unremarkable observation that "Spike Lee is one of the four or five most significant figures in current American cinema." Lee has long since established himself as a vivid presence on the national mediascape, as a canny business-artist, and an ambitious filmmaker. If sympathetic critics have glossed over his tendency toward shrill or awkward schematization, his humor (visual and verbal), inventive narrative economy, and skill with actors are far more often underestimated.

Lee is a force to be reckoned with: one, because he invented "Spike Lee," and two, because (like *Crooklyn*'s father, Woody) he's determined "to play his own music." The X on Lee's cap stands as much for experimentation as it does for exploitation—even more for existential. *Crooklyn* is full of love and confusion and a certain amount of score settling—a televised Knicks game affords the opportunity to rag on then player Phil Jackson. But it also suggests something willed on the screen because Lee wanted to see what it would look like and learn just what it was about.

The overt family involvement in *Crooklyn* (with its implied family rescue fantasy) serves to push the movie away from individual autobiography and personal psycho-drama toward the collective expression of myth. Perhaps because it sublimates his own sense of importance, Lee is comfortable as the socially responsible spokesperson for some entity larger than himself. In the context of *Crooklyn*, it's the involvement of his sister and brother that enables him to treat the material as though it had the same monumental significance as *Malcolm X*.

From the implied low angle of the movie's childhood perspective, Woody and Carolyn are the flawed giants who define the universe—assigning roles, making laws, defending (or attacking) their heedless brood, collapsing when one least expects it. They are prime causes, fierce and remote and ultimately inexplicable: "Why did Daddy have his concert tonight—the same exact night of the NBA Championship?" Clinton wails. That cry of revolt and incomprehension is truly universal. The tree that grows in *Crooklyn* isn't rooted in Lee's life so much as ours.

Also reviewed in:
CHICAGO TRIBUNE, 5/13/94, Friday/p. A, Michael Wilmington
NATION, 6/20/94, p. 882, Stuart Klawans
NEW REPUBLIC, 5/23/94, p. 34, Stanley Kauffmann
NEW YORK TIMES, 5/13/94, p. C5, Janet Maslin
NEW YORKER, 5/23/94, p. 93, Terrence Rafferty
VARIETY, 5/9-15/94, p. 68, Todd McCarthy
WASHINGTON POST, 5/13/94, p. D1, Desson Howe
WASHINGTON POST, 5/13/94, Weekend/p. 48, Joe Brown

CROW, THE

A Miramax/Dimension Films release in association with Entertainment Media Investment Corporation of an Edward R. Pressman production in association with Jeff Most Productions. *Executive Producer:* Robert L. Rosen. *Producer:* Edward R. Pressman and Jeff Most. *Director:* Alex Proyas. *Screenplay:* David J. Schow and John Shirley. *Based on the comic book series and comic strip by:* James O'Barr. *Director of Photography:* Dariusz Wolski. *Editor:* Dov Hoenig and Scott Smith. *Music:* Graeme Revell. *Music Editor:* Richard Bernstein. *Fight Choreographer:* Brandon Lee and Jeff Imada. *Sound:* Buddy Alper and (music) Brian Williams. *Sound Editor:* Dave McMoyler and John J. Miceli. *Casting:* Billy Hopkins and Suzanne Smith. *Production Designer:* Alex McDowell. *Art Director:* Simon Murton. *Set Designer:* William Barcley. *Set Decorator:* Marthe Pineau. *Special Effects:* J.B. Jones. *Costumes:* Arianne Phillips. *Make-up:* Sharon Ilson and Herita Jones. *Special Make-up Effects:* Lance Anderson. *Stunt Coordinator:* Jeff Imada. *Running time:* 105 minutes. *MPAA Rating:* R.

CAST: Brandon Lee (Eric Draven); Ernie Hudson (Albrecht); Michael Wincott (Top Dollar); David Patrick Kelly (T-Bird); Angel David (Skank); Rochelle Davis (Sarah); Bai Ling (Myca); Lawrence Mason (Tin Tin); Michael Massee (Funboy); Bill Raymond (Mickey); Marco Rodriguez (Torres); Sofia Shinas (Shelly); Anna Thomson (Darla); Tony Todd (Grange); Jon Polito (Gideon); Kim Sykes (Annabella); Rock Taulbee (Lead Cop); Norman "Max" Maxwell (Roscoe); Jeff Cadiente (Waldo); Henry King, Jr. (MJ); Erik Stabenau (Speeg); Cassandra Lawton (Newscaster); Lou Criscuolo (Uniform Cop #1); Todd Brenner (Paramedic #1); Joe West (Paramedic #2); Tom Rosales (Sanchez); Jeff Imada (Braeden); Tierre Turner (Jugger); Tim Parati (Bad Ass Criminal).

LOS ANGELES TIMES, 5/11/94, Calendar/p. 1, Peter Rainer

"The Crow," starring the late Brandon Lee, is like one long fright night. Even though it was photographed in color, the edge-of-darkness atmosphere descends on the audience like a shroud.

The "Batman" movies were probably the first to transfer the new style in doom-and-gloom comic book fantasias to the screen, but "The Crow" makes those films seem happy-go-lucky. On its own terms it's highly effective but that doesn't mean you have to accept its terms. It's almost unremittingly grungy and overwrought—"Blade Runner" with a hangover—with an eardrum-blasting industrial rock score to go with its eyeball-popping industrial rock look.

Tortured male adolescents will probably connect with the film's agonizing, horrific, masochistic pageantry of ghoulish tortures and high-style garrotings rhythemed to resemble a berserk rock video. The director Alex Proyas is an award-winning TV commercial and rock video director, and, along with screenwriters David J. Schow and John Shirley, he puts across this adaptation of the J. O'Barr "Crow" cult comic books with grim glee. He's selling pop pubescent nihilism with a stroboscopic, rock-hero kick.

Lee, who was accidentally shot dead on the set of "The Crow" with eight days of filming left, plays a Detroit rock guitarist, Eric Draven, who returns from the dead on Halloween eve, guided by a mysterious crow, to avenge his own gangland murder and that of his fianceé. Draven is, at least in his post-dead incarnation, a feral harlequin with a mime-white face and blood-red lipstick. He goes after each member of the gang responsible for the slaughter with a hyperbolic vengeance, we're encouraged to relish the killings, "Death Wish"-style. But "The Crow" is so far removed from any social agenda that, unlike the "Death Wish" films, its squashings and torchings are pure theater. It's a reactionary movie without anything to react against.

This is one of the few recent films where the bad guys are, literally, overshadowed by the hero. This overshadowing is an achievement, since a few of the nasties, including Top Dollar (Michael Wincott) and T-Bird (David Patrick Kelly), are scenery-chomping world-class scum. With his dirty lanky hair and noxious killer smiles, Top Dollar, who couples with his half-sister Myca (Bai Ling), is the gangland crime lord as polymorphous perverse Capone. The pointy-chinned T-Bird is like an atrocious imp—a self-winding mayhem machine.

Draven overwhelms their awfulness by flaunting his fire-and-brimstone invulnerability. Protected by the crow, which functions as a kind of aviary spirit guide, he wades into the fray and boggles his victims. There's something unreasonably satisfying about seeing bullies this bad get drubbed.

The only reason for a grown person to check out "The Crow" is for Lee—and not for sentimental reasons, either. What gives the movie its mite of "heart" is that, as Lee plays him, Draven's fury comes out of an almost operatic pain. Lee has phenomenal presence, and his movements are so balletically powerful that his rampages seem like waking nightmares. Lee keeps you watching "The Crow" when you'd rather look away. His death means there won't be a sequel to "The Crow"—no loss—but his star presence was the real thing.

NEW YORK, 5/23/94, p. 72, David Denby

The beauty of making live-action movies in cartoon style is that you can do anything you want without being confined by realism. The *danger* of making live-action movies in cartoon style is ...that you can do anything you want without being confined by realism. *The Crow*, based on James O'Barr's underground comic strip, tries to out-Tim Burton Tim Burton. The basic decor of this inner-city shock toon is black on black and disgustingly wet. Director Alex Proyas, an

Australian fabricator of music videos and commercials, has created a dark, cramped city, a vile, trashed landscape lighted by fires. It is always night and always raining. (Why does the rain not put out the fires? Don't ask.) Sadistic gangs run everything, and when one of them kills a rock singer, Eric Draven (Brandon Lee), and his fiancée, Draven, heralded and accompanied by a crow, comes back from the grave seeking vengeance.

Many people die. You may recall that the star, Brandon Lee (son of Bruce), also died; he was shot accidentally during the production. The performance, I suppose, is *his* return from death. He appears in whiteface, a beautiful ghoul who jumps, tumbles, climbs, and flies. Lee seethes his way through the role. In the end, the movie appears to have both killed and immortalized him in a single blow. To say that *The Crow* gives off bad vibes is a ridiculous understatement.

In brief, *The Crow* is the pop-nihilo event of the season, a cinematic Black Mass combining stupendous music-video-style visuals, perpetual violence, and a violently dead star playing a violently dead character. That *The Crow* is also profoundly repetitive, humorless, and boring may not be the point. That Alex Proyas can hardly direct a sequence, that nothing is cleanly staged or even cleanly *seen*, that one episode after another is composed of shock cuts, with each shot exploding into the previous one—none of that may be the point, either. *The Crow* is heading straight for cult status and midnight audiences. For people too tired or stoned to demand any kind of sense, the movie may be perfect. What a coup! Proyas has pulled off a cult-hit triumph without quite making a movie. He has unified the look and mood of his extended video around darkness and death.

Considering how frenzied *The Crow* is, it's a miracle that some of the actors come through, especially Ernie Hudson as a kindly cop and, as the chief nasty, Michael Wincott doing his gravel-voiced, long-haired, long-faced Doctor Death routine. Wincott and all the other bad guys in the movie are angry. Some of the cops are angry. The hero is very angry. What are they all angry about? *The Crow* has the narcissistic pointless rage of the more naively bad grunge groups. Everyone in the movie is angry because rage, as a mood, is highly commercial. *The Crow* creates villains so vicious that no one in the audience can object when they are viciously disposed of (by sword, knife, machine gun, explosion, syringe). As in so many pop artifacts, the dirtier the violence, the more moralistic the framework for it. (The hero redeems a prostitute on drugs by literally squeezing the heroin out of her veins.) When Clint Eastwood delivered this moralized sadism 23 years ago in *Dirty Harry*, *smart* people knew what to make of it. *Dirty Harry* was American fascism. When it's done as a cartoon, it's hip, it's style, it's great. But how great an achievement is it to impose style on such degraded material?

NEW YORK POST, 5/11/94, p. 33, Michael Medved

For the late Brandon Lee, the delayed release of his last movie "The Crow" adds insult to fatal injury.

It's bad enough that the 28-year-old star (son of martial arts legend Bruce Lee) died in an on-set accident on March 31, 1993, but the wretched quality of the finished film in which he lost his life makes the tragedy seem all the more pointless.

"The Crow," based on a black-and-white comic book by cult artist James O'Barr, tells the story of a blue-collar rock musician (Lee) who is brutally murdered along with his fiance (Sophia Shinas) the night before their wedding.

A year later, he comes back from the dead, crawling out of his grave to seek revenge on each member of the hideous, drooling gang of thugs who killed him and raped his bride-to-be. The restless spirit is accompanied by a magical crow who is described as "his link between the land of the living and the realm of the dead."

The movie represents an extraordinarily primitive form of entertainment: Since Lee plays an unstoppable supernatural force, there's not much doubt as to whether he'll succeed in his errand of vengeance. The only suspense in the movie involves trying to guess the lavishly sadistic means the hero will use to dispatch the bad guys, one by one.

Thirty-one-year-old Australian director Alex Proyas has previously created commercials for Nike and Kleenex, and music videos for Sting and Fleetwood Mac, so he brings plenty of what passes for "style" to this endeavor.

That means a few gestures toward incoherent religious imagery—like the stigmata that mysteriously appear on Lee's hands, or the creepy cathedral that provides the setting for his final confrontation with arch bad guy "Top Dollar" (Michael Wincott).

It also means lots of dark sets and impressionistic visions of an unidentified urban wasteland.

Brandon Lee moves with feral grace and delivers his clunky lines ("Mother is the name of God on the lips and hearts of all children") with suitable intensity, but this part hardly represents a test of his acting ability.

Worst of all, his last role amounts to an unequivocal glorification of viciousness and sadism, since the film spends nearly all its running time showing the hero—not the villains— indulging brutal instincts. It also promotes utterly irresponsible notions of adolescent invulnerability, as Lee's character absorbs innumerable knife wounds and literally hundreds of bullets without experiencing pain or damage.

Unfortunately, many of the young people who watch the movie may well forget the sad irony that, in real life, all it took was a single shot—fired from a pistol designed to discharge blanks—to stop the star forever.

NEWSDAY, 5/11/94, Part II/p. B9, Jack Mathews

I wouldn't read an illustrated action comic book if you gave it to me, which, in the case of James O'Barr's, "The Crow," someone just did. But string together some spectacle moving pictures telling the same tale, as Australian director Alex Proyas has in adapting O'Barr's work, and I'm all yours.

Proyas' "The Crow," which made headlines during production because of the accidental shooting death of its star, Brandon Lee, is a stunning stylization piece, a blisteringly fast-paced gothic fantasy that combines the technique of rock video and neo-expressionism (i.e, it rips off "Batman" and "Blade Runner") to turn something old into something new.

Ultimately, "The Crow" is as wornout and trite as any of the vigilante movies that have been exploiting urban paranoia since Hollywood stumbled onto the formula with "Death Wish," A man whose lover is raped, beaten and murdered by a pack of cackling marauders hunts them down, one at a time, and treats them to deaths just as horrible as we figure they deserve.

What sets "The Crow" apart, besides its sinister, darkly mesmerizing look, is the fact that its hero, a gentle rock guitarist named Eric Draven (Lee), is avenging his own death, as well as his fiancee's. He had interrupted her killers in the act, and was blown away trying to stop them.

In the prologue opening, we're regaled with the myth of the crow, of how the sacred bird carries the spirits of the dead to their final resting place, and how, on occasion, the crow can return an anguished, unforgiving soul to its body to complete some mortal business.

If getting even with the guys who killed you and your fiancee doesn't rate an extension, what would?

So, a year to the day after his death, on the destructive eve of Halloween as it happens, Eric Draven's corpse is rejoined by his spirit, then rises from the grave, in mint condition and generally invincible, to settle up.

There is no avoiding the macabre irony of Lee playing a hero who returns to life after being fatally shot. There is Lee himself, a dynamic physical presence with his painted-on death mask, just about a year after he was shot to death while playing the scene in which his character was to be shot to death.

The footage of his shooting has reportedly been destroyed, and the scene in which Eric dies occurs amid a blizzard of quick cuts. Any other changes necessitated by Lee's death are not apparent. Unlike "Brainstorm," edited and released after Natalie Wood's death, the story of "The Crow" seems complete.

The movie itself, however, doesn't hold together. The first hour is such a dazzling concoction of images and driving Lollapalooza rock, I felt as if I had fallen into something very dense, and moving very quickly. The first sequence, literally a bird'seye view, sweeps us through the shadowy canyons of this make-believe city, ablaze with arson fires on Devil's Night, and leads us right up to the window of Eric Draven's attic flat.

And there he is, pre-tragedy, staring into the night.

Time and again, we follow the flight of the crow, through the graveyard, the city, over the rooftops, into the alleyways and corridors, and into the cathedral where Eric and the crow have their fateful showdown with the sadistic Top Dollar (Michael Wincott), the scum of scum.

Long before we reached the cathedral, however, "The Crow" had me worn out. It is, after all, poetic myth, and though Proyas strains mightily to develop relationships between Eric and a friendly cop (Ernie Hudson) and the young girl (Rochelle Davis) who lives downstairs, the movie's emotions remain as static as a comic-strip panel.

NEWSWEEK, 5/16/94, p. 66, David Ansen

When Brandon Lee was accidentally shot to death on the set of "The Crow" in March 1993, he had only three days of filming left. The production shut down, and the devastated Australian director, Alex Proyas, wanted to abandon the $15 million production. It took the entreaties of Lee's fiancée, Eliza Hutton, and his mother, Linda Lee Cadwell, along with others associated with the film, to persuade Proyas to complete the production. "The real issue was psychological," explains co-producer Edward Pressman. "Alex went back to Australia for a month to get his head together, and we took another month off to figure out how to continue."

The film's problems were not over. Re-shoots added an extra $8 million to the budget. In September, Paramount, the original distributor, dropped the movie, claiming that Lee's death, coupled with the dark story line, made it uncomfortable. Based on the underground comic books of James O'Barr, "The Crow" is a violent fantasy in which Lee's character, Eric Draven, a Detroit rock guitarist, rises from the dead to avenge the brutal rape and murder of his fiancee and his own death. It was during the filming of this murder that Bruce Lee's son was fatally struck by a dummy bullet. The film of the actual accident was deliberately destroyed, though footage shot just before is seen in the completed film.

Miramax, the new distributor, has been careful to market the film without exploiting Lee's death, consulting with his family and fiancée throughout. But it will be hard for anybody to see "The Crow" unhaunted by the tragedy. The "fun" of the relentless mayhem—the plot consists of little more than a series of murders, as Eric kills his killers in a fashion befitting each of their vices—may be, for anyone past their teenage years, less of a kick than intended.

The early reviews, in the Hollywood trade papers and Rolling Stone, have been raves—perhaps a reaction to the speculation, after Paramount defected, that the film was a disaster. It's a slick and evocatively designed movie with a distopian Gothic vision that owes an obvious debt to "Batman" and "Blade Runner." It succeeds in bringing O'Barr's comic-book vision to life, but there's little else going on behind the graphic razzle-dazzle and the moody, ominous soundtrack. Proyas's virtuosity as a director of music videos and Nike commercials is all too obvious here: strobe lights, fast cutting and rock-star iconography. Some welcome touches of wit are supplied by Ernie Hudson, as a sympathetic cop, and Michael Wincott, as the gravel-voiced leader of the scurvy band of nihilists Draven dispatches one by one.

But it is the graceful, gorgeous Lee whose image lingers on the retina. Dressed in torn punk black, his face painted mime white with clown teardrops and exaggerated lips, Lee got to demonstrate for the first time his sensual charisma. It is both tantalizing and frustrating to watch him buried under the expressionist makeup, in a role that offers intensity but little characterization. Knowing you won't see him again, you want more than the few glimpses "The Crow" provides of his real face. The movie leaves you with the excitement, and the sadness, of great potential lost.

SIGHT AND SOUND, 6/94, p. 44, Tom Tunney

In an unnamed inner city, Halloween is known as Devil's Night because of the amount of violent crime, especially arson, it inspires. One Devil's Night, rock guitarist Eric Draven is murdered and his fiancee Shelly raped and left for dead by a gang of four heavies—Tin Tin, Funboy, T-Bird and Skank—sent by local crime lord Top Dollar to evict them from their apartment. Shelly subsequently dies in hospital.

Exactly one year later, Eric is brought back to life by a crow which then leads him to the four culprits in turn. Confronting Tin Tin in an alley, Eric proves invulnerable to his assaults with a knife and leaves him stabbed to death. Eric is then led by the crow to a pawn shop where Shelly's effects had been sold by Tin Tin. He tells the owner to warn the others he is coming for them, before destroying the building.

Eric seeks out Albrecht, the cop who had investigated his murder and is now investigating Tin Tin's; he surprises him with the revelation that, far from being dead and buried, "I'm dead and I move!" In a dark alley, Eric rescues Sarah—a young friend and the film's narrator—from the path of a speeding vehicle. In Funboy's apartment, Eric discovers Funboy in a passionate embrace with Sarah's drug addict mother Darla. Eric shoots him in the leg, orders Darla to give up drugs and be a better mother, and kills Funboy with an overdose of morphine.

Eric asks Albrecht about the exact circumstances of his and Shelly's death. He then appears in T-Bird's car and sends it exploding off a dockside. Top Dollar convenes a meeting of his gang above the Pit nightclub to finalise their Devil's Night plans. Eric appears in search of Skank. In the fight that follows, Skank and most of Top Dollar's men are killed.

Top Dollar's half-sister and incestuous lover Myca suggests capturing the crow as a way of harnessing its mystical power and destroying Eric. In the subsequent ambush, the crow is wounded and captured, and Eric loses his invulnerability; fortunately, Albrecht arrives in time to help him. The crow pecks out Myca's eyes. Eric and Top Dollar confront each other on the roof where Sarah is held captive. Eric overpowers him and impales him on a statue. Eric returns to the graveyard, to be reunited with the ghostly Shelly. They lie under Eric's gravestone, on which Sarah puts Shelly's wedding ring, declaring, "Love is forever."

Based on a comic strip, *The Crow* adequately conveys the hard edged, two-dimensional look of comic book artwork. Unfortunately, it also conforms to the most basic kind of comic book characterisation in which psychological complexity is suppressed in favour of simply moving the hero on to the next set-piece battle.

Despite the repeated brief flashbacks to Eric's death, the story's outcome is numbingly obvious from the outset: Eric comes back from the dead and gets his revenge. The feathered how and why of his quest, indicated by the title, is blithely explained as the routine manifestation of a cosmic moral order. Sarah's opening voice-over helpfully explains that "people once believed" that a crow carried off the souls of the dead and in exceptional cases would also help a wronged person obtain justice. So, even in a crazy world beset by anarchy, violence and murderous arson, it's comforting to know that there is indeed a guiding hand—or beak—at work. That idea may give the story a semblance of logic, but it also turns Eric into one of the dullest and least complex action heroes imaginable.

The romantic strand of the plot doesn't help, either. "Little things used to mean so much to Shelley," says Eric limply at one point, and throughout, his romantic obsession is couched in language more redolent of Barbara Cartland than of the film's most obvious antecedents: *Batman* and *Escape From New York*.

Having the young girl Sarah as the narrator is perhaps the film's most curious strategy. The dysfunctional family has long been one of the staple ingredients of the horror film, and has also recently become one of the most pervasive themes in Hollywood generally. However, her yearning voice-over squares badly with the anarchic comic-book and pop video-inspired cityscape, where loud music, macho posturing and instant gratification are the main things that matter.

Also, if there's so much order in the universe that one couple's love will prevail, how come the city is such a disaster zone? More to the point, why don't all the other murdered people have their own personal crows flapping around on their behalf. The sense of a feathered morality bearing down on the city soon becomes boring and oppressive. Top Dollar's flamboyant villainy, and the art direction, which gives a luridly mediaeval quality to his lair, invigorate proceedings to an extent. But his four over-acting lieutenants could easily have walked out of a *Death Wish* film, and they do and say nothing that hasn't been done before in a thousand and one other forgettable thrillers.

Of course, *The Crow* will always be remembered as the film on which Brandon Lee was shot dead for real while filming one of its many gun battles. Sadly, the character he plays is so lacking in distinctive qualities that it hardly matters which scenes involve the real Lee and which use stunt doubles. Certainly, the film has an unusually large number of scenes featuring Eric sprinting around in long shot and being filmed from the back or in silhouette. But since the character seen in close-up is little more than a stony-faced implacable force—complete with sepulchral make-up seemingly inspired by Michael Jackson's *Thriller* video—the joins are never obvious. A hero who has all his detective work done for him and simply turns up on cue to exact revenge was always bound to be a cypher and thus ripe to be taken over at any necessary point by a stand-in.

Finally, the most intriguing aspect to the film is whether its many noisy nightclub scenes are meant to be admired and enjoyed at face value or regarded more as a deafening manifestation of just how grim, unoriginal and depressing this violent inner city world really is. Perhaps only the little crow himself knows the answer.

VILLAGE VOICE, 5/17/94, p. 58, Jeff Yang

The Crow isn't the snuff film some had feared (and others, of a ghoulish nature, had hoped for). Still, Brandon Lee's final movie is littered with disturbing resonances—eerie echoes and shadows of his tragic death. Lee plays Eric Draven, a young man on the eve of his wedding who's murdered by vicious thugs (in one of the film's typically overdetermined touches, Draven is the lead singer of a band named "Hangman's Joke"; and it's hard to overlook the fact that "Draven" is a portmanteau for "driven" and "raven"). Drawn from the grave by lost love and revenge, Draven eliminates his killers one by one, all to the crashing chords of a congress of MTV alternative Nationals—Helmet, the Cure, Rollins, NIN, and Stone Temple Pilots.

Unfortunately, there is more mood than movie here, since the flimsy plot is poor anchorage for the soundtrack and Proyas's pathetically swooping camera. But how can one not be mesmerized as Eric/Brandon and his cohorts speak lines like: "They're all dead—they just don't know it yet"; "My dad said childhood's over the moment you know you're going to die"; and "The cemetery is the safest place in the world to be"?

Young death is once more the era's obsession, and, in the brief sweep of its wings, *The Crow* secures Brandon's place in the Eternal Host of the died-pretty. One could have hoped for a better memorial—one that was not, as this is, so thin that it flickers with ghosts, teasing watchers to search for the scars of Brandon's absence.

Also reviewed in:
CHICAGO TRIBUNE, 5/13/94, Friday/p. C, Michael Wilmington
NEW YORK TIMES, 5/11/94, p. C15, Caryn James
NEW YORKER, 5/23/94, p. 93, Terrence Rafferty
VARIETY, 5/2-8/94, p. 88, Todd McCarthy
WASHINGTON POST, 5/13/94, p. D1, Desson Howe
WASHINGTON POST, 5/13/94, Weekend/p. 48, Kevin McManus

CRUMB

A David Lynch presentation of a Superior Pictures production. *Executive Producer:* Lawrence Wilkinson, Albert Berger, and Lianne Halfon. *Producer:* Lynn O'Donnell and Terry Zwigoff. *Director:* Terry Zwigoff. *Director of Photography:* Maryse Alberti. *Editor:* Victor Livingston. *Music:* David Boeddinghaus. *Sound:* Scott Breindel. *Running time:* 119 minutes. *MPAA Rating:* Not Rated.

WITH: Robert Crumb (Himself); Beatrice Crumb (Robert's Mother); Charles Crumb (Robert's Older Brother); Max Crumb (Robert's Younger Brother); Dana Crumb (Robert's First Wife); Jesse Crumb (Robert's Son from First Marriage); Aline Kominsky (Robert's Second Wife); Sophie Crumb (Robert's Daughter from Second Marriage); Robert Hughes (Art Critic); Martin Muller (Owner, Modernism Gallery); Don Donahue (Former *Zap Comix* publisher); Trina Robbins, Spain Rodriguez, and Bill Griffith (Cartoonists); Deirdre English (Former Editor *Mother Jones*); Peggy Orenstein (Journalist); Kathy Goodell (Ex-Girlfriend); Dian Hanson (*Leg Show* Magazine Editor and Ex-Girlfriend).

FILM QUARTERLY, Winter 1995-96, p. 45, Felicia Feaster

The beauty of Terry Zwigoff's bleak and cathartic documentary is the wonderful evanescence of its "message." Zwigoff's reasoned investigation of countercultural comic-book artist Robert Crumb allows the viewer to dismiss, valorize, or make something in-between of his subject's life and work. Filtering issues of fame, sexism, family, and censorship through the spectator's natural identification with the film's subject, *Crumb* forces us—through that identification—to question our own political and moral views. Having risen to prominence in the anti-authoritarian Berkeley of the 1960s and reevaluated by the often dictatorial phenomenon of political correctness, Robert Crumb becomes a theoretical barometer who tests our ideas of artistic responsibility and license.

Though his film is structured in the tradition of biographical films of the famous or notable, Zwigoff's project often yields greater, more trenchant insights at its periphery: about the 1950s family, cultural alienation, and our belief in the redemptive nature of fame. Crumb and his comic-book fame often become incidental, a mere ordering device for Zwigoff's larger, more complex project of investigating the Crumb family: older brother Charles, a medicated, suicidal recluse cocooned in his mother's Philadelphia home since his youth; and Maxon, a self-punishing former molester holed up in a dank skid row hotel where jars of peanut butter and yams share quarters with his bed of nails.

Crumb is steeped in a rich subtext that expands its mission from simple biography to include every one of us as it investigates the universal plight of childhood and how the complex relationships and experiences brewed there create the adult. The strong, fecund, female bodies of Robert's drawings again and again dwarf thc artist in a replay of childhood powerlessness. At some moments his artwork seems to represent the purgative aspect of creativity; at others, however, it suggests a stymied sense that his comics may not vent, but *fuel* unpleasant or unresolved desires.

Critics have tended to focus on Robert's triumph over the sexual and psychological quagmire of his childhood (assuming Maxon and Charles to be casualties), but *Crumb* shows that this apparent success story was not without its hidden costs. By the film's conclusion, Robert's flight to France in 1993 completes a trajectory of escape that feels anything but climactic and transcendent.

Hero and anti-hero both, Robert lures us in with his critical eye and justified disgust for the world, then dares us to identify fully with his battery-acid misanthropy. Robert presents no one definable personality; he is frustratingly conflicted and nuanced, a stew of self-loathing, chest-beating egotism, hatred, despondency, and fear. One of a battery of experts and laypeople offering opinions on the artist is former *Mother Jones* editor Deirdre English, who asserts that his drawings' "arrested juvenile vision" of the world—and especially of women—reveals a sense of powerlessness instilled by an abusive father and social rejection during childhood.

If one of the more disturbing aspects of *Crumb* is Robert's unapologetic Weltanschauung—"I have these hostilities to women, I admit it" (save his "darling daughter Sophie," who wipes away his kiss with casual disdain)—the most liberating, pleasurable aspect is Robert's venomous tirades against a manufactured, advertised life. The voice of dissent is not the crusading advocate of displaced labor in Michael Moore's *Roger & Me* or *Hoop Dreams* underprivileged African Americans pining for a piece of the American pie. Instead, *Crumb* is an all-encompassing, overwhelmingly bitter rejection of the shiny lies and sordid promises of our culture via, in John Powers' words, Crumb's role as a "nerd Messiah." A valentine to the terminal outsider, *Crumb* introduces passive, masochistic rebels (in the reclusive Maxon and Charles and their misanthropic brother) who fly in the face of a popular imagination built on the brutal sexual rebellion of Brando or Dean or Kerouac. Rebellion here is not an enviable stance or fashionable pose, but a bruised life-long affliction that "attests to the playground brutality of our society.

On an intrinsic level, *Crumb* rejects culture as defined by Hollywood: the Rocky myth that we succeed through what we overcome and that there is an ultimate reward for endurance. The film shows the inescapable, deeply impacted nature of the Crumb brothers' hemlock-laced childhood which is not conquered, but merely momentarily exorcised in Robert's panels or Charles' scathing soliloquies. What *Crumb* illustrates is the continual process of a phrase Robert penned in his childhood diary "I decided to reject conforming when society rejected me."

R. Crumb's mordant, satirical art is translated by Zwigoff into storyboard scrolls of San Francisco's seedy Mission district and the eclectic clutter of Robert's California bungalow, deconstructed by the ironic, sandpiper-abrasive presence of Robert or Charles. Zwigoff retains the spirit of underground comics like *Zap* and *Weirdo* by foregrounding their autobiographical hellfire; the farrago of self-loathing and social criticism which defines the genre is translated from the comic panel to film.

Zwigoff's cynical editing captures the dour mood of the underground comic as it penetrates the central mystification of the American family as a protective, nurturing shelter from the world. By juxtaposing the richly saturated archival footage of the "ideal" 1950s home life with the Crumb brothers' own grubby, sepia-tinted remembrances of life with father, the "overbearing tyrant," the film-maker exposes the profound discrepancy between thc fact of the Crumb home life and thc television fiction as thc seed of thc brothers' mistrust and malaise.

"I'm sort of shocked at this whole buildup in the press of how crazy this family is. You know, 'the craziest, most dysfunctional family in America' type of thing," says Zwigoff. "I never thought of them that way. My own family is every bit as weird, they're just not as interesting."

Though Zwigoff may be underplaying the definite peculiarities of the Crumb family—the medicated, cottony slur of Beatrice Crumb, her body melding with thc couch beneath her, the smothering, entombing blankets and quilts she drapes on the walls; the fleshy, obsessive "wrinkles" of Charles' drawing style; the contorted, threatening female bodies in Robert and Maxon's work—his point is evident. In reading the Crumbs as some kind of entertaining perversion of family life or freak show anomaly, we fail to see the commonality we might have with them: the harsh, affection-withholding father (a legacy of emotional distance that, *Crumb* suggests, Robert is continuing with his own son); a mother in denial, soothing her children against thc paternal maelstrom; and children unable to meet their father's expectations.

In giving a voice to two of the family's more marginal members (Maxon and Charles), the film enriches our often cinematically truncated visions of society. While Zwigoff chose the title *Crumb* to acknowledge all three brothers, critical reviews of the film have tended to dismiss or patronize Maxon and Charles as "characters" in the cruelest sense, as mere set pieces to the central drama of The Famous Crumb. At least one critic has gone so far as to label Zwigoff's use of the "secondary" brothers "exploitive," an ironic remarginalization of men already ground into dust by the remorseless machinery of high school. "Try to imagine Terry Zwigoff's film without R. Crumb's thoroughly loony brothers," said Gary Dauphin, writing in the *Village Voice*. "Now ask yourself what consent might mean given their own mental states and relationship to their famous, always autobiographical brother."

Dauphin's preposterous infantilization of Charles and Maxon as being without the agency (or celebrity) necessary to give their consent to be interviewed on film plays again into the critical centrifuge that separates Robert, as the brother made good, from the "failed" brothers. In making *Crumb*, Zwigoff strove to avoid what he saw as the anthropological curiosity value of films like *Grey Gardens* (which the director recalls walking out on). The director establishes a rare intimacy with his intelligent, introspective subjects that invites collusion with Charles' or Maxon's perspective.

Part of *Crumb*'s power is its contention that fame and art may not bc the simplistic "escape" our myth of success assumes. While critics can identify with Robert's rage and may not question the misogyny or racism vision, it seems to have been a greater stretch to extend that identification to characters without the gloss of success and money to validate their self-and-society-loathing, so much so that *Sight and Sound*'s Michael Eaton can express "almost a relief to discover that [Charles] committed suicide after the film was shot." In the same issue Jonathan Romney claims that "it's easy to forget that we're marveling at real people with real problems."

If anyone is exploited by *Crumb* it's the audience member and critic who—even amidst increasing revisionism of the form—believes in documentary as unvarnished truth. Zwigoff is brutally frank about the degree of manipulation film-makers engage in to arrive at the "truth"—the editing, marketing, and aesthetic choices that are heavily modulated by the subjectivity of the director and by the demands of the narrative. The director defies the reputed "objectivity" of the documentary, compromised from the outset by his 25-year friendship with Robert. He makes no secret of his manipulations, as with the marketing of the film and the "certain commercial concessions" made in the provocative poster design of a nubile blonde flashing her panties. Fully conscious of certain effects he wanted to create in the viewer, the film-maker has described his placement of Robert sketching on the street in front of a billboard of a winsome young woman as "ironic"—for its contrast of an emotional effusiveness and feminine ideal next to the impervious, introspective Robert. Zwigoff also admits to using discontinuous reaction shots from one part of the film inserted into another. Such tampering counters at every turn the notion of distanced observation and objectivity proffered by forefathers of the genre like Frederick Wiseman, which Zwigoff dismisses as "bullshit." "Everytime you choose even what to include, or what to film or what music to put in, any of those decisions has an incredible amount of weight to it."

Just as Robert is something of a revision of the heroic, transcendent artist we expect in our biographies, and just as his brothers dispute our perception of the outsider, the brilliance of Zwigoff's film lies in its challenge to and contestation of our notions of what documentary is capable of revealing.

FILMS IN REVIEW, 11-12/95, p. 101, Andy Pawelczak

R. Crumb was a comic book artist who first gained fame in the mid-Sixties with such countercultural comics as "Fritz the Cat" and "Mr. Natural." Crumb's comics were violent, lewd, and subversive. They featured women with huge bottoms and bulging chests and men with penises as sturdy and preternaturally erect as Hindu lingams. He probably wouldn't have put it so solemnly, but Crumb and his cohorts at Zap Comix were engaged in a sly guerrilla war against an homogenized, telegenic America. It's as if he were saying this is what happens when your mother is a TV set and your father is a clone. *Crumb*, Terry Zwigoff's brilliant documentary about the artist and his family, would be an important film even if Crumb had never become a marginal art-world celebrity. It's the dark-around-the-edges story of a genuine American eccentric.

The film consists of interviews with Crumb and members of his family crosscut with shots of his comics. Zwigoff films the comics lovingly with tinkly piano blues on the soundtrack, and the result, far from being static, is stunning—*Crumb*'s Walpurgis Night processions of misfits and humanoids are like an old-fashioned vaudeville show viewed on LSD. Crumb himself comes across as surprisingly non-demonic. A skinny, middle-aged, bespectacled man dressed in a baggy suit, bow-tie, and straw boater, he variously suggests a country rube, an absent-minded professor, a carnival barker, and one of those furtive men who lurk in the tenderloin districts around urban bus terminals. Whether walking down a San Francisco street and inveighing against America's commercial civilization or participating in a photo shoot for a porn magazine with scantily-clad girls (Zwigoff treats this sequence as sweet-tempered low comedy), *Crumb* has a weird, spacey charm and the acid intelligence of a born satirist.

The center of the movie is a series of interviews with Crumb and his two brothers. Charles, the older brother, is a big, slow-talking, broken-toothed recluse who lives with his mother and her numerous cats in a house with sheets over the windows and blankets nailed to the walls. Charles is candid about his mental illness (he's on various drugs) and wryly articulate about his lifelong emotional deprivation. He was the first one in the family to draw comics, specializing in home-made comic books about Long John Silver and Jim Hawkins with whom he was erotically obsessed. As his illness progressed, the texts slowly supplanted the drawings until he ended up producing whole notebooks of tiny, closely-spaced squiggles on the page, mad black writing.

Maxon, the other brother, a startlingly good looking man possessed of laser-beam intensity, is as mad as a hatter too. In one stunning sequence, we see him in his SRO hotel room sitting in the full-lotus position on a bed of nails as he ingests a 30-foot-long cloth cord to clean out his intestines. Crumb doesn't say much in these sequences. He laughs his trademark, compulsive giggle and makes a few sympathetic observations, but you can feel the permanent bonds of love and rivalry between the brothers. It's as if Charles and Maxon were Crumb's alter-egos, the dark side from which his grotesque comic characters emerge.

The Film Forum is one of the few venues in New York City where you can see a film like *Crumb*. I saw it for the first time on a Saturday night with an audience of sophisticated filmgoers who appreciated the movie's dark humor. The second time I went on a weekday afternoon and there were only a few people in the audience. It was a subtly different kind of experience. These were the people you used to find in the old Thalia on West 95th Street in the late afternoon or in the Apollo on 42nd Street-stragglers in the rat-race, out-of-work handbill distributors, loners with brown paper-bag lunches—in short, Crumb's people. They laughed in different places than the upscale Saturday night crowd, and they added an edge to an already edgy movie.

LOS ANGELES TIMES, 4/28/95, Calendar/p. 1, Kenneth Turan

As shocking yet haunting as a Diane Arbus photograph, disturbing because it is so unmistakably human, "Crumb" makes it difficult to look away. Not even Leo Tolstoy's dictum that "Every unhappy family is unhappy in its own way" is adequate preparation for the unsettling personal dramas that unfold in this remarkable film.

Though Terry Zwigoff's documentary begins as an examination of the art and career of the celebrated cartoonist R. (for Robert) Crumb, it is considerably more than that. Because it provides an intimate view of Crumb's singular background, it ends up dealing with larger, more complex issues, from the impact of family in shaping personality to the concept of the artist as a messenger to society from a scathing personal hell.

Considered the key figure in the underground comic movement, Crumb is responsible for such outrageous creations as Mr. Natural, Fritz the Cat and the catch phrase "Keep on Truckin'." In the view of Time magazine art critic Robert Hughes, his scabrous monsters of the id drawings make Crumb "the Breughel of the last half of the 20th Century," and comparisons to Daumier and even Goya have not been lacking.

Though Crumb is often the centerpiece of his drawings, little has been known about him personally. Shy, bemused and seriously eccentric, a devotee of bow ties and old 78 records, Crumb is hardly eager to let the world interact with what he calls "the little guy that lives inside my brain."

But documentarian Zwigoff, who worked on this film for six years, has known Crumb for 25 and even played alongside the artist in the Cheap Suit Serenaders, his old-timey string band. Only an intimate of such long standing could have gotten this kind of privileged view of a subject's life, and only a talented and experience filmmaker, which Zwigoff is as well, would have been able to handle material this unnerving.

Unwilling to drive, uneasy with people, described by his wife, Aline, as someone who'd "rather be a brain in a jar than have a body," Crumb is initially presented in a typical mode of ironic self-disgust. "If I don't get to draw, I feel suicidal; if I do, I feel suicidal, too," he says, paralleling his general belief that "words fail me, and pictures aren't much better."

In fact Crumb is an engaging monologuist when he gets going, willing to reveal more about his tangled sex life (with his ex-wife and, girlfriends providing corroboration) than many people may want to hear. And his graphic, straight-from-the-unconscious artwork, which Crumb says began to flower after a particularly weird LSD experience, can be so unapologetically misogynistic that Zwigoff, appropriately devotes time to feminist critics of his sensibility.

But the biggest shock of "Crumb" is not what he draws but finding out that this man is the most normal, functional member of his family. The artist is one of five children of a violent ex-Marine who wrote and taught on "Training People Effectively" while physically terrorizing both his trio of sons and their amphetamine-abusingmother. (Crumb's two sisters refused to cooperate with the film and are not interviewed.)

Robert's oldest brother, Charles, got the brunt of the physical punishment and his presence on film has an unusually disturbing quality. Witty, painfully sad, someone who is on easy terms with Kant, Hegel and the great 19th-Century novelists, Charles has lived with his mother in their shambles of a home since high school and is only tenuously linked with reality.

As far as artistic expression in the Crumb family, however, Charles was the acknowledged trailblazer. He was the first of the children to become interested in comics, the one who insisted that Robert draw and get good at it. The film shows him dependent on tranquilizers and anti-depressants, too detached from the human race to ever so much as set foot outside the front door.

Equally arresting, but not quite so poignant, is brother Max, who sleeps on a bed of nails in a San Francisco flophouse, remembers every childhood slight and performs off-putting yoga cleansing rituals for the benefit of the camera.

Taken together, the tale of these three brothers functions as a textbook example of the way horrific family conditions can nurture an artistic sensibility. Resistant to fame, congenitally unable to sell out, Crumb draws because he has to, because it is the only way he can find to make the strain and madness of his upbringing manageable.

Last glimpsed about to move his family to France because it's "slightly less evil than the United States," Crumb also says at one point that he doesn't consider himself an exciting subject for a movie. Maybe not exciting, but when it comes to unflinching, riveting looks at a compulsive artist who can't be other than who he is, nothing comes close to "Crumb."

NEW YORK, 5/1/95, p. 65, David Denby

R. Crumb, the underground-cartoon artist who devised such "comix" as *Weird* and *Zap* and then received international renown and critical comparison to Brueghel and Daumier, is a rail-thin geek with a lower-middle-class brush mustache, a faded tweed jacket, and a small hat, all worn as a uniform in a display of ironic counter-dandyism comparable to William Burroughs's black-suited rig. In Terry Zwigoffs extraordinary documentary portrait *Crumb*, there is shockingly little separation between life and art. Crumb complains that he was ignored by girls in high school, and he still exudes the resentments and fears of a cranky, put-upon kid. So does his art, and that's its glory, but it's disconcerting to discover that the successful artist, having transcended nothing, is as devoted to surly, other-annihilating rancor as a teen nerd burrowing in a basement. That's rather funny, but it's also rather sinister. Crumb shares the same awful childhood with his wrecked older brother, Charles, who lives at home with their mother, and his kid brother, Max, who sits in a San Francisco SRO on a bed of nails, yet Crumb turned the semi-psychotic material of bent adolescence into art, while they were consumed and destroyed. The artist becomes black magician here, drawing strength from the dismay of others and giggling over his victory. *Crumb* should turn into the midnight-movie sensation of the decade: Robert Crumb is a remorseless man, and the movie, in a coolly ambiguous way, revels in the grotesque appropriateness of his triumph.

NEW YORK POST, 9/17/94, p. 35, Thelma Adams

"Crumb"—screening tonight at the New York Film Festival—is a hilarious and heart-breaking documentary about Robert Crumb, an American artist who tests the boundaries of freedom of expression within the shadow world of underground comics.

Art critic Robert Hughes once called Crumb "the Breughel of the 20th century." The LSD-inspired comic genius is best known for "Keep on Truckin'" and the sexually predatory Fritz the Cat.

What emerges from director Terry Zwigoff's probing, candid portrait of the Philadelphia-born outsider is a new American gothic. Crumb's dysfunctional family, particularly his brothers Charles and Max—the ones that didn't make it big—are as fascinating as the often-offensive cartoonist's art and its roots.

Zwigoff places the budget for this must-see documentary—nine years in the making—"somewhere between 'El Mariachi' [$7,500] and [the multimillion-dollar] 'True Lies.'"

"If you feel weird about yourself because you're different," Zwigoff told a Film Festival press conference, "hopefully this film will make you feel better."

NEW YORK POST, 4/21/95, p. 48, Thelma Adams

"How perfectly goddamn delightful it all is, to be sure," is the killjoy catch phrase of the unforgettable Charles Crumb.

Who the hell is Charles? He would be a complete unknown if Terry Zwigoff hadn't decided to make a documentary about the granddaddy of the underground comic scene, R. (Robert) Crumb.

"It's all because of my brother Charles," R. Crumb says of his artistic accomplishments. The irony is that while Crumb has gone on to international recognition, the brother who shares the frame with him is hollow-eyed, haunted, overweight, agoraphobic and flattened by antidepressants and downers.

Destiny is played out in that shabby Philadelphia bedroom: one brother channeled insanity into marketable art, the other withdrew from the world entirely. It's a shocking, insightful discovery revealed by Zwigoff with the unflinching honesty Crumb reserves for his drawings.

He despises the artwork which made him famous: the Keep on Truckin' logo that kept head shops in cash for years; the "Cheap Thrills" album cover for Big Brother and the Holding Company with Janis Joplin; and the character Fritz the Cat, immortalized by Ralph Bakshi in the first animated X-rated feature.

The latter, Crumb tells an audience of Philadelphia art students, will be an embarrassment to me for the rest of my life."

Bordering on the pornographic, frequently offensive, and darkly funny, Crumb's comics contain the fantastic vision of the high school reject who carried his soul in his fountain pen. Where did these wildly original artwork come from? Zwigoff sets out to unmask the man, show the progression of his art, and dig up the roots of his twisted psyche.

One ex confronts Robert, You really hated women then. Do you think it's improved?"

"I hate them a little less now," the artist coyly replies.

Crumb emerges as a complex, conflicted, impishly charming figure whose self-hatred easily eclipses his hostility toward women. His self-portraits are of a skinny, round-shouldered, myopic wimp in a constant sweat.

Crumb trades on an uncensored honesty in his stream-of-consciousness artwork. Crumb explains: "Not everything's for children. Not everything's for everybody."

As for being the subject of a documentary, the comic king responds with a drawing: A camera points at a bed-ridden Crumb while the words "I'm nauseous" float over his head.

NEWSDAY, 4/21/95, Part II/p. B7, Jack Mathews

Any reasonably well-balanced person who's happened onto the ranker volumes of underground artist Robert Crumb's comic books in the last three decades might have—*must* have—wondered what kind of sick mind was at work, and whether it was receiving proper medical attention.

The Crumb image that has taken root in main-stream American culture, and is seen on everything from T-shirts to mud flaps, is his "Keep on Truckin" cartoon, showing a guy with gigantic feet and a satisfied grin marching in single-file with himself, as if going out to conquer the world. Crumb is also the creator of Fritz the Cat, the horny feline who inspired Ralph Bakshi's notorious X-rated animated movie.

But those whimsical creations don't even hint at the dark nature of Crumb's signature work, his misogynistic and often pornographic comics in which women with sensationally exaggerated shapes appear as sacrificial sex objects. It's the mind behind those images we get to know in Terry Zwigoff's intimate, funny, and ultimately troubling documentary "Crumb."

Zwigoff had known Crumb for 20 years before talking him into participating in a film that ended up taking six years to complete. And his subject was gamey enough to allow the filmmaker to record it all, the genius and the weirdo. The portrait that emerges is that of a raw talent giving expression to an iconoclastic, angry, perverse, sex- and anatomy-obsessed world view.

Crumb, a slouching beanpole who wears thick glasses and a seasoned fedora, is what he draws, and clearly relishes both his outsider status and his own outrageousness. A compulsive masturbator (others may whistle while they work ...) and womanizer, he is also a caustic social critic and a jovial companion. You may not want to know him yourself, but he's great fun to follow around in a documentary.

We go with him to San Francisco's Haight-Ashbury district where he gained fame in the '60s and where he remains a legendary counterculture figure, we see him with his current wife and an old girlfriend, and see him horsing around with colleagues (he has the strange habit of leaping onto the backs of people and clinging to them with his tentacle-like limbs).

The thing that pushes "Crumb" to another level of biography is the recorded conversations between Robert and his dysfunctional family, particularly between him and his older brother Charles. As children, Charles was the most imaginative and talented of the Crumb brood, but has spent his entire adulthood as a medicated schizophrenic living in social isolation in their mother's house.

The nagging specter of exploitation hangs over these sessions; Zwigoff and Robert are clearly hitching a ride on Charles' memories to revisit the Crumb children's freaky childhood. Charles is a physical mess—his upper dentures are in a drawer somewhere, and you don't doubt when he says he hasn't bathed in five or six weeks—but he is remarkably lucid, even good-humored, about his wasted life. The most poignant moments come when the brothers thumb through Charles' own body of early comic book work and we see his mind literally unravel on the page.

Zwigoff doesn't offer much perspective on why the Crumb brothers (the child has done time for child molestation, and now meditates on a nail bed) grew up with such weirdly twisted views of the world, except to note that their father was an abusive alcoholic and that throughout school, they were unpopular nerds who retreated into shared comic book fantasies.

What the film does accomplish is showing how Robert Crumb, through exceptional talent and even more exceptional timing, was able to channel his antisocial views into a safely commercial outlet. He was there when the '60s counterculture bloomed, when irreverence and pornographic nose-thumbing at the establishment were viable cultural products.

In his case, art hasn't been necessarily therapeutic. He has married two women and slept with scores more, but still hates women because of the girls who snubbed him in high school. On the other hand, it has kept him off the streets, and after seeing "Crumb," you'll know there's value in that.

NEWSWEEK, 4/24/95, p. 64, Jack Kroll

The failure of "Crumb" to gain an Oscar nomination for best documentary is as unfathomable as the more publicized case of "Hoop Dreams." Terry Zwigoff's portrait of R. (Robert) Crumb, the freak underground cartoonist, is a marvelous movie, an instant American classic. Filmed on a shoestring over six years, "Crumb" has an amazing intimacy in its depiction of Crumb (now 52) and his hair-raisingly dysfunctional family. Only Zwigoff, a friend for 25 years, could have gotten so close to the blatantly furtive artist. The presence of Crumb turns the screen into giant living Crumb panels; the artist skinny, gulch-chested, bottle-glassed, goofy-grinning, flat-hatted. But his hands, popping out of too short sleeves, are the big mitts of a jazz pianist or a master draftsman.

Crumb's genius transcended the underground comics (or comix) of the '60s, when he became famous for such characters as Mr. Natural, Flaky Foont and Fritz the Cat, who marched out of his stoned head like his famous image "Keep on Truckin'." That big-footed parade became the ubiquitous "Kilroy Was Here" of the counterculture. But Crumb was no hippie; he hated rock and flunked out as a flower child. Still, it was LSD, he says, that gave him the "visionary change, the revelation of some seamy side of the American unconscious."

His forays into those sordid seams, his sexual fantasies involving Amazonian women, have offended plenty. The movie scans his strip "Joe Blow," the satirical tale of an Ozzie-and-Harriet type family that zips cheerily into incest. His African character, Angelfood McSpade, is seduced by white guys into coming to the United States, where she winds up cleaning johns (don't ask how) and being sexually humiliated. Crumb is a Swiftian satirist; Swift's "Modest Proposal," with its deadpan suggestion of relieving poverty is converting poor children into food for the rich, is a very Crumbian concept: you can imagine the outrage if it had been Crumb's graphically depicted idea.

As art critic Robert Hughes says in the movie, Crumb, "the Brueghel of the second half of the 20th century," works in the tradition of graphic artist as social protester. Crumb is also our Bosch; he sees modern life as a kind of hilarious hell. He walks through San Francisco's Haight-Ashbury, the bivouac of the '60s hippies, and is appalled by the jumbled urban jungle, half squalid, half gentrified. He rails against the commercialized, "market-research culture" and turns down a Hollywood offer.

The most powerful and moving scenes in the movie are the visits he makes to his brothers, Charles and Max. We learn about their late father, a tyranical ex-Marine who once broke Robert's collarbone. Charles, himself a brilliant cartoonist in youth, became suicidally depressed and has been living with his mother since high school. Max suffers from epileptic fits and lives in a fleabag hotel, meditates on a bed of nails and paints surreal visions. Zwigoff's searching but compassionate approach raises profound questions about the dark, tangled sources of creative power. "Robert would rather be a brain in a jar than a person in a body," says his wife, Aline. But "Crumb" has shown us the brain, the body, the mind of a key artist of our time, w ho keeps on truckin'.

SIGHT AND SOUND, 7/95, p. 44, Jonathan Romney

Cartoonist Robert Crumb, pioneer of 60s underground comics and creator of such characters as Fritz the Cat and Mr Natural, is filmed by his old friend Terry Zwigoff. Crumb is seen talking about his work to students, and at home in California with his wife Aline Kominsky, complaining about their neighbours. He reminisces about high school crushes, and shows his collection of 1920s jazz records.

Crumb visits his brothers, who share his artistic talents but not his social skills. His older brother Charles is chronically depressed and reclusive, and lives in squalor with their mother Beatrice; Charles' own comics were fired by his obsession with *Treasure Island*. Younger brother Maxon lives in a hotel, paints and practises yoga techniques; he has a history of molesting women.

On the occasion of a gallery retrospective, art critic Robert Hughes acclaims Crumb as a contemporary Breughel or Goya. Crumb reminisces about the late 60s, and insists that he never hung out with the fashionable Haight-Ashbury crowd. He recalls his beginnings in underground comics and explains how his characters first emerged after a LSD experience; fellow artists Trina Robbins, Spain Rodriguez and Bill Griffith comment on his work, but Robbins and journalist Deirdre English criticise its misogyny.

Crumb's former girlfriend Dian Hanson, editor of *Leg Show* and other porn mags, invites Crumb to take part in a photo shoot with models, and discusses his sexual predilections, above all his taste for receiving piggybacks. Another ex-girlfriend, Kathy Goodell, accuses Crumb of being callous and ends up hitting him. At home, Aline talks about her own comic art and her hatred of her mother. Crumb gives his son Jesse a lesson in drawing Victorian mad-women. The Crumb brothers recall their childhood in 50s suburbia and their tyrannical father. The sexist and racist aspects of Crumb's strips come under scrutiny.

Robert and Aline and their daughter Sophie prepare to move to France; Crumb winces as his beloved record collection is moved. Titles tell us the family now lives in southern France; that Charles committed suicide the year after being filmed; and that the Crumb sisters Sandra and Carol declined to be interviewed.

The most worrying aspect of *Crumb* is that it carries the credit "David Lynch presents". For sure, the Crumb family is as grotesque and disturbing as any of Lynch's own creations. From their 50s suburban background—described by Robert as an "*Ozzie and Harriet* hell"—to Charles' adult existence with his mother in a dingy house, the family could be a textbook illustration of that "dark underbelly" of American normality that was once Lynch's stock-in-trade. The credit, though, does lead us to expect some sort of invented weirdness, whereas everything we see is real.

It's the discomforting ugliness of this reality that makes Terry Zwigoff's portrait so fascinating and so oddly moving. As Robert Crumb's friend, publisher and musical collaborator over 25 years—he played in Crumb's band the Cheap Suit Serenaders—Zwigoff had unique access to less public parts of his subject's life. The result is something rare, a genuine psychobiography in which the subject is revealed less by what he says about himself than by his difference from the people around him. The most important fact about Robert is that somehow he has avoided being Charles or Maxon, just as this late-60s alternative-society icon has always refused to be a part of the culture that celebrated him.

Crumb is more than a little voyeuristic. It's one thing that the cartoonist should lay his psyche open to the camera, but you wonder how much his brothers and mother were prepared for, when they let Zwigoff into their homes. (That the Crumb household appears as a domain of warped maleness is partly to do with the fact that Sisters Sandra and Carol declined to appear.) Charles and Maxon, who seem possessed of acute cerebrality and bitter self-loathing in equal quantities, offer lacerating auto-critiques; but the lucidity of their despair doesn't preempt the camera's ability to frame them as surreal oddballs. Many of their revelations produced hearty but nervous tittering in the screening theatre—not unlike the anxiously amused "Oh my Gaaad" reaction Robert himself greets them with. It's easy to forget that we're marvelling at real people with real problems; that is, until the end of the film, when we learn that Charles killed himself the year after being filmed.

Unlike his brothers, Robert has been able to function in society, partly by designing an armour for himself—a public persona as cartoonish as his self-portraiture on paper. Pebble glasses, straw boater and sandals make this toothy, prematurely venerable scarecrow as distinctive a caricature of Mr Middle America as William Burroughs' patented square-john act, and serving much the same function. Like Burroughs, Crumb proclaims his marginality by pushing anachronistic 'normalness' to an extreme. He is insistent on his non-alignment with the hippie culture that adopted him as its flag-bearer.

Crumb's high-school reminiscences, and glimpses of a blatantly self-pitying autobiographical comic strip, demonstrate that he rescued himself by assuming in extreme form the label inflicted on him—he became a transcendent geek, adopting a fogeyish demeanour. Robert found a way to make his art communicate to the world, unlike his no less talented brothers—Maxon, whose extraordinary paintings are committed to an extreme formalising of the female body, and Charles, whose sexualised obsession with *Treasure Island* sublimated itself in an increasingly abstract comic art that eventually devolved into hermetic graphomania. Robert, however, comes across in speech as the least self-aware of the three: Charles, for example, is capable of a ruthless self-analysis: "I'm never constipated—that's about all I can say for myself."

In the scenes with his brothers, Robert plays an amused, almost disbelieving observer, collaborating in our, and the camera's, tendency to view them as freaks. When Maxon recounts his history of molesting women, Robert just sniggers like a teenager being told a gross but innocuous locker room yarn. He similarly seems to cast himself as an observer of his own life: when an ex-girlfriend lays into his infidelity and emotional dishonesty, he grins like a bashful *This is Your Life* subject—until she's driven to slap him.

One thing that seems to have saved him is his ability to dispense with sublimation in his work; as Aline puts it, "He just depicts his id in its pure form." Certainly, his art from the late 60s to the present is marked by its consistent expression of lust and rage, and seems to display a tenderness towards the world only in its freer-flowing, more realistic mode: in his portraits of 1920s blues heroes, or in his versions of Victorian photographs of madwomen.

For the most part, his cartoons present an obsessive loathing of the world and of himself. Many of his strips display in fairly undiluted form the conventional demonology of racism and misogyny—a horde of monstrous, variously deformed odalisques or, least defensible of all, the African character Ooga Booga. The purity of his bile doesn't necessarily make Crumb a Breughel or a Céline, as Robert Hughes implies, nor does it make him a debunker of such hatreds. However, one woman defends his gargantuan broads as empowering images: "He made it possible for me to have a butt."

The most concise image of Crumb, drawn for the film, has him lying in bed, surrounded by cameras and lights, muttering, "I'm nauseous." Zwigoff's great achievement is to make that nausea tangible. The strangest sequence of all is of Crumb's photo-session at his ex's porn mag, receiving mock discipline and real piggybacks from a selection of wholesome high-school majorette types, clearly having the time of his life and riding high on another absurd image of his own abjection.

TIME, 5/1/95, p. 85, Richard Corliss

Ask Robert Crumb's wives and girlfriends about the Brueghel of underground comics, and they'll say he's morose, withdrawn, almost socially autistic. Crumb agrees, and adds dryly, "That's why I'm such an exciting subject for a movie."

Well, he is. He's the subject of a spooky spellbinder called *Crumb*. With all due respect to *Hoop Dreams*, and with none to the inbred documentary-screening-committee clan of the Motion Picture Academy, which handed this year's Oscar to a former chair of that committee, *Crumb* is the one that should've won.

For director Terry Zwigoff, an old friend, Crumb and his family sit for an unvarnished portrait of an artist whose comic strips reveal modern man at his most screwed up. Slouching through celebrity life with the same gravity-defying posture as the guy in his famous "Keep On Truckin'" cartoon, Crumb presents no apologies or explanations for his work. "Maybe I should be locked up," he says, "and my pencils taken away from me."

Growing up in Philadelphia, in a family that mocked the fantasy life of '50s sit-coms, Robert was the anti-Beaver, the original geeky guy. At 17 Crumb wrote a Valentine to himself that reads like the précis for a Dostoyevsky tale: "Girls are just utterly out of my reach. They won't even let me draw them." He became a cult sensation—and got lots of girls—by drawing them as monuments to his awe and fear of women. They are mammoth fertility totems; they dare the cringing Crumb cartoon male to deify or defile them. In his work Crumb does both, which has earned him no end of scorn from people with protective sensibilities.

Then we meet Crumb's brothers Charles and Max, and we realize with a shudder that Robert is the *normal* one. Charles was the one who encouraged—forced, really—Robert to draw. Gradually Charles' own comics became choked with words, rantings in a minute hand. For 30 years now he has hardly left his mother's house. Max eats string, sits on a bed of nails, then goes begging. He felt that his elder brothers never encouraged him to create art. He finally did, saw that it was good, and had an epileptic seizure.

How can one react to this apocalyptic rubble of a '50s childhood—or to the sexual atrocities limned in Crumb's work? With the only two reactions that modern life demands: a laugh or a scream. The title on one page of a Crumb sketchbook reads,"Words Fail Me (Pictures Aren't Much Better)." But pictures allow Crumb to tell his own truth. To him, as to any artist who ascends deep into the bizarre, his work looks like reality. With care and wit, he draws his own demons and goddesses. One thing he never draws his conclusions. That is for the viewer to do, and be horrified or edified.

Or to declare, as Charles did to any of Robert's enthusiasms, "How perfectly goddamned delightful it all is, to be sure." Irony aside, that's how to respond to this magnificent study in ink and blood.

VILLAGE VOICE, 4/25/94, p. 52, Georgia Brown

So, here I am in Forbidden Planet perusing the R. Crumb rack. A roly-poly fellow I take to be police to the jerkoffs in the Adult Comix Section asks if he may help. I ask for *Self-Hatred* wanting to check out a strip Crumb's cartoonist wife, Aline Kominsky, draws on the family's daily life in the south of France. It's not in. I feel slightly bad at scaring off patrons of hard-core fare—they seem not to take to my, shall I say, motherly presence—but the young man seems happy to have me here. Come to think of it, I used to park the kids here while I rummaged in the Strand. Anyway, I've been leafing through Crumb's collected works for maybe 20 minutes when this friendly clerk nudges me with an open book. "Do you do this?" is what I think he murmurs, pointing to an unadorned line drawing of a tongue licking a giant dick.

Ah, such are the line-of-duty assaults one endures for the privilege of reviewing *Crumb*, Terry Zwigoff's heartbreaking, and, by now, justly celebrated (though not Oscar-nominated) documentary. As a longtime friend of Crumb's—even a recruit in Crumb's rinky-tink '70s string band—Zwigoff presumably works from an intimate understanding of his subject and, more crucially, is granted access to most of the Crumb family.

The film employs three general strategies. One, we follow Crumb on his daily rounds—participating in routine family life, strolling California boulevards, drawing the natives, and chatting in cafés. Two, we revisit Crumb's past through photos, artwork, and family interviews. The third avenue— probably Zwigoff being dutiful—might better have been omitted: These are talking head interviews with critics. Robert Hughes sticks up for Crumb in a way that underlines the ridiculous side of criticism. Feminists, principally Deirdre English, tackle the thankless task of examining content (she offers a strip featuring incest that she says "crosses the line between satire ... and pornography"). I'm not saying such arguments don't have a place, just that *Crumb* doesn't need them.

The heart of the picture is the Crumb family, an eccentric unit (to put it mildly) totally out of sync with the fastidious Fifties they were fated to endure. Mom was a housewife and amphetamine addict, and Dad a sadistic career Marine who died heartbroken, says Crumb, that he'd sired three "wimpy nerdy weirdos." Beside the two brothers we see, Crumb has two younger sisters who declined to participate in the documentary.

At the movie's dead center sits Crumb's brother, the pasty, blob-shaped Charles, on medication for many years and living with his mother. He never sees the sun. "Give me one good reason for going outside." (He reminds me of several film critics.) Every bit as talented as Robert, Charles was the one first obsessed with drawing comics (in sync with Walter Benjamin, he called one comic book series *Arcade*). Touchingly, the cover of his first juvenile comic, *Chuck and Bob*, shows Bob in a boat and Chuck in the water calling on Bob to save him. (Today, I might interject, Robert resides in Sauve, France, though he was not able to save Charles.) Obsessed with the 1950 *Treasure Island*—especially Jim Hawkins's relation to Long John Silver—Charles's teenage oeuvre gradually gets swamped by text, eventually to degenerate into pure graphomania. (May I suggest a double bill of *Crumb* and *Treasure Island*?)

Charles speaks of having stifled deep urges to kill Robert. Robert says he draws with Charles in mind. For both brothers, and for the younger Max, sex, or lack thereof, was their driving force. It's still their topic. The surprisingly good-looking Max, who sits Yoga-style on his homemade bed of nails, recounts episodes of molesting women. Max's sexual experiences were complicated by seizures.

Although Robert had escaped the house and married before his work took shape, becoming famous gave him license to carry out sexual fantasy. The volume I fled Forbidden Planet with has a cover depicting the nerdy Crumb, bulge in his pants (in the movie, an ex-girlfriend advertises Crumb's penis as "one of the largest in the world"), squirting ink into—blotting out—the face of a woman whose T-shirt reads, "Our Bodies, Our Shelves." "Ooh this gets me so excited," reads the character's bubble. Crumb candidly admits he draws those Amazon bodies—redwood thighs, mighty butts, shoes made for stomping—to jerk off to. His running gag: the headless female torso.

We watch him draw from yearbook photos the girls he had crushes on in high school. He salivates over Winona "the Shelf" Newhouse. (Shelves are to pile things on; a self, ooh, that would be so messy.) *Love*, Crumb confesses to an ex-girlfriend, is a word he's only abused; *lust* is what he means. (As she speaks, he paws her in a persistent childlike way a woman might easily mistake for need.) The only girl he can say he's loved is daughter Sophie. Cut to Sophie on Daddy's lap, manipulating a Game Boy.

A crusty misanthrope, Crumb says the only time he feels "love for humanity" is listening to the '20s records he collects. (The film has a marvelous score, much of it played by pianist David Boeddinghaus.) I was struck by a number of things Crumb has in common with Woody Allen—a resemblance that only emphasizes Wood's sanitizing.

It's hard to recount much of Crumb's harrowing story without sounding flip—or, as Crumb himself sounds, blithe and bemused. I guess that's why they call them comics.

Also reviewed in:
CHICAGO TRIBUNE, 5/26/94, Friday/p. K, Michael Wilmington
NATION, 5/22/95, p. 733, Stuart Klawans
NEW YORK TIMES, 4/21/95, p. C6, Stephen Holden
NEW YORKER, 5/1/95, p. 91, Terrence Rafferty
VARIETY, 9/19-25/94, p. 79, Todd McCarthy
WASHINGTON POST, 5/26/95, p. F1, Hal Hinson
WASHINGTON POST, 5/26/95, p. 42, Desson Howe

CURFEW

A New Yorker Films release of an Ayloul Film Productions & Angus Film Produktie, 1993 coproduction with WDR and ARTE. *Producer:* Hany Abu-Assad, Samir Hamed, Henri P.N. Kaupers, Peter van Voegelpoel. *Director:* Rashid Masharawi. *Screenplay (Arabic with English subtitles):* Rashid Masharawi. *Director of Photography:* Klaus Juliusburger. *Editor:* Hadara Oren. *Music:* Said Mouraad/Sabreen. *Sound:* Roni Berger. *Art Director:* Sharif Waked. *Running time:* 75 minutes. *MPAA Rating:* Not Rated.

CAST: Younis Younis (Radar); Salim Daw (Abud Raji/Father); Na'ila Zayaad (Um Raji/Mother); Mahmoud Qadah (Akram/Unmarried Brother); Assem Zoabi (Raji/Married Brother); Areen Omari (Houda/Raji's wife); Salwa Naqara Haddad (Salma/Sister); Lotaf Nweser (Khalil); Rana Saadi (Amal); Souheila Abu-Assad (Um Yousif); Roula Michaël (Sabaah).

NEW YORK POST, 12/7/94, p. 36, Thelma Adams

A boy is born, a girl dies from gas inhalation. A letter arrives from Germany; Israeli soldiers announce a curfew. Neighbors play backgammon; a couple bickers. A mother rations food; a father cuts his son's hair; another son toys with taking radical action while a third son is arrested. A family prepares for bed; a house is bulldozed. Rubber bullets fly.

This is the eventful day in the life of the fictional Rajis, a Palestinian family stuck in a Gaza refugee camp. "Curfew," which begins a two-week run at the Film Forum today, was written and directed by Rashid Masharawi.

Born in 1962 and raised in a Shati, a refugee camp on the Gaza Strip, Masharawi assumes a spare style that is cool but not detached. For most of the movie, he frames the images low, denying the sky. The result is that the exteriors are as claustrophobic as the interiors where the characters pass time under house arrest.

The Israeli soldiers remain largely on the periphery, disembodied voices or menacing faceless figures.

"Curfew" is largely a story of how the growth of a family tree is stunted by political events. The senior Raji (Salim Daw) becomes impotent and indolent, reclining but not resting on a couch. His wife (Na'ila Zayaad) is the family's brave center, whether she is making a life or death decision over the simple task of drying the laundry outside or sneaking out at night to fetch a midwife for a neighbor in labor.

For the beautiful teen-age daughter Salma (Salwa Naqara Haddad), in a way the curfew is business as usual, an extension of the social limitations Arab women face. "I don't care if there is a curfew. I'm not allowed to leave the house anyway," she laments.

Curfew weighs heavier on the angry Akram (Mahmoud Qadah). He has taken to donning a ski mask and committing acts of protest. The movie's sympathies are not with the hot-headed radical, although his anger is made understandable. Twelve-year-old Radar (Younis Younis)—an adorable boy who could star in a Middle Eastern version of "The Wonder Years"—is the filmmaker's alter-ego. Radar makes a game out of passing secrets from cell to cell or playing the lookout while a neighbor's house is razed. This is thc only life he has known.

In the end, the camera retreats. The audience can finally see the sky for the first time in 75 minutes. A weight lifts.

"Curfew" serves as a reminder that even as the audience watches the movie, there are refugees in Gaza who lack the freedom to stay or walk out at will; the simple ability to go to the movies becomes an act of freedom. The movie's grace is that it gives the audience a window on the struggles of Palestinian refugees without telling them what to think.

NEWSDAY, 12/7/94, Part II/p. B11, Gene Seymour

Set in 1993, just before talks between Israel and the PLO led to the present uneasy truce, "Curfew" presents a rueful, poignant picture of life during wartime. Writer-director Rashid Masharawi deals with the tense, cramped lives of a Palestinian family forced into confinement by a open-ended curfew imposed by the Israeli army. Yet, he manages to bring a rich, expansive view, both visually and thematically, within this claustrophobic setting.

As the film opens on a sunlit morning in a Palestinian refugee camp in Gaza, life seems to drift along in mundane, leisurely ways not often found in evening news clips of Middle East strife. People cook, gossip, hang out. Kids play soccer. Among them is quick-witted, fleet-footed Radar (Younis Younis). While playing, he gets a letter from an older brother who's studying in Germany. He's about to read it to the rest of the family when loudspeakers blare announcements of a curfew.

Why? No one in Radar's family knows, but they've been through enough of these things to know it could last a day, a week, a month, maybe more. They have plenty of onions around the house to counteract the effects of a tear gas attack. But Radar's mother (Na'ila Zayaad) is figuring out how to ration the rest of the food. Also she isn't sure whether she'll be risking her life by hanging her clothes outside to dry. His father (Salim Daw), already in fragile health, sees himself slowly wasting away from the strain of living under siege.

Meanwhile, of the two older brothers living at home, one (Assem Zoabi) is married with a small child and is trying as best he can to cope with the situation. Not so the other brother

(Mahmoud Qadah), who smolders with rage and frustration, not just with the curfew but with his constricted life.

Radar possesses the coolest head in the household, able to tell what kind of bullets are whizzing outside the house by just their sound. He's also able to carry out emergency errands for his family and for the next-door neighbors, one of whom's about to give birth. But he can't finish reading the rest of his brother's letter from Germany because of interruptions like electricity being cut off or Israeli soldiers rounding up all men in the camp for ID checks.

Masharawi stages his scenes of desperate tedium with the authority of someone who grew up in a refugee camp and spent 40 days confined with his own family during the 1990 Gulf War. He keeps everything, even the exterior sequences, contained within the point of view of the family, which heightens both the film's gnawing tension and its humane, if melancholy vision.

VILLAGE VOICE, 12/13/94, p. 72, Amy Taubin

Restrained but immensely persuasive, *Curfew*, a first feature by Palestinian director Rashid Masharawi, depicts 24 hours in the life of a family living in a refugee camp on the Gaza Strip in 1993, a few months prior to the peace treaty. Of the current political situation, Masharawi writes: "(It) is like guards leaving a prison; they open the doors to the cells but keep the exits locked." In any event, the film isn't rendered obsolete by symbolic political actions. Indeed, its purpose is to show how what we perceive as the immediate, concrete present is bound by history and memory.

Curfew is shot mostly in a single interior space, a large, sparsely furnished "family" room that opens onto a kitchen, a cluster of bedrooms, and an interior courtyard. The space is claustrophobic, but offers neither privacy nor security. A curfew has been imposed by the Israeli military; no one knows how long it will last. The family members—mother, father, three sons, a daughter, and the wife and child of the eldest son—try to go about their routines—cooking, cleaning, making conversation, speculating, reminiscing as if these were "normal" circumstances. A complex network of communication has been developed among neighboring families: food and money are passed window to window; visitors climb across the courtyard walls. Anyone going in the street, however, even to fetch a doctor, risks being shot by the Israelis. Living under such a calculatedly capricious military regime results in a permanent state of anxiety and anger. Fearful that the Israelis will take vengeance on his family if he joins the *intifada*, the middle son sulks in his room, poring over leaflets. *Curfew* shows how, in that sense, the Israeli policies have worked in the short run—leaving the Palestinians hopelessly paralyzed.

Masharawi, who has amazing formal authority for a relatively inexperienced filmmaker, knows how to build dramatic tension from swallowed words and broken gestures. There's not a single forced moment. As the father confined to his bed with what may be a mortal illness, Salim Daw centers the film with life-or-death urgency, What one feels is the end is not only sorrow and pity for people who've been robbed of their future, but abiding respect for their ability to survive—with grace.

Also reviewed in:
NEW YORK TIMES, 12/7/94, p. C17, Janet Maslin
VARIETY, 5/16-22/94, p. 41, Lisa Nesselson

D2: THE MIGHTY DUCKS

A Buena Vista release of a Walt Disney Pictures presentation. *Executive Producer:* Doug Claybourne. *Producer:* Jordan Kerner and Jon Avnet. *Director:* Sam Weisman. *Screenplay:* Steven Brill. *Based on characters created by:* Steven Brill. *Director of Photography:* Mark Irwin. *Editor:* Eric Sears and John F. Link. *Music:* J.A.C. Redford. *Music Editor:* Michael T. Ryan. *Sound:* David Kelson and (music) Andy Bass. *Sound Editor:* Robert L. Shepton. *Casting:* Judy Taylor and Lynda Gordon. *Production Designer:* Gary Frutkoff. *Art Director:* Dawn Snyder. *Set Decorator:* Kathryn Peters. *Set Dresser:* Karin L. McGaughey and Cory Schubert.

Special Effects: John E. Gray. *Costumes:* Grania Preston. *Make-up:* June Rudley Brickman. *Make-up (Emilio Estevez):* Kim Carrillo. *Running time:* 107 minutes. *MPAA Rating:* PG.

CAST: Emilio Estevez (Gordon Bombay); Kathryn Erbe (Michele); Michael Tucker (Tibbles); Jan Rubes (Jan); Carsten Norgaard (Wolf); Maria Ellingsen (Marria); Joshua Jackson (Charlie); Elden Ryan Ratliff (Fulton); Shaun Weiss (Goldberg); Matt Doherty (Averman); Brandon Adams (Jesse); Garette Ratliff Henson (Guy); Marguerite Moreau (Connie); Vincent A. Larusso (Banks); Colombe Jacobsen (Julie); Aaron Lohr (Portman); Ty O'Neal (Dwayne); Kenan Thompson (Russ); Mike Vitar (Luis); Justin Wong (Ken); Scott Whyte (Gunnar); Kai Lennox (Olaf); Vicellous Reon Shannon (James); Noah Verduzco (Hector); Marcus Klemp (Fanger); Jon Karl Hjelm (Norbert); Michael Ooms (McGill); Casey Garven (Larson); Brock Pierce (Young Gordon); Robert Pall (Young Gordon's Father); Leah Lail (Terry at Party); Wayne Gretzky (Himself); Jeannette Kerner (Woman at Boutique); Mary Brill (Woman at Boutique); Jack White and Michael Francis Kelly (Referees at Game); Bob Miller (Game Announcer); Joe Fowler (Reporter at Anaheim); Harve Cook (Trinidad Counch); Rodney Louis Johnson ("Mr. Alley Oop"); Laura Lombardi (Photo Shoot Art Director); Nancy Stephens (Coliseum Reporter); Tajsha Thomas (Coliseum Reporter); Kevin Womack, Bryant Woodert, and Adam A. Labaud, Jr. (Doo-Wop Singers).

LOS ANGELES TIMES, 3/25/94, Calendar/p. 10, Kevin Thomas

"D2 the Might Ducks" isn't nearly as mighty as the 1992 original in which hotshot Minneapolis attorney Gordon Bombay (Emilio Estevez) regains his values coaching a peewee ice hockey team. "The Mighty Ducks" cleverly managed to have it both ways: a movie that suggests winning isn't everything but for sure lets its underdogs come out on top. By the finish of "D2" the message seems pretty clear. Winning is everything, after all.

At the end of that deservedly successful picture, Bombay and the mother (Heidi Kling) of a team member who stands up to him over the issue of cheating to win are involved in a budding romance.

Logically, any sequel would have to do with the flowering of that love, but writer Steven Brill brutally writes her out of the script in order to get the Mighty Ducks team back on skates as rapidly as possible.

Her total absence from the sequel is tossed off as Gordon, on the road playing hockey himself in a minor league, nonchalantly remarks on his failure to write to her and that her son doesn't see much of his mother now that she's remarried. This casual dismissal in the ongoing story of such a major, pivotal figure, a caring individual of warmth and strength, starts the film out on a sour note.

Brill, who also wrote the first film, is on to something valid when, a la "Rocky II," he deals with the commercialism that engulfs successful athletes; you just wish that he had stuck with making this point and developed it fully. When an injury sidelines Bombay from the minors just as he's about to make the move into the majors, he's in a mood to listen to an offer from Tibbles (Michael Tucker), an official sponsor of Team USA, for him to gather up his Mighty Ducks, let Tibbles add a few more talented youngsters from around the country, and enter an international competition to be held at the brand-new Anaheim Arena.

The idea is that the coach and kids are to bc tempted by the sponsor's blandishments—and the high end of the L.A. lifestyle epitomized by Rodeo Drive.

Such moral concerns come across this time as mechanical and secondary as director Sam Weisman piles on the stunts and pranks while the Ducks prepare to take on Iceland's Vikings, whose coach (Carsten Norgaard) is so villainous that he seems to have stepped right out of a silent melodrama. Despite the earnestness and energy Estevez once again brings to Gordon Bombay,"D2" plays like a caricature of the original. The urge to cash in on a film's success by making a sequel is perfectly understandable, but "The Mighty Ducks," by its very concern with values, provided a special challenge. In not meeting it by a long shot, "D2 the Mighty Ducks" smacks of a sellout.

NEW YORK POST, 3/25/94, p. 37, Michael Medved

Part of the fun in watching "D2: The Mighty Ducks" comes from jotting down all the goofy "inspirational" lines of dialogue that keep popping up at regular intervals. For instance:

"Just when "you think they're going to break apart—ducks fly together!"

Or, "I don't want to spend the rest of my life sharpening skates in this rinky-dink town. I want something better!

Or, "Compared to other countries, America is still young. Still forming its own identity. A teenager, like all of you. A little awkward at times, but always close to greatness!"

"D2: The Mighty Ducks" is also a little awkward at times, but no one could ever claim it's close to greatness. It is, rather, an unapologetically insipid sequel that can provide 90 minutes of undemanding entertainment if you're in a sufficiently silly mood.

The story begins with former hot-shot lawyer and peewee hockey coach Emilio Estevez skating for a minor league franchise when he suffers a devastating injury. He retreats to a skate sharpening shop until a slick manufacturer of hockey equipment (Michael Tucker) persuades him to coach Team USA at the coming Junior Goodwill Games.

Naturally, Estevez reassembles eight of the original Ducks from the first movie and soon supplements their might with a Cuban-American speedster (Mike Vitar); a lasso-twirling cowpoke (Ty O'Neal); a girl goalie from Maine (Colombe Jacobsen) a Korean-American Olympic figure skater (Justin Wong) and a street-smart survivor from South Central L.A. (Kenan Thompson). It is, in other words, your basic bomber crew from any World War II movie.

And make no mistake—the Ducks must go to war to defend our national honor against an invincible arrogant foe representing a menacing world power, Iceland. The struggle for the championship is described as "a classic David and Goliath story" with the USA (population 20 million) as David and Iceland (population less than 300,00!) as a most unlikely Goliath. Isn't there an Icelandic anti-defamation league to prevent the kids of America (who are this movie's prime audience) from growing up thinking that this pleasant, peaceful land is populated entirely by black-suited sadists who cheat at hockey and sneer at mere Americans?

The final showdown between Team USA and the Icelandic brutes (led by the formidably forbidding Carsten Norgaard) is filmed with all the apocalyptic intensity of the celebrated Battle on the Ice in "Alexander Nevsky." The reason it's nonetheless watchable is that this film, unlike its predecessor, seems ready to laugh at its own excesses.

There's little attempt at serious uplift, as the Ducks skim happily across a very shallow pond. In the first picture Estevez had to leave his high-powered career to find redemption with misfit kids he's assigned to coach. This time he "loses his way" once again lured by the prospect of earning big bucks through product endorsements, but his Ducks, together with beautiful team tutor Kathryn Erbe, manage to remind him that "a game is supposed to be fun. It's about more than just winning or losing!"

Of course, the picture shamelessly indulges the same crass commercialism it pretends to condemn, and serves as one huge plug for the Disney company's new hockey franchise called (what else?) the Anaheim Mighty Ducks. The real-life team, by the way, is enjoying better-than-expected success. The film promoting them is also bound to put some impressive numbers on the box-office score board, despite well-deserved skepticism from critics and sophisticates.

NEWSDAY, 3/25/94, Part II/p. B7, Ira Robbins

Have they begun teaching the art of hypocrisy in grade school yet? If not, it's unlikely the prepubescent hockey fans for whom "D2: The Mighty Ducks" is geared will enjoy the rich irony of the film's righteous stance against runaway sports commercialism. Almost a year to the 1992 day after Disney's charming original "Mighty Ducks" movie—essentially "The Bad News Bears on Ice"—opened, the company's real-life Mighty Ducks NHL expansion team skated onto the ice of a newly built stadium in Anaheim, two miles from Disneyland. Sports, movies, money, culture, merchandise—it *is* a small world after all.

Irony was probably the last goal of "D2: The Mighty Ducks," yet this simpleminded sequel gives Coach Gordon Bombay (Emilio Estevez) his comeuppance, for being seduced by the fame and fortune promised by the equipment company sponsoring his team. The reiteration of amateur sports ideals is fine, but the real Mighty Ducks remain hockey's most extraordinarily cynical cross-marketing effort.

Such well-intentioned pedantry is typical of a self-conscious kids' film whose socially responsible political correctness identifies Iceland as the post-cold war evil empire, fields a national team of incredible multi-cultural inclusiveness and relies on a secret weapon found in a graffiti-covered Los Angeles playground.

But that's what formulaic sports fantasy is all about: our side finding a way to overcome long odds, foul play and temptation while learning about team effort, hard work and the ultimate purpose of playing for fun, not money.

The story—which, in outline if not sport, is virtually the same as "Above the Rim"—again follows Coach Bombay, who grew from promising athlete to sharkish lawyer to mature coach in the heart-melting slapstick slapshot of the first "Mighty Ducks." For the purposes of this streamlined sequel, he gets injured on the verge of his long-awaited NHL break and returns to Minneapolis to sulk, under the patient gaze of wise old skate-shop owner Jan (Jan Rubes), a replacement for the first film's Hans.

When Bombay is coaxed out of his funk to coach Team USA in the Junior Goodwill Games, he reunites most of the first film's Ducks, a rambunctious and adorable collection of archetypal moppets, augmented by some demographically broadening newcomers.

In Los Angeles for the tournament (which eventually finds its way to the Ducks' Anaheim stadium), the squad—which includes a cowboy, a Cuban, a heavy-metal thug and a Korean figure skater—engages in some mild hijinks and plays some impressively choreographed hockey. Then comes the lopsided confrontation with the brutal, Aryan-looking Iceland team and Wolf, its oily, vicious coach (Carsten Norgaard). A resultant loss of confidence, corresponding with a loss of faith in Coach Bombay, leads the team to South Central L.A., where local kids playing roller-hockey add crucial street seasoning to their game. Of course.

Thus armed with new strategies, new resolve, a new player and new regard for their coach, Team USA meets the dastardly Icelanders in the climactic finale, a rough-and-tumble cinematic set piece pumped up with a symphonic score and whooshing sound effects. It would be too much to expect "D2" to depart from its game plan, but two periods in, a surprising break with jingoist tradition trumps patriotism as a rallying cry.

If family values are an emblem of the right and political correctness a foible of the left, then "D2: The Mighty Ducks" is a center, skating towards an empty net. Take the kids and leave the thinking to them.

SIGHT AND SOUND, 1/95, p. 44, Tom Tunney

Soon after his success in coaching the Might Ducks pee wee league ice hockey team, Gordon Bombay's brief career as a professional player comes to a premature end when he's badly injured during a game. He returns to his home town of Minneapolis and to a job in the sports shop run by his friend Jan. One of the players in the Mighty Ducks team, Charlie, also works in the shop as Jan's apprentice.

Sports promoter Tibbles asks Gordon to coach 'Team USA' in the Junior Goodwill Games in Los Angeles. Charlie sets about gathering together the rest of the old Mighty Ducks team, adding further players from Texas, Miami and elsewhere. The squad is also assigned a teacher, Michele. After initial training, the group arrives in Los Angeles where Gordon is distracted by his luxurious seaside apartment and by the numerous sponsorship deals set up by Tibbles. The team's first games go well, but they are decisively beaten by the tournament favourites, Iceland, who are coached by the ruthless Wolf. Taunted by Russ, a young spectator from South Central LA, the team accept a challenge to play his team at a roller blade version of the sport on an inner city recreation ground, picking up several valuable tips in the process.

Gordon meanwhile is persuaded by Jan that team spirit, not the simple desire to win, is the main thing that counts. Reinvigorated, team and coach—with the addition of Russ, who specialises in a unique style of spinning shot—go on to play Iceland again in the tournament final. The game goes on to penalties and when Iceland's final shot is saved, victory goes to 'Team USA'.

Hollywood sports movies depressingly proffer the same plot over and over again: the underdogs gradually get themselves organised and win against a ruthless opposition, victory inevitably being achieved in the closing moments of the game. In the process, these films fulsomely assert the cliché that it's not the winning but the taking part that counts, and the cynical notion that nice guys finish last is replaced by the cosy idea that perhaps they can finish first after all. That's Hollywood and that, above all, is the Disney world view. Seasoned filmgoers may long have tried of this formula, but a new generation of easily-pleased youngsters emerges every few years to avidly consume the same recipe over and over again.

The original *The Mighty Ducks*—retitled *Champions* for UK release—adheredto this structure, delivering a lively ration of slapstick humour, crisply-edited rink action and wide-eyed homilies. This threadbare sequel regurgitates the same scenario on a larger, international stage. The result is a ludicrous display of xenophobic Americanism. The nice guys finish first, but only when they're American, and the bad guys reside in, of all places, Iceland. In years gone by, the USSR and East Germany would have been the prime sporting targets against which to define heroic American prowess. With the end of the Cold War and the opening of these markets to its product, the Disney marketing team obviously picked on Iceland not only for its metaphorical aptness, but because of its tiny population—and hence minimal potential for lost revenue.

This pantomime level of villainy is the most revealing indication of the film's steadfast refusal to engage with any recognisable reality, sporting, social or otherwise. In their neo-fascist black outfits, these ice stormtroopers represent everything soulless, militaristic and supposedly un-American. By contrast, the easy-going Americans depend on teamwork for their success. Always referred to as 'Team USA', the group triumphs only when it learns to bond together and switches its USA shirts for their (trademarked) Mighty Ducks outfits. With the team's too obviously careful ethnic and geographical balance, this is a patriotic fantasia that wouldn't have been out of place at the height of World War Two—especially the scene where the kids proudly stand up in turn and announce which states they're from. The message is that natural talent, positive thinking and team spirit can overcome any disadvantage. But it can only sustain that message by not actually showing us any disadvantages: the kids are never more than smiling ethnic and geographical ciphers who exist in a social and economic vacuum. Russ takes the team back to south Central LA, but we never see his parents or home environment.

The characters remain no more than limp mouthpieces for the film's Horatio Alger view of the world; also lost is any sense of sport as an activity involving luck, huge variations of skill and the possibility of losing on a regular basis. There is a queasy undercurrent to all the noisy statement, which suggests that this USA is a fundamental insecure place which needs its enemies to define its identity much more than it needs its friends. The original *The Mighty Ducks* at least provided some token social context for Bombay and his child players. That film's moral trajectory saw him casting off his grasping yuppie pretensions and passing on the values of teamwork and solidarity to his young charges—values embodied in the team's war cry, "Ducks fly together!" Here he is once more seduced by materialism, confronts another nasty coach, and makes good when he's reminded yet again of his late father's ideals.

The film's double-edged attitude sponsorship and business is also revealing. In its wish-fulfilment world, they are presented as innately dangerous, and yet in real life the Disney organisation has itself created a professional ice hockey team, the Mighty Ducks, to promote these two films and sundry merchandising spin-offs. It's a significant new stage in the bland Disneyfication of the American dream—the proud individualism and ruthless killer instinct of the Bald Eagle is implicitly replaced as national symbol by gullible, gregarious and non-threatening fowl. As Bombay keeps saying ducks do fly together. But they also tend to get shot down in huge numbers by greedy hunters who lure them to their doom with decoy quack whistles. Early in the film, Jan gives Bombay a quacker whistle which is presented as a kind of mystic talisman. Interpret that whistle as a symbol of how business and the media manipulate and mould society to profit-driven ends, and the film is much more truthful than it can know.

Also reviewed in:
CHICAGO TRIBUNE, 3/25/94, Friday/p. C, Michael Wilmington
NEW YORK TIMES, 3/25/94, p. C17, Caryn James
VARIETY, 3/28-4/3/94, p. 68, Leonard Klady
WASHINGTON POST, 3/25/94, p. D7, Desson Howe

DAYS, THE

A Shu Kei's Creative Workshop Ltd. production. *Executive Producer:* Wang Xiaoshuai and Zhang Hongtao. *Producer:* Liu Jie, Zhang Hongtao, and Wang Yao. *Director:* Wang Xiaoshuai. *Screenplay (Mandarin with English subtitles):* Wang Xiaoshuai. *Director of Photography:* Wu Di and Liu Jie. *Editor:* Jin Jin. *Music:* Liang Heping. *Sound:* Yu Yuezhong and Meng Jianwei. *Running time:* 80 minutes. *MPAA Rating:* Not Rated.

CAST: Yu Hong (Chun); Liu Xiaodong (Dong); Lou Ye (Friend in Bar); Wang Xiaoshuai (Narrator).

SIGHT AND SOUND, 3/95, p. 36 Tony Rayns

Dong and Chun are tutors in the Beijing art school from which they both graduated; they met and fell in love as students and have lived together ever since. But their relationship has grown stale and their day to day lives, from the early morning lovemaking to her housework and his late night drinking, have become routine. Both are aware that their time together is coming to an end, but both are very careful not to raise the issue.

Dong is crushed when a buyer from Hong Kong reneges on a commitment to buy his paintings. Chun, more realistic and more cynical, tells him to stop dreaming, but indulges him when he tries to drown his sorrows. One night he overhears her placing a collect call to someone in New York. Dong withdraws into himself and is unresponsive when Chun mentions the idea of emigrating. He begins a life-size portrait of her, representing her on a long-ago summer excursion to the Great Wall. A letter from abroad arrives for Chun. Dong discusses mutual acquaintances with a friend who is himself planning to emigrate.

Chun tells Dong that she is pregnant and he urges her to get an abortion. When it's done, she suggests a trip together to visit his family in North-East China. The break from routine slightly quickens their pulses, but Dong's need to show Chun off to his parents (and to prove himself dominant in the relationship) makes for awkwardness and embarrassment. Dong shows Chun sites from his childhood. Chun tells him that she wants to see her own family (with whom she severed contact during the Cultural Revolution) before going abroad, and intends to leave the next day. Dong becomes angry and resentful. But Chun leaves as planned.

Back in the Beijing apartment, Dong receives many excited letters from Chun but can never formulate a reply. He locks himself away and never sees anyone, slowly losing touch with reality. After breaking all the glasses in the art school one night, he is sent for psychiatric tests. His friend, narrating the story on the soundtrack, reports the doctor's comments: five out of ten people are like Dong, and his case presents no cause for concern.

There has never been a Chinese film like *The Days* before, but it has much in common with other 'outlaw' movies and videotapes made in Beijing in the last two years. The emergence of an independent film and video culture in China reflects the country's new social and economic realities: the refusal of the impoverished state film studios to employ new directors, the sudden proliferation of relatively wealthy entrepreneurs in the cities, and the rise of a post-Cultural Revolution generation with attitudes, ideas and interests very different from their fifth generation predecessors. Like He Yi's *Red Beads (Xuan Lian)* and Zhang Yuan's *Beijing Bastards (Beijing Zazhong)*, *The Days* was made on a shoestring—around £7,000, raised from private investors—and produced entirely outside the system, without permission or approval from the authorities. All of these films remain unseen in China, but their 'illegal' international distribution has led the Film Bureau to blacklist their directors, in a conspicuously unsuccessful attempt to stop them from making more independent films.

Wang Xiaoshuai's film goes to the heart of experiences and states of mind shared by many people of his age and background. Dong and Chun (played by a real life couple, who are also real life stars of the Beijing art world) are typical Beijing artist/intellectuals of the 90s; pathetically dependent on a system from which they feel completely alienated, struggling to find ways to supplement a meagre state salary, repressed and careful not to show their feelings. The art college that is their 'work unit' evidently has no actual work for them (not an unusual situation in China, where overstaffing remains the norm in the public sector); the only advantage they have over their self-employed contemporaries is the dingy, cold-water apartment that comes with the non-jobs. Like all such people in present day China, they understand that they are on their own economically but still subject to all the old political controls. For Dong, like many, the only real challenge is survival, at whatever cost to his self-esteem and mental health. For Chun, like many others, the only way up is out: she cannot envisage things getting any better if she stays in China. Their predicaments, in short, are legion.

At first sight, Wang's approach to the final days of their relationship is scrupulously naturalistic. Most scenes limit themselves to quotidian routines; there is no attempt to inject phoney 'drama' into the situation. But many of the compositions and visual/aural details have resonances that can only be described as poetic: the squads of students in military training who jog past the apartment block when Dong comes down in the mornings to fetch hot water, for example, or the gatehouse keeper who teases Dong with fantasies of receiving letters from abroad before telling him that no mail has come for him. None of these details (and there are countless other examples) has a metaphorical thrust, but their allusions to things strange and sinister coalesce a mood of unreality which gently undermines the surface naturalism.

Wang finesses this process by himself speaking a novelistic narration, ostensibly from the point of view of an unidentified friend of the couple (is he the guy who drinks with Dong in a bar one night?) but in fact offering psychological insights beyond the reach of any friend. The narration provides relevant background information about the couple (their relations with their respective families, recollections of the day trip that inspired Dong's portrait of Chun), but the wry, semi-detached tone of its analyses of their problems achieves a deeper level of truth.

There is a simple pun in the film's Chinese title. *Dong-Chun de Rizi* means literally Winter and Spring Days, but of course Dong (Winter) and Chun (Spring) are also the names of the protagonists. The story does indeed begin in winter and end in spring, setting the couple's final separation in the snows of the former Manchuria and Dong's relapse into mild schizophrenia in a room lit by spring sunlight. By this time, Chun herself is absent, or rather present only in Dong's unfinished painting, in which she stands on the Great Wall in a floral jacket peering through binoculars at what might be Russia in the distance. Here, finally, is a suggestion of metaphor: 'spring', the film implies, remains elusive for China's artists.

If this is a metaphor, it's nothing like the ones found in movies such as *Yellow Earth, the Big Parade* and *Raise the Red Lantern*. Chen Kaige, Zhang Yimou and the other leaders of the fifth generation have always seen themselves as fated to carry the burden of Chinese culture, a perception which obliges them to reconstruct over-arching visions of the state of the nations politics and social dynamics. Infinitely more modest, Wang Xiaoshuai contents himself with an intimate account of day to day life as he and many like him live it. Indeed, if he and Beijing's other new generation independents have anything in common beyond their resourcefulness and lack of money, it's their absolute commitment to rooting their work in the street-level realities they have had to cope with all their lives.

In *The Days*, this results in a delicately understated—but piercingly moving—account of the end of a relationship, which at the same time pinpoints a mood of dread and incipient defeat that Wang clearly sees as endemic in China's present political climate. But the film is not at all depressing. On the contrary, the freshness of its modesty and the unconfected immediacy of its emotions make its analysis of a kind of 'everyday madness' curiously cheering.

Also reviewed in:
NEW YORK TIMES, 8/31/94, p. C14, Caryn James
VARIETY, 11/22/93, p. 34, Ken Eisner

DEATH AND THE MAIDEN

A Fine Line Features release in association with Capitol Films Ltd. of a Mount/Kramer production in association with Channel Four Films/Flach Films.. *Executive Producer:* Sharon Harel and Jane Barclay. *Producer:* Thom Mount and Josh Kramer. *Director:* Roman Polanski.

Screenplay: Rafael Yglesias and Ariel Dorfman. *Based on the play by:* Ariel Dorfman. *Director of Photography:* Tonino delli Colli. *Editor:* Hervé De Luze. *Music:* Wojciech Kilar. *Music Editor:* Andrew Glen. *Sound:* Daniel Brisseau. *Sound Editor:* Laurent Quaglio. *Casting:* Mary Selway and Patsy Pollock. *Production Designer:* Pierre Guffroy. *Art Director:* Claude Moesching. *Set Dresser:* Martina Skala. *Special Effects:* Gilbert Pieri. *Costumes:* Milena Canonero. *Make-up:* Linda de Vetta and Didier Lavergne. *Running time:* 103 minutes. *MPAA Rating:* R.

CAST: Sigourney Weaver (Paulina Escobar); Ben Kingsley (Dr. Roberto Miranda); Stuart Wilson (Gerardo Escobar); Krystia Mova (Dr. Miranda's Wife); Jonathan Vega and Rodolphe Vega (Dr. Miranda's sons); Sergio Ortega (String Quartet Manager).

FILMS IN REVIEW, 7-8/95, p. 54, Andy Pawelczak

Who is Roman Polanski? Besides a hack writers dream, that is. His life seems made for the tabloids—childhood victimization by the Nazis in his native Poland, early success as a director, then the murder of his wife Sharon Tate by Charles Manson, and in 1977 his conviction for "unlawful sexual intercourse" with a 13-year-old girl and subsequent exile in Europe. The Manson connection in particular has made Polanski into a part of pop demonology—people have always assumed that Polanski has a secret life, that he's a habitue of an international, decadent demimonde, perhaps something like the society of Parisian vampires portrayed in *Interview With The Vampire*. Polanski himself reinforced the image with his cameo role in Chinatown as the sadistic thug who slashes Jack Nicholson's nostril with a switchblade. So it's not surprising that each new Polanski movie is an occasion for the popular parlor game of spotting the raw slices of Polanski psyche displayed on the screen.

To render Caesar his due right at the beginning—yes, *Death and the Maiden* does obscurely resonate with the facts of Polanski's life. Guilt, misogyny, rape, fascist oppression—the themes are all there. And when Sigourney Weaver appears alone in an isolated house in a storm, I suppose many viewers will think of Sharon Tate and Manson, the latter our very own gothic monster. But the surprising thing is how becalmed the movie is, how little the material activates Polanski's filmic imagination.

It's not entirely his fault. Based on a play by the Chilean Ariel Dorfman, the screenplay (written by Dorfman and Rafael Yglesias) is full of lifeless dialogue and too pat reversals. The film takes place in an unnamed South American country with a new democratic regime. The reformist president has appointed a human rights commission to investigate the atrocities of the previous regime, but Paulina Escobar (Sigourney Weaver) knows it will be a whitewash. When her husband brings home a man who helped him when his car broke down, Paulina thinks she recognizes the doctor (she was blindfolded and only heard his voice) who tortured and raped her in a fascist prison. She clubs him into submission and then ties him to a chair and tapes his mouth—she has now become the interrogator and he's the victim. The rest of the film, which takes place during a single night and is largely confined to the Escobar house, is a three-way psycho drama as Paulina tries to extract a confession from Dr. Miranda (Ben Kingsley) and convince her husband (Stuart Wilson) to go along with her.

Dorfman's play is theme besotted—it's the kind of writing in which the characters seem like afterthoughts designed to illustrate ideas. And every time some new narrative information or a new theme is introduced, you can hear the gears grind as the whole mechanism shudders and jerks forward. Among the themes are the banality of evil, the connection between fascism and misogyny, and the tendency of people what they behold. The man who tortured Paulina liked to play Schubert's "Death And The Maiden" while he raped her, and this provides both a neat emblem for the whole drama and another theme i.e., that the humanities, such as music and literature, don't humanize. (As George Steiner once pointed out the commandants of the Nazi death camps were cultivated men who listened to Bach and read Goethe during their off-hours.) Unfortunately, Dorfman doesn't bring anything new to these ideas, so we're left with the acting and Polanski's visual treatment to provide whatever bite the film has.

Polanski both mythicizes and humanizes Sigourney Weaver's screen persona. As in the *Alien* movies, she's once again fighting a monster, but this time it's an all too human monster. Weaver, with her big-boned body and fierce intensity, is like an ancient Fury come back to avenge all the crimes committed against women. Her eerie monomania also has overtones of her performance as Diane Fossey in *Gorillas in the Mist*, and in Paulina's more deranged moments she recalls the paranoid, homicidal Catherine Deneuve character from Polanski's *Repulsion*. In one quietly powerful scene, Paulina strips to the waist, and Polanski shoots the scene in such a way that instead of prurience it invites our compassion. Her naked body is somehow unutterably sad and vulnerable—she's really exposed—and when her husband nuzzles her breasts, Polanski focuses on her grief-haunted face. Weaver's performance doesn't have an ounce of audience ingratiation, and if it misses the high notes of classic tragedy which the role clearly implies, I think that's due to the weakness of the script.

As Dr. Miranda, Ben Kingsley doesn't have much to do—for a good deal of the film he's bound and gagged. The movie pretends to make a mystery out of Miranda's guilt or innocence, but enough clues are dropped that the alert viewer won't be very mystified. Kingsley does have one good speech at the end during which you can see reflections of the sulphurous fires within. As Paulina's husband, Stuart Wilson is convincingly confused and uncertain about everything—his feelings for his wife, the situation with Dr. Miranda, and his role as the head of the human rights commission.

Polanski overtly paid homage to Hitchcock in *Frantic*, but this film has Hitchcockian overtones too. Hitchcock was a master of this kind of cat and mouse game played out on a single set with a small cast of characters. He famously shot *Rope* in eight long takes, each shot taking us deeper into a labyrinth of twisted motives and delusional hubris. Polanski can't match that performance, and his visual style in this film never quite jells. In past films, he was able to make us feel voyeuristically complicit with his material, but his style here is too cold, too distant and analytic, to draw us in. The film is a respectable effort, perhaps too respectable—it doesn't have that knife slash to the nose.

LOS ANGELES TIMES, 12/23/94, Calendar/p. 16, Peter Rainer

"Death and the Maiden" is about the consequences of torture, and it never lets up. Essentially a three-character drama in a single location, it's an expert piece of claustrophobic cinema, but after a while you may want to break away from it. The film bears down on the audience with an almost sadistic relish. It's an unsettling experience, but not a particularly rich one. It's too schematic and self-important for that.

Ariel Dorfman's play, produced on Broadway in 1992 and from which the film is adapted, has its roots in the playwright's exile from Chile in 1973 during the coup that overthrew President Salvador Allende. Like the play, the film, adapted by Dorfman and Rafael Yglesias and directed by Roman Polanski, is set in an unnamed country in South America after the fall of a right-wing dictatorship.

It begins with Paulina Escobar (Sigourney Weaver) pacing like a tigress within the confines of her cliffside home as a rainstorm strikes and the power goes out. Then her husband, Gerardo Escobar (Stuart Wilson), a lawyer newly appointed by the President to head up a commission investigating the human rights violations of the overthrown fascist regime, is dropped off at home after his car has broken down in the flood. His Good Samaritan is a Dr. Roberto Miranda (Ben Kingsley), a convivial physician who professes his admiration for Gerardo's leftism. Paulina—who was blindfolded, tortured and raped repeatedly by a fascist physician 15 years earlier—overhears Miranda's voice and freezes in horror. Is this the voice of the man who brutalized her?

The film is about what happens when Paulina turns the tables on the man she believes is responsible for the horrors she still lives with. Strapping him to a chair, bludgeoning him, stuffing his mouth with her panties, she demands he confess to his crimes—that's the only way he'll be allowed to survive. Her husband, willing at first to believe Miranda's protestations of innocence, assumes the role of his defender.

And that's about it, for 103 gruesome minutes. As we hear more and more details of Paulina's torture and Miranda's denials, the film turns into a grindingly creepy whodunit. (Even the closed-off, candle-lit set is reminiscent of a murder mystery.) But the characters are so ideologically drawn that they lose our sympathies—they're stand-ins in Dorfman's existential morality play about justice and revenge.

Polanski, who no doubt connected up to this material on personal levels of his own, does a very good job of keeping the creepiness at full boil; there's never a moment in this film when you don't feel the threat of sudden violence. But if there's a larger dimension to be found in all this, Polanski didn't find it (and perhaps it's a good thing he didn't go looking). "Death and the Maiden"—the title comes from the Schubert string quartet played repeatedly while Paulina was raped—works best as a horror movie.

Weaver plays the role in high-style heroic fashion. She's overwrought with vengeance. There's nothing frail or damaged about this woman—she has become pure will. Kingsley, in the film's most difficult role, keeps you guessing about Miranda's motives.

Miranda has such a wheedling, flabbergasted, enraged presence that a few of his scenes with Paulina play like a nightmare parody of a bad marriage. She accuses him of lying, he pleads innocence, she tortures him. The batterer gets battered. Wilson's Gerardo, caught in the middle, has all the ineffectuality of a spurned suitor. He wants to believe his wife, but he also—perhaps out of cowardice—wants to believe Miranda.

Polanski has rightly resisted the urge to "open up" the play by bringing it outdoors. When he finally does move the action cliffside, the ocean vistas are as intimidating and closed-off as the Escobar's living room/torture chamber. Everything in this film works up to its final ambiguous image, and yet Polanski may have overvalued its inexorability. We're supposed to get a case of the cold creeps, but a response of "So what?" would be equally appropriate.

NEW YORK, 1/9/95, p. 49, David Denby

In *Death and the Maiden*, Roman Polanski's adaptation of Ariel Dorfman's international theatrical success, Ben Kingsley gives a brilliant performance as a Latin American doctor who may be hiding his past as a torturer for a brutal military regime. Kingsley cloaks himself in conventional locutions and good-guy body language; all his character wants is not to be drawn out of his sheath of mediocrity. The person drawing him out is Sigourney Weaver, who plays a former victim of torture into whose hands he has fallen. Now that she has the upper hand, will she become a torturer herself. The material, with its drama of sadish and ethical instincts at war, its undertone of erotic loathing, is right up Polanski's alley, and he makes their intimacy fearfully exciting and unclean. Weaver's performance, though, is misconceived: She is physically powerful but flat and unconvincing. She doesn't live inside this Latin woman so much as project an American's rage at the possibility of complete powerlessness.

NEW YORK POST, 12/23/94, p. 54, Thelma Adams

"Death and the Maiden" finds director Roman Polanski in a spare, straightforward mood. The exiled director of "Knife in the Water" and "Chinatown" has put himself almost humbly at the service of Ariel Dorfman's award-winning Broadway play. Rather than opening the drama up, Polanski has burrowed into the characters of Paulina Escobar (Sigourney Weaver), her husband, Gerardo (Stuart Wilson), and Dr. Roberto Miranda (Ben Kingsley).

Set in an unnamed Latin American country (presumably Chile), a dark and stormy night brings Miranda to the Escobar's remote beach house. Convinced that the doctor is the man who tortured her 15 years before, Paulina sets up a kangaroo court—appointing herself as judge, her husband as defense attorney—and tries the doctor for crimes against her body and soul.

Was the mild-mannered doctor, who protests his innocence, really Paulina's torturer? Has Paulina lost her wits? In taking the law into her own hands, has she become the very thing she hates and alienated her husband forever?

Who are we to believe? Polanski's "Death and the Maiden" is a claustrophobic psychological thriller where the audience finds their allegiances shifting between Paulina, Miranda, and Paulina's rational, but weak, husband.

Weaver's performance is the film's driving force, and occasionally its weakness. For the most part, the tall, athletic actress delivers the performance of a lifetime, at one point removing her underwear and shoving them in the bound doctor's mouth in a brutal—and sexual—assault. She conveys the frightening intimacy of torture.

Emotional peaks are movingly captured by Weaver, who reveals piece-by-piece the extent of the atrocity that she relives daily. In a quiet moment of foreplay, she says to Gerardo "I want us to live like suburban idiots"; the talk is poignantly punctuated by the image of her breast, marred by round burn marks, torture scars.

But Weaver falters in the less intense moments, delivering lines in a clipped, stagy manner that removes us from the moment and reminds us that this is Sigourney Weaver, hard-working actress, and not Paulina, the shell of a beautiful woman whose spirit is trying to reclaim its turf with a mongrel's tenacity.

Kingsley, on the other hand, is dependable as always. Glassy-eyed behind his self-deprecating humor, he quietly plays his role on the razor's edge. Bound and gagged, blood seeping from a wound on his naked scalp, we empathize with Miranda. uncertain, until the very end, if he is an innocent man trapped in a tortured woman's hell or a demon getting his comeuppance.

NEWSDAY, 12/23/94, Part II/p. B7, Jack Mathews

The accused, his accuser and his accuser's husband. Three people—two at war, one looking on in profound confusion—spending one long night together in an isolated bluff-top cottage along the South American coast.

You can't set up a political drama much simpler than that, but the themes of Chilean playwright Ariel Dorfman's three-character "Death and the Maiden," and director Roman Polanski's filmed adaptation of it, are anything but simple.

At the root of this story, a sort of post-mortem on the national conscience of Chile during the military dictatorship of Augusto Pinochet, is that flawed gene in human nature that, nudged on by political passions or opportunism, enable seemingly decent people to behave monstrously. In its tight little universe, "Death and the Maiden," about a former political prisoner trying to squeeze a confession out of the man she believes tortured and raped her 15 years earlier, deals with the same issues that drove Steven Spielberg's sweeping Holocaust drama "Schindler's List."

The location here is identified only as "a country in South America, after the fall of the dictatorship," but Dorfman was a political exile during the early Pinochet years, when more than 4,000 Chilean citizens were murdered, tortured or made to disappear, and those crimes are piled, like so many logs, on the fires of Paulina Escobar's rage.

That fire is already burning in Paulina (Sigourney Weaver) when her husband Gerardo (Stuart Wilson), the newly appointed head of the government's human rights commission, arrives home in the midst of a storm, accompanied by Roberto Miranda (Ben Kingsley), a doctor who'd stopped to help him after his car had broken down on the road. Though she was blindfolded while being abused all those years ago, Paulina is certain from Miranda's voice, mannerisms and other memory clues that he was her tormentor, and her fury is unleashed.

With shocking swiftness, the terrified doctor finds himself pistol-whipped, and bound and gagged to a chair, looking down the barrel of Paulina's gun and being given a choice: Confess or die. The tense mock trial that follows, with the bewildered Gerardo acting as Miranda's attorney, attempts not only to answer whether she has the right man, but whether the three of them—and, by extension, their country—have any chance of overcoming the past.

Paulina, played on the New York stage by Glenn Close, is one of the year's few strong women's roles and Weaver gives her a strenuous aerobic workout. But it is essentially a one-note performance, played loud and dissonant, leaving the subtler moments to Kingsley, whose character may be a victim or a sadist or both, and Wilson, whose Gerardo has his fundamental belief system turned inside out.

Dorfman, who co-wrote the script with author/screenwriter Rafael Yglesias ("Fearless"), has said he was eager to entrust his work to Polanski partly because the director, like Dorfman, has been in exile. I hope he was referring to Polanski's experiences as a child, when he was tormented by German soldiers after escaping the Jewish ghetto in Cracow, and not to Polanski's self-imposed exile from the United States, where he was convicted of drugging and having unlawful sex with a 13-year-old girl.

That would make it difficult to understand which of the characters Polanski best identifies with.

In any event, the director has accomplished a marvelous balancing act, preserving the play's structure while moving it into a completely realistic setting. "Death and the Maiden" (the title comes from the ominous Franz Schubert piece Paulina's captor played while abusing her) remains dialogue-driven, and as claustrophobic as the inside of a pressure cooker, but it is a movie, beautifully photographed and edited, and a worthy expansion of the play.

SIGHT AND SOUND, 4/95, p. 40, Nick James

Paulina Escobar prepares a meal in her beach house, in an anonymous South American country, while a storm brews. She hears on the radio that her husband Gerardo has been appointed to head a government commission of inquiry into human rights violations committed under the country's former military regime. The electricity supply cuts out. Lighting candles, Paulina takes her meal into the bedroom, having thrown away her husband's. Hearing an approaching car, she extinguishes the candles and gets an automatic pistol. She hears her husband thanking someone, and the car pulls away. Gerardo explains that he had a flat tyre and was lucky enough to be picked up by a near-neighbour. He tells her he has not yet made up his mind about the commission; she knows he is lying. It is revealed that Paulina herself was a victim of torture. They go to bed.

Shortly afterwards, Paulina hears a car again and then a knock on the door. Gerardo answers, it is the neighbour, Doctor Roberto Miranda, returning the spare tyre Gerardo left in the boot of his car. Unnoticed while the two men are getting acquainted, Paulina dresses, packs a small bag with the gun, and drives the doctor's car away. Gerardo assumes she has left him and begins to get seriously drunk, while Miranda offers sympathy.

Paulina rolls the car over the edge of a cliff and returns to the house. She finds Miranda asleep on the couch, cracks him across the head, rolls his unconscious body onto a chair, ties him up, removes her knickers and stuffs them in his mouth. She talks to him about her torture, occasionally adopting the voice of her torturer, whom she believes to be Miranda. Reminding him how he used to play Schubert to her, she plays a cassette of 'Death and the Maiden' she found in his car. The music wakes Gerardo, who moves to untie Miranda. But Paulina threatens him with the gun. She says she knows, by his voice and his smell, that Miranda is the same doctor who had raped and tortured her.

Gerardo argues that Paulina's behaviour is no better than that of her torturers. However Paulina intends for Miranda to have a fair trial in their house with Gerardo as his defence attorney. They ungag Miranda; he claims that at the time of Paulina's torture he was working in a Barcelona hospital. He asks Gerardo to check, but the phone line is down.

Paulina promises to let Miranda go once he confesses. She insists that Gerardo owns up to an affair he was having while she was being tortured (it was Gerardo's identity that she was protecting). She tells the full extent of her multiple rape, withheld until now, and then feeds him details for Miranda to sign. Gerardo bullies Miranda into complying, and his 'confession' is videotaped. Paulina reveals that she has trashed Miranda's car and intends to throw him over the cliff after it. While she marches Miranda off to the cliff-edge, Gerardo makes the call to Barcelona, and the story is verified. He tells Paulina, but she knows it's a set-up because she had told Gerardo lies that Miranda amended in his confession. On his knees at the cliff edge, Miranda confesses all. Paulina walks away.

At a concert of Schubert's 'Death and the Maiden', Paulina sees Miranda with his family in a balcony box. As the theme swells, they exchange looks.

That *Death and the Maiden* is probably Roman Polanski's most restrained film to date might not sound like much of a recommendation. After all, Polanski is admired as much for a flamboyant visual style as his occasional mastery of psychotic and suspenseful moods. Given the wilful tastelessness with which the director approached his last film, *Bitter Moon*, admirers of Ariel Dorfman's play—already a modern classic in terms of its international fame—could be forgiven for fearing the worst. In Polanski's hands a subtle and intricate ensemble piece, with a serious political and moral debate at its core, might be turned into high-anxiety slasher melodrama. Would not the combination of an unravelling guilt-ridden mystery and a possibly unhinged but fully-armed woman prove too tempting to the director of *Repulsion* and *The Tenant*?

Happily, the reverse is true. Polanski is almost too respectful of the play, hoarding just a few shocks for maximum effect: a sudden call from the President when the phone has been dead, a night-shattering blast of heavy metal music when the power comes back on which prompts a struggle for the gun. The problems of mobility, action and imagery associated with adapting plays are dealt with deftly. Dorfman's text has its own share of bombshells and Polanski is properly respectful of these, taking care to give Paulina's more inexplicable actions equal significance to her normal behaviour so that a sense of disquiet builds in momentum.

Dorfman's overarching theme is about whether it is possible to reintegrate not only the victims of a military regime into a new democracy but also their victimisers. His proposition is that torture is first and foremost an invasion of the body, yet he uses a familiar suburban milieu of burst tyres and talk of "my wife's marguerittas" to suggest a wider invasion zone. Paulina says at one point: "I want us to live like suburban idiots," but you sense the impossibility of such a life for her.

After the present-day concert footage under the titles and a single shot of surf pounding at the cliff bottom, we see Paulina waiting for Gerardo while a lightning storm builds. There's a neurotic edge to her preparations, as if every task is somehow an imposition. Years after her torture, she still anticipates the knock on the door in the middle of the night. Throughout this lengthy, dialogue-free sequence, her dread and hopelessness is suggested only by Sigourney Weaver's routine actions and Polanski's fluid and beautiful use of montage.

In this way, Polanski removes *Death and the Maiden* at once from its stagebound origins. If at times he does get stuck with a shot/reverse shot format (for example, during the couple's mutual confession scene on the terrace), it is only when the dialogue is critical enough to carry the film.

There are many significant departures from the play, most of which improve on it. The timescale is squeezed into one night, giving a tense, real-time pace to the proceedings. Paulina is more decisive, immediately trashing Miranda's car instead of hiding it, and her lines are sharper, finding a vicious wit within the politics of suffering. There's a more conclusive and plausible climax, with Miranda's admission that he had really loved what he was doing and was sorry when it was over—a more extreme admission than the play allows. Shifting the play's location ("probably Chile") to a generalised South American one is the only change that seems a concession.

Having the couple's domestic setup become the site for reenacting Paulina's ordeal is not just a clever conceit; it allows for multiple ironies. Thus Miranda arrives twice as an apparent Good Samaritan: in the present as the helpful motorist and in the past as the doctor whose job it was to prevent any death by torture—to clean up wounds and play soothing music—before the invitation to join in became intoxicating. The second time around reverses the roles of the powerful and the powerless, with the possibility of Miranda's innocence meant to hang in the air to the very end.

Unfortunately, from the moment that shaven-headed Ben Kingsley walks into the house, acting all weasly with wobbly eyes (and quoting Nietszche to boot), there's little doubt he will be proven guilty. But thriller mechanics are hardly at issue here. The drama comes from internal contradictions alive in each of the three characters and the unstable desires thrown up by them. Miranda craves forgiveness in the same way that Paulina craves revenge and neither can be truly satisfied. Similarly, the great liberal reconciler, Gerardo, is fighting for a future normality that it is impossible for his wife to accept.

The three actors walk a fine line between speechifying and naturalism, relishing the moral niceties of the screenplay (co-written by Dorfman and Rafael Yglesias who wrote the wonderful, under-rated Peter Weir film *Fearless*). It is Sigourney Weaver's superb portrayal of Paulina, however, that carries the drama into movieland. She is utterly plausible as a torture victim, and she makes Paulina's mental instability thoroughly logical, eschewing the skittishness that Juliet Stevenson brought to the part on stage. Her gestures and actions command the screen as resolutely here as they did in *Alien* or *Aliens*. As for Polanski, mordant material is meat and drink to him, although in his other films it has not always been as well thought-out as it is here. Restraint becomes him.

VILLAGE VOICE, 12/20/94, p. 60, Georgia Brown

Having recently encountered many nasty dames—from Linda Fiorentino's gorgon to Demi Moore's corporate snake to Mrs. Parker—I'm happy to sing of a warrior woman who picks on those who deserve it. Or those who look like they do. In Ariel Dorfman's play-turned-movie, *Death and the Maiden*, it's technically never certain whether the respected professional and family man whom Paulina Escobar (Sigourney Weaver) chooses to torture—well, not extensively—is actually the villain she thinks he is. (This is one of those tricks that play like to pull.) I myself had no doubts as to the clarity of Sigourney's instincts.

Anyone who blew $60 on *Death's* 1992 Mike Nichols-directed Broadway production starring Glenn Close, Richard Dreyfuss, and Gene Hackman probably will run screaming at the mere mention of the title. In fact, *Death and the Maiden* has had a curious and instructive history, having lent itself—I'm speaking from reports, not personal experience—to both the worst and best of theater. Covering Nichols's fiasco, most American critics blamed the play, except for a few who questioned Nichols's transformation of a political and psychological thriller into domestic comedy. ("History should record," scoffed Frank Rich, "that Mr. Nichols has given Broadway its first escapist entertainment about political torture.") What made it logical to blame the interpreter and not the text was a simultaneous London production, directed by Lindsay Posner and starring the fascinating Juliet Stevenson, that left viewers both wrung out and viscerally informed on the lasting repercussions of political torture.

Anyone who's seen Stevenson can imagine a passionate, on-the-verge performance. Weaver's Paulina is quite different: tough but less wild, intense, permanently wary, competent in physical matters—Ripleyesque. You don't know why in the world this woman is behaving this way—eating her dinner alone on the floor of a closet, for example—but you know she has a full storehouse of terror. Ten minutes into the movie, I felt like sobbing.

Action opens in "a country in South America, after the fall of a dictatorship." Radio news comes on in English—a mini-shock that swiftly passes. On this dark and stormy evening, Paulina waits impatiently, tensely, for her husband Gerardo (Stuart Wilson) to come home. She's learned from the radio that he's accepted a presidential appointment to chair a hearing on terrorism under the previous regime. When she hears an unfamiliar car approaching the deserted seaside cottage, she gets out her gun. Gerardo, it turns out, had a flat driving home and was picked up by a genial Dr. Miranda (Ben Kingsley), who now drops him off. Later that night Miranda returns with the tire—just a good deed for the country's new savior, he says. Gerardo persuades him to stay for a cognac.

He'll wish he hadn't. It turns out that Paulina recognizes Miranda as the prison doctor who raped her on several occasions to a tape of Schubert's "Death and the Maiden." Having been blindfolded, how can she be sure? His voice, his smell, the feel of his skin: She finds the same tape in his car. Now she ties up Miranda for a "trial," with her unconvinced husband as judge. Mindful of her instability, Gerardo is inclined to take Miranda's side, though he's wary of that gun in her hand. In Dorfman's play, Paulina doesn't know how to use a gun; in Polanski's movie, she does.

From Lawrence Weschler's astute *New Yorker* profile of the director, it's clear that although Polanski didn't take writer credit, the real hand behind the revisions is his. He's mercilessly pared the text, speeded up the opening, and dealt with the play's various implausibilities, making events more logical in some instances, the characters more compulsive in others. Although Polanski is the project's director-for-hire, this is definitely his territory: two-men-and-a-woman triangle; closed doors; a densely layered claustrophobic struggle of damaged psyches.

Right off it's clear that Paulina and Gerardo inhabit two separate realms. He's trying to hold on to her but knows she's long gone. In the beginning this is put in terms of female inscrutability/male bewilderment. Because he's in awe of her, Gerardo is content to trail after. But the real drama is between her and Miranda. "I told you he'd always be between us," she says to her husband. She wants to exorcise Miranda, but is it possible?

Occasionally, Dorfman's need to ask timely questions—like how can the victims of a regime coexist with their victimizers under a new order?—gets a tad insistent. The uncomprehending but well-meaning Gerardo clearly represents democracy with its rule of law, as well as the wish to get over the past and on with things. In playing the judge's role, he's bound to protect Miranda and betray his wife. Dorfman reminds us that in fledgling democracies everywhere, fascism's victims are plotting revenge and the victimizers are protecting their asses.

The movie's very last scene contains a true Polanskian twist. There's the same cul-de-sac dilemma as at the end of *Knife in the Water*, the same nod to radical evil informing the last of *Rosemary's Baby* or the jaundiced ending to *Chinatown* that Polanski imposed on Robert Towne. In one little gesture, one curl of the lips, the representative of evil says "Baby, you lose." Or worse: "Whatever you do, you are still my baby."

Also reviewed in:
CHICAGO TRIBUNE, 1/13/95, Friday/p. J, Michael Wilmington
NEW YORK TIMES, 12/23/94, p. C3, Caryn James
NATION, 1/23/95, p. 107, Stuart Klawans
NEW YORKER, 1/16/95, p. 88, Anthony Lane
VARIETY, 12/12-18/94, p. 75, Todd McCarthy
WASHINGTON POST, 1/13/95, p. B1, Hal Hinson

DEATH WISH V: THE FACE OF DEATH

A Trimark Pictures release a 21st Century Film Corporation production. *Executive Producer:* Menahem Golan and Ami Artzi. *Producer:* Damian Lee. *Director:* Allan A. Goldstein. *Screenplay:* Allan A. Goldstein. *Based on characters created by:* Brian Garfield. *Director of Photography:* Curtis Petersen. *Editor:* Patrick Rand. *Music:* Terry Plumeri. *Sound:* Valentin Pricop. *Casting:* Kathy A. Smith and Anne Tait. *Production Designer:* Csaba A. Kertesz. *Running time:* 95 minutes. *MPAA Rating:* R.

CAST: Charles Bronson (Paul Kersey); Lesley-Anne Down (Olivia Regent); Michael Parks (Tommy O'Shea); Saul Rubinek (Tony Hoyle); Kenneth Welsh (Lt. Mickey King).

LOS ANGELES TIMES, 1/17/94, Calendar/p. 3, Chris Willman

The character "arc" of every "Death Wish" film is the same: Charles Bronson, as Paul Kersey, starts each installment as a peace-loving architect with a good, doomed woman by his side, and ends up having added so many baddies to his cumulative body count you'd think he was competing against Ho Chi Minh's all-time league record for kills-batted-in. The theme of all these movies is pretty much beating plowshares back into swords, as it were.

It's not street thugs incurring Bronson's wrath this time in "Death Wish V: The Face of Death" but Mafioso. Seems deadly crime lord Tommy O'Shea—played by Michael Parks, who, coincidentally, starred in TV's "Then Came Bronson" 25 years ago—is also the ex-husband of the vigilante's new squeeze, Lesley-Anne Down. She hasn't heard that dating Kersey portends chances of survival roughly akin to a Spinal Tap drummer's, and gets it into her pretty (for now) head to testify against her mobster ex, predictably, bad things happen to good Bronson mates.

Even fans of "Wish" fulfillment—now celebrating the 20th anniversary of the original—will find the cheap, Canadian-made "V" a snoozer. Parks, at least, attacks the role of an Irishman heading New York's Italian Mafia with all the relish such an idiotic part demands. But no one can say "I love you" to an ill-fated fiancee or feign a slow burn with quite the absurd stoicism of Charles "Vengean is Mine, Sayeth the Bored" Bronson—who, it *is* good to know, even in his early 70s can leap off tall buildings in a single bound and emerge unscathed.

NEW YORK POST, 1/14/94, p. 39, Larry Worth

Times Square's brand-new "Gunfighters' Deathclock" records each bullet-related murder in America. But if it tallied revolver-related demises from "Death Wish 5," the gizmo would be kaput in minutes.

Not that all the stomach-churning violence in the series' latest entry is courtesy of a firearm. In the first half-hour, one man's cheek is ripped open with a knife, the heroine is horribly disfigured, a hefty man's stomach gets unstitched with a sewing machine's needle and his cohort is steam-pressed in a dry-cleaning unit.

In addition, neophyte writer/director Allan Goldstein lets audiences monitor damage control via closeups of the resulting gore. Let's just say the makeup staff earned their money on this one.

Natch, it's all an excuse for Charles Bronson's recurring character, Paul Kersey, to strap on the holster again and bring vigilante justice back to the streets.

What passes for a plot concerns Kersey's romance with a dress designer (Lesley-Anne Down). But he has no sooner proposed than her ex-husband-cum mobster muscles in on their happiness. Like every woman in Kersey's past, she's quickly disposed of, giving the alleged hero a reason to turn the tables on his enemies.

And as we've seen before, hell hath no fury like a scorned Bronson. But that's not to say he offers anything other than his standard flat performance. He's just a little puffier.

The challenge is distinguishing his wooden castmates from the mannequins in the garment-industry setting. As Kersey's intended, Down delivers most of her lines behind bandages—out of shame, no doubt. Michael Parks lumbers through his duties as the villainous hubby while Saul Rubinek wastes time as the district attorney.

Clearly, the "Death Wish" series has been on life-support for the last four episodes. Pulling the plug at this point would be a mercy kill.

NEWSDAY, 1/15/94, Part II/p. 23, Terry Kelleher

As I trudged through the multiplex lobby toward "Death Wish V," I passed under a banner advertising "Grumpy Old Men." And I thought, "Whoa. charles Bronson's in the wrong movie."

Ageism? Not at all. We need lots more films with lead roles for actors over 70. What we don't need is another one with Bronson jumping off roofs in slow motion (the stunt man didn't look old, but he had a right to be grumpy).

Clearly, Bronson lacks the talent, the will or the opportunity to attempt other kinds of roles at this point in his career. So he accepted producer Menahem Golan's gold to do a fourth sequel to his 1974 blockbuster.

"Remember Paul Kersey, vigilante killer a few years back?" a minor villain reminds his fellow vermin. My, how time has flown."You're not going back to your old ways, are you?" a cop (Kenneth Welsh) asks Paul. Try and stop him, flatfoot. "Paul, you can't take the law into your own hands," the D.A. (Saul Rubinek) warns. Stow the technicalities, pal. How would you feel if a cross-dressing hit man (Robert Joy) invaded the powder" room at a posh restaurant and repeatedly smashed *your* lady friend's lovely face into the mirror?

Angry, that's how Paul feels. So he goes home and slowly loads his gun while dialogue from previous scenes is needlessly replayed on the soundtrack. Then he avenges the disfigurement of his lover (Lesley-Anne Down) by going after her ex-husband, Tommy O'Shea (Michael Parks), a mumbling mob boss with a bad haircut. Tommy and his henchmen are especially vicious characters, and writer-director Allan Goldstein loves to linger over their acts of torture. But the hero tops them again and again in the sneering-sadism department. Well, either Bronson's sneering or his mustache, itches.

"Death Wish V" is yet another movie in which Toronto tries to impersonate New York and winds up looking like Toronto with trash. Welsh, Rubinek and Joy are among cast members providing the proper Canadian content, but only joy gets to howl in agony when his character's head bursts into flames.

Also reviewed in:
NEW YORK TIMES, 1/17/94, p. C18, Stephen Holden
VARIETY, 1/17-23/93, p. 105, Joe Leydon
WASHINGTON POST, 1/15/94, p. G5, Richard Harrington

DECEMBER BRIDE

An MD Wax Courier Films release of a Little Bird production presented by Film Four International/CTE/British Screen. *Executive Producer:* James Mitchell. *Producer:* Jonathan Cavendish. *Director:* Thaddeus O'Sullivan. *Screenplay:* David Rudkin. *Based on the book by:* Sam Hanna Bell. *Director of Photography:* Bruno de Keyzer. *Editor:* Rodney Holland. *Music:* Jürgen Knieper. *Sound:* Peter Lindsay. *Casting:* Noala Moiselle and Susie Figgis. *Production Designer:* Adrian Smith. *Art Director:* Steve Simmonds. *Special Effects:* Maurice Foley.

Costumes: Consolata Boyle. *Make-up:* Tommie Manderson. *Stunt Coordinator:* Terry Forrestal. *Running time:* 88 minutes. *MPAA Rating:* Not Rated.

CAST: Donal McCann (Hamilton Echlin); Saskia Reeves (Sarah); Ciaran Hinds (Frank Echlin); Patrick Malahide (Sorleyson); Brenda Bruce (Martha); Michael McKnight (Fergus); Dervla Kirwan (Young Martha); Peter Capaldi (Young Sorleyson), Geoffrey Golden (Andrew Echlin); Cathleen Delaney (Agnes); Gabrielle Reidy (Birdie); Frances Lowe (Victoria); Catherine Gibson (Mother Pentland); Julie McDonald (Molly); Roy Heaybeard (Auctioneer); Karl Hayden (Andrew); Miche Doherty (Joe); Peadar Lamb (Registrar); George Shane (Orator); Mal Whyte (Shuey); Raymond Barry (Petey); Maurice Hunter (Owen); Maureen Hunter (Egg Lady); Michael Wallace, Christopher Wallace, Catherine O'Hanlon, Michaela O'Hanlon, and Megan O'Hanlon (Dineen Children); George Jeffers (Boatman).

LOS ANGELES TIMES, 11/25/94, Calendar/p. 7, Kenneth Turan

"December Bride" doesn't seem terribly ambitious, unless you understand how difficult the creation of an authentic, self-contained world can be. Its accomplishments can seem likewise modest, unless you've seen enough film to realize the rarity of its avoidance of false steps and false emotions.

A film of beauty and restraint, thoughtful, intelligent and completely assured, the Irish "December Bride" is an experience to cherish. The winner of a Felix Special Jury Prize at the 1990 European Film Awards, the continent's version of the Oscars, the fact that it's late coming to domestic distribution is a function not of its qualities but of the perceived feebleness of American audiences.

For "December Bride," beautiful and luminous though it is, does not have a recognizable star or trendy subject matter. And unlike the face-licking, over-eager lap dogs of Hollywood, this is a film that takes its time and keeps its distance, that has the confidence to tell its passionate story with measured dignity and unhurried delicacy. All it has to offer is damn fine filmmaking, and where box office is concerned, that is often not enough.

"Bride's" opening shot, of a woman standing alone on a lonely, wind-swept bit of Ireland, signals what is to come. It showcases the beauty of the cinematography, the presence of the land as a character in its own right, and the centrality of that woman to everything that is about to transpire.

She is Sarah (Saskia Reeves), forced by poverty to join her mother (Brenda Bruce) and work as a live-in servant in the house of Andrew (Geoffrey Golden), a small landowner with two grown sons.

The house is on the shores of Strangford Lough and is part of a fiercely Protestant community in turn-of-the-century Northern Ireland. The rhythms of farming, the harvesting of kelp and potatoes and the keeping of sheep are the stuff of life in this harsh, rain-swept and muddy land, and director of photography Bruno de Keyzer's exquisite photography and handsome compositions recognizes the beauty amid the drudgery.

After a terrible accident sours Sarah on the power of the almighty, she finds herself attracted to both of Andrew's sons, different though they are. Frank (Ciaran Hinds) is younger, moodier and more impulsive, while Hamilton ("The Dead's" Donal McCann) is reasonable, responsible but still attractive.

Though Sarah's solution to this dilemma and the reaction of the community to her choice is the central business of "December Bride," what makes this film memorable is not so much what Sarah decides as the personality traits that shape that decision.

For that young woman, played with convincing passion by Reeves, is a natural radical, a fiercely independent spirit of the type common to literature but not often portrayed this effectively on screen.

Director Thaddeus O'Sullivan, whose clever short film "The Woman Who Loved Clark Gable" played briefly over here, has handled his material with a sure regard for nuance and gesture that is more than welcome. The result is a small-scaled labor of love that audiences can embrace as much as the people who made it.

MONTHLY FILM BULLETIN, 2/91, p. 43, Mark Kermode

At the turn of the century in the remote Presbyterian community of Strangford Lough, Northern Ireland, Andrew Echlin and his two sons Frank and Hamilton take an elderly woman, Martha, and her daughter Sarah into their home as servants. One stormy day, the three men and Sarah travel across the lake to the Petlins', to borrow a stud ram. On the journey home, the small boat capsizes, and Andrew sacrifices himself to save his sons and Sarah, whom he has accepted as a surrogate daughter. Back at the Echlin home, Sarah is visited by a suitor, Fergus, who is mortified that in her hour of distress Sarah did not call out his name. The local minister, Sorleyson, complains to the Echlin boys of their repeated absence from church, causing tension with the godfearing Martha. That Sunday, Frank enjoys a romantic liaison with Sarah, and consequently neglects to collect Martha from church; calling Sarah a Jezebel, Martha turns her back on the Echlin household. In the coming months, Sarah learns the way of the Echlins, who are expanding their land-holdings, and following a day trip to Belfast becomes romantically involved with Hamilton. Now rivals for Sarah's affections, the brothers fight, but soon resolve to live in harmony as a threesome. One evening, Fergus visits the Echlin household, but leaves in disgust after spying Sarah and the two brothers revelling to the accompaniment of a jew's-harp. When Sarah becomes pregnant, Sorleyson insists on behalf of the church,that she marry one of the brothers, but Sarah (whose mother has recently died) refuses. Hamilton tells Sorleyson that he would marry Sarah, but that she would never consent. Desolate, Sorleyson demands that the child must have a name, to which Sarah replies, "It does ... mine". Sarah's mother's old house, which stands on land now owned by the Echlins, is purchased by a disapproving Catholic woman, to Sarah's distress. Disenchanted with the threesome, and jealous of Hamilton's role in Sarah's affections, Frank attends the local Orange Day Parade, and despite the hostility of the locals, courts the affections of a young woman, Molly. After walking her home, Frank is attacked by a gang and left crippled for life. Eighteen years later, Sarah's daughter, Martha, begs her mother to marry, for without a recognised father she herself cannot marry. Remembering the sacrifice of Andrew Echlin, Sarah surrenders her long-held principle and marries Hamilton, with Frank as her best man.

Adapted by playwright David Rudkin from Sam Hanna Bell's novel, this economic vision of warring social systems nimbly avoids becoming merely a tangled tale of romantic intrigue set amidst breathtaking scenery. By astutely demoting the sexual theme to the role of incidental sub-plot, director Thaddeus O'Sullivan to some extent belies his claim that this is a "sensual, double love story". *December Bride* is notable for its resolutely dispassionate portrayal of passion (only during Frank's brief liaison with Molly, in which she surrenders a kiss and agrees secretly to meet him again, is there the electric tension of cinematic sex). Instead, our attention is focused throughout on the different ways in which members of this divided community have struggled to make order of their lives, an endeavour thrown into harsh relief by the hostile beauty of the landscape and the elements against which the action is played out and which are superbly captured by Bruno de Keyzer.

The randomly destructive potential of the elements is indeed the factor which sets the action in motion, when Andrew Echlin's boat is capsized, forcing him to decide which of the four should live. Crucially, Andrew's decision to sacrifice himself for the sake of his children is motivated not by a belief in the salvation of martyrs, but an autonomous (and entirely rational) assessment of the problem at hand. Wisely eschewing the emotional browbeating which could prefigure such an event, Rudkin's screenplay has Andrew simply turn and swim away from the boat, apparently making for the shore. (A finely written pivotal moment, the scene is undercut somewhat by the obvious use of an indoor set, which makes a jarring contrast with the otherwise exceptional lighting and photography. It is the one moment in which the televisual shortcomings of *December Bride* are unfortunately apparent.) Back on land, Sarah for the first time confronts Sorleyson, whose reaction to the tragic events is to ascribe them to God's masterplan, entirely denying the possibility that man in general, and Andrew in particular, could shape his own destiny. "God has taken the ripe, and spared the green", he concludes piously, to which Sarah retorts that Andrew sacrificed himself, of his own free will.

Although passed over with underplayed ease by O'Sullivan, this first confrontation is crucial, and indeed lays the philosophical ground for the subsequent drama. With Andrew gone, and the reins of control taken up by his extended family, Hamilton, Frank and Sarah must now make their own decisions, with no higher guiding authority than the knowledge that they are their own masters. However, the critical difference between Sarah, who comes from devout and servile Presbyterian stock against which she is rebelling, and the Echlin boys, whose father had always demonstrated a fierce independence, is the degree to which rebellion against community standards itself motivates their decisions and actions. While the mature Hamilton tells Sorleyson quietly, "It's our own way, and it works", he has no innate hostility towards the practices of either Presbyterians or Catholics—he is simply not part of their milieu. Sarah, on the other hand, despite her constant and vociferous condemnations of the community, feels inextricably bound to it, and struggles throughout to free herself from a past from which she cannot escape. "All your lives you slaved for rich folk", she tells her mother harshly. "Well, I'll not do it".

Similarly, Sarah's hostility towards the church extends beyond a rejection of its practices to an active assault on them, as she berates Sorleyson for desiring everything to be "all botched inside, but smooth to the eye". Played with aplomb by Patrick Malahide, Sorleyson becomes a portrait of religion in retreat, fired into active life by Sarah's attacks, but ultimately defeated by the indifference of Hamilton. Malahide deftly portrays this by switching subtly between anger and exhaustion, while O'Sullivan juxtaposes fiery confrontational scenes with melancholic moments in which a haggard Sorleyson gazes at his surroundings, bemoaning the lateness of his years. The crucial difference between Sarah's fight with her community and the Echlins' distance from it is further emphasised in one brief but telling scene in which Sarah inadvertently serves a Catholic labourer meat on a Friday, to the disdain of Frank and Hamilton. While the Echlins have no time for the Church, they are aware of the customs by which their fellow labourers live, respecting Catholic and Protestant alike, and priding themselves in always providing "good kitchen" as a reward for the honest toil of the farmhands. Sarah, however, has not escaped the anti-papist prejudices of her Protestant upbringing, and while rejecting her own religious customs, retains an active and racist disdain for Catholics.

It is in finally learning to exert her 'freedom of will', by ironically sacrificing a principle for the benefit of her daughter, that Sarah learns the lesson taught by Andrew on the stormy waters of the lake. Evoking the ghost of her grandfather, Martha tells her mother to remember that "He let go", suggesting that she must now have the courage to do the same. Having attained power over man ("I have two men", she smiles contentedly) and asserted her authority within the Echlin household, Sarah realises that just as man has created his own gods to make order out of the chaos of his existence, so she has defined her own 'principles' to order her life; rather than being answerable to a higher authority (the need to rebel against the conventions of society or religion) she is answerable ultimately only to herself. Rudkin and O'Sullivan again keep this revelation low-key, allowing Saskia Reeves to convey her dawning acceptance of Andrew's example through a series of brief conversations with her daughter, and in quiet monologues in which Sarah states simply that the young must be allowed to love.

Treating the climax with laconic humour, Rudkin's script has Sarah declare with delightful irony, "You young ones are all for marrying now!", but declines to drive home the reversed-order theme any further. Similarly, Sarah's wedding ceremony is cleverly directed as a silent point-of-view shot gazing outward from the altar. Looking down the aisle at the threesome, with Sarah flanked on either side by a brother in uniformly sombre attire, O'Sullivan plays with the funereal tone to wry effect, and also leaves the audience confused as to which of the brothers Sarah has actually married. In a memorable image, O'Sullivan creates (and holds) a portrait of Sarah, her obedient men beside her, ceremonially accepting her own death (she has sacrificed herself for her daughter), yet staring boldly into her daughter's future, having triumphed over the rigours of her community's hostility.

NEW YORK POST, 9/9/94, p. 46, Thelma Adams

Turn-of-the-century Ireland. A beautiful woman "lives in sin" with two brothers. She becomes pregnant. Who's the father?

In Thaddeus O'Sullivan's "December Bride," paternity becomes less important than why the homespun radical Sarah (Saskia Reeves) defies the pressure of her rural Presbyterian community to single out a brother—any brother—and marry.

In a passionate drama about the circle of life and one woman's staunchly individualistic course, the question becomes: When does one generation's act of defiance become the very thing the next generation rebels against?

In this visually lush picture, the camera is bewitched by Ireland's beautiful, occasionally brutal, landscapes—but it's the landscapes of the characters' faces that have the most impact. Initially nearly mute, a pale, big-featured servant girl with downcast eyes, Reeves' Sarah emerges as a stubborn, steely woman with a luminous, riveting beauty. Reeves ("Antonia & Jane") delivers an outstanding performance.

The craggy-faced Donal McCann ("The Dead") plays the elder brother who assumes responsibility as the household head, while ceding any real power to Sarah. The sensual Ciaran Hinds, best known in America for his role in "Prime Suspect 3," speaks barely five words but stamps out a striking character as the younger, conceited and weaker brother.

"December Bride" is no rural idyll. In a memorable scene, a short trip to a nearby island taken by the brothers, their father and Sarah becomes a moment of high drama. The rain-swollen sea rises against their small boat. The father, solidly played by Geoffrey Golden, lets go of the upturned hull to save his sons and adopted daughter.

The otherwise leisurely paced, engrossing movie takes a misstep when it makes a jarring, 20-year leap near its conclusion.

Thematically, this jump allows the family to come full circle. As the father released the boat to allow the next generation to continue, the time arrives for Sarah to decide whether she will abandon her rebellion to ease the way for her grown children.

Structurally, the movie loses its momentum when it ties up its loose ends in a pretty bow. This rich, atmospheric movie merits an ending as complex and compelling as Sarah and her two lovers.

NEWSDAY, 9/9/94, Part II/p. B7, Gene Seymour

A fixture in Irish film festivals worldwide in the four years since it was made, "December Bride" finally gets to show off its near-spectral storytelling in limited theatrical release. This first feature by Thaddeus O'Sullivan may come across as too bleak for audiences accustomed to weightless summer fare. But even they should be seduced by "Bride's" dark beauty and smoldering intensity.

The film's molten core is Saskia Reeves as Sarah, a young servant girl living in rural Northern Ireland at the turn-of-the-century. At the start of the film, Sarah's restlessness and passions are barely contained by a shy reserve buttressed by her pious mother (Brenda Bruce), who helps her get a job tending house for a farmer (Geoffrey Golden) and his two sons: gentle, expansive Hamilton (Donal McCann) and brooding, volatile Frank (Ciaran Hinds.)

Sarah finds unexpected joy and possibility in working for the clan. So much so that when the father dies in a boating accident, she chooses to stay on at the farm—even after she makes love to both brothers and becomes pregnant.

Such a living arrangement guarantees sporadic tension between Hamilton and Frank over the baby's parentage. It also sets forth a reaction from the surrounding community as forbidding as the coastal landscape photographed with stunning mastery by cinematographer Bruno de Keyzer. The scenery breathes, sighs, weeps as much as any character in the film.

Still, Sarah's determination to keep things status quo will not be shaken, especially not by the whimpering pleas of the local pastor (Patrick Malahide, who played a similar role in the BBC production of "Middlemarch") to give the baby a surname other than her own. Her flashing eyes, a marked contrast from her bland beginnings, give testament to the spirit and energy she derives from taking such a bold risk.

O'Sullivan's subtle orchestration of gesture and sound delivers its more haunting and evocative moments. McCann, Hinds and the rest of the cast excel, but it is Reeves who glows most from within whenever she's on screen.

The story, adapted from a 1951 novel by Sam Hanna Bell, takes an interesting turn towards the end when a daughter of this *menage a trois* grows to adulthood deciding she needs something more conventional. Such a development gives this film a timeless quality that will make "December Bride" a retrospective fixture well into the next century.

VILLAGE VOICE, 9/13/94, p. 70, Laurie Stone

Thomas Hardy meets Barbara Taylor Bradford in this visually austere but ultimately opaque first feature, completed in 1990, by Irish director Thaddeus O'Sullivan. *December Bride*'s opening shot shows a woman alone, peering out to sea on a windswept coast—a romance novel book jacket without the airbrushing. She is Sarah (Saskia Reeves), daughter of servants, looking for a leg up in turn-of-the-century Northern Ireland. She joins her mother in service to a family of farmers, the Echlins, where patriarch Andrew governs grown sons Hamilton (Donal McCann) and Frank (Ciaran Hinds). After Andrew dies, Sarah dispatches her mother back home and takes both men as lovers. She declines to marry either, insists that the two children she bears be registered in her name, and challenges the surrounding community of tight-laced Ulster Presbyterians, who feel aggrieved by the kinky ménage.

Though these events are charged and unconventional, the movie stares at the characters, blinking mutely, like one of the sheep on the farm. The camera glances, refusing to penetrate. It pokes through windows without recording dialogue. It watches lovers enter a bed and leaves before they do or say anything. Scenes continually end before anything substantive has happened, while suggesting, by their stark minimalism, that something has happened. We're meant to fathom the characters' depths by the way they flash looks at one another: the furtive peek, the brooding glare, the defiant gaze.

The actors try to add flesh to the skeleton they're given, but the pileup of reaction shots and the paucity of interaction comes off mannered, suggesting that the story is so elemental it transcends articulation. It's a lazy approach to characters, who are obviously complicated, whether or not they can explain themselves. Does Sarah love either man? Does she prefer thinking that one of them fathered her children? She craves to be established in the Echlin household but finds marriage anathema. Couldn't she tell someone why she's freer remaining legally untied? We're meant to divine the answers, as if they were written on the wind, the moody clouds, the churning surf. They never are.

Also reviewed in:
NEW YORK TIMES, 9/9/94, p. C6, Caryn James
VARIETY, 5/23/90, p. 66
WASHINGTON POST, 3/3/95, p. B7, Rita Kempley

DESPERATE REMEDIES

A Miramax Films release of a James Wallace Productions Ltd. production in association with the New Zealand Film Commission/Avalon NFV Studios/NZ on Air. *Producer:* James Wallace. *Director:* Stewart Main and Peter Wells. *Screenplay:* Peter Wells and Stewart Main. *Director of Photography:* Leon Narby. *Editor:* David Coulson. *Music:* Peter Scholes. *Sound:* Graham Morris and (music): John Neill. *Casting:* Mari Adams. *Production Designer:* Michael Kane. *Art Director:* Shane Radford. *Costumes:* Glenis Foster. *Make-up:* Abby Collins and Dominie Till. *Stunt Coordinator:* Robert Bruce. *Running time:* 94 minutes. *MPAA Rating:* Not Rated.

CAST: Jennifer Ward-Lealand (Dorothea Brook); Kevin Smith (Lawrence Hayes); Cliff Curtis (Fraser); Lisa Chappell (Anne Cooper); Michael Hurst (William Poyser); Kiri Mills (Rose); Bridget Armstrong (Mary Anne); Timothy Raby (Mr. Weedle); Helen Steemson (Gnits); Geeling Ching (Su Lim); Irene Malone (Bar Singer).

LOS ANGELES TIMES, 7/20/94, Calendar/p. 6, Kevin Thomas

With their delirious "Desperate Remedies," which premiered at the recent Los Angeles International Gay & Lesbian Film & Video Festival, New Zealand filmmakers Stewart Main and Peter Wells have written a heady, operatic Victorian romance and played it on the screen absolutely straight. The result is high-camp pathos, alternately hilarious and poignant, in which the most elaborate artifice evokes a surprising, ever-increasing degree of genuine emotion.

Artistically, this is risky business indeed, like walking a high wire: a single misstep in tone and control and the entire fragile enterprise collapses. Happily, Wells and Main never stumble, and their film emerges as a glittery triumph, as amusing as an especially fanciful wedding cake or Rose Parade float.

"At a distant point of empire ... in a town called Hope"—with those words the filmmakers take us into their stylized universe as the regal, imperious Dorothea Brook (Jennifer Ward-Lealand), dressed in blood red, proceeds swiftly by horse and buggy to meet a boat loaded with immigrants. She aims to spot a likely man to marry her younger sister (Kiri Mills), who has fallen into the clutches of her half-caste, onetime lover (Cliff Curtis), who keeps the sister, pregnant with his child, doped up on opium.

She locks gazes with a sexy, handsome, hairy-chested stud (Kevin Smith), seeking his fortune in the fictional New Britannia. Their mutual attraction is instant—never mind that Dorothea's current lover is her beautiful companion (Lisa Chappell), her assistant at her ritzy dress and hat shop. Meanwhile, an impoverished, ambitious local politico (Michael Hurst) is eager to marry Dorothea, promising in return a contract for 4,000 army uniforms needed for a land war that's under way.

In short order Main and Wells have turned loose a screen full of passionate, ruthless people quickly caught up in a series of power plays, with sex and the promise of riches as key weapons, that bring to mind the more sophisticated manipulators of "Les Liaisons Dangereuses." The appearance-is-everything dictates of Victorian propriety merely intensify the games these people play, giving them an extra kick. Yet each maneuver brings the relentlessly practical Dorothea to a moment of truth requiring her to make the choice she has so relentlessly avoided: whether to follow the dictates of her heart or her mind.

Main and Wells stir up unbridled passion in a world of deliberate artifice—primarily in the elegant black-and-red drawing room of Dorothea's mansion and Hope's seedy, rowdy waterfront saloon-bordello—and even an exotic opium den. Cinematographer Leon Narby, production designer David Coulson and costume designer Glenis Foster—some of her creations are notably naughty—have collaborated with Main and Wells to create a triumph of visual bravura, accompanied by Peter Scholes' suitably stormy score, which incorporates passages from Verdi's "La Forza del Destino," a key inspiration for the entire film.

The cast never falters in sustaining the extravagantly dramatic roles. Ultimately, through near-surreal means, Main and Wells elicit in "Desperate Remedies" a sense of psychological validity in regard to the entire rapacious colonial experience that rings truer than in more straightforward conventional depictions.

NEW YORK POST, 5/21/94, p. 27, Thelma Adams

Heaving bosoms. Quivering lips. Hearts throbbing.

"Desperate Remedies" is a gay gothic romance so desperately in love with itself that it forgets there's an audience watching.

This overheated melodrama opens tomorrow at the Quad Cinema in Greenwich Village after closing the 1994 New York Lesbian and Gay Film Festival. Co-directors co-writers Stewart Main and Peter Wells set their first feature in the 19th century in a port colony that may as well be the filmmakers' native New Zealand.

The duo's intentionally overwrought script seems to have been written by one of those crazed women-in-the-attic that are a fixture in Victorian novels.

The tormented soul comes out of the closet—oh, the attic to dispense such howlers as: "We are all strangers in this land called love," or "In a world turned upside down, we will walk on stars."

The forthright heroine, Dorothea (Jennifer Ward-Lealand), loves Anne (Lisa Chappell), marries William (Michael Hurst), and makes eyes at Lawrence (Kevin Smith) after aborting Fraser's (Cliff Curtis) child. Dorothea's opiated sister Rose (Kiri Mills) loves Fraser but marries Lawrence ...

The wires of desire get crossed in this picture-perfect but oddly sexless sextet. Who's the fairest one of all? The art decoration, a lush spree with other people's money by costumer Glenis Foster and designer Michael Kane, artfully shot by Leon Narby.

While the generally able actors do their best to uphold the directors' stylized vision, every scene is heightened, every meeting a climax. When Dorothea and Lawrence lock eyes, it's as if their overripe lips could leap off their faces and wiggle together, suspended in the air between them.

The script leaps from crescendo to crescendo. There's nowhere to go but exhaustion, although a gun displayed in reel one ensures a desperate remedy to love's problems—and a bloody corpse—in the final reel.

"You are so beautiful I ache" Lawrence tells Dorothea. "Desperate Remedies" is achingly beautiful and an achy breaky bore.

NEWSDAY, 5/20/94, Part II/p. B9, John Anderson

Visually thrilling, dramatically arch, "Desperate Remedies" begins at overwrought and makes a beeline for hysterical. Bodices bulge, bodices rip, opium is eaten and homoerotica rages, all in a riot of color, mostly blood red: This is not your father's 19th-Century novel.

It may be your mother's, though. The heroine is Dorothea Brook (Jennifer Ward-Lealand), and if her name is a nod toward George Eliot, the dialogue is strictly Bulwer-Lytton: Characters are described as "not unkind"; "We are all strangers in this land called love," says one. Little of this makes any difference. For all their posturing about love and female empowerment and sapphic desire, what New Zealand filmmakers Stewart Main and Peter Wells seem to be about is the visualization of the nearly unthinkable.

The town where Dorothea lives—she's a "draper of distinction," according to her card—is the port of Hope, and if Bill Clinton takes it personally, he might: It's a steaming, fetid, tubercular, rancid hole, full of disease and devoid of right angles. The directors, Wellesian in their contempt for the orthodox frame, also recall Derek Jarman in their use of space (the film was shot in one Aukland studio) and Peter Greenaway in their pure invention. They give the inhabitants of Hope the gleaming look of madness. In many ways, what they've created is hell.

And hell, as we've always suspected, is fascinating. Dorothea, red-haired, red-veiled and cracking a whip, rides to the docks, where life is cheap and various unsavory male qualities are on display. She likes what she sees in Lawrence Hayes (Kevin Smith), however, and makes overtures of employment, and more. But what she really wants is for Lawrence to marry and save her sister Rose (Kiri Mills), who is under the sexual sway of the "half-breed" Fraser (Cliff Curtis) and the drugs he feeds her.

Dorothea has her own history with Fraser, of course. In keeping with its vaguely Dickensian heritage, everyone and thing is intertwined in "Desperate Remedies." Dorothea will marry the rodentlike merchant William Poyser (Michael Hurst) for financial convenience, even though she really loves her loyal companion Anne Cooper (Lisa Chappell), and despite the lust she feels for Lawrence and the lust he feels for her, which will drive him to help her rid their lives of Fraser.

You straight on this? Well, you might then want to forget it. For all the rococo plot lines, the ornate speeches backed up by orchestral crescendos and some enthralling set design rich in anachronism and incongruity, the best way to enjoy "Desperate Remedies" is to simply let the colors and startling imagery wash over and drown you.

SIGHT AND SOUND, 2/94, p. 52, Claire Monk

In the imaginary 19th-century colonial port of Hope, an imperious red-veiled woman rushes to the dock and silently hands a handsome disembarking immigrant her card, offering him "a most singular opportunity". She is Dorothea Brook, beautiful, independent and a 'draper of distinction'—but her life with her 'companion' Anne is being soured by her sister Rose's opium habit and excessive sexual activity with her Latino supplier Fraser. Desperate to get Fraser out of her life, Dorothea plans to pay the young immigrant, Lawrence Hayes, to marry Rose. After much delay, Lawrence visits as instructed; in Dorothea's absence, Anne demands references but refuses to tell him what the job is. William Poyser, an ambitious, unattractive MP, calls on Dorothea and hints that a contract for army uniforms may come her way. When his bank calls in his debts, he sees Dorothea as a solution and claims it will only be seemly for her to deal with the army if she becomes his wife.

An attempt to pay Fraser to leave fails. Lawrence reappears and, ignoring the class gulf between him and Dorothea, declares his passion for her. Disappointed to learn that the 'job' on offer is not as her kept man, he demands to meet Rose before agreeing to the marriage. In case the plan fails, Anne proposes bribing Fraser to sail for San Francisco two days hence. Visiting the opium den, Dorothea shows him the rubies he'll receive if he goes, but he taunts her. Running into Lawrence, she enlists his help, and he suggests murdering Fraser instead.

Jealous at Dorothea's attraction to Lawrence, Anne takes him the rubies in Dorothea's place, hoping to discover his intentions. Disappointed that she isn't Dorothea, Lawrence responds rudely. Anne agrees to let him meet Rose later that day, but warns Dorothea that Lawrence is not co-operating and urges her that it would be expedient to marry Poyser. Lawrence doesn't turn up, and Dorothea rushes distraught into the streets. Unable to find him, she goes to Fraser's room, unaware that Lawrence is hidden there and listening. Fraser taunts her about her past affair with him and her resulting abortion; Dorothea offers herself to him again if he will then leave, but he refuses. The two men fight; Lawrence, wounded, leaves Fraser on the ship to San Francisco but keeps the rubies. Claiming to have disposed of Fraser, he offers himself to Dorothea for money; she refuses and, in a passionate farewell, reveals she is marrying Poyser.

At a ball two years later, Dorothea is disturbed to meet Fraser, who insinuatingly tells her Lawrence kept the rubies. Lawrence writes with news that Rose and her child by Fraser have died of typhoid; again declaring his love for Dorothea, he encloses the rubies, formed into two rings. As the Poysers watch an opera, a red-veiled woman shoots Fraser dead in front of the stage. She is Anne. Declaring that she is now free, Dorothea leaves Poyser. At the docks, she is reunited with Anne.

"This film is about transgression," *Desperate Remedies*' co-director Peter Wells pronounced almost seriously just before his lavish-looking £700,000 first feature unwound at the London Film Festival. After a decade as collaborators on documentaries and shorts, writer-directors Wells and Stewart Main have loosened their corsets with a sexy, queer spoof costume melodrama that's better off without such stale self-justifications. At once luxuriantly overdressed and disconcertingly *deshabillé, Desperate Remedies* heaves with costumes and art direction that Gainsborough Studios would either have died for or died at the sight of—from Dorothea's startling arrival at the docks in a swirling scarlet chiffon, to the closing homage to *Queen Christina* in which she and Anne sail away dressed in a 'Scope-width of primary-coloured taffeta.

The film's frenzied pace owes less to its deliberately disjointed plotting than to manic editing, frenetic frock changes—tartan, striped, puritanical, risque—and, most hilariously, a frantic orchestral accompaniment from the Auckland Philharmonia which, at moments of high emotion, cuts from one famous movie score to another (often, bizarrely, the theme from *Jean de Florette*). Its thin claim to subversiveness is that it heaves with the erotic excesses which costume drama traditionally both promises and denies.

Standard-issue debauched dago Fraser has pierced nipples, a penchant for lace-edged French knickers and a habit of pleasuring the insatiable Rose under Dorothea's nose while issuing dark threats about what the former might do if deprived of his "affections". In Dorothea's haughty encounters with the pouting, bare-chested Lawrence, the pair's curt, class-ridden exchanges ("I believe the tradesman's entrance is at the back!" she snaps) clash with languorous eye contact, while intercut shots of writhing flesh reveal their true desires. Even the sets ooze sensuality, from Dorothea's red velvet drawing room to the orgiastic decadence of the 'Chinese House' opium den.

That *Desperate Remedies* succeeds as something more than overblown camp spectacle is due to its exact understanding not just of genre conventions but of the ideology they represent. Its stock characters are at once pastiched to perfection by the excellent cast and thoroughly subverted. The wealthy, haughty, morally indignant heroine Dorothea has a past abortion to hide; the cool, Jane Austenish wit whom she's rescued from the grind of governessing is her lesbian lover; and the lustful opium fiend Fraser functions ambiguously as both arch-villain and exposer of the sexual hypocrisy of others. Kevin Smith is less successfully cast: the joke of a piece of *Querelle*-ish jailbait who acts more like a super-vacuous male model soon wears thin.

The S/M thrill inscribed in cross-class and inter-racial desire in the film's models is hilariously fore-grounded in Dorothea's feverish whip-cracking during her carriage ride to the eroticised squalor of the docks to check out the disembarking male convict flesh. Her ostensibly high-minded motives—moral probity and the desire to 'save' her addicted sister—are undermined from the start by Fraser's taunts about her hypocritical denial of her past ("You once regarded me in a less gothic light," he sneers), the overt sexuality of her costumes and numerous double entendres. "I need a man," she explains to Lawrence when elaborating her enigmatic work offer—whereupon sounds of female orgasm can be heard in the background.

The cumulative effect is to make costume melodrama's classic preoccupations with strict social hierarchy and sexual propriety seem hilariously gratuitous, irrational and redundant. But *Desperate Remedies*' self-conscious reinvention of the genre's pleasures is also its shortcoming: for all its verve and visual excess, it's ultimately a one-joke parody which never makes the imaginistic transgression into, say, the deep cod-historical weirdness of Canada's Guy Maddin. Its ironic achievement is to end up looking more authentic than the real thing: Hope's sweaty, dirty docks with their slaves and rough sex make Hitchcock's recreation of Sydney Harbour in the recently restored *Under Capricorn* look like the tacky toy-town model it probably was.

Also reviewed in:
NEW YORK TIMES, 5/23/94, p. C14, Stephen Holden
VARIETY, 6/7/93, p. 42, David Stratton

DEVIL, PROBABLY, THE

A Film Society of Lincoln Center re-release of a Sunchild/Gaumont Films production of a 1977 film released by Robert Bresson. *Executive Producer:* Stephane Tcholgadjieff. *Director:* Robert Bresson. *Screenplay (French with English subtitles):* Robert Bresson. *Director of Photography:* Quasqualino de Santis. *Editor:* Germaine Lamy. *Music:* Philippe Sarde. *Running time:* 95 minutes. *MPAA Rating:* Not Rated.

CAST: Antoine Monnier (Charles); Tina Irissari (Alberte); Henri de Maublanc (Michel); Laetitia Carcano (Edwige); Regis Hanrion (Psychoanalyst); Nicolas Deguy (Valentin); Geoffrey Gausson (Bookseller); Rogert Honorat (Commissioner).

NEW YORK POST, 11/4/94, p. 54, Thelma Adams

Factories pollute the air. Tankers dump oil in the ocean. Crushed seal pups leave pink smears in the snow.

Love disappoints. Drugs depress. The new church is nothing new and revolution revolts.

Who's playing this cruel joke on humanity? "The Devil, Probably." The Film Society of Lincoln Center is reviving Robert Bresson's sculpted, earnest drama about despair among the Parisian hip-hugger set in the '70s. Running through Thursday at the Walter Reade Theater, it was shown to New Yorkers only once before, at the New York Film Festival in 1977.

Born in France in 1907, Bresson began as a visual artist. With such films as "Les Anges Du Peche" (1943) and "Pickpocket" (1959), he established a reputation as an austere, painterly and original talent. Surrealist Jean Cocteau said of the director, "Bresson is a loner in this frightful profession. He expresses himself in film like a poet with his pen."

Suicides figure frequently in Bresson's films and "The Devil, Probably" is no exception. His penultimate movie opens with the news of a suicide in Pere Lachaise cemetery—and then raises the possibility that the death of a winsome youth could have been murder.

Bresson gracefully loops back in an extended flashback to flesh out the story (based on a real event) behind the headline.

Doomed mathematician Charles (Antoine Monnier) is the off-center of a pretty circle of searching adolescents: the environmentalist Michel (Henri de Maublanc); Michel's ex and Charles's current live-in, the earth mother Alberte (Tina Irissari); and the racy brunette Edwige (Laetitia Carcano).

Bresson deftly structures his exploration of a wasted youth sacrificed to an unfeeling society. His four teens glow, acne-free, like marble angels.

But the '70s weigh on "The Devil" is like a '60s hangover. A shrink asks Charles on the eve of the boy's destruction, "Your disagreement with society began how?" The waifish slacker, luxuriating in his despair, later replies "My sickness is seeing clearly."

"The Devil, Probably" has not aged well. I can appreciate Bresson's artful brush strokes of beautiful angst, but it's not my cup of cyanide.

NEWSDAY, 11/4/94, Part II/p. B8, John Anderson

Unseen here since the 1977 New York Film Festival, "The Devil Probably" contains much of what has made Robert Bresson one of the most respected and enigmatic lights of modern French cinema: a disregard for moviemaking conventions, a preference for interaction over isolation of dramatic elements, and a more-than-discreet distance from his subjects.

Made when he was 70 years old, The Devil, Probably" is evidence that the artist is never too old to mourn the ardor and waste of youth, even while doing a number on adolescent self-absorption. His four principals—Alberte (Tina Irissari), Edwige (Laetitia Carcano), Michel (Henri de Maublanc) and, chiefly, the mordant Charles (Antoine Monnier)—are in high dudgeon over the polluted state of the world, the cavalier tainting of their natural resources, the pointlessness of it all. Charles will die—from the opening of the film we know it's either suicide or murder—but his personal tragedy taxes our tolerance, because he's so easy to dislike. The others will probably adjust, and take their own advantage of the earth's exploitation. Bresson—whose "Diary of a Country Priest" and "A Man Escaped" are among world movie milestones—makes Charles' narcissistic despondence an art in and of itself. Ever callow, he takes Alberte away from his more conformist counterpart, the charming Michel, but discovering no way out of his depression through her body, dumps her for Edwige. All are oblivious to their own hypocrisy, while bemoaning that of the world.

Bresson plays the trickster with his quartet, subjecting them to an embarrassing joke: None of the leaking oil tankers or A-bomb tests or polluting vehicles are seen anywhere but on the video screen. Theirs remains an unsullied world and, although the anger and indignation they manifest may be sincere, their pure-world sentiment is artificially created.

VILLAGE VOICE, 11/8/94, p. 59, J. Hoberman

An unexpected gift, Robert Bresson's *The Devil, Probably* rematerializes here 17 years after its lone local screening at the 15th New York Film Festival. The wait is not entirely inappropriate: Like every feature this now 87-year-old French master has directed, *The Devil, Probably* is a drama of faith so uncompromising as to border on the absurd.

Chic yet austere, as flat and stylized as a medieval illumination, *The Devil, Probably* is a vision bracketed by the void. It's a movie that begins (and ends) in total darkness, presenting itself as an interlude during which abstract creatures flounce purposefully in and out of frame. As these Yves St. Laurent angels flit through Paris on predestined missions of celestial mystery, the youthful hero, Charles (Antoine Monnier), rushes headlong toward his end—suicide or murder?—in the star-studded Père Lachaise cemetery.

Bresson's near-classic *j'accuse* begins with Charles's death; the rest of the narrative is an extended flashback covering the past six months. The movie is set in a generic student milieu where long-haired panhandlers play their flutes and bongos by the Seine while sinister political activists plant pornographic photos between the pages of books sold in a church concession stand. A university dropout, the androgynous, aristocratic Charles has captivated a posse of grave young hippies with the purity of his despair. (Nonactors all, the principals are all extraordinarily beautiful objets d'art, with Monnier himself the great-grandson of Henri Matisse.)

Bresson may loathe the notion of a mechanical world, but each action in his film provokes an equal and opposite reaction. The oddly named Alberte leaves her doggedly adoring Michel, an ecological activist, to comfort Charles. Her sacrifice prompts Charles, who is nothing if not a studied sybarite, to take up with Edwige—but, really, he's in love with the idea of death. Although Alberte becomes concerned when she finds a vial of cyanide in his backpack, not everyone is so tolerant: Charles has a casual tryst with a third girl who kicks him out of her apartment upon discovering that he tried to drown himself in her bathtub.

For his circle, Charles exudes a magnetic passivity. With his blank, accusatory look, he's a living reproach to a corrupt, polluted world. Viewers may find him insufferable because, in implacably rejecting the social order, he's repudiating them as well. On the other hand, however mopey and sanctimonious, he's transfigured by the purity of his adolescent rejection. Press reports suggest that, when first released in France, *The Devil, Probably* was seen as so dangerous an incitement to suicide that it was nearly prohibited for those under 18. Indeed, this evocation of glamorous youth cult nihilism could be Bresson's belated, caustic answer to Antonioni's *Blow Up*. (Alternately, as Richard Roud pointed out, the entire movie could be read as a case study of homosexual panic.)

The Devil, Probably maintains its formal rigor through Bresson's geometric interest in fragmenting his actors—isolating their feet or truncating their gestures. The close-ups of hands trafficking in drugs by the Seine affords the sort of transaction he revels in. Still, the movie is not altogether devoid of acerbic humor: Charles adopts a heroin addict and brings him (along with a portable phonograph and a record of Monteverdi) to crash on the floor of Notre Dame; the junkie immediately takes the opportunity to rob the poor box. The greatest scene has Charles and Michel riding a city bus—their trip interspersed with cutaways to the inner working of the exit door, the machine for collecting money, the rearview mirror. They are talking, of course, about It (death, despair, the end of the world) and, as if scripted by Bertolt Brecht, the other passengers join in the conversation. "Who's in charge?" someone finally asks, setting up for the inevitable punch line, "The devil, probably." The sequence is majestically punctuated—it ends when the bus hits something, we never know what.

The Devil, Probably is a fiercely irascible movie and part of its kick is watching Bresson invoke the modern world. Mainly this takes the form of eco-disaster. Michel's involvement with the Association for the Safeguard of Man and His Environment allows for the interpolation of 16mm documentary footage of air pollution, oil spills, garbage mounds, and the deformities of Minimata—not to mention the clubbing of a baby seal. At the same time, the film is contemptuous of politics. Charles turns his back on an underground meeting at which the youthful speaker opens his oration by proclaiming "destruction"; it hardly seems coincidental that, when the movie begins, Charles is found lying dead beside the tomb of France's postwar Communist leader, Maurice Thorez. (One wonders if Bresson was cognizant of the Jim Morrison cult also centered on the Père Lachaise.)

The corruption of the adult world is absolute. Politicians lie, professors obfuscate, priests hypocritically try to make themselves relevant. At Edwige's request, Charles visits a stylishly grim shrink who questions him about his sex life and childhood, then makes a few facile pronouncements. The inference is that Charles is too smart for this disgusting world: "My sickness is seeing clearly," (Is this the voice of the filmmaker?) In a burst of transcendent sarcasm, Charles pulls out an advertising flyer and—announcing that in "losing life, I would lose ... "—begins to recite a litany of consumer catchphrases.

When Charles expresses his fear of killing himself, the shrink taunts him with the observation that, in ancient Rome, the suicidal hired their own assassins. Meeting him after this session, his friends think that Charles has been cured—and in a sense, he has been. Logic prevails. Like a rocket burning off its heat shield as it plunges to earth, *The Devil, Probably* incinerates all affectation in tracing Charles's single-minded march toward oblivion. That we never know his final interrupted thought only underscores Bresson's voluptuous pessimism: Charles is us.

Also reviewed in:
NEW YORK TIMES, 9/29/77, p. C19, Vincent Canby

DIALOGUES WITH MADWOMEN

A Light-Saraf Films release. *Producer:* Allie Light and Irving Saraf. *Director:* Allie Light. *Director of Photography:* Irving Saraf. *Editor:* Irving Saraf and Allie Light. *Sound:* Deborah Brubaker, Sara Chin, and Jeff Roth. *Running time:* 90 minutes. *MPAA Not Rated.*

WITH: Deedee Bloom; Allie Light; Mairi McFall; Karen Wong; Susan Pedrick; Hannah Ziegellaub.

LOS ANGELES TIMES, 5/26/94, Calendar/p. 4, Kevin Thomas

In Allie Light's absorbing, "Dialogues With Madwomen," seven highly articulate women of superior intelligence tell us their stories of enduring and eventually overcoming mental illness. Neither a downer nor a dry series of case studies, the documentary is a warm, encouraging experience shot through with survivors' humor. What's unsettling—and properly so—is that so much of what these women have gone through is what countless others have gone through; by and large the only difference is that these interviewees' ordeals conspired to trigger mental breakdowns.

That Light, a veteran Oscar-winning San Francisco documentarian, picked an array of women who vary widely enough in age, education, race, ethnicity and sexual orientation reinforces the impact and implications of the substantial commonality in their experiences.

Most had nightmarish childhoods at the hands of crazed, sometimes alcoholic parents, several were sexually abused by fathers or stepfathers; several suffered as members of minority groups; a number are clearly highly creative and imaginative; and the majority had truly terrible, even devastating, initial experiences with the mental-health care establishment until they at last received the help they needed—even so, you have the feeling that they all had a great deal to do with their own healing.

On the whole, you're left with the feeling that their negative environments in childhood, rather than organic causes, had far more to do with precipitating their ordeals. Even so, you wish that Light had asked her subjects whether doctors had ever found any physical conditions that might have rendered them more vulnerable to what in their own persuasive words were terrible conditions.

They are an engaging group of individuals capable of speaking of themselves with wit and detachment. One young women, sexually abused by a father who enforced nudity and no privacy within his home, speaks on her multiple personality disorder and what it was like when she was finally able to integrate all 25 of them into one. A young African American, as brilliant as she is lovely, speaks of taking a leave of absence from law school to relieve tension only to become the victim of a rape at a spa where she had gone to unwind.

Two of the women own up to continuing vulnerability, one still working out rage, especially toward her abusive father, the other a thoroughly engaging free-spirited woman who once heard voices and believed she and her great dream love, Bob Dylan, would save the world together. At 44, this woman admits she has never experienced the passionate love relationship she has always craved. She says she would end her life if she didn't believe it could still happen to her.

Light is especially inspired in the ways in which she ends "Dialogues With Madwomen"—first with a genuine and positive surprise revelation and then with a heart-wrenching coda on the tragic fate of one of the women in her film.

NEW YORK POST, 8/3/94, p. 34, Larry Worth

Hollywood depictions of mentally ill women have been undeniably manic, ranging from the highs of "Woman Under the Influence" and "Snake Pit" to" the dregs of "The Bell Jar" or "Nuts." Then there's Allie Light's documentary, "Dialogues With Madwomen," which falls somewhere in between.

Actually, her interview footage of seven troubled ladies is moving, illuminating and haunting. But Light's attempts to visualize their travails needlessly hampers the production.

For instance, when a schizophrenic discusses her 25 personalities the screen fills with glass-shard shapes, containing fragments of her nose, eyes and mouth. Another woman describes her nightmare of fingernails that grow after death. Sure enough Light segues to a gnarled hand rising out of the dirt.

You'd think the Academy Award-winning director (1991's "In the Shadow of the Stars") would recognize such gimmicks' hokeyness. Not the case. In fact, she graduates to full-fledged reenactment which prove even sillier.

Thankfully, Light has retained her touch with interview subjects resulting in some fascinating monologues. With most of the subjects, problems brought on by the likes of rape, bias, abuse, religion or family problems, their tales are especially horrifying.

In one woman's case, a Catholic school upbringing—filled with nuns' sadism and the glorification of stigmata—resulted in a desire "to sit down in a corner of the room, turn off the lights and slice myself up."

Yet another tells of being coaxed by her doctor to sleep with men. One can't help wondering who the "crazy" one is.

And while Light inserts enough humorous anecdotes to catch viewers off guard, it's balanced by the tragic murder of one interviewee before the film's completion.

But the most astounding revelation comes from director Light who, it turns out is one of the seven protagonists. Having been locked in a mental hospital for depression she recalls a psychiatrist stomping on her career dreams.

She responds: "I would like to say to you, Dr. Schwartz, I went on to school, I spent 11 years teaching and I became a filmmaker."

That's why—despite the flaws of "Madwomen"—one can't help applauding Light's hard-earned victories.

NEWSDAY, 8/3/94, Part II/p. B9, Jack Mathews

The least interesting of the seven troubled women featured in Academy Award-winning documentarian Allie Light's "Dialogues With Madwomen" is Light herself. That's because, as she tells us on camera, she has always tended to think in metaphors, and metaphors are a far cry—make that a heartbreaking wail—from the unadorned horror stories told by the others.

Most of the women Light chose as her co-subjects were horribly abused as children, either sexually molested or psychologically deprived, and as they peer back through the veils of pain, confusion, suffering, institutionalization, drug therapy and analysis, the common denominator that emerges is their early loss of identity.

Like Mairi, who was raped by her father and passed among his pedophile friends before she was 10, or Susan, whose alcoholic stepfather made her a sexual partner when she was 3, most had no chance to develop functional self-images, because their sense of self was destroyed by the environment they were born into.

The women vary in age, race, religion, social background and sexual orientation, and their diagnosed diseases run the gamut from schizophrenia to manic-depression to multiple personality disorder. But as they speak, revealing abuses both in the home and in the mental health care system, we learn that each was forced to seek an identity outside herself in order to survive.

Mairi's elaborate defense mechanism included the development of 25 different childhood personalities. Deedee, a Catholic conditioned by nuns to believe in the sanctity of physical suffering, fell into a pattern of self-mutilation. Susan, absent any sexual orientation, gave herself to anyone who expressed an interest. Hannah sought a soulmate in Bob Dylan, with whom she shared the same birth date, and developed a life-long obsession. R.B., the beautiful daughter of a jazz drummer, dropped out of law school and became a barefoot bag lady on the streets of San Francisco.

Light had her own identity problem. She was a 28-year-old housewife and mother driven into deep depression by her inability to find expression for her creative energy. Though her paternalistic therapist prescribed mild doses of housekeeping and cooking as outpatient therapy, she reclaimed her sanity with productive careers as a teacher, writer and filmmaker.

Light, whose 1991 documentary about the San Francisco Opera won an Oscar, is her own best success story, and sort of the odd woman out in the film. She alone can claim recovery. Still, it is her honesty and poetic vision that link the stories and give "Dialogues With Madwomen" its compelling strength. The movie offers no professional perspective or guidance; there are no experts on hand to explain or elaborate on the women's experiences. These are self-told profiles in desperation, there for us to draw our own conclusions.

To overcome the "talking heads" problem inherent in the film's title, and to dramatize the feelings being expressed by her subjects, Light uses a variety of visual devices, blending still photos, news footage, drawings, reenactments and symbolic imagery to turn it into a sort of multimedia documentary. Most of the devices work, but having some of the women portray themselves in reenacted events and dramatized fantasies seems wildly inappropriate.

It is okay for Light to fiddle with her own life on film—remember, she relishes metaphor—but to use the others as props in their own stories smacks of cheap exploitation.

VILLAGE VOICE, 8/9/94, p. 44, Georgia Brown

Allie Light's packed, rough-hewn documentary, *Dialogues With Madwomen*, is anything but decorative and predictable. Her effaced interviews with seven women who have had, shall we say, serious problems coping, are deeply affecting, sometimes harrowing.

Initially, it's difficult to grasp the film's structure. Without editorializing, Light lets the women speak, while filling out their stories with some hallucinatory visual passages. (Some of these images are more effective than others.) Eventually, a vague chronology emerges: After describing the genesis of their illnesses, early years of trauma and confusion, the women go on to the horrors of hospitalization and medication, the difficulty of finding anyone who understands; finally, in all but one case, they speak of recovery.

Since the women's identities aren't immediately distinct, their stories tend to overlap and sometimes merge. Most were physically and sexually abused; most came from flagrantly pathogenic homes. Their great accomplishment, we gather, is that with some effective help, they're now able to talk, to tell their stories. Here are a few vignettes:

A round-faced woman with a tiny smile and the helmet-type haircut of a nun says, "If you were Catholic, two things were really good: dying and self-mutilation." It takes a while to realize her hair is dyed a bright grape. "We would cut ourselves a lot," since, for bearing the pain, "you would get time off in purgatory."

A woman with the voice of a man recalls, "My mother always said my first words were, '*Shut that door!*' " We're shown a photo of this woman when she was 10 or so, with deep bleeding slices in her arms. She did it to herself. You have to wonder, Who took that picture?

A young woman sensuously stroking a cat recalls that her father refused to allow any door in the house to be closed. You couldn't wear any clothes in the house either. Not only did Daddy read her diary but he wrote in it. Daddy belonged to a group of pedophiles who believed it their mission to initiate children into sex.

An animated dark-haired woman describes an obsession with Bob Dylan, whose birth date she shares: "I was his soulmate. Baez hadn't been equal to it. Together we were going to save the world." A video love letter she created for him was broadcast on the Five O'Clock News. After significant therapeutic help, she's still waiting for a soulmate and sometimes feels hideously lonely.

A beautiful young African American woman describes her one short step from Stanford Law School—studying along with "the sons of the ruling class"—to going barefoot and sleeping in public toilets.

Only late in the film do we learn that one of these women is the filmmaker, and that another, the Asian American sitting in front of her painting, was raped and murdered before her segment was finished, *Dialogues* is saturated with grief, but makes abundantly clear that grief is a condition of hope.

Also reviewed in:
CHICAGO TRIBUNE, 6/3/94, Friday/p. J, John Petrakis
NEW YORK TIMES, 8/24/94, p. C20, Bruce Weber
VARIETY, 11/29/93, p. 37, Dennis Harvey
WASHINGTON POST, 7/15/94, p. B6, Hal Hinson

DINGO

A Greycat Films release of a Gevest Australia Productions/A.O. Prods./Dedra Films/Cine Cinqu coproduction, with the participation of the Australian Film Finance Corporation. *Executive Producer:* Giorgio Draskovic and Marie Pascale Osterrieth. *Producer:* Rolf de Heer and Marc Rosenberg. *Director:* Rolf de Heer. *Screenplay:* Marc Rosenberg. *Director of Photography:* Denis Lenoir. *Editor:* Surresh Ayyar. *Music:* Michel Legrand and Miles Davis. *Sound:* Henri Morelle. *Production Designer:* Judi Russell. *Costumes:* Clarissa Patterson. *Running time:* 108 minutes. *MPAA Rating:* Not Rated.

CAST: Colin Friels (John Anderson); Miles Davis (Billy Cross); Helen Buday (Jane Anderson); Joe Petruzzi (Peter); Bernadette Lafont (Angie Cross).

NEW YORK POST, 11/11/94, p. 48, Chip Defaa

In the last year of his life, jazz legend Miles Davis made his acting debut in an Australian-French film directed by Rolf de Heer, "Dingo." For fans of Davis this 1990 production, only now being released in New York, will come as one final posthumous gift.

Davis is so charismatic a presence, it is a pity he was never used in films before. Although he actually appears in a fairly small percentage of this one, he deserves the co-star billing he received for he gives the film its piquant tone.

He plays an enigmatic, reclusive, world-weary jazz legend named Billy Cross (who seems very much like Miles Davis). En route from France to Japan in 1969, his plane touches down in a remote part of Australia. On impulse, he gives an impromptu performance on the airstrip.

A boy on the verge of adolescence is awe-struck. That's the best thing I've ever heard," he tells Davis who suggests the boy take up music because "you seem tuned into it," adding after a beat: "If you're ever in Paris, look me up."

Davis quietly rasps his lines with the same focused emotion that marks his best trumpet playing, so that even such seemingly casual remarks take on near-oracular import.

Davis' words never leave the youth. Twenty years later, as an adult unhappy with his life of trapping dingoes (wild Australian dogs) and playing trumpet on the side, he finally opts to realize his dream of going to Paris, seeking out Cross and the jazz life.

The film takes too long to get to its climax. and if you're not a jazz fan you'll find its unhurried pace a trial. While Colin Friel gives a convincing performance as the frustrated, indecisive John "Dingo" Anderson—I found myself wanting to shake him and say, "What are you waiting for? Go to Paris!"—the film fully comes alive only when the camera is on Davis.

Davis improvised upon the lines in the script, offering utterances that are so quintessentially him it seems unthinkable that another actor could have essayed the role. When he mutters he never wanted to "become a jazz museum piece," he might as well have been offering a real-life epitaph.

There is so much of Davis' magnificent horn both in performance scenes and in subtle underscoring that fans of his will want to see the film more than once to fully savor it. If you're not enthralled by Davis' music or persona however, you're left with a wish-fulfillment story of the sort that Frank Capra knew how to tell more deftly.

NEWSDAY, 11/11/94, Part II/p. B9, Gene Seymour

Why did it take so long for Miles Davis and the movies to figure out they were meant for each other?

Anyone who's seen him in concert, live, filmed or taped, can attest to his magnetism and mastery of dramatic tension. Yet it wasn't until just a year before his death, at 65, in 1991, that Davis, modern jazz' biggest star, was given a major role in a feature film. So "Dingo" is all there is to the great trumpeter's acting filmography.

There should have been more. Even with all the stark, beautiful vistas of the Australian outback and the vivid, twilight scenes of Paris that provide the backdrop for "Dingo," Davis' haunting, enigmatic presence reduces everything around it to a blur.

Davis' wet-sandpaper voice, coarsened by age and recurring illness, may not always present the lines with the proper inflection—or even intelligibility. But just as Davis the musician could convey several levels of emotion with just a few notes, Davis the actor was able to use only a few gestures to keep an audience riveted.

The performance, rough edges and all, is enough to justify the existence of this otherwise muddled saga of a outback dweller (Colin Friels), who as a boy was inspired by an impromptu desert-tarmac performance by jazz legend Billy Cross (Davis) to pick up the horn himself.

The boy grows up to become a dingo trapper, a poor, but loving family man and the leader of a weekend "bush band." He dreams of someday flying off to Paris to take up Cross' long-ago invitation to visit and maybe even play alongside his hero.

At times, this fusion of "Rocky" and "Young Man With a Horn" comes closer than any film to conveying what it's like for a jazz musician to forge his art and play by the seat of his pants. But though Friels' brooding performance matches Davis' in cumulative wattage, the film becomes as gauzy and maudlin as some of Michel Legrand's music—which, like the rest of the film, is rescued by Davis' spare, bold conceptions.

VILLAGE VOICE, 11/15/94, p. 68, Beth Coleman

Loved the soundtrack, could have done without the rest of the movie. Miles Davis comes out with a haunting album called *Dingo* that recalls not only some of his old blue grooves but the air of the Australian outback to boot. We wait three years for a visual worthy of the sound. (What's your name?" "John Anderson." "Nice to meet you, John Anderson. If you ever come to Paris look me up"—a short exchange wrapped in pure brass, which teases with a retro-romance of jazz and the city.) We have all the ingredients of the tried and true story, young artist burning to emerge and mentor trying to rediscover his creative roots. *Dingo* takes that promise and delivers the maudlin over the sublime.

Ignore the single white man playing trumpet to the overgrown desert that opens the film and for a moment Dingo looks like it might deliver the goods. Three children playing in poor, white, sheep-farming land; a plane flies close overhead and the locals pile into pickups to go see. Out of the plane steps the blackest man under the sun looking more ancient than stone. He asks the people of Poona Flat if he can play for them. The hugeness of the plane, the expanse of sky and land, and the idea of Miles showing up like a Greek fury are so fine. But director de Heer has no clue how to shoot a live gig, nor can he get a rise from a generally dense cast, and the editing is too bad to be tragic. Et voilà, the transcendent brought to ground by good intentions and bad craftsmanship.

For His Largeness's most dogged fans, you do get to see Miles Davis, in bright yellow suit and shades, drive around nighttime Paris and drop philosophy—corny but thrilling.

Also reviewed in:
NEW YORK TIMES, 11/11/94, p. C19, Stephen Holden
VARIETY, 10/14/91, p. 244, David Stratton

DISCLOSURE

A Warner Bros. release of a Baltimore Pictures/Constant c production. *Executive Producer:* Peter Giuliano. *Producer:* Barry Levinson and Michael Crichton. *Director:* Barry Levinson. *Screenplay:* Paul Attanasio. *Based on the book by:* Michael Crichton. *Director of Photography:* Tony Pierce-Roberts. *Editor:* Stu Linder. *Music:* Ennio Morricone. *Music Editor:* James Flamberg. *Sound:* Steve Cantamessa. *Sound Editor:* Marc Fishman and Harry Cohen. *Casting:* Ellen Chenoweth. *Production Designer:* Neil Spisak. *Art Director:* Richard Yanez-Toyon and Charles William Breen. *Set Decorator:* Garrett Lewis. *Special Effects:* Steve Galich. *Costumes:* Gloria Gresham. *Make-up:* Cheri Minns and Tom Lucas. *Running time.* 128 minutes. *MPAA Rating:* R.

CAST: Michael Douglas (Tom Sanders); Demi Moore (Meredith Johnson); Donald Sutherland (Bob Garvin); Caroline Goodall (Susan Hendler); Dylan Baker (Philip Blackburn); Roma Maffia (Catherine Alvarez); Dennis Miller (Marc Lewyn); Allan Rich (Ben Heller); Nicholas Sadler (Don Cherry); Rosemary Forsyth (Stephanie Kaplan); Suzie Plakson (Mary Anne Hunter); Jacqueline Kim (Cindy Chang); Joe Urla (John Conley, Jr.); Michael Chieffo (Stephen Chase); Jo Attanasio (Furillo); Faryn Einhorn (Eliza Sanders); Trevor Einhorn (Matt Sanders).

CHRISTIAN SCIENCE MONITOR, 12/9/94, p. 12, David Sterritt

When you're a best-selling author like Michael Crichton or a popular Hollywood director like Barry Levinson, plugging into the latest cultural brouhahas is part of your job description.

Never have these savvy entertainers pushed more hot buttons in a single project than they do in "Disclosure," the new suspense film starring Michael Douglas as a likable computer executive and Demi Moore as his treacherous new boss. The picture serves up megadoses of sexual harassment and computer-biz backstabbing, spiced with feminist issues and antifeminist backlash—not to mention a hyperbolic sex scene, enough anatomically graphic dialogue to fill a dozen tabloid-TV shows, and a burst of virtual-reality special effects in the homestretch.

What makes the movie compulsively watchable is the sheer momentum of its story, its acting, and its images. What makes it borderline sleazy is its over-the-top sexuality, which stretches the R rating to its limits. What makes it provocative is its backward-looking view of female progress in the business world. Turning the usual gender-politics scenarios on their heads, the villain is a woman obsessed with sex and power, while the victim is a man whose career goes kerflooey when he rejects her advances.

Could it happen? Of course it could, and unquestionably it often has. But have men undergone sexual harassment nearly as often as women? Not according to any statistic I've seen. And does justice now call for a big-budget movie to make audiences weep over the sufferings of oppressed white corporation men? Many will say no, and they'll be the ones hissing as "Disclosure" hits its controversial high points.

The hero is Tom Sanders, a family man, computer engineer, and all-around nice guy whose comfy life is about to get even comfier, thanks to a much-deserved promotion he's certain to receive. Imagine his dismay when the boss passes him over, bestowing the big VP-ship on Meredith Johnson, a woman from another branch of the corporation. Is she really the best-qualified person, or is the company's honcho overeager to "break the glass ceiling" by elevating a woman at any cost?

And what's the chemistry between Tom and Meredith, who had a tempestuous affair years ago? It's been ages since Tom thought about this long-past relationship, but Meredith seems eager to revive it during an after-hours appointment in her newly acquired office.

Confronted with her aggressive sexuality, Tom caves in for a while but eventually finds the strength to just say no, regaining his dignity and storming furiously out the door. The next day Meredith retaliates with a wildly false charge of sexual harassment, damaging his career and vowing to ruin his life if he won't fall in line with her wishes.

"Disclosure" uses this story to pitch a couple of different messages. The first, stated directly and reasonably, is that sexual harassment has more to do with power than with sex.

The second, stated indirectly and insidiously, is that feminist gains have spawned a new breed of predatory woman, as dangerous as any power-abusing man *and* shielded from discovery by her ability to exploit bleeding-heart notions of female vulnerability. Meredith is a "spider woman" as surely as the evil-doing females of countless films noir in bygone decades.

What's new is the cloak of sociocultural victimhood in which she wraps her nasty schemes—and the movie's eagerness to exploit this particular brand of villainy, poignantly aimed at a hero who never abused a right or flaunted a privilege in his middle-class-white-male life.

Not surprisingly, "Disclosure" covers its postfeminist tracks. A couple of strong and honorable women play important roles, including Tom's understanding wife and the attorney who guides him through legal quicksand. And much of the tale steers in other directions altogether, through related subplots about a corporate merger and technical glitches at the computer factory. Still, there's no mistaking the movie's glee in constructing and then humiliating a corporate woman who rivals Cruella de Ville ("101 Dalmatians") for wickedness. Foes of gender harmony will find much comfort here.

On the level of pure craft, "Disclosure" is first-rate in every department. Levinson's directing is cogent and colorful, and cinematography by camera wizard Tony Pierce-Roberts is dazzling.

Paul Attanasio's screenplay is full of surprises, and while it resolves one of its major plot lines with a trite detective-story flourish, it gets a second wind and delivers a new batch of unexpected twists before the finale. The excellent supporting cast includes Donald Sutherland as the company boss, Caroline Goodall as Tom's wife, and Roma Maffia as his tough-talking lawyer.

LOS ANGELES TIMES, 12/9/95, Calendar/p. 1, Kenneth Turan

Like the hotel chain that promises "no surprises," the film version of the best-selling "Disclosure" has little use for the unexpected, with one exception. Albeit unintentionally, it increases appreciation for the storytelling skills of novelist Michael Crichton.

One aspect of Crichton's talent, his ability to spin out glib tales that are pantingly close to today's headlines, has been much commented upon. "Disclosure." with its *au courant* topic of sexual harassment in the workplace is high concept pulp fiction. The latest in a successful string that has included "Jurrasic Park" and "Rising Sun."

But not until you see "Disclosure," starring Michael Douglas and Demi Moore and directed by Barry Levinson from a script by Paul Attanasio will you appreciate a humbler aspect of Crichton's craft. Although literary critics understandably fulminate about his characterization and his writing style, Crichton knows how to write a coherent plot, something his movie versions tend to have trouble with. "Disclosure" is hardly a great mess. It is rather standard Hollywood fare, adequately entertaining if, lacking in the over-the-top enthusiasm someone like Paul Verhoeven ("Basic Instinct") would have brought. But its preoccupation with snazzy computer-generated special effects has left key plot points so unclear at least one baffled viewer had to retreat to the book to find out why some things happened and others did not.

Of course "Disclosure's" money scene, the lurid sexual encounter between Tom Sanders (Douglas) and his glamorous boss (and former girlfriend) Meredith Johnson (Moore), has not been allowed to languish in uncertainty. Crisply shot by "Howards End's" Tony Pierce-Roberts, it is presented as a high-gloss clash of the titans with the unscrupulous Johnson trying to force her dastardly will on a plainly confused Sanders.

Sanders confusion is understandable. When this particular day began, he and his svelte wife. Susan (Caroline Goodall) were looking forward to some positive results from the merger of DigiCom, the high-tech Seattle firm Sanders works for, with a bigger outfit. He might even be promoted to the plum job of vice president of Advanced Operations and Planning.

But when Sanders gets to office, he eventually finds out (in a typically murky bit of exposition) that DigiCom's mercurial boss, Bob Garvin (Donald Sutherland), has given the promotion he thought he earned to Johnson, an ambitious old flame who he feels "doesn't know the difference between software and a cashmere sweater."

As played by Moore, Johnson is a classic villainess with a heart as brittle as a silicon chip. Rapacious and conniving, she insists on getting her own way or knowing the reason why. Although Moore does not bring the brio to the part that Linda Florentino imparts to "The Last Seduction," she is perfectly adequate to the film's single-dimension sensibility.

Thc same is true for Douglas, whose character depends much of the movie rushing around with jaws clenched and a harried look on his face after Johnson has the cheek to accuse *him* of harassing *her*. As DigiCom lines up behind Garvin's favorite and problems develop with a new gizmo he is supposed to be supervising, Sanders decides to duke it out and ends up with harassment expert Catherine Alvarez (Roma Maffia, who makes the same strong impression she did in "The Paper") as his lawyer.

All this is certainly clear enough, but other things that should be are not. What, for instance, is the nature of the hold Johnson has over Garvin, and is there anything besides pure lust motivating what happens behind her locked office doors. The book tidily clears up these problems, but the film leaves them uncomfortably hanging around.

More effective, and a surprising highlight of the film, are "Disclosure's" visuals. Production designer Neil Spisak, art directors Richard Yanez-Toyon and Charles William Breen and set decorator Garrett Lewis have created an exciting office environment from scratch for the folks at DigiCom. And the ever-reliable gremlins at Industrial Light & Magic have come up with a vivid representation of the possible future of virtual reality technology.

Although Levinson has done a plausible job of directing, "Disclosure" suffers from what feels like a lack of creative passion. After "Toys" and "Jimmy Hollywood," back-to-back personal projects that misfired, it's hard not to feel that he took this film on largely to strengthen his commercial credentials, and it shows.

Similarly, screenwriter Attanasio, who dealt thoughtfully with ethical dilemmas in "Quiz Show," works in a more limited moral palette in "Disclosure." where questions of who is right and who is wrong are plainly obvious. The idea that sexual harassment is about power, not sex and that a woman in power can potentially misbehave just like a man may be news to certain segments of the population, but they are not news enough to light a much-needed fire under this production.

NEW YORK, 1/2/95, p. 66, David Denby

I never imagined my services would be required in support of a commercial thriller starring Michael Douglas and Demi Moore. But such is the case with Barry Levinson's *Disclosure*, an intelligent and entertaining movie that has been reviewed priggishly by people who should have known better. The fault goes beyond reviewers. Too many bright people of my acquaintance have written off the picture in advance. A Michael Crichton potboiler about a woman harassing a *man*? Sighing loudly—hissing, even—they begged to be excused. It was *Fatal Attraction* all over again, the old Hollywood trick of reversing a common outrage by turning a victim into an aggressor.

But there's one problem: *Disclosure* isn't really about sexual harassment. The ads for the movie, with Demi Moore doing her darkly-angry-woman-with-moss-in-her-throat routine and Michael Douglas looking puffy and implosive, promise something "hot," but *Disclosure* delivers something else. The movie is a paranoid thriller set in a Seattle computer company that is about to merge with another high-tech outfit. Tom Sanders (Douglas)—an ace electronics engineer—loses the promotion he had hoped for, only to have an old girlfriend of his, Meredith Johnson (Moore), get the job. Tom, who isn't clever about people, can't read the situation; in an instant, he plummets from big shot to a man in a total panic. Douglas, who specializes in put-upon-white-guy roles, gives his best performance in years. He keeps the spouting tirades to a minimum and actually creates the character. His mouth is drawn, even a little pursed, in tension; his voice, at first, subdued. Tom isn't so young anymore; he's a little slow on the uptake, and not nearly as adept at "personal" skills (i.e., ruthless flattery followed by shafting) as the corporate killers around him. For once, Douglas's anger seems firmly planted in a situation, not an aggressive statement ladled on top of it.

Levinson and screenwriter Paul Attanasio (*Quiz Show*), reshaping Crichton's material, have made a fascinating movie about the paradoxes of modern paranoia. Everyone in the company is genial and seemingly candid—particularly Donald Sutherland's charming CEO, who disingenuously acknowledges what's self-serving about his methods so as to better serve himself. Everyone can see everyone else—the offices have glass walls. Yet what appears transparent is entirely opaque. Even the ostensibly helpful messages on Tom's E-mail are so elliptical they seem designed to make communication impossible. Friends turn into enemies; allies spring up out of nowhere. The day she's promoted, Meredith improbably jumps Tom in her office, and when he pulls away, she accuses him of harassing *her*. What's going on—lust or calculation? What does she want out of him? Demi Moore, aflame or passive, is a proudly humorless actress, a Joan Crawford for the postfeminist age; she's not flexible enough to explore the role's latent possibilities, but at least she has the sense to make use of what's most dislikable in her style—a huffy self-righteousness. Tom hires a tough feminist lawyer to represent him, and winds up taking on the company's entire management. The little episode with his boss, we realize, was part of a much larger intrigue. In the end, the question of who grabbed whom is an interesting but relatively trivial matter. It's power and money that are at stake.

Which is why it's absurd for critics to complain that the picture doesn't live up to its come-ons—as if *Disclosure* had somehow failed in its ambition to be Basic *Instinct*. What the movie actually promises, it delivers: narrative speed and tension, teasing ambiguity, a complexly enfolding structure of hints and appearances with as many corners and levels as an M. C. Escher drawing. This is the best of the corporate thrillers—better than *Rising Sun* or any of the Grisham adaptations. Levinson's direction is crisp and lively, and he makes brilliant use of the amazing set (designed by Neil Spisak), a cavernous office with a hollowed-out center, glass-walled offices perched at mid-level, insinuating catwalks and ramps , and an executive office sitting high above. There's no place to scratch yourself or even wink at a secretary without the whole world knowing about it. Enemies conceal themselves in the most ominous place of all—the open.

But I can guess what skeptics are thinking: Whatever else is going on in *Disclosure*, the movie would never have been made without the scene of the woman pulling the man on top of her. Granted. But the scene is so carefully placed, argued with, interpreted, reinterpreted, it becomes—forgive my momentary lapse into academese—a "text" within a larger text. Give this movie a break: It's not nearly as stupid as the ads, or the critics, have made it look.

NEW YORK POST, 12/9/94, p. 50, Michael Medved

Some thrillers keep you guessing with their ingenious plots; others will hook you and hold you solely on the strength of their characters.

"Disclosure" travels the character route, with superb acting and classy direction that make up for a flimsy story line that fails apart in the final third of a movie.

These plot problems arise directly from Michael Crichton's controversial best seller which despite all the hype, isn't really an exploration of sexual harassment; instead, it's an attempted expose of all-out, survival-of-the-foulest corporate welfare, in which harassment charges represent only one weapon among many.

Michael Douglas plays a hard-working executive and devoted family man who hopes to win a key promotion in his Seattle computer company. On the day he's not only passed over for the job, but his successful rival (and new boss) turns out to be Demi Moore—an amoral corporate climber with whom he'd conducted a torrid affair in the years before his marriage.

At the end of her first day on the job, Moore invites her old flame to her new office and tries to seduce him in one of the most sexually specific scenes ever shown in a mainstream studio film.

He resists at the last moment, provoking rage, promises of revenge, and a life-shattering charge of sexual harassment. With the help of a tough feminist lawyer (Roma Maffia) Douglas fights back to establish his innocence, while discovering that the allegations against him are only part of a larger plot to find a scapegoat to hide some of the company's dark secrets at a sensitive time when its suave, but nervous owner (a perfectly cast Donald Sutherland) stands to make millions in a timely merger.

Unfortunately, the story's climactic resolution is in every sense mechanical, involving not only artificial plot devices but the absurd intervention of various convenient gadgets.

Despite such high-tech flim-flam, screenwriter Paul Attanasio (who did the taut, intelligent script for "Quiz Show") still relies at a key moment that someone else just happens to be listening, unseen, at an open door.

Nevertheless, the passionate, gutsy performance by Michael Douglas keeps you caring about his character 'til the bitter end.

Moore makes an even stronger impression in her finest movie role to date, giving full-blooded new life to the old misogynist stereotype of the hard-driving businesswoman as a vicious tiger lady.

She makes her villainess surprisingly believable and oddly sympathetic, almost admirable, in her sleek and perfect ruthlessness, giving unforgettable intensity to her on-screen hungers as a ravenous female sexual predator.

Director Barry Levinson handles even minor characters with artful humanizing touches, marking a notable comeback for this gifted filmmaker after his embarrassing detours with "Toys" and "Jimmy Hollywood."

On balance, "Disclosure" may be a far cry from "Rain Man"—or "Bugsy" or "Avalon"—but it is an undeniably absorbing entertainment that will pack audiences into theater seats and, for the most part, give them their money's worth.

NEWSDAY, 12/9/94, Part II/p. B2, Jack Mathews

Pardon me, I know sexual harassment is a serious subject, and that women executives are sometimes guilty of chasing powerless men around their desks, too. But Demi Moore chasing Michael Douglas? Catching him? Fondling him? Arousing him? And then being rejected by him?

Hello?

Everything in Barry Levinson's slick and overheated "Disclosure," like everything in the convoluted Michael Crichton novel upon which it is so earnestly based, is nonsense, a male nightmare fantasy about a corporate world gone topsy-turvy, where the power has shifted to women, and where men who once answered the call to "put up or shut up" now must fear being told to "put out or get out."

It's nonsense, but not unwatchable nonsense. Levinson, anxious for a commercial hit following two personal disasters ("Toys" "Jimmy Hollywood"), has given the trashiest elements of the book their due and concentrated on the other plot, a corporate melodrama that takes us on a tour of state-of-the-art computer technology.

It's not that the corporate intrigue is so compelling—I've read the book and seen the movie and still can't explain exactly what happens—but the toys are fun, particularly virtual reality, a computer program that puts the user inside a three-dimensional world where he can travel about with the use of a magic glove and a wired walking pad.

But there's no getting around the fact that "Disclosure" exists, as a book and movie, because of recent headline news about gender politics and sexual harassment.

Crichton, who has the literary commitment of a moist finger held up to the wind, is repeating the cathartic experience of "Rising Sun," in which he set a murder mystery inside a Japanese-run corporation in order to do a little jingoistic Japan-bashing. In "Disclosure" he is speaking for those who are frustrated with the extremes to which American society is going to protect women from men in the workplace, and mocks that movement by turning the typical sexual harassment case on its head.

"Disclosure" is the story of a married man whose career at a cutting-edge Seattle computer firm is threatened when he refuses the sexual demands of his female boss.

It is on Monday morning of the week that is to end with a profitable merger of DigiCom and its deep-pockets suitor that Douglas' Tom Sanders learns the promotion he expected has gone to his old girlfriend, Meredith Johnson (Moore). That night he goes to her office to "bring her up to speed" on department projects, and instead has her bring him up to speed on his new duties as her sexual drone.

"Here, boy!"

Douglas has been made a sex object, by predatory women before. First he had that one-night-stand from hell with Glenn Close in "Fatal Attraction," then became Sharon Stone's vibrator in "Basic Instinct." Now, with a wife, two kids and dinner waiting at home, he finds himself pinned back on a drafting table by Meredith and, with Seattle's landmark Space Needle looming in the distance, begs her to stop.

This is the date movie we've been hearing about? Sure, couples will watch anything that brings up sex. But the mauling that Tom endures in Meredith's office hardly qualifies as erotic, even though he—it is made clear in numerous clinical discussions of the event—is of two minds about it. If anything, "Disclosure" is anti-sex, full of that ultimate spoiler of mood, *discussions* about it.

And here are the issues being discussed: Exactly when does behavior between a boss and his or her employee become sexual harassment, and do the rules apply equally to men and women?

It's a fair question, and the answers are provided in speeches plentiful enough to fill a couple of pages in the Congressional Record. But what occurs is too definitive to cause many arguments on the drive home. Meredith's sexual assault is so extreme, and she is such a one-dimensional villain, you just sit back and wait to savor whatever punishment comes her way.

It may be faint praise to say that screenwriter Paul Attanasio ("Quiz Show") has greatly improved Crichton's story, but he has, dumping some extraneous characters and subplots and lacing it with crisp scenes and sharp dialogue.

Douglas and Moore are fine as Tom and Meredith, though Douglas is getting a little long in the tooth to be playing corporate boy wonders. The most memorable work is put in by Roma Maffia as the feminist lawyer helping Tom restore his soiled reputation, Donald Sutherland, the DigiCom boss under Meredith's spell, and Caroline Goodall, who brings both intelligence and humor to the obligatory role of the suffering wife.

NEWSWEEK, 12/19/94, p. 62, Jack Kroll

If there were a novel prize for literary Opportunism, Michael Crichton would have accumulated thousands of frequent-flier miles to Sweden. Crichton, a supersmart cookie, bones up on trendissimo topics ("Rising Sun," "Jurassic Park") and then uses the best-seller list as a trampoline to vault into blockbuster movies. "Disclosure" spins the hot topic of sexual harassment into reverse. Here the victim is a man, computer executive Tom Sanders (Michael Douglas), who's the target of a power-lust commando assault by his former lover and new boss, Meredith

Johnson (Demi Moore). Sanders has a hard time fending off the relentless Johnson, but he rezips his virtue in the nick of time. When the vengeful Johnson and the shocked Sanders trade harassment charges, the two become combatants in a convoluted game involving their own careers and the fate of their high-tech company, DigiCom, run by the Machiavellian Bob Garvin (Donald Sutherland).

Crichton is both gutsy and smart to brave political incorrectness (he knows it pays off in the marketplace): "Disclosure" roiled some feminist circles. Although he has said that his book was based on a real incident, it's clear he wasn't drawn to the male-female switch as a pop sociologist. (In some quarters his book was known as "Harassic Park.") That's fine; Crichton isn't Ibsen, he's a storyteller, and at some middling level "Disclosure" is fun. But the stakes aren't high enough: who really cares that these high-pay techies are trying to ace each other out of their plum jobs? At least those dinosaurs were trying to kill people.

Even as a storyteller Crichton blows it, and neither screenwriter Paul Attanasio ("Quiz Show") nor director Barry Levinson ("Bugsy") can seal the loopholes. In this world of Information Highway sophistication and virtual-reality marvels, the pivotal plot points are all rickety coincidences: an overheard conversation, a fortuitous phone call. Technology, proclaims Johnson, will bring "what religion and revolution have promised but never delivered," a future in which "we can relate to each other as pure consciousness." Sounds like an interesting woman, but she's never developed as a character, only as the female counterpart to male phallocentrism. (Her name, "Johnson," is macho street slang for the male organ—Crichton's little joke?) Moore is lusciously lubricious, and Douglas by now can play the victim of a fatal attraction in his sleep. The most engaging character is Catherine Alvarez, Sanders's tough lawyer, a role played with wit and style by Roma Maffia. But "Disclosure" provides very little that's really worth disclosing.

SIGHT AND SOUND, 3/95, p. 35, Lizzie Francke

Tom Sanders works in Seattle as a division manager for computer corporation Digital Communications, which is due to be merged with Conley-White. Tom is assuming he will be promoted to vice-president of the division once the negotiations are completed. An e-mail note from Arthur Kahn, overseeing the new line of hardware in Malaysia, informs Tom of a problem with a crucial chip. Having learned from DigiCom's counsel Philip Blackburn that he has been passed over for promotion, Tom visits company head Bob Garvin and finds him with Meredith Johnson, Tom's ex-lover of 10 years before, who is to be the new VP. Meeting up with his creative team: Stephanie Kaplan, Don Cherry and Mark Lewyn, Tom promises to call Lewyn when he knows more about the faulty chip. Garvin announces Meredith's promotion and she asks Tom to meet her later in her office. He receives an anonymous e-mail message implying that he desires Meredith.

At the meeting, Meredith attempts to seduce him with expensive wine and sexual demands. While she is distracted by a call from Garvin, Tom tries to call Lewyn, getting an answer machine at the very moment Meredith returns to get intimate. Tom protests, but Meredith begins fellating him. He succumbs angrily to foreplay, all the while saying "no", then extricates himself and returns home feeling humiliated. Susan, his wife, tells him that Meredith called to inform him that an 8:00 am meeting has been put back to 8:30. When he arrives the next morning he finds that in fact it started at 7:30. Meredith berates him, and Lewyn claims he did not ring that night before. Cherry demonstrates the new virtual reality hardware to the Conley-White executives.

Tom goes to explain his difficulties with Meredith, only to find himself accused of sexually harassing her. Another e-mail message arrives from 'A Friend'. Tom hires Catherine Alvarez, a brilliant lawyer, and files his own sexual harassment suit against Meredith. At a secret arbitration hearing Catherine's cross-examination reveals that Meredith had premeditated the seduction. Tom realises that he didn't ring Lewyn, but another associate named Levin, and is acquitted when the harassment conversation is played back from Levin's answer machine. Later Tom overhears Meredith plotting to make him the fall guy over the faulty chip. He hacks into the virtual reality network to find the files which will exonerate him, just as Meredith is wiping them. Tom manages to get the hard copy files from Mohammed, a colleague in Malaysia. At an important presentation, Tom reveals that Meredith ordered the cost-cutting changes which resulted in the faulty chip, and she is dismissed. The merger is completed. Kaplan is appointed VP and is revealed as the 'Friend'.

Packaged as the "thriller that opened the new chapter in the sex wars" Michael Crichton's novel *Disclosure* is an engagingly provocative essay about corporate power as manifested through sexual politics. If you invert Tom's discovery that "sexual harassment is all about power", then power is all about who fucks over whom. Thus in this instance, the real victims might be the workers who provide the cheap labour in Malaysia that make DigiCom's expansion possible.

However it is sexual politics which made the book a *cause célèbre*. Crichton acknowledges in the afterword that the majority of harassment claims are brought by women against men. Nevertheless, he claims that the "advantage of a role reversal story is that it may enable us to examine aspects concealed by the traditional responses and conventional rhetoric." The film tries hard then to appear analytical about sex and power, but—like DigiComs' stunning glass office building, which enables everyone to see each other without knowing what's going on—there is a sense here of show but don't tell.

The glass ceiling is also very much in evidence. Garvin announces that he is proud to appoint Meredith as VP to show that such an obstruction can be shattered for women, but it is he who holds the hammer. Donald Sutherland plays Garvin as part-schemer and part-paternalist, but there's also something of the pod-person about him. The real power belongs to the anonymous men on the Conley-White team. Joining them on the top floor, Meredith (even her name is masculinised) is the phallic woman supreme. When first we see her in Garvin's office, it is her glistening legs alone that are in the frame, high-heeled shoes reflecting a thin dagger of light—a perfect if rather too obvious case study in fetishism. Slickly dressed and gravelly voiced, Demi Moore plays her as though she had a sneak preview of Linda Fiorentino in *The Last Seduction*, but turning down the voltage, as if knowing that she hasn't the conviction to get away with such bad behaviour. There is a certain irony as Meredith tells Sanders in the finale, "I'm only playing the game the way you guys set it up," only to be met by the smug riposte, "did it ever occur to you that *I* set *you* up?" For Meredith is a fantasy spiderwoman, product of the patriarchal power system, dreamt up and subsequently destroyed by men because they find her just too scary.

As the put-upon Sanders, Michael Douglas makes a predictable foil. Although hardly as slick a creation as his Gordon Gekko who pronounced that "lunch is for wimps", Douglas still borrows from such previous *zeitgeist* testing roles in *Wall Street* and *Fatal Attraction*. In the opening shot, the endangered homely domain is aglow, voices off-screen are busy with domestic rituals while a computer blinks with the morning's e-mail. You almost expect that pet bunny to leap into frame. As the plot congeals, Douglas begins to rehearse his familiar mutton-to-the-slaughter look. In this respect, *Disclosure* seems a very calculated attempt to tap the *zeitgeist*. However such moments cannot be manufactured so self-consciously. Thus *Disclosure* never succeeds in being more than an average conspiracy thriller.

TIME, 12/19/94, p. 75, Richard Schickel

Sexual harassment is a good subject for legal briefs, psychological studies and outraged essays. It is not a natural topic for popular entertainments. Typically (to put it mildly), the protagonist lacks heroic stature, and it is hard to spin a plot of page-turning intricacy from such a crude offense.

Clever Michael Crichton understood all that when he wrote his best seller *Disclosure*. That's why he made the aggressor a female executive, her victim a happily married man who has been passed over for her job—and with whom, a decade earlier, she had a hot affair. The role reversal alone gives the story some curiosity value. It may even be, as people connected with the movie version keep insisting in interviews, that the shoe-on-the-other-foot approach to this situation will Make You Think.

Maybe so. Or then again, maybe not. For when Meredith Johnson (Demi Moore) charges Tom Sanders (Michael Douglas) with harassment after he rejects her advances and then risks his future at DigiCom, the software company where they're jostling for position, by leveling the same charge at her, their case starts to become more singular than paradigmatic. For it develops that she has something more than a desktop (or should one say laptop?) frolic in mind when she invites him up to her office for an after-hours meeting. In essence, she's trying to turn him into a corporate fall guy.

Their sexual encounter teeters on the brink of both risibility and improbability. It's hard to accept that an experienced man would permit a completely obvious seduction to proceed as far as this one does if it was unwanted; fellatio has begun before he starts emitting virginal squeaks of protest. As the movie develops, we are meant to perceive a causal link between Meredith's sexual voraciousness and her incomprehensible, corporate schemings. Eventually they begin to feel like a lot of plotting for plotting's sake, something to do for the second half of what would otherwise have been a very short and simple tale.

But it must be said that director Barry Levinson and screenwriter Paul Attanasio are great guys to waste time with. As he's proved with *Quiz Show*, the latter has a real flair for writing strong, confrontational scenes—brisk, needling, well shaped—and the former stages them with coolly concentrated intensity. And the cast is terrific. Douglas, with *Fatal Attraction* and *Basic Instinct* behind him, knows all about playing male victimization without total loss of amour propre. Moore's ferocity is totally unredeemed, therefore totally riveting. Donald Sutherland as their boss is computer-like: he has an almost-human brain and a silicon chip where his heart should be. They and a very good supporting cast often ground *Disclosure* in some kind of behavioral honesty, almost turn it into a realistic portrait of the modern workplace—full of false camaraderie, anxious rumors and secret-status warfare. But not to worry. When truth and cheap thrills compete in a movie, you know what must win out in the end.

VILLAGE VOICE, 12/13/94, p. 68, Georgia Brown

Tuned to public discourse, *Disclosure* begins at home and ends with a sickening plug for the family. When we meet The Family, they're four snug bugs in a tidy, traditional bungalow on Bainbridge Island, a commuter colony to nearby Seattle. Mom (Caroline Goodall) is having trouble making time for her lawyering but she puts family harmony first. The whole group piles into the four-wheel drive to rush Dad (Michael Douglas) to the ferry. But no family is an island, and once Tom Sanders crosses the sound to the city and his DigiCom workplace—a vast steel and glass cage—he better watch his butt.

On the morning in question, Tom reports to the office expecting a promotion to VP and by evening he's getting his cock sucked by the babe in black who stole his job. (The bitch is back; but it's okay, darlings, she doesn't bite.) This virtual rape of Tom by Meredith Johnson (Demi Moore looking like Barbie on Valium, a spider out of *Charlotte's Web*) is *Disclosure*'s showpiece, and, filmed step by gruesome step—her grabbing his crotch, her unzipping his zipper—it looks not unlike the usual sex scene. The guy murmurs no 31 times—as in "No no no no no Meredith no"—and it doesn't deter her. Did I say rape! He's forced by his hard-on and interrupts when he feels like it, something women in this position often haven't the option to do,

Sorry, but I haven't delved into Crichton's novel (life is too short), and thus have no idea if all this comes off as cartoonish on the page as it does on screen. The surprise, given the author's heartfelt pontifications on the subject, is that sexual harassment turns out to be a ruse. Meredith it's revealed, isn't driven by lust or any crude exercise in power; she's executing a complex plot to take over DigiCom. She's using the sex to neutralize Tom so he can't expose her machinations. Or something like that.

Another surprise is that someone has felt a need for p.c. content. Like those ubiquitous Dale Chihuly glass polyps, the film puts on display several knowing ironies: a pointed glance at a Native American woman dusting one of the office's conspicuous Indian artifacts; Tom's Asian secretary who feels Tom touches her inappropriately but isn't free to say so; the company's smart-but-older woman who gets routinely passed over, even while its founder proclaims his intention to help women "break the glass ceiling." Probably the film's most likable character is Alvarez (Roma Maffia), the right-on New Yorker-ish lawyer Tom hires to take his harassment case to mediation.

A few sops to common sense hardly make a dent in the badly skewed main plot. For instance, there's the firm's slimey, silverhaired boss, Bob Garvin (Donald Sutherland), who behaves nearly as contemptibly as Meredith, yet while she gets her comeuppance, he's suddenly redeemed as a jolly good fellow.

There's nothing scary here. Locating its main suspense scene in virtual reality seems a mistake given that it's a dull and rather empty space with a shock that amounts to a teensy Boo! Director

Barry Levinson, whose best work has been intimate comedy situated in his native Baltimore, seems to have no affinity for the genre.

Because Meredith is such a stick, Tom becomes the sympathetic human bean by default. Perhaps Douglas has been put in this position so many times, he 's expected to glide in on the wings of previous roles. Whatever, it's a man's point of view, again. At least in *Fatal Attraction*, for all Glenn Close's bunny-boiling, we felt something of the woman's great raging, infantile hurt, her doomed loneliness. What was so tormenting was seeing her demonized and wanting a stake in her heart.

Back to Crichton. Judging by his title, he seems to think he's revealing a dirty little secret about female predators in the workplace. The wonder is he didn't take his fantasy a step further and have Tom get pregnant. Oh, but that's another movie.

Also reviewed in:
CHICAGO TRIBUNE, 12/9/94, Friday, p. C, Michael Wilmington
NEW REPUBLIC, 1/9 & 16/95, p. 32, Stanley Kauffmann
NEW YORK TIMES, 12/9/94, p. C1, Janet Maslin
NEW YORKER, 12/19/94, p. 107, Terrence Rafferty
VARIETY, 12/5-11/94, p. 73, Todd McCarthy
WASHINGTON POST, 12/9/94, p. D1, Hal Hinson
WASHINGTON POST, 12/9/94, Weekend, p. 55, Desson Howe

DOUBLE DRAGON

A Gramercy Pictures release of an Imperial Entertainment & Scanbox presentation of a Greenleaf production. *Executive Producer:* Sundip R. Shah and Anders P. Jensen. *Producer:* Jane Hamsher, Don Murphy, Sunil R. Shah, Ash R. Shah, and Alan Schechter. *Director:* James Yukich. *Screenplay:* Michael Davis and Peter Gould. *Story:* Paul Dini and Neal Shusterman. *Director of Photography:* Gary Kibbe. *Editor:* Florent Retz. *Music:* Jay Ferguson. *Music Editor:* George Martin. *Sound:* Patrick Hanson. *Sound Editor:* Gregory M. Gerlich. *Casting:* Harriet Greenspan and Annette Benson. *Production Designer:* Mayne Berke. *Art Director:* Maya Shimoguchi. *Set Designer:* Louisa Bonnie. *Set Decorator:* Kristan Andrews. *Set Dresser:* Grant Sawyer and John Bradley. *Special Effects:* Paul Lombardi. *Costumes:* Fiona Spence. *Make-up:* Teri Blythe. *Stunt Coordinator:* Gil Arceo. *Running time:* 99 minutes. *MPAA Rating:* PG-13.

CAST: Robert Patrick (Koga Shuko); Mark Dacascos (Jimmy Lee); Scott Wolf (Billy Wolf); Kristina Malandro Wagner (Linda Lash); Julia Nickson (Satori Imada); Alyssa Milano (Marian Delario); Nils Allen-Stewart (Bo Abobo #1); Henry Kingi (Bo Abobo #2); John Mallory Asher (Smart Ass Mohawk); Leon Russom (Chief Delario); Jeff Imada (Huey); Al Leong (Lewis); Cory Milano (Marc Delario); Michael Berryman (Maniac Leader); Vanna White (Herself); Deanthony Langston (Tower); John Grantham (Torpedo); Garret Warren (Rich Kid Opponent #1); Ken McLeod (Rich Kid Opponent #2); Andy Dick (Smogcaster); Bruce Strickland, Donald Nugent, and Verle Majied (New Angeles Police); Rohr Thomas (Tour Guide); Patrica Cascino, Chuck Gillespie and Mark Brazill (Reporters); David Early (Security Man); Rio Hackford (Male Power Corps. Kid); Irene Tanaka (Female Power Corps. Kid); Edward Feldman and Joe L'Erario (Jack City Salesmen); Vincent Klyn (Wild One); Roger Yuan and Ron Yuan (Ninja Wraiths); Jim Aleck (Newscaster); Danny Wong (Mohawk); Brian Imada (Referee).

LOS ANGELES TIMES, 11/4/94, Calendar/p. 13, Kevin Thomas

"Double Dragon," a clever and lively adaptation of the popular video game, takes its title from an ancient Chinese talisman that has been broken in half. Rejoin the two pieces, and you can turn yourself into a veritable Superman.

That's just what evil tycoon Koga Shuko (Robert Patrick), who possesses one half, has in mind. It's 2007, several years after the Big Quake, and Shuko needs the whole talisman to bring "New Angeles'" roving gangs under his control. "I just want total domination of one American city," he whines to an aide. "Is that too much to ask?"

You have to wonder why he's bothering, because "Double Dragon" does a dynamite job of envisioning our city largely in ruins, so much of it submerged in water that Hollywood Boulevard is now a river. In any event, the other half of the talisman is in the possession of two teen-age martial-artist brothers, Jimmy (Mark Dacascos) and Billy (Scott Wolf) Lee, whose late father was an archeologist.

This Gramercy release, expertly aimed at youthful audiences, is another instance of an exceedingly elementary plot played against production design and special effects of awe-inspiring imagination and sophistication. Indeed, "Double Dragon," which marks the stylish, zesty directorial debut of Jim Yukich, a prize-winning maker of music videos and TV specials, envisions the future so boldly and dramatically that it could sustain more plot and character development; its ending especially could easily sustain more plot and character development; its ending especially could use a couple of more involving twists.

But the film, which has a light, humorous touch, is fun anyway, and most likely we haven't seen the last of the "Double Dragon" Lee duo.

NEW YORK POST, 11/4/94, p. 52, Bill Hoffmann

The characters are disposable, the plot is minimal and the special effects overshadow everything.

Still, "Double Dragon," based on the popular video game of the same name, is a double blast of fun that'll keep kids (and enlightened adults) entertained for its full 99 minutes.

The year is 2007. The big quake has hit Southern California and high tide brings the water all the way up to Hollywood and Vine in Los Angeles (now called New Angeles).

George Hamilton and Vanna White are the TV news anchors and the city is so polluted the weatherman gives forecasts for black rain.

Mohawked youth gangs terrorize the city at night, necessitating a curfew for decent citizens.

Into this nightmare come the kick-boxing brothers Jimmy and Billy Lee (Mark Dacascos and Scott Wolf), out to save the city with a group of grunge-attired, do-gooders called the Power Corps.

The brothers are also entrusted with half of a powerful Chinese medallion, the other half of which is owned by an evil tycoon (Robert Patrick), who wants their half in his quest to rule the world.

All of this leads to an entertaining, high-energy mix of goofy dialogue and intensive, cartoon-style fighting that's played strictly for laughs.

Ninety percent of it is mindless, but director James Yukich, with tongue planted firmly in cheek, knows that, and supervises the action with a distinctly light touch.

OK, parents, so "Lassie" it's not.

But for the tuned-in, computer-generation kids of today, "Double Dragon" is a gas!

NEWSDAY, 11/4/94, Part II/p. B7, John Anderson

[*Double Dragon* was reviewed jointly with *Floundering*; see Anderson's review of that film.]

Also reviewed in:
NEW YORK TIMES, 11/4/94, p. C19, Stephen Holden
VARIETY, 11/7-13/94, p. 47, Brian Lowry

DREAM GIRLS

A Women Make Movies release of a Twentieth Century Vixen production. *Executive Producer:* Alan Bookbinder. *Producer:* Jano Williams. *Director:* Kim Longinotto and Jano Williams.

Director of Photography: Kim Longinotto. *Editor:* John Mister. *Sound:* Claire Hunt. *Running time:* 50 minutes. *MPAA Rating:* Not Rated.

NEW YORK POST, 8/17/94, p. 36, Larry Worth

Is a good man hard to find? Not if you're enrolled at the exclusive all-girl Japanese school where students' goal is *becoming* the boy next door.

That's the mind-boggling subject of "Dream Girls," one of two new Japanese films indicating that you can't get around the male-female dynamic, even in same-sex, platonic relationships.

Paired with the male-oriented drama "Work on the Grass," "Dream Girls" is slightly more rewarding, simply because its revelations come in documentary form. The setting is Japan's Takarazuka Music School, which features the phenomenally popular Takarazuka Revue.

It's the flip side to "Farewell, My Concubine," with women playing all roles in the shows. But only those assuming the male parts achieve superstar status.

With close-cropped, slicked-back hair, the "men" sing and dance as Japanese Victor/Victorias, romancing their leading ladies in a manner that leaves the predominantly female audience drooling. Teen-age girls'—and grown women's—adulation is evidenced by love letters, gifts and a permanent camp of screaming groupies.

The secret of the attraction. according to one devotee, is that the women create "an ideal man," complete with the sensitivity and allegiance to family that's lacking in typical husbands and fathers.

Equally fascinating is interview footage with those chosen to play female parts. Cheerfully acknowledging that only their "male" counterparts command respect, they see their purpose as "making 'the men' look good."

Directors Kim Longinotto and Jano Williams flesh it all out by widening their focus to the school's obsessive code of discipline—which includes having freshmen clean the building's rooms with Q-tips.

The film's major flaw is its length, which—at just under an hour—only whets the appetite. Contrarily, the companion piece, "Work on the Grass" is perfectly paced at 42 minutes.

It's a brilliant treatment of how two twenty something men evolve from alienated co-workers to intimate friends during a day's work. And as the title implies, that work is cutting an unending valley's waist-high weeds down to size.

Prior to the first blade getting hacked, the men's differences in physique, work habits and temperament become obvious. One is a strong, arrogant hunk; the other, a timid, effeminate would-be writer. In the world of lawnmower men, it's veteran vs. virgin, leader vs. follower, stud vs. sissy.

Though subtlety reigns, writer/director Tetsuo Shinohara charges his tale with an undeniably homoerotic air. Innuendo-laced actions speak far louder than any words.

Collectively, "Dream Girls" and "Work on the Grass" is more than a superbly paired double-feature; it's Japan's proof-positive that the battle of the sexes will always be waged—and never won.

VILLAGE VOICE, 8/23/94, p. 58, Amy Taubin

A tantalizing backstage glimpse of Japan's Takarazuka revue, *Dream Girls* gives a high-kick in the face to Japanese men, husbands in particular. Founded some 75 years ago, the Takarazuka is an inversion and popularization of traditional all-male theater (Kabuki or Noh). The exclusively female company specializes in exuberant revisions of Western musical melodramas from *Tosca* to *West Side Story*.

The "Top Stars" of the Takarazuka are the women who play male roles. With red or platinum slicked-back hair, wearing sequined tuxedos or broad-shouldered pink sharkskin suits, they swagger like lounge lizards, bounce and buck as wide-leggedly as Elvis (or k.d. lang), and gaze at their dance partners as ardently as Astaire. Although their reign is short, they accumulate thousands of adoring women fans who shower them with protestations of undying love and shopping bags filled with newly purchased goodies.

Takarazuka performances are sold out months in advance; the audience is exclusively female and as rapturous as at a Michael Jackson concert. "They are the ideal man," explained one married fan. "If you think about real men it's the horrible, dirty things that put you off. Real men only care about work, they don't value their wives. For Takarazuka men, the most important thing is their partner."

Paradoxically, the directors of the Takarazuka school (all of them male) insist the training is good preparation for marriage because those who play female roles learn how to be subservient to men ("Our role is to make the men look more manly," says one performer) and those who play males will empathize more with their husbands. Or, as a father says about his "Top Star" daughter, "She will be better at helping her husband put on his jacket because she's put one on herself."

At 50 minutes, *Dream Girls* barely scratches the gender-and culture-bent surface of the Takarazuka cult. The most obvious omission is any reference, in an atmosphere suffused with female desire, to lesbianism. We have to read between the lines of one amused "Top Star": "Is there a man big enough to marry someone as selfish as me? I don't think so."

Playing with *Dream Girls* is Tetsuo Shinohara's *Work on the Grass*, a tour de force of erotic and psychological subtlety. Two men, meeting by chance at an outdoor work site, have an experience that neither is likely to forget. Someone should program *Work on the Grass* with Christopher Munch's evocative John Lennon biopic *The Hours and Times*.

Also reviewed in:
NW YORK TIMES, 8/17/95, p. C12, Stephen Holden
VARIETY, 5/9-15/94, p. 86, David Rooney

DREAM LOVER

A Gramercy Pictures release of a Polygram Filmed Entertainment presentation of a Propaganda Films production. *Executive Producer:* Steve Golin and Edward R. Pressman. *Producer:* Sigurjon Sighvatsson, Wallis Nicita, and Lauren Lloyd. *Director:* Nicholas Kazan. *Screenplay:* Nicholas Kazan. *Director of Photography:* Jean-Yves Escoffier. *Editor:* Jill Savitt and Susan Crutcher. *Music:* Christopher Young. *Music Editor:* John LaSalandra. *Choreographer:* Michael Darrin. *Sound:* Larry Hoki and (music) Rick Winquest. *Sound Editor:* Anthony R. Milch. *Casting:* Johnny Ray. *Production Designer:* Richard Hoover. *Art Director:* Bruce Hill. *Set Decorator:* Brian Kasch. *Set Dresser:* Jenny Baum. *Special Effects:* Michael Schorr. *Costumes:* Barbara Tfank. *Make-up:* Carmen Willis. *Stunt Coordinator:* Jerry Spicer. *Running time:* 103 minutes. *MPAA Rating:* R.

CAST: James Spader (Ray Reardon); Mädchen Amick (Lena Reardon); Bess Armstrong (Elaine); Fredric Lehne (Larry); Larry Miller (Norman); Kathleen York (Martha); Blair Tefkin (Cheryl); Scott Coffey (Billy); Clyde Kusatsu (Judge #2); William Shockley (Buddy); Michael Milhoan (Ray's Lawyer); Robert David Hall (Dr. Shteen); Archie Lang (Judge #1); Janel Moloney (Alice, The Temp); Talya Ferro (Cora's Sister); Lucy Butler (Ray's Secretary); Gretchen Becker (Celine Rogers); Erick Avari (Dr. Spatz); Sandra Kinder (Piru); Joel McKinnon Miller (Minister); Jeanne Bates (Jeanne); Paul Ben Victor (Clown); Joseph Scorsiani (Martha's Lawyer); Shawne Rowe (Debby); Cassie Cole (Tina, 6 years); Timothy Johnston (Bob, 4 years); Alexander Folk (Oscar); Michael Chow (Mr. Mura); Eleanor Zee (Nurse); Harriet Leider (Carnival Lady); Ava DuPree (Check-Out Girl); Kate Williamson (Mrs. Sneeder); Tom Lillard (Mr. Sneeder); Armando Pucci (Bernardo); Peter Zapp (Ticket Taker); Carl Sundstrom (Officerr #1); Irwin Keyes (Officer #2).

LOS ANGELES TIMES, 5/6/94, Calendar/p. 8, Peter Rainer

Ray Reardon (James Spader) is an upscale architect, just divorced, who appears to be leading the perfect life. He's highly successful, handsome, smart and on the prowl.

Then he encounters a woman who is so eminently his "type"— moody and darkly attractive—that he's hooked. Lena (Mädchen Amick) is alternately blunt and full of ah-sweet-mystery airs, and Ray spends most of his courtship in a state of deep ga-ga.

"Dream Lover," the first feature directed by the talented screenwriter Nicholas Kazan, is about how Ray is drawn into a marriage with a woman he realizes, to his horror, he doesn't even begin to know. Although Kazan draws on the femme fatale conventions of film noir, he's trying to tap a wider range of meanings. At its best, the film plays like a shadow play on the themes of marriage and fidelity—on the limits of really knowing the person you share your life with.

It's a tricky, harrowing little film. Kazan keeps things fairly schematic—every plot point is secured, every look is "knowing"—but the overall effect is ambiguously unsettling. Most of the movie is taken up with how Ray slowly—incrementally—learns and then unlearns practically everything he knows about his wife's past (and present). The suffocation of their burnished, perfectly appointed life is made even more suffocating by the up-close specimen-like way Kazan frames the couple. He keeps a microscopic eye on their torments.

One of the sick jokes played out in "Dream Lover" is that the characters' worst fears get realized again and again. Kazan is a sophisticated sadist; he sets up situations with multiple escape routes and then closes off all the exits. And even though you recognize what is happening before Ray does, the dread is still there.

Ray isn't a bad guy, and he's on the receiving end of most of the anguish. But Kazan doesn't give all his sympathy to him. There's something too buffed and yuppieish about Ray. Ray is so smoothly narcissistic that, despite his decency, you almost want to see him brought down—his frictionless good fortune is an indignity.

Despite Kazan's sophistication, there's a narrow, moralistic edge to his approach. (The classic Hollywood film noirs from the '40s and '50s, once you cleared away the drizzle and the fog, often thumped for "traditional" values too.) Ray is drawn to Lena primarily because of her "look" and he must be punished for his superficiality. Even though Lena, too, is drawn to Ray, the film seems more concerned with Ray's defects—and redemption.

Spader can't provide all the emotional levels the part requires—beneath all those burnished surfaces of his are still more surfaces. We're periodically shown Ray's nightmares—he dreams he's in a circus—and we can't connect up the imagery to the man.

Mädchen Amick, however, is a real find. In her first full-scale film role, she manages to give Lena's surface blankness some depth. Lena has a way of looking both vague and fixated. It's the look of someone who is constantly reinventing herself.

Kazan recoils from her but coddles her too. He understands that Lena is too fragrant a monster to squash.

NEW YORK POST, 5/6/94, p. 36, Bill Hoffmann

Searching for the perfect mate isn't easy, as wealthy young architect Ray Reardon (James Spader) discovers.

Freshly divorced and ultimately depressed, Ray's dodging desperate women his friends want to set him up with and wondering if the girl of his dreams will ever come along.

Then—poof!—she arrives in the form of the sultry, pouty-lipped Lena (Mädchen Amick) who adores Ray and has an insatiable appetite for sex.

There's a catch, as Ray finds out two years—and two kids—into their lightning-quick marriage: Lena's loving nourishment is part of an intricate plot to steal Ray's fortune, as well as his sanity.

That's the setup by first-time director Nicholas Kazan in his new psychological thriller, "Dream Lover"—a kind of lite version of "Basic Instinct," "Fatal Attraction" and all the other crazed-femme movies you've seen in recent years.

This one adds nothing new to the genre.

Both Spader and Amick have spunk. But they can't overcome a script that has them sluggishly going through the paces, only to get to a surprising, if ultimately lackluster, climax.

The movie also has a split personality. One moment, it's dramatic. Another, comedian Larry Miller, playing one of Ray's best pals, takes over doing a kind of frenzied standup that's funny yet bothersome.

Confusing things further is Kazan's inclusion of several ridiculous nightmare sequences in which Ray is tormented by an evil circus clown. These scenes are incredibly stupid, out-of-place and not even up to the standards of usual TV movie schlock.

Kazan is no slouch—he's written some fine screenplays including "Reversal of Fortune" and "Patty Hearst."

In the production notes for "Dream Lover," he say's he got the idea 15 years ago, after his girlfriend went berserk at a dinner party, turning into someone completely different for a few brief and "chilling" moments.

That must have been just like a bad dream. In most cases, bad dreams are best forgotten.

NEWSDAY, 5/6/94, Part II/p. B9, John Anderson

In his "Essential Film Guide," the British film critic Simon Rose includes a "Star Satisfaction Score" which rates movie actors by how often they've appeared in good movies, and at the very bottom of the list is "Twin Peaks" alumna Mädchen Amick. Is this fair? I think so. What I'm sure of is that Amick's latest, "Dream Lover," has ensured itself of at least one fan, since it won't be forcing Rose to make any changes in subsequent editions of his book.

In this combo platter of "Body Heat" and a gender-reversed "Gaslight," Amick plays the lovely Lena, the latest in a long line of lethal vamps who execute their nefarious schemes by duping poor, hormone-befuddled males: in this case, James Spader, as her husband-to-be, Ray. That she does it with such heartlessness will prick the more festering misogynistic fantasy. That she does it all so easily—Ray is consistently surprised to find out she's lied to him, which is sweet in a way, but mostly just dumb—makes the entire experience a muscle-straining exercise in belief suspension. Add to this director Nicholas Kazan's faux-Fellini-isms (Ray's recurring carnival dream sequence and its taunting clown), and an Obsession-ad esthetic (in one scene, Ray and Lena are splayed in post-coital perfection, hair, pearls and bedclothes arranged in strategic good taste), and a plot that makes "Basic Instinct" seem like "The Big Sleep."

Ray, who practices the current yuppie-movie profession of choice—architecture, which allows one to be manly without actually getting dirty—is wildly successful. He meets and marries Lena, and then begins peeling away, layer by deceptive layer, the identity she's created for herself. Without giving away much, nothing she said either before or during the marriage turns out to be the truth. The only question the audience will have is when Ray's going to wake up.

And it takes a long, long time. So long, in fact, that by the last quarter of the film, when the plot picks up some steam, it's reasonable to assume most viewers will have expended their patience. Neither Spader nor Amick are particularly intriguing performers, and subplots involving Ray's friends Elaine (Bess Armstrong) and the obnoxious Norman (Larry Miller) go nowhere. Single women are portrayed as thick-headed or predatory, men as innocent dupes, and the script, with the exception of the final, O'Henry-esque twist makes us more aware of its own flaws than the characters' improbable selves.

SIGHT AND SOUND, 12/94, p. 45, Mark Kermode

Successful yuppie Ray Reardon is beset by dreams in which a booth advertising 'The Girl of Your Dreams' taunts his romantic unhappiness. In court, Ray negotiates a divorce settlement with his wife, with whom relationships have broken down. At work, Ray's friends attempt to find him a new suitable companion, but Ray remains distracted by dreams of meeting his perfect partner. A chance encounter with sophisticated beauty Lena Mathers leads to the snaring of Ray's affections. The couple court and are swiftly married, take up residence in Ray's exotic apartment, and start a family.

As time progresses, Ray begins to doubt the credibility of his wife's alleged past. When her credit card bill arrives at his office, Ray uncovers regular appointments at a local hotel, and accuses Lena of adultery with his friend Larry. In the ensuing argument, Ray (who now doubts even his fatherhood of his own children) strikes Lena. Later, a badly bruised Lena (whose injuries are wholly disproportionate to her confrontation with Ray) charges her husband with assault. Ray traces Lena's true past to a backwater town where her devious reputation and abusive former partner are renowned. At a judicial hearing, Ray is unable to control his frustration, and is deemed mentally unstable. Lena wins from Ray possession of his house and children, driving Ray to further extremes. The court orders him to be placed in compulsory psychiatric care. Some time later, Lena visits Ray at the psychiatric home in which he is incarcerated. Asking her to walk with him in the gardens, Ray praises Lena's portrayal of him as a madman before strangling her—since he has been deemed insane, he will evade prosecution for murder.

Writer/director Nicholas Kazan attributes the inception of this chaotically quirky shambles to an incident at a dinner party at which "my wife said something very strange, very unlike herself, and just for that instant, her face was turned and she didn't look like herself—she seemed like a complete stranger." From this single mundane but uncanny incident flows an elaborate fantasy which raises questions of how much we ever really know about our loved ones, and how much we merely project onto them our own aspirations. As the writer of *At Close Range, Frances* and *Reversal of Fortune* (as well as 'script doctor' on Rowdy Herrington's excellent but underrated *Gladiator*), Kazan should have been more than able to take this fertile premise, brim full of paranoid promise, and tease from it a script of structural elegance and psychological depth. Sadly, what he has produced is, like Ray and Lena's marriage, merely an unstable union of warring elements which soon reach implosive critical mass.

The most glaring problem is one of overstatement; Kazan describes Nick's torment as "an exaggeration" of the fate of those who seek perfection, but as any genuine paranoiac knows, such exaggeration brings with it emotional release rather than involvement. It is the little details (Lena's occasional uneasy smiles) and the constant suspicion, rather than knowledge, of conspiracy which bear the frisson of emotional reality. Once it becomes apparent, about 30 minutes into the movie, that Lena is little more than a pathological fraud, our interest in her deception dissolves. From then on, the increasingly bizarre catalogue of revelations about Lena's behaviour remains intriguing only on the level of a hokey 'Tale of the Unexpected': will Kazan pull a clever concluding explanation from the hat, to turn what we have seen on its head and prove Lena the perfect wife after all? (Answer: No.) By the time we reach the final showdown, intrigue has turned to exasperation, understatement to hyperbole, and black comedy to farce.

Perhaps another director would have fared better with this material, which clearly suffers from having been both written and directed by the same person. Certainly, any second reader worth their mettle would have swiftly excised the cringe-worthy dream sequences which serve only to undercut the psychological reality into which Kazan hopes to tap. On the positive side, Frost/Lynch graduates James Spader and Mädchen Amick are well cast, and our knowledge of their earlier screen and TV work helps to establish their characters with the minimum fuss. Amick in particular benefits in this respect; like Lara Flynn Boyle, her former life as a resident of *Twin Peaks* has forever lent her face an air of mystery and intrigue which she uses to full effect. Spader, on the other hand, replays the 'slimy yuppie' role to which his drawling voice and college-boy haircut seem to have consigned him permanently, but which seems never to wear thin (he recently essayed the same role alongside Nicholson and Pfeiffer in *Wolf* where he more than held his own ground). With such potential in terms of concept, casting, and scriptwriter, it's a genuine shame that the most disturbing aspect of *Dream Lover* is its resolute failure to succeed as the sexy psychological thriller it was so clearly destined to be.

VILLAGE VOICE, 5/10/94, p. 62, Amy Taubin

Lacking as art and/or entertainment, *Dream Lover* comes up strong in the symptomatology department, although the film is not nearly as revealing as its press kit, sprinkled with quotes from screenwriter and first-time director Nicholas Kazan. A foolish waste of trees, press kits are perks for critics, tangible little-nothing rewards for sitting through, let's say, *three* male sexual paranoia opuses—*Bitter Moon, China Moon*, and *Dream Lover*—in as many months. Actually, *Bitter Moon* is several cuts above the latter two, not only because Polanski knows how to bend the rules, but because his target is coupledom as an institution of mutual destruction rather than women as duplicitous bitches whose perfect tits camouflage hearts of stone.

The press kit informs us that: the idea for *Dream Lover* came to Kazan after an unsettling experience at a dinner party: "My girlfriend started to say things that were completely outlandish and offensive to me. And for an instant she was a totally different person, someone I hated. And then she turned her head and smiled, explained what she meant a bit more, and went back to being herself. But that moment was so chilling that it sparked the screenplay."

The screenplay that Kazan nurtured for 15 years is not about a guy who thinks his girlfriend's out to murder him every time she says something that's not in the script he's written for both of them. In that film, the problem would have been obviously his. Instead, *Dream Lover* is a revamped *Body Heat* in which a guileless, though vastly successful, architect (James Spader), whose worst failing is to envision his sex life as if art-directed for an Obsession commercial, falls in love with a pathological man-hater (Mädchen Amick) who marries him in order to steal his money and destroy his reputation. The au courant element here is the legal system's supposed indulgence of women who claim spousal abuse—even when they're lying. Ergo, the wife punches herself in the face and the husband wakes up in a mental institution. I wouldn't want to give away *Dream Lover*'s predictably shocking ending. Let's just say that, anxious as he may be, Kazan is not going to let his man not come out on top.

Also reviewed in:
CHICAGO TRIBUNE, 5/13/94, Friday/p. F, Michael Wilmington
NEW YORK TIMES, 5/6/94, p. C11, Janet Maslin
VARIETY, 4/11-17/94, p. 36, Todd McCarthy

DREAM AND MEMORY

A C&A release of a C & A production. *Producer:* Ann Hu. *Director:* Ann Hu. *Screenplay (Mandarin and English with English subtitles):* Ann Hu. *Based on a story by:* Zhang Hongnian. *Director of Photography:* Brian Clery and Tu Jiakuan. *Editor:* Debbie Ungar and Zheng Jing. *Music:* Zhang Lida. *Sound:* Stu Deutsch, Li Yongjie, George Leung, and Gu Quanxi. *Art Director:* Liu Yuan and Duan Zhenzhong. *Running time:* 91 minutes. *MPAA Rating:* Not Rated.

CAST: Bing Yang (Hong Yuan in U.S.); Shao Bing (Hong Yuan in China); Li Wei (Village Secretary); Kathleen Claypool (Aunt Sara); Adina Porter (Janet); Wang Shuo (Ai Cheng); Ren Yan (Lanzi); Shi Ke (Gaixiu).

NEW YORK POST, 5/6/94, p. 38, Thelma Adams

There's a reason people attend film school—and it's not just to spend their parents' money.

The school environment gives fledgling filmmakers the chance to take risks, make mistakes, and suffer their first humiliations before their peers.

In "Dream and Memory," producer/writer/director Ann Hu takes an end run around the process with her first feature, an agonizing but earnest drama about Hong Yuan (Bing Yang), a blind Chinese emigre coming to terms with his past and facing his future on American soil.

Hu was among the first wave of students to come to America in the wake of China's Cultural Revolution. She studied business at NYU, made a killing, and funded her debut feature.

"Dream and Memory" falls easily into two parts. Two young Beijing painters, Hong Yuan (played in the China sequences by Shao Bing) and Ai Cheng (Wang Shuo), are sent to the countryside in the late '60s to paint propaganda pictures—Mao in red and black.

The two boys, well-acted by the cream of China's crop, quickly discover their differences. Ai Cheng believes "you should use art to please the people." Hong Yuan paints to please himself.

Hong Yuan falls for a local girl who is betrothed to her cousin. The love leads to tragedy, blindness, exile, and a funk that still immobilizes Hong 15 years later when he finds himself without art, unable to love, and virtually under house arrest in his Aunt Sara's New Jersey condo.

Meanwhile, it's no surprise that Ai Cheng achieves artistic success under the existing regime.

The memory sequences, filmed in China, have a naturalness the American scenes lack. Hu employs separate teams for the foreign and domestic segments. Cinematographer Tu Jiakuan, senior director of photography of the Beijing Film Studio, creates a unified prettiness in the China hills and easily finds the young actors' best sides.

If Hu had been satisfied with a short film set in China, she could have been justifiably proud. The story of two artists at the point where their lives radically split is nicely played.

The professional gloss of the Chinese action contrasts with the amateurish American portion, shot by Brian Clery ("Scent of a Woman"). Unfortunately, the movie hinges on the stateside plot.

The scenes between the adult Hong Yuan and his aunt (Kathleen Claypool) are embarrassingly stilted. Bing Yang's performance is wooden. Claypool flounders.

The transformation of Hong Yuan from a man crippled by his past to an artist embracing the future on new shores—the movie's emotional core—is completely bungled.

Hu's vanity production is not to be confused with the many films premiering in the U.S. from the so-called Fifth Generation of Chinese filmmakers.

These filmmakers, like Chen Kaige, whose "Farewell My Concubine" was nominated for a Best Foreign Film Oscar this year, are mostly graduates of the Beijing Film Academy's fifth class in 1982. They grew up during the Cultural Revolution and bloomed after its fall. Influenced by Fellini, Bergman, and Antonioni, they make films within the Chinese studio system.

The Fifth Generation movies that have reached U.S. audiences have been accomplished works of mature filmmakers. Hu, who works independently, has a way to go on that score. Money talks—but not always eloquently.

NEWSDAY, 5/6/94, Part II/p. B7, John Anderson

The cultural Revolution as presented in "Dream and Memory" isn't so much a response to the films of China's Fifth Generation (Zhang Yimou, Chen Kaige, Tian Zhuangzhuang) as it is the production of a parallel universe: Benign, full of smiling villagers and relocated artists not unhappy to be there, a generally contented *tout le Mao*.

Meanwhile, back in the states ... we meet "Hong Yuan (Bing Yang), a blind, embittered onetime painter living with Sara (Kathleen Claypool), his uncle's western widow, and awaiting word about his long-pending operation. You can't give up hope, Sara says, to which Hong responds, "You've been saying that for ten years, ever since you brought me here to cure my blindness"—the kind of line that, while providing background, sits there like a lump.

Just in time, a letter arrives from Hong's friend Ai Cheng (Wang Shuo) and provokes a crisis: Unable to read it, Hong reminisces about the time when, as young artists, he and Ai were sent into the countryside as part of the Cultural Revolution ("Wasn't that the time when the world first saw you as an artist?" Sara asks. Aaarrgghh). There, they would paint a public portrait of Mao, fall in love with local girls, and forge their artistic identities: Ai Cheng as a compromising populist, Hong as a modernist maverick.

Throughout his flashbacks, his time with Sara, and his budding romance with Janet (Adina Porter)—Hong doesn't know she's black, which is asking a lot of us—Hong tortures himself about what might have been. And eventually, he reconciles himself to art, helped, in the end, by the contents of the letter.

Director/writer Ann Hu's sequences in China are naturalistic, poetic; we watch time pass in the growth of chicks to chickens; lines of dialogue assume haiku form; a bird in the hand signifies so much. Her New York scenes are stilted to the point of paralysis. If this dichotomy is intentional—in her press material, Hu emphasizes that she is Chinese, not Chinese American, and seems to be an apologist for the Cultural Revolution—it's simply wrongheaded.

Hu may be a promising director, but "Dream and Memory" is a very small story set amid world-shaking events—unlike other recent Chinese films, which have used the seemingly insignificant to become transcendent.

Also reviewed in:
VARIETY, 6/6-12/94, p. 42, Derek Elley

DROP SQUAD

A Gramercy Pictures and Spike Lee release of a 40 Acres and a Mule Filmworks production. *Executive Producer:* Spike Lee. *Producer:* Butch Robinson and Shelby Stone. *Director:* David Johnson. *Screenplay:* David Johnson, Butch Robinson, and David Taylor. *Based on an original story by:* David Taylor. *Director of Photography:* Ken Kelsch. *Music:* Mike Bearden. *Sound:* Matthew Price. *Casting:* Jaki Brown. *Production Designer:* Ina Mayhew. *Art Director:* Paul Weathered. *Set Decorator:* Judy Rhee. *Set Dresser:* Kimberly Buckley and

Marshall Davis. *Costumes:* Darlene Jackson. *Make-up:* Harriet Landau. *Running time:* 86 minutes. *MPAA Rating:* R.

CAST: Eriq LaSalle (Bruford Jamison, Jr.); Vondie Curtis-Hall (Rocky); Ving Rhames (Garvey); Leonard Thomas (XB); Michael Ralph (Trevor); Billy Williams (Huey); Eric A. Payne (Stokeley); Crystal Fox (Dwania Ali); Nicole Powell (Lenora Jamison); Vanessa Williams (Mali); Kasi Lemmons (June Vanderpool); Afemo Omilami (Berl "Flip" Mangum); Tico Wells (Fat Money); Fran Carter (Ruth Jamison); Donna Biscoe (Rosette Johnson); Ed Wheeler (Counterman); Maggie Rush (Detective Atkins); Ray Aranha (Bruford Jamison, Sr.); Jay McMillan (Reverend Beekins); Ellis Williams (Frankman); Paula Kelly (Aunt Tilly); Tim Hutchinson (Detective Johnson); Gary Yates (Lucas "Stink" Jones); Mark Kennerly (Chris Burgess); Dawanna Kyles (Janet Evans); Arthur French (Vernon Dobbs); Charnele Brown (Kyra Washington); Rod Garr (Willie Morris); Charlie Brown (Uncle Frank Jamison); Charles Weldon (Uncle Omar); Michael H. Moss (Mr. Griggs); Iris Little Thomas (Desiree); Kimberly Hawthorne (Harriett).

LOS ANGELES TIMES, 10/28/94, Calendar/p. 6, Kevin Thomas

"Drop Squad" turns upon a reprehensible, indefensible dramatic device; an illegal deprogramming team dedicated to kidnaping and brainwashing self-centered upwardly mobile blacks to reconnect them with their roots.

But the presence of this Deprogramming and Restoration of Pride Squad detonates a provocative, emotion-charged melodrama that deals with complex and contradictory intra-racial issues as few films have. This is one of those unwieldy and improbable pictures that ends up touching upon more crucial bases than if had it been a more realistic, better structured film.

In the film's best-written role, "ER"s Eriq LaSalle really shines. He's Bruford Jamison Jr., a handsome young ad executive so ambitious that he supports and helps create the most demeaning campaigns imaginable aimed at African American consumers. It's hard to believe that in today's corporate America he'd actually have to be so totally an Uncle Tom. But the film nevertheless powerfully conveys the isolation and repressed anger experienced by so many blacks who succeed in overwhelmingly white-dominated American institutions.

On the one hand, Bruford believes he has to overlook so much that he loathes in order to survive and get ahead and, on the other, feels resentful toward what his family insists are his obligations and responsibilities. The flash point is his sweet-natured, uneducated and impoverished cousin (Afemo Omilami), who was his best friend in childhood. The cousin wants his help in landing an entry-level job at the ad agency, but Bruford feels that he will be an embarrassment to him if he's hired in any capacity.

For Bruford's sister (Nicole Powell), this is the last straw, and she directs the DROP Squad to kidnap her brother to straighten him out.(That this is the reason is not immediately clear, so poorly is the film structured.) Alas, its leader, Rocky (Vondie Curtis-Hall), and his key aide, Garvey (Ving Rhames), are in a philosophical conflict: Rocky wants to stick to his nonviolent principles while Garvey insists that nowadays physical force is in order. The deprogramming sequences are convincing only as displays of protracted, dangerous and degrading brutality, and both Rocky and Garvey are made to seem nothing more than misguided, none-too-bright thugs steeped in presumptuous, half-baked ideology.

In terms of morality and realism, the squad is a bum device, for any number of normal occurrences in his life could force Bruford to reappraise his values. Yet this film is so charged with ambivalence in almost all its aspects—that's its fascination, as is the case with most Oscar Micheaux films—that you have the feeling that first-time director David Johnson and his co-writers have a lingering wish that a humane form of the DROP Squad actually existed. In any event, the film evokes the dilemma that any member of a minority experiences to varying degrees: Where does your responsibility to yourself and your family and your community begin and end?

It falls to LaSalle, of TV's "E.R." series, to carry the picture through its bumpy course, and he does so with aplomb; his Bruford in fact could be more sympathetic than the filmmakers intended. With his talent, LaSalle is likely to go on to better films, but "DROP Squad" will surely remain among his most challenging assignments.

NEW YORK POST, 10/28/94, p. 49, Thelma Adams

"DROP Squad" is an acronym for Deprogramming and Restoration of Pride, the name of a vigilante thought police. The group kidnaps wayward African-Americans and gives them a brutal crash course in "being black."

Ad exec Bruford Jamison, Jr. (Eriq LaSalle of TV's "E.R.") is the embodiment of the assimilated Buppie. Consumed with getting ahead, he's forgotten what he's left behind. Bruford's' dreadlocked sister, Lenora (Nicole Powell), calls on the DROP Squad to bring her brother back to his roots.

Lenora doesn't realize there's a conflict within the Squad itself. Founder Rocky (Vondie Curtis-Hall) and his deputy, Garvey (Ving Rhames of "Pulp Fiction") , are locked in a battle over whether the group should maintain a non-violent approach or become more aggressive.

While the ideas behind this uneven satire are provocative, director David Johnson hamstrings himself by bulldozing caricatures around in a series of disjointed vignettes.

With Spike Lee as the executive producer of "DROP Squad," it's no wonder that the treatment of infra-racial strife is heavy-handed. And Johnson lacks the skill to make it engaging or entertaining.

Particularly disturbing are the deprogramming scenes. A crooked assemblyman is made to crawl on all fours wearing Klan regalia with a chain around his neck. Lashed to a dentist's chair, Bruford is beaten about the face and neck by Garvey and his violent cronies.

Should that be the punishment for wearing suits and promoting a "Gospel Pak" at a fried chicken chain?

Rocky delivers the movie's moral, lecture-style, to the bound Bruford: Climb up the wall, throw a rope back. Move up the ladder, but don't sell out your heritage. This is sensible advice, but the audience doesn't need to be bound and gagged by inept filmmaking and two-dimensional characters in order to get the message.

NEWSDAY, 10/28/94, Part II/p. B7, John Anderson

Being provocative is no trick, if all you want to do is be provocative. In the '90s, however—thanks to Madonna, and soundbites, and MTV and what would amount to a litany of other cultural malignancies—provocation itself has become a valid excuse for celebrity. And box office. And being.

Resolution, or even point of view, may eventually become entirely superfluous, as it already is irrelevant to commerce. Take "DROP Squad," a film ostensibly about black pride and upward mobility, directed by the debuting David Johnson and executive-produced by Spike Lee. The "DROP" refers to Deprogramming and Restoration of Pride; the "Squad" refers to a near-mythic black vigilante organization that kidnaps and basically brainwashes those it considers enemies of the people. These include a preacher who's fleecing the flock, a writer of self-help books who endorses wife abuse, a crooked politician, a drug dealer.

But it also includes Bruford Jamison Jr. (Eriq LaSalle, of television's "ER"), a rising star in a racist advertising agency, and a "traitor" whose crimes are defined, but whose case isn't quite resolved. Bruford is the brain behind both the Mumblin' Jack Malt Liquor campaign ("Available everywhere black people are served") and the General Otis Fried Chicken "Gospel Pak" (his commercial features kerchief-headed waitresses, enormous female gospel singers, and Spike Lee). To the DROP Squad, he's exploiting his race. To Bruford, he's just playing the game.

From the film's perspective? The moral universe remains nebulous. For all the passion of Rocky (Vondie Curtis-Hall), the group's founder who's lost touch with the streets, and Garvey (Ving Rhames of "Pulp Fiction"), who knows that the squad's non-violent techniques are becoming ineffectual, it's never clear what they're after. During the two weeks of brutal deprogramming Bruford endures, it's never stated what they want him to do. Recant? Atone?

There's also the question of Bruford's crimes. The ads might be funny, but they're so cartoonish as to demean the argument of the film.

And what is that? That Bruford's job "was earned for you by a lot of people you're trying to forget," as Garvey puts it. But Bruford is a pioneer too, a player in the white corporate world that, yes, promotes racist attitudes, but is going to do it with or without Bruford. What "DROP

Squad" never confronts is the question of what progress can be made in the corporate world if the powers that be never see a black face.

Bruford may not be the best one to put forward, but at least he's changing the complexion of the place.

VILLAGE VOICE, 11/1/94, p. 64, Gary Dauphin

Based on an incisive indie short called *The Session, Drop Squad* is a black "what if" satire about how best to teach buppies the errors of their sellout ways. Bruford Jamison Jr. (Eriq LaSalle) goes about his shuffling day at La Drone Advertising in a black middle-class fog: uttering banalities like, "Hey, my only responsibility is to myself," art-directing sexist-racist malt liquor ads ("Mumblin' Jack Malt Liquor: It Gits Ya Crazy!"), undermining conscience-stricken coworkers, and so on. When Bruford disses a relative in need of work, his right-on, braid-wearing sister Lenora (Nicole Powell) decides she has to call in the Drop Squad. One-named ciphers who answer to Rocky, Garvey, XB, Huey, Stokeley, *and* Mali, the Squad has apparently been rounding up and reeducating folks whose brand of groupthink didn't jibe with theirs for years, thus setting the audience up for two hours of meandering flashbacks, one-note agitprop, and "lean-on-me-black man" subplots straight out of George C. Wolfe's "Mama on the Couch" sketch, minus the irony.

While there's plenty of individual talent floating around on screen (director David Johnson knows his craft but should have moved on to something new after scoring with *The Session*), *Drop Squad*'s basic problem is that its politics are, well, kind of stupid. The short's original wicked sense of humor was its link to any claim of moral authority, but that's all been stretched past the breaking point by the transition to feature length. When the Squad finds they're having trouble making an impression on Bruford, the scene shifts from the content of Bruford's character to a rehash of the ever-popular By Any Means Necessary debate. Squad founder Rocky (Vondie Curtis-Hall making the best of a bad situation) wants to keep remaking detainees via a stern pop psychoanalytic talking-to, whereas black gestapo new jacks Garvey and XB figure tough times call for tough measures, like a good crack across Bruford's living mouth. Help yourself, I say, but besides the fact that none of the players have the gravity to pull off the Martin-Malcolm thing, one can't help but remember that Drop's executive producer Spike Lee covered this territory with more intelligence and humor a few pictures ago in *School Daze*. DROP stands for Deprogramming and Restoration of Pride, but the reeducation set pieces are straight out of Lee's vision of black fraternity hell week: rote repetition of slogans coupled with garden-variety humiliation and, of course, those good cracks across the mouth.

All of which left me wondering if there's a squad out there grabbing folks who peddle muddled politics under the cover of next-wave black filmmaking, because if there is, the makers of *Drop Squad* had better start watching their backs.

Also reviewed in:
CHICAGO TRIBUNE, 10/28/94, Friday/p. M, John Petrakus
NEW YORK TIMES, 10/28/94, p. C19, Janet Maslin
VARIETY, 10/24-30/94, p. 67, Leonard Klady
WASHINGTON POST, 10/28/94, p. F7, Hal Hinson

DROP ZONE

A Paramount Pictures release of a Nicita/Lloyd production. *Executive Producer:* John Badham. *Producer:* D. J. Caruso, Wallis Nicita, and Lauren Lloyd. *Director:* John Badham. *Screenplay:* Peter Barsocchini and John Bishop. *Story:* Tony Griffin, Guy Manos, and Peter Barsocchini. *Director of Photography:* Roy H. Wagner. *Editor:* Frank Morriss. *Music:* Hans Zimmer. *Music Editor:* Laura Perlman. *Sound:* Russell Williams II and (music) Jay Rifkin. *Sound Editor:* Willilam L. Manger. *Casting:* Carol Lewis. *Production Designer:* Joe Alves. *Art Director:* Mark W. Mansbridge. *Set Designer:* Thomas Minton, and John Leimanis. *Set*

Decorator: Richard C. Goddard. *Set Dresser:* Kurt Beckler, Michael D. Fitzgerald, and Jeremy A. Read. *Special Effects:* Danny Cangemi. *Visual Effects:* Chuck Comisky. *Computer Effects:* Todd Aron Marks. *Costumes:* Mary Vogt. *Make-up:* Kimberly Felix-Burke. *Aerial Stunt Coordinator:* B.J. Worth. *Stunt Coordinator:* Shane Dixon. *Running time:* 102 minutes. *MPAA Rating:* R.

CAST: Wesley Snipes (Pete Nessip); Gary Busey (Ty Moncrief); Yancy Butler (Jessie Crossman); Michael Jeter (Earl Leedy); Corin Nemec (Selkirk); Kyle Secor (Swoop); Luca Bercovici (Jagger); Malcolm-Jamal Warner (Terry Nessip); Rex Linn (Bobby); Grace Zabriskie (Winona); Sam Hennings (Torski); Claire Stansfield (Kara); Mickey Jones (Deuce); Andy Romano (Tom McCracken); Rick Zieff (Mike Milton); Clark Johnson (Bob Covington); Charles Boswell (Glenn Blackstone); Natalie Jordan (Lena); Ed Amatrudo (Detective Fox); Melanie Mayron (Mrs. Willins); A. J. Ross (Roslund); Al Israel (Schuster Stephens); Steve DuMouchel (Walsh Matthews); J. P. Patrick (Jump Master); Tim A. Powell (Gordon Maples); Steven Raulerson (Commander Dejaye); D.D. Howard (Norma); Dale Swann (747 Captain); Keith Leon Williams (747 Flight Engineer); Lexie Bigham (Big Man Passenger); Ron Kuhlman and Jerry Tondo (DEA Guards); Kimberly A. Scott (Joanne); Keith MacKechnie (Night Desk Sergeant); Jan Speck (Flight Attendant #1).

LOS ANGELES TIMES, 12/9/95, Calendar/p. 6, Peter Rainer

The best thing about "Drop Zone" are the stunt sky-divers who dive-bomb through the air at speeds of 200 m.p.h. or float together in formation. These jumpers are juiced by pure adrenaline and they juice the audience too.

Director John Badham is a techno-whiz at this sort of stuff, and he's smart enough to keep the stunt divers at the center of the action. And a good thing too: The script by Peter Barsocchini and John Bishop, is so preposterously contrived and tone-deaf that any attempt to play it straight would be laughed off the screen. It's no use picking away at "Drop Zone"—the filmmakers have done that for you.

Wesley Snipes plays Pete Nessip, a U.S. marshal tracking down a team of stunt sky-divers who have cooked up a plan to swoop down on the Drug Enforcement Agency headquarters in Washington during the Fourth of July celebrations and abscond with their entire computerized roster of undercover drug agents. The team's asking price for the DEA list—$2 million a month. (No doubt a bargain compared to this film's budget.)

Pete first gets wind of these jumpers when he and his brother Terry (Malcolm-Jamal Warner) are transporting a convicted computer whiz (Michael Jeter, in his best flibbertigibberty mode) to a federal prison on a commercial 747. Posing as terrorists, the jumpers, led by the truly bad Ty Moncrief (Gary Busey), yank the master hacker off the plane, killing Terry in the process. Later Pete goes to another sky-diver—the good-bad girl parolee Jessie (Yancy Butler)—for help in cracking the case. Whereupon Ty offs her highflying boyfriend. So their motives for revenge are *personal*.

The ground-level action is mostly filler for the highflying jamborees. Parachute-equipped but untutored, Pete learns how to sky-dive after Jessie throws him horrified out of a plane. It's not exactly Meet Cute time. When he joins Jessie's team of avengers, his participation is played mostly for comic relief.

Snipes is very funny at acting scared in the sky. His performance starts out tough-edged but he seems to have decided early on that "Drop Zone" didn't really need an actor. He's more like a stunt double comic, yet his charisma is so strong that he holds the movie together whenever it isn't airborne—quite an achievement.

There are a few good scenes involving the wiggy camaraderie of jumpers (Grace Zabriskie and Corin Nemec stand out) and Busey once again demonstrates that he's the best heavy in the business. But you could skip everything in "Drop Zone" except, perhaps, for the aerial wingdings and still live a full and complete life. (It would be different, of course, if the film had included the Flying Elvises.)

A side issue: Pete, who is black, and Jessie, who is white. clearly have a budding attraction—plus they save each other's lives. So why doesn't the film allow them a single kiss?

This is the same question a lot of us asked in the Denzel Washington-Julia Roberts starrer "Pelican Brief," which was also kissless. Now that a new generation of black superstars like Snipes and Washington are figuring in interracial romantic scenarios, is it too much to ask that these performers be allowed to be romantic?

NEW YORK POST, 12/9/94, p. 41, Thelma Adams

Call it Airspeed. "Drop Zone" is a surefire actioner set in the world of sky diving—and if anybody has any doubts about Wesley ("Passenger 57") Snipes as an action star, drop them now.

Snipes, who plays U.S. Marshal Pete Nessip, has what it takes: He's attractive, charismatic, throws a good punch and a good punchline, and he's not afraid to laugh at himself.

Directed by John ("Saturday Night Fever," "Stakeout") Badham, "Drop Zone" has a familiar setup. Two marshals, Nessip and his brother (a beefy Malcolm-Jamal Warner) are escorting a convicted computer hacker (jittery Michael Jeter of "Evening Shade") to a federal prison.

Will the prisoner get there? No way.

The twist? When the inevitable gang busts the hacker loose, they grab him on an airborne 747 at 38,000 feet and make an impossible leap to freedom, Nessip's brother gets killed in the process. For Nessip, this time it's personal—he's going to find his brother's killers even if he has to fall out of the sky to do so.

Hollywood has discovered that not only does sky diving offer thrilling stunts—and plug into national feelings of vertigo—but they're cheaper than car chases.

No sooner docs Nessip hook up with smoky-voiced ex-con and sky-diving wild woman Jessie Crossman (Yancy Butler), than he's falling through the blue without a parachute and the audience is gasping for air. Maybe he shouldn't have made that wisecrack to the pilot!

Nessip's freefall is just the first in a series of increasingly daring adventures on the way to the drop zone, the term for the area where sky divers land.

The fit Butler matches Snipes stunt-for-stunt and, in the latest trend in action thrillers—female slugfests—gets her chance to throw punches at a female baddie. No copycat stunt, Butler finishes her foe on a Xerox machine.

Gary Busey is bad-to-the-bone as the ringleader of a sky diving crew who needs Jeter's skills to crack Drug Enforcement Administration computers in a deadly money-making scam. Busey ("Under Siege") has made a cottage industry of the sharp but amoral villain and he doesn't disappoint.

For fans of Hong Kong action movies, check out the climactic reference to John Woo's "The Killer" (1989).

Snipes and Busey face off pistol-to-pistol with five feet between them in a scene that's cut to match the supercharged original.

Thc Asian invasion may not have reached broad American audiences yet, but movies from Hong Kong have become required watching for directors from Badham to Oliver Stone to Quentin Tarantino.

NEWSDAY, 12/9/94, Part II/p. B7, Jack Mathews

If skydivers were as stupid as the movies made about their sport, there would be no surviving graduates of skydiving school, no such thing as a second jump, no need for parachutes. They wouldn't remember to open them.

The problem with "Point Break," "Terminal Velocity" and the new "Drop Zone," in which a U.S. marshal (Wesley Snipes) attempts to stop a gang of skydiving computer hackers from breaking into government offices from the sky (I kid you not), is that their plots are literally made out of thin air. That's where the action is, that's where the cameras are, that's where the story must unfold.

The attraction up there is the sight of people in vertical flight, up close and personal, falling at 180 to 200 mph and appearing to execute some sort of acrobatic ballet, as the Earth, suspended below like the back of a great whale, rises up to catch them. But before we join the divers, we must be given a reason, and any reason, the writers of "Drop Zone" seem to think, will do.

In this first screenplay by writers Peter Barsocchini and John Bishop, Snipes plays a U.S. marshal who, to avenge the death of his brother in a skyjacking tragedy, seeks out a skydiving instructor (Yancey Butler), and in about a week of accelerated training, is ready to challenge Gary Busey and his skydiving bandits at a game of aerial tag that ends up, for reasons too preposterous to explain, in the Drug Enforcement Agency headquarters in Washington, D.C.

Director John Badham has a history of making do with bad action scripts ("WarGames," "Blue Thunder"), and the movie's opening skyjacking sequence is one of the best set pieces he's ever directed. But neither Badham nor the immensely likable Snipes can save this story from the whims of its authors.

Maybe they should take up golf.

SIGHT AND SOUND, 4/95, p. 41, Geoffrey Macnab

US Marshals Pete Nessip and his brother Terry are assigned to escort notorious computer hacker Earl Leedy to a Federal Prison. Halfway through their journey on a commercial 747, there is what appears to be a terrorist attack. In the ensuing mayhem, Terry is killed, the plane door flies open and several passengers, including Leedy, go missing, presumed dead.

Back on the ground, the FBI suspects that the Nessip brothers bungled the operation. Pete's badge is suspended, pending investigation. Nobody believes his theory that the attack on the 747 was orchestrated by skydivers, in order to kidnap Leedy. Pete resolves to investigate on his own. His first contact is a professional skydiver, Jessie Crossman. He has a hunch that her ex-boyfriend may have had something to do with the kidnapping. Sure enough, a little girl who survived the hijack recognises his face.

Meanwhile, Ty Moncrief, the leader of the criminal gang, is forcing Leedy to learn how to skydive. In one such session, he engineers the boyfriend's murder. He intends to swoop on the Drugs Enforcement Agency offices, and then utilise Leedy's computer talent to discover the identities of undercover DEA agents. He hopes to sell this information for a fortune to gangster bosses.

Pete realises that if he is going to solve this mystery, he's going to have to learn how to skydive himself. Jessie agrees to help him if he fixes matters with her probation officer and subsidises her team at a prestigious skydiving exhibition in Washington. Ty Moncrief and his gang have also entered the exhibition and intend to use it as a smokescreen for their most daring stunt yet, a raid on the headquarters of the DEA.

Jessie correctly suspects that Ty was responsible for killing her boyfriend. She hides in his plane and surprises him and his gang just as they are about to parachute. They overpower her and try to bungle her out of the plane. Pete manages to rescue her. He and the rest of her team follow Moncrief and colleagues to the DEA building. After multiple fist fights and shoot-outs, Moncrief ends up dead, Leedy is recaptured by the authorities, and Pete's reputation is restored.

Drop Zone masquerades as a cop thriller. It opens in a state penitentiary with the attempted murder or a convict; veers off into *Midnight Run* territory, as US Marshalls, Wesley Snipes and Malcolm-Jamal Warner, accompany the convict to trial, and even looks like turning into an *Airport*-style disaster movie when terrorists hold up a 747. But such intricate plotting is deceptive: this is really a film about skydiving which just happens to have a narrative and characters attached. It's director, John Badham, takes his cue from his daredevil stunt artists: while they pull their parachutes at the last instant, he falls back on a storyline only as a last resort. Sheer vertiginous excitement is his primary aim. The few earthbound sequences between the many, dizzy swoops out of aeroplanes are the mechanics, nothing more. That they function so smoothly, despite flimsy, erratic scripting, is a testament both to Badham's economy of style and the urgency with which he always want to hurry onto the next bit of aerial derring-do.

Slick and exhilarating the movie may be, but it is also disappointingly superficial. While it succeeds in giving a documentary-like account of its featured sport, with Snipes as the novice who only very gradually gains his wings, its attempts at capturing the essence of skydiver subculture are lamentable. (Scenes of off-duty parachutists drinking and brawling in bars hardly offer an insight into what makes otherwise rational people want to jump out of aeroplanes from 15,000 feet.) There's certainly none of the metaphysical undertow of such surfing sagas as *Point Break* and *Big Wednesday* in which the heroes are clearly driven by a death wish, and spend their time searching for the "big wave". Here the protagonists are straightforward sorts who simply see their sport as a way of expressing a rugged individualism that everyday urban life denies them.

Although the storyline cobbles together elements from just about every genre imaginable, its terrorist villains are clear descendants of western outlaw gangs. They use parachutes instead of horses, and have a computer hacker instead of a safe breaker. This character, Earl Leedy, is depicted as weedy and effete. His virtuosity as a systems analyst is seen as a facet of his neurosis. Like Holly Hunter in *The Piano*, he even has the tip of one of his fingers cut off. New technology may be revolutionising people's existences, the film seems to argue, but real heroes don't spend their days sitting in front of terminals. (Such implicit technophobia is slightly surprising when you consider that Badham numbers *WarGames*, one of the earliest computer films, among his credits.)

Drop Zone could never be accused of pretentiousness. It's far too brisk—so much so that you get the feeling that Badham is trying to conceal something. Perhaps, this is the pusillanimous way in which the relationship between Wesley Snipes and Yancy Butler is treated. Generic convention all but demands they become a couple: they share the same parachute twice, save each other's lives and swap endless smouldering glances. However, *Jungle Fever* and *Love Field* apart, it's hard to think of many recent Hollywood films that have dealt with interracial romance. *Drop Zone* shirks from the task, even at the risk of making an already strained plot yet more ridiculous.

As the improbabilities pile up, the film inevitably takes on a comic air. It lifts its frenetic, skyscraper shootout direct from *Die Hard*, and even borrows motifs from old B-movie matinees. Given Badham's recent output, in particular the self-mocking *The Hard Way*, it's tempting to think that the absurdities are deliberate. The acting hardly clarifies matters. Whereas the villains, led by Gary Busey as Moncrief, play for real, Snipes' action hero is at least half parody. As US Marshall Pete Nessip, he matches his competence as cop against his extreme incompetence as fledgling skydiver. He's the city slicker in among the rednecks who must learn their culture and codes if he is to get by. It's a neat, witty performance which lends a little, much needed human interest to affairs and prevents *Drop Zone* from being no more than the sum of its stunts.

VILLAGE VOICE, 12/20/94, p. 65, Gary Dauphin

Wesley Snipes says he wants to be the black action hero of the '90s, get his own franchise like Bruce or Arnold or Sly—only deep fried, the better to buy his son mocha-colored Wesley dolls with kung fu grips (hi-YAA!), but none of it'll ever happen if he keeps doing drivel like *Drop Zone*. If *Drop Zone* sinks, which it does, it isn't because Wesley isn't up to the task of playing onscreen supernegro. Snipes can hi-YAA it with the best of 'em and his Pete Nessip—U.S. Marshal cum, uh, trick skydiver—has the facility with quips, kicks, and falls-off-of-high-rises that's required of any action figure worth his molded plastic. Moreover, as Snipes has pointed out in just about every interview he's done regarding the parachute stunts for *Drop Zone*, "I screamed like a woman on the way down," and if that isn't dramatic range, I don't know what is.

Nope, *Drop Zone* sucks because thc five or so guy's responsible for the script and story couldn't come up with the spark of an original concept if you gave 'em a pile of dry tinder, a gallon of gasoline, and an army-issue Zippo lighter to work with. Nessip's brother (Malcolm-Jamal Warner, who also happens to be Wesley's partner in the Marshals) predictably buys it while the two of them are transferring an Alan Dershowitz-looking computer hacker (an appropriately nervous Michael Jeter) via 747. Faster than you can say, "It's personal now," Nessip has handed in his badge and is secretly investigating the wild and wooly world of high-performance skydiving, with aerial babe-parole violator Jessie Crossman as his guide (Yancy Butler looking beguiling in her spandex jumpsuit and not much more).

After a decent opening straight out of any *Airport* movie, Nessip spends the next 90 minutes discovering that former DEA agent Ty Moncrief (Gary Busey, doing his usual thanks-but-no-helmet-for-me villain) broke hacker dude out of the 747 in order to help his nylon-chuted gang steal data from high-tech office towers, a plotline with elements basically lifted from *Die Hard, Cliffhanger, Point Break*, and Snipe's own (and much more enjoyable) *Passenger 57*. The stunts, you ask? Well, besides the fact that there are only about six good jumps in *Drop Zone* (two of which are really first-and third-act reprises of a classic James Bond opening), director John Badham has an annoying habit of shooting everything from medium distance, giving stunts a rear-projection look even when the camera's actually plummeting earthward from 20,000 feet up. Snipes deserves better handling, and if his action career can survive a flop like *Drop Zone* and the projected drag minstrel show *To Wong Foo*, that'll be some real derring-do, albeit not the kind that rates a kung fu grip.

Also reviewed in:
CHICAGO TRIBUNE, 12/9/94, Friday/p. I, Michael Wilmington
NEW YORK TIMES, 12/9/94, p. C12, Stephen Holden
VARIETY, 12/12-18/94, p. 76, Joe Leydon
WASHINGTON POST, 12/9/94, p. D7, Hal Hinson
WASHINGTON POST, 12/9/94, Weekend/p. 55, Desson Howe

DUMB AND DUMBER

A New Line Cinema release in association with Motion Picture Corporation of America. *Executive Producer:* Gerald T. Olson and Aaron Meyerson. *Producer:* Charles B. Wessler, Steve Stabler, and Bradley R. Krevoy. *Director:* Peter Farrelly. *Screenplay:* Peter Farrelly, Bennett Yellin, and Bobby Farrelly. *Director of Photography:* Mark Irwin. *Editor:* Christopher Greenbury. *Music:* Todd Rundgren. *Music Editor:* Joe E. Rand. *Sound:* Jonathan Stein and (music) Todd Rundgren. *Sound Editor:* Craig Clark. *Casting:* Rick Montgomery and Dan Parada. *Production Designer:* Sidney Bartholomew, Jr. *Art Director:* Arlan Jay Vetter. *Set Decorator:* Bradford Johnson. *Set Dresser:* Gary Sivertson, Michael Budge, and Kelly Hernsdorf. *Special Effects:* Frank Ceglia. *Costumes:* Mary Zophres. *Make-up:* Sheryl Leigh Ptak. *Stunt Coordinator:* Rick Barker. *Running time:* 106 minutes. *MPAA Rating:* PG-13.

CAST: Jim Carrey (Lloyd Christmas); Jeff Daniels (Harry Dunne); Lauren Holly (Mary Swanson); Teri Garr (Helen Swanson); Karen Duffy (J.P. Shay); Mike Starr (Joe Mentalino); Charles Rocket (Nicholas Andre); Victoria Rowell (Beth Jordan); Cam Neely (Sea Bass); Felton Perry (Detective Dale); Jim Baker (Barnard); Hank Brandt (Karl Swanson); Brady Bluhm (Billy); Brad Lockerman (Bobby); Rob Moran (Bartender); Kathryn Frick (Cashier); Zen Gesner and Lawrence Kopp (Dale's Men); Clint Allen (Coroner); Connie Sawyer (Elderly Woman); Lin Shaye (Mrs. Nuegeboren); Mike Watkis (Reporter); Harland Williams (State Trooper); Diane Kinerk and Hilary Matthews (Waitresses); Lisa Strothard (Bus Stop Beauty); Sean Gildea (Sea Bass Friend); Charles Chun (Flight Attendant); Heln Boll (Swanson Maid); Fred Stoller (Anxious Man at Phone); Karen Ingram (Nicholas' Girl); Jess Borja (Martial Artist); Bruce Bowns (Barber); Denise Vienne (Concierge); Nancy Farrelly (Diner Gawker); Catalina Izasa (Manicurist); Samanta Pearson (Masseuse); Ken Duvall (Mutt Cutts Boss); Cecile Krevoy (Airport Bystander); George Bedard (Peeing Man); Bill Beauchene (Peeing Man's Friend); Gary Sivertsen (Aspen Police Officer); Traci Adell (Sexy Woman); Clem Franek (Wallbanger).

LOS ANGELES TIMES, 12/16/94, Calendar/p. 1, Peter Rainer

"Dumb and Dumber" is a heap o' gags about dumbness. Most of the jokes are dumb dumb but some of them are actually smart dumb. The film seems to have been made for precocious 7-year-olds and their parents—at least the type of parents who stay up to watch "Beavis and Butthead."

Bathroom humor isn't exactly an acquired taste. Either you think it's funny or you walk. "Dumb and Dumber," which stars Jim Carrey and Jeff Daniels as two low-wattage buddies, Lloyd and Harry, abounds in pottyjokes and gross-out gags. The real joke is that grown men are actually doing this stuff. And Carrey and Daniels go all the way with the ridiculousness: they really get inside the buddies' euphoric blankness.

Director Peter Farrelly, who co-wrote the grab-bag screenplay with Bennett Yellin and Bobby Farrelly, doesn't stage the gags particularly well, and a lot of comic payoffs misfire just because the camera isn't in the right place at the right time. But Farrelly isn't trying to pull our heartstrings either. He has the good sense to stand back and indulge the two actors' nutball riffs.

The pedigree for this scattershot, anything-for-a-laugh movie has already been set for a new generation by the "Naked Gun" films, and many others. And, in only his third starring vehicle, Carrey is already such an established comic presence that he holds the audience even when he's just mugging or making screwy little movements with his mouth.

With his bowl cut and chipped tooth, and his jointless gyrations, Carrey is like a more elasticized Jerry Lewis; he may be the most freakishly cartoonish of all the star comedians (which is why he was so well cast in "The Mask"). Lloyd is a variation on the characters Carrey has played in "Ace Ventura" and "The Mask," but he's more triumphantly dim. And Lloyd is never so dim as when he thinks he's being smart: The spark in his eye is greater than the spark in his brain.

Lloyd starts out as an airport limo driver; his roomie, Harry, runs a canine grooming operation out of his truck, which is outfitted to look like a shaggy puppy. Harry (Daniels) is pretty shaggy himself. He's unkempt in a blotto kind of way; he's not concerned with his appearance because he's not really aware that he has an appearance.

The two guys spend half the movie traveling in circles from Rhode Island to Colorado in order to return a misplaced briefcase containing a fortune in ransom money to a socialite (Lauren Holly) who has stolen Lloyd's heart. (He took her to the airport and she actually *listened* to his inane banter.)

Along the way there are run-ins with rowdy roughnecks and cops and a kidnaping team (Mike Starr and Karen Duffy) who think Lloyd and Harry are actually master criminals.

A lot of the movie hinges on this smart-dumb misperception: It's "Being There" for the kiddies. When both boys take turns romancing the socialite, the film totters into its full tastelessness. Just before his big date, Harry is slipped a bottle of laxative by his jealous friend. Guess what happens? He also sticks his tongue on a frozen ski-lift pole. Lloyd, who is more debonair, accidentally assassinates a snow owl at an endangered species benefit with a popped champagne cork.

"Dumb and Dumber" isn't exactly the sort of movie you can recommend to people—at least not to people you don't know *really* well. But it's got more laughs than "Junior" or "Speechless"—granted, no great achievement. It also has a love of silliness that isn't all that dumb.

NEW STATESMAN & SOCIETY, 4/7/95, p,. 49, Jonathan Romney

If it were true that only the French loved Jerry Lewis, then by rights it should also be the case that only they loved Jim Carrey. But Carrey, star of *The Mask* and a quite shameless emulator of Lewis' geeky mugging, was last year's biggest international overnight success—even bigger than Hugh Grant, and what an odd pairing that would be if anyone chose to test it out.

As you'll have read repeatedly of late, dumb is the thing to be in movies this year. The appalling *Forrest Gump* swept the Oscars, Beavis and Butt-head have long been established arbiters of American youth culture, there are further celebrations of witlessness around the corner, The Stupids and God knows what else. All in all, simpleton inanity is so triumphant in the American zeitgeist (have you ever seen the Conan O'Brien talk show?) that it's like that nice Mr Reagan never went away.

The failure of the Clinton regime to make its ideological weight felt has given a fresh boost to America's cult of anti-intellectualism. The liberal tenet that social problems can be relieved with patient, compassionate scrutiny is being heartily pilloried by the Newt Gingrich culture. Dumb is thus a way of throwing up your hands and saying, if there's no way of understanding the world, then to hell with it—let's have louder music, brighter colours, more fart jokes.

But there's dumb and there's dumb, and different kinds of dumb have different uses. *Forrest Gump* is a wilful blinding to the complexities of the present. It argues that if only we could see today in the simple(ton) terms in which the film sees the past, then we would know where we were; the traumas and aspirations of the 1960s are written off as an adolescent fit, discredited through the clear view of hindsight, embodied in childlike, therefore lucid Forrest.

Fred Schepisi's smarmy *IQ,* genuinely dimwitted because it thinks it's smart, is a palliative in the face of a crumbling intellectual culture, demonstrating that intelligence is just another form of dumbness with a couple of initials after its name. In it, Albert Einstein and his boffin chums disport themselves like the Bash Street Kids while trying to engineer a romance between brainy but diky Meg Ryan and slow but warm-hearted Tim Robbins. Dumb is, you know, healthier, and the only character in the film whom you'd conceivably want to have a conversation with is mercilessly derided throughout as a limey tight-arse. He's played by Stephen Fry—wouldn't *you* want to do a runner?

Then there's *Dumb and Dumber*. I can't honestly say it's the least funny film I've seen this year (there's a new Peruvian *Crime and Punishment* that is quite short on yuks.) It did raise a snigger or two, but not even a snigger you get from *Viz*, more from *Zit* or *Snot* or one of its single cell imitators. It's a film about the misadventures of a pair of cretins, and the trailer—all mugging, dribbling and remedial haircuts—suggested it might be rather offensive and just the thing to write a huffy think piece about. But the film's so slapdash in its definition of dumb that there's nothing to get upset about. It doesn't suggest that its heroes might have learning difficulties, not exactly—although at one moment Jim Carrey's Lloyd can't read the word "the". It's rather that they're so imbued with the will to gross out that they bypass conventionally intelligent action. They're like punchline-seeking missiles—Ren and Stimpy in human form, or the Three Stooges after they've accidentally killed the bald guy.

Lloyd and Harrry (Jeff Daniels) are morons, but curiously, they're depressive morans—like US college radio listeners gone too far. They do hopeless jobs hopelessly—Lloyd's a chauffeur, Harry drives a car that looks like the *Banana Splits* dog—and live in a squalid apartment with one pin-up on the wall and an ant farm. One-dimensional and deracinated: in a way, they're like the existential heroes of Jean Pierre Melville movies, but without the neat hats. Through some absurd accident, Lloyd falls in love with an impossible goddess and decides to pursue her across America to return her lost briefcase. *En route*, he and Harry have many accidents (mostly scatological), play many pranks (mostly scatological), and generally court abjection in all its guises.

The film is entirely unlovable, largely because Carrey is so obnoxious, so obviously a hip clown on a roll and trying out his luck. His frenetic goofing comes across as so much attention-grabbing, joyless and self-promoting: he probably thought if he mugged twice as much, they'd bump up his fee even more for the sequel. Daniels, acting against type (we've always seen him as sensible Brooks Brothers fellows), is actually quite charming, as long as he stays melancholic. But there's no comic principle behind the film, no consistency to its dumbness. It should be called *Dumb As Required*. If it wants dumb to mean helpless and pathetic, it gives us the boys in their flat; if it wants dumb to mean goat-like and libidinous, it wheels on ingénue Lauren Holly to be dribbled over; if dumb is monstrous, Carrey reveals his hideous claw-like toenails; if dumb is vindictive in an outrageous Machiavellian way, it has the boys play horrific, convoluted pranks on each other (there's the dead budgerigar joke, which is the film 's best gag, just because it's so unequivocally mean-spirited). Director Peter Farrelly will do anything to get a laugh, and call it dumb; but to paraphrase an old *National Lampoon* LP title, that's not dumb, that's expedient.

There are no rules. It's as if someone had decided that Superman could be vulnerable to red, green and gold kryptonite, *and* Fun-Size Mars Bars.

NEW YORK, 1/16/95, p. 57, David Denby

With his chipped front tooth, monk's bangs, and sizable jug ears, the maniacal Jim Carrey, in *Dumb and Dumber*, bears some resemblance to Moe, the great slobbo of the Three Stooges. Spazzing around the sets, he may also remind you of the young, many-elbowed Jerry Lewis. But Carrey has a physical volatility that is all his own. His body moves as fast as Robin Williams's mouth, and like Williams, he's immensely knowing, making reference to a dozen things in pop culture—only doing it physically rather than verbally. A speed freak. In the funniest bit in *Dumb and Dumber*, Carrey dreams of impressing a beautiful woman he has met. They are dining together at a posh restaurant. Some thugs enter, and he dispatches them kung fu-style. Then the restaurant's cook—a person of indeterminate Asian birth—comes out of the kitchen and engages in some preliminary Ninja whirling and hissing. Not to be outdone, Carrey spins, pinwheels, prances, pirouettes, falls to his knees, pulls on his ears, all the while screeching in Korean (or some such tongue)—and the chef is undone before he even begins to fight. Carrey goes so far into physical comedy he seems to leave normal body movements behind: His work is a free-form slapstick fantasia rather than a set of routines. In *Dumb and Dumber*, he exudes demented self-approval, a certainty of suavity that cannot be defeated. He's a comic without reserve, without protective nets of any sort beneath him.

Carrey's brows go straight across his forehead and then fall in commas on the sides of his eyes. Literally a lowbrow, he's got a born clown's face and temperament. But Jeff Daniels, his fellow defective in *Dumb and Dumber*, isn't naturally uninhibited. Daniels projects an actor's dissatisfaction. His blond hair, worn long and straight in this movie, hangs disconsolately around the sides of his face and along his big nose and jaw. In *Dumb and Dumber*, he has the sadness, the remoteness, and near-masochistic doggedness of a heavy-bodied man without grace. Perhaps Daniels, who has never quite made it as a leading man, thought, "What the hell? Nothing to lose. Let's squirt some ketchup." But he isn't fast and volatile like Carrey, and one senses that he's pushing himself into it; occasionally, his disgust shows.

As you may have gathered, *Dumb and Dumber* is a crude, wallowing-in-the-mud, occasionally very funny comedy about two men who don't have a clue. Nothing works for these guys. Unlike that other ninny, Forrest Gump, they don't receive love or respect; when they lose, they really *lose*, and they fall all the way into humiliation. The movie is big on physical punishment and bodily functions. Major quantities of excreta flow about, and serious punitive work is performed on genitals and tongues and other tender body parts. *Dumb and Dumber* goes low and lower into some sub-burlesque nirvana that makes teenage boys giddy. The most recognizable human emotion in the movie is the bottom-dog loyalty the two doofuses feel toward each other.

Some grown-ups are getting giddy as well. What accounts for this amazing nineties phenomenon of put-on stupidity? Idiocy has become the educated person's chosen form of relaxation. A wild guess: Despite a healthy economy, many of us are ruled by job anxiety, the sense that skills laboriously acquired and vigorously defended may soon appear outmoded. The pressure to *keep up* can be intolerable. Who wants to be smart all the time? Stupidity can be a release. Not only are the two men of *Dumb and Dumber* in no way a threat, they may represent a form of wished-for freedom—Jim Carrey as the ultimate liberated id, seeking not erotic bliss but the greater, wilder bliss of being completely out of it.

NEW YORK POST, 12/16/94, p. 65, Thelma Adams

Are movies getting stupider and stupider—or just "Dumb and Dumber"?

Lloyd (Jim Carrey) and Harry (Jeff Daniels) arc the overgrown poster children for the dumbing down of America in an unabashedly silly road movie that's a sturdy vehicle for "The Mask" star. The surprise is that Daniels, who was caught on "Speed" last summer and can switch hit from comedy to drama, matches Carrey mug for mug and gag for gag.

Carrey, sporting his real chipped front tooth and a bowl-shaped do that screams geek, is the person we all fear we might have been in high school. With his elastic face and Gumby body, there isn't an emotion he can conceal—and that's what makes him annoying and charming simultaneously.

Daniels plays the role of second doofus in blankface, lost within a haze of frizzy yellow hair. Together, they are two wild-and-crazy Stooges without Moe to keep them in line.

The two devoted yokels-in-crime take a road trip from Providence to Aspen in an '84 van tarted up like a sheep dog (sight gag alert!), delaying their dream of opening a pet store called "I've Got Worms" in order to return a briefcase to a beautiful stranger named Mary (Lauren Holly).

Along the way to Carrey's dream destination—"a place where the beer flows like wine"—they best a bully (hockey star Cam Neely), deep-six pro thug Joe Mentalino (Mike Starr) who would kill for what's in the case, and offer a state trooper a beverage he should've refused in a gag inducing gag.

On the road, the laughs chug along at a steady pace whether the two clueless campers are soaking together in a heart-shaped tub at the Second Honeymoon Motel, pulling childish pranks at a truck stop or annoying Mentalino with their rendition of "Mockingbird."

"Dumb and Dumber" stalls when the guys hit Aspen and a romantic subplot separates them. When Lloyd slips Harry a super-charged laxative to ruin his pal's romantic rendezvous with Mary, it's over the top and out the bottom. Like much of the movie's potty humor, whether you enjoy it is a matter of taste—or tastelessness.

No one will ever rank Peter Farrelly's "Dumb and Dumber" with "Casablanca" (or even "Faster, Pussycat! Kill! Kill!"), but it's mindless entertainment, a relative high point in low-brow humor. Todd Rundgren's buoyant score adds a consistent comic backbeat to the zany goings-on.

Did I laugh? Duuuh!

NEWSDAY, 12/16/94, Part II/p. B7, Gene Seymour

What better way to wind up the Year of the Dimwit in American movies than with "Dumb and Dumber"? (Don't answer, OK? The question's rhetorical.) The numbers that this thing will pile up should be fat enough to ensure that the next year will see a rich bounty of morons-as-heroes.

Much of what makes "D & D's" success inevitable, of course, is Jim Carrey's hot hand. Carrey's rise to the status of America's goonybird has been so meteoric that the blue meanies who chart the movie business now make it their first priority to wait for the other shoe to drop.

Sorry, guys. But "Dumb and Dumber" will only enhance Carrey's standing as a franchise player. As Lloyd Christmas, a geeky loser with a huge heart and a pea brain, Carrey is much the hyperactive toy he was in "The Mask" and "Ace Ventura, Pet Detective." His character's first encounter with damsel-in-distress Mary Swanson (Lauren Holly) is so reminiscent of Jerry Lewis' over-the-top reactions that you almost expect him to howl, "Pretty Lady! Pretty Lady!" To his credit, he doesn't.

Lloyd meets Mary while driving her limo to the airport. As he drives away, he notices she's left behind her briefcase. He runs out of the limo—which he's already wrecked, natch—and snatches the case before it can be intercepted by two thugs. Her plane's already left for Aspen. Hey, no problem! She's the woman of his dreams and the least he can do is drive out there to return it.

His best friend, Harry Dunne (Jeff Daniels), is skeptical. But then, he's so dim he thinks Aspen's in France. Which is why he goes along with Lloyd on the open road. Just before they go, however, those two goons, one of whom is an ulcer-ridden brute named Joe Mentalino (Mike Starr), decide to send them "a message" by decapitating Harry's beloved parakeet. Lloyd thinks the head fell off by itself. "It was getting old," he tells a grief-stricken Harry.

That's about as sophisticated as "D & D's" humor gets. (One should add that Lloyd tapes the dead bird back together and sells it to a blind kid living in their building.) What follows is a seemingly endless series of scatological bits that leave no bodily function (short of sex) untouched. Freezing mucous humor receives what may be its most definitive treatment on the big screen. This paper's a tad too polite to mention the beer bottles filled with ... naah, forget it.

After a while, you just have to come to terms with the prevailing boneheadedness in your own way. Depending on how this process goes, you can even start finding things here and there to like. Daniels, it turns out, makes a surprisingly capable dolt—though, in hindsight, one realizes that Harry's just a broader version of the awkward smoothies he's played in the past. Holly, best known as the spunky, smoldering deputy on "Picket Fences," also shows a gift for well-timed reaction. Anyone who's up on funny business knows that's a lot harder than it looks.

And the bad news? Well, there's a Kung Fu parody that falls way short of the one in "Wayne's World 2." Teri Garr is wasted in the role of Holly's wealthy, flighty mom. It should also be said that, once in a while, one's inner child gets a little overloaded with the unrelenting silliness.

But "Dumb and Dumber," while no classic, does little to slow the momentum of the Carrey phenomenon. If anything, it'll prove to the suits that not only is he a franchise player, he's an effective team player as well.

NEWSWEEK, 1/16/95, p. 67, Jeff Giles

Dumb and Dumber is a spectacularly dumb, but you can't say you weren't warned. This is Jim Carrey's third star turn—"Ace Ventura" and "The Mask" made $200 million combined—and it's been the highest-grossing movie in the country for three weeks. Some have attributed the movie's success to a new cult of dumbness, which is just plain stupid: dumb is, and ever was. The simple truth is that Carrey gives his funniest performance here, if you've got the stomach for it. He plays Lloyd Christmas, a sweetly moronic limo driver who gets fired early in the movie ("They always freak out when you leave the scene of an accident"). As it happens, Lloyd's sweetly moronic roommate Harry (Jeff Daniels) has just lost his job as a dog-groomer. So he convinces Harry to join him on a cross-country trek to Aspen. He plans to return a briefcase that a beautiful socialite named Mary Swanson (Lauren Holly, from TV's "Picket Fences") left behind when he chauffeured her to the airport. It turns out the briefcase is full of ransom money. Then there's some stuff about kidnappers and the FBI—we couldn't follow it all, but we weren't trying very hard, either.

Daniels isn't entirely convincing as a moron, but Carrey was born to lose. He does a wonderfully elastic turn that owes debts to Jerry Lewis's various descents into idiocy and to the great down escalator that was Steve Martin's "The Jerk." Let's be clear about the level of the humor here: there's a scene in which Lloyd sets fire to a certain bodily emission. (Rhymes with art.) Still, in its most inspired moments—such as when Harry and Lloyd hit high-society Aspen and spend the cash in the briefcase on orange and powder-blue tuxes—"Dumb" made us convulse with laughter and we're not going to lie about it now. Carrey is planning sequels to "Ace" and "The Mask,"and surely there's a movie called "Dumbest" in our future. All that's a bit much, but Carrey's role as the Riddler in "Batman Forever" should put some meat on the bones of his career. Meanwhile, "Dumb" is a pleasure in its dopey way. We've seen it before, but we'd see it again.

SIGHT AND SOUND, 4/95, p. 42, Chris Darke

Rhode Island limousine driver Lloyd Christmas picks up Mary Swanson, an attractive fare. Taking her to the airport to catch a flight to Aspen, Colorado, Lloyd tells her the story of his hopeless life. Noticing that she has left her briefcase in the lobby, he rushes to retrieve it. Meanwhile his limo is towed away, for which he is sacked. On the same day, Lloyd's roommate Harry Dunne, a dog groomer with a "Mutt Cutts" van resembling a giant dog, also loses his job. Lloyd enlists Harry to drive him to Aspen with the briefcase in the hope of following up his romantic interest in Mary. Unknown to either of them, the briefcase is stuffed with dollar-bills, a ransom for Mary's husband who has been kidnapped by Nicholas Andre, a family friend of Mary's wealthy parents. Andre's thugs, Joe Mental and J. P. Shay, are now in pursuit.

On the road, Lloyd and Harry encounter numerous misadventures, including run-ins with a vicious gay trucker and a Pennsylvania State Trooper. Joe Mentalino is finally and accidentally despatched after a red hot chilli pepper-eating contest. Arriving in Aspen, they fight over the briefcase, knocking it open to reveal the money. On a spree they rent a Presidential suite, buy tasteless new clothes and a Lamborghini Diabolo, dutifully replacing each dollar bill they remove with an IOU note.

They meet up with Mary at an Aspen Preservation Society benefit gala for the Icelandic Snow Owl, hosted by her parents with Andre. Romantic confusion ensues, in which Harry, rather than Lloyd, takes up with Mary. A jealous Lloyd spikes Harry's drink with laxative to ruin his planned evening with Mary and arrives to tell her that the briefcase is in his hotel room. They go back to the room together, only to be captured by Andre. Kitted out with a bullet-proof vest, Harry arrives in the nick of time. He and the FBI save the day. Mary and her husband are reunited. Lloyd and Harry hit the road.

Dweeb, dork, geek, nerd: American slang luxuriates in the vocabulary of stupidity, and judging from its recent output, so does the American cinema. *Dumb and Dumber* arrives wearing its no-brow credentials on its sleeve and inherits from a rich, if hardly reputable, vein of dumb that stretches in various generic directions, including the *National Lampoon* series and the *Porky's* movies. *Dumb and Dumber* inherits much from these motherlodes of low comedy, in particular a taste for fraternity-house scatology, showcased in reruns of the old piss-for-beer switch gag and the laxative micky finn routine—the latter played out with bowel-contorting exaggeration by Jeff Daniels.

However it is Jim Carrey who is on show here, albeit with less panache than in either of his two previous roles. In *Ace Ventura* there was a brash and breezy novelty to his manic mugging, while *The Mask* took Carrey's contortions to extreme yet logical limits through computerised prostheses. Here, with his toothy gurning and pie-bowl haircut, Carrey seems stuck in Jerry Lewis mode. There is a slightly other-than-human quality to his facility for shape-changing and conceptual free-forming. More in evidence than before, however, is the malevolence lining

Carrey's comedic persona (to be fully exploited, one hopes, in his role as the Riddler in the forthcoming *Batman Forever*).

Dumb and Dumber may not be a step forward for Carrey, but it does provide more evidence that the Dumb Club is growing; Wayne and Garth, Beavis and Butthead, Bill and Ted and Forrest Gump are now joined by Lloyd and Harry. The film's poster has them sitting, à la *Forrest Gump*, on a bench, staring vacantly, expectantly, utterly gormlessly at something off-frame. Thus it promises a parodic take on the culture of dumb which it fails to deliver. The film ends up collaborating with the wider culture that will face up to its internal horror and anomie only through dazed and confused slacker-chic or a pernicious glorification of freedom-through-lobotomy.

On the road and at large in the playground of the rich and famous that is Aspen, *Dumb and Dumber* revels in a comedy of confusion. For me, the laughs were few, yet at the packed preview screening, it was evident that Carrey has his own audience that laughs as much in sympathy with his character's misfortunes as with the performer himself.

TIME, 1/9/95, p. 66, Richard Schickel

High in the Himalayas lives the Guru of Low Comedy, surrounded by his tapes of Laurel and Hardy, W.C. Fields and the brothers Zucker. "Great Master, what is the secret of a hit?" ask Hollywood's best and richest when they are ushered into his presence. "Make 'em laugh," is the inevitable reply, "any damn way you can."

It is said that fastidious filmmakers retreat in dismay muttering, "Does he mean, like, bathroom jokes?" Ignoring the advice, they end up dying out there with cute, cautious comedies like *Speechless* and *I.Q.* (not to mention spineless farces like *Mixed Nuts*). Meanwhile, *Dumb and Dumber* becomes the most popular movie in America. "Grossout grosses," its rivals may sniff, and they would not be wrong. But so what? The fact is that *D and D*—in comparison with which Jim Carrey's other pictures look as if they were scripted by Oscar Wilde—makes you laugh out loud for almost its entire running time.

Lloyd, the lead moron in Peter Farrelly's film, is played by Carrey, sublimely confident that he knows what he's doing as he attempts to return a briefcase full of funny money to a woman (Lauren Holly) with whom he is smitten. This involves a cross-country journey with Harry (Jeff Daniels), Lloyd's equally dense roommate, in a truck that looks like a gigantic sheep dog. In order to enjoy the pair's company, adult viewers must regress to those thrilling days of yester-year when bodily dysfunction represented the height of hilarity. But Carrey (ably abetted here by the woofly Daniels) is both symbol and satirist of our apparently irresistible dumbing down. Astonished attention must be paid.

VILLAGE VOICE, 12/27/94, p. 74, Jeff Salamon

I didn't check out *The Mask* on the grounds that any movie that required special effects to make Jim Carrey's face look like a cartoon wasn't worth my $7.50. *Dumb and Dumber* is more like it; sporting nothing more elaborate than a dogbowl haircut and a chipped front tooth, Carrey is Goofy, in living, breathing color.

A matching pair of I'M WITH STUPID T-shirts, best friends Lloyd (Carrey) and Harry (Jeff Daniels) are stuck in dead-end jobs and nonexistent social lives. Lloyd is the happy-face moron, utterly oblivious to how stupid he is; Harry is the sad sack who one day might just give up and stop putting his left foot in front of his right if he could only figure out which was which. After Lloyd loses his job as a livery driver ("They always freak out when you leave the scene of an accident"), he and Harry travel across the country to return a briefcase full of money to the beautiful Mary (Lauren Holly). To get to Aspen ("Where the beer flows like wine"), the pair, a half-wit retread of *Easy Rider*'s Billy and Captain America, traverse America first in a van decorated like a giant sheepdog and then on motorscooter.

Fans of modern farce will note a slight resemblance to 1986's *Ruthless People* (which, like this film, was put together by two brothers and a pal), but there's no denying that screenwriters Peter and Bob Farrelly (who wrote a couple of *Seinfeld* episodes—presumably the early, funny ones) and Bennett Yellin have come up with one of the more efficient laugh machines Hollywood has turned out in a while. A few extended set pieces go nowhere, and the screenplay relies on too many piss, shit, spit, and snot gags ("Lots of body-function jokes," I scribbled in my notepad—and this was before I suffered through an overlong laxative sequence), but the only fluid that truly offends is the third-rate brand of beer that makes numerous appearances in the film. *Where the Coors flows like wine* would be more like it.

Also reviewed in:
CHICAGO TRIBUNE, 12/16/94, ArtsPlus, John Petrakis
NEW YORK TIMES, 12/16/94, p. C10, Stephen Holden
VARIETY, 12/19/94-1/1/95, p. 72, Leonard Klady
WASHINGTON POST, 12/16/94, p. F7, Rita Kempley
WASHINGTON POST, 12/16/94, Weekend/p. 49, Desson Howe

EAT DRINK MAN WOMAN

A Samuel Goldwyn Company release of a Central Motion Picture Corporation production in association with Ang Lee Productions and Good Machine. *Executive Producer:* Feng-Chyi Jiang. *Producer:* Lik-Kong Hsu. *Director:* Ang Lee. *Screenplay (Chinese with English subtitles):* Ang Lee, James Schamus, and Hui-Ling Wang. *Director of Photography:* Jong Lin. *Editor:* Tim Squyres. *Music:* Mader. *Sound:* Tom Paul and (music) Eric Liljestrand. *Sound Editor:* Steve Hamilton. *Production Designer:* Fu-Hsiung Lee. *Set Decorator:* Hsi-Chien Lee. *Costumes:* Wen-Chi Chen. *Make-up:* Wei-Min Lee. *Running time:* 123 minutes. *MPAA Rating:* Not Rated.

CAST: Sylvia Chang (Jin-Rong); Winston Chao (Li Kai); Chao-Jung Chen (Guo Lun); Lester Chen (Raymond); Yu Chen (Rachel); Ah-Leh Gua (Mrs. Liang); Chi-Der Hong (Class Leader); Gin-Ming Hsu (Coach Chai); Huei-Yi Lin (Sister Chang); Shih-Jay Lin (Chief's Son); Chin-Cheng Lu (Ming-Dao); Sihung Lung (Mr. Chu); Cho-Gin Nei (Airline Secretary); Yu-Chien Tang (Shan-Shan); Chung-Ting (The Priest); Cheng-Fen Tso (Fast Food Manager); Man-Sheng Tu (Restuarant Manager); Chuen Wang (Chief); Jui Wang (Old Wen); Yu-Wen Wang (Jia-Ning); Chien-Lien Wu (Jia-Chien); Hwa Wu (Old Man); Kuei-Mei Yang (Jia-Jen).

LOS ANGELES TIMES, 8/3/94, Calendar/p. 1, Kenneth Turan

By all means see "Eat Drink Man Woman," but not on an empty stomach. Filled with so many spectacular Chinese dishes it reduces "Like Water for Chocolate" to a Pritikin Diet promotion, this wise and rueful romantic comedy about those unavoidable human desires, food and sex, looks tasty enough to incite a monk to abandon the simple life.

The latest work from director Ang Lee (who co-wrote with Hui-Ling Wang and James Schamus), "Eat Drink" shares an empathetic sensibility with Lee's Oscar-nominated hit, "The Wedding Banquet." A look at the intertwined lives of a father and his three live-at-home daughters, this is more than anything a personal-scaled film, funny, emotional and compassionate toward the human comedy, Taiwan-style.

For unlike the New York-based "Wedding Banquet," "Eat Drink" is set in Taipei, Taiwan's capital, an upscale up-to-date but rarely seen metropolis where your women often have Western names like Sophia and Rachel and are comfortable in both miniskirts and Buddhist temples.

The three beautiful sisters "Eat Drink" is concerned with, however, all have traditional Chinese names, because their father, Master Chu ("The Wedding Banquet's" father, Sihung Lung), is a believer in the old ways.

A wizardly chef, perhaps the greatest in Taipei, Chu is crusty and brusque but a national treasure behind the stove. "Eat Drink" opens with an engaging sequence where the great man, chopping, slicing and dicing like a Vegamatic gone wild, prepares a series of knockout dishes,

It looks like the feast of a lifetime (and in fact "Eat Drink" utilized three master chefs full-time, plus several consulting food specialists) but Chu does this every Sunday for his daughters, who, not surprisingly, are tired of the fuss.

Referring to the meal as "the Sunday dinner torture ritual," they spend most of it bickering with each other and their father, who has been a widower for so long he can't accept that his children are all grown women.

The daughters, for their parts, though old enough to be out on their own, stay at home partly for financial reasons but also because their desire for independence is balanced by the Chinese tradition of filial responsibility, the desire to give their father, irritating though he is, the respect and attention his position as head of the family merits.

Most likely to leave first is middle daughter Jia-Chien (Chien-Lien Wu), a career-oriented executive with a Taiwanese airline. Still involved sexually with an ex-boyfriend but with her eye on a married co-worker (Winston Chao, the co-star of "Wedding Banquet"), she is eager to move into an about-to-open condominium complex known as the Paris of the East.

Most likely to be stuck taking care of Chu (and not particularly pleased about it) is oldest daughter Jia-Jen (Kuei-Mei Yang), a serious Christian who teaches chemistry at an all-boys high school. Still fixated on her long-gone first boyfriend, she can't help but notice the school's muscular new volleyball coach.

Not even thinking about romance is Jia-Ning (Yu-Wen Wang), the 20-year-old baby of the family who works behind the counter at Wendy's and amuses herself by chatting up a co-worker's Dostoevsky-reading boyfriend whose credo is "love is suffering."

As for Chu, when the master chef is not performing emergency "have wok will travel" culinary rescues at elaborate hotel banquets, he relaxes by cooking tasty lunches for the grade-school daughter of a neighbor (top Taiwanese star Sylvia Chang) who is involved in a messy divorce.

"Eat Drink" cuts back and forth between the daughters' interaction with each other, their father and the other men around them, watching with fond but clear-eyed sympathy as they cope with the confusions and misapprehensions of their lives.

Similar to the Chinese banquet it will make all but the most resolute hungry for, "Eat Drink Man Woman" is a leisurely affair, not in any hurry either to dole out the amusing surprises writer-director Lee is fond of or to resolve its conflicts.

This is a film that trusts us not to get impatient and also trusts us to appreciate the humor and poignancy in its situations without having to be force-fed. Though it is only Ang Lee's third feature, it is a strikingly confident one, and viewers will be understandably eager for the next course to appear.

NEW STATESMAN & SOCIETY, 1/20/95, p. 33, Jonathan Romney

Maybe it's because I'm congenitally a slow eater, but films about food never seemed that exciting to me. One comes along every two or three years, but invariably the same things get said—about how food is a metaphor for all human appetites, how directors are like cordon bleu chefs forever having to concoct new delights for jaded palates, and how after seeing that, I could murder a special fried rice. Well, we know that Chabrol used to film in different parts of France just to sample the local cuisine, and that the sex scene in Juzo Itami's *Tampopo* did wonders for egg sales in the US. What more is there to say? Where's the pleasure in coming out of *Babette's Feast* knowing that nothing more exciting awaits you than a chicken dansak? Once the link between protein and passion has been pointed out, the only direction to go is sideways, which is why films about culinary disgust—*La Grande Bouffe, The Cook The Thief...* always seem more interesting propositions, if not as cinema, then at least as dietary aids.

The thing that strikes you about Ang Lee's *Eat Drink Man Woman* is what hard work it all seems. In this story of a Taiwanese cook and his three daughters, three world-class chefs were working full-time, plus any number of specialists on hand for particular dishes, with hours required to prepare food for individual shots; this is surely the *Fitzcarraldo* of food movies. The press kit comes bound with chopsticks, and contains recipes for such delights as Steamed Deer Spare Ribs with Ginger in a Pumpkin Pot and Dragon Playing in the Sea.

The remarkable thing about the film, though, is that it's anything but a lip-smacker. In fact it gives you a sense of the futility and transience of haute cuisine—food that can never taste as good as it looks, or look as good as it sounds. Mr Chu (Sihung Lung) may spend his Sunday mornings chopping and paring and blowing down the necks of geese so that his daughters can have a full, traditional family meal—the "Sunday dinner torture ritual", one calls it—but the only character who absolutely relishes her food is a schoolgirl, who has it served up unceremoniously in a little tin jar.

The joke is that Mr. Chu's food tastes awful—or at least that its taste is in the mouth of the consumer. Once the peerless master chief of Taipel, Chu is losing his taste buds and taste for life. "Everything tastes the same", he complains, "even slop can pass as Joy Luck Dragon Phoenix." But really he's venting his self-disgust. He's unable to understand why his beloved daughters are slipping out of his control. One is a schoolteacher who's turned to Christianity, one works in Wendy's Burgers, and the third, Jia-Chien (Chien-Lien Wu), is a driven airline executive who's never forgiven him for keeping her out of the kitchen. Every Sunday they turn up at Chu's, gaze in horror at Busby Berkeley extravaganza of sea carp and carved melon shells that await them—and wince discretely at the first mouthful.

The metaphor is obvious from the start—Lee gives us all the ingredients that the film is going to work with, and we can see how the problem will have to be resolved. There's this discrepancy between the ritual of food presented with love and the difficulty of actually tasting the love in it. All the Chu family, one way or another have their appetites repressed; they all must get back their taste for life, learn to squeeze the flavour out. For us non-cooks, it's encouraging that the film's ultimate message is that we might as well throw away the *Larousse Gastronomique*—a peanut-butter sandwich prepared *con amore* may be just as good. Chu does a deal with the small daughter of a family friend, supplying a daily package of delicacies in exchange for her official lunch of grisly spare ribs. When he tucks into the foul meat with disbelief, he finds relief from the burden of "quality".

In his New York comedy *The Wedding Banquet*, Ang Lee proved himself a dab hand at light social farce, with an eye for ritual and its embarrassments. *Eat Drink Man Woman* benefits enormously from its sitcom factor, the fact that once it strays from its rather restrictive central metaphor, it has plenty of strands to keep you interested, and not just the noodles. There's the school intrigue between Kia-Jen and the gym teacher; the teenage romance between Jia-Ning and her best friend's guy and the subplot about fearsome Mrs Liang, back from New York and with nothing she likes more than coming round and blowing smoke in Mr Chu's face.

Conventional though it is, the most effective strand is the one about Jia-Chien, who embodies the new cosmopolitan Taiwan. Up for the big post abroad, she's embroiled with an international smoothie at the office, has inadvertently bought a flat on a toxic dumping ground, and is trying to reconcile career with love life and the pull of family tradition. The twist on western sexual conditioning is that the one thing she's never been allowed to do is cook; she gets to feed her lover surreptitiously.

As a statement about modern Taiwan, by a director grappling with his own cosmopolitanism, *Eat Drink Man Woman* displays a gentle touch and isn't quite as ambitious or complex as Edward Yang's similarly themed *A Confusian Confusion.* But it's enjoyable from start to finish, with an unashamedly feel-good ending that even cynics can relish. It isn't slop, and it isn't Joy Luck Dragon Phoenix either—nor, thank God, is it *The Joy Luck Club*—but as light, satisfying international cuisine, it goes down a treat.

NEW YORK, 8/29/94, p. 110, David Denby

In the wonderful new Ang Lee comedy, *Eat Drink Man Woman*, we're meant to be aroused by the extraordinary food—the steamed deer in a pumpkin pot, the lotus-flower soup, and all the other flamboyantly traditional Chinese dishes that lie hot, gurgling, and ready. *Eat Drink Man Woman* has the best porno-culinary sequences since *Babette's Feast*, and the food is used even more centrally than in that movie. Food as life, food as communication, food as sex. To our amazement, however, the characters pick disconsolately at the superb dishes or complain about minor flaws; they express their fears and uncertainties by not eating. Appetite and withdrawal battle it out. The movie asks, Why not join the banquet of life? The meal is never over. Yet it respects the people who hold back from the table.

This abundant yet disciplined work is a huge step forward for Lee, the Taiwanese-American director whose previous film (his second) was last year's relaxed comedy of sexual manners *The Wedding Banquet*. Lee is now working on a much grander scale. He makes his way around the prosperous, upper-middle-class life in Taipei with a shrewd, humming self-assurance; his movie is formally elaborate but lucid, handsome, and utterly accessible. Though Lee lives in New York, he obviously knows many of the actors (and chefs) worth knowing in Taipei, because the people in this movie are almost as great-looking as the food. One dish after another: the women, slender, exquisite, volatile; the men, handsome but languorous, waiting to be awakened by the women.

In form, *Eat Drink Man Woman* might be called a domestic *King Lear*. The greatest chef in Taipei, Mr. Chu (Sihung Lung), still grieving over his long-dead wife, busies himself by cooking for his three grown daughters, who live at home. Working with the two screenwriters Hui-Ling Wang and James Schamus, Ang Lee offers not the titanic family struggles of *Lear* but the routine yet mesmerizing anguish of love and romance and filial piety. Which of the daughters will leave for her own life, and which will stay at home and take care of the apparently declining father? Chu, perhaps 60, is on the verge of retirement from a posh restaurant, and like many aging, proud, and fastidious men, he has withdrawn from emotional engagement with his life. He performs his tasks with professional energy but without satisfaction. Having lost all sensation in his taste buds, he now lives for the responses of another old chef at the restaurant, a dying man.

The Sunday family banquet, which Chu has been preparing every week for years, is both a unifying ritual and an ordeal. Silently and alone, the great man properly kills and guts the animals, then, in a superbly edited sequence, gives himself over to violent bursts of dicing, chopping, ladling, broiling. By the time he serves the food, however, everyone is in too much of a funk to eat. The recurring orgies of non-eating hold the movie together: Every plot development passes through the comic family banquets, a formal device that brings order to flux. The daughters take surprising risks. The brilliant and beautiful middle daughter (Chien-Lien Wu), a fast-moving executive at an airline, devastating in a short-skirted business suit, wows the other executives with her analytic expertise. But like many smart people, she has terrible luck in those two puzzling enterprises real estate and love—she's taken in by her own shrewdness and makes awful mistakes. Unconsciously, she needles her repressed older sister (Kuei-Mei Yang), a high-school chemistry teacher whose emotional life has gone into retirement, hiding behind old memories and her Christian faith. When the teacher falls in love at last, she does so with a violence and speed that causes uproar at the banquet table.

The characters seem Western in their attitudes yet Asian in their behavior. In *The Wedding Banquet*, the geographical and emotional movement flowed from Taiwan to America, but here both things are going in reverse: People return home to Taipei, and from our point of view, they wind up with the best of both worlds. They live in an orderly society that still honors traditional forms of respect, yet there's nothing drab or limited about it. They consume Western culture (a morosely handsome boy reads Dostoevski) but without the Western restlessness and hollowness. They're still rooted.

East and West, activity and repose—everything flows together in a crisp, decisive, yet tender and liquid style. The story moves quickly, but there are pauses, rapt moments of contemplation, the traffic flowing in almost abstract patterns, the huge restaurant where Chu works glowing at night like a floating palace. The movie suggests that eternal recurrence and flux work together—a deeply conservative view, perhaps, but conservative in ways that may make even radical Americans sigh with pleasure. The young men are recruited for family duties with immense seriousness: Food must be cooked, daughters fed. Yet the plot boils over. The penultimate family banquet explodes in a messy and scandalous scene that is both a big surprise and completely logical. Life, it turns out, isn't like cooking after all. Life cannot be made by recipe. Even old Chu says so. Something greater than a perfect meal is at stake, and that is the force to continue, to carry on, which works like God in mysterious ways.

NEW YORK POST, 8/3/94, p. 33, Michael Medved

The title "Eat Drink Man Woman" is meant to invoke the two most basic elements in the survival of our species: food and sex.

There is nothing in the least bit crude or rudimentary, however, in the culinary delicacies or the delicately delineated relationships presented by this remarkably moving motion picture.

Taiwanese-American director/co-writer Ang Lee follows up his triumph with last year's much-loved (and Oscar-nominated) "The Wedding Banquet" by providing an even more lavish and satisfying feast for moviegoers.

His central character here is played by Sihung Lung, who was so memorable in "The Wedding Banquet" as the aristocratic Taiwanese general visiting his gay son in New York City.

Here Lung plays a different sort of unbending authority figure: a commander of the kitchen who has devoted his life to preserving age-old culinary arts as one of Taiwan's leading chefs.

Even though he is officially retired, this gruff widower spends most of his time preparing elaborate Sunday dinners as a means of expressing his love for his three beautiful daughters.

The scenes showing him cooking these meals are utterly spell-binding—even more hypnotically fascinating than similar sequences in "Like Water for Chocolate" or "Babette's Feast"—but they will also provide encouragement for all vegetarians with their depiction of the handling of various fish and fowl.

The problem for Sihung Lung's deeply sympathetic character is that he can't handle his daughters as efficiently as he takes care of Chi-Ling Fish or Lotus Flower Soup.

One of them (Kuei-Mei Yang) is a lonely high school teacher and passionately devout Christian, who is still recovering from a disastrous college romance. Another (the spectacularly lovely Chien-Lien Wu) is a hard-driving, yuppie airline executive who is secretly planning to leave her father's home and move to Europe.

The youngest (Yu-Wen Wang) is a ditzy romantic who is only occasionally distracted from her active social life to spend time on her studies at school.

Director Ang Lee makes us feel the father's ferocious love for each of his girls—at the same time we can understand his difficulty in showing it.

The plot contains numerous surprises involving all three daughters as well as the family patriarch—not to mention a chain-smoking widow with designs on the retired chef and an amorous (but married) airline efficiency expert (played by Ah-Leh Gua and Winston Chao, respectively, both of whom also played leading roles in "The Wedding Banquet").

Even the most minor characters in "Eat Drink Man Woman" emerge with passion and persuasiveness; no movie this year has boasted a more accomplished ensemble cast.

The exotic flavors in this cinematic repast include salty wit, sweet romance, sour melancholy, bittersweet remorse and joyous, tangy surprise.

Ang Lee has created another sure-thing Oscar nominee, and his glamorous star, Chien-Lien Wu, unquestionably deserves a nomination as best actress. Her heart-breakingly vivid and complex performance as a woman torn between career, filial duty and romantic yearning is easily the finest work by an actress I've seen so far this year.

"Eat Drink Man Woman" is, in other words, delicious. You come away from the film with a ravenous appetite for good food—and for life.

NEWSDAY, 8/3/94, Part II/p. B9, John Anderson

Lotus flower soup. Chi-Ling Fish. Chin-Hua Chicken. Glistening bass, hissing peppers, steaming buns, sculpted melons and voluptuous dumplings. Yes, it's hard sometimes to tell where sex stops and food begins in Ang Lee's "Eat Drink Man Woman." But any theater owner who replaces the popcorn with dim sum will make a killing.

As the title implies, life has two basic drives and sometimes they blend. In the kitchen, and world, of master chef Tao Chu (veteran actor Sihung Lung, the father in Lee's 'Wedding Banquet'), food is all. A seemingly lonely widower and father of three maturing and conflicted daughters, Chu is an artist—steaming, frying, baking, basting, wokking, not talking, and rendering as sumptuous a meal as has ever hit the screen ("Babette's Feast" included). While it's been written that the creation of art has never been satisfactorily portrayed on film, what we feel when one of Chu's meals is ready seems visceral enough to me.

Incredibly, everything he's prepared is for a single Sunday dinner, a weekly ritual at which we meet his daughters: Jia-Jen (Kuei-Mei Yang), the "old maid" professor who's been nursing a broken heart for nine years; Jia-Chien (Chien-Lien Wu), the sexually liberal airline executive who announces at dinner that she's finally leaving home, and the youngest, Jia-Ning (Yu-Wen Wang), a student and full-time romantic.

Director Lee instructs in classically simple morality, and one of his basic laws is the vast human capacity for dissatisfaction. While the viewer may be drooling, the three daughters, having had thousands like it, immediately criticize Chu's meal; the ham, for instance, is too salty. But this is no "King Lear." If anything, the struggle at the table is about expressing the love they all feel for each other, while coping with distinct but similar problems of life and love.

Structured like a meal itself, "Eat Drink Man Woman" begins with appetizers—a sparkling montage of kitchen, office, church, bed and then a return to the kitchen. What this all means isn't yet clear, but it's captivating, because of the freshness of Lee's eye and his gift for visual storytelling.

When Chu is called away from dinner to solve a crisis at his hotel kitchen, the scene plays out with all the high drama of an emergency room: the chef/surgeon being helped on with his white coat, assessing the situation, making split-second culinary decisions and bringing a dinner for hundreds back from the brink of death. It's an electric bit of filmmaking, but also an integral part of the movie's dual themes: the importance of a life's work, and how one directs his or her finite capacity for passion.

Even when mottled by Lee's omnipresent shadows, the pictures Lee creates keep the viewer enthralled, especially when the story itself bogs down in soap bubbles: Jia-Chien, for instance, wrestling with the guilt she feels about leaving not just her father, but her older sister, who apparently hasn't had sex since being dumped in college. Jia-Chien, meanwhile, is falling in love with the handsome executive Li Kai (Winston Chao, the son in "The Wedding Banquet"), while the older Jia-Jen has her eye on Ming-Dao (Chin-Cheng Lu), her school's goofy volleyball coach. At the same time, the youngest sister Jia-Ning is sabotaging her best friend's romance with Guo Lun (Chao-Jung Chen). And Chu—who is so attentive to his neighbor Jin Rong (noted Taiwanese actress Sylvia Chang) and her daughter Shan-Shan (Yu-Chien Tang)—is being matched up by everyone with Jin Rong's abrasive mother Mrs. Liang (Ah-Leh Gua). Chu has other ideas.

Whew. Co-writer and producer James Schamus, who also helped script "The Wedding Banquet," has said that in his mind, the characters in "Eat Drink" are Jewish. This may be true, but their story is also Shakespearean. As in several of the Bard's comedies ("A Midsummer Night's Dream" in particular), closure comes when all the lovers find their proper mates, none of whom were matched up at the beginning of the play. That the same thing happens in "Hannah and Her Sisters" probably means that we're both right. And it may help explain the universal appeal of Ang Lee.

NEWSWEEK, 8/22/94, p. 62, Jack Kroll

A worldwide feeding frenzy seems to have overtaken the movie business. We've had "Fried Green Tomatoes" (U.S.A.), "Like Water for Chocolate" (Mexico), "The Scent of Green Papaya" (Vietnam), "Babette's Feast" (Denmark) and others from all hemispheres. This cinematic food fetishism is either a sign of some deep spiritual hunger or a conspiracy by a global grub cartel (Oliver Stone, are you listening?) Now we have "Eat Drink Man Woman," which is as basic as a movie title can get. This charming movie by the rising Taiwanese-American director Ang Lee uses food as a metaphor for the primal human connections of family and love. Lee's last film, "The Wedding Banquet," had a similar theme: it was also the most profitable film of 1993, beating "Jurassic Park," based on cost-to-earnings ratio ("Wedding Banquet" was made for $1 million and earned $30 million).

"Eat Drink Man Woman" opens with a whiz-bang montage sequence of a cook preparing a lavish meal: it's the culinary counterpart of an action sequence as he slices, spices, dices, steams and sizzles, executes a chicken, and inflates a duck with frenetic precision. He's Mr. Chu, the foremost chef in Taipei, making the regular Sunday dinner for his three daughters. The irony is that Chu has lost his taste buds. This is Lee's metaphor for the erosion of tradition and rituals in modern Taiwan. The Sunday dinners are no fun for Chu, a widower, or his daughters, who have so many problems they barely touch their Lotus Flower soup.

Jia-Jen, the oldest, is a schoolteacher whose pupils make fun of her as an old maid. Jia-Ning, the youngest, works in an American-type fast-food restaurant, a stir-fried symbol if there ever was one. Jia-Chien, the middle sister, is an airline executive and a frustrated chef herself who is a severe critic of her father's cuisine. Meanwhile other appetites boil up as the three young women get into various romantic entanglements. Old Chu himself investigates recipes for foods designed to stimulate the sexual function.

Things work out, with some clever twists, as they should in a savory soup opera. The screenplay, by Lee, Taiwanese writer Hui-Ling Wang and the American James Schamus, is something of a multicultural feat. In an introduction to the published script Schamus tells how Lee complained that the characters' psychology wasn't Chinese enough. Schamus gave up and wrote the scenes as Jewish as he could make them. "Ah ha," said Lee reading the new scenes. "Very Chinese!" What the movie is is very human, especially in the appealing actors, notably Sihung Lung as Chu and the stunningly beautiful Chien-Lien Wu as Jia-Chien. If Ang Lee sometimes piles on the sugar, he has made a truly sweet movie in a bitter time. It leaves a bracing aftertaste.

SIGHT AND SOUND, 1/95, p. 63, Lizzie Francke

Taipei. Master chef Mr. Chu has raised three daughters on his own. They live with him even though they are now adult. The youngest, Jia-Ning, is a student who also works part-time at a fast food restaurant; school-teacher Jia-Jen is a recent convert to Christianity; and Jia-Chien is an airline executive. Each night, Chu cooks elaborate meals for them which he cannot enjoy, as his sense of taste has disappeared.

Jia-Chien announces that she is moving out to her own apartment. Mr Chu visits his brother and fellow chef Wen at their restaurant. Jia-Jen's old friend and neighbour Jin-Rong — who has a small daughter, Rachel—is getting divorced and her mother Mrs Liang is coming to stay. Chu meets Rachel while out jogging and promises to prepare her daily meals. Jia-Ning takes a shine to Guo Lun, a friend's neglected boyfriend. Jia-Chien is attracted to Li Kai, a new recruit at her company.

Jia-Chien learns that she is up for promotion to work in Amsterdam. Chu visits Wen and gives him a new sauce to try, but Wen has a seizure and is taken to hospital. Jia-Ming goes out on a date with Guo Lun. Jia-Chien finds out the real estate company that she bought her apartment from was trading fraudulently. Jin-Rong and Mrs Liang visit Chu and his family. At school, Jia-Jen—still getting over a heartbreak years earlier—is receiving anonymous love letters, but is also asked out on a date by Ming-Dao, the school's new sports coach. Jia-Chen and Li Kai also go out together.

One evening, Jia-Ning announces that she is pregnant and will be moving out to live with Guo Lun. Chu can hardly say good-bye. Later he visits Mrs Liang. Jia-Chien and Li Kai seem to be getting it together, but then she starts suspecting that he might be the man who broke her sister's heart nine years ago; however, it turns out that Jia-Jen invented the story. Meanwhile, Wen returns to work only to collapse and die.

At school, Jia-Jen makes a public announcement about the love letters and discovers that some pupils have been sending them; she is comforted by Ming-Dao. Jia-Chien visits her occasional lover, Raymond, and learns that he is getting married. She turns down the job promotion. Later, at the family meal, Jia-Jen announces that she and Ming-Dao have married. Only Jia-Chien now remains at home with Chu. At a family get-together, Chu announces that he is marrying Jin-Rong and is going to sell the family home. Months later, Jia-Chien is settled in the family home. Chu, now expecting a child by Jin-Rong, visits for a meal, and finds his sense of taste restored.

"Eat, drink, man, woman, food, sex —the basics of life," so declares Mr Chu. Ang Lee's second film follows *The Wedding Banquet* in arguing that the simple ingredients of life are not always a given in contemporary society. Shots of traffic-ridden Taipei are a recurring motif, indicating the modernising and westernising of a culture. Lee gently develops and ironically underpins this contrast with tradition. Jia-Ning works part time at a fast-food restaurant, yet goes home to her father's ample meals each night. Jet-setting Jia-Chien's plans to buy a New York-style apartment are destroyed by fraud. Jia-Jen, the Baptist convert, listens to choral music on a Walkman. Lee highlights such cultural juxtapositions and elucidates their impact on tradition within the family. However, the 'Man, Woman' part of Mr Chu's equation proves not to be so simple. Just as the parents in *The Wedding Banquet* must learn to accept that their son is gay, the widower Mr Chu has to acknowledge that his career-minded daughters will not jump to perpetuate the family line.

But these generational differences are not all that separates Chu from his children. Like every fairy story that starts "Once upon a time, there was a king with three daughters", *Eat Drink Man Woman* is rooted in parental anxieties. Apart from her portrait hanging in the dining room, the deceased mother is a conspicuous absence. Chu himself is set awkwardly apart from his female progeny. In doing their laundry, he lumps together all their underwear. When he knocks on their bedroom doors each morning, he seems almost frightened to go in. Such events stand for his general unease with their sexuality. In this respect, his surprise marriage to Jin-Rong, his eldest daughter's oldest friend, seems almost taboo-breaking — the repressed erupting in a most revealing manner.

Affection is displayed in the fetishistically lavish feasts that Chu prepares for his daughters (the recipes for which he writes down, as if to inscribe them in law), but even this culinary currency is devalued. Chu's loss of his sense of taste is matched by his daughters' lack of appetite. Thus the plumping of glistening dumplings, the filleting of succulent fish and the sizzling of crisp vegetables—all brilliantly choreographed as a frenzied musical cum action spectacle — becomes empty ritual, a literal flash in the pan. The film hints at the relationship that the cinema audience might have to such a delectable but flavourless and odourless sight. The vision of food being prepared provides the *mise en scène* of desire deferred. But without the actual satisfaction of our noses and palates, we are put in the same position as Chu.

It is the emotional release at the end which neatly ties together the film's disparate strands. With Jin-Chien — who earlier demanded to know why a woman could not be considered a real chef — now installed in the family home and kitchen, the film modulates its mood from the comic to the pensive and emotional. It's as if a magic spell has been broken, Chu finds his sense of taste and smell restored by her cooking, signifying a moment of reconciliation between the two. Less mouth- than eye-watering, the scene makes manifest the various needs that bind a family by setting a mother back at the heart of it.

TIME, 8/15/94, p. 61, Richard Schickel

The year's best action sequence? Easy. It's Mr. Chu (Sihung Lung), a master chef, slicing, dicing, chopping, boiling, broiling, steaming the ingredients of the dinner he prepares every Sunday for his three not entirely grateful daughters. It's the culinary arts rendered as thrillingly as the martial arts, with a middle-age Taiwanese cook appearing as deft and graceful in his peaceful trade as Bruce Lee ever was in his more violent one.

Eat Drink Man Woman presents Mr. Chu's morality as simple—feed the body artfully, and the soul will take care of itself—but the chef is not without cunning outside the kitchen. His children are not aware of that, nor can they see that his meals are metaphors for love; they see them as a form of torture added to their other torments. The eldest, Jia-Jen (Kuei-Mei Yang), is a spinster schoolteacher, pining for a lost love but beginning to moon over the cute new gym teacher. The youngest, Jia-Ning (Yu-Wen Wang), is rebelling by working in a fast-food restaurant and taking a lover who reads Dostoyevsky and rides a motorcycle. In the middle is Jia-Chien (Chien-Lien Wu), interrupting her yuppie bustle for liaisons that can't go anywhere.

As things work out in this comfortably intricate comedy by Ang Lee (who directed last year's *The Wedding Banquet*), their father, despite his obsession with food, does better than any of them romantically. This is perhaps because cooking at his level has taught him to blend the practical, paradoxical gifts of calculation and improvisation, while his children are—until they finally right themselves—befuddled by abstractions and distractions. Like the cuisine it celebrates, this movie is tart, sweet, generous and subtle.

VILLAGE VOICE, 8/9/94, p. 44, Georgia Brown

Just as Hollywood relies on formulae and pet ingredients (mad bombers, holy fools), so do art movies, and it's no secret that right now food is in. During the past year we've been treated (pictorially) to a variety of national cuisines: Laura Esquivel and Alfonso Arau's sumptuous *Like Water For Chocolate* jumps to mind; there were also the delicate Vietnamese concoctions in Tran Anh Hung's *The Scent of Green Papayas*, and, in my favorite indie, Nancy Savoca and Francine Prose's *Household Saints*, an extended treatise on sausage and peppers. Last year's most profitable movie, Ang Lee's *The Wedding Banquet*, while not quite living up, gustatory-wise, to its title, probably fits the category as well.

Hard on the heels of this recent success, Lee now follows up with *Eat Drink Man Woman*, a film that raises the culinary motif almost to the level of parody. Bring Maalox. You won't believe the sheer quantity of steaming platters. Apparently, the production employed three top chefs full-time. The problem, though, is that for all the tasty scenery, the characters barely touch the stuff. A movable feast is laid out with no appetite to match.

Someone recently told me that in 1941 when Marcel Carné was making *Les Visiteurs du soir*, he ordered his chefs to lace the set's food with strychnine so it wouldn't disappear before the camera could capture it. Desperate times, despotic remedies. Think, if an actor got too much into his role and took a bite, Well, for all the onscreen munching you see in *Eat Drink Man Woman*, you'd think that all these picture-perfect platters were poisoned, too.

The cook in Lee's story is Mr. Chu (Sihung Lung, who played the groom's father in *The Wedding Banquet*), father to two grown daughters and one who is nearly grown. Each night, and especially on Sundays, Mr. Chu prepares the girls a gigantic feast. The movie opens with his elaborate, time-consuming preparations. Then, finally, to table, where the three daughters merely push the food around their plates. The most svelte, Jai-Chien (Chien-Lien Wu), makes a face: "The ham is oversmoked," she offers. Like Dad, she's a born cook, or food critic. Mr. Chu himself has lost his taste buds.

Midway through the meal, Mr. Chu, Taipei's number one chef, rushes off to the city's palatial hotel where he's been called to solve a crisis. (He enters the vast series of kitchens the way Ray Liotta enters the Copa in *Goodfellas*.) At the hotel, Mr. Chu works wonders, but back home his cooking casts a pall. Marking the end of another morose meal, his daughters bicker and shovel the copious remains into Tupperware.

I suppose it would have been too obvious to depict a father who cooks so sumptuously that his daughters cannot bear to leave his table. But it would have made more sense. In this case the father's talent seems, pardon the expression, a red herring. What's it doing there? You begin wondering if all this chopping and dicing isn't visual filler—or a cynical imitation of a tried and true recipe. In *Like Water For Chocolate*, all those robust dishes had a sensual connection to the heroine's character and destiny; here the food seems merely for looks.

Cutting between the four family members' daily rounds, Lee efficiently lays out the not exactly riveting issues: Pop is ready for a new life but can't say so; sexually-repressed-schoolteacher daughter is ripe as well; overly-controlled-exec daughter needs to reorder priorities; last but not least, overlooked-youngest starts up a promising flirtation. All the while, no one communicates with any one else in the house. The usual. With each sister following the blueprint for a type, the movie asks expected questions, Who will marry? Who will leave? And with whom? Lee and his two cowriters, James Schamus and Hui-Ling Wang, prepare a few surprises, but predictable ones.

Like the immensely popular *Wedding Banquet* (*Eat Eat Man Man*), *Eat Drink Man Woman* is a smooth, genial soap opera, but it lacks the former's serious message. In the end, I admit to finding it edifying to watch a soap situated in another culture: we see how they live—what they sit on, what they wear to bed at night, what their supermarkets stock. The answer (I might have known!): As the world turns here, it turns there, too.

Also reviewed in:
CHICAGO TRIBUNE, 8/19/94, Friday/p. J, Michael Wilmington
NEW REPUBLIC, 9/5/94, p. 36, Stanley Kauffmann
NEW YORK TIMES, 8/3/94, p. C16, Janet Maslin
VARIETY, 5/23-29/94, p. 57, Leonard Klady
WASHINGTON POST, 8/19/94, p. G1, Hal Hinson
WASHINGTON POST, 8/19/94, Weekend/p. 42, Desson Howe

ED WOOD

A Touchstone Pictures release. *Executive Producer:* Michael Lehmann. *Producer:* Denise Di Novi and Tim Burton. *Director:* Tim Burton. *Screenplay:* Scott Alexander and Larry Karaszewski. *Based on the Book "Nightmare of Ecstasy" by:* Rudolph Grey. *Director of Photography:* Stefan Czapsky. *Editor:* Chris Lebenzon. *Music:* Howard Shore. *Music Editor:* Ellen Segal. *Sound:* Edward Tise and (music) John Kurlander and Keith Grant. *Sound Editor:* John Nutt. *Casting:* Victoria Thomas. *Production Designer:* Tom Duffield. *Art Director:* Okowita. *Set Designer:* Chris Nushawg and Bruce Hill. *Set Decorator:* Cricket Rowland. *Set Dresser:* Erik Polczwartek. *Special Effects:* Howard Jensen. *Costumes:* Colleen Atwood.

Make-up: Ve Neill. *Bela Lugosi Make-up Design:* Rick Baker. *Stunt Coordinator:* John Branagan. *Running time:* 120 minutes. *MPAA Rating:* R.

CAST: Johnny Depp (Ed Wood); Martin Landau (Bela Lugosi); Sarah Jessica Parker (Dolores Fuller); Patricia Arquette (Kathy O'Hara); Jeffrey Jones (Criswell); G.D. Spradlin (Reverend Lemon); Vincent C'Onofrio (Orson Welles); Bill Murray (Bunny Breckinridge); Mike Starr (Georgie Weiss); Max Casella (Paul Marco); Brent Hinkley (Conrad Brooks); Lisa Marie (Vampira); George "The Animal" Steele (Tor Johnson); Juliet Landau (Loretta King); Clive Rosengren (Ed Reynolds); Norman Alden (Cameraman Bill); Leonard Termo (Makeup Man Harry); Ned Bellamy (Dr. Tom Mason); Danny Dayton (Soundman); John Ross (Camera Assistant); Bill Cusack (Tony McCoy); Aaron Nelms (Teenage Kid); Biff Yeager (Rude Boss); Joseph R. Gannascoli (Security Guard); Carmen Filpi (Old Crusty Man); Lisa Malkiewicz (Secretary #1); Melora Walters (Secretary #2); Conrad Brooks (Bartender); Don Amendolia (Salesman); Tommy Bertelsen (Tough Boy); Reid Cruickshanks (Stage Guard); Stanley Desantis (Mr. Feldman); Lionel Decker (Executive #1); Edmund L. Shaff (Executive #2); Gene LeBell (Ring Announcer); Jesse Hernandez (Wrestling Opponent); Bobby Slayton (TV Show Host); Gretchen Becker (TV Host's Assistant); John Rice (Conservative Man); Catherine Butterfield (Conservative Wife); Mary Portser (Backer's Wife); King Cotton (Hick Backer); Don Hood (Southern Backer); Frank Echols (Doorman); Matthew Barry (Valet); Ralph Monaco (Waiter); Anthony Russell (Busboy); Tommy Bush (Stage Manager); Gregory Walcott (Potential Backer); Charles C. Stevenson, Jr. (Another Backer); Rance Howard (Old Man McCoy); Vasek C. Simek (Professor Strowski); Alan Martin (Vampira's Assistant); Salwa Ali (Vampira's Girlfriend); Rodney Kizziah (Vampira's Friend); Korla Pandit (Indian Musician); Hannah Eckstein (Greta Johnson); Luc De Schepper (Karl Johnson); Vinny Argiro (TV Horror Show Director); Patti Tippo (Nurse); Ray Baker (Doctor); Louis Lombardi (Rental House Manager); James Reid Boyce (Theatre Manager); Ben Ryan Ganger (Angry Kid); Ryan Holihan (Frantic Usher); Marc Revivo (High School Punk); Charlie Holliday (Tourist); Adam Drescher (Photographer #1); Ric Mancini (Photographer #2); Daniel Riordan (Pilot/Strapping Young Man); Mickey Cottrell (Hammy Alien); Christopher George Simpson (Organist).

FILMS IN REVIEW, 1-2/95, p. 60, Kevin Lewis

A few miles away from where Norma Desmond was writing her comeback movie with Joe Gillis in *Sunset Boulevard*, Edward D. Wood, Jr. was using Bela Lugosi to create his "place in the Hollywood sun." Though Billy Wilder created the ultimate movie about broken Hollywood dreams in that fictional drama, director Tim Burton and screenwriters Scott Alexander and Larry Karaszewski achieve a worthy companion piece in the real (or should we say reel) life drama *Ed Wood*.

Like that landmark movie, *Ed Wood* (a Touchstone release) shows what happens to an icon when nobody wants it anymore, and what an outsider will do to achieve his or her own immortality. Edward D. Wood, Jr. was a striving, artistically ambitious but untalented film and stage director in Los Angeles in the early 1950's. Wood's artistic vision consisted of the rag ends of American post-World War II pop culture. He was a devotee of sci-fi comic books and horror movies, and was obsessed with women's clothing, especially angora sweaters. In these interests, he almost represents a sexual and cultural pioneer for the '90s, but back in the conformist '50s he was definitely regarded as a fringe lunatic. His linkup with Bela Lugosi, the legendary screen Dracula but by then discarded Hollywood figure, sealed his ticket to the bad cinema pantheon. The drug addict Lugosi, unable to be hired by the major studios, was forced to parade himself in Wood's transvestite and horror nightmares.

Burton, Alexander and Karaszewski, who based their film on *Nightmare Of Ecstasy: The Life And Art of Edward D. Wood, Jr.* by Rudolph Grey, have brilliantly re-created a significant but largely undiscussed period in American life. The 1950's are remembered as the time of conformity, but it was also the era when the counterculture movement was emerging (a la Kerouac, Ginsberg, Pollack, Marcuse) and when sexual neurosis was overtaking American society even in the suburbs. The civil and sexual rights movements were in the grassroots stages at this time. *Ed Wood* is an artistic triumph because it replicates the tone, look and emotions of the cultural players of that time without creating a false hindsight sensibility. The freakish actors in Wood's films all represent forces which are now part of our collective psyche: Vampira, Criswell, Bunny Breckinridge, Dolores Fuller, and of course Lugosi. The superb black-and-white high contrast cinematography of Stefan Czapasky achieves the look of the documentary and avant garde films of the era.

As Wood, Johnny Depp is magnificent in a role which could be a caricature. He is sly, endearing and an ingenious Horatio Alger folk figure as the director scratching his way along the Hollywood bottom. Wood had no shame in his life and business dealings, and Depp makes Wood a likeable and even sexually fascinating character.

Martin Landau is unforgettable as the down-on-his luck middle European Lugosi and should receive the additional acclaim due this distinguished actor. He creates sympathy for an outcast character in brilliant pantomime scenes with his rich old theatrical voice.

Sarah Jessica Parker as actress Dolores Fuller, the confused girlfriend of Wood, Jeffrey Jones as the TV seer Criswell, Lisa Marie as the pioneer TV horror queen Vampira, Bill Murray as the wannabe woman Bunny Breckinridge and Rosanna Arquette as the gentle, accepting love of Wood's life give notable performances.

Ed Wood is one of the best conceived, most entertaining movies in many a year and should create a cult as potent as Wood's Freudian horrors. Though Wood, a true artistic primitive, was voted the Worst Director of Ail Time, Tim Burton may become one of our finest.

FILMS IN REVIEW, 9-10/95, p. 55, Peter N. Chuma II

Films about Hollywood filmmaking tend to fall into two general categories. Movies like *Sunset Boulevard* take a dark look at the Hollywood system, while others like *Singin' In The Rain* celebrate with great joy and energy the moviemaking process. Tim Burton's *Ed Wood* straddles the thin line between these two approaches as it tells the story of the real-life 1950's filmmaker often considered the worst director ever.

Ed Wood has achieved cult status in the past few years for the sheer ineptitude of his filmmaking, which is so bad it can be enjoyed for its amateurish acting, bad writing and overall cheap production values. Tim Burton, however, finds a kind of transcendence in Ed Wood's (Johnny Depp) indomitable spirit, his ability to remain optimistic and even excited about the very act of filmmaking itself.

The film follows Wood's career in the 1950's and the making of his three most famous films, *Glen or Glenda* (Wood's highly personal plea for understanding of transvestites), *Bride of the Monster* and *Plan 9 From Outer Space*. Throughout his struggles, Wood demonstrates an enthusiasm for filmmaking and his fierce determination to overcome all obstacles and get his stories on the screen.

At the heart of the film is the friendship between Wood and Bela Lugosi (brilliantly played by Martin Landau), an honest cross-generational relationship between two men so rare in movies today. At first Lugosi is a figure who legitimizes Wood's career, such that it is. As old and forgotten as Lugosi may be, a stark reminder of Hollywood's tendency to use people up and then discard them, he is a linkage to the Old Hollywood that Wood idolizes. He is in fact a kind of Norma Desmond figure, a relic from the past always presumed dead and thrilled to be given a second chance in movies. However, he lacks Norma's insane desire for a return to the movies—he is simply honored that Ed wants to work with him.

When he first meets him, Wood shows him all the respect a fan would have for his idol, but they soon develop a very personal, quite moving relationship as Wood not only helps Lugosi through the trauma of his morphine addiction but also gives him his final triumphs in front of the camera. One speech in particular that Wood writes for *Bride of the Monster* even has a Shakespearean majesty that lets Lugosi merge his real life status as a Hollywood has-been with the ludicrous mad scientist he plays: "Home—I have no home. Hunted. Despised. Living like an animal. The jungle is my home. But I shall show the world that I can be its master." It is nothing short of a tribute to the cockeyed grandeur that can come from B-movie trash.

The emotional core of the film is the Wood-Lugosi relationship, but the actual work of filmmaking is the most important thing to Wood himself. It drives him beyond all reason to keep plugging away. Despite ail his struggles to obtain financing and keep working in Hollywood (even at the margins), Ed Wood makes filmmaking a kind of party, an activity in which a small troupe of outcasts that includes a Swedish wrestler and a TV psychic can band together to put Ed's weird science fiction concoctions on the screen.

The scenes of actual filmmaking are among the funniest since Gene Kelly and Jean Hagan struggled with microphone placement in *Singin' In The Rain*. Where that film, though, depicted people trying to overcome the obstacles to making a decent film, *Ed Wood* celebrates the sheer joy of filmmaking without any regard to quality. Instead of struggling to get the scenes just right, Wood characteristically declares every shot "perfect" (no matter how bad it is) and cheerfully moves on to the next.

Burton suggests the making of these B-movie curiosities is ultimately a redemptive act, and when the film presents a kind of mythical meeting between Orson Welles (Wood's hero to whom he compares himself since they both act, write, direct and produce) and Wood, it is a tribute to Hollywood itself, a vision in which the best and the worst can both participate in the crazy world of moviemaking. Welles's encouragement, "Visions are worth fighting for," actually spurs Ed in his making of *Plan 9 From Outer Space*, often dubbed the worst film of all time. As ludicrous as the pairing may be, the film makes clear that Wood was not a hack but a man, like Welles, truly dedicated to filmmaking and to his own personal vision.

There are many filmic representations of the director as a tortured and tormented artist (think of Fellini's *8½*). Burton presents a different view of the movie director: a jolly optimist in love with the movies and thrilled every time the cameras roll to put his "visions" on the screen.

LOS ANGELES TIMES, 9/28/94, Calendar/p. 1, Kenneth Turan

Though most Americans manage to shuffle through their lives without having heard of him, to a devoted few (a very few) the name of Edward D. Wood Jr. is worthy of veneration.

A 1950s filmmaker of such unstoppable ineptitude that people who ponder extremes consider him the worst director ever ("Glen or Glenda," "Plan 9 From Outer Space"), Ed Wood had a strange personality and a startling lack of talent that turned him into a cult figure for those fascinated by the *outre* and aberrational.

There is, for instance, a loving biography called "Nightmare of Ecstasy," whose author scorns Wood's critics as "jackals of bourgeois sensibility"; a set of 36 trading cards with realistic portraits of him and his cohorts, even a video on his life, "Ed Wood: , Look Back in Angora," the title referring to the director's trademark fetish for women's angora sweaters.

The strangest chapter of Wood's singular life, however, is still being written. Director Tim Burton, no slouch himself when it comes to the bizarre ("Beetlejuice" and the "Batman" films), has just spent $25 million to celebrate in loving detail the story of a cross-dressing *cineaste* for whom $25,000 was a top-of-the-line budget.

Even more unexpectedly, the black-and-white "Ed Wood" turns out to be a thoroughly entertaining if eccentric piece of business, wacky and amusing in a cheerfully preposterous way. Anchored by a tasty, full-throttle performance by Martin Landau as Bela Lugosi, "Ed Wood" is a fantasy for the terminally disaffected, proof for those who want it that an absence of convention and even talent need not be a bar to happiness or immortality.

An additional component of "Ed Wood's" cracked charm is that it realizes how its hero and his beyond-the-fringe cohorts are simply a reduction way past absurdity of the classic Hollywood story. As one of the film's executives put it, "What if someone had the drive and ego of Orson Welles and none of the talent?" What indeed.

Though the original idea was not his, Burton was captivated by the clever Scott Alexander & Larry Karaszewski script. He was especially taken by its notion, similar to his own "Edward Scissorhands," that Wood (played by "Edward" star Johnny Depp) was an almost holy innocent, an unnaturally optimistic Pollyanna who thought that being a director was a wow beyond words.

"Wow" turns out to be one of Wood's favorite expressions, along with wonderful and similar terms of enthusiasm. So what if his play, "The Casual Company," is showing to just about nobody as the film opens, or if his actress girlfriend Dolores Fuller (Sarah Jessica Parker) keeps wondering why her angora sweaters are so stretched out. "We're all doing great work" is Wood's mantra, and he sees no reason to let reality change his mind.

This blithe spiritedness in the face of frequent disasters is the touchstone of Wood's character. And though Depp captures the gee-whiz-kid quality of a man who smiles winningly while relating that he wore women's underwear as a parachuting World War II marine, he is probably too hellaciously cheerful to support a feature by himself. That's not necessary, though, because Wood soon stumbles upon one of his idols, the great horror actor Bela Lugosi. Trying out a coffin.

No, the star of "Dracula," isn't dead yet, just terminally cranky about being forgotten by the business he was once big in. Arrogant, blasphemous (which the real Lugosi apparently wasn't) and addicted to morphine with a Demerol chaser, Lugosi gives Landau the opportunity for a wonderfully rousing yet poignant performance and gives "Ed Wood" the kind of passionate energy Burton films have been known to lack.

The real Lugosi was an opportunity for Wood, too, who used the actor's name to help finance skimpily budgeted four-day wonders, a process that "Ed Wood" relates in tongue-in-cheek detail. The films range in madness from "Glen or Glenda," about a regular guy who (surprise) likes to wear his girlfriend's angora sweaters, to the legendarily inept science fiction "Plan 9," which, as Wood himself predicts, is "the one I'll be remembered for."

These films starred more than Lugosi, for Wood had almost a radar for has-beens and never-weres wayward enough for Nathanael West. With friends and stars like Tor Johnson (George "The Animal" Steele), a professional wrestler who could barely grunt English, and Criswell (Jeffrey Jones), a suave psychic who specialized in end of the world predictions, it's no wonder that Wood's girlfriend Fuller ends up screaming "I need a normal life."

With these roles and others, including Bill Murray as one of "Plan 9's" stars and Patricia Arquette as a more understanding woman, this film has been cast with an eye toward physical resemblance. And its beautifully stylized black and white look, masterminded by cinematographer Stefan Czapsky, production designer Tom Duffield and art director Okowita, has exactly duplicated the details of Wood's more celebrated films, though, in an irony he would have appreciated, it has cost a whole lot more this time around.

Undoubtedly a labor of love by a director who had a relationship with Vincent Price similar to the one Wood enjoyed with Lugosi, "Ed Wood" is a lot more enjoyable than its subject's films and also smoothly avoids dealing with the real Wood's unhappy descent into pornography, alcoholism and unrealized projects with names like "The Day the Mummies Danced" and "I Awoke Early the Day I Died." Wood died at age 54 in 1978, almost completely forgotten, a fate this sweet and goofy film insures will never happen again.

NEW YORK, 10/17/94, p. 71, David Denby

In the ironic pantheon of film-trivia schlock, the films of Edward D. Wood Jr. inhabit a special place. Such Wood movies as *Glen or Glenda* and *Plan 9 From Outer Space* are so bad that they seem to undermine the film medium altogether. For people who attend festivals of "worst films," Wood may be no more than a proud hero of terribleness, but for film intellectuals, he's almost a saint, a kind of unwitting deconstructive genius. In Wood's "high" period, which lasted only a few years in the fifties, he shot everything so quickly and sloppily that he literally disillusioned the medium. In his hands, the cinematic myths of coherent time and space dissolve, and mimesis (acting) seems a mere presumption.

What Tim Burton, the director of *Ed Wood*, sees in this hapless man is the purity of the artistic aspiration—the longing of the artist to create his own imaginative world. Ed Wood (Johnny Depp) was an obsessive without taste, an artist without art, and Burton, forgoing irony, celebrates the innocence, the energy, the perfection of ineptitude. Wood and his friends—gathering around the hulk of an ancient star, Bela Lugosi (Martin Landau)—managed to complete movies that achieved their own kind of immortality. But Ed Wood is too sweet-natured, and, almost inevitably, it betrays its peculiar subject. Johnny Depp, blandly enthusiastic, is just a pleasant guy who means no one any harm. That's Burton's little joke: Wood, who liked to dress up as a woman, had no dark side. But in that case, how interesting is he? The movie cancels itself out: The demon of Wood's terribleness has been tamed and "placed," for what we see is not Wood's movies but perfectly lighted Tim Burton scenes of some nice people fooling around in movies. Burton achieves what Wood triumphantly avoided: banality.

NEW YORK POST, 9/23/94, P. 53, Michael Medved

Tim Burton's film biography of legendary director Edward D. Wood Jr. screens tomorrow night at the prestigious New York Film Festival.

Fourteen years ago, however, Wood figured prominently in a celluloid celebration of a very different sort, when my brother Harry and I hosted thc World's Worst Film Festival at the Beacon Theater. We had already anointed Ed Wood as the Worst Director of All Time in our book "'The Golden Turkey Awards"—and some 20,000 patrons who discovered his incomparable body of work as part of our retrospective enthusiastically confirmed the validity of that choice.

Wood's films (most notably "Glen or Glenda," "Bride of the Monster" and "Plan 9 From Outer Space") offer an endearing combination of innocence, ambition and appalling ineptitude.

In this tender retelling of thc hilarious story behind these movies, Johnny Depp plays the immortal schlockmeister with a chirpy, unshakable optimism and manic energy that represent his best work as an actor; "Ed Wood" marks it welcome departure from the sad-eyed Sensitive Sam roles that Depp has played in nearly all his previous films, from "Cry Baby" to "Edward Scissorshands" to "What's Eating Gilbert Grape."

His hero here is an All-American go-getter with a few unconventional twists: a former Boy Scout and Marine Corps veteran who arrived in California in the late '40s with flamboyant dreams of cinema glory and an uncontrollable urge to dress in women's clothes. Depp, it must be said, looks far more fetching in these feminine outfits (particularly the director's signature angora sweaters) than Wood himself ever did.

The heart and soul of this movie involves Wood's friendship and collaboration with Bela Lugosi during the "Dracula" star's deluded, drug-addicted final years, and Martin Landau's magnificent performance provides this story with unexpected dignity and power.

Landau, who's now an obvious front-runner for the supporting actor Oscar he's been denied twice before, delivers much more than an electrifying impersonation; his Lugosi is a hugely satisfying blend of pathos and hilarity, madness and nobility. The movie's additional real-life characters (portrayed by Bill Murray, Sarah Jessica Parker, Jeffrey Jones and others) are solidly, if less spectacularly, handled.

The black-and-white photography is both handsome and haunting, and for once Tim Burton's predilection for eerie, expressionistic atmosphere seems fully justified by the material; "Ed Wood" provides an oddly affectionate view of the seedy, "Day of the Locust" subculture of striving wannabes that's always festered in the shadow of Tinseltown.

In fact. the film's only false move involves its own flimsy, fraudulent Hollywood ending, which ultimately undermines the integrity of this sad little tale.

Sorry, fans, but "Plan 9" never enjoyed a glamorous 1957 premiere at the Pantages Theater, and this movie's happily-ever-after romantic fade-out ignores the far more interesting pain and eccentricity of Wood's final 20 years.

Nevertheless, Burton has created a funny, cheerfully weird. curiously captivating film, and in so doing he's achieved singular irony: centering one of the best-ever big screen biographies of a filmmaker on the worst director of all time.

NEWSDAY, 9/28/94, Part II/p. B2, Jack Mathews

Ever since Harry and Michael Medved announced the results of a write-in poll in their cheeky 1980 book "The Golden Turkey Awards," Edward D. Wood Jr. the cross-dressing ex-Marine who made such '50s shlock as "Plan 9 From Outer Space" and "Glen or Glenda," has been referred to, with growing affection, as the "worst director of all time."

Now, with affection bordering on veneration, Tim Burton has resurrected the auteur d' odeur in a $20-million major studio movie, and given us an "Ed Wood" as wondrously eccentric and lovable as "Edward Scissorhands."

Shot in black and white, the riotous "Ed Wood" takes us through the director's "heydays," the decade of the '50s, beginning with his fateful meeting with has-been "Dracula" star Bela Lugosi and the making of "Glen or Glenda," and ending with Lugosi's death and the making of "Plan 9 From Outer Space."

Though its tone is relentlessly tongue-in-cheek, Burton and his marvelous cast—headed by Johnny Depp, playing Wood as a sort of Andy Hardy in drag, and Martin Landau, as the proud, decrepit and morphine-addicted Lugosi—never mock or belittle their subject. It wasn't easy making the worst movies of all time, and Burton is clearly in awe.

As we all should be. Try to imagine directing movies while wearing women's clothes during the Eisenhower years, having to scrape up budgets from soft-porn distributors, meat packers and church groups, and using casts made up of friends, lovers, wrestlers, and such fringe TV celebrities as the psychic Criswell and the monster movie hostess Vampira.

Burton makes no attempt to examine Wood's life or the psychology behind his fetish for satin panties and angora. "Ed Wood" is a mad stew of passionate obsessions—Wood's love for women's clothes, for his girlfriend Dolores (Sarah Jessica Parker) and his eventual wife, Kathy (Patricia Arquette), for his friends Lugosi and Bunny Breckinridge (Bill Murray), and, above all, for his and Burton's love for movies.

All you have to bring to the party is an appreciation for the kind of compelling optimism it would take for a man whose greatest gift was a blindness to his own incompetence to get any movie made, let alone ones that would be remembered 40 years later.

If you haven't seen "Plan 9," about an alien invasion of Hollywood, or "Glen or Glenda," an autobiographical tale in which Wood plays a heterosexual man owning up to his transvestism, "Ed Wood" will fill you in. Not just on the cheesy subject matters, but on their immense tackiness. Wood used painted paper plates for flying saucers in "Plan 9," and the best scene from "Glen or Glenda"—Wood confessing his angora fetish to his girlfriend, and her pulling off her sweater and handing it over is re-enacted in loving detail.

Most of the events depicted in "Ed Wood" actually happened, which gives its "Strike Up the Band" tone a perverse verisimilitude. You watch Wood, in his wig and sweater, directing Lugosi, the obese Swedish wrestler Tor Johnson, Criswell and Vampira knowing that it is no more bizarre than with the original cast.

There isn't a false note among all the false notes. Jeffrey Jones has to strain to be as over-the-top as the real Criswell was, and Tor Johnson could not have been stiffer and less natural on camera than George "The Animal" Steele, the retired wrestler hired to portray him. As Vampira, whose black-clad hourglass figure and bursting cleavage drew more than horror movie fans to her TV show, Lisa Marie is a perfect fit, in all respects.

The least believable character, understandably, is Wood himself. There's no precedent for such behavior and Depp overinflates him with a heightened enthusiasm that seems to intentionally evoke the mood of those MGM/Mickey Rooney musicals. But given the zaniness of the story, it's an inspired performance, the helium that holds the balloon aloft for two hours.

"Ed Wood" does have its sober side, thanks to the stunning performance of Landau, who has not only mastered the Hungarian actor's signature accent ("Be-vare! Be-vare!"), but provides dark insights into his profound loneliness, and his despair over the grave condition of his fame.

"Nobody gives two ___ for Bela," Landau says, in a moment that is both sad and funny.

Ed Wood did, and whatever we think of his movies, that was just part of his charm.

NEWSWEEK, 10/10/94, p. 71, David Ansen

Edward D. Wood Jr., a writer-director who inhabited the outermost margins of Hollywood, died in alcoholic obscurity in 1978. Soon after, he was rediscovered by connoisseurs of kitsch and semiofficially dubbed "the worst director of all time" for such grade-Z '50s epics as "Plan 9 From Outer Space" and "Glen or Glenda." The latter, a bizarre *cri de coeur*, was a plea for compassion for transvestism in which the director—a heterosexual cross-dresser with a serious angora fetish—appeared in drag as the doubly eponymous hero. The singular nuttiness of that 1953 film—far ahead of its time in content—comes from its mind-bogglingly random shifts between pseudodocumentary earnestness and gothic delirium. The passion of the film is as undeniable as its ineptitude; that potent combination gives it its distinctively unhinged Woodsy flavor.

Tim Burton's sweet, sad and very funny *Ed Wood* takes its cue from that passion. It's a valentine to the tenacious spirit of an artist who will do anything to see his vision realized on screen. But this would-be Orson Welles's vision is, unfortunately, unredeemed by talent. He pronounces every take he shoots "perfect," no matter if the acting is hopelessly rank, the special effects straight from the five and dime. It would be easy to turn Ed Wood's strange life into a condescending freak show. Instead, Burton and his screenwriters, Scott Alexander and Larry Karaszewski, reinvent Wood as a sibling of Burton's other outcast innocent heroes—he's as single-minded as Pee-wee chasing his bicycle, as unearthly as Ed Scissorhands. Johnny Depp, brimming with deluded can-do brio, plays Wood as a holy huckster, a cockeyed optimist with a "hey, kids, let's put on a show!" spirit right out of Andy Hardy. Though this is the first Burton film from a true story (based on Rudolph Grey's oral history "Nightmare of Ecstasy"), Burton's no more interested in the real world than he ever was. "Ed Wood's" Hollywood, poetically evoked in Stefan Czapsky's black-and-white images, is only slightly less a dream than "Batman's" Gotham City. But it's a giddier dream, emotionally closer to home.

The movie follows Wood through his benighted struggles to make "Glen or Glenda" and "Plan 9," stopping before his decline into booze and soft-core skinflicks. Narrative is not the point here; nor does Burton care to psychoanalyze his subject. Though most of the facts are accurate, his Ed Wood is more metaphor than man, a Pied Piper in angora who presides over the creation of an oddball alternative family made up of the most outré inhabitants of Hollywood. Wood befriended and employed Bela Lugosi (Martin Landau) when the drug-addicted horror star was down and out, and their relationship is the heart of the movie. Landau's Lugosi is a towering, touching creation—a hilarious, pathetic, imperious old pro, imprisoned by opiates and his "Dracula" persona, still gamely pursuing the limelight. It's tempting to say that Landau does Lugosi better than Lugosi.

The whole motley Wood crew is here. There's "Bunny" Breckinridge, a powdered queen who dreams of a sex-change operation, played by the wistfully funny Bill Murray. Jeffrey Jones uncannily captures the peroxided glory of fake TV seer Criswell. There's Ed's girlfriend and wooden leading lady, Dolores Fuller (Sarah Jessica Parker, a vision of blond cheesiness), and Kathy. Wood's wife, played with whispery delicacy by Patrica Arquette.

There's cranky late-night tube ghoul Vampira (Lisa Marie), the hulking wrestler turned actor Tor Johnson (George "The Animal" Steele) and "Bride of the Monster" star Loretta King (Juliet Landau, Martin's daughter), who gets the part when she invests all her savings in the venture.

At the end, "Ed Wood" lifts off into fantasy: there's an encounter with Orson Welles (eerily caught by Vincent D'Onofrio), and "Plan 9" gets a triumphant premiere at the Pantages Theatre, where Wood is granted a cinematic apotheosis in life that he got, backhandedly, only in death. Now he's honored with this movie, a crazily entertaining celebration of his hapless career made with an artfulness he could only dream of possessing. The dizzy ironies of it all would have blown his already twisted mind.

SIGHT AND SOUND, 5/95, p. 44, Kim Newman

Hollywood, 1951, Edward D. Wood Jnr, a studio flunkey with ambitions to be a writer-director-star, stages an unsuccessful play starring his girlfriend Dolores Fuller. Learning that producer George Weiss plans a film about Christine Jorgensen, Ed pitches to direct *I Changed My Sex*, claiming to be qualified because, like Jorgensen, he is a transvestite and can persuade the washed-up Bela Lugosi to appear in the film. Ed uses his script to reveal his fetish for angora sweaters to Dolores, who is shocked but agrees to appear in the film in a role based on herself.

When the retitled *Glen or Glenda* fails to land him a Studio contract, Ed tries to run up finance for a horror film, *Bride of the Atom*, to star Bela, Dolores and wrestler Tor Johnson. Ed casts Loretta King, an actress he meets in a bar in Dolores' role because she appears to offer to invest $60,000. It turns out that Loretta only has $300, forcing Ed to raise the money from a meat packer who insists his son is cast as the hero. When the retitled *Bride of the Monster* opens, Dolores walks out. Ed persuades Bela to admit himself to hospital to be treated for morphine addiction. There he meets Kathy O'Hara, who falls in love with him though he admits to his transvestism. Bela leaves hospital and Ed shoots footage with him for a future movie, but the actor dies.

Ed's landlord mentions that his Baptist Church wants to finance religious films. Ed persuades them to invest in his science fiction script *Grave Robbers From Outer Space*, which is built around the Bela footage. Ed has his whole cast (including flamboyant homosexual Bunny Breckinridge, bogus prophet Criswell and unemployed horror hostess Vampira) baptised, and casts Kathy's chiropodist Tom Mason as Bela's double. During filming, the Baptists insist the title be changed to *Plan 9 From Outer Space*. Pressure forces Ed to flee the set to a bar where he runs into his idol Orson Welles, similarly despondent at career reversals, and is inspired to finish the film he is confident he will be remembered for.

The bravura credits sequence of *Ed Wood* perfectly evokes the look and sound of *Plan 9 from Outer Space*, complete with cast names on tombstones and a cheesy black and white mock-up model of a rainswept Hollywood. It follows a mock intro by Jeffrey Jones cum Criswell in the first of the films many uncanny impersonations/interpretationsof bizarro real-life characters. But a secondary layer of reference is touched on as the camera swoops over the model, evoking memories not only of the real Ed Wood's fondly-remembered but mainly boring pictures but also of the similar opening of Tim Burton's *Beetlejuice*. Though nurtured as a project by executive producer Michael Lehmann, and based on a strange, anecdotal biography *Nightmare of Ecstasy: The Life and Art of Edward D. Wood Jr* by Rudolph Grey), Ed Wood has been thoroughly infiltrated by the Life and Art of its own director.

Continual evocation of Burton's previous films intermingles with the recreation of *Glen and Glenda* and *Bride of the Monster*: the central thread of Ed's relationship with Bela Lugosi is a clear echo of Burton's own well-documented (in *Vincent*) relationship with Vincent Price. The presence of Johnny Depp, like the tract house exterior and gothic cluttered interior of Lugosi's last home, evokes *Edward Scissorhands* while Ed's hyperactive, monomania and peculiar high voice echo the first of Burton's feature length alter-egos Pee-Wee Herman. Burton shares with Wood a lack of interest in conventional Hollywood notions of construction and character, compensating for the waywardness of his films with a bizarre, unreplicable flavour. It is ironic that for all its anecdotal and elliptical approach, Ed Wood is Burton's most successful piece of proper storytelling, its visuals never overwhelming its emotions, its consistent strangeness never interrupted by the second unit action stuff that flaws the Batman movies.

Given the Grey book as source material, the technical veracity of *Ed Wood* is often in doubt: Loretta King and Dolores Fuller give diametrically opposed accounts of how one came to replace the other in the lead role of *Bride of the Monster*, prompting screenwriters Scott Alexander and Larry Karaszewski to pick the interpretation that offers the most humour and the strangest side detail (Loretta's no liquids diet). Much is omitted that would contradict the film's takes on Wood and Lugosi, including unmentioned marriages for each of them and important professional contacts (Wood's with producer Alex Gordon and Lugosi's late role in *The Black Sleep*). Wood's meeting with Welles is an inspired fiction given life by an uncanny Vincent D'Onofrio performance. His self-involved Welles is just as much a movie-struck outsider as Ed, fitting in perfectly with the film's other eccentrics by holding a casual conversation without once questioning why Ed is dressed in women's clothing.

Although the film does not resist the temptation to score easy laughs from Ed's eccentricities and the shortcomings of his films ("Perfect", he snaps after every botched take, "print it"), Burton and his collaborators invest them with a skewed dignity that is ultimately very moving. There is a touch of contemporary irony in Lugosi's proud claim "I'm the first celebrity that ever checked into rehab" but the film is as smitten as Ed with the old ham.

Marvellously incarnated by a crusty Martin Landau (himself a talented veteran of too many dreadful horror programmers) Lugosi sadly admits in his first scene that "Nobody gives two focs for Bela" and goes from wistfully explaining his hypnotic finger waving with "You have to be double-jointed and you have to be Hungarian" to fulminating against an old rival by claiming "Karloff doesn't deserve to smell my shit". The cast is perfect down to the walk-ons; from Bill Murray's Bunny Breckinridge, who returns from a failed sex change in Mexico with whole mariachi band in tow, alleging "Without these men, I would be dead", to Lisa Marie's Vampira, resisting induction into Wood's circle but finally swamped by her own invented Morticia Addams character.

Tim Burton remains a reticent director, unwilling to show his hand even as he continues obsessively to experiment with autobiography. This is reflected in a strange void at the centre of the film, as he refuses to examine the sources of Wood's insane, naive, ruthless drive or his off-centre integrity (in its own cracked way, *Glen or Glenda* is an art movie) or even his transvestism. All the emotional highs of the film come from Ed's devotion to his associates (when told he's "the only guy in town who doesn't pass judgement", he says "If I could, I wouldn't have any friends") or from their unexplained devotion to him (Bela envies Ed the love of Kathy, saying none of his wives would ever have jumped onto a moving car for him).

When Kathy, played with sweetly subtle seriousness by Patricia Arquette, presses Ed about his past, he talks not about himself but his love for pulp magazines and radio serials. Like Kathy, we are charmed, entertained and introduced to unforgettable people, but left no wiser about the Lives and Art of either Ed Wood or Tim Burton.

TIME, 10/10/94, p. 82, Richard Corliss

Come on, now! Edward D. Wood Jr. is not *nearly* the world's worst director. Lots of people made movies that were even more desperately inept and ludicrous. It's true that Wood's cheap '50s exploitation films—the heartfelt exposé *Glen or Glenda*, the octopus-wrangling horror movie *Bride of the Monster* and the sci-fi anticlassic *Plan 9 from Outer Space*—boasted floridly awful dialogue and actors who seemed terrified to be on camera. But Wood had passion, ambition and, as a heterosexual who enjoyed wearing women's clothes, a very chic identity crisis. His films were *about* something: man's need to create a monument to himself, even if it ends up as a smirk on the face of posterity.

After his death in 1978, Ed Wood got the last laugh: his films were rediscovered, first as camp and now as fodder for a light industry in cultural revisionism. The shaggy hagiography includes a breezily lurid documentary, *Ed Wood: Look Back in Angora*; a second documentary on the making of *Plan 9*; and even a porno homage—*Plan 69 from Outer Space*. And now there's Tim Burton's surprisingly listless biopic, known simply as *Ed Wood*. Once a never-was, Wood is now a brand name.

The *Ed Wood* script, by Scott Alexander and Larry Karaszewski (based on Rudolph Grey's excellent 1992 biography, *Nightmare of Terror*), posits Wood as a classic American optimist a Capraesque hero with little to be optimistic about since he was also a classic American loser. That's a fine start but the film then marches in staid chronological order: Ed made this bad film, then this one, then a third. It focuses on the director's curious cast of hangers-on (played here by Bill Murray, Jeffrey Jones, Lisa Marie and others). They were all, as Wood's psychic sidekick Criswell intones in the 1965 *Orgy of the Dead*, "monsters to be pitied, monsters to be despised, from the inner-most depths of the world!" But Burton treats them with stone-faced sympathy.

Primary among these was the aging, decrepit but still majestic Bela Lugosi. Martin Landau does a handsome turn as Lugosi—so strong that when he disappears, *Ed Wood* loses its momentum and continues its death march on the shoulders of Johnny Depp, in the title role, an exemplary actor who can't do much more than smile heroically in the face of every humiliation, Sometimes this is funny. "Really?" Depp says, sounding like Jon Lovitz's Master Thespian on *Saturday Night Live*. "Worst film you ever saw? Well, my next one'll be even *better!*"

Most of Burton's films have been better than better. One wonders why this one is so dishwatery—why it lacks the cartoon zest and outsider ache of *Beetlejuice, Edward Scissorhands* or *Batman Returns*. Could it be he gave the material too much respect? The real Ed Wood would have known how to do it: with oddball twists and goofy stock footage, with no brains and a lot of heart. It would have been dreadful, and it would have been better—more desperate, more daring. But this *Ed Wood* is dead wood.

VILLAGE VOICE, 10/4/94, p. 51, J. Hoberman

Only in America: Tim Burton, one of the most bankable filmmakers who ever lived, expends the credit of his success in sincere, black-and-white tribute to the tawdry vision of Ed Wood, the alcoholic, transvestite sometime pornographer known affectionately as "the world's worst director."

As nothing can be truly said to exist outside the media's glare, there is no such thing as negative publicity. And as Wood, who specialized in horror schlock exploitation, well knew, the value of celebrity is absolute. There's a moment in Burton's Ed Wood where an incredulous Hollywood producer, amazed by the most grotesque of Wood's bargain-basement productions, *Glen or Glenda*? (1952), anachronistically proclaims that it has got to be a "put-on." That's what they said of Van Gogh, schmuck. We always knew he was great—didn't we?

Just as the distributor who obtained posthumous rights to Wood's 1959 *Plan 9 from Outer Space*, a movie constructed around a few shots of Bela Lugosi taken shortly before Lugosi's death, proved his business acumen by making a small fortune over the last decade of Bad Movie festivals, so the dank aroma of skid-row that clings to the Wood oeuvre evaporates in the simulated sunlight of a Hollywood biopic with a hot young cast. Ed Wood as Johnny Depp, loved by Sarah Jessica Parker and Patricia Arquette and, if only platonically, Bill Murray. Ed Wood, recovered failure, subject of a feel-good movie ... for creeps!

Playing both ends against the middlebrow, Burton's opus arrives bearing the imprimaturs of both Walt Disney and Lincoln Center. There's no mistaking it for anything but an art film, yet it's sweeter than *Cinderella* and nearly as sexless. (That Disney seems to be positioning *Ed Wood* as a potential *Rocky Horror Picture Show* is hardly inappropriate. *Glen or Glenda*?, which played on interest in Christine Jorgensen's sex change operation as well as Lugosi's name, is a nutty monster movie meditation on gender blur and thus a *Rocky Horror* precursor.) *Time* and *Entertainment Weekly* should have no problem riding the Wood bandwagon; more enjoyable will be the prigs and flipsters of New York's two glossy weeklies explaining Wood to their readers. Most poignant, perhaps, will be the anguish of the hardcore auteurists confronted with the "travesty" of Burton's exaltation of Wood's presumed artistic integrity.

Written by Scott Alexander and Larry Karaszewski from Rudolph Grey's 1992 oral history, *Nightmare of Ecstasy*, the film is nothing if not knowing. *Ed Wood* opens with an extravagant pastiche of Wood's *Plan 9 from Outer Space*—tombstone credits illuminated by lightning, a crescendo of thunder yielding to mad bongo drums—and thereafter there's scarcely an Ed Wood joke that isn't made. "Gosh, where's my pink sweater?" is his girlfriend's first line. "Why, if I had the chance, I could make half a movie out of this stock footage," the aspiring filmmaker tells a friend.

Wood may be a joke, but he's a great one. The chasm his movies open between intent and realization, the rich realism induced by their failure to convince, are of incomparably greater aesthetic interest than the seamless naturalism of conventional narrative films: The big lie of chronology is confounded by Wood's imperfect continuity, as the myth of invisible editing is ruptured by his mismatched shots, the nature of acting foregrounded by cloddish bits of business, the notion of originality undermined by the interpolation of stock footage. As bad filmmakers go, Wood is less provocative than Oscar Micheaux, but at his best (which is to say, his worst), his mysterious illogic deforms the simplest clichés so absolutely that you're forced to consider them anew.

Moreover, Wood established himself in a fringe Hollywood beyond the imagining of Nathanael West. In addition to the burnt-out, pitifully emaciated Lugosi, B-movie workhorse Lyle Talbot, and sundry veterans of '30s westerns, his impoverished productions feature such showbiz oddities as Criswell the TV psychic, Tor Johnson the 400-pound Swedish wrestler, Vampira the beatnik ghoul girl, and a defective prop octopus stolen from Republic studio. No more oddball than his entourage, Wood was a heterosexual crossdresser with a fetish for angora: The unconvincing magic, crackpot logic, and decomposing glamour of his films mirror his own.

Gary Indiana once called Wood "John Waters without irony" and that's how Depp plays him. He's a wide-eyed, wired enthusiast at once suave and disjointed, lips accentuated by pencil-line mustache, teeth bared in a ventriloquist dummy's idiot grin, illuminated by faith in his own dream. Depp aside, the *typage* is remarkable: Jeffrey Jones's Criswell, Lisa Marie's Vampira, George "the Animal" Steele's Tor Johnson, Vincent D'Onofrio's Orson Welles are all impressively hyperreal and Martin Landau's Lugosi is a good deal more. "Now no one gives two fucks for Bela," he says sadly upon meeting avid fan Eddie Wood. Thanks to Landau's performance, a mixture of wounded pride and agonized gratitude, *Ed Wood* is as much footnote to the Lugosi oeuvre as it is celebration of Wood's. Condemned to self-parody, resurrected by the camera, Lugosi functions as the pure essence of negative stardom—he's a successful failure, Ed Wood's Ed Wood.

Skirting the sleaze and pathos of its subject's life, *Ed Wood* is heavily dependent on Wood's films—naturalizing, in a sense, the Rhino video *Look Back in Angora*, which uses clips from the Wood oeuvre as the basis for a biography—while intermittently puzzling over the miracle of how these films happened. The most thematically apposite sequence has Ed and his cast submitting to mass baptism (true story!) to secure the Baptist Church of Beverly Hills's backing for *Plan 9 From Outer Space*. In the gospel according to Burton, Wood is so solicitous of his actors that he shoots every scene in one take; his mantra is "That was perfect." *Ed Wood*, of course, is flawlessly crafted—as fastidious as any previous Burton production. The painstaking replication of Wood's haphazard compositions suggests the Buena Park Palace of Living Art—where the Mona Lisa or Whistler's Mother are reproduced as garish wax dioramas—only in reverse.

No less than its subject, albeit in a different way, *Ed Wood* is deeply solipsistic. As with *Natural Born Killers*, the entire world—however ostensibly mediated by film or TV—is subsumed to the director's vision: Everything in *Ed Wood* is stippled with noir lighting and awash in studio rain, a lavish version of a cheap horror movie. The most elaborate gag involves the mechanism of an amusement park spook house; the most powerful moment has Lugosi reprise his tormented speech from *Bride of the Monster* ("Home? I have no home!") on a Hollywood street corner; the most inspirational sequence allows Ed to meet his idol Orson Welles in a cheap bar and thus draw strength to finish his "masterpiece," *Plan 9 From Outer Space*.

Opening in a graveyard, *Ed Wood* evokes Hollywood as a mansion haunted by a gaggle of unquiet ghosts, but it's a Hollywood haunted mansion just the same. Unlike *Look Back in Angora*, which includes footage documenting Wood's bloated, befuddled descent into softcore porn, Burton ends his story on a positive note. *Plan 9 From Outer Space*, a movie that never had an L.A. theatrical release, is given a premiere at the packed Pantages Theater on Hollywood Boulevard so Wood (recognized in the movies as he never was in life) may be feted by an ecstatically appreciative audience. Us!

Thanks to Burton, the Ed Wood story makes the leap from cult to religion. I read in *Premiere* that there's a campaign underway to get Wood a star on the pavement of Hollywood Boulevard. The movie's greatest irony is the liquidation of irony itself.

Also reviewed in:
CHICAGO TRIBUNE, 10/7/94, Friday, p. C, Michael Wilmington
NATION, 10/17/94, p. 433, Stuart Klawans
NEW YORK TIMES, 9/23/94, p. C34, Janet Maslin
VARIETY, 9/12-18/94, p. 39, Todd McCarthy
WASHINGTON POST, 10/7/94, p. B1, Hal Hinson
WASHINGTON POST, 10/7/94, Weekend, p. 50, Desson Howe

8 SECONDS

A New Line Cinema release of a Jersey Films production. *Executive Producer:* Cyd LeVin and Jeffrey Swab. *Producer:* Michael Shamberg. *Director:* John G. Avildsen. *Screenplay:* Monte Merrick. *Director of Photography:* Victor Hammer. *Editor:* J. Douglas Seelig. *Music:* Bill Conti. *Music Editor:* Steve Livingston, Ken Johnson, and Eric Cowden. *Choreographer:* Mark Sellers. *Sound:* Michael Scott Goldbaum and (music) Lee DeCarlo. *Sound Editor:* Steven D. Williams. *Casting:* Caro Jones. *Production Designer:* William J. Cassidy. *Art Director:* John Frick. *Set Decorator:* Jenny C. Patrick. *Set Dresser:* Michael Leonard, Mike Kocurek, Adam Braid, and Elizabeth Jane McNamara. *Special Effects:* Bart Dion, Dennis Dion, and Bill Wynn. *Costumes:* Deena Appel. *Make-up:* Desne J. Holland. *Stunt Coordinator:* Mike McGaughy. *Running time:* 104 minutes. *MPAA Rating:* PG-13.

CAST: James Rebhorn (Clyde Frost); Cameron Finley (Young Lane); Carrie Snodgress (Elsie Frost); Dustin Mayfield (Teenage Lane); Luke Perry (Lane Frost); Stephen Baldwin (Tuff Hedeman); Red Mitchell (Cody Lambert); Gabriel Folse (Amarillo Cowboy 1); Joe Stevens (Amarillo Cowboy 2); Clint Burkey (Travis); Cynthia Geary (Kellie Frost); Ronnie Claire Edwards (Carolyn Kyle); John Swasey (Drunk Cowboy); Jim Gough (Official Nacogdoches); Mike Hammes (Police Officer); Jonathan Joss (Medic Del Rio); Danny Spear (Kellie's Father); Paul Alexander (TV Reporter); Daniel Ramos (Bartender); George Michael (Himself); Linden Ashby (Martin Hudson); Tonie Perensky (Buckle Bunny 1); Coquina Dunn (Buckle Bunny 2); Renee Zellweger (Prescott Motel Buckle Bunny); John Growney (Himself); Ed Kutts, Boyd Polhamus, and Hadly Barrett (Rodeo Announcers).

LOS ANGELES TIMES, 2/25/94, Calendar/p. 8, Peter Rainer

If only the filmmakers responsible for "8 Seconds" were half as good at riding the bull as their rodeo hero Lane Frost. It's an inspirational bio pic without a trace of inspiration.

Frost—played here by Luke Perry—as the youngest world champion bull-rider ever, before he died in a rodeo accident in 1989. (The end credits feature clips from his career.) He had worked his way up the small-town circuits, married a stand-by-your-man sweetheart, Kellie Kyle (Cynthia Geary), endured an on-the-road life of cheap-jack motels and finally made it to the top at the National Finals Rodeo in Las Vegas.

Frost must have been a crackerjack character, but the movie turns him into a cardboard good guy. He's squeaky clean even when he's straying with a groupie or having a honky-tonk snit. The hellbent passion that would keep a man retro-fitted atop a bounding 2,000-pound bull for the competitive minimum of at least eight very long seconds is nowhere in evidence in Perry's aw-shucks posturing. Neither is the effects of the commercialization of the sport. That's been purified too. The inspirationalism goes down easier that way.

Director John Avildsen, who directed "Rocky" and The Karate Kid," knows something about inspirational movies—and he appears to have forgotten most of it here. Frost never sinks low enough to make his rise exciting; his ordeals—wife problems, father problems, etc.—are standard. The screenwriter, Monte Merrick, must have recognized this—at one point he has one of the characters remark on how much their lives resemble a country-Western song. Actually, their lives resemble a *bad* country song. The good ones don't indulge in all this *processed* heartbreak.

Stephen Baldwin, as Lane's bull-riding buddy "Tuff" Hedeman, has a few swaggering good moments and James Rebhorn, playing Lane's father Clyde, has an acrid edge that de-sudses his scenes. (The filmmakers intend Clyde's competitiveness with his son to be his way of showing love, but that's not how it plays.)

The most solid presence in the film, though, is the great bull Red Rock, Lance's perpetual nemesis. He has a gravity lacking in the rest of the movie. He should have bucked a few more of its honchos.

NEW YORK POST, 2/25/94, p. 43, Michael Medved

If you're a devoted rodeo fan who agrees with the producers of "8 Seconds" that the sport of professional bull-riding represents humanity's "ultimate thrill," then it's vaguely possible you might find a few moments of passing pleasure in this listless and ludicrous picture.

For the rest of us, however, the film fails to make a convincing case for honoring the ability to stay seated on a wildly bucking bull for the regulation eight seconds (hence the title) as a major step forward for Western civilization.

Fourteen years ago, "Urban Cowboy" treated John Travolta's commitment to similar endeavors (riding a mechanical bull in a Houston bar) with a wry, affectionate sense of humor, never losing sight of the fundamental idiocy of his obsession

The biggest problem with "8 Seconds" is that it lacks any skepticism about the bizarre sport it dramatizes so reverentially, while outsiders will see the endeavor as so much bull.

The movie improbably stars Luke Perry (the sulky heartthrob of "Beverly Hills 90210") in telling the true story of Lane Frost, the Babe Ruth of Bull Riding.

Director John Avildsen ("Rocky," "The Karate Kid") follows this good-natured Oklahoma kid from his days in high school rodeo competitions in the '70s, to his many national championships in the '80s.

Along the way, Frost makes time to marry a pretty blonde rodeo rider, who's played with surprising depth and delicacy by Cynthia Geary, best known as waitress Shelly Tambo in TVs "Northern Exposure."

The entire second half focuses on the slow, sad disintegration of their marriage, as Perry spends all his time on the road, traveling from rodeo to rodeo with his hard-drinking, bull-riding buddies, cruelly ignoring the patient little woman he leaves behind at home.

This hero-with-feet-of-clay bit seems especially out of place since the movie never gives us any persuasive reason to see the main character as a hero in the first place: uncanny success at riding a previously unconquered 2,000-pound bull named Red Rock isn't enough to make this smiling, cardboard nobody into an admirable or sympathetic character.

Luke Perry's stale, stick-figure performance doesn't help. His washed-out screen presence suggests that the young star may have recently undergone charisma by-pass surgery and should end all the talk about his resemblance to James Dean.

Stephen Baldwin, the youngest and perhaps the most talented of the four movie star Baldwin brothers, offers a striking contrast to Perry's posing. As the hero's best friend, "Tuff" Hedeman he's a salty, edgy, earthy character who nearly steals the movie. "

The bulls also make a strong impression—these massive, impossibly meaty beasts flailing away with desperate intensity to throw off the cowboys so precariously straddling their backs.

The problem is that the camera can never get too close during these sequences, for fear of revealing the fact that the stunt doubles bare only the slightest resemblance to the actors with whom they're paired.

As a result, all the bull-riding scenes look like a segment of "Wide World of Sports" that's gone on too long, and "8 Seconds" begins to feel like "8 Years" to the audience.

NEWSDAY, 2/25/94, Part II/p. 67, John Anderson

This movie is full of bull, and that's the best thing about it.

Teen heartthrob Luke Perry leaves the 90210 zip code for crusty, dusty Oklahoma to play Lane Frost, champion bull rider and, if this film is to be believed, the most polite human who ever lived. He's kind to children, he loves his parents. Yes, his ex-rodeo-star father (James Rebhorn) might be a little more demonstrative toward his son, maybe just once say how proud he is of him. And OK, Lane cheats on his wife Kellie (Cynthia Geary), but she cheats on him, too. They really love each other though, which is something you have to emphasize when the surviving spouse is looking over your shoulder.

No, as you've probably guessed, Lane doesn't make it till the closing credits. But while he's here on Earth, Earth is a little better place. Not for bulls, of course. But they really do much more damage to the men than the men do to them. And the sequences in which they do it are thrilling.

"8 Seconds" is not an unpleasant or offensive film, just a very unsophisticated one. Perry is as convincing as he can be in a role that's basically a tribute, or maybe a country song (there are cameos by several country-music acts, including Vince Gill, McBride and the Ride and Brooks & Dunn). Geary, usually found waiting tables on "Northern Exposure," shows her range, which turns out not to exist. Stephen Baldwin, as Lane's best friend Tuff, smiles too much but provides the acerbic counterweight to Lane's Boy Scout. And Rebhorn, who is currently playing another insensitive father in "Blank Check," does basically the same bit here. Carrie Snodgress is virtually invisible as Lane's mother.

Director John Avildsen has been over this kind of emotional territory before, in "Rocky" and "The Karate Kid," and there's not much new here. We never doubt for a minute that Lane won't realize his dream. In fact, it all happens rather matter-of-factly. Lane's showdown with Red Rock, the unrideable bull that's thrown more than 300 riders off his back? C'mon, you know, just as you know that, despite their mistakes Kellie and Lane will get back together, enabling him to ride that bull. Only Lane's death seems surprising, and the way it happens is presented so bluntly and cruelly the effect is like fresh air. It's a little late at this point for "8 Seconds" to start flirting with reality, but it certainly brings you up short.

SIGHT AND SOUND, 11/94, p. 43, Andrew Pulver

As a small boy in Oklahoma, Lane Frost is introduced to rodeo culture by his parents Elsie and Clyde. He develops into a skilled bull-rider and determines to become a professional champion. He goes on the tour circuit with his friends Tuff Hedeman and Cody Lambert. They are all successful, but Lane is clearly the one heading for fame and fortune. Lane meets and falls in love with Kellie Kyle, a trick horsewoman who comes from a wealthy Texan family, and eventually they marry.

Lane's career goes from strength to strength until he is finally crowned world bull-riding champion. However, after an idyllic start, his life with Kellie begins to turn sour. The road takes its toll on their marriage, and when Lane sees his wife innocently talking to a childhood boyfriend, he freaks out. He takes revenge by entertaining rodeo groupies in his motel room. The marriage fails and Kellie moves back with her family, while Lane's career subsequently hits the rocks. He collapses into depression and bouts of drinking, to the disapproval of his taciturn father.

With the help of his friends, Lane recovers and after riding Red Rock, a reputedly unbreakable bull, he goes on to regain the championship and win back Kellie's love. But at the height of his success, Lane is crushed to death in the ring. A year later, Tuff dedicates his championship win to Lane.

8 Seconds is little more than a vehicle for television star Luke Perry, a teen favourite from *Beverly Hills 90210*. It's not his debut—he had a supporting role in the sparky but dumb *Buffy the Vampire Slayer*—but it is his first major part and, on this evidence, he will be lucky to get another.

The opening titles try to sell the movie as restatement of Western mythology: "The old West may be dead, but its spirit lives on". The trailer-park, ten-gallon rodeo culture that is the story's focus has proved a rich source of material in the past in films such as Nicholas Ray's *The Lusty Men* and Sam Peckinpah's *Junior Bonner*, which tap into the rodeo star's fixation with a mythology of transient fame; but *8 Seconds*' treatment of it is so relentlessly superficial that it emerges as a debased and hollow version of the original Hollywood dreamscape. It comes as no surprise that the inspiration for *8 Seconds* was a television sports item about Lane Frost's life, but what might have been an insight into a unique corner of American culture has here turned into a TV movie-style pot-boiler complete with soggy script and perfunctory performances. Perry is not the worst offender—he's game, though sorely limited in range. That privilege is reserved for *Northern Exposure*'s Cynthia Geary, who as Frost's wife gives an embarrassingly wooden rendition of what is already a cipher of a part.

The presence of Stephen Baldwin is a partially redeeming feature. The third member, with Alec and William, of the Baldwin acting clan, his gormless physiognomy enlivens the character role of Tuff Hedeman, who has most of the decent lines and a number of fist fights and drunken rages along the way. *Rocky* director John Avildsen skilfully captures the golden sunscapes and bull-riding action, but even his finesse cannot rescue what is fundamentally a flawed conception.

VILLAGE VOICE, 3/1/94, p. 58, Natasha Stovall

In a tacky motel between rodeos, hard-livin' Tuff (Stephen Baldwin) lectures innocent Lane (Luke Perry) on the key elements of cowboy life. "Drinkin', lovin', and fightin'," he drawls, shitfaced, as Lane flosses his teeth, wide-eyed. Based on the life of contemporary bull rider Lane Frost, *8 Seconds* tracks Frost's swift ascent from tossin' hay on his phlegmatic father's ranch to the pinnacle of rodeo success, while ramming Frost's aw-shucks goodness down the collective throat at every turn. But in case you didn't catch the plot's subtext, refer to the adverts: "The sport made him a legend. His heart made him a hero." Yes, folks, he's just too good to live.

With a misguided Okie accent, shaggy bowl haircut, and plaintive puppy eyes, Perry plays Lane as the quintessential American sweetheart. Honest, devoted to fans and family, hardworking, and sober—"I don't chew tobacco or nuthin'"—he's Brandon Walsh to Baldwin's Dylan McKay. *8 Seconds*'s obsession with Lane Frost as a knight in spangly country-and-western armor negates Perry's ability to be intriguing, or even sensual; when the camera Pans down Perry's bare chest to his championship belt buckle, there's serious sex object potential, but director John G. Avildsen (*The Karate Kid*—'nuff said) and screenwriter Monte Merrick are too busy boosting Lane's Dudley Do-Right disposition for any of Perry's bad-boy magnetism to slither through. Too bad. Luke Perry as a mortally reckless cowboy would have buttered my muffin. Instead, *8 Seconds* tasted like a stale piece of Wonder Bread.

Also reviewed in:
CHICAGO TRIBUNE, 2/25/94, Friday/p. G, John Petrakis
NEW YORK TIMES, 2/25/94, p. C14, Stephen Holden
VARIETY, 2/14-20/94, p. 40, Todd McCarthy
WASHINGTON POST, 2/25/94, p. D6, Richard Harrington
WASHINGTON POST, 2/25/94, Weekend/p. 38, Joe Brown

EVEN COWGIRLS GET THE BLUES

A Fine Line Features release of a New Line Cinema/Fourth Vision production. *Producer:* Laurie Parker. *Director:* Gus Van Sant. *Screenplay:* Gus Van Sant, Jr. *Based on the book by:* Tom Robbins. *Director of Photography:* John Campbell and Eric Alan Edwards. *Editor:* Curtiss Clayton. *Music:* k.d. lang and Ben Mink. *Choreographer:* Ruby Burns and Jann Dryer. *Sound:* Jon Huck and (music) Mark Ramaer. *Sound Editor:* Kelly Baker. *Casting:* Pagano Bialy Manwiller. *Production Designer:* Missy Stewart. *Art Director:* Dan Self. *Set Decorator:* Nina Bradford. *Set Dresser:* Damon Baird Sullivan, Sean Robert Fong, Jennifer Pray, and Phred Palmer. *Special Effects:* Jim Doyle. *Costumes:* Beatrix Aruna Pasztor. *Make-up:* Leonard MacDonald. *Stunt Coordinator:* Jake Crawford. *Running time:* 90 minutes. *MPAA Rating:* R.

CAST: Uma Thurman (Sissy Thurman); John Hurt (The Countess); Rain Phoenix (Bonanza Jellybean); Noriyuki "Pat" Morita (The Chink); Keanu Reeves (Julian Gitche); Lorraine Bracco (Delores Del Ruby); Angie Dickinson (Miss Adrian); Sean Young (Marie Barth); Crispin Glover (Howard Barth); Ed Begley, Jr. (Rupert); Carol Kane (Cowgirl Carla); Victoria Williams (Cowgirl Debbie); Bee Fowler (Cowgirl Kym); Arlene Wewa (Cowgirl Big Red); Judy Robinson (Cowgirl Gloria); Heather Graham (Cowgirl Heather); Betsy Roth (Cowgirl Mary); Heather Hershey (Cowgirl Donna); Roseanne Arnold (Madame Zoe); Buck Henry (Dr. Dreyfus); Alan Arnold (Lionel); Ken Kesey (Sissy's Daddy); Ken Babbs (Sissy's Uncle); Grace Zabriskie (Mrs. Hankshaw); Michael Parker (Pilgrim Driver); Suzanne Solget and Scott Patrick Green (Pilgrims); Udo Kier (Commercial Director); Tom Peterson (Crewman); Wade Evans (Cameraman); Oliver Kirk (Sheriff); Greg McMickle (FBI Agent); Treya Jeffrey (Young Sissy); Alexa (Rubber Rose Bird Expert); Eric Hull (White House Undersecretary); Joe Ivy (FBI Director); Lin Shaye (Rubber Rose Maid); Chel White (Brain Surgeon); Molly Little (Salsa Singer); William Burroughs (Himself); Tom Robbins (Narrator).

LOS ANGELES TIMES, 5/20/94, Calendar/p. 2, Kenneth Turan

Like many films that arrive on screen more dead than alive, writer-director Gus Van Sant's version of Tom Robbins' "Even Cowgirls Get the Blues" contains its own built-in epitaph. "Playfulness ceases to have a serious purpose when it takes itself too seriously," someone says, a theory this unfortunate movie goes way out of its way to prove.

Certainly Robbins' original novel, which followed the exploits, hitchhiking and otherwise, of Sissy Hankshaw and her oversized thumbs, has playful to the point of suffocating cutesyness. Whatever charges can be made against a book that comes up with a philosophy of "Ha Ha ... Hoo Hoo ... Hee Hee" and dialogue like "You can tune a guitar but you can't tuna fish," excessive seriousness is not one of them.

Though millions apparently found this sort of thing appealing, that doesn't ensure that its gossamer spirit would benefit by or even survive the translation to flesh-and--blood reality that turning words into film makes inevitable.

And even if Robbins' book could possibly have been made into a successful picture, getting Van Sant to do it, the ideal hipster-meets-hipster combination though it must have seemed at the time, has turned out to be a recipe for a fiasco.

For what Robbins' smug whimsy doesn't need is a dose of Van Sant's deadpan aesthetic of knowing, way hip boredom. Though the director's sensibility worked extraordinarily well when applied to hard-edged subject matter like "Drugstore Cowboy" and even "My Own Private Idaho," combining it with Robbins' filmsy jokiness has resulted in a film whose tedium is painful.

Postponed for six months of tinkering after lackluster screenings at last fall's Toronto Film Festival, "Cowgirls" stars Uma Thurman as Sissy, the proud possessor of thumbs the size of Hebrew National kosher hot dogs. A former model for the Yoni-Yum line of feminine hygiene products, Sissy finds that her true calling is the open road. Nothing that moves, up to and including airplanes, can resist those thumbs, a situation that causes Sissy to declaim, in a typically leaden monologue, "I have the rhythms of the universe inside me. I am in a state of grace."

A letter from Yoni-Yum magnate the Countess (John Hurt), one of Robbins' androgynous characters, brings Sissy to New York City, where she resists the notion of riding in a taxi and paying for transportation and has an abortive date with artist Julian Gitche (Keanu Reeves) and his decadent friends.

Then it's off to the Countess' Rubber Rose Ranch way out West to film yet another commercial, this one inspired by the flock of whooping cranes who stop off there. Also in the neighborhood is the Chink (Noriyuki "Pat" Morita), an enigmatic spiritual leader without portfolio, and the ranch's assorted lesbian cowgirls, led by the whip-cracking Delores Del Ruby (Lorraine Bracco) and the equally boisterous Bonanza Jellybean (Rain Phoenix, River's sister), who can't help falling in love with Sissy.

Because both the Robbins novel and Van Sant himself are such pillars of trendiness, any number of celebrated folks ended up with bit parts in the film, including a brief but puzzling glimpse of William Burroughs, a particular favorite of the director's. Former Merry Pranksters Ken Kesey and Ken Babbs play Sissy's relatives, Roseanne Arnold is a fortuneteller named Madame Zoe and Buck Henry plays an aphorism-spouting surgeon, all to not much effect. Though it is possible to pin various philosophical labels on "Cowgirls," loaded as it is with undeveloped notions about feminism and individuality, nothing about it is really memorable except the appealing musicality of the fine k.d. lang/Ben Mink score, which deserves better. So do those poor whooping cranes, who look great in their close-ups but would have been wise to follow Sissy's motto: "When in doubt, keep moving." It's that kind of film.

NEW YORK POST, 5/20/94, p. 41, Michael Medved

All in all, it's been a terrible season for cowgirls. First came the hard-riding hookers (or pistol-packing putas) of the abysmal "Bad Girls."

Then came "That's Entertainment III" with two (count 'em—two!) embarrassing outtakes of Judy Garland as a cowgirl. Now comes "Even Cowgirls Get the Blues," the most unspeakably awful all-star extravaganza of this (or any other) season: a movie so breathtakingly bad that it actually leaves the viewer in a state of numbed disbelief.

Based on Tom Robbins' hippie-dippy novel of 1976, the movie tells the story of Sissy Hankshaw (Uma Thurman, in the worst performance of her career), an innocent free spirit with two horrible handicaps: a thoroughly unconvincing Southern accent and a pair of freakishly large thumbs.

What is one supposed to do with these overdeveloped appendages? Sissy resists the natural temptation to become a TV movie critic and instead concentrates on hitchhiking, crossing the continent (we're told) 400 times.

She also finds time to work as a model for Yoni-Yum feminine hygiene spray, under the loving supervision of The Countess, a preening, cross-dressing tycoon played by John Hurt (in the worst performance of his career).

The Countess eventually dispatches Sissy to the Rubber Rose Ranch, a glitzy healthy-spa administered by steely authoritarian Angie Dickinson, where our heroine quickly falls in with a gang of rebellious cowgirls led by Delores Del Ruby (Lorraine Braco, in the worst performance of her career) and Bonanza Jellybean (Rain Phoenix, in the worst performance of her career—but hey, it's her debut!)

The charisma-free screen presence of Phoenix contributes mightily to the failure of the film, since Sissy is supposed to fall hopelessly in love with this wild, passionate character. Phoenix (younger sister of the late River Phoenix) reads all of her lines with such flat, uncomprehending inflection that you can hear every single dash and comma.

It hardly helps her cause that those lines include doozies like "the example of your life has helped me in my struggle to be a cowgirl" and "better no cowgirls at all than cowgirls compromised."

Tom Robbins' novel won admirers with its inventive word play and its whimsical humor, but the movie version feels as playful and whimsical as a medicine ball. Director Gus Van Sant ("My Own Private Idaho") has fashioned His Own Private Fiasco, full of in-crowd titters and uncredited cameos by the likes of Gregory Hines and Edward James Olmos.

Van Sant's usual visual flair is missing in action and by the end of this putrid picture, it's not just the cowgirls but the entire audience that will get the blues.

NEWSDAY, 5/20/94, Part II/p. B7, John Anderson

In transferring an unfilmmable book into an unwatchable film, director Gus Van Sant has performed like one of the whopping cranes that play so prominent a role in "Even Cowgirls Get the Blues"—plunging down, skimming along and flying away with only the clammy stuff stuck to his feathers.

The result, Van Sant's delayed and apparently troubled adaptation of the '70s cult novel by Tom Robbins, contains little of the author's occasional prose magic—much less about the "lipstick criminal moonlight" than about feminine hygiene and sexual versatility. (It does have Robbins' voice, who sounds self-satisfied delivering his uninspired narration, none of which should have been necessary.) There's none of the free-wheeling attitude and all of the self-absorption of late '60s-early '70s counter-cultural posturing; if Van Sant wanted to spoof the period—a lot of the acting, for instance, recalls the "Billy Jack" movies—he's done a good job,

But that's not what he wanted to do, even if what he did intend is unclear. In Uma Thurman, who plays the guileless, virginal, world-traveling Sissy Hankshaw, child of the '50s and child of the enormous thumbs, he has an actress who can, and does, embody goofy, wide-eyed innocence. That she has to read lines that seem better meant for fortune cookies is a handicap, but with the right tone, a consistent tone, at least, it might have worked. "Cowgirls," however, reels so recklessly from the earnest to the camp you could get whiplash.

And the viewer comes away from the film with the distinct sense that the director had lost his vision and decided to make light of his own project. There are moments of sweet, ethereal and perhaps winsome Van Sant: the moon rising to one of the k.d. lang songs that ennoble the film, or a sky-full of clouds in a time-lapsed race, or a White House-Woodstock montage—but where and why they occur seems sophomoric. What the book portrayed as mischievous or spirited generally comes off as rude, and the lyrical has become ponderous.

The story—which concerns Sissy's sexual self-discovery, her adventures with the radical cowgirls of the Rubber Rose Ranch and her relationship with her unusual thumbs, which can control the flow of road traffic or the flight of falling stars—was never of overriding importance. The performances from his principal actors—with the exception of John Hurt, who camps it up outrageously as the oyster-white Countess, accent on the second syllable—are amateurish. The chief offender is Rain Phoenix, sister of River (to whom the film is dedicated) as Sissy's love interest, Bonanza Jellybean. But she's hardly alone. Lorraine Bracco, for instance, as Delores the peyote queen, looks like she needs some sleep, and her Big Valley Brooklynese is abrasive. Pat Morita, as the shaman, is funny but pointless.

If the principal cast is making you laugh, what can you do with the numerous cameos? Crispin Glover, Sean Young, Roseanne Barrnold, OK: when you see them you chuckle anyway. But the giggle factor gets out of hand. By the time Keanu Reeves appears, you don't know what to do.

Thurman's intonation is as flat as the prairie, and the wide open spaces, via Van Sant, are claustrophobic. Dark and drained, "Even Cowgirls Get the Blues" looks like a film that's trying to crawl inside itself.

NEWSWEEK, 5/30/94, p. 64 Jack Kroll

Writer-director Gus Van Sant ("Drugstore Cowboy," "My Own Private Idaho") has become a one-man counterculture in the movie industry. That's a tough job, as his new film, "Even Cowgirls Get the Blues," demonstrates. Based on Tom Robbins's 1976 best-selling novel, the movie was scheduled to open last fall, but went back into the editing room when it was received coolly by film-festival audiences. Van Sant has not been able to pull it together. The story, about Sissy Hankshaw (Uma Thurman), a virginal innocent whose outsize thumbs make her the world's greatest hitchhiker, and her encounter with a rebel band of lesbian cowgirls, comes through as a scrappy and anachronistic remnant of the hippie days.

There are just too many half-cooked ingredients in this utopian stew of a movie: the gender-bending Countess (John Hurt), who markets feminine-hygiene products; the cave-dwelling guru called The Chink (Noriyuki "Pat" Morita); Delores (Lorraine Bracco), who leads the cowgirl revolt at the Rubber Rose Ranch, run by Miss Adrian (Angie Dickinson); Bonanza Jellybean (Rain Phoenix), the lesbian cowgirl with whom Sissy finds true love, and lots more. As his movies become bigger, the gifted Van Sant is losing control of their form and meaning. "Cowgirls" is like a counterculture piñata scattering messages—freedom, feminism, love—all over the place. Moments of lyric sweetness are swamped by moments of malarkey. As The Chink would say, Van Sant needs to find his true center.

SIGHT AND SOUND, 1/95, p. 45, Ben Thompson

Born in the American South with abnormally large thumbs, Sissy Hankshaw grows up through the 1950s to become both a beautiful woman and the world's greatest hitchhiker. Aged 16, she runs away from home and exults in the freedom of movement her primary digit brings her. Despite the perils and temptations of the road, she reaches her late 20s still technically a virgin. In one of the obscure spots where she picks up mail, she gets a letter from New York, from The Countess, the Mississippi transsexual feminine hygiene tycoon who has employed her as a model—The Yoni-Yum dew girl. The Countess wants Sissy to meet Julian Gitche, a handsome young Native American artist and a worthy prospective mate; but he succumbs to an asthma attack on being introduced to her, leaving Sissy to be partially debauched by two of his louche friends.

Sissy sets off for The Countess' Rubber Rose Ranch health farm at the Western end of the Dakotas to film a commercial for him. There she finds a rebellious group of cowgirls — led by the delectable Bonanza Jellybean and inspired by the peyote visions of whip-cracking Delores Del Ruby—and the Chink, a mysterious and lecherous Chinese seer who lives in a cave, guarding a time machine. With the aid of a powerful show of feminine unhygiene, the Cowgirls take over the Ranch, and Sissy and Bonanza Jellybean become lovers.

On her travels again, Sissy (who has one thumb amputated but continues to hitchhike with the other) keeps in touch with Jellybean and the Ranch by letter. Fed brown rice and then peyote buttons by sympathetic ranchers, the last surviving flock of American whooping cranes have extended their annual migratory stop-over at the Rubber Rose, and Sissy returns there to find an armed stand-off developing between the ranchers and the federal authorities. Inspired by the last of Delores' peyote visions, the ranchers decide to give in peacefully, but Bonanza Jellybean is shot and killed in the act of surrender. The cranes fly away. After a suitable period of mourning, Sissy sets up house with Delores and The Chink, and has The Chink's baby.

"The *idea* of cowgirls prevails in our culture," Bonanza Jellybean observes to Sissy Hankshaw in an analytical moment. "Therefore, it seems to me, the *fact* of cowgirls should prevail. Otherwise we're being ripped off again." Who can now deny the prophetic nature of Tom Robbins' writing? These lines were penned almost two decades before *Bad Girls*.

Even Cowgirls Get the Blues was originally conceived by its author as a screenplay for a low-budget film, but Robbins journey to the screen has been anything but an easy ride. In the early 80s, Shelley Duvall owned the rights and tried in vain to get the film made with herself in the lead role. Then Gus Van Sant's big Hollywood break-through version had to be re-edited—an unexpected ravine in a steady upward career slope—after less than rapturous receptions at last year's Toronto and Venice film festivals. Now *Even Cowgirls* is finally here, a year after the release of k.d. lang and Ben Mink's superb soundtrack might have drawn people in to see it, and the general feeling seems to be that the whole idea of the film promised more than it could deliver. Van Sant has clearly learned this lesson, having already gone on to make a Nicole Kidman vehicle, *2 Die 4*.

What remains is an authentically picaresque cameo movie—a sort of *Those Magnificent Men in Their Flying Machines* relaunched as eco-feminist horse-opera. There's William Burroughs, looking around as he crosses the street and observing (appropriately enough, as things turn out), "ominous"; there's Roseanne as Madame Zoe telling Sissy's future ("There vill be vimmen—lots of vimmen"); and that is only the beginning. It is possible to have enough of trying to spot Buck Henry, though, and the celebrity over-load turns out to be rather gratuitous in view of the high calibre of the lead casting.

Uma Thurman as Sissy (described in the book by The Countess as having a mouth "like a mink's vagina at the height of the rut") and Rain Phoenix as Jellybean, that "bundle of wild muscle and baby fat", seem to have emerged straight from Robbins' pages. Phoenix's exuberant performance is not overshadowed by the idea of her brother as Mike in *My Own Private Idaho,* but the rest of the film is. Campfire intimacies, road-warriorhood, same-sex bonding, the central character who is so much an object that he or she becomes a subject—all these elements were integral to Van Sant's previous film too, and that one, for all its Shakespearian indulgences, hung together rather better.

Even Cowgirls' sombre dedication—"For River"—poignantly undermines the original story's simple faith in sexual and narcotic salvation (cf. the whooping cranes: "the peyote mellowed them out"). That sort of innocence has been if not lost for ever, at least tainted with fear, and even a filmmaker of Van Sant's skill and power cannot whiten that stain out. Steps have however been taken in the re-editing process to soften the impact of the film's other stand-out 70s anomaly—the profoundly irritating hokey mysticism of Noriyuki "Pat" Morita's benighted "Chink". He is still profoundly irritating, but at least not for so long now.

Rarely in a literary adaptation have an author's voice and vision come through so clearly (Robbins even narrates his own epigrams: "the brown paper bag is the only thing civilised man has produced that does not seem out of place in nature") and yet to so muddled an overall effect. And never has a book supplied a better epitaph for its cinematic incarnation: "Playfulness ceases to serve a serious purpose when it takes itself too seriously."

VILLAGE VOICE, 5/31/94, p. 55, J. Hoberman

Gus Van Sant loves to get the show on the road, but *Even Cowgirls Get The Blues* seems to have exhausted its narrative libido during the course of its tortuous, amply documented path to the screen. Adapted by Van Sant from the 1976 paperback bestseller by hippie nostalgist Tom Robbins, drenched in k.d. lang, and flecked with cameos ranging from Ken Kesey and William Burroughs to Roseanne Arnold and Edward James Olmos, the movie is less a rolling stone than a pet rock—friendly but inert.

Originally serialized in *High Times,* Robbins's novel quickly inspired four songs and a gaga endorsement by Thomas Pynchon. ("This is one of those special novels—a piece of working magic, warm, funny, and sane—that you want to just ride off into the sunset with.") Like its contemporary mass-cult objects, *The Rocky Horror Picture Show* and *Close Encounters of the Third Kind, Cowgirls* offered a homogenized compendium of postcountercultural wisdom: The meandering, extravagantly literary saga of Sissy Hankshaw, gifted with two monstrous thumbs and consequently the world's greatest hitchhiker, is the acid head's *On the Road,* a Paul Bunyan story from the era of stoned raps and self-invented identities, Third World gurus and psychedelic VW buses.

Lanky and voluptuous, Uma Thurman's Sissy is iconographically perfect—an innocently slack-jawed, cow-eyed kewpie doll in a shapeless Stetson whose opposable appendages miraculously balance an otherwise ungainly figure. When this buckskin-clad apparition cocks her hips and, with a windup worthy of Dizzy Dean, sticks out her thumb, she can freeze a Greyhound in its tracks or bring a plane down from the sky. Daughter of a sometime Buddhist monk and one of Timothy Leary's ex-wives, born in Woodstock (the year after the "Aquarian Exposition" that appropriated the town's name), Thurman infuses the part with her own kozmic karma; the movie gains additional piquance by casting her opposite a sister Day-Glo diaper baby, Rain Phoenix, who brings jovial, gap-toothed assurance to the role of militant cowgirl Bonanza Jellybean.

In the Robbins schemata, Sissy is the site of women's liberation—a struggle he casts in conventional American male terms. Initially, Sissy is the corporate embodiment of feminine hygiene, exploited as the Yoni-Yum Dew Girl by the Countess—a prissily gynephobic cosmetic queen (John Hurt in clownish whiteface) who is the total embodiment of the effete East. In keeping with the novel, the movie's New York sequences are suavely claustrophobic, a humid terrarium of decadent geeks and cultural references (Andy Warhol, *Portnoy's Complaint*). Trapped in someone else's scene, Sissy passes out and wakes up being groped by a Manhattan sophisticate (Crispin Glover), the ash of his cigarette poised over her face; later, she will be liberated by her adventures among the cowgirls of the Countess's western health spa, the Rubber Rose Ranch.

While Robbins can surely turn a phrase ("the Countess had a smile like the first scratch on a new car"), the least to be said for Van Sant is that he deranges the novel's eccentricities with his own. Wholesome and trippy, basically an increasingly dull series of riffs against an intermittently busy background, the movie cuts back the book's male characters, including the macho, narrative-controlling shenanigans of authorial stand-in "Dr. Robbins," and represses almost all of the heterosexual relations. Thurman's nominal costar Keanu Reeves was largely edited out even before the movie's less-than-epochal Toronto premiere, while the tiresome antics of the resident Mr. Natural ("Pat" Morita) have since been excised, thus displacing the R. Crumb-like appreciation of female pulchritude onto the cowgirls.

Revolting, first against the Countess and his surrogate (Angie Dickinson, her face stretched so tight she can barely talk), then against the federal government, ultimately against Robbins himself, the Rubber Rose cowgirls espouse lesbian love, armed ecofeminism, and strategic consciousness expansion. As the cowgirls are identical with the counterculture, it seems hardly coincidental that the mournfully apocalyptic finale should be explicitly set during the Aquarian death throes of 1972-73; holding hostage the last flock of whooping cranes, they feed the birds peyote. (In one of the more evocative bits of Woodstock logic, Bonanza Jellybean argues that food and air are also drugs,) "The peyote mellowed them out, made them less uptight," says Jelly of the cranes and so it is with the movie.

That *Cowgirls* is likely too laidback for the MTV-habituated is a function of its period naturalism—best personified by the cowgirl shamaness, Dolores Del Ruby (Lorraine Bracco). Daringly puffy-faced and bedraggled, Bracco appears in a ratty Persian lamb cloak that might have been purchased in a purple haze on St. Marks Place from the mother of hip used clothing stores. With her dentalized diction and pungently nasal accounts of Yucatán epiphanies, she's an authentic flashback of an extinct type—the acid queen of St. Marks Place, the sybil of Bensonhurst.

Also reviewed in:
CHICAGO TRIBUNE, 5/20/94, Friday/p. H, Michael Wilmington
NEW YORK TIMES, 5/20/94, p. C10, Caryn James
NEW YORKER, 5/30/94, p. 99, Anthony Lane
VARIETY, 9/20/93, p. 26, Deborah Young

EXIT TO EDEN

A Savoy Pictures relase of an Alex Rose/Henderson production. *Executive Producer:* Edward K. Milkis and Nick Abdo. *Producer:* Alexandra Rose and Gary Marshall. *Director:* Garry Marshall. *Screenplay:* Deborah Amelon and Bob Brunner. *Based on the book by:* Anne Rice. *Director of Photography:* Theo Van de Sande. *Editor:* David Finfer. *Music:* Patrick Doyle. *Music Editor:* Roy Prendergast, Craig Pettigrew, and Scott Grusin. *Sound:* Jim Webb, Keith A. Webster and (music) Paul Hulme. *Sound Editor:* Alan Robert Murray. *Casting:* Valorie Massalas. *Production Designer:* Peter Jamison. *Art Director:* Margie McShirley. *Set Designer:* Steven Schwartz, Darrell J. Wight, Evelyne Barbier, and Ann Harris. *Set Decorator:* Linda Spheeris. *Set Dresser:* Troy Peters, Ken Wilson, Mark Little, Tom Kaltsas, Louis Terry, and Jim Jackson. *Special Effects:* Gary Zink. *Costumes:* Ellen Mirojnick. *Make-up:* Robert J. Mills. *Make-up (Dana Delany):* Marilyn Carbone. *Stunt Coordinator:* Glenn Wilder. *Running time:* 113 minutes. *MPAA Rating:* R.

CAST: Dana Delany (Lisa); Paul Mercurio (Elliot); Rosie O'Donnell (Sheila); Dan Aykroyd (Fred); Hector Elizondo (Martin); Stuart Wilson (Omar); Iman (Nina); Sean O'Bryan (Tommy); Stephanie Niznik (Diana); Phil Redrow (Richard); Sandra Korn (Riba); Julie Hughes (Julie); Laurelle Mehus (Heidi); Tom Hines (Nolan); Allison Moir (Kitty); Deborah Pratt (Dr. Williams); Laura Harring (M.C. Kindra); James Patrick Stuart (James); Deborah Lacey (Sophia); Lucinda Crosby (Claudia); Janet Turner (Zara); Tom Wrightman (Mike); Joey House (Velvet); Real Andrews (Andre); Rene Lamart (Roger); Rod Britt (Mr. Brady);

Rosemary Forsyth (Mrs. Brady); Shannon Wilcox (Mary); Diane Frazer (Bettiann); Leslie Sank (Evelyn); Barbara Marshall (Shy Student); Diana Kent (Tehani); Bud Markowitz (Ben-Wa Juggler); Nancy Debease (Nancy); Lynda Goodfriend (Linda); John Clayton Schafer (Lars); Tanya Reid (Naomi); Pola Maloles (Angela); Rachel Levy (Christine); Emily Smith (Durelle); Jame Curreri (Dominick); Sam Denoff (The Confused Golfer); Arnold Margolin (Mr. Vanderway); Kristi Noel (Fantasy Secretary); Alex Rose (Hostess); Jane Morris (All Tied-Up Shop Clerk); Kathleen Marshall (Stewardess Susan); Julie Paris (Immigration Security); Steve Restivo (Immigration Clerk); Ira D. Glick (Immigration Passenger); Joe Torry (Baggage Cop); Ronny Hallin (Airport Cleaning Lady); Frank Campanella (Wheelchair Walker); Mel Novak (Walker's Henchman); Lou Evans and Rio Hackford (Topless Customers); Allan Kent (Det. Anderson); Dawn Lovett (Officer Martha); Mariana Morgan (Rachel); Judith Baldwin (Priscilla); Joyce Brothers (Herself); Julia Hunter (Tour Guide); Scott Marshall (Latte); Donna Dixon (Fred's Ex-Wife); Elsie Sniffin (Police Woman); Ed Cree (Street Fiddler); Lisa LaNou (Street Girl); Ralph Martin (Hotel Manager); Sheila Hanahan (Fan Lady); Lori Marshall and Bill Fricker (Tourists); Zachary Bogatz (Brother); Mandy Ingber (Sister); Cassandra Leigh (Unhappy Wife); Bonnie Aarons (The Prostitute); Rajia Baroudi (French Maid); Brian Davila (Young Elliot); Gloria Hylton (Angry Girlfriend); Patrick Collins (Priest); Don Hood (Lisa's Father); John Schneider (Professor Collins); Diane Frazen (Bettiann); Stephen Perkins and Danya (Drummers).

LOS ANGELES TIMES, 10/14/94, Calendar/p. 12, Peter Rainer

The advance publicity for "Exit to Eden," loosely based on the Anne Rice novel about S&M, might lead you to expect a torrid kinkfest. But not to worry. Despite its free-love trappings, Hollywood has always been a deeply conservative place. No matter how many clamps and tweezers and harnesses are on display in its movies, no matter how much epidermis is evidenced, sexual wayfarers are routinely punished and true love touted.

"Exit to Eden" is the kind of erotic comedy that Doris Day might have snuggled into. It's such a dopey fizzle that it's kind of fascinating: Did the filmmakers really think they could get away with making a *wholesome* movie about the S&M scene? Director Garry Marshall seems to specialize in making denatured movies about red-hot subjects—remember "Pretty Woman"? Like that film, "Exit to Eden" gambols across sexual minefields before finally plumping for true-blue romanticism. Nothing in it is convincing—not even the whips.

The comic premise—not without possibilities—has L.A. cops Sheila Kingston (Rosie O'Donnell) and Fred Lavery (Dan Aykroyd) going undercover at a tropical resort that caters to S&M fanciers. (Sheila is assigned her own "slave," played by Sean O'Bryan in the film's only funny performance.) They're trying to entrap a pair of diamond smugglers (Stuart Wilson and Iman) on the trail of Elliot (Paul Mercurio), a photojournalist with incriminating evidence against them. Running Club Eden is Mistress Lisa (Dana Delany), who develops a dewy-eyed, against-the-rules hankering for Elliot.

Imagine what Pedro Almodóvar could have done with this! But, then again, he might not have had the gumption to depict Club Eden as a pastel-colored consciousness-raising fantasy island for squeaky-clean libertines. Marshall and screenwriter Deborah Amelon are far bigger teases than anyone in their cast: They set up an erotic roundelay and then run for cover. This is the kind of sex comedy that Dr. Joyce Brothers would endorse. (In a sense, she already has—she makes a cameo appearance.)

O'Donnell huffs and puffs her way through her Sgt. Joe Fridayish role while Aykroyd acts aggravatingly strait-laced. (She rankles him by constantly updating him on her ovulation cycles and feminine hygiene problems—perhaps the worst running gag in any movie so far this year.) It might have been funny if these two had been sorely tempted into kinkdom but the film never really explores their psyches. They don't seem to have any. Elliot and Mistress Lisa don't fare much better, despite a lot of pop psych blather about how love means losing control. This might be funny if that lack of control were touted in an S&M context, but, no, the filmmakers just want us to know that being in love means being vulnerable—without the leather outerwear, that is.

Since the Hollywood romantic comedy is still reeling from the smudging of sex roles in the past two decades, "Exit to Eden" might have worked as a free-for-all compendium of '90s love play.

(All entrants to Club Eden are given blood tests—*whew.*) But there's so little erotic heat in this movie that it gives sex a bad name.

Now *that's* an achievement.

NEW YORK, 10/31/94, p. 98, David Denby

Exit to Eden may very well mark Garry Marshall's exit from filmmaking. Searching for a way to deal with this embarrassing mess—it's a limp comedy about sadomasochism—I will take the high road and remind the reader that Marshall, the director of *The Flamingo Kid, Nothing in Common,* and *Frankie and Johnny,* has over the years given audiences a fair amount of pleasure (of the non-tingling variety). He may yet do so again, God willing. Most of *Exit to Eden* takes place on a resort island off the coast of Mexico where people pay a great deal of money to enact their fantasies—to be chained or spanked or treated as dogs, and to do the same unto others. The island is presided over by Dana Delany, a dominatrix on horseback. Occasionally naked, Ms. Delany possesses an admirably long-waisted body, but apart from one moment in which she caresses with her breasts the molded bottom of Paul Mercurio (the hero of *Strictly Ballroom,* here chained rather than dancing), I felt not even the beginnings of a warming flush. Neither, I imagine, will you—unless you find uniquely arousing the many scenes of well-built men and women larking under palm trees and swatting the behinds of the hotel staff in a perverse game of ping-pong.

A friend should have advised Marshall as politely as possible that sadomasochism and verbal comedy don't always go together—that nothing, in general, ruins the heated trance of lustful fantasy more rapidly than nattering, sitcom-style jokes (porn and black comedy might go together, but that combo is not in Marshall's repertory). Marshall makes a movie about fantasy in which there isn't any fantasy—most of the movie has the stimulating atmosphere of a deluxe dental clinic. Dan Aykroyd and Rosie O'Donnell, as two cops searching for diamond smugglers, show up at the island, where they find themselves fending off the submissive resort attendants. Joke, joke, joke—the two non-swingers appear to be in a state of panic, and of course they are meant to represent us, the normal people, who are presumably alarmed and disgusted by such goings-on. Garry Marshall titillates us and then ridicules what turns him on: He's a dirty old man with a guilty conscience—not the best state in which to direct a comedy.

NEW YORK POST, 10/14/94, p. 46, Michael Medved

Novelist Anne Rice recently drew national attention with her outspoken condemnation, and subsequent endorsement, of the upcoming film version of her book "Interview With the Vampire."

Why, then, has the opinionated writer remained so silent over this abominable adaptation of her erotic novel "Exit to Eden"?

Her book is a graphic, literate, compulsively entertaining tour-de-force about a surprising love affair that develops within the confines of an ultra-exclusive sex resort called The Club.

The movie, however, is a tour-de-worst, retaining almost nothing from the novel other than the names of three of the characters: even The Club is now known as "Eden."

The ruler of this decadent island domain is Mistress Lisa (Dana Delany of TVs "China Beach"), who falls for an Australian photographer (dancer-actor Paul Mercurio of "Strictly Ballroom") who comes to her risque resort for a week's vacation.

Unfortunately for him (and for us), he's carrying a role of film that is coveted by two murderous diamond smugglers (Stuart Wilson and Iman) who follow him to the island.

They are, in turn, followed by dedicated police officers Dan Aykroyd and Rosie O'Donnell, who go under cover in pursuit of the crooks.

None of this cops-and-robbers stupidity makes the least bit of sense and it's a great tribute to the comedic professionalism of O'Donnell and Aykroyd that they nevertheless manage to milk their pathetic parts for a few good laughs.

Dana Delany, meanwhile, displays her shapely body In a variety of outrageous outfits, but still can't shake her Betty Crocker, girl-next-door image: It comes as no surprise when this supposedly tough-minded dominatrix is transformed, through one night of love, into a docile and domesticated playmate.

"Babies and bondage," she coos "You mean I can have them both?"

Paul Mercurio is the movie's biggest bust: an embarrassingly blank screen presence whose bare buns (the object of innumerable closeups) make a far stronger impression than his face or his voice.

The movie falls flat, in fact, on every level: as a "daring" exploration of S&M indulgence, it's a silly tease, with only one brief (and unseen) allusion to playful paddling with a hairbrush to justify all the black-leather posing.

The supposedly glamorous sex resort comes across like a sad, seedy nudist camp, with it's "five-star" facilities (actually filmed on the Hawaiian island of Lanai) resembling a run-down Holiday Inn.

The movie represents a career low-point for director Garry Marshall ("Pretty Woman," "Nothing in Common") though the anonymous authors of the movie's press kit deserve some special recognition.

They composed unintentionally hilarious, deadpan declarations like, "The male-female interplay between the two villains and the two cops is a comic commentary running on the precarious balance of the power struggle between men and women."

There's also my special favorite: "The storyline of 'Exit to Eden' achieves the classical structure of a Shakespeare comedy ..."

Unfortunately, no lines in the movie itself are nearly so amusing as these pompous pronouncements to the press.

NEWSDAY, 10/14/94, Part II/p. B8, Jack Mathews

Say, do you dream of being tied up and spanked? Does the smell of leather make you tremble with desire? Like to crawl on your hands and knees, to be treated like an animal, and made to beg for love?

Cancel your subscription to Whips and Chains Monthly, don't waste another dime on nipple clamps and riding crops, and get yourself down to the multiplex for Garry Marshall's R (for ripe)-rated "Exit to Eden," where you will see the finest display of bondage accessories, tethered beauties, bare breasts and bottoms, and picturesque backdrops Hollywood has to offer.

On the other hand, if you answered no to these questions, there is a different kind of pain in store for you. The pain of seeing actors Dana Delany and Paul Mercurio try to maintain their dignity while romping around in the nude, pretending to be getting excited by the sight of ropes and hairbrushes. And the pain of seeing Rosie O'Donnell and Dan Aykroyd log as many S & M and genitalia jokes they can get off in an hour and 50 minutes.

O'Donnell and Aykroyd, playing L. A. cops working undercover at a Club Med for bondage freaks, give the movie what little amusement value it has, and O'Donnell, quite a sight in a dominatrix outfit, is actually very funny at times. But it is essentially a skin flick.

The story, adapted from an Anne Rice novel, takes place at Eden, an island off the coast of Mexico where guests pay large sums to be treated as sex slaves. It is here that an Australian photographer (Mercurio) has come to indulge a spanking fetish, followed by a pair of criminals (Stuart Wilson, and the model Iman) after some photos he took, and the cops chasing them.

Marshall, who made his fortune in TV ("Happy Days," "Laverne and Shirley") before turning to films ("Pretty Woman"), has taken Rice's dark psychosexual undercurrents and churned them all up to the surface in a giddy froth. His Eden is a sunny resort for orgies among aerobicized, HIV-negative *turistas*, and pain has nothing to do with it.

I don't mind the filmmakers' fooling around with this novel—I'd hate to see a serious movie on the subject—but the whole exercise reeks of exploitation. Not only is the background filled out with near-naked men and women, but scenes are choreographed to give us the best views of the stars' bodies—full 360s of the voluptuous Delany, and numerous lingering close-ups of Mercurio's Big Whopper buns.

There is a love story here, as there was in the book, between a slave (Mercurio) and his mistress (Delany), but it as unbelievable as the club itself, and even for those who appreciate candor on the screen, their lovemaking is less erotic than vulgar.

Marshall should have settled for a good whipping.

SIGHT AND SOUND, 8/95, p. 48, Nick James

As a small boy in Australia, Elliot Slater used to deliberately misbehave until his family's French maid would spank him. Now, as a full-grown successful photojournalist in California, he wants to get to the bottom of his peculiar need. He signs up for Club Eden, a tropical island dedicated to S&M role-play, as a slave.

Before going, however, he photographs a master diamond smuggler, Omar, in the act of pocketing contraband. As LA police detectives Sheila Kingston and Fred Lavery soon discover, there is no other picture of Omar in existence. They reason correctly that Omar and his sadistic henchwoman Nina must be keen to get back the film. Both parties are therefore after Elliot. At the island, Elliot's cockiness incurs the wrath of Club Eden's boss, Mistress Lisa. Omar, Nina and Sheila fly in disguised as guests while Fred goes undercover as a maintenance man. Elliot continues to be bare-faced in his admiration of Lisa. She decides to take him in hand personally, tying him up and spanking him with a hair brush until he confesses that he likes it. Afterwards, she allows him to sleep on the floor next to her bed, and in the night he pleasures her.

Detective Sheila constantly requests the presence of Slave Elliot. He finally arrives on sports day but confesses that he wants to go immediately to take part in the rollerblade race because the prize is a night with Lisa. He wins and Lisa realises that she loves him and that he has become a threat to her job. She orders him off the island but instead he persuades her to come away with him for a weekend in New Orleans. Sheila and Fred arrest Nina, but Omar gets away and goes after Elliot. Omar tracks the lovers down to Tara, the mansion house from *Gone with the Wind*, where they have slipped away from a guided tour to make love in the bedroom. There Omar tries to shoot Elliot but is prevented by Sheila and shot by Fred. Lisa abandons Elliot and returns to her island but Sheila brings him back to Club Eden and he proposes marriage to Lisa while strung up in bondage.

Whatever the merits of the Anne Rice novel from which *Exit to Eden* was adapted, none can have survived here. This film is a barren concoction: like a Carry On film (*Carry On Cuffing*?) but with the toned-down fantasies of Hollywood executives replacing the picture postcard vulgarity of prurient Brits and with *double entendres* conspicuous by their absence. The script's purpose seems to be to deflect attention away from the sex and punishment theme and towards S&M psychobabble. Mistress Lisa boasts of having put many people in touch with their true selves. There are encounter groups where nice middle-aged women are encouraged to talk dirty: "Put your thing in my thing," ventures one.

Most of the comic lines are given to Rosie O'Donnell. She tries for the come-hither tone of a Mae West, but sounds more like she's speaking a foreign language—scriptese rather than pricktease. No one pays her any mind except for her allotted slave (who asks her to name her fantasy. "Paint my house," she replies). Apart from the cops, everyone else is dressed for a raunchy party that never takes place. The most painful act between consenting adults shown is a gentle spanking with a hairbrush. If the point was to send up the ludicrous appearance of fetishistic gear then why be so po-faced about those who wear it? There is plenty of substance for satire in the average fetish manual but *Exit to Eden* doesn't seem to want to offend potential users.

Such contradictions find their focus in the performance of Dana Delany as Mistress Lisa. While Lisa is bareback riding about her fantasy island, we are never quite sure whether her constant female companion is more than just a domestic slave. Delany uses this and other ambiguities in Lisa's character with a skill that obliterates Paul Mercurio in their scenes together. While he remains a charmless buffoon throughout, Delany is clearly an actress of some talent and there are bizarre echoes here of her performance in Paul Schrader's *Light Sleeper* as the equally hard-to-fathom former lover of drug dealer Willem Dafoe.

But there are also many scenes in which she is ill at ease. Indeed, most of the cast appear to know that they're appearing semi-naked in a major turkey. *Exit to Eden* belies the effectiveness of the sort of talent packaging that Hollywood has gone in for over the past few years. Putting Garry *Pretty Woman* Marshall with Paul *Strictly Ballroom* Mercurio for an Anne *Interview with the Vampire* Rice story might be an A-list troilist encounter made in paradise, but the outcome is pure torture.

VILLAGE VOICE, 10/25/94, p. 57, J. Hoberman

Attempting to go the wholesome smarminess of *Pretty Woman* one better, affable Garry Marshall charges in where Michael Tolkin fears to tread, adapting *Exit to Eden*, Anne Rice's softcore romance, pseudonymously published in 1985, of a Club Med-style resort where the beautiful people go to spank and be spanked. There's no ambivalence here. Marshall is a happy popularizer. A boatload of "submissives" make their thunderous entrance into Eden like a cattle call off *The Love Boat*.

Exit to Eden, which has been banned in Saskatchewan, features a fair amount of nudity (many perfect butts encased in gold-studded bondage thong ensembles). But, as Marshall reconfigured Rice's novel to infiltrate Eden with a pair of paradigmatically normal undercover cops (Rosie O'Donnell and Dan Aykroyd) and cast the terminally "G" Dana Delany as Eden's administrator, Mistress Lisa, it's a movie of insane mood switches. Adventure comedy gives way to sentimental romance. Pornless porn inserts and glosses on *The Story of O* are interrupted by sit-com shtick ("we're the only two People on this island without handcuffs") or scenes designed to wrap the constantly yakking O'Donnell in a black vinyl muumuu. Perhaps honoring some obscure contractual agreement, the movie's last reel is played out in Rice's hometown, New Orleans, everything converging on a simulacrum of Scarlett O'Hara's boudoir.

Unlike *Clerks, Exit to Eden* lacks the wit to be tasteless. Even when brushing her actual nipples over the cleft in Paul Mercurio's body-double butt, Delany is less Queen of Outer Space than the puppy-eyed Dominatrix Next Door; as one gleans from the spectacle of Dr. Joyce Brothers explaining s/m on TV; *Exit to Eden* sees its mission as basically therapeutic, burdening its mild titillation with a massive load of I'm O.K., You're O.K. reassurance, time-tested recipes (Mercurio spreading butter and sprinkling cinnamon on Delany's heaving bosom), and even older bromides: "True love is still the ultimate turn-on."

Given the movie's lax direction and programmatic insistence on acting out one's desires, one can't but notice the performers living theirs: exotic villainous Iman pretends that she's in a James Bond film, Mercurio that he's the lead in a romantic comedy. O'Donnell, who really belongs with the cool kids in *Clerks*, acts as though she thinks she's Dan Aykroyd in *Dragnet* while the actual Aykroyd appears to imagine himself playing anything somewhere else.

Dana Delany's fantasy is the most poignant. She not only told *Premiere* that *Exit to Eden* gave her a chance to show the real her—she seems to believe that Garry Marshall is going to make that creature the next Julia Roberts.

Also reviewed in:
CHICAGO TRIBUNE, 10/14/94, Friday/p. L, Johanna Steinmetz
NEW YORK TIMES, 10/14/94, p. C20, Janet Maslin
VARIETY, 10/17-23/94, p. 37, Leonard Klady
WASHINGTON POST, 10/14/94, p. F9, Richard Harrington

EXOTICA

A Miramax Films release of an Ego Film Arts production with the participation of Telefilm Canada and the Ontario Film Development Corporation. *Producer:* Atom Egoyan and Camelia Frieberg. *Director:* Atom Egoyan. *Screenplay:* Atom Egoyan. *Director of Photography:* Paul Sarossy. *Editor:* Susan Shipton. *Music:* Mychael Danna. *Music Editor:* Paul Shikata. *Choreographer:* Claudia Moore. *Sound:* Ross Redfern and (music) David Bottrill. *Production Designer:* Linda del Rosario and Richard Paris. *Set Dresser:* Doug McCullough, Brent Kelly, Linda del Rosario, Richard Paris, and Garth Brunt. *Special Effects:* Michael Kavonaugh. *Costumes:* Linda Muir. *Make-up:* Nicole Demers. *Stunt Coordinator:* Ted Hanlon. *Running time:* 103 minutes. *MPAA Rating:* Not Rated.

CAST: Bruce Greenwood (Francis); Mia Kirshner (Christina); Don McKellar (Thomas); Arsinée Khanjian (Zoe); Elias Koteas (Eric); Sarah Polley (Tracey); Victor Garber (Harold);

Calvin Green (Customs Officer); David Hemblen (Inspector); Peter Krantz (Man in Taxi); Damon D'Oliveira and Billy Merasty (Men at Opera); Jack Blum (Scalper); Ken McDougall (Doorman).

LOS ANGELES TIMES, 3/3/95, Calendar/p. 10, Kevin Thomas

With "Exotica," whose title refers to a Toronto nightclub, Canada's venturesome Atom Egoyan has made one of his most accessible films to date, a haunting and complex fable of loss and desire with wide implications. An immense place with lush, kitschy tropical decor, the fictional strip club is the principal setting of this mesmerizing, genuinely original work that has something of the dreamy, darkly humorous fatalistic quality of another Canadian film dealing with interconnecting lives, "Atlantic City." "Exotica" took the International Critics' Prize at Cannes and was recently voted best foreign film of 1994 by the French Film Critics Assn.

The film's key relationship is between a bearded, nice-looking thirtysomething tax auditor named Francis (Bruce Greenwood), who regularly patronizes the club, always requesting the same table dancer, Christina (Mia Kirshner), who invariably starts out her routine dressed as a schoolgirl, a very convincing Lolita who in fact is not too many years past her own minority. Their relationship is intensely ritualized, and it is only with the film's gradual unraveling that we understand its meaning, a notion of why it could be of importance to Christina as well as to Francis.

This relationship emerges as a powerful metaphor for contemporary sexuality, where immense latitude as to what can be shown in public still conflicts with what can be touched; "Exotica" suggests in this way that a lingering, deeply embedded Puritanism nourishes the voyeurism so emblematic of our lonely, isolating society. Voyeurism has concerned Egoyan in such previous films as "The Adjuster" and especially "Speaking Parts."

Francis, who has suffered overwhelming personal tragedy, and Christina form the film's linchpin, where a number of othel lives intersect. On the one hand, Christiana is caught up in a complicated situation with the club's macho emcee/deejay (Elias Koteas) and the club's elegant owner (Arsinée Khanjian), whose sense of pride and propriety could not be greater if she were running an exclusive finishing school for upper-crust girls. On the other, Francis, as a government tax auditor, is zeroing in on the books of a pet shop owner, an uptight young gay man (Don McKellar) who will become caught up in Francis and Christina's lives: meanwhile, Francis has his own complicated relationship with his brother (Victor Garber) and his young niece (Sarah Polley).

With the unexpected awaiting us with each new sequence, Egoyan has the imagination and stamina to go the distance, following the destinies of his people, which reveal themselves with a forceful sense of inevitability—and in turn reveal Egoyan's grasp of the often quirky workings of human nature. Heightening the film's sensuality and mystery is Mychael Danna's lush score, inspired by Indian music.

Clearly, Egoyan inspires trust in actors, and "Exotica" is replete with selfless portrayals, with Kirshner bringing to Christina a remarkably persuasive blend of experience, vulnerability and intelligence. As a stylist, Egoyan could have been a bit more assertive, bringing more of a sense of shape to this film, but his sensibility is so fresh, so unique, that it scarcely matters.

NEW YORK, 3/13/95, p. 63, David Denby

Atom Egoyan's *Exotica* also [the reference is to *Before the Rain*] has a convoluted structure, but this movie doesn't really come together in your head afterward. While you're watching it, however, *Exotica* is quite an experience. Egoyan, who is of Armenian descent but was raised in Canada and continues to work there, sets much of *Erotica* in a lush, palm-treed, pasha-palace strip club, where mysteriously significant rituals are enacted for our amazement. A spectacular young table-dancer (Mia Kirshner), opening her schoolgirl's white shirt, works for her special "client" (Bruce Greenwood), teasing and rubbing up against him. Yet he is forbidden by the rules of the place to do anything more than suffer. For most of the movie, we don't know what their hold on each other is. Their relationship is sex but not sex, love but not love. Egoyan uses the erotic for rapt moments of suspension, and for some of the niftiest jokes in years. A customs inspector, examining an incoming passenger through a one-way mirror, later seduces him and examines him a lot closer. In the morning, he confiscates his bed partner's smuggled goods—some rare macaw eggs. *Exotica* is a rare egg itself, odd, speckled, and precious.

NEW YORK POST, 9/24/94, p. 18, Larry Worth

Voyeurism is always a hot topic. But writer/director Atom Egoyan goes way past titillation with his wonderfully complex "Exotica." As his most accomplished film to date, it's a striking addition to the New York Film Festival lineup.

Most of the action takes place in a strip-tease parlor where entertainers drape themselves all over the customers. Thc trick is that thc men can't touch the ladies.

Into this environment comes one client with a fetish for a "naughty schoolgirl" dancer. Seems they have a history together. But she's the seedy announcer's object of affection, even though he just impregnated the club's lovely owner, And that's just for starters.

The labyrinthian screenplay brings another half-dozen quirky characters into the mix, then lets their lives criss-cross for a couple hours as their secret pasts—and hidden longings—spill out with each new twist of the tale.

Freud would have a field day. Thanks to a wonderful cast and Egoyan's genius, so will viewers.

NEW YORK POST, 3/3/95, p. 44, Thelma Adams

"Exotica" is a Canadian "Twin Peaks" with a tweaked I.Q.—hold the dwarf and cue the strippers.

Writer/director Atom ("Calendar") Egoyan's hothouse mystery orbits the upscale strip joint, Exotica. A school-girl worshipping accountant (Bruce Greenwood), a smuggling pet shop owner (Don McKellar), a dissatisfied deejay (Elias Koteas) and a disrobing honor student (Mia Kirshner) fall into the club's gravitational pull.

The pregnant lesbian owner (Egoyan's mate, Arsinee Khanjian) monitors the burlesque, as well as her identity crisis. Secrets abound among the characters: a purloined egg, a sexual kink, a voyeuristic bent, an unrecoverable past, an innocence cast off, a sexual betrayal, an unacknowledged paternity.

What brought the person to this point?" asks the deejay in one of his smoky-voiced ramblings intended to get customers to pony up for private table-side dances. It's Egoyan's question.

He plumbs what's hidden in the exotic characters he's created with a chill detachment partially camouflaged by steamy atmospherics and soft-core porn.

In this Chinese puzzle-box of a movie, secrets are gradually revealed, hidden links between characters come to light, until the final image solves the interpersonal mystery in an epiphany where the whole movie clicks into place.

Or at least it should. It's a clever moment that throws a new light on what's gone before, but it's neither satisfying enough to dispel the boredom that preceded it nor does it answer remaining questions about dangling sub-plots.

Like Exotica's customers, I should be hot and bothered by the show. I wasn't. I respect Egoyan the morning after, but I'm not impassioned about "Exotica."

NEWSDAY, 9/23/94, Part II/p. B5, John Anderson

A winner at Toronto and an extraordinary film, set in a strip club called Exotica where lush horticulture, strange lushes and stranger stories intertwine. Using his usual nonlinear, almost circular storytelling technique, director Atom Egoyan ("Calendar") ultimately imbues his characters—the true exotica of the title—with damaged nobility. But first he leads us up detours and dark alleys, blurring the lines between " Exotica's" voyeurs, the movie audience and himself.

NEWSDAY, 3/3/95, Part II/p. B5, Gene Seymour

People do a lot of looking through two-way mirrors in "Exotica." The first sequence, in fact, has two customs agents peering intently at a fidgeting nerd named Thomas (Don McKellar) from behind a mirror at a Toronto airport.

Both we and the agents only suspect that there's something suspicious about this meek little cat. There is. But as with everything else in this brilliant, insinuating film (which won a major prize at last spring's Cannes Film Festival), writer-director Atom Egoyan takes his sweet time telling us about it.

There are also two-way mirrors at Exotica, a gaudy strip joint where, as the club's serpentine disc jockey, Eric (Elias Koteas), repeatedly says, five bucks buys a patron his own private dance. Eric saves his more evocative calls for Christina (Mia Kirshner), who's as dark, sultry and mysterious as the club.

That Christina dances, dresses—and partly undresses—in parochial school clothes seems to be of special fascination for a sad-eyed tax auditor named Francis (Bruce Greenwood) who, night after night, performs a tearful dialogue with her that suggests deep torment in his life. Eric, who was once Christina's lover, seethes as he watches their intense, yet mostly chaste ritual from behind ... a two-way mirror.

In these scenes, Egoyan may be saying that we are *all* two-way mirrors—gazing furtively at each other from behind the walls of our selves, collecting assumptions about what we see in the hope that they'll add up to a complete picture.

Egoyan's elliptical, allusive storytelling gives the bum's rush to this fragile notion. The characters and circumstances in "Exotica" never remain what we believe them to be at first, or even second, glance.

Francis' emotional baggage stays more or less concealed when he audits Thomas' business records, but how much does he know about the strange eggs Thomas smuggled in at the airport?

Just how intimate is the relationship between Christina and Exotica's owner (Arsinee Khanjian), who's having Eric's baby? And why does Francis' wheelchair-bound brother (Victor Garber) let his teenaged daughter babysit every night at Frances' house, where there's nobody to babysit?

Some of these questions are answered. Some are not. Part of what makes Egoyan's film such a spellbinding marvel is that he is able to make even its unresolved enigmas whirl his tangled, shadowy plot toward an unexpectedly tender conclusion.

As with other gifted young filmmaker's today, Egoyan finds near-miraculous ways of bringing wit, intelligence and grace to material that, in lesser hands, would be tawdry at best, conventional at worst. In his hands, a quirky story laced with sleaze leaves one's head buzzing with such weighty issues as: How do we know what's in our best interests? Or each other's?

You may have similar questions when "Exotica" is over. Though small in scope, it's large enough in achievement to inspire as many questions—of whatever dimension—as the mind can conceive.

SIGHT AND SOUND, 5/95, p. 45, Amanda Lipman

Thomas, a pet show owner, is watched through a two-way mirror by airport customs officials. He shares a cab from the airport into town with a stranger who, alighting by an upmarket strip club called Exotica, gives him two ballet tickets instead of his share of the fare.

The club is presided over by Zoe, a pregnant madame, and Eric, a smooth-talking DJ who has fathered her baby in a contract agreement. Christina does an act in which she plays a Lolita-ish schoolgirl, watched jealously by Eric. Every night she dances privately for Francis, an auditor whose schoolgirl daughter and wife are dead. While he visits the club, his niece, Tracey, 'babysits' at his empty home.

Eric recalls his first meeting with Christina, when hunting for Francis' missing daughter. At the ballet, Thomas picks up a young male escort, but goes home alone to the macaw eggs he smuggled through customs. Francis comes to Thomas' shop to audit his accounts. Christina discovers Zoe's pregnancy contract with Eric and is furious. After many opera/ballet visits, Thomas, finally takes a male escort home—one of the customs officials. When he wakes up, the man has confiscated the eggs. In Exotica's men's room, an unseen Eric persuades Francis to touch Christina, but when he does so, Eric throws him out and has him barred. Having discovered Thomas' smuggling activities, Francis agrees not to go to the authorities if Thomas will go to Exotica and talk to Christina.

Christina tells Thomas that Francis never got over the murder of his teenage daughter and that his wife died in a car crash a few months afterwards. Eric tries to persuade Thomas to touch Christina, telling him that he used to be her lover. Zoe finds out what Eric is up to and sacks him. The next night, Thomas goes back to the club and talks to Christina again. Francis waits outside, determined to shoot Eric. Eric approaches and tells him that it was he who found his daughter's body. Francis embraces him. Inside the club, Thomas puts his hand on Christina's leg. She removes it slowly. In a flashback, we see a young Christina arriving at Francis' house to babysit his daughter. When Francis takes her home, she hints at how unhappy she is. He comforts her kindly.

Atom Egoyan returns on magnificent form to the themes he knows and loves: sex, love, relationships and the voyeuristic nature of all of these. Where his last film, *Calendar*, emphasised the most anal aspects of his obsessions, this sympathetic group piece is far more relaxed and much more enjoyable and intriguing for it. Almost every member of this group mythologises who and where they are through play acting and ritual. Zoe plays the part of dispassionate matriarch. Christina is crystallised into the schoolgirl she acts onstage. Francis turns his mourning for his dead daughter into a fetishistic, psychosexual relationship through Christina's striptease character. Thomas, a pet shop owner, would rather see himself as a smuggler of exotic goods.

In keeping with the "look but don't touch" maxim of the club Exotica, the characters are all alienated by their personas: Eric and Zoe, both obsessed with Christina, content themselves with watching her through secret windows; Francis can only look at Christina dancing—even his memories of his wife and daughter are video images. And Thomas on his first, tentative trips to the opera can only sit next to the men he picks up, but cannot take them home. Egoyan skilfully weaves voyeurism deep into the film: there are mirrors everywhere, from the club's spyholes to Thomas' glass tanks to the two-way customs official's mirror. Voyeurism, the watchword of Egoyan's postmodern world, is a symbol of both aloneness and a strange kind of togetherness. The watchers collaborate in their spying, and are finally bound together not through love but through another's transgression (the murder of a child) in the past.

They turn out, in fact, to be members of a complicated, oedipally disrupted 'family' with Zoe, Eric and Francis all as symbolic parents/lovers to Christina. Family metaphors run even deeper: Zoe and Eric are about to parent a child; Eric and Christina meet while seeking a (dead) child. Even Thomas is nesting his macaw eggs. Egoyan's avowed desire for *Exotica* to unfold like a striptease, with every scene revealing just a little bit more, turns the audience. too, into tantalised voyeurs. Characters enter the film enigmatically, leading us to guess at their roles and identities, and to construct our own scenarios. (Who do we think Tracey is when we first see Francis take her home and hand her money? A child prostitute? A girlfriend?) But this is not just the director at his most brilliantly perverse, for *Exotica*'s game-playing is also fleshed out with real human sympathy. Francis, for example, trapped in an incestuous fantasy, is also seen in another relationship as a kindly, rather philosophical uncle. The brooding, almost satanic Eric is recalled as a fresh-faced, more optimistic student, capable of selflessness.

The film's playful teasing is not confined to its characters. The variously 'exotic' settings have the same effect, whether they be the club, where disco is replaced by Leonard Cohen as striptease music, Thomas' subterranean-inspiredpet shop, or the colourful chaos of Harold's place ('exotic' birds loom large in all locations). It is only from the moment of Christina's explanation of Francis' past to Thomas, achieved with the flourish of a detective announcing his denouement, that *Exotica* starts to lose its ingenious, languorous way. The film then seems to redirect its energy towards tidying up loose ends. But perhaps this is only one more metaphor—mirroring the way in which the titillation of the striptease can be more exciting than its final, naked flourish.

VILLAGE VOICE, 3/7/95, p. 49, J. Hoberman

A disturbing and ultimately heartbreaking erotic reverie, Atom Egoyan's *Exotica* lifts this gifted young Canadian filmmaker to a new level of achievement. Egoyan's previous movies were suffused with a powerful sense of his own voyeurism, but there's a vivid immediacy to this haunting, sensuous film that pushes it past self-consciousness—ithas the quality of spooky, tragic porn.

Steeped in shame and limned with foreboding, *Exotica* is a movie made under the sign of the superego. The opening scene has a pair of airport cops spying through a two-way mirror on the customs procedure at the Toronto airport. The subject of their interest, a painfully meek pet shop owner named Thomas (Don McKellar), isn't busted until later in the movie, but in *Exotica*, the search for secrets is universal. Everyone has something concealed in their psychological baggage;

no one is precisely who they seem to be. ("You're invited to misperceive as well," the filmmaker enthusiastically confided in *Interview*.)

Exotica is more supple and accomplished than its predecessors but is still the characteristic Egoyan nexus of tangled relationships and crisscrossing narratives. The story unfolds at several sites at once, each with its own distinctive ambient music. The most spectacular location is the nightclub Exotica. Almost a parody of Egoyan's previous sinister, sexually charged films, it's a mock jungle harem of Roman pillars and potted palms, wailing Asian music, and lushly naked women voguing under the blue lights. Humid as the environment seems, the patrons are impassive business types, cool to the point of frozen solid. The gaze rules. The iron law here (as in the movies) is look but don't touch.

Given his longstanding fascination with surveillance and guilty pleasures, technologically enhanced sexual relations and video simulation, dysfunctional patriarchy and incestuous families, Egoyan has always balanced on the knife edge of exploitation. In *Exotica* that aspect of his project is articulated by the club's smarmily insinuating master of ceremonies, Eric (Elias Koteas, the manipulative insurance man in *The Adjuster*). From his aerie above the dance floor, Eric watches and narrates over the revels. What is it that gives a schoolgirl her special innocence?" the tormented MC asks his listeners as a lithe, solemn dancer, dressed in a schoolgirl's uniform to look even younger than she is, wanders out under the lights and breaks into a slow-motion, spastic performance, raising her tartan skirt and gyrating her hips to the unlikely accompaniment of Leonard Cohen's sepulchral drone.

Thus presented, the enigmatic Christina (Mia Kirshner) is Exotica's focal point. She obsesses Eric, her former lover (who claims that it is "therapeutic" for him to offer long and personal introductions to her act). She has some sort of liaison with Zoe (Arsinée Khanjian), the woman who owns the club. And, night after night, she is hired to dance at the table of the markedly melancholy customer, Francis (Bruce Greenwood). As spied upon by jealous Eric, Christina exhibits herself for Francis with an angel's tender solicitude. They even have their rehearsed dialogue. "How could anyone want to hurt you?" he asks while she solicitously reassures him that "You'll always be there to protect me."

While the nature of Francis's desire remains, for much of the movie, something of an unknown, it develops that, in the daytime world, he himself is an investigator—arriving at Thomas's pet store to audit the company books. The pet store provides a dusty, comic analogue to the Club Exotica. It, too, is a family business, as well as both a repository of unusual fetishes and a kindred terrarium in the orderly if anxiety-charged nighttown Egoyan has made of bland Toronto. Like the nightclub, the store is eerily entropic—a greenish light emanating from the rows of fish tanks waiting to encompass who knows what fantasy.

Employing a typically prismatic Egoyan structure, *Exotica* is a series of repeated set pieces, connected by dreamy sound bridges and interspersed with flashbacks in which more youthfully innocent versions of Eric and Christina meet while combing a rural field for a missing child. The narrative inches simultaneously forward and backward as Francis engages in his nightly ritual at *Exotica*. Thomas, meanwhile, has developed his own primal scene, using an extra ballet ticket to pick up a succession of racially "exotic" one-night stands.

Such role playing and compulsive behavior are scarcely unusual in the Egoyan cosmos. The hero of his first feature, *Next of Kin*, presented himself to a bereaved family as their long-lost son; the heroine of *Speaking Parts* obsessively rented movies on videotape in order to attack the career of a particular film extra. In last year's *Calendar*, Egoyan himself played a photographer who, having separated from his wife, invites a different woman home for dinner each month, then eavesdrops as she makes an impassioned phone call to her lover in a foreign language. But no previous Egoyan film has been as founded as *Exotica* on the use of repetition to assuage trauma and conjure absence—raising the compulsion to repeat to the level of ceremonial performance.

Exotica is also a movie about parents and children—something clearly on the filmmaker's mind. (Exotica's heavily pregnant proprietress is played by his wife and frequent star.) Every house has its ghosts; each love is founded upon some sort of spiritual possession. As Francis has constructed a complicated neurotic scenario around his own lost family, so Zoe has inherited the club from her late mother, whose clothes and wig she habitually wears. Eric was contracted to father Zoe's child; even Thomas, left his shop by his father, has smuggled in a rare egg. Christina is the only central character without evident family relations, although that which Eric advertises as "the mystery of her world" is finally revealed as well.

Egoyan has always shown a greater interest in structure than narrative, but *Exotica* is less stilted and more emotional in its development than his earlier features. A hissing snake, Eric sets up unhappy Francis for the further shock of expulsion from Exotica's ersatz Eden. The narrative tension builds through the gradual elucidation of the various characters' connections—including past and present blackmail, murder, and adultery—to a climactic flashback offering a revelation at once powerfully ordinary and extraordinarily sad.

While earlier Egoyan films were set in a video phantom zone, *Exotica* takes as its subject the loneliness of life amid a paradise of paid surrogates. As Zoe tells Christina, "We're here to entertain, not to heal," The taboos are never broken on screen; the film's argument is only played out in images or the imagination. For the audience as much as for the characters, *Exotica* expresses a longing beyond its frame, beyond words.

Also reviewed in:
CHICAGO TRIBUNE, 3/3/95, Friday/p. J, John Petrakis
NEW REPUBLIC, 4/3/95, p. 29, Stanley Kauffmann
NEW YORK TIMES, 3/3/95, p. C12, Caryn James
VARIETY, 5/16-22/94, p. 40, Leonard Klady
WASHINGTON POST, 3/10/95, p. C7, Hal Hinson
WASHINGTON POST, 3/10/95, Weekend/p. 37, Desson Howe

FAUST

A Zeitgeist Films release of a Heart of Europe Prague K Productions/Lumen Films/Athenor coproduction in association with Pandora Film/BBC Bristol/Koninck Film, with financial support from the French Ministry of Culture and Communication and The State Foundation of the Czech Republic for the Support and Development of Czech Cinematography. *Executive Producer:* Karl Baumgartner, Keith Griffiths, Michael Havas, Hengameh Panahi, and Colin Rose. *Producer:* Jaromir Kallista. *Director:* Jan Svankmajer. *Screenplay:* Jan Svankmajer. *Based on "Faust" plays by:* Johann Wolfgang Goethe, Christian Dietrich Grabbe, and Christopher Marlowe. *Director of Photography:* Svatopluk Maly. *Editor:* Marie Zemanova and Alan Brett. *Music:* Johann Sebastian Bach and Charles Gounod. *Choreographer:* Daria Vobornikova. *Sound:* Ivo Spalj. *Art Director:* Eva Svankmajerova and Jan Svankmajer. *Set Decorator:* Martin Kalous, Tomas Kalous, Milos Chlustina, and Petr Bruna. *Animation:* Bedrich Glaser, Martin Kublak, and Ondrej Beranek. *Costumes:* Ruzena Blahova. *Make-up:* Tomas Kuchta, Vaclav Frank, Eva Capkova, and Jirina Bisingerova. *Running time:* 97 minutes. *MPAA Rating:* Not Rated.

CAST: Petr Cepek (Faust); Josef Podsednik and Jaroslava Zelenkova (Puppet Actors); Jan Kraus, Vladimir Kudla, Antonin Zacpal, Jiri Suchy, Viktorie Knotkova, Jana Mezlova, Miluse Strakova, Josef Fiala, Martin Radimecky, Ervin Tomendal, Frantisek Polata, Josef Chodora, Karel Vidimsky, Peter Meissel, Rudolf Ruzek, Milan Vyskocil, Pavel Marek, Dalibor Fencl, Robert Blanda, Michaela Tyllerova, Vendula Pecova, Berenika Strettiova, Zita Moravkova, Gillian Wood, Zuzana Drazilova, Karel Vild, Martin Kublak, Monika Chlustinova, Jiri Liska, Joseph Vedral, Vaclav Svankmajer, and Pavel Valenta (Voices).

NEW STATESMAN & SOCIETY, 9/23/94, p. 33, Jonathan Romney

The opening minute of Jan Svankmajer's *Faust* give us the expected engravings of skeletons and succubi cavorting at a sabbat. But it also gives us the tantalisingly mundane spectacle of dowdy crowds pouring out of a Prague subway entrance. If you've seen the dizzying animation films made by this massively influential Czech master—thick with self-devouring clay heads, and household objects in the throes of entropic implosion—you know how nightmarish and otherworldly his imagination is. But in *Faust*, although he takes us into the depths of a material hell where the presiding phantoms are wood, clay and rusty metal, what's really arresting is the ghastly light Svankmajer casts on the visible world above.

This *Faust* takes literary adaptation to delirious excess. Not only does Svankmajer follow the texts of Goethe and Marlowe—large chunks of which are read *as* playscripts—but he also throws in the lesser-known German Romantic writer Grabbe, a sample from Gounod's opera, borrowings from folk puppet versions of the Faust myth, and also (uncredited but definitely readable between the lines) Mikhail Bulgakov's novel *The Master and Margarita*. In Bulgakov's rewrite of thc Faust myth, Satan and a crew of whimsical minions turn Moscow inside out like a party hat. And in the most fascinating parts of the film, it's Bulgakov's anarchic disregard for the coherence of the urban world that really dominates.

Because Svankmajer packs all this into his film, along with a wide range of echoes from his own past work (traditional marionette puppetry, knockabout Punch, *guignol*, alarmingly liquid clay animation), there's an inescapable feeling that we've seen this all be fore.

Some critics have indeed complained that *Faust* shows us nothing new. But that's the nature of myth—it takes us to places we already know, but can't always recognise. That's also the nature of dream, and *Faust* is particularly dream-like in its apparently random mix of tones—the stuff of blood-curdling nightmare and the flippant absurdity of drunken reverie. It mixes thc blackest comedy with occasionally cloddish farce. A bizarre opera sequence with soup-guzzling ballerinas could have been taken from an early *Monty Python* show (it has that same washed-out pastel look of 1970s TV). And the moment at which thc legend reaches its highest moral seriousness—with salvation abandoned for a quick roll with Helen of Troy—is done as a speeded-up chase sequence, with Faust scuttling after Helen (actually a tarted-up wooden demon with a hole drilled in) like a metaphysical Benny Hill.

Mounted as a mad variety show (much of the action takes place backstage at a hellish theatre), the film is an extremely patchy selection of turns—some spine-chilling, some mind-boggling, some tedious beyond endurance. There's one long sequence in which Faust's Punch-like page learns the words with which to summon and dismiss a burbling devil—and goes on summoning and dismissing and summoning and dismissing until the devil collapses in sheer exhaustion, and we do too. (Svankmajer claims that the scene is actually intended to test our patience). But the film's rambling, heteroclite nature makes perfect sense—it feels like a dream, in which we intermittently drop off and wake up again.

But the film's real power lies not in its revelation of the underworld, or even of the unconscious—but in the way it rearranges the conscious world for us. Svankmajer is, famously, a card-carrying Surrealist, the Czech Surrealist group being the last surviving doctrinaire cell to adhere to a philosophy that is generally regarded as having been long since domesticated beyond redemption. But *Faust* reveals him also to be something of a Situationist in his fascination with the city and its "psychogeography". The film begins with the weary, middle-aged Faust-to-be (Petr Cepek) walking through the streets—a rain-coated, saggy-jowled cross between Tony Hancock and Peter Falk's Columbo. He picks up one of the leaflets being distributed by two sinister men; they contain what looks like a map of the city, but could also be a diagram of some hitherto uncharted section of the human aorta. The map eventually leads him to a cellar, and thence to a theatre, where he dons robes and false beard, and reads the opening of Marlowe's play, setting the whole diabolical show in motion.

But what fascinates most throughout Faust's misadventures is his recurring sorties into the real world. Nonchalantly puffing on a fag, he keeps wandering out of his encounters with ten-foot puppets and sitting down for a beer and a plate of dumplings in the park, only to find more marvels awaiting him. Shot almost *Candid Camera*-style, with panicky demons scaring the wits out of passers-by, such criss-crossing between puppet hell and the street outside suggests that Svankmajer is not only a master alchemist of inanimate matter, but a wizard of street theatre too.

It's the everyday presence of Prague—always, in its legends, a haunted city—that gives *Faust* its special dimension. Svankmajer stages his drama in the unconscious, but also in the unconscious of the city itself, with its hidden parks, seedy restaurants, and courtyards in which old women peer conspiratorially out of windows. As a mapping-out of the infinitely expandable urban topography that haunted Kafka, Svankmajer does for Prague here what Rivette did for Paris in *Céline and Julie Go Boating*, and what Tarkovsky did for time and space altogether in *Stalker*, still the most geographically disorienting film ever made. It's when *Faust* hits the street—and more to the point, when the street hits Faust—that the film most invokes Marlowe's great contribution to the hit parade of literary catch-phrases: "Why, this is hell, nor are we out of it."

NEW YORK POST, 10/26/94, p. 38, Bill Hoffmann

If you like your animation with funny cartoon animals and Road Runner-like speed. then Jan Svankmajer's "Faust" is not for you.

But anybody willing to take a chance on what 1990s animation should be about will want to catch this eye-popping, seductive homage to the Faustian legend.

Using puppets, clay and other three-dimensional animated techniques—as well as live action—Svankmajer leads us into a haunted world of evil imagery and supernatural shenanigans underneath the streets of Prague.

Like so often happens in our city, a commuter (Petr Cepek) emerges from the subway to accept a handbill from a hawker. It features a map with an address and nothing else.

Making his way to an old building, the commuter finds a deserted dressing room and a dog-eared copy of Goethe's "Faust."

Dressing in a caped costume. he suddenly becomes Faust and enters a world of black magic and betrayal.

It's here that Svankmajer's unique animated trickery takes off.

Parents should be forewarned, this is not the stuff of which the Cartoon Network is made of:

A baby forms out of clay and its head frighteningly ages from infant to skeleton; pieces of ripe fruit suddenly turn moldy and maggot-ridden; an old man carries a bloody, severed human leg wrapped in newspaper.

These stark, free-form images will stay with you long after the often confusing plot has faded.

But that's the point. Svankmajer isn't interested in bringing us a coherent story in real time or space.

Here, imagery is the key and Svankmajer is the magician, living up to the age-old adage that the hand is quicker than the eye.

In the genre of grand illusion, "Faust" is a small miracle.

NEWSDAY, 10/26/94, Part II/p. B9, Gene Seymour

Maybe it's the water. Or some kind of exotic air current found only in Central Europe. Whatever the reason, Prague, Kafka's hometown and citadel of Bohemian magic, seems to summon the strangest visions from its artists.

Among the more notable living progenitors of the Czech imagination is animator Jan Svankmajer, who got his start more than 40 years ago in puppetry and, through a series of mixed-media productions, has established an international reputation for his surreal, visionary films.

"Faust" is Svankmajer's first feature since 1988's "Alice" and, as with that bizarre, often grotesque take on Lewis Carroll's fantasy, it is a daunting combination of live-action, claymation and puppetry. Borrowing heavily from Goethe, Gounod, Christopher Marlowe and others who have had a crack at telling this familiar tale, the film uses as its Faust a rumpled Everyman (Petr Cepek) who blandly accepts an enigmatic leaflet as he steps out of a Prague subway station.

At first, Faust ignores the leaflet, a map leading to a red-marked destination somewhere in the city. Yet, at home he encounters a malevolent chicken and an egg, concealed in a loaf of bread, that has no yolk, no white, but packs a heck of a wallop. Somehow this convinces him to seek this place out.

He arrives to find a deserted building that apparently once housed a theater. In the dressing room, he finds a copy of Goethe's "Faust" and everything he needs to play the title role—including the ability to cross dimensions, make magic and seal his ill-fated deal with the Devil. Mephisto, by the way, assumes many forms in this tale. At times, he's a life-sized wooden puppet. At others, he's a disembodied clay face that often takes on the features of Faust himself.

The only humans encountered by this Everyman-Faust include an old man carrying a severed leg and these two sinister characters who goad him to revel in his newfound powers. (Maybe, *they're* Satan.) Svankmajer insists on nothing except the audience's freedom to make whatever it wants of the imagery.

And what imagery! Puppets who take a break in the privy. Ballet dancers who appear and reappear out of nowhere. A clay fetus whose head ages rapidly. Even the pastries are scary in Svankmajer's universe, where time and space seem to melt into the distended shape of a Salvador Dali watch.

There aren't many filmmakers around who are capable of convincing the audience of magic's presence in everyday life. Svankmajer succeeds at this—and much more. He uses the alchemy of his dark, rich imagination to illuminate the emptiness within man's grandest aspirations.

SIGHT AND SOUND, 10/94, p. 40, Philip Strick

Prague, 1994. A businessman sees two men handing out leaflets containing a street map. At his flat, a chicken has roosted overnight; it escapes into the street where the two men capture it in a briefcase. The businessman finds an egg inside a loaf of bread; when opened, it unleashes a thunderstorm. Another copy of the map leads him to an ancient courtyard, where he sees a man running in panic from a doorway. Investigating, he finds a cellar full of costumes and stage furniture. Picking up a scorched copy of Goethe's *Faust*, he assumes the title role, complete with wig and cloak.

As the opening curtain is signalled, 'Faust' finds himself in a theatre, a performance about to begin. Ripping off his costume, he breaks through the stage backdrop into a vault where an alchemist's laboratory is revealed; with the aid of a book of spells, he brings to life a clay child which grows horrifyingly into his own image before he smashes it. Warned by a marionette angel not to experiment further but encouraged by a demon to do as he pleases, he is sent by a wooden messenger to a café meeting with the two street-map men, identified as 'Cornelius' and 'Valdes', who give him a briefcase of magical devices. Returning to the vault, he uses these to summon Mephisto, offering Lucifer his soul in return for 24 years of self-indulgence.

At another cafe, 'Faust' is entertained by Cornelius and Valdes, who provide a fountain of wine from a table-top. He watches as a tramp, carrying a severed human leg, is pestered by a large black dog until he throws the limb into the river. 'Faust' finds a key in his food, uses it on a shop-front shutter, and is dragged back on stage by waiting stagehands. He mimes a scene from Gounod's opera, in which Mephisto returns and the pact with Lucifer is signed in blood. After the interval, 'Faust' visits Portugal to demonstrate his supernatural powers to the King; when a requested restaging of the David and Goliath contest is poorly received, he drowns the entire Portuguese court.

'Faust' is distracted from repentance by Helen of Troy, whom he seduces before realising she is a wooden demon in disguise. Lucifer arrives earlier than expected to claim his soul, and 'Faust' rushes in panic from the theatre, meeting a newcomer in the doorway as he bursts into the street. He is felled by a red car, and Cornelius and Valdes watch in amusement as a tramp carries away a severed leg from the scene of the accident. A policeman checks the car, but it is without a driver.

As Svankmajer's 'ordinary man', manipulated into perdition, becomes increasingly a masked and tethered marionette, his misadventures are interrupted at some length by the figure of Punch. Stridently bombastic as ever, this intrusive clown carries a wealth of meanings, not least in reminding us that the Faust story has long been a favourite among puppeteers throughout the world and would have been known to Svankmajer since his earliest days as a student of puppetry at the Prague Academy. Punch's interventions serve much the same purpose as the 'clownage' scenes in the original *Faustbuch*, supposedly based on fact, which provided Marlowe with the basis for his play *Doctor Faustus* in 1588; these stand-up comedy routines, largely scorned by Marlowe but firmly incorporated in the well-padded 1616 version of the play (published after his death), offer an ironic comment on Faust's plight, as well as linking it to events of the period. As Svankmajer uses them, they form the equivalent partly of a Chorus, partly of a sorcerer's-apprentice parody, partly of an alter-ego for Faust himself.

When Punch first appears in the film, dithering over a book of magic he can make little sense of (finally despairing, he sits on it: "What poor brain cannot comprehend/May well go in the other end"), he seems to be speaking for the bewildered passerby who finds himself cast in the Faustian role. During the visit to Portugal, however, when Punch raids the tea-table and stuffs cream cake into his mouth, he has become Faust's manservant, and it is he who rushes into the Prague streets at crisis time in search of guards to protect his master against the arrival of Lucifer.

Ironically, it is the most tedious of the Punch scenes, in which he orders a demon to and fro until it is exhausted, that prepares the way for Faust's death. The demon escapes in a red car, which fatally reappears at the end.

Although the English-language version of his film quotes directly from Marlowe, Svankmajer has borrowed freely from other sources—including Goethe, Gounod and the more obscure Grabbe—to shape a narrative that is all his own. A cascade of improvisation springs from each borrowing, as when the ballerinas raking hay to Gounod's music pause for soup and a siesta and get ogled by a farmhand, or when a volley of tiny demons dismember the equally minuscule angels who are trying to prevent Faust from signing away his soul. So much of it is Svankmajer, in fact, that the story of Faust only really gets started halfway through the film: the introductory scenes, in which the enigma of the map slowly exerts its fascination, provide a new and sinister dimension to the Marlovian characters of Valdes and Cornelius, who function like secret police, steering their victim to his doom with many a knowing nod.

One of them is played by Jan Kraus, who was the victorious diner in Svankmajer's previous film *Food* (in which two men, ignored by their waiter, consume the restaurant table and chairs before turning on each other). This link would seem jokingly deliberate were it not that so much of Svankmajer's work is about the process of eating. True to form, a series of unappetising snacks punctuates the drama of Faust, often with Valdes and Cornelius in attendance, their most unsettling complicity being accorded to the tramp who clearly regards Faust's mangled leg as a potential feast. And yet the hunger in Svankmajer's obsessive consumers is not so much for food itself as for destruction, a recycling of raw materials (as at the end of *Dimensions of Dialogue*, in which a succession of heads disintegrate while spewing out their own duplicates). Hoping to halt the process—"I seek the force," he says, "the reason governing life's flow"—Faust is eventually torn apart like all the rest.

Wandering like a somnambulist into an unforeseen obligation to act out the familiar legend, Svankmajer's contender derives little benefit from his bargain—which, given Mephisto's ingenious likeness, is actually with his own image. The promised tour of Heaven and Hell never materialises, there is not so much as a glimpse of the Seven Deadly Sins, and the trip to Portugal signally fails to amuse. It seems odd that Faust's demand to "live in all voluptuousness" remains unpursued until the cynically explicit coupling with a wooden Helen. There is an undoubted currency to the idea of an unending procession of Fausts, drawn off the street by curiosity and boredom to hand over their souls like mortgage payments in return for what they will never be permitted to enjoy; but it is disappointing that Svankmajer finally renders their quest so inconsequential, deflecting himself time and again into other rituals and amusements.

Which is not to say that his macabre humour has lost any of its usual alchemy. In one of his asides, the Golem materialises from a mound of clay inside a glass retort and grows at alarming speed until crushed by its creator; in another, fragments of clay scuttle off independently, sprouting eyeballs to help them on their way. Alongside Svankmajer's life-size puppets, and familiar surrealist images of neglect and decay, are appealing tricks like the egg that appears inside a loaf, and the tabletop fountain of wine. The authentic Faust in all this, one is tempted to conclude, has to be the film-maker himself.

VILLAGE VOICE, 11/1/94, p. 53, J. Hoberman

Did the Velvet Revolution set Jan Svankmajer free? Or did it provide the 60-year-old Czech animator the chance to renegotiate his deal with the devil? For his second feature, the world's preeminent object-animator, the maestro of dank whimsy and morbid tactility, a card-carrying member of Prague's surrealist cell and an alchemist whose own formula (per countryman Milos Forman) is "Buñuel + Disney," essays a modern day version of modernity's exemplar, Faust.

Svankmajer's "civil version of the myth," now at Film Forum for a two-week run that coincidentally overlaps with Nada Theater's ambitious Faust season, may surprise his own admirers as well as those familiar with the Fausts created by Marlowe, Goethe, and Thomas Mann. Svankmajer's *Faust* is largely live-action; his Faust, is neither a punk voluptuary nor a romantic intellectual, and certainly not a possessed artist. but a garden-variety ordinary opportunist—curious yet passive, perhaps one of Prague's low-level bureaucrats or aspiring business wheels. This everyman has no agenda; his main characteristic is that he never resists

Mephistopheles's blandishments. Selling his soul merely facilitates his transformation (often literally) into a puppet.

The mysterious map that Svankmajer's Faust is handed as he bops through downtown Prague might equally be an advertising handbill or a trap organized by the secret police. After several false starts, the movie's generally blank and unsurprised protagonist (played by veteran film actor Petr Cepek) winds up in the moldy tenement basement that routinely, metamorphoses into an alchemist's laboratory or theatrical dressing room. Faust dresses in costume, wanders around backstage, and then stumbles out in front of an audience to start quoting Marlowe in what looks like a production of Gonoud's *Faust et Marguerite*. He knows the play: the end has been preordained. Thereafter the stage set is intercut with the street as clattering antique puppets turn human and vice versa.

An ironic populist, Svankmajer draws on Czech folk plays and doggerel verse. (He also parodies Socialist Realism by having a scene of ballerinas bringing in the harvest.) At times, *Faust* might be an uninflected remake of *Un Chien Andalou*—with a similar emphasis on dismemberment, slapstick, and street theater, and a kindred use of a shifting invented geography—although, in tracking a human protagonist's enigmatic transformations, the movie also seems a kind of adult equivalent to Svankmajer's creepy-crawly *Alice*. *Faust*'s wonderland is less completely magical, but more memorably spiced with instances of virtuoso claymation and casual sleight of hand. Apples rot into maggots, a doll dragged downstairs gets its head squished by a closing door.

As suggested when Faust cracks the egg he finds baked into his loaf of bread and day is instantly changed to night, much of the animation is specifically alchemical. Svankmajer has Faust use an actual medieval spell to call on Mephistopheles—then creates his own form of magic by making brooms dance in formation or hands sprout from the ground. To add to the general sense of self-reflection, the shape-shifting demon assumes Faust's face before dissolving into blobs of clay, each with its own eyeball.

If the effects are reduced—"I use animation only when I need it to bring alive certain objects through metamorphosis," Svankmajer says—*Faust* is characteristically his in its fondness for disconcertingly gross close-ups (mainly people eating) and boldly tactile juxtapositions. Faust finds a rusty key in his dumpling, a dead bee in his beer, chicken shit on the sole of his shoe. At one point, he drills a hole in a café table to release a geyser of wine. When Faust must sign his compact with the devil, he gouges a wound in the arm of a wooden puppet to draw "real" blood; when he makes love to Helen of Troy, it's a human raping a puppet (who turns out to be a devil in disguise).

Svankmajer's British exegetes point out that his *Faust* seems underscored by the post-1989 transformation of Prague from a depressed, moldy ruin into a booming, sanitized tourist mecca. Vain and vindictive Faust meets his doom in the form of a shiny new sports car. As his erstwhile comrade, Vaclav Havel (author of his own version of Faust, *Temptation*) has linked the fall of communism to the dawn of postmodern times, so Svankmajer has taken a central modern myth, stripped it of heroism, and represented it in terms of ordinary corruption. If Svankmajer was an opponent of the old regime, one can scarcely call him an apologist for the new.

Also reviewed in:
CHICAGO TRIBUNE, 2/24/94, Friday/p. K, Michael Wilmington
NEW YORK TIMES, 10/26/95, p. C15, Caryn James
VARIETY, 7/11-17/94, p. 45, Lisa Nesselson
WASHINGTON POST, 3/24/94, p. C7, Richard Harrington

FAVOR, THE

An Orion Pictures release of a Nelson Entertainment presentation of a Lauren Shuler-Donner production. *Executive Producer:* Barry Spikings, Rick Finklestein, and Donna Dubrow. *Producer:* Lauren Shuler-Donner. *Director:* Donald Petrie. *Screenplay:* Sara Parriott, and Josann McGibbon. *Director of Photography:* Tim Suhrstedt. *Editor:* Harry Keramidas.

Music: Thomas Newman. *Music Editor:* Bill Bernstein. *Sound:* Stephan Von Hase and (music) John Vigran. *Sound Editor:* Victoria Rose Sampson. *Casting:* Bonnie Timmerman. *Production Designer:* David Chapman. *Art Director:* Mark Haack. *Set Decorator:* Clay A. Griffith. *Set Dresser:* Elliot Lewis Backerman, J. Edgar Bowen, and Greg Wilkinson. *Special Effects:* Ron Nary. *Costumes:* Carol Oditz. *Make-up:* Ronnie Specter and Kathryn Bihr. *Stunt Coordinator:* Ernie Orsatti. *Running time:* 97 minutes. *MPAA Rating:* R.

CAST: Harley Jane Kozak (Kathy); Elizabeth McGovern (Emily); Bill Pullman (Peter); Brad Pitt (Elliott); Larry Miller (Joe Dubin); Ken Wahl (Tom Andrews); Ginger Orsi (Gina); Leigh Ann Orsi (Hannah); Felicia Robertson (Carol); Kenny Twomey (Mr. Lucky); Florence Schauffler (Museum Docent); Elaine Mee (Chunky Woman); John Horn (Pastor); Wilma Bergheim (Lady at Church #1); Mary Marsh (Lady at Church #2); Marilyn Blechschmidt (Mrs. Konzulman); Sharon Collar (Clerk at Drugstore); Carl King (Man at Drugstore); Deborah White (Professor Allen); Lisa Robins (Stewardess); Arthur Burghardt (Hotel Clerk); Michael Anthony Taylor (Bootsie); Steve Kahan (Helpful Fisherman); Robert Biheller (Fisherman); Gary Powell (Fisherman); Moultrie Patten (Peter's Cabbie); Giuseppe Tortellini (Kathy's Cabbie); Joel Beeson and Paul Beeson (Young Tom Andrews); Kim Walker (Jill Topial); Jordan Christopher Michael (Alex); Claire Stansfield (Miranda); O'Lan Jones (Mrs. Moyer); Milt Oberman (Mr. Moyer); Mindy Sterling (Debbie Rollins); Heather Morgan (Linda); Holland Taylor (Maggie Sand).

LOS ANGELES TIMES, 4/29/94, Calendar/p. 11, Kevin Thomas

"The Favor" is a pleasant romantic comedy, aimed at thirtysomethings and younger, and it affords solid roles for Harley Jane Kozak and Elizabeth McGovern. Bearing a 1991 copyright, the film had been held up by the bankruptcy filing by Orion Pictures, which has since reorganized.

Married 10 years to Peter (Bill Pullman), a nice, but often preoccupied, guy, Kozak's Kathy finds that as her 15th high school reunion approaches she starts dreaming of her high school boyfriend, a macho football player with whom she did not go all the way. She and Peter, who live in Portland, have been married long enough to have two small daughters and busy lives loaded with responsibilities, and to discover that both are often too tired to make love.

Kathy realizes she's got what might be called a 10-year itch, but is not about to scratch it. However, there's no reason why her best pal Emily (McGovern) can't look up her old boyfriend Tom (Ken Wahl) while she's in Denver on business. Emily is a single, definitely liberated woman who says she's getting tired of her younger lover (Brad Pitt) anyway. Indeed, Kathy thinks that she might just get Tom out of her system if Emily ended up in bed with him. Predictably, Kathy's cockamamie logic backfires spectacularly, even beyond her being driven crazy by Emily's description of Tom's awesome sexual prowess.

"The Favor" is as American as apple pie, perhaps in its way as puritanical as "The Scarlet Letter." Kathy is a healthy, attractive young woman with a completely natural and understandable sexual longing, which Kozak expresses with much good humor. But you suspect strongly that writers Sara Parriott and Josann McGibbon and director Donald Petrie aren't going to let Kathy have her fling with Tom. In any event, there's much elaborate contrivance to bring the film to its finish.

The cast, however, does sparkle, and Kozak and McGovern play off each other smartly. Pullman's a likable nerd and Pitt is especially good as a young man who has to struggle mightily to be taken seriously by his elders—elders by six or seven years. Wahl finds hilarity in the hunky Tom, even though he's been arbitrarily given a nasty side. Larry Miller contributes one of his insidious pompous types as the worst possible man Peter could take as a confidante. There's a bit of sadness, too, underlying "The Favor" in that people still in their 30s actually believe they're getting old.

NEW YORK, 5/16/94, p. 89, David Denby

In the casual little sex comedy *The Favor*, Elizabeth McGovern plays a woman whose intelligence and sense of freedom determine her choices in life. So *what*, you say. Well, yes, there *should* be no reason for a critic to make a fuss over a normal grown-up appearing in a movie. Unfortunately, the phenomenon has become as rare in our infantile movies as the appearance of a Martian in Central Park. McGovern plays a gallery owner in Portland with a boyish lover (Brad Pitt) and a serious interest in other men, and though she changes her mind a lot, you can actually see her thinking. She's distressed by her life, and amused by her own distress. Consciousness—what a concept!

This is another of the Orion films made a few years ago and shelved when the company hit the skids. Written by Sara Parriott and Josann McGibbon, the movie was directed by Donald Petrie (*Mystic Pizza*), who seems to be genuinely fond of women (which makes him a rare bird, too). Friendship between two women is the motor of the plot. A wife and mother played by Harley Jane Kozak, vaguely dissatisfied with her harmonica-blowing, math-prof husband (Bill Pullman), commits adultery in her head with her old boyfriend. She sends her best friend (McGovern) off to Denver to look up the guy (Ken Wahl) and becomes outraged when the friend spends the night with him. The plot is all screwball twists and misunderstandings, but what keeps it moving is a sense of the shifting irritations and intimacies of women's friendships. These two may be competitive, but they're also candid with each other in a way that men cannot be. That's a small insight for a grown-up movie, but at least it's a start.

NEW YORK POST, 4/29/94, p. 42, Michael Medved

Like last year's wretched "Indecent Proposal," "The Favor" is a far-fetched sex fantasy that wants to have it both ways: trying to titillate the audience with naughty notions while sanctimoniously (and unpersuasively) upholding ideals of marriage and monogamy.

Harley Jane Kozak (who handled significant supporting roles in "Parenthood" and "When Harry Met Sally") here plays a wife and mother who starts thinking about her upcoming 15th high school reunion.

She wonders if she'll cross paths with the macho muscle boy (Ken Wahl) she dated as an innocent teen-ager, and she fantasizes about the torrid sex they might enjoy.

When her best friend, single Elizabeth McGovern, announces a business trip to the city where Wahl lives Kozak suggests that her pal look up her former steady, go to bed with him, then report on the experience.

The plot is supposed to come across as good-natured farce, but the characters are all such despicable creeps—so utterly spoiled and shallow and self absorbed—that you end up wishing none of them well.

Kozak's character is a particular problem, risking the welfare of her two adorable daughters and her sweet, hard-working husband simply because, as she herself says, "I just wanted to feel like a hot babe."

The screenwriting team of Josann McGibbon and Sara Parriott ("Three Men and a Little Lady") claim that the story has been inspired by their own friendship and offers a "female buddy movie for the '90s."

Actually, most of "The Favor" seems no more contemporary than an R-rated version of the adventures of Lucy Ricardo and Ethel Mertz. As Ricky himself might wisely and appropriately conclude, "Somebody's got a whole lot of es'plainin' to do!"

NEWSDAY, 4/29/94, Part II/p. B7, John Anderson

Can the modern woman have it all, and still be miserable? More important—for the purposes of movie comedy—can the modern woman *almost* have it all, and still be miserable?

Of course she can, as housewife-mother Kathy (Harley Jane Kozak) and fashionable art dealer Emily (Elizabeth McGovern) prove so decisively in "The Favor," Donald Petrie's ultra-modern domestic comedy about infidelity, and a film that poses a rather delicate question: Do you actually have to get undressed to be unfaithful? Or can you do it by proxy?

Wracked by red-leather dreams about her high school boyfriend Tom (Ken Wahl)—with whom she never technically had sex—she asks her best friend Emily to look him up and sleep with him while on a business trip to Denver. "Complete the mission," she pleads, figuring that a vicarious affair is better than none. But Emily completes the mission so successfully—"You did *me* the favor," Emily says—it drives Kathy up the Wahl, so to speak, complicates her marriage, and throws her friendship with Em into flux.

And they're certainly good friends, the kind who exchange sex histories and reflect candidly on the relative merits of their respective Caribbean vacations: "You came home with a plastic shark," Emily sighs. "I came home with crabs." If Emily's love life is overactive and unsatisfying—her biological clock is fairly thundering—Kathy's is simply unsatisfying: She and Peter (Bill Pullman), her math professor-equals-nerd of a husband, schedule sex like the week's menu plan, and they seem to be starving.

"The Favor" is the kind of comedy that has to work from the inside out—if you believe the details, you'll go for the jokes. Should a pending 15th high school reunion prompt such psycho-sexual disturbance in Kathy? (How old can she be, 33?) Would anyone put up with Joe (Larry Miller), Peter's oleaginous colleague, for more than a minute, much less accompany him on a reconnaissance mission to see if Kathy's cheating? Would Peter really ramble on obliviously about fractal geometry while Kathy, in a baby doll nightie, stands in the refrigerator doorway rubbing ice cubes on her chest, and sucking peanut butter off her fingers?

Uh, no. And by accessorizing an already outlandish premise the way he does, director Petrie is asking a lot of us. In addition, "The Favor" is a movie that can be depressing, in the way "It's a Wonderful Life" can be depressing. On the one hand, the human capacity for dissatisfaction is portrayed as enormous—why, for instance, does Emily make so much of the age difference between her and her painter boyfriend, Elliott (Brad Pitt), a man who can apparently give her everything, including the bod of the Gods? At the same time, happiness—for Kathy, ultimately, her children and husband—seems to have been predestined. In other words, since you can't do anything about your life anyway, be content.

Still, "The Favor" does give us the grossly underappreciated and underexposed Harley Jane Kozak in a starring role, and everyone else acquits themselves admirably, too, particularly Brad Pitt, who for once gets to do something besides vogue. He does go shirtless in one scene, however, lest you were concerned.

Also reviewed in:
CHICAGO TRIBUNE, 4/29/94, Friday/p. E, Michael Wilmington
NEW YORK TIMES, 4/29/94, p. C8, Janet Maslin
VARIETY, 5/2-8/94, p. 89, Leonard Klady
WASHINGTON POST, 4/29/94, p. C6, Desson Howe
WASHINGTON POST, 4/29/94, Weekend/p. 46, Joe Brown

FEAR OF A BLACK HAT

A Samuel Goldwyn Company release of an Oakwood Films production in association with the ITC Entertainment Group. *Executive Producer:* Wm. Christopher Gorog. *Producer:* Darin Scott. *Director:* Rusty Cundieff. *Screenplay:* Rusty Cundieff. *Director of Photography:* John Demps, Jr. *Editor:* Karen Horn. *Music:* Larry Robinson. *Music Editor:* Jay Bolton. *Choreographer:* Jimmy Locust. *Sound:* Oliver L. Moss and (music) Eric Hoeschen and Bryan Gladstone. *Sound Editor:* Hari Ryatt. *Casting:* Jaki Brown and Kimberly Hardin. *Production Designer:* Stuart Blatt. *Set Decorator:* Penny Barrett. *Special Effects:* Kevin McCarthy and Sandra McCarthy. *Costumes:* Rita McGhee. *Make-up:* Stacye Branche. *Stunt Coordinator:* Steve Lambert. *Running time:* 86m minutes. *MPAA Rating:* R.

CAST: Mark Christopher Lawrence (Tone Def); Larry B. Scott (Tasty-Taste); Rusty Cundieff (Ice Cold); Kasi Lemmons (Nina Blackburn); Howie Gold (Guy Friesch); G. Smokey Campbell (Backstage Manager #1); Bob Mardis (Promoter #1); Tim Hutchinson (Reggie Clay); Moon Jones (Jam Boy #1); Faizon (Jam Boy #2); Deezer D (Jam Boy #3); Darin Scott (Security Head); Devin Kamienny (Vanilla Sherbet); Jeff Burr (Chicago Cop); Kenneth J. Hall (John Liggert); Don Reed (Daryll in Charge); Reggie Bruce (Video Director); Shabaka (Geoffrey Lennox); Kurt Loder (Himself); Mark Selinger (Right Winger); Lamont Johnson

(MC Slammer); JJ Hommel (White Punk #1); Jeff Pollack (White Punk #2); Monica Tolliver (Fine Woman Back Stage); Laverne Anderson (Sage); K Front (Parsley); Deborah Swisher (Rosemary); Doug McHenry (Promoter Doug); George Jackson (Promoter George); Lance Crouther (Street Vendor); Doug Starks (Rev. Brother Pastor Deacon); Nancy Giles (Loreatha); Penny Johnson (Re-Re); Billy Elmer (Security Guard #1); Joseph Anthony Farris (Security Guard #2); Daryl Savid (Teacher); Rosemarie Jackson (Cheryl C.); Barry Heins (Marty Rabinow); Eric Laneuville (Jike Spingleton); Clyde Jones (Rico); Rochelle Ashana (Tiffini); Homeselle Joy (Mabel Ann Jackson); Brad Sanders (Promoter #2).

LOS ANGELES TIMES, 6/3/94, Calendar/p. 4, Peter Rainer

"Fear of a Black Hat" is designed to be a rap version of the classic mock rock documentary "This is Spinal Tap," and the idea is so funny that for a long time the film coasts on our good will. But it should be funnier than it is. Writer-director Rusty Cundieff, who also stars, along with Larry B. Scott and Mark Christopher Lawrence, as one of the three members of the rap group N.W.H., has a loose-limbed comic sense, and there are hilarious bits poking through the tedium. What the movie lacks is any kind of smart, sociological sense. It's a defanged spoof.

The biggest in-joke about gangsta rap, after all, is that its largest audience is white. Black rappers, many from middle-class backgrounds, market the white audience's worst racial fears. Instead of getting into this kind of material, Cundieff goes for more obvious (and safer) targets: Vanilla Ice types and cringing money-grubbing managers.

The rap group's numbers aren't particularly well-staged, or funny, but a few of the MTV clips are almost indistinguishable from what's really on the network. (That's the joke.) There's a funny interview with one of the rappers about the meaning of the group's name where he goes into a long diatribe about how slaves weren't allowed to wear hats, and another where the group's recurring use of the word *butt* is explained away as a social statement.

The titles for their rap hits are the most inspired thing in the movie, but you'll have to see the movie—or read something besides a family newspaper—to find out what they are. The tamest one is "Guerrillas in the Midst."

NEW YORK POST, 6/3/94, p. 40, Thelma Adams

Rusty Cundieff's "Fear of a Black Hat" does for rap what Rob Reiner's "This Is Spinal Tap" did for rock. Both movies celebrate the music scene they parody in a good-natured, unsparing, and entertaining way.

The similarities are not coincidental. Producer Darin Scott (Menace II Society") said in production notes, "Rusty [Cundieff] was always telling me he wanted to be the black Rob Reiner. We see this film as a rap version of that classic."

"Fear of a Black Hat" follows "Spinal Tap's" rockumentary style. But "Spinal Tap" wasn't the first or, as great as it was, even the best.

The granddaddy of the genre was "The Rutles," starring and created by Monty Python's Eric Idle and ex-Bonzo Neil Innes.

Amid cameos by everyone from Mick Jagger to John Belushi, Idle traced the phenomenon of Rutlemania (read Beatlemania) in this 1978 profile of the pre-Fab Four, "a musical legend that will last a lunchtime."

In "Fear of a Black Hat" sociology grad student Nina Blackburn (Kasi Lemmons) scours rap's underbelly for thesis material and discovers hip-hop's answer to The Rutles, N.W.H. aka Niggaz With Hats. Rappers Tone Def, Tasty-Taste and Ice Cold form a trio as cartoony and endearing as the hats they wear.

Why hats? Band philosopher Ice Cold, smoothly played by Cundieff, theorizes: During slavery, blacks worked hatless in the fields. When they returned to the plantation, the slaves were too tired to rebel.

"We've got hats," says Ice.

When Blackburn questions Ice about N.W.H.'s "Kill Whitey" album with its inflammatory subtitle, "don't shoot until you see the whites," the rapper cries censorship.

Ice Cold wonders how anyone could listen to the title song and think his group is advocating killing all whites. He had one man in mind: the bands former manager Whitey DeLuca.

Like the running gag of combustible drummers in "This Is Spinal Tap," death by gunshot is an occupational hazard for N.W.H. managers. This phenomenon provides a slick answer to why the band's managers are usually white—the band members wouldn't want any brothers getting caught in the crossfire.

Joining Ice Cold on the mean-but-profitable streets of "Tough Neighborhood, U.S.A." is gun freak and former "pharmaceutical distributor" Tasty-Taste, played with comic fury by Larry B. Scott, a veteran of the "Revenge of the Nerds" comedies. Mark Christopher Lawrence rounds out the strong cast as the band's spiritual center, Tone Def.

Writer ("House Party II"), star and first-time director Cundieff aptly juggles many hats. If "Fear of a Black Hat" pales in comparison to "The Rutles" it's partly because the blasphemy was still fresh.

While the rapumentary strings along hilarious bits, it never quite achieves "Spinal Tap's" frenzied peaks. For instance, who can forget the debacle of the miniature Stonehenge sets?

Still, from its music video takeoffs to white rapper Vanilla Sherbet, "Fear of a Black Hat" is a loving, laughable lark. Does it entertain? "Damn skippy."

NEWSDAY, 6/3/94, Part II/p. B7, Gene Seymour

A shaggier "CB4"? a hip-hopping "This is Spinal Tap"? However you look at it, there's no way for "Fear of a Black Planet" to avoid such comparisons at the outset.

Especially "Spinal Tap," given that this chronicle of a year in the life of an addle-brained rap trio—N.W.H. (Niggaz With Hats)—has the same pseudo-documentary trappings of that giddy 1983 lampoon of heavy-metal histrionics.

Also, as with "Tap's" running gag of spontaneously combusting drummers, "Fear of a Black Hat," weaves in a riff of N.W.H.'s managers getting bumped off in sometimes mysterious, sometimes purely circumstantial ways.

So are we talking rip-off? Not at all. For one thing, writer-director Rusty Cundieff, who also plays the group's leader, Ice Cold, has made no bones about his admiration for "Spinal Tap," giving his first feature the glow of a bonafide homage.

For another—and more important—thing, you can't accuse a film as inventively rude or relentlessly funny as "Fear of a Black Hat" of being wholely unoriginal. Less prone to slickness or sentimentality than last year's "CB4," "Fear of a Black Hat" rips the scattershot excesses of hard-core rap with knowing, affectionate glee.

This loose-fitting collection of set pieces and video parodies tracks the shaky camaraderie joining Ice Cold, Tasty-Taste (Larry B. Scott) and DJ Tone Def (Mark Christopher Lawrence) in their rise to stardom. They are interviewed, together and separately, by a sociologist (Kasi Lemmons), who's following the group around as part of her doctoral dissertation on the "underbelly of gangsta rap."

What she and we find beneath the new jack bluster are three preening egos in outrageous headgear. The hats, they explain, signify a protest against the way the brains of their enslaved, hat-deprived ancestors were unhinged by the hot sun. From the looks of things, *some*body's been out in the sun too long.

It could be the pseudo-messianic Ice, who promotes his philosophy, such as it is, in a manifesto entitled, "F.Y.M.," which stands for "_______Y'All Mother_______." It could very well be the wild-eyed, short-fused Taste, who stockpiles Uzis in the basement of his posh estate. It could even be the relatively easygoing Tone Def, who, after the group splits, opts for a hippy-dippy transcendence of color-consciousness in a lite-rap ditty, "I'm Just a Human."

Which isn't nearly as ... um, let's see ... evocative as the stuff N.W.H. does collectively like "Wear Yo' Hat," "____the Security Guards," "Booty Juice" and their double-platinum "Guerrillas in the Midst." And these are just the *titles*.

Cundieff's parodies are assembled with rough-edged flair. He is attentive, without being mean, to the hubris that never hovered far from even the most potent rap music of the last decade. After all, it's not Cundieff's intention to bury the genre, but, in a backhanded way, to praise its raw energy. Still, this film's arrival suggests that, while rap isn't coming to an end, its frisky adolescence is.

SIGHT AND SOUND, 11/94, p. 45, Kodwo Eshun

Film director Nina Blackburn has just completed her documentary on rap group NWH, Niggaz With Hats. As she reminisces, we return backstage before a show where members Ice Cold, Tasty-Taste and Tone Def explain the concept behind their outsize hats. Their rivals The Jam Boys argue with them over who will headline. Nina interviews them about their new album *Guerrillas In the Midst*, and on a video channel, Kurt Loder reports controversy over the title. Interviewed, the group state their intransigence, but then defer to their manager.

Newsreel shows platinum sales for the record and the group on the cover of *Newsweek* and *Billboard* magazines. They are denounced by right-wing senators and preachers alike. Nina interviews each of the newly wealthy group in their new surroundings. Tasty-Taste shows her around his garden and displays his gun collection. Leaving the house Taste is pulled over by security guards who pin him to the ground; the incident becomes the subject of NWH's new video. NWH are invited to talk on the theme of Rappers Against Violence at a local school with long time rivals The Jam Boys, and a fight breaks out.

Cheryl C., Taste's new girlfriend, pushes him to ask for more money; arguments ensue within the group. In a hotel, Taste finds Cheryl in bed with Ice Cold. Everyone pulls their guns and the band's new manager is accidentally shot. NWH split up and each of them goes solo. But on finding themselves billed below their rivals at a show, the band members decide to reform.

Produced in 1992 but released here a year after Tamra Davis' weak rap satire *CB4*, Rusty Cundieff's writing and directing debut quickly becomes predictable. Promoted as a parody of the archetypal West Coast gangsta group NWA, the film is more ambitious than this suggests, sniping vaguely at pop nationalism—Public Enemy's album *Fear of A Black Planet* (hence the title), Da Lench Mob's album *Guerrillas in the Mist*—as well as such diverse targets as PM Dawn, John Singleton, *New Jack City*, Run DMC and 2 Live Crew. As those titles suggest though, *Black Hat*'s musical moments are never anything but parasitically obvious. There is never any sense of why anyone would enjoy any of these groups or why better music would make for a stronger parody.

Cundieff's target is videogenic rap—how hip-hop looks on MTV. He is good on the channel's image repertoire picking up on the Pucci Buddha swirls of a PM Dawn set, and the claustrophobically underlit interiors of the 'Guerillas' video, even including the director's credits in the corner of the frame MTV-style. In fact, he is interested less in specific types of rap than in deflating the discursive strategies and photo-opportunities through which NWH justify their awful records.

As documentarist Nina, Kasi Lemmons starts off bright and eager, her interview technique gradually becoming more pointed and her smile more weary as she comes to realise NWH are a pack of morons. It is a surprise, therefore, when the closing titles reveal that Nina marries Ice Cold, as if the escalating stupidity of each episode has somehow drawn her into romance. Cundieff plays Cold as a roly-poly Benny Hill, an eye-popping doughboy and an absurd reduction of the messianic roles so many rappers adopt. Slaves were forced to work in the sun without hats, Cold carefully explains—therefore the group wears huge Dr. Seuss hats to remember this degraded past. While the band's name parodies NWA (Niggaz with Attitude), this interpretation captures both militant and Afrocentric rap's *faux*-historicist strategies, also catching the fiercely emphatic tone of the genre's pedagogic hubris. The joke is that NWH's programmatically hare-brained zeal should excuse but only ends up emphasising every pragmatically gross whim they have, whether that is Ice Cold proclaiming his manifesto 'F.Y.M. (Fuck Y'All Motherfuckers)' or Larry B. Scott's wolfish Tasty-Taste losing himself in a convoluted exposition of their video 'Booty Juice'. It's a neat gag—the mind contorting itself over the body's drives—but then it is the only one Cundieff knows.

His only way out of this locked groove is to introduce Cheryl C., a standard-order gold-digger who manipulates Tasty-Taste into leaving the group. Here the film finally succumbs to a misogyny it has flirted with throughout. An early scene in which NWH overreact to a gay dance instructor has a homophobic glee to it that is similarly hard to take. Cundieff thinks he has fearlessly revealed gangsta rap as a theatrical fraud, militant rap as a masquerade; but from 1985's *Krush Groove* onwards, parodies of rap groups have been the norm, rather than the outrageous exception. Imagine a film which, like Godard's *One on One*, never strayed from the studio, which meditated on the glass screen and the mixing desk and took the formal implications of hip-hop seriously in order to criticise it more emphatically. Now that really would be funny.

VILLAGE VOICE, 6/14/94, p. 56, Selwyn Seyfu Hinds

Nowadays most Black comedy is a precarious high wire act over divided ground. To one side sits the relatively safe, mainstream, consumable stuff of which Huxtables and Fresh Princes are made. On the other sit the maligned (yet still safe and consumable), near minstrel-like antics of the *In Living Color* and *Def Comedy Jam* children. True Black comic genius needs to inch along without tumbling into the rigid mediocrity at either extreme. I thought *Fear of a Black Hat* might be able to negotiate the wire—Black comedy meets hip hop, shades of *Spinal Tap*, etc., etc. The movie certainly seemed to have enough of a premise to be meaningful. But it turns out to be a condescending, hostile (if admittedly funny) film.

This "mockumentary" chronicles the rise, fall, and resurrection of fictional rap group N.W.H. (Niggaz With Hats). A young sociologist, Nina Blackburn (Kasi Lemmons), goes on the road with the group's members Ice Cold (director and screenwriter Cundieff), Tasty-Taste (Larry B. Scott), and DJ Tone Def (Mark Christopher Lawrence) to garner material for her doctoral dissertation on rap. Along the way every conceivable negative hip hop stereotype is wrung for laughs: misogynistic behavior, scheming groupies, gun worship, uncaring and manipulative label presidents, ignorant rantings masquerading as profundities.

Now, a spoof is supposed to exaggerate stereotypes, but *Fear of a Black Hat* thrusts hip hop into minstrel territory entirely too often. What are we supposed to make of DJ Tone Def's demonstration of his ability to use his dick to scratch records? Of Ice Cold's earnest (and retarded) philosophizing, cultivating pearls of wisdom like, "A 'ho is woman who fucks everybody. A bitch is a 'ho who fucks everybody but you"? There are some genuinely funny moments in *Fear*—MTV's Kurt Loder (playing himself) and his deadpan newscast delivery is bound to be a crack-up. But *Fear of a Black Hat* makes this young black man and hip hop fan cringe. Not because hip hop isn't in need of harsh examination, but because this film, for all its humor, comes across with one mean-spirited message: "Ain't these stupid niggas pitiful, America? Laugh all you want. They ain't no real threat."

Also reviewed in:
CHICAGO TRIBUNE, 6/17/94, Friday/p. J, John Petrakis
NEW YORK TIMES, 6/3/94, p. C15, Janet Maslin
VARIETY, 2/8/93, p. 76, Emanuel Levy
WASHINGTON POST, 6/17/94, p. B6, Richard Harrington

FEDERAL HILL

A Trimark release of an Eagle Beach Productions film. *Executive Producer:* Ron Kastner, Randy Finch, and Leroy Leach. *Producer:* Michael Corrente, Libby Corrente, and Richard Crudo. *Director:* Michael Corrente. *Screenplay:* Michael Corrente. *Director of Photography:* Richard Crudo. *Editor:* Kate Sanford. *Music:* Bob Held and David Bravo. *Sound:* Matt Sigal. *Sound Editor:* Tony Martinez. *Production Designer:* Robert Schleinig. *Running time:* 97 minutes. *MPAA Rating:* R.

CAST: Nicholas Turturro (Ralph); Anthony De Sando (Nicky); Libby Langdon (Wendy); Michael Raynor (Frank); Jason Andrews (Bobby); Robert Turano (Joey); Frank Vincent (Sal); Phyllis Kay (Gail); Biagio Conti (Max Haven); Vinny Gugliotti (Mr. Russo); Barry Blier (Barry); Nance Hopkins (Fat Girl); Bates Wilson (Yuppie); Lea Goldstein (Dancer); Dave Gianopoulos (Steve); Michael Corrente (Fredo); Martin Dimartino (Benny).

LOS ANGELES TIMES, 2/24/95, Calendar/p. 6, Peter Rainer

The Italian American buddies in "Federal Hill" spend a lot of time joshing and jawboning. They like to touch off little hostilities in each other—it's a way to pass the time and let off steam away from their mates, their parents.

It must be a right of passage for young filmmakers to emulate Martin Scorsese's "Mean Streets." Who would have predicted back in 1973 that it would become the touchstone for an entire generation of independent filmmakers? Its influence has been primarily thematic rather than stylistic, and not always a boon. At worst, in a film like "Laws of Gravity," we're reduced to watching a bunch of punks mouth off and shove each other—all in the name of "personal" filmmaking.

"Federal Hill" isn't awful. There's energy in the joy-riding scenes and the first-time director, Michael Corrente, who wrote the script based on his experiences growing up in the Italian American enclave of Federal Hill, R.I., brings out the snap in his performers. But there is nothing terribly different or exciting about what he shows us, the film is gripping in a conventional, formulaic way. The characters go through their motions in a fashion that seems equal parts "Mean Streets" and the Dead End Kids.

Nicky (Anthony De Sando) is the handsome smoothie who wants to rise out of Federal Hill by romancing a co-ed from nearby Brown University, Wendy (Libby Langdon), who first approaches him to buy some cocaine for a party. He's smitten by her upscale glamour; she's turned on by his wrong-side-of-the-tracks appeal. He seduces her at his apartment by making spaghetti *a l'olio*. They have sex standing up in the stacks at the Brown library. Wanna bet this all comes to a bad end?

Nicky's best friend, Ralph (Nicholas Turturro, of "NYPD Blue"), is a hothead burglar who only calms down when he's sitting in with his father, a near-catatonic bricklayer who can't take care of himself. Ralph stays with Nicky, even sleeps in his bed. This bed-sharing is meant to be platonic but there's a vicious gay-baiting scene involving Ralph and a street hustler that indicates Corrente had more ambitious things on his mind. Ralph is constantly trying to douse Nicky's infatuation with Wendy, and his reasons are not wrong, just his motives.

The Nicky-Ralph duet is equivalent to the Harvey Keitel-Robert De Niro confab in "Mean Streets." The peacemaker and the hot head. And, of course, the Mob figures big in all of this. One of their friends, Frankie (Michael Raynor), has a capo for a father—Frank Vincent's Sal—and Ralph, unconcerned, crosses him. Sal is the kind of guy who carries on a one-sided conversation with his cowering son while punching a heavy bag.

Shot in black and white on an $80,000 budget, "Federal Hill" is best when it keeps to what it knows: the street rhythms of these despairing toughs. When it ventures into social consciousness, as in the scenes with Nicky looking forlornly through a fence at the well-off Brown students gamboling across a campus he'll never attend, it's clunky. There's something antiquated, almost Depression-era, about Corrente's take on these guys' lives. He's so intent on keeping them downtrodden that he skimps on their flair. They don't seem as bad off as they're made out to be.

NEW YORK POST, 12/9/94, p. 51, Thelma Adams

With so many debutante directors chasing after the pulp fiction of Quentin Tarantino, it seems almost nostalgic for newcomer Michael Corrente to worship at the temple of Martin Scorsese in "Federal Hill."

The title refers to the blue-collar Italian neighborhood of Providence, R.I., where Corrente grew up. Located only a mile from effete Brown University, the difference between town and gown could be measured in light years—and Corrente sets out to survey the territory with a perspective as black and white as his film stock.

"Federal Hill" starts confidently. Ralph (Nicholas Turturro) gleefully robs a house, pausing to feed the cat and masturbate over the lingerie of the missus. An upbeat, jazzy score accompanies his actions and cinematographer Richard Crudo's black-and-white images have the clarity of ebony and pearls.

"I just got off work," Ralph quips to his best friend, Nicky (Anthony De Sando), afterward.

So far, so good. Turturro—actor John's brother and a regular on "NYPD Blue" has the stumpy, aggressive energy to carry off the Harvey Keitel role.

Ralph's the unpredictable force in a quintet of arrested-development cases who have their heads stuck in Federal Hill. Call central casting—here's Nicky the Romeo, Franky the fixer, Bobby the weakling and Joey the husband who's really married to his pals.

Shock waves rock the insular gang when Nicky (who has the looks of a young John Travolta) starts to romance a Brown blonde named Wendy (Libby Langdon) and, for the sake of dramatic catharsis, the affair threatens life as the young men know it.

Soon, Ralph's unpredictability becomes all too predictable. The little tough guy with the shadow mustache crosses Nicky and the local mob; a gun that was brandished in the first act starts smoking in the last.

Corrente, who based the semi-autobiographical script on his stage play, starts humming that stock tune: love and the Mafia are breaking up that old gang o' mine!

The movie's nicest moments have little to do with the jerry-rigged plot: Ralph gently bathing his depressed and incompetent father or Joey's wife giving her poker-playing husband an authentic tongue-lashing.

Crudo's cinematography, Turturro's acting, and the solid appearance of Frank Vincent as the local Mafia kingpin bolster "Federal Hill." But, we've wandered through these mean streets before—although maybe not in this particular zip code—and it all seems too familiar.

NEWSDAY, 12/9/94, Part II/p. B7, Jack Mathews

"Mean Streets" moves to Providence, R.I., in Michael Corrente's fine debut feature "Federal Hill," and in co-star Nicholas Turturro, audiences will be either looking at the next Joe Pesci or at an amazing one-shot impersonation.

Corrente, a Providence native who has been doing theater in New York for the past 10 years, has an obvious feel for the Italian-American neighborhood known as Federal Hill, and for the lively interplay of the five young men whose friendship forms the nucleus of the story.

These are familiar guys—Bronx, Brooklyn, Providence, wherever they show up—and the mobsters who lurk in the margins are, by now, generic movie figures. But Corrente, who originally conceived the piece as a one-act play, freshens it all up in colorful ways, and with the aid of some solid performances and Richard Crudo's deftly lighted black-and-white cinematography, has turned out something much more than a low-budget calling card.

"Federal Hill" drops in on the lives of its five lifelong friends just as adulthood is finally applying pressure to their mutual loyalties. Nicky (Anthony De Sando), who peddles drugs on the street, is fantasizing serious romance with a customer from nearby Brown University. Joey (Robert Turano) is getting heat from his wife because of his mandatory attendance at the guys' weekly poker game. Frank (Michael Raynor) is about to follow dad into organized crime, whose bill collectors are chasing Bobby (Jason Andrews) all over town trying to collect $30,000 in gambling debts.

Then, there's Ralph (Turturro), a free-lance burglar who, like Joe Pesci's character in "GoodFellas," has a crazy fearlessness of "made men" (mob assassins) and a temperament that fluctuates between benign joviality and volcanic tantrums. Ralph moves through the movie like a string of cherry bombs on a timer, set to go off about every 15 minutes.

What sets Ralph off most are slights to his father, a retired mason suffering from Alzheimer's, and Nicky's infatuation with Wendy (Libby Langdon), the affluent college girl he figures is out slumming for thrills. Ralph, however, is more worried about losing his friend than seeing him hurt, and Corrente suggests something even more—that Ralph, who goes out of his way to find and torment gay men, and even further out of his way to interrupt Nicky and Wendy's relationship, wants Nicky for himself.

Corrente has done a better job setting up his issues than in resolving them, and in the end, succumbs to the urges of conventional melodrama. But "Federal Hill" is a showcase first feature, for the director and most of his cast.

VILLAGE VOICE, 12/13/94, p. 63, J. Hoberman

Another quasi-autobiographical bildungsroman, [The reference is to *The Buddha of Suburbia*; see Hoberman's review.] Michael Corrente's independently produced *Federal Hill* is set on and around the mean streets of Providence, Rhode Island, a few miles up I-95 from the realm of

Mystic Pizza. Like Kureishi, albeit with a good deal less self-consciousness, Corrente reworks his coming-of-age as generic ethnic shtick amplified through the boombox of media cliché. Thus, the working-class urban Italian American world of shakedowns and street toughs is given added movie authenticity by the Scorsese-certified presence of Frank Vincent as the local Mafia don.

Familiar as *Federal Hill* feels, it does have a look: The glossy black-and-white cinematography and small-city location shooting suggest the Phil Karlsen crime exposés of the early '60s: The actors rule; that writer-producer-director Corrente doesn't always know where to position his camera adds to the earnest, haphazard feel. A lazily, if lovingly, undifferentiated, mainly male ensemble eventually boils down to the relationship between dope dealer Nicky (Anthony De Sando), the relatively good kid, and his crazy, risk-taking, fucked-up best friend, cat burglar Ralph (Nicholas Turturro sounding like Jerry Lewis doing Joe Pesci). The friendship is strained when good-looking Nicky gets involved with the slumming Brown senior Wendy (Libby Langdon); the scene in which he seduces her with a tour of his turf and a home-cooked pasta dinner is a tango of smooth moves up until the moment Ralph wanders in. That Ralph and Nicky sometimes share a bed adds an extra frisson to the latter's jealousy (and subsequent queer bashing).

Although, in Ralph's pungent phrase, "this broad [Wendy] comes from the middle of the country somewhere and shits vanilla ice cream," smitten Nicky can't give her up—he even insists on meeting her haute WASP parents when they visit town. Their dinner together is played on the edge of stone-age absurdism; actor-driven as it is, *Federal Hill* keeps threatening to burst from glum intimations of failure into some sort of crazy comedy. Alas, Corrente opts for rote violent tragedy—like Ralph and Nicky, his movie is too superficially slick and doggedly literal-minded to escape the familiar surroundings of the hood.

Also reviewed in:
CHICAGO TRIBUNE, 2/24/94, Friday/p. H, Michael Wilmington
NEW YORK TIMES, 12/9/94, p. C6, Caryn James
VARIETY, 2/21-27/94, p. 46, David Stratton
WASHINGTON POST, 3/3/94, p. B7, Hal Hinson

FIORILE

A Fine Line Features release of a Filmtre-Gierre Film production in association with Pentafilm/ Florida Movies/La Sept/Cinema Canal + Roxy Film/K.S. Film. *Executive Producer:* Karl Spiehs, Jean-Claude Cecile, and Luggi Waldleitner. *Producer:* Grazia Volpi. *Director:* Paolo Taviani and Vittorio Taviani. *Screenplay (Italian with English subtitles):* Sandro Petraglia, Paolo Taviani, and Vittorio Taviani. *Story:* Paolo Taviani and Vittorio Taviani. *Director of Photography:* Giuseppe Lanci. *Editor:* Roberto Perpignani. *Music:* Nicola Piovani. *Sound:* Danilo Moroni. *Sound Editor:* Alessandra Perpignani. *Art Director:* Gianni Sbarra. *Set Dresser:* Luca Gobbi. *Special Effects:* Ditta Battistelli. *Costumes:* Lina Nerli Taviani. *Make-up:* Mario Michisanti. *Running time:* 118 minutes. *MPAA Rating:* Not Rated.

CAST: Claudio Bigagli (Corrado/Alessandro); Galatea Ranzi (Elisabetta/Elisa); Michael Vartan (Jean/Massimo); Renato Carpentieri (Old Massimo); Lino Capolicchio (Luigi); Constanze Engelbrecht (Juliette); Athina Cenci (Gina); Chiara Caselli (Chiara); Giovanni Guidelli (Elio); Norma Martelli (Livia); Pier Paolo Capponi (Duilio).

CHRISTIAN SCIENCE MONITOR, 1/27/94, p. 11, David Sterritt

The first weeks after Christmas tend to be a slow time in the film-reviewing trade.

Hollywood releases its would-be blockbusters before the holidays to capitalize on school vacations and the festivity-prone atmosphere of the season. It puts its "prestige pictures" into the marketplace around the same time, since movies don't qualify for Academy Awards unless they open commercially by the end of the year.

So if a Hollywood film arrives in your local multiplex during January, there's a strong chance the studio regards it as a weak commodity, both commercially and artistically. There are exceptions to this rule, of course, and sometimes a studio loses faith in a film not because it's bad, but because it's too demanding or offbeat. Still, it's hard to work up much anticipation for most studio releases between New Year's Day and mid-February or so.

The bright side of this situation is that it creates a particularly large window for non-Hollywood fare to enter the theatrical circuit. International movies, independently produced films, and revivals take on special importance as the big studios brood over their upcoming superproductions and await the Memorial Day blitz.

Most of these "specialized" pictures open first in New York, spreading to additional markets if they're applauded by critics and audiences. Offerings slated for early 1994 include reissued films by Stanley Kubrick and Robert Altman, documentaries on Beat Generation poetry and the AIDS crisis, and imports from Latin America and Southeast Asia.

Perhaps the most eagerly awaited off-season movie is "Fiorile," a new Italian drama by Paolo and Vittorio Taviani. The film was given its American premiere at the New York Film Festival last fall. While it's a sweeping and ambitious film, it doesn't have the emotional impact of such Taviani works as "Padre Padrone" and "The Night of the Shooting Stars," which have acquired near-classic status since their release. In short, it's just the sort of picture that might be swamped by Hollywood competition at a busier time of year, but may be able to find an audience in the post-holiday period.

"Fiorile" begins with a journey by two children and their parents to visit the youngsters' aging grandfather. Telling the kids about the Tuscan countryside they're traveling through, the father mentions a "family curse" that supposedly haunts their relatives in the region, and he decides to explain the history of this situation.

This leads to a series of lengthy flashbacks that make up most of the film. The first, set in the late 18th century, recounts the sadly ironic tale of a young soldier who allows infatuation to distract him from a chest of gold he's been ordered to guard. He incurs the death penalty for this dereliction, and the family curse commences when his lover fails to take revenge on the blackguard who stole the treasure from him.

The next flashback, set in the early 1900s, focuses on domestic intrigue—a scheme to foil a marriage, discovery of this plot, and a murderous outcome—in the clan that was made wealthy by the purloined gold.

The third flashback, set during the World War II era, shows another family member fighting against the Fascist cause, escaping death because of his family position, and trying to break the curse by sending his own son to another country. The film's ending brings the story full circle.

It's clear from this outline that "Fiorile" is large in scope, covering two centuries and a long list of characters. Credit goes to the Taviani brothers for sustaining a fairly intimate tone throughout the film, despite the many settings and incidents they've crowded into its two-hour running time.

Yet none of its plots and subplots are very memorable, and the action has less urgency than such dramatic material would lead one to expect. "Fiorile" is an interesting and sometimes compelling work, and followers of the European art-film scene can be happy it has reached American theater screens. But it doesn't show these talented *cinéastes* at their inspired best.

LOS ANGELES TIMES, 2/16/94, Calendar/p. 4, Kevin Thomas

Paola and Vittorio Taviani's "Fiorile" is as passionate, lyrical and ravishingly beautiful as any film they have ever made. It has moments of pure enchantment, of exquisitely expressed emotion, and it is often fairly absorbing, although drawn-out. It is also faintly silly, as grand romantic sagas can so easily seem, and it doesn't travel as well as such Taviani masterpieces as "Padre Padrone" and "The Night of the Shooting Stars."

As a tale of misbegotten gold that has cursed a family for two centuries, it is the kind of highly emotional material that might have made a great silent film—by Italy's own Giovanni Pastrone ("Cabiria," 1913), for example, or even by Cecil B. De Mille. In any event, the Tavianis have brought to the screen a legend handed down over the generations in their native Tuscany, which provides the gorgeous settings for their film.

Luigi Benedetti (Lino Capolicchio), a native Tuscan reared and based in Paris, decides to visit his father, Massimo (Renato Carpentieri), whom he hasn't seen in more than 10 years, to introduce him to his French wife (Constanze Engelbrecht) and their two small children (Athina Cenci, Giovanni Guidelli, both remarkable). As they travel through the countryside, Luigi starts telling his children the reason why the Benedettis are so often referred to as the "Maledettis."

With the gracefulness that characterizes the entire film, the Tavianis whisk us back to the late 18th Century, when Napoleon's soldiers, young men filled with idealistic revolutionary fervor, were invading Tuscany. One of them, Jean (Michael Vartan), handsome and blond, becomes swept away in a rapturous encounter with a pretty peasant girl, Elisabetta Benedetti (Galatea Ranzi), whom he nicknames "Fiorile," which is the name for the month of June in the Napoleonic calendar.

While the young couple are making love, Elisabetta's brother Corrado (Claudio Bigagli) steals Jean's donkey, which has a trunk strapped to its back. Much to his astonishment, Corrado discovers that he has made off with a regimental chest crammed with gold coins. When he lets Jean be executed rather than returning the stolen treasure, both the fortunes and misfortunes of the Benedettis are set in motion, as the Tavianis jump ahead to 1903 and finally to World War II for episodes illustrating the persistent curse that plagues the Benedettis through the generations.

The Tavianis again reveal a profound grasp of human nature in all its sensuality and in its eternal conflict between good and evil, greed and generosity, Yet all their warmth, compassion and eloquence cannot disguise the fact that the curse exerts itself over the centuries in a decidedly schematic manner, an impression heightened by the fact that Bigagli, Ranzi and Vartan reappear to portray members of subsequent generations of Benedettis. (It must be said that at one point it is impossible to accept Carpentieri and Vartan as the same man, in old age and youth, respectively, since they do not resemble each other physically in the least.)

While the Tavianis create a sense of genuine ambiguity in the blurring of legend and reality over a vast period of time, they take the working out of a seemingly arbitrary fate awfully seriously. When the Benedettis—none of whom, unfortunately, is very interesting—speak dramatically of their family curse, you want to tell them to come off it and take responsibility for their own destinies.

If "Fiorile" seems a bit much, like an overly rich Italian meal topped off with spumoni, it certainly has been made, in its leisurely way, with much care and artistry. More than anything it makes you wish you could see a really first-rate film—there was a mediocre TV movie version—on the dire fates meted out to the genuinely fascinating array of owners of the legendary Hope Diamond.

NEW STATESMAN & SOCIETY, 3/24/95, p. 23, Jonathan Romney

It's hard to think of film-makers as refractory as Paolo and Vittorio Taviani ever being in vogue, but for a while they were. From 1977's *Padre Padrone* to their own transatlantic film *Good Morning Babylon* ten years later, they occupied a special niche in the world cinema's map. That niche is cinema's hermitage—that secluded spot in film-goer's imaginations that tends to be occupied by one film-maker every decade, the one who is generally held to be the most "authentic" or "primitive", who supposedly abandons the fripperies of the world and of cinema language to engage gnomically with the bigger, simpler mysteries. It/s currently occupied by Kieslowski, whose films people scan like crystal balls for metaphysical revelations.

Taviani films offered more earthy attractions. You could connect with the fable-like directness of their narratives, the economy of their style; or you could revel in their ruralist mystique of new-mown hay and sheep shit. With *Good Morning Babylon*, though, the brothers wore out their welcome: a story of two Tuscan brothers who went to Hollywood to help D W Griffith invent movie spectacle, it was the Tavianis' one genuine naive film—awkward, and awestruck by the myth of the movies and of themselves (the film's message was, "Look, even such simple souls as us can be cathedral builders!").

For their next film, *Night Sun*, they symbolically returned to the windswept heights, with the story of an 18th-century anchorite tussling alone with his demons. By then, no one much cared, but in a way this was the perfect Taviani film—it was pared-down as ever, but this time they were even more obviously playing their own games with the conventions of cinema. If it had previously escaped you what worldly artificers the Tavianis really were, you couldn't miss it here—it takes a particularly sophisticated sensibility to cast Julian Sands as a saint and get away with it.

The brothers latest film *Fiorile* made next to no impression at Cannes two years ago; now that it's released here (and you'll have to dig hard to see it), you can see why—it's a film out of time. Coming to the Tavianis in the current climate of world cinema is like reading a Tolstoy fable after the latest Martin Amis (*Night Sun* was based on one of Tolstoy's sterner yarns). As befits a film about slippages in time, it's completely anachronistic—humanist, a touch sentimental (or it would be if it weren't so austere), playing its faith in all awareness of told history and a belief in symbol. It's cinema reduced to its most straightforward storytelling function: like nearly all the brothers' films, it's structured so as to make you sit down and be told what happened—but it's easy to miss how smart and streamlined it is.

Fiorile is a portmanteau story. An Italian family travel by car from France to Tuscany, to revisit cranky old grandpa in his retreat (the brothers can't resist these scarred hermit patriarchs). En route, Papa gives a lesson in family history, telling how the family curse caused the Benedettis to be renamed "Maledetti". It's all about love and death, inevitably. In the Napoleonic wars, a young Benedetti girl falls for a French soldier guarding a consignment of gold; her brother steals the gold, the soldier is executed, doom descends. A hundred years later, a descendent of the girl, played by the same actress, has her romance wrecked by her brothers, she takes revenge. In the second world war, an idealistic descendent of the Frenchman tries to join the Resistance. He ends up as the bitter, isolated grandfather of the present day, and we're back with the new generation to see whether the old knot unties itself.

The story equates redemption with alchemy: the antique gold has been turned to evil, but all it takes is a good heart somewhere along the
line to cut the chain of misadventure and betrayal and turn the evil back to spiritual gold. Characteristically, the Tavianis place their faith in children—the two terrified grandchildren who explore the barren Maledetti house in the final scenes. In the closing sequence, as they return home, they illustrate the film's moral dichotomy—the boy claps a gold coin while the girl writes on the steamed-up car window the world "Fiorile "—the name of her ancestor, "spring" in the French Revolutionary calendar.

It's all fairy-tale imagery—the gentle maiden, the brave soldier, the wicked brothers—but the Tavianis have absolute confidence in this language, for them, the simpler it is, the more redemptive. Simpler here doesn't mean naive: they use deliberately two-dimensional techniques to draw us into the story and remind us that we're in the position of attentive children. As the children look out of the window of their speeding car, the camera tracks off the road and into a field to reveal a squad of Napoleonic soldiers parading past. The trick's so familiar it's corny, but fairy-tale telling *has* to be, and it works on two fronts; it supports the film's philosophy that history is something lived, which persists in memory, through storytelling; and it reminds us that film is about dressing up. We know these aren't really Napoleonic soldiers—just a bunch of actors dropped into the field to illustrate Papa's tale. But the minute we recognise that, we accept the story's spell—so that when soldier Jean later appears in 1940s dress, we can see him simultaneously as a timeless spirit in an epic about historical destiny, and as a player in the Tavianis' puppet theatre. (For a wonderfully brazen example of this sort of trickery, see the Tavianis' 1981 film *The Night of San Lorenzo*, now re-released on Art House Video.)

The one moment in *Fiorile* that evokes the supernatural is pure puppetry—I won't spoil it for you, but it comes at the end, and it's all about dressing up.

NEW YORK, 1/31/94, p. 64, John Powers

For all their Brechtian flourishes and left-wing rebelliousness, Paolo and Vittorio Taviani never do anything just for effect. Even their misfires have integrity. Fiorile harks back to the glory days of *Night of the Shooting Stars* and reaffirms the revolutionary dream of "Liberty! Equality! Fraternity!" that has always been their North Star. This lovely new film is something of a comeback—the brothers' most enjoyable work in a decade—and I hope the audience that felt steamrollered by *Kaos* or tittered at *Good Morning, Babylon* will give them another chance.

Fiorile opens with a family driving through the Tuscan countryside. To pass the time, the father tells his children the family history, a legend-laced saga of how a poor peasant family named

Benedetti came to gain the mocking nickname Maledetti— "the accursed." The story starts back when Napoleon's army invades Italy and an idealistic French lieutenant, Jean, falls in love at first sight with a young peasant girl, Elisabetta Benedetti, whom he dubs "Fiorile," after the French Revolutionary calendar's name for May. Yet even as these lovers make splendor in the grass, her brother Corrado steals a chest of gold coins that Jean is guarding. His thievery launches the Benedettis on the road to fabulous wealth but also unleashes a mad history teeming with firing squads and ghosts, cross-dressers and poisonous mushrooms. The Maledetti curse is played out over and over—in a 1903 fratricide redolent of early Calvino, in a chilling massacre of World War II partisans, in the saturnine solitude of a grandfather who lives as a hermit in the family's run-down manor house.

With its bright, dreamy style and grandiose passions, *Fiorile* has the hallucinatory directness of a folktale. But the Tavianis have always insisted that "real" history is inseparable from the aureole of legend and myth that surrounds it. As the Maledetti saga moves closer to our own time, we recognize that it isn't simply a tale about a family that learns that "wealth is a hunger that can't be cured." It's a sly, quietly optimistic fable about the continuous struggle in the modern world between those who'll do anything for gold and those willing to die for the ideals of freedom. The whole movie builds to the scene where the present-day Benedetti children tiptoe up to their grandfather's attic looking for gold and wind up confronting the specter of their ancestor the idealistic French lieutenant. Although brother and sister take different lessons from this encounter, you can tell where the movie's heart is. Its final image, written on a pane of misty glass, is the word FIORILE—a name offering a glimpse of Utopia.

The Tavianis orchestrate everything so movingly in the final half-hour that I wish I could say they've made another masterpiece. But it's always been one of the cruelties of the movies that a junky, money-minded Hong Kong gangster pic can have more sheer vibrant life than a conscientious work of art. *Fiorile* has every virtue that tact, taste, honesty, intelligence, compassion, historical knowledge, and love can bring to a film. But it sometimes runs dry of the one thing that no amount of hard work can force into being: inspiration. In the three great movies that ensure their reputation—*Allonsanfan, Padre Padrone*, and *Night of the Shooting Stars*—the Tavianis' intellectualism was suffused with an effortless sense of enchantment. *Fiorile* has many transcendent moments, including some camera moves so thrilling that only an Italian would dare them, but you can feel the brothers straining to recapture the old magic. And because no filmmakers in the world are more honorable, you exult each time they get a hand on it.

NEW YORK POST, 2/2/94, p. 29, Michael Medved

A stolen chest of gold bring a family curse that lasts two centuries ... Greedy, conniving brothers try to restrain their ardent, impetuous younger sisters ... A brief, passionate forest encounter alters destiny for all time ...

"Fiorile" has all the elements of a corny, compulsively readable, intergenerational historical novel. But in the hands of two master filmmakers, this material sings and glows in a spectacularly satisfying motion picture.

The Taviani Brothers, Paolo and Vittorio, have been directing together for some 50 years, but despite the international acclaim for "Padre Padrone" (1977) and "The Night of the Shooting Stars" (1981), they have never won the wide American following that they deserve. "Fiorile" should change all that, and it may well emerge as the most popular Italian import since "Cinema Paradiso."

The story, inspired by folklore in the Tavianis' native Tuscany, involves a prominent family named Benedetti (which means "the blessed") that has become universally known in the region as Maledetti ("the cursed").

As the movie opens, the Paris-based scion of this ill-fated clan is taking his two children to Tuscany for the first time to meet their hermit grandfather who lives on the ancestral estate. When local residents greet the visitors with murmurs about the family's fate, the father tells the children about the local legends surrounding their heritage.

Those legends begin at the very end of the 18th century, as Napoleon's army invades Northern Italy. A young French lieutenant (Michael Vartan) with a fiery commitment to the ideals of the revolution falls instantly in love with a local peasant girl, Elisabetta Benedetti (Galatea Ranzi, in an unforgettable film debut). While they're busy making love, not war, the regimental gold he's been assigned to guard mysteriously disappears.

His commanding officer decrees that the young lieutenant must be shot at sunrise if no one returns the missing gold—the very morning after he's discovered the love of his life.

The tangled tale then skips forward through the centuries—with an ambitious brother of the now wealthy Benedettis scheming to shatter his sister's unsuitable romance in 1903, and leading to grim attempts at revenge.

Forty years later, the family produces a lonely, sensitive cellist and university student who is drawn irresistibly into a dangerous assignment for the anti-Fascist underground in the dark days of World War II.

The Tavianis use some of the same actors to play family members in different generations, adding to the sense of haunting familiarity—and inevitability—in the family curse. One of those performers, Michael Vartan (who plays the French lieutenant in the 1790s and the shy student in the 1940s) is actually an American actor so hugely effective and so impossibly handsome, that it's hard to understand how he could have (so far) avoided discovery by Hollywood.

The lush, heartfelt music by Nicola Piovani (who also scored some of Fellini's last films) lends weight to the story as it unfolds, while the Tavianis present such luscious views of the Tuscan countryside that these images alone are worth the price of admission.

All in all, "Fiorile" is a cause of celebration—the first film of the new year that merits serious consideration as one of the very best of '94.

NEWSDAY, 2/2/94, Part II/p. 59, Jack Mathews

The first of the three related stories making up Paolo and Vittorio Taviani's family saga "Fiorile" is as rich and enchanting as anything in "Padre Padrone" or "The Night of the Shooting Stars," the 1977 and 1981 films that brought the Italian brothers into international renown.

The movie has nowhere to go from there but down, and the drop is precipitous. But seeing the Tavianis back in form, if for only a half-hour or so, is cause for some celebration.

Returning to the social and historical lore of their native Tuscany, the Tavianis here dramatize a local legend about a family living for two centuries under what might be called "The Curse of Napoleon's Gold."

How the Benedettis, whose name translates as the "blessed" came to be known by their neighbors as the Maledettis (the "cursed") is told by Luigi Benedetti (Lino Capolicchio) to his young son and daughter during a long car ride from their home in Paris to the children's reclusive grandfather's villa in Tuscany.

Luigi's stories pick up the Benedetti clan at three junctures, in the late 18th Century, when circumstances provoked their ancestors to steal a fortune in gold coins from Napoleon's army; in 1903, when corruption was rank among the beneficiaries of that ill-got wealth; and in the 1930s, when fascism forced a crisis of conscience on Massimo Benedetti, the melancholy grandfather the children are going to meet.

It all began, says dad, as if spinning a tall tale around a campfire, when Napoleon's army invaded Italy, and the lives of a French lieutenant named Jean (Michael Vartan) and those of the Benedettis intersected one fateful afternoon in the hills of Tuscany.

As the children scan the woods from the back seat of their minivan trying to imagine the scene described by their father, the French soldiers suddenly appear, and we fall in step with them.

With marvelous ease, the Tavianis lead us to the characters and through the events that will spawn the legend It is a tall tale, but a dandy, a romantic fable about a virginal farm girl named Elisabetta Benedetti (Galatea Ranzi) who wanders too close to a battle scene, is wounded by a stray bullet, then falls instantly in love with the young Frenchman who comes to her aid.

It is while Elisabetta and Jean are locked in each other's arms that her brother Corrado (Claudio Bigagli) arrives, and makes off with the chest of gold Jean was assigned to guard. That night the villagers are told that under French law, Jean will be shot at sunrise if the gold is not returned to them, and after making a passionate plea for the boy's life, Elisabetta's father learns what happened to her in the woods and changes his mind.

The lieutenant is shot, and Elisabetta, unaware that her family copped the coins, dies in childbirth, swearing a curse on those responsible for Jean's death. It is not the last time a

Benedetti will die in childbirth. It becomes part of the Benedetti curse, along with the betrayals, conspiracies, frauds and murders.

The Tavianis are reworking some favorite themes, not least the notion that history cannot be untangled from legend. The conflicts between greed and conscience, and between individual idealism and community needs, also get a warming over here.

But the second and third episodes, and the epilogue where the most recent Benedettis meet their mysterious grandfather and find out whether the curse is fact or fiction, don't add up to much more than a good TV anthology, "Amazing (Tuscan) Stories."

Using the same actors for roles a century apart, as the Tavianis do with Vardan, Ranzi and Bigagli, is not only a banal device to show family resemblance, but if you recognize each one the second time around, it gives away the ending. Still, "Fiorile" gets off to such an enchanting beginning, and the Tavianis' affection for the Tuscan landscape and its people is so affectionately and elegantly conveyed, you may feel a full surrender is the only way to respond.

SIGHT AND SOUND, 4/95, p. 43, Peter Aspden

An Italian family—the Benedettis (the blessed)—are speeding along the motorway from France. The two young children are on their first visit to Florence to meet their grandfather, who lives alone in a remote farm. During a break in the journey, the children overhear some local people refer to the family as the "Maledettis"—the cursed. Their father explains that the taunt comes from an old family legend.

In the story recounted by the father, Napoleon's army reaches Tuscany and a regimental coffer is placed in the custody of a young, handsome French officer, Jean. A young peasant girl, Elisabetta, comes across Jean in the woods and they fall in love; he names her "Fiorile" from the revolutionary name for the month of May in which they met. But while the couple are distracted, Elisabetta's brother, Corrado, steals the coffer. Jean's punishment for losing it is death by firing squad; Corrado never comes forward to rescue him. Elisabetta discovers her brother's role in Jean's execution and swears revenge, but she dies while giving birth to Jean's child.

100 years later one of Elisabetta's descendants completes the task for her. The Benedetti family now owns a sumptuous Medicean villa—its members have become lords of the area. The ambitious Alessandro wants to go into politics; his brother, Renzo is simple; his sister Elisa bears an extraordinary resemblance to her ancestor Elisabetta. She falls in love with a local boy, Elio, but the brothers secretly conspire to send him abroad because his background is too humble. When Elisa finds out, she poisons her two brothers, remembering Elisabetta's vow.

Another couple of generations pass, and young Massimo has been trying to shake off the curse of the "Maledettis". He identifies with the heroic Jean, and he joins his lover Chiara in the resistance against the Nazis. But they are captured; Massimo is spared because of his family connections, Chiara gives birth to a son as she dies. Massimo—the present day children's grandfather—becomes convinced that anyone near him will be cursed, and goes off to live the life of a hermit. That is why he sent his son to France, and why he does not receive the family well when they arrive.

That night, the two children explore their grandfather's house, and find a dummy of Jean in the attic. They climb inside it as a game, but Massimo interrupts them, and believes Jean has come alive. He speaks to the dummy, confiding all his fears and disappointments. But then he finds out what has happened. The family is forced to leave. In the car on their return, the boy is fingering a gold coin he found in the attic, while the girl sadly draws the name 'Fiorile' on one of the windows.

After the metaphysical intensity of their last work, *Night Sun*, Taviani brothers return to familiar themes in *Fiorile*: we are once more in the moral universe of the fable, in which curses and spells resonate over centuries, romantic love is denied by bitter blood feuds and the rolling Tuscan countryside provides the backdrop for murder and passion. The story of the Benedetti/Maledetti family as it unravels over a 200-year span also makes some telling socio-political points about Italian history; the touchingly innocent love stories of three generations are all ultimately destroyed by the political ruthlessness which remains constant over the whole period in question. The Tavianis offer little consolation; indeed the film's closing scenes imply a kind of eternal recurrence which gives this very moral tale an added dimension of grimness.

The directors are by now very experienced at telling this kind of story. Their immaculate control of pitch and pacing is meticulous, almost too much so: there is little humour to help us on our way. From the starry, whimsical mood of the first episode, the tone darkens appreciably as we enter the modern era. The countryside around Florence, from its initial pastoral lushness, gradually becomes more and more alienating; it is transformed from the welcoming refuge for Jean and Elisabetta's passionate tryst to the site of Elisa's callous mushroom-poisoning of her brothers. Nature, as in the Tavianis' previous work, is never the blissful retreat of retired Chiantishire addicts; as the wind howls on the soundtrack, we are made to feel the harshness of an outside world which is capable of delivering so many unwelcome surprises.

The old man's eventual retreat from this world, prompted by the fear that the family curse will inexorably devour anyone with whom he comes into contact, is a bleak conclusion to the previous generations' tragedies; but the Tavianis provide an extra twist of the knife with the reactions of the two children as they listen to their grandfather's moving address to the resuscitated Jean.

As the girl breaks down in tears, the boy finds it hard to stifle his giggles; the cycle of good and evil, in other words, does not end here. We come to realise that the delicate balance between love and money, nobility and greed is not something which can be resolved by any individual's actions, but is instead a never-ending dialectic which will ever afflict the human condition. This, suggest the directors, is the real curse of the Benedettis.

What is missing from *Fiorile* is a really memorable visual scene, such as the church massacre from *La Notte di San Lorenzo*; it is as if the Taviani brothers are stripping down any virtuoso excesses from their work in the fear that they might be distracted from delivering their powerful, and increasingly sombre message.

VILLAGE VOICE, 2/8/94, p. 58, Georgia Brown

The Taviani brothers, bless them, hold a quaint notion of mercenary greed. Essentially it's that gilt begets guilt. A cautionary tale on the subject, *Fiorile* (which, like *Aileen Wuornos*, played in the New York Film Festival) seems to be a personal story, taking place in their native Tuscany and inspired by a local folktale passed on by their mother.

In the movie's present-day frame, a family travels down from Paris to the father's ancestral home. Luigi (Lino Capolicchio) has a French wife and two children, a boy and a girl who've never been to Italy. When they stop overnight in a hotel, the kids overhear two chambermaids gossiping about their family—saying that instead of Benedetti (blessed), they ought to be called Maledetti (cursed). On the rest of the journey, their father tells them a multigenerational tale in which love and greed war for the souls of each generation.

The Tavianis have always liked short stories (with frames around them) and this is another of their multilayered concoctions. The first tale begins in the late 1700s, when Napoleon sent forces into Italy. A band of French soldiers stop to bathe in a pond when they're attacked by local partisans. In the melee, a peasant girl, Elisabetta Benedetti (Galataea Ranzi), is wounded and lovingly tended by a handsome French lieutenant overflowing with ideals of liberty and equality. Jean (Michael Vartan) is also keeper of the troop's chest of gold coins. When the gold is stolen by Elisabetta's brother, Corrado (Claudio Bigagli), Jean is executed at dawn. Elisabetta dies giving birth to his child, heir to the family's wealth and to his mother's curse on the traitors—her own family.

Cut to another century, another generation, with Ranzi and Bigagli once more playing Benedetti sibs. Again, brother betrays sister—again, getting rid of her lover—but this time sis takes revenge, with poison mushrooms. Once again, she dies in childbirth (the curse of Eve, I guess). The big difference now is the family's wealth and power.

On to the perfidy of the mid 20th century—1944 to be precise. A young scholar, Massimo Benedetti (played by Vartan, the original Jean), is caught aiding the Resistance, but his family's name, its cachet with the Fascists, saves him from a firing squad. Meanwhile, his arrested lover, a true Resistance fighter, lives long enough to give birth to Luigi. Massimo becomes a recluse, retreating to the original peasant family's house, where Luigi and his family find him. The story concludes in the present, with the children as the new protagonists, wresting secrets from their troubled grandfather.

The Tavianis have made two of my favorite films, *Padre Padrone* and *Night of the Shooting Stars*, but *Fiorile* is neither as consistently powerful nor as penetrating about patriarchy as they are. Although it makes a psychological point, the multigenerational strategy dilutes the narrative. It's hard to care deeply about characters who come and go so quickly. Still, the movie does contain several exquisite Taviani-type moments.

Contrasting Jean's tragic fate with Massimo's (easy to do since they're played by the same actor), the Tavianis render a harsh judgment on the rich. The ghost of Jean—his ideals of equality and fraternity—appears beyond the echoing figure of Massimo, however. With just a few gestures, one of the young laborers awaiting execution alongside Massimo becomes fully real; in a few frames, his death is weighed against all the Benedettis' empty, cursed lives, their repeated betrayal of ideals. All the film's meaning seems to lie in this subtle revelation of a doomed peasant's humanity, and for the moment it is stunning.

Also reviewed in:
CHICAGO TRIBUNE, 3/18/94, Friday/p. I, Michael Wilmington
NEW REPUBLIC, 2/28/94, p. 30, Stanley Kauffmann
NEW YORK TIMES, 2/2/94, p. C20, Stephen Holden
NEW YORKER, 2/7/94, p. 86, Terrence Rafferty
VARIETY, 3/29/93, p. 82, Deborah Young
WASHINGTON POST, 4/8/94, p. C7, Rita Kempley
WASHINGTON POST, 4/8/94, Weekend/p. 45, Joe Brown

FLINTSTONES, THE

A Universal Pictures release of a Steven Spielrock presentation of a Hanna-Barbera/Amblin Entertainment production. *Executive Producer:* David Kirschner, Gerald R. Molen, William Hanna, Joseph Barbera, and Kathleen Kennedy. *Producer:* Bruce Cohen. *Director:* Brian Levant. *Screenplay:* Toms S. Parker, Jim Jennewein, and Steven E. de Souza. *Based on the animated series by:* Hanna-Barbera Productions. *Director of Photography:* Dean Cundey. *Editor:* Kent Beyda. *Music:* David Newman. *Music Editor:* Laurie Higgins-Tobias. *Choreographer:* Adam M. Shankman. *Sound:* Charles Wilborn and (music) Tim Boyle. *Sound Editor:* Mark "Cro-Magnon" Mangini. *Casting:* Nancy Nayor. *Production Designer:* William Sandell. *Art Director:* Jim Teegarden, Nancy Patton, and Christopher Burian-Mohr. *Set Designer:* Paul Sonski, Elizabeth Lapp, and Erin Kemp. *Set Decorator:* Rosemary Brandenburg. *Set Dresser:* Jim Meehan, Mark Weissenfluh, Nicholas Parker, Robert Greenfield, Edward J. McCarthy III, and Jonathan Bobbitt. *Special Effects:* Michael Lantieri. *Visual Effects:* Mark Dippe. *Costumes:* Rosanna Norton. *Make-up:* Cynthia Barr-Bright. *Body Make-up:* Julie Steffes, Cindy Baggett, and Gina Rylander. *Stunt Coordinator:* Gary M. Hymes. *Running time:* 92 minutes. *MPAA Rating:* PG.

CAST: John Goodman (Fred Flintstone); Elizabeth Perkins (Wilma Flintstone); Rick Moranis (Barney Rubble); Rosie O'Donnell (Betty Rubble); Kyle MacLachlan (Cliff Vandercave); Halle Berry (Sharon Stone); Elizabeth Taylor (Pearl Slaghoople); Dann Florek (Mr. Slate); Richard Moll (Hoagie); Irwin "88" Keyes (Joe Rockhead); Jonathan Winters (Grizzled Man); Harvey Korman (Dictabird); Elaine Silver (Pebbles); Melanie Silver (Pebbles); Hlynur Sigurdsson and Marino Sigurdsson (Bamm-Bamm); Sheryl Lee Ralph (Mrs. Pyrite); Jean Vander Pyl (Mrs. Feldspar); Janice Kent (Stewardess); Jack O'Halloran (Yeti); Becky Thyre (Roxanne); Rod McGary (Store Manager); Kate Pierson, Fred Schneider, and Keith Strickland (BC-52s); Jim Doughan (Maitre d'); Laraine Newman (Susan Rock); Jay Leno (Bedrock's Most Wanted Host); Alan Blumenfeld (Fred Look-a-Like); Sam Raimi (Cliff Look-a-Like); Alex Zimmerman, Tommy Terrell, and Tabbie Brown (Accusers); Andy Steinfeld (Aerobics Instructor); Bradford Bryson (Foreman); Dean Cundey (Technician); Lita Stevens (Woman at Chevrox); Joe Barbera (Man in Mersandes); Bill Hanna (Executive in Boardroom).

LOS ANGELES TIMES, 5/27/94, Calendar/p. 1, Kenneth Turan

Welcome to Bedrock, a town proud of being "First With Fire." The locals eat at Roc Donald's ("Over 18 Dozen Sold"), watch George Lucas' "Tar Wars" at the drive-in, get their gas at the Chevrock station and their information via the Cave News Network.

You were expecting maybe "Middlemarch"?

Whatever else people say about "The Flintstones," no one will claim that a chance to make a truly great motion picture was frittered away here. A live-action cartoon in every sense of the word, this re-creation of the long-running television series about suburban life in 2,000,000 B.C. has been carefully designed to be as bright and insubstantial as a child's toy balloon.

Like "The Addams Family" before it, this is one of those clever, lively and ultimately wearying pieces of showy Hollywood machinery where a glut of creativity has gone into the visuals with only scraps left over for the plot and the dialogue. But then, given its source material, what more could anyone have expected?

Actually, someone must have at least hoped for more, because press reports indicate that somewhere between 32 and 35 writers ("almost as many people as signed the Declaration of Independence," mocked Daily Variety) had a hand in the script. It was finally credited to Tom S. Parker & Jim Jennewein and Steven E. de Souza, but any piece of writing where the most notable words are "Yabba-Dabba-Doo!" is not going to be up for any Writers Guild awards any time soon.

That, as anyone who watched the 1960s TV series remembers, is the war cry of Fred Flintstone (John Goodman), devoted family man, operator of a Bronto-crane at the Slate & Company quarry and mainstay of the Water Buffalos bowling team. Though Fred (who both here and in the cartoon strongly resembles Jackie Gleason in "The Honeymooners") likes to say, "In my cave, I reign supreme," really his wife, Wilma (Elizabeth Perkins), calls the shots. And best friends and neighbors Betty (Rosie O'Donnell) and Barney Rubble (Rick Moranis) also have sizable places in his heart.

The best thing the film that bears his family name has done is to whimsically imagine and create a world where everything, up to and apparently including Fred's head, is made from stone. Production designer William Sandell, "Jurassic Park" special-effects supervisor Michael Lantieri and the entire production team have done splendid work in this area, turning Bedrock into a shiny place that always diverts the eye.

Most fun are a host of animatronic beasties designed by Jim Henson's Creature Shop to do everyday tasks, like a lobster lawn mower, a woolly mammoth shower and something called a pigasaurus that replaces the TV series' vulture as a heavy-breathing garbage disposal unit.

If these devices are unexpected, "The Flintstones" plot devices are less so. The main idea, identical to the one that powers "The Hudsucker Proxy," has Slate & Co. evil-doers Cliff Vandercave and Sharon Stone (Kyle MacLachlan and Halle Berry) searching for "an ignorant stooge" to help them fleece the firm. Fred is obviously their man. But his bogus elevation to vice president turns him into a dreadful snob and causes a rift between the Flintstones and the Rubbles. From such acorns do $45-million films grow.

Though "The Flintstones" won't disappoint those who've been looking forward to seeing the venerable cartoon made human, its pleasures are not substantial or lasting enough to convince those who lean toward thinking it all sounds rather feeble.

Under the direction of Brian Levant, whose most notable previous credit was "Beethoven," the acting in the movie, from star Goodman to Elizabeth Taylor's well-publicized cameo, is, not surprisingly, cartoonish, with svelte and sexy villains Berry and MacLachlan registering best, as villains often do in animation.

And even the gaudy and amusing production design, winning though it is, can hold one fascinated for only so long. Even at a lean 92 minutes, "The Flintstones" eventually makes you want to change the channel and see what else is on.

NEW STATESMAN & SOCIETY, 7/29/94, p. 35, Jonathan Romney

The ides of "theme park" cinema caught on with critics a couple of years ago as a useful notion to describe a certain type of Hollywood escapism. These were the films that *took you there*, to some all-enveloping fantasy world, and made sure you bought the T-shirt on the way out. It soon transpired, come *Jurassic Park*, that Hollywood was one step ahead: films were now being made literally about theme parks, and as blueprints for them as well. There's no doubt that Steven Spielberg will get round to opening a real Jurassic Park—just as soon, that is, as he finishes working on his current project, an underwater restaurant (true!).

Until then, we'll have to make do with his production (under the *nom de chisel* Steven Spielrock) of *The Flintstones*. It's a theme park to the hilt: not only because of the ride it will inevitably spin off (a Flintstones house was in place on the Universal Studios tour well before the film was completed), but also because it clings doggedly to a single concept.

As in the cartoon series, everything must have a prehistoric gag attached: "Albert Einstone", "George Lucas presents *Tur Wars*", that sort of thing. It's done with the laborious tenacity of the jokes on fun-pub menus. No fewer than 32 writers worked on the script (only three officially take the rap). I like to think of them all having to wear little paper hats and say "Have a nice day" at the end of every brainstorming session.

Considering the results, you wonder why they didn't just run an old *Dick Van Dyke* script through a computer programme that randomly drops in the suffix "rock" every 32nd word. Still, there's one good gag, and it's an agreeably dark one. Wilma's mother (Elizabeth Taylor: one might well ask what *is* the point?) laments: "When I think of all the sacrifices your father made for you—lambs, oxen, your brother Jerry ..."

The unknown screenwriter who contributed that gag was clearly in tune with the sinister sensibility that pervades the film. Unfunny, lumbering dollar-waster that it is, Brian Levant's vision of Bedrock is not merely depressing. It is *depressive*, a cry of despair. This is Hollywood in an iron-in-the-soul moment, breaking down and confessing that there are no more ideas in the well, no more decent gags in the book. Consequently, the film is actually set in Hell.

It opens with a live-action recreation of the TV show's opening sequence—a panorama of slaving, sweating masses breaking rocks in the Bedrock quarry where Fred Flintstone (John Goodman) and his buddy Barney Rubble (Rick Moranis) are merry wage slaves. Under a lowering sky, the toilers in Mastodon-hide togas have the beetle-browed anthropoid sullenness of inmates in 1930s chain-gang movies. In fact, the whole vista uncannily resembles the infernal Brazilian goldmines so terrifyingly photographed by Sebastião Salgado.

The peculiar dinginess of Dean Cundey's photography gives these weird landscapes the purgatorial look of Mars on a Thursday afternoon. But live action cartoons are, in any case, always set in Hell. However charming film-makers intend the result to be, there's nothing reassuring about cartoon images transmuted into the forms of 3-D verisimilitude. Imagine Donald Duck recreated in animatronic form and placed among recognisable humans. He wouldn't look like a happy Disneyland host at all, but a monstrous alien mutation. (The comic book *Howard the Duck* brilliantly exploited this premise, which the inept film based on it signally failed to fathom.) Its effect is quite the opposite of Mary Poppins dancing with cartoon penguins; it simply looks as if demons have invaded our world.

The Flintstones goes a step further. Its humans seem to have slipped into an arcane music-hall circle of Hell, where they are forced to act as stooges to funny animal acts. There are horrible creatures here, but they're not *Jurassic Park* horrible, just excruciating. This is the circle of Bad Humour. The house pet Dino is a monster of winsomeness: a bouncy purple bag of polymorphous perversity, it just lollops around ingratiatingly. A zillion dollars worth of animatronic and it still looks like a rubber bag. There's a snooty-voiced Dictabird that you'd love to throttle—a cruel joke by the demon of anthropomorphism. The repellent garbage-gobbling Pigasauras is the film's one endearing species, perhaps because it looks so much like the tabloid reporters on *Spitting Image*.

The film really gets desperate in its attempts to make the humans more cartoon-like. For once, it doesn't use prosthetic jowls and brows. It buys in funny-looking people like John Goodman and Rick Moranis instead. You can see why: transforming the human body has more disturbing implications than a film like this would be prepared to entertain. Robert Altman's inspired, melancholic *Popeye* was the first live cartoon to remould its actors into Bendy toys. In so doing, it opened up a strange new vein of body horror, followed up in the grotesques of *Dick Tracy, Batman* and the forthcoming *The Mask*.

Here, though, we have to make do with cartoon motions, to bizarre effect. When Goodman roars, "Yabba dabba doo!" he *actually levitates*. When he trips along twinkle-toed at the bowling alley, he floats on balletic points. These moments make no sense; they just don't *look* like proper gags. It's not because they're impossible actions. Once Chaplin staged a gag in which a bathing beauty floats down from a diving board with the zig-zag motion of an autumn leaf, and it *remains* one of the most perfect visual puns in cinema. They jar, rather, because we know they're *translations* of visual puns that worked better in another context. They're like jokes transliterated syllable by syllable from a dead language.

In fact, the original *Flintstones* really is a dead language. Its jokes are no longer funny, except through the optic of nostalgia. They're too mechanical, too reliant on verbal rather than visual conceits. And the idea that dead humour can be reanimated through an expensive celebration of its obviousness is hopelessly misguided.

But there's another level of deadness. This *Flintstones* doesn't work because it's an anachronism within an anachronism. When the series originally started in 1960, its viewers were watching a joke about contemporary American mores. Today, the suburban banalities it lampoons—drive-in movies, lunch pails for blue-collar workers, sitcom arguments about who wears the trousers at home—look as distant to us as the Pleistocene daily news.

If the film is at all aware of that double optic, it's purely on a design level. The humour itself retains more of that early 1960s spirit than its makers might have bargained for when Wilma (Elizabeth Perkins) upbraids Fred over the "Neanderthal friends" he hangs out with, he replies: "For your information, the lodge no longer accepts Neanderthals."

That might have been funny once; today, it strikes us as a 1960 *joke*, with all the attendant undertow of routine racism and pay-packet snobbery. Main Street 1960 is no longer a norm to us; we're more likely to picture it as Hell on earth. It would take a Velociraptor to laugh at some of this stuff.

NEW YORK, 5/30/94, p. 58, David Denby

John Goodman, as Fred Flintstone, leaps into the air, hanging there for a couple of seconds like an immense swinging chandelier, and triumphantly Yabbilates. Fred feels good to be alive, and as he smiles, Goodman's huge jowls broaden at the bottom like a butternut squash. Goodman fits perfectly in the sun-drenched, plastic-rock sets of *The Flintstones*, which look like a corner of Disneyland that has never seen rain. A roaring actor with many teeth, a long, pointed nose, and a heart the size of an elephant's hindquarters, Goodman was born to play Fred Flintstone—yet he doesn't bring anything special to it.

How could he? This $45-million movie is the product of slavish devotion to a sixties cartoon sitcom, and all the money, love, and dedication have been expended on keeping it faithful—which means, despite the huge sets, keeping it trivial and small. Goodman roars and roars, a big, happy goof bouncing things off his head, but if I'm not mistaken, there's a bored actor inside the ebullient clown. Goodman doesn't show us anything new about Fred. What is there to show? Well, I don't really know. But one possible reason to make a huge movie out of a TV show is to discover something new in the material. That possibility was rejected by the filmmakers. *The Flintstones* is pleasant, and for a while I enjoyed it, but the colossal kiddie-dumbness of it wore me out, and I forgot it while I was still watching it.

The Flintstones is a case of media scholasticism taken to extremes, and it didn't have to be that way. When Barry Sonnenfeld made the two *Addams Family* movies, he emphasized the mordant wit, the kidding ghoulishness, and Sonnenfeld's sophisticated approach gave the actors room to fool around and the audience something to connect with. But the director of *The Flintstones*, Brian Levant (*Beethoven*), and the many, many writers who worked on the project carry on as if the original show were the Book of Genesis. Nothing has been allowed to intrude on the audience's memories—no extra awareness, no sense of anything around or after the show. When watching *The Flintstones*, you have to pretend, in other words, that you're still a kid. Levant lives in a Los Angeles house that has been called a pop-culture museum, complete with Mr. Peanut statues and Pebbles and Bamm-Bamm dolls. It doesn't seem to have occurred to him that anyone who enjoyed *The Flintstones* 30 years ago might have lived a little since then.

When the Hanna-Barbera series kicked off in 1960, it was the first cartoon sitcom to air in prime time. Fred and Wilma Flintstone and their friends Barney and Betty Rubble were the Kramdens and the Nortons projected into the Stone Age—two squabbling lower-middle-class families living in Bedrock, a paleolithic version of fifties suburbia. Working with a cadre of designers and builders, Levant has blown up the cute rock-world into huge sets, and the scale of the silly jokes is entertaining. There's a mastodon outside the Flintstone kitchen that sprays water on the lettuce, and a whole selection of claw creatures working at domestic tasks—shaving Fred's face in the morning, using their pincers to mow the lawn. The visual puns come fast and furious. They're all the same pun, of course, and I might have enjoyed the joke a lot more if I weren't aware of the $100-million marketing campaign designed to convert the creatures into toys. It can't be a coincidence that Bedrock has been designed to look like a theme park; every part of the movie is exploitable.

A sitcom always returns to the same point, but a full-length film, even a comedy, needs characters placed at risk in some way. The movie *The Flintstones* is a huge sitcom episode. Fred, momentarily convinced he's smart and successful, fights with Barney and has to be made to realize that he's no better than anyone else. Scads of writers are on hand, and all they do is offer the eternal depressing message of television: Don't get above yourself or you'll lose your friends.

As Wilma, Elizabeth Perkins, in a red-dish-blonde beehive, is adorable, but Rosie O'Donnell is wasted, and Rick Moranis, a deft comic in other circumstances, curls his upper lip and looks stupid (even when the character is supposed to be smart). Elizabeth Taylor has been brought in—apparently to entertain us senior citizens—as Fred's mother-in-law. It's the screen legend all right, all flashing eyes and heaving decolletage. The performance is in her snarling "Listen, Buster" mode and exactly like a guest appearance on an old TV show. Irony, I'm afraid, has never been part of Taylor's repertoire. It's not part of the movie's repertoire, either.

NEW YORK POST, 5/27/94, p. 43, Michael Medved

From its opening title ("Steven Spiel*rock* Presents ...") to the last credit that appears on the screen ("No dinosaurs were harmed in the making of this motion picture"), "The Flintstones" projects a playful and infectious sense of fun.

This picture not only delivers the dazzlingly inventive sets, props and special effects inevitably associated with a Spielberg kiddie productions, but it is unexpectedly packed with witty gags that you'll be describing to your friends at the coffee machine the morning after you see the film.

For instance, Fred's nagging mother-in-law Pearl (played in campy, hilarious style by Elizabeth Taylor) says to daughter Wilma: "When I think of all the sacrifices your father made for you! Lambs, goats, oxen ..."

On another occasion, Fred prepares to step up to the lane for his lodge bowling team as Barney asks him, "Do you think you can make a strike?" In response, our hero confidently snorts, "Is the earth flat?"

John Goodman plays Fred as something more than just a lovable Yabba-Dabba-Doofus. He brings an earthy, big-hearted dignity to the role that recalls the fact that 34 years ago the original TV series Fred was, after all, inspired by Ralph Kramden of "The Honeymooners."

The rest of the cast is similarly well-chosen, with Elizabeth Perkins as Wilma doing spot-on imitations of her familiar cartoon character. Neighbors Barney and Betty Rubble bear less resemblance to their TV prototypes, but Rick Moranis and Rosie O'Donnell are both so funny in their own right that it hardly matters.

Director Brian ("Beethoven") Levant, reportedly working with a large team of writers (only three of whom are credited), steers these people through a plot that must have felt like a fossil even in the Neanderthal era.

Barney secretly helps his best friend Fred pass a test for a coveted executive trainee position at the quarry where they both work. As he begins to climb the corporate ladder, (with snazzy dinners at Cavern on the Green), Fred forgets his old friends and once sturdy paleolithic values, surrounded as he is by a scheming boss (Kyle MacLachlan) and a seductive secretary named Sharon Stone (the lovely Halle Berry).

Levant and Company take this "Will-Success-Spoil-Fred-Flintstone?"plot in a darker direction than seems appropriate in a film so obviously aimed at young kids, even featuring a bitter separation (complete with crashing crockery and stoneware) between Fred and Wilma.

Nevertheless, the inevitable Hugs 'R Us, Feel-Good-Ending arrives on schedule and small fry will be happily distracted from the movie's more somber moments by Fred's slobbery house pet

Dino, his sardonic office Dicta-Bird, and other critters cunningly designed by Jim Henson's Creature Shop.

The old Hanna-Barbera cartoon vision of the prehistoric town of Bedrock offered a beguiling combination of middle-class Wonder-Bread suburbia and Shtone Age Shtick; since those 1950s suburban certainties now seem almost Stone Age themselves, this movie Bedrock becomes an even more exotic and appealing place to visit.

With the movie's rock-solid entertainment value combined with its implacable marketing campaign, it doesn't take an Albert Einstone to figure out that "The Flintstones" will be a brontosauraus-sized hit.

NEWSDAY, 5/27/94, Part II/p. B5, John Anderson

As funny as it was, "The Honeymooners" was basically a one-joke show: Ralph Kramden, '50s Brooklyn caveman, can't get a break. Its Hanna-barbera alter ego, "The Flintstones," which came along in 1960 was a one-joke show, too: same caveman, flashed back to the Stone Age.

The solitary gag that propels the big-budget feature film version of "The Flintstones" is the translation of cartoon humor into live-action: The mastodon as kitchen faucet (and Greek chorus); the large-beaked bird as Victrola; the giant crab as pin-changer at the Bowl-o-Rama, and Fred, as embodied by the lovably cartoonish John Goodman, suspended in mid-air during an ecstatic yabba-dabba-doo.

Directed by Brian ("Beethoven") Levant and produced by Stephen Spielberg's Amblin Entertainment (yes, there's a "Jurassic Park" plug in here, too), "The Flintstones" makes relentless puns on the words "rock" and "stone," offers proof that product placement knows no particular millennium (Cavern on the Green, RocDonald's, Rolling Rock beer) and gets mileage out of gags that were old when Dino was a pup. The intro, the music, the finale, they're all straight out of the original Bedrock. In other words, if you loved the cartoon show, you'll probably love the movie.

And did we love the cartoon? As Fred might say, "Is the Earth flat?"

The TV "Flintstones" was never that funny, perhaps because it didn't have a Gleason. The "Flintstones" movie doesn't have one either, but it has Goodman, who plays the anti-Kramden on "Roseanne" and has done some memorable work in the Coen brothers' movies. No one's ever been more physically right for a role than Goodman is for longtime Slate & Co. brontosaurus-operator Fred Flintstone, and he's a lot more Ralphy boy than Fred, but he remains throughout the movie an oddly unengaging presence; rather than flesh out the cartoon, Goodman is sucked into the animation vortex.

So is the rest of the cast. As Fred's little buddy, Barney Rubble, Rick Moranis creates a more original character, but he's mugging, too. Elizabeth Perkins as Wilma and Rosie O'Donnell as Betty have the right giggle, Perkins certainly has the right look, but the actors seem to be striving toward a Saturday morning-style one-dimensionality that's epitomized by Elizabeth Taylor's hammy cameo as Fred's mother-in-law, Pearl Slaghoople.

Although nearly devoid of what's usually defined as wit, "The Flintstones," will probably amuse both young children and older set designers. The town of' Bedrock may look parched and inhospitable, but it contains a lot of ingenious sight gags, as well as gaps in logic: They have television, for instance (on which Jay Leno hosts "Bedrock's Most Wanted") but they still write with hammers and chisels. In any event, the animals—which are the products of either Jim Henson's Creature Shop in London, or Industrial Light and Magic in California—are engaging, more so than the actors. Certainly, the pigasaurus garbage disposal has personality, and the Dictabird (voice of Harvey Korman) has as pivotal a role in the story as any human.

It's the Dictabird who gets Fred out of the jam he finds himself in—his own bombast, as usual, being partly the cause—after the nefarious Cliff Vandercave (Kyle MacLachlan) promotes him to vice president at Slate & Co. Cliff, a Stone Age yuppie embezzler and one of the two more interesting characters in the film—the other being Fred's secretary, Sharon Stone, played by the scene-stealing Halle Berry—needs a dupe to perpetrate the liquidation of Slate & Co. So he invites all employees to take an aptitude test, which Barney aces, and Fred fails. But Barney owes Fred big—Fred having lent Barney money so the Rubbles could adopt Bamm-Bamm (twins Hlynur and Marino Sigurdsson). (It was easier on the cartoon, if you recall, when Bamm-Bamm was left on the doorstep.) So Barney switches their papers. Fred gets the job and becomes insufferable. Barney, with the lowest score, is fired. Friendship, of course, will triumph, as will Fred.

You may ask yourself: If Cliff needs a stooge to take the rap for his insidious scheme, why give the job to the highest-scoring applicant? But the script by Tom S. Parker, Jim Jennewein and Stephen E. de Souza makes no pretense of intelligence. Basically, "The Flintstones" simply wants to plagiarize itself, and the only thing missing is the laugh track.

Ultimately, "The Flintstones," like many cartoons these days, is little more than a marketing tool. That the movie is as insubstantial and vacuous as the products it's designed to sell is appropriate: Why else would it have been made? There's certainly no broadening of the original material, no irony, no reflection. Eventually, the people who make these things will realize that there's really no need for a movie at all, just an advertising campaign, the right poster-friendly image (in this case, Goodman/Fred) and tie-ins with companies like McDonald's. A lot of money will be saved, a lot of eye-strain avoided.

NEWSWEEK, 5/30/94, p. 64, Jack Kroll

"The Flintstones" should really be reviewed by an 8-year-old. But NEWSWEEK's 8-year-old movie critic took early retirement last year. If you think that gag is bad, wait till you take *your* 8-year-old to see "The Flintstones." It seems as if every "rock" pun from the 1960s animated TV show is in the movie. The boulder barrage begins with the credit for producer "Steven Spielrock." Yes, that's you-know-who announcing his petrified participation in this live-ation version of the cartoon. Alas, live action has deadened the fun for this Stone Age knock-off of "The Honeymooners," with Fred Flintstone and his buddy Barney Rubble as prehistoric variants of Ralph Kramden and Ed Norton.

A cartoon is a cartoon, but John Goodman and Rick Moranis are not Jackie Gleason and Art Carney. Goodman blusters and Moranis dweebs through a formulaic script about how Fred almost comes a cropper through his ambition to rise from his job driving a brontosaurus at the quarry. Fred and wife, Wilma (Elizabeth Perkins), dream of the sweet life, but as Barney's wife, Betty (Rosie O'Donnell), says, "Fred's no Albert Einstone." Director Brian Levant gives us 90 minutes of this gravel. The actors are outcharmed by the dinosaurs, pterodactyls and mammoths created by the special-effects wizards (although Elizabeth Taylor looks smashing in a cameo as Fred's bitch mother-in-law, Pearl Slaghoople). "The Flintstones" is a lot of Yabba-Dabba-Doo-doo.

SIGHT AND SOUND, 8/94, p. 39, Geoffrey Macnab

Bedrock, 200,000,000 B.C. Fred Flintstone donates the family savings to his next-cave neighbour Barney Rubble, so that Barney and his wife Betty can afford to adopt a child. Fred's mother-in-law, Pearl Slaghoople, is aghast at such an extravagant gesture, but his wife Wilma applauds him.

Fred and Barney both work in the local quarry. When the foreman, Cliff Vandercave, sets all the employees an aptitude test, Fred struggles, but Barney springs to his dim-witted friend's rescue, swapping exam slabs with him. As a result, Fred comes out with top score and wins a promotion. He is made Vice-President of the company, little realising that he is being used as fall-guy in an embezzling conspiracy between Vandercave and secretary Sharon Stone.

As Fred enjoys executive status, Barney is sacked. Relations between the neighbours soon deteriorate: while Fred and Wilma are leading the high life, Barney and Betty struggle to make ends meet. The employees at the quarry are laid off, seemingly on Fred's orders. Wilma walks out on him. When Fred confronts Vandercave, he learns that he has been framed. With the police after him, Fred goes into hiding, but his cover is blown and his former workmates vow to lynch him.

Just as he is about to be roped up, Wilma appears on the scene with Fred's office Dictabird, which tells the mob about Vandercave's scheming.

Vandercave, meanwhile, has kidnapped the Flintstones' daughter Pebbles and the Rubbles' adopted son Bamm-Bamm, and refuses to release them unless he is given the Dictabird. Fred and Barney meet him in the quarry and hand the bird over. Vandercave tries to double-cross them, leaving the children to be bludgeoned to death in the quarry machinery. Fred improvises a catapult to rescue them; in the process, he sets off a landslide and accidentally invents concrete.

The company boss, Mr. Slate, is so delighted that he offers Fred another executive position. Fred turns it down, asking only that he and his colleagues be reinstated in their old jobs.

As you might expect of a film that made $37.5 million on the weekend it opened in the USA, *The Flintstones* is by no means as bad as certain critics ("Yabba-Dabba-Don't") have suggested. It is held together by a bravura, chest-thumping central performance from John Goodman as Fred, and boasts the usual stunning chicanery from Industrial Light and Magic, who fast seem to be collapsing the boundaries between live-action and animation. Given that most of ILM's recent work has been done on 'boy's own' sci-fi pics like *The Abyss* and *The Terminator*, or, most famously, *Jurassic Park*, it is interesting to see the computer wizards in action on a comedy. The array of eccentric animals conjured up by the Jim Henson Creature Shop—among them, a swill-guzzling pigasaurus, a lobster lawnmower and a fussy, pedantic Dictabird—is also intriguing, even if the cutesy anthropomorphism wears after a while.

Given the sophistication of the puppetry and special effects, it is perhaps a surprise that the script should be quite so threadbare and witless. There were reputedly 32 writers involved in cobbling together the screenplay. Director Brian Levant organised mass round-table sessions where the hacks fired off gags at each other in the grand tradition of much American TV writing. Unfortunately, nearly all their jokes land, on stony ground. The Bedrock news is relayed by CNN (Cave News Network), the man who invented the wheel is called Firestone, there are references to the great intellectual Albert Einstone, the local drive-in cinema is showing the new George Lucas film *Tar Wars*, and a certain producer/director is credited as Steven Spielrock. As if this not-so-wise-cracking were not enough, the production and costume designers also chip in with a welter of visual puns, fashioning stone-age bowling alleys, stone-age, foot-powered automobiles, stone-age office toys and stone-age shopping malls. It is little wonder that the narrative is all but submerged in the landslide of rocky humour and detail. The plot, which involves Fred becoming a yuppie executive and treating his old pal Barney with contempt, might have been borrowed wholesale from *The Simpsons*. Whatever the case, it is hardly enough to sustain a 20-minute Hanna-Barbara cartoon, let alone a 90-minute feature. This is not necessarily a problem, though. Like other recent examples of 'sitcom cinema', such as *The Beverly Hillbillies* or *The Addams Family*, *The Flintstones* is predicated on the familiarity of the characters. There is no need for them to change or develop because, it is assumed, the audience already knows them inside out. The storyline is not of major importance in its own right; rather, it works to draw a series of self-contained sequences together in a semblance of unity.

Levant is, by all accounts, a die-hard *Flintstones* fan. His film may come replete with all the old songs and catchphrases, but in some ways this is not an especially faithful adaptation of the cartoons. It is much darker in tone than its source material: however cuddly all the animals seem, one knows that it would only take a little digital fiddling to transform them into blood-thirsty, human-chomping monsters. Goodman, as bluff, genial Fred, still carries a hint of that menace the Coens unearthed so skilfully in *Barton Fink*. And Liz Taylor, dusting down her star persona after an absence of 15 years from the screen, doesn't fit at all comfortably into the all-American stone-age family the series used to celebrate. As Wilma's brash, blowzy mother, the aptly named Pearl Slaghoople, she looks as if she might have stumbled out of the nearest Edward Albee or Tennessee Williams play. Rosie O'Donnell, Elizabeth Perkins and Rick Moranis are more successful in capturing the ingenuous, one-dimensional quality of their cartoon characters, and all give likeable performances, blending soap style naturalism with gentle caricature: they're ordinary, blue-collar Americans who just happen to live in the year 2,000,000 B.C.

As former animator Frank Tashlin showed in his Jerry Lewis films, it is quite possible to make a live-action comedy with all the anarchic crackle of a *Tom and Jerry* cartoon. Unfortunately, *The Flintstones* is so overloaded with laboured visual and verbal gags and in-jokes, so keen to display its own attractions (many of them sure to spawn tie-in toys) and so short on narrative drive, that it seldom takes wing This is theme-park film-making, at once torpid and energetic, but singularly bereft of a sense of direction.

TIME, 5/30/94, p. 60, Richard Schickel

[*The Flintstones* was reviewed jointly with *Maverick*; see Schickel's review of that film.]

VILLAGE VOICE, 6/7/94, p. 60, Joe Levy

Suck? You bet, How? Mightily!

Just as the real thrill of *Jurassic Park* was spotting the merchandising *in the movie itself* (featured in the filmic park's gift shop), the real thrill of *The Flintstones* comes with a pan past RocDonald's. My memory gets a bit hazy here—*The Flintstones* isn't a movie you watch; it's a movie you survive—but I think that RocDonald's is right around the corner from a playground called Jurassic Park. How's that for a marketing tie-in?

Look, as live-action versions of cartoons go, *The Flintstones* lies somewhere in the gulf between Altman's *Popeye* and the Ice Capades' *Disney on Ice*. A pretty big gulf, I'll admit—I think *Howard the Duck*'s in there somewhere—so to be more specific, what we have here is *The Ten Commandments* for six-year-olds; that is, a sacred text writ large upon the silver screen. Will kids like it? Like I care. The sets *are* pretty nearly as impressive as *Pee-Wee's Playhouse*, but the whole film's so damn cheesy you can't be sure whether it's projected on celluloid or Kraft Singles.

As far as the live acting goes—assuming we can call the stilted clowning that takes up so much time here live *acting*—while Rosie O'Oonnell's triumph cannot be overstated (she *sounds* like Betty Rubble, she *actually sounds* like Betty Rubble, though there's nothing she can do about having eyelashes even when she's not blinking), you can't listen to Rick Moranis for one second without thinking, "Geez, the Fruity Pebbles guy sounds more like Mel Blanc than this." Elizabeth Taylor cameos to tremendous effect as Fred's mother-in-law, at some point yelling, "Conga line!" and dancing with Dino. Clearly she picks her film appearances with the same care as her husbands.

Which leaves us with John Goodman. Never has a talent quite so large been quite so thoroughly wasted—at least not since *Flintstones* director Brian Levant coaxed a leaden performance out of no less a comic genius than Charles Grodin in *Beethoven*. (If you're still wondering if kids will like it, there's your answer.) A gig as spokesperson for a big and tall outlet would have been a step up for Goodman. Granted, with John Candy gone and Brian Dennehy doing TV, Goodman should have his pick of roles—which means, no doubt, we'll see him in something up to the standards of *Uncle Buck* real soon.

One more thing—listen, if I keep going, this puppy's gonna be on cable, no, fuck that, *Fox*, by the time you're done reading: Just as the real thrill of summer 1989 was seeing how much like Michael Keaton the new Batman dolls looked, the real thrill of summer 1994 is seeing how much like John Goodman the new Fred Flintstone ...

Also reviewed in:
NEW YORK TIMES, 5/27/94, p, C1, Caryn James
VARIETY, 5/23-29/94, p. 51, Todd McCarthy
WASHINGTON POST, 5/27/94, p. D1, Desson Howe
WASHINGTON POST, 5/27/94, Weekend/p. 42, Joe Brown

FLOUNDERING

A Strand Releasing release of a Front Films production. *Producer:* Peter McCarthy. *Director:* Peter McCarthy. *Screenplay:* Peter McCarthy. *Director of Photography:* Denis Maloney. *Editor:* Dody Dorn and Peter McCarthy. *Music:* Pray for Rain. *Sound:* Aletha Rodgers. *Casting:* Jeanne McCarthy. *Production Designer:* Cecilia Montiel. *Set Decorator:* Lisa Monti. *Costumes:* Keron Wheeler. *Running time:* 97 minutes. *MPAA Rating:* Not Rated.

CAST: James Le Gros (John Boyz); John Cusack (JC); Ethan Hawke (Jimmy); Lisa Zane (Jessica); Steve Buscemi (Ned); Sy Richardson (Commander K); Billy Bob Thornton (Gun Clerk); Kim Wayans (Unemployment Clerk); Maritza Rivera (Elle); Nelson Lyon (Chief Merryl Fence).

LOS ANGELES TIMES, 11/25/94, Calendar/p. 2, Peter Rainer

In the all-too-aptly named "Floundering," James Le Gros plays John Boyz, an unemployed Venice layabout whose life, with the L.A. riots as backdrop, is unraveling. He shambles through life as a kind of activist voyeur. He keeps apart from the street life around him but the life keeps messing up his own anyway. He walks in on his sometime girlfriend (Lisa Zane) making love to another man; he watches home videos of the riot and then gets chummy with some crackhead revolutionaries on his apartment stoop. He fantasizes constantly, chugs beer, tries to talk his crazed brother (a surprisingly powerful Ethan Hawke) into going back into drug rehab. The IRS seizes his savings.

Peter McCarthy, the producer-writer-director of this micro-budgeted swatch of anomie, is better at dry, deadpan wit than righteous rage. But the wit is in short supply. (And sometimes it's leaden, as in the repeated interviews with bad-guy L.A. police chief "Merryl Fence"—guess who?) McCarthy produced Alex Cox's "Repo Man" and "Sid and Nancy" and he's trying here for some of the same funky, desultory poetry, along with a healthy dollop of Social Consciousness. He doesn't quite have the skills for the job.

When John, in one of his frequent voice-over diary entries, tells us, "I'm a rationalist and I'm a romanticist," you may be tempted to offer your own assessment. John is a drag. Le Gros is very good at playing draggy characters, so at least "Floundering" has a real actor at its center. Without him it would be pretty rough going.

NEW YORK POST, 11/4/94, p. 52, Thelma Adams

Anarchy in L.A.

Venice Beach boy John Boyz (James LeGros) is "Floundering." He's unemployed. The IRS is squeezing him; his girlfriend isn't. His brother escaped from rehab and John, due to insomnia, can't escape from his own incessant voice-over. If that isn't bad enough, post-riot L.A. isn't the riot it once was.

Peter McCarthy dips into the vein of white guy alienation mined in "Falling Down" and "Jimmy Hollywood" for a post-Woodstock comedy that tries to revive peace, love and understanding long after the flower children have wilted.

The low-budget producer ("Repo Man," "Sid and Nancy") directs from his own seat-of-the-pants script about a few blue days in the life of a good guy who's no hero.

Le Gros, ("Drugstore Cowboy") is hamstrung by a narration filled with adolescent ramblings better locked in a journal. We are deep in the land where "like" is not a conjunction but a form of punctuation.

Cameo appearances enliven "Floundering." A scruffy John Cusack offers Boyz spiritual advice and marijuana. Steve Buscemi tells him, to "wise up." Ethan Hawke throws a drug-induced paranoiac fit as Boyz's brother, Kim Wayans cracks herself up as a social worker while crackheads offer stoopside revolution with the sage motto, "The problem is the solution."

Also memorable is the visit from beyond the grave by John's parents, a painfully normal pair who walk the earth to remind their son to pray and phone more often.

But the bits don't add up to enough. This Boyz life flounders with its anti-hero. McCarthy claims to have written the script in five days—and it shows. Spontaneous and ultimately sweet, with music by Pray for Rain, "Floundering" proves that not every slacker's merits a feature-length movie.

NEWSDAY, 11/4/94, p. B7, John Anderson

It may subsist on sunshine, but California's image *du jour* is that of a well of dark humors, just waiting to be uncorked by earthquake or riot. Fortunately for the tottering local economy, none of this latent malevolence is so stark or terrifying that it can't be used in a major motion picture.

Or a minor one. Or two. In both "Floundering," producer Peter McCarthy's debut directorial effort, and "Double Dragon," which is supposed to be a kid's movie based on a video game, we get the same post-apocalyptic vision of Los Angeles—bombed out buildings, malignant homeless streets overrun by mutant droogies and the uneasy sense that no matter what happens, it's all fresh meat for the gaping entertainment maw.

"Floundering," a trite meditation on spiritual bankruptcy, is about the idealistic but disconnected John. (James Le Gros) having a 90-minute anxiety attack in the wake of the '91 riots. This is not just disequilibrium; John asks the kind of naive questions—mostly about man's inhumanity to man—that would embarrass most 10-year-olds. And his various encounters/humiliations—with his girlfriend, Jessica (Lisa Zane), his drugged-out brother Jimmy (Ethan Hawke), his beer-guzzling philosopher pal J. C. (John Cusack), an unemployment office clerk (Kim Wayans)—are absurdist episodes, in a pretentious exercise.

Like "Where the Day Takes You," the star-studded runaway homeless movie (which, coincidentally, also featured the talented and misdirected Le Gros), "Floundering" seems to be an opportunity for the young and the beautiful to do something socially conscious, without getting their hands dirty.

"Double Dragon," on the other hand, is standard adventure fare—two brothers, Billy Lee (Scott Wolf and Jimmy Lee (Mark Dacascos), try to keep their half of the mystical Double Dragon medallion out of the nefarious hands of Joga Shuko (Robert Patrick). Set in the year 2007, after L. A.'s suffered "the big one," the film again casts the city, which stands in for the country, as a crumbling, disabled heap except that all the high-tech weaponry still works.

The significance of these films is negligible, and "exists only in pointing out what barely exists: a dividing line between reality and entertainment. It's all amusement, you see, whether it arrives in a white Bronco or a derelict's shopping cart.

VILLAGE VOICE, 11/8/94, p. 70, Ed Morales

It's amazing how quickly L.A.'s image has metamorphosed from vapid, sterile phoniness to edgy, burnt-out analogue of the rotting, sleazy New York. I find myself feeling more and more at home out there, especially after the 1992 riots. Seizing on the aftermath of this decade's defining moment, erstwhile producer Peter McCarthy (*Repo Man, Roadside Prophets, Sid & Nancy*) makes his directorial debut with *Floundering*, a low-budget, comfy, ratty old couch of a movie that brings a new dignity—and a political edge—to the slacker dilemma.

Softening the nihilist bent of his leading role in *Guncrazy*, James be Gros gives life to McCarthy's self-deprecating, left-liberal musings through the character of John Boyz, a twentysomething Venice Beach denizen whose world is imploding. Unable to sleep for days because of a "pervasive feeling of doom," Boyz's prophetic vision is suddenly confirmed in spades. In one day, his bank account is attached by the IRS, his brother flips out on amphetamines, his unemployment benefits run out, and he catches his girlfriend cheating on him. His descent into hell begins, and only the damned can offer any hope for transcendence.

As political satire and social commentary, *Floundering* is often hilarious, if at other times preachy and obvious. While Boyz's jaunts down the riot-scarred streets of South Central are grim reminders of unresolved problems, the spoof of Daryl Gates is wickedly funny. The movie is filled with celebrity cameos, but the best stuff comes from unknown actors: Biff Yaeger as Boyz's back-from-the-dead father, and Maritza Rivera, playing Boyz's object of desire like Rosie Perez in a mellow stupor.

Most enjoyably, *Floundering* depicts a '90s muddle-class bohemia free of the high-gloss shallowness of *Reality Bites or Singles*, that enteracts with people of color in a relatively unstilted way—and people fuck with a giddy sense of abandon that almost feels like the '70s. While the movie's utopian ending doesn't really improve on the coda to Lizzie Borden's *Born in Flames*, its ultimate charm lies in the form of redemption it serves up to the hapless Boyz: a blow job in a rest area in the middle of the desert. Pomo alienation has never looked this sexy.

Also reviewed in:
NEW YORK TIMES, 11/4/94, p. C15, Stephen Holden
VARIETY, 1/24-30/94, p. 65, Leonard Klady

FORBIDDEN QUEST, THE

A Zeitgeist Films release of an Ariel Film production. *Producer:* Suzanne van Voorst. *Director:* Peter Delpeut. *Screenplay:* Peter Delpeut. *Director of Photography:* Stef Tijdink. *Editor:* Menno Boerema. *Music:* Loek Dikker. *Sound:* Paul Veld. *Running time:* 75 minutes. *MPAA Rating:* Not Rated.

CAST: Joseph O'Conor (J.C. Sullivan); Roy Ward (Interviewer).

NEW YORK POST, 1/5/94, p. 31, Bill Hoffmann

Take stunning archival footage of man's early expeditions to the South Pole, weave in an intriguing plot and a dash of "The Twilight Zone" and you have the basis of the unique adventure film "The Forbidden Quest."

This compelling new movie by Dutch director Peter Delpeut pays off in two big ways.

First, it's a creepy, often riveting, mystery. Second, it's a wonderful tribute to the pure art of cinema.

The way the movie was made is just as absorbing as the tale it tells.

Delpeut began his project by scouring the Netherlands Film Museum for footage shot by such pioneer cinematographers as Frank Hurley and Herbert Ponting. These men (with back-breakingly heavy cameras in tow) accompanied many of the early polar expeditions from 1905 to 1930, taking breathtaking shots of our planet's final frontier.

Delpeut has craftily edited the old footage and structured a fictional plot around it.

In 1905, we're told, a majestic Norwegian sailing ship set out for the South Pole on a secret mission with disastrous results.

Thirty-six years later, a journalist travels to Ireland to interview the only surviving member of that ill-fated crew—a softspoken haunted man named J.C. Sullivan, who was the ship's carpenter.

The old man (beautifully played by Joseph O'Conor) describes in hushed, pained tones how the ambitious mission to find a rumored passageway through the middle of the Earth turned into a horrific voyage in which his fellow mates resorted to murder and cannibalism.

Sullivan's somber musings are partly based on the writings of Poe and Verne—with a nod to "The Flying Dutchman" thrown in—giving them an eerily authentic feel.

The old footage accompanying his tale is fabulous: There are wonderful panoramas of the harsh, frozen Antarctic, dramatic shots of an Eskimo tribe and a sad scene of a proud white bear being shot dead (something that inevitably spells doom for other fictional explorers).

The ending, which I won't give away, left me a bit unsatisfied, But it's nothing sci-fi and fantasy fans won't be able to stomach.

Of course, what Delpeut has done in "The Forbidden Quest" goes well beyond simple manipulation.

Who knows what these men were really thinking when they were photographed? What would they have thought had they known that—75 or 85 years later—they would be turned into dramatic actors?

That misgiving aside, "The Forbidden Quest" is a marvel.

For years, avant-garde filmmakers have stolen footage from other filmmakers, bastardized it and called it their own. Most of these efforts, in my opinion are a crime.

Delpeut, on the other hand, treats most of his purloined footage with great respect, often adding subtle tints and hues to heighten the effect.

At the same time, some of this film is so old (often it appears to be falling apart right before your eyes) that its use in "The Forbidden Quest" assures its survival for another hundred years.

But don't wait that long. This is a wonderfully executed bit of magic that's not to be missed.

NEWSDAY, 1/5/94, Part II/p. 47, Gene Seymour

There's a so-old-it's new excitement about "The Forbidden Quest," similar to the spell cast on contemporary readers by Jorge Luis Borges' old-fashioned fables. In fact, were Borges himself disposed to write sea epics, thus tale of an ill-fated 1905 journey to the South Pole could very easily bear his name, though it would be considerably shorter in length.

But then, Dutch writer-director Peter Delpeut's pseudo-documentary carries many echoes: Kafka, Melville, Hawthorne, Poe, Conrad, London and, of course, the grizzled, spaced out grandaddy of all sea survival epics, Coleridge's "The Rime of the Ancient Mariner." You feel the presence of these spirits just as surely as you feel the cold dread and terror in the soft, intense voice of Joseph O'Conor, as Sullivan, who claims to be the only survivor of the doomed mission.

Sullivan, an Irish fisherman and carpenter, is being interviewed in 1941 by a historian (an off-camera Roy Ward) seeking information on the Hollandia, a Dutch vessel to which he's signed on as a carpenter. To Sullivan's surprise, he and his mates find themselves heading south to Antarctica in search of a mythical "passage" between the North and South Poles.

Once the ship arrives at its foreboding destination, its crew encounters such unlikely sights as polar bears and Eskimos, both of which belong at the other end of the globe. The crew also encounters hardship, hunger, madness, cannibalism and something resembling the Convergence of All Space and Time—which Sullivan, with just the proper deadpan pitch, calls "the other side."

What gives this deep-freeze "Heart of Darkness" its narrative authority is the understated elegance of Delpeut's language, which mitigates some of the more outrageous improbabilities of Sullivan's tale. O'Conor, by the way, is a wonder. He's the reason you become almost as convinced by the story as the unseen interviewer, though it's never explained how, exactly, Sullivan returned from the abyss.

The real excitement in this film comes in Delpeut's creative use of footage from actual polar expeditions from the early 20th Century to augment Sullivan's tale. Much of what Delpeut managed to save has an ethereal beauty to which contemporary enactments of the same events could only aspire.

Even though he submits to the temptation to colorize or tint some of the footage for dramatic effect, Delpeut achieves, with a relatively simple strategy, what most films about the past should: the convincing simulation of memory and dreams. Who says archivalism has to be boring?

VILLAGE VOICE, 1/18/94, p. 45, J. Hoberman

In *Lyrical Nitrate*, the Dutch film archivist Peter Delpeut re-presented an hour's worth of gorgeously tinted, voluptuously deteriorated silent film. Although more mannerist than need be, the material was shown basically for its own sake. In his follow-up, *The Forbidden Quest*, currently at Film Forum, Delpeut uses a framing narrative to transform an hour's worth of pre-World War I exploration footage into an overwrought tale of supernatural disaster at the South Pole.

A series of startling images (a desolate harbor clogged with dead whales, a ship collapsing while frozen in the ice) is drafted to serve a cosmology based on the lost continent of Mu. I's a stunt that opens uncanny and winds up irksome. As the onscreen storyteller, the monotonous Joseph O'Conor renders the use of silence—or music—all the more welcome. *The Forbidden Quest* is alternately a clever jigsaw puzzle and an unconvincing crock of blarney. The footage might have been perfect left alone.

Also reviewed in:
NEW YORK TIMES, 1/5/94, p. C15, Janet Maslin
VARIETY, 3/1/93, p. 61, Philip Kemp

FOREIGN STUDENT

A Gramercy Pictures release of a Silvio Berlusconi Communications/Carthago Films/Libra UK/Holland Coordinator production in association with Featherstone Productions. *Executive Producer:* Tarak Ben Ammar, Mark Lombardo, and Peter Hoffman. *Producer:* Tarak Ben Ammar and Mark Lombardo. *Director:* Eva Sereny. *Screenplay:* Menno Meyjes. *Based on the book "The Foreign Student" by:* Philippe Labro. *Director of Photography:* Franco Di

Giacomo. *Editor:* Peter Hollywood. *Music:* Jean-Claude Petit. *Sound:* Brit Warner and Daniel Brisseau. *Sound Editor:* Peter Horrocks. *Casting:* Bruce Newberg. *Production Designer:* Howard Cummings. *Art Director:* Jeffrey McDonald. *Set Decorator:* Jeanette Scott and Patrice Renault. *Set Dresser:* Jamie Bishop, Rick Gruber, Mike Harrell, and Steve Shifflette. *Costumes:* Carol Ramsey. *Make-up:* Ellie Winslow. *Stunt Coordinator:* Spike Silver. *Running time:* 96 minutes. *MPAA Rating:* R.

CAST: Robin Givens (April); Marco Hofschneider (Phillippe); Rick Johnson (Cal); Charlotte Ross (Sue Ann); Edward Herrmann (Zach Gilmore); Jack Coleman (Rex Jennings); Charles S. Dutton (Howlin' Wolf); Hinton Battle (Sonny Boy Williamson); Anthony Herrera (Coach Ballard); Bob Child (Counselor); David Long (Mr. Baldridge); Ruth Williamson (Mrs. Baldridge); Michael Reilly Burke (Harrison); Michael Goodwin (Assistant Coach); Jon Hendricks (April's Father); Andy Park (Sheriff McLain); Brendan S. Medlin (Hans); Kevin A. Parrott (Buster Dubonnet); Cliff McMullen (Preacher); Jane Beard (Doris Jennings); Sutton Knight (Editor); John Habberton (William Farrikner); Jonathan Sale (Herbie Clemson); Allan Pleasants (Tough Guy); Jonathan Orcutt (Alabama Tech Coach); Martin Sowers (Lewis); Brian Lindsey (Jock); Holley G. Procter (Belle #1); Jennifer Ray (Belle #2); Kate Hoffman (Rebecca); Linita Corbett (Girl in Red); Jean Raoul Cassadoure (School Supervisor); Gerard Duges (Postman).

LOS ANGELES TIMES, 7/29/94, Calendar/p. 10, Kevin Thomas

"Foreign Student" has such a good, offbeat premise and such winning performances from Marco Hofschneider and Robin Givens, it's a shame that it's only so-so when it could have been terrific.

Hofschneider was the charismatic young star of "Europa, Europa," in which he played a Polish Jew who winds up in the German army during World War II. Here he plays Phillippe, an 18-year-old Frenchman who wins a one-semester scholarship to a Virginia university. Hofschneider captures perfectly the culture shock experienced by the young man upon his arrival in a small college community in the beautiful Shenandoah Valley.

Not long after his arrival he encounters Givens' April, a schoolteacher who also works as a cleaning woman for one of Phillippe's professors. Their mutual attraction is instant, and why not? Both are exceptionally attractive and bright individuals. But it's 1956, the South, and the very notion of an interracial romance is fraught with peril. Still, Phillippe is the only white man who has ever looked April straight in the eye, and April is not only beautiful but as lonely as Phillippe—it's not likely that April has any friends trying, as she is, to learn French via a correspondence course.

Adapted by Menno Meyjes (who also wrote the script for "The Color Purple") from Phillippe Labro's autobiographical novel, the film is best and strongest when it sticks to Phillippe and April, whose romance develops with credibility and tenderness. From his sophisticated world of Paris, Phillippe is baffled by naked racism and segregation while April is at once intrigued and wary of this very different kind of white man. Director Eva Sereny does capture the aura of danger confronting the couple—anyone who attended a college within a stone's throw of the Mason-Dixon Line in the '50s could tell you how daring and risky their affair is.

When the film moves away from the loves by themselves, "Foreign Student" becomes decidedly uneven, Rick Johnson is outstanding as actually a sensitive, caring and courageous individual behind his breezy jock demeanor. There's also a lovely cameo by Charles Dutton as a blues singer who comes to Phillippe's rescue when the youth dares to go to a blues joint in a black neighborhood, a venue decidedly off-limits to white college boys, and a brief, effective appearance by jazz vocalist Jon Hendricks as April's father. But Edward Herrmann, so often a fine actor, emerges as a caricature of the tweedy, pipe-smoking professor, and Charlotte Ross, a game young actress, is stuck with what may well be the worst role of 1994: a Bostonian who passes herself off as a Southern belle and then suffers a nervous breakdown when she discovers Phillippe has a "black mistress." (None of this curious behavior is explored.)

In her feature debut, Sereny, a Hungarian-born Englishwoman, displays more sincerity than style, and she has a hard time imposing any kind of firm shape or form upon her material. Not helping matters are the film's syrupy score, banal theme song and unctuous soundtrack narration.

NEW YORK POST, 7/29/94, p. 43, Thelma Adams

"Foreign Student" is one of the year's funniest movies—unintentionally.

Fledgling director Eva Sereny harvests pure corn in an interracial love story that casts "Europa Europa"'s Marco Hofschneider and Playboy uncover girl Robin Givens as star-crossed lovers in the segregated '50s.

Menno Meyjes' screenplay, based on Philippe Labro's novel, takes a nostalgic look at an exchange student's coming-of-age at a small Southern college. Meyjes' previous credits include the syrupy adaptation of Alice Walker's "The Color Purple" for Steven Spielberg.

The result is "Americaine Graffiti," a dangerous liaison set against big cars, poodle skirts and pressed khakis. Phillippe (Hofschneider) and April (Givens)—a church-going, French-speaking, school teacher-cum-housekeeper with a great wardrobe—conjugate amour on the wrong side of the tracks.

As Southern gent-slash-alcoholic Cal (Rick Johnson) says in a movie brimming with characters ladling advice, "If you're gonna risk your neck for a colored girl, it might as well be her."

Givens and her co-star play their parts with moist sincerity. Their brown eyes compete under the ticker lights; it's anybody's guess whose lips are poutiest.

If the dewy, peachy-cheeked lad is the prettier of the two, April looks a bit wiser—and a decade older.

Nothing very grave ever happens to Phillippe and his Avril. They disrobe and make love on their second date (you'd think it was the '60s, not the '50s) in a shack where daylight slashes through timbers in white beams and dust motes swirl atmospherically.

The biggest indignity the lovers experience is the clunky lines they are forced to speak.

"You and I come from very different worlds," April says.

"The rain makes us both wet," Phillippe replies.

The intruding voice of the narrator—the older, wiser Phillippe looking back at his Southern pastoral through a veil of years—makes it a bumper year for the cinematic corn crop.

The narrator offers such pearls as "youth is a gift wasted on the young" and "I was at that blissful age when bad things only happen to others."

Even dyed-in-the-wool romantics will snicker when Phillippe writes "April" in his Thanksgiving mashed potatoes.

This French kiss of a movie becomes all the more laughable when it attempts larger statements about American race relations.

After all the blubber that precedes it who can take Phillippe seriously when he describes himself and April as "two foreigners traveling side-by-side in this great land called America"?

NEWSDAY, 7/29/94, Part II/p. B9, Jack Mathews

First-time director Eva Sereny's "Foreign Student" is a memory piece, adapted from an autobiographical novel by a Parisian who, as an exchange student at a Virginia college in 1956, had a hopelessly mad romance with a black maid.

Like many memory pieces, this one feels as if it has been reshaped and idealized while collecting brain dust over the years, and it is delivered as a series of gauzy recollections wrapped in '90s sociology. As we watch this story of naïve passion bashing itself against a wall of racism, a narrator—the middle-age Phillippe Le Clerk looking back—lays on the perspective.

I don't know who "Foreign Student" was made for, but American audiences don't need help understanding the tension in a southern town when a white college student ("Europa, Europa's" Marco Hofschneider) wanders across the tracks to spark the daughter (Robin Givens) of a train porter. Not in 1956, not in 1994.

Sereny, a Hungarian still photographer who has worked with many of Europe's great filmmakers, seems almost puzzled by the circumstances she's trying to depict. The relationship between Phillippe and April is both an interracial and a cross-cultural affair, and the focus keeps shifting from one to the other.

Working with a screenplay by Menno Meyjes ("The Color Purple"), Sereny creates a portrait of an innocent abroad, a sexually inexperienced French youth whose heart nearly stops at the sight of one of his university professor's housekeepers. Because he is from France, where black-white romance is tolerated and news of U. S. race relations is apparently ignored, he throws himself into the courtship of his life.

It's hard to take any of this as genuine biography because it is so rich in clichés. A colorblind Frenchman who digs the blues meets a college-educated black maid who speaks *un peu Francais*? Man, if it isn't love, it's an omen!

Hofschneider, in his first English language role, seems as lost in the movie as Philippe is in the Shenandoah Valley, or in the arms of Givens, who hasn't had a lover this foolish since Mike Tyson. The couple is a mismatch, all right, but not because of race.

VILLAGE VOICE, 8/9/94, p. 41, J. Hoberman

More innocents abroad: In *Foreign Student*, a wide-eyed 18-year-old (Marco Hofschneider) comes all the way from Paris, France, to study something or other at a bucolic college in Virginia's Shenandoah Valley. Because the year is 1956, his arrival is greeted with "Sh-Boom."

In due course, Hofschneider (who played another sort of chameleon in *Europa, Europa*) discovers American football and sexual repression, drive-ins and Southern hospitality, J. D. Salinger and the blues, pumpkin pie, and interracial romance in the person of Robin Givens—a housecleaner and school teacher who reads poetry, speaks correspondence-course French, and makes many overwrought exits, cheekbones aquiver. Given her fashionable perm, fuchsia lipstick, and clingy faux country-gal wardrobe, the warily kittenish Givens seems far more anomalous than Hofschneider—she might have been carried back to old Virginny in the same DeLorean that propelled Michael J. Fox to 1955.

Foreign Student's script, from Philippe Labro's self-regarding memoir, is by Menno Meyjes, an apparent specialist in segregationist Southern mores, having adapted *The Color Purple* for Steven Spielberg. Neophyte director Eva Sereny adds a few preposterous fillips to an inherently dramatic situation already pushed into the ridiculous through repeated quotations from Lord Byron and goofy lyrical interludes of hot sex in an abandoned shack, the passion accentuated by glamorous dissolves, cathedral lighting, generic Vegas soul, and a climatic plea to "Say my name in French!"

Moderately interesting as a fish out of water film, with diminutive Hofschneider capering among a cast of American beached whales (many of them culled from daytime soaps), *Foreign Student* grows increasingly maladroit and inadvertently wiggy, It's not every movie whose hero gets to sit at the feet of both William Faulkner and Howlin' Wolf, to whom he says: "You show me magic tonight I will never forget." *Chapeau Bas!* Charles S. Dutton makes an almost credible Wolf but there's no way he can keep up with the film's howlers.

Also reviewed in:
CHICAGO TRIBUNE, 7/29/94, Friday/p. F, John Petrakis
NEW YORK TIMES, 7/29/94, p. C10, Caryn James
VARIETY, 5/9-15/94, p. 92, Lisa Nesselson
WASHINGTON POST, 7/29/94, p. D6, Lloyd Rose

FORREST GUMP

A Paramount Pictures release of a Steve Tisch/Wendy Finerman production. *Producer:* Wendy Finerman, Steve Tisch, and Steve Starkey. *Director:* Robert Zemeckis. *Screenplay:* Eric Roth. *Based on the book by*: Winston Groom. *Director of Photography:* Don Burgess. *Editor:* Arthur Schmidt. *Music:* Alan Silvestri. *Music Editor:* Ken Karman. *Choreographer:* Leslie Cook. *Sound:* Randy Thom and (music) Dennis Sands. *Sound Editor:* Gloria S. Borders. *Casting:* Ellen Lewis. *Production Designer:* Rick Carter. *Art Director:* Leslie McDonald and Jim Teegarden. *Set Designer:* Erin Kemp, James C. Feng, Elizabeth Lapp, and Lauren E. Polizzi. *Set Decorator:* Nancy Haigh. *Set Dresser:* William F. Alford, Edward J. McCarthy III, Frank

M. Fleming, James P. Meehan, and Mark Weissenfluh. *Special Effects:* Allen Hall. *Costumes:* Joanna Johnston. *Make-up:* Daniel C. Striepeke and Hallie D'Amore. *Stunt Coordinator:* Bud Davis. *Running time:* 140 minutes. *MPAA Rating:* PG-13.

CAST: Tom Hanks (Forrest Gump); Rebecca Williams (Nurse at Park Bench); Sally Field (Mrs. Gump); Michael Conner Humphreys (Young Forrest); Harold Herthum (Doctor); George Kelly (Barber); Bob Penny and John Randall (Cronies); Sam Anderson (Principal); Margo Moorer (Louise); Ione M. Telech (Elderly Woman); Christine Seabrook (Elderly Woman's Daughter); John Worsham (Southern Gentleman); Peter Dobson (Young Elvis Presley); Siobhan J. Fallon (Bus Driver); Alexander Zemeckis (School Bus Boy); Logan Livingston Gomez (School Bus Boy); Ben Waddel (School Bus Boy); Elizabeth Hanks (School Bus Girl); Hanna R. Hall (Young Jenny Curran); Tyler Long (Red Headed Boy); Christopher Jones (Boy with Cross); Grady Bowman (Fat Boy); Kevin Mangan (Jenny's Father); Fay Genens (Jenny's Grandmother); Frank Geyer (Police Chief); Robin Wright (Jenny Curran); Rob Landry (Red Headed Teen); Jason McGuire (Fat Teen); Pete Auster (Teen with Cross); Sonny Shroyer (College Football Coach); Brett Rice (High School Football Coach); Ed Davis (High School Football Coach); Daniel Striepeke (Recruiter); Bruce Lucvia (Kick Off Return Player); David Brisbin (Newscaster); Kirk Ward (Earl); Angela Lomas and Timothy Record (Black Students); Deborah McTeer (Woman with Child on Park Bench); Mark Matheisen (Jenny's Date); Al Harrington (Local Anchor #1); Jed Gillin (President Kennedy's Voice); Bob Harks (University Dean); Don Fischer (Army Recruiter); Kenneth Bevington (Army Bus Driver); Michael Flannery and Gary Robinson (Bus Recruits); Mykelti Williamson (Bubba Blue); Marlena Smalls (Bubba's Mother); Kitty K. Green (Bubba's Great Grandmother); John Worsham (Landowner); Afemo Omilami (Drill Sargeant); Matt Wallace (Barracks Recruit); Danté McCarthy (Topless Girl); Paulie DiCocco (Emcee); Mike Jolly, Michael Kemmerling, John Voldstad, and Jeffrey Winner (Club Patrons); Russ Wilson (Pick-up Truck Driver); Daniel J. Gillooly (Helicopter Gunman); Gary Sinise (Lieutenant Dan Taylor); Calvin Gadsden (Sargeant Sims); Aaron Izbicki (Dallas); Michael Burgess (Cleveland); Steven Griffith (Tex); Bill Roberson (Fat Man at Bench); Michael McFall (Army Hospital Male Nurse); Eric Underwood (Mail Call Soldier); Stephan Derelian and Byron Minns (Wounded Soldiers); Stephen Wesley Bridgewater (Hospital Officer); Bonnie Ann Burgess (Army Nurse); Scott Oliver (National Correspondent #1); John William Galt (President Johnson's Voice); Hilary Chaplain (Hilary); Isabel Rose (Isabel); Jay Ross (Veteran at War Rally); Richard D'Alessandro (Abbie Hoffman); Dick Stilwell (Policeman at War Rally); Kevin Davis and Michael Jace (Black Panthers); Geoffrey Blake (Wesley); Tim Perry (Hippie at Commune); Vanessa Roth and Emily Carey (Hollywood Boulevard Girlfriends); Paul Raczkowski (Man in VW Bug); Valentino (Chinese Ping Pong Player); Dick Cavett (Himself); Joe Stefanelli (John Lennon's Voice); Marla Sucharetza (Lenore); Tiffany Salerno (Carla); Aloysius Gigl (Musician Boyfriend); Jack Bowden (National Correspondent #4); Joe Alaskey (President Nixon's Voice); Lazarus Jackson (Discharge Officer); W. Benson Terry (Stanley Loomis); Matt Rebenkoff (Drugged Out Boyfriend); Peter Bannon (Local Correspondent #2); Joe Washington (Local Anchor #2); Nora Dunfee (Elderly Southern Woman); Natalie Hendrix (Local Anchor #3); Hallie D'Amore (Waitress in Cafe); Jim Hanks (Running Double); Chiffonye Cobb, Juan Singleton, and Bobby Richardson (Hannibal Reporters); Michael Mattison (Taxi Driver); Lenny Herb (Young Man Running); Charles Boswell (Aging Hippie); Tim McNeil (Wild Eyed Man); Haley Joel Osment (Forrest Junior); Lonnie Hamilton (The Minister); Teresa Denton (Lieutenant Dan's Fiancée).

CHRISTIAN SCIENCE MONITOR, 7/7/94, p. 10, David Sterritt

"Forrest Gump" is a hard movie to dislike. In some respects, though, it's even harder to like. Its main assets are a richly sentimental story, an eye-pleasing visual style, and an all-stops-out performance by Tom Hanks that combines the outward mannerisms of an ugly duckling with the inner sweetness of a natural-born innocent.

But the movie supports its optimistic agenda by evading or overlooking many hard realities of the historical period it supposedly wants to explore and understand. The result is a winning but ultimately dishonest portrait.

The film begins in the 1950s. We first meet Forrest as a boy in Alabama, where the local school won't accept him because his IQ is below normal. His concerned mother solves this problem by sleeping with the principal, enabling Forrest to enter the real world despite his peculiarities.

From here on, Forrest's life slips into a pattern whereby difficult challenges always turn into rosy opportunities for his special qualities to shine triumphantly through. Running from schoolyard bullies, for instance, he discovers that his legs—once strapped into braces meant to straighten his back—are the best in town, allowing him to run farther and faster than anyone he knows. Later, a hospital stay helps him discover a similar talent for Ping-Pong, of all things.

These abilities bring him a college scholarship, help him survive as a Vietnam soldier, and come in handy when he's recruited for the diplomatic Ping-Pong team that renews Chinese-American relations in the '70s.

Later episodes find him a successful seafood entrepreneur, a cross-country runner with a hero-worshiping fan club, and ultimately the father of a son with all his virtues and none of his failings.

What makes "Forrest Gump" more than just a sugary coming-of-age tale is the way its hero comes into direct contact with many of the social forces and political leaders of his time. Using the trickiest sort of Hollywood technology, the movie shows him looking on as Alabama Gov. George Wallace grudgingly allows black students into the state university; shaking hands with President Kennedy after an athletic victory; and bantering with President Johnson about his Vietnam adventures.

And since one person can't experience *everything*, the movie gives him a girlfriend named Jenny who confronts more controversial phenomena—free love, radical politics, drug abuse—that almost magically steer away from Forrest himself.

"Forrest Gump" has an emotional power that can't be denied, especially when Hanks is going full steam as the lovable schlemiel with an inexhaustible reserve of goodness and common sense.

Movie buffs may also enjoy its allusions to earlier films—a long parody of "Midnight Cowboy," among others—and its clever exploitation of strategies borrowed from all kinds of prior productions. Its antecedents range from the 1980 comedy "Being There" to the Bill Clinton campaign video "A Place Called Hope," which also depicted a bright-eyed country boy having an all-American encounter with the president himself.

The problems with "Forrest Gump" arise from its depiction of American society and recent American history. This plays a major role in the movie, yet rings dreadfully hollow most of the time.

For one major example, most youngsters with subnormal IQ scores don't slip cutely through the bureaucratic cracks and wind up with scholarships, college degrees, and great business opportunities. Of course, it would be fine for a fairy-tale movie to show all this happening, despite its improbability in real life. But the history-based plot and documentary-style interludes in "Forrest Gump" are meant to convey the feeling that this isn't a fairy tale at all, just a good-natured portrayal of how great life would be if we'd stop fretting about improving the world and put our money on old-fashioned gumption.

Still more questionable is the movie's habit of raising tough social problems that it has no intention of dealing with forthrightly. The film even treats such tragedies as war, civic strife, and political assassination as little more than colorful backdrops for the hero's charmed life.

This evasiveness reaches its high point reaches its high point when Forrest is coaxed into addressing a huge demonstration against the Vietnam War. At last, it appears, the film is going to take a stand on something, one way or another. But a saboteur knocks out the amplifiers just as Forrest begins to talk, so neither the people *in* the movie nor those *watching* the movie can hear a word he says. If the immortal Charlie Chaplin had tried a stunt like this in "The Great Dictator," where the hero delivers a forceful speech against fascism, he wouldn't be remembered for his social commitment as well as his artistic brilliance. Too bad the makers of "Forrest Gump" aren't in his league, or even playing the same sport.

Other examples crop up throughout the film, as when a character becomes ill with a mysterious "virus" that's apparently meant to be AIDS, but gets identified only through vague euphemisms because to speak its name wouldn't suit the movie's tasteful tone.

At a time when many observers are rightfully concerned about screen depictions of violence, it's also hard to applaud a Vietnam episode that uses the horrors of combat mainly to showcase Forrest's personal heroics.

Why do the filmmakers go out of their way to address things like war and racism and death and AIDS when they lack the courage to face up honestly to them? Such dodging and weaving give escapism a bad name.

This said, director Robert Zemeckis deserves congratulations for drawing a tremendous performance from Hanks, who emerges as the year's first sure-fire contender for the next Oscar race.

Sally Field is warmly engaging as Forrest's mother, and Gary Sinise has effective moments as his best friend, whose battle-scarred body brings a touch of horrific realism to the film. Robin Wright is solid and unpretentious as the love of Forrest's life.

Don Burgess did the attractive camera rink, and Alan Silvestri composed the gushy score. Eric Roth wrote the screenplay, which is based on a novel by Winston Groom.

FILMS IN REVIEW, 11-12/94, p. 60, Harry Pearson, Jr.

I don't think we need tarry nor linger long over Forrest Gump. It is, at heart, a fairy tale about American Innocence, i.e., our belief that an unspoiled child lives at the center of each of us. Ordinarily, that child gets snuffed out as we age; though, it is said, it is he who sees us through the critical periods in our life and he who represents our creative energy. By extending this conceit to include a narcissistic child who never really grows up and who never has to part with this innocence, director Robert Zemeckis is able to show, by means of not subtle contrasts, America's loss of its innocence. But, in *Forrest Gump*, this does not mean the loss of values, since American values are what this picture is out to triumphantly trumpet, down to success as a jock and success in building upon that vestige of the free enterprise system, the small business.

Tom Hanks is a marvel as Forrest Gump. He did not, absolutely, deserve the Oscar for his makeup job performance in *Philadelphia* last year; but this time he does and, in all probability, will. Without Hanks, Zemeckis' carefully constructed soufflé, which sags more than a little in the middle, would fall flat as a crepe. He brings a believability, integrity and otherworldllness to this role that no other young actor of his generation could even begin to suggest—could you, e.g., imagine Christian Slater as Forrest Gump? (Director Zemeckis told members of the National Board of Review at a special screening that he would not have done the picture if he could not have had Hanks.)

Much has been written about the special effects used in the construction of this film, and some (critics) have damned the movie, wrongly, for being effects-driven (certainly true of Zemeckis' *Death Becomes Her*. The insertion of Hanks into historic newsreels, which is what most of the critics were thinking of, witty though these moments are, are clearly effects, and transparently so, but effects dominated by the wit behind them, The same is true for the famous floating feather at movie's beginning and end. Witty in that (I think) it suggests Doonesbury and is implicitly making its point about our collective attention span. (We are, the movie seems to be saying, like our fine feathered politician, turning into a nation of Gumps.) To me, the most impressive effect in the entire film is the elimination of actor Gary Sinise's lower legs. Now *that* looked real. It was, in fact, scary. And bodes ill for the future: How will we, as this technology is subtly perfected, ever know for sure anymore if anything is real?

Seeing this movie is like having your life pass before your eyes. Weren't we, like Forrest, unaware of the consequences of the assassinations of our leaders during the sixties, of the consequences of the flower power "liberation" and the Vietnam War? We, like the feather, drifted through these events without realizing their significance and/or being able to understand the impact they might have upon us and the life of the nation. Combine these flashbacks with most of the best tunes of the era and a genuinely felt sense of the time and place (save the Vietnam sequences which look like South Carolina, effects or no) in subdued color and crystalline widescreen photography and you get to feeling a kind of melancholia, a regret for all the things that you have, unwittingly, let pass you by. A regret for the roads not taken. And in Gump's and our case, not even recognized.

LOS ANGELES TIMES, 7/6/94, Calendar/p. 1, Kenneth Turan

Forrest Gump may have an IQ of 75, but don't be telling him he's slow. What does normal mean anyway?" his mama always used to say, among other things. "Stupid is as stupid does." A kind of holy fool who succeeds brilliantly in life while nominally wiser folk get all bollixed up, Forrest's story offers a bemused chance to view the most turbulent decades of recent American history through a particularly harebrained lens.

There is magic in "Forrest Gump," but almost by definition magic can't last and it doesn't here. In many ways a sweet piece of work with a gentle and eccentric sensibility, this Robert Zemeckis-directed film stumbles whenever it attempts what Forrest never did—forcing its charm in search of obvious sentimentality and grander points about society. Forrest would have been horrified, and, as usual, he would have been right.

Coming after "Being There," "Rain Man" and what seems like every film starring Johnny Depp, "Forrest Gump" is a further example of Hollywood's fascination with the mentally challenged. Given how cutthroat and dismissive an industry the movie business is, unlikely to so much as return Gump's phone calls in real life, this determination to celebrate slowness as wisdom and to confuse the ability to make nice with moral profundity is certainly food for thought.

Convincingly played by Tom Hanks, Gump comes into view at his ease on a bus bench in Savannah, Ga., in 1981, talking away to whoever's handy, oblivious as usual to the fact that some people are not in a mood to listen. His deliberate but charming Southern-accented voice-over (scripted by Eric Roth from a novel by Winston Groom) runs throughout the entire film, telling his story, and, not quite coincidentally, the story of America from the 1950s through the 1980s.

As a child in Alabama, Forrest (named after Confederate Gen. Nathan Bedford Forrest) is shepherded through life by his fierce mother (Sally Field, inevitably). Set apart from other children by his need to wear leg braces, he forms an instant attachment to a little girl named Jenny who asks him to sit next to her on the school bus. Like Androcles and that lion, a Gump doesn't forget.

Although Forrest never pushes himself forward, it is "Gump's" amiable conceit that sheer happenstance frequently puts him in a position to either witness or influence history. Even as a child, in one of the film's most engaging sequences, he ends up having a considerable impact on the career of Elvis Presley.

Forrest's knack for being around great events eventually results in multiple newsreel appearances, a situation that has given director Zemeckis, who can't seem to make a film anymore without special effects ("Back to the Future," "Who Framed Roger Rabbit," "Death Becomes Her"), a chance to once again grandly feed his habit.

Related to the newsreels in Woody Allen's "Zelig," only much more elaborate and impressive, the effects—created by Industrial Light & Magic—are showstoppers, presenting Forrest convincingly interacting with several Presidents, including John F. Kennedy and Lyndon B. Johnson. Clever and light-fingered without being overdone, these effects (as well as a later subplot involving a double amputee also done on computer) are "Gump" at its best.

From Elvis, Forrest goes on (don't ask how) to a football scholarship at the University of Alabama just when George Wallace made a last stand for segregation, and then to service in Vietnam ("a whole other country"), where he meets two men who have lasting influence on his life. One is fellow grunt Benjamin Buford (Bubba) Blue (Mykelti Williamson), who knows more than Forrest thought there was to know about shrimping, and the men's superior officer, Lt. Dan (Gary Sinise), the direct descendant of a long line of military losers.

Through all of this and more Forrest can never put sweet Jenny (Robin Wright) out of his mind, While he proceeds tortoise-like through life, she is the scattered rabbit, involving herself in every *au courant* movement from topless folk singing to radical politics and heavy drugs. While Wright makes it easy to understand why Forrest remains fixated on Jenny, she has been so transparently made into Everyperson, and the film is so willing to milk the pathos in their relationship, that not enough naturalness makes it into their connection.

And as its 2-hour and 22-minute length and the care expended in capturing the period make clear, "Gump" is also too eager to see itself as making larger and more important points about what America went through both pre- and post-Vietnam. How else to explain its awkward habit of having Gump mention, in a way that relates to nothing else in the film, whenever an assassination takes place.

Compared to this overreaching, Hanks is one of the film's strengths, the look of deadpan comic determination on his face never wavering as he works to unify the movie's diverse strands. Although Hanks never breaks through to the point where we forget that we are watching a performance, however expert, "Forrest Gump" would be in serious trouble without him.

Finally, it is as a wacky tall tale about some pretty unbelievable adventures that "Forrest Gump" works best, ironically commenting on what it takes to be a success in today's America. It's most successful when it is being off-center, a state of grace it doesn't quite have the nerve to maintain.

NEW STATESMAN & SOCIETY, 8/12/94, p. 33, Jonathan Romney

You can tell when an art form or a technology is reaching its highest point of sophistication. It starts trying to dazzle you with the last work in spectacle: simplicity itself. Robert Zemeckis' *Forrest Gump* begins with a long tracking shot of a feather, which floats in close-up across silky blue skies all the way through the opening credits. Flipping over gently as it goes, it hovers vertiginously above an old-world small-town square in the American South ... until coming gently to rest at Tom Hanks' feet. At which point the audience breathes a sigh of awed relief.

The shot would, of course, be quite impossible, if not for the miracle of digital compositing and the services of Industrial Light and Magic. Directors with enough budget to spare can now order anything they want, untrammelled by verisimilitude. You can have feathers, or dinosaurs, or both legs off one of your actors, as happens with Gary Sinise in *Forrest Gump*.

In his last feature, the luridly macabre *Death Becomes Her*, Zemeckis used digital illusion to twist Meryl Streep neatly at the waist and place a gaping hole clean through Goldie Hawn. In *Forrest Gump*, his big trick is discretion—illusions you don't really notice. There's some showy tampering with newsreel footage, so that Tom Hanks shakes hands with JFK, but that's just Woody Allen's *Zelig* routine being given a slicker spin.

The real *tours de force* are so seamless you're barely aware of their impossibility. For all we know, that really could be Tom Hanks playing table-tennis at lightning speed, and Gary Sinise really could have had both his legs amputated for the part of a Vietnam vet (after all, Robert de Niro would have done).

Every new advance in cinematic illusionism raises anew the old ethical and aesthetic questions about fooling the viewer; but so many barriers have now come down that it is almost as if the problem had never arisen before. Zemeckis has forecast a brave new aesthetic in which digitals can enhance the telling of a realistic story, rather than distract from it. And for the most part, it's easy to watch *Gump* without suspecting that anything is amiss. In terms of realism alone, there's no reason why that tracking shot could not be of a real feather, except that no one would ever have the patience required to shoot it.

But what's being proposed is a very particular type of illusionism. When Georges Méliès started chopping heads off his performers at the turn of the century, his cinema worked from the conventions of stage illusion. It didn't try to convince the public they were watching real mutilations but simply proposed a new magic, with the audience dared to guess how it was done.

And the public fascination with film technique that grew up over the next decades arose out of viewers' desire at once to be deceived and to see through the deception. Hence the privileged status given by cinephiles to artificial matte shots, which revel in the artfulness of the effect even as they bring it off. "If David Lean were making movies today," Zemeckis has claimed, "he'd say, 'Where has this been all my life?'" But anyone who has seen the extraordinary painted sky at the start of *Great Expectations* knows he probably wouldn't.

After *Jurassic Park*, you can't help gasping at the possibilities that digital cinema offers. What better way, for example, to boot new life into the moribund horror genre? With digital demons, the abyss is the limit—although I suspect that horror buffs, with their weird fetish for the messily tactile, could never bear to say goodbye to all that gooey latex. The depressing thing about *Forrest Gump* is that, ultimately, it proposes to strip the mirage of its magic and place it predominantly at the service of the real.

That's precisely what happens in James Cameron's new Schwarzenegger vehicle, the neo-Bond barnstormer *True Lies*, Cameron, who runs his own IBM-backed concern, Digital Domain, is one of the front-runners with this stuff. Although his *Terminator 2* was one of the most bombastic movies ever made, it was bombast with finesse. The immaterial alchemy of the effects cut through the film's too, too solid structure. In the flesh corner, Big Arnie and Linda Hamilton flexed those pecs like there was no tomorrow (indeed, the plot was that there *was* no tomorrow); in the light corner, the shape-shifting mercury man T2. No contest.

True Lies, though, is about muscle and blood and steel reasserting their sway over mere pixels, and the effects are used purely to give an enhanced sense of a lumbering, mechanical reality. Motorbikes leap from skyscraper to skyscraper, characters hang suspended from jump jets, and it is entirely without affect. We can't see how the tricks are being done, but we know they're being done. Behind the crunch of every girder, we're aware of the cool, distant crunching of numbers at some studio console. The harder Arnie and Jamie Lee Curtis struggle to remind us that they are real physical organisms, and not the computer-generated androids they appear to be, the more joyless the film becomes.

You may detect a Luddite sniffiness about this argument. Not so—it's just that I'd prefer to see the new technology placed in the service of delirium rather than the monomaniacal efficiency that Cameron achieves in *True Lies*. For that reason, I'd like to be able to recommend *The Mask*, which looks as though its digital crew consisted of glue-crazed nerds rather than white-coated algebrists.

Alas, it's a fairly witless film (although it has more to offer kids than the stolid *Flintstones*) and its star, the ingratiating grimmer Jim Carrey, is a royal pain. But there's a whiff of genuine irresponsibility in the visuals that hints at the pleasures we may soon expect. Every time Carrey dons his magic mask, he's transformed into a lime-faced loon, a half-animated, half-human version of the mercurial genie in Disney's *Aladdin*.

This protean prankster's repertoire is cribbed from Tex Avery cartoons, but at least the film countenances no respect whatsoever for verisimilitude. This isn't the painstaking, academicism Zemeckis strives for, nor Cameron's industrial functionality—this is closer to spray-can graffiti. When you can turn a Jack Russell terrier into a fanged, eye-popping, avocado-tinged hell-hound, a feather somehow doesn't seem like such a big deal.

NEW STATESMAN & SOCIETY, 10/14/94, p. 41, Jonathan Romney

Forrest Gump is the film you'll go and see if you can't get into *The Lion King*, and vice versa. The two extraordinary Hollywood phenomena of the year are a perfect match. Both are deeply reassuring and deeply anthropomorphic; the Disney film takes a conservative myth of universal order and natural monarchy and rolls it up into a cute furry cub; *Forrest Gump* conflates some 30 years of recent US history into the figure of a doe-eyed man-cub, played by America's favourite puppy-face, Tom Hanks.

Since its US release a few months ago, *Forrest Gump* has become one of the most discussed films of recent years, its box-office success fuelling, and in turn fuelled by, a thousand think pieces. Gump is tailor-made to spawn a theory for each observer—about its endorsement of the "holy fool" myth, its take on disability, its historical revisionism, its supposed liberalism or conservatism, the implications of its uncanny digital illusionism ...If Robert Zemeckis' film holds together as anything other than a package of concepts, it's only through the figure of Gump, the consistently hopeful survivor and the repository for our emotions and theories (if we warm to him at all, the logical next step is to wonder what he means). But the narrative seems random and inconsistent—a stream of picaresque siphoned off from a larger and conceivably more coherent original (a novel by Winston Groom).

Born in 1950s Alabama, with an IQ of 75 and a fiercely protective mother (liberal Hollywood's universal momma, Sally Field), Forrest passes through Vietnam and the tenures and terminations of several presidents, unscathed, hopeful and ultimately revered as a simpleton sage. The film begins and ends with an extraordinary, lyrical shot of a feather floating on the breeze. Forrest, we twig instantly, will be as free as that feather, as he bobs on the breezes of history. He'll also, however, be as lavishly artificial and airily bogus a construction, this being a very costly computer-generated feather.

It's not immediately obvious what the moral of the story is, other than, "What a long strange trip it's been." *Forrest Gump* invokes a shared experience of modern US history, but signposts its events painstakingly, so that everyone knows where they are. It's made to appeal to just about every age group (sorry, demographic): the very young, who'll get the rudiments of a *Look and Learn* history lesson; the class-of-1967 Deadheads, forever congratulating themselves on making it this far; and older conservatives who'll look on its gently piqued view of the 1960s and 1970s with a muttered "told you so" through pursed lips.

Forrest Gump himself is not so much a character as an intersection of best-loved *idiot savant* myths. He's Pinocchio without the mischief; he's Candide, and accordingly ends up cultivating his garden—but where Candide took a few blows before reaching his pragmatic conclusion, Gump has a relatively easy time and drifts through life protected by a quiverful of Mom-given mottoes: "Stupid is as stupid does", "Life's like a box of chocolates". These are already collected in a best-selling book of *Gumpisms*, which only serves to illustrate the film's droll point about the adulation Forrest receives when, aimlessly running to and fro across America, he's acclaimed as a sort of mobile Simon Stylites, an oracle spouting bumper-sticker wisdom. In this, Gump is comparable to Chance the gardener, played by Peter Sellers in *Being There*—a figure whose utter vacancy is taken as gnomic omniscience. But unlike Chance with his scary, leaden blankness, Gump is imbued with absolute infantile goodness, a global caritas which has its visual sign in the crisp gingham shirts he wears throughout. You could eat your apple pie off them.

Uncomprehending faith sees Gump through life, while those unlucky enough to grow up must take their trashings. Little Jenny is fated to be the very incarnation of beaten, debased modern America, a fallen Liberty Belle who has to have her virginity redeemed in the end. Gump's lieutenant in Vietnam (Gary Sinise) has both legs blown off and must seek his redemption on disarmingly realistic digitally airbrushed stumps. This is the film's hardest, or easiest conceit to buy, depending on how much you crave cosy reassurance: the idea that a simple soul can go through life unhurt, except by aw-shucks melancholy. In this sense, Gump is a complete departure from the tradition of the "simpleton" *Bildungsroman* from Voltaire to Vonnegut. Gump swallows what little grief an essentially benevolent world throws at him, and thrives on it. His passivity makes him a millionaire, and finally the perfect father. He doesn't have to lift a finger, only his table-tennis racket, and even then he's a natural. You could come out of Gump sincerely believing the meek inherit the earth.

But Gump's sexless purity depends on Jenny's agonised promiscuity to give it resonance. An allegorical cipher for the mad, bad times, she drifts through protest folk, sex and drugs, finally yielding to an unnameable virus at the start of the 1980s. She's an excruciating sacrificial virgin, but she's psychologised too. Her waywardness is attributed to paternal abuse as a child. This is partly the film lazily hitting whatever button of *Oprah* psychology it thinks will work on the audience; but it is also attributing America's own waywardness to the influence of bad fathers—to the presidents whose image Gump lightly mocks (he's airbrushed into LBJ and JFK footage, and unwittingly shops Nixon over Watergate). All that America needs, the film seems to argue, is a good father—which Gump symbolically becomes.

At heart, *Forrest Gump* is nothing if not an open letter to Oliver Stone. For all their Ringling Brothers bluster, films like *Platoon* and *JFK* presented a powerful vision of modern America as a collage of hacked-together footage, incoherence, rupture, cacophony. Zemeckis' hyper-sleek film papers over the cracks, takes the sting out of the harsh redemption therapy of Stone's Viet-vet drama *Born on the Fourth of July*, it smooths out chaos into a string of gently satiric gags. All Stone's films about chronically disabused patriots here find their corrective. Have faith and laugh it off, Gump argues. It wants to persuade us that America may never be innocent again, but at least it can be calmer, wiser, nicer. After Stone's strobe-light lectures, Zemeckis soothes America's brow with those gently curving long takes of a feather drifting in clear blue skies. From the opening shot, *Forrest Gump* is neither man nor boy nor saint, just Jonathan Livingstone Seagull without the beak.

NEW YORK, 7/18/94, p. 50, David Denby

Can a movie triumph over bad ideas? *Forrest Gump*, starring Tom Hanks, celebrates—and I mean celebrates—a heroic fool, a retarded young man with tremendous innate decency, unthinking courage, and "true" intelligence. Forrest is the only sane man in the country, the one refined and self-contained person in the American circus. Understanding nothing, he flies through the worst events of the sixties, seventies, and eighties untouched by experience, his heart and soul intact; and in the end, he is superior to everyone. We could be as good as he, the movie suggests, if only we had the courage to be simple.

In brief, *Forrest Gump* is another idiot-savant picture, in the commercially lucrative line of *King of Hearts*, *Being There*, and *Rain Man*; and like those movies, it's marred by sentiment and cant and much flattery of the audience. (A smart film hero, of course, would risk offending the many Americans who now get angry if there's even a hint that they've been out-classed.) If it's better than any of those movies—and at times it's a jaunty, high-flying cinematic experience—that's because the director, Robert Zemeckis, has the shrewdness and skill to turn what's most dubious about his ideas into poetic comedy. Zemeckis has made a fast movie about a slow hero; he transforms Forrest's daffy misperceptions into lyrical flights. *Forrest Gump* has a softer, more delicate touch and a richer current of feeling than any of the other holy-innocent movies.

And a better star. In the past few years, Tom Hanks has become the central American movie actor, and here he sits on a city bench, narrating expansively, telling Forrest's life story to anyone who will listen. Hanks's curly hair is cropped around the sides, causing his face to appear longer and narrower than usual; he keeps his lower lip tight, his brow furrowed, his body tensed, like a cat with nowhere to spring. He looks dumb but far from insensible, and he holds the character firmly in place, an eccentric but unforced comic creation. Forrest, puzzled by the world but determined to meet it without flinching, feels every personal slight or welcome; Hanks makes him limited in consciousness but unlimited in feeling, and the audience is with him every inch of the way. This kind of transformation—stupidity gentled into soulfulness—is one of the things commercial entertainment is all about. The southern-gothic male lout, the man of foreshortened brain developed by writers like William Faulkner and Flannery O'Connor, has now been domesticated (via the novel *Forrest Gump*, by Winston Groom) into the character of a sweet-tempered Everyman.

Hanks speaks to us directly. I sighed when I first heard the voice—slow and Deep South mulish—because he sounds like a literal-minded child. Two hours of that voice, I thought, would be intolerable. But I was wrong; the voice grows in authority, and visual material echoes it, or plays against it; the voice holds the movie together. *Forrest Gump*, it turns out, is a picaresque comic epic. As a boy, Forrest the natural child receives training in gumption (get the title now?), mainly from his mom, played by Sally Field, who is correctly cast (for once) as a rigid southern lady; and Forrest has the luck to find an angel, a little blonde girl, Jenny, who has been abused by her father and who understands, out of her own experience, how awful Forrest feels. The angel, who grows into Robin Wright, a severe beauty with elegant bones and a long waist, will burn her wings and fall but always return to Forrest, who makes her feel safe.

All in all, Forrest has a lucky childhood. Local bullies jeer at him, but he runs away from them, his legs churning, and as crowds go mad, he keeps on running, racing down high-school and college football fields. Forrest, who becomes a famous athlete, could be the Road Runner in Chuck Jones's great cartoons, with a touch of Buster Keaton added—his face is always fixed, no matter how fast he's moving, in an expression of baffled consternation. Forrest's imperceptiveness protects him; he will run through chaos and never notice it.

In Vietnam, which he enjoys as a nice time in the country (too much rain, though), he becomes friends with another man as limited as himself—Bubba (Mykelti Williamson), a black shrimper from Louisiana who talks of nothing but shrimp. The two solipsists make a communion, and Zemeckis turns the sequence into volatile absurdism, with Forrest's incomprehension and Bubba's weird shrimp obsession playing off the violence of the war like butterflies flitting at the mouth of hell. Even when Forrest's unit is under attack and men are being shot all arund, and Forrest, without thinking, runs into the jungle and pulls wounded men out of trouble, the war scenes remain buoyant, even slightly giddy. War may be a bad dream for Forrest, but it's still a dream.

Zemeckis gives the material a lift by heightening it past realism but not *too far* past realism. Zemeckis has a good touch now. He's dropped the noisy low farce, the ridiculous clowning of the *Back to the Future* series and the disastrous *Death Becomes Her*. Much of this movie has a lulling dreaminess to it a near-poetry of innocence pierced by sadness—a commercialized American version of magical realism. Zemeckis projects Forrest into the celebrity-media culture, where he exists happily amid disaster. He meets presidents who are shot or forced out of office, and Jenny, his inamorata, turns into a victim of the sixties, a flower child who takes up drugs and abusive men. As he narrates, always missing the point, we see her in one depression after another. She's feeding on the *Zeitgeist* but gets nothing; he's out of it but gets everything—he's the true flower child. Zemeckis keeps the conceits fast and light, playing tricks with documentary footage so that Forrest is inserted into scenes with Kennedy and Johnson and Nixon, a Zelig who keeps his own soul.

We're not meant to "believe" any of this; we know we're being taken for a ride. The film techniques are so smart and funny that many in the audience will forget the sanctimonious and reactionary element in the movie. Forrest Gump is packaging innocence as a higher state of being. Forrest may be slow, but the smart, ambitious, trendy people are meant to be the real fools—presidents, anti-war protesters, military heroes, Black Panthers. Anyone who's angry or passionate about anything is a jerk. The men are aggressive and predatory, while Forrest treats his Jenny as if he were a knight holding a flower. (You might get the impression from this movie that a man has to be retarded in order to respect a woman.) Of course, Zemeckis and screenwriter Eric Roth have made it awfully easy for us to like Forrest. He's not aggressive or sexual; he's not even *large*. Jenny, overwhelmed by his goodness, finally goes to bed with him, and when he has a son, his voyage is complete; he becomes a man.

Zemeckis can't stop mythicizing his hero, and he goes too far. There's a long sequence of Forrest running and running across the American landscape, followed, at a respectful distance, by people who also run, though never knowing why—the sequence has the dreadful Pied Piper religious whimsy of the hippie era that the rest of the movie is putting down. The filmmakers turn Forrest into a saint, an unconscious inventor, a child of destiny. They've tried to create a new myth for the media age—Chaplin's Tramp but without the mischievous, anarchic streak. In the end, Forrest's withdrawal doesn't mean much of anything. His kind of innocence can't be imitated. You have to be lucky enough to be born dumb to attain it. Yet people may grab on to him as a symbol and icon—as a release from knowingness, from sophistication, from the alarmingly crowded information highway. Clueless, he becomes a happy man.

NEW YORK POST, 7/6/94, p. 33, Michael Medved

"Life is like a box of chocolates," Mama Gump (Sally Field) tells her only child, Forrest (Tom Hanks). "You never know what you're gonna get."

That quality of unexpected delight is one of the chief strengths of this extraordinary motion picture, where all the flavors in director Bob Zemeckis' colorful party assortment seem delicious and satisfying.

Based on a rollicking, bittersweet novel by Winston Groom, "Forrest Gump" manages to combine some of the more appealing elements of "Fried Green Tomatoes," "Zelig" and "Being There" into a unique concoction that's difficult to describe but impossible to resist.

The heart of the movie's appeal is its unforgettable hero, a slow-witted, pure-hearted country boy from Greenbow, Ala., whose unshakable innocence gives him a unique perspective on America's loss of innocence during the 1960s and '70s.

Sitting on a bus bench in Savannah one fine spring day, Forrest talks non-stop to various passersby and narrates his own far-fetched, frisky and funny adventures. His anecdotes tell how this sincere and solemn kid with an IQ of just 75 became a football All-American for the University of Alabama, a Medal of Honor winner in Vietnam, an international ping-pong star, millionaire shrimp boat captain, and a popular guru of long-distance running and new age philosophy,

The one connecting thread in his various endeavors is his loyal, touching love for the troubled but free-spirited Jenny (Robin Wright), the only child in school back home who never made fun of him, and who's followed her own tortured path through the rough edges of the counterculture.

Robin Wright has been poised at the verge of stardom for several years now, but this perfectly nuanced tour-de-force performance should once and for all win her a place near the top of anyone's list of today's most enchanting and accomplished actresses.

Similarly impressive is Gary Sinise (who attracted well-deserved attention in "Of Mice and Men") playing Forrest's passionate, gung-ho commanding officer in Vietnam, and subsequent friend and partner.

For director Bob Zemeckis, "Forrest Gump" represents as much of a departure as "Schindler's List" did for his friend and colleague Steven Spielberg.

Until now, Zemickis has been associated with movies like the "Back to the Future" series, "Who Framed Roger Rabbit" and the lamentable "Death Becomes Her," that all used technical razzle-dazzle in the service of cartoonish content.

Here, he deploys the same sort of special effects wizardry for more notable purposes: offering astonishingly lifelike newsreel footage of his hero interacting with real-life images of Richard Nixon, John Kennedy, Lyndon Johnson, John Lennon, George Wallace and others,

There's also a breathtakingly beautiful title sequence in which the camera follows a feather drifting aimlessly for several minutes over scenic Savannah, before it finally settles decisively right at Forrest's feet.

This magical moment dramatizes the principal question which Forrest asks himself (and the rest of us): "I don't know if we each have a destiny, or we're all just floating around accidental like, on a breeze."

Hanks' performance, a triumph of dignity, decency, and warm-hearted humor, infuses such lines with an urgent intensity. Even more than his Oscar-wining achievement in "Philadelphia," this is a role that will be remembered as long as people care about great acting, as he creates a complete and utterly compelling human being who we come to know more intimately for a few hours than our own friends and family.

"I'm not a smart man," Forrest says, "but I know what love is."

You'll know what love is too, when you go to the theater to meet Forrest Gump.

NEWSDAY, 7/6/94, Part II/p. B2, Jack Mathews

In the timeless debate over whether human beings are basically good or evil, the evidence from wars, genocide, racism, intolerance and the evening news presents what appears to be an airtight case for evil. But those anxious to argue the other side, that we are born innocent and only learn how to behave badly, might call as their first witness the title character of Robert Zemeckis' magical, romantic, funny, fabulous "Forrest Gump."

Forrest (Tom Hanks), a man with a low IQ and high ideals, is as pure an innocent as the white feather that floats lazily across the screen during the opening credits, leading us to the bus bench in Savannah, Ga., where he is about to regale a series of dubious strangers with details of a life as random and fanciful as that feather's flight.

It's the story of a simple-minded southerner who, equipped with an inherent optimism and his mother's survival kit of philosophical maxims, becomes a college All-America football star, Vietnam War hero, international Ping-Pong champion, seafood mogul and—to those who literally begin to follow him—a potential messiah.

Along the way, he has eventful meetings with Presidents Kennedy, Johnson and Nixon, gives a still-undiscovered Elvis Presley some choreographic inspiration, joins black students marching past Gov. George Wallace into the University of Alabama, and, without ever understanding any of it, becomes the catalyst in some of the landmark cultural and political events of his time.

"Life is like a box of chocolates," Forrest quotes his mother, in explaining the curious twists and turns in his life. "You never know what you're going to get."

What Forrest wants most from his box of chocolates is Jenny (Robin Wright), the childhood friend who follows a much darker trail through the tumultuous '60s and '70s. The daughter of an abusive, alcoholic father, she grows up searching for love and compassion, and instead enters a downward spiral of bad relationships and drug abuse, from which only Forrest's dogged loyalty might rescue her.

"Forrest Gump" is a career milestone for Zemeckis, whose sense of whimsy and patience for elaborate visual effects have produced such blockbuster popcorn features as "Romancing the Stone," "Who Framed Roger Rabbit" and the "Back to the Future" trilogy. The images in "Forrest Gump," which place Hanks in the middle of archival newsreels and TV shows, and playing Ping-Pong with the proficiency of a piston engine, are as fantastic as any he has attempted before. But on this occasion, he also has something to say.

Adapted from the Winston Groom novel by Eric Roth, a writer whose past credits ("Mr. Jones," "Suspect") didn't predict anything as fine as this, "Forrest Gump" manages to examine some of the basic questions of human life and to add perspective to the two most disruptive decades in modern history.

Zemeckis uses Forrest as a counterpoint to the anger and confusion of America's social revolution, a sort of benign moral compass in the midst of the storm. Forrest hasn't the ability to form political opinions, nor even to comprehend the issues dividing the nation. He just takes life as it comes, from the Civil Rights Movement and political assassinations of the '60s to Vietnam, Watergate and the onset of the still-unnamed plague of AIDS, some of which leaves him puzzled and saddened, but never frustrated or discouraged.

In ways, Forrest reminds us of Peter Sellers' Chance the gardener in "Being There," a retarded man whose simple observations about the seasonal changes in his garden were taken as wise political metaphors. But Forrest isn't mistaken for a genius; he actually possesses a quality that people intuitively recognize envy. He is incorruptible.

"Being There," "Rain Man" and "Zelig" are the movies to which "Forrest Gump" will be most often compared but the movie closest to it in tone is "Field of Dreams." Fantastic in the extreme, both films cut to a deeper reality, one of the spirit, and if you surrender to them, you walk out of the theater on a little cushion of air.

There are wonderful performances throughout the film, particularly from Field as Forrest's concerned, headstrong mother, Gary Sinese as the bitter Vietnam veteran and amputee who becomes his friend and business partner, and Mykelti Williamson, as Bubba his equally unsophisticated war buddy: But it is Hanks, with faint echoes from his performance as a child-man in "Big," who gives the movie its soul and buoyancy.

Narrating and speaking in a halting southern accent, as if his words were being called up from some sluggish computer bank, Hanks draws us into his limited world and disarms us with his deadpan innocence. His stories are fantastic from the beginning—from the miraculous moment when the young Forrest (Michael Conner Humphreys) has his leg braces disintegrate while fleeing rock-throwing bullies and is suddenly freed to run "like the wind."

The discovery of his speed is the first in a series of events that, while seemingly random, also make the case for destiny and fate. Everything that happens to Forrest, and to the society around him, shapes his life in some way, just as he affects the people and world around him. When it comes to understanding and accepting the wisdom of that philosophical brain-twister, Forrest Gump may be better equipped than any of us.

NEWSWEEK, 7/11/94, p. 50, David Ansen

In the course of "Forrest Gump" you will discover how it came about that the title character, a sweet-natured simpleton from rural Alabama with a two-digit IQ, taught Elvis how to move. That's just for starters. Forrest (Tom Hanks) is an idiot for all seasons, and his life story encompasses—and sometimes brings about—most of the major events of four stormy decades of American Life. You'll see how this boy with braces on his legs became a Crimson Tide football star and a Vietnam War hero. How he met JFK, LBJ and inadvertently caused the downfall of Richard Nixon. How he came to be playing Ping-Pong in China, met the Black Panthers and ended up on the cover of Fortune. You'll see him chatting with John Lennon on "The Dick Cavett Show." Forrest was even the guy who inspired the bumper sticker S--T HAPPENS.

As Hollywood summer movies go, this picaresque fable is definitely not the same old same old. Adapted from Winston Groom's comic novel by Eric Roth, directed with great flair and technical brilliance by Robert Zemeckis, "Forrest Gump" is inventive, sometimes hilarious, and it pushes so many nostalgia buttons you can't help but stay engrossed even when the tale starts to ramble. Yet the whole seems less than the sum of its parts.

Forrest himself is like a combination of Candide, Rain Man, Zelig, Chauncey Gardiner and the guy from "Regarding Henry." Hanks, who can do no wrong as an actor, turns this fantastical conceit into funny, touching flesh and blood; even his elbows are eloquent. As the troubled, beautiful Jenny, the abused hometown girl he loves with doggish devotion throughout his life, Robin Wright gives a sketchy role grace and gravity. And in a season top-heavy with special effects, "Forrest Gump's" are truly remarkable. Everyone will be astonished by the "Zelig"-like insertions, which place the hero inside archival footage, shaking hands with Kennedy, popping up next to George Wallace, talking with Tricky Dick. No less impressive are the effects you may not recognize : using digital computer technology to create vast crowds at a Washington anti-war rally, or to amputate the legs of Gary Sinise's embittered Lieutenant Dan, the officer Forrest saves in battle and later teams up with in the shrimping business. Zemeckis, Ken Ralston and Industrial Light & Magic did state-of-the-art effects together in "Who Framed Roger Rabbit" and "Death Becomes Her," and their work here is groundbreaking. And a little scary—we've entered an era where photographic reality can't be trusted.

But what does "Forrest Gump" add up to? For all its ambition, the movie ends up using great historical events in the service of a dubious sentimentality. As satire , it's surprisingly toothless, especially coming from the man who directed the gleefully savage "Used Cars" (1980). As a tear-jerker, which unfortunately is what it ultimately becomes, it left me unmoved. Roth's screenplay significantly departs from the Groom novel in its maudlin resolution of the love story, and the more it focuses on the lovers the less psychologically credible it becomes. The movie wants to use Forrest Gump every which way—as dunce, as idiot savant, as the one pure soul in an impure world, as faithful lover. It's a tribute to Hanks and Zemeckis that this all-purpose symbol is as fetching as he is. The world according to Gump is certainly an enjoyable place to visit. But its core is disappointingly soft and elusive.

SIGHT AND SOUND, 10/94, p. 41, Leslie Felperin Sharman

At a buss stop in the American South, Forrest Gump tells his story to passers-by ... As a child in Greenbow, Alabama in the 1940s, Forrest has to wear braces on his legs and has a 'sub-normal' I.Q. score, but his widowed mother strives to make him feel no different from anyone else. His only friend is Jenny, a girl in his class whose father is sexually and violently abusive. Throughout their lives, Forrest and Jenny meet and part, as each pursues very different destinies. While being chased by bullies, Forrest discovers an uncanny ability to run fast. He is picked for his high school football team, and goes on to play for both his college and the All-American team, through which he meets President Kennedy.

Next, he joins the Army and is sent to Vietnam, where he meets Bubba, another Alabaman who dreams of becoming a shrimp boat captain. Their patrol unit leader is Lieutenant Dan Taylor, who comes from a long line of war heroes felled in combat. When the unit is attacked, Forrest single-handedly saves everyone, though Bubba dies in his arms and Lt. Dan loses both his legs. Recovering in hospital, Forrest discovers a talent for ping-pong. Back in the States, Forrest is decorated by President Johnson, and accidentally comes to speak at a peace rally where he meets up with Jenny, now a hippie. Later, Forrest runs into a deeply embittered Lt. Dan. After a celebrity career as a ping-pong player and a meeting with President Nixon, Forrest buys a shrimp boat in honour of Bubba, and with the help of Lt. Dan and a fortuitous storm, becomes a millionaire. However, he continues to pine for Jenny, who has been led astray in California by the hedonistic lifestyle of the 70s and is in a state of profound despair.

After Forrest's mother dies, he retires to Greenbow where one day Jenny shows up. They live together for a while, and have sex, but then Jenny runs off again. Forrest begins running incessantly around the country, picking up a cult of followers, then suddenly stops. Back in Greenbow, he receives a letter from Jenny, and goes to meet her, and finds that they have a son, Forrest Junior. The three of them all return to Greenbow and live happily until Jenny dies of an unspecified 'virus'. Forrest goes on to raise his son alone.

Southern-accented, intellectually-challenged and fixated on his wild-spirited quasi-sister, Forrest Gump is a distant, in-bred cousin to Benjy in Faulkner's *The Sound and the Fury*. Robert Zemeckis's film ambitiously spans 40 years of American history, but defeated by its own glibness, ends up signifying less about the times it describes than the back of a chewing gum wrapper.

The problem is that Forrest Gump wants to perform two opposing projects simultaneously. On the one hand, it strains at being a picaresque satire in the tradition of *Candide*, depicting the triumph of innocence in a corrupt world. Unfortunately, the necessity of irony for this project is fatal to its other goal, which is to tell a standard sentimental love story. Truly effective satire requires a more neutral narrator than offered here, like the holy idiot Chance in Hal Ashby's *Being There*, or the chameleon *Zelig*, so that he can be at least a little complicit with the forces of evil. With such a nauseatingly likeable protagonist, *Forrest Gump* can only bark at the darkness of its times (racism, war, etc.) without venturing to bite. Thus, despite its constant invocation of history, represented by clever retouching of archive footage, world events are never more than a flickering spectacle behind the unvarying constant that is Forrest.

In fact, having Tom Hanks, the personification of cuddliness, as its star, the closest *Forrest Gump* can come to satire is showing that Forrest's stupidity makes him the perfect soldier. In a rather misogynistic displacement, the character of Jenny becomes the vessel which carries all the 'nasty' habits of her generation, like drug abuse and promiscuity, so that Forrest can seem all the more unbesmirched in comparison. It is typical of the film's back-handedness that it should kill her off with a mysterious virus that seems linked to her sordid past— thus maintaining topicality—but cop out of naming it as Aids, which would have cast too dark a shadow on the love story. This retributive treatment of the victim is oddly at variance with the banal morality of randomness espoused throughout, encapsulated in Forrest's mottoes, such as, "Life is like a box of chocolates— you never know what you're going to get."

Like his former mentor, and now rival in the blockbuster field, Steven Spielberg, director Robert Zemeckis is clearly in the process of redefining his image. After such features as *Who Framed Roger Rabbit* and the *Back to the Future* trilogy, big at the box office but short on major Academy awards outside the technical categories, Zemeckis has been attempting to up his quality credibility. *Death Becomes Her* was a poor start, but *Forrest Gump* is just the sort of mushy, faintly liberal stuff the Academy likes. Yet despite its weaknesses, the film still demonstrates Zemeckis' finer strengths as a director. He has a sure touch for light comedy, and an especially strong sense of rhythm, beautifully interpreted by editor Arthur Schmidt.

With so much story to explicate and an intentionally chaotic perspective on world events, Zemeckis and Schmidt craft a strong sense of narrative coherence out of repetitive framings and neatly handled temporal shifts. Even more impressive is the use of special effects, for which Zemeckis has always been noted. In collaboration with Industrial Light and Magic, Zemeckis innovatively uses effects here to enhance the film's realism rather than to create the unbelievable. In addition to crowd scenes and the aforementioned archive treatments, computers seem to have been used to 'erase' Gary Sinise's calves in order to make a more convincing double amputee and make Tom Hanks look like a brilliant ping pong player. Sadly, ILM have not yet perfected the computer programme that can write better scripts.

Like its hero, Forrest Gump as a film runs around quickly, covers a lot of ground, but seems to have no particular destination. It's too specific to be a proper allegory, and too vague to provide a satisfactorily millennial perspective on the last 50 years. Neither is it caustic enough to make one cry, nor soppy enough to make one laugh. In the end, it is a feel-good movie for which it is hard to feel anything at all.

TIME, 7/11/94, p. 58, Richard Corliss

Forrest Gump is nobody special, but he meets special people. In his 30-year odyssey through recent American history, this crippled Alabama lad with a 75 IQ bumps into Elvis and John Lennon, J.F.K. and L.B.J., Nixon and Mao. Forrest is an innocent on loan to a cynical world, and in the movie bearing his name he would make little sense if he were played by anyone but Tom Hanks.

Hanks, 38 this week, is the actor who takes dangerous themes or re-cycled plots and, with his craft and decency, makes them esteemed hits. The rare flops (*Punchline, The Bonfire of the Vanities*) don't stick to him, and his past three films (*A League of Their Own, Sleepless in Seattle, Philadelphia*) have earned $310 million at the domestic box office. Now Hollywood routinely assigns its Missions Impossible to Captain Nice.

Nice is not a quality often associated with movie actors. Today's typical film star—Arnold, Jack or post-modern Keanu—radiates danger; he's a wild guy to take a wild ride with. The nice guy is on TV: he's the genial, comfortable friend you want to invite into your home each week. They are two distinct breeds, the domesticated husband of TV and the movies' demon lover. One does the dishes, the other smashes them.

Hanks is a TV type who made a big splash in movies (first in *Splash*, then in *Big*). He is a throwback to old Hollywood, when everybody went to the movies, when movies were the world's TV, when the norm was more ... normal. Back then, quiet types like Henry Fonda and Gary Cooper played the extraordinary ordinary man. That's Hanks. Offscreen, apparently, he leads a calm, happy life. Onscreen, he is less likely to explode than to simmer and smile. With his suburban niceness and elusive, rubberized features—any photo of him is bound to look smudged—he is a '40s fella for the '90s.

Nearly any Hanks character is an intelligent guy who wants to make sense out of the chaos of his life, trying to sustain his dignity when everything has gone horribly weird. He's your best self having your worst day. You are, for example, a man who must dress in drag (in Hanks' 1981 TV series *Bosom Buddies*). You're a 12-year-old kid who literally grows up overnight (*Big*). You're a detective whose top informant is a slobbery dog (*Turner & Hooch*). You're the manager of a baseball team, and your players are all girls (*A League of Their Own*). Or your girlfriend is a fish (*Splash*). Your wife has died (*Sleepless in Seattle*). You think you're dying (*Joe Versus the Volcano*). You are dying (*Philadelphia*). Whether the dilemma is fantastic or tragic, Hanks gives it an apt, gentle heft.

Like the best movie actors, Hanks is a superb reactor. His theater-trained voice often breaks into gentlemanly whining. His fretful brow expresses perplexity—a thoughtful "Huh?" And then, in the subtlest shift, comic exasperation plummets into agony. Hanks justified his *Philadelphia* Oscar in one early scene outside Denzel Washington's law office: With no more than a long, longing look, he registers the despair of a dying man who feels utterly bereft, unheard, dismissed. This lovely little revelation was an antecedent in *Big*, when the over-grown kid sits alone in a creepy hotel room and ponders his dreadful solitude. He's wonderful at portraying someone who's just been sucker-punched by fate.

Hanks is a kid again in director Robert Zemeckis' *Forrest Gump*. Slow-witted and likable, Forrest races through the rubble of the '50s, '60s and '70s. Thanks to novelist Winston Groom's cunning plot (Eric Roth wrote the script) and some nifty visual effects, Forrest pops up in many a historic venue: with George Wallace at the schoolhouse door, in the seared rice fields of Vietnam, along the Great Wall of China, at the Watergate Hotel during a third-rate burglary. As his mother and his pals die around him, he pursues his life's love; the movie might be called *Four Funerals and a Wedding*.

Like the new *Wyatt Earp*, this episodic ersatz epic feels more like a mini-series than a movie. It's a long drink of water at the fountain of pop-social memory. It wants to find an optimism in survival: if we somehow got through the past 35 years, we must be O.K. So Forrest comes across as a sweeter Zelig, a candied Candide, as the film strains to find America's inner child. But Hanks holds it together because he is working to discover Forrest's inner adult—the mature man under his infantile guilelessness. This effort pays off magnificently in Forrest's climactic declaration of love. Hanks' tone is both operatic and judicious; he makes passionate sentiment seem the highest form of common sense.

Other stars attract audiences by saving the world or stopping a runaway bus. A Hanks movie deals with more mundane imperatives: doing your job, staying alive, getting the girl. Simple things seem unattainable; when attained, they feel sublime.

In *Splash*, Hanks sits at a bar and pours out his lace-valentine heart: "I wanna meet a woman and I wanna fall in love and I wanna get married and I wanna have a kid and I wanna go see him play a tooth in the school play. It's not much." But to ordinary, unique people—the folks Hanks appeals to, and the folks he so smartly plays—it's everything.

VILLAGE VOICE, 7/12/94, p. 41, J. Hoberman

A boy from a small town in the deep South, born soon after World War II, is raised by a single mother. He learns to identify with Elvis, he witnesses the desegregation of the state's schools, he is chosen to go to Washington and shake hands with President Kennedy, he ambiguously speaks out against the Vietnam War, and he eventually attracts a mass movement because he gives people "hope." These days, he's tele- ubiquitous. America, please say hello to ... Forrest Gump!

Forrest Gump freely adapts (and improves upon) Winston Groom's 1986 novel, an autobiographical monologue delivered by an American Candide with an IQ of 70. As directed by Robert Zemeckis, *Forrest Gump* is a would-be generational saga-ranging from sweet home Alabama to Vietnam and back—as well as an ambitious F/X comedy and a veritable unicycle for Tom Hanks, who plays the backward backwoods lad with a bad haircut, a glazed look, and a delivery that ponderously enunciates every swallowed syllable.

There's an undeniable kick to the idea of recapitulating the Boomerography as a tale told by an idiot—and Zemeckis invokes the inanity of the boob tube by mixing Forrest up with a host of real media phantoms—but the thrill inexorably fades. H. L. Mencken himself might not have dreamt up a more moronic representation of We-the-People than Forrest as he plants himself on a park bench to regale whoever sits down with the story of his life. Still, Zemeckis and screenwriter Eric Roth lack the requisite misanthropy to make Forrest more than a figure of c&w bathos, just another good ol' boy out looking for love.

Albeit named for the founder of the KKK, Gump grows up a deprived victim. He's slow, he's fatherless, he has braces on his legs. His town could have been photographed by Walker Evans during the Depression, and the family mansion has devolved into a rooming house. If this South, at least initially, seems surprisingly Caucasian, it may be because Forrest has been conceptualized as a sort of White Negro. Inevitably, young Elvis passes through the movie so that young Forrest can teach him some trademark spastic gyrations.

The Elvis routine parodies the scene in Zemeckis's *Back to the Future* wherein Michael J. Fox invents Chuck Berry, but Forrest is a more stolid time-traveler—particularly once he bursts his braces. Chased by a pickup truck full of high-school bullies he stuns onlookers with his mad charge through an ongoing football game: "Could you believe it—I got to go to college too!" Evoking *Zelig* as well as *Being There, Forrest Gump* next contrives for its hero to peer over Governor George Wallace's shoulder as he attempts to bar black students from the University of Alabama and then meet JFK when his football team is invited to the White House. (Later, he'll encounter the next two presidents, as well as John Lennon and Mao Zedong.) The effects are painstaking but a bust as parody. More than anything else they mark a step toward the day when *Casablanca* will be remade as a vehicle for Jack Nicholson and Marilyn Monroe, with Little Richard at the piano.

The movie comes closest to social satire when Forrest is drafted and sent to Vietnam; thanks to his low intelligence, he's the best private in boot camp. The war lacks all texture, signified by a flat, second-hand iconography of choppers, rice paddies, and wall-to-wall classic rock. Even the confusion is given in stunted shorthand. "We were always looking for this guy named Charlie," Forrest explains. The mise-en-scène is a cartoon. When the monsoon stops, a fire-fight begins and Forrest, saving soldier after soldier with the tenacity of an animated creature, is wounded in the "buttocks." (When LBJ gives him a medal, they get to compare scars.)

Forrest's devotion to his childhood playmate Jenny (a haggard Robin Wright) aside, his emotional constant is an allegiance to his Vietnam buddy—Bubba Blue (Mykelti Williamson), a Louisiana black man even dumber than him—and his commanding officer Lieutenant Dan (Gary Sinise). After Vietnam, the movie turns mawkish and tiresome; its affect, like Forrest's, could be classified as "dull normal." Forrest re-encounters the now legless Lieutenant Dan. (As the quadriplegic, Sinise's stunt performance may be the most mystifying special effect in the movie. Magician Ricky Jay gets a credit for his wheelchair.) The hero makes a fortune in shrimp, reunites with Jenny for a romantic idyll coinciding with the Bicentennial and, abandoned again, jogs across the U.S.A., oblivious to the followers and bumper stickers that trail in his wake. This promising *Rocky* travesty is aborted; the movie ends with Reagan president and Forrest a grown-up.

Greening America as he jogs toward eternity, Forrest is the perfect embodiment of Consciousness III, the place where countercultural and conventional Hollywood wisdom meet: "The hippies were taught by their parents, their neighbors, their tabloids and their college professors that faith, instinct and emotion are superior to reason," wrote pop philosopher Ayn Rand in one of my favorite anti counterculture rants. This bleak, yet saccharine tale of simple goodness triumphing over retardation, amputation, assassination, exploitation, intolerance, child abuse, and AIDS embodies a sentimental populism that suggests Oprah as well as Capra. History does really dissolve—there's never a point where you can't see the Forrest for the trees.

Also reviewed in:
NATION, 9/5-12/94, p. 249, Stuart Klawans
NEW REPUBLIC, 8/8/94, p. 28, Stanley Kauffmann
NEW YORK TIMES, 7/6/94, p. C9, Janet Maslin
NEW YORKER, 7/25/94, p. 79, Anthony Lane

VARIETY, 7/11-17/94, p. 41, Todd McCarthy
WASHINGTON POST, 7/6/94, p. B1, Rita Kempley
WASHINGTON POST, 7/8/94, Weekend/p. 38, Desson Howe

FOUR WEDDINGS AND A FUNERAL

A Gramercy Pictures release of a Polygram Filmed Entertainment and Channel Four Films presentation of a Working Title production. *Executive Producer:* Richard Curtis, Tim Bevan, and Eric Fellner. *Producer:* Duncan Kenworthy. *Director:* Mike Newell. *Screenplay:* Richard Curtis. *Director of Photography:* Michael Coulter. *Editor:* John Gregory. *Music:* Richard Rodney Bennett. *Sound:* David Stephenson and (music) Dick Lewzey. *Sound Editor:* Sue Baker. *Casting:* Michelle Guish and David Rubin. *Production Designer:* Maggie Gray. *Set Decorator:* Anna Pinnock. *Costumes:* Lindy Hemming. *Make-up:* Ann Buchanan. *Stunt Coordinator:* Wayne Michaels. *Running time:* 118 minutes. *MPAA Rating:* R.

CAST: Hugh Grant (Charles); James Fleet (Tom); Simon Callow (Gareth); John Hannah (Matthew); Kristin Scott Thomas (Fiona); David Bower (David); Charlotte Coleman (Scarlett); Andie MacDowell (Carrie); Timothy Walker (Angus the Groom); Sara Crowe (Laura the Bride); Ronald Herdman (Vicar); Elspet Gray (Laura's Mother); Philip Voss (Laura's Father); Rupert Vansittart (George the Boor at the Boatman); Nicola Walker and Paul Stacey (Frightful Folk Duo); Simon Kunz (John with the Unfaithful Wife); Rowan Atkinson (Father Gerald); Robin McCaffrey (Serena); Kenneth Griffiths (Mad Old Man); David Haig (Bernard the Groom); Sophie Thompson (Lydia the Bride); Corin Redgrave (Hamish); Donald Weedon (Master of Ceremonies); Nigel Hastings (Tea-Tasting Alistair); Emily Morgan (Vomiting Veronica); Amanda Mealing (Naughty Nicki); Melissa Knatchbull (Mocking Martha); Polly Kemp (Miss Piggy); Anna Chancellor (Henrietta); Hannah Taylor Gordon (Young Bridesmaid); Bernice Stegers (Shop Assistant); Robert Lang (Lord Hibbot); Jeremy Kemp (Sir John Delaney); Rosalie Crutchley (Mrs. Beaumont); Ken Drury, Neville Phillips, and Richard Butler (Vicars); Struan Rodger (Best Man); Lucy Hornack (Married Woman); Randall Paul (Chester); Pat Starr (Gareth's Dance Partner); Tim Thomas (Doctor); Susanna Hamnett (Deirdre); John Abbott (Polite Verger).

LOS ANGELES TIMES, 3/9/94, Calendar/p. 1, Kenneth Turan

"Why am I always at weddings," wonders the boyish Charles, "and never get married?" "Four Weddings and a Funeral," a cheerful and witty bit of business that belies its no-nonsense title, not only answers Charles' question, it offers the kind of sly pleasure only British comedy seems to provide.

Deftly written by Richard Curtis (who wanted some revenge after attending 65 weddings in 11 years) and directed by the versatile Mike Newell (responsible for everything from "Dance With a Stranger" to "Enchanted April"), "Four Weddings" is as good as its word, breezily following a small circle of friends through every one of the events the title promises.

Three couples make up the core group, but none of them are particularly in an altar frame of mind. Fiona and Tom (Kristin Scott Thomas and James Fleet) are brother and sister, Gareth and Matthew (the ebullient Simon Callow and John Hannah) are gay, and Charles (Hugh Grant) and Scarlett (Charlotte Coleman) are good friends more than passion's playmates.

Though we occasionally catch a glimpse of these folks outside the weekend wedding whirl, it is the playful conceit of "Four Weddings" to tell us almost nothing about the group that doesn't come to light at one of those social events. So while we learn that the endearingly oafish Tom is "the seventh-richest man in England, more or less," we never see the rest of the comfortably well-off characters' lives or even find out how anyone earns a living.

First among equals is the boyish Charles, a man of considerable if chaotic charm who is invariably late to these weddings, even when he is the best man and has to apologize by promising, "I'll be killing myself after the service if its any consolation."

As played by Hugh Grant (best known for "Maurice," but now in "Sirens" and Roman Polanski's forthcoming "Bitter Moon"), Charles is suave but scattered, using his considerable wit to compensate for his lack of focus. A handsome pixie with something of the look and verve of a youthful British Kennedy, Grant gives a sunnily self-confident performance that anchors the film in the good spirits it never loses.

At the film's first wedding, Charles catches a glimpse of Carrie (Andie MacDowell), an American who used to work for Vogue. Actually, wearing an enormous black hat, she is difficult to miss, but the tart Fiona warns him "she went out with very glamorous people. She's quite out of your league."

But Charles, though a sturdy bachelor "in bewildered awe" of married people, is clearly smitten, and Carrie, temperamentally bolder than he, is interested as well. But it is the gift of screenwriter Richard Curtis to find endlessly clever ways to alternately bring these two together and then push them apart as they try to sort out what they want out of romantic love and how much commitment they can handle.

Curtis, who wrote the script for the little-seen but seriously funny "The Tall Guy" starring Emma Thompson and Jeff Goldblum, is concerned not just with romance. He and polished director Newell are fascinated as well by the humor to be found in ritual situations, by the crazy way people act in public emotional moments.

So "Four Weddings" is rife with matrimonial madness, everything from a grotesque version of "Stand by Your Man" to the nightmare of being seated at a table filled with old girlfriends to a classic bit involving a newly minted priest (the dead-on Rowan Atkinson) who can't seem to get the words of the ceremony out of his mouth.

As Atkinson proves, when you are doing delicate farce it helps to have actors who can pull this kind of business off, and, with the exception of MacDowell, who could do with a bit more animation, the cast here is peerless.

Not only do Grant, Scott Thomas, Callow and company handle the sprightly dialogue with aplomb, they are also adept at the doubletakes and befuddled looks that make '"Four Weddings," both amusing and irresistible all the way through the not-to-be-missed final credits.

So when screenwriter Curtis notes in the press material that perhaps "in the passing of time I'll write a screenplay called "Four Funerals and a Wedding,'" one can only hope that it turns out as well as this tasty, sophisticated romp, a romantic comedy that wears its skill lightly and garnishes its humor with style.

NEW YORK, 4/4/94, p. 78, John Powers

Fired up by the rave reviews, I raced to see *Four Weddings and a Funeral*, which proved to be little more than a dim British version of *Groundhog Day*: It has alarm clocks, repeated events (in this case weddings), and a hero, played by cutely bespectacled Hugh Grant, who must shake off his narcissism in order to win Andie MacDowell (also the female lead in *Groundhog Day*!). Although it promises to be a frothy tour de force—a man and woman pursuing a private romance during four weddings and a funeral—this Mike Newell movie can't live up to its formal conceit. It cheats on its premise (one sequence takes place at neither a wedding nor a funeral) and falls back on the most sodden clichés of English comedy: malaprop-spouting vicars ("the Holy Spigot"), idiot Yanks who think Oscar Wilde is still alive, clumsy aristos who step into every available cow pie. Richard Curtis's script has a few genuinely amusing moments, but like Kenneth Branagh's *Peter's Friends*, it celebrates the Oxbridge complacency of a circle of yuppies. (If an American made a movie like this about prosperous Harvard grads, the audience would scream bloody murder.) *Four Weddings and a Funeral* is less a cinematic triumph than a yardstick of critics' increasingly indiscriminate Anglophilia.

NEW YORK, 5/2/94, p. 81, David Denby

His hair parted in the middle and falling into his face, Hugh Grant, the star of the English romantic comedy *Four Weddings and a Funeral*, has a careless school-boy charm that is most appealing. Grant's character, Charlie, stammers and dithers; he's a man trapped by his own decency. Expected to say nice things to Hen (short for Henrietta), his dreary, dark-eyed former girlfriend—a woman who could make Casanova feel guilty—he looks so stricken that we wonder if he will not expire at her feet. Charlie is perhaps too attractive for his own good. He can't commit himself to any of the girls who want him, and in the end he's unwittingly cruel. But then he meets an American, Carrie (Andie MacDowell), who uses him and leaves him, and he falls in love with her—one of the many things in the movie that don't quite make sense.

This British movie has become an American phenomenon—possibly one of the most successful British imports ever—and obviously Grant has a lot to do with it. Exceptionally good-looking in a smooth, hairless, almost nubile way (more deer than goat), he's appealing to women, I would guess, because he's so clearly nonthreatening. He pursues Andie MacDowell through the London streets in a pair of shorts that expose his skinny legs. Catching up with her, he's too tongue-tied to do anything but blurt out his love. In modern terms, the power is all with the woman: Charlie can win only if his uncertainty is more charming than anything else around. In other words, Hugh Grant is a romantic hero for the feminist era—as much a fantasy dreamboat as Harvey Keitel was (in a vastly different style) in *The Piano*, in which Keitel played a primitive man with complete respect for his woman, waiting for her to signal that sex was okay.

The style of male irresistibility here owes little to the arrogant tradition of, say, Rex Harrison or the young Peter O'Toole. In spirit, Grant is closer to the bumbling, stumbling Henry Fonda in *The Lady Eve*, a young man who did not know he was handsome; or to the bashful, romantically appealing young James Stewart. Mention of those classics should suggest another reason the movie is a hit here: The American audience is starved for romantic comedy. This country, you may recall, once led the world in such films. But romantic comedy requires some sort of formal aesthetic style and the artifice of manners and even, perhaps, a touch of refinement. In a country where conventional elegance is now considered contemptible and exclusionary—at least in art—comedy turns into slapstick romping. The spirit of the frat house and the shopping mall overwhelms the form.

Look at the appalling *Threesome*, which is about a sexually mixed trio (two men, one woman) who share a college dorm room. The story depends on sexual ambiguity, homosexual feelings unacknowledged or half acknowledged—and suddenly, just when a mood is developing and something interesting might happen, the writer-director, Andrew Fleming, has a character announce what he's feeling: *Now I'm attracted to* ... Heaven forbid someone in a sixplex should be puzzled for even an instant! Fleming's timidity has been rewarded with a disaster. He attempts to play with "advanced" ideas about the pleasures of companionship (the movie is an *hommage* to *Jules et Jim*), but he does it TV-sitcom style, converting the actors into clowns: Stephen Baldwin, in a turned-around cap, bares his big teeth and big rump and looks like a talking mule; Lara Flynn Boyle has an orgasm on a library table; and so on.

By contrast, Mike Newell, the director of *Four Weddings*, etc., knows what he is doing. The movie is about a group of friends, vaguely situated in London, who go from one wedding to the next, each of them hoping to meet the right partner among the other guests and get married. With the exception of a gay couple (Simon Callow and John Hannah) who are already happily married, they have become increasingly morose about their chances. And then things begin to happen. By the end, in a triumphant coda, they are all hooked. The movie has the formalized frame of an old Hollywood masterpiece: Each wedding is introduced with an engraved invitation seen in close-up; Newell and the writer, Richard Curtis (from British TV), show us virtually nothing of the group but their attendance at weddings.

An odd existence, of course. No one in this morning-coat-and-carnation life of perpetual nuptials seems to work or to care about anything besides social life. And what an unlikely group they are: Stupid, amicable Tom (James Fleet) and his elegant sister Fiona (Kristin Scott Thomas), society swells of uncountable wealth;, apparently spend all their time with near-impoverished intellectuals (like Hugh Grant's Charlie) and shopgirls. We wonder: Has the British class system been dissolved overnight? At first it seems that Newell and Curtis have also engaged in Hollywood-style calculation, putting in something for everyone. As well as the gay couple, there is Charlie's brother, who is deaf and who signs a devastating message at the movie's climax. But here's the surprise: The movie has a genuine good spirit, a democratic appreciation of erotic possibilities in unlikely situations. And Newell and Curtis convince us that the people in this odd group actually do like one another—certainly an immense change from the sour, chilblained nastiness that English movies have featured for years (this movie was made, after all, by the director responsible for that pale-blue drop of smoking acid, *Dance With a Stranger*).

Curtis provides a steadily ripening banter, and the actors take mighty bites: Simon Callow gives his most extroverted performance yet as a sort of drunken Pan, leading the revels. Tilting his beard up and caressing ordinary lines so lavishly that they seem covered in suavity, Callow creates whirling eddies of merriment all around him. The fascinating Kristin Scott Thomas brings a mannequin's surface to the role of a sarcastic beauty hiding her feelings. Scott Thomas's lines seem chilled in the dry-martini atmosphere of earlier periods of elegance—a Noel Coward play, perhaps.

It's an immensely companionable movie. (But who can remember the title? *Three Coins in a Shower? Four Weddings And a Bris*?) There is time for jokes, for nonsense, for old memories and a fine funeral speech, including a long recitation of W. H. Auden, when one of the group unexpectedly dies. The great comic Rowan Atkinson has a good bit as a nervously unctuous clergyman who buggers the words of the marriage service. Some of the sex play is crude, but none of it is mean-spirited, as it was in that excruciating Kenneth Branagh thing *Between Friends*, in which people who could not conceivably be imagined as buddies embarrassed themselves and us, and every scene died a thousand deaths.

The only problem is Andie MacDowell. Her Carrie is supposed to be a smashing, ruthless American adventuress—a sexy clotheshorse—who uses men for her own convenience and pleasure and is somehow, at the same time, a good person. American actresses like Veronica Lake, Gene Tierney, and Lauren Bacall used to be adept at this good/bad girl stuff, but MacDowell plays Carrie sincerely and flatly. When Grant looks at her as if she were his dream woman, we don't understand him. Why is a longtime bachelor who can have anyone falling for this woman? Is he a masochist? How is he going to keep her in clothes? The movie doesn't always make sense, but it's still awfully pleasant.

NEW YORK POST, 3/9/94, p. 31, Michael Medved

Admittedly, the year is still young, but it's hard to imagine that 1994 will bring a more charming or seductive romantic comedy than "Four Weddings and a Funeral."

The seduction begins with the opening sequence, in which the hapless hero (Hugh Grant) finds himself in a situation with which many of us can identify: He has overslept one Saturday and must now make a desperate dash from his London, flat to a country church where he's due to serve as best man at a lavish wedding.

The first nine words of the script are all obscenities as Grant, in the company of his eccentric, henna-haired nose-pinned flatmate (Charlotte Coleman) fights various mishaps to get them to the church on time. Once he's arrived, with clothes only slightly askew, he breathes normally until someone asks him if he has brought the wedding rings.

Grant survives the ceremony, but at the reception that follows he meets a woman who changes his life: an irresistibly brash, breezy American, played by the appropriately irresistible Andie MacDowell.

Through the rest of the film, Grant attempts uncertain pursuit of this alluring vision as he and his dearest friends gather for three more weddings and, yes, a funeral.

Those friends include a bored aristocrat (Kristin Scott Thomas), her dim-witted eager-to-please, obscenely wealthy brother (James Fleet), and a deeply devoted gay couple comprised of earthy, exuberant Simon Callow and his shy partner John Hannah.

Each of these performances is a triumph, as the actors make us feel intimately acquainted with people about whom we actually know next to nothing—not even what they do for a living or how they happen to know one another.

It hardly matters as the movie sweeps you up in its joyous embrace, and director Mike Newell offers sumptuous, summery, glad-to-be-alive images reminiscent of his magnificent "Enchanted April"

He makes the most of every moment in the witty script by Richard Curtis (who wrote the underrated 1989 Jeff Goldblum-Emma Thompson comedy "The Tall Guy"), wringing belly laughs out of James Fleet's embarrassing speech as best man in wedding No. 2, and the stumbling performance of rookie priest Rowan Atkinson, who pronounces the bride an "awful wedded wife."

If the movie stumbles at all, it's in the funeral sequence, following the sudden death of one of the characters. Newell tries too hard to provoke tears, darkening the emotional tone to lend depth to the big romantic finale.

Hugh Grant deserves primary credit for the rousing effectiveness of this conclusion and for carrying the rest of the movie as well. He's previously been typecast as an annoying, upper-crust twit, (in "The Lair of the White Worm," "Sirens," "Bitter Moon," or as Chopin in "Impromptu.")

Here, he comes into his own as one of today's most appealing leading men. He combines the elegant appearance and self-deprecating wit of an earlier Grant (Cary), with the sheepish fumbling, Everyman appeal of a Jimmy Stewart. It's a spectacularly effective combination.

The lush, lyrical score by Richard Rodney Bennett (next year's Oscar voters, please take note!) adds a touch of poetry, as does the perfectly chosen theme song, "But Not for Me," by a pretty fair composer named Gershwin.

The climax of a plot/Should be the marriage knot/But there's no knot for me," warbles Elton John on the soundtrack, expressing the hero's lonely ache as a perennial guest, but never a groom.

This stylish romp can satisfy that ache (at least temporarily) for any moviegoer, and in the process provides as much fun as legally possible in a movie theater.

NEWSDAY, 3/9/94, Part II/p. 63, Terry Kelleher

The thought occurs during the first reception in "Four weddings and a Funeral": The main characters may not be as likable as director Mike Newell intended.

Charles (Hugh Grant), the thoroughly English best man, delivers a funny pre-toast speech that principally concerns himself—his favorite topic, one suspects—rather than the happy couple. As the festivities wind down, he encounters Carrie (Andie MacDowell), the attractive American guest with whom he fell in love at first sight earlier in the day. "Great speech," she offers, indicating self-involvement is no flaw in her book.

In Newell's "Enchanted April," mismatched married couples rekindled romance a little too easily. In "Four Weddings and a Funeral," the degree of difficulty is supposed to be romantic in itself. The plan calls for viewers to melt every time Charles and Carrie lock eyes across a crowded lawn or banquet hall, though their behavior sometimes borders on the abominable.

After failing to follow up on the marvelous sex he enjoyed with Carrie the night of that first wedding, Charles is delighted to run into her at the nuptials of another friend, then crestfallen when she introduces her fiancé. Of course, he picks himself up in time to have sex with her again that evening, but he steals away with a wistful smile that seems to say, "Alas, 'tis not to be."

To her credit, Carrie does not have sex with Charles on the very night of her marriage to someone else, but her speech to the guests contains a clear signal that bonnie Charlie may have another shot at her quite soon. When a freshly separated Carrie shows up at Charles' wedding 10 months later, who (besides the unfortunate bride) would begrudge him a slight change of heart?

Although the nervous charm of Grant's Charles is not to be denied, it's insufficient to cover what his English forebears might call a caddish streak. Frankly, we'd sooner make friends with other members of the film's floating wedding party— the endearingly clumsy Tom (James Fleet), say, or the Falstaffian Gareth (Simon Callow): And we wouldn't mind seeing more of that newly ordained priest (Rowan Atkinson) whose way of mangling a sacred vow brings a touch of hilarity to the second wedding.

If this handsome production were more of a farce, we'd give less thought to the wounded feelings of those who, through no fault of their own, block the path of true love between Charles and Carrie. But Newell and writer Richard Curtis shouldn't have interrupted the weddings with a funeral if they didn't want the audience to ponder life as more than the impulsive pursuit of happiness.

NEWSWEEK, 3/21/94, p. 74, David Ansen

Hugh Grant, who has graced the margins of many an English film, gets to step front and center in the romantic comedy "Four Weddings and a Funeral" and proves himself a deft and debonair leading man. He plays Charles, a handsome, diffident bachelor with a lethal wit who's dated every woman in his set without finding a proper mate. What Charles does for a living we never find out. What occupies his leisure hours is his friends' incessant nuptials. True to its title, Mike ("Enchanted April") Newell's movie follows Charles and his friends through four elaborate, very funny wedding ceremonies. At the first, Charles is smitten by the beautiful, elusive American Carrie (Andie MacDowell). But after they spend a blissful night together, she vanishes back to the States.

We know he's found the woman of his dreams. But the sophisticated screenplay by Richard Curtis piles clever comic roadblocks in their path, not the least of which is the third wedding Charles attends—Carrie's marriage to another man. If this breezy and bawdy tale has a flaw, it's in the depiction of its enigmatic heroine. Actually, she's incomprehensible, and the winsome MacDowell hasn't enough resources to flesh her out. Fortunately, there are too many other delicious distractions to make this a serious bother. There is Rowan Atkinson's priceless farcical turn as a bungling novice priest. There is Simon Callow's rude, acerbic gusto as the gayest member of the set; Charlotte Coleman's punkish ebullience as Charle's flatmate Scarlett, and the unexpected poignance of that one funeral. Fluff with an edge, "Four Weddings" brings a venerable old genre delightfully up to date.

SIGHT AND SOUND, 6/94, p. 47, Caren Myers

Charles is a frequent wedding-goer, along with his urban *haute bourgeoisie* friends—the sharp-tongued Fiona and her wealthy brother Tom, his own deaf brother David, his punky flatmate Scarlett and the effusive Gareth and his lover Matthew. None of them, however, have ever risked marriage themselves. But at a wedding in Somerset, Charles is struck by a beautiful stranger, Carrie. Fiona promptly tells him that Carrie is a slut and out of his league anyway, but Carrie surprises him by taking him to bed. The next morning, Carrie goes back to America, leaving Charles befuddled.

At a London wedding two months later, Charles sees Carrie again, but his hopes are dashed when she introduces her new fiance, Hamish. Charles spends the rest of the evening beleaguered by vengeful ex-girlfriends; he is particularly embarrassed to see the over-emotional Henrietta, who bursts into tears. But Carrie rescues him. Hamish has left for a business trip, so they spend a second night together.

A month later, Charles receives an invitation to Carrie's wedding. As he dutifully goes to buy her a gift, he runs into her. Over coffee, Carrie enumerates the 33 men she has slept with. Charles makes her a fumbling declaration of love, but nevertheless finds himself at her wedding shortly afterwards. At the party, Fiona admits to him that she has always loved him, and Henrietta, who has a new boyfriend, seems much more together. Then Gareth suddenly has a heart attack. The friends reconvene at his funeral. Afterwards, moved by Matthew's speech, Charles wonders if he will ever feel that way about anyone himself.

Ten months later, however, Charles is to marry Henrietta. As his friends, apart from Fiona, meet their ideal mates, Carrie reappears, conveniently separated from Hamish, throwing Charles into confusion. He decides to go through with the wedding anyway, but with David's encouragement he jilts Henrietta at the altar. Carrie and Charles agree not to get married 'til death do they part.

Weddings, those microcosmic maelstroms of greed, snobbery and unwise tailoring, provide fertile ground for comedy, but countless temptations to slide into sitcom humour. Indeed, by the time Rowan Atkinson's Father Gerald (Mr. Bean had he graduated from the seminary) has stepped out to garble the second couple's wedding ceremony, there doesn't seem to be much to choose between this and Yorkshire TV's David Jason vehicle *A Bit of A Do*. With a wealth of easy-target caricatures to lean on (ghastly ex-girlfriends, drunken bores, senile old men—and this film doesn't miss one), a movie about a wedding can often feel like a wedding itself—two hours stuck in a crowded room with a lot of people you don't know very well and don't particularly like.

But *Four Weddings And A Funeral*, which is structured like a film student's senior project, strives to be more than that and ends up as something worse: a smarmy little fable about the magic of true love. This is a lazy, *Sleepless in Seattle*-style romanticism, the kind that assumes that if we're told often enough that the two dull protagonists are meant for each other, we'll eventually believe it and care sufficiently to be warmed by the inevitable hearts-and-flowers finale.

Of course, it would help if there were a single spark of chemistry between the two leads. Andie MacDowell looks ravishing enough for anyone to be smitten at first sight, but as a light comedienne she is disastrous. Her idea of sprightly repartee is to pronounce every syllable, and she can't quite hide the furrows of perplexity around her eyes—she doesn't seem to grasp her own witticisms. You can't help remembering how she was dubbed by Glenn Close in *Greystoke*, and thinking how much livelier this film would be if she were dubbed by Helen Lederer. She is not helped, either, by having to pretend that she has fallen for someone who looks like a chipmunk. Hugh Grant, his hands full playing repressed-and-hesitant, does not exactly radiate sex appeal here (and the fact that he looks all of 22 hardly lends credence to his fretting about ending up a sad old bachelor). The fact that a post-credits photomontage shows them with a baby does little to assuage our suspicions that the affair will last six months.

The film does score points with those of the supporting cast that it graces with personalities. Kristen Scott Thomas makes a marvellously brittle Fiona; when she confesses to an elderly lady that she has never got married because she is in love with someone who never thinks of her, she makes us feel how much this admission has cost her, how morbidly proud and secretive she is beneath her icy exterior. And the film has a pleasingly matter-of-fact way of establishing Gareth and Matthew's relationship—they're a convincing couple, and you wish you could see more of them, because the brief glimpses of their affectionate rapport ring true.

But too much time is taken up with the spectacle of Charles and his improbably alternative flatmate (Scarlett appears to be a 'Sarf' London punkette, so you wonder just how she got in with the independently wealthy crowd) racing to various churches, and people making boring speeches after dinner. You can feel how earnestly the film-makers tried to vary the visual aspect of the ceremonies—posh London wedding, Somerset country church, draughty Scottish castle—but the fact remains that by the time Charles' own wedding rolls around, you wish they had left it two weddings and a funeral.

TIME, 3/14/94, p. 101, Richard Corliss

There are movies so breezy, even flimsy, that you can enjoy them as genial providers of an evening's entertainment yet forget all about them by the time you leave the multiplex. Such a film is *Four Weddings and a Funeral*, a British romantic comedy with not much inside its pretty head but the spinning out of an ancient Hollywood riddle: How long will it take the two leading characters to realize that they are destined to be together?

Mike Newell's film finds its premise in one of modern life's minor truths: if you are a sociable specimen of the yuppie breed, you spend many of your Saturdays and much of your spare income suiting yourself up for friends' weddings. Charles (Hugh Grant), a 32-year-old Londoner, has made a second career out of being a supporting player in these archaic rituals. For him it's like attending a rugby match without having to get muddy. Until, that is, he meets Carrie (Andie MacDowell), a pretty American. The movie being a nostalgia piece—remember the '80s?—the two have sex, then love, then a marriage. But not to each other. That's why this is a comedy.

Grant, who can soon be seen in *Sirens* and *Bitter Moon*, is every inch the blithe aristocrat. MacDowell imports her *Groundhog Day* sweetness to a role that is more a fantasy than a character. And Rowan Atkinson has a cute turn as a tongue-tied cleric. Richard Curtis (*The Tall Guy, Blackadder*) has stocked his script with transatlantic gags (How many times has Carrie had sex? "Less than Madonna, more than Lady Di"). The movie strains a bit to prove it's all a lark, but because the mood is cunningly sunny, and the cast is so relaxed in its empyrean of casual sex and restorative love, you can bet the sterling silverware that America will give a warm reception to ... what's the name of this picture?

VILLAGE VOICE, 3/15/94, p. 53, Beth Coleman

Going from the understanding that weddings make everyone belligerent, *Four Weddings and a Funeral* brings us love American style in Britain. David Cassidy is invoked as the patron saint of the proceedings. Hugh Grant, charming as the sensitive yet profligate Charles, takes us on a tour: from a suburban wedding in Somerset to a grander London cathedral and on to lords in their lairs in Scotland. The fourth wedding cannot be listed as such; it's more of a state of mind than place, as it is Charles's. Marriage has always been about property, that much is clear. Its other aspect, the one that starts with *L*, with which director Mike Newell and writer Richard Curtis clutter up the scenery like so many bad wedding bouquets, is less dependable.

Charles and his pals, among them several Brit faces old and new, are dutiful hecklers at any state affair. Rowan Atkinson of *Blackadder* fame presides over wedding two, taking the ham-handed script to a surprising level of hilarity. The lovely Kristin Scott Thomas plays opposite Grant as his true love manqué, as she also does in the forthcoming *Bitter Moon*—how he missed her twice (and this time for the attractive and dull Andie MacDowell) is beyond me, but such is love. Or marketing.

It is the funeral that breaks our hearts. Gareth (Simon Callow) and Matthew (John Hannah) are the actual couple subset within the gang of happy malcontents, and, as the filmmakers know in some bizarre fashion, when the world is divided between those who get married and those who cannot, the funerals of our darling boys make us weep with recognition. Auden explains it all in a eulogy delivered with great generosity by Hannah.

In the end, everyone shacks up with his or her mate in proper sitcom manner. Andie looks great in the rain—so does Hugh, for that matter. The film's rather an awful thing as Hollywood grotesques go, and it isn't even actually an H-town gig (yet, and there must always be a qualifier, I went out and got engaged afterward). Weddings, no matter how badly shot, remain fascinating and unnerving till death do us part. Or until Danny Bonaduce's arrival, transforming all into an episode of *Married ... With Children*.

Also reviewed in:
CHICAGO TRIBUNE, 3/18/94, Friday/p. C, John Petrakis
NEW REPUBLIC, 4/4/94, p. 24, Stanley Kauffmann
NEW YORK TIMES, 3/9/94, p. C15, Janet Maslin
VARIETY, 1/24-30/94, Todd McCarthy
WASHINGTON POST, 3/18/94, Weekend/p. 48, Desson Howe
WASHINGTON POST, 3/19/94, p. D1, Megan Rosenfeld

FRANÇOIS TRUFFAUT: STOLEN PORTRAITS

A Myriad Pictures release of a Chrysalide Films presentation coprouced by France 2 Cinema/INA Enterprise/Maecenas Films/Premiere with the participation of Canal Plus. A documentary in French with English subtitles. *Producer:* Monique Annaud. *Director:* Serge Toubiana and Michel Pascal. *Director of Photography:* Maurice Fellous, Jean-Yves Le Mener, and Michel Sourioux. *Editor:* Dominique Martin. *Running time:* 93 minutes. *MPAA Rating:* Not Rated.

WITH: Gérard Depardieu; Ewa Truffaut; Claude Chabrol; Jean-Louis Richard; Jean Gruault; Alexandre Astruc; Claude de Givray; Jean Aurel; Annette Insdorf; Olivier Assayas; Marcel Berbert; Madeleine Morgenstern; Eric Rohmer; Robert Lachenay; Janine Bazin; Bertrand Tavernier; Marcel Ophüls; Monique Lucas; Albert Duchesne; Liliane Siegel; Laura Truffaut; Marie-France Pisier; Yann Dedet; Claude Miller; Nathalie Baye; Fanny Ardant.

LOS ANGELES TIMES, 1/10/95, Calendar/p. 3, Kevin Thomas

Francois Truffaut, who died of cancer 10 years ago at age 52, was a charmer. He had an enduring boyishness and a passionate, encyclopedic knowledge of world cinema to which he contributed substantially, beginning with his internationally acclaimed, semi-autobiographical 1959 "400 Blows."

Serge Toubiana and Michel Pascal, in their illuminating, engaging "Francois Truffaut: Stolen Portraits," acknowledge the charm of both the man and his films, but they also provide a glimpse of a darker side in him and his work through the candid remarks of his friends and colleagues, interspersed with appropriate clips from his films.

In their documentary, which launches a retrospective of 10 Truffaut films at the Sunset 5, Toubiana and Pascal aren't out to denigrate Truffaut but are attempting to see him in the round.

The entire film is suffused with the characteristic French respect for emotions and for precision of expression. Truffaut tended to be a bit hazy about his childhood, which involved a brush with the law. He once wrote that his parents meant no more to him than strangers.

The filmmakers are especially good at digging out his troubled youth, shaped by a remote, seemingly indifferent mother and stepfather (who were stunned, nonetheless, by their far-from-flattering alter egos in "The 400 Blows"). Truffaut, it seemed, came to an understanding of his mother only when it was too late and hired private detectives to try to locate his real father.

Whereas such fellow filmmakers as Alexandre Astruc and Eric Rohmer and various actors speak with affection, gratitude and insight into the complex Truffaut and his films, it's left to director Bertrand Tavernier to provide the film's real zinger. Forty years ago, Truffaut, who at age 17 had attempted to start a film club, wrote in Cahiers du Cinema a famous attack on the French traditional "cinema of quality" that paved the way for the Nouvelle Vague.

Tavernier reveals that Truffaut had befriended the veteran screenwriter Pierre Bost (subsequently rejuvenated by Tavernier himself) only to attack him in his article. Truffaut then wrote Bost, saying he secretly admired him but that he was a journalist with a reputation to make. While pointing out that Truffaut should have instead attacked some of the directors who filmed Bost and his partner Jean Aurenche's scripts, Tavernier remains deeply impressed that Bost always resisted making public Truffaut's letter to him.

There's a certain detached sadness in Madeleine Morgenstern, Truffaut's ex-wife, but she insists that the help from her and her producer-father hastened Truffaut's success only about a year, insisting that he would have made it without them. Described by his daughter Ewa as a "man using himself up," Truffaut, a smoker—he loved to pass out cigars—apparently always believed he would die young.

In the film, we miss the presence of Jean-Luc Godard, Jeanne Moreau and especially Jean-Pierre Leaud, Truffaut's frequent screen alter ego, starting with "The 400 Blows." But there's an interview clip of his friend and hero Jean Renoir, who says that upon seeing "Jules and Jim," he thought, "Gosh, that's good. I wish I had done that myself.

NEW YORK POST, 7/15/94, p. 38, Thelma Adams

"I miss his laughter," says a shaggy Gerard Depardieu about the legendary French director in "Francois Truffaut: Stolen Portraits."

Serge Toubiana and Michel Pascal's fine revealing documentary focuses on the director of "Jules and Jim" and the 1972 Academy Award winner for foreign language film, "Day for Night." Truffaut died at 52 a decade ago.

Toubiana and Pascal rely primarily on talking heads—and their broad access to the cream of French film is outstanding.

Sources include: directors Eric Rohmer, Claude Miller, Marcel Ophuls and Bertrand Tavernier; actresses Fanny Ardant, Marie-France Pisier and Nathalie Baye; wife Madeleine Morgenstern and daughters Ewa and Laura and Columbia University professor Annette Insdorf.

The stolen portrait referred to in the title is a view of the director behind the image he created, an image that was as potent as his films. Because "The 400 Blows," "Stolen Kisses," and others were autobiographical—using Truffaut's alter-ego Antoine Doinel (Jean-Pierre Leaud)—audiences often believed they knew more about the director than the truth warranted. These were fictions, not transparent histories.

But who was the man behind the myth?

As one source says, "Like all men, he was a lie."

Truffaut's daughter Ewa felt that the care and feeding of his image was a conscious act. "He looked very trim on the outside," she tells the camera, "but inside he was different."

Drawing from clips of the Antoine Doinel series and the talking heads, a portrait emerges of a delinquent Paris brat with an early love for film which blossomed into a lifelong passion and a successful career that planted Truffaut firmly in the French bourgeoisie.

The director had an unhappy childhood. His mother, busy with his stepfather and outside activities, did not give her son the love he craved—a gaping hole in Truffaut's emotional makeup that he would try to fill for the rest of his life.

As an adult Truffaut embarked on a search for his biological father, who he had never met. The detective he hired to assist him is featured in "Stolen Portraits." They discovered the man was alive and living in Paris, a Jewish dentist. But while Truffaut watched his real father walk his dog from afar, he never contacted him.

The desire to be loved, the search for the lost father, the ripple of violence that exists in his movies just below the charming surface—all are explored in this documentary, a must-see for any Truffaut fan.

The documentary's delight is that the director surrounded himself with intelligent and articulate people; their collective wisdom shines on the screen.

For those new to Truffaut, or less in-the-know about French cinema in general, the film's reliance on talking heads identified strictly by name without further explanations is frustrating.

In the end, beautiful Truffaut star Fanny Ardant ("The Woman Next Door") says that there are two types of film: "[Those] that make you want to live and those that don't."

Truffaut's films made us want to live; "Stolen Portraits" makes us want to see Truffaut's films—again.

NEWSDAY, 7/15/94, Part II/p. B11, John Anderson

Nothing obscures like biography, and the people who pique our curiosity are usually the most mysterious. So it is with Francois Truffaut, the late and much-missed French director, screenwriter, critic and New Wave cipher, whose films were never quite the autobiographical confessionals his worshippers made them out to be.

So it appears, at least from Serge Toubiana and Michel Pascal's homage-cum-bio "Stolen Portraits," which parades a Olympian cast of actors, Gerard Depardieu, Fanny Ardant; directors, Marcel Ophuls, Bernard Tavernier, Claude Chabrol, Eric Rohmer; family, daughters, aunts, ex-wives; and friends, who erect an affectionate if a slightly askew monument in tribute to a filmmaker for whom simplicity was a goal, not a characteristic.

By the time of his cruelly premature death from a brain tumor at the age of 52 in 1984, Truffaut was the most famous French filmmaker and one of the world's best known directors, who had propelled the French New Wave to international prominence through such remarkable early films as "The 400 Blows," "Love at Twenty," and "Jules et Jim." Later would come "Stolen Kisses," "Small Change," "The Wild Child," "Day for Night" and "The Last Metro." And through film clips and interviews with the principals in these films, as well as with Truffaut's peers—who are far from gushing, and occasionally quite critical—we get insight into this work methods, his inspirations, his influences and his drive, which one witness ascribes to his premonition of early death.

Do we get Francois himself. Probably not, but for that, we should return to feast on the films themselves, "Stolen Portraits" having whetted our appetites.

VILLAGE VOICE, 7/19/94, p. 50, Georgia Brown

François Truffaut had his secrets. According to screenwriter Jean Gruault, he "lied in a thousand ways." "It's not that he was Bluebeard," says Truffaut's ex-wife Madeleine Morgenstern, "but there are closets I'm still afraid of opening."

The filmmaker had his reasons, and these are the subject of Serge Toubiana and Michel Pascal's fascinating documentary *François Truffaut: Stolen Portraits*. Made up simply of talking heads and film clips, this modest film manages to serve up a real bombshell: It tells who the filmmaker's real father was. You'd never guess.

Although he was given the name of his mother's husband, Truffaut later found out that she'd become pregnant, before marriage, by another man. Mother and stepfather promptly farmed out the infant to his grandmother, who kept him until she died. He was eight when they unenthusiastically took him back. (His daughter says he liked to reverse the cliché: "Other mothers are saints; mine was a whore.") An unwanted child, literally nurtured by the movies, Truffaut conducted a lifelong search for love that left him prey to serial fixations. Almost all of his films fit the *l'amour fou* genre.

"I'm a young journalist and I have to make a career," he once wrote in a private apology for a ruthless critique. As a *Cahiers* turk, he took some of his elders to task; others he became son to. Recounting the first meeting between Truffaut, Rivette, and his father Max, Marcel Ophuls quotes Balzac's maxim, "The best way into the house is on the coattails of masters." Truffaut's genius, of course, let him pick the true masters.

There was also the class factor. Whereas New Wave colleagues had alternate careers or family money to fall back on, Truffaut was always the urchin scrambling to keep from being tossed into the streets on his behind. Touchingly, Morgenstern, whose father bank-rolled Truffaut's first film, admits that, after so many references to her as "the producer's daughter," she began to accept her role in his biography. "We saved him maybe a year," she murmurs.

Early on, Truffaut's reputation with cineasts began to wane. His craving for "universality" was held against him. The publicized break with Godard (conspicuously absent here) led some to believe it was necessary to choose. And it was easy for Godardians to write off Truffaut as bourgeois when, more and more, he was compelled by character and story, less and less by innovative form. He was becoming, critics said, the kind of filmmaker he'd warned against. The irony wasn't lost on him.

Personally, I don't doubt that one day Truffaut will be valued as a great filmmaker—and to the very end. (*The Man Who Loved Women* and *The Woman Next Door* are vastly underrated.) In his critic's hat, he once pointed out that "Chaplin helped people to live." A man for whom cinema was life, Truffaut did this, too.

Also reviewed in:
NEW REPUBLIC, 8/8/94, p. 28, Stanley Kauffmann
NEW YORK TIMES, 7/15/94, p. C27, Stephen Holden
VARIETY, 5/24/93, p. 47, Todd McCarthy
WASHINGTON POST, 7/30/94, p. D5, Hal Hinson

FREEDOM ON MY MIND

A Tara Releasing release of a Clarity Film Productions film. *Producer:* Connie Field and Marilyn Mulford. *Director:* Connie Field and Marilyn Mulford. *Screenplay:* Michael Chandler. *Director of Photography:* Michael Chinn, Steve Devita, and Vicente Franco. *Editor:* Michael Chandler. *Music:* Mary Watkins. *Sound:* Don Thomas, Larry Loewinger, and Curtis Choy. *Running time:* 105 minutes. *MPAA Rating:* Not Rated.

CAST: Ronnie Washington (Narrator).

CINEASTE, Vol. XXI, Nos. 1-2, 1995, p. 81, Paul Arthur and Janet Cutler

Near the end of *Freedom on My Mind*, a white male volunteer in the Mississippi voter registration project of 1964 attempts a summary statement of the enduring significance of 'Freedom Summer,' affirming the value of "ideas that speak to something larger than the individual." It is a fine and, in context, utterly persuasive sentiment; yet it is to the genuine credit of veteran political documentarists Connie Field (*The Life and Times of Rosie the Riveter*) and Marilyn Mulford (*Chicano Park*) that neither this nor any other personal or authorial perspective is granted the status of 'final word,' the privileged and unimpeachable core of historical truth. Instead, the narrative shape given to this famous and often idealized chapter in the struggle against racism and political disenfranchisement is made all the more cogent by its admission of contrasting motivations, analyses, and implications.

It is easy to underestimate *Freedom*'s complexity of design and nuanced account of historical process since the film rarely deviates from the standard practices of the interview/archival footage documentary, a ready-for-PBS-primetime format which has dominated social issue filmmaking since the late Seventies. Indeed, the intercutting of compelling testimony offered by engaging personalities with remarkable images culled from TV news clips, still photos, and an unfinished film diary (shot by actor Richard Beymer) imparts a seamless chronological and emotional flow that only gradually reveals underlying gaps and frictions. At the start, a backdrop of rural social oppression is sketched through vivid childhood recollections of humiliation, anger, and alienation by ex-sharecroppers L.C. Dorsey and Curtis Hayes and former prostitute Endesha Ida Mae Holland (raped at age eleven by her white employer). Intermittent narration provides a wider context of Jim Crow laws and the more urban confrontations over lunch counters and schools.

With the introduction of Bob Moses, a northern college student who for five years served as Student Nonviolent Coordinating Committee (SNCC) field secretary and principal architect of the drive to register black voters, the film locates an organizational focus for collective action and a human link between the interwoven stories of local activists and northern students recruited to draw national media attention to a flagging campaign—by 1963, only five percent of Mississippi's potential voters had been enrolled—and hopefully to lure the federal government into the struggle. Moses is exceptionally candid about the intended role of these volunteers and, at least in retrospect, they too are clear about their own achievements and limitations. As Marshall Ganz, a Harvard undergraduate moved by JFK's challenge for public service, remarks, the goal of securing civil and constitutional protections meant that SNCC "had to bring the people who the law covered to the South"—namely white middle-class educated youth.

Throughout the film, the recountings of personal, cathartic anecdotes are carefully balanced by discussions of political strategy. While Moses provides much of the latter, nearly every participant contributes something to the overall understanding of how the cause was defined and advanced, particularly how the negotiation of daunting racial, cultural, and gender differences figured in the mobilization of 'communal' work and trust. In this regard, both black and white participants comment on the reciprocity of cultural and formal education; the volunteers' learning about local customs and institutions took place alongside their teaching of reading and history, overcoming initial mistrust on both sides. In the best Newsreel tradition, a filmic training ground for Loth Field and Mulford, *Freedom* implicitly lays out a blueprint for organizing that is as applicable to current political realities as it was to voting rights in the Sixties.

For both outsiders and locals, the risks were abundantly clear from the beginning. The chilling and potentially disruptive murder of Chaney, Goodman, and Schwerner is treated not only as a cataclysmic event (documentary footage captures a group of northern students pausing to rededicate themselves to the struggle despite the palpable danger), but as the extension of systemic violence exercised in the maintenance of white power. What distinguished it from the killing of Herbert Lee (a black farmer who was among the first to register) or Medgar Evers was the national attention it garnered and its use as a rallying tool when the scene shifted to the Democratic Convention and the effort to seat the Mississippi Freedom delegation failed. Recognition by Moses and others of the crucial weight of media coverage in the process of legitimation, and of the thorny relationship between direct action (voter registration) and essentially symbolic representation in the party system (unseating the Dixiecrats), anticipates predicaments yet to be faced by the antiwar movement.

"Where do you go next?," asks one participant. Given the hard-won regional, and largely micropolitical, successes achieved in the South, the decision to head north to, as one activist puts it, "take on the system at the highest level"—the "power base" that props up the people who murder and burn churches—functions as the film's turning point and conceptual crux. Trying to exploit what Moses calls a "great theater for empowerment" brings the movement into truly alien terrain, the obdurate and more subtly racist infrastructure of national party politics. Although this move is made to appear both logical and inevitable, there is a certain unreflective naivete expressed about "the profound sense of betrayal" by Lyndon Johnson and his minions when they block the group's righteous petition for inclusion. Oddly, the exposition and analysis of what happened in Atlantic City is *Freedom*'s weakest section, as if the goals and machinations of electoral empowerment, "the undermined faith in democratic process," remain after thirty years a source of ambivalence and confusion.

The well-rehearsed story of the preempting by LBJ of Fannie Lou Hamer's national television address, and the deceptive "deal" cut to grant token representation to the 80,000 member Freedom Democratic Party, deflect the energies of the film as, historically, they taxed the resolve and resources of the movement. Moses has it right when he says that the Democrats were willing to make room for the professional organizers but were adamantly opposed to embracing "grass roots people," the farmers and housewives and domestic workers stirred to action—and, not incidentally, to self-realization—by the registration campaign. But Moses is almost surely wrong when, at the end of the film, he inflates the failure in Atlantic City, asserting that it triggered the accelerating political polarization and escalation of violence by radicals in the Black Power and antiwar movements; he concludes, "The Democratic Party missed an opportunity to capture the energy of a young generation."

Unfortunately that claim, left unchallenged in the film's broader discourse, fails to account for the urban eruptions which *preceded* the convention and for the insuperable grievances of economic and social inequality which the party system could not accommodate. Even the film's recognition that seizing the national spotlight in Atlantic City undoubtedly ensured the 1965 passage of the Voting Rights Act seems an aside given the deeper problems broached by the film—including the history of violence and death that was so much a part of Mississippi's place as "the last stand of the South."

The desire to represent 'Freedom Summer' as a crucial historical moment and to treat Moses reverentially is perfectly understandable, yet it has the effect of flattening out other contradictory, and in a sense more admirable, impulses. The interview/archival footage documentary is frequently caught in the dilemma of focussing either on ordinary 'rank and file' observer/agents of events—selecting the most vivid characters and elevating their stories into dramatic exemplars (as in *Union Maids*)—or relying on the socially-constructed authority of, and presumed audience interest in, celebrity 'experts' or acknowledged leaders (as is the case in the often opportunistic *Baseball*). *Freedom* pursues the former approach, yet cannot refrain from making Bob Moses a central figure. He is the only participant—apart from Fannie Lou Hamer—referred to by other speakers and the only one to enjoy two separate interviews. His importance to the narrative is not quite that of a Great Man intercession, but nonetheless unbalances the film s political and historical vision.

It is indeed felicitous that the soft-spoken Moses, for all his considerable insight and personal charisma, assumes the appointed role with marked self-doubt and more than a hint of corrosive bitterness. Like other magnetic figures of the Sixties at the forefront of social transformation, Moses (at least in retrospect) displays a poignant ambivalence over the burdens of leadership itself, the dynamics of direct and communal action versus hierarchical organization. If the film in some ways privileges Moses, his presence is eloquently counterbalanced by an array of compelling and memorable protagonists each of whom offers up rewarding revelations. In fact, the editing often creates a heady unity between the participants; as the interviews address similar topics, the film enlists its subjects in a present-day, dynamic 'conversation.'

There is, as it were, a punchline to *Freedom* and it tends to support both the extraordinary vitality of the segments devoted to the registration campaign in Mississippi and the political lessons embodied by its narrators. In the opening sections, interviewees address their personal backgrounds but their positions in the movement—even their names—are withheld. We learn gradually who they are, how they joined, what they did, and what they have concluded about their experiences. Indeed, one of the pleasures of the film comes with the growing recognition that the color images of interviewees in the present are juxtaposed with black and white images of them shot thirty years earlier. We hear Endesha Holland talk about a confrontation with a white law enforcement officer, then realize we are watching her, much younger, experiencing that same event. We hear Marshall Ganz talk about his motives for coming to Mississippi, then see him go over the same ground in the three-decade-old footage.

Only at the coda, however, do we discover the subsequent course of their personal lives and political commitments. One of the revelations of the film is its concrete depiction of the ways in which 'Freedom Summer' was a transforming experience for the participants—a period that indelibly shaped future identities and goals. Among the film's unforgettable figures, Endesha Ida Mae Holland alternates humorous and energetic accounts of crucial events in the civil rights movement with horrific tales about her childhood rape, her conversion from prostitute to civil rights activist (having initially tried to solicit customers among the volunteers, she found "the movement said to me I was somebody"), and the death of her mother (her family's home was fire-bombed as a result of her civil rights activities). In a dramatic turnabout she went on to earn a doctorate and pursue a career as a dramatist and professor of American Studies.

Curtis Hayes recounts how he used to "go into the woods and hit trees and pretend they were white folks"; he saw the Freedom Riders on television and thought "they looked magnificent." From sharecropper to SNCC organizer, Hayes formed bonds with the college students—black and white—and despite their many differences concluded, "I was in heaven for a minute."

That statement speaks to the inspirational quality of the film—the sense of personal fulfillment and community ties forged in meetings and marches and the singing of freedom songs. The lives of the northern college students may not have been 'rescued' in the same way, but as Marshall Ganz explains, "The movement gave us hope." The film then shows how much was risked—just registering to vote meant losing a job, beatings, burnings, even death—while asserting the power of organized political struggle.

It turns out that every speaker in *Freedom* has a continuous record of activism but in widely diverse venues and causes: healthcare, legal aid, playwriting, migrant labor, education. Moses is the only one who turned his considerable energies elsewhere; he taught in Africa for a number of years but has since returned to lead an inner city math program. And significantly, virtually all the activities that currently engage the veterans of 1964 are localized, community-oriented; there is not an electoral functionary in the bunch.

An unstated agenda in many, if not most, recent historical documentaries containing a political edge is not only to expose and celebrate a 'forgotten' moment of social consciousness but also to map a relationship between past and present that demonstrates the continuing viability of activism in our conservative climate. *Freedom on My Mind*, in its deft emphasis on strategy and process and in its invigorating linkage of personal fulfillment with the myriad pathways to "ideas that speak to something larger than the individual," performs this task with a singular grace and intelligence.

NEW YORK POST, 6/22/94, p. 35, Bill Hoffmann

After you've gotten your action fix from "Speed," your comedy fix from "The Flintstones" and your horror fix from "Wolf," how about settling back for a power-packed dose of mind-enrichment?

It's delivered with remarkable skill in the brilliant new documentary "Freedom on My Mind."

Already a winner for best documentary at this year's Sundance Film Festival, "Freedom" begins today for a limited run at the Film Forum.

The film chronicles one of the most shameful periods of the modern-day South, that era in the early '60s when blacks, despite a federal civil rights law, were denied the most basic of human dignities.

The scene is Mississippi, where blacks couldn't vote, couldn't eat at "whites-only" restaurants, had to sit at the back of the bus and were discouraged from going to school and urged to make cotton-picking a career.

Any deviations from this behavior could result in beatings, or burnings or lynchings.

As Dr. Henry Garrett, a past president of the American Psychology Association, is seen saying emphatically echoing every redneck from Biloxi to Yazoo City:

"Like it or not, this is a European civilization, a white man's civilization and it should remain that, with the Negroes considered to be, more or less, guests."

It was this outrageous situation that planted the seeds of discontent.

They grew to such proportion that the controversial Mississippi Voter Registration Project was born, in which a thousand predominantly white college students were bused into the state to try to register blacks to vote.

The huge influx of "rabble-rousers" fueled the hatred of the Ku Klux Klan, the racist network of good ol' boy politicians and the state's "no-niggers-need-apply" mentality.

The documentary's directors, Connie Field and Marilyn Mulford, do a magnificent job of presenting their material by using one tried-and-true trick: letting it speak for itself.

Presenting nearly two hours of gripping archival footage along with the modern-day remembrances of those who were there, Field and Mulford hammer home the terrible lessons of one of the 20th century's greatest shames.

The scenes of poor black sharecroppers living in squalor in shacks that aren't fit for barnyard animals are heartbreaking.

But the film has a living breathing high to it as it beautifully describes a revolution taking place one that slowly but surely will exchange the course of American, and particularly Southern history.

Sure, the summer blockbusters are in Dolby sound and wide screen with special effects galore, but "Freedom on My Mind" has something the big boys don't have: heart and soul and one big history lesson that has never been told this well before.

NEWSDAY, 6/22/94, Part II/p. B9, Gene Seymour

Despite its conventional, ready-for-PBS trappings, "Freedom on My Mind," a documentary chronicling the epochal four-year campaign in the early 1960s to register black voters in Mississippi delivers both the intellectual rigor of sound history and the emotional rush of absorbing storytelling. Besides, any film that revives the magnificent presence of the late great activist Fannie Lou Hamer should be seen immediately.

Much of the glow in "Freedom on My Mind" is registered on the faces of those who took part in what culminated in the so-called "Freedom Summer" of 1964. In both the archival black-and-white footage and in present-day interview that make up this saga, you feel the transfiguring energy of what went on in those scary, yet exalting days when it was possible to feel, as one activist recalled, "I was in heaven—for a while."

If the movement was heaven, one didn't have to look far for the other place. Pre-1960s Mississippi is depicted by producer-directors Connie Field and Marilyn Mulford and writer-editor Michael Chandler as a nightmarish dystopia for blacks whose dehumanization was rigidly enforced by whites.

Once racial segregation was openly challenged in the courts and the streets, Mississippi's enforcement of racial hegemony became more brutal. A black farmer who tried to vote in 1961 was shot and killed by a state legislator, thus becoming the first casualty in the Mississippi Voter Registration Project, led by a remarkable Harvard mathematics student named Bob Moses. The quiet intensity of Moses, still one of the unsung heroes of the civil rights era, helped galvanize and mobilize poor black citizens and middle-class white students into a determined, nonviolent army taking siege against injustice.

All of which, and much more, is included in this film, which is likewise unsparing in its depiction of how the Lyndon Johnson-led Democratic Party sold out the insurgent Mississippi delegation, made up of Freedom Summer activists, seeking to oust the segregationist regulars from the 1964 convention.

Even with the depiction of such sorry events, it isn't disillusion you take from "Freedom on My Mind," but the afterglow of personal and collective transformation. In those days, as many in the film are moved to recall, one believed anything was possible. This sense of possibility is the most profound legacy of both Freedom Summer and the smart, moving film that tells its story 30 years later.

VILLAGE VOICE, 6/28/94, p. 59, J. Hoberman

Opening at Film Forum to mark the 30th anniversary of Freedom Summer, the feature doc *Freedom on My Mind* recounts the drama of the Mississippi Voter Registration Project with a focused intensity that's alternately sobering and exhilarated.

The civil rights movement was a real-life analogue to the ponderous biblical spectaculars with which America congratulated itself in the 1950s. If the fight against segregation provided the most clear-cut moral combat in our postwar history, Mississippi was that struggle's most dangerous arena—"a state like no other," the voiceover tells us, "a kind of little South African enclave ... the battleground for the South's last stand."

Unlike Henry Hampton's epic *Eyes on the Prize, Freedom on My Mind* is less an overview than an oral history. Abetted by some remarkable archival footage, its subjects recollect the conditions of their childhood and the transformations of their youth. The film's central presence is Bob Moses—the amazingly coolheaded and low-keyed Harlem-born Harvard graduate, who taught math at Horace Mann before relocating to Mississippi in 1961 to coordinate the Student Nonviolent Coordinating Committee. The protagonists, however, are his disciples—children of sharecroppers and domestics, a young prostitute, and the white college students whose lives were changed through their work with SNCC.

"They looked so magnificent," Curtis Hayes remembers thinking of the Freedom Riders when he saw them first on television in the early '60s. *Freedom on My Mind* is a similar source of essential imagery. White mobs scream as U.S. marshals escort a black child into a segregated school; a five-year-old cries as a beefy cop snatches the American flag out of his fist; dignified church matrons march toward a mass arrest. That the Mississippi Delta is also an appropriately primal American landscape is reinforced by the bottle-neck guitar and wailing harmonica that underscore the black-and-white newsreel footage of sultry main streets and dirt-floor shacks.

As the civil rights bill was debated in Congress, Mississippi segregationists ran amok, staging open Klan rallies and committing unpunished murders—an NAACP official shot point-blank by a white state legislator who'd known him from boyhood, Medgar Evers assassinated by a sniper ... 30 years later the perp was convicted. Blacks were unprotected in what was essentially a foreign country; Moses planned to draw more attention to Mississippi by bringing a thousand Northern college kids to help with the registration drive. (Local police armed themselves for "self defense" against 50,000 "invaders," but a secondary drama concerns the culture shock experienced by the white students and the people of Mississippi, black and white.)

Freedom Summer began with the passage of the civil rights bill—held up by the longest filibuster in American history—and the disappearance of the civil rights workers Chaney, Goodman, and Schwerner. The summer climaxed, two weeks after their bodies were discovered in a Mississippi swamp, at the Democratic Convention in Atlantic City, where, as the representative of 80,000 newly registered Mississippi voters, the Mississippi Freedom Democratic Party challenged the credentials of the state's segregated official Democrats.

Once Lyndon Johnson eliminated Robert Kennedy as a possible running mate, the MFDP provided the convention's only drama. *Freedom on My Mind* shows the optimistic MFDP delegates singing, lobbying, and camping out under pictures of the three martyrs—even displaying their burnt-out station wagon on the boardwalk. LBJ unsuccessfully tried to preempt testimony given by the indomitable Fannie Lou Hamer, then assigned Hubert Humphrey to defuse the situation. (Humphrey delegated the dirty work to his protégé Walter Mondale.) A paternalistic compromise was rejected by both delegations. The whites walked out and the MFDP staged a bitter demonstration by temporarily filling their empty seats.

The makers of *Freedom on My Mind* blame the failure to seat the MFDP for the whirlwind that followed—a montage of demos, riots, and Black Power salutes—as if the storm weren't already evident. Alabama's governor, George Wallace, had run strongly in the Wisconsin, Indiana, and Maryland primaries as the personification of white "backlash." Senator Barry Goldwater, the leading non-Southern opponent of the Civil Rights Act, was the Republican nominee; there were racial disturbances that summer in New York, Rochester, Jersey City, and Philadelphia. The failure to assimilate the MFDP presaged the schisms that would convulse the '68 and '72 Democratic conventions.

Because Freedom Summer was also an ongoing media event, *Freedom on My Mind* adds another chapter to that celluloid Boomerography that has been a distinct part of Clinton Culture. While *Maverick* was fading when Bob Moses left for Mississippi, the prime-time heyday of The *Flintstones*—presenting suburban white America as a page, pace Marx, out of prehistory—coincided with that of the civil rights movement.

Freedom on My Mind recalls the vivid images of violent injustice, the gutsy idealism of civil rights organizers, and the seemingly innocent fervor of the aroused black underclass, which reenergized the American left. It hardly seems coincidental that Connie Fields (maker of The *Life and Times of Rosie the Riveter*) and Marilyn Mulford are both veterans of Vietnam-era newsreel collectives. In more ways than one, *Freedom on My Mind* is about their roots as well.

Also reviewed in:
CHICAGO TRIBUNE, 10/28/94, Friday/p. Q, John Petrakis
NEW REPUBLIC, 6/27/94, p. 27, Stanley Kauffmann
NEW YORK TIMES, 6/22/94, p. C13, Caryn James
VARIETY, 2/14-20/94, p. 39, Emanuel Levy
WASHINGTON POST, 8/12/94, p. F7, Hal Hinson
WASHINGTON POST, 8/12/94, Weekend/p. 38, Desson Howe

FRESH

A Miramax Films release of a Lumiere Pictures presentation. *Executive Producer:* Lila Cazes. *Producer:* Lawrence Bender and Randy Ostrow. *Director:* Boaz Yakin. *Screenplay:* Boaz Yakin. *Director of Photography:* Adam Holender. *Editor:* Dorian Harris. *Music:* Stewart Copeland. *Music Editor:* Michael Dittrick. *Sound:* Michael Barosky and (music) Jeff Seitz and Joseph McGee. *Sound Editor:* Geoffrey Rubay and Curt Schulkey. *Casting:* Douglas Aiabel. *Production Designer:* Dan Leigh. *Set Decorator:* Ronald von Blomberg and Stephanie Carroll. *Sound Editor:* Geoffrey Rubay and Curt Schulkey. *Set Dresser:* Dennis Causey and Jeff Naparstek. *Special Effects:* Al Griswold and Bill Traynor. *Costumes:* Ellen Lutter. *Make-up:* Anita Gibson. *Stunt Coordinator:* Jeff Ward and Peter Bucossi. *Running time:* 115 minutes. *MPAA Rating:* Not Rated.

CAST: Sean Nelson (Fresh); Giancarlo Esposito (Esteban); Samuel L. Jackson (Sam); N'Bushe Wright (Nichole); Ron Brice (Corky); Jean LaMarre (Jake); Jose Zuniga (Lt. Perez); Luis Lantigua (Chuckie); Yul Vasquez (Chillie); Cheryl Freeman (Aunt Frances); Anthony Thomas (Red); Curtis McClarin (Darryl); Charles Malik Whitfield (Smokey); Victor Gonzalez (Herbie); Guillermo Diaz (Spike); Robert Jimenez (Salvador); Jerome Butler (James); Cortez Nance, Jr. (Reggie); Anthony Ruiz (Hector); Jacinto Taras Riddick (Enriquez); Alfi McClendon (Hilary); Natima Bradley (Rosie); Daiquan Smith (Tarleak); Jason Rodriguez (Nicholas); Mizan Ayers (Curtis); Zakee L. Howze (Mattie); Davenia McFadden (Mrs. Coleman); Iraida Polanco (Rosa Vasquez); Danielia L. Cotton (Juana); Tracy Vilar and Tonye Patano (Girls) Randy Ostrow (Mr. Cohen); Shahid Ali (Fat Freddie); Scott Nicholson (O'Toole); Matthew Faber (Long-haired Teenager); Elizabeth Rodriquez (Pregnant Woman); Lawrence Bender (Yuppie); Belinda Becker (Fiona); Mateo Gomez (Mexican); Elsie Hilario (Aida); Paul J.Q. Lee (Tommy Lee); Joseph Pentangelo (Transit Cop); Martin Shakar (Detective Abe Sharp); Christopher Scott (Devon); Terri Vargas (Chuckie's Mother).

LOS ANGELES TIMES, 8/31/94, Calendar/p. 1, Kenneth Turan

"Fresh" isn't. Glibly shocking, it would like you to think it deals with the hard realities of urban life, but in fact it uses its patina of social consciousness as a come-on for the most conventional kind of violent commercial filmmaking.

Set in the Bushwick section of Brooklyn and revolving around the life and hard times of 12-year-old Michael, Fresh to his friends, Boaz Yakin's debut film as a writer-director does have several effective acting performances, especially Sean Nelson's in the title role.

But no amount of eye-catching acting can disguise the fact that this film is a masquerade. Despite its attempt at an authentic setting, "Fresh" has more in common with earlier Yakin writing projects like the Clint Eastwood actioner "The Rookie" than with something like "Boyz N the Hood."

Initially, however, "Fresh" has a promising air to it. Fresh's encounter with a kindly Latino lady who provides chocolate chip cookies while she gets some heroin ready for him to deliver has an intriguing quality. Who is this stone-faced youngster, so sure of himself in such an unnerving world?

Perhaps because he lives with a saintly aunt and no less than 11 cousins in a crowded group home, Fresh spends much of his time out on the street working for a cross-section of drug dealers.

Esteban (Giancarlo Esposito) is the elegant local heroin connection, given to rhapsodizing about "the land of H" and talking about his work as more secure than banking. By contrast, Corky (Ron Brice) and Jake (Jean LaMarre), the crack establishment, are much more volatile and bad-tempered individuals.

All parties agree, however, that Fresh is a stand-up little guy, smart, ambitious, the very picture of responsibility. Corky speaks for the entire neighborhood when he says, "Only reason you not the man, you too ... little."

Adept at looking after himself, Fresh is, not by choice, estranged from his family. His mother is not around, his sister Nichole (N'Bushe Wright) is a heroin addict who the married Esteban is drawn to, and Fresh's father, Sam, is a story all by himself.

A speed chess wizard who (like the Laurence Fishburne character in "Searching for Bobby Fisher") hustles the unwary in Washington Square Park, Sam only meets with his son to tutor him in the game. A believer in values despite his dissolute lifestyle, Sam is given a smart and powerful presence by Samuel L. Jackson that emphasizes the ambivalent place he has in his son's life.

Sean Nelson, who has done some previous TV and theater work, holds his own with Jackson as a boy whose face gives nothing away. Esposito, Wright, Brice and LaMarre also provide vivid performances, but even early on the uncomfortable sense that things are being artificially over-amped is present.

That artificiality soon takes permanent hold when a calculated-to-shock act of random violence turns Fresh's world around and motivates him to attempt a plan of such complexity that it takes the rest of the picture just to work itself out.

Though "Fresh" wants us to believe that the boy's chess-playing skills enable him to concoct such an intricate scenario, in fact the idea is so far-fetched and unlikely that audiences will have trouble following it, let alone believing that any kid could've come up with it.

As Fresh's plan unfolds, the film's attempts at realism are revealed as no more than jive-talking window dressing. Like any exploitation film, "Fresh" turns out to want nothing more than to titillate and make us gasp, and everything authentic in the film is sacrificed toward that end.

As violent scene follows violent scene, it is possible to notice how phony even the film's painstakingly constructed macho dialogue starts to sound. And "Fresh's" willingness to use legitimate social problems as nothing more than an excuse for cheap thrills gets increasingly off-putting. Fresh and his father may be able to push those chess pieces around at breakneck speed, but audiences will want to be treated with more respect.

NEW YORK POST, 8/24/94, p. 35, Michael Medved

"Fresh" takes one of the most tired, two-dimensional subjects in contemporary films—a bleak inner-city hell dominated by charismatic, amoral drug dealers—and makes those elements remarkably compelling and, well ... fresh.

The secret is that the movie presents its brutal world through the horrified eyes of a child. The title character is a bright, quiet 12-year-old (played with understated integrity by newcomer Sean Nelson) who lives in Brooklyn with his aunt and 11 cousins.

While worrying about homework and getting to school on time, Fresh earns a few extra dollars by running errands for crack and heroin dealers in the neighborhood. One of these drug merchants is Esteban—a reptilian creep unforgettably played by Giancarlo Esposito—who hopes to adopt the kid as his protege.

At the same time, Esteban seduces the boy's adored older sister (N'Bushe Wright), a beautiful haunted junkie who's casually passed from man to man as she attempts to assure herself a steady supply of drugs.

Though many of these characters seem familiar, or even formulaic, they come across with utter conviction on screen thanks to the superb quality of the acting, where even the smallest roles are brilliantly played.

Samuel L. Jackson is especially effective as the main character's father—a troubled loner who lives in an abandoned trailer and who Fresh is forbidden to see. Nevertheless, they meet secretly, and Jackson, an obsessed master of speed chess, tries to teach his boy the game's fundamentals.

Fresh later uses those principles to devise an elaborate strategy playing off various drug dealers against one another in an effort to destroy them all.

His calculations are so brilliant, and his execution so flawless, that in its last 10 minutes the movie for the first time begins to lose credibility, though it remains intensely watchable to the end.

Cinematographer Adam Holender brings the same gritty lyricism to the film that he brought to "Midnight Cowboy" 25 years ago, and composer Stewart Copeland (formerly of the rock group the Police) provides a rich, evocative, edgy musical score that makes a major contribution to the picture's emotional impact.

Chief hero of the project, nonetheless, is its first-time director Boaz Yakin an NYU film school product who previously wrote the disappointing Clint Eastwood vehicle "The Rookie."

Here, he shapes every scene with extraordinary subtlety, handling his virtually all-black cast with such assurance and authenticity that some viewers may be shocked to learn that the writer-director is white.

Talent, however, has nothing to do with ethnicity, and Yakin has fashioned a stunning debut that's good enough to recall Truffaut's "The 400 Blows" in its heart-breaking account of an embittered childhood and the tragic loss of innocence.

NEWSDAY, 8/24/94, Part II/p. B7, John Anderson

In the winsome opening sequence to his directorial debut "Fresh," Boaz Yakin builds his Brooklyn out of thin air, on an empty plain, a house at a time, adding streets, some cars, some people, congesting his once-mythic landscape until he arrives at a borough that's the Brooklyn we know and we have to ask: What the hell happened?

You might ask the same, and will, about Fresh, the 12-year-old street hustler, drug-runner and chess player who's portrayed so heartbreakingly by young Sean Nelson. As worried about getting to school on time as about making drops and buys, he's a child/man in the failed-promise land. And he turns a natural gift for strategy into a homemade weapon to right all the wrongs in his small hard world.

Does he succeed? Does Yakin? It depends on what that means.

Fresh's brilliant scheming, which begins after he witnesses a vicious schoolyard murder, certainly succeeds in changing the film from what it had appeared to be—a street drama/character study—and into a far more conventional though thoroughly satisfying sort of caper movie. And Fresh succeeds in getting revenge on those he feels deserve it—although sacrificing a lot of the men on his metaphoric chessboard, as well as a good bit of himself.

To Yakin's credit, we get what we want out of "Fresh" without feeling exhilarated. Because there's no way it's not going to be a sad story.

Fresh lives with his 11 cousins at the home of his Aunt Frances (Cheryl Freeman), who despite her best efforts can barely keep things together. His slack-jawed older sister Nicki (N'Bushe Wright), a beautiful junkie, is juggling an abusive boyfriend, James (Jerome Butler), and the local heroin kingpin, Esteban (Giancarlo Esposito). Fresh splits his workday between the paternal Esteban, who calls smack a "gentleman's operation," and Corky (Ron Brice), the younger crack dealer who tells Fresh, "Someday, you gonnna be the man."

Fresh is sucked into none of this. He hides his swelling wad of money in a coffee can near the train tracks and spends what's left of his time hustling speed chess at a nearby park. Here, he gets to visit his father, Sam (Samuel L. Jackson), a true chess genius and vagrant whom he is forbidden to see, and learns the lessons in chess and life that will help him weave the delicate web of betrayal he uses to bring everyone down.

Yakin's city can be oddly cool, strangely aloof. We see what we're supposed to see, but it's a kid's world; we view many things the way Fresh does, as if he's watching an episode of "Cops." When reality reaches up and slaps him, the sting is doubly sharp, because the way young Nelson plays him—taciturn, slightly intolerant of stupidity, and with the accumulated indignities of his life roiling just under his skin—makes him both an intellectual hero and a warning shot.

Yakin gets solid performances out of all his actors, and not just Nelson, who's a wonder, or the reliable Esposito and Jackson, but Ron Brice, who's always good and too rarely seen, and Jean LaMarre, who as the belligerent, homicidal drug-dealer Jake provides all we need to see about where Fresh might be going, and what happens when you make all the wrong moves.

NEWSWEEK, 9/5/94, p. 69, David Ansen

"Fresh," the debut film of the talented writer-director Boaz Yakin, generated a lot of buzz at the Sundance Film Festival. This inner-city drama, set amid the drug-ravaged streets of Brooklyn, contains shocking scenes, none more so than a brutal playground shooting that claims innocent children's lives. And its title character, the 12-year-old Fresh (Sean Nelson), is certainly a disturbing protagonist. A precocious survivor, he works for crack dealers and the local heroin kingpin, Esteban (Giancarlo Esposito), a surrogate father who has a passion for Fresh's strung-out older sister (N'Bushe Wright). He's forbidden, for reasons never adequately explained, to see his own father (Samuel L. Jackson), a gifted chess hustler who has imparted to his son a keen sense of chessboard strategy.

This setup suggests that "Fresh" is a slice of violent urban realism. Not quite. As Fresh witnesses the destruction of those he loves, he decides to fight back, using his analytical chess-whiz mind. Pitting bad guy against bad guy in a disinformation campaign as elaborate as Dashiell Hammett's "Red Harvest," Fresh becomes a pint-size combo of Superfly, Bobby Fischer and Dirty Harry. Suddenly we're in an action-movie fantasy, and it's not easy to swallow. It takes nothing away from young Nelson's watchful, poised performance to say that Fresh himself is bogus. From scene to scene he's whatever the screenwriter wants him to be; by the end, he's no longer flesh and blood. Though well acted, and handsomely shot by veteran Adam ("Midnight Cowboy") Holender, "Fresh" sacrifices real emotion for thriller contrivances. It's a tourist's drive through inner-city hell.

SIGHT AND SOUND, 6/95, p. 42, Verina Glaessner

Fresh is a 12-year-old black New Yorker living with his Aunt Francis and 11 young cousins in a cramped apartment in Brooklyn. In his out-of-school hours he runs drugs, scrupulously secreting his earnings in an empty can hidden in a railway siding. He meets his father, an alcoholic and brilliant speed chess player, in Washington Square, where the elder man passes on to his son the finer points of the game, how to get the measure of his opponent and how to find his weak points.

At school, Fresh is keen on Rosie, who indulges in fantasies about her absent mother who she says is white and wealthy. Fresh is disturbed when his elder sister Nichole moves out of Aunt Francis' crowded apartment. She has developed a heroin dependency, is living with James and working the streets. She has also attracted the sexual attentions of Esteban, a heroin pusher for whom Fresh works, who is married and has two young children. Esteban sees a future for Fresh as a key player in the heroin trade—as long as he does not dabble in crack—while Sam wants him to excel at speed chess.

The sad repetitiveness of Fresh's life is given a tragic focus during a basketball game when Jake, a sidekick of cocaine dealer Corky, is tauntingly out-played by an unprepossessing kid half his size. In a flash Jake draws a gun and shoots the youngster dead. As the court instantly clears, Fresh is left as the sole witness to the fact that a stray bullet has passed through Rosie's throat. Rosie dies and at the police station, Fresh refuses to name the killer.

Fresh conceives a game plan in which Rosie's death will be avenged and Jake will get his just deserts. He begins to set up Esteban, Corky and James—with his friend Chuckie's help. He uses his own money to buy cocaine saying that the drug is for Corky. He replaces Esteban's heroin with cocaine so that Corky will be convinced that Esteban is moving into his territory. After he and Chuckie are attacked by Corky's men he convinces Corky that Jake has been dealing on his own account. Sceptical at first, Corky finally believes the boy and beats Jake to death with a chain.

James, Fresh claims, is in with Jake. He then lets Esteban fall into the trap. He takes Fresh along with two henchmen on their raid of the shop, which is virtually blown up before Fresh's eyes. Afraid of what Esteban might do to his sister, Fresh slips off and phones Lieutenant Perez telling him that Esteban is at the flat and attacking Nichole. Before the Lieutenant arrives, Fresh plants a gun and drugs on the unwary Esteban. As he is taken away Esteban realizes who has betrayed him. Perez promises Fresh and Nichole that he will find them a place of safety. Sometime later, Sam is shocked to see tears in his son's eyes as they begin their regular game.

If *Fresh*'s territory of drugs and violence in the New York black and Hispanic ghetto is familiar, the way it is approached is not. The film's tone is resolutely dark and devoid of the celebratory, cartoon-like violence or street sassiness that is endemic in Hollywood exploitations of black street culture. Fresh, the 12-year-old protagonist, is dispassionate and withdrawn. The characters with whom he interacts are grotesques of various kinds. Mercifully without 'attitude', they are shown as warped, like the fabric of the city they inhabit, and wounded by their circumstances. Deprived of language (Fresh's father apart, no one else seems to have access to a vocabulary of more than 25 words except for expletives), their minds are limited to only the most rudimentary of thought processes, so the terrified Fresh is able to run intellectual rings around his elders while putting his master plan into action. However, unlike the screen heroes whom both Jake, the frustrated basketball player, and Esteban, 'body-built' in the Van Damme mould, seem to emulate physically, these characters are not shown in quasi-heroic high relief, stripped of their social ties, but instead are depicted as part of a community.

As Fresh does his pre-school drug round he is offered those talismanic tokens of All-American suburban wholesomeness, milk and chocolate chip cookies, by a grandmotherly sort who passes him that day's stash of drugs. Esteban (a notably strong performance from Giancarlo Esposito as a character descended half from the films of Jean-Pierre Melville and half from the morally ambiguous Antonio of Shakespeare's *Measure for Measure*) thoughtfully gets his youngest child off to sleep while advising Fresh on how to become 'the man' in the heroin trade in a room which contains both an elaborate family altar and numerous crucifixes. The film's weaknesses stem from Yakin's reluctance to fight himself loose of his own slightly over-written script. Need Sam's instructions to his son over the chessboard signal the plot of the film so clearly? Need, in fact, Samuel L Jackson be handed quite such a theatrical old war-horse of a part as Fresh's father, chess genius and philosopher of the bottle? And in stopping short of the grinding pain of the father-son reconciliation that Sergei Bodrov allows his child protagonist in the similar *Freedom is Paradise*, Yakin lets his own film peter out in tears.

Time, 9/12/94, p. 86, Richard Corliss

[*Fresh* was reviewed jointly with *Clerks*; see Corliss' review of that film.]

VILLAGE VOICE, 8/30/94, p. 48, Beth Coleman

Fresh (Sean Nelson) is the young G with the cool, the little money man with the smarts and savvy to run with the big men—the base dealer, the horse jockey, and their muscled minions. This 12-year-old slides in for his first pickup before breakfast, but there are always hassles along the way, so the kid is mad late by the time he rolls in to homeroom. The difference between Fresh and the young Henry Hill is that this small hood works all sides of his education. Part *Menace II Society*, part *Searching for Bobby Fischer*, *Fresh* sits between after-school special and after-school bloodbath (it's produced by *Reservoir Dogs*'s Lawrence Bender), weighing honor among thieves against a singular strategy that would make Machiavelli weep.

Director-writer Yakin's feature debut, *Fresh* owes as much to West Coast *Boyz* as it does to Little Italy. The drug runners and pimps of this black demimonde share the particularity and paranoia of goodfellas. What they lack is the mob's family air—the weddings, the meals, the knives in the back. Yakin, by choosing a child as our scout through the burnt-out cars and bloodstained ball courts, makes it clear that this is no place to grow up. Did someone give Fresh a choice?

Fresh is offered his own dynasty, particularly persuasively by the smooth Esteban (Giancarlo Esposito), if he continues as is—down, smart, and quiet. His pops (Samuel L. Jackson), the Washington Square chess king, instructs him in a game of mastery that Fresh expands on with human pieces. All the while, the lad seems to be dreaming about a rosy household in the suburbs.

Yakin shoots New York like it's a forest. The dark alleyways and messed-up crack women are part of its topography, almost indistinct, as Fresh bustles around like a busy dwarf. Every now and then Fresh makes his escape across the river into a field where the weeds and empty train tracks have never looked so much like a playland for lost boys. Markedly, Fresh never, ever gets to play. Without any pleasure, some smiles from the hardworking little G, he's more equipped for an action film where the heroes are self-winding.

The music (by Stewart Copeland), a gliding, Ry Cooder-esque groove, underscores a time-lapse opening where clean buildings get crowded with graffiti and garbage as the day grows hotter. Not to have a hip hop-driven soundtrack for a film about black, urban, criminal lives upends certain expectations as it raises other questions. A white director, Yakin steps unabashedly into Spike Lee territory, leaving his own mark. Visually, *Fresh* is often startling and lofty (through the slatted light shifting across the ceiling we know the train is running past Fresh's window. The train is part of the boy's dream, as he is part of the train—a little nut, a cog in the wheels of the city's machine). The artful distance from which it's shot works at cross-purposes with the earnestness and eagerness of its involved story. The results are surprisingly chilling—way past cool into frigid.

When Fresh finally breaks he is already more than monstrous, trying to do the right thing and all, making the film a disturbing allegory on goodness. *Fresh* stretches the genre—the morbid and melancholy urban black boy's movie—but Yakin's passion for the material doesn't match the filmic nuance and moral spin he brings to it.

Also reviewed in:
NEW YORK TIMES, 8/24/94, p. C13, Janet Maslin
NEW YORKER, 9/12/94, p. 98, Anthony Lane
VARIETY, 2/7-13/94, p. 38, Todd McCarthy
WASHINGTON POST, 8/31/94, p. C1, Hal Hinson
WASHINGTON POST, 9/2/94, Weekend/p. 38, Desson Howe

FROSH: NINE MONTHS IN A FRESHMAN DORM

A Horizon Unlimited release of a Geller/Goldfine procuction. *Producer:* Daniel Geller. *Director:* Daniel Geller and Dayna Goldfine. *Director of Photography:* Daniel Geller and Dayna Goldfine. *Editor:* Dayna Goldfine, Daniel Geller, and Deborah Hoffman. *Music:* Don Hunter. *Sound:* Stuart Dubey and (music) Stuart Dubey. *Running time:* 99 minutes. *MPAA Rating:* Not Rated.

LOS ANGELES TIMES, 4/28/94, Calendar/p. 2, Kevin Thomas

In an era when we're constantly bombarded with messages of despair, Daniel Geller and Dayna Goldfine's "Frosh: Nine Months in a Freshman Dorm" offers real hope. The bright, reflective young people who are living in Stanford's Trancos dorm—it is the 1990-91 academic year—are caring, inquiring individuals who mature before our very eyes. This wonderfully refreshing film, full of humor and compassion, leaves us with the feeling that if there are sufficient numbers of such people, this country may just continue to survive, maybe thrive.

For most anyone who ever was a college freshman, the film has an irresistible nostalgic pull. Some things don't change, after all: the tug of bidding parents goodby; the adjustment to a new and challenging environment; the forging of friendships, some of which may last a lifetime, the bull sessions; the high jinks amid hard study; the struggle to maintain emotional equilibrium.

Freshman year is the best of times, the worst of times, but you can't help but feel how much better, how much richer an experience it is for these young people than it was for those of us who underwent it decades ago.

Trancos is not only co-ed—40 men, 40 women—but strongly multiethnic, with many African Americans and Asian Americans (but, oddly, few Latinos). How good it is for young people from all over the country and from widely differing backgrounds to get to know one another, how good it is, in this era of paranoia between the sexes, for men and women to get to know one another by living in the same building and sharing the same facilities.

Ironics abound. The highly intelligent and mature Brandi, an African American, admits she grew up in an upper-middle-class neighborhood so white that she didn't have any black friends. It's Brandi, however, who's supportive of Monique, a black woman from Oakland, born out of wedlock to a woman who is now addicted to crack. Monique is every bit as smart and competent as Brandi but lacks Brandi's confidence and feels so out of place she threatens to drop out.

Other students we get to know are Shayne, who finds her views increasingly in conflict with the rigid doctrines of her Catholic upbringing; Debbie, who is an outspoken feminist; Cheng, who discovers Stanford to be academically tougher than he expected; and Sam, who is as close to being average or ordinary as these young people get. Significantly, he's the most thrilled to be accepted by a fraternity, admitting frankly to his need to be liked.

We find ourselves hating to bid farewell to these young people and cannot help but wonder what has become of them, especially Monique, We'll eventually get our chance to find out, for the filmmakers are at work on a sequel, centering on the graduation of this class this year.

NEW YORK POST, 10/5/94, p. 33, Thelma Adams

Holy multiculturalism! Alumni Dan Geller and Dayna Goldfine returned to Stanford University with their cameras and all but showered with a group of mixed-race, coed, randomly bisexual students over a school year. Their documentary—"Frosh: Nine Months in a Freshman Dorm"—isn't pregnant with insight.

The crises are few. No one drops out, commits or suffers date rape, gets caught in a drug deal gone bad, or crashes their BMW. A student agonizing over switching to feminist studies from pre-med is no great drama.

On the other hand, the painful generalizations are many. As the clean-cut kids discuss politics, sex and God before dining on London broil in the cafeteria, they offer such nuggets as:

"John Stuart Mill—my messiah," and "Aristotle is always wrong."

The discussion is all pretty tepid p.c. chatter. It's much more fun to be a freshman—living the life on Mom and Dad's money—than to listen to one.

VILLAGE VOICE, 10/11/94, p. 74, Jason Vincz

The readiest recollections of freshman year are often the most pathetic, That time comes back to me as a buzzing cloud of dread: I was asphyxiatingly afraid of social missteps, paralyzed in the presence of my professors (who now look like pretty mundane fellows) and guilty of mumbled clods of text with theses like "Socrates Was Wise" and "Salinger Is Good." It's a pretty dreary time to recall.

But to relive it, as Dan Geller and Dayna Goldfine would have us do, with the help of a good-natured group of Stanford frosh, is a different and more pleasant story. Geller and Goldfine spent the 1990-91 school year in Stanford's Trancos Hall, recording the lives of a smilingly, diverse bunch of students. This cross-cultural gang includes, among others, a sensitive future fratboy, a beachy blond bisexual, a bourgeois Afro-Hoosier whose black friends accuse her of acting white, an Oakland homegirl with a crack-addicted mother, and a Chinese-Ohioan boy who calls John Stuart Mill "my messiah."

With such a rainbow swirl of humanity to portray, *Frosh*'s biggest problem is mathematical: 10 individuals, times nine months of self-discovery, equals a lot more than 90 minutes of Super-8 footage. Still, Geller and Goldfine pack in most of the personal grapplings and psychological struggles that confront the young and bespectacled. They read, they write, they bitch, they moan, they question other people's moral convictions, as well as their own, they find their way to kegs (and bongs), and all the while lament the existence of other prodigies. "I'm sick of all these people being smarter than me," says one. *Smarter than I*, he means. Most everyone already knew about sex, however some struggle with the fact that (surprise!) not all of it is the hetero-kind.

Geller and Goldfine won't win any technical awards—blindingly bright windows and invisibly dark subjects seem not to faze our intrepid camera-persons, and the synthetic soundtrack grates—but they do capture the giddy anxieties and laughter of rookie scholars. If *Frosh* has you cringing in empathetic embarrassment, it's still a charming document of thoughtful youth, and a time when brains are small, but rapidly expanding.

Also reviewed in:
NEW YORK TIMES, 10/5/94, p. C18, Caryn James
VARIETY, 1/17-23/94, p. 106, Dennis Harvey
WASHINGTON POST, 9/23/94, p. F7, Hal Hinson

GERMINAL

A Sony Pictures Classics release of a Renn Productions/France 2 Cinema/DD Productions/Alternative Films/Nuova Artisti Associati production with the participation of Nord-Pas-de-Calais Region/Ministère de la Culture et de la Francophonie Centre National de la Cinématographie/Ministère de l'Education Nationale/Sofiarp/Investimage2/Canal+/Groupe Pinault. *Executive Producer:* Pierre Grunstein. *Producer:* Claude Berri. *Director:* Claude Berri.

Screenplay (French with English subtitles): Claude Berri and Arlette Langmann. *Based on the book by:* Emile Zola. *Director of Photography:* Yves Angelo. *Editor:* Hervé de Luze. *Music:* Jean-Louis Roques. *Choreographer:* Nicole Deshayes. *Sound:* Pierre Gamet and Dominique Hennequin. *Sound Editor:* Michel Kochendler. *Casting:* Gérard Moulevrier. *Production Designer:* Thanh At Hoang and Christian Marti. *Special Effects:* Jean-Pierre Maricourt, Philippe Sylvain, and Christophe Messaoudi. *Costumes:* Sylvie Gautrelet, Caroline De Vivaise, and Bernadette Villard. *Make-up:* Joël Lavau and Nathalie Louichon. *Running time:* 158 minutes. *MPAA Rating:* R.

CAST: Renaud (Etienne Lantier); Gérard Depardieu (Maheu); Miou-Miou (Maheude); Jean Carmet (Bonnemort); Judith Henry (Catherine Maheu); Jean-Roger Milo (Chaval); Laurent Terzieff (Souvarine); Jean-Pierre Bisson (Rasseneur); Bernard Fresson (Deneulin); Jacques Dacqmine (M. Hennebeau); Anny Duperey (Mme. Hennebeau); Pierre Lafont (M. Grégoire); Annik Alane (Mme. Grégoire); Frédéric Van Den Driessche (Paul Négrel); Gérard Croce (Maigrat); Thierry Levaret (Zacharie Maheu); Albano Guaetta (Jeanlin Maheu); Séverine Huon (Alzire Maheu); Jessica Sueur (Lénore Maheu); Mathieu Mathez (Henri Maheu); Alexandre Lekieffre (Maxime); Yolande Moreau (La Levaque); Georges Staquet (Levaque); Sabrina Deladeriere (Philomène); Maximilien Regiani (Pierron); Joel Petit (Bébert); Anne-Marie Pisani (La Mouquette); André Julien (Mouque); Yvette Petit (La Veuve Désir); Solenn Jarniou (Mme Rasseneur); Fred Personne (Pluchart); Cécile Bois (Cécile Grégoire); Delphine Quentin (Lucie Deneulin); Alexandrine Loeb (Jeanne Deneulin); Fred Ulysse (Dansaert); Frédérique Ruchaud (Honorine); Maryse Moutier (Mélanie); Jenny Clève (Rose); Nathalie Hequet (Amélie); Bruno Tuchszer (Capitaine des Gardes); Fernand Kindt (Secrétaire de la Cie); Andre Chaumeau (Caissier de la Cie); Philippe Desboeuf (Le Docteur).

CHRISTIAN SCIENCE MONITOR, 3/11/94, p. 14, David Sterritt

The ambitions of French filmmaker Claude Berri have grown more sweeping in recent years. In earlier movies such as "One Wild Moment" and "The Two of Us," he told straightforward stories that retained their modest dimensions while showing unexpected depths of meaning and emotion. In his most widely celebrated films of the mid-1980s, however, he took a different approach—spreading the tales of "Jean de Florette" and "Manon of the Spring" over several hours of screen time, allowing audiences to feel like inhabitants of their worlds rather than mere observers of their characters and plots.

Berri's latest film, "Germinal," returns to this expansive narrative approach. Closely based on the muckraking French novel published by Émile Zola in 1885, it takes considerable time to spin out its tale, incorporating a wide range of incidents and unfolding its sense of time, place, and atmosphere with a multitude of carefully wrought details.

The film is exemplary in its historical awareness and its concern for inequities of wealth and opportunity in a nation that could afford much better if it cared to try.

There's a lurking contradiction, though, in its insistence on making social and political points through traditional Hollywood-style spectacle. One wonders if Berri ever noticed the paradox at the heart of his project: It champions the anonymous masses over the privileged elite, but it does this through old-fashioned movie formulas, complete with swarming crowds of anonymous extras who serve as backdrops for the luminous movie stars in the leading roles.

To its credit, the screenplay by Berri and Arlette Langmann takes reasonable care not to sentimentalize the poor or demonize the rich in ways not justified by the historical facts as conveyed through Zola's novel. The book uses conventions of 19th-century naturalism and scientific analysis in chronicling a violent conflict between oppressed coal miners and the pit owners.

To a degree, all the individuals involved in the story are seen as products of the mining and manufacturing system, which rewards one kind of risk (financial investment) with profits and privileges while pushing another kind of risk (labor in the mines) with relentless danger, physical damage, and psychological decay.

True to the French Revolution that helped form them, the exploited masses are as capable of horrific excess as the wealthy capitalists they're driven to oppose; and the bosses often seem more insensitive and unthinking than evil or brutal. Still, it's always clear where Berri's sympathies lie, and there's no questioning his basic stance in favor of the toiling workers and against the system.

The shortcoming that dogs "Germinal" despite its dramatic authenticity and sometimes powerful acting is rooted not in its ideas but in its cinematic style. While this isn't slick or glossy, it's always calculated to glean maximum impact from the photogenic presences of the stars and the eye-beguiling detail of their historically correct surroundings. Zola's novel is intensely critical of abuses in 19th-century capitalism.

Yet the film version of "Germinal" mirrors some of that system's core values—most notably a glorification of wealth, reflected by the movie's expensive production and an obsession with individual heroics.

In sum, Berri's film is easy to enjoy as a saga of underdogs against fat-cats; but one looks in vain for more incisive social or historical analysis, and one finds little sense that its interests are rooted in the imperfect present as well as the troubled past.

As so often happens, Gérard Depardieu—as Maheu, a foreman in the mines—manages to dominate much of the film even though others have more time on the screen. The same goes for his female counterpart Miou-Miou, as Maheu's long-suffering wife.

The folk singer known as Renaud makes a strong impression in his first movie role, playing Etienne, a newcomer to the mines who becomes an activist on behalf of the workers cause. Laurent Terzieff gives a standout performance as Souvarine, a glowering anarchist so radical the he thinks the local Marxists are a bunch of right-wing wimps.

"Germinal" was filmed in the northern French region of Lille, an appropriate location with a history of mining activity; about 800 inhabitants of the area were employed as extras and much of the action was shot in an actual mining village rebuilt for this production.

The set was designed by Thanh At Hoang and Christian Marti, and Yves Angelo did the sumptuous cinematography.

LOS ANGELES TIMES, 12/14/93, Calendar/p. 4, Kevin Thomas

Claude Berri's soaring, magnificent film of Emile Zola's "Germinal" cuts right to the movies' unique, paradoxical power of rendering human misery at its most unrelenting with images of surpassing grandeur and meaning. Pictures don't get much bleaker than this 158-minute epic saga of the grinding existence of 19th-Century French coal miners—but they don't get much more beautiful either.

Berri and his formidable yet understated cinematographer, Yves Angelo, aided by Jean-Louis Roque's subtle yet stirring score, bring a unifying, majestic lyricism to their contrasting views of the few ultra-rich and the many desperately poor. "Germinal," France's official entry in the Oscars glows with the humanism and passion for authenticity that were Zola's hallmarks, and is a worthy successor to Berri's similarly powerful "Jean de Florette" and "Manon of the Spring."

The story is set roughly a century ago, but it's actually unfolding, with varying degrees of severity, around the world right now. As a leader in the international Naturalist literary movement, Zola believed that the destinies of most people, especially the poor, were dictated—and usually harshly—by environment.

In any event, the Maheu family and their friends and neighbors, who labor mightily at the Voreux pit in Northern France, could scarcely be more trapped. Times are bad, which means that the miners must concentrate on loading their carts as fully and as often as possible at the expense of properly securing the mine's tunnels with timber; if they complain, they risk losing all payment for timbering.

Maheu (Gerard Depardieu) and his wife, Maheude (Miou-Miou), have seven children, more than they can support, but doubtlessly religion—and quite possibly ignorance as well—have made birth control out of the question. Besides, as the community's resident anarchist (Laurent Terzieff, who bears more than a passing resemblance to Lenin) remarks. "Capitalism allows workers only to eat dry bread and make babies."

But now pay cuts threaten to take away the bread and to starve the babies. A quiet, reasonable man, Maheu, a foreman, emerges as the leader of a strike movement after management has refused his modest plea for enough pay to provide daily bread.

What keeps cuts between the Maheu's barren table and that of the mine's managing director (Jacques Dacqmine) with its elaborate, abundant fare from seeming heavy-handed is that

Zola—and Berri—are able to perceive that the haves are actually vulnerable to the same economic system as the have-nots.

Zola may have had a passion for social reform, but thankfully it is tempered by a healthy pessimism that keeps it from seeming like self-righteous ax-grinding. "Germinal," which has too profound a vision of life to be a mere message movie, is no Marxist tract—just a simple urging for the privileged to share more generously with the needy, i.e., you shouldn't be eating brioche when your workers can't afford bread.

In an actual abandoned mining community, restored for the film down to the last detail, Berri has gathered a large and superb ensemble cast that includes Jean Carmet as the Maheu grandfather stricken with black lung. Judith Henry as their grown daughter and Jean-Roger Milo as her hot-tempered, homely suitor.

Triggered by the arrival of the idealistic, dangerously naive, labor-organizing machinist Etienne Lantier (Renaud), the plight of the Maheus and everyone else at Voreux goes from bad to the unspeakably worse, culminating in multiple tragedies characteristic of ancient Greek drama.

Since "Germinal" is "so determinedly grim and the socioeconomic ills and injustices it depicts so depressingly familiar, one might well ask why one should submit to it—and submission, make no mistake about it, is precisely what is required. The answer is that we can see ourselves in the film's people and be moved by their plight, buoyed by their warm, earthy spirit and thrilled by how vividly Berri has brought the past back to life. "Germinal" offers only the most tentative note of hope, but that it was made in the first place is in itself an affirmation.

NEW STATESMAN & SOCIETY, 5/6/94, p. 33, Jonathan Romney

Emile Zola's *Germinal* is one of the few great novels to be remembered not its opening sentences, but for its ending. As its hero, Etienne Lantier, trudges away from the defeated mining community of Montsou, he hears the sounds of the miners hammering away beneath the countryside. The very earth is thick with the sound, quite literally pregnant (*grosse*) with it. Lantier is aware of "a black avenging host ... slowly germinating in the furrows, thrusting upwards for the harvests of future ages. And very soon the germination would crack the earth asunder."

It's a marvellous, millenarian vision, a flourish of apocalyptic triumphalism to redeem the day after a seemingly unmitigated defeat. The excessive imagery makes perfect sense in what is only nominally a naturalist novel, partly because of the book's chthonic theme, which belongs to Zola's discourse of cyclical renewal—a discourse as much cosmological as political. But it makes sense in historical terms too. The rising socialism that motors *Germinal*'s conflicts may meet a temporary defeat, but it was bound to make a spectacular comeback.

The ending, of course, makes *Germinal* perfect material for cinema, a form we tend to see in terms of endings rather than beginnings. (We don't think of cowboys riding out of the sunset.) Zola's last line alone makes the book a movie; it's up there with "Forget it, Jake, it's Chinatown" and "Nobody's perfect". Director-producer Claude Berri surely thought this, and his respectful film still has the subtext that we're watching *Germinal* as it was always meant to be: if Zola were alive today, he'd be mounting 160-million-franc epics.

Zola's ending, which is Berri's too, ought to have acquired a powerful ironic thrust after 110 years' hindsight. With the notion of popular revolt soured and a massive miners' defeat still echoing across the Channel, Berri's film ought to carry a resonance of the embittered optimism that Zola's ending now suggests. But we're not in 1994 here; the film wants us to imagine that we're still in 1885, when the novel was published.

Historical distance lends it a frisson of nostalgic poignancy—the nostalgia being for a particular myth of French community that owes as much to Jean Renoir and Marcel Carné's crowds as it does to 1968, the Popular Front or the Commune. But this nostalgia itself enforces the illusion that we're getting the original novel unmediated; the historical distance is meant to remain invisible.

I enjoyed *Germinal* thoroughly, but that's not the point. It's the cinematic equivalent of a good read and mercifully free of the softness you associate with Berri. He has come to represent in French cinema as much of a knee-jerk bogeyman as Merchant and Ivory do in Britain, for the marshmallow ruralism of his *Jean de Florette* diptych and his production of Jean-Jacques

Annaud's cretinous *The Lover*. The late, great French critic Serge Daney would periodically greet a film as the harbinger of the death of cinema; more than once, it was one of Berri's.

Germinal's spectacle is far from glutinous prettification, but it's certainly a prime example of the literalist cinema that deadens imagination. It's what Daney, by analogy with "filmed theatre", used to call "filmed cinema". The celluloid simply captures what's imagined to be already there in the text and the *mise en scène*. It's a cinema of transparency that takes the materials provided—text, sets, actors—as a template for what we see, as if the minds of film-makers and viewers alike were exempt from doing any work. Hence *Germinal* is exactly as you picture a film of the novel to be. What we admire is the thoroughness of the research, the smoothness with which it has seemingly been decanted straight into the frame.

Among the actors, Berri resorts to what they call *valeurs sûres*—safe institutions who bring their own connotations to the parts they play. As the mining couple, Maheu and Maheude, we have Gérard Depardieu and Miou-Miou; he a national economic resource and a landmark as unshakeable as the Eiffel Tower, she a long-standing icon of intransigent feminist toughness. As Lantier, the observing catalyst, there's the singer Renaud: a much-loved post-1968 non-conformist. The gargantuan *bon viveur* Depardieu doesn't convince for a moment as an impoverished miner, but they all emote their butts off.

A lesser-known name—Jean-Roger Milo, playing the treacherous slob Chaval—is the only figure who quite catches the volatility of Zola's melodrama. Gargling, twitching and rolling his eyes like some crazed Pulchinello, he has a touch of that great slippery Renoir villain Jules Berry. Of course, the performance goes wildly against the grain of the film—that's why *Germinal* needs it so much.

Otherwise, everything is too easy. *Germinal* guides us around its horrors without making us experience any discomfort. When it takes us down the mine, we feel the rush we might on a virtual-reality theme ride—but we don't land anywhere really grim. The tunnels are filled not with tangible darkness, but a sort of impoverished daylight. Berri makes it easy for us to see what's going on. We're never left without a guide.

Zola is similarly scrupulous, but you'd think Berri would be interested in giving us a late 20th-century perspective on 19th-century narrative. As the wary mine owner, faced with a strike, learns he has been cuckolded, he sighs and mutters "You think bread is enough?". Berri sees this as simple poignancy; he seems unable to read it as melodrama and to take that as his starting point. He wants us to experience such moments as if Zola had never written them first.

This one-dimensionality makes *Germinal* a formidable national monument, but not much cop as a film. Joao Botelho's modern-day Portuguese *Hard Times* (1988) showed how displacement and anachronism could amplify a classic text. Even Christine Edzard's conservative two-part *Little Dorrit* played off knowingly against the familiar tradition of tea-time TV Dickens. *Germinal* simply invokes a great literary and cinematic "academy" and bids us nod respectfully. This is back-to-basics cinema *par excellence*.

A key piece in France's recent Gatt-inspired debate about the future of European cinema, *Germinal* was seen as a national leviathan sent to do battle with *Jurassic Park*. It too aspired to revive dinosaurs—French cinema, and mining too, or at least a memory of it. But it's far more saurian and lumbering than Spielberg's sleek DNA beast. The future of a rational cinema isn't to be found in invoking the "universal" or the "civilised", nor in reimagining cinema as if it merely superseded literature. *Germinal* may not be the end of cinema, as Daney might have seen it, but it's certainly a dead end.

NEW YORK POST, 3/11/94, p. 45, Michael Medved

"Germinal" opens in pre-dawn darkness, with coal mines belching flame into the chilly air and weary miners changing shifts like streams of worker ants. A stranger wanders onto the other-worldly scene, searching for warmth and employment, and we soon explore this nightmarish reality through his eyes.

It's the north of France in the 1880s, and the newcomer (played by popular French social protest singer Renaud) brings with him radical ideas that ultimately lead to a life-and-death struggle between the workers and their bosses.

As dry and distant as this material may seem, director Claude Berri ("Jean de Florette" and "Manon of the Spring") presents it with a passionate intensity that is altogether riveting.

In the manner of "Schindler's List" visual and dramatic artistry combine to create a series of scenes that are simultaneously cruel and beautiful.

The story line follows the Emile Zola novel that inspired the film, focusing on the tribulations and tragedies of one miner's family. Gerard Depardieu (who else?) plays the head of this hard-working clan, which consists of seven children and a wheezing grandfather (Jean Carmet) whose lungs have been ruined by 50 years of toiling below ground.

In order to bring in a few extra sous, Depardieu and his long-suffering wife (Miou-Miou) welcome the idealistic stranger (Renaud) as a lodger in their already crowded hut. He inevitably develops an interest in their soulful-eyed oldest daughter (Judith Henry), who is regularly abused by her drunken and loutish lover (Jean-Roger Milo).

The personal concerns of all characters fade into insignificance, however, when the mine's management, facing increased competition, asks the workers to accept more dangerous conditions together with lower pay.

The bitter strike that follows brings unexpected consequences for all the principals, forcing the hearty, good-natured Depardieu into an unlikely (and dangerous) position of leadership.

Director Berri clearly intended "Germinal" as a timeless anti-capitalist statement—a special irony in view of the movie's reported status as the most expensive and lavish French film ever made. Berri is, however, too fine an artist—as was Emile Zola—to allow this story to degenerate to the level of brightly colored two-dimensional left-wing poster art.

The members of the ruling class that we meet in the course of the film may be shallow and short-sighted, but they are never vicious; "Germinal" emphasizes the vulnerability and insecurity they share with their workers.

Moreover the agitators and revolutionaries who influence the miners are hardly storybook heroes, and their activism brings disastrous results to each of the major characters.

Some members of the movie audience may grow vaguely nostalgic over the righteous simplicity of the strikers in their struggle but Berri's stunningly detailed, utterly convincing evocation of daily life for the 19th-century working class will make most viewers feel gratitude (and wonder) at the distance the western world has traveled in the last 100 years.

Released in Los Angeles in December for Oscar consideration, "Germinal" has already appeared on my "10 Best" list for '93. Now that it's finally making its way to New York, many more moviegoers will come to share my astonishment that this spell-binding epic failed to receive the Academy Award foreign-language nomination it so obviously deserved.

NEWSDAY, 3/11/94, Part II/p. 79, Jack Mathews

For their adaptation of "Germinal," Emile Zola's ambitious novel about class warfare in a 19th-century coal-mining community, director Claude Berri and co-writer Arlette Langmann seemed determined to leave no character or nuance unexplained, and through their own ambition, condemned themselves to a certain degree of failure.

Even in a film that runs more than two and a half hours, it is impossible to retell a novel in every detail, particularly one as specific to a time and place and social condition as "Germinal." In their attempt, they've turned one entire level of the story—that of the ruling class—into a shallow stream of "arrogant rich" cliches.

Still, "Germinal" is as noble a failure as you're apt to see. Berri, director of the magnificent adaptations of Marcel Pagnol's "Jean de Florette" and "Manon of the Spring," shares Zola's passion for the working poor and, let's face it, before the labor movement got up to speed, the lords of industry were often the worst sort of villains.

Zola studied the class conflicts that led to a massive strike of French coal miners in 1884, and used that material in writing "Germinal." The epic tale is built around two families, the hard-pressed Maheus, three generations of miners sharing a two-room cottage in a company-owned compound, and the wealthy Gregoires, who own and operate the mine.

Berri brings absolutely no life to the Gregoires. But when he's focused on the Maheus and the problems of the miners, "Germinal" approaches the intensity and power of John Ford's "The Grapes of Wrath."

Gerard Depardieu, when he isn't trying to become a Hollywood leading man, is a great character actor, and as the head of the Maheu clan, he seems to have crawled right out of a coal mine. Maheu is a simple man leading a complicated life, trying to be a good father, husband and worker, but faced with the growingly difficult task of surviving.

There's a recession in the coal industry, and to make up for lost profits, the owners of the mines are cutting the miners' already low pay and deducting fines for their mistakes. Unable to earn enough even for food, the miners' families are forced to go begging, while the workers themselves ignore safety procedures to haul out more coal each day.

When the organizer Etienne (Renaud) has accumulated what he thinks is an adequate strike fund, and after one of Maheu's sons is seriously injured in a mine accident, the workers walk off their jobs, pushing over the first domino in what management fears is the beginning of a nationwide strike.

After a long, sometimes tedious first half, "Germinal" sets a blistering second-half pace. Berri used the first section to introduce his large cast of characters and their intricate relationships, and the second to show us what becomes of them in the ensuing labor battle.

It is melodrama of tragic proportions, with accidental deaths, murders, riots and workers pitted against the militia with management looking on from a distance. The realism of the coal community, of the lives of the miners, is almost suffocating. Every performance, at least among those actors playing coal miners, is exceptional.

"Germinal" is not an easy movie to watch, nor at times is it easy to follow. There are so many characters and subplots, so much greasepaint and roaring of crowds, that it's hard to keep track of who's who.

Berri might have condensed the coal miners' world and devoted more time to developing their opposition. There is no way to mitigate the actions of the mine operators, but as Zola knew, and demonstrated to his readers, those characters were not tyrants in the eyes of anyone other than the workers they tyrannized. They were simply management.

For today's movie audiences, they come off in "Germinal" as monsters, unsympathetic and inhuman, and their artificiality diminishes an otherwise brilliant piece of work.

SIGHT AND SOUND, 5/94, p. 43, Keith Reader

Northern France, during the Second Empire. Etienne Lantier, a machinist, seeks work at the immense Voreux coal mine, and is taken on in place of a woman miner who has just died. His team leader is Maheu, the father of seven children who all work (or will work) in the pit. His wife Maheude asks for food and clothing from the wealthy Grégoire family, the mine's principal shareholders, whose daughter Cécile is to be married to Négrel, the nephew of Hennebeau, the mining company's general manager. The family give Maheude clothing but refuse her food, forcing her to extend her credit with the sexually blackmailing shopkeeper Maigrat.

Etienne, a self-taught socialist, is horrified at the conditions in which the miners live and work. These threaten to become even worse when management, after an accident, talk of imposing a change in the method of calculating workers' pay. Etienne finds himself attracted to the Maheus' daughter, Catherine, who is also being courted by the boorish Chaval; this attraction increases when Etienne moves in with the family. He sets about organising a strike fund, and shortly afterwards the workers, at a mass meeting, decide to go on strike. Hennebeau refuses to negotiate with them, agonised by his discovery that his wife has been having an affair with Négrel.

The nearby Jean-Bart mine is still working, and Catherine joins Chaval (with whom she is now living) in working there, to the disgust of her family. Men and women alike march on the scab pit, which is shut down when Maheu opens the steam valves that provide its power; his daughter and her lover are among the miners who climb out and run the gauntlet of their old workmates. Maigrat climbs onto his roof for safety, falls to his death, and is jubilantly castrated by the women.

When the miners march on the Voreux, they are met by soldiers who open fire at random, killing among others Maheu and the young woman miner Mouquette. The strike is taking its toll and talk begins of a return to work. Etienne's Russian anarchist friend Souvarine warns him against going back down the pit, but, prompted by tender feelings for Catherine, who has been thrown out by Chaval, he joins her in a return to work. Souvarine has sabotaged the mine, which is flooded; Catherine, Etienne and Chaval are trapped underground together, and Etienne kills his rival in a fight. Catherine dies in his arms, not before their true feelings for each other have been recognised.

Meanwhile, Maheu's father, the old, now retired and almost catatonic miner Bonnemort, has strangled Cécile who has come on a charity visit. Etienne is rescued from the pit, and finds Maheude—the staunchest of the strikers—getting ready to go back to work. She wishes him well; he leaves in the April sunshine, reflecting on how seeds are growing underground which will grow stronger and flourish like the miners' struggles to secure a better life and a more just society.

Germinal is inescapably a film of its time, because of the period setting rather than in spite of it. The most expensive French film ever (with a budget of more than 160 million francs, and a set that took seven months to build on location near Valenciennes), it stands—and will, I suspect, do so increasingly with time—as a monument to the end of the Mitterrand years and the vicissitudes, in France and worldwide, of socialism during that period. Gérard Depardieu is a well-known admirer of the President, who earned much criticism for making a special journey to Lille for the film's premiere on board a high-speed train on which a fabulously expensive champagne buffet was served. The film was excoriated by Gérard Lefort in *Libération*—erstwhile Maoist broadsheet, now effectively the house daily of the designer social-democratic Left in France—for its "Soviet hue" and theme-park presentation of the working class, whose very textural realism he sees as confining it to an unthreateningly distant past.

This reviewer was not so sure; a year (more or less) to the day before seeing *Germinal* for the first time in Paris, I had been marching through London in support of real-life British miners, and my first response on seeing the film was that for them at least it had come just too late. Claude Berri has given us a lavish socialist-realist canvas, taking over aesthetically where the French Left has come to a halt politically, so that the film in a sense enacts the eclipsing of the more narrowly political by the cultural that has been a major legacy of the Mitterrand years. He remains faithful to the extraordinary visual richness of Zola's text, though inevitably the bi-gendered charge of the Voreux pit, at once phallic and castratory, loses in 'translation' (Maheu's assertion that he "loves his pit" hardly does as a replacement). It is also puzzling that Berri chose to bowdlerise the sequence in which Mouquette 'moons' the soldiery by having her keep on her bloomers— the more so as the film has a self-consciously painterly quality that often evokes artists of the bawdy, such as Breughel, Rembrandt, Caravaggio, Monet are all likewise at different times brought to mind, notably in the 'set-pieces' of the Voreux, whose epic sweep is at the opposite pole to, say, Godard's alienatory and deconstructionist use of painting.

Budget and spectacle rather over-shadow the performances. The singer Renaud seems somewhat overawed in his first screen role, while Depardieu is exactly as one might have expected (unless one had taken note of Zola's description of Maheu as "*petit*" surely the film's major departure from the literary text). The women, on the whole, upstage the men; Judith Henry, hitherto unknown to British audiences, carries a convincing (and disturbing) undernourished sensuality as Catherine, and Miou-Miou's Maheude—compared by the actress herself to Mother Courage—may well be the performance of her career. Jean-Roger Milo, finally, gives Chaval a savage, almost deranged sneering quality reminiscent of Robert Le Vigan, who played the suicidal painter in Carné's *Quai des Brumes* and the actor in Renoir's *Les Bas-Fonds* before fleeing France for his life at the Liberation. Chaval's 'collaboration' with the employers thus acquires troublingly wider overtones.

Germinal, then, succeeds where the French Communist Party has failed (*mutatis mutandis*, the same might be said for *Les Visiteurs* and Eurodisney). Even for audiences unfamiliar with current developments in France, however, it offers a full-blooded committed spectacle unlike anything in British cinema, and for that alone deserves to do well.

TIME, 4/4/94, p. 80, Richard Corliss

The quality merchandise label is stamped all over *Germinal.* Gérard Depardieu, who heads the film's huge cast is the one French actor with worldwide heft and clout. Director Claude Berri is among France's toniest auteurs and producers. Now he and Gerard Brach have adapted Emile Zola's sprawling indictment of a novel. The result is dispiriting: a minor work on a huge canvas.

For 160 claustrophobic minutes, Berri locks viewers inside Zola's 19th century coal mines, where death by cave-in seems only slightly worse than the 12-hour-a-day life sentences that are the miners' jobs. Aboveground too, everything seems a dark metaphor for exploitation. Sex, marriage, even motherhood are tainted by capitalist precepts: a woman's basic job is to keep the workers sated and breed more of them.

In this determinist bleakness, where is the lamplight of hope? In a union of the workers against the bosses? Dream on. The miners endure such harsh lives that when they start a strike, they must brutalize the workers who oppose it. The workers have lost the victim's halo; now their hands will be soiled by blood as well as coal dust.

Excepting a few scenes of adulterous frivol among the ruling class, the film is remarkably fair-minded in doling out bad hands to workers and bosses. But because the theme is that the Industrial Revolution ground human beings into human beasts, Berri can't explore the very individual perfidy that was at the heart of *Jean de Florette*. *Germinal*, with its climactic mine disaster and bitter lamentations, is finally buried in its fidelity to its source.

VILLAGE VOICE, 3/8/94, p. 54, Georgia Brown

On the day of the big snow, I fluffed the pillows and curled up with Zola's *Germinal*. The window was a Robert Ryman canvas, the page an Ad Reinhardt. If *Moby Dick* is an ode to whiteness, *Germinal*—the stirring 1885 epic of life in the coal mines—is a great piece of blackness, its miserable heroes toiling in pitch darkness, breathing foul dust, and turning black even on the inside. If the title (like *Fiorile*) comes from one of the spring months on the French Revolution's calendar, it's because Zola was thinking in terms of the coming century. The miners are just emerging from their sleep. What have been sown are seeds of workers' self-consciousness. In the novel's stirring last lines: "a black avenging army was slowly germinating ... And soon this germination would sunder the earth." Well, that was the dream and it was a great one.

Now here's the movie, directed, adapted, and produced by Claude Berri. (Actually, this is at least the seventh in a line of film adaptations.) During the recent GATT go-rounds, Berri's *Germinal* was pitted by the French press against Spielberg's *Jurassic Park*. The scales, predictably, were tipped: The home product was based on a beloved classic, the intruder on a corny contemporary blockbuster. The one possessed a deep and serious theme; the other was an escapist adventure story. The trash, of course, threatened to bury the national treasure.

Now, I'm all for those protections against Hollywood dreck, but in this localized *guerre*, gimme *Jurassic Park* anyday. At least it is what it is and doesn't pretend to be art or good for you. And it does what it does very well. Berri's film isn't art and doesn't do what it does well at all.

Germinal is a perfect example of what Truffaut as a young *Cahiers* turk (notably in his seminal "Une Certaine Tendance du cinéma français") scornfully referred to as France's "tradition of quality." It's what Rivette meant by a "prestige film." A "faithful" adaptation of a literary property, it uses iconic actors and more or less demands national *hommage*. And I've not even mentioned Berri's mise en scène, which is perfectly vulgar. In short, *Germinal* is pallid, ponderous, and, at two hours and 38 minutes, as stifling as a mine shaft.

Like the novel, the film opens with the arrival of a young stranger, Etienne Lantier, at the fire-breathing Veroux (voracious) mine, (Etienne is played by the popular singer Renaud, but since he can't act it's imperative you know from the novel that the character is bright and sensitive, not stupid and vacant as he seems here.) Etienne meets old Bonnemort (Jean Carmet)—infelicitously translated as "Goner" in the subtitles—patriarch of the Maheu family. Filling in the young man on the dismal work situation, Bonnemort wheezes and hawks and spits a liquid coal gunk that dribbles round his mouth.

A worker just died, and thanks to Bonnemort's son, Maheu (Gérard Depardieu, hardly looking malnourished), Etienne gets her job. Women work the mines, too, as the young man discovers his first time down, and the most appealing is Maheu's gaunt, saucer-eyed daughter, Catherine (Judith Henry, the girl from *La Discrète*). She is vigorously claimed, however, by the brutish, shovel-faced Chaval (Jean-Roger Milo), who looks straight out of *Dick Tracy*. In fact, everyone here—except Miou-Miou playing Maheude—looks more than a bit cartoonish, thanks partially to some bizarre makeup. (The most hilarious caricature is the Kropotkin-style anarchist Souvarine, who looks like the demented composite of about five Russian revolutionaries.)

Briefly, Etienne is the catalyst who sparks off a hugely destructive strike. Though a political novice, he becomes the miners' de facto leader. But the starving, desperate mob gets out of hand and turns vengeful. Berri's pièce de resistance is a graphic castration when raging mothers take revenge on the village's lecherous shopkeeper. (Unlike John Wayne Bobbitt, the victim is dead when mutilated, having fallen from the roof trying to escape.) Zola was occasionally sentimental about workers, but he was also crystal clear about the monstrous effects of despair and deprivation.

It's odd that a film fiercely condensing its source should end up with so much dead time (and space). It's odd too that Berri and cowriter Arlette Langmann ignore so much of the novel's most cinematically promising material—like the flocks of youngsters breeding in the slag heaps or the juvenile delinquency proceeding directly out of poverty. (In the movie, of course, the Maheu urchins look like picture-book tots instead of sickly, stunted creatures with oversize heads.)

Updating Rivette's 1957 statement above, British cinema today—with Leigh, Jarman, Davies, Greenaway, Loach, etc.—is *far* more vigorous and audacious than French cinema. Combine this with the fact that Americans like James Ivory and now even Scorsese are doing the old Brit-lit stuff better than anyone. At present the French haven't much at all to put up against *Jurassic Park*. Still, they'd be more credible touting Leos Carax—or even Cyril Collard—over Claude Berri.

Also reviewed in:
NEW REPUBLIC, 3/21/94, p. 26, Stanley Kauffmann
NEW YORK TIMES, 3/11/94, p. C1, Janet Maslin
NEW YORKER, 3/14/94, p. 90, Anthony Lane
VARIETY, 10/4/93, p. 39, Lisa Nesselson
WASHINGTON POST, 5/6/94, p. B1, Desson Howe
WASHINGTON POST, 5/6/94, Weekend/p. 47, Joe Brown

GETAWAY, THE

A Universal Pictures release of a Largo Entertainment presentation in association with JVC Entertainment. *Producer:* David Foster, Lawrence Turman, and John Alan Simon. *Director:* Roger Donaldson. *Screenplay:* Walter Hill and Amy Jones. *Based on the book by::* Jim Thompson. *Director of Photography:* Peter Menzies, Jr. *Editor:* Conrad Buff. *Music:* Mark Isham. *Music Editor:* Craig Pettigrew. *Sound:* Richard Bryce Goodman and (music) Stephen Krause. *Sound Editor:* Jay Boekelheide. *Casting:* Michael Fenton and Allison Cowitt. *Production Designer:* Joseph Nemec, III. *Art Director:* Dan Olexiewicz. *Set Designer:* William Law III. *Set Decorator:* R.W. "Inke" Intlekofer. *Set Dresser:* Larry D. Koszakovszky, Syd Moore, and Herb Morris. *Special Effects:* Phil Cory. *Costumes:* Marilyn Vance. *Make-up:* Robert Norin and Carl Fullerton. *Make-up (Kim Basinger):* Jack Freeman. *Stunt Coordinator:* Glenn R. Wilder. *Running time:* 110 minutes. *MPAA Rating:* R.

CAST: Alec Baldwin (Doc McCoy); Kim Basinger (Carol McCoy); Michael Madsen (Rudy Travis); James Woods (Jack Benyon); David Morse (Jim Deer Jackson); Jennifer Tilly (Fran Carvey); James Stephens (Harold Carvey); Richard Farnsworth (Slim); Philip Hoffman (Frank Hansen); Burton Gilliam (Gollie); Royce D. Applegate (Gun Shop Salesman); Daniel Villareal (Mendoza); Scott McKenna (Red Shirt); Alex Colon (Ramon); Justin Williams (Soldier); Peppi Sanders (Bookkeeper); Jo Ann Soto (Woman on Train); Louis Martinez (Train Station Cop); Boots Southerland (Cab Driver); Maurice Orozco (Customs Official); George Dobbs (City Jail Guard); Kenny Endoso (Sheriff's Van Driver). Don Pulford (Guard in Counting Room); Rick Taylor (Porter); Phil Allen (Newscaster #1); Bill Mosley (Newscaster #2); Debbie Dedo

(Newscaster #3); Gary Kirk (Policeman); J.W. "Corky" Fornof (Pilot); Peter Donaldson (Boy in Cafe); Michele Hawk (Waitress); Sam Hernandez (Bartender).

LOS ANGELES TIMES, 2/11/94, Calendar/p. 1, Kenneth Turan

Though it began life as an unpretentious paperback original by pulp icon Jim Thompson, "The Getaway" has turned into a lovers' lane for hot Hollywood couples. Steve McQueen and Ali MacGraw starred in the first version, Alec Baldwin and Kim Basinger headline this one, and for all we know Macaulay Culkin and Anna Chlumsky are already planning another a ways down the road.

A perfectly respectable thriller that mostly manages to be as crisp and efficient as the crimes it depicts, this Roger Donaldson-directed "Getaway" compares favorably with the Sam Peckinpah original. In fact, if this version has a problem it's that, with the same screenwriter (Walter Hill, now collaborating with Amy Jones) and two of the same producers, its smooth surface sticks so close to its predecessor's that the oomph originality can bring is lacking.

The best thing about this "Getaway" turns out to be that Baldwin-Basinger pairing as Doc and Carol McCoy, partners in crime and concupiscence. Though McQueen and MacGraw may have been just as crazy about each other, the new couple is much better matched in terms of on-screen charisma. Not only in the glamorous love scenes, which will make interesting viewing for future grandchildren, but also in angry confrontations and even quiet moments, Baldwin and Basinger's palpable chemistry brings a pleasant buzz to the proceedings.

First glimpsed on a firing range playfully bickering as to who gets to keep which gun, Doc and Carol are kind of a renegade Nick and Nora Charles who never miss an opportunity to crack wise. While she handles the driving, he is a practiced safecracker and explosives expert, a stand-up guy who does the jobs others say can't be done. "It's a hell of a way to make a living, Doc," she says. "You should have married a dentist," he agrees.

The serpents in this particular garden are plentiful, starting with the grungy Rudy (Michael Madsen), a low-class career criminal who brings Doc a set-up he says can't miss. But "The Getaway" is barely under way before Doc is seen languishing in a Mexican prison, trying to figure a way out.

Enter Snake No. 2, Jack Benyon (James Woods), a disreputable businessman oozing power, influence and unctuous depravity. Benyon has always wanted to use Doc's talents, and the imprisoned man sends Carol, wearing a dress that is practically painted on, to cut a deal: Get out of prison and I'll sign on for one last job.

Doc gets out, but nothing is simple after that. Grudges and suspicion soon proliferate, double- and triple-crosses become commonplace and everybody ends up chasing everybody else, heavy-duty weapons in hand. Though many of "The Getaway's" most intriguing twists duplicate the original, they still retain the ability to engage audiences.

Aside from greater explicitness in the love scenes, also marking this "Getaway" as up-to-date is an off-putting increase in the amount of sadism present in bad boy Rudy's relationship with a young woman named Fran (Jennifer Tilly reprising the Sally Struthers role). "It's been my experience that having a friend is overrated," Rudy says, and with a friend like him it's easy to see why.

Director Donaldson, whose last film was the neo-thriller "White Sands," rides out all these storms, doing a solid, unruffled job with the step-by-step crime re-creations and in general bring a bit more style than usual to this violence-begets-violence tale. If nothing else, they don't make many movies with guys named Doc as heros anymore, and it's nice to see another one come around.

NEW YORK, 2/21/94, p. 48, John Powers

Maybe I don't get out enough, but I seem to have missed the public outcry for a remake of *The Getaway*. When the Steve McOueen-Ali MacGraw version of this chase picture came out in 1972, it was both a box-office hit and a depressing anomaly— one of the Vietnam era's few well-made pictures with violence that had no moral or psychological weight. Of course, these days casual, flashy slaughter is almost obligatory in Hollywood thrillers; in that unhappy sense, Roger

Donaldson's remake is probably truer to its time than Sam Peckinpah's original. But the new movie is still disheartening: Just as it was difficult to watch Bloody Sam use his peerless technique to put over a piece of thuggish doodling, it's lousy to see Donaldson, the New Zealand director who once made the remarkable marital drama *Smash Palace*, sink deeper into barbarous impersonality. *Cocktail, White Sands*, and now this: He's become less a filmmaker than a cautionary tale about selling your talent to people who are buying only your proficiency.

Except for a few changes up front, the new movie is a scene-by-scene copy of the original—a Road Runner cartoon sponsored by the NRA. Alec Baldwin and Kim Basinger are Doc and Carol McCoy, professional crooks who rob a dog track and then kill their boss, an Arizona crime czar played by the cockroach Olivier—James Woods. Fleeing to El Paso, they're stalked by assorted goons, including their wounded ex-accomplice Rudy (Michael Madsen); he kidnaps a veterinarian and his bovine wife, who instantly prefers the gunman to her husband. (This sluttish role, thoughtlessly played here by Jennifer Tilly, is even more degrading today than it was twenty years ago.) Nothing if not an efficient machine, *The Getaway* keeps jerking you along, even though you've seen it all before: the steamy-shower sex scene, loving close-ups of triggers being squeezed, Madsen laughing sadistically as he wastes the next person.

While the original movie was sold as a star vehicle, the new version's ads play up the sex-and-gunplay angle because Baldwin and Basinger can't pull anyone into the theater. Her poor image has rubbed off on him—they're the first couple of bimbodom. I've begun to feel sorry for Basinger, who started out as a gifted comedienne and has become a painful example of how bad taste can do in a beautiful actress; though the comparison may smack of faint praise, I'm happy to report that she makes a far more compelling Carol than did Ali MacGraw. For his part, Alec Baldwin is a better actor than Steve McQueen, but he's not one tenth the movie star. McOueen was often as inexpressive as a piece of beef jerky, but he always exuded a peculiarly American calm, the cool that comes from knowing how to hot-wire a car. He did nothing, but he held the screen. The handsome Baldwin strikes all sorts of macho poses as Doc (he's always fiddling with his sunglasses), but he lacks a leading man's effortless authority. He has to work hard to make us notice him, which is why he's most enjoyable in hammy character roles like the bullyboy doctor in *Malice*.

When I heard Donaldson was redoing *The Getaway*, I felt sure he'd restore the best thing in Jim Thompson's original novel, the ending: The McCoys wind up in a Mexican village that's actually hell—forbidden to leave, they spend eternity stewing in misery and mistrust. Instead, this remake preserves the Hollywood ending, which replaced metaphysical desolation with twinkly good feelings. It asks us to believe that despite everything Doc and Carol do—commit armed robbery, beat faces bloody, blast people with twelve-gauge shotguns—they remain essentially decent people who deserve an old man's blessing as they get away with their swag. On the worst day of his life, Jim Thompson was never that cynical.

NEW YORK POST, 2/11/94, p. 31, Michael Medved

The biggest problem with the glossy new thriller "The Getaway" is the disastrous casting of Alec Baldwin in the central role.

In previous movies, he's done capable work playing silky smooth good guys ("Prelude to a Kiss" and "The Hunt for Red October") or silky smooth bad guys ("Malice" and "Glengarry Glen Ross"), but he's all wrong here as a rough, tough, battle-scarred ex-con named Doc McCoy.

Even in his scenes in a Mexican jail, the well-groomed Baldwin looks like he's striking poses for "Gentleman's Quarterly"; a small biceps tattoo and a shoulder holster aren't enough to dispel the air of bored yuppie smugness he so powerfully projects.

Twenty-two years ago, Steve McQueen played this earthy part to perfection in Sam Peckinpah's taut adaptation of Jim Thompson's novel, but asking Alec Baldwin to take the role makes as much sense as getting Woody Allen to play Stanley Kowalski in a future remake of "A Streetcar Named Desire."

Unfortunately, Baldwin's shortcomings undermine the occasionally intriguing efforts by his wife and co-star, Kim Basinger. In contrast to Ali MacGraw, who came across as little more than a sleek piece of set decoration in Peckinpah's "Getaway," Basinger creates a compelling character—a passionately adoring wife who is simultaneously excited and horrified by her husband's life of crime.

Their big adventure begins when she visits him in jail and he begs her to go to an all-powerful crime boss (the memorably vicious James Woods) to persuade him to arrange his release.

The dutiful wife does everything that's necessary —and perhaps more—and when Baldwin is turned loose, they must both pay the price: working for Woods in bringing off a fiendishly complicated scheme to steal several million dollars from an Arizona dog track.

Of course, this ingenious heist develops more than a few glitches in the execution, and before long Baldwin and Basinger find themselves careening through the Southwest toward the Mexican border, carrying a valise stuffed with money and simultaneously pursued by the cops, James Woods' murderous associates, and one of their own double-crossing fellow thieves, Michael Madsen.

Along the way, Madsen kidnaps a veterinarian (James Stephens) and his dizzy wife (Jennifer Tilly), who finds the gun-wielding thug a good deal more interesting than her stuffy husband.

The script is co-written by director Walter Hill (who also wrote the 1972 version of the story), and it follows the previous movie in nearly all its details.

In place of Sam Peckinpah's gritty intensity, however, director Roger Donaldson goes for big, splashy shootouts, indulgent love scenes and screeching, over-produced car chases.

In all of this, Donaldson displays the same sort of exaggeration and artificiality that's characterized the worst of his previous work ("Cocktail," "White Sands," "Cadillac Man").

Here, villains just don't die from gory gunshot wounds; they fall four stories, crash through glass ceilings and land on scaffolding with their mangled corpses splattered by red and black paint.

Some of these excesses are impressively staged but what got away from this "Getaway" is any sense of passion, conviction or realism—in either the action or the characters.

By the end of this long, mindless chase, the journey seems hardly worth the trip.

NEWSDAY, 2/11/94, Part II/p. 74, Jack Mathews

You won't see many movie remakes as faithful to the original as Roger Donaldson's updating—recasting really—of Sam Peckinpah's 1972 "The Getaway." The two pictures, both written by Walter Hill (the second with an assist from Amy Jones), are nearly scene-for-scene, often line-for-line, identical, and neither one has anything important to say.

When the project and cast were first announced, it seemed as if a parody were in the works. If you're going to make fun of Steve McQueen and Ali MacGraw; the real-life lovers who played the outlaw couple Doc and Carol McCoy in Peckinpah's film, who better to play them this time than Alec Baldwin and Kim Basinger?

And if you can remember how insufferably ditzy Sally Struthers was playing Fran Carvey, a veterinarian's wife who falls in love with the killer who kidnaps her and her husband the casting of Jennifer Tilly seems no less than inspired.

The truth, with the remake now among us, is that the new cast— which includes Michael Madsen as a sadistic thug and James Woods as a vicious mob boss—*is* inspired and with those improvements, Donaldson has turned one of Peckinpah's worst movies into a fast-moving, reasonably entertaining action picture.

Baldwin may not have the brooding intensity (or was it just disinterest?) of McQueen, but his aggressive style suits the mood better, and no one who remembers how stunningly bad an actress MacGraw was can deny that Basinger is an improved version of Carol McCoy.

Since one of the selling points of both movies is the heat generated in love scenes by the practiced couples, a big edge goes to the Baldwin-Basinger team. More nudity, more enthusiasm, more often.

"The Getaway," one of the first films adapted from a Jim Thompson novel, is a nihilistic road movie, one of a rash that followed "Bonnie and Clyde" into theaters in the late '60s and early '70s. It tells the story of a married pair of crooks who, after an armed robbery goes bad, are chased across the American Southwest by the partner they'd left for dead, the mob they'd double-crossed, and the dumbest assortment of cops since the Mack Sennett days.

The moral dilemma has nothing to do with the number of people, innocent and otherwise, slaughtered along the way. It's the revelation to Doc that Carol had slept with mob sleaze Jack Benyon (Woods), as part of a deal to spring Doc from a Mexican prison, and the dark hint that she may have moaned "Oh, God!" a time or two while she was at it.

There is a hilarious scene, played as tragedy, where Doc and Carol, oblivious to the death and carnage left behind them, debate the morality of her deed, and for the rest of the movie—while guns are blazing, bodies flying, cars exploding—the only suspense is whether Doc's ego can survive the insult.

(If it reminds you at all of last year's "Indecent Proposal," it's no coincidence. Hill's co-writer, Amy Jones wrote "Indecent Proposal" all by herself and along with Heidi Fleiss, is now one of Hollywood's resident experts on sexual bargaining.)

Donaldson has out-Peckinpahed Peckinpah in the blood and action sequences, and he has certainly populated the story with more interesting actors (besides regular heavies Woods and Madsen, David Morse is a terrific mob hit man). But the question remains whether many people will be interested in the remake of a story that didn't seem worth doing the first time.

SIGHT AND SOUND, 7/94, p. 41, Jill McGreal

Carter 'Doc' McCoy and his wife Carol plan and execute a job with partner-in-crime Rudy Butler, which involves springing a prisoner from jail and returning him to his family in Mexico. Everything goes according to plan, but when the felon is delivered to his family, he is summarily executed for dishonourable behaviour. McCoy is allowed to leave with his payment, but on his arrival at the airport the police are waiting for him. Carol and Rudy get away but McCoy is jailed for robbery. In jail, McCoy reaches breaking point and instructs Carol to make contact with Jack Benyon. Benyon has the means to buy back McCoy's freedom in return for his involvement in Benyon's next heist. Doc is freed, but in the meantime Carol has started a relationship with Benyon as part of the price of Doc's release.

Rudy is recruited by Benyon for the greyhound track robbery, which is successfully carried out. However, the third member of the gang gets jumpy and shoots a security guard. In the getaway, Rudy shoots him and arrives at the rendezvous to wait for Doc and Carol, intending to shoot them too. Anticipating the double cross, Doc shoots Rudy first, and he and Carol head for Benyon's ranch. There, Benyon tells Doc that he has been set up and that he and Carol are having an affair; but Carol shoots him, and she and Doc leave with the money.

Meanwhile, the injured Rudy drives to an isolated veterinary surgeon's and demands medical attention and transport to the border town where he expects to catch up with Doc and Carol. The vet, Harold Carvey, is forced to comply, but his bored wife Fran helps Rudy, relishing the excitement of being a gangster's moll. On the journey south, Harold commits suicide while Rudy and Fran have sex in a cheap motel.

Doc and Carol are also heading for the border hotel where their false passports are waiting. On the way, they fight about Carol's relationship with Benyon, but are reconciled and decide to continue their journey by train. At the station, Carol drops off the money in the left luggage lockers, but is the victim of a con man who steals the bag.

Doc and Carol spot the thief boarding a train and Doc goes after him. After a struggle, Doc retrieves the money and returns to pick up Carol. Later, the thief is picked up by the police, who realise that Doc is behind the greyhound track robbery and Benyon's death. Doc's picture is released to the press; he is subsequently recognised and he and Carol have to escape in a stolen car. They stop to buy guns but are chased by the police.

When they finally arrive at the hotel, they are unaware that Rudy is waiting for them. However, Doc becomes suspicious and is prepared when Rudy comes for him. Benyon's mob are also on Doc's trail; in the ensuing shootout, they and Rudy are all killed. Doc and Carol escape and hijack a truck belonging to an old man known as the Cowboy; with his help, they drive over the border into Mexico. Doc and Carol drive off to freedom and a new life together without crime.

Amor vincit omnia is the moral behind this heist-gone-right tale, but all the force of the Sam Peckinpah original is missing. The first screen appearance of the crime-does-pay theme caused moral outrage in 1972, but while this theme is still and always will be an issue, something has gone wrong in the remake. In Peckinpah's hands, the audience is brought to a point of genuine sympathy and identification with the two central characters, the trembly Ali McGraw and the bullish, inarticulate Steve McQueen; the ending thus gets a satisfying and uncomplicated emotional uplift. Under Roger Donaldson's direction, crime is glamorised by the use of sweaty Kim Basinger and hunky Alec Baldwin. The result—moral confusion.

In the original version all the elements come together—the script, the McQueen/McGraw partnership, the Clinton/Butler relationship, the journey south and the heist itself. The chalk-and-cheese contrast in directorial styles is nowhere more apparent than in the prison scenes, which in the Peckinpah version open the action. Peckinpah's film is shot in semi-documentary style: animals graze on scrub land and the camera rises to reveal some long low institutional buildings. There is little dialogue and much of the sequence is in long shot, with McQueen's no-acting acting style perfectly complementing the director's intention to create a believable portrait of the dreariness of prison life. In the remake, Donaldson goes for broke with barbed wire, armed guards, prison rats, mistreatment and big close-ups. The whole show is over-dramatised and heavy-handed in its attempt to enhance the original—a directorial strategy which continues throughout the entire film.

By using Basinger and Baldwin, two of the most bankable Hollywood stars, Donaldson presumably hoped to create an equivalent to the earlier film's star partnership; but with the camera lingering on cleavage and biceps rather than the global picture, the real drama is reduced. Donaldson also fails to understand that sexual chemistry is not the same as love. Peckinpah, paradoxically for the man who made *The Wild Bunch*, not only recognises the difference between physical and emotional responses but also manages to convey it by contrasting the Doc/Carol relationship with its degenerate and corrupted form in the Fran/Rudy coupling. And like all great directors, Peckinpah makes the comparison apparently effortlessly.

Peckinpah's reputation has always, perhaps unjustly, been linked with the violence of his movies. But, again paradoxically, his version of *The Getaway* is not as ugly as Donaldson's. And yet Al Lettieri's original Rudy is by a long stretch a more unpleasant and menacing character than his 1994 ponytailed equivalent. Similarly, Donaldson loses his nerve in Harold Carvey's suicide scene, having Rudy discover him hanging in the bathroom. In Peckinpah's film, Rudy and Fran are filmed making love through the dangling legs of Harold, who in ghoulishly voyeuristic style is strung up next to their bed. The contrast gives real force to that overworked notion of gratuitous violence which characterises the Donaldson version. Again, it is the big close-up which does the damage.

The most astonishing link between the two films is Walter Hill's script. The 1994 *Getaway* is, in this sense, a faithful remake, with Hill leaving in chunks of dialogue lifted straight from his original screenplay. There is some attempt to bring the script up to date, particularly in the scene where Doc and Carol fight about Benyon. McGraw's dialogue portrays the female as defenceless against raging male jealousy, while Basinger is given feisty lines that meet the macho challenge of her partner. But in the ensuing reconciliation, love not desire is the key to the film's trajectory; McQueen's ability to overcome his emotions speaks love more eloquently than Baldwin's defeat by the feminist argument.

Generally the new mix of Donaldson with the Basinger/Baldwin couple is at odds with Hill's ploy, and the reworked script is, at times, leaden and uncompelling. The big question is, why remake *The Getaway*? When Martin Scorsese remade *Cape Fear*, he stood it on its head for the 90s, desanctifying the good and pathologising the bad. This version of *The Getaway* fails to make any such contemporary statement. If you think you've seen it before, that probably has more to do with the fact that this is just another routine heist movie than the fact that you've seen the original.

VILLAGE VOICE, 2/15/94, p. 56, Georgia Brown

I wasn't one who knocked Sam Peckinpah's 1972 *The Getaway* for not being echt Peckinpah—or true Jim Thompson for that matter. There was a whole other (tender, romantic) Peckinpah anyway that many never wanted to see. As a gritty but lyrical love-on-the-run story, a mythic journey into the underworld and back, *The Getaway* was truer than most movies in depicting the woes of marriage, the vicissitudes of difficult love. (The nasty "Rudy, the Vet, and the Vet's Wife" subplot served to caricature demons released by infidelity.) Anyway, romance rubbed off on the two leads, and the short, unhappy union of Steve McQueen and Ali MacGraw was born. (Reviewers made fun of MacGraw's scared-rabbit "acting," but Steve's endorsement counted for something.)

Peckinpah's ashes have long since scattered on the wind. The new *Getaway* is terrible. The pits. It wouldn't be worth talking about if its flaws weren't symptomatic of Hollywood's worst tendencies. How easy it is for those guys to ruin a solid property. An imitation of the first movie (not a fresh adaptation of Thompson), a vehicle for two new embattled lovebirds—Baldwin and Basinger—*The Getaway II* manages to bore and infuriate at the same time.

Walter Hill, who wrote the screenplay for the first film, is credited as cowriter here, but this may be simply because elements are lifted directly from the original movie. (The garbage truck was not in the novel, for example. Nor was Rudy's kitten, the french fry fight, the pickup into Mexico.) When I called Universal to ask about Hill's 1994 contribution, they referred me to Largo Entertainment (the development company), which in turn transferred me from one person to the next. No one seemed to understand the question.

In Thompson's novel, Doc and Carol may be inseparable but they're a pair of doomed paranoiacs. A cold-blooded killer with a genial surface, Doc hooks up with a woman in search of a center and the two are stuck for life. They manage to escape the (local) law but there's no escape from themselves. Thompson concludes his chill squirt of acid with one of the bleakest epilogues ever: Holed up in a tropical hell-on-earth, Doc and Carol end up prisoners of each other. There is no getaway.

Compared to this, Peckinpah's film is positively mellow. His Getaway is about home and family and trying to reach a safe haven, a place to rest. The point is that havens hover all around, yet Doc, a chronic loner, a knot of distrust, can't connect. Most touching are the color-saturated, wistful visions of normality—lyric passages showing wholesome families enjoying leisure, kids at play, a small-town parade. The point is that Getaway I had a vision of its own. Not Thompson's, but one consistent with Peckinpah's all along. (Straw Dogs, after all, is the story of a man protecting his home.) The only vision the new Getaway, directed by Roger Donaldson, has is of dollar signs. Compare the openings: One meaningful, the other empty. Getaway I opened with a super over-the-titles montage establishing just how sick and desperate Doc McCoy (McQueen) was becoming in the pen: "free" deer roaming outside the walls, white jumpsuits in the yard, Doc's parole hearing, Ben Johnson's sour puss, petition denied, Doc crushing the model bridge he's built, fleeting memories of his wife Carol (MacGraw). And over all this, the clackety-clack of the automated shuttle loom, the sight of cogs engaging, silent lint accumulating. The new *Getaway*—whose it is really, we don't know—starts with a fuzzy close-up of a trigger. Focus and pull back slightly and we have a gun, a finger pulls the trigger. Another gun takes its place. Subtle? Doc (Alec Baldwin) and his wife (Kim Basinger) are target-practicing, blowing rusty cans off a fence and smooching between rounds.

Getaway II's idea of invention is to start with the job Doc is initially busted for. Working with Carol and Rudy, Doc springs a Mexican from an Arizona prison, flies him down to his uncle's place in Mexico, where the kid gets plugged and Doc gets caught—betrayed both by the uncle and Rudy—and ends up rotting in a Mexican jail. (The intention seems to be to give viewers an early jolt of violence.) Then Doc sends Carol to Benyon, an operator who has influence over border matters.

This movie adheres to the Book of Type Casting: James Woods embodies a no-nuanced Benyon, pure sleaze from the get-go; *Reservoir Dogs* sadist-psycho Michael Madsen plays sadist-psycho Rudy. Inserting Jennifer Tilly into the Sally Struthers role (the vet's wife) shows a bit more finesse.

Getaway II is a hyperactive string of quick cuts of thoroughly vapid material. The dialogue is all one-two-punch stuff—repartee as filler. As when Doc shoots Rudy the first time and intones, "That's what I like about Rudy"—one-beat—"He was predictable." Predictable. That's the word.

Differences between *I* and *II* are of this order: When Harold the Vet hangs himself in *I*, Rudy sits on the pot; in *II*, he stands to piss. In *II*, when Doc slaps Carol, she slaps back. In *II*, the big heist takes place at a dog track (there's a "Dog Races in Juarez" sign in the hotel lobby in *Getaway I*, so maybe this is an homage). The real differences are: no character, no dialogue of substance, no shots held over a few seconds, no scenes—except sex, chases, and shoot-outs—of any appreciable length.

Also reviewed in:
CHICAGO TRIBUNE, 2/11/94, Friday/p. A, Michael Wilmington
NEW YORK TIMES, 2/11/94, p. C12, Caryn James
NEW YORKER, 2/21/94, p. 110, Terrence Rafferty
VARIETY, 2/14-20/94, p. 38, Todd McCarthy
WASHINGTON POST, 2/11/94, p. B7, Rita Kempley
WASHINGTON POST, 2/11/94, Weekend/p. 48, Desson Howe

GETTING EVEN WITH DAD

An MGM/UA release. *Executive Producer:* Richard Hashimoto. *Producer:* Katie Jacobs and Pierce Gardner. *Director:* Howard Deutch. *Screenplay:* Tom S. Parker and Jim Jennewein. *Director of Photography:* Tim Suhrstedt. *Editor:* Richard Halsey. *Music:* Miles Goodman. *Music Editor:* Nancy Fogarty. *Choreographer:* Michelle Johnston. *Sound:* Agamemnon Andrianos and (music) Joel Moss. *Sound Editor:* Bill Phillips and John Phillips. *Casting:* Richard Pagano, Sharon Bialy, and Debi Manwiller. *Production Designer:* Virginia L. Randolph. *Art Director:* Clayton R. Hartley. *Set Designer:* Edward L. Rubin. *Set Decorator:* Barbara Munch. *Set Dresser:* Don Weinger. *Special Effects:* Chuck Gaspar. *Costumes:* Rudy Dillon. *Make-up:* John M. Elliott, Jr. *Make-up (Glenne Headly):* Ronnie Specter. *Stunt Coordinator:* Jack Gill. *Running time:* 108 minutes. *MPAA Rating:* PG.

CAST: Macaulay Culkin (Timmy); Ted Danson (Ray); Glenne Headly (Theresa); Saul Rubinek (Bobby); Gailard Sartain (Carl); Sam McMurray (Alex); Hector Elizondo (Lt. Romayko); Sydney Walker (Mr. Wankmueller); Kathleen Wilhoite (Kitty); Dann Florek (Wayne); Ron Canada (Zinn); Ralph Peduto (Chapman); Bert Kinyon (Guard); Melvin Thompson (Guard); Danny Hunter (Armored Car Driver); Suzanne Lime (Secretary at Elevator); Mary Dilts (T.V. Reporter); Scott Beach (Wino); Wil Albert (Docent); David Kagen (Little League Coach); Dick Bright (Father at Golf Course); Barbara Scott (Dog-walking Mother); Seth Smith (Boy in Bathroom); A.C. Griffing (Italian Waiter); Richard Koldewyn (Italian Waiter); Barrett Lindsay Steiner (Italian Waiter); Barbara Oliver (Nun); Charles Dean (Policeman at Church); Nick Scoggins (Scary Prisoner); Heather Bostian (Chatty Woman); Pamela Khoury (Woman on Subway); Sam Horrigan (Boy on Subway); Cheryl Lee (Leggy Blonde); Jarion Monroe (Ticket Seller); Joe Lerer (Bus Driver); Karen Kahn (T.V. Anchorwoman); Susan Hopper (Waitress at Lunch Counter).

LOS ANGELES TIMES, 6/17/94, Calendar/p. 12, Peter Rainer

Kiddies longing for a Mac attack this summer won't be enlivened by the tepid shenanigans and mushy maunderings of "Getting Even With Dad." Macaulay Culkin plays the estranged 11-year-old son of an ex-con, and he doesn't bare his tonsils once.

His eyes moisten on cue, however. Such acting range! Culkin's Timmy, motherless, has been living with his aunt for the three years his father, Ray (Ted Danson), has been in prison for stealing VCRs. (A "cute" crime.) Dad, a baker by trade, is out of the clink now and planning a rare coin heist in San Francisco with two bumbly accomplices (Saul Rubinek and Gailard Sartain) when Timmy is deposited on his doorstep for a week's visit. The boy quickly figures out a way to blackmail his father into loving him—he hides the stolen coin cache and won't reveal its whereabouts until his father takes him to the amusement park and the aquarium and the ballpark.

It's difficult to determine what's more unbelievable—Culkin as an unhappily neglected boy in need of male bonding or Danson as a tough-talking, tattooed ex-con. Actually, Ray is a softened good/bad guy from the start, which leaves no doubt about the ultimate fate of his fathering. He's a *baker*, after all—how terrible can he be? He can't keep the plant in his apartment watered, but it's clear he's a closet nurturer.

Ray has a lot to learn about feelings and his life teacher is Timmy. Ray may be useful to his son showing him how to catch a fish or shoot a basket, but "Getting Even With Dad" is all about—apologies to William Wordsworth—the son being the father to the man. The title for this film should be taken literally: Timmy gets even with his errant dad by transforming him into his emotionally caring equal.

Any movie that asks us to glean life lessons from a character played by Macaulay Culkin is asking for a lot—and asking for trouble. His tyke fans probably won't connect with the film's civics lesson tone or its touchy-feely bond-a-thons. (When Culkin's character was stung to death by a bee in "My Girl" it sent shock waves through kiddieland.) So, as insurance, the filmmakers—director Howard Deutch and screenwriters Tom S. Parker and Jim Jennewein—toss in a lot of stoogey shenanigans involving Rubinek and Sartain. These guys drip chili dogs on their shirts, get crunched in garbage dumpsters, fall down flights of stairs. Now *that's* entertainment. Timmy is allowed only one comparable moment: He sips a soda through straws in his nostrils. Interestingly, in a movie clogged with product tie-ins, the soda goes unlabeled. (This could be a commercial miscalculation since kids will want to try this at home.)

Culkin's acting, such as it is, is deadpan minimalist. Has he been looking at early Clint Eastwood movies for inspiration? He doesn't seem to have much inner life to draw on for this film, which bollixes its meaning. Timmy's blackmailing of his father, which is supposed to come out of an inner pain, instead seems like a species of torture. Culkin's flat line readings have Bad Seed vibes.

But maybe this is the fantasy level that will put "Getting Even With Dad" over the top. Timmy gets to torture his dad in the process of defusing him. Isn't this what every kid wants? He even maneuvers to get a smitten undercover cop (Glenne Headly) to romance his father, and they all go out together to fancy restaurants and museums. In the kid-power universe of this film, the boy gets to pick his parent's suitors—another big-time child fantasy. It's all a bit smug and suspect. You get the feeling that, by the time Timmy hits his teens, dad and he will be double-dating.

NEW YORK POST, 6/17/94, p. 38, Michael Medved

In 1993, Macaulay Culkin made two brave attempts to expand his career and broaden his acting range.

In "The Good Son," Little Mac tried his hand at playing the part of a twisted, psycho kiddie killer. And in "The Nutcracker" he tried his foot at dancing classical ballet. I happened to like both films, but the public stayed away in droves. So what's a poor little 13-year-old superstar to do?

The answer, apparently, is to return to familiar turf, because "Getting Even With Dad" is a shameless recycling of all the elements that made the two "Home Alone" movies so popular.

Once again, the young star plays an amazingly resourceful kid who, forced to act entirely on his own, easily outwits some bumbling adults—including a pair of dim-witted thieves who provide the slapstick comic relief.

But "Getting Even With Dad" also features a new element along with the old formula: a shockingly effective and heartfelt performance by Ted Danson. This often misused and undervalued actor is so touching and funny, so thoroughly inside his character, that he single-handedly breathes some life into this tired material.

Danson plays a small-time crook who has just been released from prison but dreams of pulling one last heist so he can retire from his life of crime.

At the very moment he's about to make these dreams come true, he gets a most unwelcome visit from the son (Macaulay Culkin) he left behind years before when he went to jail. The boy realizes that the only way to get his old man's attention is to hide the stolen loot from the big robbery.

He then refuses to give it back until Danson and his two goofball accomplices (Saul Rubinek and Gailard Sartain) accompany him to what seems like every roller coaster, ballgame, aquarium and miniature golf course in Northern California.

Director Howard Deutsch ("Pretty in Pink," "Some Kind of Wonderful") creates lots of pretty, polished scenes full of boyish fun and gets many amusing turns from veterans Sartain and Rubinek. Glenne Headly also shines as an undercover cop assigned to keep an eye on Danson who finds herself uncomfortably touched by the growing closeness between father and son.

Culkin does little to make that relationship believable: He seems unmistakably bored by the part. His moussed hair and heavily rouged lips are all wrong for the kind of hard-luck kid he's supposed to be playing.

Danson, on the other hand, is so riveting in all their scenes together that you hardly notice his co-star's inadequacy.

As a Father's Day gift, this "Dad" leaves lots to be desired. In contrast to the splendid "The Lion King," which actually shows a father helping and teaching his son, this movie resorts to the unfortunate kids-know-best cliche, in which sensitive, all-knowing tykes teach their bone-headed parents about integrity, love and the meaning of life.

Now if only Ted Danson could, in return, have taught Macaulay Culkin about committed and credible acting, the entire film might have been something more than a harmless, barely watchable trifle.

NEWSDAY, 6/17/94, Part II/p. B2, Jack Mathews

To be a successful child actor—no, to be the most famous child on earth—you have to do something better than any other child can do. For Shirley Temple, that was singing and dancing. For Macaulay Culkin, it's making life hell for thieves.

Culkin made life hell for thieves in "Home Alone," the most popular comedy in history, and in "Home Alone 2," Hollywood's third most popular comedy, then stubbed his toe playing the prince in "Nutcracker" and a sociopath in "The Good Son."

In Howard Deutch's "Getting Even With Dad Culkin is back to form in a story so blatantly derived from the "Home Alone" movies that you just groan and wait for heavy objects to start falling on the heads of the really stupid but genuinely lovable bad guys.

The unwitting thieves are hot-tempered Bobby (Saul Rubinek), food-obsessed Carl (Gailard Sartain) and Ray (Ted Danson), a genial ex-con hoping to make one final score so he can buy a bakery and spend the rest of his life decorating cakes. The three are on the eve of a risky heist of rare coins when into their lives drops Timmy (Culkin), Ray's precocious and highly principled 11-year-old son.

Father and son have been estranged since Dad went to prison, but now that Timmy's mother is dead and his aunt is getting married, it's time for a reunion and, for Dad, a crisis of conscience. Risk another prison sentence or become a good father? And does he have any choice? Timmy hides the stolen coins and holds them hostage while Dad takes him to every museum, sports event and amusement park in San Francisco.

Add to the mix a sentimental cop (Glenne Headly) who, while trailing the thieves, falls in love with the boy and his dad, and you've got the potential for a restored family unit and a last-scene gusher. But all this business about a child showing a parent the way is secondary to the film's real purpose, which is to get Culkin into position to drive the thieves crazy, to play Roadrunner to their Wile E. Coyotes. For Culkin's fans, those broad physical scenes do pay off with some big laughs.

The bozos are mulched in garbage, thrown down flights of stairs and sent on wild goose chases that land them in jail..The scenes aren't as violent as their counterparts in "Home Alone," and Bobby and Carl are so accident-prone they don't need much help from Timmy. But it's all the same idea.

Culkin can't play this cute, little troublemaker much longer. His voice is going to change any minute, and once he's got hair under his arms, there goes the underdog status that makes his triumphs so satisfying. If he's smart—check that, if his stage father from hell, Kit Culkin, is smart—he will take a cue from Shirley Temple, whose acting career peaked before puberty, and start studying for the foreign service.

SIGHT AND SOUND, 8/94, p. 41, Geoffrey Macnab

San Francisco, Ray Gleason, a small-time crook, plans one last heist. He intends to steal a consignment of valuable old coins, sell the hoard to a gangster contact, and use his share of the proceeds to buy his own bakery store. Shortly before the robbery is due to take place, Ray's sister Kitty turns up at his apartment. While he was away in jail, she looked after his son, Timmy. Now she is about to go on honeymoon with her new husband, and needs to leave the boy in San Francisco for a week.

The robbery goes ahead as planned. However, Timmy eavesdrops as Ray and his accomplices, Bobby and Carl, conceal the coins on the roof. He is left at home when they go out to celebrate. Exasperated at being ignored by his father, he hides the money himself and refuses to give it back until Ray meets his demands. For the next few days, he insists on being pampered—taken out to ball games and fun fairs, to ice skate, play crazy golf and visit aquariums.

Gradually, Ray and Timmy rebuild their relationship. The boy sends Bobby and Carl off on a wild goose chase by dropping a few false clues, and is able to spend 'quality time' with his father. Ray chats up a woman called Theresa, little realising she is a detective assigned to follow him, and romance begins to blossom.

There is still the matter of the stolen coins. Unless Ray renounces the robbery, Timmy says he will walk out on him for good. Ray refuses. He puts the boy on a bus back to Aunt Kitty and is about to unlock the locker where he thinks the money is hidden when he has an attack of conscience. He stops the bus and is briefly reunited with his son. However, Bobby and Carl, convinced they are being double-crossed, force him to open the locker at gunpoint. As soon as he does so, the police, who have been staking out the entire operation, swoop. Fortunately, the money in the locker turns out to be worthless. The real coins are in a bag in a local department store. Ray is released, resolves to go straight, and sets up house with Timmy.

"You've been watching way too much Oprah," Ted Danson snaps at Macaulay Culkin halfway through *Getting Even With Dad*, and it's not hard to see why—the boy does indeed have an unhealthy obsession with solving other people's problems. As if to compensate for his brief flirtation with evil in *The Good Son*, Culkin returns to the screen scrubbed squeaky clean and on the side of the ministering angels. Here, grown-ups are dysfunctional, confused beings while he is a paragon of common sense. *Sorting Out Dad* might have been a more appropriate title: his father is the delinquent, not him. In the course of the film, he tries to wean the poor man off cigarettes, teach him about family responsibility, convince him of the drawbacks of a life of crime, and match-make him with a suitable woman. He even tells him to change his toothbrush. It's a heroically smug effort, but ends up costing Culkin dear. Rather than steal scenes from the adults (the usual prerogative of the child actor), he has them plucked from under his own nose instead. Danson's character, petulant, vain and not a little dim—he has just served a prison sentence for stealing a haul of Betamax VCRs—is infinitely more likeable than that of his manipulative, do-gooding son.

Getting Even With Dad may tout itself as a paean to family values, but the marked shortage of female characters suggests it is more a variation on the buddy movie. At times, given their differences in age, Culkin and Danson make a very odd couple indeed. although there are token attempts at providing Danson with a girlfriend (and hence Culkin with a surrogate mother), Glenne Headly's character, dowdy detective Theresa, plays a relatively insignificant part in the story. Presumably, developing her role further would have meant shifting the focus away from Culkin. As he was paid in excess of £5 million for appearing, this wasn't a risk the scriptwriters could comfortably take. Instead, the relationship between father and son is foregrounded throughout, and with sometimes bizarre consequences. The film's finale, where Danson chases after and stops a bus to prevent Culkin leaving him, may be a cliche of romantic drama, but is slightly jarring when a middle-aged man and his 12-year old kid are the parties concerned.

Howard Deutch directs in brisk fashion. The occasional moments of severe mawkishness (for instance, Culkin staring plaintively at a photograph of himself by his mother's grave) are counterpointed with chases (In one scene, which seems to be borrowed wholesale from *The French Connection*, Culkin is pursued across the subway, darting in and out of trains and up and down escalators as he goes) and splurts of slapstick comedy. These are largely provided by Saul Rubinek and Gailard Sartain as Danson's little and large stooges, but are strained and only fitfully funny.

Danson is more effective. It's hardly his most taxing role. As the feckless father and two-bit thief, he still seems to be playing a certain Boston bartender, but at least he does so with the usual quota of smug charm. Given that the storyline demands Culkin be taken on trips to every conceivable San Francisco tourist attraction, it's little wonder that watching the picture sometimes seems akin to looking at a stranger's holiday snaps.

There's a certain irony to the title, if not to the film as a whole. Getting even with Dad is something many Hollywood executives have been wanting to do ever since Culkin's success in *Home Alone* gave his father and business manager, Kit, such leverage with the studios. What they need is for Mac to have a series of clunking failures. This moralistic, saccharine fable, which sees the young star at his most self-satisfied, may just be one of them.

TIME, 6/27/94, p. 71, Richard Schickel

Now that Macaulay Culkin is a teenager, vulnerability, the quality that has prevented his wise child from turning into a wise guy, comes harder for him. Now that Ted Danson is a movie star, or thinks he is, stupidity comes harder for him. Danson's character in *Getting Even With Dad* is supposed to be an inept thief, but the actor doesn't want to dig into dumbness, which is where the laughs, if any, might be. Untutored is the worst he'll allow himself to seem. Untutored, but capable of sensitivity, of love, of being a '90s beau ideal, if given a chance.

Providing that chance is the job of the half-pint, in a movie so desperately maneuvered that it's possibly unfair to blame Danson for defending himself against it. Culkin plays Timmy, the son whom widowed Ray hasn't seen for three years, and he arrives just as his dad and two confederates are about to rob a coin collection. This they manage with a cleverness that belies their alleged incompetence. But the boy steals the loot, and will give it back only if Ray will act the good father for a week—you know, ball games, amusement parks, miniature golf. Father and son bond, of course, and along the way Timmy does a little matchmaking, helping Pop and the cop who's trailing him (Glenne Headly) fall in love.

Timmy is a calculating little guy, the creation of calculating big guys. Like everyone else in the movie, he appears to have been morphed into existence by people who aren't writing or directing in the usual sense of those words but are operating a computer whose keypad is marked with a few simple signs: SENTIMENT, SWEETNESS, LOVABLE MISCHIEVOUSNESS. The coldness with which these filmmakers pursue warmth is—no other word for it—bone chilling.

VILLAGE VOICE, 6/28/94, p. 66, Beth Coleman

You figure for the title alone it's worth the $8. But *Getting Even With Dad*, though star-studded and perfectly timed for "Dad's day," should wait its turn on the new-release shelf like any other movie acquired to satisfy highly specialized drives. If, for instance, you're having a Mac attack, or need to know about Ted Danson's hair, or want to keep the seven-year-old away from the adult *animé* shelf.

The concept is sound enough: all 11-year-old whiz kid Timmy (Macaulay Culkin) wants is dad's undivided attention, but father Ray (Danson), an ex-convict, is too busy planning a heist to even look at Timmy—what to do? Well, junior's got a video camera and he knows how to use it. Quickly dad's armed robbery (Mace, not guns, parents) turns into son's blackmail of the heart. What follows is pure kiddy formula, without the Disney animation, a madcap week of father-son hoops, father-son date—with the same girl no less—and father-son seafood banter. The stockpiling of amusement park, ice skating, and ice cream parlor is enough to give every preteen in the theater a cavity.

As much as I relish the sight of Culkin's inhumanly berry-bright, puffy little mouth, *Getting Even* only just chugs along until the closing hug. Take the kids to an amusement park this summer, the Cyclone is only $3 and an F train away.

Also reviewed in:
CHICAGO TRIBUNE, 6/17/94, Friday/p. H, John Petrakis
NEW YORK TIMES, 6/17/94, p. C12, Caryn James
VARIETY, 6/13-19/94, p. 56, Brian Lowry
WASHINGTON POST, 6/17/94, p. B6, Rita Kempley
WASHINGTON POST, 6/17/94, Weekend/p. 38, Desson Howe

GO FISH

A Samuel Goldwyn Company release in association with Islet Pictures of a Can I Watch Pictures/KUPI production. *Executive Producer:* Tom Kalin and Christine Vachon. *Producer:* Rose Troche and Guinevere Turner. *Director:* Rose Troche. *Screenplay:* Guinevere Turner and Rose Troche. *Director of Photography:* Ann T. Rossetti. *Editor:* Rose Troche. *Music:* Brendan Dolan, Jennifer Sharpe, and Scott Aldrich. *Sound:* Lisa Hubbard and Elspeth Kydd. *Sound Editor:* Missy Cohen. *Running time:* 87 minutes. *MPAA Rating:* Not Rated.

CAST: V.S. Brodie (Ely); Guinvere Turner (Max); T. Wendy McMillan (Kia); Migdalia Melendez (Evy); Anastasia Sharp (Daria); Mary Garvey, Danielia Falcon, and Tracy Kimme (Students/Jury Members); Jennifer Allen, Walter Youngblood, and Arthur C. Stone (Students); Elspeth Kydd (Angry Student); Brooke Webster (Mel); Mimi Wadell (Mimi); Scout (Haircutter); Susan Gregson, Carolyn Kotlarski, and Joanna Brown (Brides/Jury Members); Betty Jeannie Pejko (Evy's Mother); Alfredo Troche (Junior); JoAnne C. Willis (Sam); Jonathan T. Vincent (Boy); Jamika Ajalon and Michele Cullom (Jury Members); Marianna (Herself); Shelly Schneider-Bello (Bella); Stephanie Boles (Alice); Julia LaFleur (Andy); Lisa Raymond and Nina Von Voss (Dinner Guests); Dorothea Reichenbacher (Della).

LOS ANGELES TIMES, 7/1/94, Calendar/p. 12, Kevin Thomas

The most important remark in Rose Troche's quirky lesbian romantic comedy "Go Fish" occurs when, leaving a theater, a woman says she didn't think the filmmaker was trying to "represent the entire gay community ... that's a lot to ask."

This observation applies directly to Troche, who's introducing us to a close-knit group of young women living in Chicago, many of whom like to dress like boys, a grungy look that isn't going to appeal to all lesbians, nor should it have to.

The irony is that the low-budget "Go Fish," which exhilaratingly proclaims Troche and her co-writer and star Guinevere Turner as fresh and lively talents, could just turn out to be a crossover success. Troche and company have an amusing but sensitive take on human nature that transcends sexual orientation and a consistently original and witty way of expression. Surely, straights as well as gays can identify with the vicissitudes of dating that plague the film's pretty but tart heroine, Max (Turner), who's as pert as a young Debbie Reynolds. Max is the woman who doesn't like the unidentified movie, and defending it is her new acquaintance Ely (V. S. Brodie).

It has taken a certain amount of good-natured maneuvering and pressuring on the part of mutual friends to get the two women to go out together. First of all, Max, who's aptly described by a pal as a "total babe," spells out her initial response to Ely: U-G-L-Y. Beanpole thin and long nosed, Ely is decidedly plain and shy to boot. Besides, she considers herself attached; never mind that her lover has been living in Seattle for two years and that Ely has seen her only three times in that time. But Ely has a radiant smile and a sweet, gentle nature. Besides, Max finds it so unexpectedly easy to talk to Ely.

Their friends couldn't be more caught up in matchmaking than the women in Jane Austen's "Pride and Prejudice," and their bemused but loving concern allows us to get to know them as well. Principal are Max's roommate, her onetime professor Kia (T. Wendy McMillan), who specializes in women's studies and is an ample, formidably but humorously intellectual black woman who has just commenced a romance with an attractive Latina, Evy (Migdalia Melendez). Then there's Darla (Anastasia Sharp), the playgirl of the group, a bartender who unapologetically constantly moves from one woman to the next but is as convinced as Kia that Max and Ely are made for each other.

A delightful storyteller, Troche comes up with wholly unexpected and consistently effective bits of visual punctuation—there's much cutting to expressive shots of hands—and she has a subtle way with sensuality and a secure touch with non-professional actors. Admittedly, Max's growing sexual attraction to Ely is a stretch, which could have been slackened helpfully by Ely merely ditching the world's clunkiest eyeglasses at the same time she goes in for a radical new hairstyle. But then "Go Fish's" parting shot is, that "the girl you're going to meet doesn't look like any girl you know."

NEW STATESMAN & SOCIETY, 7/15/94, p. 32, Jonathan Romney

You could almost talk about *Go Fish* as if it weren't a lesbian film at all. You could still say how fresh Rose Troche's film looks, that it's enough of an anomaly to make you want to wave the flag for it. It's about a bunch of friends who hang out together, discuss their lives and loves, share gossip, get supportive but not so much that the air doesn't sometimes crackle with argument—all in grainy fast-edited black-and-white set to an insouciant jazzy soundtrack. Funny, confident and made on a shoestring, it's the sort of film that gets applauded at festivals but rarely slips through the net of mainstream releasing. So it's something of an event that it has.

But, as Troche says, "*Go Fish* is different because of its sexuality. If it wasn't a lesbian film, it would be a film about twentysomething gals who are just living their lives." If that were the case, *Go Fish* might be no big deal—another US indie that struck lucky. Certainly, it never apologises either for its low-rent production values or for its very personal motivation. Although directed by Troche, the film belongs as much to Guinevere Turner, who stars, co-wrote and co-produced.

She plays Max, a young woman in search of a lover, who is set up by friends for an encounter with Ely (V S Brodie), who to all appearances, is her exact opposite. Max—funky, style-driven, a boots-and-baseball-cap girl—is none too taken at first with gawky, bespectacled Ely, with hair, glasses, speciality teas and absentee partner in Seattle. It doesn't take much to bring them together. A few sly looks and pithy comments from friends, and a drastic new haircut for Ely break the ice (this is the only on-screen haircut I can remember outside an army film). The duo soon make out to cheers all round.

Go Fish isn't so much about the meeting-cute but the endless mating dance of come-ons and deferrals that fuels most straight cinema, *Sleepless in Seattle* and *When Harry Met Sally* being the most extreme examples. The point of *Go Fish* is that it's futile to mess around: what's moving the lovers is lust and love, and the deal is to tackle them. Their no-nonsense courtship is set about with discourse from friends, who lie around arranged in geometric patterns, talking about Max and Ely's style choices, or about the vocabulary of genitalia ("Love mound is so Victorian!").

The film has no patience with courting the mainstream either in form or subject. It doesn't have to make a case about being or becoming "different", but presents an almost Utopian picture of a republic of gay women. Despite the Chicago location, it's very much set in a free-floating, multiracial woman-world. Only at one point does one of the women face off against her grieving Latino mother and ex-husband in a too-familiar scene of family conflict, which comes across as a cursory nod to genre conventions.

Troche's community is by no means shielded from its own tensions. The film is a communal bulletin board, avid to cram in every topic. It begins with a blackboard rollcall of famous gay and maybe-gay names, a step towards the unwritten history of lesbians. Later, Max and Ely debate gay cinema, and the pressures on film-makers to speak for themselves or for their entire community. In a stylised night tribunal scene, one woman confronts accusers who complain that, by sleeping with a man, she has lost her right to call herself a lesbian. No, she says, I'm a lesbian who slept with a man. This assertively undoctrinaire film is very much angled not at a viewer but at an audience, with one eye on the arguments in the bar afterwards.

Together with the public debate, there's a personal feel that belongs to Troche and Turner equally. Turner seems to provide her own musings in the form of the diary that Max scribbles furiously at the start, narrating it in a gabbled voice-over; she also provides the film's cartoon-style credits, embellished with little sketches: smiling fish, spirals and suns.

All this gives the film a scratchy, scrapbook-collage feel: at the very least, you sense that the makers have spent many argumentative nights working on it. As a debut independent feature, the closest analogy to *Go Fish* is probably Spike Lee's debut *She's Gotta Have It*, which was equally fast and reckless in as much as it had maximum fun with minimal resources. Lee's film achieved the same mix of personal adventure and communal debate.

But black cinema has its own history and its own difficult relationship with the mainstream, whereas to most people lesbian cinema doesn't exist. So *Go Fish* can't be simply a film; it's consciously an entry into an arena, new girls strutting in to boot some life into the place. And because it has won a mainstream release, it's in a very peculiar position. Made for gay women, it will be reviewed predominantly by straight men, some of whom will write it off as of minority interest, while others will strain to damn with faint praise. The real story of its success will have to be told in the box-office queues.

NEW YORK POST, 6/10/94, p. 42, Thelma Adams

"Go Fish" is a frisky, low-budget, girl-meets-girl comedy shot in grainy black-and-white.

The movie playfully poses questions about a lifestyle that often remains hidden from the mainstream because the participants rarely chronicle their own lives.

Was Eve the first lesbian? Was comic-strip tomboy Peppermint Patty bent?

"Go Fish" is less interested in outing than "ining," showing what it's like to be a twentysomething woman loving women amid the urban brick-and-boards bookshelf, apartment-dwelling set.

When Kia (T. Wendy McMillan), Evy (Migdalia Melendez), and Daria (Anastaia Sharp) meet for weekly talk sessions, the conversation turns to Max (Guinevere Turner), "a carefree single lesbian looking for love," and the progress of her budding romance with Ely (V.S. Brodie).

One of the joys of Rose Troche's directorial debut, which she co-wrote and co-produced with Guinevere Turner a.k.a Max, is the warmth and affection the team bears for all their characters and their resistance to making them role models or even dream dates.

These women—teachers, nurses, bartenders, veterinary aides, and students—tend to be more tortured by what to wear on a date than AIDS or self-hate.

A scene in which Daria is confronted by a gaggle of lesbians about the fact that she slept with a man raises the issue of lesbian purity while showing the pressure to conform amid the lesbian community.

The pressure of the lesbian thought police (big sister is watching) exerts a tidal pull against the strain to conform to the mainstream.

A sequence in which Max imagines what it would be like to don a wedding dress, marry a man, and fit into family and social dynamics is artfully played with the light touch and roguish good humor that characterizes Turner and Troche.

If there's a fault to "Go Fish" it's that the girl-meets-girl, girl-gets-girl structure stints on dramatic tension. Whatever happened to girl-loses-girl?

NEWSDAY, 6/10/94, Part II/p. B13, Gene Seymour

Ely (V.S. Brodie) is an aging flower child, terminally shy and hesitant in speech. Max (Guinevere Turner) is a captivating, sassy Generation X type, who runs off at the mouth. They don't seem to have much in common except that they're both ruminative, both gay, both looking for a lover.

Well, *Max* is, anyway. Ely insists she's tied to someone else who's now living in Seattle, roughly 2000 miles away from their Chicago home. Meanwhile, Max shields her nascent attraction to Ely's fetching reserve with a smokescreen of gibes about Ely's hair, taste in movies and comprehensive selection of herbal teas.

To the women who make up their overlapping social circles, Ely and Max are Meant To Be. "The little relationship that could," is how it's characterized by Kia (T. Wendy McMillan), a wise—and wisecracking—African-American college instructor who's attached to Evy (Migdalia Melendez), a sweet, sensual Hispanic nurse who hasn't yet "come out" to her conservative family. Another mutual friend, Daria (Anastasia Sharp), has no attachments. Or rather, she has five or more at various times of the week.

This is the tableau of "Go Fish," a free-wheeling, low-budget romantic comedy of ideas, filmed in beautiful black and white and paced with jazzy insouciance by co-writer, co-producer and co-star Turner and co-writer, co-producer, director and editor Rose Troche. Having been screened at a few festivals before its general release, "Go Fish" has already become a legend for the triumphant way it celebrates lesbianism with a spirited, ingratiating lack of didacticism or self-consciousness.

Through the film's zesty, seamless flow of jaunty banter and glow-in-the-dark insight, you are told more about the longings, apprehensions and epiphanies of lesbian life than you'd believe was possible in such an unassuming film. Indeed, you become so caught up in the lives of these altogether likable characters you almost forget what a break-through "Go Fish" is.

And by "breakthrough," one isn't just talking about the lesbians-in-love angle, but the film's relationship to the prevailing cultural atmosphere of hair-trigger uptightness. Put another way, it's a fresh kick to see any movie in any era that dares to embrace both romantic love and sexual passion without making a big deal about it.

NEWSWEEK, 6/27/94, p. 53, David Ansen

It's a measure of how starved the lesbian audience is for films that reflect their lives that "Fried Green Tomatoes"—a surprise hit most people regarded as a heartwarming Southern period piece—became a lesbian cult favorite and even won an award from GLAAD (Gay & Lesbian Alliance Against Defamation). All this for a movie that avoided any overt references to its heroines' sexual orientation for fear of alienating mainstream audiences.

When Rose Troche and her girlfriend Guinevere Turner sat down to brainstorm the lesbian movie they'd like to make, they never considered it might have mainstream appeal. But they knew what they didn't want it to be. It would not be another agonized tract about coming out or, in director Troche's words, a movie in which women "only have sex under excruciating circumstances." It would not be about upper-middle-class lesbians with spike heels (not to mention murder in their hearts, à la "Basic Instinct"). Says the 30-year-old Troche: "We wanted to make something we'd want to go out and see." "We're writing a happy script," Turner kept reminding her partner. "We want to just for once have a movie that's plain old tra-la-la."

"Go Fish" is it. This black-and-white movie, shot in Chicago on a minuscule budget, is a blithe and funkily stylish celebration of community—a twentysomething girl-meets-girl comedy whose charm is in its matter-of-fact disregard for what a straight audience might think. Turner, the co-writer, stars as Max, given to baggy shorts, baseball caps and writing romantic entries in her journal about meeting the girl of her dreams. Her friends fix her up with Ely (V. S. Brodie), an androgynous, shy veterinary assistant who strikes the hip Max as much too '70s crunchy granola for her taste. The gist of the tale is how these two improbable mates become lovers. But Troche and Turner surround them with a chorus of kibitzing friends that includes Max's roommate Kia, a teacher never at a loss for a pedagogical point; Kia's lover Evy, whose ex-husband outs her to her mother; and Daria, a waitress so promiscuous she even sleeps with man. The movie's most radical stroke may be casting the homely Brodie as a leading lady—a rebuke to Hollywood romantic conditioning. Once you adjust to the no-budget, anti-glamour style, Troche' s artistry sneaks up on you. True to her mission, she leaves you smiling.

The angst that isn't in "Go Fish" occurred in the three-year struggle to get the film made. Using money out of their own pockets and borrowed equipment, and filming mostly on weekends to accommodate their nonpro actors, Troche and Turner ran out of money with only 60 percent of the movie shot. John Pierson, a veteran angel of the independent scene, came through with the necessary funds, but by the time filming resumed Turner and Troche had split up.

The filmmakers figured that at best the movie would play the gay and lesbian festival circuit. But "Go Fish" became a sleeper sensation at the Sundance Film Festival last January and was picked up by the Samuel Goldwyn Co., which knew there was an audience for lesbian films but also felt the comedy had crossover appeal. "To have it supposedly appealing to a heterosexual audience is fascinating to us," says Turner, 26, a Sarah Lawrence graduate. "It makes us a little nervous because neither of us would want any lesbian to think we made it as some public-service announcement to the heterosexual world or to cash in on lesbian chic."

Two weeks after Sundance, Troche got a call asking if she'd like to direct a film of "The Brady Bunch." She said no. She'd rather stay independent; she's now developing a movie about the pioneering woman director Dorothy Arzner. "It's turned into a lesbian period piece, Hollywood in the late '30s." Turner has no illusions about a major career playing gay roles but she speculates about being cast in heterosexual parts. "People like Tom Hanks and William Hurt got Oscars for playing a sexual orientation that's not their own. I wonder if I'm going to get an Oscar for playing a straight person," she jokes. "Is the press going to ask me, 'What was it like to kiss a man?'"

SIGHT AND SOUND, 7/94, p. 42, Lizzie Francke

Chicago the beginning of summer. Max, a young aspiring writer, is looking for love. She shares a house with Kia, a college lecturer, who is happily ensconced with her girlfriend Evy. Max confides to Kia and Evy that she is having problems meeting the right person. Kia suggests to Max that she might like to meet one of her old students, Ely, and sets the two up. Max thinks she is attracted to Ely but the date goes awry when Ely's girlfriend, who now lives in Seattle, calls.

Ely confides to her flatmate Daria about the poor state of her relationship. Days later, Max and Ely meet in a bookshop and shyly talk. The two women become a hot topic of conversation for Kia and her friends. Meanwhile Evy, who has been living with her mother since she split up with her husband, is kicked out of the family home when her mother discovers that she is a lesbian. Consequently she moves in with Kia and Max.

Daria decides to start plotting on Ely's behalf and holds a dinner party to which Max, among others, is invited. The party goes to plan—Max gets on with Ely and asks her out. Later, Ely tells her girlfriend's answering machine that their relationship is over. The night of Max and Ely's big date arrives. Ely arrives at Max's and the two end up making out. The following day their respective flatmates want to know all about the date. As the summer unfolds, Max and Ely fall in love.

Go Fish might be described as a low-budget *When Sally Met Sally.* A perky love story filmed with wonderful elan in black and white, it marks a significant debut for the director Rose Troche and her co-writer and lead Guinevere Turner, who brings an exuberant charm to the role of Max. Filmed over a couple of years on a minuscule budget pulled together by the two from their own and their friends' pockets, it has a freshness and energy that belie its long drawn-out inception.

Troche, who also edited the film, has created a piece that flickers with cinematic possibility as she juxtaposes imagery to both lyrical and humorous effect. Thus the director meshes a love scene with one in which a meal is being prepared, cutting away to shots of bread being broken open by hungry hands as the couple start to climax. It is a brazen take on the cliched connection between food and sex. Troche's flip style works well with Turner's effervescent script, which makes a punchy rap out of girl talk and thoughts. This is typified in the opening scene in which Max bubbles with a stream-of-consciousness musing about a girl she has seen on a bus.

Certainly Troche and Turner follow in the Queer Cinema tradition of their executive producers Christine Vachon (who produced *Poison* and *Swoon*) and Tom Kalin (who directed *Swoon*), in that there is nothing straight about the film's form. The manifest desire to be cinematically different should eclipse the more obvious point that Troche and Turner have come up with a lesbian story that departs from the coming-out narratives of films such as Donna Deitch's *Desert Hearts*. In *Go Fish* the women are happily already assured of their sexuality. They are very much out and about. Indeed, this is a hanging-out sort of film, which makes much use of the irreverent girl rap, with frequent intermissions in the story devoted to Kia and an ever increasing circle of friends gossiping about Max and Ely. Their talking heads provide a festive chorus with many asides on the way to the anticipated consummation of Max and Ely's 'will they or won't they?' affair.

This approach creates a strong sense of a lesbian community, while the flexible digressive style enables Troche and Turner to dive a little deeper under *Go Fish*'s seemingly light, shimmery surface and ponder on some weightier questions about lesbian identity—but without letting the movie get too hung up on them. Kia gives a lecture on lesbians hidden in history, but also ponders on the many euphemisms for the vagina—her favourite being "honey-pot", since "it's sexy without being vulgar". Meanwhile, the roving-eyed Daria defends her decision to sleep with a man for one night, berating a lesbian politics that suggests such an act might mean "her whole life choice becomes suspect".

Indeed, the film acknowledges the shifts in concerns over the last couple of decades for different generations of lesbians by setting up a wry dialogue between the slightly older and politically active Kia and the younger women. There is even a passing discussion about lesbian films. In such a way, *Go Fish* anchors itself in a particular history while marking a new wave in film-making, of which one hopes there will be much to follow.

TIME, 9/12/94, p. 86, Richard Corliss

[*Go Fish* was reviewed jointly with *Clerks*; see Corliss' review of that film.]

VILLAGE VOICE, 6/14/94, p. 47, J. Hoberman

Talk is the handmaiden of action rather than vice versa in Rose Troche's *Go Fish*, but it's no less of a cool breeze.

As a suspense drama, *Go Fish* could have been titled *Stasis* or maybe *Off Speed*. Will the young and eager Max (Guinevere Turner), a pensive cutie who looks like a '40s starlet masquerading as a member of the Little Rascals, ever get down with the older and less outgoing Ely (V. S. Brodie), a recovering hippie with a long-distance lover somewhere in Seattle?

This low-budget, character-driven, regional independent production may be *Speed*'s antithesis—although there's a sense in which the often comically sexualized *Speed* is a narrative based on the extended foreplay of getting two characters together. Indeed, *Go Fish* is an equally assured first feature and—taken on its own terms—just as much a technical tour de force.

A weekend project begun in Chicago during the summer of 1992 by writer-producer-director-editor Troche and writer-producer-star Turner, *Go Fish* feels like a collective enterprise fueled by a marked sense of mission. The characters cross a variety of ethnic and generational lines but, from the opening sequence in which the movie's intellectual queen bee and her university class speculate on the identities of history's closeted lesbians (Eve, Marilyn Quayle, Dennis the Menace's neighbor Margaret) to the final montage of a half-dozen couples kissing, the movie is set in a totally lesbian milieu.

As befits a film not altogether unconcerned with issues of personal style, *Go Fish* is well shot in glamorous black and white—the 16mm original blown up to 35mm—and imaginatively edited. Given the project's lengthy, stop-start shoot, Troche has made particularly canny use of voiceover and lyrical montage to bind together her fragmentary material. (The panoply of insouciant new wave tricks are proof of adept problem solving.) Interspersed with all manner of domestic vignettes and lively exchanges, jazzy camera moves and mega close-ups, the movie manages to be both self-conscious and playful. Every few minutes the narrative takes a break to reflect upon itself or permit the characters to debate the nature of lesbian "positive images," stage an impromptu inquisition, or dramatize a fantasy of middle-class "normality."

Clearly, *Go Fish* is a movie with an agenda. But with all the talking and making out, the overall effect is less didactic than it is light-hearted—the overlapping dialogue manages to sound natural as well as declamatory, the tone is simultaneously romantic and matter-of-fact sexy. A crowd pleaser at Sundance, Berlin, and, most recently, the Lesbian and Gay Film Festival, the movie seems destined for a healthy run at the Angelika. With its jaunty chic, inside moves, and breakthrough attitudinizing, *Go Fish* seems most reminiscent of *She's Gotta Have It*. It's a film that bops along, secure in its own hipness.

Also reviewed in:
CHICAGO TRIBUNE, 7/1/94, Friday/p. M, John Petrakis
NATION, 7/25-8/1/94, p. 137, Stuart Klawans
NEW YORK TIMES, 6/10/94, p. C6, Janet Maslin
VARIETY, 1/31-2/6/94, p. 66, Emanuel Levy
WASHINGTON POST, 7/2/94, p. D1, Rita Kempley

GOLDEN GATE

A Samuel Goldwyn Company release in association with American Playhouse Theatrical Films. *Executive Producer:* Lindsay Law. *Producer:* Michael Brandman. *Director:* John Madden. *Screenplay:* David Henry Hwang. *Director of Photography:* Bobby Bukowski. *Editor:* Sean Barton. *Music:* Elliot Goldenthal. *Sound:* Andy Wiskes. *Casting:* Risa Bramon Garcia, Juel Bestrop, and Mary Vernieu. *Production Designer:* Andrew Jackness. *Art Director:* Edward Rubin. *Costume:* Ingrid Ferrin. *Running time:* 95 minutes. *MPAA Rating:* R.

CAST: Matt Dillon (Kevin Walker); Joan Chen (Marilyn Song); Bruno Kirby (Ron Pirelli); Teri Polo (Cynthia); Tzi Ma (Chen Jung Song); Stan Egi (Bradley Ichiyasu); Jack Shearer (FBI Chief); Peter Murnik (Byrd); George Guidall (Meisner).

CHRISTIAN SCIENCE MONITOR, 2/9/94, Marilynne S. Mason

Written by playwright David Henry Hwang (who wrote "M. Butterfly"), director John Madden's *Golden Gate* is parodistic and stylized—an intense, beautiful film that's entirely artificial and strange. The dialogue is hilarious because it so closely parallels the language of 1940s and '50s B movies without ever imitating them.

A young FBI agent frames a Chinese immigrant suspected of communist activity in the 1950s. The innocent man spends 10 years in prison and is disgraced among his people. His suicide makes the FBI agent remorseful, and he sets about trying to help the man's daughter. Matt Dillon plays the agent and Joan Chen the Chinese-American woman he tries to protect and with whom he falls in love.

"An impossible love is love nevertheless," one character tells us.

The tragicomedy is about having the courage to choose justice over injustice and doing well instead of just doing what is expected of one, but the filmmakers squander this message with a totally implausible (and unsatisfactory) ending.

"Golden Gate," may not be a big commercial success. Its style defies Hollywood realism and its vision of love is not a popular one. Neither is its take on expiation—paying for one's sins. But popular or not, "Golden Gate" is an American original, full of excellent little theatrical twists—as natural, surprising, and predictable as a mountain stream.

LOS ANGELES TIMES, 1/28/94, Calendar/p. 10, Kevin Thomas

"Golden Gate" is as ambitious as it is disastrous. David Henry Hwang, who wrote "M. Butterfly," one of the most provocative and successful American plays in recent years, has taken an important premise only to let it lapse into a protracted soap opera. The question Hwang poses implicitly is this: How many of us are aware that Chinese Americans were subjected to persecution by the FBI because the Communist Revolution in China happened to coincide with the McCarthy era?

In its opening sequences, "Golden Gate" would seem to be illuminating this injustice in promising fashion. It's San Francisco, 1952, and J. Edgar Hoover has ordered the local bureau to ferret out commies in Chinatown. Brand-new agent Kevin Walker (Matt Dillon) hits upon an idea: Go after a laundryman, Chen Jung Song (Tzi Ma, in the film's most eloquent performance), who has collected funds to send via Hong Kong to his and his friends' impoverished relatives in the recently formed People's Republic of China.

In the climate of anti-communist hysteria it's not hard to get him sent to prison for 10 years for "trading with the enemy." Upon his release he's shunned by his community, and since Walker is ordered to hound him some more, the laundryman jumps to his death off a promontory overlooking the Golden Gate Bridge. Walker at long last commences to get a serious case of guilt.

So far OK, but darned if Walker, concealing his identity, proceeds to court the dead man's beautiful daughter Marilyn (Joan Chen), now a Berkeley law student involved in a campaign to clear her father's name, which fits right in with the mood of the anti-war activist '60s.

Since Dillon and Chen look like movie stars, their mutual attraction is certainly credible, and what Hwang attempts is to stir up a love between them so overpowering that it overrides both Walker's well-deserved sense of shame and Marilyn's horror when she inevitably finds out that her lover is the man who systematically and unjustly destroyed her father. Tempestuous emotions trigger lots of scenery-chewing, leading to increasing ludicrousness. In danger of drowning in the suds is Hwang's important point that there's a tendency to regard Asian Americans as "perpetual foreigners."

Chen and especially Dillon are gallant, but they don't seem to get much help from director John Madden, whose first theatrical film was "Ethan Frome." Madden directs everything head on, without a trace of subtlety or understatement. Thanks to Hwang's writing, compounded by Madden's heavy hand, Bruno Kirby, as Walker's straight-arrow superior, and Stan Egi, as a fiery '60s activist, emerge as caricatures. "Golden Gate" looks great, thanks to the meticulous, evocative contributions of production designer Andrew Jackness, costume designer Ingrid Ferrin and cinematographer Bobby Bukowski, but it's pure dross.

NEW YORK POST, 1/28/94, p. 45, Michael Medved

"Golden Gate" begins with intriguing narration by Joan Chen declaring that "this is the story of a man who transformed himself into an angel," but the sodden earthbound movie that tells his tale never sprouts heavenly wings.

Matt Dillon plays the main character, an ambitious young FBI agent assigned to the bureau's San Francisco field office in 1952. We're told that J. Edgar Hoover wants his G-men to clamp down on residents of Chinatown who provide aid or encouragement to the Commies back home. Dillon and his lonely, insecure partner Bruno Kirby do their best to comply with these directives.

Eventually, they focus their attention on a local laundry man (Tzi Ma), whose left-wing politics and efforts to forward Chinatown money to impoverished relatives in Red China make him a likely target.

Dillon's idealistic blonde girlfriend (the radiant other-worldly Teri Polo) is appalled at the way the feds pursue the innocent laundry man. And after they succeed in putting him behind bars she leaves the young agent forever.

The story then shifts 10 years forward, as Dillon feels deepening guilt over his role in the whole sordid affair. The Chinese immigrant he once persecuted meets a tragic death shortly after his release from prison and Dillon feels irresistibly drawn to the funeral.

The day after the ceremony, he tries to comfort his victim's beautiful daughter (Joan Chen), and the obligatory love affair quickly develops. Of course, Dillon lies to the bereaved young woman—trying to make her believe he was actually her father's friend and protector rather than his chief accuser.

The pairing of Dillon and Chen in this haunted romance suggests rich dramatic—or at least melodramatic—possibilities, but the movie never develops them. Instead, screenwriter David Henry Hwang concentrates on some of the same themes of East-West cultural conflict he developed so famously in his triumphant play (and horribly disappointing movie) "M. Butterfly."

Once again the focus is a tormented Western bureaucrat simultaneously attracted and terrified by the potent mysteries of Chinese culture.

In addition to heavy-handed political point-scoring, incoherent attempts are made at deepening its shallow story with mythic elements. Eerie lighting, for instance, suggests that Dillon's vanished girlfriend is some sort of heavenly messenger, while Chen may be an incarnation of the Chinese goddess of mercy, representing Dillon's only hope of escaping a dead man's curse.

Director John Madden seems especially ill-suited to bring such enchantment to the screen. In last year's impressive "Ethan Frome," his intense, almost flat-footed style seemed perfectly suited to the rough-hewn material. But the magic element in this script definitely demanded a lighter, more whimsical touch.

Thanks to a cast full of capable actors, "Golden Gate" is never outright embarrassing. But it remains little more than a plodding period piece, far more earnest than ethereal.

NEWSDAY, 1/28/94, Part II/p. 63, Jack Mathews

A movie is charting itself a tough course when it promises a story about a "man who turned himself into an angel," and then identifies that man as a young FBI agent so anxious to please the paranoid urges of J. Edgar Hoover he's willing to frame and destroy an innocent man.

John Madden's "Golden Gate," a sociopolitical soap opera written by playwright David Henry Hwang ("M. Butterfly"), is really the story of a man who sells his soul for a career, then feels just awful about it. And if having a guilty conscience and redemption are the same thing, I guess he earns his wings.

At the core of this ultimately dopey saga which takes us from the era of anti-Communist hysteria to the student protest movement of the late '60s, is a serious, and perfectly believable accusation, that in the early 1950s, the FBI paid off witnesses and planted evidence to convict innocent Chinese-Americans of conspiring to aid Red China.

Hwang's story opens in 1952, with 22-year-old rookie FBI agent Kevin Walker (Matt Dillon), having failed to find any Communist spies in San Francisco's Chinatown, framing laundryman Chen Jung Song (Tzi Ma) and using the conviction to impress his superiors.

Madden sets this story up as a kind of romantic political fantasy, with Walker's horrible misdeed carried out amid lush dream sequences in nightclubs, alleyways and courtrooms. We see him fall in love with the idealistic Cynthia (Teri Polo), who makes him pass a pop quiz ("If you had to choose between law and justice, which would you choose?") before going to bed with him, then dumps him when his actions belie his answer.

There are some striking sequences in this first section, particularly a nightclub scene where Kevin and Cynthia seem to be dancing to an altogether different tune and beat than the jitterbuggers surrounding them. Bobby Bukowski's cinematography, like the rest of the film 's production, is first-rate throughout.

The story is a disaster, however. It falls apart after leaping forward to 1962, when Chen Jung Song, freshly released from prison but unable to return to his old life, commits suicide and Walker, wracked with guilt, seeks out the man's daughter and tries to make amends.

Walker is either the dumbest FBI agent in bureau history or simply the most glaring victim of Hwang's script. But instead of telling Marilyn (Joan Chen) how he knew her father, he passes himself off as a friend full of anecdotes about what a wonderful guy dad was, and when his lies help make her fall in love with him ... well, the plot doesn't thicken as much as it congeals.

Madden, a British television filmmaker who made his feature debut with last year's subtly erotic "Ethan Frome," will see better days, and almost certainly better scripts. There is a nice grace to his visual compositions, and given the impossible task he had here (they weren't kidding about a man turning himself into an angel), the movie isn't quite as easy to dismiss as it should be.

VILLAGE VOICE, 2/1/94, p. 59, Manohla Dargis

As thrilling and animated as the make-believe land in *Mr. Rogers Neighborhood, Golden Gate* is distinctive only for being the first worst movie of the new year. Directed by John Madden and written—if, indeed, that is the right word—by *M. Butterfly*'s David Henry Hwang, the film tracks the rise and inevitable fall of a white FBI agent (er, Matt Dillon) whose manifest destiny comes to screeching halt in San Francisco's Chinatown.

It's 1952 and as Joe McCarthy rages vitriolic in subcommittee, fresh Bureau meat Kevin Walker is doing his patriotic bit by sniffing out the local Maoists. Problem is, the only thing that smells is special agent Walker. If you think that cliché is tired, get these:

The name of the country is Red China.

Yeah, there's this thing called the Bill of Rights.

I guess you just didn't realize what you were doing.

I feel I got off on the wrong foot.

The jaws of godless anarchy.

They say miracles really do happen.

Not here they don't. To please Hoover, Walker frames an innocent (Tzi Ma), only to then fall for the guy's very fetching daughter, Marilyn (Joan Chen), years later. Needless to say, it's a bumpy ride. Walker lies, Marilyn cries, and the goddess of mercy spares no one—on screen or off. Madden, who showed a squeak of promise with last year's *Ethan Frome*, tries to cop some nor by swirling the smoke and tilting the camera but it only looks like his tripod is taking a tumble in the fog. By the time '68 rolls around and Grace Slick is belting "White Rabbit," it's clear Madden's hat of tricks is empty.

Apparently *Golden Gate* and its promising revisionist romance was one of those legendary unproduced scripts that had Hollywood panting (or so the press kit claims). Given the results it's hard to believe, scenery and good intentions notwithstanding. There's plenty of blame to spread around here but special mention must go to the folks in casting. While it's tough to imagine any actor emoting inspirational with Hwang's dialogue (Walker: "He couldn't take the, uh ... what did you call it?" Marilyn: "Shame"), it's particularly cruel and unusual punishment for Dillon and Chen. Only Bruno Kirby, as an unlikely FBI operative, gets the joke, veering dangerously, tantalizingly, close to the parodic. Too bad he never gets there.

Also reviewed in:
CHICAGO TRIBUNE, 1/28/94, Friday/p. C, Clifford Terry
NEW YORK TIMES, 1/28/94, p. C10, Janet Maslin
VARIETY, 1/31-2/6/94, p. 68, Leonard Klady
WASHINGTON POST, 1/28/94, p. C7, David Mills

GOOD MAN IN AFRICA, A

A Gramercy Pictures release of a Southern Sun presentation of a Polar Entertainment production in association with Capitol Films. *Executive Producer:* Joseph Caracciolo, Jr., Jane Barclay, Avi Lerner, and Sharon Hare. *Producer:* John Fiedler and Mark Tarlow. *Director:* Bruce Beresford. *Screenplay (based on his novel):* William Boyd. *Director of Photography:* Andrzej Bartkowiak. *Editor:* Jim Clark. *Music:* John du Prez. *Sound:* Frank Garfield. *Sound Editor:* Les Hodgson. *Casting:* Billy Hopkins and Susie Figgis. *Production Designer:* Herbert Pinter. *Art Director:* Graeme Orwin. *Set Decorator:* Vic Botha. *Special Effects:* Rick Cresswell. *Costumes:* Rosemary Burrows. *Make-up:* Tracy Crystal. *Stunt Coordinator:* Roly Jansen. *Running time:* 93 minutes. *MPAA Rating:* R.

CAST: Colin Friels (Morgan Leafy); Sean Connery (Dr. Murray); John Lithgow (Arthur Fanshawe); Diana Rigg (Chloe); Lewis Gossett, Jr.(Sam Adekunle); Joanne Whalley-Kilmer (Celia); Sarah-Jane Fenton (Priscilla); Maynard Eziashi (Friday); Jeremy Crutchley (Dalmire); Jackie Mofokeng (Hazel); Daphne Greenwood (Duchess); Themba Ndaba (Kojo); David Phetoe (Isaiah); Dambuza Mdledle (Sonny); Lillian Dube (Innocence); Peter Thage (Peter); Patrick Mynhardt (Muller); George Lee (Highlife Singer); Aubrey Molefi (Customs Official); Jerry Mofokeng (Ezekial); Kedibone Diamini (Ijeoma); Thapelo Mofokeng (Officer); Sophie Mgcina (Hospital Sister); Putso Diamini (Heavy in Car); Trilby Beresford (Christmas Girl); Fiona Fraser (Lady in Waiting); Fats Dibeco (Roadside Barman); Yule Simone (Adekunle Double); Peter Se-Puma (Shack Barman); Oliver Tambo, Jr. (Christmas Boy); Russel Savadier (Jones); Patrick Shai (Femi); Vivian Ingrid Pinter (Christmas Girl); Russel Savadier (Jones).

LOS ANGELES TIMES, 9/9/94, Calendar/p. 8, Peter Rainer

Morgan Leafy (Colin Friels), the mid-level British diplomat who has been stationed for three years in the emerging West African nation of Kinjanja, has the hangdog look of someone who knows he's in a rut. As ruts go, it's not the worst: Kinjanja is a tremendously colorful and spirited country, and he gets to spend much of his time drinking and womanizing.

But the discovery of vast oil reserves off the coast complicates Leafy's position. As put to him by visiting British High Commissioner Arthur Fanshawe (John Lithgow), Leafy's mission is to ingratiate the Crown with Prof. Sam Adekunle (Lou Gossett Jr.), the likely African president in the upcoming elections. But Adekunle isn't easily wooed: He needles the Brits and exacts tribute from them. He enjoys being top dog.

"A Good Man in Africa," scripted by William Boyd from his novel and directed by Bruce Beresford, has so many good things in it that it's a little disappointing it's not terrific. But it's a far more daring movie than its flip jauntiness might at first suggest. Beresford and Boyd are trying for a comic tragedy about both the colonialists who once ruled Africa and the Africans who have replaced them. It's a vision of a mercenary culture where the corruption has worked its way through white *and* black. In "A Good Man in Africa," even near-absolute power corrupts absolutely.

Leafy is a standard-issue British imperialist of a very minor sort. He has an African mistress but won't be seen in public with her; when he visits the doctor he unthinkingly cuts in front of a long line of black patients, He doesn't involve himself in the culture of Kinjanja in any real way.

When Fanshawe's servant is struck and killed by lightning, the Africans in his employ refuse to have her body moved from the front of his house until one of their tribal spirit leaders appeases the gods. Leafy can't comprehend this ritual. Neither, of course, can Fanshawe, who is a high parody of imperialist nincompoopery. (Lithgow doesn't overdo the archness. He's just being accurate.)

Leafy and Fanshawe live in the teeming, brightly colored thick of things and yet they are apart from their surroundings—that's the source of the film's comedy and tragedy. And ultimately Adekunle is apart from his people too. He just talks a better game.

The only resolute man in Kinjanja—the only incorruptible person we see—is the Scots doctor Alex Murray, played by Sean Connery. It's one of the most perfectly cast roles Connery has ever had: He even gets to play golf with the rich earth tones of Africa as his backdrop. Murray is a deliberately heroic, larger-than-life character, he's in the movie to test Leafy's resolve but he's also our guide through the thickets of political intrigue in Kinjanja. His worldly cynicism cuts through the maneuverings and posturings of both the Brits and the Africans, and he enjoys taunting them both.

If Leafy's transformation from a drowsy rake to a man of principle had been fully accomplished, "A Good Man in Africa"' might have been great. But despite Friels considerable gifts, the filmmakers don't really shape his ascent, we don't quite spot in him the emotional resources that are called upon in the end. And the rollickiness of Beresford's style is a shade too goofy for the depths he's also trying to plumb. Sections of the film are like Graham Greene or Evelyn Waugh as reimagined by Blake Edwards. (Not a terrible combo by any means.)

What complicates the assessment is that a lot of this goofiness is integral to the story. The collisions of cultures may have many sorrowing effects on the Africans (most of which we don't see), but they also produce a state of high levity. Power—and the loss of it—turns the ruling class of both camps into caricatures of themselves.

Because he is above thc allurements of power politics, only Dr. Murray is not a figure of fun. He's been in Africa for more than 20 years and he's planning to leave—to Portugal, perhaps—but he has a sense of what has been lost in his adopted country. He's the Good Man in Africa and the film does justice to his goodness. It doesn't soften it.

NEW YORK POST, 9/9/94, p. 45, Michael Medved

There are fleeting moments in Bruce Beresford's new film "A Good Man in Africa" when you're reminded of the sensitive, humanistic director of "Driving Miss Daisy," "Tender Mercies," "Breaker Morant" and "Black Robe."

Far more frequently, however, this misguided and mediocre comedy brings to mind Beresford's clumsy, empty-headed embarrassments like "King David" or "Her Alibi."

Despite handsome camera-work (by Andrzej Bartkowiak, of "Terms of Endearment" and "Speed"), and the skillful exertions of a stellar cast, the film feels slack and stilted, amounting to little more than pointless piffle.

Based on a 1981 novel by William Boyd (who also wrote the screenplay), the story centers on a bored, perpetually frazzled, junior-grade British diplomat (Colin Friels) in a fictional West African country who's far more interested in women and alcohol than in representing the interest of Her Majesty's government.

His pompous new boss (John Lithgow) wants Friels to cozy up to a nationalist presidential candidate (Louis Gossett Jr.) in order to secure special concessions of the nation's oil reserves.

But the African leader has priorities of his own. He wants to enlist the aid of the English in removing the one obstacle standing in the way of a huge construction project that will make him rich—which means eliminating the opposition of the idealistic Scottish doctor who is supposed to be the "good man" of the title.

Since this part calls for a Scotch accent, it was inevitably handed to the one and only Sean Connery, who presents his character like an uneasy blend of Albert Schweitzer and 007.

The main point of the story is that a few short conversations with this heroic figure lead Friels' diplomat to reconsider his selfish, hedonistic ways; but Connery's indestructible charisma isn't nearly enough to make this transformation even briefly believable.

Similarly unconvincing are the many scenes showing the central character's hectic love life; we're given no basis at all for understanding why this shallow time-server proves so irresistible to every gorgeous female in the cast.

He effortlessly seduces his boss' adventurous daughter (Sarah-Jane Fenton) and neglected wife (Diana Rigg), Gossett's moody spouse (Joanne Whalley-Kilmer), and a spectacularly statuesque local girl (Jackie Mofokeng).

The implausible elements in each of these relationships undermine the biting topical humor which the filmmakers intend for the entire piece: When the personal relationships make so little sense, it's impossible to credit the post-colonial political shenanigans which the story is supposed to be satirizing.

The casting of familiar American actors as both the moustachioed arch-English imperialist (Lithgow) and the fiery, berobed African nationalist (Gossett) further undermines authenticity.

Like Beresford's little-seen 1990 project "Mr. Johnson," this new film is an intermittently intriguing African excursion with some pretty scenery, a few colorful characters and a flimsy storyline that's hardly worth the time for the trip.

NEWSDAY, 9/9/94, Part II/p. B7, Gene Seymour

The lean, sure-footed grace that made William Boyd's novel, "A Good Man in Africa," a model for contemporary comedy-of-manners is all but absent in this clumsy, awkward film adaptation. How this happened is a mystery, especially given the fact that Boyd himself wrote the script.

It's even more inexplicable given the charismatic talent on hand: Sean Connery, Colin Friels, John Lithgow, Diana Rigg, Lou Gossett Jr., Joanne Whalley-Kilmer. How could you lose with a lineup like this? Yet somehow director Bruce Beresford, so adroit with his performers in "Driving Miss Daisy," has made lumpy, sour stew out of Boyd's subtle, spicy recipe.

Only Connery, in the title role of a tough, tender doctor battling disease and corruption in the emerging West African nation of Kinjanja, evokes the cool cunning so enjoyable in Boyd's book. And Connery, for all practical purposes, is little more than a supporting player in this tale of low-ranking British diplomat named Leafy (Friels), who is the disillusioned and dissolute *yin* to Connery's compassionate and honorable *yang*.

At least Leafy comes by his cynicism honestly, given the morally questionable, things he's asked to do by varied loathsome persons. For instance, the British High Commissioner (Lithgow in an overplayed impersonation of John Cleese) wants Leafy to convince Kinjanja's newly elected president (Gossett) to give England dibs on the country's huge oil reserves. The president, upon discovering Leafy leaving the boudoir of his wife (Whalley-Kilmer), presses the luckless sap to bribe the good doctor to vote for additions to a local college.

Everybody, it seems, wants something from Leafy, even the commissioner's stiff-backed wife (Rigg), who gets an inexplicable case of the hots for the younger man. The only person who hasn't got an angle is the doctor, who knows the president is the contractor for the new campus buildings and wants to plunder his electorate.

Despite the many complications and sub-plots in Boyd's tale, it couldn't have been so hard to make them flow smoothly on celluoid. Yet even the more original set pieces, like the death-by-lightning of Lithgow's Kinjanjan maid and its lingering aftermath, are handled with heavy hands and fumbled fingers.

Indeed, while the film is respectful to the African characters, one can't really call any of them characters, except for the president and Leafy's cook (Maynard Eziashi from "Bopha!"). The rest seem little more than pieces of scenery used to dramatize how noble, nutty or craven the whites are. This skewed perspective proves once again how a good story ends up embodying some of the values it's supposed to condemn.

SIGHT AND SOUND, 12/94, p. 48, Robert Yates

Morgan Leafy, a mid-ranking diplomat in the West African state of Kinjana, feels his career is stagnant and wants to move elsewhere. As Kinjana prepares for a presidential election, Leafy's superior, High Commissioner Arthur Fanshawe, sets him the task of charming the election's likely winner, Sam Adekunle. There are oil reserves off the Kinjanan coast, and Britain would like a stake in them. Leafy meets Adekunle's beautiful wife Celia, who promises to introduce him to her husband. Fanshawe has also asked Leafy to show his newly arrived daughter Priscilla around.

Leafy attempts to seduce her but fails. In the morning, bent double with pain, Leafy visits the hospital, and gives a urine sample to Dr. Alex Murray, known locally as the "good man". Meanwhile, Priscilla has thawed and asks Leafy to take her home. As they are leaving, Leafy runs into Murray, who tells him the tests show he might have a sexually transmitted disease, ruining his night with Priscilla.

Later Innocence, a member of Fanshawe's staff, is struck dead by lightning. Local custom insists she cannot be moved until a juju man performs a ceremony. Fanshawe is especially anxious that the body should be moved, since he is expecting a visit from a minor royal. Murray, sensitive to local custom, refuses to help. He tells Leafy, however, that the tests proved negative, allowing him to take advantage of Celia's sexual overtures. But, as Leafy leaves the Adekunle home after spending the night with Celia, Sam catches him. As punishment, he gives Leafy the job of bribing Murray, the only member of a local board blocking one of Adekunle's building projects.

Leafy and his employee Friday move Innocence's body in the night, but Fanshawe's staff refuse to work when they see the body gone. To add to Leafy's problems, Murray refuses his bribe. Adekunle wins the election, and comes to an understanding with the British over the oil. Kinjana's radicals are unhappy and gather menacingly outside a reception attended by Adekunle and the British. When they threaten to attack, Leafy offers to don Fanshawe's clothes and make a run for it in the official car, providing a diversion. Fanshawe's wife insists on going with him; they manage to escape from the rioting crowd. As they return to town, they discover that Murray has been seriously injured in a road accident. Before Murray dies, Leafy tells him that he too will try to be a good man. Returning to the embassy, Leafy gives Innocence's family the money for the juju man.

Bruce Beresford gives the impression that he directs with his mind on other things. If there is any tempo to the writing—and there are plenty of scenes here which ought to be knockabout—he manages to lose it. Sometimes, it seems we are watching one of those guide-to-the-production packages, '*The Making of a Good Man in Africa*' perhaps, the camera furtively picking up the action a beat behind.

William Boyd adapted the screenplay from his own novel of the same name. Its concerns are twofold—to satirise the political games played both by the British and the locals, and to trace how Leafy gains wisdom and a moral conscience. Central to both is Dr Murray, possibly, it's said, the last good man in Africa. The character so matches the way we assume Sean Connery to be—honourable, strong, no-nonsense—that he might almost be making an in-person appearance, striding boldly into the fiction. At one point, Murray/Connery tells Leafy that his ambition is to go somewhere warm and play golf. He's already made his judgement on the film, you think, and is itching to get back to his Marbella course.

In adapting, Boyd has stuck pretty closely to his novel, resulting in some sketchiness in the necessary compression. We only discover in the film's second half how sensitive Leafy is about his lowly roots, from a drunken speech he makes about his dear old dad. This sensitivity informs Boyd's novel from the start, contributing to a more complex character than the one we see on screen—one who attempts to quieten any moral qualms by reminding himself of the benefits of getting on. Despite an affably rumpled Colin Friels, the screen Leafy's changing of his ways comes as something of a surprise.

The sketchiness is heightened by Leafy's continually running about from sexual encounter to embassy mess. This perpetual motion ends up illustrating the adaptor's problems. How do you fit the whole novel into a 94-minute film? Apparently, by having the characters run at top speed from start to finish. With all this scurrying, and the line of women queuing up for Leafy (partly, it seems, because he has a large penis—a running joke), this could be a *Carry On* film.

Boyd was brought up in Ghana and Nigeria, and Beresford lived in Nigeria for two years. Even so, much of the picture of Africa, both in the novel and film, seems dated and stereotypical, and would surely have done so in 1981, when the novel was published. Speech from Friday—yes, *Friday*—is of the "Masta e never come home yet" sort. (As balance, there is the sharp Adekunle, who doesn't need Western lessons in scheming.) On the British side, Fanshawe is essence of upper middle-class diplomatic duffer. In this company, no wonder Connery seems like the real thing.

VILLAGE VOICE, 9/13/94, p. 70, Amy Taubin

Several first-rate actors, among them Sean Connery, Colin Friels, Diana Rigg, Louis Gossett Jr., and John Lithgow, are wasted in *A Good Man in Africa*, a predictable and rather pointless comedy of manners set in a fictional post-colonial African state. Director Bruce Beresford once again revels in the sentimentality about race relations that helped his *Driving Miss Daisy* win a Best Picture Oscar. The stolid script is an adaptation by William Boyd of his own tougher, more amusing novel.

The film is a kind of pale version of Ousmane Sembène's ferociously funny *Xala* (1974), which exposed the construction of property, sex, and power in the then newly emerged Nigerian bourgeoisie. *A Good Man in Africa* makes similar connections, but here the Africans are merely background against which their white former oppressors can behave wisely (Connery, as the local doctor and eponymous good man), behave foolishly (Lithgow, as the fatuous British ambassador), or evolve from foolishness to wisdom (Friels, as a beleaguered career diplomat who absorbs Connery's lessons with a little help from the gods) .

What makes *A Good Man in Africa* trivial is not only the short shrift given to the Africans, but also that so much of the comedy is a function of personality clichés rather than structures of power. Special mention must be made of the film's treatment of all the women characters, who are variously carriers of disease, manipulative gold diggers, and frustrated nymphomaniacs. Implicit in the m.o. of the "good man" is that he wants nothing whatsoever to do with them.

Also reviewed in:
CHICAGO TRIBUNE, 9/9/94, Friday/p. C, Michael Wilmington
NEW YORK TIMES, 9/9/94, p. C6, Janet Maslin
VARIETY, 8/15-21/94, p. 43, Leonard Klady
WASHINGTON POST, 9/9/94, p. D7, Hal Hinson
WASHINGTON POST, 9/9/94, Weekend/p. 43, Desson Howe

GOOD TIME SUNDAY

Producer: Paula Ballan, Gary Keys, and Philip Pearle. *Director:* Gary Keys. *Director of Photography:* Kevin Keating. *Running time:* 83 minutes. *MPAA Rating:* Not Rated.

NEW YORK POST, 12/23/94, p. 35, Thelma Adams

The underused Anthology Film Archives, situated on a cold corner of the East Village, is the site of one of the city's most heart-warming programs of holiday cheer. For two weeks beginning today, the Anthology is hosting a gospel Christmas program.

Mixing film and performance, the show's centerpiece is Gary Keys' movie "Good Time Sunday." The feature documentary chronicles the Salt and Pepper Gospel Choir from New Haven, Conn. The interracial choir is known for bringing its message of unity and the healing power of its music to schools, hospices, prisons and churches.

Each screening is preceded by live music. Among the featured local gospel groups are Kathy Farmers Gospel Explosion, Deverell Smith Group, Randy Jones & Special Edition and the Victor Jones Trio.

Whatever one's religious persuasion, gospel music cuts to the bone with an emotional message of hope, healing and redemption

The gospel performances boost a movie that already inspires audiences to leave the theater singing. The Museum of Modern Art has recognized Gary Keys' talents in directing bio-performance films by adding his award-winning documentaries, "Memories of Duke [Ellington]" and "Give Peace a Chance," to its permanent collection.

The highlights of "Good Time Sunday" are the soaring performances of Salt and Pepper. Interviews with choir members reveal the road the "salts" and "peppers," the whites and blacks, traveled to shed their nervousness about entering each other's lives and hearts.

You'll laugh when you see the footage of a performance at a white church which shows that white men can't jump—or clap. There are also poignant moments. During a visit to a Connecticut prison—one young black singer recognizes a number of inmates from his old neighborhood.

At 83 minutes, "Good Time Sunday" could have been shaved shorter without losing any of its zest. The filming has the homemade feel of the gospel amateurs: sound booms bop at the top of the frame and the occasional black hair curls on the margin.

Fortunately, the movie also shares the choir's ability to soar above its limitations and provide a vision of what it would be like if more people took small steps toward racial harmony.

Gospel, says one chorister, "is not the prescription for all the world's ills." But it has the spiritual power to show the commonality among men and women, blacks and whites, Christians and Jews, sick and well, free and imprisoned.

NEWSDAY, 12/31/93, Part II/p. 58, Esther Iverem

At one point in "Good Time Sunday," a sign for the "Connecticut Hospice" appears on the screen. Having just seen the gospel choir Salt and Pepper visit a prison and then a center for AIDS victims, you might feel you just can't bear to see another institution filled with despair.

But then when one patient, then another, and then another is wheeled into the Hospice's makeshift concert room in beds or wheelchairs, apprehension quickly melts. The rocking, tears or simple smiles of those bereft of hope bear witness to the uplifting power of gospel song.

This documentary about the interracial gospel choir Salt and Pepper is strongest when it shows this outreach of gospel, beyond its stronghold in the churches of black America. The film focuses particularly on the experiences of white choir members who have found meaning in the singing. And it documents the choir's trips around Connecticut, from community centers to Yale University, and shows how all these different cultures come together around something so personal as the worship of God.

We see Salt and Pepper singing before a reserved white congregation that routinely never joins in with its church choir. But before the end of the concert, people are standing on their feet, clapping and swaying. White choir members admit initial fears of driving into black neighborhoods. Black members admit initial doubts at the ability of their white fellow members of the choir to sing, clap and sway with the beat.

But this is not a study of the best of gospel music and performance. The lead singers are strong, but the choir is not made up of polished vocalists. Rather the power and spirit their songs evoke, especially those led by the husky-voiced founder, Mae Gibson-Brown, are a powerful example of the talent found in scores of churches throughout the country.

This music film does not raise the roof, and it does not convince us that gospel music, by itself, can heal the rifts between races. But it does show how uplifting song can mend a few links.

GREEDY

A Universal Pictures release of an Imagine Entertainment presentation. *Executive Producer:* David T. Friendly and George Folsey, Jr. *Producer:* Brian Grazer. *Director:* Jonathan Lynn. *Screenplay:* Lowell Ganz and Babaloo Mandel. *Director of Photography:* Gabriel Beristain. *Editor:* Tony Lombardo. *Music:* Randy Edelman. *Music Editor:* Tom Carlson. *Choreographer:* Jennifer Nairn-Smith. *Sound:* Robert Anderson, Jr. and (music) Dennis Sands. *Sound Editor:* Michael Hilkene. *Casting:* Karen Rea. *Production Designer:* Victoria Paul. *Art Director:* Dan Webster. *Set Designer:* Lauren Polizzi and Cheryl T. Smith. *Set Decorator:* Anne H. Ahrens. *Set Dresser:* John H. Maxwell. *Costumes:* Shay Cunliffe. *Make-up:* Felicity Bowring. *Make-up (Michael J. Fox):* Bron Roylance. *Stunt Coordinator:* Charlie Croughwell. *Running time:* 109 minutes. *MPAA Rating:* PG-13.

CAST: Michael J. Fox (Daniel); Kirk Douglas (Uncle Joe); Nancy Travis (Robin); Olivia d'Abo (Molly); Phil Hartman (Frank); Ed Begley, Jr. (Carl); Jere Burns (Glen); Colleen Camp (Patti); Bob Balaban (Ed); Joyce Hyser (Muriel); Mary Ellen Trainor (Nora); Siobhan Fallon (Tina); Kevin McCarthy (Bartlett); Khandi Alexander (Laura); Jonathan Lynn

(Douglas); Francix X. McCarthy (Daniel Sr); Tom Mason (Actor); Austin Pendleton (Hotel Clerk); Lowell Ganz (TV Director); Bea Soong (Assistant TV Director); Beau Byron (Little Danny); Ronnie Prettyman (Little Carl); Sean Babb (Dennis); Adam Hendershott (Joe, 9 years old); Eric Lloyd (Joe, 6 years old); Kirsten Dunst (Jolene); Lisa Bradley (Joette); Rita Gomez (Yolanda); John LaFayette (Wayne); Rich Barretta (Beefy Worker); Vince Morton (Uncle Vince at the Piano); Chris Schenkel (Himself).

FILMS IN REVIEW, 5/6/94, p. 56, Nathaniel Bird

The latest clunky comedy from British director Jonathan Lynn (who also did the shallow, lackluster *The Distinguished Gentleman*) has only one glimmer of sly intelligence—but it's only in the title allusion, for those conversant with film history. The film is entitled *Greedy*, and the main character is named McTeague—presumably from Erich von Stroheim's classic *Greed*, taken from the novel with the eponymous anti-hero McTeague.

This time, the movie plot revolves around the crotchety, manipulative patriarch of the McTeague family (Kirk Douglas), whose various unappealing relatives flock around him sycophantically, drawn by the possibility of inheriting his accumulated wealth. The four third-generation households are all scrambling for footholds in the most contemptible ways, largely focusing on mutual character assassination. Their interests are threatened when the codger develops a fond attraction for the nubile young Olivia d'Abo, his new companion, so the warring relatives join forces to track down the black sheep family offshoot for whom Douglas once had a soft spot, played by Michael J. Fox. Fox's high minded, ethically pure father had raised him to be above the lure of filthy lucre, but once ensconced in the McTeague mansion, Fox finds the lure stronger than expected.

The film plays out the machinations of the rival factions, which could have made for some good comedy. Unfortunately, although there are a few enjoyable plot twists, acting is largely abandoned in favor of mugging, repartee is abandoned in favor of scatological insults. (It's particularly nice to see Kirk Douglas, but he seems to belong to some entirely other film.) Perhaps the major Hollywood studios are too close to the subject to be able to say anything sincerely critical about greed.

LOS ANGELES TIMES, 3/4/94, Calendar/p. 4, Kevin Thomas

Kirk Douglas is so good in "Greedy" that you're tempted to forgive this wildly uneven satire its overkill script and often ponderous direction.

Douglas is cast as an aged but vigorous self-made scrap-metal tycoon whose declining health neither prevents him from going to work nor taking tremendous relish in watching his various nephews and nieces currying slavish favor in hopes of inheriting his $20-million fortune.

It is gratifying to see a great veteran star in a major role—no cameo this—in which he brings a lifetime of experience in a portrayal rich in sly, deft nuances and details. Douglas' sheer presence holds the film together when all else flounders. Ironically, with a tough-minded rewrite and a lighter touch, "Greedy" might have been as good as Douglas.

What's wrong here is crystal clear from the start. Writers Lowell Ganz and Babaloo Mandel, who should have know better, load up Douglas with three craven nephews—Ed Begley Jr., Phil Hartman and Jere Burns—and an equally grabby niece, Colleen Camp, and caricature them to the extent that they don't seem to be in the same film with Douglas' long-lost grandnephew, Michael J. Fox, his girlfriend, Nancy Travis, or Douglas' gorgeous but honorable new companion, Olivia d'Abo. (Douglas, luckily, is able to play off them all.)

The relentlessly one-dimensional cousins and their awful spouses become tiresome and stupendously obvious even before they've completed their first scenes; one or two cousins would have sufficed.

There are moments when you wonder why anyone would pay to see a money-isn't-everything lecture from two of the most successful screenwriters in the history of the movies, and Ganz and Mandel's bursts of moralizing tend to overshadow their valid point of how even the nicest people—i.e., Fox's none-too-successful pro bowler and d'Abo's decent care-giver—can be tempted by vast sums without even realizing it.

The writers also don't overlook the tycoon's own responsibility in the degrading, endless manipulation of his relatives. The film doesn't shy away from the tycoon's darker side and neither does Douglas.

Ultimately, however, director Jonathan Lynn cannot impose any kind of evenness of tone upon "Greedy," which wants too hard to be a ruthlessly honest and bouncy mainstream entertainment at the same time.

As with Douglas, Lynn and the writers do very well by d'Abo and especially Fox, who holds on to our sympathies even when his well-meaning character is in danger of selling out. Travis, who is able to be simultaneously funny and beautiful in the stylish tradition of Sally Kellerman and Carole Lombard, is most welcome as a consistent moral force and reality check.

"Greedy," which is slick and shiny-looking, isn't up to par with either Lynn's "My Cousin Vinny" or Ganz and Mandel's "A League of Their Own," "City Slickers" and other hits reaching back to "Splash."

NEW YORK, 3/14/94, p. 75, John Powers

The clumsily staged *Greedy* starts out as a black comedy about a group of relatives who wheedle, cajole, grovel, and connive to inherit the fortune of their crusty uncle Joe (Kirk Douglas). But once Michael J. Fox turns up, this appealingly ruthless premise starts to go muzzy and soft. (*Only Saturday Night Live*'s Phil Hartman achieves the necessary razor-stropping glee.) As genial and corrupt as Louisiana politician, *Greedy* mainly serves to answer the question "How does a Michael J. Fox comedy made in the chastened nineties differ from one made in the avaricious eighties?" It's simple, really: In this decade's model, Fox has to spend a few minutes feeling guilty about wanting lots of dough before it lands in his lap.

NEW YORK POST, 3/4/94, p. 37, Michael Medved

What can you say in defense of a movie that offers as its dramatic and emotional high point a long musical number in which Michael J. Fox presents his earnest impersonation of Jimmy Durante singing "Inka Dinka Doo"?

Fox isn't bad exactly—it's just that in comparison to the real Durante (who appears in the title sequence in 50-year-old footage from "Two Girls and a Sailor") he seems like a pallid wimpish substitute. By the same token "Greedy" isn't bad either—it's just lifeless, stale and relentlessly unfunny.

The story centers around an aging, wheelchair-bound scrap metal tycoon played by Kirk Douglas—who seems to be the only member of the cast who's actually enjoying himself. Since he has no children of his own his various cousins, nieces and nephews each hope to inherit his millions.

They grovel shamelessly before him, and constantly try to discredit one another in order to gain' some advantage in the old man's will, but they briefly manage to form a united front when confronted with a common threat: an outrageously attractive 20-something pizza delivery girl with a fetching cockney accent (Olivia d'Abo) who has suddenly moved into Uncle Joe's mansion as his "nurse" and confidante.

To counteract this menace, the relatives resolve to locate Uncle Joe's long-lost favorite nephew: a luckless professional bowler played by Michael J. Fox.

For years, he's been the only family member with no interest in cashing in on the old man's gold but his failing career on the bowling circuit leaves him ready to respond to his cousin's pleas that he help them persuade Kirk Douglas that his relatives, rather than his seductive new companion, deserve the bulk of his estate.

The script for "Greedy" represents a career lowpoint for the gifted team of Lowell Ganz and Babaloo Mandel, who previously wrote "Night Shift," "Splash," "Parenthood," City Slickers" and "A League of Their Own."

In the past, their comedies worked because even when they set up bizarre situations, they gave us characters who seemed both sympathetic and real. By contrast, no one in "Greedy" comes across as the least bit believable; these people are about as vivid and complex as the performers in an inferior sketch on "Saturday Night Live."

Perhaps it's no accident that SNL veterans Phil Hartman and Siobhan Fallon portray two of the ruthless relatives (together with Ed Begley Jr., Bob Balaban, Colleen Camp, and others). Part of the problem is that there are simply too many of these overacting plotters, so that most moviegoers will find it impossible to keep their identities straight.

Director Jonathan Lynn ("My Cousin Vinny," "The Distinguished Gentleman") brings neither bite nor energy to this musty material, nor to his smirking on-screen role as Uncle Joe's sardonic butler.

With nothing else to sell to the movie-going audience, he resorts to innumerable leering views of Olivia d'Abo's exposed flesh, as this engaging, gorgeous, easygoing actress parades her talents in various states of undress.

Film buffs will no doubt note the fact that the family name here is McTeague which is the same moniker featured in the Erich von Stroheim silent classic "Greed"—a great film with which this tired trifle otherwise has nothing in common.

NEWSDAY, 3/4/94, Part II/p. 81, Jack Mathews

Michael J. Fox told an interviewer recently that working with screen legend Kirk Douglas on Jonathan Lynn's "Greedy" was an experience he'll never forget. Let's hope he'll have better luck forgetting the movie."

"Greedy" is a real porker, a film so broad and badly developed, greed is about the only explanation for having so many talented people feeding at the same trough. Screenwriters Lowell Ganz and Babaloo Mandel, who have blue-printed such winsome comedies as "City Slickers" and "Splash!," have written what amounts to a feature-length "Saturday Night Live" sketch and Lynn, who last gave us the cleverly riotous "My Cousin Vinny," directed it like an episode of "Married ... With Children."

What passes for a moral theme in this tale about a band of parasitic nephews, nieces and in-laws bowing and scraping before scrap-metal baron Joe McTeague (Douglas) is the cynical notion that, faced with the opportunity for undeserved wealth, anybody will do anything.

The brood of cartoonish scavengers assembled for a death watch at Uncle Joe's mansion includes cousins Ed Begley Jr., Colleen Camp, Phil Hartman and Jere Burns and their accompanying spouses and children, the latter bearing names like Jolene and Josephene that conveniently abbreviate in honor of their great uncle.

When the clan gets a load of Uncle Joe's new companion, Molly (Olivia d'Abo), a vivacious English nymphette who dropped by with a delivery of pizza and stuck around to massage his ego and compete for his riches, they send away for Daniel McTeague (Fox), the long-lost cousin who used to thrill Uncle Joe with his Jimmy Durante impressions.

Daniel, a second-rate professional bowler with an arthritic wrist, is appalled by his cousins' behavior, but as soon as he gets a whiff of Uncle Joe's dough, he is doing his old Durante act and trying to beat both his relatives and Molly to it. The only character in the sorry affair with a conscience is Daniel's girlfriend, Robin (Nancy Travis), who stands around scowling, shaking her head and threatening to leave if his decency doesn't return.

There is too much talent involved for "Greedy" to be a total failure. Ganz and Mandel are funny writers and their script contains a few good lines. And Lynn, who cast himself as Uncle Joe's insincere British butler Douglas, knows how to set up to a punchline.

Douglas actually comes off better than anyone, hamming it up as the conniving, wheelchair-bound Uncle Joe. Fox was right to be impressed. Douglas is one of the last in the breed of old Hollywood stars, and Fox, who is stuck playing the same human money clip in every movie, can only marvel at the diversity that kind of stardom brings.

NEWSWEEK, 3/14/94, p. 72, David Ansen

In the new comedy "Greedy," avaricious horde of relatives schemes, deceives and grovels in hopes of winning its rich uncle's huge inheritance, while the uncle takes sadistic delight in their humiliation. In the comedy "The Ref," a snarlingly ill-matched husband and wife are taken hostage by a thief, but it's the crook who's dying to escape after exposure to their toxically dysfunctional family. In "The Hudsucker Proxy," corporate greed incites a tycoon to hire a witless dolt to head his company so that stock prices will fall and the grasping board members can buy up the shares.

Bile, as a comic ingredient, is back. Hollywood seems to be gambling that the best cure for our national distemper is a blast of nasty humor. Both "Greedy" and "The Ref" find comic pay dirt in the spectacle of blood relations uncorking their revulsions and resentments in open insult. You could read them as belated tantrums against the patriarchal, money-obsessed Reagan '80s.

The trouble with "Greedy" is that it lacks the courage of its crankiness: director Jonathan Lynn leavens bile with moralism, meanness with sentimentality, and it's not a palatable brew. The relatives who descend on wheelchairbound Uncle Joe McTeague (Kirk Douglas) have tough competition in the inheritance game: Uncle's luscious British live-in "nurse" (Olivia d'Abo). Desperate, they dig up Uncle Joe's long lost favorite nephew (Michael J. Fox), a professional bowler whose idealism is severely compromised when it dawns on him how much money he could rake in. Any film written by Lowell Ganz and Babaloo Mandel ("Splash," "Parenthood") is bound to have its share of laughs (many supplied by Phil Hartman), but they get bogged down in soul-searching. The have-your-cake-and-eat-it-too ending says a lot about Hollywood: naturally, this ferocious attack on avarice can end happily only if someone gets filthy rich.

One of the reasons "The Ref" is a funnier, more trenchant comedy than "Greedy" is that it's cast better. Judy Davis and Kevin Spacey play the bickering couple jewel thief Denis Leary has the misfortune to kidnap. Their bone-deep mutual disgust gives the farce a bracing edge of verisimilitude. They snap and squabble from the moment they're hijacked, driving their frustrated captor to moan, "I've hijacked my f-----g parents!" And he has yet to meet their screwed-up, blackmailing son Jesse (Robert Steinmiller Jr.) or Spacey's rich monster mom (Glynis Johns) and the rest of the bickering brood descending for Christmas Eve dinner.

If "Greedy" takes its cue from Ben Jonson's "Volpone," "The Ref" owes an obvious debt to O. Henry's "The Ransom of Red Chief." The script, by Richard LaGravenese and Marie Weiss, veers unevenly between sharp, sophisticated malice and crowd-pleasing low humor, but director Ted Demme (Jonathan's nephew) keeps the laughs coming at a brisk pace. Stand-up comic Leary holds his own as a felon whose values prove more decent than those of the indiscreet, uncharming bourgeoisie. But "The Ref's" venom is ultimately more bark than bite: its feel-good wrap-up seems rushed and unearned. The great bilious black comedies arose from a singular vision—from a Billy Wilder, a Buñuel, a Polanski. In both "Greedy" and "The Ref" you can feel the footprints of studio committees. Hollywood will never be comfortable with true misanthropy, preferring to hedge its bets.

You can't say that about the Coen brothers Joel and Ethan. Though "The Hudsucker Proxy" had a much bigger budget than "Barton Fink" or "Raising Arizona," this highly stylized comic extravaganza bears their unmistakably independent stamp. This big-business satire is a post-modern pastiche of the Capra, Hawks and Sturges rat-a-tat social comedies of the '30s and '40s. Though set in 1958, everything about it—from its rube Midwestern hero (Tim Robbins) to its fast-talking reporter heroine (Jennifer Jason Leigh) to its cigar-chomping villain (Paul Newman) to its spectacular sets (by Dennis Gassner)—reeks of those earlier decades.

Robbins is the dolt Newman plucks from the Hudsucker company mailroom and makes president. Hot-shot reporter Leigh, smelling a rat, poses as Robbins's secretary and wins his heart while pillorying him in print. But the idiot is a savant: his simple-minded invention—the hula hoop—becomes a national obsession, forcing Newman to found new ways to crush him.

"The Hudsucker Proxy," which the Coens co-wrote with Sam Raimi, has sequences as dazzling as anything they've done. It also has pages that are unusually strained and shrill: gags that only reveal the effort that went into them. Movie buffs will lap up the inventive variations on old conventions and revel in Leigh's astonishing mile-a-minute amalgam of Katherine Hepburn and Rosalind Russell. But even by the Coens' cool standards, "Hudsucker" is a chilly experience (you don't go to the Coens for the milk of human kindness). Brilliant as its artifice is, there's something hollow at its core. In the past, the Coens took old genres and twisted them into distinctive new shapes. Here they seem as much imprisoned by old movies as inspired. This supremely self-conscious comedy is both delightful exhausting. But never for a moment do you doubt that it's exactly the movie they wanted to make. Its gleeful, cartoon heartlessness is for real.

VILLAGE VOICE, 3/15/94, p. 54, Anne Glusker

Straight from the dreck factory to you. No focus groups, no test screenings—nope, the makers of *Greedy* just went directly to the agency and ordered up that extra-big type for their subway ad posters, because they knew—without one moment's hesitation—that what we all needed to relieve our end-of-winter doldrums was this movie, as banal, crass, and unengaging as it is.

What makes all this so puzzling is that the writers, Babaloo Mandel and Lowell Ganz, have produced some good stuff: *Splash* and *City Slickers* (or was that Billy Crystal's doing?). Even *Parenthood* had more than a few moments. Here we have a movie that's utterly reducible to its advertising slogan: "Where there's a will ... there's a relative." The moronic scenario (which the filmmakers maintain was "borrowed" from Dickens's *Martin Chuzzlewit*) is this: Uncle Joe is mean, nasty, and very rich. (Kirk Douglas, unshaven and in a wheelchair, just looks sad—he can't have *needed* this job.) His passel of relatives are shallow, duplicitous, and grasping. They want what he's got. Two things stand in their way. One is Molly (Olivia d'Abo), who came to Joe's manse to deliver pizza and stayed to lie around the pool, displaying what must be the best waxing job in history. D'Abo makes a great 007 blonde, but in this she looks as if she know exactly how ridiculous her part is. The relatives' second obstacle is long-lost, sweet-faced cousin Daniel (Michael J. Fox). He arrives on the scene, a sad-sack pro bowler (don't ask), broke and honorable but—here's a plot point for you—perhaps a bit corruptible. As his girlfriend, Nancy Travis has "moral center" emblazoned on her forehead.

If I hadn't been watching this movie in order to write this, I would've walked after the first 20 minutes (something I've done only once: *Pocket Money* with Paul Newman). So save your money, and go for something a tad less witless. Don't even rent it.

Also reviewed in:
CHICAGO TRIBUNE, 3/4/94, Friday/p. H, Mark Caro
NEW YORK TIMES, 3/4/94,p. C15, Janet Maslin
VARIETY, 2/28-3/6/94, p. 69, Leonard Klady
WASHINGTON POST, 3/4/94, p. C9, Hal Hinson
WASHINGTON POST, 3/4/94, Weekend/p. 44, Roger Piantadosi

GRIEF

A Strand Releasing release of a Grief Productions film.. *Executive Producer:* Marcus Hu. *Producer:* Ruth Charny and Yoram Mandel. *Director:* Richard Glatzer. *Screenplay:* Richard Glatzer. *Director of Photography:* David Dechant. *Editor:* William W. Williams and Robin Katz. *Music:* Tom Judson. *Sound:* Thomas Jones. *Sound Editor:* Alberto Garcia. *Production Designer:* Don Diers. *Set Decorator:* David Carpender. *Set Dresser:* Ethan Pines. *Costumes:* Laser N. Rosenberg. *Make-up:* Isabelle Pilliere. *Running time:* 87 minutes. *MPAA Rating:* Not Rated.

CAST: Craig Chester (Mark); Jackie Beat (Jo); Illeana Douglas (Leslie); Alexis Arquette (Bill); Carlton Wilborn (Jeremy); Lucy Gutteridge (Paula); Robin Swid (Kelly); Bill Rotko (Bill No. 2); Shawn Hoffman (Ben); Frank Rehwaldt and Greg Bennett (Movers); Mickey Cottrell (Judge); Catherine Connella (Beverley/Ginger); Jeffrey Hilbert (Antonio); Johanna Went (Marleen); Kent Fuher (Harvey); Joan Valencia (Tutti); Beatrice Manley (Loretta); Ian Abercrombie (Stanley); John Fleck (Ben/Chaz); Sloane Bosniak (Susie).

LOS ANGELES TIMES, 4/1/94, Calendar/p. 6, Kevin Thomas

"Grief" may be an unlikely title for a comedy, but a large part of its appeal is in its willingness to take its people seriously amid much laughter. In a nifty feature debut, writer-director Richard Glatzer makes hilarious use of his experiences as producer of "Divorce Court" as he takes us into the crazed world of the writers for a lurid daytime courtroom TV show. The staff runs the gamut of sexual orientation from gay to straight, from an individual uncertain about his orientation to another of indeterminate gender.

Glatzer picks a particularly tumultuous week in the production office of "The Love Judge," headquartered in Hollywood's Art Deco Montecito. Central among six key characters is Craig Chester's Mark, a pleasant, preppie-looking story editor considered to be among the most gifted of the series writers and one of the operation's more mature presences. However, he's facing the first anniversary of the death of his lover from AIDS. Meanwhile, Jo (Jackie Beat), the show's producer, announces she's leaving to get married. This doesn't mean she still isn't thrown into a tizzy every time she discovers evidence that her office's couch has been used for some off-duty lovemaking.

Other key figures are Jo's man-crazy assistant Leslie (Illeana Douglas), who's eager to break into writing; Bill (Alexis Arquette), who's just broken up with his girlfriend, the muscular Jeremy (Carlton Wilborn), as wise as he is sexy, and the ambitious Paula (Lucy Gutteridge).

Drawing upon his personal as well as professional experiences—like Mark, he has also lost a lover—the insightful Glatzer is a filmmaker of humor and compassion, He also brings a sure sense of structure and makes the most of an opportunity to display a gift for sharp, witty dialogue. "Grief" takes place virtually entirely within "The Love Judge" offices, yet it is always cinematic, never stagy.

Whenever "Grief" threatens to get too emotional, Glatzer deftly cuts to glimpses of outrageous "Love Judge" episodes, which feature cameos by Mickey Cottrell (as the judge), Mary Woronov, Paul Bartel and performance artists Johanna Went and John Fleck. The stories the writers concoct border on the delirious as do their inevitable mutations. The hefty Beat, most appropriately described as a male actress, to borrow Charles Pierce's self-description, shines under Glatzer's direction, as does everyone. Douglas is especially sparkling as the vibrant, self-deprecating Leslie, and Chester, who made his film debut as Nathan Leopold in "Swoon," once again conveys exceptional intelligence and perception. Made on a low-low budget, "Grief" has been resourcefully designed (by Don Diers) and photographed (David Dechant). "The Love Judge" may be laughably outlandish, but the people of "Grief" prove to be real and endearing.

NEW STATESMAN & SOCIETY, 4/1/94, p. 41, Jonathan Romney

Over the past few weeks, I have detected a worrying tendency in myself. I've started to praise films for their ordinariness, to like them for not being heart-rending and Hollywood and demonstrative—simply for not making a fuss. I liked *Philadelphia* precisely because it was no big deal, unmemorable and workaday, and gave Hollywood Aids movies a blueprint for being as ordinary and un-tub-thumping as they need to be. And I grudgingly approved of *Shadowlands* for being so stiff-upper-lip and recalcitrant about love and death and middle-aged *Weltschmerz*.

I can see myself slipping into kind of a minor groove here, praising all things so-so—but I'd probably get away with this rather better in France, where it's still cool to turn out manifestos with titles like *Pour un cinéma mineur* or maybe a nice gnomic *L'Ordinaire*. Over here, though, you look as if you're arguing for more Julie Walters *Screen Two* movies. Great. Next week, I'll be writing encomiums to *The Rector's Wife*.

All right: this is the last time I do it. *Grief*, which closed this year's Lesbian and Gay Film Festival and opens at the ICA Cinema, is a new gay comedy by Richard Glatzer. It's really no big deal whether you see it or not, but if you do, you'll be glad you did. This sounds like damning with faint praise, but it fits the film's feeling of jaunty camp amusement.

Grief is very much about life going on without the carpet being torn from under you, and its title is particularly acute. It's grief in the sense of regret, anguish and mourning, but also as in "Don't give me *grief*"—worrying about what deli to eat in today, the daily grind of jockeying for office position, how unfathomably dumb your favourite soap opera seems to be getting week by week.

The film lasts only 87 minutes, but you almost wish it could run all day, so that you could walk in for ten minutes every couple of hours and find the characters still bickering, still worrying about the stains on the sofa, still snogging under the desk. Someone ought to figure out a way to make a soap movie so that it would reproduce the familiar, disorientating effect of tuning into the *Archers* omnibus midway through, after you've already heard half the week's episodes.

Grief is set in the production office of an implausibly ropey TV soap called *The Love Judge*, loosely based on *Divorce Court*: a long-running purgatory on which director/writer Glatzer served time. An astounding, stilted show, which we get to see in lurid fragments, *The Love Judge* is clearly the work of intelligent minds turning to porridge out of boredom and using outrage as a last-ditch tactic against encroaching dementia.

They're not rash-addled subversives, just a regular crew of nice fresh smart sexy boys and girls who happen to be wasting away with boredom and fatigue from daily jousting with boorish network bosses. You can tell how desperate they are to distract themselves from the daily choosing between pastrami or tuna on rye.

The production office is located in a former brothel; the work's okay, says the producer Jo, it's just "a different kind of prostitution". The team are "a terrific bunch of maladjusted underachievers".

There's Mark (Craig Chester), whose lover died with Aids a year ago; Bill (Alexis Arquette), who just split up with his girlfriend and seems to be on the verge of a little identity experimentation; wild-girl-turned-celibate Leslie (Illeana Douglas); and dandyish, aggressive Jeremy (Carlton Wilborn), who has ambitions to shake the show up, but can't see why no one takes to his lepers-in-love plot line.

Ruling over them is Jo, played by the monumental Jackie Beat, a drag artist who must be tired by now of being hailed as the new Divine. As Divine was wont to do, she appears briefly in court in her male persona, as a horrific barking slob.

The film is broken up into day-by-day slices from the working week. Its interspersed soap episodes are the weak link: the design is to show false, spectacular crises against the ordinary ones in the office, and to demonstrate how things in real life rarely come to a head, but simply go on, fitting themselves around off-the-cuff sexual encounters or the photocopier breaking down.

But the extracts don't quite work either as contrast, or as a satire of the US image bucket. Whether it's just Glatzer's fevered imagination playing tricks or a reflection of the kind of mad, meaningless show his bored characters would *like* it to be, *The Love Judge* sticks out as too wilfully wacky, as if a little chunk of John Waters had landed in *Rhoda*. It's funny, but not that funny, although larded with great one-liners ("He beat me with my copy of *The Feminine Mystique!*" rages a circus lesbian).

In any case, this imbalance of flavours tends to be what makes good soap. We love a soap most when it veers madly between downbeat realism and no-holds-barred melodrama—when we're constantly asked to zap in imagination between, say, little Billy's cat being taken ill, troilism among the young doctors on the new estate, and ritual decapitations at the housing co-op.

So on this level of madcap diversity, *Grief* works rather well. There's blatant unreality in the *Love Judge*, with its circus lesbians, Tourette's cases, rock'n'roll dog trainers. And then there's reality, which gets its gravitas from Craig Chester—whose suavely jowly demeanor (he was wonderfully dapper and lofty in *Swoon*) makes light work of grappling between mourning and lust.

Grief carries its seriousness as lightly as it does its sense of camp, without ever doing a big Life's Rich Tapestry number. Its sex context is gleeful and mischievous. You know from the start that the film can't wait to get the pants off Alexis Arquette, but it doesn't make a meal of it. The cast helps too, nicely pitched between pantomime cattiness and languid Californian ennui.

Illeana Douglas, last seen getting a horrific love bite in *Cape Fear*, is the funky secretary who's just a little weary being funky. With her nice nervy style, expect her to turn up in a Woody Allen picture one of these days. And Jackie Beat gives the film a sardonic oomph: Beat's great trick is the way she changes registers, flicking from distracted fussiness in a whispering-pines purr to a welling-up mania couched in the sort of can-do confidence that speaks of a thousand self-help manuals: "Now they can threaten me, make sumo wrestler jokes—I'm impenetrable!" She's great when the Prozac calm breaks and the rage erupts: "Someone has been jerking off on my new sofa!" Nothing in *The Love Judge* can quite compete.

NEW YORK POST, 6/3/94, p. 39, Bill Hoffmann

Bill just broke up with his girlfriend Kelly, and now his good friend Mark. whose male lover recently died of AIDS, wants to hook up with him, except that Bill begins having an affair with their mutual friend Jeremy, all while their tank-sized female boss Jo plans a quicky marriage and getaway to Prague.

With us so far? If so, you've got a taste of the wacky plot of "Grief," a comedy-drama that's got its heart in the right place but its funnybone strictly on a banana peel.

"Grief" shows us five wild days behind the scenes at a trashy daytime soap opera called "The Love Judge."

A handful of writers crank out hackneyed over-the-top scripts involving circus lesbians, Tourette's syndrome victims and schizoid opera singers on trial before a cantankerous old judge who disapproves of it all.

The crazed TV courtroom scenes have an energized life all their own and they boast some great cameos by cult stars like Paul Bartel and Mary Woronov (both of "Eating Raoul" fame).

But the TV shenanigans play second fiddle to the rather strained office politics being played by Bill, Mark and Jeremy.

Director Richard Glatzer's comedy tries to show us that beyond the corporate facade and camaraderie of the office setting, there are real human beings with real problems more stirring than any soap could dish out.

What's wrong here is that much of the film's rag-tag, anything-goes humor is simply lame. The actors toss off line after line hoping they'll get a laugh. Only a few do.

Toward the end, Glatzer does bring a genuine pathos to his players' predicaments. But, alas, it's just too late.

But one big high note is the performance of Jackie Beat, a.k.a. drag actor Kent Fuher, as the compassionate Jo. Fuher may succeed Divine as the world's most lovable transvestite.

But despite his/her presence, "Grief" is one production the "Love Judge" himself would probably dismiss.

SIGHT AND SOUND, 4/94, p. 42, Leslie Felperin Sharman

One working week n the production office of *The Love Judge*, a daytime television show about a divorce court. Video clips from the series are interspersed with scenes showing the office workers interacting with each other. Mark, a story editor for the show, is still grieving for his lover Kenny, who died of Aids a year ago this week. He confides to his friend Jeremy, a scriptwriter for the show, that he is strongly attracted to Bill, an apparently heterosexual writer who has just broken up with his girlfriend Kelly. Jeremy warns Mark off Bill, insisting that he couldn't be interested in him. Jo, the series' producer, announces over the course of the week that she is leaving to go and live in Prague with her new husband and that she has nominated Mark and Paula, another story editor, as candidates for her successor. Leslie, the secretary, develops a flirtation with Ben, the photocopier repairman, and tries to interest Mark in her script for the show.

As the week progresses, it is revealed that Jeremy and Bill have been having a torrid affair for three weeks. Bill, confused about his sexuality, is hesitant about coming out to everyone else, especially since he still has feelings for Kelly, who is now dating a rich performance artist, also named Bill. Mark and Paula endure grilling interviews with the network for Jo's job. Bill comforts a distraught Mark after his interview, which leads to a passionate kiss. Mark runs away confused.

Later, Jo catches Bill and Jeremy in an embrace in her office. Mark and Jeremy have a confrontation about each other's relations with Bill. Mark goes missing and everyone fears that he may have committed suicide, but Jeremy tracks him down. Jo manages to have both Mark and Paula appointed co-producers for the show. Leslie's script is produced, Jeremy and Bill become an official item, and Jo takes everyone out to lunch.

Grief is a deeply likeable movie. Deftly remixing elements of John Waters-style camp and *thirtysomething* yuppie melodrama, art-house aesthetics and pulp fiction, it adds up to much more than the sum of its parts, and marks the debut of talented first-time writer-director Richard Glatzer. His script is as taut as the lycra shorts on Carlton Wilborn, who plays the strutting Jeremy, and as fresh as a transvestite's new lipstick. You have to hear lines like "I don't have time for circus lesbians and neither should you" in context in order to appreciate how well Glatzer handles situational comedy. The counterpointing between scenes from the ridiculous *The Love Judge* and the 'real life' of the people who produce it neatly illustrates the soapy quality of office passions and politics. *Grief* was partly inspired by Glatzer's stint as producer of *Divorce Court*, a series to which *The Love Judge* bears an uncanny resemblance. Yet despite its autobiographical origins, *Grief* is elaborately structured, almost glib in the way that bad TV can often be. For example, an avant-garde video artist who films empty rooms is passingly mentioned early on, and lo and behold, the closing shots show the office, vacated at last. This also neatly alludes to the work of Ozu, whose *Tokyo Story* is instrumental to the plot. Like Gregg Araki's *The Living End*, *Grief* has an air of film-school cleverness, but its allusions and reworkings are more motivated and controlled than Araki's.

Though clearly made on a low budget, nothing seems cut-price about *Grief*'s other qualities, especially where the acting is concerned. The ensemble cast of semi-knowns turn in excellent performances, especially Craig Chester as Mark (last seen in Tom Kalin's *Swoon*), Alexis Arquette as Bill, and drag artist Jackie Beat, aka Kent Fuher, who plays both Jo the lady boss and a minor role as the jilted husband of a circus lesbian in one of the excerpts from *The Love Judge*. Comparisons will be inevitable between Beat and Divine, the Maria Callas of drag, but Beat holds her/his own very well. Watch out also for cameo appearances from Paul Bartel and Mary Woronov of *Eating Raoul* notoriety.

After we have been lulled into a false sense of security by the cheerful fun of its other storylines, the film's cold central theme of bereavement sneaks up on us unexpectedly. Mark's grief at the loss of his lover Kenny from Aids has cast an numbing chill over his life, and throws all the humour, especially his, into sharper relief. Afraid to take a chance on a new relationship, hesitant about pursuing promotion, too scared even to take the test for HIV, Mark has put his life on hold ever since Kenny died. In contrast, many of the other characters have reacted to his death by exuberantly seizing the day. Despite all its distractions, *Grief* deals more squarely and honestly with Aids and its effects than most films that focus directly on HIV-positive protagonists. Indeed, it points out that Aids has victims beyond the people who die from it. *Grief* illustrates issues like this well but avoids becoming that stodgiest of film genres, the issue-based movie. It well deserves the cult status for which it seems destined.

VILLAGE VOICE, 6/14/94, p. 52, Georgia Brown

Richard Glatzer's oddball comedy *Grief* is a lot more about loss than it lets on most of the time. In fact, the film's title only really registers—with a lump in the throat—at the end. Most of the time in the five-day workweek represented here, things in the L.A. production office of the daytime TV show *The Love Judge* are wacky, tacky, and downright raunchy.

Jo (Jackie Beat) is the big, and do I mean big, boss. She literally dwarfs her five employees: somber Mark (Craig Chester, who played Nathan Leopold in *Swoon*), muscular Jeremy (Carlton Wilborn), pretty boy Bill (Alexis Arquette, brother of Rosanna and Patricia), Leslie (Illeana Douglas), the dizzy secretary who longs to break into the creative end, and the relatively recessive Paula (Lucy Gutteridge).

First, there's a running gag of the mysterious stains on the boss's new sofa. Then there's Jo's announcement that she's finally found happiness and relief from "fat jokes" in Eastern Europe. With Jo moving to Prague with her fiancé Milos, either Mark or Paula stands to succeed her. This week's questions: Who will get the nod from above and who is screwing whom, leaving a white stain and a red condom on the blue couch? Meanwhile, we get to watch five weird *Love Judge* episodes straight from the team's collective' imagination. (Two of these, the opera diva sequence and the circus lesbians sequence, feature Mary Woronov and Paul Bartel.)

For five years a producer on *Divorce Court*, Glatzer evidently knows whereof he speaks. He has also lost his companion to AIDS, as has his main protagonist, Mark. This is the real loss that *Grief* refers to in an honest, valiant attempt to say that the soaps, they are our lives.

Also reviewed in:
CHICAGO TRIBUNE, 7/15/94, Friday/p. K, John Petrakis
NEW YORK TIMES, 6/3/94, p. C6, Caryn James
VARIETY, 7/19/93, p. 72, Dennis Harvey

GUARDING TESS

A TriStar Pictures release of a Channel production. *Producer:* Ned Tanen and Nancy Graham Tanen. *Director:* Hugh Wilson. *Screenplay:* Hugh Wilson and Peter Torokvei. *Director of Photography:* Brian J. Reynolds. *Editor:* Sidney Levin. *Music:* Michael Convertino. *Music Editor:* Kenneth Wannberg. *Choreographer:* Mary Ann Kellogg. *Sound:* James Sabat and (music) Dennis Sands. *Sound Editor:* Victoria Rose Sampson. *Casting:* Aleta Chappelle. *Production Designer:* Peter Larkin. *Art Director:* Charley Beal. *Set Decorator:* Leslie Rollins. *Set Dresser:* Paul Bowman, Tom Scruggs, and Elizabeth Weber. *Special Effects:* Doutlas Retzler and Conrad Brink. *Costumes:* Ann Roth and Sue Gandy. *Make-up:* Selena Miller. *Stunt Coordinator:* Jery Hewitt. *Running time:* 98 minutes. *MPAA Rating:* PG-13.

CAST: Shirley MacLaine (Tess Carlisle); Nicolas Cage (Doug Chesnic); Austin Pendleton (Earl); Edward Albert (Barry Carlisle); James Rebhorn (Howard Shaeffer); Richard Griffiths (Frederick); John Roselius (Tom Bahlor); David Graf (Lee Danielson); Don Yesso (Ralph Buoncristiani); James Lally (Joe Spector); Brant Von Hoffman (Bob Hutcherson); Harry J. Lennix (Kenny Young); Susan Blommaert (Kimberly Cannon); Dale Dye (Charles Ivy); James Handy (Neal Carlo); Stephen S. Chen (Jimmy); Katie O'Hare (Barbara); Mark Conway (Caleb Harrison); David L. King (Derrick Hastings); Jane Beard and Michael Gabel (Kidnappers); Kelly Williams (Mr. Porter); Beverly Brigham (Autograph Seeker); Teman Treadway, Kyle Duvall, Andrew C. Boothby, Sharief Paris, and Gary Glaesser (FBI Men); Brian Deenihan (Plainclothes Guard); Julie Kurzava and Michael Consoli (Opera Singers); Hugh Wilson (President's Voice); Brenna McDonough (Doctor); John Leonard Thompson (Young Doctor); Saige Spinney (Waitress); Gerald Gough (Store Manager); George Gomes (James Carlisle); Bob Child (Shaeffer's Assistant); John Louis Fischer (Crew Member); Diana Sowle (Hairdresser); Maggie Linton (Carlo's Secretary); Jim Hild (Helicopter Doctor); Will Bellais (Major Domo); Matilde Valera (Yvonne Hernandez); Marie McKenzie (Nurse); Al Cerullo, Jr. (Helicopter Pilot); Michael A. Echols (Orderly).

FILMS IN REVIEW, 5-6/94, p. 55, Nathaniel Bird

Guarding Tess has the flattened out, small scale look of a movie made for TV. In Nicolas Cage it has a great, manic comic actor whose talents are thrown away in the role of Doug Chesnic, an uptight, buttoned down Secret Service agent assigned to guarding Tess Carlisle, a president's widow. And Shirley Maclaine, as the Nancy Reagan-like widow, is, predictably, Shirley MacLaine: a bitchy grande dame who turns out to have a heart of gold.

The plot is the stuff of TV sitcoms. Doug wants a more exciting, glamorous job than guarding the reclusive, difficult Mrs. Carlisle, but she likes him and uses her influence to prevent his reassignment. For most of the film, Doug goes a slow burn while Mrs. Carlisle makes demands and the audience waits for something to happen before the inevitably heart warming ending. Not much does. Mrs, Carlisle plays golf, goes to the opera, undergoes a CAT scan for a possible brain tumor, visits with her crassly opportunistic yuppie son, mischievously gives the agents the slip. Early on she tells Doug that he should try being crazy for once, and it's not long before they achieve a rapprochement over drinks in a country and western bar, a nod to the audience's populist instincts I suppose. The movie never decides if it's a comedy, a sentimental domestic drama, or even, in the last twenty minutes, a thriller. The comedy might summon a laugh or two out of a couple on a first date anxious to have a successful genial evening, but in general it's pretty tepid. The funniest bit comes from an actor who doesn't even appear on screen when Doug gets a call from the current president who sounds like the endearingly vulgar, irascible LBJ.

It's not hard to apportion blame for this misconceived project—the buck stops on the desk of Hugh Wilson who wrote the screenplay and directed the film in a style as blandly pictorial as a Kodak snapshot. There's so little happening here that I found myself pondering the contradiction between product endorsing shots of a Marlboro poster and the heroine's prohibition of smoking—Hollywood cynicism at its best.

LOS ANGELES TIMES, 3/11/94, Calendar/p. 9, Kenneth Turan

Unlike the often troublesome academic subject, nothing is more welcome or elusive in pictures than Hollywood's version of chemistry, the sparks two actors set off when they mix on screen. Sometimes, too, the most unlikely combinations prove effective, and so it is with Shirley MacLaine and Nicolas Cage in "Guarding Tess."

Though they've never acted together and most likely never even met before this pairing , these disparate performers find common ground in this delicately funny chamber comedy about the war of nerves that develops between a formidable First Lady and the dissatisfied Secret Service agent assigned to protect and serve.

But aside from demonstrating how far a pleasing acting mixture can take you, "Guarding Tess" also shows its limitations, Though set up beautifully, "Tess" has difficultly delivering on its promise, taking an unexpected and unsatisfactory turn that undercuts rather than emphasizes all the good things that have come before.

And as good as its performances are, "Tess" also benefits from the unmistakable stamp of Hugh Wilson, whose playful sensibility created television's "WKRP in Cincinnati," "Frank's Place" and "The Famous Teddy Z." In addition to co-writing (with Peter Torokvei) and directing, Wilson plays a crucial voice-only role that helps set "Tess'" comic tone.

Tess Carlisle (MacLaine) is the widow of a President, a take-no-guff figure ("Don't Mess With Tess" reads a Time magazine cover) who is much beloved by the great American public. But guarding this termagant, Doug Chesnic (Cage) tells his boss, is without doubt "the worst assignment there is in the Secret Service."

Doug feels free to express these thoughts because after three years of living in deeply tedious Ohio and being the agent in charge of Tess' detail, he thinks he's on the verge of another, more cutting-edge assignment.

Then comes a phone call from the current President, a Carlisle protege (done in great unctuous/enthusiastic style by Wilson himself) who says that Tess has requested another tour for her favorite agent and that he as Chief Executive would consider it a personal favor if Doug agreed to return.

For it turns out that the tough, formidable woman enjoys nothing better than engaging in wars of words with the strictly-by-the-book Agent Chesnic. Their always polite, always deadly verbal duels are invariably engaging, and though the President of course exaggerates when he suggests "maybe you two have some kind of sicko thing going on," their acerbic, ironic battles inevitably binds them into a "Driving Miss Daisy"-type relationship.

Though his work is problematic at times, there is perhaps no actor of his generation who does better in ridiculous situations ("Moonstruck," "Honeymoon in Vegas") than Cage. Neither he nor the equally adept MacLaine forces or flaunts their characterizations; rather they underplay their parts as much as the situation allows, and though neither breaks any new ground, they succeed in bringing "Tess'" light-on-its-feet humor to life.

After facing off in a number of whimsical situations (a mid-winter golf game, comic trips to the opera and the supermarket), Tess and Doug begin to bring other colors to their interaction, and for a brief while it seems as if this film will be able to gracefully segue to a more serious emotional level.

Instead, "Guarding Tess" takes a sharp hairpin turn, as if Miss Daisy's house were suddenly burned to the ground by a vengeful pack of Klansmen, a plot twist out of character with what's gone before and one that seems to have come from a totally different movie.

While it's understandable that it was thought that "Tess" needed something more, that it couldn't go on merely being clever and fragile, this solution goes too far in the opposite direction. It turns "Guarding Tess" into a movie Tess herself would have seen through, and that is not a good sign.

NEW YORK POST, 3/11/94, p. 44, Thelma Adams

Shirley MacLaine has reincarnated herself as the post-menopause poster woman. Ask her to do a Shelley Winters and she'll shriek and shrew it up. Ask her to play Betty Ford and she'll build you a clinic.

In "Guarding Tess," MacLaine is as crusty as an old loaf. And, since this is Hollywood, a golden heart is buried in the doughy center.

Tess Carlisle (MacLaine) is a frustrated former first lady who gets her kicks out of tormenting her seven Secret Service agents. Her chief whipping boy is special agent Doug Chesnic (Nicolas Cage).

It's a classic sitcom situation (very "Benson"). Director/writer Hugh Wilson ("Burglar") squeezes the material for all the obvious laughs with help from co-writer and Second City alumnus Peter Torokvei.

On an impromptu mid-winter golf trip, Tess cheats and Doug raises his hackles when she asks him to retrieve her ball. "I'm a Secret Service agent not a caddy," he says.

Cage, an actor who never rises above his material, does a binary performance. He is either completely buttoned-up or out-of-control and throwing things.

After the setup, there's nowhere to go in this one-gag movie. Suddenly, it shifts from Snow Gray and the Seven Gunmen to a far-fetched thriller.

Kidnappers pop out of nowhere and the plot—which has more loose ends than a Rastafarian—takes a grisly turn.

Of course, there's an eventual reconciliation between the crusty old broad and her gofer-with-a-gun. Doug emerges as a hero and Tess gets to shine her heart of gold.

Aa long as Wilson and Torokvei were going to be far-fetched why not go all the way? Why not have Tess and Doug fall in love and at least give an otherwise bland outing a "Harold and Maude" twist?

NEWSDAY, 3/11/94, Part II/p. 72, John Anderson

Roles for older actresses are scarce, I know, but do they all have to involve torturing Nicolas Cage? Diane Ladd wanted him dead in "Wild at Heart." Olympia Dukakis gave him the hairy eyeball in "Moonstruck." Anne Bancroft—playing his *mother*—haunted him in "Honeymoon in Vegas." And now, just when he should be catching his breath, he's got to go back out there and face the champ.

Yes, Shirley MacLaine is the source of his pain in "Guarding Tess," as the iron-willed former first lady to his beleaguered Secret Service agent. But Shirley MacLaine is also the reason to watch this Hugh Wilson comedy, even if it's not for the humor.

You can't really laugh *with* MacLaine; she's too weighty, too sober, and almost totally incapable of self-deprecation. And you certainly can't laugh at her, for all the same reasons. Given that Cage is mostly a reactive comic actor, this doesn't create a lot of light-hearted fun. But in creating Tess, a public figure who's lost the limelight, a gifted political player who's been put out to pasture, and the woman death has left behind, MacLaine can and does, deliver the bitter, lonely, mean-spirited goods.

And before it dissolves into an Oedipal soap opera, "Guarding Tess" is well on its way to becoming a witty and thoughtful film with something to say about women, their second-class position in public life and the weird plight of first ladies. It chickens out halfway, collapsing into a highly improbable kidnap scenario that involves the contentious Tess and Doug realizing just how much they mean to each other, blahblahblah. But until it does, we get the strong feeling that maybe Tess should have occupied the Oval office.

Tess Carlisle, national treasure, possesses the qualities of several recent White House wives. The simple human warmth of Nancy Reagan. The impenetrable facade of Barbara Bush. The common touch of Hillary Clinton. But her public image is unimpeachable, even if Special Agent Doug Chesnic (Cage), who had been a member of her husband's Secret Service detail, considers her nothing more than a selfish and demanding dead-end to his career.

Doug has completed a three-year hitch at Camp Tess and immediately fled to Washington when he's told she wants him back. It would be, he's told, "a personal favor to the president," whom we never see, but whose voice (director Wilson's) comes off as a combination of Bush, Clinton and Ross Perot. The chief executive wants to maintain the Teflon bequeathed him by Tess' late husband, and keeping Tess happy and safe is all part of it.

So Doug goes back to Ohio and tries to rein her in, with predictable results. You wonder why such a domineering woman would want a strong-willed agent like Chesnic assigned to her—until a rather sad scene where she reruns her public life on her VCR and we found out why: Doug had been among the few who wept at her husband's funeral.

Tess is a talent unfulfilled, half dignity, half pathos. She drinks a little. She has a son (Edward Albert) who only visits because he has a project that needs her endorsement. She has a brain tumor—one of the inexplicable and unresolved aspects of Wilson and Peter Torokevei's script—and she has a nagging doubt about the significance of her life. We might not all identify with her, but we can certainly sympathize.

SIGHT AND SOUND, 7/95, p. 49, Philip Strick

Thankful to have completed a three-year assignment guarding former First Lady Tess Carlisle in Summersville, Ohio, Secret Service agent Doug Chesnic returns to Washington for his next posting. His Director, Neal Carlo, breaks the news that at the personal request of the President he is to continue to head the seven-man Ohio team, a job which, thanks to the petulance of Mrs Carlisle, consists of a daily battle of wills. While Doug takes his duties very seriously, Tess treats her guards like domestic servants, subject to petty household rules and innumerable menial tasks. Grimly resuming his role as chief target for Tess' moods, Doug announces that he and his men will no longer run trivial errands; the immediate result of his defiance is a call from the President, to whom Tess has complained, asking him to be more co-operative.

Tess decides to go to the opera in Columbus, Ohio. Their departure is delayed when Doug insists on the correct seating arrangements but the trip is otherwise uneventful until, in the middle of the show, Tess falls noisily asleep. When Doug discreetly tries to wake her there is even more noise; Tess is angry and humiliated but the warm acclaim of her public restores her good humour. On the way home she orders her chauffeur, Earl, to give their Secret Service escort the slip, and Doug has to request the help of the local sheriff to trace her car. He attempts to get Earl dismissed but after a blazing row Tess orders Doug and his men out of the house. On the phone from Air Force One, the President orders him to restore harmony as soon as possible.

Locked out, Doug gloomily maintains surveillance from the perimeter of the Carlisle estate. After a visit from her son Barry, who hopes to gain her support for a dubious business project, Tess at last relents, recognising that Doug is the only reliable person in her life, and an evening at the local bar marks the start of a new friendship between them. There is news of an intended Presidential visit, causing much fluster and planning, but when this is abruptly cancelled Doug is saddened to see Tess lose some of her vitality. After a period of inertia, she decides to have a picnic, although snow is forecast; afterwards, Earl again drives off with Tess unguarded, leaving Doug, marooned. It becomes apparent that Tess has been kidnapped.

When Doug alerts Washington to Tess' disappearance, an army of government men arrives to take control and Doug's team is sidelined in disgrace. Tess' car is found, with Earl beaten up beside a ransom note, and Doug realises that the chauffeur had to be an accomplice. Accompanied by top F.B.I. official Harvard Shaeffer, Doug visits Earl in hospital and threatens to shoot him; terrified, Earl admits that Tess was kidnapped by his own sister and her husband. They have her hidden under the floor of a barn, and Doug insists that he and his men are the rescuers who dig her out. In turn, although barely conscious, Tess demands that her Secret Service team be the ones to accompany her to hospital. When she is fully recovered it is on Doug's orders that she accepts a wheelchair for her departure from hospital, cheered on by the patients and staff.

Since the peculiar risks of riding shotgun over a celebrity are known to every showbiz bouncer and press attache, as well as to every journalist assigned to dodge the defences and hit the story target, there is a certain familiarity about *Guarding Tess*, not least thanks to its echoes of *The Bodyguard*. While few may previously have given much thought to the fate of past Presidents and their families, said to exist in greater numbers than ever before in Stateside history, the haunting spectacle of (for example) Coppola's Godfathers with their self-sacrificing retinue of shadows have increasingly accustomed audiences to households blighted with an excess of armed staff. Looking for a fresh slant on the inherent parallel themes of domestic power struggle and generation gap animosity, embodying an irrefutable hint of *Driving Miss Daisy*—and, for that matter, of Miss Haversham, the matriarch of eccentricity—the creators of *Guarding Tess* have nothing much more to offer than Shirley MacLaine who has become, in entertainment terms at least, about as First a Lady as could be hoped for.

To her credit, hers is a relievingly underplayed Norma Desmond, all termagant qualities well under control. Although required to rail against the Secret Service stranglehold that represents the residue of her share of history, and although incarcerated with a pack of protectors whose evident instability would be the envy of Roderick Usher, she refrains from hurling furniture, unleashing obscenities, or ravaging the wine cellar. Instead, even when the script requires her to cheat against herself at golf, she maintains an assertive dignity, a poise which serves her well when her odious son is unmasked as an unscrupulous conman, or—with particular pathos—when her face hardly changes at the news that there will, after all, be no Presidential visit. Against this delicacy, Nicolas Cage can show little but exasperation, resorting to a series of frenzied outbursts (some, admittedly, sounding like an attempt to be heard above the blare of the music soundtrack) which only serve to emphasise that his role is curiously without substance or background. If we might guess, by the time of their reconciliation, that he is intended to be a replacement for both son and husband in a life without much future, it is hard to see what contribution other than a unquestioning devotion he will be able to make to Tess' welfare.

Given that Hugh Wilson was responsible for *Police Academy*, the film's indulgence towards its minor players is to be expected. Even so, the abrupt miming to Mozart by Richard Griffiths seems to have strayed in from some other show, and Austin Pendleton's contribution as the wimpish chauffeur is so lugubriously comical that the whole kidnap episode, with its parodied C.I.A. musclemen, appears destructively close to farce. Wilson himself provides the voice of the beleaguered President, whose phone calls make a wonderfully unsettling intervention: "I've got the most important job in the world," he complains to the incredulous bodyguard, "so maybe you two have some kinda sicko thing goin' on but you gonna help me out on this one, okay?" This bizarre Dr Strangelove tone works absurdly well, as does the visit to the supermarket when the manager checks nervously whether or not the First Lady wishes to be incognito and the agents mutter into their handsets about the special offer on peas. But it drains all vestigial realism from Tess' predicament, despite being set among superb production designs by Peter Larkin, and reduces it to the vaguely sentimental, a daft and muddled homage to those whose fame may painfully have overtaken their usefulness.

VILLAGE VOICE, 3/22/94, p. 54, Lisa Kennedy

They have, in the past, crossed that line, hurrying toward that scary island called self-parody, but not here. Here Nicolas Cage and Shirley MacLaine rein it in, and in doing so give their best performances in quite a while for the benefit of the funny if slightly confusing, though not confused (director Hugh Wilson's hand seems mighty sure), *Guarding Tess*.

Why confusing? Possibly because the humor's just too darn smart and nuanced, especially if you're expecting an out-and-out spoof on the burgeoning personal security guard genre. Instead of lampooning *The Bodyguard* or *In the Line of Fire*, Tess sidles up beside them, suggesting a more absurdist and likely truer vision of the relationship between the body and the guard. One of the cleverest send-ups in the movie has former first lady Tess Carlisle (MacLaine) and her resentful secret service man Doug Chesnic (Cage) sharing a drink and a chat in a c&w bar; remember Whitney and Kev with Dolly playing in the background. It's so subtle you could miss the joke, but the nice thing is the filmmaker gives it to you as a perk: you get it—good; you don't—that's okay too, it just furthers the characters' development.

There's something dumbfounding in Wilson and cowriter Peter Torokvei's approach to their script: Much could have been played for easy belly laughs, but they opt instead for comedic discipline and inject the leads with equal measures of charm and infuriating weaknesses. While the latter is not necessarily an original gesture, with the help of the two leads, Wilson manages to it an act of deft humanism. Yes, Tess is crotchety, but she's also lonely and cramped by this mandated sentinel. Yes, one can relate to Special Agent in Charge Chesnic's desire for a "real" detail (he too had guarded a president, the one whose wife he now serves—breakfast on a tray—and protects) but also be a little frustrated with his sense of values, his desire for guts and glory. With not too many trite shenanigans, Wilson imparts the unavoidable lesson in all of this: that while taking care of this cranky national treasure, agent Chesnic gets both the glory and the guts.

Also reviewed in:
CHICAGO TRIBUNE, 3/11/94, Friday/p. A, Michael Wilmington
NEW YORK TIMES, 3/11/94, p. C12, Janet Maslin
VARIETY, 3/7-13/94, p. 59, Leonard Klady
WASHINGTON POST, 3/11/94, p. G6, Richard Harrington
WASHINGTON POST, 3/11/94, Weekend/p. 42, Desson Howe

GUNMEN

A Dimensions Films release. *Executive Producer:* Lance Hool and Conrad Hool. *Producer:* Laurence Mark, John Davis, and John Flock. *Director:* Deran Sarafian. *Screenplay:* Stephen Sommers. *Director of Photography:* Hiro Narita. *Editor:* Bonnie Koehler. *Music:* John Debney. *Sound:* Fernando Camara. *Casting:* Terry Liebling. *Production Designer:* Michael Seymour. *Art Director:* Hector Romero, Jr. *Set Decorator:* Ian Whitaker and Enrique Estevez. *Special Effects:* Jesus Duran. *Costumes:* Betsy Heimann. *Running time:* 90 minutes. *MPAA Rating:* R.

CAST: Christopher Lambert (Dani Servigo); Mario Van Peebles (Cole Parker); Denis Leary (Armor O'Malley); Patrick Stewart (Loomis); Kadeem Hardison (Izzy); Sally Kirkland (Bennett); Richard Sarafian (Chief Chavez); Robert Harper (Rance); Brenda Bakke (Maria).

LOS ANGELES TIMES, 2/4/94, Calendar/p. 6, Kevin Thomas

"Gunmen" is the kind of picture people are talking about when they express concern over excessive screen violence. Murky in plot, sketchy in characterization, routinely crafted—except for Hiro Narita's fine noirish camerawork—it exists only as an excuse to depict the piling up of bullet-riddled corpses. Considering its relentless mediocrity, it is amazing that it was actually previewed for critics rather than opening cold.

All you really need to know about its needlessly convoluted story is that it struggles in vain to play as a buddy movie, teaming up a straight-arrow bounty hunter (Mario Van Peebles), under contract to the Drug Enforcement Agency, and a goofy, small-time smuggler (Christopher Lambert) who inadvertently may hold the key to the location of a huge drug fortune. The film's locale is the fictional South American country of Boa Vista—it seems lots like Colombia—and was filmed in Puerto Vallarta.

Van Peebles manages to work up a modicum of credibility, but Lambert's part is so underwritten that his attempt to play it like Jean-Paul Belmondo in a comic action caper of the '60s makes the guy come across as merely being stupid rather than amusing.

Anyway, there is a slew of bad guys who throughout the movie are constantly trying to gun down or otherwise eliminate Van Peebles and Lambert—and lots of other people as well. Patrick Stewart is a drug kingpin so nasty that he buries his bride alive, Denis Leary is a gleeful killer, and Sally Kirkland is vivid but wasted in a small part as an arms dealer. The real culprits of "Gunmen," however, are director Deran Sarafian and writer Stephen Sommers.

NEW YORK POST, 2/4/94, p. 36, Michael Medved

What's the point of a gory, gut-spilling action film if the violence is so poorly shot and sloppily staged that most of the time you can't even tell who's supposed to be doing what to whom?

Most of the big fight scenes in the dismal dud "Gunmen" take place at night, and the images on screen are much too dark and hazy to follow the tide of battle. Even more important, these scenes provide so little light that unless you have a glow-in-the-dark dial you can't even check your watch.

The muddled plot has something to do with evil drug lords in a fictional South American country called Boa Vista which bears an uncanny resemblance in many scenes to the Jungle Cruise ride at Disneyland.

Patrick Stewart (the noble hero of "Star Trek, the Next Generation") here plays a crippled creep who isn't exactly thrilled when one of his associates steals $400 million of his ill-gotten gains and hides the money in a boat in some unknown harbor.

To recover the loot, Stewart hires sadistic, sarcastic enforcer Denis Leary (playing essentially the same part he handled effectively in "Judgment Night") to track down the one man who may know the key to the mystery.

That man is jailed, bug-munching drug smuggler Christopher Lambert, but before Leary can get to Lambert, the prisoner is kidnapped by yet another interested party: Mario Van Peebles, a daring commando who's working as a sort of free-lance supporter of the Drug Enforcement Agency because, we're told, he's upset over the impact of drugs in his neighborhood back home. Despite these idealistic intentions, Van Peebles soon joins the hunt for the hidden cash, working in an uneasy alliance with Lambert.

The movie tries to focus on their relationship—where, amid much insipid banter, they can't decide whether to kill one another or try to work together. Many of these scenes are apparently supposed to be humorous, but the featured twosome comes across like an achingly unfunny blend of "The Defiant Ones" and "Beavis and Butt-head."

For Lambert, this teeth-gnashing, eye-rolling performance marks his worst film to date—which is saying quite a bit for the star of such past triumphs as "The Sicilian" and "Highlander II."

Van Peebles is, as always, an appealing screen presence. Unfortunately, in nearly half his scenes he seems to be trying his best in difficult circumstances, so the real shame here is that he didn't direct the film.

As creator of "New Jack City" and "Posse," he might at least have brought some edge and energy to the wake-me-when-it's-over "action" scenes, which are woefully mishandled by director Deran Serafian (whose previous credits included "Death Warrant" and "Back in the USSR").

Van Peebles did, however, produce the soundtrack album, which features the music of Big Daddy Kane, Kid Frost, Dr. Dre, and Christopher Williams (who appears briefly in the film's obligatory whorehouse scene) and that album will, almost certainly, do better business than this altogether miserable movie.

NEWSDAY, 2/4/94, Part II/p. 66, John Anderson

"Do you think I'm overreacting?" asks the drug-dealing archvillain Loomis (Patrick Stewart), just after having his unfaithful wife buried alive. I was shaking my head furiously, but I though he said "overacting."

"Gunmen" uses a bit of the theme to "The Good, the Bad and the Ugly" to get the credits rolling, which is more than appropriate: The music is good; the rest of the film is bad or ugly. Considering the amount of vulgarity and violence to be found in so many mall-oriented movies, for "Gunmen" to be so glaringly offensive is something of an accomplishment. But that's probably because these qualities aren't hinged to anything like a plot, or a script. The scene in which Big Daddy Kane is found rapping in the middle of a South American jungle makes more sense than the rest of the story line.

But what, after all, are we to expect from a movie starring Mario Van Peebles and Christopher Lambert, two of the more voracious scenery chewers in the business? Or Stewart, as their wheelchair-bound nemesis, or the equally villainous Denis Leary, direct from "Judgment Night"? Or Brenda Bakke, star of "Hot Shots Part Deux," as Leary's female henchman (henchwoman?). Or, in a cameo, Sally Kirkland? The mind reels.

Down in South American—Boa Vista, to be precise—Cole (Van Peebles), an agent with the Drug Enforcement Administration, is looking for Loomis, because "his poison took half my neighborhood out." Right. Shortly thereafter, the political climate changes and Cole's cut loose by the DEA, which frees him up to violate every law known to God and man. And by explaining his entire history, and that of every other character, in one breathless conversation with a superior who should have known it all before—he frees the movie up to indulge its violently adolescent sensibilities.

As it trips merrily along, ripping off every other buddy movie, action flick and western—including what must be the 500th shameless lift of the cliff-jumping scene from

"Butch Cassidy"—"Gunmen" focuses on the love-hate relationship between Cole and Dani (Lambert), whose brother was killed by Leary's character (yes, folks, Armor O'Malley) and spends the movie trying to cheat Cole out of the missing money his brother left behind. And vice versa. Their wisecracking gets on your nerves though, and you begin hoping that considering the abundance of automatic-weapons fire, one of the bad guys would at least get lucky.

VILLAGE VOICE, 2/15/94, p. 64, Henry Beck

Gunmen is a new take on the goofy Chef Boy-Ar-Dee spaghetti westerns that came in the wake of Leone, generally featuring James Coburn or Henry Fonda in the front seat alongside a circus tentful of dubbed character clowns like Bud Spencer and Terence Hill. Here you've got Chris Lambert as a goonybird South American with a French accent who chews on beetles, and prettyboy Mario Van Peebles as an urban cop in the jungle trying to make the hood back home safer from the usual blah blah blah. The two guys chase around, jump off cliffs à la Butch and Sundance, shoot each other for kicks, and nearly make out together in a tender campfire moment.

Squat in the middle of this tropical cocaine neverland, they stumble onto a joint where Big Daddy Kane, Dr. Dre, and other rappers just happen to be hanging, like maybe the Hip Hop Tour Bus From Hell got its tires stuck in the backwater's purgatorial muck. Denis Leary (the Dice Clay memorial cancer-poster boy of the '90s) runs around acting mean; Sally Kirkland deals guns from her own private Silicone Valley; and Patrick "Picard" Stewart has fun barking Royal Shakespearean lines like "Don't toy with me, you fuck!" and reciting the Lord's Prayer with a faceful of dirt as he is buried alive.

Former Tarzan Lambert has found his niche, playing Daffy Duck to Van Peebles's Bugs in a movie that rightly wears its abundant stupidity like a medal. Homeboy at the KISS-FM screening sees me taking notes and tells me to give it two and a half stars, but entertaining and charming nonsense like this deserves nothing less than three.

Also reviewed in:
CHICAGO TRIBUNE, 2/4/94, Friday/p. N, Michael H. Price
NEW YORK TIMES, 2/4/94, p. C8, Caryn James
VARIETY, 2/7-13/94, p. 41, Emanuel Levy
WASHINGTON POST, 2/4/94, p. C6, David Mills

HANS CHRISTIAN ANDERSEN'S THUMBELINA

A Warner Bros. release. *Producer:* Don Bluth, Gary Goldman, and John Pomeroy. *Director:* Don Bluth and Gary Goldman. *Screenplay:* Don Bluth. *Animation Director:* John Pomeroy. *Sequence Animation:* Cathy Jones and Ralf Palmer. *Computer Animation:* Jan Carlée. *Editor:* Thomas V. Moss. *Music:* William Ross and Barry Manilow. *Songs:* Barry Manilow, Jack Feldman, and Bruce Sussman. *Music Editor:* Jim Harrison. *Sound:* Martin Maryska. *Sound Editor:* John K. Carr. *Production Designer:* Rowland Wilson. *Art Director:* Barry Atkinson. *Special Effects:* Dave Tidgwell. *Make-up:* Maria Farrell. *Running time:* 85 minutes. *MPAA Rating:* G.

VOICES: Gino Conforti (Jacquimo); Barbara Cook (Mother); Jodi Benson (Thumbelina); Will Ryan (Hero); June Foray (Queen Tabitha); Kenneth Mars (King Colbert); Gary Imhoff (Prince Cornelius); Joe Lynch (Grundel); Charo (Mrs. "Ma" Toad); Danny Mann (Mozo); Loren Michaels (Gringo); Kendall Cunningham (Baby Bug); Tawny Sunshine Glover (Gnatty); Michael Nunes (Li'l Bee); Gilbert Gottfried (Mr. Beetle); Pat Musick (Mrs. Rabbit); Neil Ross (Mr. Fox/Mr. Bear); Carol Channing (Ms. Fieldmouse); John Hurt (Mr. Mole); Will Ryan (Reverend Rat).

LOS ANGELES TIMES, 3/30/94, Calendar/p. 5, Kevin Thomas

Don Bluth's "Hans Christian Andersen's Thumbelina" casts its spell so effectively that you don't even have to be a child to be swept away to its magical never-never land. Another success from Bluth and his partner Gary Goldman, whose previous animated hits include "The Secret of NIMH" and "An American Tail," it is a work of lilting pace and charm with an array of enjoyable rather than memorable songs, with lyrics by Jack Feldman and Bruce Sussman and music by Barry Manilow.

As a work of animation, it is securely in the Disney tradition of simply designed whimsical characters set against painterly landscapes and interiors. Bluth's script, in fact, is so sturdily constructed that he actually could have gotten away with a more venturesome, contemporary style and still appeal to family audiences.

A lonely woman (voice of Barbara Cook) living in a cottage on the outskirts of medieval Paris so longs for a child that she visits a "good witch," who gives her a barley seed, revealing, when it blossoms, a tiny living creature, a pretty young woman whom her new mother names "Thumbelina" (voice of Jodi Benson) because she's no bigger than her thumb.

Thumbelina brings joy to her mother, but she soon grows lonely, longing to enter the world of fairy tales because the figures in her mother's book are the same size she is. Magically, her wish is granted, and she soon meets and falls in love with the handsome prince Cornelius (voice of Gary Imhoff), whose wings leave trails of stardust and who rides a bumblebee for longer journeys.

Naturally, the young lovers are not about to get to live happily ever after so early in the game, and, sure enough, Thumbelina is kidnaped by the amorous toad Grundel (voice of Joe Lynch). She escapes only to land momentarily in the arms of Mr. Beetle (voice of Gilbert Gottfried) and finally winds up for the winter in the care of Ms. Fieldmouse (voice of Carol Channing), who thinks she'd be the perfect bride for the homely, sightless but rich Mr. Mole (voice of John Hurt), whose underground quarters possess a movie palace splendor. At times, Thumbelina seems as imperiled as a heroine in a Samuel Richardson novel.

Although not innovative, Bluth and company are certainly imaginative, taking us into their enchanting world so completely its people actually become real for us.

NEW YORK POST, 3/30/94, p. 31, Michael Medved

When a picture relies for its musical interludes on eight contagiously catchy songs by the one and only Barry Manilow, you can safely assume that the filmmakers aren't exactly aiming for cutting-edge intensity.

Instead, the new animated extravaganza, "Hans Christian Andersen's Thumbelina" tries for safe, soft family entertainment. And it succeeds handsomely.

Despite its saccharin elements (and all those maddeningly hummable Manilow tunes), "Hans Christian Andersen's Thumbelina" maintains just enough of the dark, dangerous tone of the original tale by the Danish master to keep young moviegoers utterly absorbed.

The title character (given rich voice by Jodi Benson, who won previous acclaim by singing the part of "The Little Mermaid") is a tiny, thumb-sized teen-aged girl, born out of a flower to provide companionship to a lonely, good-hearted old woman (Barbara Cook).

Thumbelina despairs of ever meeting someone her own size. But one night, her sweet singing attracts the attention of the handsome fairy prince (Gary Imhoff) who flies in through her window. Almost immediately, they begin talking marriage, but before he can win his parents' consent or arrange a caterer, Thumbelina is kidnapped and taken far from home by the scheming Mrs. Toad (Charo).

This unfortunately insulting Latina stereotype hopes to use the girl in her traveling show ("Singers de Espana") and wants her to marry her grotesque son. Thumbelina manages to escape this cruel fate but like many another single woman she seems to be plagued by a long succession of unsuitable suitors.

In addition to the toad, there's a raspy-voiced nightlife-loving beetle (Gilbert Gottfried) and a wealthy, middle-aged mole (John Hurt), whose cause is pleaded by a worldly wise fieldmouse (Carol Channing).

Meanwhile, Thumbelina meets a kindly French swallow (Gino Conforti) who tries to help her get home to reunite with the intrepid prince and repeatedly urges her to "follow her heart."

The movie relentlessly reinforces this lesson—that you should obey your own emotions above any commitment to a higher code or other people— as if it represented the deepest wisdom of the ages.

The luminous, gorgeously detailed animation marks a welcome comeback for producer-director Don Bluth, following his truly disastrous outing with "Rock-A-Doodle." "Thumbelina" approaches the quality of his Spielberg collaborations, "An American Tail" and "The Land Before Time," which means it's one of the better non-Disney animated films of recent years.

In contrast to Disney's peerless and thrilling adventures in "Beauty and the Beast" and "Aladdin" however, the pacing here is easy-going, almost sedate. But small children respond beautifully to these gentle rhythms, as evidenced by the worldwide popularity of Mister Rogers or even Barney.

My own flawless barometers of juvenile taste (Sarah, age 7, and Shayna, age 5) both loved this movie and watched every moment at the literal edge of their seats, while their restless old man checked his watch only three or four times.

In other words, this is above-average family fare that deserves to score solid success.

NEWSDAY, 3/30/94, Part II/p. B9, John Anderson

Be careful what you wish for, the old adage goes, 'cause you just might get it. Take Thumbelina. Longing for love, she winds up being chased by two suitors at the same time, and they turn out to be a fairy and a toad.

Thumbelina (voice of Jodi Benson), the enchanted girl born fully grown from a flower bud, really loves Cornelius (Gary Imhoff, the handsome Prince of the Fairies. But before they can wed, she's kidnaped by Grundel (Joe Lynch), the plug-ugly son of Mrs. Delores Toad (Charo), who wants to put Thumbelina in their singing act, Los Sapos Guapos. This sets up the requisite series of adventures, escapes and encounters with an assortment of colorful characters, as well as various musical interludes in which Barry Manilow attempts to prove he can be as pointless as Andrew Lloyd Webber.

Animator Don Bluth has remained fairly faithful to the Hans Christian Andersen story, although the results could have been titled "Gidget Goes to Arden Forest." She's an amorphous and overly animated entity; her face, which seems to mutate before our eyes, is never really defined, nor is her personality. But lack of dimension is always a problem with Don Bluth's characters.

His animation—seen most recently in "Rock-a-Doodle" and "All Dogs Go to Heaven"—always begs the comparison with his old employer, Disney, and always suffers. There is a distinct lack of warmth, and a frenetic need to amuse. Any involvement on the part of the audience is strictly voluntary.

But "Thumbelina" moves along quickly enough to keep younger children interested, and provides a raft of colorful characters. Besides the Toad Family Singers, there's the insidious Berkeley Beetle (Gilbert Gottfried), who drafts Thumbelina into the floor show in his club; Jacquimo the swallow (voice of Gino Conforti), who sounds like Maurice Chevalier and has a kick-line of Folies Bergère birds accompany him on one number, and Ms. Fieldmouse (Carol Channing), who rescues Thumbelina from the snow but then maneuvers the poor girl into marriage with the myopic mogul Mr. Mole (John Hurt). The best musical number, in fact, is titled "Marry the Mole" and features Channing singing the enchanted forest equivalent of "Diamonds Are a Girl's Best Friend."

SIGHT AND SOUND, 8/94, p. 54, Andrew Pulver

A lonely woman asks a good witch to give her a daughter, and receives a barleycorn seed. When the seed grows and opens, a tiny child is revealed sleeping inside. The child, named Thumbelina, is treated by the woman as if she is her own. One night, however, Thumbelina meets a fairy prince and, before he can return to become acquainted properly, she is kidnapped by a troupe of toads.

Thumbelina manages to escape quickly, but she is now isolated and vulnerable in a hostile world. Jacquimo, a swallow, proves friendly; but Berkeley Beetle is less so, and, after singing at the Beetle Ball, Thumbelina is forced again to flee.

Meanwhile, the prince is searching for his lost love, racing against the onset of winter. A blizzard arrives, and the prince is frozen into a block of ice. Thumbelina is luckier—she finds shelter with a mouse, but is soon under siege again, this time from a mole. She refuses to become his wife and escapes the wedding ceremony. She is soon reunited with her prince, who is thawed out of the ice and returns to defend her.

With children's animation fare currently doing all the talking at the box-office, one-time Disney animator Don Bluth has recently sewn up a production and distribution deal with Twentieth Century Fox to try and break his resurgent employers' all-conquering performances. Projects like this Hans Christian Andersen adaptation for Warners will be judged and compared directly with the likes of *Aladdin* and *Beauty and the Beast*, and the evidence points to the inescapable conclusion that Bluth has not yet managed to capture either the visual or narrative sophistication with which the Disney workshops impregnate their output.

The advances made in computer-generated imagery, as well as an increasing appreciation of cinematic style, has led Disney towards more gothic, fantastical material. *Thumbelina*, on the other hand, is grounded firmly in traditional methods of animated story-telling: from the page-turning story-book introduction, to the cute but game cast of insects and small animals who assist the heroine. Whether Bluth simply does not have access to the kind of technology that made the flying carpet or the ever-changing Genie in *Aladdin* possible (and it is impossible to believe he does not) is a moot point; what is much more disappointing is the uncertain exploitation of even the most basic devices—rushing through set-pieces, underplaying one dramatic crux after another, frequently ill-judged shot choices.

That said, there are some genuinely impressive passages—the trail of golden dust left by the fairies' progress through the autumn woods, Prince Cornelius' ice prison which leaves just a fingertip free—which go some way to counter-balance the pedestrian quality of the film as a whole. Admittedly, the songs (by Barry Manilow) are no worse than those in *Aladdin*, but since both are less than inspired examples of the most mediocre form of MOR show-tunes, there is nothing positive to be found there. It is particularly ironic, given the importance that the animators currently ascribe to music in their films, that an increasing proportion of a film's running time is given over to less and less adventurous songs.

Still, *Thumbelina* delivers its story with some measure of efficiency, and does just enough to keep a child interested, even if the over-stuffed plot risks losing and confusing its younger audience. There is not much here for their adult companions, though, with little in the way of gags or thematic idiosyncracy. Bluth left Disney at their lowest ebb in 1979 and it looks increasingly as though it might have been better to stay. His erstwhile employers are going from strength to strength while, on the evidence of *Thumbelina* at least, Bluth is merely marking time.

Also reviewed in:
CHICAGO TRIBUNE, 4/1/94, Friday/p. B, Jennifer Mangan
NEW YORK TIMES, 3/30/94, p. C19, Stephen Holden
VARIETY, 3/28-4/3/94, p. 69, Steven Gaydos
WASHINGTON POST, 3/30/94, p. B10, Rita Kempley

HEAVENLY CREATURES

A Miramax Films release of a Wingnut Films/Fontana Film Productions coproduction in association with the New Zealand Film Commission. *Executive Producer:* Hanno Huth. *Producer:* Jim Booth. *Director:* Peter Jackson. *Screenplay:* Peter Jackson and Frances Walsh. *Director of Photography:* Alun Bollinger. *Editor:* James Selkirk. *Music:* Peter Dasent. *Sound:* Michael Hedges. *Sound Editor:* Michael Hopkins and Greg Bell. *Casting:* John Hubbard, Ros Hubbard, and Liz Mullane. *Production Designer:* Grant Major. *Art Director:* Jill Cormack.

Set Dresser: Meryl Cronin. *Costumes:* Ngila Dickson. *Make-up:* Marjorie Hamlin and Debbie Watson. *Running time:* 98 minutes. *MPAA Rating:* R.

CAST: Melanie Lynskey (Pauline Parker); Kate Winslet (Juliet Hulme); Sarah Peirse (Honora Parker); Diana Kent (Hilda Hulme); Clive Merrison (Henry Hulme); Simon O'Connor (Herbert Rieper); Jed Brophy (John/Nicholas); Peter Elliott (Bill Perry); Gilbert Goldie (Dr. Bennett); Geoffrey Heath (Rev. Norris); Kirsti Ferry (Wendy); Ben Skjellerup (Jonathon); Darien Takle (Miss Stewart); Elizabeth Moody (Miss Walker); Liz Mullane (Mrs. Collins); Moreen Eason (Mrs. Stevens); Pearl Carpenter (Mrs. Zwartz); Lou Dobson (Grandma Parker); Jesse Griffin (Laurie); Glen Drake (Steve); Nick Farra and Chris Clarkson (Boarders); Ray Henwood, John Nicoll, and Mike Maxwell (Professors); Raewyn Pelham (Laura); Toni Jones (Agnes Ritchie); Glenys Lloyd-Smith (Miss Digby); Wendy Watson (Mrs. Bennett); Jean Guerin (Orson Welles); Stephen Reilly (Mario Lanza); Andrea Sanders (Diello); Ben Fransham (Charles); Jessica Bradley (Pauline, age 5); Alex Shirtcliffe-Scot (Juliet, age 5); Barry Thomson (Farmer/Policeman).

CHRISTIAN SCIENCE MONITOR, 11/29/94, p. 14, David Sterritt

[*Heavenly Creatures* was reviewed jointly with *Ladybird Ladybird*; see Sterritt's review of that film.]

FILM QUARTERLY, Fall 1995, p. 33, Luisa F. Ribeiro

The 1950s, Christchurch, New Zealand. An era and place that conjure up an atmosphere of stifling Anglican propriety and reserve. On a cold late June day in 1954, teenagers Pauline Parker and Juliet Hulme dashed the serenity of that image by bludgeoning to death Pauline's mother, Honora Rieper, with a brick as the three walked through Victoria Park. Why Parker and Hulme felt driven to commit what became one of New Zealand's most scandalous crimes is vividly recounted in the film *Heavenly Creatures* (1994), written by Frances Walsh and Peter Jackson and directed by Jackson. The film's exuberant style and humor belie its equally serious and deeply disturbing tone that is weirdly empathic to the girls while paradoxically never undercutting the brutal nature of their crime. By turns comic, tragic, fantastic, and romantic, the film, much like its true-life source, defies simple interpretation, yet leads inescapably to an unsettling awareness of a guilt rarely untouched by innocence and an innocence not untainted by some degree of guilt.

Jackson and Walsh based their screenplay on transcripts and psychiatric reports from the Parker/Hulme murder trial, interviews with the girls' classmates, and the diaries from 1953 and 1954 of Pauline Parker. Jackson has indicated that he and Walsh were particularly drawn to and influenced by the girls' own witty and irreverent humor as evidenced in Parker's diaries, which were quoted liberally at the trial and which serve as voice-over material throughout the film.[1] Although publicity for the film brought to light the identity of Juliet Hulme (changed after her release from prison in 1959) as mystery writer Anne Perry, Jackson and Walsh avoid all mention of the fact in the film and did not attempt to contact Hulme/Perry in the course of their research or after the film's release. Jackson, whose previous work includes the gory cult favorite *Braindead* (U.S.: *Dead Alive*, 1993), is aided by his fascination for the inexplicable and grotesque, plunging viewers into a visually vivid world of adolescent imagination, racing along with Pauline and Juliet's sweeping fantasies into sand castles and fanciful kingdoms. Jackson and Walsh temper these audacious visual extremes with an abstruse quality by framing the girls' relationship within distinctively religious parameters and a sense of immutable destiny that characterize their association as a reach for the sublime and mark their fall as all the more tragic.

Jackson and Walsh play up this fateful sensibility with thematic and dramatic devices that shape the ties between the Riepers and the Hulmes into a mythical bond.[2] In one of several self-reflexive moments, Pauline remarks about an opera she is writing, describing is as "a three act story with a tragic end," thereby punctuating Jackson and Walsh's structure as mirroring that of the classic tragedy. The bare facts of the tragedy are that teenage outcasts Pauline Parker and Juliet Hulme meet in school, are drawn together by mutual childhood illnesses, become extraordinarily devoted to one another, so much so that when their respective parents grow concerned and try to separate them they become desperate enough to murder Pauline's mother, whom they perceive to be the major obstacle to their remaining together. Jackson, in a radical departure from New Zealand's legendary view of Parker and Hulme as monstrous deviants, calls their tale "[a] murder story about love. A murder story with no villains."[3]

Pauline Parker and Juliet Hulme are literally in continual flight from their respective fates, Pauline (Melanie Lynskey) from a despised, dull, working-class background and unremarkable parents (Honora and Herbert Rieper, played by Sarah Peirse and Simon O'Connor), Juliet (Kate Winslet) from ill health, careless parents (Hilda and Herbert Hulme, played by Diana Kent and Clive Merrison) and repeated periods of abandonment. Jackson and Walsh intimate that disaster is brought about not so much by the girls' avoidance of destiny as by their determination to shape it themselves. Juliet's own definition of heaven, "a paradise of music, art, and pure enjoyment," fashions the narrative arc, with the girls' constant imaginative creativity implicated as a major source of their undoing. Although the murder of Honora Rieper is depicted as the nightmarish calamity it indeed was, there is no doubt that an equal part of the horror of the story lies in the unaccustomed positioning of desire and determination in the hands of two adolescent females. The deceptively mild, even playful tampering with gender, class, and age expectations delineated in the film gives an added twist to the odd symbiosis of the sullen, introverted Pauline and the precocious, extroverted Juliet, and unexpectedly provides much of the discomfiture about their association and raises germane questions of past and continuing expectations of gender, especially female, roles.

Although *Heavenly Creatures* explores both girls' lives two years before, up to, and including the murder, ultimately the film concentrates on Pauline's story and her unique tragedy. Surrounded by identically guileless classmates and implacable teachers at school, and overly solicitous parents and insipid male boarders at home, Pauline is emblematic of the Flaubertian heroine in her longing to escape to a world of romance. She is mortified by her family's working-class background, her gregariously simple fish store manager father, and her unimaginatively practical mother who takes in boarders. Jackson parallels the Rieper's home life and the staid, pragmatic qualities of Christchurch with such disarming (if droll) ingenuousness that they immediately assume the loathsome blandness discerned by the restless Pauline. When pitched next to Juliet's vivaciousness, posh home, and glamorous parents, Pauline' s dissatisfactions and romantic hopes appear palpable.

While a common enough predilection, what makes Pauline's discontent unusual is her seeking salvation so fiercely through Juliet. What might otherwise be neatly categorized as a normal, if perhaps hyper, extension of a passing phase of the tumultuous extremes of adolescence in this instance amazingly unfolds instead into matricide. Jackson's running fantasy motif of Pauline happily chasing Juliet across a cruise-liner deck toward Hilda and Henry Hulme perfectly captures Pauline's yearning for/to be Juliet, as well as her wish for the autonomy of the upper-class and the proper family who could provide her with that ideal. Pauline is constantly shown throughout the film in literal pursuit of Juliet (significantly reversed in the walk through Victoria Park). Jackson's near obsessive focus on legs and feet suggests an attempt by the characters to find a bearing, to direct a mercurial fate that eventually proves beyond even Pauline and Juliet's most determined retreats. Juliet, as Pauline's link to this dream, is consequently placed, by her own supreme confidence and Pauline's fervent loyalty (traditionally masculine values), in a position of preeminence rarely allotted women and for which, not surprisingly, she and Pauline—and, tragically, Honora Rieper—will suffer. The consequence, blithely but knowingly painted by the film-makers, is that acumen, desire, and the feminine are an inherently dangerous mix.

The film's lingering and often irreverently humorous religious tone, meant to echo the girls' gradually prospering view of themselves as indeed superior "heavenly creatures," is built upon their constant association with creativity and art (the two meet in art class). Pauline and Juliet's drawing, sculpting, writing, and musical proclivities are interwoven into the narrative diegetically and nondiegetically in impressive fashion, with perhaps the strongest empathic tone gained through an astute use of music, associated with the spiritual and emotional. Peter Dasent's mesmerizing original score is augmented by Jackson's shrewd employment of prerecorded music, the importance of which is emphasized by its actual reference in the script.[4] In the initial musical motif, the framing reference of the divine is established under the opening titles with a girls choir's crisply enunciated rendering of the hymn "Just a Closer Walk with Thee." The hymn's lyric foreshadows Pauline and Juliet's association, emphasizing a strong element of longing: "Just a closer walk with thee, grant if Jesus, it's my plea, daily walking close to thee, let it be, dear Lord, let it be ..."

The virtuous tone of the ongoing hymn is contrasted with the pointedly physical introduction to Pauline. The red (danger?) school door is matched by a pan across a clothes-filled clothesline to the red door of a small cottage, which opens to reveal a schoolgirl's coat and skirt hiked up, exposing a thigh and gloved hands pulling up hose to a garter belt before the girl hastens off to join the throng of students heading to school. The emphasis on the corporeal immediately connects Pauline with the erotic and also with death, as a hose stocking will cover the brick used to kill Mrs. Rieper. Combined with the reverential mood set up by the hymn (significantly intoning "Thro' this world of toil and snares ... who with me by burden shares?"), Pauline is established within a distinctly religious parameter of yearning and, further, within a traditional Christian definition, of seeking life through death (the ultimate object of desire). Her ripeness for "conversion" is underscored as, sullenly silent amongst her booming classmates, Pauline is eyed by an ever-vigilant teacher and then hastily mutters the last line to the hymn, the markedly supplicate words, "let it be." "It" arrives immediately thereafter, in the form of the supercilious Juliet. As the coolly British Juliet is introduced to Pauline and the class, the girls choir is just barely discernible, angelically, in the background connecting her with the divine, a literal answer to Pauline's prayer.

A more blatant if distinctive musical motif is established with the boisterous tunes of Juliet's idol, Mario Lanza, whose resonant style captures her some what manic energy, while also serving as a (humorously campy) link to her insistence on seeking refuge within romantic fantasy. Lanza's singing comes across as antiseptic "pop opera," particularly in contrast with the poignancy of the Puccini arias used in the darker second half of the film. Amusingly, Lanza is the first and most significant of the girls' self-ordained "saints," and the only figure to traverse between their customized version of paradise, the "fourth world" ("It's sort of like heaven—only better, because there aren't any Christians"), and their more licentious fantasy kingdom (described in a jointly written novel), Borovnia. As such, Lanza literally functions as the primary mediating symbol displacing the girls' burgeoning desire, yet is always held in the realm of the emotional and romantic, in direct contrast to his opposite "cast out" saint, discussed below.

Lanza and his enthusiastically rendered melodies also serve as a barometer of Pauline's emotions, in the girl's initial captivation with Juliet (prophetically, with "Be My Love"), in her uncertainty over Juliet's flights of fancy (swept aside when Juliet propels a startled Pauline into her own ebullience by whisking her off to "The Donkey Serenade"), and in Pauline and Juliet's eventual romantic consummation ("The Loveliest Night of the Year"). Significantly, once the girls commit to their plan to murder Honora Rieper, they burn all their Lanza records, indicating a complete break with the world of enchantment. Lanza's return over the end credits with "You'll Never Walk Alone" provides a powerful backdrop that elicits a particularly ironic pathos after the desolation of the final scenes.

The obvious correlation between musical excess and Pauline and Juliet's emotions is paralleled by the connection between their more tangible artistic pursuits of writing, drawing, and sculpting as further displacements of their simultaneously mounting mutual self-absorption and familial frustrations. This culminates with a startling joint creation of darker consequence, that Jackson and Walsh again fix against a religiously ritualistic backdrop. When Juliet ordains pictures of (exclusively male) film stars as fourth world "saints" one night at a homemade brick altar, renaming them ("He," "Him," "This," "That"), Pauline offers her own "saint," Orson Welles, declaring him "It." Juliet hurls away the picture ("Absolutely not! Orson Welles—the most hideous man alive!"), then immediately grasps the startled if still enraptured Pauline by the hands to give praise to her preferred saints. Juliet's attempts to fling away the unmanageable reality of desire, incorporated in the "hideous" It—Jackson and Walsh's transparent but shrewd allusion to the Id—with a more aesthetic, if egocentric illusion, denies her literal clinging to It in the form of Pauline. The use of Welles, as the darker "outcast saint," delightfully plays upon his wunderkind reputation as well as his cinematic image as the mysterious, complex, sinister, and very often outside the law rogue, whose most famous role, not uncoincidentally, involves the loss of maternal love. The shot of the dismissed picture of Welles floating down the stream before being swept over a tiny fall, as ominous music swells, suggest that It/desire will not be long denied. Shrouded within the humor of the scene is the uneasy but clear reinforcement of the combination of ego and desire in the feminine as unnatural and unpredictable.

This notion is made even clearer with the girls' vision of the fourth world (prompted by the Hulmes' decision to go abroad for a lengthy stay, without Juliet), realized through morphing effects, described by Pauline's diary entries in voice-over as distinctly edenesque ("full of peace and bliss"), righteously exclusive ("only ten people have [the key]"), and pointedly anti-Christian ("we only recognized it on the day of the death of Christ"). Emphasizing this moment of genesis, the sequence immediately following has Pauline and Juliet assuming the identities of Borovnian royalty, Charles and Deborah, and hilariously enacting the birth of Charles/Pauline and Deborah/Juliet's "heir"—Diello. Diello's literal appearance, first as a tiny clay figurine, then as a lifesize one with distinctly Wellesian features that reveal his identity as It, is immediately connected with excess. Juliet's abrupt recurrence of tuberculosis and four-month quarantine and the girls' resulting frustration at separation prompts Diello's emergence in Pauline and Juliet's daily exchange of letters. The royal heir goes on imaginary, if vivid, killing rampages "to alleviate (Pauline's) boredom (of the dull lower classes)," and to dispense with vexatious adults, such as the sanctimonious minister ("Jesus Loves You") who comes to visit Juliet at the sanitarium and the clumsy doctor ("Do you like your mother?") to whom the Riepers eventually take Pauline. With the conception of Diello the ecstatic exuberance of the Lanza-inspired cavortings and whimsical fantasy of the celestialized fourth world give way to a more ominous indication of desire spinning out of control and, more disquietingly, to the growing regard of the girls for violence as a potential solution to ward off unpleasant realities. This reversal of conventional female prodigality is unsettling in its inference that the only possible outcome of any union between women is horror, excess, and death. Yet Jackson and Walsh's somewhat dark intimations do not lead inexorably to matricide, serving instead as provocative endeavors at interpreting the unfathomable depth and complexities of Pauline and Juliet's involvement and their remarkable inward-looking capacity for self-fulfillment.

Themes of transformation and rebirth are suggested by the multiple names given Pauline throughout the film (significantly, the two holidays mentioned in the film are religious and mirror these themes: Christmas/birth, when Pauline gets her diaries, and Easter/rebirth through death at Port Levy where the girls have their "revelation" of the fourth world). Pauline's family, John the boarder, and Dr. Bennett use her middle name, Yvonne. To schoolmates, teachers, and the Hulmes she is Pauline Rieper. Juliet calls her Paul, then Charles, and finally Gina, a Borovnian gypsy clay figurine that Pauline tells John is Juliet's creation. Only as Gina does Pauline find satisfaction, however fleeting. The film's undercurrent of Juliet as the focus of desire, as "divine," and Pauline as her pliant "disciple" seeking salvation and transformation, is stressed as Pauline refers to herself for the remainder of the film as Gina—as does Juliet. Even in the closing moments of the film, with the grisly murder intercut with Juliet on the fantasy cruise ship pulling away and Pauline trapped on the pier, Juliet calls out to Pauline as Gina. Juliet's last words, "I'm sorry," seem an apology for her ultimate inability to sustain the girls' shared paradisiacal delusions and for in fact destroying all their creations, primarily Pauline herself.

However persuasive the film-makers are at weaving a weird if uneasy empathy for Pauline and Juliet's exhilarating alliance, they carefully refrain from demonizing the girls' parents (if not the other adults in the film, who are waggishly presented exclusively from the girls' point of view). The Hulmes are initially bemused, the Riepers confused by Pauline and Juliet's intense mutual devotion, seemingly never fully aware of how their own ordinary deficiencies drive the girls ever closer. Jackson and Walsh characterize the Hulmes' growing domestic misfortunes in a sensitive if sparse manner, focusing more harshly on Henry's trepidation over the fervor of Juliet and Pauline's friendship. Henry's anxiety easily mirrors that of the patriarchal social milieu of the decade, scandalized at impermeable, uncontrollable feminine excess. Both the Riepers' and the Hulmes' inability to grasp the magnitude of their respective daughter's individual and combined alienation and emotional needs decidedly propels the situation towards catastrophe.

Honora Rieper especially finds her daughter's emotional withdrawal and hostility incomprehensible, as is made apparent by her completely guileless response to Dr. Bennett's declaration that Pauline may be (in his terms) homosexual: "But she's always been a normal, happy child." Honora Rieper encroaches on hallowed ground. Juliet's excessive longing for dependable, unwavering parental love and Pauline's absolute rejection of her own parents as deficient creates a tremendous emotional void the girls fill with a frighteningly powerful faith in each other which leaves no room for their hapless parents. Rather than a crime *of* passion, Honora's murder becomes a crime *for* passion, a sacrificial act binding Pauline and Juliet together forever, a reach for the exaltation of mutual faith that ends in damnation with their shattering the most sacred of taboos, matricide.

The film falters slightly in bridging the gap between Pauline and Juliet's leap from emotional desperation at the threat of separation (the Hulmes' breakup precipitating Juliet's relocation to South Africa) to murder. Juliet's enforced separation from Pauline as the latter's homelife crumbles is confused, although the final musical shift to opera stabilizes some of these choppier sections, recalling the theme of mythical and unalterable predetermination. Forbidden to see Juliet, a despondent Pauline considers suicide ("Life seems so much not worth living") as "E lucevan le stelle" from *Tosca* plays on her phonograph ("My dream of love is now destroyed forever, my hour is fleeting and I must die despairing!"). The sense of immutable destiny is augmented by the narrative rupture of Juliet's poignant a cappella rendering of "Sono andati" from *La Boheme* after she agrees to help Pauline murder Honora. Significantly, the fantasy cruise-liner sequence is completed during this scene, as Pauline and Juliet, calling "Mummy," rush into the welcoming embrace of Henry and Hilda, connecting sacrifice/death with fulfillment. The operatic motif is concluded by Pauline, Honora, and Juliet's "last supper" and their fateful walk in Victoria Park to Puccini's haunting "Humming Chorus."

The extravagance linked with opera is indicative of delirium, yet given the somberness of the pieces utilized, it promotes a bleaker tone in sharp contrast to the earlier ebullience of the Lanza music. The musical sense of threatening delirium is articulated when Pauline tells Juliet as the two sit in the bathtub together, "I think I'm going crazy." Juliet (significantly up to her neck in water) replies, "No you're not, Gina, it's everyone else who's bonkers." In her diary Pauline claims she and Juliet must be mad, as are the saints and even Henry Hulme, which asserts—breaking somewhat with the narrative's constant insinuation of female desire as insanity—that as reality around them sinks into madness they have no choice but to respond in kind. This implicates the girls' surrounding circumstance as at least partially responsible for the coming disaster, reiterates thc preordained theme, and subtly insists that female madness is indeed a constructed designation.

The link between feminine desire and madness is reestablished with the film's climax. Parker's diary indicates a sexual relationship with Hulme ("We enacted how each saint would make love ... It was wonderful, heavenly, beautiful and ours ... We have learned the peace of the thing called bliss, the joy of the thing called sin") that Jackson and Walsh artfully and touchingly translate to the screen, fulfilling the augur of Orson Welles/It as the surrogate of desire. Nevertheless, in discussing thc film's lesbian content, Jackson states he believes the issue is something of a red herring,"[5] despite his own heavily romanticized construction of Pauline and Juliet's relationship. Psychiatric reports given at the trial arc contradictory in reaching a conclusion as to whether or not thc girls did indeed have a physical relationship, although homosexuality, then categorized as a mental illness, was part of the girls' unsuccessful insanity defense. Jackson's veiled implications that the girls were merely playing out conventional romantic fantasies disregards the fact that they would have had little else but heterosexual prototypes against which to play out nascent longings, lesbian or otherwise. The linking of lesbianism and mental illness falls into a similar psychological tendency of associating any powerful feminine drive with the unnatural and the problematic and therefore needful of a "cure." Placing the girls' romantic fulfillment immediately before their decision to murder Honora completes thc connection of sex and death, while stressing their own revered desire to be united on a higher, inviolate plane.

Heavenly Creatures is a startling, brilliantly rendered love story of faith and loyalty that was misguided and misunderstood in its own era perhaps as much as today. Pauline Parker and Juliet Hulme, each catalogued as outsider, as other, dared to find and believe in the grandeur of their difference. Their overwhelming, ferocious emotional unity was both audacious and terrifying in its dimensions. Film-maker Peter Jackson and co-screenwriter Frances Walsh rise to the bizarre and dazzling demands of portraying Parker and Hulme's relationship as one that is as peculiarly admirable and touching as it is horrifying. It remains one of the strongest of the all too infrequent cinematic representations of women's interrelationships as capable of passion, intelligence, and fidelity, basking in rather than condemning the extremes of distinctive feminine emotional possibilities, and hauntingly tragic in its revelation of the depth of human frailties when attempting to reach beyond the sublime.

Notes

1. Interview with Peter Jackson and Francis Walsh by Terry Gross; "Fresh Air," National Public Radio, December 22, 1994.
2. An end title explains Honora and Herbert Rieper were never legally married and so Pauline was charged under her mother's maiden name of Parker.
3. *Heavenly Creatures* press notes.
4 .A draft of the screenplay indicates scenes were always built around the use of specific Mario Lanza songs. Jackson and Walsh were guided in their musical selections by Parker's own stated preferences in diary entries mentioning *Tosca* and psychiatric reports that state one of her novels was entitled *The Donkey's Serenade*.
5. Gemma Files, "Those Difficult, Murderous Teenage Years," *Eye Weekly*, January 19, 1995, Toronto, Ontario.

LOS ANGELES TIMES, 11/23/94, Calendar/p. 1, Kenneth Turan

"Heavenly Creatures" is what Pauline Parker and Juliet Hulme called each other, but those are just words, and words, no matter how passionate and adoring, can only hint at the intensity of the attachment these two teen-age girls felt.

Inseparable real-life schoolmates and soul mates in Christchurch, New Zealand, in 1952, Pauline and Juliet inhabited a symbiotic world that was giddy, euphoric and chilling. Frightfully self-absorbed, their conduct unnerved the adult world and led, with horrible inevitability, to what is still considered the most celebrated criminal case in New Zealand history.

New Zealand director Peter Jackson, best known for the cult fright favorite "Dead Alive," has nervily translated the Parker-Hulme case into film terms, and an adventurous, accomplished piece of business, burning with cinematic energy, it turns out to be.

Utilizing a thoughtful, thoroughly researched script he co-wrote with Frances Walsh, Jackson directs in a way that is both tightly controlled and highly emotional. Photographed by Alun Bollinger, "Creatures" has a witty, overwrought visual style that the girls themselves would probably favor, and it makes good dramatic use of state-of-the art special effects.

Related in voice over taken from a diary kept by Pauline, "Creatures" begins with a newsreel of Christchurch Girls High School, a classically prim establishment that insists on proper uniforms and sensible shoes.

Pauline (Melanie Lynskey), her sullen face framed by dark curly ringlets, is a bright but quietly resentful ninth-grade student who comes from undeniably lower-class stock. Her feckless father, Bert (Simon O'Connor), is prone to silly sight gags involving fish, and her hard-working mother, Honora (Sarah Peirse), has to take in boarders to pay the family expenses.

All this ceases to matter to Pauline the day Juliet (Kate Winslet) arrives from dreamy England. Totally upper class, knowing more about the intricacies of the French subjunctive than her teachers and not shy about proving it, Juliet may be outwardly glamorous and confident, but she is as high strung and emotionally needy as Pauline. Almost immediately, they bond with a fierceness that no one knows quite what to make of.

Starting with a shared passion for Mario Lanza, "only the world's greatest tenor," Pauline and Juliet progress to creating elaborate candle-lit shrines to their idols. Determined to either go to Hollywood ("It's better than heaven; no Christians") or have a novel published in New York, they begin to jointly work on a project.

Realizing "how hard it is for other people to appreciate our genius," the girls retreat more and more to an imaginary place they call "the Fourth World," which includes a medieval kingdom named Borovnia. With fine use of up-to-the-minute effects like morphing, "Creatures" makes it possible for audiences to physically enter these worlds with Pauline and Juliet, to experience the surrender to fantasy as completely as they do.

This ability to get inside hysteria and obsession, the skill to make us feel sensations as intensely as its protagonists, is what makes "Creatures" memorable.

Helped by remarkable performances by its young actresses (Winslet has worked in theater and TV in England, Lynskey is pretty much an absolute beginner), "Creatures" insidiously encourages us to side with these two young women. Clearly they are so much fresher, more radiant and energetic than their elders, who begin to dully suspect that something as mundane as sexual attraction is holding these two together.

So when Pauline and Juliet teeter at the edge of sanity, when their infatuation becomes uncontrollable, their willfulness frightening, we go over the top with them, horrified co-conspirators almost to the end. "Heavenly Creatures" does not romanticize or excuse, it merely presents the inevitable and leaves us to shake our heads in wonder.

NEW STATESMAN & SOCIETY, 2/10/95, p. 39, Jonathan Romney

This is what you call a drastic career turn. New Zealand director Peter Jackson made his name with no-budget sci-fi splatter and zombie bloodbaths. His new film, *Heavenly Creatures*, is about the intimate passion between two teenage girls in 1950s New Zealand, and features some lovely frocks and gardens.

Jackson's specialty to date has been to leave nothing to the imagination, so It is understandable that he should come a little unstuck now that his central concern is imagination itself. The heroines of his true murder story—Juliet Hulme and Pauline Parker who killed Parker's mother in Christchurch in 1954—are driven to their crime of passion by febrile over-creativity. They meet at school, and gradually develop what Juliet's father calls "an unwholesome attachment". They come to inhabit a hallucinatory universe that begins as a shared cult venerating Mario Lanza and Orson Welles, and blossoms into obsessional creative activity that generates a vast epic novel and accompanying plasticene figures depicting the mythical kingdom of Borovnia. Their world finally becomes Borovnia, as the entire screen around the girls digitally moves into a celestial garden of unicorns and giant butterflies, their own private Narnia.

Quite apart from whether Jackson has a firm ironic handle on this fairy kitsch, it's his desire to *take us there* that is the problem. The more he wants to take us inside the girls' heads, the more we find ourselves outside them, because we are at once outside the recognisable universe and outside the film itself. We are transported into a world of digital delights, and our reference points are no longer Hitchcock or *Picnic at Hanging Rock*, or whatever else may come to mind; instead we find ourselves making comparisons with *Jurassic Park* and *The Mask*. We are in the unreal, but it doesn't feel like the unreal that the girls have generated in their worlds (words we hear in Pauline's diary, and taken verbatim from the original). *Heavenly Creatures* is immensely ambitious, but not really challenging, because it makes it too easy to sit back and marvel. Borovnia, a medieval world inhabited by plasticene giants, is not that much stranger than the 1950s Christchurch that represents the norm. For the newsreel that opens the film (a panorama of ersatz little Englishness straight out of Harry Enfleld's Cholmeley-Warner routine) to the oddness of everyday home life ("Pikelets"! squeals Pauline's brother at teatime, "Yum!"), Jackson can't resist the opportunity to make it all exotic. Everything from the shape of Juliet's father's hat and glasses to the cut of the gymslips, is droll and wonderful to Jackson's eye. By setting up 40 years' time and cultural distance as an absolute imaginative distance, he simply makes it look as if the girls are fleeing one world of irreducible weirdness for another.

There's no sense of a revolt against dead suburban banality—Jackson can't do banality except through the filter of the bizarre (for example, Pauline's dad spoiling her Lanza reverie by singing to a mackerel).

You almost wish Jackson had done without imagination. A less fanciful film could have presented the very fact of the girls' extravagance as being something far more marvelous and enviable, simply by excluding us from it. But Jackson seems to be competing with his heroines for the wild whimsy medal, and ends up slavishly scurrying to make their visions literal.

This could have worked brilliantly as a much more prosaic film, it need not have been dead literal, but it could have been more coolly forensic, and it is the forensic moments that work best. This is an extraordinary case that begs for ordinary telling—a furiously intense teenage pash that can't be pinned down simply as a lesbian romance, although the girls do sleep together. But there are so many factors—the girls' fever for a pantheon of heartthrobs; parental rage that greets Pauline's affair with a gormless boarder, Juliet's jealousy at the sexually overcharged world of her glam, cosmopolitan mother. Theirs is a passionate twindom, a consensual rage channelled into the creation of a fetishistically detailed dream universe, the only universe in which they can really be together. But their telepathic understanding is taken for granted: by keeping those visions at arms' length, the film could have left some doubt as to how much they simply shared the one vision, as opposed to each doing her own embroidery on the common frame.

Jackson is on another plane entirely in the Hitchcockian ticking away of tiny details. The run-up to the murder is brilliant—a stilted teatime of giggling and one more piece of cake, time counting down on a dainty little green clock; then the awkward trudge down a muddy slope, before the brick comes out of the satchel where it's been neatly stashed.

There is actually—and I hate to say this—a fine, self-effacing realist drama stashed away between these luscious folds of imagery. It thrives on precise, nervy playing for the two leads, Kate Winslet and Melanie Lynskey. The rest is caricature and frenzy. Jackson can't keep still for a minute, forever rushing us in and out of the undergrowth. In the title sequence, the camera scurries in and out between schoolgirls' legs like an overexcited terrier. Jackson wants too much to be in the thick of it. A view from the outside might have been another view entirely.

NEW YORK POST, 11/18/94, p. 31, Thelma Adams

"Heavenly Creatures" is divinely wicked. It's so fun and full of life I nearly forgot it was about two teen-agers who commit matricide.

Writer/director Peter Jackson ("Dead Alive") focuses on the intense friendship between Pauline Parker (Melanie Lynskey) and Juliet Hulme (Kate Winslet). Few movies have captured the giddy highs and deep emotional bonds between best girlfriends. The duo's intimacy creates a pleasurable retreat for two otherwise outcast and unhappy children.

The setting is Christchurch, New Zealand, in the '50s, a "Blue Velvet" kind of town. Shy, dark-haired, downcast Pauline lives in her parents' grim boarding house. Juliet, a cheeky outspoken golden girl, has just arrived from England with her parents, cultured professionals both. The girls bear childhood scars: Pauline has a bum leg and Juliet has not completely shaken TB. Both actresses are completely compelling.

"Heavenly Creatures" revels in Juliet and Pauline's girlish passions: a crush on Mario Lanza, novel-writing and molding clay figures. Together they invent an imaginary "Fourth World," a color-saturated paradise with its own religion and "Borovnia" a medieval fantasy as lusty and violent as the Middle Ages.

Adept at special effects, New Zealander Jackson enters Borovnia, placing the flush-cheeked girls amid life-sized chunky clay villagers. At one point, Mario Lanza stops in to serenade the Borovnians; at another, after a screening of Carol Reed's "The Third Man" in Christchurch, the menacing, erotic figure of Orson Welles chases the girls home until they scream hysterically, on the razor's edge between terror and ecstasy.

By sucking the audience into the girls' fantasy world, Marshall makes their terrible act more understandable without blunting the horror. When the teen-agers' parents become threatened by Pauline and Juliet's exclusive closeness—and suspected "unhealthy" activities—they try to separate them.

Complications arise; the Hulmes plan to ship the tubercular Juliet to South Africa. Pauline sees her mother, Honora (Sarah Peirse), as the one impediment to her accompanying Juliet.

"Only the best people fight against all obstacles in pursuit of happiness," says the blonde.

Like a latter-day Juliet and Juliet, the girls' star crossed love leads to violent tragedy. Pauline prepares for her mother's murder "keyed up as if planning a surprise party." Juliet says brightly, "I'm so looking forward to it."

Based on New Zealand's notorious Parker-Hulme affair, the movie ends with the brutal bludgeoning of Honora Parker in 1954. The shocking act that was intended to join Juliet and Pauline together forever yielded swift murder convictions.

In 1959, Juliet and Pauline were released from prison on the condition that they never meet again. As it happens, the popular British murder mystery writer Anne Perry had first-hand experience in her art; she was born Juliet Hulme.

NEWSDAY, 11/16/94, Part II/p. B9, Jack Mathews

In 1959, five years after committing one of the most notorious crimes in New Zealand history, Pauline Parker and Juliet Hulme were released from prison, on the condition they never meet again. Peter Jackson's hauntingly fine "Heavenly Creatures" leaves no doubt in the viewer's mind why that ruling was necessary.

Their crime was murder—premeditated, brutal, and personal—but what focused a stunned nation's attention on it were the ages of the killers, 16 and 15, the fact that the victim was one of their mothers, and the general presumption of a lesbian relationship.

It is worth noting that since the movie was made, Juliet Hulme's identity has been revealed as the British mystery writer Anne Perry, and that Pauline Parker has been said to be working in a New Zealand bookstore. It was literature and their overly developed imaginations that brought these unlikely friends—Juliet, the outgoing, cultured daughter of affluent British immigrants, and Pauline, the withdrawn working class New Zealander—together in the first place.

"Heavenly Creatures," which begins and ends at the murder scene, totally avoids the tabloid phase of the story—the arrests, trial, and inevitable hand-wringing over the collapse of moral values—and, by blending fantasy and reality throughout, takes us on an almost enchanted tour of the obsessions and shared delusions that led the girls to their, irrational act.

Using Pauline's detailed and unguarded diary entries, Jackson goes behind the wall the girls build between themselves and society and create their own fantasy world.

At first, their fantasyland is an eden o£ manicured gardens, pools, unicorns and kite-size butterflies. But the more they feed each other's imaginations, the darker the world becomes, eventually evolving into a violent medieval kingdom that they preside over as king and queen. Eventually, their fantasy lives spill into their real lives, and they begin making both love *and* decisions based on the characters they are playing.

By dramatizing their fantasies, through living versions of the clay models Juliet sculpts, Jackson invites us to experience the intoxication of the friends' growingly dangerous obsession. It doesn't make us sympathize with them, exactly; they are too antisocial for that. But when circumstances in the real world threaten to permanently separate them, we can at least understand *their* logic for killing.

Jackson has a tendency to oversell the exhilaration of the friendship. Half the time they are together, usually delirious over the music of their idol Mario Lanza, Pauline and Juliet are leaping around, shrieking and clutching each other like cheerleaders celebrating a winning touchdown. As the story progresses, with the parents becoming increasingly concerned, it becomes harder to think of the girls as real people.

That may be Jackson's intention. He says in the production notes that his film is a "murder story with no villains." But, in fact, the teenagers become so grotesquely self-absorbed, especially compared to the woman they plan to kill, and the murder is carried out with such cold-blooded brutality, they end up, in the final scene, looking like "The Bad Seed" times two.

Still, "Heavenly Creatures" is a powerful, troubling film, a horror fantasy constructed from real life, and featuring a host of terrific performances, particularly from Sarah Peirse, as Pauline's heartbroken mother, and Diana Kent, as Juliet's mother, a psychologist whose philandering ways with a patient indirectly inspires a murder.

SIGHT AND SOUND, 2/95, p. 45, Stella Bruzzi

The 1950s. Two blood-spattered schoolgirls run into the garden of a suburban house, crying out "mother's terribly hurt". The true story of how Pauline Parker and Juliet Hulme got to this traumatic point begins in 1953, with Juliet's first day at Christchurch Girls' High School. Pauline, a native New Zealander who has been at the school some time, is a loner until she is put with Juliet, a new girl from England. Despite their very different backgrounds, the two strike up an immediate and exclusive rapport. They are linked by their childhood illnesses, their adulation of the tenor Mario Lanza and the fantasy world they create together: the non-Christian Fourth World of "music, art and pure enjoyment".

For Christmas, Pauline is given a diary in which she documents her life with Juliet and the imaginative realm of the "novel" that they embark on together. The mythical Borovnia, a medieval tale of King Charles and Queen Debora, soon consumes their real existence. When they discover, as Juliet puts it, the "key" to the Fourth World, the extra part of the human brain that only ten people possess, this is where they escape to as fantasy and in actuality become interchangeable.

At school one day, Juliet is rushed to a clinic to be treated for a recurrence of her TB. Despite their daughter's illness, the Hulmes spend the summer months in England, leaving Juliet alone. Separated for two months, Juliet and Pauline write to each other as Charles and Debora, and when Pauline is allowed to visit she tells her that John, the student lodging in her house, is madly in love with her. Despite Juliet's protestations that this has broken her heart, Pauline allows John into her bed, only to be discovered by her father, who throws him out. However, she later loses her virginity to John.

On their return to New Zealand, Juliet's parents begin to sense that the friendship with Pauline may be unhealthy. The girls' time together is rationed and Pauline is sent to a psychiatrist. Due to the separation from Juliet, Pauline's schoolwork suffers. She decides to train as a typist, but meanwhile the two plot their escape to Hollywood where they hope to sell the rights to their novel. Juliet finds her mother in bed with another man, precipitating divorce proceedings from her father. It is decided that Juliet will stay with South African relatives; the girls' anguish at the prospect of separation reaches hysterical proportions. Pauline stops speaking to her parents and Juliet begs for Pauline to be allowed to go with her to South Africa. As compensation, Pauline is permitted to stay at the Hulmes' house; the girls sleep together and plan the murder of Honora, Pauline's mother. When the day arrives, the girls take Honora out to a local park where they hit her repeatedly over the head with a brick.

Captions tell us that the girls were found guilty of murder in what came to be known as the Parker-Hulme affair They were released in 1959 on the condition that they never meet again.

When she arrives at Christchurch High School, Juliet is brought into Pauline's French class, superciliously eyeing a sea of pupils with cardboard name tags tied around their necks—a penchant of the mistress who makes her classes use French names rather than their own. This kooky small-town 50s, with its obsolete rituals and garish pastel shades, forms the backdrop for what is essentially an exploration of the captivating and bizarre world of that even kookier phenomenon, the imaginative, pubescent schoolgirl. Like Tom Kalin's *Swoon*, Peter Jackson's film abandons the conventional investigative route and approaches a true-life murder case via the obsessive, private relationship between its central characters. Juliet and Pauline shroud themselves in a world of ritual and fantasy which increasingly severs its ties with the conformity of what lies outside, eventually repositioning 50s Christchurch as one of the characters in their jointly conceived novel. Juliet and Pauline, the self-designated Heavenly Creatures of the title, script their own rites of passage, from kneeling at an altar to worship-worthy men to solemnly burning their Mario Lanza record collection on a funeral pyre after hitting upon the idea of killing off Honora.

Heavenly Creatures is a beautifully choreographed descent into the realm of the personal and therefore (to an outsider) the inexplicable. Initially we observe with curious detachment as the girls strip down to their underwear and dance around trees to a lush Lanza soundtrack proclaiming, "She's the one for me"; but we are then jolted into their 'Fourth World', the real hills dissolving into their ornamental fantasy paradise. Such literalising of characters' fantasy worlds can have embarrassing results, as it did in *Sirens*, which made one wish that people never allowed their deepest sexual desires to surface at all. What disciplines the excesses of *Heavenly Creatures* is that the subconscious sequences are always clearly located within the teenage imaginations that concoct them; they're not some abstract, ashamedly adult vision of what Peter Jackson might assume constitutes dreamland.

It's significant, for instance, that Borovnia surfaces in both everyday life and the life of fantasy. In one evocative scene, Juliet and Pauline—as Charles and Debora—are going through the birth of their son in the prosaic setting of Juliet's bedroom, a scene reminiscent of many a childish piece of role-playing. Scenes such as this (and the use of Pauline's diary entries as voice-over) ground the more outrageous flights of fancy into the animated Borovnia, a medieval castle populated by plasticine figures. Perhaps most compelling and disquieting are the sequences in which the two worlds collide, as when Juliet imagines a figure decapitating a visiting vicar.

Whereas most films that deal with the relationship between the real and the unconscious (from *Spellbound* to *Sirens*) never lose sight of the dividing line between the two, *Heavenly Creatures* dwells on the smudging of those boundaries. The film's most intense, lyrical and absurd moment comes near the end, when Juliet mouths along to a Lanza aria, as a monochrome sequence shows her family united and happy. Although the film assiduously avoids making any definite comment about the girls' morality, their sanity or their motivation for the killing, such scenes capture the strange euphoric loneliness of their world of sword-bearers, matinee idols and self-glorification. As the girls repeatedly pummel Honora on the head, the vibrantly coloured violence is intercut with more black and white, now showing Juliet on a ship, joyous cocooned between her parents and waving to Pauline on the quayside. These are the last shots of the film, which ends therefore not with a neat return to where it began but with an enigmatic, elliptical allusion to an emotional and psychological turmoil that remains unresolved.

The single idealised image sums up the strange sense of distance which pervades *Heavenly Creatures*: a distance which extends beyond the obvious separation between reality and fantasy, to touch on such diverse things as Pauline's detached third-person diary descriptions of "these lovely two" or the way in which the camera, although often showing the girls in extreme close-up, always gives the impression of observing, of trying to understand but never quite getting there. Accompanying the details of the girls' sentence and subsequent release is Lanza's rendition of "You'll Never Walk None", at once poignant and puzzling. For all its sensuousness, its detail and its affection, *Heavenly Creatures* leaves Juliet and Pauline as mysterious as they were at the beginning. Although difficult to attribute, this is somehow the source of the film's brilliance; without casting judgment over the girls' actions, it never seeks to explain them. After Pauline and Juliet sleep together, the diary entry refers to "the joy of that thing called sin", which could be read as being specifically about sex or about everything besides. The whole film is a breathtaking blend of the particular and the opaque, a deft juggling act with the two undefinable notions of joy and sin.

TIME, 11/21/94, p. 110, Richard Corliss

Obsession, when it takes hold, is not a fragrance but a lethal gas. It envelops and consumes us; it is all the air we breathe. It should make for an ideal film subject. But moviemakers rarely know what to do with obsession. They make it trivial, cartoonish. A superfiend itches to blow up the planet—big hairy deal. An id-monster like Freddy Krueger dices and slices kids as they sleep. *Zzzzzz*!

Those scenarios are timid next to the real thing: the power one person has over another—the puppy love, say, that turns rabid as two souls merge in a toxic rapture. For most kids this is just a part of growing up; somehow they learn to cope with the glandular and emotional convulsions that accompany the transformation from child to teenager. Yet the threat of surrender is always there. The teenage girls in the wonderfully unsettling movie *Heavenly Creatures* create their own fantasy world out of youthful obsession, and then it spins out of their control. The result is murder.

You should know—actually, for complete, suspenseful enjoyment of the film, you very much should *not* know, but the word is out, so we're obliged to tell you—that *Heavenly Creatures* is based on a notorious murder case. In 1954 in Christchurch, New Zealand, Pauline Parker and Juliet Hulme were convicted of bludgeoning Pauline's mother Honora to death. The girls were "detained at Her Majesty's pleasure" until 1959, when Juliet left New Zealand and Pauline went into hiding. It was recently revealed that Juliet became a best-selling mystery novelist who lives in Scotland and writes under the name Anne Perry. Perry claims to remember little of the murder; the hero of several of her novels is a detective, William Monk, who occasionally suffers from amnesia.

Pauline (Melanie Lynskey) and Juliet (Kate Winslet) are children of two different cultures. Juliet's father is an English canon, and the girl is blond, worldly, brash; she was hospitalized for lung disease, and has been brought to New Zealand for the climate. Pauline, whose father manages a fish store, is dark and broody; she has leg scars from the ravages of osteomyelitis. Juliet sees their wounds as badges of spiritual aristocracy: "All the best people have bad chests and bone diseases. It's all frightfully romantic."

Heavenly Creatures is frightfully romantic too, and romantically frightening. It ascends and plummets with the girls' mercurial moods. As they fall into a conspiracy of affection, the film lures the viewer into the girls' fantasy world, as elaborate as that created by the Bronte sisters: a kingdom called Borovnià, where the clay statues they have molded come to life as blue-blooded versions of their favorite "saints" (Mario Lanza and James Mason) and demons (Orson Welles, "the most hideous man alive").

But demons can also be sexy. When a fellow makes clumsy love to Pauline, she pays him no heed and imagines herself ravaged by her fantasy Welles.

Director Peter Jackson, whose three earlier features (*Bad Taste, Meet the Feebles* and *Dead Alive*) make clever use of puppetry and guignol splatter effects, here is like a physician who assumes a patient's fever in order to understand her illness. He visualizes the landscape of Pauline's and Juliet's minds as a fetid garden, where fairytale plots of courtly love and castle intrigue blot out their edgy lives at home and school. The girls' vision of Borovnia utterly mesmerizes them. Anyone who would break the spell—like Pauline's sweet, anxious mum—must be a witch. Must be sentenced to death.

Screenwriter Frances Walsh based the script she wrote with Jackson on interviews with those who knew the girls and on the bits of Pauline's diary that were submitted in court. As quoted in *Heavenly Creatures*, the daybook is a monologue of a fertile mind racing gaily toward madness. At first Pauline takes some blinkered notice of the outside world: "We have decided how sad it is for other people that they cannot appreciate our genius." Later, after the girls make love to their saints (and each other), she writes, "We have learned the peace of the thing called bliss, the joy of the thing called sin." And the morning of the murder, she notes, "I felt very excited and night-before-Christmasy last night."

The film's triumph is to communicate this creepy excitement with urgency and great cinematic brio, while neither condescending to the girls nor apologizing for their sin. The film's serendipitous stroke was to find Winslet and, especially, Lynskey, a first-time actress. They are perfect, fearless in embodying teenage hysteria. They declaim their lines with an intensity that approaches ecstasy, as if reading aloud from *Wuthering Heights*. The giggles that punctuate the girls' early friendship are not beneath Winslet and Lynskey. The screams that end the film are not beyond them.

In her diary Pauline wrote this verse: "It is indeed a miracle, one must feel,/ That two such heavenly creatures are real." In *Heavenly Creatures* the sad creatures whom Pauline and Juliet must have been in real life are alchemized into figures of horror and beauty. They become the stuff of thrilling popular art.

VILLAGE VOICE, 11/29/94, p. 59, J. Hoberman

No stranger to bad taste, the 33-year-old Jackson is a master of ooze and ahs—legendary among gore aficionados for such gooey exercises in matricidal splatstick as *Bad Taste, Meet the Feebles* and *Dead Alive*. He's taken for his subject two teenage schoolgirls who, 40 years ago last June in a peaceful Christchurch park, broke free of the reality principle and exercised *their* "festive freedom" by wielding a brick in a stocking to bludgeon one of their mums to death. If print ads are any indication, Miramax seems to be positioning *Heavenly Creatures* as this year's *Crying Game*. But, in treating a notorious youth crime with such madcap brio, *Heavenly Creatures* is a cerebral grossout—the respectable equivalent to those teen-o-centric laff-riot screamfests William Paul takes as his meat.

Dead Alive, in which a chaste lad's first kiss triggers the transformation of his already formidable mother into a flesh-eating zombie, was a cartoon with guts—literally. *Heavenly Creatures*, which opened last week to near universal raves (*The New Yorker* which used to dote on precisely this sort of edgy frolic, was a sniffy exception), is no less knowingly overwrought. Where a sophisticate like Claude Chabrol might have treated this tabloid material with languorously lip-smacking cynicism (as, in fact, he did in his account of another real-life teen parricide, *Violette*), Jackson opts for a feverish delirium of widescreen close-ups, scenes begun mid-dolly, and breathless subjective camera swoops. *Heavenly Creatures* opens by overlaying a staid 1952 travelogue, Christchurch in Kodachrome, with a tumult of splatterific frenzy—two blood-drenched girls run shrieking through the woods before Jackson cuts back in time to their initial meeting.

The dumpy, working-class Pauline (Melanie Lynskey) is introduced garter first en route to French class, glowering like the Bad Seed at golden girl Juliet (Kate Winslet), self-dramatizing, supercilious, and just arrived from England. Pauline is fascinated, despite herself, by Juliet's contempt for school authorities; their bond solidifies when the new girl ignores an art class assignment to produce instead a detailed drawing of Mario Lanza, MGM star and "the world's greatest tenor," as a triumphant St. George; the friendship is consecrated when it turns out that both suffered debilitating childhood illnesses: "All the best people have bad chests and bone diseases—it's frightfully romantic," Juliet enthusiastically sighs.

These frightful romantics constitute an aristocracy of two. *Heavenly Creatures* gives full vent to the manic mood swings and obsessive fetishism of adolescent passion, but is otherwise populated by the gargoyle teachers, grotesque parents, and geeky swains who are the stock figures of teenage comedy. Pauline's parents may be embarrassingly drab while Juliet's are glamorously well-off and self-preoccupied—nevertheless, the movie derives much of its punch from the spectacle of these boisterous schoolgirls bounding past their ineffectual progenitors, hurtling through space, high on the energy of the latest Lanza opus, hysterical maenads who rip off their school uniforms to cavort and cuddle in some handy meadow.

Together, Pauline, and Juliet cultivate their secret garden. A helicopter shot swooning over the hills suggests a travesty of *The Sound of Music*; at one point they traipse into a hilarious hormone-fueled Hallmark hallucination of snow-white unicorns and gigantic butterflies. This so-called Fourth World, detailed in Pauline's remarkably uninhibited diaries (the source for much of the script) and as a sort of grandiose children's pop-up book, comes complete with a religion whose deities include Lanza, James Mason, and "the most hideous man alive," Orson Welles. After the girls see *The Third Man*, an apparition of the diabolical Welles chases them, laughing screaming, back to their bedroom.

Like more than a few teenagers, Pauline and Juliet regard themselves as geniuses; the film's title is a self-description. In his *Voice* review of *Dead Alive*, James Hannaham ventured that "only someone from a very bad home could have made a film at once so inventive and stupefyingly gory." Empathetic Jackson celebrates even as he parodies his Creature's adolescent creativity. (Indeed, one of *Heavenly Creatures* side effects has been Juliet's outing as the bestselling mystery writer Anne Perry.) The girls compose an epic romantic fiction set in the imaginary world of Borovnia and sculpt clay figurines to illustrate their mythology, which, in his most bravura sequences, Jackson brings lurching to life. As the Borovnian cosmos grows increasingly vivid, the girls' affair—basically a form of *l'amour fou*—becomes ever more intense. Ultimately, they not only correspond but also make love in character.

Accompanied by a suitably gothic thunderstorm, Juliet's father arrives chez Pauline to report on this "unhealthy" and "unwholesome" friendship and "wayward" Pauline is sent to a wheezing shrink who terrorizes her mother with a vintage '50s sex-ed lecture on the dangers of homosexuality. But, despite the twisted Freudianism Jackson demonstrated in *Dead Alive, Heavenly Creatures* offers no particular psychological explanation for how this particular adolescent fantasy came to fruition. *Heavenly Creatures* climaxes once Juliet's high-class but highly dysfunctional family disintegrates; meanwhile, down in the trenches, Pauline 's struggle with her mother (played by Sarah Peirse as a living reproach) becomes hand-to-hand combat.

Like *Heavenly Creatures* giddy lack of tonal modulation, Pauline's near generic loathing for her parent is a factor of the movie's unconditional sympathy for its teenage monsters. Still, the murder, which has been well-rehearsed in fantasy, is filmed for naturalistic horror—and bleak finality. As the court's stipulation that blood sisters Juliet and Pauline be forever separated is also a kind of death, so the credit-roll coda of Mario Lanza yowling "You'll Never Walk Alone" is suffused with unexpected pathos. *Heavenly Creatures* is kitsch with a pang.

Also reviewed in:
CHICAGO TRIBUNE, 11/25/94, Friday/p. M, John Petrakis
NEW YORK TIMES, 11/16/94, p. C17, Janet Maslin
NEW YORKER, 11/21/94, p. 131, Terrence Rafferty
VARIETY, 9/12-18/94, p. 44, David Rooney
WASHINGTON POST, 11/23/94, p. D1, Hal Hinson

HELAS POUR MOI

A Cinema Parallel release of a Vega Film/Les Films Alain Sarde, Peripheria production. *Producer:* Ruth Waldburger. *Director:* Jean-Luc Godard. *Screenplay (French with English subtitles):* Jean-Luc Godard. *Director of Photography:* Caroline Champetier. *Editor:* Jean-Luc Godard. *Sound:* François Musy. *Running time:* 84 minutes. *MPAA Rating:* Not Rated.

CAST: Gérard Depardieu (Simon Donnalieu); Laurence Masliah (Rachel Donnadieu); Bernard Verley (Abraham Klimt); Jean-Louis Loca (Max Mercure); François Germond (The Pastor); Jean-Pierre Miquel (The Other Pastor); Anny Romand (The Pastor's Wife); Roland Blanche (The Teacher); Marc Betton (The Doctor).

CHRISTIAN SCIENCE MONITOR, 2/5/94, p. 12, David Sterritt

French cinema is divided into two main branches nowadays. One branch, growing like mad, consists of commercialized ventures that aim for Hollywood-style profits with Hollywood-style methods. Examples are the thriller "La Femme Nikita" and the comedy "Three Men and a Cradle," which were so Hollywooden that big studios promptly bought the rights to remake them as "Point of No Return" and "Three Men and a Baby," respectively.

The other branch, bravely hanging in there, consists of thoughtful productions in the great tradition of European art cinema. Examples are recent dramas like "Un Coeur en hiver" and "The Accompanist," which combine sensitive acting and picturesque cinematography with stories about human relations in the world of classical music.

Glimmering through both branches meanwhile, are occasional flashes of the inventiveness and wit that characterized the most exhilarating of all phases in modern French cinema: the New Wave movement, which burst forth around 1960 in the early films of five young directors associated with Cahiers du cinéma, the renowned French movie magazine.

Cahiers du cinéma still exists today, and exerts a strong influence on the art-minded enclaves of France's film community. Since the magazine's outreach is international in scope, it's fitting that New York's adventurous Film Society of Lincoln Center has begun a policy of inviting the publication's editors to choose their favorite French movies for an annual New York minifestival.

Now in its third year, "*Cahiers du Cinéma* Selects..." has become a valuable showcase for films and filmmakers that might otherwise be hidden from view by the busy parade of commercialized releases with large-scale advertising budgets and promotional campaigns.

This year's program features net works by no fewer than three of the original New Wave filmmakers, all of whom refined their aesthetic views as Cahiers critics before starting their directorial careers more than 30 years ago. Of the three, Jean-Luc Godard is the one who has clung most tenaciously to the energy, imagination, and iconoclasm that made this movement so vital during its glory days in the '60s and '70s.

His latest film, "Hélas pour moi," finds him as challenging, innovative, and all-around ornery as he ever was in the past. Also going strong is his enduring interest in religious and philosophical matters, which found its strongest expression in "Hail Mary," released in 1984 and still his most controversial film.

"Hélas pour moi," which translates as "Woe Is Me," stars Gérard Depardieu as a stranger in town who falls in love with a beautiful woman and engages her in a series of enigmatic dialogues on deep and complex issues: What is the purpose of suffering? How is human experience related to awareness of spiritual realities? And above all, how can the sublimities of transcendent love be glimpsed by creatures bound in the imperfections of fleshly life?

Godard has no easy answers to these questions, nor does he have easy ways of *posing* these questions. As in his recent "Nouvelle Vague" and "Histoire(s) du cinéma," the content of "Hélas pour moi" is fractured into countless fragments of word, picture, and gesture, calling on each spectator to decide how these pieces should be assembled and what conclusions might be drawn from them.

Dealing with subjects that soar beyond quick human understanding, Godard refuses to confine them within the ready-made structures of conventional cinema. His new film is as hard to grasp as the ineffable issues it calls to our attention. It is also stunningly beautiful in its radiant images, its densely layered soundtrack, and its evocative use of music.

Also in top form on the "Cahiers" program is Eric Rohmer, another New Wave veteran with strong religious interests. For the past few years he's been working on a quartet of films called "Tales of the Four Seasons," and "A Tale of Winter" is the best in the series to date. It tells the story of a young woman who was separated from her new boyfriend by a silly mistake in communication and hasn't seen him in four years; now she's raising their child and refusing to accept the notion that she'll never see her lover again.

This story works delightfully well as a romantic comedy with a mellow mood and a warm sense of humanity. On a less obvious level, Rohmer makes it clear that his heroine's sense of confidence is not mere optimism. Instead, it grows from an intuitive confidence that faith in the ultimate rightness of the world will bring rich rewards, no matter how unlikely this may seem to those around her. Rarely has this great filmmaker been so successful at blending his most serious concerns with such engaging entertainment.

Claude Chabrol, the third Cahiers graduate on the program, is represented by a less characteristic work: "The Eye of Vichy," a densely constructed documentary using newsreel footage and other archival sources to explore the collaboration between French officials and German occupiers during the dark days of the Nazi regime. Exploring the ways Nazi sympathizers used mass media to promulgate their ideologies, the movie casts a smart and skeptical eye on the negative capabilities of cinematic expression itself.

If there is a young filmmaker in the "Cahiers" series who best exemplifies the still-living legacy of the New Wave movement, it is Leos Carax, whose latest film has generated much heated discussion even before making its way into general American distribution.

"Les Amants de Pont-Neuf" centers on two homeless people who develop a relationship at once hostile and romantic, undergo a series of arduous trials and mutual betrayals, and finally sail toward the sunset in a finale as touching as it is preposterous.

Carax's visual inventiveness seems almost limitless, especially in a bravura sequence that finds our destitute hero power-boating down the Seine while a spectacular fireworks show celebrates the French bicentennial all around him. Yet the story-telling style of this much-debated young filmmaker is so eclectic and unpredictable that even some admirers of flamboyantly artistic cinema find his work more studied than inspired.

My own view is very much in favor of Carax's nonstop inventiveness, even though I don't always like the results of his experiments. I'm delighted to see all three of his features on the "Cahiers" program—especially the explosive "Bad Blood," one of the most provocative pictures to come from France during the past dozen years. Daring, difficult, and even daunting, it's exactly the sort of ruckus-raising work that Cahiers du cinéma and the Film Society of Lincoln Center were born to champion.

LOS ANGELES TIMES, 6/30/94, Calendar/p. 7, Kevin Thomas

Jean-Luc Godard's "Hélas Pour Moi" ("Oh, Woe is Me") is beautiful, terse, perplexing, allusive as it is elusive—and a stunning experience if you're prepared to bring to it near-total alertness and openness. It helps a lot if you're an admirer well versed in the films of the ever-evolving New Wave pioneer, one of the giants of the cinema.

Not a lot can be said for certain about what's going on in this most elliptical of films. It is set in an idyllic Swiss lakeside community both in the present and in unannounced flashes back to an incredible event said to have occurred there in July, 1989. A burly, middle-aged publisher, Abraham Klimt (Bernard Verly), has come to find out whether the body of Simon Donnadieu—which means God-given, hmm—(Gérard Depardieu), proprietor of the local inn, was in fact inhabited briefly by God.

Godard has helpfully stated that his shimmering fable of emotional and spiritual longing in the face of the remorseless decline of faith was in part inspired by Zeus' impersonation of Amphitryon so as to seduce Amphitryon's wife, Alcmene. Yet, there is a decidedly Christian cast to Godard's retelling. (The film's Zeus, barely glimpsed, arrives accompanied by a Mercury carrying a tennis racket.) "Hélas pour moi" is what Simon's beautiful wife, Rachel (Laurence Masliah), exclaims when she realizes that she has discovered the "weakness of the flesh" when she was tempted to submit to God in the form of her own husband (who in the meantime may have set off on a trip to Italy to buy a small hotel). But Rachel, *hélas*, is not interested in the promise of immortality in return for her favors.

Godard seems to be creating a paradox, expressing a belief on the one hand that the spirit must be made flesh if we are to know God and a suspicion on the other that such an experience, should it actually happen, may ultimately be merely transient rather than transforming for those who experienced it. The irony here is that the film can evoke an actual sense of spiritual awakening for those watching it, but then Godard insists that the best we can do is to arrive at an image of truth rather than truth itself.

"Hélas Pour Moi," so radiantly photographed by Caroline Champtier, unfolds on two levels of reality while alternating between past and present. As in Eugene O'Neill's "Strange Interlude," the film's people, as they go about their daily routines, speak conversationally but also let loose with a sort of stream-of-consciousness barrage of Godard's trademark aphorisms (which also are heard on the soundtrack and written in intertitles on the screen). The film is a tantalizing miracle of economy: Godard will hold a moment as long as it has meaning; otherwise, he has assembled his film as a brisk flow of fragmented images. Yet no one can charge an image with so much emotion, so much thought.

Depardieu and Masliah bring to Simon and Rachel understated portrayals of absolute concentration and passion. Depardieu's God is deep-voiced, and trench-coated like Bogart—that is, if he actually manifests himself as one is tempted to believe he does.

As ferociously demanding as "Hélas Pour Moi" is, it is not without Godard's characteristically dry, throwaway humor. Amid a plethora of religious and philosophical propositions, one line pretty much summons up the bemused, confounding spirit of the enterprise: "All the perfumes of Araby cannot remove a nonexistent stain."

NEW YORK POST, 3/18/94, p. 37, Bill Hoffmann

Jean-Luc Godard's latest effort, "Helas Pour Moi," ultimately fails.

But like any Godard film, it's loaded with rich cinematic texture to nourish fans of the brilliant, eclectic director—one of the French New Wave's few living legends still grinding them out.

"Helas Pour Moi" is based on the Greek legend of Amphityron and his wife, whom the god Zeus seduces by impersonating her husband.

Amidst the backdrop of the breathtaking Swiss countryside, God (Gerard Depardieu) arrives to learn the truth about human desire.

Don't expect a conventional narrative form. Rather, Godard gives us a series of fragmented "Twilight Zone-like" vignettes, further disjointed by overlapping dialogue, title cards and up-to-the-second political references.

It makes for an intriguing, if somewhat cold and uninvolving experience. With even a barebones structure, Godard would have hooked the audience.

Fans of the early Godard will be delighted by glimpses of the master's past works.

One of the narrators sounds like the voice of the maniacal computer in the sci-fi classic, "Alphaville."

And several of the young, nubile women suggest the waif-like innocence of Jean Seberg in "Breathless."

Most of Godard's contemporaries are long gone and others have sold out, so the fact that he's still spouting about Communism and tackling new issues like AIDS and Bosnia is comforting and reassuring.

It's just that his style and lack of structure seem a bit tired and uninvolving in the fast-and-furious '90s.

Ah, Jean-Luc Godard, you can be so frustrating, at times—but we still love you.

NEWSDAY, 3/18/94, Part II/p. 75, John Anderson

The world-weary and film-weary Jean-Luc Godard draws on Greek mythology for his latest film, "Helas Pour Moi," namely the story of Alcmene, who was impregnated by Zeus when he visited her in the form of her husband, Amphitryon.

Zeus wanted to taste desire in human form; Godard, not the first director to harbor delusions of divinity, would like to as well. "Helas Pour Moi," a wildly personal and wildly obscure film, seems resigned to the fact that not only can humans not capture the essence of love, cinema can't possibly express their plight.

He's right, if "Helas Pour Moi" (roughly, Woe is Me) is any indication. With resignation, Godard delivers excruciatingly pretty places and people within suffocating frames, fracturing the whole with existential sloganeering and Beckettian adornments—which is an oxymoron, as is romantic filmmaking about the impossibility of human love. The presence of the ubiquitous Gerard Depardieu, who plays Simon, the man embodied by God(ard), is a nicely perverse touch: A man of action standing in for the captive of his own intellect, the actor serving a director whose films serve only themselves.

VILLAGE VOICE, 3/22/94, p. 43, J. Hoberman

Polanski is a genius of life; Godard a genius of film. As perverse in its fashion as *Bitter Moon* [see Hoberman's review], *Hélas Pour Moi*—the title can be translated as "Oy Vey"—is inspired by the Greek myth in which Zeus impregnates Alcmene, taking the form of her husband, Amphitryon, while he is out avenging the murder of her eight brothers. The fruit of this union is Heracles, although Godard's main interest is in "the desire of a God to feel human desire."

Which deity is that, I wonder? Even given its classical premise and Godard's own biases, *Hélas Pour Moi* seems inordinately male supremacist—although not without its humorous aspects. God, whose divine consciousness is represented by the vomit-voiced croak of the computer from *Alphaville*, crassly manifests himself amidst the placid beauty of a perfect Europe. The crisply photographed Swiss landscape is populated by a variety of ripe and tawny young women, self-conscious film characters ("present but not here"), and official star Gérard Depardieu. Appreciating the fidelity of the russet-haired beauty who plays Depardieu's wife, God duplicitously assumes the star's stolid form.

At 85 minutes, *Hélas* is even more tightly wrought and accomplished than Godard's last commercial feature, *Nouvelle Vague*. Moment to moment, it's a dazzling performance. Although blatantly producing a movie about the ineffable, Godard has no compunction about stopping short to ponder the way (for example) a bicycle falls to earth. And like Polanski, he hasn't ceased to be a wiseguy. "*The Communist Manifesto* was published the same year as *Alice in Wonderland*," the titles note; where Polanski throws a quote from *1900* into *Bitter Moon*, Godard has God watching Straub and Huillet's ethereal *From the Clouds to the Resistance* on TV and offhandedly referring to it as a horror film.

Stately and fragmented, given to all manner of sudden emotional outbursts, TV inserts, and F-stop flickers, *Hélas Pour Moi* is at once fast and slow, beautiful and infuriating, stupid and smart. ("The deepest human instinct is to wage war against the truth" is one of its more memorable aphorisms.) With the possible exception of Stan Brakhage, there is no other living artist so utterly in command of his particular film vocabulary.

Who else could create so elegantly layered, rhythmically complex, and willfully impenetrable a celluloid construction? But where the young Godard made movies seemingly authored by a combination of all previous movies, he now produces obscurantist masterpieces that refer only to themselves. The paradox of Godard is that of an artist who has regressed from postmodern to modern.

Also reviewed in:
NATION, 3/21/94, p. 390, Stuart Klawans
VARIETY, 9/20/93, p. 26, David Stratton
NEW YORK TIMES, 3/18/94, p. C15, Caryn James
WASHINGTON POST, 11/11/94, p. D7, Hal Hinson

HIGH LONESOME: THE STORY OF BLUEGRASS MUSIC

A Tara Releasing presentation of a Northside Films production. *Producer:* Rachel Liebling and Andrew Serwer. *Director:* Rachel Liebling. *Screenplay:* Rachel Liebling. *Director of Photography:* Buddy Squires and Allen Moore. *Editor:* Tody Shimin. *Running time:* 95 minutes. *MPAA Rating:* Not Rated.

WITH: Bill Monroe; Ralph Stanley; Mac Wiseman; Jimmy Martin; Earl Scruggs; Jim McReynolds; Osborne Brothers; Seldom Scene; Sam Bush; Alison Krauss & Union Station; Nashville Bluegrass Band.

LOS ANGELES TIMES, 6/8/94, Calendar/p. 3, Kenneth Turan

It is an indelible sound, soulful yet streamlined, often overlooked but once heard never forgotten. It is bluegrass, a.k.a. "folk music with overdrive," as vibrant an American musical synthesis as jazz and the subject of a thorough and thoroughly entertaining documentary titled "High Lonesome" after the haunting melodies it calls its own.

Written and directed by Rachel Liebling, "High Lonesome" is an exploration of bluegrass's roots, an almost poetic evocation of the world from which it sprang, a celebration of its greatest practitioners and a biography of the man who started it all, Bill Monroe.

This may sound like a sizable order, but because it's been made with simplicity and care, "High Lonesome" carries it off. Liebling's film will please the initiated and introduce the subject to the uninformed, as well as providing a chance to hear parts of more than 100 songs with evocative titles like "Blue Moon of Kentucky" and "I Wonder How the Old Folks Are at Home."

Kentucky native Monroe is "High Lonesome's" centerpiece and understandably so. The man who did the final combining of bluegrass's diverse elements back in 1930, Monroe at age 83 is still playing and touring, a courtly yet indomitable legend whose trademark high country tenor voice and swift mandolin playing fingers have lost none of their emotional power.

The first of bluegrass's components were the Scottish-Irish ballads carried by immigrants to the hills of Appalachia. Gradually added to the mix was white gospel music, and, brought in by the railroad, African American rhythms in general and the banjo, a plantation instrument, in particular.

Pushing everything together was the Great Depression, which drove people like Monroe, one of eight children who took up the mandolin because it was the only instrument not already spoken for, to the modern, industrialized north. There, exposure on radio stations like Indiana's WJKS ("Where Joy Kills Sorrow") and ultimately the Grand Ole Opry led to the music's increasing popularity.

Aside from its scintillating sound, what makes "High Lonesome" so effective is the footage the music is placed against. Writer-director Liebling scoured more than 50 archives, finding historical material (some so combustible it had to be transported in an armored car) that almost poetically evokes the physical world of chores, churchgoing and quiet beauty the music grew out of.

Of course there is rare performance footage as well, including country pioneers like Uncle Dave Macon, "the Dixie Dewdrop"; classic groups like the Stanley Brothers and Jim & Jesse; and folks like Jimmy Martin and narrator Mac Wiseman, who began as Monroe sidemen. For, as the great man likes to point out, his band has been through more than 65 fiddle players, as many on the banjo, "but there's been only one mandolin."

Bluegrass was nearly killed by the rock explosion, but it stayed alive long enough to inspire a current generation, like John Duffey and the Seldom Scene and Alison Krauss and Union Station, both of whom pay tribute to Monroe as the great progenitor.

"High Lonesome" seems so thorough, in fact, that it's a bit disappointing that Liebling doesn't find time for the classic citybilly bands of the 1960s—the Charles River Valley Boys, the Kentucky Colonels and the influential Greenbriar Boys—that provided a crucial link between Monroe and today's gang.

Finally, though, the music wins out over everything. Everyone will have a favorite moment, from the great Lester Flatt and Earl Scruggs performing with Monroe when their careers began as members of his Bluegrass Boys, to Monroe and his current band breaking into a impromptu version of "I'm Going Back to Old Kentucky" on their bus. Beautiful and spirited, these songs represent the music at its best, and we are fortunate that Liebling has packaged its history so thoughtfully.

NEW YORK POST, 4/29/94, p. 43, Larry Worth

Bluegrass music is an acquired taste. But that needn't extend to a documentary on the subject.

Unless the director is Rachel Liebling and the film is "High Lonesome: The Story of Bluegrass Music."

Actually, the title identifies the main problem: Liebling tries squeezing the entire history of bluegrass into 95 minutes. Unfolding like a pedantic history lesson the music's appeal gets lost in the shuffle.

Another wrong note: letting events unwind through the eyes of bluegrass legend Bill Monroe, 82, whose talent on string instruments doesn't translate into verbal skills.

Nonetheless, Monroe puts his perspective on bluegrass' circuitous path from the British Isles to Appalachia, charting its popularity during the Depression to its "death" from '50s rock 'n' roll and subsequent resurrection in the '80s.

Unfortunately, both Liebling and Monroe barely touch on the two bluegrass selections with the widest appeal: the "Dueling Banjos" scene in "Deliverance" and "The Ballad of Jed Clampett," which made Lester Flatt and Earl Scruggs into household names.

Instead, a clip from "The Beverly Hillbillies" is included only to mention how bluegrass fans are often depicted as "hayseeds." But Liebling does little to dispel the stereotype when she keeps returning to two elderly farmers who practically liken Elvis to Satan.

And when time comes to showcase the music, it's often in a silly package. For example, when "Blue Moon of Kentucky" is warbled on the sound track, a big ol' you-know-what races like a cardboard cutout across an inky sky. Welcome to Filmmaking 101.

Redeeming the production is a collection of photos that beautifully captures the poverty and hardship characterizing the '30s.

Clearly, there's still a wonderful story to be told here. But before setting her sights on "High Lonesome II," Liebling should give more thought to technique. And a man named Jed.

NEWSDAY, 4/29/94, Part II/p. B9, Jack Mathews

Bluegrass, that distinct varietal of "hillbilly" music that echoed out of the southern Appalachians in the '40s and '50s to join the mainstream of popular American folk, has a rhythmic, relentlessly driving pace that is nicely matched by "High Lonesome," Rachel Liebling's fine documentary on the subject.

"High Lonesome" opens with snapshots taken in the hills of Kentucky in the early days of this century, dissolves to a pan shot of mountain peaks silhouetted against a purple sunset, then, with the molasses-thick Virginia drawl of singer Mac Wiseman narrating the way, takes off on a 96-minute chronological tour of bluegrass history. You pretty much have to love the music to enjoy the tour. Bluegrass hasn't always had that harmonious sound we're familiar with now.

In the beginning, when Bill Monroe, the now 82-year-old father of bluegrass, began pickin' and strummin' his way through the assortment of musical influences permeating rural life in the Appalachians, hillbilly folk sounded about as pleasant to outsiders as the cry of a trapped possum.

"High Lonesome," deftly blending Depression Era photos, archival home movies, clips from TV shows, concerts and the Grand Ole Opry, and interviews with Monroe and other bluegrass masters, tracks the musical form from its immigrant Scots-Irish antecedents to the sophisticated sound of today's popular Nashville Bluegrass Band.

In rich detail, we learn how the railroads, built largely with African-American labor, brought the sounds of gospel and blues to the hills, how traveling shows introduced jazz and ragtime, and radio and phonographs added the melodic compositions of swing. We see how mass production and the Sears catalog flooded the hills with $3.95 guitars and mandolins, and how the Depression drove Bill Monroe and others into the big cities, where they began spicing the airwaves with their special blend of mountain music.

When Monroe's Blue Grass Boys were joined in the late '40s by Earl Scruggs, who'd adopted his unique banjo style from the old minstrel players, the sound we've come to know as bluegrass entered the popular culture. It began hitting the country charts in the early '50s, flamed out during the Presley-driven mania for rock and roll, then was revived in the late '60s, when its acoustic purity made it the musical granola of the counter-culture.

Liebling, a New Yorker, had the sense to let the musicians tell their own story and sell their own music. She calls her film a living history, and that's about right. She's caught it all, from its roots to its legends, and has told it with an editorial style as simple and pure and joyful as the bluegrass sound itself.

NEWSWEEK, 5/16/94, p. 67, Malcolm Jones, Jr.

Near the beginning of "High Lonesome," Rachel Liebling's documentary about bluegrass music, the screen suddenly explodes with energy illustrating the period in the '20s when industry invaded the bucolic Appalachians, Liebling shows old footage of huge logs plummeting down a flume and steam trains hurtling down the tracks. As counterpoint, she fills the soundtrack with Bill Monroe's "Jerusalem Ridge," a driving instrumental that marries the skirling fiddles of his Scots-Irish heritage to the streamlined rhythms of modernity. The cinematic fusion of sound and image precisely evokes the passage of old-time mountain music into quick-tempoed bluegrass.

There are few moments quite so fine in this film, but for anyone curious about bluegrass, this is a fine place to start. Intercutting performance footage with interviews, Liebling spotlights the music's principal figures, including Mac Wiseman, Ralph Stanley and Jimmy Martin. She slights no one, but after a while you wish she hadn't fretted about fairness, because when she obeys her instincts and points the camera at her heart's darling—82-year-old Bill Monroe—the movie takes wing. A Kentucky country boy, Monroe came out of a homemade world ("My mother, she used to walk through the house singing, and she could play the fiddle," he proudly recollects); with audacious genius he singlehandedly forged country songs, blues and early jazz into the music we call bluegrass. Eavesdropping on this old autocrat as he muses on his triumphs, Liebling leaves no doubt that we are beholding a true American original. "High Lonesome" gives him his due.

VILLAGE VOICE, 5/17/94, p. 58, Jeff Salamon

Bluegrass is a rural-based, acoustic music that appeals to a small niche audience—which is to say, it's not rock. But bluegrass is also a genre that emphasizes velocity, arrives in catchy three-minute bites, and grew out of a midcentury Southern encounter between blacks, whites, and mass culture—which is to say, it's not rock, either. But the closest Rachel Liebling's documentary *High Lonesome* gets to MTV is decades-old found footage of a baptism. The film stock has deteriorated oddly, and as the faithful get dipped in water, the sky and foliage strobe like a Metallica video by Matt Mahurin.

Most of *High Lonesome*'s pleasures are more straightforward. Telling the story of this "folk music on overdrive" by tracing the career of the genre's father Bill Monroe, Liebling treats us to much fine music, great concert footage, thumbnail social history, and pleasant if not revelatory interviews. A few moments stand out: Two aged farmers are so eager to describe the horrors of the Great Depression that they can't stop talking over each other, their impromptu polyphony the speech equivalent of dueling banjos. Or giddily absurd footage of a '60s bluegrass revival concert at San Francisco's Avalon Ballroom, featuring Flatt and Scruggs picking and strumming while a psychedelic light show is projected on top of them. (Ironically, the hippie audience is dressed like the very "hayseed stereotype" Bill Monroe tried to overturn by insisting that his musicians wear suits.)

Underneath *Lonesome*'s pleasant surface, though, Liebling builds a definite and problematic argument. Though she makes clear that bluegrass contrary to popular belief, was a mongrelized and very 20th-century music—born when Gaelic folk styles met up with black labor shouts, minstrelsy, Hawaiian guitars, jazz, commercial ditties, and even the movies (old time musician Jimmy Martin admits that his first guitar featured Gene Autry's signature)—she has trouble shedding fannish notions of authenticity. Time and again, she conveys the rapture of the music but misses the tension between its conservative and progressive tendencies. After the original story gets told, for instance, the question of race disappears entirely, as if the uniform whiteness of the performers and audience was a natural fact and not a result of specific historical causes. (The closest we get to commentary is a quick glimpse of a 1938 Monroe Brothers concert poster that features a blackface performer kneeling between them.) Similarly, Liebling gives more recent developments in the music short shrift. We get to hear young star Alison Krauss sing Monroe's praises, but we don't learn how she's wed bluegrass playing to Nashville-style song-writing. And though mandolist David Grisman can be spotted in the background of a still photo, neither his name nor the newgrass school he invented are mentioned. Also neglected are Jerry Douglas, Russ Barenberg, Tony Trischka, Andy Statman, Alison Brown, Fiddle Fever, the Modern Mandolin Quartet, and any of the other musicians who have wed a bluegrass sensibility to world musics, rock, jazz, or even classical. Of course, any two-hour history of a 50-year-old music will have some omissions, but these form a pattern, a pattern that's completed when the film ends as it began: with Bill Monroe walking through the ruins of the house where he was raised, as if bluegrass were an arrow that travels from the '40s to the '90s only to point right back where it started.

Also reviewed in:
CHICAGO TRIBUNE, 7/10/92, Friday/p. H, Lynn Van Matre
NEW YORK TIMES, 4/2 9/94, p. C8, Janet Maslin
VARIETY, 12/6/93, p. 39, Dennis Harvey
WASHINGTON POST, 4/8/94, p. C1, Richard Harrington

HIGH SCHOOL II

A Zipporah Films release. *Producer:* Frederick Wiseman. *Director:* Frederick Wiseman. *Director of Photography:* John Davey. *Editor:* Frederick Wiseman. *Running time:* 220 minutes. *MPAA Rating:* Not Rated.

LOS ANGELES TIMES, 9/7/94, Calendar/p. 9, Robert Koehler

Frederick Wiseman makes films in which patterns and meanings gradually emerge. But a pattern is also emerging in Wiseman's career, and his latest work, "High School II," confirms it.

The early Wiseman films, while seemingly removed from their subjects, were considerable social critiques of institutions, from mental hospitals and the welfare system to the meat industry—and public schools, which come off rather badly in Wiseman's 1968 "High School," about Philadelphia's Northeast High.

As Wiseman grows older, he seems to grow more hopeful. His recent "Near Death," "Central Park" and "Zoo" showed mostly good people doing goof work (yes, even in zoos). "High School II" documents success in an East Harlem public school, Central Park East Secondary, where drug use is as rare as dropouts and where 67% of the graduates attend private colleges (and only 10% don't go to college at all).

The old rules that dominated in the first "High School" silent classes dominated by a yammering teacher, bureaucratic mini-dictators, few visible parents, rampant boredom—are tossed out in the new "High School."

The contrast immediately hits you. Students confer with teachers in one-on-one discussions, co-principals Paul Schwartz and Deborah Meier appear to be constantly available for individual meetings with students and their families, and intellectual rigor in a lab-like atmosphere is so dominant that it's like breathing. Only at the end of the nearly 4-hour film does Meier sum up what we've been watching: A pedagogy that blends kindergarten's sense of active play with the Oxford-Cambridge tradition of a student setting his or her academic course with a tutor.

For a good stretch of "High School II," all we know is that we're not in the typical public school anymore. The school's full name and neighborhood are never mentioned, and its academic program of doctoral-style papers in lieu of standard tests is never articulated. Wiseman's adherence to a *cinéma vérité* that resists factoids doesn't help him here.

The film, though cleverly plays on viewer presumptions of both what a public school looks and sounds like, and what a school with predominantly minorities should be. Where arc the rigid audiences of students impassively staring at a lecturing teacher? Where are the drugs, the guns, the gangs?

Somewhere, out on the street, but not in here. Here, Central Park East kids sit in small groups, puzzling through engineering or math or literary problems, prodded by friendly but very serious teachers—and deeply concerned parents,

The guiding ethic at Central Park East is what Schwartz and Meier call five "habits of mind": Show evidence, analyze whose point of view is being expressed, examine alternative solutions, show how ideas are connected to each other and prove their relevancy. But the umbrella value above this school's "habits" is that endangered species, critical thinking. Wiseman has found it alive and well and living in East Harlem.

NEW YORK POST, 7/6/94, p. 33, Bill Hoffmann

There are few documentary filmmakers who can tackle a subject like Frederick Wiseman.

Not only does his camera never blink, but the subjects being filmed give no indication they know it's there.

In 1968, Wiseman wowed the world with his brilliant portrayal of a day in the life of Northeast High School in Philadelphia.

Now a mind-blowing time capsule, Wiseman's film showed us the towering strengths and glaring weaknesses of an urban school ruled by crew-cutted teachers and a staunch curriculum.

Twenty-six years later, in "High School II," Wiseman has tackled another high school, this one 180 degrees different—the Central Park East Secondary School at 106th Street and Madison Avenue in Spanish Harlem.

It's a successful alternative public high school; 95 percent of its graduates go on to four-year colleges.

The difference at Central Park is that the teachers are merely guides to the students' independent interests and studies.

As one teacher says, "It's a high school that works best if you want to be here."

Some traditionalist educators would go berserk seeing the structureless school at work: students putting their feet up on desks, calling teachers by their first names, and teachers and students alike using profanity.

Compare the sex education here (proper use of a condom) with the sex education in thc original "High School" (diagrams of diseased reproductive systems).

But it all seems to work, as the results show.

Unfortunately, the fast-paced cinema-verite magic of the first film is missing here.

The camera often seems to be stationary, a bit lazy. Scenes plod on, seemingly without the help of an editor's eye.

And at 3½ hours, "High School II" seems less accessible to a general audience than its predecessor.

The production is more of a educational tool for city teachers in the '90s.

The original "High School" was only 75 minutes. I suspect the new one could be a mean and lean entry at that length.

VILLAGE VOICE, 7/12/94, p. 48, Beth Coleman

Central Park East Secondary School, 1994, the location of *High School II*, should have reached Planet Reebok by now, light years away from the large, generic Philadelphia school of 1968's *High School*, documentary innovator Wiseman's first foray into the training of the American citizen. Made soon after the King assassination, with Vietnam still raging, the first *High School* works as sly joke and serious filmmaking, using the country's love of order and status quo (what better place to find it than high school?) against itself by simply shooting the scene, with no commentary and a light hand on the editorial juxtaposition.

That the same filmic techniques are used over 25 years later, in a culture moving at warp speed, illustrates the limitations of this style more vividly than the ostensible subject: a progressive, public high school in Spanish Harlem with a majority white teaching staff and a student body of many different colors. The teachers at CPESS are incredibly decent and successful in their efforts (the school has a 90 per cent college continuance rate and Wiseman is publicizing this good thing). But Wiseman ignores that high school as social structure is not what it used to be, which makes the sequel more human-interest story than iconic wrestling match.

Though *90210* might represent Satan (and I'm not talking about Shannen), it revels in high schoolness, like David Lynch, who I hate but cannot deny is a master of this paradigm. Despite or because of its resolute whiteness and reeling cash fantasy, it catches the noise of youth culture in the hallways better than the well-intentioned documentary.

Also reviewed in:
NATION, 7/25-8/1/94, p. 136, Stuart Klawans
NEW YORK TIMES, 7/6/94, p. C14, Caryn James
VARIETY, 3/14-20/94, p. 56, Daniel M. Kimmel

HOOP DREAMS

A Fine Line Features release of a Kartemquin Films and KTCA-TV production. *Executive Producer:* Gordon Quinn and Catherine Allan. *Producer:* Frederick Marx, Steve James, and Peter Gilbert. *Director:* Steve James. *Screenplay:* Steve James, Frederick Mark, and Peter Gilbert. *Director of Photography:* Peter Gilbert. *Editor:* Frederick Marx, Steve James, and Bill Haugse. *Music:* Ben Sidran. *Sound:* Adam Singer and Tom Yore. *Running time:* 171 minutes. *MPAA Rating:* PG-13.

WITH: Steve James (Narrator); William Gates; Arthur Agee; Emma Gates; Curtis Gates; Sheila Agee; Arthur "Bo" Agee; Earl Smith; Gene Pingatore; Dennis Doyle; Isiah Thomas; Sister Marlyn Hopewell; Bill Gleason; Patricia Weir; Marjorie Heard; Aretha Mitchell; Luther Bedford; Shannon Johnson; Tomika Agee; Joe "Sweetie" Agee; Jazz Agee; Catherine Mines; Alicia Mines; Alvin Bibbs; Elijah Ephraim; Willie Gates; Spike Lee; James Kelly; Michael O'Brien; Dick Vitale; Kevin O'Neill; Bo Ellis; Bobby Knight; Joey Meyer; Frank DuBois; Bob Gibbons; Clarence Webb; Stan Wilson; Derrick Zinneman; Tim Gray; Myron Gordon.

LOS ANGELES TIMES, 10/19/94, Calendar/p. 1, Kenneth Turan

Basketball is just a game. The quintessential city sport, played with reckless passion on random patches of concrete, it classically offers a way out of poverty for its best players, but there is more.

When it's used right, basketball can also provide a way in for those who have the wit to use it, a chance to dramatically combine the excitement of competition with a provocative look at the complexities of urban life. And "Hoop Dreams" certainly does it right.

A 2-hour, 49-minute epic that zips by like a fluid fast break, "Hoop Dreams" has taken a simple concept and, by a Horatio Alger combination of luck, pluck and pure hard work, turned it into a landmark of American documentary film.

By focusing on the personal side of the city game, "Hoop Dreams" tells us more about what works and what doesn't in our society than the proverbial shelf of sociological studies. And it is thoroughly entertaining in the bargain.

The trio of filmmakers (Steve James, Frederick Marx, Peter Gilbert) responsible for "Hoop Dreams" made it the old-fashioned way: refusing to stint on time spent with their subjects, a pair of promising teen-age Chicago basketball players, they shot some 250 hours over a five-year period, staying with the young men from before their high school careers to what transpired after graduation.

The result is a film as rife with incident, with the ups and downs of outrageous fortune, as any Victorian triple-decker novel. By adroitly eavesdropping on reality, the "Hoop Dreams" team rooted out the kind of unvarnished home truths that make for the most engrossing viewing.

Where luck enters the equation is with the players selected. Both William Gates and Arthur Agee are but 14 years old when "Hoop Dreams" begins, just out of grade school but already good enough to dream of the money and glory of an NBA career. And the cameras are present when Earl Smith, a neighborhood talent scout, discovers Arthur on a local court. "I don't know anything about him," Smith says, "but I'll bet you a steak dinner in four years you'll be hearing about him."

Either or both of these kids could have proved to be duds on the court as well as ciphers as human beings, but it is the great good fortune of "Hoop Dreams" that the reverse is true. Explosively talented players who are willing to be honest in the face of the camera, their life paths turn out to be unpredictable and intensely human, with the agonizing drama of victory and loss on the court always present to add zest to the mixture.

Both William, a smooth natural leader, and Arthur, whose talent is undeniable but rawer, are actively recruited by St. Joseph High School and its cantankerous coach, Gene Pingatore. The alma mater of the NBA's Isiah Thomas and a perennial basketball power, St. Joseph's tranquil suburban location requires adjustments for both boys that range from three hours of commuting time to demanding academics and the novelty of spending time with white people.

Since the pleasure of "Hoop Dreams" lies in discovering what happens to William and Arthur as their lives unfold, giving away any more of their stories wouldn't be fair. Interspersing interviews with parents, siblings, friends, coaches, counselors and others with talks with the boys themselves (plus liberal amounts of game footage), each subject's particular mixture of disappointment and joy becomes involving in a way fiction often is not.

What is worth pointing out are the meaty themes "Hoop Dreams" touches on, one of the pivotal ones being the thoughtless way these kids are fed into the omnivorous machine that is big-time sports.

While bringing talented city kids out to St. Joseph's may seem like a win-win situation, it soon becomes obvious that both the school and the boys' mentors have agendas that do not necessarily put the welfare of their players first. "We don't understand what we're really doing to these kids," says a rival coach, and the truth of that is much in evidence.

But though the pressures placed on these kids are severe, "Hoop Dreams" emphasizes why they try to endure. For both William ("This is my ticket out of the ghetto") and Arthur ("Nobody is going to take my dream away from me"), basketball is the only thing they can have pride in, the only place where they can see their presence making a difference.

In plain contrast to the sense of hope basketball engenders is the grinding nature of the poverty the boys' families, both their fierce and protective mothers and their troubled fathers, have to contend with. Without any sense of special pleading, "Hoop Dreams" underlines the difficulties of making something of yourself in an indifferent system, helping us to understand Arthur's mother when she bares her heart and says, "Do you wonder sometimes how I am living? It's enough to make you want to lash out and hurt someone."

In the end, we feel we know both William and Arthur and their lives in a way only a film like this can manage. When the final crawl lets us know just what both men are up to today, audiences talk, marvel and express concern, just as they would with their own friends, and there is no better gauge of "Hoop Dreams'" considerable accomplishment than that.

NEW YORK, 10/24/94, p. 60, David Denby

Arthur Agee, 14 when we first see him, is a knife-thin black kid from Chicago who explodes from a motionless stance on a cement court, darts, fakes and takes the ball to the basket. Off the courts, Arthur is shy and languid, collapsing in on himself, hardly speaking or moving. William Gates, also 14 and an African-American from Chicago, is more solidly built, not as fast as Arthur, but graceful and liquid in his movements. William has the glowing, lion-eyed handsomeness of an admired high-school athlete—a natural—relieved by a sheepish smile.

The two boys stand at the center of the documentary *Hoop Dreams*, which is an extraordinarily detailed and emotionally satisfying piece of work about American inner-city life, American hopes, American defeat. The boys want to be NBA players. That is their only desire. They have no fallback position, no middle ground, nothing else they would settle for. The movie follows them through the ups and downs of their high-school years and then into college, and much of it takes place off the courts, among coaches, parents, and friends, who apply an annihilating pressure on the young men to succeed. What is so frightening about *Hoop Dreams* is how cruelly the dreams fall away—how suddenly and absolutely they sheer off into failure and nowheresville. Whatever else it is, the movie is a portrait of a wounded culture that, at the moment, can imagine very few ways to bind and heal itself.

Hoop Dreams, chosen by the New York Film Festival as its closing-night feature, was initiated in the late eighties as a rather modest affair—a short film about playground basketball in Chicago. But the three documentary filmmakers Steve James, Frederick Marx, and Peter Gilbert, realizing that they had got hold of something, stuck with the subject for more than four years, and their movie grew into an American epic. Kartemquin Films, a Chicago documentary outfit, became involved, as did public-television station KTCA of Minneapolis and many foundations and individuals. In the end, the 250 hours of footage were edited down to a very absorbing 171 minutes. *Hoop Dreams* will stand, I believe, as one of the more significant attempts in this period by white Americans to understand black life. As such it may not always be successful, but it is nevertheless a many-sided work of documentary art, emotionally rich, disturbing, unresolved.

In the beginning, the boys are seen watching the NBA on television with their families. What they want—celebrity, wealth, power—is all there on the tube, and they are held by the images in silence. Who would have the courage to warn them against so dangerous a dream? (Would I? I would not.) Although they both read at a fourth-or fifth-grade level, Arthur Agee and William Gates are "discovered" while still in grammar school, and both are sent out of the city, with partial scholarships, to St. Joseph's, a mainly white Catholic school in the suburb of Westchester. St. Joseph's has a strong basketball tradition—the great Isiah Thomas, of the Detroit Pistons, is a graduate. William, initially the more promising of the two, remains at St. Joseph's through graduation, his way paid for by a wealthy woman, Patricia Weir, the president of Encyclopaedia Britannica. But Arthur, smaller and less impressive, cannot survive a tuition rise and is sent, unwilling and depressed, back to the city, where he attends Marshall High School.

As the boys play basketball, dubious angels move in the background, arranging and controlling; a fantasy of rescue and transcendence is put in place. The great pot of media gold, even though it remains years away and may never be reached, somehow governs the lives of boys not yet out of the eighth grade. The whites want to be benefactors and kingmakers—that's *their* fantasy. They feed the boys' hopes without equipping them for anything else. And so William and Arthur are caught in a cruel and ridiculous contradiction. They are constantly shamed by their low grades, which they must improve in order to qualify for college, yet no one we see takes full responsibility for educating them—that little detail somehow gets overlooked.

O America! William's older brother Curtis, a high-school star himself a few years earlier, mysteriously came apart in college; now, barely employable, and full of bitter accusations and excuses, he sits around the house sinking into his own flesh. Arthur's father, Bo, another school athlete who didn't make it to the NBA, has become an older, slickly self-justifying version of Curtis; a frequent drug abuser, he disappears into the slammer on a burglary charge in the middle of the movie.

He returns, with new religious faith, and then leaves again. Both men are economically useless, the object of mockery among the women. Somehow the two boys are expected to redeem all that defeat, and to make whole the two broken men, who both love and resent them. Only the boys' mothers seem to have a grip on the actualities of the situation. They dare not oppose their sons' dreams, but they are full of foreboding.

From the point of view of technique or narrative strategy, there's nothing startling here. The camera is often extraordinarily well placed, the many basketball games rapidly summarized and highlighted; but really, the principal technique of such a film is *waiting*. I am not being facetious. The filmmakers hang out, and if the people trust them, eventually the moment ripens, and the apple of truth falls. About five times a decade this method works well. The editing of *Hoop Dreams* accentuates the emotional and narrative continuities. These boys are situated within their families (the movie is a better argument for the family than 100 neoconservative sermons), and we see the growth and happiness within the families and also many things that don't work. The family members become characters in their own right, especially Arthur's mother, Sheila Agee, one of the more intelligent and heroic women in recent American movies.

At St. Joseph's, William falls under the tutelage and control of the longtime coach Gene Pingatore, a heavy-set wall-slammer with a huge temper. Athletic coaches may be the last personalities in America unburdened by self-consciousness; Pingatore dominates and bullies his players like a charmless John Wayne. A boy like William will be successful and rich, but only if he does exactly what his coach says. *Then* that boy will have tears in his eyes thinking of his old high-school coach. Oh, yes. But now William does nothing but fail his coach. Fail and fail. Pingatore creates William Gates and at the same time destroys him, driving him too hard when his knee is injured, browbeating and humiliating him, raising him up and casting him down. By the end, at college, William has rejected Pingatore as a false god.

If the high-school athlete survives the taunting and undermining pressures, the relentless challenges, he escapes gravity; he becomes awesome. We do not know what will happen to Arthur Agee or William Gates, but *Hoop Dreams*, which is graced by much sweet struggle and several euphoric moments, is nevertheless tragic in its implications. America is interested in making these boys into stars but not into men. They will grow older and possibly suffer the mockery of their hopes, at which time, defenseless, they may join the many *others*, the ones on the outskirts of their dreams. The movie takes a long enough look at those others to see how forlorn, and unprotected, they will always be.

NEW YORK POST, 10/7/94, p. 46, Michael Medved

"Hoop Dreams" introduces some of the most vivid characters you'll meet anywhere in films this year—people who emerge with even more striking impact and intimacy because they happen to be real.

This remarkable documentary (which closes the 32nd New York Film Festival) tells the true story of William Gates and Arthur Agee, two sweet-tempered inner-city kids in Chicago who are incurably obsessed with dreams of basketball glory.

At age 14, both boys are plucked from the streets when a celebrated scout arranges athletic scholarships to a prestigious Catholic prep school.

There, the two kids get the chance to play for the same legendary coach (a hard-driving monster with an impossible temper and bad toupee) who once shaped the skills of NBA superstar Isiah Thomas.

The filmmakers (veteran documentarians Steve James, Frederick Marx and Peter Gilbert) cover the boys and their struggles for 4½ years and allow us to share every aspect of their lives—on the court, in the classroom and, most movingly, at home, where their loving families make painful sacrifices to sustain their athletic ambitions.

The emotional range of the film is extraordinary: Both families experience so many shocks and surprises, such rich moments of heartbreak and triumph, that any screenwriter who dared create such an overloaded plot would have been criticized for making his tale too melodramatic.

At one point, for instance, Arthur Agee's unemployed father—a singularly handsome and engaging presence in his family—goes to jail for dealing crack cocaine. Much later, he returns from prison transformed by a new commitment to Christ: The scene in which he goes to church to reconsecrate his marriage and renew his life moved this critic to free-flowing tears.

Similarly affecting is a sequence in which one of the boys (it would give too much away to say here which one) suffers a career-threatening injury at the height of his success: His knee surgery and its aftermath are presented in excruciating, edge-of-your-seat detail.

Unlike other celebrated documentaries of recent years "The Thin Blue Line," "Roger and Me," "Hearts of Darkness"), the filmmakers never upstage their characters, or allow the real-life voices to be drowned out by the whirring sound of a grinding ax.

The story emerges with startling, fly-on-the-wall immediacy, leaving the viewer to draw his own conclusions. You can see the cruel, exploitative aspects of the sports obsession at the same time you can easily understand its appeal as an escape route from poverty and the projects.

The two-hour-and-50-minute running time (edited down from 250 hours of raw footage) never feels slow—though the film's concluding section, as the boys' high school careers wind down without final surprises or big emotional payoffs, does seem a bit anticlimactic.

Nevertheless, "Hoop Dreams" remains an astonishing experience, and far more than a superior sports movie: With its epic scope and dozens of indelible portraits, it's one of the most moving and thought-provoking portrayals—in any form—of America's ongoing inner-city tragedy.

NEWSDAY, 10/14/94, Part II/p. B7, John Anderson

To say that "Hoop Dreams" is "simply brilliant" would do the film a disservice. Yes, it possesses every quality a documentary should: breadth, drama, social conscience. Subjects who demand the emotional investment of their audience. A story with an irresistible momentum. But there's nothing simple about it.

Directors Steve James, Frederick Marx and Peter Gilbert intended their first film to be a 30-minute short, but the journey of William Gates and Arthur Agee—from their last year of Chicago elementary school to their first year of college—took on a life of its own. What they ended up with was five years out of their subjects' lives, condensed into a little less than three hours, much of which has a tension similar to the last five minutes of a Knicks-Bulls playoff.

That the NBA equals El Dorado for a large segment of the young, male black population in this country is nothing new. But for Gates and Agee, it's actually attainable. Both show enough prodigious talent in grammar school to be recruited by St. Joseph's prestigious suburban prep school with a long basketball tradition and a celebrated alumnus—perennial NBA all-star Isiah Thomas. William, with a similar build and similar style, becomes coach Gene Pignatore's designated Isiah-to-be—much to Gates' detriment. Arthur Agee, the gangly, awkward-seeming but passionate player, is set on a different track entirely.

Pursuing a dream is strenuous enough. Doing it under the conditions imposed on Arthur and William is cruel, although both young men show inspiring resilience and character—something they bring to the court, rather than learn there. The pressure comes from everywhere: William's brother Curtis, for instance, who was himself a college star, fouled out of a promising career, and sees in William the last gasp of his frustrated dream. We see Arthur's father, Bo, migrate, from abusive husband to crackhead to missing-in-action to a born-again, but always an overweening factor in Arthur's life. Their dynamic—Bo speaks, Arthur rolls his eyes—is one of the film's more powerful subplots.

Watching "Hoop Dreams," one suspects the filmmakers lived in the boys' closets. They miss very little, and their access to the two households is so free it can be disconcerting. The families aren't alone in their open-door policy. Pignatore, for instance, reveals himself as a prime example of both the exploitive and the incompetent.

When Arthur doesn't progress or grow quickly enough, the coach loses interest in him and Arthur eventually drops out, owing the school money. That we're allowed to see the scene of Arthur's parents ransoming back his academic records so he can graduate from his city high school—the smiling bursar is practicing extortion—is an amazing example of public-relations suicide on the part of St. Joseph's.

William, meanwhile, is put under such pressure as Pignatore's great black hope, and by the coach's relentlessly intimidating style, it's as if he were shooting a 400-pound basketball. How can he win?

They both do, though. Perhaps not entirely, and certainly not until after numerous twists and turns in the plot—it is a plot, although it couldn't have been written or filmed by Hollywood (Spike Lee, though, is supposed to produce a fictional remake for TNT). This isn't any fairy tale; it leaves the fabled American Dream downcourt and shoeless, and presents troubling questions about our priorities. But "Hoop Dreams" also resonates, like a final buzzer echoing in an empty arena.

NEWSWEEK, 10/17/94, p. 80, David Ansen

Not too many filmmakers are determined enough, or crazy enough, to devote seven years of their lives to the making of a movie. A movie that has no stars, no script, and was made on a budget that would barely cover the catering costs on "True Lies." Indeed, the odds against "Hoop Dreams" ever seeing the light of day were overwhelming, for it is a documentary, and the term itself carries such a commercial stigma that only a few are lucky enough to get a theatrical release.

But "Hoop Dreams" has more than good luck on its side: it's one of the richest movie experiences of the year, a spellbinding American epic that holds you firmly in its grip for nearly three hours. Chicago filmmakers Steve James, Frederick Marx and Peter Gilbert spent four and a half years following two inner-city kids with dreams of NBA glory, William Gates and Arthur Agee, basketball prodigies whose hopes of escaping the hazards of the ghetto rest on their hardwood performance. With an intimacy that never seems intrusive, "Hoop Dreams" tracks them through high school up to the brink of college. We watch two boys turn into young men before our eyes. And we see a portrait of inner-city struggle and survival shorn of the sound-bite clichés of TV and the sensationalist reductionism of Hollywood 'hood flicks. "Hoop Dreams" has all the suspense of a soap opera, but without the manipulation. It lets us draw our own conclusions, never forcing the story to fit a preordained agenda, never making easy generalizations out of the lives it examines with such cleareyed generosity.

At 14, Gates and Agee are given financial aid to attend St. Joseph's, a suburban Catholic high school that prides itself for producing superstar Isiah Thomas. The quiet Gates, who lives in the Cabrini Green project and enters school at a fifth-grade academic level, is the blue-chip prospect, in whom coach Gene Pingatore sees a glimmer of the Thomas magic. Agee is the gangly speedster, a diamond in the rough. He has to make a three-hour round trip to St. Joseph's, where there are more white faces than he's ever seen. By sophomore year, Gates is on the honor roll, and Agee, whose father has been laid off, is forced to transfer to all-black Marshall High School.

Blasted fantasies: You think you can see which way fate's arrows are pointing, but life isn't so predictable. One kid is felled by a knee injury, and has to undergo surgery. we're startled to learn that, in his junior year, Gates becomes a father. Agee's father deserts his family, and we see him on a playground where Arthur is shooting hoops, a stumbling figure scoring drugs. We get a haunting view of Gates's older brother, Curtis. A former basketball whiz deemed "uncoachable," he invests all his blasted NBA fantasies in his younger brother. There are heartbreaking, exhilarating ups and downs—a family plunged into darkness when their electricity is cut off; the pride of Arthur's mother when she graduates from a nurse's assistant's course; the nail-biting state championships.

The movie captures the meat-market frenzy of the basketball camps, where college recruiters come to salivate over the hot prospects, and the hard-sell pressure they put on the boys. A friend succumbs to the temptation of drug dealing and gets caught. The stakes in this movie couldn't be higher. When Mrs. Agee celebrates her son's birthday, her gratitude is not for his accomplishment on the court, but that he's managed to live to 18. This is a portrait of inner-city America as complex, moving and surprising as any film has given us.

When James and Marx—later joined by cinematographer Gilbert—conceived of this project, in 1987, they thought it would be, a 30-minute film about the culture of inner-city playground basketball. With $2,500 in grants and the producing help of Kartemquin Films, they began to look for their subjects. The first week of shooting they met Agee and Gates, and quickly realized that their plans had to be drastically revised: these were kids they had to follow, wherever it led.

It led them eventually to shoot 250 hours of film, almost every game and major event in the boys' lives. The project struggled through the first three years on only $2,500. (Later they got $70,000 from the Corporation for Public Broadcasting and a $250,000 MacArthur Foundation grant.) Everyone had a second job. Marriages were strained, debts accumulated and the filmmakers grew more and more attached to their subjects. Peter Gilbert's wife, Dru, recalls: "What really got to me was when things were not going well with the families. Peter would come home adding misery to the pile. But then our problems would look minuscule in comparison to theirs."

"There were times when it was difficult to separate the roles of filmmaker/observer and extended family friend," admits Steve James. When the Agees' power was shut off, the filmmakers pulled some money together to restore it. It was the one moment when they clearly stepped beyond their roles as documentarians. "We weren't just going to exploit their pain and suffering. They say that to be a great documentary filmmaker you have to be cutthroat and not get involved. But if that's what it takes, then we don't want to be great documentary filmmakers.

"Hoop Dreams" had its triumphant première at the Sundance Film Festival, where it won the audience award and found a distributor, Fine Line Features. It was the first documentary ever chosen for closing night at the New York Film Festival. (And recently St. Joseph's and coach

Pingatore brought a lawsuit against the film, claiming it depicts the school "in a false and untrue light.") It's even generating spinoffs: there's a book and possibly a fictionalized TV movie; an album, single and video of Ben Sidran's fine jazz and rap score are in the works, and hats and T shirts will be sold to benefit inner-city programs.

The bitter irony is that William Gates and Arthur Agee have not been able to share in the glory. Because they are college players, the NCAA has forbidden them from sharing in the proceeds or talking about the movie: their comments would be considered commercial endorsements. "We are in an appeal process to get them to let us compensate the families for their involvement," says James. So far, the NCAA is holding firm. "Do they want to play basketball or do they want to be movie stars?" says the NCAAs Mike Racy. "Under our rules they can't do both." The NCAA, which ought to have better things to worry about, has an odd idea of what a movie star is. But "Hoop Dreams" has shown us that the rules of the game are stacked against kids like Gates and Agee. Even better, it shows us how they fight back with inside moves of hope.

SIGHT AND SOUND, 4/95, p. 44, Amanda Lipman

This documentary follows four years in the lives of two black teenage boys from the Chicago housing projects. William Gates and Arthur Agee, just graduated from junior high, dream of becoming basketball players. Spotted by talent scouts, the boys are offered semi-scholarship places at the prestigious St. Joseph's College out in the largely white suburbs. Arthur fails to fulfil his potential, cannot make the academic grades and falls behind with fee payments. He is asked to leave, and joins Marshall, the local public high school. William, who receives funding from the director of Encyclopaedia Britannica as well as his school scholarship, stays on at St Joseph's battling with the academic work and shining at basketball. What looks like a potentially brilliant career becomes more erratic, however, when he injures his knee badly and has to undergo two operations. Meanwhile William has had a baby, Alicia, with his girlfriend, Catherine.

Arthur's father leaves his family. When he returns a year later, a reformed man and an ardent church-goer, it transpires that he was beating his wife, addicted to crack, and had been imprisoned for burglary. While Arthur's academic record remains poor, his basketball goes from strength to strength. Eventually his unfancied school team comes third in the state championships.

By William's final year, his school team does worse than it ever has, but he is offered a scholarship to Marquette University in Wisconsin, providing he passes his final SAT exams. After five tries, he passes and graduates from St. Joseph's. Arthur repeatedly fails his SAT and has to settle for a basketball scholarship to a junior college. He finally passes his summer school exams and gets to college. The film ends explaining William's disenchantment with Marquette and basketball. He tries to leave but is persuaded to stay on and is faring averagely. Arthur has gone on from his college to Arkansas University. He now has two children and is still hoping to become a professional basketball player.

A three-hour film about basketball may seem like a long haul, and there are ways in which this could have been made tighter and shorter. In the end, it turns out to be a largely fascinating document of the real lives of its two teenage protagonists.

What William and Arthur share overwhelmingly is a love of the game and the perception that it could lead them out of the Chicago ghetto. But as the film shows, just being good is not enough. To become professional players the boys have to get to college, and to do that, they have to pass academic exams. Of the seven black boys at Mineral Area, the junior college to which Arthur finally goes, six are basketball scholars.

When Spike Lee makes an appearance at William's summer school for basketball hopefuls, he states the only consciously political point in the film: that this is all about money. College talent scouts come in order to entice players they hope will make money for the school and these black boys serve their purpose. Later, the scouts somewhat bashfully agree with him.

Hoop Dreams shows how the system uses Arthur and his family. Swept up by the prestige of going to St Joseph's, a private school with a reputation for creating basketball players, they get caught in a financial trap. After Arthur leaves, his family is forced to find a way of paying off the $18,000 they owe or Arthur will lose the academic credits he received. As it happens, Arthur ends up doing as well through the rowdy but surprisingly helpful and supportive school system as William does with private education.

Understated as they are, there are some extraordinary family sagas here. Without making any judgment, the cameras watch Arthur's father develop and then kick his crack dependency, all the time claiming that he is trying to do his best for his son. Despite the physical and emotional damage done to her, we see Arthur's mother striving to keep the family together, providing for them on a pittance and determined that her son will get to college. On Arthur's 18th birthday, without a trace of irony or melodrama she says that she feels lucky he has reached that age: a lot of sons do not. There are plenty of issues here about class and race, but the film is careful to let them emerge through the voices and daily concerns of the protagonists.

Other problems are revealed in the same way. William's brother, Curtis, was once the great basketball hope of his year, but he could not conform to the system, failed college and dropped out. Now he invests his own dreams in his brother. The philosophical, rather gentle William is all too aware of and troubled by this. In a feature film, this would be the big issue. Here it simmers below the surface of barely stated conflicts with which he seems unable to come to terms. His efforts to seek help in a man's world are in vain: his father is not around, his brother is too caught up in basketball daydreams and his bear-like coach is almost brutally unhelpful. Arthur seems more shiftless, less willing to think about things. Asked if he thinks he might end up going through the same troubles as his father he replies no, then "well, maybe, who knows?" Sassier than William, he also seems weaker, matures less over the four years, and certainly appears more dependent on the basketball ticket dream.

Documentaries can never really be objective because they are, by definition, intrusive. Yet this one does appear to have a disarming honesty about it. It rarely seems self-conscious, obligingly presents contradictory viewpoints of people and issues, and, despite frequent tears and declarations of love, is never sentimental. It might be argued that there is too much basketball to allow the really important games to work dramatically, but these endless matches are, after all, the stuff of the boys' lives. And although *Hoop Dreams* is hardly innovative in combining to-camera interviews with fly-on-the-wall scenarios, there is something about the film's upfront rawness that pitches it engagingly somewhere between home movie and drama.

TIME, 10/24/94, Richard Corliss

Making it to the NBA: it's the worst dream a boy can have. Even if he's one of the 50,000 or so high school phenoms in a year, his chances are only one in 2,000 that he will play NBA basketball. And once there, the kid is more likely to be a bench jockey, a Harthorne Wingo, than an idol-of-millions type like the Detroit Pistons' Isiah Thomas.

But people will dream the implausible dream, especially if they are agile black boys in a neighborhood ravaged by crime, and their only other options are fast-food chef and drug runner. *Hoop Dreams*, the powerful new documentary by Steve James, Fred Marx and Peter Gilbert, follows two basketball players from the Chicago projects as they pursue their calling through full or partial scholarships to suburban St. Joseph High School, which is a three-hour round trip and social light years away from home.

It's a grueling life for William Gates and Arthur Agee; they can make poetry of a jump shot, but to them algebra looks like Chinese. At school they are hired guns, set apart by their race and their athletic gift. And when they get on the court, thrill and fear pump through their veins like high-grade heroin. In class you can get a B or a C; in basketball you get an A or an F—win or lose, period—and everyone's watching. These kids must perform under pressures that would break most adults. "It became more of a job," William says, "than a game to play."

Arthur soon slips that noose, but at a hefty price. When tuition is raised at St. Joseph, he transfers to local Marshall High, where he becomes a star player. But until his parents pay St. Joseph what they owe, the school refuses to release Arthur's records, thus threatening him with loss of a full school year. By then his dad has left home, done drugs and jail time; his mom has to hold things together in the dark (literally—the electricity's been turned off). But she, the film's heroine, does it; then she gets the top grade in a nurse's-assistant course. At her graduation, all we see are tears of joy and rows of empty chairs.

William is the one marked for stardom, and the burden of anticipated glory weighs heavily on him. His brother Curtis, once a junior college star, is now a has-been in sports and an ain't-gonna-be in life; he wants his brother to make it for him, but William says, "I always felt that Curtis should not be living his dream through me." The St. Joe coach can't afford to bring

William along slowly. In the '70s he had refused to play a gifted freshman—Isiah Thomas—and "it cost us the state championship." William's teachers, classmates and family all want him to make it—their way. As he notes wanly, "It's like everybody I know is my coach."

By the end of his four-year high school tour, William is an old man with a damaged knee, a child to support and some rueful wisdom: "When somebody said, 'When you turn NBA, don't forget about me' and all that stuff, I should've said to them, 'If I don't make it, well, don't you forget about me.'"

You won't soon forget him. You may be bored by basketball, and maybe you don't much care about black kids. But *Hoop Dreams* isn't mainly about sport, or even about life and death in the inner city. It's about families hanging tough on nerve and prayer. It's about what passes for the American dream to people whose daily lives are closer to nightmares.

Oh yes, and it's about three hours long. But it moves like Isiah, fast and smooth, and it's over in a heartbreak.

VILLAGE VOICE, 10/18/94, p. 49, J. Hoberman

The sports inspirational may be the purest of feel-good entertainments, inviting us to work up an imaginary sweat and vicariously participate in the justified pay-off. Success is preordained, everyone leaves a winner, America works. But *Hoop Dreams*, the remarkable documentary that closed the New York Film Festival and opens theatrically Friday, makes that payoff problematic by putting athletic prowess in a wider social context and implicitly asking what it takes for a disadvantaged black kid from an urban ghetto to become a star in the media firmament.

Between 1987 and 1991, filmmakers Steve James, Fred Marx, and Peter Gilbert—members of the venerable, Chicago-based documentary collective Kartemquin Films—shot some 250 hours of film and videotape tracking the progress of two teenage basketball prospects out of the hood and into the burbs and beyond. Originally intended as a 30-minute short, *Hoop Dreams* developed an irresistible momentum, which is precisely why, impeccably blown up to 35mm, it's a terrific movie—as well as a great documentary, a textbook in camera placement, a how-to guide in hacking a narrative through a thicket of incidents.

Hoop Dreams opens with the principals transfixed by a televised NBA all-star game and repeatedly makes the analogy between the enthusiasm of a basketball crowd and the expressive jubilation of the African American church. The film's operative word is "dream." The ruling metaphor is the player defying gravity and soaring to the hoop. Basketball is a secular faith—a force that unites families, raises hopes, and, when it fails, blights lives. William Gates and Arthur Agee are plucked from the playgrounds of South Side Chicago and receive basketball scholarships to St. Joseph's, an overwhelmingly white and seemingly well-off Catholic high school where, at least as the filmmakers show it, the image of superstar alumnus Isiah Thomas is more prominent than that of Jesus Christ.

Up at 5:30 a.m. for their reverse commute, both William and Arthur enter St. Joseph's reading on a fourth-grade level. Moreover, William has been cast, by the media as well as coach Gene Pingatore, in the impossible role of Isiah redux. Still, the serious and dogged William makes an initial adjustment—jumping through hoops, as it were. Arthur doesn't, and after his father Bo is laid off has to leave St. Joseph's for a neighborhood school. (Money is the issue, although there is also the disturbing implication that he hasn't grown quickly enough to play varsity basketball.)

Hoop Dreams juxtaposes the American Dream with the precarious nature of black working-class life. As previous Kartemquin documentaries have dealt with social problems ranging from sexism to gentrification, so this one is a study of the struggle against marginality. The debt owed St. Joseph's exacerbates the disintegration of the Agee family. Arthur's parents have to ransom his transcripts from St. Joseph's so that he can receive credit for the year he spent there. As he attends remedial summer school and works in a Pizza Hut, so William is invited to the Princeton campus for the annual Nike camp of top high school players, complete with Spike Lee cameo. (It's all business, he tells them.) William is recruited by the basketball cathedral Marquette; Arthur's mother celebrates his birthday by expressing gratitude that he's even made it to age 18. Not for nothing does he knock out a science paper on the life cycle of the butterfly.

Among other things, *Hoop Dreams* suggests the paradoxical nature of success. Arthur, whose life is in tumult and whose attitude alternates between wary and carefree, is most himself when on the court, where the more stable William may be too introspective and self-conscious. Midway through his high school career, basketball has become "more a job than a game." The pathology of racism and the stresses of urban poverty only accentuate the fantastic pressure on these kids. In his junior year, William (a father by now himself) injures his knee and has to have arthroscopic surgery. In one of the most amazing sequences, Coach Pingatore inserts his recuperating star into a crucial game. The whole season comes down to one basket and William misses—the first of a series of startling reversals.

Although *Hoop Dreams* kicks in during its second hour with an underdog championship run (and a narrative trajectory that could not have been scripted), its mode is admirably contemplative. The texture is rich. The filmmakers may be outsiders but, over the years, they enjoyed tremendous access. The movie is filled not only with excellent basketball but revealing vignettes; not simply do William and Arthur emerge as complex individuals, so do the members of their immediate families. Indeed, to an intriguing degree, the kids prove products of temperaments inherited from their respectively depressed and mercurial clans.

William's older brother—a one-time college basketball star, now a chunky security guard whose affect matches that of his sad, doughy mother—emerges as a tragic figure, telling the filmmakers that William embodies all of his remaining aspirations: "I want him to make it so bad I don't know what to do." Arthur's parents undergo their own dramatic evolutions over the course of the movie, His mother Sheila is forced on welfare—"Do you ever wonder how we are living?" she asks the camera with typical vivacity—and reinvents herself as an assistant nurse. Bo turns to crack, crime, and then religion. (Arthur's unresolved struggle with his erratic, desperately posturing father he so much resembles is one of the movie's more compelling subtexts.)

An earlier version of *Hoop Dreams* cast a revealing light on the great American long shot that is *Rocky* with the following statistics: Of the half million high school kids who play team basketball each year, only 14,000 (2.8 per cent) manage to play in college, and a mere 25 of those (.005 per cent) ever make it, for even one season, to the NBA. (The filmmakers dropped this information because the numbers have gotten even worse.) Ultimately, *Hoop Dreams* questions a system where schools promote themselves, and practice a spurious form of integration, by importing inner-city athletes to staff their basketball teams. While Pingatore is a smug cog in a large machine, the bitterness of the coach at Arthur's all-black school is palpable. Invited to Missouri's Mineral Area Junior College, Arthur discovers that there are seven black students, six of whom bunk together and are on the basketball team.

After experiencing this movie, you may never see professional basketball quite the same way again. William and Arthur could be thinking of careers as TV sneaker salesmen, but it's striking that when they're each asked what they want to study (besides basketball), both answer "communications." *Hoop Dreams* makes the two fields seem identical.

Also reviewed in:
NATION, 11/14/94, p. 590, Stuart Klawans
CHICAGO TRIBUNE, 10/21/94, Friday/p. C, Michael Wilmington
NEW REPUBLIC, 10/31/94, p. 39, Stanley Kauffmann
NEW YORK TIMES, 10/7/94, p. C1, Caryn James
NEW YORKER, 10/17/94, p. 113, Terrence Rafferty
VARIETY, 2/14-20/94, p. 39, Todd McCarthy
WASHINGTON POST, 11/4/94, p. F1, Hal Hinson
WASHINGTON POST, 11/4/94, Weekend/p. 43, Desson Howe

HOUSE OF THE SPIRITS, THE

A Miramax Films release of a Neue Constantin Film production in association with Spring Creek Productions/House of the Spirits Film/Costa do Castelo Filmes. *Executive Producer:* Edwin Leicht, Paula Weinstein, and Mark Rosenberg. *Producer:* Bernd Eichinger. *Director:* Bille August. *Screenplay:* Bille August. *Based on the book by:* Isabel Allende. *Director of Photography:* Jorgen Persson. *Editor:* Janus Billeskov Jansen. *Music:* Hans Zimmer. *Sound:* Michael Kranz and (music) Malcolm Luker. *Sound Editor:* Niels Avild. *Casting:* Billy

Hopkins, Suzanne Smith, Kelly Barden, and Anne Goulder. *Production Designer:* Anna Asp. *Art Director:* Augusto Mayer. *Set Decorator:* Søren Gam. *Stunt Coordinator:* Miguel Fredecosa. *Running time:* 132 minutes. *MPAA Rating:* R.

CAST: Jeremy Irons (Esteban Trueba); Meryl Streep (Clara); Glenn Close (Ferula); Winona Ryder (Blanca); Antonio Banderas (Pedro); Vanessa Redgrave (Nivea); Maria Conchita Alonso (Transito); Armin Mueller-Stahl (Severo); Jan Niklas (Satigny); Sarita Choudhury (Pancha); Antonio Assumiçio (Man at Cattle Market); Julie Balloo (Young Lady); Frank Baker (Intelligence Officer); João Cabral, Miguel Guilherme, José Mora Ramos, and Victor Rocha (Soldiers); Carlos César and Alexandre de Sousa (Drivers); Rogérjo Claro (Man in Club); Edith Clement (Midwife); Miriam Colon (Nun); Oscar A. Colon (Sheriff); Franco Diogent (Man at Party); Pedro Effe (Immigration Officer); Fran Fullenwider (Elmer Trueba); Vincent Gallo (Esteban Garcia); Jane Gray (Young Clara); Sasha Hanau (Alba); Denys Hawthorne (Politician); Frank Lenart (Interviewer); Lone Lindorff (Maid); Josh Maguire (Pedro as a Child); Joaquin Martinez (Segrado); Steve Mason (Maestro); Jean Michael (Musician); Luis Pinhão (Woodcarver); Teri Polo (Rosa); Vivianna Reis (Indian Girl); Carlos Rodrigues (Postman); Manuela Santos (Saleswoman); Joost Stedhoff (Father Antonio); Hellmuth O. Stuven (TV General); Hannah Taylor-Gordon (Clara as a Child); Jaime Tirelli (Oliver); Martin Umbach (TV Reporter); Hans Wyprächtiger (Dr. Caevus).

FILMS IN REVIEW, 7-8/94, p. 55, Pat Anderson

A bowl of fruit moving through the air; a shifting table; Meryl Streep, as Clara, claiming to be in touch with the spirits and superficially forecasting a few disasters, much like a fairground fortune teller. Nothing like the mysterious and joyous spirits we have grown to know through Latin American culture as described in the book. And Jeremy Irons plays Esteban Trueba, Clara's husband, as a tight lipped, spurious Latin version of Claus von Bulow. Glenn Close plays his sister Ferula, a dowdy spinster ridden with sexual desires that have more in common with textbook Freud than South American sensibilities: The international all star cast includes Vanessa Redgrave and Armin Mueller-Stahl as Clara's parents. Not one has any sense of the passion of the Latin American country in which the story is set.

Although the events take place in this unnamed country, on one level, Isabel Allende's intention in her acclaimed novel (on which the film is loosely based) is to provide an allegory of her native Chile at the time of the coup that overthrew and assassinated her uncle, President Salvador Allende. The other level is the saga of a wealthy family chronicled from the 1920's to the 1970's. The movie, though, is an episodic soap opera.

Jeremy Irons plays Esteban as an autocratic, overbearing, insensitive man whose word is not only law, but not to be questioned. Which does not sit well with his daughter Blanca (Winona Ryder, who looks and sounds like a fluffy Gidget). And when she falls for the son of his farm foreman, he really turns up the acrimony. Added to this, the young man, Pedro (Antonio Banderas), is a revolutionary who tries to organize Esteban's farm workers into a union.

Well, can you guess what happens when a left wing government is democratically elected? And whose daughter and boyfriend are caught in the coup organized by whose father? Did you shout the Truebas?

It is sad that Bille August, who wrote and directed *The House of the Spirits*, is so out of his depth here. His direction of *Pelle The Conqueror* and of Ingmar Bergman's *The Best Intentions* was marvelous; but they took place in Scandinavia, not Latin America.

LOS ANGELES TIMES, 4/1/94, Calendar/p. 1, Kenneth Turan

Bille August's version of Isabel Allende's internationally best-selling novel "The House of the Spirits" had no trouble attracting a celebrated cast. So many stars signed on, in fact, that their names barely fit together on the same frame of the opening credits.

By the time this lumbering oaf of a movie is over, however, the wonder is not that Jeremy Irons, Meryl Streep, Glenn Close, Winona Ryder and Antonio Banderas (plus Vanessa Redgrave and Armin Mueller-Stahl) were involved, but that their efforts added up to so little. Inert from its opening moments to its too-long-delayed close, this lackluster production is an example of international filmmaking at its least attractive, and a misstep in the careers of pretty much everyone involved.

A multigenerational story covering half a century of personal and political turmoil in a South American country modeled on Allende's native Chile, "Spirits" has unaccountably been placed in the hands of a Danish director whose reputation was made in Sweden and who decided to deploy his multinational cast in Portugal and Denmark. Is it any wonder that things ended up confused?

In fairness, Allende's novel probably is too dependent on outlandish incidents of the Gabriel Garcia Marquez magic realism variety to be handled effectively in any form shorter than a miniseries. To squeeze it into a feature, major characters have had to be combined, the barest bones of plot carved out and the narrative in general flattened into an exhausted soap opera.

"Spirits" is narrated by Blanca (Ryder), the daughter of the film's main characters, fun couple Esteban Trueba (Irons) and his wife Clara (Streep). It opens in 1923, with the child Clara getting her first glimpse of Esteban, who she knows is going to be her husband even though he is in the process of proposing to her older sister.

Clara is right about Esteban, as she is about many things, because she is gifted with psychic powers that enable her to see into the future as well as move objects across tabletops. An angelic, ethereal woman who every now and again decides to remain mute for years at a time, Clara does not seem to have much power in the present, where lots of situations could use her help.

Most pressingly, as the years go on (and on), is the way husband Esteban, never a very likable individual, turns from a poor landowner to a sour and flinty oligarch, a whip-first-and-ask-questions-later type who oppresses peasants just for the heck of it. He also fathers an understandably grumpy illegitimate son and engages in a blood feud with his sister Ferula (Close), whose chaste passion for Clara he can't abide.

Coming into a family like this, is it any wonder that Blanca chooses to love Pedro (Banderas), a boy of hearty peasant stock who becomes a revolutionary. This not surprisingly causes all kinds of trouble in the last part of the film, when a coup modeled on the one that drove Salvador Allende (the author's uncle) from power in Chile disturbs the Truebas' cloistered lives.

Though the strength of the novel was in its long passages of narrative description, the film has no choice but to lean heavily on dialogue, which even in the book was unremarkable. Sadly, August, screenwriter as well as director, has made things worse: The script for "Spirits" is an unbroken string of clichés lacking even a whiff of originality.

Probably seduced by the book and then unexpectedly mired in this dismal swamp of a production, the film's performers are uniformly energyless and plodding. Though most of the actors are content to be forgettable, Irons comes off worst due to a choice of accent that can most charitably be called baffling.

Though it's always risky to try to assess blame in a bankrupt picture like "The House of the Spirits," the across-the-board failure of usually reliable actors does suggest writer-director August's responsibility.

Winner of a best foreign film Oscar for "Pelle the Conqueror" and the Palme d'Or for "Best Intentions," both intensely Scandinavian projects, August has been promoted into an arena where he lacks competence, with this bland epic as the result. When Irons' character wonders late in the film, "How could I have been so wrong?" he's asking the question that will be on a lot of minds.

NEW YORK, 4/11/94, p. 56, John Powers

The House of the Spirits is based on Isabel Allende's first novel, a sprawling multi-generational saga that is, in equal measure, a celebration of women's strength, an allegory about the author's home country of Chile, and a highbrow romance for the sort of reader who'd sooner die than pull Rosemary Rogers off the supermarket rack. Although far less imaginative than its model, *One Hundred Years of Solitude*, the novel is teeming with mood, character, incident, metaphor—it gives you a big, bright, enchanted world to wander around in. By contrast, Bille August's screen adaptation feels like a ride on the world's slowest Ferris wheel. It's a strangely benumbed epic about magic, rebellion, and overwhelming passion.

The movie traces the 50-year arc of the Trueba family from its patriarch's discovery of gold through the military coup that threatens to destroy it. Jeremy Irons plays Estaban Trueba, an ambitious miner who buys the abandoned estate of Tres Marias and becomes a rich, cruel, and reactionary landowner. He marries Clara (Meryl Streep), a dreamy, willful woman endowed with psychokinetic powers and a head swarming with visions—she has a hot line to the world of the spirits. The offspring of their peculiar union is Blanca (Winona Ryder), who falls in love with the revolutionary son of her father's foreman. Enraged, Esteban does everything in his power to thwart their romance and their dreams of social justice, unaware that history is delighted to hand him the petard on which he's later going to be hoisted.

Boasting half a dozen movie stars and a number of prominent European craftsmen, *The House of the Spirits* takes place in that eerie limbo known as "international cinema," with its deracinated settings (the exteriors were shot in Portugal, the interiors in Denmark) and actors who come from everyplace but where the story is set. I've never been one to insist on ethnic purity in casting, but don't the producers care that nowadays it seems clueless to populate a Latin American romance with northern European actors? Vanessa Redgrave and Armin Mueller-Stahl beget Meryl Streep, who marries Jeremy Irons and begets Winona Ryder—who chirps her lines like a cheerleader talking about her Rollerblades. By the time Antonio Banderas turns up as her lover, Pedro, you can only laugh: With his olive skin, black hair, and thick Spanish accent, the poor guy seems to have stumbled into the wrong movie.

Such commercially minded miscasting is nothing new, of course, and it's actually no more exasperating than the clashing sensibilities of novelist Allende and August, the Danish writer-director who made *Pelle the Conqueror* and *The Best Intentions*. While Allende's novel features all the Technicolor flourishes of magical realism (green-haired women, time swooping back on itself like a homing pigeon), August's cinematic style is achingly Scandinavian: literal, linear, restrained. There's too much blue to his palette. Keeping us removed from passions we want to experience up close, he loses the emotional richness of events in his rush to get them all onscreen. When Clara dies unexpectedly, August evokes Esteban's anguish at the news in a lovely, understated shot of him smashing a car window in the distance. But the movie doesn't pause to let us see how her death affects Esteban's sense of life—August's already moving doggedly on to the coup.

Nailed to the cross of his unbending masculinity, Esteban is the sort of overbearing, tragic dynamo who demands a performance as majestic as Al Pacino's in the first two *Godfather* films. Jeremy Irons has previously done some extraordinary work, from his Karloffian hamminess as Claus von Bulow to the sly, tiptoeing precision of his brother act in *Dead Ringers*. Still, he's a bizarre choice for the part of a fiery Latino patriarch; he's an actor most comfortable with edgy, angst-riddled roles that ask him to devour his own liver. As Esteban, he flaunts all the vices of machismo but displays no manly strength: He rapes a peasant girl, exploits his workers, and abuses his sister Ferula, a devout spinster played by, of all people, Glenn Close. For us to care about the poignant futility of Esteban's life, Irons must make us see the essential decency beneath his phallocratic hubris. But everything about his gimmicky performance puts us off—his swarthied-up English features, his oddly distended upper lip (a dental prosthesis?), and his inexplicable grits-in-the-craw Dixie accent apparently borrowed from Foghorn Leghorn.

Underlying Allende's novel is faith in the enduring suppleness of women, who are bearers of continuity in family life and know how to treasure the fullness of each passing moment. August doesn't scuttle the book's feminism, but he waters it down, treating Blanca's political commitment as little more than a love affair with a good-looking radical, and largely ignoring Allende's ideas about women and the spirit world. A protege of Ingmar Bergman's, August obviously feels more comfortable with the swirling psychological currents of every day life. Most of the film's strongest scenes are small ones, like the shared moments of affection between Clara and her downtrodden sister-in-law, Ferula. While Winona Ryder walks around looking lost and Glenn Close seems terribly oppressed—she obviously senses the movie's in trouble—Meryl Streep is pleasingly subdued as the otherworldly Clara. There was a time when this kind of saintly role threw her into such frenzies of mannerism that she seemed to be being paid by the tic; yet her quiet self-possession here comes closer to putting across Allende's ideas than do any of the film's melodramatics. Whether smiling enigmatically or letting her soul rise to greet ghosts that no one else can see, Clara's an ethereal counterweight to the grasping violence of men.

Allende brought out *The House of the Spirits* in 1982, nine years after her uncle, President Salvador Allende, was killed during the military coup in Chile. The novel's urgency came from her desire to capture a vanishing world and find some source of hope for the future. There's no such idealism behind August's movie, which seems like a misguided effort to entice the audience of *Like Water for Chocolate*. But that cheesy little crowd-pleaser was bursting with things that people enjoy—sex and food and magic and love. This picture is prosaic and glum. A well-upholstered star vehicle headed straight to the video store, it offers little more than handsome cinematography and the spectacle of expensively dressed gringos taking the magic out of magical realism.

NEW YORK POST, 4/1/94, p. 39, Thelma Adams

I can't resist family sagas, those perfect blends of gossip and romance where interpersonal power struggles are rivalled, but never eclipsed, by the rising and falling of governments.

In Isabel Allende's best-selling magic realist novel, "The House of the Spirits," the Trueba clan wages love and war against the backdrop of the struggle between right and left in an unnamed South American country which strongly resembles the author's native Chile.

Swedish director Bille ("Pelle the Conqueror") August brings the novel to the screen with an old-fashioned "Gone with the Wind," "Dr. Zhivago" sweep that's rare in contemporary movies.

At first I resisted the movie's plodding grandness, its Merchant Ivory attention to detail in set and costume, its portrayal (without a hint of irony) of all women and revolutionaries as good, conservatives as suspect, the clearly-drawn battle line between head and heart. But, I was ultimately seduced, in large part by a cast that is nothing short of magnificent.

Meryl Streep glows as Clara, the ethereal clairvoyant married to landowner and conservative politician Esteban Trueba (Jeremy Irons). Esteban's passion for Clara is mirrored by his churlish treatment of his spinster sister, Ferula (Glenn Close).

The masterful pairing of Streep and Close as sisters-in-law is one of the movie's greatest gifts and underscores the theme that women's bonds cement civilization (even if they don't build monuments to themselves).

In their first encounter, Clara treats Ferula with affection. "No one has ever shown me any tenderness," Ferula responds.

The emotional barrenness of Ferula's life to that point, and the way it has twisted her personality, is completely believable, the bond between the two women immediate. While Streep is not quite the dewy twentysomething she is intended to be at that point, both actresses project deep emotions that sweep the plot forward.

Irons fares less well. Trueba is nothing less than an ogre, an authoritarian and rapist, who seeks to control Clara and is threatened by her closeness with Ferula. When the role is at its most two-dimensional, Irons often comes across as if his mouth was full of marbles, his movements constricted by the cardboard construct of his character.

As an old man, in his final scenes, Irons poignantly opens up, redeemed by Clara's love and his affection for their daughter, Blanca (Winona Ryder).

With the popularity of Allende's novel, the actors seem to have come to the material like pilgrims to a shrine. In addition to Antonio Banderas as Blanca's proletarian lover, Vanessa Redgrave plays Clara's mother, Maria Conchita Alonso plays a prostitute, and Sarita Choudhury is the mother of Trueba's bastard child. The supporting cast's strength enriches the saga.

While "The House of the Spirits" starts off precious, it accumulates weight over its lengthy course.

The magical past—where even an autopsy is shot with the golden glow of a Raphael madonna crossed with the visceral impact of Mexican artist Frida Kahlo—is in sharp contrast to the squalid scenes of torture at the movie's close.

The tension between beauty and brutality, love and politics— the sins of the fathers visited upon the daughters—gives "The House of the Spirits" its edge.

NEWSDAY, 4/1/94, Part II/p. B3, John Anderson

Maybe it was a bad marriage of temperaments, or climates: The full-blooded passion of the Latin American novelist meets the ice-blue esthetic of Scandinavian director, the result a tepid puddle of unrealized intentions.

Maybe it was the top-heavy cast, the clash of the titans that turns out to be the crash of the titans.

Maybe it was simply too much narrative, too much sweeping territory, too much magical realism, too much elusive spirituality.

Whatever it was, "The House of the Spirits," Bille August's adaptation of Isabel Allende's novel, should be declared unfit for human habitation.

Less an epic than an outline for an epic, "House" tells the story of the Trueba family, a wealthy Latin American clan peopled by fascists, bastards, clairvoyants and misanthropes. And it does so with neither the spiritual power of Allende's book, nor the cinematic sensitivity and control August displayed in "Pelle the Conqueror" or "The Best Intentions."

Covering six decades, innumerable crises and one bloody counter-revolution, "House of the Spirits" caroms from episode to episode in the life of its troubled characters without once coming to rest long enough to let us catch our breath and care. Certainly, there's little reason to care about Esteban Trueba (Jeremy Irons), who after losing his fiancee to poison and himself in work emerges as one of his country's wealthiest and powerful men, as well as a brutish rapist and petulant child. But we should care about the rest of the tribe, and would, if they didn't seem like strangers who've found themselves riding the same runaway bus.

Clara, the psychically gifted sister of Esteban's dead betrothed who ultimately becomes his wife, is the moral cornerstone of the story, just as Esteban is the moral wrecking ball. But as played by Meryl Streep, gauzy and ethereal, Clara comes off more like Aunt Clara on "Bewitched." Possessing the gift of prophecy and the ability to move inanimate objects, Clara progresses from young womanhood to old age, but she remains an eccentric cipher, her existence a vapor.

Glenn Close's Ferula, Esteban's beleaguered sister, is a more skittish and ultimately more moving character. "House of the Spirits" has been anticipated as the first screen pairing of Streep and Close, two of our more prominent actresses, and it's a less than climactic moment. But even when fighting bad lines, Close makes Ferula—who cared for their horribly obese mother until her death, but is treated with contempt by her brother—convincingly bitter, and possessed, and then grateful, when Clara offers her first milk of human kindness. It's a gratitude, however, that lasts beyond the grave, and Ferula's post-mortem appearances are campy apparitions.

Esteban's moral decay—he is August's standard-bearer of fascism, racial bigotry and economic oppression—parallels his country's barrel-roll into purgatory. Early on, he sees the romance between his thoroughbred daughter Blanca (Winona Ryder) and the peasant unionizer Pedro (Antonio Banderas) as a sign of the corruption destroying his way of life. He flogs Pedro, shoots at him, tries to have him killed.

But like his attitude toward Ferula—he hates her, presumably because he's jealous of her closeness with his wife—it's all wildly unsubstantiated emotion. There is no objective correlative here, and its absence makes Esteban, for all Irons' valiant efforts, simply a banality.

Just as events in the country begin to move swiftly—from "people's revolution," to military takeover—the film decides to slow down and tell a story. The concluding episodes, in which Clara dies, Esteban helps initiate the dictatorship and then saves Pedro, and Blanca is taken prisoner and tortured by Esteban's illegitimate son, hint at the novelistic qualities and dramatic tension it has lacked for the previous two hours.

By this time, of course, two hours or so into the film, it's too late for redemption, or for blame.

NEWSWEEK, 4/11/94, p. 74, David Ansen

If you could judge a movie on its credentials alone, "The House of the Spirits" would already be halfway to heaven. The prestige cast couldn't be more enticing: Jeremy Irons, Meryl Streep, Glenn Close, Vanessa Redgrave, Winona Ryder, Antonio Banderas and Armin Mueller-Stahl. The writer-director, Bille August, made the award-winning "Pelle the Conqueror" and "The Best Intentions." The story, a tumultuous 50-year family saga encompassing politics, passion, mysticism and revenge, comes from the acclaimed novel by Isabel Allende. It's handsomely shot, sumptuously produced, nobly intentioned. And it unfolds, sadly, like the longest trailer ever made.

What went awry? The simplest answer is that you can't tell this story—the chronicle of a South American family from 1926 into the '70s—in one rushed two-hour-and-11-minute movie. The greatest actors in the world can't overcome a script that boils everything down to the Esperanto of cliché. A brutal right-wing patriarch (Irons)! A clairvoyant, ethereal earth mother (Streep) and a lonely spinster aunt (Close)! A handsome revolutionary rabble rouser (Banderas) and the rebellious daughter who falls in love with him (Ryder)! Though set in a mythical South American country, this story is rooted in the tragic history of Chile. (The novelist is the niece of President Salvador Allende Gossens, who died in a coup d'etat much like the one in this story.) But one never feels the rhythms or smells the scents of a particular culture. This German-produced movie, shot in Portugal and Copenhagen by a Danish director with an English-speaking cast, aims for universality. What it achieves, too much of the time, is inauthenticity.

SIGHT AND SOUND, 4/94, p. 43, Amanda Lipman

Chile, 1973. A young woman, Blanca, drivers her elderly father, Esteban Trueba, to a deserted hacienda. In voice-over, she recalls her late mother Clara, and the film flashes back to Clara's childhood. While her parents and sister Rosa entertain Rosa's beau Esteban, Clara exerts magic powers. Meanwhile, her father Severo has been made mayor. At the celebrations, Clara foresees a death in the family and Rosa dies from poison. Clara blames herself and stops speaking. Esteban, who has been working in the gold mines to earn money to marry Rosa, returns wealthier. His dour sister Ferula, who looks after their invalid mother, begs him to stay, but he leaves to set up a hacienda in the hills. Working himself and his workers hard, he is soon rich.

One day, Esteban rapes one of his women workers, Pancha. On another occasion, he lends money to an ambitious prostitute, Transito. Returning to town, he catches sight of Clara and woos her; agreeing to marry him, she starts to speak again. Ferula comes to live on the hacienda and the two women become friends, although Esteban is cruel to Ferula. Clara becomes pregnant and foresees her parents' death in a car accident. She takes the police to the spot where her mother's head has been torn from her body. Esteban, meanwhile, is becoming an important right-wing political figure. Clara gives birth to a girl, Blanca. One day, Pancha comes to the hacienda with a son she claims is Esteban's. He gives her money and sends her away. Later, Esteban Jr creeps into the house and starts to molest Blanca but is disturbed by Ferula's arrival.

When Blanca becomes friendly with the hacienda foreman's son, Pedro, Esteban sends her off to school. However, she and Pedro eventually become lovers. After an earthquake, Esteban rushes home to find Ferula sleeping with her arms around Clara. In a rage, he throws his sister out of the house. When Pedro rallies his fellow workers about fair pay and conditions, Esteban has him whipped and sent away. One night, Ferula's ghost walks through the door, and Clara correctly announces her death. Esteban invites a French count, whom he considers a possible husband for Blanca. The count, seeing Blanca slip off to meet Pedro, tells Esteban. He drags her home and beats her and Clara, who has come to her defense. Clara vows never to speak to him. Blanca discovers that she is pregnant, and mother and daughter leave for their home in the town. Esteban drags the count there to force him to marry Blanca but she refuses him.

Esteban puts a price on Pedro's head. Led by Esteban Jr, he finds him but the young man escapes him. Esteban rises through the political ranks, but his life is empty and he goes to beg Clara's forgiveness. They live together again and he accepts his granddaughter Alba, though Clara will speak to him only through an intermediary. At Alba's birthday party, Esteban Jr turns up and asks for money to join the army. In the election, Esteban loses and Pedro's party, the People's Front, wins. Pedro meets his daughter. At Christmas, Esteban and Blanca are out shopping when Clara falls ill. As she dies, she asks Alba to give her diaries to Blanca. After a military coup takes place, Pedro hides in the Trueba house. The police arrest Blanca who asks her shocked father to help Pedro escape. Blanca is tortured over Pedro's whereabouts by Esteban Jr and sees her mother's ghost. Realising that he has been wrong about so much, Esteban smuggles Pedro into the Canadian embassy. Eventually, with the help of the now-influential Transito, Blanca is released. They leave the town house and drive back up to the hacienda, where Esteban dies after Clara comes to him in a vision.

Worried that it would be trivalised by Hollywood, Isabel Allende held firmly onto her best-selling novel *The House of the Spirits*, seeing off all prospective movie offers. She only relented when Bille August proved to her how seriously he took it. Indeed, like August's other films, this is the proverbial 'serious movie with a touch of the epic'. That would be fine but for the fact that Allende's novel is less of a weighty epic than a romantic soap opera told with an engagingly deft touch, painted against a background of rather crudely drawn politics and sprinkled with a sweep of magic realism borrowed from other Latin American writers.

But epic is how August would have it. He treats us to big wide shots of workers building, growing and fetching on Esteban's hacienda; to tanks rolling into towns, scattering crowds of bystanders; and—always important—to lavish use of make-up effects as the characters age. Jeremy Irons is pretty convincing as the tanned, youthful Esteban, but by the time he has turned into an old man, it is the quantity of padding in his mouth that arouses most interest.

Epic movies usually demand big names, and this one does its duty in that respect. Unfortunately, that only proves that it doesn't matter who is on them. Here, the prime culprit is the music. Hans Zimmer's score drowns out any feeling the actors might be hoping to bring to the scene. It doesn't take long to work out the code—syrupy violins for impending love, urgent poundings for impending disaster—and even less time to find its clichés tiresome. Streep and Irons, as the youngish Clara and Esteban, manage a few convincing moments in depicting their passionate lifelong love affair but the music gets them in the end.

Although August would have us find this all overtly serious, the film simply comes across as stodgy. It deals with the simplistic politics with a faithful but heavy hand, giving a textbook impression of good versus bad, and leaving a space where the human involvement should be. The forbidden passion between Blanca and Pedro is a very sparkless affair, and the potential sexual tensions between Blanca's relationships with Pedro and with her sadistic, twisted half-brother Esteban are left unexplored.

Allende's central theme—that women are positive forces for change who have to drag reactionary, ignorant men into the present— has not been lost, but the focus does appear to have shifted. Streep's Clara is a fey Christmas-tree fairy, while Ryder's Blanca is so strenuously earnest that it is hard to engage with her. Consequently, Irons' Esteban dominates. Because he is viewed largely through his different relationships with different women, he is allowed a multi-faceted existence that those women lack. The exception is the film's one really strong performance, Glenn Close's Ferula. Initially played almost as a caricature, she reveals a capacity for love, guilt, repression and fantasy that provide a dimension of conflict lacking in the wiser Clara and Blanca.

The tricksy, mystical, magic-realist elements are another hazard. Perhaps recognising that he is no Raul Ruiz or Ruy Guerra, who might delight in these as an end in themselves, August plays down the supernatural occurrences, simply allowing the odd squawk of a sixth sense from the coyly ethereal Streep, or the glimpse of a ghostly appearance. This is a wise move in some ways but, given the way the film works, it also leads the narrative to the wrong side of pedestrian. Echoing the title of August's own previous film, *The House of the Spirits* comes with the best of intentions. But goodwill alone cannot make it sparkle.

TIME, 4/18/94, p. 73, Richard Schickel

When Esteban the patrón (Jeremy Irons) wakes up horny, saddles his horse and goes out to rape a peasant, you just know this isn't going to turn out to be an idle incident. A little later, when he is outraged at discovering his prepubescent daughter Blanca skinny-dipping with Pedro, his *estancia* foreman's son, you sense that moment too is going to have its consequences somewhere down the plot line. For from its opening frames, *The House of the Spirits* announces itself as one of those sagas in which there are no accidents, only portents of big-time ironies to come.

Sure enough, Blanca grows up to be a rebellious Winona Ryder, and Pedro turns into a revolutionary played by Antonio Banderas (of *Philadelphia*)—enemy of the privileges Esteban holds dear, progenitor (out of wedlock) of the granddaughter he holds dearer still. When the fascists stage their inevitable coup, it is, of course, the bastard Esteban begot in that long-ago dawn who turns up trying to torture Blanca into revealing Pedro's whereabouts.

For this two-hour film, Isabel Allende's complex, stylish novel has of necessity been stripped to its working parts. Yet the thing works in its goofy way, mainly because Bille August (of *Pelle the Conqueror*) is a man of apparently dauntless conviction. He has written and directed every scene with serene authority, somehow compelling your belief in what he's doing through his own sublime self-confidence.

His spirit is especially infectious to actors. Take Meryl Streep, for instance. In the early passages she's obliged to play a woman half her age, and one blessed with precognitive powers too. Later on, she turns up as a ghost. But she just sails gloriously through both incarnations, utterly untroubled by doubts in herself or August's enterprise. That's true of her co-stars too. When Irons ages, he adopts an oddly strangled tone that should make you want to laugh. But it doesn't—at least while the movie's on. Glenn Close as his ferociously virginal sister has to work pretty near Mel Brooks country (Remember Cloris Leachman in *Young Frankenstein*), but she keeps burrowing toward the character's repressed pain—and quite touchingly reveals it. And if Ryder is the headstrong heiress of a thousand movies, the simple clarity of her playing redeems the cliché.

So it goes—on through fortune-hunting playboys and good-hearted whores, down to the last oppressed peon. Everything they do and say has been done and said before. But they simply refuse to admit it. The result is not epic cinema as David Lean defined it but as Bette Davis used to play it at Warner Bros.—where history was a branch of melodrama and the subtler emotions were Xed out on the second-draft screenplay.

VILLAGE VOICE, 4/12/94, p. 56, Georgia Brown

"Memory is fragile" are the first words of *The House of the Spirits*, Bille August's disastrous adaptation of Isabel Allende's epic novel. In truth, memory looks like a tough old bird next to an engaging book in the hands of a well-meaning filmmaker. Galloping through 433 richly detailed pages (paperback edition), August has laid waste the territory.

What it looks like is that he shot maybe an eight-hour epic and then edited it down to 130 minutes by reducing each scene to one line of required exposition. The result: a series of probably the shortest scenes on record, punctuated occasionally by printed notifications that another 10 years have just zipped by. In speeding up events, trying to include the whole range of Allende's plot, August jettisoned practically all of the novel's lively details as well as its distinctive South American texture. As it is—and especially with the predominately American and British cast—the movie, with its elegant period interiors, could be set almost anywhere on earth. August has done his own English screenplay and the prose is as flat as a Nevada highway.

What's left? Well, at the beginning and almost to the very end, there's Jeremy Irons with his hair permed and something stiff under his upper lip. This mouthpiece recalls Brando's in *Godfather II*, although the real role model for Irons's Esteban Trueba, the story's troubled patriarch, seems to be Burt Lancaster in *The Leopard*—another work about the end of an old order, the beginning of the new. Irons's patrón, however, has none of the Sicilian's authority. As the movie goes along, the performance becomes more and more wooden. The part simply isn't written. There are no scenes here that stretch out until you see the inner workings of a soul. Everything we learn we are summarily told.

In a similar vein, but more comfortably, Meryl Streep plays Esteban's gentle wife, Clara, who moves vases around tables and foretells the future. (Clara's clairvoyance certainly is annoyingly selective.) Cinematographer Jorgen Persson has done a superb job with the lighting, and Streep looks as glowingly fresh as a young bride; then she grows older until in one scene she actually resembles Vanessa Redgrave, who plays her mother.

Perhaps the most striking performance here is Glenn Close's as Esteban's creepy sister, a woman on the verge of some bloody act until Clara offers friendship. Swathed in black, Close doesn't overdo the witchiness, however; she merely intimates the great longings underlying her deprivation. (Close is the one actor who gets to conduct an extended interior monologue.) As Clara and Esteban's daughter, Blanca, Winona Ryder is rather jarring: It's like Generation X goes to the coup d'etat. I enjoyed glimpses of Antonio Banderas as Pedro the fiery peasant organizer, though he was always running offscreen, chased by Blanca's papa.

The stars come, the stars go. Here we are seeing stars rather than characters—or the house's spirits.

The question is how could a skilled director like August (*Pelle the Conqueror, The Best Intentions*) have let this happen? Frankly, my dear, I have no idea. We must await some candid future interview. In the meantime, I imagine he must be beating a chagrined retreat back to Denmark and material he knows far better.

Also reviewed in:
CHICAGO TRIBUNE, 4/1/94, Friday/p. A, Michael Wilmington
NEW REPUBLIC, 5/2/94, p. 28, Stanley Kauffmann
NEW YORK TIMES, 4/1/94, p. C1, Janet Maslin
VARIETY, 1/3-9/94, p. 53, Todd McCarthy
WASHINGTON POST, 4/1/94, p. D1, Desson Howe
WASHINGTON POST, 4/1/94, Weekend/p. 38, Joe Brown

HOUSE PARTY 3

A New Line Cinema release in association with Doug McHenry and George Jackson. *Executive Producer:* Doug McHenry, George Jackson, and Janet Grillo. *Producer:* Carl Craig. *Director:* Eric Meza. *Screenplay:* Takashi Bufford. *Story:* David Toney and Takashi Bufford. *Based on characters created by:* Reginald Hudlin. *Director of Photography:* Anghel Decca. *Editor:* Tom Walls. *Music:* David Allen Jones. *Music Editor:* Jay Bolton. *Choreographer:* Russell Clark. *Sound:* Darryl Linkow. *Casting:* Robi Reed, Tony Lee, and Andrea Reed. *Production Designer:* Simon Dobbin. *Art Director:* Renee Faia. *Set Decorator:* M. Claypool. *Set Dresser:* Don G. Smith and Joel Osborne. *Costumes:* Mel Grayson. *Make-up:* Judy Murdock. *Stunt Coordinator:* Jophery Brown. *Running time:* 94 minutes. *MPAA Rating:* R.

CAST: Christopher Reid (Kid); Christopher Martin (Play); David Edwards (Stinky); Angela Means (Veda); Tisha Campbell (Sydney); Immature (Himself); Ketty Lester (Aunt Lucy); Bernie Mac (Uncle Vester); Michael Colyar (Showboat); Chris Tucker (Johnny Booze); Tionne "T-Boz" Watkins, Lisa "Left Eye" Lopes, Rozonda "Chilli" Thomas (Sex As A Weapon); Khandi Alexander (Janelle); Anthony Johnson (Butcher); Freez Luv (Ex Con Caterer); Michel Andrew Shure (Hotel Waiter); Shireen Crutchfield (Shireen); Shayna Bridges (Catholic School Girl #1); Mayah McCoy (Catholic School Girl #2); Bee-Be Smith (Party Girl #1); Mikki Val (Party Girl #2); Yvette Wilson (Esther); Gilbert Gottfried (Luggage Clerk); Simply Marvalous (Veda's Mom); Reynaldo Rey (Veda's Dad); Vanessa Hampton (Female Cop #1); Joe Torry (D-Trick); Daniel Gardner (Chill); Katrina McNeal (Tough Type); Lazarus Jackson (Night Heat); Kevin Stockton (Male Cop #1); Jimmy Woodard (M.C. Cane); Bobby Mardis (Master Cataract); Roy Fegan (McCan't C); Bigga Don and Soul Gee (R.A.S. Posse); Sam McCullough (Crazy Sam); Joyce Tolbert (Woman #1 Night Club); Kyler Richie (Teen #1); Odell Jones (Transvestite); Neisha Folkes-Lemel (Miss Pain); Thomas Le Ottis (Backstage Doorman); Chuckii Booker, Russell Hawkins, and Derek "Doa" Allen (Hotel Band Members).

LOS ANGELES TIMES, 1/14/94, Calendar/p. 8, Chris Willman

Hair of the dog that bit hip-hop fans? Nope. "House Party 3" is as much hangover as holdover, a relatively spiritless sequel that puts the law of diminishing returns to the groggy proof again. The great fun that was the first one is as forgotten as a blackout by now.

Kid'N Play (Christopher Reid and Christopher Martin) are back and now living in L.A., apparently retired from their own rap careers and running a management company so fledgling they resort to slight scams for cash flow. A minor one, they pull on a seedy music-business bigwig, Showboat (Michael Colyar)—who seems to have been lifted wholesale from a "Superfly" flick—again gives the pair the prompting they need to spend much of the movie on the run from potential castrators.

Aside from hulk-avoidance and creditor-dodging, the other half of any "House Party" movie is the romantic entanglements of Kid, the charmer shoe high-rise hair is in elevator dreads now. This time he's engaged, not to saucy Sydney (Tisha Campbell, making a brief, tempting return), but to the sweetest of sweethearts, Veda (Angela Means).

The well-intentioned Kid is, of course, utterly beset by females in heat now that he's wearing an engagement ring—and suffers the inevitable nightmare in which he's married by a winking preacher with cleavage deeper than the Grand Canyon—while both he and his intended are surrounded by naysaying friends and family. Call it "Posse of the Bride."

Kid 'N Play are still OK, but their squabbling seems pretty half-hearted this time around. The picture *is* periodically resuscitated by some of its supporting players—especially the very funny Bernie Mac as Uncle Vester, who more or less stands in here for the first film's Robin Harris as the lovably loud-mouthed authority figure, and who intermittently shouts the movie out of its slumber. The rap trio TLC, as the hot female act the heroes pretend to represent, also brightens up the affair in two fleeting scenes.

Most of the performers, professional thesps and cameo rappers alike, come through with charisma enough that it's not the most disagreeable hour and a half out, though you keep wishing they'd been given some business to do. (The best bits play like asides, not set pieces.) Scripter Takashi Bufford and director Eric Meza—making a feature debut after a run of music videos—aren't much help, resorting with alarming regularity to stereotypes that well pre-date hip-hop, from the ageist (look out for that senile aunt who digs porno movies) to the mildly blaxploitative.

The producers don't seem to have much faith in their own waning franchise, begun so promisingly by the long-gone Hudlin brothers four scant years ago. Shot by Anghel Decca, "HP3" looks a lot shoddier than both its predecessors, overstocked with under-lit extreme close-ups that suggest all involved expected a payoff on VHS rentals. "Home Video Party," indeed.

NEW YORK POST, 1/13/94, p. 41, Bill Hoffmann

"House Party 3" may be the first rap movie that needs a spoonful of Geritol. Boy, is this one tired effort!

It seems like only yesterday when goofy rappers Kid 'N Play burst onto the scene in the hip, energized and hysterically funny "House Party."

As produced and directed by the Hudlin brothers, the first movie was a refreshing, up-to-the-second slice of life revolving around a pair of wide-eyed black teens whose immediate goals were to throw a party and have sex, not necessarily in that order.

But while the debut effort was original, spontaneous and rudely witty, "House Party 3" is derivative, predictable and just plain rude.

This time, Kid is getting married and Play is determined to throw him the definitive bachelor party.

Before that can happen, the pair has to deliver a hot female rap group, Sex as a Weapon, to Showboat—a foulmouthed record producer who strong-arms his business partners with a pair of switchblade-wielding beauties always aiming for the crotch.

Christopher Reid and Christopher Martin, who were so engaging four years ago in their debut, are simply going through the motions here.

They might have gotten away with it if the rest of the production had shown even the slightest effort.

But the material plays like a second-rate sitcom, the pacing is off and the editing is sloppy.

The script is loaded with profanity to cover up for the lack of wit. Even the rap tunes seem sadly sapped of energy.

When Kid 'N Play finally do their big climactic rap number, director Eric Meza can think of nothing more original than repeatedly zoom his camera in and out.

Reid and Martin are talented comic players who'll be back on top again when they get some good material.

In the meantime, guys, bail out of this series while you can— it has run out of gas and is operating on fumes.

NEWSDAY, 1/13/94, Part II/p. 63, John Anderson

If "House Party 3" were actually a party—which it's not—it would be 4 a.m., the police would be at the door and someone would have just thrown up in your shoes.

It's time, in other words, to turn out the lights and go the hell home. The freshness is as long gone as the Hudlin brothers, who produced the original "House Party." And even executive producers George Jackson and Doug McHenry, who directed the harmless "House Party 2," have handed off the third like an unwanted child. Director Eric Meza the bemused new parent, isn't expected to turn out anything new, and doesn't.

Like "House Party 2," the latest installment begins with a dream sequence involving Kid, whose upcoming wedding to Veda (Angela Means) provides the movie's loose dramatic framework. In the dream he's in the church, shackled and chained, and surrounded by a church full of women who want him very badly. Why are all these gorgeous people, much less the beautiful and classy Veda, so enchanted by an overweight rapper whose head looks like a party favor? Well, that's why they call 'em dream sequences.

But this is the very young-male-oriented thrust of the film: That once a man, even Kid, is engaged, he becomes irresistible to other women. No, "HP3" isn't the most enlightened film. It's more blaxploitation than innovation, promoting racial and sexual stereotypes in a pandering for laughs that's a little desperate. It also subscribes to the belief men and women cannot coexist anyway, and so may as well engage in the kind of vicious verbal sniping that makes "HP3" so sour. The truly amusing bits in "HP3," are provided almost exclusively by the marginal characters especially Bernie Mac as Kid's explosive uncle. A routine involving "Ex-Con Catering" is a fairly hilarious celebration of bad customer service, and the blind rap group (featuring M. C. Cataract) whose license plate reads LOOKOUT also was pretty funny. And the pint-size preteen rap group Immature provides much of what charm "House Party 3" actually has.

Also reviewed in:
NEW YORK TIMES, 1/13/94, p. C17, Caryn James
VARIETY, 1/17-23/94, p. 104, Emmanuel Levy
WASHINGTON POST, 1/13/94, p. C2, David Mills

HUDSUCKER PROXY, THE

A Warner Bros. release in association with Polygram Filmed Entertainment of a Silver Pictures production in association with Working Title Films. *Executive Producer:* Eric Fellner and Tim Bevan. *Producer:* Ethan Coen. *Director:* Joel Coen. *Screenplay:* Ethan Coen, Joel Coen, and Sam Raimi. *Director of Photography:* Roger Deakins. *Editor:* Thom Noble. *Music:* Carter Burwell. *Music Editor:* Todd Kasow. *Choreographer:* Wesley Fata. *Sound:* Allan Byer and (music): Michael Farrow. *Sound Editor:* Skip Lievsay. *Casting:* Donna Isaacson and John Lyons. *Production Designer:* Dennis Gassner. *Art Director:* Leslie McDonald. *Set Designer:* Gina Cranham, Tony Fanning, and Richard Yanez. *Set Decorator:* Nancy Haigh. *Set Dresser:* Paige Augustine, Claire Gaul, Tinker Linville, Linda Cathey, and Kip Bartlett. *Visual Effects:* Michael J. McAlister. *Mechanical Effects:* Peter M. Chesnsey. *Costumes:* Richard Hornung. *Make-up:* Jean A. Black and Lydia Milars. *Make-up (Paul Newman):* Monty Westmore. *Stunt Coordinator:* Jery Hewitt. *Running time:* 115 minutes. *MPAA Rating:* PG.

CAST: Tim Robbins (Norville Barnes); Jennifer Jason Leigh (Amy Archer); Paul Newman (Sidney J. Mussburger); Charles Durning (Waring Hudsucker); John Mahoney (Chief); Jim True (Buzz); William Cobbs (Moses); Bruce Campbell (Smitty); Harry Bugin (Aloysius); John Seitz (Benny); Joe Grifasi (Lou); David Byrd (Dr. Hugo Bronfenbrenner); Christopher Darga (Mail Room Orienter); Pat Cranshaw (Ancient Sorter); Robert Weil (Mail Room Boss); Mary Lou Rosato (Mussburger's Secretary); Ernie Sarracino (Luigi the Tailor); Eleanor Glockner (Mrs. Mussburger); Kathleen Perkins (Mrs. Braithwaite); Joseph Marcus (Sears Braithwaite of Bullard); Peter Gallagher (Vic Tenetta); Noble Willinghma (Zebulon Cardozo); Barbara Ann Grimes (Mrs. Cardozo); Thom Noble (Thorstenson Finlandson); Steve Buscemi (Beatnik Barman); William Duff-Griffin (Newsreel Scientist); Anna Nicole (Za-Za); Pamela Everett (Dream Dancer); Arthur Bridges (The Hula-Hoop Kid); Sam Raimi and John Cameron (Hudsucker Brainstormers); Skipper Dune (Mr. Grier); Jay Kapner (Mr. Levin); Jon Polito (Mr. Bumstead); Richard Whiting (Ancient Puzzler); Linda McCoy (Coffee Shop Waitress); Stan Adams (Emcee); Karl Mundt (Newsreel Announcer); Joanne Pankow (Newsreel

Secretary); Mario Todisco (Norville's Goon); Colin Fickes (Newsboy); Dick Sasso (Drunk in Alley).

CHRISTIAN SCIENCE MONITOR, 3/15/94, p. 13, David Sterritt

The filmmaking career of Joel and Ethan Coen has had plenty of ups and downs, from the critical success of "Blood Simple" and "Raising Arizona" to the failure of "Miller's Crossing" at the box office. But one fact stands out: These talented brothers have more *fun* with cinema than anyone else around.

Their new picture, "The Hudsucker Proxy," is an excellent case in point. Set in a fairy-tale version of New York in the 1950s, it blends fable, fantasy, and nostalgia into an entertainment so smooth that the wildest implausibilities of plot and character don't slow it down for a second. At once a screwball comedy, a sardonic romance, and a cheerfully phony history of the Hula Hoop, it's nothing if not ambitious. Yet it's never too busy to poke fun at it's own logic, or to leave that logic completely behind and enter the rarefied realm of pure comic imagination.

The hero of the tale is Norville Barnes, a young Midwesterner who's eager to apply his business-school education to Manhattan's corporate world. Hired by the mighty Hudsucker Industries, he starts plugging away in the mail room while dreaming of the moment when he'll spring his first brilliant idea on President Hudsucker and skyrocket to the executive suite.

Little does he know that President Hudsucker has just ended his own career by leaping from the 44th floor, and that the board of directors wants to protect its power by discouraging new investors from purchasing the late executive's stock. Their plan: to install a foolish nonentity as the company's new chief, thus confusing Wall Street and disguising the huge profit potential of the business. Their patsy: none other than the innocent Norville.

In outline, this plot sounds more like melodrama than farce. Ditto for the main subplot, about a tough-talking newspaperwoman who romances Norville in order to spy on him and expose his empty-headedness for all to see.

It's true that Hollywood cranked out zillions of business-world dramas between the 1930s and the '50s with story lines and character types very much like these, and the hokey seriousness of those pictures is exactly what the Coen brothers aim to demolish with their affectionate but acerbic wit. "The Hudsucker Proxy" is to Hollywood melodrama what Norville is to the corporate world: hard to take seriously at first, but smarter than its straight-faced competition and just as savvy about looking after its own interests.

If the spirit of any single filmmaker hovers over "The Hudsucker Proxy," it's that of Frank Capra, whose most popular movies—one thinks of "It's a Wonderful Life" and "Meet John Doe" in particular—have a similar ability to mix dewy-eyed optimism with thinly masked anguish, and a similar willingness to steer away from realism in order to score an emotional or ideological point. While the Coens lack Capra's resonance as a mythmaker, they avoid the inconsistency and opportunism that dog his films, and at times they surpass Capra as outrageous visual comedians.

What keeps this movie short of first-class status are some miscalculations in its writing and acting. The subplot about the hard-boiled reporter goes on much too long, stretching its ironies perilously thin and pushing the performances into needless repetition.

In other scenes, too, the acting is less varied than it ought to be, even in a film based on caricatures. Tim Robbins succeeds as Norville by virtue of sheer energy, but Jennifer Jason Leigh has no idea how to modulate her wisecracking character and even the great Paul Newman is more cartoonish than credible as Hudsucker's crafty board chairman.

"The Hudsucker Proxy" is less brilliant than the Coen brothers' best movie "Barton Fink," because of these problems and also because it's less persistent in pursuing its most inventive impulses. This relative conservatism is probably a wise commercial decision, given the difficulties of marketing a surrealistic comedy-drama like "Barton Fink," but it's disappointing for those of us who value the Coens precisely for their audacious approach to cinematic style.

Still, the new comedy has moments of great humor and terrific visual appeal. It's a solid achievement for Joel Coen, who directed; Ethan Coen, who produced; Sam Raimi, who wrote the screenplay with the brothers; Roger Deakins, still one of the most gifted cinematographers in the movie world; and their many collaborators—especially Charles Durning, whose portrayal of president Hudsucker is one of the movie's most hilarious assets.

LOS ANGELES TIMES, 3/11/94, Calendar/p. 1, Kenneth Turan

You have to admire what the Coen brothers have accomplished in "The Hudsucker Proxy," but actually enjoying their achievement is a little more difficult.

Pristine perfectionists who delight in the craft of filmmaking, director Joel and producer Ethan have come up with a visual extravaganza, a series of gorgeous, technically dazzling set pieces impeccably conceived, designed and photographed. But impressive as all this is, it is great filmmaking only from the wrists down.

For if "The Hudsucker Proxy is a triumph, it is a zombie one. Too cold, too elegant, too perfect, more an exhibit in a cinema museum than a flesh-and-blood film, "Proxy's" highly polished surface leaves barely any space for an audience's emotional connection.

Though set in 1958, "Hudsucker" is intended as an *hommage* to several different kinds of 1940s films, from fast-talking comedies like the Howard Hawks-directed "His Girl Friday" to the jaunty populism of Frank Capra's "Meet John Doe" and "It's a Wonderful Life." But this film is so concerned with giving just the right tongue-in-cheek twist to its story line it ends up, to quote a very different 1940s vehicle, "a little cold around the heart."

It is in fact a kind of perverse tribute to how icily controlled the Coens' world is that "Hudsucker" persists in remaining uninvolving despite a pair of brash comic performances from stars Tim Robbins and Jennifer Jason Leigh that could have brought life to another film.

Robbins plays Norville Barnes, a recent graduate of the Muncie College of Business Administration who is so boyishly eager to make his mark in commerce that his cheeks literally gleam as he steps out of the bus from Indiana in bustling New York City.

A trusting naif, Norville manages to land a job in the hellacious mailroom of mighty Hudsucker Industries, assuring his co-workers that he has impressive plans for the future involving a mysterious invention intended, he says with a grin, "you know, for kids."

Meanwhile, unbeknownst to Norville, big things are happening higher up. There is a sudden vacancy at the very top of Hudsucker Industries that leaves the company vulnerable. But crafty No. 2 man Sidney J. Mussburger (Paul Newman, trying perhaps too hard) has a plan.

The idea is to install a dunce as CEO, someone guaranteed to drive the stock price down so the board of directors can buy the company for a fraction of what its worth. "I want a Grade-A ding-dong," Mussburger roars, and, naturally, when Norville wanders up from the mailroom, it's clear that the appropriate victim has been found. Though Norville thinks this good fortune is simply his due, others are not so sure, especially the folks at the Manhattan Argus, the kind of newspaper where the reporters call the editor "chief." "The human angle, that's what sells papers," this worthy opines and he assigns his ace reporter, the fast-talking Amy Archer (Leigh), to get the scoop on unsuspecting Norville.

Amy, showing the form that's already won her a Pulitzer Prize, finagles her way into a job as Norville's secretary, and soon the Argus is running headlines like "Imbecile Heads Hudsucker." Naturally Norville is hardly pleased about this and, Amy discovers to her chagrin, she is starting to rethink her attitude toward the big galoot as well.

Sprinkled through this story are great visual set pieces, starting with a gorgeous opening tracking shot over a mock-New York skyline and continuing with that cavernous mailroom and assorted high jinks involving open skyscraper windows. Production designer Dennis Gassner, working with exquisite effects (visual by Michael J. McAlister, mechanical by Peter M. Chesney), has matched if not exceeded the wonders he accomplished with "Barton Fink" and "Bugsy," both Oscar nominated in the same year.

And even in a brief retelling it is possible to see how much of a kick the Coens (who co-wrote the script with Sam Raimi) get out of fooling around with venerable movie conventions. They love the old dialogue, lines like "Is this guy from Chumpsville?" and "What gives?" and they love the old movie types, like Buzz the gabby elevator operator (Jim True) and Smitty the cynical reporter (Bruce Campbell).

Maybe they love it all too much. Despite the best and often entertaining efforts of Robbins and Leigh, whose zippy comic impersonation of Katharine Hepburn doing Rosalind Russell is extraordinary, there is an air of self-satisfaction about this excessively derivative project that carefully keeps audiences at a distance.

The Coens seem to have learned all the lessons old Hollywood had to teach except the most important one: You gotta have heart.

NEW STATESMAN & SOCIETY, 8/26/94, p. 32, Jonathan Romney

If Joel and Ethan Coen were'nt such retiring guys—if they were more like the rampaging studio boss in their *Barton Fink*—then they'd have a coat of arms emblazoned with the motto "What do you *mean*, you've seen it all before?" The sense of over-familiarity in most Coen movies is built into the very fabric of what the brothers do, as the most studious and overt *pasticheurs* currently working in American cinema. They're not alone, of course. Just about everyone making films in America today—no, make that the world—is stitching together copied fragments of the old repertoire.

The difference with the Coens, however, is that they apply themselves to pastiche with absolute seriousness and with no sense of distance. They immerse themselves as no one else does. In *The Hudsucker Proxy*, they take us to the heart of the screwball comedy and tune up its rusted workings. Then they perform a sort of anachronism-therapy by transplanting it from its roots in the 1930s (Frank Capra) into the 1950s, when it degenerated gloriously into brash cartoon (Frank Tashlin).

The borrowings are all there—the two Franks, Preston Sturges, Lang, Welles, Daffy Duck—but sewn together so seamlessly that they merge into a meta-screwball that takes on the dimensions of a self-contained reality. The result is self-reflexive to the hilt, yet without a hint of the cool, narcissistic distancing you might expect. Against all odds, we buy the illusion whole—we're not outside a movie, but inside Movieland.

The Hudsucker Proxy is the best shaggy dog story I've heard or seen all year. It ends, suitably, with a climactic twist to make you groan with delight; in fact, it's stacked with such twists. And yet, as is the way with shaggy dog stories, you not only forget it as soon as it's over but faintly resent your time being wasted so spectacularly, at such length, and to such bathetic effect.

It's a good yarn, while it lasts: the story of why, on a snowy New Year's Eve in New York, 1958, one Norville Barnes (Tim Robbins) is about to throw himself 45 floors ("counting the mezzanine") to the street below. A breezy, bushy-tailed hick in town, Barnes falls victim to a piece of Machiavellian finagling by the patrician cigar-chomper Sidney J Massburger (a terrifyingly steely Paul Newman).

Barnes, an amiable, indefatigable bungler, is the perfect stooge to be made puppet chairman of the monolithic Hudsucker Industries and so bring its share prices crashing down. Jennifer Jason Leigh comes on his trail as a cynical newshound with Hepburn inflections and Howitzer repartee, and the scene is set for rare fun.

Fun, though, is what the film doesn't quite give you, although it affords any number of discrete pleasures. (Not least are those provided by Roger Deakin's photography and Dennis Gassner's design, which take a sense of the turban monolith to delirious new extremes.) But somehow they don't add up to an overall pleasurable experience. That seems to be because the Coens are more concerned with testing the calibrations of their remarkable machinery than letting it roll of its own accord. They leave nothing to chance; so rigorous is *The Hudsucker Proxy* that it practically intimidates you into being impressed. It's massive and solemn and somehow professorial.

The Coens don't allow their imaginations to skate off the surfaces of things. Rather they want to get to grips with their whole construction, right down to the inner workings. You have to see the film to realise quite how thoroughly this metaphor of "inner workings" runs through it. Suffice to say (at the risk of giving away its most ingenious tricks) that a huge clock plays a very important part. It's the film's central manifestation, among many others, of providence and predestination, circularity and repetition. You rarely see mainstream movies in which the thematics are so densely worked or so suggestive. That's the trouble. This isn't a film to laugh at, but to write theses about.

The Hudsucker Proxy comes across with the cumulative effect of a light, frothy diversion. Yet it's instilled with all the metaphysical solemnity of a full-blown Pilgrim's Progress. This is a massive joke told in stentorian tones. The film has its own draconian rhythm, and wants us to dance to it, to laugh on cue. But we're more likely to recognise gags as gags and draw the line there. Even the slimmest conceits resound to this clockwork beat.

When the gaggle of wheezy financiers discuss their plan, you begin to wonder whether the script has actually been in verse all along: "It could work"—"It should work"—"It would work!" The leitmotif of "Say ... what gives?" similarly marks a beat each time it comes round, but does no more. The trouble is that nothing here *gives* in the other sense. There's no give, no "play" in the machinery. Nothing can get loose and work of its own accord. At its worst, this means that each joke arrives on cue: the punchline to a visual gag about duration is marked out by the reading of *War and Peace*. This is satisfying only in a rhythmic sense, because it turns out to be as predictable and as punctual as we fear.

One of the film's key themes is the music of chance; but the Coens' densely composed rhapsody actually drowns out chance. Leigh's snarly staccato delivery steals the film, like abstract modernist music pitched against the lushness of the main Khatchaturian theme (*The Onedin Line*, strange to say). It never seems to matter that her lines aren't entirely comprehensible; but we're also very aware of how precisely she's "getting" the cadences of 1930s/1940s wiseacre-spiel.

There's no denying that this is an extraordinary film, but it doesn't inspire anything other than admiration. When you' re watching it, it seems unthinkable that the film fared so little debate at Cannes this year. Five minutes after leaving the cinema, you already see why. The Coens have again proved their brilliance as master machinists, but they're no longer the crafty watchmakers of their fiendish debut *Blood Simple*. Here they have become the Isambard Kingdom Brunels of the gag. Like his notable steamship, the *Great Western, The Hudsucker Proxy* is a beautiful monumental thing that just doesn't float so well.

NEW YORK, 3/14/94, p. 74, John Powers

Literary adaptations, collections of Yoruba masks, secretaries with British accents—Hollywood has always had a taste for anything that seems classy. Consider the instructive case of Joel and Ethan Coen, whose work is lavishly admired in Manhattan and West Los Angeles but mostly ignored everywhere in between. While such box-office duds as *Millers's Crossing* and *Barton Fink* would have ruined most other filmmakers, they have only increased the Coens' special allure: Like the post-comedic pre-tabloid Woody Allen, the brothers offer their patrons the cachet of artistic respectability. The latest to hitch his vanity to their talent is producer Joel Silver, godfather of the flying-lass school of cinema, whose movies include *Die Hard* and *Lethal Weapon*. Silver recently gushed to Charlie Rose about how honored he'd been to be involved with the Coens' new movie, *The Hudsucker Proxy*, and how thrilling it was to work with genuine artists. He didn't appear to be sweating whether the picture would make back its rumored $40-million cost.

I'm afraid there's not a lot of glory to go around in *The Hudsucker Proxy*, a muffled, miscalculated attempt to inject a corny Capraesque fable with the break-neck cynicism of Preston Sturges. Tim Robbins stars as doofusy Norville Barnes, an idealistic graduate of the Muncie College of Business Administration who comes to make his fortune in 1958 New York. Hired to work in the mailroom of Hudsucker Industries, he's promptly taken up by Sidney J. Mussburger (Paul Newman), a corporate Machiavelli who's looking for "some jerk" to play the patsy in a Byzantine stock scam. Before he knows what's hit him, Norville is named company president, becomes celebrated as both an imbecile and a genius, and gets romantically involved with a reporter, Amy Archer (Jennifer Jason Leigh), who talks with the voice of Katharine Hepburn but sprays out her lines like an Uzi. Though this hard-bitten newshound starts out trying to nail him, she's won over by his innocence and his battles to keep his integrity when unexpected success threatens to corrupt him.

The Coens began writing this movie in the mid-eighties along with their friend Sam Raimi, and the years of work pay off in some classic movie moments: a fake newsreel about Hula Hoops, a loopy monologue about Rorschach blots, and a hilariously gratuitous flashback to a discussion of double-stitching as Sidney Mussburger dangles from the ledge of a skyscraper. Yet for all its laughs, *The Hudsucker Proxy* was probably too long in gestation: It has no spontaneity, no forward momentum. It's all marginalia. Director Joel Coen is hooked on self-congratulatory flourishes—he goes into his home-run trot before every joke—and his lead-pipe comic touch only accentuates the arid cleverness of a movie that asks us to snicker at arch tracking shots, references to his *Girl Friday*, and the lambent wit of naming someone "Hudsucker."

Virginia Woolf once cracked that the novelist Arnold Bennett seemed to think that if he described a house in enough detail, readers would believe that somebody lived there. The same could be said of the Coens, who have lost the human dimension of Norville's story in their control-freak obsession with the Hudsucker building's elegant spareness, set pieces about admen and knuckleheaded veeps, and the governing motif of the circle, which shows up everywhere—in Hula Hoops, clocks, and even the plot's 360-degree shape. Like *Miller's Crossing*, *The Hudsucker Proxy* knocks you out with its externals but is so dead inside that you spend entire scenes recalling how much more you enjoyed these urban-nightmare sight gags when you first saw them in *Brazil*.

The Coens' style demands juicy performances for its lifeblood—think how John Goodman lifted *Barton Fink*—but here even the stars are trapped in one-note roles that don't let them breathe. At first it's amusing to see Jennifer Jason Leigh doing her motor-mouth-journalist bit, but five minutes later you're praying she'll stop. And why cast Paul Newman as a scheming boardroom assassin if you aren't going to make hay with his blue-eyed seductiveness and bleeding-heart image?

Norville Barnes is a goofier version of the naive small-town heroes winningly played by homespun charmers like Jimmy Stewart and Gary Cooper. But Tim Robbins is nobody's idea of a likable actor (his specialty: thin-lipped, rodent-eyed bastards), and he's lost the gawky-sweet boobishness that made him endearing in *Bull Durham*. As Norville, he does the dumbest thing you can do if you're playing dumb—he keeps making sure we know that he's actually a lot smarter than his character. Yet even as he looks down on the young man from Muncie, he's not up to the part's comic demands: When Norville's foot gets stuck in a burning wastebasket, Robbins flails around ineptly, hoping to wring some laughs with sheer exertion, as we think wistfully of Jim Carrey's slapstick brilliance in *Ace Ventura*. Robbins's icy, self-admiring performance confirms the bad news suggested by his condescending turn as the motorcycle cop in *Short Cuts*: He now wears an aura of smugness that makes one long for the self-effacing humility of Ted Koppel.

His complacency feeds what's worst in the Coens, a smirking sense of superiority that is antithetical to a fable's generosity of spirit. *The Hudsucker Proxy* tries to play its story both ways at once, but it leaves the audience with nothing—neither a sentimental heart-warmer like *Mr. Deeds Goes to Washington* nor a savvy, snide send-up of Hollywood's prized chestnuts. Of course, you don't actually have to feel human sympathy to please the mass audience—Frank Capra was a great resenter, Sturges a practiced whore—but you must at least know how to fake it well enough to make your movies inviting. With a perverse integrity, the Coens have never bothered to learn such fakery, which may be why their work so often feels sealed off and inert, like the gimcrack-filled Xanadu after Charles Foster Kane dies. The great irony is that the brash, crass, audience-chasing Joel Silver is precisely the kind of producer who might have given this picture the transfusion of show-biz vitality it so desperately needs. But he stood in such awe of the Coens' artistry that he didn't lift a finger as they turned out *The Hudsucker Proxy*, the most expensive bad art film in motion-picture history. I wonder if anyone will tell Silver the truth, that there's more glory—and more art—in *Die Hard* and *Lethal Weapon*.

NEW YORK POST, 3/11/94, p. 45, Thelma Adams

Joel and Ethan Coen are running in circles.

In "The Hudsucker Proxy," the hula hoop and a giant clock figure prominently and are as perfectly circular as the plot. And, like the circle, the brothers' latest movie is completely empty in the center.

In tracking down their big theme—power—the klepto Coens have stylishly mooched elements from more movies than I can recognize. "Hudsucker" strikes me as a strange mutation of "His Girl Friday" and "How to Succeed in Business Without Really Trying," with a few dramatic camera swoops borrowed from Tim Burton's "Batman" extravaganzas.

But after such offbeat excursion as "Blood Simple," "Raising Arizona" and "Miller's Crossing," director Joel and producer Ethan have given faithful fans the equivalent of a movie-star map to the hallowed halls of Better Hollywood Filmmakers.

The brothers, with co-writer Sam Raini ("Darkman"), have set their oversized saga about big business not at the Worldwide Wicket Co. of "How to ...," but at Hudsucker Industries. The place is an art deco Gotham, the fast-talking and big-shouldered characters cry 1940s, but the year is 1958. Stylistic overkill!

Waring Hudsucker himself played by the rotund Charles Durning, makes an early leap from the plot when this captain of industry commits suicide from the Hudsucker Building, leaving his Machiavellian right-hand, Sidney Mussberger (Paul Newman), to make a power grab.

A board member drolly comments, "Every step he [Hudsucker] took was a step up except, of course, this last one." Such snappy dialogue is part of the film's pleasures—if only the Coens weren't too clever for their own good.

Mussberger schemes to drive down the value of Hudsucker Industries in order to seize control on the cheap. He replaces Hudsucker with an imbecile, Norville Barnes (Tim Robbins), fresh off the bus from Muncie.

Ace reporter Amy Archer (Jennifer Jason Leigh) smells a rat and takes time off from polishing her Pulitzer to go undercover as Barnes' secretary.

As a cigar-chomping industrialist Newman seems to have the young Coens cowed. He delivers a villainous performance so two-dimensional it's as if he walked out of Toon Town (another reference alert, "Who Framed Roger Rabbit").

Jennifer Jason Leigh is always a surprising actress—but not all surprises are good ones. Her hair swirled and dyed chestnut, the petite actress gamely crosses Katharine Hepburn and Rosalind Russell, two icons who couldn't be more uncomfortable sharing the same pair of shoes.

Newman, Robbins and Leigh act past each other, talking over each other's shoulders. There's so little emotional heat that if romantic leads Robbins and Leigh could kiss over each other's shoulders, they would.

Even a Coen disaster has its delights—an excess of cleverness is a rare complaint about a Hollywood movie.

Unfortunately, "Hudsucker" is so hollow it echoes.

NEWSDAY, 3/11/94, Part II/p. 72, Jack Mathews

On Sept. 12, 1991, reader Louis Awamy of South Huntington wrote a letter to the editor of this newspaper complaining about the buffoon— me!—who gave a rave review to the Coen brothers' "Barton Fink."

"Based on your rating I went to see this garbage," Mr. Awamy wrote, "and anyone who considers this a 4-star movie should stand up so as to not induce any more brain damage!!!"

Well, I tried standing, Louis, and it only made my feet sore. So, please pay attention when I say, if you didn't like "Barton Fink," there is no chance of your liking their latest movie, "The Hudsucker Proxy."

The Coen brothers—Ethan directs, Joel produces, they co-write—make weird films, offbeat comedies mostly that parody old movie genres. They don't tell conventional stories, they barely tell stories at all, and they seem to have nothing whatsoever to say about the human condition. What they do is make the most inventive, unpredictable, visually interesting films out there today, and for critics watching 150 or so paint-by-the-numbers pictures a year, we appreciate their effort.

"The Hudsucker Proxy," though Warner Bros. is gamely trying to peddle it as the Coens' first mainstream movie, is their most bizarre genre concoction yet, a simultaneous send-up of Preston Sturges' screwball comedies and Frank Capra's sentimental rise-of-the-common-man melodramas, all decked out in gorgeous Art Deco settings inspired by Fritz Lang's "Metropolis."

The story, about a Midwest rube (Tim Robbins) who becomes the accidental head of a corrupt conglomerate, is set in 1958 New York, the giddy era of Eisenhower, Howdy Doody and hula hoops. But everything from the clothing to the cars to the tabloid journalists digging for scoops springs straight from the fantasies of Old Hollywood.

The movie opens with echoes of "It's a Wonderful Life," with the voice of a godlike narrator (William Cobbs) introducing us to Norville Barnes, who is perched on the 44th-floor ledge of Hudsucker Industries, about to jump and "jelly up" the sidewalk below.

To find out how he got there, we have to go back to another suicide at Hudsucker, to the hilarious leap (this is the Coen brothers, remember) of its previous president (Charles Durning) and learn why the board of directors plucked Norville from the mail room to succeed him. They figured with an idiot running the company, stock values would plunge, they'd buy 'em up, kick him out, and own the whole show.

But Norville turns out to be an idiot savant, carrying around an idea for what will become the most popular toy of the 20th Century, and the Hudsucker board, led by cigar-chomping windbag Sidney J. Mussburger (Paul Newman), has to figure out how to get rid of him before his success destroys them.

There isn't a real person anywhere in the movie, just cartoon versions of people who were caricatures the first time around. Robbins plays Barnes as a sort of cross between John Doe and L'il Abner, and the Abner side is as annoying as the John Doe side is charming. Newman and some of the others—notably Jim True's shrill elevator operator—start out over-the-top and spin into orbit from there.

The transcending graces of "The Hudsucker Proxy" are Jennifer Jason Leigh's hyperkinetic performance as the fast-talking newspaper reporter who falls in love with Norville while trying to expose him (she talks like Katharine Hepburn on speed) and the Coens' constantly dazzling imagery.

To Mr. Awamy, who has since become my pen pal, no, stunning sets, clever photographic effects and eccentric characters aren't enough to recommend a movie as a mass audience entertainment. The Coen brothers haven't shown yet that they can, or care to, come up with stories or characters outside of their own movie references.

But for those who appreciate an occasional break from the humdrum predictability of most Hollywood comedies, even a failed Coen brothers picture is a worthy event.

NEWSWEEK, 3/14/94, p. 72, David Ansen

[*The Hudsucker Proxy* was reviewed jointly with *Greedy*; see Ansen's review of that film.]

SIGHT AND SOUND, 9/94, p. 39, Kim Newman

New York, New Year's Eve, 1958-9, Norville Barnes, Chairman of Hudsucker Industries, climbs out on a ledge at the top of the Hudsucker Building, contemplating suicide. A month earlier, Norville arrives in the city from Muncie, Indiana, and gets a job in the Hudsucker mail room on the day company founder Waring Hudsucker jumps to his death. Sidney J. Mussburger, Hudsucker's aide, reasons that if an idiot is appointed to the chairmanship, the stock will plunge to a point when the board can buy it up and gain control. Norville is entrusted with a last letter from Hudsucker to Mussburger but so flounders in his attempt at delivery that Mussburger makes him Chairman.

Amy Archer, a cynical journalist, poses as Norville's secretary to research an expose of his appointment. When Mussburger approves Norville's stupidest idea, the company unexpectedly makes a killing by marketing the hula hoop and begins to trade extraordinarily high. Success goes to Norville's head and he becomes self-satisfied and corrupt just as the hard-boiled Amy is on the point of warming to him. Mussburger leaks to the press that Norville, depressed now he has found out Amy has been fooling him, is on the point of going insane. On New Year's Eve, Norville evades the men from the asylum and climbs out on the ledge. He falls but Moses, the Hudsucker Building's mysteriously beneficent clock-keeper, halts time by jamming the giant clock. Suspended in mid-air, Norville is visited by an angelic Waring Hudsucker, who reminds him of the undelivered letter; it decrees his personal stock be deeded to whoever becomes Chairman. Moses struggles with Aloysius, his evil opposite number, and time starts again, but Norville makes it safely to the ground. Mussburger is committed, Norville and Amy are engaged and Norville announces his new stupid idea, the frisbee.

In style, this expensive item recalls the other broad comedy collaboration between the Coen Brothers and Sam Raimi, Raimi's compromised living cartoon *Crimewave*. Here again is a fantasy world stranded between a real and an imagined past, populated by slightly caricatured stereotypes, where innocence is constantly threatened by irrational, violent evil. There are obvious elements from classic Hollywood, with touches of *Meet John Doe*, *Mr Deeds Goes to Town* and *It's a Wonderful Life*, although the setting of 50s big business is subtly different from the Depression or World War One arenas favoured by Frank Capra. Given Raimi's debt to EC horror comics, it would seem that the touchstone here, for subject matter as well as approach, is EC's other great achievement, *MAD* magazine. The hard-boiled newsroom and the ominously oppressive boardroom are less like the originals of *His Girl Friday* or *Executive Suite* than like the sort of movie satires *MAD* published in its heyday. Even the lampooning of fads like beatniks, the hula hoop and the Organisation Man harks back not only to the jokes of *MAD* but to its late 50s targets.

The strand of the demonic which threads through the Coen oeuvre recurs here, with a literal battle of devils and angels in the background. Harry Bugin's barely-glimpsed but unsettling character Aloysius (the little man who chips names off the office doors of the departed) succeeds the literally hellborn demons played by Randall 'Tex' Cobb, John Turturro and John Goodman in *Raising Arizona*, *Miller's Crossing* and *Barton Fink*. But here, the upfront villainy of a nattily-suited Paul Newman is more in line with the comical fiends of Raimi's pictures than with the subtler, more rounded grotesques played by Jon Polito or Michael Lerner in those last two films. In the character of Moses, there is an angelic answer to these rampant demons. His beneficence provides a literal *deus ex machina* for the breathtaking time-stop finale, and allows Charles Durning to appear as a ludicrous but touching pantomime angel drifting down through swirling snow as he strums a ukelele.

If this is somehow not a pinnacle masterpiece to equal the all-round perfection of the last two Coen films, perhaps it is because the actual story (written shortly after *Blood Simple*) is too deeply indebted to its movie precursors to form its own identity. *Blood Simple* and *Miller's Crossing* might have grown from the seeds of Dashiell Hammett, but they have an obsessive, perfectly-plotted identity of their own. *The Hudsucker Proxy*, which has some of Raimi's knockabout looseness and even a few plodding stretches, is essentially a simple Faust tale, while the earlier films were complex examinations of the Devil's Bargain. Tim Robbins manages the change from sweetness to superficiality with expert ease but always seems to strain to evoke Jimmy Stewart or Gary Cooper. Jennifer Jason Leigh, meanwhile, goes against the odds by taking bits from Jean Arthur, Barbara Stanwyck, Katharine Hepburn and Rosalind Russell and scrambling them into a genuine, original performance (it's not often noted, but Joel Coen is an extraordinarily sensitive director of interesting actresses).

While the earlier Coen films went beyond pastiche, this wholly delightful urban parable is content simply to juggle much-loved elements and present them with a cinematic verve that easily equals the originals. Few filmmakers today are capable of moments as perfect as the little hitch-and-smile Durning makes before beginning his running jump along the boardroom table and through the window. And the superbly orchestrated sequence (all credit to composer Carter Burwell and editor Thom Noble) which follows the initial failure and snowballing success of the hula hoop is a set piece to rank beside the 'Danny Boy' shoot-out from *Miller's Crossing*, with the added advantage of charm. Though they have never made a commercial crossover hit (and this seems an unlikely prospect), the Coens are the most exciting, imaginative and confident movie-makers in America.

TIME, 3/14/94, p. 105, Richard Schickel

So far it's been a great year for Art Deco. The hype for Barbra Streisand's auction of her extensive Deco collection has been almost as impressive as the objects themselves. And now the Coen brothers, Ethan and Joel, have made a movie in which the massive moderne settings by production designer Dennis Gassner and the glowing light cast on them by cinematographer Roger Deakins make you wonder how a decorative style at once so sleek and warm could ever have fallen out of favor.

But therein lies the trouble with *The Hudsucker Proxy*, which is the handsomest American movie in years. You really shouldn't be lost in the history of architecture and home furnishing at the movies. Nor should you be wondering why a film supposedly set in 1958, when classic Deco pieces were mostly to be found at the Goodwill, actually evokes aspects of the previous three decades. Most especially you should not be musing about why a movie that wants to be a funny social commentary—the press kit hopefully evokes the names of Frank Capra and Preston Sturges—is shot in the impersonal expressionist manner that was literally foreign to these American masters, a style that was favored by glum and self-important German directors like Fritz Lang.

This choice is particularly odd since the film is about the kind of naïf Capra adored and Sturges affectionately satirized. His name is Norville Barnes (Tim Robbins) and he's plucked out of the mailroom and made president of Hudsucker Industries when its founder (Charles Durning) commits spectacular suicide. You can imagine either Jimmy Stewart or Eddie Bracken in the part, but Robbins has a tricky modernist charm all his own. And you can just as easily imagine Edward Arnold as the evil genius of the board of directors, Sidney J. Mussburger, although Paul Newman brings a sprightly spite to the role.

Mussburger's plan is to let dopey Norville, an all too recent graduate of Muncie College of Business Administration, run the company into the ground so that he and his colleagues can pick up shares in a basically sound company on the cheap. The tough newspaper gal (Jennifer Jason Leigh) who's supposed to expose the fraud and falls for Norville is distinctly Capraesque too. There's even angelic intervention and a touch of time warping, devices Capra employed in *It's A Wonderful Life*.

But despite such fanciful touches, Capra, a master of motion within the frame, never lost touch with reality, which is sadly not the case with the stylish but bloodless *Hudsucker Proxy*. Most important, he and Sturges, ever the sentimental wise guy, were at heart children of the light. The Coens (Joel directs, Ethan produces and they write together, this time with Sam Raimi) are creatures of darkness. At their best (the great *Miller's Crossing* or the dizzy *Raising Arizona*) they are brilliant satirists of the national propensity for violence. But here they have deliberately cut themselves off from their best subject. Try as they will to create a vision of corporate (and urban) hellishness through sheer stylishness, theirs is a truly abstract expressionism, at once heavy, lifeless and dry.

VILLAGE VOICE, 3/22/94, p. 48, Georgia Brown

Pressed by proximity, you might even see the influence—via various intermediaries—of *Triumph of the Will* on *The Hudsucker Proxy*, the chilly new, silly new $40 million (Look ma, no shoestrings) movie by Joel and Ethan Coen. Ostensibly, their sources are Capra and Sturges as well as other snappy comedies starring Gary Cooper and Jimmy Stewart as shy young hicks threatened by the machinations of slick, big-time operators (Edward Arnold, et al.) and saved by the love of a competent dame—like Claudette Colbert or Katharine Hepburn. But *Hudsucker*, for all its ultrasavvy referencing, its generalized nostalgia (the film is set in a 1958 that feels like '48), has none of its sources' simplicity or charm. More parody than homage, *Hudsucker* is replete with attitude, atmosphere, and decor.

A huge toy company housed in a vintage Midtown tower, Hudsucker Enterprises is ruled over by a heartless tyrant (an icy Paul Newman). Tim Robbins plays Norville Barnes, the jerk from the provinces who works in the mailroom until called on to deliver an important missive to the chief. After passing through a series of mammoth portals—low-angle shots—the quaking Norville comes upon the exec seated at a sleek desk at the far end of a monumental space. All the cartoony fascist trimmings suggest the evil empire. (The Coens' longtime friend Sam Raimi cowrote *Hudsucker*.)

But *Hudsucker* is not really anticapitalist. As usual with the Coens, a baroque circular plot—everything, in fact, comes back to the figure of the circle here—seems merely an excuse for a series of rococo sidebars. My favorite filigree involves the first kid on the street to try out the new hula hoop—Norville's contribution to Hudsucker product development. Trust the Coens to dispense at least a couple genuine thrills. I also like Jennifer Jason Leigh's jaded, fast-talking reporter. This may be because several times Leigh simply looks panicked—trapped in the languor of her lingo, the pitter of her patter—and thus less a grotesque than those around her. (Robbins is so goofy, I could barely watch.)

Except for tiny hooks, though, there's nothing' to hold on to in this vast assemblage. Oh, there's this phantom darkman tending the giant clockworks—Ole' Mose (William Cobbs) prattling on like some Uncle Remus of the metropolis. The ghost in the machine? Biding his time you might say? Only the shadow knows.

Also reviewed in:
CHICAGO TRIBUNE, 3/25/94, Friday/p. A, Michael Wilmington
NATION, 3/21/94, p. 390, Stuart Klawans
NEW YORK TIMES, 3/11/94, p. C8, Caryn James

VARIETY, 1/31-2/6/94, p. 65, Todd McCarthy
WASHINGTON POST, 3/25/94, p. D1, Desson Howe
WASHINGTON POST, 3/25/94, Weekend/p. 44, Joe Brown

HUMAN RIGHTS WATCH INTERNATIONAL FILM FESTIVAL (FIFTH)

CHRISTIAN SCIENCE MONITOR, 5/4/94, p. 16, David Sterritt

"I wonder how people used to remember when they didn't film, when the didn't take pictures..."

This statement by Chris Marker, a socially aware filmmaker of near-legendary reputation, overstates the case for cinema and photography as conveyors of "truth" about human affairs. But one readily sympathizes with the sentiment behind the remark, since movies and television have become the modern world's most powerful tools for recording, recalling, and interpreting its own ideas and behaviors.

Quoted at the beginning of "Starting Place," a new documentary by Robert Kramer about the Vietnam War and its legacy, Marker's words make a good starting place for thinking about this year's edition of the annual Human Rights Watch International Film Festival, now playing in New York and soon embarking on an extensive American and European tour.

The artists who made the festival's dozens of offerings are actively engaged in the task of providing visual memories for all of us to share. These memories will have enduring value in future years, when we look back on the current era and try to understand what made it tick. But they have a special urgency right now, since most of them deal with real-world issues in desperate need of understanding, amelioration, and correction.

The centerpiece of the program is the first-ever retrospective of movies by Margarethe von Trotta, one of the few female filmmakers to emerge from Germany and establish a strong international reputation. It's hard to imagine a more appropriate artist for this equality-minded festival to honor, given the magnitude of her achievement as a woman in a male-dominated industry, and the consistency of her concern with social and political problems.

Such problems are at the heart of her latest work, "The Long Silence," a highlight of the filmfest. Made as a German-Italian coproduction, it centers on an Italian woman whose husband, an enterprising and controversial judge, is investigating a flagrantly illegal weapons-dealing operation run by figures from government and organized crime.

When he is assassinated, his wife must come to terms with her grief and anger. She chooses to do this by continuing the judge's work, despite the physical and psychological dangers this decision brings with it. The movie's title refers to the silence of decent but inactive citizens faced with threats to their liberty and well-being, and also to the silence of women who are expected to support the powerful men in society rather than taking action of their own. Both silences are resoundingly broken in the course of von Trotta's film, although it avoids any hint of easy answers or simplistic solutions for the troubling social questions it raises.

The festival includes many documentaries alongside its fictional movies, and Kramer's unconventional "Starting Place" is likely to be one of the most talked-about offerings. Shot in 1992, the film chronicles Kramer's return to Vietnam more than two decades after his first journey there.

Much of the film presents fragmentary interviews with such persons as Kramer's first Vietnamese guide—now a respected translator of Western literature—and an American woman imprisoned in the United States for radical activism that had its original spark when she joined the antiwar movement years earlier. Other portions of the movie depict Vietnam itself as seen through Kramer's highly subjective camera eye.

In a sizable list of films including such respected efforts as "Ice" and "Milestones," which he co-directed, Kramer has worked for years to combine the personal and the political into a seamless and humanitarian whole; the outcome of his labor has been extremely uneven in quality, but his seriousness and sincerity have always been clear. "Starting Point" leans toward the personal end of his artistic spectrum, even including footage of the birth of his daughter. As a result, the movie is more impressionistic than instructive.

It serves up some powerful images, however, often avoiding the merely photogenic to concentrate on the unexpectedly poetic instead. And it has a touchingly human dimension that makes it a fitting selection for a film festival that's named after *human* rights in the broadest sense.

Other attractions in the festival range from features to shorts, covering an impressively broad swath of intellectual and emotional territory. Some noteworthy items:

■"Shadow Puppets," directed by Chuck W. Gamble (US). This allegorical cartoon focuses on a charming little misfit who lives in a sort of factory-prison run by a totalitarian state. After work each day, every laborer's hands are locked in a box to keep them out of mischief, but our hero finds a secret key that allows him to open the box and amuse himself by making funny finger-shadows on the wall. When caught, he's brutally punished—this is a cartoon for grownups, not young children—but he manages to triumph in the end. Drawn in strikingly bold black-and-white strokes, Gamble's animated tale is an effective parable of the human urge to maintain individuality and humor under even the most awful circumstances.

■"A Street Under Siege," made by the Sarajevo Group of Authors (former Yugoslavia/France/United Kingdom). Shot late last year in Sarajevo by a collective of filmmakers, writers, artists, and students, this compilation of short videos gives harrowing evidence of such atrocities as the shelling of schools and hospitals. It also includes revealing conversations with overworked physicians, children who pass the time by playing war and survival games, and others who choose either to stay in their city or find a way to escape it. One poignant segment even shows the homeless dogs and cats of the city, finding in this seemingly small detail a subtle dimension of the inhumanity of Sarajevo's horrific situation.

■"Satya: A Prayer for the Enemy," directed by Ellen Bruno (US). This poetic documentary is a tribute to the Buddhist nuns of Tibet for mounting courageous opposition to Chinese suppression of their religion and culture. Interviews with women who endured appalling ordeals of torture and maltreatment are juxtaposed with moving evocations of the ancient Buddhist tradition.

■"The Imperial's Ism," directed by Alexander Kort, Michael MacIntyre, Shay Nichols, and Chet Fenster (US). Thomasi Macdonald vigorously recites a poem about a notorious explosion and fire in a North Carolina chicken-processing plant, which killed 25 people and injured 53 more. The carnage took place because the plant's doors were locked—or as Macdonald puts it, because "a stolen chicken is counted for more than an endangered human life." Recounting and protesting this tragedy, his words are intercut with documentary shots of the plant and its surrounding community, and accompanied by Todd Bayshore's wailing saxophone. The film is brief, spontaneous, and completely to the point.

Additional items range from "Are They Still Shooting?" by Tomislav Novakovic, a roughhewn but inventive meditation on the war in former Yugoslavia from an American perspective, to "*L'homme sur les quais*" by Raoul Peck, a moody and picturesque French drama billed as the first feature film about Haiti's recent history.

Of special interest is a reprise of the powerfully political "Life on Hold" by Lebanese director Maroun Bagdadi, a film about Middle Eastern terrorism that was shown in the 1992 festival and is being brought back this year as a tribute to Bagdadi after his recent accidental death.

NEW YORK POST, 4/29/94, p. 42, Larry Worth

Geographically speaking, Rome Saigon, Warsaw, Port-au-Prince and Belgrade are as diverse as you can get. What unites them is the constant rattle of gunfire that served (or serves) as a Greek chorus in each city.

The screams of the innocent, the onslaught of totalitarianism and the use of physical and/or psychological torture have become part of each locale's history. Now, as the fifth annual Human Rights Watch International Film Festival addresses, they're also part of cinema's history.

The lineup, debuting tonight at Loews Village VII, is incredibly diverse.

The high point may be the U.S. premiere of Janusz Kijowski's "Warszawa Year 5703," In her best role since "The Marriage of Maria Braun," Hanna Schygulla stars as a middle-aged woman hiding two refugees from Nazi storm troopers.

Almost as powerful is Margarette von Trotta's "The Long Silence." It's a thriller about an Italian judge and his wife, whose lives are ruined by threats of violence.

In view of deposed Haitian President Jean-Bertrand Aristede's attempts to return to power, one of the timeliest offerings is "Man by the Shore."' Under Raoul Peck's flawless direction, the film is a complex reflection on Papa Doc Duvalier's reign of horror.

Documentaries also get their due, best exemplified by the striking "Starting Place." "It takes audiences to Vietnam 25 years after the country was turned into a battlefield.

Among the other must-sees:

■"Betrayal," Radu Mihaileanu's disturbing tale of a Romanian dissident writer who is released from prison in exchange for an agreement to spy on his wife and friends.

■"Shadow Puppets," American Chuck W. Gamble's heart-wrenching, animated take on the brutal oppression of freedom of expression, and the indomitability of the human spirit.

■"Why Have You Left Me?" a remarkable effort by 25-year-old director Oleg Novkovich on his generation's reaction to war.

Aside from its embarrassment of riches, the fest's only real sticking point is an unrelentingly bleak nature. Sure enough, there are no happy endings to be found here. But ignoring such important films—and their messages—seems sadder still.

VILLAGE VOICE, 5/3/94, p. 54, Georgia Brown

Let's go back to *Schindler's List*. In the *New Republic*, Stanley Kauffmann ended his second review of the movie favorably comparing Spielberg's shot of the kid hiding in the privy to the famous German army photo of an older boy, hands raised in surrender, being hustled out of the Warsaw ghetto. Now, Kauffmann opines, Spielberg's child "may join that earlier photo in the world's memory."

The world's memory, if there is such a thing, is glutted with images. I assume the reviewer means *his* memory. We would probably argue, too, that he's not just upholding the single shot (think of a movie still with its crisp focus against the grainy authority of the vintage photo) but that whole mad, movie dash to find a hiding place: The boy looks here, he looks there, every cubby is closed to him, until finally he ducks into the (remarkably clean) privy, claims a remote corner, and huddles quaking in the gray foam. It's a piquant shot. Spielberg has picked the most adorable of munchkin faces. The face is in my mind now, as I imagine it is in yours if you've seen the movie.

Actually, I'd like to get it out of my mind. It has no weight. It's unbearably cute. Whereas the other image—of the boy in the cap who didn't find a hiding place—will never diminish in impact. Its hard to imagine anyone not granting its moral and aesthetic (i.e., emotional) priority. (That the anonymous photographer was probably a Nazi raises provocative questions about the genesis of a great photograph.)

The issue of Holocaust fiction versus Holocaust documentary comes up because the excellent new Human Rights Watch International Film Festival raises it. The first movie screened for the press was a searing Polish documentary on the subject, a film far more wrenching, I think, than *Schindler's List*. Jolanta Dylewska's *Chronicle of the Uprising in the Warsaw Ghetto According to Marek Edelman* uses, almost entirely, archival footage of the ghetto's gradual liquidation. (True to her material, Dylewska didn't go seeking a catchy title.) In the second half of the film, Dylewska introduces Marek Edelman, a Warsaw ghetto survivor, recounting his own experience leading the uprising,

The footage Dylewska uses comes from the anonymous German army films now in Polish archives. The footage here begins in 1940, with the Jews being moved into the ghetto: people carrying bedding, a row of children in single file, each with a chair on his head. It goes up until 1943 and seems to record several evacuations—although no explanatory data is provided. Much of the footage shows orderly crowds being hurried along, people carrying small suitcases; at times we see them being stashed into trucks or trains.

Dylewska has blown up certain areas of the original film to emphasize details—a toddler racing to keep up, the adult hand trying to reach hers, a child's fist going to his eye. We see some terrible things this way. Most effectively, she slows the film at varying rates. Sometimes she repeats sequences. The effect of the manipulation, this slowing into dream time, is to bring subjects into something like eternity and to emphasize their innocence.

An eloquent witness, Edelman provides a matter-of-fact, day-to-day account of the doomed uprising. Again, the emphasis is on particulars and identities. He tells who died and how. (A woman flees with two children. Outside the wall, they're shot. The children die but the mother, who crawls into some bushes, survives—"but she's been mentally unstable since.") Only a handful escaped in the end. The very arbitrariness of survival is continually reinforced: you were in the right place at the right time, but it could just as easily have been the wrong place.

Janusz Kijowski's *Warszawa Year 5703*, also from Poland, is an example of a wrongheaded fiction. (When it comes to the Holocaust, former East Bloc filmmakers have been working in a peculiar artistic vacuum.) Kijowski's very creepy melodrama is based roughly on the same materials as *Chronicle*, the last weeks of the Warsaw ghetto, and, oddly enough, it begins with the issue of photographs.

As the Nazis storm the ghetto (in a sequence that mixes archival footage with re-creations), a Jewish resident with a camera clicks away at his window. A young man, Alek (Lambert Wilson), is entrusted with getting the film out, to show the world what's happening—a purpose that gets entirely lost in what follows: a sex triangle involving Alek, his wife, and an older Aryan woman. (In *Chronicle*, Edelman addresses the subject of love, or sex, among the rebels: It was a matter, he says, of having "someone to put their head on your shoulder, someone to cuddle.")

So, Alek sneaks out through the sewers (making it look easy) and almost immediately starts cuddling, and coupling, with Stephania (Hanna Schygulla), who takes him in. The fly in the ointment is that he's brought along Fryda (Julie Delpy), whom he first presents as his sister but later admits is his wife. The fugitives hide out in Stephania's apartment, which happens to be just across the wall from the ghetto. The infamous carousel barrel organ grinds away. (Edelman: "People were dying here and people were playing there.") Fryda understandably goes bonkers; as for Alek, it's hard to know just what he's thinking. Ditto for the filmmaker.

Coincidentally, still another film in the festival, *Betrayal*—rich and complex fiction by Romanian director Radu Mihaileanu—employs a still from the same footage used in *Chronicle*. (It's the shot of the Nazi officer rudely pushing his whip under an old woman's chin.) This is part of an opening history montage showing the series of betrayals befalling Romania before, during, and since the war.

A poet (played by Dutch actor Johan Leysen, speaking French), is imprisoned in '48 for an article critical of the regime. After 11 years in solitary, he's offered a deal by a sympathetic, and sinister, Securitate inspector: Collaborate and be released. The state will even guarantee publication of his poems. Eventually he agrees, but only to confirm information that the secret service already has. "We already know everything," the man assures him. And it seems they do, with so many informers.

In prison, the poet laments later, lines are clear, "You know who you are, victim or executioner." On the outside, you can be both. Nothing is as it seems. Indeed, the film itself often seems maddenly cryptic. (Westerners might think of a workplace, or family, where one's superiors are pathological and only the compatibly pathological thrive.) Former East bloc residents will recognize the milieu only too well. Milhaileanu himself is an exile who has lived many years in Paris.

Raoul Peck (*Lumumba: Death of a Prophet*) is a Haitian who's spent his adult years in France and Germany. His powerful film, *Man on the Shore*, a relentless portrait of a thug state, played in the main competition at Cannes last year, and I'm not sure why it hasn't opened here in the interim. Maybe it would be too upsetting for Americans, given that we've elected to let Haiti sink.

The story is told through Sarah, a woman we never see, looking back on her childhood 30 years ago when papa Doc and the Tonton Macoutes ruled—a time, one imagines, not so different from now. This coming-of-age-into-terror tale weaves past, present, and future as Sarah the child (played indelibly by young Jennifer Zubar) tries to piece together the horrors she's witnessed in her short life. Peck is an extremely skilled filmmaker and his placid pastel compositions pack a wallop.

Now to that present-day genocide that everyone, while welling up over *Schindler's List*, is quietly evading. Of the festival's films from the former Yugoslavia, only one was available for screening by my deadline, but this one, *Why Have You Left Me*?, is an eye-opener. Astonishingly, it's the Belgrade Academy of Dramatic Arts thesis film of a 25-year-old. His name is Oleg Novkovic and may he find his way safely through the land mines. The film's charismatic male star, I've heard, is now in jail.

In the summer of '91, two friends, Ljuba and Pedja, are drafted and sent to Vukovar where one is shot. The dying Ljuba is taken in by an extended family who huddle catatonically around their bombed-out premises wearing homemade yellow caps (Grandma is still knitting). Soon after, the teenaged daughter, Vera (Milica Mihajlovic), is raped and the rest of the family massacred, their bodies floated down the river. Back in Belgrade on leave, Pedja (Zarco Lausevic) spies the traumatized Vera scrounging, still in her yellow hat, and, much to his Paris-bound girlfriend's dismay, becomes obsessed with helping her. But Vera keeps eluding his grasp.

This is just the beginning. Novkovic stuffs his anecdotal film with a mix of punky new waveish intermissions, Greek choral figures, surreal flourishes, and some closely observed, endearing details. At the same time it's impressively reticent—the words *Croat, Muslim, Bosnia*, never show up in the subtitles, and *Serb* just once, in a World War II song sung by an old woman. *Why Have You Left Me?* reeks of youthful despair, adult guilt, and premonitions of early death.

Each spring, some of the best films of the year play in the Human Rights Watch festival. In this grave year, judging by the films I've seen so far, the quality seems especially high.

Also reviewed in:
NATION, 5/2/94, p. 606, Stuart Klawans

I AM MY OWN WOMAN

A Cinevista release of a Rosa von Praunheim Filmproduktion production in association with Scala Z film GmbH and René Perraudin. *Producer:* Rosa von Praunheim. *Director:* Rosa von Praunheim. *Screenplay (German with English subtitles):* Valentin Passoni and Rosa von Prauheim. *Based on the book by:* Charlotte von Mahlsdorf. *Director of Photography:* Lorenz Haarmann. *Editor:* Mike Shepard. *Music:* Joachim Litty and Cello Familie. *Sound:* Mike Shephard. *Production Designer:* Peter Kothe. *Costumes:* Joachim Voeltzke. *Running time:* 91 minutes. *MPAA Rating:* Not Rated.

CAST: Jens Taschner (Charlotte, age 15-17); Ichgola Androgyn (Charlotte, age 20-40); Charlotte von Mahlsdorf (Herself).

NEW YORK POST, 4/30/94, p. 16, Thelma Adams

From storm troopers to skinheads, "I Am My Own Woman" chronicles five decades of homosexual oppression in Germany.

Rosa von Praunheim's docudrama fixes on the life and times of the transvestite Charlotte von Mahlsdorf, nee Lothar Berfelde. Born in 1928 in the German village from which he took his name, Charlotte/Lothar tells the camera "even as a child. I liked to dust and clean."

It takes a filmmaker as brave as von Praunheim, known as "the bad boy of the German gay scene," to undertake this ambitious biography. But the director of the AIDS comedy "A Virus Has No Morals" has tried here to substitute courage for discipline, brashness for structure, and his sheer artlessness undercuts fascinating material.

In the pervasive voiceover, Charlotte tells the story of his life. It's like sitting next to an old woman on Amtrak—drone, drone, drone. This technique, or lack thereof, blunts the drama of a life that spans *Kristallnacht* and the fall of the Berlin Wall.

Mixing dramatic recreations and documentary footage in a way that fractures the narrative and tries the patience, there is no shortage of striking material. Under the Nazi regime, young Lothar risked death in a camp for wearing dresses and tumbling in haylofts with other boys.

Lothar's storm trooper father tried to beat the young boy's femininity out of him. When Lothar's mother tried to divorce his father, the Nazi threatened to kill the family. Lothar preempted the attack by beating his father to death with a wooden stick.

Von Praunheim presents the murder and its consequences off-camera with Charlotte nattering away on the soundtrack. When we are finally hooked on the dramatic recreations, the real Charlotte steps in to chat with the actors who ask leading questions to hook one segment to the next.

The director leaps over significant relationships and dallies in scenes of explicit sex. Little is shown of Charlotte's 27-year relationship with a dominant male, but the S&M sex play that began their pairing is lovingly re-created, whack by whack.

I would like to see Charlotte's story retold in more competent hands. Still, the transvestite remains a compelling figure in his granny shoes, housedress, and hair scarf—his mother's eldest daughter, as he calls himself "I feel that I'm a female being in a male body," he tells the camera.

Soft-spoken, good-natured and generous, Charlotte has found happiness by being true to himself. He gives the movie its title when he says, "I am my own woman."

NEWSDAY, 4/29/94, Part II/p. B15, John Anderson

As we see in Rosa von Praunheim's "I Am My Own Woman," Charlotte von Mahlsdorf—born Lothar Berfelde in 1928, "a female being in a male body"—has spent her life being true to herself: dressing as a woman, living as a woman, and yet being perfectly comfortable with her male anatomy. And the fact that the world she's lived in—under the threat of Nazis, Stasis and now skinheads—has been so tragically true to its own basic instincts makes her life that much more remarkable and inspiring.

Composed with the same gentle dignity that distinguishes its subject, "I Am My Own Woman" maintains its tone whether von Mahlsdorf is talking about the turn-of-the-century antiques she collects so passionately, or about beating her brutal Nazi father to death in his sleep. Or about her near-execution as an alleged deserter near the end of World War II, or "swishing my way through the last battle of the war in my fitted overcoat," or working on a swine farm, or having kinky photography sessions with a randy aristocrat who employed her as a housemaid.

Always keenly aware of her sexual orientation, von Mahlsdorf is portrayed at various ages by actors—Jens Taschner as a youth, Ichgola Androgyn as a 20-something cruiser—who then assume the role of von Mahlsdorf's interviewer. The sensation is jarring, but unifying in a way, making von Mahlsdorf both a link in the chain of worldwide homosexual independence, and its exemplar.

Having survived while assorted regimes have not, the seemingly mild von Mahlsdorf remains contentious. Feted by the government—she received Germany's Federal Order of Merit Cross in 1992—she also had to divest herself of antique treasures rather than allow bureaucratic interference with her private museum. She's been through it all before, though. Neither Charlotte von Mahlsdorf nor the world has changed very much during the course of this century, which may be a cause for both celebration and tears, but is certainly the stuff of a fascinating film.

VILLAGE VOICE, 5/3/94, p. 58, Randy Gener

She is Mrs. Doubtfire with a lot of fire and little doubt. East German Lothar Berfelde, a/k/a Charlotte von Mahlsdorf, is a transvestite and proud of it. She's not looking for a place at anyone's table—she's not hetero-impaired like Bruce Bauer, and frankly, if anyone offers, she isn't interested. Like the late-1800s *Gründerzeit* bric-a-brac she privately collects and passionately dusts in her own museum, she's been smacked and pawed for decades by a gallery of rogues and brutes (her gun-toting father, the Nazis, the Stasis, and the neo-Nazi skinheads), and she's resisted. In drag. When an East German officer, threatening to strip her of her archival duties, inquires if it's true that she's been seen all dolled up at parties, she replies with matter-of-fact aplomb: "Yes, it is true. I wore a sky-blue dress with edging, a bead necklace, and a gold-blond wig." During an openly persecutory period, going from boy to girl or girl to boy is also a day trip. Open and unapologetic, Charlotte doesn't disguise that she's a man. For in Rosa von Praunheim's *Ich Bin Meine Eigene Frau* (I Am My Own Woman), it is not the trans-gendered soul that is perverse, but the situation in which it lives.

The movie is a lovely hagiography about a man whose wonderful, sissy self remains undamaged and bravely intact. Charlotte serves as a guide through her own life story; Von Praunheim's technique mingles interviews with her and dramatized sequences in which she coaches younger actors playing her younger selves (handsome Ichgola Androgyn and humdinger Jens Taschner). The effect allows Von Praunheim to establish the moving allegory of the Three Ages of Transvestitism, and invoke the iconoclastic charm of androgyny as a playful historical icon. Although Von Praunheim's attempt to seal Charlotte as both simple *Hausfrau* and heroic queen tends to be redundant, the film has an irrepressibly deft touch; there is a comic piquance to Charlotte's idyllic remembrance of a youthful roll in the hay, of her escapades in park toilets in search of light s/m, and even to the revelation that the only time she contemplates suicide is in 1974, when the East German government finally tries to confiscate every furnishing she owns. In the end, she decides to give it all away—the gramophones, 18 pianos, the shellac records, the 10,000 volumes of books—and her refusal to surrender to the maneuvers of a repressive regime beautifully, gracefully links up with Von Praunheim's radical activism. The movie is a young gay man's heartwarming hymn to drag pioneers. It smells like queer spirit.

Also reviewed in:
NEW YORK TIMES, 4/29/94, p. C15, Stephen Holden
VARIETY, 12/7/92, p. 72, Eric Hansen

I DON'T WANT TO TALK ABOUT IT

A Sony Pictures Classics release of an Oscar Kramer/Aura Films S.R.L. coproduction. *Producer:* Oscar Kramer. *Director:* Maria Luisa Bemberg. *Screenplay (Spanish with English subtitles):* Maria Luisa Bemberg and Jorge Goldenberg. *Based on a short story by:* Julio Llinás. *Director of Photography:* Felix Monti. *Editor:* Juan Carlos Macias. *Music:* Nicola Piovani. *Sound:* Carlos Abbate. *Art Director:* Jorge Sarudiansky. *Special Effects:* Tom Cumdom. *Costumes:* Graciela Galán. *Make-up:* Jorge Bruno. *Running time:* 102 minutes. *MPAA Rating:* PG-13.

CAST: Marcello Mastroianni (Ludovico D'Andrea); Luisina Brando (Leonor); Alejandra Podesta (Charlotte); Betiana Blum (Madama); Roberto Carnaghi (Padre Aurelio); Alberto Segado (Dr. Blanes); Jorge Luz (Alcalde); Monica Villa (Señora Zamudio); Juan Manuel Tenuta (Police Chief); Tina Serrano (Widow Schmidt); Veronica Llinás (Myrna); Susana Cortinez (Señora Blanes); Maria Cecilia Miserere (Romilda); Hernán Muñoa (Celestino); Walter Marin (Mojamé); Jorge Ochoa (Señor Peralta); Jean Pierre Reguerraz (Mr. Poussineau); Fito Paez (Musician); Jorge Baza De Candia (Señor Zamudio); Nene Real (Celina); Guillermo Marin (Sarrasani); Marta Lopez Lecube (Gladys); Micaela Rosa (Charlotte as a Child); Miguel Serebrenik (Mojamé as a Child).

FILMS IN REVIEW, 1-2/95, p. 60, Eva Kissin

This small exquisite film was created by a woman who had never made a film until she was 55. It must have been perking on her stove for a long time.

The scene is a small, uptight Argentinian town in the 1930's where things are rarely what they seem. Behind the refined surfaces, the kindly priest is in bed with a Protestant woman and the town brothel thrives on the regular weekly visits of its best local gentlemen.

Leonor, a handsome young widow, has been left with a permanently dwarfed child as a result of her short, unhappy marriage. The horror of anything or anyone different is unacceptable to her, and she handles her sorrow by denying it. She steals out secretly at night to destroy the graveyard monuments of dwarfs lest her daughter come upon them. In her home, she consigns all literature about dwarfs (*Snow White* included) to the fire lest her daughter read about them. Dwarfs do not exist for her, and when her neighbors or the local priest attempt to share her problem, her inevitable reply is, "I don't want to talk about it."

Nevertheless, Leonor does a great deal more than merely deny. Her total capacity for love is focused on the bright, eager-to-please little girl whom she shapes into a well read, multilingual, musical young woman whose charm and intelligence provide a particular attractiveness in spite of her obvious physical liabilities.

When a mysterious Italian charmer, Ludovico, magnificently played by the aging Marcello Mastroianni, arrives in town and becomes involved with the widow and her daughter, relationships change and become increasingly complex. Something has to be talked about now.

The impact of the world on this bizarre situation creates a fascinating tangle with an interesting open-ended denouement about people who want to be different.

However, it is not merely the fairy tale aspect of the story and the remarkable acting of Mastroianni (hurray for older actors!), Luisina Brando as the widow and Alejandra Podesta as her daughter, that create the magic. The substance of the film itself—the Magritte-like lighting, the music (Nicola Piovani) and the female warmth and almost perfumed scent of the brothel—create a sensual experience that only a really good film can supply. The feminine sensibility throughout—the choice of clothing, the color of painted doorways, the little girl dancing before the mirror in her mother's clothes and the bursting quality of the laced uptown do-gooders all supply the somewhat surreal aspect of a South American novel. Only here, where a thousand pages of a Garcia Marquez type of romance can be condensed into a small, deep, super realist film, do we realize that the art of cinema has arrived.

FILM QUARTERLY, Winter 1994-94, p. 52, Karen Jaehne

If Buñuel had been a woman, he might have made *I Don't Want to Talk About It (De eso no se habla)*, but would he have engendered controversy over his feminism? The feminist who did direct it, Argentinian Maria Luisa Bemberg, wears the Buñuel mantle lightly, but has been hit by friendly fire from feminists for her vision of woman as dwarf. Indeed, *I Don't Want to Talk About It* reflects such a complex view of mothers, daughters, freaks, artists, and decadents—without coming to any happy or definitive statement—that we are forced to talk about it and all the things it says we don't want to discuss. In an Age of Political Correctness, Bemberg challenges our beliefs in assimilation, shows us the absurdity of suppressed speech, and rebukes a society in which only men can be tolerated as outsiders. And she takes on freaks. She traps us between denial and voyeurism.

When Bemberg declares that her film must be understood as a fable or fairy tale and in the next breath claims it as her most autobiographical work, you need to know that Bemberg was brought up in a stiflingly proper and wealthy Argentinian family, married, and raised four children before she broke out, divorced, began writing screenplays in 1971, and debuted as a director in 1981 at the age of 56. In 1984, her elegant historical love story, *Camila*, received an Oscar nomination for Best Foreign Film. She was a success by artistic standards, but she had lost the position she once enjoyed in the innermost circle of Argentina's elite, where respectable women were neither workers nor artists. And she is harshly criticized (particularly by the Church) as an artist and frequently ostracized as a mad feminist. "But I don't like talking about it," she finds herself saying, laughing at herself, then explaining, "It's not the interesting part of my life."

By its title alone, *I Don't Want to Talk About It* cleverly forces us out of the denial it proclaims for its subject. It is the story of a widow who will not acknowledge that her only child will never "grow up." Set in a South American town where the locals drift into a kind of collusion with the mother's denial, the film moves through the points-of-view of the three protagonists with subtlety and tolerance of their extreme differences. Carlotta is a dwarf in a society hidebound by normalcy. The telling achondroplastic features of a dwarf do not age in the usual sense; although we watch her "grow up," Carlotta is forever young. The intrinsic danger here is that we, the viewers, continue to see her as a child and commit the same mistake as her loved ones—from whom she must escape in order to enjoy any kind of autonomy.

We enter the fictional San Jose de los Altares (filmed in the historic old city of Colonia on the Uruguayan shore opposite Buenos Aires) on Carlotta's fifth birthday. Her mother, Leonor, is giving her a party. As the camera pans the faces of the other mothers, caricatures in exaggerated 1930s hats and prim expressions, their whispers and averted gazes betray the potential for scandal in a colonial backwater. And when one woman, who is herself the mother of a deaf-mute child, tries to sympathize with Leonor, Leonor distances herself from any such "recognition" of Carlotta's deformation. Although Bemberg utilizes a village priest to his full comic and dramatic potential, she never touches on superstitions that used to see in a deformed child some form of divine retribution on the mother; or an even earlier association of dwarfism with witchcraft and devilry. An amusing social defiance marks Leonor's motherhood: late at night she purges the town of every symbol that might reflect her daughter, destroying a neighbor's garden dwarf and burning children's books about little people.

Leonor perfects her imperfect child in every possible way, giving Carlotta a prodigious education and cultivating her musical and linguistic talents so that she is living proof that Leonor is a perfect mother. The child learns French so well—the very measure of civilization—that she prefers to be called "Charlotte." Voilá, her transformation is complete. She becomes such an exemplary product of bourgeois ideals that her physical otherness seems trivial. By the end of the first act, we are ready to side with Leonor for insisting on her daughter's normalcy.

Charlotte is so accomplished that when her mother arranges for her to perform a piano recital (to the horror of other mothers), Charlotte acquits herself of the task elegantly. But it is here that we see the seeds of defiance. Leonor advises Charlotte to be already seated on the piano bench when the curtain rises. But the child proudly prances on stage, minces as any young girl would, scales the piano bench, and demonstrates that Schumann is impervious to size. She has learned more from her independent-minded mother than Leonor may have intended.

Enter Ludovico D'Andrea, man of the world, an Italian, and an outsider capable of seeing Charlotte as someone who, like himself, exists apart from the crowd. In the scenes of them together, the camera is restless until the inevitable close-up of Charlotte's wide-eyed trust. Ludovico tells her of faraway places and she listens avidly, accepting his every tale and fantasy. Marcello Mastroianni in the role of eligible bachelor appeals to all the women in town (nor can the audience forget Mastroianni's stock-in-trade as cinema's most ambivalent seducer).

Leonor turns to Ludovico when she needs help in getting her daughter a birthday present—a horse. Ludovico brings back a Shetland pony, and Leonor erupts: the mini-horse nearly breaks the taboo of silence. Ludovico apologetically backtracks and gives Charlotte a beautiful palomino. In a world of magical realism, it is this white horse, this Pegasus, that endows sexuality and empowers Charlotte. In many ways, Ludovico plays her liberator, and that he gives her the horse rather than riding in on it himself deftly foreshadows the way she will, in the end, ride off with the circus.

His first sight of the girl training the horse stirs an uncontrollable passion in Ludovico. He attempts to flee her power over him, but some indeterminate number of years later, he returns to ask for her hand in marriage. This request sends her mother, the priest, and the entire town into fits of objection. Charlotte's response, however, has no giddy nervousness about it. In her quiet, self-possessed way, she accepts.

The old mayor, who is to give the girl away, dies in the middle of the marriage ceremony—threatening to foil Leonor's ambitions. But with the help of her shop assistant, she packs the body in ice, so as to keep the death a secret until the next day. There is no obstacle Leonor cannot overcome in order to present her daughter as perfection. (Leonor's power of denial is surpassed by that of the film's publicists, who had no photos made of Alejandra Podesta, who plays Charlotte, lest we learn the "secret" of the movie.) When the musicians announce that it is time for the bride and groom to dance, we cut to Leonor's grim reaction—yet another obstacle for her, and we share her panic. But Mastroianni saves the moment by lifting little Charlotte up to his height as he swirls her away. It is a mystical moment of wedding dress and white sand and blazing light as they leave the wedding guests and embark on the great adventure of marriage. At once romantic and sly, this scene plays out the archetypal happy ending with a sleight of hand learned from Fellini. It's only the end of the second act; could this be love?

The fetishization of the dwarf is an inevitable risk of a picture like this, and Bemherg steers a discreet course around it. She makes it quite clear that Charlotte herself is a sexual creature: the young girl prances before a mirror; we see flirtation in her eyes; the palomino is the symbol of her sexual prowess. Mastroianni's love is the linchpin of the fairy tale that Charlotte is a full, complete woman with a psyche as strong as an Amazon.

Yet we never hear much from the object of desire. Is her silence that of the town, whose speech has been suppressed by Leonor? Or is she keeping the peace until the right moment? Bemberg comments on the girl's passivity by citing the French critic Roland Barthes' observation that "the amorous object never talks." "I thought that was quite interesting," notes Bemberg, "to have the girl like a catalyst to make his story appear. And I gave my character the name of Charlotte, the object of Werther's love in Goethe's *The Sorrows of Young Werther*." Most of Charlotte's dialogue is given over to questions in which she explores others (most deftly when she asks her mother if she's thought of marrying Ludovico herself. Yet the girl's silence is not sadness, nor even, I would argue, resignation. It seems much more the reticence of someone with the faith that freedom is something gained in stages rather than revolutions. Someone like Maria Luisa Bemberg. For women who have lived both kinds of lives, this metaphor is not as offensive as for women born liberated.

I Don't Want to Talk About It is also a film about getting out from under the thumb of a well-intentioned mother in order to claim one's individual identity. A dedication is scrawled across the screen over the opening of the film, declaring its intention: "This tale is dedicated to all people who have the courage to be different in order to be themselves." A physical deformity, however, is not the same as a talent or a gift. It might be flattering to make the parallel between physically challenged people and the artist, and there's no reason any individual dwarf would not be as sensitive or talented as any particular artist, but there is a definite temerity in comparing a physical handicap to a social or psychological condition.

The separate reality of "freaks," known to us previously in Werner Herzog's *Even Dwarfs Start Small* or Todd Browning's *Freaks*, or in the characters played by the actor Michael Dunne, is the source of the discomfort created by the film. Carlotta *is* a dwarf, and moreover, "the end" is not the end of the story. The woman who plays Carlotta, Alejandra Podesta, is not a Meryl Streep with a good accent, but a non-actress who lives and works in Buenos Aires. Her achondroplastic image is on the screen more than half the time, and we have ample opportunity to measure her humanity against her freakiness. And tenderness outdistances any quality that could be exploited by P.T. Barnum.

"I suppose," Bemberg speculates, "if the film had been directed by Buñuel or Fellini, it would probably have been much funnier. And maybe more ferocious. But I never wanted to make fun of her. Art and ethics go hand in hand. It would have been wrong to be cruel with this young girl, who was doing her very best to make her first movie, and in which reality and fiction are so painfully criss-crossed. She finishes at the end of her day and goes back to her poor little house with her lonely mother. And she still is the character, still a little dwarf. I was very maternal with her. I still am."

The final sequence begins with the fictional mother tending her husband's gravestone. As we watch her polish his plaque, we can't help but reflect on how well she has managed her mission to steer her daughter into a moribund society. Leonor's will and power are impressive; but fate is impervious to human design, and in the distance we hear the caterwaul of trumpets and drums. (This inimitable circus sound cannot be heard without thinking of Fellini's *8½*, a daunting comparison to invoke in the final flourishes of a movie.)

Bemberg doesn't even take us inside the circus, a decision that maintains the "silence" imposed by Leonor, who forbids her daughter to attend the circus. At this point it is not only suppression of expression and freedom; it is "structured absence." We are forced to consider what in the circus could change Charlotte: a caged lion? a trapeze artist? a midget act? It is no particular person or thing, of course, but the circus as a concept. This is the place where Leonor would least like to see her daughter, because any possible comparison with a freak of nature would be in bad taste. A "mother's instinct," as she calls it, warns her of an unknown hand that could claim an unknown part of her daughter.

The shocking loss of a closely watched maiden is the driving mechanism of Demeter and Persephone, Madame de Volange and Cecile (*Les Liaisons Dangereuses*), Eliane and Camille (*Indochine*), or Cocteau's *Orpheus*. The mythic tenor of the film's final sequence is reinforced by a narrator describing the marriage of Ludovico and Charlotte: "Time went by slowly, like that which is forever." When Charlotte slips from bed and we see her in the darkness of the circus grounds, moving stealthily but surely among the tents, wagons, and cages, there is no doubt she is at home. Another achondroplastic face is seen dimly in the half-light; although it is not clearly a dwarf, it smiles and welcomes her.

"Running away with the circus" is not just the classic escape; the circus is for Charlotte a place where—whatever she is, she is the norm. The malformations of the circus can be a mirror of our "secret self," as Fellini intended in his pageantry of ever-present freaks. Bemberg wisely refrains from speculating on the potential lurch into melodrama and only shows Charlotte riding away on her white horse, wearing a crown. The paradox is that the less said, the more metaphoric and less pathetic is the creature.

General Tom Thumb, who was a Connecticut Yankee put on display in the English court of Victoria and Albert, wrote, "God has given me a small body, but I believe He has not contracted my heart, nor brain, nor soul ..." Given the rich tradition of little people, what's not to talk about? Speech insists on Charlotte's reality; silence is the secret to the poetry of a Charlotte. Bemberg has made a film that makes us choose.

LOS ANGELES TIMES, 10/14/94, Calendar/p. 8, Kevin Thomas

Argentine filmmaker Maria Luisa Bemberg's "I Don't Want to Talk About It," a fable of unexpected love and its equally unpredictable consequences, unfolds with the subtlety and irony of an Isak Dinesen tale. A beautiful, leisurely period piece set in a small South American town in the '30s, it begins as a droll, engrossing story that builds to a stunning, utterly surprising climax that adds yet another layer of meanings to an already illuminating revelation of character.

In an idyllic, ancient town, Leonor (Luisina Brando) is the community's most dominant personality; a beautiful, well-off widow who's confronted with the truth that her daughter will be a dwarf.

Once she has worked out her rage and pain, she becomes determined that her Charlotte (Alejandra Podesta) will be happy and accomplished. Bemberg and her co-writer Jorge Goldenberg, in adapting a short story by Julio Llinas, find considerable humor in the sheer imperiousness Leonor exerts over everyone to ensure that Charlotte's diminutive size is never mentioned in her daughter's presence.

By the time Marcello Mastroianni's Ludovico, an elegant, slightly mysterious, endlessly charming man of the world arrives in the community, Charlotte is 15 and an outstanding scholar and a skilled pianist. The formidable Leonor warms enough to Ludovico to ask him the favor of selecting a horse for her daughter's birthday. All it takes is a glimpse of Charlotte, who is already the only educated person with whom Ludovico can converse, riding her new horse to make Ludovico feel transfixed by love.

Bemberg brings to the working out of this astonishing development the same detached humor and compassion with which she views Leonor's zealously protective mother, but she has much more in mind than a tale of the transforming power of love. She goes on to suggest that love cannot be enough if there's a failure to acknowledge that which makes an individual different from others.

It is impossible to imagine anyone but Mastroianni, with his legendary savoir-faire, in the role of Ludovico. Even as he grows older, Mastroianni remains the eternal Casanova/Don Juan-like object of desire; in playing Ludovico, he reminds us that it rarely occurs to us to consider what a lady-killer may really need or be attracted to in a woman. Brando brings a moving heroic, even noble, quality to the frequently unintentionally humorous yet finally tragic Leonor. From start to finish Podesta's Charlotte rightly remains a smiling enigma.

When Maria Luisa Bemberg dedicates "this tale to all people who have the courage to be different in order to be themselves," she in effect is speaking more of herself than anyone in her film. At 56 in 1981, Bemberg made her directorial debut and accrued international acclaim with the romantic tragedy "Camila" in 1984. With "I Don't Want to Talk About It" and the superb but unreleased "I, the Worst of All," starring Assumpta Serna as a brilliant 16th-Century Mexican nun, Bemberg has come fully into her own as a screen artist.

NEW YORK POST, 9/30/94, p. 43, Larry Worth

Legendary directors Federico Fellini and Luis Bunuel have gone to their greater rewards. But you'd swear one of them had returned to lens the deliciously offbeat "I Don't Want to Talk About It," which serves as an homage to them both.

Surreal imagery that blends the beautiful and the grotesque suffuses the screen in this fractured fairy tale about a handsome older man's obsession with a mesmerizing dwarf.

But director/co-writer Maria Luisa Bemberg never exploits the situation. Instead, she gently moves from dark comedy to romance to the bittersweet, leaving viewers with a liberating commentary on the need to be true to oneself.

In addition, Bemberg has given superstar Marcello Mastroiani his best role in years as a sentient man of letters who defies the world to be with the woman he loves. Even if she's the size of a yardstick.

But height isn't the biggest hurdle. Not compared to the dwarfs towering mother, who refuses to acknowledge—or let anyone speak of—her daughters stature. That extends to destroying every plaster gnome within the towns boundaries and burning copies of "Snow White" and "Gullivers Travels."

As played by the luminous Luisina Brando, she may be a regimental horror hut never a monster. Strutting down the street in her stiletto heels, Brando's defiant glare would make Torquemada flinch. Yet, her strength lies in showing the pain underneath.

She's matched only by the exquisite Mastroianni, who brings grace, charm and infinite sadness to his confused professor. The emotional fireworks in his world-weary eyes, balanced with an adroit flair for comic nuance, is the stuff of Academy Awards.

And comprising the isosceles triangle's third side, Alejandra Podesta's dwarf is positively incandescent. It's a lovely, lovingly understated performance.

Still, Bemberg comes off as the star. Her self-assured direction is sheer magic: at once delicate and hard-edged, straightforward and complex, enchanting and disturbing. But what's not conflicted is the end result: "I Don't Want to Talk About It" is one of 1994's best.

NEWSDAY, 9/30/94, Part II/p. B7, Gene Seymour

It's easy for filmgoers to take Marcello Mastroianni for granted the way New Yorkers are casual about the Brooklyn Bridge. We assume such landmarks will always be around, so it isn't necessary to appreciate the subtle, wondrous ways they fit into the landscape.

Still, after 30 years and more than 150 films, Mastroianni does the most amazing things with seeming effortlessness. When you see Mastroianni in "I Don't Want to Talk About It" gazing at the unlikely object of his character's long-dormant passion, he makes his face into a relief map of conflicting emotions: terror, longing, grief, ecstasy. It's a pleasure to watch such a master film actor playing his face within the frame so well.

Like Mastroianni's performance, "I Don't Want to Talk About It" is a mix of subtle pleasures. Adapted from a short story by Jorge Goldenberg, the movie is a dreamlike saga conceived with warm cunning and loving austerity by Argentine director Maria Luisa Bemberg.

Mastroianni portrays the enigmatic Ludovico D'Andrea, a sophisticate who lives with elegant indolence in a small Argentine town. One of his most prominent neighbors is a wealthy widow named Leonor (Luisina Brando), who has never been able to accept the fact that her daughter Charlotte (Alejandra Podesta) is a dwarf. So intent is she on reconfiguring reality that she destroys anything within miles that alludes to small people, going so far as to burn copies of "Gulliver's Travels" and "Snow White and the Seven Dwarfs."

D'Andrea becomes friendly with Leonor and Charlotte, regaling them with stories of intrigue and romance in faraway places. When Charlotte turns 15, he gives her a white stallion for her birthday. Upon seeing her ride the horse, D'Andrea feels an overpowering love for the young girl, a development which stuns her mother and baffles the rest of the town. Nevertheless, they marry.

Imagine what Federico Fellini, Mastroianni's late mentor, would have done with this situation. Then imagine the opposite. That's how Bemberg guides this story. In the process, she navigates it to a middle range between gentle humor and soft-edged poignancy. She also draws an affecting performance from the neophyte Podesta and a compelling one from Brando, whose barely-contained passion works as a perfect counterpoint to Mastroianni's slow-melting containment.

Bemberg's austere, polished style proves a perfect fit for the story. The wedding sequence, especially the part where the newlyweds dance, is touching and sweet. But if Bemberg's intention was to show the triumph of the individuals who, in her words, "have the courage to be different," why couldn't she have had D'Andrea and Charlotte kiss as lovers do?

But that's a minor quibble. True, "I Don't Want to Talk About It" could have taken a few more chances with its material. Upon reflection, though, you wonder what that would have done to its delicate, enchanting aura.

SIGHT AND SOUND, 9/94, p. 39, Lizzie Francke

In a small town, Leonor, a widow runs a store and looks after her young daughter Charlotte. She employs Mojame, a young orphan. On Charlotte's second birthday, Leonor comes to terms with the fact that her daughter's growth will be restricted. Consequently she obliterates every reference to 'dwarfs' and small people, even burning fairy tales. Meanwhile Charlotte grows up to be an elegant and intelligent young woman. The arrival in town of the mysterious Ludovico D'Andrea arouses Leonor's interest. He becomes a regular guest both at Leonor's tea parties and at the local brothel. Plans are made for a fund-raising concert and Leonor suggests that Charlotte give a piano recital. Later she asks D'Andrea to find a horse for her daughter and is upset when he turns up with a Shetland pony. He returns with a horse and is mesmerized by the sight of Charlotte riding it.

Visiting the brothel that night, D'Andrea gets into an argument with the local doctor. They duel, and D'Andrea is injured. He goes away for a few months to recuperate, and on returning invites Leonor out. She believes that he will propose to her; but he asks to marry her daughter. Though shocked, Leonor agrees; D'Andrea proposes to Charlotte and she accepts.

The wedding goes ahead, although the mayor dies in the middle of the ceremony. Later, D'Andrea is made mayor and enjoys married life with Charlotte. One night, however, the circus comes to town. Leonor is horrified and begs D'Andrea to ban it. He refuses, but concedes to her demand that Charlotte should not be allowed to go. That night a storm brews. D'Andrea releases Charlotte's horse from the stable. Later, Charlotte steals away and visits the circus. The following day the circus leaves town with Charlotte joining them. Devastated, Leonor shuts herself away, while D'Andrea disappears. Some believe that he drowned, while there are stories of him being seen prowling around the circuses in Hamburg.

For her sixth feature, Argentinian director Maria Luisa Bemberg has turned away from the concerns with her country, its history and the place of women within it that have marked her previous films. In *We Don't Want to Talk About It*, there is no particular sense of time or place. The costumes and cars are of the 30s, but such period details do not seem to carry any great weight. They may be there to allude to a particularly classic and decorative moment in cinema history, or to the time of Bemberg's own childhood. Meanwhile the small, isolated port town in which the story is set could be on the out-reaches of Never-Never Land. It's an appropriate setting for a tragi-comic fable which gently lampoons Leonor's *petit bourgeois* values but more significantly touches on the universal and timeless theme of parent-child relationships.

Leonor may burn such books as *Tom Thumb, Gulliver's Travels* and *Snow White and the Seven Dwarfs*, but Bemberg creates an uneasy fairy tale of her own. Leonor and Charlotte are the focus of the narrative, but their predicament is fleetingly echoed in the relationship between one of Leonor's friends and her deaf and dumb daughter, and also between the decrepit Mayor and the son who has to translate his father's mumblings. The other child that is important to the story is Mojame, the young lad whom Leonor employs to work at her store. An orphan cut off from his background, he has no parents to cast a protective shadow over his life. One character suggests that he might be of Arabic descent, that an all-revealing 'd' has been lopped off from the end of his name. Indeed, the end of the film seems to confirm this, when the story's occasional narrator announces his name as Mohammed Ben Ali. One can only presume that Mojame has finally made claim to his origins, accepted who he is. In this respect, Bemberg treats the familial ties with a certain ambiguity. For Mojame, his absent family becomes his fortunate destiny.

Of course, Mojame is also 'different' from the community around him, and the notion of accepting one's difference is at the heart of the film. Charlotte's physical 'deviation' is that which is not talked about as Leonor represses the truth. On one level the story provides a critique of a 'politically correct' desire to banish certain images rather than open them up for understanding. Certainly the bookburning scene has a particularly eerie resonance—signifyingthe triumph of the literal over a symbolic and more imaginative interpretation of myths and fairy-tales. Certainly Bemberg would like the audience to embrace the romantic sensibility. The dashing D'Andrea (Marcello Mastroianni continues to work his particular charm) is an unreliable fabulist who accepts Charlotte for what she is. Yet, once wedded to her, he becomes subsumed to convention; their married live is lifeless. As Charlotte runs away with the glittering circus, fantasy appears to triumph, as the repressed returns with a vengeance. Meanwhile Leonor is left bereft in a cold, dark cell—punishment meted out to the mother who attempts to exercise some influence over her child even in her adult years.

In this respect, Charlotte's diminutive size takes on a symbolic meaning within the film. Leonor would prefer her daughter to be her little girl for the rest of her life. In one scene Leonor spies the adolescent Charlotte dressed up as Carmen and admiring herself in front of the mirror. It is a sight that patently disturbs the mother, who goes to her room and starts screaming. But Leonor's fears that her daughter will usurp her place are confirmed when D'Andrea confesses to her his love for Charlotte. It is a wryly observed moment as Leonor and D'Andrea talk at cross purposes, with her believing he is about to propose to her. The fact that Bemberg also wants the audience to believe that this is about to be the case suggests that Leonor is a figure for whom one should have a degree of sympathy rather than mocking. If her attempts to remove every reference to dwarfs and midgets seem a little extreme—she steals into a neighbour's garden at midnight to knock down some gnomes, and later removes the marzipan bridal figures from the wedding cake and munches them in one gulp—she believes that she has the best intentions. Luisina Brando portrays Leonor as a woman with a great many foibles, but at least with some heart. As she walls herself at the end of the tale, looking as grey as her stone house, there is a sense of great pity for the spellbound woman who could not let the magic of change into her life.

TIME, 10/10/94, p. 83, Richard Corliss

Perhaps we are all blind to the limitations of those we love. Dona Leonor (Luisina Brando), a proud widow in a South American town in the '30s, certainly loves her daughter Charlotte (Alejandra Podesta). She is beguiled by Charlotte's grace, her easy imperiousness, her ease with languages, her virtuosity at the piano. And she refuses to accept what is evident to all: that Charlotte, now on the cusp of womanhood, is a dwarf. The townspeople pretend to ignore it. But one fellow, the aging stranger Ludovico D'Andrea (Marcello Mastroianni), sees Charlotte's disability as a sweet eccentricity, like a birthmark or an overbite. Ludovico has been courting Dona Leonor in his fashion, and someday he will be a doting stepfather to the girl. He will propose, won't he? Of course he will ...

The first thing to note about *I Don't Want to Talk About It*, Maria Luisa Bemberg's Argentine film (which she and screenwriter Jorge Goldenberg based on a short story by Julio Llinas) is that this is no freak show. It is a poignant, often funny fable, unfolding like a cautionary bedtime tale. It skips delicately among the ruins of passion, obsession and propriety. As in the novel and movie *Like Water for Chocolate*, family matters are treated in a mode balanced between magic realism and tragic surrealism.

The superb cast is led by Mastroianni, whose world-weary charisma so comfortably bears every man's crimes and charms. But finally it is the film's images that seize the memory. You won't soon forget the bleached radiance of a seaside wedding reception, the shadows caressing Dona Leonor on her midnight raid to smash dwarf statues on a nearby lawn, the face of a girl who wonders if she is the pawn of a lady's possessiveness or the beneficiary of a gentleman's genial lust.

VILLAGE VOICE, 10/11/94, p. 66, Georgia Brown

It's hard to know whether to be delicate or clinical here. I really don't want to talk about *I Don't Wont to Talk About It*. (The English title has you singing along with Rod Stewart. The original, *De Eso No Se Habla*, translates more ominously, "Of this one doesn't speak.") I could say that this film by Maria Luisa Bemberg (director of *Camila, Miss Mary*, and *I, the Worst of All*) is about the human ability to create a force field of fog around a fact. Here fact is a 15-year-old dwarf, and pathos, or is it horror, makes us dumb, and dumbness, complicity in silence, can translate as another form of cruelty, I could quote Eliot: "Human kind cannot bear very much reality."

Every bit aware of the subject's intricate nature, Maria Luisa Bemberg has fashioned her story—set in an unnamed Latin American town that looks like Bemberg's native Argentina—so it can be read three ways, as a mother's story, a lover's story, or, only at the very end, as the child's story. The point of the structure perhaps is that viewers can take their choice or be led, unsuspectingly, from one to the next.

So we begin with the mother and her recognition around the time of her daughter Charlotte's second birthday—"the apple of her eye" is a dwarf. Twisting in torment, the widow Leonor (Luisina Brando) sets out in the middle of the night to smash several kitschy ceramic dwarves that guard the home of a German couple. Then she buries the fragments in a pit—a sign to the town that she won't tolerate "notice" of her daughter's condition. (At the birthday party earlier, Leonor curtly rejected overtures—with intimations that they should be soulmates—from the chipper mother of a deaf child.) Now we watch as copies of *Snow White, Gulliver's Travels*, and *Tom Thumb* are thrown into the fire. There is no censor like a protective parent. Protective of whom, is the question.

Years pass. In her mid-teens, Charlotte (Alejandra Podesta), classically educated by a tutor, has quiet dignity, a sweet disposition, and curiosity about faraway lands. At a piano recital, her mother has ordered Charlotte to stay seated at the instrument, but she insists on standing to take her bow. The mortified mother is ever on the alert to breaches in her elaborate fortress of reticence. She stalks a narrow precipice.

The movie has the crispness, and logic of a fable or fairy tale; it's told with little embellishment, and occasionally through a voiceover (we discover the narrator's identity only at the end). Although the subject has vast psychological implications, characters are treated less as rounded beings than as embodiments of particular passions. Of the three central characters, the one we know least is Charlotte. For most of the movie we observe her from outside, watching the effect she has on others. We see her poise, never her pain.

After the mother's story comes the lover's. An older man in town, a rich, mysterious Italian, Ludovico D'Andrea (Marcello Mastroianni), falls in love with Charlotte the first time he sees her riding her white horse. Until then, let's say, he has "belittled" her. At first, the perversity of his passion shocks him—not the least because he has already been many places and seen many strange things—and he tries to evade it, even to the point of trying to get himself killed. Finally, he succumbs and the two are married. (Who but Mastroianni could make this man so credible?) D'Andrea's monumental self-possession makes everyone around the pair seem stunted, stupid, and provincial.

If the story ended here, it would be a charming, rather quaint curiosity. But another ending, almost a coda really, makes the film unforgettable. Bemberg—who raised four children before divorcing and becoming a filmmaker in her fifties—takes us out of the "happy ending" of marriage and into the wilder hills of self-definition. This end is risky and not politically correct, and whether it succeeds in the immediate experience or in the memory, I'm not sure.

But for a few moments, thanks to a point-of-view camera, Charlotte becomes a subject in her own right. She observes beasts—an elephant, a lion—dreaming of the faraway places they came from. This dream of a stranger reality, we realize, has always beguiled her, and at last we comprehend why and what she'll do next.

Also reviewed in:
CHICAGO TRIBUNE, 11/4/94, Friday/p. K, Michael Wilmington
NEW YORK TIMES, 9/30/94, p. C12, Janet Maslin
VARIETY, 3/21-27/94, p. 60, David Stratton
WASHINGTON POST, 10/21/94, p. C7, Hal Hinson

I LIKE IT LIKE THAT

A Columbia Pictures release of a Think Again production. *Executive Producer:* Wendy Finerman. *Producer:* Ann Carli and Lane Janger. *Director:* Darnell Martin. *Screenplay:* Darnell Martin. *Director of Photography:* Alexander Gruszynski. *Editor:* Peter C. Frank.

Music: Sergio George. *Music Editor:* Nicholas Myers. *Sound:* Rosa Howell-Thornhill. *Sound Editor:* Wendy Hedin. *Casting:* Meg Simon. *Production Designer:* Scott Chambliss. *Art Director:* Teresa Carriker-Thayer. *Set Decorator:* Susie Goulder. *Set Dresser:* Jerry Pineo, Doug Fecht and Willie Roache Greco. *Costumes:* Sandra Hernandez. *Make-up:* Joseph Cuervo. *Stunt Coordinator:* Manny Siverio. *Running time:* 94 minutes. *MPAA Rating:* R.

CAST: Lauren Vélez (Lisette Linares); Jon Seda (Chino Linares); Tomas Melly (Li'l Chino Linares); Desiree Casado (Minnie Linares); Isiah Garcia (Pee Wee Linares); Jesse Borrego (Alexis); Lisa Vidal (Magdalena Soto); Griffin Dunne (Stephen Price); Rita Moreno (Rosaria Linares); Vincent Laresca (Angel); E.O. Nolasco (Tito); Sammy Melandez (Victor); Jose Soto (Chris); Gloria Irizarry (Mrs. Gonzalez); Emilio Del Pozo (Mr. Soto); Donald Jackson (Jack); Gary Perez (Father Jaime); Scott Jarred Cohen (Ritchie Soto); Martha Speakes (Hefty Woman); Marina Durell (Cookie); Lou Ferguson (Joe); Juan Cruz (David); Michael McKinney (Tour); Casey E. Rodriguez (Freddy); Joe Quintero (Pawnbroker); Daphne Rubin-Vega (Modeling School Director); Tookie A. Smith (Val); Fat Joe Da Gangsta (Biker Inmate); Luis A. Marrero (Tony Mendez); Freddy Correa (Ricky Mendez); Jerry Rivera (Pablo Herrera); Billy Lux (Photographer); Larry Attile (Dispatcher); Marta Vidal (Santera).

FILMS IN REVIEW, 11-12/94, p. 59, Maria Garcia

I Like It Like That represents the first effort of filmmaker Darnell Martin, touted by Columbia as the first African-American woman to "make a major studio movie." While one wishes such tokenism was a thing of the past, it isn't, so Martin's achievement is something to celebrate. However, the writer/director has more guts than experience, and while her film is spirited and authentic, it's short on dramatic structure.

I Like It Like That is a woman's plea for understanding and acceptance in a cultural and socio-economic milieu that is both sexist and racist. Martin's hero is Lisette (Lauren Vélez), a mixed race Latino/African-American married to a Latino man (Jon Seda). They live in the Bronx neighborhood where Martin grew up. Tired of living on the edge, on Chino's salary as a bicycle messenger, Lisette sets out to find a job and an identity. In the process, she confronts all the dilemmas of a working mother, and many of the barriers faced by poor working class women of color.

Martin's dialogue is well-written—it captures the patios of Bronx English—but her screenplay has no emotional arc which would allow the viewer to establish intimacy with the characters. The film's pivotal incident, Chino's attempt to steal a stereo for Lisette, and his subsequent incarceration, is handled in three or four anticlimactic shots, less time than it takes the reader to complete this sentence. Chino's incarceration is significant because it secures Lisette's determination to establish financial independence. But the incident comes so early in the film, and it happens so quickly, it's difficult for the viewer to perceive the change in Lisette.

Martin maintains some directorial control though most of the first half of the film, but loses it in the second half, which is composed of dramatic subplots that detract from rather than enhance our involvement with the main characters. In one sequence, Chino realizes that his anger with Lisette is affecting his relationship with his children. "C" (Tomas "Tommy" Melly), their eldest child, refuses to dress for school, and Chino pushes him out into the hall naked. Our empathy is naturally with the child, when it should be with Chino, who is in the throes of a significant revelation which will make him a better father and a more loving husband.

Like many first efforts that are also autobiographical, Martin's film encompasses too much and achieves less than it should. Although the main characters and the setting of *I Like It Like That* appear to be unlike those of other Hollywood films, the director relies on some of the same racial and gender stereotypes perpetuated by Hollywood. Alexis (Jesse Borrego), Lisette's "sister," is the stereotypical transvestite who desperately craves acceptance and a baby. Rosaria (Rita Moreno), Lisette's angry mother-in-law, is a gender stereotype that someone should declare extinct, especially a woman filmmaker. Magdalena (Lisa Vidal), the neighborhood's beautiful woman of easy virtue, is also sadly discarded as a depraved and jealous witch.

Lisette seems, at first, to have possibilities, but when we realize she aspires to every middle class notion of success and femininity, it's tough to distinguish between her and any other woman in the same situation. If that's Martin's intention, to have us perceive her heroine as we would a white woman in a Hollywood movie, one wonders why she bothered making a film with a black heroine. If Martin wished to portray a powerful woman of color on the path toward self-actualization, we need to experience the heroine's *internal* struggle—the one that would distinguish her—not just her difficulties in overcoming social or class barriers.

Almost all of the actors in *I Like It Like That* are excellent, a quality which elevates an otherwise unexceptional film. The one extraordinary performance comes from Melly, a 10-year-old with no previous acting experience, who nearly snatches the movie away from the main characters. His eyes possess the same sensuality and expressiveness that we find in Ben Kingsley's or Omar Sharif's. It is in Melly's haunting face that we sense the pain and the heroic striving of the people who inhabit the mean streets of Martin's birthplace.

LOS ANGELES TIMES, 10/14/94, Calendar/p. 4, Kenneth Turan

Debut films, and debut directors, tend to arrive and fade away with a depressing frequency, but "I Like It Like That" and writer-director Darnell Martin are going to be around for a while.

Lively, assured and practically vibrating with color and excitement, "I Like It Like That" marks the emergence of a passionate new film voice. Though it is rough around the edges and overreaches at times, it has the great benefit of a filmmaker intimately connected to her material who knows how to convey its essence to an audience.

Set in the Bronx neighborhood where Martin herself grew up, "I Like It Like That" is a gritty Cinderella story that moves easily from comedy to romance to unblinking reality without compromising its integrity. Touted by Columbia as the first African American woman to make a major studio movie, Martin has bitten off a great deal gracefully touching on the pressures poverty and misfortune put on parents and children, husbands and wives, yet she handles it with humor as well as compassion, heart as well as soul.

Most of all, "I Like It Like That" is the story of Lisette Linares and her fight to he both self-reliant and in love, a life and mother as well as a woman with a business plan, a fight to be, most difficult of all, simply herself.

Conveyed with striking confidence and sass by Lauren Velez in her feature debut, Lisette's plight as a person with an independent spirit caught in a culture that does not necessarily value what is obviously the situation writer-director Martin is most invested in.

But Martin (like her character, the child of a mixed marriage) also has such an affinity for the Latino culture the story is awash in that this slice of city life seems to erupt on screen with a special vibrancy and volatility.

For openers, the film's gaudy look, its meticulous eye for exactly the kind of streets and apartments its people inhabit, is directly on target. The same is true for Martin's take on her characters' psychological texture, their thoughts on the vagaries of love and marriage, respect and fidelity.

Best of all is Martin's vivid ear for street language. Unlike dialogue in films like "Fresh," which pretend to realism but feel false, "Like" is bracingly authentic, brimming with juicy, profane talk that combines arch put-downs ("Lisette, why do you think my last name is 'lend me'"?) with a saucy sexual frankness, "Like It's" opening scene is a case in point. It has Lisette in bed with her husband, Chino (Jon Seda), but the moment is not exactly romantic. The macho Chino is so intent on extending his personal record for sexual endurance that the entire neighborhood is in an uproar, from the broom-wielding Mrs. Gonzalez downstairs to a raucous crowd on the stoop to the couple's three ever-rambunctious children.

Even at its best, Lisette's life is chaotic. Not only does she have this immediate family to deal with, but fussy mother-in-law (Rita Moreno, a transvestite brother (an effective Jesse Borrego) who owns the local *botanica*, and neighborhood hot-number Magdalena (Lisa Vidal), who has an out-of-wedlock child and a serious eye for Chino. No wonder Lisette often flees to the bathroom for stolen moments of glorious solitude.

Yet despite all these obstacles to their happiness, Lisette and Chino, who has pictures of his children tattooed on his arm, have managed to stay married and in love for 10 years. His job as a bicycle messenger supports the family, and though outsiders are dubious, Lisette insists that "what Chino and I got is spiritual."

Then a sudden blackout (the film's original title) and some subsequent looting changes everything. Chino finds himself in the Bronx House of Detention, his $1,500 bail looming impossibly large, and Lisette becomes unexpectedly responsible for supporting her family, keeping her oldest boy (Tomas Melly) from an infatuation with crime and trying to get her husband out of jail.

Out of this crisis, however, Lisette sees a glimmer of opportunity. A chance encounter leads her to slightly obnoxious record producer Stephen Price (Griffin Dunne) who wants to sign Latino acts but knows nothing from the culture. Can Lissette's hustle and street smarts lead her at last to a cubicle to call her own, or will Chino's die-hard machismo and the machinations of neighborhood busybodies be too much for even her to handle?

As even this skeletal outline indicates, "I Like It Like That" has a crisis-a-minute feel to it that can be tiring, as can the realistically cacophonous quality of its dialogue. But is one film whose minor missteps are easy to forgive, for though its situations may get out of hand, the feelings behind them are always real. With strong and vivid acting from all the principals, including little Tomas Melly, an orphan discovered at a public audition, I Like It Like That" ends up as savvy as its writer-director, which is good news indeed.

NEW YORK, 10/31/94, p. 96, David Denby

Chino (Jon Seda), the young and ripely attractive working-class Puerto Rican husband in *I Like It Like That*, is seen in a way that's startlingly new. I don't favor gender explanations for quality in the arts, but surely part of the reason for the freshness of the portrait is that Chino's creator, writer-director Darnell Martin, is a woman. Making her first film, Martin charges into the sexual and romantic heart of a penny-pinched Bronx marriage on the verge of falling apart. Chino's wife, Lisette Linares (Lauren Veléz), is besieged by noise and clamor—by the children, the malicious "friends" who live nearby, the downstairs neighbor who thumps with her mop against the ceiling. Lisette hides in the bathroom, where she escapes not into silence but into greater clamor: She turns on the radio and dances away her anguish. Chino is her chief obsession and trouble, and Darnell Martin (working with cinematographer Alexander Gruszynski) photographs Seda's Chino for his dark, liquid eyes and handsome flesh—and also for his infantile selfishness and showing off. Macho has rarely appeared so sensually appealing and so exasperating at the same time.

This is a vibrantly entertaining debut film. Darnell Martin's hammering, brightly colored style has been compared to Spike Lee's, but Martin may already possess the innate emotional coherence that has eluded Lee, whose films whirl about brilliantly without any center. No doubt about it: *I Like It Like That* makes more noise than the Seventh Avenue express. Martin has conceived the material in broad, popular terms as slam-bang marital comedy and feminist drama, with everyone shouting and carrying on at once. Even if a scene starts quietly, it explodes sooner or later, with profanities and a lot of other things flying around the room or the street. Some of the anger wore me down, but I never for a second doubted that it was genuine. And for all the noise, *I Like It Like That* is a sweet-natured and true-hearted representation of love and family life, coarse in speech but never in feeling. This woman can direct: The pumped-up volume of the movie shouldn't prevent us from noticing the beauty of the camera movements and the way the blended colors inside the couple's shabby apartment soften the many furious arguments. Set in squalor, the movie is still great to look at.

Lauren Vélez, new to me, is a sensational presence. A beautiful woman with bow lips and luscious skin, she slams around the room in a rage—a domestic Tina Turner—and then suddenly goes slack, her features swollen with grief. The talent is busting out of her Lisette. Trapped by her pretty but feckless husband, her misbehaving kids, and a variety of neighborhood layabouts—female as well as male—who all have vested interests in failure, she runs downtown and hustles her way into a job at a recording company. She reinvents herself and, of course, almost loses her husband as a reward. Will Lisette and Chino stay together or not? The issue hangs in the balance, and we root for them because they're a good match, hot-tempered, with matching eyes and lips. They seem destined for each other, like a couple in a fairy tale.

NEW YORK POST, 10/14/94, p. 47, Thelma Adams

With "I Like It Like That," Darnell Martin makes the most exciting directorial debut of 1994. The Bronx tale about a mother of three who takes control of her life is confident, funny, emotionally direct, character-driven, energetic and juicy.

Martin, who wrote the script, is the first African-American woman to direct a major studio feature (Columbia Pictures picked up the tab).

If that seems to make this a "should-see" movie, forget about it. Who needs tokenism? This is a must-see for the picture that landed on the screen, not the back story about how it arrived.

Unconventional beauty Lauren Velez plays the vivacious, overwhelmed Lisette Linares. It's summer. Life in her Bronx box seems as suffocating and deadly as the still hot air.

When the movie opens Lisette's husband Chino (Jon Seda) is making love with his wife. Their three kids bang at the door. The downstairs neighbor thumps on her ceiling with a broom. Chino's curvaceous girlfriend Magdalena (Lisa Vidal) steams on the street below.

Lisette's world has become too loud, and her voice too small. There's no privacy. The bathroom is her only refuge.

Everything changes one night when Chino takes advantage of a black-out, steals a stereo Lisette wants, and gets caught red-handed.

With Chino in jail, Lisette has a chance to change her life. Unskilled and cash-poor, she miraculously lands a job as an assistant to a Latino record label weasel (Griffin Dunne). Her husband, the provider, would rather she go on welfare than work.

While keeping the plot bouncing along in unexpected and comic directions, Martin deftly sets up a mesh of conflicts that explore class and color tensions, machismo and homophobia. But the tail never wags the dog, the issues she explores are always rooted in the characters.

The director's secret weapon is empathy. Alexis is a woman trapped in a man's body, a soul with faith in family values whose own parents have violently rejected him, Chino's mother is a hardass, but the death of her other son, a cop, in the line of duty, explains why she tries so desperately to control her remaining son's life.

The sole weak link is the Griffin Dunne record exec. Unlike the others he's a shallow creation lacking his own history, a character merely in service of the plot.

But that's a minor lapse in a major movie. "I Like It Like That" is that rare laugh 'til you cry, cry 'til you laugh experience that will have you leaving the theater uplifted and satisfied.

NEWSDAY, 10/14/94, Part II/p. B2, John Anderson

In addition to the energy, intelligence and hormones of Darnell Martin's "I Like It Like That," there's a concrete sense of place. The Bronx of her film, specifically 167th Street and Findlay Avenue, is not some way station, or forbidden planet. It's where the important things happen to the important people. Where the ethos and attitudes are dealt with, not cured. It is, in other words, home.

And trying to keep her small piece of it together is Lisette Linares (Lauren Velez) whose bike-messenger husband, Chino (Jon Seda), gets arrested for looting during a blackout, leaving her to play his number and raise his kids. With no money and few prospects, Lisette scams her way into a job with record producer Stephen Price (Griffin Dunne), starts her progress up the company ladder and always comes back to the Bronx. "You live here?" Price asks incredulously after driving her home. "No, I'm vacationing," she says, which wouldn't be so funny if Martin hadn't made the place, and the woman, so real.

There's an electricity about "I Like It Like That" beginning with the opening street/circus scene that sets up a crazy-summer ambience and throbs with color. Martin's talents for rendering urban anarchy will probably prompt comparisons with her old boss, Spike Lee (for whom she was a camera operator), but Martin's tack is more unfettered, sexier. As if to emphasize, she segues from sidewalk to bedroom, where Chino is timing their lovemaking, the kids are trying to break down the door and Lisette is wearing a look of increasing impatience with everyone. It's classic.

And Lisette's is a classic woman's story, too much responsibility, not enough help. Martin keeps it funny, but the humor is just a side dish to the movie's real meat—the relationships among Lisette and Chino and their 10-year-old son (Tommy Melly), who's getting seduced by the rewards of drug dealing while his parents do their infantile dance over money and sex and the local macho mores.

Magdalena (Lisa Vidal), a hot babe with a lot of local history, wants Chino and nearly gets him because of pride and stupidity. And part of Lisette's education is finding out what she wants, and what she can live without. It's something like maturity, which Darnell Martin, if not her characters, has in abundance.

NEWSWEEK, 10/17/94, p. 78, Jack Kroll

Darnell Martin is a thinking woman's street fighter. The 29-year-old Bronx-born writer-director bobs and weaves with weaves with ideas, words, gestures. She hates being called the first African-American woman to direct a major studio feature, as Columbia did in its publicity for her movie, "I Like It Like That." To single me out takes away from all the new black women directors like Julie Dash, Leslie Harris, Euzhan Palcy," says Martin angrily. "And it suggests we're not part of the mainstream. When you look in the Yellow Pages, do you see African-American Women Dentists?"

Martin gets angry a lot, but anger is just one of her innumerable energies. Those energies have lifted her from poverty to make her the first—well, let's just say she caused a stir at the Cannes and Toronto film festivals with her first feature. "I Like It Like That" comes from the place and people where Martin grew up as a kid who didn't know where her next plate of watered-down macaroni and cheese was coming from. The movie follows a young black/Puerto Rican married couple, Lisette (Lauren Vélez) and Chino (Jon Seda), and their three children through their toughest summer. When Chino impulsively joins the looting during a power blackout, he lands in jail, and Lisette fast-talks her way into a job with a white record executive (Griffin Dunne) to help bail out her husband. Martin gets beautiful performances from her young actors. Her take on sexuality is at once wise, tender and funny—the movie opens with a scene in which Chino makes pneumatic love with Lisette while timing his staying power with an alarm clock. Brrrinnng! New record!

Martin shot her movie where she was raised, a Hispanic section in the heart of the Bronx. She's the child of an interracial marriage that broke up in her infancy, leaving her white (Irish) mother to raise her and her two sisters. "My mom is the most amazing woman," says Martin. "We only bought furniture once when I was 10 years old. Before then we'd find stuff in the street." She recalls how her tiny mother would carry heavy chairs up five flights of stairs. And how they'd share everything with the Puerto Rican family next door, food and even electricity. "If the lights were turned off in someone's house, we'd pass an extension cord through a hole we made in the thin wall."

Her Irish mother's gift of blarney helped her to talk the Barnard School for Girls in upper Manhattan (it closed in 1993) into accepting the precocious Darnell as a scholarship student. She won a scholarship to Sarah Lawrence College and later at graduate film school at New York University. "Sarah Lawrence was where I grew the most," says Martin. "It took the lid off you creatively. And despite its rich-kids reputation, it was more democratic than NYU, which made things easier for kids with money." Martin got into NYU through the recommendation of Spike Lee, whom she met after she got a job as assistant to Lee's cinematographer Ernest Dickerson on "Do the Right Thing." "One time I was sick and throwing up blood but I refused to go home," she says. "They wanted to hire someone else for that day but I said, 'No, this is my job; I don't want anyone else to do my job'."

When New Line Cinema accepted her screenplay (which she wrote while at NYU), she turned down their offer of a $2 million budget and a seven-week shoot. When Spike Lee offered to produce it at his studio, Universal, she turned that down, too. She didn't want even Lee calling the shots. Then Columbia offered $5.5 million and a nine-week schedule, and Martin was off. But she still stuck by her guns when Columbia insisted on cutting out some of the "grittier" scenes in what they saw as a romantic comedy. Martin refused, saying she would take her name off the picture. "That made them back down," says Martin. "That and the test screenings, when the audience applauded the very scenes they wanted to cut."

The workaholic Martin has found her proper mate. She lives in New York's East Village; her Italian artist husband lives in Rome. "We're both alike—'Now I work. Now I eat. Now I love.' We get together every two or three months. It's great." She's written the screenplay for her next project, a psychological horror film involving an interracial family in the Bronx. "I think Columbia is excited about my work," says Martin, "but maybe not about me. Sometimes I'm not easy to cop to. I don't have much of a diplomacy filter." Filtered or straight, Martin is on her way.

SIGHT AND SOUND, 3/95, p. 39, Joanna Berry

Lisette and her husband Chino live in a small apartment in the Bronx with their three children, trying to survive on Chino's meagre wages as a bicycle messenger. Lisette is unhappy with her life, as her husband seems to pay too much attention to Magdalena, the unmarried mother living next door, and spends what little money he earns playing the numbers. She also has to cope with the problems of her transvestite brother Alexis, who is not accepted by their parents.

During a blackout in the neighbourhood, Chino goes looting to get a stereo. He is arrested, and Lisette cannot raise the $1,500 bail. Meanwhile her eldest son, eight-year-old L'il Chino, decides to raise some money himself, even if it means stealing and doing errands for the young drug dealers in the neighbourhood. In desperation, Lisette tries to get some modelling work, but instead gets offered money to babysit a hot young Latino band called The Mendez Brothers for an evening. She goes to visit her husband in prison; he tells her he doesn't want her to take the job, that he would rather she go on welfare. The evening turns out to be a meal with The Mendez Brothers and the record executive, Stephen Price, who wants to sign them. Initially, he doesn't like Lisette, but she convinces him that she knows a lot about Latino music, and he decides to hire her as his assistant.

Price drives Lisette home in his sports car. Chino's friends lie and tell him that they saw her having sex with Price. Magdalena's father bails Chino out of jail, after she says that the father of her baby is Chino. Thinking Lisette is unfaithful, Chino moves in with Magdalena. Lisette begins a brief sexual affair with her boss, but grudgingly lets Chino move back into their apartment after Magdalena confesses that the baby is not his. Lisette and Chino keep separate lives while her career gets more successful, until, on a visit to the beach to film The Mendez Brothers latest video, the pair are reunited.

Darnell Martin's directing debut is a Cinderella tale with a twist. Her protagonist doesn't need a fairy godmother or a Prince Charming to achieve a happy ending, she does it all by herself. This is a test indeed, since writer/director Martin gives Lisette as difficult a start in life as Cinders ever had—no money, no job, delinquent children and a good-for-nothing husband (expertly played with full Latin machismo by Jon Seda).

Although this romantic comedy-drama could have taken place in any borough of New York, Martin sets it in a community of South Bronx Latinos. Their fiery outbursts, touching on everything from the stigma of welfare to sexual politics in the office, give it a refreshingly zany feel. Unlike Spike Lee, who of late has tended to ram his opinions down our throats, Martin manages to say much about race, sexuality and life in New York without resorting to shock tactics.

Instead, her central characters address these issues tangentially. Lisette's humiliation when having to go on welfare is movingly portrayed by Lauren Velez, while a scene in which Alexis deals with the hurt of being rejected by his parents comes across as an almost accidental aside. Martin also works plenty of humour into her film, most often through the chauvinistic Chino, who refuses ever to admit his mistakes, and L'il Chino, who seems dangerously close to following in his father's footsteps.

The one character not well drawn is record executive Stephen Price. Griffin Dunne plays him as a parody in the *Spinal Tap* mould. Price's only function is to prove the point that males are not to be trusted unless they are under 20 or transvestite. Indeed, the scene in which Lisette discovers during sex that Price is even more self-obsessed than her husband may induce men in the audience to look away. But Price is also there to show that white, middle-aged record company executives are the wrong people to be choosing the ethnic music we get to hear, and that there should be more opportunities in the music business (and for that matter, the movie industry) for people who know what they're talking about—a point reinforced by the salsa and samba soundtrack.

The film demands to be taken on its own terms as a romantic comedy. The message that Lisette can do much better on her own without the help of any of the men in her life is well argued. It is only spoiled during the end-credits sequence when we get to watch the making of The Mendez Brothers' video, and Chino and Lisette are reunited.

VILLAGE VOICE, 10/18/94, p. 49, J. Hoberman

A related success story [the reference is to *Hoop Dreams*] by virtue of its very existence, Darnell Martin's assured and flashy *I Like It Like That* opens in an ambiguous tribute to the erotic vitality of the working poor: Bronx bicycle-messenger Chino (Jon Seda) clocks a 60-minute fuck with his less-than-ecstatic wife, Lisette (Lauren Velez), in a noisy apartment in a frantic neighborhood overrun by kids, pulsating with music, and otherwise vibrating in electric local color.

The harried Lisette has, it would seem, a different definition of making it. What she craves is not prolonged sex but greater sublimation. (She has aspirations—even if she decides that she wants a turntable when the culture is dictating CD.) A power blackout that amounts to the first of a capricious deity's several jokes affords gallant Chino the opportunity to loot one for her and thus wind up in the Bronx House of Detention, leaving the initially scattered protagonist to attempt to cope on her own.

I Like It Like That looks like a tropical bouquet, but it's not a movie to soothe a headache. Martin, who makes her feature debut, worked as an assistant camera operator on *Do The Right Thing*; for manic cuteness, built-in music videos, and choreographed disorder, her 167th Street manages to outclamor Spike. Unlike Lee's more somber and conflicted street scenes, however, Martin's is genuinely carnivalesque. The motor-mouthed ensemble, including Jesse Borrego as Lisette's snap-queen brother, Rita Moreno as Chino's tightly-wound mom and Griffin Dunne as the white record-producer boss whom Lisette consistently manages to outwit, doesn't inhabit the movie so much as parade through it—sometimes on floats that carry a surprising amount of emotional baggage.

A comedy of errors, the script (which Martin also wrote) wiggles through contrivances equally suggestive of William Shakespeare and *I Love Lucy*, spinning a surplus of family, gender, and social conflicts, to pivot on the issue of Lisette's confused identity. Is she a mother or an independent woman? One thing this aptly titled movie never doubts is that Lisette is the authentic voice of underclass desire—a confidence that nearly equals Martin's own.

Also reviewed in:
CHICAGO TRIBUNE, 10/14/94, Friday/p. J, Johanna Steinmetz
NATION, 11/14/94, p. 592, Stuart Klawans
NEW YORK TIMES, 10/14/94, p. C23, Janet Maslin
VARIETY, 5/23-29/94, p. 55, Todd McCarthy
WASHINGTON POST, 10/14/94, p. F9, Rita Kempley

I LOVE TROUBLE

A Touchstone Pictures release in association with Caravan Pictures. *Producer:* Nancy Meyers. *Director:* Charles Shyer. *Screenplay:* Nancy Meyers and Charles Shyer. *Director of Photography:* John Lindley. *Editor:* Paul Hirsch, Walter Murch and Adam Bernardi. *Music:* David Newman. *Music Editor:* Tom Kramer, George A. Martin, and Tom Villano. *Choreographer:* Peggy Holmes. *Sound:* Richard Bryce Goodman and (music) Bruce Botnick and Robert Fernandez. *Sound Editor:* Mark P. Stoeckinger and Larry Kemp. *Casting:* Bonnie Timmermann. *Production Designer:* Dean Tavoularis. *Art Director:* Alex Tavoularis. *Set Designer:* Sean Haworth, James J. Murakami, Nick Navarro, William O'Brien, and Nancy Tobias. *Set Decorator:* Gary Fettis. *Set Dresser:* Kurt Hulett, Eric Hulett, and Edson C. Moreno. *Special Effects:* Stan Parks. *Costumes:* Susan Becker. *Make-up:* Bradley Wilder. *Make-up (Julia Roberts):* Richard Dean. *Stunt Coordinator:* Jack Gill. *Running time:* 120 minutes. *MPAA Rating:* PG.

CAST: Nick Nolte (Peter Brackett); Julia Roberts (Sabrina Peterson); Saul Rubinek (Sam Smotherman); James Rebhorn (The Thin Man); Robert Loggia (Matt Greenfield); Kelly Rutherford (Kim); Olympia Dukakais (Jeannie); Marsha Mason (Senator Gayle Robbins); Eugene Levy (Justice of the Peace); Charles Martin Smith (Rick Medwick); Dan Butler (Wilson Chess); Paul Gleason (Kenny Bacon); Jane Adams (Evans); Lisa Lu (Virginia Hervey); Nora Dunn (Lindy); Hallie Meyers-Shyer (Little Girl in Barn); Boone David Cates (Little Boy in Barn); Richard Brown (Minister); Clark Gregg (Darry Beekman, Jr.); Anna Holbrook (Woman in Sportscar); Cindy Katz (Wire Editor); Jay Wolpert (Passing Writer); Andy Milder (Copy Person); Dorothy Lyman (Suzie); Dafidd McCracken (Midrail Assistant); Keith Gordon (Andy); Jim Pepper (Reporter #1); Lisa Cloud (Reporter #2); Larry Margo (Reporter #3); Marianne Murciano ("Good Day Chicago" Anchor); Sally Meyers Kovler (Woman at Newsstand); Jody Gottlieb, and Kathryn Weiss (Friends at Newsstand); Jonathan Kovler (Cop reading *Globe*); Bruce Block (Man at Newsstand); Joseph D'Onofrio (Sully); Barry Sobel (Delivery Person); Laura Mae Tate (Nadia); Brian Fenwick (Museum Bartender); Frankie R. Faison (Police Chief); Stuart Pankin (Society Photographer); Mike Bacarella (Train Station Engineer); Kimo Wills (Danny Brown); Oscar Jordan (*Globe* Secretary); Megan Cavanagh (Mrs. Beekman); Patrick St. Esprit (Assassin); Michael Edgar Myers (Skycap); Paul Hirsch (Man on Plane); Jessica Lundy, Maura Russo, and Blaire Baron (Flight Attendants); Nestor Serrano (Pecos); Mary Seibel (Woman Walking Dog); Annie Meyers-Shyer (Student Librarian); Doug Spinuzza (Senator Robbins' Assistant); Eric Poppick (Steak House Waiter); Rebecca Cross (Chess Chemical Tour Guide); Lisa Roberts and Lucy Lin (Kim's Friends); Bill Worley (Ruby's Bartender); Chad Einbinder (Dixon); Mike Cargile (Sabrina's Dance Partner); Karl Plouffe and Matthew Lindvig (Ranger Scouts); Robin Duke (Sandra); Michael Quill (Security Guard).

FILMS IN REVIEW, 7-8/94, p. 59, Harry Pearson, Jr.

What we have, in the instance of *I Love Trouble*, are two widely differing concepts, indifferently melded, of what this movie ought to be.

On the one hand, and its best, we have a most mild version of *All The President's Men*: or the paranoid political thriller, with two savvy reporters investigating a train wreck, stumbling on things much darker and much worse (the poisoning of our drinking milk, certainly no laughing matter). On the other, we have an attempt to resurrect the thirties screwball comedy, imposing the attitudes of Cary Grant and Katherine Hepburn in *Bringing Up Baby* upon the journalistic archetypes created in *His Girl Friday* by Cary Grant and Rosalind Russell. In other words, superimposing the anarchic style of *Baby*, a bone in search of a plot, upon the almost mechanically-driven plot devices of the prototypical film about daily journalism. The two cancel each other out, naturally, and what you're left with is a summer movie that underestimates the sense and savvy of its intended audience.

For about the first third of its length, we are entertained, and credibly at that, by the competition between a cub reporter (Julia Roberts) and one of the senior statesmen of Chicago journalism (played in, as is his wont, stolid Sequoia style by Nick Nolte), a Mike Royko-like columnist who wouldn't normally be caught dead covering a daily news story. (We know we're in cloud cuckoo-land when we see Roberts at the scene of what is supposed to be a messy accident in stiletto-thin spiked heels. And that's our first shot of her, from the heels up, with wonderfully beautifully colored sparks illuminating the velvet-rich night air. So right away, we feel the tug between a kind of hyper reality (the scenes in real locations and a real newspaper office and cotton candy land). We learn, over the credits, that the train wreck has been arranged. A guy who looks like an executive has packed his briefcase with documents and inside his pen, some microfilm; he has been directed to the last car in the train (by the bad guy, whom you can practically smell, he's so obvious). It's that briefcase the bad guys, CIA-like types, are after. They've managed, we'll find out, to de-couple the last car (saves money that way for the producers in recreating the wreck site) so that it will crash. Not, if you think about it, entirely logical, since the car should just roll to a stop. We see, at the site, some kids stealing stuff from the wreck, including the briefcase the meanies are after, but, fear not, our assassin gets (in the dark no less) a great look at their departing license tag.

Because Roberts scoops Nolte, he loses face back at his office and the competition is on. With each new story, both begin to see that all was not as it appeared. Fine, high heels and all; it's got you going, thanks in no small part to the production design by the gifted Dean Tavoularis [*The Godfathers*, *Apocalypse Now*, et al] and the most handsome photography using the standard widescreen as if it were Panavision. Looked at simply as pure film, and as a study in art design, this is a most beautiful work, surely worthy of Academy attention. You feel, when watching it, as though you've broken into a Haagen Dazs store. With subtitles, the movie would, perhaps, seem profound.

So far, so good. But when Nick and Julia are in deep enough to realize that the wreck was probably an assassination staged to look like an accident, the film goes haywire. First, Julia stumbles across a dead body (one of the kids who swiped the briefcase) but, little if anything is made of this. No headline stories, *nada*. It isn't even clear if Nolte knows about this (surely) traumatic episode. Then, both try to interview the dead man's wife, and find that a hit man is after them. He nearly succeeds (in what has to be one of the least suspenseful rooftop chases in the long history of flashy, star vehicles). And still no headline stories, no big official investigations; we never even learn what happened to the wife. If anyone had pulled a pistol on Woodward and Bernstein during Watergate, it would have been an historic journalistic event. And it would have invited the intervention of the Big Boys of law enforcement—curiously absent throughout the plot—and their taking over of the investigation. Resulting, of course in the end of this movie. And so nothing comes of these events; there are no consequences. (This is becoming a major problem in Hollywood movies of late: actions without consequences.)

And from here, we wind up with Roberts and Nolte on the road, having combined forces (sort of, being pursued by assassins deft enough to wreck a train but not at all apt when it comes to getting rid of Nick and Julia, who bounce around in plain sight. And then the really cutesy pie stuff starts. Julia naked in front of a lascivious Boy Scout troop (don't even bother to ask how; you wouldn't believe me if I told you). Then, the writers would have us believe that these two, who exhibit less chemistry together than Ma and Pa Kettle, get married in a Las Vegas chapel (and without a license) simply to escape the assassin, who has grown more incompetent at his job as Roberts and Nolte have become increasingly star-like. The problem here is that Nolte is a presence, not an actor, and a self-involved one; you can practically hear the brain ordering the face to change expressions, and, atop this, not a particularly likeable one. He's been given no character (not that it would matter), just characteristics. And poor Roberts, she's hardly even given those.

And so we sit and wait for the plot to snap back in, which it does about ten minutes before the end, and that finale is meant to be dazzling, but it's too little and too late. So we can gather up our depleted popcorn bag and head for the trash can, where we dump it and most of what we may remember about the film.

LOS ANGELES TIMES, 6/29/94, Calendar/p. 1, Kenneth Turan

It's a good thing "I Love Trouble" loves trouble, because trouble is just what it's in.

Although Julia Roberts and Nick Nolte beaming out at the world from "Trouble" posters everywhere point to a light and frothy concoction, that's not what filmmaking team Nancy Meyers and Charles Shyer (she produces, he directs, they both write) have delivered. On screens instead is a stab at the kind of thriller/romance combination that Alfred Hitchcock turned out in treats like "North by Northwest."

But, instead of the charm and the suspense complementing each other in the classic manner, they drag each other down. The film's jeopardy sequences are ineffectual and cast a pall over the romantic comedy aspects, which are not especially entrancing despite the star power. Instead of synergy, what "Trouble" achieves is more like disappointment squared.

No one expects movies like this one, set as it is in the largely mythological world of fiercely competitive daily newspapering, to be realistic. But neither should they be as flaccid and unconvincing as what we are presented with here.

After a *pro forma* opening setting up the thriller parts of the plot, Peter Brackett (Nolte) makes an appearance kissing a willing blonde in a fancy convertible. "Meet the Press" indeed. Although he still pulls down the big bucks as the city columnist for the Chicago Chronicle, Brackett is clearly more interested in promoting his new novel and chasing skirts than corralling a Pulitzer Prize.

What changes his mind is meeting Sabrina Peterson (Julia Roberts), the new face at the rival Chicago Globe. The two meet when both are assigned to cover the same train wreck, and Brackett feels all his instincts, competitive and otherwise, start to go into action. Peterson, however, is business personified and gives Brackett such a chilly brushoff it's surprising the movie doesn't end right there.

Instead, to no one's surprise but their own, these two find their lives increasingly intertwined. First they go toe to toe on the wreck story, snarling at each other and trading scoops on a story their papers inexplicably view as bigger than the sinking of the Titanic.

Then, when developments lead them to a more complicated and dangerous situation, Brackett suggests they pool their skills. "If you knew what I knew and I knew what you knew," he theorizes in a rare moment of logic, "maybe we could live through this story." Peterson grudgingly sees his point and a reluctant collaboration is on.

There are clever moments in "I Love Trouble," odd times when the concept that amused Meyers and Shyer, a pair of rascals trying to both cooperate and out-con each other, is fleetingly visible. But mostly what we see is an unconvincing attempt at entertainment that is not good enough any way you look at it.

Just one glance at the gripping opening elevator scene in "Speed," for instance, illustrates how ineffectual a similar situation in "Trouble" is. Neither Meyers nor Shyer has any previous experience turning out jeopardy material, and this is not an area where on-the-job training is successful.

What this team has been good at, most notably in the perennially underappreciated "Irreconcilable Differences" as well as their successful "Father of the Bride" remake, is writing glib, amusing dialogue. Here, however, perhaps because they were sidetracked coping with the thriller aspects, the repartee is mostly lackluster, something that not even the inordinate number of editors involved in the project can remedy.

And, for the second time in two movies, Roberts finds herself thoughtlessly misused. An actress with an unbeatable smile who can effortlessly project warmth and good cheer, she spends far too much of this movie, as she did in "The Pelican Brief," looking somber and glum when she isn't being the focus of sporadic and insipid ogling. Unless everyone concerned wakes up and remembers what her celebrity is based on, Roberts' career could end up in considerable trouble itself.

NEW YORK, 7/18/94, p. 51, David Denby

Was the pairing of Nick Nolte and Julia Roberts in *I Love Trouble* intended to light up the skies, like Tracy and Hepburn in *Adam 's Rib* or *Pat and Mike*? My own response was to write a check to the National Organization for Women. Nolte, a terrific actor but long enough in the tooth to take Jack Nicholson's place in *Wolf* without makeup, is supposed to be a great ladies' man and newspaper columnist; Roberts is a cub reporter with moxie. The two journalists fight over a story, then fight their way into bed. They even speak some of the same lines as Tracy and Hepburn. But Nolte must be twice Roberts's age, and their relationship is far from delicious; it's closer to scandalous. Nolte, embarrassed (I would guess), gives a distanced, grinning performance, the first hackwork he's done in years; Roberts is charming but rather wan. The filmmaking team of Nancy Meyers (writer-producer) and Charles Shyer (writer-director) has miscalculated before: Meyers & Shyer (*Baby Boom, Father of the Bride*) have a tendency to revive old Hollywood genres only to kill them. Here, they fill out the battling-professionals formula with clichés from standard action movies. Corpses fall out of closets; cars go hurtling through the night; people crash through glass and fall off catwalks. Ah, the journalist's life! If Meyers & Shyer made a film about movie critics, they'd have us wrestling with alligators in the sewers below the screening rooms.

NEW YORK POST, 6/29/94, p. 35, Michael Medved

"I Love Trouble" tries to combine two very different movie formats—light-hearted romantic comedy and paranoid thriller—but only one of the two rises even to the level of mediocrity.

The nearly indestructible charisma of the two stars (Julia Roberts and Nick Nolte) makes their flirtatious, bickering byplay occasionally entertaining, despite the sort of sparkling repartee that seems more appropriate to a fourth grade playground than to a sophisticated Hollywood production.

Nolte, for instance, raises his eyebrows and inquires, "Where did you say you're from? Bitchville?"

Even these feeble attempts at wit, however, are quickly swallowed up by an appallingly illogical plot about a gigantic corporate conspiracy that pursues the two leads through a seemingly endless series of contrived, overproduced chase scenes.

The best you can say about this half of the picture is that it represents the finest (and the first) movie Hollywood has produced so far on the sizzling issue of bovine growth hormone.

That hormone stands at the center of a dark secret which Nolte and Roberts, as rival newshounds for two competing Chicago papers, are determined to uncover. He's supposed to be a smug, celebrity columnist; she's the upstart cub reporter whose dedicated pursuit of the truth forces Nolte to get off his apathy and try to beat her to the story.

"Because of you," he tells her, "I remembered how much I loved newspapering." Unfortunately, the "newspapering" invoked here might as well refer to the layer of protection placed beneath an incontinent puppy; "I Love Trouble" lacks even the vague whiff of authenticity that Ron Howard brought to "The Paper."

The most surprising aspect of "I Love Trouble" is that it's the product of the respected team known in Hollywood as "The Shmyers"—writer/director Charles Shyer and writer/producer Nancy Meyers.

In the past they've specialized in warm, witty character-driven comedies like "Private Benjamin," "Baby Boom" and the "Father of the Bride" remake, but here they seem determined to prove that they can do big high-tech action scenes in the Renny Harlin style. Unfortunately, these surprisingly dark sequences serve only to undermine the atmosphere of charming screw-ball banter they try to set up between their stars.

Julia Roberts further destroys any attempt to pass off this new couple as a '90s answer to Tracy and Hepburn. She is, as always, an appealing screen presence with a delicate aura of vulnerability, but she totally lacks the tough, energetic edge that could give her relationship with Nolte some zing. As it is, he seems like a cad for even trying to do anything other than cuddle and coddle the poor baby who's supposed to be his formidable competitor.

Meanwhile, the filmmakers try to draw attention from all the shortcomings in their work with repeated and leering views of Ms. Roberts legs, accompanied by hubba-hubba saxophone music; the camera seems to do everything but lick her. This may help to lure some die-hard fans, but "I Love Trouble" still seems like big Trouble at the box office, and it will inspire very little Love.

NEWSDAY, 6/29/94, Part II/p. B2, Jack Mathews

Husband-wife filmmaking team charles Shyer and Nancy Meyers (he directs, she produces, they co-write) have carved out a nice Hollywood career making the kinds of movies older people complain don't get made anymore, and younger ones generally don't want to see. Amiable, dialogue-rich, star-driven comedies like those the studios turned out with regularity before television cam along in the '50s and appropriated the form. In fact, two of the movies made from Shyer-Meyers scripts, "Private Benjamin" and "Baby Boom," were so much like the movies TV appropriated that TV appropriated them, too, in follow-up sitcoms with more affordable stars than Goldie Hawn and Diane Keaton.

Their last film, a remake of Vincente Minnelli's "Father of the Bride," found such an appreciative audience that Shyer and Meyers will next remake Minnelli's '51 sequel, "Father's Little Dividend."

In the meantime, we have "I Love Trouble," a romantic thriller starring Nick Nolte and Julia Roberts as rival Chicago newspaper reporters falling in love while covering the same story, and the nostalgia this time doesn't quite work. While borrowing freely from the comedies of Howard Hawks and the mysteries of Alfred Hitchcock, the filmmakers failed to either match the pace of the former or the tensions of the latter.

It's two hours of coy repartee, interrupted by sporadic chases and dull exposition, followed by more coy repartee. Nolte and Roberts are a handsome couple, but in roles that might have been played 40 years ago by Cary Grant and Grace Kelly, they don't exactly send you away feeling you can now die happy.

The movie gets off to a crisp beginning, at the site of a train wreck where Nolte's Peter Brackett, a legendary columnist and ladies man who has long since begun living on his reputation, and Roberts Sabrina Peterson, a feisty young reporter for a competing newspaper, show up for what Brackett assumes is a routine story. When he wakes up the next morning to discover he has been scooped and embarrassed by her, he rekindles his journalistic fire and throws down the challenge.

While the two are one-upping each other on the train wreck story and rubbing their noses in each success, "I Love Trouble" does recall the spunk of "His Girl Friday" and some of the other early newsroom classics. But as Brackett and Peterson follow their leads from Chicago to Wisconsin to Las Vegas, getting deeper and deeper into a scandal involving microfilm, politicians, scientists and a carcinogenic, genetically engineered hormone for dairy cattle, the story is like a paper boat taking on water.

Hitchcock would have used the hormone, LDF, as an excuse to introduce Brackett and Peterson into the midst of dangerous people, and not even bothered to explain what it means or how it works. Shyer-Meyers go to such lengths to develop the environmental sub-plot you feel as if you've tuned in late to a biology class on "Mind Extension University," or worse, in the middle of an Al Gore speech.

It doesn't matter that the reporters are solving a crime police don't even know occurred, or that they seem to lose contact with their editors and readers the minute they're out of town. The point is to get them out there, like Cary Grant and Eva Marie Saint in "North by Northwest," to find love literally on the edge of danger. But we keep being pulled out of that fantasy for the boring details about LDF.

Brackett and Peterson are the only interesting characters in the film, and we can't take too much of them. Though the age and experience differences are crucial to their relationship, Nolte and Roberts seem to be delivering dialogue—or rather putdowns—written for the same person.

In their eagerness to invoke the styles of romantic thrillers from old Hollywood, Shyer and Meyer have forgotten the key to their own success, which is making an old-fashioned story seem altogether fresh. Nostalgia, in this instance, feels awfully stale.

NEWSWEEK, 7/4/94, p. 71, Jack Kroll

Damon Runyon had a character called "Waldo Winchester, the half-smart scribe." *I Love Trouble* is a half-smart movie. Well, maybe one-third. Pairing Julia Roberts and Nick Nolte was smart. He's Peter Brackett, a hotshot columnist; she's Sabrina Peterson, a cub reporter just starting to heat up her shot. Assigned to a mysterious train wreck by their rival Chicago papers, they take turns scooping each other and finally decide to join up, following a tangled trail that leads to the worlds of big industry and big politics. All the while Roberts smirks as she watches Nolte womanize, and Nolte smirks as he watches Roberts smirking. Finally, kiss, bang, boom, and everything comes out just as it always has in that classic genre, the romantic thriller.

The team of writer/producer Nancy Meyers and co-writer/director Charles Shyer ("Private Benjamin," "Father of the Bride") has put together an anthology of genre moves that takes no risks and scores no surprises. We know that Nolte and Roberts are going to pretend mutual unattraction. We know that they're going to try to outmaneuver each other. All we ask is that our foreknowledge be fulfilled with style, wit and goose bumps.

Only the goose bumps come through in reasonable numbers—when, for example, Nolte and Roberts are trapped in an elevator shaft, scrambling up cables as the elevator pursues them. Unfortunately, the convoluted story produces the opposite of goose bumps, sort of goose depressions. And the bad guys have less personality than the elevator cables.

Most serious is the failure of the Shyer-Meyers team to get the most out of their stars. Instead of the crackling repartee of a "His Girl Friday," we get stock exchanges, updated now and then by the new sexual frankness, as when Roberts outmachos Nolte. Nolte (referring to a bulldog he's sent to Roberts): "Does he remind you of me?" Roberts: "Yeah, I've grown awfully fond of little Dick." Nolte and Roberts are greatly appealing presences; the movie's mistake is to swaddle them in niceness, especially Roberts. After her two-year sabbatical, she's returned in two unremarkable films, "The Pelican Brief" and this one. Roberts is the anti-Sharon Stone; one uncrosses her legs, the other doesn't. But at 26, Roberts needs roles with some edge and grit. Maybe we'll see some of that in Robert Altman's upcoming "Prêt-à-Porter." If anyone can de-nice Roberts, it's Altman.

SIGHT AND SOUND, 12/94, p. 49, Nick James

Chicago. Ace author, columnist and womaniser Peter Brackett reports to work at the *Chronicle*. His editor knows that Brackett's latest column is a rehash of something he wrote many years before. News of a fatal rail crash comes in and Brackett, who hasn't had to do leg-work in years, is the only available reporter. At the crash scene, Brackett waits to find out when the train was last serviced. He sees an attractive young cub reporter, Sabrina Peterson, from a rival paper, the *Globe*; she rebuffs his patronising attentions. Meanwhile a gang of youths steal some luggage from the crash, including a briefcase.

Next day, Peterson has scooped Brackett with a story about the suspension of an engineer with a drink problem. This begins a tit-for-tat war in which Brackett rediscovers his newsman's instincts. The two reporters vie for each new break, sending each other ironic gifts, and laying down false clues. The trail leads them both to the young gang leader's lair, where they find his body next to a scribbled note showing the letters: LD. Sabrina picks up a pen that was in the briefcase and absent-mindedly keeps it.

The pair are attacked by assassins; after escaping they agree to team up for research. Brackett discovers from a wedding group's video footage that the train was sabotaged. One of the victims is discovered to be the son of a recently deceased scientist who was working on a new hormone called LDF that increases the speed with which cows produce milk. Separate leads take Brackett and Peterson to a Wisconsin company that is developing the hormone. After looking around, the pair are kidnapped but Bracket manages to crash the car and disable the assassin. They get a lift to Las Vegas, where they are again the targets of an assassin. They evade him by entering a wedding parlour and have to go through the ceremony; later in a honeymoon hotel, they confess their attraction for each other.

Back in Chicago, Brackett finds out that Peterson has gone undercover as a tour guide at the LDF plant. Realising that she is in danger, he breaks in and finds her about to be executed by the company's chief hitman. Brackett saves her and microfilm is discovered, revealing that the hormone has disastrous side effects.

The writer-director/writer-producer team of Charles Shyer and Nancy Meyers have devoted themselves to reviving the classic form of Hollywood romantic comedy in films such as *Irreconcilable Differences* and their remake of *Father of the Bride*. But their take on the genre represents something of an indulgence in false memory syndrome. While *Pretty Woman* and *Sleepless in Seattle* have shown that there are ways to effectively update the 'women's picture' of the 30s, 40s and 50s, *I Love Trouble* by-passes the updating process by referring not to romantic comedies as they actually were but to the way we nostalgically remember them to be. Apart from occasional bursts of high-tech thriller violence, the narrative offers an idealised, ungrounded form of romance that belies the sheen of world-weary sophistication initially presented in the character of Peter Brackett. Yet such a sophistication is at the core of the model that Shyer and Meyers so fondly and regularly allude to.

Amoral news hacks desperate for a story have been a cinema staple since Hecht and MacArthur's play *The Front Page* was first adapted for the screen in 1931. With each new incarnation, however, the portrayal of professional duplicity and cynicism has been progressively less shocking. Figures from the news media are now so relentlessly demonised that any sign of decency is now likely to be thought unreasonable—a trope knowingly exploited in Ron Howard's recent newsroom hit *The Paper*. But Brackett and Peterson are too pleasant to be journalists from any era. Nolte oozes a knowingly hokey charm, while Roberts wears a nervous smile that insists that she's really a *nice* girl. Their romance is a cornball dance, one that Shyer and Meyers' idols—Hawks, Cukor, Lubitsch—would surely have subverted.

The characterisations in *His Girl Friday* and *Trouble In Paradise* (the most obvious models here) are more hard-bitten than any recent romantic comedy. The idea that *I Love Trouble* is just too naive for today's more cynical era therefore doesn't hold up. Rather, the film fails either to tap into modern anxieties or to arouse our empathy. *Sleepless In Seattle* and *Pretty Woman* at least acknowledge issues such as single parenthood and social alienation. Without a recognisable hook into the present, *I Love Trouble* exists instead in a junkshop limbo of hybridisation, joining the Coen brothers' *The Hudsucker Proxy* in demonstrating that lovingly collected spare parts cannot keep a classic form on the road forever.

As for the machine-gun attacks and car chases that interrupt the reporter couple's banter, these are desultory motors of a plot that lacks any hint of humanity. The film seems to be pieced together in such a way that rumours of on-set difficulties between the two stars would appear to be born out. Julia Roberts is so concerned to look vulnerably wholesome that her constant reciprocal pickpocketing of Nick Nolte looks more like kleptomania than ruthless one-upmanship. Still, it's a useful metaphor for the jackdaw mentality currently infesting Hollywood.

TIME, 7/4/94, p. 73, Richard Corliss

Julia Roberts is the oddest of star commodities in Hollywood: a Lamborghini that few people know how to drive. Her soft good looks, easy glamour and megawatt, kilo-tooth smile give her a box-office appeal unique among today's actresses. Yet filmmakers seem blind to these qualities. Roberts so often has to mope and so rarely gets to be her famous radiant self.

Say this, at least and at most, for the jovial new suspense movie *I Love Trouble*: it knows what to do with its star. Screenwriters Charles Shyer (who also directed) and Nancy Meyers (who also produced) realize that adventure with a comic twist is the most suitable genre for an actress who is no great shakes in the emoting department but has brightness and vulnerability to burn. So they made her character a cub reporter who hasn't figured out how attractive, resourceful or brave she is—a heroine in the process of becoming. It's a nicely contoured outfit for Roberts to wear to the Hitchcock ball. And Nick Nolte, displaying his dimpled machismo, is a knowing escort.

Nolte plays a Chicago columnist (with something no Chicago newspaperman has: a deep tan). Roberts is his rival on a hot story involving murders, environmental hazards and this summer's obligatory movie thrill, an elevator in jeopardy.

With its semisnazzy repartee and would-be ebullience, *I Love Trouble* strains for the style of the grand old movies (the *Thin Man* capers, the Tracy-Hepburn comedies *Adam's Rib* and *Pat and Mike*, half a dozen Hitchcocks) from which it borrows plot, dialogue and ambiance. But style is a Hollywood commodity even rarer these days than a pretty woman. Films don't breeze; they wheeze. Directors aren't pastry chefs anymore; they are construction foremen. Watching *I Love Trouble*, you can see the erection of a new Julia Roberts statue. The monument is eye-catching but bland, and Lord, it must weigh a ton.

VILLAGE VOICE, 7/5/94, p. 49, J. Hoberman

Julia Roberts only recently rivaled Kevin Costner as the most powerful performer in Hollywood but her cultural aspirations come lower in the clumsily titled *I Love Trouble*, the latest feature by Nancy Meyers and Charles Shyer, the husband-wife team responsible for such canny sitcom pilots as *Private Benjamin* and *Baby Boom*.

Splicing genres with abandon, *I Love Trouble* opens as a hard-boiled newspaper yarn with a hot-shot columnist (Nick Nolte) battling to outscoop a self-possessed cub reporter (Roberts, repeatedly introduced gams first) in the investigation of a suspicious train derailment. Albeit presented with less cornball pow than the tab wars in *The Paper*, the contest hypnotizes the public—which apparently loses all interest once *I Love Trouble* shades into faux Grisham (sources offed, corpses found, chases through spooky office buildings and sinister industrial complexes). Meanwhile, rivals Nolte and Roberts play out an extended comedy of romantic antipathy.

The macguffin has something to do with genetic engineering, although this newfangled dairy whatsit seems hardly more synthetic than the chemistry between the stars—both handling their lines (and the cute character tics the script assigns them) with more dignity than the situation warrants. Action slowly bounding from Chicago to rural Wisconsin to downtown Las Vegas and back, *I Love Trouble* builds to a mildly boffo closer, which affords Meyers and Shyer a stretch, and breaks with generic convention mainly by providing the occasion for multi-gender heroics.

Also reviewed in:
NATION, 7/25-8/1/94, p. 138, Stuart Klawans
NEW YORK TIMES, 6/29/94, p. C15, Caryn James
VARIETY, 6/27-7/3/94, p. 85, Todd McCarthy
WASHINGTON POST, 6/29/94, p. D1, Rita Kempley

I ONLY WANT YOU TO LOVE ME

A Leisure Time Features release of a Bavaria Atelier GmbH production for Westdeutscher Rundfunk (WDR). *Producer:* Peter Maethesheimer. *Director:* Rainer Werner Fassbinder. *Screenplay (German with English subtitles):* Rainer Werener Fassbinder. *Based on the book "Life Sentence" by:* Klaus Antes and Christine Erhardt. *Director of Photography:* Michael Ballhaus. *Editor:* Liesgret Schmitt-Klink. *Music:* Peer Raben. *Production Designer:* Kurt Raab. *Running time:* 104 minutes. *MPAA Rating:* Not Rated.

CAST: Vitus Zeplichal (Peter); Elke Aberle (Erika); Ernie Mangold (Mother); Alexander Allerson (Father); Johanna Hofer (Grandmother).

LOS ANGELES TIMES, 6/2/94, Calendar/p. 5, Kevin Thomas

R.W. Fassbinder's superbly understated "I Only Want You to Love Me," made for German TV, arrives 18 years after its completion and nearly 12 years after its prodigious maker's untimely death, at once underlining it's own timelessness and the great loss to world cinema in general and to German films in particular caused by Fassbinder's passing.

There are many talented German filmmakers, but none has had quite the unique, sustained and far-ranging impact of Fassbinder. The consolation is that at his death at 36 he left behind an incredibly rich legacy of 28 plays, three radio plays and no less than 43 films, a number of which have, yet to surface in America.

Fassbinder was one of the first openly gay filmmakers in the world, but his strength lay in his ability to empathize no less with straights than with gays. Based on a true incident, "I Only Want You to Love Me" is a perfect case in point, a study of a young married man Fassbinder views with the utmost compassion as he proceeds to his fate with a remorseless inevitability.

In flashback we witness the stark childhood of a boy born in a small Bavarian town to hard-working parents—they run a restaurant and live above it—who are both perfectionists and severe disciplinarians, absolutely lacking in any capacity for affection for their only child. Their son Peter grows up obediently to be an understandably shy young man (Vitus Zeplichal) but with a quiet determination not to be the failure his father predicts he will be.

At first it looks as if Peter will prove his father wrong. A pleasant-looking young man, he attracts a young woman, Erika (Elke Aberle), as ordinary in appearance as he, but capable both of appreciating him and of making the initial overtures between them. A first-rate bricklayer who in his spare time has built his parents a sizable home (for which he receives no thanks), he marries Erika and dares to seek his fortune in Munich, where he quickly finds employment in construction and where his zeal and ability are recognized by his boss and co-workers.

Peter seemingly has the wherewithal to make something of his life, but his arrival in Munich coincides with West Germany's economic miracle. Munich is one the most beautiful and sophisticated of European cities, but it's also a shoppers' paradise. Material goods abound, along with inducements to buy them. Peter, starved for love his entire life, believes that the way to secure his wife's love is to keep buying her things. Erika is at once more mature and sensible than Peter, but it's beyond her ability to comprehend or to control her husband's compulsive spending. Surely, something's going to have to give.

Fassbinder draws from his cast, in particular Zeplichal and Aberle—and also from esteemed, veteran actress Johanna Hofer as Aberle's gentle grandmother—the remarkably complete and selfless portrayals that are his trademark.

NEW YORK POST, 4/15/94, p. 38, Larry Worth

In 1979, Rainer Werner Fassbinder became a bonafide art house superstar after directing his masterpiece, "The Marriage of Maria Braun".

Granted, the German director was still developing his talents in 1976. But with earlier films like "Fox and His Friends" and "The Bitter Tears of Petra van Kant," Fassbinder had demonstrated cinema savvy. At least enough to avoid the pitfalls of "I Only Want You to Love Me."

Twelve years after his death the "lost" film is finally being released in America. The decade-plus delay was supposedly due to legal problems. But the tie-up might simply have entailed quality control.

Like the bulk of Fassbinder's canon, the saga is set in Germany and involves a misfit drowning in a vortex of angst and depression. Based on a true incident, the script concerns a man whose lack of parental love ultimately drove him to murder.

At the outset, twenty-something Peter is in prison, reviewing his troubles with a counselor, and leading to his stream-of-consciousness reflections. They begin with Mum beating his 6-year-old body with a coat hanger for presenting flowers from a neighbor's garden.

But before it becomes "Mommie Dearest Does Munich," Fassbinder switches gears and shows how Peter's marriage to a sweet gal pal amounts to too little, too late. That also sums up the film, with the power generated in the final reel—involving the climactic killing—seeming like a waste of effort.

The majority of Fassbinder's dialogue and work behind the camera is amateurish at best, with a light, airy look lending a washed-out feel. Paired with the plot's disjointed telling, no discernible mood builds, making it impossible to relate to Peter or his problems.

Fassbinder's use of title cards to explain the story's machinations indicates more trouble, specifically, a recognition of his actors' inabilities.

Eschewing regulars like Hanna Schygulla or the star power of Dirk Bogarde in "Despair," Fassbinder went with unknowns, who've since managed to retain that status.

As the lead, Vitus Zeplichal is a human cipher while Elke Aberle, playing his well-intentioned spouse, could double as a mannequin. Only Ernie Mangold and Alexander Allerson's turns as the icy parents make a palpable impression.

Maybe that's enough for Fassbinder devotees. For others, "I Only Want You to Love Me" offers firsthand knowledge of quiet desperation.

NEWSDAY, 4/15/94, Part II/p. B9, John Anderson

Although dead a dozen years, Rainer Werner Fassbinder remains perverse, at least in his timing. "I Only Want You to Love Me," his 1976 plea for understanding the motivations of a murderer, has languished in legal limbo for years. Now, this made-for-German-TV movie finally makes its U.S. debut, just as the American public's patience with poor, misunderstood killers has been exhausted.

This isn't Fassbinder's fault, of course, but his dogged naivete dates the film. So does its very era-specific look; the hair, the clothes, the furniture, they all scream mid-'70s, which isn't an attractive habit. And yet, the director's exploration of his twin obsessions—power and alienation seems as potent as his subject's doom seems predestined.

Peter (Vitus Zeplichal) is a bricklayer whose childhood has been devoid of love and who therefore lives to please. His mother (Ernie Mangold) and father (Alexander Allerson) are unyieldingly oblivious to Peter's existence; in one of Fassbinder's chronologically skewed flashbacks, we watch as each avoids punishing the boy—out of mutual disinterest, not affection—until Mom finally takes a wooden coat hanger and beats him with it till it breaks. Despite all this, Peter builds them a house. And as one of the occasional subtitles tells us, "Two weeks after the house was built, they seemed to forget it was Peter who built it."

Their cruel legacy will infect Peter's marriage to Erika (Elke Aberle), who lacks the strength to remedy Peter's emotional neediness, and who will get caught up in his compulsions—to work, and to buy—which lead to debt, exhaustion and eventual murder.

Fassbinder frames his two principals as aliens in a hostile environment. Peter, particularly, has no moorings; he feels that love can be bought, and must constantly be renewed through fresh payments. As played by Zeplichal, Peter's shoulders are constantly hunched, as if he's expecting a blow. That Peter delivers one first simply emphasizes his powerlessness; He can't control his compulsions, and the world in constructed to feed them.

VILLAGE VOICE, 4/19/94, p. 49, J. Hoberman

The formerly pervasive influence of R.W. Fassbinder, once cited by Waters as "the most talented filmmaker of his day," has lain dormant since his death a dozen years ago. Terminally independent, socially astute, and openly gay, Fassbinder is overdue for reevaluation. A straw in the wind may be the Public Theater's premiere of a hitherto locally unseen telefilm, *I Only Want You To Love Me* (1976).

The nakedly poignant title sums up Fassbinder's sense of childhood. The movie opens with the adult Peter (Vitus Zeplichal) building a new house for his cold, rejecting, supremely unappreciative parents and soon after flashes back to his being beaten by his mother for making her a gift of stolen flowers. From that, everything follows. The depressed bricklayer takes a comparably stolid wife (she tells him that he reminds her of a beloved pet dog) and moves with her to Munich where, exploited by his bosses, he labors overtime to furnish his home on credit. (Waters would doubtless appreciate the decor but, because this is a Fassbinder film, the flat is on Dachauerstrasse.)

Set in a bland world edged with paranoia, this painful tale is made all the more so by Fassbinder's skillful evocation of life's daily grind and Peter's johnlike belief that one must pay for love. (Zeplichal trudges through the movie, branded with a wide-eyed expression of perpetual fear.) His wife gets pregnant, which means he has to work that much more—seeking refuge in drink but paralyzed by the prospect of asking his parents for money. Ultimately, Peter displaces his rage onto a friendly bartender whom, in a rare moment of spontaneity, he bludgeons to death with the very telephone on which he had been trying to call his father.

Albeit relatively minor, *I Only Want You To Love Me* is enlivened by the blank reaction shots, lugubrious humor, stagy mise-en-scéne, and endless parody of German uptightness that are Fassbinder trademarks (and have been further refined by Aki Kaurismäki). What's most powerful about the movie is also what's most banal: The source of Peter's rage is his traumatic family romance. Trapped in a world of phantoms, he's a murder waiting to happen. The climax is completely overdetermined—Peter's parents (and an indifferent society) act, so to speak, through him.

Fassbinder based *I Only Want You To Love Me* on interviews with convicted killers but informed it with memories of his own unhappy childhood. (Zeplichal even looks like a diminished Fassbinder.) Thus, it shares the skewed autobiography of *Katzelmacher, Beware of a Holy Whore, The Merchant of the Four Seasons, The Bitter Tears of Petra Von Kant, Ali: Fear Eats the Soul, Fox and His Friends*, or *In a Year of Thirteen Moons*. In a year as devoid so far of cine-sustenance as this, any would be a welcome revival.

Also reviewed in:
CHICAGO TRIBUNE, 12/8/95, Friday/p.14, Michael Wilmington
NEW YORK TIMES, 4/15/94, p. C10, Stephen Holden

I.Q.

A Paramount Pictures release of a Sandollar production. *Executive Producer*: Scott Rudin and Sandy Gallin. *Producer:* Carol Baum and Fred Schepisi. *Director:* Fred Schepisi. *Screenplay:* Andy Breckman and Michael Leeson. *Story:* Andy Breckman. *Director of Photography:* Ian Baker. *Editor:* Jill Bilcock. *Music:* Jerry Goldsmith. *Music Editor:* Kenneth Hall. *Sound:* Danny Michael and (music) Robin Gray. *Sound Editor:* Peter Burgess. *Casting:* David Rubin. *Production Designer:* Stuart Wurtzel. *Art Director:* Wray Steven Graham. *Set Decorator:* Gretchen Rau. *Set Dresser:* David Scott Gagnon, Bryon Lovelace, Mike Leather, Martin Lazowicz, and Victor Zolfo. *Special Effects:* Stan Parks. *Costumes:* Ruth Myers. *Make-up:* Michael Laudati and C.Romania Ford. *Stunt Coordinator:* Joe Dunne. *Running time:* 96 minutes. *MPAA Rating:* PG.

CAST: Tim Robbins (Ed Walters); Meg Ryan (Catherine Boyd); Walter Matthau (Albert Einstein); Lou Jacobi (Kurt Godel); Gene Saks (Boris Podolsky); Joseph Maher (Nathan Liebknecht); Stephen Fry (James Morland); Tony Shalhoub (Bob Watters); Frank Whaley (Frank); Charles Durning (Louis Bamberger); Keene Curtis (Eisenhower); Alice Playten (Gretchen); Danny Zorn (Dennis); Helen Hanft (Rose); Roger Berlind (Duncan); Arthur Berwick, Timothy Jerome, and John McDonough (Academics); Lewis J. Stadlen (Moderator); Jeff Brooks (Reporter); Rex Robbins and Richard Woods (Suits); Daniel Von Bargen (Secret Service Agent); Jack Koenig (Reporter); Sol Frieder (Professor Loewenstein); Michelle Naimo Bird (Nurse).

LOS ANGELES TIMES, 12/23/94, Calendar/p. 12, Kevin Thomas

"I.Q." has one good idea: to cast Walter Matthau as Albert Einstein. Put a shuffling, German-accented Matthau in a sweat shirt, a silvery mustache and a lion's mane, and you've got an amusingly convincing take on the man who devised the theory of relativity. Matthau's Einstein, however, dotes on a relative, his pretty mathematician niece Catherine (Meg Ryan), not relativity.

Alas, it's writers Andy Breckman and Michael Leeson's notion to have Einstein play matchmaker for Catherine. It's the kind of news that automatically makes you wary and "I.Q." wastes no time in confirming your suspicion that we're in for a lot of contrived foolishness.

It's nice to see Matthau make Einstein a mensch, but it's off-putting to watch him and his three elderly genius pals (Lou Jacobi, Gene Saks and Joseph Maher) indulge in exceedingly elaborate ruses to steer Catherine away from an obtuse experimental psychologist (Stephen Fry, Peter in "Peters Friends") and toward an ace Princeton auto mechanic (Tim Robbins).

Matthau himself takes a subtle, gentle nudging approach, but the script calls for him to indulge in major interference in his niece's life and to perform acts of credibility-defying dishonesty, such as passing off Robbins as a scientific genius, not just to Catherine but to the entire world. (The script also requires him to come right out and say the deathless phrase, "Don't let the brain get in the way of your heart," and it could have emphasized a bit more that Einstein wants to prevent Catherine from making the mistakes he made.)

Breckman and Leeson are dexterous in plotting out a finish that's clever scientifically, but they've not been able to banish the specter of predictability that hangs over the entire film.

The way the film, which tries hard to evoke '30s romantic screwball comedy, tells it, Robbins is a smart, likable guy for whom an encounter with Ryan really is love at first sight. Ryan, on the other hand, feels that she must make a "sensible" marriage—well, it is the '50s—while not completely acknowledging to herself just how intellectually daunted she is by her loving uncle, how obligated she feels to marry a genius.

Matthau has the best role, but Robbins and Ryan are finally simply too good for their material, which is not nearly inspired enough to do justice to their talent.

The same goes for director Fred Schepisi, who makes the most of each and every situation, but should be expending his efforts on a picture, whether comedy or drama, that's more worthy of his proven gifts.

NEW STATESMAN & SOCIETY, 4/7/95, p. 49, Jonathan Romney

[*IQ* was reviewed jointly with *Dumb and Dumber*; see Romney's review of that film.]

NEW YORK, 1/16/95, p. 57, David Denby

The new Fred Schepisi romantic comedy, *I.Q.*, is filled with the kind of awful packaged whimsy—Albert Einstein on the back of a motorcycle, and so on—that I thought had gone out of our movies sometime around 1946. Set at Princeton in the fifties, *I.Q.* turns Einstein and four of his colleagues into harmless old sillies playing Cupid for mathematician Meg Ryan and garage mechanic Tim Robbins, and its message is that "the heart" is more important than "the mind"—an idea forever consoling to people untroubled by much of the latter. *I.Q.* patronizes everybody, intellectual or not, and the movie is so fussily overstructured and unspontaneous that it appears at times to be chucking itself under the chin.

NEW YORK POST, 12/23/94, p. 52, Michael Medved

When the characters played by Meg Ryan and Tim Robbins first meet in "I.Q.," they exchange such dazed, longing glances that it shouldn't take an Einstein to figure out that they belong together.

But in this film it does, because it's Meg's "Uncle Albert" (Einstein, that is) who's the only one who understands the urgency of helping true love run its course. It's 1955, spring is in the air in that green country town of Princeton, N.J., and the great physicist has already won his Nobel Prize, so what the "hey? Why not try something relatively new and play Cupid for your niece?

The problem is that she's supposed to be a brilliant mathematician who won't even consider Tim Robbins because he's just a lowly auto mechanic. So it's up to Einstein (Walter Matthau) to make the grease jockey look like a genius.

Together with some eccentric academic emigre colleagues (Gene Saks, Joseph Maher, Lou Jacobi), Uncle Albert teaches his new protege how to wear loose-fitting button-up sweaters and floppy bow ties like any self-respecting man of science. Even more important, they tutor him in the details of "cold fusion" and give him one of Einstein's old, unpublished papers to present so that he's instantly hailed as a giant intellect.

This certainly helps distract Meg Ryan from her fiance (Stephen Fry), a snobbish psychology professor. But it also attracts attention from President Eisenhower, who suddenly shows up to enlist Tim Robbins' supposedly formidable mind for the national defense.

This goofy, good-natured plot unmistakably invokes the spirit of old-time screwball comedy—particularly 1941's "Ball of Fire," a Gary Cooper-Barbara Stanwyck vehicle with a similar academic setting and the same sort of cute, cuddly professors.

The main problem here is that neither Robbins nor Ryan project the energy and edge they need, and the powerful chemistry they're supposed to generate (with lots of talk, naturally, about neutrons and electrons circling one another) is never convincingly displayed.

By contrast, Walter Matthau has a ball with this role; with the assistance of cunning makeup, he's a dead ringer for Einstein but his unfailingly warm-hearted performance is always a characterization rather than merely an impersonation.

Purists may protest that this angelic, fun-loving old man bears little resemblance to the real Einstein, who we know was a far darker, more tormented genius, but no one will come to "I.Q." expecting a serious treatment of the history of science.

In fact, the movie's at its worst when it tries for deeper moments (with Einstein twice invoking his famous line "God doesn't play dice with the universe") so it's appropriate that versatile director Fred Schepisi ("A Cry in the Dark," "The Russia House") generally keeps things light and breezy. The scenic Princeton locations lend the same seductive, June-is-bustin' aura that Schepisi brought to his previous romantic comedy, "Roxanne."

That charming surface helps make the film a pleasant trifle, though when you pause even for a moment to think about it, this particular "I.Q." definitely falls at the lower end of the bell curve.

NEWSDAY, 12/23/94, Part II/p. B2, Jack Mathews

If you're going to make a period romantic comedy about Albert Einstein's attempt to help his niece find love in the arms of an amiable garage mechanic, it had better be relatively smart. And Fred Schepisi's "I.Q." is one of the smartest romantic comedies of the year.

For those who say Hollywood can't make them like they used to, check it out. "I. Q."is a direct descendant of the line of screwball comedies turned out with enviable regularity in the early years by such directors as Howard Hawks and Preston Sturges, and though audience tastes have changed—we have a tougher time suspending our disbelief—Schepisi offers a credible reminder.

The gimmick in Andy Breckman's original story is that Einstein's niece (Meg Ryan) is an overachiever, a mathematician too concerned with being smart and marrying smart to even dream of falling in love, and that Einstein (played in a white fright wig by an otherwise subdued Walter Matthau) is determined to get her to follow her heart.

When we meet her, Catherine is engaged to a brainy psychologist (Stephen Fry) so oblivious to real life he can't figure out why the rats in one of his experiments consistently choose an electrical response that simulates an orgasm to one that simulates a full stomach.

Tim Robbins' Ed Walters would understand. He's a romantic to his soles, and when Catherine shows up at his garage needing service on her sports car, it's love at first sight. But how does he even begin to pursue a woman who thinks the phrase "garage monkey" is a literal description?

In this case, it does take Einstein to figure it out.

How the scientist and his gang of elderly Princeton cronies meet Ed and take up his cause is as delightful as it is fanciful, and soon they've hatched a plot to pass him off with Catherine as a working-stiff savant, an intellectual diamond-in-the-rough who's capable of knocking off theories every bit as impressive as e=mc2. But the scheme backfires when Ed delivers a paper on nuclear fusion, an old discarded theory of Einstein's, and President Eisenhower seizes on it as a power chip in the emerging Cold War with the Soviet Union.

Eventually, the story falls back on basic values, as Ed and Uncle Albert realize deception is a fool's game. But getting there is full of pleasures, large and small.

This is all spectacularly silly, but Robbins and Ryan have the chemistry to draw us in and take us the distance, in roles that play naturally to their strengths. Robbins' intelligence is hard to hide (that was one of the problems with "The Hudsucker Proxy," you couldn't believe he was stupid), and we know that sooner or later, Ryan's effervescence is going to explode through Catherine's cool facade.

"I. Q." is not exactly a physics lesson, but in a season currently dominated by a comedy called "Dumb or Dumber," I'd go for the one that mentions the theory of relativity.

SIGHT AND SOUND, 3/95, p. 42, Chris Darke

Princeton, NJ. The mid-50s. Celebrated physicist Albert Einstein is concerned about his niece, Catherine Boyd, who is engaged to be married to James, an accomplished but uncaring experimental psychologist. Catherine and James stop in a local garage, where Ed, a mechanic, instantly falls in love with Catherine. Finding her pocket watch in the garage, Ed takes it to her address, where he encounters her uncle. Einstein introduces Ed to his three friends, Godel, Liebknecht and Podolsky, and asks him to help them retrieve some objects they have lost up a tree while playing badminton. Einstein and Ed strike up a friendship that the professor seeks to cultivate further as soon as he realises Ed's feelings for his niece.

Einstein and his friends contrive to meet Ed regularly at his garage. They hatch a plan whereby Ed will masquerade as a physicist and deliver a paper on nuclear fusion at a forthcoming international symposium at Princeton. Catherine is surprised by Ed's hidden capabilities and is further intrigued after his success at the symposium, where he is hailed as a genius. After the reception, Einstein fakes a heart tremor to divert Catherine away from James. She and Ed take Einstein home, but he recovers and they stop at a cafe where Catherine and Ed dance.

The press get hold of the nuclear fusion story and Ed becomes a celebrity. James, out to humiliate Ed, stages a public test of his IQ. With the surreptitious assistance of the scientists, Ed scores an IQ of 186. On a sailing trip without James, Catherine admits to Ed that she loves him.

President Eisenhower visits Princeton to encourage Ed to start work on a nuclear-fusion powered space rocket to compete with the Russians. En route to a press conference, Ed confesses the truth to Catherine, who has found the flaw in Ed's paper on nuclear fusion. James announces at the conference that the paper was in fact a plagiarism of an unpublished paper by Einstein. Einstein asserts that, with the help of Ed's hoax and Catherine's calculations, he has conclusively disproven Soviet claims of possessing cold fusion technology. Ed and Catherine unhappily part but are bought together at last by the final machinations of Einstein and his friends.

With heartwarming homilies such as "never lose your sense of wonder" and "don't let your brain interfere with your heart", I.Q. pitches its self-consciously sentimental charm as if it were a *Readers Digest* story illustrated by Norman Rockwell and bought to you courtesy of Forrest Gump Enterprises Inc. Like *Forrest Gump*, *I.Q.* works on the simple conceit of juxtaposing the small town humdrum with the global-historic (and cosmic), but does justice to neither.

Because the film's purblind sentimental register bleeds into historical nostalgia, all potential comic moments are neutered. For example, the scene where Ed, having been made over into a stereotypical approximation of a dishevelled physics genius to address the symposium, is played for tooth-rotting sweetness rather than for the comedy of embarrassment such a moment could present. Cue shots of Ed haltingly delivering the paper, gazing misty-eyed at his muse and instantly finding the confidence to fake it successfully.

Such moments are not helped by the constant presence of Einstein's three comic stooges—Godel, Podolsky and Liebknecht—each progressively more of a caricature of the Jewish Eastern European émigré intellectual than Matthau's Einstein, who is played as an unkempt, caring uncle with a talent for self-deprecating one-liners. If nothing else, *I.Q.* will be of paradigmatic value to students researching a thesis on the Representation of Scientists in Popular Cinema. Gags about funny foreigners getting culturally acclimatised are far too familiar. See Einstein on a motorbike! Observe the three stooges in a convertible digging Chuck Berry! Its not that these gags could not be funny, its just that the film is so unimaginative it cannot muster the required degree of irony .

This is part of the larger problem with *I.Q.*; it refuses to mine the incongruencies around class and the status of intellect that might have made it more interesting. Instead, we become so accustomed to the spectacle of four venerable old gentlemen spying on Catherine, that the scenario starts to look a little creepy. Schepisi fails to foreground the subtext of voyeurism and remote control that underwrites the film's sexual politics. "She doesn't know what she wants", Einstein says of Catherine at one point. Ryan's interpretation of the character as a ditsy bobbysoxer with a Maths degree is little more than a blank centre to the film, focusing and absorbing the varieties of male desire. In fact, the film's intense and wearing sentimentality might be read as symptomatic of denial in the face of this latent meaning.

It is difficult to say exactly when *I.Q.* becomes so insufferable that one seeks solace in the more interesting reading, but it is not difficult to suggest why. More remarkable, but equally indicative of the film's complacency, is the underuse of its cast. Matthau, a great master of truculence, is denied any chance to exhibit jowly disdain. Robbins is exclusively a good-natured grease monkey who wears his windcheater well, and Fry is recognisably anal as the petulant scheming British lab-geek. One joke, one note.

VILLAGE VOICE, 1/3/95, p. 72, J. Hoberman

I.Q.'s unrelenting cute premise posits Meg Ryan, America's sweetheart, as the ditsy physics genius Catherine Boyd, for whom Walter Matthau, cast as her adorably rumpled guardian uncle, Albert Einstein, must play cupid. Meg, here a platinum blond, rolls her eyes, curls her lips, and pertly scrunches up her face. Matthau twinkles endearingly behind his bushy mustache and tells her things like "Don't vorry, *Liebchen*—it vill all vork out." If Matthau wins the lovability contest, it's in part because he's inexplicably been given the better hair.

Given that Catherine's father has gone to Heaven (where she identifies him with a particular comet), it is up to Uncle Albert, the vorld's nicest und shmartest man, to help the garage mechanic Ed Walters (Tim Robbins, no mean cutie himself) rescue Catherine from her dreadful British fiancé, a behavioral psychologist known, in an unacknowledged Freudian joke, as der Rat Man. Ed bonds with Al by taking him for a spin on his motorcycle and then helping him to transform his auto into a convertible; Einstein consequently returns the favor by passing off his young friend as the self-taught genius who has discovered a method for cold nuclear fusion.

Directing this variation on a venerable screwball theme (see *Ball of Fire*, 1941), Fred Schepisi manages a reasonable impersonation of Robert Zemeckis. As the opening blast of generic '50s rock 'n' roll makes clear, *I.Q.* is taking us back, Back to the Future. The 1955 mise-en-scène is twinkly enough to induce sugar shock; the special effects include a desiccated-looking President Eisenhower. Princeton is the paradise of fools where Uncle Albert's whimsical musings on chance, chaos, and the nature of the universe are echoed by a vaudeville posse of comic, Middle European sidekicks named for actual mathematicians and scientists. Naturally, much self-congratulatory mileage is derived from their incongruous luff for American popular culture.

Indeed, *I.Q.* can be read as a happy version of *Quiz Show*, in which a sympathetic Charles Van Doren reveals that he lied on TV to protect national security and is rewarded with a more attractive, less ethnic version of Herbie Stempel's wife. The myth of Einstein, Roland Barthes observed, is that the secret of the universe can be reduced to a single magic formula. In *I.Q.*, this ultimate wisdom comes straight from the Steven Spielberg songbook: "Don't let your brain interfere with your heart."

Also reviewed in:
CHICAGO TRIBUNE, 12/25/94, Tempo/p. 5, Michael Wilmington
NEW YORK TIMES, 12/23/94, p. C8, Janet Maslin
VARIETY, 12/29/94-1/1/95, p. 73, Leonard Klady
WASHINGTON POST, 12/23/94, Weekend/p. 36, Desson Howe

I'LL DO ANYTHING

A Columbia Pictures release of a Gracie Films production. *Executive Producer:* Penney Finkelman Cox. *Producer:* James L. Brooks and Polly Platt. *Director:* James L. Brooks. *Screenplay:* James L. Brooks. *Director of Photography:* Michael Ballhaus. *Editor:* Richard Marks. *Music:* Hans Zimmer. *Music Editor:* Sally Boldt. *Sound:* David M. Kelson and (music) Jay Rifkin. *Sound Editor:* Dennis Drummond. *Casting:* Paula Herold. *Production Designer:* Stephen J. Lineweaver. *Art Director:* Bill Brzeski. *Set Designer:* Mindi R. Toback and Cosmos A. Demetriou. *Set Decorator:* Cheryl Carasik. *Special Effects:* Bill Myatt. *Costumes:* Marlene Stewart. *Make-up:* Robert Ryan. *Stunt Coordinator:* Phil Adams. *Running time:* 116 minutes. *MPAA Rating:* PG-13.

CAST: Nick Nolte (Matt Hobbs); Whittni Wright (Jeannie Hobbs); Albert Brooks (Burke Adler); Julie Kavner (Nan Mulhanney); Joely Richardson (Cathy Breslow); Tracey Ullman (Beth Hobbs); Jeb Brown (Male D Person); Joely Fisher (Female D Person); Vicki Lewis (Millie); Anne Heche (Claire); Ian McKellen (John Earl McAlpine); Joel Thurm (Martin); Angela Alvarado (Lucy); Dominik Lukas-Espeleta (Ricky); Justina Hardesty (Essa); Robert Joy (U.S. Marshal); Maria Pitillo (Flight Attendant); Suzzanne Douglas (*Rainbow House* Star); Joseph Malone (Assistant Director); Jake Busey (Burke's Fired Driver); Harry Shearer (Audience Research Captain); Rosie O'Donnell (Makeup); Ken Page (Hair Person); Chelsea Field (Screentest Actress); Justine Arlin (Studio Executive); Amy Brooks (Shannon); Ian Deitchman (Popcorn Pictures P.A.); Maria Kavanaugh (Secretary on Telephone); Peter Kwong (Popcorn Pictures Intern); Roz Baker (Taxi Driver); Courtney Perry (Audition Child); Perry Anzilotti (*Rainbow House* Supporting Actor); Wren T. Brown (Floor Manager); John D. Schofield (Screentest Director); Steve Vinovich (*Rainbow House* Director); Chloe Brooks (Child Actress in the Street); Andy Milder (Warm-up Man); Ron Perkins (Victor); Aaron Lustig (Jack); Elisabeth Boyd (Elisabeth); Kate McNeil (Stacy); Patrick Cassidy (*Ground Zero* Villain); Woody Harrelson (*Ground Zero* Hero); Hannah Nielsen and Ingrid Nielsen (Baby Jeannie).

CHRISTIAN SCIENCE MONITOR, 2/8/94, p. 12, David Sterritt

"I'll Do Anything," an amusing satire of Hollywood and its denizens, has the most fascinating behind-the-scenes story so far this year.

Written and directed by James L. Brooks, whose credits include the popular "Terms of Endearment" and "Broadcast News," it was planned as an old-style Hollywood entertainment with eight musical numbers. But a test screening indicated that the music interludes were weighing down the story's effectiveness, so Brooks postponed the picture's release for a couple of months—it was originally slated for the Christmas season—to do additional shooting and editing.

This piqued more curiosity than usual from the show-business press, which drummed up more interest than usual in the production's bottom-line question: Did its last-minute changeover transform it into a sleek and streamlined winner or into a reconstructed patchwork that's neither musical-comedy fish nor straight-comedy fowl?

The answer lies somewhere in between. "I'll Do Anything" is a likable picture with breezy dialogue and a couple of first-rate performances. Yet its atmosphere wobbles between comparative realism—moments when we're meant to be seriously caught up in the lives and loves of the characters—and stylized touches left over from its earlier incarnation as a song-and-dance movie.

While this inconsistency isn't disastrous, the film also has another problem, unrelated to the tribulations before its release. Brooks can't seem to decide whether his tongue-in-cheek depiction of the movie business is intended to skewer Hollywood unmercifully—as movies like "The Player" and "All About Eve" have memorably done—or to poke gentle fun while simultaneously depicting Tinseltown as a fairyland with a happy ending around every corner. There's a sense of indecision within "I'll Do Anything" that doesn't bode well for all-out success at the box office.

Nick Nolte plays the main character, a struggling actor with personal and professional problems. As if it weren't already hard to land meaningful roles in a business that values sex appeal over serious talent, his ex-wife gets arrested for financial skullduggery, and he inherits the time-consuming job of raising their six-year-old daughter.

He loves the child dearly, but he's ill-prepared for adding full-time fatherhood to his hectic and erratic schedule. Then she complicates their relationship further by succeeding at something he's never accomplished for himself: landing a juicy part in a TV series, which promises fame and fortune if she can only memorize her lines and learn to cry on cue.

If it were written more decisively and directed more smoothly, "I'll Do Anything" might do for Hollywood what the hilarious "Broadcast News" did for television—expose hypocrisy and deflate pomposity via sharply defined characters in clearly focused situations. As it stands, the new movie is a hit-or-miss affair, alternating moments of superbly conceived parody with underdeveloped scenes that promise more than they deliver. It generates some hearty laughs and intelligent observations, but its ambitions outstrip its achievements.

Nolte gives a skilled and amiable performance as the hero, and young Whittni Wright couldn't be more feisty as his bratty-but-adorable daughter.

The most memorable acting comes from Albert Brooks, though, as a money-driven producer who oscillates between comic peevishness (an Albert Brooks specialty) and uproarious outbursts of self-centered buffoonery. Julie Kavner is thoroughly winning as his girlfriend. Rounding out the cast with varying effectiveness are Tracey Ullman as the arrested ex-wife, Joely Richardson as an aspiring mogul, Angela Alvarado as a helpful neighbor, and Ian McKellen as a European filmmaker.

Michael Ballhaus did the cinematography, which is sometimes quite vivid and sometimes too pretty for its own good. Hans Zimmer composed the score, which drenches much of the action.

LOS ANGELES TIMES, 2/4/94, Calendar/p. 1, Kenneth Turan

Just about the first thing anyone says to struggling actor Matt Hobbs, the center of James L. Brooks' idiosyncratic and entertaining "I'll Do Anything," is this heartfelt declaration from the woman who is briefly to be his wife: "Your feeling toward your work is one of the things I love most about you."

It's an admiration that writer-director Brooks not surprisingly shares. Because many of the traits that characterize actors, from a focus on insecurity to unapologetic emotionality and the willingness to take huge risks in front of as wide an audience as possible, can be applied to his work as well, especially to his marvelous last two films, "Terms of Endearment" and "Broadcast News."

So it's also no surprise that while his first feature since 1987 is in part a warm tribute to the acting profession, Brooks would hardly leave it at that. "I'll Do Anything" is also a two-couple romantic comedy, a study of an especially prickly father-daughter relationship and a gleeful skewering of aspects of modern Hollywood. It was even at one point supposed to be a musical, but something like nine songs by Prince, one by Sinead O'Connor and choreography by Twyla Tharp got very publicly left by the wayside when test audiences balked at their inclusion.

What's left after the music is what audiences have always responded to in Brooks' work: the cockeyed sense of life, the daring and quirky comedy, the great torrents of words that practically explode out of the air. No one writes characters quite like this, in fact no one since Joseph L. Mankiewicz decades ago has so consistently put such smart dialogue on the screen.

But in trying to do so much, Brooks inevitably runs the risk of stumbling. His films have always been loose-limbed balancing acts, with audiences wondering whether he'll manage to stay on the wire or not. With "I'll Do Anything," Brooks doesn't actually fall off, but he does slip.

For though it includes many laugh-out-loud moments and fine and lively performances by stars Nick Nolte, Albert Brooks, Julie Kavner, Joely Richardson, Tracey Ullman and tiny dynamo

Whittni Wright, this film falls short of holding together. A triumph of individual parts more than a coherent whole, "Anything" has a ragged, haphazard feel, possibly rooted in the way it was conceived, that ends in dissatisfaction despite the considerable pleasures it provides along the way.

Probably the film's greatest pleasure is its cast of characters, all of whom (including clever cameos by Ian McKellen, Robert Joy, Harry Shearer and Rosie O'Donnell) manage to be thoroughly engaging despite being burdened, in typical Brooks fashion, with more than their share of neurotic, obsessive behavior.

In fact, it's a measure of how psychologically shaky everyone in "I'll Do Anything" is that unemployed actor Matt Hobbs (Nolte) comes off as almost stable by comparison. When the film's main action begins, Matt is divorced from ex-wife Beth (Ullman) and hasn't seen 6-year-old daughter Jeannie (Wright) in three years, a situation that is about to change.

For though the out-of-work Matt pleads that "the only full-time job I seem to have is not showing how scared I am," Beth, a fanatical mother who believes "there is no such thing as spoiling a child," has compelling reasons why Jeannie simply has to spend an indefinite period of time with her father.

Terrified at the thought, Matt in desperation calls up Cathy Breslow (Richardson), an attractive production company executive he'd met at an acting class to see if she knows of any jobs. Through Cathy he ends up working for her boss, producer Burke Adler of Popcorn Pictures (Albert Brooks), and Burke's trusted market research associate, Nan Mulhanney (Julie Kavner).

Though it probably wasn't planned that way, the relationship between Burke and Nan turns out to be the most involving part of "Anything. " While not related, the two Brookses have always been on the same wavelength, and Albert's role as the tortured, tyrannical schlock producer who can't have lunch because "that's when everyone returns my calls because they're trying to miss me" is even stronger than the one in "Broadcast News" that won him an Oscar nomination.

With the looks of his face rapidly changing from horror to befuddlement to desperation, Brooks' Burke gleefully raises the energy level of the film whenever he's on screen. And Kavner's Nan does a beautiful job opposite him as the doyenne of test screenings who is compelled by virtue of an unlikely, combination of prescription drugs to tell all the truth all the time.

While Burke and Nan think they have a difficult relationship, the most torturous ones in the film are the interactions Matt has both with his daughter and with Cathy, a bright but overmatched executive who means well but, as the personification of the uncertain nature of the movie business, has to carry rather more metaphorical baggage than is good for the part.

As for young Jeannie, she turns out to be a remarkably self-possessed, intensely bratty little person who totally flummoxes her dad without half trying. Wright, an amazing performer who had just turned 4 when she auditioned for this complex child's role, has no difficulty holding her own against Nolte, who in his turn delivers one of the most relaxed and natural performances he's given recently.

As funny and moving as it all can be, laced with the cockeyed grace of struggling humanity, even this brief retelling of the film's diverse story lines shows why it was difficult to pull together. Though all its plots deal with relationships, they do not have much of a relationship with each other, and in the absence of a strong narrative through line, "I'll Do Anything" can do no more than offer a glimpse of the promised land, not a trip inside.

NEW YORK, 2/7/94, p. 64, John Powers

If today's Hollywood has a siren song, it is the old-fashioned technicolor musical, which has seduced and shipwrecked everyone from Francis Coppola and Martin Scorsese to Spike Lee and whoever it was who made *Swing Kids*. The latest to hit the reef is Jim Brooks, who wrote and directed *Broadcast News*. His new movie started out as a full-fledged musical with the actors singing and dancing to choreography by Twyla Tharp. Later, these numbers were expunged, and songs by Prince and Sinéad O'Connor were played over the action. Now those songs are gone too, and *I'll Do Anything* comes into theaters as what Brooks is calling a "romantic comedy"—an optimistic term for not-a-musical. A pleasant enough shambles, it's compulsory viewing for film critics, industry insiders, Albert Brooks fans, and connoisseurs of disaster.

I'll Do Anything is set in a benevolently corrupt Hollywood that owes more to *Singin' in the Rain* than to *The Player*. Nick Nolte plays Matt Hobbs, a talented, down-on-his-luck actor who is torn between two females: his bratty 6-year-old daughter, Jeannie (Whittni Wright), whom he hasn't seen since his divorce, and Cathy Breslow (Joely Richardson), a lovely but weak-willed movie executive who wants to boost his career. Cathy helps Matt land a chauffeur's job with her boss, Burke Adler (Albert Brooks), the thuggish head of Popcorn Pictures, who seeks out the lowest common denominator as the hog does the truffle. As insecure as he is insensitive, Burke is having an affair with his test-screening analyst, Nan Mulhanney (Julie Kavner), who anatomizes his character defects even as she joins him in bed.

When he decided the movie didn't work as a musical, Jim Brooks went back and shot some extra scenes to clarify the action. But this is like repainting the bricks from a house collapsed in an earthquake. Song-and-dance numbers aren't window dressing—they're a musical's meaning. When you pluck them out, the dramatic rhythm goes kerflooey, the characters become dinky and hollow, the performances have a bogus, dinner-theater bonhomie. Nolte and Richardson keep grinning and giving little head shakes as if to cue the showstopping tune that's going to rocket our spirits into the stratosphere. But *I'll Do Anything* never takes off, and without the larky good humor of musical numbers, Brooks's genial satire of Hollywood seems lame, almost clueless. He sends up easy targets like test screenings and studio execs who wear their smugness as a rapper does his 24K neck chain. But the barbs have no sting. How could they? Brooks cut the music from his own musical after bad test screenings.

It speaks eloquently of Hollywood's disarray that Columbia would green-light a big-budget musical with actors who can't sing (Haven't the studio heads ever seen *Paint Your Wagon*? Probably not) and a director who can't properly stage a conversation between Matt and his daughter, let alone pull off a bright, swirling dance number. What Jim Brooks *can* do is write funny dialogue, and the movie comes fluttering to life in the hugely enjoyable scenes between vulgar Burke Adler and his conscientious Nan. As in *Broadcast News*, Jim Brooks does for the actor Albert Brooks what Albert Brooks the director won't do for himself—he makes him adorable. With his pitbull neck and raspy bluster, Burke's a hilariously affectionate caricature of producers like *Die Hard*'s Joel Silver, guys so crassly narcissistic they think you're not being "real" unless you behave as atrociously as they do. And while only a Hollywood movie could make a pollster into a symbol of integrity, Julie Kavner's Nan is the perfect counterpoint, wading off her lover's self-congratulatory cynicism with ripostes all the more lacerating because they're expressed with such earnest, Marge Simpson matter-of-factness: I think it's so wonderful," she tells him, "that you don't worry about even trying to act strong." Their scenes together culminate in a marvelous, painfully funny sequence at a chichi restaurant: Nan walks out in horror as Burke works the room with a sweaty, groveling self-hatred that may keep you from ever again stopping by the table of someone who scares you.

Although we're expected to identify with honest Matt Hobbs, who has the gumption to tell off know-nothing industry phonies, he's too openhearted to hold our interest. All the movie's ambivalence about Hollywood goes into the slippery Cathy, an essentially decent person who wants to make good movies (or at least a remake of *Mr. Deeds Goes To Town*) but also wants to succeed so badly that she mistrusts her own instincts: What if they're wrong and it hurts my career? It's clear that Jim Brooks identifies with her anxiety, for even when she commits a hideous betrayal that most of us would never forgive, he doesn't really want us to dislike her. She gets her comic come-uppance, and we're supposed to think, "Cathy's not bad, just weak. That's just the way she is. That's just the way this business is."

Whether it's *The Mary Tyler Moore Show*, *Terms of Endearment*, or *Broadcast News*, Jim Brooks's work is forever urging the wry acceptance of life's limitations; there are no heroes or villains, only flawed, likable people. This attitude is often called "generous," but it's actually small-minded—a sitcom writer's genteel version of Burke Adler's pleasure in reducing everyone to the same primeval loutishness. I'd wager that Brooks secretly resents those who don't compromise: His climax subtly betrays Matt, the movie's one honest artist, by having him make a wry, accepting joke as he settles for a part too small for his talent. More revealingly, the movie betrays what Brooks surely knows to be true about Hollywood kids. He knows that the squalling Jeannie may be the most obnoxious child ever in a medium that specializes in loud, preening, smart-alecky little monsters—and yet he proceeds to sentimentalize her. He also knows it's a sick joke that Jeannie should become a child TV star, but he still douses her ascent in saccharine to give his not-a-musical an upbeat ending. Evidently, Brooks will do anything to help Columbia recoup the film's $43-million budget.

NEW YORK POST, 2/4/94, p. 37, Michael Medved

"I'll Do Anything" is a mess, but if writer-director Jim Brooks had kept the musical numbers he originally shot for the film it might at least have been an interesting mess.

We can't say for sure, since no critics have seen these interludes (featuring songs by Prince, Carole King and Sinead O'Connor) which Brooks removed from his picture when test audiences reacted to them with near-universal hostility.

In its current form, the film could never provoke such an intense reaction; in fact, it fails to generate emotion of any kind. This is a picture that's simultaneously gloomy and gooey, a formless fizzle that tries to blend satire and sentiment without bite, energy, or redeeming wit.

Nick Nolte plays a veteran character actor who, despite an Emmy nomination some 15 years ago and a bit part in "Platoon," can't get work in today's Hollywood. His sad situation takes a definite turn for the worse when a disaster in the life of his former wife forces him to take sudden charge of the emotionally disturbed 6-year-old daughter he hardly knows.

The reliable Nolte brings warmth and conviction to his long-suffering nice guy role, but he is totally surrounded by appallingly obnoxious characters—from his shrieking, horrifically hostile ex-wife (Tracey Ullman), to his outrageously spoiled, borderline schizophrenic 6-year-old-from-hell (played by pretty 5-year-old Whittni Wright), to a neurotic junior executive and fluff-brained flake (Joely Richardson) who becomes his love interest.

Richardson's boss is a crass, egomaniacal producer of body-count action films (Albert Brooks, with an unnaturally deep-throated growl) who gives the desperate Nolte a job as his driver.

When this misanthropic mogul begins an unsatisfying affair with a sad-sack, drug-dependent audience response researcher (Julie Kavner), their attraction to one another makes no sense at all—but neither do any of the other relationships, which serve as mere script conveniences rather than growing organically out of the characters.

This weakness is especially apparent in the central father-daughter connection, where Nolte and his impossible little girl come to adore one another in a sudden, arbitrary and inexplicable way that's dictated more by the need for artificially uplifting conclusion than by any demonstrated developments in their relationship.

Beyond manipulative melodrama, "I'll Do Anything" makes some feeble attempts to expose the prevailing nuttiness of Hollywood in the style of "The Player," but its soggy spitballs are aimed exclusively at obvious targets and display none of the satirical sting (or diabolical undercurrents) that Robert Altman brought to his vastly superior film.

NEWSDAY, 2/4/94, Part II/p. 60, Jack Mathews

The question facing writer-director James L. Brooks after research audiences rejected the musical numbers in "I'll Do Anything" was whether the film could possibly work without them.

After all, they weren't just rock video montages inserted to draw the youth audience and enhance soundtrack album sales. The numbers were inherent to his script, which he wrote as a musical satire about Hollywood. To eliminate them after the fact is a little like cutting the jokes out of a failed comedy in hopes of ending up with a ripping drama.

The answer, after months of re-editing and understandably gloomy speculation, is ... yes, well, it sort of works without the music. The movie has the same rich dialogue and humor we've got from Brooks in such TV series as "Mary Tyler Moore" and "Taxi," and his two Oscar-nominated films, "Terms of Endearment" and "Broadcast News." And Brooks has closed the wounds left by the excised numbers with surgical perfection.

If you didn't know it had once been a musical, you wouldn't know where the songs and dances had been located.

But we do know of his intentions, and we can't help thinking that the hollowness at the center of the story, and some of its characters, might have been filled with music.

As it is, "I'll Do Anything," the story of a broken-down actor (Nick Nolte) having to choose between his own career and the well- being of the 6-year-old daughter (Whittni Wright) suddenly entrusted to him, is a modestly amusing movie that reveals no good reason for consuming three years of Brooks' valuable time.

Nolte gives a smart, heartfelt performance as an actor, unlike himself, facing constant rejection and champing at the bit for a juicy role, such as the lead in a remake of "Mr. Deeds Goes to Town" that his production executive girlfriend (Joely Richardson) is pushing him for.

Though Nolte is not in the film's best scene, a casting meeting where women executives are asked to gauge Hobbs' appeal by their willingness to sleep with him, he has created such a strong profile of an actor's fragile ego you feel the pain for him.

We'll never know (unless Brooks does a director's cut later on) how that scene would have fit into a musical, but its satirical bite stands out in sharp relief from the rest of the movie. That is the main problem. There are a half-dozen scenes that—for being too serious or too silly or too sentimental—don't seem to be working to the same end.

Richardson's Cathy Breslow goes through a personality change unsupported by anything we see, and though Wright might have seemed another Shirley Temple in those missing musical numbers, she comes off now as just another cute movie brat.

Still, there is plenty to appreciate in the rubble. Brooks doesn't savage Hollywood as viciously as he did television in "Broadcast News," but the bites he takes will be felt. And he got a wonderful performance from Julie Kavner, as a blunt researcher having a tentative affair with the insecure head (Albert Brooks) of Popcorn Pictures.

"I'll Do Anything" refers, of course, to the cry of all out-of-work actors, but as Brooks learned after that disastrous research screening, directors sometimes know exactly how they feel.

NEWSWEEK, 2/7/94, p. 61, Marc Peyser & Mark Miller

Considering how successful director James Brooks is, he sure takes a long time to wake up and smell the double decaf cappuccino. A year ago, Brooks had sold so many people on his movie-musical "I'll Do Anything" that apparently no one thought much about the bizarre artistic team: music by Prince, Sinéad O'Connor and Carole King, choreography by Twyla Tharp—all performed by utterly unmusical, utterly undubbed Nick Nolte, Albert Brooks and Julie Kavner. But it's hard to ignore 100 people marching out of a test screening, which is what happened last August. So Brooks removed much of the music in order to work out minor details like plot and characters. Audiences liked it; Brooks still wanted to play Stephen Sondheim. He tried putting the music in the background and leaving the singing to the songwriters. But after a few more unsuccessful screenings and $10 million beyond the original $35 million budget, Brooks finally surrendered. "I'll Do Anything" is officially the first nonmusical musical. What was he thinking? "I had in mind," says the man behind "The Mary Tyler Moore Show," "Terms of Endearment" and "The Simpsons," "to destroy myself."

There's enough irony in all this to make a Robert Altman movie. "I'll Do Anything" is itself a behind-the-scenes look at the machinations of movie development, from cut-throat casting to test-screening hell. Nolte plays Matt Hobbs, an unemployed actor who will "do anything" to get a part. What he gets is custody of his 6-year-old daughter, Jeannie (Whittni Wright), the kind of child who slaps herself to make everyone think she's being beaten. She arrives as Hobbs's career is flickering, thanks to his new girlfriend, a ladder-climbing studio exec (Joely Richardson), and a carnivorous studio chief (Albert Brooks) for whom Hobbs works as a chauffeur. When Jeannie gets cast in a TV show, it further tests a deeply troubled parent-child relationship.

Even more amazing than the parallels between on-screen and behind-the-scenes Hollywood is that Brooks has somehow pulled it all together. "I'll Do Anything" is both wickedly funny and surprisingly touching, part "The Player" and part "Kramer vs. Kramer." Some of the fun is guessing where frog-voiced Nolte was to sing Prince songs with frightening titles like "Be My Mirror." But except for a few spots where the music gallops and dies abruptly, Brooks has done a miraculous job of sandpapering and spackling the holes left by the 10 songs (only King's sweet one remains). Which brings us back to our original question: if the movie works this well a cappella, what was he thinking? "I wanted to render Hollywood and this 6-year-old emotionally. I thought the music would help me make it more real. I just made a mistake."

But we may still get to hear Nolte Sings Prince. Danny DeVito wants to help put the music and dance numbers on laser disc. And fresh on the heels of disastrous movies-turned-Broadway-musicals like "The Red Shoes" and "The Goodbye Girl," Brooks says he's received several calls from producers eager to bring "Anything" to the stage. Some people never learn.

VILLAGE VOICE, 2/8/94, p. 53, J. Hoberman

I'll Do Anything isn't quite as shameless as its title would suggest—but not for lack of effort. The story of an actor who fails to win an Emmy and falls into a 12-year funk, TV maestro James L. Brooks's first movie since *Broadcast News* (1987) is an ode to misunderstood talent and misappreciated fatherhood, appropriately cued with sentimental mood music and embellished with inside Hollywood one-liners.

As the actor, Nick Nolte is honesty personified—meant to be a shambling, natural method type. (The press notes call him a "talented New York character actor.") When first introduced, he sports a Prince Valiant haircut and is living with Tracey Ullman in picturesque squalor; seven years later, the no-less-squalid house has been accessorized with a crying infant. Ullman walks out with the kid, leaving Nolte nobly clinging to the shards of his career. Years pass. Encouraged by a former acting student, now script reader (Joely Richardson), and desperate for a part, Nolte falls into the hands of a crass, obnoxious producer of crass, obnoxious action films, played (how else?) by Albert Brooks.

Nolte doesn't get the role he reads for, winding up as Brooks's chauffeur and therefore an integral part of the Popcorn Movies ensemble that includes Richardson and audience research expert Julie Kavner. Compounding his misery, Ullman resurfaces to stick him with their now six-year-old daughter (Whittni Wright). This shrill and attitudinous kid is a weird sort of brat—so blatantly actressy that her own TV break-through seems preordained. Indeed, Nolte is deemed a successful father precisely when Wright learns to "act" on TV. In the movie's context the child's motivational problem is that she can't cry on demand. So much is made of this that it's an unavoidably Brechtian moment when she does.

For all his Oscars, Brooks remains a television director writ large. *Terms of Endearment* used cancer to sanctify canned laughter; *Broadcast News* was *The Mary Tyler Moore Show* for people who claimed to never watch television. As those who do watch know, the sitcom staple is the functional dysfunctional family, workplace or actual. *I'll Do Anything* draws on both. While Nolte plays an updated version of *The Bachelor Father*, Albert Brooks presides over Popcorn Movies as a combination of Ted Baxter and Mr. Grant—at once the butt and the head.

Unable to modulate, actor Brooks defines in-your-face. The character is meant to be a spoof of megaschlockmeister Joel Silver, but Brooks tears into the role as though he's the one whose career has fizzled. His energy is disorienting; it doubles up the movie like a stomach spasm. When Brooks rants, he's coked up on ego—his features clench, eyes beam a kryptonite gaze on the spittle flying from his mouth. But (speaking of misappreciated talents) Brooks can only play a fully realized character in his own movies. For director James, actor Albert is either an abrasive jerk or a lovable neurotic, paired cute with bighearted Kavner, who explains that she's with him "for the same reason that 86 per cent of all older women love *Beauty and the Beast.*"

With her compulsive truth-telling, Kavner might be the movie's most explosive character were she not also so blatantly therapeutic. *I'll Do Anything* assumes the sitcom mandate to educate as well as entertain. The workplace mantra is "I am being real," and *I'll Do Anything* is all but bursting with realness. Nolte erupts when Popcorn's pompous development droid mindlessly disses half the name actors in the Academy of Motion Picture Arts and Sciences: "Where did they find you?" he yells with righteous indignation.

Nolte's passion inflames Richardson to pitch her pet project to Brooks. His response is appropriately formalist: "Very excellent presentation." But what else can he say? Her dazzling idea is to remake Frank Capra's 1936 comedy about a naively benevolent millionaire, *Mr. Deeds Goes to Town*. It's also Richardson's idea to cast Nolte in the Gary Cooper role of Mr. Deeds. She, however, is something less than a Capra heroine—a creature so other-directed that even her libido is ruled by focus-group consensus.

That *I'll Do Anything* is fixated on the idea of movies as a form of audience feedback is scarcely inappropriate given the film's (or Brooks's) production history. Although the producer-writer-director is a man with an internalized laugh track, *I'll Do Anything* was born in a burst of mad love. It was conceived and shot as a musical—eight songs by Prince, no less— and reverted to straight sitcom only after a series of less-than-enthusiastic test screenings. (Strikes me that signing Nick Nolte to sing and dance is booking passage on the Titanic, but Albert Brooks did execute a hilarious cover of "Something's Gotta Give" in *Real Life*, and Joely Richardson seems capable of anything.) "The music undermined the reality of the film," is how Brooks subsequently explained his movie's degenrefication to *Variety* editor Peter Bart. Brooks must be thinking of all the Hollywood movies whose verisimilitude was enhanced by the spectacle of performers bursting into song.

Thus denuded, *I'll Do Anything* may be realistically "real." As satire, however, it's pretty mealy-mouthed and toothless. Why is the shamelessly pandering Albert Brooks character any worse than his creator? *I'll Do Anything* outdoes *The Player* in flattering the industry it pretends to expose. What does it mean to evoke Oliver Stone as a Hollywood savior? That the movie's official dream project is a Frank Capra remake might be a form of courage. I don't think Brooks would have the nerve to even suggest redoing *Mr. Deeds* on television.

While the Nolte character is a beacon of integrity, everyone else on screen is presented as just one or another sort of failed actor. In the realm of *I'll Do Anything*, this basically means that they haven't learned to sublimate their hypocrisy. So is it Pirandello or schizophrenia? Taken at face value, *I'll Do Anything* is like a primer on how to be a sincere phony.

Also reviewed in:
CHICAGO TRIBUNE, 2/4/94, Friday/p. A, Michael Wilmington
NEW REPUBLIC, 3/7/94, p. 30, Stanley Kauffmann
NEW YORK TIMES, 2/4/94, p. C3, Janet Maslin
NEW YORKER, 2/28/94, p. 99, Anthony Lane
VARIETY, 1/31-2/6/94, p. 65, Brian Lowry
WASHINGTON POST, 2/4/94, p. C6, Rita Kempley
WASHINGTON POST, 2/4/94, Weekend/p. 43, Desson Howe

IMAGINARY CRIMES

A Warner Bros. release of a Morgan Creek production. *Executive Producer:* Gary Barber, Ted Field, and Robert W. Cort. *Producer:* James G. Robinson. *Director:* Anthony Drazan. *Screenplay:* Kristine Johnson and Davia Nelson. *Based on the book by:* Sheila Ballantyne. *Director of Photography:* John J. Campbell. *Editor:* Elizabeth Kling. *Music:* Stephen Endelman. *Music Editor:* Christopher Kennedy. *Sound:* Mark Ulano. *Sound Editor:* Skip Lievsay. *Casting:* Deborah Aquila and Jane Shannon. *Production Designer:* Joseph T. Garrity. *Art Director:* Pat Tagliaferro. *Set Decorator:* Dena Roth. *Set Dresser:* Michael Moran, Roman Guenther, Carl Winter, Damon Sullivan, and Nina Bradford. *Costumes:* Susan Lyall. *Make-up:* Kelcey Fry. *Stunt Coordinator:* David Boushey. *Running time:* 105 minutes. *MPAA Rating:* PG.

CAST: Harvey Keitel (Ray Weiler); Fairuza Balk (Sonya); Kelly Lynch (Valery); Vincent D'Onofrio (Mr. Webster); Diane Baker (Abigale Tate); Chris Penn (Jarvis); Amber Benson (Margaret); Elisabeth Moss (Greta); Richard Venture (Judge Klein); Seymour Cassel (Eddie); Tori Paul (Young Sonya); Melissa Bernsten (Gigi Rucklehaus); Annette O'Toole (Ginny Rucklehaus); Bill Geisslinger (Bud Rucklehaus); William Shilling (Mr. Garrity); Luke Reilly (Everett); Peggy Gormley (Mrs. Cole); Chad Burton (Vern); April Henderson (Roxie); Rebecca Long (Theater Manager); Diana Van Fossen and Kitty Larsen (Mothers at Tea); Carol Povey (Nona); Kelsea Aryn Graham (Young Greta); Jefferson Davis (Test Center Teacher); Pirrko Haavisto (Finnish Housekeeper); J. R. Knotts (Foreman); Greg Germann (Mr. Drew); Robert Blanche (Policeman #1); Ken Gillam (Policeman #2); Steven Clark Pachosa and Roger Wilson (Reno Men).

LOS ANGELES TIMES, 10/14/94, Calendar/p. 12, Peter Rainer

"Imaginary Crimes," set in the early '60s, is about the family life of con man. It's a terrific subject for a movie but, the way it's been done here, the story is mildewed with good intentions. It's a respectable piece of work, well acted, but it's not terribly exciting. The filmmakers seem to be flaunting what sensitive souls they are—more sensitive, even, than the characters in their movie.

Harvey Keitel plays Ray Weiler, whose wife (played, in flashbacks, by Kelly Lynch) has died, leaving him in charge of two young daughters, Sonya, the elder (Fairuza Balk), and Greta (Elisabeth Moss). Ray is the kind of guy who is constantly cooking up get-rich-quick schemes and then wheedling out of the inevitable fallout. Landlords, moneylenders and partners dog his elusive tracks, his daughters are schooled in keeping creditors at bay with well-rehearsed ruses.

The emotional core of the film is Ray's abiding love for his daughters despite his responsibility in damaging their lives. The one thing he does not do—at least not voluntarily—is desert them. In his own way he wants to do right by them—he wants them to be princesses. But he's hopelessly mired in a small-timer's mind-set. Compared to Ray, Willy Loman was a slickster.

Keitel doesn't pull out all of his stops, and his nuanced reticence is intriguing. (As a change of pace from his recent movies, he doesn't drop his pants, either.) As usual, he takes chances—clearly this is a role he cares about. Ray speaks in bookish cadences, as if he had memorized his words: it's the actor's unstressed way of bringing out Ray's insecurities.

But Keitel overvalues Ray's lumpishness: he's such a Common Man that, after a while, you long for something a bit more uncommon. Keitel is very good at getting at the self-hatred in Ray's weaselly soul—Ray even exploits his dead wife's name in order to get Sonya into a prestigious girls' school. What makes the scene work is that we can tell Ray still loves his wife.) But the film surrounds Ray in a nimbus of heartfelt intentions, and it tenderizes what might have been a great character—a great performance.

(And, for a film this well-acted, there are some shocking missed opportunities throughout, like the blink-or-you'll-miss-them cameos by Lynch, Diane Baker and Annette O'Toole.) The relationship between Sonya and Greta is sensitively played; the two actresses share the kind of rapport that can't be faked. Balk's Sonya, whose "poetic" voice-overs sugar the soundtrack, is shell-shocked, yet almost frighteningly vulnerable. She hates her father's consmanship and yet, like him, she holds out for golden opportunity. (In her case, the opportunities, like a college education, are far less pie-in-the-sky than Ray's.) Balk manages the difficult feat of creating a character who is both grimly resilient and fragile, and that combo seems true to the experience of abused children.

Director Anthony Drazan and his screenwriters Kristine Johnson and Davia Nelson based the film on an autobiographical novel by Sheila Ballantyne, and the film has the tentative self-consciousnessof "personal" reminiscence movies. Would a real look back to a childhood this ravaged appear so sedate and nostalgic?

Drazan manages the period setting convincingly, and he slides smoothly in and out of the flash-backs, but he doesn't want to take the audience over the edge-into the kind of emotional experience we can't sort out as soon as we leave the theater.

NEW YORK POST, 10/14/94, p. 47, Michael Medved

Every father is, at one time or another, a hero to his kids—no matter how little he may deserve their admiration.

As teen-agers, however, we all tend to cut our parents down to size—at times feeling bitterly betrayed by all the shortcomings we suddenly discover.

This process of adolescent disillusionment is the focus of "Imaginary Crimes," a powerful, poetic movie about a well-intentioned loser who ultimately squanders all the trust and affections his daughters once felt for him.

Harvey Keitel, an actor not generally celebrated for the restraint and delicacy of his performances, strikes a remarkable balance in the lead role, evoking pity and disgust in just about equal measure.

He plays an irresponsible dreamer in 1950s Oregon who believes so fervently in his own far-fetched inventions and mining schemes that he manages to fool a series of gullible investors.

His 17-year-old daughter (played by Fairuza Balk of "Gas Food Lodging") comes to realize that he is a fraud, but because her mother died of cancer years before, she and her little sister feel trapped in his shabby, crumbling world.

Keitel does manage to keep his word to his late wife by enrolling his oldest daughter in an exclusive Portland girls' school where her English teacher (beautifully played by Vincent D'Onofrio) encourages her to write down her painful recollections.

Based on the eloquent autobiographical novel by Sheila Ballantyne, the film brings these compositions to life in a series of flashbacks focusing primarily on the girl's dead mother—played by an appropriately ethereal and angelic Kelly Lynch.

These warm, vivid memories, of weekly trips to the movie palaces or maternal cheers as the child learns to ride a bike, bring the movie to brief bursts of vitality, so that it's painful for both the audience and the characters to return to the drab, doomed reality of life with father.

The problem is that we're aware of Keitel's flaws long before his daughters are and it becomes tedious to watch them slowly catching up to us.

With its atmospheric evocation of the Pacific Northwest in the Eisenhower era, and its focus on a troubled father who passes on his unhappiness to his helpless kids, "Imaginary Crimes" bears a striking resemblance to last year's critical favorite "This Boy's Life."

Keitel, like Robert De Niro in the previous movie, rails against "pinko intellectuals." But unlike De Niro's character he never comes across as a vicious monster: His unintended cruelties inspire sympathy and sadness rather than horror.

The best actor in the movie, aside from Keitel, happens to be a lovely 9-year-old newcomer named Elisabeth Moss, who portrays the younger daughter with such effortless energy and sweetness in the face of family adversity that she can just about break your heart.

Director Anthony Drazen (whose one previous film was the intriguing, uneven "Zebrahead") makes the most of these moments, helped immensely by a splendid, moving musical score by Stephen Endelman.

Though it never quite reaches the level of high tragedy which it strains to achieve, "Imaginary Crimes" powerfully projects pathos, and it's impossible to remain altogether unmoved.

NEWSDAY, 10/14/94, Part II/p. B8, John Anderson

Director Tony Drazan's first feature, "Zebrahead," which was a novel riff on high school race relations, may have been a bit earnest, but it was kinetic. His second "Imaginary Crimes" is basically inert. The fabled sophomore jinx? The result of working with someone else's script? Whatever, the two movies might have been made by two different people.

The malignant centerpiece of "Imaginary Crimes" is Ray Weiler (Harvey Keitel), a bourbon-drinking, Ralph Kramden-esque dreamer with a million schemes, a habitual liar who lacks the self-delusion that might make him sympathetic, or the enthusiasm that might make him successful. His older daughter Sonya (Fairuza Balk), who's been burdened with de facto motherhood of her younger sister, Greta (Elisabeth Moss), greets each episode of his verbal fantasies with a look of venomous disdain.

Balk and Keitel do what they can with the script, but there's never any sense of love between them, or even love lost. Sonya's dead mother, Valery (Kelly Lynch), seen in numerous flashbacks, is the sole object of affection. But since we know from the start she's already dead, her repeated appearances aren't so much bittersweet as anticlimactic, and even irritating.

"Imaginary Crimes," in which Ray's and Sonya's destinies diverge—hers toward college, his toward jail—is like a yellow photograph, somebody else's memory. A kind of female version of Geoffrey Wolff's "The Duke of Deception," it adopts the point of view of the child of the deceiver. But it keeps us at arm's length, which is fatal: None of us wants to watch misery, unless the director can make it our own.

SIGHT AND SOUND, 6/95, p. 44, Philip Strick

Typical of Ray Weiler, as recalled in later years by his daughter Sonya, is the time he takes her out to buy ice cream on the coldest night of the year. The cost goes on the tab while Ray excitedly outlines a scheme of partnership with the weary shopkeeper. This was Ray's style. When the Weiler's home-help walks out, complaining she hasn't been paid, Sonya and her younger sister Greta reckon this is the twelfth home-help they've lost since their mother died, but their father's buoyant spirits are seemingly undampened. He takes Sonya for enrolment at Edgemont School where her mother, Valery, was once a pupil, and charms the Headmistress,

Miss Tate, into disregarding both the fact that term has already started and that he has forgotten to bring his chequebook. Sonya remembers how she and her mother would be similarly charmed by Ray's eloquence and as quickly disillusioned.

At Edgemont, Sonya is encouraged by Mr Webster, the English teacher, to work on her writing skills; her essays are about what she knows best—life with father. While dodging the landlord's rent demands, Ray has developed a mining project with his friend Eddie that will, he says, make them all rich. The promise has been heard many times before: Valery used to escape from it by taking Sonya to Joan Crawford movies. Cultivating the other Edgemont parents, Ray manages to meet with local banker Bud Rucklehaus and Sonya overhears him launching into the familiar chance-of-a-lifetime assurances. She is reminded of the summer when her mother was found to have cancer; somehow Ray managed to arrange for Valery to live in a new house before she died.

Just in time to pacify the landlord, Ray suddenly has bundles of cash, but their affluence is soon dissipated. Taking its place is a growing hostility between Ray and Sonya, whose maturing literacy is regarded uneasily by her father. As Sonya learns she has been accepted by the University of California, Ray's creditors close in and he is put behind bars until Webster quietly pays his bail. Ray collects his daughters and sets out for Reno in the car, but Sonya refuses to accompany him and takes the reluctant Greta back home. Soon a social worker separates them both. In Reno, Ray and Eddie are offered the chance of a shady get-rich-quick scheme, but Ray realises this is a dangerous turning point and goes back to face his punishment. As Sonya celebrates with the Edgemont Class of 1962, cheered on by Mr Webster, she is reunited with Ray and Greta. Years later, as she describes in a novel, her father—still hunting his fortune—goes into the mountains and dies in the winter snows.

The courage of the single parent makes a convenient cinematic peg for displaying colourful nostalgia. The format of *Imaginary Crimes*, close on the heels of *Gas, Food, Lodging* and *A Home of Our Own* and close in spirit to *Housekeeping*, also emulates *To Kill a Mockingbird* in attempting to recapture the mood of a specific period of parenting, its look, its sound, and its ethics. Where *Mockingbird*'s Atticus, however, was the ultimate in father-figures, encased in an unyielding integrity, the floundering Ray Weiler is fascinatingly fallible, to be trusted only in his resilience and his fierce loyalty to his family. Interpreted through his daughter's eyes he is part-myth, part-Micawber, offered in exasperated affection as a miscast mystery, constantly striving to do the right thing in the wrong place at the wrong time.

Of this obsessive figure, marooned on the edge of fiction by a biographer who admitted to having no idea for most of their life together what he did all day, Harvey Keitel fashions an enjoyable complexity, a bad lieutenant without the lapses. The strutting, the fast talking, and the intensity of gaze are standard Keitel tricks, but the transparency is something new: vulnerable and Chaplinesque, perpetually within a few days' reach of the jackpot, he is a dreamer because without dreams his would be an intolerable predicament. Offsetting the scenes of blatant bluster—the neatly negotiated thawing of the headmistress, the verbal seduction of a whole tea party of impressionable ladies, the inventive disarming of a hostile creditor—are times when the rhetoric runs dry and Ray can only resort to near-speechless pleading which finds in Keitel a powerful orator.

Underlying these helpless hesitations is the unmentioned, dimly recognised, sexual tension between the father and the daughter who has slowly taken over her mother's role. Disconcertingly shifting around on the timescale *Imaginary Crimes* is uncertain of its 'present', which at the end even appears abruptly to be some years in the future, but its primary reminiscences, right from the early childhood glimpse of Sonya imitating Carmen Miranda for her father's entertainment, are all concerned with emotional crisis points. There is the outing in the woods when Sonya's patience with Ray's 'basic rules of the forest' routine snaps into furious revolt and they stand trembling at each other in an edgy physicality. There is the incident when Ray finds a copy of *Lady Chatterly's Lover* in Sonya's room and protests with an inarticulate panic. And most revealingly to them both there is his response to the news of her acceptance by the University: "Your Daddy knows about Professors—they'll ruin everything you and your Daddy hold precious..." This is biography as catharsis, unfolding in glances and movement rather than in words.

With his second film (his first, *Zebrahead*, appeared at the Sundance Festival in 1992), Anthony Drazan plays safe by concentrating on Keitel and using Sonya's commentary with lashings of orchestral emphasis to tell us what we're watching and how we should be feeling about it. His piecemeal structure forgets at times to paper over the joins, particularly when dealing with Sonya's schooldays and her encouragement by the altruistic Mr Webster (Played by Vincent D'Onofrio with an appealing dignity) whose affection for Walt Whitman has no discernible effect—his pupils mostly prefer Frankie Avalon—and who is mysteriously spied upon in one episode without preamble or consequence. For the account of Greta's deafness, Drazan shifts into subjective monochrome, an irrelevant experiment which, like the peculiar intrusion of a dancing-class, is at odds with a generally more careful formalism. The occasional awkwardness is also echoed by Fairuza Balk who, repeating her wide-eyed and slightly aggrieved appearances in *Gas, Food, Lodging* and *Murder in the Heartland*, imparts an understandable, if oddly dispassionate, stoicism. Even if she could, she is clearly not about to steal Keitel's thunder.

VILLAGE VOICE, 11/1/94, p. 64, Kathy Deacon

Ray Weiler (Harvey Keitel) is a con man who believes passionately in his own harebrained land investment schemes. With the rent perpetually in arrears, he's always insisting he's going to make his family rich in a day or two. When his dreamy wife's brief life of smoking and solitaire is cut short by cancer, Ray finds himself raising his two daughters on his own.

Zebrahead director Anthony Drazan has based his latest work on Sheila Ballantyne's novel, set in the late '50s and early '60s. It's constructed of flashback scenes narrated by Ray's elder daughter, Sonya (Fairuza Balk). Keitel's paterfamilias has a fierce commitment to his girls and a determination that Sonya will graduate from tony Edgemont high school, her mother's alma mater. When she mentions she'd like to go to college, though, he tells her she's too young to know what she's talking about: "Those pinko intellectuals will distort your values." Complaining if his daughters' "Hi Dad" is too low-key ("I deserve a little more enthusiasm than that"), Ray is unintentionally hard on his daughters.

Sonya is a budding writer with a talent for spare and moving description; her adolescence engenders a painful ambivalence toward her father and her sister, and her voiceover leaves the necessary things unsaid. Unfortunately, the flashbacks seem to occur somewhat randomly, and it's never really clear when "now" is, from what point in time Sonya is speaking.

Imaginary Crimes climaxes in 1962, and the film strains to evoke the tackiness of those years of the beehive hairdo and *Hawaiian Eye*. It's a small film about sacrifice, about how three people's lives play out because they are a family. The girls' roles are sensitively acted. Keitel's performance is a bit one-dimensional, but manages to elicit grudging sympathy. As a con he thinks he knows the way the game is set up: without money you are nothing, without family you have nothing. This is a film about lower-middle-class life that could have been made anytime.

Also reviewed in:
CHICAGO TRIBUNE, 10/28/94, Friday/p. O, Johanna Steinmetz
NEW YORK TIMES, 10/14/94, p. C16, Caryn James
VARIETY, 9/12-18/94, p. 42, Daniel M. Kimmel
WASHINGTON POST, 10/28/94, p. F6, Hal Hinson

IMMORTAL BELOVED

A Columbia Pictures release of an Icon production. *Executive Producer:* Stephen McEveety. *Producer:* Bruce Davey. *Director:* Bernard Rose. *Screenplay:* Bernard Rose. *Director of Photography:* Peter Suschitzky. *Editor:* Dan Rae. *Music:* Georg Solti. *Music Editor:* Dean Beaville. *Sound:* Peter Glossop. *Sound Editor:* Nigel Holland. *Casting:* Marion Dougherty. *Production Designer:* Jiří Hlupý. *Art Director:* John Myhre. *Set Decorator:* Olga Rosenfelderová. *Set Dresser:* Marek Hlupy. *Special Effects:* Garth Inns. *Costumes:* Maurizio Millenotti. *Make-up:* Fabrizio Sforza. *Running time:* 203 minutes. *MPAA Rating:* R.

CAST: Gary Oldman (Ludwig van Beethoven); Jeroen Krabbé (Anton Felix Schindler); Isabella Rossellini (Anna Marie Erdödy); Johanna Ter Steege (Johanna Reiss); Marco Hofschneider (Karl van Beethoven); Miriam Margolyes (Nanette Streicher); Barry Humphries (Clemens Metternich); Valeria Golina (Giulietta Guicciardi); Gerard Horan (Nikolaus Johann van Beethoven); Christopher Fulford (Caper Anton Carl van Beethoven); Alexandra Pigg (Therese Obermayer); Luigi Diberti (Franz Josef Guicciardi); Michael Culkin (Jakob Hotscevar); Donal Gibson (Karl Holz); Matthew North (Young Karl van Beethoven); Geno Lechner (Josephine von Brunsvik); Claudia Solti (Theresa von Brunsvik); Rory Edwards (Wenzel Robert von Gallenberg); Hannes Flaschberger (Joseph Deym); Leo Faulkner (Young Ludwig van Beethoven); Fintan McKeown (Johann van Beethoven, Sr.); Everton Nelson (George Bridgetower); Sandra Voe (Marie Frolich); Bernard Rose (Elector Max Friedrich); Jindra Petráková (Lilo Braun); Marek Vašut (Custody Policeman); Hugo Kiminsky (Magistrate); Stanislav Behal (Ignaz Schuppanzigh); Arnoštka Mohelská (Suzanna Guicciardi); Štěpán Hlatky (Zoltan); Gordon Lovitt (Metternich's Flunky); Anna Kolińská (Fritzi Erdödy); Ruby Rose (Mimi Erdödy); Johan/Josef Kolińský (August Erdödy); Jan Kuželka (Country Policeman); Barbora Srncová (Erdödy's Servant); Bruce Davey (Artillery Captain); Jan Censky (Captain); Tomas Hanak (Jacob Raicz); Jiři Patocka (Pock-marked Tramp); Stanislav Hybler (Sergeant); Michael Arthur Miller (Toothless Drunk); Petr Pospicahl (Thin Man); Pavel Vondruska (Aristocrat); Ladislav Kazda (Landlord).

FILMS IN REVIEWS, 3-4/95, p. 58, Maria Garcia

Bernard Rose's *Immortal Beloved* is the story of an unsolved mystery involving the German composer Ludwig van Beethoven. After Beethoven's death, an undated and unaddressed letter was found among his papers, a passionate love letter written to an unknown woman. Maynard Solomon, one of Beethoven's biographers, conducted an extensive investigation into the recipient's identity, which he articulates quite convincingly in his book (*Beethoven*, 1977). Solomon's conclusion is very different from Rose's. (Attempts were made to reach the director in order to discover this sources.) In fact, *Immortal Beloved* ignores the four most likely recipients, the ones Solomon identifies as candidates according to the evidence he and other biographers have discovered.

Sacrificing historical fact in the name of poetic license isn't new; in fact, in Hollywood, even in this era of historical revisionism, it is entirely acceptable, especially if the film is brilliant but obviously fabricated, if it provides a new twist to an old story, or if it's well-directed and controversial (like *JFK*). Unfortunately, despite all extraordinary performance by Gary Oldman (playing Beethoven), *Immortal Beloved* isn't any of these things. The supporting roles are poorly acted, the direction is uninspired at its best and amateurish at its worst, and the screenplay, leaving aside for a moment the issue of poetic license, frequently distances us from the main character through the narrative voice, which is not Beethoven's but Schindler's, the composer's secretary.

Beethoven never married, and Solomon claims that despite his appeal to women, and the intrigues or affairs he was supposedly involved in, he was a misogynist and actually engaged in very few intimate relationships with women. That makes the letter to the *Immortal Beloved* an important document, but in order to comprehend its significance we must understand it in the context of Beethoven's life or his life's work. Otherwise, it's a tempest in a teapot, which is exactly what it becomes in this film. Rose chooses to tell the singularly anticlimactic story about the search for the identity of the *Immortal Beloved*. One can't help feeling that the director/screenwriter sacrificed cathartic storytelling in order to indulge himself, to tell us about *his* research into Beethoven's life. That sacrifice is painfully evident in the disparity between the lavish sentiment such a story could have invoked, and the overwhelming blandness with which it is actually presented.

Failing an interesting portrayal of events, one may hope for historical accuracy. But even that's not forthcoming in this movie. Schindler, through whom the story is told, was not a friend of Beethoven's, nor did he remain a secretary for very long—in fact, Schindler destroyed 260 of Beethoven's approximately 400 conversation notebooks, and he forged entries into those notebooks. He published the *Immortal Beloved* letter in 1840, forging the date, an offense which was later discovered by Ludwig Nohl, another of Beethoven's early biographers. Actually, much of what we know about Beethoven is based on the contemporary accounts of two of his close friends and associates, Franz Wegeler and Ferdinand Ries.

Contrary to Rose's version of events, Beethoven's estate was not willed to the *Immortal Beloved*. According to Solomon, when the composer sued for guardianship of his nephew, Karl, a key event in the film, he was acting out of a deep psychological conflict with women, one manifested in his relationship with his sister-in-law, Karl's mother. That conflict, Solomon explains, is also evident in his lifelong indecision over intimate relationships with women, a sentiment that is clearly expressed in the three-part letter to the *Immortal Beloved*.

Beethoven was the first composer to raise orchestral music to the status of choral or operatic music. In other words, his greatest achievement was realized in the absence of language and of lyrics; his hearing loss eventually precluded him from engaging in conversation. Beethoven left only one letter expressing physical passion, a letter which probably never reached its intended reader. These facts lead us to wonder whether his exquisite music was composed from a well of frustration, suppressed passion, unexpressed emotion, and unrequited love—the stuff of great movies, but not *this* movie.

LOS ANGELES TIMES, 12/16/94, Calendar/p. 6, Kenneth Turan

It is a classic mad maestro look, half-rabid, half-rhapsodic, and seeing it on Gary Oldman's face unmasks "Immortal Beloved" even before you read the breathless prose on the rest of the poster: "The genius behind the music. The madness behind the man. The untold love story of Ludwig van Beethoven." Oh, brother.

Yes, this is another one of Hollywood's silly symphonies, an unintentionally amusing bit of piffle that allows mortals a privileged glimpse into the private life of a legendary composer, letting us watch in awe as the great man indulges in passionate romantic liaisons and says things like, "I am writing a new symphony. It will cause a scandal."

And great he was, worthy of the somber funeral oration delivered in 1827 by Beethoven factotum Anton Schindler (Jeroen Krabbe): "He was an artist and who will stand beside him? The thorns of his life wounded him deeply, but he held to his art. He carried the music in his heart even when he could no longer hear it." And so on.

Devoted as Schindler was to the maestro, he is as shocked as the next person when a hidden document reveals that Beethoven left everything to the great love of his life, the never identified "Immortal Beloved." "The maestro was nursing a secret passion," Schindler all but gasps. "Who could this be?"

Armed with a list of likely suspects, Schindler ignores the composer's gruff surviving brother who wants the big bucks for himself, and sets off on a grand tour of former girlfriends, determined to solve this musical mystery because, and you can quote him, "There can be no peace without the truth."

The first stop is a sprawling hotel in Carlsbad where Beethoven and the I.B. were scheduled to have a rendezvous years before. But the lady mysteriously stormed out mere seconds before the maestro's arrival, causing the bereaved man to smash furniture and heave armchairs out the window like a rampaging rock star.

Next is Vienna and a visit to the Countess Julia Guicciardi (Valeria Golino), an early Ludwig groupie who locks the door and insists, "What I shall tell you will never leave this room." Though Beethoven had the personality of a common oaf, she reveals, he first became her piano teacher and then won her heart. But her snooty father, upset at the maestro's increasing deafness and his humble birth, nixed the match.

Deafness also forged a bond between the composer and another woman in the I.B. sweepstakes, the countess Anna Marie Erdody (Isabella Rossellini), encountered by Schindler in a roadside tavern knocking a few back with the hearty peasants of her Hungarian estate.

She met the composer at the first performance of one of his concertos when Beethoven's hearing disorder, which made the world sound like a jet, was forever revving its engines, causing him to act strangely and provoking audience laughter. "His fire offended their small brains," the countess grumbles, still upset at the tyranny of petty minds.

The last important woman in thc composer's life is his sister-in-law Johanna (Johanna Ter Steege), a no-nonsense, self-reliant type who got on Beethoven's bad side by running off with his favorite brother.

Given how over the top he's been recently, Oldman is actually restrained (for him) as the romantic composer who storms through life railing against the commonplace, but the role is conceived in such a formulaic way, it can't arouse much interest.

"Immortal Beloved" does have a few things to look forward to, especially the snippets of the man's splendid music, here played by soloists Murray Perahia, Emanuel Ax and Yo Yo Ma and the London Symphony Orchestra conducted by Sir Gcorg Solti.

But though Bernard Rose's interest in Beethoven is doubtlessly genuine, that has not stopped him from taking liberties with history and turning out an inane piece of work, the kind of movie where you can actually see the irate master scratching Napoleon's name off what came to be known as the "Eroica" Symphony. Those wild and crazy composers, they really knew how to live.

NEW YORK, 1/9/95, p. 48, David Denby

In the most familiar piece of music in the world—the last movement of Beethoven's Ninth symphony—something happens that no one really understand. As the hymnlike "Ode to Joy" theme reaches its first thundering apotheosis, the chorus and orchestra break off, and Beethoven suddenly throws in a variation in the form of banal military march. Tenor and chorus join the triangle, bass drum, and twittering piccolo, and the march builds to an almost hysterical climax. What's going on here? The rude, bang-the-can march is followed by a superbly exhilarating orchestral passage—pure scampering energy—that eventually leads back to another statement of the elevated "Ode to Joy" theme and the symphony's jubilant conclusion. But why the military episode? Just a bit of darkness and mockery before the inevitable triumph?

In *Immortal Beloved*, the stone-deaf Beethoven (Gary Oldman) stands up beside the conductor at the 1824 premiere of the symphony in Vienna, and as the march passage begins, a faraway look comes into his eyes. The music continues, and in a flashback we see Beethoven's loutish father in a military bicorne, pawing the local whores in an alley and staggering into his house; the young Beethoven, afraid of a beating, escapes through a window (beginning of scampering orchestral passage), jumps into a pond, and looks up at the stars. It's that memory of boyhood escape that inspired the two musical episodes. Or so we're meant to believe.

Silly? Of course it's silly. As all of us learned in school (in those long-gone days when they taught music in school), music is never simply "about" a series of real-life happenings or ideas. As an interpretation of Beethoven's music, *Immortal Beloved* is repeatedly embarrassing; to take another example, the great storm in the *Pastoral* Symphony gets reduced to a temper tantrum. But then, no movie about Beethoven—or Homer or Michelangelo or Shakespeare—is likely to be anything less than kitsch, since the genius's work is sure to outclass whatever interpretive context the filmmaker can provide for it. Some subjects really should be left alone. Having said that, I should also say that *Immortal Beloved*, which was written and directed by Bernard Rose, is nothing like such florid miseries as *Song Without End* (the life of Liszt). Parts of the movie are stirring, even moving, and Gary Oldman is a fiery, sullen Beethoven. This is kitsch of a high order.

Like *Citizen Kane, Immortal Beloved* takes the form of a posthumous investigation: The great man dies, and Anton Schindler (Jeroen Krabbé), the composer's devoted friend, amanuensis, patsy, and eventual biographer, travels around Austria and Hungary, visiting B's former mistresses. Which one of them is the "Immortal Beloved" to whom Beethoven once addressed a passionate love letter? Is it the rapturous, worshiping Giulietta Guicciardi (Valeria Golino), to whom Beethoven gave piano lessons? Or the sublime Countess Erdödy (Isabella Rossellini), whom Beethoven consoled after the death of her son by playing the piano for hours (a true story)? Along the way, Schindler touches on nearly every aspect of Beethoven's emotional life, including the other great mystery that stirs every biographer's lust: Why was Beethoven so obsessed with his nephew Karl? Beethoven spent the greater part of five years fighting his sister-in-law for control of the boy. Was Beethoven a repressed homosexual? Some have thought so. The shining-eyed Marco Hofschneider certainly makes a luscious Karl. But Rose chooses to ignore all the pressures of queer theory and instead ties these mysteries together into a single, improbable, and decidedly hetero package.

Rose, who has made music videos and a few minor movies, says he has been obsessed with the subject for years, and I believe him, since no one could make a folly like this cynically. I mean, what does Rose think he is telling us? In *Citizen Kane*, the mystery of Rosebud, when it is finally explained, explains nothing; the same is true here. Rose doesn't come close to the real conundrums, such as how this boorish, deaf, slovenly man could compose one masterpiece after another, or how the staggering ethical and aesthetic idealism evident in, say, the Ninth symphony could have consorted with a shocking personal ruthlessness.

The movie's externals are impressive. Prague, standing in for imperial Vienna, looks beautiful, and the music on the soundtrack is powerfully (if heavily) performed by Sir Georg Solti and the London Symphony Orchestra. To its credit, *Immortal Beloved* is neither fey nor pompous. Beethoven rages and suffers and curses, and people treat him as if he were a man and an artist, not some demigod; the women are both fleshy and intelligent. Like almost everyone who makes movies now, Rose fears dullness, and he whips up a tempest when plain statement would have sufficed. Sometimes the roaring composer acts like a rock star tearing up a hotel room in Cleveland; at other times the Beethoven myth of tempestuous brilliance gets merged into the Mozart myth of neglected genius, which in Beethoven's case is nonsense. Beethoven was immensely famous in his own lifetime, and there's no need for Rose to create special sympathy for him; the director is already dramatizing one of the most painful stories in the history of the arts—Beethoven's increasing deafness—in all its horror, dementia, and excruciating comedy. Beethoven fakes his way through conversations and rehearsals, storming out when he can't figure out what's going on. Conducting the *Emperor* Concerto, he cues in the sections at the wrong time; the result is chaos. It is a tragic moment, the disharmonizing of the universe. For all its hubris and awkwardness, *Immortal Beloved* shakes its fist at the heavens often enough to capture the spirit of its outsize hero.

NEW YORK POST, 12/16/94, p. 66, Michael Medved

Anyone who pays even the slightest attention to the world of classical music knows that the biggest rage of recent years has been the fascination with original instrument performance: using museum-piece equipment to approximate the sound that composers heard themselves when they wrote their great music.

With so many original instrument ensembles enjoying worldwide popularity, and with antique instruments prominently displayed on screen, then why did the bumbling producers of "Immortal Beloved" fill the soundtrack with the spectacularly incongruous, inauthentic sound of today's London Symphony Orchestra?

It's just another wasted opportunity, and altogether typical of this maddening, misguided motion picture.

The focus is one of the great mysteries in musical history; the identity of the "Immortal Beloved" addressed in a passionate letter found with Beethoven's papers after his death in 1827.

Stylish writer-director Bernard Rose ("Paper House") explores the riddle with the help of an absurd plot twist in which the composer wills his fortune to this mystery woman and it's up to long-suffering secretary Anton Schindler (played by a bespectacled, appropriately understated Jeroen Krabbe) to find out who she is and give her the money.

The story then unfolds with flashbacks as Schindler interviews two elegant aristocrats (Valeria Golino and Isabella Rossellini) who had been involved with the maestro.

Gary Oldman, assisted by world-class makeup transformations, does a magnificent job portraying the lonely composer at various stages of his troubled life. He is so good, in fact, as the surly, shabby, willfully eccentric, ferociously independent, tormented deaf genius that the strength of his performance works against the script's most absurd supposition; that this notoriously solitary sufferer was actually a "Casanova" (a term used in the press notes) who bedded innumerable women like some contemporary rock idol.

These dumb distortions need not have been fatal to the project: after all, "Amadeus" (which also used gorgeous Prague locations) took comparable liberties with Mozart's life but made so much dramatic sense on its own terms that it remained a superbly satisfying motion picture.

The problem with this picture is that even for those who know nothing about Beethoven, the elements don't add up, and when filmmaker Rose gets around to his ludicrously far-fetched "solution" to the "Immortal Beloved" mystery, audiences will groan with distaste and disbelief.

Meanwhile, other elements of the great man's personality, clearly preserved in his letters, are altogether ignored by the film including his close, obsessive but agonized relationship with a God who had cursed him with progressive deafness. That deafness itself, however, is portrayed with frightening effectiveness—occasionally rendering the roaring racket that filled Beethoven's head and obscured the sounds of speech or music.

An inventive montage of bitter childhood memories, perfectly and ironically coordinated to the music of the Ninth Symphony's "Ode To Joy," shows how powerful the whole movie might have been had it not been stretched and distorted to fit its framework of mediocre melodrama.

At points, the film is so strong, in fact, that its failures aren't just disappointing: They are downright infuriating, leaving a project that is hardly immortal, and will be beloved by few.

NEWSDAY, 12/16/94, Part II/p. B7, Jack Mathews

After his death in 1827, at the age of 56, three letters wee found among the effects of composer Ludwig van Beethoven, addressed but never mailed to a woman identified only as "Immortal Beloved." For 167 years, the woman's identity has remained a mystery to historians and biographers, but it couldn't elude the deductive powers of writer-director Bernard Rose.

"It is not the solution that any of the Beethoven biographies have come up with," Rose says, of the jaw-dropping revelation of his "Immortal Beloved," but I defy any of them to prove me wrong.

I would defy any of them to stay awake. Rose has turned his version of the mystery into such a convoluted mess, and made such a poor case for his theory, it isn't compelling as fictional drama, let alone biographical insight.

It is too bad. Rose is obviously a talented director; the scenes within his scrambled context are vibrant with energy and demonstrate a genuine feel for the madness of Beethoven and the emotional impact of his music. He also got a smart, passionate performance from Gary Oldman, who portrays the deaf and ill-tempered genius over the last three decades of his life.

But in choosing to tell the story in the style of a cheap whodunnit, teasing us with clues and red herrings, and setting up the revelation as if it were the last act of a Sherlock Holmes tale, Rose defused the real power of his story. He kept Beethoven's secret lover such a secret, we gasp out of disbelief, not sweet surprise.

Beethoven's letter—there's just one in the movie—is the lone piece of evidence leading his secretary, Anton Schindler (Jeroen Krabbe), to the hotel where the maestro's lover had apparently stayed, then to three different women in his life—the Countess Guicciardi (Valeria Golino), to whom Beethoven had proposed as a young man; the Countess Erdody (Isabella Rossellini), who rescued him from embarrassment at a court concert where his deafness was exposed, and his brother's widow Johanna (Johanna Ter Steege), whose child he had legally taken from her and raised to become his hearing alter ego at the piano.

Had Rose told the story as linear, straightforward biography, critics might be comparing it to "Amadeus." It has the scale and human dimension, a similar father-son dynamic, spectacular costumes and settings (it was shot in the pristine palaces and cobbled streets of Prague), and a sound track that would drown out an Italian opera.

The truth is that even if Rose hadn't "solved" the romantic mystery, he had a fascinating subject. What is it, Beethoven wonders at one moment, about music that alters the chemistry of the brain, shifts moods, communicates feelings from the author to the audience, and where does that creativity come from?

While careening through his own maze, Rose begins to answer those questions, and in those moments the film soars. But it is a maze, and when you finally get to the center, all you remember is the trouble you had getting there.

SIGHT AND SOUND, 3/95, p. 41, Nick Kimberley

Ludwig van Beethoven is dead. Vienna is in mourning. Even in death, mystery surrounds the composer, whose will bequeaths his worldly goods to his "Immortal Beloved". No-one—least of all his relations who are incensed by their treatment—knows who this woman can be, but Schindler, the composer's secretary, vows to uncover her identity.

In a series of encounters, each occasioning its own flashbacks, Schindler attempts to unravel the strands of Beethoven's tangled love life. He meets the countess Julia Guicciardi. Years earlier, a beautiful adolescent, she gave Beethoven access to the Viennese *beau monde* which, she recalls, was suspicious of the composer's political views: was he not an admirer of Napoleon? Bewitched by her beauty, Ludwig had dedicated a piano sonata to Julia: perhaps she was his Immortal Beloved.

Schindler also travels to Hungary to meet the Countess Anna Marie Erdody. She remembers seeing Beethoven for the first time at a performance of his music, when his deafness first became apparent to his public. She comforted Beethoven, living with him through one of his life's few periods of contentment, but was she his greatest love?

Schindler is more and more intrigued by Beethoven's relationship with Joanna, wife of the composer's brother, Caspar. Another brother, Johann, maintains that Beethoven hated women; as proof he cites an incident when Beethoven first met Joanna. She flirted with him; he denounced her to Caspar as a common whore. No man who behaved like that could ever truly love a woman.

But Schindler learns more: about a fight between Caspar and Ludwig which only ended when Joanna told Ludwig that his brother was dying of consumption; and about the legal battle after Caspar's death, when Ludwig won custody of Joanna's son Karl. Intent on turning him into a concert pianist, Beethoven bullied the boy mercilessly, refusing to allow him to see his mother. Schindler realises that Beethoven thought Karl was his own son. The composer had an affair with Joanna and beneath his protestations of hatred lay a lifelong love. Joanna was Beethoven's Immortal Beloved, but this knowledge, and the rewards that go with it, cannot compensate for the way the composer had treated her. Great art cannot obliterate her painful memories.

When, in Julien Temple's *The Great Rock'N' Roll Swindle*, Sid Vicious brings his rendition of 'My Way' to a rousing climax by pulling a gun and shooting into the audience, he gives a sardonic twist to the Romantic figure of the artist as an outsider, tormented by the demands of the public and the marketplace. Even punk preferred its artists to be tormented and to show it. The agony guarantees their genius, their separateness from us.

As Benjamin Britten once remarked, the rot started with Beethoven. He was the prototype of the tortured genius, his deafness an emblem of that condition of being in the world, but not of it. Bridging the gap between the eighteenth and nineteenth centuries, between Classicism and Romanticism, Beethoven prefigured generations of misunderstood geniuses who could only be sullied by contact with the *vulgus*, the mass audience. Gunslinging Sid Vicious reduced the stereotype to absurdity while at the same time subscribing to its power.

Gary Oldman played Sid Vicious in Alex Cox's *Sid and Nancy*, and now plays Beethoven in *Immortal Beloved*. While not quite portraying the composer as a proto-punk, Gary Oldman invests him with something of the rock star's sneery truculence. The script provides its own gloss, at one point demanding that Beethoven indulge in that quintessential act of rock 'n' roll bravado, throwing furniture through a hotel window. Pouting and strutting, his accent sliding across vast swathes of Central Europe, Oldman gives us the artist in self-destruct mode. Thus Beethoven underwrites the film, but to what end if the composer is portrayed as just an irritating little fart?

Everything about *Immortal Beloved*—not least its title—is judiciously old-fashioned. Declining to follow the current trend for performing Beethoven's music on instruments of his period, the film-makers obstinately choose a modern orchestra playing modern instruments—which is no longer the modern way. No doubt it suits the soundtrack, which favours volume throughout. Every footfall, every scrape of a chairleg, is magnified, as if such hyper-realism could take us into a realm beyond the merely human.

Not that the film overlooks the minutiae that make for a worldly authenticity. The composer is variously called van Beethoven, von Beethoven, Ludwig, Luigi and Louis, all of which are authentic. At another level, the many forenames suggest that he is a man for all Europe, which suits the film's mythifying. Beethoven was indeed impressed by the new pianos being made in England—his Broadwood recently toured concert halls throughout Europe. It's an obscure logic that has a coachman say "Ja mein Herr" when everyone around him is speaking English, but the range of accents on display is not only a product of multi-national casting: it can also be taken to represent the variety of accents in a nineteenth century capital before mass travel had begun to eradicate regionalisms.

Such tiny details show that someone has done their homework, yet they never add more than decoration, knowing nudges that try to convince us that this is how it really was. The narrative requires Beethoven's genius to guarantee it, but that cannot obscure the fact that this Beethoven—authentic or not—is repressed, thuggish and a boor. Shades of *Amadeus* haunt *Immortal Beloved*, but the zest that enlivened Peter Schaffer's play and Milos Forman's film is not in evidence here.

VILLAGE VOICE, 12/20/94, p. 65, Amy Taubin

Not to lose perspective: *Immortal Beloved*, which stars Gary Oldman as Beethoven, is a ridiculous movie in search of the sublime. It is, however, my guilty pleasure of the year. Basically, the combination of Oldman and Beethoven got me the way Elvis Costello singing "Almost Blue" does. Which is to say, feeling tight in the chest and twitchy between thc legs. (Is that what those guys mean by "two thumbs up"?)

In movies, less Beethoven is always more. Think of how Godard fuses a fragment of the Opus 135 string quartet with a shot of Marina Vlady washing the dishes in *Two or Three Things I Know About Her* or how a bit of the Seventh Symphony works with Eddie Constantine shuffling along the lakefront in *Germany Nine Zero 90*. The quotidian is charged with "oceanic feeling," as Freud so gracefully put it. In *Immortal Beloved*, director-writer Bernard Rose gives us extended passages from a dozen of Beethoven's biggest hits (soundtrack extravagantly packaged by Sony), but sound and image seldom cohere. The movie doesn't lack for sensuous elements: Peter Suschitzky's cinematography, the architecture of Prague (standing in for Vienna), and of course the music and Oldman doing an extension of his yearning, world-weary Dracula (minus the camp edge). But here, it's not the protagonist but the script that sucks.

Among the papers discovered after Beethoven's death were several letters addressed to his "Immortal Beloved." Since Beethoven was as much a misogynist as a womanizer, there was a flurry of interest about who this special lady could be. (No biographer has come up with a satisfactory answer.) Rose gives his biopic a mystery twist by structuring it around the search for the "Immortal Beloved." Thus, Beethoven's life is reconstructed through his involvement with three women (played by Isabella Rossellini, Valeria Golino, and Johanna Ter Steege), one of whom might be his "Rosebud." Unfortunately, Rose treats Beethoven a lot more reductively than Welles did Charles Foster Kane. As in the most formulaic of Hollywood's great artist bios, Beethoven's genius is defined through his love life and his physical disability.

In *Paperhouse*, Rose showed he had a talent for evoking both tender and terrifying childhood memories. Here, a scene of the young Beethoven being beaten by his father, and another of him floating, at night, in a pond that turns into a field of stars suggest what *Immortal Beloved* might have been had it not been burdened by its silly story.

That Oldman, despite the latex wrinkles and impossible dialogue, gives something close to a great performance is pretty amazing. Whether he's playing the ruttish young Beethoven, tearing up hotel rooms like Sid Vicious, or the stone-deaf old man, lost in the music inside his head, he makes anguish seem like perfect bliss.

Also reviewed in:
CHICAGO TRIBUNE, 1/6/95, Friday/p. C, Michael Wilmington
NATION, 1/23/95, p. 108, Stuart Klawans
NEW YORK TIMES, 12/16/94, p. C4, Janet Maslin
VARIETY, 12/12-18/94, p. 77, Todd McCarthy
WASHINGTON POST, 1/6/95, p. C7, Rita Kempley
WASHINGTON POST, 1/6/95, Weekend/p. 37, Desson Howe

IN THE ARMY NOW

A Hollywood Pictures release. *Executive Producer:* Nicholas Hassitt and Cyrus Yavneh. *Producer:* Michael Rotenberg. *Director:* Daniel Petrie, Jr. *Screenplay:* Ken Kaufman, Stu Krieger, Daniel Petrie, Jr., Fax Fahr, and Adam Small. *Story:* Steve Zacharias, Jeff Buhai, and Robbie Fox. *Director of Photography:* William Wages. *Editor:* O. Nicholas Brown. *Music:* Robert Folk. *Music Editor:* Tom Villano. *Sound:* Mary Hopkins McNabb and (music) Eric Tomlinson. *Sound Editor:* John Phillips and Bill Phillips. *Casting:* Mary Jo Slater and Steve Brooksbank. *Production Designer:* Craig Stearns. *Art Director:* Randy Moore. *Set Designer:* Thomas Reta. *Set Decorator:* Ellen Totleben. *Set Dresser:* Amy Durose. *Special Effects:* Paul Lombardi. *Costumes:* Michael T. Boyd. *Make-up:* Daniel C. Striepeke. *Stunt Coordinator:* Eddy Donno. *Running time:* 91 minutes. *MPAA Rating:* PG.

CAST: Pauly Shore (Bones Conway); Andy Dick (Jack Kaufman); Lori Petty (Christine Jones); David Alan Grier (Fred Ostroff); Esai Morales (Sgt. Stern); Lynn Whitfield (Sgt. Ladd); Art LaFleur (Sgt. Williams); Fabiana Udenio (Gabriella); Glenn Morshower (Recruiting Sargeant); Beau Billingslea (Sgt. Daniels); Peter Spellos (Mr. Quinn); Barry Nolan (Stu Krieger); Coleen Christie (News Anchor Person); Paul Mooney (LTC Peter Hume); Richard Assad (Col. Babaganousch); Allen R. Stokes (Drill Sgt. Stokes); Earl M. Nicholson (Drill Sgt. Nicholson); Kenneth O. Kilgo (Drill Sgt. Kilgo); Anthony H. Humphreys (Drill Sgt. Humphreys); Derek C. Zackery (Drill Sgt. Zackery); Vincent Marotta (Reserve Soldier #1); Carlton Wilborn (Reserve Soldier #2); Daniel C. Striepeke (Barber); Maurice Sherbanee (Camel Salesman); Tom Villard (Obnoxious Salesguy); Justin Simons and Christopher B. Duncan (Soldiers); Kirk Fox (Corporal); Brian Fenwick (Classroom Soldier); Howard J. Von Kaenel (General); Daniel Petrie, Jr. (Lieutenant Colonel); Dan Wolfe (Special Forces Major); John Larsen (Radio Operator); Keith Coogan (Stoner #1); Matthew Walker (Stoner #2).

LOS ANGELES TIMES, 8/12/94, Calendar/p. 6, Kevin Thomas

There's not a whole lot to be said about "In the Army Now" or its star, Pauly Shore. If Shore's comic genius eludes you or if you find the film something less than a constant laugh riot, you may still be willing to agree that it's amiable enough and not begrudge in the least the likelihood that Shore fans will be pleased.

It's a service comedy, reminiscent of may others—Bill Murray's funnier and more inspired "Stripes" is the first to come to mind. Shore and his sidekick (Andy Dick) are goofy guys trying hard to be cool but wind up signing up with the Army Reserve when they're fired from their video store jobs. They opt for the water purification team, believing it to be a safe choice, only to find themselves charged with destroying a Libyan Scud base hidden in a desert in Chad.

Shore, who first scored on MTV, is pleasant-looking and disciplined. His sense of timing is well-honed and his delivery droll—there's a childlike quality to his way of speaking that finds you imagining him doing a scene with sound-alike Melanie Griffith. Like other comedians in the film—Christine Jones and Fred Ostroff in particular as his water purification teammates—Shore can draw laughs even in these fairly uninspired circumstances—witness his miming a trip to the dentist.

Eight writers, including the film's director Daniel Petrie Jr., haven't freshened up very much a plot that's been around since the silent era. Petrie, however, compensates with consistently brisk, crisp direction; there's a refreshing lack of self-indulgence throughout. Even if you're not particularly amused by "In the Army Now," you may agree with one admirer who summed it up as "a nice, clean job."

NEW YORK POST, 8/12/94, p. 47, Michael Medved

"In the Army Now" represents the greatest performance of Pauly Shore's motion-picture career.

Of course, that's not saying much, considering the nature of his two previous starring vehicles, "Encino Man" and "Son-In-Law." There, the long-haired star merely provided sleepwalking approximations of the space-case caricature that originally won him fame on MTV's "Totally Pauly" bits.

This time, however, he actually plays a character—a dim-witted eccentric character to be sure, but nonetheless a fictional personality with feelings, endearing moments and even traces of believability.

Shore portrays a goofball sales clerk at a Southern California electronics store, who loses his job and then signs up for the Army reserves. He persuades his sidekick from the stereo store (the capable Andy Dick of the old Letterman show) that the few months of training will be an easy way to get the money they need to achieve their dream of one day opening an audio shop of their own.

Of course, the adjustment to Army life turns out to be more of a challenge than expected—especially when their water purification unit is dispatched to handle an emergency in the North African desert of Chad, which its threatened by a Libyan invasion.

There, Pauly and pal team with two other ill-prepared GIs: a neurotic black dentist (amusingly acted by David Alan Grier) and a gung-ho, muscular Rambo-ette wannabe (played by the always excellent Lori Petty).

This odd squad soon finds itself thrust into the center of the global crisis, as they're stranded in the desert, captured by the Libyans, and ultimately represent Uncle Sam's only hope for knocking out Uncle Khadafy's menacing Scuds.

As the silly plot unfolds, surprises are as scarce as shade trees in the desert sands (actually shot near Yuma, Ariz.). At least the eight well-established writers who contributed to the story and script managed to come up with "A Few Good Lines" for "the Few Good Men (and Women)" in the story.

As Pauly tries to rally the fighting spirit of his fellow GIs, he tells them: "If our American soldiers acted like this in Desert Storm then Saddam Hussein would still be running Iraq!"

Director Daniel Petrie ("Toy Soldiers") makes the most of the occasional funny moments and keeps the action scenes surprisingly crisp and watchable.

Meanwhile, the same Arab-American interest groups who've been protesting "True Lies" will have a fit over the one-dimensional bad guys in this film, through someone ought to remind them that a ruthless, irresponsible and murderous regime in Libya is, unfortunately, no Hollywood invention.

One group that will not complain, however, is the U.S. Army, which couldn't ask for more sympathetic treatment—or a more effective recruiting ad—than they get here.

Unlike most misfits-joining-the-service comedies, from "No Time for Sergeants" to "Gomer Pyle" to the recent "Renaissance Man," this film never suggests that its oddball hero can teach the Army a thing or two; instead it's the military that has the answers and can, in the most traditional sense, "make a man out of you."

Watching the main character's transformation is unexpectedly satisfying, due to the similarly remarkable transformation of Pauly Shore into an actor who, though not quite ready for the Anthony Hopkins roles, nonetheless displays surprising charm and self-assurance.

NEWSDAY, 8/12/94, Part II/p. B7, Jack Mathews

With "In the Army Now," comedian and MTV personality Pauly Shore completes his three-picture deal with Walt Disney's Hollywood Pictures division, and for critics out of their teens, the long national nightmare would seem to be over.

Would that it were so. Shore's first two films, "Encino Man" and "Son-in-Law," stripped indiscriminating viewers of almost $80 million, making his presence in at least a couple more movies an undeniable reality. But he's 26 now, with a receding hairline, and he'll either upbrain his act or deadpan his way into obscurity.

In the meantime, he's in the Army now, a one-man Bud Abbott and Lou Costello show on the road in North Africa, taking on the desert rats of Moammar Khadafi,and the dumb jokes are flying like enemy scuds. Here comes one now ... Whoops, missed by a mile.

Let's face it, you either like this guy, in which case every gesture and impertinent wisecrack knocks your socks off, or you pass the time noticing how pronounced his frontal lobe appears with his GI buzzcut. Director Daniel Petrie Jr. refers to Shore's Pvt. Bones Conway as a knucklehead, and we can see why.

Shore's one-note act is that of the passive rebel, mocking authority with a manner that is too laid back and affable to be truly mean-spirited. He attacks and withdraws in the same breath, and, to the squealing delight of his fans, leaves his targets—square peers, school officials, bosses, parents—off-balance and befuddled.

The military, of course, offers Shore a mother lode of uptight authority figures to tweak, and so he does, after Bones and his best friend, Jack (Andy Dick), are fired from their stereo store jobs and decide to enlist in the Army reserves. From bootcamp, where Bones and Jack buddy up with fellow grunts Christine (Lori Petty) and Fred (David Alan Grier), to the desert dunes of Chad, where U.N. troops are sent to take out a camouflaged Libyan Scud base, it is Bones & Co. kicking sand in the faces of both Khadafi's men and U.S. military brass.

I laughed hard once during the movie, but only because the scene showing Libyan soldiers monitoring troop movements on American TV reminded me of my favorite Desert Storm joke. "Do you know how many Iraqis it takes to fire a Scud? Three. One to aim, one to fire and one to watch CNN to see where it lands."

You don't get that kind of humor from Pauly Shore.

VILLAGE VOICE, 8/23/94, p. 58, Arianna Pavia Rosati

You're broke, you're bored, you're irreverent, you're in Glendale. All you want to do is open that rad stereo store with your best friend Jack, throw keggers, and screw your busty Italian girlfriend. Sucks to be you, buddy, cuz not only are you broke, you've just been fired. But that's cool—a most fortuitous encounter at the mini-golf inspires you and Jack to be all you can be (and earn a cold $5000) in the army reserves.

Bones Conway is totally Pauly Shore, the genius behind this get-rich-on-the-weekends scheme. Army life for these yahoos is an at ease sitcom breeze, from the de rigueur buzz cut montage sequence (where I confess I caught myself thinking, hmmm, he actually looks a little like Keanu ...) and the drop-and-give-me-20s from the sexy boot camp sergeant to the war they (egads) are sent to fight in desert Chad. Rounding out the Bones and Jack (Andy Dick) excellent adventure posse are Fred (David Alan Grier), a neurotic dental student whose real mission is to teach nameless Africans how to floss, and Christine (Lori Petty), a cutesy-voiced babe eager to defy that no-women-in-combat clause. These are the few good men our military had in mind?

Pauly packs yuks aplenty, and even manages some lofty philosophical rehistoricizing: "Would America have won the Civil War if Ben Franklin hadn't gotten along with Eleanor Roosevelt?" War à la dingbat is full of affectionate camels, SCUD missiles, unpeeled potatoes, and Libyan prisons run by the evil Babaganousch, whom Pauly affectionately calls "Babagadouche." Don't ask; let's simply say the film's Third World political awareness sucks. But my expectations for the next installment in the Pauly oeuvre were so sketchy to begin with I was kinda charmed. Maybe I'm just a sucker for a tight butch haircut.

Also reviewed in:
CHICAGO TRIBUNE, 8/12/94, Friday/p. D, Michael Wilmington
NEW YORK TIMES, 8/12/94, p. C6, Janet Maslin
VARIETY, 8/15-21/94, p. 43, Brian Lowry
WASHINGTON POST, 8/12/94, p. F7, Rita Kempley
WASHINGTON POST, 8/12/94, Weekend/p. 37, Desson Howe

IN CUSTODY

A Sony Pictures Classics release of a Merchant Ivory Productions film in association with Channel 4 Films. *Executive Producer:* Paul Bradley and Donald Rosenfeld. *Producer:* Wahid Chowhan. *Director:* Ismail Merchant. *Screenplay:* Anita Desai and Shahrukh Husain. *Based on the book by:* Anita Desai. *Director of Photography:* Larry Pizer. *Editor:* Roberto Silvi.

Music: Zakir Hussain and Ustad Sultan Khan. *Sound:* Mike Shoring. *Sound Editor:* Colin Miller. *Production Designer:* Suresh Sawant. *Costumes:* Lovleen Bains. *Make-up:* Norma Webb. *Running time:* 123 minutes. *MPAA Rating:* PG.

CAST: Shashi Kapoor (Nur); Sameer Mitha (Manu); Neena Gupta (Sarla); Rupinder Kaur (Mrs. Bhalla); Om Puri (Deven); Shahid Masood (Dhanu); Tiblu Khan and Afzal Khan (Students); Manzoor Ahtesham (Jaidev); Alakh Nandan (Trivedi); Tinnu Anand (Murad); Amit Goswani (Street Urchin); Sushma Seth (Safiya Begum); Umer Sahib (Young Deven); Gopal Janum (Deven's Father); Ramratan Sen (Ali); Samir Feroz (Nur's Son); Syed Zaheer Ul-Hasan (Servant); Shabana Azmi (Imtiaz Begum); Sulbha Chaurasia (Asiya the Tampura Player); Mustafa Taj (Man in Audience); Nasir Mirza (Man in Audience with Rose); Siddarth (Tea Boy); Shashank Mukherjee (Sahay); Ajay Sahni (Siddiqui); Prashant Khirwadkar (Registrar); Razzak Siddiqui (The Principal); Mohamad Ali (The Chief Guest); Prayag Raj (Jain); Sagar Arya (Chiku); Kaynat Kauser and Parveen Rehman (Imtiaz Begum's Attendants); Afzal Hussein (Babu); Ishak Khan, Nikhil Das, and Jamil Mansoor (Babu's Musicians); Habib Bhopali (Burly Man); Nafisa Sharma (Brothel Madam); Sajid Mitha (Pimp); Humayan Khan (Customer at Brothel); K.S. Mehta (Contractor).

LOS ANGELES TIMES, 5/4/94, Calendar/p. 4, Kevin Thomas

With the wise and rueful comedy "In Custody," Ismail Merchant, the producing half of the distinguished Merchant-Ivory team, turns director.

Merchant and his longtime partner, director James Ivory, have been responsible for such celebrated films as "Howards End" and "The Remains of the Day," and he brings to his film of the Anita Desai novel the same kind of civility and sophistication that has characterized Merchant Ivory productions for 30 years.

The primary point of this leisurely and engaging film is to celebrate Urdu, a Northern Indian language cherished by poets and writers for its beauty, that is on the verge of extinction. In selecting Desai's novel to adapt to the screen, however, Merchant has wisely chosen humor as the most effective way to protest a great cultural loss. Indeed, his film is at times almost literally excruciatingly funny, striking a perfect balance between laughter and pain.

Om Puri stars as Deven, a poorly paid, badly treated professor of Hindi at a backwater college in the ancient town of Mirpore. He has had a lifelong passion for Urdu and would love to devote his life to writing poetry in that language, but has a wife (Neena Gupta) and small son (Sameer Mitha) to support. When a friend (Tinnu Anand), the publisher of a journal devoted to Urdu culture, suggests that he interview Nur Shahjehanabadi, the man widely regarded as the greatest living Urdu poet, Deven cannot resist.

Deven inadvertently has embarked upon a journey fraught with comic peril. After no small difficulty he finds Nur (Shashi Kapoor) living in a crumbling Bhopal palace with his two wives, (Sushma Seth, Shabana Azmi), who detest each other ferociously.

As for Nur himself, he has slid into a life of indolent despair, surrounded by freeloading admirers who drink and feast at the poet's expense far into the night. As soon as Nur is convinced of Deven's sincerity, he agrees to the interview, but Deven doesn't reckon with the wives; worse luck, he lets himself get carried away with the possibility of videotaping the master reciting his own work, settling for a used tape recorder.

At every turn Deven meets fresh, costly complications, and the humor of these encounters makes bearable the massive indifference he faces without exception. Even those fully aware of Nur's stature are so immersed in their own petty concerns they actually tend to hinder rather than help Deven in his modest but important quest.

With his gallery of beautifully observed characters Merchant has evoked a genuine sense of the human comedy. The smallest role is sharply, comically defined, and Om Puri's heroically patient Deven, a much put-upon middle-aged man, offers a sharp contrast to Shashi Kapoor's selfless, majestic portrayal of Nur, a man only too well aware of his own sad decline.

NEW YORK POST, 4/15/94, p. 38, Thelma Adams

Ismail Merchant's "In Custody" is easier to defend than to watch.

Until now, the one-two punch of Merchant as producer and James Ivory as director has brought such lush and literary movies as "The Remains of the Day" and "A Room With a View" to international audiences.

For his directorial debut, Merchant has chosen literary material and returned to India, the setting of earlier Merchant Ivory outings, "Heat and Dust," and "Bombay Talkie."

Working from an Anita Desai novel (adapted by Desai and Shahrukh Husain), Merchant tackles nothing less than the death by strangulation of Urdu poetry—in a comedy of manners!

Indian star Shashi Kapoor ("Heat and Dust," "Sammy and Rosie Get Laid") plays Nur, the greatest living Urdu poet—and arguably the last in a long line of Muslim poets in India.

Nur's characterization is magnificent. The corpulent bigamist is pampered, spoiled, gluttonous, drunken, irresponsible, loud, self-absorbed and, with his spit curls and soulful eyes, irresistible.

In contrast, Deven (Om Puri) is a dour, pock-marked, henpecked, joyless academic. Tired of teaching Hindi at a backwater college, he grabs the opportunity to travel to nearby Bhopal to interview the great master. The meeting changes Deven's life—but not before Nur turns it inside out.

Perhaps a more experienced director would have made this ambitious project pay off. Merchant never raises a head of steam. Scene after scene rolls by bringing hardly more than a limp smile and furtive time-checks.

"In Custody" has memorable moments. Chief among them is a poetry recitation by Nur's gorgeous second wife. Dressed in gold-embroidered red silk, her hands ritually streaked with henna, her performance is mesmerizing.

But, like unstrung pearls spilled across a marred table, these stirring set pieces don't hold together.

"In Custody" is a snore—and that's a shame.

NEWSDAY, 4/15/94, Part II/p. B9, Jack Mathews

Urdu, an Indo-Aryan language that originated in northern India during the Muslim dynasty of the 16th and 17th Centuries, is spoken by about 5 percent of today's Indian population, and for political and social reasons fluency in the poetic language declines every year.

That troubles Ismail Merchant, a native of India and the producer half of the extraordinary Merchant-Ivory filmmaking team, and so Merchant has made a movie about it. Not a movie that many non-Urdu or non-Hindi speaking people in the West will have any reason to see, but as passionate a piece of personal filmmaking as you're likely to skip.

"In Custody," adapted from a novel by Anita Desai, tells the contemporary story of Deven (Om Puri), a teacher of the common Hindi language at a Bhopal university who allows his admiration for the work of one of India's last great Urdu poets to nearly ruin his life.

Invited by a publishing friend to interview the famed recluse Nur (Shashi Kapoor) for an all-Urdu edition of a poetry magazine, Deven searches out his idol and finds him an obese, burned-out alcoholic, trying to satisfy two feuding wives and a band of incorrigible sycophants.

The passive Deven, with his job, his marriage and various friendships on the line, has to insinuate himself into the midst of this clamorous crowd and coax Nur to trust him with his last unpublished poems.

Merchant, making his debut as a feature-film director, has propped up this fragile tale with layers of leaden humor. Deven, in his bumbling attempts to lobby his university for expenses, to make peace with Nur's nagging wives and to capture the poems themselves on an antiquated second-hand tape recorder, is reduced almost to a Third World clown.

Merchant doesn't have the directing skill to balance the tragic and comic elements of Desai's story. Deven's numerous failures are pathetic and saddening, and only in those moments when he's intoxicated on Nur's Urdu verse does the humorless Om Puri allow an expression other than pained desperation to cross his face.

There are other problems for those of us speed-reading the English subtitles. Most of the dialogue is in Hindi, and as lyrical as Urdu may be to those who speak and love it, the untrained ear has trouble detecting when the dialogue shifts from one language to the other. Also, if Nur is an Indian version of Keats, something is seriously lost in the mundane subtitled translations.

To his credit, Merchant didn't attempt to turn "In Custody" into a plea for outside understanding of India's cultural upheaval. He barely hints at the sociopolitical conflicts between the Muslims and Hindus, and though his underlying theme may be the universal need to preserve culture, he doesn't pause to hammer us with that message.

Still, "In Custody" provides better evidence of Merchant's gifts as a producer than as a director, Not many people could have found financing and U.S. distribution for a story of such limited appeal and while he has directed his first feature with persuasive passion, he shouldn't give up his day job.

SIGHT AND SOUND, 6/94, p. 50, Christopher Bray

Deven, a teacher at a provincial Indian college, is commissioned to interview a famous Urdu poet, Nur, who lives in Bhopal. Seeking out his great hero, Deven finds him old and broken, surrounded by hangers-on who lead him into drunken excesses, and harassed by his two wives, a homely older one and a beautiful younger woman who claims to be a poet herself.

Borrowing money from his college, Deven buys a tape recorder and hires a young technical assistant. But the interview, which takes place in a brothel, is a series of disasters, and when Deven tries to edit the tape, all he gets are some drunken ramblings. Deven returns to Bhopal for another interview but this time is intercepted by the younger of Nur's wives; she wants him to record her poetry instead. Again he returns home. Troubled by the debts he has incurred in purchasing the tape deck, hiring its operator, and paying for his journeys to and from Bhopal, Deven is in despair. Unexpectedly, however, he receives a package from Nur, who fears that death is nigh: hence he is leaving all his work in Deven's keep. Nur's funeral, far from being mournful, is a joyous occasion.

Ismail Merchant has always wanted to make a film about Urdu, "a language that is gracious, grand, poetic" and "fast disappearing". Hence *In Custody*, an adaptation of Anita Desai's Booker-shortlisted novel about the need for tradition and cultural continuity through language. The early parts of the film are stuffed full of threats to this continuity. There are references to Disney movies, the awful *Dead Poets Society* and feminism, all three in their different ways working against the integrity of the mother tongue. Even Deven, whom Nur describes as "a devotee of Urdu", teaches Hindi. Asked why this should be, Deven shamefacedly admits that he has to do so in order to make a living. When he buys his tape recorder, the salesman speculates, "if only we were as clever as the Japanese: how we would have progressed".

Yet all this emphasis on cultural integrity sits uneasy in a movie that is unashamedly designed for western audiences. Hollywood aesthetics dominate the production. Will it wash? I'm not sure. On the one hand, Merchant—whose first feature as director this is—has clearly learned everything he knows about film-making from watching James Ivory in action. On the other hand, it's an odds-on bet that anyone who liked *Howards End* will want nothing at all to do with the 'Johnny Foreigner' types running around in this movie.

The whole affair is very tasteful, discreet, humourless, glossy and inconsequential. Just as Ivory serves us up a picture of heritage Britain that is stiflingly offensive, Merchant offers us India as a colour supplement feature. Most of the time, the film looks as if it has been constructed out of overmatter from a travel show. There is no attempt made to get at the reality of contemporary India.

Over and over again we are fed glorious compositions—silhouettes, sunsets, sunrises, white walls against burning blue skies—that could have come from the pages of a teach-yourself-photography manual, or an advert for a new type of curry powder. Unlike Gurinder Chadha's recent *Bhaji on the Beach*, however, which had the courage or confusion to accept the notion of cultural integration, *In Custody* postures about continuity but by means of techniques that everywhere undermine the project.

All this might not matter so much were the film at all entertaining. Instead, it's a drizzle. Deven's problems with his tape deck, for example, which last for half an hour or so, have all the subtlety of a brick dropped on a toe. How many times must we see a shot of Nur's young wife's disapproval of the interview before we get the point? *In Custody* is dull, repetitive and enervating—at the press screening I attended both people I was sat between fell asleep within 10 minutes of the curtains parting.

VILLAGE VOICE, 4/26/94, p. 51, J. Hoberman

Is it inevitable that all ambitious first features would take as their true subject the conditions of their own making? Ismail Merchant's *In Custody* and Dan Algrant's *Naked in New York* are, each in its way, meditations on the artistic vocation. If the latter feels brash and opportunistic and the former seems worshipful and discreet, it may be that young Algrant is fresh out of film school while middle-aged Merchant has been the long-time faithful producer of the James Ivory oeuvre.

Adapted from the well-received novel by Anita Desai, *In Custody* is scarcely more than a sardonic anecdote—a timid, downtrodden university instructor becomes involved with the old and dissolute poet he once lionized in an unpublished monograph. Still, it's packed with subtext. For one thing, the movie features three major stars of the Hindi-language cinema, although it is devoted to Urdu, court language of the Indian subcontinent's former Moslem rulers, dying in India but official in Pakistan. For another, it's Merchant's opportunity to explore all manner of creative symbiosis. For a third, it's a meditation on the vicissitudes of mechanical reproduction.

Deven (Om Puri), a devotee of Urdu compelled by economic necessity to teach Hindi, struggles along in a provincial milieu of impoverished intellectuals, dismissive students, and rough academic politics. A meeting with a former schoolmate, now the editor of an Urdu literary journal, saddles him with the assignment to interview Nur, the greatest living Urdu poet. Deven takes the bus to Bhopal (Delhi in the novel) and is guided through the back alleys of the City's Moslem quarter to the ruined palace where Nur lives in flamboyant squalor, attended by two irate wives and a gaggle of shameless hangers-on.

As played by onetime matinee idol Shashi Kapoor, Nur is bloated with charm. He's a Falstaffian figure—not only fleshy, but tragic, absurd, and sensual in equal measure. Deven is properly appalled by the antics of Nur's drunken acolytes, who appear at dusk like harpies to the feast, but he is even more horrified when Nur's furious and beautiful second wife, Imtiaz Begum (Shabana Azmi), mistakes him for one of these "hyenas." Enacting a parody of academic criticism, Deven is ordered to sponge the poet's puke—he's so stunned that he only realizes later that he may have used a precious manuscript to wipe up the mess.

This initiation is only the beginning. *In Custody* tells a very Indian story in which a small matter becomes increasingly, and ultimately bewilderingly, complicated. Deven is soon summoned back to Bhopal to hear Imtiaz recite *her* verse. Humiliated by this performance, Nur actively woos Deven as his disciple, and Deven gets the bright idea to videotape the poet as he reminisces and recites—thus Urdu will be preserved. Haplessly trying to raise money for a video camera from some university slush fund, he winds up with barely enough capital to buy a secondhand tape recorder; the academic intrigue required to fund that acquisition is more than complemented by the various schemes and backdoor alliances he needs to form within Nur's household.

Part Bengali, part German, Desai has a distinctive inside-outside perspective on India. Her novel has the fiery aftertaste of Chekhov vindaloo but, in keeping with what the blurbs call "the Merchant Ivory stamp of supremely good taste," the stolidly workman-like Merchant manages to bland things out. His mode is laid-back and picturesque, the action served with a dollop of keening sitar and garnished with local color (mainly electric orange and hot lavender). Merchant is extremely fortunate in his choice of actors but his camera placement can be somnolent and, while he doesn't wish to cut, he lacks the brio for long takes. The image is consistently underexposed, the movie isn't as funny as it means to be, and there are several endings too many. (Completely unexplored, however, is the perspective of Imtiaz, who ultimately confronts Deven with her own literary claims and accuses him of sexism for not taking her seriously.)

There is only one sequence where *In Custody* rises from the merely interesting to the truly inspired. Back in Bhopal, a crew in tow, Deven rents a cramped room in a seedy brothel to record Nur's recitations. The "studio" is sub-standard; the star is increasingly demanding. In the course of the taping, Deven must cater meals, telephone backers for additional funds, deal with faulty equipment, coddle inept technicians, endure abuse from the star's entourage, and, in general, cope with all manner of unforeseen accidents. (Afterward, he has to save the tape in the editing.) In the novel, Deven is ultimately a holy fool, in the movie, he's ... a heroic producer.

Also reviewed in:
CHICAGO TRIBUNE, 8/19/94, Friday/p. L, Michael Wilmington
NEW YORK TIMES, 4/15/94, p. C6, Caryn James
VARIETY, 11/22/93, p. 33, Derek Elley
WASHINGTON POST, 4/30/94, p. G2, Rita Kempley

IN THE LAND OF THE DEAF

An International Film Circuit release of a Les Films d'Ici/La Sept Cinema/Le Centre Européen Cinématographique Rhône-Alpes coproduction in association with Rhône-Alpes region/Canal Plus/the CNC/ La Foundation de France/the Ministry of Foreign Affairs/RAI-3/BBC/RTSR and support from the Gan Foundation. *Producer:* Serge Lalou. *Director:* Nicolas Philibert. *Screenplay (French sign-language and French with English subtitles):* Nicolas Philibert. *Director of Photography:* Frédéric Labourasse. *Editor:* Guy Lecorne. *Sound:* Henri Maikoff. *Running time:* 99 minutes. *MPAA Rating:* Not Rated.

CAST: Florent (Boy on Poster); Jean-Claude Poulain (Sign Language Teacher).

LOS ANGELES TIMES, 1/18/95, Calendar/p. 7, Kevin Thomas

French documentarian Nicolas Philibert's tender, lyrical "In the Land of the Deaf" takes us into the world of the hearing impaired, showing its richness of possibilities and the warmth of its community, and above all, celebrating the beauty and expressiveness of sign language.

Although it introduces us to hearing impaired individuals of all ages, it spends too much of its time with adorable small children and their infinitely patient, loving and dedicated teachers.

To be sure, several deaf adults reveal past horrors overcome and a sense of isolation endured, but Philibert is so determinedly affirmative that he skirts dealing with the strain of everyday life in a household where one of its members is severely hearing impaired.

More important, he fails to suggest that unless such an individual accepts him or herself, he or she will always view a hearing loss as a handicap—a handicap with the potential for both destruction of self and of family life.

NEW YORK POST, 9/14/94, p. 40, Thelma Adams

"In the Land of the Deaf" is a rather pedestrian, shapeless French documentary notable for providing a passport into a rarely explored subculture—the world of the severely hearing-impaired.

The audience for Nicolas Philibert's film, which opens today at the Film Forum, is primarily the "silence-deprived," although the Film Forum will be providing listening devices on a first-come, first-served basis.

Director Philibert pursues the philosophy that the millions of hearing-impaired worldwide are more a community, a culture with its own norms and method of communication, than a handicapped minority.

This is an increasingly popular viewpoint and Philibert presents it seductively. With their rich communication through sign language and their expressive faces and bodies, the deaf subjects are striking on film, often demonstrating the power of silent movie actors. "Talking head" interviews are greatly enhanced with the grace of talking hands.

Philibert follows school kids just learning to make the oral sounds they cannot hear, young adults turning to each other for comfort while trying to make their way in the hearing mainstream, and sign language teachers. He avoids discussions with hearing family members.

"In the Land of the Deaf" would have been improved by economy. For example, segments that include the wedding of a deaf couple, and the awarding of prizes at a school for the deaf at year's end go on for much longer than necessary.

The strongest presence is a natural-born ham named Jean-Claude Poulain, a deaf sign-language teacher with strong opinions about the place of the hearing-impaired in the world. He calls for bilingualism in the schools—French and sign language—and rails against the hearing people in power.

The most radical of the bunch, Poulain expresses his disappointment at the birth of his hearing daughter. Communication would have been easier if she were deaf, he says, "but I love her just the same."

NEWSDAY, 9/14/94, Part II/p. B9, Jonathan Mandell

Right in the middle of the wedding, as the bride marches toward the altar in full and stately white, a young woman sitting by the aisle suddenly sticks out her hand and fidgets with the bouquet, as if the bride is somehow holding it wrong.

It is the smallest of gestures, undoubtedly well meaning, and in it is contained a history of condescension and contempt—the history of the hearing world's attitudes toward the deaf; both the bride and the groom cannot hear. They are two of the lives that too briefly inhabit "In the Land of the Deaf," a French documentary about deaf life and culture that is full of such subtly observant moments.

But the true visual music of Nicolas Philibert's film is not in the body language of the few hearing people, but in the sign language of the deaf. Indeed, the film begins with a signing quartet, performing poetry in front of music stands like classical artists.

If the film is a poem, it is lyric, not linear. There is no narration, few of the people appear on camera very long, fewer still are named and for a long time the film seems to be a clutter of random encounters. Eventually, though, three stories come into focus: the marrying couple (including a priceless scene with their new landlord); a young student named Florent and his classmates in a school for the deaf; and Jean-Claude Poulain, an energetic mensch of a sign language teacher who talks of his triumphs and disappointments in a world that might to outsiders seem turned upside down. "I had dreamt of having a deaf child; communication would be easier. But," he signs, in a gesture of magnanimity, "I love her all the same."

Interspersed are quick comments to the camera from other deaf people, primarily young adults, that manage to touch on most of the major issues of deaf culture and deaf rights, though far too faintly: the central, century-old debate over deaf education ("oralism" vs. sign) is only obliquely presented. "In the Land of the Deaf" can be seen as a quick first tour through the Deaf Nation. The specific information is familiar to anybody who has followed the modern deaf-rights movement since its explosive inception on the campus of Gallaudet University six years ago.

But the advantage this film has is that, thanks to the director's intelligence and sensitivity—and to the subtitles that help make French sign language seem like just another (if especially beautiful) foreign language—we are able to enter more fully the visual world of the deaf, as respectful and curious tourists, rather than pitying voyeurs.

VILLAGE VOICE, 9/20/94, p. 58, Georgia Brown

Nicolas Philibert's eloquent documentary *In the Land of the Deaf* couldn't be more timely. This is a heady, progressive moment for the deaf because their condition is finally engaging the hearing—those who, in ignorance and prejudice, usually create and manage the institutions of the nonhearing.

Although not deaf himself, Philibert has made a movie for the deaf and hearing alike using subtitled French sign language (different countries and even regions have their own sign languages). He doesn't lead with a thesis or stick with any particular individual throughout, but instead takes us into a series of gatherings of the deaf, giving us some brief sense of lives lived in profound silence. The film includes interviews with deaf subjects but uses no explanatory voiceover—by its nature inimical to signing.

For example, we're shown a class of deaf six-year-olds learning to speak and read. All are appealing, but one in particular, Florent, captures the heart because the first time we see him his large eyes are dropping tears on the page. (A teacher then calls him a baby.) The movie shows how physically expressive the deaf are—and what it signifies is that our own voices are invisible. A deaf teacher of sign, Jean-Claude Poulain, impresses us with the sort of extraordinary acting we recognize from mime and the great silent clowns. Except that there's no character; he's expressing himself.

At the airport, a group of teenagers taking leave of some American visitors cry and hug and hold on tight—boys just as ardently as girls. If they were hearing, you'd think they were mourning for the dead. (We might call such expression exaggerated.) The scene teaches how little we show, how emotionally impoverished our language, even how cold our love is. Contemplate deafness long enough and you begin to glimpse how verbal communication conditions feeling itself.

Coincidentally, I just read the obituary of the deaf South African poet David Wright. Wright's achievement reminds me that soon a great deaf filmmaker will come along, and her films will be a revelation.

Also reviewed in:
CHICAGO TRIBUNE, 8/5/94, Friday/p. L, Michael Wilmington
NATION, 10/17/94, p. 435, Stuart Klawans
NEW YORK TIMES, 9/14/94, p. C16, Caryn James
VARIETY, 6/7/93, p. 43, Lisa Nesselson
WASHINGTON POST, 10/7/94, p. B1, Richard Harrington
WASHINGTON POST, 10/7/94, Weekend/p. 50, Desson Howe

INEVITABLE GRACE

A Silverstar Pictures release. *Executive Producer:* John Canawati Sr. *Producer:* Christian Capobianco. *Director:* Alex Canawati. *Director of Photography:* Christian Sebaldt. *Editor:* Grace Valenti. *Music:* Christopher Whiffen. *Sound:* Sean Sullivan. *Production Designer:* Marc Rizzo. *Art Director:* Christina Shellen. *Set Decorator:* Allison McVann. *Costumes:* Alison Edmond. *Running time:* 104 minutes. *MPAA Rating:* Not Rated.

CAST: Maxwell Caulfield (Adam Cestare); Stephanie Knights (Lisa Kelner); Jennifer Nicholson (Veronica); Tippi Hedren (Dr. Marcia Stevens); Sylvia B. Suarez (Simone); John Pearson (Philip); Samantha Eggar (Britt); Andrea King (Dorothy).

NEW YORK POST, 9/30/94, p. 46, Larry Worth

Jack Nicholson is one of Hollywood's best actors. But he clearly spent no time teaching the tricks of the trade to daughter Jennifer. At least if her performance in "Inevitable Grace" is any indication.

Sadder still, she's the highlight. Or at least her scene "with dad." It takes place in the first five minutes as a sexpot dressed like a '40s femme fatale enters a movie theater and watches a scene of young Jack Nicholson heading for trouble in Roger Corman's "The Terror." She lets out a bloodcurdling scream before collapsing on the floor.

One can only assume she saw what was coming: a hopelessly muddled script about sanitariums, locked basement doors, mother fixations, lesbian therapists, cross-dressing, demented husbands, incest and murder.

The dismal results beg three questions:

■ How did writer/director Alex Canawati turn such lurid trapplngs into such a colossal bore?

■ What enticed screen veterans Tippi Hedren and Samantha Eggar (both of whom are aging beautifully) into the proceedings, along with suitably campy Maxwell "Grease II" Caulfield?

■ And—most importantly—why didn't this cinematic Sominex go straight to your nearest video store?

NEWSDAY, 9/30/94, Part II/p. B9, Jack Mathews

During the brief close-ups we get of Jennifer Nicholson, who is making her acting debut in first-time writer-director Alex Canawati's incompetent psychological thriller "Inevitable Grace," you can spot vague similarities to her famous father, Jack. Something around her mouth when she smiles, a look in her slightly hooded eyes.

That's the extent of the detectable genetic links. From her stiff reading of lines to her ungainly physical movements, Nicholson demonstrates none of pop's acting talent. But then, no one seems particularly gifted in this relentlessly amateurish production, and the cast includes such veterans as Maxwell Caulfield, Tippi Hedren and Samantha Eggar.

Nicholson is luckier than the others, in that her character, a woman driven mad by her rich, depraved husband (Caulfield), dies early on, banging her head on a bedpost after a raucous lesbian encounter with her overly accommodating psychiatrist.

This is one of those overheated stories in which the shrinks are more vulnerable than the patients. Young Dr. Lisa Kelner (Stephanie Knights), our real heroine, has barely reported to her first job at a mental hospital when she becomes involved with the couple from hell. The wife wants the doctor's body, the husband wants to transform her into his fantasy woman, and the husband's mother (Andrea King) is lurking in the background like the absent relative from "Psycho."

Talk about on-the-job training!

Canawati, a recent film-school graduate, seems most inspired by Roman Polanski, but the film is such a hash of imitated styles, bad writing and clumsy direction, it's hard to know what he had in mind. Harder still to care.

Also reviewed in:
NEW YORK TIMES, 9/30/94, p. C8, Stephen Holden
VARIETY, 2/21-27/94, p. 42, Emanuel Levy

INKWELL, THE

A Buena Vista Pictures release of a Touchstone Pictures presentation of an Irving Azoff production. *Executive Producer:* Jon Jashni. *Producer:* Irving Azoff and Guy Riedel. *Director:* Matty Rich. *Screenplay:* Tom Ricostronza and Paris Qualles. *Editor:* Quinnie Martin, Jr. *Music:* Terence Blanchard. *Music Editor:* Alex Steyermark. *Choreographer:* Tyme Kennedy. *Sound:* Robert L. Warner and (music) James Nichols. *Sound Editor:* Bobbi Banks. *Casting:* Chemin Sylvia Bernard. *Production Designer:* Lester Cohen. *Art Director:* Daniel Talpers. *Set Decorator:* Karen Wiesel. *Special Effects:* Joey DiGaetano. *Costumes:* Ceci. *Make-up:* Ellie Winslow. *Stunt Coordinator:* David Lomax and Sonja Darling. *Running time:* 112 minutes. *MPAA Rating:* R.

CAST: Larenz Tate (Drew Tate); Joe Morton (Kenny Tate); Suzzanne Douglas (Brenda Tate); Glynn Turman (Spencer Phillips); Vaness Bell Calloway (Frances Phillips); Adrienne-Joi Johnson (Heather Lee); Morris Chestnut (Harold Lee); Jada Pinkett (Lauren Kelly); Duane Martin (Junior. Phillips); Mary Alice (Evelyn); Phyllis Yvonne Stickney (Dr. Wade); Markus Redmond (Darryl); Perry Moore (Moe); Akia Victor (Charlene); Aaron Griffin (Boy w/Lauren); Reggie McFadden (MC Madman); Greg Leevy (Man at Party); Stacie Davis (Girl at Party).

LOS ANGELES TIMES, 4/22/94, Calendar/p. 6, Kevin Thomas

"The Inkwell" takes its title from a Martha's Vineyard beach, an African American enclave since the turn of the century. The film is at once a coming-of-age story, set in the summer of 1976, and a satire on the affectations of the black bourgeoisie. That's a conceivably viable mix, but unfortunately it proves too great of a stretch for director Matty Rich, who created a stir with his raw, powerful debut film, "Straight Out of Brooklyn," made when he was only 19, and for his writers, Tom Ricostronza and Paris Qualles.

The problem is simple enough: The writers and the director cannot resist caricaturing black conservatives to ludicrous extremes, thus botching a rare instance in which we're able to witness a believable conflict of values between classes within black society. Worse yet, the film, which tends to drag, ends up pouring a syrupy sentimentality over both its emotional and social issues.

Incredible as it may seem, an attractive wife and mother (Suzzanne Douglas) insists she did not anticipate trouble when she urges that she and her husband (Joe Morton) and their 16-year-old son (Larenz Tate) spend two weeks with her sister (Vanessa Bell Calloway) and brother-in-law (Glynn Turman) at their place in Martha's Vineyard.

Morton is a former Black Panther and Turman is so ardent a Republican that he has oil paintings of Richard Nixon and Gerald Ford on his living-room wall. Not helping matters is that Douglas' mother (Mary Alice), who lives with Calloway and Turman, addresses Douglas with cruelty and contempt apparently only because of her husband's past Panthers affiliation, something that is never explored.

Against this tense background the shy, troubled Tate, urged on by his playboy cousin (Duane Martin), commences to spread his wings ever so tentatively. Where the film is at its most deft and subtle is in the way in which it credibly involves the awkward (but handsome) Tate, first with the imperious queen of the beach (Jada Pinkett), a beauty whose frosty and cynical veneer hides considerable vulnerability, and then with a gorgeous woman (Adrienne-Joi Johnson), married to a compulsive philanderer (Morris Chestnut). (In a way, the film is a black "Tea and Sympathy.")

The film is on sufficiently sure ground in depicting Tate's gradual, sometimes funny, sometimes painful, path to maturity that it's a shame that it otherwise misfires so badly.

Everyone in the large cast is game but understandably only Tate, Pinkett and Johnson are fully persuasive. Let's hope that the talented Rich will get back on track the next time around.

NEW YORK POST, 4/22/94, p. 41, Michael Medved

Despite strong acting and obvious good intentions, "The Inkwell" feels uncomfortably close to a contrived African-American version of "The Summer of '42."

Gifted and sensitive director Matty ("Straight Out of Brooklyn") Rich provides the same nostalgic tone, the same focus on coming-of-age trials of a shy teen-ager on seaside vacation with his family, the same crush on a conveniently sympathetic older woman.

The accomplished ensemble cast makes these elements watchable, but can't hide the fundamentally derivative nature of the material. The title here refers to a celebrated beach on Martha's Vineyard once exclusively populated by prosperous people of color. In the bicentennial summer of '76, a nerdy, nervous 16-year-old from upstate New York (Larenz Tate) makes his first trip to this vacation paradise with his parents.

His father (Joe Morton) is a former Black Panther who doesn't like the idea of staying at the comfortable beach house of his nouveau riche Republican brother-in-law (Glynn Turman). While Tate's lady-killer cousin (Duane Martin) tries to introduce him to some of the teen-aged beauties at the Inkwell, the newcomer is so socially inept that he invariably embarrasses himself.

Ultimately, his very awkwardness begins to endear him to the haughty and gorgeous Jada Pinkett and, even more important, to a glamorous, warm, hearted married woman played by Adrienne Joi-Johnson.

Each of these characters comes across as vivid and endearing—so much so that you can almost overlook the fact that his script lacks all shape or forward momentum.

Inspired by an autobiographical story by talented young novelist Trey Ellis, the final screenplay bore so little resemblance to his actual recollections that he allowed his name to appear on the credits only under the pseudonym "Tom Ricostronza."

The movie never feels heartfelt or authentic, as the fine performers struggle constantly against the danger of caricature. The Glynn Turman character may be a committed conservative, but would he really have a portrait of Richard Nixon on his wall—more than a year after he resigned in disgrace?

The culture clash between this GOP die-hard and his militant brother-in-law plays itself out on a sub-sitcom level, with the activist declaring, "Malcolm X told it like it was!," while the businessman responds, "America—love it or leave it!"

Young star Larenz Tate, who made such a chilling impression as the ruthless "O-Dog" in last year's "Menace II Society," is almost unrecognizable here as the painfully vulnerable protagonist, but the unfocused script undermines even his superior performance.

Intriguing details about the character, like his obsession with a crude doll that functions as his one confidante, and his possible involvement in pyromania, are awkwardly jettisoned as the plot lurches toward its contrived tale of sexual initiation.

Director Rich provides his movie with a handsome, glowing surface, and will receive some appropriate praise for his refreshing focus on a world of functional, intact black families.

In the final analysis. however, "The Inkwell"'resembles too many real-life summer vacations: pleasant enough while it's happening, but hardly memorable as you look back on it.

NEWSDAY, 4/22/94, Part II/p. B7, John Anderson

After his incendiary debut with "Straight Out of Brooklyn," one expected a lot of things from director Matty Rich. Clichés, superficiality and haughty superiority were not among them.

But in "The Inkwell," a comedy set in the bourgeois-black enclave on Martha's Vineyard in 1976, Rich leaves what he knows—the anger and grit of the Brooklyn projects—for something he doesn't—the African-American upper middle class—and shows what he lacks: a sensibility big enough to deal emotionally with something foreign, and perhaps personally troubling, without resorting to outright derision.

What he does have, and what almost saves the film, is a leading man with the opposite approach: Larenz Tate, the *enfant homicidal* of "Menace II Society" (and a star of TV's "South Central"), who makes the picture more than just a vehicle for cheap laughs and superior attitude. As Drew Tate, a sweetly immature 16-year-old with several socialization problems, he pulls off the thankless task of bestowing humanity on a geek, and in the process creates a sympathetic and gently funny hero—one who may not get the girl (the snooty Lauren, played by Jada Pinkett), but who discovers himself nonetheless.

Rich might deserve some credit for Tate's performance, but the way he handles the rest of the movie—which takes place during Drew and his parents' two-week summer vacation with their rich relatives tends to belie this. Operating from a sniper's position, he blows holes in his characters from discreet distances. Drew's uncle Spencer (Glynn Turman), for instance, who plays host to the Tates—Kenny (Joe Morton) and Brenda (Suzzanne Douglas)—is presented like the black Thurston Howell III, complete with cigarette holder, tennis whites and a picture of Richard Nixon on his living room wall. His wife, Frances (Vanessa Bell Calloway), is merely a caricature of the social-climbing spouse.

And while Spencer's volatile exchanges with Kenny, a former Black Panther, are electric, if clichéd—Spencer actually tells him "Love it or leave it" at one point—what makes Spencer Spencer is summarily dismissed; social or economic aspirations, much less achievement, are something to be snickered at.

The things Rich genuinely seems to care about—the relationship between Kenny and Brenda, or their concern for Drew—never get the attention they deserve. Why does Brenda break down at one point, asking Kenny whether their marriage can be saved? It's a scene that implies much greater problems than we've had reason to believe exist.

But the story line in general has more holes than Albert Hall: Why does Brenda's mother, Evelyn (Mary Alice), treat her so contemptuously? Why is Drew's only friend a carved wooden totem named Iago? Why is he so socially inept when he hangs out with his cousin Junior (Duane Martin) and his Stooge-like pals? Why does the island psychiatrist, Dr. Wade (Phyllis Yvonne Stickney), put dreads in Drew's early-Michael-Jackson Afro?

The making of this film was awash in controversy: Trey Ellis, who wrote the original screenplay, thought Rich unsuitable to the story and wound up taking his name off the film (Tom Ricostronza is an alias). And he seems to have been right. Shifting wildly from broad comedy to pathos to weak sociology, the film often seems like a cross between an episode of "What's Happening!!" and "Summer of '42." It should have been more. It's maddening that it's not.

VILLAGE VOICE, 5/3/94, p. 58, Selwyn Seyfu Hinds

It's about goddamned time someone finally realized it's possible to make a viable feature about Black folk that's not chock-full of fucking guns. What do Hollywood insiders think we do, eat hollow tips for breakfast and crack for dinner? You think I wanna see that shit all the time? Black *don't* mean monolithic, my man. Black is full range of expression. In other words, we got mad amounts of stories. Listen harder! (Props to whoever heard *The Inkwell.*)

The setting is 1976, and Drew Tate (Larenz Tate) is on a two-week vacation at Inkwell Beach on Martha's Vineyard with his parents, Kenny and Brenda (Joe Morton, Suzzanne Douglas), who hope the time spent with their wealthy relatives, the Spencers (Glynn Turman, Vanessa Bell Calloway, and Duane Martin) will help pull their introverted 16-year-old son out of his shell. Drew manages to come through very well on his own, through his experiences with a local princess-type, Lauren Kelly (Jada Pinkett); Dr. Wade, a concerned psychiatrist (Phyllis Yvonne Stickney); and Heather Lee (Adrienne-Joi Johnson), an older woman who's more than just a friend. Drew's *quite* a bit more mature by the end of his vacation.

Conflicts inherent in the black middle-class experience lie at the heart of *The Inkwell*, The film positions Kenny Tate ("*Common Harlem hoodlum!*) and Spencer Phillips ("*Bourgie Nigga!*") as the embodiments of the forget-where-you-come-from-sellout-bastard and the ghetto-conscious-fuck-capitalism-ex-Panther-militant-idealist.The interplay between the two men, though initially a bit pat, provides some of the film's funniest and sweetest moments.

The Inkwell is a heartwarming film with a powerful Black narrative; yet it has a universal quality. From the cinematography, to the acting, to the excellent period work, *The Inkwell* simmers with an authenticity that comes across as far more affecting than the recent flood of celluloid AK-47s.

Also reviewed in:
NEW REPUBLIC, 5/23/94, p. 34, Stanley Kauffmann
NEW YORK TIMES, 4/22/94, p. C8, Stephen Holden
VARIETY, 1/31-2/6/94, Todd McCarthy

INTERSECTION

A Paramount Pictures release. *Executive Producer:* Frederic Golchan. *Producer:* Bud Yorkin and Mark Rydell. *Director:* Mark Rydell. *Screenplay:* David Rayfiel and Marshall Brickman. *Based on the book "Les Choses de la Vie" by:* Paul Guimard. *Based on the screenplay by:* Paul Guimard, Jean-Loup Dabadie, and Claude Sautet. *Director of Photography:* Vilmos Zsigmond. *Editor:* Mark Warner. *Music:* James Newton Howard. *Music Editor:* Jim Weidman. *Sound:* Eric Batut and (music) Shawn Murphy. *Sound Editor:* Kay Rose. *Casting:* Lynn Stalmaster. *Production Designer:* Harold Michelson. *Art Director:* Yvonne Hurst. *Set Designer:* Marco Rubeo. *Set Decorator:* Dominique Fauquet-Lemaitre. *Special Effects:* Michael Vezina. *Costumes:* Ellen Mirojnick. *Make-up:* Jan Newman. *Make-up (Richard Gere):* Tom Lucas. *Make-up (Sharon Stone):* Tricia Sawyer. *Stunt Coordinator:* Mic Rodgers and Brent Woolsey. *Running time:* 98 minutes. *MPAA Rating:* R.

CAST: Richard Gere (Vincent Eastman); Sharon Stone (Sally Eastman); Lolita Davidovich (Olivia Marshak); Martin Landau (Neal); David Selby (Richard Quarry); Jenny Morrison (Meaghan Eastman); Ron White (Charlie); Matthew Walker (Surgeon); Scott Bellis (Van Driver); Patricia Harras (Van Driver's Wife); Keegan Macintosh (Van Driver's Son); Alan C. Peterson (Semi-Driver); Sandra P. Grant (Receptionist); Barney McFadden and Kevin McNulty (Developers); Jay Brazeau (Businessman); Betty Phillips (Edwina); Mikal Dughi (Mrs. Krask); Paul McLean (Pappas); Mark Roberts (John Graham); Marlene Worrall (Kirsten Graham); Ted Deeken (Auctioneer); Bill Finck (Man at Auction); Carol Whiteman (Auction Cashier); Stacy Grant (Hostess); Andrew Guy (Bartender); Suki Kaiser (Diner Waitress); Tom Heaton (Grandfather); Christine Hendra (Little Girl); Timothy Webber (Truck Driver); Christopher J. Tuck (Passenger in Pick-up Truck); Garry Chalk (Paramedic); Veena Sood (Intern); Tim Battle (Draftsman); Nancy Cawsey and Katherine McLaren (Trauma Nurses); D'Arcy Lawrence (Radiologist); Ron Chartier (Resident); Denise Beaudry (Anesthesiologist); Jon Cuthbert (Cop); Susan Astley (Woman in Waiting Room); Margaret Nelson (Nurse at Desk).

FILMS IN REVIEW, 3-4/94, p. 58, Andy Pawelczak

The advertising copy for *Intersection*—"Make every move as if it were your last"—suggests a desperation that might apply more to the filmmakers than to the movie's characters. As directed by Mark Rydell (*The Rose, On Golden Pond*) and written by the high powered David Rayfiel and Marshall Brickman (Woody Allen's collaborator), the movie, marketed as a noir thriller, is really a throwback to the women's pictures of the forties, but it lacks the belief in its trashy conventions that made those films into frequently compelling exercises in sudsy hysteria.

The film is structured as a long flashback—with flashbacks within the flashback—as Vince Eastman's Mercedes skids out of control on a country road. (We don't learn the result of the accident until the end of the movie.) Vince (Richard Gere) is an architect married to Sally (Sharon Stone), a cold, rich WASP whose family connections helped Vince get started in business. The marriage is on the rocks; as Vince says to a friend, they're not a family but a corporation with a kid. Enter Olivia (Lolita Davidovich), a magazine columnist who is every misunderstood husband's dream, sympathetic, earthy, good humored, and, as the therapists, those high priests of the culture of narcissism, have taught us all to say, very supportive. Vince and Olivia meet cute at an auction at which she bids against him for an antique clock, and before long they're exchanging heartfelt dialogue about the missing element in Vince's marriage. The rest of the film, reversing the usual gender roles in such movies, is about Vince's dilemma in choosing between family and mistress.

As Vince, Richard Gere, with the fabulous hair and cute sexy overbite, is the apotheosis of narcissism, which the film underlines in a scene in which he and Stone, in a state of semi-nudity, admire each other in a mirror. Not that this is a film with an ironic Sirkian subtext (in Sirk's *Imitation of Life*, mirrors always have a charged semantic presence). Clearly we're meant to take Vince's sensitivity and moral agonizing at face value, but I couldn't help thinking of a Hemingway remark that American men never grow up. As Sally, Sharon Stone, in her coming out role as a serious actress, fares a bit better—she's quite convincing as the masochistic object, choice, as the Freudians would say, of an eternally adolescent male. In the film's most talked about, and silliest, scene, Vince and Sally make love fully clothed in a sitting position during a party at her father's house, and she's more concerned with her makeup and dress, and with the rich potential patrons in the next room, than with poor Vince's unrequited passion. Lolita Davidovich as Olivia is appropriately warm and huggable, though she's burdened with some of the movie's soggiest dialogue.

At one point in the movie, Vince, enthusing over an article Olivia wrote, says he particularly loved the last line, "Hell is other people." It's characteristic of the movie's pretensions and condescension that this line, which is absolutely unrelated to the film's theme, is not identified as a quote from Sartre's *No Exit*. The filmmakers have aspirations to non-generic seriousness—particularly in the film's closing moments—but ultimately the picture is like the American Indian museum that Vince designed, a sleek glass palace that calls more attention to itself than to the artifacts it houses. *Intersection*'s packaging—an affluent dream of cars, houses, boats, and furniture—fails to disguise the fact that its characters are cliches all dressed up with nowhere to go.

LOS ANGELES TIMES, 1/21/94, Calendar/p. 1, Kenneth Turan

"Hell is other people," one of the characters in "Intersection" allows in a philosophical moment, but that isn't quite accurate. Hell is other people in movies like this.

A dithering romantic drama about a self-absorbed dolt of a husband going through yet another midlife crisis, unable to choose between two stunning women who throw themselves at him and inexplicably put up with his whiny indecisiveness, "Intersection" in truth isn't intense enough to be called hell. Purgatory would be more like it.

Based on a French novel that director Claude Sautet turned into his 1970 film "Les Choses de la Vie," "Intersection" as directed by Mark Rydell is riddled with miscalculations. It is miscast, filled with characters who are incapable of eliciting sympathy, and relates a story so unsatisfying one can only wonder that it got made at all.

Vincent Eastman (Richard Gere) is the man with too many women. The architect of choice in Vancouver, B.C., prone to peering over half-glasses and muttering about fenestration, Eastman designs buildings that cause an admiring associate to say, "somewhere Frank Lloyd Wright is eating his heart out."

What Vincent lacks, to steal a title from a far better film, is a design for living. He has been married for 16 years to his high-powered partner Sally (Sharon Stone), an ambitious woman who wears her hair in a bun and cares more about clients than carnal pleasures. "It's not a family," Vincent grouses, "it's a corporation with a kid." That would be 13-year-old Meaghan (Jenny Morrison) who is the apple, pear and peach of her dad's eye.

The other woman is the free-spirited Olivia Marshak (Lolita Davidovich, a counterculture journalist so bursting with youthful joi d'vivre you want to hide under a rock, and so understandingof Vincent's inability to truly commit she makes Dr. Joyce Brothers look like Rush Limbaugh.

Most of the movie is made up of Vincent equivocating about whom he really loves and remembering the good times with both women, trying to balance how much Sally has meant to him with how good Olivia makes him feel. Problems, problems, problems.

All the principals certainly look glamorous in Vilmos Zsigmond's glossy cinematography, with Gere's windblown hair nicely setting off his Armani clothes and Stone looking regal in jewels precious enough to get a screen credit. The only thing the three stars can't do is get anyone involved in the David Rayfiel and Marshall Brickman script.

For one thing, though the story's dynamics and the Eastmans' 16-year marriage tell you that this is at least in part an older-woman, younger-woman situation, Stone and Davidovich are in reality only a few years apart in age and putting Stone's hair up in that bun does not go a long way toward making her look like Grandma Moses.

For another thing, Gere is about the last actor you want to see having a crisis of conscience on screen. Handsome and talented though he is, he is also too self-absorbed to be empathetic while searching his soul, and his most successful roles, from "An Officer and a Gentleman" to "Internal Affairs" and "Pretty Woman," have wisely not called on him to be the kind of audience surrogate he is supposed to be here.

Already burdened with distant actors and an artificial script, "Intersection" does not need its peculiar central plot contrivance, which starts with the film's mysterious opening scene and closes with a leaden finale. Midlife crises are invariably a bore on screen, but this one is worst than most.

NEW YORK POST, 1/21/94, p. 39, Michael Medved

As the central character of "Intersection," Richard Gere, plays a brilliant architect whose daring buildings have won him wide acclaim. He lives in a luxurious mansion in one of the world's most appealing cities (Vancouver), drives a slick, spiffy Mercedes and enjoys a warm relationship with his lovely, gifted 13-year-old daughter (Jenny Morrison).

The only shadow on an otherwise perfect existence is that he feels torn between his brilliant, stunning and adoring wife (Sharon Stone) and his sexy and equally adoring mistress (Lolita Davidovich).

Poor baby!

The big problem with "Intersection" is that the picture actually wants us to feel sorry for this pampered putz, treating his self-imposed, utterly indulgent adolescent angst as if it represented one of mankind's most significant dilemmas.

Gere is most certainly suave and sexy (especially since he spends nearly half his role with his shirt off), but his opaque performance helps create a character so devoid of wit, charm or even the slightest hint of self-awareness that he inspires neither respect nor affection.

Frankly, both women in his life seem too good for him.

Sharon Stone is cast against type as the efficient, frigid ("Don't get your fingers on my dress!") wife who has faithfully run her husband's architecture business for 16 years.

"We were never a family," Gere whines to his partner, Martin Landau. "We were a corporation with a kid!"

Ms. Stone presumably took this role to demonstrate her dramatic range by playing a woman thoroughly lacking in basic instincts; unfortunately, she still projects a tough, dangerous femme-fatale edge that undermines the sympathy we're supposed to feel for the spurned spouse.

The character of the mistress remains even more unfocused. She's supposed to be a brilliant, incisive columnist for a local newspaper, but she comes across more like the earthy, good-hearted bimbo Davidovich played so well in "Blaze."

Her lack of on-screen chemistry with Gere is downright embarrassing, in sad contrast to his persuasively passionate interaction with Jodie Foster in last year's "Sommersby."

The script hardly helps, bringing Davidovich and Gere together in an idiotic "cute meet," bidding against one another for the quaint clock at an antique auction. The resulting relationship seems so boring and shallow that it's tough to imagine missing a good football game for its sake, let alone walking away from a long-term marriage.

Bud Yorkin, producer of "Intersection" previously produced and directed the fine film "Twice in a Lifetime," which dramatized a mid-life affair far more effectively; Allen Parker searingly explored the same territory in "Shoot the Moon."

Unlike such earthy, honest portrayals, director Mark Rydell ("On Golden Pond," "For the Boys") here seems preoccupied with picturesque poses and shimmering surf aces, showing pretty, petty people who feel little poetry or pain.

This movie's flawed structure most certainly contributes to the twisted wreckage that piles up at this "Intersection." Loosely based on a 1970 French picture called "Les Choses de la Vie" ("The Things of Life"), it begins with Gere speeding along a misty British Columbia highway in his hot Mercedes, then going into a scary spin at a country crossroads.

The movie moves through 90 minutes of meandering flashbacks before answering the basic questions raised by that suspended skid. Does the main character live or die? And where was he driving in such a desperate hurry?

But the picture makes no attempt to answer the even more basic question: Who cares?

NEWSDAY, 1/21/94, Part II/p. 70, Jack Mathews

We're on a rain-soaked country road somewhere near Vancouver, B.C., cruising along at about 80 mph in a Mercedes 280SL with day-dreaming architect Vincent Eastman (Richard Gere) when we spot a stalled VW van blocking our lane ahead, and, just beyond it, a huge tractor trailer coming toward us from the other direction.

Startled from his reverie, Vincent hits the brakes and throws the gunmetal-gray sports car into a sideways slide, like a hockey puck loose on the ice, and we see the panic on the faces of the occupants of all three vehicles. Then ... freeze!

Before we learn the outcome of this crafty opening sequence in Mark Rydell's otherwise uninvolving "Intersection," we will travel back through Vincent's daydreams to see what got him here and meet the two women—his estranged wife Sally (Sharon Stone) and his new girlfriend Olivia (Lolita Davidovich)—who have him so preoccupied.

The backdrop of the story, told in confusing layers of flashbacks, is nowhere near as compelling as the accident it interrupts. Vincent, presented as a sort of updated version of "The Fountainhead's" Howard Roark, is a man too obsessed with his work and his own interests to play the pivotal role in a love triangle, and the women don't make up for what he lacks.

Stone plays Sally as an ice goddess, a frigid socialite cum career woman who rations sex between business calls, and the open passion of Davidovich's Olivia, a magazine columnist specializing in the singles lifestyle, is tempered by a massive penchant for nagging.

Based loosely on the French novel "The Things of Life" and the 1970 Claude Sautet movie made from it, "Intersection" is leaden romantic melodrama in the guise of existential reckoning, one man's attempt to rescue himself from emotional mediocrity. "Intersection." "Introspection." Take your pick.

There are some promising ideas in the script, by David Rayfiel (Sidney Pollack's long-time collaborator) and Marshall Brickman (who co-wrote "Annie Hall" with Woody Allen), but to embrace them with any enthusiasm, you have to have more feeling for the characters than we can muster for these three.

The harder the film works to fill us in on the characters' lives, the more off-putting they become. The passion hasn't exactly gone out of Vincent's and Sally's marriage, we learn, it was never there. And rather than being shaken out of his complacency by some irresistible romantic urge, we see Vincent and Olivia meet at a country auction (they get into a bidding match for an English clock) and blithely date their way into a domestic crisis.

The casting of Gere, and Stone, Hollywood's preeminent sexual predators, figured to produce as much huffing and puffing as a mating in the rhino pen. But Vincent and Sally don't even work up a sweat. One of their two "love scenes" is interrupted by a telephone call, the other—a quicky conducted in evening wear on a couch back in their courtship days—is played as comic relief.

Rydell, a former actor who often relies on star power to carry his films ("On Golden Pond," "The Rose"), doesn't have the right people in the right places here. There is too cool and emotionally distanced an actor to warm up an ordinary soul like Vincent, and by having her play a woman with no interest in sex, they've taken Stone's fastball away from her.

As for Davidovich, she plays the other woman with such a fury of childlike emotions, we half-suspect suicide as a motive for Vincent's reckless driving. Certainly, by the time we return to the highway to see how Vincent makes out in that accident (an event, by the way, that provides the film's only moment of realism), he doesn't seem like a man with much to lose.

NEWSWEEK, 1/31/94, p. 58, David Ansen

Vincent Eastman (Richard Gere) is a man who can't make up his mind, which doesn't exactly make him Hamlet. A successful 42-year-old Vancouver architect, Vincent is at a crossroads in his life—hence the title "Intersection," of Mark Rydell's movie. Though separated from his wealthy, coolly beautiful wife (Sharon Stone) and living with an adoring and warmly beautiful journalist (Lolita Davidovich), Vincent is unwilling to let go of his old life or fully embrace his new one. Since the film opens with Vincent's catastrophic car crash—the outcome of which is withheld until the end—the subsequent account of our hero's glamorously disheveled life and loves is meant to achieve poignancy in the shadow of mortality.

Actually, it's hard to know what to make of this glossy romantic triangle, or to work up much concern about its selfish and opportunistic hero. In transposing Claude Sautet's 1970 French movie "The Things of Life"—a film about the banality and allure of bourgeois comforts—into Hollywoodese, director Rydell and screenwriters David Rayfiel and Marshall Brickman seem uncertain of their own point of view. Are we meant to find Vincent as irresistible as the women do, or to criticize his waffling? Gere's movie-star presence confuses the issue further. His "sensitive" mannerisms—linking and closing his eves to convey deep thoughtfulness, rippling his jawbone to connote inner turmoil—are so familiar and so self-regarding it is impossible to tell whether the narcissism he radiates is an aspect of Vincent's character or simply Gere posturing for sympathy. From the way Rydell's camera dotes on his moods, we guess the latter.

"Intersection" pretends to be a movie of grown-up, middle-aged concerns, but it plays like a rather dull and pointless soap opera. Everything that should be precise, matter-of-fact and quotidian is made slightly larger, and falser, than life. There's a moment of epiphany that enables Vincent to realize his heart's true calling, but it is hard to imagine the viewer who will swallow it with a straight face. The one very pleasant surprise of "Intersection" is Stone's sharply etched portrait of Gere's wife and business partner, a brittle, unspontaneous woman in whom one can see the spoiled, giggly rich girl she once was. Stone alone creates a character—Gere and Davidovich just want to win us over. To what, we have to wonder?

SIGHT AND SOUND, 7/94, p. 47, Geoffrey Macnab

America, somewhere on the open road. A car spins out of control. As it crashes, we flash back a few weeks in the life of its driver. Vincent Eastman, a successful architect, has recently separated from his wife Sally and started an affair with young journalist Olivia Marshak. However, he can't make up his mind whether or not he wants a divorce. He is still drawn to Sally, who has played a crucial, administrative part in furthering his career, and he doesn't want to lose contact with his 14- year-old ballet dancer daughter Meaghan.

Matters come to a head on the evening the trustees of one of his new buildings, a museum of American Indian culture, throw a reception in his honour. Olivia turns up, drunk and uninvited. He is furious with her and only reluctantly introduces her to his wife. Rather than go home with her, he drives off into the night to think about his future. Eventually, he writes her a letter, telling her their affair is over. As dawn breaks, he stops off at a store to mail the letter. A chance encounter with a little girl and her grandfather makes him reconsider his decision. He decides he does love Olivia after all, leaves a message on her answering machine telling her he wants to marry her, and then drives at high speed to get back to her.

En route, he crashes. He is rushed to the local hospital, but dies shortly afterwards from his injuries. Sally is presented with his personal effects, which include the unposted letter. She reads this. Believing her husband was on the verge of returning to her, and not wishing to hurt Olivia's feelings, she rips it up. Olivia, for her part, makes no mention of Vincent's last call to her.

An architect is really just a cowboy with cultural capital. This at least, was an idea King Vidor seemed to endorse when he cast Gary Cooper as the lead in his absurdly overblown version of the absurdly overblown Ayn Rand novel, *The Fountainhead*, which celebrated the lawless, freewheeling individualism of a Frank Lloyd Wright-like visionary. A little less gung-ho than Vidor's picture, *Intersection* also subscribes to the architect-as-hero myth. Here, though, the protagonist is not so much concerned with designing startling new buildings as with sorting out his tangled love life. Take away the veneer of sophistication which his profession gives him, and we're left with a commonplace saga about a self-indulgent man who treats the women in his life with contempt.

Perhaps fearful that their flimsy narrative would otherwise be revealed for the powderpuff concoction it is, the film-makers pile flashback upon flashback, telling the story in as oblique a way as possible. To remind us of the fact, Vilmos Zsigmond lights the picture in restrained autumnal hues, Mark Rydell directs in his leaden, lugubrious, terminally tasteful *On Golden Pond* fashion, and the actors pause and sigh meaningfully wherever possible. One might have expected the central pairing of Richard Gere and Sharon Stone to give off at least a few sparks, but the gunpowder here is definitely damp. Emotions are what we are dealing with: the transitory nature of time, the big things of life (the whole project has its origins in a French novel filmed by Claude Sautet back in 1969). Even the architect's teenage daughter is caught up in the earnest, highbrow conspiracy. She seems completely unaware of popular culture. Rather than chewing gum and listening to Pearl Jam, she follows ballet with a passion.

As the characters ponder the metaphysical monstrosity of existence, there are frequent, excruciating cutaways to a rococo clock with a marble at its base, which slides further down a maze with every passing tick. It's hard to think of a more clumsy metaphor, short of having the Grim Reaper turn up with his chess set on the beach.

Despite its longueurs, *Intersection* begins and ends arrestingly enough. Connoisseurs of cinema car crashes will find much to admire. The central narrative conceit of telling the story from the perspective of a character lying in his mangled automobile, halfway beën life and death, is at least initially intriguing (J.G. Ballard's classic sci-fi novels *Crash* and *The Concrete Island* start from a roughly similar premise). And even the hoary old plot-line about the man torn between his lover and his wife has some mileage still left in it. The picture might have worked if the film-makers had cranked it up into an out-and-out Sirk-style melodrama. Unfortunately, they do the reverse, aiming for subtlety and nuance, and utterly eviscerate their material in the process.

TIME, 1/31/94, p. 108, Richard Schickel

Intersection is—earnestly, self-consciously—a movie for grownups. It is made by veteran adults (director Mark Rydell; writers Marshall Brickman and David Rayfiel). It takes up a "mature" (if not exactly original) theme, that of a man torn between the responsibilities of marriage and the delights of a young mistress. It comes to an ending that is both tragic and neatly ironic. And it is a movie that does not for one minute draw you into its life, make you believe in its reality.

Instead, it creates the curious impression that its actors worked against a blue screen projecting handsome views of a nameless Pacific Northwest city (actually Vancouver) and glamorous lifestyles. They never seem to be in touch with their environment, their ostensible professions or, for that matter, one another.

Richard Gere, playing an architect, doesn't act as if he could read a blueprint, much less draw one up. He's also supposed to be a loving father, but the scenes with his daughter are played as if he fears a charge of child molestation. His wife is meant to be a frigid business-woman, but you can practically hear Sharon Stone's joints pop as she attempts the stretch. The other woman

(Lolita Davidovich) is said to be a witty journalist, but looks as if she might need help booting up her word processor.

It's not important, really—just another banal triangle. Though based on a 1969 French film, *Les Choses de la Vie, Intersection* made at least one viewer think of *Blue*, the 1993 French movie that's also about infidelity and life's sad ironies. There was a felt reality in the intimacy of *Blue*'s textures, and its elliptical style kept the eye puzzled and alert. Not for the first time one wonders why American moviemakers can't get the hang of, the fun of, the higher trivia.

VILLAGE VOICE, 2/1/94, p. 56, Georgia Brown

For women who love married men too much, *Intersection* too is about beautiful things. British Columbia's coastal highways, its snowcapped mountains, may as well be an extension of the hero's designer outerwear. As the connoisseur, snowcapped Richard Gere has to choose between the rich, frigid object of beauty he's married to and the tacky-but-lively journalist (now there's a messy profession) he's been romancing on the side. The regal, blond WASP is played by Sharon Stone, the sloppy, ethnic redhead by Lolita Davidovich. Everything surrounding the former is crisp, beige, and elegant; everything around the other is garishly patterned or more than a bit off.

But this lifestyle movie's real object of desire is the silver fleece himself. (Once, when Vilmos Zsigmond backlights Gere's locks, I actually believed a new woman had entered the plot.) Gere's Vincent Eastman is a famous architect (profession of choice for the new sensitive/creative hero) doted on by three women—the third is his 13-year-old ballet-dancing daughter—each of them waiting impatiently for him to make up his mind.

Intersection may be shot, scored, and advertised as a thriller, but it's really a romantic melodrama—what used to be called "a woman's picture" from a man's point of view. The plot is minuscule. (I kept waiting for someone to get bumped off, in the old sense, but no such luck.) In the beginning, Vincent and his silver (natch) Mercedes approach a dangerous crossroads (get it?) where things fly out of control. What happens when the car goes into a spin is held in abeyance, while the movie presents—flashbacks within flashbacks—the mundane, consumer-oriented events bringing Vince to this juncture in the road. It finally reveals what he is on his way to do—i.e., which woman he picks.

Directed by Mark Rydell and written by David Rayfiel and Marshall Brickman, *Intersection* is based on *Les Choses de la Vie*, a 1970 film directed by Claude Sautet. I don't recall having seen Sautet's film (though I may well have), but I do remember his icky *César and Rosalie* an ultra-lyrical ménage a trois movie with devoted fans among the married and the restless. Clearly, *Intersection* is an attempt to appeal both to the single woman on a string as well as the guy who dangles it. Its carpe diem message will appeal more to her. He, after all, already is seizing the day.

The movie has one memorably tasteless comic moment: It comes when Stone, wearing a Hillary headband, mounts Gere's lap for a quickie in her parents' library. (The scene though is uncomprehending of the woman and smugly deferential to the male.) Since she's otherwise looking either starry-eyed or hurt, it's Stone's best scene (she's a comedian). As for Davidovich, her tousled Olivia Marshak—a magazine columnist whom people recognize from her photo—is so forgiving even of Vincent's nasty snobbery, she's a male fantasy of infinite tolerance. Since all along the two women humor and tolerate this narcissist, it wouldn't be surprising if they were left to clean up his mess at the end.

Also reviewed in:
CHICAGO TRIBUNE, 1/21/94, Friday/p. K, Johanna Steinmetz
NEW YORK TIMES, 1/21/94, p. C8, Janet Maslin
VARIETY, 1/24-30/94, p. 63, Todd McCarthy
WASHINGTON POST, 1/21/94, p. G6, Rita Kempley
WASHINGTON POST, 1/21/94, Weekend/p. 38, Desson Howe

INTERVIEW WITH THE VAMPIRE

A Geffen Pictures release distributed by Warner Bros.. *Producer:* David Geffen and Stephen Wooley. *Director:* Neil Jordan. *Screenplay (based on her novel):* Anne Rice. *Director of Photography:* Philippe Rousselot. *Editor:* Mick Audsley and Joke van Wijk. *Music:* Elliot Goldenthal. *Music Editor:* Michael Connell. *Choreographer:* Micha Bergese. *Sound:* Clive Winter and (music) Stephen McLaughlin and Joel Iwataki. *Sound Editor:* Eddy Joseph. *Casting:* Juliet Taylor, Susie Figis and Sandy Dawes. *Production Designer:* Dante Ferretti. *Art Director:* Malcolm Middleton. *Set Designer:* Stella Furner and Munroe Kelly. *Set Decorator:* Francesca Lo Schiavo. *Special Effects:* Yves de Bono. *Costumes:* Sandy Powell. *Make-up:* Carol Schwartz, Nick Dudman, Sarah Monzani and Morag Ross. *Vampire Make-up:* Stan Winston. *Stunt Coordinator:* Greg Powell. *Running time:* 120 minutes. *MPAA Rating:* R.

CAST: Brad Pitt (Louis); Christian Slater (Malloy); Tom Cruise (Lestat); Stephen Rea (Santiago); Antonio Banderas (Armand); Kirsten Dunst (Claudia); Virginia McCollam (Whore on Waterfron); John McConnell (Gambler); Mike Seelig (Pimp); Bellina Logan (Tavern Girl); Thandie Newton (Yvette); Lyla Hay Owen (Widow St. Clair); Lee Emery (Widow's Lover); Indra Ove and Helen McCrory (New Orleans Whores); Monte Montague (Plague Victim Bearer); Nathalie Bloch (Maid); Jeanette Kontomitras (Woman in Square); Roger Lloyd Pack (Piano Teacher); George Kelly (Dollmaker); Nicole Dubois (Creole Woman); Sara Stockbridge (Estelle); Laure Marsac (Mortal Woman on Stage); Katia Caballero (Woman in Audience); Louis Lewis-Smith (Mortal Boy); Domiziana Giordano (Madeleine).

CHRISTIAN SCIENCE MONITOR, 11/14/94, p. 13, David Sterritt

Horrors! A new generation of movie monsters is stalking the screen—or rather an old generation, since most of the currently popular creatures come from the same venerable lineage as the original Count Dracula and Baron Frankenstein, whose exploits have spanned many hits, flops, remakes, and sequels dating back to the early decades of film.

"Interview With the Vampire: The Vampire Chronicles," based on the first volume in novelist Anne Rice's best-selling series, comes hot on the heels of "Mary Shelley's Frankenstein," directed by Kenneth Branagh with a manic energy that breathes new life into the old story. Both movies are clearly inspired by "Bram Stoker's Dracula, directed two years ago by Francis Ford Coppola and still the best entry in the 1990s horror sweepstakes.

In terms of old-fashioned gothic horror, "Interview With the Vampire" is the creepiest of the three pictures. Coppola and Branagh load their movies with the free-flowing gore that's a staple of the genre, but distract our attention with cinematic stunts having more Tinseltown than Transylvania about them.

By contrast, "Vampire" director Neil Jordan plunges us into a dark-toned abyss of predatory evil, revenge, and misogyny, creating a persistently morbid atmosphere that's relieved only by an occasional outburst of unexpected camp. You may chuckle when the centuries-old antihero decides to take in a few movies, or when the story's final shockeroo is accompanied by a blast of cleverly chosen rock and roll. But you may feel outrage rather than cinematic chills when you notice how vicious the picture is toward women.

The unremitting darkness of "Interview With the Vampire" is a reflection of Rice's novel, which relies more on sepulchral mood-spinning than on original plot development or three-dimensional characterization. Readers of the book will recognize almost everything on screen, including the narrative twists that seem designed merely to provide another excuse for hyperbolic suffering and gratuitous gore-mongering.

What the novel's fans may not expect is the manner and appearance of the main characters, Louis and Lestat, as embodied by Brad Pitt and Tom Cruise respectively. The picture's public-relations got off to a rocky start when Cruise's participation was first announced, prompting Rice into a widely reported statement that the good-looking star was wildly wrong for a leading role. She has since recanted that position—in yet another statement, this one proudly reprinted in a newspaper ad by the film's distributor—but moviegoers may think she had it right the first time.

While he has plenty of his usual handsome charm, Cruise has none of the feral coarseness that characterized Lestat in the novel, where his vampiric career mixed cruelty and crudity in equal measure.

Pitt tackles his part with enthusiasm, but he hasn't acquired the acting skills required by this important role , which carries the picture for long stretches. Other parts are handled with more panache; performers include Christian Slater as the interviewer, Stephen Rea and Antonio Banderas as vampires with a theatrical bent, and Kirsten Dunst as the little girl who becomes a vampire in one of Rice's most outlandishly ghoulish conceits.

Dante Ferretti did the funereal set designs, and cinematographer Philippe Rousselot has managed to capture many striking images with some of the dimmest lighting in memory. Elliot Goldenthal composed the intermittently effective music. Rice wrote the wordy screenplay.

FILMS IN REVIEW, 1-2/95, p. 57, Harry Pearson, Jr.

There is no way to be kind about this. So why try? *Interview With the Vampire* is a mess. It is, by turns, talky and then gory, aimlessly staggering the slow distances between "set" scenes with hardly a provocative thought in its pretty little head.

Well, I staggered out of the packed opening day show wondering whether 'twas better to be abducted by *X-Files* aliens than in the company of those who brought this conglomeration to the screen. It's the kind of experience that can leave you feeling somehow dirtied, and not just because there are one too many rat blood cocktails, but rather for an unrelenting and narcissistic self-absorption

Of one thing I now stand convinced: There are two Neil Jordans. Number 2 authored *The Company of Wolves* and *The Crying Game*, and Number 1, who, when handed a Hollywood-sized budget turns out abominations like this, *High Spirits* and *We're No Angels*. I can't say that I understand treating this entertaining morsel of pulp fiction as if it were a literary classic and abandoning most of the language of cinema to do a "Classics Illustrated" job. For *Interview* to have been a great entertainment, as opposed to a great film, it would have needed—say—the directorial hand of a Jane Campion, who would have injected the heavy doses of romantic eroticism it needed to take off. The Anne Rice original had it in spades, with more than a passing nod to De Sade and Masoch.

What the filmmakers have done to make this commercially palatable to a mass audience is intellectualize (I use the word almost oxymoronically in this context) the book's homoeroticism, so that its inherently gay subtext becomes deconstructed. In other words, they talk circles around it. Without this core of the forbidden, the outlaw sexual eroticism, and a commanding star turn, the movie becomes dispossessed of a center, that core of interest that would engage more fully our deeper attentions. Tom Cruise's turn as Lestat surprises because the actor brings more energy to this performance than he has since his early days in *Taps*, *The Outsiders* and *Risky Business*; he seems rejuvenated (so to speak) by the opportunity to play the barely caged beast. But what he either cannot or will not bring to Lestat is that sexual charisma, without which the motivating engine behind the plot fails to putter. Here he gets to play the part of the upstaging second banana—the guy who steals the show from the role of the immoral Puritan, which is how Brad Pitt, trancelike, glides through the motions of being Louis. Granted that Louis could not be an easy play. He willingly chooses to become a vampire and then spends his evenings for the next 200 years bitching over his fate. (Better for all concerned had Rice changed this, as she did the book's ending—the better to set up a sequel, m'dear—so that Louis could have been taken by force.) This leaves Louis as a self-righteous slaughterer of the innocent (from rats to chickens to children), who lacks *even* the courage of his homoerotic convictions.

Once in Paris, in the movie's second part, he falls passionately in love with Armand (though you'd never know this from any chemistry between Pitt and actor Antonio Banderas). In the novel, as in the movie, Louis turns his back on Armand for reasons that made no sense in the Rice original, but which do, commercially, make sense upon the screen. In one scene, the farewell, he moves his lips close to Armand, letting them drift about his head and face, as if aiming for a kiss upon the mouth (while sitting near me, a teenage boy, baseball cap reversed, murmured a series of "ohs" and "nos") and then the kiss didn't happen (much to the satisfaction of our child of the nineties). Given the makeup job on Banderas, his fanny-length black hair (auburn in the book), the filmmakers have accomplished the impossible—they've made him a wallflower. And catch his voice; it sounds like the dubbing of Fernando Rey in a spaghetti Western.

Aside from all this, what's left? Well, there's always the existential angst of the undead: "What am I going to do with the next 73,050 nights?" Which goes on at length and which might be compelling were it a metaphor for something, but such is hardly the stuff of a 122-minute David Geffen production. (I am, kindly I think, overlooking the possibility that *Interview* might be a metaphor for life in the LA movie colony: where we, the audience, are viewed as the vampires view us, as victims, human sushi rather than folks like you and me with soul, character and fascinations of our own making. I thought the color photography lacking in contrast (maybe a rush job to get all the prints to the theater in time?) without the depth and kind of high gloss stylizing it needed considering how much of the movie takes place in near darkness. (It will be a beast to reproduce on home video, for sure.) Credits? A solid score by Elliot Goldenthal, a first rate, even brilliant, performance by a child actress (Kirsten Dunst) and imaginative production design by Dante Ferretti.

The movie does have its moments. But if you thought the hard core gore days were over and that Freddie and Jason had been tamed by the MPAA, then I'm here to tell you they are not and it isn't safe just yet to go back into the theater. Many of the major critics ate *Interview* up, so to speak, while demeaning Kenneth Branagh's vision of *Frankenstein*, the better and better made film, and one that takes more chances with its material. One of the more jejune objections to Branagh's version is that it wasn't scary. This overlooks the fact that Frankenstein never has been scary. Vampires, on the other hand, are. And so was the book upon which this film was based. Here we don't have a single scare. Unless you can't separate being revolted from being frightened.

LOS ANGELES TIMES, 11/11/94, Calendar/p. 1, Kenneth Turan

"Interview With the Vampire" is half alive, which for a movie about the undead is not as bad as it sounds.

Directed by "The Crying Game's" Neil Jordan from the brooding, sweepingly popular book about how "the dark gift" of eternal life is passed on from the vampire Lestat to a handsome young aristocrat named Louis, "Interview" has been the subject of considerable. speculation because of the divergent public positions author Anne Rice has taken about the film version.

Rice broke with protocol more than a year ago to lambaste the selection of Tom Cruise as Lestat and Brad Pitt as Louis, scathingly comparing it to "casting Huck Finn and Tom Sawyer" and reserving special scorn for Cruise, "who is no more my Vampire Lestat than Edward G. Robinson is Rhett Butler."

Then, about a month ago, Rice appeared to reverse herself, saying the finished product "surpassed my maddest expectations" and stunned her with how faithful it was "to the spirit, the content and the ambience of the novel." Now that the film is here, these seemingly contradictory positions turn out to be both correct.

For director Jordan, whose elegantly gory 1984 version of Angela Carter's "The Company of Wolves" can be seen as a dress rehearsal for "Interview," has a feel for the supernatural and a gift for establishing creepy mood and atmosphere that this film fully exploits.

Whatever else it lacks, "Interview" does a gorgeous job of recreating not only 18th-Century New Orleans and 19th-Century Paris but also the book's genuinely weird, disturbing, almost unimaginable world of those who can never die.

Put together by a superior team, including Oscar-winning "A River Runs Through It" cinematographer Philippe Rousselot (who lit the film with Chinese paper lanterns), "The Age of Innocence" production designer Dante Ferretti and "Orlando" costume designer Sandy Powell, "Interview's" visual strength does all that can be done to convincingly set the stage for drama. That element, however, almost never arrives because "Interview With the Vampire" is fatally anemic in terms of emotional weight and attachment.

Although the book was originally written out of Rice's agony at having lost a young daughter and consequently has a powerful air of despairing melancholy about it, the movie version (with a script credited to Rice alone, although Jordan is known to have contributed) has little sense of love or loss for an audience to connect with.

The reason is the casting, where the filmmakers made a pact with the devil and have paid the price. After Daniel Day-Lewis, who would have made a memorable Lestat, turned the role down, it went to Tom Cruise, he of the $2-billion and counting worldwide gross, while Louis' part went to the equally photogenic Pitt.

And why not? Jordan and company insisted as the outrage mounted. The vampires were young and handsome and the actor's playing them should be likewise. Thc dramatic reality, however, is subtler than that. What make's Lestat and Louis such involving characters is that they have ancient minds and souls in their lithe bodies, and neither Pitt nor Cruise has the persona or the acting range to convey that critical age-within-beauty quality.

Pitt has an easier time of it with Louis, the young Louisiana plantation owner turned vampire with a conscience who despairs at having to take human life to live. As he tells his story in today's San Francisco to a young journalist (Christian Slater, who replaced River Phoenix), Louis remembers back to Louisiana in 1791, when he was a 24-year-old widower who longed to be gone himself because of his wife's recent death.

Instead of expiring, Louis is turned into one of the brotherhood of darkness by the sinister Lestat, the cold and hateful vampire's vampire who kills for revenge against life and whom the book describes as "masterfully clever and utterly vicious."

Although he works his hardest at the part and doesn't embarrass himself, even with the help of Stan Winston's vampire makeup Tom Cruise is plainly miscast as Lestat. He is determined and has his moments, but it is simply too much of a stretch even from his Oscar-nominated role in "Born on the Fourth of July" to play a hateful l8th-Century French fop with the fey habit of bringing his handkerchief to his mouth. And with Lestat softened, the fury Louis and Claudia, the 5-year-old turned into a vampire by Lestat's whim, come to feel toward him makes less emotional sense.

While the movie eliminates several of the book's characters, it wouldn't dare do without Claudia and Armand, a Parisian vampire met during the next century when Louis goes abroad on a kind of fact-finding mission. Both 12-year-old Kirsten Dunst and the magnetic Antonio Banderas bring the kind of delicately eroticized menace to their parts that Cruise and Pitt ought to be conveying but can't manage, and "Interview" is better for it.

Although Hollywood will never lose its lust to turn bestsellers into film, "Interview" demonstrates why they can be tricky. Some things are better imagined than seen, and while it's one thing to read "the blood flowed like water," it is quite another to actually sit through as much bloodletting (much of it inflicted on women) as the film puts on screen.

Another place where actually seeing things changes the emphasis is in "Interview's" homoerotic qualities. Although the men mad about men subtext, is in Rice's book (where Louis mourns his brother, not his wife), scenes like a frenzied Cruise passionately burying his head in Pitt's neck give parts of this film as much male-male sexual energy as Hollywood has ever allowed.

But for every part of "Interview" that is effective, there are others that are not; witness the gimmicky ending and the campy humor that sporadically comes out of nowhere. Like the vampires themselves, the film occupies a kind of nether world, sporadically coming alive just when you think it has gone away for good. Perhaps that is appropriate, after all.

NEW YORK, 11/21/94, p. 74, David Denby

Perhaps the undead are among us, restlessly turning the pages of Anne Rice's "Vampire Chronicles." So many readers! Can they all be ghouls? Well, pleasure to their coffins. But if you don't have a thing about vampires—if you're a wine drinker—you may find *Interview With the Vampire*, an adaptation of Rice's first vamp book, exceptionally boring, parochial, and remote. This spectacular but interminable movie, directed by Neil Jordan and starring Brad Pitt and Tom Cruise, assumes that we're all obsessed with the minutiae of a vampire's existence—his hunger, his "death," his passions, his loneliness, his relations with other vampires, even his epistemological relation with the modern world. The movie makes everything that happens to vampires unspeakably important while reducing the world around the creatures to a playground and killing field. People are murdered and drained by the dozen, but no one resists or pursues the vampires; no one even notices them. The world remains as oblivious of them as it does of the actors in a pornographic movie.

Interview With the Vampire is perhaps the most expensive and beautiful cult movie of all time—a film of great technical distinction but no dramatic interest whatsoever. In the opening shots, Philippe Rousselot's camera glides into San Francisco at night, and the gleaming darkness of the swank electric city is literally enchanting—we're more than willing to be put into a trance. The whole movie plays off the color black. Flames or candles, or mysteriously diffused light, appear to be the only illumination in the night world, a world in which the light of humanity has gone out. The vampires themselves can be physically astonishing, rising, floating, disappearing like creatures in some silent film from 70 years ago. When two of them—a grown woman and a little vampirette—face the sun, their flesh smokes, burns, and chars like paper under a magnifying glass. The hallucinatory creepiness can bc quite stunning. Yet for all the beauty and strangeness, and despite Neil Jordan's emotionally saturated evocations of longing and despair, this is a fundamentally senseless movie. Unless we're Anne Rice buffs, we don't know what's going on or why we should care.

Adapting the 1976 best-seller herself, Rice retained the book's principal narrative conceit. She frames the entire narrative as a flashback, a tale told by an unhappy vampire, Louis de Pointe du Lac (Pitt), to a young interviewer (Christian Slater) in contemporary San Francisco. Poor, morose Louis—200 years of bloodsucking and not one moment of guilt-free pleasure! His story begins near New Orleans in 1791. The young master of a plantation, he's bitten and turned into a vampire by Lestat (Cruise), an effete southern gentleman/vampire in ruffles. Lestat initiates Louis into what is literally a blood brotherhood—they have a mutual orgasm or a mutual something—and they then join in unholy rites, prowling the humid bayous, biting prostitutes and other ladies of the night. Vampire movies, of course, have always "really" been about erotic domination and submission, and Jordan makes that metaphor literal. The women don't resist; they present their bosoms and necks passively, happily, and then, quivering in ecstasy, they receive the bite as if it were the horn of plenty itself. Throughout the movie, the eager, dummy women are virtually anonymous—just bodies waiting to be drained and cast away. Only the relationships between the men mean anything. So what is *this* movie really about? After a while, one begins to wonder.

We have to watch the mythic moment—the bite—over and over. Visually, the movie is nothing like pornography, but emotionally, the similarities ate striking. Chomp, chomp, again and again, until there are rivers of blood flowing in an obsessional circle leading nowhere. The ravaging of women and children is relieved now and then by piquant jokes involving rats and dogs—squeezing a rat's blood into a glass as if it were a lemon, for instance. My feeling about such jokes is that you can laugh easily at them if you aren't much afflicted by self-respect. The mock-debonair tone of all this is rather pathetic. Tom Cruise, draining some woman's blood into a goblet, appears to be imitating a foppish actor from long ago (Louis Hayward in *The Man in the Iron Mask*?); he lets his voice go high and indulges giggling fits. Cruise tries hard to be saturnine and witty, but his manner isn't rich enough for pompous "ironic" lines. He's just that callow American boy in eyeteeth. (Daniel Day-Lewis would have been a little more like it.) As for Brad Pitt, different vampires may tell him he's beautiful, but actually he looks awkward in period costume—an unsmiling, inhibited actor with puffy lips and a dead voice. These two are amateurish together.

Traditionally, vampire movies have concentrated on the horror of alien creatures, a loathsome presence, preying on the normal. But in this movie, we're supposed to be all caught up in the vampires' existential dilemma, their need to go on killing in order to survive—a prospect that causes Lestat to make cynical jokes and Louis to mourn his lost humanity. Louis always hates himself in the morning. Once again, Neil Jordan has made a fable of forbidden or hopeless love. In *Mona Lisa*, the gentle ex-con falls in love with a black prostitute who's a lesbian; in *The Miracle*, the boy loves a woman who turns out to be his mother; and in *The Crying Game*, of course, the reluctant IRA member thinks he's in love with a girl. But this time Jordan, stuck with someone else's junk obsessions, can't resolve the material dramatically. For a while, Louis tries to build a paternal relationship with the little girl (Kirsten Dunst) whom he and Lestat vampirize. But once afflicted, she's just a killer, too, a little devil doll-like Linda Blair in *The Exorcist*, only more talented—and when Jordan makes grotesque jokes about the three of them as a bizarre, dysfunctional family, the touching emotions get cast overboard. Is *Interview With the Vampire* so irresolute—so muffled and baffling—because Jordan can't quite say what he means? He appears to have reinvented the love that dare not speak its name. If he wants to make a gay movie, he should go ahead and make one.

The scene shifts to a gothically enhanced Paris, where Antonio Banderas turns up as Armand, the oldest living vampire and master of the sinister Theater of Vampires. In a cathedral, which is also a stage, Sadean rituals are performed for the public. The vampires strip a beautiful girl, reassure her, and then devour her. This is genuinely erotic in a nasty sort of way—the girl is utterly vulnerable—although Banderas, who seems to have a hairball in his mouth, dissipates the tension by making eyes at Brad Pitt and burbling such things as "We must be powerful, beautiful, without regret." The Paris scenes grow more and more spectacular—and incomprehensible. Creatures we don't care about get sliced or burned—the movie collapses into sheer sensation.

Interview With the Vampire is tedious and fairly disgusting, and my advice is to avoid it: Let the undead bury the undead. Yet I fear that people will want to be bitten. Massive publicity can silence a lot of doubt; it can even make revulsion seem unhip. The folly could go on forever, with endless sequels. Common sense and judgment seem to be hiding in that coffin along with the ghouls.

NEW YORK POST, 11/11/94, p. 39, Michael Medved

There's always been an odd contradiction in Hollywood's portrayal of vampires. They're supposed to be suave, impeccably elegant creatures even though they get their nourishment (and their kicks) from biting victims to death and draining their blood—a gross messy, decidedly inelegant business to be sure.

Director Neil Jordan ("The Crying Game," "Mona Lisa") uses "Interview With the Vampire" to address this contradiction more honestly than ever before, but few filmgoers will thank him for it—unless they're longing to see veins opened in gory detail, or enjoy watching unwitting victims tormented in scenes of unspeakably blood-soaked sadism.

There's nothing prettified about Jordan's vampires: though they still get to wear great clothes, their blue veins throbbing beneath white faces and pale green, feral, see-in-the-dark eyes make them far more bestial than aristocratic. They even pause for between-meal-snacks of chickens and rats, in scenes so grotesque that the merest memory of them serves to obscure other aspects of the film that are incontestably impressive.

The screenplay by, Anne Rice follows the general outlines of her justly popular 1977 novel. A skeptical young interviewer (Christian Slater) turns on his tape recorder to preserve the life story of an odd loner (Brad Pitt in a disappointing, pouting, one-dimensional performance) who claims to be a weary bloodsucker.

His account begins on a Louisiana plantation in 1791, when our moody, death-obsessed hero is selected by the ruthless vampire Lestat (Tom Cruise) first as a meal, then as companion and colleague. They conduct a bickering love-hate relationship as they feed together, night after night, on a varied menu of Creole delicacies, but their loneliness eventually leads to an odd act of adoption—bestowing the "dark gift" on a little girl (played by formidable 11-year-old actress Kirsten Dunst) who becomes their surrogate daughter and an ageless, insatiable child vampire.

(Warning: An unpleasant whiff of kiddie porn arises from the romantic passion between her character and Brad Pitt's, adding to the fetid aura of decadence that surrounds the entire story.)

Actually, it's Tom Cruise who unwittingly ruins the project, but not for reasons anyone predicted. It turns out he's so good as Lestat, so fiendishly fascinating as a figure of all-knowing evil, that when he disappears from the plot midway through the film, "Interview" suddenly loses its bite.

The second half suffers from additional burdens, with Antonio Banderas (as a Parisian vampire and theatrical impresario) who delivers all his lines in an unintelligible accent, and drab French locations that lack the over-ripe, moonlit atmosphere that characterize the earlier New Orleans settings.

"God kills indiscriminately and so shall we," Lestat declares, "for no creatures under God are as like him as we are." For brief stretches, this ambitious film manages to convey the power of this diabolical, nihilistic vision, but those fleeting moments are quickly buried under heaps of pointless and poorly-paced indulgence.

Even without a stake through its heart, this tired "Vampire" does itself in and dies before dawn.

NEWSDAY, 11/11/94, Part II/p. B2, Jack Mathews

Before it was announced that her 1976 novel "Interview With the Vampire" would become a movie, before she made and retracted those nasty comments about the casting of Hollywood heartthrob Tom Cruise as the vicious vampire Lestat, author Anne Rice said three things would have to come together to make the story work on film.

First, it would have to feature classical vampires, "cape-wearing creatures of the night," who blend elegance with wile and seductive charm. They would have to be feeling creatures, as well, with philosophical and psychological dimension; the ability to suffer pain and guilt is a must! Above all, they would have to be heroic, "a bit quicker, faster, better, and smarter than human beings."

Well, the movie has arrived, under the fine direction of Neil Jordan ("The Crying Game") and with a script by Rice herself, and the essential ingredients are all there, *plus* a wonderful sense of humor, another tour de force of period set design by Dante Ferretti ("Age of Innocence"), and a passably maleficent performance by Cruise. If the movie isn't as compelling as the novel, the fault is more that of the medium than of the stars or the filmmakers.

"Interview," the introductory book in Rice's homoerotic "Vampire Chronicles," is considerably more ambitious mythology than Bram Stoker's "Dracula," and most other supernatural monster stories. By going into the minds of her vampires, and letting us see that they think and feel in human terms, she forces us to view and inhabit their world, to share their desire, hunger, pain, loneliness and the sheer boredom of eternity.

Some of that magic is lost in the movie, because what was implied is now explicit, and because seeing Rice's vampires on screen—their protruding canines, blushed lips, catlike eyes, pasty skin, and veins that stand out like lines on a Transylvanian road map—eliminates all subtleties of the imagination, reminding us that what we're seeing, after all, is a large-scale genre horror movie.

But it is a far more sophisticated horror movie than we've come to expect, and with particular resonance for our time. Not only is there the obvious AIDS metaphor, the blending of desire and danger, but it also taps into our collective paranoia, the sense of dread about becoming the unprotected prey of real-life creatures of the night.

"Interview," however, is less a monster show than a quest for identity, companionship and the meaning of life. Lestat, ancient and soulless, is a loathsome villain, but Louis (Brad Pitt), Lestat's tormented companion, and Claudia (Kirsten Dunst), the corrupted infant, may be the warmest and fuzziest mass murderers in modern literature.

Their story, which takes place almost entirely in the dark, is told by Louis to a young magazine reporter (Christian Slater) he has picked up and brought to his hotel room in contemporary San Francisco. It begins in 1791 in Louisiana where Louis, while grieving over his dead wife, is seduced and turned into a vampire by Lestat, then faced with an eternity of vile lifestyle and eating habits.

For a while, Louis cannot force himself to kill humans, instead surviving on the gamey juice of birds and rodents and an occasional goblet of blood drained from one of Lestat's plump, aristocratic victims. When he finally succumbs to his aching thirst, Louis chooses to drink from a young child orphaned by the plague, and his guilt is so immediate and profound that Lestat rescues the girl, transfuses her with his own blood, and makes her their immortal "daughter."

"Just one happy family," Lestat says, with even more irony than he knows. Soon, Claudia, an angry woman trapped in a child's unchanging body, is plotting her maker's destruction.

"Interview" breaks down into two distinct sections, with radically different tones. The first, dealing with Lestat's creation of the perpetually reticent Louis and aggressive, strong minded Claudia, and their eventual betrayal of him, plays almost as black comedy. The second part follows Louis and Claudia to Europe in their search for other, older vampires, who might teach them things Lestat never did.

The two sections of "Interview" are also defined by two love triangles, the first between Lestat, Louis and Claudia, the second replacing Lestat with Armand (Antonio Banderas), the magnetic leader of a vampire brood that performs ritualistic murders every night on the stage of the ghoulish Theatre des Vampires in 1870 Paris.

The erotic impulses between the characters are palpable. Vampires don't have sex, of course, they have dinner. But the distinctions blur. When Lestat plunges his teeth into the pulsing neck of the compliant Louis, and takes him to the other side, it is an embrace ending in something very like an orgasm, and you won't need a Freudian guide to interpret the meaning of Lestat's predilection for the blood of pubescent boys.

The filmmakers did make a serious casting error, not with Cruise but with Pitt. Louis is the pivotal character in every relationship, but Pitt seems to inhabit that role rather than fill it, and comes off more as a whiny pacifist than the story's anguished conscience.

Still, given the complexity of the novel, and the task of condensing two centuries into two hours, Rice and Jordan, who seasoned horror with sensuality in his little-seen 1984 film "The Company of Wolves," have done a remarkable job. "Interview" is not the scariest vampire movie ever made, or the best looking (that honor goes to Francis Coppola's otherwise inane version of Bram Stoker's "Dracula"), but it is the most intelligent, and, in a world of increasingly arbitrary violence, perhaps the most relevant.

Vampires, muggers, what's the difference?

SIGHT AND SOUND, 2/95, p. 46, Kim Newman

San Francisco. Louis, a vampire, is interviewed by Malloy, a young man who collects taped reminiscences. Louis reveals he lived in Louisiana in the eighteenth century, the master of a plantation. Grieving for a dead wife, Louis wanders around New Orleans and is saved from a robber by Lestat, who offers him the chance to become a vampire. Louis, drinking Lestat's blood as he dies, is transformed, but rebels against the predatory Lestat's cruelty and tries to subsist on the blood of animals. Louis's slaves are on the point of rebellion when he frees them and burns down the plantation.

In New Orleans, Louis finds Claudia, a newly-orphaned child of a plague victim, and cannot resist drinking her blood, whereupon Lestat turns her into an unageing vampire. As decades pass Claudia resents Lestat for robbing her of the chance to grow up. With Louis's tacit approval, Claudia tries to murder Lestat by tricking him into drinking laudanum-laced blood, cutting his throat and dumping him in the swamp. Claudia prepares to depart for Europe, but the withered Lestat attacks them and Louis sets fire to him, burning down their town house.

Years later, in Paris, Louis encounters other vampires. Armand, 400-year-old proprietor of a theatre where vampire killings are passed off as illusions, recognises Louis as a kindred soul and asks him to be a bridge to the modern world. Santiago, a clownish sadist, suspects Claudia of the murder of a vampire—the only crime among their kind. Claudia, feeling rejected by Louis' interest in Armand, insists Louis turn Madeleine, a woman she has chosen to be her companion, into a vampire. Santiago seizes Claudia and Madeleine and executes them by exposure to sunlight. Louis destroys Santiago and his brood with scythe and fire, and burns down the theatre. Parting from Armand Louis experiences the twentieth century by compulsive cinema-going. In 1988, he returns to New Orleans and encounters Lestat, still injured, living as a pathetic recluse. Malloy begs Louis to make him a vampire, but Louis leaves in disgust. Driving away, Malloy is attacked by Lestat, rejuvenated by young blood, who promises to turn the interviewer into a vampire.

Instantly alter publication in 1975, Anne Rice's *Interview with the Vampire* was optioned for filming, and has been in development ever since. It is easy to see what made the property so attractive, as it is to see the snags that have delayed production for nearly 20 years. The novel has roles uniquely suited to male film stars (defending his controversial casting of Tom Cruise and Brad Pitt, Neil Jordan correctly points out that Rice's glamorous, self-regarding, luminous monsters demand to be played by bigger-than-life name actors) and contains set-pieces which read like spectacular movie scenes (several of which Jordan has omitted).

It also has the historic sweep of a TV mini-series, combined with perverse material that could never be done on American network television and an all-in-one-night narrative frame that would resist serialisation even though the straggling plot might provide a working description of the term 'episodic'. The thorniest problem of all, though, is Rice's use of the vampire myth not for horror but for philosophical enquiry, with Louis maundering on at length about his place in the universe under God.

In the event, after much public argument and kiss-and-make-up between author and film-makers, the film of *Interview* is perhaps as strong as it could be, given concealed but inherent weaknesses in the original material. Sometimes, as it trips through two centuries, the film overdoses on montage: decades are encapsulated with a flurry of impressions that can never convey the changelessness that so frustrates Claudia. However, the kitsch-sounding summation of the twentieth century in terms of movie sunrises (*Sunrise, Nosferatu et al*) is surprisingly effective, even to the throwaway punch line that has Louis re-encountering Lestat after wasting an evening on *Tequila Sunrise*. Exposed by the adaptation are some astonishingly ramshackle plot transitions, papered over by clever banter in the novel, but shown up for arrant melodrama here. By the time Louis has ended a third episode by burning down the set, the device becomes tiresome.

Fortunately, Jordan's work here is more in keeping with the fantastical *The Company of Wolves* than the *echt*-Hollywood of *High Spirits*. Never allowing make-up effects to swamp character as he did in his werewolf outing, Jordan achieves tiny moments of inexplicable creepiness (the stone eyes of the tomb-image of Louis' dead wife closing as he dies) and genuinely shocking scenes of physical horror (Lestat's blood pouring from his throat in a tide that threatens Claudia's delicate pumps). While the first half sometimes seems cramped for an historical epic, the trip to Paris allows for marvellous full-blooded decadences such as the vampire theatre with its Jean Rollin-like ritual cruelties. Sadly, the last-minute reversal, as Lestat pops up magically in Molloy's car without any narrative justification, reduces the grand vision to just another horror movie.

Though Louis is given an unusual interior life, and Lestat and Claudia remain among the most striking vampire characters in fiction, everyone else who passes through the overpopulated story is stuck with being a one-scene victim or a plot contrivance. Stephen Rea's Santiago, who has a neat Chaplinesque introduction as he teases Louis on a Paris street, suffers especially from an ill-thought-out subplot. He first declares it unforgivable for one vampire to murder another. Then he kills Claudia merely on suspicion, incidentally destroying Madeleine and thus violating his own rule. Antonio Banderas' gloomy Armand suffers from playing stooge to tiresome stretches of religious debate, then allows his life work to be wrecked for no real reason and steps out of the story, presumably to sulk for a few more centuries.

The subtitle, which Rice has retroactively stuck on new editions of her book, indicates an ambition to chronicle all of vampire-kind, but the strength of the film is the uneasy, eroticised, disturbing relationship between Louis and Lestat. The elder vampire tries to nudge his prissier pupil into indulging a capacity for sin, and their shared crime—the creation of Claudia—is the event which ends the stasis of their lives, consigning Lestat to the past and pushing Louis out into the world in search of answers.

While the import of *Interview* is in Louis' quizzing of human and inhuman nature, the novel's lasting appeal lies with Lestat and Claudia, and Jordan's film is less likely to be remembered for its philosophy than for its action. Pitt's pouting Louis signals modernity by confessing his confused alienation, which Armand marks as the characteristic of the age, but the devils get all the best tunes. Remarkably, 12-year-old Kirsten Dunst plays Claudia as an embittered woman in a pre-teenage body, a uniquely childish monster who kills her dressmaker or piano teacher on a whim and then nuzzles up to her 'parents' for approval.

In subsequent much inferior novels, Rice has recanted her depiction in *Interview* of Lestat as a dashing monster, infusing him with Louis' conscience and introspection, but the character works best as a villain. Using an effeminate version of his *Far and Away* accent, Cruise is a fine narcissist monster. Demonstrating a wit rarely seen in his earlier work, he justifies his atrocities ("God kills indiscriminately and so shall we") and complains after the Louisiana purchase that he dislikes the taste of democratic American blood. By contrast with Pitt, and following Gary Oldman's lovelorn Dracula, it is refreshing to find a screen vampire who truly relishes being a monster.

TIME, 11/21/94, p. 112, Richard Corliss

Why would Tom Cruise be playing Lestat, a gaunt, suave European vampire with a taste for young men? Because a big movie star can do whatever he wants. And why would Neil Jordan be directing *Interview with the Vampire: The Vampire Chronicles*? Because his signature films, *Mona Lisa* and *The Crying Game*, are gay fables with mass appeal. Once again he has a sympathetic fellow (here it's Brad Pitt as Louis, a New Orleans landowner in the 18th century) falling in with a charismatic homosexual (Cruise's Lestat). Louis tells his story to a young interviewer (Christian Slater) in a sort of *Donahue* with spooky flashbacks.

So far, so promising. In Anne Rice's screenplay, which she adapted from her megaselling 1976 novel, Lestat and his crew are displaced aristocrats, glorious anachronisms. They are enslaved by bloodlust: every night a little death. They lean into the victims' necks and give them the hickey from hell, the infernal overbite—the kiss that bleeds. The nightly rampages of these putty-faced predators suggest an AIDs metaphor: voluptuous sexuality with fatal consequences. And after a couple of hundred years, the vampires get the edgy sourness of people married too long.

It's a cute idea to have Cruise, the movies' all-American guy, gussied up like Pierre Clementi, protopunk of French art films. It's a bad idea to let Cruise vanish for almost an hour in the middle of his picture. But by then the film's central flaw has been exposed. A vampire story needs vampires, sure, but it also needs a human victim to lead the audience into the vortex and help them escape it. Otherwise, the fear factor evaporates, and you get this mishmash: an interview in a void, a vampire movie with underbite.

VILLAGE VOICE, 11/22/94, Film Special/p. 64, Georgia Brown

To die, to become really, *really* dead, is a condition for vampires to obsess on. But who would have thought it could be so bloody complicated? In my book, losing a five-year-old to leukemia gives the mother the right to enter whatever mode of funereal discourse she chooses, but why have so many followed Anne Rice into this creepy esoterica?. It may be that devotees of *Interview With the Vampire*, the novel, will gulp down this campy extravaganza—particularly now that it has the author's full-page blessing—but for those of us who couldn't get past page 51, the pleasures of hearing Rice's private theology explicated ad nauseam are as thin as strawberry Kool-Aid.

As a Rice novice, I was interested to find *Interview* a bit short on adult females. The mother, you might say, is too busy at her writing desk, but then not many of her charges seem in search of a mother. Men sucking, or suckling, men are the primary turn-ons, though several anonymous, usually nutty and slutty, women are on hand to provide fresh blood when the rat supply dwindles. One of the movie's more erotic images has the story's two chief vampires—the elder, natural born killer Lestat, (Tom Cruise) and the reluctant, queasy (more effeminate) Louis (Brad Pitt)—simultaneously drinking from a single swooning mulatta.

Director Neil Jordan—always strong on atmospherics as well as psychosexual flavoring—provides any number of juicy morsels to savor. Some of the more perverse scenes involve an aggressive nymphet-vampire, Claudia (12-year-old Kirsten Dunst), a hardened preadolescent with the massive ringlets of Velazquez's Infanta. The only principal capable of being thoroughly dispensed with, she is got rid of once her shock value wears off.

Though it's *him* on the magazine covers, the newly thin, blonde, tall, blue-eyed Cruise isn't the movie's star but more of a supporting played to Pitt's depressive, rosy-lipped beauty. (Perhaps seeing Cruise effaced and professionally humbled is what changed Rice's mind about the film.) Both actors, with their blue networks of capillaries substituting for facial hair, grow an even whiter shade of pale once our story moves to Paris and Antonio Banderas and Stephen Rea inject the more robust, grown-up aura of Old World evil. As the implausible interviewer, an impish Christian Slater probably provides a comic edge that the more preternatural River Phoenix, originally slated for the part, might not have shown. finally, a spoofy ending to this very pretentious gorefest gives a nice little lift, though this is thanks to the Rolling Stones.

Also reviewed in:
CHICAGO TRIBUNE, 11/11/94, Friday/p. C, Michael Wilmington
NEW REPUBLIC, 12/12/94, p. 24, Stanley Kauffmann
NEW YORK TIMES, 11/11/94, p. C1, Janet Maslin
NEW YORKER, 11/21/94, p. 128, Terrence Rafferty
VARIETY, 11/7-13/94, p. 46, Todd McCarthy
WASHINGTON POST, 11/11/94, p. D1, Rita Kempley
WASHINGTON POST, 11/11/94, Weekend/p. 48, Desson Howe

IRON WILL

A Buena Vista Pictures release of a Walt Disney Pictures presentation. *Producer:* Patrick Palmer and Robert Schwartz. *Director:* Charles Haid. *Screenplay:* John Michael Hayes, Djordje Milićević, and Jeff Arch. *Director of Photography:* William Wages. *Editor:* Andrew Doerfer. *Music:* Joel McNeely. *Music Editor:* Curtis Roush. *Sound:* Richard Lightstone. *Sound Editor:* Fred Judkins. *Casting:* Jennifer Shull. *Production Designer:* Stephen Storer. *Art Director:* Nathan Haas. *Set Decorator:* Hilton Rosemarin. *Set Dresser:* Elliot Berlovitz, Jeffrey DeBell, and Jeff Angus. *Special Effects:* Paul J. Lombardi, Robert G. Willard, Chuck E. Stewart, Parry Willard, John Fagan, and Stanley T. Bielowicz. *Costumes:* Betty Madden. *Make-up:* David Atherton and Quinn Atherton. *Stunt Coordinator:* R.A. Rondell. *Running time:* 104 minutes. *MPAA Rating:* PG.

CAST: Mackenzie Astin (Will Stoneman); Kevin Spacey (Harry Kingsley); David Ogden Stiers (J.P. Harper); August Schellenberg (Ned Dodd); Brian Cox (Angus McTeague); George Gerdes (Borg Guillarson); John Terry (Jack Stoneman); Penelope Windust (Maggie Stoneman); Jeffrey Allen Chandler (De Fontaine); Michael Laskin (Simon Lambert); James Cada (Peter Swenson); Rex Linn (Joe McPherson); Allan "RJ" Joseph (Albert Carey); Alvin William "Dutch" Lunak (Gabriel Carey); Tony Griffin (Mike Riley); Jeff Hochendoner (Groven); Rusty Hendrickson (Devereaux); Richard Riehle (Burton); Paige Litfin (Becky); Marcus Klemp (Ward); Richard Hughes (Conductor Brawley); Dan Chambers (Camerman Reporter); Wayne A. Evenson (Potter); Stan Garner (Brakeman); Ed Dallas (Gunnar Tveit); Jerry Allan (Remy); Karl Randa (Thordur Thorenson); Jim Olsen (Mayor of Winnipeg); David Nason, Ron Winters, and Gerald DePerry (Spirit Guides); Aaron Houseman (Guard); Henry Novotny (Kaiser Bill); Karen Clift (Soprano Singer); Benjamin Salisbury (Scout #1); Brian Grussing (Scout #2); Don Maloney (Sergeant); William John Murphy (Reporter #2); Davio Dakotablu (Waiter); Brittany Haid (Young Woman); Elisabeth Harmon-Haid (Blacksmith's Wife); McKegney Barr (Pretty Woman); Marvin Defoe, Jr. (Native American at Train Depot); Sheldon Aubut (Man); Beau (Gus).

LOS ANGELES TIMES, 1/14/94, Calendar/p. 1, Kenneth Turan

Like the earnest young man it's named after, "Iron Will" would blush and protest if any kind of fuss were made over it. Just doing my job, sir, this film would say if it could talk, no need to make me out to be more than I am.

True enough, but it is "Iron Will's" double charm that its aspirations are humble and straightforward and that it fulfills them so completely. Not as slick as "Free Willy" or as sophisticated as "Searching for Bobby Fischer," this is a throwback to the sweet and sentimental Disney family films that Walt himself loved, a live-action fairy tale about a boy, his dogs and a darn tough race.

Set in 1917 and "inspired by" a real event, "Iron Will" shrewdly does not attempt to modernize its story or make it hipper for the nominally more sophisticated kids who are its core audience. It sees the world the same way its open and innocent protagonist, Will Stoneman (Mackenzie Astin) does, as a manageable place where enthusiasm and heart are enough to solve any problem.

A passionate dog-sledder who lives deep in snowbound South Dakota, Will, who has just been accepted to college, is ambivalent about going and no wonder: who would want to leave a dad like Jack (John Terry), the most understanding guy in 12 states who speaks only in aphorisms like "Don't let fear stand in the way of your dreams" and "If there's something you really want, you've got to go out and grab it."

But then, in a cruel moment that probably accounts for the film's PG rating, Jack dies in an accident and Will must face not only the lack of money for college but the family's financial ruin. Then he remembers the Carnival Derby, "the longest, toughest, richest dog race ever," with a problem-solving $10,000 going to the first team to cross the 500 miles from Winnipeg, Manitoba, to St. Paul, Minn.

Under the tutelage of medicine-ball-throwing family friend Ned Dodd (August Schellenberg), a Native American whose store of tribal aphorisms rivals those of the late Jack, Will toughens himself up for a race across "the meanest stretch of land God ever put together."

And a good thing, too, because in addition to horrendous weather and topological features with names like Heartbreak Hill and Devil's Slide, Will has to face his other competitors. This fierce lot includes Borg Guillarson (George Gerdes), who looks like the Hannibal Lecter of cross-country sledding.

Will also contends with Kevin Spacey's cynical, jaded journalist, who dubs him Iron Will and says things like "This kid will put me on the front page." And he has to earn the respect of the redoubtable Gus, his father's old lead dog that has a heart, not to mention a bite, as big as all outdoors.

All this can be made to sound quite silly, and in some ways it obviously is. But even though a mix-and-match trio of disparate screenwriters (74-year-old John Michael Hayes, who counts "Rear Window" and "To Catch a Thief" among his credits; "Runaway Train's" Djordje Milicevic and "Sleepless in Seattle's" Jeff Arch) are involved, "Iron Will" is unified and made endearing by the simplicity and belief that director Charles Haid and those in front of the camera bring to the personal drama and the pounding races.

Mackenzie Astin, whose first theatrical feature this is (as it is for director Haid), is perfectly cast as Will, bringing to the part not only the ability to look good on a sled but also a convincing rugged innocence and an ease with emotion, a quality he shares with his brother, Sean ("Rudy"), and their mother, Patty Duke.

And don't forget those dogs. Brightly and vividly shot by cinematographer William Wages, the assorted huskies and malamutes look inexpressibly cheerful as they mush through the snow, a good humor that those who embrace the decidedly old-fashioned pleasures of "Iron Will" can easily share.

NEW YORK POST, 1/14/94, p. 39, Michael Medved

Last year brought the Disney company a long string of box-office busts, interrupted by the startling success of "Cool Runnings"— a funny, feel-good movie about Jamaica's bobsled team in the Winter Olympics.

Now it's 1994 and the cunning crew at the Magic Kingdom is selling another underdog adventure involving an even more exotic winter sport: long-distance dog-sled racing.

Even if this form of athletic endeavor has never been one of your consuming passions, you can have a fine time with "Iron Will." This is rousing family fare, a straightforward boy-against-the-odds epic that delivers two solid hours of excitement and uplift.

The teen-age hero is Will Stoneman (Mackenzie Astin), a South Dakota farm boy in 1917. He dreams of going away to college but his family has no money to pay for education. The situation gets even worse when his loving father (John Terry) drowns in a frozen river after a nasty accident with his dog sled, and the mother (Penelope Windust) struggles to save the farm from impatient creditors.

Barring some miracle, she'll even have to sell the cherished dog teams that represented papa's pride. There's only one desperate chance for our hero to save the farm: entering a 522-mile dog-sled race from Winnipeg to St. Paul, taking on the world's most illustrious mushers for a $10,000 prize.

"Iron Will" is every bit as corny as this sounds, but the big race itself—which takes up three-quarters of the movie's running time—is go engrossing that all reservations disappear with the exhilarating whoosh of sleds on snow.

The story is loosely based on an actual race and the filmmakers wisely stress colorful period details: We accept the movie's old-fashioned values more comfortably in the innocent Midwest of 77 years ago than we would if they had tried in any way to update the story.

Leading man Mackenzie Astin (best known for his role on TVs "Facts of Life") resembles a young Matt Dillon more than he does his talented brother Sean—not to mention parents Patty Duke and John Astin.

His gee-whiz line delivery suggests that he may not be ready for Shakespeare, but he's a consistently likable screen presence and well-suited to the physical demands of his role.

The formidable August Schellenberg does virtually the same part he played in "Free Willy", as a kindly, all-knowing Native American mentor to the youthful hero.

Kevin Spacey is the hard-boiled newspaperman who first dubs the kid "Iron Will," and whose sentimental dispatches make the boy an overnight hero.

George Gerdes is the villain of the piece, a shaved-headed, snarling "Scandavanian champion" of dog-sledding who will stop at nothing to put the American upstart in his place.

The script for "Iron Will" originated 23 years ago with John Michael Hayes (screenwriter of "Rear Window" and other Hitchcock classics), then received more recent contributions from both Djordje Milicevic ("Runaway Train") and Jeff Arch ("Sleepless in Seattle").

With these three distinguished scribes each doing his bit, it's no surprise that the final screenplay seems overloaded with incident—containing more than a few thrown-in kitchen sinks.

This makes for a conclusion so manipulative (complete with contrived climax in extreme slow motion) that it begins to tax the audience good will the film has earned up to that point.

Nevertheless, first-time feature film director (and former actor) Charles Haid fills his picture with so many vivid storybook images and so much youthful energy that you still want to overlook its absurdities; with all that snow and speed, this tired material seems illogically fresh.

NEWSDAY, 1/14/94, Part II/p. 78, Jack Mathews

On the time-honored assumption that all clichés are fresh to those seeing them for the first time, Walt Disney pictures has strung some beauties together for youngsters drawn to "Iron Will," an adventure story about a South Dakota teenager's attempts to win the $10,000 first prize in a 1917 dogsled race and save the family farm.

The movie, shot about this time last year in the frozen wilds of Wisconsin and Minnesota, won't provide any relief from our own miserable weather, but the unwavering resolve of Will Stoneman, who becomes a national folk hero during the tortuous 522-mile race from Winnipeg, Manitoba, to Minneapolis-St. Paul, should warm your heart.

Mackenzie Astin, the son of John Astin and Patty Duke, and younger brother of Sean Astin ("Rudy"), makes a strong feature film debut as Will, a farm boy whose dream of going to college seems to vanish with his father's death and the prospect of bank foreclosure looming for his widowed mom.

In the depth of his grief, Will spots a circular about the international Carnival Derby, which his father was preparing to enter, and with the start of the race just a month away, talks the family's American Indian friend Ned Dodd (August Schellenberg) into teaching him how to mush a team of dogs.

The outcome of the race is about as predictable as last year's Super Bowl, and from the moment we meet Will's spirited lead dog, Gus, we know the two are going to spend some time saving each other's lives along the trail. But what the film lacks in suspense it makes up for in the stunning choreography and composition of the race sequences.

You get a sample of what's to come in the scene where Will and his father (John Terry) are sledding near their farm, and his father falls through the ice into a river. Knowing they will both die if Will jumps in after him, his father cuts loose the line connecting them and disappears into the raging current. (Dad's wise voice, like that of "Star Wars" Obi Wan Kenobi lives on, urging Will in mid-race to "let the creator guide you ... trust the dogs, trust yourself.")

Charles Haid, a TV director getting his first shot at a feature, has a real feel for this kind of action and with the considerable help of cinematographer William Wages, another TV veteran, manages to keep the race zipping along, even as Will and his rivals seem ready to quit.

The drama on the sidelines is far less interesting. The script's three writers came up with a cartoon assortment of supporting characters. Among them: Kevin Spacey's jaded newspaperman Harry Kingsley, who pressures the sponsors to admit the inexperienced boy in the race, but only to turn him into a career-making story; David Ogden Stiers and Brian Cox as the rival sponsors, making sporting side bets with Will's life on the line; and Will's rivals, who will do anything to keep him from reaching the end of the trail.

"Iron Will" is a throwback in many ways to the wilderness adventures turned out by Disney in the '50s, the indomitable spirit of Americans overcoming long odds. It's old hat to most of us, very old hat, but to that new generation Disney courts better than anyone, it will seem fresh as the driven snow.

Also reviewed in:
CHICAGO TRIBUNE, 1/14/94, Friday/p. I, Clifford Terry
NEW YORK TIMES, 1/14/94, p. C6, Janet Maslin
VARIETY, 1/17-23/94, p. 104, Joe Leydon
WASHINGTON POST, 1/15/94, p. G1, David Mills

IT COULD HAPPEN TO YOU

A TriStar Pictures release of an Adelson/Baumgarten and Lobell/Bergman production. *Executive Producer:* Gary Adelson, Craig Baumgarten, and Joseph Hartwick. *Producer:* Mike Lobell. *Director:* Andrew Bergman. *Screenplay:* Jane Anderson. *Director of Photography:* Caleb Deschanel. *Editor:* Barry Malkin. *Music:* Carter Burwell. *Music Editor:* Todd Kasow and Thomas Drescher. *Choreographer:* John Carrafa. *Sound:* Gary Alper. *Sound Editor:* Michael Kirchberger. *Casting:* John Lyons. *Production Designer:* Bill Groom. *Art Director:* Dennis Bradford. *Set Decorator:* George DeTitta, Jr. *Special Effects:* Albert Griswold and William Traynor. *Costumes:* Julie Weiss. *Make-up:* Lizbeth Williamson. *Stunt Coordinator:* Jeff Habberstad. *Running time:* 101 minutes. *MPAA Rating:* PG.

CAST: Nicolas Cage (Charlie Lang); Bridget Fonda (Yvonne Biasi); Rosie Perez (Muriel Lang); Wendell Pierce (Bo Williams); Isaac Hayes (Angel); Victor Rojas (Jesu); Seymour Cassel (Jack Gross); Stanley Tucci (Eddie Biasi); J.E. Freeman (Sal Bontempo); Red Buttons (Walter Zakuto); Richard Jenkins (C. Vernon Hale); Robert Dorfman (Walter); Charles Busch (Timothy); Beatrice Winde (Judge); Ginny Yang (Mrs. Sun); Rene Rivera (Julio); Angel David (Esteban); Anna Lobell (Korean Deli Customer); Claudia Shear (Muriel's Customer); Jimmy Sabater (Fry Cook); Merwin Goldsmith (Bankruptcy Judge); Vincent Pastore, Barry Squitieri, Phil Stein, and Jerome Turner (Bowling Team Members); George J. Manos (Lotto Official); Edward Goldstein (Candy Store Owner); Emily Deschanel (Paint Throwing Fur Activist); Willie Colon (Mayor); Ranjit Chowdhry (Mr. Patel); Pedro Pietri (Homeless Man in Coffee Shop); Frank Pellegrino (Water's Edge Maitre D'); Charles B. Lowlicht and Jed Krascella (Passersby at Subway Station); Bob Sheppard (Yankee Stadium Announcer); Kathleen McNenny (Plaza Desk Clerk); John Louis Fischer and Kaipo Schwab (Plaza Bellhops); Candece V. Tarpley (Bo's Wife); Emena C. Santiago (Bo's Daughter); Angela Pietropinto (Jury Foreperson); Mina Bern (Muriel's Neighbor); Feiga Martinez (Jesu's Mom); John Norman Thomas (Mr. Muktananda); John R. Russell (Blind Beggar).

LOS ANGELES TIMES, 7/29/94, Calendar/p. 1, Peter Rainer

Charlie Lang (Nicolas Cage) is a New York cop with an overdose of decency. He's sweet and affable and he believes in keeping his word—he's like Forrest Gump with an elevated IQ.

When Charlie finds himself in a diner short of a tip, he makes a pie-in-the-sky promise to his waitress (Bridget Fonda) to give her half of any possible winnings on his just-purchased lottery ticket. When the ticket pays $4 million, Charlie, moving against his aghast, social-climbing wife (Rosie Perez), does the right thing.

"It Could Happen to You" is a romantic comedy about the consequences of doing the right thing. It's slight but sweet: It might have been made by Charlie Lang himself. It's not easy to make a movie about a character—particularly an adult of some intelligence—who is all good. Goodness in the movies is often a guarantee of blandness. Goodness usually means a civics lesson is lurking in the brush.

But even though "It Could Happen to You" has its tenderized, good citizenship side, it's been written (by Jane Anderson) and directed (by Andrew Bergman) with an embracing cheer. It's blissfully uncynical. When Yvonne, the wide-eyed waitress who came to New York from Pittsburgh five years ago, tells Charlie that what he did is "like a fairy tale," she's also cuing the audience what to expect.

Cinematographer Caleb Deschanel keeps the New York cityscapes delicately soft—the grime has a pastel shimmer. Turning New York into a magical aerie where ordinary folk can win millions and sweet-hearted romance can bloom may seem as far-fetched a goal as actually lucking into the lottery. But in its own modest, beseeching way, the urban transformation in this movie works.

Of course, the filmmakers cheat a bit. They draw their romantic feeling from a sugared '40s conception of the city, with Sinatra and Tony Bennett doing their versions of "Young at Heart" on the soundtrack. The nostalgia isn't as gummy as it was in "Sleepless in Seattle," a movie that also went in for a those-were-the-days romanticism. The romanticism in that movie seemed forced. In "It Could Happen to You," it just wafts off the screen.

Cage and Fonda are perfectly paired. Cage, for that matter, also seems perfectly paired with Perez, and with Wendell Pierce, who plays his partner, and just about everybody else in the film. He's become a remarkably generous and versatile performer. Is there any other actor who can play zigzag dementia as well as he can—in films like "Wild at Heart" and "Vampire's Kiss"—and then turn around and play zigzag normality—as in "Moonstruck" and Bergman's "Honeymoon in Vegas" and now "It Could Happen to You"—with equal conviction? It could be that, for Cage, these ordinary guys are the weirdest of incarnations—normality as the ultimate masquerade. But he doesn't condescend to these characters or turn them into schmoes. He respects their tiny dreams and so, of course, when the dreams pay off big, they don't seem so ordinary anymore. These characters become figures in a fable.

Fonda shares Cage's grace and gift for simple gestures. Her Yvonne, bankrupt and on the outs from a crumbum husband (Stanley Tucci), still manages to cling to her romantic illusions. She's untarnished: Her white waitress uniform looks angelic on her. Fonda lets Yvonne's emotions out "slowly; as the inevitable romance with Charlie develops, her eyes grow wider and her smile radiates. She's the emblem of happiness, and we can see why the married Charlie would be drawn to her—even though it messes with his rectitude.

All our sympathies are with Charlie, though, because Perez plays his wife like a gold-digging chatterbox. ("I'm a person who needs money," she squeals.) She's a cartoon Emma Bovary: Stuck with her dull, decent husband in Queens, she craves shopping sprees at Saks. Perez's life-of-the-party spiritedness and rat-a-tat locutions give the film a buzz. Post-lottery, she twinkles like a 44-carat diamond, and she's just about as hard. Her redecorated apartment is such a gaudy-tacky wonder that it's practically an amusement park.

Bergman eases into conventionality a bit too cozily in "It Could Happen to You." It lacks his trademark nut-ball inspirations: like that scene in "The Freshman" where Bert Parks serenaded Marlon Brando with Bob Dylan's "Maggie's Farm," or the parachuting Elvis impersonators in "Honeymoon in Vegas." But he pulls off the central romantic conceit in this film without a hitch, and that's not easy. Charlie and Yvonne are each other's lucky charms. They don't need to win a lottery. They're *already* rich—they have hearts of gold.

NEW YORK POST, 7/29/94, p. 48, Michael Medved

"A promise is a promise."

That's the code that good-guy New York cop Charlie Lang (Nicolas Cage) has always tried to live by, and he's willing to take that idea to unusual extremes.

One day, when he finds that he doesn't have the cash to leave a tip for a cup of coffee, he shows the harried waitress (Bridget Fonda) the lottery ticket he's just bought for his wife and tells her that if he wins, he'll give her half the pot. Even if he doesn't win, he promises to come back the next day to bring her a tip.

Fonda doesn't even expect that tip, much less 50 percent of $4 million that Cage ultimately wins in the lottery, but he's determined to keep his word—despite the angry protests of his hairdresser wife, played by Rosie Perez.

If this story sounds vaguely familiar, it's because it's loosely based on the actual incident which provoked the classic New York Post headline: "Cop Tips Waitress $2 Mil." That headline nearly replicated the original movie title, before producers inexplicably replaced it with the bland, meaningless label "It Could Happen to You."

Fortunately, that last-minute switch represents one of the few major mistakes in a charming comedy that will play particularly well to incurable romantics. The main focus of the movie is, of course, the relationship that develops between the cop and the waitress after they split the big prize, and Cage and Fonda generate a sunny, easygoing chemistry that can't fail to win a smile.

The script (by playwright and TV writer Jane Anderson) makes it easy on these lovers by showing that Cage's marriage is already dead before he meets the waitress. In fact, the screenplay depicts the wife as a selfish, materialistic little shrew; it's only the innate likability and in-your-face spunk of Perez that makes this character funny rather than hateful.

As in his previous films ("So Fine," "The Freshman" and "Honeymoon in Vegas") director Andrew Bergman wins our affection for slightly off-center, nice guy heroes who must suddenly cope with outrageous situations. Here, he maintains a gentle, once-upon-a-time touch, recounting his odd urban fable with a series of splashy Post headlines; in fact, this newspaper serves as one of the movie's uncredited stars.

The warm-hearted spirit of Frank Capra hovers over the entire project which even features a vintage Capra moment in which all the "little people" of the city deluge the heroes with letters to show appreciation for their indestructable decency. It's surely no accident that Cage who becomes a more appealing leading man with each new project, here displays an unmistakable resemblance to Capra's favorite star Jimmy Stewart.

Perhaps this film goes a bit overboard in showing the cop's admirable qualities and there may be some in the audience who will agree with Perez when she tells him I'm sick of it! Your saintliness! Your decency!" Nevertheless every fairy tale needs its Prince Charming, and most of us still manage to believe in good people and happy endings.

As Isaac Hayes, the all-knowing, angelic figure who narrates the film declares of the characters: "They live in a city where people pray for miracles every day. And sometimes they happen."

NEWSDAY, 7/29/94, Part II/p. B2, John Anderson

"Once upon a time in New York City ... " our movie tells us, there were good people, clean streets, heroic skylines, Tony Bennett and a cop who split his $4 million in Lotto winnings with a waitress 'cause he didn't have a tip. Or a clue, apparently. But that's just cynicism, cultivated by watching Andrew Bergman's "It Could Happen to You."

The film, which was shot all around New York, wants desperately to be old-fashioned and romantic. And it often is. But from the opening scene—in which a string of shirts are stripped off a Queens clothesline to reveal the promised land of Manhattan—this movie is about money. Not just the symbolic fiscal chasm of the East River, or even the big bucks that Police Officer Charlie Lang (Nicolas Cage), shares with down-on-her-luck waitress Yvonne Biasi (Bridget Fonda). It's about the power of money, the impotence of those without it, the money involved in making a movie and the money that can be made by making a movie.

Recalling a slew of films, but none so much as "It's a Wonderful Life," "It Could Happen" introduces its hero George Bailey-style: Angel (Isaac Hayes), our faux-divine narrator (a lot like the one in "The Hudsucker Proxy"), shows us Charlie at work: carrying a confused blind man across a street, delivering a baby on a bus, nabbing a fleeing felon without using his gun. He's "just a good cop," Angel says. And a good guy. But unlike George Bailey, who got to see the miserable state of Bedford Falls without him, it's Charlie's real life that's the nightmare. His wife, Muriel (Rosie Perez), a greedy shrew, holds Charlie in contempt. "If he was on the take," she says, "I could say, 'OK, he's got initiative.'" When they win the jackpot and Charlie tells her about his promise to Yvonne—twice the tip, or half his lottery win—Muriel starts spitting rivets.

If Charlie is Jupiter, Muriel is Shoemaker-Levy, and as a couple they're an astronomical stretch. Charlie and Yvonne, on the other hand, are—hold onto your seats—made for each other. And while both Cage and Fonda can be so understated they disappear, they're a perfect match here, almost too perfect. Cage has always been best as a border-line nutball ("Raising Arizona," "Moonstruck") but as the downbeat Charlie, he's brought to life by love. Fonda shines as well. In the scene where Charlie tells her about the money, Yvonne's wordless response is moving, and very real.

Bergman, who co-wrote "Blazing Saddles" way back when and directed Cage in "Honeymoon in Vegas," tries to avoid cliché while at the same time striving for a "Sleepless in Seattle"-style coziness. What he does with Muriel, though, is borderline racist. Rosie Perez is basically an ethnic joke. Her delivery, Jose Jimenez-meets-Carmen Miranda-meets-Speedy Gonzales, is only funny if you find the stereotypes she embodies funny. So, it's difficult to say whether she succeeds as Muriel Lang. She does attain a monumental tackiness—plucking a dollar out of a beggar's cup after Charlie drops it in, or hanging a grotesque portrait of herself in their newly refurbished, Liberace-on-Mescaline living room. But her base social climbing is rendered not just ridiculous but predatory in light of Cage and Fonda's white-on-white universe.

Muriel uses her money to buy things; Charlie and Yvonne use it to feed the poor, hand out free subway tokens during rush hour, take a bunch of kids to Yankee Stadium. The morality is a little obnoxious: Animal activists paint Muriel's fur on Fifth Avenue; Charlie and Yvonne eat in the nonsmoking section.

This PC posturing wouldn't be so offensive if "It Could Happen to You" were not a virtual parade of product endorsements, from the macadamia nuts that are Yvonne's only indulgence (the brand is obvious) to the irritatingly ubiquitous headlines from a certain New York tabloid (the original, better, title of this film was "Cop Gives Waitress $2 Million Tip"), which devotes one Page One after another to what is really a pretty trashy story.

And it does turn trashy: Muriel sues for divorce and wins, at which point the film turns terribly dark. Everything that's looked golden before is made tawdry. Yvonne and Charlie are humiliated and impoverished. The result is that, rather than proclaim the superiority of love over money, the film makes one realize how important money is: Not to buy things, but to fend off the wolves, the lawyers, a court system that can be bought, and to ensure a little security in an otherwise ugly world.

This bleakness is probably not what Bergman set out to evoke, although it does, again, recall "It's a Wonderful Life": When the hero's eventual salvation comes, it's not as a result of his own goodness, but through the capricious generosity of others. Frank Capra knew this was a black joke. Bergman doesn't seem to. "It Could Happen to You" ends with triumphs and comeuppances delivered via a tidy series of postscripts, and we're left with the echoes of Charlie's mantra: "A promise is a promise." Yes, and a con job is a con job, even if the director is pulling one on himself.

NEWSWEEK, 8/1/94, p. 56, Katrine Ames

Things don't always go bump—or *kaboom*—in the night, even in this season of "True Lies" and "Speed." The only thing that explodes in "It Could Happen to You" is Muriel Lang (Rosie Perez) when she discovers that her husband, Charlie (Nicolas Cage), has promised half their lottery ticket to a bankrupt waitress, Yvonne Biasi (Bridget Fonda), as a tip. When the ticket turns out to be worth $4 million, Muriel, a beautician with ambition (those golden talons are no accident), insists that Charlie, a New York City cop who bleeds true blue, renege on the deal. "Do you love me? Then stiff her." Charlie won't.

Loosely based on a true story, the movie poses a lot of familiar questions, among them: Does money corrupt? and How honest are you? Muriel drops a bundle in Tiffany's, commissions a large, garish portrait of herself and has her breasts enlarged. Charlie buys his partner (Wendell Pierce) season tickets to the Knicks. Yvonne takes over the coffee shop, dispensing free food to the indigent and good cheer to the ailing. Her big indulgence is a jar of macadamia nuts, which she'd rather not share with her lout of an estranged husband, who wants a chunk of her fortune. Altruism unites Charlie and Yvonne, whose idea of fun is giving subway tokens to commuters. They are tabloid darlings, but when the unscrupulous Muriel, instigates dramatic divorce proceedings, they become media goats.

Fifty years ago, Jimmy Stewart and Margaret Sullavan would have played them. "It Could Happen to You" (changed from "Cop Gives Waitress $2 Million Tip," the new title surely plays on "It Should Happen to You," George Cukor's lovely, little-known 1954 comedy) is shamelessly old-fashioned: it shouldn't float, but it does. Director Andrew Bergman, a sometime novelist who first made a name co-writing "Blazing Saddles," and screenwriter Jane Anderson (HBO's "Positively True Adventures of the Texas Cheerleader-Murdering Mom") have just enough edge to stave off sentimentality. Perez, with a whine like a high-speed drill, quickly wears out her welcome, but Fonda and Cage exhibit an endearing lightness. This is a perfect summer souffle.

SIGHT AND SOUND, 12/94, p. 50, Andrew Pulver

Charlie Lang is a lowly cop, living in Queens, New York City. His beautician wife Muriel is discontented with life in the suburbs, and not at all pleased with Charlie's insistence on staying honest. Meanwhile Yvonne Biasi, a waitress, is declared bankrupt after her unpleasant husband runs up thousands of dollars on her credit card and refuses to pay.

Charlie and his partner have a coffee at the cafe where Yvonne works. Unable to afford a tip, Charlie offers her half of whatever he wins that day on his (and Muriel's) lottery ticket. The number comes up, and the Langs win four million dollars. To Muriel's disgust, Charlie offers Yvonne her share. The three become instant celebrities, but their emotional paths begin to diverge. Muriel goes on a shopping spree, Charlie gives money to beggars, Yvonne buys the cafe where she works, establishing a table where tramps (like the narrator Angel) can eat for free. Then her rat-fink husband turns up.

Charlie interrupts a hold-up at his local grocers. He is then feted even more and earns a decoration. Charlie and Yvonne see little of each other, until, as lottery winners, they are invited to a party on a boat. The increasingly avaricious Muriel is besotted by smooth-sounding financial advisor Jack Gross; Charlie gets stranded on shore just as Yvonne arrives and the boat departs. While they eat together, the first sneaking romantic feelings arise; they agree to see more of each other when they realise the unpleasantness of their respective spouses. Yvonne's husband materialises again and she leaves her flat to get away. Meanwhile, Charlie and Muriel decide to split up, and by chance Yvonne and Charlie spend the night at the same hotel, where their romance is consummated.

Muriel fights a nasty divorce, taking all the money (including Yvonne's share). Despite the public mud-slinging, Charlie and Yvonne remain in love, winning public acclaim (and a few thousand dollars) when Angel turns out to be an undercover newspaper photographer and publicises their picture.

This latest from the Hollywood school of contemporary chaste romance focuses with great tenacity on the twin archetypes of the American Dream and the Ordinary Guy. In fact, one of the Guys is a Gal, and in tandem Charlie Lang and Yvonne Biasi prove durable symbols of US white blue-collardom. The film's original title *Cop Gives Waitress $2m Dollar Tip* spells out the iconography and the milieu. That phrase pops up in the movie as one of a series of *New York Post* headlines which chronicle the plot moves in an appropriately downmarket manner. The movie has a cute but superficial point to make about the public consumption of such stories and the press's intervention to make them come true: in this case the phrase is a response to the final loving scene, after the central couple's ultra-nice reputation has been blackened in court.

Bland good-guy characterisation causes what few problems there are in the script. Most of the time, however, director Andrew Bergman gets the tone of fresh-faced romance right. Cage and, in particular, Fonda are on good form and produce characters that are ingenues without the generic self-consciousness that might have unravelled the whole. They're aided by a screenplay that draws a simple universe of harmless, stickball-playing kids, unsmelly tramps and swindlers you can spot a mile away.

Compared to *Forrest Gump*, which also buys into the Capra-esque innocent's state of mind currently inspiring Hollywood, *It Could Happen To You* is utterly unapologetic about its fairy-tale aspirations: it's less of a parable than a cosy fireside tale. (Incidentally, both films refer to AIDS with a curious reticence, as if they are anxious to acquire its weight as a modern moral symbol, but are worried about accusations of tub-thumping).

For all that, the film's strength is in its portrayal of the love intrigue. Suspense derives not from whether it will happen but when. The romance barnstorms its way through uncertain portrayals of ethnicity, and easy sentiment. There are some moral surprises, no doubt intended to shore up the idea that this is a totally modern love match— like the fact that both lovers are technically adulterers—but as the court scene is designed to demonstrate, in the end, love is all you need.

VILLAGE VOICE, 8/2/94, p. 43, J. Hoberman

It Could Happen To You was inspired by the true story of a cop who split his lottery winnings with a waitress in lieu of a tip but its real antecedents are Depression-era Capra fables like *Lady for a Day* and *Mr. Deeds Goes to Washington*. The title not only suggests a missing link between

It Happened One Night and *You Can't Take It With You*, the movie actually begins, "Once upon a time in New York," a city where, a narrator named Angel (Isaac Hayes) reports, "people prayed for miracles every day."

You know you never know, but the miracle here isn't so much a $4 million payoff as the pained honesty of police officer Charlie Lang (Nicolas Cage), the guy who bought the winning ticket ... and shared with a stranger. Sufficiently resourceful to foil a grocery-store stickup, the tab-dubbed LOTTO cop is a version of the hayseed philanthropist played by Gary Cooper in *Mr. Deeds*. Decency is more important than money. No less than Cooper, Cage seems at once goofy and formidable: "I made a promise and I kept it, most people would have done the same."

Charlie's purity is reinforced by marriage to his high school sweetheart, Muriel. Played by Rosie Perez as a motormouthed shrew, the characterization opens in high and accelerates past self-parody—Perez's caricatured Latina so quickly burns up the movie's reservoir of good-faith that the comic engine simply fuses. Transparently calculating every second, Muriel is a crasser version of *Barcelona*'s sveltely deceptive senoritas: "Maybe I could get some commercial endorsements out of this," is her response to Charlie's insane integrity.

Of course, as the bankrupt waitress Yvonne, Bridget Fonda provides Muriel's antithesis. Muriel storms Fifth Avenue like Donald Trump in hot pants; Yvonne, whose big splurge is a tin of macadamia nuts, needs no breakfast at Tiffany's. Slim and blond, she's an old-fashioned sort of deserving little person, a priori the American Dream. With her too-perfect nose, endearing square jaw, and million-dollar smile, Yvonne is everything Muriel can never be. Complete with a sense of noblesse oblige, she's kind to people with AIDS and helpful to the homeless.

There is something uniting Bergman's working class and Stillman's ruling one. In the sexual realm at least, Fred, Ted, and Charlie all prove to be equally upwardly mobile. While greedy Muriel is vamped by a sleazy chiseler named Jack Gross (Seymour Cassel), Charlie and Yvonne strike up a hot platonic friendship based on the shared simple pleasures of rollerblading in Central Park and distributing tokens to rush-hour commuters: "Hey, the Cop and the Waitress are treating everybody!" one New Yorker exults. Such crazy behavior cannot go unpunished, although, in the inevitable courtroom scene, *It Could Happen To You* compromises its neo-populism by managing to be both antilawyer and antijury.

Sensationally photographed by Caleb Deschanel, New York (Queens included) is the romantic City of Dreams. (The best running gag makes the *New York Post* an instrument of divine intervention—not even the Fox 5 news has given Rupert Murdoch so generous a plug.) Thanks to the ethnic vaudeville provided by the background antics of various Koreans, Pakistanis, and Hasidim, Bergman's city is more naturalistically pluralistic than, say, Woody Allen's. *But It Could Happen To You* supports its unnatural sweetness by displacing cynical realism onto its characters of color. Similarly, the movie maintains its yuppie populism ("If only rich people had kids we wouldn't have public schools," is Charlie's strongest bon mot) by identifying the déclassé Muriel with vulgar taste, parvenu greed, and the worst excesses of the legal profession. The movie's bias comes into focus as soon as one imagines casting Perez in Fonda's role.

The pity is that, in its details and premise, *It Could Happen To You* comes closer to authentically spurious Capracorn than any recent attempt. The problem is that it presents a "New York" of which *New York* magazine would be proud. In this town, the dusky, accented Muriel is the social climber. Charlie and Yvonne merely receive their due.

Also reviewed in:
CHICAGO TRIBUNE, 7/29/94, Friday/p. C, Michael Wilmington
NEW REPUBLIC, 9/12/94, p. 26, Stanley Kauffmann
NEW YORK TIMES, 7/29/94, p. C10, Caryn James
NEW YORKER, 8/1/94, p. 74, Terrence Rafferty
VARIETY, 7/18-24/94, p. 38, Brian Lowry
WASHINGTON POST, 7/29/94, p. D1, Hal Hinson
WASHINGTON POST, 7/29/94, Weekend/p. 36, John F. Kelly

IT'S HAPPENING TOMORROW

A Sacis release of a Sacher Film/Sofina coproduction in association with RAI-TV, Channel 1. *Producer:* Nanni Moretti and Angelo Barbagallo. *Director:* Daniele Luchetti. *Screenplay (Italian with English subtitles):* Daniele Luchetti, Franco Bernini, Angelo Pasquini, and Sandro Petraglia. *Director of Photography:* Franco Di Giacomo. *Editor:* Angelo Nicolini. *Music:* Nicola Piovani. *Art Director:* Giancarlo Basili and Leonardo Scarpa. *Costumes:* Albert Barsacq and Marina Sciarelli. *Running time:* 92 minutes. *MPAA Rating:* Not Rated.

CAST: Paolo Hendel (Lupo); Giovanni Guidelli (Edo); Ciccio Ingrassia (Gianloreto). Angela Finocchiaro (Duchess); Agnese Nano (Allegra); Margherita Buy (Vera); Ugo Gregoretti (Count Lucifero); Dario Cantarelli (Abbott).

NEW YORK POST, 4/1/94, p. 38, Larry Worth

Sergio Leone movies became a thing of the past with the director's premature death in 1989. But his spirit clearly lives on in the likes of Daniele Luchetti.

Making his big screen debut with "It's Happening Tomorrow," the Italian filmmaker has tapped into the time and place of Leone's spaghetti-westerns, then peopled his tale with sad sacks harkening back to Vittorio De Sica classics.

But despite its inspirations, this doesn't boil down to "The Bicycle Thief" meets "The Good, the Bad and the Ugly." It's more of a pleasant picaresque, in the tradition of Mark Twain's "Roughing It."

And roughing it is just what the two principals experience in the Tuscan Maremma of 1848. Lupo and Edo (nicely played by Paola Hendel and Giovanni Guidelli) are two handsome but hopelessly naive cowboys who commit a robbery to aid a sick crony.

Typical of the pair's bad luck, their gun doesn't work and the victim of their holdup instantly outsmarts them. And it's all downhill from there.

The pair are suddenly on the run from avenging Austrian mercenaries and stumbling through a comedy of errors, meeting up with love, death and everything in between as they traverse the gorgeous countryside.

For the most part, Luchetti keeps matters pretty light, flitting between the heroes' charmingly comic capers. But just when you least expect it, violence punctuates the bonhomie, keeping viewers from taking things for granted. Its matter-of-fact presentation proves effectively haunting.

Unfortunately, Luchetti—who collaborated on the screenplay with Franco Bernini and Angelo Pasquini—loses his grip in the film's final third.

Themes concerning the aristocracy vs. the proletariat get too heavy-handed. Things bog down again after the action moves to a utopia that's long on symbolism and short on necessary social satire.

OK, so "It's Happening Tomorrow" can't bring off utopia. But it still manages enough stabs at perfection to do Leone and company proud.

NEWSDAY, 4/1/94, Part II/p. B20, John Anderson

When people say Italian cinema has gotten goofy over the last decade or so, they're usually talking about films like "It's Happening Tomorrow," a late '80s comedy about two fugitive cowherds making its American debut at the Public Theater today. The broad humor and outright silliness mask a deeper political sentiment, although it neither intrudes on the fun, nor makes itself fully felt until the film's final moments.

Traversing gold-dusted landscapes and several historical eras, the minimally savvy Lupo (Paolo Hendel) and the blitheringly innocent Edo (Giovanni Guidelli) find themselves on a Swiftian odyssey disguised as a buddy movie. Fleeing their insular village after a botched robbery. the two suffer a world that's part Italo Calvino, part Mel Brooks, and encounter a philosophical and allegorical cross-section of pre-evolutionary Italians, the Mediterranean equivalents of Houyhnhnms and Yahoos.

There are the ruthless kidnapers led by the Vincent Price look-alike Gianloreto (Ciccio Ingrassia), who plans, matter-of-factly, to kill both Edo and Lupo when they first happen upon him. ("Let's show him how a cowherd dies," Lupo says bravely, then crumbles: "Pity!!!! ..."). There are the inhabitants of a ruined, chicken-infested abbey, who use Lupo and Edo as lab rats in an experiment to settle their free will vs. predestination debate. There is the Harmony Community, where everyone is allowed to indulge his or her whims, including the children, who eventually burn the place down. And there are the three relentless Austrian mercenaries—symbolic of the yoke Italy will soon be shrugging off—who pursue the pair. "Who *are* those guys?" you expect them to say; they're a cross between Butch and Sundance, and Mario and Luigi.

"If we don't go, we won't see," is the recurring mantra of "It's Happening Tomorrow." If it were a movie ad, it would be just about perfect.

Also reviewed in:
NEW YORK TIMES, 4/1/94, p. C12, Stephen Holden
VARIETY, 5/11/88, p. 23

IVAN AND ABRAHAM

A New Yorker Films release of a Hachette Première & Co. production. *Executive Producer:* Bernard Bouix. *Producer:* René Cleitman and Jean-Luc Ormières. *Director:* Yolande Zauberman. *Screenplay (Yiddish, Polish, Russian and Romany with English subtitles):* Yolande Zauberman. *Director of Photography:* Jean-Marc Fabre. *Editor:* Yann Dedet. *Music:* Ghedalia Tazartes. *Sound:* Jean-Pierre Duret. *Set Designer:* Alexandre Sagoskin. *Costumes:* Marina Kaishauri. *Running time:* 105 minutes. *MPAA Rating:* Not Rated.

CAST: Roma Alexandrovitch (Abraham); Sacha Iakovlev (Ivan); Vladimir Machkov (Aaron); Maria Lipkina (Abraham's Sister); Hélène Lapiower (Abraham's Mother); Alexandre Kaliaguine (Abraham's Father); Rolan Bykov (Abraham's Grandfather); Zinovi Guerdt (Aaron's Father); Daniel Olbrychski (Stepan); Aïlika Kremer (Ivan's Cousin); Oleg Iankovski (The Prince); Malina Iablonskaïa (Bada); Alexeï Serebriakov (Andrej); Armen Djigarkhanian (Slava); Alexeï Gorbounov (Pavel); Valery Ivtchenko (The Old Rabbi).

CHRISTIAN SCIENCE MONITOR, 2/9/94, p. 17, Marilynne S. Mason

Ivan and Abraham, shows us life in a Jewish settlement in pre-Hitler easter Poland. Two little boys, a Christian and Jew, survive together despite prejudice and persecution. The simple tale is so layered with sociopolitical undercurrents, and so elegant in its storytelling, that the viewer finds genuine insight into another time and culture.

CHRISTIAN SCIENCE MONITOR, 3/28/95, p. 14, David Sterritt

Ivan and Abraham, was directed by Yolande Zauberman, the daughter of Polish Jews who endured first-hand experiences of Nazi terror. Set in a Polish village during the 1930s, her film centers on a nine-year-old Jewish boy and his closest friend, a 14-year-old gentile who lives with a Jewish family as an apprentice.

The adventures of these youngsters begin when the proprietor of their village, an irresponsible prince, stirs up anti-Semitic sentiment by abandoning his estate and leaving the townspeople prey to severe financial troubles. Unhappy with the prospects awaiting them in their devastated community, the boys flee to the countryside, where they encounter new and old acquaintances, including Abraham's daringly independent sister and her lover, a man who has earned the suspicion of their village by daring to be a Communist.

Filmed in black-and-white, "Ivan and Abraham" has strong performances and imaginative music that lends an extra measure of dark-toned excitement to several of its episodes. While its storytelling strategies aren't always successful, it provides a poignant reminder of not-so-distant events, and paints an evocative portrait of the region where it was made—largely in Ukraine, in a Jewish town that has survived from the prewar period. The film has been acquired for distribution by New Yorker Films, and has its theatrical opening shortly after its ND/NF screenings.

LOS ANGELES TIMES, 10/13/94, Calendar/p. 8, Kenneth Turan

It is a time of madness, with every aspect of society, from the personal to the political, veering toward collapse. Mystics, racists, pragmatists, idealists and young people in love collide on the 1930s streets of the nameless town on the eastern Polish frontier that is the setting for an impressive new work called "Ivan and Abraham."

The first fiction film by French documentarian Yolande Zauberman, "Ivan and Abraham" is ambitious in all its aspects. An attempt to re-create the lost world of Eastern European Jewry between the two World Wars, it is a well-crafted document that captures the chaotic spirit of the times with a Brueghl-like texture and density.

Sensitively photographed (by Jean-Marc Fabre) in wide-screen black and white, "Ivan" is more than anything a visual pleasure. Shot in small villages in Belarus and the Ukraine, it uncannily brings to life the crowded courtyards, the winding paths and byways, the cluttered study houses that characterized life in the long-gone *shtetls* of Poland.

Writer-director Zauberman, whose parents were Polish Jews who survived the war, has also laced the visuals with a moodiness that emphasizes the melancholy that cut across all aspects of society, as the apocalypse that no one could name but everyone felt hovered just out of reach.

"Ivan and Abraham" tells its story through a single family. The grandfather, the pious but rigid Nachman (Rolan Bykov), has trouble managing the estates of the area's dissipated prince (Oleg Iankovski), but worrying him just as much are two problem grandchildren.

Rachel (Maria Lipkina) is a marriageable teen-ager, but she is terribly in love with a man her family considers unsuitable, the renegade Communist Aaron (Vladimir Machkov), who is on the run from the authorities but returns to the town because Rachel is on his mind.

Rachel's 9-year-old brother Abraham (Roma Alexandrovitch) is just as much of a trial to Nachman. Too wild to be considered an acceptable Jewish child, he would rather ride horses than pray and spends most of his time with his best friend, the older, non-Jewish Ivan (Sacha Iakovlev), who has been apprenticed to Abraham's family.

Overlaying all of this is the wariness with which Jews and non-Jews regard each other. The local peasantry both hate the Jews and are frightened of them, their superstitiousness making them ready to scapegoat any outsiders. So when the reckless prince loses everything to gambling debts, he sets a whirlwind into motion that soon sweeps up Aaron and Rachel, Abraham and Ivan.

Concerned with verisimilitude, writer-director Zauberman went to some lengths to make everything feel right. Since most of the film's dialogue is in Yiddish, she had her non-Jewish cast learn the language from scratch, and, helped by a tutor who was a student of the great Soviet Yiddish actor Solomon Mikhaels, they do a surprisingly good job speaking it, as well as the Russian, Polish and Gypsy languages that add to the babble of tongues.

In her eagerness, Zauberman does allow some of the film's dramatic scenes to drift into awkwardness, and the overall pacing is not unexpectedly slow. But standing in strong compensation is the way "Ivan and Abraham" conveys a sense of silent witness to this seething world, half-medieval, half-modern, that was soon to be no more.

NEW YORK POST, 3/25/94, p. 36, Thelma Adams

The most striking part of "Ivan and Abraham" is the black and white photography. Every rut in the road, leaf on the vine, shutter off its hinge, has character and definition.

"Ivan and Abraham" opens with a blithe coming-of-age moment that is seductively simple: two boys compare their members in an attic. One's circumcised, the other isn't. Meet Abraham (Roma Alexandrovitch) and Ivan (Sacha Iakovlev)

As relations between Christians and Jews deteriorate in their Polish shtetl circa 1930, the two boys flee into the woods. They are pursued by Abraham's sister Rachel (Maria Lipkina) and her beloved, Aaron (Vladimir Machkov), a Marxist on the lam.

These tangled relationships should provide enough plot momentum for a soap opera on shtetl life. The boys are fleeing from a situation that, seen with the clarity of hindsight, is already unraveling. The door to the past is swinging shut. The Jews will be driven off the land. It is only a matter of time.

French newcomer Yolande Zauberman (the child of Polish Jews) ably shows the roots of anti-Semitism and puts them into the context of anti-Gypsy sentiment. Zauberman cut her teeth on documentaries. Her keen eye for detail, use of Yiddish and local dialects, and the beautiful cinematography lend authenticity to the plight of the runaways.,

It's as if Zauberman smothers her leads with too much maternal love. What she loses in dramatic friction she gains in two appealing performances. Both Abraham and Ivan are charmingly played by non-actors: Alexandrovitch was plucked from a Gypsy camp, Iakovlev from an orphanage.

Too much authenticity, not enough fiction—that's the problem in this ambitious first feature that recently played New Directors/New Films at MoMA. While Zauberman is at ease sketching the larger tensions between Christians, Jews and Gypsies, she falters when her fictional characters must speak for the whole community.

Unable to bridge the gap between fact and fantasy, Zauberman fails to build tension or create a gripping drama.

NEWSDAY, 3/25/94, Part II/p. B7, John Anderson

A holocaust drama without a Holocaust? Sure. Create a world full of anger, love and insanity, peopled by believable characters who are almost too beautiful, place them in compelling situations, and, and lull your audience into a false sense of dramatic conclusion. And then remind us that none of what we see matters, because it will all be gone, and soon.

"Ivan and Abraham," set on the eastern Polish border "sometime in the '30s," is no Jewish costume drama, no "Yentl"-esque caricature. Its characters aren't all Jewish, and aren't at all perfect, although the film's black and white photography often makes them look so. Their faces are haunting, rather than haunted, and their problems foreshadow disaster.

Shot in a shtetl in Ukraine, the film occasionally lapses into the obvious: The title characters are introduced during a show-me session in which Ivan (Sacha Iakovlev) wants to see the circumcised member of Abraham (Roma Alexandrovitch). So we know, having been hit over the head, that Abraham is Jewish and Ivan is not, and that all men, or at least boys, are created equal.

But Yolande Zauberman, a first-time French film director who's picked up a thing or two from Francois Truffaut (including the freeze frame that ends the film), also knows that Ivan and Abraham are of an age when their mutual feeling is the fiercest love they've yet to taste. And love, or lack thereof, is at the heart of this moody, starkly gorgeous movie.

Passion in general runs wild in Ivan and Abraham's troubled little village, a small but remarkably diverse one in its ethnic and political makeups. The chief landowner is a dissolute prince (Oleg Iakovski) who plans to sell his property out from under his workers and flee. The prince 's manager, Nachman (Rolan Bykov), who's also Abraham's grandfather, is a despised figure among the Catholic working population, and a domestic despot: Having arranged a marriage for his granddaughter, Rachel (Maria Lipkina), he tells her, "I won't let anyone else have you," implying any number of things. Rachel, however, loves Aaron (Vladimir Machkov), a jailed communist who escapes and takes her away. Abraham and Rachel's parents, Mardoche (Alexandre Kaliaguine) and Reyzele (Helene Lapiower), are a lustful but lost middle generation.

Zauberman loads up her film with omens. "Why didn't you go to Palestine?" Aaron asks his father (Zinovi Guerdt), who has waited for Aaron to escape. "It's going to be terrible," a woman screams, referring to life after the prince, but meaning so much more. The peasants' rage at Nachman, who, they assume, was aware of the prince's pending desertion, focuses on his ethnicity as much as his avariciousness; in actuality, the prince has taken all of Nachman's money, too, leaving him with nothing but Rachel's dowry. The workers, who have less, don't really care.

Abraham and Ivan flee to the countryside, where they find not safety but more cruelty. Abraham, a beautiful, darkly Sephardic-looking child, passes himself off as Gypsy, but Gypsies, too, are hated. They return, but they find nothing and no one.

"We're going away together, you and me," Ivan tells an inconsolable Abraham, in one of the film's final, fatalistic moments. And then, Ivan speaks for the director. "Open your eyes, please ..." If you don't, it certainly isn't her fault.

VILLAGE VOICE, 3/29/94, p. 56, J. Hoberman

Hectic and sultry, *Ivan and Abraham* skitters across the screen in the ominous wind of an impending storm. It's a movie of gusts as much as scenes. Shot, with forceful elegance, in widescreen black and white by French director Yolande Zauberman, this accomplished first feature—showing twice at "New Directors" before opening at the Lincoln Plaza—offers a panorama of Euro tribalism on the brink of catastrophe.

Ivan and Abraham is programmatically polyglot. Actors speak Russian, Polish, Romany, and Yiddish (the latter in a variety of accents); Zauberman's camera rolls and tumbles against a keening, babbling undercurrent of sound. The movie was shot on the former Pale of Jewish Settlement, in and around the remnants of ramshackle market towns, but it is set "somewhere on the Polish border in the 1930s." Topography and chronology are intentionally vague. There are no cities and, were it not for the presence of a single automobile belonging to a dissolute Polish prince, the entire movie could easily be taking place in the 19th century. Indeed, it has the millennial feel of a century's end.

Ivan and Abraham's protagonists are the raw and unkempt revolutionary Aaron, Rachel, the shtetl gamine, and her no-less-exquisite brother Abraham, a 10-year-old child of nature who spends so much time with the household's Russian apprentice, Ivan, that his autocratic grandfather pronounces him "worse than a goy." The movie's first half is the hectic prelude to a dark, turgid *shabbes* night, roiled by hysterical rumors and anti-Semitic agitators; the second half follows the children's escape to a chaotic freedom beyond the Pale.

Ivan and Abraham, Aaron and Rachel flee out into the fields, where horsemen whip the boys to make them dance, where the churches are decorated with paintings of bloodsucking Jews, where Gypsies and dissolute Russian bards sleep under the sky. Aaron, a devoted Communist, and Rachel want to go to France. (Zauberman is the daughter of Polish Jews. Is this the imagined story of idealized parents surviving the storm in an escape to the West?) Abraham and Ivan, who only want out, briefly connect with a gallant Polish "madman" (Wajda star Daniel Olbrychski).

At once gritty and abstract, and far less naturalistic than it might appear, *Ivan and Abraham* practices a new sort of anti-romantic romanticism by placing traditional East European Jews (here played by a variety of Russians, Poles, Armenians, Gypsies, and more) in situ—amid the clamor of muddy marketplaces and decrepit rural inns, a teeming wooden shul or a disorderly study-house presided over by a mystically vacant *melamed*. The movie is a kind of self-conscious conjuring act suggesting one of the tropes in Philip Roth's *Operation Shylock*: Roth invents a counterfeit "Philip Roth" who, fearing a second Holocaust in Israel, proclaims that "Zionism has outlived its historical function" and proposes a counterforce, Diasporism, that "seeks to promote the dispersion of the Jews in the West, particularly the resettlement of Israeli Jews of European background in the European countries where there were sizable Jewish populations before World War II."

Ivan and Abraham is a prime example of a Diasporist or neo-shtetl-izing cinema that would also include Judit Elek's 1989 *Memoirs of a River* and Eleanor Antin's 1991 *The Man Without a World.* In these films, too, a dreamy East European past replaces the lost ideals of socialism and Israel, not to mention the Talmud, as the source of tribal values and positive otherness. Neo-shtetl-ism celebrates Jews in rebellion (largely against being Jews). *Memoirs of a River*, locating Jewish shepherds and woodsmen in a rustic Carpathian landscape of natural piety, is more pastoral than *Ivan and Abraham*, but it exudes a kindred sense of Jews as Europe's internal Third World.

More blatantly postmodern, *The Man Without a World*, a faux silent feature purporting to have been made in Poland in 1928, augments familiar shtetl types—scholars, paupers, fishwives—with a troupe of performing Gypsies. It alludes to the variety (the confinements and instability) of East European Jewish life by setting much of the action in a tavern where artists mix with artistes and an assortment of Zionists, anarchists, and socialists argue politics. Similarly, Zauberman's shabby, disheveled Jews are surrounded by heartless nobles and a hard-drinking, superstitious peasantry, not to mention their own tousled, unmanageable children.

Ivan overemphasizes its lyrical soul, but there's an eerie familiarity to the supercharged atmosphere. The movie's two recurring lines are the free-floating observation that "You've all gone mad" and the hostile command to "Speak in our language." The story could easily be transposed to present-day Bosnia. Of course, there would be no place in that film for an idealistic internationalist like Aaron. The final freeze-frame of brotherhood, however, would hardly seem more hopelessly doomed.

Also reviewed in:
CHICAGO TRIBUNE, 6/22/95, Tempo/p. 9, Michael Wilmington
NEW YORK TIMES, 3/23/94, p. C17, Janet Maslin
VARIETY, 5/17/93, p. 96, Lisa Nesselson
WASHINGTON POST, 7/22/94, p. C7, Rita Kempley

JACK BE NIMBLE

An Essential Productions Ltd film in association with The New Zealand Film Commission. *Executive Producer:* Murray Newey and John Barnett. *Producer:* Jonathan Dowling and Kelly Rogers. *Director:* Garth Maxwell. *Screenplay:* Garth Maxwell. *Director of Photography:* Donald Duncan. *Editor:* John Gilbert. *Music:* Chris Neal. *Sound:* Dick Reade. *Sound Editor:* Dick Reade, Paul Stent and Graeme Myhre. *Production Designer:* Grant Major. *Art Director:* Jackie Gilmore. *Special Effects:* Kevin Chisnall. *Costumes:* Ngila Dickson. *Make-up:* Viv Mepham. *Stunt Coordinator:* Peter Bell. *Running time:* 95 minutes. *MPAA Rating:* Not Rated.

CAST: Alexis Arquette (Jack); Sarah Smuts-Kennedy (Dora); Bruno Lawrence (Teddy); Tony Barry (Clarrie); Elizabeth Hawthorne (Clarrie's Wife); Brenda Simmons (Mrs. Birch); Gilbert Goldie (Mr. Birch); Tricia Phillips (Anne); Paul Minifie (Kevin); Sam Smith, (Little Jack); Hannah Jessop (Little Dora); Nicholas Antwis (Jack, age 7); Olivia Jessop (Dora, age 8); Ricky Plester (Young Sean); Rohan Stace (Sean); Bridget Armstrong (Typing Teacher); Bridget Donovan (Carlene); Caroline Lowry (Trish); Tina Frantzen and Vicky Haughton (Matrons); Helen Medlyn (Orphanage Nurse); Grant McFarland (Metalwork Teacher); Celia Nicholson (Motel Woman); Chris Auchinvole (Gordon); Peter Bell (Thief).

NEW YORK POST, 6/10/94, p. 46, Larry worth

If the budget for "Jack Be Nimble" was $10, there must have been $9.95 left over.

This cheap attempt to create a gothic fairy tale-cum-horror story for the '90s makes those low-budget Roger Corman-Vincent Price frights from the '60s look like "The Shining."

The main claim to fame of "Jack Be Nimble" is rising star Alexis Arquette. The brother of Rosanna and Patricia first astounded viewers with his knockout work as a transvestite in "Last Exit to Brooklyn." Then he earned kudos as a two-timing TV writer in the recently released comedy "Grief." The buzz is even louder about his part in Quentin Tarantino's "Pulp Fiction," which won the grand prize at Cannes last month.

Without doubt, "Jack Be Nimble" will be the skeleton in Arquette's closet, the one he forgets to put on his resume. And who could blame him?

He plays Jack, one half of a pair of orphans. But while sister Dora is adopted by loving parents, Jack enters the home of a sadistic couple and their four menacing daughters.

After years of constant abuse, Jack takes drastic means to reteam with Dora. But tragedy isn't far behind as the various elements—including a quartet of mop-topped harpies—coalesce for a stomach-churning finale of death and mutilation.

Director/writer Garth Maxwell, who lensed this "Harvest Home" wannabe on his home turf in New Zealand, never creates the dark mood and creepy ambience necessitated by the genre. Further, his meandering, unrealistic screenplay fails to convince on any level.

Amateur day continues with Arquette's somnambulistic efforts as Jack. But he doesn't have an exclusive on monotoned recitations. Sarah Smuts-Kennedy's Dora could pass as a lobotomy victim.

Meanwhile, the rest of the cast led by Bruno Lawrence as Dora's tough-talking lover—masquerades as cartoon creations, with out-of-control histrionics reigning supreme.

Accordingly, "Jack Be Nimble" comes off as a thriller haunted by a major contradiction: Though never scary, it's the stuff of moviegoers' nightmares.

NEWSDAY, 6/10/94, Part II/p. B13, John Anderson

With its harpies, furies, child abuse, suggestions of incest and inexplicable bursts of rage, "Jack Be Nimble" has all the accessories of Greek tragedy, without the archetypal underpinnings. So it's rather a free-floating thing, technically equipped but unnavigable.

Which is not to say that this tale of a brother and sister—who grow up to be played by the Alexis Arquette and "Angel at My Table's" Sarah Smuts-Kennedy—isn't occasionally moving, or frightening. Director Garth Maxwell tries a bit too hard to imbue inanimate objects with dread—the kids' jack-in-the-box is a horror cliché—but he does attain a kind of dizzying, "Black Narcissus"-style sense of vertigo. The opening scene, for instance, with its eerie wind, eerie music, the sheets on the clothes line and the slap of wet linen against the hysterical woman's face, all carries with it some delightful creepiness.

And that's a quality that follows the woman into the nearby house where two children's fates will be decided: Jack (Sam Smith) and Dora (Hannah Jessop), very small, domestically outraged and soon to be sent off to an indifferent adoption agency, where they'll be sent to wildly different destinations.

Dora goes home with a nice middle-aged, middle-class couple who raise her in a state of domestic torpor; Jack is taken by a brutish farming couple who already have four cretinous, thick-maned daughters and need a strong male back. Jack will, despite his manure-encrusted environment and severe beatings, grow up to be sensitive, and intelligent enough to create an electric device that hypnotizes his parents so he can kill them off. His mistake is sparing the lethal sisters, who spend the rest of the movie pursuing him.

Dora, meanwhile, has, like Jack, been pining for years for her lost sibling. Both are distinctly weird, but Dora also has developed keen psychic powers and communicates with others—including her lover, Teddy (Bruno Lawrence), via telepathy. One gets the feeling, though, that somewhere along the line, Maxwell started spreading things a bit thick.

The director's visual sense is highly developed, even if what he accomplishes with it is suspect. We virtually reel back and forth between Jack and Dora's childhoods, for instance, on a seesaw of overheated imagery: the plastic pig adorning Dora's birthday cake cuts to a slaughtered pig on the farm which is dripping blood into a bucket which becomes the blood red icing of Dora's next birthday cake. It's disgusting, but that's not everything.

SIGHT AND SOUND, 2/94, p. 54, Geoffrey Macnab

New Zealand. After their mother has a nervous breakdown, largely brought about by their father's philandering, Jack and Dora, two young children, are deposited in an orphanage, and end up being adopted by different families. Dora is taken to live with a kindly, middle-aged couple, deep in the heart of suburbia, while Jack finds himself in a grim farmhouse with tyrannical step-parents. As he grows up, he is taunted by his step-sisters, made to work hard at menial tasks, and faces random, brutal punishment from his stepfather for any perceived misdemeanour. Dora's childhood is also unhappy. She is constantly thinking of her brother. In a typing lesson, when she is supposed to be drafting a specimen business letter, she writes to him instead. The teacher victimises her, reading her letter aloud to the rest of the class. On the way home, when she is teased by her school mates, she gets into a scrap, and almost dies when she is pushed off a precipice by one of her assailants.

One evening at supper, after his step-parents have upbraided him for his poor college results, Jack fetches the piece of equipment he has been building in metalwork—an electrical appliance which somehow hypnotises the entire family. Jack leads his step-father, still in a trance, to the middle of a country road, and causes him to be mown down by a bus. Jack then makes his stepmother imagine she is a cat, and causes her to drown in a river. Leaving his step-sisters asleep, Jack heads off to town with the vague intention of finding his long-lost sister. Dora, meanwhile, has discovered she is psychic. With the assistance of her much older boyfriend, Teddy, she manages to track Jack down. They have an emotional reunion, but she is alarmed by his bitterness and tendency to violence. Teddy and Jack take an immediate dislike to each other.

Jack wants Dora to go with him in pursuit of their parents. She agrees, helping steal Teddy's car keys. They track down their mother, now re-married, in a small town, and Jack forces her to admit she never loved them. Dora has been hearing voices in her head. Jack's step-parents are in contact with her from beyond the grave, and want revenge. His four step-sisters have already set out in pursuit of him, and have tracked down and killed Dora's blind stepmother. Jack and Dora, next visit their father, an overweight man with a weak heart and a drink problem. He is unsympathetic, and Jack reacts by hypnotising him and making him do a thousand situps, knowing the effort will kill him. He and Dora drive out into the open country.

After a chase, the step-sisters overtake Jack and Dora, forcing them off the road. Knocked unconscious, Dora wakes to find Jack gone. She rushes back to Teddy and asks for his help in finding her brother. Teddy takes her to the farmhouse where Jack was brought up. There, somebody leaps out from behind a door and slits Teddy's throat. Dora flees into the back yard, where she is confronted by the four sisters. Driven on by the spirit of their dead parents, they try to kill her. But Dora proves psychically too strong for them, and is able to turn their malevolence on themselves. Once the sisters are all dead, she rushes into the woods, where she finds Jack hanging bound and gagged from a tree. She lets him down, but it is too late to save him.

After several months, Dora is now pregnant, and is being looked after by her mother. By the nursery rhyme she sings, she makes it apparent she believes the child she is carrying is, in fact, Jack.

New Zealand, judging by the way it has depicted itself in recent films, must be a daunting place. Peter Jackson's *Braindead* suggested a land full of murderous zombies; Alison Maclean's *Crush* showed a soggy, grey country, with dark emotions simmering away as turbulently as the geysers of Hell's Kitchen. Now writer-director Garth Maxwell's debut feature adds to the litany: this latest slice of 'New Zealand Gothic' is a mercurial, grisly modern fairy tale, which skips across genres with alacrity, borrowing from Hollywood and art-house cinema alike. Despite its obvious, polite nods in the direction of Jane Campion, its influences, according to Maxwell, also include *The Silence Of The Lambs* and Edgar Allan Poe, and it manages to combine elements of the horror film, the road movie and the suspense thriller with a lyrical, if brutal, evocation of childhood. The script was apparently inspired by a story Maxwell once heard about a boy who was beaten with barbed wire. With such an image at its core, it's little wonder that *Jack Be Nimble* errs on the bleak side. The mood of foreboding is evident right from the opening shot, where a storm is brewing, and a mother's sense of nervous anxiety seems to affect the landscape itself. As she approaches the end of her tether, her two little children sit huddled inside, waiting for the worst to happen.

We start on familiar ground. This appears to be another anguished family fable about a brother and sister separated from their parents, and then from each other, at an early age. Predictably, the narrative bifurcates as Jack and Dora are taken into different foster families, and their personalities change to fit their new environments: one child is hardened and made bitter by his experiences while the other withdraws into a cocoon. Thematically, *Jack Be Nimble* sometimes seems like a rustic counterpart to Alan Rudolph's *Equinox*, where the two main characters, who are twins, also lose track of each other in infancy, and only come together as the film ends. As in Rudolph's picture, there is an emphasis on symmetry and balance, with frequent cutting between the two stories to emphasise moments where the children's lives correspond. For instance, when Dora is given a birthday cake with a toy pig on the icing, Jack is simultaneously being forced by his stepfather to watch a real pig be slaughtered. Maxwell has described the siblings as being "like two halves of one personality," and deliberately makes their lives mirror each other. The film differs from *Equinox*, though, in that the duo are re-united relatively early on. Having found each other, they must search for their parents.

As in *An Angel At My Table*, there is a seamless transition from childhood to adolescence, with youthful actors giving way to the stars, Alex Arquette (he of the famous sisters) and Sarah Smuts-Kennedy. Even if there is nothing very original about the material, Maxwell handles it all delicately enough, at least in the early scenes. However, as *Jack Be Nimble* progresses, and as he foregrounds the bloody, supernatural elements in the script, the film loses much of its subtlety. Rather than offering a sympathetic account of Jack's plight, he begins to crank the picture up into a full-blown revenge tragedy. His attempts at leavening his grim tale with a little humour backfire: the comedy ends up undermining the horror, and vice versa. His ambivalent attitude is highlighted in the acting: whereas the three leads, Arquette, Smuts-Kennedy and Bruno Lawrence, play for 'real', giving intense, humourless performances, the supporting cast offer cheerfully overblown caricatures. Nemesis, for instance, comes to Jack in the unlikely shape of his four step-sisters, who bear more than a passing resemblance to St Trinians fourth formers, and look as if they should be armed with lacrosse sticks; Jack's brooding, bad-tempered stepfather is likewise a virtual pantomime figure. The gallows humour is certainly intentional, and there are moments—notably when Jack hypnotises his step-parents and lures them to unlikely deaths—where it works wonderfully well. Still, if Maxwell's intention is, as he rather grandly puts it in the production notes, "to confront issues of the beast and violence in humanity," you can't help feeling he is shooting himself in the foot by being so light-hearted about it. Leaping hither and thither, shifting mood and style with alarming frequency, *Jack Be Nimble* may underline Maxwell's quicksilver imagination, but it's hardly a coherent piece of work.

VILLAGE VOICE, 6/14/94, p. 56, Julie Lang

What's frustrating about this artsy thriller is that the images are so damn good: four psycho stepsisters having permanent bad-hair days, wafting through the New Zealand countryside looking to find and cold hard kill their adopted brother Jack (Alexis Arquette). Or Jack's big and shiny silver machine, which hypnotizes all, especially his various daddies, with these maniacal lightbulbs blink, blink, blinking you toward deadly encounters with Mack trucks, thunderous black water, or sit-ups. (Death by sit-ups? Yeah, you go and try a thousand of 'em when you're half-conscious, buddy.) Or those cockamamie Laurie Anderson-type voices screeching through Dora's (Sarah Smuts-Kennedy) synapses. Dora, by the by, is Jack's biological sister, who happens to be psychic as well. Stop the insanity!

But, Alexis, you're a far cry from *Last Exit to Brooklyn*. You used to be so fey and delicate, I could have just taken you home and fed you hot chocolate. Here, you're a regular trauma drama. Mummy's a crazy lush, you're whisked off and separated from beloved Dora, and your new folks, with those hillbilly sisters, are straight outta *Texas Chainsaw Massacre*. Alexis, you've got to be strong, you've got to be mean, you've got to find Dora, (pronounced DOE-rah), but I think you're better off with sequins and tweezers. In other words, I don't buy your macho act.

This psycho-horror shindig attempts to enmesh blood-red gore with *Persona*. I crave to grasp the intensity seizing both Jack and Dora, but the Freudian slapstick always gets in the way of the characters' emotional development. Take the moment Jack believes, deeply believes, Dora will not abandon him like the others; they're in a stolen Mercedes, their fingers entwine and grip tight, they are together, truly, after all these years—and then those freaky inbreds come barreling down the country road in a rusty old Ford pickup, staring comatose into the camera. And sure, they actually run down the Mercedes. Dora's nature might be elucidated by those bizarre squeals from hell that only she hears. But then along comes your generic extraneous well-oiled guy, Teddy (Bruno Lawrence), who speaks to her like *The Next Generation's* Counselor Troi. And within a good 10 minutes, they're squirmin' like worms between the sheets, if you know what I mean.

What I mean is that I give two thumbs up for the sex scenes, especially the phonetic conflations between, let's say, a woman's painful cries from winds whipping wet clothes against her skin and the yelpin' and meowin' of some she rompin' in the sack with a man, any man. But for that, you can just switch to channel 35 late at night, flog yourself with a sweaty pair of socks, and save yourself a nickel.

Also reviewed in:
NEW YORK TIMES, 6/10/94, p. C21, Stephen Holden
VARIETY, 6/14/93, p. 58, David Stratton
VARIETY, 10/25/93, p. 83, Leonard Klady

JASON'S LYRIC

A Gramercy Pictures and Jackson/McHenry Company release in association with Propaganda Films. *Executive Producer:* Suzanne Broderick and Clarance Avant. *Producer:* Doug McHenry and George Jackson. *Director:* Doug McHenry. *Screenplay:* Bobby Smith, Jr. *Director of Photography:* Francis Kenny. *Editor:* Andrew Mondshein. *Music:* Afrika and Matt Noble. *Music Editor:* Andrew Silver. *Sound:* David Yaffe and (music) Tim Boyle. *Sound Editor:* David McMoyler. *Casting:* Jaki Brown-Karman and Kimberly Hardin. *Production Designer:* Simon Dobbin. *Art Director:* David Lazan. Set Decorator: Tessa Posnansky. *Set Dresser:* Charles Scaife. *Special Effects:* Bob Williams. *Costumes:* Craig Anthony. *Make-up:* Judy Murdock. *Special Effects Make-up:* Phillip Nichols and Melissa Nichols. *Stunt Coordinator:* Eddie Smith. *Running time:* 119 minutes. *MPAA Rating:* R.

CAST: Allen Payne (Jason Alexander); Jada Pinkett (Lyric Greer); Forest Whitaker (Maddog); Bokeem Woodbine (Joshua Alexander); Suzzanne Douglas (Gloria Alexander); Treach (Alonzo); Eddie Griffin (Rat); Lahmard Tate (Ron); Lisa Carson (Marti); Clarence Whitmore (Elmo); Asheamu Earl Randle (Teddy); Rushion McDonald (Fast Freddy); Bebe Drake (Ms. Murphy); Kenneth Randle (Leroy); Wayne DeHart (Street Preacher); Sean Hutchinson (Jason, 11 years old); Burleigh Moore (Joshua, 8 years old); Olivia Gatewood (Carjack Victim); Ronald Lee (Jelly); Ambrosio Guerra (Latin Man); Michon Benson (Black Girl); Erma DeMart (Erma); Curtis Von Burrell (Darryl); Jaye Delai Robinson (Clown); Suzanne Mari (Lola); Dwain Woodfork (Bus Driver); Avery Dale Goodman (Jazz Player); Sandra Denton (Sandy); Bill Travis (B.T.); The Mad Hatter (Himself); Big Black (Herself).

LOS ANGELES TIMES, 9/28/94, Calendar/p. 6, Peter Rainer

"Jason's Lyric" is a terribly earnest melodrama with king-size ambitions. Set in the inner cities of Houston, it bulges with biblical pretension.

Joshua (Bokeem Woodbine) and Jason (Allen Payne) are the Cain and Abel of the piece. We first see them in flashback as two carefree lads romping in the fields with their doting dad (Forest Whitaker). But that was before he was shattered and deranged by Vietnam. In an in-your-face sequence that has more power than anything else in the movie, the father breaks into the family home and attacks his wife (Suzzanne Douglas) and is then shot by one of his young sons.

The memories and guilt surrounding this event have gnarled the boys' lives. Joshua has spent time in prison; Jason, while seemingly hard-working and law-abiding, is plagued by nightmares.

Director Doug McHenry and screenwriter Bobby Smith Jr. frame the story as a redemptive fantasy. Jason, who turns down an out-of-town job promotion because it would leave his mother living alone with Josh, finds his dream woman in the form of Lyric (Jada Pinkett), who works in a soul food restaurant and plays extremely hard-to-get. She has seen too many boyfriends gunned down—her half-brother ("Naughty by Nature's" Treach) is a local gangsta—and she doesn't want any more pain.

Of course, Jason woos her and wins, and their communions are alternately pastoral (lots of soft-focus, outdoorsy, smell-the-roses stuff) and heavy-duty (graphic couplings that seem inserted to boost the film's commercial temperature). The notion that two good-hearted soul mates could thrive in this jungle is, no doubt, important to the film's polemic. But the lovey-dovey material doesn't have much substance; neither does the criminal sequences involving Josh, who is so perpetually out of control that it's a miracle he's able to make it through a day without getting offed.

The filmmakers attempt to temper the good son/bad son plot by making each boy a variation of the other: Jason is supposed to internalize Josh's rage. But Jason is too bland to sustain the comparison, and Josh doesn't transcend his scary trappings. The film seems overextended and unbelievable both as love story and as urban tragedy. There are a few good scenes, such as the birthday homecoming of a drunken Josh, or the sassy-sincere interplay between Lyric and her co-worker/buddy (Lisa Carson). But most of "Jason's Lyric" tries to force its cooked-up sensitivities on us. Greatness is more hard-won than this.

NEW YORK POST, 9/28/94, p. 34, Thelma Adams

Cain and Abel meet Romeo and Juliet in the Houston Wards.

That's "Jason's Lyric," a corny ghetto romance that occasionally cooks.

Jason (Allen Payne) sells TVs. Joshua (Bokeem Woodbine) pushes dope. Lyric (Jada Pinkett) serves soul food—literally and figuratively.

The brothers' lives are overshadowed by the memory of their father, Maddog (Forest Whitaker), who returned from Vietnam a broken man.

The growing love between Lyric and Jason threatens the tangled sibling bonds fused by their dark secret about the night their father died. Can love break the cycle of violence and substance abuse in the inner city?

Director Doug McHenry, in tandem with producing partner George Jackson ("Krush Groove," "New Jack City" and "House Party 2") , uses Hollywood cliches and conventions to tell a commercial black story that pits good eggs against gangstas, love against despair.

The results are mixed. The awkward-but-attractive Jason makes courtship seem fresh when he follows the slim, pearly toothed Lyric home and riffs, "If you're going to the market, I want to be in the same aisle." But their romantic rendezvous in the bayou couldn't be more Hallmark.

The lovers, dressed in matching peach—she in a whimsical hat—row through a swan-filled pond while butterflies cavort on shore and the afternoon light glows gold.

And yet, when the two make love al fresco, there's a power and intensity to their liaison, Payne and Pinkett have chemistry.

The movie wavers between truth and cliche. In voiceover, Jason utters the clunker, "Memories don't let you forget." But the jaw-jutting tower of anger Josh strikes a humorous chord when he says he's "waiting out the recession" to justify his unemployment.

The script, penned by Bobby Smith Jr., doesn't glamorize violence and alcohol but shows their cyclical nature. Both Maddog and Joshua have vomit-spewing, violent, drink-induced rages.

The underlying pain and anger, the feelings of being cut off from love and the mainstream, are wrenched to the surface.

The universally strong cast has Woodbine soaring as a frightened, angry boy in a man's body, and Payne holding the center as a man straining to reject violence as the only expression of manly courage.

NEWSDAY, 9/28/94, Part II/p. B7, Gene Seymour

Two brothers grow up hard in Houston's predominantly black Third Ward. Jason (Allen Payne) is smart, sensitive, generous. His hobby of building model airplanes bespeaks a thwarted urge to fly away from the inner city. Joshua (Bokeem Woodbine) is confused, volatile, embittered. He's been in and out of jail ever since the boys' father Maddog (Forest Whitaker), an alcoholic Vietnam vet, was killed in a fight with their mother (Suzzanne Douglas).

Jason feels obliged to look after his brother and long-suffering mom. But his resolve wavers when he beholds Lyric (Jada Pinkett), an enchanting young woman who shares Jason's dreams of escape. They fall truly, madly, deeply in love. But Jason can't pull himself away from his family obligations—especially when Joshua seems headed for the biggest trouble of his life.

As the above indicates, the familiar, inexorable elements of the ghetto tragedy genre are much in evidence in this directoral debut by Doug McHenry, who, along with co-producer George Jackson, helped jump-start the revival of African-American commercial film with, "Krush Groove" and "New Jack City." With these elements, McHenry and screenwriter Bobby Smith Jr. have mixed in the broad-brush passions of the young-adult street romance (Think "West Side Story," sort of), seasoned with lushly erotic love scenes that, according to published reports, nearly slapped the movie with the dreaded "NC-17" rating.

But Payne and Pinkett's lubricous clinches aren't the only thing that make "Jason's Lyric" more absorbing and less predictable than one would expect. Smith's screenplay carries a sweet, deftly handled sense of airborne imagery rarely attempted in commercial movies. The "rainmaker" sequence, with the biplane showering Maddog and his young sons, is redolent of the sweeping technicolor melodramas of the late '50s and early '60s.

There's also a gallery of lively supporting characters like Marti (Lisa Carson), Lyric's gaudily coiffed friend, whom Carson brings to life with warm insight and admirable restraint. And comedian Eddie Griffin sets off ticklish anticipation whenever he appears as one of Joshua'a corner buddies. Indeed, the emotions of "Jason's Lyric" are orchestrated to such a pitch that, at times, logic tends to be drowned out. Most in the audience will wonder, after a while, where the cops are, especially after a bloody bank robbery that accelerates events to their inevitable denouement.

Loose ends and all, however, there's something about "Jason's Lyric" that makes you stay with it, rooting for the appealing Payne and Pinkett to chase their dreams. The film braces the customary despair of the "'hood" subgenre with the notion that True Love Conquers All. It's a risky mix that McHenry and company just barely pull off without lapsing into bathos, thanks largely to their tough-minded energy.

SIGHT AND SOUND, 9/95, p. 53, Nick James

Houston, Texas. Jason Alexander sells television sets: his younger brother, Joshua, is fresh out of the State Penitentiary. Jason is troubled by nightmares from his childhood when his father Maddog—a once-magical figure, crazed and crippled by army service in Vietnam—was shot dead after breaking into the family home. Joshua, too young to remember his father's better days, suppresses his memory of the death with booze. His wilful criminality soon causes the boys' mother, Gloria, pain and anxiety and Jason refuses promotion to another store because he feels his brother needs minding. A self-possessed young woman, Lyric, visits the television shop and gently rebuffs Jason's interest. They meet again at the restaurant where she works and he follows her home, winning the promise of a date. Their relationship blossoms. Lyric tells Jason her dream is to board a bus and get away from the ghetto.

Lyric's brother Alonzo, a local gang boss, recruits Joshua for a bank robbery. Wise to their plans, Lyric warns Jason who confronts Joshua on the morning of the crime. Joshua leaves his gun with his brother, but then blunders late into the robbery, causing the alarm to be set off. When Joshua arrives home bleeding from Alonzo's punishment, Jason swears revenge. He waits until Alonzo is alone and beats him up. He then keeps an appointment to escape the ghetto with Lyric, confesses what he's done and explains his bond with his brother: it was Jason who accidentally shot Maddog after wrestling the gun away from Joshua. Stricken with renewed grief, Jason returns to his mother. Joshua shoots his way into Alonzo's house, but Alonzo is elsewhere. Finding Lyric upstairs, Joshua holds her hostage. When Jason arrives, Joshua's gun goes off, accidentally wounding Lyric. As Jason carries her out to an ambulance, Joshua shoots himself. Later, Jason and a recovered Lyric make their getaway.

An uneven patchwork of Greek tragedy, melodrama, parable and crime thriller, *Jason's Lyric* goes for broad strokes and big emotions that remain indistinct nevertheless. Certainly there is a big love to celebrate between the protagonist Jason and his hard-to-impress paramour Lyric. However, for the rest of the characters it's a mixed diet of anguish, confusion and self-hatred. That the cast are for the most part able to convey this confusion through the grand gestures of a near-epic form is the film's major strength.

Jason's Lyric is built around one moment of trauma that explicitly connects the Vietnam war and African-American ghetto life. The spectre of Forest Whitaker, as the war-damaged Maddog, drunkenly manhandling Gloria before he gets shot by one of his sons—an image which haunts the film throughout—suggests that young black males caught up in violence today are as much victims of a war as Maddog. Yet theirs is a war with invisible enemies. The struggle between Maddog's two sons, the painfully responsible Jason and his disturbed brother Joshua, remains an internalised family matter rather than a reaction to forms of oppression coming from outside the ghetto. Were it not for Lyric's dream of escape, inspired by the Greyhound buses she sees passing in the distance from a ruined railway bridge, Vietnam would be just about the only point of contact with the world outside the ghetto represented in this film. Thus the idea that the ghetto is a state of mind is refuted—it's the place itself that must be escaped at all costs.

This breakaway-or-die theme is reinforced by the film's Dallas setting (showing that a Texan ghetto differs little from one in South Central Los Angeles), and by the yearning quality of its more romantic sequences with their well-chosen segues of aching soul music. Southern countryside is used in strange and sometimes powerful bucolic contrast to the cyclical despair of the Dallas cityscape. The colour-saturated, 60s back-to-nature album cover feel might have been expected for the brief interludes of togetherness between Jason and Lyric. But the pre-war mural decorating the deserted bus depot that Jason takes Lyric to as a treat to seal their relationship is used more ironically: there on the wall is Lyric's dream personified by beaming crowds of satisfied Greyhound customers, and nearly every face is white.

A more unsettling image, though, occurs near the beginning when we see a healthy, pre-Vietnam Maddog hugging his boys amid a dazzling carpet of wild flowers. A crop-spraying aircraft swoops down and, to their delight, completely douses them. For quite some time the audience is left wondering if the family are somehow addicted to DDT before we learn that the local farmer encouraged wild flowers by spraying them with water. Doug McHenry (producer of *New Jack City* and director of *House Party II*) is engagingly fond of such sweeping gestures of surprise, so even if the constant switching of tone between romantic bliss, ancient sorrows and reactive aggression does become irritating after a while, it ensures that the confusion expressed by the characters is physically felt by the audience.

VILLAGE VOICE, 10/4/94, p. 62, Beth Coleman

The outer wards of Houston run the same inner wars as Compton, Bushwick, Watts, any place where black communities have been reduced to drive-thru soul food and guns. Jason (Allen Payne) picks up his younger brother Joshua (Bokeem Woodbine) from prison in the honorably earned pickup truck (hard-top removable for the cool ride with the honeys) ready to recommence their particular game of responsible Abel minding the shiftless Cain.

Jason's Lyric works that parable along with the more American myths of ghetto life and Vietnam. Forest Whitaker appears as Maddog, the good father who lost his leg and, in effect, his life in the war. He comes back as the original madness in the boys' lives by which the sins of the father are endlessly visited on the sons.

Mom (Suzzanne Douglas) is a bulwark of black fashions—love those Afro puffs—and black female suffering—the figure of emotional blackmail that keeps Jason in the trenches and Josh, like dad, coming back home. But the drama, what a surprise, is between the men. (Lyric, played by Jada Pinkett, is the love interest, a role as corny and wishful as a Mariah Carey video.

McHenry makes this psychological drama a subgenre of Gangsta, with the diffusive results of trying to get everything in there from Rosebud to *Apocalypse Now* and a happy ending to boot. You walk away with the residue of dreams gone bad like those proverbial raisins in the sun and more nigga realness—which, of course, is not real anywhere except for on the screen.

Also reviewed in:
NEW YORK TIMES, 9/28/94, p. C14, Caryn James
VARIETY, 9/19-25/94, p. 81, Deborah Young
WASHINGTON POST, 9/28/94, p. C1, Hal Hinson

JIMMY HOLLYWOOD

A Paramount Pictures release of a Baltimore Pictures production. *Executive Producer:* Peter Giuliano. *Producer:* Mark Johnson and Barry Levinson. *Director:* Barry Levinson. *Screenplay:* Barry Levinson. *Director of Photography:* Peter Sova. *Editor:* Jay Rabinowitz. *Music:* Robbie Robertson. *Sound:* Steve Cantamessa and (music) Pat McCarthy. *Sound Editor:* Marc Fishman. *Casting:* Louis Di Giaimo. *Production Designer:* Linda DeScenna. *Set Decorator:* Ric McElvin. *Special Effects:* John E. Gray. *Visual Effects:* John Mesa.

Costumes: Kirsten Everberg. *Make-up:* Cheri Minns. *Make-up (Joe Pesci):* James Sarzotti. *Stunt Coordinator:* Billy Lucas. *Running time:* 110 minutes. *MPAA Rating:* R.

CAST: Joe Pesci (Jimmy Alto); Christian Slater (William); Victoria Abril (Lorraine); Jason Beghe (Detective); John Cothran, Jr. (Detective); Hal Fishman (Anchorperson); Jerry Dunphy (Anchorperson); Andrea Kutyas (Anchorperson); Robert LaSardo (ATM Robber); Richard Kind (Angry Driver); Marcus Giamatti (BMW Preppy); Ralph Tabakin (Fan in Hospital); Blanche Rubin (Autograph Woman); Lopez (Spanish Fan); Cynthia Steele (Waitress in Coffee Shop); Helen Brown (Elderly Woman in Deli); James Pickens, Jr. (Cook); Lou Cutell (Meyerhoff); Tom Rosales, Jr. (Tough Guy); Chuck Zito (Tough Guy); Earl Billings (Police Captain); Sterling Farris, Jr. (Drug Dealer); Chris Stacy (Car Radio Thief); Kathy M. Hartsell (Beautician); Joe Kurodo (Festiva Driver); Rob Weiss (Rob Weiss); Chad McQueen (Auditon Partner); Robbi Chong (Casting Secretary); Jodie Markell (Casting Assistant); Adrian Ricard (Receptionist); Jill Holden (Receptionist in Life Story); Barry Levinson (Director of Life Story); Leslie Darwin (Screaming Lady).

FILMS IN REVIEW, 7-8/94, p. 55, Andy Pawelczak

Jimmy Hollywood tries hard to be an apocalyptic vision of Hollywood à la *The Day of The Locust*, but the effort is all too visible. In a big chase scene I couldn't help squinting at the Joe Pesci character to confirm that the scene was done by a stand in—Pesci seems much too tired in this somnolent movie to sprint across a mall as he ostensibly does in this scene. Barry Levinson, who wrote and directed the film, has made another movie, like his *Tin Men*, about a lower middle class dreamer in a mid-life crisis; but time is catching up with him and he can't hide the sour, disappointed feeling that clings to the film like L.A. smog.

When we first see Jimmy Alto, a refugee from a job in the east as an aluminum siding salesman, he's reciting the names of the stars emblazoned on the pavement of Hollywood Boulevard. Dressed in loose short pants and sporting long blond hair, he looks vaguely, and alarmingly, like Brando in drag in *The Missouri Breaks*. Jimmy is an unemployed aspiring actor who has spent his girlfriend's savings on a bus bench sign that promotes him as an "actor extraordinaire." He now spends his time lounging around the cracked pool in his run-down apartment complex waiting for the phone to ring announcing his big break. But when his girlfriend gets mugged and his car radio stolen, something in the already on-the-edge Jimmy snaps, and he embarks on a second career as a vigilante. He and his pal William (Christian Slater) stalk the streets of L.A. armed with a video camera and a gun loaded with blanks, catching bad guys in the act and leaving them tied up at the door of the police station with a video tape of their criminal activities and a message from the half visible Jimmy.

The film's central comic conceit has Jimmy getting more and more obsessed with his role as Jericho, the vigilante leader—it's his role of a lifetime, and he wants to play it to the hilt. He tells William that, like a method actor, he has to reinvent himself to really be Jericho, and by the end he's a kind of Don Quixote of Lala Land. Levinson pours on the Hollywood one liners, but once we get the main joke we just wait for the movie to arrive at its preordained absurdist conclusion.

As Jimmy, Pesci does his New York motor mouth number leavened with some wistfulness—the film wants us to see Jimmy, as he eventually sees himself, as the little man with a tough guy facade and the soul of a poet, who makes one last desperate stab at greatness. Victoria Abril is exotic looking and convincing as Jimmy's devoted, slightly dotty girlfriend, though she's the only character with even a shred of rationality. Christian Slater, with a glazed look on his face and an American flag bandanna on his head, doesn't have much to do as Jimmy's dim bulb pal who's so dumb that he names the make believe vigilante gang the SOS after David O. Selznick, producer of the revered *Gone With the Wind* as Jimmy points out, he has confused Selznick with Steven Spielberg. A shot of the three principals in sunglasses, animatedly discussing their plight, gives a sense of how loony the picture could have been if Levinson hadn't waylaid it with a pretentious, theme mongering plot—they're three strangers in a strange land, members of a different species from the rest of us.

Levinson mixes several genres—the vigilante movie, film noir, the Hollywood movie—but the seams show and the film ends up feeling like a too-clever-for-its-own-good academic exercise in pastiche. It's characteristic of the picture's labyrinthine references to other movies that its dominant influence is Scorsese's *Taxi Driver*, a film in which Pesci doesn't appear but with whose director he's indissolubly associated. As Jimmy drives around the city complaining, like Travis Bickle, of the scum who have taken over his beloved Hollywood, Levinson echoes Scorsese with shots through the windshield of a neon underworld populated by whores, freaks and drug dealers. And the film's ironic, mock happy ending is lifted right from Scorsese's *The King of Comedy* though without that film's sense of the deep freeze effect of popular culture. Levinson has a few surprises for us before this, but the characters' quirky humanity is irretrievably lost once the script turns them into sentimental emblematic figures in a post-modernist parable about celebrity and the movies and the plight of the forgotten little guy in Clinton's America. *Jimmy Hollywood* starts out with big ambitions, but by the end it's a melancholy record of missed opportunities—*The Day of The Med Fly* rather than *The Day of The Locust*.

LOS ANGELES TIMES, 3/30/94, Calendar/p. 1, Kenneth Turan

Directors offering tribute to the acting profession has become a mini-trend lately. and why not: Where would these auteurs be if the performers weren't there for them? However, in an ironic but inevitable twist, in each case the acting process and lifestyle are filtered through that director's distinctly personal lens.

So while writer-director James L. Brooks' "I'll Do Anything" stressed the wildly neurotic comic insecurity of the profession. Abel Ferrara's "Dangerous Games" (scripted by Nicholas St. John) was a lacerating look at its darker psychological corners. And writer-director Barry Levinson's "Jimmy Hollywood" turns out to be just the kind of flimsy doodle of a movie, amusing but small in scale, you might expect from the director of "Diner" and "Tin Men."

What "Jimmy Hollywood" isn't reminiscent of is the elaborate films Levinson has done most recently, big-ticket items like "Bugsy" and "Toys." with stars like Warren Beatty and Robin Williams attached. While Levinson tends to go too far in the opposite direction here, often ending up with minimal emotional effects, "Jimmy Hollywood" does have its shambling pleasures, starting with Joe Pesci in the title role.

Given the name Jimmy Alto, but known to pals back in New Jersey as Jimmy Hollywood because of his passion for the movies, he is one of those self-absorbed "Day of the Locust"-type characters who hover around the edges of the industry in sunglasses, dyed-blond hair and loud tropical shirts waiting for that one break.

Though success as an actor has easily eluded him (he seems, in fact, never to have actually gotten a part), Jimmy retains full confidence that he knows all the angles and all the answers. Didn't he blow Andy Griffith off the screen in a reading, only to lose the role because of "politics"? And hasn't he just made the shrewd career move of investing in an ad on a bus bench at a particularly high-profile corner of Sunset Boulevard. Like the Energizer Rabbit, Jimmy never ever runs out of steam.

And since the two people in Jimmy's life—his hairdresser girlfriend Lorraine de la Pena (Spanish actress Victoria Abril in her American debut) and his best friend William (Christian Slater), a mentally challenged Hollywood Boulevard street urchin, accept Jimmy the way he is, things probably would have gone on this way forever. Except for the burglary.

One unfortunate night Jimmy's car gets broken into and his radio stolen. Vowing revenge, Jimmy and William stake out the neighborhood with a video camera. One amusingly implausible turn of events leads rapidly to another and suddenly these two find themselves mistaken both by the media and the police for a powerful vigilante organization dedicated to retaking the streets of Hollywood for decent folk.

But before he is anything else, Jimmy is an actor, and the best parts of "Jimmy Hollywood" (curiously reminiscent of "General Della Rovere," the Italian classic starring Vittorio De Sica as a petty criminal whose life changes when he impersonates a resistance leader) involve the way this man embraces vigilante leadership as the role of his life, enabling him to use all the "deep acting stuff" he's been working on for years.

Considerable care has been lavished on Pcsci's character, on detailing all the foibles of a man who is so endearingly self-deluded his darkest threat is "you're out of the Oscar speech." Pesci, himself an Oscar winner for "GoodFellas," has a fine time with the part, commanding the screen and almost hypnotizing you with his brash patter.

One of the problems with "Jimmy Hollywood," paradoxically, is that there is too much of Jimmy in it and too little of anything else. Writer-director Levinson appears to have been mesmerized by his title character, to the point where Victoria Abril and especially Christian Slater have had to make do with undernourished roles.

The film's plot has related problems, first taking its time to kick in and grandly bypassing plausibility when it does. Still, Jimmy Hollywood is such a determined character that the cockeyed fable he's lent his name and story to manages to carry you along even as it gets further and further out of hand. Maybe the guy can act after all.

NEW YORK, 4/4/94, p. 77, John Powers

With his vacuum-cleaner whine and incorrigible mugging, Joe Pesci is nobody's idea of a movie star. But he's every producer's idea of a reliable actor: He does exactly the same thing every time. In his new movie *Jimmy Hollywood*, he's cast as an East Coast blowhard who lives in L.A. It's another Pesci-out-of-water comedy.

Wearing a long, blond wig even sillier than his salmon-colored job in *JFK*, he plays Jimmy Alto, a wannabe actor who has memorized all the stars on the Walk of Fame and come to Hollywood in pursuit of his dream. His days are spent hanging out with his pal William, an addlepated drifter played with low-key charm by Christian Slater, and waiting in vain for the phone to ring.

When not boasting bitterly about his failed auditions ("I blew Andy Griffith off the screen"), Jimmy is railing against the crooks who besmirch Hollywood's legendary streets. After his car radio is stolen, he forms an imaginary vigilante group called the SOS ("Save Our Streets"), and he and William start catching robbers and drug dealers, leaving them tied up for the cops. In the process, Jimmy adopts the persona of "Jericho," the group's mysterious leader, who talks to the public in a series of videotaped communiqués broadcast on local TV. It's the acting role of a lifetime, and Jimmy becomes a minor folk hero—a kind of dopey Angeleno Curtis Sliwa. His, anger has been turned into street theater.

Jimmy Hollywood was written and directed by Barry Levinson, who says it's partly based on his own experiences as a young actor living in an apartment off Hollywood Boulevard. That was back in 1970, which may explain the heavy scent of mildew that saturates this whole project. Not only is Pesci far too gamy to play a naive dreamer like Jimmy—with his sagging chin and peevish mouth, he'd be better cast as his character's father—but the movie's perceptions are a good two decades out of date. While Levinson keeps pointing out the abyss that separates Jimmy's idealized Hollywood from the guttersnipe reality of its streets, we keep wondering how this could be news to anyone. Didn't Jimmy (or, for that matter, Barry) ever turn on the tube? They could have learned all they needed to know about Hollywood Boulevard from those noted urban theorists Starsky and Hutch.

In the dozen years since he made *Diner*, Levinson has lost touch with what he used to know—the raggedy give-and-take of everyday life. Looking at life from out a limousine window, he now does sharper work on nakedly commercial star vehicles like *Rain Man* or *Bugsy* than he does on such "personal" films as *Avalon* or *Toys*, which bring out his woolly self-importance. In *Jimmy Hollywood*, he wants to make a big statement about urban anger, but his portraits of Jimmy Alto and Hollywood street life aren't precise enough even to be wrong. The movie's only spark comes from the contrast between Jimmy's red-hot bluster and the amnesiac cool of William, who's forever dredging up childhood memories of watching *The Mummy*. Levinson has always had a knack for capturing camaraderie, and whenever this duo sits by the swimming pool, their patter drifting in goofy circles, the movie briefly loses its hammering obviousness and achieves the pleasantly brain-dead drollery of beach-blanket Beckett.

Levinson's too good a liberal to crank out a movie like *Death Wish*; yet he's too attracted by the idea of vigilante justice to give it up altogether. His ambivalence makes *Jimmy Hollywood* a peculiar hodgepodge, a feel-good version of *Falling Down* that can't decide how serious it's being. Even as Jimmy's transformation into Jericho is played as a broad comic fantasy, Peter Sova's cinematography gives Hollywood the grim, dark, realistic look suitable to streets filled with graffiti and hookers, crack addicts and thieves.

Levinson's notion of Jimmy is afflicted with the same uncertainty. In one scene, he's a street-smart wiseacre, braying out one-liners in pure New Jersey dialect; in the next, he's a deluded "little man," dreaming his big, sad dreams and repeatedly watching a nostalgic documentary about Hollywood's Golden Age. As he sinks ever deeper into his fantasy of the heroic Jericho, the movie loses its moorings. Are we supposed to admire Jimmy's absurd chutzpa or decide that his anger has left him unhinged? Levinson's made a career of fudging such bottom-line questions, and just as he did in *Good Morning, Vietnam,* he leaves everything up to his star. Pesci works like a galley slave to keep *Jimmy Hollywood* afloat—he speaks very loudly and carries a big shtick—but his performance is so hectoring that theater owners may start selling blindfolds and earplugs. No doubt sitcom producers are already swimming around him in circles.

NEW YORK POST, 3/30/94, p. 32, Michael Medved

In his new movie, "Jimmy Hollywood," writer-director Barry Levinson wages war against himself. He inexplicably employs a gritty, hard-hitting, cinema verite style that fatally conflicts with his fanciful, feel-good plot about the triumph of the little guy.

After working hard to establish realistic down-and-out characters, he then places them in situations so contrived and preposterous that you'll want to throw your popcorn at the screen.

The first part of the movie plays like "I'll Do Anything" meets "Midnight Cowboy," with a few touches from "Of Mice and Men" thrown in for good measure.

Joe Pesci plays Jimmy Alto, a loser in bleached hair and Bermuda shorts who can't even hold a job as a waiter at a Hollywood Boulevard greasy spoon.

He talks obsessively of his acting career but has never come closer to professional success than once reading for a small part on "Matlock." The only human being on the planet who believes in his prospects for stardom is William (Christian Slater), a sweet-but-slow-witted street person who becomes Jimmy's confidante and sidekick.

Together, they roam the grimy streets of the once-glamorous movie capital while Jimmy's hairdresser girlfriend (played by Victoria Abril, Spanish star of "High Heels" and "Tie Me Up! Tie Me Down!," in her American debut) unselfishly pays the bills,

In the first third of the picture, Levinson evokes some compassion for these eccentric lost souls, but then disastrously veers off into tall tales about vigilantism and media manipulation.

After Jimmy succeeds in capturing the punk who ripped off the radio from his battered used car, he decides he's discovered the role of a lifetime. He reinvents himself as "Jericho," the leader of a non-existent army of anti-crime avengers called "S.O.S." for "Save Our Streets."

Through a series of daring deeds and videotapes to the police in which he appears only in profile, Jericho becomes a media sensation and cult hero.

The main problem with all this is the outrageous ease with which Jimmy/Jericho apprehends a series of big-time drug dealers and gang leaders, armed only with a stage pistol that fires blanks.

The movie offers no real sense of the risks in the dangerous game he plays, or any reason to believe in his overnight success in cleaning up Hollywood's mean streets.

Pesci, of course, could play this sort of role in his sleep, and that's just about what he does here—offering a performance with no surprises and no depth.

Slater is so uncharacteristically understated that he's all but invisible on screen—a vague blur that seems unhappily reminiscent of Yogi Bear's cartoon sidekick, Boo Boo. Abril is fiery and effective in her few scenes, but the script gives no hint at all of what she sees in Jimmy.

The only kind word one can offer on "Jimmy Hollywood" is that it represents at least a small step up from Levinson's appallingly unwatchable 1992 Robin Williams fiasco, "Toys."

After two such films in a row, it may be time to hope that this superbly accomplished filmmaker (of "Diner," "Avalon" "Good Morning, Vietnam," "Rain Man," "Bugsy," and other impressive films) will return to form and stay away from social-comment comedy-fantasies that remain both incoherent and painfully unfunny.

NEWSDAY, 3/30/94, Part II/p. B3, Jack Mathews

In the last three years, there has been a rash of introspective Hollywood movies, or at least of films taking the filmmaking process as their subject, and both the quality and ambitions of these pictures have been in rapid descent

Robert Altman's "The Player," a masterfully cynical look at the modern studio system, kicked off the trend, followed by Barry Primus' modestly clever "Mistress," about some has-been filmmaker's attempts to round up money for a low-budget picture. Then came "Dangerous Game," Abel Ferrara's egocentric psychodrama about a screwed-up director, and "I'll Do Anything," James L. Brooks' whopping misfire about an actor in conflict over his career and his relationship with his young daughter.

Now, Barry Levinson "weighs in" with "Jimmy Hollywood," a pittance of a comedy-drama starring Joe Pesci as a New Jersey wretch obsessed with making it as an actor in Hollywood, Instead, he becomes the inadvertent star of a series of vigilante videos, produced on the streets by himself and his brain-damaged pal, William (Christian Slater), and shown almost nightly on the local TV news.

Levinson's interest with this cockeyed story is in showing the contrast between the dreams of those who come seeking fame in Hollywood, and the almost Third World conditions they live under there. The joke is that Jimmy gets his big break from the burglar who steals his car radio and turns him into a vigilante, and that crime, whichever side of the law you're on, is an easier avenue to stardom than casting calls.

To anyone who has driven the side streets of Hollywood, past the rundown apartments, street walkers and vagrants just a block from the Walk of Stars, the milieu is as real as it is ironic. But the irony doesn't sustain a full-length feature, and the characters never come alive.

Pesci, wearing a ridiculous blond wig, is as addled and near-dangerous as Robert De Niro's Rupert Pupkin in "King of Comedy," but he plays it like "My Cousin Vinny in Hollywood." He's a lovable loser, a pillar of self-deception who steals his girlfriend's savings to promote himself on a Beverly Hills bus bench.

The force of Pesci's personality reduces his co-stars Slater and Victoria Abril to animated props, and he overwhelms Levinson's slight dramatic premise. It is fun watching this wiseguy chew scenery in a town that manufactures the stuff by the (box office) gross, but you've got a tough sale when your biggest mistake is also your only asset.

NEWSWEEK, 4/11/94, p. 74, David Ansen

Jimmy Alto (Joe Pesci) is a manic middle-aged runt with dyed blond hair and an obsessive ambition to be a Hollywood actor. A former aluminum-siding salesman from New Jersey, he's got the actor's jargon down pat, but his biggest claim to fame is the ad he's paid for on a bus bench: JIMMY ALTO—ACTOR EXTRAORDINAIRE. If you saw this guy approaching you on Hollywood Boulevard, where, lacking work, he hangs out most days with his loyal, simple-minded pal William (Christian Slater), you'd duck, put off by his tacky clothes, his aggressive self-promotion, the pungent whiff of cocky desperation.

It takes some daring for Barry Levinson to build his quirky comic drama "Jimmy Hollywood" around such a loser. He's a funny guy, but he's a pest, and Levinson presents him with an affectionate ambivalence that keeps the viewer slightly off balance. Is he a hero or a schmuck? The director of "Rain Man" and "Good Morning, Vietnam" is back in the small, low-budget, personal mode of "Diner" and "Tin Men," but those movies were about close, cohesive communities. "Jimmy Hollywood" is set in a deracinated dreamland, a Hollywood gone sour. The legendary boulevard is awash in crime and drugs; it's a place where nobody really belongs and all relationships are tenuous. Jimmy doesn't even know William's last name. And he seems to have nothing in common with the Spanish woman he lives with—the volatile but sensible Lorraine (Victoria Abril)—except her desire to be a hairdresser to the stars.

The ironic twist is the backhanded way Jimmy falls into fame. Enraged by a thief who's broken into his car, he and William apprehend the felon, videotape the capture and dump the guy on the police-station steps. Through a fanciful turn of events, the cops think a well-organized vigilante organization is at work. Jimmy has found his role: as the shadowy figure Jericho, whose videotape pronouncements against street crime make him a media legend. It's one of the better jokes of the movie that as Jimmy/Jericho becomes a vigilante hero, it's only his videotape performances he really cares about ("What do you think of the work?" he grills Lorraine. "I thought there was vulnerability.") It's the acting exercise, not the social cause, that really excites him.

Both a character study of a colorful failure and an elegy on the rotted dream of Hollywood glory, Levinson's atmospheric movie both fascinates and frustrates. The lack of connection between the characters may be the director's point, but it makes for dramatic sketchiness. It's essentially a solo piece, and good as Pesci is (as all the actors are) you begin to weary of Jimmy Alto's hypersolipsism. The vigilante conceit strains credulity, and the climax in the empty expanse of a once grand movie palace is portentously protracted. Yet you keep rooting for "Jimmy Hollywood," 'because it has the bittersweet, unexpected flavors of a personal vision. It may not be Hollywood's idea of a socko entertainment, but, unlike many a hit, it follows you home.

VILLAGE VOICE, 4/12/94, p. 60, Lisa Kennedy

Barry Levinson's latest, *Jimmy Hollywood*, with Joel Schumacher's *Falling Down* on a double bill—now that's a rich pairing. Each has, after all, a central character that falls into vigilantism, and each depicts a debilitated Los Angeles, an L.A. that immediately reminds us that certain visions of the City of Angels are completely repressed by its homegrown industry (except, of course, in the case of L.A.'s neoreality, 'n-the-'hood fare).

Nope, not a bad bill at all: last year's L.A.-in-crisis oddity meets this year's at a revival house near you. And, given Hollywood's stunning conventionality, oddity is never a bad word. Indeed, it often suggests the filmmaker was trying to tell us a more ambitious tale. In *Falling Down*, Schumacher tried and, depending on your identification threshold, did or didn't fail to fathom a kind of explosive white male rage. In the end, most audiences couldn't seem to quash their own desire to embrace the hyperfrustrated, hyperentitled vigilante. Levinson stays with what he knows—living and breathing flicks in a real and imagined burg—and has a sweeter, if still vaguely confounding, movie for his effort.

Making things much easier from the get-go, however, is the fact that Levinson's eponymous hero is a different sort of nut: a goofball. Joe Pesci is Jimmy Alto is Jimmy Hollywood, an actor-in-waiting (by the peeling pool, at the diner, near the phone), whose sense of his town has been greatly impaired by his love of the Hollywood of yore. His best buddy, and audience of one, is William (underplayed winningly by Christian Slater), a strung-out-sans-drugs video savant. Completing this triangle is Victoria Abril as Lorraine, Jimmy's hairdresser girlfriend. With a hint of his own movieland nostalgia, Levinson gives this absolute girlfriend great presence of mind; she is the only person with any sense in the film.

Jimmy's slide into a soft, techie vigilantism begins when he and William capture—on video and in reel life—a thief, whom they promptly deliver to a precinct house trussed with the Hi-8 recording. Without much ado, or thought, Jimmy creates and then latches on to "his greatest role" ever, à la Tanya and the SLA, as the SOS (Save Our Streets) spokesman. Needless to say, Jimmy and William get deeper and deeper until they're faced with an impossible run-in with the LAPD. What makes *Jimmy Hollywood* so endearing, finally, is its desire to address the relationship between the impossible (life) and the fantastic (movies). If Levinson doesn't quite pull off the *Sullivan's Travels* of our generation it might be that Hollywood itself has made Sturges's resolution impossible. No longer is the great satisfaction of entertaining the masses enough. Indeed, *Hollywood*'s finale is at once happy and hollow, a sign less of Levinson's limits (he's pretty smart) than of a time where directors are both victims and perps in the problems of dire reality and its funhouse images.

Also reviewed in:
NEW REPUBLIC, 5/2/94, p. 28, Stanley Kauffmann
NEW YORK TIMES, 3/30/94, p. C15, Janet Maslin
NEW YORKER, 4/4/94, p. 97, Anthony Lane
VARIETY, 3/28-4/3/94, p. 68, Todd McCarthy
WASHINGTON POST, 3/30/94, p. B1, Desson Howe
WASHINGTON POST, 4/1/94, Weekend/p. 38, Joe Brown

JUNIOR

A Universal Pictures release of a Northern Lights production. *Executive Producer:* Joe Medjuck, Daniel Goldberg and Beverly J. Camhe. *Producer:* Ivan Reitman. *Director:* Ivan

Reitman. *Screenplay:* Kevin Wade and Chris Conrad. *Director of Photography:* Adam Greenberg. *Editor:* Sheldon Kahn and Wendy Greene Bricmont. *Music:* James Newton Howard. *Music Editor:* Jim Weidman. *Choreographer:* Marguerite Derricks. *Sound:* Gene Cantamessa and (music) Shawn Murphy. *Casting:* Michael Chinich and Alan Berger. *Production Designer:* Stephen Lineweaver. *Art Director:* Gary Wissner. *Set Designer:* Barry Chusid and Dawn Snyder. *Set Decorator:* Clay A. Griffith. *Set Dresser:* Greg Wilkinson, John H. Maxwell, Edward J. McCarthy III, Brana Rosenfeld, and Elizabeth Ragagli. *Special Effects:* David M. Blitstein. *Costumes:* Albert Wolsky. *Make-up (Arnold Schwarzenegger):* Joseph W. McKinney. *Make-up (Danny DeVito):* Ve Neill. *Make-up (Emma Thompson):* Valli O'Reilly. *Stunt Coordinator:* Joel Kramer. *Running time*: 110 minutes. *MPAA Rating*: PG-13.

CAST: Arnold Schwarzenegger (Dr. Alexander Hesse); Danny DeVito (Dr. Larry Arbogast); Emma Thompson (Dr. Diana Reddin); Frank Langella (Noah Banes); Pamela Reed (Angela); Judy Collins (Naomi); James Eckhouse (Ned Sneller); Aida Turturro (Louise); Welker White (Jenny); Megan Cavanagh (Willow); Merle Kennedy (Samantha); Mindy Seeger (Alice); Christopher Melond (Mr. Lanzarotta); Antoinette Peragine (Mrs. Lanzarotta); Cassandra Wilson (Singer); Ellen McLaughlin (Chairwoman FDA); Stefan Gierasch (Edward Sawyer); Alexander Enberg (Arthur); Judy Ovitz (Stewardess); Kevin West and Ira Newborn (Lyndon Executives); Misa Koprova (Lyndon Receptionist); Jodi Knotts and Michelle Abrams (Waiting Room Women); John Pinette (Clerk); Fred Stoller (Waiter); Kathleen Chalfant and Anna Gunn (Casitas Madres Receptionists); Lisa Summerour and Kristina Hardee (Casitas Madres Exercise Attendants); Leah Teweles (Mrs. Logan); Maggie Han (Lab Assistant); Maggie Han. Charmaine Alicia Mancil (Scanner Guard). Lawrence Tierney and Matt Mulhern (Movers); Lawrence T. Wrentz (Campus Security Guard); Monika Schnarre (Angelic Nurse); Allen Walls (Banquet Waiter); Kevin Sifeuntes (Banquet Valet); Tom Dugan (Lobster Man); Holly Wortell (Lobster Woman); Susan Dills and Maggy Myers Davidson (Campus Gals); Peter Chen (Taxi Driver); Dean Jacobson (Turkel); Mary Gordon Murray (Betty); Julie Vasquez (Ticket Agent). Dayna Winston (Stewardess at Boarding Gate).

LOS ANGELES TIMES, 11/23/94, Calendar/p. 1, Kenneth Turan

Accomplished farceurs specialize in making the ridiculous plausible, and certainly few films can claim to be as unlikely as "Junior. " In cheeky defiance of the laws of nature, it presents us with the spectacle of ultimate male Arnold Schwarzenegger heavy with child. If the French had thought of it first, it might've been called "One Man and a Baby."

"Junior," however, is quintessentially studio American, which means it is as slickly commercial as the audience-pleasing proclivities of director Ivan Reitman ("Ghostbusters," "Dave") can make it. The jokes in the Kevin Wade and Chris Conrad script flow smoothly, and everything is as polished and smooth as a ballroom dance floor.

And in Schwarzenegger, Danny DeVito and Emma Thompson, the film has an expert cast whose comic gifts are always complementary. Schwarzenegger's deadpan delivery, DeVito's insistent miniature swagger and Thompson's practiced slapstick clumsiness play off each other in satisfying three-part harmony.

The result is, of course, effective, but despite the trio's fine efforts "Junior" can't get past lightly amusing, never manages to work up a sustained comic head of steam. It is a farce without staying power, partly because of the traditional way it deals with its central theme.

Initially, however, it is fun to watch these three develop their characters. Schwarzenegger plays the bookish, barely human Dr. Alexander Hesse, a research scientist at San Francisco's Lufkin Biotec Research Center whose motto is "Luck is for the ill-prepared." His partner, gynecologist Dr. Larry Arbogast (DeVito), is frantic, effusive and perpetually exasperated with Hesse, who he sees as having "all the warmth and charm of a wall-eyed pike."

Together, however, these men have developed what they consider a breakthrough drug that prevents miscarriages. But when the FDA refuses to sanction Expectane, Lufkin administrator Noah Banes (Frank Langella) cancels Hesse's grant and gives his lab space to the daft, socially maladroit Dr. Diana Reddin (Thompson), who specializes in freezing eggs.

Hesse is ready to head back to the fatherland, but Arbogast is more stubborn. Why not, he asks his partner, test the drug on yourself, as did Jenner, the discoverer of vaccination, by having a fertilized embryo implanted in your abdomen? "Come claim your place in the pantheon," he cries, and Hesse, unable to resist such eloquence, begins one of the most cockeyed experiments in medical history.

While Schwarzenegger and DeVito improve on the comic timing they began in Reitman's "Twins," Thompson, an Oscar winner for the very different "Howards End," shows she hasn't forgotten the antic comic roots she displayed in 1989's unappreciated "The Tall Guy." And it is always satisfying to see the underutilized Pamela Reed, here cast as Arbogast's pregnant ex-wife.

Given how well these actresses do, it is surprising that one of the things "Junior" stumbles over is how he treats Alex Hesse's character when he does become pregnant.

Simply put, the stiff doctor melts into a compilation of clichéd female behavior, crying at sentimental TV commercials, complaining about having nothing to wear and whining, "Does my body disgust you?" to anyone who will listen.

On one level, helped by Schwarzenegger's performance, this is certainly innocent fun. But if it's no longer acceptable for white folks to don makeup and mimic black behavior, or for males to prance around being clichéd, limp-wristed gays, it is an interesting question why this kind of comedy remains more than acceptable.

To put this in a different perspective, it is helpful to remember back to Dustin Hoffman's deft role in "Tootsie." He, too, wore a dress and came to understand things about the opposite sex he hadn't before, but that film treated him as a most unusual woman, not as a nonstop cliché. "Junior" doesn't have the wit or the vision to try for something like that, and the feeling is inescapable that it would be a stronger film if it had.

NEW STATESMAN & SOCIETY, 12/9/94, p. 34, Jonathan Romney

Junior is what you call a high concept movie: that is, it has one measly idea and milks it for all it's worth. It's a comedy about a man getting pregnant—surely a droll enough conceit to keep us amused for 90 minutes or so—but make that man Arnold Schwarzenegger and you're upping the ante somewhat. Not only do you provide punters with a visual paradox to make the head spin—those biceps, that jaw, that belly!—but you instantly send critics everywhere scurrying off to bash out think pieces about the Crisis of Masculinity. Everybody's happy ... or would be if *Junior* weren't such a dreary piece of work—shoddy, smug and a little late in the day. Late because *True Lies* already proved that there was no fun to be had out of Arnie as a big soft family man; and because *Mrs Doubtfire* said all there was to say about boys being girls with the aid of funny rubber attachments.

The trouble with high concept movies is that they invariably boil down to a single sentence—"What if ... ?"—and so you invariably end up with a single sentence answer. What if a man got pregnant! Why, then he'd start eating pickles, wearing pastel colours and getting all soppy.

Junior reunites Schwarzenegger with Danny DeVito, his partner in *Twins*, as a pair of scientists working on a pregnancy wonder drug, Expectane. When their grant is cut off and a rival project, headed by Emma Thompson, hustled into their lab, they decide to carry on research anyway. Schwarzenegger is injected in the gut with a cocktail of Expectane and eggs from an unknown donor.

The pay-off is a long time coming, but it comes with heavy inevitability. Arnie is pregnant, and grows a huge prosthetic belly. He also starts complaining of sore nipples and a bad back, develops an odd waddling gait, and starts getting testy when DeVito is late home for work. What starts off in effect as a drag act finally becomes one literally, when Arnie has to don a floral smock and a wig and pass himself off as a former East German athlete zapped up on hormones.

It's easy to say why the film falls flat—because the jokes are obvious, lamely executed and telegraphed miles ahead; because Schwarzenegger now takes himself so seriously as a comic turn instead of the rumbling cyborg he should ever have remained; and because director Ivan Reitman has taken too much inspiration from the baby theme, cloaking the whole film in nursery pastels that lull the eye into a queasy languor. But why the central joke itself fails is more of a problem. What seems like a surefire gag, backfires and leaves us feeling curiously uneasy, as if we're being asked to laugh at something we'd really rather not be seeing.

What makes *Mrs Doubtfire* an entertaining charade is that it announces itself from the start as a charade, a variant on the pantomime dame tradition, with a thoughtful bit of spin in the direction of the decline of the nuclear family. *Junior* has no such spin. It has no questions to ask about the structure of the family, about what makes men men and women women or vice versa. Its premise stands or falls entirely on the question that haunts all Schwarzenegger films, whether he's a cyborg, a Cimmerian or a civil servant—the question of his *impossible* body. The idea of his being transformed by prosthetics is from the outset a redundant one, because that excessive frame is already prosthetic. Arnie with a little extra, male or female, isn't remarkable; Arnie with a little less *would* be, and the day he gets to play a hunger striker, we should all sit up and take notice.

In *Mrs Doubtfire* Robin Williams' character proves himself in some ways to be a "better" woman, more maternal than his own ex-wife. But the film wasn't so much about challenging modern ideas of womanhood; rather, in a roundabout, very 1990s-Hollywood gooey liberal way, it was about a guy learning new ways to be a guy. So you want to be a real man! Go and be your granny for a week. Gay themes notwithstanding, I suspect the same may be true, although I haven't seen either, of the drag comedies *The Adventures of Priscilla* and the forthcoming *To Wong Foo*...(Snipes and Swayze in wigs).

Junior seems to be about this too, but only up to a point. On the surface, it's about dry, academic Dr Hesse becoming a complete person, getting in touch with his body and his emotions, learning to lighten up and, you know, love life (the many awestruck glimpses of babies on scanners make this a pro-life film in more senses than one). But at the same time, he' s actually made incomplete—he starts acting irrationally, feeling all manner of physical discomforts, losing his sense of himself as a man. As he says to DeVito, "I feel so humiliated, I feel I've lost control over my body." *Junior* is effectively a horror story, a male nightmare about how being a woman means being debilitated in some way. (See Arnie's look of coy bemusement on the poster—what is it but sheer terror?)

The film's two principal female characters are represented as out of control in different ways. Thompson's Dr Reddin—a surprisingly gamey turn in her briskest Joyce Grenfell mould—is a scatty boffin-buffoon, who invariably has cheese smeared over her face and a 100 roll hanging off her shoe; while Argobast's ex-wife Angela (Pamela Reed) is herself pregnant as a result of an extreme lapse of control (or at least taste) with a member of Aerosmith's entourage. They're both oddly defeminised—Angela because she's played by Reed, who brings to the film a history of asexual-buddy tough cookie cop roles; and Reddin by virtue of being so common-sense and English public school, with her stout-chap jumper and slacks (also, of course an allusion to Katharine Hepburn's typical garb in her screwball comedies). Effectively, Arnie is the *only* woman in the movie—the crowds of fluttery moms-to-be wafting around in neat frocks are simply there as so much flowered wallpaper.

When Dr Reddin learns what's been going on she angrily complains, "You think men don't hold enough cards! You're trying to take this away from us!" The line falls flat; it's a well-meaning bit of tokenism whose implications the film has no intention of following up. In one sense, Arnie does have all the cards—he's so much more than a man that he can also be that much more of a woman. The film can operate on its light, engaging level precisely because we see Arnie as a superbody and not as a person at all. If the film had starred any actor who appeared vaguely human, that actor's body *would* be at issue. By the flip wheeze of featuring Arnie, the film refuses to acknowledge that there are questions to be asked about how men's and women's identities are defined by their bodies. But it's actually that refusal that makes *Junior* rather uncomfortable to watch, as if it were repressing something it didn't want to think about. That something is the fact that, if not for Arnie, it would have to take itself more seriously. It would have to be a David Cronenberg film with gags.

NEW YORK, 12/5/94, p. 110, David Denby

For more than fifteen years, ever since *Pumping Iron* came out, Arnold Schwarzenegger's body has functioned in the world's fancy as a spectacular example of Western technology. The wedged and bulging shape is not only a super-developed male envelope but a veritable free-world payload, right up there with the Abrams M-1 tank, the Mercedes-Benz factory in Stuttgart, and Bob Hope's favorite golf course. *Junior*, the new Ivan Reitman comedy starring Schwarzenegger, makes use of an obvious premise: What if a man were to carry a baby to term? But the obviousness turns into something strange, and strangely moving, for the baby is carried not by any male body but by *the* male body—now 47 years old, and less clearly defined than before, but still massive and alarming in its shifting buttes, clefts, and promontories. The joke is an unsettling one. When quizzed by a lady of his acquaintance on the differences between men and women, Oscar Wilde is alleged to have said, "Madam, I can't conceive." Well, Arnold Schwarzenegger can't either, but in *Junior* he's injected with a cryogenically preserved egg that has been fertilized by his own sperm. The embryo takes hold, and Arnold, after a few months, "shows" in a style rather different from that of his old greased-trapezius days.

In form, *Junior* is just a conventional commercial comedy—director Ivan Reitman can't make anything else—but women all around me were leaning toward the screen, laughing and amazed, so something is going on here. This is the kind of lovably stupid movie that gets to people. The screenplay was written by Chris Conrad and Kevin Wade, and I can't say it shows any great genius. Once you've heard the basic premise, you could probably write most of the jokes yourself (Arnold wears sensible shoes, Arnold eats pickles with his moo goo gai pan, etc.). But in movies, when the word becomes flesh,obvious ideas can be transformed into something else. *Junior* has surprises and little expansions of feeling. When Arnold's stomach swells and jabbering Danny DeVito as his doctor friend shuts up for a second and listens with his stethoscope, the silliness is too weird for simple laughter.

The filmmakers made a number of shrewd strategic choices. The academic setting seems to put Reitman in a gentle mood, just as it did in the early scenes of *Ghostbusters*. Schwarzenegger plays a human-fertility researcher, a dour bachelor repelled by the thought of fatherhood. For once he's supposed to be Austrian; he doesn't fight his accent, and in the early stages of the movie he lets himself go wooden and remote. Together with DeVito, Schwarzenegger has developed an experimental drug Expectane, that helps ensure healthy pregnancies. When their lab is closed down by a suave villain—Frank Langella, the head of the research institute—it gets taken over by Emma Thompson, a bachelorette researcher who freezes female eggs, including her own. It's one of Thompson's eggs that gets put into Arnold's tummy along with Expectane and female hormones.

Carl Reiner, in his *Man With Two Brains* phase, would have had wild dirty fun with the plot premise, bouncing absurd jokes off the walls. That way would have been funnier. But sometimes placidity isn't the worst fate to befall a comedy: The commonplace mediocrity of the settings and direction in *Junior* actually makes the freakish central idea easier to take. *Junior* is unhurried and easygoing. For a long time the movie is a quieter version of such gender-reversal farces as *Victor/Victoria, Tootsie, All of Me, Switch*, and *Mrs. Doubtfire*. Male directors seem to like making these gender-benders; this new genre allows them to draw on the old (now vanished) stable sex roles without committing the error of putting them on the screen: That is, the movies can refer to what a "woman" is, or is supposed to be, by having a man play her—and vice versa—thereby refreshing the clichés. It's a way of first goosing and then soothing the audience—and everyone comes out feeling better. In the end, all these movies aim at reconciliation between the sexes, a melding of allegedly separate gender traits. *Junior* domesticates the feminist complain—Why can't a man be more like a woman?—with an absurdly specific answer. A man becomes more like a woman and he likes it.

Reitman also makes a sweet pass at romantic comedy. Emma Thompson, who started her acting career (at Cambridge) as a comedienne, turns out to be a real sport. Her dedicated scientist is a lovely, fresh creation—a fogged, physically hapless dear thing, with both the integrity and rich dottiness of an English village librarian. Thompson's scientist wants to be crisp and tidy, yet she's too literal-minded to understand anything, and she has frequent misadventures with pieces of cheese and paper that get attached to her face or shoes. She has adhesive sympathies. Naturally, her stern goodness is shocked by Arnold's getting pregnant. As a fact of nature, she doesn't seem to find it all that strange, but the arrogance of it puts her off: She feels—what?—effeminated? The two of them become a very strange couple

With female discomforts come new female glories. Arnold's back hurts, and he can't seem to get out of a car, but he's not humiliated by becoming a woman; on the contrary, he develops a new kind of pride. The best part of Schwarzenegger's performance is that he plays the situation straight, without winking a parody. The stiffness and the imposingness don't disappear. Instead, he puts them to use as the armature of a massively dignified maternity. Even though technology allows him to carry the baby, Arnold leaves technology behind at last and joins nature—no longer a tank but a huge moving mountain. Weird as it may seem, the birth of his child is actually an emotional moment. Ridiculous? Maybe so, but I dropped a tear or two, like almost everyone sitting around me.

NEW YORK POST, 11/23/94, p. 41, Michael Medved

"Junior" takes a single silly premise—Arnold Schwarzenegger's pregnancy—and stretches it out to fill an entire movie. Even though the stretch marks remain visible throughout the project, the obvious enthusiasm of the all-star cast makes for a pleasant if predictable two hours.

Schwarzenegger plays a brilliant research scientist at a fictional Bay Area university (exteriors were actually shot on the Berkeley campus) who, together with an earthy gynecologist played by Danny DeVito, has been working on a wonder drug to prevent miscarriages.

When the FDA and a suave, scheming academic administrator (gorgeously well-played by Frank Langella) shut down their experiments, the two scientists take desperate measures: They fertilize a frozen egg with Arnold's own sperm, and then implant it in the big guy's abdomen where they can test their new formula for a few months.

Of course, Schwarzenegger is gradually transformed by the growing presence in his belly and by the hormone injections he receives, and he decides to carry the baby to term. Meanwhile, he finds himself powerfully drawn to a rival scientist who's taken over his lab space at the university—played by Emma Thompson as a sweet, endearing but utterly hopeless klutz.

In this unlikely role, the always elegant actress displays formidable slapstick gifts apparently well-known to British audiences from her stage and television work, but that may come as a pleasant surprise to moviegoers on this side of the pond.

There's also a subplot involving DeVito's ex-wife (Pamela Reed) who turns up pregnant with another man's child but wants Dr. Danny to take care of her. He, however, has his hands full with his buddy Arnold, who's begun saying things like "I never get to go out in public anymore" or "does my body disgust you?"

There's a consciousness-raising purpose to all this, attempting to sensitize men to the discomforts of childbearing; "Junior" is like an expectant "Tootsie," with a "walk a trimester in my hormones" theme. Many of the gags would have miscarried with any other actor than Arnold; nevertheless, to see this icon of masculinity go through unpredictable mood swings, irrational food cravings and a self-conscious waddling walk is certainly good for a few laughs.

Schwarzenegger plays his part with appropriate innocence and aplomb—including a few scenes where he appears in full drag, and bears a passing resemblance to Janet Reno. He also generates surprising chemistry with Emma Thompson, and does the bickering buddy bit with DeVito even more effectively than they did in "Twins."

Ivan ("Ghostbusters") Reitman, who directed them in that previous smash hit, creates the big, bright, handsome images that always characterize his comedies, though he expends a bit too much effort trying to make the medical details seem plausible; at times, all the scientific information threatens to upstage the likable characters.

Like any pregnancy, "Junior" seems to drag a bit toward the end, but for the most part it meets the modest expectations of its audience. In other words, Schwarzenegger delivers.

NEWSDAY, 11/23/94, Part II/p. B3, Jack Mathews

The challenge of Ivan Reitman's "Junior" is the challenge of all star-driven, high-concept comedies. How to take what is essentially a whopping sight gag—Whoopi Goldberg as a nun, Robin Williams as a nanny, Arnold Schwarzenegger as a pregnant man—and stretch it out to feature length.

The success of these films is measured by the ratio of laughs per joke attempted, which in turn is dependent on the ingenuity shown by the filmmakers in exploiting the premise. In "Sister Act," Goldberg had all those wonderful Motown tunes to divert us, and whenever things got dull in "Mrs. Doubtfire," Robin Williams simply flew off on a comic riff.

In "Junior," there are no diversions, no riffs. Schwarzenegger may be the most lovable mesomorph to ever fill out the frame of a movie camera, and he is becoming a master of self-parody. But he is no comedian, and strong as he is, he cannot carry one joke for an entire movie.

That's not to say "Junior" doesn't deliver some big laughs. It does. I'll leave it to women to decide whether it's insulting for the ultimate screen action hero to be turned into a mass of weepy, dependent female stereotypes, but Schwarzenegger, and his co-stars Danny DeVito and Emma Thompson, have plenty of good moments.

The pregnancy? Ah, yes, well it comes about when Arnold's Dr. Alexander Hesse agrees to let his university research partner (DeVito) use him as a guinea pig in a surreptitious fertility drug experiment. By implanting a fertilized egg in Hesse's abdominal cavity, and keeping it alive for three months with hormones and their magic drug, DeVito's greedy Dr. Arbogast figures they can make a fortune selling the formula to pharmaceutical companies.

Two problems. After three months, Dr. Mom refuses to abort his fetus, even though his breasts are unbearably sensitive and he can't watch a TV commercial without blubbering. And he has fallen in love with a colleague (Thompson) whose baby, unbeknownst to either of them, he is carrying. Her frozen egg was stolen by Arbogast from the "dairy section" of her lab, and fertilized with Hesse's sperm. Talk about a blind date!

You don't want to think too much about the clinical probabilities of all this. "Junior" is strictly about Arnold going to term, getting big as a house, and suffering every pregnancy symptom from morning sickness to hypersensitivity to back pains. People comment on his radiance, if not his girth, and his moods swing from exhilaration to mopey "Does my body disgust you?" self-pity.

The film is at its best playing off Hesse's physical changes—for once, an expectant father feels more than sympathy pains—and the lengths to which he and his partner go to cover his condition. The sight of Arnold in maternity drag, checking into a home for third trimester moms, is a howl, as is the explanation Arbogast gives the center's director for his friend's enormous size. She was forced to take steroids while on the East German Olympic team.

"Junior," like Reitman's "Dave" and "Twins" before it, is too good-natured and silly to arouse much passion for or against it. The actors certainly all got into the spirit. Emma Thompson, before she won her Oscar and arthouse rep, did some wonderful light comedy in a movie called "The Tall Guy," and as Arnold's love interest and egg donor, she makes the most of this role. DeVito is perfectly cast as an opportunist hoisted on his own petard. And memorable relief is provided by Pamela Reed, as DeVito 's pregnant ex-wife, and Frank Langella, playing an administrator determined to claim the tabloid baby as university property.

Given the one-joke nature of "Junior," however, it all comes down to how much—rather, how *long*—you can appreciate the sight of the Herculean Schwarzenegger being governed by his feminine side. It's a game and often engaging performance, but the repetition eventually gave me a pain. Not in the back. Lower.

NEWSWEEK, 11/28/94, p. 66, David Ansen

Arnold gets pregnant. There it is, the height of high concept, a gimmick so sure-fire—that no matter how hilarious or horrible "Junior" turned out to be, anything less than a $25 million opening weekend would be a scandal. Add Midas-touch director Ivan Reitman ("Ghostbusters," "Twins") to the package, cover your bets with reliable second fiddle Danny DeVito, soften up the critics with tony Emma Thompson as the romantic interest and make sure you get Schwarzenegger in drag before the comedy is over, and you've got yourself a product any self-respecting Hollywood executive would kill his children to produce.

The nice thing is, "Junior" isn't exactly the movie you'd imagine it to be. It's broad, but not that broad. It has pratfalls, but farce is not the tone Reitman's after. Since "Dave," he's become a more discreet, understated director, and the best scenes here don't go for knee-slapping responses. There's the pregnant Arnold pigging out with DeVito's pregnant ex-wife Pamela Reed at the dinner table, overcome by strange food cravings, or the funny/lovely moment when Arnold becomes teary-eyed watching a sappy Kodak commercial.

The script, by Kevin Wade and Chris Conrad, takes its time setting up the joke. Arnold's a grim, cold-fish scientist working with DeVito on a new miracle drug to guarantee healthy pregnancies. When the FDA and the university pull the plug on the project, Arnold secretly tries it out on himself, using a frozen egg from scientist Emma Thompson's lab. These first 40 minutes don't bode well. Thompson's character, the brainy klutz, seems a tired stereotype. The villain of the piece, Frank Langella's spiteful research administrator, is utterly perfunctory. The graphic pseudo-science of the impregnation—injecting Arnold's muscle-bound abdomen—is more a turnoff than a riot.

But the wait pays off. When the Big Guy starts showing, and begins to get that radiant glow, "Junior" hits its mellow, endearing comic stride. The "message" is the old "Tootsie" roll: Arnold becomes a better, more sensitive man by experiencing life as a woman. Some people (not men, I'd bet) may be offended: is there nothing those guys won't co-opt? But the fantasy's intentions seem benign. Who ever imagined they'd see the former Mr. Universe, his belly extended, shouting "My body, my choice!"? This is Schwarzenegger's most adroit comic turn: relieved of his macho duties, he seems looser and subtler. Thompson, an agile physical clown, plays off him deftly. They make odd romantic sense. Neither hilarious nor horrible, "Junior" is the first would-be Arnold blockbuster that coasts on charm.

SIGHT AND SOUND, 1/95, p. 46, Howard Feinstein

San Francisco. Two men of science, cold researcher Dr. Alexander Hesse and earthy Dr. Larry Arbogast, lose university funding and facilities after the Federal Drug Administration refuses to approve Expectane, a fertility formula they have developed. Their boss and nemesis, Noah Banes, replaces them with clumsy female scientist Dr. Diana Reddin, who is working on a different fertility project for which she has frozen some of her own eggs. Arbogast unknowingly steals them and combines them with Hesse's sperm. Desperate to validate the discovery and obtain funding from a pharmaceutical company, Arbogast injects Hesse with the mixture. The two men agree that they will terminate the pregnancy after the first trimester, but Hesse, who has begun to change both emotionally and physically, insists on carrying the baby to term. They continue to use the lab on a part-time basis, due to Reddin's generosity. Hesse and Reddin fall in love, and he decides to tell her of the condition that he has been successfully hiding. Initially angry, she becomes supportive, and they decide to raise the child together. When the opportunistic Banes discovers the scheme, Hesse, in full drag, checks into a home for unwed mothers, where he participates in all of the women's pre-delivery activities. Trying to appropriate the men's accomplishment, Banes calls the media to the delivery room, but the press find only Arbogast's pregnant (by Aerosmith's personal trainer) ex-wife Angela, with whom he is affecting a reconciliation. Arbogast delivers Hesse's baby by caesarean section, while Angela, with Reddin's assistance, gives birth in the next room. A year later, the two couples — Hesse with a pregnant Reddin, Arbogast with Angela — celebrate their offspring's first birthday on the beach. Hesse and the two women propose that Arbogast carry his and Angela's next child.

Junior is clearly keyed to the mood of America. A pro-life ode to the nuclear family. Ivan Reitman's film opened in the wake of the recent conservative Republican sweep of both Congress and the Senate — and yet another assassination attempt (in Canada) on a pro-choice doctor.

The fact that a man can carry a child might be a good subject for sophisticated parody or political theatre, but here it only a joke stretched very thin. That the man—a bespectacled, brilliant scientist with tortoiseshell rims—is portrayed by Arnold Schwarzenegger, keeps the laughs coming far longer than the script deserves. Only a film archivist could withhold yucks when he explains his torrent of tears upon watching a schmaltzy TV commercial to surrogate father Danny DeVito: "She was Daddy's little girl!" Or when, in dress and blonde wig, he clarifies the reason for his enormous size to the head of a fancy home for unwed mothers (played by 60s counter-culture folk-singing queen Judy Collins): "The East Germans pumped up female athletes like me with anabolic steroids the way they dispense Gatorade here—but, I'm all woman!"

What seems at first merely a weakly-directed movie with more than enough juvenile humour to pull in the weekend dating crowd (closeups of oversized urine cups, references to Schwarzenegger's large load, comments like "My nipples are sensitive") soon becomes egregious. The scene in which Schwarzenegger and DeVito lovingly examine in detail a foetal sonogram smacks of the ubiquitous anti-abortion commercials ("Life: what a beautiful choice") running on American television. Conservative Republican Schwarzenegger takes on the most insulting external trappings of femininity and pseudo-wifeliness: nagging DeVito, berating his enlarged body, cooking obsessively — but the film refuses to push their relationship any further. Instead,

Schwarzenegger's nascent sensitivity and his increased sexual drive lead him into an affair with fellow scientist Emma Thompson.

At first, Thompson chastises the two men for appropriating pregnancy from women, but this token feminism does not balance out the adorably bumbling traits given her (not to mention lines like "a woman's life is a nightmare"): she falls regularly, she dances with toilet paper sticking to her shoe, she flips a lobster shell onto an adjacent table in a restaurant. She is a sort of British Mary Tyler Moore who metamorphoses from a no-nonsense, quasi-masculine, trouser-attired researcher into a softly coiffed caricature of conventional womanhood.

Junior reunites the team that made *Twins*, Reitman, Schwarzenegger and DeVito. Given his more typical screen personae, it's obvious why such a passive role might appeal to Schwarzenegger, and DeVito (recently charted in *The New York Times* as one of the best-connected people in Hollywood) has never been too choosy about his parts. What is unclear is why Thompson would play such a retrograde character.

TIME, 11/28/94, p. 80, Richard Schickel

His favorite nosh is the pickles-and-ice-cream combo. He's delighted with his suddenly glowing complexion. He gets anxious and whiny when his significant other leaves him home alone too much. He is, of course, pregnant. But you've probably guessed all that. The marketing campaign has left little doubt about *Junior*'s central joke. Sure, this is formulaic, describe-it-in-one-sentence moviemaking, but nevertheless, there is a certain irresistible curiosity about seeing Arnold Schwarzenegger mime the rituals of expectant motherhood. Go ahead, surrender to it. It won't make you a better person, but it might, very briefly, make you a happier one.

Schwarzenegger is a scientist named Dr. Alex Hesse. With hustling Larry Arbogast (Danny DeVito, Schwarzenegger's *Twins* costar), he has developed a drug that promises to help women carry difficult pregnancies to full term. The Food and Drug Administration refuses them permission to test it, so they steal an embryo, fertilize it and implant it in Alex's abdomen. After which nature—if that's the word we want—takes its course. The Kevin Wade-Chris Conrad screenplay takes some humorless pains to make this science fiction plausible, and it's smart of director Ivan Reitman to be patient with all that. The more that Schwarzenegger's predicament seems real, the funnier it is.

Schwarzenegger gives a soberly befuddled performance as a man pleasantly surprised, and ultimately transformed, by the play of alien hormones to which he's host. Giddiness (and most of the film's knockabout comedy) is left to Emma Thompson as a bright, klutzy fellow scientist, and she is a lovely reminder of our screwball yesteryears. Like all concerned with *Junior*, she refuses to let it rest lazily on its concept. The result is a high-energy farce that is more endearing and, yes, more believable than it has any right to be.

VILLAGE VOICE, 11/29/94, p. 73, Ben Greenman

Fast-talking gynecologist Larry Arbogast (Danny DeVito) and button-down researcher Alexander Hesse (Arnold Schwarzenegger) have spent years perfecting an anti-miscarriage drug on chimps, only to have the FDA quash the project at the last minute. Distraught and defiant, Arbogast vows to continue the trials with a human subject. But who!

In the world of high-concept king Ivan Reitman (*Twins, Kindergarten Cop*), the answer is simple: pregnant Arnold. Though *Junior* has an evil villain (Frank Langella) and some love interest (Pamela Reed and jumpier-than-thou Emma Thompson), its real promise lies in exploring the feminine mystery of pregnancy through *übermensch* numero uno. The formula is a sturdy one: Arnold plus morning sickness plus mood swings equals laughter. And it drives plot as well as character—when Arbogast wants to end his groundbreaking research after a few months, the pregnant Hesse refuses to say "hasta la vista, baby" to his unborn child. Did someone say Full-Terminator!

Though Reitman's steady hand sometimes falters, *Junior* avoids the Scylla and Charybdis of shrillness and corn that sunk its two closest progenitors, Joan Rivers's *Rabbit Test* and the saccharine *3 Men and a Baby*. As Alex and Larry struggle with intellectual paternity (the research trials) and biological parenthood (the pregnancy itself), the film asks entry-level questions about creation and responsibility, and answers them far more successfully than, say, *Mary Shelley's*

Frankenstein. Superficiality is *Junior*'s saving grace; musings on anatomical essentialism don't deliver what they promise—where have you gone, Thomas Laqueur?— and there's thought of early termination until an abysmal final sequence at a maternity resort. In the end, the pleasures of *Junior* are the small ones: the implausibilities and one-liners ("My body, my choice," thunders Hesse), and the irresistible sight of Der Arnold cradling a baby tinier than his bicep.

Also reviewed in:
NEW YORK TIMES, 11/23/94, p. C9, Janet Maslin
VARIETY, 11/21-27/94, p. 37, Leonard Klady
WASHINGTON POST, 11/23/94, p. D1, Rita Kempley
WASHINGTON POST, 11/25/94, Weekend/p. 60, Desson Howe

JUST LIKE A WOMAN

A Samuel Goldwyn Company/Rank Film Distributors/LWT release with the participation of British Screen of a Zenith Productions film. *Executive Producer:* Archie Tait, Fred Turner, and Nick Elliott. *Producer:* Nick Evans. *Director:* Christopher Monger. *Screenplay:* Nick Evans. *Based on the book "Geraldine" by:* Monica Jay. *Director of Photography:* Alan Hume. *Editor:* Nicolas Gaster. *Music:* Michael Storey. *Choreographer*: David Massingham. *Sound:* Neil Kingsbury and (music) Richard Whaley. *Sound Editor*: John Poyner *Production Designer:* John Box. *Art Director*: Michael White. *Set Decorator*: Peter Howitt. *Costumes:* Suzy Peters. *Make-up*: Fae Hammond and Sarah Monzani. *Running time:* 102 minutes. *MPAA Rating:* Not Rated.

CAST: Julie Walters (Monica Jay); Adrian Pasdar (Gerald Tilson); Paul Freeman (Miles Millichamp); Gordon Kennedy (C.J.); Ian Redford (Tom Braxton); Shelly Thompson (Eleanor Tilson); Togo Igawa (Akira Watanabe); Susan Wooldridge (Louisa); Jill Spurrier (Daphne); Corey Cowper (Erika Tilson); Mark Hadfield (Dennis); Joseph Bennett (Jocelyn); Brooke (Linda); Eve Bland (Betty); Jeff Nuttall (Vanessa); Sayo Inaba (Interpreter); David Hunt and Rupert Holliday Evans (Policemen); Albert Welling (Priest); Edwin Hock Thong Low (Waiter); Tim Stern (Hypnotist); Rohan McCullough (Mrs. Millichamp); John Shin (Embassy Attaché); David Tse and Harumi Okada (Kabuki Actors); Brigid Major (Gerald's Secretary); Laura Gouldesbrough (Lille); Gareth Heale (Tom Tilson); Chloe Skew (Emily Tilson); Damian Hunt (Young Gerald); Sam Wise (Millichamp's Son).

LOS ANGELES TIMES, 7/22/94, Calendar/p. 8, Kevin Thomas

"Just Like a Woman," a romantic comedy with a decidedly different twist, finds a young American (Adrian Pasdar) rushing home from the London merchant bank where he is working on a half-billion-dollar deal with a Japanese company. Unfortunately, he arrives just in time to witness his wife, who has unexpectedly returned early from a trip with their two small children, throwing a large amount of women's clothing out the master bedroom window.

She won't let him explain, and she very well might not be able to understand if she gave her husband the chance to do so. Naturally, she assumes the clothing belongs to some unknown other woman. The truth is that Pasdar's Gerald is himself the other woman, for he is a transvestite who calls himself Geraldine when he dresses in feminine attire.

In looking for new digs, Gerald has the good fortune to end up at the doorstep of Julie Walters' Monica, a recent divorcée who's just decided to take in some boarders to afford staying in her large and comfortable Edwardian row house. Gerald is such an ideal tenant, thoughtful and considerate, and Monica is such a warm, good-humored woman, that it's not surprising that mutual attraction occurs.

"Just Like a Woman," which was written and produced by Nick Evans and directed by Christopher Monger, is resolutely buoyant. Although not without pathos, it avoids any probing of what may cause transvestism, content to make the point that many transvestites are straight. It does a good, credible job in depicting Gerald gathering strength to confess his predilection—a first for him—to Monica, whose stunned response is laughter, but who proves strong and caring enough to accept Gerald the way he is. She even encourages Gerald to dare to transform himself into Geraldine for a daytime outing, urging him to be less fearful in the guise in which he seems so comfortable.

Having drawn from a true story (based on a book by Monica Jay) up to this point and thereby setting the stage for some serious considerations, the filmmakers nevertheless plunge ahead with a giddy farce plot that involves Gerald's escalating clashes with his bombastic boss (Paul Freeman).

Although "Just Like a Woman" becomes increasingly contrived, it offers splendid performances from its stars. The film itself may proceed gingerly at times but Pasdar, tall and strapping, wisely plays Geraldine with a bold display of confidence. Despite his husky physique and strong jaw, Pasdar manages to be convincingly feminine. As Monica, Walters has never looked so attractive or underplayed so effectively, even though she thrives in the showy parts afforded her in "Educating Rita" and the current "Wedding Gift."

Although "Just Like a Woman" strains a bit in emphasizing what a likable, emphatically masculine guy Gerald is, it is nevertheless a landmark in mainstream movies for its compassionate view of a straight transvestite.

NEWSDAY, 7/22/94, Part II/p. B6, Terry Kelleher

"Some Like It Hot," "Tootsie," "Mrs. Doubtfire"—forget that Hollywood stuff about guys who don women's clothing because desperate times call for desperate measures.

Gerald Tilson (Adrian Pasdar), one of the two principal characters in the British-made "Just Like a Woman," is a handsome young investment banker from America who cross-dresses because he enjoys it. Now, isn't that daring for a mainstream movie?

Rather. Monica Jay (Julie Walters), his middle-class London landlady and lover-to-be, does go slack-jawed at the wonder and mystery of it all the first time Gerald allows her to behold his transformation into the glamorous night creature who prefers to be called Geraldine. With its arty, slow-motion photography and ethereal music, the scene may leave viewers a bit stunned as well. On the other hand, Monica takes remarkably little time to grow comfy with the whole concept of cross-dressing. Quickly discarding her misconception that transvestites are uniformly gay, she assures her best friend that Gerald is "a perfectly heterosexual man [who] likes dressing up in frocks." On her maiden visit to a drag club, she scans the room full of gents in evening gowns and remarks to Geraldine), "It's not like I expected at all—it's all so normal!"

If Monica is too understanding to be true—although "Just Like a Woman" is "inspired" by a true story—it's only because she's serving as spokeswoman for a writer (Nick Evans) and director (Christopher Monger) who are at pains to assure the average filmgoer that transvestism is *perfectly* OK, albeit entertainingly exotic. Their concern for conveying this message sometimes gives "Just Like a Woman" that dreaded TV-movie quality.

Plausibility problems notwithstanding, we're exceedingly fond of Monica for the simple reason that Walters plays her. Her warmth, natural wit and salt-of-the-earth appeal undoubtedly would win us over even if her character were a trifle less broad-minded. Pasdar's Gerald is something of an enigma emotionally. We'd like to get more of a sense that the fun he derives from dressing up compensates for the anguish brought on by social disapproval and the fear of discovery. The moviemakers would have been better advised to concentrate on developing the main characters instead of spending time on a subplot involving Gerald's bigoted, bombastic boss (Paul Freeman) and his deceptive dealings with a benign Japanese tycoon. The story lines intersect in a protracted boardroom climax that wants to be a crowd-pleaser but amounts to a credulity-strainer.

Despite the film's title, Bob Dylan is nowhere to be heard on the soundtrack. But Gerald and Monica do share a fondness for golden oldies.

NEW YORK POST, 7/22/94, p. 40, Bill Hoffmann

LONDON HOUSEWIFE FALLS FOR TRANSVESTITE!

That's how the London tabloids might trumpet the new film "Just Like a Woman," in which a middle-aged London divorcee falls head over heels for a London banker who loves heels *and* dresses *and* wigs *and* makeup.

Refreshingly, there's not the least bit of sensationalism in this offbeat British entry based on Monica Jay's bestselling biography about what it's like to live with a cross-dresser.

Instead, "Just Like a Woman" is a charming, witty and warmhearted romantic comedy about falling in love under the most bizarre circumstances.

Adrian Pasdar (who played a hunky pilot opposite Tom Cruise in "Top Gun") is Gerald Tilson, a successful mid-level investment banker with a gorgeous blonde wife and two lovely kids.

Tilson is also a secret cross-dresser who's got trunk loads of women's clothes stashed at home. When his wife stumbles upon his frilly panties and garters, she throws him out, convinced he's having a torrid affair.

Too ashamed to tell the truth, Gerald moves into a boarding house run by Monica Jay (Julie Walters), a divorced middle-aged woman bordering on full-fledged hausfrau.

She and Gerald are instantly drawn together, a fact that has Monica torn with emotion when she sees a "woman" sneaking into his room every night in the wee hours.

When he decides to confess his secret, she greets the news with howls of uncontrollable laughter. Still, these two sad souls are inevitably made for each other.

Director Christopher Monger has his hands planted firmly on our emotional buttons as the couple grasps and gropes through the pains of living with transvestitism.

What makes this film credible is that Gerald's obsession is treated with great dignity and respect. There are occasional hints of the broad comedy of "Tootsie" and "La Cage Aux Folles," but they're only hints.

Unfortunately, Jay's fascinating story is intermingled with a fictional subplot concerning Gerald's attempts to stop his greedy banking firm from cashing in on a get-rich-quick scheme.

This bit of forced intrigue stretches credibility much too far, especially during the weird conclusion in which cross-dressing is used to save the day.

It mars what otherwise is a small, feel-good movie with a heart of gold.

SIGHT AND SOUND, 9/92, p. 53, Tom Charity

Gerald is a young, high-flying American merchant banker living in London with his wife and two children. He's about to pull off a multi-million-pound deal with a big Japanese corporation when his wife finds another woman's underwear in their bedroom and throws him out of the house. Meanwhile, London housewife Monica, divorced after twenty-two years of unhappy marriage, is looking for lodgers to fill her large home. When Gerald moves in, she is delighted and surprised when a relationship begins to develop; but after they make love for the first time, he starts to avoid her.

Eventually, he confesses his secret: he is a transvestite, and before her eyes, he transforms himself into "Geraldine". He takes her to the élite Pembrook Club, where she meets his friends and some of their wives. She encourages him to go out in the daytime as Geraldine, and they go shopping together. They enjoy humorous role-playing games, and the relationship proves liberating for both of them. At work, meanwhile, Gerald and his colleague C.J. suspect that their racist, arrogant boss Miles Millichamp is undermining their Japanese deal for reasons of his own.

On his way home from the Pembrook one night, "Geraldine" is pulled over by the police, arrested and humiliated. Miles fires him, and he resolves to go back to the US. But Monica and C.J. hatch a plan that could help Gerald rebuild his life and save the Japanese deal. At the crucial meeting, the Japanese surprise Miles by calling in two independent financial advisers: Monica and Geraldine. They expose Miles' fraudulent plan; Gerald's original deal is saved, and the lovers leave the boardroom in triumph. "Life isn't really like this" worries Gerald. "It is tonight" Monica assures him.

When Monica opens her front door and sees Gerald standing there with a pamphlet entitled "Resurrection" under his arm, she assumes he is with the bible-bashers who are working in the neighbourhood and gives him short shrift ("If it's the end of the world, I've got to pop down to the shops, you see"). In fact, Gerald has just been presented with the booklet himself; he's there as a prospective lodger. The scene is a familiar comic 'meeting cute', and it comes with an equally banal sub-text: appearances can be deceptive. But it is also indicative of two impulses behind this romantic comedy; a duality that is appropriate enough in the circumstances.

In the first place, there is an evangelical aspect to the production, carried over, presumably, from Monica Jay's autobiographical novel. Within the mainstream tradition of transvestite movies (from *Some Like It Hot* via *La Cage aux folles* to *Victor/Victoria* and *Tootsie*), this is by far the most prosaic and the least camp. The script, for instance, is at pains to spell out that transvestites are not necessarily gay, and that, in Japan, "a man dressing as a woman is not seen as posing the same social or moral threat". The opening credits sequence features a boy watching, fascinated, as his mother makes up, with Doris Day singing "Que Sera Sera", while the film closes with an end title to the effect that one in twenty men feel the need to dress in women's clothing. The comparison that immediately comes to mind is far out of the mainstream: Ed Wood's labour of love, *Glen or Glenda?*.

Then there is the middle-aged divorcée, Monica. That initial put-down to the stranger on her front doorstep calls on a peculiarly British, female(?), down-to-earth sense of humour which is Julie Walters' forte. It's a humour with a keen sense of the ridiculous, but no desire to ridicule. When Gerald tells Monica about Geraldine, his other half, she cannot help laughing, but she is soon gently asking his forgiveness, seeking to understand. Accompanying Geraldine to a transvestite club, she compares notes with the other wives and girlfriends, and is soon exclaiming, "It's so normal!"; for all the world like Walters' Cynthia Payne in *Personal Services*.

There is inevitably something reductive about espousing the normalcy of perversity, but it's hard to argue with the film-makers' liberal political correctness. And to give director Chris Monger his due, while the sex scenes are 15-certificate coy, he does pull off a remarkably sensual transformation scene, in which Gerald becomes Geraldine in a series of slow, enveloping fades. Incidentally, the merchant-banking sub-plot which supplies a feeble narrative motor is remarkable not only for giving us a yuppie hero of sorts, but for what is surely the first happy ending in British cinema to celebrate a Japanese buy-out of a parochial English firm. The times they are a-changin'.

VILLAGE VOICE 8/2/94, p. 51, Bethany White

It is the telling last words, "Life isn't like this," spoken by leading man/woman Gerald Tilson (Adrian Pasdar) in Christopher Monger's *Just Like a Woman*, that point to the frustrating insecurity laced about this latest U.K. gender bender, whose mission is to depict the lives of cross-dressers as being as normal as golf.

Tilson, a young American, is a mild-mannered investment banker by day, but enjoys dressing up in women's togs at night. His wife leaves him when she comes home early from a trip and finds their bedroom littered with undies and cosmetics that are just not hers. Gerald goes off to seek alternative housing and falls into the bed of his middle-aged landlady, Monica (Julie Walters), who has recently sawed the ring representing 22 years of married blisslessness from her own finger. (Point emphatically made: Many cross-dressers are not gay.)

The oddly flat narrative does manage a few deliciously voyeuristic moments such as when Gerald metamorphoses into Geraldine before Monica's stunned gaze. Of course, Gerald demanding "What's my name?" as he stares hungrily into her eyes could put even the most jaded at attention. When Monica whispers "Geraldine" before her own lips are crushed beneath Geraldine's now cherry-red pair, well, the audience is left wondering where it's all going to go from here. Unfortunately, deeper into a weak corporate subplot that one supposes writer Nick Evans felt needed to be included to pump up Gerald's hetero-masculine side.

Also reviewed in:
NEW REPUBLIC, 8/22 & 29/94, p. 34, Stanley Kauffmann
NEW YORK TIMES, 7/22/94, p. C12, Caryn James
VARIETY, 9/28/92, p. 82, Joe Leydon
WASHINGTON POST, 8/12/94, p. F7, Rita Kempley

KIKA

An October Films release of an El Deseo S.A. presentation of an El Deseo S.A.-and CIBY 2000 coproduction. *Executive Producer:* Agustin Almodóvar. *Director:* Pedro Almodóvar. *Screenplay (Spanish with English subtitles):* Pedro Almodóvar. *Director of Photography:* Alfredo Mayo. *Editor:* José Salcedo. *Sound:* Jean-Paul Mugel and Nic Lemussurier. *Sound Editor:* Graham V. Hartstone. *Set Designer:* Javier Fernandez and Alain Bainée. *Special Effects:* Yves Domenjoud, Olivier Gleyze, and Jean-Baptiste Bonetto. *Costumes:* Jean-Paul Gaultier and José Maria Cossio with the collaboration of Gianni Versace. *Make-up:* Gregorio Ros. *Running time:* 115 minutes. *MPAA Rating:* Not Rated.

CAST: Verónica Forqué (Kika); Peter Coyote (Nicholas); Victoria Abril (Andrea Caracortada, "Scarface"); Alex Casanovas (Ramón); Rossy de Palma (Juana); Santiago Lajusticia (Pablo); Anabel Alonso (Amparo); Bibi Andersen (Susana); Jesús Bonilla and Karra Elejalde (Police); Manuel Bandera (Chico Carretera); Charo López (Rafaela); Francisca Caballero (Dona Paquita); Mónica Bardem (Paca); Joaquín Climent (Killer); Blanca Li (Murdered Woman); Claudia Aros (Model).

LOS ANGELES TIMES, 5/6/94, Calendar/p. 6, Kevin Thomas

In the title role of "Kika," Pedro Almodóvar's latest darkly outrageous attack on propriety, Veronica Forque emerges as an adorable innocent, as giddy as Geena Davis in "Thelma & Louise" but as buoyant as a rubber duck in a bathtub. She's sweet, sex-loving and kind, but it's her naivete that protects her like a suit of armor.

Had not Almodóvar seriously overplayed his hand by stretching out a clever and ironic finish interminably, "Kika," which needs to lose at least 10 minutes, might well have been his most substantial picture since "Women on the Verge of a Nervous Breakdown." As it is, "Kika" most likely will please primarily only die-hard Almodóvar fans.

Kika can use all the protection she can get. A Madrid makeup artist, she's involved with Ramon (Alex Casanovas), a commercial photographer and collage artist who feels compelled to photograph himself making love to Kika; this is surely the sequence that originally pulled down an NC-17 rating (it's now unrated). Since Ramon, who worships the memory of his mother, an apparent suicide, is so kinky, Kika is also involved with his stepfather, Nicholas (Peter Coyote), an American writer and ardent womanizer (who's much like the character Coyote plays in Roman Polanski's "Bitter Moon").

One of Nicholas' discarded lovers calls herself Andrea Scarface (Victoria Abril)—she had scarred her face in a crazed attempt to hold on to Nicholas—and stars in a tabloid TV show, dressed in Jean Paul Gaultier futuristic garb, that makes Geraldo Rivera seem like Mary Worth. Kika, in turn, has a lesbian housekeeper, Juana (Rossy de Palma, an Almodóvar regular, a comedian with a regal hatchet nose) who's mad for her and whose brother Pablo (Santiago Lajusticia) is an escaped convict, a rapist and ex-porn star (who also makes love to his sister).

As Almodóvar catches up all these individuals—and others—in a freewheeling farce plot, he creates a contemporary parable on violence that's become so random and sex so bizarre that both have lost meaning; he perceives the relationship between sex and violence as constantly evolving and treacherously complex. Although Almodóvar can actually get a laugh from a rape scene, he's seriously concerned with an increasingly perilous and arid world in which people tend to connect destructively if they connect at all.

Almodóvar's exuberant style remains intact; he's one director who's intensely verbal yet always keeps his films moving, always inspiring trust in his actors to cast away virtually all their inhibitions. They in turn reward him with terrific comic portrayals. "Kika," which has Almodóvar's characteristic high gloss, may not be a vintage film but it's nevertheless indelibly idiosyncratic. Nobody but Pedro Almodóvar could have made it.

NEW STATESMAN & SOCIETY, 7/1/94, p. 33, Jonathan Romney

There's only one decent joke in John Waters' recently released *Serial Mom*—an *Oprah*-style TV show on "Serial Hags: women who love men who mutilate". It's funny because it encapsulates in a pithy headline the mix of tabloid sensationalism and suburban banality that the rest of the film strives to elaborate.

It also shows up the redundancy of Waters' brand of satiric outrage, so effective in the days of *Pink Flamingo* and *Female Trouble*. There's no longer anything strange about the idea that such a show might exist on American TV, or that the "straight" media might resort to such flagrant camp-speak. What's "weird" in *Serial Mom* is no longer the outrageous behaviour of Waters' former cast of anti-social freaks. Instead the freak is Mom herself, who is monstrous not because she murders, but because she's excessively normal.

The reason that Waters' barbs now seem so directionless is that the very institution of camp has become redundant. Reading Susan Sontag's 1964 "Notes on Camp" in the reissued *Against Interpretation* (Vintage), you're struck by how many facets of what was once a marginal stance have become, 30 years later, deeply embedded in the mainstream.

The intervening developments of gay politics and theory make it hard now to celebrate camp as purely "dandyish", what Sontag calls "a victory of 'style' over 'content', 'aesthetics' over 'morality', or 'irony' over 'tragedy'". The political needs of gay communities and mainstream recuperation have changed camp's meaning. If it can still have value, it is most likely to be as a rhetorical weapon, no longer divorced from morality.

Camp, like any counter-culture language, tends to be not only assimilated, but also institutionalised. Whatever is brought from the margins into the light risks being canonised, and often actively pursues a parodic canonisation. Hence, on one hand, the cults surrounding John Waters or *The Rocky Horror Show*; on the other, the path from Warhol's Factory to the Warhol Museum. The latest example of this tendency is the Madrid company El Deseo SA (Desire Ltd), which presents itself as an industry selling a particular generic product: the "Almodóvar Film".

The "Serial Hag" joke has an exact counterpart in Pedro Almodóvar's *Kika*. Andrea "Scarface" (Victoria Abril) is the presenter of a TV "reality show" *The Worst of the Day*, which features real-life atrocities. Andrea is public voyeurism incarnate—Shaw Taylor in bondage drag, peddling a familiar brand of titillating moralism. Before the latest hot-off-the-street sleaze, she warns, "It'll shock your sensibilities—if you still have any."

On one level, this is a straightforward critique of the excesses of tabloid TV. But at the same time, Andrea's taunt is an anxious wink to *Kika*'s audience. Almodóvar is asking us whether *our* sensibilities are dulled yet—whether we can still be galvanised by his films or whether their power has worn off.

Alas, it has: On paper, *Kika* appears rich in perverse conceits; as Almodóvar's tenth feature, it is a retread of tropes already threadbare in *Tie Me Up! Tie Me Down!* Now the flouting of narrative coherence and the courting of shock value are so transparent that it looks as though El Deseo is running a sort of market survey to see which tricks work.

Kika's remarkably cluttered plot concerns an irrepressibly jolly make-up artist (Veronica Forque, whose toothy sexiness is pure Barbara Windsor), her cataleptic beau, his American stepfather writer (Peter Coyote), a brain-damaged porn stud, a lesbian maid (the ineffably beaky Rossy de Palma) and as many other oddballs as Almodóvar can cram onto his stylishly garish posters. In fact, *Kika* seems to have been created not so much to exist as a film as to generate its own promotional impedimenta—poster, funky trailer, fashion stills with Abril modelling Jean-Paul Gaultier's cyber-splatter collection.

Almodóvar has described the film as a "jigsaw", and indeed the narrative appears almost random. It starts off as a false whodunnit, in which the original crime is either unstated or forgotten. A baroque construction of flashbacks and inserts, the plot seems capable of going anywhere, and by all accounts nearly did. One abandoned storyline involved Rossy de Palma in a wax museum, dressed up as Morticia Addams.

Rather than the "depth" provided by narrative and character, we get Almodóvar's superficiality. Alfredo Mayo's photography and the designs of Javier Fernandez and Alain Bainee flatten everything out. Expanses of blue and orange push us out of the picture; in one shot, characters are separated by flamboyantly obtrusive red and yellow orchids.

Not only the film's look is all surface. *Kika* is a make-up artist, and her world is "made up" in every sense. Andrea wears her scar, the badge of her badness, like a tattoo; the lesbian maid, when dragged up in glam gear, declares "I'm authentic!" No matter how momentous, what we get are also cartoon events. The controversial scene in which Kika is raped by the escaped porn star is neither shocking nor funny; it's entirely without effect, a farcical gesture as empty of meaning as the film's incidental references to Sarajevo.

"Real" experience transmutes into glib commentary on media gloss: Kika's ordeal happens simply so that she can protest about it being used to sell milk. The film's most representative moment is its full-frontal shot of glamorous transsexual Bibi Andersen. A "scandalous" spectacle that isn't, it is a *reductio ad absurdum* of striptease. On display is the very fact that there's nothing to see.

It's true that aspects of *Kika*—the TV satire, notions of identity and "authenticity"—gain in meaning if we apply them to a specific Spanish context. Yet outside Spain, of course, the "Spanishness" of these films functions as a particular kind of exoticism. But the apparent emptiness of *Kika* seems to be a function of the film's anxiety about its effectiveness as a political gesture. What is Andrea's show—perverse curiosity incarnate—if not a demoralised representation of Almodóvar's own flashy scandal tactics?

In that case, *Kika*'s own audience may prove as desensitised as hers. *Kika* finally offers its heroine's indefatigable optimism as an antidote to Andrea's cynicism. But it seems an empty gesture in the face of the film's underlying anxiety that Almodóvar might have ended up selling milk like the rest of them.

NEW YORK POST, 5/6/94, p. 37, Thelma Adams

Pedro Almodovar has pulled off another bigger-than-life, over-the-top, sex-and-death romp—"Kika."

Will the Spanish director of "Tie Me Up! Tie Me Down!" offend American audiences?

Sure. Why should he stop now?

Almodovar, who also scripted this cheekily demented comedy, creates a variation on Goldilocks and the three bears as seen through a keyhole.

Over the course of two wild summer days, the life of a vivacious makeup artist named Kika gets tangled up with three darker souls: her brooding fiance Ramon (Alex Casanovas); his seductive stepfather, Nicholas (Peter Coyote); and Andrea Scarface (Victoria Abril), a video vigilante.

Suicide, murder, rape, passion: Welcome to Almodovar country.

"Kika" swings from moments of cartoonish sex to sensibility-shocking violence pedaled on "Today's Worst," a Spanish tab-TV Scarface and sponsored by a milk company.

"Kika"'s kicker is completely taboo and, before I saw this movie, presumably impossible to pull off—a comic rape scene.

American viewers are prepared for comic murders. Who can make a case against "Arsenic and Old Lace"?

But rape's another matter. Almodovar readies viewers with a sex scene between Kika and her fiance that is simultaneously arousing and ludicrous.

Ramon a photographer, insists on shooting Polaroids during climax. It gets him clicking, but it leaves Kika studying the ceiling lamp.

Escaped rapist Pablo (Santiago Lajusticia) needs no artificial stimulation. Stupid and enslaved to an overactive libido, the former porn star is brutish, pathetic and comic.

Almodovar paints the rape with broad strokes. The scene edges on satire, but Kika's pain is real. The rape changes the course of her life, and brings out the true (if lurid) colors of those around her.

How do the other major characters respond? Wretchedly. Ramon is self-obsessed. Nicholas worries that his own misdeeds will be revealed. Andrea Scarface compounds the crime by airing a tape of the rape on "Today's Worst."

Kika is aptly described as "so mistaken but so charming." Still, in a world of bears and bores, it's Kika who knows when to bail when life gets too complicated.

In the end, this Goldilocks takes the high road in search of her"own happiness. Her character—and a superlative cast—makes "Kika" a buoyant dark comedy, best seen by those with the most open of minds.

NEWSDAY, 5/6/94, Part II/p. B7, John Anderson

If myopia were a crime, the Motion Picture Association of American would be wearing a scarlet M. Having refused to budge from its NC-17 rating on Pedro Almodovar's "Kika"—Presumably over the film's ludicrous rape scene—the MPAA has played right into Almodovar's hands. "

Because "Kika," like the rape itself isn't about sex. It's about a world in which everyone is a voyeur, projecting sexual fantasies onto any visual media (including this film), with a corresponding blindness to facts.

From the opening, a silhouetted keyhole that opens up the rest of the film—and through which we watch an increasingly aroused photographer shooting a beautiful, bored-to-tears fashion model—it's about seeing what we want to see, and how images are manipulated, and manipulate.

The photographer is Ramon (Alex Casanovas), who becomes engaged to Kika (Veronica Forque), a beautician sent to make up Ramon's body after he's suffered a heart attack, and whose makeup brushes bring him back from the dead. Kika clearly has a streak of the divine running through her; unabashedly sexual—and why not?— she's really an innocent, and as such is betrayed by everyone around her. That she maintains her naivete has as much to do with her own blinkered approach to life as it does her innate sweetness.

She becomes engaged to Ramon, but the sex is wrong: He spends most of their time in bed taking pictures, so she dallies with their upstairs neighbor, Nicholas (Peter Coyote) a mysterious American writer and roamer who was married to Ramon's dead, suicidal mother (Charo Lopez), and who, with Ramon, inherited her estate. Nicholas, of course, is cheating on Kika, with her best friend Amparo (Anabel Alonso) among others, and they're all being watched through a telescopic lens across town.

This sex chain has many links: Andrea (Victoria Abril), who was unceremoniously dumped by Ramon and slashed her cheek in a desperate gesture of love, has become Scarface, whose television news magazine show "Today's Worst" ("sponsored by Royal Milk!") presents the most lurid, sordid and violent stories, improvising facts whenever necessary.

Abril's Andrea is a fabulous creation: With a camcorder mounted on her motorcycle helmet, and a Barbarella-style bustiere, she has cops on her payroll and arrives wherever a story breaks. Her technique is a harbinger of "Geraldos" to come: After showing a tape of a man killing his wife at the grave of her daughter, whom he raped, she interviews the man's mother, who says he didn't do it.

Scarface has it in for Ramon—the vendettas, like the sexual network, intermesh like macrame—and so when she gets a tape of Kika being raped, she runs it, and then tries to interview the victim, asking all the questions lawyers don't ask anymore.

The rape itself is a prolonged, darkly comic sequence that's in extremely bad taste, but devoid of eroticism, which is the point. Pablo (Santiago La Justicia), the retarded, sexually insatiable rapist brother of Kika's maid, Juana (Rossy De Palma), has been granted a one-day leave from prison to go home to attend a religious ceremony, complete with ritual self-flagellation—closeups of the bloodletting being an Almodovar dig at his censors. Pablo escapes amid the confusion and arrives at Kika's intending to rob. He stays to rape, and rape, and rape, until the police have to drag him off Kika, who's then subjected to more humiliation and abuse.

The rape, along with the sexual antics and frenetic subplotting, distract from what becomes a much more conventional storyline—and that we've been so distracted is another subtle Almodovar joke. Subtlety, however, is lost on some people, including the MPAA. In fighting censorship—and what is an NC-17 rating if not veiled censorship?—"Kika" has joined some celebrated and notorious company, Ice T's "Cop Killer" record, for instance, or "The Merchant of Venice" or "Huckleberry Finn." Works which, for the crime of not representing social evil in the broadest way possible, are judged to be evil themselves.

SIGHT AND SOUND, 7/94, p. 48, Rikki Morgan

Kika is an ever-optimistic beautician living with Ramón, an introspective and uncommunicative underwear photographer she met when summoned to make up his cataleptic 'corpse'. Returning from abroad, Ramón's stepfather, American novelist Nicholas Pearce, moves into the flat above. Ramón and Nicholas jointly own a country house ('Youkali') bequeathed them by Ramón's mother, with whom Ramón has been obsessed since her suicide. Unsatisfied by her relationship with Ramón, Kika secretly enjoys occasional sex with the mysterious and seductive Nicholas.

Ramón also has his secrets: before Kika, he had been involved with Andrea Caracortada (Scarface), an ex-psychologist turned crime reporter. Their relationship ended dramatically, leaving Andrea with a sizeable grudge and a scar on her face. Equipped with a motorbike and customised black rubber suit, Andrea specialises in on-the-spot crime reports and sensationalist interviews with victims and perpetrators for her TV 'reality show' *The Worst of the Day*.

Andrea encounters Kika when pursuing mentally-deficient convicted rapist Pablo, who escaped while on parole from prison to attend a religious festival in his home village. Unknown to Kika, her maid Juana is Pablo's sister and Kika's flat is his first port of call on the run. Juana, a plain-speaking lesbian who is in love with Kika, does her best to protect her sleeping mistress from Pablo's voracious sexual appetite by promising to satisfy his needs herself. She decides to send Pablo into hiding and tells him to steal some of Ramón's cameras, concealing her role in the theft by getting Pablo to slug her and tie her to a chair. While Juana is bound and unconscious, Pablo repeatedly rapes Kika until the police arrive and pull him away. He escapes as Andrea arrives on the scene. Kika angrily refuses to answer Andrea's intrusive questions and tries to put the incident behind her, only to be further humiliated by the TV screening of a video recording of the rape sent in by a neighbouring voyeur. Discovering that Ramón is the source of the video, she moves out.

Andrea's continuing scrutiny of Ramón's video and Nicholas' latest manuscript lead her to suspect Nicholas of multiple murder and, desperate for the scoop, she pursues him to Youkali, where Ramón has already discovered a dead body and confronted him with the evidence of his mother's murder. While Ramón lies in another cataleptic swoon, Andrea forces her way in and dies in a struggle with Nicholas. Kika, drawn by a letter from Ramón, turns up in time to hear Nicholas' dying confession and revive Ramón. Following the ambulance taking him to hospital, however, she picks up a hitcher, with whom she drives off into the sunset.

Following the relatively disappointing *High Heels* (1991), this latest offering from Spain's iconoclastic *enfant terrible* clearly attempts to reprise the more provocative tone of Almodóvar's stylishly outrageous work of the mid-80s. Such characteristically challenging films as *What Have I Done To Deserve This?* (1984), *Matador* (1986) and *Law of Desire* (1987) rode exquisitely roughshod over traditionally divisive notions of high and low with their defiant subversions of rigid social structures and gender binaries. But, although *Kika* reassembles the familiar ingredients of these explosive generic cocktails of dark melodrama, wacky comedy and colourful visual flamboyance, the film is marred by two major irritants: a poorly crafted and fragmented plot which abandons characters and narrative threads mid-stream, and a recurrently nagging feeling that we have been here before.

In a self-conscious pastiche of its classic precursors, voyeurism and obsession dominate the film, serving up a veritable voyeur's gallery of referential camerawork, dialogue, clips and posters which recall *The Prowler, Rear Window* and, most persistently, *Peeping Tom*. Substituting Michael Powell's psychopathic protagonist with a parade of obsessives, Almodóvar focuses on the postmodern world of the surface, creating a world of urban violence and media exploitation in which his characters experience life through a series of personal fictions and obsessions. For the introspective, oedipally stunted Ramón, pleasure is only possible through the camera lens that mediates both his private and professional pursuits, including his sexual relationship with Kika; fiction and reality merge for Nicholas, whose darkly 'mysterious' activities are recorded by the alter ego protagonists of his novels; half-witted rapist Pablo regards his porn-star credentials as a licence for sexual abuse; and Kika's naive faith in the transformative power of cosmetic artistry celebrates the enhancing effects of eye make-up on intelligence ("Long live eyelashes!") and revitalises corpses—quite literally in the case of the cataleptic Ramón.

Some of Almodóvar's most memorable parodies revolve around merciless send-ups of the media, and in *Kika*, where sensation and sensationalism are all grist to the media mill, this preoccupation moves centre-stage. Sponsored by La Real Milk (a linguistic play on the sexual connotations and associations with violence and absurdity of the Spanish word for milk, 'leche', meaning both 'a blow' and 'the absolute limit'), Andrea's TV 'reality show' epitomises the worst excesses of media exploitation with grotesquely intrusive interviews and her obsessive pursuit of the ultimate exclusive: a head-to-head with a serial killer. The raw-edged effect of their presentation through the video medium lends a more caustic edge to these parodies of victim harassment, and to Almodóvar's customary critique of Catholic ritual in the more sinister, Buñuelian tone of Andrea's graphic recordings of the 'Los Picaos' festival of flagellation and self-mortification.

Always sailing close to the wind of controversy, *Kika* has provoked from the Spanish press the most vitriolic accusations of rampant commercialism, media hype, exploitation of homosexuality and gratuitously sensationalist misogyny. Whether or not this is deserved, it is certainly not entirely surprising. There seems little narrative justification, for example, for the much-publicised first on-screen full-frontal nude shot of transsexual Bibi Andersen, and the lengthy protraction of Kika's rape scene suggests less a distancing effect than a reluctance to recognise when enough is enough. *Kika*'s indignant distress at the television broadcast of her videoed violation ("I'm not prepared to have my rape used to sell milk") invites a presumably unintentional—or perhaps perversely deliberate—ironic reflection on Almodóvar's own treatment of the subject. As a shock tactic, the impact of the device is weakened by its obvious reworking of the post-rape interrogation of Eva in *Matador* and the exhibitionist 'trick' in *What Have I Done To Deserve This?*.

Almodóvar's famed centrality of strong female roles is one of *Kika*'s strengths. Kika's maid Juana (enhanced by the striking features of Rossy de Palma) offers one of the most originally-crafted characters of the film—the love-struck lesbian who fiercely defends her right to sport a moustache, which is "not a solely male prerogative"—though she regrettably becomes a casualty of the abrupt plot swerve halfway through the film. Victoria Abril displays her customary versatility as the predatory Andrea, introducing a futuristic element hitherto unseen in Almodóvar with her much-commented on costume—a Jean-Paul Gaultier creation featuring camcorder headgear and breastplate spotlights. In her role as dizzily pragmatic Kika ('Our Lady of Optimism; as the director has dubbed her), Verónica Forqué also offers an impressive performance, but her style, whilst highly amusing, is shot through with *déjà vu* from *What Have I Done To Deserve This?*, and her work with other comic directors.

Although some of the set pieces display Almodóvar's capacity for originality—such as Kika's second revival of the 'dead' Ramón by plugging his big toe into a light socket and the characteristic 'bad taste' of Pablo's lascivious orange-sucking gag—unfortunately many of the comic strategies are over-familiar. Perhaps significantly, even Almodóvar's elderly mother is wheeled out yet again in the previously-exploited gag of the monotone TV presenter (*Women on the Verge Of a Nervous Breakdown*), this time as a chat-show host, to deliver the film's most glaringly auteurist conceit: "My son is directing this programme." Some of the dialogues distractingly echo earlier films and the opening credits themselves—spotlight, keyhole, scantily-clad mannequin cut-outs—betray their origins: *Law of Desire* and *Pepi, Luci, Bom, and Other Girls On the Heap* (1980). The film's main strength lies in its visual exuberance (even more glossily extravagant than usual, thanks to a relatively big budget by Spanish standards), but here many of the effects are more striking for their recall of previous films than for their own inventiveness.

Almodóvar's highly referential register seems to have come full circle, feeding cannibalistically off his earlier work and devouring much of its originality in the process. If the list of guests at *Kika*'s Gran Via opening night knees-up provides a measure of Spanish institutionalisation of the 'Almodóvar phenomenon'—a concept ironically at odds with the director's declared anti-establishment position—one is tempted to wonder whether Almodóvar has not become a victim of his own notoriety, losing the sharpness of his critical edge and recycling of his own style and ideas into a disappointing imitation of its former self.

VILLAGE VOICE, 5/10/94, p. 53, J. Hoberman

One of *TE! III*'s (*That's Entertainment! III*) first bits—lifted from the 1946 *Ziegfeld Follies*, itself a celebration of entertainments past—has the pre-Lucy Lucille Ball taming a gaggle of spangled cat women. [See Hoberman's review of that film.] Hollywood put out "imaginative, outlandish images," the narrator opines by way of explanation, ' "and audiences loved it." Audiences still do—and as a purveyor of the hot, the hyperbolic, and (recently, alas) the aggressively superficial, Pedro Almodóvar may be the only European auteur who can compete with Hollywood on its own pleasure-principle terms—a thought reinforced by the MPAA decision to brand *Kika* with an NC-17.

Life in its Almodóvariety is most often a carnival for actresses—but who is the butt of the joke? *Kika*'s eponymous heroine (Verónica Forqué, the cheerful hooker in *What Have I Done To Deserve This*) is a professional beautician and a world-class chatterbox. In the press notes, her creator calls her "a naive girl, like Marilyn at her best ... a figure of almost surreal optimism." For Kika, things are never as bad as they seem. She meets her lover Ramon when called upon to make up his apparently dead body—as she babbles away, the corpse wakes from his cataleptic trance and they fall in love.

A dizzy dame with wide eyes and a corona of upswept hair, not so different from Playboy's cartoon innocent Little Annie Fanny, Kika is Almodóvar's notion of a goddess and, as such, is too much for any one individual. She is adored by her dour lesbian maid Juana (Almodóvar axiom Rossy de Palma) and occasionally sneaks upstairs to tryst with Ramon's dissolute American stepfather Nicholas (Peter Coyote), who is himself simultaneously involved with one of her best friends, as well as a statuesque blond played by the transsexual talk show hostess Bibi Andersen.

Kika's opposite and nemesis is Andrea Scarface (Victoria Abril), the celebrity host of a morbidly voyeuristic tele-tabloid news show called *Today's Worst*. If Kika is the spirit of MGM, Scarface is pure TV. Sponsored by a milk company, she delivers her scoops amid the stylized ruins of an empty stage to the enthusiastic applause of a nonexistent audience. Almodóvar's hatred of television has been a career-long running gag—still, as designed by Jean-Paul Gaultier, La Scarface is the movie's prime conception. Her working clothes include a latex bodysuit embellished with an eye-catching pair of faux nipple-exposing rips. Zipping around Madrid on her motorcycle, armored with a movie-light breastplate and a crash helmet topped by revolving camcorder, she's a literal and metaphoric follower of fashion.

The male element in this largely female world is Juana's hunky brother Pablo. A parody of the already parodic character played by Antonio Banderas in *Tie Me Up! Tie Me Down!*, Pablo is pure id; having escaped from prison, he is diverted from his objective, namely burglarizing Kika's apartment, by the aroma of her sex. In the movie's set piece (the source of its scarlet rating), Pablo ravishes the sleeping beautician. Kika resists but Pablo won't stop fucking even when two cops hold guns to his head—an expression of the life-force comparable only to the victim's nonstop chatter.

The scene suggests that Almodóvar has a similar heedless quality, although, unlike its heroine, his movie runs out of fizz well before it ends, in the manner of a Jacobean tragedy, the stage littered with corpses. *Kika*'s crazed soap-operatics are first enlivened but ultimately embalmed by the fantastic couture and museum-quality kitschscape. As Sternberg was to cinematography, so Almodóvar is to production design. And, as was said of Sternberg, "when a director dies, he becomes a cameraman.

Also reviewed in:
NEW REPUBLIC, 6/6/94, p. 26, Stanley Kauffmann
NEW YORK TIMES, 5/6/94, p. C8, Janet Maslin
NEW YORKER, 5/16/94, p. 106, Anthony Lane
VARIETY, 11/8/93, p. 26, Peter Besas
WASHINGTON POST, 5/27/94, p. D7, Desson Howe
WASHINGTON POST, 5/27/94, Weekend/p. 44, Joe Brown

KILLING ZOE

An October Films release of a Davis Film production. *Executive Producer:* Becka Boss, Quentin Tarantino, and Lawrence Bender. *Producer:* Samuel Hadida. *Director:* Roger Avary. *Screenplay:* Roger Avary. *Director of Photography:* Tom Richmond. *Editor:* Kathryn Himoff. *Music:* Tomandandy. *Sound:* Giovanni Di Simone. *Sound Editor:* John Larsen. *Casting:* Rick Montgomery and Dan Parada. *Production Designer:* David Wasco. *Art Director:* Charles Collum. *Set Designer:* Michael Armani. *Set Decorator:* Sandy Reynolds-Wasco. *Set Dresser:*

Michael Malone and Patia Prouti. *Special Effects:* André G. Ellingson. *Costumes:* Mary Claire Hannan. *Make-up:* Ashlee Petersen. *Special Make-up Effects:* Tom Savini. *Stunt Coordinator:* Al Jones. *Running time:* 96 minutes. *MPAA Rating:* R.

CAST: Eric Stoltz (Zed); Julie Delpy (Zoe); Jean-Hugues Anglade (Eric); Tai Thai (François); Bruce Ramsay (Ricardo); Kario Salem (Jean); Salvator Xuereh (Claude); Gary Kemp (Oliver); Martin Raymond (Cab Driver); Eric Pascal Chaltiel (Bellboy); Cecilia Peck (Martina); Gladys Holland (Sub Lobby Teller); Gian Carlo Scandiuzzi and Gerard Bonn (Assistant Bank Managers); Bernard Baski and Michel Jean-Phillippe (Policemen); Elise Renée (Patchoo); Ron Jeremy Hyatt (Concierge); Chris Tragos (Sub Lobby Assistant); George Hernandez (Stodgy Customer); Richard Turner (American Tourist); Kimberly Beck (Customer); Sandra Larédo (Teller); David Thompson (Burnt Vault Guard).

LOS ANGELES TIMES, 8/26/94, Calendar/p. 4, Peter Rainer

The bank heist genre has made it into a new generation with its nose bloodied. "Killing Zoe" is a raucous, arty little neo-film-noir that comes equipped with a bucket of blood to splatter the halls of convention. It's not terribly good but you keep expecting it to take off in unexpected directions. Writer-director Roger Roberts Avary does have a genuine gift for hysteria—not exactly the most welcome gift these days—but his film finally collapses into a hyper-driven snit fit.

We're introduced in the beginning to Zed (Eric Stoltz), a stringy-haired American safecracker recently arrived in Paris to hook up with a childhood friend, Eric (Jean-Hugues Anglade), who is planning a bank robbery with his heroin-hooked gang on Bastille Day. Zed starts things out with a languorous tryst with a peppy prostie, Zoe (Julie Delpy), who, post-passion, informs Zed they both have "Z" names. (This film should carry a bumper sticker, Warning: We Brake for Symbolism.)

Even though Avary is American, as well as a few of his actors and his co-producers (one of whom is Quentin "van Gogh" Tarantino), and even though an L.a. bank doubled for most of the interiors, the film at its worst still has the luridly vapid tone of a *real* French neo-noir like "Subway." (A lot of it is subtitled into English.) Avary converts his in-your-face attitude into an aesthetic. Oliver Stone's "Natural Born Killers," which has a story credited to Tarantino, has the same swagger, but it's much bossier about buzz-sawing you with its bad ideas. At least "Killing Zoe" swaggers to a simpler beat.

It's jazzy and hot-footed in its early sequences, when Zed goes on a robbery-eve joy ride that turns into a druggies' delirium. Avary keeps things loose and wiggy in these opening sequences, and so it's a letdown when the bank heist kicks in and we're left with a lot of hollering and gunplay and cornball Theater of the Absurd theatrics. Anglade, in particular, seems hellbent for glory. He's trying to turn his character into Antonin Artaud with an Uzi.

The film sides with Zed throughout, and when he begins to realize that his old friend is a raving psychopath, the action takes on some resonance. But, for someone as wised-up and world-weary as Zed appears to he, this realization comes painfully late, (If it came earlier there wouldn't be a movie.) And since the bank robbers—who also include Gary Kemp, who was chilling as Ronnie Kray in "The Krays"—are such out-of-control incompetents, there's not much suspense about how it will all turn out. The heist rapidly becomes existential—i.e. boring.

Maybe that's why Avary juices the screen with ultra-violence. He couldn't figure out a clever way to get his guys out of there.

NEW YORK POST, 8/19/94, p. 48, Thelma Adams

Roger Avary's ultra-violent bank caper, "Killing Zoe," is a bloody comedy of excess.

The talented 17-year-old co-authored Quentin Tarantino's "True Romance" and "Pulp Fiction," which will open next month's New York Film festival after scoring the Palme D'Or in Cannes.

Tarantino, who became the reigning king of intelligent splatter with the cult fave "Reservoir Dogs," served as one of Zoe's three executive producers.

Eric Stoltz, who appears in "Pulp Fiction," plays an American safecracker. Zed travels to Paris at the request of an old friend, Eric (Jean-Hugues Anglade), for a daring Bastille Day robbery.

The freckle-faced star—who exposed himself in "Naked in New York"—is the movie's sole American "name" actor.

Stoltz seems intentionally miscast as the world-weary, divorced, Camel-sucking safecracker. When he manipulates the complex tools of the trade in an underground bank vault, he seems hardly capable of toasting a Pop Tart.

And yet, it is this miscasting, this opposition, that makes Zed's tough talk funny. Whenever he mentions his ex-wife, it seems almost impossible that this baby boy would have a dark past and it gets a laugh.

When Zed beds down on his first night in Paris with bank-clerk-by-day, hooker-by-night Zoe (Julie Delpy), he attempts cynicism, confessing, "Sometimes you need the honesty and security of a whore."

The boy-next-door line readings of hard-boiled dialogue is played for laughs, like children talking dirty. "Killing Zoe"'s red-headed hero is clearly no Harvey ("Reservoir Dogs") Keitel, though the actors share a penchant for full-frontal nudity.

Waifish seductress Delpy ("Europa Europa") does a deft turn on the whore with a heart of gold (neither Tarantino or Avary are blazing a trail of invention on the female front so far), but the scene stealer is French actor Anglade ("La Femme Nikita").

Anglade plays a hopped-up Rasputin, a heroin-shooting son-of-the-bourgeoisie, a terrorist-manque. Violent and charming by turns, this greasy-haired rogue is a criminal mastermind without a plot.

Eric leads Zed and a junkie-gang into the bank with a wisp of a plan and plenty of firepower, a recipe for disaster that will reap the splashes of blood and chunks of gore essential to pulp film fiction.

When the inevitable face-off arrives, Zed must choose between Eric and Zoe, between male buddy and bust, between an out-of-control machismo and an equally improbable romanticism.

Avary places his extreme characters in a Bermuda triangle of cultural references, ranging from F.W. Murnau's 1922 "Nosferatu" and British TV's "The Prisoner," to Viking marauders who set their beards ablaze before battle and "Beowulf."

Precocious? Yes. But the writer-director is saved by his willingness to poke fun at his own pretentions.

Avary's directorial debut is madcap mayhem. Call it "Reservoir Puppies."

NEWSDAY, 8/19/94, Part II/p. B7, John Anderson

Like a warning shot that grazes your skull, "Killing Zoe" marks the arrival of Tarantino Season, a time when blood will be spilled across movie screens nationwide, perhaps in vain.

If one wanted to do an Oliver Stone, one could concoct a conspiracy theory. The executive producers of Roger Avary's "Killing Zoe"—Quentin Tarantino, the primeval genius behind the volatile "Reservoir Dogs" and partner Lawrence Bender—are involved in several upcoming projects that are sure to inflame the debate over violence in film. In fact, both the Tarantino-scripted Stone-directed "Natural Born Killers" which arrives next week and Tarantino's second feature, "Pulp Fiction"—which will open the New York Film Festival in September—have already done just that. So why not use "Zoe" as chum to bait the critical waters? Why not get some of the more mindless slaughter out of the way early? And why not use a film that will only firm up Tarantino's own reputation as the thinking person's postmodern Peckinpah?

The comparisons between "Reservoir Dogs" and "Killing Zoe"—in which a dissolute American safecracker named Zed (Eric Stoltz) arrives in Paris to help his childhood friend Eric (Jean-Hugues Anglade pull an allegedly foolproof heist and falls in love with a part-time prostitute named Zoe (Julie Delpy)—are inevitable, and lopsided, Both are about heists, both strive to shock with violence and both feed off a sense of soullessness.

And yet, I was thrilled by "Reservoir Dogs," and repelled by "Killing Zoe." The former had an artfully constructed narrative, some memorable characters and used violence as icing; "Zoe," for all its French-filtered American nihilism, seems not only to be about violence for violence's sake, but both patronizing and opportunistic.

When, during the robbery, a bank employee has a gun put in her mouth and her brains blown out, it's shocking, and useless, but it makes a kind of sense. When a robber extinguishes his cigarette in her puddling blood, we're just being tickled, and we're not laughing.

Avary, clawing at Tarantino's coattails, accelerates the bloodletting until all becomes a wet red blur. But he does achieve one thing he intends: a sense of terror rooted not just in violence but sociopathy.

Anglade, as the reputed mastermind, begins by roughly throwing Zoe out of Zed's room—where, in a nod toward Baudelaire's "Metamorphosis of the Vampire," shots of Murnau's "Nosferatu" have been intercut with the lovemaking. Eric tells Zed not to shower because people will respect him if he smells like sex, takes him first to his gang's fetid apartment and then on a nightlong heroin binge and bar crawl. When robbery time arrives, everyone is strung out and Eric, who constantly claims the crime cannot fail, executes it like a suicide mission. That Eric has AIDS is a bit of news that arrives like a sucker punch.

Stoltz, an actor who lately seems to be everywhere, and nowhere, is well cast as Zed, the bemused American, and Avary's stand-in for the audience. Despite Zed's occasional wry observation, he's simply caught up in a current of anarchy and can't get loose. While the gang is slaughtering customers and employees, he's down below, cracking the vault. He surfaces to find that hell, literally, has broken loose. And that Zoe, whom Delpy presents as perhaps the only partially aware human in the film, is one of the employees Eric is itching to waste.

The problem, ultimately, in "Zoe" is that the killing gets out of hand before we have time to care who gets it. And so, we're simply awash, both in gore and a feeling we haven't seen the last of this kind of slaughter.

SIGHT AND SOUND, 1/95, p. 47, Geoffrey Macnab

Zed, a young American man, arrives in Paris. En route to his hotel, he gets into conversation with his cab driver, who offers him "a wife for the night". Zed has barely booked into his room when this "wife" arrives. She is Zoe, a beautiful Parisian student, who works sporadically as a prostitute to pay her tuition fees. The couple make love and are developing a rapport when Eric, Zed's childhood friend, arrives. Eric unceremoniously throws Zoe out, and tries to get Zed to concentrate on the job in hand. The next day, Bastille Day, Eric and his gang are going to rob a bank; Zed is to be their safe-breaker.

Zed is taken to meet the rest of the thieves. He spends a wild evening with them, drinking and smoking heroin. They end up in a cellar watching a band play Dixieland jazz; this, Eric explains, is the real Paris. The next morning, Zed awakes feeling groggy. The gang storms the bank and takes everyone hostage, including Zoe, who has a part-time job as a bank secretary. When a cashier refuses to open the vault, he is promptly shot, as is an elderly woman employee. Zed seems shocked by this wanton violence, but sets to work in the basement, breaking the safe's combination. On the main floor of the bank, a hostage reaches for a gun and shoots two of the robbers. This provokes more bloody carnage before the gang gets matters under control again. Eric, high on drugs and adrenaline, is becoming seriously unhinged. The police, alerted to the heist, surround the building. Eric wants them to provide an aeroplane for the gang's escape, but they refuse to bargain.

Meanwhile, Zed manages to open the outer door of the vault. There is a security officer guarding the inner vault; Eric blows him up with dynamite. There is money and gold aplenty, but the chances of escaping with any of the loot seems slender. Eric decides to use Zoe as a human shield, but she grabs his machine gun and breaks free, running toward the basement. Zed and gang member Claude, on their way up, bump into her. Claude wants to shoot her, but Zed prevents him. When Eric learns what has happened, he slits Zed's face open and boots him down the stairs. The police break in and overcome the remaining gang members. Eric catches up with Zed and Zoe; the ensuing fight ends when police burst onto the scene and blow him to pieces. Zoe pretends that Zed is a bank customer and escorts him from the building. They drive off to safety.

Nicknamed a little unkindly by one French journalist as "Reservoir Frogs", *Killing Zoe* sometimes seems like a Tarantino film gone continental. With a script organised round a bungled heist, plenty of comic camaraderie between the thieves, and enough blood haemorrhaged in 96 minutes to fill a small swimming pool, it covers similar territory to Tarantino's debut (indeed, Tarantino is one of the film's executive producers). There is a basic difference, though: the action has been transplanted to Paris. Instead of Mr Blond, Mr Pink and co, we have a gang of bohemian anarchists who listen to Billie Holiday records. One even keeps a monkey as a pet.

Writer/director Roger Avary — who co-wrote *Pulp Fiction* — harnesses the elements of the conventional B-thriller, but gives them a distinctly European art-house spin. This lends to some stylistic confusion. *Killing Zoe* tries to be rarefied and downbeat at the same time. It aims for the strong narrative pulse of the typical heist caper, but also has a dilatory, improvised air. It's never quite clear whether we should take the story seriously or not.

Locations and characters are sketched in perfunctory fashion. The Paris here is the arty demi-monde of popular imagination. Zoe is the most contrived figure of all. Appearing as if out of nowhere at Zed's door, she is a composite of clichés — at once a kind-hearted prostitute, an indigent student at the school of fine arts, and a secretary at the bank which the gang plans to rob. Zed is an equally unlikely creation, a twentysomething poet-philosopher who just happens to be an expert safe-cracker. There's a suspicion that the random, muddled quality of the script, which was written in under a week, must be deliberate. It certainly lends the film a giddy sense of dislocation.

The plot creaks, but it's really nothing more than a framework for the visuals. In this department, at least, Avary is always prepared to take risks. When Zed and Zoe meet in the hotel room, their love-making is intercut with scenes from Murnau's *Nosferatu*, showing on the hotel TV. The bald, macabre-looking vampire, rising from his coffin, is treated in comic fashion as some sort of phallic imp. This little bit of self-referential, cinematic expressionism is soon followed by an even more extraordinary sequence in which Zed and the rest of the gang go on a pre-heist drink and drugs binge. They end up in a cellar, listening to a Dixieland band. In their delirium, they see cartoon notes coming out of one of the trumpets. It is the heart of the "real Paris", Eric tells Zed, but the club — decadent, smoke-filled, and full of garishly lipsticked prostitutes — seems more like something out of Weimar Berlin than anything in contemporary France. Jump-cuts, distorting lenses and odd camera angles add to the phantasmagoric quality of the scene.

Avary also quotes from more conventional sources. He shares Tarantino's jackdaw-like enthusiasm for garnering ideas and motifs from other heist movies. There are nods in the direction of everybody from Don Siegel to Godard, and the central conceit of the bungled bank siege echoes *Dog Day Afternoon*. The borrowing is perhaps at its most brazen in a splendidly ridiculous denouement which tries to out-trump *Scarface*, as Eric is caught in a fusillade of bullets. He is hit 42 times but, like Al Pacino in De Palma's film, he takes an eternity to hit the ground. His dying pirouettes are shot in comic-poetic slow motion.

Throughout the film, Avary leavens the random eruptions of violence with incongruous humour. The body count is high. Minor characters are dispatched with alacrity. When a loud-mouthed American tourist complains about being detained, he is promptly killed for such imperialist arrogance. Even the sweet-natured old woman who works in the bank is unceremoniously murdered. The siege itself is confidently handled. As Zed goes about opening the safe, the sepulchral calm in the bowels of the building makes an effective contrast to the chaos with the hostages and their trigger-happy captors above.

One thing Avary lacks, however, is Tarantino's ear for dialogue. There is none of the street patois or sense of milieu that characterised *Reservoir Dogs*. Conversation here comes in a mish-mash of French and English, and often takes on a grating veneer of pseudo-sophistication. The narrative is propelled by coincidence. It can't be said that film is about very much. The director's claims in the production notes that he is trying to portray the "nihilism" of his generation are laughable. This really isn't more than a formal exercise, but it's a virtuoso one. Exhilarating camera work, fluid direction and a gloriously overblown performance from Jean-Hugues Anglade—as a gang leader who seems modelled in equal parts on Rasputin and Al Capone — compensate for any portentousness in the script.

TIME, 9/12/94, p. 86, Richard Corliss

[*Killing Zoe* was reviewed jointly with *Clerks*; see Corliss' review of that film.]

VILLAGE VOICE, 8/23/94, p. 49, J. Hoberman

France invented the movie machine that the U.S. perfected and, ever since, our films have enjoyed a special relationship. Take, for example, two shrewd first features opening this Friday:

Café au Lait, written and directed by 75-year-old Mathieu Kassovitz [See Hoberman's review] and *Killing Zoe*, written and directed by 27-year-old Roger Avary. In the former, an ambitious young French auteur draws inspiration from the American independent movies that were themselves stylistic descendants of cinema vérité and the Nouvelle Vague; in the latter, an ambitious young American indie riffs on the very French gangster flicks inspired by Hollywood noir.

The spirit of Spike Lee informs *Café au Lait* as that of Jean-Pierre Melville does *Killing Zoe*. Each of these ultrafashionable movies spins out of the Franco-American fascination and, however different they are in affect and intent, both open with the camera moving at breakneck speed through the streets of Paris, as if to galvanize the City of Light to the very edge of an aggressively with-it present.

Confidently happening, *Killing Zoe* credits Quentin Tarantino as an executive producer. This smart and bloody caper flick is thus part of the Tarantino summer that began with *Pulp Fiction*'s victory at Cannes, gathered momentum in the revival of *Reservoir Dogs*, should receive a jolt with the premiere of *Natural Born Killers*, and climaxes in gala fashion when *Pulp Fiction* opens the New York Film Festival. Tarantino's onetime colleague behind the counter of a Manhattan Beach video store, Avary contributed to the script for *True Romance* (which suggests nothing so much as the shared daydream of two clerks) and co-wrote *Pulp Fiction*. Not surprisingly, *Killing Zoe* plays itself out in a kindred fantasy zone of bang-bang action, badass attitude, adolescent misogyny, and high-octane gibberish.

Avary's humor is appropriately nihilist: *Killing Zoe* is the sort of movie that exacts a callous frisson from the fate of an obnoxious American tourist trying to exchange his dollars mid-bank heist or revels in the amplified sizzle produced by a Gauloise flicked into a pool of blood. "I hope you enjoy it until it hurts," one of the film's producers told the audience last February at the Sundance Film Festival, where, following in the footsteps of *Reservoir Dogs, Killing Zoe* had its American premiere.

That the Sundance response was severely, if predictably, mixed is not inappropriate. *Killing Zoe* is a movie that courts, as well as illustrates, disorientation. Zed, a young American safecracker played by Eric Stoltz—amusingly reconfigured to suggest a punk version of *le gran* Mickey Rourke—deplanes in Paris to find himself at the mercy of the locals. "I don't speak French," is his first line. Despite his patina of tough-guy grunge, Zed is one more romantic American in Paris. A helpful African cab driver fixes him up with a "wife for the night" and Zoe (Julie Delpy) materializes in his hotel room, snapping her chewing gum and chattering away in unsubtitled French. By default, the ensuing tryst is the most tender sequence in the movie. Avary's cinephilia runs rampant, intercutting Zed and Zoe's lovemaking with a telecast of F. W. Murnau's Nosferatu—a source of free-floating poetry and lewd visual puns.

Their sex may be *kundalini* cool—Zoe has her first orgasm ever with a trick, she says, even though Zed seems perfectly immobile—but the movie is filled with jokes on the hero's passivity. Indeed, the laid-back American is helpless to prevent Zoe's being booted out of his room, still naked, by Eric, his manic French partner in crime. As the caper's lunatic mastermind, Jean-Hugues Anglade, erstwhile lover of Betty Blue and La Femme Nikita, puts on an astonishing show, fulfilling every Anglo-Saxon prejudice about French funk. "In Paris, it's good to smell like you've been fucking—people respect you," he says to dissuade Zed from taking a post-Zoe shower, escorting him to a fetid apartment reeking of hash fumes and dirty dishes, inhabited by a dead cat, a pet monkey, and a quartet of scruffy confederates.

Opinionated and loquacious, Eric has an existential maxim for every occasion: "Before we do the job, we live life—it is better that way." In the most hilarious sequence, the gang takes off on a prolonged magical mystery tour—the eve of Bastille Day, yet—driving around Paris in a state of drugged inebriation. No less than *Café au Lait*'s wannabe homeboy Kassovitz, Avary has a ball designing his own French demimonde. But whereas *Café au Lait* celebrates a local hip-hop culture, *Killing Zoe* contrives a 24-hour Dixieland cavern for Eric's dissolute confreres to shoot heroin and pop pills while engaging in appropriately rancid bonding. In the best vid-store tradition, friendship is founded on arcane connoisseurship. The British member of the gang is not only a total Dixieland freak ("I live for this music—it has total purity of essence") but a passionate fan of Norwegian Viking films.

Shot with an inventively mobile camera, Zed's journey to the end of the night is a jagged smear of blurred sensations. There's a comic Kafkaesque quality to the sequence. The American who has been unsuccessfully trying to find out what time it is since his arrival—is always at least one step behind the action. His jet-lagged, hungover befuddlement escalates the next morning when the gang, now armed with automatic weapons and disguised behind carnival masks, storms the French National Bank to a berserk jungle beat, taking hostages, generating hysteria, and generally posturing like mad rock stars of total power.

If the heist is a debacle from the moment it begins, the horrific details of the ensuing catastrophe are better seen than read. Suffice it to say that Zoe's reappearance is as sublimely romantic as Eric's ABC formula—"We go in, we get what we want, we come out"—is wildly optimistic, and that the movie's wiseass punch line is the best so far this year.

Also reviewed in:
CHICAGO TRIBUNE, 2/9/94, Friday/p. E, John Petrakis
NEW REPUBLIC, 9/12/94, p. 27, Stanley Kauffmann
NEW YORK TIMES, 8/19/94, p. C3, Janet Maslin
NEW YORKER, 8/22 & 29/94, p. 113, Anthony Lane
VARIETY, 1/24-30/94, p. 64, Leonard Klady
WASHINGTON POST, 9/9/94, p. D1, Hal Hinson
WASHINGTON POST, 9/9/94, Weekend/p. 43, Joe Brown

KINGDOM OF ZYDECO, THE

A Mug-Shot Productions presentation. *Executive Producer:* David Steffan. *Producer:* Robert Mugge. *Director:* Robert Mugge. *Director of Photography:* David Sperling. *Editor:* Robert Mugge. *Sound:* William Barth. *Running time:* 71 minutes. *MPAA Rating:* Not Rated.

WITH: Boozoo Chavis; Beau Jocque.

LOS ANGELES TIMES, 7/6/94, Calendar/p. 10, Kevin Thomas

The leaders of bluegrass express the need to preserve its traditional form yet continue to grow, and we're given the impression that both impulses are being accommodated harmoniously.

Judging from the 75-minute "Kingdom of Zydeco," that's not the case with the black Creole music scene in southwestern Louisiana. The music may be irresistible but the crowning of veteran accordionist Boozoo Chavis as zydeco's new king in April (following the deaths of the legendary Clifton Chenier in 1987 and his successor, Rockin' Dopsie, last August) sparked a controversy.

Chavis was crowned zydeco's new king by Lou Gabus, founder and president of the Louisiana Hall of Fame, who insists that Dopsie designated Chavis as his heir. However, many African American Creoles disagree with the selection and believe they should have been able to vote for the new king. It is believed that if they had been allowed to vote, the title would have gone to the young and burly Beau Jocque, currently the most popular zydeco musician on the scene. Jocque sings in English and has a much faster tempo than the still enormously vigorous 63-year-old Chavis.

NEW YORK POST, 7/1/94, p. 45, Larry Worth

Once upon a time in a faraway land, a king lay on his deathbed, whispered his successor's name and passed on. But the people wanted a different ruler to inherit the throne. Thus began the battle for "The Kingdom of Zydeco."

Thankfully, no lives were lost as Boozoo Chavis marshalled his forces and faced down Beau Jocque for the crown and scepter. Then again, it's hard to draw blood when your only weapon is a funky accordion and your breastplate is a pieee of corrugated metal to run spoons across.

Welcome to the world of black Creole music, where truth is definitely stranger than fiction and filmmaker Robert Mugge found a goldmine of entertaining subjects for his new documentary. Indeed, the effort has more colorful characters than all of Hollywood's summer offerings combined.

Watching the elderly Boozoo engage in petty politics to become zydeco's leader puts any presidential debate to shame, while seeing the laidback Beau Jocque's effect on a roomful of two-stepping dancers singlehandedly justifies the production.

But the real pleasure rests with the supporting players; radio jocks, record store clerks or—best of all—the late King Rockin' Dopsie's bleached blonde acolyte engaging in verbal fisticuffs. They serve as tour guides to Southwest Louisiana's version of "The Twilight Zone."

And that's not even mentioning the cornucopia of musical highlights, which will put zydeco fans in seventh heaven, and turn the uninitiated into foot-stomping devotees.

However, director Mugge is surprisingly unimaginative behind the camera, settling for grainy photography and failing to make the most of the surroundings' potential. Further, he includes scenes that have nothing to do with the dueling musicians, then cuts short on the long-awaited appointment.

Put such drawbacks pale next to the pleasures, which should put "Kingdom" on the map for summer moviegoers.

NEWSDAY, 7/1/94, Part II/p. B7, Gene Seymour

"The Kingdom of Zydeco" is both a cunning little comedy of manners and a sweet-tempered celebration of American roots music. It chronicles the sea change that took place in the black Creole music scene of southwest Louisiana with the deaths of both Clifton Chenier and Rockin' Dopsie, king and crown prince, respectively, of zydeco music.

Who, then, assumes titular leadership of this righteously rocking, washboard-driven sub-genre of rhythm-and-blues? Writer-director Robert Mugge begins the story a year ago when Boozoo Chavis, a feisty old coot and veteran accordionist, makes his claim on the crowd. Chavis believes he owns the crown, if only by virtue of having been present at the creation of zydeco, along with Chenier.

Yet if sheer popularity alone comprised the true measure of zydeco royalty, then the title should belong to Beau Jocque, a big, strapping accordionist who's got youth and sex appeal to match Chavis' eminence and experience.

Nowhere is this topic hotter than in the town of Lafayette, La., zydeco's capital. A colorful, engaging cast of disc jockeys, club owners, record dealers and other zydeco artists have their own opinions and biases in the matter. Even Dopsie's opinion, expressed posthumously by his friends, comes into play. His vote was for Chavis.

Who, it turns out, is given the crown in a climactic ceremony filmed in April. (You can be sure they're still arguing about it down there.)

The Chavis-Jocque tussle is prototypical American status buffoonery painted in folk-miniature. After all, as some in the film point out, there wouldn't even have been a dispute of this kind if Chenier, the first and greatest of zydeco's masters, hadn't proclaimed himself king in the first place.

In fact, it is Chenier's spirit that presides most conspicuously over this film, especially in the dance hall performances of both Jocque and Chavis. Both these men kick out the jambs in thrilling performances filmed with blissful authority by Mugge, a specialist in roots music documentaries such as 1991's "Deep Blues."

After watching "Kingdom of Zydeco," you may be scratching your heads wondering whom you would pick for king. And then you may wonder why a crown is needed in the first place. It's Chenier's legacy—and Mugge's observational skills—that triumph in the end.

VILLAGE VOICE, 7/19/94, p. 56, Jeff Salamon

When Beau Jocque, Boozoo Chavis, and their respective accordions blew through town a few weeks ago, I rather brusquely—and perversely, since my toes were tapping and my hips a-shaking—declined to dance with a young woman I would have been happy to dance with. What could account for this self-denying, mean-spirited behavior? Since I am by nature a rather sweet-hearted fellow, I guess that old devil zydeco must have made me do it. Though zydeco, the Creole music of southern Louisiana, is usually thought of as good-time dance tunes, there's no denying that when your body starts swaying and jerking, shadowy aspects can shake loose—dancing feet kick up all sorts of psychological dust. (Working title for a musical self-help book: *Zydeco-Dependency No More*.)

Some of that dust collects around the edges of Robert Mugge's documentary *The Kingdom of Zydeco*. Focusing on the silly rivalry between old-timer Chavis and young lion Jocque for the title "King of Zydeco," Mugge digs up some pretty good oedipal dirt. "I'm the daddy!" Chavis proclaims at one point, and though he gets really worked up about his putative heirs aspirations, you'd have to be more deeply immersed in the zydeco scene than I am to figure out if his bluster is sincere or just so much Hulk Hoganesque spiel. In one monologue that could have been lifted from a Monty Python sketch, Chavis insists that in the old days "I played on the porch by myself, didn't need no drummer—I played with my foot! I didn't have no socks!"

But the heart of a film like this is the concert footage, and unfortunately Mugge hasn't figured out how to capture zydeco live. His camerawork is static, and for long stretches we don't see the dancing audience at all. Since it only occurs to Mugge late in the film to shoot from behind the performers' shoulders, when we do see the crowd, it's almost exclusively in cutaway shots that don't include the band. The result is weirdly disassociative, as if the footage were spliced in from another event. At moments like this, which are supposed to be joyful, if not ecstatic, you feel instead a creepy sort of dread, as if you've suddenly found yourself in the faded, ghostly future musician John Delafose alludes to midway through the film, when he ruefully predicts that zydeco's "gonna last for a while and then die out."

Also reviewed in:
CHICAGO TRIBUNE, 7/15/94, Friday/p. H, Lynn Van Matre
NEW YORK TIMES, 7/2/94, p. 13, Jon Pareles
VARIETY, 8/8-14/94, p. 77, Leonard Klady
WASHINGTON POST, 11/11/94, p. D6, Richard Harrington

L.627

A Kino International release of a Little Bear production. *Executive Producer:* Frédéric Bourboulon. *Producer:* Alain Sarde. *Director:* Bertrand Tavernier. *Screenplay (French with English subtitles):* Michel Alexandre and Bertrand Tavernier. *Director of Photography:* Alain Choquart. *Editor:* Ariane Boeglin. *Music:* Philippe Sarde. *Sound:* Michel Desrois, Gérard Lamps, and (music) John Timperley. *Casting*: Daniel Mallet and Bobby Pacha. *Production Designer:* Guy-Claude François. *Set Decorator:* Marie-Pierre Mercier-Bourboulon. *Costumes:* Jacqueline Moreau. *Make-up:* Agnès Tassel. *Running time:* 145 minutes. *MPAA Rating:* Not Rated.

CAST: Didier Bezace (Lucien "Lulu" Marguet); Jean-Paul Comart (Dominique "Dodo" Cantoni); Charlotte Kady (Marie); Jean-Roger Milo (Manuel); Nils Tavernier (Vincent); Philippe Torreton (Antoine); Lara Guirao (Cécile); Cécile Garcia-Fogel (Kathy); Claude Brosset (Adore); Jean-Claude Calon (Longuet); Jean-Louis Benoit (Gardacier); Eric Savin (Inspector Lefort); Hervé Laudiere (Inspector Biere); Didier Castello (Willy); Isabelle Noah (Philomène); Shériff Scouri (Norredine); John Arnold (Addict "L.627"); Jeanne Dubois (School Director); Patrick Rocca (Division Inspector Caron); Eric Dufay (Mr. Propre); Francis Lax (Commisar); Adrienne Bonnet (Receptionist); Alain Frerot (Man in Hat); Thierry Desroses (Inspector Antillais); Fabrice Roux (Toulouse); Small Mekki (Miloud Amrani); Bruno Raffaelli (Inspector Ricard); Jacques Boudet (Raymond); Jacques Rosny (Tulipe 4); Cyliane Guy (African); Laurentine Milebo (Alimata); Alain Lechaus (Chief Brigadier); François Levantal (Inspector of Police); Jéan Le Mouel (Aussenac); Denis Cherer (Minister); Boris Napes (Man in Blue Shirt); Frédéric Pierrot (René); Rémy Riflade (Developer); Luc Palun (Brigadier); Laurence Roche (PErvenche); Jean Luisi (Toussaint); Joséphine Kouam (Housewife);

Christian Bazir (Black Rasta); Jean Odoutan (Mamadou Diop); Idriss Lanrichi (Hotel Manager); Alexandra Scherpereel (Travesti); Thierry Maricot (European Dealer); Bruno Therasse (Carpet Delivery Man); Didier Harlmann (Plant Delivery Man); François Lescurat (Usher); Gilette Barbier (Old Woman); Thien-Nga Fabre (Chinese Woman); Emmanuelle Bataillle (Spanish Woman); Fabienne Pascaud (Elegant Woman); Jean Granger (Man with Dog); Kamel Cheriff (Said); Yasmine Abdi (Tunisian Chambermaid); Karen Rancurel (Woman in Apartment Block); Eugene Collombat (School Caretaker); Marcelle Barreau (Old Woman Dealer); Carole Africa (Prostitute); Jean-Charles Dumay (Man at Undertaker's); Syvlie Van Den Elsen (Corsican Woman); Frédéric Bourboulon (Client Plume); Françoise Miquelis (Nurse); Amandine Chelon (Moaning Woman); Bobby Pacha (Café Owner); Michel Charvaz (IML Employee); François Decaux (Priest); Francis Girod (Married Father); Alain Sarde (Intruder); Jean-Claude Mino (Maître d'); Marc Peronne (Accordionist); Michel Alexandre (Chef); Jean-Luc Abel (J.P.); Olivier Martial (Rambo); Jacques Pratoussy (Mario); Bruno Lopez (Delinquent); Fayçal Ghrir (Hotel Owner); Victor Ahianor (Bodyguard); hassan El Barnoussi (Old Arab); Dany Logan (Lulu's Mother); Simone Pheto (Couliba); Giséle Torterolo (Shot Young Girl); Uche Aniagolu (Berthe); Fathia Said (Malika); Alban Odil (Italian); Jean-Claude Lagniez (Man Falling from a Taxi-Bus); Ben Braklhia (Cigarette Addict); Corinne Nabet (Young Addict Who Falls); Jean-Paul Pitolin (Vomiting Dealer); Samir Bouadi (Beur); Roberto Montoya (Taximan 77); Tikka (Dead Senegalese Man); Thérèse Moumani (African's Sister); Catherine Abecassis (Beur's Sister); Didi Duprat (Guitarist).

LOS ANGELES TIMES, 9/30/94, Calendar/p. 10, Kevin Thomas

With "L.627," a classic police procedural, France's formidable Bertrand Tavernier puts his mastery of storytelling to a severe test, yet succeeds triumphantly in involving us completely in a story with virtually no exposition or plot and that takes 145 minutes to tell.

He straightaway plunges us into the grinding everyday existence of a veteran Parisian narcotics cop nicknamed Lulu (Didier Bezace), a quietly dedicated man who becomes part of a small, ill-equipped drug squad headquartered in a cramped prefab structure, a site that speaks volumes about the status of their operation.

On the surface Lulu is like his colleagues, who are good-humored, ordinary-looking, conscientious blue-collar guys. There's also a feisty woman (Charlotte Kady). Their camaraderie is warm and solid in the face of their hotheaded, lazy and cynical boss (Jean-Paul Comart). As we follow them on the job, enduring stakeouts in a stuffy van, collaring suspects—sometimes brutally—interviewing countless citizens, we gradually learn that Lulu has a beautiful, devoted wife (Cécile Garcia-Fogel) and small daughter who see little of him—and a tender, loving concern for a waif-like young prostitute/junkie (Lara Guirao).

Lulu, in short, is a wonderful guy, and his life unfolds rigorously with Tavernier's typically acute powers of observation and attention to nuances and details.

"L.627" exudes the vitality and humor so characteristic of the director's work and glows with its ensemble portrayals. Tavernier's inspired cinematographer, Alain Choquart, takes us on a distinctly non-tourist trip through Paris' seamiest, most dangerous areas with their ancient narrow streets. In fact, "L.627," which takes its name from the French drug law, could be transferred intact to New York City.

Always one to speak his mind in his films, Tavernier is here modestly saluting a decent cop—and thereby such men everywhere—intent upon doing his job despite a demoralizing police bureaucracy and widespread public indifference to the war against drugs. Tavernier, reportedly inspired by a brief brush with drugs experienced by his son Nils (who plays one of the cops), has made one of his best films.

NEW YORK POST, 7/15/94, p. 40, Thelma Adams

Don't expect to see the Eiffel Tower in Bertrand Tavernier's Paris Vice—"L.627."

The title refers to the French public health code that covers narcotics. Tavernier, who directed "Round Midnight," intends his portrait of a narc to be as stark and literal as the title. This is reality, mon chere, and it's not pretty.

Didien Bezace plays Lucien Marguet a.k.a. Lulu, the narc. With his mustache and thick brown hair, Bezace resembles Post critic Michael Medved rather than Clint Eastwood.

Lulu, a low-level street detective, is not moving up the police ladder. What sets him apart from his superiors is his zeal—Lulu's a junkie for the street beat.

Tavernier lives for texture, working from a script he co-authored with Michel Alexandre, a veteran French cop. When Lulu's team stakes out a drug dealer in a claustrophobic mini-van, we feel like a bored cop in a can.

Amid broken typewriters and a carbon shortage, Lulu's lazy boss kills time in their shabby trailer/office by playing Risk with his men. "And I invade Greenland," a player calls out.

When the squad chases down a dealer, Lulu forces the suspect to throw up and removes drug balloons from the vomit. This is not a glamorous job.

Three women play a role in Lulu's life. He has a sexless affair with one of his stoolies, Cecile (Lara Guirao). An HIV-positive prostitute, she is caught in a vicious cycle: she hustles to get drugs, she does drugs so she can hustle.

Fellow narc Marie (Charlotte Kady) manages to be one of the boys while remaining an attractive woman, and she's a good cop. Lulu's homebound wife, Kathy (Cecile Garcia-Fogel), laments that all of her husband's home movies feature drug dealers and not one picture of their daughter.

Because Kathy's character is not fully realized a triangular tension between cop, wife and mistress fails to develop. This isn't the only situation that the director sets up which doesn't pay off.

Tavernier's portrait of an impassioned cop who gets results, but must bend the rules to do so, is dynamic—unfortunately, the plot isn't. The director sacrifices structure for texture.

"L.627" pales in comparison to more satisfying TV cop fare, like the excellent "Prime Suspect" with Helen Mirren—or even "Hill Street Blues." These were shows that managed to wed texture and plot, to get you inside the anxiety-ridden, adrenaline-driven minds of their characters, to show their often-neglected personal lives, and still maintain dramatic tension.

At 145 minutes, "L.627" is long enough to feel like an all-night stakeout. Maybe a cop's daily life isn't a thrill, but I prefer my police movies to be one.

NEWSDAY, 7/15/94, Part II/p. B7, Gene Seymour

Those with conventional expectations of how cop movies are supposed to behave may be put off by "L.627."

Mostly, they should be warned that this nearly 2½-hour saga of a Paris narcotics squad delivers no cathartic payoffs comparable, say to "Lethal Weapon's" rain-soaked karate fight. The satisfactions offered by this rambling, anecdotal film are closer to the subtle kicks provided by such TV genre-breakers as "Hill Street Blues" and "Homicide."

"L.627" (the title refers to the French statute prosecuting illegal drug sales) is told from the rueful perspective of a narc named Lulu, short for Lucien, played with appealing world-weariness by Didier Bezace. With his bushy hair style, floppy mustache and tortoise-shelled specs, Lulu looks more like a struggling community college instructor than the street-hardened veteran cop he is.

When one of Lulu's alleged superiors pulls him off a stakeout so the boss can use a department van to get home, Lulu gives the supervisor an earful. This outburst gets him busted down to a mundane desk job for a while before he's moved to a special narcotics strike force operating out of a couple of chintzy trailers in a headquarters' back lot.

Lulu is very much at home among the squad's motley assortment of streetwise sensibilities, among them a wily, sexy woman inspector named Marie (Charlotte Kady). Dodo (Jean-Paul Comart), the aptly named squad leader, is a jaded bungler who seems more interested in making cheap collars than penetrating deeper into the drug trade.

The rest of the cops are, by turns, funny, high-strung and so embittered by their soul-depleting war that they often reduce everyone who isn't on their side—dealers, users and bureaucrats alike—to subhuman status. The fact that those rousted are either Arab or African was a source of controversy when the film was released a couple years ago in France. But the steady-rolling humanism of director Bertrand Tavernier ("Round Midnight," "A Sunday in the Country") gives both authenticity and balance to the unpleasantness "L.627" depicts.

This is a "police procedural" in the most literal sense. Stakeouts, busts (botched or otherwise), interrogations, street chases and office in-fighting are depicted with unflinching, documentary-like literalness. The density of detail may weigh too heavily for some. But when "L.627" is over, you'll feel as if you've done more than just see a movie. You'll feel as if you've lived through it.

SIGHT AND SOUND, 1/93, p. 49, Chris Darke

Thirty-five-year-old Lucien "Lulu" Marguet has worked for fifteen years as an investigator in the Seventh Division of the Paris Police. During a surveillance operation, Lulu makes contact with "un cousin" (police slang for informer), Willy, to gather information about a forthcoming crack consignment. The stakeout is interrupted by Lulu's superior, who calls in the one observation vehicle at Lulu's disposal before the operation can be completed. Furious, Lulu returns to headquarters where he accuses his chief of drunken incompetence. As a result, he is transferred to a desk job at another station.

While in clerical limbo, Lulu receives a call from another 'cousin', Cécile, a young drug-addicted prostitute who is HIV-positive, and for whom Lulu feels a protective affection. They arrange to meet at the Père-Lachaisse cemetery where, facing a memorial stone to the victims of a terrorist attack on an airliner, Lulu makes it clear to Cécile that he considers dealers to be terrorists and that they should be dealt with accordingly. Through the intervention of Commissioner Adore, Lulu is transferred to a neighbouring division where he is integrated into a newly established team dealing exclusively with drug-related crime.

The chief of "les stupes" (from the French for narcotics, *stupefiants*), Dominique "Dodo" Cantoni, is concerned more with filling a quota of convictions than with the penetration of trafficking rings. In the course of a series of raids, Lulu discovers that his commitment is at odds with the lackadaisical approaches of Dodo and his colleague Manuel, but he is supported by Marie, the deputy-chief, and Antoine, who becomes Lulu's partner. The differences within the group come to a head when Dodo, Manuel and Vincent, the youngest 'stupe' and a police-college graduate, carry out a raid on a squat without their colleagues' knowledge. Although intended to net a dealer, the raid succeeds only in unearthing a user, a young immigrant mother, whom Dodo arrests. Lulu and Antoine hurry to the scene where they attempt to placate the inhabitants, while berating Dodo.

Soon afterwards, Lulu learns that Willy, his key informant, is hiding in fear for his life. Lulu seeks him out to assure him of his protection, but later learns that Willy has suffered a savage knife attack after his whereabouts is divulged by Dodo to a gang of dealers. Still in pursuit of the same dealers, the team is staking out a café when Lulu, inside an observation van, spots Cécile on the street. Having been unable to locate her for over a year, Lulu abandons his post to speak to her. She is with her new-born child and informs Lulu that she intends to leave Paris. The team is about to set out after the dealers, and Lulu, hurriedly bidding Cécile goodbye, rejoins them. Back in the van, he realises that he has forgotten to ask Cécile for her new address.

Taking its title from the article of the French Code of Public Health that forbids "all offences linked to the possession, traffic and consumption of narcotics", *L.627* was co-written by an ex-'stupe' Michel Alexandre, whose collaboration presumably ensures an authenticity of detail and tone in the film's study of Parisian plain-clothes drug investigators. Released in France the same week as the Maastricht Referendum, Tavernier's film is an ambitious examination of 'the state of the nation' in the guise of a *policier*. As such, *L.627* occupies the same territory as Bob Swaim's *La Balance* (1982), Maurice Pialat's *Police* (1982) and Catherine Breillat's *Sale comme un ange* (1991), although it is, by comparison, occupied by resolutely 'second-string' performers.

Didier Bezace is outstanding as Lulu, the tenacious and committed investigator whose calm resourcefulness and often sentimental attachment to his 'cousins' succeeds where the blustering tactics of the team's chief, "Dodo" Cantoni—played by Jean-Paul Comart as an overgrown adolescent, complete with hyena cackle and water pistol—fail to do anything other than fulfil the statistical requirements imposed by the Ministry of the Interior. This casting strategy is of a piece with the film's overall style, which opts for an anti-climactic, quasi-behaviourist realism, which concentrates on context and milieu rather than on a lone-vigilante cop.

Doggedly unglamorous, both in terms of character and location, *L.627* studies police procedure at the desk, on the street, in interrogations, and has several strong set-pieces, all of them emphatically focused on the *work* of surveillance and raids. Tavernier adopts the point of view of the police, a tactic carried over from his previous film *La Guerre sans nom* (1991), a documentary on the Algerian War seen from the perspective of French soldiers. But he does so unindulgently, concentrating on "les stupes" as a unit existing between official indifference and street-level trauma.

What defines *L.627*'s realist method—as well as its shortcomings—is Lulu's video-camera. Used off-duty to film weddings, it becomes an instrument of surveillance on stakeouts. The video images mark a kind of zero-degree realism that the film can only aspire to and approximate in a scrupulous and unflinching pursuit of the authentic details of street-level police procedure. The video image acts as a reflexive comment on the difficulties of simplicity, a directorial acknowledgement of the drawbacks of realism.

Tavernier's method is, on the whole, judicious; putting the hot subject of drugs, and the racial networks associated with them, in the 'cool' frame of a procedural *policier*. When Lulu comments, "I have the impression that filming helps me understand things better", it is tempting to take this as the director's own statement of intent"—that audiences will confront their prejudices through his film. *L.627* is a consciously micro-political exploration of urban France at a point when the grand idea of 'Europe' no longer conceals the absence of political will to deal with domestic social devastation.

VILLAGE VOICE, 7/19/94 p. 47, J. Hoberman

Bertrand Tavernier's *L.627* is named for the French statute prosecuting the sale of illegal drugs and was written in collaboration with a Paris police detective, but it might have been set in downtown Bucharest. The backdrop for this rambling exercise in *nouveau* grit is an unfamiliar Paris of slum alleyways, crumbling hotels, and rubble-strewn lots.

Opening, like *The Conjugal Bed*, *L.627* is a film of handheld street photography and vaguely comic-opera interludes; it's engagingly jaunty and discursive and, in its context, perhaps something of a breakthrough. Called in from a stakeout so that his drunken supervisor can use the unit van, the good cop Lulu (Didier Bezace) squawks and finds himself transferred first to a grubby desk job and then to a newly formed narcotics squad. Operating out of a Quonset hut, this querulous bunch of jokers includes an improbably saucy femme inspector (Tavernier favorite, Charlotte Kady) and, somewhat more realistically, manages to bungle most of its operations despite the hyper-focused Lulu's best efforts.

A rumpled little guy whose horn-rimmed glasses match his fuzzy mustache, Lulu looks more like a cinematographer than a cop and, indeed, he turns out to be something of a frustrated *cineaste*, making video documents of dealers in action and using the camcorder on his day off to tape a wedding. Dedicated to his work, genuinely concerned with the welfare of his mainly African and Arab informers, Lulu cherishes the sort of sentimental relationship with the most beautiful of these "cousins," the junkie hooker Cécile (Lara Guirao), that a director might cultivate with a star. The setup reeks of doomed love-affair but, here as elsewhere, Tavernier's movie confounds genre expectations.

Unlike a Hollywood *policier, L.627* eschews gunplay for an abundance of ickier rough stuff: When one dealer swallows his stash, zealous Lulu kicks him in the stomach until he pukes, then scoops up the evidence. The spectacle of white cops beating on Third World criminals has evidently been criticized in France as racist—although, however unpleasant, the attitudes seem naturalistic enough. What may confound American audiences is the absence of relief. Despite his mounting frustration in the face of red tape and collegial ineptitude, Lulu is no Dirty Harry. Running nearly two and a half hours, the film has ample insouciance but insufficient catharsis.

Also reviewed in:
NEW YORK TIMES, 7/15/94, p. C14, Stephen Holden
VARIETY, 9/14/92, p. 49, David Stratton

L'ENFER

An MK2 Productions USA release of an MK2 Productions SA/CED Productions/France 3 Cinéma/Cinémanuel coproduction with the participation of Canal+. *Producer:* Marin Karmitz. *Director:* Claude Chabrol. *Screenplay (French with English subtitles):* Henri-Georges Clouzot, José-André Lacour and Claude Chabrol. *Director of Photography:* Bernard Zitzermann. *Editor:* Monique Fardoulis. *Music:* Matthieu Chabrol. *Sound:* Jean-Bernard Thomasson. *Art Director:* Emile Ghigo. *Set Decorator:* Denis Seiglan, Claire Amoureux-Nicole, Jean-François Corneille, Bernard Camus, Marc Barroyer, Frédéric Bersani, Pierre Galliard, and Claude Vincent. *Costumes:* Corinne Jorry. *Make-up:* Marie Lastenet-Fournier, Stéphanie Lemaire, and Jean-Pierre Berroyer. *Stunt Coordinator:* Michel Thiriet. *Running time:* 100 minutes. *MPAA Rating:* R.

CAST: Emmanuelle Béart (Nelly); François Cluzet (Paul Prieur); Nathalie Cardone (Marilyn); André Wilms (Doctor Arnoux); Marc Lavoine (Martineau); Christiane Minazzoli (Mme. Vernon); Dora Doll (Mme. Chabert); Mario David (Duhamel); Jean-Pierre Cassel (M. Vernon); Sophie Artur (Clothilde); Thomas Chabrol (Julien); Noel Simsolo (M. Chabert); Yves Verhoeven (Young Boy); Amaya Antolin (Mariette); Jean-Claude Barbier (M. Pinoiseau); Claire de Beaumont (Mme. Rudemont); Pierre-François Dumeniaud (M. Lenoir); René Gouzenne (M. Ballandieu); Marie-Thérèse Izar (Mme. Pinoiseau); Dominique Jambert (Young Woman); Louis de Léotoing d'Anjony (Vincent); Jérôme le Paulmier (La Flèche); Vincent Mangado (Young Man); Françoise Meyruels (Plump Woman); Laurent Nassiet (Little Boy at the Café); Catherine Tacha (Mme. Point).

NEW STATESMAN & SOCIETY, 10/21/94, p. 35, Jonathan Romney

L'amour toujours, in French cinema at least, means nothing more than "business as usual". Thirty-five years after Jeanne Moreau's definitive display of the art of ooh-and-aahing ln Louis Malle's *Les Amants*, French film-makers still can't seem to get enough of the tropes of grand passion. Some impressionable young critic in the bowels of the Paris Cinematéque must have gawped at Jean Gabin's pithy imprecation, "Tes beaux yeux ... ", taken it literally, and rushed out to spread a gospel that has lasted generations. From François Truffaut building an entire career on indulging his Svengali syndrome, to Patrice Leconte's weedy gentleman of a certain age convulsing themselves over fantasy odalisques, or Diane Kurys' interminable *trentaine*-something entanglements for mature professionals ... You can see why the *Germinal* school is there, with their blustery historical theme-pageants. It's something else to do.

Of course this is a narrow, stereotypical view of French cinema, but then it's a view that UK distributors tend to cater to. What used to be called "continental passion" sells, and has done since at least the 1950s, while other European waves come and go. One film that did effectively deflate Anglo-American notions of Gallic passion was Roman Polanski's massively underrated *Bitter Moon*. An acute, if indulgent, study of male hysteria, and of the Svengali complex itself, *Bitter Moon* was so finely tuned in its ironic use of romantic excess that when I saw it, half the audience was rocking with laughter—and I'd like to think that half of them were doing so out of discomfort. *Bitter Moon* had an embittered would-be Hemingway in Paris regaling a deeply embarrassed Bertie Wooster type (Hugh Grant in best "steady on!" mode) with the saga of his tormented passion for Emmanuelle Seigner—Polanski's own current muse, whose whole persona is almost a parody of Anglo-American fantasies of simmering Frenchness. *Bitter Moon* was a cruel dismantling of the myth of *amour fou*, and it proved that even such a dead topic could come alive, given attention to the finer points of story-telling. In fact, Polanski's elaborately constructed trick box didn't so much tell the story as untell it. Only a deconstructive love story could have been so exquisitely embarrassing.

Claude Chabrol's *L'Enfer* comes nowhere near. The laziest of all the Nouvelle Vague veterans, Chabrol here resorts to filmmaking as ghost-writing, taking on a script by the late and indisputably great Henri-Georges Clouzot, maker of *Le Corbeau* and *Les Diaboliques*, and at his best, a filmmaker to out-Hitchcock Hitchcock (Clouzot died before he could film *L'Enfer*).

It's the story of Paul, a hotelier (François Cluzet) and his young wife Nelly (Emmanuelle Béart). At first, he's crazy about her, then he's just crazy, and starts storming around their rural idyll, convinced she's screwing every guy in sight. Love is hell, warns this blackest of scenarios, but Chabrol's lost the grip on the infernal that he once had. He gives us dual optics, so that we see could either be the evidence of our senses, or the non-evidence of Paul's perceptions. Eventually we reach the point where the optics jar with each other so much that we're no longer certain if we're seeing anything at all, and we end up with a trick ending that isn't one: It looks like a poignant twist, but it might just be that Clouzot never completed the original and Chabrol is simply respecting the final dotted line.

But there's nothing here to grip us, much less worry us. Too much of the film rides on Cluzet's ability to pop his tightly crammed cork at short notice, and on Béart's ability to reduce her considerable acting range to just the cheesecakey moves and shimmies. Considering how hard-edged she was in *La Belle Noiseuse*, it's odd to see her staking all on her pout. But then Clouzot had already done full justice to the theme of "pouting women, doubting man" in his 1960 film *La Vérité*, in which an absurdly kittenish Brigitte Bardot worried several older men rigid. With *L'Enfer*, he got out when the going was good.

NEW YORK POST, 10/19/94, p. 36, Thelma Adams

Some people can watch French actress Emmanuelle Beart break baguettes and be satisfied. A cross between Brigitte Bardot and Julia Roberts, the voluptuous free spirit of "Manon of the Spring" stars in "L'Enfer."

This muddled mess of a movie has a fine pedigree. Claude Chabrol ("Madame Bovary") directs his own adaptation of Henri-Georges Clouzot's long-dormant script. In 1964, Clouzot cast Romy Schneider to star in this jealousy-themed thriller, but a heart attack forced the "Diabolique" director to abandon "L'Enfer" ("Hell").

In this updated version of Clouzot's script Paul (Francois Cluzet) seems to be verging on paradise. He buys a lakeside inn and marries Nelly (Beart). They soon have a son and a successful, if demanding, business.

Paradise is lost for Paul after he catches Nelly in the dark with a smarmy but studly mechanic. Whether the liaison is real or imagined, jealousy consumes Paul. His descent into a self-made hell is the psychological thriller's spine.

Is Paul a cuckold or simply cuckoo? Unless watching mother Nelly disrobe into sexy lingerie or water-ski with her body tense and cleavage pronounced distracts you, the plot sickens along with the increasingly paranoid Paul.

While the defenders of French culture rail against Yankee cultural imperialism and decry box-office behemoths like Schwarzenegger and Stallone, we free-trade Americans have nothing to protect us from high-toned French trash.

NEWSDAY, 10/19/94, Part II/p. B11, Jack Mathews

The history of French director Claude Chabrol's "L'Enfer" (Hell"), a psychological drama of jealousy and madness, is a lot more interesting than the movie, so I'll talk about that a little first.

The original screenplay, from which Chabrol adapted it, was written more than 30 years ago by the late Henri-Georges Clouzot, who had previously written and directed the classic thrillers "Diabolique" and "Wages of Fear." Clouzot even began filming the story, with Romy Schneider in the role taken up by Emmanuelle Beart, but illnesses—first of one of the stars, then of Clouzot—shut it down.

Just what Clouzot intended is not made very clear by the production notes, or by the film Chabrol made of it. Certainly, there is nothing in the finished "L'Enfer" to suggest the range of psychological complexities that must have inhabited Clouzot's original 1,000-page script. In fact, after its awkward jump-cut opening, which covers the first few exhilarating years of the marriage between Paul (Francois Cluzet), a workaholic provincial innkeeper, and the beautiful Nelly (Beart), "L'Enfer" follows the dramatic arc of a body dropped out of an airplane.

From the moment Paul first suspects Nelly of infidelity, finding her and a handsome young guest looking at slides in a room off the inn's foyer, it is clear that (a) she is innocent, and (b) that he is deluded to even suspect her.

Chabrol goes to great effort to make sure there are no misunderstandings about Paul's mental state. He allows us to watch Nelly's behavior through both the disinterested camera's eye, and through Paul's paranoia. We see her as a model of devotion to both him and their young son, yet he sees her every gesture, every trip to town to visit a friend or relative, every conversation with another man, as the flagrant betrayal of a wanton nymphomaniac.

Somewhere in the development of the story, Chabrol made a conscious decision to turn it away from a study in jealousy and to concentrate instead on a man's unbroken fall into madness, whizzing past pique and jealousy on the way. That is the filmmaker's prerogative, and he has gotten fine performances from Cluzet and Beart. But it is a less interesting subject, and even as an interior view of psychosis, not very illuminating.

Though we spend a lot of time inside Paul's troubled mind, seeing those distorted images and listening to his inner voice egg him on, we feel less informed than imprisoned. Maybe there were clues to his condition in those gaps from the early years of his marriage. Some earlier infidelities, perhaps, or at least suggestions of a pattern of insecurity in his background. Anything that might explain why, on one sunny day, he would suddenly decide Nelly is providing guests with more than a free continental breakfast.

In the end, maybe Clouzot's from-the-grave collaboration with Chabrol wasn't such a great idea. Clouzot was a master of morbid psychological suspense—Hitchcock without a sense of humor, he has been called—and I suspect that he intended for Paul to create his own hell by allowing his imagination to run wild.

But Chabrol is less interested in psychological than social malaise, and "L'Enfer" seems to be struggling to comment on some larger, life-is-hell among the bourgeoisie, issue.The result is a compromised, and ultimately unsatisfying melodrama.

SIGHT AND SOUND, 11/94, p. 44, Phillip Kemp

In south-west France, while supervising the building of his country hotel, Paul Prieur meets Nelly, a beautiful young woman. They fall in love, marry and have a son, Vincent. The hotel prospers and for some years the couple are idyllically happy. But gradually Paul starts to detect discrepancies in Nelly's accounts of where she's been and what she's been doing, and comes to suspect her of having an affair with Martineau, the local *garagiste*.

Paul takes to following Nelly into town. Catching him at it, she is initially amused and even flattered by his jealousy. But after seeing Nelly and Martineau water-skiing together, Paul goes missing for hours, and on returning hurls wild accusations at his wife. Protesting her innocence, she bans Martineau from the hotel and promises never to go into town again. Paul's jealousy only increases, and he begins to suffer from hallucinations. During a film show organised by Duhamel, an elderly guest at the hotel, Paul screams insults at Nelly and hits her. The guests start to check out.

One evening, during a power cut, Paul becomes convinced Nelly is having sex with every man in the hotel, both staff and guests. He beats and rapes her. When she visits the local doctor, Dr Arnoux, Paul follows her and insists she is mad. Talking ambiguously about a stay in a clinic, Arnoux sends them both back to the hotel to await an ambulance the next morning. During the night, Paul, believing Nelly is plotting against him, ties her to the bed. In the bathroom he falls and hits his head. He thinks he has untied Nelly, and imagines slitting his own throat. As dawn breaks Nelly is still tied up, while Paul gazes bleakly out of the window.

A mix of sex, food and violence, simmered in the pressure-cooker of French provincial claustrophobia, has furnished some of Chabrol's best films—*Le Boucher*, to look no further. So a study of psychotic marital jealousy set in a gourmet Auvergnat hotel should in theory have provided ideal material. If this time the dish seems disappointingly underdone, it's maybe because the chef is working to a recipe not his own. The script of *L'Enfer* was originally written by Henri-Georges Clouzot, director of *The Wages of Fear* and *Les Diaboliques*, who started shooting it in 1964, but suffered a heart attack and had to abandon the project. Chabrol, while keeping "the main framework" of Clouzot's screenplay, has "brushed it up a lot" and updated the action to the present, "lightly modernising the dialogue".

On balance, he might have been wiser to leave it in period. Set in 1964 in the depths of the provinces, the plot might have just about passed muster; but that an intelligent young woman of today would stick with an increasingly deranged husband, meekly submitting to his whims, strains belief past the limit. Emmanuelle Béart, perhaps uneasily aware of the credibility gap, rather overdoes the innocent girlish frolics. François Cluzet (Dexter Gordon's French minder in Tavernier's *Round Midnight*) is well cast as the paranoid Paul—even at his most relaxed there's a nervous tension about his neck muscles—but he too by the end is reduced to desperate mugging as the plot falls away beneath his feet.

Yet to begin with, *L'Enfer* promises well. Chabrol has always had the knack of injecting small notes of disquiet into seemingly placid situations, and the first half of the film abounds in off-hand, off-key details: giggles in a darkened room, warplanes soaring high overhead, a video store displaying a poster, "Les Infideles". There's one weirdly unsettling moment while Paul is tracking his wife through the streets of the town: as he passes the open doors of a cathedral, a wedding procession suddenly swoops at him out of the darkness. We even get a hint that his state of mind may be deliberately drug-induced: "I'm the queen of sleeping-pills," announces Nelly, blithely dosing her insomniac husband from a well-stocked drawer.

Some at least of these intimations ought to pay off in due course. Were this pure Clouzot, a fiendish scam would be revealed, with Nelly, say, plotting to destroy Paul in cahoots with the fatherly Dr Arnoux. Were it Chabrol on good form, we could expect some violent emotional catharsis, blood dappling the *haute cuisine*. Instead *L'Enfer* flounders, stumbles and in the end falls abjectly apart. Paul ties Nelly up or he doesn't, he slits his own throat or he doesn't, switching in and out of hallucinations till we neither know nor care what's true. As a bleak dawn breaks, the title comes up—"SANS FIN". Paul, we're to understand, is trapped in an endless hell of his own devising. But there's a more literal interpretation: that the film simply lacks an ending. More's the pity, when it started so well.

VILLAGE VOICE, 10/25/94, p. 62, Georgia Brown

The title of Claude Chabrol's tense, claustrophobic new film may translate as hell, but the setting of *L'Enfer* is anything but hellish—a tranquil lakeside inn, the sort of low-key family-run establishment that has loyal guests reserving their favorite room for the next season. This being Chabrol, however, can *la rupture* be far behind? The placid lake-pictured sans human contamination—will surely be ruffled by some foul and ominous wind. Indeed, by the end of *L'Enfer*, the modest resort has become as nightmarish as that mountaintop hotel in *The Shining*: guests flee, insects screech, the patron has lost his marbles.

First, think what it would be like to run such a hotel: always having to set the tone, keep up a front, hide the cranky moods. The question is whether the dogged, good-looking Paul (François Cluzet, the wimpy POW husband in Chabrol's *Story of Women*, the husband who runs off to Africa in Agnieska Holland's *Olivier, Olivier*) has the gifts—the expansive nature, the ability to anticipate the needs of others, He thinks he does. At 35, the ambitious Paul buys the hotel where he's been working. Now, of course, he needs the proper wife: cheerful attractive, hardworking. Perhaps the one he takes, Nelly (the ever stunning Emmanuelle Béart), is too beautiful, but she has stamina, courage, and an upbeat disposition.

Chabrol once taught us to look at Hitchcock (in his and Eric Rohmer's 1957 *Hitchcock: The First Forty-One Films*) and then proceeded to teach us to look at Chabrol. It's neat to watch *L'Enfer* set in motion: click, click, click. In the first few minutes years fly by with no palpable transition: proposal, wedding, baby boy, the child starts to walk. Crucial information slips like little notes into your pocket, to be read later. For instance, Paul no sooner announces his son's first steps than Nelly pops out to say he's walked before. Is Paul out of touch? Is Nelly smug? Answers suggest themselves only at the end.

Periodically, training jets shatter the hotel's tranquility. You get used to it, Paul tells the new guest. The child cries in the night. When Nelly gets up, Paul is annoyed—almost, you might say, jealous. The family doctor warns Paul about the pills he takes to sleep and about his drinking. One day Paul catches Nelly looking at slides with a guest, Martineau (Marc Lavoine), a slick young blade who runs a garage in town. When Martineau takes Nelly waterskiing in his boat, they stop to rest on an island. Are they or aren't they? This oldest of stories is told nearly entirely from Paul's perspective. Point of view is everything here, making the film almost unrelievedly painful.

Originally *L'Enfer* was a project of Henri-Georges Clouzot, one he began filming in 1964. First, the production was interrupted by star Serge Reggiani's pneumonia; then, after they'd begun filming again with Jean-Louis Trintignant opposite Romy Schneider, Clouzot himself had a heart attack. Production never resumed. The script Chabrol has adapted here was Clouzot and José-André Lacour's first draft, a chronological, simplified version of the one Clouzot wanted to make. It's a pared-down anatomy of jealousy that seems almost punishingly straightforward.

Use is made of a tactic elaborated on in the Hitchcock book—something Truffaut first noticed in *Shadow of a Doubt*—"the principle of rhyme," or doubling. Images or actions are repeated for emphasis. Happening twice here: a happy couple pedaling a boat; a child getting his throat examined; a mysterious light glowing in a dark room; a wedding party bursting from a church. A shot of the flickering lake begins and ends the movie. Partially, repetition is a way of inviting reflection, but there's also a sense of reflection as mirroring. Paul is always looking into mirrors, sometimes talking to himself.) According to Chabrol's law, two beings always inhabit one body, the beast and the man.

Originally developed (by Clouzot) in close collaboration with psychologists, *L'Enfer* still has a clinical edge. If the couple were more charismatic, the film might be richer, like *Le Boucher*, Chabrol's great, sympathetic portrait of a serial killer. But Cluzet's Paul isn't a sad, wounded beast like Jean Yanne's Popaul. He's too uptight; his shortcoming as a hotel manager works against him as a hero. Nor does Béart's Nelly grow into a luminous or compelling victim (or accomplice). Seen from her husband's vantage—licking an ice cream, coltishly prancing down the rue—she's merely a luscious morsel, a ravishing fruit that men would love to pick.

Tantalizingly, Chabrol includes one achingly tender interlude in which Paul makes a rent in his madness. For one night anyway, sanity is restored. It's just after this that we're shown the couple in their pedal boat for the second time (the first was just after their wedding). Their legs are churning furiously, but the boat viewed from the rear looks like its going nowhere.

Hovering over all this unrealized idea of the hotel as haven. What Paul desperately wants is what his guests want: quiet, rest, calm. He craves peace, yet he's the one to violate it. Inevitably, his sanctuary turns into an asylum in the perverted sense, a loony bin.

Also reviewed in:
CHICAGO TRIBUNE, 11/25/94, Friday/p. C, Michael Wilmington
NEW YORK TIMES, 10/19/94, p. C17, Caryn James
VARIETY, 2/21-27/94, p. 42, Lisa Nesselson
WASHINGTON POST, 2/24/95, p. C7, Hal Hinson

LA SCORTA

A First Look Pictures release of a Claudio Bonivento Productions film. *Producer:* Claudio Bonivento. *Director:* Ricky Tognazzi. *Screenplay (Italian with English subtitles):* Graziano Diana and Simona Izzo. *Based on an idea by:* Stefano Sudrié and Giovanni Romoli. *Director of Photography:* Alessandro Gelsini. *Editor:* Carla Simoncelli. *Music:* Ennio Morricone. *Sound:* Danilo Moroni and (music) Franco Patrignani. *Sound Editor:* Filippo Bussi. *Production Designer:* Mariangela Capuano. *Costumes:* Catia Dottori. *Make-up:* Stefano Fava. *Running time:* 92 minutes. *MPAA Rating:* Not Rated.

CAST: Claudio Amendola (Angelo Mandolesi); Enrico Lo Verso (Andrea Corsale); Carlo Cecchi (Judge Michele De Francesco); Ricky Memphis (Fabio Muzzi); Leo Gulliotta (Policeman); Tony Sperandeo (Raffaele Frasca); Angelo Infanti (Judge Barresi); Ugo Conti (Nicola); Francesca D'Aloja (Anna Spano); Lorenza Indovina (Lia Corsale); Rita Savagnone (Angelo's Mother); Giovanni Alamia (Squealer); Giovanni Pallavicino (Padre Virzi); Benedetto Raneli (President Caruso); Luigi Maria Burruano (Informer); Claudia Bonivento (Roberta De Francesco); Francesco Sicillano (Policeman Marchetti); Giacinto Ferro (M.P. Nestore Bonura); Davide Gavine Cannas (Davide Corsale); Nunzia Greco (Bonura's Wife); Guia Jelo (Rosalia Carabba); Salvo Mangione (Magistrate); Mimmo Mignemi (Maresciallo); Marco Magnesia

(Mattia Corsale); Antonino Pensabene (Vice-Prevect Scavone); Ninni Picone (Janitor); Elda Alvigini (Milena); Maurizio Romoli (Judge Pollara); Santi Bellina (Salvatore Genna); Claudio Spadaro (Farina); Tony Sperandeo, Jr. (Igor Corsale).

CINEASTE, Vol. XX, no. 4, 1994, p. 47, Hank Heifetz

In American gangster movies, the Mafia usually appears in loud, showy images. Within approaches as different as the high opera of the first two *Godfather* films (or the feeble comic book of *The Godfather, Part III*) or Martin Scorsese's sprightly dance-of-death realism in *GoodFellas*, the dons and soldiers of La Cosa Nostra parade their brutality and vulgarity, sentimentalize their feelings for their domestic and their criminal 'families,' and essentially draw the viewer's emotional interest to themselves, not to their victims or to the society they manipulate through their primary resource: the fear of death. In *La Scorta* (*The Bodyguards*)—set in the Sicilian port city of Trapani—director Ricky Tognazzi has produced a film about the Mafia from which the killers themselves are almost totally absent—except for distant figures fleeing on a motorbike and a single turncoat gunman, briefly interviewed and glamorless. The power that can kill exists as tension and fear in those who are threatened, compliance and fear in the bureaucrats and politicians who bow to it.

Tognazzi—son of comic actor Ugo Tognazzi—dealt in his last film, *Ultra*, (winner of the Golden Bear at the 1991 Berlin Film Festival) with a grim contemporary problem, both Italian and European—the neo-fascist youth culture energized by racism and marked by fanatic devotion to local soccer squads. *La Scorta* springs from another major Italian process—the wave of investigations of the Sicilian Mafia (and to a lesser degree other organized crime groups in southern Italy) fueled by recent years of crisis over governmental corruption. The Mafia has responded with a wave of public assassinations, the most famous and flamboyant being the killing, two years ago, of Judge Giovanni Falcone, his wife, and three police bodyguards through a bomb in a highway tunnel, detonated by remote control as his car was on its way to the Palermo airport. Tognazzi's film loosely draws its story from an earlier situation (in 1989) of a northern magistrate assigned to a Sicilian investigation; but clearly, for the filmmaker and writers, the film is charged with the memory of those three bodyguards, blown to bits, their names remembered only by families or within the police.

The bodyguards of *La Scorta* are four *carabinieri*, members of the militarized national police, assigned to provide the protective escort (scorta) for Judge De Francesco, who has arrived in Trapani to replace another investigative judge murdered along with his single *carabinieri* guard. They are the focus of the film—their feelings, their personal lives, their growing, almost filial, solidarity with the judge from the north who treats them with respect and who, when it becomes clear that the local authorities cannot be trusted, turns them into his investigative team.

Three of the *carabinieri* are Sicilians, the other a mainland southerner, reflecting the traditional preponderance within the force of southerners from relatively poor families. All of them understand the extreme danger of their assignment, but come into it at first from different angles and with different levels of commitment. Only the passionately angry Angelo has requested it, because his friend was the murdered police guard. Fabio, the non-Sicilian, begins as the least enthusiastic, seeing only the prospect of a meaningless death and asking for reassignment. He and Angelo live in the *carabinieri* barracks while Andrea, who commands the unit, is a family man with young children, assigned an apartment not quite large enough for them all. Played by Enrico Lo Verso—who was also the well-meaning young *carabinieri* in Gianni Amelio's sensitive update of neorealist style, *Il Ladro di Bambini*—Andrea is a tender husband and father but one for whom, at the outset, family considerations outweigh higher loyalties. He is at first willing to pass on some information about the judge's investigation to a local bureaucrat, who dangles the promise of a better apartment before him. Later he will confess his action to the judge and be forgiven and respected for his honesty.

Raffaele, the fourth bodyguard, is looking forward to his marriage to a woman who works in a pastry shop. The two times he meets with her—one by night, one by day—begin with a brightly lit panning shot of a showcase of sparkling Sicilian pastries. The second appearance of the pastries is followed by the only long sequence in bright sunlight, the bodyguards relaxing at a beach with

Andrea's family and Judge De Francesco's young daughter. They are among the very few moments in the film where light prevails.

Otherwise the film is almost all shadows, night, interiors, overcast skies in normally sun-drenched Sicily. *La Scorta* begins in the darkness of a rainy season twilight, with clouds gathering over the ocean, and it ends in the darkness of night. Threat from the skies—in the scene before the credits—hangs over an old man in a dark room who is preparing a meal. As gunfire sounds outside and the old man runs downstairs in anguish, we find that he is the father of the police guard who has been killed along with the judge he was protecting—the event that will bring De Francesco to Sicily. Not only does this scene initiate the kind of symbolic lighting which runs throughout the film but it also sounds the motif of domesticity threatened. For in *La Scorta*, the dinner tables around which friends commune are the province not of the Mafia but of the honest people they menace.

Tognazzi's most powerful achievement in this small but strong film is the creation of a mood of relentless menace, without melodrama and without strain. Pulsing through the constant shadows and the threat of rain are the hair-trigger reflexes of the bodyguards and the dance of their deployment as, automatic weapons at the ready, they spring from cars or survey the open sidewalks that must rapidly be crossed. Driving at high speed—sirens blaring amid traffic because any slowdown is dangerous—they are seen in tense close-ups within their cars or followed through aerial shots that give a sense of unavoidable destiny surveying and dominating the trapped scurrying of human beings. Ennio Morricone's throbbing, restrainedly percussive score accentuates the restless, unsettling drive of the film.

The expressive device of seemingly humdrum events triggering terror provides some of the film s most frightening moments. Passing a car parked by the side of a country road becomes an ordeal, since it may contain a bomb. When there is a malfunction of a hand-held remote control device that normally raises the garage gate of the judge's office building so that they can speed inside without slowing down, it feels like possible sabotage intended to force them out of their cars into open space. The editing quietly suggests threat in sequences that at first seem calm interludes: Andrea's small son strikes his father and mother, as they stand kissing, with the cork bullet of a play gun; a shot of a bodyguard sitting and smiling cuts to a menacing view of police weapons being fired on a practice range; the doorbell rings during a dinner at Andrea's house which marks a new level of comradeship between the judge and his *carabinieri* and, when the door is guardedly opened, the camera closes in on a clip of bullets taped outside the door as a Mafia threat.

But the viewer's apprehension, maintained with a breathless, unremitting elegance, never finds the expected violent release. The final, successful assault on Judge De Francesco and his remaining bodyguards is accomplished not through bullets but through words on paper. They have discovered the name of the local *capomafia* and his illegal control of water rights in the city (one of the traditional goals throughout Sicily of Mafia power politics) and De Francesco has initiated seizures of documents when, in turn, a document is delivered to his office ordering his transfer out of Sicily. As Andrea, the head of the escort, reads the words, the camera moves up over a partition and in a long, continuous tracking shot that follows one person, then another, it reveals most of the bureaucrats we have earlier met who, through self-interest and fear, permit the Mafia to flourish, and who have now helped to close off De Francesco's mission.

The reading continues over future time—quiet words that do the work of gunshots—as the judge and bodyguards are seen, by night, leaving the bunker-like apartment into which De Francesco has moved. Then they set off on their final ride together, with the music mourning, for the harbor, where they embrace with strong, restrained feeling and we learn that the bodyguards have been reassigned to menial, tedious duty. We see them through De Francesco's eyes, growing smaller, on the dock in the darkness. In a practical sense, nothing has been accomplished—only the creation of human bonds and the memory of them retained.

They have been defeated by the modern Mafia, skilled not only in hogging water rights, in terror and in murder, but also in technology. (One anonymous mafioso has earlier amused himself by telephoning Angelo at a wiretap location to show that he is overhearing everything.) In this regard, the recent election of a rightist coalition in Italy—with Mafia support (for the straight-forward reason of getting opponents out of power) apparently going to the neofascists in the south—is likely to turn back the tide of Mafia investigations.

La Scorta takes a very contemporary place among the body of Italian films on crime and corruption in the South. Within probably the greatest of them, Francesco Rosi's *Salvatori Giuliano* (1962), its action set in the Forties and early Fifties, the bandits and Mafia of Sicily moved in clear black and white through the sharp visual contrasts of the island—bright sun and dark clothes, blinding white houses and tiny darkened alleys—carrying their complex motives and loyalties. In *La Scorta,* motives and loyalties are clear or become clear, but everything else—hope, safety, honest memory—is tangled in shadows, true perhaps now not only of the South but also of Italy itself.

LOS ANGELES TIMES, 7/8/94, Calendar/p. 11, Kenneth Turan

The worst of times for a particular country may end up the best of times for its filmmakers. Witness "La Scorta,"a taut, expertly made political thriller that confronts Italy's pervasive institutional corruption with a surprising combination of energy and sensitivity.

Slickly directed in the best sense by Ricky Tognazzi, whose father Ugo was a celebrated actor ("La Cage aux Folles"), "La Scorta" offers more than the expected squealing tires on rain-slick pavement. It is also a thoughtful film, concerned with character to an extent most melodramas don't think is worth their while.

Set in Sicily, where the Italian government and the Mafia have been engaged in a bitter, violent power struggle, "La Scorta" is freely adapted from the experiences of a real-life investigating magistrate and the escort of *carabinieri*, the state police, designated to protect his life.

An expensive film by Italian standards, "La Scorta" ended up being a huge hit in its home country and was we'll received as well at last year's Cannes Film Festival. The factors that helped make it popular, qualities like carefully controlled tension and unself-conscious heroism, should translate easily to this country as well.

"La Scorta" focuses on a pair of *carabinieri*, part of a detail assigned to a magistrate who has vowed to at least begin to clean up the city of Trapani. One, Angelo Mandolesi (Claudio Amendola) has come back to Sicily because his best friend was killed trying to protect the city's last magistrate. The other, Andrea Corsale (Enrico Lo Verso), never left, and now has a wife and three children who are strongly affected by the kind of work he does.

When Judge De Francesco (Carlo Cecchi) arrives, he doesn't feel comfortable with the idea of protection. And his escort, it turns out, has to make do with an ancient Alfa that barely runs. There are so few bullet-proof vests that the detail has to draw straws to determine who gets one.

Gradually, however, the seriousness of the problem becomes clearer to both the judge and his protectors. It is a venality so nearly all-inclusive that it makes almost everyone, even many of its supposed opponents, an accomplice in the evil to one degree or another.

To meet this challenge, the previously faction-ridden escort, including the uncommitted Fabio (Ricky Memphis) and the easy-going Raffaele (Tony Sperandeo), coalesce into one of those cinematic band of brothers, united in their determination to protect the judge and see that at least an attempt at justice is made.

A lot of the elements of the script by Graziano Diana and Simona Izzo are extremely traditional: wiretaps, gutless squealers and midnight rendezvous. But director Tognazzi, helped by one of the best of Ennio Morricone's recent scores, makes the scenes crackle and doesn't fall victim to excessive histrionics.

Watching these obsessed men shiver with uncertainty as they enter a building or climb a flight of stairs knowing that something could go wrong at any time, that even a momentary lapse could mean death, is as intense an experience as it sounds. Operating on the theory that if you're not scared, you're not doing your job, they make us feel the realism of their story.

Essential here is the work of the excellent actors, most of whom are not well known to American audiences.

NEW YORK POST, 5/4/94, p. 33, Thelma Adams

Ricky Tognazzi has guts.

Actor Ugo Tognazzi's son has taken on the Mafia in "La Scorta," which opens today at the Film Forum. The thriller's title literally means the escort but has been translated as "The Bodyguards" (catching the Whitney Houston wave?).

The Mafia has become movie-of-the-week material in America. John Gotti, the Teflon Don, is in a sticky situation. He's behind bars and his organization is showing the downside of the survival of the fittest.

In Italy, the Mafia retains the power to topple governments. Two years ago, a Mafia-related scandal led to the indictment of five prime ministers.

Tognazzi, with screenwriters Graziano Diana and Simona Izzo, have ripped their story from recent headlines. Jurors are threatened. Judges are killed. The mayor of Corleone, Siciiy, finds a calf's head on the threshold of his fiancee's house.

If the Mafia can intimidate judges and jurors, bishops and senators, why not filmmakers? In Tognazzi's case, he shares the fervor of the young men he raises up as heroes: four working-class Italians who risk their lives to protect one crusading judge (Carlo Cecchi).

Tognazzi refuses to be a "fence-sitter," an individual who collaborates with the Mafia through his inaction. The strength of "La Scorta" is in its perspective. By focusing on the judge and his bodyguards, and leaving the Mafia figures in the shadowy background, Tognazzi creates a profile in terror without resorting to a cops-and-robbers plot.

Driving the winding Sicilian roads, the five are like Spam in a can—dead meat that doesn't know it's dead yet. The tension is not whether they will be killed, but who will die first.

As in Brian De Palma's "The Untouchables," the movie's emotional center is the bond that develops between the five men. What begins with squabbles over who will wear the two bullet-proof vests allotted to the group, ends with a corps of young men united around a father figure on an impossible quest.

The cast is led by the handsome Claudio Amendola, who plays devoted bodyguard Angelo Mandolesi. The strong-but-silent actor projects his good looks with a Franco Nero swagger.

While the supporting cast is strong, the thriller fails to be gripping in one key area. By keeping the Mafia figures at arms-length and choosing a dullish plot about water rights, the mystery never fully hooks the audience.

The interaction between the squad and their terror becomes everything. We begin to wait for the final assassination attempt; the corruption issue becomes as muddy as an abandoned well.

What redeems Tognazzi's movie is his refusal to go for the Hollywood ending.

In "The Bodyguard," love conquers all. Houston and Kevin Costner get their big embrace and out come the handkerchiefs.

In "The Untouchables," Costner's Eliot Ness prevails over Robert De Niro's Al Capone, and good conquers evil, law routs disorder.

In "La Scorta," the victory is in surviving to fight another day, in finding the strength within oneself to battle the odds. Justice doesn't prevail. but in some small corner of Sicily, it struggles to exist at all.

NEWSDAY, 5/4/94, Part II/p. B9, John Anderson

Forget it, Jake, it's Sicily.

The bark of the gun, the fading whine of a motor scooter, the car spattered in blood, the bullet-riddled bodies, it's all part of a landscape—political, spiritual and ballistic—that's never going to change. Not, at least, according to Ricky Tognazzi's "La Scorta," a fast-paced Italian thriller based on recent, real-life events in the war against the Mafia, a film in which corruption and violence are never quite as horrible as the resigned, complicit acceptance of both.

The Sisyphean plight of the man who pursues a moral course—in this case, a judge named De Francesca (Carlo Cecchi) and his four *caribiniere*—is just one of the ways "La Scorta" recalls Roman Polanski's "Chinatown" (the others include a political scandal involving the public water supply, and an Ennio Morricone score that evokes Jerry Goldsmith's moody noir music). Like Polanski, Tognazzi at no time hints that the investigation ia anything but futile, that the trail won't lead far higher on the power chain than the heroes can pursue it, or that good people won't die so the banal, evil ones can profit. And yet Tognazzi, his nervously roaming camera constantly scanning the bushes for gun muzzles, still makes us hope. And squirm.

"La Scorta" is in many ways standard-issue, both as a revenge tale—the carabiniere Angelo (Claudio Amendola) has returned to Sicily ostensibly to take a slain friend's place as a bodyguard, but also to avenge his death—and as an exposé of Mafiagate—there seem to be as many government officials involved in the water scheme and coverup as not.

But in a film that's as much about the emotional growth of its characters as about their adventures, Tognazzi performs a delicate balancing act, giving equal emphasis to the investigation and to the paternal bond between De Francesco and his four bodyguards, who grow tighter as the conspirators around them bear down.

The four include Andrea (Enrico Lo Verso, of "Il Ladro Di Bambini"), the head of the bodyguard detail, whose happy family life provides counterpoint to the constant peril of his job; Angelo, who clashes and then bonds with Andrea; Fabio (Ricky Memphis), who begins his duty yearning to transfer out, and then finds he can't, and Raffaele (Tony Sperandeo), who's the first to go.

The story is told from the bodyguards' perspective, with their extreme concern with security and constant state of apprehension. In one scene, as the judge's two-car caravan makes its way through the country, a parked car is spotted on the roadside. It is assumed to contain explosives—assumed, like everyone and everything the escorts encounter, to be malevolent. The drivers go into a practiced routine, protecting the judge's car at the expense of the one containing only bodyguards. And does the parked car explode? Well, in a film like "La Scorta," the best kind of thrillers, you kind of wish that terrible things would happen, and be over with, almost as much as you wish they wouldn't happen at all.

SIGHT AND SOUND, 5/94, p. 54, Phillip Kemp

Trapani, Sicily. Special investigator Judge Rizzo is assassinated along with his escort, *carabiniero* Pietro Virzi. Angelo Mandolesi, a colleague and friend of Virzi's, requests a transfer from Rome back to his native Sicily to take the dead man's place. In the barracks he meets a younger policeman, Fabio Muzzi, who is hoping for a safe posting. But both Angelo and Fabio, along with the easy-going Raffaele Frasca, are detailed to escort the newly-arrived investigator, Michele de Francesco. The team is headed by a sergeant, Andrea Corsale, a family man whose wife Lia fears for his safety. The escort's jumpiness is exacerbated by the inadequate equipment they have been issued with.

Promised every assistance by local prosecutor Caruso and his assistant Polizzi, de Francesco starts to investigate a scam involving water-wells controlled by a local landowner, Mazzaglia. He sequestrates the wells, but when a water shortage hits the town he incurs widespread criticism and the hostility of Caruso and his staff. Angelo angrily confronts Andrea, who he realises is secretly reporting to Caruso. Andrea shamefacedly confesses his duplicity to de Francesco, who forgives him. At dinner at Andrea's apartment, the judge and all four of his escort are united in a bond of loyalty.

Relying solely on his escort for assistance, de Francesco unearths evidence implicating the vice-prefect Scavone and the local senator Nestore Bonura in the Mafia-led corruption. Vital documents go missing from the judge's desk, but Polizzi and his colleagues indignantly deny responsibility. While de Francesco is busy, the escort take his daughter Roberta, plus Lia and her children, to the seaside; as they prepare to return, Raffaele's car blows up, killing him. Fabio, whose transfer has come through, elects to stick with the team, and together with the judge they move into a bunker-like concrete apartment.

Through an informer, Angelo traces one of Rizzo and Virzi's killers, who accuses Mazzaglia and Senator Bonura. De Francesco raids the offices of everyone involved, the senator included. Soon afterwards, Bonura and his escort are gunned down. Caruso holds de Francesco responsible for the killing and contrives to have him transferred away from Sicily. On the quayside the escort team, all now assigned to menial duties, take an emotional farewell of the judge.

For a film so concerned with death, *La Scorta* has a modest body count: a mere two killings, barring the pre-credit sequence. The judge, the supposed target, doesn't once come under attack; and the expected climax, the big set-piece shoot-out where the escort lay their lives on the line to protect their charge, never happens. Instead, director Tognazzi maintains the tension by conveying a constant sense of *potential* death, showing through the escort's eyes how the most innocuous objects—a parked car or an old lady at a window—can seem a source of latent menace. At moments of maximum stress, the camera itself joins the escort team, panning wildly from side to side, checking every angle for hidden danger. The one time they relax—the seaside trip—is when violence strikes.

We're also deprived of another expected big scene, the triumphant round-up of all those involved in the conspiracy. Bonura dies, Caruso takes early retirement, and we never learn what happens to Mazzaglia, the local *capo di mafia*—the implication is, not very much. Danger is omnipresent but so too is complicity, subverting authority and justice and seeping like a noxious gas into every crevice of society. At one point Angelo, busily phone-tapping, calls de Francesco to report a conversation he's just overheard. A moment later his own phone rings, and a voice contemptuously corrects a detail he got wrong. The tappers are being tapped, the watchers are being watched, and *La Scorta* is too honest a film to pretend that the efforts of five individuals will have more than minimal impact on the all-pervasive corruption. Their only achievement is personal, in terms of their own maturity and emotional development.

For what *La Scorta* is about, no less than the battle with the Mafia, is family. "I don't like this family business," says de Francesco, referring to the way Caruso's staff close ranks against the outsider; but what he does in response is form a surrogate family of his own. The film's key scene is the dinner to which Andrea invites his fellow escorts and the judge, whose own private life is in tatters. (His wife has left him, and we see him dolefully trying to cook according to phoned instructions from his mother.) Around the domestic table, laden with pasta and wine, a new extended family is created, and once Andrea's wife and children are safely out of the way the men forge an even closer bond: the good father and his four loyal sons. When the going gets still tougher, they even set up house together.

Tognazzi himself describes the film as "a great love story between men". Nothing gay, of course; sound, if sketchy, hetero attachments are provided for the unmarried team members, and the only openly gay character, an informer, is depicted as a cringing sleazeball. But despite lip-service to traditional Italian machismo ("To have kids with balls, only kiss them when they're asleep"), the men are tender with women and children as well as with each other. In this, they're opposed to the bad family of the Mafia that subsists on greed and cruelty, and it's only through relationships like theirs, Tognazzi implies, that the sickness at the heart of Italian society can eventually be overcome. Though it ends in a defeat, *La Scorta*'s long-term message is one of cautious optimism.

VILLAGE VOICE, 5/10/94, p. 58, Georgia Brown

Italy's largest grossing indie last year, *La Scorta*, is certainly timely. The subject is Italy's mafia-related corruption scandals, and director Ricky Tognazzi (son of actor Ugo) has a promising angle: He focuses on the lowly bodyguards assigned to protect the crusading judges. When magistrates are killed, their "escorts," in close proximity, usually get it too, though they get none of the glory.

Based on a true story, *La Scorta* is set in a port town in Sicily, where a judge and his bodyguard are gunned down in an ambush. Shortly after, a young policeman, Angelo (Claudio Amendola), returns to his hometown where he has asked to be transferred. The guard killed was his friend and mentor. Angelo's mission: to redeem his death. But the crew he joins, at least initially, seems not to share his zeal. The youngest, Fabio (Ricky Memphis), still in his babyfat, only wants out of the region ASAP. Another (Enrico Lo Verso, the patient policeman in *Il Ladro di Bambini*) has three kids and is worried about securing better housing—a concern that renders him potentially corruptible.

But then bonds begin to form. Apparently, Tognazzi, whose prizewinning *Ultrá* was about the misplaced violence of roving soccer fans, has a thing for male friendships. Here, the silver-haired, blue-eyed judge (Carlo Cecchi) who arrives to continue the slain magistrate's work has the mien of a martyr, the demeanor of a father. In the midst of a messy divorce, he seems careless of his own safety. (Later his young daughter arrives and he seems somewhat careless of hers, too.) The bodyguards—three of them single young men—end up taking on the judge's cause with the selfless devotion of surrogate sons.

Tognazzi and his scriptwriters appear more concerned with honoring their factual source than crafting a taut political thriller. Right up to the inconclusive, anti-climactic ending, *La Scorta* is more like an "investigative fiction" than a tense action picture. All of which could be refreshingly mature, of course. Except that it's difficult to follow the local intrigue—a plot revolving *Chinatown*-style around water rights and a dam—and, more crucially, the main characters never develop sufficient weight. Under Tognazzi's toothless direction, Cecchi's judge looks increasingly clueless, while the movie's nominal hero, Angelo, helplessly waves his semi-automatic weapon. Now that I'm getting to brass tacks, even Ennio Morricone's score drags. Poor Italy could use more of a kick in the pants than this.

Also reviewed in:
NEW REPUBLIC, 5/20/94, p. 28, Stanley Kauffmann
NEW YORK TIMES, 5/4/94, p. C16, Caryn James
VARIETY, 5/24/93, p. 47, Deborah Young
WASHINGTON POST, 9/2/94, p. D6, Hal Hinson

LADYBIRD, LADYBIRD

A Samuel Goldwyn Productions release of a Parallax Pictures and Film Four International production. *Producer:* Sally Hibbin. *Director:* Ken Loach. *Screenplay:* Rona Munro. *Director of Photography:* Barry Ackroyd. *Editor:* Jonathan Morris. *Music:* George Fenton. *Sound:* Ray Beckett. *Production Designer:* Martin Johnson. *Art Director:* Fergus Clegg. *Costumes:* Wendy Knowles. *Make-up:* Anne Spiers. *Stunt Coordinator:* Lee Sheward. *Running time:* 102 minutes. *MPAA Rating:* Not Rated.

CAST: Crissy Rock (Maggie Conlon); Vladimir Vega (Jorge); Sandie Lavelle (Mairead); Mauricio Venegas (Adrian); Ray Winstone (Simon); Clare Perkins (Jill); Jason Stracey (Sean); Luke Brown (Mickey); Lily Farrell (Serena); Scottie Moore (Maggie's Father); Linda Ross (Maggie's Mother); Kim Hartley (Maggie, aged 5); Jimmy Batten (Karaoke Compere); Sue Sawyer (Foster Mother); Pamela Hunt (Mrs. Higgs); Alan Gold (Neighbor); James Bannon (Fast Food Manager); Christine Ellerbeck (Moira Denning).

CHRISTIAN SCIENCE MONITOR, 11/29/94, p. 14, David Sterritt

The news is that a trend continues: An increasing number of responsible films are exposing and exploring problems of domestic abuse and family troubles.

The latest examples are "Ladybird Ladybird," an English movie now opening in American theaters after debuting at the New York Film Festival, and "Heavenly Creatures," a New Zealand drama due on United States screens next month.

The bad news is that Hollywood isn't playing much part in this activity. In the main, American filmmakers take a superficial view of family, exploiting domestic distress for its melodramatic value but generally failing to probe the causes and consequences of abusive behaviors in the home.

It may be argued that fuzziness and fantasy have always been Hollywood's stock in trade, and they are to be expected even where serious subjects are concerned. While this is true, it's an attitude that gives us wish-fulfillment fabrications that suggest social and historical forces will slip obediently into line if we just think positively.

It's worth noting that "Heavenly Creatures" contains more vivid fantasies than any scene in "Forrest Gump," yet manages to examine key aspects of modern-day malaise with an honesty that puts Gumpishness to shame.

"Ladybird Ladybird" is the most urgently relevant to current social issues. This is especially true after the recent elections in the US, which could lead to new attitudes regarding government's role in helping disadvantaged people.

Based on actual events, "Ladybird Ladybird" centers on a woman named Maggie who was the victim of physical and psychological abuse during childhood, and has re-created this pattern by gravitating toward abusive men in her adult life.

Now the mother of four children, she is forced to put all of them into foster care after one is injured in a household accident caused partly by her own negligence. She wants desperately to regain custody of the youngsters, but finds herself thwarted by a number of factors. These range from her continuing poverty to an uncontainable rage that erupts at undiplomatic moments, such as during interviews with social workers.

Matters are complicated further by Jorge, the new man in her life—a gentle and compassionate fellow in all respects, but also an illegal Paraguayan immigrant.

"Ladybird Ladybird" tackles this troubling tale with documentary-style realism, showing profound sympathy with the protagonists while dispassionately revealing the enormous divide that exists between ideals of harmonious family life, on one hand and a network of inadequate social policies, on the other.

Watching the film is like being on an emotional roller coaster, and the ride becomes almost overwhelming when Maggie's desperation reaches such heights that she begins having new babies in order to regain the active motherhood that society has taken away from her.

The movie was written by Rona Munro and directed by Ken Loach, a clear-eyed filmmaker with a long record of socially committed work. Heading the excellent cast, Crissy Rock gives an explosive performance that deserves dozens of awards. Easily one of this year's 10 best pictures, it's one of the rare films that make you think and feel with equal fervor.

Also based on real events, "Heavenly Creatures" takes place in a New Zealand city during the 1950s, a decade still regarded as a time of untroubled "Ozzie and Harriet" contentment by some who don't remember the period too accurately.

The main characters are Pauline and Juliet, teenagers whose friendship is anchored in a shared love of pop culture—the songs of Mario Lanza, American movie stars, and especially romance novels, which prompt them to invent their own imaginative realm populated by kings, commoners, and tempestuous passions.

So deep is the companionship of Pauline and Juliet that they can't bear to be separated, even when their families try to split them up.

Driven to distraction by this and other problems, including Juliet's uncertain health, they decide to flee their homes—after murdering Pauline's mother, perceived as the biggest hurdle to freedom.

Two elements of "Heavenly Creatures" which was directed by Peter Jackson, raise it above the level of a lurid melodrama.

One is the movie's clear criticism of the girl's fantasies for failing to look beyond their own prejudices and assumptions about adolescence—a mistake that clouds their perception of the girls' troubles.

The other is the remarkable fact that while the later history of the real-life Pauline is not known, the real-life Juliet left prison five years after the murder, moved to a community in Scotland, and earned international respect as Anne Perry, a popular mystery-novel author whose works are known for their recurring interest in repentant murderers.

"Heavenly Creatures" delves into the mysteries of adolescent angst and anómie less deeply than the recent Canadian movie "Fun," to which it bears amazing similarities.

Still, this inventive drama from Down Under conveys a powerful impression of the hazy line that may be drawn between imagination and reality by immature minds. And considering that the real Juliet has lived a decent and productive life since her years in prison for the crime, the film makes a potent argument for rehabilitation at a time when "tough on crime" ideologies threaten to eradicate that concept.

CINEASTE, Vol. XXI, Nos. 1-2, 1995, p. 84, Leonard Quart

Ken Loach is not a fashionable or commercial director. His films remain rooted in a social-realist esthetic which eschews formal virtuosity and postmodern ironies for a straightforward camera style and a fidelity to the authentic texture of everyday life. From his early films like *Cathy Comes Home* (1966) and *Kes* (1970), to his most recent films, *Riff-Raff* (1991) and *Raining Stones* (1993), Loach's socially committed films give voice to the class entrapment and economic despair that lies at the heart of much of English working class life.

His latest film, *Ladybird, Ladybird,* is based on a true story. It centers around the agonizing plight of a West London unmarried mother, Maggie (Crissie Rock), who has four children, two black and two white, from four different men. Maggie is a product of an abused childhood, and has predictably chosen men who are as abusive and sadistic as her father. She is chain-smoking, angry, self-destructive, and on the dole, but clearly loves and is deeply committed to her children.

Still, she is able to irresponsibly go off one night to sing in a pub, leaving her children alone and locking the door of their room. A fire breaks out, and her oldest child is severely burned and sent to foster care. The decision by the welfare authorities sets the stage for Maggie's protracted, raging conflict with them which is at the center of the film. The authorities classify her other three children as "At Risk," and take them away as well.

Maggie may be emotionally distraught and feel "that love isn't for her," but she's resilient and hopeful enough, even after the loss of her children, to develop a loving relationship with Jorge (Vladimir Vega), a gentle, empathetic Paraguayan political refugee. The relationship with Jorge brings positive changes to her life—she is with a man who is compassionate rather than sadistic—and she has two children with him. But the government remains unconvinced that any change has taken place in her life, and intervenes each time, abruptly and brutally taking the children away from her. Given the outlines of this story, *Ladybird, Ladybird* could have easily become a heavy-handed social message film about a luminous victim of a working class mother who is callously destroyed by an unfeeling, impersonal welfare bureaucracy. And Loach, of course, has made films where his anger towards, and commitment to changing, social institutions like the family and labor unions has imposed itself on the action, forcing the films into a too polemical form (e.g, *Family Life's* commitment to R.D. Laing's theories of mental illness).

With *Ladybird, Ladybird*, however, Loach has consciously made a less predictable, more balanced and ambiguous work than one would have imagined (given some his earlier films) from these raw materials. Maggie is a social victim, but she is also a volatile and angry woman who has become her own worst enemy. In the extremity of her anguish, she rants and curses at the social workers and the court that decides on her childrens' custody, reinforcing their notion of her as an unfit mother, and losing any chance of gaining their support. Loach does not portray the social workers as ogres or oppressors. They are, in the main, soft-spoken men and women who come from varied ethnic and racial groups, acting according to what they think is in the children's best interest. In fact, only one of them indulges in obtuse psychobabble, talking to Jorge and Maggie about "supportive relations." It's the system and "the flaws in its design," not the individual social workers, that Loach blames. Loach's point is not that Maggie is an exemplary mother. Though much of her mothering seems tender and forbearing, it's hard to believe that some of her rage doesn't spill over towards the children. The real problem in Loach's eyes is that the bureaucracy treats Maggie as an abstraction, and pays little attention to the particulars of her situation and the person behind the harangues.

Crissy Rock (a Liverpudlian stand-up comedienne and first-time actress) gives a riveting, emotionally wrenching, totally natural performance as Maggie. It's the kind of acting that prevents an audience from ever seeing Maggie as merely a dire social statistic or some stereotype of the feckless, self-destructive, single mother. Maggie may be abrasive, and, at moments, out of control, but Loach suggests that it's her relentless suffering at the hands of the welfare bureaucracy that causes much of her explosive behavior. She's a vital, intelligent woman with loyal friends and a capacity for love who is also an emotionally wounded, flawed human being. And it's these wounds that are exacerbated by the authorities' trampling all over her.

Maggie's powerful, turbulent, indomitable presence dominates the film, making everyone else who shares the frame with her seem a touch diminished and undefined. Even sweet, patient Jorge, who gives Maggie his unconditional love, lacks a clear shape and is a bit too saintly to be true. He endures not only having his two babies wrenched from him, but Maggie using him as a whipping boy for her own near-suicidal desperation. Vega makes Jorge a convincingly caring lover. But the fact that Jorge is a Third World political refugee who had provided refuge to children whose parents had been killed by the Paraguayan government, and was passionately opposed to the exploitative, murderous state there, obviously affects the left-leaning Loach's depiction of him. The sympathetic Jorge is ultimately inflated into a virtuous icon, a somewhat airless figure who loses a great deal of his nuance and complexity as a character.

Loach's welfare bureaucracy in *Ladybird, Ladybird* is an oppressive one. And Maggie s traumatic situation is treated as the kind of case that displays the system at its most unseeing and inhumane. But Loach is not engaging in an outright condemnation of the social services. He's not a Thatcherite committed to cutting social spending, and dismantling the welfare state. In fact, he has asserted in interviews that there is a necessity for "more social workers with the time and skills to respond sensitively to people in distress. " What *Ladybird, Ladybird* does is confront the whole question of the standards that welfare authorities use to define a mother's capacity to raise her children. In this film their standards seem arbitrary and surreal, and the victim, a woman whose humanity can't be subsumed under some psychosocial category, is left utterly bereft.

The film, however, holds back from suggesting that a mother, no matter how abusive or neglectful, has the absolute right to raise her child. There are clearly cases where the authorities must be draconian, and wrest children away from their mother. Still, the film—which is the dramatization of an individual case and not a social policy position paper on single motherhood—provides a cautionary warning to welfare authorities contemplating that form of ultimate action. Obviously, all things being equal, it's better for a child, emotionally and economically, to make its claims on two adults rather than one, but intruding on motherhood is an emotionally charged and treacherous business. Even if the mothers are callow teenagers who don't have the strength of Maggie and who lack a compassionate man like Jorge for support, this sort of social engineering can be dangerously counterproductive.

Though *Ladybird, Ladybird*'s main focus is on Maggie's travails, its treatment of race (especially for an American audience) is noteworthy. In the world Maggie moves in, race is treated as a given, not a problem. Maggie's having two black children may have an influence on the court's adverse custody decision (though nothing is ever made explicit), but it causes not a ripple in the interracial world she moves in. That is not to say that racism—polite or violent—doesn't exist or play a powerful role in English life. It's just that in pockets of the urban working class, sexual and social relations among the races are more open and less self-conscious than they would be in parallel American cities. Class more than race is still what separates people in England from each other.

Loach has made a film whose visual plainness and emotional directness operates in a far different world from most films that elicit critical applause and garner large audiences today. *Ladybird, Ladybird,* centers on performance, character, raw emotion, and social reality. It does that by using close-ups and two shots, framing the scene to get at the center of action, and doing little outdoor shooting, except the exhausted-looking, red brick council estate Maggie and Jorge live in. Loach makes no fetish about the cinematic methods he uses, and that's both the strength and a limit of his work. His films are rarely interesting on a formal level, and one recalls few distinctive images or camera movements from his work.

Nevertheless, at a time when genre parody, stylized dialog and violence, special effects, self-reflexivity, and ironic distance have become staples of much of both independent and studio-produced American films, a director who is committed to the unadorned emotional and social truth is a rarity. Like Mike Leigh, a very different kind of English director, Ken Loach is an artist who, rejecting all that is cinematically modish, has stuck to the realist esthetic for close to thirty years. In both their cases the commitment to detailing the particularity of individual and social realty has paid off in powerful works of art.

LOS ANGELES TIMES, 12/30/94, Calendar/p. 1, Peter Rainer

Ken Loach's "Ladybird, Ladybird" is so unrelievably grim that it's remarkable the filmmakers had the strength to get on with it. It's not an inspirational downer or a call-to-action. Even though it's based on a true story, it's not even an exposé.

The horror story of a woman, Maggie (Crissy Rock), who loses six of her children to the state authorities is almost too painful to experience. Loach, and his screenwriter, Rona Munro, don't attempt to distance the audience from the pain. They don't even try to modulate it. It's just *there* on the screen, like a thick, suffocating fog.

Loach is perhaps the least compromising—and least commercial—of major British directors. It's not just his use of non-actors and newcomers, or his semi-documentary style, or his guerrilla left-wing political sympathies. Loach doesn't offer audiences a helping hand, and that can sometimes seem like a rebuff. With "Ladybird, Ladybird," the rebuff at least makes stylistic sense—it places us in the same trapped, enraged position as Maggie.

Her character is not softened or sentimentalized for us. Rock, a Liverpool stand-up comedian acting in her first movie, gives her an ornery, block-like force. She has been battered by a series of men—the four children she takes care of at the beginning of the movie all have different fathers—but she's something of a battering ram herself. All the punishment she has received has given her a chunky fortitude. She's wary not only of other people but of herself—of her ability to *feel* anything.

When she meets Jorge (Vladimir Vega), a Paraguayan refugee, in a pub, his doting unconditional tenderness is like an affront to her. Jorge is almost too good to be true: He needs a reason to love and Maggie is it. It takes her most of the movie to recognize his goodness. In other words, it takes that long for her to comprehend her *own* goodness.

Maggie's long slide with the social service authorities in west London begins when one of her sons is accidentally burned at the women's shelter where she is holing up. Because she left the boy unattended with her other children, and because she has in the past exposed them to domestic violence, the state takes them away from her.

It's a vicious cycle: The more enraged Maggie becomes at what the authorities have perpetrated, the more they regard her as dangerously unfit for motherhood. When she and Jorge have children of their own, the same cycle is repeated. Did Dickens ever dream up anything this ghoulish?

But Loach, for all his docu-realism, isn't quite the even-handed chronicler he pretends to be. When Maggie and Jorge first make love, for example, the soundtrack tinkles with soft guitars and pan-pipes. The social service types, especially the judges, are mostly implacable. Surely, they must have felt in their own minds that what they were doing was best for the children. But Loach doesn't extend his sympathies to them. To do so would be to disrupt the film's neat arrangement of concerns.

It may appear that we are getting a more "real" take on life with Loach, but his realism lacks the flavors that give drama its richness. Nobody in "Ladybird, Ladybird," not even Maggie, grows very much in the course of the film. Their unvarying quality is probably meant to be taken as mythic—these people are acting out a primal drama in which the drama is much more pertinent than the people.

The power of "Ladybird, Ladybird" is inseparable from its weaknesses. Loach brings us up close to the misery but, in a larger sense, he stands back.

NEW STATESMAN & SOCIETY, 9/30/94, p. 50, Boyd Tonkin

Saturday night at the movies in suburban Madrid. It's a brisk February evening, with seats at all prices in the local multiplex—except for one screen. Oliver Stone's latest bag of piss and wind plays to half-empty cinemas. But try to buy seats for *Raining Stones*, as I did, and you find that the house is definitely *completo*.

Ken Loach's international comeback shows that, even in the film business, reputations can go up as well as down. A decade ago, he turned out ads for bitter while his four-part trade-union series, *Questions of Leadership*, languished on the shelves of TV schedulers who handled it as if it were a snuff movie. Now he commands the sort of pre-release publicity that Spielberg wouldn't despise.

Because of that, you probably know that *Ladybird, Ladybird* tells the true story of a woman who had six children brutally taken into care—though not by "social services" alone. We'll deal with that later, as it matters. It's also likely that you will have picked up the row about the extent to which Loach and his writer, Rona Munro, have glossed over the reasons for those care orders. Loach assures us that the film contains "all the evidence" that was used against the woman whose life inspired it, even the worst.

He richly deserves the revival that began with a Cannes prize for *Hidden Agenda* in 1990. But it does mean that his stories of struggle against the system no longer amount to some good lost cause that everyone to the left of Michael Winner must support without a murmur. They rightly ask tough questions about our social institutions. And now, perhaps, it's time to question them.

What makes this especially hard is that most viewers will (like this one) glimpse much of *Ladybird, Ladybird* through a mist of tears. As Maggie, the irascible but loving Scouser who was abused in her own painful childhood, club comedienne Crissy Rock gives a stupendously fiery and involving performance. It seems that only Loach can coax work of this calibre from novice film actors. In March 1995, some other actress will probably lift an Oscar for a much less compelling role.

In a karaoke pub, Maggie meets the tender Paraguayan exile Jorge (Vladimir Vega, whose quiet dignity makes a crucial foil for Rock's histrionics). As their affair develops, she tells him about her four lost children, all by different fathers.

Her sister Mairead, so Maggie reports, says that "I smell trouble and then I go to bed with it." Eventually, she does leave the thuggish Simon (Ray Winstone). In a women's refuge, she locks two children in her room, but fire breaks out. Their injuries provoke the first care order, after Rock delivers a hospital scene of utter visceral panic. Has any actress done as much for thwarted motherhood since Barbara Stanwyck pined for her daughter in Vidor's *Stella Dallas*?

Maggie returns to Simon, and the courts take the children for good. Now her and Jorge's story proper starts. A paperless émigré, he takes a lousy chip-shop job but gives her unconditional love. They move to a damp flat on a sink estate full of nasty imps and sour old bats. (Perhaps, for Loach the Marxist, these dregs aren't working-class but lumpen proles).

The pair have a daughter, but Maggie loses her rag when the health visitor comes round. The nightmare recommences. Social services damn her on past form. They listen to neighbours' malign gossip. The new baby goes into care fast; a sixth is snatched at birth. Jorge endures her tide of rage; the film ends in their reconciliation. The real Maggie and Jorge have since had three more kids, and kept them. But the other six stay stuck in care.

Let's agree that Loach and Munro have merely simplified the facts. We should still ask how far their emotionally wrenching naturalism can foster understanding, not just empathy. Loach's output divides into two broad types. One is the drama of social combat, from *Days of Hope* to his forthcoming film about the Spanish civil war, which sets clued-up rebels against sell-outs and reformists.

The other strand, from *Cathy Come Home* to *Ladybird, Ladybird*, views injustice through the lens of family breakdown. It focuses on individuals trapped by class and by the red-taped cruelty of welfare bureaucracy. Both, of course, are equally "political". Here, the link is made by Jorge. Once a rural activist in Paraguay, he tells Maggie that "suffering has a job to do for the government".

But can this victim's-eye perspective explore the ties between one woman's pain and a state of general inequality! I doubt it. Maggie becomes the kind of female martyr beloved of 19th-century Naturalist writers: a plaything of fate, buffeted by the gales of heredity and environment. Whereas Zola or Hardy could track their heroines' trouble to its roots, Loach's narrative can't even do that.

Instead, we only see the front rank of her persecutors. Loach has stressed that "it's no part of our intention to vilify social workers". Still, his close-focus methods give no real sense of the child protection laws as a system that can spin wildly out of control. Yes, the police, doctors and lawyers all flit through the odd scene like grim soldiers of an occupying power. The harshest blow comes when a judge believes the bad neighbour's lies. Yet what do we see at crucial turning-points? One black social worker who can't pronounce the word "statutory". Or a woman spouting lame-brained platitudes. You could call it blaming the messenger.

"The social took your baby," some local kids tell Jorge in the chip shop. Wrong: only a magistrate's authority can do that. But naturalistic melodrama needs some visible villainy. And who better than the tabloids' favourite punch-bag to provide it? Some of Ken Loach's best friends may well be social workers. The point is that his style acquires its own momentum. Few spectators will give a damn about the law's inflexibility or the courts' wayward decisions. Most will treat *Ladybird, Ladybird* as yet another plea to get those interfering half-wits off our backs.

Some 28 years ago, the curiously similar *Cathy, Come Home* flayed the official neglect that pushed a homeless woman's family into care. Now the same story returns with its poles reversed. Then the state was damned for not doing enough. Now it' s damned if it does anything at all. Loach detests the political weather that set in around 1979. His work seems to have acclimatised to it all the same.

NEW YORK POST, 10/7/94, p. 46, V. A. Musetto

"Ladybird Ladybird," by the acclaimed British director Ken Loach, is an unrelentingly grim, superbly crafted film about a middle-aged, working-class woman abused by her father, by a string of lovers and, finally, by the social-service bureaucracy that should *help* her.

Crissy Rock, a stand-up comic, makes her acting debut as the woman Maggie, and turns in a dynamic performance that won her the best-actress award at the 1994 Berlin Film Festival.

When we first encounter Maggie she has had four children by four men only to have the kids taken away by the authorities who consider her an unfit mother. ("I smell trouble and I go to bed with it," Maggie confides.)

At a London pub, she meets the gentle Jorge (Vladimir Vega), who will become one of the few men (if not the only one) in her life not to abuse her. They settle into a stable relationship and have a child. But—in Rock's most riveting scene—police and social workers barge into Maggie's hospital room and rip her newborn child from her.

The impersonal bureaucracy is unable to believe that Maggie might have changed her ways. The moment is as traumatic for the viewer as for her.

NEWSDAY, 10/7/94, Part II/p. B7, Gene Seymour

The word "searing" is one of those adjectives overused by reviewers, to the point that it doesn't mean anything. But it seems tailor-made for a movie like this latest from British director Ken Loach ("Raining Stones," "Riff Raff"). It's about a *lumpen* girl from Liverpool named Maggie (stand-up comic Crissy Rock in a knockout performance), who's had "four different kids from four different dads."

Every man she's been with has been mean and abusive, which is why she can't quite believe her good fortune in meeting a gentle South American poet-exile Jorge (Vladimir Vega).

The social services department can't believe it either. They've placed her other four kids up for adoption and believe the couple's newborn will be better off away from their care. For a film that is intended to show how, in Loach's words, "anger kills," it certainly makes one agitated—or, at least, deeply affected.

NEWSDAY, 12/9/94, Part II/p. B7, Jack Mathews

Before he starts rounding up welfare children and sending them all off to Boy's Town with Mickey Rooney, incoming Mouth of the House Newt Gingrich ought to take a look at Ken Loach's new film, "Ladybird, Ladybird." It's British and not likely to change Newt's glib political views. But it's about a real person having her babies taken from her, and the sight of a mother's anguish might at least soften his rhetoric.

Not that "Ladybird," which is based on a true story, offers any solutions to welfare motherhood. It just tells a chilling story, a representative story on many levels, about a woman virtually consigned at birth to the bureaucratic guardianship of the social services system and being unable to free herself from it.

Born into poverty, poorly educated, severely abused as both a child and an adult, Maggie Conlon (Crissy Rock) is entering middle age as a single mother with four children, by four different men, little money and only one prospect—the gentle South American political refugee, Jorge (Vladimir Vega), who enters her life determined to calm her rage and build a stable family.

The title refers to a nursery Americans know as "Ladybug, ladybug, fly away home, your house is on fire, and your children will burn."

It is such an incident, an electrical fire in her apartment while she's out drinking, that puts Maggie in the grip of the well-intended but overextended British Social Services System and causes her to lose forever not only those four children, but the first two she later has with Jorge, as well.

Crissy Rock, a Liverpool nightclub comedian making an astonishing acting debut, was herself an abused child and plays Maggie with an emotional fury that is at once heart-breaking and terrifying.

All Maggie wants is to be independent and raise her children, but a lifetime of abuse—she was raped by her father and beaten by a string of violent lovers—has left her running in place on a treadmill driven by rage.

Loach, who has made a career of reform-minded dramas about the British underclass, originally set out to do a documentary on a single mother struggling within the welfare system, and changed his mind, fearing the film itself would get tangled up in the bureaucracy.

With Rock, who has given the most emotionally honest performance seen anywhere on the planet this year, and Vega, who is in fact a Chilean refugee living in London, Loach seems to have had it both ways. "Ladybird" is a tightly written human drama that seems, in its most intimate moments, to have been captured on the fly.

In the end, "Ladybird" seems to be taking what is, for Loach, a fairly ambivalent position. It's critical of the social system for failing to adjust to changes in "trouble" cases; at the same time, Maggie's unstable personality is so clearly defined, you cannot be sure her children—at least, the first four—would be safe with her.

Where people are concerned, whether on welfare or in high political office, nothing is ever as simple as it seems, or as they would like.

SIGHT AND SOUND, 10/94, p. 46, Lizzie Francke

Maggie is a Liverpudlian living in London. One night, out with friends at the pub, she meets Jorge, a political exile from Paraguay; she ends up going home with him, and in the small hours, tells him her life story ... She has been in a series of abusive relationships; her last boyfriend, Simon, was so violent that she sought a place for herself and her four children at a women's refuge. While she is out one night, there is a fire at the refuge and her eldest son Sean is seriously burnt. It transpires Maggie might be partly to blame, as she locked them into the room without leaving a key with one of the other women. Consequently her children are taken away from her and placed in care with the social services.

Maggie is told that she can be reunited with her children if she stays at a family centre. Instead, she insists on being given a flat, but without success. Sent to the family centre with her children, she walks out and returns to Simon. She persuades him to run away, but the social services chase them; after an argument, he drives away with the children. The police intervene, and the social services accuse Simon of abusing the children. Maggie goes to court hoping to get the children back, but is refused custody.

Meanwhile, Maggie starts a new life with Jorge. She becomes pregnant and the couple move into a council flat. Jorge gets a job as a fast food cook; Maggie has the baby and everything seems happy. But when a health visitor and then a social worker come to see them, Maggie refuses to let them in. The social worker confers with a cantankerous neighbour, who tells lies about Maggie and Jorge. The police take the baby away, and the couple's relationship is scrutinised by the social services. When their case comes up, the neighbour gives evidence and falsely claims that Jorge hits Maggie. It transpires that Jorge might have a wife in Paraguay; he is served with a deportation order, but later has his passport returned. Maggie gets pregnant again, but in hospital her baby is taken away from her straight after delivery. Maggie is furious that Jorge didn't do more to prevent this. Despite the tension in their relationship, they stay together. A post-script tells us that Maggie and Jorge have been allowed to have three other children, but they have no access to their first two, nor to the children from Maggie's previous relationships.

Based on a true story, *Ladybird Ladybird* dramatises harrowing events that would seem incredible in fiction. But Ken Loach's film, a return to the more specific female subject matter of *Family Life* or *Poor Cow* offers little insight into the character under scrutiny. It should be a fierce indictment of a state that attempts to pathologise Maggie, who, as the working-class 'unmarried' mother who just keeps 'breeding', is the archetypal bugbear of Majorite policy. But the film itself ends up pathologising her, and violence against women is again portrayed as endemic to the working class. In the present political climate, this is a very dangerous move.

In Crissy Rock's unnerving and powerful performance, Maggie is presented as a raw, visceral force, larger than life. The scene in which her newly-born baby is wrenched away from her is traumatic to watch, especially when she is met with the final indignity of being sedated as if she were some breeding animal. The trouble is that, although there is no excuse for what the social services put her through, she is not always an easy person to sympathise with. In a fiction film, this would be something to applaud (the more difficult and unsympathetic women in films the better), but the case-study nature of *Ladybird Ladybird* makes it a more complicated matter. One can imagine the details of Maggie's life playing into the hands of the present government rather than providing ammunition against it.

Though there is never any question about Maggie's ability to be a good mother—the brief scenes of her and her children have a sweetness which gives the film its respite—her absolutely justified anger implodes on her and renders her a passive force.

She is presented as victim of her own emotional state, as much as of the state's interventionist methods. In this respect, an understanding of her character is needed, rather than just a depiction of it. Her early life receives the glibbest of glimpses; the brief flashbacks to Maggie's childhood show that her father was as violent towards her mother as her partners were to her, and she later mentions that she was sexually abused as a child. There is something perfunctory about the way that this information is conveyed, as though it were not organic to the rest of the film but simply tacked on.

Given the spectacular wall of anger that is put up around Maggie, it is the pacifying character of Jorge that we are given space to identify with. He is the one who attempts to co-operate with the social services, who brings his intellect to bear on the case. This is a revealing move on the film's part. It compounds Loach's thesis, which seems increasingly to be true, that the United Kingdom shares, much in common with despotic countries (cf. the liberation theology of *Raining Stones*); in Britain too, those tainted by the state's ideology end up snitching on their neighbours.

Jorge knows too well how to negotiate with dictatorial authorities; one tries to be accommodating and play them at their own game, not out of cowardice but in order to survive. It is deplorable that these skills should not be out of place when dealing with the British social services. But it is problematic that Jorge, the middle-class intellectual poet who ran shelters for the homeless before being forced to leave his country, becomes the softly-spoken voice of sanity, as the railing Maggie is pushed beyond any reason of her own. It may be honest to the facts of the case, but it is none the less smug.

One can imagine a Hollywood remake with Sally Field and Raul Julia, in which Maggie would end up going to night school to study law so that she can fight in the high court for her right to see her children again. Sometimes it's worth remembering that fiction can have a utopian purpose as well.

TIME, 1/30/95, p. 88, Richard Corliss

Boys Town is not the movie to see for the inside view on child-welfare problems. *Ladybird, Ladybird* is. This English drama about a worst-case child-custody scenario may show those who make social policy how hard it is to legislate love, lust, neglect, despair and other real-family values. Ken Loach's film, written by Rona Munro and based on a true story, horrifies and edifies in equal measure.

Maggie Conlon (Crissy Rock) is a working-class mess. She has had four children by four men. She does care for her lads and tries her best to take care of them, but she has also lived with a man who beat her in front of her children. ("He never, ever touched the kids," she says defensively. "You gotta give him that.") Once, when she and her brood were staying in a welfare hotel, she locked them inside the flat and went to a pub; there was a fire, and the children were injured. Social Services removed them to foster homes.

Maggie catches a break when she meets Jorge (Vladimir Vega), a gentle Paraguayan refugee. But as they try to create their own family, Maggie's past haunts them. So does her bad temper. Brutalized as a child, she has a vicious streak and a suspicion of Jorge's goodness. Any man who doesn't strike her—and strike out at the system that she believes oppresses her—well, he can't be a real man, can he? Heroically, Jorge endures Maggie's depressions, rages and physical abuse. All he can do is love her. All Maggie can do for her children is love them—from a distance. Assuming that Jorge is another of Maggie's brutal mates, the welfare state abducts their first child from their home and their second child straight from the maternity ward. By now Maggie is afraid to let her babies out of her sight, or even out of her body. "No!" she screams as she goes through labor." It's stayin' where it is!"

Ladybird, Ladybird opens one naked wound of the welfare dilemma. Should a loving mother be allowed to raise her children? But of course. And what if she is unable to protect them from her crippling weaknesses? Motherhood is a craft as well as a passion; it requires competence, ingenuity, common sense."Children need more than love," a welfare worker testifies at one of Maggie's humiliating hearings. "They need support, and they need stability." In other words, the parent can't also be a child.

A social tract however, can also be a movie. *Ladybird, Ladybird* is a good one—more painful to watch than any slasher film, because its emotional violence literally hits home. And however close Jorge comes to being fitted for the halo worn in *Boys Town* by Spencer Tracy's Father Flanagan, the new film rarely sentimentalizes its scorching situations.

That is due largely to Rock's fine ferocity. A Liverpool club comic who never acted before, but who has survived an abusive marriage, Rock asks for no quarter and gives none. Here is a mother, she says, dishing it out and taking it. Now you decide what to do with Maggie, and the millions of women like her, in England, America and around the world.

VILLAGE VOICE, 12/13/94, p. 68, Georgia Brown

Deeper, richer and scarier by far [The reference is to *Disclosure*; see Brown's review of that film] is Ken Loach's *Ladybird, Ladybird*, based on a true story of a west London mother spinning way, way out of control. Like this grueling picture or not—no one will *enjoy* it—you probably won't come away with the same conclusions as the friend beside you.

When we meet Maggie Conlon (Crissy Rock) singing her heart out in a karaoke bar, she already has four kids by four dads and they've all been taken away by social services. What has Maggie done to deserve this? Quite a lot, actually, as we find out in flashbacks. Aside from favoring abusive men, one night she's left her kids alone, to sing with a band in a bar, and a fire starts in their locked room. The children are hospitalized, two with severe burns, and are not returned to Maggie's care.

So far so good! Some might protest right off that Maggie's been wronged. (Not I.) You might argue that she's made a really bad mistake, that she realizes it, indeed has paid for it in grief and anguish, that she truly loves her kids who undoubtedly miss her. At any rate, now this woman who's prone to violent tantrums has a tormentor in social services to focus on. This ladybug's house is always on fire.

While Loach and writer Rona Munro stick to Maggie's point of view, they don't shirk from showing how warped her perceptions are. For example, when she visits the home where her eldest, Sean, is recovering, she insists on pulling at his bandages to show that she, Maggie, and not that sweet miss reading in the corner is the real mum. Hurt is love in Maggie's lexicon.

On the other side, while showing us this comfy house where Sean is being cared for, the filmmakers remind us that one day, when his burns are healed, social services will put up this 10- or 11-year-old traumatized black boy for adoption. Who will take him then?

Sick with grief but stifling her guilt, Maggie meets Jorge (Vladimir Vega), a political refugee from Peru whose initial desperation, his relentless pursuit of her, is enough to arouse one's suspicions. Why does he fix on this stormy, chunky blond who seems to see her only profession as breeder? At any rate, he takes a menial job and finds them a decent apartment. "It's like a palace," says she, hanging photos of the four lost children. Jorge grows snapdragons on the balcony. Maggie starts another baby.

Now the fun starts again. Deducing that Maggie has found another abusive mate, services take away the new child when she's a few months old. They push into the home, with cops to subdue anyone who objects. The more babies are removed, the madder Maggie gets. (Though Loach couldn't have anticipated it, the movie arrives just in time for our own debate over orphanages.)

Loach doesn't demonize the social workers. Most look like perfectly intelligent, right-thinking beings. They just participate in rotten acts. Counterproductive, too. The more babies they take away, the more Maggie fixates on pregnancy. Most frustrating, whatever's troubling Maggie hasn't begun to be addressed. Much of the time, she's howling and flailing, picking fights all around, often slugging and berating Jorge. "You want me to be one of those men who beat you up," he observes.

Would she treat a child differently? The movie fudges some issues, like this one. It seems to assume that she's not violent—or minimally violent—with her kids:

However brilliant Rock's performance as this valiant, perfectly maddening woman, it isn't a mystery. What I'm afraid to ask is how Loach got certain reaction shots—one of a little girl playing child—Maggie watching her father batter her mum; others of the kids playing Maggie's children watching a man stomp their mother on the pavement. What's on these children's faces is beyond acting. They're *seeing* something and their pain is almost too much to bear. This is the heart of the matter and Loach, to his credit, knows it.

Also reviewed in:
CHICAGO TRIBUNE, 1/20/95, Friday/p. C, Michael Wilmington
NATION, 1/23/95, p. 107, Stuart Klawans
NEW REPUBLIC, 12/12/94, p. 24, Stanley Kauffmann
NEW YORK TIMES, 12/9/94, p. C23, Janet Maslin
VARIETY, 2/28-3/6/94, p. 69, Derek Elley

LASSIE

A Paramount Pictures release of a Broadway Pictures production. *Executive Producer:* Michael Rachmil. *Producer:* Lorne Michaels. *Director:* Daniel Petrie. *Screenplay:* Matthew Jacobs, Gary Ross, and Elizabeth Anderson. *Director of Photography:* Kenneth MacMillan. *Editor:* Steve Mirkovich. *Music:* Basil Poledouris. *Music Editor:* Curtis Roush. *Sound:* Stacy Brownrigg and (music) Tim Boyle. *Sound Editor:* Beth Sterner. *Casting:* Gretchen Rennell. *Production Designer:* Paul Peters. *Art Director:* David Crank. *Set Decorator:* Amy Wells. *Set Dresser:* Paul Louis Perry, Stephen Shifflette, Cliff Eubank, James D. Bishop, Jonathan Dunham, and Andrew Eifert. *Special Effects:* Joseph Di Gaetano III. *Costumes:* Ingrid Price. *Make-up:* Hariette Landau. *Stunt Coordinator:* Michael Adams. *Running time:* 95 minutes. *MPAA Rating:* PG.

CAST: Brittany Boyd (Jennifer Turner); Thomas Guiry (Matthew Turner); Helen Slater (Laura Turner); Jon Tenney (Steve Turner); Earnest Poole, Jr. (Highway Patrolman #1); Jeffrey H. Gray (Highway Patrolman #2); Richard Farnsworth (Len Collns); Joe Inscoe (Pete Jarman); Yvonne Brisendine (Mrs. Jarman); David Bridgewater (Customer); Frederic Forrest (Sam Garland); Jody Smith Strickler (Mrs. Garland); Margaret Peery (Mrs. Parker); Michelle Williams (April); Charlie Hofheimer (Jim Garland); Clayton Barclay Jones (Josh Garland); Robert B. Brittain (Grommet Foreman); Rick Warner (Timid Neighbor); Kelly L. Edwards (Smoking Girl); Jordan Young (Smoking Boy).

LOS ANGELES TIMES, 7/22/94, Calendar/p. 13, Peter Rainer

Laaaseeeee ...

It's the mantra that sends a primal shiver up and down the spines of oldsters who remember "Lassie Come Home" when it opened in 1943. It makes the boomers who grew up on the TV show, which ran from 1954 to 1971, get all warm and fuzzy.

But do we need a new Lassie movie? Apparently the studio marketeers think so. There's been a revival in animal movies—we'll see seals and stallions before the summer is through. And the New Wholesomeness in family entertainment was tailor-made for a movie about a silky, fluffy collie who teaches kids (and adults) the importance of togetherness. You take your soothsayers where you find them these days. Woof woof.

Lassie is picked up at the beginning of the film after surviving a car wreck on a rain-swept highway. She's a wanderer—kind of like Richard Kimble. The Turner family, en route to Virginia from Baltimore to start a new life on a farm in the glorious Shenandoah Valley, picks up the dog. But the bonding doesn't begin right away. Seven-year-old Jennifer (Brittany Boyd) takes an instant shine to her—after all, we've already seen her watching "Lassie" reruns on television. And her stepmother, Laura (Helen Slater), is all for keeping the dog too. But 13-year-old Matt (Thomas Guiry) and his dad, Steve (Jon Tenney), take a while to be convinced. Is this some sort of Male thing?

Would Matt, the "Power Ranger" fan, have liked Lassie better if she'd been a he—if Lassie were a pit bull or a Doberman? (Actually, this Lassie, like all the Lassies in the previous TV shows and movies, is a male and a direct descendant of Lassie No. 1.)

But this "Lassie" is, after all, a story about a boy and his dog, and it's not long before Matt is cajoled by Lassie into romping with her across the lush countryside. This Lassie is as preternatural as her forebears: Matt is constantly being rescued by Lassie from wolves and bad weather and spoiled rich kids on tractors; she even gives him a knowing look when he sets up a telephone date for the Livestock Expo with a local cutie (Michelle Williams). Lassie is all things to Matt: Savior, Tutor, Matchmaker. And, oh yes, Dog.

The Virginia landscape is post-card pretty—no, make that post-card gorgeous. And Lassie is pretty gorgeous too. The fairy-tale charm of the story works fitfully whenever the dog and the scenery come together, which is not often enough. There's something lulling—no, make that boring—about the way this film ladles out the homespun homilies. It's just not as easy making movies about childhood innocence as the filmmakers of "Lassie" want to believe it is.

Director Daniel Petrie and screenwriters Matthew Jacobs, Gary Ross and Elizabeth Anderson don't bring anything fresh to this old warhorse—or wardog. And that may be their point. "Lassie" is an attempt to apotheosize the clichés of the collie myth. When Lassie jumps into a raging waterfall to save Matt, or grapples with a wolf, the suspense isn't real suspense because we're supposed to already know how it all turns out.

One of the drawbacks of the film's syrupy approach—at least from a family-entertainment point of view—is that you keep waiting for danger and bad guys to liven things up. And, sure enough, the presence of Frederic Forrest as Sam Garland, the biggest and baddest sheep farmer in the state, turns out to be a boon. Perpetually scowling and sunglass-clad, Sam is a rude dude; he looks over his flock of sheep and sees only lamb chops on the hoof. His two young sons (Charlie Hoffheimer and Clayton Barclay Jones) are a pair of range-riding homunculi. You keep expecting the Garlands to get seriously nutty and take over the picture—maybe try to mate Lassie with a lamb, or spike the ol' swimmin' hole, or force-feed Matt's kindly granddad (Richard Farnsworth) Puppy Chow. The producer of "Lassie," after all, is Lorne Michaels, executive producer of "Saturday Night Live." But even the Garlands are ultimately redeemed by the love of a dog. Their bark is worse than their bite. (On the other hand, Lassie's bite is worse than her bark. Go figure.)

Still, children may find themselves transported by the images of Lassie rippling in the chill wind. Their adult chaperons may too. But more likely, they'll be thinking about the price of real estate in the Shenandoah Valley.

NEW YORK POST, 7/22/94, p. 41, Michael Medved

For those of us who feel an abiding, irrational love for dogs, the most appealing aspect of these creatures isn't their resemblance to human beings, but their clear superiority to people in terms of selflessness and character.

This is certainly true for Lassie, who, in the handsome new movie that bears her name, emerges as a veritable Messiah with Paws. America's canine sweetheart not only performs the courageous rescues you'd expect, but she also teaches values to a troubled kid, repairs a family's wounded spirits, and ultimately sacrifices herself for those she loves.

This heavenly hound is also capable of a miraculous resurrection—approximately three days after her apparent death.

This movie, in short, has the courage to be corny—and veteran director Daniel Petrie ("A Raisin in the Sun" "Lifeguard") makes the sentimental material glow with unmistakable affection and sincerity.

The plot centers on a sullen 13-year-old punk (flawlessly played by Thomas Guiry of "The Sandlot") whose mother has died four years before, and who now moves with his father, his kid sister, and his new stepmother (the radiant, affecting Helen Slater) from big city Baltimore to Virginia's scenic Shenandoah Valley.

They plan to refurbish the weathered farm house where the children's late mother grew up with their kindly grandpa—played by Richard Farnsworth who worked as a stunt man on the "Lassie" TV show some 40 years ago. On the way to the country, the family adopts a remarkable collie whose previous owner just died in a highway accident, and the little girl inevitably names the dog "Lassie."

This new member of the clan soon leads her brooding teen-age master to exchange grunge rock and an angry attitude for family chores and the local swimming hole. She also persuades the father (Jon Tenney) that he can make a living as a sheep rancher, and defeats the nasty schemes of a greedy neighbor played by Frederic Forrest.

Amazingly enough, the dog who plays the title role is such an accomplished animal actress that she makes you believe in her supernatural powers: this drop-dead gorgeous collie is, in fact, the most charismatic and expressive new star of the entire summer.

She's an eight-generation descendant of the dog who co-starred in the 1943 "Lassie Come Home" with Roddy McDowall and Elizabeth Taylor, and this current collie has been trained by Robert Weatherwax—son of the legendary trainer who worked with the original dog.

Cynics might complain that the new Lassie looks a bit too perfectly groomed and blow-dried even in her most rugged action scenes, but there's good reason for all the special care in combing her fur—particularly around the hindquarters where it serves to obscure her private parts. The startling fact is that this Lassie is the most convincing male masquerader since "The Crying Game," like all of her/his predecessors, the dog is actually a guy, since male collies are purportedly easier to train.

This effective imposture (never disclosed in the movie's official press material) does nothing to undermine the loving, old-fashioned values the story so effectively conveys.

The production values are also first rate—especially the luminous camera work by Kenneth MacMillan (Branagh's "Henry V") and the lush, sweeping score by Basil Poledouris. These elements help "Lassie" do for dogs what "The Lion King" did for big cats; it's a family treasure that will produce thrills, tears and a warm, satisfied glow in moviegoers of all ages.

NEWSDAY, 7/22/94, Part II/p. B6, John Anderson

That she's one of Hollywood's most durable leading female roles, and is still played by a male, says something about the movies. And so does the fact that, for no discernible reason, "Lassie" has returned to the screen for yet another romp through our hearts, leaving big wet paw prints behind.

Beginning with "Lassie Come Home," the 1943 film starring Roddy McDowell, Lassie has whelped a number of feature films, several television shows, and seems to have never gone away. Why? Because those old-fashioned values that never die can best be represented by a dumb animal. Even so, the latest "Lassie" does take some tentative steps into the present, although there's some unpleasantness involved.

Chiefly, Thomas Guiry, who as Lassie's designated-human Matthew Turner—the role first played by McDowell and perhaps most famously by Tommy Rettig in the CBS series—is a headphone-headband-earring wearing pubescent malcontent who resents his stepmother Laura (Helen Slater) and really hates the fact he's had to move from Baltimore to very, very rural Virginia. Sheep ranching is the major industry; cigarettes are the major vice. Matthew is a major pain.

"So there's no TV!" he says as they arrive at their new home, where a storm has downed the electric wires. "That means there's no MTV! Why don't we just kill ourselves?" Besides screaming "Yes! Yes!" audiences might wonder if Matt really has emotional problems this severe, or if his outburst is just shrewd product placement.

But each time he sulks in his room—about his dead mom, or Virginia, or whatever—Lassie barges in to cheer him up, when she's not running along a hillside to the sound of shimmering strings and heroic horns (the rest of the sound track ranges from Bob Dylan to Primal Scream).

There's no connection between this Lassie and any other—June Lockhart didn't drop her off at the pound, for instance—which is itself a kind of tribute to the dog star's recognition factor. Coming upon an accident site en route to Virginia, they find tractor-trailer full of sheep, a dead driver and a dog. "It's Lassie, Dad," says Matt's sister, Jennifer (Brittany Boyd), to their father, Steve (Jon Tenney). And though Dad tries to ditch the mutt, she's tenacious, and they wind up taking her home.

The Turners' new home is the house where Matt's mom, yes, Steve's late wife, grew up—as if Laura didn't have enough to worry about. Steve's father, Len (an elfin Richard Farnsworth), lives in town, and all is bucolic except the neighbors: The Garlands, a family of wealthy cretins headed by Sam (Frederic Forrest), are the biggest sheep ranchers in the area, because they let their sheep graze on land owned by others—who, because Sam is nuts and usually armed, let 'em.

If this sounds like a film that should have been set in Montana, you're right—the set-up is strictly Old West, and Lassie even has her inevitable battle with a wolf—which not only maligns wolves, but is more than geographically improbable. When Steve the contractor's big job falls through the family decides to get into the ranching business, too, which sets up the crisis, climax and some shaggy moments.

Let's face it: This is a kid's movie, and if they love animals they're likely to love "Lassie." Adults, however, will prefer Primal Scream.

Also reviewed in:
CHICAGO TRIBUNE, 7/22/94, Friday/p. K, John Petrakis
NEW YORK TIMES, 7/22/94, p. C1, Janet Maslin
VARIETY, 7/25-31/94, p. 57, Steven Gaydos
WASHINGTON POST, 7/22/94, p. C1, Richard Leiby
WASHINGTON POST, 7/22/94, Weekend/p. 41, Kevin McManus

LAST KLEZMER, THE

A Maelstrom Films release. *Producer:* Bernard Berkin. *Director:* Yale Strom. *Screenplay:* Yale Strom. *Director of Photography:* Oren Rudavsky. *Editor:* David Notowitz. *Music:* Leopold Kozlowski. *Production Designer:* Yale Strom. *Running time:* 84 minutes. *MPAA Rating:* Not Rated.

NEW YORK POST, 8/12/94, p. 53, Michael Medved

"There isn't a professor in the world that can teach you to become a klezmer, A klezmer has to be born. It had to come from the mother, in the stomach where she fed him the feeling of klezmer."

So says Leopold Kozlowski, the 70-year-old Polish composer, pianist, conductor and Holocaust survivor who is the subject of the remarkably moving and meaningful new documentary "The Last Klezmer."

His insistence that authentic klezmer musicians arc born, not made, helps to justify the film's surprising title—at a time when so many young performers in the U.S. and Israel are mining the rich vein of emotional Jewish "soul" music performed for centuries at family and public celebrations.

One of those young musicians is a violinist named Yale Strom, who grew up in San Diego, Calif.—not exactly known as a flavorful center of Eastern European Jewish culture. As part of his personal rediscovery of his roots, Strom traveled to Poland, befriended Kozlowski, and wrote and directed this superb film about his life and work.

Mostly the movie focuses on Kozlowski's emotional return to his Ukrainian home town for the first time since the war. He is determined to revisit the precise locations where the Germans murdered his father, mother and brother.

He also goes back to the site of the concentration camp where the Nazis forced him to play a "death tango" that accompanied the torments of other prisoners, before he escaped to the forest to join the Jewish partisans.

These recollections are almost unbearably affecting, especially after Kozlowski reunites with one of his partisan comrades for the first time in 50 years and they travel together through the wintry landscape of their bloody youth.

In presenting these memories, director Strom takes care to spice the nostalgia and tragedy with the bracing flavor of irony. The editing, and the video camera work are magnificent, conveying an elegiac but surprisingly upbeat mood that mourns the past while it celebrates survival, and fits perfectly with the haunting soundtrack.

"Klezmer music wasn't written" insists Kozlowski. "It came from the heart! From the blood." In the same sense, this astonishing film comes from the heart and blood—and celebrates, in incomparable style, the bittersweet music of Jewish life.

NEWSDAY, 8/12/94, Part II/p. B7, Jonathan Mandell

I once asked Luciano Pavarotti what opera meant. He looked completely baffled. Opera is ... life, he said; opera is clear to everybody: Why, dairy farmers play opera in the barns to produce more milk; even cows understand opera.

In Yale Strom's modest and moving documentary, Leopold Kozlowski is asked a similar question about the Jewish folk music known as klezmer. Klezmer, he answers, is happy occasions, tragedies, pogroms, inquisitions—in other words, Jewish life. And, he says, only Jews can understand klezmer.

"The Last Klezmer" is, in a way, an attempt to explain— not just klezmer music, not just Kozlowski's life, but, through klezmer and Kozlowski, Yiddish culture and Jewish life.

Before World War II, the filmmaker says, there were some 7,000 klezmer musicians throughout Eastern Europe. Now there is Leopold Kozlowski. Born Leopold Kleinman into a family of several generations of *klezmorim*, Kozlowski, now 72, has been a resident of Poland for about half a century, a conservatory-trained conductor and composer, and an accomplished pianist. Nevertheless, he teaches eager Polish opera singers how to sing klezmer; he instructs one pianist to add "the Jewish twist—from here, in your heart."

Equal parts Jewish jazz and Yiddish soul music, klezmer, he says, "wasn't written. It came from the heart, from the blood."

We see what blood he is referring to when he returns for the first time in 50 years to the small village in Ukraine where he was born. He goes to the home of his first piano teacher, he meets a friend he hasn't seen since the 1940s—and he visits the forest where his father and more than 300 other Jews were shot dead. As villagers look on, he travels to other personal landmarks from the Holocaust: the forest where he lived for a year with a group of Jewish resistance fighters (men, women and children), his Kalishnikov rifle slung on one shoulder, his accordion on the other; the concentration camps where his music literally saved him (he played "death tangos" while camp guards marched other Jews to the ovens). Every place he goes, he lights a candle, collects a small bag of dirt as a sacred reminder, prays, weeps, reminisces. It should be no surprise that Kozlowski was an actor and consultant on Steven Spielberg's "Schindler's List" (though the documentary does not mention this).

"The Last Klezmer" follows by three years Yale Strom's first documentary, whose lofty title, "At the Crossroads: Jews in Eastern Europe Today," hinted at its ambition. The earlier film tried to do too much with too many people. Now Strom, a young American musician and passionate Yiddishist, has chosen to focus narrowly on just one of his original interview subjects, which makes for less confusion and more affecting encounters. But now there is too little context, too few details, and we hear the music too fleetingly (mostly as background score).

The optimism is more muted "too. "Jewish culture cannot be destroyed," Kozlowski said in the first film. In "The Last Klezmer" he adds, "as long as I'm alive." But the hope is still there: Maybe, he says, some American watching this will create a museum of Jewish music?

VILLAGE VOICE, 8/16/94, p. 50, Leslie Camhi

"My hut, my little hut," lilts an old Yiddish melody, longing for lost sites of Jewish abjection. *The Last Klezmer*, an ebullient and moving film, suggests that the current shtetl revival is only the most recent expression of a relentlessly nostalgic people. Yale Strom's documentary focuses on Leopold Kozlowski (ne Kleinman), born in the Ukraine into a long line of distinguished Kleinman klezmorim, who continues to ply his now lonely trade in Poland. Klezmorim are born, not made, the fervent Kozlowski informs us; in the womb they're fed the emotional influences that make great klezmer musicians. This impassioned, largely improvised music of personal feeling was formerly played all across Eastern Europe by countless small bands, frequently made up of tailors and kosher butchers.

Well, we know what ended that. Kozlowski's family was murdered under German occupation; he survived in part by playing for the inmates and jailers of a forced labor camp; escaping execution, he played and fought alongside Jewish partisans in the Ukrainian forest. After the war he went to Poland, changed his name, and for 23 years (before anti-Semitic purges in the '60s) directed the Polish Army Symphony Orchestra.

"If you were so important, why didn't you call me sooner?" chides an old ghetto friend with whom he's reunited. With Strom, Kozlowski returns to his native village, where they test the uncertain waters of contemporary Jewish culture and anti-Semitic sentiment. The president of the Lvov Jewish community, asked to sing a melody, offers the camera a striking rendition of "Hello, Dolly." A cross marks the site in the forest where Kozlowski's father, with 300 Jews, was murdered—though the Ukrainian hospital workers who've led him there weep as he collects a bit of earth to bury at home. Still, as we watch Kozlowski bustling about his daily business—conducting "Sunrise, Sunset" with the State Theater Orchestra in Warsaw or teaching young Polish divas old Yiddish songs—his fabulous vibrancy almost belies the film's sad title; it's hard to imagine he's the last of his kind.

Also reviewed in:
NEW YORK TIMES, 8/12/94, p. C6, Stephen Holden
VARIETY, 5/9-15/94, p. 92, Eric Hansen
WASHINGTON POST, 1/14/95, p. C3, Pamela Sommers

LAST SEDUCTION, THE

An October Films release of an ITC Entertainment Ltd production.. *Producer:* Jonathan Shestack. *Director:* John Dahl. *Screenplay:* Steve Barancik. *Director of Photography:* Jeffrey Jur. *Editor:* Eric L. Beason. *Music:* Joseph Vitarelli. *Music Editor:* Allan K. Rosen and Patty Von Arx. *Sound:* Mark Deren. *Sound Editor:* Jon Johnson. *Casting:* Debra Zane. *Production Designer:* Linda Pearl. *Art Director:* Dina Lipton. *Set Decorator:* Katherine Lucas. *Set Dresser:* Thierry "T.T." Labbe and Andrea Berty. *Special Effects:* John Hartigan. *Costumes:* Terry Dresbach. *Make-up:* Camille Henderson. *Stunt Coordinator:* Bill Erickson. *Running time:* 110 minutes. *MPAA Rating:* R.

CAST: Linda Fiorentino (Bridget Gregory); Peter Berg (Mike Swale); Bill Pullman (Clay Gregory); J.T. Walsh (Frank Griffith); Bill Nunn (Harlan); Herb Mitchell (Bob Trotter); Brien Varady (Chris); Dean Norris (Shep); Donna Wilson (Stacy); Mik Scriba (Ray); Michael Raysses (Phone Sales Rep); Zack Phifer (Gas Station Attendant); Erik-Anders Nilsson and Patricia R. Caprio (Boston Passersby); Renee Rogers (Receptionist); Bill Stevenson (Mail Boy); Walter Addison (Detective); Mike Lisenco (Bert); Serena (Trish Swale); Michelle Davison (911 Operator); Jack Shearer (Public Defender).

LOS ANGELES TIMES, 10/26/94, Calendar/p. 1, Kenneth Turan

"She can't be all bad, no one is," is the best anyone can manage about Jane Greer's malevolent Kathie Moffett in the classic film noir "Out of the Past," but Robert Mitchum's Jeff Bailey isn't buying. "She comes the closest," is his curt reply, but then he never met Bridget Gregory.

As played with career-making gusto by Linda Fiorentino, Bridget Gregory is a virtuoso of venom. Nasty, brutish and short to all concerned, her cold amorality leaves bystanders gasping. "You're not human," is a typical response, and even her lawyer has to ask, "Anybody check you for a heartbeat?"

Fiorentino's diabolical performance is the delectable heart of "The Last Seduction," the latest film by the polished John Dahl, whose "Red Rock West" was this year's most unexpected (and well-deserved) independent film hit.

Both "Seduction" and "Red Rock" had to overcome the hurdle of prior showings on HBO before getting theatrical distribution, and although "Red Rock" is the more satisfying film, "Seduction" is pure Dahl and that is reason enough to pay attention.

With only three features to his credit (the first was the Val Kilmer/Joanne Whalley-Kilmer-starring "Kill Me Again"), Dahl has made a reputation for himself as a modern master of a much imitated and overworked genre, the dark-end-of-the-street film noir.

While most directors approach noir from the outside, taking a paint-by-numbers approach to its components, Dahl intuitively penetrates to the heart of the beast, luxuriating in its fatalism, duplicity and despair, not to mention its baroque plot lines. And he also understands that laughter and shivers can be bedfellows, that being true to the spirit doesn't preclude having a little fun on the side.

Gregory, on the other hand, is all business. "The Last Seduction" opens with a glimpse of her at work, so pitilessly castigating the telephone solicitors under her charge that the word "eunuchs" is as mild as it gets.

Meanwhile, her unsavory doctor husband Clay (Bill Pullman) is out setting up a drug deal, making what he thinks is the score of a lifetime for both of them by selling a large quantity of pharmaceutical cocaine. Bridget, however, has other ideas.

Coolly absconding with the cash and headed as far out of town as she can get, Bridget stops for gas in the Upstate New York hamlet of Beston. With some time to kill, she wanders into the local bar and there, all unknowing, sits Mike Swale (Peter Berg).

A Boston native just returned after an unhappy stint living in nearby Buffalo, Mike is looking for someone or something to give him the nerve to leave town again. Bridget's abrasiveness fascinates him, and the more abusive she gets, for instance advising him to "make nice little cow babies and leave me alone," the more pleased he becomes.

Although Beston's friendliness makes Bridget want to throw up, circumstances force her to stick around for a while, making such cold-bloodedly carnal use of Mike he feels "like a 4-H experiment." Meanwhile, back in Manhattan, Clay is plotting revenge, and Bridget is coming up with a few new wrinkles of her own.

In part a tribute to "Double Indemnity" (an insurance company figures prominently, and Bridget at one point calls herself Mrs. Neff), "Seduction" is the first Dahl film the director himself didn't co-write.

First-time screenwriter Steve Barancik definitely works in the Dahl spirit, maybe too much so. Even "Last Seduction's" admirers will have to admit that the film's ornate plot goes more seriously haywire than usual, dispensing with plausibility early on and never bothering to look back.

Helping to counteract the plot's dizziness is Dahl's feel for the genre and his skill in making scenes that sound like clichés, for instance passionate sex on a rainy night to a muted jazz score, play like they're supposed to. Dahl also works well with actors, and in addition to Fiorentino he has fine support from the devious Pullman and Berg's perfect dupe.

With its brisk audacity and the deliriousness of its plotting, "The Last Seduction" must have tickled its director as much as it pleases audiences. Like its amoral protagonist, this little item likes to play with people's minds and has the panache to pull it off.

NEW STATESMAN & SOCIETY, 8/5/94, p. 33, Jonathan Romney

John Dahl may be the last film-maker in America to have preserved the art of the true B-movie. I say, *maybe*, but then I don't get to see that much straight-to-video stuff, and who knows what unsung auteurs of neo-*noir* are yet to be discovered in that murky Sargasso. Still, if we're talking celluloid, Dahl's our operator—clean execution, fast getaway and no sentimental qualms.

What makes him a true B-man is that he hasn't yet made his masterpiece, or anything aspiring to be one. You suspect that, if he tried, this would entail bigger budgets, starrier names, flashier design, and somehow the result wouldn't be half as thrilling. You'd end up with something mainstream and clever that was enjoyable because it was a cut above, but no more he'd be making films as good but as ordinary as *Jagged Edge*, or Harold Becker's *Sea of Love*, or the better latterday efforts of Sidney Lumet. Since Dahl is also one of the least-interviewed of new filmmakers, he may well be making the films he does purely as a calling-card to land that prestigious new Alec Baldwin vehicle; but let's hope not, and celebrate him while he still has an eye for the wild and tawdry.

Dahl has so far written and directed two films. *Kill Me Again* was a cat-and-mouse game for dumb dick and *femme fatale*, and *Red Rock West* brought to light the hitherto unsuspected affinities between a Jim Thompson paperback and a Road Runner cartoon. The new Dahl, *The Last Seduction*, is something of a departure: less comic-book in tone, it feels more like a "real" film, which means it sacrifices some of the throwaway pleasure that Dahl's so good at. But you also gain a certain seriousness—this is a film that is not afraid to be nasty. It's scripted not by the Dahls, but by one Steve Barancik, whose eye for sharp plotting, mean lapidary dialogue, and the pleasures of unremitting amorality, allow Dahl to get more ruthless, more acerbic in his direction—it's a less stylised film than his others, but you feel it means business.

The Last Seduction achieves a rare coup in creating a screen monster who's completely believable and completely unbelievable all at once. Bridget Gregory, played by Linda Fiorentino, is a law to herself, a completely unrelenting amoralist, and you can hardly believe how far she'll go or the purity of her motives—she's after money and power, and will brook no complications. She's unbelievable because she follows her own rules in a world that isn't made to accommodate them; yet everything about her is completely credible because she doesn't waver from her path. She's a shark—she has to keep swimming in blood because she's wired that way, and wouldn't have it any different.

She's more complex and rounded than the last big-time *femme fatale*—Sharon Stone's preposterous Catherine Trammell in *Basic Instinct*. Trammell wasn't a woman at all, but a projection of male fears and desires wrapped around a playboy centrefold. Paul Verhoeven kept us at a distance from his creation (and she was entirely that: no less a creation than the girl robot in *Metropolis*), and provided Michael Douglas' smitten cop as a safe conduit for our fears and fantasies. In *The Last Seduction*, too, there's a fall guy who wants Bridget, and our apprehensions of her are partly channelled through him; but he's a rank outsider, and we always know more than he knows. It's entirely Bridget who carries us along on her joyride.

We recognise her immediately: stalking with undisguised contempt along her ranks of minions in a telesales business, spurring them on with small humiliations, she's Thatcher-era woman born again in New York.

She believes in survival of the fittest and knows there's no one fitter than her—certainly not her husband, whom she promptly divests of the money he's got them in a perilous drugs deal. When she lifts the loot she seems, as much as anything, driven by impatience at having to deal with someone who's not in her league.

Taking off, she starts a new life in a distant hick town. Here the film works a neat variation on B-movie conventions. Usually, when a guy hits town, with something to hide, he drifts in out of the dust and stays dusty, becomes a handyman or something and takes up with the shady dame in town (which was exactly what *Red Rock West* was about). Bridget, however, walks straight into the local insurance business and lands a plum job in five minutes flat. When her hapless bar-room pick-up Mike (a wonderfully vain, hurt, confused characterisation by Peter Berg) is surprised to see her in his workplace, she delivers a brisk putdown: "I work here now—don't fuck with my image."

Fiorentino works twists on the *fatale* template with venomous brio—Bridget's into sex and playing on men's emotions, but it's a side order to her real business, which is getting the money and outmanoeuvring everyone, staying on top of the pile. She's the eternal castrating dame of *noir*, but she'd probably see her 1940s precursors, the Hayworths and Stanwycks, as mere amateurs, acting out of confusion and appetite instead of really getting their act together—she's probably on the way to publishing her own Five-Point Castration Business Plan. She shows byzantine cruelty in manipulating the sappy Mike, playing every turn with absolute transparency, and marvelling derisively that he falls for it. It's her New Yorker impatience that gives her a truly distinctive touch: Fiorentino wears a beautifully peppery don't-mess-with-me demeanour, seething with big-city distaste when someone greets her with a cheery "Morning, beautiful day".

But you can't help feeling that Bridget deserves some opponent who's actually on her level. That's what makes the film almost tragic; she's so much smarter than anyone else that victory seems futile—there can't be that much fun in it for her. The fun's all ours, watching her prey squirm.

Yes, the film appeals to our basest instincts, but then Bridget's victims are so appalling that we can't grieve too much for them. Her husband is a slow-burning eye-rolling mass of weasly dementia (it's good to see perennial nice guy Bill Pullman play a creep for once), while Mike's puppy-dog vulnerability is mitigated by stud vanity (his pick-up line is "I'm hung like a horse").

Only the relationship between Mike and Bridget tips us off that we've been here before. He's a claims adjuster, she wants to get him embroiled in an insurance scam. It's when you notice a distinctive touch of Fred MacMurray around his eyes that the coin drops ... and then the film goes and spoils it all by actually using the words "double indemnity". We could have managed without it, and since the film has the temerity to namecheck such an illustrious precursor, we're bound to respond that *The Last Seduction* just isn't in that league. It's a little too mechanical, a little too crossword puzzle in its construction. But it's a mean try.

NEW YORK, 10/31/94, p. 96, David Denby

The Last Seduction, the new neo-*noir* thriller directed by the talented John Dahl (*Red Rock West*), moves with the devastating energy of its viciously inventive dark lady—a lying, cheating tramp, played by the amusingly tough Linda Fiorentino. Before it goes sour at the end, most of this little movie is fast and exhilarating—not radical in form, like *Pulp Fiction*, but erotically ravenous, exceptionally witty, and impressively knowledgeable about all the dirty deals and low maneuvers that keep a corrupt world going. Dahl and his writer (in this case Steve Barancik) may have created their villainess with malice in their hearts, but there's love here, too, and appreciation. Fiorentino's Bridget Gregory is a murderer, a thief—and, hilariously, a feminist who gets huffy if a guy looks at her the wrong way. She's so determined and indefatigable that—as a character—she escapes male paranoia and goes right over the top into Camille Paglia-land, in which any kind of supreme power in women is something to cherish. With superb performances by Bill Pullman and Peter Berg as two different kinds of helpless saps.

NEW YORK POST, 10/26/94, p. 38, Thelma Adams

Bridget (Linda Fiorentino) is impolite—but that's not the worst of it. She's the wickedest screen brunette since Lena Olin smashed a windshield with stiletto heels and slithered to freedom in "Romeo Is Bleeding."

John ("Red Rock West") Dahl has fashioned his latest hip noir, "The Last Seduction," around a femme fatale who takes the money and runs.

The cash happens to be drug money. Bridget steals it from her doting but dotty husband, Dr. Clay Gregory (Bill Pullman). The smitten schlemiel is left to face a loan shark who lent him $100,000 for a one-time-only cocaine deal that would net Clay and Bridget the condo of their yuppie dreams.

There's no condo in the cards for the lovesick Dr. Gregory when Bridget double-crosses him.

Things aren't going to pan out much better for Mike (Peter Berg) of Beston, N.Y. The slack-jawed claims adjuster wants to escape his up-state berg in the worst way and Bridget fulfills his desires in spades.

Until now, Fiorentino has never quite fulfilled the promise she showed in Martin Scorsese's "After Hours." Carnivorous cranked and deadly, the sexy actress makes Bridget's soft-hearted patsies beg for their own destruction.

"You are a criminal mastermind," says Bridget's chumpy hubby. "Just a hobby," she coolly replies.

Whether the rabid minx is making love to Mike while hanging from a chainlink fence outside his favorite bar or planting murderous thoughts by pitching life insurance on fickle husbands to their heartbroken wives, she's one woman for whom love means never having to say you're sorry.

Newcomer Steve Barancik's script is part role-reversal comedy, part twisted thriller. It harks back to "Double Indemnity," but its amorality and wicked humor have a '90s sting.

Without a self-conscious wink at the audience, Dahl gets away with movie murder in this darkly delicious entertainment. Just don't try Bridget's tricks at home—they could be hazardous to the health of someone you love.

NEWSDAY, 10/26/94, Part II/p. B7, John Anderson

In "Red Rock West," his neo-*noir* cult hit of early this year, director John Dahl put Nicolas Cage in a trap that might have been set by Billy Wilder, in league with Jean-Paul Sartre: Every time Cage had a chance to get out of town, and escape the intra-marital murder plot that was sucking him in, he found himself back in Red Rock. He was a free-floating thing; evil was a whirlpool in a Hitchcockian shower drain.

In Dahl's new film, "The Last Seduction," the feral, venomous and sex-soaked Bridget Gregory (Linda Fiorentino) is the vortex and there is no escape—not for her husband, Clay (Bill Pullman), whom she rips off for $750,000 after sending him on a near-fatal drug-money swap; not for Mike Swale (Peter Berg), the hapless claims adjuster she meets and beds in her upstate New York hideout, not for anyone who tries to separate her from her money.

But is she a vessel of evil? Not if you consider that always-elusive quality as something beyond human control. Whether she's undulating with Mike behind a bar, or sending an unzipped private detective through the windshield of her car, or telling Mike she'll be a good girl, or plotting by phone with her attorney (J.T. Walsh), Bridget—a worthy descendant of Brigid O'Shaughnessy ("The Maltese Falcon") and, perhaps, Medea—is beyond good and evil. She merely is.

And just what she is will be, should be, a matter of large discussion among moviegoers this season. As played by the rivetingly earthy Fiorentino, Bridget is a force of nature, rough and seductive. When she bounces along in heels, her perkiness is chilling. And her character is pure, in a perverse sort of way. Although the plot of "The Last Seduction" is akin to "Body Heat," the hook there was in the revelation of just how corrupt Kathleen Turner's character was. The only surprise in "Last Seduction" is how often we expect Bridget to melt, knowing from the start that she's a cold-hearted bitch with a soul packed in dry ice.

We're not alone in our illusions, though; with Bridget, guilt by association means a conviction for stupidity. Clay comes home from his near-fatal meeting under the Brooklyn Bridge—where he's traded, at gunpoint, pharmaceutical cocaine for a case full of money—leaves the money in the living room while he takes a shower, and comes out to find wife and currency gone. He doesn't seem mentally deficient, but he must be.

En route to Chicago, Bridget stops in Beston, N.Y., where she meets Mike, a local with a secret who introduces himself with an anatomical boast ("Let's see," she says, and does). She finds a job at his office, and they couple on a regular basis, but he begins to crave more conversation, a real *relationship* (the italics are Bridget's). Just as her movie ancestors include every love-'em-and-leave-'em hero to ever warm a theater seat, Mike can count among his progenitors Debra Winger in "An Officer and Gentleman": He's too good for his one-horse town, and he sees Bridget as his ticket out. God help him.

Dahl, who creates a cool, jazzy atmosphere for a steamy storyline, clearly loves the genre, and constantly plays with his audience's expectations regarding gender and plot. Asked by Mike why she's in Beston at all, Bridget answers, "I don't know, Mike. You're so damned intuitive, you tell me." Male intuition? An interesting concept, and a totally fallacious one given the evidence in "The Last Seduction."

SIGHT AND SOUND, 8/94, p. 44, Kim Newman

New York. Intern Clay Gregory sells a cache of pharmaceutical cocaine for $700,000, and his wife Bridget runs off with the money. She goes to ground in the small town of Beston, where she picks up local man Mike Swale in a bar. Bridget's lawyer advises her to stay hidden while she applies for a divorce and she takes a job with an insurance company, assuming the name Wendy Kroy. Mike, who also works for the firm, pushes her for a deeper relationship but she holds back until Clay's private eye neighbour Harlan tracks her down. After staging a car accident in which Harlan is killed, Bridget sets about manipulating Mike into attempting the murder of Clay. First, she shows how actuarial tables and credit ratings can be used to single out heavily insured men who cheat on their wives, then she suggests they can turn a profit by hiring themselves as hit men to the wives.

Mike is appalled but Bridget manages to persuade him that she really loves him despite her outward hard-boiled indifference, and pretends that she has taken a trip to Miami and committed a murder for money. To introduce equality into their relationship, Mike consents to a contract killing and Bridget convinces him that Clay is a foreclosure lawyer who deserves to be murdered. Mike breaks into Clay's apartment but is unable to go through with the murder, whereupon Clay shows Mike his wedding photograph and deduces that he has been duped. Bridget arrives to find Mike in a rage. She kills Clay, then taunts Mike—with her knowledge of his deepest secret, that he briefly and accidentally married a transvestite—into raping her as she phones the police. Mike is unable to prove his version of events and Bridget keeps the money.

From the modestly effective *Kill Me Again* through the minor but highly satisfying *Red Rock West* to this perfect example of grunge *noir*, John Dahl has developed an interesting subcategory of medium-budget, moderately starry trick thriller. Without the baroque overkill of *Basic Instinct* or the top-shelf sleaze of Gregory Hippolyte's direct-to-video silicone slashers, Dahl redeems the 'erotic thriller', not so much in the explicitness of the sex scenes but in his revamping of the classic *noir* theme of the woman who uses all her sexual powers and any other psychological advantage to bend weaker-willed men to her avaricious purpose. *The Last Seduction* is the first of Dahl's films not to be scripted by the director, though the mix of Chinese-puzzle plotting and face-slapping cynicism found in Steve Barancik's outstanding screenplay is in keeping with the first two films. With a running time 15 minutes longer than those faster-paced, more explosively violent melodramas, *The Last Seduction* has a little more room to breathe, which allows the three central characters to develop beyond their functional roles as components in a fiendishly cunning plot.

Dahl always gets the best from his actors, and the playing here is excellent, with Peter Berg and Bill Pullman, whose doggily dumb decency and half-smart cringing are expertly contrasted, redeeming their uneven careers with funny, touching, creepy performances. The always interesting but lately neglected Linda Fiorentino avoids pastiching the 40s *femme fatale*, portraying Bridget as a contemporary monster heroine who effortlessly eclipses Sharon Stone's Catherine Trammell as villainess of the decade. Hard-faced and appallingly direct (her meeting-cute line with Mike is "fuck off"), Bridget occasionally overplays her sweetness act when manipulating lesser men, but Fiorentino always stirs in enough underlying contempt to signal the character's belief that the fools she dupes are not worth the effort of a really convincing imposture.

Like *Blood Simple*, *The Last Seduction* offers the pleasures of an intricate and gradually unfolding story of misunderstanding and murder, but here we are always a few steps behind Bridget, who is in complete control and able to turn any opportunity to her advantage. Because her motives are never fully explained, the implication is that Bridget really is the thoroughgoing bitch she claims to be. It is entirely due to Fiorentino's performance that she is as fascinating as she is rotten, and Barancik and Dahl capitalise on the audience's grudging sympathy for her by pulling an ending with no last-minute reprieve for the dim Mike, in which Bridget is driven away in a limousine with the loot.

TIME, 11/14/94, p. 82, Richard Schickel

As usual, conventional wisdom has it all wrong. The problem is not that they don't write good roles for women anymore; it's that they only write roles for good women. Actresses still get to suffer nobly and ignobly. They are even allowed to be brave and capable. But down-and-dirty wickedness is denied them. It's not nice.

It's all part of the new prissiness. But evil has traditionally been an equal-opportunity employer. Where would Barbara Stanwyck and the other ladies of the *noir* have been if their only subtext had been female victimization? Every once in a while a girl has to stop brooding over gender injustice, start thinking about sexual revenge, and slip into her thigh-highs and stiletto heels to lure a few dopes to destruction.

There has always been something bracing about such creatures, especially when no whiny attempts are made to justify their malignity. The grace that redeems a wretch like Bridget Gregory (Linda Fiorentino) in *The Last Seduction* is her breathtaking lack of hypocrisy. She's economic woman on an intricate and divinely sociopathic rampage. She just plain wants the money she steals from her husband (Bill Pullman), who obtained it in a drug deal that she had urged on him. She just plain needs to create a new life so she can hide from his wrath. And she just plain must enlist simple Mike Swale (Peter Berg) as an accomplice in murder when her mate finally catches up with her.

There's no guise—fighting feminist or yuppie careerist, prudish housewife or pouty adolescent, barroom slut or abused bride—that Bridget won't assume to win this game. Her quick changes are funny. So is her chilly single-mindedness. And so is the eagerness of males, stupefied by lust, to be taken in by her. Fiorentino is ferociously good in the role. If first-time screenwriter Steve

Barancik conceived it as a parody of have-it-all feminism, this actress doesn't acknowledge it" She's after the humor of humorlessness, the nuttiness of self-interest untrammeled by sentiment—and she nails it.

Similarly, director John Dahl is after something more than a nostalgic evocation of the old film noir style. He can light a mean street, a smoky barroom or a morning-after bedroom in the best tradition of the genre. But these venues are no longer situated in a big city. Dahl's *Red Rock West*, released earlier this year, was set in a dour little Western town. *Seduction* mostly takes place in a small, upstate New York town. What Dahl is saying is that you can perhaps avoid becoming a crime statistic by living in the boondocks, but that evil, in the larger sense, is everywhere and inescapable. Not that he would ever put that point so crudely. Dahl is a cool, even reticent filmmaker, however complicated his plots, however hot and basic the emotions that drive them. But that's a virtue these days. A lot of directors are drawn to the classic genres, but few of them seem to have any real confidence in their strengths. Their tendency is to overheat, and in the process overexpand, these projects. Dahl lets his loony material speak for itself. He understands that overdirecting is like overacting; it pushes us away instead of drawing us in.

VILLAGE VOICE, 11/1/94, p. 56, Georgia Brown

Turn to the so-called male genre, film noir: no self-sacrificing sufferers here. Noir, of course, harbored spider women and dragon ladies, desperate dames out to get what they can. But real noir came out of a historical time and place, provable by the fact that none of the neo-, or shall I say *color*, noirs really get it right. The first wave of imitators (*Chinatown*, perhaps *Klute*) had panache, but then there was a tapering to a cool tease like *Body Heat* and finally a drastic plummet to the commercial cynicism of *Basic Instinct*.

Welcome to more or less the pits, John Dahl's *The Last Seduction*, a willed, synthetic pastiche, primarily of *Body Heat* and *Basic Instinct*. From the first comes the bones of the plot; from the second, the lineaments of the bitch.

The Medusa here is Bridget (Linda Fiorentino), who gets her kicks from being mean. An Aunt Ginny in this script would get tossed off her terrace. In the New York opener, Bridget cons her bumbling hubby Clay (Bill Pullman), out of the cash he's just made in a drug deal. Fleeing toward Chicago, she pulls off in the sleepy upstate burg of Beston and decides to hide out for a while. For a few moments Beston seems appealingly sinister in the way of the dusty crossroads Nick Cage stumbles into in *Red Rock West*, but no, it's a collection of genial halfwits, none of them any match for Bridget. (The movie has a couple of good laughs on the yokels—as when a black man comes to town.) Bridget takes up with one of the dumber citizens, the well-hung Mike (Peter Berg), who serves as her "designated fuck" and designated fall guy. Poor Mike didn't catch *Body Heat*, not to mention *Double Indemnity*.

"Where you from?" asks Mike. "A galaxy far, far away," answers Bridget. So true. She's an alien, a cartoon. Judging by the chortles and guffaws at the press screening, many will find her outrageously funny.

The Last Seduction has already played on HBO. It's being promoted as the new John Dahl on the basis of the modest success of his *Red Rock West*—also a neo-noir but one with some appeal. I'm not sure Dahl deserves my ire here since he was just doing a gig and makes Steve Barancik's script more interesting, certainly classier, than it should have been. Who I really blame is anyone taking this for the real thing. It wants so bad to be trash but it's really hash.

Also reviewed in:
CHICAGO TRIBUNE, 11/18/94, Friday/p. L, Michael Wilmington
NATION, 11/14/94, p. 592, Stuart Klawans
NEW YORK TIMES, 10/26/94, p. C13, Janet Maslin
NEW YORKER, 10/24/94, p. 100, Anthony Lane
VARIETY, 2/28-3/6/94, p. 70, David Stratton
WASHINGTON POST, 11/18/94, p. F7, Rita Kempley
WASHINGTON POST, 11/18/94, Weekend/p. 50, Desson Howe

LATCHO DROM

A Shadow Distribution Inc. release of a K.G. Productions production with the participation of the CNC/Sofiarp/Investimages/Canal Plus/The Sacem Fund. *Producer:* Michèle Ray-Gavras. *Director:* Tony Gatlif. *Screenplay (Romany with English subtitles):* Tony Gatlif. *Director of Photograhy:* Eric Guichard and Claude Garnier. *Editor:* Nicole Berkmans. *Musical Adviser: Alain Weber*. *Sound:* Nicolas Naegelen. *Production Designer:* Denis Mercier. *Running time:* 103 minutes. *MPAA Rating:* Not Rated.

LOS ANGELES TIMES, 10/31/94, Calendar/p. 2, Kevin Thomas

Tony Gatlif's rapturously beautiful "Latcho Drom" ("Safe Journey"), celebrates the sustaining power of music in Gypsy culture, as he retraces the migration of the Rom people from India that began 1,000 years ago.

As he moves through the Mideast to Eastern and Western Europe, he films Gypsies singing and dancing amid vignettes of their nomadic existence, marked by hardship and discrimination to this day. The images are as glorious as the music, which is alternately joyous and mournful.

Most memorable is an older woman's haunting lament for the Gypsies who died at Auschwitz.

NEW YORK POST, 7/20/94, p. 31, Thelma adams

"Latcho Drom" is the year's most off-putting title. Is it a misspelling? A bizarre sporting event? A saga about a Romanian idiot savant with an IQ of 75?

The words mean "safe journey" in Romany. Tony Gatlif's musical odyssey offers a mesmerizing voyage through Gypsy territory from India to Spain, with stops in Egypt, Turkey, Romania, Hungary, Slovakia and France.

Scratching beneath the surface of Gypsy life, the movie—neither documentary nor fiction—reveals a cultural wealth that belies the rags and poverty often associated with Romany-speakers.

While writer/director Gatlif, a Frenchman of Rom extraction, captures the tribe's nomadic nature as it migrates north and west from India, he also shows what is constant: the compelling and sophisticated music and dance that these dark-skinned, dark-eyed people carry with them.

Without dialogue or narration, the movie shifts between ethno-graphic scenes of Gypsy life set against the backdrop of exotic locales, and "raves"—gatherings where Gypsies congregate to sing and dance. Both the sound recording and Eric Guichard's cinematography are impeccable.

The music speaks for itself, assisted by expressive lyrics translated from Romany in subtitles. In Rajasthan, a turbaned tenor sings of love to a woman under a full moon: "I have placed my bed in a delicious spot; how can I sleep alone without you?"

In Romania, the horrors of Ceausescu find their way into the lyrics of a ragged Rom playing a violin with calloused fingers; riding on a train, a woman in a babushka sings, "The whole world hates us. We're chased. We're cursed. We're condemned to wandering throughout life."

The theme of persecution exists alongside an unquenchable joie de vivre. The spirit of the Egyptian who sings, "the fire that burns inside me drives my soul crazy," runs through the impassioned music from India to Spain.

"Latcho Drom" could be improved by adding a subtitle identifying each country and shaving 10 minutes in the second half. But these are quibbles.

The movie, which won the Prix Gervais at the 1993 Cannes Film festival, is a sensual, stirring, visual treat.

NEWSDAY, 7/20/94, Part II/p. B9, John Anderson

About halfway through "Latcho Drom" Tony Gatlif's wonderfully sad-eyed celebration of Gypsy music and woe, a neighborhood string band leaves its minor-key drone for something that might be described as bohemian bluegrass: Harmonics shift, fingers fly, smiles break on faces, a horse gallops across a field, a train rockets down a track and the audience lifts off. There's no narrative connection, necessarily, between what we see and what we hear, but the whole is a rollicking, visceral thrill. And "Latcho Drom" just might be the ultimate music video.

Gatlif set out to pay tribute to his people—he is French, with Rom (Gypsy) roots—and he does so, in a film that's part travelogue, part documentary, part staged vignettes and part lament for a welcome the Gypsies have never known. "The whole world hates us," are typical words to a typical dirge. Ever since the Rom people's inexplicable flight from India a millennium ago, they have been ever wandering, ever persecuted (the title, somewhat ironically, means "safe journey" in Romany), victims of Hitler's death camps and, since the fall of communism, the targets of increased racism in Eastern Europe. Like the stream we see course through the opening moments, and like the smooth stones over which it runs, the Gypsies have been ever-moving, ever-static, unchanging and changing.

A result of this amorphous status has been a reliance on music both as a source of solace and a means of recording history. Gatlif charts the music from India, Egypt and Turkey, through Europe using virtually no words, just the music and the landscape, which he makes synonymous: A couple taking their family on a journey through the desert find music in water; hammering on an anvil, they create a rhythm that causes their daughter to dance. She in turn becomes an older girl, in traditional costume, singing a courtship song. We move, in turn, to the wedding, where pastel turbans dot the parched landscape, and polyrhythms percolate under a subtext of sorrow. Music and life are inseparable.

Occasionally, a character from one episode—an episode consisting of a song, or a style of Gypsy music—will lead us to another. A child from that bohemian bluegrass episode watches a ship, the ship carries a family to a city where the mother and daughter sell flowers amid enormous flocks of pigeons; a father on a side street teaches a son to play the drum, the beat of a shoeshine punctuated by a child's scream and Gatlif has melded sight and sound into one beautiful moment.

The film makes its way both musically and geographically across Europe, with the instrumentation and music becoming progressively sophisticated, until we meet a guitar-violin ensemble in France who play the kind of jazz associated with violinist Stephane Grappelli and the legendary Gypsy guitarist Django Reinhardt. Crossing the Pyrenees to Spain, Gatlif leaves us with a startling woman whose words of remorse—"Why does your wicked mouth spit on me?" ... "I find myself envying the respect you give your dog"—are made ironic by the defiant strength of her look, and her voice. These are qualities of survival. The music, Gatlif strives to tell us, is what helps make the survival worthwhile.

VILLAGE VOICE, 7/26/94, p. 47, J. Hoberman

The sensibility of Tony Gatlif's *Latcho Drom* may be explicitly Gypsy or, rather, Rom; but instead of familiar, the effect is spectacularly exotic. The title of this lush music documentary is the Romany equivalent of "bon voyage," and the movie affords an often terrific trip.

Journeying through time as well as space, *Latcho Drom* traces, more or less, the road that, beginning a thousand years ago, the Rom took from India to Iberia. The movie begins with a caravan—complete with dogs, chickens, and children, not to mention bangled women and mustachioed men, crossing the orange sands of Rajasthan, singing of their wandering fate. All the stereotypes are in place, amplified by Cinema-Scope and India's abundance of hot pinks and electric yellows.

For Gatlif, *Latcho Drom* is "neither a documentary nor a fictional film." Basically, it's an anthology of Gypsy music as played by an assortment of professionals in a half dozen countries on a variety of stringed instruments—sitars, zithers, violins, guitars—against means of percussion that range from small drums to brass vases to paired spoons to castanets. The vocals are as wailing and soulful as the rhythms are hypnotic and infectious. Gatlif puts music at the center of Rom culture. All performances are communal, musicians, invariably watched by a gaggle of kids intent on learning the beat.

Music also helps determine *Latcho Drom*'s structure. In the Rajasthan sequence, Gatlif match-cuts on tempo so that a young girl dancing to amuse herself, as adults set up camp around her, suddenly becomes a nubile maid, whirling to the same cautionary song ("protect yourself from the evil eye") without missing a step. Typically, the scene develops into a sort of staged revue—the Rom preparing for a show by painting a bull's horns, combing their hair, tuning up instruments. Musicians beneath a tree transformed into a massive candelabra begin a clanging, driving, keening piece, while dancers execute synchronized gestures under the improbably full desert moon and a sky filled with impossibly bright stars. This consciously primal image gives way to another. As children frisk beside the Nile, their elders gather in a courtyard for another sensationally kinetic number.

With its fairy-tale landscapes, *Latcho Drom* has an undeniable kitschy quality, but the performance level and production values are so high that it's irresistible. Eventually, the early *National Geographic* locales yield to bleaker terrain. Gatlif crosses the Bosporus and, suddenly, ragged kids are shining shoes in run-down back alleys. Istanbul is like the entrance to the fallen world. It is in Europe, after all, that the Rom enter into history. (And, it is in post-Communist Eastern Europe, where Gypsies are now the most persecuted and impoverished of ethnic minorities.)

Romania, where Gypsies were enslaved, is signified by two old men on the rainy outskirts of a muddy village singing a ballad about the fall of Ceauşescu. The sense of desolation increases as another band of Gypsies takes a train across the gray expanse of the Hungarian *puszta*: "We're cursed ... condemned to be alone." In an even more barren Slovakian field, marked by a closeup of barbed wire and snow, a middle-aged Gypsy woman offers a haunting a cappella lament about her experience of Auschwitz.

The mood lightens once the movie reaches France. The villages are picturesque and the fields are green—finally, it's spring. A musician drives his late-model car along a bucolic road, guitar stowed in the backseat. (As opposed to Hungary and Romania, the performers look as if they get paid.) The movie finally crosses the Pyrenees to the streets of a picture-postcard Spanish town where a lone flamenco guitar prompts ever more elaborate vocal ululations as a variety of Gypsy women take turns executing a stomping, sensual dance—the harsh, stinging sound mitigating all sentimentality.

Gypsies have hardly been ignored by the movies; still, few, if any films, have been made from a Rom perspective in the Romany language. (Yolande Zauberman's romantic *shtetl* drama *Ivan and Abraham* is an exception—mainly in Yiddish, it includes a number of Romany passages.) An Algerian-born Frenchman of Andalusian Rom origin, Gatlif embarked on *Latcho Drom* as a personal quest. The final song, which he wrote, is a denunciation of prejudice and persecution from Ferdinand and Isabella through Hitler and Franco.

As seen here, the Rom have some history but no particular economy. They are children of nature inhabiting their own planet. The locations are unidentified and there's a paucity of titles—most frustratingly in the sequence visiting the shrine of Sara the Black Virgin in southern France. Latcho Drom is more an appreciation than an explication of Rom culture. But if the film projects a half-imaginary world, it's still a marvelously seductive one.

Also reviewed in:
CHICAGO TRIBUNE, 2/3/94, Tempo/p. 3, Michael Wilmington
NEW YORK TIMES, 7/20/94, p. C18, Stephen Holden
VARIETY, 6/21/93, p. 42, Lisa Nesselson
WASHINGTON POST, 8/32/94, p. C2, Hal Hinson

LEGENDS OF THE FALL

A TriStar Pictures release of a Bedford Falls/Pangaea production. *Executive Producer:* Patrick Crowley. *Producer:* Edward Zwick, Bill Wittliff and Marshall Herskovitz. *Director:* Edward Zwick. *Screenplay:* Susan Shilliday and Bill Wittliff. *Based on the novella by:* Jim Harrison. *Director of Photography:* John Toll. *Editor:* Steven Rosenblum. *Music:* James Horner. *Music Editor:* Jim Henrikson. *Sound:* Douglas Ganton and (music) Shawn Murphy. *Sound Editor:* Per Hallberg and Lon Bender. *Casting:* Mary Colquhoun. *Production Designer:* Lilly Kilvert. *Art Director:* Rick Roberts and Andrew Precht. *Set Designer:* Greg Papalia and Peter Kelly. *Set Decorator:* Dorree Cooper. *Special Effects:* Mike Vezina. *Costumes:* Deborah Scott. *Make-up:* Jean A. Black. *Special Effects Make-up:* Gordon J. Smith. *Make-up (Anthony*

Hopkins): Christine Beveridge. *Stunt Coordinator:* Gary Combs, Brent Woolsey, and Doug Seus. *Running time:* 133 minutes. *MPAA Rating:* R.

CAST: Brad Pitt (Tristan); Anthony Hopkins (Ludlow); Aidan Quinn (Alfred); Julia Ormond (Susannah); Henry Thomas (Samuel); Karina Lombard (Isabel Two); Tantoo Cardinal (Pet); Gordon Tootoosis (One Stab); Paul Desmond (Decker); Christina Pickles (Isabel); Robert Wisden (John T. O'Banion); John Novak (James O'Banion); Kenneth Welsh (Sheriff Tynert); Bill Dow (Longley); Sam Sarkar (Rodriguez); Nigel Bennett (Asgaard); Keegan Macintosh (Boy Tristan); Eric Johnson (Teen Tristan); Randall Slavin (Teen Alfred); Doug Hughes (Teen Samuel); Sekwan Auger (Young Isabel Two); David Kaye (Samuel Decker); Christine Harder (Isabel Three); Charles Andre (Federal Officer); Weston McMillan (Noel); Aaron Goettel (Corporal's Friend); Brian Stollery (Captain); Bill Croft (Bartender); Ray Godshall (Businessman); Marc Levy (Butler); Ken Kirzinger (O'Banion Thug); Winnie Hung (Chinese Woman); Simon Sherwood (Officer); Rob Hrdlicka and Channing Knull (Canadian Soldiers); John D. Cameron (Proprietor).

FILMS IN REVIEW, 3-4/95, p. 58, Andy Pawelczak

Legends of the Fall is a neo-Western soap opera, the kind of movie the ads call epic, sweeping, romantic. Well, it has some wide-screen shots of Montana, enough soap to stimulate the tear ducts about once every half hour, and a hero named Tristan played by Brad Pitt with luxuriant shoulder length hair, gluey eyes and the kind of scruffy beard that signifies rugged masculinity these days. Based on a novella by Jim Harrison, the movie is a do-it-yourself American Studies kit for mythomaniacs, a refurbishing of Cooper's Hawkeye tales with a few Biblical motifs thrown in.

The film is about a tightly knit family on the receding frontier in the early years of the twentieth century. Anthony Hopkins is the standard-issue patriarch, an ex-cavalry officer who retired from civilization in protest against the government's treatment of Indians. His cultivated wife returned to the East and he has brought up his three sons with the help of an Indian whose off-screen voice narrates the movie, thus adding a dash of Native American mysticism with a New Age spin. Tristan, the favorite son, is the Hawkeye character; as a child he went mano-a-mano with a bear, and, as the narrator frequently reminds us, ever since he has been driven to peripatetic excesses by the inner voice of the bear—it's his totem, just as the wolf is Jack Nicholson's totem in *Wolf*, also based on a Harrison novella.

Like Hawkeye, Tristan occupies a no-man's land between civilization and the wilderness. The film's director, Edward Zwick, underlines this point with frequent shots of the prodigal riding in from the wide open spaces as watched by the family from the porch of the homestead. If that sounds familiar, it's because it's lifted from John Ford's *The Searchers*, a film that explores both the ascetic heroism and pathology of the Hawkeye figure in a genuinely mythic mode. But where John Wayne, in Ford's film, is a chthonic presence, an emanation of the primordial Western landscape, Brad Pitt is all posturing and flouncing hair. Before the film is over, in a veritable delirium of narcissism and myth-mongering, Tristan becomes a kind of tormented Conradian hero traveling up rivers never seen by a white man—with his long hair he looks like somebody's idea of Rimbaud as played by a rock-n-roll star maudit.

The source of Tristan's angst is the death of his younger brother Samuel (Henry Thomas of *E. T.*) in World War I—the film, intent on touching all the bases, wants to remind us of the magnitude of the trauma inflicted by the Great War. In an overwrought crane shot, we see him cradling his brother's body and cursing God—the fall referred to in the title, I suppose. We're free to speculate that the real cause of his anguish and guilt is an unconscious death wish for Samuel with whose fiance (the Eve in this frontier Eden, played by the blandly beautiful Julia Ormond) Tristan is secretly in love. So is Aidan Quinn in the thankless role of the comparatively plodding, bourgeois brother, Alfred, with whom Tristan carries on a Cain and Abel-like rivalry. There's enough muscular, brotherly agony here to satisfy even a Sam Shepard.

Legends of the Fall isn't actively offensive—it's predictable but harmless. Harrison's novella mobilizes all the archetypes—its narrative structure is by the numbers—but the book is redeemed by his conviction and the poetic power of his prose. The movie's equivalent is pictorialism—it was nominated for an Academy Award for cinematography—but placing its characters in stunning landscapes doesn't bring them to life. Like Robert Bly's tom-toms and masculinist rituals, the movie might fulfill a psychological need in some viewers. Watching it is like hoisting a few with the guys on a weekday night and engaging in some mild chest-thumping, leavened by New Male sensitivity, before returning to the routines of domestic life. But what a fall from genre grace and potency the picture represents.

LOS ANGELES TIMES, 12/23/94, Calendar/p. 1, Kenneth Turan

Everything about "Legends of the Fall" shouts epic filmmaking and it is not an altogether unpleasant sound.

Bursting with big country Montana landscapes, big music, big emotions, even big hair, this is highly romanticized, old-fashioned sentimental filmmaking of a type we haven't seen in a while, the kind of movie where ringlets turn white overnight and no one rides in quietly on a single horse when leading a galloping herd is an option.

Slow moving and at times foolish, too conscious of its ambitions as an epic for its own good, "Legends" does present an easy target. But director Edward Zwick has infused it with so much sheer watchability, it believes so earnestly in its high-gloss doings, that it's difficult to pull the trigger.

Although it retains the name of the Jim Harrison novella, as admired a piece of American writing as the last 20 years has produced, the most telling thing about "Legends" is how little it has to do with its nominal source material.

For while the Harrison novella is primarily concerned with men, their loneliness and their relationship to each other, the movie has smoothly turned this on its head, both feminizing and Hollywoodizing the narrative by recasting it as a story about three men competing for the same woman.

Expanding some things, condensing others, tossing out a lot of material and adding a heap of invention, screenwriters Susan Shilliday and Bill Wittliff have, in a way that is almost engaging in its audacity, turned the masculine Harrison into a latter-day Edna Ferber, the patron saint of panoramic Western romances.

In fact, what "Legends" will remind veteran moviegoers of most is the 1956 George Stevens-directed version of Ferber's "Giant," with Brad Pitt, Aidan Quinn and Julia Ormond standing in nicely for James Dean, Rock Hudson and Elizabeth Taylor.

Pitt, Quinn and Henry Thomas play the Ludlow brothers—the wild Tristan, the stodgy Alfred and young idealist Samuel—all sons of a rugged colonel (Anthony Hopkins, as usual making the most of a small role) who retires to a remote corner of Montana when he can no longer stomach U.S. Cavalry policy.

With their mother in permanent retreat back East, the boys grow up under the watchful eye of a venerable Cree named One Stab whose tribal affiliation was probably changed from Cheyenne to accommodate Gordon Tootoosis, the Cree actor who has the role.

One Stab is also responsible for much of the film's voice-over narration, delivered in classic venerable Native American sage fashion. It is One Stab who gets to recite "Legends'" topic sentences: "Some people hear their own inner voices with great clearness and live by what they hear. Such people become crazy. Or they become legends."

On the eve of World War I, Samuel gets the plot in gear by returning home from Harvard with his fiancée, the beautiful Susannah Fincannon (Julia Ormond). While Alfred and the Colonel dutifully meet the couple at the train station, the ponytailed Tristan, a major hunk who has been outdoors forever doing god knows what, rides up glistening with dirt and sweat.

As soon as Susannah eyes him and archly comments, "So this is Tristan, and does he speak English?" it doesn't take a Native American sage to realize that trouble will soon be brewing between these previously inseparable sons. All too soon One Stab will be moved to wax aphoristically and say, "You cannot blame the water that freezes in the rock and splits it apart."

Susannah, only lightly sketched in the novella and described by Harrison as "a frail, lovely girl" is turned by the film into a robust natural woman who is soon roping and riding with the gang. Ormond, whose previous credits include the odd mixture of "Nostradamus," HBO's "Stalin" and Peter Greenaway's "The Baby of Macon," is the film's major surprise. An energetic actress, she brings vigor, charm and reality to a part that might have been no more than decorative.

Brad Pitt's trademark virility is not a surprise, though it is a relief to see him looking so alive after the gloom, doom and pale makeup of "Interview With the Vampire." An instinctive actor who must emotionally feel a role to be successfully in it, Pitt is perfectly cast in a traditional heartthrob way as the spirited masculine animal whose idea of fun is waking up hibernating bears and seeing what happens, and the screen is more alive whenever he is on it.

What happens to these three brothers, all of whom covet Susannah in their own way, is what "Legends" uncovers, and what a story filled with tears, curses, passion, suffering and any other larger-than-life emotion you can imagine it turns out to be.

Director Zwick orchestrates everything with welcome gusto, and though the result is not as meaningful as it would have you believe, it is undeniably pleasant to have this kind of production to kick around.

NEW YORK POST, 12/23/94, p. 52, Michael Medved

Some movies, like some people, can win you over on the strength of good looks alone.

It doesn't matter that your better judgment tells you there's no substance there: The sheer visual impact is so strong that you're impressed in spite of yourself.

"Legends of the Fall" is that kind of movie, a gloriously good-looking epic full of eye-popping vistas of Montana mountains (actually shot in Western Canada) and featuring, in Brad Pitt and Julia Ormond, one of the more spectacularly attractive couples of recent years.

At the same time. when you strip away all the gorgeous human and wilderness scenery, and the overwrought intensity of the acting, what you're left with is soap opera: a plodding, preposterous tall tale of three brothers in love with the same woman.

The three boys are the sons of a crusty curmudgeon of a retired cavalry colonel (an uneven though impressive Anthony Hopkins) who left the Army because he disapproved of the government's Indian policy. His former Cree Indian scout (Gordon Tootoosis) joins him on his sprawling ranch and helps to raise the boys with an abundance of tribal lore.

Brad Pitt plays Tristan, the nature boy who's most influenced by this material; with his flowing, shoulder-length blonde locks and his other-worldly, walk-on-water ways he comes across like an odd combination of Wild Thing and Jesus of Montana. Aidan Quinn plays his far more conventional brother, a hard-working businessman and aspiring politician, while Henry Thomas is the youngest, and most idealistic of the brood.

This sweet-spirited kid kicks the plot into gear when he returns to the ranch from an East Coast education accompanied by a stunningly beautiful and sophisticated fiancee, played by the British newcomer Julia Ormond, who deploys the most dazzling smile in the known universe.

By the time the three brothers march off together to fight in World War I (over their father's strenuous objections) they're all understandably smitten with this ethereal creature.

The story's based on the moody 1970s novella by Jim Harrison and for the first half of the movie, up through some genuinely horrifying battlefield scenes in France, it works splendidly. The problem comes with the picture's second half, dramatizing the tragic "fall" of the title, when the family begins to suffer a run of bad luck that crushes credibility.

Unfortunately, these random disasters don't feel like the hammer blows of fate as much as they seem like arbitrary and malign manipulations of straining screenwriters. The behavior of the protagonists makes little sense and Brad Pitt's character in particular seems not so much "unpredictable and unknowable," as out-of-focus and confused.

Director Ed Zwick (still best known as co-creator of TV's "thirtysomething") previously showed his skill at historical epics with 1989's "Glory." But that Civil War masterpiece had intelligence and integrity to go along with its seductive surfaces.

"Legends of the Fall" boasts similar ambition and sweep, but ultimately, like its main characters, it's just a pretty face.

NEWSDAY, 12/23/94, Part II/p. B19, Jack Mathews

It is hard to pinpoint the exact moment when Edward Zwick's "Legends of the Fall" crosses over from frontier epic to soggy family melodrama, but once it does, it picks up speed and never looks back.

Adapted from a Jim Harrison novella, "Legends" busts a gut reaching for the kind of passionate sweep of George Stevens' "Giant," and on its surface—Lilly Kilvert's detailed western sets, John Toll's spectacular cinematography—it does attain a certain level of grandeur. But the story of fraternal strife, spiritual quests, political corruption and romantic jealousy during the taming of the West, is a soap opera with saddle sores.

Narrated by the 100-year-old Cree Indian (Gordon Tootoosis) who lived with them, "Legends" is the story of the Ludlow family of men. Col. William Ludlow (Anthony Hopkins) is the patriarch, a former cavalry officer who has turned his back on the government because of its treatment of Indians, and gone into cattle ranching in Montana with his three sons—Alfred (Aidan Quinn), the oldest and most reliable; Tristan (Brad Pitt), the untamable spirit, and their idealistic baby brother Samuel (Henry Thomas). Mrs. Ludlow, we learn, couldn't take the hard winters and left them.

Two events occur that strain the bonds between the brothers and set the melodrama in motion. First, young Samuel returns from his freshman year at Harvard with Susannah, the fiancee (Julia Ormond) of his brothers' dreams. And for reasons not particularly clear, Samuel then decides to join the British in the emerging war with Germany in 1913, and his brothers tag along in a failed effort to keep him alive.

The events in Europe drive a wedge between Alfred and Tristan, and send Tristan off on the first of two around-the-world spiritual quests, between which he comes home for an affair with Susannah, further alienating the love-sick Alfred, whose decision to run for Congress alienates the colonel, who has a stroke and ... on it goes.

Zwick, who created the TV series "thirtysomething" and directed the fine civil War movie "Glory," is a director in search of a style. He clearly has the eye to go with his passion for the epic form, but this tight and over-cooked family drama doesn't expand to that scale. There simply isn't enough story to go around, and co-writers William Wittliff ("Lonesome Dove") and Susan Shilliday ("thirtysomething"), seem to have vamped entire sections. The last act of the movie, filled with murders, suicides, beatings and family redemption, plays like a very bad imitation of the "Godfather" movies.

There are some sincere performances on display, particularly from Ormond, a British actress who will have better days, and Pitt, who certainly has the movie star presence to hold the center. But once the story crosses the line of credibility—for me, it was when Tristan, looking like Jeffrey Hunter's Jesus in "King of Kings," is shown meeting with ash-covered natives somewhere in Africa—you begin to feel for the actors and not for their characters.

It is an indication of the kind of year Hollywood is having that TriStar is opening "Legends" for one week before the end of year, to qualify for the Academy Awards.

NEWSWEEK, 1/23/94, p. 68, David Ansen

So many damn things happen in "Legends of the Fall," an attempt at epic filmmaking from Edward ("Glory") Zwick, that you just might be persuaded you're watching something momentous. In the course of this saga, set in the Montana Rockies, the three sons of rugged iconoclast Col. William Ludlow (Anthony Hopkins) will all fall in love with the same woman; the first world war will break out, claiming the youngest brother, Samuel (Henry Thomas); the wild middle brother, Tristan (Brad Pitt), haunted by guilt that he didn't protect his sibling in the war, will abandon his dead brother's fiancée and roam the South Seas; the oldest brother, Alfred (Aidan Quinn), will marry the woman who loved both his brothers and become a politician: There will be shoot-outs, bootlegging, politics, a tragic accident, a debilitating stroke, a suicide, vengeance and a wise old Indian narrator explaining it all to you in metaphorical aphorisms.

A lot of activity, however, is not the same thing as a great story. Screenwriters Susan Shilliday and Bill Wittliff, taking big liberties with Jim Harrison's novella, transform his terse text into a glossy romantic melodrama best described as macho Edna Ferber. At the center of the erotic turmoil is Susannah (Julia Ormond), a Boston beauty who lives at the Ludlows' picturesque ranch engaged to the idealistic Samuel. Director Zwick was wise to cast the beguiling Ormond in the role, for it's easy to see why the three boys go gaga for her. But Ormond's charm can't quite hide the fact that Susannah is a cipher. Why would this sophisticated woman spend half her life hanging around waiting for various Ludlow boys to come riding back from their adventures?

"Legends of the Fall" can't afford to delve too deeply into the women in the story, for it must save all its mythmaking energy for the wild-thing hero, Tristan, the movie's true love object. Tristan is untamed Natural Man, the kind of guy who wrestles bears, runs bootleg liquor and, when he's not breaking hearts, is literally tearing them out of dead bodies (it's an Indian warrior thing). His government-hating father dotes on him, Susannah is undone by him, the halfbreed Indian girl Isabel vows she'll marry him, Samuel looks up to him and the family's old Indian retainer, One Stab, reveres him. Understandably, his dutiful, responsible older brother Alfred builds up quite a resentment; his virtue can't begin to compete with the wild thing's dangerous glamour.

Zwick give Pitt the full star treatment. The camera worships his melting smile, his golden locks, his tormented James Deanish bravado. When he's on screen, it's hard to watch anyone else. This has little to do with great acting, but it bodes well for his future as a Hollywood leading man.

The movie, like Pitt, is easy on the eyes, but it's more successful at striking epic poses than at conjuring up any real emotion. "Legends of the Fall" is fun"in a grandiloquent, guilty-pleasure sort of way, but underneath its pretty surface it's peddling a lot of stale old notions about the unfettered West, when men were men—and we are asked to worship their brutal self-absorption. In the Ludlow clan, the guys earn each other's respect by blowing people away, a rather bloody form of family therapy. Does Zwick, the man who made the touchy-feely "thirtsomething," really believe this macho hooey?

SIGHT AND SOUND, 5/95, p. 48, Ben Thompson

At the turn of the century cavalryman Colonel William Ludlow leaves the army and settles on a ranch in the Montana Rockies. His cultivated wife Isabel leaves to live in the city, but his three sons—Alfred the eldest, wild impetuous Tristan, and young idealistic Samuel—grow up with him in the stern but beautiful countryside, Tristan is especially close to Ludlow's old Cree Indian scout One Stab, and from an early age is a fierce and reckless hunter.

Samuel returns from the city with a beautiful fiancee, Susannah, who makes an impression on both of his brothers. Europe is on the brink of war and Samuel insists on enlisting. His brothers go with him, hoping to protect him from harm. Amid the horror of the trenches, Alfred is injured and Samuel killed. Tristan blames himself; he cuts out Samuel's heart for an Indian-style burial and takes to scalping Germans.

Alfred returns home, limping, and goes into business. He professes his love for the grieving Susannah, but she refuses to marry him. When Tristan comes home, he and Susannah become lovers; but Tristan's restless, unhappy spirit carries him away again. He travels the world as a hunter, eventually telling Susannah to marry another.

Tristan returns home to find the farm run down, his father crippled by a stroke, and Alfred a successful congressman in Alberta. Tristan falls in love with Isabel Two, who had sworn to marry him even as a child. They have children, and Tristan builds up a bootlegging business, flouting the authority of his brother and the racketeering O'Banion family who back him. Their second attempt at scaring off Tristan culminates in Isabel Two's death. Mad with rage and grief, he kills one of the brothers, and when they come to the ranch for revenge is forced to go on the run, living in the wild as a hunter. He lives for many years before being killed by a bear.

First *Glory* and now this deliciously overheated saga of brothers wrestling in the great outdoors for the love of a good woman: a pattern is beginning to emerge here. The feature films of Edward Zwick seem to show a conscious effort to leave behind the *zeitgeist*-bound whinging of his television shows *thirtysomething* and *My So-Called Life* for a widescreen world of larger-than-life heroism. Lavishly inflated onto celluloid from Jim Harrison's novella, *Legends of the Fall* doesn't just aspire to the elevated condition of ripping yarnhood, it actually attains it.

It does so largely thanks to an epic performance from Brad Pitt. The first time we see him riding across the plains as a full-grown adult, his brother tells him "you smell". He doesn't just smell, he positively reeks—his machismo all but fogs up the screen. In the same way that Esther Williams was a goddess when wet, Brad Pitt is a god on horseback. He ropes steers, he steers ropes, he prowls the high country in a selection of beautifully starched fabrics. And when things go wrong for him emotionally, he does what all men long to do: he grows his hair, and goes out into the world to kill things.

Raised in the Native American tradition to be a one man environmental catastrophe, when Tristan is around every species is endangered. "There are creatures here that cannot even be found in books," he writes from his travels—that is until he kills them all. Humans too have an unfortunate tendency to die around him, especially after he has promised to protect them. Even amid the hellish carnage of Ypres, his scalp-taking causes the soldiering community to sit up and take notice.

Wisely, the supporting cast do not try to compete in the untamed spirit stakes. Aidan Quinn—"I followed all the rules, man's and God's, and you followed none of them"—seems nobly reconciled to second-lead status. Anthony Hopkins starts out engagingly, with one less button undone then usual, and is delightfully moustachioed and raffish in a series of absurd carcoats. It's a shame the story obliges him to have a stroke and write all his subsequent dialogue on a slate. The role of Susannah ("she was like the water that freezes in a rock and splits it open") is potentially the most problematic, because the pleasures this film offers women—unlike the romances of Barbara Cartland which it resembles—are more in spectating than participation. Julia Ormond carries it off, however, Her still centre gives the malestrom a focus; for well over two hours it rages, the swirl rarely slackening, and when Brad Pitt finally succumbs to the bear's embrace, it's a hard man or woman who can suppress a sniffle.

TIME, 1/23/94, p. 57, Richard Schickel

Legends of the Fall teaches us an important lesson: do not impose a mythically resonant name on a child. The responsibility is likely to make him surly, if not downright bloodthirsty. And his tormented thrashings are likely to bring misery, if not downright death, to all who—mysteriously—love him.

Old Colonel Ludlow (Anthony Hopkins) and the wife who has very sensibly left him named their firstborn Alfred and their last born Samuel, and both are pretty normal, boring American boys—the former (Aidan Quinn) perhaps a little too priggish and self-serving, the latter (Henry Thomas) perhaps a little too simpy and idealistic. But in the middle there's Tristan (Brad Pitt, with a long, irritating mane of hair, doing his James Dean imitation).

As a young man growing up on a vast Montana ranch early in this century, Tristan is unduly influenced by One Stab (Gordon Tootoosis), the Native American who narrates the tale in movie Indianspeak—stilted language with many references to nature ("It was in the moon of the red grass," he says solemnly when he wants to date something). Tristan takes to cutting out the hearts of fallen prey to free their spirit and develops a lifelong, mutually unhealthy relationship with a grizzly bear. He never fully escapes the call of the primitive, but at a certain point he does begin carrying on like his Wagnerian namesake, giving himself over to romantic brooding, hopeless love, careless violence and long sea voyages.

When Samuel gets himself killed in World War I, Tristan, of course, blames himself, curses God and scalps a few Germans in order that they may share his pain. After that? he and Alfred get to squabbling over their brother's fiancee, played, thankfully, by the lovely Julia Ormond, who gives the movie s only unaffected performance. At this point your thoughts may turn back to *East of Eden*, which was a gloss on the biblical tale of Cain and Abel. When the Colonel suffers a stroke, just as the patriarch in that film did, you may begin to entertain suspicions of ripoff—not to mention thoughts of escape from this tangle of portentous cross-references.

Edward Zwick, the director, and Susan Shilliday and Bill Wittliff, the screenwriters, are under the impression that they are bringing forth a tragic epic, not a silly melodrama, and therefore much blood must be spilled before whoever is left standing at the end is granted peace and wisdom. That most of the dying results from a bootlegging operation Tristan starts up during Prohibition tends to short-circuit whatever impulses toward terror and pity we might still have. Running hooch in from Canada is not an occupation we usually associate with profound drama, especially when it is centered on a figure who is literally a deadly bore.

Unless you happen to be a tribal elder with a taste for geological metaphors. To the old chief, Tristan is the rock everyone "broke themselves against," and a good thing too, since from their suffering he gains "his honor and a long life." Swell, but we're left with our stifled laughter and a very long movie.

VILLAGE VOICE, 1/3/95, p. 74, Ben Greenman

At the beginning of Ed Zwick's gusty frontier saga *Legends of the Fall*, callow Samuel Ludlow (Henry Thomas) returns to Montana from the Northeast with his fiancée Susannah (Julia Ormond). means only to introduce her to his family—older brothers Alfred (Aidan Quinn) and Tristan (Brad Pitt), and father (Anthony Hopkins), a former colonel in the Indian wars. But Susannah's presence unbalances the Ludlow clan. After Samuel's death in the first World War—Zwick (*Glory*) hasn't lost his talent for harrowing battle scenes—she becomes the pinball in the family machine, bouncing from man to man as the Ludlows confront madness and memory.

With breathtaking Western vistas reminiscent of the *other* Montana period piece (*A River Runs Through It*?), *Legends of the Fall* has no shortage of plot or energy. But the years the film spans *seem* like years, as Zwick lashes his characters to fate's whipping post and flogs them repeatedly with the grandest of grand themes (infidelity, corruption, salvation, race, sex, love, and death). Measured performances from Thomas and Ormond offset the narrative excesses, and Quinn is wonderfully understated, playing Alfred as a man embittered by his own misunderstanding of the rewards of honesty. Only Hopkins slips character for caricature, riffing wildly on filial piety like a Big Sky Lear.

But the real focus of the film is Pitt's Tristan. Deeply divided—lover and loner, brutal warrior and spiritual introvert—Tristan toes the line between rugged hero and a man whose appetite for solitude borders on the pathological. And while Pitt was anemic in *Interview*, he proves here that he can inhabit a character without sacrificing his own charisma. With the physicality of the young Brando he dominates not only the screen but the audience, and even the clutter and cliché of the film's final hour cannot dim the power of his performance.

Also reviewed in:
CHICAGO TRIBUNE, 1/13/95, Friday/p. L, Michael Wilmington
NATION, 1/23/95, p. 108, Stuart Klawans
NEW REPUBLIC, 1/2/95, p. 26, Stanley Kauffmann
NEW YORK TIMES, 12/23/94, p. C10, Janet Maslin
NEW YORKER, 1/9/95, p. 84, Terrence Rafferty
VARIETY, 12/19/94-1/1/95, p. 72, Leonard Klady
WASHINGTON POST, 1/13/95, p. B7, Rita Kempley
WASHINGTON POST, 1/13/95, Weekend/p. 39, Desson Howe

LEPRECHAUN 2

A Trimark Pictures release. *Executive Producer:* Mark Amin. *Producer:* Donald P. Borchers. *Director:* Rodman Flender. *Screenplay:* Turi Meyer and Al Septien. *Based on characters created by:* Mark Jones. *Director of Photography:* Jane Castle. *Editor:* Richard Gentner and Christopher Roth. *Music:* Jonathan Elias. *Sound:* Oliver Moss. *Casting:* Linda Francis. *Production Designer:* Anthony Tremblay. *Art Director:* Claire Kaufman. *Special Visual Effects:* Paolo Mazzucato. *Costumes:* Meta Jardine. *Leprechaun Make-up:* Gabe Z. Bartalos. *Special Visual Effects:* Paulo Mazzucato. *Costumes:* Meta Jardine. *Running time:* 84m minutes. *MPAA Rating:* RATED R.

CAST: Warwick Davis (The Leprechaun); Charlie Heath (Cody); Shevonne Durkin (Bridget); Sandy Baron (Morty); Adam Biesk (Ian); James Lancaster (William O'Day); Clint Howard (Tourist); Kimmy Robertson (Tourist Girlfriend).

LOS ANGELES TIMES, 4/1//94, Calendar/p. 6, Kevin Thomas

The 1992 original "Leprechaun" proved that if you've got a good enough gimmick you can get away with minimal proficiency in all other aspects of a film. The gimmick was, of course, a leprechaun from hell, a diminutive figure with an evil simian countenance and a crazed sense of humor as jaunty as his quaint period attire. He was played with unstinting panache by British actor Warwick Davis.

"Leprechaun 2" has it all over the first film, for its makers have been smart enough to plow back profits from the original into a better script, stronger cast and richer production values. This time all the elements are much nearer Davis' own bravura level.

Once again the Leprechaun is enraged over one missing gold coin, but this time he's also concerned with getting married and starting a family, heaven forbid. In a prologue set in Ireland a millennium earlier a father, who'd been foolish enough to be tempted by the Leprechaun's pot of gold, has sacrificed his own life to spare his daughter from becoming the Leprechaun's bride.

Now the Leprechaun has tracked down that daughter's direct descendant, a pretty teen-ager named Bridget (Shevonne Durkin) who lives in L.A. and whose enterprising boyfriend Joe (Charlie Heath) works for his shrewd but boozy uncle Morty (Sandy Baron), the proprietor of Darkside Tours, one of those tourist magnets that purport to guide you to the sites where Hollywood celebrities died, preferably in a macabre fashion.

"Leprechaun 2" unfolds in a classically mythical manner with the young suitor determined to save his lady fair from a fate worse than death. Faced with an inevitable plot, writer Turi Meyer and Al Septien have balanced with considerable humor, well-drawn and engaging characters and some smart one-liners.

Heath and Durkin are a totally believable, down-to-earth young couple coping gamely with horrendous supernatural events. Best of all, Meyer and Septien have written one of the best movie roles ever for Baron, that protean veteran who's perfectly cast as an outrageous yet endearing sharpie, a relentless con man with a Charles Bukowski seediness and street smarts who nonetheless genuinely loves his orphaned nephew.

"Leprechaun 2" is especially gratifying for us longtime Sandy Baron admirers. Although not for little kids, "Leprechaun 2" in its gore is in the theatrical, comically obvious Grand Guignol tradition. Its pace never flags, thanks to director Rodman Flender, a Roger Corman alumnus.

NEW YORK POST, 4/9/94, p. 20, Thelma Adams

When I finally got around to seeing the original "Leprechaun" on cable, it wasn't nearly so bad as all those 1993 bottom 10 lists made it out to be. It was awful in a good way.

Hell—it wasn't "Leprechaun 2!"

This sequel is pond scum—the precise skin shade of that midget of mayhem, the leprechaun.

Displeasingly played (in a good sense) by Warwick Davis, the imp returns to LA. to satisfy his sexual urges. It's been more than 2,000 years since he got lucky, so perhaps he's justifiably cranky.

According to legend, and inane screenwriters Turi Meyer and Al Septien, the little lad has an opportunity to take a bride once every millennium. If his dream wench sneezes thrice and no one says "bless you," the lass is his.

Robbed of the opportunity to wed 1,000 years before by an unfortunate Irishman the magical misanthrope has fixed on the man's unlikely heir, a bland blonde named Bridget, limply played by Shevonne Durkin under Rodman Flender's lackluster direction.

Love may be in the air, but the point of leprechaun movies' (hopefully, a limited genre) is to gross us out. So be it:

■The mean-spirited imp licks Bridget's cheek and a river of spittle rolls towards her eye.

■A weasly talent agent wearing a gold ring offers the lep a card; the little beast rips off the ring, finger and all, tongues the red gore and says, "finger lickin' good."

The comedic high point occurs when the green meanie chases Bridget's boyfriend into a pub well-stocked with midgets celebrating the holiday of the little people, St. Patrick's Day—and that's the high point!

Always grousing about the theft of his pot of gold, in this sequel the greedy leprechaun was robbed of the most precious cinematic treasure of all—a decent script.

NEWSDAY, 4/9/94, Part II/p. B4, Terry Kelleher

Irish-Americans, be thankful for small favors: "Leprechaun 2" originally was scheduled to open the day after St. Patrick's Day, but Trimark Pictures had the good grace (or bad timing) to delay its infliction upon the New York area.

Otherwise, this crummy horror sequel gives no grounds for gratitude. The few—maybe two—chuckles it offers aren't nearly enough to relieve the tedium. The movie leaves you with a dull headache, as if you'd just come to after a night of chugging green beer.

The ageless title character (Warwick Davis) apparently resides in Killarney, but he's determined to cause trouble in America, with or without a green card. He tore up North Dakota in his first outing; now he's in Los Angeles looking for a bride. See, he gets the mating urge every thousandth birthday (March 17, natch).

The Leprechaun zeroes in on Bridget (Shevonne Durkin); a blond teen with a nice boyfriend named Cody (Charlie Heath). When the wee devil snatches Bridget and imprisons her in his lair, it's up to Cody to effect her rescue, an enterprise in which he's alternately helped and hindered by his boozy, scamming Uncle Morty (Sandy Baron).

Talking in uninspired rhymes and maiming with a mirthless cackle, the Leprechaun ranks well behind Chucky of "Child's Play" in the diminutive-demon department. Director Rodman Flender makes far too little effort to exploit the comic potential in the villain's L. A. culture shock, though it is mildly amusing to see the undersized Hibernian slumped in an espresso bar, nursing a post-St. Paddy's Day hangover.

The gore quotient in "Leprechaun 2" is too low for horror enthusiasts and too high for the rest of us. Where's the customer satisfaction in that? Suspense is nil, even when Cody and Bridget are trapped in the Leprechaun's cave. "There's got to be a way out of here!" the laddie cries, fairly defying the audience not to eye the exit signs.

Bitter irony: Producer Donald Borchers attended the University of Notre Dame.

Also reviewed in:
VARIETY, 4/18-24/94, p. 63, Leonard Klady

LIFE AND TIMES OF ALLEN GINSBERG, THE

A First Run Features release. *Producer:* Jerry Aronson. *Director:* Jerry Aronson. *Director of Photography:* Jean de Segonzac, Roger Carter, and Richard Lerner. *Editor:* Nathaniel Dorsky and Jerry Aronson. *Music:* Tom Capek. *Sound:* Lori Loeb, Michael Harrison, Erik Houseman, and Greg Poschman. *Running time:* 83 minutes. *MPAA Rating:* Not Rated.

WITH: Allen Ginsberg; Jack Keruac; William Burroughs; Ken Kesey; Norman Mailer; Timothy Leary; Joan Baez; Amiri Baraka; Abbie Hoffman.

LOS ANGELES TIMES, 2/17/94, Calendar/p. 3, Peter Rainer

Allen Ginsberg is a great camera subject, but he's mostly been a subject in documentaries about other people, like Jack Kerouac or William Burroughs. "The Life and Times of Allen Ginsberg." directed by Jerry Aronson, redresses the balance. It's a deeply affectionate portrait of the poet-guru, and the affection seems appropriate to Ginsberg's becalmed, hypersensitive presence. The paradox of Ginsberg's life, as the movie demonstrates, is how someone so gentle could still be a major countercultural force.

The gentility of the '60s countercultural warriors was often a pose—those flower-power types had stems of steel—but with Ginsberg the peace gestures and Buddhist chanting didn't seem faked. Aronson had access to Ginsberg's home movies and family photos from adolescence, and one can see the same languid, beseeching quality in the young wiry, bespectacled Ginsberg as in the Beat visionary and the later, bearded, love-beaded '60s guru.

The connection to all of these selves lies in Ginsberg's poetry, and it's to Aronson's credit that he keeps the poetry front and center. We hear Ginsberg reading from "Howl," perhaps the most famous of postwar American poems, and "Kaddish." which was Ginsberg's attempt to reclaim the shock of his mother's anguish and lay it to rest.

His mother spent her later years in a sanitarium. As a child, Ginsberg, according to his stepmother, "saw more than any little boy should." By his own admission, the pain of watching his mother's breakdown preempted the pains that followed: Nothing could quite shatter him in the same way, and perhaps this helps to explain the unflappable, pacific way he rose up against the baton-wielding police during the 1968 Democratic Convention. Despite Ginsberg's aestheticism, his confrontations with conservative orthodoxy were at always based on political principles. If he's a visionary, he's a practical-minded one. He's a political activist for the spirit.

Aronson spent 10 years putting together the footage for the film. Even though it's only 83 minutes, it has an epic scope because Ginsberg's life seems to take in the most highly charged history of the past 50 years. His progression from scrawny Columbia University student to Beat to hippie to Buddhist to Grand Old Man is a great American story. His homosexuality links him to a Whitmanesque tradition that he revels in. (This is one of the few current films where homosexual love is discussed without sniggering or special pleading.)

Is it also a bit too hero-worshippy toward Ginsberg? Perhaps, but the worshipfulness doesn't seem out of place. Aronson recognizes that Ginsberg can't be approached as a film subject in half-measures. When we see Ginsberg being interviewed by William Buckley in a '60s "Firing Line" show, the high comedy of the pairing gives way to something inexplicably touching. Buckley, eyebrow raised, lip curled, asks Ginsberg if "hippies are the new order," and the poet replies by intoning one of his poems. As the words roll out, the sensual imagery takes hold and even Buckley seems entranced. Now *that's* the power of art.

NEW YORK POST, 2/18/94, p. 49, Larry Worth

In 1956 Allen Ginsberg's "Howl" shocked the world. Aside from "obscene" passages resulting in the poem's censorship, it was a volcano of rage against a society filled with ugliness, injustice and insanity.

Almost 40 years later, filmmaker Jerry Aronson explores—in a powerful documentary, "The Life and Times of Allen Ginsberg"—what provoked that rage.

And while the pre-eminent voice of the Beat Generation is the center of attention the supporting cast is of near-equal interest: Jack Kerouac, William Burroughs, Neal Cassady, Timothy Leary, Abbie Hoffman, Ken Kesey and Norman Mailer.

Whittling 100 hours of film to 83 minutes, Aronson has created a separate segment for each decade, cross-cutting from interviews with Ginsberg's family and contemporaries to archival footage. It starts with the pained expressions of a pre-teen Ginsberg—looking like a young Jeff Goldblum—reacting to his beloved mother's commitment to a madhouse.

Ultimately, the youth found catharsis in writing. Seguing to the adult Ginsberg reading "Kaddish," a poignant tribute to his late mom, Aronson pulls off the first of many emotional highlights.

Ginsberg's comments on other loved ones prove similarly insightful, as in tales of unrequited amour for best friend Kerouac. Also touching are anecdotes about poet Peter Orlovsky, the man Ginsberg "married."

In each segment, Aronson communicates Ginsberg's attempts to transform society, much as he transformed himself from Flower Power guru to pacifist icon to Buddhist student.

However, the sneering asides of William F. Buckley Jr. are the only words to paint Ginsberg in a negative light. Couldn't Aronson find one of Ginsberg's more reasonable detractors to strike a balance?

But even if the documentary isn't to film what "Howl" is to poetry, both showcase the rhythm behind Ginsberg's enduring appeal.

NEWSDAY, 2/18/94, Part II/p. 81, John Anderson

One of the more amusing fragments of media gathered together in Jerry Aronson's "The Life and Times of Allen Ginsberg," is a 1968 clip from "Firing Line." In it, William F. Buckley, eyebrows arching toward heaven, introduces the poet as "the hippie's hippie, the bohemian prototype."

"He is unconventional," Buckley intones, implying as much as possible between gleaming teeth, "in all matters ..."

If, behind all the teeth, Buckley seems slightly aghast, then he represents mainstream America's general reaction to Ginsberg, master flouter of form, perpetual hipster, chanting Buddhist peace marcher, heir to Whitman and son of mad Naomi. Matter-of-factly homosexual, a questioner of every authority, an intrepid psychic explorer and a veteran practitioner of consciousness-altering, Ginsberg has been a thorn in conformity's side for five decades. And, almost incidentally, he's written poetry of consistent, uncompromising honesty and craft.

Had Aronson's film been a fraction as unconventional as its subject, it might have been a more spirited journey through a great American life. But even with its compulsive chronology, photo-album sensibility and reliance on talking-heads for illumination, it provides an entertaining story, and perhaps some insight into a major literary mind.

"Get married Allen, don't take drugs." Famous words, uttered by a mother on her asylum deathbed and immortalized in the much celebrated poem "Kaddish." But even while Ginsberg ignored Naomi's edict—with abandon—he was "a good son," according to his stepmother, the ever-charming Edith Ginsberg. We get a sense of it: Family, along with death and life, inform his poetry; the snapshots of Allen and brother Eugene and their father, the poet Louis Ginsberg, are full of affection. So is a father-son poetry reading, in which Louis and Allen trade verse. Naomi, we see, was a combination nightmare and muse.

Ginsberg's "other" family, the friends he met at Columbia University in the '40s and with whom he traded aid and comfort, make their entrances and exits. The photos they took together reveal a prescience about their own coming celebrity; many look like they were conceived as album covers. There's William Burroughs, Jack Kerouac, Neal Cassady. There's Peter Orlovsky, with whom Ginsberg shared an all-but-state-sanctioned marriage, seen in glorious youth, and shattered age—and a reminder that while many of those around him were drinking their lives away, Ginsberg kept a safe distance from the edge of the abyss.

The most cogent point of Aronson's film, even if it's delivered indirectly, is that for all the cacophonous countercultural claptrap that surrounded Ginsberg and his history, it's his writing that was, and is, important. He's seen with Bob Dylan (in the "Subterranean Homesick Blues" bit from "Don't Look Back"), with Timothy Leary, with protesters at the '68 Democratic Convention in Chicago, as the honorary King of May at a spring '68 celebration in Prague. Joan Baez, Ken Kesey, the late Abbie Hoffman and Amiri Baraka weigh in on his public self; less time is spent examining his words, unfortunately. But the viewer is left with the somehow satisfying conclusion that while his erstwhile associates were fading, either artistically or in their celebrity, Ginsberg has always been the real thing.

VILLAGE VOICE, 2/15/94, p. 56, Georgia Brown

Jerry Aronson's *The Life and Times of Allen Ginsberg* is a work of zero pretensions. This modest documentary seeks to honor its subject, not to bury or compete with it. Humility is an effective strategy: I laughed a little, I cried a little. The spirits were lifted.

Though Aronson has a formidable list of filmmaking credits, *Life and Times* is simple, formally conventional, and straightforwardly chronological. For the past, 10 years he's been conducting talking-head interviews, collecting archival footage and stills, all with Ginsberg's cooperation. The end product is frankly adulatory. No reason why it shouldn't be.

Ginsberg was born in Newark in 1926 to a poet-teacher father, Louis, and an emotionally disturbed mother, Naomi. As a child, Allen was close to her suffering and felt responsible. As the poet recites at the film's opening, "The weight of the world is love."

Aronson makes economical use of family photos and a couple of charming home movies of young, gawky Allen at the beach. He has a lively relation to the camera, appearing both aware of observation and unafraid. A sort of amused curiosity comes across in the stills. Luckily, Ginsberg was also a talented photographer who persisted in recording visits of friends through the years.

When he went off to Columbia, the fabled friendships with Burroughs, Kerouac, Herbert Huncke, and Neil Cassady developed. His stepmother, reminiscing, wonders if Burroughs had been "a little too old for Allen." Burroughs himself remembers, "His father thought I was a decadent millionaire corrupting his young son." Ginsberg says Burroughs was acquainted with analysis and, quite without qualms, sat down in a chair and put Ginsberg on the couch. The analysis was productive; one day, he reports, he came to the core recognition that "nobody loved me." By now he was loved by his friends, who became a new family. As for coming out of the closet: "Kerouac was the first person I told." He describes meeting Peter Orlovsky when he was 28 and Orlovsky 21 or 22 and exchanging vows in a Village café: "It was the first time I felt accepted in my life completely."

As a cameraman, Aronson shot the riots at the 1968 Chicago Democratic convention, so it's not surprising that the film covers this event in more detail than any other. Ginsberg—shown chanting "Om" amid the chaos—took a nonviolent stand against many demonstration leaders, and later went on to blame the violent left for getting Nixon elected and extending the war another six years.

If, with Peter and friends, Ginsberg created a new family, he didn't forget the old. Probably the most touching section of Aronson's movie concerns the relation of Allen and his aging father. His stepmother's moving assessment—"Allen was a good son"— might well be the one that Ginsberg, with his vast accomplishments, may value most.

Also reviewed in:
NEW YORK TIMES, 2/18/94, p. C10, Janet Maslin
VARIETY, 4/26/93, p. 70, Emanuel Levy
WASHINGTON POST, 2/25/94, p. D6, Hal Hinson

LIGHTNING JACK

A Savoy Pictures release of a Lightning Ridge/Village Roadshow production. *Executive Producer:* Simon Wincer, Paul Hogan, Graham Burke, and Anthony Stewart. *Producer:* Greg Coote. *Director:* Simon Wincer. *Screenplay:* Paul Hogan. *Director of Photography:* David Eggby. *Editor:* O. Nicholas Brown. *Music:* Bruce Rowland. *Music Editor:* Roy Prendergast. *Sound:* Bud Alper and (music) Robin Grey. *Sound Editor:* Tim Chau. *Casting:* Mike Fenton and Julie Ashton. *Production Designer:* Bernard Hines. *Art Director:* Lisette Thomas and Virginia Bieneman. *Set Designer:* Andrew Gartner and Kelley Graham. *Set Decorator:* Lynn Wolverton Parker and Susan Maybury. *Set Dresser:* Robert Alcala, Wren Boney, Dan Miller, Leonard Vigil, Andrew Trujillo, Frederic Lopez, Edie Douglass, Siri Singh, John Kretschmer, and Margie Rahmann. *Special Effects:* Greg Curtis. *Costumes:* Bruce Finlayson. *Make-up:* Judy Lovell, Bonita DeHaven, and Margaret Stevenson. *Stunt Coordinator:* Bill Burton and Guy Norris. *Running time:* 101 minutes. *MPAA Rating:* PG-13.

CAST: Paul Hogan (Lightning Jack Kane); Cuba Gooding, Jr. (Ben Doyle); Beverly D'Angelo (Lana); Kamala Dawson (Pilar); Pat Hingle (Marshall Kurtz); Richard Riehle (Reporter); Frank McRae (Mr. Doyle); Roger Daltry (John T. Coles); L. Q. Jones (Local Sheriff); Max Cullen (Bart); Sandy Ward (Mr. Curren); Roy Brocksmith (Junction City Tailor); Douglas Stewart (Junction City Shopkeeper); Kevin O'Morrison (Old Man in Alley); Mark Miles (Luke); Clif Stokes (Bully Cowboy); Bob Sorenson (Clem); Ramond O'Connor (Pat); Robert Guajardo (Bank Manager); Tom Noga (Bank Clerk); Ed Adams (Cole Younger); Bruce Miles (Man); Grace Keagy (Mrs. Franks); Jess Franks (Auctioneer); Kenny Jacobs (South Fork Bank Teller); Ben Cooper (Shopkeeper in Bank); Sandy Gibbons (South Fork Sheriff); Larry Sellers (Comanche Leader); Patrick Augure (Young Comanche); Michael E. Wells (Man in Wayside Flats Saloon); Ben Zeller (Old Timer); Paul Blott and Steve Schwartz Hartley (Deputies); Mark Coffey and Etienne Fourie (Saloon Cowboys).

LOS ANGELES TIMES, 3/11/94, Calendar/p. 8, Peter Rainer

What can you say about the very dull "Lightning Jack"? "Unforgiven" it's not. "Cat Ballou" it's not either. It's not even "Quigley Down Under."

Paul Hogan plays Jack, a—har, har—nearsighted Aussie gunslinger in the Old West. He's on the run from the law in Junction City for a botched robbery. Ben (Cuba Gooding, Jr.), a mute, is his all-too-obliging hostage who becomes his all-too-obliging accomplice.

The pairing does not begin auspiciously, as Ben prepares to suck rattlesnake venom from Jack's rear quarters. This could be the first "Beavis and Butt-head" Western, except it's not as witty.

The so-called resurgence of the movie Western in recent years is mostly studio hype—for every "Unforgiven" there's a "Posse." But "Lightning Jack" doesn't even attempt to ut a spin on the genre. It just dawdles along in amiable imbecility. It looks as if it were made because everyone involved felt like kicking up some dust and spitting tobacco juice.

Hogan, looking trim and leathery—like a cross between Johnny Carson and a shank of beef jerky—doesn't exactly stretch his modest skills. Gooding overdoes the mute business with so much mugging that he makes Holly Hunter's overactive overacting in "The Piano" seem restrained by comparison. (The problem with mute characters in movies is that their muteness invariably leads to miming, and miming rightly provokes bloodlust. When Dustin Hoffman punched out that mime in "Tootsie," the audience's cheers rocked the rafters.)

Beverly D'Angelo and Pat Hingle put in some old-pro cameo appearances, just long enough to make you moon for some real acting.

At least there won't be a sequel.

NEW YORK POST, 3/11/94, p. 44, Michael Medved

"Lightning Jack" Kane is supposed to be the Fastest Gun in the West, but the movie that dramatizes his adventures could be the slowest (and dumbest) picture of the year.

Its cartoon characters stagger through long, arid stretches of plotless cinematic emptiness, interrupted only by smutty gags that embarrass the audience as much as the actors.

Paul ("Crocodile Dundee") Hogan plays the title character, an aging outlaw who robs banks not for the money but for the publicity. He says he came to the American west from Down Under some 30 years before, but the film makes nothing of his Aussie origins; it's only a way of explaining his accent.

After a bungled bank robbery, Lightning Jack takes a hostage: a mute clerk from a dry goods store, played by Cuba Gooding, Jr. of "Boyz N The Hood." Since Jack's gun works faster than his brain, it seems to take 10 minutes of strenuous charades before Gooding succeeds in explaining that he can't talk—a process that's painfully repeated with each new character he meets.

Meanwhile, Gooding decides to saddle up as Lightning Jack's new partner, and they ride aimlessly from town to town, robbing a few banks, avoiding posses and Comanche war parties, and visiting Jack's old friend Lana (played by an uncomfortable-looking Beverly D'Angelo), the inevitable prostitute with a heart of gold.

Paul Hogan has never been noted for spectacular dramatic range. But here, his performance is so flat, featureless and absolutely wooden that he makes Al Gore look like Al Pacino.

Cuba Gooding tries harder and fares worse; his bug-eyed, open-mouthed, wildly gesticulating terror at each new danger brings us uncomfortably close to Stepin Fetchit country, reducing this gifted actor to an insulting stereotype.

One of the movie's supposed comedic highlights shows the hero bitten by a rattler on his rear end, so he tries to force Cuba Gooding to put his mouth on the wound and suck out venom.

It's also supposed to be hilarious when, as a touching token of his growing esteem, Jack presents his new partner with a necklace of dried testicles. These, and many other gratuitously raunchy touches, make this PG-13 picture inappropriate even for the undemanding kiddie audience at which its ads seem aimed.

Ironically, director Simon Wincer recently worked on the fine family film "Free Willy," and previously showed that he could handle westerns by creating the justly acclaimed "Lonesome Dove" miniseries. Here, however, he's at the mercy of Paul Hogan who produced the movie, wrote the inane script, and even devised a novel means to raise money for it.

Instead of approaching studios, Hogan sold shares on the Australian stock exchange and drew more than 6,000 investors who put up an average stake of some $4,000.

In view of the incompetent fiasco that resulted from these good faith contributions each of the investors should now demand his money back, forming one huge, angry posse that "Lightning Jack" doesn't deserve to escape.

NEWSDAY, 3/11/94, Part II/p. 79, Terry Kelleher

Paul Hogan makes comedy look easy—and it is, if you don't bother to make it funny.

The leathery Aussie's laconic act worked fine when he was playing off New York crazies in "Crocodile Dundee." But "Almost an Angel" was as listless as it was innocuous, and the torpor continues in his new movie, a tongue-in-cheek western called "Lightning Jack."

Hogan wrote the script and portrays the title character, an outlaw from down under who barely escapes with his life when his American gang rides into an ambush. Forced to operate solo, Jack discovers that gunslinging gets you only so far in the bank-robbing game. Faulty eyesight and poor planning skills limit his profit potential.

Jack botches a holdup, and his only way out is to take bystander Ben Doyle (Cuba Gooding Jr.) hostage. The audience knows Ben is mute, but Jack doesn't. So naturally we're expected to crack up when Jack snarls to Ben, "One word and you're dead." And when an embarrassed Jack has to don spectacles to read Ben's note of reply—well, it's gut-busting time.

The humor in "Lightning Jack" isn't just unsophisticated. It's virtually undetectable. Gooding probably needed a stiff drink before he could go through with the scene that calls for Ben—by now Jack's partner in crime—to shoot himself in the foot and hop around doing the silent-scream routine. But at least that lame gag required effort. For most of the movie, director Simon Wincer ("Lonesome Dove," "Free Willy") falls into a rhythm of long setup, no payoff, repeat.

Jack and Ben happen on a group of settlers. Much discussion of how Jack will "charm" these "real folks" into selling him a horse at a bargain price. Cut to Jack complaining to Ben that he was overcharged. In this movie, it takes forever to get from A to C even when we bypass B.

Beverly D'Angelo is on hand as Lana, a gold-hearted hooker who has been waiting nine years for Jack to keep his promise and whisk her away to a better life. Having waited an hour and a half for the punchline, we know pretty much how she feels.

Pat Hingle plays a politically ambitious marshal in cahoots with an evil newspaperman (Richard Riehle) to spring headline-making traps for outlaws. The marshal sends a contingent of fearsome bounty hunters after Jack, but the anticipated showdown, like the rest of the picture, never comes off.

Every once in a while, Wincer invites us to feast our eyes on a scenic western vista and listen to some Marlboro Man music. He doesn't seem to realize that feeble little jokes can get hopelessly lost in the great outdoors.

SIGHT AND SOUND, 9/94, p. 41, Verina Glaessner

1870. Lightning Jack Kane is the only member of the Younger Brothers gang to escape a botched bank robbery they attempt to pull off in Junction City. When he reads the newspaper report of the robbery and the gang's capture, he is disappointed to note the decline in his reputation. He stages another robbery and during the getaway takes hostage a mute boy, Ben Doyle, who, although initially terrified, is glad to escape the patronising attitude of the customer in the general store in which he works. Doyle soon proves his worth by helping Jack elude a posse of pursuing riders. To impress his young partner, Lightning Jack allows him to read his press cuttings, and Doyle is delighted to learn Jack is a genuine outlaw.

Fleeing another bungled robbery, Lightning Jack and Doyle find themselves under observation by a large group of Comanches. They escape after an extended chase through mountainous terrain and a network of caves. After instructing the innocent Doyle in sexual techniques, Jack takes his young sidekick to the saloon where his old flame Lana is still nursing hopes of Jack fulfilling his promise to her to take her away. After a night with her, Jack extricates Doyle from an incipient conflict with a gunman in the bar. Meanwhile, Marshall Kurtz of Junction City has hired a number of bounty hunters to track him down and kill him. When Lana learns of their arrival in town, she warns Jack and Doyle. Disappointed at the slim bounty on offer, Jack decides to pull off another job where it will be least expected, back at Junction City. Before he can put this plan into effect, however, he is captured and imprisoned. Evading capture, Doyle manages to spring Jack from the sheriff's office.

Back in Junction City, Lightning Jack has noticed a rival gang's presence in the town. He alerts the town's vigilantes and watches them walk into the trap. As the town celebrate the gang's capture, he and Doyle rob the bank themselves before setting off in disguise to reward the faithfully waiting Lana. As Doyle, Lana and Jack set off, he reassures her that there are no Indians in the territory through which they are passing; two puffs of smoke then appear on the horizon.

The role of ageing outlaw whose reputation is on the slide proves uncomfortably close to Paul Hogan's own position as an actor who seems to have got whatever mileage there was from his *Crocodile Dundee* persona. That persona was, not accidentally, most at home within the knockabout but bland confines of Australian television commercials, perhaps in the end the most appropriate medium in which to both re-invent and send up a soft-centered version of post-imperial Australian masculinity. *Crocodile Dundee* played on notions of national identity. Here, a single reference apart, Hogan's character of Lightning Jack is entirely detached from those antipodean roots, but Hogan is not an actor of sufficient range to maintain credibility without them. He is not helped by the rambling script he wrote for the project (he is decidedly not a master of the witty one-liner) nor by Simon Wincer's lacklustre direction. The comic line between sending up incompetence and simply being incompetent needs a sharp eye for mood and a fine sense of timing to observe. There is little sense of either quality here. There are also signs of last-minute cuts which waste the presumably expensive use of a troupe of genuine Cheyenne riders and an elaborate set-up involving settlers, tents and a large herd of cattle.

If Hogan's own performance seems jaded, that of Cuba Gooding, from *Boyz N the Hood*, is never encouraged to develop beyond that of eye-rolling stereotype. The gags, mining a familiar homoerotic vein, stimulate embarrassment rather than laughter, most painfully in the scene in which Lightning Jack mimes the sex act by way of instructing Doyle. A presumably equally embarrassing scene involving a horse harness in the brothel appears to have been excised—the harness is brandished without explanation. While nothing can dim the splendour of the panoramic shots of Monument Valley, there seems slim reason for their inclusion. As is the case in so many Australian period productions, props are strewn about as if for a fashion shoot. If Paul Hogan, whose personal project this seems largely to have been, is genuinely keen on Western comedy, he could do worse than take a look at the Terence Hill/Bud Spencer 'Trinity' films, which, despite their unevenness, prove that broad comedy and cinematic boldness can go hand in hand. The most interesting thing about *Lightening Jack* remains the way it was funded, through floating the Lightning Jack Film Trust on the Australian Stock Exchange.

Also reviewed in:
CHICAGO TRIBUNE, 3/11/94, Friday/p. B, John Petrakis
NEW YORK TIMES, 3/11/94, p. C8, Stephen Holden
VARIETY, 3/14-20/94, p. 54, Leonard Klady
WASHINGTON POST, 3/14/94, p. D9, Richard Harrington

LION KING, THE

A Buena Vista release of a Walt Disney Pictures productiion. *Executive Producer:* Thomas Schumacher and Sarah McArthur. *Producer:* Don Hahn. *Director:* Roger Allers and Rob Minkoff. *Screenplay:* Irene Mecchi, Jonathan Roberts, and Linda Woolverton. *Editor:* Tom Finan and John Carnochan. *Music:* Hans Zimmer, Tim Rice, and Elton John. *Music Editor:* Adam Milo Smalley. *Sound:* Doc Kane, Vince Caro, Weldon Brown, Andrew Morris, Steve Hellaby, and (music) Jay Rifkin. *Sound Editor:* Richard L. Anderson and Mark Mangini. *Casting:* Brian Chavanne. *Production Designer:* Chris Sanders. *Art Director:* Andy Gaskill. *Visual Effects:* Scott Santoro. *Special Sound Effects:* John Pospisil. *Supervising Animator:* Mark Henn (Young Simba); Ruben Aquino (Adult Simba); Tony Fucile (Mufasa); Andreas Deja (Scar); Anthony Derosa (Adult Nala); Aaron Blaise (Young Nala); Tony Bancroft

(Pumbaa); Michael Surrey (Timon); James Baxter (Rafiki); Ellen Woodbury (Zazu); Russ Edmonds (Sarabi). *Running time:* 87 minutes. *MPAA Rating:* G.

VOICES: Rowan Atkinson (Zazu); Matthew Broderick (Simba); Niketa Calame (Young Nala); Jim Cummings (Ed); Whoopi Goldberg (Shenzi); Robert Guillaume (Rafiki); Jeremy Irons (Scar); James Earl Jones (Mufasa); Moira Kelly (Nala); Nathan Lane (Timon); Cheech Marin (Banzai); Ernie Sabella (Pumbaa); Madge Sinclair (Sarabi); Jonathan Taylor Thomas (Young Simba).

CHRISTIAN SCIENCE MONITOR, 6/15/94, p. 12, David Sterritt

Some mighty talented people, such as Steven Spielberg and Don Bluth, have challenged the animation wizards at Walt Disney Pictures in recent years. They've made some pleasant little cartoons—the "American Tail" movies, for instance—but they have yet to put a dent in Disney's reputation as the unquestioned king of animated filmmaking.

What's the secret behind Disney's success? Simply stated, it's the studio's willingness to stick with a cluster of winning formulas that have been around for decades—relating to plot, character, and drawing style—and to deploy these with such energy, variety, and panache that they don't *seem* like formulas at all.

When this trick is pulled off properly, it gives us movies like "Beauty and the Beast" and "Aladdin," with their uncanny knack of appearing fresh and familiar at the same time. The same quality charges through "The Lion King," the latest Disney triumph.

Although it differs from most of the studio's feature-length cartoons in that it's an original project, not based on a well-known fairy tale or children's book, "The Lion King" partakes so strongly of time-tested Disney methods that all but the youngest moviegoers will find it as instantly recognizable as an old friend.

Yet it manipulates those methods with such skill and imagination that you can't help surrendering to its spell—even if you wish it were a little more surprising for the grownup portion of the audience, which has been down this road so many times before.

At heart, "The Lion King" is a family story, focusing on the relationship between Mufasa, literally the king of beasts in his corner of the African wilderness, and Simba, the monarch's little son. Also in the picture is Mufasa's brother, Scar, a petulant type who resents his second-place status in the royal household.

Scar's envy turns deadly when he lures young Simba into a den of hungry hyenas who'd dine on him as readily as look at him. When this nasty trick fails, the evil uncle enlists his hyena pals to murder Mufasa himself—and succeeds in claiming the kingdom, with Simba doomed to a life in exile among unglamorous beasts on the lower links of the food chain.

As often with Disney animations, the most memorable figures in "The Lion King" are the youngsters, the villains, and the comical sidekicks. Simba is a superbly realized character, especially in the first half of the movie when he's still a little cub; when he faces discipline by his dad after his adventure with the hyenas, for instance, his round and teary eyes are as heartbreaking as they are hilarious.

Just as winning are the lowly critters who become his companions in exile: a slow-witted warthog and a sharp-tongued meerkat, whose artfully mis-matched personalities make them the funniest comedy team to hit the screen in ages. And a special nod goes to the heinous hyenas—Shenzi, Banzai, and Ed—for the quickness of their banter and the absolute idiocy of almost everything they say. Bad guys don't come more menacing or more laughable.

Visually, the movie is an example of Disney animation at its supple best. Directed by Roger Allers and Rob Minkoff, it's packed with thoroughly individualized characters moving gracefully and efficiently through a variety of eye-beguiling settings and situations.

Verbally, it's a bravura display of cleverly written dialogue interpreted by a superb cast. Standouts include James Earl Jones, who provides Mufasa's voice, and the team of Jonathan Taylor Thomas and Matthew Broderick, who speak the words of Simba as a child and young adult, respectively. Jeremy Irons is positively brilliant as Scar, at once insinuating and insufferable. Ernie Sabella and Nathan Lane are a riot as Simba's low-life buddies; and similar energy springs from the trio of Whoopi Goldberg, Cheech Marin, and Jim Cummings as the hyenas.

In sum, "The Lion King" is another first-rate effort from the world's most gifted animation studio. With this affirmed, however, it's worth taking a moment to note a few shortcomings that prevent the picture from achieving the stature of a truly significant art work.

While the familiarity of the story helps give the production its patented Disney ring, there are too few twists or variations to distinguish it from a long list of predecessors. The music score is sprightly, but it's so steeped in pop-music clichés that it seems ordinary compared with other aspects of the film.

And above all, why can't the Disney writers and artists approach the animal kingdom in a way that doesn't totally anthropomorphize it?

There's something limited and limiting about the cartoon tradition of turning every species into a stylized version of the human race.

An animal fable that taught us something about animals as well as people, bringing multiculturalism to a whole new realm—now there's an original project the Disney folks might think about tackling someday.

FILMS IN REVIEW, 9-10/94, p. 60, Sonny Pearson

This is only going to sound weird if you don't know Harry Pearson; but he asked if I, his inner kid, would write this review, and promised to if he won't make me sit through any more of Lawrence Kasdan's "serious" pictures. (Larry's inner kid, Danny, is fun, though. Remember *Silverado* and *Raiders*?)

H. thought I might bring a fresh viewpoint to the latest Disney effort, *The Lion King*. He didn't trust himself. Personally, it's been downhill with him ever since *Bambi*, which, come to think of it, *The Lion King* owes a lot to.

I hate to confess it, but Harry and I see eye-to-eye on at least one thing: We both like surprises. We like the unexpected. And that is exactly what you don't get from *The Lion King*.

I think Harry himself came to see this when Nathan Lane's character, the meerkat, said something about getting into drag (to distract the hyenas, who had Harry distracted for a while earlier in the picture because he has a soft spot in his head for Whoopi. That's my influence); there's a jump cut, and the Lane animal is in a hula skirt (but no coconuts, drat!), and Harry laughed out loud—for the first time, And the last.

And that's what's wrong with this film. No spontaneity, nothing original, nothing to take your breath away. Even the animation looks a little cheesy, computer recycling, I call it. None of those three and four dimensional impressionistic effects, like *Bambi*, even though they ripped the story right off Felix Salter's back.

Don't tell the guys at the CD Club this, but I couldn't tell one song from the other; I could tell when they were coming—so could you—but after they were over, I pulled H's sleeve and said, "That's my boy Elton writing that Muzak stuff?" H. told me that they weren't ever going to do another animated film without music because the last one they did that way didn't make a bundle of dough. We both liked *The Little Mermaid* (H. was surprised he laughed so much). I had my doubts about *Beauty and the Beast*, and H. actually was happy with *Aladdin*, at least when the Genie was on. Well, it just goes to show, the more predictable things get in this world, the less you know what to expect.

H. and I agreed on one more thing. There wasn't much (H. says any) magic in *The Lion King*. Maybe magic and surprise go together. I was curious, though, about the lady lions and why there weren't any other guy lions around anywhere, except that sissy old Jeremy Irons. It looked to me like the lady lions did all the work, hustled up all the grub and stuff, and the guys, kings they call themselves, just sat back on their buttocki and grew hair.

Oh yeah, and I didn't think it was scary at all, Both H. and I had a fit when Bambi's mother was shot. And when the hunters came into the woods. But we sat through this one without battling back a single tear. We weren't even scared, or sad, or much of anything. In fact, we left the theater remembering all the good stuff Disney used to do, and wondering if they just don't know how anymore, or whether they're so interested in money now they just play everything sàfe, right down the middle. H. was in a fury, but I was sad. If you can't trust Disney to make something for us kids, then who can you trust?

LOS ANGELES TIMES, 6/15/94, Calendar/p. 1, Kenneth Turan

A movie's heroes may have their names above the title, but often as not it's the sidekicks who get the real work done. And sometimes, as in "The Lion King," it's those under-appreciated little people who steal the spotlight and provide the best reason to see something in the first place.

While in many ways a worthy successor to "Beauty and the Beast" and "Aladdin," this latest in Disney's string of animated extravaganzas is less of a piece than its revered predecessors and the first to have a core story noticeably less involving than its scintillating peripheral characters.

Set in an African landscape where man is not in evidence, "The Lion King" opens with a gorgeous set-piece, a gathering at Pride Rock of animals from ants to elephants to pay homage to Simba, newly born son and heir to the great king of beasts, Mufasa (voiced by James Earl Jones).

Young Simba (Jonathan Taylor Thomas) turns out to be an irritatingly callow cub who talks ("It would be so weird") rather like a hip kid from the Valley and always wants to go exploring in just the places his father says are forbidden.

He's encouraged in this by his uncle Scar (Jeremy Irons), a sullen, manipulative beast, passed over for the king's slot, who is given to pouting that he's "surrounded by idiots." Not surprisingly, listening to Scar's oily advice gets Simba into all kinds of trouble with his regal senior.

This father-son relationship, and the parallel tale of a young man's growth to adulthood, is "The Lion King's" central story and for the first time in Disney's 32 animated features, outside source material was not used as its dramatic basis.

But even though three different writers (Irene Mecchi, Jonathan Roberts, Linda Woolverton) were involved, none of them were able to convey this part of the tale in a way that doesn't feel its step.

But just when things are looking darkest, the first of the film's clever sidekick teams appears, a trio of wild and crazy hipster hyenas who serve as Scar's henchmen. Whoopi Goldberg and Cheech Marin as Shenzi and Banzai have a lot of fun trading riffs about "dangling at the bottom of the food chain," while Jim Cummings is equally strong as a goofy hyena who really does love to laugh.

Though he is the hero, Simba needs sidekicks as much as anyone, especially after, in the film's darkest moment (and one that will probably unnerve small children), his father, the regal Mufasa, tragically dies.

Fleeing Pride Rock as a result, Simba has the good fortune to run into a couple of mellow dudes, a tender-hearted but evil-smelling wart hog named Pumbaa (Ernie Sabella, animated by Tony Bancroft) and a fast-talking meerkat named Timon (Nathan Lane, animated by Michael Surrey) who have gaily dropped out of the jungle rat race and encourage the young lion to do the same.

Lane and Sabella, who played together as Nathan Detroit and Harry the Horse in the recent New York revival of Damon Runyon's "Guys and Dolls," form a completely hysterical team. Working off each other as smoothly as practiced athletes, they provide the film with an uncontainable—and essential—comic sass. Their "Hakuna Matata" (Swahili for "no worries") is the score's liveliest song, and to hear them break into a spontaneous chorus of "The Lion Sleeps Tonight" is the purest joy.

"Lion King" needs every bit of this gleeful anarchy because the film's final section, with its somber talk of guilt, responsibility, confronting the past and even a hint of recovered memory syndrome, threatens to turn the proceedings into a Serengeti therapy session.

Likewise the adult Simba (Matthew Broderick) seems at times on the verge of becoming the only lion ever to seek psychiatric help, though he settles instead for an amusing encounter with Rafiki the shaman baboon (an engaging Robert Guillaume).

Essential in keeping things lively throughout is "Lion King's" companionable soundtrack, with songs by Tim Rice and Elton John and score and arrangements by Hans Zimmer. It was Zimmer, in fact, who added the irresistible African rhythms and Zulu chanting that give the music much of its impact and style.

So big technically it needed two directors (Roger Allers and Rob Minkoff) and the hard work of more than 600 artists, animators and technicians, "The Lion King" also features its share of computer-generated wonders, including a dazzling stampede of thousands of wildebeests.

The greatest wonder of all, however, is how approximately 1 million drawings ultimately turn into a film that lives and breathes. For even with its flaws, this latest Disney animated feature once again delivers what its audience wants. Too bad flesh and blood films can't be this consistent.

NEW LEADER, 7/4-18/94, p. 19, David Bromwich

The Lion King, an ecological-paternalist romance from Disney, is witty and generous in unexpected ways, and registers the influence of (in no particular order) Kipling, Caravaggio, United Airlines, Sergio Leone, Leni Riefenstahl, and several generations of Disney pictures. The message is delivered succinctly by Mufasa, the good king of the lions, who tells his son and heir Simba: "Everything you see exists in a delicate balance." And Mufasa explains: "We are all connected in the Great Circle of Life." The film betrays a touching assent to the popular Tory creed that any disruption in the order of things will draw down violence, sudden plague and the wide waste of anarchy. All the creatures know this. It is the wicked usurper-lion, Uncle Scar, a silky Oxonian relativist, who announces "the dawning of a new era in which lion and hyena come together." As Mufasa warns, you just don't do that with hyenas.

They are the most finely drawn of the animals. With their dark eyes, sharp ears and small, mean heads that almost touch the ground when they snuffle and run, these creatures recall young Richard Widmark in *Kiss of Death,* who bellied into the same crazed skids of laughter. At rest, they annoy each other with miscellaneous dietary grouses and cravings. "Why are we dangling at the bottom of the food chain?" "I'm so hungry, I just gotta have a wildebeest." An unsavory influence on the lion child, the hyenas are countered with pluck by the king's counselor, a bird named Zazu who carries on the Jiminy Cricket tradition of sage sexagenarian air-borne sidekick. Zazu is crafty and reserved—he, too, knows his place in the Great Circle—but he urges preemptive action against Scar: "He'd make a very handsome throw-rug."

Mufasa is set up by Scar to be killed in a stampede, and young Simba, convinced that one of his practice-roars caused the disaster, retreats to the parched earth outside the pridelands. For half an hour or so the film now climbs to a pitch of genuine invention. Simba is rescued by an oafish, good-natured warthog and his master, the African equivalent of a prairie dog. They bring him to a region of lush forests and waterfalls, and nurture him to adolescence in their—relatively—lotus-eating way of life, subsisting on insects and slugs ("slimy yet satisfying"), and teaching postmodern apothegms ("The past doesn't matter"). The warthog, Pumbaa, a cross between Mrs. Malaprop and Ernest Borgnine in one of his benigner roles, turns out a daily quota of worthy but twisted platitudes. "You gotta put your behind in your past," he sweetly admonishes Simba, and the prairie dog Timon cuts in with exasperated tenderness: "No no no *no*! Why don't you lie down before you hurt yourself."

The pastoral interlude closes with a baboon-trickster discovering Simba in exile and reminding him of his duties with the aid of history, anecdote, riddle, and a shamanistic invocation of his father. After a lost-ark allusion for the groundlings, the plot turns around with Zen economy as Simba, still intractable, mutters "The past doesn't matter," and the baboon cracks him on the skull with a walking-stick. "Ouch! Why'd you do that?" "It doesn't matter, it's in the past." Point taken. The land of Simba's father has changed, under the hyena-rule of Scar and his minions, from a Great Circle of Life to a heap of charred stumps and rotting bones. Zazu is glimpsed pining away in a cage—actually a ribcage made from an antelope carcass—singing "Nobody knows the trouble I've seen."

It will be a "nice little job" to renew the pridelands, as one character ruefully observes. But with Simba's guilt expiated, his uncle cashiered at a single stroke, and the hyenas back where they belong, nature is ready to be reborn; a hefty chorus of zebras and giraffes agree, and it would be churlish to dissent from this harmony, coming as it does from the silent middle of the food chain. My only regret was that the last fight of Simba and Scar is done in slow motion, in the manner of football highlights and Sam Peckinpah—an evasion on more than one count, since a battle of wits, as well as claws, has been promised that the lions never perform.

In the older Disney pictures, the songs were occasionally memorable and the lyrics were permitted to be clever—more so at times than the script. This has now altered in what seems a premeditated decision by the studio. The songs of *The Lion King* are a saccharine pastiche of the Fifth Dimension and Elton John—There's more to see than can ever be seen,/ More to do than can ever be done"—though we are spared a set-piece as drawn-out and insipid as "A Whole New World" in *Aladdin*. The real music is in the words of Mufasa spoken by James Earl Jones—the irresistible father, for good or evil, in this genre of movie—whose inflections prove him deeply versed in the superego. Jeremy Irons, the voice of Scar, suggests an ease in the inner reaches of lolling, languid cruelty, as accomplished as if he had spent 20 years in a cave with James Mason. He has shown his face in parts like this—in *Dead Ringers* and *Reversal of Fortune*—but too seldom and too sparingly given the resonance of his gift.

NEW STATESMAN & SOCIETY, 10/7/94, p. 35, Jonathan Romney

Once the world was young and things were simple, and there just two points of view about Walt Disney cartoons. They were as natural a part of childhood as gripe water or Marmite soldiers; or they were the Great Satan, importing poisoned ideology into young minds under cover of cute button noses and goo-goo eyes. Bambi was a propagandist for the nuclear family, Dumbo an apologist for the imperatives of conformity, and Snow White taught little girls that while waiting for their Prince to come, they could do worse than tend to the everyday needs of any seven pint-size patriarchs they happened to meet.

Yet sooner or later, even the most devout Disneyphobe would break down and admit that as a child, they'd shed an elephant tear or two for Dumbo's mummy; or felt their nose growing Pinocchio-style every time they fibbed about the dog eating the homework; or simply swooned at some gouached sunset. We've *all* ingested Disney along with a lifetime's E-additives and carbon monoxide. Besides, these days, we're too sophisticated to be paranoid about Hollywood brainwashing; as long as we don't spend good money at EuroDisney, then our ideological purity can rest unimpaired.

With *The Lion King*, though, things get a little complicated, and it's probably safe—or, at least, salutary—to start worrying about Disney again. Disney's biggest hit in aeons is very weird, not to say stomach-turningly kitsch. It's best to forget the press kit rhetoric about its "powerful, allegorical story", and all you've heard about its timeless echoes of *Hamlet*—it's best summed up as described early on in its inception: "Bambi in Africa".

Here's the tale: Simba, a little boy lion cub, is born and his daddy Mufasa, King of the Beasts, waves a paw at the veldt and tells him, one day, son, all this will be yours. But evil Scar, Simba's uncle, has his eye on the throne, and lures Mufasa into a wildebeest stampede, killing the king and traumatising his rightful heir, who slopes off into the jungle. There—shades of Prince Hal—he lives a leisurely, bug-eating life in the company of an insouciant meerkat and a flatulent warthog, while Scar and his hyena coterie lord it over the now-crestfallen noble cats. Soon, of course, Simba must return to save the day, so that a new king will reign, a new cute boy cub will be born, and the glorious hymnal of Elton John's and Tim Rice's "Circle of Life" will ring out, filling the air with the chime of a thousand candyfloss machines.

In a curious volte-face from the cautiously PC-ish trio of *The Little Mermaid, Beauty and the Beast* and *Aladdin*, all the things we expected to find in classic Disney are back In force: anthropomorphism, sexism, the divine right of kings. Homophobia, too: wicked Scar, voiced by a magisterially sneery Jeremy Irons, is camp to the hilt and the only lion who doesn't mate, who therefore impedes the Circle of Life ("You're so weird," marvels the cub; "You have no idea," smirks Uncle). The racism is textbook stuff, too: of Scar' s trio of mad, bad hyenas, one is characterised as black (voiced by Whoopi Goldberg), one as Hispanic (Cheech Marin), the third as a gibbering crackhead. When Simba gets lost in the elephants' graveyard where they hang out, he's a little white kid who's wandered into the bad part of town: like Sherman McCoy in *The Bonfire of the Vanities* taking the wrong turn and finding himself in the Bronx.

The film seems to outwit itself, though, when it has Scar's ranked hyenas doing a goosestep. Is Disney trying to alert us to a black, gay Nazi conspiracy? Does this make any sense? No, and it's not supposed to. The only rule of the exercise is to use whatever image will be most powerful. *The Lion King* is out to appeal to everyone's cherished myths and pet paranoias. The Disney studio, aspiring to milk the widest possible demographic, here thinks nothing of placing all its oldest reactionary commonplaces alongside its overtures to a black audience; for this is, in effect Disney's first black film.

Hence the discrepancy of the film's appeal, on the one hand, to an exotic European dream of Africa as lush Safariland, and on the other to post-*Roots* Africanism. Throughout, the messages jar: Simba's dad, who shares his unmistakable Caucasian features, is voiced by that icon of black gravitas James Earl Jones. Simba's speaking voice is pure babyWASP; but when he sings, it's with the hiccuping lilt of a Michael Jackson.

What's more, *The Lion King* takes its moral rhetoric straight from the codes of the new black US cinema, with its recurrent themes of the absent father and the need for young men to wise up, get serious, Be King. Like the home boys in *Juice*, Simba wants to cruise through life fuelled on testosterone ("I Just Can't Wait to be King"); but Mufasa, King of Pride Rock, explains that with power comes responsibility, just as super-patriarch Furious Styles does in *Boyz 'N' The Hood*. Later, when it's time for Simba to leave his hip hedonistic friends—bug-eaters and therefore not his people—it's his girlfriend who reads him the riot act, just as in *Straight Out of Brooklyn* and *Menace II Society*.

The reactionary clichés may be more transparent, because familiar, but it's these borrowed black codes that dominate the film and make it readable in a way that's more current—and to a young African-American audience, far more "archetypal"—than *Hamlet* or *Ulysses* or whatever grand precedents the Disney script analysts claim for it. This really is Bambi in Africa.

NEW YORK, 6/20/94, p. 78, David Denby

Joy is not an emotion one associates with Jeremy Irons, but in the new Disney animated feature *The Lion King*, Irons, speaking the part of the lazy, bitter Scar—a loser lion—sounds like he's having a better time than he's ever had in movies before. Scar hates his brother, the overbearing king of beasts Mufasa (who is spoken by James Earl Jones in his deep-resonating sub-woofer style), and he wishes everyone ill. He's like some huffpot working in the costume department of a small theater, a guy who never made it and now sees through everyone. He's sour and disobliging, and Irons, drawing on the British theatrical traditions that he's often ignored, gives his lines fey, nasty twists.

The big Disney animated films are soaked in show business now—filled with ethnic humor and references to old movies and TV shows as well as famous actors doing riffs on their normal tones. They've become multifaceted entertainments. In *The Lion King*, the bad guys—three toothy hyenas with dark-circled eyes who work for Scar—are spoken by Whoopi Goldberg, Cheech Marin, and Jim Cummings, and the three of them are like nasty comics slagging one another on late-night cable. *The Lion King* is fine entertainment—solid family stuff with a shrewd sense of how the grown-up audience might need a little goosing to stay interested in an animal fable.

Unlike the Disney films, *Lion* is not based on a famous fairy tale; it's an original, which means nothing in this case, since the story is entirely generic. *The Lion King* is a patriarchal narrative: As Scar mutters to himself, ready to destroy the king and seize control, Mufasa holds his young cub, Simba, aloft for the other animals to see. Mufasa is a pro-ecology king of beasts who believes in "the circle of life," and he introduces his son to his responsibilities. But through Scar's machinations, Mufasa is killed and Simba sent into exile, and Scar and the hyenas ravage the earth. Will Simba become himself—that is, become his father, and claim the kingship? Will the health of the land be restored? Feminists will no doubt have a field day deconstructing the tale (to disguise its essential boss-daddy ethos, Disney has made Simba's childhood friend Nala the lioness a better wrestler than he).

The Lion King is set in the folkloric East Africa of Western imagination, and it features a medicine man/prophet type of baboon, Rafiki, who shakes a stick and makes wise remarks. An unpleasant thought rises up: Is this the only kind of movie that can now be set in the chaotic continent of Africa? *The Lion King* is almost nostalgic for a prehuman existence.

Elton John has composed some pseudo gospel music, which is a bizarre waste of time, since there's plenty of heart-pounding African music the filmmakers could have used. John allegedly spent no more than twenty minutes finding the basic melody of each song, all of which sound as if he spent ten. But the movie looks beautiful. Director Rob Minkoff and his army of animators have mimicked photographic effects—shimmering backlit landscapes and overhead shots of bird flocks cruising through the daylight. The ecological bent they've given the material isn't a total fake: The grandeur of the Serengeti Plain comes through the animation, and the young audience may actually feel something like amazement.

NEW YORK POST, 6/15/94, p. 29, Michael Medved

"The Lion King" rules.

As lyrical and gorgeous as "Beauty and the Beast," as witty and inventive as "Aladdin" this new Disney triumph boasts animation even more breathtaking than its immediate predecessors.

Every scene contains some new splendor to delight the eye or refresh the spirit, and to advance the film's higher purpose: inspiring a sense of wonder at "the circle of life" in which we all play our part.

That "endless round" is celebrated in the unforgettable opening sequence, already famous from the trailers that have been playing in theaters for several months.

As the sound track throbs with the African-flavored hymn "Circle of Life" (one of five catchy new songs by Elton John and Tim Rice) animals of every species make their pilgrimage to Pride Rock to pay homage to the newborn lion cub, Simba, son of the great King Mufasa (the voice of James Earl Jones).

Unfortunately, this heir apparent provokes jealous resentment from Mufasa's evil brother, Scar (brought to life by the marvelously modulated tones of Jeremy Irons) who enlists the assistance of some nasty, low-on-the-food-chain hyenas (voices of Whoopi Goldberg, Cheech Marin and others) in a plot to kill the king and seize the throne.

In one sense, "The Lion King" follow's the old death-of-a-parent format so common in children's classics, but here the tragedy plays out more like "Hamlet" than "Bambi"—especially when the grown Simba (voice of Matthew Broderick) sees his father's ghost urging him to "Remember" and to take the kingdom back from his usurping uncle.

Other Shakespearean overtones turn up when the self-exiled Simba denies his royal origins like a reluctant Prince Hal, and spends his time in the company of a decidedly Falstaffian wart hog who teaches him the hedonistic philosophy of "Hakuna Matata" (no worries).

That wart hog and his meerkat companion (played by the voices of Broadway veterans Ernie Sabella and Nathan Lane) all but steal the movie with their zesty singing and snappy one-liners; they could be the most hilarious characters ever to appear in a Disney-animated film.

Part of the magic of the animation is an uncanny ability to make these and all other animals move with astonishing grace and realism, even as their faces subtly suggest the famous human actors who provide the voices.

For all its raucous humor and sweeping grandeur, "The Lion King" remains a tender love story, though, unlike other recent Disney offerings, the central relationship here is father-and-son, not boy-and-girl.

The notion that his inter-generational connection is durable enough to survive evil schemes and death itself will prove profoundly moving to both parents and children.

At the screening I attended, the crowd greeted the conclusion of the movie by rising in their seats for a two-minute ovation; in 14 years of reviewing films, I've never seen a comparable reaction.

Actually, you'd have to have a hyena's heart not to join the joyous shouts of "Long live the King!" greeting this new monarch of the box office, and the most Oscar-worthy film that Hollywood has released so far this year.

NEWSDAY, 6/15/94, Part II/p. B2, Jack Mathews

The plotline reads like Greek tragedy, the story of a young king who, having been convinced that he is responsible for his father's death, is forced to live in guilt-ridden exile while his kingdom is laid to ruin by the real murderer, his father's own brother!

But "The Lion King," the latest creation from the Second Golden Age of Disney Animation, is also the funniest, hippest, liveliest and most exhilarating family picture we're apt to see this year. The act of fratricide is a formidable downer in a children's movie, but there is far more comic relief than grief.

In fact, there's a little of everything. Cleverly written, hummable show tunes by Tim Rice and Elton John, a trio of hilariously mischievous hyenas, a jaunty vaudeville team starring a flatulent warthog and a glib meerkat, a reggae baboon witch doctor, and the loathsome Uncle Scar, who takes his place among Disney villains as the Cruella de Vil of the veldt.

Throw in a love story between the homesick King Simba (adult voice by Matthew Broderick) and his childhood sweetheart Nala (Moira Kelly), connect it all with a coming-of-age theme about individual responsibility and the cycle of life, and parents will be answering questions for weeks.

"The Lion King" is the 32nd animated feature film from Walt Disney Studios, the first ever to be based on an original story, and, in terms of technical brilliance, the best of them all. Disney's animation department, on the brink of creative default just a decade ago, has crafted such a seamless blend of classic and computer animation that it is hard to imagine where it can go from here.

With the aid of computers, the animators have long-since overcome the two-dimensional constrictions of flat cell paintings, finding ways to create the illusion of a camera moving through a cartoon universe, as if on a dolly or crane, to match angles and shots routine in live-action adventure films. But it has never been done on this level of grace and scale, and there are other scenes—one of a herd of loping zebras, another of stampeding wildebeests—whose detail and movement verge on photo-realism.

None of this techno-artistry will mean anything to kids, whose sense of wonder will be stimulated by the same things that have stimulated children in Disney movies since "Snow White and the Seven Dwarfs" started it all nearly 60 years ago. It's an irresistible tale, filled with wondrous characters, sparkling wit and honest emotion, a supermarket of old-fashioned family values.

Some may find "The Lion King" a little too old-fashioned. The world of Simba, King Mufasa (James Earl Jones) and Scar (a wonderfully malign Jeremy Irons) is dominated by males. They are the leaders, teachers, and protectors, and though it is mentioned in passing that lionesses do all the serious hunting in Pride Lands, Nala and Simba's mother, Sarabi, are passive victims under the reign of Scar. There is not so much as a Good Witch around to serve as a role model for girls.

So, take it in the spirit of Father's Day and enjoy the relationship between Simba, the impetuous son, and Mufasa, the kindest, bravest, gentlest, most patient dad in the land.

Parents who remember the killing of Bambi's mother as a terrifying childhood experience should disregard the benign G rating given "The Lion King." The murder of Mufasa (he's crushed trying to save Simba from a wildebeest stampede started by Scar) is a scary and violent sequence, and Simba's panicked attempt to revive him ("Get up, Dad, we have to go home") is heartbreaking.

Children who identify with the cub may also be troubled by his journey away from Pride Lands and his mother and into the dark shadows his father had warned him against, where he nearly dies.

But the time devoted to these events is brief, and writers Linda Woolverton ("Beauty and the Beast"), Irene Mecchi and Jonathan Roberts never let us go far without a relaxing laugh. The hyenas Shenzi (Whoopi Goldberg), Banzai (Cheech Marin) and Ed (Jim Cummings) chasing Simba are deliriously goofy and seemingly too stupid to be of any real danger to him. And once Simba is rescued by Pumbaa and Timon, the warthog and meerkat (voice-acted by Broadway veterans Ernie Sabella and Nathan Lane), the movie adopts their problem-free philosophy of "Hakuna Matata."

That phrase, the Swahili equivalent of Bobby McFerren's "Don't worry, be happy," will drive you crazy before the summer's over, but you will be singing it on your way out of the theater.

This is the first animated Disney musical in five years to be without the services of Oscar-winning songwriter Alan Menken. But Elton John and Tim Rice, who worked with Menken on "Aladdin," have come up with their own memorable, African-tempo songs. Besides the whimsical "Hakuna Matata," the least shakable are "Circle of Life," a huge choral piece, and "I Just Can't Wait to Be King," which accompanies the film's one big production number.

My only disappointment with "The Lion King" is the mundane showdown between the forces of Simba and Scar. After all its allusions to nobility, and so much originality, the movie descends to the level of all modern action films, with the villain facing the most violent end the writers can imagine.

For kids who haven't yet developed a taste for screen retribution, Scar's fate, though tastefully done in shadows, offers a hint of what's to come in movies exploiting real violence. There is little nobility in that.

NEWSWEEK, 6/20/94, p. 62, Peter Plagens

Disney movies speak to the kid in all of us. And since kids like the same healthful stuff—mother love, frolicking in the grass with other kids and pretending to be heroes—the Disney appeal is nearly universal. But when Walt was alive, the old Disney studio occasionally advocated as well as entertained. "Victory through Air Power" (1943) promoted strategic bombing of enemy cities as opposed to mere air support for ground troops. And a '50s TV documentary-cum-cartoon, "Our Friend the Atom," lobbied for atomic power. Now the new mega-Disney enterprise—on a roll from "The Little Mermaid" (1989), "Beauty and the Beast" (1991) and "Aladdin" (1992)—has released "The Lion King."

It's Disney's 32d animated feature and first ever from an original story. Generously filled with love, play and heroism—not to mention very pop songs by Elton John and Tim Rice—it's sure to draw a huge audience from among the great American mosaic. The film is also what used to be called a message movie, containing lessons about everything from the environment to why strong women shouldn't be considered a threat by men. "The Lion King" is especially concerned with issues of family and responsibility. And much in the movie points to where in our society they burn most fiercely: the inner city, the place of despair for young black males.

The studio's press material calls "The Lion King" an "African-based coming-of-age story." The monarch Mufasa (the voice of James Earl Jones) wisely rules a vast animal kingdom from a place pointedly called Pride Rock. Cuddly cub Simba is the heir apparent. He's ceremonially presented to a panspecies gathering at the end of the movie's rousing choral overture, "Circle of Life." Continuity of both royal rule and the father-son relationship would be a cinch if it weren't for Scar, Mufasa's sinister brother, who covets the throne. Equipped with Jeremy Irons's dulcetly evil intonations and the allegiance of hyenas (who seem to stand for the dangerous lowlifes of street culture), Scar hatches a plot in which Mufasa is killed and Simba is sent into guilt-ridden exile. In the press booklet, codirector Roger Allers sums up Simba's predicament: "When his father is taken away from him too soon, he feels unworthy and inadequate." A counselor at PS 1 in the Bronx couldn't have put it straighter.

Simba is rescued in the desert by a lemurlike animal named Timon (borscht-belt voice: Nathan Lane), and Pumbaa the wart hog (who, in the movie's rainbow of archetypes, fills the role of the goodhearted, somewhat dim white ethnic). The adult Simba (Matthew Broderick) tries to put what he sees as his tainted heritage behind him. But a ghostly visit from his father persuades Simba to set things right. He returns to find the kingdom in leafless ruin, with the indolent hyenas complaining that the lionesses aren't bringing home enough food. The climactic battle for the neighborhood isn't just a lion thing: Timon and Pumbaa have rushed to Simba's side. Instructively, Scar's demise comes at the hands of the very gangstas he rode to power. Simba accepts the responsibility of being a lion and eventually, with a cub of his own, of being a father. While the cumulative effect of "The Lion King" is majestically Afrocentric, it's one (coupled with such supporting voices as Cheech Marin and Whoopi Goldberg) with a distinctly American glint.

"The Lion King" does have some problems, and they're in the art. Animation leans toward cartoon comedy, so "The Lion King" needed a boost in naturalism to make it serious. The lions have muscle and—accompanied by the booming soundtrack—weight. But the skinny, villainous Scar is actually the most realistic. Mufasa and the adult Simba look too much like wrestlers with manes. "The Lion King's" 1,197 painted backgrounds are disappointing, even though they've been inspired by Old West artists like Frederic Remington and Charles Russell. The backdrops of Disney animated features are always a torrent of clichés from romantic painting made bearable only by their moving so fast. These just don't have the character of the characters.

Nevertheless, it's been more than 50 years since those racially caricatured crows taught Dumbo how to fly, and a little less than that since the NAACP criticized "Song of the South" for its "idyllic" view of slavery. And Disney still possesses a little of Walt's Midwestern sense of doing well by doing good. With the culturally confused Euro Disney needing a bailout and the proposed Disney's America park in Virginia peppered by protest, this isn't a bad time for a good deed. "The Lion King" will likely be slipped into urban school VCRs for generations to come. That's because the film also speaks to the responsible grownup in all of us kids.

SIGHT AND SOUND, 10/94, p. 47, Caren Myers

At Pride Rock in the African plains, Mufasa, the king of the lions, presents his new-born heir Simba to all species of local subjects. Everyone is happy except for Scar, Mufasa's embittered younger brother, who burns with thwarted political ambition.

As the months pass, Simba grows into a mischievous cub, rough-housing with his best friend Nala, blithely ignoring Zazu, the king's officious major-domo, and looking forward to the day when he too will rule the land. But Scar is waiting to make his move, and after an unsuccessful attempt to dispose of Simba by sending him off to explore an elephant graveyard, deep in hyena territory, without adult supervision, he hatches a dastardly plot to murder Mufasa and usurp the throne.

Enlisting the help of the hyenas, Scar lures the unsuspecting Simba into the path of a wildebeest stampede; Mufasa is killed trying to save his son. Scar then convinces the shocked Simba that the tragedy was his fault, and that he should go into exile. Narrowly escaping Scar's hyena henchmen, Simba collapses in the desert. There he is found by Pumbaa, a friendly warthog, and his wisecracking meerkat sidekick Timon. Adopting their 'no worries' philosophy, Simba grows into a bug-eating slacker. One day, he saves Pumbaa from being eaten by a lioness; it turns out to be Nala, who brings bad news from Pride Rock. Scar's reign has brought famine and devastation to the plain, and she urges Simba to return and put things right.

But Simba shrinks from the task, and it isn't until Rafiki, a witch doctor mandrill, seeks him out, that he resolves to face his past. He returns to do battle with Scar and learns the truth about his father's death. Galvanised with righteous anger, Simba saves himself but lets Scar be torn to pieces by the hyenas.

A year later, the ecological balance is restored, and, above the flourishing plain, Rafiki the mandrill presents the new-born son of Simba and Nala—the future lion king.

The Lion King, Disney's thirty-second full-length animated feature, has already been phenomenally successful in America, as well as extremely controversial for certain elements that are supposedly traumatic for the very young. Despite this, it maintains a consistently saccharine tone; it is also, as might be expected, unconscionably pompous.

Disney's first cartoon feature to be based on an original story, *The Lion King* purports to be no less than "a unique allegory about each new generation being a torchbearer for its ancestors". Since Disney have always been at their best when bastardising well-loved children's stories, it seems a shame that they have suddenly felt the need to start weaving unique allegories, particularly ones that prop themselves up on such well-worn themes. From the opening scene, the film clearly aspires to a kind of Shakespearian grandeur. It begins with the hordes of furry faithful applauding the arrival of Simba to a song entitled 'Circle of Life', which is deafening and platitudinous in about equal measure (and just what are the gazelles and zebras so happy about—(there's a new predator in town). The *Hamlet* parallel is earnestly laboured, and there's a bizarre moment when Scar, like a hairier Richard III, sings of his coup d'état while the cave he's in mutates into the phallic towers of fascist architecture and the hyenas start goose-stepping.

The film's emphasis is on flashy, computer-generated effects (like the senssurround wildebeest stampede) to the detriment of the cartoonish sprightliness that usually makes Disney's version of the animal kingdom so endearing. There is a jolly interlude (as well as a jarring change of pace) with the fast-talking meerkat Timon, and Jeremy Irons does a creditable George Sanders impersonation as Scar, but the fun loses out to the portentousness. And despite all the money lavished on it' the stylisation looks cheap and rather nasty—the lions are peaky, the zebras beaky, and the warthog has a nose like an electrical socket.

Nonetheless, *The Lion King* has been so popular that Disney are pulling it out of US theatres so that they can rerelease it for Thanksgiving—the kind of shameless marketing exercise only Disney can get away with. But their latest is not a patch on *The Jungle Book*.

TIME, 6/20/94, p. 59, Richard Corliss

The modern Disney cartoon feature is an adventure of the spirit—a guided tour through eruptive emotions. *The Little Mermaid* plunged briskly into the growing pains of a creature that felt as isolated from the shimmering haut monde as any Afghan peasant or Harlem street kid. *Beauty and the Beast* took a stroll in the woods with a fellow who needed lessons in the civilizing power of love. The *Aladdin* carpet ride revealed a whole grownup world of pleasures and perils to a young thief who started out in search of only a quick spin with a pretty princess.

Out of these excursions came show-business magic. Disney's handsome fantasies satisfied as master lessons in the storytelling craft. They rekindled the art and emotion of the studio's classic animation style; they showed Broadway what it had forgotten about integrating popular music into a potent story; and they reassembled the fragmented movie audience—these are pictures all races and ages enjoy. Fifty years from now they will probably be enthralling the grandchildren of kids who thrill to *Dumbo* and other Disney relics today.

In the process they have made enough money to please even Scrooge McDuck. Everybody from Disney renegades to Steven Spielberg tries making cartoon epics; Disney alone consistently succeeds. The studio, which issued (or reissued) only 12 of the 42 animated features that were released in the past five years, has grabbed 83% of the North American box-office take for the genre. (*Aladdin* has earned $1 billion from box-office income, video sales and such ancillary baubles as Princess Jasmine dresses and Genie cookie jars.)

At heart, though, *Aladdin* and its kin were the merest, dearest emotional travelogues. They alighted on a dream here, a resentment there; they poked at a feeling until it sang a perky or rhapsodic Alan Menken tune. Nothing was lacking in these terrific movies, but something was missing: primal anguish, the kind that made children wet the seats of movie palaces more than a half-century ago as they watched Snow White succumb to the poison apple or Bambi's mother die from a hunter's shotgun blast. Disney cartoons were often the first films kids saw and the first that forced them to confront the loss of home, parent, life. These were horror movies with songs, Greek tragedies with a cute chorus. They offered shock therapy to four-year-olds, and that elemental jolt could last forever.

Get out the Pampers, Mom. Get ready to explain to the kids why a good father should die violently and why a child should have to witness the death. And while you're at it, prepare to be awed at the cunning of a G-rated medium that brings to bright life emotions that can be at once convulsive, cathartic and loads of fun. In *The Lion King*, premiering in New York City and Los Angeles this week primal Disney returns with a growl.

The studio's 32nd animated feature tells of a lion cub who loses his birthright to an evil relative before regaining both his pride and his, er, pride. The film has jolly moments, delicious comic characters and five songs (by Elton John and Tim Rice), all so simple and infectious that you could immediately commit them to memory even if you weren't destined to hear them on tie-in commercials this summer for Burger King, Nestle, Kodak and General Mills. And yes, there's the hilariously extravagant production number that climaxes with whirlwind editing and a stupendous pyramid of pelts. With all this, *The Lion King* is almost guaranteed to be one of the huge hits of this bustling movie season.

Directed by Roger Allers and Rob Minkoff, *The Lion King* is a film of firsts for the studio. "It is our first cartoon feature not based on a fable or "a literary work," says Disney movie boss Jeffrey Katzenberg, who has overseen the animation unit since he joined the mouse factory in 1984. "It's the first where there's no human character or human influence. Our animators went back on all fours, and they'll tell you it's 10 times harder to make an animal talk and be expressive than it is to do that with a human." Nor is it easy to study a 500-lb. lion close up, as the directors and animators did ("The handlers tell you not to wear cologne," says Minkoff, "and not to dress like a zebra"). But the real challenge was to relate a moral tale of aristocratic dignity, and to do this in a pop-cultural era when feel-good facetiousness reigns. Comedy is easy these days; majesty is hard.

Not since *Bambi* has so much been at stake in a Disney tale. There are kingdoms to be sundered, deaths to be atoned for. The father of a prince is killed, and his conniving uncle seizes the throne; driven from the kingdom, the lad leads a carefree life until the father's ghost instructs him to seek honorable revenge. Put it another way: a boy leaves home, escapes responsibility with some genially irresponsible friends, then returns to face society's obligations. *The Lion King* is a mix of two masterpieces cribbed for cartoons and brought ferociously up to date. On the grasslands of Africa, Huck Finn meets Hamlet.

The hero s Simba (voiced as a child by *Home Improvement's* Jonathan Taylor Thomas and as an adult by Matthew Broderick). This cub is the headstrong son of lion king Mufasa (James Earl Jones) and nephew of the green-eyed Scar (Jeremy Irons), who with oleaginous irony hides his intentions to kill Mufasa and Simba and become a low-down, schemin', lyin' king. After Scar engineers Mufasa's downfall in a wildebeest stampede, Simba slinks into exile and away from duty, until at the urging of his father's spirit and of his friend Nala (Moira Kelly), the young lion returns home to challenge Scar and renew the circle of dynastic life.

Every Disney cartoon drama is laced with intoxicating comedy, with harlequins and hellcats. From *Pinocchio* on, the villain makes use of a sly sense of humor and a few goofy abettors. Scar, whom Irons plays with wicked precision as the purring offspring of Iago and Cruella De Vil, hires a pack of hyenas as his goons: clever Shenzi (Whoopi Goldberg), giddy Banzai (Cheech Marin) and idiotic Ed (Jim Cummings), who says little but is happy to chew voraciously on his own leg. The hero's helpers, who save Simba in the desert and teach him their live-for-today philosophy, *Hakuna matata*— Swahili for "What, me worry?" are Timon (Nathan Lane), a streetwitty meerkat, and the lumbering warthog Pumbaa (Ernie Sabella). They chew beetles.

Lane and Sabella, veterans of the *Guys and Dolls* revival on Broadway, make up in dynamite comic camaraderie what they may lack in marquee value. "I have no idea if they considered major motion-picture stars for our parts," says Lane pensively. "Do you suppose they were thinking of the Menendez brothers?" Lane loved the work, which involved mainly "acting silly for several hours and trying to make the directors laugh." Irons also enjoyed the spontaneity of the process. In animation, words come before pictures, so improvising actors help develop characters and dialogue. "It's extraordinary,"Irons says. "It's as though the animators, the writers and the performers are all creating at the same moment."

The directors and animators, though, create for years. That takes teamwork, discipline and sustained passion. "The creative process is usually thought to be an individual inspiration," says Michael Eisner, who runs the Disney empire. "And that's true if you're sitting on Walden Pond writing an essay or a poem or short story. But this is a different kind of creative form, even more so than a regular movie. I can't point to any one person and say, 'If it were not for him, we wouldn't have this movie.' But I can point to a series of people." Even the stars and directors are treated differently in a Disney animated feature, having traded huge salaries and profit participation for a chance to create dazzling popular art.

Eisner might have cited Katzenberg as the one man—the modern Walt, who does not create the story or draw the pictures but whose imprint is indelible in a million questions and suggestions, in his noodging and kibitzing, in refusing to be quickly pleased. Yet Katzenberg denies authorial status. "This is not me having a humility attack," he says. "It's just that the characterization isn't true. If you want, you can call me the coach. When Pat Riley coaches a basketball team, they do pretty good. Yet the absolute reality is that Riley did not put one ball through one net for the Knicks this entire year."

The Knicks reference is revealing. Katzenberg grew up in Manhattan, and in the Disney cartoons he has brought one of its institutions west. To state it bluntly: Broadway died and went to Disney. Pop went sour, and Disney smartly sweetened it. With Menken and lyricist Howard Ashman importing their Broadway savvy for *The Little Mermaid* and *Beauty and the Beast* (which completed the circle by opening as a Broadway show this spring), Disney reopened the franchise that Walt founded with *Snow White*'s dreamy *Some Day My Prince Will Come*. Last year the Menken-Rice *A Whole New World* from *Aladdin* won the Oscar for best song—the third time in four years that a Disney cartoon theme has won the award.

In *The Lion King*, Rice and John follow the Menken-Ashman formula. Music dramatizes moods (the first-act "I Want" song, when the young protagonist proclaims his or her dreams, is Simba's bouncy, Michael Jacksonish *I Just Can't Wait to Be King*) and prods the action (*Hakuna Matata*, which carries Simba from boyhood to manhood). The album just couldn't wait to be a hit. Two weeks before the movie opens nationwide, the soundtrack is already No. 13 on *Billboard's* pop-music chart.

Music can break hearts and make the Top 40. But a cartoon's narrative imagination is first and finally in the images. Animation is a supple form; it can be as free as free verse, as fanciful as a Bosch landscape. *The Lion King*'s palette (blinding yellows and blooming greens to portray the savannah and high grass) cues subtle or seismic shifts in tone and character. Thanks to the devotion of nearly 400 artists, each shot registers its beauty and simplicity.

Seeming simplicity, that is. "When we do a film well," says Walt's nephew, company vice chairman Roy Disney, "we make it look easy, like a good golf swing. People say, 'I can do that'."

Someday somebody will; Disney's way is not the only way. Says Katzenberg: "On this planet today is another Walt Disney, waiting for that moment when his or her genius is going to produce something great, and competitive to us."

Not as long as Disney monopolizes cartoon royalty with the likes of Simba and his ingratiating menagerie. In the world of feature cartoons, everybody else is a mere cat. Disney is the lion king.

VILLAGE VOICE, 6/21/94, p. 45, J. Hoberman

Not yet a part of our genetic material, *The Lion King* wastes no time irradiating the universe. A blood orange sun rising o'er the awesome perspective of an African savannah, this latest Disney animation opens with the apocalyptic pow of an atomic bomb bursting upon Yucca Flats.

If you've got it, flaunt it. *The Lion King*'s pretitle sequence is a hothouse blend of stately hysteria and quasi-religious splendor. The sky is aflame, the peaceable kingdom runs amok. Shafts of light illuminate a geometric gaggle of giraffes. Elephants and gazelles cast fast-moving shadows. There's a mock rack-focus from an army of purple termites to the blinding moiré pattern of a zebra herd. A gibbering baboon capers atop the cliff. Behold: The lion cub Simba is born!

Clearly, *The Lion King* celebrates itself. The movie is both a newly minted corporate mythos (the first Disney animated feature based on an original story) as well as the megabuck ultimate in animated smoke and mirrors. Cosmic and craggy, The Lion King revels in natural phenomena. There are rainstorms and rock slides, lava flows and geysers, shimmering waterfalls and sparkly mists—not to mention an exuberant surplus of computer-animated aerial perspectives, vertiginous chase sequences, and a wildebeest stampede with the thunderous symmetry of an M. C. Escher brain-twister.

Closer to *Bambi* or even *Dumbo* than it is to *The Jungle Book*, *The Lion King* has little Simba frolic in his habitat, endure the death of his father Mufasa (dubbed by the voice of America, James Earl Jones), retreat into exile, grow up, and return to his people. That he's obviously traumatized—in part, by life inside a Disney cartoon—contributes to a lack of sentimentality accentuated by comic references to various creatures' respective positions on the food chain. *The Lion King* is populated by the regulation Disney galaxy of buzzy li'l sidekicks and epicene villains, all prone to British accents. If the most elegant vocal performance belongs to Jeremy Irons as Simba's treacherous Uncle Scar, the wittiest character animation is reserved for the trio of rabid hyenas (Whoopi Goldberg, Cheech Marin, Jim Cummings) who serve as his henchmen.

Since *Roger Rabbit*, Disney has become the grand repository of animation styles—its own brand of Zoo Parade quasi-naturalism now encompasses a measure of neo-Warners bug-eyed stretch, as well as a taste of Fleischer surreal vaudeville and the sort of landscape luminescence practiced in Japanese sci-fi. During his retreat, Simba falls in with a modified Ren and Stimpy team—a flatulent warthog and a shrill, streetwise meerkat. When this degenerate pair bring him to the jungle to munch on multicolored bugs, it's a plunge into one of Tex Avery's Raid commercials; a bit later, the dopey duo are dancing a hula as frantic and free-associational as any choreographed for Daffy Duck.

That two stars from the Broadway revival of *Guys and Dolls* supply the warthog and meerkat voices underscores *The Lion King*'s extravagant theatricality. (This is the first animated feature that actually feels as though it were lit.) All pretense to "naturalism" is abandoned for the two designated showstoppers—kid Simba's "I Just Can't Wait To Be King" and the warthog and meerkat's "Hakuna Matata." Both designed by Chris Sanders, the numbers are characterized by stridently flashing patterns, radical color shifts, and roving spotlights. The bilious yellow rally in which Scar addresses his hyena followers is another exercise in animated stagecraft—the would-be dictator rising like a Ziegfeld showgirl on the fiery cloud of a mechanical volcano.

Though not without a certain amount of static preening, embodied on the narrative level by granite-faced Mufasa, *The Lion King* is relaxed enough to reference *Triumph of the Will* (Uncle Walt was one of the few not to snub Leni Riefenstahl on her 1938 trip to Hollywood) and riff on the horror of "It's a Small World After All." The movie isn't as inspired as *Aladdin*, nor is it as unexpectedly funny; instead of Robin Williams's spritz there's a glitzy patina of New Age mysticism and a greater degree of corporate sensitivity. Like the ghastly *Beauty and the Beast*, *The Lion King* is programmatically nonsexist; what's more remarkable, however, is just how black it is.

The voices of Jones and Goldberg give lions and hyenas a shared negritude—and the baboon shaman has a heavy Caribbean accent. The songs, by Tim Rice and Elton John, incorporate Swahili expressions; the orchestration uses South African choirs; there are jokes predicated on "The Lion Sleeps Tonight" and "Nobody Knows the Trouble I've Seen," and "I Just Can't Wait To Be King" would have made credible filler on an early Jackson 5 album. (Indeed, the number is sung by Jason Weaver, who played the young Michael Jackson in a 1992 telefilm.) It's as if Disney just now realized Mickey's color—or the basic black-and-white dynamic of American show biz.

The Lion King might have been made to celebrate the new South Africa but, four years in the works, its release marks the 10th anniversary of the Michael Eisner era. Indeed, the movie is dedicated to the late Frank Wells, Eisner's managerial partner in the corporate resurrection that followed the thwarted hostile takeovers of the early '80s.

Jeffrey Katzenberg, Eisner's head of film production, spins *The Lion King* as "a love story between a father and son" that concerns "the responsibility we have as torchbearers from one generation to the next." When Mufasa tells his son that "everything the light touches is our kingdom," and, later, the shaman Rafiki assures Simba that Mufasa "lives in you," it's impossible not to think of Walt Disney World and Walt's reincarnation in Eisner.

After all, Disney is our most human corporation—the drama of "Disney After Disney" is that of "Family Business and the Business of Family," to take professor Jon Lewis's felicitous phrase. *The Lion King* produces additional human interest in the crucial realm of meta-entertainment as Disney battles Universal-Spielberg for the summer's most lucrative franchise. *The Lion King*'s primeval world is virginal compared to *The Flintstones*'s ersatz Stone Age suburbia. Still *The Lion King* hopes to best *The Flintstone*'s 550 licenses with an unprecedented marketing blitz. This ancillary war not only includes T-shirts, breakfast cereals, and candy bars but industrial titans as well—*The Lion King* having mobilized Kodak, Toys 'R' Us, and Burger King against *The Flintstone*'s Sega, Mattel, and McDonald's.

Is there an underlying anxiety that *The Lion King* will fail to spawn a new American trademark? Universal, after all, has gone Disney one better in treating the presold *Flintstones* as the recyclable by-product of a whole new dimension in the Universal Studios theme park. Disney, though, advances on many fronts. In the past few weeks, the made-for-video *Return of Jafar* has sold 1.5 million units sight unseen, while the critically disdained *Beauty and the Beast* rules Broadway (101.3 per cent capacity per *Variety*). The autobiography of mouseketeer Annette Funicello has been reviewed everywhere as the scholarly *Disney Discourse: Producing The Magic Kingdom* is naturally ignored. Meanwhile, such rival pop historians as Shelby Foote, Arthur Schlesinger Jr., and David McCullough unite to attack the proposed Virginia theme park "Disney's America."

Let Fred crow and the intellectuals rant. Everyone knows that Disney is already America's official culture. The nation's problems are almost identical with the corporation's. Disney proposes to bail out 42nd Street even as the floundering Euro Disney is itself bailed out by Prince Al-Waleed Bin Talal Bin Abdulaziz Al Saud. (Wonder how he liked *Aladdin*'s faraway place where they cut off your hands if they don't like your face"?) Disney makes room in the Magic Kingdom for MGM, acquires Miramax to become the unlikely sponsor of Quentin Tarantino, Krzysztof Kieslowski, and even Bernardo Bertolucci, author of the eccentric European entry in the summer kiddiefest, *Little Buddha*. (Exploiting a promisingly underleveraged trademark, Bertolucci was sufficiently yabba-dabba-doo to take Spielberg for his directorial model, but insufficiently visionary to cast Macaulay Culkin in the title role.)

Earlier this month, the unofficial celebration of Gay and Lesbian Pride Day at Walt Disney World even produced a Magic Queendom where, according to *The New York Times*, "the proportion of outwardly gay men and lesbians at the amusement park made [its] streets resemble those of Greenwich Village." Perhaps all Americans should be issued Disney stock certificates at birth. The corporation's secret motto has changed from Mickey Über Alles to Disney 'R' Us.

Also reviewed in:
CHICAGO TRIBUNE, 6/24/94, Friday/p. C, Michael Wilmington
NEW YORK TIMES, 6/15/94, p. C11, Janet Maslin
NEW YORKER, 6/20/94, p. 86, Terrence Rafferty
VARIETY, 6/13-19/94, p. 52, Jeremy Gerard
WASHINGTON POST, 6/24/94, p. B1, Hal Hinson
WASHINGTON POST, 6/24/94, Weekend/p. 42, Desson Howe

LITTLE BIG LEAGUE

A Castle Rock Entertainment release of a Lobell/Bergman production.. *Executive Producer:* Steve Nicolaides and Andrew Bergman. *Producer:* Mike Lobell. *Director:* Andrew Scheinman. *Screenplay:* Gregory K. Pincus and Adam Scheinman. *Story:* Gregory K. Pincus. *Director of Photography:* Donald E. Thorin. *Editor:* Michael Jablow. *Music:* Stanley Clarke. *Music Editor:* Lise Richardson. *Sound:* Bob Eber and (music) Dan Wallin. *Sound Editor:* George Simpson. *Casting:* Mary Gail Artz and Barbara Cohen. *Production Designer:* Jeffrey Howard. *Set Decorator:* Ethel Robins Richards. *Set Dresser:* Richie Cline, Robert F. Shaw III, and Joel Benton. *Special Effects:* Danny Gill. *Special Visual Effects:* Walter Hart. *Costumes:* Erica Edell Phillips. *Make-up:* Pamela Westmore. *Running time:* 119 minutes. *MPAA Rating:* PG.

CAST: Luke Edwards (Billy Heywood); Timothy Busfield (Lou Collins); John Ashton (Mac Macnally); Ashley Crow (Jenny Heywood); Kevin Dunn (Arthur Goslin); Billy L. Sullivan (Chuck Lobert); Miles Feulner (Joey Smith); Jonathan Silverman (Jim Bowers); Dennis Farina (George O'Farrell); Jason Robards (Thomas Heywood); Wolfgang Bodison (Spencer Hamilton); Duane Davis (Jerry Johnson); Leon "Bull" Durham (Leon Alexander); Kevin Elster (Pat Corning); Joseph Latimore (Lonnie Ritter); Bradley Jay Lesley (John "Blackout" Gatling); John Minch (Mark Hodges); Michael Papajohn (Tucker Kain); Scott Patterson (Mike McGrevey); Troy Startoni (Larry Hilbert); Antonio Lewis Todd (Mickey Scales); David Arnott (Little League Manager); Jeff Garlin (Opposing Little League Manager); Allan Wasserman (Little League Umpire); Teddy Bergman (Lowell); Cammy Kerrison (Shelly Hogeboom); Allen Hamilton (Mr. Patterson); Lavin Erickson (Margaret Sullivan); John Beasley (Roberts); Joe Johnson (Whitey); John Gordon (Wally Holland); Jason Wolf (Wally's Stat Guy); O'Neil Compton (Major League Umpire); Steve Cochran (Reporter #1); Tim Russell (Reporter #2); Mark McGann (Agent); Peter Syvertsen (Hotel Manager); Jodie Fisher (Night Nurse #1); Jodi Russell (Night Nurse #2); Kristen Fontaine (Night Nurse #3); Gary Groomes (Doctor); Charlie Owens (Patient); Tony Denman (Phil); Vinnie Kartheiser (James); Robert Schiel and Dean Wittenberg (Trainers); Brock Pierce (Sidney); Ronald J. Wojcik (Doctor, Twins Team); Ryan Anderson, Marc Gittleman, Clint Parnell, and Eric Jeffrey (Batboys).

LOS ANGELES TIMES, 6/29/94, Calendar/p. 5, Peter Rainer

In "Little Big League," 12-year-old baseball maven Billy Heywood (Luke Edwards) inherits the general managership of the Minnesota Twins from his grandfather (Jason Robards) and ends up becoming the team's manager too. It's yet another Hollywood high concept in the burgeoning baseball movie cottage industry. But think about it—is it really every boy's fantasy to *manage* a ball club?

What seems more likely is that "Little Big League" is an adult's baseball fantasy retooled for tykes. After all, a boy would more likely fantasize himself a slugger who wins the game for his team with a bases-loaded home run; the adult fantasy is to be that team's CEO. "Little Big League" tries to reconcile two conflicting scenarios: It gives us baseball as a game for the child within all of us but then it makes that child a corporate honcho. It's the perfect split for the '90s.

Billy, of course, isn't much of a player on the field—we can identify better with him that way. But this Little Big Man knows every bit of baseball lore since the days of Abner Doubleday and he's a master tactician, too; he even knows how to psych out the troublemakers on his team and cajole their prowess. He brings the Twins from the cellar to pennant contention and he does it by making baseball fun again. That's his philosophy—forget winning or losing, forget the money, just have fun. Of course, the filmmakers have it both ways on this, too: All this baseball-as-fun stuff points toward fame and fortune.

Director Andrew Scheinman and screenwriters Gregory Pincus and Adam Scheinman don't really delve into what it might be like for a 12-year-old to own and manage a baseball team; they don't really get into the ways in which the sport has been corporatized and how that would affect what a manager can do. Some of the players are surly, and one—Billy's childhood idol—has to be let go, but you won't be seeing any Darryl Strawberrys on this club. "Little Big League" isn't really in a position to jab the corporate sports culture because a movie with this hard a sell implicitly endorses that culture. It's Hollywood hardball masquerading as whiffle ball.

Billy would have been more interesting if he demonstrated some surly sides of his own, but he's drearily saintly and precocious. This fatherless boy has a weak spell when one of the players (Timothy Busfield) woos his mom (Ashley Crowe) and finds himself inexplicably benched. But that's about as petty as Billy gets—oh yes, he also forgets to go fishing with his buddies (Billy L. Sullivan and Miles Feulner) when he gets a lunch offer from Reggie Jackson. *Excuuuuse* me.

Billy picks up a few life lessons along the way—not much mention is made of the school lessons he'll have to make up—but most of the wisdom emanates from the boy. And if he seems wise beyond his years, that's because baseball here is employed as a metaphor for life. He who masters the game masters life. The field of dreams is soggy with sentiment.

First-time director Andrew Scheinman—one of the partners in Castle Rock Entertainment—may have too much of the Billy in himself to bring out the true roisterousness of baseball. He manages the movie with too soft a touch. The film's injected pathos isn't true to what most adults respond to in the sport—let alone children. It's a movie about "growing up"—i.e., becoming responsible. But the best, the least pretentious baseball movies have always been about how the game can make you blessedly irresponsible.

NEW YORK POST, 6/29/94, p. 34, Michael Medved

If you care about baseball and faithfully follow the fortunes of a favorite team (as I do with my beleaguered Philadelphia Phillies) then you've entertained the notion that you could do a better job running the club than its current management.

"Little Big League" makes that universal fantasy come alive for a 12-year-old boy with mediocre athletic skills but an encyclopedic knowledge of the games past and present.

Billy Heywood (played by bright, likable Luke Edwards, who previously appeared in small parts in "Guilty by Suspicion" and "Newsies") is one of those pre-pubescent baseball fanatics who can tell you in a flash which left-handed catchers are best at nailing runners at second base. or how many homers the notorious "Boom Boom" Beck allowed in 1842.

The boy's devotion to the game delights his kindly, crusty grandfather (Jason Robards, in the sort of standard-issue role he could perform in his sleep) who just happens to own the Minnesota Twins.

When Grandpa dies suddenly, he leaves a will that designates his beloved Billy as new owner of the team, and the plucky lad quickly uses that authority to fire floundering, short-fused manager Dennis Farina and to take over management duties himself.

It's a silly premise, of course, but on screen it plays out as far more believable than last years' similarly themed little-boy-in-the-big-leagues hit "Rookie of the Year"—about a star relief pitcher who's just 12.

In part, that's because it's much easier to imagine a kid besting major leaguers with his brain rather than beating them with his arm, but it also reflects the very different emphasis in "Little Big League."

The movie focuses on adventure, emotion and baseball authenticity rather than broad comedy, and the decision pays off handsomely. The on-field sequences are the most convincing, flavorful bits of big-screen baseball since "Bull Durham," aided immensely by an all-star assemblage of current players appearing as themselves (Ken Griffey Jr., Randy Johnson, Paul O'Neill, Raphael Palmiero and others), pius a cast full of actors with significant professional and semi-pro experience.

The best of these are one-time Cincinnati Reds reliever Brad "The Animal" Lesley, as a ferociously intense and obnoxious hurler who tries to intimidate his new manager, and especially Jonathan Silverman as an eccentric, philosophical, head-case hurler in the tradition of Boston's Bill "Space Man" Lee.

Silverman is so endearingly off-kilter that he effortlessly walks away with every scene in which he appears; it's a shame that the script never made more of his juicy part.

Timothy Busfield of "thirtysomething" fame (and a semi-pro player for the Sacramento Smokeys) enjoys a more substantial role as the solid, professional, nice guy third baseman with eyes for his young manager's winsome, widowed mother (Ashley Crowe).

The movie ambles along at a gentle pace—more like a self-satisfied home run trot than a dash to first. Scenes tend to go on too long and lines of dialogue fall to earth like lazy bloop singles, with little punch or energy—sowing the occasionally clumsy touch of a first-time director.

Andrew Scheinman is that nervous rookie behind the camera, but he's certainly no stranger to feature films; he co-produced "A Few Good Men," "When Harry Met Sally," "Misery" and other notable titles. Here, he brings such obvious affection to all his colorful characters and to the grand old game of baseball, that it's easy to overlook his occasional stumbles.

He also delivers an ending of uncommon intelligence and integrity—far more satisfying than we have any right to expect from such formula fare. All in all, "Little Big League" may not be one for the record books, or any sort of cinematic grand slam, but it deserves attention as a clean, solid hit.

NEWSDAY, 6/29/94, Part II/p. B9, Jack Mathews

In Andrew Scheinman's "Little Big League," a 12-year-old baseball trivia buff inherits the Minnesota Twins from his grandfather and, seeing as how the manager can't rouse the team to victory, decides to run the club himself. It looks as though the kid might have directed the movie, too.

In fact, the whole project might have been dreamed up by a bunch of kids sitting around at a baseball card trading fair, arguing about the relative worth of the autographs of Cobb and Ricky Henderson, and imagining how much better they'd be at managing a team than some of those beer-bellied geezers spitting on their feet out there.

"Hey, what if one of us was to become the owner of a team and could do whatever we wanted ... "

That kid is Billy Heywood (Luke Edwards), the worst player and best strategist on his little league team, and, as it happens, the grandson of Twins owner Thomas Heywood (Jason Robards). Thomas and Billy, whose father died years before, are as close as a hot dog and relish, and when the old man dies, he leaves his team to the kid.

Soon, Billy fires his insubordinate manager (Dennis Farina) and, with the blessings of the league, his mom (Ashley Crow) and school officials, takes over the job and begins lecturing his dismayed players about the joy of baseball. Geez, guys, if you'd just remember how much fun this is, you'd win. And, of course, they do.

Meanwhile, Billy is on the road, staying up late watching "Night Nurses From Jersey" on his hotel room TV, engaging in water balloon fights with the team, and otherwise learning about life in the big leagues.

This fantasy is at least as plausible as a little leaguer having his broken arm mend with a 100-mph fastball, which was the premise of last summer's baseball hit "Rookie of the Year." And "Little Big League," with its real team names, real players (look for the Yankees' Paul O'Neill), real ballparks, and actual historical anecdotes, offers up a lot more baseball savvy than we've come to expect from Hollywood movies.

Once it's set up, however, the story is about as much fun as "Rhubarb," a 1951 comedy about a major league team owner who dies and leaves the club to his cat, There are a couple of funny scenes, one involving a hidden ball trick in a crucial game, but the movie mostly just ambles from one flat-footed episode to another, as Billy turns his players back into kids, then has to stop taking himself so seriously.

The most noticeable rookie around is Scheinman. The producer turned director hasn't a clue how to set up the dramatic turns in the story, or how to develop the relationships between Billy and his friends and players, one, of whom (Timothy Busfield) is his mother's new boyfriend. For all the implied sentimentality, the movie plays out in an emotional vacuum.

In the end, I'm not even sure the fantasy has much appeal to little leaguers. No matter how much they know about the game, kids don't start dreaming of becoming managers until they're too old to dream of becoming players.

SIGHT AND SOUND, 4/95, p. 45, Trevor Johnston

12-year-old Billy Heywood, a keen baseball fan but mediocre player regularly attends matches with his grandfather, the wealthy owner of local major league outfit the Minnesota Twins. On the day that they are due to travel to an away game, Billy arrives home to some shock news: the old man has died, and in a video adjunct to his will he announces that he's left the Twins team to his grandson. Almost immediately Billy is pitched into a crisis when he's forced to dismiss team manager George O'Farrell over the latter's unwillingness to countenance a deal with a potential new player. Billy faces a press conference with the revelation that—school vacation permitting—he's about to take over as the game's first owner-manager in decades.

With the players initially resentful of Billy's inexperience and coaching assistant Mac Macnally doubting his man-management skills, the team loses its first four games, but after his inspirational speech extolling them to rediscover a childlike fun in their playing, the revitalised Twins go on to record six wins in a row. At the same time, the pressure starts to mount: Billy neglects his schoolchums; he has to fire wornout veteran hitter Jerry Johnson; and then his mother (who has been dating first baseman Lou Collins) grounds him for using bad language in front of an umpire. Only after enjoying a simple game with some street kids is his faith in baseball reaffirmed.

Billy faces the closing stages of the season with new resolve. Four wins on the trot sets them up for a playoff decider against the Seattle Mariners, where an ingenious setpiece move brings victory tantalisingly within their grasp. His mid-match marriage proposal already accepted by Billy's mom, Collins hits what looks like the clinching home run, but a brilliant catch on the boundary brings the Twins defeat by the slimmest margin. Against the players' wishes, Billy relinquishes his managership, but not before he's called back onto the diamond by the crowd and thrust a triumphant fist in the air.

Having produced, among others, such smart but solidly improving fare as *Stand By Me* and *The Princess Bride*, Castle Rock Entertainment partner Andrew Scheinman makes his directorial debut with this less nimble but similarly well-intentioned baseball picture, patterned specifically to appeal to a narrow band of pubescent male sports fanatics. Scheinman offers them a carefully-assembled blend of adolescent wish-fulfilment (fantasy baseball made flesh), with plentiful action interspersing a raft of real-life Major League stars, and an all-important respect and delight for the statistical heritage of the modern game. As a sports movie, *Little Big League* is more interested in remaining a credible entertainment for its core market than it is in the knock-about crossover potential of *The Mighty Ducks* films, *Cool Runnings* or the recent Daniel Stern-directed effort *Rookie of the Year*. For instance, the Minnesota Twins' last gasp defeat goes against the grain of the post-*Rocky* crowd-pleaser to underline, sentimentally if perhaps unfashionably, that it's the taking part, not the winning that's the most important aspect of sporting competition. But you really do need some knowledge of the intricate workings of the game to be able to get the most out of the film.

There's little else that rises much above the workmanlike. Scheinman's inexperience in longer term structural manipulation results in a rather one-paced affair, broken up by a series of serio-comic baseball montages cut to easy-to-follow R 'n' B standards. The eminently predictable contours of the plotting (kid teaches players childlike innocence, kid in turn learns adult responsibility, divorced mom hooks up with the first baseman) and the rather underpowered casting (ex-*thirtysomething* regular Busfield signals his graduation to romantic lead by shaving off his ginger beard) wouldn't be out of place in a television movie, though the location shooting in the Minnesota stadium and the highly convincing big match atmosphere indicate considerable big screen production expertise.

Also reviewed in:
NEW YORK TIMES, 6/29/94, p. C21, Stephen Holden
VARIETY, 6/20-26/94, p. 42, Brian Lowry
WASHINGTON POST, 6/29/94, p. D2, Rita Kempley

LITTLE BUDDHA

A Miramax Films release of a CiBy 2000 production in association with Recorded Picture Company. *Producer:* Jeremy Thomas. *Director:* Bernardo Bertolucci. *Screenplay:* Mark Peploe and Rudy Wurlitzer. *Story:* Bernardo Bertolucci. *Director of Photography:* Vittoria Storaro. *Editor:* Pietro Scalia. *Music:* Ryuichi Sakamoto. *Music Editor:* Michael Connell. *Sound:* Ivan Sharrock and (music) Steve Price. *Sound Editor:* Eddy Joseph. *Casting:* Howard Feuer, Priscilla John, and Joanna Merlin. *Production Designer:* James Acheson. *Art Director:* Andrew Sanders. *Set Decorator:* Bruno Cesari and Rondi Tucker. *Special Effects:* Richard Conway. *Costumes:* James Acheson. *Make-up:* Peter Frampton. *Stunt Coordinator:* Franco Fantasia. *Running time:* 123 minutes. *MPAA Rating:* PG.

CAST: Keanu Reeves (Prince Siddhartha); Chris Isaak (Dean Konrad); Bridget Fonda (Lisa Konrad); Alex Wiesendanger (Jesse Konrad); Ying Ruocheng (Lama Norbu); Jigme Kunsang (Champa); Raju Lal (Raju); Greishma Makar Singh (Gita); T.K. Lama (Sangay); Doma Tshomo (Ani-la); Khyongla Rato Rinpoche (Abbot); Mantu Lal (Mantu); Rudraprasad Sengupta (King Suddhodhana); Santosh Bangera (Chana); Kanika Panday (Queen Maya); Bhisham Sahni (Asita); Raj Kaur Sachdev/Rajeshwari (Yasodhara); Anupam Shayam (Lord Mara); Tsultim Gyelsen Geshe (Lama Dorje); Sogyal Rinpoche (Kenpo Tenzin); Jo Champa (Maria); Thubtem Jampa (Punzo); Surehka Sikri (Sonali); Rinzin Dakpa (Oracele); Vijay Kashyap (Vizir); Madhu Mathur (Prajapati); Ruchi Mathur (Queen's Assistant); Rashid Mastaan (Beggar); S. S. Pandey (Old Musician); Tarana Ramakrishnan (Saddiya Siddiqui); Anu Ehetri (Anita Thakur); Mahana Amar (Nagabab Shyam); Narmadapuree Kumar Lingeshewer (Chritra Mandal); Nirmala (Village Girl); Ailsa Berk (Elephant).

FILMS IN REVIEW, 7-8/94, p. 57, Keith Edwards

Little Buddha is a visually stunning Fortune Cookie which may find a home in Buddhist indoctrination centers around the globe as a layman's guide to enlightenment.

In this age of legal battles to retrieve children abducted into assorted religious cults, it is inconceivable that this synthetic American couple would readily surrender their little blonde progeny to the first aliens, in sheets and sandals, to ring their doorbell. They are told by the rotund senior half of this odd couple that their mighty mentor has left their sainted world to be reincarnated as a young child and that their frisky offspring is number one candidate. After a moment's hesitation, Daddy decides to take junior to Tibet to collect his booty. As the journey commences they are joined by two additional contenders for the throne; a darker hued lad closer in class to the militant monks and a spunky little feminist.

Bernardo Bertolucci has chosen to interweave this contemporary narrative with the mystical saga of the God Siddartha (portrayed by a caramelized Keanu Reeves) and the two takes do not mesh well. Just as one settles into the magical world of Siddartha, which evokes felicitous memories of Sabu and Turhan Bey in the writing and playing, you are suddenly jolted onto the Seattle freeway. Since the modern sections are so absurd, one yearns for the fantasy flashbacks, even though Keanu Reeves is not a very convincing actor, not that he tries, and might be more comfortable as a Gianni Versace model. The two other leads are the parents played by Bridget of the famed Fondas, and Chris Isaak, a neophyte actor who should return to his world of music, wherever that may be.

In the final scene, the elderly disciple, having completed his quest, goes to the bosom of Siddartha, and as his eyes close, we cut to Mother Fonda pregnant once again in Seattle with what one expects will be Rosemary's Buddha.

LOS ANGELES TIMES, 5/25/94, Calendar/p. 1, Kenneth Turan

When the editor of Tricycle, the Buddhist Review, one of the few journalists allowed on the set of "Little Buddha," the new Bernardo Bertolucci film, wrote about her experience, one question continued to trouble her. What was the word *Little* doing in the title?

None of the filmmakers, it turned out could give her a satisfactory answer, but now that the picture itself is here, the reason seems obvious. Despite its illustrious pedigree, "Little Buddha" turns out to have the sensibility of a children's film, the most elaborate and expensive "Afterschool Special" ever to make it to the big screen.

Being a children's film, of course, is not necessarily a negative thing, and aspects of "Little Buddha" do linger pleasantly in the memory. But what lingers as well is the suspicion that this is a children's film at least partly by default, the product of too much goofy New Age reverence and too little nuance and sophistication.

Those who remember such Bertolucci films as "The Conformist" and "Last Tango in Paris" may be surprised at this turn in his career, but those pictures are deep in the director's past. More recently we've seen the likes of "The Last Emperor," which, its many Oscars notwithstanding, is best remembered for how everything looked, not for what anyone said.

In fact, especially when, as here, Bertolucci collaborates with Vittorio Storaro, one of the world's preeminent cinematographers, the director has a tendency to become a prisoner of his own particular gift for luscious images, to assume that the dramatic side of things will more or less take care of itself.

Story, however, can be neglected only at great risk, especially when two parallel tales are being told. The first begins in a Tibetan Buddhist monastery in modern day Bhutan, where Lama Norbu (Chinese actor Ying Ruocheng) gets a telegram he's been waiting for for nine years, a message that soon puts him on a jet headed for Seattle.

Though all Buddhists believe in reincarnation, only Tibetan Buddhist believe that specific people, invariably great teachers, can be identified in their next incarnation. And Lama Norbu has reason to believe that his own teacher, admittedly a man with a hell of a sense of humor, has been reincarnated as an 8-year-old American named Jesse Konrad (newcomer Alex Wiesendanger).

Not surprisingly nonplussed by this news are Jesse's parents, Lisa (Bridget Fonda) and Dean (singer Chris Isaak), a sprightly young couple who don't quite know what to make of all these robed and shaven monks appearing suddenly in their lives.

They don't object, however, when Lama Norbu gives Jesse a child's life of the Buddha. This little book forms the basis of "Little Buddha's" second narrative strand, a film-within-a-film set in Asia 2,500 years ago that details how the fun-loving Prince Siddhartha transformed himself into a great spiritual being.

Though it plays at times like an infomercial on Eastern religions, this half of "Little Buddha" is the most successful. For one thing, this is where Storaro's photography and James Acheson's production and costume design are at their best, making good use of the never-before-seen streets of Bhutan and creating opulent set pieces.

And though eyebrows and even entire faces were raised when it was announced that Keanu Reeves was going to play Siddhartha, in fact, he does what the part calls for as the golden youth shielded from misery and death who takes the path the enlightenment. Hewing closely to traditional texts, this part of "Little Buddha" comes off closest to the fable quality the filmmakers were apparently after.

In the modern half, however, the lack of texture that is the film's weakest link is most evident. The Mark Peploe and Rudy Wurlitzer plot, from a story by the director, seems determined to take the drama out of every situation.

Being blissed out may be an enviable state for a human being, but it is not necessary the best one for a film.

NEW STATESMAN AND SOCIETY, 4/29/94, p. 33, Boyd Tonkin

If you seek the wisdom of the east, listen to this Zen parable. In a wealthy country there lived a story-teller called Liu Chi. The angry son of a famous poet, young Liu's tales scandalised the mighty. He told of lust. He told of power. He told, above all, of the hidden links between lust and power. States banned his stories. Priests cursed his name. Falsely accused of immorality and nihilism, he gave an honest voice to the quest for truth and faith in an age bereft of gods.

Then the heretical sages that Liu had followed fell from grace. Adrift,he turned to the lore of distant lands. He took on a pompous manner. His style grew fancier; his message, cruder. Now the authorities applauded him. But his new yarns hid a terrible emptiness. The old, pious Liu was much more a decadent materialist than the young, outrageous Liu. And the moral? Don't expect salvation from a guru who makes a costly song-and-dance about it. For real enlightenment lies in the gutter, not among the clouds ...

Clouds loom large in Bernardo Bertolucci's *Little Buddha*—the last wagon in a three-part spiritual caravan that began in the Forbidden City of *The Last Emperor* and then trekked across the Sahara of *The Sheltering Sky*. Here, the clouds roll in first over the familiar towers of Seattle, everyone's favourite 1990s location. In that trim, grey city, a trim, grey couple played by Bridget Fonda and the singer Chris Isaak digest the news that some visiting Tibetan monks suspect their small son Jesse may be the reincarnation of a revered lama.

Later, those clouds swirl around the Himalayan valleys of Nepal and Bhutan. There, Isaak and his boy learn about Buddhism in a cliff-hanging monastery, meet the other child claimants and await the surprise verdict. The world of Capra's *Lost Horizon* adjusts to the age of the Gameboy, played—and named—by the street urchins of Katmandu. (Could that really be a product placement?)

Meanwhile, lavish flashbacks to ancient India depict the pilgrimage of young Prince Siddhartha (incarnated by Keanu Reeves, left). Learning of age, sickness and death, the spoilt royal brat changes first into a grunge-haired ascetic and then into the serene and neatly-coiffured teacher known as Buddha.

Each of the "oriental" epics that preceded *Little Buddha* took someone else's book as source. Here, Bertolucci brazenly makes autobiography into spectacle. The film splashes his agony and ecstasy over a vast and glowing canvas. In a recent *Sight & Sound* interview, he frankly admitted that "Buddhism saved me from a big depression at a time when I had been deprived of the right to dream of utopias after the fall of the Wall".

With the convert's zeal, he now wants to shake everyone—especially children—out of our own big depressions. In fact, much of *Little Buddha* comes across as a budget-busting live-action Disney—a wholesome fairy-tale about the strange adventures of some ordinary folk, taken from a book crammed with sumptuous pictures. It begins, ominously enough, in a schoolroom, as a monk reads his class an illustrated fable.

Now, I don't mind becoming Bertolucci's wide-eyed pupil. Deluxe didactic cinema often calls for a child-like credulity. And *Little Buddha*, like earlier works in his canon, shows not just a revolt against the father's law but a process of conversion. Helped by the curiosity of young Jesse, the melancholic Isaak half-opens his heart to Buddhism. As a construction engineer in Seattle, he had built a domed skyscraper that stayed emblematically empty. In Katmandu, he visits a domed temple throbbing with life and faith.

The trouble is that Bertolucci wants to win our assent exclusively through top-of-the-range production values. Yes, we can relish the gorgeous cinematography of his perennial sidekick Vittorio Storaro, the fabulous 500BC-frocks from designer James Acheson and £33 million of blockbuster trimmings—from the sacred sites opened up by decree of the King of Nepal down to the 150 pairs of specially-made anklets. It's not enough.

And in the flashbacks, stone-faced Siddartha withstands all the scares and seductions that Maru, prince of darkness, can chuck at him. Typically the SFX are great; the emotions perfunctory. When it comes to hi-tech devilry, from giggling houris to fiery phantom archers, Bertolucci outguns the feeble Satanic cabaret in Scorsese's *Last Temptation of Christ*. But Scorsese coaxed from his Jesus, Willem Dafoe, a moving, baffled rage in the face of destiny that has no parallel here.

We get a very sketchy sense from the impassive Reeves of the Buddha-to-be as a protestant reformer, who cleared out the Hindu pantheon and planted the way to truth firmly in the human mind. This ought to matter for Bertolucci, since Buddhism makes a less violent break with his Marxist-Freudian background than any other creed. Yet the lush iconography betrays the very inwardness he tries to show, The film delivers Buddhism through a Hollywood-style Hindu lens.

All this scenic frippery massages the eye but leaves the mind unmoved. No one in *Little Buddha*—not Reeves and certainly not the terminally bland Fonda and Isaak—know how to act the drama of transformation. When, at the end, Isaak drones that "It's been a kind of emotional time for all of us," you can only conclude that if he acted calm, he'd be carted off to the nearest morgue. It's the very young and old who save this cast from bathos: the poised Alex Wiesendanger as Jesse (watch your back, Macaulay) and the Chinese veteran Ying Ruocheng, oozing an unworldy but alert charm as Lama Norbu.

Did Bertolucci mean to make his big names so soporific? After all, mention Seattle and nirvana in the same breath, and most people will think not of Keanu, but of the late Kurt. Perhaps he sought to summon up the anomie of what ad-men call Generation X. Or maybe he just chose a trio of cute but insipid stars. Since he views the film as a sort of scripture lesson with slide-show, a "dramaturgy without conflicts", the latter seems more plausible.

This urge to circumvent conflict in favour of a healing spectacle began at the fag-end of his Marxist phase. His political epic *1900* closed with a soft-focus idyll that bestowed a spurious grace on the short-term and cynical "historic compromise" between left and right in Italy. Here, the reunited family drop a deceased lama's ashes into the harbour from their boat; the camera comes to rest on Fonda's pregnant belly. This cosy image tries to reconcile all those polarities—east and west, spirit and flesh, death and birth—that script and acting have failed to explore.

This is a film punctuated with evasions, its fuzziness masked by cosmetic art direction. Selling the gain of faith without its pain, it flogs off-the-peg uplift to New Age consumers. And faced with Isaak's zombie-like performance, it's hard to credit that his director once nurtured (or, at any rate, unleashed) one of the finest ever incarnations of spiritual crisis. Marlon Brando's dark night of the soul in *Last Tango in Paris* plumbed a metaphysical depth that Bertolucci has never touched again. We should pray, chant (or simply hope against hope) for him to take his head out of the clouds before it's too late.

NEW YORK, 6/6/94, p. 53, David Denby

Why has Bernardo Bertolucci made *Little Buddha*? Stillness, detachment, and wisdom—the essence of Buddhism—may be the worst possible ideals for a movie director with a luscious camera style and a taste for intellectual melodrama. *Little Buddha* is about an elderly Tibetan monk, Lama Norbu (Ying Ruocheng), who becomes convinced that his dead teacher and spiritual guide has been reborn in the body of a towheaded American boy living in Seattle. He travels there and persuades the boy's parents (Bridget Fonda and Chris Isaak) that the child should come back with him to Bhutan, where he lives in exile. Along the way, he reads to the boy the story of the Buddha, born in great luxury as Prince Siddhartha (Keanu Reeves), and we see Siddhartha's journeys and trials and final enlightenment. Working against his strengths, Bertolucci can't do much with nirvana except photograph it. And he's too respectful to exploit reincarnation for the creepy thrills a horror director would find in it. He's left making pretty pictures—and whimsical jokes about the ineffable.

Little Buddha isn't a travesty: Ying Ruocheng, a deeply charming gentleman, speaks English with rounded musical perfection (he's Chinese), and his articulate spirit—penetrating, gentle—controls the entire movie. The picture offers relief from the noise and clamor of the commercial cinema. But it's a work of no dramatic interest whatsoever. Bertolucci and his great cinematographer Vittorio Storaro make the American scenes gray-blue and cold, reflecting the emptiness—dear God—of our souls, while the sequences set in Bhutan, Kathmandu, and Siddhartha's ancient India are ripely golden, like an ad for Bain de Soleil. As Siddhartha, Keanu Reeves goes through the three phases of what appears to be a pretentious magazine spread. At first, he's a honey-colored, nearly naked prince stroked by beautiful young ladies of the court. Later, In his ascetic period, sitting in the woods surrounded by followers, he becomes a hairy Indian, with hair growing out of his nose and who knows where else. He's very hairy. Finally, enlightened, he chooses "the Middle Way," and sits with his hair in a bun; he has become the Buddha.

Which means very little. The enlightenment of the Buddhists, if it is to signify anything, must be experienced as a series of trials, not as a pictorial cavalcade. When Siddhartha achieves "compassion," he's still just a handsome young man sitting under a tree, and we can't get away from the thought that Reeves looks like a bulimic model. Some of the movie is extremely beautiful, but Bertolucci appears to have little interest in dramatizing his ideas. The vibrant young director who made *The Conformist* has vanished.

NEW YORK POST, 5/25/94, p. 35, Michael Medved

Keanu Reeves playing Buddha?

At first blush, this bit of unorthodox casting seems to make as much sense as asking Ethan Hawke to play Mohammad, or choosing Sean Penn to star as Jesus Christ.

But despite fears that Reeves might turn Bernardo Bertolucci's ambitious "Little Buddha" into "Prince Siddhartha's Excellent Adventure," the much-maligned star of the Bill-and-Ted pictures does a surprisingly effective job in one of the most difficult roles imaginable.

Reeves (who descended from Hawaiian, European and Chinese ancestors) projects an appropriately universal—and other-worldly— innocence as the pampered Prince Siddhartha in India in 500 B.C., who rejects his life of privilege and pleasure for a path of self-denial and spiritual exploration.

The luscious, magical scenes dramatizing Siddhartha's struggle for enlightenment and his eventual transformation into the Buddha represent the most compelling moments of "Little Buddha." Unfortunately, they are surrounded—and ultimately overwhelmed—by a current-day tale that offers far less conviction and energy.

"This contemporary story centers on a yuppie family in Seattle (mother Bridget Fonda, father Chris Isaak, and 9-year-old son, Alex Wisendanger) whose life is disrupted by dream-driven Tibetan monks who announce that the boy has been tentatively identified as the reincarnation of a revered Buddhist lama.

They want to take the child to the mountain kingdom of Bhutan to test his identification but first they provide the boy (and American moviegoers) with a rudimentary education in Buddhism. They present the lad with a handsome picture book called "Little Buddha" that gives the movie its title and provides an excuse for the regularly interspersed scenes about Siddhartha's life 2,500 years ago.

Bertolucci—whose other films include "The Last Emperor," "Last Tango in Paris" and "The Spider's Stratagem"—is noted for the shimmering sensuality of his imagery, but here the visual seduction can't hide the shallowness of the characters. It's especially hard to accept the decision of the American parents to go along with a plan that takes the boy and his father to one of the most remote and exotic corners of Asia. These sections of the movie come across a bit like solemn PBS travelogue.

The entire film, in fact begins to feel like an earnest Buddhist tract—perhaps reflecting the consultation and encouragement of the Dalai Lama at every stage of the project. When the narration provides lines like, "The five ascetics witnessed these miracles with wonder and they became Siddhartha's first disciples," the movie communicates an unapologetic, childlike reverence not seen in films about Western religions since the days of old-fashioned sandals-and-sandstorms Biblical epics.

Is Bertolucci's vision transforming and inspiring? Not really, but it is consistently watchable and intriguing. "Little Buddha" may deserve no thunderous ovations but surely it has earned the sound of one hand clapping.

NEWSDAY, 5/25/94, Part II/p. B9, John Anderson

Bernardo Bertolucci may not know anything more about eastern religion that I do, but I don't care. This is not to say his "Little Buddha" is inaccurate, either in its portrayal of Tibetan

Buddhist thought or the life of Siddhartha (Keanu Reeves), only that it doesn't really matter. What matters is what happens on screen, and Bertolucci's direction alone is the stuff of religious conversion.

The director, whose philosophical questing has taken him to China and North Africa in recent years (for "The Last Emperor" and "The Sheltering Sky"), has filmed his latest in the holy lands of Nepal, Bhutan and Seattle. And in telling his based-on-real-lifestory—about a blond 9-year-old who is suspected of being a reincarnated lama—and juxtaposing it with an epic recounting of the life of Prince Siddhartha—who will become the Buddha—Bertolucci reverses the tired conventions about ancient religions and religious life and in the process evokes a very contemporary yearning for spirituality.

That he cannot sustain the tone of serene momentum that opens the film is perhaps inevitable; once the seduction of the viewer is accomplished there's a certain leveling-off of passion. But the beginning of "Little Buddha" has moments so full of magic it's surprising how much of it is accomplished through simple humor. The Buddhist temple in Bhutan, where the film opens, is not the forbidding place of popular imagination. It is a center of learning, of warmth and of children instructed by Lama Norbu (Ying Ruocheng), who invites questions and makes jokes. His beatific demeanor changes only after he gets a letter saying that the reincarnated spirit of his late teacher, Lama Norje, has been located. In Seattle.

"Lama Norje had a great sense of humor," says Kenpo Tensin (Sogyal Rinpoche), one of the jolly monks who have determined that blond, Gameboy-playing Jesse Conrad (Alex Wiesendanger) has been chosen by Norje for his reappearance. Jesse likes the idea, likes the gentle Lama Norbu, and gives signs that he may actually be Lama Norje. But it's no joke to his parents (Bridget Fonda and Chris Isaak), who have made no provision in their yuppie life-plan for a Buddhist invasion.

Where "Little Buddha" falters, and it does, lies in the casting. As Jesse's father Dean, who takes Jesse to Bhutan, Isaak has the unformed face and personality to make him truly American, and truly flat. Likewise Reeves, whose lighter-than-air screen presence is appropriate for the young, naive Prince Siddhartha, but who in the end doesn't provide anything very substantial. The ancient Indian sequences are full of miracles, outlandish visuals and ornate religion, but the modern world defines the film's spiritual impact. Bertolucci says that godhead isn't about myth and trappings, but about yearning—as defined by the faith of monks, or perhaps the unfilled need of secular Americans. "Little Buddha," in its gentle way, probes that cavity.

SIGHT AND SOUND, 6/94, p. 53, Phillip Strick

A telegram arrives for Lama Norbu at the Paro Monastery in the Himalayan kingdom of Bhutan. Although in failing health, he sets out immediately for Seattle, where Dean and Lisa Conrad are disconcerted to learn from him that their young son Jesse may be the reincarnation of Lama Dorje, one of the Monastery's most respected teachers, who died in Seattle nine years ago. In order to confirm this, Jesse would have to travel to Bhutan. As the Conrads know nothing about Buddhism, Norbu introduces them to the story of Siddhârtha, born 2,500 years ago in Kapilavastu (Nepal) to King Suddhodhana and his wife Mâyâ. After a miraculous birth, the future Buddha was fiercely protected by his father until, insisting on seeing the world, he discovered the existence of suffering and death. Promptly abandoning his former indolence, he adopted a life of self-deprivation, with five Ascetic disciples.

Shaken by the news of the death of a business partner, Dean Conrad decides that he should take time off to reassess his future while accompanying Jesse to Bhutan. Another possible candidate for Lama Dorje's reincarnation has been identified in Kathmandu, and Norbu leaves Seattle with Dean and Jesse. During the journey, he tells how, after six years as an Ascetic, the emaciated Siddhârtha recognised that the path to enlightenment lay not in austerity but in meditation. At the *stupa* (temple) at Bodnath, Jesse befriends Raju, the boy acrobat Norbu has been sent to approve, who joins them to find a third candidate, Gita, a girl who lives near the banyan tree in Bodh-Gayâ (Bihar, India) where Siddhârtha's titanic struggle with Mâra, the Lord of Darkness, took place. At the base of the tree, the three children relive the spectacular events that transformed Siddhârtha into the Buddha.

Returning to the Paro Monastery with his three acolytes, Lama Norbu awaits the decision of the Oracle as to which is the true reincarnation of Lama Dorje. The verdict is that the reincarnation is in all three of them, and they are prepared for a ceremony of acceptance and enthronement. His work accomplished, Norbu placidly resigns himself to death, reappearing to the children after the ceremony with final words of wisdom. When they return home, they take Norbu's ashes with them; on a boat with Dean and the pregnant Lisa, Jesse places his share of the ashes close to the shores of Seattle.

Continuing the symmetry of me *The Last Emperor* and *The Sheltering Sky*, Bertolucci completes his oriental trilogy with another tale of innocents abroad. While it will doubtless come as no surprise to committed Buddhists, the journeys of Pu Yi and the ill-fated Moresbys from lives of useless luxury to the informative extremes of destitution turn out closely to parallel the path taken by Siddhârtha, whose serene childhood—lotus flowers sprouting at every footfall—left him ill-prepared for the inevitabilities of adulthood.

Conveniently, Bertolucci's own preference for privation, venturing where no camera has gone before in his attempts to evade Western consumerism, echoes the same learning process, the need for reassurance growing more acute with the advancing years. Borrowing from Paul Bowles, he concluded *The Sheltering Sky* (where survival proved more valuable than death) on a note of gloomy hope, recommending that we savour every minute of the final countdown. With *Little Buddha*, in effect a post-countdown story of the after-life, he puts his faith in recycled humanity, with rebirth on the agenda as a comforting, if necessarily unproven, prospect. In his final images, which for a moment seem set to repeat the miraculous (and confirming) instant when Siddhârtha's bowl flows *against* the current, he offers reincarnation like a kind of plague dust, destined to convert us all to the living dead.

In aiming his film at a young audience, on the pretext that we are all like children when learning about Buddha (who also achieved wisdom through innocence), Bertolucci creates an inevitable tension. The fear of death can easily be lifted by the promise of resurrection, but it's the promise that needs substantiating. Up to a point, the world of an adult is authority enough, but beyond that, attainment of enlightenment by the Four Noble Truths and the Eightfold Path, the essentials of Buddhism, involves painfully complex, and decidedly non-filmic, considerations. Avoiding complication, Bertolucci has had to resort to simple mythology, staging a pantomime that will excite curiosity but provides no answers. Even so, his self-denial only goes so far; he underpins the splendid melodrama of Siddhârtha with a strange, fragmentary story of his own (plus recognisable grace-notes from Wurlitzer and Peploe) which almost reverses the riches-to-rags legend by taking average all-American boy Jesse on the adventure of a lifetime to be hailed as a near-deity on the other side of the world. This Spielbergian premise certainly achieves the right flavour for juvenile audiences, but at the same time it introduces ingredients for which Buddhism seems more placebo than panacea.

Were it not for the excellent humour with which Lama Norbu and his companion monks conduct their quest, as if fully aware of its more unlikely aspects, the whole exercise would seem irredeemably farcical. Instead, the general tone of incongruity as the small flock of monks tours the museums and monorails of Seattle, sitting on the floor instead of the furniture, acquires a fantastical charm of its own. More dissonant, as a result, is the Conrad family, occupying a house of breathtaking simplicity which sprouts from the ground in a jolt of computerised conjury to survey the entire city like a watch-tower of ominously tinted glass. The Conrads are clearly suspicious of the Tibetans, yet leave their son alone with them for hours, and although the family's financial future seems bound up with the unseen partner, whose death leaves Dean curiously distraught, it is Jesse's mother who stays in Seattle while the boy and his father go to the Himalayas.

Whole chapters of the Conrad story, with its hints of the same incestuous triangle as *La Luna*, seem to have been denied us, leaving unexplained the hovering camera over Dean as he stares suicidally at a motorway or later the intense scrutiny with which he studies Norbu's demise, as if awaiting a major revelation. Played by Chris Isaak in a state of high anxiety, by contrast with Bridget Fonda's immaculate poise as his wife, his concluding appearance as castaway in the Seattle bay seems to leave Buddhism very much at sea. This despite the orange sunset (as we may expect from Storaro, the whole film is a dialogue of blues and oranges) and the implied correlation between Norbu's ashes and Lisa's pregnancy.

The other paradox of *Little Buddha* is, of course, its own magnificence. Where the eponymous nontheist, reasonably enough after six years as a ascetic, opted for moderation in all things,

Bertolucci and Storaro provide panoplies of costume, landscape and construction that are seldom less than sumptuous. The palace home of Siddhârtha is lavish in the crowds and colours of a children's fable, and even when the prince discards the excesses of ignorance and settles for the wilderness, the majesty of the riverside and the gleeful intrusion of special effects lends his mental struggle an overwhelming grandeur. With frequent sky-high shots of patterns and movements, Bertolucci makes spectacle a theme in its own right, celebrated interminably by Sakamoto's drifting score, at first a marvel of foreboding, later a shapeless package of crescendos. As Siddhârtha, Keanu Reeves confronts himself with an affable authority; for a refreshing change, this is a philosophical hero who only has to sit and think, and whether or not his example offers any kind of inspiration, it is unarguably fascinating to watch.

TIME, 6/6/94, p. 66, Richard Corliss

Any old hack can direct movies that make you cry. It's a simple matter of putting onscreen some wrenchingly sentimental image (sad-eyed dog with broken leg, widow on deathbed, noble peasant gunned down by soldiers) while a dozen violins tremble on the sound track. A filmmaker's real challenge is to create what German director Wim Wenders has called "emotion pictures": films that move you in a fresh way, with images that speak to the intelligent heart. Bernardo Bertolucci makes emotion pictures. He illustrates complex issues with indelible, seductive, ravishing images. And in his 12th film, *Little Buddha*, the Italian director has created his clearest statement of what it means to see things—literally see them—his unique way.

Little Buddha hopscotches the world from the kingdom of Bhutan to Seattle, Washington, and leapfrogs millenniums from the Buddha's birth in 2500 B.C. to today. In Bhutan a Tibetan monk named Lama Norbu (Ying Ruocheng) hears that an American boy, Jesse Conrad (Alex Wiesendanger), may be the reincarnation of an important lama. Incredulous at first Jesse's parents (Chris Isaak and Bridget Fonda) are sufficiently impressed by Lama Norbu's otherworldly sweetness that they allow the boy to keep company with him, and eventually to journey to Bhutan with his father and two other candidates for the exalted position of reincarnated holy man.

This could turn into a story of Moonie-like brainwashing or, at least, a Spielbergian audition for spiritual star quality. But Bertolucci is remarkably open-minded; he is eager to entertain and then to accept the beliefs and rhythms of another, older culture. The film's loveliest sections are those that concern the life of Siddhartha the Indian prince who renounced worldly pleasures and religious extremism to find the Middle Way of Buddhist truth. Siddhartha is played with improbable persuasiveness by Keanu Reeves, another of Bertolucci's eccentric choices in *Little Buddha* that pay off.

Bertolucci has always been less interested in telling a predictably coherent story than in evoking strong feelings. His political epics (*The Conformist, The Last Emperor*) are really interior melodramas about small people overwhelmed by sweeping events; his intimate studies of sexual desperation (*Last Tango in Paris, The Sheltering Sky*) are really about the places—Paris apartments or the depths of the Sahara—where troubled people get lost. *Little Buddha* is a story of quite small people, three modern kids, who rise to great spiritual demands, and of Jesse's parents, who come to terms with truths that are much greater than their problems.

After 30 years of making passionately skeptical movies, Bertolucci has made a film of the most sophisticated simplicity. His triumph is to make you see the Buddhist world through his eyes. It shines like innocence reincarnated.

VILLAGE VOICE, 5/31/94, p. 58, Georgia Brown

Bernardo Bertolucci begins his gentle *Little Buddha* with an illustrated parable. A clever goat talks a priest out of slitting his throat by reminding him of the implications of reincarnation; their positions could be reversed one day. When the old teacher presenting the story, Lama Norbu (Ying Ruocheng), asks his class what the moral is, the children chant in unison, "No living creature should be sacrificed."

Perhaps this is Bertolucci's reply to Mao's warning about egg breaking. At any rate, it seems that after a lifelong teetering between Freud and Marx—the family and the party, as *Before the Revolution* put it—Bertolucci may be revising the equation once more. As the refreshingly unguarded Bertolucci told *Sight and Sound*: "Buddhism saved me from a big depression at a time when I had been deprived of the right to dream of utopias after the fall of the Wall." Not a very sexy position, that. "Maybe I'm insane, but I had this desire to be simple and childlike," he told *The Hollywood Reporter*. This spring, *Little Buddha* was greeted in Rome and Paris with critical sneers.

It may do better here. I hope so. As a children's story, the film is obviously directed to the childlike West, and specifically to the U.S. Even an American family, *Little Buddha* implies, can harbor highly evolved beings. It's *E.T.* told alternately in the manner of Antonioni and Michael Powell. The Antonioni part takes place not in Ravenna or Milan but in Seattle; the Powell, or Korda-produced, sections in ancient India (actually Nepal and Bhutan).

A Seattle nine-year-old, Jesse Konrad (Alex Wiesendanger), is discovered by a local Tibetan monk (played by the revered Sogyal Rinpoche, author of *The Tibetan Book of Living and Dying*) who believes him to be a *tulku*—the incarnation of a deceased Lama. The monk writes to Lama Norbu, living in exile in Bhutan, saying that the dead lama appeared in a dream, wearing jeans and pointing to a vacant lot. (A pricey property, it has a view of the sound and the space needle.) Sometime later the site was built on and a young couple with a son moved in. The jovial Seattle monk approaches Mrs. Konrad (Bridget Fonda), a math teacher, and paves the way for a visit from Lama Norbu. The Konrads, a "nice" but opaque couple, are hardly thrilled. "Where's our little reincarnation today?" asks Dad (Chris Isaak).

Vittorio Storaro shoots Seattle as though the city's cloud cover is a state of mind. It's as if the city is already in mourning for its own Nirvana's son. Visual emphasis is not on mountains and water but on cars and freeways. Except for a surreal cleanliness, this could be anywhere in the greater U.S. The Konrads' house, a sleek boxy structure decorated in minimalist style, resembles a dental health clinic, and Mom and Dad drift around inside as if on novocaine. Taking a seat on the white carpet, the visiting monks admire the "emptiness." Having presented Jesse with a picture book called Little Buddha, the red-robed visitors take their leave.

Now the movie's parallel plot kicks in: the story of Siddhartha Gautama as read to a child. (The prince is played by a beatific Keanu Reeves. Bertolucci: "I wanted a face just like a photo I'd seen of Satyajit Ray at 21.") Following a simple, straightforward design, writers Mark Peploe and (practicing Buddhist) Rudy Wurlitzer alternate the story of Jesse's candidacy with that of Siddhartha's birth, his decision to leave his father's court, and certain adventures on the path to enlightenment. Unlike the austere, underpopulated Seattle sections (asphalt blues and grays, bleached skys), the India and Bhutan scenes are loaded with swirling human activity and vibrant, saturated color (whole spectrums of reds and yellows). Storaro filmed the Seattle scenes in 35mm, the Indian in 65mm. The implication, I take it, is that in the 2500 years since Buddha, humans have suffered radical sensory deprivation as well as a diminution in consciousness.

When Jesse's dad confronts a friend's suicide, his attitude toward Tibetan lamas changes and he decides to accompany Jesse to Bhutan. "Think of it as a career opportunity," Dad says to Mom. Because of *her* career, Mom can't leave and feels thwarted: "He's never been away from me." To a degree, each of the Konrads faces the pain of leaving the womb. Perversely, however, Bertolucci refuses to give the Konrads, including Jesse, much specificity; they're almost generic.

In Bhutan, a nominal narrative tension is created by the discovery that Jesse has two rivals for the lama's seat—a cute street urchin as well as a snobbish Indian girl with her very own Bo tree. Which one will the fountain bless?

As far as the movie's attitude toward reincarnation goes, it seems a quite practical one. Boiled down, reverence for the living is its own justification. Similarly, the practice of choosing *tulku* appears to be self-fulfilling in that the chosen almost invariably will live up to the call. More radically, the film implies that all children ought to be nurtured as *tulku* since they come into the world special beings with unique qualities. Who wouldn't respond to such respectful treatment?

Bertolucci the seeker has always been viewed as torn between the comfortable world he was born into and various ideologies. In the early years, the poles tended to be bourgeois and revolutionary, traitor and partisan. More recently, it's easy to see his affinity with Pu Yi, China's last emperor, thrust into a treacherous world outside the imperial gates, or, on a more intimate scale, with Port and Kit Moresby confronting a vastly foreign culture in *The Sheltering Sky*. Siddhartha and little Jesse too are heroes who leave the sheltered world, the illusion of family, to enter the larger world of suffering and death.

But there's another Bertolucci split brought up by *Little Buddha*: the one between Hollywood palaces and lowly European art houses. In the '60s, when attention was focused on the latter, the choice was easy. But art films long ago lost cachet, and Bertolucci has more and more, perhaps unintentionally, devised his own middle way, making art house extravaganzas—sumptuous epics that are still too esoteric, too "dry," to compete commercially with the Hollywood product, Whether finding himself in this limbo disturbs him or not hasn't been clear.

Now, though, Bertolucci is being very candid about an anxiety he's been feeling. In the *Sight and Sound* interview he almost sounds in crisis: "I want desperately to communicate. I don't want to pursue a monologue, I want to have an exchange ... But I demand so much from this relationship with the audience, I want it so badly and am so nervous about it, and afraid that I won't get it, that I prefer to stay in a safe zone, let's say, in the Godard galaxy." He describes an affinity with two kinds of cinema as if it's an affliction: On the one hand he appreciates an experimental film by an Italian, Tonino Di Bernardi; on the other, he's enthusiastic about *Close Encounters of the Third Kind*. And obviously there's embarrassment about loving the latter. "I suspect that underneath I was always like this without being able to express it, because in the '60s I would have been considered a traitor."

So. Does *Little Buddha* have Spielberg on the brain? As in *E.T.*, an ordinary boy in an ordinary family is visited by an evolved being from a benign, far more advanced world; both films end with the kid's sadder, wiser goodbye to a beloved mentor. But fortunately Bertolucci can't make a Spielberg movie any more than, back in the '60s, he could make a Godard or Rossellini movie. The most obvious difference is that Spielberg compulsively milks audience emotion, whereas Bertolucci, despite those ravishing surfaces and grand baroque flourishes, tends to stay cool, almost passive, even while depicting powerful events. It's as if he's embarrassed by feeling, or by requiring it of others.

Still and all, it is emotion—a sort of ecstatic serenity—that carries *Little Buddha*. The informal spirituality of the monks, and particularly the tenderness of Lama Norbu, are immensely seductive. The final scenes in Bhutan show a love of death that is anything but morbid. The epilogue back in Seattle glows with an eerie, other-worldly light. This certainly is the most quietly moving film Bertolucci has made—also the strangest.

Also reviewed in:
NEW REPUBLIC, 6/13/94, p. 32, Stanley Kauffmann
NEW YORK TIMES, 5/25/94, p. C13, Janet Maslin
NEW YORKER, 5/30/94, p. 97, Anthony Lane
VARIETY , 12/13/93, p. 37, Todd McCarthy
WASHINGTON POST, 5/25/94, p. C1, Desson Howe
WASHINGTON POST, 5/27/94, Weekend/p. 42, Joe Brown

LITTLE GIANTS

A Warner Bros. release of an Amblin Entertainment production. *Executive Producer:* Walter F. Parkes and Gerald R. Molen. *Producer:* Arne L. Schmidt. *Director:* Duwayne Dunham. *Screenplay:* James Ferguson, Robert Shallcross, Tommy Swerdlow, and Michael Goldberg. *Based on a story by:* James Ferguson and Robert Shallcross. *Director of Photography:* Janusz Kaminski. *Editor:* Donn Cambern. *Music:* John Debney. *Sound:* J. Paul Huntsman. *Production Designer:* Bill Kenny. *Costumes:* April Ferry. *Running time:* 106 minutes. *MPAA Rating:* PG.

CAST: Rich Moranis (Danny O'Shea); Ed O'Neill (Kevin O'Shea); John Madden (Himself); Shawna Waldron (Becky O'Shea); Mary Ellen Trainor (Karen O'Shea); Matheuw McCurley (Nubie); Susanna Thompson (Patty Floyd); Brian Haley (Mike Hammersmith); Sam Horrigan (Spike Hammersmith); Todd Bosley (Jake "Ther Berminator" Berman); Devon Sawa (Junior).

LOS ANGELES TIMES, 10/14/94, Calendar/p. 6, Kevin Thomas

"Little Giants" happily arrives just as football season goes into high gear to cheer audiences of all ages. This comedy about a small Ohio town getting a chance to field a Pop Warner junior team is genuinely funny, more so than you might expect, because it is also smarter than many of its ilk. Clearly a great deal of care and thought has gone into making special a picture that could so easily have been routine family fare.

Not surprisingly, the mayor of idyllic Urbania, Ohio, chooses the local football hero, Kevin O'Shea (Ed O'Neill), to coach the team. A car dealer with "Heisman" on his license plate, Kevin has his name emblazoned on the town water tower, the "Welcome to Urbania" billboard and even has a hamburger named after him at the Coffee Cup Cafe (where a hearty group of older men hang out and become the film's kibitzers). A big, loud husky guy, he has a gentle, nebbishy younger brother Danny (Rick Moranis), who has a teenage daughter, Becky (Shawna Waldron), who takes after her uncle to the extent that she's the town's best football player. Danny, a gas station proprietor and single father, has lived his entire life in Kevin's formidable shadow.

Push comes to shove at last when Kevin, in a burst of male chauvinism, rejects Becky for his team—along with a bunch of boys whose liabilities are lots more obvious. That does it for Danny, who assembles the misfits, with Becky as the team star, to compete with Kevin's lineup for the chance to represent Urbania. Based on his own negative childhood experience, Danny believes all kids should get a chance to play football. Of course, the film is about winning, the healthiness of honest competition, but it's above all about getting a chance to play in the first place.

The film's shrewd script is a collaboration between first-timers James Ferguson and Robert Shallcross, Chicago ad execs whose Super Bowl commercial centering on Pop Warner football prompted a call from Steven Spielberg's Amblin Entertainment, and Tommy Swerdlow and Michael Goldberg, who did such a good job with last year's "Cool Runnings." There's equally knowing direction from Duwayne Dunham, who made a nifty feature debut himself last year with Disney's "Homeward Bound: The Incredible Journey."

Since the filmmakers realize full well they're spinning a classic underdog tale whose outcome is not exactly impossible to predict, they concentrate on characterization as well as humor. In this light, Moranis' Danny is pivotal, the little guy who in sticking to his guns effects changes not only within himself but also his overbearing brother and his daughter, a budding beauty experiencing the onset of puberty.

Wisely, Kevin is not presented as an all-out heavy, just as someone reflexively used to getting his way but who's also capable of humor and reflection. O'Neill, a star of TV's "Married ... With Children," overdue for a big-screen breakthrough, is an actor of wit and nuance as well as imposing physical presence.

A well-made film actually shot largely up the coast in Arroyo Grande (by "Schindler's List's" Oscar-winning Janusz Kaminski), "Little Giants" reveals its subtlety and awareness in an opening sequence introducing Kevin and Danny as youngsters. All the children on view are white, but when the picture moves to the present we discover a modest rainbow coalition among the aspiring peewee leaguers.

NEW YORK POST, 10/14/94, p. 45, Michael Medved

After churning out successful movies about Little League baseball (the "Bad News Bears" trilogy) and recent epics about peewee hockey ("The Mighty Ducks" I & II), it was only a matter of time before Hollywood turned its attention to kiddie football.

While "Little Giants" may have been inevitable, it didn't have to be so appallingly predictable, so shamelessly derivative. Every single element of the script (by four credited writers) feels stale and secondhand. There's the multi-cultural group of underdog kids who somehow discover the courage to stand up against arrogant opponents.

There's the lost, lonely coach who finds redemption by working with these spunky challengers. There's even a flatulent fat kid (borrowed directly from "The Mighty Ducks") and an attractive tomboy who represents the misfit team's secret weapon (straight from "The Bad News Bears").

To be fair, there's also one new twist: a silly brother-against-brother struggle that sets up the inevitable climactic game. Ed O'Neill (of TV's "Married ... With Children") plays a local football hero and former Heisman trophy winner who coaches the local Pop Warner football team in his

Ohio town and ruthlessly eliminates the less talented players—including his own niece (played by likable newcomer Shawna Waldron).

The girl's father, gas station owner and single parent Rick Moranis, feels a natural kinship with the rejected players and agrees to organize them into a team that will challenge his brother's over-confident all-stars.

Director Duwayne Dunham, who previously created the delightful family adventure "Homeward Bound: The Incredible Journey," does the best he can with the tired material and the big game sequence comes to life with surprising energy and emotion.

Not even the gifted Mr. Dunham, however, can make the California locations look anything like rural Ohio. (Why does Hollywood insist on setting these stories in the Midwest? Is there the assumption that we will only accept such corn if it unfolds in an area where the crop is actually grown?)

Despite its Middle-American, squeaky-clean pretensions, the movie offers several surprises some parents may find offensive. The constant resort to rude language by both grownups and kids, and frequent slapstick gags involving private parts, are hardly necessary in a movie aimed so squarely" at 7-year-olds. There's also a dumb, time-consuming sub-plot about a developing romance, with detailed talk of deep kissing, between the team's male and female stars.

These kids are supposed to be just 10 or 11 years old: Do we really need so much attention to their budding sex life?

Whatever the reservations of parents, children can still have a reasonably good time with this picture—especially since the climactic athletes contest (following a brief "inspirational appearance" by John Madden and some real-life NFL stars) is so nicely staged.

Nevertheless, it's surprising to see that this silly project emerged from Steven Spielberg's celebrated Amblin Entertainment. Of course, no one expects a movie about peewee football to compare to "Schindler's List," but I'm not even sure that "Little Giants" can play on the same field as "The Flintstones."

NEWSDAY, 10/14/94, Part II/p. B7, John Anderson

Football is forever, apparently, as are bad sports, overly competitive parents chewing up the sidelines, and pretty girls in dirty jerseys who suddenly discover boys. And while we're contemplating the verities, Ed O'Neill is always going to be cast as Al Bundy and Rick Moranis a good-natured nebbish.

But while all these things may be true, "Little Giants," a feminist, anti-sports movie masquerading as sports movie, proves it's all a question of degrees—a game of inches, separating the truly bad sports movie from the decent one, and the stock characters from the customized.

Moranis, for instance, who plays tow-truck-driving single parent Danny O'Shea, isn't quite the superdweeb he was in "Honey I Shrunk the Kids," although both characters would certainly be the last ones picked for football. And Danny *was* the last one picked. In fact he wasn't picked at all, and it was his own brother, Kevin (O'Neill) doing the picking. This kind of stuck in his craw, the way Kevin is stuck on himself.

It's easy to see why. Football legend and Heisman winner Kevin O'Shea's name is on the Urbania, Ohio, watertower, on the local park, on signs leading into town and on a burger at the local cafe, and it's Kevin who coaches the local Pee-Wee football players. When it comes time for the town to field a Pop Warner team—one team per town is the rule—Kevin is the only candidate. On purely sexist grounds, he doesn't pick his own niece, Danny's daughter Becky (Shawna Waldron), who's known as the Icebox and is the best player Kevin's got. So the athletically challenged Danny fields his own squad.

Not since Spanky and Alfalfa played Butch and Woim has there been such a motley assortment of players and equipment on one field. An ethnically diverse and physically distressed group of wheezers, whiners and wackos—40-pound Todd Bosley as Jake (The Berminator) Berman is particularly droll—the Little Giants wouldn't stand a chance of finding the field much less winning, but this isn't the real world. Plus, they do have the Icebox, and Junior (Devon Sawa), who throws passes and catches Becky's eye, and Nubie (Matthew McCurley), the small blond brainiac who devises plays with names like "The Annexation of Puerto Rico."

Kevin, on the other hand, has Spike (Sam Horrigan), a 10-year-old serial killer-to-be. "I've been cultivating him," says his dad, Mike (Brian Haley). It's training like this that makes pit bulls lethal.

Two things separate "Little Giants" from, let's say, "D2," the Mighty Ducks film. One is a lunatic sense of comedy, a flair for the totally inappropriate and incongruous. The other is Becky. Torn between being a cheerleader and a player, she could be a real inspiration for 10- and 11-year-old girls, who are in that crisis stage of self-confidence. She's as good or better than any of the boys, she stands up for herself, and she's no pre-adolescent caricature. "Little Giants" may play out like every other sports movie, with heroic music and an unlikely ending, but it does have the Icebox, and she's cool.

Also reviewed in:
CHICAGO TRIBUNE, 10/14/94, Friday, p. L, John Petrakis
NEW YORK TIMES, 10/14/94, p. C12, Stephen Holden
VARIETY, 10/17-23/94, p. 44, Joe Leydon
WASHINGTON POST, 10/17/94, p. B4, Hal Hinson

LITTLE RASCALS, THE

A Universal Pictures and King World release. *Executive Producer:* Gerald R. Molen, Deborah Jelin Newmyer, and Roger King. *Producer:* Michael King and Bill Oakes. *Director:* Penelope Spheeris. *Screenplay:* Paul Guay, Stephen Mazur, and Penelope Spheeris. *Story*: Penelope Spheeris, Robert Wolterstorff, Mike Scott, Paul Guay, and Stephen Mazur. *Director of Photography:* Richard Bowen. *Editor:* Ross Albert. *Music:* William Ross. *Music Editor:* Steve McCroskey. *Choreographer:* Nancy Gregory. *Sound:* Susumu Tokunow and (music) John Richards. *Sound Editor:* Richard L. Anderson and David Whittaker. *Casting:* Judy Taylor and Lynda Gordon. *Production Designer:* Larry Fulton. *Art Director:* Gae Buckley. *Set Designer:* Richard Yanez. *Set Decorator:* Linda Spheeris. *Special Effects:* Rick Zarro, Ron Zarro, Rick Hill, Richard M. Bisetti, Michael Roundy, Paul Sabourin, and George Zamora. *Costumes:* Jami Burrows. *Make-up:* James Lee McCoy. *Stunt Coordinator:* Shane Dixon. *Running time:* 80 minutes. *MPAA Rating:* PG.

CAST: Travis Tedford (Spanky); Bug Hall (Alfalfa); Brittany Ashton Holmes (Darla); Kevin Jamal Woods (Stymie); Zachary Mabry (Porky); Ross Elliot Bagley (Buckwheat); Sam Saletta (Butch); Blake Jeremy Collins (Woim); Blake McIver Ewing (Waldo); Jordan Warkol (Froggy); Courtland Mead (Uh-Huh); Juliette Brewer (Mary Ann); Heather Karasek (Jane); Petey (Himself); Elmer (Himself); Mel Brooks (Mr. Welling); Whoopi Goldberg (Buckwheat's Mom); Daryl Hannah (Miss Crabtree); Reba McEntire (A.J. Ferguson); Ashley Olsen and Mary-Kate Olsen (Twins); Raven-Symone (Stymie's Girlfriend); Lea Thompson (Ms. Roberts); Donald Trump (Waldo's Dad); George Wendt (Lumberyard Clerk); Dan Carton (Alfalfa's Dad); Eric "Sparky" Edwards (Spanky's Dad); John Ashker (Chauffeur); Charles Noland and John Wesley (Amish Men); Alexandra Monroe King and Zoë Oakes (Darla's Friends); John Ashker and Michael Matzdorff (Race Announcers); Gary Johnson (Race Official).

LOS ANGELES TIMES, 8/5/94, Calendar/p. 1, Kevin Thomas

Between 1922 and 1944 producer Hal Roach turned out countless "Our Gang" comedies, featuring the antics of a beloved bunch of youngsters engaged in everyday exploits that were as endearing as they were hilarious. The series received new life with the advent of TV, where they were shown as "The Little Rascals" since MGM owned the rights to the title "Our Gang."

"The Little Rascals" has now become a stylistically venturesome but uneven new film by Penelope Spheeris, who brought "The Beverly Hillbillies" to the big screen with a successful blend of sophistication and affection. She brings those same qualities to this film, but it isn't as funny as it ought to be. Even so, it is unmistakably the work of a distinctive filmmaker whose work is always worthy of attention and rewarding in one aspect or another.

In the opening shot, which shows Alfalfa (Bug Hall) sitting on the front steps of a modest white clapboard cottage of the early '20s, you detect a TV antenna on the roof, Surely, an oversight, but no: This "Little Rascals takes place in the present. What Spheeris has done is to dress her Gang in more or less vintage attire and film largely but not slavishly in older L.A. neighborhoods. This tactic really pays off, and is the film's key strength, which is to evoke the past in such a way as to suggest an innocence lost, for those locales have faded surely from the time when Roach might well have used them himself.

The plot line is rightly simple. The boys have formed their "He-Man Woman Haters Club" just as the sweet-natured Alfalfa has developed a crush on pretty little Darla (Brittany Ashton Holmes). From Alfalfa's conflicting loyalties comes a string of skirmishes, misunderstandings and adventures culminating in a lively go-cart race.

The problem with "The Little Rascals" is one of content rather than form. What the film needs is lots more classic slapstick, sight gags and pranks and lots less adult repartée. We need more chances to laugh out loud, as when Alfalfa and his best pal Spanky (Travis Tedford) are forced to disguise themselves as ballerinas and then proceed to wreak havoc on a little girls' "Nutcracker Suite" recital. Too much of the film is too reminiscent of the kiddie faux-gangster movie "Bugsy Malone," which had the strength of being entirely a period piece. Since Spheeris' film is set, more or less, in the real world, it's creepy when Alfalfa and Darla, 9 and 5, respectively, carry on like romantic teen-agers. But then even Shirley Temple's vintage impersonation of Mae West probably wouldn't play as innocently as it did 60 years ago.

On the plus side are the film's many surprise cameos by adult celebrities (most of which are amusing), its great look, its terrific pacing and its punchy eclectic soundtrack. Many of the film's 13 key Rascals are as appealing as Hall, and as Buckwheat, Ross Elliott Bagley reveals an especially live-wire personality. "The Little Rascals" is such an emphatically well-shaped, well-crafted picture that you wish you could have enjoyed it more than you did.

NEW YORK POST, 8/5/94, p. 42, Michael Medved

As the movie opens, the sound track pumps out a richly orchestrated version of the old "Little Rascals" theme song (officially known as "The Good Old Days"), and this nostalgic (and endlessly repeated) music provides one of the few sources of warmth in a misguided and joyless project.

The concept and characters originated in 1922 with movie pioneer Hal Roach, resulting in 221 "Our Gang" comedies over the next 22 years. (They were ultimately released under the "Little Rascals" title for TV.)

Director/co-writer Penelope Spheeris ("Wayne's World," "Beverly Hillbillies") faced an obvious and fundamental dilemma in adapting such venerable material for the big screen: She and her four co-writers could either treat the story as a period piece, complete with 1930s sets and costumes, or else try to update everything and bring Our Gang into today's world.

Instead of facing this decision honestly, the filmmakers try a dim-witted compromise: The setting has been updated, complete with shots of today's Los Angeles skyline and references to Milli Vanilli. But the characters remain firmly rooted in the Depression era, wearing beanies and bow ties and expressing 60-year-old attitudes.

As a result, we're left with a collection of unquestionably cute kids (between the ages of 4 and 9) who mug for the camera and remember their lines, but seem lost in the middle of absolutely nowhere.

The plot features the members of the "He-Man Woman Haters Club," led by president Spanky McFarland (Travis Tedford), trying to rescue lovesick Alfalfa (Bug Hall) from his infatuation with the sweet-faced Darla (Brittany Ashton Holmes).

The macho munchkins want to bring Alfalfa back to the fold because his driving skills are needed for their big go-cart race against neighborhood bullies Butch and Woim (Sam Saletta and Blake Jeremy Collins) and spoiled rich kid Waldo (Blake McIver Ewing).

Adults appear in cameo roles only, but some of those walk-ons provide the movie's best laughs—such as the moment when we discover that bratty Waldo's father is Donald Trump, or that Buckwheat's loving mom is none other than Whoopi Goldberg.

Some of the other grown-ups fare less well: for instance Reba McEntire (still recovering from her equally embarrassing bit part in "North") greets Alfalfa at the go-cart race by asking, "Is that a cowlick, or are you just glad to see me?"

Such tastelessness turns up repeatedly—and pointlessly—in a movie whose entire selling point is sweetness and innocence.

There's a long scene with Spanky and Alfalfa in drag, participating in a girl's ballet class; perhaps this dance-a-mile-in-my-tutu bit is supposed to set up the politically correct resolution of the plot, in which the He-Man Woman Haters Club learns to accept female members far more cheerfully than real-life male bastions such as The Citadel.

The movie's key lines occur at the very center of the story, as Alfalfa turns to Spanky and emphatically declares, "I'm bored!" He surely speaks for many in the audience—especially youngsters, who won't even have fond memories of the old "Little Rascals" to help keep them interested.

NEWSDAY, 8/5/94, Part II/p. B2, John Anderson

When human landmark Hal Roach produced the original, silent Our Gang comedies back in the early '20s, the idea was "kids being kids." That he succeeded rather gloriously over the next couple of decades was what made the series the cultural icon it is. Years later, though, after he and others had failed on numerous occasions to resurrect the series, Roach wrote off his original success to some kind of genetic blip: The right kind of kids, he said, just weren't around anymore.

Well, if anything is apparent from "The Little Rascals"—the spanky-new, Penelope Spheeris-directed amalgamation of the classic series—it's that the right kind of adults aren't around anymore.

Would it be an irrelevant cheap shot to point out that Spheeris, who made the "Wayne's World" movies and "The Beverly Hillbillies" for a 5-year-old mentality, is now actually directing 5-year-olds? No, it's relevant.

The paradox of the Roach series, as directed by the likes of Robert F. McGowan and Gus Meins, was that the cast—George (Spanky) McFarland, Carl (Alfalfa) Switzer, Darla Hood, Stymie Beard—always came across like real kids, while performing like professionals. The paradox of Spheeris' cast, a fatally appealing group of children, is that they're less polished actors, but their stiffness also makes them seem less sincere.

As does the material. With almost as many writers as Rascals, Spheeris' film is short—not just in mean height, but in originality and taste. When the members of the He-Man Woman Haters Club, led by Spanky (Travis Tedford), sabotage a lunch date between Darla (Brittany Ashford Holmes) and the quisling Alfalfa (Bug Hall), they sprinkle old cat litter in the couple's sandwiches. When the stage-bound Alfalfa, who sings worse here than he ever did, is slipped a soap solution by his romantic rival Waldo (Blake McIver Ewing), the bubbles don't just pop out of his mouth, they escape from his pants. Petey the dog helps extinguish a clubhouse fire by lifting his leg. And when Darla gives Alfalfa a kiss, his famous cowlick pops up in a phallic salute.

Dressed like the originals in Depression-era garb, the new Rascals never-the-less live in contemporary Los Angeles, which seems not only cruel but contrary: Unlike the real-kid originals, how can such transplanted characters seem anything but cartoonish?

Spheeris also fills in the gap between borrowed plotlines with some Enlightened New Age sloganeering. "I'm a sensitive male," Alfalfa tells a doubting Darla. "I'm in touch with my feminine side." Waldo is not just a rich snob but a male chauvinist. Spanky, dressed in a tutu—he and Alfalfa having infiltrated the ballet school recital, and being pursued by Butch and Woim (Sam Saletta and Blake Jeremy Collins)—is denied sanctuary at a local Boys Club. Thankfully, though, the complaint the girls have about the boys, and the boys have about the girls, is the same: "They smell weird!"

While the adults involved act like idiots, the kids are all attractive little performers, who create many genuinely funny moments. Five-year-old Travis Tedford grimaces a a bit, but he's a charmer. The wonderfully named Bug Hall, 9, is appropriately goofy as Alfalfa, and more appealing than Switzer in many ways. Brittany Ashford Holmes, 5, seems barely out of infancy, making her siren's role a bit strange, but amusing. As Buckwheat, Ross Elliot Bagley, 5, steals every scene he's in.

With the exception of Whoopi Goldberg, whose fleeting appearance as Buckwheat's mother is inspired, the cameos are jarringly out of synch with the child's world we're supposed to be watching. Sometimes, they're just unpleasant: Mel Brooks as a rude banker, Reba McIntire as the overbearing host of the climactic go-cart derby, and, as Waldo's father, Donald Trump, proving that there are certain things to which children should not be exposed.

Despite its cute cast, "The Little rascals" won't be replacing the originals, known alternately as Our Gang (the name of the first film) or the Little Rascals ("Hal Roach's Rascals" was the original series title) and who, through the wonder of television syndication, have become household names to several generations of Americans. (Contrary to an apparently popular rumor, Bill Cosby did not buy up the series to keep it off the air; King World owns it and licenses it market-by-market. No New York station currently has it, but cable's TBS does). Let's face it: Daryl Hannah as Miss Crabtree?

SIGHT AND SOUND, 4/95, p. 46, Verina Glaessner

Spanky, Alfalfa, Porky, Buckwheat, Froggy and Uh-Huh are members of the He-Man Woman Haters Club which is based in a ramshackle hut on a hillside. Their prize possession is their homemade go-kart, The Blur, much envied by neighbourhood bullies, Butch and his side-kick Woim—two slightly older boys who terrorise the gang whenever they can. Loosely attached to the gang are neighbourhood pets, Petey and Elmer, a mongrel and monkey respectively. Spanky, the gang's leader, insists on a policy of total apartheid against women. All are horrified when, eavesdropping on an assignation between Alfalfa and Darla, they discover him protesting undying love. By way of revenge they successfully sabotage a candlelit lunch he arranges for her at the club house when the others are due to be absent. However, Darla has met the neighbourhood new boy, the super rich Waldo, and it takes only the disastrous meal and Alfalfa's obvious unwillingness to acknowledge his relationship with her to his fellow gang members, to give her an excuse to transfer her affections to Waldo. Even worse, she plans to enter a local talent contest and sing a duet with him.

Alfalfa's punishment is guarding The Blur following a fire at the hut. Schemes to collect money to rebuild the club house, including taking out a bank loan, fail. An attempt to see Darla secretly ends in disaster when Alfalfa is pursued by Butch. Disguised in tutus, Spanky and Alfalfa cause mayhem during Darla's ballet recital. At the talent contest, Waldo sings to Darla onstage and Alfalfa, his pre-performance drink spiked by Waldo with detergent, humiliates Darla by protesting his love for her onstage while blowing bubbles. Meanwhile, Butch and Woim steal The Blur which Alfalfa has left unguarded. Undaunted, the gang build themselves another go-kart from discarded junk. At the go-kart championship the gang find themselves up against not only the repainted Blur driven by Butch and Woim, but also Waldo and Darla in a slick new machine. The race goes far from smoothly thanks to a mis-positioned signpost and the contestants' devious hi-jinks, but by crawling onto the bonnet Alfalfa is able to ensure the gang's new kart's victory in a photofinish—by a hair. Spanky is shocked to discover that his race hero A. J. Ferguson is in fact a woman, and head of the prize-giving ceremony. Alfalfa and Spanky are further shocked to discover that the driver of Waldo's car who saved them from disaster is not Waldo himself but none other than Darla. The gang reconstitute themselves on a new basis, deciding that from now on women are welcome.

Hal Roach's *Our Gang*—originally titled *Hal Roach's Rascals*—series was a major success between 1922 and 1944 when some 221 films were produced, all based around the daily activities and adventures of a neighbourhood gang of children aged between about four and nine. Despite the gang's racial integration, they were never politically correct—one episode involved a pint-sized chapter of the Klu Klux Klan. Produced for a while in tandem with the films of Harold Lloyd, who had a cameo in one episode, they initially mobilised the same kind of slapstick. The series produced an undoubted feelgood factor during the Depression and, in the words of one book on the subject, it pitted "scrappy have-nots" against "rich... sissy kids... who embodied the class-conscious adult world."

Director Penelope Spheeris has her own agenda, and as co-writer ensures its visibility. Her strengths are those of the caricaturist. She is unsubtle, abrasive and unafraid of vulgarity. In many ways she seems ideal for a project with inbuilt freckle-faced cuteness and sepia toned nostalgia. Although the modest bungalows she shows recall those of Laurel and Hardy, Keaton and Lloyd, her kids inhabit neither the comforting world of Lake Woebegone nor the stereotypical ghetto saturated with drugs, pimps and guns.

Instead, like the characters in Todd Browning's *Freaks*, they live in a micro-cosmic world whose chauvinism is a parody of that prevailing in the city overlooked by the kids' shantytown-like, hillside club house. If Spheeris disapproves of the buddies "dumping on" Alfalfa's romance, while maintaining an acerbity about romance itself (the girls at the end are happy to commence a more level-headed relationship) she is equally sour about the pastel frills and frou-frou of Darla's bedroom. Saccharine sweetness of these dimensions has not been seen on screen since the last *My Little Pony* movie. "Change," as a slightly older and certainly wiser Spanky admits in the feminist flag-waving of the film's closing moments, "has to come sooner or later."

While the denouement may offer moral support to weary mothers seeking suitable outings for their young charges, the film hardly does more. *Bugsy Malone*, with its kids playing adult characters, offered more thoroughly drilled entertainment, despite its mawkishness. Here, an uneven script and uncertain handling of a very diverse group of infants, some already marked by experience on the commercial audition circuit, proves a challenge not always successfully met. Nine-year-old Bug Hall as Alfalfa is, however, on another level, relishing his role despite its gaucheries, he drives the action along with considerable aplomb. Very slim cameos are offered by Mel Brooks as a bank manager and Whoopi Goldberg as Buckwheat's mother. That the series is revived now, at a time of still chimerical economic revival and an American lurch to the Right, is understandable. However, changed times, new viewing habits and Bart Simpson might have pre-empted its success.

VILLAGE VOICE, 9/6/94, p. 62, Meredith Brody

Neither slavishly nostalgic nor heedlessly revisionist, *The Little Rascals* is unexpectedly charming, its chief delight being the convincingly relaxed and unspoiled performances of virtually all its 13 main characters, especially Spanky—now merely sturdy instead of fat, with a delicious dimple and a sweet Southern drawl—seductive Darla, and Buckwheat, who improvises bits of songs.

Director Penelope Spheeris (previous chronicler of such boys' tribes as punks and metalheads in *The Decline of Western Civilization I* and *II*, serial killers in *The Boys Next Door*, and doofuses in *Wayne's World*), though working for Amblin Entertainment, doesn't move the gang out to a soulless Spielbergian suburb, but opens in the exact same Echo Park neighborhood that Hal Roach used back in 1922, grown shabby, with cracked sidewalks. Now the background includes the '90s L.A. skyscraper skyline, and the He-Man Woman Haters Club is surrounded by piles of the urban trash from which it's cobbled together.

Alfalfa, of course, horrifies the He-Men by telling Darla that he's "a sensitive male—sharing, caring, feeling," and crooning "You Are So Beautiful," setting in motion the slender plot. Which amounts to the repair of Spanky and Alfalfa's damaged friendship ("You only make a once-in-a-lifetime buddy, once in a lifetime!") and a go-cart race in which Darla is literally a deus ex machina, paving the way for the Womun Haters to add a "Womun Welcome" sign to the clubhouse. The best set pieces are a wittily intercut pair of boys' and girls' slumber parties and a *Nutcracker* ballet recital in which Alfalfa and Spanky look amazingly fetching in pink tutus and curly wigs, cross-dressing being as much a part of the Little Rascals as it is of Bugs Bunny—or Ed Wood.

Also reviewed in:
CHICAGO TRIBUNE, 8/5/94, Friday/p. C, Michael Wilmington
NEW YORK TIMES, 8/5/94, p. C21, Janet Maslin
VARIETY, 8/8-14/94, p. 75, Brian Lowry
WASHINGTON POST, 8/5/94, p. C6, Hal Hinson

LITTLE WOMEN

A Columbia Pictures release of a DiNovi Pictures production. *Producer:* Denise DiNovi. *Director:* Gillian Armstrong. *Screenplay:* Robin Swicord. *Based on the book by:* Louisa May Alcott. *Director of Photography:* Geoffrey Simpson. *Editor:* Nicholas Beauman. *Music:* Thomas Newman. *Music Editor:* Bill Bernstein. *Choreographer:* Trudi Forrest. *Sound:* Eric Batut and (music) Shawn Murphy. *Sound Editor:* Peter Townend. *Casting:* Carrie Frazier and Shani Ginsberg. *Production Designer:* Jan Roelfs. *Art Director:* Richard Hudolin. *Set Designer:* Richard St. John Harrison. *Set Decorator:* Jim Erickson. *Special Effects:* William Orr. *Costumes:* Colleen Atwood. *Make-up:* Jan Newman. *Make-up (Susan Sarandon and Gabriel Byrne):* Marilyn Carbone. *Make-up (Winona Ryder):* Naomi Donne. *Running time:* 115 minutes. *MPAA Rating:* PG.

CAST: Winona Ryder (Jo March); Gabriel Byrne (Friedrich Bhaer); Trini Alvarado (Meg March); Samantha Mathis (Older Amy March); Kirsten Dunst (Younger Amy March); Claire Danes (Beth March); Christian Bale (Laurie); Eric Stoltz (John Brooke); John Neville (Mr. Laurence); Mary Wickes (Aunt March); Susan Sarandon (Mrs. March); Florence Paterson (Hannah); Robin Collins (Carriage Boy); Corrie Clark (Belle Gardiner); Rebecca Toolan (Mrs. Gardiner); Curt Willington (Red Haired Young Man); Billie Pleffer and Louela Pleffer (Naughty Girls); Janne Mortil (Sally Moffat); Sarah Strange and Ahnee Boyce (Sally's Friends); Michele Goodger (Hortense); Marco Roy (Mr. Parker); Janie Woods-Morris and Patricia Leith (Boston Matrons); Christine Lippa (Mrs. Hummel); Kristina West, Nicole Babuick, and Jenna Percy (Hummel Children); Alan Robertson (Dr. Bangs); Mar Andersons (Fred Vaughn); Cameron Labine (Averill); Matthew Walker (Mr. March); Bethoe Shirkoff (Art Teacher); Marilyn Norry (Mrs. Kirk); Andrea Libman (Kitty Kirk); Tegan Moss (Minnie Kirk); Janet Craig (Miss Norton); Beverley Elliott (Irish Maid); James Leard and Charles Baird (Officer Workers); Jay Brazeau (Dashwood); Demetri Goritsas (Bhaer's Student); Kate Robbins (Opera Singer 'Leila'); David Adams (Opera singer 'Nadir'); Donal Logue (Jacob Mayer); Scott Bellis (John McCracken); John C. Shaw (Charles Botts); Irene Miscisco (French Maid); Peter Haworth (Male Secretary); Natalie Friisdahl and Kristy Friisdahl (Daisy); Bryan Finn and Sean Finn (Demi); A.J. Unger (Ned Moffat).

FILMS IN REVIEW, 3-4/95, p. 59, Eva H. Kissin

Little Women, published in 1868, has been around so long, translated into so many languages, put out into so many editions, and read and reread by so many "girls" (I use the word respectively and descriptively as Alcott would have), that it is as much a part of our childhood as a mother's touch.

Earlier versions of the book have been made into film for the hungry young readers aching to see Meg, Jo, Beth and Amy fleshed out into real people. I recall standing in the rain for an hour waiting to see what Katherine Hepburn would do playing Jo. She did enough to satisfy us—at that time.

The new film is far more elaborate. The photography of the changing New England seasons is a wonderful parallel to the four March daughters coming of age during the Civil War. Everything is somewhat heightened in the way of contemporary filmmaking. Amy is more beautiful, Laurie handsomer, and Aunt March richer than in the book or our imagination.

If the film begins with a Christmas-cardy look of snow scenes and carriages, it grows richer in its depiction of the genuine warmth of the household, the deep caring relationship between the little women and their mother, Marmee, solidly played by Susan Sarandon. She would have made Bronson Alcott proud in her understated but direct feminist statements of his best principles.

Jo (Alcott herself), played by Winona Ryder, is as intense and ardent as one would hope to find her. Trini Alvarado makes a proper Meg, and young Amy, Kirsten Dunst, supplies her own variety of charm and humor. Samantha Mathis does an exceedingly good older Amy. Claire Danes, as Beth, always heaven bound, makes you pull out another handkerchief.

If you've wondered why still another *Little Women* should be made, go see Gillian Armstrong's version. The family affection, and the underlying values of decency and equality that are not only preached but acted on, are as nourishing as ever.

A newly discovered unpublished manuscript by Louisa May Alcott is coming out this spring. *A Long Fatal Love Chase*, reputed to be a thriller and a page turner, was far too sensational for its era. Although it may be fun to read and learn the other side of Jo, it can't possibly compete with the dog earred copies of *Little Women* we all kept next to our pillows for so long.

LOS ANGELES TIMES, 12/21/94, Calendar/p. 1, Kevin Thomas

Gillian Armstrong's beguiling new version of Louis May Alcott's "Little Women" brings alive the past so vividly but perceives it through a contemporary sensibility so acute that you have the feeling that you're watching life unfolding before you.

Armstrong, screenplay adapter/co-producer Robin Swicord and their colleagues have got everything just right: You really believe you're observing New England family life in the 1860s, yet you're almost subliminally aware that you're seeing it from a present-day perspective.

In their vision, Alcott's alter ego/heroine, Jo March (played by Winona Ryder), is not a modern-day feminist but rather points the way to the future in her unladylike ambition and outspoken free thinking. The filmmakers acknowledge the second-class status of Victorian-era women without making a federal case about it: indeed, if this "Little Women" reveals what women needed to gain for themselves it even more shows us what has been lost in much of middle-class American society: the love of and respect for family and ethical conduct in everyday life. In its charmingly persuasive way, "Little Women" suggests that such matters still count, no matter how we may tend to neglect them.

With her radiance and quizzical spirit, her courage and vulnerability, Ryder is perfectly cast as Jo, the most intellectual of the four March daughters of Concord, Mass. They live with their mother, Marmee (Susan Sarandon, just the actress to leaven Mrs. March's sweetness with a dash of earthiness) in a spacious picture-book house of homespun warmth and well-worn beauty—it has, that look an Ethan Allen catalogue promises.

But they're hard put to make ends meet, and not just because Mr. March (Matthew Walker) is off fighting in the Civil War. The Marches ladies are Transcendentalists, who—like fellow Concord resident Ralph Waldo Emerson—thought that reality may be perceived through spiritual intuition. They are such do-gooders, in fact, they're poor.

"Once they were a fine family," sniffs their rich, grand next-door neighbor Mr. Laurence (John Neville)—but that's before he really gets to know them through his handsome grandson Laurie (Christian Bale), who becomes virtually a part of the March family. The other sisters, also captivating, are the demure, traditional Meg (Trini Alvarado), the gentle Beth (Claire Danes) and lively young Amy, who's played by Kirsten Dunst at age 12 and Samantha Mathis at 16. Living nearby is Mr. March's rich, selfish aunt (an amusing turn by Mary Wickes, one of the last great Hollywood character actors).

While fully recognizing the restrictions of genteel poverty and the female condition, Marmee, as an enlightened woman, encourages her daughters to make the most of themselves, especially Jo, who eventually goes off to New York to make her way as a writer, a daring act for a young woman of little means and fewer connections in the 1860s—and not one to be taken lightly today.

Among the men in their lives, Mr. March remains shadowy, even upon his return from war; Eric Stoltz is a prim but decent teacher. Bale's Laurie and, later on, Gabriel Byrne's German professor, a boarder in the Manhattan rooming house where Jo lodges, emerge as major figures, romantic, to be sure, but also as reflective as the March women.

Bale has an extraordinary scene in which we're able to feel the full force of the pain of rejection upon a truly worthy young man—deeply in love, devoted, good-looking, rich, Harvard-educated, open-minded, with a future of limitless promise; you do have to wonder if a woman wouldn't be just a little crazy to refuse him. Yet Armstrong makes such a turn of events as understandable as she did in her stunning, not dissimilar Australian 1978 debut film, "My Brilliant Career."

"Little Women" is an affectionate, superbly acted group portrait of female strength and solidarity as four young women come of age and how, despite natural clashes and differences of temperament, they are ultimately always supportive of each other. The great thing about the film is its accessibility. It invites thought but plays like a sure-fire, heart-tugging Christmas season entertainment. And it looks glorious, alternately summoning up memories of Currier & Ives prints and illustrations from Godey's Ladies' Magazine.

In evoking the past, Armstrong is here even better served than in her "Mrs. Soffel," set in turn-of-the-century Pittsburgh. Anachronisms are nearly nonexistent in this exquisite period piece, the creation of production designer Jan Roelfs and costume designer Colleen Atwood, whose crucial contributions have a burnished glow, thanks to cameraman Geoffrey Simpson's care with lighting. Completing the picture is Thomas Newman's lovely score.

Finally, "Little Women" says a great deal about Gillian Armstrong's own character and integrity as an artist. As she has proceeded from one distinctive accomplishment to the next, alternating between America and her homeland, Armstrong has remained uncompromised among those Australians who have heeded Hollywood's siren call.

NEW YORK, 1/9/95, p. 49, David Denby

The latest version of Louisa May Alcott's *Little Women*, by Gillian Armstrong, is so beautiful that one wishes it were more interesting. The winter light is dry and grayish; the New England interiors are brownish dark, lit by a fireplace and candles—there's not a trace of brightness or glare, no obvious "cinematic" effects. Period movies have become much more authentic than they used to be, and the decor and colors of this one are just about perfect. I was held by *Little Women*—by the March girls arguing and fighting against illness and taking care of one another, by Armstrong's courage in sticking with American Victorian manners in all their genteel sweetness. She cast the right actresses, too, especially Winona Ryder as Alcott's ardent and ambitious heroine, Jo. *Little Women* is filled with generosity and high ethical and feminist sentiment. It's about a mother and four daughters surviving in hard times; it's about the endurance of goodness.

Afterward, though, the glow fades. If only the family longings were shadowed by darker impulses; if only the feminist consciousness of the mother (Susan Sarandon) were sullied by doubt or error; if only the men (including Christian Bale and Gabriel Byrne) weren't always so gentlemanly. When the girls' much-longed-for father comes home from the Civil War, they hardly seem to notice him. The men are little more than vessels into which the women project their pride, their energy, their idealized feelings. This is a lovely movie, but it's also a complacent one, a world ruled by women in which traditionally masculine energies have been tamed or eliminated.

NEW YORK POST, 12/21/94, p. 39, Thelma Adams

Better get out your handkerchiefs. Resist, rationalize and refuse to surrender—but Gillian Armstrong's "Little Women" will melt even the most granitic of hearts.

Neither reverent nor revisionist, Armstrong ("My Brilliant Career") has created 1994's warmest movie by taking a rich, surprisingly traditional approach to the gilded feminist classic Louisa May Alcott published in 1868.

Screenwriter Robin Swicord hews closely to the autobiographical novel while opening the script up to include details from Alcott's life, such as the influence of transcendentalism on her philosophy and writing from the opening Christmas card of snowy New England to the closing lovers kiss under a canopy of spring rain, Armstrong embraces the March family of Concord, Mass.

The rest you no doubt know. While Papa March (Matthew Walker) fights Rebs down south, his four daughters—tomboy/writer Jo (Winona Ryder), proper beauty Meg (Trini Alvarado), gold-hearted Beth (Claire Danes) and spoiled Amy (Kirsten Dunst/Samantha Mathis) orbit around their Marmee (Susan Sarandon), while keeping a watchful eye over those less fortunate than themselves.

What takes this "Little Women" out of the rote is the acting. In a year when critics and Oscar voters are scratching parched ground for best and supporting actresses, the ensemble acting in "Little Women" sings out. Ryder's Jo (Katharine Hepburn's role in George Cukor's memorable 1933 version) is vivacious, headstrong and delicious. And while Hepburn (oh, sacrilege!) tended to upstage her co-stars with her butchy bluster, swishing them out of the frame with her hoop skirt, Ryder galvanizes the actresses around her.

As the plain pianist Beth, Danes (the star of TV's "My So-Called Life") performs with quiet strength, a wallflower whose shining virtue keeps her from fading into the wallpaper. Dane's intimate deathbed speech delivered to Ryder will reduce the last hard-hearted holdout in the audience to tears.

But "Little Women" isn't sentimental slosh. It wouldn't be such an enduring sisters story if there weren't sibling rivalry. When the selfish Amy burns Jo's cherished manuscript in a childish snit, the pain is searing. It doesn't hurt that Dunst, fresh from playing the littlest bloodsucker in "Interview With the Vampire," retains her cool-heart-in-blonde-curls edge. Samantha Mathis doesn't lose a crooked stitch when she picks up the role of Amy as a young woman and steals Jo's boy, Laurie (Christian Bale).

Sarandon's Marmee is the role model of the wise, nurturing, moral-center-of-the-universe mother. Occasionally, though, the actress slips in a sanctimonious slice of Marmee's maternal wisdom with a tinny modernity that jars with the movie's rich, even tone. Still, Sarandon seems like a woman who would give great hug.

Of the little men in Jo's life, Bale ("Henry V") is a standout as Laurie, the perfect prince of a man whose passionate love Jo can never return. Gabriel ("Miller's Crossing") Byrne is more problematic as German professor Friedrich Bhaer, whom Jo meets when she goes to New York to establish herself as a writer.

Byrne fails to convey Bhaer's trustworthiness and warmth; in the floundering New York scenes, I found myself fearing for Jo in the worldly professor's clutches, rather than seeing safety in the intellectual haven Bhaer offers the young novelist.

Beautifully designed by Jan ("Orlando") Roelfs, "Little Women" balances humor, heartache and timeless homilies for living. It's as toasty and inviting as fireside bedtime stories, a near-perfect movie to be shared with the family on Christmas Day and Christmases to come.

NEWSDAY, 12/21/94, Part II/p. B2, John Anderson

For the iconoclastic director Gillian Armstrong, bringing Louisa May Alcott's 1868 novel "Little Women" back to the screen meant confronting two memorable if unremarkable predecessors—one with Katharine Hepburn, the other with June Allyson—and a sentimental dilemma: Make it mawkish, and you lose. Make it strident, and you lost.

But Armstrong ("My Brilliant Career," "The Last Days of Chez Nous") possesses that rare thing in movies today, a purpose, and has realized it—not by projecting herself onto Alcott's autobiographical story and turning it into a modern parable, but by unashamedly mining its vein of emotional sincerity. Yes, one might construe "Little Women" as a greatest hit of women's lit, but Alcott's agenda wasn't sexual/ political, and she wasn't pandering to a market share. She wrote about her family, which she loved unconditionally, and her audience has lasted 126 years. Armstrong is smart enough not to muck around with that kind of success, and brave enough to let the emotional current have its head.

The result is not just the best family movie of the year, but one of the better movies.

In Winona Ryder, an actress who consistently seems in search of the proper part, Armstrong has her big gun. And Ryder has her best role. Properly youthful, delicate enough for a pre-Freudian period piece, the actress also has the right degree of barely contained spunk to play proto-feminist Jo March, whose pursuit of a writing career serves as the modern motor hitched to an otherwise horse-drawn vehicle. She and her sisters—conservative Meg (Trini Alvarado), retiring Beth (Claire Danes) and unrestrained Amy (Kirsten Dunst of "Interview With the Vampire" as a child, Samantha Mathis as an adult)—live a life of intoxicating affection with Marmee (Susan Sarandon) while their abolitionist-transcendentalistand virtually invisible father (Matthew Walker) is off fighting the rebs. Together, they comprise a poor but cozy household that's heady with generosity and potential.

All the young are wonderful, but particularly Claire Danes of the TV's highly acclaimed but ratings-anemic "My So-Called Life"), who has at least two moments of true brilliance—her horror at the neighboring Hummels' sick baby, which is an ominous glimpse at her own fate, and her radiant gratitude at the gift of a piano from her wealthy neighbor, Mr. Laurence (John Neville). His nephew, Laurie, the earnest youth-cum-callow man, is given a sturdy enough portrayal by Christian Bale, but the goateed, sunglasses-wearing Eric Stoltz is not—surprisingly—quite unctuous enough as Laurie's tutor and Meg's husband-to-be, John Brooke. Susan Sarandon is the picture of self-righteous virtue.

But besides distilling the nectar of familial affection out of Alcott's book, Armstrong, in her use of the outdoors and Jan Roelfs evocative production design, creates an America of spirit and grandeur. And reinforces our suspicion that the truly American is being rendered on screen most consistently by non-Americans.

NEWSWEEK, 1/9/94, p. 57, David Ansen

In a movie world dominated by aggressive male fantasies such as "Disclosure" and "Dumb and Dumber," "Little Women" seems daringly unfashionable. Louisa May Alcott in the era of Courtney Love and Sharon Stone? Fortunately, neither director Gillian Armstrong nor screenwriter Robin Swicord seems the least bit daunted presenting the March sisters to a '90s audience, with all their 19th-century New England virtues and vanities intact. This lovely, lived-in "Little Women" confidently settles into the domestic rituals of the March household, paying loving attention to the details, sure that these four sisters' journey of self-discovery will seduce us anew.

Winona Ryder holds center stage as headstrong Jo, the aspiring writer. Trini Alvarado is responsible, conventional Meg, who falls for the stiff young tutor played by Eric Stoltz. Claire Danes has an otherworldly calm as sickly, good-hearted Beth: she makes virtue so natural it takes the sappy curse off the role. And Kirsten Dunst perfectly captures the blond prima donna Amy at 12—before the older, spookier Samantha Mathis takes over as Amy grown up.

Ryder is captivating—so much so that she throws the emotional balance a bit out of whack. She's sexier and more vulnerable than the tomboy Jos we're used to, like Katharine Hepburn's coltish Jo in the 1933 movie. Viewers who remember director Armstrong's "My Brilliant Career," in which the fiercely independent Judy Davis rejects Sam Neill to pursue her writing, will be reminded of that scene when Jo turns down the marriage proposal of her best friend Laurie (Christian Bale). Most people will be nonplused by her decision, because Ryder and Bale seem so right for each other. But the disappointment is proof that the movie is alive: the filmmakers have made us members of the family, and we want to argue with their romantic choices.

The small role of mom remains a problem. Susan Sarandon's transcendentalist Marmee isn't sickly sweet—she's been turned into a 19th-century feminist, and Sarandon gives her as much haggard reality as she can—but she's little more than a dispenser of progressive platitudes.

"Little Women" may seem poky initially, but it has a strong, lyric emotional undertow that gathers force. By the time the story expands to New York (where Jo meets Gabriel Byrne's Friedrich Bhaer, an itinerant German philosophy professor) and France (where Amy is studying art), you're caught up in its epic intimacy. Alcott's sense. sensibility and sentiment find new life in this handcrafted valentine.

TIME, 12/19/94, p. 74, Richard Schickel

The March family is Santa Clueless. They are transcendentalists, so there are no angels in their outfield—maybe just Ralph Waldo Emerson out for his evening stroll. They are the creation of a 19th century New England lady who never heard the phrase "family entertainment" but in her innocence imagined that by telling the story of one family going about the ordinary business of life, she could divert and instruct other families.

You have to worry about *Little Women*. As a movie, it is exotic in all the wrong ways for today's market—all hoopskirts, candlelight and genteel language. In Louisa May Alcott's world, heavy snowfall was a big-time special effect, sausages for breakfast made for a woozily joyful Christmas, and it was omnipresent death, not omnipresent divorce, that threatened childhood's serenity. Can a movie that faithfully reflects this life—at once harder and more innocent than ours—and does so without condescension, preachment or gross sentiment, make its way in our times ?

It deserves to. For director Gillian Armstrong and writer Robin Swicord have fashioned an entrancing film from this distinctly unfashionable classic. They do not so much dramatize the passage of the four March sisters from girlhood to womanhood as let it unfold. Over the years the sisters must cope with a father's absence (when he's not off fighting the Civil War, he's lost in philosophical musings), a mother's bustling idealism, romances appropriate and inappropriate, the constant threat of poverty and illness. Eventually Jo (the luminous Winona Ryder) embraces art and an older man (Gabriel Byrne); Meg (Trini Alvarado) embraces domesticity; Amy (played as a child by Kirstin Dunst of *Interview with the Vampire*, as a young woman by Samantha Mathis) embraces—and shapes up—the boy next door. And poor retiring Beth (Claire Danes, who stars in the TV series *My So-Called Life*) embraces death—with exemplary courage.

Armstrong and Swicord have made the girls' mother (Susan Sarandon) something more of a feminist exemplar than she originally was; still, her social activism and her insistence that her children must claim their freedom do not seem anachronistic for a Concord woman of her time and class.

Little Women gently but firmly asks us to penetrate its 19th century disguises and discover something of ourselves hiding in the dim past. There has always been a kind of awkward exuberance in the way this story looks life straight in the eye and sweetly, soberly embraces its basic experiences and emotions. It is this unspoken moral strength, which is not to be confused with the vulgar, politicized moralism of our time, that permits it to transcend its gentilities of expression and its lack of structural grace. And grants this lovely cast, these intelligent and passionate filmmakers, the year's unlikeliest triumph.

SIGHT AND SOUND, 3/95, p. 42, Amanda Lipman

Christmas Eve in mid-nineteenth century Concord, Massachusetts. In Orchard House, four teenage girls, Meg, Jo, Beth and Amy, wait for their mother to come home from distributing food to the poor. Their father is away, fighting in the Civil War. The next morning, a modest Christmas feast awaits the genteelly poor household but instead the girls take their food to a starving German family. On the way, they see their neighbour, the grumpy Mr Laurence and his newly arrived grandson, Laurie. Later Laurie watches wistfully from his window and hears the girls play-acting together. At a dance, Jo stumbles into him and they become friends. Meg meets and falls for Laurie's tutor, John Brooke. After a night at the theatre with Laurie and John, Jo discovers that Amy, jealous at not being invited, has burnt the manuscript of a story she has been writing. She is furious with her little sister. Soon after, however, she rescues Amy from drowning and the two make it up.

A telegram brings news that Mr March is in a Washington hospital, wounded, and his wife decides to go to him. Rather than ask her sulky Great Aunt March, for whom she acts as a companion, for the train fare, Jo sells her long hair. While their mother is away, Jo then sells her first story to a newspaper but her joy is marred when Beth contracts scarlet fever. With her mother's return, Beth starts to recover, although she is left with a weak heart. The following Christmas, when Beth comes downstairs for the first time, Mr March arrives home. Four years later, Meg and John Brooke get married. Laurie declares his love for Jo. She refuses him, and he leaves for England, hurt and angry. Jo is miserable and goes to New York to be a governess in a boarding house. Amy, meanwhile, is taken to Europe by Aunt March. In Nice, she meets Laurie who now professes his love for her. Rebuffed, he goes back to England to prove himself worthy of her by working hard.

In New York, Jo meets Friedrich Bhaer, a German tutor. A romance develops between them, but when he is critical of her first novel, she is hurt. That day, she receives a letter from her mother, saying that Beth is very ill, and goes back home without saying goodbye to Friedrich. Soon after she reaches home Beth dies. In her grief, Jo writes a novel based around her life with her sisters. Meg gives birth to twins and Laurie returns, bringing his new wife, Amy. Aunt March dies, leaving Jo her huge house. Her mother suggests she turn it into a school. One day, Jo comes home to find a package. It is a proof copy of her soon-to-be-published new novel, left for her by Friedrich. She finds him and begs to him to stay and teach at her school. Kissing her, he accepts the offer.

The fourth film version of Louisa May Alcott's novel (and its sequel, *Good Wives*) is oddly pitched. In some ways, it reruns the stuff of director Gillian Armstrong's debut film, *My Brilliant Career*, by making a broadly feminist drama out of a period piece. In others, it is imbued with what enough movies have caused us to define as decent, all-American family values and loving relationships in spite of hardship. For a cynical modern audience, that could be a little archaic.

After the prickly *The Last Days of Chez Nous*, Armstrong is also back in the mushier visual land of her third feature, *Mrs Soffell*. There is something unnerving about a family that cannot be shown without being bathed in a warm sepia glow, or without an orchestra of violins to back up their every emotional exchange. In a similar fashion, a film that spends so much time lingering on gorgeous New England scenery, whether crisp snow, red and golden autumns, or lush green summers, is trying very hard to get a message across about the essential goodness and innocence of the place. What is odd is that these are neither innocent nor good times. There is war, poverty and disease. Yet despite *Little Women*'s apparent political intent, there is no irony here. Atrocities simply drop out of focus as soon as they have provided a gauzy backdrop to the goodness of the women in question.

There's no question where the gender emphasis lies: the film resolutely sticks with its little women. Although much is made of Mr March and his return, he barely opens his mouth during the whole film. John Brooke, rather admirably played by Eric Stoltz in the circumstances, is a duffer. Even Laurie is only really seen as a reflection of the women he loves: first Jo, then Amy.

Yet the film runs into problems because its women are so polarised that they never cease to be mere representations. Beth, for example, is the Victorian ideal: the shy, home-loving, angelic victim who talks and lives in greeting card clichés. At the other end of the spectrum, her "Marmee" is a maternal blue stocking. Susan Sarandon's Mrs March is much less sentimental than her literary counterpart, who is forever praising her dear husband for helping her become such a good person, but she is also less human. In the novel Mrs March admits to having to deal with anger and frustration. Here Mrs March is the ultimate earth mother, healing the sick, soothing the angry, and all the while spouting sensible feminist dictats to her daughters (women should be self-reliant, use their talents, not waste themselves simply on being decorative, and so on). It is upsetting to be irritated by an actress of Susan Sarandon's calibre, but that is the cumulative effect of this mother-machine.

As the most contemporary character, it is Jo with whom we are expected to be most in tune. Independent, gawky, tomboyish and rebellious, she finds it hard to fit in (and who wouldn't, surrounded by these paragons of perfection?). She is also always trying to please and can never understand why, she cannot succeed. Winona Ryder runs around eagerly in a most unladylike fashion but— unlike Katharine Hepburn in the 1933 version, and even June Alyson 16 years later—she misses a vital ingredient. Her Jo is not wild and difficult and clumsy; she is doe-eyed and rather mournful, with a mother who can solve every problem for her. Ryder may have made her name playing mixed-up teenagers, but they were altogether of a more sophisticated bent than earnest Jo.

For just one moment, as Jo, talking to Friedrich about her parents' transcendental beliefs, comments ruefully on how hard it is to grow up as a flawed person with "perfect" parents, the film alights upon what might have been its true dramatic centre. But the moment passes and we are sucked instead into idealism: not just about the March family but now also through a conventional screen romance between two rather beautiful people many miles away from the novel's ungainly lovers. Following the pattern it has set throughout, the film brushes away conflict and, almost magically, puts pat harmony in its place.

Once upon a time, this was a sentimental but often charming story about four girls growing up at a point in history when ideas about 'womanliness' were starting to enter a difficult period of flux. Now it has become a film with a mixed message; one that is both simplified political dogma and bland, wholesome sentiment. The question is: why did they bother?

VILLAGE VOICE, 12/27/94, p. 68, Georgia Brown

A new classic, a classic renewed: As you please. The new *Little Women*, directed with grace by Gillian Armstrong, adapted with tact by Robin Swicord, and starring an extraordinary ensemble, has made my holiday. I'm hard-pressed to tell you how the movie works because *Little Women* doesn't so much tell a story as draw you into a vortex, hold you suspended, and, when the time is up, gently let you drop.

Whereas Alcott's novel has become a ripe text for feminist academics, I doubt that it still casts a spell on girl readers. (According to the movie's production notes, the only cast member who'd read the novel as a child was Gabriel Byrne!) No doubt the deportment lessons are outmoded. Obviously it will be hard for any child raised on the Republican book of virtues to identify with a heroine who turns down a handsome young man with a large fortune. Former adaptations were products of their eras: There was George Cukor's timely mid-Depression production starring the nervy Katharine Hepburn, and Mervyn LeRoy's semi-hysterical post-World War II I'll-never-eat-yams-again recovery vehicle. This one was notable for Elizabeth Taylor's Amy, a flouncing, pouting materialist in the spirit of Vivien Leigh's Scarlett.

With Civil War hardships in the background, the Marches of Concord were to be pitied because their children were all girls. Perhaps because he has no sons to give, Mr. March (modeled on Louisa's Transcendentalist father, Bronson Alcott) has gone to war as a chaplain, leaving wife and four daughters to fend for themselves. The theme of women's self-sufficiency is central, with the four girls "complete" in character and talents: the domestic Meg (Trini Alvarado) likes theater; tomboy Jo (Winona Ryder) writes fiction; shy, altruistic Beth (Claire Danes) plays the piano; and fashion-conscious Amy (Kirsten Dunst, later Samantha Mathis) draws and paints. The presiding conscience and teacher is the wise, patient Marmee (Susan Sarandon). Something of the same isolated female community exists in Wilder's *Little House* books, except that Pa is necessary for hard labor.

Trying to reconstruct Armstrong's *Little Women*, what I remember is a feverish series of tableaux, glowing windows onto rich, almost utopian, harmony. In the beginning, all is fruitful energy; later, in encounters with the outside, complications arise. Swicord has modulated the sibling rivalry and tempered the novel's didacticism. Representing near perfect authority, Sarandon brings along her own reputation for social consciousness, enhancing the fervor when she recommends "moral courage." If perfect control is hard to take, at least she's not glorifying repression and self-sacrifice like the book's Mrs. March. Unlike *The Wizard of Oz*, *Little Women* is not about the failure or treachery of adults but more or less a lesson in good nurturing. Real inhibitors to destiny lurk outside the immediate environment.

A product of a freer generation than mine, Ryder has little to do with crude tomboy antics; her Jo seems naturally bold, ardent, and focused. Also marvelous is Claire Danes as the plain, soulful, and terminally selfless Beth—the masochist in all of us. (Margaret O'Brien's Beth in the 1949 version was particularly good as well.) That naughty vampyrette from *Interview*, Kirsten Dunst, is riveting as the young Amy; her every expression is interesting. It's impossible that Amy would grow up into a bland, bloodless Samantha Mathis unless, in the four year interim, she'd suffered some unmentioned trauma.

For the boys—outsiders, yearning to join the Marches' matriarchal fun—Christian Bale (child star of *Empire of the Sun*) makes a fine Laurie, the poor little rich boy next door, and Eric Stoltz is a bonus as the dandyfied tutor attracted to Meg. I'm sad to report that even Gabriel Byrne, sexiest man alive, isn't sufficient to alleviate the depressed aura clinging to Professor Bhaer. We must accept that Alcott blundered in matching fiery Jo with a fatherly intellectual helpmate, an emigrant Leonard Woolf. It may work in life, but here we're talking true romance.

Two other commendations: Nowadays when characters are rubbed out with nary a second thought given their absence, it's rare for a movie to take time, past a few sniffles over the corpse, to mourn the dead. *Little Women* even takes the time to show that out of grief comes something besides revenge killings. I also love the way the movie's characters speak in quaint archaisms, reenforcing the sense of a foreign realm accessible only to those with literary memories.

I hope I've convince you that *Little Women* is not only a children's film. but it may be woman's picture. I'm not sure.

Also reviewed in:
NATION, 1/23/95, p. 107, Stuart Klawans
NEW YORK TIMES, 12/21/94, p. C13, Janet Maslin
NEW YORKER, 1/9/95, p. 83, Terrence Rafferty
VARIETY, 12/19/94-1/1/95, p. 71, Todd McCarthy
WASHINGTON POST, 12/21/94, p. C1, Rita Kempley
WASHINGTON POST, 12/23/95, Weekend/p. 36, Joe Brown

LIVING PROOF: HIV AND THE PURSUIT OF HAPPINESS

A First Run Features release of a Short Films production. *Producer:* Kermit Cole, Beth Tyler, and Anthony Bennett. *Director:* Kermit Cole. *Screenplay:* Jameson Currier. *Director of Photography:* Richard Dallett. *Editor:* Michael Gersh. *Music:* James Legg and Mark Suozzo. *Sound:* Richard Brause, Kira Smith, Felix Andrew, and John Murphy. *Running time:* 72 minutes. *MPAA Rating:* Not Rated.

NEW YORK POST, 1/28/94, p. 44, Thelma Adams

"Pain and suffering is life," Ross Johnson tells the camera. "Misery is choice. I choose not to be miserable."

That's the guiding spirit behind "Living Proof: HIV and the Pursuit of Happiness." Kermit Cole's uplifting documentary suggests that death is inevitable—living is the challenge.

"Living Proof" began with a photo history project conceived by George DeSipio and photographed by Carolyn Jones. Exhibited at the World Trade Center last November the portraits of people infected with the virus inspired Cole's documentary.

The people in the movie affirm life in death's shadow: a cowlicky Eagle Scout who would be president—in 2008; a pixieish painter who abandoned commercial art for oils, her nimble fingers creating new worlds while the camera peeks over her shoulder; and a bony drag queen who holds forth on political power adorned in feathers and curls.

It's hard for me to be objective. Over the holiday season, I buried a 40-year-old man who had aged 50 years in 15 months. For me, in mourning, the movie's optimism is bittersweet.

I'm not ready to set aside my black cloth and put red ribbons in my hair. In the documentary portraits of attractive men and vital women, I see the sunken cheeks to come.

I remember a fall afternoon when my friend and I shared a bench in Prospect Park and though he was slightly weary, it seemed like death wouldn't overtake him. He still hadn't decided what he wanted to be when he grew up; now that was no longer an issue.

The months passed in long subway rides to Lenox Hill Hospital, glaring white hallways, and a glimpse of two old men, spooned around each other in a hospital bed, wrapped in each other's lives to the very end.

"Living Proof: HIV and the Pursuit of Happiness" captures its subjects in a moment of healthy denial. They are mothers, policemen, athletes, activists, dentists, designers, blue-collar workers, street people, teachers, lovers and caught for a bright moment in Carolyn Jones' airy photography studio, they are vibrantly alive.

Embrace their courage for considering AIDS a life sentence rather than a death knell.

NEWSDAY, 1/28/94, Part II/p. 69, Terry Kelleher

Prior Walter, the reluctant PWA ("prophet" with AIDS) in Tony Kushner's "Angels in America," has a remarkably short wish list when all is said and done: "More life, I want more life."

The people interviewed in "Living Proof: HIV and the Pursuit of Happiness" have been granted more life since receiving a diagnosis widely regarded as a "death sentence." And they're not counting the days. They're using them.

That's the simple message of this film, and producer-director Kermit Cole obviously believes it bears repeating. For a while, "Living Proof" threatens to be an endless series of upbeat sound bites. But all these expressions of optimism, resiliency and matter-of-fact courage have a cumulative effect on the viewer. Whatever your brand of misfortune, you're bound to come away in a *carpe diem* mood.

No, this isn't another film about AIDS that announces it's "not about AIDS." "Living Proof" has a legitimate claim to universality, only it doesn't make a big deal about it. "I don't have a lot of time to waste," says one of the film's most winning personalities. "None of us do, really. But I'm just reminded of it every day."

"Living Proof" grew out of a photo exhibit designed to dispel a little of the AIDS-related gloom by showing a variety of people coping with the virus. While photographer Carolyn Jones took still pictures, Cole and cinematographer Richard Dallett shot film of her subjects as they posed, conversed and reflected. In several instances—not enough, it must be said—photo-session interviews are supplemented by glimpses of the individuals at work or play. Not surprisingly, watching someone "living in the moment" beats listening to him or her advocate it.

The filmmakers may not strike the perfect balance between personal stories and general truths. Nonetheless, their test results on the human spirit are convincingly, hearteningly positive.

VILLAGE VOICE, 2/1/94, p. 58, Lisa Kennedy

After my brother (heretoafter the Swimmer because he was wonderfully strong in the water) was diagnosed with thrush, he admonished me for obsessing about his mortality when my own life came with no factory guarantee.

"*You* could be hit by a bus, you could die before me," he said, not angrily, just clearly. And while the MTA might not appreciate the metaphor, it's one that is reiterated more than a few times in the bittersweet and lovingly rendered *Living Proof.* Organized around a photo project conceived by George DeSipio and photographer Carolyn Jones to document HIV-infected people and PWAs, the film's mission is to give good face and voice to those "living positively." And as people speak less and less about cure but tentatively about disease management, living positively becomes its own vital, humanist activism.

The stars of *Living Proof* are Jones's subjects: the people who have agreed to have their portrait shot (the film's own flexibility allows us to follow some of them outside the artist's space and into their own). They outline the contours of the virus's demographics: gay men (of color and white), straight men and women (of color and white), maybe a lesbian, an effervescent little girl.

As with all talking-head documentaries, this one has people you crave to see again and again. My own attachments ran the gamut: the recovering addict whose son, Isaac, is now testing negative; the taciturn artist in her studio, vaguely monotone and deeply thoughtful. as she assiduously avoids the camera; the Brooklyn gal who chats matter-of-factly about dosages and combination therapies; and Ross, beautiful, bald, swimming Ross whose name, by the way, we only learn by an accident no doubt of the filmmaker's design. (One of the curious strategies of the film is the absence almost entirely of names. This is not a names project. Unless a name is spoken within the context of interviews, we do not learn them. It's a compassionate and compelling gesture toward the equal status and footing that these willing subjects share.)

There's so much more to be said about this marvel of simple filmmaking, some of it very difficult for those of us who are happy to extrapolate lessons about living well from the dying, but also confused and ashamed about the arbitrariness of the MTA. The final scene is a little existential poem to all of us: Ross smiling broadly, squatting at the bottom of a pool, a few bubbles drifting toward the surface.

VILLAGE VOICE, 2/15/94, p. 66, Marco Spino

With the agility of a messenger and the Lands' End look of an academic, Kermit Cole arrived on a bicycle and extended a gentle greeting. Among the packages in his arms were the freshly printed posters for his documentary *Living Proof: HIV and the Pursuit of Happiness.* He unveiled the posters only to find a small typo in the production studio's name. "Oh well, I'll just white it out," he shrugged.

"On all 4000 copies," I joked.

"No, only on the one I give to the studio." With that line Cole gave up a laugh that expressed the typo's triviality and the idea that life is too short to waste worrying over small details.

The characters in *Living Proof* maintain a similar perspective. Summoned by a flyer asking those "living positively" with HIV to come forward and change the face of AIDS, they were photographed by Carolyn Jones for a traveling exhibit and book. Asked by the project's creators, George DeSipio and Michael Libertore, to document it, Cole accepted. He started without knowing where the money would come from; "Once you've decided to make something because you realize the sooner the message gets out, the sooner it will help people; you can't wait for the money to roll in," he says. The list of benefactors is surprisingly long. Remarkably, Cole completed the film within a year.

Cole doesn't consider himself an AIDS expert. His previous work, a short called *Before Comedy*, looks at a clan of prehistoric clowns who teach a tribe of Neanderthals to laugh. *Living Proof* puts similar structures in play: one clan (tied together by a photo project) aims to teach another clan—we, the audience—about enjoying life. When asked to draw parallels, Cole explains that both films deal with groups unappreciated by their societies. "People with AIDS have been made to feel less than free to express themselves publicly, less than valued," he laments. "In the past, they have been at best pitied and usually worse than that." But rather than guilt-trip or preach us into caring, Cole uses envy. "I want people to envy these people not for having the virus but for their community and sense of support," he explains.

The 29-year-old director, who once performed as a mime, saw the film as a chance to champion a positive philosophy. He found making the film therapeutic. "I didn't grow up in an environment where I felt very much at liberty to feel my emotions or express them. What drew me to this project was the hope that I would learn how to do this," he comments. "And I have."

Though he wouldn't name names, Cole felt that the media and movies have concentrated too much on negative images of people with HIV, that they've festered hopelessness and paralysis. One of his aims was to challenge misconceptions and empower a group of people who have been "subordinated." The film's poster of seven lean, wet swimmers illustrates how he hopes to change people's thinking. These swimmers—who could signify Everymen—display a remarkable amount of resilience and courage. Cole hopes that everyone in the film will be perceived as the heroes they are. "The most important thing is that people leave the theater with the hope that people can be prized for their differences and embraced," he says.

He slicked up the look of *Living Proof* so that Middle America wouldn't have reason to doubt its importance. "The point was to get others to accept these people's perspectives as social truths and one of the most effective ways of doing this is through the appearance of commercially packaged reality," he says. The jazzy background melodies by James Legg and Mark Suozzo were an intentional effort to co-opt mainstream culture and evoke an era when people rallied together to fight another battle—World War II. "I meant for big-band music to infuse a sense of joy and freedom and exuberance from a time before AIDS," he says.

Taking the film's subtitle from the Declaration of Independence was Cole's way of advocating that everyone—whether HIV-positive or -negative—has the right to pursue happiness. By showing how we all share this dream, he hopes to combat phobias and stereotypes associated with the virus. "Hopefully, the film will engender a certain universal view that leaves people with the thought that it's really possible to save your life," Cole says. "That considerations of the amount of time you or somebody else might be allotted are a ludicrous thing to evaluate." Being mortal, we can all relate.

Also reviewed in:
NEW YORK TIMES, 1/28/94, p. C8, Janet Maslin
VARIETY, 11/1/93, p. 43, Daniel M. Kimmel
WASHINGTON POST, 72/2/94, p. D1, Hal Hinson

LONDON

A Zeitgeist Films release of a Koninck/BFI production in association with Channel Four Television. *Executive Producer:* Ben Gibson. *Producer:* Keith Griffiths. *Director:* Patrick Keiller. *Screenplay:* Patrick Keiller. *Director of Photography:* Patrick Keiller. *Editor:* Larry Sider. *Sound:* Hugh Strain. *Sound Editor:* Kate O'Neill. *Running time:* 84 minutes. *MPAA Rating:* Not Rated.

CAST: Paul Scofield (Narrator).

NEW STATESMAN & SOCIETY, 6/17/94, p. 33, Jonathan Romney

If documentary is film-making *about* subjects, another kind of cinema—one that doesn't really have a name—is film making *around* subjects. The grand master of this approach is Chris Marker, whose 1983 film *Sans Soleil* is its classic example, being most manifestly not a film *about* Japan.

Godard is another great exponent, most recently in his *Histoire(s) du cinéma*—largely since he couldn't talk directly *about* anything if he tried. This school is not quite what you'd call "essay cinema" either. That suggests something too lucid and sure of its own aims, with a definite point to make. Really, this is a cinema that toys distractedly with the facts, mixes in a shade of fiction, speculates vaguely, circumvents, lands wide of the mark. It takes the risk of boring or mystifying us outright, but may achieve the ultimate pay-off of *reinventing* its subject as if it had never existed before.

Patrick Keiller's *London* is a brave shot at such non-documentary. Ostensibly a film "about" our majestically sordid capital, *London* is really a film "around" it, in the most literal sense: a peripatetic portrait, an assemblage of postcards from a walk around the city's known and unknown landmarks. The one-word title implies a vast, unified single cell, but Keiller's film breaks the monolithic metropolis into a million shimmering mirror-ball fragments.

It's concerned with the dizzying challenge of reconciling 17th-century Fleet Street churches with the Brent Cross escalators, Betjeman's Metroland with Apollinaire's Brixton. Keiller tells his story as a shuffled set of still shots, and sets them to the tune of a narrative about conspiracy, cultural archaeology and long walks.

London has a thesis of sorts: that, as Montaigne (a one-time Londoner) put it, "It is good to live in depraved times", and ours are more depraved than most. But it's crippled by Paul Scofield's voice-over, which gives it an air of pedagogic solemnity, and drags into bathos its already unilluminating lament on London's political fate. (I think we already knew that John Major is not a good thing for the capital and the Routemaster bus was).

Scofield's melancholy intonation gives the film a single voice it otherwise strives to break away from. What makes *London* interesting, rather, is its sense of fragmentation and displacement—the feeling of no longer knowing where and when we are, despite the postmark on the cards. This is a foreign city, the stamping ground of Poe, Rimbaud and Verlaine. Its Imperial War Museum was once Bedlam (strange but true), and it's thick with unfamiliar sights and sites—like the beautiful Harrods Furniture Depository, looming strange and golden over the Thames.

What makes London a disappointing example of the genre is its single-minded determination to plunge to the *heart* of London's mystery—to represent the place.

NEW YORK POST, 9/28/94, p. 34, Larry Worth

If "My Dinner With Andre" had taken place on Great Britain's highways and byways, the result would be pretty close to "London."

Writer/director Patrick Keiller makes an astonishing feature film debut with this faux documentary about two intellectuals' journey through the heart and soul of not-so-merry old England. To hear these men's story, London Bridge isn't all that fell down, not with IRA bombs' devastation, House of Windsor scandals and the government going to hell in a hand basket.

Neither character is ever seen. For that matter, only one is heard. Instead, the crumbling splendor of Europe's biggest island—ranging from fog-shrouded Tower Bridge to lesser-known environs—consumes the screen as the two ex-lovers follow in the footsteps of French poets Paul Verlaine and Arthur Rimbaud. But the scenery merely complements the narrative.

And what a narrative. Subjects segue from the arts (William Hogarth and Joshua Reynolds' paintings, Charles Pierre Baudelaire's verses) to history (the Battle of Waterloo, Guy Fawkes' Gunpowder Plot) to current affairs (John Major's re-election, the Maastricht Treaty).

Believe it or not, that's just the warm-up. A cavalcade of deliciously wry anecdotes follows, seamlessly blending with real-life footage that includes a protester excoriating the Queen Mum by yelling "Pay your taxes, you scum!"

With Paul ("Quiz Show") Scofield's soothing if slightly condescending narration, director Keiller subtly makes his points about the city's demise by showing sex ads in phone booths, the

Thames drowning in pollution or a giant Ronald McDonald figure sitting atop a McDonald's franchise.

The results are fascinating, informative, poignant and undeniably amusing, giving cineastes ample reason to fly to "London."

SIGHT AND SOUND, 6/94, p. 54, Robert Yates

London is a documentary portrait of the capital which reflects the concerns of a fictional male character called Robinson during 1992. The images are accompanied by an unnamed male narrator, a friend and former lover of Robinson. Neither Robinson nor the narrator is seen. Apart from the narration and occasional music, the film is shot without sound.

The narrator tells us he has just completed seven years as a photographer on a cruise ship. He was asked to return to London by Robinson, whom he describes as an autodidact who teaches a day or two a week in the University of Barking's School of Fine Art and Architecture. Robinson has told him that he is nearing a breakthrough with his 'investigations'. These seem to involve an attempt to research the city's artistic past and to suggest alternative paths the city's history might have taken. Also, Robinson would like to find a place where he can become a *flâneur*. When abroad, Robinson enthusiastically wanders the streets; in London he seldom leaves his home.

The film consists of the narrator and Robinson undertaking three 'expeditions', and other mini-journeys, across London by foot. The first is from the house in Strawberry Hill, Twickenham, where Horace Walpole wrote the first English Gothic fiction, *The Castle of Otranto*, to Robinson's home in Vauxhall. The second begins outside the Stockwell house where poet Guillaume Apollinaire once came in search of a former lover, and continues, via London Bridge and the City, to Stoke Newington, where Edgar Alan Poe attended a school. There is no trace of the school, but close by stands the house where Daniel Defoe wrote Robinson Crusoe. The third tracks the River Brent, through outer north-west London, looking for 'city' life in the suburbs.

On these travels, the narrator and Robinson are repeatedly distracted by contemporary events, routine and extraordinary, which include IRA bomb attacks, the General Election, and the huge October 1992 march in support of the miners. They also take time out, spending a night in the Savoy suite where Monet had stayed when painting his views of the Thames, and visiting the Notting Hill Carnival. Throughout, the narrator reports his own and Robinson's reflections on the past and their opinions on how political decisions might impact upon the city's future.

It is tempting to consider *London* as primarily a piece of writing. In itself, the narration is an elegant achievement, accommodating history and fantasy, polemic and wit, and a good deal of well-turned rhetoric. There are plentiful references to Robinson's favourite writers, who also inspire the majority of the journeys. Even the jokes are literary ones, including the name given to the principal character: the lover of the French *flâneurs* recalls their spiritual opposite, Robinson Crusoe, that emblem of 'protestant isolationism' in the words of the narrator.

But to read the script alone would be to hugely reduce its impact. The words do not relate to the images as presentation might to supporting slides. Rather, both are involved in a sort of jazzy piece of social investigation which moves between theory and research: Robinson has his ideas about London which the journeys put to the test. The camera—a lightweight Eclair Cameflex, favoured, as director Patrick Keiller's notes explain, by the French New Wave—works as the eyes of the *flâneurs*, of Robinson and of the narrator, and drifts with them.

London is Keiller's first full-length film, although he has made several short films since 1981 which reveal an interest in contemporary Britain that is informed by literary and artistic ideas. He notes that he was originally motivated to make *London* by reading from the memoirs of Alexander Herzen, the exiled Russian socialist who arrived in the city in 1852. "There is no town in the world which is more adapted for training one away from people and training one into solitude," wrote Herzen. Robinson, presumably something of an autobiographical figure since Keiller also teaches architecture and fine art, thinks that Herzen's assessment still holds.

Robinson's thesis seems to be that London took a wrong turn in the nineteenth century. Cities became the site of modernism, but Britain chose the suburban, perhaps through governments' fear of the mob, or of socialism, and London became a place to pass through, not to linger in. If only London were more like Paris, is the implicit sigh, which partly explains Robinson's interest in

French moderns, including Baudelaire, the quintessential poet of the city. The Walpole excursion is presumably in homage to a native surreal romanticism.

With research into the past diverted by present-day events, the narration integrates aesthetic and political concerns. When the subject under scrutiny is a city, the relationship between the two cannot be ignored, *London* suggests. Robinson is angered by the outcome of the General Election, which he reads as a hammer blow to London that will result in more degradation, and this anger feeds in turn back into the research and the historical neglect of the city.

The investigations are offered at one remove. The narrator, although an informed and very close companion to Robinson, is not as committed. This allows Paul Scofield, as the narrator, to read with a voice that is somewhat detached, and wry when appropriate. Indeed, the narration takes pleasure in playing off images. "Everywhere we went there was an atmosphere of conspiracy and intrigue," we hear as the two *flâneurs* approach the new MI6 building in Vauxhall. In search of a cafe society, they end up in the IKEA furniture supermarket in suburban north-west London, and find somewhere to drink, but "the atmosphere was tainted by the ill-humour that often accompanies questions of interior design". So persuasively do image and commentary work together that it is easy to forgive the epigrammatic irony—the film at its most 'writerly'—with which *London* ends, the city, Robinson claims, revealing finally its modernity in its absence.

VILLAGE VOICE, 10/4/94, p. 62, Leslie Camhi

The bridge still stands, but the rest of the city is falling, in *London*, an oddly engaging, exhilaratingly articulate faux documentary and first feature by British architect-turned-director Patrick Keiller. Our fictional narrator (Paul Scofield), a francophilic Londoner suffering from "horror of home," returns after a seven-year absence to assist Robinson, his friend and former lover. Robinson's, quixotic project of "psychic landscaping" involves "searching the surface of the city for the molecular basis of historical events"; it leads our unseen protagonists on forays through the urban streets and into the London suburbs.

Like his namesake Mr. Crusoe, Robinson is also shipwrecked, but on the ruined shores of home instead. With a strange indifference, London bears all the blights of a late imperial metropolis; a prefab box that has served for 30 years as a family's "temporary" housing; an IRA-bombed office building, its shredded venetian blinds waving; rampant homelessness; reelected Tories; and the splendid, stolid trappings of monarchy moving about a city of squalor.

French flaneurs and surrealists mined Parisian street culture for its radical aesthetic and political potential, but the English tend to dread their cities out of a fear of urban rebellion and a love of monarchy and landed gentry. Yet Keiller's London is not only re-politicized but funny. Consider the narrator's account, accompanying images of John Major entering office, of Robinson's reflection on the manifold ills that will now befall him: "his flat would continue to deteriorate and its rent increase...he would drink more, he would be ill more often, he would die sooner."

Melancholy used to be called "the English malady" and, though it seems to be one of Keiller's infirmities, his sharpest nostalgia is reserved for the city's present, and his task is to reenvision it.

Also reviewed in:
NEW YORK TIMES, 9/28/94, p. C14, Stephen Holden
VARIETY, 6/13-19/94, p. 63, Derek Elley

LOST WORDS, THE

A Film Crash release of a Scopix production. *Producer:* Scott Saunders, Vanessa Baran, and Katrina Charmatz. *Director:* Scott Saunders. *Screenplay:* Dan Koeppel, Scott Saunders, and Michael Kaniecki. *Director of Photography:* Marc Kroll and Scott Saunders. *Editor:* Scott Saunders. *Music:* Michael Kaniecki, Chris Burke, Neal Sugarman, George M., and Red Sedan. *Sound:* Michael Greene. *Art Director:* Carmen Einfinger. *Running time:* 85 minutes. *MPAA Rating:* Not Rated.

WITH: Michael Kaniecki (Charles); Bob McGrath (Sid); Zelda Gergel (Marcie): Brian O'Neill (Jeff); Deborah McDowell (Louise); Rini Stahl (Judie); Fred Tietz (Fred); Salley May (Bettina); George M; Joe Litto.

NEW YORK POST, 9/21/94, p. 38, Thelma Adams

Some things are better off lost, "The Lost Words" included. This self-conscious, whiny East Village soap aspires to be "sex, lies, and videotape."

Pock-marked auteur Charles (Michael Kaniecki) is an unemployed filmmaker/musician. Marcie (Zelda Gergel) is his soon-to-be ex. Sid, Jeff and Fred are his buds. Welcome to Charles' fish bowl.

"The Lost Words" falls prey to the idea that since the filmmaker finds his friends (and his navel) so interesting, we will, too. It ain't necessarily so. There's an art to making the banal universal.

The sad-sack saga has occasional flashes of self-deprecating humor. Kaniecki and Gergel turn in natural performances. (Marcie honestly admits, "I'm not even photogenic.")

First-time feature director Scott Saunders' ambition and drive outstrip his talent. "The Lost Words" is closer to home-movies-as-therapy than popular entertainment.

VILLAGE VOICE, 9/27/94, p. 66, James Hannham

Hey, Chris Isaak! The next time you're shooting a video, look up a guy named Scott Saunders, the director of a film called *The Lost Words*. Shot in Hi-8 and transferred to film, it still has that re-verby you-are-there-but-you'd-rather-not-be video quality, but Saunders and crew manage to make it gorgeous and seductive, especially the heavily edited sequences during which there's no dialogue. You'd pick up one of those little MTV astronaut statues for sure. However, it might not be a good idea to have him direct you in an actual full-length film.

The Lost Words follows an East Village nebbish named Charles, an unemployed commercial editor with dyed black hair, played with a flat, whiny deadpan by Michael Kaniecki. His last attempt to save his relationship with live-in girlfriend Marcie is to make a cinema verité video about all his friends' miserable (and tediously similar) relationships. Naturally, this makes the film feel like spending 85 minutes getting harangued by an irate ex-boyfriend. Seeing only the pain of breakups without the reasons why "we need the eggs," as Woody Allen put it, you almost want to cheer when characters who obviously couldn't get along break up two by two. Even the guys, who all play poker together, harbor deep resentments. "I don't know why the hell I hang around with you anyway," Charles tells his buddies. Saunders's formal conceits don't help, either. Having characters refer to "Charles's film" and point at the camera feels fake, like a ripoff of *sex, lies and videotape*, especially since the film gets interrupted by "real people" monologues (including one by the Voice's own Beth Coleman). They're intended, I guess, to prove that relationships suck. But they don't. Bad relationships between selfish, immature people do.

Also reviewed in:
CHICAGO TRIBUNE, 1/20/95, Friday/p. E, Michael Wilmington
NEW YORK TIMES, 9/21/94, p. C18, Stephen Holden
VARIETY, 10/10-16/94, p. 85, Godfrey Cheshire

LOVE AFFAIR

A Warner Bros. release. *Executive Producer:* Andrew Z. Davis. *Producer:* Warren Beatty. *Director:* Glenn Gordon Caron. *Screenplay:* Robert Towne and Warren Beatty. *Based on the motion picture "Love Affair" screenplay by:* Delmer Daves, Donald Ogden Stewart. *Story:* Mildred Cram and Leo McCarey. *Director of Photography:* Conrad L. Hall. *Editor:* Robert C. Jones. *Music:* Ennio Morricone. *Sound:* Jim Tannenbaum. *Casting:* Marion Dougherty. *Production Designer:* Ferdinando Scarfiotti. *Art Director:* Edward Richardson. *Set Designer:*

Al Manzer. *Set Decorator:* Dan L. May. *Costumes:* Milena Canonero. *Running time:* 107 minutes. *MPAA Rating:* PG-13.

CAST: Warren Beatty (Mike Gambril); Annette Bening (Terry McKay); Katharine Hepburn (Ginny); Garry Shandling (Kip DeMay); Chloe Webb (Tina Wilson); Pierce Brosnan (Ken Allen); Kate Capshaw (Lynn Weaver); Paul Mazursky (Herb Stillman); Brenda Vaccaro (Nora Stillman); Glenn Shadix (Anthony Rotundo); Barry Miller (Robert Crosley); Harold Ramis (Sheldon Blumenthal).

CHRISTIAN SCIENCE MONITOR, 12/21/94, p. 11, David Sterritt

A man and woman meet during an ocean cruise. Each is engaged to marry someone else back home, but when you're glamorous enough to be played by a top Hollywood star, it's hard to keep romantic sparks from flying

After a nostalgic side-trip to visit the man's elderly grandmother, they head for New York and vow to reunite as soon as they've broken off their current entanglements. They'll meet again in a few short months, at the top of the Empire State Building—if they still feel the same way about each other, and if fate doesn't intervene with some nasty surprise. The weeks pass, the important day arrives, and then ...

If that sounds familiar; you've probably seen the 1939 romance called "Love Affair" or the 1957 remake called 'An Affair to Remember," both of which used this story with popular results.

Or maybe you heard characters discussing 'An Affair to Remember" in last year's comedy "Sleepless in Seattle," where the Meg Ryan character goes misty-eyed whenever she watches the 1957 picture—starring Cary Grant and Deborah Kerr, two of Hollywood's most dependable charmers—in one of its interminable TV showings.

Or maybe you've just seen a coming-attractions trailer for Warren Beatty's new "Love Affair," which marks the third go-round for this unkillable tale. The new version is so faithful to its source material that you'd almost think your multiplex had entered a time warp—whisking you back to an era when stars had conversations instead of gunfights, romance meant lasting love instead of instant sex, and Manhattan looked as homey as the Pacific island where the hero's aging relative live's in her steadfastly old-fashioned world.

The conservatism of the new "Love Affair" comes as a mild surprise, considering that a thoroughly modern type like Beatty is producer, cowriter and star. Following the trend of most contemporary remakes, such as the new adaptation of "The Browning Version" that just arrived in theaters, the "Love Affair" team might have updated the old yarn in one way or another—perhaps reflecting how male-female relationships have evolved over the years, and how these changes have affected modern society.

As directed by Glenn Gordon Caron from a screenplay by Beatty and Robert Towne, the new picture does have a '90s look, at least in its big-city scenes. It also has a glimmering awareness of contemporary issues—making the Beatty character not just a popular socialite like Grant in the '57 version, for instance, but a full-fledged media star who knows the eyes of the nation are always upon him.

In most respects, though, the filmmakers have opted for the most backward-looking approach possible, serving up their time-tested story with a minimum of new trimmings. Fans of traditional tear-jerkers will adore it. Others will wonder what's happened to the adventurous spirit Beatty possessed in years gone by. If you expected the bold screen artist who produced "Bonnie and Clyde" and directed "Reds" to meet you at the Empire State Building this year, get ready for a rendezvous with his much duller twin.

This doesn't mean his "Love Affair" retread is identical to its predecessors, of course. The lovers meet on an airplane this time, moving to the ocean liner only when an emergency landing strands them far from home. The elderly granny has become an elderly aunt. The action and dialogue are spicy enough at times to earn a PG-13 rating. And two of the most resonant touches in the 1957 version—a scene where the lovers unwittingly take adjoining tables in the ship's restaurant, and a loving gesture Grant bestows on Kerr as she greets her soon-to-be-abandoned fiancé—have been inexplicably pruned away.

The stars are different, too. Beatty and Annette Bening, known for their chemistry on and of the screen, have a reasonably spunky rapport that keeps their scenes engaging. Garry Shandling livens up the show as a wise-cracking friend. And the great Katharine Hepburn brings every bit as much warmth, dignity, and style to the aging aunt as the similarly legendary Cathleen Nesbitt brought to thc granny in 1957. Chloe Webb and Kate Capshaw show their usual professionalism in smaller supporting roles.

Conrad L. Hall did the cinematography, which is consistently pleasing to the eye, and Robert C. Jones is credited with the movie's efficient editing. The only real disappointment among the film's secondary contributions is the music by Ennio Morricone, a towering figure working well below his usual lofty standard.

LOS ANGELES TIMES, 10/21/94, Calendar/p. 1, Kenneth Turan

In his latest film, Warren Beatty has loved wisely but not all that well. His infatuation with the 1939 "Love Affair," one of the great romantic weepies of its time, is well-placed, and his decision to faithfully remake such an openly sentimental and old-fashioned film is almost a brave one.

But though it is effective in fits and starts, this third version of that sturdy tale (the fourth, if you count "Sleepless in Seattle," which it in part inspired) never manages to be more than a reasonable facsimile of its progenitor.

For like all things light and airy, romantic fantasies turn out to be more difficult to construct than they seem. The memorable ones are as delicate and ephemeral as champagne bubbles, defying logic and gravity as they infiltrate our sensibilities.

The first "Love Affair," directed by Leo McCarey and starring Irene Dunne and Charles Boyer, managed this feat, and Beatty (who also produced and co-wrote with Robert Towne while Glenn Gordon Caron did the directing) has attempted to recapture the magic by closely following the original script.

But not even the kick husband and wife Beatty and Annette Bening must have gotten from reenacting one of the screen's memorable liaisons has been enough to bring this "Love Affair" totally to life.

One of the intriguing aspects of this "Love Affair" is watching Beatty and Bening in what can be read as a version of their own relationship, acting out a kind of valentine to their own personal success as a married couple.

Beatty plays Mike Gambril, former NFL star and now a sportscaster best known, if the TV tabloid shows are to be believed, as either an "aging playboy" or "an aging sports stud."

At the film's opening, Mike's engagement to powerful and glamorous talk-show host Lynn Weaver (Kate Capshaw) has just become announced, and the man himself is off to Australia for what is supposed to be a quick few days of work.

On the plane over, however, he encounters Terry McKay (Bening) when he drops his little black book and she archly comments, "I thought those things were extinct."

Herself engaged to lord of Wall Street Ken Allen (Pierce Brosnan), a financier whose yacht she is flying off to decorate, Terry is both attractive and seemingly immune to Mike's heavily practiced line of chat, a combination he finds intriguing.

Since most of the original "Love Affair" took place on an ocean liner, some fancy plot footwork is employed to get Mike and Terry onto a goofy Russian cruise ship, but the feat is managed and in the few days they have together, a kind of bond is forged.

Helping in the bonding is a quick visit to Mike's Aunt Ginny (Katharine Hepburn in her first feature appearance in nine years) who conveniently lives on a nearby island. A font of ancient wisdom, as was the delightful and elfin Maria Ouspenskaya in the 1939 version, Ginny opines that her nephew may not be the philanderer he appears to be. He may just have not met the right woman.

Terry and Mike can see the conflict between their increasing attachment to each other and their commitments to other people but what neither they nor the audience can imagine are the other kinds of roadblocks the film's shameless plot will put in their path.

"Love Affair" wisely does not try to update things too much. A simple kiss is as explicit as things get romantically, and venerable devices like pages flying off a wall calendar to indicate the passage of time are lovingly employed.

But all this care is not enough to bring "Love Affair" to life. Beatty and Bening, though they do have their moments, mostly seem to be acting as opposed to inhabiting their parts, and

Hepburn, gamely battling against the encroachments of age and disease, has a particularly tough time of it. Magic cannot be willed into existence, and despite everyone's best intentions, this film remains earthbound.

NEW YORK, 11/7/94, p. 67, David Denby

Not to put too fine a point on it, Warren Beatty has wasted long stretches of his time considering one movie project after another, demanding rewrites, changing his mind, and in general displaying a spectacular talent for high-style Hollywood dithering. As a result, this talented man has appeared in exactly twelve movies in 25 years. True, he directed three of these movies and produced a few others, but in the same 25-year span (ages 33 through 57), Cary Grant appeared in 44 movies, and the late Burt Lancaster—a torrent of energy—appeared in 48 (including one that he directed). I wonder: Now that Beatty has married Annette Bening and has attained considerable influence over her career, will Bening also begin this strange disappearing act? For a Hollywood power, the only greater vanity than appearing in a movie is not appearing in a movie. Unmade projects fashionably consume entire careers.

After much fussing, Beatty and Bening have together brought forth *Love Affair*. Directed by the modestly accomplished Glenn Cordon Caron, it is not a disaster, but it's not good, either—in fact, it's not much of anything. *Love Affair* is the third go-round for maudlin material first conceived almost 60 years ago, and some of the plot devices no longer make much sense. What are these two intelligent people—plus screenwriter Robert Towne—doing with this retro weepie plot? Trying to make tasteful popular romance, I guess. But in that case, why not find a fresh story? *Love Affair* is kitsch derived from old "woman's film" formulas but put together without the conviction or the moral urgency that once made such stuff irresistible.

Leo McCarey first directed the material, charmingly, in 1939, as *Love Affair*, with Charles Boyer and Irene Dunne, and then again, with less sparkle but more depth and emotion, in 1957, as *An Affair to Remember*. This latter version starred Deborah Kerr as a very elegant and well-spoken Boston nightclub singer and kept woman and Cary Grant as an impeccable, ironically classy gigolo. Dressed to the teeth, lighting cigarettes in the gentle breezes, they bantered gracefully on shipboard and fell (chastely) in love. The movie, dedicated to the many states of longing, has become a kind of genteel romantic classic among women—teasingly commemorated as such by Nora Ephron in *Sleepless in Seattle*. In the new version, Beatty is Mike Gambril, a ladies' man and ex-football star who has lost his way as a broadcaster. Mike is about to be married to a powerful network on-camera personality—a very avid and appealing Kate Capshaw—when he meets Bening's Terry McKay, who is also set to be married, to a wealthy financier (Pierce Brosnan). The movieness of the plot is amusing for a while: Beatty and Bening don't exactly dig into their roles; the movie is less about Mike and Terry than about Warren and Annette as a couple—a man "who's never been faithful to anybody" falling for an elegant and willful woman who would never allow herself to be taken for granted.

The bantering intimacy between these two—the sense of very smart, glamorous people playing intricately pleasurable games with each other—makes us feel that we've joined very swift company indeed. I wouldn't have much minded if *Love Affair* had turned into a kind of extended home movie: Annette Bening is altogether charming—crisp, self-possessed, amused—and Beatty's longtime screen habits of modesty, diffidence, and light irony take the camera very well. But right from the beginning, there are certain embarrassments. As you may have heard, Beatty appears in half-shadow and is generally lighted more discreetly than Joan Crawford in her later years. A quick look in the mirror should have told him that something was wrong with this project: Warren Beatty should play characters his own age. Unlike Cary Grant, whose age was always indeterminate—neither young nor old but mature perfection in a suit—Beatty looks his 57 years. There's nothing wrong with that: He has a fine, weathered face, and he looks like a man, not like someone pickled in tanning lotions. As usual, I realized how much I had missed him. He's one of the few actors who easily suggest intelligence, just by the way he listens.

For McCarey, a Catholic, the story was about sin, punishment, and redemption, and Towne has remained insanely faithful to the clammily virtuous scheme. But why? In a contemporary context, it no longer makes any particular sense that Bening atone for her nonexistent sins by teaching underprivileged children to sing "The Farmer in the Dell." (Quite a scene, let me tell you.) Nor do we understand why everyone goes off to Bora-Bora, or Kon-Tiki, or wherever it is—in any case, a significantly primeval place, where the clouds and landscapes are rich and dark, and only the deepest truths are spoken. Out there in Polynesian never-neverland, Warren and Annette encounter Katharine Hepburn, who utters indecipherable wisdom about love. Something about ducks, horses—they mate, they don't mate ... Anyway, it's profound.

Later, running for her rendezvous with Warren at the Empire State Building, Annette gets clipped by a car, which is no longer a punishment enmeshed in a religious mythos of sin and redemption but a mere stupid accident. Nevertheless, it sets up a reprise of the famous, unendurable final scene, in which he comes to her, not knowing, and speaks oh, so bitterly, and she's too proud, too proud ... well , you must experience it for yourself. I pray that the maiming Bening undergoes in this movie won't serve as a metaphor for her career after meeting Warren Beatty. If he doesn't want to work very much, he might at least turn her loose now and then. She used to be a very funny wicked lady. I hardly think God intended her to hide her light under a bushel—or sit with her legs under a blanket.

NEW YORK POST, 10/21/94, p. 39, Michael Medved

Can an aging playboy notorious for his innumerable conquests suddenly mend his wandering ways and find monogamous bliss with a strong-willed beauty many years his junior?

This question has not only been posed by gossip columnists reporting on the private life of Warren Beatty, but it also arises in the course of Beatty's new movie, "Love Affair."

The deliberate blurring of fiction and reality is part of the fun of this picture; it's impossible to forget for even a moment that Beatty and his co-star Annette Bening are off-screen husband-and-wife. Fortunately for them (and for us) these two charming stars project a potent, passionate, yet comfortable chemistry that helps their movie overcome many of its shortcomings.

The story, of course, has been kicking around Hollywood for more than 50 years, serving as the basis for two previous films, "Love Affair" (1939), with Charles Boyer and Irene Dunne, and "An Affair to Remember" (1957), with Cary Grant and Deborah Kerr. The latter film became an important point of reference in last year's smash hit "Sleepless in Seattle," leading inexorably to this latest remake.

Unlike "Sleepless," which viewed the old movie as a cornball classic, absurd but endearing, this new "Love Affair" treats the material with, if anything, too much reverence and respect. Beatty (who wrote the script together with Robert Towne) seems intent on preserving all details of the previous films. Since they focused on shipboard romance, and no one crosses the ocean on luxury liners anymore, one of the few changes in the plot involves the two lovers meeting on a plane, which makes an emergency landing on a tiny atoll, and then a cruise ship picks them up.

Meanwhile, both Beatty and Bening arc promised to others (Kate Capshaw and Pierce Brosnan, respectively) but they fall in love anyway. When they say goodbye after their adventure they agree to give each other three months of space to straighten out their lives and then meet at the top of the Empire State Building, On the day of their scheduled reunion, however, fate intervenes with tragic effect.

As in previous versions of the story, the romantic comedy atmosphere of the first half works much better than the tear-jerking melodrama of the conclusion—though the old story can still produce misty eyes for moviegoers who are especially vulnerable to this sort of manipulation.

This new movie tries to milk an additional few tears by casting 87-year-old Katharine Hepburn as Beatty's free-spirited aunt, heavy-handedly reminding us that this may (God forbid) be the great actress' last movie role. In any event, Hepburn's scenes produce a different sort of sadness than the producers intended since many of her lines are all but unintelligible.

The one aspect of "Love Affair" that is an unmitigated triumph is the heart-tugging score by Ennio Morricone, which should win the composer his fifth Oscar nomination. Like the movie itself, the music is shameless schmaltz (evoking the tunes of the 1957 version), but it's nonetheless difficult to resist.

NEWSDAY, 10/21/94, Part II/p. B5, Jack Mathews

If it was absolutely necessary that someone do another remake of "Love Affair," Leo McCarey's classic 1939 romantic melodrama, they could have done worse than cast Warren

Beatty and Annette Bening in the roles played in the original by Charles Boyer and Irene Dunne, and in McCarey's 1957 remake, "An Affair to Remember," by Cary Grant and Deborah Kerr:

Beatty, in certain roles, approaches the charm and urbanity of Grant. And as a lady's man, he has established a reputation—on and off the screen—that would make Boyer's famous bedroom eyes light up with envy. As for the woman whose simple honesty and love would humble such a worldly rake, who better to play her than Bening, who seems to have actually done it?

Of course, another remake of "Love Affair" was not necessary, or even advisable, despite the renewed interest after the recurring references in last year's "Sleepless in Seattle." In fact, it must have taken all of Beatty's persuasiveness as a producer to get Warner Bros. to pony up the money for such an old-fashioned hanky soaker, and despite the earnest performances of the married co-stars, the story is too fragile to shoulder the baggage they bring along.

"You know, I have never been faithful to anyone in my life," Beatty tells Bening early in their characters' relationship. The line is such an obvious nudge in the ribs, that you have no choice but to consider it—and the other allusions to his character's philandering past—in the context of Beatty's own legendary love life, and middle-age reform. It's hard to surrender to a story in which the actors keep showing you their clippings, and if you cannot suspend disbelief in a melodrama this ripe, it has no chance.

The new version of "Love Affair," directed by Glenn Gordon Caron and co-written by Beatty and his old friend Robert Towne ("Shampoo"), is steeped in contemporary culture—at least, in contemporary television culture—but it faithfully follows the original story line.

Beatty's Mike Gambril is an ex-football star now working in TV, and engaged to one of the country's most popular talk show hostesses (Kate Capshaw). Bening is Terry McKay, a music teacher engaged to the head (Pierce Brosnan) of a Wall Street investment firm. They meet on an airliner bound for Australia, but engine trouble causes a forced landing in the South Pacific. After spending a few hours with Mike's wise-in-the-ways-of-romance aunt (Katharine Hepburn), who just happens to live on an island in the area, they begin a romance aboard a Russian cruise ship headed for Tahiti.

Months later, while rushing to keep a date with Mike on the observation deck of the Empire State Building, Terry is struck by a car, and left paralyzed, determined not to let him know what happened until she can walk again. Meanwhile, he's hurt, bitter and almost broke, having shucked his TV career for a small college coaching job, only to be left alone up there where King Kong last saw Fay Wray.

Can fate bring them back together?

NEWSWEEK, 10/24/94, p. 76, David Ansen

Like every movie Warren Beatty has produced, *Love Affair* is made with skill, the participation of topnotch talents and considerable taste. There are times, however, when good taste can get in your way. Why do another remake of the sentimental classics "Love Affair" and "An Affair to Remember" (both directed by Leo McCarey, in 1939 and 1957) if you're not prepared to wallow in four-hankie heaven? Beatty, who stars and co-wrote the script with Robert Towne (Glenn Gordon Caron directs), follows the originals' plot line with great fidelity, with a sprinkling of contemporary details to drag it into the '90s. He's a former pro quarterback and notorious womanizer engaged to a TV talk-show host (Kate Capshaw). On a flight to Australia he meets the woman of his dreams—piano teacher Terry McKay (Annette Bening), herself engaged to marry a wealthy financier (Pierce Brosnan). The plane crash-lands on a Pacific island; the two embark on a ship for Tahiti, fall in love and vow to meet in three months atop the Empire State Building. If you don't know what happens next, you didn't see "Sleepless in Seattle."

Aside from the autobiographical echoes—famous philanderer discovers monogamy late in the day—Beatty offers no fresh take. The movie, bathed in soft focus, is as reticent about sex as the Cary Grant/Deborah Kerr version, and half as romantic. The only fun is in the lively first third: Beatty and Bening are at their best in push-pull seduction mode, when they can be a bit naughty. But once the couple clinch their bond—just when the story gets really shameless—the life drains out of the movie. "Love Affair" takes such pains to dodge vulgarity it forgets to put anything in its place.

TIME, 10/24/94, p. 76, Richard Schickel

Handsome couple, swell clothes, upper-crust settings, smart, sexually sparring dialogue and a plot device that contrives to keep the pair apart until you think you—and they—are about to burst. It worked in 1939. It worked in 1957, when it was retitled *An Affair to Remember*. It even worked last year when it was extensively quoted in *Sleepless in Seattle*. How is it then, that *Love Affair* doesn't work in 1994?

Probably because it's been postmodernized. Previously Terry (Annette Bening in the new version) was a virgin, perkily defending that status while the threat to her innocence, Mike the Playboy (Warren Beatty), was shadowed by Catholic guilt about his careless ways. (Remember those poignant visits to his wise old auntie's chapel?) These scruples served two functions: they heated up forbidden desires, and they gave a certain bent logic to the three-month hiatus the couple imposed on their affair, ostensibly to shed other commitments, really for the chaste contemplation of this one's radical implications.

You can see why Beatty (who produced the film and co-wrote it with Robert Towne) was drawn to this story; for a famous womanizer, it must have emotionally autobiographical elements. But he also recognized that maidenly virtue and religiously inspired guilt are tough sells these days. Under Glenn Gordon Caron's uninflected direction, there are no chapels (though a distressingly feeble Katharine Hepburn appears as the aunt), the couple consummates quickly, and the 90-day wait for their famous date atop the Empire State Building is motivated by no more than a postcoital fear of rushing into something. Not much suspense in that. Some of us religious and romantic skeptics have always thought this was a loathsomely pious and sentimental tale, but in a way we were wrong. Shorn of those qualities, it just dries up and blows away.

VILLAGE VOICE, 11/1/94, p. 56, Georgia Brown

Just before the lights went down an usher led three blind people into the sneak preview for *Love Affair*. A gentleman, he carried their popcorns. Afterward the blind fended for themselves, wending their way out hand-to-shoulder, choochoo style. If I were a real reporter I'd have leapt across the theater and asked how they liked the movie. Since I'm no reporter at all, I'll rely on what looked like blissful countenances.

Someone has called Beatty's new *Love Affair* the movie with the most expensive trailer ever, meaning *Sleepless in Seattle*. But the fact is that, thanks to video, Leo McCarey's *An Affair To Remember*—itself a remake of his own less well known but superior *Love Affair*—has achieved the status of 20th century, fairy tale and classic of kitsch. Unlike Kundera, I don't mean the word as a put-down.

The movie's first half is about the domestication of a Don Juan. Presumably—since Beatty has cast himself and wife Annette Bening in the starring roles—the story hit a nerve. But more compelling is the second half, where, following the rules of melodrama, the woman is struck down, becomes a cripple, and then utilizes her injury to obtain a substantial prize. "I was looking up," she says, and we can see very well what she was looking at—that giant imperial phallus in the sky.

Beatty turns his hero into L.A.-based sportscaster Mike Gambril, a national celebrity whose announced engagement to a fellow TV journalist (Kate Capshaw) hasn't stopped him from screwing around. Ensconced in the first class cabin of a flight to Australia, Mike quickly puts the make on the cool, aloof Terry McKay (Bening), a singer and decorator. Her engagement—to a rich, handsome investment banker (Pierce Brosnan)—gives her the strength to resist the irresistible, and even to tease the seducer a bit.

Mike's reformation isn't really convincing in terms of Terry's appeal. It's the agency of a fairy godmother—a visit to her magical realm—that works this charm. After their plane makes an emergency landing on an island in the Pacific, they're put on a Russian freighter, and at some point it's just a hop-skip to the island home of Mike's Aunt Ginny (the game Katharine Hepburn). The Beatty-Bening *Love Affair* does away with her chapel, the religious component to conversion. There's just aged Ginny's blessing and her estate's green serenity (her wealth?) that changes them.

Now they have to divest themselves of their respective fiancés and those frivolous careers. The idea is that, becoming better people, they now value obscurity and downward mobility. Sure. In Beatty's version (written by Beatty and Robert Towne), Mike becomes a football coach at a Pennsylvania teachers' college, resuming painting on the side. As in the old version, she becomes a music teacher for slum kids.

As he is on Larry King, Warren-in-shadows is lit the way Fassbinder lit Armin Mueller-Stahl in *Lola*, with a nostalgic, religious beam straight into the eyes, a sign of divine grace no doubt. Sometimes Warren throws the spot on Annette, whose usual brittle style serves her well as a valiant sufferer.

My theory is that *Love Affair* was conceived by McCarey as a follow-up to Lloyd Douglas's best-selling *Magnificent Obsession*, made into a film in 1935 (directed by John M. Stahl) and remade in 1954 by Douglas Sirk. (Note that *Love Affair* came out in 1939 and then again in '57.) In *Magnificent Obsession* a drunk-driving playboy blinds a woman and kills her husband, and then becomes a doctor in order to heal her. Being blind, she doesn't know the identity of her benefactor, thus setting up emotionally charged scenes where the audience knows crucial info the characters don't.

This business of gallantly bearing affliction—Terry doesn't tell Mike that she's crippled—allows (requires?) the audience to feel the self-pity she denies. In the old war pictures men stoically bear their wounds; in melodramas, women bear theirs. The brave silence of women was especially pathetic since they usually wouldn't be heard anyway, and because they had so many wounds to bear. Call melodrama the sufferers' revenge.

All this exquisite pathos culminates in the scene where he finally finds her and she still refuses to talk. Reclining under her lap robe, she's one blithe spirit while he circles, hurt and oblivious. (Recognizing his betters, Beatty more or less reproduces Daves and Stewart's original dialogue here.) Mock it, lament it, scorn it, resent it, it still works.

Also reviewed in:
CHICAGO TRIBUNE, 10/21/94, Friday/p. C, Michael Wilmington
NEW YORK TIMES, 10/21/94, p. C3, Janet Maslin
VARIETY, 10/10-16/94, p. 84, Todd McCarthy
WASHINGTON POST, 10/21/94, p. C1, Hal Hinson
WASHINGTON POST, 10/21/94, Weekend/p. 48, Desson Howe

LOVE AFTER LOVE

A Rainbow release of an Alexandre Films/TF1 Films/Prodeve with the participation of Sofiarp/Investimage 3/Canal Plus. *Executive Producer:* Robert Benmussa. *Producer:* Jean-Bernard Fetoux. *Director:* Diane Kurys. *Screenplay (French with English subtitles):* Diane Kurys and Antoine Lacomblez. *Director of Photography:* Fabio Conversi. *Editor:* Hervé Schneid. *Music:* Yves Simon. *Choreographer:* Chris Gandois. *Sound:* Bernard Bats, Claude Villand, Bernard Le Roux and (music) William Flageollet. *Sound Editor:* Michèle Boehm. *Casting:* Pierre Amzallag. *Art Director:* Tony Egry. *Costumes:* Mic Cheminal. *Make-up:* Paul LeMarinel. *Stunt Coordinator:* Roland Neunreuther. *Running time:* 104 minutes. *MPAA Rating:* Not Rated.

CAST: Isabelle Huppert (Lola); Bernard Giraudeau (David); Hippolyte Girardot (Tom); Lio (Marianne); Yvan Attal (Romain); Judith Reval (Rachel); Ingrid Held (Anne); Laure Killing (Elisabeth); Mehdi Iossen (Simon); Florian Billon (Olivier); Eva Killing (Caroline); Ana Girardot (Juliette); Jean-Claude de Goros (Langwood); Chrystelle Labaude (Christine); Philippe Chany (Manager); Pierre Amzallag (Babysitter); Renée Amzallag (Rebecca); Jean Grecault (Factory Watchman); Dominique Stablo (Hospital Receptionist); Philippe Yarache (Birthday Guest); Franco Tonfoni (Concierge).

LOS ANGELES TIMES, 7/8/94, Calendar/p. 14, Kevin Thomas

As Diane Kurys' wise and graceful "Love After Love" opens, Lola (Isabelle Huppert), a popular Parisian novelist, is celebrating her 35th birthday at a festive gathering in the spacious high-rise apartment she shares with her longtime lover, David (Bernard Giraudeau), an equally successful architect. Lola would appear to have everything, but by the time she celebrates her next birthday, her entire life has changed.

Lola and David have been together since she was 15, and their determinedly open relationship has survived David's fathering two children with another woman. An autobiographical novelist, Lola is experiencing writer's block, apparently for the first time. It is not lost on her that her own new lover, a rock musician (Hippolyte Girardot), is also the father of two children who make legitimate claims upon his time and attentions. Lola is beginning to be no longer content playing second fiddle in the lives of the men with whom she is involved.

Through Lola's quietly intensifying search for renewal, Kurys evokes an acute sense of contemporary urban life as it is lived in most major cities of the world. Lola and David may be more sophisticated in regard to the vicissitudes of amour than most couples, yet Kurys suggests that traditional French worldliness in affairs of the heart may be wearing a tad thin in the competitive, economically depressed '90s.

Kurys puts major importance on the relationship between David and his younger half-brother Romain (Yvan Attal). Handsome and debonair in his 40s, David reflexively responds to the overtures of gorgeous women, including his ambitious but naive new secretary (Judith Reval) and regards such encounters as merely casual sex. A workaholic who accepts all the commissions that come his way, David is an irascible hard-driving employer. He is everything that Romain does not want to be; Romain wants to strike out on his own and also to establish a stable marriage.

Although central to the story, Lola is also a point of departure for Kurys in exploring with wry humor and compassion the longings and frustrations of all the key people close to the novelist. Kurys gets reflective portrayals from her first-rate cast, and "Love After Love" has the easy flow and intimacy typical of Kurys, who has always seemed the most natural and spontaneous of filmmakers. Indeed, this lovely and thoughtful film proceeds with so much effortlessness that you may be in danger of overlooking its considerable substance.

NEW YORK POST, 10/14/94, p. 46, Thelma Adams

In "Love After Love," the sedately beautiful French actress Isabelle Huppert plays Lola—a successful author who "has nothing to say" in her novel-in-progress, but she has lovely handwriting. Writer/director Diane Kurys appears to be noodling as well, concentrating on characters who tell lie after lie and never developing a larger truth.

Huppert who starred in Kurys' "Entre Nous," is a highly watchable actress. She can make floating along, free, white and 35, in slim ebony outfits and black flats seem initially interesting.

A sophisticated Parisian with no apparent history or family, but a substantial stash, Lola has a live-in love, David (Bernard Giraudeau), and a musician lover, Tom (Hippolyte Girardot).

David, a tense yuppie architect, also has divided loyalties. He splits his time between Huppert and the mother of his two children. The spouse, Marianne (Lio), is a demanding and dependent female whose desperation seems to fill a need that the self-sufficient Lola cannot.

David also dallies with Rachel (Judith Reval), his scheming assistant. Tom's no free ride either. He threatens to leave his wife and two children for Lola and becomes unhinged when he discovers his spouse is also having an affair.

Urbane and accomplished, this upscale French soap plays like "thirtysomething," with one significant difference—the self-involved characters hardly care for themselves (ah, ennui), much less each other.

The net result is that we don't care for Lola and her crowd. They make love; I think about defrosting pork chops.

Let this attractive cast of husbands and wives, artists and professionals, scratch for pleasure, mate and betray who they will, attempt suicide, regroup, write a page and wrinkle it into a ball, design a building, record a pop song, wear black leather or eat Japanese. They don't give a damn. Why should we?

NEWSDAY, 10/14/94, Part II/p. B8, Jack Mathews

I don't know how a thorough survey of the sex lives of the French would square with that shocker announced last week about us 80 percent monogamous Americans, but Dianne Kurys' bittersweet soap opera "Love After Love" makes a pretty good case for the concept of mating for life, even in Paris.

Kurys has made a career of dramatizing her personal crises, her teenage years in a rigid private school ("Pepperment Soda"), her involvement in the '68 student revolt ("Cocktail Molotov"), and the impact on her of her parents' divorce ("Entre Nous," "C'est La Vie"). In "Love After Love," she examines how coming of age in the '70s, with its emphasis on self-gratification and noncommitment, affects some members of that generation in the '90s.

Isabelle Huppert, who played Kurys' fictionalized mother in "Entre Nous," takes on the role here of Lola, a popular diarist (a writer, as opposed to filmmaker) who is advancing toward middle age with two lovers, no children and one gigantic heartache. Her writing has become brittle and meaningless, her once keen sense of observation is now trained on the hollowness of her own existence, and though she does little to conceal her own affairs from the architect with whom she has lived most of her adult life, she is becoming increasingly closed-minded about his sleepovers with the suicidal mother of his two sons!

To compound Lola's agony, her rock musician lover Tom (Hippolyte Girardot) is married, with a couple of kids and a wife he genuinely loves, and her architect lover (Bernard Giraudeau) is also being tempted by his predatory secretary (Judith Reval).

If this sounds like a Mad Magazine parody of "One Day at a Time," it doesn't miss by far. Kurys has built her story inside a tight universe of worst-case scenarios, a cartoon panel of philanderers, and a sex survey pollster working their neighborhoods is likely to get a yes to everything.

The movie opens and closes with birthday parties at which the honoree is elsewhere having sex when the flaming cake arrives. And while a bride at a wedding reception is sobbing with happiness indoors, her new husband is out in the greenhouse consummating one of the guests.

I'm sure Kurys expects us to be amused by some of these goings-on, but there is way too much anguish, guilt and remorse on display throughout the movie for it to be taken even remotely as bedroom farce. Lola is a wreck, clinging to her '70s fantasies about pain-free love and non-commitment, as if to feel anything else would be an act of self-betrayal.

Huppert is an actress whose face always seems to be masking some major turbulence, and as pathetic and insecure as Lola often is, we follow along willingly, hoping she finds her way. By the end, we do learn some of what Kurys presumably has learned about trust and romantic companionship, and Lola's life does begin to take on shape and meaning.

But, of course, we're Americans, and we mate for life. You can look it up.

SIGHT AND SOUND, 9/93, p. 39, Amanda Lipman

During her thirtieth birthday part, Lola, a successful novelist, slips outside to make love with her musician lover, Tom, in his car. After the party, Lola and David, the architect she lives with, argue in a desultory fashion. That night, they are woken up by a phone call from David's ex-wife Marianne, who says that one of their children is ill. David rushes over to find that the child is well, but decides to stay the night with Marianne anyway. Lola is having problems with her latest novel and finds herself day-dreaming exaggerated sequences from her life. She and David are not getting on. She goes to stay with Tom in a hotel while he records a new album. Meanwhile, David falls out with his brother and partner Romain, and is seduced by his secretary. Tom takes Lola to Italy. But when his wife Elisabeth turns up, Tom abandons Lola, who returns to France by herself. She asks David to meet her at the airport but he sends his secretary, who admits to Lola that she slept with David.

Meanwhile, David is dining with Marianne and ends up sleeping with her. Marianne asks David to take their children. The boys move into Lola and David's apartment where Lola, after initial difficulties, grows to love them. But when Marianne attempts suicide, David and his sons go back to her. Now that she's alone, Lola's lifestyle becomes sloppier and more relaxed. Tom turns up one night and persuades her to accompany him to a hotel, where he claims Elisabeth is being unfaithful to him. A fight ensues and Lola leaves. She writes in her diary that she is still seeing David occasionally and that she is pregnant. She decides to keep the baby. Romain marries his girlfriend. At the wedding, Marianne is friendly towards Lola, David's secretary tries to seduce Romain, and Lola tells Romain about the baby. At Lola's thirty-first birthday party she tells

David that she is pregnant and he makes no response. But when it is time to cut the cake, Lola and David have disappeared.

Diane Kurys' promising career has turned out to be surprisingly patchy. It was four years before she made a follow-up to the hugely successful *Coup de foudre*—and that was the disappointingly rambling *A Man in Love*. *La Boule-les-Pins (C'est la vie)*, her last film, saw a return to form with the chirpy observations of rites of passage reminiscent of her debut feature, *Diabolo Menthe*. This time, however, she's tackled the adult *drame de passion* again—with more success.

As if in search of good omens, Kurys brought back *Coup de foudre* star Isabelle Huppert to play Lola. Huppert as a 30-year-old? That's par for the odd generational course here; it's almost as if Kurys, having written about a group of fortysomethings, had worried about her characters being too old and sliced ten years off their ages. The preoccupations here—love and liberty—seem to be those of children of the 60s, not the more materialist 70s.

That aside, Huppert 's calm magnetism serves her well as the successful, self-controlled woman who almost falls apart when not one, but two men leave her. (There's a neat parallel in the good-time girl resonance of her name; in her own, more cerebral way, this solitary Lola also goes for exactly what she wants.) Without labouring the point, the film slips between what other people see in Lola (a controlled, unemotional woman), what she would like to see in herself (in her written flights of fancy), and what we actually see. Huppert pulls off the tricky feat of retaining our interest while dividing our sympathies. While she flits smugly between David and Tom, not even bothering to disguise her telephone conversation with Tom in front of David, or disappearing during her birthday party to have sex with Tom, she is the woman we love to hate—one who takes a kind of careless revenge on what is seen here as an equally cynical *man*kind (after all, David is still secretly seeing Marianne and Tom is cheating on Elisabeth).

And when she is rejected by both of them (each man returning to a 'hysterical' woman in need of protection), Lola appears to have got what she deserves in both senses of the word: punishment and freedom. But this isn't a simple 70s feminist tale of loving and leaving them; Huppert's Lola is at once liberated, miserable and still determined to get her own way—to the extent that she carries on seeing David as before, except without living with him. If she learns anything, it is that she wants to have a child. An easy way out of the man/woman conundrum, perhaps, but a perfectly acceptable transferral of love.

If Lola is the strong point at the film's centre, everyone else is characterised by weakness, from the brash, arrogant David (weak enough to let himself be seduced by his ex-wife and his secretary) to the gentle, impressionable Romain. But these weaknesses are largely the observations of Lola; for her to be strong, she has to see others as weak. The suggestion is that this is the reason she writes: to make sense of them or contain them by moulding them as she would like them, glamorising situations in glossy black and white versions of reality. (At the same time, Lola's distance can be seen as a sign of her own weakness, and a good example of the ways in which the film gets at the cracks in her armour: in Italy, she is forced into voyeurism, watching Tom and his wife through their window after he has rejected her.) Lola also discovers that despite, or perhaps because of, their weaknesses, others do just fine. Marianne and Elisabeth get what they want by retreating into sickness; the men find the fragile women they seek.

Kurys seems to have learned some lessons from *A Man in Love*: the over-the-top-sexual high jinks, currently characterising Hollywood's 'psychosexual' movies, have been replaced by lower-key verbal encounters. And while the other film churned out ravaged clichés in French, English and Italian, *Apres l'amour* seems much more at ease with itself. It copes with agony, bluster, lies and voyeurism in a cynically relaxed spirit that places it firmly in the French 'relationship movie' genre; though with the difference, outdated as it may seem anywhere except in France, that it is a woman through whose eyes we look.

VILLAGE VOICE, 10/18/94, p. 61, Lisa Katzman

Love After Love is one of those French films where well-dressed Parisians who carry on affairs are treated as though they are exercising an ontological imperative rather than a bourgeois prerogative. In the opening scene of Diane Kurys's new film, the pretty and successful writer Lola (Isabelle Huppert) slips away from her 35th birthday party for a breathless rendezvous with a musician named Tom, moments after her lover, dapper architect David, puts the moves on another woman. Kurys captures the lemming-like compulsion that fuels polygamy, but disappoints by making neither of Lola's men worthy of the contained intelligence Huppert brings to her role. In this Gallic soap opera, a chilly Cartesian logic rules the emotions. These people think, therefore they fuck. The problem is, what they think is unbelievably banal; consequently, so are their sex scenes.

Kurys's suggestion that for women polygamy is trouble extends the premise of *Entre Nous* (1987) that men are cads. While in her earlier film, the women discover the healing power of love for each other, in *Love After Love*, Lola is bereft even of female friendship; she's at odds with Tom's wife, David's ex, and his vixenish secretary. When Tom proves he is first a coward, then a sad sack, she is left with few choices. David's subsequent character reversal is as unconvincing as the generic portrayal of his bastardliness was. When he takes on a crumpled sensitivity as the film nears its end, it's a relief not to have to stick around for love *after* love.

Also reviewed in:
CHICAGO TRIBUNE, 10/14/94, Friday/p. M, Michael Wilmington
NEW YORK TIMES, 10/14/94, p. C10, Caryn James
VARIETY, 9/7/92, p. 50, Lisa Nesselson
WASHINGTON POST, 11/11/94, p. D6, Hal Hinson

LOVE & A .45

A Trimark Pictures release of a Darin Scott/Trimark production. *Producer:* Darin Scott. *Director:* C. M. Talkington. *Screenplay:* C. M. Talkington. *Director of Photography:* Tom Richmond. *Editor:* Bob Duscay. *Sound:* Bill Fiege. *Production Designer:* Deborah Pastor. *Art Director:* D. Montgomery. *Set Dresser:* Marcus Brown. *Special Effects:* Randy Moore. *Costumes:* Kari Perkins. *Make-up:* Kate Shorter. *Special Effects Make-up:* David Whitley. *Stunt Coordinator:* Russell Towery. *Running time:* 101 minutes. *MPAA Rating:* R.

CAST: Gil Bellows (Watty Watts); Renee Zellweger (Starlene); Rory Cochrane (Billy Mack); Jeffrey Combs (Dino Bob); Jace Alexander (Creepy Cody); Anne Wedgeworth (Thaylene); Peter Fonda (Virgil); Tammy Le Blanc (Stipper); Wiley Wiggins (Young Clerk); Jack Nance (Justice Thurmar); Charlotte Ross (Mary Ann); Michael Bowen (Ranger X); Todd Conner (Young Cop).

LOS ANGELES TIMES, 11/23/94, Calendar/p. 6, Kevin Thomas

C. M. Talkington's "Love & a .45" sends up the gun-toting lovers-on-the-run genre with a gleeful wit, nonstop energy and a refreshing honesty. It's a low-budget, stripped-down "Natural Born Killers" that comments on the role of the media in making celebrities of criminals without all the hypocritical hyperbole of the Oliver Stone film.

Right at the start, Talkington, in a potent debut, pinpoints the appeal of such pictures: Audiences can enjoy condescending to those they consider rednecks—and such couples invariably are none-too-bright hicks—while vicariously experiencing the thrill of a wild spree of reckless adventure and passionate sex.

"My granddaddy told me the only two things you need to get by in this world is never to believe anything anyone says and never point a loaded gun," remarks Gil Bellows' Watty Watts, petty career criminal, to a wide-eyed 14-year-old (Wiley Wiggins) clerk at an East Texas convenience store he has just robbed. Watty, however, soon disregards his grandfather's wisdom.

Actually, he's on the verge of settling down. He's fallen in love with Renee Zellweger's giggly, squirmy Starlene, and they're living in a trailer on the outskirts of town, not so far from that convenience store. He has his treasured '72 Pontiac, and Starlene, despite her demeanor, is more sensible than he is. She tries to curb him from doing anything too stupid—especially with his skittish, drugged-out fellow ex-con Billy (Rory Cochrane).

There's this hitch, though: Watty, carried away with love, has secretly purchased a $2,000 engagement ring for Starlene with funds borrowed from an underworld type whose crazed, sadistic strong-arms (Jeffrey Combs, Jace Alexander)—who could be right out of "Pulp Fiction"—are intent upon Watty's repayment of the loan in timely fashion. As a result, Watty and Starlene are swiftly fugitives, wanted for three murders—never mind that Billy is responsible for one of them and that the other two are in self-defense, Billy and the strong-arms seem far more intent than the law in catching up with the couple, who in time-honored fashion are heading for Mexico. There's a stopover in San Antonio to visit Starlene's hilarious suburban hippie parents, played gloriously by Ann Wedgeworth and Peter Fonda.

Although Talkington has roots deep in Texas himself, he writes, as part of his satire, quaintly exaggerated dialogue that nobody would speak in real life. "Love & a .45" is a comic book, not to be taken seriously, yet Talkington's people are real, well-drawn, even though they're caricatures. Talkington not only has style but also a terrific way with actors, giving them the confidence to go over the top while having fun doing so. Shrewdly, he keeps Watty and Starlene as a pair of ultra-sexy innocents in a cold, brutal world. He doesn't ask us to like them, but don't be surprised if you find yourself wanting them to make good on their getaway.

As Watty and Starlene become hyped on TV and in the press, Starlene deliriously compares herself and Watty to Faye Dunaway and Warren Beatty, but Watty says it all when he quietly replies "Everybody gets caught and killed in those movies."

NEW YORK POST, 11/23/94, p. 51, Thelma Adams

"My Daddy said there are only two things you need to get by on in this country: Love and a .45," says the lethal cutie Watty Watts (Gil Bellows).

That seems to be the low-budget anthem in a recent breed of "Reservoir" puppies nipping at the heels of Quentin Tarantino.

First-timer C.M. Talkington has returned to his native Texas from the hallowed halls of Brown University to write and direct a joyous psychedelic splatterfest that steals from the video convenience store, most prominently but not exclusively from "The Getaway."

In "Love & a .45," the slacker Robin Hood Watty steals from the speedy mart and enriches himself and his love kitten Starlene (Renee Zellweger). He lives by a code: "Never rob a store with a loaded gun.

For the lovers, trailer park life is nothing like a box of chocolates.

In order to get to the increasingly wild scenes of carnage that are this type of movie's bread and bloodshed, a gun must go off. Enter Billy Mack, a volatile, drug-addicted ex-con, played with wall-eyed gusto by Rory Cochrane (the waifish Slater in "Dazed and Confused").

When Watty and Billy team up, the latter breaks the golden rule—and the body count begins. "Love & a .45" offers a meaty scene with a fork and knife, but the set piece is the use of a tattoo needle as an instrument of torture. Remember how you felt about dentists after "The Marathon Man"? If you're even considering getting a teeny butterfly drilled onto your ankle, don't see this movie!!

Talkington laces the gore with humor. As Starlene's dad, Peter Fonda spoofs his generation as a handicapped suburban hippie who ripped his own throat out on a bad acid trip, but hasn't given up the Stuff.

The dizzy Starlene declares her undying love for her Texas robber, proclaiming: "Baby, I'd follow you to Oklahoma."

"Love & a .45" is the kind of movie that makes me yearn for the return of the drive-in.

NEWSDAY, 11/23/94, Part II/p. B12, John Anderson

"I'd follow you to *Oklahoma*," coos the blond, bodacious and lethal-as-she-has-to-be Starlene (Renee Zellweger), who may or may not know where Oklahoma is, or even that she's currently in Texas.

She's too busy—swapping spit with Watty (Gil Bellows), her career convenience-store-bandit boyfriend, or wondering when the cops and homicidal speed freaks are gonna catch up to them. Or, perhaps, wondering where the next bag of Cheetos is coming from.

But, name aside, Starlene is not quite the echt-bimbo. She's smarter than all that, as is "Love & a .45." Garbagey, bloody, facetious and occasionally hair-raising, C.M. Talkington's horror-western follows a couple of natural born something-or-others on a road trip from hell, taking side trips to media criticism, hallucinatory visuals and cut-rate Raymond Chandler mood swings. If this sounds familiar, though, don't blame the director. The zeitgeist occasionally just burps these things up in six-packs.

"I'd always considered myself happy," Watty says, between tosses of the I Ching. "I had a beautiful girlfriend, a car, a trailer home ... " All is lost, however, when Watty's old cellmate, crazy Billy Mack (Rory Cochrane, the memorable pothead of "Dazed and Confused") lets his drug appetite override his better instincts, shoots an equally coked-up store clerk, threatens Watty, gets a fork in the neck for his trouble, and shaves his head. After Watty and Starlene accidentally kill two malicious cops, they take off—pursued by police, Billy and two lethal loansharks named Creepy Cody and Dinosaur Bob (Jace Alexander and Jeffrey Combs), who keep Billy supplied with amphetamines as they all chase each other across Texas.

For all its mayhem and marked-down sensibility, "Love & a .45" is truer to what Oliver Stone set out to do in "Natural Born Killers" than Stone would probably realize. The tone is more consistent, the dialogue cheaper, the tongue firmer in cheek, the violence less choreographed and more believable—thus making a stronger point about murderers as celebrities. And it's cognizant of what makes so-called "white trash" trashy—a flamboyant lack of self-respect—and what comprises the white-trash nightmare—someone trashier than you. In "Love & a .45," the characters are clawing their way to the bottom.

VILLAGE VOICE, 12/6/94, p. 66, Gary Dauphin

Yet another entry in the recent white-trash-kids-shoot-up-Southwest sweepstakes, *Love & a .45* might have lost its summer zeitgeist hook when its release was rolled back to now, but it also avoided the embarrassment of having to stand in *Natural Born Killers*'s shadow. Mickey and Mallory without a decent script, Watty Watts and Starlene (Gil Bellows and Renee Zellweger) share a rural prefab house and argue about Watty's crime sprees, their hunk'-a 'burnin' love declaimed over their bed in multicolored Lite Brite pegs.

After one of Watty's convenience store holdups goes awry, the pair bang-bangs its way from losers to cop-killing media darlings, fitfully pursued across East Texas by the cops, some recessive-gened loan sharks, and Watty's onetime stickup partner Billy Mack (Rory Cochrane, last seen in *Dazed and Confused*). There are requisite stops along the way for a road-side wedding and a visit to Starlene's folks (Peter Fonda plays dad, an ex-hippie with a voice box), but the only thing worth watching is Cochrane's Billy Mack. Standing between Watty and Starlene and that mythical land of nonextradition—Mexico—Billy Mack is the one live body on screen, a speed-popping knot of hyperkinetic nervous tics and hick-scenery-chomping plopped down in a cast whose basic concern isn't acting but the consistent maintenance of their accents.

Directed by first-timer C.M. Talkington, *.45*'s main debt isn't to *NBK* but to the look and feel of *Liquid Television*, especially the subuniverses of the Dog Boy and Winter Steele segments. The folks swirling around Watty and Starlene are slick gobs of pink goo straight out of MTV's white-Southerner-as-special-effect aesthetic, itself borrowed from biker flicks and the white, window dressing in blaxploitation. In the end, that look and feel will be the only thing you'll remember about *Love & a .45*, as the cartoonlike quality of certain classes of white people goes from Northern in-joke to something even an East Texas native like Talkington can laugh about.

Also reviewed in:
NEW YORK TIMES, 11/23/94, p. C14, Janet Maslin
VARIETY, 6/6-12/94, p. 34, Todd McCarthy

LOW DOWN DIRTY SHAME, A

A Buena Vista release of a Caravan Pictures presentation. *Executive Producer:* Eric L. Gold and Lee R. Mayes. *Producer:* Joe Roth and Roger Birnbaum. *Director:* Keenen Ivory Wayans.

Screenplay: Keenen Ivory Wayans. *Director of Photography:* Matthew F. Leonetti. *Editor:* John F. Link. *Music:* Marcus Miller. *Music Editor:* Earl Ghaffari. *Sound:* Willie Burton and (music) Alan Meyerson. *Sound Editor:* Gregory M. Gerlich and Gary S. Gerlich. *Casting:* Robi Reed-Humes. *Production Designer:* Robb Wilson King. *Art Director:* Richard L. Johnson. *Set Designer:* Ron Yates. *Set Decorator:* Lance Lombardo. *Set Dresser:* Kinney Booker. *Special Effects:* Bruno Van Zeebroeck. *Costumes:* Francine Jamison-Tanchuck. *Make-up:* Stephanie Cozart Burton. *Stunt Coordinator:* Charles Picerni and Billy Burton. *Running time:* 108 minutes. *MPAA Rating:* R.

CAST: Keenen Ivory Wayans (Andre Shame); Charles S. Dutton (Sonny Rothmiller); Jada Pinkett (Peaches); Salli Richardson (Angela Flowers); Andrew Divoff (Ernesto Mendoza); Corwin Hawkins (Wayman); Gary Cervantes (Luis); Gregory Sierra (Captain Nunez); Kim Wayans (Diane); Andrew Shaifer (Bernard); Christopher Spencer (Benny); Devin Devasquez (Mendoza's Girl); John Capodice (Mob Boss); Craig Ryan Ng (Chun Yung Fat); Donald Diamont (Chad); Randy Hall (Hank); Doug Kruse (Skinhead Speaker); Michael Bofshever (Mr. Gold); Renee Hicks (Hooker); Robert Schimmel (The John); Kristina Wagner (Lisa); Bob Hughes (Cop #1); Mike Echols (Cop #2); Luanne Crawford (Cop #3); Dominique Jennings (Funeral Guest); Lisa Mende (Chad's Agent); De-Andre L. Russell (Mailman at Post Office); Derek Woolley (Maitre'd); Diane Little (Waitress); Erika Monroe (Customer #1); Gloria Pawlak (Customer #2); Shawn Lusader (Female Lovemaker); Mark Ian Simon (Male Lovemaker); Rafael H. Robeedo (Heavy); Pillow (Body Builder); Michael Wheels Parise (Man in Bath); Twist (Young Police Officer); Bobby Jen (Hotel Thug); Nikki Fritz (Exotic Dancer); Andrea Evans (Denise).

LOS ANGELES TIMES, 11/23/94, Calendar/p. 2, Kevin Thomas

Although humorous and energetic, "A Low Down Dirty Shame" is about as routine as a private-eye action-adventure can get, but it does have a secret weapon: Jada Pinkett, a feisty and funny comedian, as witty as she is pretty, who lights up the screen. She has already been seen to advantage in "Menace II Society" and "Jason's Lyric," having established herself in TV's "A Different World," and she's the best reason to see this film.

She has been cast as Peaches, secretary extraordinaire, at once sassy and devoted to Keenen Ivory Wayans' Andre Shame, a seedy L.A. private detective, an ex-cop down on his luck. Things seem to be looking up, however, when a DEA agent (Charles S. Dutton) hires Shame to track down $20 million in missing drug money. At every inevitably convoluted turn, Shame is going to need Peaches' endless resourcefulness and spunk.

Wayans, who also wrote and directed the film, seems to have overreached. He's fine directing others, but could have used some guidance and reassurance in his own portrayal. He has presence but seems self-conscious and uncertain in a role that ranges from the serious to the comic, with plenty of action and a little romance thrown in. What works best is Shame's slow realization that it's Peaches who's worthy of his love rather than Salli Richardson's glamorous Angela, his lost love, newly resurfaced and about as reliable as Mary Astor's Bridget O'Shaughnessy in "The Maltese Falcon."

As a writer, Wayans might well have started telling his story earlier, since so much of it has already happened by the time the picture actually begins. Dutton, Andrew Divoff as a key heavy and others shine in support. Smartly produced and certainly lively, "A Low Down Dirty Shame" is diverting while you're watching it, but you're liable to start forgetting it by the time the end credits start to unroll.

NEW YORK POST, 11/23/94, p. 50, Bill Hoffmann

Stand aside, Shaft and Superfly, the latest black superhero has arrived and his name is Shame.

He's the cavalier cutup and all-around good-guy detective in Keenen Ivory Wayans' hysterical '90s sendup of those awful, but awfully entertaining, blaxploitation movies of the '70s.

Wayans—the comic genius behind Fox TV's breakthrough series "In Living Color"—has created a character who's just as likable and lovable as he is off-color and offensive.

And if "A Low Down Dirty Shame" is the hit it should be, there should be countless sequels ahead.

The comedy here is both tastefully sharp and crassly cruel. It's black-on-black humor with a vengeance.

Wayans plays Andre Shame, a hunky, hard-nosed private eye, who takes big risks for his exorbitant fees. Along for the ride is Shame's smart, sassy and smutty-mouthed sidekick Peaches (Jada Pinkett), whose love for Shame is second only to her continual wisecracks.

Shame's got a smart mouth, too. When Peaches finds him black-and-blue after a rough fight, she demands to know what happened.

"I went partying with Rodney King and Reginald Denny," he says.

There's also a fiercely mean—and brilliantly funny—routine about the intelligence levels of Mike Tyson and Muhammad Ali.

The plot involves Shame's attempt to track down $20 million in missing drug money and face off his old nemesis, crime king Ernesto Mendoza (Andrew Divoff).

The main and basically inescapable problem with Wayans' film is that in between the jokes, it slips into the familiar trappings of the films he's parodying.

There are endless shootouts, brutal fights and an abundance of gratuitous foul language, which becomes mind-numbing after a while.

Perhaps if Wayans had gone more towards the constant satire of the "Naked Gun" movies, he'd have hit his highs more often.

The most that can be said of the nearly non-stop action sequences is that Wayans has obviously studied the movies of John Woo. Here, every cough and splatter is gloriously choreographed and filmed in slow motion for maximum screen time.

Interestingly, "Shame" comes along just as Eddie Murphy's Axel Foley character runs out of gas in now abysmal "Beverly Hills Cop" series, the previous giant of black-hero parody films.

We hope Wayans will remember to keep Shame fresh and exciting in future ventures.

NEWSDAY, 11/23/94, Part II/p. B9, John Anderson

Keenen Ivory Wayans' caustic sense of humor is an equal-opportunity corrosive—sort of. In "A Low Down Dirty Shame," gays, immigrants, the handicapped, postal workers and Gary Coleman all feel the bite of his wit. Not so filmmakers who feign parody because they need something else to hang their one-liners on.

Writing, directing and starring—as ex-cop-cum-private-eye Andre Shame—Wayans is walking a familiar beat, and showing some signs of premature fatigue. In "I'm Gonna Get You Sucka," his well-received 1988 directing debut, Wayans skewered the "blaxploitation" films of the '70s with good-natured humor. "Shame's" target, though, is less specific—everything from "Stick" to "The Specialist"—and while genre-busting is still Wayans' game, this is a much more casual and less focused effort. Basically, "Shame" can't decide whether it wants to really be a thriller with a sense of humor, or a satire with a sense of adventure.

It's definitely funny, if unevenly so. Wayans, who created "In Living Color" and made it, at the outset, TV's freshest comedy, knows how to milk the clichés for maximum effect. So does Jada Pinkett, who plays Peaches, Shame's girl friday/little sister who's eager to kick some butt, eager to get closer to Shame, and who takes the concept of "sassy" to ridiculous new extremes. She steals the picture.

The plot, of course, is immaterial, but here goes: The down-on-his-luck Shame, who lost his job after a drug bust went bad, is approached by his old DEA colleague Rothmiller (Charles S. Dutton) and asked to track down Mendoza (Andrew Divoff, the pockmarked (aren't they all?) Latino gangster he thought he'd killed, find millions in drug money and be reunited with Angela Flowers (Salli Richardson), the bombshell he loved and lost to Mendoza. In the course of all this, the film gives us massive explosions, insane shootouts in hotel rooms, blood-gushing fistfights, ugly skinheads, soap opera stars, and two of what have become staples of cheesy '90s thrillers: the topless bar scene, and the shootout in the mall. In short, something for everyone.

It's a good thing Wayans' can write a joke, a good thing he's got Jada Pinkett watching his back, and a good thing there are so many bad movies he won't have to come up with anything original for years. But like a one-man "Mystery Science Theater 3000," he may be looking at the screen one day, and see himself.

SIGHT AND SOUND, 10/95, p. 52, Max Schaefer

Expelled from the Los Angeles Police Department after a botched drug bust, Andre Shame works as a private investigator undertaking dangerous work for low pay with the help of his secretary and feisty Girl Friday, Peaches. Sonny Rothmiller of the Drug Enforcement Agency, also involved in the failed bust, announces that Shame's ex-girlfriend Angela Flowers is back in town. He believes she is living with Ernesto Mendoza, the drug baron whom Shame thought he had killed during the raid. Shame agrees to find them. Shortly into his investigation, he is captured by Mendoza, who bruises him but lets him go with a warning. Peaches tends to his wounds and makes advances to him which he rebuffs.

Shame surprises Angela at her hotel and informs Rothmiller. When Angela reveals that she has left Mendoza he realises that Rothmiller is in Mendoza's pay, but too late: his men are already at the door. They escape and he leaves Angela at Peaches' house. Alone, the two women fight and Angela walks out. Meanwhile, Shame confronts Mendoza in his nightclub, but loses him.

Rothmiller kidnaps Peaches. Shame finds Angela retrieving $20 million that she stole from Mendoza. He agrees to an exchange—Peaches for Angela and then money—but manages to overcome both Mendoza's henchmen and Rothmiller's DEA troops. He takes Mendoza alive but Angela shoots him. She threatens to kill Shame since she knows he will never let her keep the money, but Peaches intervenes and triumphs over Angela. As the police take Angela away, Shame realises that Peaches is the woman he really wants.

A Low Down Dirty Shame is an action-comedy, but so is every other action movie these days. From its roots in the James Bond series, the genre as a whole has increasingly embraced tongue-in-cheek humour, a trend which reaches a peak in *Demolition Man* and blows itself to pieces, memorably, in *The Last Action Hero*. So established is this in the minds of western audiences that when faced with genuine romanticism in action, as in John Woo's movies, they are inclined to read it as camp. Self-parody undermines our ability to read the clash of good and evil innocently. Thus, in this summer's blockbusters Judge Dredd is well-meaning but none too bright, the lads in *Bad Boys* are suspected of being lovers, and Batman has a rubber fetish and needs to see a shrink.

These films survive—when they do—in a delicate balance: comedy makes the adrenaline rush safe without lessening the pleasure. *A Low Down Dirty Shame*, however, is unevenly weighted. Writer/director/star Keenan Ivory Wayans' debut feature *I'm Gonna Git You, Sucka* was an out-and-out parody of blaxploitation films and *Shame*, too, is a very funny film. But whereas in *Sucka* Wayans deliberately chose stunt doubles that looked nothing like his cast, here he performs most of his stunts himself: for much of the time *Shame* (like Shame the character) wants to be taken seriously but, as an action director, Wayans has neither the technique nor the budget to deliver. The use of slow motion, for example, is so hackneyed that it looks like another joke: as yet another thug moves towards him with the grace and precision of an action replay, Shame's wide-eyed gaze is embarrassingly reminiscent of Leslie Nielsen in the *Naked Gun* films. Wayans insists, "It's not a parody. It's taking a step in a different direction". But only the logic of parody enables him to switch from disgusted alarm on waking in the arms of Peaches' gay housemate Wayman to pouting camp bitchiness when he tries to convince Wayman's lover that he has replaced him in order to blackmail Wayman into doing him a favour. Frank Drebin could get away with such a quick change; James Bond never could (or would). In such an atmosphere, the pretensions to action in earnest— already weak—cannot survive.

This uneasiness is partly redeemed by the central performances: Wayans' Shame is attractive and assured. Jada Pinkett, of *Menace II Society* and *Jason's Lyric*, takes naturally to comedy and plays Peaches with a slightly manic charm. As Wayman, Corwin Hawkins (who died last year and to whom the film is dedicated) manages a surprising amount within the stereotype to which he is confined. Only Charles S. Dutton, as Rothmiller, is out of place: bizarrely self-righteous, as if he'd developed too much sympathy for his character.

Dutton and Hawkins' performances could stand for the worst and best aspects of the movie as a whole. When it begins to take its own clichés seriously, and plays them for drama or romance, it remains unconvincing; but for much of the time it relaxes and baits these clichés them with an amiable wit that is never less than watchable. *Shame* cannot do straight action—if it could only come out and admit this it would be a lot more comfortable.

VILLAGE VOICE, 12/6/94, p. 66, Tom Kertes

The setup: a hotel maid startles a guest sitting on the toilet. "Do you know how to spell 'Do Not Disturb'?" shrieks the victim. "Do *you* know how to spell Lysol? " our sassy heroine retorts. "It stinks in here."

Before you can recover from such heavy-duty hilarity, you must get out of the way of all the falling bodies. Keenen Ivory Wayans, leaps out of the maid's cart and mows down every baddie in sight, in Sam Peckinpahesque slow-mo, no less. Eyes fall out of sockets (slowly), blood spurts out of foreheads (copiously), innumerable body parts are parted from bodies (ponderously). All this before the credits.

As the gay movie critics on Wayans's *In Living Color* would shriek: *Hated it!!!*"

Disgraced ex-cop Andre Shame is now a seedy private eye with a not-so-private eye for the ladies who gets involved in an inexplicable mess that has something to do with drugs, diamonds, mob-men, and mobette-molls. The baddie is a guy with a Spanish accent—except when he has a Russian accent. Don't ask.

Shame, a blatant mutation-ripoff of *Lethal Weapon I, Die Hard II*, and *Beverly Hills Cop III*, isn't funny enough to be a comedy. (See putative joke above) There's not a hint of mysteriousness about its mystery. Is it a parody? By the end of the interminable two hours, no one cares.

Still, of all the shameful things about *Shame*, the most annoying must be the ludicrous "action" sequences. After applying their own pitifully ineffective blows, the meanies just stand there and visibly *wait* for Wayans to crush their thoraxes into teeny bits. Nice of them, no?

Also reviewed in:
NEW YORK TIMES, 11/23/94, p. C18, Stephen Holden
VARIETY, 11/28-12/4/94, p. 94, Brian Lowry
WASHINGTON POST, 11/24/94, p. B14, Rita Kempley

LUNA PARK

A Northern Entertainment release of an Ima Productions/Ciby 2000/L Productions co-production in association with Canal Plus, Blues Films, CNC.. *Producer:* Georges Benayoun. *Director:* Pavel Lounguine. *Screenplay (Russian with English subtitles):* Pavel Lounguine. *Director of Photography:* Denis Evstigneev. *Editor:* Pavel Lounguine. *Music:* Isaac Schwartz. *Art Director:* Pavel Kaplevitch. *Set Designer:* Vladimir Pasternak. *Running time:* 107 minutes. *MPAA Rating:* Not Rated.

CAST: Andrei Goutine (Andrei); Oleg Borisov (Naoum Kheifitz); Natalia Egorova (Aliona); Nonna Mordioukova (The Aunt); Mikhail Goloubovich (The Mute).

LOS ANGELES TIMES, 3/27/94, Calendar/p. 13, Kevin Thomas

"Taxi Blues'" Pavel Loungine returns with the equally messy, passionate and irresistible "Luna Park," a sprawling, revved-up tale about a skinhead thug (Andrei Goutine) who hangs with an ultra-nationalist gang, headquartered by a Moscow amusement park, dedicated to terrorizing gays and Jews. Then Goutine discovers his father not only is Jewish but a famous, popular, singer-composer (Oleg Borisov), an official Soviet hero living in a vast, luxurious flat where he gives boisterous, seemingly endless parties.

NEW YORK, 1/24/94, p. 56, John Powers

"Can't a Russian get drunk in his own country anymore?" So bellows Andrei (Andrei Goutine), the callow neo-Fascist at the center of *Luna Park*, a forceful but wildly uneven glimpse into the crazier shadows of post-Communist Moscow. first shown at the 1992 Cannes Film Festival, and pretty much ignored thereafter, Pavel Lounguine's movie has taken on a creepy new resonance since Vladimir Zhirinovsky's strong showing in the recent parliamentary elections and he began fitting himself for a Hitler mustache. As one of the film's characters puts it, "Russians scare even themselves."

Angry, dark-eyed, and tense as a cramped muscle, Andrei is a leader of the Clean-Up Squad, a group of iron-pumping thugs who live in Moscow's Luna Park, growl darkly about conspiracies against "real" Russian people, and look for chances to thrash Jews, homosexuals, and Westernized types who drink Coca-Cola. Andrei 's hateful self-confidence is shaken when he learns that he's actually half Jewish, and it shatters when he finds his long-lost father. Naoum Blumstein (Oleg Borisov) is a frowsy, Oscar Wilde-quoting musician whose apartment serves as a way station for hookers and gangsters, artists and Eskimos; he's as lax as his son is tightly wound. Though Andrei thinks he should despise such an icon of decadence, he can't keep himself from being drawn to the twinkly old bohemian. Suddenly torn by an identity crisis, his life is perfectly expressed by the film's recurring image of him hurtling alone through the night on the Luna Park roller coaster.

Luna Park takes pride in snatching us by the lapels (every few minutes there's another beating or gaudy explosion), but Lounguine isn't really interested in right-wing violence. Rather, he's obsessed with Mother Russia's rawest psychic truth, the ongoing dance of love and hate that binds working class and intelligentsia, anti-Semite and Jew. Here, as in his earlier film *Taxi Blues* (about an up-tight cabbie and a drunken Jewish saxophone player), Lounguine insists that opposites don't merely attract; they create each other. For all his sly, life-affirming charm, Naoum is an irresponsible gadabout who feels no qualms about letting the whole world go to hell; for all his narrow-minded brutality, Andrei is a soulful young man who would rather clean up his country than trash it.

Naoum and Andrei mark the latest chapter in the eternal Russian saga of liberal-minded fathers siring radical sons, but Lounguine can't quite figure out what to do with them—he's a creator of sizzling moments, not satisfying stories. In love with showy detail, his work is a veritable Baedeker to the dismal textures of Moscow life: the concrete barrens and Stalin Gothic towers, the oyster-gray skies and blindingly dim light bulbs, the mechanical joy of the amusement parks and the cheesy elegance of the nightclubs where every single patron drinks to get plastered. Drunkenness, of course, is one of Russian art's gloriously enduring leitmotivs, and Lounguine never tires of pulling out the stopper. *Luna Park*'s characters are forever buying booze, scrounging money for booze, bemoaning broken bottles, distilling the hard stuff in their free-standing bathtubs. "Anyone can get drunk at night," Naoum says, smiling, over a liquid breakfast, "but to get drunk in the morning, to toss the whole day out the window—that takes talent."

It's a talent that Pavel Lounguine celebrates. He makes movies like a man on a five-day bender, lurching crazily between flights of inspiration and incoherent maundering, whipping every scene toward spiraling cadenzas of emotion or exasperating bouts of actorly self-indulgence. When in doubt, he has somebody smash a chair. His gift is for chaos, and *Luna Park* is full of bodies crashing through windows and cameras roaring down corridors like runaway bobsleds. Never truer to its creator's vision than when most out of control, this is a delirious movie about the delirium of Yeltsin's Moscow, a city where lost souls pursue healing moments of love and centuries-old hatreds rise from the pavement, breathing vodka and shrieking.

NEW YORK POST, 1/21/94, p. 39, Bill Hoffmann

Andrei has just been knocked for a loop.

For years, the handsome, musclebound tough has had a ball, terrorizing Moscow with a tough-as-nails gang of nationalists who want to cleanse Russia of its "human garbage."

This ultra-violent group of young skinheads, "The Clean-Up Squad," beats up on Jews, homosexuals, foreigners and anybody promoting Western lifestyles.

But Andrei, who's enjoyed night after night of stalking and bashing, has been sucker-punched by the news that he's half-Jewish.

Stunned and disbelieving, Andrei breaks from the crowd in search of the father he's never known.

And here's where Pavel Lounguine's captivating new drama, "Luna Park," really takes off, turning from an ultra-violent "A Clockwork Orange"-type actioner into a poignant tale of a lost young man bonding with the father he's never known.

Andrei's dad, Naoum, is an eccentric old musician who runs a decaying apartment house full of lovable misfits, including hookers, artists, gangsters, bums and revolutionaries.

Naoum is a cross between Woody Allen and Roberto Benigni, forever rattling off priceless one-liners about life, liberty and the pursuit of dodging bread lines.

Knowing there's no way to fight the ever-changing, economically disastrous system in modern-day Russia, Naoum is content to take one day at a time, schmoozing and boozing his way through life.

He's the antithesis of his son whose soulless, cement-cold ideals have no foreseeable future.

The old man instantly recognizes his son's seething anger and slowly, tries to bring him around to enjoy life.

Naoum, as played by Oleg Borisov, is a riot, spewing endless sarcasm with the sensibility of a Borscht Belt comic.

At the breakfast table, he cracks open a bottle of champagne, toasting: "Anybody can get smashed at night. But to drink in the morning, to toss the whole day out the window, now that takes talent!"

Naoum's gentle humor and warmth are a perfect antidote to Andrei's angriest of angry young men.

Unfortunately, just as the two misfits begin their heartfelt and tremendously entertaining bonding process, the film ends!

I could have watched at least another hour of Naoum using his wisdom to teach Andrei how to forgive the shortcomings and sins of modern-day Russia.

And it would have been fascinating to see Andrei jolt his old man out of his growing malaise and force him to nurture his musical talents once again.

But alas, we'll never know how this endearing pair made out, unless we can convince director Lounguine to make the first Russian sequel in movie history.

I'm quite sure "Luna Park 2: The Bonding," would be a smash.

Yes, there are 10 bad sequels for every good one, but here's one flick whose story deserves another go-round.

For now see "Luna Park" and then pray for more.

NEWSDAY, 1/21/94, Part II/p. 75, John Anderson

"WE ARE THE CLEANERS!!!" Andrei cries, just before he and his fellow Russian-nationalist Droogies-with-a-cause bang heads with a leather-clad biker hoard, in a borscht-colored fight to the death. And after some rather nasty exchanges, the whole thing concludes with Andrei using a bulldozer to pile bikes and riders under ground, leaving the earth freshly scraped.

It's an overblown end to an overblown scene, one that's almost as overblown as Andrei's anger. And it's almost as pointless: The roots of the clash are never explained, nor does the scene figure in the rest of Pavel Lounguine's "Luna Park." But it opens the film on an appropriately skewed note: The violence is heroic in its way, but more theatrical than dangerous. And Andrei, who's definitely dangerous, is no hero.

Lounguine ("Taxi Blues") made "Luna Park"—which appeared at the 1992 Cannes festival—while communism was in mid-fall. So what might seem like Zhirinovsky-inspired vitriol is really prescience, a foreshadowing of the current bloom of international Andrei-ism. The sentiments, though, are timeless.

For all his physical presence and passion, Andrei—played by Andrei Goutine, a real life gang member Lounguine recruited from a Russian gym, is still a pretty loathsome character. The Cleaners, too, are little more than thugs and petty thieves; they may rationalize their brutal treatment of Jews and gays as part of a necessary ethnic cleansing, but they never fail to rob their victims.

Lounguine, though, is never dismissive of these overheated steroid cases. The combined failures of communism and capitalism, he acknowledges, have produced a Russian youth with no discernible identity other than what they create for themselves—which includes the myth of Russian ethnic purity.

But he also takes the defensive tack in dealing with this skinhead mentality, which is laughing at it. You start by snickering at the overfed, vodka-swilling blonde, Aliona (Natalie Egorova), who with Andrei runs the Cleaners out of the Luna Park fairground (Aliona, who might have starred in a Siberian "Seven Beauties," begins by blaming Jews for her aborted singing career, and ends the film lip-synching Wagner). You continue by chortling at the muscle-headed ravings of the musclebound Cleaners. And you finally have to hoot at Andrei's kick in the head: While riding the Luna Park bumper cars together, the sloppy-drunk Aliona tells the self-appointed savior of the Motherland that his father was a Jew. That he's a "half-yid." A "bastard son of Abraham."

Andrei doesn't find this funny, of course. But he's a resilient lad. Having been abruptly and genetically disenfranchised by his lethal boys' club, he goes off looking for Dad, whom he finds in the urbane and quite liberal Naoum Heifetz. Played with crusty panache by the veteran actor Oleg Borisov, Naoum is a musician and singer who long ago sold out his talent writing Brezhnev-era patriotic songs. But in solidarity with his Soviet brethren, he uses his massive apartment as a combination haven/ hostel/halfway house for prostitutes, dropouts, rootless academics and occasional passersby of indeterminate religion or race. And so, Andrei's rocky re-education begins, as does his campaign to keep Naoum safe from both the Cleaners and an even more sinister force behind the scenes.

Lounguine's mix of social commentary with a distinctly Russian tone of black comedy is successful, even if the symbolism—the roller coaster at Luna Park, for instance, representing the almost-inescapable and directionless tracks of communism—may be a bit broad. The two main characters sometimes seem like refugees—Naoum from the circus, Andrei from a Schwarzenegger movie (Arnold is the butt of a Western-directed joke.) But even in its low-energy moments, "Luna Park" remains electric. And even though it took a couple of years to get here, it has nonetheless arrived—like the train that carries Naoum and Andrei away—right on time.

VILLAGE VOICE, 1/25/94, p. 61, Amy Virshup

Luna Park, like Pavel Lounguine's 1990 *Taxi Blues*, features a good many more explosions than one expects in a Russian movie. But then, this is the New Russia. The movie's central question—Who are we?—is posed in its first seconds by Andrei, one of the Cleaners, a Russian nationalist body-building gang not unlike the actual *Lubertsy*. These thugs, headquartered in an old amusement park, especially delight in beating up Jews. They're led by Aliona, a fleshy blond clown/chanteuse who seems to have ridden the Luna Park roller coaster a few too many times.

When working-class anti-hero Andrei comes to believe his father is Jewish, he goes off in a haze of hatred, searching out Naoum Blumstein, a Brezhnev-era hack composer now, like Russia herself, greatly reduced in circumstances. He too is a clown—a joker with a chestful of Soviet medals; a rambling apartment filled with musicians, hangers-on, and whores; and well-placed former lovers who make sure he gets enough yogurt. As in *Taxi Blues*, these opposites form an uneasy attraction, though brooding Andrei can't even pick up on Naoum's Chekhov references, and Naoum can't see Andrei's "polite" friends for what they are. Eventually, Andrei must choose which side he is on—who he is.

Luna Park's Moscow is almost surreally squalid, and filled with characters reaching toward the Fellini-esque: a mute arms-dealing moonshiner, a band of drumming Inuit, and Aliona herself, last seen lip-synching to Wagner as the roller coaster goes up in flames. The camera always seems to be sliding past drunken multi-ethnic celebrations in dingy hallways, moth-balled trolley cars, and sad cafés. The only ones not invited to the party are the ethnic Russians like Andrei and Aliona.

That may seem true to these poorly educated hooligans (all played by nonactors discovered in gyms), but Lounguine's own thinking on Russia's ethnic and ideological battles seems muddled. And by giving Naoum his Soviet medals and a Great Artist plaque on his door, the writer-director glosses over the real history of Communist anti-Semitism.

Also reviewed in:
NEW YORK TIMES, 1/21/94, p. C6, Janet Maslin
VARIETY, 5/25/92, p. 50, Deborah Young

MADNESS OF KING GEORGE, THE

A Samuel Goldwyn Company release in association with Channel 4 Films of a Close Call Films production. *Producer:* Stephen Evans and David Parfitt. *Director:* Nicholas Hytner. *Screenplay (based on his stage play "The Madness of George III")*: Alan Bennett. *Director of Photogaphy:* Andrew Dunn. *Editor:* Tariq Anwar. *Music:* George Fenton. *Music adapted from the works of:* George Frederic Handel. *Sound:* David Crozier. *Sound Editor:* Christopher Ackland. *Casting:* Celestia Fox. *Production Designer:* Ken Adam. *Art Director:* Martin Childs. *Set Decorator:* Carolyn Scott. *Costumes:* Mark Thompson. *Make-up:* Lisa Westcott. *Stunt Coordinator:* Wayne Michaels and Gareth Milne. *Running time:* 105 minutes. *MPAA Rating:* Not Rated.

CAST: Rupert Graves (Greville); Helen Mirren (Queen Charlotte); Amanda Donohoe (Lady Pembroke); Charlotte Curley (Amelia); Rupert Everett (Prince of Wales); Julian Rhind-Tutt (Duke of York); David Leon, Dan Hammond, Nick Irons, and Martin Julier (Footmen); Nigel Hawthorne (George III); Anthony Calf (Fitzroy); Matthew Lloyd Davies (Papandick); Adrian Scarborough (Fortnum); Paul Corrigan (Braun); John Wood (Thurlow); Nick Sampson (Sergeant at Arms); Jeremy Child (Black Rod); Nicholas Selby (Speaker); Julian Wadham (Pitt); Jim Carter (Fox); Barry Stanton (Sheridan); Struan Rodger (Dundas); Janine Duvitski (Margaret Nicholson); Caroline Harker (Mrs. Fitzherbert); Iain Mitchell (Farmer); Roger Hammond (Baker); Geoffrey Palmer (Warren); Celestine Randall (Lady Adam); Cyril Shaps (Pepys); Michael Grandage (Amputee); Ian Holm (Willis); James Peck, Clive Brunt, Fergus Webster, and Joe Maddison (Willis' Attendants); Selina Cadell (Mrs. Cordwell); Dermot Keaney (Footman); Peter Woodthorpe (Clergyman); Robert Swann and Alan Bennett (MPs).

CINEASTE, VOL. XXI, NO. 3, 1995, p. 47, Harvey Roy Greenberg

A mental malady afflicting the chief of state poses its own peculiar menace to the health of the realm. It may be cynically suggested that narcissism and paranoia often constitute the native soil for rulership to flourish. When these traits ripen into frank delusion, what Stalin or Mao will label himself unfit towards the general good, quit his dominion, and seek paltry treatment? Determining whether an emotionally troubled ruler is too troubled to rule may constitute an even more daunting task than assessing the degree to which physical illness limits the capacity to govern. Shakespeare's Claudius averred that "Madness in great ones should not unwatch'd go." But Claudius's case is a signal illustration of the ancient warning: *quis custodiet ipsos custodes?*—Who watches the watchers? History affords ample evidence of physicians compelled by 'watchers' of whatever intention to perform questionable appraisals of a ruler's physical/psychiatric fitness. (A notable modern instance was the suppression of Woodrow Wilson's incapacity due to a stroke by his wife, with his doctor's assistance.) Other quondam healers have been motivated by their own beliefs or ambitions to render inappropriate judgments and dubious cures, or have even acted as hired assassins. But the most upright practitioner may still be overswayed by the sheer power of the patient's office, the siren song of fame and wealth attendant upon successful treatment, or the awful consequences of failure.

The political and personal vicissitudes spun out of the aberrations of the great were interrogated in Alan Bennett's 1991 drama, *The Madness of George III*. The current film version, also directed by Nicholas Hytner, lacks the original's keen edge, hut still features Nigel Hawthorne's astonishing depiction of the manic monarch and retains enough of the play's other virtue's to recommend *The Madness of King George*. (The original title was changed from the dim fear that audiences would think it designated a sequel; the decision would seem to speak volumes to the deficit of producers rather than viewers.)

The narrative's action is set in 1787, a problematic time for the English monarchy and its conservative Tory regime. The king has been popular, has reigned long and—for the day—reasonably well. But now France is frighteningly ablaze with republican sentiment, and an opposition Whig party clamors impatiently for massive reform in Parliament.

A personage of vast, obsessive energy who takes particular delight in knowing the name of his pettiest appointee; a stickler for decorum; an avid balancer of budgets and, above all, a passionate agriculturalist, the king imagines himself the nation's 'Farmer-in-Chief.' Scorning his court's frantic debauchery, he embodies the family values he enthusiastically recommends to his subjects; dotes upon Charlotte (Helen Mirren), his teutonic, frazzled wife, who has given him nineteen children. The couple happily refer to each other as "Mr. and Mrs. King."

But serpents are astir in George's garden. His fat, foppish, oldest son, the dissolute Prince of Wales (Rupert Everett, burdened with an absurdly mobile artificial paunch), chronically short of cash and grown weary of incessant waiting in the wings, has thrown his lot in with the Whigs to undermine his father's reign. The American debacle of 1776 continues to abrade George's sensibilities. And he lives with the queasy knowledge that on several previous occasions his faculties have inexplicably been thrown into frenetic disorder.

Hawthorne's craft reveals that, underneath the king's bluff facade, hides an insecure man who harbors the peculiar horror of lunacy that haunted the Enlightenment ("O God, let me not lose my reason!," prayed Dr. Johnson, terrorized by a small stroke). As the story opens, even the mere mention of the new United States precipitates even more excessive explosions of choler. Bennett acutely intimates the unconscious articulation in the king's mind between the amputation to the body politic and the onset of his physical distemper. Soon George's thoughts race hurtfully ahead of his ability to speak them. He's wracked by attacks of violent pain in his abdomen and extremities. Then the behavior of this model of propriety turns erratic, gross, lewd, even as his urine turns blue. As a lunatic, his discourse—previously stamped with blustering "Hey! Hey!"s and vapid "Wot! Wot!"s—also turns remarkably searching and witty (a convention unfortunately more likely to be encountered on the stage than in the clinic).

The watchers of this majestic decline respond with despair or delight according to their lights and loyalties. The queen's solicitude is viciously spurned by her consort: with the lid now thoroughly blown off the royal id, George is exquisitely sensitized to his son's Oedipally tinged competitiveness, elaborating it into a delusional fixation that Charlotte has been bedding the Prince. The dour Tory Prime Minister, Pitt the Younger—whose own father went instructively mad—tries to downplay the depths of the king's lunacy. The Whigs push a bill to have George set aside so that his viper offspring can rule as Regent. With the Prince's help, they conspire to separate him from the queen George yearns for despite his psychotic ire, thus further spurring his deterioration. Meanwhile, the allegiances of assorted toadies and hangers-on in high places shift uneasily, according to whatever wind blows from the sickroom.

It is a curious fact that the patient with megaclout is frequently joined by associates in manipulating and intimidating physicians, who are frequently drawn from a cadre of 'society' practitioners more notable for an unctuous bedside manner than professional skill—the so-called 'VIP syndrome.' The king's doctors are as sorry a clutch of sententious bunglers as ever serviced a VIP with substandard treatment. His personal physician seizes upon the occasion to stroke his purse and reputation; another consultant is a Whig hireling, eager to sneak reports about his patient's relapses to his devious masters. Still another savors every quiddity of the king's stool: this learned boobie disdains examining George's colorful urine, declaring that as a man of science he only values what he can observe. Yet unseen under his nose lies the very signature of acute intermittent porphyria, a rare hereditary metabolic disorder characterized by episodes of fulminating abdominal pain, epileptic seizures, and discoloration of the urine. (While experts have demonstrated with a fair degree of certainty that George III had some form of porphyria, ample documentation suggests that he also may have suffered from bipolar disorder, formally known as manic-depressive psychosis.) Spouting Galenic mumbo jumbo at extravagant cross purposes, the triumvirate of charlatans heap hellish torments upon their already tormented charge. The babbling king is bled and purged, scourged and blistered to utterly unwholesome effect.

At length, over the quacks' protests, the king's supporters bring in Dr. Willis (Ian Holm), a pragmatic Lincolnshire specialist and parson. He scorns the establishment's archaic humoral theories, barbaric remedies, and confinements. His sanitarium is a farm where patients—whatever their station—are set free to perform simple labor, as he instructs them in recovering their wits through diligent exercise of their native powers of reason. But even Willis's humanism is tempered by a cold severity that comprised the Age of Reason's harsher side. Confronted with the king's weak Ego and rampant Id, the doctor opts to align himself with his patient's beleaguered Superego. He believes George cannot rule others until he learns to rule himself again. To that end, the king must obey Willis s every command towards rational behavior, or be gagged and strapped into a curious half-throne, half-instrument of the torture chamber.

Observers of the day report that Willis was known for the eerie, mesmeric penetration of his glance. "I have you in my eye, sir!," he warns George. Held in that intransigent gaze and confined by Willis's horrible chair, the recalcitrant king relents, gropes his way back to the light. As much as George rages at Willis, the film implies that his cure is facilitated by his identification with the feisty little doctor, who mirrors his patient's bullish strength of will, obsessive concern for appearances—and agrarian pursuits. (Holm admirably captures Willis's fierce self-confidence and crusty compassion.)

Film scholars have cogently addressed the pitfalls of converting fiction to film. It is less clear why juicy dramas should so resist translation. *The Madness of George III* is essentially a chamber piece with a minimum of bright, brisk pageantry, propelled by dazzling argument. The play simply does not sustain the weight of cinematic expansion. Bennett's exhilarating language is curiously vitiated amidst a surplus of sumptuous decor, impressive exteriors, and a plethora of extras. The lucid potency of Handel's music, sparingly quoted in the original, is diluted by its almost nonstop employment as sonic wallpaper.

The screenplay (also written by Bennett) considerably elides the play's acid sendup of medical politics, presumptuousness, and stupidity. A subtler reflective ending has been discarded. The now merely triumphalist finale dwells instead upon George's return to the public eye, with a rather patronizing recommendation clumsily directed at the royals of our day to eschew their scandals and take up their responsibilities to look down upon us with renewed dignity ("Wave to them!," says George to the disgruntled Prince, "That's what we're here for!"). Also lost to the film viewer is the irony of discovering that George would eventually sicken again, to be superseded by his vindictive son, and spend the rest of his days in demented obscurity.

These objections aside, several moments which were profoundly moving on the stage are even more affecting on screen. In a scene mingling pathos and paradox, Handel's mighty coronation anthem, "Zadock the Priest," swells up as the protesting king is bound for the first time, Christ-like, into Willis s infernal throne. Later in a sunlit garden, George prompts his chancellor and a lackey through an unexpectedly delicate reading of King Lear's return to reason. At its conclusion, he recognizes his renewed ability to conceal his inner life as ambiguous evidence of healing: "I have always been myself, even when I was ill. Only now I seem myself. That's the important thing. I have remembered how to seem."

The film also retains the play's mordant cautionary message to those too intimately regarding majesty in disarray. Upon the king's recovery, the young officer and servants who faithfully nursed him back to health are immediately sent packing, while other supporters removed from the brute particularities of his madness—the raving abuse, the soiled underclothes—are handsomely rewarded. Willis himself is dispatched back to his farm with a hefty annuity and scant thanks (to his credit, he has no illusions about being owed more). A restored king, safe from his demons, now regards his healer with contempt and fear.

More to the point, George III cannot abide Willis's presence because he has conflated his healer with his disease. Willis reminds the king of that terrifying moment when this dominating, obsessive personality was confronted with the unmasterable disorder lurking within his own being—and forgot how to seem.

LOS ANGELES TIMES, 12/28/94, Calendar/p. 1, Kenneth Turan

Late in 1788 in the 28th year of the reign of England's King George III, something extraordinary happened. As one modern historian tactfully puts it, "The king's mind broke down." A bizarre kind of dementia overtook the monarch who had already lost the American Colonies, and everyone who was anyone in the country's ruling circles was faced with a crisis beyond all imagining.

As if to prove that the unlikeliest material can make for the best films, "The Madness of King George," directed by Nicholas Hytner from Alan Bennett's prize-winning play, has taken this footnote to history and transformed it into one of the triumphs of the year—potent. engrossing and even thrilling to experience.

This is due in great measure to Nigel Hawthorne's work as the deranged monarch, a heroic performance that enlarges our understanding of what acting can accomplish. A recent arrival at celebrity, the 65-year-old Hawthorne swept his country's major theatrical awards when he played the part on the London stage. And Hytner, who directed that version as well, has ensured that his interpretation was transferred to the screen with its intensity intact.

Although not as celebrated here as he is back home, writer Bennett (who has a brief cameo as a mild member of Parliament) is one of Britain's most respected men of letters. Discerning folk will remember him as the screenwriter for the Joe Orton biography, "Prick Up Your Ears," and the Alan Bates-starring "An Englishman Abroad," as well as for being one of the nonpareil quartet (along with Peter Cook, Dudley Moore and Jonathan Miller) that made the Beyond the Fringe satirical troupe so brilliant.

What Bennett has done in "Madness" is to powerfully re-imagine the atmosphere of George's royal court, giving the dialogue a modern twist while keeping it from sounding anachronistic.

The pleasure he takes in the spoken word, his ability to etch characters in both acid and compassion, to write such lines of dialogue as "the state of monarchy and the state of lunacy share a frontier" set this film thankfully apart.

Confessing, the play's introduction, that he has "always had a soft spot for George III," Bennett introduces the monarch at the height of his powers. A genially choleric man, bluff, gruff and plainspoken, he is proud of his popularity with the common folk but is a trial to his 15 children, especially his bored-to-death heir, the Prince of Wales (Rupert Everett).

Setting a hectic pace and ending most sentences with a speedy "What, what?" the king's energy looks even greater than it is because he is surrounded by effete whiners and smooth careerists.

Except for Greville (Rupert Graves), his loyal equerry, everyone, including ice-cold Prime Minister William Pitt (Julian Wadham), is both irritated and comforted by the knowledge that they are more sophisticated than their ruler.

George's most heartening and moving relationship is with his Queen Charlotte, beautifully played—albeit with welcome dramatic license—by Helen Mirren. Never apart for so much as a day in their 28 years of marriage, they call each other "Mr. King" and "Mrs. King" in private and still seem very much in love.

Then, with almost no warning, the madness begins, difficult to detect at first because, as one character asks,"Who can say what is normal to a king?"

But after bouts of waking everyone up at 4 a.m. screaming fits about nonexistent floods and zealous sexual attacks on the attractive Lady Pembroke (Amanda Donohoe), one of the queen's attendants, there can no longer by any doubt that the monarch is not himself.

When the king's condition becomes known, the political maneuvering begins in earnest. For if Parliament declares Gorge unfit to rule and the noxious Prince of Wales is installed as regent, Pitt will be out and the hungry opposition, led by the troublesome Charles James Fox (Jim Carter), will take power.

In the meantime, George's condition is made worse by the barbaric treatments, verging on medieval torture, that his crackpot Three Stooges medical team inflict on him. Finally, as a last resort, he is put in the hands of Will (Ian Holm), a former clergyman with unusual ideas about the treatment of the mentally ill.

It is a measure of Hawthorne's performance in the title role that, like King Lear (who is pointedly referred to), the worse his condition becomes, the more he inspires our sorrow and pity.

His madness adds to his moral stature by making him increasingly human, and we root for him with a surprising passion to recover his wits.

Meanwhile the looks of confused horror and self-loathing that flits across his ravaged face express torment as heartbreakingly as acting is able to.

Director Hytner, known for his stage work on "Miss Saigon" and "Carousel," is so at home with film that it is difficult to believe this is his feature debut. Working with cinematographer Andrew Dunn and Oscar-winning production designer Ken Adam ("Barry Lyndon"), he has faultlessly opened up the play and made a distant world seem physically real.

Down to its final footnote on modern theories about the cause of the royal illness, every aspect of "The Madness of King George." keeps us amused, surprised and delighted. Who wouldn't wish long life to a film as worthy as this?

NEW YORK, 1/2/95, p. 66, David Denby

The Madness of King George achieves that state of theatrical blessedness that lies halfway between farce and tragedy—in this case, between Monty Python and *King Lear*. This marvelous movie, a full-scale historical recreation based on Alan Bennett's play, is about the very human George III—the George of schoolboy jokes, the one who reigned for 60 years, taxed the colonies so unpleasantly, and occasionally went out of his head. The movie picks him up in mid-reign, in 1788, as he is growing more and more unstable. Nigel Hawthorne, who played the role onstage for nearly three years, renders the king as a virile, fiftyish sport with a bullying voice, a frantic gait, and sudden, convulsive movements. The king lacks repose. Rampant, violent, exhausting, George is a philosophical and temperamental vitalist ruling over a court that insists on languor. Hawthorne looks a bit like Mel Brooks, but he's taller and more imposing, and his ranting fancies give way to the most abject suffering.

Nicholas Hytner, the distinguished stage director (*Carousel* and many others), begins his first film with a seemingly conventional spoof of the monarchy. The king, seated, relishes Christmas carols played by somnolent bell ringers, while the rest of the court, standing in wigs, breeches, brocades, and jewels, nearly faints with boredom. Ultimately, the crown gets tossed to a retainer. The Prince of Wales (Rupert Everett) is a nasty popinjay, and George's prime minister, Pitt the Younger (Julian Wadham), a manipulative cold fish. But as George drifts off into madness, the movie moves in two directions at once—outdoors, to the lawns and heaths around the royal castles, where George rages like a Lear beset by sunshine instead of storms ; and indoors , into a greater physical intimacy with the king, whose fits and starts and digestive turmoils are subjected to the high quackery of the royal physicians. The flesh is tormented, the spirit harrowed, and something like poetry takes over.

Doctor Willis (Ian Holm), a kind of proto-psychoanalyst, is summoned by the king's friends, who don't want to lose control of the government; the authoritarian Willis brazenly eyeballs the raving monarch and straps him into a chair. Oddly enough, Alan Bennett seems to support Willis's theory, if not his methods: The king is mad because he has too much freedom. He can do whatever he wants, say whatever he wants. He possesses an immense strength and even goodness, but he is never checked or thwarted. In a paradox, he has to submit to humiliation—and find his limits—before he can rule again. He has to learn as well to "seem" the king. Royalty is all about playacting—the movie acknowledges as much—yet there's something else going on, the expression in the monarch of the nation's sturdiest and best character. Bennett and Hytner openly revive the Shakespearean dimension of royalty; George finally remembers that the English want the king to be a king, that anything else would be an embarrassment. It is by acting Lear in a garden before his ministers that he is restored to sanity. This may sound fanciful, but it's so delicately played, it is instead comical and ineffably moving.

NEW YORK POST, 12/28/94, p. 31, Michael Medved

What do you do when a popular, all-powerful head of state suddenly loses his mind? We're not talking about just a few oddball decisions on health care policy or a weird appointee as surgeon general.

For 18th-century England, the situation with reigning monarch George III involved full-blown lunacy—sudden bursts of violent, embarrassing public behavior, accompanied by unstoppable, incoherent chatter that exhausted his courtiers, as well as his wife and 15 children.

As the crazed king (Nigel Hawthorne) pathetically admits to his devoted, long: suffering queen (the splendid Helen Mirren) in the course of this profoundly moving (and occasionally hilarious) film: "I hear the words and I have to speak them. I have to empty my head of the words ... Something is not right."

Everything is right, however, with an extraordinary cast where even the smallest parts emerge with indelible artistry.

Julian Wadham is unforgettable as William Pitt, the slick prime minister who will do anything to minimize the seriousness of the king's condition; if power passes from George's fumbling hands then Pitt's government will fall.

Meanwhile, the king's eldest son, the foppish Prince of Wales (Rupert Everett) conspires to enact a parliamentary bid declaring his father unfit and proclaiming himself regent.

The only hope for the mad monarch lies with Dr. Willis (played by the ferociously formidable Ian Holm), who has developed radical new means for treating insanity.

As a pioneering behaviorist, the good doctor subjects the poor king to appalling torments and indignities, but his treatment finally begins to show small signs of working.

The question is whether it can it work in time to save George's throne, and allow him to return to the arms of his loving wife.

No matter how little or how much of this fascinating history you may know, you come to care deeply about what happens to each of these people—who certainly seem more human and appealing than the current royal family.

Nigel Hawthorne, a veteran stage actor little known in this country, gives one of the finest cinematic performances I have ever seen, expressing the unimaginable pain and startling transformations of a gruff, decent man who can still understand just enough of his situation to comprehend its tragedy.

Every detail of this characterization such as the king's obsessive mourning for the American colonies which his own misguided policies helped to lose, or his odd, endearing habit of adding the words, "what what?" to the end of most sentences, is historically accurate.

Based on a brilliant play by Alan Bennett, "The Madness of King George" is directed by Nicholas Hytner, an acclaimed London theater director who here makes a startlingly accomplished motion picture debut.

Nothing about the lush, sumptuous recreations of the royal court feels like a filmed play, and the story gallops along in a brisk, breathtakingly cinematic style.

The original play featured an "Upstairs/Downstairs" element involving the confusion of various loyal members of the royal household (played here by Rupert Graves, Amanda Donohoe and others), but director Hytner wisely shifted the focus of the film almost entirely to George and his immediate family.

The result is unequivocally one of the year's finest films, immeasurably enriched by the splendid (and splendidly appropriate) music of Handel, who happened to be court composer to George's grandfather.

Altogether, no moviegoer, whether noble or commoner, should be permitted to miss what is in every sense a regal entertainment, what, what?

NEWSDAY, 12/28/94, Part II/p. B9, John Anderson

When one declares " I am the Lord's anointed!" the diagnosis is generally swift, the treatment long-term, the restraints secure. And so it is with George III, who proves among other things that it takes a bit of madness just to think oneself the monarch.

"The Madness of King George," Nicolas Hytner's robust adaptation of Alan Bennett's allegorical tragi-comedy ("The Madness of George III") is about the king who lost the colonies and his mind. But while it draws obvious parallels between the Hanovers of the 18th Century and the media-besieged Windsor descendants, George is more than just a metaphor for kingly obsolescence. As portrayed by the marvelous Nigel Hawthorne who also played him at the Brooklyn Academy of Music last year under Hytner's direction—he becomes a pathetic, tortured and ultimately regal model of a man in the throes of an undefined illness and redefinition.

Beautifully shot, and possessed of a cinematic vitality that leaves its stage origins far behind, "The Madness of King George" applies the same patina of lushness and luxury to a base, venal world that the ermine-wearing royals did. Their role, as it is today, was symbolic, and creeping democracy was already eating away at their station. Hytner's visual references to this are plentiful and pointed: One attendant spit-polishing the crown; the under-employed, resentful Prince of Wales (the marvelous Rupert Everett, in an unavoidable Prince Charles burlesque) sucking a flask between rude asides. Basically, George III, the protector of the crown, is shoveling sand against the sea.

And it's tough to maintain one institution while you're trying to avoid another. Devastated by the Revolution in "that place we mustn't mention"—not so much because of the "paradise lost" but because the idea of a United States itself rebukes him—George is losing control of his regal propriety, his bowels, his hands—groping the bountiful Lady Pembroke (Amanda Donohoe) in the presence of his loyal queen, Charlotte (Helen Mirren)—and his crown as well.

Despite the efforts of Prime Minister Robert Pitt (Julian Wadham) to shore up the monarchy, his parliamentary nemesis Fox (Jim Carter) is maneuvering to have the idle and impatient Prince installed as regent and the crown eventually abolished. With his only ally his ill-used aide Greville (Rupert Graves), the king, his condition worsening, is then subjected to the rustic psychotherapy of the dictatorial Dr. Willis (Ian Holm), who is established as George's tyrant and institutes a regiment of restraint and abuse that sorely tries the royal will. George's recovery will come, but only after a reunion with Charlotte, whose steadfastness is far more reliable than Mirren's transient accent (although her acting is, as usual, superb).

Hawthorne is spectacular, and spectacularly unrestrained as the ailing king, whom modern doctors have determined was suffering from porphyria. It's a condition that turns the urine blue and the mind to mush—and which George's descendants are no doubt pleased to know is hereditary. The ridicule heaped on an archaic medical profession and its primitive treatments seems cheap—I mean, it's not as if what doctors think *today* won't be obsolete tomorrow. But that is really the only discordant note in a remarkable film, one that ennobles while it demolishes.

NEWSWEEK, 3/6/95, p. 68, Jack Kroll

The unlikeliest hit of the year is *The Madness of King George*. This British film about the bizarre syndrome that afflicted George III in 1788 is being shown in some 300 theaters (compared with nearly 2,600 for "Dumb and Dumber" at its peak), but since its release on Dec. 28 it has been a top box-office performer on a per-screen average. And it's garnered four Oscar nominations: leading actor Nigel Hawthorne, supporting actress Helen Mirren, screenwriter Alan Bennett and production designer Ken Adam. The Oscar nods are helping kick the take higher as "George" moves to an eventual 700 screens. Call it the "Smart and Smarter" of the year.

How come a British historical costume movie, with no American stars—and not even Anthony Hopkins—is so popular? Because it's such a good film, right? Ummm, maybe. Or maybe because U.S. audiences are having fun making parallels between those wacky royals of yore and those of today. "To be Prince of Wales is not a position, it's a predicament," says Rupert Everett as George's clueless son and heir. Poor Charles couldn't have said it better today, And Dr. Willis (Ian Holm), who's been called in after the king has apparently gone bonkers, sagely observes that "the state of monarchy and the state of lunacy share a common frontier."

Bennett's script, based on his 1991 play, sees kingship as an ordeal—absolute power is a pathology. George speaks gibberish, defecates in public, refuses to admit the loss of the American colonies, attempts carnalities with his wife's lady-in-waiting, ordering poor, patient Queen Charlotte (Mirren) to "mind your own business!" when she interferes. Meanwhile, the opposition schemes to have the prince take over. It's a Keystone Kings spectacle, directed galvanically by Nicholas Hytner (who staged the play) in his film debut. Hawthorne's poignant George is a ruler who's lost power over himself. In a key scene he reads from "King Lear" with his retinue, and Shakespeare cures what his quack doctors couldn't. "We must be a model family for the nation," he says at the end. Bet this movie doesn't make it to a royal command performance.

SIGHT AND SOUND, 4/95, p. 47, Geoffrey Macnab

England, 1788, King George III's relations with his idle, pampered son, the Prince of Wales, are fast deteriorating. He isn't entirely popular with his subjects either, one of whom tries to stab him to death with a fruit knife after the State Opening of Parliament. The King's eccentric personal behaviour also gives cause for concern. One evening, he has a mild fit and is prescribed senna by his incompetent doctor. He seems to recover, but his antics subsequently grow ever more wilful. Prime Minister Pitt knows that if the King is declared unfit to rule, his own government will topple and he will be replaced by his arch-rival, the Whig leader, Fox, who has the support of the Prince of Wales.

Three quack doctors do their best to cure the King of his distemper, blistering him, taking his pulse and studying his stools. The Prince refuses to allow his mother, Queen Charlotte, anywhere near the King. However, the Queen's Lady-in-Waiting, Lady Pembroke, tells Pitt about a new physician, Dr Willis, who is reputed to be able to cure diseases of the mind. Willis is summoned to oversee George's treatment away from the court. Although the King's condition slowly improves, a bill has already been drawn up to declare the Prince of Wales as Regent. Queen Charlotte realises what this implies: if the bill is passed, George will never be able to regain power. She manages to smuggle herself into his chambers and warns him what is at stake. George pulls himself together, shaves off his beard and hurries to Westminster to prove in person that he is recovered. He arrives in the nick of time and is given a rousing welcome by government MPs. The Royal family is reunited.

As the film ends, an intertitle reveals that George may not, strictly speaking, have been mad at all, but was possibly suffering from an hereditary metabolic disorder known as porphyria that produces chemical changes in the body and symptoms similar to dementia.

Whether it be Anna Neagle deliciously prim as Queen Victoria, Charles Laughton in bellowing form as Henry VIII, or Laurence Olivier doing his Shakespeare turns, British cinema has always enjoyed basking in the shadow of monarchy. *The Madness of King George*, latest addition to the royal genre, is the kind of movie that will go down well in what American showmen used to call "the better class of neighborhood". Adapted from an award-winning play, it comes complete with rolling countryside, castles, pageantry and court ritual. Characters are decked out in full Georgian finery, with frock-coats and periwigs to the fore. *Mise-en-scéne* is lovingly detailed.

Tear away the regal trappings, though, and you find a microscopic drama of the kind that Alan Bennett is famous for. In writing the original play, he acknowledged his debt to Roy Porter's *A Social History Of Madness*. The film works almost as a case study; the story of an individual subjected to the rigours of eighteenth-century medicine. That individual just happens to be the King, "the engine of the nation". When he falls ill, government stalls and a power vacuum is created.

Alan Bennett and director, Nicholas Hytner, are determined to destroy the mystique of majesty. By focusing intently on George's condition, they make him a sympathetic character, but hardly one who seems divinely ordained to rule. Private functions are the key: the King's deteriorating condition is first announced by his inability to fart. Doctors treat him with laxatives; spend much of their time poring over his faeces ("I've always found the stool more eloquent than the pulse" one quack proclaims), and make great play of his urine, which mysteriously turns blue.

Even when he is in robust health, he's an earthy sort, delighting in his nickname Farmer George. Pigs (something of a leitmotif in Bennett's work) are his favourite animals, and he has a ripe way with language which is utterly at odds with conventional courtly discourse. Nigel Hawthorne's exceptional performance never allows George to become an empty figure of fun. Although he blusters and rages, he is more victim than despot. The real comedy (and the film is often very funny) comes from the political feuding between Fox and Pitt, and the absurd pomposity of the Prince Regent, a louche, fat figure played with typical conceit by Rupert Everett.

There are many stilted set-pieces in the picture; depictions of everything from the State Opening of Parliament to Handel renditions and bell-ringing concerts. But Hytner takes a Hogarthian pleasure in disrupting the excessive formality of such scenes. Jarring comic business is always going on at the edge of the frame. For instance, while the King and Queen sit complacently listening to music, the camera pulls back to reveal their courtiers behind them, fidgeting and sweating with boredom: convention demands that they must remain standing throughout the recital (even if pregnant), however long it lasts.

In a way, madness is a king's prerogative. For republicans, certainly, the very notion of monarchy is crazy by definition. Bennett laces his screenplay with constant, sly digs at Britain's current crop of beleaguered Royals. "To be the Prince of Wales is not a position; it is a predicament," the Prince Regent is heard to complain. "We must be more of a family," George tells his squabbling relatives as they make an all too transparent show of unity at the end of the film. We see disgruntled princes waving languidly at the crowds from the balcony, or from inside their carriages.

The Madness of King George is perhaps intended as a barbed, ironic vision of monarchy and manners, but the sharpness of its critique is somewhat blunted by all the English Heritage style imagery on display. At least, it's far from a filmed play. Thanks to Hytner's brisk, confident direction, which accommodates some eccentric, very actorly performances from the likes of John Wood and Geoffrey Palmer without sacrificing tempo, it manages the rare feat of being both cinematic and theatrical.

VILLAGE VOICE, 1/3/95, p. 72, Georgia Brown

It's 1788 and George the III (Nigel Hawthorne) is behaving oddly. It's rather hard to tell when royals go round the bend because their behavior seems batty most of the time. Perhaps the blue urine clinches matters. (You've heard of blue blood?) The Queen (Helen Mirren) calls the royal quacks, who are of no use at all since they have trouble viewing their sovereign as mortal. The

Queen's Mistress of the Robes (Amanda Donohoe) recommends a Dr. Willis (Ian Holm), a fearless, stubborn sort who begins treatment by daring to look the king in the face. Can the monarchy survive such insolence, or will a trip to earth do some good?

Even before Alan Bennett's dazzling script for *The Madness of King George* gets to its own dear, heartrending *King Lear* scene, the image of that poor, fork'd creature on the heath will probably rise to mind as his majesty is reduced to a howling, diapered infant with no power over anything at all. In the halls of Parliament, his ungrateful eldest son, the priggish Prince of Wales (Rupert Everett), plots with a surly Tory minister, Mr. Fox (Jim Carter), to seize the reins of government.

Bennett—formerly of Beyond the Fringe, now one of Britain's most treasured writers—presents his history lesson as a comedy while making sure we understand how very pathetic it all is. Directed by Nicholas Hytner with some distracting camera pirouettes, the film starts out silly, turns ghastly, and by the end is simultaneously hilarious and rueful. It's also consistently provocative.

"God rot all royals," growls Mr. Fox after witnessing a princely tantrum. But Bennett seems at times to extend his critique to all the English in their smugness and cozy isolation. It's not only the royals who look defective here—everyone, outside of a couple of pretty courtiers (played by Donahoe and Rupert Graves), looks like a grotesque, drawn by Hogarth or Phiz. Still, far out at the forefront of this collection of pinheads, airheads, and fatheads stands the pink, pampered, pompous Prince of Wales (a stretch for the handsome Everett). Obviously, we're meant to be reminded of present-day royals, their Dumbo ears and horsey features. But we might also think of anyone—Hollywood moguls, for example—who insulates himself from the common herd.

The title of Bennett's play during its London run was *The Madness of George III*. Movie execs changed it, fearing doltish Americans would expect a sequel to some horror pic. It's that, too.

Also reviewed in:
CHICAGO TRIBUNE, 1/27/95, Friday/p. H, Johanna Steinmetz
NATION, 1/23/95, p. 107, Stuart Klawans
NEW YORK TIMES, 12/28/94, p. C11, Janet Maslin
NEW YORKER, 1/16/95, p. 86, Anthony Lane
VARIETY, 12/19/94-1/1/95, p. 71, Emanuel Levy
WASHINGTON POST, 1/27/95, p. C1, Hal Hinson
WASHINGTON POST, 1/27/95, Weekend/p. 36, Desson Howe

MAJOR LEAGUE II

A Warner Bros. release of a James G. Robinson presentation of a Morgan Creek production. *Executive Producer:* Gary Barber. *Producer:* James G. Robinson and David S. Ward. *Director:* David S. Ward. *Screenplay:* R. J. Stewart. *Story:* R. J. Stewart, Tom S. Parker, and Jim Jennewein. *Director of Photography:* Victor Hammer. *Editor:* Paul Seydor and Donn Cambern. *Music:* Michel Colombier. *Music Editor:* Thomas Milano, Terry Delsing, and Tom Kramer. *Sound:* Robert Anderson and (music) Clark Germain. *Sound Editor:* Larry Kemp. *Casting:* Ferne Cassel. *Production Designer:* Stephen Hendrickson. *Art Director:* Gary Diamond. *Set Designer:* Kyung Chang. *Set Decorator:* Leslie Bloom. *Set Dresser:* Clark Hospelhorn, James M. Bloom, Jr., and Patrick M. Stare. *Costumes:* Bobbie Read. *Make-up:* Allan A. Apone and Jeanne Van Phue. *Stunt Coordinator:* James Arnett, Eddie Braun, and John Moio. *Running time:* 105 minutes. *MPAA Rating:* PG.

CAST: Charlie Sheen (Rick Vaughn); Tom Berenger (Jake Taylor); Corbin Bernsen (Roger Dorn); Dennis Haysbert (Pedro Cerrano); James Gammon (Lou Brown); Omar Epps (Willie Mays Hayes); Eric Bruskotter (Rube Baker); Takaaki Ishibashi (Isuro Tanaka); Alan Doody (Flannery); Michelle Burke (Nikki Reese); David Keith (Jack Parkman); Margaret Whitton

(Rachel Phelps); Bob Uecker (Harry Doyle); Steve Yeager (Coach "Duke" Temple); Kevin Hickey (Schoup); Skip Griparis (Monte); Kevin Crowley (Vic); Bill Leff (Bobby); Michael Mundra (Frankie); Courtney Pee (Steve); Farajii Rasulallah (Tommy); Edward Woodson (Tim); Ted Duncan (Ron); Marie-Louise White (Lisa); Saige Spinney (Big Woman); Michael Willis (Airport Photographer); Jason Kravitz (Accountant); Alan Wade (Psychiatrist); Keith Johnson (Vaughn's Valet); Jay Leno (Himself); Susan Duvall (Lou's Nurse); Ron Meadows, Jr. (Orderly); Jesse Ventura (White Lightening); Keith Uchima and Kurt Uchima (Groundskeepers); Richard Salamanca and Harold Surratt (Reporters); Daniel O'Donnell (Suit); Richard Shiff (Director); Louis Tureene (Distinguished Gentleman); Patrick Smith (Clapper Boy); Dan Kilday (Slider); Dick Stilwell (Cleveland Trainer); David Sherrill (White Sox Centerfielder); J. Michael Sarbaugh (Pirate Shortstop); Jeff Sheaffer (Pirate on 2nd Base); Tom Quinn (Red Sox Manager); John Millsitz (Red Sox Catcher); Jim Dedrick (White Sox Pitcher); Bob Hopkins (Toronto Shortstop); Bobby Joe Brown (Ballplayer Playing Cards); Wayne Crist (Vendor); Julia Miller (Stadium Control Room Announcer); Ashton Smith (Black Hammer Announcer).

LOS ANGELES TIMES, 3/30/94, Calendar/p. 6, Peter Rainer

Except for the fact that it was a commercial hit, the 1989 baseball movie "Major League" was not thc sort of film that cried out to be sequelized. But a lot can happen in five years—for one thing, baseball movies seem to be hanging in there. (So are sports movies in general.) So here's another go-round with the cloddy, come-from-behind Cleveland Indians sluggers who once again stumble in pursuit of thc American League Eastern Division championship. Want to bet they make it again? The people behind "Major League II" are no dopes: They must already be cooking up "III."

Many of the same players from the first film put in repeat appearances. Charlie Sheen's Rick "Wild Thing" Vaughn is now a superstar with a seven-digit salary. a stretch limo, a fancy girlfriend and a groomed GQ look to replace his former punkishness. Dennis Haysbert's Pedro Cerrano has gone Buddhist: he chants in the locker room and compliments opposing pitchers on their fastballs. Willie Mays Hayes, played in the first film by Wesley Snipes and here by Omar Epps, has been making Hollywood movies in thc off-season as the action hero Black Hammer. Tom Berenger's Jake is back as the manager, replacing James Gammon, who spends his best moments in the film cheering thc Indians from a hospital bed while he's pretending to watch "Masterpiece Theatre." Bob Uecker, as the Indians' perpetually bedraggled play-by-play radio announcer, puts in another appearance, dressing down from his Liberace-like duds to a T-shirt as the Indians slide into the cellar. (His aghast expostulations are the film's highlight.)

If only the "Naked Gun" folks had stepped in to really shake things up! Baseball movies are ripe for a full-out lampoon but "Major League II" keeps pumping up its "heart." We learn all sorts of homiletic life lessons about the value of sportsmanship and Being True to Yourself. Why do sports movies always have to devolve into civics lessons. To its credit, "Major League II" doesn't go in for a lot of moony sentiment about America's Pasttime but it ends up tenderized anyway.

NEW YORK POST, 3/30/94, p. 33, Michael Medved

If the characters in a movie sequel keep shouting out lines like, "I can't believe it's happening again!" then it's a clear sign that the filmmakers know that they're in trouble. When the fictional people who populate the picture can't believe what's going on then how is the movie-going audience supposed to buy it?

That's the problem with "Major League II." It takes a silly story that was merely far-fetched the first time around and makes it both ludicrous and lifeless by trying to repeat its key elements. The result feels patched together and mechanical, despite a number of genuinely funny gags and some likable performances.

The sequel opens as spring training begins for the Cleveland Indians, an assemblage of lunatics and losers who miraculously won their division last season (and last film).

This time, it looks like success may have spoiled the returning players. Star pitcher Rick "Wild Thing" Vaughan (Charlie Sheen), the ex-con who once favored leather jackets and a Harley, is now a cautious yuppie in a limousine.

Willie Mays Hayes, the speedy outfielder played in the first film by Wesley Snipes and now portrayed in a surprisingly seamless transition by Omar Epps, began pumping iron in the off-season so he has foolishly decided he's a power hitter.

The Cuban slugger (perfectly played by the very gifted Dennis Haysbert) who once used voodoo rites to focus his intensity has abruptly replaced that faith with Buddhism; it helps him to glow with inner calm and contentment, but makes him hopeless as a ballplayer.

Aging catcher Toni Berenger is also back with the team, but this time his love interest, Rene Russo, makes only the briefest uncredited cameo appearance.

Inept third baseman Roger Dorn (Corbin Bernsen) has taken over as the team's owner, but then he passes that ownership back to ruthless, scheming Margaret Whitton in a series of transactions that make no dramatic or logical sense and will bewilder anyone who's paying attention.

In addition to these returning veterans, the team boasts a few standout newcomers, including a marvelous young actor named Eric Bruskotter as a big-hearted, dim-bulb farmboy and rookie catcher, and David Keith, playing an impossibly arrogant, perpetually scowling, high-priced free-agent slugger who directs malice at his own teammates as much as the opposition.

In the original "Major League" (as well as the recent, college football saga "The Program") director David S. Ward re-created big-time sporting events and wildly cheering crowds with energy and conviction.

Here, the slickly edited game scenes generate a level of electricity that is surprising, especially since the entire arc of the story (where the Indians turn suddenly terrible, but just as suddenly they're contending for the pennant again) is simultaneously arbitrary and predictable.

If nothing else, the actors seem to enjoy themselves, and the picture is good for a few laughs. In the rush of optimism and gratitude that stirs the hearts of all baseball fans each year at Opening Day, "Major League II" will probably receive a warmer reception than it rightly deserves.

NEWSDAY, 3/30/94, Part II/p. B9, Jack Mathews

Sitting through "Major League II," the sequel to David S. Ward's 1989 comedy hit, is like sitting through a highlights film from the Mets' 1993 season. The only thing funny about it is how bad it is.

The first "Major League" was not great, but at least its story, about a ragtag Cleveland Indians team pulling together in defiance of its cynical owner, and its characters—a voodoo-practicing slugger, an ex-con pitcher with a lethal fastball—were fresh. That film set in a city that almost never has a winning team, also captured some of the fickleness and civic craziness that comes with an unexpected championship season (recall the Miracle Mets of '69?).

"Major League II" picks the first story up where it left off, then essentially repeats it. It's the following spring, and as the players reassemble, they're a bunch of losers again. Rick "Wild Thing" Vaughn (Charlie Sheen) has changed his image, and lost his fastball. Pedro Cerrano (Dennis Haysbert) has given up his voodoo for Buddhism and sees spiritual beauty even in defeat And Omar Epps' Willie Mays Hayes (in an apparent slap at Wesley Snipe who played Willie in the first film) has become an off-season action movie star with an ego.

The team's insipid third baseman (Corbin Bernsen) is the new owner, and its bum-kneed catcher Jake Taylor (Tom Berenger),is about to become its manager. Ward, and co-writer R. J. Stewart, added a couple of new characters—a hayseed catcher (Eric Bruskotter) with a fetish for Playboy centerfold bios and a Japanese outfielder (Takaashi Ishibashi) who keeps knocking himself out chasing fly balls into the fence—but the plotline is the same. The Indians are so bad, their radio announcer (Bob Uecker) has to get drunk in order to call the game, and only when their old owner (Margaret Whitton) returns are the players inspired to make another run for the pennant.

Ward and the actors repeating their roles seem to have been inspired by nothing so much as an easy payday. Sheen, whose creation of the myopic Vaughn was the best thing about "Major League," barely gets a chance to parody the character this time, and there is no one else to pick up the slack.

The baseball sequences, the inevitable last-inning-of-the-last-game heroics with everyone back in character, are crowd-pleasers, but there is a cheaper way for you to experience the same thrills. Rent the first movie on video, and watch it again.

SIGHT AND SOUND, 11/94, p. 48, Leslie Felperin Sharman

After their Cinderella winning season last year, the Cleveland Indians baseball team begins another season of spring training. Former shortstop Dorn has bought the team from Rachel Phelps at an inflated price. Taylor fails to make the final line-up because of his age and becomes a coach instead. New players include mercenary free agent Parkman and a gormless rookie nicknamed Rube, while fame and success has gone to the heads of most of the original star players. Rick 'Wild Thing' Vaughn has forsaken his trademark haircut and motorcycle for lucrative sponsorship deals and a limo. He is dating a sleek agent instead of his old girlfriend Nikki, who works with underprivileged children. Willie Mays Hayes has made a film, and Cerrano has forsaken voodoo worship for Buddhism. The team lose their first game of the season when Cerrano hits a bird with a fly ball and neglects to run home out of grief-stricken guilt. As the season progresses, they fail to improve and their once-optimistic fans lose faith in their team.

Parkman is traded to the White Sox for a Japanese outfielder, Tanaka. The team begins to lose so much money that Dorn is forced to sell them back to Rachel Phelps, who plans to sack everyone and move the team to Florida when they come bottom of the league as she predicts. At their lowest ebb, Tanaka's slanders of their masculinity and an impassioned speech by Rube fire them to improved performances. Vaughn starts to see Nikki again and resumes riding motorcycles. After a cycle of victories, the *Indians* make it to the playoffs against the White Sox, despite many misfortunes including Lou the manager having a heart attack.

At the top of the ninth inning, the Indians are barely ahead. Taylor puts Vaughn on, dressed in his old attire, and the crowd cheers wildly. Vaughn is so determined to defeat his old rival Parkman that he risks walking the batter before him. Pitching faster and better than he has done all year, Vaughn strikes Parkman out, thus winning the game and a place in the World Series.

While all over Hollywood male leads are waxing sensitive and even Arnie is getting in touch with his feelings, in the world of *Major League II* some things never change. Even though in the real world play has been indefinitely suspended due to a players' strike, these Indians still have their balls—the standard leather ones weighing 5 oz. and measuring 9-9¼ inches in circumference. Rarely does the cinema witness such an unbridled display of testicular preoccupation and pride. Gonads of all sorts are the film's central trope, whether as objects of derision and thus the impetus to improvement, or lovingly framed by the camera as the catchers signal the next pitch over their crotches. Though the comedy may be lame as an undrugged British athlete, the plot as predictable as Gazza's next meal, there is still something quaintly comforting about the unquestioned certainties of masculinity displayed here. Like the slow, oddly dressed game itself, baseball movies are best when they stick to the old rules and refuse to clutter the game with girls and too much stuff about relationships.

The best thing about *Major League II*—like its predecessor, to which it sticks closely in structure—is that it captures the soggy hot dog flavour of the game undiluted. Interspersed with regrettably necessary bits of drama about the players' private lives, the bulk of the film consists of ball play. Crisply edited so as to make the game intelligible even to the most baseball-illiterate Brit, the film utilises slow-motion in a truly cinematic way, recalling Riefenstahl's *Olympia*. Tongue, loosely in cheek, it recycles all the standard devices of the sports movie, such as montage sequences of victories with spinning sports-page headlines and a "Win this one for Lou" speech. In addition, the film regroups most of its original cast list, with Tom Berenger wasting his time, and Charlie Sheen just looking wasted, Now the big star, Wesley Snipes has traded up to lead parts, so his old character of Willie Mays Hayes is taken over by Omar Epps. However, the film exacts revenge by placing Hayes in a parody of Snipes' current action films, in which he does "both his own stunts *and* his own acting!"

The chorus of fans commenting on the team's progress, led by homophobic announcer Harry Doyle and counterpointed by a yobbish trio on the bleachers, embodies the white working-class culture which makes up the bulk of its fan base. Compared with most sports movies, the film is unusually swollen with crowd shots, partly as a means of interpellating the viewer, and partly because the game itself is more marked than any other by the intense rivalries of local patriotism.

Also reviewed in:
NEW YORK TIMES, 3/30/94, p. C16, Caryn James
VARIETY, 3/28-4/3/94, p. 69, Emanuel Levy
WASHINGTON POST, 3/30/94, p. B11, Rita Kempley

MAKING UP!

A Seventh Art Releasing presentation of a Vela-X Filmproduction in asociation with Munich Film and Television School and The Bavarian Broadcasting Corporation. *Producer:* Ewa Karlström. *Director:* Katja von Garnier. *Screenplay (German with English subtitles):* Benjamin Taylor, Katja von Garnier, and Hannes Jaenicke. *Director of Photography:* Torsten Breuer. *Editor:* Katja von Garnier. *Music:* Peter Wenke and Tillmann Höhne. *Sound:* Rainer Plabst. *Sound Editor:* Achim Hofmann. *Casting:* Carola Höhne. *Costumes:* Birgit Aichele. *Make-up:* Denise Marx and Rita Absmeier. *Running time:* 90 minutes. *MPAA Rating:* Not Rated.

CAST: Katja Riemann (Frenzy); Nina Kronjäger (Maischa); Gedeon Burkhard (René); Max Tidof (Mark); Daniela Lunkewitz (Susa); Peter Sattmann (Editor); Jochen Nickel (Party Animal); Carola Höhne (René's Sister); Stefan von Moers (Man with Iniative); Jophi Ries (Bartender); Sybille Hamm (Woman in Pink); Giovanni Mangano (Bodybuilder).

LOS ANGELES TIMES, 10/21/94, Calendar/p. 10, Kevin Thomas

German filmmaker Katja von Garnier's effervescent, 55-minute "Making Up!" and Louis Venosta's distinctive 35-minute "The Coriolis Effect" add up to an amusing commentary on the state of relations between men and women today. We most certainly are going to hear more from both von Garnier and Venosta.

Von Garnier's vignette, which won a student film Oscar, is a witty farce about what even the most attractive and vibrant young women have to put up with in the search for suitable men. Maischa (Nina Kronjäger), a blond cartoonist, has pretty much retreated from the fray, drawing inspiration for her comic strip from the romantic exploits of her vivacious best friend, a tall brunette nurse nicknamed Frenzy (Katja Riemann, who recalls Geena Davis in her looks and infectious giddiness).

At the moment Frenzy has set her sights on the handsome René (Gedeon Burkhard), who on their first date asks her to bring along a friend for *his* best pal Mark (Max Tidof). Pressed into going, Maischa realizes immediately that she and Max have literally crossed paths before—and not fortuitously.

Nothing that develops can be said to be unpredictable, but von Garnier manages to make every turn seem fresh and wryly funny. She's a sharp, stylish observer of the challenge modern women face in squaring away their freedom and independence with their attraction to the opposite sex and their longing for love. She has a sure way with both the camera and her cast, which sparkles under her direction.

The people of "The Coriolis Effect," which was named the best short film at Venice this year, are not as sophisticated as those of "Making Up!," but Venosta is every bit as assured a director as von Garnier.

Ray (Dana Ashbrook) and Stanley (James Wilder) are best friends, U.S. Weather Service scientists working in the Texas Panhandle and specializing in chasing tornadoes. Just as Ray's girlfriend (Corinne Rohrer) has admitted, in a burst of unwelcome honesty, that she's slept with Stanley, a tornado starts brewing.

In his film debut, Venosta manages to make turbulent emotions and weather echo each other without lots of heavy-handed symbolism or rigid symmetry. As Ray and Stanley begin working out the crisis in their friendship, they encounter the alluring and mysterious Ruby (Jennifer Rubin, always a radiant presence) who's a force of nature herself.

NEW YORK POST, 9/16/94, p. 45, Larry Worth

German comedy has long been an oxymoron, what with auteurs like Rainer Werner Fassbinder, Werner Herzog and Wim Wenders at the cinematic forefront. But all that's changed with the emergence of Katja von Garnier.

The twentysomething first-time director is the country's wunderkind, thanks to her 55-minute romp about two young women seeking romance.

And the secret to its international triumph in 26 countries? Well, the vagaries of love translate into every language, here brought to fruition in von Garnier's near-perfect script.

The tale concerns a nurse and her cartoonist friend's weekend manhunt. One gallery opening later, the nurse has found her dream hunk—and arranged a blind date for her pal.

The director's gimlet eye for detail wittily captures the mating dance, from nagging self-doubts to endless costume changes, from hopeless small talk to bare essentials.

Heartfelt performances from a cast of newcomers will make viewers think they've been guided through every facet of '90s relationships. Until the double-feature's second part: "The Coriolis Effect."

This 30-minute black-and-white look at two men and two women facing down a tornado—and a minefield of metaphors—is a hilarious, creepy, completely original examination of infidelity and its rainbow of repercussions.

Writer/director Louis Venosta opens with a couple making violent love atop a kitchen table as a storm moves in. But the real thunder breaks when she admits to having slept with his co-worker/best friend.

And that's just the beginning. It's part "Twin Peaks" and part "Wizard of Oz," all fanned by sterling turns from a quartet of rising stars, never mind the vocal talents of Quentin Tarantino.

Separately, "Making Up!" and "The Coriolis Effect" would justify a trip to the cinema. Together, they're fall's best movie bargain.

NEWSDAY, 9/16/94, Part II/p. B5, John Anderson

Besides its fiscal implications, the term "date movie" describes a film with that squooshy, gooshy, hand-holding, "Four Weddings and a Funeral" kind of feeling. The sort of movie you can take someone you don't know so well, without fear of insult, embarrassment, or too much post-credits conversation.

That said, "Making Up!" and "The Coriolis Effect" would have to be considered the anti-date double bill of the millennium. Both pry into secrets of the sexes that neither wants the other to know. They strip the veneer off the romance game, the dignity off the ego, and promise to keep arguments going deep into the night.

They're also both witty and honest in their own ways, particularly "Making Up!" I hesitate, for obvious reasons, calling it a "woman's movie" but certain experts of my acquaintance thought that it exposed (affectionately, of course) how women allow themselves to be driven crazy by men.

Maischa (Nina Kronjager) is all set to go off for the weekend with the unseen Claus, when her cartoonist pal Frenzy (Katja Riemann)—who uses Maischa's romantic antics as fodder for her comic strip—gets her to ditch Claus and attend a gallery show and cocktail party. There, Maischa spots the hunky Rene (Gedeon Burkhard), a date is soon arranged, and the already ennui-ridden Frenzy is dragged along on a blind date with Rene's friend Mark (Max Tidof).

Director Katja von Garnier does tend to belabor things a bit— Maischa's pre-date preening, for instance, is funny, but we get it already. But she also shows us things we don't usually see. The emotional surrender of women to love, for instance; the way each date means the life and death for their self-image; how nothing ever works out the way you expect it to. And all the time, you believe it.

Louis Venosta's quirky "The Coriolis Effect" is a far more manic movie, opening with a swarm of clouds in a silver-toned black and white sky and the sound of bodies moaning, furniture groaning, dishes breaking, and some unmistakable hostility. The couple on the kitchen table, Ray (Dana Ashbrook) and Suzie (Corrine Bohrer), have just made angry love, Suzie having told Ray she slept with his best friend Stan (James Wilder), and Ray not taking it at all well.

Stan and Ray are tornado chasers—they chart the path of twisters—and one is on the way. Stan comes by to pick up Ray, not knowing about the recent revelation, and the two head off amid various types of storms. Their conversation is one of-those things you never hear: male territorality laid bare, uncensored sexual propriety. It's more than a bit pretentious, but the photography is gorgeous and the ideas are the kind you seldom hear discussed. Not in mixed company, anyway.

SIGHT AND SOUND, 12/94, p. 40, Lizzie Francke

Frenzy is a cartoonist; her best friend Maischa is a nurse. Maischa is boy crazy; Frenzy, who is single, is more worried about her work as she is having a creative block. One weekend Maischa ditches her boyfriend so that she can go out on the town with Frenzy. At an exhibition opening, Maischa spots an eligible young man (who she subsequently learns is called René) and tries to talk to him. The next day she co-opts Frenzy into helping her track him down. They go to the park where he plays football. While Maischa jogs around the track, Frenzy waits on the sidelines, and bumps into a man that she thinks is a bit of a jerk.

That night the two women go to a party. René is there and Maischa finally has a date for the next day. She persuades Frenzy to come along with her since René has a friend, The friend transpires to be the man in the park, Mark. Maischa goes off with René and ends up in bed with him. Frenzy and Mark spend the day horsing around. When Frenzy returns home, she finds a distraught Maischa, who now feels rejected. Frenzy, however, plans on a second date with Mark. She becomes anxious about when he will call, but at the same time starts having new ideas for her cartoon strip. Maischa resolves that she doesn't need to have men in her life for the moment. Mark does call and since he is in the army, Frenzy looks forward to an occasional relationship with him.

Katja von Garnier's featurette has already won much acclaim, with Hollywood offers apparently flooding in for the young director. It started out as a graduation project but, mindful of a more commercial approach, von Garnier persuaded a handful of German television stars to work on it. In this respect, it is not surprising that it feels like a well-crafted episode of some television series—*thirtysomething* springing to mind, particularly the 'Melissa' chapter. Consequently *Making Up* does not feel that strikingly original, with its themes as tired and obvious as the rather dreadful soft rock soundtrack. Certainly Frenzy is little different from the young photographer in the 80s American show. She pursues her career as a comic strip artist, working on 'Rubi'—The Mosquito Woman'. But this visual motif is not exploited—a shame since a 'Rubi' story could have been used to counterpoint the film's rather simple narrative.

Predictably, Frenzy's male boss is not very encouraging, suggesting that the cartoon should be "more up-beat" and that her Rubi character should "have bigger tits". There is the sense that her involvement with her work precludes relationships with men. Frenzy is resolutely independent and tired of life's struggles with the opposite sex. Yet at the same time, *Making Up* concludes with a rather cheap payoff, with Frenzy overcoming her artistic anxieties just when love—or at least the possibility of some relationship and, ideally, a casual one at that— seems to be around the corner.

Maischa provides a rather obvious contrast. She is a nurse who acquires boyfriends to do things around the house such as putting up shelves. With an ever optimistic attitude, she sets out to 'conquer' men but ends up being used by them. While she is being subjected to the narcissist René's workout-style love-making, which in the end makes her feel hollow "as a doll". Frenzy is having fun in a playground getting to know Mark.

Von Garnier is hardly subtle as she cross-cuts between the two scenes. The two women's different experiences resolve in one learning to put up shelves herself, while the other proves to be just as dependent on that phone-call as her friend, checking, as countless women have done before her, that the line works when the call seems overdue. At the end, the friends joke that they should set up a business to make women immune to men. For, of course, it is the men who are the mosquitos, and women need them like a case of malaria. It's the old story. While von Garnier is certainly an accomplished director, she should be a little more inventive with her story-board.

VILLAGE VOICE, 9/27/94, p. 66, Amy Taubin

A crowd-pleasing double bill, *Making Up!* and *The Coriolis Effect* treat the anxieties of romantic attachment with blithe irreverence. Both films played at the Sundance film festival, where they were perceived as welcome relief from the prevailing gloom.

In Louis Venosta's *The Coriolis Effect*, Ray (Dana Ashbrook, immortalized as Bobby in *Twin Peaks*) and Stanley (James Wilder of *Melrose Place*) work as tornado chasers. Just before they head out after a big one, Ray discovers that Stanley poached his girlfriend for a one night stand and, to add insult to injury, that they'd done it while Ray lay next to them, drunk and passed out. Stanley and Ray are satiric variations on the Neanderthal male: Stanley believes that women are nothing but trouble while Ray views them as prime property—which means that Stanley can't understand why Ray's so upset, and Ray's so blind jealous he can't even keep his truck on the road.

Director-writer Louis Venosta has a sharp ear for studly dialogue; he also knows how to mine his bad-weather metaphor for comic visual effect. *The Coriolis Effect* takes a wrong turn, however, with the introduction of a female twister chaser (Jennifer Rubin) whose Oz obsession makes absolutely no sense at all.

Comic repartee is also the strong suit of Katja von Garnier's *Making Up!*, which follows the infrequent amorous adventures of Maischa and her droll girlfriend Frenzy. Maischa's a nurse with a weakness for narcissistic men; Frenzy falls for a country bumpkin who inadvertently pisses on her foot before they've been properly introduced. "I wonder if *he's* going through the agony of picking out clothes. 'Maybe an orange loincloth would be right,'" Frenzy says mockingly as she watches Maischa try on everything in her wardrobe in preparation for a first date. *Making Up!* is best when it sends up sexual difference. Ultimately, however, it loses track of everything except romantic infatuation, becoming in the process a bit of a bore.

Also reviewed in:
NEW YORK TIMES, 9/16/94, p. C8, Janet Maslin
VARIETY, 11/15/93, p. 32, Eric Hansen

MAN OF NO IMPORTANCE, A

A Sony Pictures Classics release of a Majestic Films presentation in association with Newcomm and BBC Films of a Little Bird production. *Executive Producer:* James Mitchell. *Producer:* Jonathan Cavendish. *Director:* Suri Krishnamma. *Screenplay:* Barry Devlin. *Director of Photography:* Ashley Rowe. *Editor:* David Freeman. *Music:* Julian Nott. *Sound:* David Stephenson. *Casting:* Michelle Guish. *Production Designer:* Jamie Leonard. *Art Director:* Frank Flood. *Set Dresser:* Fiona Daly. *Special Effects:* Gerry Johnson. *Costumes:* Phoebe De Gaye. *Make-up:* Ken Jennings. *Stunt Coordinator:* Martin Grace. *Running time:* 98 minutes. *MPAA Rating:* R.

CAST: Albert Finney (Alfie Byrne); Brenda Fricker (Lily Byrne); Michael Gambon (Carney); Tara Fitzgerald (Adele Rice); Rufus Sewell (Robbie Fay); Patrick Malahide (Carson); David Kelly (Baldy); Mick Lally (Father Ignatius Kenny); Anna Manahan (Mrs. Grace); Joe Pilkington (Ernie Lally); Brendan Conroy (Rasher Flynn); Joan O'Hara (Mrs. Crowe); Eileen Reid (Mrs. Rock); Eileen Conroy (Mrs. Curtin); Maureen Egan (Mrs. Dunne); Paddy Ashe (Mr. Ryan); Pat Killalea (Phil Curran); John Killalea (Jack Curran); Pascal Perry (Mr. Gorman); Joe Savino (Breton-Beret); Paudge Behan (Kitty); Jimmy Keogh (Treasurer); Ingrid Craigie (Waitress); Enda Oates (Garda); Damien Kaye (Foley); Catherine Byrne (Woman at Canal); Dylan Tighe (Landlady's Son); Stuart Dunne (John); Jonathan Rhys-Myers (1st Young Man); Vincent Walsh (2nd Young Man); Paul Roe (3rd Young Man).

LOS ANGELES TIMES, 12/22/94, Calendar/p. 3, Kevin Thomas

"A Man of No Importance" takes us to an early '60s Dublin neighborhood, where a jolly bus conductor, Alfie (Albert Finney) entertains his riders, regulars all, with impassioned recitations from his favorite author, Oscar Wilde. At his local church he has staged "The Importance of Being Earnest" with his passengers and neighbors and now he wants to tackle "Salome"—especially since he feels he's found the perfect young woman to play the title role, a country girl named Adele (Tara Fitzgerald), newly arrived in town.

Alfie is an exuberant fellow, well-liked by his passengers, and he manages to get "Salome" past the parish priest by pointing out its biblical source. Trouble starts early on, however, when he casts his landlord, Ivor (Michael Gambon), as King Herod. Ivor swiftly declares the work immoral. Alfie soldiers on, but in doing so, is actually triggering an inevitable confrontation with himself.

Writer Barry Devlin and director Suri Krishnamma allow us to realize that Alfie is gay so gradually and so discreetly that we're able to understand what a jolt it would be for those around him to learn the truth about his sexual orientation. That's because at the same time they're filling out Alfie's life they're showing us a pious, blue-collar world in which the very existence of homosexuality is denied.

Although enthusiastic to the point of bombast in regard to the sacredness of art and the greatness of Oscar Wilde, Alfie is such a burly, hearty, kindly middle-aged guy that the unsophisticated people who surround him do not suspect his true sexual orientation. Late marriage is not all that uncommon in Ireland, and Alfie's sister, Lily (Brenda Fricker), with whom he lives above Ivor's butcher shop, continues to hope that he will find the "right girl." At times the film is so contrived and theatrical—those constant bus recitations are a bit much—that it comes as a surprise to discover it was not based on a play. Such an objection matters little alongside its signal and deeply moving accomplishments, the most important of which is to convey with force and accuracy just how isolating life in the closet can be—and how justified a gay individual is to try to stay there in an environment as hostile to homosexuals as Alfie's is. There's just no way Alfie can declare his love for the likable young bus driver (Rufus Sewell), for example, with whom he works.

Autodidact that he may be, Alfie has a grasp of the nature and function of art as fully developed as that of Wilde himself. As amusing as his rehearsal's of "Salome" are, he shows himself to be a true artist, making the most of what his unlettered, awkward friends have to give to the play and drawing an inspired portrayal from Adele, who is not quite the innocent Alfie so dearly wants her to be in his heart. But the very nature of "Salome" demands that Alfie defend it increasingly to one and all; in doing so he discovers how hard it is to keep separate art and truth.

Alfie is not the only person who evolves. As Ivor and Lily's suspicions of Alfie grow, the more hateful they become, revealing minds as cramped as the quarters in which they and Alfie live but eventually becoming figures of pity in their ignorance. Gambon and Fricker manage to bring some humanity to this miserable duo, and Fitzgerald convinces us that the sweet, troubled Adele really could play Salome.

Towering over one and all, not surprisingly, as Finney as the increasingly tormented but brave Alfie.

NEW YORK POST, 12/22/94, p. 63, Michael Medved

The title "A Man of No Importance" is supposed to be an ironic reference to Oscar Wilde's sparkling 1893 play "A Woman of No Importance," but the atmosphere of this sad and profoundly touching film is light years away from Wilde's sparkling comedy.

The movie's main character is Alfie Byrne (Albert Finney), a middle-aged bus conductor in Dublin in the early '60s who lives above a butcher shop with his crotchety spinster sister (Brenda Fricker). He's become obsessed with the life and work of Wilde, his fellow Irishman, as the only source of joy or color in a singularly drab life.

Every day, he recites Wilde's poetry to the bemused passengers on his bus route, and he recruits those acquaintances to join him in an outrageously amateurish production of his hero's "scandalous" drama "Salome" to be staged at a church social hall.

Alfie even follows the great writer's example by suffering the pangs of a deep, guilty, infatuation with a much younger man—in Alfie's case, his partner, a good-looking bus driver and salt-of-the-earth bloke played by Rufus Sewell.

Meanwhile, a shy passenger who's recently arrived from the country (the lovely Tara Fitzgerald of "Sirens" and "Hear My Song") agrees to play the lead role of Princess Salome in Alfie's play; she seems powerfully drawn to the older man but she's also troubled by some guilty secrets of her own.

The 1960s setting turns out to be crucial to the movie's dramatic core, which involves the main character's truly terrifying loneliness. In that time and place, it feels entirely credible that Alfie would encounter not a single giving soul with whom he could share— or even discuss— "the love that dare not speak its name."

Albert Finney has made something of a specialty in recent years of playing doomed, lonely characters forced to suppress their longings ("The Playboys," "The Browning Version") but he's never handled such a role as brilliantly as it's handled here. "

For all his tragic moments, Alfie is hardly a depressing character; his warmth, energy, and intoxicating passion for "art" (particularly, of course by Wilde) make him one of the year's more endearing and memorable film characters.

His collaborator in this unusual project is a debuting director with the grand old Irish name of Suri Krishnamma. This Londoner (of mixed Indian and English ancestry) infuses his first feature film with a wonderfully flavorful feel of both the warmth and claustrophobia of Dublin life.

The screenplay (by a successful Irish rock musician named Barry Devlin) is often poetic but never pretentious: The movie's better lines ("My hands are innocent of affection") have a lilt to them that leaves a lasting impression. Though the climax to this generally understated slice-of-life drama seems a bit forced and illogical, the superb cast nonetheless manages to bring it off.

Even the most minor characters emerge with intensity and integrity, creating a rich ensemble of earthy personalities, each of whom strike the viewer as men (and women) of great importance.

SIGHT AND SOUND, 5/95, p. 50, Geoffrey Macnab

Dublin, 1963. Bus conductor Alfie Byrne, is mounting a production of Oscar Wilde's *Salome* in the local church hall. He earmarks Adele Rice, a young girl he spots on the number 34 route, for the title role, and tries to persuade Robbie, the driver he works with, to take the male lead. At the first rehearsal, Mr Carney, the butcher, makes a great show of moral indignation. He doesn't like the idea of being cast as King Herod and complains to Alfie's sister, Lily, that the play is blasphemous. She agrees to help him halt the production.

Alfie is warned by his friend, Baldy, that Carney is campaigning against him, but he refuses to abandon the play. During rehearsal, Adele breaks down in tears, and explains that she is pregnant. Alfie goes to confession to ask advice about what Adele's lover should do. The priest recognises his voice and wrongly presumes that Alfie is the father. Exasperated, Alfie storms out of the church and heads off to Adele's bedsit. Here, he stumbles in on her making love with her boyfriend.

That night, Alfie puts on make-up and a big cape, and cruises the streets of Dublin. He enters a gay bar, approaches Kitty, a handsome young man, and asks him for a cuddle. The episode ends violently with Alfie robbed and assaulted by Kitty and his friends. As a policeman escorts him home, he is spotted by Carney and Lily. His secret is out. Ashamed, he makes a bungling attempt to commit suicide by jumping in the canal, but the water is only knee-deep. The next day at work, his homophobic boss, Carson, tells him that Robbie is so disgusted that he has had himself transferred to another bus route. He is also harangued by Carney, but his passengers stay loyal to him. Adele, who is off to England, comes to say goodbye to him.

Alfie goes back to the church hall. As he sits musing over events, Robbie bursts in and announces that he wants to join the play. He explains he was taken off the bus route against his will. The two friends read an Oscar Wilde poem together.

A Man of No Importance is set in 1963, the year of the Profumo scandal and also of Albert Finney's famous performance in Tony Richardson's *Tom Jones*. Not that the swinging 60s have much bearing on the events here. The action is set in a close-knit Dublin community where everyone knows everyone else's business, and where the outside world hardly ever intrudes. Finney's role is very different from the roistering Jack-the-lad he created for Richardson. He plays Alfie Byrne, a wistful, charming but sexually repressed bus conductor, much given to reciting poetry to his passengers.

Barry Devlin's script borrows motifs, names, and even incidents from the life of Oscar Wilde. Initially, it seems to be aiming for comedy. Alfie, the surrogate Wilde figure, may be an aesthete but he lives above a butcher's shop. Nobody understands his witty aphorisms. Whereas Wilde had London high society, Lord Alfred Douglas and the Cadogan Hotel, Alfie must cope with the cramped little flat he shares with his sister, the pub, the church hall and the bowling green.

Suri Krishnamma's naturalistic approach makes Alfie's grand notions about life and art seem all the more ridiculous. When Alfie embarks on flights of poetic fantasy, domestic details always threaten to drag him back down to earth. We see the offal, the pigs' heads and the strings of sausages in the butcher's shop. Characters eat in close-up, and their chewing never fails to register on the soundtrack. Alfie's sister regards his liking for cooking as a sure sign of his effeminacy, and his many books as evidence of his decadence. "If I can produce only one beautiful work of art, I shall be able to rob malice of its venom, cowardice of its sneer and pluck out the tongue of scorn by the root," Alfie tells himself as he sets about mounting his amateur production of *Salome*, but his cast is comprised of grizzled old Dubliners who forget their lines or turn up at rehearsal dressed as vikings.

Early on, as the number 34 bus bumbles across town with Alfie doing his cabaret turn, events unfold in whimsical fashion. Even the two villains, Michael Gambon's hunched, malevolent butcher and Patrick Malahide's sneering bus inspector, are comic, ineffectual figures. At times, the film seems like a Norman Wisdom comedy with a little bit of blarney and high culture grafted on for good measure. If not exactly feeble, it certainly errs on the winsome side. The only hints of something more sombre come when Alfie's homosexuality is referred to. (He resists his sister's attempts at matchmaking him with his Salome, Adele, and is seen kissing a photograph of his handsome young bus driver, Robbie.) This makes the sudden, belated shift in mood all the more surprising. It climaxes when Alfie finally acknowledges that "the only way to get rid of temptation is to yield to it," dresses up in cape and hat like a latterday Wilde, and tries to pick up a man in a local pub. His subsequent humiliation is brutal in a way that seems entirely out of keeping with the rest of the movie. What had started as a gentle piece of whimsy threatens to turn into full-blown tragedy. However, even at the bleakest moment, *A Man of No Importance* preserves its mood of benevolence. "What a funny little man you are," Alfie murmurs to himself after a ludicrous suicide attempt.

VILLAGE VOICE, 12/27/94, p. 78, James Hannaham

Even people who actually read the *Voice* (none of my hip acquaintances will admit to it, even though they do) always complain to me, of all people, that they never know whether or not reviewers like the subjects of their reviews. Though I know that "loved it" or "hated it" have the stamp of certain thumb-happy TV film critics, I feel compelled to give the people what they want in some form or another.

What I Hated About *A Man of No Importance*:

1. It's another narrative featuring a homosexual who doesn't get to have any sex (in fact, he gets gay-bashed by hustlers when he attempts to get laid) and winds up unfulfilled, yet with his dignity intact. Dignity schmignity. The excuse for this nonsense is, as usual, the setting, this time Dublin 1961. Let's please bury the romantic and false notion that in the face of zero tolerance, all pre-Stonewall queers were as pathetic as Alfie Byrne (Albert Finney), a Wilde-idolizing bus attendant who can't play snooker (does that count as "not good at sports"?) and tries to drown himself in a foot-deep creek. That screenwriter Barry Devlin tells *No Importance* from Alfie's viewpoint is less consolation than it is in *Threesome*. Loserdom knows no sexual orientation. It sure hasn't stopped heterosexual loser filmmakers from ruling out gay PDA because they don't think het audiences can handle it.

2. It celebrates the most annoying equation for a film that affirms the redemptive qualities of art: COMMON FOLK + HIGH ART = HILARIOUS MISINTERPRETATION x JERKING OF TEARS. The first time Alfie pronounces *Salomé*, the Wilde play he plans to direct at the local church, with the accent on the second syllable, it earns a chuckle, maybe. The *eight billionth*, no.

3. Albert Finney. So disgustingly earnest.

4. The film has that made-for-U.K.-TV-but-theatrically-released-in-the-U.S. look. The shots are claustrophobic and grimy for good reason.
5. The music. After 12 or so minutes of "Let's Do It (Let's Fall in Love)" at both ends, I nearly blew chow. And, by the by, to *whom* could this shameless Muzak possibly refer? Not Alfie, who retains the friendship of his beloved co-worker Robbie Fay (Rufus Sewell), but God forbid they should ever touch each other. Not Adele Rice (Tara Fitzgerald), the bus rider Alfie hounds into taking the lead in the play who turns out to be playing hide the Salomé for a living...
6. Albert Finney. Just thinking about him again.

What I Liked About *A Man of No Importance*:

1. Brenda Fricker's fat and sour portrayal of Alfie's sister Lily.
2. The fact that I never have to see it again if I don't want to.

Finney may not manage to get full comic mileage out of his role, but he offers dignity and pathos aplenty. It is a surprisingly gentle performance, in its own quiet way as impressive as his drunken diplomat in *Under the Volcano* or his Shakespearean actor gone to seed in *The Dresser*. The film, though, is as diffident as its title suggests. Rather than acknowledge that Alfie is a victim of a prejudiced, repressive society, it persists in portraying its little corner of 60s Dublin as a picture postcard community, full of loveable eccentrics.

Also reviewed in:
CHICAGO TRIBUNE, 2/3/95, Friday/p. K, Michael Wilmington
NEW REPUBLIC, 1/23/95, p. 31, Stanley Kauffmann
NEW YORK TIMES, 12/22/94, p. C11, Caryn James
VARIETY, 9/19-25/94, p. 78, Leonard Klady
WASHINGTON POST, 1/27/95, p. C7, Hal Hinson
WASHINGTON POST, 1/27/95, Weekend/p. 36, Desson Howe

MAN IN UNIFORM, A

An I.R.S. Releasing Corporation release of an Alliance Communications and Miracle Pictures presentation of a Miracle Pictures production with the participation of Telefilm Canada and the Ontario Film Development Corporation. *Executive Producer:* Alexandra Raffé. *Producer:* Paul Brown. *Director:* David Wellington. *Screenplay:* David Wellington. *Director of Photography:* David Franco. *Editor:* Susan Shipton. *Music:* Ron Sures and The Tragically Hip. *Music Editor:* Alastair Gray. *Sound:* Bryan Day and Ao Loo. *Sound Editor:* Jane Tattersall. *Casting:* Susan Forrest. *Production Designer:* John Dondertman. *Set Decorator:* Megan Less. *Special Effects:* Ted Ross. *Costumes:* Beth Pasternak. *Make-up:* Judy Murdock. *Stunt Coordinator:* Larry McLean. *Running time:* 97 minutes. *MPAA Rating:* Not Rated.

CAST: Tom McCamus (Henry Adler); Brigitte Bako (Charlie Warner); Kevin Tighe (Frank); David Hemblen (Father); Alex Karzis (Bruce); Graham McPherson (Mr. Pearson); Daniel MacIvov (Director); Wendy Hopkins (Casting Director); Kirsten Kieferle (Anita); Pauline Gillis (Janet); Dana Brooks (Marilyn); Steve Ambrose (Bank Robber); Michael Hogan (Detective Rich); Mark Melymick (Lt. Edam); Cynthia Gillespie (Crimewave A.D.); Jack Nichols (Archer); Dick Grant (Sgt. Robin); Victor Ertmanis (Alley Cop); Rino Romano (Clyde); Maureen McKay (Bonnie); Matt Cooke (Sgt. Cheddar); Ken MacNeil (Dirt Bag); Mark Wilson (Butch); Matthew Ferguson (Edward Nichols); Albert Schultz (Businessman); Richard Blackburn (Bullet Salesman); Henry Czerny (Joseph Riggs); Nancy Cser (Sheila Riggs); Graham Losee (Jack Riggs); Von Flores (Kenny); Jhene Erwin (Tara); Christopher Marren (Sgt. Brown); Nereen Virgin (Radio Voice); Rafal Mickiewick (Stand In).

LOS ANGELES TIMES, 6/24/94, Calendar/p. 16, Peter Rainer

A good idea is hard to find—particularly in the movies. "A Man in Uniform" has a pretty terrific one: Henry Adler (Tom McCamus), a mousy bank clerk and sometime actor, gets a role as a brutal cop in a TV series and allows the role to take over his personal life. He wears his police duds at home and on the streets, where he's accepted by real officers and baited and cajoled by unknowing citizens. He takes part in a robbery and drug bust, all the while detaching more and more cleanly from what paltry reality he once possessed.

A lot of the film, which was written and directed by David Wellington, plays out in long slow shadowy passages where we're supposed to enter into Henry's fugue state. The problem is that Henry—whose cop name is Flanagan—is a blank; his fixations and emotional contradictions, such as his passive demeanor and livid temper, are too clinical to engage us. Wellington thinks that by training his camera on Henry's closed-off mug he'll open up his mind for us, but it doesn't happen.

The filmmaker's model is undoubtedly Scorsese's "Taxi Driver," to which it owes a large debt, but that film was raw where this one is freeze-dried. When Henry talks to himself menacingly in a mirror or speaks to an actress playing a prostitute (Brigitte Bako) about the "scum" in the city, he's not palpably scary the way De Niro's Travis Bickle was. McCamus is a capable actor, but he's given very little to work with. He's playing a strenuous cipher.

What makes the film watchable is the way it portrays the creepy, powerful feeling a weak man can acquire wearing a police uniform. Henry is a Method actor in the extreme: He lets the Method take over his matter. And there are a few sequences, such as the one where he comes upon a scene of police brutality and stands there fixated—simultaneously fascinated and sickened—that have real power. "A Man in Uniform" is best when it's not trying to hook us with fancy life-imitates-art philosophizing and just gets into Henry's uneasy mimicry. The film brings out the pathology in play acting.

NEW YORK POST, 8/19/94, p. 48, Bill Hoffmann

"A Man in Uniform" is not a good movie, but it at least reminds us of a real good movie, one it shamelessly rips off.

Broody-faced actor Tom McCamus plays Henry, a bored banking cxec who hopes to quit the biz to be a full-time actor.

He lands a role as a do-gooder cop on a violence-ridden TV police drama and begins practicing the role at home, in uniform, staring into a mirror.

"Don't push your luck, sc--bag!" is his favorite line. The line actually plays OK—it's just that the whole act seemed a lot more convincing a couple of decades ago when Robert De Niro uttered "You talkin' to me?" in "Taxi Driver."

McCamus' Henry and DeNiro's Travis Bickle have a lot in common.

They're both on the edge. They both love women they can't have and they're one step from exploding into unspeakable violence.

But Henry goes a step further. He begins playing "real" cop with his TV uniform, going out in broad daylight and the dead of night to fight bad guys.

The problem with this film is that Henry is a boring guy. He's a cliched-right-winger through and through and writer-director David Wellington tells us little of his background or why he relates to women so weirdly.

Brigitte Bako, while similarly underdeveloped, (character-wise at least), does an interesting turn as the TV actress playing a good-hearted hooker who first likes the cop, then rejects him with shattering results.

This film was lensed in Toronto, which is a wannabe New York for producers who can't afford the real thing.

It's the antithesis of why "Taxi Driver," beautifully filmed on our mean streets, worked so well.

Avoid "A Man in Uniform." It's strictly second-rate.

NEWSDAY, 8/19/94, Part II/p. B7, John Anderson

Virtually the first thing we see in David Wellington's cooly claustrophobic "A Man in Uniform" is a police officer being shot dead. Not quite dead, actually: He's caught mid-blast while the opening credits roll, and only collapses when they finish.

But by freeze-framing his first victim, Wellington immediately asserts his omnipotence: No one dies without my say-so, he declares. And, of course, he warps reality. Is this a murder? No, it's a movie. But there are movies within movies, aren't there? And various kinds of control? Five minutes haven't elapsed, and Wellington has already completed the overture for a neat little psychodrama, in which control and reality constantly blur and shift.

The film's human hotbed of mutating realities and lost control is Henry Adler (Tom McCamus), a bank teller and aspiring actor who is wound tighter than a pack of hundreds. Henry observes the bloodshed, and digests it: He has an audition that afternoon for the role of a cop on a "reality-based" TV show called "Crime Wave," and the cop's death turns out to be fortuitous. At the tryout, Henry is aggressive and convincing. "You ever play a cop before?" the director asks. No, Henry says, but I saw one shot this afternoon.

As Henry slowly but inevitably surrenders his identity to the fictional character Flanagan (first, he wears the uniform around town, then he walks a beat, then he gets a gun, then ...) we have to ask, just what did we know about Henry to begin with? The answer is nothing. He's a creature solely of this film; he has no past, outside of a father (David Hemblen), whose illness and death may be Henry's wish fulfilled. He attaches himself to his female co-star Charlie (Brigitte Bako), because just as he protects her in the show, he wants to protect her in real life. He becomes prone to law-and-order diatribes. He quits his job. Eventually, he joins the very criminal element he claims to detest.

Henry as buttoned-down Travis Bickle—there are electric scenes of him alone in his room, reciting his lines and getting progressively furious—is not all that Wellington is after. He's also making a sly case against the fraud perpetrated by "reality" programs—and the way media sucks the identity out of all of us—by creating one of his own.

Henry's life becomes a kind of entertainment, the gun a substitute for his manhood, the TV show a substitute for his life. The bank is robbed one day by a huge Marilyn Monroe look-alike, who thrusts her gun barrel in and out of his mouth and has her skirt blown up "Seven-Year Itch"-style. This really happens; others witness it. Later, when Henry disappears after helping a policeman subdue a suspect, and the officer looks around to find him, there's nothing left in his wake but a whirl of vapor. Henry's police radio says there's a body in the river; the one they dredge up is a cop. Henry's fantasy is an all-consuming vortex.

A Canadian, Wellington might be particularly sensitive to the imperialism of the U.S. media, but he's also made a thriller. And unlike most of the "entertainment" he skewers, his film works on more than one level.

SIGHT AND SOUND, 3/95, p. 40, Ben Thompson

A policeman is shot and killed in a Canadian city street. Among the crowd of onlookers is 31-year-old Henry Adler, an unsuccessful actor who works in a bank where he is under pressure to give up his thespian aspirations. With little social contact in his life other than an unhappy relationship with his father, the chance of a part as cop Flanagan—in a television drama series called *Crimewave*—appears to be a lifeline. A combination of unexpected vehemence and dedicated preparation wins him the role.

At a costume fitting, Henry meets Charlie Warner, who plays a prostitute in the show. Henry persuades the wardrobe mistress to let him take his uniform home to practice in. There is a robbery at the bank, a security guard is killed and, at gun point, Henry is forced to open the vault by a vicious robber. It is then a small step from rehearsing at home to walking the streets. He helps a real policeman subdue someone resisting arrest, using dialogue written for his fictional character.

On set, the intensity that Henry brings to his role is well received, and he starts rehearsing with Charlie, who seems to like him. However, at the bank he threatens a customer and in the ensuing argument with his boss, he quits his job. When a stroppy motorist refuses to submit to his dubious authority, he is humiliated. Ever more confused between his different roles, Henry takes Charlie to a hospital, to see his father who has had a stroke. When she points out to him that they are not having a relationship, he comes close to threatening her.

As Henry finishes filming his role, his father dies. He steals his costume and walks the streets, finding a police car in an alley, with one of the drivers inside receiving favours from a prostitute. Frank, the other policeman, asks him for help and Henry finds himself collecting bribes from a drug dealer. When the dealer flaunts his authority, Henry shoots him dead. He goes to Charlie's flat and terrorises her. Then he too picks up a prostitute. Back home, watching the death of his character on television, Henry shoots himself. Next morning, his body is found by a policeman who thinks he is a colleague.

This edgily fetishistic debut from Canadian writer-director Wellington opens with a cliché—the brutal murder of an unnamed man in uniform. There is a slightly more point to the standard public servant slaying sequence here than usual. The idea that a policeman walks a thin line between authority and violent death is integral to the almost sexual fascination the role begins to exercise over downtrodden anti-hero Henry Adler.

Wellington allows the odd flashy moment—the camera following a torn fragment of the dead cop's uniform as it is carried away on the wind—but otherwise he focuses on Henry's developing obsession with such a stern discipline that an atmosphere of authentic perversity is created. The swing of a night stick and the flash of a handcuff become visual punctuation marks. Dialogue is sometimes all but drowned out by the creak of leather. As the production notes assert breathlessly, the costume designer Beth Pasternak "wanted to design uniforms that looked so good the crew would be fighting over them after the shoot." She succeeded. Identification did not end there. "The director and (lead) actor not only sound alike", we are informed with unnerving cheerfulness, "they actually look very much alike."

At first, all this is fun to watch. Tom McCamus—his features exactly half way between Lou Reed and John Cale—is a compelling presence in the lead role. As long as he is poised between tragedy and comedy—acquiring an unaccustomed potency by acting the hardass in auditions, or introducing snippets of absurdly overheated cop dialogue into life at the bank—he is very funny and engaging, like Travis Bickle with a mortgage. Once he goes over the brink of madness however, he just becomes pathetic, and without another strong character for the viewer to identify with, the whole thing becomes depressing.

Brigitte Bako's role as Charlie is seriously underwritten. She starts out as a reasonably sassy actress disillusioned with victim roles, but in a sinister dramatised example of real life imitating fiction, a victim is exactly what she turns out to be. As is often the way of these things, the more inexorable Henry's inexorable spiral into personal degradation becomes, the less interesting it gets. Wellington's sense of mischief—shown off to worthy effect early on in such fine lines as: "chuckles here is out of commission"—rather deserts him as the film builds towards its inevitably messy climax. Hopefully it's not gone for good.

VILLAGE VOICE, 8/23/94, p. 54, Georgia Brown

Another story of a basket case is David Wellington's claustrophobic *A Man in Uniform*. It's hero, Henry (Tom McCamus), is a creep and a loner, a lowly bank clerk who gets a semblance of a life after auditioning for a popular TV police drama, *Crimewave*. At first, just those lines he goes about rehearsing—"Don't push your luck, *scum*bag!" "Don't push your *luck*, scumbag!"—give Henry a lift. Once he's cast as Officer Flanagan, even the director notices, "Henry, you were born to play this part." By then our man has secretly become Flanagan. Having persuaded the wardrobe girl to let him take home the uniform (just to help him get into his part, you know, he begins wearing it around town. Watching Henry's tentativeness on the street, you do get a sense of how uniforms bestow identity on the wearer—but only if he's equipped to play the part.

Henry, however, finds that role-playing isn't as simple as on TV. Although troublingly aggressive in civilian life—sometimes Henry comes on like a closet maniac—walking his self-appointed beat he's a Milquetoast. When a parking violator berates him, Henry runs away. (Although many of these situations are intrinsically comic, it's a strain to laugh given the film's own creepiness.) He can't seem to fit in with the other patrolmen. Helping a fellow officer subdue a suspect, he asks if he should read the perp his rights. "You been watching too much TV, kid," scoffs his new partner. Here and elsewhere, Wellington detours into muckraking, showing what seems like the entire force as mean, venal, and corrupt.

With its synthetic dialogue and stage-set look, *A Man in Uniform* is reminiscent of Mamet films like *House of Games*. But Wellington hasn't Mamet's ability to spin a web and baffle the senses. After the first half hour, Henry simply isn't very interesting. Details tend to be pointedly clinical—as when Henry visits the actress cast as the TV show's hooker (she's played by Brigitte Bako) and keeps marveling how *clean* her place is.

By the end, Wellington has painted himself into a corner and, not knowing how to dispose of his nutcase, takes the easiest way out. My companion's verdict on the film, "the poor man's *Taxi Driver*," seems as succinct a description as any I can think of.

Also reviewed in:
CHICAGO TRIBUNE, 8/5/94, Friday/p. L, John Petrakis
NEW YORK TIMES, 8/19/94, p. C10, Janet Maslin
VARIETY, 6/7/93, p. 41, Leonard Klady

MANHATTAN BY NUMBERS

A Rising Star/Pardis Inc./International Film & Video Center production. *Executive Producer:* Bahman Maghsoudiou and Behrooz Hashemian. *Producer:* Ramin Niami. *Director:* Amir Naderi. *Screenplay:* Amir Naderi. *Director of Photography:* James Callanan. *Editor:* Amir Naderi. *Music:* Gato Barbieri. *Sound:* Judy Karp. *Running time:* 88 minutes. *MPAA Rating:* Not Rated.

CAST: John Wojda (George Murphy); Branislav Tomich (Chuck Lehrman); Mary Chang Faulk (Ruby); Matt Friedson (Fabric Store Assistant); Frank Irwin (Floyd); Lou Galiardo (Man in Bar); Lee Crogham (Fabric Store Owner); William Rafal (Mouse Man); Gerard Small (Shining Star).

LOS ANGELES TIMES, 11/18/94, Calendar/p. 10, Peter Rainer

Iranian-born director Amir Naderi, who has been living in New York City since 1987, has a fine eye for the city's avid, woebegone landscape. In "Manhattan by Numbers," his first American feature, he lets his camera roam from Washington Heights to the Lower East Side, and he always finds fresh ways of seeing things.

The film might have been better if Naderi, who made the acclaimed "The Runner," had made a documentary. He has such a lyrical, free-flowing feeling for the city that the story he comes up with seems forced and perfunctory by comparison. It's about a laid-off Daily News reporter, George Murphy (John Wojda), who spends a long day trekking around the city trying to stir up $1,200 to avoid eviction. His wife and daughter are staying with his father-in-law in Queens.

As George rifles through his address book calling friends from pay phones and getting nowhere, you begin to get a sinking feeling: This is going to turn out to be an Odyssey. When George tries to locate an old despairing friend who appears to have dropped out of sight, George's money hunt turns into a Samuel Beckett escapade: It's Looking for Godot.

Wojda's overwrought acting jars with Naderi's naturalism. Perhaps Naderi agrees, since long stretches of the film show the actor in medium and long shot wandering the streets wordlessly. But he manages to work in a range of New York "types"—homeless people, reporters, landlords—who resonate as more than types.

"Manhattan by Numbers" is listless but Naderi is a true filmmaker. His evocation of the city deserves a better movie, but this one's not bad.

NEW YORK POST, 11/11/94, p. 48, Bill Hoffmann

There's nothing quite as bad, or as emotionally draining, as being down and out in New York City.

It's a deep urban angst, a feeling of being trapped and without hope in a city that doesn't love you.

If you've ever walked the Big Apple's streets on a cold autumn day, worrying about money or aching over a broken heart, then you've lived a part of "Manhattan by Numbers."

Filmed on the streets of Manhattan with an unflinching camera, Iranian writer-director Amir Naderi's movie has a powerful realism that hasn't been matched in any other movie in recent years.

The main character is George Murphy, a lanky, middle-aged newspaper reporter who's been laid off and has to pay $1,200 in rent within 24 hours, If he doesn't pay, it's out on the street.

In a desperate bid to get cash, Murphy embarks on a Harlem-to-Wall-Street search, appealing to friends for money.

He gets a rueful lesson on just how cruel the world can be as friend after so-called friend turns him down.

His one hope rides on his childhood pal and longtime friend Tom Ryan, who everybody seems to know but nobody knows where he is.

After some intense sleuthing, Murphy finds that Ryan is somewhat of a souse, working sporadically at a parking lot, leading a Tompkins Square revolt, making friends and enemies on the Bowery and owing plenty of money to everybody along the way.

Murphy's hope of solving his own dilemma fades further and further until ... ah, but that would be giving away the film's great hand.

And Naderi's final resolution, lovingly filmed at the start of Broadway and using the famed bronze bull as a character is a reminder that just when you sink to your lowest point, miracles can happen in New York.

With his stark images gritty cast and thoughtful direction, Naderi delivers a thoughtful parable.

NEWSDAY, 11/11/94, Part II/p. B7, John Anderson

Manhattan runs on numbers. Streets. Phones. Bank balances. Sometimes your number comes in. Sometimes your number's up.

It is for George Murphy, a writer left destitute and directionless by the "bloodbath" at the Daily News, who needs $1,200 immediately to avoid eviction and homelessness. His wife and child, to whom he makes occasional and dispirited phone calls, are staying with her father. His friends have evaporated. His city is uninterested.

George's tale—seen here in the 1993 New Director/New Films series—is a kind of "Looking for Godot," a picaresque search for the unfindable. Having exhausted every other avenue for borrowing the money he needs, George sets out to locate an old friend-cum-phantom named Tom Ryan. But from his imperiled Inwood apartment to the funhouse-mirrored canyons of Wall Street, his quest becomes a way of losing himself. And George doesn't need much help, because his identity is flying away faster than the last subway stop. He just doesn't have the numbers.

There isn't much plot, but throughout his sidewalk detective story, Amir Naderi—the expatriated Iranian director of "Water, Wind and Sand" and 1985's spectacular "The Runner"—presents Manhattan as perhaps only a recent arrivee might with a haunted fascination. One of the more wondrous things about "Manhattan by Numbers," in fact, is just how wondrous he finds the place. How he revels in showing the city from every obscure angle, in blight and untouchable bounty and not-so-benign neglect; as a sensory assault and general heartbreak. Naderi eschews almost every cinematic cliché and, like every good immigrant, makes the city his own.

John Wojda, in his feature film debut, takes George through a labyrinth of unpleasant emotions, from desperate dignity to Lower Manhattan-induced delirium, never the hero, or charmer, but an object of pity—and because he's so ordinary, fear. That Wojda can make such an impression in a movie like this is an accomplishment, because the real star is the city, and the city is a shameless scene-stealer.

VILLAGE VOICE, 11/15/94, p. 55, Georgia Brown

Pity poor George (John Wojda), owing $1200 back rent. A former *Daily News* reporter, George can't come up with anyone flush enough to spare even a few bucks, so he sets off on an extended journey from his Washington Heights apartment downtown. Inexplicably, his quest soon turns into a quixotic search for a former colleague, an elusive boozer named Tom Ryan. Not a practical move obviously, considering that Tom's circumstances seem far more desperate than George's.

Accomplished Iranian filmmaker Amir Naderi, a New York resident since 1986 takes a risk in trying to write American and use an American protagonist in this one-character meditation. His strong, poetic Iranian film *The Runner* followed a single character too, but it was a boy based on himself and the story took place in a milieu he knew well. Nothing about the beleaguered George, a sulky saint confronting the capitalist dragon (or, as it turns out, the market's bull), or his predicament strikes me as authentic. George is an anxious body to hang a fable, or a socio-political critique, on.

The essence of this mood piece is a brightly colored tour of the borough in a cheerless, charityless Christmas season. The title's "numbers" are streets and their subway stops, phone numbers dialed futilely from pay phones, the forbidding denominations on those missing bills. James Callanan's camera travels from the bleaker reaches of Harlem, through the madly reflecting glares of Times Square, into the funk and stress of Alphabet City, to wind up finally (symbolically) at the base of those impenetrable ramparts of Wall Street—the high green wall.

The director has an eye for New Wavish commercial sign language, but these are images you've seen before. The Lower East Side looks like one long painted stage set. *Manhattan by Numbers* doesn't look like the city I know, nor does it show me a city I don't know. The numbers don't add up.

Also reviewed in:
NEW YORK TIMES, 11/11/94, p. C12, Vincent Canby
VARIETY, 4/5/93, p. 178, Fred Lombardi
WASHINGTON POST, 10/29/94, p. D1, Hal Hinson

MARY SHELLEY'S FRANKENSTEIN

A TriStar Pictures release in association with Japan Satellite Broadcasting, Inc. and The IndieProd Company of an American Zoetrope production. *Executive Producer:* Fred Fuchs. *Producer:* Francis Ford Coppola, James V. Hart, and John Veitch. *Director:* Kenneth Branagh. *Screenplay:* Steph Lady and Frank Darabont. *Based on the novel by:* Mary Shelley. *Director of Photography:* Roger Pratt. *Editor:* Andrew Marcus. *Music:* Patrick Doyle. *Music Editor:* Roy Prendergast and Gerard McCann. *Choreographer:* Stuart Hopps. *Sound:* Ivan Sharrock and (music) Paul Hulme and Geoff Foster. *Sound Editor:* Campbell Askew. *Casting:* Priscilla John. *Production Designer:* Tim Harvey. *Art Director:* Martin Childs. *Special Effects:* Neil Farrell. *Costumes:* James Acheson. *Make-up:* Paul Engelen. *Make-up (Robert De Niro):* Ilona Herman. *Creature Make-up and Effects:* Daniel Parker. *Prosthetics Make-up:* David White and Mark Coulier. *Stunt Coordinator:* Simon Crane. *Running time:* 128 minutes. *MPAA Rating:* R.

CAST: Robert De Niro (Creature/Sharp Featured Man); Kenneth Branagh (Victor Frankenstein); Tom Hulce (Henry); Helena Bonham Carter (Elizabeth); Aidan Quinn (Walton); Ian Holm (Victor's Father); Richard Briers (Grandfather); John Cleese (Professor Waldman); Robert Hardy (Professor Krempe); Cherie Lunghi (Victor's Mother); Celia Imrie (Mrs. Moritz); Trevyn McDowell (Justine); Gerard Horan (Claude); Mark Hadfield (Felix); Joanna Roth (Marie); Sasha Hanau (Maggie); Joseph England (Thomas); Alfred Bell (Landlord); Richard Clifford (Minister); George Asprey (Policeman); Richard Bonneville (Schiller); Ryan Smith (William); Charles Wyn-Davies (Young William); Rory Jennings (Young Victor); Christina Cuttall (Young Justine); Hannah Taylor-Gordon (Young Elizabeth); Susan Field (Frau Brach); Jimmy Yuill (Grigori); Lonnie James (Rough Woman); Jenny Galloway (Vendor's Wife); Peter Jonfield (Rough Man); Edward Jewesbury (City Official); Siobhan Redmond (Midwife); Francine Morgan (Assistant Midwife); Sue Long (Woman in Labor); Angus Wright (Guard); Michael Gould (Stablehand); Max Gold (Servant).

FILMS IN REVIEW, 1-2/95, p. 58, Harry Pearson, Jr.

Sometimes I find myself looking, with bemused detachment, upon the writings of what I fear we must call movie critics shopping to find a rationale, an aesthetic or intellectual perspective that will frame their work, giving it context, depth and meaning. Without this, we are all reduced to TV movie "commentators," subject to the whim of audience grosses and/or studio manipulation. Without standards, our criticism becomes the "taste" or "flavor" of the month club and without enduring value. We all become, in other words, Jeffrey Lyons, Rex Reeds and Caryn Jameses.

If you pour through the word of the critics, like some ancient Druid trying to decipher the runes, on movies like *Mary Shelly's Frankenstein* (more aptly entitled Kenneth Branagh's) and the loathsome and emotionally dishonest *Interview With the Vampire*, you'll find Branagh's reimagining of an ancient myth trashed for its romantic excesses (and this, no less, in its depicting the era of Byron, Keats and Shelley), while *Interviews* de-constructivist reimagining of the world 200 years ago couldn't be more contemporary in its existential angst and studied narcissism: LA in 1790. Neither film is frightening; both are capable of either terrorizing or revolting the nineties audience. Branagh's excesses are flogged, especially among the urban critics, while Neil Jordan's are embraced, even though they depend upon the kind of gore we used to keep locked up in drive-in theaters down south.

Branagh's career as a director is nowhere near as mixed a bag as is Jordan's, although *Peter's Friends* certainly gives *High Spirits* competition in the Worst Major Picture I've Seen category. But Branagh's time for uppance has come. Jordan is just off the high of *The Crying Game*, while Branagh has not quite gotten his balance back after *Friends* and the mixed bag that was *Much Ado About Nothing*. Read through the criticisms of Franky and you'll get, toward the end of the review, the grudging respect for all those things that do work in *Frankenstein* which far outnumber those that don't. Yes, I could do without ever seeing the camera do 360 degree waltzes around swooning lovers (it worked brilliantly when Hitchcock originated it, and with reason, in *Vertigo*, and it has worked with decreasing effectiveness ever since). Yes, I am aware that there is no way the interior room and staircase of the Frankenstein manor would ever be consonant with the building's exterior (and since when has that been skillfully accomplished in horror movies—remember *The House on Haunted Hill*, with its Frank Lloyd Wright Ennis House exterior and its Victorian innards?). And yes, Branagh should have kept his shirt on, instead of displaying his gym-built abs when he was supposed to look gaunt and haggard. And no, I shouldn't have been able to bring his bride back to life quite so quickly (a dramatically effective, but jarring, departure from the film's up-to-then faithful translation of the word and "feel" of the book.

But look at what we do get. The ethical issue raised in thoughtful terms: Who will take the responsibility for the genetic creation of a human-like creature? Who will be its father? We get Robert De Niro's best performance in more than a decade. He is so heavily clad with make-up that all he can do is move his right eye, and so must convey all feelings and comprehensions with but that. None of the little tics and cute smiles, mannerisms he has let overcome his acting over the years. Here he actually manages to convey, visually, not just the soul, but the thought inside a deformed creature. You get epic production design (an entire and ancient looking town built for the university sequences) from Tim Harvey, and color photography by Robert Pratt that suggests how Technicolor might look today, had it evolved (check out that long, velvet red train being pulled up the blue and white marble circular staircase). You get a scene between De Niro, Branagh and Helena Bonham Carter that is just about worth the price of admission. And you get a retelling of what has become a cultural myth with meaning to spare as we enter the era of deliberate genetic engineering.

What you don't get, and here perhaps we have Branagh's narcissism to blame, is a Frankenstein who has *gravitas* and a streak of obsessional madness that would rivet our attention. He's just a bit too much the nice guy; better he had been played as Henry V. As a consequence, it's an unmatched battle between him and his monster, with De Niro left out to sea (as it were) because Branagh cannot match him in the fury of the delusion. (And how I wished Branagh had ended the movie with the pyre burning instead of continuing on for a few fatally self-indulgent minutes more; he undercut his own ending.) Nevertheless, this is a film, at the moment underrated, whereas *Interview* is a movie, and nothing more.

So why do i think it works, viewed in toto? Because the film has a point of view, a highly moral one at that (in part, that you must accept the responsibility and consequences for the acts of your creations) that lends it a kind of formal structure, nowhere to be found in the self-pitying solipsism of the vampires in *Interview*. If Frankenstein doesn't quite jell in the way we have grown used to expecting in the genre film, it does engage our imaginations by making explicit not only the conventions of the horror movie, but also the underlying motifs that lend it timelessness and the ability to fascinate.

LOS ANGELES TIMES, 11/4/94, Calendar/p. 1, Kenneth Turan

They're calling it "Mary Shelley's Frankenstein," but with apologies to the former rock group, "Frankie Goes to Hollywood" is more like it.

That was the idea, of course. Why not join the verve and artistic intelligence director Kenneth Branagh brought to Shakespeare ("Henry V," "Much Ado About Nothing") to this most durable of fright tales, continuously in print since 1818 and the subject of several dozen films, ranging in seriousness from the 1931 James Whale/Boris Karloff classic to the iffier "I Was a Teenage Frankenstein," "Frankenhooker" and "Frankenstein Created Woman"?

But like the creature itself, this notion rapidly got out of hand. Seduced by a $40-million budget and the chance to do things like use a million gallons of water to create a storm and build the biggest exterior set ever constructed at a British studio, Branagh, who also stars as the doctor who dared create life in the lab, soon lost perspective.

In what feels a bit like slumming, the director, abetted by screenwriters Steph Lady and Frank Darabont ("The Shawshank Redemption"), decided that mass audiences didn't need wit or discernment but wanted things broad and slapdash. Presumably concurring in this analysis were the same trio of producers who turned "Bram Stoker's Dracula" into a similar mess.

As a result, "Mary Shelley's Frankenstein," like the creature itself, is awkwardly stitched together from a number of thematic elements. there is a bit of passionate romance for the doctor and his adopted sister Elizabeth (Helena Bonham Carter), a quiet country interlude for the creature (Robert De Niro) he builda and abandons, but mostly there is the kind of frantic frenzy that creates headaches rather than arouses emotions.

Full-bore hysteria is the ruling passion here, infecting everything from Patrick Doyle's thumping score to eye-widening performances from most of the cast. Hardly a sequence goes by without someone, usually the director himself, operatically bellowing "Noooooo" like a fiend in torment.

While it's traditional for the creature to come off best in these films, De Niro's character earns our special affection by not screaming at maximum volume like everyone else. Looking like "Raging Bull's" Jake La Motta after losing a close decision to a Cuisinart, the creature is not as tearfully articulate as he was in Shelley's original, where lines like "I am well satisfied that abhorrence and opprobrium should load my memory" fell from his lips.

Still, well-played by De Niro under supple foam latex makeup devised by Daniel Parker, the creature is the most convincing and sympathetic thing in the movie, a misunderstood nice guy who would prefer philosophical discussions to physical violence. Karloff's laurels, as well as those of makeup pioneer Jack Pierce, are not in danger, but at least the creature isn't an embarrassment, which in this film is an accomplishment

Before the creature gets to put in an appearance, however, "Mary Shelley's Frankenstein," which is fitfully faithful to the original, follows the book by sketching in a complex back story for the doctor. He is kind enough to relate it himself to Captain Robert Walton (an uncomfortable-looking Aidan Quinn), an explorer he chances to meet in 1794 while chasing the creature in the vicinity of the Arctic circle.

Back we go to sunny Geneva, where young Victor grows up under the eye of his doctor-father (Ian Holm), an earnest young man with a passion for books and a belief in the power of science that the unexpected death of his mother only intensifies. "No one need ever die," is one of his favorite phrases, with "I will stop this, I promise" in second place.

At medical school in Ingolstadt, Victor makes a solid friend in fellow student Henry Clerval (Tom Hulce, in knee-breeches perhaps left over from "Amadeus") but falls under the sinister influence of Professor Waldman (an uncharacteristically somber John Cleese), also fascinated with the possibilities of artificially creating life.

Tearing around his spacious attic lab in an enormous robe, Victor is successful in his experiments, but, oh, what a price must be paid. Like more conventional children, the creature is far from grateful at being brought into the world, and between the bloody troubles it causes and those visited upon it, its prime mover—Victor—would be forgiven if he wished he'd stayed home and gone into the cheese business.

Even if the vivid Whale/Karloff version had never been made, this treatment of the Shelley novel would be a loud and tacky disappointment. It lacks the gravity, the dignity, even the humor of its illustrious predecessor, and director Branagh, with his wearisome fascination with swooping, disorienting camera movements (Roger Pratt is the cinematographer) acts like this is his first feature, not his fifth. "God forgive me," his Victor says at one point, and though the deity may oblige, others may find it more difficult.

NEW STATESMAN & SOCIETY, 11/4/94, p. 32, Jonathan Romney

You expect Frankenstein to be stitched together from many parts, but *Mary Shelley's Frankenstein*, directed by and starring Kenneth Branagh, is so heteroclite it hurts. A ragbag of medievalism, modernism and by-the-book Romanticism, this is a Shakespearean's Shelley—tragical-historical-pastoral-farcical. Parts of it work (well enough), but that's like Frankenstein looking on his botched creation and concluding that, after all, it has a rather fine pancreas.

The most singular thing about the film is the title, which seems to be telling us that this isn't just any Frankenstein, but the real thing, the original, with the creator's name stamped large on it. *MSF*—if I may—is produced by Francis Ford Coppola, who recently gave us his own essay in monster-movie revisionism, *Bram Stoker's Dracula*, Coppola's *Dracula*, however, was anyone's but Stoker's; it was driven by a set of contemporary obsessions—Aids, homophobia, xenophobia—that Coppola presented as simply being filtered through the vampire myth. However messy that film was, there was never any notion that the return to source meant working off a blank slate—Coppola was adapting the novel complete with a century's worth of theoretical and ideological jottings in the margin.

Branagh's *Frankenstein*, though, takes itself in deadly earnest as the definitive unsullied version, Shelley's first edition faithfully replaced—in a glossy new binding—among the respectful shelves of Eng Lit. Apart from a ghoulish major deviation at the end, Branagh's idea of respecting the text is very literal. He restores the original narrative frame, a showdown in the howling Arctic, as well as the original Swiss setting, peopled with a cast of minor characters, all so unfamiliar that we can't help after a while getting itchy and wondering where faithful old Igor's got to.

Branagh also tries to give us an *echt*—1816 notion of what the Gothic was really about—not the ghoulish apparatus of castles and coffins that only truly came into its own a full century *after* Mrs Radcliffe's prime, but the Gothic as was, a mix of high Romantic morbidity, sentiment and landscape description, with lashings of pathetic fallacy.

Branagh dearly wants us to forget the history of *Frankenstein* that we can't help bringing with us. He wants us to leave behind Karloff's flat-top and Elsa Lanchester's high-voltage coiffure.

This is not Frankenstein as we've never seen it before, but Frankenstein *as if* we'd never seen it before. Of course, that's impossible, and the film can't help but assemble itself from a whole history of horror images. But each one has its own singular resonance removed, like scraps of stolen clothes with the labels torn off. It's appropriate, in a sense—after all, Frankenstein uses limbs and organs that aren't marked with the names of their original bearers. Thus, you can find remnants of Poe, Roger Corman and Hammer in here—but they all seem empty borrowings, present in the design rather than the text of the film.

In addition to the resonances of *Faust* and Milton that come ready programmed into the story, in the opening alone, there's some *Moby Dick*, Doré's illustrated *Ancient Mariner*, and incongruous echoes of *Alien* and John Carpenter's *The Thing*, as the unseen Creature briskly rends a few huskies.

But there's never any sense that Branagh is in control of his material. Too many inadvertent meanings seem to be beyond his control. Take the casting. It quite possibly never occurred to him that you can't put Tom Hulce into 18th-century garb without everyone immediately thinking of *Amadeus*.

Similarly, you can't put John Cleese in a funereal straight part without making sure you ruthlessly expunge your script of the slightest *soupçon* of Basil Fawlty. However, among the plentifully clangers penned by Steph Lady and Frank Darabont comes this peerless exchange between De Niro, shortly to be reconstituted as the Creature, and Cleese, who's trying to vaccinate him against cholera: "You're not sticking that in me!"—"Yes, I am, it's the law."

Presumably Branagh doesn't see, either, that when Frankenstein and his jolly family go running with kites through a gorgeous, menthol-fresh Alpine landscape, our first thought is that Julie Andrews can't be far behind. When the Creature is dewy-eyed in the cabin, gazing on family tenderness, it's a wonder he doesn't break into "Where is Love?" from *Oliver!* In fact, there are moments when Branagh might as well have done what he did with *Much Ado About Nothing*, and turned the book into a full-blown musical—the Frankenstein family hoedown on a *trompe l'oeil* ballroom set is straight out of a Royal Ballet panto of *Beauty and the Beast*.

Much Ado and *Peter's Friends*, relentless in their chums-together conviviality, showed that Branagh does have one recurrent obsession that may conceivably give his work some *auteur* coherence, and that's his thing about happy families. It's a dirty rotten shame that Mama Frankenstein should die in childbirth, leaving dear Victor, such a serious, promising boy ("All these strange and ancient books! You'll be a greater doctor than your father") to topple over the edge.

It's a commonplace to observe that *Frankenstein*, and indeed all Gothic narratives, are really about crises of the family. A consistent theme in all versions of *Frankenstein* is that the hero is defying nature not only by aping the divine patriarch but by usurping matriarchal power as well. It's the one theme that Branagh brings to light with any consistency. In Frankenstein's animation of the creature through a method involving acupuncture, amniotic fluid and electric eels, you could hardly have a stranger mix of the maternal and the phallic.

The film's most original touch is the Creature's birth agony—a huge burst of slime, then a ballet of stumbling and tumbling as Frankenstein and naked "son" flail like landed trout on a floor of gunge.

But Branagh is at pains to undermine any excessive femininity that might have crept into the creator's role, by making Victor excessively male. The creation scene is a riot of rattling chains and slamming gears, macho-fast-cutting and shirt-off shots, as Ken flashes his newly acquired pecs. It's almost as if he's butching it up to show who's the real author of this text—neither the "Lady" who's co-written it, nor the one who has her name above the title.

Branagh's frantic energy throughout makes him seem more irrepressibly the actor-manger than ever. Playing Victor as a well-meaning fresher gone barmy from too much study, he overdoes it, giving himself far more presence than the curiously muted De Niro. But then, the Creature has a mighty weight to carry—he's not only the first monster of modern horror, but he seems intended to be the last, the one who's going to make us forget Karloff, Freddy and all the rest.

De Niro is a serious, sullen *golem*; lumbering, wincing and emitting heavy sighs of *Weltschmerz* from under an oily greatcoat, he looks like a skinhead version of Rodin's Balzac. He's charged with the onerous task of restoring language to the Incredible Hulk; and he does a remarkably convincing job of his evolution from monosyllabism to expounding—albeit in terms less florid than Shelley's—on the enigma of identity and knowledge,

He may still carry a touch of vintage De Niro, hanging on Branagh's trail like vengeful hood looking for the guy who carved him up bad in a knife-fight, but that's all to the best. There's a great moment when he almost wordlessly arrives to summon Victor to a showdown, and we suddenly relish the prospect of a to-the-death between two styles of acting—Rada meets the Method.

As it surely must, the film goes off the rails at the end. Having uneasily skirted around the incestuous implications of Victor's romance with his "sister" Elizabeth, it at last has to find an interesting turn for Helena Bonham-Carter, who until then has been a troublesome posh girl, the Fiend of Roedean. It's as if, having held back the full flood of the Gothic until now, Branagh has to pull out all the stops—but too radically, and too late. We're suddenly thrown into pure genre horror, but we don't feel we have a guide who knows his way around. It's a relief when we get to the Arctic epilogue, and weary explorer Walton (Aidan Quinn) decides to ditch his polar quest and head for home. Feeling as exhausted as he is, you rather wish we'd stayed in Switzerland with Julie Andrews.

NEW YORK, 11/14/94, P. 76, David Denby

In the most astonishing moment in *Mary Shelley's Frankenstein*—a movie not lacking in astonishments—the monster (Robert De Niro) rises out of an electrified caldron, spilling his nourishing broth of amniotic fluid to the floor, and wrestles with his creator, Dr. Victor Frankenstein (Kenneth Branagh), in the gleaming and sticky wet. A momentous birth, both disgusting and inspiring. The huge stitched-together creature is naked; his creator (Kenneth Branag) is almost naked; and the two men grapple in silence, sliding and falling in the muck. The strangeness of this event is almost Michelangelesque—so powerful it hurts. Much of *Frankenstein* is spectacular and hyperbolic, but in a good way. Kenneth Branagh has made a very fleshy and visceral movie, though not a horror movie in the normal sense. Branagh is fascinated by the liquid slosh and filth of creation, the moldering decay of death. There are very few conventional jolts; instead, the whole movie is shockingly vivid.

The shock is there in the original—in Mary Shelley's novel, one of the evil flowers of English Romanticism. When she was only 19 years old, in 1816, Mary and her husband, Percy Bysshe Shelley, spent the summer with Lord Byron and other friends at Lac Léman, near Geneva; the weather turned bad, and they all stayed indoors reading and writing ghost stories. After listening to the two poets talk one night about the principle of life, and how life might be sustained after death—speculation among the scientific avant-garde at the time—Mary Shelley had a nightmare about a reanimated corpse. By the following morning, she knew what her ghost story would be about; *Frankenstein* was published as a novel in 1818. How much did Mary's portrait of Dr. Frankenstein take its critical edge from her intimacy with the two flamboyant and over-reaching poets? The book is animated—and appalled—by the follies of genius.

Working with director of photography Roger Pratt and screenwriters Steph Lady and Frank Darabont, Branagh has tried to create the cinematic equivalent of Mary Shelley's feverish mind—the tenor of literary romanticism at its most ripe and expressive. *Frankenstein* is intentional borderline kitsch: Everyone rushes about wildly, the camera deliriously whirls and rises, and there is much mist, storm, and gloom. Yet the overstatement all works. As his Shakespeare films have demonstrated, Branagh is a popular storyteller—he likes things to be clear. He doesn't go in for the kind of clotted visual gibberish that made, say, Coppola's *Bram Stoker's Dracula* so exhausting and dull. In *Frankenstein*, Branagh doesn't get lost in the misty woods: He tells the story *through* hyperbole, and one realizes that the high-romantic filmmaking, the tempest-tossed, electrified space, is, for him, a good narrative mode-intensity and clear dramatic purpose save the visual style from cliché.

It's very much Branagh's show. In his Victor Frankenstein, romantic faith and madness are intertwined. A little boy in ruffles, Victor grows up in a Genevese great house so empty of furniture that it seems almost a stage set for dislocation. His mother dies giving birth to his brother, and Victor becomes obsessed with preserving life. Not as a doctor, though—as an inventor and god. After Gene Wilder's hysterical (in both senses) parody in Mel Brooks's *Young Frankenstein*, no one can do Dr. Frankenstein straight, and Branagh's fervency—the genius mop of hair, haggard brow, and ironlike voice (is Beethoven his next role?)—goes a little over the top. This young Frankenstein puts his hand in the flame of a candle and tempts lightning on icy, preposterously exciting Swiss mountaintops. He displays a dangerous avidity for experiment, a penchant for the grandiose, the thrilling, the improbable—talents that attract his idealistic stepsister Elizabeth (Helena Bonham Carter). Their love is borderline incest. With her pale coloring, abundant hair, and faraway look, Bonham Carter is hard to imagine in a non-period role; she excels at grand emotions—dedication, faith, erotic rapture.

When Victor abandons Elizabeth for life as a medical student at Ingolstadt, he goes off the rails. The town, built at Shepperton Studios in England, is a triumph of old-fashioned film craftsmanship (Tim Harvey is the production designer), with enough cobblestones to lame a team of stallions, huge medieval walls and exaggerated perspectives, and a lecture theater that goes straight up like the inside of a well. The style isn't quite expressionistic. I would call it studio-set megalomaniacal, with naturalistic details—the rot and disorder of a town during the plague; the charnel-house pallor. Everything in Victor's loft laboratory is wonderfully revolting. I love the clunky old James Whale *Frankenstein*, from 1931, with Boris Karloff, but let's not kid ourselves: Modern technology allows filmmakers to achieve textures and tonalities not possible in 1931. You know dirty things are going on in this room because you can almost smell the formaldehyde.

Branagh and his crew have purposely revised the most famous image in the old film—the Monster himself, square-topped, lumbering Karloff. De Niro's Monster is nearly bald, with a strong nose and blackened eye sockets (the eyes are of different colors), and he moves rapidly but unsteadily on legs of different length, darting at times like a nervous animal. Robert De Niro, making amends for his ridiculous excess in *Cape Fear*, consistently underplays. At first, his speech is thick and halting, as if he were still the retired, drunken Jake LaMotta in *Raging Bull*. But as the Monster grows into his capabilities and speaks in rational sentences ("Who are these people of whom I am composed? Do I have a soul?"), De Niro becomes more and more moving. This Monster wants to be a man; he howls and turns into a killer only when denied the human community. His crimes follow rationally from his nature. In all, Frankenstein'sMonster is a more moral creature than Frankenstein, just as man is perhaps a better creature than God.

Frankenstein hurtles forward to the amazing climax of Victor and Elizabeth's wedding night, which I will not attempt to describe for you. The final scenes are grotesque and complexly upsetting. But no matter how bizarre, the movie sticks to a simple underlying meaning: You must live with what you create, and if you do not, you also destroy.

NEWSDAY, 11/4/94, Part II/p. B2, Jack Mathews

Timing is everything. If Sigmund Freud had been born a century and a half earlier, if there had been a good plastic surgeon in Ingolstadt, if his father weren't the ultimate deadbeat dad, the creature we've come to know as Frankenstein's monster might have become a gentle aristocrat, or a priest.

Instead, the hideous reanimated corpse of Mary Shelley's classic 1818 novel became a vengeful killer, and literature's most celebrated victim of unchecked science and psychological rejection.

Alas, in "Mary Shelley's Frankenstein," Kenneth Branagh's epic and spectacularly overheated film version of the novel, the monster, his maker, and the story itself are victims of bad timing. It arrives, in the most glorious Gothic dress and louder than the howl of the damned, when mad scientist stories are passé and Dr. Frankenstein's surgical skills seem about as sophisticated as Lorena Bobbitt's.

In Shelley's day, the idea of assembling a man from spare parts and turning him on with electricity wasn't too far-fetched a concept—and it was still to captivate movie audiences in the early 1930s. But since the two James Whale classics, the 1931 "Frankenstein" and 1935 "Bride of Frankenstein," the monster has been more of a comic than tragic figure, and that, inadvertently, is his and actor Robert De Niro's fate here.

Branagh, with a screenplay by Steph Lady and Frank Darabont, frames the story as Shelley did, with a dying Dr. Frankenstein (Branagh) telling his incredible tale to an ambitious ship captain (Aidan Quinn) leading his men on a seemingly suicidal mission to the North Pole. With a couple of glaring exceptions, the movie hews closely to Shelley's sweeping two-part story, the first about Dr. Frankenstein's obsession to create life, the second chronicling the horrors that come after he rejects his own creation.

The sequence where the monster is brought to life is both the film's action centerpiece and its most hopeless conceit. The lab is a marvelous blend of Industrial Revolution architecture and Hollywood Gothic set design, all pulleys and chains and electromagnetic sparklers. But it also looks like the most ungainly Rube Goldberg device ever made, and when De Niro's monster pops out of his metal womb, covered in some amniotic house dressing, and into the arms of his revolted maker, one doesn't immediately think of the miracle of birth.

Branagh doesn't attempt to give the story a contemporary spin. He treats it as the flamboyant period opera it is, and nearly every character —certainly, his own—is given to ghastly spasms of histrionic excess. A tortured soul is indeed a hammy soul.

De Niro's monster, who looks like a reanimated Max Cady from "Cape Fear," is, of course, the most tortured of them all, a man driven to evil by rejection, and De Niro is only effective when conveying his rage, when he becomes a traditional horror villain. In attempting to show the monster's civilized side, his heartsick search for love and companionship, the best De Niro can do is slink across the screen like a beaten dog.

He has a couple of truly frightful scenes, including one with Frankenstein's bride, Elizabeth (Helena Bonham Carter), that will send the squeamish up the aisles, but the movie rarely achieves the suspense and tension it's aiming for. At its best, it strikes a kind of theatrical grandiloquence that overwhelms your senses—it is the most visually stunning movie of the year, and features the best staircase—and at its worst, it is laughably camp.

Its silliest scene, a variation from the novel, has Frankenstein racing to reanimate his dead bride, who is then asked to choose between him and his first creation. Carter is wonderful here, peering out through a train wreck of a face and managing to seem both dead and alive. But the situation is such a glib Hollywood cheat, Shelley will be spinning in her grave.

Her novel, intended as both a Gothic nightmare and a cautionary tale about the power of science, has come down to a love triangle. A monster and his maker are fighting over the woman of both of their dreams and wouldn't you know she can't make up her mind.

NEWSWEEK, 11/7/94, p. 73, David Ansen

Romantic with a big and a small R, Kenneth Branagh's hyperventilating version of *Mary Shelley's Frankenstein* strains for grand theatrical effects at every turn. The camera, and the actors, are always in a mad dash from here to there. If the lovers, Victor Frankenstein (Branagh) and his future bride, Elizabeth (Helena Bonham Carter), settle down for a moment, the airborne lens will swirl around them like a hornet contemplating a sting. You can see what Branagh is after in this umpteenth retelling of Shelley's Gothic classic: he wants to restore the passionate emotional scale of the early 19th century to a tale that most people remember as a 1930s horror flick. But with his other eye firmly on the marketplace, he also wants to wow the MTV generation. What we get is Romanticism for short attention spans; a lavishly decorated horror movie with excellent elocution. His strategy undermines itself—there's a lot of sound and fury, but all the grand passions are indicated rather than felt. Watching the movie work itself into an operatic frenzy, one remains curiously detached: the grand gestures are there, but where's the music?

Branagh's two Shakespeare films have been triumphs—meaty, moving and fun. Bardless, the director flounders. His "Frankenstein" gives off the same hollow echo that "Dead Again" did, the same mixture of stylistic flair and insincerity. We should be simultaneously terrified and moved by the figure of the monster (Robert De Niro), who turns to destruction only after he's been rejected by his creator and society. But while De Niro cuts a striking figure with his stitched face and Nosferatu-style coat, his tragedy remains rhetorical. (Bizarrely, the movie omits the crucial moment when he first sees his own reflection.) But there is one near-great scene: when the monster, naked as a newborn, first escapes his metallic womb, he and his appalled creator grapple in the slime of the laboratory in a struggle for survival. It's a memorably horrific image of patricidal rejection.

The title implies, like "Bram Stoker's Dracula," that this will be a faithful adaptation. While it's certainly closer to Shelley than the Karloff version is, there are plenty of Grand Guignol embellishments—screenwriters Steph Lady and Frank Darabont add an abbreviated "Bride of Frankenstein" variation in which Victor decides to bring his own slaughtered wife back to life. It has a certain ghoulish excitement, but by this point the storytelling has become almost incoherent (a number of crucial scenes appear to have been cut) and Branagh's performance as the tragic scientist has come to resemble the Master Thespian on "Saturday Night Live." For a much more provocative, original retelling, someone should resurrect the 1973 TV movie "Frankenstein: The True Story," written by Christopher Isherwood. In that version, the monster comes out perfect, beautiful—and then, to his enamored creator's horror, slowly begins to rot.

SIGHT AND SOUND, 12/94, p. 51, Amanda Lipman

The Arctic, 1794. An explorer's ship, commanded by the intrepid Captain Walton, is stranded in frozen sea. A strange, exhausted man comes on board and tells Walton his story. He is Victor Frankenstein, born in Geneva, We see his childhood in a happy house with his parents and adopted sister, Elizabeth. But some years later, his mother dies giving birth to his brother, William. Victor, by now a serious young student, leaves to study medicine in Ingolstadt, promising to marry Elizabeth on his return.

Victor's questioning outlook allows him to befriend a Dr Waldman, who tells him how he once tried to reanimate dead life. When the doctor is murdered, Victor steals his work journal and sets about constructing a living being from body parts he steals, including Waldman's brain and parts of his killer's body. Elizabeth comes to find him. But neither she, nor the cholera epidemic that is raging in the city, can drag him away from his work. Having completed his experiment, Victor is horrified by what he has done. The creature comes to life and escapes. Victor falls ill from pneumonia. When he recovers, he persuades himself that the creature must have died from cholera and decides to go back to Geneva and marry Elizabeth.

Meanwhile, the creature, hounded by the townspeople, runs to the countryside where he shelters in a peasant family's pig pen. The blind grandfather befriends him but the family, thinking he is harming the old man, drives him out. The creature resolves to take revenge on Victor and journeys across country to Geneva. There he kills William and has the blame pinned on Justine, the housekeeper's daughter. She is hanged by a mob of townspeople. The creature asks Victor to make him a female partner. In return, he will never trouble him again. Victor agrees, but then decides to marry Elizabeth and escape from Geneva instead. The creature finds them and tears out Elizabeth's heart.

Grief-stricken, Victor reanimates a woman using parts of Justine and Elizabeth. The creature claims her for himself, but she sets fire to herself and to the house. Victor follows the creature to the Arctic wastes. Having told Walton his story, Victor dies. The sea melts again and the ship sails off for home, leaving the creature, mourning, to set fire to himself on Victor's funeral pyre.

Kenneth Branagh continues his apparent quest to turn works of English Literature into adaptations-made-easy with this rip-roaring version of Mary Shelley's novel, probably the most famous Penguin Classic no-one has read. Branagh's version of a book mythologised by cinema is easily the most faithful to the original, leaving out the book's more irrelevant departures, and adding Gothic moments that Shelley might be proud of. Of course, it should have been obvious that Branagh would do this tale justice: his only non-adapted film so far, *Dead Again*, was another overloaded Gothic drama.

Branagh plays the hapless doctor obsessed as a Marlovian figure, to whom he adds his *Henry V* modus operandi: big hammy gestures, exaggerated emotions and loud speech. In the context, it works rather well, vying with a thunderous musical score that never lets up for one moment. This Frankenstein also has a dollop of contemporary action hero about him. When he conducts his experiments, the pace accelerates to breakneck speed, with an alarming array of whizzbang effects. Moreover, at this point, Branagh strips down to a pair of leggings, hoisting a well-toned and certainly well-oiled torso around the screen as he grapples his creation into life. His apparel, or lack of it, adds a sexual dimension to the birthing proceedings—particularly as he only sports this attire again on his wedding night. This quasi-sexual male labour is an alarming contrast to the film's images of women actually giving birth—both bloody, screaming, grim affairs. These could be a nod to feminist readings of the novel, which point to Mary Shelley's own gruesome experience (her mother, Mary Wollstonecraft, died of septicaemia after giving birth to her, and Shelley herself had a miscarriage just before she wrote *Frankenstein*).

Certainly, the film is full of body horror, the preserve of many contemporary horror movies: not only does this include the monster itself but corpse dissection, body parts being cleavered off and sewn together, two hangings, and the cholera epidemic that leaves dead bodies strewn everywhere. Elizabeth's murder is a nasty piece of Hannibal Lecter-style heart-ripping. And the whole movie is drenched in blood.

Helena Bonham Carter's Elizabeth echoes Victor's ever-dancing mother in character. Even though neither Elizabeth nor Justine gives birth, both meet a nasty end as a result of Victor's (literal) labour. The dancing of the past is also echoed, to great effect, when Victor waltzes pathetically with his second monstrous creation: the lolling rag doll made from Justine and Elizabeth. These women are born (and reborn) to suffer, and that makes the image of the burning female monster rampaging through the house particularly potent, expressing just as much of the pain of the new-born as the rages of De Niro's male creature.

De Niro is in good form, loping and howling at the horror of his dilemma. His nameless monster, bearing little relation to Boris Karloff, turns from a grunting animal into a pained, articulate psychopath who wants to be "normal" but cannot help his nature. He ends up a strangely modern creation, understanding psychological conflict where others, including Victor, can only show it. This combination of old and modern permeates the film. The language is colloquially contemporary; the mechanics of the re-animation are fleshed out with intricate-sounding discussions about acupuncture and electricity; and much is made of the scientific nature of Victor's lightning-conducting experiments to convince a knowing latter-day audience who will not be content simply with flashing buttons, sparks and bubbling potions.

The film also seems at pains to get to the heart of the nurture-vs-nature argument. Its conclusion rests on the fact that the monster has been made out of criminals, and must therefore be inherently evil. But the film never asks why Victor, a happy little boy from a happy family, turns out as he does. If his obsession was brought about by losing his mother so gruesomely, then surely there is more to be said about the nature of evil, or of messing with the "natural state of things".

Between the crashing opening and closing as the sea ices up then melts again, every episode is a drama in some genre. The only unsatisfactory character is Aidan Quinn's Walton, more of a book-end than the glory-seeking explorer he is meant to be. The film is simply not large enough to have more than two big boys in it. Even so, after years of somewhat mistaken identity, it does the job of restoring Mary Shelley's book to its real place in the literary archive, while adding a touch of modernity that embraces its true horror and its sense of the bizarre.

TIME, 11/7/94, p. 73, Richard Schickel

The exterior of the Frankenstein house, as it is presented in *Mary Shelley's Frankenstein*, is well proportioned and nicely balanced; the mansion appears to be an entirely suitable residence for a prosperous, rational 18th century doctor and his cheerful, loving family. But the interior is something else again. It includes a vast, vaulting staircase that couldn't possibly fit inside the house we have seen from the outside and that seems completely at odds with the family's sensibility. The house is rather too obviously meant to act as a metaphor for the character of the Frankensteins' son Victor, played by Kenneth Branagh, who also directed. On the surface he seems to be quite a reasonable fellow, a medical student eager to follow in his father's footsteps. On the inside, though, it turns out he's as loopy and out of scale as that staircase. Chap wants to play God, create life in his laboratory. Mortality, which took away his beloved mother, seems to him a dirty trick he must do something about.

But you know all that, don't you? Even if you haven't actually read *Frankenstein*, you have seen the classic horror movies based on the novel. From these sources you will have gathered that no good can possibly come of messing around with the secrets of life and death. You probably don't need half an hour of talky, tedious back story, as you get in this screenplay by Steph Lady and Frank Darabont, explaining why Victor is driven to reanimate a corpse. They used to dispense with his hubris in half a dozen lines of hysterical dialogue, the better to get on to the good stuff.

Unfortunately, the good stuff here isn't so good. Branagh doesn't evoke terror, only repulsion. Frankenstein's laboratory is a mess, with amniotic fluid sloshing all over the place (never mind why). Even lovely Helena Bonham Carter, playing the doctor's wife, is not spared hideous disfigurement. The most authentically bizarre thing about the film is that John Cleese appears as a heavy and does a very nice job.

As the monster, Robert De Niro looks like an aging Marlon Brando with his head stitched together. And De Niro acts like Brando too—fake intellectual mumblings and unsuccessfully suppressed rage. His creature is somewhere between Shelley's monster, who quoted Milton and Goethe, and Boris Karloff's, who was a pre-literate child. There is much to be said for the latter conception. The fact that his depredations stemmed from clumsy innocence made the monster sympathetic in a way.

This is not to suggest that a bunch of 1930s scenarists were better writers than Mary Shelley, only that they had a clearer sense of their medium's imperatives than her present servants do. James Whale, who made the 1931 version and its even stronger sequel, *The Bride of Frankenstein*, certainly was a better director than Branagh. The latter has just created isolated sensations that aren't even frightening. Whale had real style. He understood that if it was too late to take this tale completely seriously, it was too soon to camp it up or make it an exercise in empty disgust. Delicately poising irony, dark sentiment and terror, he drew you into his web. Branagh never weaves one. He's too busy serving his own expansive ego.

VILLAGE VOICE, 11/8/94, p. 64, Georgia Brown

We all have our Frankensteins. And now Kenneth Branagh has his. So why must he call it Mary Shelley's? One reason certainly is to make bookends with his producer Francis Ford Coppola's *Bram Stoker's Dracula*.

Before getting to *Mary Shelley's Frankenstein*, a few words are in order about Mary Shelley's *Frankenstein*. (I mean, since they brought it up.) This is the novel by an 18-year-old unwed mother whose own mother—the truly astonishing Mary Wollstonecraft—died giving birth to her.

It's very much about a rejecting parent and an ugly, rejected child who, in the search for love, commits monstrous crimes ("I have strangled the innocent as they slept ...").

Anyone who reads the novel recognizes that Victor Frankenstein, the scientist who creates the monster, is the real beast. (The best filmed *Frankenstein* is still James Whale's 1931 version, opening Friday at the Cinema Village, with Boris Karloff's beloved monster as the emotional center.) In Branagh's Frankenstein, Victor, played by you know who, is the center and tragic hero—his flaw lying all in his Faustian or Promethean daring and not at all in his cruel desertion of his creation. Victor's is the passionate love story: He and his childhood companion Elizabeth (Helena Bonham Carter) are dying for consummation but that confounded *thing* keeps getting in the way. Here the poor monster (Robert De Niro, sort of peeking in) has his story taken from him.

Of course, all's fair in adaptation-land, if you make it work. But Branagh's *Frankenstein* is a grandiose fiasco—manic, lurid, bombastic, as well as unintentionally comic where it ought to be, as Whale's modest movie is, deeply affecting.

Writers Steph Lady and Frank Darabont (director-writer of *The Shawshank Redemption*) pay tribute to Mary Shelley's origins by having Victor's attractive mother die towards the beginning, not of scarlet fever as she does in the novel, but in childbirth. Actually, this gives Branagh an excuse for the first of several visceral and graphic deaths (including two gratuitous public hangings where the victim is dropped from such great heights it's a wonder we don't see their heads ripped off). Anyway, the gory death of his mother invigorates Victor and sets him off on his mission to bring back the dead.

The next birth (also with complications) is the monster's. Now a driven med student, Victor follows the manual left behind by a sinister professor (John Cleese), undertakes a series of sordid preparations, and finally delivers a pretty pathetic babe. Father and full-grown son (De Niro looks reptilian, more like the creature from the black lagoon) proceed to wrestle in a puddle of slippery amniotic fluid that Victor has stolen from female prisoners apparently forced into labor. Not present in the delivery room, but implicated in these proceedings is Victor's timid sidekick (Tom Hulce), a conventional figure of comic relief.

The screening audience laughed more at De Niro. With his hurt, or menacing, eyes peering out of that clumsily stitched hide, he really does seem isolated and pathetic. But in this case it is less that the wretch is supposed to be isolated and pathetic, and more that De Niro is patently outside the loop. Though I can't say Branagh intends it, De Niro comes off as a freakish Yank who won't let the grown-ups get on with their Fine Performances. Whenever Branagh and Bonham Carter get together, the film's frantic exposition shudders to a halt for a stint of heavy-duty give-and-take. The real suffering is theirs, says Branagh's *Frankenstein*. Mary Shelley knew better and, if I'm right about how flat this picture will fall, she'll have her revenge.

Also reviewed in:
CHICAGO TRIBUNE, 11/4/94, Friday/p. C, Michael Wilmington
NEW REPUBLIC, 11/28/94, p. 56, Stanley Kauffmann
NEW YORK TIMES, 11/4/94, p. C1, Janet Maslin
NEW YORKER, 11/14/94, p. 141, Anthony Lane
VARIETY, 10/31-11/6/94, p. 88, Brian Lowry
WASHINGTON POST, 11/4/94, p. F1, Hal Hinson
WASHINGTON POST, 11/4/94, Weekend/p. 43, Desson Howe

MASK, THE

A New Line Productions release in association with Dark Horse Entertainment. *Executive Producer:* Mike Richardson, Charles Russell, and Michael De Luca. *Producer:* Bob Engelman. *Director:* Charles Russell. *Screenplay:* Mike Werb. *Story (based on the characters in Dark Horse Comics):* Mark Verheiden and Michael Fallon. *Director of Photography:* John R. Leonetti. *Animation Photography:* Brian Adams. *Editor:* Arthur Coburn. *Music:* Randy Edelman. *Music Editor:* John La Salandra. *Choreographer:* Jerry Evans. *Sound:* Mark Hopkins McNabb and (music) Andrew Boland and Elton Ahi. *Sound Editor:* Craig Clark and Steven Williams. *Casting:* Fern Champion and Mark Paladini. *Production Designer:* Craig Stearns. *Art Director:* Randy Moore. *Set Decorator:* Ellen Totleben. *Set Dresser:* Julie Sexsmith, Terence Doherty, and James Gregory Evans. *Special Effects:* Thomas L. Bellissimo. *Visual Effects:* Ken Ralston. *Costumes:* Ha Nguyen. *Make-up:* Michael "Mic" Tomasino and Sheryl Leigh Ptak. *Special Make-up Effects:* Greg Cannon. *Stunt Coordinator:* Rick Barker. *Running time:* 102 minutes. *MPAA Rating:* PG-13.

CAST: Jim Carrey (Stanley Ipkiss/The Mask); Cameron Diaz (Tina Carlyle); Peter Riegert (Lieutenant Mitch Kellaway); Peter Greene (Dorian Tyrel); Amy Yasbeck (Peggy Brandt); Richard Jeni (Charlie Schumaker); Orestes Matacena (Niko); Timothy Begley (Irv); Nancy Fish (Mrs. Peenman); Johnny Williams (Burt); Reginald E. Cathey (Freeze); Jim Doughan (Doyle); Denis Forest (Sweet Eddy); Joseph Alfieri and Robert Keith (Police Officers); B. J. Barie, Debra Casey, and Bullet Valmont (Alley Punks); Catherine Berge (Cigarette Seller); Phil Boardman (Guard); Krista Buonauro (Cop); Blake Clark (Murray); Christopher Darga (Paramedic); Suzanne Dunn (Reporter); Joely Fisher (Maggie); Kevin Grevioux, Richard Montes, and Daniel James Peterson (Henchmen.); Peter Jazwinski (Park Policeman); Howard Kay and Scott McElroy (Niko's Thugs); Beau Lotterman (Megaphone Cop); Ivory Ocean (Mayor Tilton); Robert O'Reilly (The Figure); Louie Ortiz (Coco Bongo Valet); Jeremy Roberts (Bobby the Bouncer); Eamonn Roche (Mr. Dickey); Randi Ruimy (Screaming Woman); Benjamin J. Stein (Dr. Neuman); Nils Allen Stewart (Orlando); Chris Taylor (Coco Bongo Cop); Wendy Walsh (Herself); Meadow Williams (Pebbles).

LOS ANGELES TIMES, 7/28/94, Calendar/p. 1, Kenneth Turan

This is the summer Hollywood has decided Cartoons-R-Us. First "The Flintstones" had actors re-create cartoon roles, then "The Lion King" offered pure animation, and now comes "The Mask," in which a flesh-and-blood performer is turned into an elastic, living cartoon.

Much of the early buzz about "The Mask" involved the wizardly computer-generated special effects that allow kick-sand-in-my-face bank clerk Stanley Ipkiss to turn into an off-kilter superhero whose India rubber body contorts like Spiderman and absorbs punishment like something out of Looney Tunes.

And, masterminded by the imps at Industrial Light & Magic, who ought to just wrap the visual effects Oscar and take it home, the tricks in "The Mask" are something to see. When the Mask's body recovers from being flattened like a tortilla and his eyes literally pop out at the sight of a beautiful woman, audience eyes are likely to roll as well.

Yet despite all this technology it is heartening to report that "The Mask's" sine qua non, the factor it would be hard-pressed to live without, is the actor who plays both the cartoon and alter ego Ipkiss, Jim Carrey.

Best known as the lucky man whose salary made a Roadrunner leap to millions per picture after the unexpected success of "Ace Ventura: Pet Detective," Carrey is revealed here as a comic actor of charm and talent.

Not only is he adept at physical humor, the kind of knockabout stuff that recalls the classic silent clowns, but Carrey also has a bright and likable screen presence, a lost puppy quality that is surprisingly endearing.

And when he plays the Mask, wearing a supple and non-confining latex facial apparatus designed by Greg Cannom, Carrey displays a manic side as well, doing riffs from old movies and dishy impersonations of everyone from Elvis to Clint Eastwood to Sally Field accepting her Oscar.

Amid all these amusing elements, it may not matter very much that "The Mask" runs out of energy faster than its star does. Though director Charles Russell knows how to keep things loose and playful, the movie doesn't aspire to be more than a gaudy showcase for Carrey's ability and ILM's magic, and anyone looking for something else is open to disappointment.

In line with this, Mike Werb's screenplay, based on a story by Michael Fallon and Mark Verheiden and before that on a comicbook character, is less a sturdy narrative than an extended premise on which all these assorted antics can be hung like ornaments on a tree.

The pre-Mask Ipkiss lives and works in Edge City and wonders why nice guys finish last. A shy pushover and dupe whose primary emotional attachment is to his clever terrier Milo (one of the more entertaining of recent dog performances), Ipkiss just about stops breathing when sultry Tina Carlyle (Cameron Diaz) stops by his desk at the bank.

A headliner at the chic Coco Bongo Club, Tina is also the girlfriend of mobster Dorian Tyrel (Peter Greene), but Ipkiss can't get her out of his mind. And though the movie presents Tina as little more than the scantily clad physical embodiment of Roger Rabbit's wife Jessica, model Diaz, in her first screen role, has enough presence to help us see past the tinsel.

At a particularly morose point in his life, Ipkiss comes across a nondescript green wooden mask, which, he later learns, is probably of Scandinavian origin and carved to represent Loki, the Norse god of mischief, permanently banned from Valhalla for his pranks.

Not surprisingly, then, when Ipkiss puts the mask on, havoc breaks loose. Normally timid, he becomes an amoral live wire out of one of the Tex Avery cartoons he admires, a party animal with a face the color of key lime pie capable of robbing banks and whirling off like a pastel tornado.

That robbery aside, the Mask isn't really a bad guy, and his most memorable moments are song-and-dance riffs so antic that in interviews Carrey has taken to calling his character "Fred Astaire on acid." Whether passionately twirling with Tina in a canary-yellow ensemble, playing the maniac French *boulevardier* in beret and loud pants or turning a SWAT team into a conga line with his Cuban Pete impersonation, Carrey is a treat on his feet.

While no one wants to look this kind of gift horse in the mouth, it is hard to watch "The Mask" without wishing its pluses were attached to a story even a trifle more inventive or involving. But in the glory days of Cartoons-R-Us, that is an awful lot to ask.

NEW STATESMAN & SOCIETY, 8/12/94, p. 33, Jonathan Romney

[*The Mask* was reviewed jointly with *Forrest Gump*; see Romney's review of that film.]

NEW YORK, 8/15/94, p. 55, David Denby

In *The Mask* Jim Carrey, a schlump pushing paper in a bank, can't speak to a girl or do anything else right until he puts on a mystic ancient mask and instantly becomes a species of pure prancing id—a green-faced, demonic superhero, dashing around like liquid fire. Once transformed, the normally gangly, big-toothed Carrey draws on the duded flourishes of African-American macho, and then, in taunting combinations, the intonations and moves of Paul Lynde (you heard me) and José Greco (again). The director, Charles Russell, adds goony special effects—bulging eyes, popping tongues—and some of the little shocks are amazing: like pinpricks on your hand, only fun. There's no script to speak of, and the other characters hardly matter. Russell stays fixed on his star. That's the right thing to do.

NEW YORK POST, 7/29/94, p. 43, Michael Medved

"The Mask" may not qualify as a great contribution to our civilization, but it does keep both of its principal promises to its audience—delivering stunningly inventive special effects together with a weird, wacked-out, Jekyll-and-Hyde performance by its star, Jim Carrey.

In this story (based on a cult comic book of the early '80s) Carrey first shows up as Stanley Ipkiss, a timid bank clerk who can't get a date and is regularly abused by auto mechanics, parking attendants, and the rest of the humanity.

This downtrodden dip can only fight back after he pauses one night to pull an ancient mask out of the river, then tries it on and undergoes a supernatural transformation. The Mask (which we later learn is associated with "the Scandinavian god of mischief") unleashes the green-faced, grinning, invincible, zoot-suited, sexually super-charged beast that's been raging in the depths of Stanley's id.

Carrey is good at both halves of his role, bringing a surprising sweetness to the soft-spoken Stanley, and an oddly debonair ferocity ("like Fred Astaire on acid," Carrey himself says) to The Mask.

Throughout his comedy career, Carrey's been trying to turn himself into a cartoon character; here, with the help of the computer animation wizards at Industrial Light and Magic, he has finally achieved that ambition.

Carrey also offers a series of stream-of-consciousness imitations, invoking Sally Field, Clark Gable and even Desi Arnez (singing "Cuban Pete" in a campy chorus line) in dizzying and mind-numbing succession. His performance is free, faster and funnier than it was in "Ace Ventura"; anyone who enjoyed that previous movie (which I loathed) will probably love this one.

As in "Ace," the plot is merely a feeble excuse for the comic contortions of the star—in this case some forgettable nonsense about a gang of vicious thieves (led by Peter Greene) who battle The Mask over a million-dollar heist from the bank where Stanley works.

This competition causes confusion for a bumbling police lieutenant (Peter Riegert), but gives our hero, in both halves of his personality, the chance to pursue a relationship with a sultry singer (Cameron Diaz) who works in a swanky, '40s style nightclub owned by the gangsters.

Diaz, a fashion model making her movie debut, is a major find; the camera loves her (she looks a bit like a more voluptuous Ellen Barkin) while projecting an accessible, girl-next-door charm.

The most impressive member of the supporting cast is s Jack Russell Terrier named Max who plays Stanley's devoted dog,

They previously worked together on "Nightmare on Elm Street III" (easily the finest—and funniest—offering of that series) and in their capable hands "The Mask" is fanciful, and strange, but never disgusting; in fact, its success should make other practitioners of the difficult format of horror-comedy turn green with envy.

NEWSDAY, 7/29/94, Part II/p. B2, Jack Mathews

Stanley Ipkiss, like most comic book superheroes in disguise, is a square. He's a bank clerk who wears generic gray suits and nerdy ties, talks like a Boy Scout, and can't get the girls at the office to see him as anything but a gentle twerp.

What distinguishes Stanley from a Clark Kent or Billy Batson is that he doesn't know what a stud he actually is until he dons a green mask burped up from some Norse treasure at the bottom of the sea. then, he is, to use his own word, *smokin'!*

The masked Stanley, tailored to the extraordinary physical comedy skills of "Ace Ventura's" Jim Carrey, is more of a comic Mr. Hyde than a traditional superhero. He's Jerry Lewis'"The Nutty Professor" on an acid bender, an introvert whose wild and crazy side needs a little supernatural lift to be brought to the surface.

With the mask on, Stanley becomes a dashing, whirling dervish of energy, a combination live action/animation figure in screaming yellow and aqua zoot suits, with a face and body that fold, bend, stretch and are transmogrified like a Chuck Jones character in a Warner Bros. cartoon.

When Stanley starts giving wolf whistles to the sultry nightclub singer Tina Carlyle (Cameron Diaz), his head billows into the shape of wolf and his lips flutter like flags in a breeze. At other times, his eyes pop out, as if on springs, his jaw drops to a table top where his tongue unspools like a roll of carpet, and his heart leaps out of his chest to throb in mid-air.

Directed by Charles Russell ("Nightmare on Elm Street III"), "The Mask" is a singular work of cartoon comedy. Jim Carrey is often as annoying as Jerry Lewis, and he has given no signs yet of being a better actor. But you have to go back to Buster Keaton to find a more interesting physical comedian, and as wildly imaginative as they are, the effects designed for him by George Lucas' Industrial Light & Magic merely extend and exaggerate his natural moves. ILM does for Carrey what the magic mask does for Stanley.

I don't know what percentage of the film's 102 minutes is taken up by these cartoon sequences, but the moments are golden. Whether Stanley is eluding police, by putting a spell on them and turning a massive stakeout into a Busby Berkeley conga line, or taunting the mob with his plastic invulnerability, the screen is a colorful blur of happy surprises.

For those of us who didn't get the humor in "Ace Ventura," however, the rest of "The Mask" is hard going. Carrey can convince us he is made out of rubber, but he can't convince us he is human. Though the wimpy Stanley doesn't like what the mask does to him, he figures it's the only chance he has with Tina Carlyle, and it's a good thing. He and the movie only come alive when it becomes a cartoon.

The story, what little there is of it, has Stanley caught between the police, led by a befuddled Lt. Kellaway (Peter Riegert), and Tina Carlyle's mobster boyfriend Dorian Tyrel (Peter Greene), whose planned bank heist is upset when Stanley beats his gang to it.

The other actors are little more than props for Carrey, though model Cameron Diaz has some fun on her own, as a live action version of Jessica Rabbit. The second-best performance, however, was given by Max, a Jack Russell Terrier playing Stanley's faithful pet. Max gets one of the film's biggest laughs when, in the midst of a nightclub riot, he dons Stanley's mask and becomes a superhero in his own right.

Comic book aficionados may be offended by the film's relentless spoofing of the genre, but if you have to choose between the summer's two superheroes, the broodingly somber "The Shadow" or the manically goofy "The Mask," it's no contest.

NEWSWEEK, 8/8/94, p. 54, Jeff Giles

It'd be easy to hate Jim Carrey, but where's the fun in that? Sure, his superstar-making turn in "Ace Ventura" was an aria of obnoxiousness. (Ben Kingsley was born to play Gandhi; Carrey was born to play Woody Woodpecker.) But if you limboed down to its level, you glimpsed what might be the second coming of Robin Williams. Like the young Williams, Carrey's a pole-vaulter: no matter how high they set the bar, he goes over the top. In "The Mask," he plays Stanley Ipkiss, who finds an ancient mask that transforms him from a trembling bank clerk into a libidinous superhero. The plot's a throwaway: something about warring mobsters, a bank heist and a bombshell chanteuse (model Cameron Diaz, who's pretty good once the camera stops feeling her up). Still, the movie's so invincibly silly you've got to get on board or get out of the way. The masked man spins like a Tasmanian devil and rolls his tongue out like so much red carpet, but the real special effect is Carrey. He's a fine mimic and a frenetic physical comedian, who ricochets through wacko character bits and sly movie references. Accused of pulling the bank job, he moans, "It was the one-armed man!" Then he leads the cops in a rumba nunber. "The Mask," says the ad, is about going "from zero to hero." Carrey himself has made that trip, and there'll be no turning back.

SIGHT AND SOUND, 10/94, p. 48, Michael Atkinson

Underwater workers in the harbour near Edge City stumble upon an ancient chest and accidentally open it, releasing an ancient wooden mask. That day, dweebish bank clerk Stanley Ipkiss finally gets a break—or seemingly so—when the beautiful Tina Carlyle walks into his bank and requests his help. As she flirts with him, however, she secretly aims a camera at the bank's vault, watched far away by Dorian, a gangster planning a robbery. Ipkiss agrees to accompany his friend Charlie to the Coco Bongo, a new elite nightclub. After work, Stanley find his car dismantled in the sleazy auto repair shop where he left it, and must use instead the shop's antiquated 'loaner'. He is left out in the cold by the club's surly bouncers, and humiliated in front of Tina, who is the Coco Bongo's star chanteuse. On the way home, Stanley spots what looks like a body floating in the river; it turns out to be a mass of flotsam, in which he finds the mask.

Back in his apartment, Stanley tries the mask on, and is instantly transformed into The Mask, a zoot-suited, green-faced cartoon figure with the superhuman ability to do just about anything. Stanley/The Mask wreaks havoc on his landlady, his car mechanics, Dorian's bank-robbing cohorts, and the dance floor of the Coco Bongo.

By day, Ipkiss is hung over, addicted to the mask's power. By night, The Mask rules fearlessly; when the police eventually corner him, he dives into a swinging mambo number, hypnotising the massed cops. Eventually Stanley is kidnapped by Dorian, who tries the mask on, becoming a green-headed, intensely evil version of himself. Dorian's thugs then deposit Stanley at the police station, where he is quickly arrested. Later at the Coco Bongo, Dorian plans to blow up the nightclub and Tina with it, but Stanley—with the help of his Jack Russell terrier Milo—escapes from custody, steals the mask back and saves the day. United with Tina, he flings the mask into the river, only for Milo to retrieve it ...

Every inch the comic book, *The Mask* bears witness to both the glories and the shortcomings of that literary genre more eloquently than any movie ever has. As dull-witted and straitjacketed by cliché as it is visually hellzapoppin, the film may be a watershed moment in the cultural current that looks to loot the baby-boomer memory banks for recyclable cinematic ideas. Cartoons have breached the reality web of live-action movies once and for all, but to what end? No sooner does Jim Carrey don his magical mask than the ghosts of Tex Avery and Chuck Jones are summoned from the void and given hi-tech life; still, the result is curiously unamusing. Regardless of its astounding computer-animated effects, *The Mask* seems mundane, half-hearted and less engaged by its own chaos than your average eight-year-hold, for whom the movie seems particularly intended. It's more *Beethoven* than *Beetlejuice,* and no matter how much The Mask himself advocates gleeful anarchy, the film is as safe and routine as an afternoon with Lamb Chop.

It seemed a sure thing. Suddenly a major commodity since the unforeseen success of *Ace Ventura: Pet Detective*, Jim Carrey is a rapturously idiosyncratic film persona, all double-jointed weirdness and mock game-show host delivery. In *Ace Ventura*, and in his extraordinary TV work (notably in the comedy series *In Living Colour*), Carrey has already revealed himself to be as close to the free-associative tornado of *The Mask*'s central conception as any actor alive (he makes Robin Williams look constipated by comparison). So the casting seemed fortuitous, and this fully-morphed adaptation of the Dark Horse comic was anticipated with understandable eagerness.

All the more disappointing, then, that here Carrey is dishwater-dull and, as The Mask, is so cluttered up with computerised accoutrements that we barely recognise him. At times, anybody at all could be behind the make-up and exploding props. More vitally, director Charles (aka Chuck) Russell, whose previous credits include *A Nightmare on Elm Street 3: Dream Warriors* and the already-forgotten remake of *The Blob*, seems lost at sea trying to shape the simple material into comedy. Most of *The Mask* is ruefully unfunny: the jokes are strained ("That doesn't sound good to me"—"What does sound good to you?"—"Breakfast"), the sight gags are Tex Avery retreads, and the timing is way off. The result is uninspired and witless, no matter how cyclonic the visuals. Indeed, the effects themselves are hopelessly derivative. Unlike the crack creative team behind *Who Framed Roger Rabbit?*, Russell and co rarely bother to instil new life into the 40-year-old tropes of Avery at his peak. Avery's bulging eyeballs, howling wolves and entropic action are simply aped here. If you've seen 'Swing Shift Cinderella' (1945), you've already seen *The Mask*'s most furious visual fillips, but in two dimensions.

If you're eight, these are all pointless quibbles—*The Mask*'s simple story and goofy showboating are bound to excite the tyros in the audience without ever interesting their parents. Similarly, the brazen set-up for a sequel may get the pre-teen demographic slavering in anticipation. Adults, however, will know better.

VILLAGE VOICE, 8/9/94, p. 48, Arianna Pavia Rosati

Holy transmorphography, Batman! The loser's the hero again!

And this time, he's Stanley Ipkiss (Jim Carrey), a too-nice guy schlemiel with a nasty landlady and an adorable pooch, who spends his days toiling in a bank, and his rainy nights outside the Coco Bongo lounge getting sprayed by passing Porsches. Sound familiar? It should. He's the next member of the Superman-Popeye-Mighty Mouse-Charles Atlas club for wimps who wanna be men. Or, in this twist, cartoons.

The irreverent lunacy Stanley's superego holds in tight rein explodes when he dons an innocuous-looking ancient mask, and his body goes nuts. The green-faced beast within lies a Tasmanian devil dance away, wearing a dapper turquoise zoot suit. Within a minute, the Mask has tortured his landlady, trashed his technicolor apartment, annihilated a gnarly leather-clad gang, and rhumba'd the dame in his life, the luscious torch singer Tina (lovely Cameron Diaz), a sashaying Jessica Rabbit. Poor unsuspecting Stanley—should he take credit or go on the lam? *The Mask* is your typical Saturday morning fare—a dazzling spectacle of eyeball-popping, head-smashing visual effects—until you realize, wait, this is not a cartoon!

Carrey may be wacky without the enhancement, but, oh, what a little computer generation can do. This film is so much fun to watch, and that from a viewer nursed on *Star Wars*; jaded by techno-whizardry. (Another touchdown for Industrial Light & Magic, who helped rush it into post-production hot off Carrey's *Ace Ventura* coup.) For film noir or animation junkies, *The*

Mask is a referential smorgasbord: from Bogart and Cagney to Dick Tracy and the Incredible Hulk. For everyone else, it's just looney 'toons.

Also reviewed in:
CHICAGO TRIBUNE, 7/29/94, Friday/p. C, Michael Wilmington
NEW YORK TIMES, 7/29/94, p. C1, Janet Maslin
VARIETY, 8/1-7/94, p. 44, Leonard Klady
WASHINGTON POST, 7/29/94, p. D1, Rita Kempley
WASHINGTON POST, 7/29/94, Weekend/p. 35, Joe Brown

MAVERICK

A Warner Bros. release of an Icon production in association with Donner/Shuler-Donner Productions. *Producer:* Bruce Davey and Richard Donner. *Director:* Richard Donner. *Screenplay:* William Goldman. *Based on the TV series "Maverick" created by:* Roy Huggins. *Director of Photographer:* Vilmos Zsigmond. *Editor:* Stuart Baird and Mike Kelly. *Music:* Randy Newman. *Music Editor:* Christopher Brooks. *Sound:* Clark King and (music) Frank Wolf. *Sound Editor:* Robert G. Henderson. *Casting:* Marion Dougherty. *Production Designer:* Tom Sanders. *Art Director:* Daniel Dorrance. *Set Decorator:* Lisa Dean. *Special Effects:* Matt Sweeney. *Costumes:* April Ferry. *Make-up:* Michael Hancock. *Stunt Coordinator:* Mic Rodgers. *Running time:* 120 minutes. *MPAA Rating:* PG.

CAST: Mel Gibson (Bret Maverick); Jodie Foster (Annabelle Bransford); James Garner (Zane Cooper); Graham Greene (Joseph); Alfred Mullins (Angel); James Coburn (Commodore Duval); Dub Taylor (Room Clerk); Geoffrey Lewis (Matthew Wicker); Paul L. Smith (Archduke); Dan Hedaya (Twitchy); Dennis Fimple (Stuttering); Denver Pyle (Old Gambler); Clint Black (Sweet-faced Gambler); Max Perlich (Johnny Hardin); Art LaFleur, Leo V. Gordon, and Paul Tuerpe (Poker Players); Jean De Baer (Margaret Mary); Paul Brinegar (Stage Driver); Hal Ketchum, Corey Feldman, and John Woodward (Bank Robbers); Jesse Eric Carroll and Toshonnie Touchin (Stable Boys); John Meier, Steve Chambers, Doc Duhame, and Frank Orsati (Unshaven Men); Lauren Shuler-Donner (Bathhouse Maid); Courtney Barilla and Kimberly Cullum (Music Box Girls); Gary Richard Frank (Crooked Dealer); Read Morgan, Steve Kahan, and Stephen Liska (Dealers); Robert Jones (Bank Employee); John Mills Goodloe (Telegraph Operator); Vilmos Zsigmond (Albert Bierstadt); Waylon Jennings and Kathy Mattea (Couple with Concealed Guns); Carlene Carter (Waitress); Vince Gill and Janice Gill (Spectators); Danny Glover (Bank Robber).

CHRISTIAN SCIENCE MONITOR, 5/20/94, p. 10, David Sterritt

Based on a popular television show of the 1950s, the new "Maverick" conjures up an era when westerns exercised a ferociously strong hold on the American imagination.

Theaters were jammed with "oaters" of all sorts, ranging from "psychological" westerns by Anthony Mann to minimalist dissections of the genre by Budd Boetticher, plus an endless string of formula-bound horse operas that shared the same simple plots and the same simple repertoire of variations. You couldn't escape them on the airwaves, either, where kiddie shows with Roy Rogers and Gene Autry rubbed elbows with "adult westerns" like "Gunsmoke" and the relatively exotic "Have Gun, Will Travel," among many others.

"Maverick" stood with the most popular of the TV westerns, thanks largely to its flexible format—the presence of two handsome good guys, Bret and Bart, helped the series seem fresh week after week—and to its lively sense of humor, often poking fun at its own heroics and the situations that gave rise to them. It was a likable show, more enjoyable than much of the competition.

The studio marketeers who decided to produce a film version of "Maverick" in 1994 immediately ran against a major hurdle: Bret Maverick, the most beloved of the show's regular characters, was played by James Garner, who's still an attractive presence but no longer the fresh-faced young man who graced TV sets nearly four decades ago.

Should a different actor be recruited to play Bret, thereby calling the whole point of a "Maverick" movie into question? Or should the title role go to Garner despite his years, thereby aiming the project, at an age group considerably older than the teen and young-adult crowd?

Faced with this dilemma, the marketeers chose both solutions at once, although I can't discuss this further without giving away one of the film's many surprises. Suffice it to say that Bret Maverick is appealingly played by Mel Gibson, as much a star in the '90s as Garner ever was in the '50s, and that Garner is prominently on hand as a marshall who travels, feuds, and bonds with Bret over the course of a two-hour plot with more than its share of twists.

Aside from its clever casting, the most noteworthy thing about "Maverick" is the professionalism of the picture. It was made by a conspicuously polished group including director Richard Donner, screenwriter William Goldman, cinematographer Vilmos Zsigmond, and composer Randy Newman.

Professional doesn't mean inspired, of course, and little about "Maverick" lingers in the mind once the final image has faded from the screen. But it's cleverly crafted, and you can't help enjoying it even when you know it's manipulating you as brazenly as a poker dealer with tricky fingers and a well-stacked deck.

The story loses no time announcing its degree of subtlety: The credits have barely finished before we see Maverick astride a fidgety horse with a noose around his neck, a rattlesnake slithering in his direction, and bad guys roaring with delight at his imminent demise. A flashback tells us how our hero landed in this predicament, and then we watch the escapades that follow his escape.

The plot zings along rapidly, allowing us few chances to catch our breath and ruminate on how silly this all is. The filmmakers are eager to relieve us of any obligation to think, programming all our reactions and making up their own rules as they go along. Key dialogue is repeated over and over, to make sure we'll know what's going on even if we've spent the last 10 minutes at the popcorn counter. Lest we fail to notice that the poker dealer is cheating, the movie slips into slow-motion as he slides a card off the bottom of his deck. If a scene drags, rock music erupts on the soundtrack—a tad anachronistic, but good for a jolt to regain our attention. Gibson brings to Maverick a touch of the high-grade hysteria that he patented in "Lethal Weapon," also directed by Donner, as if his recent solemnity in "Hamlet" and "The Man Without a Face" now legitimizes all the goofiness he cares to throw at us. Garner reestablishes his status as an engaging star with one of the most winning smiles in the business.

In other important roles, Jodie Foster shows a solid flair for comedy as a beguiling woman who's no more trustworthy than the slippery men surrounding her, and James Coburn steals more than one scene as proprietor of the riverboat poker tournament that gives the story its climax. Alfred Molina, one of the most gifted characters actors around, is perfect as the most dastardly villain. And certainly not least, Graham Greene is superb as an Indian chief.

Since one of the things that drastically cut back the western genre after the '50s was the skepticism bred by ultraviolent westerns like "The Wild Bunch" and "The Good, the Bad, and the Ugly," it's encouraging to note that "Maverick" keeps its gunplay and fistfights within bounds. Credit for this goes to director Donner and screenwriter Goldman, and perhaps also to cinematographer Zsigmond, who has spoken out against excessive gore. "Maverick" has a visual appeal the small screen could never equal.

FILMS IN REVIEW, 7-8/94, p. 60, Harry Pearson, Jr.

The word "maverick" is meant to describe a nonconformist, one who stands apart from the crowd and does things in a uniquely individualistic way, perhaps even with a kind of tongue-stuck-out attitude toward the sacred cows of his times. In this respect, this Richard Donner film is truly misnamed. The spirit that motivates it is anything but a maverick one. Instead of a tongue-stuck-out iconoclasm, this movie tries for tongue-in-cheek humor, at which it fails for want of wit and a compelling plot line. To be a maverick you have to have some idea of what you're against, or, what you're making fun of. Nobody associated with this film, save Graham Greene (doing a wicked turn on the pomposity of Hollywood's politically correctly treatment of native Americans) has the slightest idea of what to satirize in the Old West, or, failing that, what to satirize about the way we'd like to think of the Old West given our "modern" sensibility.

What we get, at its best moments, is an amiable mess. And why? Because neither its director (the puzzlingly inconsistent Richard Donner), nor the scriptwriter (the normally pungent William Goldman) nor much of the cast, particularly the stars (Mel Gibson and Jodie Foster), seem to have the faintest notion of what this movie *should* be about. Consequently, what it doesn't have is style, with which they might have pulled this off, even in the absence of mordant wit. Even the fabled Vilmos Zsigmond, once the very master of the Panavision frame, has given the movie no consistency of look. One moment it's swooping crane shots, the next, rather ordinary compositions of a desert town, made to look more dusty by the indiscriminate use of a yellow filter.

Gibson starts out doing his crazy man routine from the first edition of *Lethal Weapon*, which is out of tone here: Note how flat falleth the scene with the young would-be Billy the Kid (who ought to be played as a sullen psychopath, instead of someone who'd back down in the face of Mel's alternations between cowardice—no doubt a post-echo, however faint, of the original TV series—and an ability with the fast draw). James Garner, who knows what this is all about, barely bestirs himself to do any more than is absolutely necessary. A bit of charm and he makes off with the money, in this case his equity check. Foster tries valiantly. She flounces, she pouts, she does everything but floss her teeth; she's a real actress looking in vain for a part to play. But the way it's written there's no there *there* in the character, and so Foster has nowhere to go, except, of course, to collect her percentage for stooping, but not to conquer. If anyone had thought of it, including Gibson, they might have bounced off, for starters, our neo-preconceptions of the p.c. Western hero, as say, filtered through Kevin Costner's malarkey in *Dances With Wolves*. Whoever got this to the screen should have known that a few drops of acid and bite would have given the movie the spine it so sadly lacks. So we watch and wait for something to happen, and because everybody's so darned likeable, we keep waiting.

A firm hand in the editing room would have helped, too. Every scene goes on several beats too long (and it is said that it was even longer before commercial considerations—read the studio—forced Donner to cut). The movie pokes for a considerable while after its (supposed) climactic sequence—an improbable and suspenseless poker game—while carefully setting us up for a sequel and dropping a last minute twist that has been too long in coming.

So pokey is the pace that we have time to think about the considerable holes in the plot and to wonder about things we shouldn't be thinking about, things that betray a certain contempt for the audience to which the filmmakers should be appealing. Massive fresh water lakes in the high desert country are a rarity and yet here we are, on a recognizable Lake Powell in Utah, serving as a backdrop for what appears to be a hastily constructed set of a Western town (and this, for starters, as the movie begins). The entire business with the religious folks, robbed by bandits—is that Margot Kidder in an uncredited part?—falls flat, and one of the movie's best jokes, involving Greene and an Indian attack upon this same wagon train, goes on and on and on, until it isn't funny anymore. Do animatronically fake rattlesnakes really scare us, as would the real ones, a good stunt man and some sharp editing? It's as if the director, cast and crew are so full of themselves they forget it's supposed to be us who are having the good time.

And why are even the action sequences so tame, so unthrilling? Is this because the studio wanted a PG rating, or is what seems to be the continuing devolution of Donner, once away from cars he can crash and buildings he can blow up, showing a lack of imaginative resourcefulness when stuck in the old West without the machines of modern society to explode, maul and maim?

The idea of the maverick is either to play with our expectations, or, better yet, against them. Here, Donner and Co. play to them by playing safe.

So see it for Greene's bit and for Garner, who has the right idea: He does nothing, and thus soars above everyone else.

LOS ANGELES TIMES, 5/20/94, Calendar/p. 1, Peter Rainer

"Maverick" is smart-alecky without being very smart. It's full of spoofy, har-dee-har-har ribaldries—this film practically winks at you. As sophisticated Western comedies go, it's somewhere between "Butch Cassidy and the Sundance Kid" and "The Apple Dumpling Gang." Crammed with such big-name crowd-pleasers as Mel Gibson, Jodie Foster and James Garner, "Maverick" reaches for that Feel Good feeling. It settles for Feel OK.

The most damning criticism ever leveled against "Butch Cassidy"—like "Maverick" scripted by William Goldman—is that it was a "Beverly Hills Western." This also describes "Maverick." It's *proudly* unauthentic, twinkling with high-gloss production values that make even the dust look like something you'd buy at Bijan. Watching it is like taking in a deluxe window display of hand-me-downs.

As Maverick, who spends most of the movie trying to con his way into a high-stakes poker game, Gibson is still in his hyperhectic mode from the "Lethal Weapon" films—perhaps because Richard Donner is once again the director. Gibson tumbles and scampers and issues double—and triple—takes to everything from riverboat gamblers to rattlesnakes. He's ingratiatingly and, finally, exhaustingly, goofy. He seems to be simultaneously impersonating the Road Runner *and* Wile E. Coyote.

Actors form-fitted for heroism often go a little blooey when they're encouraged to act comically anti-heroic; they bounce off the audience's expectations of glamour. Gibson manages to look glamorous anyway in "Maverick;" and that's part of the joke—just as it was with Paul Newman and Robert Redford in "Butch Cassidy." But it's not the most ample of jokes. Gibson, for all his handsomeness and hearty frivolity, is playing down to us.

Not that Maverick is a role to be played with the gravity of a Geronimo. James Garner's Bret Maverick on the original ABC-TV show, which ran from 1957 to 1962, was already pretty sporty and flip. So was the series. (A memorable parody of "Bonanza" featured Jim Backus as the baron of the Subrosa cattle ranch, with sons Moose, Henry and Small Paul.) Garner is in the new movie as lawman Zane (Coop) Cooper, and he gives the film a pedigree—and some class. (Garner walked out on the series in 1960, two years before its demise, so his appearance here is a double-edged "tribute.") In this whirligig of off-the-shelf gags and celebrity clowning, Garner's wry harrumphiness goes a long way.

Jodie Foster is playing Annabelle Bransford, a siren who spends the entire movie trying to out-con Maverick. She's the kind of woman who bats goo-goo eyes at her man while she lifts his wallet. Now how often have you seen *that* gag before? Foster tries to ventilate the tiresomeness letting us know she's too smart to be playing someone this smart-dumb. Her performance has an only-kidding coyness that's entirely in keeping with the entire movie—alas. It's integrity of a sort. Foster knows what kind of movie this is, and she at least has the courage of her own unauthenticity. What else can she do when she's required to play a character who keeps misstating Maverick's name? She repeatedly calls him Burt instead of Bret—har har.

The tiredness of the jokes in "Maverick" is supposed to be terminally hip. We're supposed to enjoy our familiarity with all the clichés. For people who enjoy having their junk memories jogged—and coddled—this kiddie connoiseurship can pass for a good time. When Maverick puts his ear to the ground as if to listen for distant hoofbeats and then lays down for a nap, we can see the gag coming a mile away, just as we can anticipate the shenanigans at the gaming tables and the horsing around with a tribal chief (Graham Greene) who dresses Maverick up as a bespangled Native American.

Goldman and Donner don't draw on Western traditions in order to tweak them into new life; they're having too much fun giggling over the corpses of old routines. Their uninspiration has above-it-all airs. They showcase a rogue's gallery of familiar faces from old Westerns and from the country-Western music world, ranging from the glorious Dub Taylor to Denver Pyle and Waylon Jennings, but that's all these people remain: faces. (James Coburn fills out smartly a somewhat larger role as the ringleader of the poker championship.) The filmmakers have no feeling for the traditions they're sending up, and the lack gives "Maverick" a hollow facetiousness.

Maverick the high-stakes gambler is proud of being spineless. He's fast on the draw, but he always opts to run from a fight. In a way, he's the perfect protagonist for this high-stakes film, which also flaunts its flimsiness.

NEW YORK, 6/6/94, p. 52, David Denby

At the beginning of *Maverick*, Mel Gibson rides into a cruddy little western town at the edge of a lake, brushes against a south-of-the-border thug in a big hat, and says, "I smell trouble—and refried beans."

So many movies have fizzled this year that we're more than ready for a smarty-pants entertainment that stays a step or two ahead of us. Taking the old James Garner role, Gibson, running around bare-chested, is lithe and powerful, a far more physical performer than the hyper-relaxed Garner, who preferred acting with his voice and smile. A cardsharp and wit, a daredevil clown and acrobat, this Maverick can beat you in a dozen ways. The movie itself is full of tricks. Screenwriter William Goldman redoes the old TV series, but faster and smarter, and director Richard Donner, unable to race cars and smash windows this time, as he did in his appalling *Lethal Weapon* series, has to invent. His way of inventing is to horse around, teasing everything and everybody, but at first the tone is friendly: Come along for the ride.

Gibson sits at a poker table with a bunch of hardbitten types, including a saloon hustler named Mrs. Bransford, played by Jodie Foster in a plunging neckline and mountains of golden ringlets. Foster smiles and simpers; she's in her proficient, workmanlike I-can-do-this-commercial-shit mode. As Annabelle Bransford, she's a sparkling little thing with sharply cut features, diamond teeth, and a stare like a laser beam. What a gal. But do we really want Jodie Foster proving that she's a sport? She's not the same kind of actor as Mel Gibson, who was made for movies like this one. Gibson does satirical macho: He shows off how modest he is. He's the flake who's really a superstud, and he can look silly because he has nothing to lose; dignity is not what he's upholding. But Jodie Foster is something else, a major actress with a talent for playing outsiders and losers who hold on to their will and integrity. In this movie, she gets the externals of a comic performance right, but then nothing happens. She can't, or won't, develop or expand the character. She's along for the ride, too.

Maverick offers the minor but distinct pleasures of cynicism; it's the bastard child of such slickly confident entertainments as *The Sting* and *Butch Cassidy and the Sundance Kid.* As he sits down to gamble, Mel Gibson is saying (in effect) to the others, "I'm hustling you—and even though you know that, you can't stop me from taking your money." We're also in the know, but we can't stop Goldman and Donner from stinging us a few times as well. Nor do we want to. *Maverick* is a series of seductions, put-ons, and reversals; it pulls out rugs we didn't even know we were standing on. In this version of the Old West, no one has any honor, bravery is a joke, and people are out for themselves. All of which, of course, has little to do with the West or with Westerns, and everything to do with Hollywood.

Gibson and Foster pick up the old pro, James Garner himself—this time playing a rather dyspeptic lawman—and the three of them head east so that Maverick can join a high-stakes poker game. Along the way, Donner gives us a frivolous black-comedy joke: An ancient, wheezing stagecoach driver dies as the coach is racing along. And then comes the first mistake. Burying the old man, the three characters sing "Amazing Grace." A soaring chorus joins them, and the camera rises to photograph the majestic buttes of Arizona. But who are Goldman and Donner to evoke grace? Theirs is a world without grace; that's why it's funny. The hymn and the heroic camera lift stick out like a Bach organ toccata at an Alice Cooper concert.

Suddenly the movie seems confused and too smart for its own good. A sequence with some Indians threatening a church community starts wittily, with Gibson and Graham Greene (as the chief exchanging remarks in mysterious Indian talk, but then it turns disastrously sour. One minute Goldman and Donner have Maverick making ironic, "liberal" pro-Indian cracks; the next, the Indians are shown to be on the take, just like everybody else. Even the religious folk have got their hands out.

The movie's debonair tone slips badly. Comedy turns to nagging and shtick. The final poker game, onboard a paddle-wheel steamer, receives an interminable, pompous setup, with dozens of extras and James Coburn's tedious courtliness rolled out like a red carpet. Why not just stage the game in a small room? *Maverick* becomes ponderous, even grandiose, and by this time we begin to notice that the same joke has been played on us too many times. The filmmakers are so pleased with their own wit that they can't stop repeating themselves. In the end, Hollywood cynicism may be indistinguishable from self-love.

NEW YORK POST, 5/20/94, p. 41, Michael Medved

"Maverick," the first of this year's summertime spectaculars, features lots of pretty scenery, three pretty superstars, pretty Randy Newman music, a spectacularly pretty steamboat, and some pretty inventive plot twists and surprises.

It also suffers, unfortunately, from a nearly terminal case of the cutes, as this slick, glossy, over-the-top picture constantly pokes the viewer in the ribs to remind him what a good time he's supposed to be having.

For instance, Danny Glover turns up in a brief, uncredited, mugging-for-the-camera cameo—intended to remind us that the same director (Richard Donner) and star (Mel Gibson) previously worked with Glover on the three hugely successful "Lethal Weapon" pictures.

Yeah, it's a mildly amusing moment, but Donner can't resist the temptation of overdoing it—rubbing it in and gloating at his own wittiness. This same smug, knowing tone mars the entire movie and will keep moviegoers from losing themselves in the characters or the story.

Gibson, nevertheless, is well-cast as Bret Maverick, the debonair gambler and con artist familiar to fans of the old TV series of the '50s and '60s.

The ageless and affable James Garner (who played Bret in the original show) here lends his reassuring presence as a straight-arrow lawman named Zane Cooper (combining Zane Grey and Gary Cooper?) who ends up accompanying Maverick to a championship poker tournament with a half-million-dollar prize.

Also on her way to the poker showdown is a seductive card sharp and pickpocket played by Jodie Foster, who not only looks heartbreakingly beautiful in all her frills and bustles. but whose conviction and intensity blow her easy-going male counterparts off the screen in all the scenes they share.

In their wanderings through the wild West, the big three encounter a series of veteran character actors, including James Coburn as the devious steamboat "commodore" who hosts the poker tournament, and Graham Greene as a Native American chief who shamelessly exploits his "noble savage" image.

Some of these sequences are genuinely amusing but they all go on much too long—even the spectacular stuntwork in a runaway stagecoach scene cries out for cutting.

Less than halfway into the film, "Maverick" begins to feel sluggish and repetitive. Perhaps the prestige of screenwriter William Goldman ("Butch Cassidy and the Sundance Kid," "All the President's Men") prevented Donner and his colleagues from making badly needed trims in the story.

None of these quibbles will keep eager audiences from enjoying the humor and star power deployed here. Yet, this empty but entertaining exercise leaves an overwhelming impression of offering audiences too much of a good thing.

NEWSDAY, 5/20/94, Part II/p. B3, John Anderson

From the minute the dandified gambling man Bret Maverick appears atop a donkey in the Mel Gibson-powered "Maverick," you know it's going to be a case of good news-bad news.

The good news? Gibson is charming, glib, funny. Jodie Foster has seldom been more beautiful or brightly unrestrained. James Garner, although unusually phlegmatic, is a warm, manly Ward Bonding agent for the whole wagon train. And while the action may not agree with director Richard ("Lethal Weapon") Donner's occasional scorched-earth policy, the film moves along at something like a gallop.

The bad news? While revisionist westerns usually have to justify mucking around with a classic genre, "Maverick" doesn't have to justify anything. It has the cast, it has the script, it has a familiar predecessor—the '50s television series in which Garner starred—and it knows it. Enter complacency.

"Maverick," isn't really a revisionist western, though. It may not even be a western: There's no moral focus, no clearly defined good or evil. Angel (Alfred Molina), Bret's nemesis, is also his stooge; the Commodore, host of the All-Rivers Draw Poker Championship to which Bret aspires, is James Coburn at his least venomous. So what "Maverick" turns out to be is a homage to another revisionist western, and as such more or less contradicts its own existence. The TV series, which premiered in 1957 and starred Garner and Jack Kelly as brothers Bret and Bart, was a pioneer in the deflation of frontier machismo, as well as being a fourth-wall-breaking sendup of other television shows. "Maverick" the movie, however, eschews the satirical edge—what could it possibly satirize?—while appropriating all the series' conventions: Bret's voiceover narration, the cameos (one of which is so predictable it's unpredictable), a sea of leathery old TV-

and movie-cowboy faces that amuse but never distract from the one face that the whole movie is riding on. And no, I don't mean Foster's.

The movie has a sense of humor and a lighter-than-tumbleweed storyline: Bret is $3,000 short of the entry fee for the Commodore's riverboat poker game, and on the way there picks up "legendary" lawman Zane Cooper (Garner) and Mrs. Bransford (Foster), while Angel tries to stop him. Nothing knotty, but Bret does begin his narration with a noose around his neck, astride a horse that's being menaced by rattlesnakes. And while he sits, very close to being hanged, we're taken back to the beginning of his story, with Bret aboard the donkey.

How the story then manages to include things Bret can't know about—his being cheated by the entrepreneurial Indian chief Joseph (Graham Greene), for instance, in the movie's funniest sequence—is one of the many lapses in logic audiences will just have to forgive.

Shot amid some breathtaking Arizona landscapes, "Maverick" has no problem establishing Bret as the slickest character this (that) side of the Mississippi; Gibson, after all, is playing Garner, not some fop on the frontier. He pays a gang of cowboys to let him beat them up. He avoids peril the way he would avoid a man with his own deck of cards. And he wisecracks incessantly, and self-deprecatingly. But he always rises to the occasion.

Not so Donner, and the opening poker game is a good example of how. Like many of the set pieces in a film made up of set pieces, it's funny but prolonged. Donner doesn't seem to know when to move on without an explosion to cue him in. The camera moves constantly, cutting around the poker table, to cards, to faces, and back again, although nothing is really happening. When the camera stops, the sense of dead air is oppressive.

But then, the longer Donner stalls, the longer he can delay facing the fact that there's nothing to "Maverick" except very attractive actors and motion itself. And a funny but arrogantly directionless script by William Goldman, which moves from card game to fistfight to runaway stagecoach to Indian raid to riverboat shootout with such blasé disregard for narrative logic the film becomes less an heir to "Destry Rides Again" than to "F Troop," or perhaps Wile E. Coyote.

But Gibson and Foster are fun to watch. Their's isn't a sexual chemistry as much as it is a comedic sympathy, but they cavort winningly around the contrivances of a film that lacks a lot, but has an abundance of what it takes to be a summer movie box-office blockbuster: Hilarity, on the range.

NEWSWEEK, 5/30/94, p. 64, Katrine Ames

The credits for "Maverick" say that it's "based on" the famous '50s TV series. Smart choice. If the filmmakers had opted for "inspired by," they might be in trouble. Bret Maverick is back, still a quick-draw coward in search of a card game, but on the big screen he seems oddly diminished—and not because Mel Gibson is a lot shorter than the original Bret, James Garner. What worked well in a one-hour format gets thin when it's stretched over two. Still, "Maverick" can charm, with a wonderful final plot twist and a mostly good cast.

Maverick is trying to raise the $25,000 he needs for a high-stakes poker tourney in St. Louis. Still a few thousand shy, he rides into a desert town (on a jackass—there may be a subtle point here) to call in a marker from the local banker. Before he can collect, robbers bust in and clean the place out. More or less undaunted, Maverick presses on to Missouri, joined by light-fingered Annabelle Bransford (Jodie Foster) and lawman Zane Cooper (Garner).

Director Richard Donner ("Lethal Weapon"), borrowing liberally from a dozen caper movies, paints with a brush wide enough to cover the Grand Canyon with one swipe. Writer William Goldman, usually better in this genre ("Butch Cassidy and the Sundance Kid"), stumbles: marauding Indians, for instance, turn out to be a bunch of white guys in war paint; the *real* ones, led by Graham Greene, are whooping it up for a visiting archduke. Gibson is right at home as the wise-cracking gambler, and Foster, though slightly squirmy in this burlesque, hints at a fine comic side. But it's the veteran's show. Garner wears his you-can't-put-one-over-on-me character like a pair of fine weathered boots. With his breaking half-smile, he's irresistible.

SIGHT AND SOUND, 8/94, p. 46, Phillip Kemp

About to be lynched by the villainous Angel and his gang, gambler Bret Maverick recalls the events that led to this predicament ... Maverick rides into the town of Crystal River, hoping to win the $3,000 he still needs for his $25,000 entrance stake to the Three Rivers Poker Championship. In the saloon he joins a poker game that includes Angel, adventuress Annabelle Bransford and young gunslinger Johnny Hardin. When he starts winning Maverick sets off a challenge from Hardin, but is about to have trouble with Angel when a gang of vengeful thugs burst in looking for him. He beats them all up, to general applause. That night Annabelle comes to his room, but only in an attempt to lift his wallet.

Maverick visits banker Eugene to collect a debt, but the bank is robbed and he loses his wallet. When the thugs show up demanding payment for their fake attack he gives them his last $100 and joins Annabelle on the stagecoach, where he finds her under the protection of Marshall Zane Cooper. En route they encounter missionaries who have been robbed by a gang posing as Indians. Maverick, Annabelle and Cooper track down the gang and restore the money—only for a war party of real Indians to show up. Volunteering as a sacrifice, Maverick is taken captive. The Indian chief, though, is his old friend Joseph, who owes him money and suggests that a Russian archduke, camped nearby on safari, might pay well to shoot an Indian. Maverick dresses up, pretends to be killed, and nets $1,000. Heading for the championship, he encounters Angel and his gang and is strung up, but contrives to escape ...

On board the championship's riverboat venue Maverick finds Angel and two sidekicks, also Annabelle who, like him, is still short of her full stake. Spotting the archduke, Maverick cons enough out of him to put them both in the game. Commodore Duval declares the championship open: 40 players put up $25,000 each, all guarded by Marshall Cooper. Round one eliminates everyone but Maverick, Angel, Annabelle and the Commodore. During the interval, Maverick and Annabelle make love. In the final round Maverick emerges the winner. Angel and his henchmen pull guns, but are shot down by Cooper and Maverick. Cooper then holds up everybody and makes off with the half million dollars. Later, encamped at night, he is joined by his accomplice, the Commodore, who pulls a gun on him—at which point Maverick appears, takes the money and leaves the other two squabbling. Maverick is relaxing in a New Orleans bathhouse when Cooper shows up, but turns out to be his father. As the two laugh over the scam Annabelle arrives and takes the money at gunpoint. After she's gone, Maverick reveals he still has half the money, and looks forward to getting the rest back.

"Nearly got hanged maself once," observes Alfred Molina's ripely villainous Angel, happily stringing up the hero in the opening sequence of *Maverick*—"Didn't much care for it." There's no mistaking the tone: we're back in the reassuringly disenchanted world of the latter-day comedy Western, where everyone's on the take and talks in laconic wisecracks. And if *Maverick* never quite exerts the cynical bite of the finest specimens of the genre—*The Missouri Breaks*, say, or Mankiewicz's neglected *There Was a Crooked Man*—it's entertaining, amiable and (thanks to Zsigmond's rich, burnished photography) consistently good to look at.

Perhaps inevitably, the film cleaned up a little—both morally and visually—from the classic television series it's based on. The TV *Maverick* originally screened from 1957 and including episodes directed by Budd Boetticher and Robert Altman, differed refreshingly from other teleoaters of the period in featuring a hero with no redeeming features beyond ingenuity and charm. Cowardly, devious, mercenary and wholly self-interested, James Garner's Bret Maverick was about as far from the upright Gary Cooper model as could be imagined—which of course was just what made him so appealing. His big-screen incarnation sets out the same way, but now and then succumbs to regrettable impulses of decency, like handing back a fairly earned $3,000 to a bunch of missionaries. TV Maverick, one suspects, might have made the same noble gesture—before sneaking round the back to retrieve the cash.

Still, those who feared, after *Hamlet* and *The Man Without a Face*, that Mel Gibson might be falling prone to Kevin-Costnerish solemnity should be reassured by his likeably self-mocking performance. If there's a hint of worry around the eyes, it's perhaps that Gibson sensed he was being upstaged by some very class acts indeed: Jodie Foster's sexy, feisty Annabelle; James Coburn, engagingly relaxed as ever and of course Garner, the original Maverick himself, deftly hitting just the right note as the seemingly principled lawman.

Unexpectedly, given a script by William Goldman, the film's weakness lies in its narrative structure. Not so much in the first half, with its picaresque one-damn-thing-after-another circling back to the opening scene; this kind of episodic plot has honourable antecedents in the genre, as *Maverick* acknowledges with a cheeky visual nod to Ford's *Stagecoach*. The problem lies with the ending or rather the endings, that follow the poker tournament, where each time the action seems to be winding down it gets kick-started with yet another plot twist. "When in doubt," Raymond Chandler famously advised, "have a man come through the door with a gun." It's a good trick, but shouldn't be reprised too often. As one armed character after another shows up to hijack the loot, the joke comes to feel mechanical and the laughter dies.

For most of its length, though, the film does not disappoint, least of all in its set-piece action sequences, secure in the practised hands of Richard (*Lethal Weapon*) Donner. Comfortably irreverent, *Maverick* hardly offers a fresh take on the genre, since most of the conventions it spoofs were thoroughly sent up years ago. But if, as seems likely, the long-heralded revival of the Western is at last upon us, a film like this bodes well for hours of undemanding pleasure to come.

TIME, 5/30/94, p. 60, Richard Schickel

Neither of the two brand-new, big-budget TV-derived summer movies will do you any harm, and one actually succeeds pretty well. The best (and worst) you can say about *Maverick* is that it does the job—it allows you to spend a perfectly agreeable evening without making you feel completely stupid or totally conned. The film offers us Mel Gibson as a new Bret Maverick, the Western gambler, as well as the old TV Maverick, James Garner, now playing a wry frontier sheriff. These two guys can make you smile contentedly even when the script is wandering and they're just sort of standing around waiting for its next good part to develop. Jodie Foster has to work harder as a gambling lady who exists mostly to bicker with Bret, but she's game.

The story is nothing much: Maverick trying to round up the money to enter a high-stakes poker game before it starts. Writer William Goldman (*Butch Cassidy and the Sundance Kid*) and director Richard Donner (the *Lethal Weapon* series) both seem to understand that the TV *Maverick* offered tinkly satirical relief from the other Western programs of the day, which took themselves so seriously. If the filmmakers lose the show's sharpness by converting it to the large screen with broad gestures, they can live with it. Doubtless all the rest of us can too.

The Flintstones fares better than *Maverick*. In Bedrock the finest restaurant is the Cavern on the Green. Down at the drive-in they're playing *Tar Wars*. People talk about spending a relaxing week in Rocapulco. Puns may be the lowest form of humor, but in this movie such wordplay is the only possible accompaniment for the pictureplay that runs throughout this merry story of "a modern Stone Age fam-il-ee": newspapers carved in stone; cars powered by feet; prehistoric creatures employed as primitive, parodic versions of contemporary labor-saving devices (dinosaurs are adapted to be lawn mowers, garbage disposals, even a bowling-alley pinsetter). Yes, it's business as it usually was on the old animated TV show. But nothing has been lost—or worse, inflated out of proportion—in translating the program to the big screen in a live-action version whose story, believe it or not, takes up white-collar crime, technology-induced unemployment and even the homeless.

John Goodman and Elizabeth Perkins as the eponymous heads of household, Rick Moranis and Rosie O'Donnell as the Rubbles, and Elizabeth Taylor, who plays Fred's insulting, overbearing mother-in-law, all tread a nice, comically persuasive line between caricature and naturalism under Brian Levant's direction. And while more than 30 writers worked on the screenplay and untold numbers labored to re-create the ambiance and effects that the animators once tossed off with a few squiggles of their pencils, *The Flintstones* doesn't feel overcalculated, overproduced or overthought. Nor, however, is it aimed solely at "the young and the thumbless" (to borrow the name of Bedrock's favorite soap opera). Once again, prehistory has been good to the film's producer, billed here as Steven Spielrock.

VILLAGE VOICE, 5/31/94, p. 55, J. Hoberman

Cowgirls is scarcely the season's lone Baby Boomerang. [See Hoberman's review of *Even Cowgirls Get the Blues*.] Indeed, to see the TV shows of one's childhood resurrected as hyped-up would-be blockbusters is to experience another sort of flashback, one founded on generational megalomania and cut with the strychnine of metaphysical dread.

In the days before *The Flintstones*, *Maverick* (ABC, 1957-62) ranked somewhere below Ernie Kovacs, *The Twilight Zone*, and foreign car commercials as a fount of tele-subversion. (In the novel *Even Cowgirls Get The Blues*, the child Jellybean Bonanza is introduced eating beef jerky and watching a rerun.) Maverick's creator-producer Roy Huggins may not have been the Tom Robbins of 1957, but his series was the most iconoclastic of TV westerns—in part because it declined to present its charming antihero as anything resembling a father figure.

Huggins, who subsequently developed such wise guy series as *77 Sunset Strip*, *Hawaiian Eye*, and *The Rockford Files*, called gambler Bret Maverick "the original disorganization man" and invited his writers and directors (who included Budd Boetticher and Robert Altman) to "live dangerously." That's not much of an issue with the new *Maverick*, a mega poker western directed with hectic indifference by hack supremo Richard Donner and, per *Premiere* puff, evincing "as close to a lock on summer-blockbuster status as Hollywood science can formulate." The movie plays its own generational card—with Mel Gibson in the role originated by James Garner, while finding room in its heart for the aged Garner as well.

Assigned the role of baby-sitting his younger self, Garner seems perpetually bemused. Gibson's Maverick is a sunny, self-deprecating, duplicitous dude—although the tacky miracle that allows him to escape sure death is the only bit that justifies *Life*'s description of the original Mav as "a lazy, sneaky, poker-playing vagrant [who] survives only through skulduggery or dumb luck [and] can be bamboozled or robbed by his best friend or his own brother or almost any passing female." Female, in this case, is a kittenish Jodie Foster, doing comedy for the first time since *Freaky Friday* and flacking the flick with the devotion another star might reserve for religious conversion, Not exactly what you'd call a cowgirl, Foster is corsetted into a sequinned Belle Starr ensemble, but, if too often reduced to a living reaction-shot, still animates Donner's somnolent compositions with a variety of flutters, flounces, twitches, squints, and wiggles.

With William Goldman's script drawing as much on his scenarios for *Butch Cassidy and The Sundance Kid* and *The Sting* as its TV namesake, nothing here is what it seems. Basically a succession of hotfoots and schoolyard gags, some suggesting a frontier *Naked Gun*, *Maverick* is one long game of charade. Everybody, including bank robbers and redskins, is some sort of cute phony. The ersatz Americana climaxes with an improbably integrated poker game on a Mississippi paddleboat; the movie winds up insisting on a magic formula so desperately simpleminded it makes Tom Robbins's formula *ha ha ho ho hee hee* seem mysterious as the cabala.

Also reviewed in:
CHICAGO TRIBUNE, 5/20/94, Friday/p. C, Michael Wilmington
NEW REPUBLIC, 6/20/94, p. 26, Stanley Kauffmann
NEW YORK TIMES, 5/20/94, p. C1, Caryn James
NEW YORKER, 6/6/94, p. 92, Terrence Rafferty
VARIETY, 5/16-22/94, p. 38, Leonard Klady

ME AND THE MOB

An Arrow Releasing presentation of a R.S.V.P. Productions Inc. production. *Producer:* Frank Rainone. *Director:* Frank Rainone. *Screenplay:* Rocco Simonelle, James Lorinz, and Frank Rainone. *Director of Photography:* Adam Kimmel. *Editor:* Michelle Gorchow. *Music:* Doug Katsaros. *Production Designer:* Susan Bolles. *Running time:* 86 minutes. *MPAA Rating:* Not Rated.

CAST: James Lorinz (Jimmy Corona); Sandra Bullock (Lori); Tony Darrow (Tony Bando); Anthony Michael Hall (Jimmy's Friend); Stephen Lee (Bobby Blitzer); Ted Sorel (George Stellaris); Vinny Pastore (Aldo Badamo); Frank Aquilino (Joey Tantillo); John Costelloe (Billy "Bink-Bink" Borelli).

NEW YORK POST, 9/23/94, p. 48, Larry Worth

At the outset of "Me and the Mob," a struggling author is trying to sell a JFK assassination book that claims Oswald was spurned by Marilyn Monroe, motivating him to shoot Kennedy.

Without doubt, that would have been a better story than anything which follows.

Instead, the lame script has the fledgling writer infiltrating the Mafia via his wise-guy uncle, with the intent of penning a firsthand account of Cosa Nostra comings and cement-shoed goings. The supposedly riotous results should have been rubbed out in the editing room.

Maybe first-time director Frank Rainone thought he was lensing the comic answer to "GoodFellas." But the closest he comes to the mob scene is having his product smell like dead fish.

Having also penned the script with Rocco Simonelle and James Lorinz (the unappealing lead actor with more forehead than Telly "Savalas), Rainone shows a distinct absence of anything akin to comic timing.

The only thing that's funny is why actress Sandra Bullock (Keanu Reeves' main squeeze in "Speed") would embarrass herself as a sex-crazed floozy. She doesn't even chew gum here with conviction. Equally awful is Steve Buscemi as a neighborhood crackpot. But at least he was smart enough to go without a screen credit.

The rest of the cast is peopled by unimpressive newcomers, like the aforementioned Lorinz and Tony Darrow's by-the-numbers bit as the hero's expletive-spouting uncle.

The only bright spot to "Me and the Mob" is that it's sure to pull a Jimmy Hoffa and disappear without a trace.

NEWSDAY, 9/23/94, Part II/p. B9, Gene Seymour

"Me and the Mob" is a mess but the ramshackle goofiness permeating director Frank Rainone's first feature saves it from being a total waste of time.

Its protagonist is Jimmy Corona (James Lorinz), a writer groping desperately for a subject, any subject. After a humiliating harangue by his agent (a pretty funny sequence), Jimmy is told by his girlfriend-muse Lori (Sandra Bullock) that she's moving out of his life. She brushes him off in the most exotic fashion possible, leaving Jimmy alone with his blocked creativity and his mounting debts. And when Bullock leaves, she takes much of the movie's electricity with her.

Jimmy's so hapless he can't even kill himself after several tries. Then just as he's about to barbecue himself in his bathtub, he remembers a job offer made by his mob-connected Uncle Tony (Tony Darrow), known to feds and fellow wise-guys as "Tony Dead Presidents" because of the prodigious wad of bills he flashes.

Figuring to get a true-crime expose in the bargain, Jimmy decides to accept Uncle Tony's offer to work as "mechanic." Tony puts Jimmy under the supervision of a thumb-breaker named Billy (Bink-Bink) Borelli (John Costelloe) who rolls dice in a Yahtzee cup to give his victims a sporting chance to save their lives. (He kills them anyway.)

Jimmy proves to be as much of a luckless klutz in the underworld as he is in the literary marketplace. After a hit goes awry, he gets nailed by a police strike force and is forced to wear a wire at the next private powwow of Tony and the "fellas."

The strike force's funds are so limited that Jimmy's sub-standard equipment picks up AM radio signals during the meeting. His cover blown, Jimmy's fate is sealed when the nymphomaniac daughter of Tony's boss reveals her night of blissful S&M with the doomed-to-sleep-with-fishes writer.

Even after all this, the story takes increasingly ludicrous turns, as if Rainone and company couldn't figure out a way to end the thing and let it run itself into a shambles. Picking one's way around the debris, however, it's possible to glimpse the kind of comic talent Rainone could become with time, more money and a better script.

VILLAGE VOICE, 10/4/94, p. 64, Evelyn McDonnell

What with Quentin Tarantino running amok in our nation's theaters, gangster movies are due for a good spoofing. The most I can say for *Me and the Mob* is it tries. One of the film's funnier scenes lampoons *Reservoir Dogs*: A bunch of thugs argue about executing a man trussed in a chair; in the pseudotense standoff, they point their guns at each other. The sudden appearance of a moving object triggers their nerves and unnerves their triggers—shots ring out. When the smoke clears a cat has been executed and the hostage has died of a heart attack.

Me and the Mob, the first feature film by New York native Frank Rainone, is told in classic detective-film voiceover by lead character Jimmy Corona (James Lorinz), a journalist whose desperate search for a good book idea leads him from hack writing to hacking. He joins his mobster uncle Tony (Tony Darrow), and after some Stooge-ish antics, finally proves himself to the bad guys, only to double-cross them. Like many of the movie's gags, the convoluted plot is almost clever.

Me and the Mob grew out of a short called *Writer's Block* conceived by Rainone and Lorinz, but the pair don't have the wit to pull off 86 minutes of satire, and take themselves too seriously for slapstick. I can't decide which makes this film more amateurish: Lorinz's Michael J. Fox-with-stubble acting job or Rainone's dank, ugly shooting. Not even a cameo by Sandra Bullock can salvage this film. Her performance as Corona's fuck-thing—I won't elevate her role with the label girlfriend—shows you the level of fantasy at which these guys operate. Lori comes home in sexy underwear and mechanical screws Corona while telling him she's dumping him because he's such a failure. Coming (so to speak) barely 10 minutes into the film, the scene is cringingly crass—even for this self-identified fan of *Kentucky Fried Movie* and *The Naked Gun*. Maybe it's up to a woman director to deflate the hypermasculinity of the gangster genre without resorting to jiggle appeal. Will a female Mel Brooks please step up?

Also reviewed in:
NEW YORK TIMES, 9/23/94, p. C10, Janet Maslin

MI VIDA LOCA (MY CRAZY LIFE)

A Sony Pictures Classics release of an HBO Showcase production in association with Cineville, Inc. *Executive Producer:* Christopher Henkeland and Colin Callender. *Producer:* Daniel Hassid and Carl-Jan Colpaert. *Director:* Allison Anders. *Screenplay:* Allison Anders. *Director of Photography:* Rodrigo Garcia. *Editor:* Richard Chew. *Music:* John Taylor. *Music Editor:* Carlton Kaller and Bill Black. *Choreographer:* Maria Leone. *Sound:* Mary Jo Devenney. *Casting:* Betsy Fels. *Production Designer:* Jane Stewart. *Art Director:* Bradley Wisham. *Set Designer:* Chris Miller. *Set Decorator:* Cindy Johnson. *Set Dresser:* Steven Rick, Scott Dangerfield, and Ryan Wilson. *Costumes:* Susan Bertram. *Make-up:* Jay A. Wijebe. *Stunt Coordinator:* Eddie Perez. *Running time:* 92 minutes. *MPAA Rating:* R.

CAST: Angel Aviles (Sad Girl); Seidy Lopez (Mousie); Jacob Vargas (Ernesto); Marlo Marron (Giggles); Jessie Borrego (El Duran); Magali Alvarado (La Blue Eyes); Julian Reyes (Big Sleepy); Bertilla Damas (Rachel); Art Esquer (Shadow); Christina Solis (Baby Doll); Rick Salinas (Efren); Gabriel Gonzalez (Sleepy); Danny Trejo (Frank); Rosa Segura (Dimples); Salma Hayek (Gata); Noah Verduzeo (Chuco); John Rangel (Snoopy); Panchito Gomez (Joker Bird); Maurice Bernard (Creeper); Eddie Perez (Sir Speedy); Marita De Leon and Alexis Midrano (River Valley Girls); Leigh Hamilton (Social Worker); Terri Phillips (Trendy Girl); Carlos Rivas (Sad Girl's Day); Kid Frost (Mousie's Dad); Nelida Lopez (Whisper); Brittany Parkin (Gracilla); Guy Boyd (Priest); Cesario Montano (Squeaky), Sissy Boyd (Tia Elena); Jessica Estrada (Young Sad Girl); Gloria Gibson (Young Mousie); Eliana Alexander (Mousie's Mother); Tomassa Santiago (Ernesto's Aburlita); Carlos Rivas (Sad Girl's Father); Gloria Vargas and Rubens Valenzuela (Big Sleeping Kids); Alexis Midrano (Crystal); Adrian Amano (Jennifer); Alexander Stephano (Mailman).

LOS ANGELES TIMES, 7/22/94, Calendar/p. 4, Kevin Thomas

Within the first few minutes of the well-meaning but misguided "Mi Vida Loca," we've come to know two appealing Latinas, Sad Girl (Angel Aviles) and Mousie (Seidy Lopez), who've been friends from childhood, growing up in Echo Park and joining a gang, a kind of ladies' auxiliary for the local male gang. But now Sad Girl and Mousie have become deadly enemies, all set for a potentially fatal showdown to resolve their rivalry for the same young man, Ernesto (Jacob Vargas), who has fathered a child out of wedlock with each of them.

Ernesto, who's moved from grocery clerking to drug dealing, however, is shot fatally by a disgruntled customer, one of the "white" women he holds in such contempt, before his own women can gun each other down. They mourn Ernesto, but their mutual relief is tremendous: Now they don't have to try to kill each other anymore and can go back to being best friends.

What's going on here? Two life-long friends, both with infants prepared to snuff out each other's lives all because of their love for a glib charmer whom we have every reason to assume would take up with yet another woman in a flash. Can their gang's code of behavior have them in such an iron grip that they cannot conceive an alternative to such a drastic course of action?

Writer-director Allison Anders, who made such a mark with the knowing "Gas Food Lodging," has treated this entire episode with a deft, rueful, suspenseful humor, but goes on to confirm rather than dispel our impression that these two young women and all their friends are none too bright. One young woman, a college student who's avoided gang life, goes off into delirious flights of romantic fancy over her epistolary romance with a prisoner she has never even met. With all good intentions, Anders has ended up confirming a decidedly negative stereotype of young Latinos as aimless, dangerous, and incapable of thinking for themselves, not to mention welfare-dependent. As a result, "Mi Vida Loca" is downright offensive.

What Anders meant to do is clear enough: to show a bunch of young Latinos gradually grasping that they can only count upon each other in the face of the dire mortality rate of their young men and to start considering questioning those men to whom they are so blindly obedient. Yet when one of their friends, Giggles (Marlo Marron), comes out of prison after four years for having taken a rap for her boyfriend, saying self-consciously that "Computers are the key to the future," the effect of her statement is comical when it should seem serious to us, if not her friends.

You respect Anders' impulse not to judge, but her context and characters are simply too shallow not to make most everyone seem foolish. While it has gorgeous camera work (by "Danzon's" Rodrigo Garcia) and some great music, "Mi Vida Loca" desperately needs to suggest the impact of the historical, social, economic, religious and cultural forces that shape the lives of these young women and their behavior and values. It just isn't enough to depict their touching loyalty to each other and their loving devotion to their children.

Do they have dreams or aspirations? Did they ever have jobs or want them? (None seem to be employed.) How much pressure is there on them to join gangs? Is criminal activity an individual affair or organized or both? Is there no viable alternative to gangs in the community? How easy or difficult is it to leave them? Do these homegirls and homeboys ever do much of anything except hang out? In the entire group is there not a single individual capable of making a concentrated effort to escape gang life and its perils? Or are the forces of discrimination, the lack of opportunity, chronic poverty, so overwhelming that they feel their situation is hopeless?

You sense that Anders wanted to make another film like "Gas Food Lodging" in praise of female solidarity in the face of male unreliability, but when the women are Latina gang girls she trivializes them by avoiding all the questions their identity and situation inescapably raise. (Curiously, the press book for the film has far more substance, more enlightenment, than the film itself).

More than anything else, "Mi Vida Loca" makes the case for how important it is that ethnic and minority filmmakers get the opportunity to tell the stories of their own people.

NEW YORK POST, 7/15/94, p. 39, Michael Medved

"Mi Vida Loca/My Crazy Life" is a solemn, slice-of-life, inner-city melodrama that wants you to accept its major shortcomings as courageous virtues.

In her comments about the film, writer-director Allison Anders seems to suggest that the lack of a coherent plot, the clumsy dialogue and occasionally amateurish acting all advance the cause of authenticity. She even includes a special category in the credit: "Real Homegirls" and "Homeboys' Playing Themselves."

Despite the Spanish title, the script is entirely in English and focuses on a group of Latina single mothers and gang members living on welfare in the colorful Echo Park neighborhood of Los Angeles. "Sad Girl" (Angel Aviles) and "Mousie" (Seidy Lopez) both bear children to the same charming teen-aged drug dealer (Jacob Vargas). But only after he's gunned down are the two women able to forget their rivalry and renew their friendship.

They spend most of the rest of the film trying to decide what to do with "Suavecity," the lovingly customized and brightly painted van that represents the dead boy's major legacy.

Later, their circle of sisterhood is strengthened when a slightly older woman, "Giggles", (Marlo Marron) gets out of jail and inspires her friends with her wisdom and insight. "Men come and go," she declares. "We girls need new skills because by the time our guys are 21 they're dead or in prison or disabled or sh _ _."

One of the problems with the picture is that it never helps you to understand why its bright and attractive female characters are in any way drawn to the lazy, selfish, stupid, gross and worthless men in their lives.

Is Anders suggesting that such pathetic losers are the only males to be found in the Mexican-American barrios of Los Angeles?

Though most of the cast of virtual unknowns seem awkward in front of the camera, two of them display real star power. Puerto Rican-born Magali Alvarado plays an innocent college girl known as "La Blue Eyes" with extraordinary delicacy, while Marlo Marron as "Giggles" not only delivers her preachy lines with panache, but ignites every scene in which she appears with her extraordinary beauty, grace and intensity.

As in her prior effort, "Gas Food Lodging," an overpraised film festival favorite from 1992, director Anders (who grew up in rural Kentucky) displays a rare eye for color and nuance and establishes a sense of place so flavorful you can almost taste it.

It's a shame that her laudable determination to explore the world of the barrio led to one-dimensional cliches of thugs-and-drugs—which continue to be the only way that Hollywood seems ready to confront the hugely varied, and far more hopeful, lives of this country's nearly 20 million Latinos.

NEWSDAY, 7/15/94, Part II/p. B10, Jack Mathews

In "Mi Vida Loca My Crazy Life," writer-director Allison Anders continues the highly personal examination of single motherhood she began with her award-winning first feature "Gas Food Lodging," which revolved around the lives of truck stop waitress and her two teenage daughters in New Mexico.

Anders, who grew up in a fatherless family and has been alone in raising her own children, knew the emotional terrain, and though she adapted "Gas Food Lodging" from a novel, it had a raw, unsentimental honesty about it that seemed to spring directly from her heart to the screen.

For her second film, Anders simply looked around her, at the young women pushing strollers through her predominantly Latino neighborhood of Echo Park in Los Angeles, mothers of children whose fathers are either dead or in prison, and saw another cycle of despair being repeated.

"Mi Vida Loca My Crazy Life" plunges us into that community, telling three interrelated stories about the struggles of some of these mothers in an environment where surviving drugs, gangs and drive-by shootings is the everyday challenge their children will face.

Anders again has a sharp, empathetic eye for what her characters are going through, and "Mi Vida Loca" gives us a different view of barrio life than we've seen before. But this time, Anders' heart got caught up on her sleeve, and her three thin stories collapse under all their earnest sociology. She's made something like a dramatized term paper.

The first of Anders' three stories is about the rivalry that develops between life-long best friends Sad Girl (Angel Aviles) and Mousie (Seidy Lopez), both of whom become pregnant by the same amiable drug dealer, Ernesto (Jacob Vargas). The second focuses on Giggles (Marlo Marron), a prison parolee determined to learn a skill and escape the barrio with her young daughter. The third introduces Giggles' sister, La Blue Eyes (Magali Alvarado), a shy loner who has idealized a pen pal romance with an imprisoned gang leader called El Duran (Jessie Borrego).

The device that ultimately ties the three stories together is a show-quality pickup truck bearing the colorful scroll "Suavecito." It's a symbol of pride to Ernesto's gang, and much desired by El Duran's. In their macho, trigger-happy world, it's literally to die for.

Anders obviously doesn't have much interest in the surface of these stories. She wants to get at the issues facing her four women, at their cultural dependence on undependable men, and the virtual inevitability of single parenthood. As a result, she talks the subject to death. The film is made up almost entirely of static voice-over scenes, or conversations, all telegraphing her dramatic punches.

You can admire her restraint in keeping most of the violence off-camera, but it is, after all, a violent world she's depicting, and to show only the reactions to those events is to defuse their power.

Anders got the title right. It is a crazy life, and pretty hopeless, one where girls and boys grow up under the rituals of gang life and follow the same self-destructive paths as their mothers and fathers.

"We've got to grow up some time," says one of the more reflective youths, "get a plan for the future."

That's the answer, all right, but having the movie's theme laid out in a line of dialogue underscores the filmmaker's immaturity. Movies aren't a show-and-tell medium, they're just show. Anders, who obviously has a lot to say on this subject, needs to overcome the urge to come right out and say it.

SIGHT AND SOUND, 4/95, p. 48, Leslie Felperin

Sad Girl and Mousie, two Chicana teenagers, are members of Echo Park Home Girl gang in Los Angeles. Once best friends, they have fallen out over Ernesto, a local drug dealer who has fathered children by both of them. Without telling either of them, he buys a custom-built Mini Truck called Suavecito, which El Duran, a rival gangster from River Valley, feels is rightfully his. Sad Girl and Mousie meet to fight a duel of honour, but they finally relent. At exactly the same moment, Ernesto is killed by a customer, and his assistant, Whisper, wounded in the leg. The boys' gang blames El Duran and swears revenge.

The girls go to collect a former gang member, Giggles, released from prison. To their horror, she talks of going straight and getting a job. Giggles soon becomes romantically involved with Sleepy, the custom car artist responsible for Suavecito's design. Mousie and Sad Girl find out where the boys have hidden the truck. At a gang meeting, they decide to sell it to raise money for their children and Whisper's hospital bills. Meanwhile, the boys' gang, who planned to enter the truck in a custom car rally, discover it is missing and assume El Duran has stolen it.

Sad Girl's sister Alicia (nicknamed 'La Blue Eyes') is devastated when her penpal, Juan Temido—a recently released prisoner—stops writing to her. Knowing him to be a notorious philander, the girls take Alicia to a dance where she will meet him and discover what a cad he really is. But Juan is really El Duran, and just as Alicia discovers his true identity, Ernesto's brother shoots him dead. Later, the gang learns that Suavecito was borrowed by a boy who wrecked it in an accident. In a drive-by hit intended for Ernesto's brother. Sleepy's young daughter is killed by El Duran's girlfriend. All assemble at the concluding funeral.

In her feature debut, *Gas Food Lodging*, director Allison Anders explored a downmarket but poetically rendered *demi monde* of trailer parks and roadside diners, located somewhere between *Bagdad Café* and *Paris, Texas* (the film on which she cut her teeth as a production assistant after deluging Wim Wenders with fan letters and requests for work). *Mi Vida Loca* finds similar territory in an urban setting, Los Angeles' Echo Park, once the home of bungalow-dwelling movie stars in the 20s and now the stomping ground of the dispossessed Hispanic Community.

As she did in her earlier films, Anders pivots the plot around the lives of single mothers and working class women, celebrating female friendship as a balm to the callous damage inflicted by men. Depicting a milieu seldom seen in mainstream films and giving voice to speakers rarely heard (voice-overs by several characters narrate the film throughout), Anders sets herself a difficult task: balancing verisimilitude with a more personal elegiac vision. *Mi Vida Loca* often comes precariously close to collapsing under the weight of these aspirations. Nonetheless, such an aesthetic tension is necessary to encode the genetic blueprint of the 'individual in conflict with neighbourhood' plot in visual terms. *Mean Streets* is the obvious template here (Far more so than the closer-to-home *Boyz N the Hood*) evoking an elliptical style of narration, indirectly through the use of voice-overs. Yet, where Scorsese's work springs from autobiography, Anders' seems to be more painstakingly constructed from pre-production research.

Anders casts members of real gangs (under whose protection the film was made) in some major roles, such as Whisper the teenage drug baroness. Consequently, certain performances are stiff and paradoxically unnatural. Yet, what it loses in performative polish, is more than compensated for by accurate dress, language, setting and car design.

Trying hard not to patronise its subjects, *Mi Vida Loca* feels at times like a dramatised article by eminent LA social geographer, Mike Davis. Poverty, discrimination, police harassment and a culture of violence are all duly noted and accounted for, resulting in such painfully preachy speeches as: "We girls need new skills 'cause by the time our boys are 21, they're either in prison, disabled or dead. That's fucked up, but that's the way it is." Yet the film is not so naïvely didactic that it forgets to show the speaker, Giggles (a fine performance by newcomer Marlo Marron), despairingly perusing an application for a job she knows she will never get. It's easy to be scathing about the banal sentimentality and confused moral sense of these and other speeches, especially the concluding lines "Women don't use pistols to prove a point, women use weapons for love", but even easier to forget that sometimes people talk like this, especially women reared on cheap romance and the religion of the gun.

Mi Vida Loca is redeemed by its many well-observed touches. When Sad Girl and Mousie remember how they were so close that even their periods were synchronised, or the gang refuses to raise their hands to signal their assent because it reminds them of school, the sense of authenticity blazes with warmth. Realism is often assuaged by an evocative use of slow-motion and contrapuntal editing. The soundtrack of classic Latin pop and original music is worth the price of admission alone. *Mi Vida Loca* manages to be a female-centered film without an overbearingly feminist political agenda. Indeed, the homegirls are often enduringly sexist, a point especially well illustrated in a witty ensemble scene in McDonald's where a discussion about men serves almost as a riposte to the 'Like a Virgin' dialogue in *Reservoir Dogs*. Anders is to collaborate with Tarantino in the forthcoming portmanteau film, *Four Rooms*. Like him, Anders has an instinctive feel for low-life dialogue and a taste for experimental narration that still needs polish, but she also shows tremendous promise.

TIME, 9/12/94, p. 86, Richard Corliss

[*Mi Vida Loca/My Crazy Life* was reviewed jointly with *Clerks*; see Corliss' review of that film.]

VILLAGE VOICE, 7/19/94, p. 54, Gary Indiana

Mi Vida Loca is another film that promises, on the face of it, to resemble a lot of other movies, namely the ubiquitous gritty urban dramas depicting life in the hood that've popped up in the past few years. I confess to a severe allergic reaction to such movies, which tend to show an assortment of vivid young black and Latino males breathing undeserved vitality into really stale, formulaic celebrations of violence, with the added, pushy insistence that they're really about race relations and poverty and therefore about America in an epic metaphorical way. This indie outpost of the apocalyptic imagination offers no worse but generally little better than the average Hollywood no-brainer, which is fine, but I think any viewer can be forgiven for finding the gangsta sensibility less than cosmically portentous. It has, for one thing, too much bilious testosterone spraying out of it to be taken that seriously.

Mi Vida Loca, then, has the depressingly rare originality to be an actual work of art, with no interest in extorting claims of political importance or other kinds of egregious critical generosity. In its quiet but very forceful way, *Mi Vida Loca* presents interwoven lives in a particular neighborhood—the predominantly Latino Echo Park area of Los Angeles—as they've developed from childhood to young adulthood, among women whose first notion of real life involves attaching themselves to men who are, in the film's words, "in prison, disabled, or dead by the time they're 21."

This is not a "girl movie," though its main characters are women and its major theme is the way these women bond, become rivals, sisters, and role models for each other; the young males in *Mi Vida Loca* are also richly drawn, sometimes remarkably sweet as well as irresponsible, violent, and driven by absurd and intractable codes of masculinity. Though it's set in a milieu that many outsiders might view as hopeless, *Mi Vida Loca* wins us over almost instantly with its display of what makes daily life interesting and pleasurable in Echo Park: youthful energy, children, cars, love, food, decoration.

Dope, guns, gang shootings, territorial codes, heartbreak, mourning, and poverty are conspicuous parts of this life as well. Director Allison Anders's approach, however, is to range over all of it with a delicate mixture of fatalism and narrative spell-casting that has less in common with, say, *Boyz N the Hood* than with Juan Rulfo's haunting montage of posthumous voices in the great novel *Pedro Paramo*. Indeed, many of the characters who speak to us in voice-over here, telling about their childhood wishes, the friends they've made and lost, and the important events of their lives, turn out to be dead, the ghosts of a neighborhood that indeed gets worse as it gets older. But life goes on.

Like *Spanking the Monkey, Mi Vida Loca* is as notable for what it isn't as for what it is. Here too, a plot synopsis would give little indication of its virtues, though *Mi Vida Loca* is quite adventurously knit together, as dreamlike in its narrative locutions as Buñuel's *The Phantom of Liberty*. It begins with two women, Sad Girl and Mousie, who successively have babies by Ernesto, a small-scale, mildly lovable dope dealer. First one and then the other woman narrates the tale of their ruptured friendship; *Mi Vida Loca* begins to look like one kind of movie, but then Ernesto narrates, too, his story segueing to another person's, and another's. Anders pulls these threads together just tightly enough that they circle the same center, leaving enough slack for the characters to grow and change slightly while they're out of frame, For a film that deals with mortal events and daily horrors, *Mi Vida Loca* is almost relaxed in its pacing, proceeding with stately assurance from an opening in a graveyard to its conclusion in the same graveyard. Most movies about life in the hood indict the fact that their characters aren't really going anywhere; this film reminds us that wherever anyone is going, we all end up in the same place.

Also reviewed in:
CHICAGO TRIBUNE, 8/12/94, Friday/p. C, Michael Wilmington
NEW YORK TIMES, 7/15/94, p. C5, Caryn James
VARIETY, 6/7/93, p. 40, Todd McCarthy
WASHINGTON POST, 8/5/94, p. C1, Hal Hinson

MIDNIGHT EDITION

A Shapiro Glickenhaus Entertainment release of a Libov/Epstein production. *Producer:* Ehud Epstein and Jonathan Cordish. *Director:* Howard Libov. *Screenplay:* Michael Stewart, Yuri Zeltser, and Howard Libov. *Based on the autobiography "Escape of My Dead Man" by:* Charles Postell. *Director of Photography:* Alik Sakharov. *Editor:* Yosef Grunfeld. *Music:* Murray Attaway. *Sound:* Palmer Norris. *Casting:* Ann Mongan. *Production Designer:* Guy Tuttle. *Costumes:* Mary-An Ceo. *Running time:* 97 minutes. *MPAA Rating:* R.

CAST: Will Patton (Jack Travers); Michael De Luise (Darryl Weston); Clare Wren (Sarah Travers); Sarabeth Tucek (Becky); Nancy Moore Atchinson (Maggie).

NEW YORK POST, 4/1/94, p. 38, Bill Hoffmann

One of the ink-stained rules of journalism is: Never get involved with the person you're writing about.

It also stands to reason you shouldn't sleep with your subject's girlfriend or help him escape from jail.

But that's exactly what Jack Travers—a troubled, egocentric reporter for a small daily paper in backwoods Georgia—does in a misguided effort to jump-start his stalled career.

He's also trying to patch up his failed marriage.

Travers' descent into unethical behavior and madness is the intriguing premise of "Midnight Edition," an unsettling, taut little thriller which is based on a true story.

Travers sets up exclusive interviews with baby-faced Darryl Weston, the town's most infamous villain, who at age 19 has just blown away an entire farming family.

He's quickly drawn in by Weston's twisted, roguish charm and sees his sick story as a ticket to stardom.

But Weston uses his new friend's weaknesses to procure drugs and booze, exchanging them for exclusives, women and eventual madness.

The reporter's obsession with Weston grows deeper and darker, until the issue becomes how far he will go to keep him out of the electric chair.

As writer and murderer, respectively, Will Patton and Michael DeLuise are solid throughout.

Unfortunately, the script is unflinchingly grim and sometimes choppy, which tends to make the picture less involving.

Just what makes Travers tick is also a bit of a mystery. We seem to know more about what motivates the killer, and that's nearly a showstopper.

One fine supporting role must be noted. Nancy Moore Atchinson, playing Travers' precocious 11-year-old daughter, Maggie, deservedly steals every scene she's in and is nearly worth the price of admission,

First-time director Libov is a graduate of New York University film school and the American Film Institute.

Like many college-trained moviemakers, Libov tends to lean too heavily on showy camera work and arty special effects.

But in handling his cast Libov does have his feet firmly on the ground. His direction is commanding and the script, which he co-wrote, avoids the cliches of the genre. I look forward to his next effort.

NEWSDAY, 4/1/94, Part II/p. B7, Jonathan Mandell

In "Midnight Edition," billed as psychological thriller, a young man holds hands in prayer—ominously—around a dinner table with the farm family that has welcomed him into their home

We know this is ominous because the scene is photographed darkly, and the score sounds like an amplified heartbeat. Sure enough, suddenly, the man gets up from the table, takes out a handgun, and, in slow motion, he inexplicably shoots them dead, accompanied by close-ups of the blood-spattered dinnerware.

At about the same time, a big-city reporter has returned to the area to work on his small southern hometown newspaper in order to salvage his marriage.

It is inevitable in movies such as this that the lives of the reporter and the killer will soon intersect. When reporter Jack Travers (Will Patton, who is usually the one to play the psychopaths, as in "No Way Out") pays the first of many visits on death row to interview the captured 19-year-old killer Darryl Weston (Michael DeLuise, heartthrob son of Dom), "Midnight Edition" makes some implicit promises. Like "In Cold Blood," which treated a similar real-life rural massacre, the film will offer some psychological insight into a murderer, and perhaps provide a statement against capital punishment. Or, like "Silence of the Lambs," it will present a gripping mind game with a murderer.

"Midnight Edition" delivers none of this. Supposedly "loosely based" on real-life journalist Charles Postell's autobiography, the film focuses not on the victims or on the murderer but on the reporter, and the ways in which he is duped and corrupted in his pursuit of the biggest story of his life. When we hear him say "I *write* about killers ... That's where I draw the line," we know he is already crossing it.

Maybe this would work better if Will Patton didn't grin so lamely all the time, or if he didn't keep on saying "I'm trying to do my job," or if by the end the plot made any sense. Unlike a thriller like "The Fugitive," the movie does not sacrifice logic for excitement—but only because there is very little excitement.

In a season that has already brought us "The Paper," how many more movies do we need in which the reporter is given more attention than anything he writes about—and far more than he deserves?

VILLAGE VOICE, 4/12/94, p. 62, Lawrence Chua

A potboiler that barely simmers, *Midnight Edition* could be an intriguing pulp thriller if it weren't so flat. This tepid first film unfolds in a discreet Southern town where very cute and very crazy Darryl Weston (Michael De Luise) effortlessly murders an entire household, disrupting the region's bucolic charm. Newspaper hack Jack Travers (Will Patton) has come back to the town to save his own failing marriage, and winds up covering the case for the local paper. After his black partner is gunned down (by—surprise—the local black police chief), 19-year-old Darryl is collared. Jack and the electric chair-bound Darryl forge a vaguely intimate relationship and discover they share several things in common. For one, both grew up without knowing their fathers. Jack continues to report the case, rejuvenating his reputation, but his association with Darryl threatens his marriage. Jack, entranced by Darryl's story, or his stylish haircut, wants to keep him alive for the book, and presumably the movie deal that will follow. Darryl manipulates Jack into helping him escape from jail.

Midnight Edition can't accommodate the richness of its premise: a writer becomes part of the story he's writing. The town's ambience, the characters' racial and sexual ambivalence, and other intrapersonal tensions are steamrolled by the film's blunt sermonizing on the evils of not belonging to a strong patriarchal tradition. "I wanted something in there, something I never had ..." Darryl oozes, remembering the night he offed that happy Southern family over a chicken and biscuit dinner. Even under the burdens of such lugubrious dialogue, the mosquito-weight characters threaten to fly away at the slightest suggestion of real depth. The voluptuous young woman who wants to have Darryl's children observes, "He's so intense, he's beautiful, he's got perfect teeth." But not even Darryl's pearly whites can save this toothless narrative.

Also reviewed in:
NEW YORK TIMES, 4/1/94, p. C18, Stephen Holden
VARIETY, 12/27/93, p. 53, Lisa Nesselson

MILK MONEY

A Paramount Pictures release of a Kennedy/Marshall production. *Executive Producer:* Patrick Palmer and Michael Finnell. *Producer:* Kathleen Kennedy and Frank Marshall. *Director:* Richard Benjamin. *Screenplay:* John Mattson. *Director of Photography:* David Watkin. *Editor:* Jacqueline Cambas. *Music:* Michael Convertino. *Music Editor:* Ken Wannberg and Richard Whitfield. *Choreographer:* Adam Shankman. *Sound:* Richard Lightstone and (music): Dennis Sands. *Sound Editor:* Alan Robert Murray and Mike Dobie. *Casting:* Mary Goldberg and Amy Lippens. *Production Designer:* Paul Sylbert. *Set Designer:* Antoinette J. Gordon. *Set Decorator:* Casey Hallenbeck. *Set Dresser:* Charlotte Garnell. *Special Effects:* Alan E. Lorimer. *Costumes:* Theoni V. Aldredge. *Costumes (Melanie Griffith):* Nava Riva Sadan. *Make-up:* Richard Arias. *Make-up (Melanie Griffith):* Naomi Donne. *Body Make-up (Melanie Griffith):* Nadege Schoenfeld. *Stunt Coordinator:* Rocky Capella and R.A. Rondell. *Running time:* 110 minutes. *MPAA Rating:* PG-13.

CAST: Melanie Griffith (V); Ed Harris (Dad); Michael Patrick Carter (Frank); Malcolm McDowell (Waltzer); Anne Heche (Betty); Casey Siemaszko (Cash); Philip Bosco (Jerry the Pope); Brian Christopher (Kevin); Adam LaVorgna (Brad); Kevin Scannell (Mr. Clean); Jessica Wesson (Stacey); Amanda Sharkey (Holly); Margaret Nagle (Mrs. Fetch); Kati Powell (Mrs. Clean); Tom Coop (Holly's Brother); Gregory Procaccino (Man/Thief); Andrea Afanador (Gaggle Member); John Alvin (Rich Old Guy); Jack Arwine (Senior Citizen on Street); Ann Baker (Checker at Grocery Store); Matt Behan (Little Kid); Michael Conn (Little Kid's Dad); Tony D. Davis (Taxi Driver); Annie Fitzpatrick (Busineswoman); Roger Grooms (Businessman); Mary Scott Gudaitis (Housewife); Lou Headley (Old Man); Aaron Jollay, Jason Mathes and Howard Newstate (Nerds); James P. Kisicki (City Official); Jacquelyn K. Kotch (Woman); Julia Montgomery (Stacey's Mom); William John Murphy (Sheriff);

Mark W. Pennell (Holly's Dad); Ann Reskin (Holly's Mom); Don Roberts (Larry the Neighbor); William L. Schwarber (Tow Truck Driver); Lisa Stephan (Little Kid's Mom); Darnell Suttles (Reporter); Lee Walsh (Matron).

LOS ANGELES TIMES, 8/31/94, Calendar/p. 2, Kevin Thomas

If there's one star who'd be a safe bet for getting away with playing an archetypal hooker, with a heart of gold, she'd have to be Melanie Griffith.

In "Milk Money," as in "Shining Through," Griffith has a mix of vulnerability, dignity and moxie that persuades you to believe in her no matter what. Here, she has a strong assist from Ed Harris in a distinctively different kind of role for him, but they and director Richard Benjamin don't get much help from first-time screenwriter John Mattson.

Harris has got to be just about the nicest guy in the world, a science teacher desperately trying to save some wetlands near his Pittsburgh suburb and single-handedly raising his 12-year-old son (Michael Patrick Carter), whose mother died during his birth.

Carter and his pals (Brian Christopher, Adam LaVorgna) have reached the age when they think it's high time they see a woman naked. A couple of plot maneuvers later, Griffith not only winds up the woman they hire but also on the lam, staying in Carter's treehouse. Pretty much from the get-go Carter thinks Griffith would be the perfect mother for him and the perfect wife for Harris.

Obviously, this premise for a comedy with both romantic and adolescent angles is a bit of a stretch, to put it mildly. It needs all the shoring up it can get, but Mattson instead keeps on stretching its credibility, throwing in some underworld caricatures (which wastes such stalwarts as Malcolm McDowell and Philip Bosco) and a number of crude, tasteless moments.

Benjamin brings to the film a graceful buoyancy and a perceptive affection for its key people that holds it together. But when it comes to hooker fantasies, "Milk Money" doesn't remotely possess the resiliency and punch of "Pretty Woman."

Since the producers went for the best in such key assignments as cameraman (David Watkin), production designer (Paul Sylbert) and costume designer (Theoni V. Aldredge), it's hard to understand why they didn't bring in a seasoned writer to bolster the script.

That's too bad, because the chemistry between Griffith and Harris is just as potent as it was between Julia Roberts and Richard Gere. Benjamin plays for strength which lies in the relationships between father, son and prostitute, and in the contrast between the brassy Griffith and the film's idyllic Norman Rockwell suburban setting. But only the least demanding audiences can be expected to buy into "Milk Money."

NEW YORK POST, 8/31/94, p. 37, Michael Medved

"Pretty Woman" meets "E.T." ...

That may have been an early pitch line for "Milk Money." in which lovable suburban kids on bicycles adopt a gorgeous hooker with a heart of gold and hide her in their tree house.

They protect this sensitive alien (from the red light district of the nearby city) and defend her from unsympathetic adults, even bringing her to school where she's displayed in a sex ed class. Meanwhile, romance kicks in with the widower dad of one of the boys.

All this is precisely the sort of high-concept stupidity that Hollywood ought to swear off forevermore, but superior acting makes this silly movie surprisingly watchable and even occasionally endearing.

Melanie Griffith, often disappointing in her more demanding roles (like "Shining Through"), is just about perfect here as the fantasy hooker heroine: sweet, sexy, vulnerable, and hugely likable.

She makes contact with her three 12-old-admirers when they pool their "milk money" and ride their bikes to the big bad city to pay a lady to display her naked body. Later she gives them a ride back to the 'burbs, but once she's there her car conveniently won't start and she stays on with Frank (played by appealing and accomplished newcomer Michael Patrick Cartet) and his absent-minded science teacher dad (Ed Harris).

Like the children of movie widowers in "Sleepless in Seattle," "Getting Even With Dad" and "Corinna, Corinna" young Frank knows just what the old man needs and meddles shamelessly—and successfully—in his romantic life.

The audience won't mind, however, because Griffith and Harris make such an effective screen couple and their touching scenes together are considerably helped by the heartfelt musical score by Michael Convertino—complete with uncredited quotations from Ravel's "Mother Goose."

Meanwhile, director Richard Benjamin hugely overdoes the Norman Rockwell bit in emphasizing the contrast between the dangers of the city and the coziness of the suburbs. The suburban scenes (shot in metropolitan Cincinnati) strongly resemble Frank Capra's Bedford Falls, complete with "howdy, neighbor" extras from 50 years ago; "Milk Money" seems blissfully unaware that Beavis and Butthead culture long ago penetrated even the most idyllic rural enclaves.

There's also an inane subplot involving Malcolm McDowell as a vicious pimp determined to track down the missing Griffith and murder her in revenge for some money he thinks she's stolen.

Despite its likable elements, it's hard to imagine which audience "Milk Money" was intended to please. Constant sexual references make the PG-13 release altogether unsuitable for young kids, and teen-agers will find it tough to relate to a comedy that focuses so squarely on the innocence of 12-year-olds.

As for adults, they may be charmed by Griffith and Harris, but even with the good will they generate, it's hard to swallow this preposterous plot.

NEWSDAY, 8/31/94, Part II/p. B7, Gene Seymour

As V, the prostitute who, in "Milk Money," stumbles into the Beaver Cleaver universe of the suburbs, Melanie Griffith carries her golden aura as if she's balancing an overburdened tray of wine glasses through a crowded room. She's confident, but a little shaky. This is the kind of wry-but-winsome-bombshell part that made her a star and she does barely enough with it to hold your attention. You can't help pulling for her. Nor can you help thinking of the eight long years that have gone by since "Something Wild."

Even a morsel of energy or imagination from that 1986 romantic comedy would have made "Milk Money" bearable. But this is a vaguely creepy comedy with no wit, a forced sense of fun and not a whole lot of romance. It's like a kid who's trying hard to be liked by being a little naughty, but is finally too uptight to act on his convictions.

A perfect description, by the way, of Frank (Michael Patrick Carter), "Milk Money's" 12-year-old protagonist, who, with two of his friends, leave their split-level cocoon for the dangerous, forbidding big city (Cincinnati, in this case) with about $100 in joint savings. Their purpose: to find a woman who'll take off her clothes in front of them. All they want is a look. Honest.

Through various improbable circumstances, the following happens: Griffith's V lets them have, you know, a look. (Two of them, anyway. Frank closes his eyes.) She steals a car belonging to her vicious pimp and takes them back to the suburbs. The car breaks down in front of Frank's house. Which fits in perfectly with Frank's plan to match V with his widowed dad (Ed Harris), a quixotic environmentalist, who's almost as awkward as Frank.

While hiding out in Frank's tree house, V finds out her pimp's been murdered by his shady boss (Malcolm McDowell's sneer now seems frozen forever), who thinks V's stolen his money. So she hides out long enough to serve as a visual aid for Frank's sex-education class (a sequence that's at once the funniest and strangest), teach the kid how to dance and awaken dad's dormant feelings of romance.

"Milk Money's" conflicted intentions are revealed during V's dance lesson with Frank. She tells him to move his hips. "No way!," Frank says. "That's where the trouble starts. The sex stuff!" This is said without apparent irony—which makes one wonder if the filmmakers are not only trying to tame Griffith's edgy, provocative persona, but the rest of us as well. If so, they chose a peculiar story to do it with.

Director Richard Benjamin's best scenes are the most intimate, especially when Harris, who always deserves better than he gets as an actor, is communicating one-on-one with Carter or with Griffith. At everything else, whether it's a dance, a car chase or a messy fight in a school gym, Benjamin's control is way off.

SIGHT AND SOUND, 5/95, p. 50, Louise Grey

Twelve-year-old Frank Wheeler and his best friends, Kevin and Brad want to know what girls look like, but Stacey, a haughty girl and her meek friend, Holly, won't even talk to them. Tom,

Frank's father, is a science master whose wife died during Frank's birth and who is now fighting to save five acres of wetland from developers. Learning that there are women who take off their clothes for money, the boys pool their milk money savings and cycle off in search of one. A thief tries to mug them, but V, a prostitute, saves them. She agrees to strip for the boys, and for $103.62, shows them her breasts. Frank keeps his eyes closed. They find their bikes have been stolen.

V visits her pimp, Cash. She spots the boys outside and takes them home in Cash's car which then breaks down. Tom arrives home and agrees to fix it. Frank surreptitiously lets V spend the night in his tree house. Frank persuades V to continue staying in the tree house. Next day, Frank's biology mistress assigns him the task of explaining female reproductive system. Cash is murdered and V learns that his boss Waltzer killed him, in the belief that V stole money that Cash took.

Locking his biology mistress out of the class, Frank uses V as a live model. Afterwards, he shows her his mother's dresses. Wearing one, V goes out to dinner with Tom. They meet Kevin with his father, Alan, who had once slept with V. Tom and V kiss and, back home, V confesses to being a hooker. Tom confronts Frank and, as V leaves, they see the weeping boy throw his secret box, containing a picture of his mother, in the trash. Tom and V recover it and make up, spending the night together. V spots Waltzer searching for her and, realising that staying with the Wheelers is too dangerous, she goes to the school dance to bid Frank farewell.

Tom and Waltzer separately follow her. V and Frank dance together; then Frank asks Holly to be his partner. Alan tells Tom that V is a slut. As they fight, Waltzer pulls a gun on V, telling her that the stolen money is in Cash's car. Frank raises the fire alarm; he, Kevin, Brad and V escape in the car, pursued by Waltzer. They crash but are unhurt; the car blows up. V asks Waltzer's boss to release her. He consents; she returns to her hotel where, to her surprise, Cash had hidden the money. As the developers move in on the wetlands, a lawyer arrives with a property deed: the land has been bought in Tom's name. V is the buyer and she has also bought the ice cream parlour in town.

In this tame romantic comedy, one of the more interesting characters never appears: Grace Kelly. V keeps a picture of Kelly in her hotel room; Tom tells Frank that his mother had a Kelly-like quality about her. Frank himself thinks of V as Kelly-like. Hell, V-as-Kelly even fits perfectly the mother-as-Kelly's clothes. Scratch the surface of *Milk Money*, and there is a story of a repressed sexual quest with Kelly as the signifier for whom both Frank (as a pubescent) and Tom compete. *Milk Money* is actually a thinly-disguised oedipal sit-com.

Yet such undercurrents as these are anathema to the family values that Richard Benjamin's film upholds. Thus, although an oedipal order must, ultimately, be upheld it is also continually fudged. The most outrageous example is V's appearance in the school biology lab, as a human model on whom Frank traces the outlines of the female reproduction system. Tellingly, the teacher manages to burst in and end the lesson just as Frank is on the brink of explaining intercourse itself.

Otherwise, comic confusion rests on three misunderstandings: Tom believes that V is a young boy's maths tutor; V believes that Tom knows she is a hooker initiating his son and, lastly, acquaintances think V is Tom's sister. Hence the illicit frisson to their kiss when an unnamed family are watching them. Resolution only occurs when Frank chooses Holly over Stacey (a *Heathers* character in the making), and V and Tom finally come together. Along with the redemption of V from an arena of perverse sexuality to a suburban life whipping up vanilla ice, these distinctions are *Milk Money*'s central dynamic. Tom differentiates between sex and making love; Frank tells V that he wants her to marry his father, she doesn't have to have sex with him. The slap-dash sub-plot, with Malcolm McDowell playing a king-sized ham of a role as Waltzer the gangster, exists only to facilitate the main storyline.

Strangely enough, this uneven quality is one of *Milk Money*'s few near-redeeming features. The boggle-eyed McDowell, the car chase and the various dancing scenes are all elements likely to appeal to viewers who may prefer to leave the romantic slant of the film well alone. Yet such neglect would be a pity, because the farcical interchanges between Harris and Carter and Griffith and the boy work well. Griffith balances her smouldering with the burgeoning maternal instinct that her interaction with Frank requires. Harris, the only character who really stands out, is a believable portrait of an all-American figure, albeit in the Norman Rockwell mould. Ultimately though, *Milk Money* is an unadventurous film, a variation on the theme of tart-finds-heart and little else.

VILLAGE VOICE, 9/13/94, p. 10, Lisa Kennedy

In the absolutely 2 per cent, if not skim, *Milk Money*, three prepubescent boys anxious to sneak a peek (in the sequel they'll cop a feel no doubt) hawk their comic books and hoard their, yes, milk money for the chance to see a naked woman. Being precocious pups raised on porn and probably a lot of movies just like this one, they recognize their success rate will increase if they procure the services of a prostitute. So Frank and his friends Kevin and Brad head into the city from their nice burbclave, fall into some deep urban unpleasantry, and are rescued, what luck, by V, a working girl with a bod for sin and a heart of gold. That this bad girl is none other than Melanie Griffith has director Benjamin chirping, "You couldn't make this movie without [her] because what you see in this incredibly gorgeous package is heart."

Titularly, so to speak, *Milk Money* is this year's *Scent of a Woman*. Though less egregiously named, hell, less egregious period, it's also more than a wee bit familiar. After the initial peep show, the movie settles down into a tale about getting Dad, here Ed Harris's absentminded professor, a wife. Forget the madonna/whore dichotomy, *Milk Money* does quite a nice job of arguing for something more akin to a continuum. After all, if everything goes according to happy-ending logic, V will make the leap from the oldest profession to the oldest non-paying position, Mom. (Yes, there will be some obstacles. Malcolm McDowell's cranky pimp for one. McDowell fans are sure to be disappointed at his too brief turn.)

Milk Money is not without some edible fluff: the scene where Dad thinks V is a math tutor and she thinks he knows she's a sexpert is nearly a who'll-get-to-first classic, and the bio lesson with V as the visible woman is worth a chuckle. Still, that this movie so comfortably sets up its parallel universes of whores and their pimps, wives and their husbands might strike some semioticians among you as either remarkably bald or deeply, subtly subversive. But the truth is this may be the oldest story line in the book.

Also reviewed in:
NEW YORK TIMES, 8/31/94, p. C11, Janet Maslin
VARIETY, 8/22-28/94, p. 55, Leonard Klady
WASHINGTON POST, 8/31/94, p. C2, Megan Rosenfeld
WASHINGTON POST, 9/2/94, Weekend/p. 38, Kevin McManus

MINBO—OR THE GENTLE ART OF JAPANESE EXTORTION

A Northern Arts Entertainment release of an Itami Films production. *Executive Producer:* Yukuo Takenaka and Nigel Sinclair. *Producer:* Yasushi Tamaoki. *Director:* Juzo Itami. *Screenplay (Japanese with English subtitles):* Juzo Itami. *Director of Photography:* Yonezo Maeda. *Editor:* Akira Suzuki. *Music:* Toshiyuki Honda. *Sound:* Osamu Onodera. *Production Designer:* Shuji Nakamura. *Running time:* 123 minutes. *MPAA Rating:* Not Rated.

CAST: Nobuko Miyamoto (Mahiru Inoue); Akira Takarada (Kobayashi); Yasuo Daichi (Yuki Suzuki); Takehiro Murata (Taro Wakasugi); Hideji Otaki (Hotel Owner); Noboru Mitani (Gang Boss); Shir Ito (Iriuchijima); Akira Nakao (Ibagi); Hosei Komatsu (Hanaoka); Tetsu Watanabe (Akechi).

LOS ANGELES TIMES, 10/19/94, Calendar/p. 5, Kevin Thomas

Juzo Itami's "Minbo—or the Gentle Art of Japanese Extortion," another lively social satire from the filmmaker best known for "Tampopo."

It's a serious comedy about how staffers at a luxury hotel are taught to stand up to *yakuza* (gangster) extortionists by a tough, smart attorney, played with her usual panache by Itami's wife and perennial star, Nobuko Miyamoto.

Akira Takarada, Toho Studio's romantic leading man of the 1960s, is perfectly cast as the hotel's suave general manager. Clearly, Itami's message hit home because the director was severely slashed in an underworld-style stabbing 10 days after the picture opened in Tokyo in May, 1992.

NEW YORK POST, 10/19/94, p. 36, Larry Worth

They're kind of like Japan's answer to the old Woody Allen-Mia Farrow pairings. Director/writer Juzo Itami keeps coming up with wonderful comedic parts to showcase his wife and leading lady, Nobuku Miyamoto.

But in their sixth collaboration. "Minbo, or the Gentle Art of Japanese Extortion," Itami has gone a step too far: he's made his wife the whole show. The good news is that Miyamoto does her part and then some; she's more enchanting then ever.

Taking a 180-degree turn from the duo's most popular successes ("Tampopo," "The Funeral" and "A Taxing Woman"), the storyline centers on a middle-aged woman's battle with the yakuza, a.k.a. the Japanese Mafia, that may not sound like a laughing matter, but Itami emphasizes mirth over murder.

Specifically, a group of yakuza thugs have made a prominent hotel into their hangout, much to the consternation of guests—and the building's hand-wringing manager.

That's where a savvy, snappily-attired attorney (Miyamoto) comes in. Armed with common sense, a winning grin and a united-we-stand philosophy, she gives the tattooed, knife-wielding gangsters a run for their scare tactics. And the war is on.

As fans of "A Taxing Woman" know, all bets should be on Miyamoto. She's a one-woman dynamo in cat-and-mouse·verbal duels, Better still, her winning demeanor is nicely complemented in scenes with co-stars Akira Takarada and Yasuo Daichi.

But things darken whenever Miyamoto isn't front and center.

Regardless, the film had an undeniable impact in Japan. Within a week of its release, yakuza goons attacked Itami, slashing him across the face, neck and shoulder.

Ironically, a film based on the incident might make a more compelling, better-rounded project than "Minbo." Especially if Itami gets wifey to star.

NEWSDAY, 10/19/94, Part II/p. B11, John Anderson

There was nothing gentle about the review the Japanese mob gave director Juzo Itami after the 1992 Tokyo opening of his "Minbo, or the Gentle Art of Japanese Extortion." Waylaid outside his home by three reputed members of the *yakusa*, Itami's carotid artery was nearly slashed. From his hospital bed, he issued a challenge to his country to resist gangsterism. Five men are currently being tried for the attack.

The *yakuza*'s reaction was, if not forgivable, understandable. Itami, one of Japan's most celebrated writers and filmmakers—"Tampopo," "A Taxing Woman," "A Taxing Woman's Return"—had committed the ultimate insult, and effected the best means of taking the starch out of a force of evil: He made them look ridiculous.

"Minbo," a kind of post-nuclear "Seven Samurai," is about little people standing, up to the powerful. Put another way, it's about the civilized becoming uncivilized in the interests of self-preservation. It's a hard lesson; a particularly 20th-Century one despite its classic models, and Itami serves it up as a palatable mix of satire and sociology.

When the film begins, the *yakuza* have taken over the lobby of the Hotel Europa, and as a result the hotel loses a bid to host an international summit. Corporate cupidity prompts the hotel to appoint two lowly, frightened employees—Suzuki (Yasuo Daichi) and Wakasugi (Takehiro Murata)—to the newly created department of *yakuza* management. Their fear, however, causes their efforts to backfire: The hotel winds up paying even more extortion, and the *yakuza* become even more entrenched.

Enter Mahiru Inoue (Nobuko Miyamoto), a lawyer who specializes in *yakuza*. By employing the same intimidating rhetoric—and aware that actual violence on the part of the mob always costs them more than it's worth—she consistently stymies their efforts to blackmail the hotel, leading to an inevitable but quite satisfying denouement.

By casting a woman as hero, the bad guys as blowhards and corporate Japan in general as feckless, Itami is stepping on innumerable toes, and seems to enjoy it. And, obviously, he paid a price. But he's created a thoroughly entertaining and intelligent film that turns out to be both an old tale and a modern parable.

VILLAGE VOICE, 10/25/94, p. 69, James Hannaham

Everyone at the Hotel Europa fears the yakuza. These loud-mouthed extortionists who dress like Kid Creole congregate in the hotel's lobby, pool, and restaurant, plotting scam after scam. They plant cockroaches in the lasagna—"Is this some Italian spice?"—and threaten to go public if they aren't paid off. They fake the theft of a suitcase, claiming it contains promissory notes and demanding compensation.

Juzo Itami's amusing simplification of these organized criminals earned him several wounds to the face after *Minbo*'s release, apparently the gangsters' attempt to prove that they're more action and less talk than the *Married to the Mob*-sters depicted. Itami, best known for his food fest *Tampopo*, dismantles the yakuza's not-so-clever extortion techniques in a comedy only as funny as their quirks seem unusual. Translated into Italian-American, the film would have the impact of a wet noodle.

However, heroine Mahiru Inoue (Nobuku Miyamoto), attorney-at-law and yakuza specialist, saves the plot and the film it encumbers. Skilled in the art of *minbo*, the special brand of intimidation and torment these *udon* dons use to get their way, the demure yet tough-as-nails-underneath Inoue battles the rude extortionists, answering their barked epithets with firm politeness. Miyamoto makes this character more than half the reason to watch the film's tarnished setups. The scenes from which she's absent seem much longer. Though the men rob her of a crowning triumph, she nevertheless retains her pride and independence. Behind every great woman, there's a bunch of blowhards.

Also reviewed in:
CHICAGO TRIBUNE, 2/3/95, Tempo/p. 5, Michael Wilmington
NEW YORK TIMES, 10/19/94, p. C17, Janet Maslin
VARIETY, 9/7/92, p. 52, David Stratton
WASHINGTON POST, 11/18/94, p. F7, Hal Hinson

MINOTAUR

A Headliner Entertainment Group release of an RFPL production. *Producer:* Kris Krengel. *Director:* Dan McCormack. *Screenplay:* Dan McCormack. *Director of Photography:* Dan Gillham. *Editor:* Martin Hunter. *Music:* William T. Stromberg. *Sound:* David Barr Yaffe and Giovanni Di Simoni. *Production Designer:* Michael Krantz and Martha Rutan Faye. *Art Director:* Ann Johnstad White. *Set Decorator:* Mary Gullickson. *Costumes:* Penny Rose. *Running time:* 55 minutes. *MPAA Rating:* Not Rated.

CAST: Michael Faella (The Minotaur); Ricky Aiello (Mink); Holley Chant (Cindy); Willo Hausman (Woman); Tom Kurlander (Paul); Jack Wallace (Father).

LOS ANGELES TIMES, 4/18/94, Calendar/p. 5, Kevin Thomas

Dan McCormack's 55-minute "Minotaur" is an arty, breathtakingly pretentious parable on the decline and fall of an Elvis-like pop star (Michael Faella) that presents an overly familiar phenomenon as if it were some kind of profound revelation.

NEW YORK POST, 6/10/94, p. 42, Bill Hoffmann

Meet the "Odd Couple" of double features. One's chillingly effective, the other's a tepid time waster.

Both are chuckfull of disturbing images, but while one fills you with the creeps, the other's simply filled with pretension.

The good one is "Some Folks Call It a Slide Blade" a project that's more of an acting exercise than a movie, but hits the mark nonetheless.

Beautifully photographed in a drab black-and-white that reminds you of a Frederick Wiseman documentary, "Slide Blade" focuses on an important day in the life of a killer (Billy Bob Thornton). He's about to be paroled 25 years after murdering her lover.

In waltzes a novice reporter (Molly Ringwald) to do her big interview. In a darkened room with just a crack of light, the wide-eyed journalist listens with goosebumps as the killer goes back to that horrifying night.

Thornton is perfectly terrifying yet ultimately sympathetic in the role and he carries the picture. It's certainly worth a look.

"Minotaur" purports to show us the last, decadent days of a pop icon on the permanent skids.

Alone in his apartment, the superstar named "Minotaur" shoots drugs into his neck, vomits on the floor and strangles a groupie in a giant champagne glass (really!). He does all these things while wearing a big white cloth diaper.

Mixed in is a ridiculous subplot in which the government seizes the rocker and tries to "cure" him of his decadent lifestyle.

Hokey dialogue and images try to push this film into a realm of self-importance it has no business going for.

As much as they've said about poor Elvis' feverish final days, I doubt they were as bad as the Minotaur's. Skip this one.

NEWSDAY, 6/10/94, Part II/p. B13, Gene Seymour

It's hard to believe anyone could get as many red herrings in a 25-minute film as director George Hickenlooper and writer Billy Bob Thornton manage to squeeze into "Some Folks Call It a Sling Blade," one of the two gut-grabbing shorts from this year's Sundance Film Festival paired for theatrical release.

In "Sling Blade," Hickenlooper, best known for the 1991 documentary, "Hearts of Darkness: A Filmmaker's Apocalypse," and Thornton, who wrote the screenplay for last year's "One False Move," have wrought a hard, brilliant little gem whose many facets send your conventional expectations down several false corridors.

Set in a mental ward, the film opens languidly with a bespectacled inmate (J.T. Walsh), sauntering into a rec room, teasing and prodding other patients before settling into a bizarre sex-stained rap with a grunting, brooding inmate (Thornton).

One of these two men is about to be released from the ward after serving time for a brutal murder. A callow, self-righteous reporter (Molly Ringwald) is convinced that this fellow, Carl, will kill again and, through an exit interview with him hopes to expose the inadequacy of the criminal justice system. Because of Walsh's twisted patter, you presume he's the one the reporter wants to talk to. But it turns out to be Thornton's character instead.

Carl is brought into a dimly lit room alone with the reporter, who's been warned that he doesn't like talking to women. This sets us up for all kinds of tension inducing possibilities. Yet Carl merely growls and stumbles his way through into a somber monologue about the misery and torment that led him to murder both his mother and her lover. Thornton makes Carl's story sound like the most heartbreaking country-western blues dirge you ever heard—and all the more convincing because of it.

So convincing that, by the time the reporter asks Carl whether he'll kill again, she does so without the conviction she had going in. What starts out as an exercise in manipulating audience expectations transforms itself—quietly, wondrously—into a plea for compassion. Or, at least, tolerance.

The other film, "Minotaur," aims at a similarly high level of thematic and technical achievement. Writer-director Dan McCormack's surreal 55-minute meditation on plenty of inspired Grand Guignol effects—notably a champagne glass big enough for the bloated title character (Michael Faella), a "pop icon" who's got Sinatra's repertoire and Presley's bad habits, to carry out a depraved, drug-induced act of violence upon a beauty queen (Holley Chant).

But McCormack's erudition gets the better of his baroque imagination. For all its highly charged language and mythopoeic trappings, "Minotaur" coasts loftily—and queasily—over the hole in the heart of American pop culture. We don't feel the presence of a real person in this film who's crashed and burned. We feel only the notion of a fallen hero.

Also reviewed in:
NEW YORK TIMES, 6/10/94, p. C12, Stephen Holden
VARIETY, 2/28-3/6/94, p. 73, Emanuel Levy

MIRACLE ON 34TH STREET

A Twentieth Century Fox release. *Executive Producer:* William Ryan and William S. Beasley. *Producer:* John Hughes. *Director:* Les Mayfield. *Screenplay:* George Seaton and John Hughes. *Story:* Valentine Davies. *Based on the 1947 Motion Picture Screenplay by:* George Seaton. *Director of Photography:* Julio Macat. *Editor:* Raja Gosnell. *Music:* Bruce Broughton. *Music Editor:* Patricia Carlin. *Sound:* Ronald Judkins and (music) Armin Steiner. *Sound Editor:* Gloria S.Borders. *Casting:* Jane Jenkins and Janet Hirshenson. *Production Designer:* Doug Kraner. *Art Director:* Steve Arnold. *Set Designer:* John Berger, Patricia A. Klawonn, Nancy Mickelberry, and Carl Stensel. *Set Decorator:* Leslie Rollins. *Set Dresser:* Troy Borisy. *Special Effects:* John D. Milinac and Rodman Kiser. *Costumes:* Kathy O'Rear. *Make-up:* Ben Nye, Jr. *Running time:* 114 minutes. *MPAA Rating:* PG.

CAST: Richard Attenborough (Kriss Kringle); Elizabeth Perkins (Dorey Walker); Dylan McDermott (Bryan Bedford); J.T. Walsh (Ed Collins); James Remar (Jack Duff); Joss Ackland (Victor Landbergh); Jane Leeves (Alberta Leonard); Simon Jones (Shellhammer); William Windom (C.F. Cole); Mara Wilson (Susan Walker); Robert Prosky (Judge Harper); Jack McGee (Tony Falacchi); Joe Pentangelo (Bailiff); Mark Damiano II (Daniel); Casey Moses Wurzbach (Grandson); Jenny Morrison (Denice); Peter Siragusa (Cabbie); Samantha Krieger (Sami); Horatio Sanz (Orderly); Lisa Sparrman (Mrs. Collins); Kimberly Smith (Court Clerk); Mike Bacarella (Santa); Harve Kolzow (Businessman); Bianca Rose Pucci (Little Girl); Jimmy Joseph Meglio (Little Boy); Hank Johnston (Boy); Margo Buchanan (Another Mother); Bill Buell (Band Director); Ron Beattie (Priest); Alexandra Michelle Stewart (Child); Paige Walker Leavell (Tricia); Rosanna Scotto, Michele Marsh, and Joe Moskowitz (News Anchors); Lester Holt, Susi Park, and Janet Kauss (Newscasters); Al Cerullo (Helicopter Pilot); Kathrine Narducci (Mother); Mary C. McCormack (Myrna Foy); Alvin Greenman (The Doorman); Allison Janney (The Woman); Greg Noonan (Cmdr. Coulson); Byrne Piven (Dr. Hunter); Peter Gerety (Cop).

LOS ANGELES TIMES, 11/18/94, Calendar/p. 1, Kenneth Turan

"Miracle on 34th Street" is one of the genuinely beloved holiday movies, winner of a trio of Oscars in 1947 and a Christmas season fixture ever since. So producer/co-writer John Hughes, the force behind this remake, has understandably tried hard to be faithful to its spirit.

Hughes has shared his screenplay credit with initial writer George Seaton, cast Alvin Greenman (who played a teen-age Santa back then) in a cameo role, and even tried to get R.H. Macy's to repeat its to repeat its role as the story's pivotal department store. Macy's declined, a decision that now looks rather wise.

The problem is not that the original (from a story by Valentine Davies) has been trashed. In truth, Richard Attenborough and Mara Wilson, taking on the roles that brought an Academy Award to Edmund Gwenn and stardom to a young Natalie Wood, do fine work and are the best things about this production.

It's rather that Hughes and director Les Mayfield have undertaken to not just remake but update "Miracle," which means making it cruder and more vulgar to match the tenor of modern times and Hughes' fatuous sensibility. Although attracted to the original's innocence, they eventually lose faith and ended up tampering with its purity in small but ruinous ways.

The basic outline of "Miracle" remains thankfully unchanged although this version is a sluggish 18 minutes longer than its predecessor. It is the day of New York City's big Thanksgiving parade, here sponsored by the C.F. Cole Department Store, a landmark on Manhattan's 34th Street. But Dorey Walker (Elizabeth Perkins), the store's director of special projects, is more frazzled than happy.

It seems the store's Santa, the parade's *piéce de résistance*, is too inebriated to do his festive duty. In desperation Dorey turns to a nearby old gent (Attenborough), who happens to look just like Mr. Claus and says that yes, he's had a bit of experience in that line.

The old gent is a big success in the parade, ditto later in the week with the customers at Cole's, where he astonishes everyone by directing shoppers to whatever store has the best prices, even if it's the dread Shoppers Express (Gimbels in the original) just across the street.

He seems too good to be true, and in fact Dorey soon uncovers a glitch. The man not only says his name is Kriss Kringle, he claims with total sincerity to be the true Santa Claus, the one with the reindeer, the elves, the whole nine yards.

Of course rationalist Dorey finds this hard to believe, as does her 6-year-old daughter Susan (Mara Wilson), who has been trained to be as skeptical as her mom. "I've known for a long time," Susan says in somber tones, "that he's not real." So Kriss' task is not only to persuade the world to have faith but to bring the spirit of the holiday back to one particular family as well.

Looking every inch the emperor of the North Pole, Attenborough, an actor before he was a director, was an inspired choice for Kringle. His eyes have an Eveready battery twinkle, his chuckle is vigorous and hearty, and he has the impressive hauteur of someone who's been important for ever so long. "If I didn't know better," a store executive says, "I'd think he was the real thing," a sentiment audiences will inevitably share.

Matching him twinkle for twinkle is Wilson—Robin Williams' youngest daughter in "'Mrs. Doubtfire"—as the doubting Susan. An engaging, cheerfully precocious cherub, she also has an affecting melancholy side that keeps sugar overload from contaminating her performance.

After this, things gets dicier. The relationship between Susan's mother and handsome neighbor Bryan Bedford (Dylan McDermott) is awkward and not even close to convincing. And the extended courtroom scenes where Kriss' claims to be the real Santa are put to a legal challenge do little to hold our interest.

Least welcome of all are the hard edges Hughes and company have felt a compulsion to add to the mix. These range from having the inebriated Santa's backside visible, to changing the force behind the trial (now it's the sinister owner of Shoppers World, an uncredited Joss Ackland), to having someone bait poor Kriss with charges of child molestation. If this is pleasant escapism and the spirit of Christmas, it will be news to most folks.

Still, when "Miracle on 34th Street" remembers that it's supposed to be a sweet piece of hokum, when it has the wit to leave Attenborough and Wilson on the screen together and forget about its rash of putative improvements, it does offer well-scrubbed family fare. Kriss himself would want us to forgive its flaws, and at this time of the year it gets harder and harder to turn the old gentleman down.

NEW YORK POST, 11/18/94, p. 49, Michael Medved

Writer-producer John Hughes has pulled off his own holiday miracle with a new version of "Miracle on 34th Street" that preserves all the whimsical humor of the original, and adds a level of emotional intensity that should make it a perennial favorite.

Hughes closely follows writer/director George Seaton's Oscar-winning script from the 1947 "Miracle," at times reproducing memorable scenes almost line for line.

Once again, a mysterious white-bearded old man is recruited as a last-minute replacement for a drunken Santa in the Thanksgiving Day Parade, and becomes a popular sensation when holding court in the toy department of a major department store.

It soon becomes evident that the reason he brings so much conviction to his role is that he actually believes he's Kris Kringle. Later, when hard-hearted bad guys get him committed to a mental institution as a dangerous nut, he has to prove his identity to the skeptical world in a courtroom confrontation.

One of the few significant changes from the original involves Hughes' daring decision to broaden the implications of the simple story, so that the movie actually resonates with deeper question of faith that will touch many moviegoers.

"I'm a symbol of the human ability to suppress the selfish and hateful tendencies that rule the major part of our lives," Kriss Kringle explains. "If you can't believe, then you'll live the rest of your life dominated by doubt."

In the hands of a lesser actor, such lines might fall to earth with an embarrassing thud, but Richard Attenborough (best known as director of ambitious films like "Gandhi" and "Shadowlands") brings such force and dignity to the role that his character becomes convincingly prophetic, rather than simply an eccentric old coot.

Edmund Gwenn won a supporting-actor Oscar as Kris Kringle in the original film and the splendid Attenborough, heart and soul of this remake, is even more deserving of Academy consideration.

Similarly effective are Elizabeth Perkins as the harried department store executive who hires Kringle in the first place, and 7-year-old Mara Wilson (Robin Williams' youngest in "Mrs. Doubtfire") as her worldly-wise daughter.

Both actresses bring a tougher edge to their roles than did Maureen O'Hara and Natalie Wood in the original, which seems appropriate for an overworked single mom and her often ignored offspring. In any event, Perkins' occasionally sour, long-suffering characterization gives larger meaning to Kringle's attempts to battle her cynicism, and to the occasionally troubled courtship by her devoted suitor.

All these actors are expertly guided by Les Mayfield, entrusted by Hughes with direction of the project, though his one previous credit ("Encino Man") gave little indication of his ability to build big scenes or to win suspension of disbelief in a film that is, after all, about a faith that defies logic.

There is, in the end, no entirely rational way to explain the way this lovely film plays upon our emotions; it's better to simply treasure it and accept it as Hollywood's first formidable gift of the holiday season.

NEWSDAY, 11/18/94, Part II/p. B2, Jack Mathews

Given its beautiful structure and timeless appeal, it would seem impossible for someone to take George Seaton's Oscar-winning screenplay for the 1947 Christmas classic "Miracle on 34th Street" and make a bad movie from it. But John Hughes has beaten the odds.

I have no way of knowing how people who have never seen the original film will respond to this version, written and produced by Hughes and directed by Les Mayfield ("Encino Man"). Hollywood has pretty much lost its knack for coming up with fresh holiday fare, so what little magic survives the updating may seem inspired.

But in virtually every instance where Hughes made changes in Seaton's story, he diminished or cheapened it. And in coming up with a "better" denouement to the Kriss Kringle sanity case, he turned one of the great film courtroom scenes into sentimental drivel.

Normally, the most controversial thing about remakes of film classics is the casting. Contemporary actors, no matter how well-suited they may be for the parts or how well they perform them, suffer in comparison to the time-gilded images of the original cast. And the first "Miracle" workers, with Edmund Gwenn as the last word in screen Santas, John Payne, and Maureen O'Hara as the couple he brings together, and Natalie Wood as the child whose doubts he overcomes, set a high standard.

But the cast of the '94 "Miracle" is the least of its problems. British actor-director Richard Attenborough is physically on the button as Kriss Kringle; his accent and size even remind us of the Welsh-born Gwenn. Dylan McDermott and Elizabeth Perkins make a fine couple, and in choosing "Mrs. Doubtfire's" Mara Wilson to play the precocious kid with the season's toughest wish list (a dad, a baby brother and a house in the 'burbs, please), Hughes exercised the one talent he does have—an eye for adorable moppets.

In broad outline, the two "Miracles" do tell the same story, that of a New York department store Santa whose insistence that he is the real thing lands him in Bellevue. With Christmas just days away, his fate is in the hands of the judge presiding over his sanity hearing and the lawyer friend (McDermott) determined to prove that he is the one and only Santa Claus.

As Seaton envisioned it in 1947, two years into a flush postwar prosperity, the real defendant of the story was the cynicism and commercial crassness of retailers subverting the spirit of Christmas in their pursuit of profits. The miracle of "Miracle" wasn't that Kriss Kringle was eventually acknowledged as Santa, but that he shamed the city's merchandising giants, Macy's and Gimbel's, into calling a Christmas truce.

Hughes has dispensed with all of these finer points and turned "Miracle" into a simple good vs. evil comedy. His department stores—C.F. Cole's (Macy's, for some reason, didn't allow the use of its name) and Shoppers Express (Gimbel's is long gone)—remain rivals to the end. In fact, it is a thug hired by Shoppers Express who provokes Kriss into an act of violence so they can have him locked up for the holidays.

Many of Hughes' changes were made to update the story's environment, which he achieves mostly by acknowledging the pervasiveness of television. But the other changes suggest he either did not understand the material or didn't think contemporary audiences would.

Seaton's overarching premise was that nobody would know for certain whether Kriss Kringle was Santa Claus or, as the young girl fears, "just a nice old man with whiskers." What people have taken away from the movie for more than 40 years is that there is more to Christmas than opening presents. Hughes, going for easy laughs at the expense of his character, has Kriss making serious references to his pals the Easter Bunny and the Tooth Fairy, passwords to the padded slammer if there were any.

Nowhere did Hughes go more wrong, however, than in the climactic courtroom scene. In Seaton's version, you'll recall, some postal workers saved the day by hauling thousands of dead-mail letters addressed to Santa Claus to the courthouse and dumping them on the judge's desk. It not only gave the judge a rationale for endorsing Santa Claus (and thus enhancing his own chances for re-election), but it was spectacularly visual. Who can forget Gene Lockhart peering over that mountain of mail and yelling "Case dismissed!"?

Hughes' version, which draws God and country into the debate, is anticlimactic, irrelevant, immaterial and visually static. The religious right may love it, but it's an affront to the late George Seaton, who, unable to protest, shares a screenplay credit with Hughes.

Movie dismissed!

NEWSWEEK, 11/21/94, p. 96, Jeff Giles

The makers of both "Miracle on 34th Street" and "The Santa Clause" claim to know Santa's secret, that he services a billion chimneys a night by slowing time to a supernatural crawl. They should know—their movies don't exactly go dashing through the snow. "Miracle" is a remake, of course. The good news is that the 1947 original (with Edmund Gwenn, Maureen O'Hara and a wee Natalie Wood) survived being one of the first movies ever colorized, and it'll survive this, too. The new "Miracle"—directed by Les Mayfield, and produced and co-written by John Hughes—stars renowned director Richard Attenborough as Kriss Kringle. the department-store Santa who insists he's the real thing. Elizabeth Perkins plays his boss, a bitter single mother, whose daughter (the flinty and charming Mara Wilson) is a grim little girl secretly looking for a reason to believe. The new 'Miracle" has a nicely old-fashioned air to it—the lighting is so warm and fuzzy that everyone's face fairly glows—but the reheated plot is joyless and wooden. There's a perfunctory love story. There's some exceedingly muddled courtroom action, in which Kringle defends his sanity (mystery of mysteries: Mayfield skips that great scene where the guards lumber into court with all of Santa's mail). Then there's a rushed, happy-ever-after ending that comes off like a big forced smile. Maybe your kid will like "Miracle." But at a screening in New York City, a boy up front started singing, "Row, Row, Row Your Boat." If his parents hadn't hushed him, he might have gotten a round going.

Santa isn't put on trial in "The Santa Clause," but he does get chased by the cops. Tim Allen, of the ABC hit "Home Improvement," makes his movie debut as a divorced toy-company executive, Scott Calvin. On Christmas Eve, Calvin grudgingly fills in for Santa when the big guy takes a tumble off his roof. Then he learns he's got the job for life, and suddenly he's sprouting a white beard and putting on 45 pounds in a week. Calvin' s ex-wife (Wendy Crewson) and her new husband (Judge Reinhold) think he's crazy and dangerous, but his son (Eric Lloyd) thinks he's a hero. "The Clause," directed by John Pasquin, makes the same musty point as "Miracle"—namely, you gotta believe. Allen is likable (if you like him), and he pulls off plenty of cute bits and sarcastic one-liners. Still, under all the gift-wrapping, this is really a story about an estranged father who loses visitation rights, kidnaps his son and becomes the subject of a manhunt. Which may or may not put you in the holiday spirit. "Mrs. Doubtfire" got away with this sort of broken-home hand-wringing because it could be helplessly funny. But "The Clause" is clunky and ramshackle. Like "Miracle," it never really takes off—and true believers are right to expect more. Heck, even reindeers can fly.

SIGHT AND SOUND, 1/95, p. 49, Philip Strick

Dorey Walker, supervisor of Special Projects at Cole's Department Store, panics when the Santa Claus hired for the Store's spectacular Christmas Parade topples drunkenly from his sleigh. Fortunately a replacement is at hand, Kriss Kringle, a specialist in the Santa Claus role, whose jovial participation renders the Parade a resounding success. This is unwelcome news to Victor Landbergh of Shopper's Express, main rival to Cole's, who assigns his henchman Jack Duff to monitor developments. That evening, Dorey shares a Thanksgiving dinner with her neighbour Bryan Bedford, an attorney, and her six-year-old daughter Susan, who decided long ago that Santa doesn't exist. Bryan loves them both, but Dorey is still smarting from the collapse of her first marriage and avoids involvement.

Next day, in his own Santa Claus outfit, Kriss takes up his duties at the Store, visited by throngs of delighted children. Their parents are furious that 'Santa' promises to deliver whatever he's asked for, until he points out that many of the gifts requested are available more cheaply at other stores. After a few qualms, this unusual altruism is welcomed as a promotional gimmick by the Store's Chairman, C.F. Cole. Reconsidering her opinion of Santa Claus, Susan consults her mother; Dorey suggests she asks for a near-impossible gift that only a truly magical Santa could deliver, and Susan accordingly tells Kriss she'd like a house, a father, and a brother for Christmas. Chances of delivery look slender when Dorey coldly turns down Bryan's offer of an engagement ring; sadly he passes the ring to Kriss to find a suitable owner.

Duff bribes the drunk 'Santa' to pretend that Kriss has attacked him; Kriss is arrested, and there are much-publicised doubts as to his sanity. Suspicious at pressure from Landbergh's attorney to have Kriss locked away in an asylum, Judge Harper agrees to Bryan's demand for a public hearing. Kriss admits to believing he is Santa Claus, hoping that his dismissal as merely a crazy old man will protect the reputation of the 'real' Santa; the hearing becomes a debate as to whether Santa Claus exists or not. Taking his cue from Bryan, Susan, and a dollar bill, Judge Harper concludes that the collective faith of the American people justifies a belief in Santa Claus — and that he exists in the person of Kriss Kringle.

Amid nation-wide jubilation, Kriss rushes off for a busy night's work, while Dorey and Bryan receive separate invitations to meet at St. Mary's Church. They arrive to find a priest in readiness, with the ring. On Christmas morning, Susan sits in Dorey's apartment, certain that Santa has failed her, only to discover that Dorey and Bryan were married overnight, that a lavishly-decorated house awaits them, and that there is every prospect of a baby brother arriving in due course.

Partly because of a musical phrase on the soundtrack which echoes a number from *My Fair Lady*, the impression initially conveyed by *Miracle on 34th Street* is that everyone is about to burst into song. At various times since it first appeared in 1947, George Seaton's story has done just that (as a Broadway musical in 1963, and a decade later on CBS), as well as undergoing revivals on American radio and television. Inscrutably disguised as *The Big Heart*, it staked a lesser claim to the affections of British audiences but remains cherished by fans of Maureen O'Hara and Natalie Wood (an irresistible 9-year-old at the time). Now refurbished for the *Jurassic Park* generation, the weight of the story has been shifted to the shoulders of Richard Attenborough whose zest for perilous magic seems unclouded by the recollection of a few undisciplined dinosaurs. His celebrity status and impermeable jolliness, while never quite other-worldly enough, render him the ideal Santa Claus, a creature of popular, and mercenary, fiction with any number of good deeds to his name.

It's a pity, though, that the songs never get sung. Offered in the exuberant form of a musical, where conventional logic can be diverted by a simple change of key and an overwhelming chorus, the 'proving' of Santa would be much less of a challenge to the attentive audience. In a non-musical, however, the moment of collision between fable and reality (always the weakest point in Seaton's screenplay) offers scant confirmation of anything. Originally, the argument ran that, as the government-owned Post Office delivered all 'Santa Claus' letters to Kriss Kringle, the government—and therefore the law—recognised him as Santa. This time around, with amendments by John Hughes, the fact that 'In God We Trust' appears on American currency is regarded as substantiating the nation's faith in the unprovable. This enables Judge Harper, displaying a clear case of bias, to assert that Santa exists in the person of Kringle — a resounding non-sequitur. The implications for any thinking British child must be firstly that Santa is American, secondly that the Bank of England would appear to be more reliable than God, and thirdly that you can legally believe in anything you like so long as nobody can prove you're wrong.

While plenty of free-thinking is to be encouraged, the irony of young Susan's education is that she regresses from a healthy cynicism into the compulsory conclusion that Kringle is what he claims to be—and that this acceptance is forced upon her by a display of rampant materialism (a sumptuous dreamhouse straight out of a department-store catalogue) and a shotgun wedding. Kringle's ability to talk in Swahili and sign-language, along with his politely ingratiating demeanour, does convey a small hint of Christmas spirit (although most religious aspects of the festive season are resolutely ignored), but since his chief function is to stimulate sales, there remains the awkward question of why he has to descend all the world's chimneys in a single night to deliver parcels that have already been purchased.

This is all something of a hoax and would be none the worse for it except that it has been filmed with a peculiar lifelessness. One might guess that director Mayfield has an interest in culture-shock themes: he was a producer on *Hearts of Darkness* (about Coppola's *Apocalypse Now*) and recently made *California Man* (a comedy about the revival of a prehistoric 'missing link'), but has yet to find an effective voice. While never less than smoothly professional, *Miracle* has a visual dullness too seldom relieved by such touches as the flash of gold from the rims of Kringle's glasses, or the array of toy soldiers on the desk of his main antagonist (an uncredited but enjoyably villainous appearance by Joss Ackland). Frozen into a mask of makeup, Elizabeth Perkins has little chance of conveying anything but disapproval, while Mara Wilson, excellently meditative as her long-suffering daughter, looks understandably eager to take on tougher assignments. They both deserve brighter and more sparkling miracles.

TIME, 11/28/94, p. 80, Richard Schickel

Santa Claus? Of course we believe in him. If we can believe in Newt Gingrich we can believe in anything. The real question is, Do we believe in Santa Claus movies? There are two on screens at the moment, and the best that can be said for them is that they offer a clear-cut choice: you can take your seasonal dose of sappy sentiment either in stuffy traditional or tacky modernist form. *Miracle on 34th Street*, as befits a remake we probably don't need, offers us a Santa Claus cut along classic lines—round, twinkly and played with a nice, comforting restraint by the redoubtable Richard Attenborough. *The Santa Clause* presents us with an Anti-Claus, Tim Allen of *Home Improvement*, hard-edged, discomfitingly frenetic and spritzing cheerless one-liners.

Certainly Attenborough has the more agreeable role, since his Kriss Kringle is utterly secure in his identity. He knows he really is Santa Claus and hasn't the slightest desire to be anyone else. How it is that he ends up defending himself in court when mean people question his sanity is a tale too familiar to relate once again: it has been available on television—in a less overbearing version—every Christmas season for almost a half-century. Given these circumstances, it betrays no secrets to say that aided by smart lawyering, shrewd media manipulation and a child's faith, he beats a bum rap.

Allen, on the other hand, is obliged to play a man named Scott Calvin, a hard-charging, fast-rising toy-company executive who is pressed into service as a substitute St. Nick in circumstances at once too complicated and too stupid to explain. He finds to his dismay that the job is his for all eternity (that—Get it?—is the Santa clause buried in some fine print he didn't get a chance to read), and he is understandably skeptical about whether taking over operations at the North Pole is a great career move. To achieve a happy resolution of his dilemma requires the intervention of insistent (and charmless) elves, much desperate plotting and a number of cheesy special effects.

Different as these movies are in tone and development, they both address the same basic issue. In *The Santa Clause*, Scott gets into trouble because he wants to rescue his son (Eric Lloyd) from the rationalism of his psychiatrist stepfather (Judge Reinhold), who keeps insisting that it is unhealthy for the boy to believe in fantasy figures. In *Miracle*, Kriss has to perform the same task for Susan Walker (Mara Wilson), whose Mom (an over-chilled Elizabeth Perkins) represents unyielding reason.

Risking Scrooginess, one might observe that commonsensical immunity to whimsy may be a bore, but even when carried to the grim lengths exhibited here, it's not a major cause of familial dysfunction. But forget that; we don't go to the movies, especially Christmas movies, expecting much in the way of useful social commentary. What's really wrong with these pictures—Attenborough's sweet, smart performance aside—is that their sentiments are completely predictable and completely unfelt. They're just the standard seasonal slush. You can get the same emotional and imaginative kick staying home and rereading your Christmas cards.

Also reviewed in:
CHICAGO TRIBUNE, 11/18/94, Friday/p. H, Johanna Steinmetz
NEW YORK TIMES, 11/18/94, p. C12, Caryn James
VARIETY, 11/14-20/94, p. 48, Leonard Klady
WASHINGTON POST, 11/18/94, p. F1, Hal Hlnson
WASHINGTON POST, 11/18/94, Weekend/p. 50, Desson Howe

MIXED NUTS

A TriStar Pictures release of a Witt-Thomas production. *Executive Producer:* Delia Ephron and James W. Skotchdopole. *Producer:* Paul Junger Witt, Tony Thomas, and Joseph Hartwick. *Director:* Nora Ephron. *Screenplay (based on the film "La Père Noël est une Ordure"):* Nora Ephron and Delia Ephron. *Director of Photography:* Sven Nykvist. *Editor:* Robert Reitano. *Music:* George Fenton. *Music Editor:* Nicholas Meyers. *Choreographer:* Lynne Taylor-Corbett. *Sound:* James Sabat. *Sound Editor:* Dan Sable. *Casting:* Juliet Taylor and Laura Rosenthal. *Production Designer:* Bill Groom. *Art Director:* Dennis Bradford. *Set Decorator:* George DeTitta, Jr. *Set Dresser:* Chris DeTitta, Steve Krieger, Paul Gaily and Anthony Dimeo. *Special Effects:* John Ottesen. *Costumes:* Jeffrey Kurland. *Make-up:* Joe Campayno. *Make-up (Steve Martin):* Frank H. Griffin, Jr. *Stunt Coordinator:* M. James Arnett. *Running time:* 97 minutes. *MPAA Rating:* PG-13.

CAST: Steve Martin (Philip); Madeline Kahn (Mrs. Munchnik); Robert Klein (Mr. Lobel); Anthony LaPaglia (Felix); Juliette Lewis (Gracie); Rob Reiner (Dr. Kinsky); Adam Sandler (Louis); Liev Schreiber (Chris); Rita Wilson (Catherine); Parker Posey and Jon Stewart (Rollerbladers); Joely Fisher (Susan); Steven Randazzo (Detective); Christine Cavanaugh and Henry Brown (Police); Garry Shandling (Stanley); Steven Wright (Man at Pay Phone); Brian Markinson (Policeman/Voice of Obscene Caller); Victor Garber (Voice of Irate Neighbor); Sidney Armus (Chris' Father); Michele Singer (Vanessa); Haley Joel Osment (Little Boy); Diane Sokolow (Chris' Mother); Michael Badalucco (AAA Driver); Joann Lamneck (Woman Doctor); France Iann and Jacqueline Murphy (Nurses).

LOS ANGELES TIMES, 12/21/94, Calendar/p. 1, Peter Rainer

"Mixed Nuts" is a farcical whirligig that doesn't whirl. It's energetically unfunny, like "Radioland Murders," and, like that film, it boasts top-flight talent. Maybe the idea of making a comedy about a suicide prevention center just got to everyone—it's a bummed-out comedy about being bummed out.

Steve Martin plays Philip, the head of a Venice, Calif.-based suicide hotline service called Lifesavers. It's Christmas Eve, and the lifesavers at Lifesavers are about to be evicted from their headquarters by their gloatingly unfeeling landlord (Garry Shandling). Philip's co-workers are Catherine (Rita Wilson), a pretty wallflower who has a simmering crush on him, and Blanche (Madeline Kahn), a no-nonsense widow with a voice like an air-raid siren.

Directed by Nora Ephron, who co-wrote it with Delia Ephron, "Mixed Nuts" operates from a single, promising comedy conceit: Suicide hotline helpmates are as miserable as the people they are supposed to be helping. (The basis for the plot is an obscure French film, "Le Pere Noel est une Ordure," or Santa Claus Is Garbage.) This could have been funny if the characters were miserable in ways that hit home—if they were flamboyantly, irresistibly miserable. But there's a dull funk about this film: it seems in need of its own suicide hotline.

It has the problem of most failed farces: Thc complications in the movie are there only to make things more complicated. Characters are introduced to keep things hectic, but the timing is off and the lines don't tingle. Anthony LaPaglia and Juliette Lewis play a dysfunctional couple—she's the pregnant owner of a secondhand clothing store: he's a sometime Santa who wants to be a "wall artist." Their nattering inspires a Kervorkian response in the audience.

Rob Reiner, in a funny cameo, is a veterinarian who occasionally works on humans. Louie (Adam Sandler) serenades Catherine with his ukulele. (Sandler seems to have wandered in from one of his unfunnier "Saturday Night Live" sketches. Ukulele Man, anyone?) Liev Schreiber plays a suicidal transvestite who seeks out Philip at the office, and ends up dancing with him, Someone like Michael Jeter in this role could have perked things up, but Schreiber plays it for heartfelt sympathy and it's a drag (pun intended).

Nora Ephron, on the basis of her journalism, is a lot sharper than the director who made the gooey, coercively insipid "Sleepless in Seattle." "Mixed Nuts" is even more insipid than that film. It doesn't draw on her talent for wiggy, softly devastating social observation. It's an old story that Hollywood devalues its brightest talents, but here the devaluation seems to be entered into freely—enthusiastically. One big reason "Mixed Nuts" doesn't work is that the people who made it are too smart for it. In comedic terms, all that Yuletide uplift doesn't suit them. They're trying for a misery-loves-company comedy with an O. Henry twist and a cheery, Capraesque finale, but the results are too tinny to carry any conviction.

Steve Martin has a few fresh moments, like the scene where he is suddenly swept onto the dance floor by the transvestite and glimmers with dumbfounded excitement. Garry Shandling is a good comic meanie—the movie could have used much more of his heartlessness. Madeline Kahn has a great scene trapped in an elevator. Her cries for help turn into rap.

But these moments would barely add up to the running time for the trailer. Even if "Mixed Nuts" were better crafted and choreographed, it would still be in trouble because of the soggy whimsy. Why start out to make a black comedy and then dump in all that whitener?

NEW YORK POST, 12/21/94, p. 41, Michael Medved

"Mixed Nuts" is an unmixed disaster, a Christmas concoction so sour and unappetizing that if you make the mistake of paying money to see it the experience may single-handedly spoil your holiday mood.

Poor Steve Martin plays the lead—a well-meaning bumbler who runs a suicide hotline base in the bohemian beachside community of Venice, Calif.

On Christmas Eve he not only learns that his fiance is dumping him, but he also hears from his smarmy landlord (Garry Shandling) that the "Lifesavers" service will soon be evicted from its offices.

Meanwhile, Martin's chief assistant, a prim, lonely social worker type played by Rita Wilson, has eyes for her boss, and the other employee (Madeline Kahn) is a whining widow with the sort of abrasive personality that would encourage any caller to the suicide hotline to go ahead and finish the job.

Juliette Lewis plays another neighborhood kvetch who's trying to dump her gun-toting, Santa-suited boyfriend (Anthony LaPaglia) despite the fact that she appears to be somewhat near her 12th month of pregnancy.

As the seasonal celebrations proceed apace, these jolly revelers are soon joined by Adam Sandler, their ukelele-strumming, falsetto-singing neighbor from upstairs, and by a depressive, muscular transvestite (Liev Schreiber) who just may be the "seaside stranger" the police are trying to catch.

Newcomer Schreiber gives the movie's only vaguely interesting performance, creating a bizarre but believable character that you actually come to care about. The rest of the cast reverts to frenetic, shallow shtick that isn't for one moment either plausible or funny.

Freely adapted from the genuinely hilarious (and nasty) French farce "Le Pere Noel est une Ordure" (loosely translated as "Santa Claus is ... er, Garbage"), this picture attempts to offer a cynical, clear-eyed antidote to the idealized Frank Capra take on Christmas.

The movie reminds us that the holiday can be hell for weird, lonely people (like most of us) who can't live up to the greeting card images—any more than Venice Beach can live up to the traditional snowy visions of Currier and Ives.

The problem is that Nora Ephron is precisely the wrong director for this project. She's a hugely talented filmmaker who's at her best with the sort of warm-hearted emotional interaction of her two fine movies "This is My Life" and "Sleepless in Seattle."

She has no gift at all, however, for the edgy, fast-moving, mean-spirited comedic material she's asked to handle here. Her timing is disastrously loose and pokey, the characters are treated with soft-focus sentimentality, and the movie's hollow core is all too obvious—as it tries to milk laughs out of knee-slapping situations like cars that won't start, elevators that get stuck, or roller-skaters who inevitably collide (on three different occasions).

In addition to the other talented performers wasted in this yuletide yuckiness, Robert Klein turns up as a lonely guy who adores his three springer spaniels and Rob Reiner plays a dapper veterinarian—appropriate roles for a picture that is in every way a dog.

NEWSDAY, 12/21/94, Part II/p. B9, Jack Mathews

Before she became a successful novelist, screenwriter and movie director, Nora Ephron made a name for herself writing witty, sharply observed essays—mostly about life on the frontiers of feminism—for various New York publications. And like everyone else who has written humor in the short form, and in high volume, there must have been times when she read her words back to herself from the printed page and wondered, "What was I thinking?!"

Movies take a long time to write and make, and studio executives are tough editors, but Ephron's latest movie, "Mixed Nuts," plays like the worst column she ever wrote, some dithering whimsy just to get her past a deadline, and if there was a ever a point to it, it's found its way to the margin and escaped.

What *was* she thinking?

"Mixed Nuts," set in a suicide hotline office in Venice Beach, Calif., takes Ephron far afield of her urban intellectual base, and gives her no room for the kind of sophisticated comedy she plied in her scripts for "When Harry Met Sally ..." and "Sleepless in Seattle." As irresistible as the flaky lifestyle along Venice's boardwalk must be to New York writers, the scene has been parodied so often it is beyond ridicule, and though Ephron seems to want us to like these people, it feels as if she's merely sharpening her teeth on them.

The story, written with her sister, Delia Ephron, takes place on Christmas Eve, mostly in the cramped Lifesavers office with bumbling do-gooder Philip (Steve Martin), virginal hysteric Catherine (Rita Wilson), and Mrs. Munchnik (Madeline Kahn), the uptight office manager whose pucker factor is ratcheted up with each successive crisis.

Into their office and lives comes a lonely, husky-voiced transvestite (Liev Schreiber), a temperamental artist wannabe (Anthony LaPaglia) and his pregnant wife (Juliette Lewis), an airhead beach balladeer (the always uninteresting Adam Sandler), a cold-hearted landlord (Garry Shandling), and, somewhere in the neighborhood, the dreaded Seaside Strangler.

Also figuring prominently in the story is a year-old fruitcake, which keeps changing hands. It's meant to symbolize the wacky environment, but it may serve better as a metaphor for the movie itself. Stale, full of weird crap, and you can't give it away.

What was Steve Martin thinking? Philip is a blank, and he has to resort to pratfalls just to attract your eye to him. Martin is a great physical comedian, and has one mildly amusing scene doing the tango with the transvestite. But even for physical comedy to work, there must be context.

"Mixed Nuts" has none. The attempt is made to link its characters as lovable losers, people helping others in order to help themselves, but that doesn't add up to a premise, a theme or a story, even in California.

VILLAGE VOICE, 12/27/94, p. 76, Laurie Stone

Steve Martin, playing his suave nincompoop, said it was hipper to be silly than cool. In myriad appearances on SNL, as well as in *The Jerk, The Man With Two Brains* and *All of Me*, he brought glory to vainglory. A number of iffy choices later, Martin stars in a movie so punishing it suggests he's sold his soul to the devil and it's payback time. Director Nora Ephron—who wrote the script, based on a French comedy, with her sister Delia—has tinted his white hair field-mouse dun and poufed it; she's accomplished the same with his persona. He plays Philip, the officious director of a suicide hot line that blithely bungles calls by disconnecting clients.

Forget plot. Instead there is locale: wacky, winsome Venice, California, where everyone is some kind of cartoon, and hey, it's set on Christmas Eve, so who needs event? Characters—among them a hard-luck pregnant lass, a lovelorn crisis worker, a neighbor with three dogs, another neighbor with a ukulele—don't so much interact as crash into each other. You don't want to know the number of pratfalls, doors slammed in faces and hurled missiles that are perpetrated. The bits in this movie, including a homophobic Philip swallowing his distaste to dance with a drag queen, veer from pointless meanness to schmaltz; *Mixed Nuts* is like some endless Don Rickles routine.

Like the recent, joylessly frantic *Radioland Murders, Mixed Nuts* screams out: WASTE. More than a dozen talents, in addition to Martin, deck the project, including Madeline Kahn, Juliette Lewis, Robert Klein, Anthony LaPaglia, Rob Reiner, Garry Shandling, and cinematographer Sven Nykvist. Given so little to do, they mostly come off like expensive party favors at a dreary bash. Lewis, playing a woman about to give birth, works in a bubble of credibility, and Shandling is hilarious as a landlord so cheap he unscrews light bulbs in the hallways to save electricity. On camera for only a few minutes, he injects the satire and assured comedy that's so sparse here. This is cynical moviemaking of an evolved order. You flash names, sprinkle concept, get Carly Simon to emote on the soundtrack, replicate the atmosphere of an aimless, insistent SNL sketch, and hire Martin for the dead-eyed, Kevin Nealon part. At the end, the cast even sways together on a soundstage.

Also reviewed in:
NEW YORK TIMES, 12/21/94, p. C18, Janet Maslin
VARIETY, 12/19/94-1/1/95, p. 73, Leonard Klady
WASHINGTON POST, 12/21/94, p. C14, Hal Hinson
WASHINGTON POST, 12/23/94, Weekend/p. 38, Desson Howe

MONKEY TROUBLE

A New Line Cinema release of a Perey Main production in association with Effe Films/Victor Company of Japan Ltd. *Executive Producer:* Ridley Scott. *Producer:* Mimi Polk and Heide Rufus Isaacs. *Director:* Franco Amurri. *Screenplay:* Franco Amurri and Stu Krieger. *Director of Photography:* Luciano Tovoli. *Editor:* Ray Lovejoy and Chris Peppe. *Music:* Mark Mancina. *Music Editor:* Chris McGeary. *Sound:* Michael Evje, Charles Kelly and (music) Bret Newman and Steven M. Stern. *Sound Editor:* Craig Clark and Marc "Leggs" Fishman. *Casting:* Karen Rea and Doreen Lane. *Production Designer:* Les Dilley. *Art Director:* Nathan Crowley. *Set Decorator:* Denise Pizzini. *Set Dresser:* Lisa Yvette Lopez. *Costumes:* Eileen Kennedy. *Make-up:* Michelle J. Buhler. *Stunt Coordinator:* Randy "Fife" and Jeff Smolek. *Running time:* 95 minutes. *MPAA Rating:* PG.

CAST: "Finster" (Dodger); Thora Birch (Eva); Harvey Keitel (Azro); Mimi Rogers (Amy); Christopher McDonald (Tom); Adrian Johnson and Julian Johnson (Jack); Kevin Scannell (Peter); Alison Elliott (Tessa); Robert Miranda (Drake); Victor Argo (Charlie); Remy Ryan (Katie); Adam Lavorgna (Mark); Jo Champa (Annie); John Lafayette (Cates); Andi Chapman (Christine, the Teacher); Julie Payne (Librarian); Kimberly Cullum (Jesse); Molly David (Kaye Weller); Harvey Vernon (Harold Weller); Tereza Ellis (Female Cashier); Frank Lugo (Mexican Park Attendant); Gerry Bednob (Mr. Rao); Aaron Lustig (Store Manager);

Bea Soong (Japanese Woman); Deborah White (Katie's Mom); Richard Reicheg (Assistant to Mr. Big); Robert A. Perry (Echo Man); Rino Piccolo (Man in Crowd); Marcy Goldman (Park Attendant); Gabriel Christopher (Bored Cashier); Diane Manzo (Jogger); Carrie Pauley (Girl with Kite); Stephen J. Todey (Rooftop Worker).

LOS ANGELES TIMES, 3/18/94, Calendar/p. 13, Peter Rainer

While it's true that great children's films work equally well for adults, what about middling kid flix? If you're over the age of 10, "Monkey Trouble" isn't the kind of film you would want to spend much time with. It's indifferently made—to put it mildly. The microphone actually drops into frame in a couple of scenes.

But it has something going for it that kids will probably eat up. It's about a 9-year-old girl, Eva Gregory (Thora Birch), who longs for a pet against the wishes of her' parents (Mimi Rogers and Christopher McDonald) and ends up with more than she bargained for—a capuchin monkey.

The monkey, whom she nicknames Dodger, literally falls into her path one day while she's strolling through the park. On the run from the Gypsy (Harvey Keitel) who trained him to pick pockets and loot homes, Dodger becomes Eva's secret playmate. She keeps her formerly messy room so spic-and-span that her parents never suspect a thing (though her stepfather, allergic to pet fur, can't explain his sudden sneezing).

Director Franco Amurri and his screenwriter Stu Krieger work in a lot of standard storybook elements: Eva has a baby brother she wishes would go away and a stepfather she can't warm up to. Keitel's Gypsy is a gold-toothed scalawag who prances after her like he was a reject from a touring company of "Peter Pan." (Keitel is once again indulging his appetite for grunge, but in kiddie-sized bites.) If the filmmakers had worked some storybook magic into the filmmaking. "Monkey Trouble" might have been a joy.

But they do all right by the monkey, whose real name is Finster and who was trained for the film by Mark Harden. He's a wizardly little performer, and he's in practically every scene. And the land that develops between Eva and Dodger feels just right. It's a convincing evocation that every kid feels about his first pet.

NEW YORK POST, 3/18/94, p. 36, Michael Medved

The way that you respond to "Monkey Trouble" will, to some extent, depend on how you feel about capuchin monkeys—the South American primates traditionally associated with organ grinders.

If you happen to adore the screechy, jumpy little beasts, then you may well find this picture intensely appealing. As for me, I've never understood the charm of these particular creatures, with their tight, twitchy, inexpressive faces and their sharp, chattering, little teeth.

At the emotional climax of this movie, when the soundtrack swells with a romantic theme and Dodger, the hirsute star of the film, leaps up toward his 9-year-old leading lady to hug her face, I found myself cringing and looking away from the screen. When it comes to animal stars who can tug at the heart strings, Dodger will never replace Lassie, or Benji—or even Spuds McKenzie.

Despite his cold, unappetizing screen presence, Dodger does come across as marginally more likable than at least one of his co-stars: Harvey Keitel, who plays the crooked organ grinder who trains Dodger to become a master picket-pocket and burglar. Keitel is entirely too menacing and intense for this light-hearted kiddie material; he seems to be acting not only in a different film but in a different universe.

His extraordinarily weird (and wired) performance suggests what might have happened had Martin Scorsese directed Disney's "That Darn Cat".

Needless to say, Dodger wants to get away from this abusive oddball and so runs away, finding himself a new home with a spunky little girl played by the pretty and persuasive Thora Birch, who has previously starred in "All I Want for Christmas," and "Hocus Pocus."

Here, she hides the run-away monkey in her room, in the style of Elliott and ET, since her mother (Mimi Rogers) and her animal-allergic, police lieutenant stepfather (Christopher McDonald) don't want her to have a pet.

While this new roommate remains her dirty little secret for weeks, Dodger keeps secrets of his own: he continues to subtly filch watches, wallets, and other items, accumulating them in a box in the closet. Mean while, his original owner is desperately trying to recover the critter so he can employ his thievery skills in a big jewel heist for the mob.

This silly plot keeps the movie chugging at a decent pace and kids of all ages will have a reasonably good time. Their parents will notice, however, that a big chase scene goes on much too long and that the picture, while explicitly condemning stealing, makes the process of lifting valuables from strangers look like a great deal of harmless fun.

The movie also shows its lovable young heroine engaging in deception of her parents that is far more outrageous—and dangerous —than the story required.

Writer/director Franco Amurri displays the same energetic, no-nonsense story-telling skills he brought to "Flashback," but the biggest name behind this project is executive producer Ridley Scott.

One can imagine that some future grad student will face a formidable task in trying to find common elements in "Blade Runner," "Thelma and Louise" and "Monkey Trouble"—and adequate entertainment.

NEWSDAY, 3/18/94, Part II/p. 69, John Anderson

As the ads for "Monkey Trouble" point out, the title character's a kleptomaniac. And the girl's a pathological liar. And Harvey Keitel's a compulsive actor. Other than that, it's your basic girl-meets-monkey, girl-loses-monkey, girl-wins-monkey-back story.

Thora Birch, a quite capable and attractive young actress ("Patriot Games," "Hocus Pocus") doesn't get quite the direction she needs, but she's winning enough as Eva, a California schoolgirl with problems: She desperately wants a pet, but her stepfather, Tom the police detective (Christopher McDonald), has severe allergies. She has an infant half-brother, Jack (Adrian and Julian Johnson), whom she can barely tolerate. And she has a mother, Amy (Mimi Rogers), who doesn't think that, all things considered, Eva's a very responsible girl.

She's right, although Eva learns responsibility—and we learn patience—after the monkey swings into her life. Naming him Dodger after his baseball cap, she soon learns he's of the artful variety: An escapee from a "gypsy" hustler named Shorty (Harvey Keitel), he's been trained to pick pockets on the Venice Beach boardwalk. Dodger's talents present considerable, predictable difficulties for Eva, an accomplished liar who gets better.

Shorty, meanwhile, is facing his own problems: two large gangsters—"Reservoir Apes"?—who have paid him a considerable down payment for Dodger's services. With the monkey gone, Shorty's looking at a long walk on a short pier.

Director Franco Amurri, who once upon a time worked as an assistant director to Federico Fellini on "City of Women," does what he can with the story, although he should have done more with the psychological aspects of Dodger's re-education. When Eva tries to redirect Dodger's larcenous tendencies, and his impulses tell him to steal, we have the makings of a hairy, banana-eating "'Manchurian Candidate."

But "Monkey Trouble" is mostly monkey business, much of it perpetrated by Keitel. With his metal teeth and mix-and-match millinery, he looks like a cross between Willem Dafoe in "Wild at Heart" and Bob Dylan in "Renaldo and Clara." And he'll apparently appear in any movie offered him. But he does get to engage in some very un-Keitel-like slapstick, and enlivens what can otherwise be rather slow-moving mirth-making

"Monkey Trouble" engages in some of the more blatant product placement you're likely to see in a major motion picture, and indulges itself in protracted sequences of Dodger being cute. Which doesn't really work: Being a Capuchin monkey, his face is cast in a perpetual grimace, a look of alarm. Audiences will have no such excuse.

SIGHT AND SOUND, 11/94, p. 49, Nick James

Venice Beach. Fingers, a capuchin monkey, performs and picks pockets for gypsy organ-grinder Azro 'Shorty' Kohn. Two mobsters want to hire the monkey for a robbery; as a demonstration,

Fingers steals some jewellery, and Azro is given an advance and told to wait for a call. The burgled house is the home of nine-year-old Eva Gregory, who feels neglected; her mother Amy and policeman stepfather Tom, busy doting on their baby son, won't let her keep a pet.

Azro returns home to find his wife and son have left him. Then Fingers runs away, and encounters Eva in the park. She takes him home and hides him in her room, not knowing that Fingers, now renamed Dodger, has stolen an elderly lady's earrings and stashed them in a bedside casket. Eva wants to tell her best friend Katie about Dodger, but she turns up with a gang of other children waiting to hear the secret; Eva refuses to tell them. Due to spend the weekend with her father near the beach, Eva tries to cry off but changes her mind when he cancels. Instead she pretends to Amy and Tom that the arrangement is unchanged, getting Katie's mother to drop her off at her father's house and reconciling with Katie on the way.

The house is locked, but Dodger is able to break in. On the beach front, Eva makes money from Dodger's antics. In a supermarket, she is accused of thieving stuff that Dodger has been taking behind her back. She is let off but then discovers Dodger's hoard from the beach, and begins re-educating him to prefer bananas to jewellery.

Meanwhile Azro has tracked his monkey to Eva's father's house. Eva and Dodger escape, but he tracks her down to the pet shop where she leaves Dodger during school. Meanwhile, Amy and Tom have found Dodger's hoard and believe that Eva is responsible. Azro brings Dodger to demonstrate his skills for the mob boss but finds he won't thieve anymore. After Azro makes a quick exit, the monkey escapes and heads back to the park where he is seen by Katie, who notifies Eva. Azro asks his son to help him retrieve the animal. Amy and Tom are about to go in search for Eva when their son wanders in and says his first word, "monkey". They realise that Eva has been telling the truth when Dodger appears. Meanwhile, Eva is rescued from Azro by Dodger. After Tom's colleagues arrest Azro, his son arrives and Eva gives him the monkey. However, he slips his leash and returns to Eva who is able to bring both Dodger and her baby brother to school for her 'show and tell.'

The Ridley Scott/Mimi Polk production axis seem determined to be eclectic in their output, following up *The Browning Version* with this resolutely Californian comedy aimed at kids. Writer/director Franco Amurri's scheme to emulate the success of *My Girl* and *Home Alone* involves a convoluted plot, driven by a relentlessly dominant electronic music score that leaves little breathing space to dwell on character and performance.

Leaving aside the question of whether or not child actress Thora Birch can handle the speedy range of emotions she is asked to (resentment = pout, fear = screwed-up eyes, embarrassment = looking from side to side), the basis of her character is anyway a rather sketchy mixture of possible anxieties. Eva's desire for a pet is both a sublimation of her jealousy of her toddler half-brother and an attempt to match her mother's joy with her own little bundle of fun, but her vague resentment seems equally shared out between toddler, mother, stepfather, father and best friend. Thus there seems no definite alternative to the bogey-man bad-fatherhood of Harvey Keitel's cartoon villain. This lack of a plausible hero belies the apparently happy ending, which seems contingent on Eva's stepfather losing his allergy to animals.

Despite the frantic pace, the educational parenting parallels tend to distract from the comedy. Attempts to match up the two, such as Eva's attempt to toilet-train Dodger, are perfunctory at best, and the rather cruel way that Azro's embittered son (the monkey's 'true' parent) loses his pet to her at the end sours whatever good humour the film has gathered. Much the saddest sight, however, is the abject gold-toothed mugging of Keitel in an unfamiliar comic role. While he manages not to be too frightening, the latent psychosis carried over from his trademark bad guy roles means that he's never laughable enough to be the butt of slapstick jokes. He lacks the vulnerability that Joe Pesci and Daniel Stern bring to ritual humiliation in the *Home Alone* movies.

Consequently the weight of the movie falls on the slender shoulders of Thora Birch and her monkey. For the film's premise to work, you need to be susceptible to the diminutive scene-stealer's doffing his cap on cue and his scampering antics among the skateboarders, body-builders, check-out cashiers and librarians of Venice Beach; it's a milieu, however, in which mere monkeying around seems relatively sane behaviour.

Also reviewed in:
NEW YORK TIMES, 3/18/94, p. C8, Janet Maslin
VARIETY, 3/21-27/94, p. 57, Emanuel Levy
WASHINGTON POST, 3/18/94, p. D7, Rita Kempley

MOTHER'S BOYS

A Dimension Films release of a CBS Entertainment film. *Executive Producer:* Bob Weinstein, Harvey Weinstein, and Randall Poster. *Producer:* Jack E. Freedman, Wayne S. Williams, and Patricia Herskovic. *Director:* Yves Simoneau. *Screenplay:* Barry Schneider and Richard Hawley. *Based on the book by:* Bernard Taylor. *Director of Photography:* Elliot Davis. *Editor:* Michael Ornstein. *Music:* George S. Clinton. *Music Editor:* Marty Wereski. *Sound:* Clark King and (music) John Whynott. *Sound Editor:* Fred Judkins and Scott Weber. *Casting:* Francine Maisler. *Art Director:* David Bomba. *Set Decorator:* Barbara Cassel. *Set Dresser:* Mark Kusy, Kevin Coyle, Don Riley, and Eric Polczwartek. *Special Effects:* Peter Chesney. *Costumes:* Deena Appel and Simon Tuke. *Make-up:* Julie Hewett. *Stunt Coordinator:* Kevin Swigert. *Running time:* 95 minutes. *MPAA Rating:* R.

CAST: Jamie Lee Curtis (Jude Madigan); Peter Gallagher (Robert Madigan); Joanne Whalley-Kilmer (Callie); Vanessa Redgrave (Lydia); Luke Edwards (Kes); Colin Ward (Michael); Joey Zimmerman (Ben); Joss Ackland (Lansing); Paul Guilfoyle (Mark Kaplan); J.E. Freeman (Everett); John C. McGinley (Mr. Fogel); Jill Freedman (Nurse); Lorraine Toussaint (Robert's Associate); Ken Lerner (Analyst); Mary Ann McGarry (Planetarium Woman); Judith Roberts (Narrator); Sachi Ena (Cynthia); Jeanine Jackson (Market Mom); Jesse Stock (Market Kid).

LOS ANGELES TIMES, 3/21/94, Calendar/p. 5, Kevin Thomas

"Mother's Boys," a scary and unsettling drama of psychological suspense, is as elegant as it is risk-taking. No wonder Jamie Lee Curtis was lured into returning to the kind of genre film with which she launched her career, for this handsome picture affords her the most bravura role of her big-screen career.

She is Jude Madigan, a beautiful, sexy wife and mother of three sons who in the throes of postpartum depression, abandons her rich Los Angeles family to wander about Europe. When her husband, Robert (Peter Gallagher), at last files for divorce, having fallen in love with a demure but resilient assistant principal (Joanne Whalley-Kilmer) at his 12-year-old son's school, Jude abruptly terminates her three-year absence and returns home. No one, even her mother (Vanessa Redgrave), is remotely glad to see her.

Our initial tentative sympathy for Jude gradually evaporates when we realize that she's not interested in merely winning visiting rights or even partial custody of her three children. She is absolutely and utterly determined to get back her entire family, including her husband. In time we realize we're in the present of a dangerously unstable woman.

Working with Barry Schneider and Richard Hawley's adroit adaptation of Bernard Taylor's novel, director Yves Simoneau dares to proceed at a languorous pace, which soon provides a fine contrast to Curtis' nervy, multifaceted portrayal of the savage—and sometimes savagely funny—Jude and ultimately sets up a jolting, literally cliff-hanging finish. The script is anchored in two sad truths about human nature: that the demons of one generation can so easily infect the next, and that nice, decent people can be exceedingly vulnerable to the clever sociopath.

Simoneau is wonderful with his actors, especially with young Luke Edwards in the pivotal role of Kes, the eldest son, the only one old enough to remember and feel abandoned by his mother, who proceeds to manipulate him for her own ends. "Mother's Boys" climaxes in an edge-of-your-seat action-filled finish, but it's actually at its scariest in its convincing depiction of the horrendous things people do to one another in the name of love.

NEW YORK POST, 3/19/94, p. 15, Thelma Adams

Mother's milk turns sour in the Mommie Dearest thriller "Mother's Boys."

The first horror flick about daddy's rights—"Mrs. Doubtfire" tickled the theme for laughs, "Kramer vs. Kramer" milked it for tears—has Jude (Jamie Lee Curtis) returning home after a three-year absence to reclaim her husband, Robert (Peter Gallagher), and three sons.

While Jude was off finding herself, Robert found Callie (Joanne Whalley-Kilmer). Wickedly unhappy about this development, Jude enlists Kes (Luke Edwards), her eldest son, to scratch the match.

Curtis returns to familiar territory. Having started off being chased by a homicidal maniac in "Halloween," the busty but androgynous actress is a second-generation blonde-in-peril. Mother Janet Leigh went under Tony Perkins' knife in Hitchcock's "Psycho."

In Yves Simoneau's "Mother's Boys," the knife turns. As the seductive stalker with a C-section scar and more than a motherly interest in Kes, Curtis shoots killer, looks. When she tells her eldest that "Mother loves you," she's one chill witch. A demon seed is born!

Gallagher (in leading man form with chin-cleft, ebony eyebrows and oh-so-blue eyes) and Kilmer play it straight while Curtis camps it up. It would all simply be a disjointed exercise in divorce horror if the plot didn't start to bubble in the last 30 minutes.

You might be able to predict what's around those dangerous curves on the way to the cliff-hanging climax, but there are some good scares en route.

When Mom's a psychokiller, father always knows best. Papa Gallagher's biggest scare is yet to come shelling out for the shrinks he's going to need to paste this dysfunctional family back together again.

NEWSDAY, 3/19/94, Part II/p. 27, Terry Kelleher

Fairness forbids our calling "Mother's Boys" a routine exploitation film. Please note that it is a little slicker, and a little sicker, than average.

Jamie Lee Curtis plays Jude, the femme fatale du jour. Three years ago, Jude callously walked out on Robert (Peter Gallagher), her architect husband, and their three small sons. But will she let him have a divorce so he can wed Callie (Joanne Whalley-Kilmer), the perfectly nice assistant principal at the boys' school? Afraid not.

Now Jude's vow is "I want my family back," and she'll stop at nothing to regain domestic bliss. She'll try to seduce Robert with provocative outfits (nothing but black underwear under the coat, nothing but nothing under the robe). She'll invade Callie's office, smash herself in the face with a framed photograph, then charge her rival with assault. She'll spray-paint "WHORE" on the side of Callie's car. ("WASH ME" wouldn't be cruel enough.)

If you've read this far—and you've seen those ads for "The 'Fatal Attraction' of the '90s!"—you probably think you need no further information about "Mother's Boys." But you really should know that Jude turns the head of Kes (Luke Edwards), her brooding 12-year-old, by parading before him in the nude and urging him to sit close while she enjoys a bubble bath. How did she develop this unwholesome concept of parenting? Well, Jude's own upbringing was less than exemplary, as belatedly revealed by her mother (a role Vanessa Redgrave inexplicably chose to fill).

Director Yves Simoneau relies on sleaze and self-conscious style to divert the audience awhile, but the fake-out shocks and moody lighting (Curtis' face seems always half-shadowed, except when she's wearing dark glasses) are poor compensation for an acute lack of logic and originality. It all leads to a ludicrous climax that cries out to be advertised as "The Perils of Pauline' of the '90s!"

SIGHT AND SOUND, 5/94, p. 45, Caren Myers

Three years ago, Jude walked out on her husband Robert and their three sons. While 12-year-old Kes, the eldest, is prone to violent rages, his younger brothers Michael, ten, and Ben, six, have settled into their new life and are fond of their father's new girlfriend Callie, the assistant principal at their school. When Jude suddenly returns to reclaim her family, even her own mother Lydia disapproves. Undeterred, Jude appears at the house, where a furious Robert tells her to stay away. But despite his misgivings, he is obliged to let her see her boys. Jude soon wins over the little ones with Nintendo Game Boys and a trip to the planetarium, and confuses the fragile Kes with her own version of events. She then attempts to seduce Robert, but he tells her he is filing for divorce.

Determined to drive Callie away, Jude spray-paints her car and makes mischief at her office. Jude and Kes go away for the weekend. Insisting that they have a stronger than normal mother-son bond because he was born by Caesarian, Jude convinces Kes that Callie is the sole obstacle to the family's reunion. She persuades him to scare Callie with a particularly hostile game, Trials. Lydia overhears Kes explaining the plan to his brothers and confronts him, but he accidentally pushes her down the stairs. Determined to protect the family, Lydia narrowly escapes being suffocated by Jude at the hospital. When Robert goes to the hospital, Kes sets up a mock trial on Jude's instructions, with the hand-cuffed Callie as the accused.

Ben trips when bringing Callie a glass of water and stabs himself on a shard of broken glass. Callie begs Kes to release her so she can drive him to the hospital, but Kes runs outside to see why the dog is barking. Callie is freed by Michael but is unable to open her car door and runs for help with Ben in her arms. Kes and Michael follow in the car. Jude, who is lying in wait for Callie's car, has tampered with the brakes and sends the family dog into the middle of the road to cause an accident. Kes and Michael drive over the cliff, and Jude watches in horror as Callie climbs down to save the boys. Jude follows, intent on finishing the job, but falls to her death.

The formula thriller's yuppie family (here Robert is an architect) has been threatened by such a barrage of psychotic interlopers—overzealous cops, mad tenants, crazed nannies, evil neighbours, wall-eyed temporary secretaries among them—that it was only a matter of time before someone placed the seeds of destruction within the family itself. *Mother's Boys* is a kind of *Fatal Attraction* in reverse, which might have been intriguing if the movie had an iota of credibility. After all, the desire of a mother to come back to her family has great emotional potential.

But in the movie's terms, Jude's running out on her family has stripped her of any maternal, feminine qualities. She is clearly a psycho even before she starts punching out windows and parading naked in front of her son. So when Robert snarls "I'll kill her" the moment she comes back, this is presented as the normal reaction of a concerned father, not as any indication that he might have played a part in her running away.

The movie is not concerned with ambiguity—it does not empathise with Jude's regret at the years she has lost, or with her rage at being excluded from the family's smug little barbecues and shopping trips. Her maternal longings are presented as a sham. It's no accident that Jamie Lee Curtis, the most androgynous of Hollywood actresses, plays Jude, and she is directed to emphasise her predatory, reckless edge. Her angular body and David Bowie-esque hairstyle make you wonder how this unnatural woman could have given birth. Jude drives a Mercedes sports car while Callie, the single career woman, drives a family station wagon—it's clear who the real mother is.

But the film is not about nature versus nurture, the snapping of biological ties; it's just an excuse to jolt us in our seats a few times. And when it comes down to it, the film-makers' nerve fails. The movie does not have anything very horrifying (or even mildly interesting) up its sleeve, and it shies away from even the most incidental of casualties— Ben gets to the hospital on time, Grandma recovers, Callie is shaken but not stirred, even Jocko the dog is unscathed.

To compensate for his singularly ineffective psychopath, director Yves Simoneau falls back on empty stylistic clichés—goldfish bowls toppling over in slow motion, *Vertigo*-style spinning shots, screeching zoom-ins. A frog swims slowly through the title sequence as a scalpel drops into a child's outstretched hand—this leads into the opening scene, where Kes goes berserk in biology class on frog dissecting day. But the frogs, like the rest of the film, have no particular significance. *Mother's Boys* offers little more than the mild amusement of watching Joanne Whalley-Kilmer struggle with an American accent and a ridiculous wig-like hairdo, and as the film creaks towards its laborious, implausible climax one barely has the energy to shrug.

Also reviewed in:
CHICAGO TRIBUNE, 4/15/94, Friday/p. B, Dave Kehr
NEW YORK TIMES, 3/19/94, p. 18, Stephen Holden

VARIETY, 3/23-4/3/94, p. 69, Emanuel Levy
WASHINGTON POST, 4/16/94, p. C4, Desson Howe

MRS. PARKER AND THE VICIOUS CIRCLE

A Fine Line Features release in association with Miramax Films of a Robert Altman production in association with Odyssey Entertainment Ltd. *Executive Producer:* Scott Bushnell and Ira Deutchman. *Producer:* Robert Altman. *Director:* Alan Rudolph. *Screenplay:* Alan Rudolph and Randy Sue Coburn. *Director of Photography:* Jan Kiesser. *Editor:* Suzy Elmiger. *Music:* Mark Isham. *Music Editor:* Steven Borne. *Sound:* Richard Nichol and (music) Steven Krause. *Casting:* Lucie Robitaille. *Production Designer:* François Séguin. *Art Director:* James Fox. *Set Decorator:* Frances Calder. *Set Dressers:* Jean Bourret and Anne Galea. *Costumes:* John Hay and Renée April. *Make-up:* Micheline Trépanier and Nathalie Trépanier. *Special Make-up Effects:* Adrien Morot. *Running time:* 125 minutes. *MPAA Rating:* R.

CAST: Jennifer Jason Leigh (Dorothy Parker); Matthew Broderick (Charles MacArthur); Campbell Scott (Robert Benchley); Peter Gallagher (Alan Campbell); Jennifer Beals (Gertrude Benchley); Andrew McCarthy (Eddie Parker); Wallace Shawn (Horatio Byrd); Martha Plimpton (Jane Grant); Sam Robards (Harold Ross); Lili Taylor (Edna Ferber); James LeGros (Deems Taylor); Gwyneth Paltrow (Paula Hunt); Nick Cassavetes (Robert Sherwood); David Thornton (George S. Kaufman); Heather Graham (Mary Kennedy Taylor); Tom McGowan (Alexander Woollcott); Chip Zien (Franklin P. Adams); Gary Basaraba (Heywood Broun); Jane Adams (Ruth Hale); Stephen Baldwin (Roger Spalding); Matt Malloy (Marc Connelly); Rebecca Miller (Neysa McMein); Jake Johannsen (John Peter Toohey); Amelia Campbell (Mary Brandon Sherwood); David Gow (Donald Ogden Stewart); Leni Parker (Beatrice Kaufman); Jean-Michael Henry (Harpo Marx); Stanley Tucci (Fred Hunter); Mina Badie (Joanie Gerard); Randy Lowell (Alvan Barach); Keith Carradine (Will Rogers); Gabriel Gascon (Georges Attends); Malcolm Gets (F. Scott Fitzgerald); Peter Benchley (Frank Crowninshield).

LOS ANGELES TIMES, 12/21/94, Calendar/p. 4, Peter Rainer

The Algonquin crowd in "Mrs. Parker and the Vicious Circle"—the film should be called "Smart and Smarter"—are a nattery bunch of smarty-pants cynics, mostly men. The only woman who holds her own with them is Dorothy Parker (Jennifer Jason Leigh).

As a Jazz Age wit in a roomful of overweening fellow wits, Dorothy is a sodden sprite. Her zingers take the form of funky aphorisms, but her line delivery is deliberately wan. It's as if she's bored by her own genius for barbs.

Directed by Alan Rudolph and co-scripted by him with Randy Sue Coburn, "Mrs. Parker" is a real odd duck of a movie. It seems to have been made both as tribute and put-down. The sporty conviviality of the Algonquin Round Table—the playwrights, critics, poets, actors, artists and hangers-on who regularly convened for lunch at New York's Algonquin Hotel for more than a decade—is celebrated, and yet; there's a hollowness to the confabs.

Rudolph doesn't really want to skewer the likes of George S. Kaufman (David Thornton), Robert Benchley (Campbell Scott), Charles MacArthur (Matthew Broderick), New Yorker magazine founder Harold Ross (Sam Robards), Robert Sherwood (Nick Cassavetes) or Alexander Woollcott (Tom McGowan). He doesn't, want to spoil the party but he doesn't want to make these people the life of the party either. Their can-you-top-this banter is full of *bon mots* that aren't all that *mot*.

Since the Algonquin Round Table has faded into America literary mythology, Rudolph's attempt to revive it seems musty and coy. It's not just a matter of "Who cares?" We are given no compelling *reason* to care. Parker, and her extended and deep friendship with Benchley, are thc movie's centerpiece, but most of the time we seem to be floating high above the proceedings. The movie is basically about writers as jawboners, as drinkers, with Parker as Queen of the Hill.

Since most of their achievements—on Broadway, in Hollywood, in the magazines—are skimped or glossed over, we're unfortunately left with their personalities. And Rudolph, as usual, puts brackets around his people: Like the Paris expatriates in "The Moderns," the Algonquin gabbers are conceits first and human beings second. They congregate in a mellifluous, boozy haze. The inauthenticity is carefully wrought—even the furniture seems to be play-acting.

Parker starts out hung over with cynicism and, by the time the film finishes up with her death in 1967, she's essentially the same way. In between she slashes her wrists, puts up with a series of disdainful husbands and lovers, goes to Hollywood and retreats to semi-anonymity in Manhattan—she's a pixie Garbo who still goes out.

Leigh manages the 30-plus year trajectory with ease and yet her performance seems like a deeply felt stunt. Her clipped archness is apparently a dead-ringer for Parker's but, as with Leigh's Katharine Hepburnish accent in "Hudsucker Proxy," the exaggerated intonations distract from the woman underneath. Leigh manages to work up a fair amount of feeling for Parker without stooping to easy pathos, and that's an achievement. At times she fulfills Alexander Woollcott's famous description of Parker as a cross between Little Nell and Lady Macbeth. But the Dorothy of this movie doesn't really live on in our imaginations. None of the characters do.

The irony of Parker's life is that, although her lifelong theme was the seductive closeness of death, she managed to outlive just about everybody in the Round Table. She squandered her considerable gifts as a poet and short-story writer and then sat in silent witness to the wreckage. Some of this material comes through in the movie, but not enough—perhaps because Parker's talents on the page are never really given their due. Instead Parker is memorialized as a misery-wracked quipster. It's too limiting a conception. Her mausoleum could use a few more rooms.

NEW YORK, 12/12/94, p. 66, David Denby

Jennifer Jason Leigh is a determined and gifted actress who grabs hold of a part the way a mastiff latches onto an intruders pant leg. Short and fierce, she has tremendous concentration and discipline—and a rather daunting taste for bleakness and misery. In such movies as *Last Exit to Brooklyn* and *Miami Blues*, Leigh has played unhappy, self-lacerating young women—the kind of women born to lose. She's almost too pure, gallant to the point of perversity, and even as one admires her, one also builds up some resistance to her work. (Perhaps even Jean Rhys would have found her use-me-and-discard-me fatalism a little disconcerting.) Jason Leigh's performance as Dorothy Parker in Alan Rudolph's *Mrs. Parker and the Vicious Circle* is a classic of defiant masochism, a distillation of bitter vulnerability. Tilting her head and sounding like a soused duchess, Jason Leigh mutters the too-famous epigrams and insults through clenched teeth. She turns Dorothy Parker's joking into a high-wire act, all tension and taut danger. She's great, but she never gives herself—or us—a break.

The real Dorothy Parker was sometimes puzzling, but as portrayed in this accomplished movie, she's virtually unfathomable. Stuck in a hopeless marriage with a morphine-addicted World War I vet, Eddie Parker (Andrew McCarthy), she has an affair with the journalist/playwright Charles MacArthur (in the appealing person of Matthew Broderick), who is also married. When she finds MacArthur in bed with another woman, she goes into a severe tailspin apparently lasting years. MacArthur seems contrite enough—he's an adulterer, so is she—yet she carries on as if he had just invented betrayal. At the same time, she adores the humorist Robert Benchley (Campbell Scott), who returns her affection but apparently finds every other woman in the world more sexually attractive. Was Dorothy Parker a masochist or just unlucky? The movie suggests both possibilities, and in Jason Leigh's performance, Dorothy leaps into unhappiness the way a bird takes flight—naturally, inevitably.

Co-written by Randy Sue Coburn, *Mrs. Parker* presents a disillusioned view not only of Parker but of the entire giddy Algonquin Round Table (Alexander Woollcott, Marc Connelly, Harold Ross, George S. Kaufman, and Edna Ferber are also in attendance). They boozed, they wasted their talents, they were funny but infantile, turning insult humor into destructive sport. The movie doesn't go anywhere dramatically, but it successfully sustains a party atmosphere of frivolous brilliance. This is incomparably Alan Rudolph's best picture. I loved the rich texture of jokes, the nattering puns in the background of scenes, one linked to the next as the show-offs—try to top one another. At a party scene, as Parker is talking to someone in the foreground, the others can been seen through a doorway down on their hands and knees, blowing tissues along the floor (a sort of race).

The characters joke and drink as their hearts break. But why are their hearts breaking? We can see why they didn't do more serious work—they had too much fun sitting around drinking and collaborating with one another on plays and revues—but is there any chance they could have? And if they couldn't, what, exactly, is being held against them? Rudolph and Coburn judge them as shallow without suggesting what depths might be there, lying unexplored. The priggish note rings false; Rudolph and Coburn are buying into precisely the atmosphere of glamorous dissipation—without it, they wouldn't have a movie. (No one would be interested in a movie about hardworking, serious writers.)

Mrs. Parker starts in black-and-white, in 1937, when Dorothy Parker is apparently a cynical Hollywood hack, married (for the second time) to Alan Campbell (Peter Gallagher), a man for whom she has little admiration; then it flashes back (in color this time) to her dissolute life in New York after World War I. In other words, *Mrs. Parker* moves from the period in which its heroine is a middle-aged broken-down alcoholic to the period in which she's a young broken-down alcoholic. It then carries her through to the squalid end, in New York, when she goes out in public clutching a lapdog and emanates, in her eyes and flesh, an unmistakable waiflike look of fear. Interspersed with the jokes and the miseries there are straight-into-the-camera sequences, also shot in black-and-white, of Jason Leigh reciting Parker's little poems. If she sounds drunk during the rest of the movie, she reads the poems as if she were biting carrot sticks—precisely, elegantly. The poems are really very small, but she turns them into mini-arias of self-mocking despair. The question the movie won't answer is How did Dorothy Parker survive to the age of 73? There must have been something besides gin and wisecracks sustaining her. We know that the actual Dorothy Parker loved books and was generous to writers. That doesn't explain much, but at least it's a beginning.

The most shocking thing about the Algonquin wits, of course, was not their drinking or time-wasting but their astonishing fame. None of them attended to the practice of literature with any seriousness. The were writer-celebrities of the twenties, working in theater, journalism, light fiction, and verse, and, later, the movies. They hyped one another, repeating one another's jokes in their newspaper columns, and created their own myth of sophistication, which often enough depended more on commercial facetiousness than wit. They were skilled entertainers, and we have nothing like so coherent a group now; indeed, the Algonquin style of debonair letters cannot be understood apart from such long-gone phenomena as the multiplicity of newspapers in New York and the relative ease of putting on a play. In its more chaste moments, the Algonquin group produced the airily arrogant tone of the early *New Yorker*; in its promiscuous ones, the wisecracking atmosphere of thirties Hollywood comedy.

The name-dropping and famous-quip-dropping gets a little thick, yet the movie does many things right. Campbell Scott, looking wonderful in his Benchley mustache, gives a sneakily glamorous performance. Scott, almost whispering, sidles into jokes, as if Benchley were evading his own talent. And there's a wonderfully evocative Long Island lawn party, at Alexander Woollcott's house. As everyone drinks and plays croquet, and Harpo Marx in a white suit runs around goosing the ladies, the whole period of thc twenties, which mixed drink, waste, and a peculiarly American high-spiritedness, comes most beautifully and heart-wrenchingly into focus.

NEW YORK POST, 11/23/94, p. 44, Thelma Adams

That accent!

It will undoubtedly be the most discussed point of Alan Rudolph's "Mrs. Parker and the Vicious Circle." In the title role, Jennifer Jason Leigh adopts a slurred, nasal mid-Atlantic lockjaw with the power to grate on audiences and send dogs squealing for cover.

The talented Leigh has said that she culled the voice from audio tapes of the famed poet, drama critic, fiction- and screen-writer, Dorothy Parker. In the case of this accent, artifice might have served Leigh better than hewing close to reality.

It's to the actress' credit then, that, voice aside, she has created one of 1994's most memorable leading ladies. As the brightest flame of the famed Algonquin Round Table, a boozy gathering of literary lights on Manhattan's 44th Street, Leigh delivers a sharp portrait in contradictions: witty and woebegone, acid-tongued and thin-skinned, sexually voracious and exceedingly loyal.

Director Rudolph, who co-wrote the script with Randy Sue Coburn, follows "The Moderns" with another sprawling tableau of an artistic set. It is not surprising that the producer, and Rudolph's mentor, is Robert Altman, director of "Short Cuts" and the coming "Pret-A-Porter."

The breakthrough performance here is not Leigh's; she can be expected to do the unexpected and make an indelible impression. Campbell Scott's Robert Benchley is a revelation.

The platonic love affair between Parker and the married Benchley, soul mates and intellectual equals who were not fool enough to ruin a good thing with sex, stands out as the most satisfying dramatic line in "Mrs. Parker and the Vicious Circle."

Scott portrays Benchley with a rare sweetness and gentility. Scott is not another young actor playing at being a grown-up. His Benchley is a man growing into his complications who takes love—but not himself seriously.

Matthew Broderick also makes an admirable career leap as Charles MacArthur, the dashing journalist and playwright who stole Parker's heart and returned it the worse for wear.

I am, in general, a Rudolph fan, and found "Mrs. Parker" entertaining, intelligent, but dramatically flawed. The danger of these big-canvas pictures is that the whole doesn't add up to the sum of the parts. But, if the parts include a vision of a fascinating, literate female with a deadly wit and a terrific, troubled soul portrayed by one of the most risk-taking actresses of her generation, it deserves admiration and support.

NEWSDAY, 11/23/94, Part II/p. B9, Jack Mathews

"You don't want to be the town drunk, Eddie. Not in Manhattan."

The line delivered by Dorothy Parker (Jennifer Jason Leigh) to her slushed husband (Andrew McCarthy) in Prohibition Era New York, points up both the best and worst of "Mrs. Parker and the Vicious Circle," Alan Rudolph's bittersweet tribute to the famed short-story writer, critic and Algonquin Hotel Round Table raconteur.

In the context of the scene, with Eddie drowning himself in bathtub gin, the line is poignantly funny, and just the sort of literary image you would expect a writer of Parker's celebrated wit to ad lib. However, taken as one line from an improbable perfect two hours of colorful banter, repartee, bon mots, puns, putdowns and dish, it feels as deliberate as a kick in a chorus line revue.

Rudolph, one of the most literary-minded film directors, has made himself the trustee of the spirit of the Algonquin lunch bunch, much as he did with the Lost Generation of 1920s Paris in "The Moderns," and try as he does to shutter some of its overblown mythology, "Mrs. Parker" makes a loving contribution to it.

"There were no giants," says Parker, looking back on the Round Table's '20s from Hollywood, where she worked in the '40s. "We were just a bunch of loudmouths spouting off." Moments later, cueing the first flashback to the early days, she says, in a voice softened by nostalgia, "I suppose it was ... colorful."

It certainly is colorful from this perspective. Though Parker is portrayed as a woman of surpassing sadness and unfulfillment, the movie is far too respectful of her legend, and those of critic/humorist Robert Benchley (Campbell Scott) and other Round Table notables, for it to qualify as biography. But as an impressionist's view of a particular time, place and attitude, it is a sublime achievement.

Rudolph and Leigh both claim to be attempting a realistic psychological portrait of Parker. If so, they must have inhaled some of the gas they were letting out of the balloon. Leigh, having spent hours listening to Parker's voice on tape, has effected the speaking style of some one reciting her own words at a book reading, with accents and inflection dead-on. The characters don't have conversations, they have routines. Even the lunch sessions at the Algonquin, where the wit sizzles like steaks, seem more idealized than spontaneous.

No giants? Well, some have at least stood tall. The novelist Edna Ferber (Lili Taylor), the playwrights George S. Kaufman (David Thornton), Robert E. Sherwood (Nick Cassavetes), and Marc Connelly (Matt Malloy), New Yorker magazine founder Harold Ross (Sam Robards). Avoiding name-dropping in this story is impossible.

Rudolph made a couple of silly choices, having Keith Carradine, direct from the Will Rogers Follies, drop by in character ("I never liked a man I didn't meet," Parker tells him), and having Harpo Marx (Jean-Michael Henry) silently running around goosing people at parties. But for the most part, he held his focus on Parker, on her struggles with being a writer and an independent but needful woman, and her unsatisfying relationships with her husbands and lovers.

Campbell Scott is wonderful as Benchley, giving a brilliant impersonation of one of the humorist's dryly hilarious stage monologues, and showing how he succumbed to the liberated era's seductive vices of booze, sex and ego. It's a performance to be remembered at Oscar time.

Leigh's work is more problematic. She goes in and out of her character, sometimes more concerned with the image she's filling than the emotions she's feeling. "Wit has truth in it; wisecracking is simply calisthenics with words," Parker wrote in the Paris Review in 1956. Leigh and "Mrs. Parker" show a little of both.

SIGHT AND SOUND, 3/95, p. 44, Philip Strick

Hollywood, 1937. Dorothy Parker and her second husband, Alan Campbell, with whom she has written *A Star is Born*, watch the film being made at Selznick Studios. Following a brief reunion with her old friend Robert Benchley, Parker recalls the days, in 1917, when they first worked together at *Vanity Fair*, recruited by editor Frank Crowninshield, who launched her as a drama critic.

Married to Edwin Pond Parker II, who returned as a drunk and a drug-addict from military service, Parker increasingly turns to the company of other New York critics and writers, who take to meeting daily at lunchtime at the Algonquin hotel. Headed by *New York Times* theatre critic Alexander Woollcott, these noisy gatherings provide the ideal stimulus for the sharply cynical shafts of humour for which she becomes quickly renowned.

Fired from *Vanity Fair*, Parker turns for sympathy to Robert Benchley who, despite having a family to support, promptly announces his resignation. The two share an office; he as a columnist for *Life* and *New York World*, she writing poems and short stories. The Algonquin lunches continue, and after a visit by famed entertainer Will Rogers, the hotel provides a special table for future meetings of the self-designated "Vicious Circle". At a festive Round Table cabaret Parker meets Chicago journalist Charles MacArthur and falls for him. A compulsive womaniser, he is soon unfaithful, and despairingly she attempts suicide. Benchley comes to her rescue and not for the first time they consider having an affair; instead, they decide to remain just good friends.

Inspired by the Vicious Circle, Harold Ross launches *The New Yorker* in 1925; contributions from Parker are to appear for nearly 30 years. A collection of poems proves a best-seller, and her reputation grows, but her life remains unstable and unfulfilling. She marries Alan Campbell, 11 years her junior, suffers a miscarriage, and moves with him to Hollywood. In 1945, while Campbell is away at the War, news reaches her of Benchley's death from cirrhosis of the liver. She remembers one of the last Vicious Circle parties, at which Benchley was drunk and Parker was persuaded to visit a psychiatrist. In 1958, on her way to receive the Peabody Award for Achievement and Integrity, she stops off at a bar and distractedly answers the questions of an eager fan. She dies in 1967 at the age of 74.

In an interview that runs behind the final credits, Dorothy Parker admits to participating in the Spanish Civil War (reporting from Madrid in November, 1937), dismissing the Beat Generation (she was scathing about Kerouac), and whispers her preferred epitaph (something along the lines, perhaps, of her ironic *Tombstones in the Starlight* verses). It is clear then that there was considerably more to her than Alan Rudolph's film has had time to tell. Although the screenplay is admirably packed with information, it is selective in emphasis. Dull and disconsolate scenes at the typewriter are sensibly excluded, but it is disappointing not to see more of Parker's film studio activities, while her co-authored play *The Ladies of the Corridor* ("the only thing I ever did that I was proud of") is firmly ignored.

Worse, in measuring the decline and fall of Dorothy Parker from the time of her affair with Charles MacArthur in the mid-20s, the film overlooks at least two vital perspectives. There is little hint of the shock-waves caused by her political views, damaging her Hollywood career to the extent that she was pronounced Communist by the Un-American Activities Committee in 1952. Instead, we are shown a promiscuous and alcoholic Parker, concerned more with dog food than civil rights. And in place of an authentic account of her stormy but remarkably durable marriage to the wealthy Alan Campbell (whom she divorced once and married twice), the

Rudolph version puts Robert Benchley firmly at the centre of her world in a grandly unconsummated *folie à deux*.

It is the reluctance of this relationship to accept its own consequences that turns Parker's story into the stuff of Rudolph's dreams. If she had been played by Genevieve Bujold, (*Trouble in Mind, The Moderns*) the resemblance to Rudolph's archetypal woman might almost have been too obvious. Incarnated by a welter of women in *Welcome to LA* and by Geraldine Chaplin in *Remember My Name*, she's the one for whom the perfect love remains inspiringly just out of reach, a source both of satisfaction and of perplexity, leading to desperation. In Parker's case, the result is partly that somnambulistic (or inebriated) condition which has infected Rudolph's heroines since *Premonition* (1972) and partly an irresistible eloquence. Rudolph has always written good dialogue and here, legitimately plagiarising Parker, he has excelled himself.

A master of the social event, Rudolph reconstructs the Algonquin as he formerly constructed Paris for *The Moderns*—in a Montreal studio, with much the same vitality of costume and decor, footnoted by much the same weary observation of parties that outlive their proper span and mornings after that last for days. The Round Table lunches are a fanfare of one-liners amid a hubbub of passing names elusively on the edge of distinction. They are filmed with exuberant swoops of the camera. The formal geometries of Rudolph's early films have been replaced by the mellow appreciation of furniture, an inclination to glide from one beautifully appointed room to another or to contemplate a lakeside garden party in a single leisurely revolve—all indolence and charm. As usual, the past is where the colour lies; for the present, which in *Mrs. Parker*'s case seems to mean everything after the mid-30s, Rudolph shifts to a prosaic monochrome.

Augmenting Mark Isham's music, set in its accustomed introspective key, the film's soundtrack is punctuated by Parker's poems. Her unexpectedly vulnerable cadences, with their bitter punch rhymes ("And if that makes you happy, kid/You'll be the first it ever did") are less crowd pleasing than her more famous asides—"I never liked a man I didn't meet", "Don't look at me in that tone of voice", "A girl can get splinters sliding down a barrister"—but they remain her salvation. However sparsely we are informed about Parker's pursuit of the unsuitable, however fictional the unexplored romance with Benchley (who has in this elegant rendering by Campbell Scott, all the dash of another Errol Flynn), a portrait of a genuine loner emerges from this melancholy commentary.

Employing accents said to be accurate (although they sound at first like a W. C. Fields impersonation), Jennifer Jason Leigh constructs a jaded and terminally wounded Parker, as inexplicable now as she must have seemed in her time with her unsteady poise, pitiless self-appraisals, and strange miscellany of distraught hats. This formidable performance, as cunning and detailed as her contributions to *Rush* and *Miami Blues*, gives Rudolph's amiably fragmented, eavesdropping agenda more than a few useful hints of plausibility. For the real Dorothy Parker, nevertheless, a dose of *Constant Reader* remains the best recommendation.

TIME, 12/12/94, p. 90, Richard Schickel

Dorothy Parker quipped her way into minor celebrity, wrote her way into modest immortality and drank herself into near oblivion. All talk and no action, she is not an ideal subject for a movie. But if you must film this life, you'd better do something more than flatly recount the failed promise and failed romances that made it miserable.

At times Alan Rudolph, the director (and co-writer) of *Mrs. Parker and the Vicious Circle*, seems to have a larger purpose, which is to challenge the supposed glamour of the bright, bibulous young writers who drew themselves up to the round table at Manhattan's Algonquin Hotel in the 1920s. Yet Rudolph remains of two minds about his subjects. He wants them to charm us, but he also wants to show how their infinite distractability stunted their lives and careers. His ambivalence creates not an intriguing thematic tension but merely confusion.

Rudolph doesn't sharply differentiate these figures—this is a movie of cameos—and his re-creations of their famously brittle conversations suffer from a desperate case of fallen archness. What's worst is that the development of the film's central character is so uninvolving. Jennifer Jason Leighs draggy performance as Parker is all studied accent (something vaguely mid-Atlantic but never before heard on Earth) and equally studied self-pity. Her sadness is attributed mainly to her failure to sexually consummate a relationship with her pal Robert Benchley (Campbell

Scott). But this is a dithery and inconsequential tragedy, and it cannot sustain our sympathy, or our interest in this inept film.

VILLAGE VOICE, 12/6/94, p. 58, Georgia Brown

"At the *center* of the world's most notorious table ... was a woman ahead of her time." So goes the poster copy for *Mrs. Parker and the Vicious Circle.* As Dorothy was wont to quip, "Bullshit." As Edmund Wilson, who was there, said in a review of one of her books, "Her wit is the wit of a particular time and place."

The time was the '20s and Parker made a splash in a journalistic genre called "light verse"—coy rhymes, deflating punch lines with tough-cookie sentiments; "do-dahs" Dorothy called them. Later she composed some heftier, mostly sad stories, of which "Big Blonde" was and is the popular favorite, Her theater and book criticism was waspish and best on the putdown. Mostly, though, she was a figure, a glib girl in a guys' town, a lady lush who nevertheless was fairly prolific and lived, while others dropped like flies, well into her seventies. But even in her success, the aura of failure and doom clung to her. Doom was the scent she gave off, her brand of perfume.

Drink and dance and laugh and lie,
Love, the reeling midnight through,
For tomorrow we shall die!
(But, alas, we never do.)

She even belittled herself for botching her suicides.

The Parker that Alan Rudolph and cowriter Randy Sue Coburn dote on is the class cynic, the game girl sitting at the Round Table with assorted menfolk—most notably the buttoned-up but soon-to-be-unbuttoned Robert Benchley (Campbell Scott)—poised to snicker, snipe, and skewer. There's no trace in the film of the D.P, of the late '20s and '30s, after her first collection, with the aptly macabre title *Enough Rope*, turned into an unexpected bestseller and she became the companion of Gerald and Sara "Living Well" Murphy.

Although *Mrs. Parker* has a frame set in her later, Hollywood years—Dorothy (Jennifer Jason Leigh) knitting on a set, coddling her pooch of the moment, bitching at her young husband, screenwriter Alan Campbell (Peter Gallagher)— most of the movie takes place in the early '20s, at the start of her career. We see her first husband, Mr. Parker (Andrew McCarthy), return unannounced from the trenches, (Dorothy, nee Rothschild, once said she married Edwin Pond Parker II for his "nice, clean name.") Eddie turns out to have picked up a morphine habit while driving an ambulance, and isn't much more help to the movie than he was to Parker. She had a taste for good-looking losers, cads who leave.

Here was a woman who made an impression early on with "Women: A Hate Song" ("I hate Women/They get on my Nerves"). Like Lillian Hellman, Parker preferred being one of the boys and didn't much take to competition. She was especially contemptuous of suburban wives like the maddeningly compliant Gertrude Benchley (here played by Jennifer Beals), wife of Dorothy's soulmate. But again and again, the boys, and even Mr. B., let her down.

The sun's gone dim, and
The moon's turned black;
For I loved him, and
He didn't love back.

Her best relationships were with dogs.

Benchley maintains his allure by not going to bed with Dorothy and being a swell friend. Like a screwball comedy couple, they call each other Mrs. Parker and Mr. Benchley, when she doesn't call him Fred: when Dorothy is rudely dismissed from *Vanity Fair*, Fred resigns in solidarity. The two chums rent a Times Square cubicle, install back-to-back desks, and carry on their droll, irreverent antics. (When Benchley did latch into a career of adultery—just alluded to here—it was with a 19-year-old Western Union clerk whom the working drama critic could find a part for on the stage. Revered for his integrity, Mr. B. was known to regularly miss the first act of plays he reviewed. Later he often missed the whole thing)

Meanwhile, their luncheon table at the Algonquin swells. These rowdy crowd scenes are used as occasions for cutesy cameos; the funnier-looking the actor the better because this was a singularly funny-looking group. Here's porky Alexander Woollcott (Tom McGowan); here's Harold Ross (Sam Robards) starting up his new magazine. "Why not call it *The New Yorker*?" someone pipes up. Will Rogers (Keith Carradine) sashays in under a Stetson. My favorite: a wry, quipping Lili Taylor as dowdy Edna Ferber.

Rudolph has affinities for artsy groups and moody milieus (*Choose Me, The Moderns*), and particularly for romantic aches and hazy nostalgia. At heart *Mrs. Parker* wants to represent a time and temperament, a national mood, as the best and brightest—or at least the brightest—lost their way. Parker's own subject is incapacity, loneliness, the publicly aching heart, and the glossy cover of wit, not grit. The circle closes for a magical time because the links don't function well independently—a critique delivered in the movie by Dorothy's analyst. Most of the revelers ended sadly. Most—even the teetotaling prohibitionist Benchley—turned into serious alcoholics.

As Mrs, P., Leigh seems physically right—a tiny, spaniel-eyed waif sulking in the shade of assorted hat brims until doing something impulsive like whacking her wrists with a straight razor. But her speech, halfway into that continental accent she put on in *The Hudsucker Proxy*, is seriously misguided. Leigh says she modeled accent and delivery on Parker. Maybe Parker soused. (She usually was.) But in recordings I've heard, Parker projects, she doesn't swallow her words in a gargley mutter. If she'd talked like Leigh talks here, none of those bon mots could've been picked up.

Leavening Benchley's mischief-making with WASP chivalry, Scott gives the sort of impressive performance that makes you think he's a seriously underused actor. Still, I'm compelled to say, Sorry, he's no Robert Benchley. And I'm not talking about the double chin. (Actually, in the *Vanity Fair* years, Benchley was trim and quite good-looking. By the time he got around to making motion pictures, he'd blown into a pudge.)

Benchley's comic persona had a wonderful befuddled klutziness, a daft humbleness, that put people in stitches. Here Scott delivers two of Benchley's most famous comedy routines, The Art of Making Motion Pictures," which opens the film, and "The Treasurer's Report," and neither of these drew a single audible chuckle at screenings. Many movie-goers will not even know what they're supposed to be watching. (Film Forum's Bruce Goldstein, who rates Benchley one of the century's great comics and will take any opportunity to trot out his collection of one reelers, has scheduled a Benchley miniseries on selected days during the Christmas holidays.) In a sanitized bio of his wayward father, Nathaniel Benchley observed of the old man's humor; "Few of the things he says were by themselves funny; they depended on the atmosphere of the moment ... and they are only funny if the mood in which they were said can be reproduced."

Atmosphere, mood, whatever, it's missing here. They got the decor down—great wallpaper, great hats, and gauzy dresses—but a whole universe of people working, thinking, self-destructing is missing. A friend says she kept wondering if she'd wandered into *Bugsy Malone*, Alan Parker's kiddie gangster pic where 12-year-olds dress up in slinky gowns and tuxes, with mustaches drawn under their noses, and the whole game is how cute they look when coarse words escape their pretty little mouths. This, I'm afraid, is the impression Leigh, Scott, and most of the other actors here make: They look adorable parading about, but they're not real grown-ups.

Also reviewed in:
CHICAGO TRIBUNE, 12/23/94, Friday/p. N, Michael Wilmington
NEW YORK TIMES, 11/23/94, p. C9, Janet Maslin
NEW YORKER, 12/12/94, p. 128, Anthony Lane
VARIETY, 5/16-22/94, p. 39, Todd McCarthy
WASHINGTON POST, 12/23/94, p. D1, Hal Hinson
WASHINGTON POST, 12/23/94, Weekend/p. 36, Desson Howe

MURDER MAGIC

A Metropolis Pictures release. *Executive Producer:* Alvin Rothkopf. *Producer:* Windell Williams and Mavis K. Fowler. *Director:* Windell Williams. *Screenplay:* Windell Williams. *Director of Photography:* John Rosnell. *Editor:* Spence Daniels. *Music:* Reginald Woods. *Running time:* 90 minutes. *MPAA Rating:* Not Rated.

CAST: Ron Cephas Jones (Buddy Dixon); D. Ruben Green (Leo Dixon); Collette Wilson (Gabrielle); Jeni Anderson (Betty); Glenn Dandridge (Gleason).

NEWSDAY, 5/6/94, Part II/p. B14, Gene Seymour

"Murder Magic" has already acquired legendary status for having been made from roughly $75,000 in T-shirt sales. The shirts bore the title of the film along with a caricature of director Windell Williams, a Long Island University grad whose previous experience was with commercials and music videos.

This contemporary African-American spin on the Cain and Abel story focuses on Leo Dixon (D. Ruben Green), a bow-tied Brooklyn buppie poised to move from the district attorney's office to City Council. From there, who knows? Governor, he thinks. So does his supportive wife, Gabrielle (Collette Wilson), who knows little or nothing about Leo's shady past.

She doesn't know, for instance, that Leo has a brother named Buddy (Ron Cephas Jones) who's just been released from three years in prison back in North Carolina. Buddy, a dry-witted hipster-magician who's got at least one extraordinary trick in his repertoire, say's he's "hungry, horny and angry."

The person he's angriest at is Leo, who's the reason Buddy was imprisoned for the murder of their father. Buddy heads to Brooklyn to confront Leo, who's not anxious to have the circumstances surrounding the murder muddying up his campaign. With eyes focused implacably on the prize, Leo is determined to make sure that the brothers' tangle past doesn't come to light—by, as it were, any means necessary.

There are times when "Murder Magic" *looks* as if it were made on a shoestring—a few awkward transitions, some scenes that on too long. But all these lapses are overcome by the insinuating cleverness and astringent bite of Williams' darkly funny tales of revenge, betrayal and the trouble black "striving" can sometimes yield.

Also reviewed in:
NEW YORK TIMES, 5/10/94, p. C19, Stephen Holden

MY FATHER, THE HERO

A Buena Vista Pictures release of a Touchstone Pictures presentation of a Cité Films/Film par Film/D.D. Productions coproduction in association with the Edward S. Feldman Company. *Executive Producer:* Edward S. Feldman. *Producer:* Jacques Bar and Jean-Louis Livi. *Director:* Steve Miner. *Screenplay:* Francis Veber and Charlie Peters. *Based on the film "Mon Père, Ce Héros" by:* Gérard Lauzier. *Director of Photography:* Daryn Okada. *Editor:* Marshall Harvey. *Music:* David Newman. *Music Editor*: Tom Villano. *Sound:* Joseph Geisinger, Les Lazarowitz, and (music) Tim Boyle and Bob Fernandez. *Sound Editor:* Dane A. Davis. *Casting:* Dianne Crittenden. *Production Designer:* Christopher Nowak. *Art Director:* Patricia Woodbridge. *Set Decorator:* Don K. Ivey. *Costumes:* Vicki Sanchez. *Make-up:* Guiseppe Campagna. *Stunt Coordinator:* Tim Davison. *Running time:* 90 minutes. *MPAA Rating:* PG.

CAST: Gérard Depardieu (André); Katherine Heigl (Nicole); Dalton James (Ben); Lauren Hutton (Megan); Faith Prince (Diana); Stephen Tobolowsky (Mike); Ann Hearn (Stella); Robyn Peterson (Doris); Frank Renzulli (Fred); Manny Jacobs (Raymond); Jeffrey Chea

(Pablo); Michael Robinson (Tom); Stephen Burrows (Hakim); Robert Miner (Mr. Porter); Betty Miner (Mrs. Porter); Roberto Escobar (Alberto); Yusef Bulos (Cab Driver); Stacey Williamson (Airport Bartender); Malou Corrigan (Ben's Girlfriend); Robin Bolter (Raymond's Girlfriend); Steve Wise (Ben's Father); Judy Clayton (Ben's Mother); Bonnie Byfield (Guest); Jennifer Roberts (Girl #1); Felicity Ingraham (Girl #2); Noa Meldy (Pablo's Girlfriend); Sid Raymond (Elderly Guest); Anthony Delaney (Hotel Bartender); Michelle Riu (Girl on TV); Dave Corey (Father at Beach); Dorian Jones (David); Tom Bahr (Guest); Eileen Santillan and Juan Santillan (Tango Dancers); Emma Thompson (Isabelle).

LOS ANGELES TIMES, 2/4/94, Calendar/p. 15, Peter Rainer

The arrival of "My Father, the Hero" begs the question: Why does Hollywood persist in remaking French sex comedies? Most of the originals—including "The Tall Blonde Man With One Black Shoe" and "Les Fugitifs," remade as "Three Fugitives"—weren't all that sexy or funny to begin with. And with the exception of "Three Men and a Little Lady," none of these remakes, which also include "The Toy," "Blame It on Rio," "Partners" and "Buddy Buddy," has been a smash hit. Or sexy. Or funny.

"My Father, the Hero," remade from a French comedy virtually unseen in this country, at least has Gérard Depardieu in the cast, which gives it a pedigree. Depardieu, who has appeared in every French film for the past 20 years, give or take a few, makes his third appearance in a Hollywood movie. (The first two were "Green Card" and "1492: Conquest of Paradise.") It's enjoyable watching Depardieu wrap his mouth around the English language; he seems to enjoy it as much as we do. Less enjoyable is watching Depardieu (or, in long shot, his stunt double) water skiing and wallowing through treacherous shoals. (A friend said he reminded her of Shamu.)

Depardieu may be fun to watch but he's not enough reason to see the movie. The plot is one of those ooo-la-la jobs that was probably pretty smarmy even in the original (except the French can get away with these things better than we can). It's about what happens when Andre (Depardieu), an errant, divorced dad, takes his 14-year-old daughter, Nicole (Katherine Heigl), to a Bahamas resort for a quality-time vacation.

When Nicole falls for a hunky local, Ben (Dalton James), she concocts a jealousy-making scheme to rope him in: She pretends Andre is actually her lover and an international spy. (The father-daughter relationship is supposed to be a ruse to get around the illegalities.) The vacationers all think Andre is a child molester and give him scorching stares; Nicole, meanwhile, with her princessy, sweet-young-thing wiles, enjoys teasing the resort's male staff and playing up her role as kept woman (or child-woman).

Does this sound like the comic premise we've all been waiting for? The screenwriters, Francis Veber and Charlie Peters, have worked on many of the previous France-to-Hollywood adaptations. (Peters contributed to the script for "Blame It on Rio," which also dabbled in incest yuks.) Along with director Steve Miner, they try to muffle the essential sleaziness of the plot while at the same time playing up to it. Nicole is ogled not only by the local guys but by the camera.

There's something sordid about the way the filmmakers offer up this—shall we say questionable—entertainment as a refreshment.

NEW YORK POST, 2/4/94, p. 34, Larry Worth

There's an old saying: Those who don't learn from history are doomed to repeat it. Sadly, such counsel never reached Gerard Depardieu.

How else to explain his appearance in the French fiasco "Mon Pere, Ce Heros," only to take on the American remake, "My Father, the Hero"?

Well, if director Steve Miner had cleaned up Gerard Lauzier's alleged farce, maybe. But this recycled nonsense actually deteriorated in the translation.

The plot is all-too-familiar, even to those who didn't suffer through the original. A 14-going-on-40 Lolita vacations in the Bahamas with her beefy dad (Depardieu). But when she spots a rich, hunky teen, she lets him think Pop is actually her lover. Faster than you can say pedophile, the resorts' inhabitants are waging war on the bumbling protagonist.

But while misconceptions mount, hilarity doesn't. With the exception of one clever gimmick keyed to a cameo, the script telegraphs all its punchlines. Further, the script, co-written by Francis Veber and Charlie Peters, has more holes in it than Sonny Corleone.

The usually reliable Depardieu's acting isn't a saving grace. His halting English and flat attempts at humor are no laughing matter.

The surprise is that young costar Katherine Heigl knocks him right off the screen. Aside from being as pretty as the Caribbean locale, she's got a teen's pouty petulance and need for acceptance down to a science.

Too bad the supporting characters didn't follow her lead. As the ardent young suitor, Dalton James has the dramatic abilities of a Ken doll while Lauren Hutton's and Faith Prince's turns as the women in Dad's life are completely one-dimensional.

So, despite the valiant efforts of newcomer Heigl, this "Hero" merits a Bronx cheer.

NEWSDAY, 2/4/94, Part II/p. 65, Jack Mathews

It's hard not to like Gerard Depardieu. Despite what should have been grave reservations, he still spends much of "My Father, the Hero," a movie with a considerable number of firm young bodies, with his shirt off. It's courageous. It's inspiring.

It's also overwhelming. But unlike the elastic in his trunks, Depardieu's talent is big enough to encompass all that it encounters. And in "My Father, the Hero," he makes bemused fatherhood as sympathetic a condition as it's been since Spencer Tracy married off Elizabeth Taylor.

If you don't mind the idea of a 14-year-old girl passing off her father as her lover—which is what Nicole (Katherine Heigl), does when she and the long-divorced Andre (Depardieu) travel to the Caribbean for some overdue quality time—then "My Father" is perfectly harmless. There's certainly nothing prurient here. In fact, the film is as conventional a confection as possible, the kind of broad comedy Disney used to turn out in the '60s. There's even an extended slapstick routine with Andre on water skis, and a tango number that interrupts the story line. Depardieu might as well be Brian Keith.

Nicole is a very mature looking 14-year-old, and island boy Ben (Dalton James) is more than willing to let her convince him she's 18. It also helps that she's such an accomplished liar: She not only tells Ben that Andre is her lover, but that her real father is in prison and her mother's a prostitute. When the story gets around, the innocent Andre becomes the object of scorn and Ben's physical abuse, much to Andre's confusion. When Nicole finally 'fesses up, he's at first appalled, but then—loving father that he is—agrees to cooperate.

There's a lot of laughter at Andre's expense, some of which is rooted in Depardieu's frequently butchered English, but there's also a sensitivity to the plight of divorced parents, and in Andre's case a willingness to do anything for his child, to the point of lunacy. Heigl makes Nicole believable, despite all the gauzy shots of her lovely face, and makes her adolescent self-absorption just as infuriating as it ought to be.

SIGHT AND SOUND, 5/94, p. 46, Leslie Felperin Sharman

Divorced André takes his 14-year-old daughter Nicole on holiday to a Caribbean resort. André is worried about his relationship with his girlfriend Isabelle in Paris; she wants more commitment from him and refuses to answer his calls. Nicole thinks the resort is boring until she spots Ben, a dishy young stud who lives on the island. To impress him, she lies about her age and pretends that André is not her father but a lover who saved her from a life on the streets. Ben tells the other guests, and soon everyone shuns André, thinking him a dirty old man. Upset at the thought that André might marry Isabelle and have more children, Nicole runs to Ben, who tries to persuade her to leave André, but André fetches her back.

Back at their hotel room, Nicole guiltily confesses her lies to André, who is furious. Nonetheless, he agrees to help her out by sticking to the story. They tell Ben that they are no longer sleeping together, so that he'll think the coast is clear for him to court Nicole. André and Nicole make up outrageous stories about André, hinting that he is a spy and mercenary.

Fascinated, Ben begins to spend more time with André than with Nicole. After seeing how lovingly she watches André play piano one night, Ben renounces his claim on Nicole, thinking that she loves André more. When André almost drowns trying to save Nicole, she inadvertently calls him Daddy in Ben's presence, and the truth comes out. Ben angrily spurns them both. André helps Nicole woo Ben with letters and a Cyrano de Bergerac-style balcony scene in which he tells her romantic things to shout up to Ben, thus winning her back. As the young lovers dance on the beach, André proposes over the phone to Isabelle, saying he wants to have children with her, hopefully all girls. Tearfully, she accepts.

Latest in the current spate of Hollywood remakes of French films comes *My Father, the Hero*, an almost word-for-translated-word remake of Gerard Lauzier's 1991 *Mon père, ce héros*. It even features the same star, Gérard Depardieu—either a spectacularly unimaginative or brilliant casting coup, depending on your perspective. One shudders to imagine what kind of financial desperation must have driven him to reprise the role—perhaps his entire vineyard crop failed last year, or maybe he needs a new Masarati. Whatever the motive, the film will do no favours for his reputation, nor for those of anyone involved with it. The fact that Emma Thompson, playing the shadowy Isabelle, doesn't appear in the credits might indicate more shame than modesty on her part. This feeble comedy generates its biggest laugh from Depardieu saying the heroine's name—Nicole—with a French accent, irresistibly recalling the Renault Clio adverts. Sadly, the joke wears off after five minutes.

The original film was hardly a masterpiece, but it had a certain effervescence and nonchalant ease with its own silliness that only French sex farces can pull off. Marie Gillain as the daughter (there named Véro) was appealingly natural, while Depardieu held the centre well, coasting on his charisma. As Philip Strick noted in this journal, it once again reworked French cinema's decade-long preoccupation with "the twin themes of nymphetology and incest" without asking any really awkward questions. Véro and André's intimacy was mainly familial, only faintly tinged with illicit desire.

For such a family-oriented film, this Touchstone remake puts surprisingly more electricity into its version of the Electra complex. The incestuous subtext becomes even more striking, especially when it is being disavowed. For example, a showy fuss is made about Nicole and André sleeping in separate rooms while their earlier incarnations were content to share. In the original, Véro wore a buttock-revealing swimsuit that André insisted she cover up. This time round, Depardieu produces a full-on eye-goggling double take. The camera, reflecting his point of view, zooms in on the even more abundant display of pubescent flesh. Later he has epileptic fits of sexual jealousy when she talks to older men. Nicole's anger with her father is born from having spotted him with his girlfriend Isabelle when he should have been at her birthday party. In true scorned-woman style, she repays him for the snub by being the most irritating, spoilt, stuckup brat to grace the screen for a long time. André's request to Isabelle to have another daughter can only be understood as a desperate attempt to get it right the next time, hopefully with the help of a less permissive European education.

Subtlety is not *My Father, the Hero*'s strong point. When it comes to the balcony scene, André even feeds Nicole lines straight from Cyrano de Bergerac. These are flagged so obviously as allusions that even the most illiterate viewer who had never seen a subtitle couldn't fail to spot the joke (again, this scene is more discreetly done in the original). The same goes for the film's second funniest moment when, upon being asked to sing something French, André launches into an exuberant rendition of "Thank Heaven for Little Girls " from *Gigi*. The cast get into the spirit of things by overacting so shamelessly they could fry bacon in the back row. Depardieu's self-parodying histrionics are more embarrassing than amusing. It's as if he were trying to do an impression of Charles Grodin in the Beethoven films.

Where Lauzier wisely aimed for the wry smile rather than the belly laugh, here director Steve Miner can't resist cranking up the slapstick volume, producing an annoying feedback whine that grates on the nerves. The result is like some bastard progeny of *Lolita* and the worst of Disney's live action 60s comedies, such as *The Absent Minded Professor*. *My Father, the Hero* ends up being so unfunny it's hilarious, but the joke is ultimately on the producers. You don't have to be a black-polo-neck-wearing francophile to see that hardly a single American remake of a French movie has been any good. Let us hope the flopping of this latest atrocity augurs the cessation of this insidious Hollywood habit.

Also reviewed in:
CHICAGO TRIBUNE, 2/4/94, Friday/p. K, Mark Caro
NEW YORK TIMES, 2/4/94, p. C10, Janet Maslin
VARIETY, 2/7-13/94, p. 37, Brian Lowry
WASHINGTON POST, 2/4/94, p. C6, Rita Kempley

MY GIRL 2

A Columbia Pictures release of an Imagine Films Entertainment production. *Executive Producer:* Joseph M. Caracciolo, David T. Friendly, and Howard Zieff. *Producer:* Brian Grazer. *Director:* Howard Zieff. *Screenplay:* Janet Kovalcik. *Director of Photography:* Paul Elliott. *Editor:* Wendy Greene Bricmont. *Music:* Cliff Eidelman. *Sound:* John Sutton, III. *Sound Editor:* Julia Evershade. *Casting:* Alan Berger. *Production Designer:* Charles Rosen. *Art Director:* Diane Yates. *Set Designer:* Harold Fuhrman. *Set Decorator:* Mary Olivia McIntosh. *Costumes:* Shelley Komarov. *Make-up:* Frank H. Griffin, Jr. *Make-up (Dan Aykroyd):* David B. Miller. *Make-up (Jamie Lee Curtis):* June Brickman. *Running time:* 94 minutes. *MPAA Rating:* PG.

CAST: Dan Aykroyd (Harry Sultenfuss); Jamie Lee Curtis (Shelly Sultenfuss); Anna Chlumsky (Vada Sultenfuss); Austin O'Brien (Nick Zsigmond); Richard Masur (Phil Sultenfuss); Christine Ebersole (Rose Zsigmond); John David Souther (Jeffrey Pommeroy); Angeline Ball (Maggie Muldovan); Aubrey Morris (Alfred Beidermeyer); Gerrit Graham (Dr. Sam Helburn); Ben Stein (Stanley Rosenfeld); Keone Young (Daryl Tanaka); Anthony R. Jones (Arthur); Jodie Markell (Hillary Mitchell); Richard Beymer (Peter Webb); David Purdham (Mr. Owett); Kevin Sifuentes (Julio); Lauren Ashley (Judy); Roland Thomson (Kevin); Dan Hildebrand (Hari Krishna); Charles Fleischer (Cab Driver); George D. Wallace (Gnarly Old Man); Cindy Benson, Tamara Olson, James Parkes, and Bart Sumner (Wedding Guests); Megan Butler (Wardrobe Lady); Wendy Schaal (Emily); Lisa Bradley (Katie); Ryan Olson and Beau Richardson (Kevin's Gang Members); Renée Wedel (Beverly Hills Matron).

LOS ANGELES TIMES, 2/11/94, Calendar/p. 6, Peter Rainer

Anna Chlumsky, the star of "My Girl 2," isn't a conventionally adorable movie tyke, and that's to her credit. She has pluck and smarts, and she doesn't mug for the camera. This sequel to "My Girl" isn't much—it's essentially for people who found that first film endearing—but Chlumsky, at 13, may turn out to be one of the few child stars to successfully it into the world of adulthood performing.

In the meantime, there are cloying entertainments like "My Girl 2" to contend with. In the first film, Chlumsky's Vada, whose mother died giving birth to her, maneuvered her way into an adult writing class because she had a crush on the teacher. Her father, played by Dan Aykroyd, was a mortician who embalmed corpses in the basement of their home.

With this kind of background, one would expect Vada to be a bit more wiggy and careworn than she is in "My Girl 2." The film, set in the spring of 1974, is about Vada's search for information about her deceased mother. (She's writing a school paper on her.) Journeying to Los Angeles, where her mother grew up, she stays with her uncle (Richard Masur) and the woman he lives with (Christine Ebersole) and her son (Austin O'Brien) and ferrets out clues. She pressures her mother's old high school friends to offer up personal tidbits. Of course, we're supposed to regard her mission as an inner voyage. Vada learns who she is by finding out who her mother was.

This dubious scenario is made even more so by the treacly approach of director Howard Zieff and screenwriter Janet Kovalcik. Everything in this film is sugared with sermons about the importance of Being Yourself. Vada doesn't experience any twinges of rage at the loss of her mother or any misgivings about her quest. She's preternaturally mature.

The processed coziness of "My Girl 2" is tolerable only because, besides Chlumsky, the performers are better than average for this sort of thing. Aykroyd once again plays well against Jamie Lee Curtis, as Vada's stepmom; they seem like a real married couple and not the usual movie put-up job. Masur is warmly expert, and Ebersole matches him. O'Brien, rebounding from "Last Action Hero," works well with Chlumsky. They all do better by this movie than it deserves. They should call themselves GooBusters.

NEW YORK POST, 2/11/94, p. 37, Michael Medved

The best news about "My Girl 2" is that nobody dies of a bee sting this time.

Two years ago, the original film featured a fatal insect attack that not only killed off Macaulay Culkin's character but helped to ruin the picture; a moment of mindless melodrama that came out of left field and made the movie pointlessly disturbing for many of the youngsters who comprised its core constituency.

In the sequel, however, the moviemakers show more respect for the family audience: This is a sweet, gentle (though shamelessly corny) picture that most children will enjoy along with their parents.

The focus is once again Vada Sultenfuss (played by 13-year-old actress Anna Chlumsky), the sensitive daughter of a mildly eccentric small-town Pennsylvania undertaker (Dan Aykroyd).

As the sequel begins, it's spring of '74 and Vada's widower father has married the free-spirited cosmetologist (Jamie Lee Curtis) he met in the first film. They're expecting a child, and while Vada adjusts to the changes in the family, she responds to a school assignment by researching the mother she never knew.

Her questions take her on a spring break visit to her mom's hometown of L.A., where her uncle (Richard Masur) works as a mechanic. Conveniently enough, his girlfriend has a teen-aged son (Austin O'Brien, Schwarzenegger's co-star from "The Last Action Hero").

He becomes our heroine's guide and companion as she seeks out various colorful Californians for information on her late mom.

Cameo roles feature a long series of embarrassingly bad actors; worst of all is Aubrey Morris as a bohemian poet and one-time college professor who sounds like Donald Duck's uncle, Ludwig Van Drake.

The climax of Vada's search is also profoundly annoying, as she tearfully views home movie footage from the late '50s (recorded in full sound, no less!) showing her late mother cavorting with friends and singing sentimental songs.

When Congress is finished with health care reform, they ought to pass a law establishing mandatory life imprisonment for any filmmaker so manipulative that he synthesizes tear-jerking home movies of fictional characters who have died.

Nevertheless, director Howard Zieff ("Private Benjamin," "The Dream Team" and the original "My Girl") brings a loving, lyrical touch to even the most treacly material that it's hard to resist this movie's serene, elegiac mood.

Zieff's blessed with a remarkable leading lady in Anna Chlumsky, who's matured from the pretty, perky child of the first film to a slightly awkward—and wonderfully vulnerable and transparent—adolescent. Unlike so many of the flawless physical specimens who commonly play such roles in Hollywood, she comes across as an appealingly ordinary kid—an uncommonly intelligent version of the girl next door,

Hardworking character actor Richard Masur is also fine as her uncle, making us care about this obtuse but endearing regular guy who can't work up the courage to propose to the woman he loves.

It's easy to find fault with this flimsy material, or to focus on many period details that don't fit with the 1974 setting, or the feeble attempts to pass off California locations as a small town in central Pennsylvania.

Nevertheless, it's hard to imagine that such shortcomings will stop most moviegoers from responding to the film's warm-hearted, sentimental appeal, or prevent them from feeling gratitude for one of those exceedingly rare sequels that is superior to the original film.

NEWSDAY, 2/11/94, Part II/p. 79, John Anderson

Most Hollywood films don't teach you anything, so consider it a bonus that you can walk away from "My Girl 2" with two pieces of wisdom; you can bury the dead, but you can't bury the '70s.

This sequel to the 1991 hit in which Macaulay Culkin was stung to death by bees (not to imply any connection) is full of '70s music and '70s faces, and in some ways it's as if nothing ever changed: Rod Stewart, for instance, is still on the radio singing "Reason to Believe." On the other hand, in the '70s, Dan Aykroyd ("Saturday Night Live") and Richard Masur ("One Day at a Time") were considered funny.

There isn't a whole lot that's remotely humorous here, and not just because Vada, played by the film's one bright light, Anna Chlumsky, spends the entire film searching for the spirit of her dead mother, Maggie (played in a home-movie sequence by Angeline Ball of "The Commitments"). The dialogue has all the grace of a car crash; the acting is almost uniformly dreadful, and director Howard Zieff, who returns from the first film, seems to have lacked the required enthusiasm. Or any enthusiasm at all.

And then there's obnoxious young Austin O'Brien, who plays Nick, the obnoxious son of Rose (Christine Ebersole), both of whom are living with Phil (Masur), brother of Harry Sultenfuss (Akyroyd), the widowed Pennsylvania mortician who learned to connect with his precocious daughter in the original "My Girl." Harry, now married to the very pregnant Shelly (Jamie Lee Curtis), has resolved his domestic dysfunction with Vada challenging the filmmakers to find a crisis upon which to build their sequel. So when her teacher assigns her class a paper on someone they admire but have never met, Vada picks her mother Maggie. And since Maggie came from L.A., and spring vacation is coming up, Shelly suggested a trip to Uncle Phil's so Vada can do the research she needs. And, of course, get out of Shelly's hair. And her taco chips.

Steve Miller, Elton John, Grand Funk Railroad and Edgar Winter provide the sound track; John David Souther, who wrote a lot of the songs that infected the radio back in the '70s, plays Maggie's first husband ... oops, I'm giving away too much. And yet, there really isn't any suspense in "My Girl 2," or any laughs, or any warmth. There is, however, on the wall of Vada's classroom, a pretty scary picture of Richard Nixon, who in 1974 was hanging on for dear life, much like the cast of this movie.

SIGHT AND SOUND, 8/94, p. 47, Leslie Felperin Sharman

1974, Vada Sultenfuss, now 13 has to write a school project on someone who achieved something and whom she never met. She decides to study her mother, who died shortly after she was born. Her father Harry can provide little information, so Vada goes to Los Angeles, her Mom's home town, where she stays with her Uncle Phil, his new girlfriend Rose, and Nick, her son from a previous marriage.

At first, Nick and Vada seem to dislike each other, but he agrees to help her. They visit assorted people who each tell her a little about her mother, including a policeman, a wedding photographer, a poet, an eccentric woman who runs a second-hand shop, and Jeffrey Pommeroy, who was briefly married to Vada's mother. He shows Vada a Super-8 film of her mother, which solves many of the mysteries that have cropped up in her search. Before Vada leaves, Phil decides to propose to Rose. At the airport, Nick and Vada kiss. Back home, where her stepmother Shelly has given birth to a baby boy, Vada decides that her mother's greatest achievement was having her.

"Part adventure, part miracle," is how Vada describes her quest in *My Girl 2*. But the greater part of it is a viscous blob of clichés, painful to endure. This is the follow-up to the only slightly less soppy *My Girl*, itself a shameless rip-off, with its use of voice-overs and nostalgia, of the TV series *The Wonder Years*, except with a female protagonist. Apart from the cockle-warming spectacle of Macaulay Culkin being stung to death by bees, the first film was mildly redeemed by patches of passable dialogue and by Dan Aykroyd and Jamie Lee Curtis in a sub-plot about middle-aged romance. Sadly, they only pass through the sequel long enough to collect their cheques.

In their place, Richard Masur and Christine Ebersole act out their parallel adult love story, to provide a suitably reactionary example for the children by having them decide to marry rather than "live in sin". The general thrust of the film is nauseatingly moralistic, with Vada shocked to learn her mother was once suspended from school for smoking. The logic behind setting the film in the 70s gradually becomes apparent. Back-to-basics ideology, which dictates that a woman's greatest achievement is having children, is safely enshrined in the golden glow of the past. This seems to be the sole purpose of a period setting only half-heartedly evoked by the odd portrait of Nixon and an incessant soundtrack of minor hits of the time. There are also such glaring anachronisms as a Benetton shop in the background, and the presence of sound on a home Super-8 camera from the 50s.

In the press release, director Howard Zieff is described as an admirer of Frank Capra, whose work was clearly a model for the first film's small-town sentiment and preoccupation with mortality. This time, death has far less sting, and with the transfer to Los Angeles, Capra's shadow has become even fainter. The crude parody of L.A. social types is just another cheap exercise in Hollywood narcissism, as well as a way to skimp on location costs.

Also reviewed in:
CHICAGO TRIBUNE, 2/11/94, Friday/p. F, Clifford Terry
NEW YORK TIMES, 2/11/94, p. C22, Stephen Holden
VARIETY, 2/14-20/94, p. 40, Joe Leydon
WASHINGTON POST, 2/11/94, p. B1, Richard Harrington

MY LIFE'S IN TURNAROUND

An Arrow Entertainment release in association with Islet presents a Third Step and Frontier Production film. *Producer:* Daniel Einfeld. *Director:* Eric Schaeffer. *Screenplay:* Eric Schaeffer. *Director of Photography:* Peter Hawkins. *Editor:* Susan Graff. *Music:* Susan Cirillo. *Running time:* 84 minutes. *MPAA Rating:* Not Rated.

CAST: Eric Schaeffer (Splick Featherstone); Daniel Lardner Ward (Jason Little); Lisa Gerstein (Sarah Hershfeld); John Dore (Shrink); Debra Clein (Amanda); Dana Wheeler Nicholson (Rachel); Sheila Jaffe (Beverly Spannenbaum); Casey Siemaszko (Himself); Martha Plimpton (Herself); Phoebe Cates (Herself); John Sayles (Himself).

LOS ANGELES TIMES, 8/12/94, Calendar/p. 4, Peter Rainer

Movies about the making of movies can be as good as Fellini's "8½" or they can be as bad as well, "My Life's in Turnaround." This micro-budgeted feature co-written, directed and starring Eric Schaeffer and Donal Lardner Ward doesn't have much going for it except the dithery rapport of its two leads, and that rapport doesn't go very far. They're trying to be a New Wave comedy team but deadbeat grunginess isn't a thrilling substitute for good humor.

Splick (Schaeffer) is a motormouth New York cabbie and Jason (Ward) is a bartender with a yen for young models. Thirtyish and worn out performing oddball theater sketches together, they decide to make a movie. All they lack is money, actors, expertise. They also lack ideas but, as Jason says, "think this whole idea thing is overrated anyway."

Given the incompetencies of this movie, Jason's line is particularly self-serving. Schaeffer and Ward seem to believe that their idea for a movie—a movie about two guys with no idea for a movie—is a great idea. The bad pacing, wayward dialogue, blotchy lighting and going-nowhere jokes can seem funky if you take the film as a put-on. But it's also meant to be hilarious.

The only halfway interesting "idea" is the way the guys keep running into well-known actresses in the city and then conning them into being in their movie. Phoebe Cates and Martha Plimpton have cameos that brighten the blandness, and John Sayles also turns up in a very funny bit as a sharky Hollywood producer type. Sayles must be sending up a real producer here; the satire is chillingly specific. But the most powerful line in the movie comes when the boys' friend and agent (Lisa Gerstein) tells them, "You have to focus. Life is short." Her advice applies equally to this film's audience.

NEW YORK POST, 6/17/94, p. 39, Thelma Adams

"Shoah" meets "Dawn of the Dead" meets "Ordinary People."

That's the description 29-year-old cabbie Splick (Eric Schaeffer) gives his buddy, bartender Jason (Donal Lardner Ward), when they decide to make "a movie about ourselves."

"My Life's in Turnaround"—a low-budget movie about making the movie that the audience is watching—is closer to "Bill and Ted's Excellent Adventure" meets Beavis and Butt-head with a twist of "Seinfeld."

Like the spate of TV shows that run on the fact that they're about nothing, co-producers, writers, directors and stars Schaeffer and Ward are the butt of their own jokes. These Woodstock toddlers prod the central Generation X dilemma: We want to express ourselves but we don't have much to say.

The filmmaker's saving grace is their sense of humor. "We're just gonna die weird and dumb."

Self-absorbed? Yes. But "My Life's in Turnaround" is also laugh-out-loud funny.

Splick, a droopy forelock in his eye, is an elastic-faced arrested-development boy-man who speaks in the hopped-up riffs of James Woods when he gets excited. Jason is the straight man, the Prozac case with the deadpan delivery. A chick-magnet for teen models, Jason can't seem to make the jump to hitting on women his own age.

Together, Schaeffer and Ward have more chemistry than Kim Basinger and Alec Baldwin in "The Getaway" or Mel Gibson and Jodie Foster in "Maverick." They're on the road to a Hope-Crosby camaraderie.

Drawn into the cast are a trio of talented newcomers, Lisa Gerstein, Dana Wheeler Nicholson and Debra Clein. Also on hand for whimsical cameos are Martha Plimpton and Phoebe Cates.

As a sleazy movie producer, director John ("Matewan") Sayles mocks himself when he delivers a hilarious rant against independent filmmakers with their character-driven stories.

Shot in 15 days on location in New York, Schaeffer and Ward have made a self-mocking indie comedy driven by two memorable anti-heroes. Who could provide a better slacker motto than Jason when he says: "My career that never happened is over"?

Maybe these guys aren't such slackers after all. In "My Life's in Turnaround," Schaeffer and Ward demonstrate shaggy talents that should return them to the screen following the trail blazed by Spike Lee, Nick Gomez, Robert Townsend and others.

What's next for the duo? Maybe "Casablanca" meets "Citizen Kane" meets "Conan the Barbarian."

NEWSDAY, 6/17/94, Part II/p. B7, John Anderson

"Turnaround" is studio-speak for the nebulous state of scripts that have been bought, but never filmed. Translate this being/nothingness into career inertia, and you have Jason and Splick—failed performance artists with a withering naiveté about their own talent—who find their metaphorical selves languishing and decide to do the only logical thing: Make a movie.

That cinema should be the last resort of the blissfully idiotic is neither far-fetched, nor a very promising premise for a first-time film.

And yet ... the writing-directing team of Donal Lardner Ward and Eric Schaeffer have two things going for them that all the screen time in the world isn't going to provide: A unique comedic sense and an instinct for translating the idiosyncrasies of their lives and story—about two lost boys making their first movie—into a universal language. "My Life's in Turnaround" is, in short, a delight in a summer season that promises very few.

The filmmakers wear their influences on their sleeves. "My Life's in Turnaround," a paradigm of low-budget cinema, most closely resembles the early Woody Allen comedies, both in laughs per minute and basic structure.

The story itself, which concerns the pair's off-handed but ultimately successful decision to abandon their bizarre theater pieces and "switch media," is little more than a vehicle for set pieces, very funny ones. But, unlike the similarly constructed scripts of Nora Ephron, for instance, which always seem like Catskills routines in formal wear, Ward and Schaeffer's comedy and the episodic nature of their film works as an organic whole.

As Jason, the good-looking, occasional bartender Ward serves as an palliative to Schaeffer's cab-driving Splick, who is given to sputtering explosions of inarticulateness, a kind of spontaneous verbal combustion that's convincingly sincere, hilarious, and original, even if it occasionally recalls the deadpanned hysteria of Jon Lovitz in his better moments.

The two pursue their scriptless, conceptless film ("The whole 'idea' thing is overrated," Jason says at one point) with dogged ineptness, and a large amount of luck. Their loyal friend Sarah (Lisa Gerstein) gets them a meeting with the actor-producer Casey Siemaszko (as himself who wants them to rewrite a heavy Polish novel. Splick picks up Phoebe Cates in his cab and exacts a glancing nod of interest in his project.

With all this circumstantial evidence that a film will actually materialize, Ward and Schaeffer are making pointed fun of the flimsiness of the corporate/creative process—the meetings, the concepts, the stars—as well as its self-importance. The big buildup the camera gives to Martha Plimpton, for instance, a good sport but an actress of only moderate celebrity, is yet another torpedo aimed at Hollywood (as is John Sayles' brilliant cameo as a thick-headed Hollywood producer).

Splick and Jason also wrestle with their love lives—Splick negotiating a "trial" relationship with his beautiful lawyer (Dana Wheeler Nicholson) and Jason finally forsaking his bevy of pubescent models for the mature Amanda (Debra Clein). The emphasis, however, remains on the process of making the film, which is actually the film we're watching. If this seems a violation of some Aristotelian unity, it's not the only one. But part of Ward and Schaeffer's charm is making their distinctly personal experiences, no matter how absurd or humiliating, recognizable and funny.

VILLAGE VOICE, 6/28/94, p. 66, James Hannaham

The really neat thing about reality, though bite it may, is, like, its complete subjectivity, especially as far as, like, the film and television industry goes. Like, wake up and decide, as the charming deadbeats of *My Life's in Turnaround* do, that you're, like, a filmmaker, then worry about learning how to, like, make a film. Splick Featherstone (Eric Schaeffer) and intrepid sidekick Jason Little (Donal Lardner Ward, only, like, the dopiest boy you'll ever have a crush on), after years as a cab driver and a bartender (at, like, Live Bait, even), suddenly realize that their lives are going nowhere. Like, duh! Their experimental theater pieces suck, girls they hit on respond by, like, spitting in their faces, they're slobs, and above all they have, like, redundant and repetitious, like, syntax that they repeat a lot. Splick worries aloud, "We're just gonna die weird and dumb!" So they, like, decide to become filmmakers. A logical choice—NOT! But good as any. And they set about it like the greats. You know—Ren and Stimpy, Beavis and Butthead, Duckman and Cornfed. Of course they make a movie about, like, themselves. A movie about, like, the fact that they don't have girlfriends or lives and stuff. A movie that's, like, sorta funny and pathetic. And, like, this is that movie. It's also, like, one of those pictures that's about two guys who chase after chicks a lot but, like, the story's really about the love between the two guys. It's, like, so self-referential and stuff that it's, like, *trippy*. I mean, hello!? Hey, tail-eating snake dude, howya doin? I got chills when I saw a shot of the street I'd just, like, walked up to get to the screening room. I freaked 'cause I thought I'd forgotten that I was in the movie. But it's kinda cool. I don't know. It was, like, inspiring and stuff? I at least, like, bopped out of the theater going, "I'm a loser baby, so why don't you film me?"

Also reviewed in:
CHICAGO TRIBUNE, 2/2/94, Friday/p. J, John Petrakis
NEW YORK TIMES, 6/17/94, p. C5, Janet Maslin
VARIETY, 5/17/93, p. 97, Dennis Harvey
WASHINGTON POST, 7/22/94, p. C7, Rita Kempley
WASHINGTON POST, 7/22/94, Weekend/p. 42, Joe Brown

NAKED GUN 33⅓: THE FINAL INSULT

A Paramount Pictures release. *Executive Producer:* Jerry Zucker, Jim Abrahams, and Gil Netter. *Producer:* Robert K. Weiss and David Zucker. *Director:* Peter Segal. *Screenplay:* Pat Proft, David Zucker, and Robert LoCash. *Director of Photography:* Robert Stevens. *Editor:* James R. Symons. *Music:* Ira Newborn. *Music Editor:* Jeff Carson. *Choreographer:* Miranda Garrison. *Sound:* Hank W. Garfield and (music): Robert Fernandez . *Sound Editor:* Terry Rodman and Joseph Ippolito. *Casting:* Pamela Basker. *Production Designer:* Lawrence G. Paull. *Art Director:* Bruce Crone. *Set Designer:* John Berger, Ann Harris, John Leimanis, and Natalie V. Richards. *Set Decorator:* Kathie Klopp. *Set Dresser:* James Randol. *Special Effects:* Jeff Jarvis. *Visual Effects:* Kimberly K. Nelson. *Costumes:* Mary E. Vogt. *Make-up:* Steve Abrums. *Make-up (Leslie Nielsen):* James R. Scribner. *Stunt Coordinator:* Phil Adams. *Running time:* 75 minutes. *MPAA Rating:* PG-13.

CAST: Leslie Nielsen (Lt. Frank Drebin); Priscilla Presley (Jane Spencer); George Kennedy (Ed Hocken); O.J. Simpson (Nordberg); Fred Ward (Rocco); Katheleen Freeman (Muriel); Anna Nicole Smith (Tanya); Ellen Greene (Louise); Ed Williams (Ted); Raye Birk (Papshmir); Matt Roe (Clayton); Wylie Small (Defense Attorney); Sharon Cornell (Stenographer); Earl Boen (Dr. Eisendrath); Jeff Wright (Store Manager); Karen Segal (Purse Woman); Lorali Hart (Melon Lady); Mallory Sandler (Grocery Mother); Brad Lockerman (Jason); Rosalind Allen (Bobbi); Charlotte Zucker (Nurse); Lois de Banzie (Dr. Kohlzak); Doris Belack (Dr. Roberts); Nigel Gibbs (Carjacker); Andre Rosey Brown (Corridor Guard); Randall "Tex" Cobb (Big Hairy Con); Ann B. Davis (Herself); Alex Zimmerman (Mess Hall Convict); Marc Alaimo (Trucker); Tom Finnegan (Priest); Hammam Shafie (Cabby); Jeffrey Anderson Gunter (Cabby); Danny D. Daniels (Cabby); Joe Grifasi (Director); Vanna White (Herself); "Weird Al" Yankovic (Himself); Rick Scarry (Security Guard); Mary Lou Retton (Herself); James Robert Scribner (Phil Donahue's Make-Up Man); Lou Felder (Presenter); Chrissy Bocchino (Mother Theresa); Pia Zadora (Herself). Joe D'Angerio (Security Guard); Gary Cooper, Christopher J. Keene and Joe Flood (Cops); Scott Evers (Umpire); Paul Hutton (Doctor); Peter Segal, Robert LoCash, and William Kerr (Producers of "Sawdust & Mildew"); Jolie Chain, Wendy Hogan, and Jeri Caldwell (Producers' Wives); Michael Ewing (Assistant Director); David "Skippy" Malloy (Maalox Boy); Vanessa Sandin (Gabriella); Julie Strain (Dominatrix); Andrew Craig (Bryce Porterhouse Guard); David Fresco (Lifetime Award Recipient); Bill Erwin (Conductor); Adam Hasart (Frank Jr.); John Capodice (Mr. Big); Glen Chin (Sumo Wrestler); Philip Yamaguchi (Sumo Wrestler); Florence Henderson (Herself); Tim Bohn (Waldo); Timothy Watters (President Clinton); Gene Geytak (Pope); Aaron Seville (Cop); Adrienne Parson (Mercedes Lady); Robert J. Elisberg (Taxi Driver); Elisa Pensler Gabrielli (Mourner); Taran Killam (Boy of Geriatric Park); Marianne Davis (Girl of Geriatric Park); Bill Zuckert (Old Man); Nicole Segal (Screaming Supermarket Baby); Burt Zucker (Clinic Patient); Susan Breslau (Train Lady); Marcy Goldman (Train Lady); David Zucker (Teleprompter Guy); Robert K. Weiss (Tuba Player).

LOS ANGELES TIMES, 3/18/94, Calendar/p. 6, Peter Rainer

Reviewing "Naked Gun 33⅓: The Final Insult" is a bit like reviewing a joke book—you don't want to give away the jokes. Some of the gags are side-splitters, some just sit on the screen.

But the film would have to be a great deal worse to prevent "Naked Gun" die-hards from lining up. It is, after all, the movie that finally confirms what we suspected all along—Leslie Nielsen's Lt. Frank Drebin looks exactly like Phil Donahue from the back.

Drebin is retired in this third series installment but a mysterious bomb plot brings him back into action. He's also having marital problems with his wife, Jane (Priscilla Presley)—and no movie hero was ever less suggestive to marriage counseling than the blank-faced Drebin.

He's in his deadpan element going undercover to root out terrorists. Stops along the way include a maximum-security prison, a sperm bank—he becomes a heavy donor—and finally thc Academy Awards show. The Oscars have never been trashed in quite this way in a movie before, though the Oscar show itself has often come close. The shenanigans go on for too long, but, then again, so does the telecast. It's hard-edged realism, "Naked Gun"-style.

The usual faces turn up again, including George Kennedy and O.J. Simpson, and a few new ones too, like Fred Ward as a square-jawed baddie: Guess? jeans model Anna Nicole Smith, whose pneumatic enticements threaten to smother Drebin: and Ellen Greene, in a way-too-small cameo. (Greene is a great comic actress in a cast of Great Pretenders.) The regulars all have the good humor of performers who know they're playing out an annuity.

Director Peter Segal is new to the series—he's new to feature-film directing—and he doesn't vary much from the formula. He keeps the gags popping, and there are always funny little doodles taking place in the corner of the frame (like the convict who pole vaults to safety during a prison yard scene). There are also a couple of misfires. We don't really need a joke involving a black prisoner in a riot imploring us with the words, "Can't we all get along?" That's the real world.

"Naked Gun 33⅓," of course, functions best in the fake one. One hopes this "Insult" won't be final.

NEW YORK POST, 3/18/94, p. 19, Michael Medved

In "Naked Gun 33⅓: The Final Insult" the redoubtable hero Frank Drebin (Leslie Nielsen) displays a more vulnerable, sensitive side of his complex personality than we've seen before.

As the story begins, he's retired from the police force to pursue a quiet life with his new wife, Jane Spencer-Drebin (Priscilla Presley), but he finds that their sex life suffers when he no longer gets to shoot people every day at work.

Meanwhile, a deadly terrorist (Fred Ward) has escaped from prison in order to destroy one of America's most beloved institutions, with the eager assistance of his statuesque girlfriend (played by "Guess?" supermodel Anna Nicole Smith). Drebin's old pals on the police squad, Hocken and Nordberg (George Kennedy and O.J. Simpson) try to coax the lieutenant out of retirement to combat this double-barreled menace, but if he returns to battling bad guys his wife may walk out on their increasingly shaky marriage.

This moral dilemma is addressed in the course of the movie with all the thoughtful intensity and probing intelligence one has come to expect from the "Naked Gun" pictures. Actually, these projects aren't so much movies aa they are fast-moving collections of gags, so the only significant question is whether the gags work. The answer here is a qualified yes.

One of the weaknesses of this "Final Insult" is this absolutely relentless emphasis on sexual (but never sexy) material. Silly, vulgar gags and references have always been part of the appeal of the series, but this time the vast majority of punch lines have some sort of off-color overtones.

Florence Henderson, Mary Lou Retton, Shannen Doherty and Morgan Fairchild have all been nominated for best supporting actress and anxiously await this overdue recognition of their prodigious thespian skills. Raquel Welch also makes an appearance, looking so spectacular in a slinky silver gown that she nearly steals the movie.

A newcomer named Peter Segal (previously associated with Tom Arnold's "Jackie Thomas Show," on TV) took over the directing chores here from David Zucker, but Zucker's continued presence as co-writer and co-producer makes for a seamless transition.

The slapstick and silliness are just as enjoyable as before— especially an Oscar night production number in which the flat-footed Drebin is forced to dance in the top-hatted chorus line backing up the incomparable Pia Zadora. "The Final Insult" may not be the finest comedy ever made—or even the finest "Naked Gun" movie—but it deserves recognition as the greatest Pia Zadora movie in cinema history.

NEWSDAY, 3/18/94, Part II/p. 62, Jack Mathews

The first joke in "Naked Gun 33⅓: The Final Insult" is a newspaper headline reading "Dyslexia for Cure." The last is in the final credits, explaining that while no animals were harmed during the making of the movie, some species did become extinct, including, the Wooly Fettered Tree Squirrel, whose last 100 members were eaten at a "Naked Gun" crew lunch.

In between, there are dozens, hundreds, maybe thousands of sight gags, double entendres, tasteless puns and cheap shots, an amazingly large percentage of which are scream-out-loud funny.

"Gun 3," we'll call it, contains stretches as hilarious as anything we've gotten from the Zucker-Abrahams-Zucker company, or its fragments, since the team's career-making hit "Airplane!" 14 years ago. David Zucker. who directed the first two "Guns," served as co-writer and producer on this one, which marks a solid directing debut by Peter Segal.

As important as the writing and directing are, however, the "Naked Gun" series is as dependent on Leslie Nielsen's Frank Drebin as the "Pink Panther" movies were on Peter Sellers' Inspector Clouseau, and Nielsen hasn't been better.

In"Gun 2,"as he has done in those terrible TV commercials, the actor was having so much fun at Frank's expense, he became a parody of a parody. Here, given an entirely new center of motivation—Frank is retired, playing impotent househusband to Priscilla Presley's ambitious attorney—he allows the humor to come out of his daffily benign character and the crazy situations he's placed in, and he's a howl.

The story, such as it is, begins when Police Squad's Ed Hocken (George Kennedy) and Nordberg (O.J. Simpson) show up at Frank's house to talk him out of retirement, to help them thwart a mercenary terrorist (Fred Ward) from escaping prison and blowing something up. Frank goes incognito, wearing iron chastity shorts under his prison garb, befriends the snarling Rocco, then follows him, his vicious mother (Kathleen Freeman) and his Amazon girlfriend (Anna Nicole Smith) to the scene of the 66th Academy Awards, where Rocco's plan and the Best Picture winner will be simultaneously unveiled.

The first half-hour of "Gun 3," which begins with a dream re-enactment of the "Potemkin"-steps homage from Brian de Palma's "The Untouchables," is funny enough to cause damage. The humor, either out of mercy or creative exhaustion, flattens out badly in the mid-section, then picks up again about the time the pretty people, if that's what you call "Weird Al" Yankovic and Vanna White, start to arrive for the Oscars.

Segal, who has directed TV and cable shows, distinguishes himself in that last act, sending up the Academy Awards higher than they've ever gone before. There are clips from such Oscar-nominated films as "Geriatric Park," a Spielbergian adventure set in a place called Seizure World, and the rollicking musical "Mother!," the story of Mother Teresa.

"The Final Insult"? Let's hope not.

NEW STATESMAN & SOCIETY, 5/27/94, p. 33, Jonathan Romney

The last thing I saw Leslie Nielsen in was an American TV special about palaeontology. There he was in his casual V-neck sweater, striding solemnly through a cavernous museum set, the gargantuan bones of *Tyrannosaurus Rex* looming malevolently above him.

As he intoned in a hushed basso about the mysteries that had been handed down to us from the dawn of time, you could lay bets that what was coming was going to be a cracker. Poker-faced, he would blithely pluck an intercostalclavicle out of the mighty beast's leg, and the whole thing would come tumbling down on his imperturbable silver head.

Reader, I waited in vain. For this genuinely was a documentary about dinosaur bones. God knows what perversity led to Nielsen being cast as compere; someone must have been under the delusion that his senatorial white tonsure can still be read as a sign of genuine gravitas. But anyone who's seen the *Naked Gun* films or the Red Rock cider ads will know that there's no possibility of taking him seriously ever again.

I wonder how *The Poseidon Adventure* would look now, with Nielsen as the stout captain of the sinking ship? They'd have to re-release it in a new cut, splicing in a shot of him shrugging sheepishly with a dangling bath-plug: "Everyone makes mistakes."

The field of parody, as we know, is where genres limp home to die. And since Hollywood has for the past decade lived entirely off the bones of spavined formulae, then it's clear that there will be genre graveyards on every corner. The current trend started with *Airplane!* and its portmanteau precursor *Kentucky Fried Movie*, and spun off into *Naked Gun, Hot Shots!, Loaded Weapon* and the rest, not to mention the frenetic self-immolation of *Last Action Hero*. As "real" movies increasingly display the flatness and disposability of comics, it's only natural that other movies should rise up in their wake that are comics, no more or less.

Such films are really only parodies for a moment; then they kick under their own steam. What we love about them is not the way they treat their models, but the cavalier way they jettison those models entirely. As a parody of *Airport, Airplane!* would have been so-so. What made it great was its insatiability in gobbling up every other movie from *Saturday Night Fever* to *From Here to Eternity*.

Straight parody in these films is something we can leave or take. What we relish is their function as a kind of sophomore bulletin board, which we plug into to share jokes that are already in the air, the more obvious the better jokes about Michael Jackson, Sharon Stone, *Thelma and Louise*. They're the nearest US equivalent to British panto's in-jokes. We see them to laugh once more (with any luck, for the last time) at what we already know is funny.

Naked Gun 33⅓ is not the first spoof to make a *Crying Game* joke; what you appreciate is that it makes it bang on cue. It's beside the point to complain that these films are tired; the point is that they reanimate dead material for one final zombie spin. Whether or not they're funny does matter, but often the laugh quotient is in direct proportion to the way they parody themselves. That's why sequels are usually better than first episodes, as witness *Wayne's World* (merely cool) and 2 (excellent!).

As with gags, so with actors whose careers have run their course, Leslie Nielsen fell into *The Naked Gun* at the right time, just when it seemed no longer possible to cast this cornily august 1950s G-man type as anything "real". But Nielsen playing pretend Nielsen is something else again. The same goes for all those others whose revived careers consist of taking the piss out of their own CVs: George Kennedy, *Mission Impossible*'s Peter Graves, young premature deadbeats like the Sheen boys and, most imposingly saurian of all, Lloyd Bridges.

In the end, these films maintain so much of their own momentum that they don't function as parody at all, in the traditional sense: they don't administer the *coup de grâce* to dying genres. No one will ever say, "we can no longer make police procedural movies because they'll look like *Naked Gun*"; no real cop thriller would ever look like it.

They can only try to make ones that look slightly less like it. *Naked Gun 33⅓: the Final Insult* chews up scrag ends of James Bond, prison drama and loads of minor Hollywood gossip, but in no way resembles any cop movie ever made. If we love it, we love it because it dares wheel out the same old larks again ("Mostly all new jokes", the ad boasts). As the title suggests, it can't resist giving us the same old whoopee cushion one more time. True to form, the series is looking a bit toothless, and has probably run its course. *Naked Gun 33⅓* is not wildly funny, but like a dose of the salts, it does what it's supposed to. See it if only for the *Beavis and Butthead* joke.

It's no problem that *Naked Gun* condemns Nielsen to being forever a joke about himself. The series has freed him from the purgatory of being a dependable player and raised him to fully fledged iconhood. Something more regrettable happens in Donald Petrie's *Grumpy Old Men*, in which Jack Lemmon and Walter Matthau are called on to redo their *Odd Couple* turn—a Greatest Hit in suspended animation. It's no accident that the film takes place in a snow-bound landscape.

Lemmon and Matthau are two feuding codgers, best buddies at heart, bickering over the new neighbour: a crazy, ditsy, new-agey free spirit played by Ann-Margret, who is an embarrassment from start to finish. They should have cast Anne Bancroft, who'd have put her foot down about the motor-sledding sequence and had the whole script rewritten to make her just as curmudgeonly as the boys—*then* we'd be working.

The lead duo click as intended, but when they trade insults ("Morning dickhead", "Hello moron"), it's too cosy. It too easily undermines the point that these crusty venerables are still little boys, warring over the playground sweetheart—hardly a major insight in psycho-gerontology.

Matthau comes out worst. Always more of a one-noter, he's ended up in recent years leaning back on his supergrouch act, as stooge to everyone from Roberto Benigni to Dennis the Menace.

Again, the jowls carry him. Lemmon fares better, because we know he's simply coasting after his show-stoppers in *Glengarry Glen Ross* and *Short Cuts*. What's interesting, though, is that he still manages to play it as a residual juvenile lead (he gets the girl, no surprises there). The lovable working stiff of *Irma la Douce* and *The Apartment* still surfaces now and then.

But let's please end the deplorable practice of sticking out-takes at the end of films to remind us that it's all a giggle and everyone's good chums really. Such illusion-puncturing frippery is fine in Godard, but unless you can come up with something better than Burgess Meredith wrapping his gums round a string of risque euphemisms, you're chancing it. Of course, the idea of Leslie Nielsen in a movie that's all about out-takes and nothing else *does* have its appeal.

SIGHT AND SOUND, 6/94, p. 56, Lizzie Francke

Lt. Frank Drebin is now married to Jane Spencer. Having taken early retirement from the Police Squad, he plays house husband while Jane practices as a lawyer. The couple are keen to have a baby but nothing has happened in that department yet. Meanwhile the head of a small disreputable state seeks the services of Rocco, a highly dangerous terrorist now residing in Statesville Prison. With the help of his mother Muriel, Rocco plans to break out so that he can carry out the mission. News of the planned bomb attack reaches Police Squad and Captain Ed Hocken persuades Drebin to return to the team to help capture Rocco.

Drebin's first priority is to follow a lead to a fertility clinic where Rocco's associate Tanya is working. He finds Tanya's address and scribbles it on a handkerchief. Later, when Jane learns Drebin is back with the Squad, she decides to leave him, but inadvertently walks off with the handkerchief. Drebin goes undercover as a prisoner at Statesville. He teams up with Rocco and the two make their escape, meeting up with Muriel later. The three then make their way to Rocco's country hide-out where they are joined by Tanya. Meanwhile, Jane decides that Drebin is not really back with the Squad, but seeing another woman. Presuming the address on the handkerchief to be that of his mistress, she also ends up at Rocco's cabin and is taken hostage. The troupe make their way to Hollywood; Rocco's bomb attack is to take place at the Academy Award ceremonies. There, Drebin is able to overpower Muriel and set Jane free. Disguising themselves as guests, the two go to the award ceremony and, after much mayhem, manage to foil Rocco and Tanya. Later, Frank and Jane get to play mom and dad.

The latest *Naked Gun* episode kicks off with a double whammy—Zucker/Abrahams do De Palma doing Eisenstein. In what might seem an inevitable scotching of *The Untouchables*' Grand Central Station steps sequence, a small flotilla of baby carriages bounces down the stairway. This apart, it bodes ill that perhaps the wryest thing about *Naked Gun 33⅓* is the ad campaign which features Leslie Nielsen's face superimposed over the infamous *Vanity Fair* picture of a nude and heavily pregnant Demi Moore. *Naked Gun*'s humour is at its best in these odd dislocations, which mostly occur in the jokes that speedily pass by.

Still, there are a few belly laughs to be found in the set pieces as the *Naked Gun* team aim at a few of Hollywood's recent fads. There's a lame *Thelma and Louise* send-up (a poor second to the French and Saunders version), that portrays Jane hitting the road and the Chanel bottle; an allusion to the sex twist in *The Crying Game* (Drebin finds that there's more to Tanya, played by the monumental model Anna Nicole Smith, than meets the eye); Drebin acting the aproned house husband; plus a rash of baby jokes—with all this, the movie would seem to be skirting around the gender agenda. The big wheeze is at the expense of the Oscar night pomposity. However, if the most recent award ceremony is anything to go by, the real thing is far more ludicrous than Drebin and co's antics, which include the scuppering of a song-and-dance extravaganza, together with the general lambasting of show-biz bonhomie. Ultimately, with the arrival of young contenders Wayne and Garth on the TV-turned-to-film-satire scene, Drebin might as well stick to his retirement plans.

Also reviewed in:
CHICAGO TRIBUNE, 3/18/94, Friday/p. H, Michael Wilmington
NEW YORK TIMES, 3/18/94, p. C14, Caryn James
VARIETY, 3/21-27/94, p. 57, Brian Lowry
WASHINGTON POST, 3/18/94, p. D1, Rita Kampley
WASHINGTON POST, 3/18/94, Weekend/p. 48, Desson Howe

NAKED IN NEW YORK

A Fine Line Features release. *Executive Producer:* Martin Scorsese. *Producer:* Frederick Zollo. *Director:* Dan Algrant. *Screenplay:* Dan Algrant and John Warren. *Director of Photography:* Joey Forsyte. *Editor:* Bill Pankow. *Music:* Angelo Badalamenti. *Sound:* Dennis Maitland. *Casting:* Bonnie Timmerman. *Production Designer:* Kalina Ivanov. *Costumes:* Julie Weiss. *Running time:* 91 minutes. *MPAA Rating:* R.

CAST: Eric Stoltz (Jake Briggs); Mary-Louise Parker (Joanne White); Ralph Macchio (Chris); Jill Clayburgh (Shirley Briggs); Tony Curtis (Carl Fisher); Timothy Dalton (Elliot Price); Lynne Thigpen (Helen); Kathleen Turner (Dana Coles); Roscoe Lee Browne (Mr. Reid); Whoopi Goldberg (Tragedy Mask).

FILMS IN REVIEW, 5-6/94, p. 54, Andy Pawelczak

It's hard to fault a movie for being smart, tasteful and charming, but that's the case with Dan Algrant's romantic comedy *Naked In New York*. It's depressing to see a first film by a talented young director/writer with all the rough edges so thoroughly sanded down. There's nothing to bang up against here, no bruises to give the comedy deeper, more varied coloration, and no invitations to the anarchic id to revel in the excesses of misrule. This is the kind of film beloved by *The New York Times*, a chronicle of the adventures and problems of attractive, privileged young people caught up in the career skirmishes of the nineties, and leave your sense of the more troubling, intractable aspects of reality at the door, please.

Not that reality is completely left out. There's a lot of low keyed angst about what to do after college, and the principal characters have confusion to spare about sexuality and marriage. Jake (Eric Stoltz) and Joanne (Mary-Louise Parker) are college lovers who end up on separate paths after graduation. Jake, an aspiring playwright, moves to New York while Joanne stays in Boston to work for Elliot (Timothy Dalton), a rich, sexy art dealer who clearly has plans for her beyond a job as his assistant. She loves Jake, but she's neurotically indecisive and can't pass up the career opportunity offered by Elliot. It's the classical, soul torturing dilemma of our time: love vs. career, the stuff out of which soap operas are made.

Meanwhile, in New York Jake is faced with his own moral conflict: to sell out or not to sell out, or, at what price glory? His Mephistopheles is a funny, fast talking producer, brilliantly played by Tony Curtis in a benign variation of his role in *Sweet Smell of Success*, who insists on miscasting a soap opera queen in the leading part in Jake's play. To complicate matters further, the actress, who plays Jake's mother in the semi-autobiographical play, sets her sights on seducing Jake, thus adding a high gloss Freudian finish to the whole situation that attests to the picture's New York/Woody Allen provenance. As the actress, Kathleen Turner does a risky, self-parodying turn as a femme fatale—she looks like one of De Kooning's women, her face an iconic, flattened out mask of feral, rapacious sexuality. She and Curtis make the picture's New York sequences something to see and suggest what might have been if only Algrant hadn't given in to the imperatives of the polite, well made movie.

As Jake, Eric Stoltz is appropriately passive and anti-charismatic, a distant relative of Holden Caufield. In one of the film's stabs at ironic, self-deprecating wit, Joanne takes a nude photo of him posing heroically atop a huge boulder. He's no hero, our Jake, but he is morally finicky enough to stand aloof from the lure of celebritydom. When he goes to parties adorned with such celebrities as William Styron and Eric Bogosian—who play themselves in cameo roles—he adopts the defensive stance of the half-ironic, half-star-struck outsider. Although there's something faintly mendacious about these scenes, a whiff of the cool insider playing the role of the hip outsider, Algrant nicely captures the sense of unreality and ambiguous abashment we feel on such occasions. Let's face it—such people excite our envy and desire, they're to us what Proust's aristocrats are to his bourgeoisie, and we feel that we deserve the little frisson of panic and joy we experience in their presence—what else do we create them for?

Mary-Louise Parker as Joanne is pretty and slightly out of focus—her Joanne is not about to commit herself to anything. She makes an absent-minded, screwball entrance into the film when she strays across the stage during a play rehearsal, and she keeps that drifting yet perversely willful air throughout. Ralph Macchio, looking like a svelte Sal Mineo, is very good as Jake's New York-dazzled actor friend, and Jill Clayburgh is convincingly ditsy as Jake's mother.

Algrant clutters up the film with Felliniesque fantasy sequences that are far too cute—a talking chimpanzee, Whoopi Goldberg in a cameo role as a talking comedy mask on the facade of a theater, a dream sequence in which the nude Jake meets the father who abandoned him years ago. He's very good with his performers in scenes that elicit delicate, reticent feelings—there's a show stopper involving Macchio and Stoltz—but in the end the film is afflicted with an almost fatal wistfulness. *Naked In New York* covers some of the same territory as the recent *Reality Bites* but without that film's reality, bite, or fun. Algrant is a talented filmmaker—perhaps in his next movie he'll strike out in riskier directions and avoid the inconsequentiality of his work here.

LOS ANGELES TIMES, 4/15/94, Calendar/p. 15, Peter Rainer

Dan Algrant, making his feature-film debut as co-writer and director in "Naked in New York," doesn't try to wow the audience with a lot of semi-autobiographical *Angst*. He's not big on wow in general. He's the kind of filmmaker who works in safe, methodical strokes, and the safeness is both calming and clotting in a filmmaker so new. He's made a friendly, disconcertingly tame debut movie.

Algrant may be short on *Angst* but his film still carries the flavor of something closer to his concerns than the latest grosses. It's about what happens when two college lovers, Jake (Eric Stoltz) and Joanne (Mary-Louise Parker), live together in Cambridge, Mass., after graduation and then apart when their careers conflict. He's an aspiring young playwright—aren't all young playwrights in the movie aspiring?—who makes the move to New York City when one of his plays is produced Off-Broadway. She's a photographer who stays behind in order to work for a well-connected gallery owner (played by Timothy Dalton, who has the kind of brittle British diction that really deserves a hearing on "Star Trek: The Next Generation" opposite Patrick Stewart's).

The film's time scheme, ranging from Jake's voice-over reminiscences in the present to flashbacks of his loopy childhood with his single mom (Jill Clayburgh) to places in between, is complicated but lucid. We're supposed to regard Jake's coming of age as a kind of tall-tale jaunt. He's an artist because he embraces his foolhardiness.

Stoltz has a shaggy grace and a couple of his confrontations with Parker's Joanne have the tang of real spats. Their living-apart situation, with Jake periodically calling her in moments of distress and getting her answering machine instead, have a familiar horror.

Algrant stages a good arty party scene, and there's a sexual moment between Jake and his best friend Chris (Ralph Macchio) that is blessedly understated where leers might have substituted. Famous artist celebs like William Styron and Arthur Penn and Eric Bogosian keep popping up, and it's fun to see them playacting in their element.

But the film is stolen by Tony Curtis, as Jake's Off-Broadway producer, and Kathleen Turner, as the soap-opera diva who, is all wrong for Jake's play—and of course is cast in the lead. These two performers dig into their parts with such campy relish that they seem to be having an actor's holiday. (This is what can happen when two studio-savvy players have a fling in low-budget land.) They burst the film's carefully stitched seams, and the bursting is all for the best.

NEW YORK, 5/9/94, p. 70, David Denby

Naked in New York, Dan Algrant's casual notebook-movie about a Harvard boy who journeys to New York to make it as a playwright mixes beginner's charm with trivial narcissism, and I'm sorry to say that narcissism wins. There's too much meaningless angst, and fatally too much of Eric Stoltz (as the hero), who puts spaces between his words like a bad Method actor from 1955. But Algrant gets richly self-parodying performances from Tony Curtis, as a still-avid theatrical producer, and Kathleen Turner, as a tempestuous soap-opera star.

NEW YORK POST, 4/15/94, p. 39, Thelma Adams

What's all this fuss about Generation X? I prefer that silly old soap "Madame X"—at least it had passion and sacrifice.

Did Rudolph Valentino have time to whine? He made "The Sheik" and "Blood and Sand" in his 20s before he faced the big bull in the sky at 31.

Did James Dean dither between skim milk and whole? He played a "Rebel Without a Cause" and died a "Giant" when he crashed his Porsche at 24.

What do the twentysomethings of Generation X have that previous generations lacked? Full male frontal nudity. "Naked in New York," Dan Algrant's precocious first feature, delivers Eric Stoltz ("Mask") as naked and pink as the day he was born.

Stoltz is a generic leading man: good, bland but a far cry from Jimmy Stewart.

Stoltz plays playwright Jake Briggs, a post-feminist with a penchant for talking to the camera and sincere voiceovers. He's reached the great leap between college and real life, between making out with his first sweetheart and making it big.

Briggs spent his youth playing the man of the house for his divorced mother (Jill Clayburgh). No longer a boy, Briggs is already tired of being a man.

Indulging in cheap psychologizing (The Post is only 50 cents; the movie $7.50), the divorce rate could account for a lot of twentysomethings dragging their heels into adulthood. After a decade or more of parenting their parents, responsibility's the last thing they want.

Briggs' live-in—a photographer named Joanne (Mary-Louise Parker), doesn't know what she wants either. But when she meets a dreamy gallery owner (Timothy Dalton) and a big-time producer (Tony Curtis) lures Briggs to New York, the couple's cozy Cambridge life unravels.

Algrant tells his story with shaggy good humor and a scratch pad of narrative tricks. Some experiments are inspired (a scene in a Chinese restaurant where the Briggs' baby is whirled around on a lazy susan while his parents argue); others annoy (various Fellini moments where Algrant literally sends in the clowns, the mariachi bands, and even Whoopi Goldberg).

Parker ("Fried Green Tomatoes") delivers a fresh performance as a sharp young lady slowly unwrapping her post-college identity. Kathleen Turner bursts onto the screen as a soap opera diva who stars in, and dismantles, Briggs' off-Broadway play.

Algrant can direct actors, but he slathers on the cameos (his former Columbia prof, Martin Scorsese, is the executive producer) in a way that overwhelms a structurally flimsy script. In the battle between the members of Generation X, Algrant lacks the comic and dramatic control Ben Stiller exerted in "Reality Bites."

"Naked in New York" builds to the big revelation (and we know it's big because Stoltz addresses it directly to the camera) that "Everything would be all right. Sometimes things just happen and it's nobody's fault."

Hey, I'm OK, you're OK, the movie's just OK. OK?

NEWSDAY, 4/15/94, Part II/p. B7, Jack Mathews

Somewhere near the halfway mark in Dan Algrant's "Naked in New York," a Broadway producer, played with knowing smarminess by Tony Curtis, tells a young writer, played with knowing smugness by Eric Stoltz, that though his new play has "lots of good things in it," its dominant feature is its self-indulgence.

The same can be said about the movie, a romantic comedy co-written by Algrant and John Warren and inspired, we're told, by the life, wit and romantic experiences of Algrant himself. There are good things in it, too, particularly in the dialogue and a couple of the performances. But given the relatively uneventful life and tepid wit of Algrant's alter-ego Jake Briggs, self-indulgence is the driving force.

"Naked in New York," executive produced by Algrant's former professor Martin Scorsese, is an expanded version of a script the 33-year-old Algrant wrote while a student at Columbia University. He said he based it on the real-life trauma of breaking up with his first love, and that, with other events and psychological detail from Jake's childhood, adolescence and college career fleshed out, is the movie.

That might be enough, if Algrant were as interesting a storyteller as Woody Allen, whose style he seems to be imitating. "Naked" is told much as "Annie Hall" is, with quick flashbacks to pivotal moments in Jake's past, and with his relationship to Joanne (Mary-Louise Parker) frequently giving way to dream sequences and hallucinations from the narrator's fertile imagination.

In one scene, Jake gets advice from a philosophical orangutan at a circus. In another, the faces on the tragedy/comedy masks outside a theater come alive and argue whether Joanne, starting her career as a photographer in Boston while Jake tries to get his first play produced in New York, is having an affair with her mentor (Timothy Dalton).

Though the movie is beautifully shot and edited, most of the fantasy sequences do nothing but emphasize the, weakness of the story, and at times, they are either ill-conceived or awkwardly introduced. Worse, they're simply not funny.

Nor did Algrant do much to showcase the talent of the actors who dropped in, at Scorsese's invitation, to do cameos. Curtis has some good moments as the tough Broadway producer, and Kathleen Turner chews the scenery as the ego-driven stage star who seduces and dumps Jake. But Dalton and Jill Clayburgh, as Jake's insecure mother, don't have much to do, and Whoopi Goldberg is barely recognizable behind the tragedy mask.

Algrant's imagination is all over the place in t his film. We go from talking apes and highway hallucinations to sunny soirees on Martha's Vineyard, attended by, and appearing as themselves, such literary lights as William Styron, Ariel Dorfman, Richard Price and Marsha Norman. (Holding cocktail glasses and feigning disinterest on movie sets is becoming a second career for some of these people.)

But the problems of "Naked in New York" all emanate from the vacuous center of Jake Briggs' personality. He's not an interesting character, despite the glib assurances of his own words and Stoltz' self-satisfied performance. Jake is a nice enough guy, if a little whiney, but if his admirers are right about him having genius, we never glimpse it.

The "truth" that we hear is such a part of Jake's writing is only evident in Mary-Louise Parker's Joanne. She's the one real person around, and her story, that of a young woman having to choose between supporting her lover's career and developing her own, gives the film what little power it has.

Life may be nothing more than a series of random events, the conclusion that Jake Briggs finally comes to, but we go to the movies expecting something more.

VILLAGE VOICE, 4/26/94, p. 51, J. Hoberman

Lacking only Hugh Grant to be fashionably insufferable, *Naked in New York* is a Generation X portrait of the artist as a young man—a smug twit cursed with an atavistic desire to write for the Broadway stage.

Reality isn't the only thing that bites in Dan Algrant's quasi-autobiographical first feature. Narrated by the sadder but wiser twentysomething Jake (Eric Stoltz), *Naked in New York* flashes back to Jake's unconventional childhood—making martinis for and listening to the Ramones with his Jewish mother (Jill Clayburgh in an equally grotesque wig hat)—and more customary Ivy League education, where he meets the nice and normal WASP Joanne (Mary-Louise Parker).

Aided by his pert principals, Algrant manages to provide a few sweet touches in delineating the campus adornments of their first love. Jake's an aspiring playwright, Joanne a would-be photographer. After college they move in together in Cambridge for more creative agony. Meanwhile, Jake's good buddy, the aspiring actor Chris (perpetual 12-year-old Ralph Macchio), is down in New York hustling Jake's plays—least believably to a tough-guy producer (Tony Curtis, seemingly dropped from the road company of *Guys and Dolls*).

When lightning strikes and Jake relocates to New York. (Joanne, meanwhile, flounces off to Santa Fe with her employer, a smarmy gallery owner played by Timothy Dalton.) Alternately flat and arch, and at one point embarrassingly literal-minded, *Naked in New York* dramatizes Jake's theatrical education, including his tangle with the production's temperamental star, a blowsy man-eater played by Kathleen Turner playing Bette Davis. As though afraid that the movie would be utterly conventional, Algrant further embellishes the action with a Woody-wannabe first-person voiceover, tricking out the plot with assorted Fellini-isms and worse. (At one point, Jake receives advice from a friendly chimp.)

Of course, while Jake's play may be a disaster, the movie is its own happy ending. Not only did Martin Scorsese sign on as Algrant's executive producer, not simply did Whoopi Goldberg provide an inane cameo, but such paradigms of artistic success as Richard Price, Ariel Dorfman, William Styron, Eric Bogosian, and Arthur Penn made themselves available to play themselves.

(The film's distributor, Ira Deutchman, is also on hand, but he was doubtless working at the time.)

So placid is the movie that one could be grateful for Turner's camping, were her performance not so blatantly donational. Indeed, given the stars and celebs Algrant puts on display, you have to wonder if some smart CPA hasn't figured out a way for them to write off their appearances as charity.

Also reviewed in:
CHICAGO TRIBUNE, 4/29/94, Friday/p. B, Michael Wilmington
NEW YORK TIMES, 4/15/94, p. C3, Janet Maslin
VARIETY, 10/25/93, p. 82, Karen Regelman
WASHINGTON POST, 5/13/94, p. D6, Rita Kempley

NATURAL BORN KILLERS

A Warner Bros. release in association with Regency Enterprises and Alcor Films of an Ixtlan/New Regency production in association with J D Productions. *Executive Producer:* Arnon Milchan and Thom Mount. *Producer:* Jane Hamsher, Don Murphy, and Clayton Townsend. *Director:* Oliver Stone. *Screenplay:* David Veloz, Richard Rutowski and Oliver Stone. *Story:* Quentin Tarantino. *Director of Photography:* Robert Richardson. *Editor:* Hank Corwin and Brian Berdan. *Music:* Budd Carr. *Music Editor:* Alex Gibson and Carlton Kaller. *Sound:* David MacMillan. *Sound Editor:* Michael Wilhoit and Wylie Stateman. *Casting:* Risa Bramon Garcia, Billy Hopkins, and Heidi Levitt. *Production Designer:* Victor Kempster. *Art Director:* Margery Zweizig. *Set Decorator:* Merideth Boswell. *Special Effects:* Matt Sweeney. *Costumes:* Richard Hornung. *Make-up:* Mathew W. Mungle and John E. Jackson. *Special Make-up Effects:* Matthew W. Mungle and Gordon J. Smith. *Stunt Coordinator:* Phil Neilson. *Running time:* 120 minutes. *MPAA Rating:* R.

CAST: O-Lan Jones (Mabel); Woody Harrelson (Mickey Knox); Juliette Lewis (Mallory Knox); Ed White (Pinball Cowboy); Richard Lineback (Sonny); Lanny Flaherty (Earl); Carol-Renee Modrall (Short Order Cook); Rodney Dangerfield (Mallory's Dad); Edie McClurg (Mallory's Mom); Sean Stone (Kevin); Jerry Gardner (Work Boss #1); Jack Caffrey (Work Boss #2); Leon Skyhorse Thomas (Work Boss #3); Robert Downey, Jr. (Wayne Gale); Corey Everson (TV Mallory); Dale Dye (Dale Wrigley); Eddy "Doogie" Conna (Gerald Nash); Evan Handler (David); Kirk Baltz (Roger); Terrylene (Julie); Maria Pitillo (Deborah); Josh Richman (Soundman); Matthew Faber (Kid #1); Jamie Herrold (Kid #2); Jake Beecham (Kid #3); Saemi Nakamura (Japanese Kid #1); Seiko Yoshida (Japanese Kid #2); Jared Harris (London Boy); Katharine McQueen (London Girl); Salvator Xuereb (French Boy #1); Emmanuel Xuereb (French Boy #2); Natalie Karp (French Girl); Jessie Rutowski (Young Girl); Sally Jackson (Mickey's Mom); Phil Neilson (Mickey's Dad); Brian Barker (Young Mickey); Corinna Laszlo (Emily/Hostage in Motel); Balthazar Getty (Gas Station Attendant); Tom Sizemore (Jack Scagnetti); Red West (Cowboy Sheriff); Gerry Runnels (Indian Cop); Jeremiah Bitsui (Young Indian Boy); Russell Means (Old Indian); Lorraine Ferris (Pinky); Glen Chin (Druggist); Saemi Nakamura (Japanese Reporter); Pruitt Taylor Vince (Kavanaugh); Tommy Lee Jones (Dwight McClusky); Everett Quinton (Wurlitzer), Steven Wright (Dr. Emil Reingold); Peter Crombie (Intense Cop); John M. Watson Sr. (Black Inmate); Joe Grifasi (Duncan Homolka); Douglas Crosby (Malllory's Guard #1); Carl Ciarfalio (Mallory's Guard #2); Marshall Bell (Deputy #1); Melinda Renna (Antonia Chavez); Jim Carrane (Smithy); Bob Swan (Napalatoni); Louis Lombardi (Sparky); Robert Jordan (WGN Newscaster).

CHRISTIAN SCIENCE MONITOR, 8/26/94, p. 10, David Sterritt

"Natural Born Killers" comes as a surprise. Oliver Stone's past movies have varied widely in quality, from the highs of "JFK" and "Wall Street" to the lows of "Talk Radio" and "Heaven and Earth," his last picture. But he always seemed to be working from a forthright set of ideas—a kind of feisty Hollywood liberalism—that gave his films a consistency one could identify and respect, whether or not one agreed with them.

What's startling about "Natural Born Killers" is that it represents the opposite of everything Stone's earlier work seemed to stand for, including the basic notion of film as a medium for sharing progressive ideas. The main characters, played by Woody Harrelson and Juliette Lewis, are a boneheaded murderer and his air-headed girlfriend, barging through life with nothing but lust and violence on their demented minds.

Why would the rest of us want to see such a spectacle? It's a question Stone and company might ask themselves when their project bombs at the box office, as I expect it will once its prerelease publicity wears off.

The most appalling thing about "Natural Born Killers" is not its story, a young-outlaw saga with roots in "Badlands" and "Bonnie and Clyde," among other respectable movies. Nor is there anything automatically wrong with Stone's stated intention of satirizing the media's glorification of illicit acts—a subject that cries out for responsible treatment after heavy TV coverage of lurid criminal cases lately.

What's upsetting about "Natural Born Killers" is the contempt Stone shows toward virtually all his characters—the murderous protagonists and everyone they run across: friends, family members, the tabloid-TV journalist who tries to exploit them, the ambitious prison warden who tries to jail them. Stone despises them all, and minor characters fare even worse, getting slaughtered like ants in scenes of astonishing misanthropy.

The audience is invited to join Stone in his smirking superiority. But if he loathes the people in his story so much, could he really think much of the audience watching it?

None of this would deserve much mention if Stone's prior reputation and pumped-up promotional machine hadn't made "Natural Born Killers" the season's most talked-about movie long before ticket-buyers had a chance to see it. Even negative reviews will add to its notoriety, but to ignore or dismiss it would be to give it a free pass it doesn't deserve.

Adding to the irony of the picture is the fact that Stone's visual imagination is tremendously impressive here. It is one of Hollywood's most stylistically adventurous films ever. What a pity its brilliant ideas are expended on a failed satire with little but rage on its agenda. Someone should tell Stone about avant-garde cinema, and steer him toward abstract films where his virtuosity could shine without the nasty attitudes he's picked up recently—and without the sad self-delusion that he's attacking media sensationalism, when he's actually playing right into its dirty hands.

CINEASTE, Vol. XXI, Nos. 1-2, 1995, p. 83, Christopher Sharrett

Although *Natural Born Killers* appears to be a sophisticated film, aware of a variety of discourses from McLuhan to Burroughs to Baudrillard, Oliver Stone's meditation on the media-scape finally looks confused and dated. After *Network*, the films of David Cronenberg, *Man Bites Dog*, and numerous self-reflexive, postmodern movies, it is a considerable stretch these days to make a film with something incisive to say about the media. The media, after all, become steadily self-parodical as they devolve. Everyone becomes a media critic as the banality of the media circus and the commercial interests that underpin it become brazenly transparent. The persistent preoccupation these days with media representation looks increasingly tiresome, but the postmodernists have created something of an intellectual cult within academe and pop culture as they rehash this topic *ad nauseam*. Are the media anything other than large corporations that continue to focus the public on wish-dreams, trash, and trivia, and serve to divert serious political discourse?

Stone's project is to push cinema's stylistic envelope by making a film that assaults not just movie conventions, but also illusionism itself. In short, Stone offers a film that is deliberately fashioned to look like what it is—a construct, like all other media products. *Natural Born Killers* wants to call attention to the media's manipulation of consciousness as well as its distortion of the public agenda. The problem is that this focus is skewed in at least several very incompatible directions. While the film forcefully calls attention to itself as a fabrication through Stone's use of various film stocks and media (super 8mm, 16mm, black and white, color, video), and by emphasizing montage over narrative, with Stone's signature barrage of imagery edited in an almost subliminal fashion, the film also depends on some very hoary conventions that take it into melodrama and away from the themes the director initially establishes.

Sometime *Natural Born Killers* is a moralistic statement about the media's perversion of reality and corruption of our other institutions. At other points, it is about the media and violence, and about the media's role in shaping the violent personality. At still other points, it is about violence itself, moving into tired issues of the nature of American character that the film seems not to be interested in addressing very substantially.

Amid the cyclone of images is a screenplay (based on a story by Quentin Tarantino) about two young-lovers-on-the-lam, *à la Gun Crazy* and *Badlands*, that looks extraordinarily conventional and inappropriate to the film's issues. The lovers, Mickey and Mallory Knox (Woody Harrelson and Juliette Lewis), are presented as media phantasms, first in a ridiculously-stylized massacre in a Southwest greasy spoon, then in a shot-on-video sitcom called "I Love Mallory" that suggests to us the bankruptcy not just of that entertainment form but also of the image of the nuclear family that it perpetuates—again, not exactly startling insights. Mallory has a loudmouthed, abusive father (Rodney Dangerfield), a numbskull mom, and a headbanger kid brother; the sequence shows Stone's talent with the heavy hand.

Even with the stylization and self-referentiality of this sequence, and even with the introduction of its main characters as mere cardboard media caricatures, the film wants us to take its characters seriously. At many points we are asked to see Mickey and Mallory as vacuous nothings, as synthetic as the rest of the mediascape through which they travel—Mickey is a piece of animation, morphed video, and a monster from hell as often as he is Woody Harrelson. But Mickey and Mallory are still young lovers in a violent chase movie: just before we see them crawling through a day-glo franchise pharmacy out of *Repo Man*, they are given solace by a Native American *shaman* (Russell Means) in a scene of high seriousness that makes us ask what the heck is going on, and not in a way that provokes or raises our curiosity.

Mickey and Mallory are supposed to be a mirror reflecting the sick appetites and expectations of the viewing public, but they too often merely replicate the formulas of the entertainment industry. Each time Stone wants to send up the devices of the media, he uses them for very prosaic purposes. In a David Lynchian scene wherein Mallory hallucinates divine intervention, Mickey says, "The world's comin' to an end, Mallory"; the idea that the media culture has stopped making sense is supposed to provide a typically postmodern, apocalyptic tenor that permits Stone to movie in and out of realistic narrative at whim—it's all just text anyway, in po-mo parlance.

Some sequences are almost Brechtian in their attempt to keep the spectator at a cool remove: we see scenes from *Scarface*, *The Wild Bunch*, and Holocaust footage not just on Mickey and Mallory's motel TV, but through the window as well. They drive their Challenger against and through obvious rear-screen projections of landscape, they have visions of angels out of *Wild at Heart* (with which this film shares more than a little), and they throw enormous knives and shoot gigantic, slo-mo bullets out of Looney Tunes. But we are still asked to empathize with our heroes, as Stone uses them as a vehicle for his ongoing moralizations—somehow they are always superior to the world they inhabit. They are beleaguered by a Steve Dunleavy-style sleazoid journalist (Robert Downey, Jr.) and by a self-promoting cop (Tom Sizemore), neither of whom ring particularly true as updated remarks on media culture tawdriness.

The function of the supporting characters is not so much to delineate further the mediascape as it is to support the basic superiority of Mickey and Mallory, even as the two are also compared (very inaccurately) to Charles Manson, John Wayne Gacy, Richard Ramirez, and other superstars of serial violence. At such moments, the lovers-on-the-run convention is a jarringly poor metaphor for the frenzy of the media spectacle. The idea of criminals made into celebrities is a commonplace, and it doesn't go very far in commenting on the media's equalizing of the horrendous with the banal.

Stone's notion of the hyperreal, of the image blending with lived experience, is the central concern of the film overcome by the road movie plot. In some sequences the film never stops cutting, bombarding us with image after image in a shocking, out-of-context editing formula. Yet other passages are surprisingly static, such as a long jailhouse sequence that becomes another platform for Stone's moralizing. Instead of saturating the sequence with random clips from *Bruce Force* or *Riot in Cell Block 11* to sustain the movie's first premises about tired conventions and media manipulation, the movie adopts its own tired conventions. We are forced to endure Mickey's recollections of an abusive father and a particularly grating set-piece that allows Juliette Lewis her singing debut. Tommy Lee Jones is fine in another over the top performance as a nosepicking, redneck warden, but the entire prison sequence is overdrawn and does little except make the meretricious leap of showing the media as collaborators, such is their amorality and pragmatism (the Downey character helps Mickey and Mallory escape).

The movie's confusion makes it enervating and passionless, surprising for an Oliver Stone project, but this flows naturally from the director's failure to find a single, focused concept and a style to carry it. The blizzard of images in *JFK* worked well in supporting Stone's premise of history as perspectival illusion, a perfectly postmodern trope that happened to bring with it a certain nightmarish fury. The irony of *Natural Born Killers* is supposed to reside in its title, suggesting that there is nothing 'natural' about our current world, both in the sense that it is perverse and that the people in it are made, not born. Mickey and Mallory are merely representative of a culture that thrives on sacrificial bloodshed and scapegoats, but this is an issue that precedes the arrival of the media.

The relationship of American violence to current media culture is the real topic of Stone's film, but there isn't a strategy in *Natural Born Killers* to tackle it adequately. The film wants to be expansive, especially in a coda that flashes images of Tonya Harding, O.J. Simpson, the Bobbitt and Menendez cases, along with the Waco tragedy, all to hammer home the media's venality and reduction of human suffering to spectacle. Stone looks especially arrogant and indulgent here, since there is little in the film to justify such broad allusions and mannered intertextuality—the director inserts these images just because he thinks they are relevant. (For some real hotshot intertext, Stone might have convinced Woody to allow a reference to his dad, Charles, a convicted professional killer fingered by some conspiracy buffs as a Dealey Plaza sharpshooter.)

Stone's very arrogance and hubris are sufficient to make the film worth watching. Those same qualities, along with his position as one of the few Hollywood filmmakers with social concerns, continue to leave us with the nagging sense of a major talent not yet fully realized.

FILMS IN REVIEW, 11-12/94, p. 57, Andy Pawelczak

Natural Born Killers, Oliver Stone's delirious meditation on violence and American culture, is like a spectacularly bad acid trip into one of the demonic bardo realms described in *The Tibetan Book of the Dead*. The movie is best viewed as a kind of exorcism—it's as if Stone is saying to us that if we survive this trip, face down these demons, we'll see the light and be reborn into the pure land. Stone uses state of the art technology to deliver us to his nirvana and seems intent on proving the truth of Blake's dictum that the road of excess leads to the palace of wisdom. Like any acid trip, the movie is alternately exhilarating and irritating, compelling and boring, funny and disturbing.

The movie's opening sequence is a piece of audacious, bravura film-making characteristic of the whole picture. From shots of the Southwestern desert, reminiscent of Terence Malick's *Badlands*, the camera moves into a diner where Mickey (Woody Harrelson) and Mallory (Juliette Lewis), two young killers on the run from the law, perform their latest act of cathartic carnage. As Mallory does a seductive dance, Stone switches from black and white to color film stock and cuts from a close up of Mickey's unsettlingly protoplasmic—the film is full of images of life forms anterior to the huma—key lime pie to the bright green of a pulsating jukebox. When some rednecks arrive, their pickup truck runs over a scorpion which Stone shoots in close up, recalling the opening of Peckinpah's *The Wild Bunch*, a film that in its time represented a new high in the depiction of violence. Eventually, Mickey and Mallory kill everyone in the diner as the camera tilts drunkenly and at one point follows a bowie knife flipping through the air in slow motion toward its hapless target. The sequence ends with the two young lovers doing a slow, romantic dance to "La Vie En Rose" as the sky explodes with fireworks. And all of this is before the credits.

The movie's plot, based on a story by Quentin Tarantino, is a permutation of the familiar tale of two outlaws on the lam, but Stone isn't interested in linear narrative in this picture and splinters the classic mythos into a thousand pieces. Piling image on image, reference on reference, he reinvents film syntax to give us a multi-layered pop collage, a spectrographic picture of certain tendencies in American life and culture. One example: when Mickey and Mallory make love in a motel room, we see rear-projected images through a window of Stalin, Hitler, writhing snakes, insects devouring each other. Though the characters are cartoon caricatures, the riotous Walpurgisnacht of images gives them, and the movie, an unexpected, vertiginous depth.

As Mickey, Woody Harrelson is a revelation in a role which is several lifetimes away from his characters in *Cheers* and *White Men Can't Jump*. Alternately winsome and frightening, eerie and as American as apple pie, He's a kind of Gary Gilmore as he writes poetic love letters from prison to Mallory and controls his own media image. In a brilliant speech at the end, he cites the New Testament parable about the seed that must die to be born again in order to explain his homicidal vocation as the messianic savior of his victims. In the movie's finale in which Mickey orchestrates a prison riot, he's simultaneously a weird Buddhist monk with shaved head and an unearthly calm in the midst of chaos, and a mythical avenger, the Lord of Death.

As Mallory Juliette Lewis picks up on the sullen, perverse side of the character she played in *Cape Fear*. Unflatteringly photographed, she's feral and corrupt, never more so than during a brief scene in prison where she fantasizes about sex. In a risky sequence that pushes excess to its limits, Stone presents her family life in a flashback which is a parody of sitcoms, with Rodney Dangerfield convincingly repellent as Mallory's foul-mouthed, bumptious father who sexually abuses his perfectly blank, Lolita-like daughter. In the supporting cast, Tommy Lee Jones does one of his gargoyle imitations as a half-crazed prison warden, and Robert Downey, Jr. is unctuously opportunistic as the Australian host of a real life TV crime show who makes Mickey into one of America's most wanted.

Natural Born Killers has generated critical anxieties similar to those occasioned by Stanley Kubrick's *A Clockwork Orange*, with some critics claiming that the movie glorifies its murderous heroes. But Stone's mise-en-scene, with its stylized ultra-violence, hyperbolic performances, and meta-cinematic deconstructions of the classic movie myths of cowboys, outlaws, and monsters, doesn't give us any point of identification with the movie's characters or allow us a catharsis. Ultimately, the film is more cerebral than emotional, its characters specimens seen through a glass darkly. The movie has its missteps and longueurs—some of the satire is heavy handed, the prison riot goes on too long, and the attempt to make Mickey's killing spree into an allegorical spiritual journey is feckless if not seriously deranged—and one can argue that the presentation of Mickey as a judgement on the violence intoxicated society that produced him is shallow and disingenuous. But still the film is shot through with resonant images that are strong enough to infiltrate your dreams. Among others, I'll remember Mickey and Mallory stumbling through a huge, nauseously green drug supermarket called "Drug Zone," a white tiled prison enclosure that looks like a bloody abattoir, a bridal veil that twists and turns as it floats down a deep gorge that might very well be the mouth of hell itself.

LOS ANGELES TIMES, 8/26/94, Calendar/p. 1, Kenneth Turan

"Natural Born Killers" is the movie Oliver Stone was born to make, and if that statement is a knife that cuts both ways, so be it.

A filmmaker celebrated and excoriated, recipient of a pair of best director Oscars for "Platoon" and "Born on the Fourth of july" as well as the contempt of the political establishment for "JFK," Stone has not exactly had a tranquil career. Yet nothing he's attempted before is adequate preparation for the over-the-top savagery and carefully controlled madness that is "Natural Born Killers."

The picaresque, satirical adventures of till-death-do-us-part serial murderers Mickey and Mallory Knox (Woody Harrelson and Juliette Lewis) and their road to international celebrity, "Natural Born Killers" is both audacious and astonishing, a vision of a charnel house apocalypse that comes close to defying description.

So unyieldingly violent and blood-splattered it took five trips to the ratings board to earn its R, "Killers" (which carries an advisory label unprecedented in its length and detail) is too consumed by carnage to be to everyone's taste. But it is also, and perhaps more lastingly, a tribute to the power of film and the skill of a director who, for the first and perhaps the only time in his career, has taken the gloves off with a vengeance.

For all of Stone's previous work can be seen as a prolonged attempt to pretend, with varying degrees of success, that he is an orthodox filmmaker. But after continuously trying to squeeze his crazed/visionary sense of the medium into Hollywood's inelastic forms, of making at times awkward films that were equal parts conventional and maniacal, Stone has found subject matter that can tolerate his style at its most outrageous and disturbing. The effect has been liberating.

Screen violence poster boy Quentin Tarantino, whose Palme d'Or-winning "Pulp Fiction" seems almost tame compared to this, wrote the original script for "Killers." But Stone, working with co-screenwriters David Veloz and Richard Rutowski, has so made this project his own that Tarantino has kept his aesthetic distance, settling for no more than a "story by" credit.

Like so many loners-on-the-loose films before it, "Natural Born Killers" opens in a bleak roadside diner. Mickey, a slight grin playing behind his rose-tinted granny glasses, is sitting at the counter deciding to "give the key lime pie its day in court," while Mallory, in a skimpy halter top that reveals her scorpion tattoo, is dancing provocatively by the jukebox when some rough-and-ready locals slam through the door.

It doesn't require much intuition to figure out that no good will come from this unforeseen meeting. But though the ensuing slaughter is inevitable, Stone, cinematographer Robert Richardson (a Stone regular) and editors Hank Corwin and Brian Berdan bring things off with so much visual panache we don't know whether to be impressed or horrified. Or both.

While this kind of "Badlands on speed" opening is outrageous, how far Stone and company are willing to go is not apparent until the next set piece, when what might have been an ordinary look at Mallory's tortured childhood is shown as a warped TV sitcom called "I Love Mallory," complete with heart symbol, laugh track and a wise-cracking, malignant Rodney Dangerfield startling as a sexually abusive toad of a father.

It is Mickey, forever after to be her knight, who shows up to deliver 50 pounds of beef and rescues Mallory from this pit. And the almost continuous murder spree that follows is intercut with juvenile protestations of endless love and a goony joining of vows that includes Mickey's wistful determination "not to murder anybody on our wedding day."

As unnerving as "Killers'" plot is, relating it can only hint at what the experience is like on film. For Stone, in a brilliant display of visual dexterity, has so heedlessly, even recklessly, piled image on top of image—color, black and white, tinted stock, video, double exposures, animation and more—that surrender to the onslaught seems the only option.

More than showing highlights of M&M's three-week murder spree and their 48 (or is it 52?) victims "Killers" is intent as well on visually taking us inside their minds. This means that a constantly changing array of images is projected on any surface that is handy, everything from shots of animals having sex to Edward Curtis' vintage ethnographic footage.

Equally eclectic, and just as essential in creating mood, is the "Killers" redoubtable soundtrack, containing more than 75 selections including Nine Inch Nails (whose Trent Reznor put it all together), Nusrat Fateh Ali Khan, the Shangri-Las and the story's poet laureate, Leonard Cohen.

Unusual for a film whose effects are so dependent on the bombardment of stimuli, the cast's satiric acting is on target as well. Not only are Harrelson and Lewis all they should be, they are matched by both Tom Sizemore as twisted criminal investigator Jack Scagnetti and Tommy Lee Jones as a feisty prison warden. Best of the lot is Robert Downey Jr, as Wayne Gale, the blabbering Australian host of TV's hottest show, "American Maniacs," intended, he fondly admits, for "the nitwits out there in zombie-land."

And the nitwits, "Natural Born Killers" amusingly and horrifically points out, are eating it up. Mickey and Mallory become the ultimate international media darlings, cover subjects for Newsweek and People and captivating fans like the wanna-be victim who holds up a hopeful "Murder Me, Mickey" sign during one of M&M's courtroom appearances.

It was, not surprisingly, the chance to examine the how and why of this kind of celebrity-hood that initially motivated Stone to make "Killers," and, aside from his technical wizardry, that is the element that makes the excesses palatable.

For unlike any number of films, the excruciating violence and gore here is not done to titillate. The idea, witness O.J. Simpson and the Menendez brothers, is to mock our societal fascination with blood-letting, to hold up a cracked mirror and literally force a reconsideration of what we're doing as a culture and where it seems to be leading. This nightmare world in flames that's making you wince, Stone is saying, it's the one we live in right now.

Does this all come off as planned? Of course not. "Natural Born Killers" lacks the vigor of the similarly themed, little seen Belgian film "Man Bites Dog," and it has twinges of its own kind of sentimentality, especially in the scenes involving Russell Means as an all-knowing (is there any other kind?) tribal shaman. Plus, if you don't find yourself on the film's often warped wavelength, the non-stop violence will sicken and offend you.

But because of the frisson of directorial energy Stone infuses this film with, we can't help but be affected by its sensory barrage. Watching "Natural Born Killers" is like sitting next to a wild man driving at 90 m.p.h. in order to convince you to wear a seat belt. You may wish he'd slow down a bit, but it's hard to argue with the effectiveness of the tools at hand.

NEW STATESMAN & SOCIETY, 2/24/95, p. 49, Jonathan Romney

A director working on a screenplay for a love story recently told me that he wished he could break the rules of the genre. If only he could bring a gun into it somewhere, then he could get finished so much faster. Produce a gun at any point in a plot, he said, and things simply happen. In fact, produce a gun and people immediately know where they are.

Violence, in real life and in cinema, is unequivocal: it sorts you out, stops you in your tracks: you know what it means. That, at least, is what Oliver Stone counts on when he uses it—both its power to repel and its box-office allure—as the basis for his satirical argument in *Natural Born Killers*. Despite the high ketchup factor *NBK* is far more violent formally than it is in what it shows. It's a hyperspeed-edited flash-fry of lurid imagery, much it sampled from TV and film.

The suggestion is that we no longer know any moral absolutes, because the onslaught of media imagery has left our judgments scrambled with a cacophony of interfering signals. His anti-hero lovebirds, psychotic killers Mickey and Mallory (Woody Harrelson and Juliette Lewis) are innocents simply looking for spiritual stillness amidst the radio noise. "They're lost in a world of ghosts," says the film's one moral centre, the wise old American Indian (Russell Means) who can read the words "Too much TV" projected on their chests.

In Britain, *Natural Born Killers* has made headline news for contingent reasons—its certification was delayed after media speculation that murders in France may have been directly triggered by the film. But films, the evidence suggests, don't trigger violence; what they do trigger, and on the slightest provocation, is media generalisations about violence. It's enough to know that *NBK* is about two young homicides who become pop heroes and that its leads play up amoral thrill-kill sexiness to the hilt—and whether or not anyone's seen the film, it's deemed unarguably Bad For You.

NBK probably is bad for you, but only insofar as it's bad for film. It certainly represents some kind of breakthrough in terms of the speed and intensity with which it marshals its images, but it does so without any sense of rhetorical complexity. By throwing enough extreme images at us, it proves we live in an extreme world. You shall know the truly evil because they're ugly and bloated and sweaty, or wear hideous houndstooth suits and demonic little moustaches. *NBK* is a clumsy, stupid, extremely tiring film that leaves you numbed and disinclined to form any complex judgements.

Its breakneck dementia is a form of violence in itself; it's the violence of bad rhetoric. But it's also a technological refinement of a basic violence that's always been fundamental to cinema. The very fact of editing images together, forcing them into incongruous promiscuity, is based on a very material violation—the severing of continuity, the cutting of the strip of celluloid that records real acts, so that it can be recut into a reality that never existed. The act of editing the film forcibly directs our sensibility, constantly prevents us from following our own attention span, goading us with the cut away from one image to another.

It's perhaps because of this symbolic mutilation that cinema has so readily embraced violence as a subject matter; but it's also always been regarded as an act to be approached with caution. The best respected action directors are the ones who cut fast and clean. And the mistrust with which some theorists have traditionally regarded montage may go hand in hand with an awareness of film's expense—there's both a formal and a financial puritanism at stake.

What makes *NBK* a case of genuinely gratuitous violence is the editing itself—Stone's use of the Lightworks system, a computer-based method that means edits can be done at lightning speed without laborious concrete cutting-and-pasting. All cuts are therefore provisional and immaterial (perhaps in more senses than one). Editing becomes something like automatic writing, or rather—a sense that Stone explicitly gives it—like zapping between channels. But the violence his editing inflicts on the viewer is also inflicted on the image itself: each image is promptly bled dry of its significance, which is invariably primary and immediate, then tossed aside.

It's easy to make the leap from distaste for this kind of MTV rhetoric to a paranoia about film's infectious power. There's a powerful fear of being affected subliminally, if not literally, by the much demonised and probably apocryphal subliminals—flash messages that only your unconscious reads. But Stone's use of comic-strip shorthand actually defuses the power of violence altogether.

There are some great films that set out to brutalise the viewer—notably Shinya Tsukamoto's two *Tetsuo* films, which make you feel you've been set upon with a sledgehammer for 90 minutes a piece. But the really artful exercise of screen violence tends to deflect the blow away from the viewer, to produce a more devastating effect than mere revulsion can produce. In the ear-cutting sequence of *Reservoir Dogs*, we never actually see the cut, because the camera veers away; we all but think we do. In the Belgian black comedy *Man Bites Dog*, a far blacker exposé of media complicity than *NBK*, the camera crew accompanying a personable killer wakes up the morning after a night of slaughter to realise that they've themselves taken part. The fact that we've missed the action only makes us feel more involved in their horrific lapse of consciousness. By being out of it, we become part of it.

But sometimes too we just have to be there. The current release *Bandit Queen*, by Indian director Shekar Kapur, features violence that is painfully hard to watch—not just the raping and beating of the heroine, but the moral opprobrium and caste discrimination that go hand in hand with it. Her ordeal explains her fate—how in real life Phoolan Devi became a feared bandit and folk heroine. Kapur's film may have the stylised feel of a spaghetti western. Yet what shakes you is that the violence doesn't end in a burst of ketchup and quip, but in suffering shock and lasting moral damage.

After several months on a diet of cartoon-bloodbath films like *Killing Zoe* and the lamebrain subtleties of *Pulp Fiction, Bandit Queen* feels like a slap in the face from the real world.

NEW YORK, 9/5/94, p. 46, David Denby

Like some madly ambitious riverboat gambler, Oliver Stone keeps upping the ante on us, and we have to keep up with his challenge or leave the game. He wants to be progressively wilder, more provocative, more excessive—and by implication more deeply and comprehensively in touch with American reality—than anyone else. And by doing that he hopes to change us, to create a new audience that will reward his assaults as art. The normal name for this, of course, is megalomania, and our response is likely to be that art requires courage but also more than courage. Stone's method now is to wildly overload the medium; his movies are like a furious electric storm that blows out the windows, kicks over the ashcans, and, still raging, roars out of town. The constant thunder and lightning leave us exhausted and baffled; after a while we don't see anything, we don't hear anything.

Natural Born Killers is a paroxysm of loathing and strangled laughter, a boldly nihilistic work, nasty, and crazy as sin. According to Stone, America is being destroyed by violence and the media, which are merely two aspects of the same thing, living off each other, whipping up the public into an unendurable mood of anxiety and revolt. A brainless poor-white-trash couple, Mickey and Mallory, kill people whenever they feel like it, and for a while no one bothers to catch them. It's as if the country were too fascinated to put them out of commission. Mickey (Woody Harrelson), with his demented smirk, his opaque, freaked, closed-off mind, says little until he begins ranting and raving like a prison-house Satanist. Mallory (Juliette Lewis) speaks in a softly wandering voice and sways to whatever music is around, her midriff bare, but she goes bad suddenly, like an elephant suffering an attack of must, and her voice turns razory and mean. Unreachable and unfathomable, they kill people from the opening scene (in a roadside diner) and always on impulse.

They kill Mallory's parents and also cops and people in gas stations and restaurants; people who offend them and people who turn from them; people who want to kill *them* and people who beg for mercy. Yet they are true to each other, longing for each other's lips, squalid in act but pure in romance. And as they rampage through the West, the media have a ball. Mickey and Mallory! The couple are featured on news-magazine covers and pursued by giggly Japanese TV reporters. Scruffy teenagers, interviewed on the tube, murmur, "Yeah, Mickey and Mallory are cool." A hysterical Australian-born TV personality named Wayne Gale (Robert Downey Jr.) closes in on them, and when Mickey and Mallory are in prison at last, Wayne puts them on the air; the broadcast, which the other inmates are watching, sets off a riot that ends with everyone shooting everyone.

Natural Born Killers is like bad sex and a bad drug trip combined. It's an ejaculatory farce, but without satiation or rest. Stone pushes well beyond plausibility, yet we are meant to take the movie seriously as the essential, rabid truth of our times we are meant to take it as satire. Stone can't successfully satirize anything, however, because he can't distance himself from his subjects. He's driven by the logic of his temperament to become what he hates, or what he claims to hate. His response to the media frenzy is to redouble it—the imitative fallacy with a vengeance. And except for one goofy moment of excess in which Harrelson, breaking out of a chain gang, jumps on a horse and rides straight toward a tornado, Stone is too bearishly sincere to be funny. He sets up a mock TV sitcom—a scabrous "I Love Mallory" version of Mallory's childhood with a red-faced Rodney Dangerfield, as her slobbo dad, spitting and pawing—but the episode is grindingly sordid, and it isn't any fun. We're moving toward apocalypse here: By the end of Stone's movie, the gap between media and subject, voyeurism and participation, has been closed. We are what we broadcast, and what we broadcast in the age of trash is annihilation.

Stone has revived the experimental film techniques that feature-film directors earlier rejected as naive and confusing. The quick, discontinuous cutting that works on MTV as mood creation is still exhausting when used in a movie. As Mickey and Mallory go on their spree, images pour in, an avalanche filling up their heads and all the space around them. At the sides of their convertible we see not the landscape passing but pictures of M&M abused as children, as well as bloody faces and horror-movie freakouts. Angry, violent cartoons, in swollen red-black superhero style, pop out of their heads and take over the screen. Children of TV-heroes of an infinitely degraded, postmodernist *Bonnie and Clyde*-Mickey and Mallory live *in* images from beginning to end.

Some of this is interesting, in the sense that no one has been foolish enough to do it in a feature film before. But none of it is pleasurable. (The only thing I enjoyed in the movie was Juliette Lewis singing the blues anthem "Born Bad" with a surprisingly strong voice.) Stone produces frenzy without emotion or sense. Since he never establishes any normal reality in *Natural Born Killers*, he has nothing to take off from, nothing to violate, and after a while the viewer stops feeling shock or outrage and just goes dead. Stone switches from black-and-white to color, from one film stock to another; he blurs and staggers the images, turns Woody Harrelson's face into a melting ectoplasmic mask. So many contexts are ripped that the collection of pasted-together fragments is the only body the movie has. *Natural Born Killers* is all commentary and no text, an editing-table folly.

Many of the scenes suggest a deep complicity with murder, which is Stone's way of upping the ante this time. He's letting us know how good it must feel to kill. Okay, I'm shocked. But what shocks me as well is that there's little regret or anguish in the scenes but instead a mood of gleeful nuttiness and play, as in a degraded Friday-night horror movie made for kids. In the opening episode, Mickey and Mallory cut up some rubes who look at them the wrong way. One man, a mere spectator, tries to escape, and Stone's camera follows Mickey's heavy knife as it turns end over end and smashes through the window and takes the sucker down. We're meant to enjoy the flight of the knife as a movieish cheap thrill: That knife, like Steven Seagal's feet, gets them every time. Since Mickey and Mallory kill virtually everyone they meet, *Natural Born Killers* lacks suspense and even horror. After a while, I stopped begging the couple (in my head) not to pull the trigger. Instead I thought, Shoot him, so we can get on to the next thing and get the hell out of here.

It's meant to be a sign of American sickness that Mickey and Mallory become style leaders. But it's Oliver Stone and no one else who encourages the audience to relish the young, lean killers with their dark glasses and modish trash clothes as they kill some groveling fat person crawling on the floor. The jeering way in which many of the scenes are staged suggests a coarsening of Stone's spirit. And I'm not happy with the cockeyed moralism by which someone like (say) Geraldo Rivera is supposed to be worse than a serial killer like John Wayne Gacy. The murderer, you see, is pure, he merely kills your body, whereas the media hustler takes your soul. This is the kind of ersatz hip perception that normally (and with good reason) dies at the first sign of daylight. The misfortune of *Natural Born Killers* is that Stone put his jangled disgust, his night thoughts, into a movie.

NEW YORK POST, 8/26/94, p. 37, Michael Medved

"Natural Born Killers" may be many things—gross, disgusting, pretentious, incoherent and excessive—but it is not for one moment dull.

It is, in fact, a cinematic assault, a sensory mugging. Director/co-writer Oliver Stone shifts inexplicably from black-and-white to color, from bloody superhero cartoons to gory special effects, flashing random surreal images in a dizzy psychedelic spin.

The visual references include footage from "Leave It to Beaver," the Super Bowl and "Night of the Lepus," plus newsreel footage of Rodney King and Tonya Harding.

The crowded soundtrack features woozy original songs by Trent Reznor and Nine Inch Nails, along with 70 other selections ranging from Orff's "Carmina Burana" to "Leader of the Pack."

All of this is used to embellish the straightforward story (originally written by Quentin Tarantino, who has long since disowned the project) of Mickey and Mallory (Woody Harrelson and Juliette Lewis), two lovesick serial killers in the "Badlands", "Bonnie and Clyde" tradition.

They begin by murdering Mallory's incestuously abusive father (Rodney Dangerfield) and then go on to slaughter some 50 others as they make their way through the parched landscape west of the Mississippi (do Hollywood serial killers ever flourish anywhere else?).

In the process, they become media darlings, especially exploited by a tabloid TV reporter with an Aussie accent (Robert Downey Jr.) and pursued by a swaggering cop (Tom Sizemore) who commits sex murders of his own.

Stone's point seems to be that the whole society is in love with violence but only the two fugitives are willing to be honest about it. Stunningly persuasive performances by Harrelson and Lewis help win our sympathy, and they display memorable chemistry in their scenes together.

The other actors are campy and cartoonish, but that seems to be what Stone wanted; Tommy Lee Jones as a psycho prison warden not only chews the scenery but literally gets to climb the walls.

As everyone knows by now, Oliver Stone is a director of prodigious gifts who seems constitutionally incapable of letting a simple story tell itself; he invariably insists on blowing his hot breath into the viewer's face.

His preachments are less profound than he pretends and the messages of this movie seem painfully muddled. If Mickey and Mallory are, indeed, "natural born killers" (as the script repeatedly declares) then how can you blame the media for their murderous rampage?

In a key scene when they visit the hut of a Native American mystic (Russell Means), glowing labels appear on them reading "Demon" and "Too Much TV." Aren't these two designations contradictory? Stone seems unable to decide whether they are born evil, made that way through childhood abuse (which they both suffer), or shaped into viciousness by television culture.

For all its flashes of brilliance, "Natural Born Killers" is less likely to inspire heartache than it is to produce a splitting headache for its weary, battered audience.

NEWSDAY, 8/26/94, Part II/p. B2, Gene Seymour

Oliver Stone takes on a project the way Peter O'Toole's Lawrence of Arabia took on the Turks: with relentless, all-out ferocity. One imagines his beginning each scene with a Lawrence-like howl of "No prisoners!" instead of "Action!"

The best ("Salvador," "JFK"), worst ("The Doors"), most overrated ("Platoon") and underrated ("Wall Street," "The Hand") of Stone's films have all been powered by a declamatory fervor whose sheer force can't be denied. What also can't be denied is that his frenetic intensity can go haywire, especially when—as was the case with his previous effort, "Heaven and Earth"—it is applied to material requiring something softer than a trowel.

Simply put, an over-the-top guy like Stone works best with an over-the-top narrative. And it would be hard to find a more perfect marriage of artist and subject than "Natural Born Killers," a hyperkinetic nightmare surfeited with gut-wrenching mayhem, antic humor and up-to-the-minute inspiration.

As you may have already divined from the thick pre-release hype, "NBK" gooses the "they're-young-they're-in-love-they-kill-people-and-they're-on-the-run" formula with heavy doses of hallucinogens.

The saga of Mickey (Woody Harrelson) and Mallory (Juliette Lewis), sexy sociopaths on a three-week murder binge, unravels in a dizzying welter of jump-cutting, mind-bending visual effects. Scenes implode, explode, stretch, subdivide from juicy color to grainy black-and-white and back again before shifting to something completely different. Slow motion, rear projection, videotape, animation ...You name it. Stone uses it to pound your senses into a near-hypnotic trance.

Stimulus overload acts as both style and substance in "NBK." Indeed, the very point of Stone's gimmickry is that even the most shocking, brutal and horrific aspects of life can be simultaneously enhanced and drained of real meaning once they become stylized and exploited.

A flashback to Mallory's meeting with Mickey, for instance, is conceived as a coarse family sitcom in which every insult, no matter how vicious, is saluted with a loud laugh track. Mallory's dad (played with alarming viciousness by Rodney Dangerfield) is a rheumy-eyed abusive lout who's just asking to have his head opened with a crowbar and jammed into a fish tank. Which is pretty much what happens as he becomes the first of Mallory and Mickey's 50 victims.

You get so caught up in Stone's whirlwind of montage that you barely notice how good Harrelson and Lewis are. The mad yet captivating glint in Harrelson's eyes that one first noticed in "White Men Can't Jump" expands to a sinister but no less entrancing glow. Lewis' feral sensuality is allowed to ripen here as never before. They are truly charismatic kids. Yet their magnetism, as with Warren Beatty's Clyde and Faye Dunaway's Bonnie, has relatively little to do with their gunplay.

(Which is why the much-expressed concerns that this flick will inspire a new generation of psycho killers don't hold water. If anything, Stone's visual excesses tend to smother the kind of glamor that made movies like "Breathless" and even "Taxi Driver" beacons for outlaw behavior.)

Cops, truckers, gas-station attendants, waitresses, even a snake-tending Native American shaman (Russell Means), who is both kind to them and hep to their jive, become part of the body count. Meanwhile, their trail is picked up by a tabloid TV show, "American Maniacs," hosted by Wayne Gale (Robert Downey Jr.), a wild-eyed, glandular Aussie. Downey is a stitch, yet one wonders if Stone's satire would have carried more resonance if the TV guy were less like Robin Leach and more like, say, Morley Safer.

Gale's segment on the pair helps make them the glam couple of the moment, even after the cops nail them in a tableau eerily (and unaccountably) reminiscent of the Rodney King video. They are pitched into a prison run by a sleazeball warden (Tommy Lee Jones as a Brylcreemed Daffy Duck with a discount wardrobe) who allows Gale and his camera crew to do a live interview with Mickey on Super Bowl Sunday. The chaos that ensues from this unfortunate decision makes for some of the most effectively harrowing filmmaking in Stone's prolific career.

At the end, film clips of a Menendez brother, Rodney King and O. J. Simpson are tacked on. (We get it already, OK?) It wouldn't be an Oliver Stone film if he didn't get carried away. You may think the whole movie constitutes wretched excess. Even reckless endangerment. But Stone's audacity and drive are what make "Natural Born Killers" the rare Hollywood movie that will stick to the back of your brain like an itch you can't reach.

NEWSWEEK, 8/29/94, p. 54, David Ansen

The best and worst of Oliver Stone are on ample display in "Natural Born Killers," a hyperactive, blood-spattered, semi-satirical visual onslaught that examines the American obsession with violence and the warped media values that turn killers into celebrities, murder into infotainment. The topic, amid O. J. fever and Menendez mania, couldn't be more timely, and Stone is, to say the least, a controversial man for the job. From the start, he's built his Oscar-garlanded career on violence, working out his own plentiful aggression on screen.

Now he wants to deconstruct the way the media present murder for our delectation.

His radical method is clear in the opening sequence, In a roadside diner, mass murderers Mickey (Woody Harrelson) and Mallory (Juliette Lewis) stab, blow away and otherwise slaughter nearly everyone in sight. From shot to shot, the style changes: from black and white to color, slow-mo to normal speed, 16mm to 35, while the background music leaps from rock to opera.

Disorienting us, Stone wants us to note how the medium alters the message—he wants to force us to watch ourselves watching a movie. But he also—make no mistake—wants to stage a really bitchin' display of ultraviolence. Which he does.

Stylistically, "Natural Born Killers" makes "Platoon" look as delicate as Lubitsch. Here, the pedal is always to the floor. Stone's satirical strategy is overkill—as if he believed that an overdose of orgiastic mayhem would be purgative. For two hours, Stone assaults us with everything in his virtuoso's arsenal: animation, video, back-projections, scratchy footage. Perhaps his most effectively unnerving ploy is to stage Mallory's recollection of her dysfunctional family in the style of a '50s sitcom, with Rodney Dangerfield as her abusive father mugging to a laugh track as he makes sexual overtures to his daughter. Soon after, Dad gets bludgeoned to death, and Mom is set on fire, commencing the young lovers' 52-person killing spree.

As the serial killers become celebrities, seen on the covers of Esquire and NEWSWEEK, Stone's main satirical target worms his way aboard: Wayne Gale (Robert Downey Jr.), the fatuous Aussie host of the tabloid TV show "American Maniacs." Wayne wants to get a live interview with Mickey, and in the second half of the movie, when the lovers have been captured, he gets his chance. Because Downey is a gifted comic, some of this stuff is quite funny. But "Natural Born Killers" suffers from the disadvantage of being made by a man with little discernible sense of humor. Satire needs breathing space, and Stone locks himself into the hammering tempo of a heavy-metal music video. Last year's Belgian black comedy "Man Bites Dog," about a film crew following a serial killer, did it first, funnier and with a greater sense of horror.

Though Stone's movie is luridly packed with shotgun blasts, beatings, rattlesnakes and prison riots, the deaths have no sting. The only murder the killers regret is that of a wise old Indian—an outburst of P.C. guilt that seems oddly out of character. All the other victims are dehumanized. Stone hasn't figured out how to make a movie *about* the estheticizing of violence without fetishizing it himself, thus aping what he's criticizing TV for. He can't help it—he loves the visceral charge too much. Nor can Stone resist glamorizing his psychos: they may be brain dead, but they're the coolest people on screen. (And expertly performed by the stars.) The Bonnie-and-Clyde, lovers-on-the-run conceit presumably comes from Quentin Tarantino's original story—thoroughly rewritten by Stone, David Veloz and Richard Rutowski. But it's a dated notion for an up-to-the-minute movie.

As it becomes more hectoring and repetitive, the satire gets crazily out of joint. Stone's deepest moral indignation is reserved for Wayne Gale and the media, whose hypocrisy troubles him a good deal more than the dead bodies Mickey and Mallory have left behind. It figures. The media have given the director a lot more grief over the years than any serial killers. But it's too easy to blame our fascination with violence on the tabloids. Stone has always viewed the world in terms of good guys and bad. There aren't any heroes this time, but by giving us an easily hissable villain he lets the audience off the hook: it's blame-the-messenger time again.

And he lets himself off too. What Stone can't acknowledge in his fitfully astonishing, ultimately numbing movie is that he and Wayne Gale are two sides of the same coin. Had he done so, "Natural Born Killers" might have gotten under the skin of the issues it tantalizingly raises. Instead, fighting fire with fire, the movie cancels itself out. You leave it more battered than enlightened.

NEWSWEEK, 8/29/94, p. 55, Jack Kroll

If Oliver Stone didn't exist, American culture would have to invent him. Throughout his career he's been a pterodactyl-size gadfly pushing our noses deep into some of our thorniest issues—Vietnam, the JFK assassination, the youth revolt of the '60s. He has been rightly called a troublemaker for our times. In "Natural Born Killers," Stone is making more trouble than ever. A creature of the media himself, he's assaulting the media for its crucial role in a process of dehumanization that seems to be an inescapable feature of mass society.

How does a filmmaker deal with the Catch-22 of presenting extreme violence without luxuriating in it? Stone handles the problem in a brutally logical fashion, by subjecting the movie medium itself to violence. In "The Wild Bunch," Sam Peckinpah made you feel violence by slowing it down to a voluptuous ballet of fleshly demolition. Stone reverses the process, speeding up his stream of images (he says "Killers" has 3,000 images) so that you have no rest, no place to collect your thoughts, to stabilize your senses, to get your bearings—physical, esthetic, moral. Stone pulverizes the murderous acts of his youthful serial killers, Mickey and Mallory, into their behavioral particles: GLAM! goes the gun, and the "realistic" image ripsaws into a grainy TV image, a black-and-white home movie, a cartoon demon, a newsreel flash, a fragment from some cesspool of dreams.

With this fission of images Stone wants you to sense that the murderous behavior is erupting from a wrenching complexity of causes. There's no pseudo-Freudian claptrap, no New Age moral masturbation, and just enough perverse pleasure so that you don't miss the horrific fun that Mickey and Mallory are having. Stone never lets you forget that these kill-crazy kids are operating in good part out of some terrible pleasure principle. What drives them to do it? Stone's answer is brilliantly nightmarish. He gives us "I Love Mallory," a savage sitcom parody with Rodney Dangerfield as Mallory's incestuous slob father—and her first victim. Casting Dangerfield was a fiendish inspiration. The no-respect comic, with the face of a paternal troglodyte, is like a character in Aristophanes, grotesquely and hilariously loathsome.

Stone doesn't use the sitcom parody to "explain" Mallory's behavior. The sitcom itself, with its cackling laugh track, is part of the cultural mindlessness he's evoking. If his killers are "brain dead," then what of the consumers of this culture? And what of the Mickey-and-Mallory fans interviewed by the local news shows, who say things like "I'm not saying I respect mass murder. But if I were a mass murderer I'd be Mickey and Mallory." These scenes predated the O. J. Simpson fans who rooted him on during his freeway fight. Stone's movie is the most all-out assault yet on American media as complicit with American violence. Even more gruesomely funny than "I Love Mallory" is "American Maniacs," the tabloid TV show run by Robert Downey Jr. as the Aussie-accented Wayne Gale (based on tab TV pioneer Steve Dunleavy, with whom Downey researched the role). Downey's performance is amazing—he's cynical, devious, narcissistic and finally suicidally hysterical as he's caught up in the blood lust of M&M's apocalyptic breakout from prison.

Stone's movie is no random spew of MTV images. He shot it in 53 days but took a year to edit it. The film's multifarious formats are as precisely placed as the planes in a cubist Picasso. The movie is in fact a portrait of a new American mind dislocated and stupefied by vicarious violence. Its extravagant surrealism reflects reality. Parts of H. R. Haldeman's recently published diaries read like scenes from a Stone movie. In one, President Nixon and Co. are watching an anti-Vietnam demonstration on TV. Police are using tear gas on demonstrators who are carrying candles. Haldeman writes that Nixon "had helpful ideas like using helicopters to blow out their candles ... Said was like watching an old movie, keep thinking something interesting will happen."

In "Natural Born Killers" something revelatory happens. The movie is enlightening, not because it transmits new information, but in the way that movies enlighten, through a synergy of images and rhythm that makes us sense the world in a new way. Stone's besetting fault is sentimentalism, here expressed in his idealization of the redemptive love between Mickey and Mallory. But even here, the performances of Woody Harrelson and Juliette Lewis produce an unsettling passion. The horror is the distortion of that passion to violence: you believe it when the slight Lewis, transfigured by nameless rage, beats the living hell out of some poor rednecks. Stone's flabbergasting movie cannot be dismissed; it must and will be fought over.

SIGHT AND SOUND, 3/95, p. 45, Nick James

In a diner somewhere in the midwest, a young girl begins dancing while her boyfriend orders food. Three roughnecks assume she's easy bait and begin to taunt her. Immediately she and her boyfriend produce firearms and begin slaughtering everyone, leaving only one witness to tell the tale. The pair are Mickey and Mallory and they're on a killing spree. A backstory in the form of a spoof television sitcom entitled *I Love Mallory* sketches out how Mallory was prey to an abusive and violent father and how she and Mickey killed her entire family.

On a high bridge over a deep gorge, the two clasp slashed hands in a blood bond. Their instant media history is then encapsulated by the television show *American Maniacs*, hosted by Australian Wayne Gayle. They are celebrity killers. As they drive along, Mickey suggests several passing candidates to take as hostage. Irritated that they're all women, Mallory leaves Mickey stranded, driving to a garage where she seduces a mechanic on the bonnet of her car before shooting him for giving "the worst head I ever had".

Together again, Mickey and Mallory run out of gas in the middle of the desert. An old Indian mystic gives them shelter in his hut. He seems to have some understanding and sympathy for them, but that night Mickey has a nightmare and shoots the Indian dead by mistake. Surrounded by deadly conjured snakes, the two both get bitten before making their getaway. They go to collect an antidote from a store, but the alarm is raised and the building surrounded. Hard-nosed detective Jack Scagnetti is soon on the scene to arrest them, hoping to consummate a perverse passion for Mallory.

A year later, Scagnetti is called in by the warden to deliberately assassinate Mickey and Mallory in prison. On Superbowl Sunday, Mickey gives an in-depth interview to Gayle and his *American Maniacs* crew. His unapologetic admission that he's a "natural born killer" sparks an instant riot among the watching inmates. While his guards are distracted by the noise, Mickey grabs a shotgun and kills several of them before leading a procession of hostages through the prison to Mallory's cell. There he finds Scagnetti trying to assault her. Mickey shoots him dead and fights his way out, via the front gate, encouraging a frenzied Gayle to join in the killing. In a clearing in the woods, the couple explain to Gayle that he must die and together they execute him before his own camera. A flash-forward shows Mickey and Mallory living in a mobile home as a nuclear family.

After the much-discussed delay to its classification by the BBFC, what's most surprising about *Natural Born Killers* is not the visceral depiction of violent acts, but that anyone could have accepted Oliver Stone's putative satire as a serious work. Not only is the film played for grim laughs throughout (albeit by a director who is clearly not laughing), with Mickey and Mallory as overblown cartoon killers, but its black humour is so strained and hysterical that all satirical intent is dissipated. There's barely a trace left of Tarantino's usual cool wit (assuming it was there in the original script), no nice domestic touches to offset the mayhem; it's a straightforward rush of inexplicably raw visual data.

Stone's proclaimed target is the pernicious levelling effect of media saturation on moral questions, but if this full-on assault of MTV blip-editing and simulated channel-surfing hits any target at all, it would be the barn door marked 'overused imagery'. For all the hallucinogenic frenzy with which this film shuffles the full range of image-gathering options, it is a curiously second-hand experience. Its pictorial exuberance feels forced, a slap-dash imitation of music video and infotainment style. In attempting a self-lacerating version of Terrence Malick's *Badlands* and the tinpot imitations that have followed that film in mythologising 'misunderstood' hoodlum youth, Stone is clearly so afraid that his audience won't get the fact that he's engaged in parody, that he restates everything over and over, repeatedly cutting from wielded gun, to reacting victim, to entry wound, to gun again. But he also sends himself up, having Mallory rant at Mickey for killing the Indian: "Bad, bad, bad, bad, bad", as if she were giving notes on his performance.

Woody Harrelson and Juliette Lewis are nevertheless superb at exaggerating the archetypes of cool psychopathology forged around the mean and moody stars of the 50s and 60s. Harrelson's cocky smirk makes a particularly apt counterpart to Lewis's method pout (she could have parodied her own performance in *Kalifornia*; instead she plays a more decisive and self-possessed version of white trash womanhood). There are blink-and-miss-'em knowing allusions to films as diverse as *Detour* and *Scorpio Rising*, which can be seen as progenitors of the standard weirdness-is-all music video approach. But while it's undoubtedly true that the image bank of rebel youth mythology—of Dean, Presley, Brando *et al*—has been plundered to bankruptcy by the endless recycling of the music promo business, it didn't need a scion of the 60s such as Stone—whose own movie, *The Doors*, is similarly meretricious—to spend millions of dollars bemoaning it. To call it overkill would be an understatement.

What is unique and remarkable, however, is for a big budget Hollywood movie deliberately to trash its narrative in favour of a nightmare logic. Perhaps Stone has no interest in telling more than a vestigal story because it's harder with narrative to predict an audience's reaction. He wants us to feel nothing but his own palpable disgust at the kind of true-crime cultural production spoofed as *American Maniacs*. But what he is holding up is a fairground's distorting mirror, to which we can only respond with a laugh or a shrug.

Of course, it will be argued that one-note-harping on one-note-harping is the whole point, that, whether or not you get the insider references, you will get the message. But Stone fails to follow his own logic. If an audience is sophisticated enough to read the stream of images then surely they deserve a coherent argument. Here the audience gets a deafening imprecation to think about every little thing from a director who seems to feel that they've already lost the ability to do so.

There might be another reason for Stone's abandoning the coherent narrative. Perhaps the least-discussed of recent new technologies is the computer-based editing systems, such as Avid and Lightworks, which enable a film to be edited digitally at speed in many different versions. Without this facility, *Natural Born Killers* would be almost unthinkable, not simply because otherwise the process of assembling such a random mass of footage would take too long, but also because linear hands-on editing arguably forces the film-maker to think the whole thing through, to keep the entire film in his or her head. No-one could possibly retain a complete and detailed picture of this film because it is so non-commital and open-ended.

As for the film's much-trumpeted ability to shock, it is set at the level of a prank, reminiscent of nothing so much as a heavy metal band adding a backwards voice track to an album simply to wind up Christian fundamentalists.

TIME, 8/29/94, p. 66, Richard Corliss

Has everybody gone nuts? Is violence the way we resolve every domestic grievance, or is it just the quickest way to get on TV? With the Bobbitts, the Jacksons, the Menendez clan and that favorite new horror sitcom, *The (O.J.) Simpsons*, the American family has entered its postnuclear stage. Talk shows offer quack catharsis from every form of spousal and parental abuse. We're shouting at each other in *National Enquirer* headlines and have promoted tabloid newspapers and TV programs, once on the fringe of journalism, up to its hot center. It's Armageddon with commercial breaks. Why, the whole bloody mess could be straight out of an Oliver Stone movie.

Now it is. *Natural Born Killers*, the new outrage from Hollywood's most audacious auteur, takes a wild look at America's infatuation with hoisted minds. The $34 million movie is so manic, so violent, so seemingly at one with the subject it satirizes, that Warner Bros. was reportedly spooked about a potential fire storm. Now the execs say they are feeling better. "I'm encouraged and excited" says marketing boss Rob Friedman. "The media response has been overwhelmingly positive."

Natural Born Killers—in shorthand, *NBK*, to echo Stone's nutsy-greatsy *JFK*—traces the odyssey of love—thugs Mickey and Mallory Knox (Woody Harrelson and Juliette Lewis) as they terrorize the Southwest and mesmerize America's couch spuds. *Like Bonnie & Clyde, Badlands* and a zillion tortured teen movies of the '50s, *NBK* creates two doomed maniacs busy mythologizing themselves. "We got the road to hell in front of us," Mickey tells his bride, and he's not lying. These kids get their kicks on Route 66; when they go traveling, the devil thumbs a ride.

Three men want them bad which is the only way Mickey and Mallory come. A brutish detective (Tom Sizemore) hopes to capture these miscreants and maybe write a best seller about it. A tabloid-TV newsman (Robert Downey Jr.) figures he can exploit their exploits, turning this Mansonized Romeo and Juliet—52 murders, no regrets—into media darlings. A crazed warden (Tommy Lee Jones) is determined to achieve fame as the man who put them to death. It's the ideal recipe for a Stone-crazy parable of greed and abuse. Shake well, pull the pin and stand back.

Except, of course, that Stone doesn't let you stand back. *NBK* plunders every visual trick of avant-garde and mainstream cinema—morphing, back projection, slow motion, animation and pixillation on five kinds of film stock—and, for two delirious hours, pushes them in your face like a Cagney grapefruit. The actors go hyper-hyper, the camera is ever on the bias, the garish colors converge and collide, and you're caught in this Excedrin vision of America in heat. The ride is fun too, daredevil fun of the sort that only Stone seems willing to provide in this timid film era. *NBK* is the most excessive, most exasperating, most ... let's just say it's the *most* movie in quite some time.

NBK took quite some time to take shape. It began as a script by Quentin Tarantino (*Reservoir Dogs*), then got spun and spindled: Tarantino is credited with the story, Stone and his collaborators David Veloz and Richard Rutowski with the screenplay. Meanwhile, *NBK* was acquiring a bizarre new resonance. "When I started," says Stone, "this was a surreal piece. Now, thanks to Bobbitt and Menendez and Tonya Harding, it's become satire. By the time I'd finished, fact had caught up to fiction. O.J. is the final blowout."

It's still on the surreal side, and not just in the carnage that almost earned the picture an NC-17 rating. *NBK* is also a blanket indictment of the American family (breeders of abuse), the justice system (sadistic and incompetent) and the avid media that find in tabloid crime the no-brain modern equivalent of Greek tragedy. And intentionally or not, *NBK* romanticizes its hero and heroine, because they are smarter and sexier than their pursuers. As the kid in the movies fake news footage says, "If I was a mass murderer, I'd be Mickey and Mallory."

Stone is always ready to defend his movies' most outlandish theses. O.K., Oliver, hit it: "Let's look at the statistics. Violent crime has remained flat over the past 20 years. But the perception of crime has changed; now it's the No. 1 enemy. Every night on the news it's back-to-back murder and body bags. Even the national news is perverted, because the news has become a profit-oriented enterprise since Tisch took over CBS. It's the old yellow journalism. Now that communism is dead, they need new demons. This virus has infected us all—the demons within us and among us.

NBK may have little new to say about those demons, but it has plenty to show, in images that mix beauty and horror, atrocity and comedy. Angels and red horses glide across the night sky. Mallory's family life is played as a grotesque sitcom that ends when her own father (Rodney Dangerfield) is beaten to death and her weak mother is set ablaze. When Mickey and Mallory visit an Indian shaman (Russell Means), the words DEMON and TOO MUCH TV are superimposed on their torsos flashes of Hitler and Stalin, insects and rhinos, *The Wild Bunch* and *Midnight Express* (the film whose screenplay won Stone his first Oscar) explode on the window of a motel room while the two make love and a hostage looks on. As the Cowboy Junkies' ethereal version of *Sweet Jane* plays on the sound track, they make a blood pact, and the drops form cartoon snakes—a big motif here.

In all three stages of the project—writing, shooting, editing—Stone encouraged everybody to go higher, wilder. "The set was intense and exciting," recalls Harrelson, a bit of a real-life brawler whose father is in prison for murder. "Oliver played an incessant barrage of wild music to get you going. The crew would jam the music, then fire shotguns into the air." All the actors felt this electricity, like a searchlight or a cattle prod. "Oliver shot at a feverish pace," Sizemore says, "54 days and no standing around. It was managed chaos."

Chaos? Perhaps. Managed? Perhaps not. "The shoot was extraordinarily angst-ridden," says Stone's superb cinematographer, Robert Richardson, "because it was anarchy in style. It wasn't planned out in the traditional sense. It was more like throwing paint at the canvas—you don't know if you're making art. The only rule was that you could change your mind." That same rule applied in the editing, which took 11 grueling months. Says co-editor Hank Corwin: "We wanted an impressionistic feeling, but there was no randomness. Every two-frame flash was thought out. This style can work on anything. It could be one of the futures of filmmaking."

One wouldn't want this to be the only future; then we really would go nuts. But most films today are afraid to try anything new. That's exactly what Stone does. He's like Mickey or Mallory careering to hell or heaven. And the viewer is like the bit-part cook in the opening diner scene. A bullet whirls toward him, stops for a split second as the victim's eyes widen in fear, then BOOM! *Natural Born Killers* is an explosive device for the sleepy movie audience, a wake-up call in the form of a frag bomb.

VILLAGE VOICE, 8/30/94, p. 41, J. Hoberman

More bombast than bombshell, *Natural Born Killers* is still sufficiently schizoid to infect the viewer with a nasty case of ambivalence. Two hours of Oliver Stone shadowboxing here should leave you impressed but unconvinced, torn between admiration and disgust, a desire to praise audacious filmmaking and the urge to laugh at rampaging idiocy.

It's hard to fault Stone's timing. *Natural Born Killers* is both an aesthetic throwback and a new advance in metaexploitation. Cosmic bummer or current affair? On the one hand, this is the most blatantly avant-garde studio release since Dennis Hopper delivered *The Last Movie* (not to mention the most solemnly ludicrous vision of evil since Luchino Visconti applied black lipstick to National Socialism in *The Damned*). On the other, it surfs into theaters on a tsunami of ancillary hype.

In theory, the movie sounded like a belated postscript to the serial killer craze. In practice it's fresher than fresh. The premise, adapted from a story by red-hot Quentin Tarantino, could have been the centerpiece of *New York*'s recent "White Trash" cover story. *The New Yorker*, meanwhile, used its Stone profile as a pretext to emblazon their cover with the magic letters "O.J," for the third time since the Night of the White Bronco.

Basically, *Natural Born Killers* posits a nouveau Bonnie and Clyde—Mickey and Mallory Knox, played to the max by Wood Harrelson and Juliette Lewis—as a pair of dada punk cartoon cracker *l'amour fou*—struck thrill-killer Mansonettes, and presents the tale of their telecelebrity beatitude as an exercise in frenzied montage. The opening desert diner massacre—a bungled jumble of pulverized scorpions and shifting angles, the film stock oscillating like an old TV between livid color and black-and-white-buriesall horror and foreboding in a welter of gimmicks, including one of Lewis's patented writhing cooch dances. The performances are beyond Kabuki. While big-jawed Harrelson seems lit from within like a jack-o-lantern, Lewis, her bulging forehead concealed beneath a blond Brunhilde wig, is so rabid she must have been bitten by De Niro on the set of *Cape Fear*.

Clearly, *Natural Born Killers* is meant to be a comedy—although Stone never fences with a rapier when he can wrap his mitts around a Louisville Slugger, presenting, for example, Mallory's life as a sitcom complete with laugh track and Rodney Dangerfield as her abusive lech of a father. As in *Badlands*, Terrence Malick's more subdued treatment of similar material, the delinquent couple begin their spree by disposing of the girl's parents—here, however, they bludgeon Dad and drown him in a fish tank, then torch Mom in her sleep, telegraphing Stone's strategy to obliterate David Lynch and beat Tarantino's premise to a hallucinatory pulp.

Shifting film stocks and formats, throwing up rearscreen projections or subliminal images of bloody horror, interpolating all manner of animation, stock footage, and stroboscopic monkey screams, Stone has no shortage of visual ideas—and, as in *JFK*, he's found the film editors to cope with them. *Natural Born Killers* is full of hellfire and Japanese movie monsters. In its creepy-crawly nature inserts and computer-distorted close-ups, *Natural Born Killers* suggests a whole culture on bad acid. With Trent Reznor's symphonic sound mix underscoring the montage hysteria, the effect is pulverizing: Stan Brakhage meets Sam Fuller, with a soupçon of Dali-Buñuel insect fear. When Mickey and Mallory take refuge in a motel room (a hostage cowering in the corner), the TV erupts with images of Hitler, Stalin, and a mountain of corpses, as well as clips from *The Wild Bunch* and *Midnight Express*. As in a Syberberg film, the window functions as yet another TV.

Stone's anthology of celluloid atrocities resembles Wilhelm and Birgit Hein's underground assemblage *Kali-Filme*—except that the Heins' flick, a homemade contraption meant for study in the affectless, half-deserted aesthetic catacombs of New York and Berlin, exhibits a certain anthropological detachment while cinema devil worship à la Stone is an overweening megamillion-dollar attempt to huff and puff and blow your house down. Every fade is the equivalent of an atomic blast.

Unlike Tarantino, Stone is obsessed with generating significance. Mickey and Mallory alternately reflect their society, represent an endless cycle of abuse, and enact timeless Jungian archetypes. Hence, the self-canceling aspect of Stone's mania. The body count rises but nothing can quite project the couple's absolute evil. The scenes in which she murders the hapless gas jockey she's seduced into going down on her or he shoots a happy snake-handling Indian shaman (Russel Means) are meant to show Mickey and Mallory's worst, most secret transgressions. But, after killing 12 cops and an unspecified number of civilians, they only achieve notoriety as the subject of the tabloid TV news show *American Maniacs*, hosted by Wayne Gale (Robert Downey, Jr.), a gross, braying Australian modeled on Steve Dunleavy and Robin Leach.

Like Bonnie and Clyde in their 1967 incarnation, Mickey and Mallory are adored by kids all over the world; bad as the Knoxes may be, society is even worse. The outlaws are caught by a lunatic cop (introduced throttling a sweet-faced hooker in another image-ridden motel) and sent to a hellish prison administered by Tommy Lee Jones. Wildly camping as the pomaded warden, Jones manipulates himself like a marionette. He's a dervish of stooped positions, enlivening every scene with his slack-jawed, rubber-faced contortions, looking like Charles Burns's Dog Boy fronting for an entourage culled from the pages of *Mad* magazine. Meanwhile, Wayne Gale contrives to make television history, following the Super Bowl with an exclusive interview with the condemned Mickey.

There's nothing new, except maybe in degree, to such Hollywood finger-pointing at big, bad TV. Still, unexpectedly improving in its final reel, *Natural Born Killers* plays to its own medium's strength to end with a blast of pure anarchy and mad release—Stone even tossing "Night on Bald Mountain" in the charnel house mix.

Among other things we've been replacing Summer of '69 for the past two months. The macho-patriotic *True Lies* is our debased, current equivalent of the Apollo Project's techno-extravagant moon landing, and if *Forrest Gump* represents the counterculture's Woodshtick yin, *Natural Born Killers* is a blatant expression of its contemporaneous Mansonesque yang. Mickey's explanation of murder as cosmic and natural is pure Charlie—as is his observation that "media's like the weather, only it's man-made."

But just as pundits will inevitably trap themselves flogging the tar baby of Stone's scenario, so Stone can't bear to separate himself from the spectacle at large—topical to the last, he winds up *Natural Born Killers* by flashing Eric and Lyle, Lorena, Tonya, Waco, and the whole sick crew (including a last-minute insert of O.J.) in our face. *Natural Born Killers* demonstrates that there isn't anything Stone won't try for an effect-including strip-mining the integrity of his own strenuously achieved paranoia. The movie doesn't achieve full amorality when Harrelson crowns Charles Manson "king," but when he trashes *JFK* with the observation that "Oswald might have been a pussy, but he was a great shot." (Even so, the joke is evil with a small *e*.)

Having produced, in *JFK*, the most baroque snuff film in American history (and the most blatant since Thomas Edison documented the electrocution of an elephant), Stone is scarcely detached from the celebrity death religion he burlesques. Indeed, given the megalomaniacal occultism that underscores Stone's enterprise, I wonder why he isn't afraid that this frenzy of subliminal "evil" images won't light some lunatic's fire. Perhaps he wants a Hinckley-style assassin to call his own.

Also reviewed in:
CHICAGO TRIBUNE, 8/26/94, Friday/p. C, Michael Wilmington
NATION, 9/19/94, p. 284, Stuart Klawans
NEW REPUBLIC, 10/3/94, p. 26, Stanley Kauffmann
NEW YORK TIMES, 8/26/94, p. C1, Janet Maslin
NEW YORKER, 9/5/94, p. 106, Terrence Rafferty
VARIETY, 8/15-21/94, p. 43, Todd McCarthy
WASHINGTON POST, 8/26/94, p. D1, Hal Hinson
WASHINGTON POST, 8/26/94, Weekend/p. 42, Desson Howe

NELL

A Twentieth Century Fox release of an Egg Pictures production. *Producer:* Renée Missel and Jodie Foster. *Director:* Michael Apted. *Screenplay:* William Nicholson and Mark Handley. *Based on the play "Idioglossia" by:* Mark Handley. *Director of Photography:* Dante Spinotti. *Editor:* Jim Clark. *Music:* Mark Isham. *Music Editor:* Tom Carlson. *Sound:* Chris Newman and (music) Stephen Krause. *Sound Editor:* Eddy Joseph. *Casting:* Linda Lory. *Production Designer:* Jon Hutman. *Art Director:* Tim Galvin. *Set Decorator:* Samara Hutman. *Set Dresser:* John Ceniceros, Lisa K. Sessions, John T. Bromell, Michael Shapiro, and Drew Sywanyk. *Special Effects:* Bob Vasquez. *Costumes:* Susan Lyall. *Make-up:* Jaren Millard. *Stunt Coordinator:* Jery Hewitt and Danny Aiello III. *Running time:* 112 minutes. *MPAA Rating:* PG-13.

CAST: Jodie Foster (Nell); Liam Neeson (Jerome Lovell); Natasha Richardson (Paula Olsen); Richard Libertini (Alexander Paley); Nick Searcy (Todd Peterson); Robin Mullins (Mary

Peterson); Jeremy Davies (Billy Fisher); O'Neal Compton (Don Fontana); Heather M. Bomba and Marianne E. Bomba (The Twins); Sean Bridgers (Mike Ibarra); Joe Inscoe (Judge); Stephanie Dawn Wood (Ruthie Lovell); Mary Lynn Riner (Janet Baring); Lucile McIntyre (Sally); Al Wiggins (Harry Goppel); Beth Bostic (Jean Malinowski); Rob Buren III (Stevie); Christ T. Hill (Jed); Tim Mehaffey (Shane); Dana Stevens (Rachel Weiss); Nicole Adair (Autistic Child); Robin Rochelle (Teacher); Susan Correll Hickerson (Administrator); Marlon Jackson (Male Nurse); Danny Millsaps (Deputy).

CHRISTIAN SCIENCE MONITOR, 12/16/94, p. 11, David Sterritt

Since the early years of Hollywood filmmaking, big-name performers have tried to boost their careers by putting up their own talent, clout, and money to support productions that offer them juicy parts. The practice continues to this day, and some of the most eager players are actresses who become producers as a way of combating the shortage of substantial female roles in American cinema.

Given these circumstances, it's not surprising that two new pictures with strong female characters were largely assembled by strong female stars working behind the cameras as well. The movies are "Nell" and "Speechless," and the actresses are Jodie Foster and Geena Davis, both of whom served as co-producers in addition to playing the leading roles. They deserve credit for widening the current range of movie heroines, even though the films themselves don't live up to the hopes that inspired them.

"Nell" is an ambitious look at a subject difficult to dramatize: the thoughts, perceptions, and experiences of a person raised in near-total separation from other human beings, then removed from isolation by well-meaning but ultimately self-serving representatives of society. Previous films on such material include François Truffaut's popular "The Wild Child" and Werner Herzog's visionary "The Mystery of Kaspar Hauser," as well as a recent episode of the "Nova" television show documenting a modern-day case history.

"Nell" follows a common trajectory for tales like this. First the half-savage young woman is discovered after the death of the disabled mother who raised her. Then she's observed by a physician and a psychologist, who find her case compelling for both professional and personal reasons. They come to appreciate her as a person rather than a specimen, but they can't protect her from snoops less altruistic and enlightened than themselves.

The climax occurs when Nell is plunged into the ordinary world with few skills and insights to protect her.

This is a fascinating topic, and the film certainly offers Foster a role worthy of her talents. The problem with the picture is that it cares less about exploring Nell's consciousness than about molding her experiences into the contours of conventional Hollywood storytelling—smoothing rough edges, sanitizing harsh details, stressing sentimentality over substance. In production notes for the movie, Foster says the story is "about defying description, about not being put in a box, and not being labeled and marketed." Yet that's precisely what "Nell" does to its remarkable heroine, who is described and boxed and labeled and marketed from first scene to last.

This is standard Hollywood procedure, of course, and that's why Hollywood should leave such challenging material to filmmakers more willing to take artistic and commercial risks. Michael Apted directed "Nell" from a screenplay by William Nicholson and Mark Handley; the fine supporting cast includes Liam Neeson and Natasha Richardson as the scientists who become Nell's friends.

"Speechless" visits a domain much closer to home for most moviegoers—the political arena where two rival speechwriters fall dizzily in love as the campaign season reaches its peak. It's an amusing situation, although it would seem more original if countless new reports hadn't publicized the real-life relationship of consultants James Carville and Mary Matalin during the last presidential race. Admirers of screen satire will also recall that Robert Altman got mileage from similar material in his "Tanner '88" miniseries six years ago.

Engagingly played by Davis and Michael Keaton, the main characters of "Speechless" are a liberal (her) and conservative (him) odd couple each willing to bend any rule or stretch any scruple to gain an extra sound bite on the evening news. Also on hand are the woman's ex-boyfriend and the man's ex-wife, a network journalist and campaign worker (respectively) who don't want to be "ex" anymore. Robert King's screenplay has some genuinely funny lines, and solid supporting players like Bonnie Bedelia and Ernie Hudson reinforce the picture's comic credibility. There's not much imagination to Ron Underwood's listless directing style, though, which drains energy from the yarn when it's needed most.

Also disappointing is the story's tediously well-balanced ideological slant, making all the politicians equally dishonest creeps so that neither liberal nor conservative moviegoers will be dissuaded from enriching the film's investors at the box office. Evenhandedness, too, is standard Hollywood procedure—unfortunately for those who'd rather be occasionally riled than perpetually lulled at their local multiplex.

LOS ANGELES TIMES, 12/14/94, Calendar/p. 1, Kenneth Turan

Deep in rural North Carolina, in a secluded cabin hidden away in an especially remote corner of the Great Smoky Mountains, a singular young woman is discovered, someone who has lived her entire life without making contact with the forces of society.

Uneasy around other people, speaking a unique language, this person inhabits a universe all her own. So the quandary for her discoverers becomes how best to integrate those special qualities with what the workaday world has to offer.

Aside from being the plot line of "Nell," this setup also summarizes the predicament the film's creators were presented with. Challenged by a remarkable performance by Jodie Foster in the title role, they were unable to construct anything that did justice to it, making the actress and her fine work seem as out of place in this movie as Nell and her naive doings are back in civilization.

Though "Nell" is a work of fiction, adapted from a play called "Idioglossia" by Mark Handley, the sudden appearance of people who have lived without human society is historically accurate. In fact, two previous films on the subject, Francois Truffaut's "The Wild Child" and Werner Herzog's "The Mystery of Kasper Hauser," were based on real situations.

Both of those films starred unknowns in the uncivilized role, and it is not difficult to understand why. The qualities that make a star a star—a familiar voice, face, acting style—are very difficult to efface, yet effacement is necessary if audiences are to be convinced that they are watching a renegade human being, not an actor playing a kooky part.

The barriers to this happening are so great that even a performer of Foster's abilities is not immediately convincing. But she works hard at making Nell come alive, using a keening vocal timbre, a gift for speaking the character's language as if it meant something, and a willingness to tap the kind of inner fury she has not shown much before. By the time "Nell" is over, Foster's passionate performance will make almost everyone believe.

The first person to discover Nell is Dr. Jerome Lovell (Liam Neeson), called to her cabin because of the death of Nell's mother, a hermit of some notoriety in the nearby town of Robbinsville. A hunky free spirit who dislikes making plans, Dr. Lovell is delighted by Nell's rural surroundings but uncertain about what should be done with this young woman who is a stranger to standard English.

Enter Dr. Paula Olsen (Natasha Richardson), an all-business scientist whose specialty is disturbed children. She has not the smallest doubt about what to do with Nell: take her out of the woods, lock her in a lab and place her under supervised clinical observation for the rest of recorded time.

Dr. Lovell, a fiend for fresh air, disagrees and goes to court, convincing a judge that until more is known about Nell and what she wants, the young woman stays where she is. Which means that both doctors end up camping out at Nell's doorstep, observing her, trying to learn her language, and, in whatever time is left over, having philosophical debates about her future.

The issues Lovell and Olsen thrash over—questions about whether it is healthy to live an entire life completely alone or how someone like Nell might handle the commotion her inevitable fame would bring—ought to be interesting ones, but they and the entire movie are hampered by several defects.

For one thing, unlike the medical controversy in, say, "Lorenzo's Oil," these two doctors arc not having a fair fight. In today's pervasive anti-science, anti-cities environment, all it takes is one vision of natural Nell dancing alone in the luminous moonlight and one glance at Dr. Olsen's officious supervisor (Richard Libertini) to figure out which way this movie has stacked the deck.

Making matters worse is the clunky, awkward dialogue playwright Handley and fellow screenwriter William Nicholson have come up with, language that makes it difficult to view the doctors as real people despite the presence of fine actors like Neeson and Richardson in the roles. Either excessively theatrical or too on-the-nose (a problem it shares with Nicholson's previous "Shadowlands"), the words here make one realize how lucky Nell is to have a language of her own.

And though Michael Apted has been dealt a hand rife with artificial crises, he has not helped things much with his unconvincing direction. Too much that might have been genuinely thought-provoking in this film has been sacrificed to enhance audience tearfulness, and that is unfortunate.

Finally, however, the strength of Foster's spooky performance makes "Nell" more effective and worthwhile than it otherwise deserves to be. And it is just because we come to care about that unusual young woman that we wish she were in a better movie, but that was not to be.

NEW YORK POST, 12/14/94, p. 37, Michael Medved

She's sweet, simple, unspoiled and Southern; though the doctors think she's mentally retarded, she could sure teach those city slickers a thing or two about wisdom and decency.

In fact, Jodie Foster's "Nell" is a forest creature who could easily be kissing cousins with that popular guy Gump. Like her counterpart Tom Hanks, Foster also seems a solid contender for yet another Oscar, since this role allows her to speak in a strange, unintelligible language, to project a mysterious, perplexing mental state and even to frolic buck naked in a mountain lake, creating numerous scenes that call to mind the fondly remembered White Rock girl from old soda bottles.

The odd story that occasions this display is based on an obscure play called "Idioglossia" that begins when an elderly hermit woman dies in her remote lakeside cabin in the mountains of North Carolina.

Her body is discovered by the delivery boy who brings her food every few weeks, but when the doctor (Liam Neeson) from the nearest small town arrives to take charge of the situation he finds that the woman's been harboring a secret for nearly 30 years; she's been living with a daughter (who was born following a brutal rape) for all this time and has scrupulously hidden the girl from the world.

Since this young woman has never had contact with any human being other than her mother, and since the old lady's speech had been crippled by several strokes. Nell speaks with exotic sounds and phrases that no one can understand. The doctor's determined to break through her defenses and to learn to communicate with her—and so is a research psychologist (Natasha Richardson) who arrives from the big city to study this homespun specimen.

The two scientists park themselves on a houseboat docked just yards away from Nell's cabin, and at that point the movie itself runs aground in shallow water. For the rest of the film, nothing much happens; Neeson and Richardson (both likable performers with little to do) simply stand back in awe, watching Jodie Foster's undeniably impressive acting, while eventually falling into a totally predictable romance with one another.

Director Michael Apted is a specialist in documentaries (the "7 Up" series and this year's superb "Moving the Mountain") and he does a good job presenting Foster's histrionics in a surprisingly believable, authentic light. Englishman Apted also has a special feeling for Appalachia (which he previously displayed in "Coal Miner's Daughter"), as does cinematographer Dante Spinotti, who gives us the same sort of breathtaking wilderness vistas he brought to "'The Last of the Mohicans."

"Nell" is obviously intended to appeal to our current national yearning for all-conquering innocence, but the movie unwittingly proves that the mere fact that you've been isolated from civilization doesn't mean that you have anything to teach the world. For all the pretty scenery and Foster's earnest, intriguing, inventive babbling, you end up leaving the theater feeling as if you've learned—and felt very little.

NEWSDAY, 12/14/94, Part II/p. B2, Jack Mathews

You won't see many movies that work as well on one level and fail as completely on another as Michael Apted's "Nell," the story of a so-called "wild child" found in the mountains of North Carolina and gradually introduced to the society down below.

The movie works "up there," with Nell (Jodie Foster) in her natural habitat, where her two visitors—the passionate small-town doctor (Liam Neeson) and an ambitious university psychologist (Natasha Richardson)—are trying to understand her fractured hillbilly language and penetrate the world of her imagination.

But when they come down from the mountain, and Nell gets a load of civilization, the movie crumples under the weight of its clichés. Honking horns, slavering rednecks, unfeeling scientists, swarming TV camera crews, cold courtroom justice. It's enough to make anyone cherish wooded isolation, which is a point that Apted and co-writers William Nicholson and Mark Handley figured could not be made too often.

Nell herself is a fascinating invention, a woman of about 30 who has spent her entire life within a few hundred yards of her mother's remote cabin in the piney woods of the Smoky Mountains. No electricity, no phone, and, except for the occasional delivery boy leaving groceries, no human sightings.

It is one of those delivery boys who finds the body of Nell's mother, and sets in motion the process of discovery and socializing of the daughter no one knew the strange old lady had. Soon, Nell is having to share her space with the opposing forces of nature and science. Dr. Lovell (Neeson) is the humanist, there to help Nell choose her environment; Dr. Olsen (Richardson) is the cool professional anxious to bring her back for laboratory study.

If you have felt insulted by Hollywood before, you know that the doctors, like bickering neighbors brought together by their concern for a wounded sparrow, will conjoin for the good of Nell, and the new family of three will attempt to ward off demon society.

"Nell," adapted from Mark Handley's play "Idioglossia," is the first of the three films to be produced by Foster's Egg Productions for Polygram, and it's easy to understand the appeal for her. The character is a shell, to be filled from the inside out, and as such, an actor's dream. How would a person with no comprehensible language—her mother's words were distorted by strokes—and no social experience behave?

As Foster plays her, Nell is exactly like a tiny orphaned animal, wary of her intruders, but intuitively dependent on them. Her private world, which we glimpse long before anyone else, is a vivid one, and the mysteries of her existence and her behavior are revealed in surprising, moving ways.

"Nell" serves almost as a companion piece to "Forrest Gump." They both promote the notion that people free of the corrupting influence of society—whether they can't understand it or aren't exposed to it maintain the innocence of newborn babies. It is wishful thinking, a reaction to our violent times, and "Forrest Gump" was able to get away with it only by treating it as a fable. There is a sincere "if only" quality to Gump's fantastic journey that lifts the spirit.

But Apted, a British director who made the wonderful biographical film about country singer Loretta Lynn ("Coal Miner's Daughter"), treats "Nell" as if it were a true story, and any wishful thinking is undone by moments of high Hollywood drama; Nell being rescued by Lovell from various institutional horrors, and being roused from her reveries to give the year's most cogent and stirring courtroom speech.

Foster is an amazingly unselfconscious actress, one who can take us into a character so quickly we forget who we're watching, and before she comes down from the mountain, Nell is one of her most fascinating characters. In the end, it isn't society that brings Nell to grief, it's bad writing.

NEWSWEEK, 12/19/94, p. 64, Jack Kroll

The "Wild Child," untouched by the corruptions of civilization, is a recurrent fantasy, from the 18th-century idea of the noble savage to Tarzan. In "Nell," Jodie Foster is a young woman who's found in an isolated North Carolina backwater after her mother dies. Because the mother's speech was impaired by strokes, Nell never learned English, and speaks in her own primitive language. Lovell (Liam Neeson), the local doctor, fights to prevent Nell from being institutionalized, which Paula (Natasha Richardson), the psychologist, thinks will protect her. Of course it's Nell who changes their lives and breaks their emotional hang-ups.

Based on a play by Mark Handley called "Idioglossia' (which means a self-devised language), the screenplay by Handley and William Nicholson ("Shadowlands") luxuriates in Nell's unpolluted spiritual radiance. And director Michael Apted ("Coal Miner's Daughter, " "Blink") makes sure we feel its every blessed ray. But so much transcendent ultraviolet produces an intense case of soul-burn. Foster is hauntingly beautiful; she exudes purity as a rose gives off its aroma. But the rest of the movie sprays us with a New Age aerosol, the fragrance of spiritual escapism. Nell remains free (the threat that she might become a glorified lab animal never seems real) so that she can continue to be the embodiment of this sentimental pantheism. Foster (who produced the movie) is a greatly compelling actress. She wrings tears from the audience in "Nell," but they come too easily. In her final rejection of civilization, Nell becomes a soft-focus saint in an all too harsh world.

SIGHT AND SOUND, 3/95, p. 46, Claire Monk

Jerry Lovell, a doctor working in smalltown North Carolina, is called out by Sheriff Todd Peterson to an isolated lakeside cabin where an old woman has died. Jerry is fascinated to find evidence of a life untouched by twentieth century developments. As he explores, he is startled by a creature who springs from the rafters, wailing and screaming in an incomprehensible language. The young woman violently ejects the two shaken men; but Jerry finds a note in an old family Bible: "The Lord led you here, stranger. Guard my Nell. "

Speculating that Nell's sole human contact must have been with her mother and that her strange language may be derived from her mother's stroke-affected speech, Jerry invites an ambitious city psychologist, Paula Olsen, to examine his discovery. Surreptitiously observing Nell's childlike rituals, he soon regrets involving Paula, who applies to have Nell committed. Jerry fights her, and the judge agrees to defer a decision for three months until Nell's behaviour has been more thoroughly studied. Jerry and Paula establish their respective observation bases and pursue different methods; while Jerry learns to imitate Nell's language, Paula is unable to reach a conclusive diagnosis.

One night, they see Nell naked on a rock in the lake, seemingly absorbed in a private ritual with another invisible person. When Nell explains one of her words, "eva'dur"—meaning both evil-doer and man—to Jerry by miming a stabbing movement towards her belly, he concludes that she has an irrational fear of rape. At Paula's suggestion, he shows Nell his naked body, but she responds with neither sexual interest nor unease. One day Nell leads them to a small skeleton sheltered in the woods. They realise that Nell had a twin, May, who died as a child and guess that the pair spoke their own private language.

Attracted to Jerry but increasingly excluded by the bond between him and Nell, Paula taunts him that he is only interested in Nell because she is not a threat to his bachelor lifestyle. They drive Nell into town. Although overwhelmed, she forms an instant, uncanny empathy with Peterson's mentally distressed wife Mary. Nell then wanders into a bar where salacious youths persuade her to expose her breasts, until Jerry angrily bursts in and saves her.

After discreet facilitation by Nell, Jerry and Paul spend their first night together. A story about the "wild woman of the woods" breaks as front-page news. The city mental hospital is now the only place where Nell can be safe. She is utterly traumatised and if she does not improve in time for the court hearing she will be institutionalised. Jerry snatches her away to a motel. His pain melts the frozen emotions between him and Paula. Seeing their embrace Nell shows signs of recovery. In court, Nell asks Jerry to act as her interpreter and speaks for herself. Five years later, the Jerry and Paula—now married with a young daughter—drive out to Nell's cabin, where she is surrounded by friends, to celebrate her birthday.

Speculation that *Nell* could cull Jodie Foster a third Best Actress Oscar has already generated cynicism among critics on both sides of the Atlantic, one even suggesting that the prospect was the only plausible motive for her production company Big Egg Pictures picking this backwoods moral tale as its first movie. Perhaps it's *Piano* envy: as US *Premiere* explained recently, "being mute won an Oscar for Holly Hunter, so there's no telling what speaking gibberish will do for Jodie Foster." Or perhaps it's just unfortunate that *Nell* comes so close on the heels of *Forrest Gump*—another back-to-basics fable whose bottom line is the triumph of homespun innocence over post-60s values. Though its intelligent liberal surface might seem some distance from *Gump*'s simple-minded homilies, *Nell* shares more of the latter's reactionary nostalgia than its makers might like to think.

Nell often looks and feels less like a movie than a showcase for a star turn. In contrast with Ada in *The Piano*, whose gestures and facial expressions surpass speech in their defiant eloquence, Nell's physical and facial language is intentionally unreadable, in keeping with her total isolation from modern society. But it is difficult to believe in that isolation when Foster gesticulates around her lakeside cabin as if she were a one woman contemporary dance class and when her painstakingly faded print frocks look like grunge chic leftovers. As her supposedly incomprehensible private language sounds very like a heavily distorted Southern drawl, it's no surprise when Neeson laboriously realises that that's more or less what it is.

From *Rain Man* to *Awakenings*, the notion that the mentally 'challenged' have in fact been blessed with a special gift has found increasing popularity in Hollywood. The most pertinent question about this trend is not whether such movies are producing positive images, but exactly whose needs these images are serving. For all its liberal noises about Nell's vulnerability to exploitation and abuse at the hands of 'civilisation', *Nell* is not really interested in its protagonist's subjective experience. The film does not require us even to begin imagining what it would *mean* to live like her, but merely to echo Jerry's response to his first sight of her cabin: "Wow! Is this for real?"

A recurring theme in several recent idiot-savant films is that the challenged-but-gifted character becomes a valid member of society not in their own right but because of their value to other (less gifted) people. In *Rain Man*, this value was literally monetary: yuppie Tom Cruise's reward for learning to love his autistic brother Dustin Hoffman instead of fleecing him of his $3 million inheritance was to gain a share of the cash. Here, Nell's right to autonomy is demonstrated entirely in terms of her value as a catalyst through whom Jerry and Paula learn about themselves.

It says plenty about the film's essential conservatism and aversion to risk that the possibility of sexual attraction between Nell and Jerry is never seriously entertained. The casting of real-life twosome Neeson and Richardson underlines the tacit assumption that Nell cannot really be a sexual contender—more so when, conveniently, Nell starts relating to the pair as if they were her parents. In this context, Paula's shows of jealousy over Jerry's fascination with Nell are merely a function of her own unadmitted desire, while Nell's joy as she gambols naked in the lake is passed off as sexless and childlike.

More insidiously, Nell's innocence functions as a benchmark of nostalgia against which urban life, psychiatry, the uncertainties of 90s relationships—and seemingly even feminism—are rounded up and denounced. You don't need to wait for her to narrowly escape rape by teenage rednecks (in a pool bar setting that toys distastefully with memories of Foster's performance in *The Accused*) to figure that the world beyond the backwoods is a menacing place; its sledgehammer visual imagery—idyllic, over-leisurely sequences of dense woodland and misty, mystical lakes edited against intimidating urban freeways and mirror-glass skyscrapers—has already done the job within minutes of the opening credits.

The connection between this backward-looking ruralism and an equally regressive take on gender roles is made clear in the film's treatment of Paula, in whom bad female ambition and bad urban values are explicitly linked. While Jerry observes Nell from a self-built hide in the woods, unreconstructed career-woman Paula spies on her via close-circuit television from a luxury houseboat and records her observations into a dictaphone. Jerry's reaction to the news that she plans to stay for three months—"Don't you have a life?"—is a surefire insinuation that a career and emotional fulfilment don't mix. It's no surprise then, that Paula ends up shacked up in the country with Jerry, an estate car and a toddler. In keeping with this film's considerable limitations, the exact nature of Nell's fulfilment is harder to gauge.

TIME, 12/12/94, p. 92, Richard Corliss

It's not fair to Jodie Foster and her sisters in cinema that Hollywood makes so few movies starring women. In dollar terms, this gender myopia is defensible, since guy pictures do bigger business. This year, for example, all eight of the films that earned more than $100 million at the domestic box office are stories of "a man who ..." Or, in one case, "a male lion who ..."

But even the moguls realize that women's pictures often have a gentility, an expanse of emotion, absent from *True Lies* or *The Mask*. And, hell, somebody's got to fill those five slots for the Best Actress Oscar nominations. So come December, when the Oscar-qualification deadline looms, the women's club is allowed in. This month will see movies starring such divas as Susan Sarandon (in two films), Jessica Tandy (two), Geena Davis, Sigourney Weaver, Anjelica Huston, Winona Ryder and Jennifer Jason Leigh.

On Oscar night they all may be applauding Foster. In *Nell* the two-time winner (for *The Accused* and *The Silence of the Lambs*) plays a North Carolina woodswoman who has grown up utterly isolated from the outside world. Now her only companion, her mother, has died, and Nell is a rich woman—but still barely a girl. She speaks her own dialect, recoiling from the doctor (Liam Neeson) and the psychologist (Natasha Richardson) who would help her, use her, perhaps destroy her, and who will be forever touched by her innocent sorcery.

Already you hear echoes of Foster's own *Little Man Tate*, as well as *The Miracle Worker, The Wild Child, Every Man for Himself and God Against All, Forrest Gump* and *Green Mansions* (the last with Audrey Hepburn memorably miscast as Rima the Bird Girl). *Nell* is a fable of emergence and transcendence. Written by William Nicholson and Mark Handley, from Handley's play *Idioglossia*, it illustrates the familiar movie moral that wounded creatures are powerful ones, with powerful lessons to teach those who would presume to educate them. It's humanism at its most Panglossian. But Michael Apted, who has directed vigorous woodland women before (Sissy Spacek in *Coal Miner's Daughter*, Weaver in *Gorillas in the Mist*), focuses on the weird wonder of Foster. Of course her portrayal is a stunt; of course the viewer is aware of the distance between the actress and her role. Yet she undercuts cliché with a fearless, fierce, beautifully attuned performance.

Foster also produced the film, which surely would not have been made (not with this care and glamour, anyway) unless a powerful star had wanted it to be. It's the worthiest kind of vanity production, welcome in any movie season.

VILLAGE VOICE, 12/20/94, p. 55, J. Hoberman

A blandly confident borderline hoot, *Nell* mainly makes sense as Jodie Foster's psychodrama. The movie's official source may be Mark Handley's play, *Idioglossia*, but the scenario of a mysterious backwoods woman who lives alone and apparently speaks her own language suggests Foster's own fantasy: Her Nell is a wondrous Other, the acme of self-anointed singularity.

Foster, who initiated and co-produced this undeniably serious project, is at once the most public and private of stars. She has spent virtually her whole life performing for the camera and yet her strongest performances are a kind of withholding. "Everyone prejudges Nell," the star is quoted in the movie's press notes. "They think she's never known any human contact that she's never known love, that she can't articulate anything, that she's dull ... This movie is about defying description, about not being put in a box, and not being labeled and marketed."

Exactly my point. Like Nell, Foster is misunderstood and unclassifiable, an innocent victim and a tenacious survivor, an intellectual and an autodidact, precocious yet backward. ("Her problem now is that she's not mattering as a woman, she lacks womanliness," Camille Paglia complained in a recent issue of *Movieline*) Having played at age 12 the most celebrated prostitute in the history of American movies, Foster has never fit comfortably into grown-up parts. Her Oscar-winning representation of "sexuality" in *The Accused* is no less an intellectual construct than her impersonation of a hussified gambling gal in *Maverick. Silence of the Lambs* was unique for allowing Foster a genre role without the glamorous burden of gender expectations.

The heroine of *Nell* is even more sui generis than was Clarice Starling. *Nell* is a sometimes touching fairy tale that gives Foster a chance to be her own version of the child genius she directed in *Little Man Tate*. Nell is part chimp, part Pocahontas, part E.T., the sprightly elf in an American Eden. Underlying Foster's self-projection is the notion of our national belief in born-again self-invention. "God, it's beautiful," sighs kindly Dr. Lovell (Liam Neeson), surveying Nell's Smoky Mountain domain—and that's before a somewhat worldlier rival scientist, Dr. Olsen (Natasha Richardson), arrives to enhance the scenery with her wardrobe of designer swimsuits and cocktail ensembles.

Soberly directed by self-effacing Michael Apted (whose résumé most relevantly includes *Coal Miner's Daughter* and *Gorillas in the Mist*), *Nell* is good-hearted, sentimental claptrap, filled with a random selection of cheery bromides. ("Life's tough but she's luckier than some," Lovell says of an angst-paralyzed matron. "She's got a good husband.") With a real-life married and hence parental couple battling for control of womanchild Nell, it's not hard to stay one step ahead of the narrative. The source of Nell-speak will be obvious to anyone who has seen Jean-Pierre

Gorin's documentary *Poto and Cabengo*. In any case, Nell's invented language soon devolves into Appalachian folk poetry.

As the characterization of Nell is predicated on Foster's self-sufficiency, so the movie has little interest in the mundane details of the wild child's existence. (It's never made clear, for example, how and what she eats or how she maintains such excellent teeth.) Foster dances through the movie like a pale flame, hoping to warm the world with her flickering glow. *Nell* is kept aloft by the force of the 32-year-old actress's search for her inner child.

We watch this delightful creature skip and giggle, pose like the White Rock girl, and swim naked in the moonlight, oblivious to the two adult spies and their hidden video camera, as the movie repeatedly flirts with allegory.

Transfixed by the closed-circuit spectacle of Nell jabbering at her mirrored reflection, the shrinks could be paraphrasing one of the seminars Foster took at Yale: "She has an object of self *and* a subject of self!" To complete the Lacanian subtext, Lovell shows Nell his penis to demystify the terror of the Phallus. What's really at stake, in Nell's life as in Foster's, despite her evident narcissism, is the unwanted exposure of potential celebrity. (The first exploitative interloper is a journalist who explains that a newsman's gotta do what a newsman's gotta do.)

"We haven't had a true wild child in this country for 60 years," one scientist exults. Make that *wise* child. Nell is Nature itself. Driven in a car through the woods, she laughs with joy. Taken to town for the first time in her life, she intuitively connects with all the bruised creatures who dwell there. Evoking *The Accused*, the local pool hall is the focus of evil. Nell is instinctively drawn to it and dispels its malignant lust with the innocence of her nonsexualized nudity. (The movie's notion of child psychology is at once post-Lacanian and pre-Freudian.) Naturally therapeutic, Nell can feel your pain; she invariably materializes when the "parents" are fighting and dissipates their negativity by making them touch foreheads.

The South these days is a primary site for American fantasy, and, like the year's other homespun Hollywood oracle, Nell is constitutionally incapable of telling a lie. Does Foster want to teach us something! *Nell* conjures up a courtroom climax where this unique creature can reproach the world with her Yoda-like wisdom. But what is that wisdom beyond the awesome fact of her own existence! The concluding vision of Nell's peaceable kingdom is like a Kodak commercial of love.

Also reviewed in:
CHICAGO TRIBUNE, 12/23/94, Friday/p. C, Michael Wilmington
NATION, 1/23/95, p. 108, Stuart Klawens
NEW REPUBLIC, 1/23/95, p. 30, Stanley Kauffmann
NEW YORK TIMES, 12/14/94, p. C15, Janet Maslin
NEW YORKER, 12/19/94, p. 108, Terrence Rafferty
VARIETY. 12/5-11/94, p. 73, Todd McCarthy
WASHINGTON POST, 12/23/94, Weekend/p. 36, Desson Howe

NEW AGE, THE

A Regency Enterprises and Alcor Films release of an Ixtlan/Addis-Wechsler production. *Executive Producer:* Oliver Stone and Arnon Milchan. *Producer:* Nick Wechsler and Keith Addis. *Director:* Michael Tolkin. *Screenplay:* Michael Tolkin. *Director of Photography:* John Campbell. *Editor:* Suzanne Fenn. *Music:* Mark Mothersbaugh. *Music Editor:* Mark Green. *Sound:* Stephen Halbert and (music) Bob Casale. *Sound Editor:* Susan Dudeck. *Casting:* Deborah Aquila. *Production Designer:* Robin Standefer. *Art Director:* Kenneth A. Hardy. *Set Designer:* Barbara Ann Jaeckel. *Set Decorator:* Claire Jenora Bowin. *Set Dresser:* Matthew Altman, Steven Hickel, Tom Kerns, Lisa K. Sessions, and Dan Spaulding. *Special Effects:* Marcus Dean, Allen Hall, Matthew Hall, Chuck Hessey, Mike Menzel, and Joe Pancake. *Costumes:* Richard Shissler. *Make-up:* Deborah Larsen. *Running time:* 115 minutes. *MPAA Rating:* R.

CAST: Peter Weller (Peter Witner); Judy Davis (Katherine Witner); Patrick Bauchau (Jean Levy); Rachel Rosenthal (Sarah Friedberg); Adam West (Jeff Witner); Paula Marshall (Alison Gale); Bruce Ramsay (Misha); Tanya Pohlkotte (Bettina); Susan Traylor (Ellen Saltonstall); Patricia Heaton (Anna); John Diehl (Lyle); Maureen Mueller (Laura); Sandra Seacat (Mary Netter); Samuel L. Jackson (Dale Deveaux); Audra Lindley (Sandi Rego); Corbin Bernsen (Kevin Bulasky); Jonathan Hadary (Paul Hartmann); Lily Mariye (Sue); Kimberly Kates (Other Katherine); Maria Ellingsen (Hilly); Kelly Miller (Carol); Dana Hollowell (Emily); Rebecca Staab (Woman Customer); Alexander Pourtash (Man Customer); Scott Layne (Swimmer); Mary Kane (Tina Bulasky); Patrick Dollaghan (Chet); Jeff Weston (Tab); Lisa Pescia (Nova Trainee); Victoria Baker (Victoria); Bob Flanagan (Bob); Nicole Nagel (Rich German); Dana Kaminski (Andrea); Cheri Gaulke (Pagan Woman).

LOS ANGELES TIMES, 9/16/94, Calendar/p. 9, Chris Willman

It's nearly impossible to put together a picture about ennui without dramatically succumbing to it in a big way. Michael Tolkin, talent that he is, isn't yet the moviemaker to meet the feat.

"The New Age," his second feature as a director, is an audacious attempt at taking a snapshot of a whole culture's moral torpor—that is, L.A.'s—in the midst of an overweening spiritual narcissism. In this it's even fleetingly successful, yet drags on so long past its point you feel as if you've missed two or three harmonic convergences.

The title's a joke, of sorts, of course. Tolkin's movie is pointedly ambivalent on matters spiritual, opening and closing with thc voices of friendly gurus, with various drumming circles and life-passage ceremonies nonjudgementally visited in-between. In these scenes he's not really spoofing *or* endorsing.

But the unhappily marrieds at the movie's center—conspicuous consumers Peter Weller and Judy Davis—don't allow all this fashionable etherealism to infringe much past the periphery of their lives, where it's a comfortable, curious accouterment to their materialism. The implicit gag is that when they flirt with New Age practices, they're still just shopping.

But the ether is about the only place their credit might still be good. In a secular sense, the "new age" represents downward mobility for the designer set, a riff on the pragmatic post-Reagan years.

In the opening scenes, Davis sees her ad agency's primary account (a failing bank, of course) fall through on the same day Weller quits his studio job, precipitating a fast decline that threatens their Hollywood hillside way of life. Vaguely terrified, they react to their dwindling resources by throwing a lavish party, separating, embarking on separate but equal affairs (though he has a good head-start on her) in the same home, and selling the Ruschas.

The picture reaches a good comic-nightmarish peak in the middle section, when Davis and Weller, dumb with desperation, resolve to use said Ruschas to fund an expensive clothing store they open together on Melrose. Not unlike the restaurant scenes in Mike Leigh's "Life Is Sweet," Tolkin smartly captures the dread in opening—and closing—a small business: the initial anxiety, the premature glee of the first sales, the torment of sidewalk browsers who won't come in, the ultimate terrible sinking feeling.

But by the time thc boutique finally goes under, our couple's financial and psychic torment has just begun. Eventually, as they wallow in their decline and even negotiate mutual suicide, the film comes to seem uncomfortably like a drugless, upper-class "Sid and Nancy." But "Sid and Nancy's" downward spiral at least had an ending. Tolkin meanders toward and through at least three or four possible finishes, none very satisfactory—least of all the real one, which sells one principal short and provides the other partner what seems like an artificially arrived-at triumph.

Part of the problem might be that Tolkin is so fair-minded he wants to have it every possible way, sacrificing a point of view in the process. In his better, first feature, "The Rapture," this ambivalence worked brilliantly (if maddeningly, for most audiences): Fundamentalist Christianity *was* true after all, but mortals *were* courageous in rejecting its stern God, the movie seemed to posit, quite an audacious bit of juggling.

"The New Age" does offer the chance to see one of our best actresses, Davis, do another funny, pathetic, lip-biting malcontent, though Weller gets woodenly stuck with no arc to follow, having to act the caddish foil to his wife's minor enlightenments. The smaller roles include some varyingly successful but fun stunt castings, including Adam West as the crude, rich playboy dad who taught Weller his bad pickup lines ("How are your morals tonight?"), performance artist Rachel Rosenthal (!) as one of Davis' chosen avatars, and Samuel L. Jackson as the phone-sales huckster Weller picks as *his* guru.

But as the underedited pacing flags, and Tolkin moves in more claustrophobically on his couple, you may feel as if you're trapped at a marathon two-person Debtors Anonymous meeting—which is to say, unforgiving. Robert Altman, who adapted Tolkin's "The Player," might have had a field day elaborating on the L.A. ensemble aspects of this script. But Tolkin is too tightly focused on two characters—and consequently, an audience—in search of an exit. After all is moped and done, "The New Age" gets old before its time.

NEW YORK POST, 9/16/94, p. 41, Thelma Adams

Peter Weller and Judy Davis are the Fred and Ginger of dysfunctional couples.

In David Cronenberg's deliciously dark "Naked Lunch," Weller's wacked-out writer shoots his drug-addicted wife, played by Davis, in a drunken game of William Tell.

The duo returns as the hip, witty, and superficial husband and wife, Peter and Katherine Witner, in writer/director Michael Tolkin's latest dispatch from the Hollywood Hills, "The New Age." The author of "The Player" sends his unhappily marrieds into a free fall when the recession sours the California miracle and they have to do the unthinkable— get jobs.

They got a "collect call from reality," says Peter, and what he'd really like to do is "reverse the charges."

Tolkin's glib, chatty script is smart and darkly humorous, well-matched by John Campbell's playful cinematography. Tolkin chides a bankrupt culture in which spiritual charlatans mix with new-age capitalists and shopping wins out as the most effective therapy.

Both Davis and Weller share an edgy intelligence that's well-suited to the material. Davis, with her Medusa curls, pale skin and stained lips, comes across as a trendy, dissolute child whose emotions lay on the surface like a rash. The skeletal but handsome Weller conceals his confusion beneath a dry delivery; when he expresses his feelings, his evasions are visible to everyone but himself.

The most honest moments come during the Witners' relationship talks. To end one entertaining sparring match, Katherine flings a final zinger at Peter: "Why don't you get in touch with your inner adult?"

Despite welcome appearances from Adam West, as Peter's swinger father, and bald Left Coast art celebrity Rachel Rosenthal, the story never widens out from the free fall of these two new-age capitalists through the vacuum of modern life.

Tolkin has plenty of style, but lacks the guts to make the plight of these two emotional cripples truly affecting. They are, in fact, two numbskulls, two people unable or afraid to feel, and because this hardly changes over the movie's arc, we never feel for them.

"The New Age" is hardly run-of-the-mill, but it's infuriatingly shallow. As much as I wanted to love the movie, it was as hollow as the Hollywood lives it so aptly skewers.

NEWSDAY, 9/16/94, Part II/p. B2, Gene Seymour

For the second time in the last few weeks, a commercial American movie has been released featuring a reckless, sexy, mixed-up couple adrift in the parched frenzy of post-Reagan America. But where "Natural Born Killers" fires white-hot crescendos in succession like a John Coltrane passage, "The New Age" spins allusion and nuance with the silky intricacy (if not quite the assurance) of a Joe Henderson solo.

As with "Killers," "The New Age" isn't built for comfort. Where a film like "Forrest Gump" almost sanctifies the notion of drift, The New Age," rubs the audience's nose in it. And the audience will either appreciate the effort or wince with scorn at writer-director Michael Tolkin's irrepressible urge to keep people's psychic antennas on yellow alert.

In both his novels ("The Player," "Among the Dead") and his previous feature ("The Rapture"), Tolkin has been concerned with how values snared by extreme circumstances lead to crises of the spirit. "The New Age" extends this inquiry as it tracks the painful, slow-motion fall of Peter and Katherine Witner (Peter Weller, Judy Davis) from L.A.'s ultra-glam fast track.

Within the same 24-hour period, Peter quits his job at a high-powered talent agency and Katherine's graphic design business goes belly-up. Both these victims of early-'90s recession respond to their crises in mid-'80s fashion: self-indulgently.

They go on shopping binges. They take up with lovers. They throw a party attended by as gaudy an assortment of mystics and hustlers as you can find roaming the hills of Hollywood. (One of the hustlers is Peter's lecherous dad, triumphantly played with cunning smarm by Adam West. No, really. *Adam West!* Batman as Robo-Cop's father!)

The morning after the party, the harsh reality of an uncertain future beats down on Peter and Katherine like the Southern California sun. Their guru (Patrick Bauchau) asks them to think of what they're good at and transform that into a step forward. "Shopping and talking!'" Katherine says triumphantly.

So naturally they open up a pricey boutique on Melrose Avenue, called "Hipocracy." It isn't long before the markdown gremlins slip through the store windows and the Witners' wealthy friends begin to avoid them, literally, like the plague. Separately and together, Peter and Katherine search frantically for ways to either escape the downward spiral or null the pain. They sample a smorgasbord of rites, both pagan and sacred. Yet they can't quite commit to anything except their own self-pity.

Set in cold type, this all sounds like "thirtysomething" with the flu. Yet what gives it bounce and verve is Tolkin's writing. His lines glow like neon in the self-obsessed fog. Many of them deserve to become catchphrases. One come-on line, "How are your morals today?" generates the response, "I'm working on them."

But for all its stylish, sinuous dialogue, "The New Age" will generate more rueful recognition than laughter. If we're left dangling at the end, it's because Tolkin both sees—and shares—the ambivalence that clings to baby boomers in this ongoing age of anxiety.

TIME, 9/26/94, p. 78, Richard Schickel

Peter and Katherine (Peter Weller and Judy Davis) are bored and careless. They lost jobs, take on lovers, futz around with guru-driven spirituality and dress to the nines. You could argue, as writer-director Michael Tolkin doubtless did when he was pitching *The New Age*, that they are perfect exemplars of chic anomie as it manifests itself in postmodern—or post-rational—Los Angeles. You could also argue, as people whose malls don't yet contain an Issey Miyake boutique might, that they are hopeless twits.

It is possible that Tolkin, who in 1992 adapted his own novel, *The Player*, for the screen, harbored satirical hopes for this project. But as a director he lacks the antic eye that (often enough to keep us interested) rescues Robert Altman from depression and pretension. Tolkin just doesn't know how to position himself—far enough from his characters to make fun of them, close enough to them to retain our sympathy. And the question of whether they will make a go of Hipocracy, the upmarket clothing store they decide to open, is not a compelling one. Shopkeeping cannot compare to moviemaking and murder (*The Player*'s topics) in dramatic interest. Peter and Katherine don't even bicker entertainingly as their marriage collapses; they just drawl withdrawal. The languid self-satisfaction of *The New Age*, the sense that its maker knows most people will hate it and doesn't care because he's issuing "a personal statement," is its most annoying quality. Don't be suckered. Your first instinct is right. It's a terrible movie.

VILLAGE VOICE, 9/20/94, p. 53, J. Hoberman

Writer-director Michael Tolkin is some kind of cowboy—at least on Rodeo Drive. In *The New Age*, as in *The Rapture* and *The Player* (which he wrote), the former journalist positions himself atop the unbroken bronco of the L.A. zeitgeist. Tolkin always gets thrown, but it's a wild ride while it lasts.

An edgier, less secure, and more ethnographic social observer than Woody Allen, Tolkin has a measure of quick wit, a knack for the phrase du jour, and a spongelike ability to soak up atmosphere. In *The Player* and *The Rapture*, he had the added advantage of sniping at such ideological billboards as Hollywood hustlers and Christian fundamentalists. In *The New Age*, however, he inflates his relatively modest targets well past their bursting point.

Reconfiguring *Naked Lunch*'s hipster leads into a slick yupscale couple, *The New Age* stars Peter Weller and Judy Davis as Peter and Katherine Witner, two cold-eyed hypersophisticates in haute designer wardrobes. Playing a smooth master of the mind fuck who calls himself "half cool, but not really" and is saddled with a swinger dad (Adam *Batman* West!) even sleazier than he, Weller sets his dial to modulated anxiety and vamps. Judy Davis is an even scarier zombie. Her clammy pallor accentuated by blood-red lipstick and a mass of damp ringlets, she seems drenched in Giorgio flop sweat.

It's one of the film's conceits that, despite their floundering marriage, the Witners are perfectly phased—they experience everything in tandem. Katherine's free-lance design studio goes belly-up just as pressured Peter quits work at his talent agency, spewing self-actualizing vitriol like the Mount St. Helen's of psychobabble. Each having had a cataclysmic day, they decide to throw a party and, voilà!, *The New Age* becomes a svelte Fellini geek show. The Witners' neo-Deco pad is packed with an evil array of friends, lovers, and mystics on the make: "Did you know that in Chinese, the word for 'crisis' is the same as that for 'opportunity'?"

It only takes one knock for the propositioned Katherine to leave her own party. Afterward, the Witners find themselves in an existential cusp—both unemployed and living in the same house while carrying on separate affairs (that their dates involve distinct theme-music is used to comic effect). Thanks to the probing of their resident guru (Patrick Bauchau), they realize that their talents are "shopping and talking." The short-range solution is a mom-and-pop luxury boutique named Hipocracy, where the Witners can be surrounded by beautiful stuff and rich, if unpredictable, customers. ("For us, shopping here is like you shopping in Tijuana," one German tourist remarks.) The fantasy lasts until the first markdown; after that, the couple's friends shun their bad karma. Facing failure, the Witners exhibit a boundless capacity for self-pity: "We were born while the economy was expanding, now it's contracting and they don't need us."

Like these two dedicated followers of fashion (and the Ed Ruscha paintings frequently alluded to *The New Age* has an airbrushed, fetishized sheen and a taste for svelte, slashing angles. The movie means to skewer the Witners' material desires to those of the audience. It begins where a more self-consciously Brechtian flick would have ended—with a bald woman yoga teacher (L.A. performance artist Rachel Rosenthal) telling us to experience ourselves sitting. At its best, *The New Age* evokes uneasy laughter as a sort of screwball comedy populated by self-indulgently tormented clichés. But, as in *The Rapture*—where he could not help but wonder *what if these religious crazies are right?*—Tolkin seems stumped by indecision. Are the Witners surrounded by spiritual masters or neighborhood yentas? Should we be looking for or laughing at this om-sweet-om? Is a Tibetan suicide ceremony a touching affirmation or an absurd affectation?

Peter winds up cruising an orgy with "the usual art and spirituality and s/m crowd"—the mood of lugubrious voyeurism and mortified sin suggesting a night spent in the company of Michelangelo Antonioni or a visit to Madame Tussaud's—even as Katherine finds herself sitting around the campfire for some sort of goddess rite. As Tolkin cuts back and forth between the two adventures, each Witner is freaked out and beats a confused retreat. So too, the film. A far more cynical (not to mention delirious) vision of mad paganism and Hollywood intimations of the apocalypse may be found in last week's Warners release, *Rapa Nui*. Indeed, as *Rapa Nui* knowingly teeters on the verge of self-parody, so *The New Age* naively trembles on the brink of self-importance.

Compelled back together, the Witners search for closure—along with Tolkin. "Why don't you get in touch with your inner adult?" That's not the filmmakers problem. Too responsible or too fearful to stick with satire, he lets *The New Age* dither into ambivalence. The movie isn't as daring as *The Rapture*, but Tolkin is no less tangled up in weirdness by the time he loses his balance and gets dumped on his seat in the dust.

Also reviewed in:
NEW YORK TIMES, 9/16/95, p. C5, Janet Maslin
VARIETY, 9/5-11/94, p. 53, Todd McCarthy

NEXT KARATE KID, THE

A Columbia Pictures release. *Executive Producer:* R. J. Louis. *Producer:* Jerry Weintraub. *Director:* Christopher Cain. *Screenplay:* Mark Lee. *Based on characters created by:* Robert Mark Kamen. *Director of Photography:* Laszlo Kovacs. *Editor:* Ronald Roose. *Music:* Bill Conti. *Music Editor:* Steve Livingston. *Sound:* Andy Wiskes. *Sound Editor:* Stephen Flick and Dave Barlett. *Casting:* Joy Todd. *Production Designer:* Walter P. Martishius. *Set Decorator:* Tracey A. Doyle. *Special Effects:* Chris Burton. *Costumes:* Carole James and Kent James. *Make-up:* Steve LaPorte. *Stunt Coordinator:* Pat E. Johnson. *Martial Arts Choreographer:* Pat E. Johnson. *Running time:* 104 minutes. *MPAA Rating:* PG.

CAST: Noriyuki "Pat" Morita (Miyagi); Hilary Swank (Julie Pierce); Michael Ironside (Dugan); Constance Towers (Louisa); Chris Conrad (Eric); Arsenio Trinidad (Abbot Monk); Michael Cavalieri (Ned); Walt Goggins (Charlie); Jim Ishida (Tall Monk); Rodney Kageyama (Monk); Seth Sakai (Buddist Monk); Eugene Boles (Mr. Wilkes); Keena Keel (School Clerk); Tom O'Brien (Gabe); Tom Downey (Morgan); Brian McGrail (T.J.); Wayne Chou (Pizza Driver); Daniel Inouye (Senator); Gustave Johnson (Wilson); Brian Smiar (O'Connor); Christopher Beam, Eric Beam, and Scott Powderly (Wescott Boys); Davis Robinson (Leon); Anthony Ejarque (Ernie); Steven Mark Friedman (Ted); Christopher Wilder (Roland); Annette Miller (Sales Woman): Bud Ekins (Jack Russel); Paul Bronk (Larry Townes); Fred Fontana (Dusty); Julie Caroline Weintraub (Girl at Prom); Johnny Melton, Chad Melton, and Scott Strupe (Bungee Jumpers).

LOS ANGELES TIMES, 9/12/94, Calendar/p. 2, Chris Willman

The overt message of any "Karate Kid" movie: Don't fight unless you absolutely have to. The implicit message: You'll always have to. Let the smitings begin!

The transparent philosophy continues in "The Next Karate Kid," wherein another petulant teen—Hilary Swank's comely Julie (replacing gray belt Ralph Macchio)—has to learn a few life lessons and the joy of Zen car washing before being granted license to knock the solar plexuses out of her tormentors.

"Julie-san right. *Now* is the time," announces Noriyuki (Pat) Morita's Mr. Miyagi (never one to use articles), waiting till just before the climax to say the words every kid is waiting to hear.

Julie's not just the cutest lass in her class, but could make dust out of your windpipe even before she meets up with Mr. Miyagi, an old war buddy of her late grandpa. Julie doesn't need martial-arts tips so much as quiet guidance to get past bitterness over the death of her parents. This she gets not only from her adoptive sage, but from sweet new boyfriend Eric (Chris Conrad), a rival of nasty Ned (Michael Cavalieri).

Both boys are members of an unlikely paramilitary group sanctioned by their Boston high school and led by Col. Dugan (poor Michael Ironside, the embodiment of evil *again*). These deadly hall monitors are contrasted with Mr. Miyagi's pacifist monk pals, who get peeved when Julie tries to kill a cockroach but are hep enough to boogie to the Cranberries and bowl.

If this installment is just slightly less laborious than "Karate Kid II" or "III," it's not from Mark Lee's surprise-free script or Christopher Cain's placid direction, but because young Swank really might be a find. Early on, she's such a convincingly testy teen that parents may flinch, but she does seem to blossom before your eyes. And doing her moves, she looks, well *suss-y*.

NEW YORK POST, 9/10/94, p. 15, Thelma Adams

Just say sayonara.

Original Karate Kid Ralph Macchio did. After three turns at bat, so did director John G. Avildsen. Pat Morita, star of "The Next Karate Kid" and the three previous wimp-to-winner movies, just couldn't say no to a fourth round.

Then again, how many lead roles are there for feisty seniors with wicked lunge kicks?

Is it feminism or opportunism that changed the kid from a he to a she in this sorry sequel directed by Christopher "Young Guns" Cain? Newcomer Hilary Swank co-stars as Julie, a moody grungester grieving over her parents' accidental death.

Enter Morita to mentor the angry teen and balance her yin and yang through karate zen. Michael Ironside, a "Total Recall" villain, turns up in a bit of heavy-handed casting as a homicidal gym teacher.

What saves the movie from bomb status (see "The Karate Kid III") is not Morita's threadbare charm, or any surprise plot twists, but the addition of a group of monks to the mix. The bald trio doing a modified hora at the monastery to Julie's boom box gets an honest chuckle.

Screenwriter Mark Lee builds on this with a whimsical scene of Morita taking the monks bowling in Boston. It doesn't move the plot anywhere, but there's more triumph in the robed guys tromping the locals at the lanes than in the inevitable showdown between Morita and Ironside.

New kid on the block Swank makes an able movie debut, although the overuse of slow motion in her action scenes makes it clear that she's no martial arts queen. Swank handles the inevitable transformation from pouter to pretty miss with a nubile charm that's reminiscent of Jane Fonda just pre-"Barbarella."

Morita seems appropriately immune to the teen's Lolita allure. If only the French remade this sorry remake! They could do a twist on the karate kid by focusing on an old man's obsession for his young protege. It might push the PG to an R, but al least it would be more kicky.

NEWSDAY, 9/12/94, Part II/p. B9, Terry Kelleher

"Who says the good guy has to be a guy?" ask the ads for "The Next Karate Kid," fairly bristling with feminist assertiveness.

But listen to the wise old sensei, Mr. Miyagi (Noriyuki "Pat" Morita). Mr. Miyagi say: "Answer only important when ask right question."

The right question about the latest "Karate Kid" sequel is: Why did they desperately need a new protagonist, regardless of sex? Important answer: Because any fool could see Ralph Macchio was too old to play the perennial-underdog teenager in 1989's "The Karate Kid Part III."

So the "Karate Kid" series is now "Equal Opportunity, M/F." Does the new policy pump life into a patently overworked concept? Only for a while.

Writer Mark Lee has contrived a way for Mr. Miyagi to act as surrogate parent to 17-year-old Julie (Hilary Swank), the alienated orphan granddaughter of the man who saved his life in World War II. OK, he instructs her in martial artistry so she can channel her anger, but he also takes her on a two-week visit to a Buddhist monastery (occupied by cute monks who are into pop music and "Zen bowling"), teaches her to waltz and buys her a prom dress. Heck, he even blinks back tears of pride when he sees her all dolled up for the big night.

Most of the movie is nonviolent and inoffensive, if a bit dull. But every good guy or girl needs bad guys to bump up against, and the villains here are especially overdrawn and unconvincing: a paramilitary band of high-school enforcers spearheaded by a sexual predator (Michael Cavalieri) and commanded by a lip-curling ex-Army colonel (Michael Ironside). Sad to report, the black hats eventually stomp Julie's boyfriend (Chris Conrad), giving the next karate kid and her mentor a long-delayed excuse to kick mucho butt.

For 10 years, Mr. Miyagi say over and over, "Fighting not good." With all due respect, we doubt sensei's sincerity.

Also reviewed in:
NEW YORK TIMES, 9/10/94, p. 14, Stephen Holden
VARIETY, 8/22-28/94, p. 56, Lisa Nesselson
WASHINGTON POST, 9/10/94, p. C3, Rita Kempley

NO ESCAPE

A Savoy Pictures release in association with Allied Filmmakers of a Pacific Western production. *Executive Producer:* Jake Eberts. *Producer:* Gale Anne Hurd. *Director:* Martin Campbell. *Screenplay:* Michael Gaylin and Joel Gross. *Based on "The Penal Colony" by:* Richard Herley. *Director of Photography:* Phil Meheux. *Editor:* Terry Rawlings. *Music:* Graeme Revell. *Music Editor:* Dick Bernstein. *Sound:* Graham Hartstone and Ben Osmo. *Sound Editor:* Jim Shields. *Casting:* Pam Dixon Mickelson. *Production Designer:* Allan Cameron. *Art Director:* Ian Gracie. *Set Decorator:* Lesley Crawford. *Set Dresser:* Beverley Dunn, Peter Foster, Michael Iacono, Alex Slater, Kris Torma, Nic Brunner, and Faith Robinson. *Special Effects:* Brian Cox. *Costumes:* Norma Moriceau. *Make-up:* Lesley Vanderwalt. *Prosthetic Make-up:* Bob McCarron. *Stunt Coordinator:* Conrad E. Palmisano *Running time:* 118 minutes. *MPAA Rating:* R.

CAST: Ray Liotta (Robbins); Lance Henriksen (The Father); Stuart Wilson (Marek); Kevin Dillon (Casey); Kevin J. O'Connor (Stephano); Don Henderson (Killian); Ian McNeice (King); Jack Shepherd (Dysart); Michael Lerner (Warden); Ernie Hudson (Hawkins); Russell Kiefel (Iceman); Brian M. Logan (Scab); Cheuk-Fai Chan (Skull); Machs Colombani (Ratman); David Argue (Cellmate); Stephen Shanahan (Screaming Inmate); Dominic Bianco (Ralph); Justin Monjo (Technician #1); Brandon Burke (Technician #2); Stan Kouros (NCO); Ron Vreekin (Biker); Scott Lowe (Skinhead); Colin Moody (Outsider #2); Richard Carter (Sleeping Sentry); Boris Brkic (Hotel Guard #1); David Wenham (Hotel Guard #2); Vic Wilson (Military Officer); Chris Hargreaves (Prison Guard); Jim Richards (Executioner); Wilfred Woodrow (Bola Thrower); Greg Robinson (Spiked Log Tree Man); Paul Witton (Knife Thrower); Steven Spinaze (Chopper Co-Pilot); Serge Dekin (Chopper Pilot); Ric Herbert (Insider).

LOS ANGELES TIMES, 4/29/94, Calendar/p. 9, Peter Rainer

"I'm not a joiner," says imprisoned Marine Capt. John Robbins (Ray Liotta) in "No Escape," and that's an understatement. After assassinating his commanding officer in the very first scene, Robbins is dispatched to a maximum security prison and then, still bucking the authorities, dumped by the don't-mess-with-me warden (Michael Lerner) into the ultimate prison—a jungle peninsula called Absolom, 200 miles from civilization. He's not much of a joiner there either.

You can't really blame him. Half the peninsula is occupied by the Outsiders, a band of 600 or so *really* grody guys, led by the snickery, very hairy Marek (Stuart Wilson). These convicts have gone tribal in a big way—they decapitate each other for sport, bare their tonsils in bloodcurdling yells and never, ever floss.

Robbins, by comparison, is a GQ model, and so it's not long before he does a back flip into raging waterfalls, which brings him into contact with the Insiders. (This flipping into raging torrents must be the latest thing: You half expect Robbins to collide in the rapids with "The Fugitive's" Richard Kimble.) The Insiders, led by a haunted-looking ex-surgeon known as the Father (Lance Henriksen), are a comparatively peaceful brood of convicts numbering less than 100; they weave and grow vegetables and ready themselves for periodic assaults from the Outsiders. Robbins could be an asset to them—he is, after all, the only guy ever to escape from the Outsiders—but he just wants out.

Robbins the loner individualist is, of course, a good guy camouflaged by a scowl and an attitude. He's a natural leader, as opposed to all the unnatural Outsider types. There's a brotherhood-of-man morality play lurking in all this underbrush, but it's best not to peer too closely. Pulp is best digested raw. (But not too raw: There is not a single woman on the entire peninsula, but the film is surprisingly chaste about any suggestion of male coupling.) It's clear that director Martin Campbell doesn't have the same feeling for the Insiders as he does for the Outsiders. The spectacle of virtuousness seems to curdle his movie-making instincts; it doesn't galvanize the Mad Max in his soul. And so we in the audience are placed in the same wait-and-see position as the Insiders bracing for another attack—except that we look forward to it.

Movie bad guys always seem to take up more space on the screen than good guys. Besides the Father, the Insiders include a jumbo-size security chief (Ernie Hudson), an inventor (Jack Shepherd) who is sort of like a jungle version of Q in the James Bond series, and a youthful, scared-stiff kidnaper (Kevin Dillon) who looks up to Robbins. None of them can hold a candle to the gross-out bullyboys from the wrong side of the falls. Stuart Wilson, in particular, is so amusingly vile as Marek that he positively glistens with dementia.

Which is not to say that spending a few hours with all their yelling and puncturing and headrolling is any great time either. "No Escape" will appeal primarily to people who thought "The Road Warrior" was a tad too intellectual. Except for all the brains it spills, it could qualify as the archetypal no-brainer.

NEW YORK POST, 4/29/94, p. 43, Thelma Adams

Marine Captain Robbins life is a mess.

It's 2022. Robbins (Ray Liotta) is stuck in a penal colony—and there's "No Escape.

Robbins harbors a dirty little military secret that led him to shoot his commanding officer. Needless to say, he has a problem with authority.

Dispatched to Absolom, a remote island for the world's most hardened criminals (shades of Alcatraz?), Robbins is always under attack: rats, blow guns, spiked log trees, flaming arrows, a guillotine, a guy named Ralph, and tooth decay.

The list is endless; add frogs, boils and the killing of the first born (no women on the island—could be a problem) and you've got the biblical plagues.

On the plus side. Robbins is cute in an intense sort of way (a Scorpio?), he's a natural-born leader—and he kills without hesitation.

Liotta is doing a Steve McQueen (it worked for Kevin Costner!), and not a bad one. If the actor wants to be an action hero, he'll do OK. But he's no Jean-Claude Van Damme.

There's more to Liotta than has been tapped since "Something Wild" and "Dominick and Eugene" and director Michael Campbell (of the forgettable "Criminal Law" and "Defenseless") overdoes the brooding closeups.

Stuart Wilson gets to blast through his scenes as the evil Marek, the leader of the wild bands of "Outsiders" on Absolom. With the bridge of his nose pierced, a gleeful response to violence, and a penchant for cutting heads without a barber's license, he has perfect villain pitch.

Lance Henriksen, who has been deliciously villainous in "Hard Target" and "Johnny Handsome," is saddled with a more groovy, new age convict-leader called The Father. Henriksen is better when he's bad but he's always fun to watch.

"No Escape" peaks when it's campiest in the "Conan"/"Red Sonya" vein. (Where is Brigitte Nielsen when you need her?)

Things sag when the convicts go confessional and the script, by relative newcomers Michael Gaylin and Joel Gross, telegraphs its central (and sole) psychological thread: coping with authority and father figures.

Comparisons will be made to "Papillon" "Escape From Alcatraz," and "The Great Escape." (It's surprising how many movies have the word escape in their titles.) There's also a touch of "Lord of the Flies" and "Mad Max Beyond Thunderdome" thrown in.

"No Escape" isn't campy enough to be a classic; Liotta is solid but still no action star.

Yet, "No Escape" arrives during an action-adventure drought. If it becomes a runaway hit, there could be no escaping a breakout movie revival.

NEWSDAY, 4/29/94, Part II/p. B7, John Anderson

What was going to make "No Escape" different from all its post-apocalyptic, jungle-warfare, prison-picture predecessors—and there are many—was Ray Liotta, the beloved psycho of "Something Wild" and the pragmatic charmer of "GoodFellas." Different, however, doesn't quite do it justice.

Recycling the wise-cracking, Schwarzenegger-Stallone approach to the action-adventure yarn, "No Escape" director Martin Campbell doesn't so much marry comedy and mayhem as drop them like grenades across his stunning Australian terrain and a thoroughly violent, thoroughly fantastic story. There's not enough humor to make it a comedy, but there's enough comedy to dilute the suspense. And Liotta, a thoroughly likeable and talented actor, is too boyish and self-aware for the hard-bitten, well-trained killer he's supposed to be playing.

The year is 2022, and to relieve prison overcrowding—the current crime bill apparently having passed both houses—the most recalcitrant prisoners are sent to Absolom, a remote tropical island run by a ruthless warden (Michael Lerner), who can read his inmates minds electronically and subjects them to horrible forms of punishment. And should they escape his high-tech torture chamber? The jungle outside is almost impenetrable, and full of Outsiders—a group of mutant escapees led by a lunatic named Marek (Stuart Wilson)—who will likely have them for lunch. With fava beans and a nice chianti.

Beyond the Outsiders live the Insiders, another, more enlightened group of escapees led by The Father (Lance Henriksen), a onetime surgeon and convicted murderer who's half Supreme Being, half Robert Bly.

Into this community, which is productive, redemptive and besieged by the Outsiders, comes Robbins (Liotta), a mix of Mad Max and Papillon who has a little trouble dealing with authority, but who's also the only person ever to escape Marek's clutches and make it to their coastal stronghold. This gives him considerable cachet among the Insiders, as does his military training, which is going to come in handy. There are Major Themes happening here: Robbins' initial resistance to the idea of community, for instance; the idea of personal redemption, among men who have been left to die on an island no one in the outside world knows exists; man's dual nature, as epitomized by the Outsiders and Insiders. And if you want to think about all that, fine. But it will distract from all the great explosions, and some really novel means of bloodletting.

One more curious thing: Remember all that commotion about the lack of women's roles in major movies? Well, in the future according to producer Gale Ann Hurd, women are not only unseen, they're unheard of. Except for the word, uttered very, very late in the film—as in "women and children killed"—the subject of female people never comes up. And this is a prison movie. About lifers. On an island.

But then, that's the nice thing about creating such a loosely defined, futuristic world—even your fictional reality becomes a malleable thing, subject to the whim of the screenwriters. This may lead to a less-than-convincing storyline, but it does allow more chaos per frame—which is really the only thing "No Escape" promises, or delivers.

SIGHT AND SOUND, 6/94, p. 57, Kim Newman

2022, John Robbins, a Special Forces commander who has taken the blame for a war crime, is removed from a maximum security facility to Absolom, a island where dangerous prisoners are secretly dumped and left to their own devices. Robbins survives an encounter with Marek, insane leader of a savage faction known as the Outsiders, and makes his way to a stockade ruled by the visionary Father, whose followers are the Insiders. Robbins, intent on finding a way of escape from the island, is initially reluctant to join the Insiders, but is befriended by Casey, a young man who idolises him.

The Insiders resist an attack by the Outsiders, but an escape ship launched by Father is destroyed, prompting the realisation that the warden, who rules over the Absolom programme, has a spy on the island. Robbins discovers the Insiders have an engine which can be used to power an escape ship but that a vital component is in the hands of the Outsiders, and he offers to retrieve it in exchange for a place on the boat. Robbins ventures into the Outsiders' camp, where the well-intentioned Casey is captured and killed, and escapes with the engine part.

Father reveals that he is dying, and wants Robbins to take his place. But Robbins feels he must escape to set the record straight on his war crime. Marek launches a final attack but Robbins' strategic abilities lead to his defeat and death. Father is killed in the battle and Robbins tells Hawkins, the Insiders' security chief, that Father wished Hawkins to become leader. It is discovered that King, the Insiders' physician, is the traitor, and he is forced to lure the warden into a trap. Robbins leaves King and the warden to the surviving savages and flies off in a helicopter, determined to blow the whistle on the Absolom scandal.

Filmed in Australia as *Penal Colony* (test marketing revealed most audiences thought that sounded like a porn film), this continues a mini-genre of shot-down-under futuristic prison movies which include *Turkey Shoot, Ghosts ...of the Civil Dead* and *Fortress.* With its *Lord of the Flies* tribal culture and Mad Maxish post-apocalypse gear, the film owes an ever greater debt to films of the early '70s which imagine futurist alternatives to conventional prison, notably Peter Watkins' *Punishment Park* and (especially) Stephanie Rothman's *Terminal Island.* Director Martin Campbell does this film no favours by ignoring the ideas about redemptive communal societies and the inefficiency of violence as an agent of control found in Rothman's film, instead opting lazily for non-stop action.

Ray Liotta, aspiring to an action hero laurel, is lumbered with a clumsy back-story signalled by *Terminator 2*-ish flaming visions and acts throughout a dispenser of carnage, without ever deciding whether his primary duty is to escape and clear his name or to talk over from Father as the saviour of the Insiders. Unwilling to stick with one plot thread, the script is cluttered with two spies who need to be unmasked (the warden's stoolie in the Insider and a man the Insiders have infiltrated into the Outsiders) and two 'evil establishment' cover-up plots (about Robbins' crime and about Absolom itself) that have to be exposed.

The first reel offers glimpses of a science fiction future with huge sets and futuristic helicopters, but when Robbins gets to the island we are stuck with a very conventional jungle adventure, kitted out with hammy British character actors and sentimentally macho Americans.

There is a hint of a theme in the character of Father, and his insistence on the redemptive powers of self-sufficiency (he is a saint believed to be innocent of the crime of which he was convicted but sadly admits that he is indeed a wife-murderer), but all the other characters are stereotypes. There is a homily here about the possibility of establishing a genuine society within the framework of a prison but it is quickly ditched in favour of a *Boys' Own* display of POW escape attempts.

VILLAGE VOICE, 5/24/94, Film Special/p. 27, Julie Lang

I'm glad there is not one single woman in this film because she would probably be raped and/or used as a bargaining chip. You see, the *No Escape* men are bona fide don't-eat-quiche types—all tough, tan, and alone on a hot and lush jungle island named Absolom and all they can do is make war, not love. It's *Lord of the Flies* with the boys grown big, so pass the conch shell to 2022, the year of *No Escape*.

In the beginning, the lights dim, the screen is blank then cuts to the words: *Prisons have become a big business.* Scary. Next, the image: Marine captain John Robbins (Ray Liotta) locked and looking sexy-intense, all chained up and on the road to Level 6 Leviticus Maximum Security Prison for offing a commanding officer, escaping two Level 5 joints, and being deemed a complete social outcast. Well, Robbins is a real trouble-maker; he threatens the life of the sadistic prison warden (Michael Lerner), and is banished to the ultimate of penile colonies, Absolom.

Absolom's divided into two camps of criminal rejects. The Insiders have created a rudimentary socialist utopian society; the Outsiders, crazed barbarian anarchy. Here's the juicy part: the Insiders are 99 per cent Ivory white, with security chief Hawkins (Ernie Hudson) as the token 1 per cent—think Billy Dee Williams. And the Outsiders are either slimy brown with tattooed faces or slimy brown with tattooed and black-painted faces. There is no black representation beyond Hawkins, only a grotesque emulation signifying ignorance and evil. Both pack leaders are white, and the Insiders chief even names himself the Father (Lance Henriksen). This is very scary.

No Escape tells an interesting moral tale: each camp—from civil society to prison to Outsiders to Insiders—dissects and re-creates an ethical structure to conform to an authoritarian ideology. Since all the characters are criminals (even the warden with his penchant for pain), these moral systems are mainly concerned with the possibility of redemption, and the proper punishment for each crime. Should redemption be sought out through physical or psychological means, and, lastly, who has the right to impose what type of punishment? The answer, my friend, is blowing through the dick-tums of the white man. The answer blows in *No Escape*. Peace.

Also reviewed in:
CHICAGO TRIBUNE, 4/29/94, Friday/p. F, Clifford Terry
NEW YORK TIMES, 4/29/94, p. C15, Caryn James
VARIETY, 5/2-8/94, p. 89, Emanuel Levy
WASHINGTON POST, 4/29/94, p. C6, Rita Kempley
WASHINGTON POST, 4/29/94, Weekend/p. 46, Joe Brown

NOBODY'S FOOL

A Paramount Pictures release in association with Capella International of a Scott Rudin/Cinehaus production. *Executive Producer:* Michael Hausman. *Producer:* Scott Rudin and Arlene Donovan. *Director:* Robert Benton. *Screenplay:* Robert Benton. *Based upon the novel by:* Richard Russo. *Director of Photography:* John Bailey. *Editor:* John Bloom. *Music:* Howard Shore. *Music Editor:* Suzana Perić. *Sound:* Danny Michael and (music) John Kurlander. *Sound Editor:* Maurice Schell. *Casting:* Ellen Chenoweth. *Production Designer:* David Gropman. *Art Director:* Dan Davis. *Set Decorator:* Gretchen Rau. *Set Dresser:* Michael Benson, David Scott Gagnon, and Byron Lovelace. *Special Effects:* Tom Ryba. *Costumes:* Joseph G. Aulisi. *Make-up (Melanie Griffith):* Naomi Donne. *Make-up (Paul Newman):* Monty Westmore. *Make-up (Bruce Willis)*; Dale Bach-Siss. *Stunt Coordinator:* Peter Bucosssi. *Running time:* 112 minutes. *MPAA Rating:* R.

CAST: Paul Newman (Donald "Sully" Sullivan); Jessica Tandy (Miss Beryl); Bruce Willis (Carl Roebuck); Melanie Griffith (Toby Roebuck); Dylan Walsh (Peter); Pruitt Taylor Vince (Rub Squeers); Gene Saks (Wirf); Josef Sommer (Clive Peoples, Jr.); Phil Seymour Hoffman (Officer Raymer); Philip Bosco (Judge Flatt); Catherine Dent (Charlotte); Alexander Goodwin (Will); Carl John Matusovich (Wacker); Jay Patterson (Jocko); Jerry Mayer (Ollie Quinn); Angela Pietropinto (Cass); Alice Drummond (Hattie); Margo Martindale (Birdy); Angelica Torn (Ruby); Richard Mawe (Ralph); Joe Paparone (Rufus); Shannah Laumeister (Didi); John Leighton (Funeral Director); Kenneth Frawley (Horace Yancy); Marcus Powell (Whit); Frank W. Inness (Garbage Man); Page Johnson (C.W. Lomax); William Raymond Calhoun (Vernon); Bob Heitman (Lawyer from Albany); Drenda Spohnholtz (Girl at the Country Club); Gerry Robert Byrne (Charlie); Elizabeth Wilson (Vera).

CHRISTIAN SCIENCE MONITOR, 12/23/94, p. 11, David Sterritt

[*Nobody's Fool* was reviewed jointly with *Ready-to-Wear*; see Sterritt's review of that film.]

LOS ANGELES TIMES, 12/23/94, Calendar/p. 1, Kenneth Turan

Moviegoing holds few pleasures greater than watching an established star completely inhabit a role that exactly suits his personality and abilities. And seeing Paul Newman in "Nobody's Fool" defines that pleasure.

"Fool" is Newman's 52nd feature (his debut was in "The Silver Chalice" 40 years ago), but it's more than the weight of accumulated experience that makes his work so satisfying here.

For Newman is so right for the role of Donald "Sully" Sullivan, an aging, stubbornly independent black Irish scamp, that he infuses it with the easy enthusiasm and sense of the new usually associated with the young and the restless. It's been so long since Newman has been this satisfying that he projects the excitement of an undiscovered new talent, the kind you can't wait to tell your friends about.

Newman is so revivified, in fact, that he has sparked his co-stars to give better than average performances. Jessica Tandy (always delightful), Bruce Willis and Melanie Griffith (both somewhat less reliable) all had to pump up the volume just to keep up with their star.

What Newman can't do, however, is turn "Nobody's Fool" into a truly memorable film. Taken from a discursive 549-page novel by Richard Russo set in the mythical upstate New York town of North Bath, "Fool" has to contend with the predilections of its writer-director, Robert Benton ("Kramer vs., Kramer," "Places in the Heart").

On the plus side is a pleasure in fine writing as well as a concern for character. "Nobody's Fool" is a film that cares about its people, addled and disheveled though the residents of North Bath may be, a film that revels in the cracked qualities of their diverse humanity.

That kind of sentiment, however, is best leavened with something a tad grittier, and "Nobody's Fool," as it meanders from one shaggy situation to another, is finally too soft and unfocused for too long to consistently hold our attention. A little more rigor would have gone a considerable way.

Described by the novel as "the uncontested master of the futile gesture" and a "case study underachiever," Sully is the center of a variety of relationships in North Bath, many of them absentee. A 60-year-old construction work gypsy abandoned his family when his son was barely a year old, he is closest to a mental case co-worker nicknamed Rub (for Rubberhead), convincingly played by Pruitt Taylor Vince.

But during this particular holiday season, "a time for normal people to do normal things," as someone puts it, Sully, always prone to misadventures, gets reinvolved in his family with a vengeance. His estranged son comes back to town burdened by a failing marriage, he attempts a relationship with one of his grandchildren, and he tries finally to deal with the memory of his own errant father, long since dead.

Though it suffers from its lack of focus, one of the paradoxes of "Nobody's Fool" is that when it tries to get more real, when it concentrates on the glum dissatisfaction of Sully's overly earnest son, Peter (Dylan Walsh), it falls in love with its own ordinary wisdom and forfeits part of our interest.

The best things about "Nobody's Fool" are its sideshows: Sully's verbal sparring with his landlady and former eighth-grade teacher Miss Beryl (Tandy), his erratic sometime-boss Carl Roebuck (Willis) and his beautiful but neglected wife, Toby (Griffith). Sully's ambivalence toward Carl, the kind of demented macho tricks they play on each other, turns out to be the film's most original and intriguing relationship.

Though, as always with Newman, we never quite feel he could have been as bad a guy as the script insists he was, he remains the reason to see "Nobody's Fool." The film's various difficulties inevitably fade from memory, but his performance lingers, as the great ones always do.

NEW YORK, 1/16/95, p. 56, David Denby

In North Bath, New York—a town so depleted that the jailbirds are employed as pallbearers—a banner hangs over the grimy main street. The banner announces that an entertainment paradise, "The Ultimate Escape Theme Park," will be build there in the near future. Escape? From North Bath? *Nobody's Fool*, an affecting chronicle of life in this dim burg, doesn't entertain any such illusions.

People stay forever, grimly attached to the boarded-up houses, the old bar, the lone diner. A number of them work for the sleazy deadbeat Carl Roebuck (Bruce Willis), who owns a local construction-and-renovation company; no one likes the cynical Roebuck, but he's the only game in town. Sully (Paul Newman), twenty years older than Roebuck but still a better man, has been working for him for years, even though he's suing him for nonpayment. Forever unsettled, a lifetime screwup, Sully lives as a boarder in the house of his former schoolteacher (Jessica Tandy) and flirts with Roebuck's wife (Melanie Griffith), a North Bath beauty developing lines around her mouth from despair, perhaps, as she waits for Sully to make his move. The movie is set from Thanksgiving to Christmas, the season of joy, when the sun never shines in North Bath, and Sully comes to terms with his past, forgiving his long-dead father and accepting forgiveness from his son.

In *Nobody's Fool*, Robert Benton achieves the mix of acerbity and sweetness, wit and sentiment, that eluded him in such earlier down-home films as *Places in the Heart* and *Nadine*. Adapting Richard Russo's novel, Benton displays a gentle yet steady touch: There's a continuity of mood, an evenness of light, a flow of mordant joking and gossip from one quiet scene to the next. The movie is a beautifully sustained piece of upstate melancholy. Nothing much is going on, but after a while the nothing much begins to seem like something, a way of life—not, to be sure, a successful way of life, but far from death.

The North Bathers are a community of kibitzers, wringing jokes from the general seedy depression. People work a little, but mostly they play poker, drink, argue, and sit around, sharing the blues. The movie recognizes sitting around for what it is—one of life's principal activities. In this town of losers, few things matter more than a successful passing remark; one's honor can be saved for a week by topping someone else's put-down. Under the joshing surface, the movie is serious about missed connections between parents and children and surrogates stepping in for the absent child, the absent parent. But Benton is very tender; he doesn't intrude on the characters too much, or reveal all their secrets for a melodramatic climax. The citizens of North Bath may be losers, but they keep their dignity. *Nobody's Fool* is an anti-*Oprah* movie, a model of stoicism; it values booze and sociability above "truth."

Sully is superior to his surroundings, and everyone knows it, but he won't make the effort to improve his situation. He'd rather be a bum, doing odd jobs; failure is central to his aging-hipster's pride. "Hang in there"—that's his motto, and it might be Newman's too. Newman's light, easy authority isn't challenged enough in this movie—no one deeply upsets Sully—but everything he does is wonderfully satisfying. He gives a coolly ironic performance: His Sully knows that he's no more than king of the scrap heap, but that's enough for him as long as no one pushes him around; he socks a stupid police officer when the man offends him aesthetically. Macho refined and macho crude, Newman and Bruce Willis match up well together. The look-at-me shmuckiness that was offensive in Willis's performances as a leading man—the sarcastic open mouth, the negligent shrug of the shoulders—work well in this supporting performance as a hollow dumbbell stud. Willis may be as effective as a character actor as he is tiresome as a star.

One problem. Sully is meant to be a screwup, but Newman projects sweetness and candor, and Sully's actual nature tends to be at odds with whatever is said about him. The allegedly selfish Sully, a man who ran away from responsibility, actually takes care of everyone in sight—his landlady; his inept, one-legged lawyer (Gene Saks); his bedraggled, resentful friend (Ptuitt Taylor Vince), who works for him and adores him. Noblesse oblige. Sully actually holds the entire town together. He's only *pretending* to be selfish. And the more we look at this passed-over town, the stranger and more unlikely it seems in some ways. The movie is set in the present, but it might as well be set in the mid-forties. Mass electronic culture doesn't exist. At night, rather than retire into their huts to watch the tube, people gather to *talk*, which must make North Bath unique among American nowheresvilles. These people also have Sully to look after them. Aren't they really living in a kind of ramshackle paradise?

NEW YORK POST, 12/23/94, p. 52, Michael Medved

"Nobody's Fool" is one of those maddening, meandering slice-of-life movies that's full of admirable artistic elements that never add up to anything at all.

Watching this indulgent, yawn-inducing and seemingly endless enterprise resembles a visit to a world-class wax museum: You can marvel at the realism of the cunningly crafted figures, or the authentic atmosphere of the exquisitely crafted little scenes, but none of it ever manages to come to life.

The setting is the fictional village of North Bath, N.Y, (actually shot in several different towns in Dutchess and Orange counties)—a gritty, blue-collar burg buried under mountains of fresh snow.

Paul Newman makes his semi-annual Oscar bid as Donald "Sully" Sullivan, one of the town's lifelong residents and a regular at the local bar—a 60-year-old construction worker with a bum knee and no work. He wants to collect money for his injury from his slimy and selfish former boss (effectively played by Bruce Willis) at the same time that he flirts shamelessly (and aimlessly) with this tough guy's estranged and restless wife (a suitably languid Melanie Griffith).

It turns out that Sully abandoned his own wife and kid some 30 years before, but now that little boy suddenly turns up as an unemployed college professor (Dylan Walsh) with a shy son and a troubled marriage all his own. With nothing better to do, Sully's boy joins his hard luck dad, his dad's feckless lawyer (Gene Saks) and other pals in hoisting a few brewskis while waiting for something—anything—to happen.

The late Jessica Tandy adds a brief touch of class to these pokey proceedings as Newman's one-time eighth-grade teacher who now rents him a room in her empty, ramshackle house.

In adopting Richard Russo's atmospheric but uneventful novel director writer Robert Benton ("Kramer vs Kramer", "Places in the Heart") faced a formidable challenge: How do you show aging characters trapped in a drab but cozy small town world without having the audience itself feeling similarly trapped?

Despite all his good intentions Benton never solves the fundamental problem. You know that a movies suffering from a fatal energy shortage when the main focus of the feeble plot is the fight over a spiffy new snow blower that Willis and Newman keep stealing back and forth from one another.

Of course, the only real reason to see this picture is Newman's astonishingly assured performance and, it's true that his Sully is an endearing and enduring creation. The character is exactly the sort of lovable rascal that Old Blue Eyes does better than anyone else—a crusty, salty, self-destructive scamp with an understated, subversive sense of humor.

He certainly makes the most out of Benton's better lines, as when his son asks Sully, "Do you know what Mom's worst fear is? That your life has been fun."

"Tell her not to worry," Newman smiles.

And on that basis, she also needn't worry about this flat and formless film.

NEWSDAY, 12/23/94, Part II/p. B2, Jack Mathews

The character of Sully, the 60-year-old lovable loser of North Bath, N.Y., in Robert Benton's warm comedy "Nobody's Fool," fits Paul Newman like a $1,000 suit, and the actor, who will actually be 70 when the occasion arrives, could wear it to the Academy Awards.

Newman has already picked off one major award, from the New York Film Critics Circle, and the performance is certain to bring him his eighth career best actor Oscar nomination (only Laurence Oliver and Spencer Tracy have had more).

"Nobody's Fool," adapted by Benton ("Kramer vs. Kramer") from a Richard Russo novel, is not a total success. It often seems aimless and overpopulated with eccentric characters and small-town mannerisms, and it strains where it shouldn't have to for both sentiment and laughs. But in a year where few filmmakers even attempted stories about life among ordinary people, its flaws are as benign as Sully's.

How refreshing it is to sit through a movie that doesn't build to some pointedly contrived resolution. Russo was writing about life in a small upstate town where stories are played out in different ways every day, not always with tidy endings, and Benton merely takes us into that environment and lets us hang around over the snow-blanketed holidays.

It's an odd place to find such sizable stars. Besides Newman, the cast includes Bruce Willis, as the philandering construction company boss with whom Sully has a running feud, and Melanie Griffith, as Willis' long-suffering wife. Yet, star power is never a distraction. Willis always does his best work in supporting roles, and is marvelous here, and Griffith, her cloying mannerisms in check, gets more done in her brief scenes than she has in a half-dozen starring roles.

But the movie belongs to Newman, who has never shown more heart or been more relaxed in a character. Sully is the real item, a soft blue-collar stiff who has sort of ambled through life, never quite achieving anything, but never giving up either. The main task is to get from here to there, from paycheck to paycheck, and keep his options open.

As we check in on him, Sully is facing a series of mini-life crises. He's trying to get paid off by Willis' Carl Roebuck for a job injury that left him with a seriously gimpy leg, he is reunited with a grown son (Dylan Walsh) who is harboring a lifetime of anger over having been abandoned by him, and his lone possession, a boarded-up Georgian home he inherited, is forcing him to deal with his bitterness toward his own father.

These evolving stories keep things moving forward, but the real pleasures of the film come from the more mundane events of Sully's daily life. His relationships with Miss Beryl (the late Jessica Tandy, wonderful as ever), the retired school teacher who has taken him in as a boarder, and with all those oddball soulmates with whom he's spent decades playing poker and knocking back drinks at the neighborhood bar.

And there is Toby (Griffith), who will eventually call his bluff and force him to stop flirting long enough to look at least a few days into the future.

The world is full of Sullys, underachievers whose lives run out before they've considered how to live or understand them, and Newman invests this one with a charm and range of feelings—reflective without being melancholy, resigned without being pessimistic—that makes you want to pat him on the shoulder and wish him the best.

There's a scene in "Nobody's Fool" where a judge tries to advise a talkative attorney to shut up by saying, "Sometimes, less is more." The same can be said of movies, and in laying his story out in gently understated layers, Benton has said a lot more.

SIGHT AND SOUND, 4/95, p. 49, Ben Thompson

Donald "Sully" Sullivan is a 60-year-old construction worker, perpetually down on his luck in the chilly small town of North Bath, NY. He lodges with his old school teacher Miss Beryl, whose banker son is determined to get rid of him. With his slow-witted friend Rub, he works on and off for Carl, a hard-headed, philandering local entrepreneur. Sully struggles with a horribly wounded knee, sustained while working for Carl without insurance, and is also bogged down in a fruitless legal quest to secure compensation. His only consolations are flirting with Carl's attractive but unhappy wife Toby, and endeavouring to steal his snow-blower.

Hitching home from a loading job that has gone wrong, Sully gets picked up on the road by his son Peter and family, who are visiting North Bath for Thanksgiving with Sully's ex-wife Vera. The atmosphere is strained—not just between Sully and Peter, whom he walked out on as a child, but between Peter and his wife, who are on the verge of splitting up—but Sully still finds himself invited to his ex-wife's house for Thanksgiving. There he encounters a level of domestic chaos which he is unable to cope with, and leaves, unaware that Peter's son Will has stowed away in his pick-up.

Sully starts to build relationships; first with his grandson, then with Peter who, it turns out, has recently lost his job teaching at a university. Sully still makes plenty of mistakes—at one point abandoning Will outside in the cold while looking over his dead father's old house, which he has let run to rack and ruin—but he finally seems to be learning to face up to the idea of family. When Peter's wife walks out, Sully offers him a job. Much to Rub's disgust he accepts. Trying to catch Rub, who has stormed off, Sully gets in the most serious of several rows with the town's policeman, and punches him in the face.

Sully's minor irresponsibility is nothing compared to that of Miss Beryl's son who, when a big property deal falls through, runs off leaving most of the town out of pocket. Miss Beryl, who does not have long to live, pays off Sully's debts on his father's old house. Toby walks out on Carl and asks Sully to go with her to Hawaii, but he eventually decides not to. Before commencing his week in jail, Sully helps Peter begin to patch up his marriage, and he is allowed out of prison to be a pallbearer at Miss Beryl's funeral.

This warm, multi-layered adaptation of Robert Russo's novel makes a worthy if unobtrusive addition to Robert Benton's blockbusting track record as a screenwriter, which includes *Bonnie and Clyde, Superman*, and *Kramer vs. Kramer*. A small town tale of dysfunctional folk learning to love, *Nobody's Fool* forsakes the showy starturns and emotional pyrotechnics of *Kramer vs. Kramer* for a low-key intelligence and an impressive attention to emotional detail. "Do you know what mum's worst fear is?" the abandoned son asks the absentee father, "That your life has been fun".

It's heartening to see a major Hollywood production focus so unapologetically on a major character who is almost eligible for his free bus-pass. Paul Newman's Sully gets to run the gamut of venerable guy emotions slightly beyond the usual A to B. He's not around just to dispense curmudgeonly but loving wisdom to the young folk. He is also allowed to have relationships with people (well, Jessica Tandy) who are even older than he is. Newman can do ornery as well as any man alive, and he manages to create an authentic sense of the poignancy of someone still scrabbling for a living when he'd be better off putting his feet up. Tandy's combination of strength and fragility, meanwhile, has never seemed stronger or more fragile. Her meditations on mortality would have been unsettlingly poignant even if she hadn't just died in real life.

Away from their accustomed centre stage, the younger generation come out of this film pretty well too. This is certainly one of Melanie Griffiths' more dignified performances—she imbues the phrase "Watch out for that mean-ass dog" with more meaning than one would have thought it was ever equipped to carry. And it's odd that Bruce Willis has been said to be less than ecstatic about having his name associated with *Nobody's Fool*, as he is unusually three-dimensional in it. Perhaps that's why: maybe he thinks he is just too convincing as a brilliantined scuzzball.

It is rare in a modern American film to see a small town setting used as more than just shorthand for nothing much in particular. But there is a real sense here of relationships—particularly between the characters of Willis and Newman—striding on down through the years, taking both animosity and fondness, success and failure in their stride. There is one strikingly beautiful shot when the camera closes in on Tandy's Miss Beryl, who has had a stroke, and the picture decays into a celluloid snowstorm. This is one of two moments when

Benton's direction steps out of the everyday and aspires to flamboyance. The other, where two little boys squabble in the toilet over who gets to pee first, we could probably have done without.

TIME, 1/16/95, p. 72, Richard Schickel

Imagine cool hand Luke, the Hustler or even Butch Cassidy somehow making it all the way to his sunset years. Then imagine him measuring out those years as an unemployed, virtually unemployable, construction worker in one of those small, featureless upstate New York towns—still a knothead, still a wise guy in revolt against the conventional wisdom, still very recognizably Paul Newman. That, in essence, is *Nobody's Fool*.

WORN TO PERFECTION, the ads for this shrewd, agreeable, ultimately dishonest movie proclaim. But they lie. At 70, the actor doesn't look worn at all; he's trim and bouncy, the blue eyes undimmed by the passing years, the gray in his hair seeming, if anything, premature. He's playing a man of 60, and it is not a reach for him. It is, however, a problem for writer-director Robert Benton's movie. Benton can't help it, and Newman can't help it, but the actor is wrong for the part of Donald ("Sully") Sullivan, a man logic tells us should look ill used by the years instead of like a movie star gorgeously defying them.

For Sully's troubles are innumerable, and, realistically speaking, they ought to make him at least contemplate the possibility of defeat. He has banged up his knee working for exploitative Carl Roebuck (Bruce Willis in another of his astonishingly good character jobs), and his amiable, incompetent lawyer (Gene Saks) can't get him compensation. Sully is long since estranged from his wife, and his relationship with his college-professor son (Dylan Walsh), who has career and marital problems of his own, is difficult. Sully rents a room from a tolerant, spirited old lady (the late Jessica Tandy) who is beginning to fail physically. His best friend (Pruitt Taylor Vince) is not quite bright and is being harassed by the town cop. Oh, yes, and he and Roebuck's wife (Melanie Griffith) are inappropriately, frustratingly attracted to each other.

None of this is permitted to get Sully down—not for long, anyway. He may occasionally rage at his narrowing circumstances, but mostly he confronts them with a cheeky joke. Or a boyish prank: he and Roebuck keep stealing a snowblower back and forth. Or some comically self-destructive behavior—he finally punches out that cop and lands briefly in jail—that doesn't do him as much harm as it would if this were real life instead of a movie determined to be cheerful at any cost.

God, it would be nice to believe life is really like that: when you get old, you'll be fit and quick like Newman; if you neglect your savings, you'll finally hit your favorite trifecta; even though you live in some nowhereplace, buried hip deep in snow for half the year, you'll be warmed by sweet, colorful friends who'll get up a game of strip poker when things turn a little dull.

By giving his movie a very effective realistic look, by helping his actors to shape strongly believable performances, even when they are doing implausible things, Benton lends credence to these inspirational fibs. And two important critical groups have rewarded Newman with their best-actor prizes. An Oscar nomination—his eighth—cannot be far behind. These are partly tributes to a long and invaluable career. But they are also rather careless obeisances to stardom's saving grace, its ability to impart a kind of unconscious glamour even to the contemplation of failure and mortality.

VILLAGE VOICE, 12/27/94, p. 68, Georgia Brown

Didactic in its own crusty way, *Nobody's Fool* holds that growing up, assuming responsibility, may take place at any age provided senility hasn't set in—as it has with one poor soul who periodically ventures into the snow in her bathrobe. As Donald "Sully" Sullivan (Paul Newman), the movie's 60-year-old fuckup, puts it, "Ya gotta start someday."

After the disastrous *Billy Bathgate*, Robert Benton returns to slice-of-life moviemaking, affectionately focusing on a circle of neighbors in a depressed upstate town. Radiating outward from Sully's center, there's his landlady and former eighth grade teacher, Miss Beryl (Jessica Tandy); her pinched but prosperous son Clive (Josef Sommer); Sully's freewheeling, philandering boss (Bruce Willis); the boss's melancholy wife (Melanie Griffith), who nurses a reciprocated crush on Sully; Sully's dimwitted friend Rub (Pruitt Taylor Vince); and his incompetent, one-legged lawyer, Wirf (Broadway director Gene Saks).

One Thanksgiving, Sully's son Peter (Dylan Walsh), a college teacher recently denied tenure, shows up with his wife and twin boys. Visiting his mother, Peter runs into Sully only by chance, but their encounter is prolonged when Peter's wife splits. Doing some construction work alongside his dad, Peter makes a mild attempt to hold the ice-bound Sully accountable for walking out on the family many years ago.

Peter: "Did you ever think about me?" Sully: "Some of the time." Peter: "Well, I thought about you *all* of the time."

As exchanges go, this is one of the movie's more effective ones. In adapting Richard Russo's novel, Benton goes just too far almost every time, spinning simple dialogue into ingratiating repartee. Most of the exchanges get mighty cute; everything gets spelled out. (One clip you're sure to see Oscar night has Jessica Tandy, who died after making the film, musing over having just seen her neighbor's birdbath knocked out by a falling tree limb. "God's moving in on me ... I have the feeling this is the year he lowers the boom.") In the year of Gump, we know there's a big audience for the collected wisdom of God's simpler creatures—all their lines thunk on laptops by people with pools. Besides the fact that Newman as he ages is increasingly luminous, it's impossible to resist the small-town, working-class ambiance—sights familiar to all of us, whether from intimate experience or from just passing through: battered pickups with one taillight out, machine parts littering driveways and front yards, steam escaping from diners at mealtimes, the coiled Doberman behind the chainlink fence. The movie makes it possible to believe that we've chanced on these folks at a particular juncture in their affairs, and that their jokes and squabbles will go on once that camera crew gets the heck out.

Also reviewed in:
CHICAGO TRIBUNE, 1/13/95, Friday/p. C, Michael Wilmington
NEW REPUBLIC, 1/9 & 16/95, p. 33, Stanley Kauffmann
NEW YORK TIMES, 12/23/94, p. C5, Caryn James
VARIETY, 12/12-18/94, p. 76, Todd McCarthy
WASHINGTON POST, 1/13/95, p. B1, Rita Kempley
WASHINGTON POST, 1/13/95, Weekend/p. 39, Desson Howe

NORTH

A Columbia Pictures and Castle Rock Entertainment release in association with New Line Cinema. *Executive Producer:* Jeffrey Stott and Andrew Scheinman. *Producer:* Rob Reiner and Alan Zweibel. *Director:* Rob Reiner. *Screenplay:* Alan Zweibel and Andrew Scheinman. *Based on the novel by:* Alan Zeibel. *Director of Photography:* Adam Greenberg. *Editor:* Robert Leighton. *Music:* Marc Shaiman. *Music Editor*: Scott Stambler. *Choreographer:* Pat Birch. *Sound:* Bob Eber. *Sound Editor:* Robert Grieve. *Casting:* Jane Jenkins and Janet Hirshenson. *Production Designer:* J. Michael Riva. *Art Director:* David Klassen. *Set Designer:* Darrel L. Wight, Dawn Snyder, Virginia Randolf, and Rob Woodruff. *Set Decorator:* Michael Taylor. *Set Dresser:* Mike Hanrahan, Philippe Rockholt, Mark Davidson, Carl Cassara, and Joseph L. Byrne. *Special Effects:* Terry Frazee. *Costumes:* Gloria Gresham. *Costumes (Bruce Willis):* Laurie Stilson. *Make-up:* Tom Hoerber and Pete Altobelli. *Make-up (Bruce Willis):* Dale Bach-Siss. *Stunt Coordinator:* R.A. Rondell. *Running time:* 87 minutes. *MPAA Rating:* PG.

CAST: Elijah Wood (North); Jason Alexander (North's Dad); Julia Louis-Dreyfus (North's Mom); Marc Shaiman (Piano Player); Jussie Smollet (Adam); Taylor Fry (Zoe); Alana Austin (Sarah); Peg Shirley (Teacher); Chuck Cooper (Umpire); Alan Zweibel (Coach); Donavon Dietz (Assistant Couch); Teddy Bergman, Michael Cipriani, Joran Corneal, and Joshua Kaplan (Teammates); Bruce Willis (Narrator); James F. Dean (Dad Smith); Glenn

Walker Harris, Jr. (Jeffrey Smith); Nancy Nichols (Mom Jones); Ryan O'Neill (Andy Wilson); Kim Delgado (Dad Johnson); Tony T. Johnson (Steve Johnson); Mathew McCurley (Winchell); Carmela Rappazzo (Receptionist); Jordan Jacobson (Vice President); Rafale Yermazyan (Austrian Dancer); Jon Lovitz (Arthur Belt); Mitchell Group (Dad Wilson); Bryon Stewart (Bailiff); Alan Arkin (Judge Buckle); Alan Rachins (Defense Attorney); Dan Aykroyd (Pa Tex); Reba McEntire (Ma Tex); Jenifer Panton (Betty Lou); Keone Young (Governor Ho); Lauren Tom (Mrs. Ho); Gil Janklowicz (Man on Beach); Maud Winchester (Stewart's Mom); Tyler Gurciullo (Stewart); Fritz Sperberg (Stewart's Dad); Brynn Hartman (Waitress); Larry Williams (Alaskan Pilot); Graham Greene (Alaskan Dad); Kathy Bates (Alaskan Mom); Abe Vigoda (Alaskan Grandpa); Richard Belzer (Barker); Ben Stein (Curator); Marla Frees, and Robert Rigamonti (D.C. Reporters); Alexander Godunov (Amish Dad); Kelly McGillis (Amish Mom); Jay Black (Amish Pilot); Rosalind Chao (Chinese Mom); George Kee Cheung (Chinese Barber); Ay Adejugbe (African Dad); Darwyn Carson (African Mom); Lucy Lin (Female Newscaster); Faith Ford (Donna Nelson); John Ritter (Ward Nelson); Scarlett Johanssen (Laura Nelson); Jesse Zeigler (Bud Nelson); Robert Costanzo (Al); Audrey Klebahn (Secretary); Philip Levy (Panhandler); Dan Grimaldi (Hot Dog Vendor); Marvin Braverman (Waiter); Wendel Josepher (Ticket Agent); D.L. Shroder (Federal Express Agent).

FILMS IN REVIEW, 9-10/94, p. 61, Andy Pawelczak

In *North*, Rob Reiner has gone back to his roots—Mel Brooks/Carl Reiner borscht belt shtick. Unfortunately, the comedy isn't very funny, and it clashes with the picture's sweet tempered moral, something about how we're all stuck with our parents—which is unexceptionable enough, God knows. Is this Rob Reiner at fifty-something still working out his problems with his father, the redoubtable Carl?

The movie follows the adventures of North (Elijah Wood), a fourth grader afflicted with parents who don't appreciate him. North is a dream kid who so excels at everything he does, from playing Tevye in the school production of *Fiddler on The Roof* to pitching on the Little League team, that other kids' parents unfavorably compare their offspring to him. North's parents are manic talkers, so absorbed in their jobs—the father is a pants inspector and the mother a travel agent—that they barely notice his existence. Early on, a distraught North falls asleep in his secret spot—it's one of the film's jokes that instead of a rustic treehouse it's a furniture display in a mall—and the rest of the movie is his dream, where he becomes a free agent with the right to choose his own parents.

The picture's dream structure allows Reiner all sorts of anti-realistic comic liberties as North travels around the world trying out prospective parents. In Texas he auditions a rancher/oil millionaire, played by Dan Aykroyd in a ten gallon hat, who buys him the Houston Astros and puts on a peculiarly uninspired, humorless musical production number in his living room with a big cast of chorus girls. In Hawaii, he stays with the Governor, who plans on using North as a poster boy with an exposed backside in an advertising campaign, a conceit that occasions a lot of dumb, puerile jokes. In Alaska, his Eskimo hosts, played by Kathy Bates and Graham Greene, send their aged parent out to die on an ice floe, all the while making bad, tasteless jokes about old age such as a remark about the unattractiveness of frozen drool. Reiner's mentor, Mel Brooks, made bad taste into high comic art, but Reiner's a long way here from such manic brilliance as "Springtime For Hitler."

A rule of thumb in Hollywood today seems to be that, when in doubt, make trivial pursuit references to other movies. *North* has a subplot involving a fourth grade school journalist named Winchell (Matthew McCurley) who parlays North's celebrity as a free agent into political power for himself. He's a pint sized, buck toothed Citizen Kane, a parallel that Reiner underlines with a low shot of Winchell delivering a demagogic, pseudo-populist speech from a high podium with a huge portrait of North behind him. Reiner begins the movie with a *Kane* reference, a shot of one of those glass spheres that snow inside when you turn them upside down. Reiner's rosebud, a hint that in some oblique way the movie is really about his own childhood? If so, he has left only traces of Fifties Jewish ethnicity—a shot of an orthodox rabbi in a clothing factory, Bruce Willis as a borscht belt comic. Otherwise the picture is firmly set in a generic Suburbia, U.S.A. 1994.

Oh yes, Bruce Willis is surprisingly appealing as North's guardian angel who turns up in a variety of incarnations and costumes, but he's not enough to save this film from the summer doldrums.

LOS ANGELES TIMES, 7/22/94, Calendar/p. 1, Kenneth Turan

Shed a tear for "North." Not for the 11-year-old boy it's named after, who thinks he has problems and doesn't, but for the movie itself, which is in more trouble than it knows.

Besides being disappointing, which it certainly is, "North" is baffling, a cause for sadness rather than anger. How could director Rob Reiner, whose touch for what pleases a mass audience is usually unfailing, have strayed this far? And how could anyone else have concluded that this languid fable about a boy who decides he needs a new set of parents was a film worth making?

Obviously Reiner's impressive commercial track record ("Stand by Me," "When Harry Met Sally ... ," "A Few Good Men") caused everyone from actors to executives to shrug and sign off on a project so lacking in sparkle that no one with less power would have had a chance of getting it made.

As for why the director himself wanted to be involved, the press material carefully stipulates that the "North" story line "echoed Reiner's own maturation process. " So, like Barry Levinson and the equally ill-starred "Toys," the director couldn't get the project off his mind for a decade, biding his time until he had the clout to get is done.

Based on a novel by Alan Zweibel, who co-wrote the lackluster script with Andrew Scheinman, the film focuses on a fourth-grader who seems to have an enviable life. North (Elijah Wood) is a scholar, an athlete and a role model, but when he sits down at the dinner table, he can't seem to get his folks' attention.

Given the difficulties children today have to face up to, living with a pair of comically self-absorbed parents (played by "Seinfeld" regulars Jason Alexander and Julia Louis-Dreyfus) may not seem unduly traumatic. But in the uncertain tradition of previous "liberate the inner child" movies, North's situation is treated as a candidate for the trials of Job.

Under the influence of a wily fellow fourth-grader (Mathew McCurley) and an unscrupulous adult lawyer (Jon Lovitz), North decides enough is enough and declares himself a free agent, intent on scouring the world for parents worthy of his exceptional gifts. After all, as his tireless guardian angel (Bruce Willis) tells him, "Parents are supposed to make kids feel better, not the other way around."

Questionable as all this may be as a premise, it's not really what sinks "North." Rather it is how incompletely imagined the alternative parenting scenarios we're presented with turn out to be.

First up are Texans Pa and Ma Tex (Dan Aykroyd and singer Reba McEntire), wealthy folk who like the biggest and the best of everything. Next comes a completely inexplicable interlude with parental wanna-bes in Hawaii, another in Alaska, and increasingly shorter ones in China, Paris, Zaire and assorted other spots.

There are a few amusing moments in "North," mainly involving jokey references to other movies, but they are overshadowed by a dubious plot turn involving a full-scale revolt of America's children inspired by North's antics.

The problem overall is not so much that the humor, especially in the parent-tryout situations, is forced, but that it simply is not there at all. So little is going on in this mildest of fantasies that it is hard to even guess what kinds of emotional effects were aimed at in the first place.

So when Bruce Willis turns to game but overmatched Elijah Wood near the finale and tells the boy, "You've realized something it takes most people a lifetime to figure out," it is hard to resist yelling something like, "Be more careful next time," at the screen. It's a lesson everyone involved in "North" ought to take to heart.

NEW YORK, 8/1/94, p. 53, David Denby

Rob Reiner's disastrously unfunny *North* features TV-sketch gags devoted to a TV-sketch idea. A little boy (Elijah Wood), disgusted with his parents, declares himself a "free agent" and searches the world for a new mom and dad. The spectacle of a famous director pandering to children might be enraging if the movie weren't such an obvious dog.

NEW YORK POST, 7/22/94, p. 41, Michael Medved

Say it ain't so, Rob!

How could Rob Reiner, the comic genius who created "This Is Spinal Tap," the sensitive director who used children's memories and fantasies to shape "Stand by Me" and "Thc Princess Bride," now offer the world such an appalling example of kiddie crud as the truly unspeakable, "North"?

Thc title character is a bright, popular 11-year-old (Elijah Wood), who feels unappreciated by his parents.

With the help of a whining weasel of a lawyer (Jon Lovitz) and a screwball judge (Alan Arkin), the kid succeeds in declaring "free agency"—enabling him to search the world to find the perfect mom and dad.

While repeatedly encountering a street-smart guardian angel (played by Bruce Willis, who appears first as a department store Easter bunny), young North meets a dazzling variety of prospective parents, including oil-rich Texans (Dan Aykroyd and Reba McEntire), Alaskan Eskimos (Graham Greene and Kathy Bates), and WASPy suburban refugees from '50s TV sitcoms (John Ritter and Faith Ford).

The silly, exaggerated sets and costumes are supposed to reflect a young boy's unsophisticated, stereotyped images of various exotic corners of the world (including bare-breasted cannibals in Africa), but the result is painfully unfunny and often downright offensive.

When North meets "Governor Ho" of Hawaii (Keone Young), that gracious politician gestures to his wife (Lauren Tom) and declares: "Hawaii is a lush and fertile land. There's only one barren area on all the islands. Unfortunately, it's Mrs. Ho."

The pathetic script is full of such knee-slappers, along with an inane subplot about a conniving schoolmate of North's (nicely played by talented 10-year-old newcomer Matthew McCurley), who uses his friend's example to inspire kids across the country to seize power from their parents and take over the country.

It wouldn't matter that none of this makes sense if Reiner's vision turned out to be entertainingly bizarre, but it's not; it is, rather, indescribably flat (and flatulent).

The only intriguing aspect of the movie is the possibility that the filmmakers intended it as some cockamamie parable about assimilation. North's original parents (Jason Alexander and Julia Louis-Dreyfus of the "Seinfeld" show) both come across as loud, obnoxious Jewish stereotypes. The various alternate parents he visits around the world all seem as far removed as possible from any Jewish flavor.

These elements may provide fodder for some future grad student investigating Reiner's images of ethnic identity, But they hardly provide a reason to subject yourself to this altogether insufficient movie.

NEWSDAY, 7/22/94, Part II/p. B6, Jack Mathews

It is ironic that the funniest moment, one of the *few* funny moments, in Rob Reiner's "North" comes in a scene set in Paris mocking the popularity of Jerry Lewis. The French may be easily amused, but even they will be hard-pressed to find the humor in "North."

This ill-conceived, startlingly mundane fable about a boy's dream of adopting a new set of parents is such a complete miss you have to wonder what anyone ever saw in it, let alone a filmmaker with the talented commercial palate of Reiner. But there it sits, with all the wit, charm and depth of a 90-minute Willard Scott weather report, daring us to check its pedigree.

Reiner has reportedly been wanting to do "North" for 10 years, ever since his friend and original "Saturday Night Live" writer Alan Zweibel wrote the novel upon which it's based. A good thing he waited; if Reiner had done "North" before he did "A Sure Thing" and "Stand By Me," there might not have been a "When Harry Met Sally ..." and "Misery."

In a performance much better than the film, Elijah Wood plays North, an 11-year-old boy who becomes so depressed by his parents' lack of appreciation for his grades (high), his Little League batting average (even higher), and his envied behavior (he is the role model for every other parent in the neighborhood) that he plops down in a favorite chair one night and dreams about divorcing and replacing them.

Within that dream, North wins his divorce and is given until Labor Day, the end of his summer vacation, to choose a new set of parents, return to his old ones or end up in an orphanage. As he hopscotches the globe road-testing couples eager to adopt so perfect a child, North's best friend, a little Nazi named Winchell (Mathew McCurley), and the sleazy attorney Arthur Belt (Jon Lovitz), organize a children's revolt, intending to lower the voting age to 7 and take over the country.

Yes, it's only a dream, but we're stuck in it, and as North (and his guardian angel, played by a wise-cracking Bruce Willis) skip from one set of would-be adoptive parents to the next, the movie takes on the momentum of a toothache.

Zweibel's experience writing those glib and often amateurish sketches for "Saturday Night Live" is evident in the script, which he co-wrote with producer Andrew Scheinman. Each of North's stops becomes a little skit, outrageously feeble on the big screen. There's the Texas millionaire couple (Dan Aykroyd and Reba McEntire) shopping for a replacement for their dead son, the Hawaiian governor (Keone Young) and his wife (Lauren Tom) hoping to use a coppertoned North to promote tourism in the islands, and the suburban New York Nelsons (John Ritter and Faith Ford), whose family life is as sublime as Ozzie and Harriet's.

"North" is laced with these kind of easy sight gags and inside movie and TV references. In a scene that probably lasts less than a minute, Alexander Godunov and Kelly McGillis appear in Amish dress, a whimsical reminder—and nothing more—of their roles in "Witness." Elsewhere, Kathy Bates and Abe Vigoda show up as Igloo-bound Alaskan natives, in a crudely racist sketch likely to amuse no one.

Lost in this morass of bad ideas are the spirited performances of Jason Alexander and Julia Louis-Dreyfus, on loan from "Seinfeld" as North's biological parents, and Alan Arkin, as the pro-choice judge who sets the kid free.

Whether Reiner made "North" to satisfy the demands of his rapidly growing Castle Rock Entertainment, or out of sincere befuddlement, it sets the standard against which his future failures will be measured. I'm no fan of Jerry Lewis, but to make fun of him in this movie takes nerve.

NEWSWEEK, 8/1/94, p. 56, Katrine Ames

You can almost hear a mogul yelling. "Get me recycling!" *North*, a mean-spirited comedy, shows just how short Hollywood can get on ideas. North (Elijah Wood), a model 11-year-old, thinks everyone but his parents appreciates him. What's a boy in need of unfettered self-esteem to do? Sue for the right to get a new family. Aided by a polymorphic guardian angel (Bruce Willis), he goes on a search. Unknown to him, kids at home are revolting in his name, led by his mini-megalomaniac best friend (Mathew McCurley), who's using North as a straw man to form a new, childcentric world order. Uh-oh, Director Rob Reiner, hampered by Alan Zweibel and Andrew Scheinman's predictable script, drowns us in references from "Citizen Kane" and "Father Knows Best" to "Strangers on a Train" and "Bonanza." Only Wood ("Forever Young"), whose range and intensity are not unlike the young Jodie Foster's, makes "North" endurable.

SIGHT AND SOUND, 8/94, p. 48, Lizzie Francke

11-year-old North decides to divorce his parents, who bicker constantly. Visiting his favourite shopping-mall hideaway he meets a man dressed up as a pink rabbit who advises him to go home. But at school North is hailed as a hero and Winchell, the editor of the school magazine, takes a particular interest in his case. With the help of Arthur Belt, an unscrupulous lawyer, North takes his parents to court. The judge tells him he must find new parents before a certain date or be put in an orphanage. On hearing the news, North's parents go into comas and are mounted as museum exhibits. North is besieged by invitations from potential parents. Meanwhile, unbeknown to him, Winchell and Belt, hoping to capitalise on North's case, are organising a children's uprising.

North's search for parents starts in Texas with Pa and Ma Tex, but they are not suitable. He ends up trekking around the world, frequently bumping into a man who resembles the pink rabbit. As the deadline draws near, North decides to settle for the Nelsons, who seem to be the perfect family. But they are still not quite right. North's real parents come out of their comas and are kidnapped by Winchell. They make a video pleading with him to come home, but Winchell re-edits it and transforms it into hate-mail. When North receives the video he despairs and resolves to run away rather than be put in an orphanage. Winchell decides he should be assassinated, and North ends up in Manhattan pursued by Winchell's henchmen. In Central Park, he meets a school friend who gives him the original version of his parents' video.

Fleeing his pursuers, North ends up in the ballroom of a big hotel where a reception is taking place. In the dressing room of the MC, who looks rather familiar, he watches the video and realises that his parents do love him. The MC arranges to Federal Express North back to his parents before the deadline expires. But he arrives home to find his parents have been kidnapped. Later they are released and race to meet North at his secret hideaway. Parents and son are reunited just in time, but Winchell's henchman is still on North's trail and takes aim at the boy. At this point, North wakes up, realising that his adventures have all been a terrible dream.

One of the first rules of film-making should be: never end a story, "She woke up and realised it was all a dream." It is a shame that Rob Reiner and Alan Zweibel ignored this edict, since North has the makings of an agreeable comic fantasy for kids along the lines of *Home Alone*. The winsome North (played by a bug-eyed Elijah Wood, who seems intent on challenging the Culkin crown), determined to divorce his unsatisfactory parents, undertakes a Cook's tour in which he checks out a range of potential adoptive families, only to find they all suck.

Unfortunately, the world he navigates owes more to Disney than to the UN. Caricatures such as Ma and Pa Tex (Dan Aykroyd and Country and Western star Reba McEntire, complete with hoe-down musical number) and the Amish family (*Witness*' Kelly McGillis and Alexander Godunov as Mom and Pop) are anarchic and engaging enough. And the depiction of Alaska as a country in which grandparents are floated unceremoniously out to sea, or France as a place which has Jerry Lewis on every television channel has a certain endearing craziness. But to portray 'Africa' as something out of a nineteenth-century missionary's picture book is unforgivable—a well-intentioned jibe at stereotypes which seriously misfires.

The problem is that North never achieves the scathing satire to which he aspires. The Nelsons, the all-American happy family with whom North briefly settles, are straight out of 50s sit-coms such as *The Donna Reed Show*. But Dad at the barbecue in his patterned sweater and Mom with her pristine apron and shiny coiffure come across as lame pastiches in comparison with the more sharply skewed portraits in *Parents*, for example. Even the casting of John Ritter, who played the beleaguered father in *Problem Child*, as Nelson *père* fails to give these scenes edge. Audiences for whom Addams family values have become the norm deserve better than bland dreams featuring Bruce Willis in a fluffy, fluorescent pink rabbit suit.

TIME, 8/1/94, p. 58, Richard Schickel

[*North* was reviewed jointly with *The Client*; see Schickel's review of that film.]

VILLAGE VOICE, 8/2/94, p. 48, Georgia Brown

You'd think that Alan Zweibel's *North* would be just too silly, too puny, a project even for Rob Reiner. Think again: It's about a boy whose parents don't appreciate him—a theme that still captures the director's heart.

Briefly, North is not a point on the compass but the given name of a picture-perfect suburban 11-year-old (Elijah Wood): 91 average in school, lowest ERA in Little League, Tevye in the class play. In fact, he's idolized by all local parents except his own (Seinfeld duo Jason Alexander and Julia Louis-Dreyfus), who, unfortunately, aren't evil—this might spice things up—but simply preoccupied with their own *tsuris*.

Anyway, North decides to take his show on the road by declaring himself a "free agent child," eliciting bids, and auditioning would-be parents around the globe. With Bruce Willis as his Jiminy Cricket, North travels from sight gag to sight gag—Texas, Hawaii, Alaska, Paris, Beijing, and then, closer to home, he stops awhile with the blond, bland Nelson family. (I admit that some tiny background stuff here and there might even be funny if the whole weren't so fantastically tedious.) Eventually, wouldn't you know, North returns to roots, which, considering the evidence, means coming to terms with his Jewishness. This you could call an in-joke.

Relentlessly vulgar, *North* can be seen as yet another plaintive cry from, or cynical appeal to, the home alone generation. It also partakes of the current tendency—most noticeable on sitcoms—to treat kids as grown-ups, and grown-ups as kids.

Also reviewed in:
CHICAGO TRIBUNE, 7/22/94, Friday/p. C, Michael Wilmington
NEW YORK TIMES, 7/22/94, p. C3, Janet Maslin
VARIETY, 7/18-24/94, p. 38, Leonard Klady
WASHINGTON POST, 7/22/94, p. C1, Rita Kempley
WASHINGTON POST, 7/22/94, Weekend/p. 41, Joe Brown

NOSTRADAMUS

An Orion Classics release of an Allied Entertainments and Vereinigte Film Partners production. *Executive Producer:* Peter McRae, Kent Walwin, and David Mintz. *Producer:* Edward Simons and Harold Reichebner. *Director:* Roger Christian. *Screenplay:* Knut Boeser. *Based on a story by:* Piers Ashworth and Roger Christian. *Director of Photography:* Denis Crossan. *Editor:* Alan Strachan. *Music:* Barrington Pheloung. *Sound:* James Corcoran and (music) Dave. Hunt. *Sound Editor:* Alan Paley. *Casting:* Joyce Gallie and Sally Osoba. *Production Designer:* Peter J. Hampton. *Art Director:* Christian Nicul. *Set Designer:* Mihai Ionescu. *Set Decorator:* Michael D. Ford. *Special Effects:* Jim Francis. *Costumes:* Ulla Gothe. *Make-up:* Christine Atar, Christiane Weber, and Samir Atar. *Special Make-up Effects:* Jens Bartram. *Running time:* 118 minutes. *MPAA Rating:* R.

CAST: Tcheky Karyo (Nostradamus); F. Murray Abraham (Scalinger); Rutger Hauer (Monk); Amanda Plummer (Catherine de Medici); Julia Ormond (Marie); Assumpta Serna (Anne); Anthony Higgins (King Henry II); Diana Quick (Diane de Portier); Michael Gough (Jean de Remy); Maja Morgenstern (Helen); Magdalena Ritter (Sophie); Bruce Myers (Professor); Leon Lissek, Michael Byrne, and Stefan Patoli (Inquisitors); Bruce Alexander (Paul); Oana Pelea (Landlady); Matthew Morley (Michel, age 11); Thhomas Christian (Cezar, age 10); David Gwillim (Michael's Father); Amanda Walker (Madame Scalinger); Richenda Carey (Countess); Razvan Popa (Scalinger's Servant); Amanda Boxer (Patient); Serban Celea (Raoul); Adrian Pentea (Doctor); Eugenia Maci (Madame Auberligne); Mihai Niculescu (Mayor); Florin Calinescu, Dan Sanulescu, and Adrian Titieni (Priests); Eugen Cristea (Scribe); Sergiu Anghel and Tomi Cristin (Students); Sergiu Anghel and Doina Anghel (Dancers); Maria Varsami (Midwife); Florin Busuioc (Commander); Rupert Holiday Evans (Pilgrim in Church); Michael Verbitky (Pilgrim in Boat); Rudy Rosenfeld (Assistant Doctor); Vasile Popa (Montgomery); Vasile Albinet (Henry's Double); Mihai Cibu (Chamberlain); Ioan Brancu (Footman); Gheorghe Visu (Ruggerio); Manuela Colescu (Chambermaid); Anca Danilescu (Margaret); Viviana Ghita (Claude); Sandu Mihai Gruia (Stretcher Bearer); Andrei Peniuc (Torturer).

LOS ANGELES TIMES, 9/16/94, Calendar/p. 8, Kevin Thomas

"Nostradamus" is a rather conventional film bio of a highly unconventional man, Michel de Nostradame, the French 16th-Century physician and astrologer whose prophecies, which he first published in 1555, continue to fascinate multitudes. Filmed largely in Romania, "Nostradamus" is a handsome, intermittently involving large-scale period epic that presents Nostradame's turbulent life and times with conviction and clarity, and it is sparked by several stunning performances.

Unfortunately, that of Turkish-born French star Tcheky Karyo in the title role is not one of them. The rugged Karyo, most familiar as the agent who trained Anne Parillaud to be an assassin in "La Femme Nikita," radiates sensitivity and concentration, but his Nostradame is so introspective and brooding as to seem glum, almost never catching fire, an approach suitable for a Rossellini or Bresson film but not such a straightforward picture as here. When such strong personalities as F. Murray Abraham, Assumpta Serna and Amanda Plummer aren't on screen, the film tends to become lifeless.

While obviously the film is most likely to please avid believers of Nostradamus, it does suggest to wider audiences how very perilous life could be in the 16th Century for intellectuals, a time when learning was severely proscribed by the Inquisition. Indeed, director Roger Christian and his co-writers have effectively suggested the ways in which Nostradame's era parallels our own. The eternal conflict between science and religion that is at the heart of "Nostradamus," for example, erupted anew in the recent world population conference in Cairo—just as the bubonic plague (which Nostradame fought with controversial natural medicines) inevitably brings to mind the AIDS epidemic.

The filmmakers depict the visions that Nostradame apparently experienced throughout his 63 years with considerable panache, most successfully when Nostradame walks down a darkened street only to be confronted with rumbling Nazi tanks. In other instances they become too literal: The poor guy can't look into a bucket of water without seeing an atom bomb mushroom or J.F.K. at Dealey Plaza or a glimpse of Saddam Hussein.

The first half of the film is charged by Abraham as Nostradame's aristocratic patron and fellow free-thinker and to a lesser extent by Julia Ormond as Abraham's feminist daughter who became Nostradame's first wife and scientific colleague. Rutger Hauer cameos as a mystic, a whimsical monk who consoles Nostradame in a period of despair.

The second half is livelier, thanks to radiant Assumpta Serna as Nostradame's supportive but outspoken Barcelona-born second wife and by Amanda Plummer as a wonderfully astringent Catherine de Medici, Queen of France, whose patronage proves a lifesaver for Nostradame. Solidly crafted, "Nostradamus" is more consistently intelligent and illuminating than exciting or imaginative.

NEW YORK POST, 11/23/94, p. 45, Thelma Adams

"The world is breaking! The world is breaking!" shrieks a prepubescent Nostradamus after a particularly nasty nightmare.

Millenarians delight! With only five years to spare before 2000 A.D., someone has finally filmed a bio pic of the life of medieval oracle Michel de Nostradame (1504-1566).

Former art director Roger Christian ("Alien") cast French actor Tcheky Karyo ("La Femme Nikita") in the pivotal role as the twice-married doctor and visionary who battled the bubonic plague with rose petal pills, dodged the Spanish Inquisition, befriended Catherine de Medici and allegedly predicted the death of her husband, King Henry II, as well as Hitler's rise, Kennedy's assassination, and the atomic bomb.

Karyo plays the role with a deadly seriousness (visions of your own death apparently limit one's sense of humor). His face hidden behind a beard his eyes are intense and, as the. years pass, red-rimmed and angst-filled.

A new-age guru, Nostradamus advocates avoiding fat and pork in the diet, is into astrology, and takes a mysterious potion laced with nutmeg to intensify his visions. As his wife goes into labor, he clears the room with the very unmedieval, "Would you please leave so we can have more space."

Nostradamus was apparently irresistible to women, if not the audience. He strips on a dime and fells women with a single, silent potent look. The sex scenes—shot with a soft porn glow are explicit without being intimate and inspire unintentional laughter.

The cast is an odd stew. As Catherine de Medici, Amanda Plummer is the least regal, most twitchy and affected of queens. The wonderful Rutger Hauer is tossed in as a twisted monk who inexplicably wears a metallic crown of candles and blows Karyo out of their brief shared scenes. F. Murray Abraham plays Nostradamus' mentor Scalinger as a medieval Carlos Castenada who introduces the young doctor to forbidden texts like the cabala and that psychedelic nutmeg potion.

Was Nostradamus a medieval acid casualty? We'll never know from this episodic, sodden movie. In the end, I felt as baffled by the man and his predictions as I did in the beginning.

"The 20th century will be especially terrible," Nostradamus predicts.

But all is not apocalypse for the medieval mystic. He also envisioned paradise in space, In "Nostradamus," it looks a lot like a "Star Trek" rerun.

NEWSDAY, 11/23/94, Part II/p. B12, Gene Seymour

You don't have to be a wild-eyed gleaner of the daily horoscope or a trafficker in Tarot cards to be fascinated with the saga of Michel de Nostradame, aka Nostradamus, the 16th-Century scientist-humanitarian-prophetwho foresaw just about every horrific event up to, and beyond, our own turbulent era.

He enjoys such legitimacy, even among some skeptics, that one is curious about what made him so convincing.

Well, according to this eponymous film, Nostradamus, as portrayed by Tcheky Karyo ("La Femme Nikita"), was a cool, sexy, sensitive-but-intense kinda guy. Think of what Dr. Kildare, or even "NYPD Blue's" John Kelly, would be like if he lived in the 1500s and had these really bad dreams.

He moves through plague, pestilence and repression with the serenity of someone who knows, pretty much, when he's supposed to die.

He was also ahead of his time in more ways than one, treating the diseased with herbs and floral essences rather than bleeding them dry. Such innovations attract the attention of Scalinger (F. Murray Abraham), a wealthy scientist who takes on Nostradamus as a close confidant. This ticks off Scalinger's protegee (Julia Ormond), who burns with righteous anger over being shut out of the men's circle of forbidden knowledge but marries the young doctor.

It's the first of a series of jolting transitions for Nostradamus, who becomes a Candide-like figure stumbling in and out of good and bad luck, despair and happiness, widowerhood and remarriage. He also keeps running into World War II battles, Vietnam fire-fights, images of Hitler, atom bombs, the Kennedy assassination.

Even rumors of such visions make the Inquisition yearn to rip Nostradamus' limbs off. But he and his family have an unexpected protector in the queen of France, played by Amanda Plummer with her trademark nerviness.

Director Roger Christian guides this epic with bland efficiency. Karyo's efforts as leading man are heroic, given the ludicrous things he has to say or do.

Otherwise, this is one of those patch-work melodramas from which you get your jollies where you can. Mine come when Rutger Hauer, playing someone known only as "the mad monk" appears out of the blue to help our hero through a rough emotional stretch. Hauer makes a terrific old hippie up to the moment he gives Nostradamus his parting words of advice: "Light the candle at the bottom of your heart." Hey, man, why the bottom? Why not the lower middle?

SIGHT AND SOUND, 1/95, p. 51, Kim Newman

Sixteenth-century France. Michel de Nostre Dame, whose family have converted from Judaism to Christianity, causes controversy at medical school by advocating herbal cures rather than bleeding, and is marked as an enemy of the Holy Inquisition. Joining the household of Scalinger, one of a cabal of heretical scientists, Michel learns the secrets of the scientist's secret library and marries Marie, Scalinger's apprentice, with whom he has two children. Fascinated by astrology as well as medicine, Michel is afflicted with visions of violent destructions that he believes will fall upon the world in the future. When Marie and the children die of the plague, the Inquisition discover one of Scalinger's forbidden books in her possession. Michel has to flee, along with the books.

Remarrying to Anne, a Spanish widow, Michel burns the books to avoid persecution but compiles and publishes his prophecies. His prediction that King Henry II will die in a jousting accident attracts the interest of the Queen, Catherine de Medici, who is humiliated by her husband's public amour with Diane de Portier. Henry and Diane try to poison Michel, but the Queen helps him survive. Michel tells Catherine that all her sons will sit on the throne of France but that she will outlive them all. Helene, Michel's sister-in-law, denounces him to the Inquisition because he has rejected her sexual advances, but the Queen intervenes and saves him from torture. Henry dies as Michel predicted, precipitating the French religious wars. Michel reveals the extent of the catastrophes (including three world wars, Hitler, the atomic bomb and Aids) he envisions for the twentieth century, but also predicts mankind. will survive to make a future in space.

After art direction and second unit work (notably on the *Star Wars* films), high profile shorts (*The Dollar Bottom* and *Black Angel*), and a striking if little-seen debut with *The Sender*, director Roger Christian hit a career stumbling block with his dreadful second feature *Lorca and the Outlaws* (omitted from his current c.v.) and has not been heard of for ten years. *Nostradamus*, a fascinating mess which alternates between provocative and ridiculous, marks a welcome return. However, its startling moments (such as an under-the-credits vision of a dark city devastated by a nightmare quake) are balanced by the kind of weird historical thigh-slapping indicated by the credit "and Rutger Hauer as 'The Mystic Monk'", which provoked such hilarity at the press show. Christian manages fairly well to integrate jarring time-slips like Michel's straying from sixteenth-century France into a World War II battle, recalling the shocking psychic bursts of *The Sender*. But he stumbles somewhat on biographical moments, such as the amazingly swift mood-shift from Marie's attempted suicide into love-making with her rescuer, Michel.

In shuffling through biography and history, *Nostradamus*—though held together by a charismatic lead performance from Tcheky Karyo—sometimes seems as if it has been cut down from a much greater length. A spirited cast makes the most of roles which end up as little more than cameos. Audiences with memories of A-level history might understand the chilling sequence when the Queen introduces Michel to her angelic coterie of children ("This is my wife," one pre-teen says of a little girl, "Queen Mary of Scotland"); he instantly is overcome by a vision of blood pouring *Shining*-style through the walls and doors over the doomed junior monarchs. When it gets into court intrigues, Amanda Plummer (who obviously accepted the role of Catherine de Medici purely for the frocks) shows off her line in sly aristocratic patronage, breezing into a Pythonesque Inquisition chamber and asking Michel's torturer whether he would care to bet his life on the superiority of the Holy Court to the temporal powers invested in the Queen.

The film slips when it turns from biography into Awful Warning, perhaps because it accepts whole-heartedly that Nostradamus was not at all a charlatan. As Michel stares into a bowl of water and sees familiar news footage of Hitler, nuclear tests, JFK, famine and Saddam Hussein, it's hard not to wonder why his visions go from sepia to colour towards the end of the twentieth century. One might also question why, until a last vision of a serene spaceship, Nostradamus never seems to foresee anything trivial or good, like Elvis on *The Ed Sullivan Show* or the life of Gandhi. Though Nostradamus declares he has revealed his knowledge to the world because it is possible to go against the visions and avoid disasters, his own slightly-advanced-for-its-day medicine is simply good sense. If he could predict events like wars and assassinations in the twentieth century, surely his duty as a physician was to concentrate on predicting discoveries, like penicillin and anaesthesia, which would have been of immediate use to his patients in the sixteenth.

Nevertheless, probably because of its sillinesses as much as despite them, Nostradamus offers a variety of pleasures and instantly eclipses the 1957 *The Man Without A Body*—in which financier George Coulouris has scientists revive Nostradamus' severed head so the prophet can give him stock market tips—as the definitive Nostradamus exploitation movie.

VILLAGE VOICE, 12/6/94, p. 66, Jeff Salamon

From his vantage point in 16th-century France, Michel de Nostradame prophesied the rise of Hitler, the assassination of JFK, and the onslaught of AIDS. *But could even he have foreseen what a botch Hollywood would make of his own life*?

Alright, alright, you saw that joke coming 400 years away. Too bad. *Nostradamus*'s narrative isn't so easily grasped; rather than establish a specific take on its protagonist, the film jumps back and forth between two characters the filmmakers can't reconcile: Nostradamus the Dutiful Husband Who Was Tragically Widowed but Found Love Again and Nostradamus the Pioneering Physician Who Stood Up to the Church and Courageously Battled the Plague. (And then there are the numerous scenes in which our hero, seized by nightmarish visions of an apocalyptic future, clutches his head and writhes like Spock undergoing the *pahnfar*.) When the two stories finally meet up—in order to save his family from the church's wrath, Nostradamus burns his private cache of outlawed scientific texts—it's a feeble attempt at thematic catch-up rather than a dramatic climax.

Made on the cheap in Romania, much of this period piece looks like outtakes from the "Losing My Religion" video—sans a nifty mandolin line to hold your attention. I could also mention how wasted F. Murray Abraham and Rutger Hauer are in this film but I won't. That would be so predictable.

Also reviewed in:
CHICAGO TRIBUNE, 12/9/94, Friday/p. F, John Petrakis
NEW YORK TIMES, 11/23/94, p. C14, Caryn James
VARIETY, 9/19-25/94, p. 77, Emanuel Levy

OLEANNA

A Samuel Goldwyn Company release in association with Channel Four Films of a Bay Kinescope production. *Producer:* Patricia Wolf and Sarah Green. *Director:* David Mamet. *Screenplay (based on his play)*: David Mamet. *Director of Photography:* Andrzej Sekula. *Editor:* Barbara Tulliver. *Music:* Rebecca Pidgeon. *Music Editor:* David Carbonara. *Sound:* Peter Kurland, Freddy Potatohead, Ryan Weiss, and (music) Tim Hatfield. *Sound Editor:* Philip Stockton. *Production Designer:* David Wasco and Sandy Reynolds Wasco. *Art Director:* Sarah Alcorn. *Set Designer:* Daniel Bradford. *Set Decorator:* Kate Conklin. *Set Dresser:* Robert Engle and Arthur A. Wood, III. *Special Effects:* Brian Ricci. *Costumes:* Jane Greenwood. *Make-up:* Lori Hicks. *Running time:* 90 minutes. *MPAA Rating:* Not Rated.

CAST: William H. Macy (John); Debra Eisenstadt (Carol).

CHRISTIAN SCIENCE MONITOR, 11/4/94, p. 12, David Sterritt

David Mamet's name is mighty prominent just now. He recently published his first novel, and his adaptation of Anton Chekhov's drama "Uncle Vanya" has become Louis Malle's latest film, the wonderful "Vanya on 42nd Street."

Most important, Mamet has directed a searing film version of his play "Oleanna," which was riveting in its Off Broadway stage production and retains every bit of its disturbing power on screen.

Mamet's currently high profile is encouraging to observe, since the 1990s have not ben turning into a very distinguished decade for thought-provoking media activity. At a time when society's idea of a Major Cultural Event is the formation of a new movie studio by mass-market wizard Steven Spielberg and two of his most crowd-conscious cronies, film producer Jeffrey Katzenberg and music magnate David Geffen, it's good to see a maverick like Mamet continue down his chosen path with hardly a glance at the box-office bonanzas he could easily earn through more conventional projects.

I had the good fortune to see the stage production of "Oleanna" in one of its first New York performances, so both its method and its message took me by surprise. If you're interested in Mamet but haven't heard the details of this drama, you'd be well advised to save this review—and any others—until after you've seen the film. I'll try not to reveal more information than necessary, but it's impossible to review the movie without referring to its subject, story, and structure.

Taking its somewhat mysterious title from a utopian community mentioned in an old folk song, "Oleanna" has two characters and a single setting. The action occurs in the office of a university professor named John, whose life is quite hectic. He gets frequent phone calls from his wife, who's closing the deal on an expensive house they're buying, and he awaits a message from the tenure committee, confirming that a higher salary and lifetime job security have been approved for him.

It's during this busy period that a student named Carol walks into his office, distressed about her classroom abilities and longing for whatever support her teacher can provide. They talk at length about Carol's trouble with school, John's theories of education, and the shortcomings they both see in the academic world.

Their conversation grows heated at times, especially when both John and Carol have trouble separating scholarly matters from more personal concerns. The first portion of the film ends inconclusively, with the characters still unreconciled and the audience still uncertain where the tale might be heading.

This becomes clear in the second scene when Carol revisits John to discuss charges of sexual harassment she has officially leveled against him. It appears some of his words and gestures during their first meeting—a touch on the shoulder, an anecdote about lovemaking—were interpreted by Carol as unwarranted liberties that degraded not only herself but all members of her gender and her "group," as she frequently puts it.

Eager to rescue his personal dignity and professional success from what he regards as a wildly unjustified assault, John engages her in an emotional debate that results in yet another round of allegations being filed against him, even more damning than the last. He fights back again during a last encounter with his contentious student trying to puncture her arguments at every turn—but revealing, in the process a violent male elitism that has indeed been lurking within his character all the while.

Who is the most aggrieved party in this increasingly furious battle of the sexists?

Mamet's text refuses to provide easy answers, and in the New York production of his original play, the program was printed with two different covers—both dominated by a target with a large bull's-eye at the center, but one showing John and the other showing Carol as the "victim" sitting behind it.

Like that production, the film version of "Oleanna" balances its dialogues so delicately that audience sympathies zigzag between John and Carol with hardly a letup, never settling on either character for long. Mamet thus indicates the dangers of self-delusion and self-righteousness in today's debates about equality, domination, and what philosopher Michel Foucault has identified as the inseparability of knowledge and power in the modern world.

This verbal tightrope act is difficult to pull off, and it seems to me that some imperfectly tuned nuances of dialogue and camera work give John a slight edge in the movie that he didn't have onstage. But other spectators may feel just the opposite.

If I'm right about this, then Mamet has again accomplished his feat with extraordinary skill—making "Oleanna" the most truly Hitchcockian film of recent years, with an uncanny ability to orchestrate moment-by-moment identification between viewers and characters.

High grades also go to the performers, longtime Mamet collaborator William H. Macy, and newcomer Debra Eisenstadt, who is as convincing on screen as Rebecca Pidgeon was onstage. Pidgeon, who originated the role of Carol but didn't participate in the movie because of pregnancy, provided the film's insinuating music. Andrzej Sekula did the precisely framed cinematography, and Barbara Tulliver did the impeccably timed editing. David Wasco and Sandy Reynolds Wasco were the picture's visual designers.

LOS ANGELES TIMES, 11/4/94, Calendar/p. 4, Peter Rainer

David Mamet's, "Oleanna," adapted from his two-character play, is about sexual harassment, but it's the audience for this movie that gets harassed. Mamet must mean for this movie to be as enjoyable as fingernails scraping a blackboard. For both men and women, watching it is intended as an act of penance for all our sexist, elitist, feminist, patriarchal ills.

But, for all his rigorous finger-pointing, Mamet may have misfired. Partly because of casting, partly because of what's in the play itself, "Oleanna" ends up as a tirade against feminist PC cruelties.

John (William H. Macy) is a prominent liberal arts college professor who is on the verge of achieving tenure—and a new home for his family. Carol (Debra Eisenstadt) has received a failing grade from him—it's never clear what exactly he's teaching. In a series of self-contained scenes, Carol challenges the smug, smarty-pants academic to explain himself, accusing him of sexual harassment after their first meeting and jeopardizing his tenure.

As the power roles slowly reverse, John's smugness turns beseeching while Carol's fury turns smug. It's clear that, on some essential level, they both relish drawing blood from each other. It's also clear that we're not meant to take either John or Carol as full-bodied human beings. They're archetypes, placards, mouthpieces.

Except that Carol's mouthpiece seems more shrill and hysterical than John's. Is this because we're meant to take her cruelty as retribution for all the ills perpetrated by the patriarchy? But then her charges of sexual harassment—and an even bigger bombshell—are obviously invented. In order for us to sympathize with Carol's destruction of John's career, we have to connect to some larger rage in her—a rage he fomented. Mamet seems to think that if we buy the archetype, we'll buy the person.

But "Oleanna," at least on film, never makes it to the archetypal stage. The actors are too in-your-face for that. And Carol isn't someone you want in your face. She may look like the epitome of the agitating, aggravating student, just as John resembles the epitome of self-impressed academia. But her insistent yammer, cadenced in Mametspeak, is enough to drive you out of the theater. (At the screening I attended, the drive up the aisle was bustling.) If Mamet was trying to give equal weight to Carol and John—to the male and female psyche—then he didn't study his movie-in-progress carefully enough.

Not that John comes across as Gandhi. He loves power—a big no-no in powerful PC circles—and it's clear that a large measure of his capitulation to Carol comes from plain old convenience. He'll do the Liberated thing if she'll withdraw her charges before the tenure board. He may be less grating than Carol, and less unfair in his charges, but he's not someone you want to be bunkered with either.

Mamet may interpret the audience's hostility to "Oleanna" as a sign he's touched a nerve. But I wonder. You don't see this many walkouts at Strindberg or Ibsen—two guys who knew a few things about dramatizing male-female hand-to-hand combat. Could it be that people turn off to "Oleanna" because it's as self-righteously phony and baselessly provocative as its characters?

NEW YORK POST, 11/4/94, p. 53, Michael Medved

It's certainly possible to create an absorbing film with just two characters, as Laurence Olivier and Michael Caine demonstrated so memorably in "Sleuth" some 20 years ago.

The key requirement is that the pair who inhabit the tightly enclosed world of the film must be well-balanced, with both of them in some way appealing or intriguing.

If, on the other hand, you're stuck for two hours with a couple of thoroughly despicable and deranged creeps, then the cinematic experience will be altogether insufferable—as it certainly is with David Mamet's "Oleanna," a claustrophobic catastrophe that will send many moviegoers running for the exits long before it wheezes its tired way to its intentionally "shocking" conclusion.

As a stage play, "Oleanna" benefitted enormously from its impeccable timing: It opened shortly after the Anita Hill-Clarence Thomas confrontation made the issue of sexual harassment into the national flavor-of-the-month. Though some critics saw the play as a stinging indictment of feminist extremists, Mamet's typically talky text tried hard for balance.

They're both right and they're both wrong (mostly) in this account of an undergraduate at a prestigious college who goes to her male professor to argue about a failing grade. The lengthy and uncomfortable meeting that follows provides her with the basis for a sexual harassment charge, and the final two acts dramatize even more disturbing encounters between the two principals.

On screen, their verbal jousting emerges in great dollops of undigested dialogue that come across as hopelessly stilted and artificial. "I saw you the entire semester exploit your paternal prerogative," she tells him. On another occasion, he declares, "They're going to discharge me!" to which she replies, "As full well they should!"

Even the stuffiest academics don't talk like that, and even the finest actors can't make such conversation come alive on screen. William H. Macy originated the professor's role onstage and played it across the country; he certainly knows how to convey his character's monstrous pomposity and egotism, but he fails in front of the camera to evoke even the briefest hints of sympathetic humanity.

The female part, meanwhile, went to newcomer Debra Eisenstadt, replacing Mamet's pregnant wife, Rebecca Pidgeon. This talented 24-year-old manages to get the most from her impossible part, making the character far more believable (and visibly vulnerable) than her male counterpart.

As a director, Mamet's made three fascinating films ("House of Games," "Things Change" and "Homicide"), but he wrote each of them originally for the screen and they are all unfailingly cinematic. Here, he seems inexplicably content to simply offer up a filmed play, providing only the briefest, no-dialogue preludes to each of the three acts as a feeble gesture toward "opening up" the project.

NEWSDAY, 11/4/94, Part II/p. B7, Jack Mathews

"There are two side to every story" is the cliché used to describe David Mamet's "Oleanna," an intended discourse on the extremes of political correctness and sexual politics. but the movie, adapted with claustrophobic fidelity to the spare Off-Broadway play, is so loaded to one side of the story—think Mamet, think male—that your mind would have to be both open and empty in order to see it as a fair contest.

The opposite sex combatants in this draining emotional war are John (William H. Macy), a patronizing, intellectually inflated liberal arts professor on the cusp of tenure at a prominent university, and Carol (Debra Eisenstadt), a reserved, confused student whose accusation of sexual harassment and attempted rape threaten to destroy his career.

That, at least, is the general arc of the story. As it actually plays, with the power being totally shifted and abused, it is like watching "The Incredible Shrinking Man" and "Attack of the 50 Ft. Woman" at the same time.

With "Oleanna," first produced onstage in late 1992, Mamet seemed intent on cutting through the obvious examples of sexual misconduct—say, a gang rape on a pool table in a public bar—to deal with those ambiguous moments between men and women when a look may or may not be a "look," a touch a "touch," and a vulgar comment about a pubic hair on a Coca Cola can be not necessarily a come-on.

It's a provocative idea exploring those dynamics in a university setting, between a self-deluded professor who prides himself on his open-mindedness and communication skills, and a student profoundly confused and antagonized by his dense academic language and paternalistic attitude.

But as the play wears on, and wears us down, it's clear Mamet isn't as interested in the subtle shadings of gender behavior as he is in ridiculing the extremes of feminist politics. Carol isn't just mistaken about John's intentions, she is paranoid schizophrenic about them, and part of a rabid movement (she keeps referring to her responsibilities to "my group") to eliminate sexual differentiation from the cultural vocabulary. In her mind he is already a convicted sexist for having used endearments when speaking with women students in class.

In the stage production there was at least a hint of doubt about John's intentions toward Carol, but with the additional information we get on film—close-ups of facial expressions, clearer views of body language—it is evident that he is guilty of nothing more than self-importance, insensitivity and bad listening habits.

Had the play been opened up to explore John's behavior with other students, and with his wife, there might have been more meat on the bones Mamet wanted to pick with feminists and the political correctness police. As it is, with an insufferable, ultimately pathetic windbag and a radfem hysteric locked in a room together, you may feel less anxious to get to the truth than to the end.

VILLAGE VOICE, 11/8/94, p. 64, Georgia Brown

David Mamet's button-pusher is now a $7.50 ticket. Since I didn't see *Oleanna* the play, I'm a bit surprised to discover that this is what all that fuss was about.

John (William H. Macy) and Carol (Debra Eisenstadt) are excruciating to spend time with. (I know this is supposed to be good for me.) Their mode of discourse: interrupting, spewing double-talk, ejecting shards of broken speech, using words as sticks and stones. Italics land like blows: *Thwack* and then again *thwack*. You wonder why they'd ever closet themselves together unless they were working some revenge on the other—which in fact they are. The play has each of them trying to leave, or pretending to try to leave, yet they're stuck.

John's the teacher, Carol's the student. She comes to his office to see what she can do for her grade, then lingers to submit to his preening pedantry. He points out right off that she's angry, which turns out to be an insight. Clearly, she has good reason to be when it comes to his class and probably his book, which is required reading. He too is angry as well as oblivious to his bullying ways, but this doesn't make the two even since he's in the catbird seat.

At first Carol seems irritatingly obtuse, struggling, dense in the pejorative sense; later—in the play's Act II—she's strident and dishonest. A whole course of indoctrination seems to have been undergone. She now has a Group and is filing charges against him, lying about his acts. By making her a thug, a witch, Mamet stacks the deck. Meanwhile, good old put-upon John seems more logical, honest, and justified. A poor man's *Master Builder*, the play would be better if both were really right instead of sort of right and if she were provocative, even destructive, but not demonized by the author. Mamet's tactics make me feel toyed with.

Oleanna is one of those "entertainments" for people who think everything is about power. Since it's meant to rile, watching it is inevitably masochistic, and you really need the physical release Mamet provides at the end. But it would probably be healthier to punch the author.

Also reviewed in:
CHICAGO TRIBUNE, 11/4/94, Friday/p. J. Michael Wilmington
NEW REPUBLIC, 11/21/94, p. 24, Stanley Kauffmann
NEW YORK TIMES, 11/4/94, p. C22, Caryn James
VARIETY, 11/7-13/94, p. 47, Leonard Klady
WASHINGTON POST, 11/11/94, p. D7, Rita Kempley

OLYMPIC SUMMER, THE

A New Yorker Films release of a Film-und Fernsehproduktionen film. *Producer:* Gordian Maugg. *Director:* Gordian Maugg. *Screenplay (German with English subtitles):* Gordian Maugg. *Based on the novel "Der Geselle" by:* Günther Rücker. *Director of Photography:* Andreas Giesecke. *Editor:* Monika Shindler and Behzad Beheshtipour. *Music:* Heidi Aydt and Frank Will. *Sound:* Guido Kühn and Omid Azmi. *Production Designer:* Günther Reisch. *Set Decorator:* Angelika Krause. *Special Effects:* Hans Moser and Thomas Rosie. *Costumes:* Klaus Geidies. *Running time:* 84 minutes. *MPAA Rating:* Not Rated.

CAST: Otto Sander (Narrator); Jost Gerstein (Apprentice); Verena Plangger (Widow); Otto Ruck (Butcher); Uwe Mauch (Student); Christoph Rapp (SA Man).

NEWSDAY, 8/3/94, Part II/p. B11, Jack Mathews

To call German director Gordian Maugg's "The Olympic Summer" an experimental film would seem to beg the question. It is a conventional drama, the story of lost innocence in Nazi Germany, and it follows a linear narrative line.

Based on a novella by Gunther Rucker, it tells of a 16-year-old butcher's apprentice (Jost Gerstein) who rides his bicycle from Pomerania to Berlin, hoping to get tickets to the 1936 Olympics, and is instead drawn into a series of events, romantic and tragic, that change and ultimately destroy him. His story is, in effect, the story of Germany itself under Hitler and the Third Reich.

What makes it an experimental film is Maugg's decision to shoot with a 1927 model hand-cranked camera, and blend his new material with archival newsreel footage and still photographs from the period, creating what appears to be a freshly minted, 60-year-old silent movie.

Maugg made the movie as a film school project, and it earned him more than a diploma. He has accompanied it to festivals from Ukraine to Japan, and is earning a few extra marks from its unexpected theatrical release in the United States and elsewhere.

"The Olympic Summer"is a remarkable thesis film, beautifully crafted and edited, and we'll give Maugg another A+ for his work here. But the film is nothing more than an exercise in style, an elaborate exhumation of obsolete motion picture technology. Except for the voice of a narrator (English translation provided), and music and sound effects synchronized to the action, "The Olympic Summer" plays like a melodrama that might have been made for the screen a decade before Hitler came to power.

Who says you can't halt progress?

NEW YORK POST, 8/3/94, p. 32, Bill Hoffmann

If you want to see some absolutely spectacular archival footage of pre-war Nazi Germany on the rise, catch "The Olympic Summer."

Because when it sticks to the beauty and uneasiness of these stark images—Hitler heiling at the games; happy beach bathers wearing swastikas—"The Olympic Summer" is dazzling.

Unfortunately, the filmmakers are up to tricks, trying to pull a cinematic rabbit out of a hat. At that, they're strictly amateur magicians. The film combines straightforward newsreel footage with newly shot black-and-white stock, which tells the story of a handsome young farm boy who travels from the countryside to see the 1936 Summer Olympics in Berlin.

On his way, he meets a wealthy 36-year-old widow who takes a fancy to him and puts him up on her estate. They begin a stormy affair which begins with dizzying champagne toasts and frenzied lovemaking.

It ends when the widow grows tired of him and he moves to Berlin, only to wind up with a lengthy jail term for being caught with another man during a misguided evening.

Will our hero ever be sprung or will he rot away before seeing his true love once again?

That question might have been a lot more compelling had the filmmakers been a little less artsy.

To match the mood of the documentary footage, director Gordian Maugg has used a hand-cranked 1927 camera to shoot the new material.

The technique makes the action appear slightly speeded up. Which would have been OK, had it been left that way.

But Maugg and company have gone one step further and used '90s optical trickery to further alter the material.

Slow motion and frame-by-frame stop motion are used freely throughout "The Olympic Summer" in most obvious and unneeded ways.

These are state-of-the-art tricks that give the film a phony, MTV edge.

Director Maugg is so into modern technique that he even changes focus from one of the characters to a condom.

Earlier this year, filmmaker Peter Delpeut used archival footage wonderfully in his fictionalized account of an arctic tragedy in "The Forbidden Quest."

Delpeut's film is an example of how it's done. Maugg shows how it's not.

VILLAGE VOICE, 8/9/94, p. 41, J. Hoberman

The Olympic Summer, which wafts into Film Forum as a belated postscript to *The Wonderful, Horrible Life of Leni Riefenstahl*, is a precise and distanced, hauntingly low-tech evocation of the Third Reich at high noon—Nazi Germany basking in the glory of the 1936 Berlin Olympiad, which legitimized the regime to its subjects and to the world.

Like our own, somewhat more confused, *Forrest Gump*, *The Olympic Summer* is an exercise in hindsight; it similarly sets loose an innocent lad in a postmodern past blatantly constructed out of newsreel footage, old popular music and archival broadcasts , all bound together with a particularly self-conscious use of technology. As its tour de force, *The Olympic Summer* was shot with a vintage, hand-cranked camera found by director Gordian Maugg in an East German animation studio.

Born 30 years after the Olympic summer, Maugg might be making a movie about his grandparents. The tone, as the title suggests, is mythological, but there's also a sense in which his technologically enhanced, imaginary landscape matches that of his subject: In preparation for the Olympic Games, the Nazis created something of a *Triumph of the Will* theme park; they not only transformed Berlin into an antiseptic Swastika World but strategically relaxed the laws against Jews in order to ease the minds of sensitive foreigners.

The Olympic Summer was Maugg's thesis project at the School of Fine Art in Kassel, and the movie's lengthy pretitle sequence is a tribute to the miracle of the medium. The first few minutes are frozen images of rural life accompanied by a hurdy-gurdy's hypnotic drone. A pig is butchered and then, as befits a magical fairground entertainment, another pig twitches into movement. *The Olympic Summer*, which has music, sound effects, and a voiceover narration but no dialogue, as suffused with movieness. The action is undercranked throughout, with the speed varied for emphasis; the shots of drifting clouds or the wind in the leaves suggest the archaic lyricism of early '30s art films.

Having saved his wages to purchase a bicycle, a 16-year-old apprentice butcher pedals from his Pomeranian village to Berlin to see the Olympics—barreling through the verdant countryside as though the camera were mounted on his bike. The capital, shown in 1936 cutaways as awash with tourists and festooned with festive swastikas fluttering in the breeze, is like a modern city on another planet. Seeking refuge from the dazzling streets in a working class bar, casually populated by raucous SA men, the butcher boy is swept into another sort of vision. As he sits slurping his pea soup, he's picked up by a wealthy widow twice his age. Like a dream, she whisks him away to her suburban villa and offers him the boat house as a place to stay.

The widow is plain but trim, good-natured and lusty. The boy is handsome and none too bright with the open, "honest" face of an Eisenstein worker. He's robust but shy—as the widow understands when, in a wonderfully tactile moment, she blindfolds herself as they first make love. The butcher's sexual initiation is echoed by the rising national excitement. The novelty song "I'm Crazy About Your Freckles" plays as the crowds stream into the vast new Olympic stadium.

Trained as a documentarian, Maugg integrates bits of Leni Riefenstahl's pompous *Olympiad*—a flash of Jesse Owens, a few glimpses of Hitler, the crowd using every opportunity to extend their arms in ecstatic salutes. As archival footage provides the mind-boggling image of ordinary Nazis cavorting on the beach, the butcher boy splashes in happy indolence with the passionate widow, learning what the narrator calls "the secret of the reeds." She has told him that it is hopeless to try to get tickets for the Olympics, although their idyll is punctuated by the repeated image of her roadster leaving on some mysterious errand in the city.

For its first 40 minutes, *The Olympic Summer* offers a measured rhythm of close-ups and long shots against a backbeat of wistful tangos, with the compassionate narration by Wenders angel Otto Sander evoking the sense of some imperfectly understood perfection inexorably slipping away. As autumn ripens, the boy moves into Berlin, placing *The Olympic Summer* in the venerable German concern with rural innocence and urban corruption. Now the city seems overwhelming. A nocturnal neon montage, at once seductive and alienating, evokes such Weimar proto-noirs as *Asphalt Tragedy of the Street*.

The widow's visits grow less frequent and, left to his own limited devices, the boy is picked up by a homosexual SS man (a tattered Olympic poster in background). Without understanding how it happens, he's involved in a killing and sentenced to two years in prison, where wordless routines are enlivened only by painful memories of the previous summer. As if to underscore these unnecessary flashbacks, a failed escape adds eight years to his sentence.

The Olympic Summer is more a fairy tale than an allegory, but the hapless butcher boy's fate is unmistakably bound up with that of the German people—even if he experiences World War II via radio from his cell. *The Olympic Summer* has a brilliant first half, followed by a slow, grim decline. (Although only 84 minutes long, the movie could afford to lose another 10.) Perhaps this pattern is itself overdetermined, for Maugg does contrive an elegantly ironic ending: Still living in the past, the principals cannot recognize the present. Their glorious Olympian summer was a fleeting illusion—they are mortal after all.

Also reviewed in:
NEW YORK TIMES, 8/3/94, p. C16, Stephen Holden
VARIETY, 10/11/93, p. 72, Ken Eisner

ON DEADLY GROUND

A Warner Bros. release of a Seagal/Nasso production. *Executive Producer:* Robert Watts and Jeffrey Robinov. *Producer:* Steven Seagal, Julius R. Nasso, and A. Kitman Ho. *Director:* Steven Seagal. *Screenplay:* Ed Horowitz and Robin U. Russin. *Director of Photography:* Ric Waite. *Editor:* Robert A. Ferretti and Don Brochu. *Music:* Basil Poledouris. *Music Editor:*

Curtis Roush. *Sound:* Edward Tise, Gordon Ecker, Jr. and (music) Tim Boyle. *Sound Editor:* John Leveque and Richard E. Yawn. *Casting:* Pamela Basker and Carol Carlson. *Production Designer:* William Ladd Skinner. *Art Director:* Lou Montejeno. *Set Designer:* Nick Navarro. *Set Decorator:* John Anderson and Ronald R. Reiss. *Special Effects:* Thomas L. Fisher. *Special Miniature Effects:* John Striber. *Costumes:* Joseph G. Aulisi. *Make-up:* Jef Simons. *Stunt Coordinator:* Glenn Randall. *Running time:* 90 minutes. *MPAA Rating:* R.

CAST: Steven Seagal (Forrest Taft); Michael Caine (Michael Jennings); Joan Chen (Masu); John C. McGinley (MacGruder); R. Lee Ermey (Stone); Shari Shattuck (Liles); Billy Bob Thornton (Homer Carlton); Richard Hamilton (Hugh Palmer); Chief Irvin Brink (Silook); Apanguluk Charlie Kairaiuak (Tunrak); Elsie Pistolhead (Takanapsaluk); John Trudell (Johnny Redfeather); Mike Starr (Big Mike); Swen-Ole Thorsen (Otto); Jules Desjarlais (Drunken Eskimo); Moses Wassille (Joseph Ittok); Nanny Kagak (Elak); Irvin Kershner (Walters); Kenji (Rook); Todd Beadle (Collins); Ivan Kane (Spinks); David John Cervantes (Stokes); David Selburg (Harold); Arisa Wolf (Make-up Woman); Carlotta Chang (Dream Woman); Reid Asato (Etok); Fumiyasu Daikyu (Maktak); Warren Tabata (Oovi); Joe Lala (Guard); Chic Daniel (Chic); Jim Farnum (Reporter); Conrad E. Palmisano (Richter); Webster Whinery (Independent); David Paris and Gary Farrell (Helicopter Pilots); Debbie Houk (Bar Woman); Brian Simpson (Mr. Bear); Peter Navy Tulasosopo and Craig Ryan Ng (Workers); Nicole Mier and Summer Holmstrand (Little Girls); Billie Jo Price (Girl's Mother); Patrick Gorman and Chris Dunn (Oil Executives).

LOS ANGELES TIMES, 2/21/94, Calendar/p. 10, Kevin Thomas

With "On Deadly Ground," Steven Seagal not only makes his directorial debut but also risks combining action with a message, a deadly serious, intelligent protest against the threat to the environment posed by the oil industry. He also does some consciousness-raising in regard to the rights of Native Americans and the spiritual values Inuit culture has to offer all of us.

Although you could certainly wish that Seagal and his writers, Ed Horowitz and Robin U. Russin, could have found less preachy ways to express themselves, "On Deadly Ground" is otherwise lively entertainment for action fans. Seagal is to be admired for using his stardom to send a warning; most people at the first show at the AMC Century 14 last Friday sat through Seagal's much-publicized long, impassioned speech. What he has to say is important, and he may succeed in reaching a segment of the audience who have never thought about the environment.

In plot, "On Deadly Ground" is simplicity itself. Seagal plays an oil rigger for Michael Caine's oil company. Caine is racing against a tight deadline in getting his Alaskan oil rig and refinery in operation. If he misses the deadline, his oil rights, which he's held for 20 years, revert to the Eskimos. Nevertheless, Seagal, a regular Red Adair when it comes to putting out oil fires, discovers that Caine has been cutting corners to the extent of endangering the environment; this knowledge, in turn, endangers Seagal's life.

"On Dangerous Ground," a handsome, big-budget production, has a comic book sensibility in which Seagal is a super-hero up against villains of the deepest hue. However, along with his own star presence, Seagal has lined up other strong pluses. The majesty of cameraman Ric Waite's images of Alaska's snowy wilderness is matched by Basil Poledouris' sweeping score. Best of all is Caine's deliciously nasty villain, hot-tempered, ruthless, his evil underlined by a dark, severe dye job. Caine's chief minion is an ultra-hyper John C. McGinley, and Joan Chen is the beautiful Native American activist with whom Seagal shares the final fade-out.

NEW YORK, 3/7/94, p. 65, John Powers

Having spent his early career killing nearly everyone on the planet, Steven Seagal is now worried about the fate of what's left. In his directorial debut, *On Deadly Ground*, he has to stop an oil baron (Michael Caine) from despoiling Alaska. Perhaps it is a failure of imagination, but I don't get why anyone takes this guy seriously. With his soft chin, black-shirted paunch, and ponytail the size of a chihuahua's penis, Seagal looks more like a schnorrer at a Hollywood party than like the toughest man in creation.

NEW YORK POST, 2/19/94, p. 19, Thelma Adams

Real men don't need critics. Ask Steven Seagal.

In "On Deadly Ground," the pony-tailed, bone-crunching leading man directed himself—and refused to screen the movie for critics before opening day.

After the monster hit "Under Siege," Seagal could write his own meal ticket. For his directorial debut, he chose a hawk-and-mouse eco-thriller set in the 49th state. Told in oil black and igloo white, it's "Billy Jack" meets "Dances with Alaskan Huskies."

Seagal plays Forrest (pun intended?) Taft, a security consultant for Aegis Oil, a company drilling the Alaska coast and run by the oily Michael Jennings (Michael Caine). Forrest falls for an environmentalist Inuit, Masu (Joan Chen), and goes on a spiritual journey—but not before he kicks some major oil rigger butt.

Seagal does a fine job directing himself. At least his performance is no worse than expected, although he's more humor-impaired than usual. Then again this is about a serious subject: THE ENVIRONMENT! Seagal waddles along with his usual beady-eyed deadpan.

Michael ("Dirty Rotten Scoundrels") Caine delivers his patented smarmy Scrooge routine, varied only by a bolo tie. It's a one-note performance that only goes from bad to bad, and raises nostalgia for Tommy Lee Jones' searing "Under Siege" villain.

Joan ("Golden Gate") Chen starts out feisty and radical but is soon reduced to running a traditional three steps behind her leading man and his chunky butt. For all the explosives set by the duo to level an offending oil rig, there's no romantic charge between Chen and Seagal.

Seagal clumsily wedges his big environmental message into the drama itself. With all the petty villains getting bones crunched, faces blasted, and bodies pureed by helicopter propellers, it's possible to forget that the big bad wolves are government and big business working in cahoots to poison the common man.

In an epilogue reminiscent of the Time-Life documentaries forced on high school civics students, Seagal spends the movie's final three minutes preaching to the converted—Indians in full native dress—about the evils of the internal combustion engine. (His speech was originally 10 minutes long but was cut at the urging of Warner Bros.)

Real men care about the environment—but, first, they like to blow things up.

NEWSDAY, 2/19/94, Part II/p. 27, Terry Kelleher

Who'd have thought Steven Seagal was not only a martial-arts master but a genuine Greenpeace warrior? Who'd have thought that for his directorial debut he'd do a big-budget "Billy Jack Goes to Alaska"? This hombre is a constant source of surprise.

"On Deadly Ground" starts out like a "National Geographic Special" (dig those peaks and polar bears), shows signs of becoming a standard Seagal butt-kicker (a protracted bar fight breaks out after a loudmouth questions the hero's heterosexuality), detours into "Dances With Wolves" territory (Inuits nurse the wounded hero back to health, dosing him heavily with mysticism) and finally resolves itself in the expected orgy of cracking bones, blazing guns and raging fires.

Through the sound and fury, however, an environmentalist message clearly emerges: America has one precious resource, one natural wonder, that the polluters and profiteers can never destroy—Steven Seagal.

From the moment Seagal first strides into view, and the awestruck camera pans slowly from his boots to his ponytail, it's obvious he will brook no serious resistance for the sixth film in a row. His oil-baron boss (Michael Caine, disguised by "Addams Family"-brand hair dye) tries to silence Seagal's dissent by arranging his death in a little explosion, but that incident merely provides the Inuit samaritans an opportunity to expand the hero's consciousness and inflate his ego. When he returns to torch Caine's refinery and slaughter his minions, Seagal's beautiful, formerly peace-loving Inuit companion (Joan Chen) urges him to give no quarter.

"On Deadly Ground" would be a more exciting movie if the secondary characters didn't keep interrupting the action to extol Seagal's toughness and spirituality. For sure, it would be a shorter movie if Seagal didn't insist on closing with a save-the-planet slide show. All hail the expressionless environmentalist.

SIGHT AND SOUND, 5/94, p. 47, Tom Tunney

Alaska. Aegis Oil Company president Michael Jennings and his top troubleshooter Forrest Taft helicopter to the scene of an oil well fire, where Taft uses explosives to extinguish the blaze. He is accused by his old friend Hughie of selling out to the company. Later, Taft intervenes in a bar-room brawl to help a Native Alaskan who has been insulted by a roughneck. Meanwhile, Jennings films a TV advert which stresses Aegis Oil's concern for the environment. It emerges that the rig and refinery have to be operational in 13 days or the oil rights will revert to the Native Alaskan population. Taft investigates the cause of the fire and discovers that defective blow-out preventers had been used. He notes that a shipment of new preventers will not make the deadline; the rig will cause a pollution disaster if it goes into operation using the defective equipment.

Jennings' henchman MacGruder and a sidekick torture and kill Hughie in a vain bid to discover the whereabouts of a computer file which details the company's malpractice. At a press conference, Jennings is questioned by the Native Alaskans and has oil thrown on him by Masu, the daughter of Chief Silook. Jennings persuades Taft to help him repair a sub-station fault. Arriving by helicopter, Taft finds Hughie's body in the plant just before it is detonated by remote control. Taft is rescued by the Native Alaskans; his wounds are treated by Silook and Masu, and the old man teaches him about the power of nature.

Silook is shot by MacGruder, who comes looking for Taft. Taking his leave of the dying old man, Taft travels to Hughie's house with Masu to recover the computer disc, running into a group of MacGruder's heavies as he retrieves it. Taft decides to destroy the new rig and heads off on horseback with Masu to his secret weapons dump. Meanwhile, Jennings has hired a group of contract assassins led by Stone. MacGruder, Stone and their team give chase, but Taft is able to blow up their helicopter. Taft and Masu escape and fight their way on to the rig. After picking off Jennings' men, including MacGruder, Taft confronts Jennings, who is still attempting to get the rig operational. Jennings falls to his death into the pool of crude oil below, and Taft and Masu make their escape as the rig explodes. At a hearing in the state capital, Taft makes a speech warning that big business will continue to pollute the environment so long as they can make a profit from it.

"We've got nothing on this guy before 1987" says one of the hired guns pursuing Forrest Taft. It could be taken as a wry reference to Steven Seagal's own rapid rise in the late 80s from obscure martial arts teacher to action movie superstar. This is Seagal's sixth film and the first in which he directs himself. However, one has to go back to his 1988 movie *Above the Law* to find a precursor of the crusading speech which concludes *On Deadly Ground*. There, just before the closing credits, Seagal's voice-over declaims sternly against those in high political office who consider themselves to be "above the law".

Above the Law was intriguing because as well as ably showcasing Seagal's martial arts skills—and including a clever autobiographical reference to his long sojourn in Japan—it pitted him against a CIA which was presented explicitly as having sanctioned mass murder both in 70s South East Asia and contemporary Central America. The shallow contours of the 80s action movie were thus deepened and given a left-of-centre slant. In *Above the Law*, Seagal effectively announced himself as a new kind of action hero with a new brand of political consciousness.

In *On Deadly Ground*, Seagal carries forward that film's subversive promise and ambitious political reach by taking on the entire system of multi-national big business. The film is remarkable for its singleminded contempt for everything business stands for, personified by Michael Caine's corrupt, nostril-flaring villain Jennings. It's a strange theme for a project financed by a major Hollywood studio and it offers a bleak vision. Of course, Taft destroys the rig, but the grim speech and archive pollution footage suggest he's merely won one battle in a near-unwinnable war.

It is a brave way to end an action movie, but Seagal's star image has always been that of crusading hero who is simultaneously on the inside and on the outside of the institutions of power. He's always a wilful nonconformist due to his (heavily implied) experiences during the Vietnam era. And invariably, he rejects conventional Western values in favour of wisdom acquired in the East. *On Deadly Ground* conforms to these requirements, with Seagal the director employing an unfussy style to showcase his character's heroic stature. However, that image is broadened to include self-consciously mythic, nationalistic and Western hero dimensions.

Like a cavalry scout, Seagal's oil troubleshooter mediates between the worlds of the white man and the Native American. The film's stark presentation of industrial relations is also straight out of a Western, with Jennings as the scheming Easterner, Taft's doomed friend Hughie blatantly wearing his frontier integrity in the form of his checked shirt, and John McGinley and R. Lee Ermey playing modern versions of the kind of callous hired guns Brian Donlevy and John Carradine would have played 50 years ago. However, as well as being a natural force and a Western-style hero, Taft is also presented as a kind of intellectualised, left-field Rambo—but with none of Rambo's self-pity and moral confusion.

Above the Law included scenes set in the jungle of 1973 South East Asia; *On Deadly Ground* brings Vietnam-style warfare to the Alaskan wilderness. In his running battle with Stone's mercenaries, Taft deploys all the paraphernalia of jungle guerrilla combat: deadly booby traps, claymore mines, an M-26 rifle and plastic explosives. Unlike Rambo, Taft isn't emotionally scarred by his past experiences but strengthened by them. The implication is that the discipline of his martial arts—and the wisdom of Eskimo folklore—have allowed him to see through the corruption and confusion of modern life to a personal salvation. That, perhaps more than anything, is the key characteristic of Seagal's star image: his confidence both in his fighting abilities and his personal moral values.

Like John Wayne in the 50s and Clint Eastwood in the 60s, Seagal is despised by middlebrow critics who don't seem to realise that the deadpan humour in his work is intentional. Here, the fawning low camera angle which heralds his first appearance, a script in which the bad guys take turns in lavishly singing his praises and, above all, the scene in which he says, "I didn't want to resort to violence," before walking in a room packed with pre-positioned weapons, point to his parch-dry sense of humour. Of course the plot is wilfully absurd—Taft explodes an oil well to stop the pollution of Alaska—but an energetically absurd storyline has always been one of the prime requirements of an action movie. Here Seagal takes the formula by the scruff of the neck and throws it into challenging new territory.

Who else of the current crop of bemuscled action stars could convincingly turn a bar-room brawl into a learning experience and who else would dare end an action movie with a long, business-bashing speech? Steven Seagal may have a limited range as an actor, but within those limits, to quote from another fiery oil well movie, *Hellfighters*, "he's "the best there is at what he does."

TIME, 3/7/94, p. 75, Richard Corliss

Steven Seagal comes to save Alaska but nearly destroys it. It *On Deadly Ground*, the art of moviemaking gets totaled too.

In his directorial debut, this pony-tailed stud—the most consistently successful action star worldwide—kicks butt in the name of political correctness. He plays Forrest Taft, the usual genius renegade from the CIA who bonds with sacred Inuit spirits and works every woodland trick in the boy scout manual. He also thwarts an oil company run by evil Michael Caine. But first a few good guys must be beaten, kicked and de-fingered, all to give Forrest an excuse to cripple his enemies and blow up most of Alaska.

This is sadism with scruples. But in all his movies Seagal snacks on villains as if they were sunflower seeds. In *Marked for Death* he broke the lead villain's body—snap!—over his knee. In *Under Siege*, by far the snazziest of Seagal's films, he got to smash Tommy Lee Jones' head through a computer screen. Faced with a bunch of thugs in *Hard to Kill*, he used his fatal grace to dispatch all but the gang leader, then tossed his weapon aside to give the gun-toting goon a sporting chance. Talk about your Zen machismo; he lets the bad guys shoot first because he knows they can't shoot straight.

Director Seagal can't shoot straight either. The choppy pace and inane plot exertions make *On Deadly Ground* a $40 million vanity epic. At least Warner Bros., Seagal's sponsor, cut the star's climactic lecture on the environment—antibusiness and boldly pro-plankton—from a reported 10 minutes to just over three. It's fine to think an audience is stupid but not to leave it in a stupor.

Also reviewed in:
NEW YORK TIMES, 2/19/94, p. 11, Janet Maslin

VARIETY, 2/21-27/94, p. 42, Leonard Klady
WASHINGTON POST, 2/19/94, p. G5, Richard Harrington

ONLY THE BRAVE

A Scorpio Film Productions release of a Scorpio Film Productions/VPRO-TV coproduction. *Producer:* Kees Rijninks. *Director:* Sonia Herman Dolz. *Screenplay (Spanish with English subtitles):* Sonia Herman Dolz. *Director of Photography:* Ellen Kuras. *Editor:* Andrez de Jong. *Music:* Leo Anemaet. *Running time:* 89 minutes. *MPAA Rating:* Not Rated.

WITH: Enrique Ponce; Manuel Tornay; Juan Antonio Maguilla; Jose Sanchez; Antonio Novillo.

NEWSDAY, 8/31/94, Part II/p. B7, Gene Seymour

The inflated macho mumbo-jumbo infesting much that's been written or filmed about bullfighting is kept to a minimum in "Only the Brave." Sonia Herman Dolz, the Spanish-born Dutch filmmaker, doubtless started out wanting to do much more than that in this documentary, which spends almost as much time with the bulls as it does with the matadors.

Dolz aims for cool balance as opposed to gaudy spectacle in this accomplished and fascinating chronicle of a bullfighting tour in Spain during the summer of 1992. She lets both the passions and processes that drive the sport speak for themselves. The sadness in the eyes of the bull breeder as he watches his charges romping around a rolling meadow is framed with as much meaning and portent as the glint in the eye of the aficionado as he reads about the up-and-coming matador Enrique Ponce.

The 20-year-old Ponce, who looks both callow and commanding, is the central figure in Dolz' travelogue. All the images of bullfighting's past, present and future (youngsters are shown learning how to move their capes) swirl around Ponce's pensive, magnetic presence as he moves towards a climactic battle in Barcelona that comes to a remarkably satisfying denouement.

Before that happens, Dolz and her talented cinematographer Ellen Kuras show us everything there is to see about the sport, even a vanquished bull being gutted, skinned and boned after a fight. Such queasy images are offset by the artistry and grace of Ponce and his peers as they carry out their spectacular moves. Whatever one's feeling about this blood sport, Dolz' level-headed approach demonstrates why it's hard to shake the faith of those who believe in its primal force.

It seems even Dolz was seduced by the death dance between man and bull. This won't make animal-rights activists very happy. But as the film's somewhat surprising ending suggests, even one's worst expectations for what can happen in a bull ring can be either fulfilled or subdued—which explains why all sports, bloody or not, exert their transcendent and enduring appeal.

VILLAGE VOICE, 9/6/94, p. 55, Georgia Brown

At one point in *Only the Brave*, Sonia Herman Dolz's entertaining, occasionally invigorating, documentary on bullfighting, a background radio barks news of the L.A. riots: Troops have been called in; a tally of the dead and wounded follows. Not so subtly, it seems, the Spanish-born, Dutch-reared filmmaker anticipates a squeamish American critique of her subject and, in response, wonders about a culture where rites of manhood often involve going mano a mano with cops. Bullfighting from this perspective could look like such a civilized ritual.

What the filmmaker probably doesn't realize is that bullfighting rarely enters Americans' minds. Especially since Hemingway stuck those double-barrels into his mouth. The more likely response to the subject: Oh, they're still doing *that*? Over here a film about bullfighting seems like an anachronism. So get out your *Death in the Afternoon* and try to remember what the fuss was all about.

If Dolz can be trusted, the corrida—in Spain anyway—is alive and well. Bulls are still bred with loving care and fanaticism. Small boys practice their passes to become young men with shapely butts working their way up in the profession. A goring in Seville triggers a national outpouring of grief. Men in bars relive the day's events in the ring. The rhetoric lives.

And now—as a sop to new sentiments—there is even talk of pardoning the rare bull who puts up an especially noble fight. This innovation seems to make everyone happy: breeders who want to improve the bloodline; matadors who can see themselves not simply as killers but as benign priests; the audience that finds its taste for excellence ratified. So for the first time, in the sport that has death written into the rules of the game, death may not take place each and every time.

Although nowhere as brash and scathing as Bigas Luna's recent *Jamon, Jamon, Only The Brave* presents the bullfight in the context of familiar Spanish obsessions: machismo, Catholicism, color, song, fiesta. There's even a sequence showing a man being shaved—shaving being a fraught masculine ritual that crops up in practically every Spanish film this century. In one nice shot (the cinematographer is *Swoon*'s Ellen Kuras) the crucified Jesus resembles a martyred torero—in the context, his wounds look like he's been gored.

For her narrative centerpiece, Dolz follows a rising 20-year-old matador, Enrique Ponce, on the summer circuit. Ponce has a soft, good-looking, but unformed face and, because we don't see much of his fighting until the very end, it takes a while to accept him as a full-fledged torero. We do watch him being outfitted—choosing between pink and blue jackets, pulling on his fuchsia stockings and garters, struggling into the tight pants, slipping into his dainty slippers. We see him set up makeshift shrines to the Virgin in his various hotel rooms. The reality of his occupation finally sinks in when, on the phone, his mother begs him to stop fighting: "It's getting too much for us. We can't take it anymore." Just after this conversation, we're finally shown Ponce's meeting with what everyone agrees is a noble bull.

In voiceover, Ponce delivers the sport's rationale and aesthetics. A few samples: "Bullfighting is the deceit of the animal by man; it's about intelligence against strength ... It's also about creating a composition, a sculpture, as the bull passes ... How can I, weighing 60 kilos, avoid an attack and create an art?"

The bull, so far as we know, has no comparable phrases to facilitate his death. (Yet it is almost always you-know-who who dies.) On the animal's behalf, Dolz exercises some visual irony, juxtaposing a speaker's rhetoric about "moment of truth" and "the death of my noble opponent" being "the most beautiful death," with footage of the stiffened carcass dragged from the arena, then hacked, skinned, butchered, and boiled, until at last the noble head is reconstructed as a noble wall plaque.

But it's the man's death, or his risk anyway, that has always given bullfighting a certain status as metaphor. Except for prefacing her film with Oscar Wilde's lines about every man killing the thing he loves (the coward doing it with a kiss, the brave man with a sword), Dolz forgoes the literary aspect of the sport. Clearly, she's not of my generation. We learned about bullfighting from *The Sun Also Rises* (" 'Funny,' Brett said. 'How one doesn't mind the blood.' "), and later perhaps from the pained convolutions of Michel Leiris in "The Autobiographer as Torero," the afterword to his magnificent *Manhood* ("I was dreaming, then, of a bull's horn").

Although her film contains any number of superfluous lyrical flourishes, Dolz's doc is strongest when taking a prosaic—almost a child's eye-view of bullfighting. I can appreciate how difficult this is with a subject so loaded with bullshit.

Also reviewed in:
NEW YORK TIMES, 8/31/94, p. C14, Stephen Holden
VARIETY, 4/25-5/1/94, p. 32, David Rooney

ONLY YOU

A TriStar Pictures release of a Fried/Woods Films and Yorktown Productions, Ltd. production. *Producer:* Norman Jewison, Cary Woods, Robert N. Fried, and Charles Mulvehill. *Director:* Norman Jewison. *Screenplay:* Diane Drake. *Director of Photography:* Sven Nykvist. *Editor:* Stephen Rivkin. *Music:* Rachel Portman. *Music Editor:* Bill Abbott. *Sound:* Ken Weston and (music) Dick Lewzey. *Sound Editor:* Michael O'Farrell and Wayne Griffin. *Casting:* Howard

Feuer. *Production Designer:* Luciana Arrighi. *Art Director:* Stephano Ortolani and Maria Teresa Barbasso. *Set Decorator:* Ian Whittaker and Alessandra Querzola. *Set Dresser:* Catherine Stanton. *Special Effects:* Dennis Dion. *Costumes:* Milena Canonero. *Make-up:* Fabrizio Sforza and Joanne Gair. *Running time:* 108 minutes. *MPAA Rating:* PG.

CAST: Marisa Tomei (Faith Corvatch); Robert Downey, Jr. (Peter Wright); Bonnie Hunt (Kate); Joaquim de Almeida (Giovanni); Fisher Stevens (Larry); Billy Zane (The False Damon Bradley); Adam LeFevre (Damon Bradley); John Benjamin Hickey (Dwayne); Siobhan Fallon (Leslie); Antonia Rey (Fortune Teller); Phyllis Newman (Faith's Mother); Denise Du Maurier (Dwayne's Mother); Tammy Minoff (Young Faith); Harry Barandes (Young Larry); Jessica Hertel (Young Kate); Rick Applegate and Marc Field (TWA Gate Attendants); Bob Tracey (Foot Patient); Gianfranco Barra (Danieli Concierge); Barbara Cupisti (Anna); Sergio Pierattini (Pension Waiter); Giovanni Di Benedetto (Pension Concierge); Domenico Pane (Le Sirenuse Concierge); Fiorenzo Fiorentini (Old Man); Francesco Romei (Flower Vendor); Buck Herron (Man with Medallion); Amanda Lohman (Girl at Pool); Shari Summers (Woman with Suede Boots); Cristina Formichi Moglia (Information Desk Attendant); Mattia Sbragia (Alitalia Pilot); Diane Jones (Alitalia Flight Attendant); James Sampson (Saxophone Player); Claudio Padovan (Boat Driver); K. J. Roberts (Airport Security Guard); Gregory Gibson Kenny (State Police Officer); Antone di Leo (Taxi Driver); Jaclyn Urso, Jessica Merlin, and Bethany Smocer (Girls at the Carnival); Gina Maria Trello (Girl in Classroom); Victor Buhler (Waiter at Party); Dina Morrone (Shoe Show Announcer).

LOS ANGELES TIMES, 10/7/94, Calendar/p. 4, Kenneth Turan

"Only You" is mostly ersatz. An implausible romantic comedy that is flimsy even by the classic standards of the genre, it counts on star power to compensate for a lack of originality, but it is not to be.

A fluffy knockoff of "Sleepless in Seattle" that makes that film's charming plot seem as rigorously logical as a mathematical theorem, "Only You" owes so much to so many movies the word derivative isn't quite strong enough.

While stars are defined by their ability to carry vehicles others couldn't begin to lift, Marisa Tomei and Robert Downey Jr., certainly an engaging couple, are not up to the task here. Diane Drake's script, directed by Norman Jewison, could strain the star power of Cary Grant and Grace Kelly, and Tomei and Downey, although they try their hardest, lack the heft to pull it off.

For a while, Tomei has the job all by herself. In a pair of brief prologues, Faith Corvatch is glimpsed as quite an impressionable young girl. First, at age 11, she and her bratty brother Larry manipulate a Ouija board to determine the name of her life's soul mate. The answer: Damon Bradley.

Then, a couple of years later, a shady fortuneteller at a carnival utters the same name, along with a bit of pivotal advice: "The truth is, you make your own destiny. Don't wait for it to come to you."

Cut to 14 years later, when Faith is a perky teacher in a Catholic school, engaged to a fussy podiatrist named Dwayne who made the ultimate sacrifice at the moment of proposing: He turned off his beeper.

But true to her name, Faith, a romantic who loves watching Ezio Pinza and Mary Martin sing "Some Enchanted Evening," has not given up on her childhood fantasy of a soul mate named Damon Bradley. All this to the scorn of best friend and sister-in-law Kate (Bonnie Hunt), married to the grown-up but still drippy Larry (Fisher Stevens), who understandably thinks love is largely an imaginary notion.

All these issues might have remained theoretical except for a phone call from a long lost-friend of Dwayne's, who talks only long enough to tell Faith he's on his way to Venice and leave his name. Yes, it's Damon Bradley.

Never mind that Faith is only 10 days away from her wedding. She has to find out if this Damon Bradley is *her* Damon Bradley, and, with a dubious but protective Kate in tow, immediately boards a plane for Italy to bring her quarry to earth.

Even if you buy this premise (a sizable if) and admire Marisa Tomei's squeaky energy (somewhat easier to do), the twists "Only You" takes in Italy are predictable, preposterous or both as Faith pursues Damon through a host of feebly imagined difficulties.

Not even the appearance of a lively Robert Downey Jr. as a New Jersey shoe salesman who claims to be Damon Bradley clears things up. Increasingly wearing and bogus obstacles arise, and the question of whether this match is destiny or not gets dragged out to unnatural lengths.

What is dragged into the mix are Kate's marital problems, as, not surprisingly, she is having Larry trouble. Trying to make her forget she even has a husband is the suave Giovanni ("Clear and Present Danger's" Joaquim de Almeida), a standard-issue Italian who doesn't miss an opportunity to say things like "the female body has always been the mystery, the essence of human life."

All of "Only You's" stars acquit themselves solidly, with Hunt making the strongest impression as the cynical Kate. But director Jewison, who covered similar territory more efficiently in "Moonstruck," does not appear to have his heart in this version.

With loving shots of swank yachts, romantic restaurants and the kind of hotels the rich and famous frequent, "Only You" plays more like a pleasant travelogue than an involving film. While those desperate for even hollow romanticism will perhaps be satisfied, put up the slightest bit of resistance to this film and it falls apart in your hands.

NEW YORK POST, 10/7/94, p. 37, Michael Medved

The company that produced "Sleepless in Seattle" (TriStar Pictures) has combined with the director of "Moonstruck" (Norman Jewison) to create a new comedy designed to delight the same diehard romantics who made the previous two films such enormous hits.

Like its predecessors, "Only You" focuses on the illogical but intractable notion that some higher power—call it deity or destiny, as you will—arranges our lives to bring us each together with our one true love.

No one cherishes this idea more fervently than this film's protagonist—a sweet, sensitive teacher at a Pittsburgh Catholic school who's appropriately named Faith and who's perfectly played by Marisa Tomei.

For most of life, she's been waiting to meet someone named Damon Bradley—since a Ouija board told her at age 11 that this was the name of her predestined mate and a carnival fortune teller later came up with the same mysterious moniker.

Now, as a young adult, she's put aside these prophecies and settled into a safe, sensible engagement to a pompous podiatrist (John Benjamin Hickey). During a fitting for her wedding dress, however, she gets a call from one of her fiance's old friends who phones while changing planes for Venice, Italy. He offers best wishes and leaves his name—which just happens to be Damon Bradley.

Stricken with the sense that she may be missing her destiny, Faith bolts to the airport to intercept the stranger, and ends up following the phantom all the way to Europe.

In the best Lucy-and-Ethel tradition, she's accompanied by her best friend and sister-in-law (Bonnie Hunt) on a chase through Italy, with gorgeous locations made richly satisfying through glorious cinematography by the great Sven Nykvist.

In Rome, they cross paths with Robert Downey Jr.—a witty shoe salesman from Boston who's instantly smitten with Tomei and feels certain, even without help from a Ouija board, that she's his predestined one.

The witty script (by first-timer Diane Drake) is so richly endowed with shocking turnabouts and cute reverses that you'll find yourself admiring the writing just as much as you do the expert performances.

Tomei, in contrast to her Oscar-winning earthiness in "My Cousin Vinnie," projects en ethereal aura that gives this fairy tale its magical glow: Her pretty feet barely seem to touch the ground and she'll remind many viewers of the late Audrey Hepburn a resemblance that's enhanced by restaging a memorable scene from "Roman Holiday."

Of course, this film never explains why a teacher owns so many high-fashion outfits, or could afford this last-minute Italian vacation at a series of five-star hotels. But breathless romances aren't really expected to make much sense.

Another problem involves the devious maneuvers of the Robert Downey character, which the audience may find more difficult to forgive than do his fellow characters.

Nevertheless, he maintains an impish appeal which like the cunning charm of the movie itself disarms resistance and should send a dazzled audience home in a pleasant mood of happily-ever-after.

NEWSDAY, 10/7/94, Part II/p. 2, Jack Mathews

You know you're biting into something awfully sweet when the major character in a romantic comedy about love and destiny is named Faith and Norman Jewison's "Only You" could rot your teeth before you even get to its caramel-topped, three-scoop, Haagen-Dazs banana-split ending.

Shamelessly derivative of "Sleepless in Seattle," "Only You" is the story of a Pittsburgh schoolteacher (Marisa Tomei) who, nine days before her scheduled wedding to a foot doctor with a swelled head, takes off for Europe to find the one man she believes she was meant to have.

At 11, already a hopeless romantic, Faith had asked both a Ouija board and a carnival fortune teller whom she would marry, and both agreed his name was Damon Bradley. Fourteen years later, as she is about to settle for a podiatrist so dull your feet would reject him, fate pays Faith a call. Literally. The phone rings, and it's ... *him!* He's an old friend of her fiance and just called to say hello on his way to Italy.

Still in the wedding gown she was trying on, and with her best friend, Kate, (Bonnie Hunt), in tow, Faith impulsively follows Damon Bradley—tall, dark and handsome, or short, fat and ugly, married or single, serial killer or CEO—all the way to Italy.

This all happens in the first 10 or 15 minutes of the movie, so romantics hoping for the sort of honest emotion of Jewison's Oscar-nominated "Moonstruck" will be quickly advised to lower their expectations. And the lower the better. There are no honest emotions in "Only You," just a series of schoolgirl fantasies—swoons, disappointments, mistaken identities and, in the end, forced sentiment.

Jewison, with a first script by Diane Drake, has lifted the romantic ideal of "Sleepless in Seattle," the endlessly appealing notion that two people among the gazillions may be fated for each other, and foregone all the work Nora Ephron did in making them seem a perfect match. Hers was a fantasy grounded by recognizable and likable people who needed things we knew each could give the other.

It was movie love, pure shmaltz liquor, but it did the trick.

"Only You" doesn't dip a toe in reality, and the romance that develops between Faith and the lovestruck Boston shoe salesman (Robert Downey Jr.) who may or may not be Damon Bradley, is so contrived and baseless their future together looks like a perennial blind date.

In fact, the movie is more a situation than romantic comedy. You have two young women, one engaged to a man she doesn't love, the other married to a man she thinks no longer loves her, wandering through scenic Italy (with cinematographer Sven Nykvist framing every gorgeous vista) because of a Ouija board prediction!

Imagine the possibilities. Faith could meet and fall instantly in love with a man who identifies himself as Damon Bradley, but who, after one moonlit stroll and a thousand kisses, announces that his real name is Peter Wright. She would be appalled, of course, and continue her search for what's-his-name, but we will know, from a script that both telegraphs and *names* its punches, that Faith didn't meet Mr. Wright for nothing.

Meanwhile, Kate could have her deflated housewife's ego bolstered by the pursuit of a honey-voiced Latin lover (Joaquim De Almeida) and have to think about learning how to say "Oh, God!" in Italian.

As goofy and uninvolving as all this is, "Only You" does have a few good laughs, most of them due to Bonnie Hunt's snappy reading of the film's best lines. There is also a terrific dinner scene, between the smitten Faith and a hilariously flaky beefcake tourist (Billy Zane) she thinks is her Ouija squeeze.

Downey, who is fairly engaging in a pathetic puppy dog role, and Tomei, playing Faith as a cranky Audrey Hepburn, make a handsome couple, and by the end you may be convinced they were made for each other. But this is love at the shallow end of the pool, and it's definitely no way to see Italy.

SIGHT AND SOUND, 2/95, p. 48, Jo Comino

Pittsburgh. Eleven year-old Faith Corvatch and her brother Larry consult her ouija board about the identity of her future soul mate. The name Damon Bradley is spelled out. Three years later, at a fair, a fortune-teller comes up with an identical name.

At twenty-eight Faith is engaged to Dwayne, a podiatrist. A few days before the wedding she receives a phone call from one of her fiancé's school friends. The caller's name is Damon Bradley. Having ascertained that he is about to board a flight to Venice, Faith rushes to the airport for a sighting of the man she feels is destined for her. She is too late but decides to follow on the next plane. Her best friend and sister-in-law Kate, on the hop from her own marriage problems, accompanies her.

Once in Italy, Faith and Kate trace Damon to an exclusive Venetian hotel only to find him gone. They hire a car and make for Rome. Their only lead, a woman who works in a boutique, tells them where they can catch up with Damon that evening. Meanwhile Kate embarks on a flirtation with the boutique's proprietor, Giovanni. At the designated restaurant they glimpse Damon but he leaves before Faith can approach him. Tantalized, she runs after him, losing her shoe in the process. The shoe is retrieved by Peter Wright, a footwear salesman from Boston. Gleaning the requisite information, he passes himself off to Faith as Damon Bradley. The pair spend the night walking the streets of Rome in a romantic haze. They discover they have much in common; in other words, they are in love. When, however, Peter reveals his true identity, Faith is furious and spurns him.

Eventually Peter manages to persuade her that he will help pick up the real Damon's trail. Driving south to Positano with Giovanni and Kate, they track him down. Although Damon turns out to be impossibly handsome, Faith's date with him turns sour when he starts groping her; he is definitely not her type. Peter, ever watchful, intervenes and in the fight which ensues, the truth is revealed: this Damon is also an impostor hired by Peter to disillusion Faith. Irate, she breaks off her engagement and departs for home, just as Larry, in conciliatory mood, arrives in pursuit of Kate. Larry tells Kate that he set Faith up with the ouija board and the fortune-teller as a boyish prank.

At the airport Faith and Peter, in queues for separate flights, hear Damon Bradley's name being paged. Simultaneously they rush for the information desk to discover the real Damon, a middle-aged businessmen. Peter explains the situation and departs; Faith realises she loves him and gives chase. Though Peter's flight is closed, sympathetic airline staff allow Faith on board and the pair embrace to the applause of passengers and crew.

It seems appropriate, if more than a little pitiable, that contemporary romantic comedies should rely so heavily on dissertations on the meaning of love. Could this film do for Rilke's 'You Who Never Arrived' what *Four Weddings and a Funeral* has done for W.H. Auden in the poetry sales stakes? More arch even than that confection, *Only You*'s central thesis is the meeting of minds. Its heroine, Faith, teaches English at high school, which allows for a generous peppering of literary references. Her first scene as an adult finds her expounding impassionedly on the ideals of platonic love. Even the names are charged with çorny significance: Faith, trusting in destiny, searches for her swain, Damon, only to find her Mr Wright under her nose.

It is cinema, however, specifically that group of romantic comedies made and set in the 50s featuring the American ingenue on vacation in Italy—anything from *Three Coins in the Fountain* to *Roman Holiday*—which provides the main body of allusions. Indeed Faith and Peter's compatibility appears to hinge on the ease with which they're able to reenact the scene in *Roman Holiday* where Gregory Peck and Audrey Hepburn put their hands in the statue's mouth. The period feel lingers over the film, from the wedding gown foisted on Faith by her prospective mother-in-law, which she is conveniently modelling when the fateful phone call arrives and is subsequently too preoccupied to remove, to the interminable sight-seeing tours of fountains. Marisa Tomei as Faith has a kind of breathless elfin quality intended to mimic the ethereality of Hepburn, while even Giovanni's patter is reminiscent of Rossano Brazzi in *Summer Madness*.

It's as if romantic love is perceived to be a much-craved but easily denied commodity for contemporary audiences. Because it is seen to be untenable it has to be delivered second-hand, self-consciously, as a parody of itself. Hence the lush location shots, the glistening moonlit streets resembling the set of some classic musical, the gushiest opera arias alongside schmaltz such as

"Some Enchanted Evening" and "O Sole Mio" plus outrageous dialogue like, "I was born to kiss you". The film's saving grace, perhaps, resides in the more cynical characters, Peter and Kate, who wise-crack their way through the gunge.

At best *Only You* has something in common with Jewison's earlier and thoroughly enjoyable *Moonstruck*, where the intensity of the passion between Cher and Nicholas Cage managed to be both touching and ridiculous, a happy coincidence of the overblown and the mundane. Here, the effect is diluted because the site for romance is firmly fixed some place else, at some other time. The happy ending is delivered by benevolent Alitalia staff incanting the word *amore*; it deals in nostalgia and escapism, but not in emotions. For a light-hearted conceit about the tribulations of mistaken identity, *Only You* dabbles too deeply and a shade too moralistically on the nature of true love.

VILLAGE VOICE, 10/18/94, p. 54, Georgia Brown

Footloose and heartbroken in Rome, Robert Downey Jr. goes to the movies but can't sit still. "Woody Allen is not funny dubbed in Italian, so I left," he explains. Not funny in English is *Only You*, a romantic comedy that has Downey straining to look comfortable.

The low concept in this Norman Jewison-directed romance comes directly from *Sleepless in Seattle*. It's those old catchwords: destiny, fate, romance. Follow your bliss wait for your soul mate, even if Mr. Right is on the other side of the world and you've never met him. Yes, show once again what besotted idiots women can be. (And if *Sleepless* can have Sven Nykvist, let's get him too.)

What's in a name? Well, if it's Faith, quite a lot. Ever since Faith was 11 and her brother manipulated a Ouija board wedge to spell Damon Bradley, she's been waiting for someone by that name to claim her. So when the grown-up Faith (Marisa Tomei), a Pittsburgh schoolteacher, becomes engaged to a podiatrist (no, he doesn't have asthma) and a mysterious Damon Bradley calls to say he's in town on his way to Venice, what can she do but pursue him in her wedding dress (she was just trying it on). Forgive me if on the page any of this sounds the least bit charming.

Towing her amiable sister-in-law (Bonnie Hunt), Faith treats Italy as a dreary obstacle between herself and the elusive Damon B. For a schoolteacher, she has a spectacular wardrobe and in Rome we find out why: The way *Sleepless in Seattle*'s soul mate was *An Affair To Remember*, *Only You*'s is *Roman Holiday*! Which makes Marisa Tomei ... Audrey Hepburn. Someone has given Tomei the haircut and gowns but no one has done anything to conceive a character. Oh, Marisa, you nabbed your Oscar and then picked the wrong project!

Cognizant that he's not Gregory Peck—not this time anyway—Downey, as a Boston shoe salesman (shoe ... Cinderella, get it?), delivers his lines as if he's just found them under a paving stone. He's embarrassed, poor thing. And who wouldn't be?

Also reviewed in:
CHICAGO TRIBUNE, 10/7/94, Friday/p. J, Michael Wilmington
NEW YORK TIMES, 10/7/94, p. C12, Janet Maslin
VARIETY, 9/19-25/94, p. 76, Todd McCarthy
WASHINGTON POST, 10/7/94, p. B7, Rita Kempley
WASHINGTON POST, 10/7/94, Weekend/p. 50, Desson Howe

OSCAR SHORTS 1993

A Strand Releasing presentation of five Oscar-nominated shorts. *Producer:* Margaret Lazarus and Renner Wunderlich ("Defending Our Lives"). *Director:* Steven Cantor ("Blood Ties: The Life and Workds of Sally Mann"). *Director:* Pepe Danquart ("Black Rider"). *Director:* Elaine Holliman ("Chicks in White Satin"). *Director:* Stacey Title ("Down on the Waterfron"). *Running time:* 130 minutes. *MPAA Rating:* Not Rated.

LOS ANGELES TIMES, 3/4/94, Calendar/p. 2, Kevin Thomas

"Oscar Shorts'93" composed of the three short documentaries and four of the five live-action shorts nominated for Academy Awards, opens today.

The quality of the documentaries is so high that it will take the wisdom of Solomon to pick a winner among them. The live-action entries are another matter: only two were available for this program, and one is as outstanding as the other is dreadful. Those not shown are: Susan Seidelman's "The Dutch Master," Didier Flamand's "The Screw," and Peter Weller's "Partners."

Steven Cantor's 30-minute "Blood Ties: The Life and Work of Sally Mann" explores the predicament of Mann), a gifted and acclaimed photographer who has incurred the wrath of some because some of the countless photos she has taken of her three young children have depicted them in the nude. (The children, age 6, 9 and 11, insist that their mother has never asked them to disrobe to be photographed.) Intent on standing up for her right of freedom of expression, Mann is clearly a serious, *responsible* artist, articulate in her own defense. There is nothing suggestive or titillating in her stunning, poetically beautiful work.

Elaine Holliman's warm and engaging 22-minute "Chicks in White Satin" introduces us to two young lesbians who have been lovers for eight years and who decide that they want a traditional marriage, with both of them wearing white gowns. This warm, graceful film becomes a dual portrait in courage as the women face rejection from some relatives and who, most important, must win over one of the women's mothers, who feels uneasy at the prospect of the ceremony.

It would be hard to imagine a film more effective in raising consciousness about the plight of battered women than Margaret Lazarus and Renner Wunderlich's 30-minute "Defending Our Lives," which intercuts the remarks of human-rights activist Stacey Kabat, herself a battered wife, with interviews with eight women who recite with absolute conviction their harrowing existence as the wives of husbands physically abusive to the extent of endangering their lives.

The film points up how ineffectual police can be in protecting such women; Kabat states that in the United States, there are three times as many shelters for animals as there are for battered women. As fine as this film is, it would have been even stronger had it delved, even briefly, into the reasons why men brutalize women.

The presence of such pros as Jason Alexander and Edward Asner in Stacy Title's "Down on the Waterfront," a talky, boring, 27-minute drama about a pair of young filmmakers meeting with union officials, is of no help whatsoever.

On the other hand, German filmmaker Pepe Danquart's 12-minute "Black Rider" is a miracle of wit and economy, as a black man (Paul Outlaw) comes up with a deft, amusing revenge upon his street car seatmate, an older German who spouts nonstop hatred and contempt of Turkish, Italian and, especially, African immigrants.

Also being screened is last year's live-action short Oscar winner, Sam Karmann's eight-minute "Omnibus," which deals with a harried office worker (Daniel Rialet) who boards his usual commuter train only to find that the schedule has changed, a surprise he regards as catastrophic. No wonder this gem walked off with top prize at Cannes as well as an Academy Award.

NEW YORK POST, 3/4/94, p. 34, Bill Hoffmann

If you're like me, you've felt left out in the cold when the Academy Awards show doles out prizes to those odd short-subject films you've never heard of.

Fortunately, Strand Releasing has assembled five of this year's nominees in one show.

While it's quite a mixed bag—you'll laugh out loud at one and be repelled at another—"Oscar Shorts 1993" is a great way to see an always-struggling art form at its best.

This grab-bag compilation features four documentaries and a screamingly funny comedy.

"Down on the Waterfront," shows how low two struggling filmmakers will stoop to do a movie. "Seinfeld's" Jason Alexander and Jonathan Penner agree to meet mob union boss (Ed Asner) who wants to make a shameless propaganda film about how great unions are.

Too chicken to disagree, they kowtow to the idea, hash out hackneyed plot lines and even improvise a bizarre scene with the mobster. It's a hysterical premise that's played perfectly.

"Chicks in White Satin" is the bittersweet story of two Jewish lesbians planning their wedding.

The usual conflicts arise. How will their parents react? Will people come to the service? It's a fascinating look at a very real difficulty.

"Blood Ties: The Life and Work of Sally Mann" looks at a photographer whose nude snaps of her pre-pubescent kids have conservatives howling in protest. The film valiantly tries but fails to crack the underbelly of this very unusual family.

"Defending Our Lives" is a shocking glimpse into the lives of battered women, Survivors give disturbing testimonials while we're shown body bags and horrific police photos.

It's hard to watch without flinching—but the graphic approach hammers how serious the problem of domestic violence is.

Recently, Academy bosses tried to eliminate the shorts category. Thankfully, they failed. This compilation proves that short independent films remain a vital, vibrant part of the American movie industry.

NEWSDAY, 3/4/94, Part II/p. 88, Joseph Gelmis

The motion picture Academy shot itself in the foot last year when it said it would discontinue the Oscar category for short films because "these films have been virtually non-existent in American theaters" for the past quarter-century.

Influential Hollywood filmmakers, independents, film schools and the media vociferously denounced the decision. Most superstar directors, the academy was reminded, learn their craft by making shorts, and it's simply self-interest for the industry to recognize and reward fledgling talent. Last month, the academy's board of governors recanted its heresy and reinstated the documentary and fiction short film categories.

To show there is a theatrical market for these films, Strand Releasing set out to assemble two packages of this year's Oscar nominees and open them simultaneously in 10 U.S cities. But good intentions don't clinch deals. Strand couldn't acquire the five animated shorts or three of the five fiction shorts. And, probably because the academy waited so long to solicit entries, there are only three documentary short nominees.

Which is why "Oscar Shorts 1993," has only three politically correct documentary shorts, two clever fiction shorts and, as filler, last year's Oscar-winning short fiction film, "Omnibus" (not screened for reviewers).

Pepe Danquart's "Schwarzfahrer" ("Black Rider"), a 12-minute fiction film—or "live-action film," as the academy labels the category—is a socially-conscious comic sketch shot in Berlin aboard a tram. A bigoted German crone rants about foreigners, until the calm African sitting next to her amusingly ends her tirade with a sudden act of non-violent sabotage. A funny film, skillfully made.

Set in the '50s, taking place on one set, a park bench, "Down on the Waterfront" demonstrates a high-degree of show-biz savvy on a low budget. It's an entertaining 27-minute riff on the 1953 masterpiece "On the Waterfront." Edward Asner's a mobster/union boss, and Jason Alexander (of "Seinfeld") and Jonathan Penner (of "Grapevine") are two shlocky short filmmakers discussing a feature film that will improve the sullied image of the longshoremen's union. Directed by Penner's wife, Stacy Title.

The three non-fiction shorts seem to have been nominated for what they have to say rather than for their filmmaking ingenuity or flair. The most impressive is "Defending Our Lives," a horrific half-hour chronicle that contends battered women don't get help from the police or justice from the courts.

"Blood Ties: The Life and Works of Sally Mann" (30 minutes) is a pastiche of interviews that makes the case for Mann's controversial nude photos of her children being art rather than a form of child abuse, as fundamentalist Christian leaders claim.

"Chicks in White Satin" (22 minutes) is a documentary about two gay women who consecrate eight years of living together with a wedding ceremony. Uninspired filmmaking, but great timing: Based on her short, former University of Southern California film student Elaine Holliman will reportedly co-write and direct a feature for Disney's Hollywood Pictures on this significant '90s trend.

VILLAGE VOICE, 3/15/94, p. 53, Howard Feinstein

Make 'em eat crow. Dropping live-action and doc shorts from Oscar consideration in late '92, the Academy announced that such works "ceased to reflect the realities of theatrical motion-picture exhibition." Filmmakers protested, so the Academy's Board of Governors granted a one-year reprieve. Testing the waters, Strand Releasing has put together five of the eight nominees in these two categories, plus last year's winner for live-action short, in a program entitled *Oscar Shorts 1993*. At least two of the films prove that the format is still feasible, fresh, and vital. All three doc-short contenders are about women, but the gem is Margaret Lazarus and Renner Wunderlich's harrowing *Defending Our Lives*, about four battered wives and girlfriends sentenced to lengthy prison terms for fighting back—in fact, for killing their abusers. The directors deftly intercut each of these women's stories with photos of nauseating bruised and bloody faces, news clips of less fortunate women being taken away in body bags, and fact-filled testimony from two impassioned advocates for victims of domestic violence—themselves former casualties.

German filmmaker Pepe Danquart's live-action *Black Rider* (*Schwarzfahrer*) is also socially committed—and it's formally flawless. In this black-and-white, multicultural update of Walter Ruttmann's 1927 *Berlin: Symphony of a Great City*, eccentric angles and hyperextreme close-ups slice up *die Stadt*. Danquart then settles his restless camera inside a moving streetcar, where an elderly white woman spews out racist rubbish. Unfortunately for her, she is seated next to a *schwarzfahrer* (a pun referring more often to a nonpaying passenger than to a black rider). He makes her eat crow, too.

Also reviewed in:
NEW YORK TIMES, 3/5/94, p. 19, Stephen Holden

PCU

A Twentieth Century Fox release. *Producer:* Paul Schiff. *Director:* Hart Bochner. *Screenplay:* Adam Leff and Zak Penn. *Director of Photography:* Reynaldo Villalobos. *Editor:* Nicholas C. Smith. *Music:* Steve Vai. *Sound:* David Lee. *Sound Editor:* Paul Clay. *Casting:* Margery Simkin. *Production Designer:* Steven Jordan. *Art Director:* David M. Davis. *Set Decorator:* Enrico Campana. *Set Dresser:* David Charles. *Special Effects:* Martin Malivoire. *Costumes:* Mary Zophres. *Make-up:* Linda Gill. *Running time:* 81 minutes. *MPAA Rating:* PG-13.

CAST: Jeremy Piven (Droz); Chris Young (Tom Lawrence); Megan Ward (Katy); Jon Favreau (Gutter); Alex Désert (Mullaney); Gale Mayron (Cecelia); Jake Beecham (Dave #1); Karin Heames (Dave #2); Matthew Brandon Ross (Raji); Stivi Paskoski (Deege); Jody Racicot (Pigman); Sarah Trigger (Samantha); Viveka Davis (Womynist #1); Maddie Corman (Womynist #2); David Spade (Rand McPherson); Thomas Mitchell (Bantam Draper); Kevin Jubinville (Carter Prescott); Jake Busey (Mersh); Ted Kozma (Kosmo); Theo Caldwell (The Giggler); Jessica Walter (President Garcia-Thompson); Colin Fox (Trustee #1); Larry Reynolds (Trustee #2); Becky Thyre (Moonbeam); Kevin Thigpen (Afrocentrist); Rob Gfroerer (Computer Geek); Jonathan Wilson (Gay Activist); Joel Bissonnette (Sanskrit Major); M.J. Kang (Physics Major); Tret McMullen (Phys. Ed Major); David Berni (Jock #1); Jeff Clarke (Jock #2); Valentina Cardinalli (Singer); Adam Bocknek (Folksinger); Zak Penn (Bathroom Patron); Freddy Proia (D. J.); Jeremy Harris (Granola #1); Jeff Feher (Granola #2); Joel Keller (Pretty Boy Dancer); Lee Hoverd (Cattle Butcher); Teresa Sherrer (Flashback Girl); Jannie McInnes (Scoreboard Flipper); Marcia Diamond (Pampers Woman); Dick Callahan (Liquor Store Guy); Stephen Jackson (Townie #1); Pierre Larocque (Townie #2); Shelley Goldstein (Gutter's Mother); Glenn Pearson (Newscaster in Video Clip); George Clinton (Himself); Greg Boyer (Himself); Gary Cooper (Himself); Bennie Cowan (Himself); Ray Davis (Himself); Louis Kabbabie (Himself); Tracy Lewis (Himself); Dewayne McKnight (Himself); Cardell Mosson (Himself); William Michael Payne (Himself); Garry Shider (Himself); Nicole Tindall (Herself); Greg Thomas (Himself); Andre Williams (Himself); Belita Woods (Herself).

LOS ANGELES TIMES, 4/29/94, Calendar/p. 8, Kevin Thomas

"PCU" stands for both Port Chester University and Politically Correct University. Actually, the spoofing of campus politics is haphazard and directed mainly at humorless feminists. The whole point of this anemic venture is to get down and party, but it comes across as a pale passé carbon of "Animal House" that's not half as much fun.

Chris Young stars as a preppy who's come to PCU for the weekend to see if he wants to enroll there in the fall. He's assigned to a good-natured sharpie (Jeremy Piven), who's the key guy in the Pit, a residence hall that's supposed to be the last bastion of independent thought on campus, waging a war on PC. This translates mainly into the students asserting their right to engage in nonstop hell-raising.

Written by Adam Leff and Zak Penn and directed by Hart Bochner, "PCU" is terrifically tedious, its people and their lives remaining relentlessly uninvolving. You're better off with the real thing, the amusing and involving "Frosh: Nine Months in a College," which reveals what it's actually like to be in college in the '90s.

NEW YORK POST, 4/29/94, p. 44, Michael Medved

A few weeks ago I gave a lecture at Yale (my alma mater) and went to dinner with some students before my speech. In the course of a pleasant conversation, I innocently used the term "freshman year" when discussing my own recollections of the campus, only to find myself instantly corrected by one of the undergraduates.

"That's your fresh-person year," she solemnly insisted.

Anyone who spends time around contemporary campuses can tell you that political correctness is no laughing matter—which, of course, makes it a ripe subject for movie satire. "PCU" takes a first shot at this juicy target, but misses the bull's-eye (or bovine-person's-eye?) by a country mile.

The title refers to the fictional "Port Chester University," a 200- year-old campus visited by a shy teen-ager (Chris Young) who's thinking of enrolling as a freshperson in September.

He's welcome at "the Pit," a former frat house now inhabited by a group of grumpy outcasts who defy the enlightened values that prevail on the rest of the campus. When university president Andrea Garcia-Thompson (Jessica Walter) visits this controversial den of dorks she declares: "So this is the sewer where you persons breed your anti-community crimes!"

She threatens to close down the Pit unless its members can come up with $7,000 to pay for past damage they've done, so the leader of the group (Jeremy Piven) invites the entire uptight campus to a big beer bust to raise the money. From this point forward the movie becomes an embarrassing rehash of "Animal House" or "Revenge of the Nerds," with radical Womynists, Vegans, militant gays and people of color conveniently substituted for the smug frat boys of those earlier films.

In fact, to make sure they've covered all their political bases, screenwriters Adam Leff and Zak Penn (who previously collaborated on the ill-fated "The Last Action Hero") even create a secret society of Reaganite preppies (called "Balls and Shaft") who implausibly collaborate with the left-wing administrators in attacking the lovable losers in the Pit.

The script suggests that for all the various protesters, the real enemy isn't the phallocracy or Eurocentrism, but good, old-fashioned fun.

Unfortunately, the movie provides little of that, since veteran actor Hart Bochner, making his clumsy debut as a director, fails to generate any spark or energy at all, even in the climactic party sequences.

The little-known cast members provide pallid caricatures rather than robust characterizations, and they nearly all look too old for their parts—especially Jeremy Piven, whose character tries to explain the discrepancy by referring to the fact that he repeated sophomore year three times.

Far more questionable is the film's affectionate portrayal of recreational drug use as the best alternative to the boring tyranny of political correctness—a point of view that may help to explain the woozy, incoherent texture of so much of the picture.

By the end of its brief running time, one can't help but conclude that the most appropriate abbreviation for this particular university isn't really "PCU"; a simple "PU" would suffice.

NEWSDAY, 4/29/94, Part II/p. B9, Terry Kelleher

With one show called "Politically Incorrect" on Broadway and another on TV, could it be that political incorrectness has become, for want of a better buzz phrase, politically correct?

Just wondering, because the new campus comedy "PCU" somehow lacks a subversive edge. Even a screenplay by Dinesh ("Illiberal Education") D'Souza might have been funnier, or at least more pointed, than this weak "Animal House" update written by Zak Penn and Adam Leff.

Penn and Leff graduated from Wesleyan University in Connecticut in 1990 and put their education to use by penning the original script for "Last Action Hero." Producer Paul Schiff took his Wesleyan degree nine years earlier. All three report chafing under rigid school codes intended to wipe out racism, sexism, etc. So have they evened the score by teaming with their first-time director, actor Hart Bochner, to make a movie Rush Limbaugh's legions will love?

Well, the dittoheads should howl when cut-ups at Port Chester University dump ground beef on a group of "vegan protesters." And they'll recognize the man-hating "womynist" radicals as nothing but a bunch of no-good "feminists."

But what's this—a secret society of lock-step preppies who revere Ronald Reagan, hate Jews, sneer at the poor and follow the lead of David Spade, doing his "Saturday Night Live" supersmug routine? Their presence establishes the moviemakers' commitment to equal-opportunity stereotyping—rather a "politically correct" concept when you think about it.

"PCU" isn't political satire, really. It's anti-politics pseudo-satire. The theme is old: College kids just want to have fun. The plot is familiar: The goof-offs residing at a former frat house dubbed "The Pit" must pay a heavy damage bill by tomorrow or the nasty university president (Jessica Walter as the multiculturally sensitive equivalent of "Animal House's" Dean Wormer) will kick them off campus.

Jeremy Piven plays the slacker-in-chief, a cross between Bluto and Otter who fires up the Pit crew with inspirational, nonsensical speeches. His emergency fund-raising plan is to throw a wild party and charge admission. Providing the music are George Clinton and Parliament Funkadelic, who get lost en route to a paying gig and decide to make themselves useful by performing long enough for "PCU" to approach a respectable running time. United by their innate desire to rock and revel, the school's warring factions resolve to put down their placards permanently.

Swept up in the events of the weekend, a visiting high-school senior (Chris Young) changes overnight from undecided preppie to PCU-bound prankster. We'd advise the admissions office to double-check his SATs.

VILLAGE VOICE, 5/17/94, p. 58, Mike Rubin

I hate to date myself, but even at my relatively tender age I'm old enough to remember with gauzy fondness the bygone days when "politically correct" was a term of indictment favored by the left, used to describe its own dogmatically disabled elements—the cause-hopping Sandalistas and Trustafarians of college campus culture, humorless guardians of piety for whom the Big Issues were No Joking Matter: Of course, then the right appropriated the phrase, turning it into a retrofitted euphemism for anything remotely progressive and positing it as the greatest threat to our nation's precious bodily fluids since the Red Menace. The joke was on us. This struggle between these two forces of unfunniness hardly seems the stuff of great comedy, at least from Hollywood anyway, and for the most part, it isn't: *PCU*, a reactionary satire scripted by *Last Action Hero* villains Adam Leff and Zak Penn, squeezes only an occasional snicker out of a subject Nat Hentoff builds whole monologues around.

Set in the mythical Connecticut campus of Port Chester University, *PCU* is *Animal House* as imagined by Dinesh D'Souza. A naive, squeaky-clean pre-frosh arrives for orientation and is indoctrinated into the toga-party system by the college's decadent, fast-talking outcasts—Bluto's now a dread-locked punk, Dean Wormer's a female tenured radical with a hyphenated Latina name—only this time the enemy isn't the fledgling military-industrial complex of snooty Greeks and ROTCs (at PCU, frats were "banned in 1967") but the chanting, protesting horde of vegetarians, "womynists," and other illin' liberal special interest groups bent on enslaving the world with their Antioch Rules. The *Larry Sanders Show*'s Jeremy Piven is hyperkinetically captivating as the Otter-esque spiritual leader of the beer-drinking hell-raisers, while *Saturday Night Live*'s David Spade is deliciously evil as the Greg Marmalard-like führer of the College

Republican-ish secret society, Balls and Shaft; otherwise, *PCU* is as flat as a tapped keg. In the end, the film's most memorable highlights come from a couple of live performances by George Clinton and the P-Funk All-Stars playing the Otis Day and the Knights role, although Dr. Funkenstein's musical Ph.D. ought to have prepped him to steer clear of such a fraudulent educational venture.

Also reviewed in:
CHICAGO TRIBUNE, 4/29/94, Friday/p. D, John Petrakis
NEW YORK TIMES, 4/29/94, p. C6, Janet Maslin
VARIETY, 5/2-8/94, p. 88, Emanuel Levy
WASHINGTON POST, 4/30/94, p. G2, Rita Kempley

PAGEMASTER, THE

A Twentieth Century Fox release in association with Turner Pictures, Inc. *Producer:* David Kirschner and Paul Gertz. *Director (Live Action):* Joe Johnston. *Director (Animation):* Maurice Hunt. *Screenplay:* David Casci, David Kirschner, and Ernie Contreras. *Story:* David Kirschner and David Casci. *Director of Photography (Live Action):* Alexander Gruszynski. *Director of Photography (Visual Effects)*: Dennis Skotak. *Editor:* Kaja Fehr. *Editor (Animation):* Jeffrey Patch. *Music:* James Horner. *Music Editor:* Jim Henrikson. *Sound:* Steve Nelson and (music) Shawn Murphy. *Sound Editor:* Lon E. Bender and Per Hallberg. *Casting:* Amy Kimmelman. *Production Designer:* Gay Lawrence and Valerio Ventura. *Art Director:* Pixote. *Set Decorator:* Ronald Reiss. *Set Dresser:* Evan Lurance. *Special Effects:* Robbie Knott. *Special Effects (Animation):* Mark Myer. *Special Visual Effects:* Richard T. Sullivan. *Costumes:* Robin Lewis. *Make-up:* Donna J. Bard. *Stunt Coordinator:* John Branigan. *Running time:* 75 minutes. *MPAA Rating:* G.

CAST: Macaulay Culkin (Richard Tyler); Ed Begley, Jr. (Alan Tyler); Mel Harris (Claire Tyler); Christopher Lloyd (Mr. Dewey/The Pagemaster); Patrick Stewart (Adventure); Whoopi Goldberg (Fantasy); Frank Welker (Horror); Leonard Nimoy (Dr. Jekyll & Mr. Hyde); George Hearn (Captain Ahab); Dorian Harewood (Jamaican Pirates); Ed Gilbert (George Merry); Dick Erdman, Fernando Escandon, and Robert Piccardo (Pirates); Phil Hartman (Tom Morgan); Jim Cummings (Long John Silver); B.J. Ward (Queen of Hearts).

LOS ANGELES TIMES, 11/23/94, Calendar/p. 8, Peter Rainer

"The Pagemaster" is a feature-length, mostly animated commercial for the pleasures of library-going. It's rare that a kiddie film makes such a show of plumping for the opposition. If the movie succeeds it could backfire for the producers. Kids might stay at home reading "Treasure Island" or "Jack and the Beanstalk" instead of trooping out to see and re-see "The Pagemaster."

That wouldn't be so terrible. Despite its admirable intentions, and some witty animated sequences, "Pagemaster" seems more like a TV animated show with grade-A names. (The voice-overs belong to, among others, Patrick Stewart, Whoopi Goldberg and Leonard Nimoy.) Ironically, the film will probably work best for children who can't yet read.

It begins as a live-action feature about Richard Tyler (Macaulay Culkin), a boy so frightened by everything that he won't even eat a tuna fish sandwich (it's the mercury). When a storm sidetracks him in the local library, he encounters an eerie librarian (Christopher Lloyd) and gets transported into an animated world of bookish adventures ranging from "Dr. Jekyll and Mr. Hyde" to "Moby Dick."

The live-action library has a moldy grandeur that accurately fits how we all felt when we first tramped through all those high-ceiling shelves in search of our first picture book. There's a wonderfully fluid effect when colors from a mural flow into the floor and sweep Richard up in its maelstrom. And Richard's book-sized buddies—the piratelike Adventure (Stewart), the sassy, ethereal Fantasy (Goldberg) and the blubbery Horror (voiced by Frank Welker)—are frisky fun.

There are a few other nice things, like the scene where Richard winds his way out the belly of a fire-eating dragon by reading "Jack and the Beanstalk." Or the way Christopher Lloyd, intentionally no doubt, is a dead ringer for Charles Dickens. But producer and co-writer David Kirschner, along with scripters David Casci and Ernie Contreras, animation director Maurice Hunt and live-action director Joe Johnston, keep the inspirationalism sticky. A little of this movie's there-is-no-frigate-like-a-book stuff goes a long way.

On the other hand, there may be no other way to get kids to read these days except to promote books as the ultimate voyage—a video game of the mind. And if it takes Culkin to introduce toddlers to Captain Ahab, I say aye, aye.

NEW YORK POST, 11/23/94, p. 51, Michael Medved

"The Pagemaster" flamboyantly flaunts its good intentions, begging for acceptance on the strength of its noble purposes alone, but inept execution prevents the picture from achieving its grand goals. This is a formless, flaccid mess that attempts to celebrate the joys of reading while providing no joy at all for its audience. It's true that parents could take their kids to see this film for the holiday season, but only if they've been very, very naughty in the year just past.

The picture begins with a brief live-action prologue, introducing a timid, bespectacled hero played by Macaulay Culkin. To the dismay of his parents (Ed Begley Jr. and Mel Harris), little Mac is afraid of absolutely everything; this fearful personality helps to explain why he's terrified by a sudden thunderstorm, despite the cheesy special effects employed to bring to life on screen.

He seeks shelter in a huge, mysterious library that looks like a combination of the New York Public Library and the haunted mansion at Disneyland. There, an eccentric librarian with a silly goatee named "Mr. Dewey" (as in decimal system, get it?), and played by an embarrassingly over-the-top Christopher Lloyd, soon hands him a library card which, for some reason, instantly transforms the lad into a cartoon.

The rest of the movie is played out in dreary animation, with Christopher Lloyd's voice returning as "The Pagemaster," the Oz-like ruler of the world of books. Naturally, to escape from this mystical realm and to make his way to the "Exit" sign that beckons like a shining, unattainable goal at the far end of the building, the cartoon Culkin is accompanied by three colorful companions—a la Scarecrow, et al.

In this case, three talking books— the swashbuckling Adventure (the voice of Patrick Stewart), the fairy-like Fantasy (the voice of Whoopi Goldberg) and the shy, deformed Horror (the voice of Frank Welker)—guide him through corresponding sections in the library.

Along the way, the filmmakers attempt an oddly selected "greatest hits" tour of world literature, briefly introducing characters from Moby Dick, Treasure Island, Dr. Jekyll and Mr. Hyde, and other works.

Each of these characters turns up as some sort of dire menace to the boy and his companions—an odd strategy to follow if you want to inspire affection for the books in question. The adventures flow into each other in such a purposeless and repetitive pattern that you feel as if you're drowning in some murky, gooey pudding. The animation is sturdy and serviceable, but never inspired, while the color has a curiously faded, and washed-out quality to it.

In the end (which seems as hard to reach as that elusive exit sign!), even the movie's positive purposes seem questionable: It's hard to imagine that any child will be encouraged to read "Moby Dick," for instance, because he's seen this lame cartoon version of the white whale. The only lasting message of the movie is to communicate the odd notion that libraries are dangerous places that may, in fact, bore you to death.

NEWSDAY, 11/23/94, Part II/p. B9, Jack Mathews

A scaredy-cat kid, ducking out of a storm, gets locked in a Gothic library where he knocks himself out, wakes up as a cartoon character, and finds his courage in battles with Moby Dick, Long John Silver and other literary villains who spill out of the musty pages of their books.

The idea behind David Kirschner's mostly animated feature "The Pagemaster" is so rich, it's a wonder there haven't been dozens of children's movies set in libraries before. But the idea was about the last inspired moment in the film's three-year journey to the screen. The story is an almost shockingly mundane chase through a spookhouse, and the animation looks as drained of color as Tom Cruise's girlfriends in "Interview With the Vampire."

"The Pagemaster" was partly undermined by the nature of movie marketing, and by the popularity, when the project was begun, of Macaulay Culkin. It is always jolting to go directly from live action to animation, and there was no reason to do it here other than to bill "Pagemaster" as a Macaulay Culkin film.

Kirschner, a writer and producer making his directing debut, squandered not only his "novel" idea, but his cast. Whoopi Goldberg, hilarious as an evil hyena in "The Lion King," is numbingly unfunny as the voice of Fantasy, one of three talking books who come to Richie Tyler's aid. And Christopher Lloyd, as both the live-action librarian and the eponymous lord of Richie's dream, has little to do.

Culkin is at his pre-pubescent cutest in the opening and closing scenes, and gives an adequate performance in between. But those live action sequences are deadly, badly written and directed, and in their attempt to catch the magic of Spielberg's suburbia, they merely point out how misguided the whole endeavor was.

SIGHT AND SOUND, 2/95, p. 49, Leslie Felperin

Richard Tyler is afraid of almost everything. When his father sends him to the hardware store to collect supplies for the tree house that he is afraid to climb, Richard is caught in an electrical storm and takes shelter in a library. Inside he meets the librarian, Mr Dewey, who tries to interest him in borrowing some books, but Richard only wants to use the telephone. Dewey advises him, that if he gets lost, he should head for the 'Exit' sign. He discovers a rotunda whose dome is covered by a mural with a wizard figure in the centre. Frightened by the storm, Richard slips and knocks himself unconscious. When he awakes, the mural begins to drip off the dome and form a tidal wave that engulfs Richard and turns him into a cartoon of himself. The Pagemaster, the wizard figure in the mural, tells Richard that, in order to get back home, he must pursue the Exit sign and pass three tests of courage. Inside the library, Richard meets three anthropomorphised books named Horror, Adventure, and Fantasy, who assist him in his quest.

The first test is entering a haunted house. Horror is afraid, and his fears seem justified when they meet Mr Jekyll, who turns into Mr Hyde and pursues them to the roof where they escape. They proceed to the Sea of Adventure by boat, but Moby Dick shipwrecks them. Richard and Horror are picked up by Long John Silver and his mercenary crew. who press-gang them into searching for buried gold on Treasure Island. Saved by Fantasy and Adventure, they follow the Exit sign which now hovers over a castle in the land of Fantasy. They meet a fire-breathing dragon. Richard engages it in battle and is swallowed whole. A handy copy of *Jack and the Beanstalk*, found in the dragon's belly, helps Richard to escape and rejoin his friends.

In the castle, Richard and company find a rotunda exactly like the one in the library. The Pagemaster, congratulating Richard on his bravery, sends him back to his old body, which involves overcoming his fear of heights by leaping into a vortex. Upon awakening, Richard heads home, ready for life's adventures, and eager to develop his reading skills. His parents, who have been looking for him, return home to find him asleep in the tree house.

With the rich seam of well-known fairy tales mined to exhaustion, animation producers have been forced to quarry deeper for stories to tell. The formerly innovative Don Bluth studio has reverted to using third division subjects like *Thumbelina*, while Disney are tentatively experimenting with original material (*The Lion King, the Nightmare Before Christmas*), albeit conventionally structured. 20th Century Fox's latest animated feature, *The Pagemaster*, can only be described as a meta-fiction. Set in a library with a librarian named after Melvil Dewey, the father of decimal classification, it brims with allusions to numerous classics of children's fiction. Three of its major characters are genres in the form of living books. Its message, drummed in none too subtly, extols the empowering pleasures of reading.

Other cinematic influences are detectable but not overpoweringly pungent: a bit of *The Neverending Story*; a dash of *The Secret Life of Walter Mitty*; an animation/live action combined structure which recalls Chuck Jones' *The Phantom Tollbooth* (the transition is beautifully executed, but over much too quickly). Yet in *The Pagemaster*'s league table of recommended art forms, the literary consistently outranks the filmic, a strangely self-effacing gesture given that this is a film. The Pagemaster even insists that Richard has been turned into "an illustration", rather than a mere "cartoon". Clearly the film-makers are eager to avert parental criticism, overtly signposting the intention to supplement rather than supplant reading. One wonders how many parents will be aware that screenwriter/producer David Kirschner, who wrote and co-produced *An American Tail*, was also responsible for the original *Child's Play*, the alleged corrupter of Jamie Bulger's juvenile killers (who probably never saw it), and if one believes the tabloids, the most evil film ever made.

The Pagemaster, however, is a very worthy film, in line with 20th Century Fox's earnest and eco-friendly *FernGully: The Last Rainforest* and *Once upon a Forest*. Like the latter, it is well-crafted, unlikely to corrupt or deprave, and faintly dull. The live action sequences book-ending the animation perfunctorily establish and conclude. Macaulay Culkin, bespectacled and restrained, has not broadened his range of facial expressions, and is still reminiscent of Harold Lloyd with a hormone problem, although not as talented. As a cartoon, he's rather more likable, speaking his lines well despite the fact that his voice broke during the three years it took to make the film.

Christopher Lloyd does his stock rent-a-loony schtick as Mr Dewey/The Pagemaster and the rest of the cast of voice actors includes a hammy Patrick Stewart, the ubiquitous Whoopi Goldberg, Leonard Nimoy, and Frank Welker—the last a Mel Blanc *de nos jours*. The animation, directed by Maurice Hunt, is pretty and suitably bookish and the whole moves along swiftly enough. My date for the press screening, seven-year-old Jay, appeared to like it, although he seemed more interested in playing with his *Lion King* toy from MacDonalds.

Also reviewed in:
NEW YORK TIMES, 11/23/94, p. C18, Caryn James
VARIETY, 11/21-27/94, p. 37, Brian Lowry
WASHINGTON POST, 11/23/94, p. D11, Rita Kempley

PAPER, THE

A Universal Pictures release of an Imagine Entertainment presentation. *Executive Producer:* Dylan Sellers and Todd Hallowell. *Producer:* Brian Grazer and Frederick Zollo. *Director:* Ron Howard. *Screenplay:* David Koepp and Stephen Koepp. *Director of Photography:* John Seale. *Editor:* Daniel Hanley and Michael Hill. *Music:* Randy Newman. *Music Editor:* Tom Kramer and James Flamberg. *Sound:* Danny Michael and (music) Frank Wolf. *Sound Editor:* Anthony "Chic" Ciccolini III and Lou Cerborino. *Casting:* Jane Jenkins and Janet Hirshenson. *Production Designer:* Todd Hallowell. *Art Director:* Maher Ahmad. *Set Decorator:* Debra Schutt. *Set Dresser:* Anthony Baldasare, Michael Lee Benson, Nancy Boytos-Amanuel, Peter Gelfman, Jerry Kadar, Daniel Boy Kenney, Raymond Murphy, Marc Simon, Mitch Towse, and Peter Von Bartheld. *Special Effects:* Hugo Cimmelli. *Costumes:* Rita Ryack. *Make-up:* Allen Weisinger. *Make-up (Glenn Close):* Jean Luc Russier. *Make-up (Robert Duvall):* Manlio Rocchetti. *Make-up (Marisa Tomei):* Fern Buchner. *Stunt Coordinator:* Jeff Ward. *Running time:* 112 minutes. *MPAA Rating:* R.

CAST: Michael Keaton (Henry Hackett); Robert Duvall (Bernie White); Glenn Close (Alicia Clark); Marisa Tomei (Martha "Marty" Hackett); Randy Quaid (McDougal); Jason Robards (Graham Keighley); Jason Alexander (Marion Sandusky); Spalding Gray (Paul Bladden); Catherine O'Hara (Susan); Lynne Thigpen (Janet); Jack Kehoe (Phil); Roma Maffia (Carmen); Clint Howard (Ray Blaisch); Geoffrey Owens (Lou); Amelia Campbell (Robin); Jill Hennessy (Deanne White); William Prince (Henry's Father); Augusta Dabney (Henry's Mother); Bruce Altman (Carl); Jack McGee (Wilder); Bobo Lewis (Anna); Edward Hibbert (Jerry); Michael Countryman (Emmett); Siobhan Fallon (Lisa); Joe Viviani (Max); Julie Donatt (Kathy); Ed Jupp, Jr. (Copy Editor); Christi Hatcher (City Editor); Gary Dourdan (Copy Guy); James Ritz and Miles Watson (A.C. Repairmen); Divina Cook (Sobbing Woman); Aloysius R. Burke (Parking Cop); Benny Benowitz (Crazy Guy); Lee Kimball (Security Guard); Michael Moran (Chuck); Jack O'Connell (Press Operator); Herb Krystall

(Pressroom Foreman); Herb Lovelle (Victor); John Bentley (Paste-Up Person); Vincent D'Arbouze (First Kid); Michael Michael (Second Kid); Yvonne Warden (Woman with Dog); Louisa Marie (Sentinel Receptionist); Stephen Koepp (German Newsperson); Victor Truro (Bernie's Doctor); Cedric Young and Wylie Weeks (Martha's Paramedics); James Golby (Alicia's Paramedic); Paul Geier (Doctor Porter); Rance Howard (Alicia's Doctor); Maureen Goldfedder (Alicia's E.R. Nurse); Karen Church (Alicia's Nurse); Diane Gnagnarelli (Pediatric Nurse); David J. Birnbach (Anesthesiologist); Amos Grunebaum (Obstetrician); Vickie Thomas (E.R. Doctor); Jacqueline Murphy (O.R. Nurse); Jean Speegle Howard (Hospital Volunteer); Joseph Pentangelo and James Nestor (Arresting Officers); Jim Meskimen (Tom); Tony Hoty (Waiter); Sally-Jane Heit (Grace); Mike Sheehan (Richie); Herbert Rubens (Tony); Cheryl Howard (Redheaded Barmaid); Carol Ann Donohue (Crying Child); Shannon E. Dnohue (Grumpy Child); Jeffrey H. Kaufman (Police Officer); Myra Taylor (Mother); Erika Johnson (Little Sister); Jan Mickens (Diner Owner); Daniel Kenney (Pinhead); Thomas Long (Bureaucrat); Harsh Nayyar (Attendant); Frank Inzerillo (News Truck Driver); Rosanna Scott (Herself); Donna Hanover (Herself); Jane Hanson (Herself); Valerie Coleman (Herself); Chuck Scarborough (Himself); Brenda Blackmon (Herself); Cynthia Carter (Herself); E. Graydon Carter (Himself); Lou Colasuonno (Himself); Bob Costas (Himself); Larry Hackett (Himself); Hap Hairston (Himself); Pete Hamill (Himself); William Kunstler (Himself); Kurt Loder (Himself); Mike McAlary (Himself); Joanna Molloy (Herself); Richard Price (Himself); John Rhodes (Himself); Jerry Rosa (Himself); Linda Stasi (Herself); Dini Von Mueffling (Herself); Jeannie Williams (Herself); John Miller (Himself); Debbie Gross Rodriguez (Herself).

LOS ANGELES TIMES, 3/18/94, Calendar/p. 1, Kenneth Turan

"Who remembers the great writers of the city room?" a disgruntled reporter was once moved to complain. "In a single generation they are one with Ninevah and Tyre." A sad fate, and one newspapers themselves, dismissed by heartless futurists as road kill on the information superhighway, may someday be forced to share.

But even if everyone else gives up on newspapers, Hollywood never will. Not for nothing has Ben Hecht and Charles MacArthur's "The Front Page" been made and remade three times. At least once a decade the movies fall in love with the romance of print journalism, and the studios' latest crush, "The Paper," directed by Ron Howard shows the reasons why.

The story of a single day in the life of a great, albeit fictional tabloid, the New York Sun (motto: "It Shines on All"), and Henry Hackett (Michael Keaton), its God-I-love-this-business metro editor. "The Paper" is rife with the motion and commotion that characterize all newspaper films. With their insistence on what's timely and their fear of time running out, deadline-crazed daily papers have a built-in thrill-of-the-chase quality that the movie business understandably finds irresistible.

That kind of manic "get-that-story" energy is especially suited to knockabout comedy and when "The Paper" relaxes and concentrates on jolt-a-minute madness, it's as crowd-pleasing as "Parenthood," Howard's most-successful ensemble venture to date.

But Howard and screenwriting brothers David Koepp & Stephen Koepp (one a "Jurassic Park" writer, the other a Time magazine senior editor) are not content to make us laugh. They are determined to thrust as many serious moments into this picture as it can take, and it can't take very many at all.

"The Paper's" breathless doings begin with a brief prologue showing a pair of black teenagers in the Williamsburg section of Brooklyn discovering a car containing two slain white businessmen and, via a bit of bad luck, becoming prime suspects for the crime.

Henry Hackett is also introduced not at his best, waking up fully clothed (don't worry, he's been chasing stories, not women) next to his extremely pregnant wife, Martha (Marisa Tomei). She's a former Sun reporter who has quit the paper for motherhood and days full of worry.

Martha is especially concerned about an interview Henry has with the tweedy New York Sentinel, an upscale place that runs headlines like "Nepalese Premier Won't Resign" while the Sun concentrates on murder and mayhem. Martha wants him to forsake his tabloid roots for security, but Henry, not surprisingly, is not so sure.

Once he gets to his office (whose tip of Manhattan location is patterned on the New York Post as surely as the Sentinel is on the New York Times), it's obvious why Henry hates the thought of leaving. For the Sun is staffed entirely by lovable comic eccentrics, zany types like a gun-toting columnist named McDougal (Randy Quaid) and a reporter who cares more about his orthopedic chair than any story he's ever worked on.

Since this makes staff meetings as hectic as a Marx Brothers movie, it's the newspaper situations that are the most consistently entertaining parts of "The Paper," never lacking for laughs even when Henry leaves the building and goes for that interview with a stuffy Sentinel editor (deliciously played by Spalding Gray).

Policing the zoo at the Sun are a particularly odd couple. Editor in chief Bernie White (Robert Duvall, engaging even when he's coasting) is Henry's mentor, a crusty troglodyte who barks more than he bites. Glamorous managing editor Alicia Clark (Glenn Close) is Henry's bete noir, a bottom line-oriented ice queen whose motto is "if everybody loves you, you're doing something wrong."

The problem of the day for this group is deciding whether that unlucky pair's arrest for thc Williamsburg murder can command the front page. Henry, who's heard rumors that even the cops disown the bust, doesn't want to ruin the boys' lives if the story is wrong. So Bernie gives him five hours to prove what thc audience already knows, that the kids didn't do it.

While this would be enough for most movies, it's not for Howard and the Koepps, who toss prominent subplots to everyone within reach. Bernie is given a malignant prostate "the size of a bagel" and an estranged daughter. Alicia has worries about her career and her looks. McDougal has a vengeful city parking commissioner on his trail, and, of course, Henry has a career crisis as well as a wife who fears, like the first Mrs. Charles Foster Kane, that she may have to name the paper as a co-respondent.

That welter of incident, helped by lively acting, especially from Keaton, who despite the ensemble nature of things really carries this picture, means that at minimum "The Paper" never stops for breath long enough to be dull.

But all this tumult also leads to a feeling of shellshock, of having every contrivance not nailed down thrown at the audience. Part of the problem is that many of these subplots, like Henry's marital difficulties, are no more than Hollywood serious, dealing with adult situations in a bogus way that would be better avoided.

Not helping is Howard's insistence on underlining everything. Though he likes the idea of mixing serious moments with his comedy, the director doesn't trust that his audience will catch the change of pace. So manipulative situations end up being milked with overly insistent music and a too-careful tone. Like a novice reporter trying to cram too much into a lead, Howard overreaches and leaves a taste of frustration along with the pleasant laughter.

NEW YORK, 3/21/94, p. 32, John Powers

After months of hemorrhoidal op-ed pieces bemoaning the evils of tabloid culture, Ron Howard's new comedy, *The Paper*, comes as a welcome relief. Set at the imaginary New York *Sun*, this is no anguished cry from the sick Menendez-dazed soul of America.

Michael Keaton stars as metro editor Henry Hackett, who's being pulled apart by all the demands upon him. His voluminously pregnant wife, Marty (Marisa Tomei) wants him to spend nights at home and is pushing him to take a less-demanding job with the snooty *Sentinel* (the stand-in for the *Times*), which arrogantly claims to "cover the world." At work, Henry's trying to stay on top of a hot story: Two African-American teenagers have been arrested for what looks like a racially motivated murder, and he's rushing to get the correct version of the story on the front page. This puts him at loggerheads with managing editor Alicia Clark (Glenn Close), who claims the *Sun* can't afford to delay its press runs—if tomorrow's headline is wrong, they'll just fix things the day after. Meanwhile, editor-in-chief Bernie White (Robert Duvall) won't mediate their squabble because he's re-evaluating his life after learning that his prostate is "the size of a bagel." This leaves Henry all alone with his problems and impossible deadlines: The movie has enough ticking clocks to push a Swiss over the edge.

Hollywood takes boundless pride in getting external details absolutely right, and *The Paper* wears its research like a Rolex the size of a hubcap. Just as the *Sun*'s newsroom has been re-created with an accuracy that will delight most reporters (and be overlooked by most civilians), so David and Stephen Koepp's script shows off their feel for daily-paper bedlam: A/C repairmen clogging the aisles between cubicles, headline writers with their 10,000 small questions, sniffy editors whining about second-hand smoke, prima donna columnists who swagger even when lying down. In love with the kick-ass lingo of tabloid life, the Koepps can't get enough of Henry yakking with five people at once, editors swapping bitchy remarks at the morning story meeting, or a smug, simpering *Sentinel* editor—played by the bow-tied and suspendered Spalding Gray—giving Henry a book about management as part of a job interview.

As long as it stays inside this journalistic hothouse, *The Paper* zips nicely toward the final showdown between Michael Keaton and Glenn Close, high-energy performers who know how to jump-start papier-mâché roles. As Henry, Keaton proves again that he's one of the few genuinely graceful actors now working in Hollywood, smoothly gliding by desks and printing presses, shuttling with impudent ease between endearments and throwaway jokes. Keaton is most entertaining when he spins out of control—he's a master at being *wired*—but he's trying to be less shticky. Here he saves his funniest manic seizure for a moment that will bring the house down. When an angry *Sentinel* editor sputters that his newspaper covers the *world*, Henry suddenly explodes: "I don't live in the fucking world! I live in fucking New York City! So shut the fuck up!" Perhaps the mayor's office could turn this into a T-shirt.

A born diva, Close steals the movie as the tense, brainy, ambitious Alicia, who holds the *Sun*'s purse strings and dreams of hobnobbing with the big shots she once covered. Early in her career, Close played earth mothers so beatific you wanted someone to smack her. These days, someone usually does (in this case, Keaton), and it's wonderful to see her get it. With her high forehead, chilly blue eyes, and aggressive beak of a nose, Close has a gift for playing Wasp monsters; if anything, she suits the *vagina dentata* stereotype too well, letting the filmmakers fudge key issues about the newspaper business. At one point, Henry yells, "Not everything is about money," and Alicia snaps back, "It is when you're about to close every six months." This is a reasonable reply (at least two of New York's three real-life tabloids lose money), but we don't take her seriously because she's the heavy.

Like all newspaper movies, *The Paper* has its roots in Hecht and MacArthur's 1928 play *The Front Page*, whose rapid-fire dialogue is pure wisecrack bebop. But where *The Front Page*'s characters have no existence outside of journalism—the whole plot's about a glitteringly amoral editor stopping his star reporter from getting married—Ron Howard's picture comes from a Hollywood whose therapy-lashed ideas of "personal growth" would have had Hecht herniating himself with laughter. *The Paper* falters when it tries to make its two-dimensional characters stop to smell three-dimensional flowers; our hearts sink each time Duvall's crusty-wise editor grows pensive about his failed family life or when Henry's wife, Marty, turns up to scold him about abandoning her to her pregnancy. I kept wishing the filmmakers had given Marisa Tomei, a marvelous comedienne, something marvelous to do. She sparkles only when she ceases to be a walking womb and helps Henry investigate his murder case.

Fred Allen once joked that to a newspaperman, a human being is nothing but a story with skin around it. If *The Paper* is missing any one thing, it's a reporter with that kind of delectable absolute truthlessness. Randy Quaid's character probably comes closest (he's a spoiled, paranoid columnist with a vendetta against the parking commissioner), but he's Charles Kuralt compared with the scoundrels on display in *Tabloid Truth*, the Richard Ben Cramer documentary that aired on *Frontline* a few weeks back. Reporters from the *National Enquirer* and *Hard Copy* have what it takes—the nose of a bloodhound, the compassion of a slot machine, the ethics of a tapeworm. Sadly, there's no one half so flamboyantly scuzzy in Howard's movie, which scrupulously avoids anything that might put the audience on edge. We're even shown from the first scene that the African-American suspects are innocent, sparing us any worry that honest Henry may be coming to the defense of murderers.

Although *The Paper* plays up the amphetamine glamour of the tabloid life, you can tell it was made by people who subscribe to the *Times*; its last half-hour goes all gooey and inspirational in a way *The Front Page* never did. Hecht and MacArthur exulted in the press's shameless antics and were right to do so—in comedy, morality matters less than vitality. Ron Howard has never learned this. A nice man but an imprecise director, he spreads good wishes all through the movie, ending with doe-eyed shots of babies and the risible suggestion that a sensationalistic paper like the *Sun* would never knowingly print something untrue. While Howard's good heart makes this movie less savage than it should be, his obvious decency will cheer up those pundits who fret that the piranha tabloids have devoured our national conscience. *The Paper* is infinitely less cynical than the Hollywood comedies of 60 years ago, back when America was supposed to be innocent.

NEW YORK POST, 3/18/94, p. 35, Michael Medved

What New York newspaper is fun, feisty and fearlessly honest—honest enough, in fact, to admit that it is perpetually teetering on the verge of bankruptcy?

In Ron Howard's ambitious new movie, "The Paper," the name of that beloved tabloid is The Sun, but regular readers of the New York Post will recognize many similarities between that fictional journal and this very real one.

A key distinction, however, is that the people who work in this building (which shows up in a couple scenes in the movie) manage to keep better control of themselves than the explosive characters who appear on screen.

There is, for instance, The Sun's tirelessly toiling metro editor (Michael Keaton), whose very pregnant wife (Marisa Tomei) is thoroughly fed up with his workaholic ways.

Keaton's boss, earthy, understanding editor-in-chief Robert Duvall, faces a potentially life-threatening case of prostate cancer and begins to question his long-standing priorities.

Managing editor Glenn Close on the other hand, never questions anything she does; she's an intensely ambitious corporate climber whose ruthless cost-cutting has made plenty of enemies at the same time it may have saved the paper.

Meanwhile columnist Randy Quaid needs a different sort of rescue: he's been in the newsroom with a gun tucked into his belt to protect himself from threatened violence by a city parking commissioner (Jason Alexander) he's shamed in print.

The movie's taut, expertly crafted script (by David Koepp, who co-wrote "Jurassic Park" and "Carlito's Way," and his brother, Time Magazine senior editor Stephen Koepp) follows these people through 24 fateful hours. In the style of Paddy Chayevsky's classic scripts to "Network" and "Hospital," it explores the guts of a high pressure institution at a moment when everything seems to be collapsing.

There's also a touch of Hecht and MacArthur's "The Front Page" as fearless news hounds try to surmount their personal conflicts to free two black kids who've been wrongly arrested for murder.

Director Howard knows how to build tension and to shape funny moments, but he's never been particularly good with actors. Here, only Duvall delivers a fresh, fully realized performance, creating a character you believe and care about.

The women, on the other hand, fare particularly badly, and the contrast between them will provide a field day for Susan ("Backlash") Faludi: Close plays her caricature of a career woman as a nasty, manipulative, adulterous bitch, while the sweet, lovable Tomei has given up her job at the paper to concentrate on her baby.

Keaton's central character remains something of an enigma but he has a few big emotional moments where he connects with the audience. When he passes up the chance for a better-paying job at the prestigious New York Sentinel (read New York Times) that paper's pompous editor (Spalding Gray) tells him, "You're giving up your chance to cover the world!"

Keaton responds with hysterical gusto: "I don't live in the f---ing world! I live in f---ing New York City!"

It's hard to resist this movie's energy and momentum, or its warm-hearted love for the desperate deadline-driven world it portrays. A rousing, soul-stirring Oscar-calibre score by Randy Newman helps portray the challenge of getting this newspaper into your hands for what it is—a miraculous act of everyday heroism.

NEWSDAY, 3/18/94, Part II/p. 62, Jack Mathews

It's hard to bore me with a newpaper movie, but Ron Howard, who put lead weights in my eyelids with the Oklahoma Land Rush in "Far and Away," has done it again with "The Paper," his slapstick drama about a day in the life of a New York City tabloid.

I don't want to seem defensive. Newspapers are great fare for Hollywood satire, and the "buy me or I'll kill your dog" tabs are the best fare of all. But "The Paper" is not satire, it's a raucous valentine to the clichéd scruffiness of big city journalism, and though it's got a lot of the newsroom nuts and nuances right, it is about the newspaper business in the same way the Road Runner cartoons are about wildlife in the American Southwest.

Howard, who is said to have hung out at the New York Post and Daily News, have been quoted as saying he found the people there "very entertaining." Sure they are. So are Mexican jumping beans, but you don't make a movie about them unless you have a good story to tell.

Here's the entire arc of "The Paper": Fictional New York Sun metro editor Henry Hackett (Michael Keaton) wakes up at 7 a.m., having slept only four hours, discovers that the Sun has been beaten on a late-breaking crime story by rival tabs, spends the day playing catch-up, then goes to war with the managing editor (Glenn Close) over her decision to run a story he knows is factually wrong.

Howard, intercutting sub-plots about Hackett's hormonally-agitated pregnant wife (Marisa Tomei) and his swollen prostate-agitated editor (Robert Duvall), starts this off beautifully, bringing Hackett and the other Sun principals together in a morning news meeting where, through what seems routine banter, we glimpse all the significant personality conflicts and get a feel for what drives the paper's news judgment.

They talk about foreign stories, national stories, even entertainment, but what they're really looking for are stories that are (a) deliciously ghastly and (b) involve New Yorkers, something they can trumpet on Page 1 with a seize-commuters-by-the-throat headline with a slammer (explanation point).

This is a particularly tense day for Hackett. The Sun not only has been beaten by the other tabs on the killing of two out-of-town businessmen in Brooklyn, but his wife is pushing him to take that high-paying job at the fat and exceedingly dull New York Sentinel (read: Times).

After creating a batch of interesting characters, including the paper's colorful star columnist (Randy Quaid), and setting up Hackett's conflicts, Howard allows his film to collapse in deadline farce, goofy physical shtick more reminiscent of Martin and Lewis than Woodward and Bernstein, even while dealing with the same fundamental question raised in "All the President's Men." How solid does a story have to be before you run it?

Howard, working with a script by the brothers Koepp (David wrote "Jurassic Park" and "Carlito's Way," Stephen is an editor at Time Magazine), is desperately trying to have it two ways, to be giddier than the comics section and smarter than the editorial page, and succeeding at neither.

The basic problem is that the murder story Hackett covets, to the point of being willing to steal a lead from a rival newspaper editor's desk, has no narrative force of its own. In the opening, we see the two black teenagers who are going to be wrongfully accused of the murder, but we never get to know them, and only through a dialogue reference thrown in late do we realize what is actually at stake.

Without that part of the story developed, Hackett's stricken conscience seems abstract, if not insincere, and this breathtaking race against time boils down to little more than a power struggle between two editors, who might do it all over again tomorrow.

Howard did give his movie a lot of energy—it goes nowhere fast—and Keaton has a real grasp of his character's conflicting emotions. He plays Hackett as if he were on a perennial caffeine-adrenaline high (the leading cause of burnout in journalists everywhere), and he has a couple of brilliantly funny scenes.

Howard's wisest move, however, may have been populating the background of the newsroom and party scenes with such New York media personalities as Pete Hamill, Bob Costas and Chuck Scarborough. Filmmakers don't get many opportunities to build their publicity campaigns into the script, and these guys have been coming through.

The director's gamble, a big one, is that audiences outside New York's tabloid world will be interested in the old-fashioned print newshounds at the Sun, who see each day in the headline business as a grand adventure, fighting off the demon urges of sensationalism while clawing their way to the truth.

In reality, these people are adventurers, civic heroes on their best days, and Ron Howard could barely manage to make them "interesting."

NEWSWEEK, 3/21/94, p. 74, David Ansen

Compressed into a furious 24-hour time frame, Ron Howard's giddily entertaining newspaper comedy "The Paper" mimics the pressure-cooker rhythms of deadline journalism. It starts with a casual, jokey tension that as the day progresses turns increasingly manic, escalating by nightfall into full-pedal frenzy. This tightly coiled farcical structure is just what Howard needed after the dull sprawl of "Far and Away." He's back on the crowded, serio-comic turf of "Parenthood," and the collective commotion of the newsroom brings out his best showbiz instincts.

The paper in question is a financially strapped New York City tabloid called The Sun. Henry Hackett (Michael Keaton), the metro editor, has been offered a cushier job at the stuffier uptown Sentinel (i.e. The New York Times) and his pregnant wife (Marisa Tomei), a reporter herself, wants him to go for the bigger bucks. Today is decision day. But what's troubling him even more is the breaking page-one story, the arrest of two young black men for the murder of two white businessmen in Brooklyn. Convinced they're innocent, he's determined to get the story for the morning edition, but it's a race against time. He has to do battle with his nemesis, the aggressively unhappy, penny-counting managing editor Alicia (Glenn Close); his increasingly freaked-out wife is convinced she'll be on her own once the baby is born; he's got a paranoid, gun-carrying columnist (Randy Quaid) sleeping in his office; and the paper's crusty editor in chief (Robert Duvall) is too preoccupied with his prostate problem and the wreckage of his personal life to help. All these pressures come to a melodramatic boil that has more to do with Feydeau than with the realities of journalism. But even when "The Paper" gets a little too slapsticky silly, it's always fun to watch.

Writers David Koepp ("Jurassic Park") and Stephen Koepp, a senior editor at Time, pay lip service to such themes as work versus family and journalistic ethics, but no one will mistake this for an in-depth portrait of tabloid journalism. (Given the current furor over the dominance of tabloid scandalmongering in all journalism—an issue the movie doesn't take up—"The Paper" is oddly *untimely*.) What they do capture, with wit and pizzazz, is the ulcer-producing surface of newspaper life—the competitiveness of the story conference, the controlled chaos, the thrill of the news chase. Their real subject is the adrenaline rush that keeps these journalists hooked to their jobs like junkies, making mincemeat of their private lives.

Howard watches over these driven, obsessive characters like a benignly mischievous master of ceremonies: there are no real villains here. His big, impressive cast (which includes Spalding Gray, Jason Alexander and Catherine O'Hara) responds in kind. Led by Keaton at his breezily manic best, the actors seem to be having almost as good a time as we are.

SIGHT AND SOUND, 5/94, p. 49, Michael Atkinson

7 a.m. Henry Hackett, metro editor of the slightly yellow *New York Sun*, wakes up in the office to find that the city's other dailies have beaten the *Sun* on a front-page story: the apparently racially-tinged killing of two white businessmen in Brooklyn. His pregnant wife Marty, a former *Sun* reporter herself, presents him with a running dilemma—how to meet the needs of his family and those of the paper? On top of that, Hackett has a job interview at the *Sentinel*, an upmarket competitor; the move would mean higher pay and less low-grade newspaper thrills. In the newsroom, Hackett tries to find a quiet moment to sort out his life, as reporters, columnists and editors inundate him with questions. At the morning meeting in editor Bernie White's office, Hackett petitions for a deeper look into the slaying—for which two innocent black youths have been arrested—and has his usual run-in with managing editor Alicia Clark.

At his *Sentinel* interview, Hackett attempts to seduce information about the slaying from that paper's editor, rather than concern himself with getting the new job. Hackett sneaks a look at the editor's notes and reads the name of a belly-up savings-and-loan bank where the murdered businessmen had been executives. Back at his office, he works with a disillusioned *Sun* columnist, McDougal, to flesh out what may turn out to be a Mafia hit, while simultaneously having the arrest of the youths covered for the front page, in case he doesn't get the real story in time. The *Sentinel* editor, apprised of Hackett's unethical tactic, angrily withdraws his job offer.

Marty, suffering from pregnancy cabin fever, plumbs her own downtown connections and glimpses a list of the failed bank's investors, which includes the name of a prominent mobster. With this information, Hackett and McDougal go downtown to get confirmation from a reluctant cop that the arrest of the two kids is purely cosmetic. Hackett rushes back to change the front page celebrating their arrest to a headline announcing their innocence. Unfortunately, he is hours past deadline. Alicia has set the presses running, and Hackett crosses all professional boundaries by stopping them, costing the paper thousands of dollars. Alicia fights with him hand-to-hand over control of the presses, and eventually fires him.

Later, Marty begins haemorrhaging and goes to the hospital. At the same time, Alicia and McDougal are in a bar wrangling over ethics when a city official disgruntled with McDougal's columns starts a fight and shoots at him. He misses and hits Alicia in the leg, just as she succumbs to a fit of conscience and tries to call the press room and get the front page switched to Hackett's headline. In the hospital, Marty gives birth to a son, and Alicia finally contacts the press room, setting the paper straight. The next day, everyone is reading the *Sun*, which for once has got the jump on the other papers.

Maintaining that Ron Howard is the most banal film-making mind in Hollywood is a bit like observing that grass is green—or at least the grass in his Irish epic *Far and Away*, which may stand as an acme of Industry muttonheadedness for some time to come. But, casting a cold eye on his films, from *Splash* through *Willow* and *Parenthood* to *The Paper*, one gets a sense that Howard is more than just a dull-witted, soap-watery Son of Spielberg whose clichéd films happen to cost $30 million plus, and often gross many times more. More than that, Howard is television incarnate: he is Richie Cunningham, the character he played in the *Happy Days* series. His is a world-view shaped by canned laugh tracks, half-hour sitcom plot structure, deadpan reaction shots and backlot hometowns. Having simultaneously grown up on both sides of the TV screen—the "glass teat", as Harlan Ellison has called it— Howard has made millions suckling movie viewers thirsty for easy answers. The rhythms and easy huggability of his movies invoke a cultural subconscious mutated by the shorthand morality of Mayberry, Howard's hometown in *The Andy Griffith Show*. Even by James L. Brooks' standards, his films are equivalent in narrative depth to an episode of *Happy Days*.

For all its big-city brouhaha and teeth-gnashing about ethics, *The Paper* is more like a paragon of Howardism than an exception, however it may leap ineffectively toward the Paddy Chayevsky shelf like a short kid jumping for the cookie jar. Mired in working-man toilet humour and New York Writer clichés (including the climactic visit to the too-famous White Horse Tavern, and cameos by Pete Hamill, Richard Price *et al*), Howard's movie paints with a broad brush, camouflaging with hard-bitten grit its inescapable cousinship to every newspaper movie since *The Front Page*. Michael Keaton's Hackett is the fast-talking newspaperman-with-ink-in-his-veins, Marisa Tomei's Marty is a loveable nag, Randy Quaid's McDougal is gruff, boozy and cynical. Robert Duvall's crusty editor with prostate problems is simply a gone-to-seed variation on Lou Grant.

Glenn Close's Alicia is perhaps the most appallingly simplistic character of all. Little more than her professional harpy of *Fatal Attraction* given a career change and a few months of therapy, Alicia is every working stiff's nightmare female boss, complete with big shoulders and a power complex. She's a paranoid, misogynistic vision from the 80s (she's even willing to sleep with Jason Robards to get ahead), and seemingly the speciality of co-screenwriter David Koepp, previously responsible for the cruel and/or laughable portraits of women in *Death Becomes Her*, *Carlito's Way* and *Jurassic Park*. But much of *The Paper* seems at least a decade old already; it's a belated twin to Brooks' own hellishly glib *Broadcast News*.

Like the Brooks movie, *The Paper* is also easy to suffer through, largely thanks to a cast that, without original characters, still manages to appear interested in the material. It couldn't have been easy, what with the annoying metrocentrism, self-satisfied pronouncements of newsroom slang, and neat, TV-style wrap-up. (A good headline seems to heal every sundered relationship in the movie.) For all *The Paper*'s ostensible realism (one New York critic said the movie was about real newspaper work as much as the Road Runner cartoons were about wildlife in the American Southwest), the ghost of Paddy Chayevsky is summoned more than once in the chaos, which only serves to dwarf whatever dubious achievements Howard and the Koepps might have managed on their own. Chayefsky at his most ludicrous wouldn't have had editors fist-fighting over the press machines (Close gets slugged several times, and takes it like a man), and at his preachiest wouldn't have tied it all up with a bow for a heart-warming climax. He certainly wouldn't have had anyone literally shout "Stop the presses!" Howard may take on large, semi-serious topics, but he always intends to make cotton candy of them in the end. In the way nearly every scene squirms free from its seemingly inevitable interface with real life, you can tell Howard is struggling to remake the world into the one he knew as a pampered, telegenic child. In a very real sense, all of Howard's films are set in Mayberry, whether he realises it or not.

TIME, 3/21/94, p. 71, Richard Corliss

Newspapers—remember them? They're where people used to get their infotainment before CNN, *Hard Copy* and the Letterman Top 10 list. Kids don't read them much anymore; newspapers are nostalgia items for the geriatric Gutenberg generation. And even more anachronistic are newspaper movies, which were nearly always about rapacious reporters chiseling bereaved losers out of their private dignity. *Five Star Final, The Front Page* (*His Girl Friday* in the Cary Grant edition) and *Ace in the Hole* were papers in nutshell, tabloid on celluloid. They gave you the headlines, the editorial and the funnies too. The subject of these movies wasn't even newspapers; it was the American urge for speed and aggression—corporate, personal, romantic.

With a smart cast and a chic patina, Ron Howard's *The Paper* reprises this theme, less to celebrate old times than to offer a skeptical perspective on career men and women. Henry Hackett (Michael Keaton), metro editor for the *Sun*, a New York City tabloid, has to worry about a local race crime—or is it a mob rubout?—on a day when he should be thinking about his pregnant, ex-reporter wife (Marisa Tomei) and the cushier job she wants him to take at an uptown daily. There are clever doses of cynicism and office politicking, but at heart *The Paper* wants to be a *Front Page* for the New Age; most of the tough talk is about ethics. "It was always the truth," intones the paper's columnist (Randy Quaid in a savvy, genial turn). And Henry snarls indignantly, "Not everything is about money."

The recipient of these sentiments—and of a righteous punch from our hero in the film's most ungainly scene—is the *Sun's* female managing editor, played by Glenn Close in a haggard, predatory tone, as if stranded between *Fatal Attraction* and *Sunset Blvd.* One can detect here the fine misogyny of screenwriter David Koepp, who had Meryl Streep and Goldie Hawn destroy themselves for vanity's sake in *Death Becomes Her*. (Koepp wrote *The Paper* with his brother Stephen, a TIME senior editor.)

Having dug up the bones of a cunning old genre, Howard lets the flesh hang like crape. There's *beaucoup* bustle but not much pulse. The pace is too slow for farce, the characters too cartoony for drama. Whereas *His Girl Friday* ran its gags on the fast track, *The Paper* often slows down to lend its galaxy of star types (Robert Duvall, Jason Alexander) a hint of dimension to their roles. But these subplots aren't much more sophisticated than those in *The Wizard of Oz*: Duvall gets a heart, Close a brain, Keaton courage. Tomei gets a baby—and gets left out.

In *His Girl Friday*, Hildy Johnson wound up with the exacta: she got to ditch her fiancé and keep her job. Back then, having it all was getting paid for work you loved doing. Maybe the old days—and the old movies—were more modern than we thought.

VILLAGE VOICE, 3/29/94, p. 60, Alyssa Katz

Never mind the stretch of casting an auteurist's eye on a well-oiled machine like *The Paper*. Ron Howard deserves a round at his movie's Bear's Head bar just for delivering so much frantic energy. A handheld, even zooming camera caroms around the offices of the New York *Sun* as if that onetime New York paper had never actually died. If all the pep talk about the "newspaperman"—the reporters wear that creaky emblem like a scout badge—and the strained scatological repartee in the newsroom come off as a tad antediluvian, well, *The Paper* is about as cutting-edge as the print tabloid itself.

In a fleet 24 hours, affable metro editor Michael Keaton butts heads with his demanding wife (Marisa Tomei, charming under a fleshy pregnancy prosthesis), fights for pennies and deadlines with his witchy managing editor (Glenn Close), wrestles with a job offer from the *Times*-y Sentinel (and later, literally, with Close). The *Sun* takes up *Newsday*'s mantle as the "respectable" tab—in fact, it casually outdoes it. Passing on the chance to run a subway disaster on page one, the editor and his variously incompetent crew set out to prove that two African American teens took the fall for a Williamsburg mob hit.

The farther the action gets from the *Sun* building, the fuzzier it becomes, like an out-of-range cordless phone. In a savory set piece, a half dozen staffers in Keaton's holding pen simultaneously break into screaming rants on ergonomic chairs, hot scoops, lost staplers, death threats. It's a moment of inspired catharsis in a piece of lean cuisine not so much about journalism as the pleasures of pressure-cooker office politics played by clever lunatics. (The low point comes late, with belabored intercutting between a bloody childbirth and the paper's hard-earned run on the presses in a harshly unimaginative play on the "creative" efforts of woman and man.)

The Paper beneficently proffers winking insiderism as if it were a canapé at a company party, but its genesis in the postliterate muck of tabloid TV is unmistakable—the paper itself remains invisible and unread behind its cover, a gesture of the thing. The unions, if there are any, don't make a peep, and, uh, do professional women, like Close, still have to prostitute their integrity to get ahead? Even the tabs rise above that kind of smug nostalgia.

Also reviewed in:
CHICAGO TRIBUNE, 3/18/94, Friday/p. A, Michael Wilmington
NEW REPUBLIC, 4/18/94, p. 30, Stanley Kauffmann
NEW YORK TIMES, 3/18/94, p. C19, Janet Maslin
VARIETY, 3/14-20/94, p. 54, Todd McCarthy
WASHINGTON POST, 3/25/94, p. D1, Rita Kempley
WASHINGTON POST, 3/25/94, Weekend/p. 44, Joe Brown

PARIS, FRANCE

An Alliance Releasing release of an Alliance Communications Corporation/Lightshow coproduction with the participation of Telefilm/Canada/Ontario Film Development Corporation. *Executive Producer:* Stéphane Reichel. *Producer:* Eric Norlen and Allan Levine. *Director:* Gérard Ciccoritti. *Screenplay (based on his novel):* Tom Walmsley. *Director of Photography:* Barry Stone. *Editor:* Roushell Goldstein. *Music:* John McCarthy. *Sound:* Erv Copestake. *Sound Editor:* Manse James. *Casting:* John Buchan. *Production Designer:* Marian Wihack. *Art Director:* Bill Layton. *Set Dresser:* Andris Molodecky. *Costumes:* Ann Tree Newson. *Make-up:* Sandra Moore. *Running time:* 111 minutes. *MPAA Rating:* Not Rated.

CAST: Leslie Hope (Lucy Quick); Peter Outerbridge (Randall Sloan); Victor Ertmanis (Michael); Dan Lett (William); Raoul Trujillo (Minter); Patricia Ciccoritti (Voice of Lucy's Mother).

NEW YORK POST, 2/4/94, p. 36, Bill Hoffmann

Just as the coldest month of winter settles in along comes "Paris France" to heat up the screen with a dizzying display of grappling bodies and sizzling hot sex.

They do it in bed, they do it on the window sill, they do it against the wall—and when that gets boring, they don leather, tie each other up and do it some more.

This new psychodrama from Canadian director Gerard Ciccoritti is an uneven, sometimes pretentious, but never boring exploration of the great obstacle authors, journalists and poets have to face: writer's block.

Moody, dour-faced author Lucy Quick (Leslie Hope), has a real case of the block.

When Lucy lived in Paris, she was a human writing machine, churning out page after inspired page of a novel called "Paris, France" while having hot, dangerous sex with a criminal named Minter.

When Minter mysteriously died, Lucy fled to Canada married an established book publisher and entered a safe, if uninspired lifestyle. But safety has killed Lucy's creativity and sex drive.

Enter Sloan, a young bisexual writer who instantly gets the hots for Lucy. They begin a wild affair.

The couple babbles (pretentiously) about life, death and deviant sex and talk about their private parts as if they were instruments of destruction.

Back in the saddle again, a reinspired Lucy dusts off her unfinished novel and begins writing nightly.

Meanwhile, Lucy's hubby starts believing John Lennon is phoning him, telling him he's going to die in three days.

The characters are all perfectly disposable but their outrageous behavior and unquenchable desires fuel the drama from beginning to end.

NEWSDAY, 2/4/94, Part II/p. 66, Gene Seymour

Much of the advance buzz surrounding "Paris, France" has been over its explicit sex scenes. And, for sure, there are many sequences in this odd little comedy-of-manners that, if nothing else, give fresh meaning to the expression "rough-and-tumble." Same goes for the language, which, like the movie, is an overheated medley of elevated passion and nervy lust.

The drive wheel for this high-speed journey along the edges of erotic excess is Lucy (Leslie Hope from "Talk Radio"), a writer of short fiction whose cult success doesn't keep her from wishing she could finish a novel she started years before: an autobiographical pastiche entitled ... "Paris, France."

She was inspired to write the book by her libido-unleashing encounter with a mysterious poet named Minter (Raoul Trujillo), who claimed intimate knowledge of everything and everybody, But Minter's dead and Lucy's passion—and creativity—have been contained by a marriage with a Toronto publisher named Michael (Victor Ertmanis), a poet-*manque* who's undergoing a severe mid-life crisis, struggling to commune with the ghost of John Lennon.

One Easter weekend, this distraught pair is introduced to a mysterious poet named Sloan (Peter Outerbridge), an ex-boxer obsessed with famed serial killer-ghoul Ed Gein. Seeing Sloan as Minter reborn, Lucy goads him into several rounds of rough love. The "rounds" metaphor is almost literal. At one point, Lucy, garbed in leather dominatrix clothing, dons boxing gloves and spars with Sloan. When she gets in a shot to the jaw, Sloan says, "I love you! " Director Gerard Ciccoritti handles such nasty little interludes with a relaxed, yet evocative touch.

His actors are likewise adept at keeping their roles from drifting into caricature. Hope is a fiery presence throughout and Outerbridge's Sloan is a supple mix of insinuation and confusion. Dan Lett's performance as Michael's publishing partner—yet another blocked writer—is dry and poignant.

If you looked beyond all the body-slamming sex, you could probably make a case that Ciccoritti and writer Tom Walmsley are trying to depict a whole generation of erstwhile hippies and bohemians struggling to retrieve their life-force through the awkwardness of middle age. But it's precisely when that subtext is brought in that the movie ends up sounding more puerile than profound. Better, maybe, to get off on the sly jokes and the shadowy mood.

SIGHT AND SOUND, 8/94, p. 49, Jill McGreal

Good Friday. Writer Lucy Quick and her publisher husband Michael entertain a new author, Randall Sloan, and their friend William, Sloan's agent. The action is intercut with black-and-white flashbacks apparently telling the story of a relationship which took place in Paris at an earlier date, between a poet, Minter, and a woman whom Lucy describes as her friend. It appears that Minter, a friend of Lucy and Michael's, has since died of cancer. At the dinner party, Lucy catches Sloan rummaging through her underwear, and later she gives him the pair of silk panties he had tried to steal. The next day, Sloan arrives at Michael's office. and he and Lucy go to a cheap hotel and have sex.

Meanwhile, Michael has returned home, where he receives a mysterious phone call which he believes is from John Lennon. When Lucy returns home, Michael has become obsessed with a parallel between his life and that of a hybrid Christ/Lennon figure, and imagines that he will die in three days. Sloan returns to William's apartment, where he is staying, and has sex with him too.

On Easter Sunday, Lucy is unable to perform at a reading of her work and is comforted by William. After a row with Michael, she returns to William's flat and plays sex games with Sloan, dressing up in Nazi-style bondage gear. Meanwhile, in Michael's office, Michael and William search for Minter's manuscript; by now it is clear that Minter is Lucy's fantasy lover, and together they are the subject of Lucy's new novel, as depicted in the flashbacks. Michael is fast disintegrating into a mass of delusions and madness, and when he collapses in the office, William kisses him.

Lucy, bored with the dominatrix role, reads to Sloan from her new novel, resolving the action by having Minter's lover (herself) take a razor to his throat. William returns unexpectedly and Lucy hides in the bedroom but reveals herself when she sees Sloan and William having sex. Lucy leaves and William, enraged by Sloan's betrayal, throws him out. Sloan goes to Lucy's flat, where she and the deluded Michael are attempting to have sex. Sloan has sex with them both, and Michael dies while being fucked by Sloan. Finally, a serene and empowered Lucy gazes out of her hotel window in Paris.

The less said about this hysterical movie the better. It abounds with literary and artistic references, starting with the title, taken, presumably, from the novel published in 1940 by Gertrude Stein, in which she mocks the behaviour of the Americans in Paris. The reference to Wenders' *Paris, Texas*, is also unavoidable, and throughout it is as if the filmmakers thought that simply by referring to these and other authors/composers/film-makers (Godard, Bulgakov, Lennon, Buñuel are all heavily present) their own film would thus be rendered more substantial. But the opposite effect is achieved, with every reference simply pointing up the deficiencies of the film in which they are embedded. The black and white flashback sequences are particularly offensive as Godard's *A bout de souffle* and Buñuel's *Belle de jour* are both plundered indiscriminately.

Mainstream movies which manage to capture the erotic are always wondrous anomalies. Genuinely erotic scenes may consist of only a look or a touch, as in *The Piano*, or in the fullest representation of love-making, as in *Don't Look Now*. But what is important is the sexual tension that is established between the characters, and here script and casting come into their own.

David Cronenberg once said that he expected his actors and actresses to "get it up for each other", the implication being that if they then chose to deliver a real sexual performance, then so much the better. He was talking about *Dead Ringers*, in which Genevieve Bujold and Jeremy Irons play out a bondage fantasy with the sort of evident pleasure which reassures the audience about the permissibility of their own fantasies. Porn movies have a different take altogether. Sexual tension is replaced by graphic sexual detail, which can itself be quite sustaining, at least arousing a natural curiosity about the sexual practice of others.

Paris France is neither one thing nor the other. Leslie Hope in Nazi bondage gear, shaving the pubic region of her shackled AC/DC lover, fails to convince when the full frontal shots are of resolutely flaccid penises. The blow jobs are discreetly hidden behind thighs and below waists, and the aggressive sexual energy of the main characters looks more like farce as the camera swings between scenes with a restless, directionless motion. In short, the erotic content is zero, and the pseudo-intellectual context will simply bewilder the dirty mac brigade who may provide the only audience for this ill-judged movie

Canadian film has achieved something of a following in recent years, with directors such as Atom Egoyan and Denys Arcand leading a new wave out of the tax shelter years in the 80s. Both these directors have tackled the erotic with conviction and integrity and within a genuinely intellectual context. *Paris, France* should not be confused with the contemporary Canadian cinema, which has struggled successfully to mobilise the vast Canadian government subsidy programmes to the cause of real film-making.

VILLAGE VOICE, 2/15/95, p. 64, Manohla Dargis

A comely duo does the nasty with choreographed facility as a woman's voiceover intones, "You have to trust your own cunt." The character who speaks these words is Lucy Quick (Leslie Hope), a writer who once upon a time fucked her brains out in Paris, France, and thought herself another Anaïs Nin. Years later, Lucy is married to dull, doughy Michael (Victor Ertmanis), a small-press publisher for whom she also works. Michael, in turn, is business partners with William (Dan Lett), a well-groomed bon vivant partial to opera and smutty pictures. Enter Sloan—a studly ex-boxer whose tribute to serial killer Ed Gein, *Under My Skin*, will soon be published by Michael and William. Sloan fondles Lucy, Lucy screws Sloan, Sloan screws

William, Sloan screws Lucy again, and Michael channels the ghost of John Lennon. Meanwhile, Lucy dreams wetly of Minter, the pouty Parisian who dripped hot wax on her sweaty, bound body and made her whimper, with pleasure, I think. (These particular scenes, shot in black and white, vaguely recall Cindy Sherman's early work but without the wit or animation. They are an attempt at style.)

At once verbal and erotically hot-wired, Lucy is a man-made churning vortex. Though terribly fond of the C-word in circumstances either savage or intimate, I'm skeptical of its deployment by members of the opposing sex. I'm especially skeptical given all the other words screenwriter Tom Walmsley (he's no Henry Miller, to put it kindly) and director Ciccoritti put in Lucy's mouth, even as Sloan and Minter probe her other orifices. Trust your cunt, sure, but girlfriend, trust your brain, too.

Also reviewed in:
NEW YORK TIMES, 2/4/94, p. C6, Stephen Holden
VARIETY, 10/18/93, p. 51, Emanuel Levy

PASSION TO KILL, A

A Rysher Entertainment release of an A-Pix Entertainment film. *Executive Producer:* Keith Samples and William Hart. *Producer:* Bruce Cohn Curtis. *Director:* Rick King. *Screenplay:* William Delligan. *Director of Photography:* Paul Rayn. *Editor:* David H. Lloyd. *Music:* Robert Sprayberry. *Casting:* Denise Chamian. *Production Designer:* Ivo Cristante. *Set Decorator*: Tim Collohan. *Costumes:* Barbara Palmer. *Running time:* 93 minutes. *MPAA Rating:* R.

CAST: Scott Bakula (David Lawson); Chelsea Field (Diana); Sheila Kelley (Beth); John Getz (Jerry Chamberlain); Rex Smith (Ted); France Nuyen (Lou Mazaud); Eddie Valez (Morales); Michael Warren (Martindale).

LOS ANGELES TIMES, 10/21/94, Calendar/p. 8, Kevin Thomas

Maybe the third time Scott Bakula plays an L.A. psychiatrist will be the charm. He got knocked off early on in "Color of Money," and now in "A Passion to Kill," a relentlessly routine psychological murder mystery, he's done in by a lackluster script.

Bakula's Dr. David Lawson receives a double whammy when he meets the beautiful, regal Diana (Chelsea Field), the bride of his best friend Jerry Chamberlain (John Getz). On the one hand, Diana rapidly displays scary mood swings that leave her consumed with brief, perplexing outbursts of rage, and on the other, she attracts David profoundly. Despite the repeated warnings of a friendly colleague (France Nuyen), David allows himself to become swiftly ensnared in an affair with the woman he's supposed to be unofficially counseling at the urgent request of her husband.

Soon the corpses start piling up, and the question becomes simple: Is Diana a crazy woman going around knocking off every man who makes an unwelcome pass at her or is she being set up? Director Rick King keeps us guessing, but he can't keep us caring; David and Diana are too underwritten, too uninteresting, to involve us despite Bakula and Field's best efforts. There's no doubt that David is caught up in a grand passion, but that's no excuse for him and Diana to be such glum characters. The result is that Sheila Kelley, as David's ex-girlfriend, becomes the film's most sparkling presence.

Improbabilities escalate in proportion to the mounting casualties, which might not matter so much if "A Passion to Kill" were as much fun as the recent and outrageous "Trial by Jury:" This is a sleek, painstaking production with great-looking stars and settings, but its Sunset 5 engagement seems but a stopover on the way to thc video store.

NEWSDAY, 11/4/94, Part II/p. B7, John Anderson

The psychosexual thriller demands a certain suspension of disbelief, and not just among the audience. What, you find yourself asking, are the characters thinking? Don't they know? Can't they see?!

In order to make a movie like "A Passion to Kill," you need characters who've never seen a movie like "A Passion to Kill"—or "Black Widow," or even "Basic Instinct"—and who are capable of ignoring the obvious. Otherwise, they'd be running for their lives as soon as the plot devices started popping up: the mysterious beauty with the emotional problems, predatory sexuality and history of violence; the love triangle; the corpses; her protestations of innocence. And, of course, the man who believes in her, even when her own mom would be ready to pull the switch.

Thankfully, "A Passion to Kill" has Scott Bakula, late of TV's "Quantum Leap," as designated dupe. Despite the fact that he's portraying a highly successful Beverly Hills psychiatrist named David Lawson, Bakula is rumpled and comfy enough to let us believe that, yes, he just might be lured into the libidinous cul-de-sac of Diana Chamberlain (Chelsea Field). And Field, who has a uniquely sexual screen presence, adds to our understanding of David's hormonal slavery.

Other aspects of "A Passion to Kill" are more difficult to handle or discuss without giving away too much. So if you want to turn the page now, let's just say the film has an appealing if not particularly inspired cast and will keep your interest.

Whether it will be entirely convincing, or whether its basic premise is unscrupulous, is another story. When we meet Diana, her name is Lily and she's stabbing her husband Ted (Rex Smith) who, in a drunken, lustful rage has struck her. Flash ahead seven years and Diana (now Diana), has married David's best friend Jerry (John Getz) after a whirlwind romance. Almost immediately, Jerry becomes concerned about Diana's mood swings and erratic sexual impulses, and engages David to act as Diana's ad hoc therapist. David and Diana, of course, have an affair, and Jerry, of course, winds up dead, after slapping Diana in a drunken, lustful rage. Yes, she knows how to pick 'em.

There's a neat little twist involving David's old flame Beth (the captivating Sheila Kelley), who gets blamed for the crimes, but we also learn, bit by agonizing bit, that Diana was sexually abused as a child and this, apparently, lets the filmmakers have it both way's. Keep her sympathetic, while manipulating the audience's suspicions for maximum mileage. As I said, this is not a bad thriller, but it may be thoroughly amoral.

Also reviewed in:
NEW YORK TIMES, 11/4/94, p. C10, Janet Maslin
VARIETY, 10/24-20/94, p. 68, Steven Gaydos

PAUL BOWLES: THE COMPLETE OUTSIDER

A First Run Features release. *Producer:* Catherine Warnow and Regina Weinreich. *Director:* Caterine Warnow and Regina Weinreich. *Director of Photography:* Burleigh Wartes. *Editor:* Jessica Bendiner and Amanda Zinoman. *Music:* Paul Bowles. *Sound:* Samantha Heilweil. *Running time:* 60 minutes. *MPAA Rating:* Not Rated.

WITH: Allen Ginsberg; Ned Rorem; Paul Bowles.

NEW YORK POST, 9/7/94, p. 32, Michael Medved

"Life isn't about other people. It's about one's self against the world. Against everything and everybody."

So say's Paul Bowles, the 84-year-old cult novelist and composer who's the focus of this spell-binding documentary. The film arrives as part of the new wave of interest in his life and work launched, in part, by Bernardo Bertolucci's lavish (but snooze-inducing) 1990 film adaptation of Bowles' acclaimed novel "The Sheltering Sky."

"Paul Bowles: The Complete Outsider" offers not a single dull moment, as its charismatic subject offers trenchant insights about writing and living.

In addition to Bowles' own observations, the film includes interviews with longtime friends (including poet Allen Ginsberg), beautifully shot sequences showing the exotic streets of Tangiers, Morocco (where Bowles has lived for 40 years), and even scenes from a surrealistic 1950s film featuring the author with his handsome, muscular Moroccan lover.

All of this is accompanied by a sound track of Bowles' own music: hugely appealing, jaunty but acerbic compositions that recall the work of the French master Francis Poulenc.

Inevitably, the film spends much of its time looking at its subject's relationship with his hauntingly beautiful wife, the novelist Jane Bowles; together they formed what one observer goes so far as to describe in the film as "the most glamorous couple who ever lived." They were both primarily homosexual, and avidly pursued same-sex relationships during the course of their stormy, doomed marriage.

Bowles himself remains largely reticent on the subject of Jane, so the filmmakers make the mistake of interviewing some of his biographers to get down the details of the relationship. These people are too young to have directly observed the long-ago incidents they describe, so their narratives are jarring.

One needn't support Ginsberg's contention that Bowles deserves recognition as "as one of the great writers of the century" to feel fascinated by the irresistible energy of this versatile, free-spirited intellect—especially when it's presented in a film that does such a subtle job of exploring the always intriguing connection between an artist's life and work.

VILLAGE VOICE, 9/20/94, p. 64, B. Ruby Rich

Paul Bowles fans from casual to obsessive have a new fetish item: an up-close look at the object of reverence himself, walking, talking, and returning our gaze. Paul Bowles is still alive! That's the inevitable subtext of this enterprise, and not the worst reason for making a documentary. Nor the best. One part pilgrimage, one part archaeology, *Paul Bowles: The Complete Outsider* is a footnote to an ongoing canon that's beginning to rival Bloomsbury.

Collaborators Catherine Warnow and Regina Weinreich use Weinreich's correspondence with Bowles as a structuring device: the letters lead us in and out of Bowles's witty ruminations and observations on the life around him. The pair are focused on Bowles the serious artist, but generally not (sadly) on the scandalous details of his marriage to Jane Bowles or relationships with scores of Tangiers youths that have occupied most of the histories. As a result, though, we get to learn about Bowles the composer, whose work even gets an onscreen plug from Ned Rorem. Bowles blames his exit from poetry on Gertrude Stein's withering judgment. Of course, what Stein most liked was to hear him read her own writing aloud. Clips from the little-seen Hans Richter film; *8 x 8*, capture Bowles in the '50s frolicking with a musician pal. But it's Allen Ginsberg who steals the show when he pronounces the Bowles style a product of "kif" consciousness, paradigm of a drug aesthetic.

In the end, there's less to *Paul Bowles* than might have been hoped for. Avoiding the familiar stories and legends, avidly pursuing the high culture route of honoring and exploring the master at work, Warnow and Weinreich overplay the reverence at the expense of the important. It's silly to think that his sexuality (and its influence on his oeuvre) can simply go unmentioned, for instance. And worse yet to exile Jane Bowles from the story with omission or patronizing attack. Still and all, it's undeniable fun to see Paul Bowles in sync sound and to relive postwar expat culture with the guys who made it buzz. Besides homoeroticism shows up on the bill in the accompanying short, *Death in Venice, California*, which updates Thomas Mann to Muscle Beach.

Also reviewed in:
CHICAGO TRIBUNE, 4/14/94, Friday/p. J, John Petrakis
NEW YORK TIMES, 9/7/94, p. C13, Stephen Holden
VARIETY, 6/20-26/94, p. 43, Ken Eisner
WASHINGTON POST, 12/30/94, p. C1, Rita Kempley

PLACE IN THE WORLD, A

A First Look Pictures release. *Producer:* Adolfo Aristarain. *Director:* Adolfo Aristarain. *Screenplay (Spanish with English subtitles):* Adolfo Aristarain and Alberto Lecchi. *Based on a story by:* Adolfo Aristarain and Kathy Saavedra. *Director of Photography:* Ricardo De Angelis. *Music:* Patricio Kauderer. *Art Director:* Abel Facello. *Running time:* 120 minutes. *MPAA Rating:* Not Rated.

WITH: José Sacristán (Hans); Federico Luppi (Mario); Cecilia Roth (Ana); Leonor Benedetto (Nelda); Gastón Batyi (Ernesto); Rodolfo Ranni (Andrada); Lorena Del Rio (Luciana); Hugo Arana (Zamora).

LOS ANGELES TIMES, 8/17/94, Calendar/p. 5, Kevin Thomas

Adolfo Aristarain's superb "A Place in the World" is at once a memory film, an exceptionally intelligent coming-of-age story, a commentary on Argentina's turbulent, harrowing, recent political history and a consideration of just how much an individual can hope to accomplish with his or her life.

Beyond all this, it is a warm and good-humored celebration of adult friendship and strong family ties. In short, it is remarkable how much Aristarain's film encompasses while involving us with the kind of density and detail we associate with the most inviting novels. Intriguingly, he has stated that his film was inspired by "Shane" and, "How Green Was My Valley."

(What a shame that this beautiful, rueful yet inspiriting picture, an Argentina-Uruguay co-production, was nominated for a best foreign film Oscar for the awards ceremony held in 1993, only to be disqualified over a conflict in regard to its country of origin.)

The film unfolds as a flashback when a young man visits a small remote town (which could easily pass as a desert outpost in the American Southwest) for the time in nine years. With the same effortless grace that Aristarain uses to introduce his various themes, he swiftly acquaints us with that man as an adolescent, Ernesto (Gaston Batyi), and a host of others who will impact upon his life. The key figures are Ernesto's parents, Mario (Federico Luppi) and Ana (Cecilia Roth); their friend, a nun named Nelda (Leonor Benedetto); and a newcomer named Hans (Jose Sacristan), a Madrid geologist hired by the local landowner to investigate the possibility of oil reserves in the area.

All in good time we learn that Mario and Ana were driven into exile during Argentina's military dictatorship. Upon returning, they struck out for Bermejo Valley, where they formed a cooperative with the local peasants, mainly sheepherders. Mario teaches school while Ana, a physician, runs a clinic.

They are in perfect sync with Nelda, a witty, devout but free-thinking activist who refuses to wear traditional nun's garb. The sheer, down-to-earth goodness of these three dedicated but embracing people will have a crucial effect upon the cynical, lonely Hans, a peripatetic two-time divorcé. Meantime, Ernesto is experiencing first love with Luciana, a local girl (Lorena Del Rio) whom he teaches how to read, despite her father's disapproval.

These people are truly charismatic, and the emotional heart of the film really is in mealtime gatherings, marked by amusing, passionate and intellectual conversation of a level heard rarely outside an Eric Rohmer film. Because Aristarain in his prologue has introduced a sense of the transitory quality of life, we soon experience that familiar feeling of the overwhelming obstacles facing those who try to make a difference, or merely to live a decent life.

Aristarain touches upon that universal, highly contemporary sense that we are powerless to control our destinies. Yet in the face of such feelings, Mario realizes that he has discovered his "place in the world," and with it the belief that it's worth standing his ground—even if that ground seems to be crumbling beneath him.

How refreshing it is to be in the company of such talented actors bringing to life people who are worth caring about. The film, which has an especially evocative score, is in particular another triumph for the handsome, silver-haired Luppi, who makes Mario a figure of unpretentious nobility. Most recently seen in the darkly humorous horror picture "Cronos," both he and

Aristarain achieved international renown in 1981 with the scathing, compelling political allegory, "Time for Revenge."

NEW YORK POST, 7/1/94, p. 44, Thelma Adams

Is the world ready for a socialist "Shane"?

Producer/director Adolfo Aristarain affectionately rips off George Stevens' classic 1953 Western to tell the coming-of-age story of a young boy searching for "A Place in the World."

Set in rural, post-Peron Argentina the movie adopts the point of view of 12-year-old Ernesto (Gaston Batyi). His parents, cosmopolitan Peronistas who have returned from Spanish exile, are committed to making their ideas work on a local level.

Mario (Federico Luppi) is a sociology professor who now teaches at a one-room schoolhouse and leads a collective for local sheep farmers. Ana (Cecilia Roth), a Jewish physician, tends to the workers ln a ramshackle clinic.

Enter geologist Hans (Jose Sacristan), a hired gun for the local "jefe" who changes the lives of Ernesto's family.

He falls in love with Ana, befriends Mario and makes a pass at a beautiful nun, Nelda (Leonor Benedetto).

Like everything else in this predictable if heartfelt and well-acted movie, it's only a matter of time before Hans switches allegiances.

Like Alan Ladd in "Shane," he soon takes up the call to defend the homesteaders—in this case the local peasants—against the exploitative landowners.

The characters are often more intelligent than the script, which telegraphs every action. A repeated motif—Ernesto racing a train in his pony cart—will always have the game outcome. Ernesto crosses the tracks a breath ahead of the engine. The audience knows the result of every horse race before it's run.

Aristarain, who also co-wrote the script, forgets that the tension in a Western is the conflict between good and evil.

Andrada (Rodolfo Ranni), the landlord, arrives on the scene after the first hour and is a cigar-smoking heavy with no history. Similarly, Aristarain, like his protagonists, apparently loves the People in theory, but he doesn't seem to think his peasant characters are worth developing.

The most interesting twist occurs inadvertently. Mario can't dissuade the collective from selling their wool crop to Andrada at a low price.

Unable to abide by the people's decision, the professor torches the wool warehouse and reduces a year's labor to burnt hair. Lurking in every collective is a tyrant—what a refreshing insight!

A more interesting film could have been made about the uneasy relationship between the intellectual idealists from out-of-town and the pragmatic peasantry, rather than a socialist fable that gives Ernesto a place in a fantasy world where landlords always wear black hats.

NEWSDAY, 7/1/94, Part II/p. B7, Gene Seymour

Most, if not all, coming-of-age stories are pervaded by wistful melancholy. Yet much of what makes "A Place in the World" more interesting than similar tales is the way such emotions are spread among both the adults and the 12-year-old Argentine named Ernesto (Gaston Batyi), whose sensitive observations nudge the movie along.

Both grownups and adolescents in writer-director Adolfo Aristarain's story are caught up in the dilemma of how one compensates for not getting what one wants. Or, *pace* the Stones, even what one needs.

Both Ernesto's doctor mom (Cecilia Roth) and teacher dad (Federico Luppi) were left-wing activists who fled to Spain when Argentina was ruled by a military dictatorship. They continue a sort-of exile in a remote village in the San Luis Mountains, keeping their populist vision alive by helping poor shepherds organize a self-sufficient collective with help from a hip, casually attired nun (Leonor Benedetto).

The nun's hipness is soon superceded by the arrival of an ultra-cool Spanish geologist (Jose Sacristan), who's doing some mysterious work for the wealthy rancher against whom the poor sheepherders are united. Ernesto is spellbound by the geologist's worldly wisdom. So is everyone else in the family—especially mom, who seems to be cultivating a serious crush on him.

Ernesto's got romantic problems of his own. He's fallen for the illiterate daughter of the greedy rancher's foreman, who is violently opposed to any effort to teach her to read, Ernesto nonetheless conducts secret reading lessons for the daughter in a barn. Inevitably, they both begin learning lessons of love as well.

While all this is going on, the geologist,who's become fond of Ernesto's family, risks his gig by revealing its purpose: He's surveying the village's rugged land mass so the government can build a dam. With the financial windfall bound to come to the town, Ernesto's dad sees both his dreams and a way of life coming to an end.

Aristarain excels at sustaining a burnished, elegiac mood and manipulating allusive dramatic devices. It's always nice to see a movie that gives its audience permission to draw its own conclusions about the characters. (Since we're seeing the film through Ernesto's eyes, we've no choice.) Yet the film seems, in the end, hamstrung by its rueful tone and wayward complexity. It dares us to care, but there's little force, or even conviction backing it up.

VILLAGE VOICE, 7/5/94, p. 56, Julie Lang

When I no longer have expectations, when my needs vanish, I can forgive what frustrates me. Yes, *A Place in the World* is not flawless: the plot crawls at times (freighted more with relentless emotion than thematic development), while the relationship between the film and the audience is cut too short—I'm right on the brink of tears, ready to let go, and then one scene just up and leaves me stranded for another.

Structurally, this Argentinian-Uruguayan film parallels George Stevens's classic western *Shane*. In the role of the former gunslinger destined for glory in the eyes of little Joe for his defense of good, all-American, Bible-thumping homesteaders, Hans Mayer Plaza (Jose Sacristan), a Spanish geologist, appears in the poverty-stricken, mountainous farmlands of the fictitious Bermejo Valley in Argentina. Although Hans works for the iniquitous land baron Andrada (Rodolfo Ranni), he befriends the struggling, Communist-bent couple Ana (Cecilia Roth) and Mario (Federico Luppi), and reveals to them Andrada's scheme to exploit the region's destitute farmers. Their world—with Hans as the beloved foreigner—is observed, respected, and narrated by their 12-year-old son, Ernesto (Gaston Batyi). More than *Shane*'s, *A Place in the World*'s relationships move beyond a strong look or a firm handshake: in a drunken fit of laughter with Mario—which echoes the seductive inebriation of *Betty Blue*—Hans turns to the sober and peeved Ana at four in the morning to confess, "I love you," and then, "I love you both," and Hans and Mario kiss and hug and stumble into each other's arms.

I could tell you more, like how Ernesto's ambiguous "you" filters throughout the opening scene to brilliantly create a direct rapport with the audience, or how political strife threatens Ana, a Perónist Jew, or even how the title itself signifies a spiritual quest for, literally, geographical self-definition. There is so much more—have patience with the film's shortcomings and instead assimilate the tender humanity that escaped me until I realized I felt no longer stranded.

Also reviewed in:
CHICAGO TRIBUNE, 11/25/94, Friday/p. M, John Petrakis
NEW YORK TIMES, 7/1/94, p. C3, Stephen Holden
VARIETY, 8/3/92, p. 40, Domingo Di Nubila

PONTIAC MOON

A Paramount Pictures release. *Executive Producer:* Jeffrey Brown, Ted Danson, and Bob Benedetti. *Producer:* Robert Schaffel and Youssef Vahabzadeh. *Director:* Peter Medak. *Screenplay:* Finn Taylor and Jeffrey Brown. *Story:* Finn Taylor. Director of Photography: Thomas Kloss. *Editor:* Anne V. Coates. *Music:* Randy Edelman. *Sound:* Kim Ornitz and Ric Waddell. *Casting:* Jane Jenkins and Janet Hirshenson. *Production Designer:* Jeffrey Beecroft. *Art Director:* Wm. Ladd Skinner. *Set Decorator:* Robert J. Franco. *Costumes:* Ruth Myers. *Running time:* 108 minutes. *MPAA Rating:* PG-13.

CAST: Ted Danson (Washington Bellamy); Mary Steenburgen (Katherine Bellamy); Ryan Todd (Andy Bellamy); Eric Schweig (Ernest Ironplume); Cathy Moriarty (Lorraine); Max Gail (Jerome Bellamy); Lisa Jane Persky (Alicia Frook).

LOS ANGELES TIMES, 11/11/94, Calendar/p. 2, Peter Rainer

"Pontiac Moon" is one of those movies in which every action is meant to be symbolic. It's so symbolic—make that Symbolic—that it never really makes you care about what it's symbolizing.

Ted Danson plays Washington Bellamy, an oddball high school English teacher who, on the eve of the 1969 Apollo moon landing, drives his 1949 Pontiac Chief 1,776 miles—as in 1776, the year of the Declaration of Independence—in order to run the mileage up to 238,857—the distance between the Earth and the moon. He's a big believer in the "one perfect act," and he's gotten it into his hare-brained noggin that this odyssey will turn his life around.

His son Andy (Ryan Todd), a moon-shot buff, is along for the trip, and there is lots of father-son bonding and unbonding and rebonding going on in that Pontiac. Washington's wife, Katherine (at least she's not named Martha), is played by Mary Steenburgen in a role that's perhaps too jarring for this frail falderal.

Katherine is intensely phobic about leaving her home—she hasn't set foot outside in seven years. But when her husband and son set off on their trek, she muscles up the courage to follow them. Her pursuit is comical—her vehicle is one of those '60s amphibious cars that floats—but it's also touching. Her fears are motivated by a past family tragedy, and only her love for her son keeps her from seizing up in terror. Steenburgen gives Katherine an addled pluckiness that makes her the movie's true hero.

Unfortunately, most of the time we're on the road with Washington and Andy, and their roadside encounters with rednecks and hard-scrabble law officers as they move through Utah and Arizona and New Mexico are enough to make similar scenes from "Easy Rider" seem almost egalitarian. For a movie that's so preachy about virtue and "perfect acts," "Pontiac Moon," directed by Peter Medak from a Finn Taylor and Jeffrey Brown script, goes in for some really crass common man caricature. Is this really the spirit of '76?

Danson is so intent on playing a kookie (yet wise) eccentric that he's not believable for a moment. He mugs and prances and tries to work up a vaudeville rhythm with Ryan Todd. They keep getting upstaged by the scenery: Monument Valley once again lights up a movie. (Shouldn't it be getting a special Oscar by now? Or maybe the Jean Hersholt Humanitarian Award?) There are some nice bits from Cathy Moriarty as a seen-it-all waitress, and Eric Shweig plays a Vietnam vet Native American with a minimum of hokum. But by the time we get to the inevitable desert-walk/moonwalk parallels, you may want to start your own trek up the aisle.

NEW YORK POST, 11/11/94, p. 48, Michael Medved

"Pontiac Moon" once more takes us back to the haunted summer of 1969 and suggests that the Apollo XI mission to the moon not only distracted America from the horrors of Vietnam and urban riots, but helped to rescue the members of one dysfunctional family from the prison of their own neuroses.

Mary Steenburgen plays a pretty but petrified young mother who hasn't set foot outside her cluttered Victorian home in seven years, following some mysterious tragedy.

Ted Danson is her exuberant eccentric, science teacher husband who worries about their bright bookish boy (Ryan Todd) who's spent all of his 11 years in their small town, on the Northern California coast, since the mother won't let him ride in cars.

Inspired by the moon mission, Danson plans a daring escape in his beloved 1949 Pontiac Chief. He'll take his son on a four-day journey to Spires of the Moon National Monument to echo the astronauts' epic expedition to the lunar surface; by the time father and son race to their destination, the odometer on their classic car will read 238,857—matching the distance between Earth and the moon.

As soon as they depart on this trek, the worried mother suddenly overcomes her stubborn agoraphobia, gets into another of her husband's odd assortment of antique cars. and does her best to catch up with them.

This script (by debuting writers Finn Taylor and Jeffrey Brown) offers up the sort of self-consciously "sensitive" material that gets "A" grades in film school, and might even win screenwriting prizes, but plays poorly on screen.

The family's adventures seem utterly contrived and the characters they meet on the way—a brooding Vietnam vet (Eric Schweig) hitchhiking back to his Indian reservation, a floozy cocktail waitress (Cathy Moriarty) with round heels but a heart of gold, plus vicious, fight-picking rednecks in cowboy hats and jean jackets—all seem to derive from other movies rather than any authentic on-the-road experience.

Hungarian-British director Peter Medak ("Romeo Is Bleeding," "The Krays") blows up his scenes of the Great American West (including, inevitably, the overused Monument Valley) to look like travel posters rather than actual landscapes, but his affection for the oddball, over-written characters nearly saves the picture.

He's also been blessed by a hard-working cast; Steenburgen gets her best role since her Oscar-winning turn in "Melvin and Howard," making her troubled character both laugh-out-loud funny and profoundly touching.

Danson cast against type, also does a nice job. As with his surprisingly strong work in "Getting Even With Dad" a few months ago, he seems doomed to deliver his most impressive performances in mundane and mediocre movies.

The particular moon mission may never get off the launching pad, but its hitchhiking Native American does offer two pieces of valuable advice: "First don't sweat the small stuff. And second, everything is small stuff."

The silly story here definitely amounts to small stuff, but still offers the gentle joys of seeing fine actors doing solid work with no sweat.

NEWSDAY, 11/11/94, Part II/p. B7, Jack Mathews

The moment we first see and hear Ted Danson in "Pontiac Moon," in a classroom full of slackjawed children listening to his overheated lecture about sperm, it is clear that some horrible decisions have been made. Not only is Danson badly miscast as a nerdy science teacher, but he has chosen to play him like some drunk spouting "Hamlet" in a neighborhood bar.

There is over the top, and there is over the moon, and apropos the subject of this peculiar road movie, about a father and son trying to mimic the imminent 1969 Apollo 11 moon landing, Danson goes all the way.

And he is not the only one. Mary Steenburgen, as an agoraphobic who braves the outdoors to follow her husband and son across country, plays her part in a full-blown Lucy Ricardo panic attack, flailing around on the screen like a raw nerve trying to stuff itself back in its sheath. It's the kind of performance that tests the resolve of reformed smokers.

Directed by Peter Medak, with a composer's wand, I imagine, "Pontiac Moon" is all about personal epiphanies and scientific miracles, which are one and the same to Danson's Washington Bellamy, a lame Korean War veteran whose passion for life has been stifled by the same tragedy that drove his wife indoors seven years earlier.

Fearing that his 11-year-old son Andy (Ryan Todd) is taking root in his mother's isolation, Washington comes up with a scheme for the boy and himself to share "one perfect act." They will hop into Washington's classic 1949 Pontiac Chief convertible, and drive a circuitious 1,776-mile (symbolism alert!) route from their home in California, planning to arrive at a landmark desert crater at the precise moment the Apollo 11 crew reaches its destination, and with the Pontiac's odometer reading exactly 238,857—the distance in miles between the Earth and the moon.

Along the way, as the landscape becomes increasingly similar to the gray, pocked surface of the moon, they encounter rednecks, a yahoo sheriff, a predatory, Mae Western-style waitress (Cathy Moriarty), a gentle American Indian Vietnam vet (Eric Schweig), a band of a soulful hippies and other denizens of an imaginary 1969 desert.

It's all very fanciful, and perfectly absurd. The script, the first feature effort by Finn Taylor and Jeffrey Brown, uses the moon landing and the juxtaposed family adventure as an excuse for some serious father-son bonding, some dubious '60s social commentary, and as a device to force Washington and his wife to confront their earlier tragedy. But you cannot do all that heavy lifting on the backs of actors whose feet never touch the ground.

In a film boiling with symbolism, they missed their best opportunity. The car should have been an Edsel.

Also reviewed in:
NEW YORK TIMES, 11/11/94, p. C18, Janet Maslin
VARIETY, 11/7-13/94, p. 46, Brian Lowry

POSTCARDS FROM AMERICA

A Normal Films Inc. production. *Executive Producer:* Mark Nash. *Producer:* Craig Paull and Christine Vachon. *Director:* Steve McLean. *Screenplay:* Steve McLean. *Adapted from the writings of:* David Wojnarowicz. *Director of Photography:* Ellen Kuras. *Editor:* Elizabeth Gazzara. *Music:* Stephen Endleman. *Music Editor:* Nic Ratner. *Sound:* Neil Danziger and Jan McLaughlin. *Sound Editor:* Tim O'Shea. *Casting:* Daniel Haughey. *Production Designer:* Thérèse Deprez. *Art Director:* Scott Pask. *Costumes:* Sara Slotnick. *Make-up:* Tim Dark, Barri Scinto, and Mandy Lyons. *Running time:* 93 minutes. *MPAA Rating:* Not Rated.

CAST: Jim Lyons (Adult David); Michael Tighe (Teen David); Olmo Tighe (Young David); Michael Imperioli (Teen Hustler); Michael Ringer (David's Father); Maggie Low (David's Mother); Les 'Linda' Simpson (Trippy); Dean 'Sissy Fit" Novotny (Port Theater Drag Queen); Tom Gilroy (Adult David's Friend); Peter Byrne (St. Sebastian); Bob Romano (Art Dealer); Oona Brangham-Snell (Little Girl); Colin Blair Fisher (Young David's Friend); Rick Bolton (Uncle); Lane Burgess (Aunt); Joyce George (Ideal Mom); Jay Nickerson (Ideal Dad); Jonathan Turner and Lea Gulino (David's Neighbors); Thom Milano (Policeman); Crosby Romberger (David's Brother); Allyson Anne Buckley (David's Sister); Augustus Goertz (Mugged Man); Todd Marsh (Son with Aids).

NEW YORK POST, 10/8/94, p. 17, Larry Worth

Before emitting a primal scram on an empty highway, the handsome gay protagonist of "Postcards From America" announces: "Something in my body is trying to Kill Me." And no, it's not AIDS.

Instead, child abuse memories, experiences as a teen-age Times Square hustler and adult years filled with anonymous sex contribute to an emotional cancer. Director/writer Steve McLean uses the soul-piercing yell as a launching pad to chapters in one man's tortured history.

Initially, McLean's stream-of-consciousness narrative style proves off-putting and confusing. But the skillfully shot tableaus—occasionally sweet, more often ugly—slowly merge into an arresting mosaic, aided by strong performances from a cast of newcomers.

The bottom line: the pictures in "Postcards" certainly aren't pretty, but the message is undeniably haunting.

NEW YORK POST, 7/21/95, p. 40, Thelma Adams

Walking through "The Decade Show" at SoHo's New Museum of Contemporary Art in 1990, the art of David Wojnarowicz stood out in a loft space crammed with flamboyant work. His function of images and text was ferocious, in-your-face and as lucid as the funny pages. He created a potent myth to parallel Huck Finn's odyssey down the Mississippi: that of the boy-next-door who swam outside the mainstream in that dark river of gay culture.

"Postcards From America," Steve McLean's fictionalized biopic of the late artist felled by AIDS, never matches the clarity and power of Wojnarowicz's artwork, although it treats its subject with mythic reverence.

McLean makes his feature directorial debut after gaining most of his experience in British music videos. He chooses a fractured narrative, intercutting three distinct stages in the artist's life: his boyhood as his father's punching bag, his teens as a New York street hustler, and his adult life. Olmo Tighe, his brother Michael, and Jim Lyons play the respective parts.

The early years are, a self-conscious effort to show the seamy underside of suburbia and the American dream—imagine if the Beaver's dad was a drunken sailor and his mom was powerless to protect him from the physical abuse. Based on Wojnarowicz's autobiographical narratives, McLean shoots a series of tawdry and trite scenes of domestic violence in a threadbare living room shrouded in a theatrical horizon of darkness.

This theme of paternal abuse in common in gay literature. It raises a troubling question: Did the boy's homosexuality arise out of the abuse? This idea is at odds with current p.c. opinion that homosexuality is innate and not a product of a child's environment—but then why all those, beastly, battering papas in gay lit?

The scenes of Wojnarowicz as a teen hustler in Times Square arise out of the foam: How did the kid with the crewcut become the scraggly youth doing the nasty with gents from New Jersey for a dime? Wojnarowicz courts abuse on the streets, as if he has escaped his father only to seek out an endless line of repetitions, brutal punishments for his own desires.

The grown Wojnarowicz, has made peace with his homosexuality but faces the ravages of AIDS. McLean sets the artist against a desert landscape, portraying him as a man who loves the open road but whose own path is finite.

These adult sections are frequently disjointed and incoherent. Two yahoos pick up the artist, threaten him with guns and then dump him at the side of the road—why? He suddenly has a lover dying from AIDS—who is he and where did he come from?

The movie's biggest hole is that the cinematic character barely reveals himself as the visual artist who blazed a trail through the New York art world. Except for a scene in which thc hustler discusses a painting with a partner before fantasizing his murder with a nearby sculpture, and a few paintbrushes soaking in a sink, there's no sense of his unique creative life, With all his worrying about his father and prowling for sex, there seems to be no time for McLean's semi-fictional Wojnarowicz to develop the talents that were so evident at "The Decade Show."

NEWSDAY, 10/8/94, Part II/p. B5, John Anderson

Based on the poetry and prose of the late artist and AIDS activist David Wojnarowicz, this frequently hallucinatory, often alarming and somewhat derivative film by debuting British director Steve McLean is another example of the fascinating things that can happen when non-Americans examine the American psychological landscape. Owing much to Terence Davies, Derek Jarman and even Todd Haynes, McLean uses riveting imagery, blackouts, black humor and the violence that marked Wojnarowicz' writing to portray the gay male experience starkly and relentlessly. Not an easy film, but nobody said it was going to be easy.

SIGHT AND SOUND, 4/95, p. 51, Paul Burston

A man wanders through a desert landscape. His face is dripping with sweat. In a voice-over, he indicates that he is in a state of intense emotional anguish. He screams. Inside his apartment, he washes his face in a sink piled high with dirty dishes and paint-brushes. He announces that there is something inside his body trying to kill him. His name is David and he begins talking through some episodes of his life, roaming back and forth between scenes of him as a boy, as a younger man, and at roughly the age he is now.

Denied the love of his mother, abused by his alcoholic father, the boy David plays in the woods, goes swimming in the lake and fantasises about growing up in a perfect American family. Escaping the suburban nightmare of New Jersey, he hitchhikes to New York, where he lives hand to mouth as a hustler, "looking for the weight of some man to lie across me to replace the non-existent hugs and kisses from my mom and dad." He meets with a variety of men—a married lawyer who sees to it that he gets a good meal; a man who offers him a lift and then rapes him; a supercilious art collector he dreams of murdering; a "rich fag" he and a fellow hustler attempt to mug with a pair of ill-concealed meat-cleavers; two young thugs who drive him into the desert and threaten to shoot him.

Death finally takes hold when David's lover develops Aids, bringing back memories of David's father's suicide. He stumbles around the desert, swearing that if he could only merge his own body with that of his dying lover, he would.

When the artist and writer David Wojnarowicz died of an Aids-related illness in July 1992, he had become a kind of American legend. His paintings, photography, installations and one-man performances made him the talk of New York's East Village art scene. But it was his two semi-autobiographical books, *Close To The Knives* and *Memories That Smell Like Gasoline*, which brought him to the attention of a much wider audience, and prompted at least one critic to label him the Jack Kerouac of the Aids generation.

In the first (subtitled *A Memoir of Disintegration*), Wojnarowicz offers a scathing account of what it means to grow up queer in America—raging against homophobia, government indifference to the Aids crisis and "the sense of death in the American landscape". In the second, he provides a moving testament to the longing for love and sexual contact in the shadow of the epidemic.

Steve McLean's visually arresting first feature draws heavily on these books for its narrative content and fragmentary structure. From a series of jumbled snapshots of David's life as an abused child, a homeless hustler and a grieving lover, we gradually piece together a portrait of a man desperately at odds with the world. "Sometimes it gets dark in here, behind these eyes", the adult David tells us at the start, and the film is an attempt to take us deep into the heart of his interior darkness.

From the blinking opening titles to the last formalised flashback to David's violent childhood, McLean employs a range of technical devices which succeed in conveying the necessary sense of dislocation, but run the risk of obscuring all points of identification beyond a personal one between the director and author. In this regard, David's mother talking directly to camera about how her husband "beat my little boy with a chain" evokes far greater sympathy than an elegantly choreographed scene in which the father is shown silently beating the child in a stylised 50s living room.

The frantic jump-cutting and choice of imagery (a boy curled up in a bird's nest, a bully transmogrified into Saint Sebastian) suggest a significant debt to Derek Jarman, while the scenes where the camera roves around the family home are reminiscent of Terence Davies. But the biggest influences are young and American. Co-produced by Christine Vachon (producer on Todd Haynes' *Poison* and Tom Kalin's *Swoon*), and featuring Jim Lyons (one of the stars of *Poison*) as the adult David, *Postcards From America* looks like a tailor-made application to the New Queer Cinema Club.

The vital components are all there—the flagrant disregard for so-called positive images, the romantic sense of out-siderdom, the love of the road and desire for dark-eyed men with dirty thoughts and feelings. But while these aspects of McLean's film are an undeniable source of pleasure, they don't necessarily serve the material well. Wojnarowicz's reputation as a queer outlaw was shaped by his own HIV status and acute awareness of how "death comes in small doses". And while *Postcards* certainly beats the designer nihilism of a film as self-consciously 'queer' as Gregg Araki's *The Living End*, it never matches the emotional intensity of a more linear Aids narrative such as *Savage Nights*.

Postcards ends, where it began, in the desert. In a sense, it's the same desert Cyril Collard found himself in at the end of *Savage Nights*— only there is no suggestion of transcendence. Nor, strangely, is there much sense of the raw anger which drove Wojnarowicz to explore such desolate territory. In a chapter of *Close To The Knives* entitled 'Postcards From America: X Rays From Hell', he wrote that, "my rage is really about the fact that when I was told that I'd contracted this virus it didn't take me long to realise that I'd contracted a diseased society as well".

For all its visual flair, McLean's film focuses on the disease of the body without really reflecting on the society responsible for it. When David's hustler friend remarks that "America is such a beautiful place, isn't it?", you can't tell whether he is being ironic or not. Watching *Postcards From America* won't make you wish you were here, but neither will it start you wondering about where that "here" is.

Also reviewed in:
NEW YORK TIMES, 10/8/94, p. 14, Stephen Holden
VARIETY, 9/19-25/94, p. 80, Todd McCarthy

PRINCESS CARABOO

A Beacon and TriStar Pictures release of a Longfellow Pictures/Artisan Films production. *Executive Producer:* Armyan Bernstein, Tom Rosenberg, and Marc Abraham. *Producer:* Andrew Karsch and Simon Bosanquet. *Director:* Michael Austin. *Screenplay:* Michael Austin and John Wells. *Director of Photography:* Freddie Francis. *Editor:* George Akers. *Music:* Richard Hartley. *Music Editor:* Jupiter Sen. *Sound:* Peter Glossop. *Sound Editor:* Eddy Joseph. *Casting:* Lucy Boulting. *Production Designer:* Michael Howells. *Art Director:* Sam Riley. *Set Decorator:* Sasha Schwetd. *Special Effects:* Ian Wingrove. *Costumes:* Tom Rand. *Make-up:* Nuala Conway. *Make-up (Kevin Kline):* Barbara Southcott. *Make-up (Phoebe Cates):* Christopher Redman. *Stunt Coordinator:* Roma Gorrara. *Running time:* 94 minutes. *MPAA Rating:* PG.

CAST: Jim Broadbent (Mr. Worrall); Phoebe Cates (Princess Caraboo/Mary); Wendy Hughes (Mrs. Worrall); Kevin Kline (Frixos); John Lithgow (Professor Wilkinson); Stephen Rea (Gutch); Peter Eyre (Lord Apthorpe); Jacqueline Pearce (Lady Apthorpe); Roger Lloyd Pack (Magistrate Haythorne); John Wells (Reverend Hunt); John Sessions (Prince Regent); John Lynch (Amon McCarthy); Arkie Whiteley (Betty); Kate Ashfield (Ella); Ewan Bailey (Ship's Captain); Annabel Brooks (Lady Neville); Anna Chancellor (Mrs. Peake); Rachel Fielding (Mrs. Benson); Anoushka Fooks (Charlotte); David Glover (Musician); Jerry Hall (Lady Motley); Jamie Harris (Tom); Peter Howell (Clerk of the Court); Barbara Keogh (Mrs. Wilberforce); Anthony Van Laast (Second Dressmaker); Philip Lester (Print Worker); Steven Mackintosh (Harold); Tim McMullan (Light-fingered Aristocrat); Murray Melvin (Lord Motley); Dougray Scott (Dragoon Captain); Andrew Seear (Mr. Peake); David Sibley (Harrison); Ed Stobart (Footman); Stromboli (Fire Eater); Pauline Thomson (First Dressmaker); Jacqueline Tong (Mrs. Hunt); Edward Tudor-Pole (Lord Neville).

CHRISTIAN SCIENCE MONITOR, 9/8/94, p. 14, David Sterritt

Another offering that pleased most Montreal [World Film Festival] observers is "Princess Caraboo" an American and British coproduction. Mingling a suspenseful story with a frolicsome mood and occasional dark undercurrents, it's based on the true story of a mysterious young woman who appeared in an English town during the early 19th century, sparking great interest with her exotic manners and unknown history.

There's much to enjoy in filmmaker Michael Austin's account of her unexplained arrival, her growing fame in British society, and her immersion in a controversy that puts her in deadly danger. Still, the movie's pleasure comes less from its plot than from its crisp performances by Phoebe Cates as the so-called princess, Jim Broadbent and Wendy Hughes as upper-crust folks who take her in, John Lithgow as a scholar who studies her, Kevin Kline as a servant who suspects her, and Stephen Rea—fresh from "The Crying Game," another keep-'em-guessing conversation piece—as a journalist who becomes a key player in her little game.

LOS ANGELES TIMES, 9/16/94, Calendar/p. 4, Kevin Thomas

Witty and hilarious, "Princess Caraboo" is at once a romantic adventure and a comedy of manners in the finest tradition of British screen humor, a sophisticated entertainment that should be a delight for older children as well with its Cinderella-like story.

An outstanding international cast, impeccable period design, a lively score and an inspired screenplay have been blended to perfection by astute director Michael Austin to create a lively and constant pleasure. Amazingly, the film is based on a true story.

The appearance of the mysterious Princess Caraboo in England on or near Good Friday in 1817 marked the convergence of two dominant social forces. Laws concerning begging, fraud and vagrancy had just been made extremely harsh while the Prince Regent, with his fanciful Brighton Pavilion in the midst of an elaborate remodeling, had made fashionable fantastic interpretations of Asian decor and clothing.

Consequently, when a proud, beautiful but dirty-faced young woman (Phoebe Cates) shows up in Bristol, wearing a turban and pants and uttering sparse phrases from a vaguely Southeast Asian dialect she is at once in mortal danger and in a position of great opportunity.

If she can be proven to be a fraud she faces death by hanging; if she catches the fancy of the nouveau riche, the aristocracy and especially thc fatuous heir (John Sessions) to the throne himself, a fabulous life of luxury and privilege awaits her.

Austin and his co-writer John Wells have succeeded on two important counts: first, in scattering the fewest possible tidbits of conjecture about the woman who calls herself Caraboo, and second, in showing just how rapidly people will weave them into a plausible, albeit far-fetched, narrative.

Very swiftly it is widely understood throughout the community that Caraboo really is a Southeast Asian princess who was kidnaped by pirates but who managed to jump ship in the Bristol Channel. Quite apart from the question of the authenticity of Caraboo's identity, the film suggests just how badly people can want to believe in someone for myriad reasons.

Caraboo, in any event, finds shelter at a handsome Adamesque country estate rented by the Worralls (Wendy Hughes, Jim Broadbent). Mrs. Worrall, who has inherited money, is kind and elegant while her husband is a comically lusty, womanizing vulgarian, a greedy entrepreneurial banker of dubious financial stability.

Only human, Mrs. Worrall can't help but take some pleasure in the social cachet that having a real princess under her immense roof has brought her. By contrast, Worrall intends to exploit Caraboo's presence to better his financial position in any way he can.

Along for the fun are such sterling players as Kevin Kline, as the Worralls' splendidly haughty Greek butler; John Lithgow, as a pedantic Oxford linguist intent on exposing Caraboo as a fraud; and, most important, Stephen Rea as a shrewd but caring Bristol journalist suspicious yet protective of her.

While it is a joy to see these and other actors create a polished, witty ensemble, "Princess Caraboo" has as its most unusual accomplishment the ability to make us conscious of the important political and financial role fashion can play in society and individual destiny, a phenomenon rarely implied outside films on Louis XIV, who deliberately gathered the rich and powerful at Versailles and then depleted their coffers via the absurdly fancy attire they were expected to wear.

To this end production designer Michael Howells and costume designer Tom Rand have made crucial, major contributions as the film charts the gradual, ever-increasing overlay of exoticism in decor and clothing inspired by the exquisite princess.

NEW YORK POST, 9/16/94, p. 44, Michael Medved

Is she princess or impostor?

The British nobility, and even one member of the royal family, believe she's the real thing—the shipwrecked daughter of a powerful king on some exotic island. One cynical journalist, on the other hand, is determined to expose her as an audacious phony—in a society where fraud is punishable by death.

Amazingly enough, the new film "Princess Caraboo" manages to keep you guessing right down to the final minutes of the movie. Whenever you're convinced that the main character must be an obvious fake, the movie turns up some new clue that leads you to believe she just might be telling the truth.

It's all based on an actual episode from 1817, when British authorities picked up a turbaned vagrant (here played by Phoebe Cates) who spoke no known language and followed bizarre religious practices in the poorhouse where they confined her.

Eventually, she was taken under the wing of a wealthy, boorish squire and his kind-hearted wife (Jim Broadbent and Wendy Hughes) who enjoyed the public attention and social prestige that Caraboo's presence brought to their country estate.

For instance, a pompous Oxford scholar (nicely played by John Lithgow) came to call for the purpose of examining the mysterious lady and using his expertise to determine her origins. Though at first dismissing her unintelligible language as mere gibberish, he quickly fell under her spell and began to believe her story.

The superb supporting cast also includes Stephen Rea of "The Crying Game" as the newspaperman who tries to prove that the girl is a fake, but remains utterly captivated nonetheless. That old scene-stealer Kevin Kline (Cates' off-screen husband) is laugh-out-loud hilarious as a curmudgeonly Greek butler with a contemptuous attitude toward his employers and, at first, to Caraboo.

Phoebe Cates, meanwhile, gets the sort of role that every actress dreams about and she certainly makes the most of it. Though the early years of her career featured dull, empty (though undeniably decorative) screen appearances, here she is nothing short of miraculous; her wondrously subtle performance works on many levels at once, making Caraboo utterly compelling even when no one understands a word she says.

Director/co-writer Michael Austin (previously best known as writer of "Greystoke" and "Five Days One Summer") takes us back in time to a world that hadn't yet lost its sense of wonder—that still expected startling discoveries from all the remote, unexplored corners of the globe. This aura of curiosity and excitement help make this an ideal film for children to enjoy with their parents. I took my 7-year-old to the screening and I'm proud to say it's the first "grownup" movie she has unqualifiedly loved.

In fact, it's hard to imagine anyone, of any age, resisting the potent charm of this very royal "Princess"; it leaves behind such a pleasant impression that it brings a smile to your face whenever you think back on it.

NEWSDAY, 9/16/94, Part II/p. B5, Jack Mathews

The fact that Michael Austin's "Princess Caraboo" is based on a true story works for the film in the same way that another historical incident worked for French director Daniel Vigne's "The Return of Martin Guerre," and "Sommersby," the American remake of "Guerre."

You watch all three period movies about confused identity with severe skepticism, confident that if you had been on the scene you'd have known the truth immediately. Yet, something like these stories did occur, and the knowledge adds a haunting quality to the dramatizations.

The "Guerre"/"Sommersby" films were based on the recorded tale of a 16th-Century French soldier who assumed the identity of a fallen comrade, and returned to the dead man's village to take up his presumably better life. "Princess Caraboo" is the story of a mysterious young woman (played by Phoebe Cates) who suddenly appears at an estate in 1817 England, wearing a black turban and pants and speaking an exotic unknown language, to turn the heads of nobles and peasants alike.

Is she an East Indian princess who escaped a slave trader's ship and swam ashore in Bristol Channel, as her wealthy hostess Mrs. Worrall (Wendy Hughes) believes? Or is she a phony playing out an elaborate hoax, as the journalist Gutch (Stephen Rea) and others suspect?

Much is at stake. If found a fraud, she will be hanged forthwith, hoaxes being capital offenses against the aristocracy. If accepted as royalty, she could blend into high society, perhaps even marry her own prince, and live out her life in splendor.

Shot on manorial grounds near London, primarily in and around an old estate dressed to blend oriental flourishes with European grandeur, "Princess Caraboo" is a visually striking film that, despite its richly comic tone, says a lot about the British class system. The more accepted Princess Caraboo becomes by the patricians, the more she is appreciated by the commoners, who vicariously relish her pampered life.

Austin, whose only previous feature was the black comedy "Killing Dad," plays his is-she-or-isn't-she? game with such skillful delicacy there isn't a chance of leaping ahead in the story. If Caraboo isn't the real thing, she possesses the best poker face in the kingdom, and with Gutch, the Oxford scholar Wilkinson (John Lithgow), and the impertinent Greek butler Frixos (a very funny Kevin Kline) all trying to trip her up, there isn't a flicker of evidence in her manner, movements or behavior to betray her.

Audiences are likely to be surprised by the outcome, regardless of how they think the mystery will unfold. With a marvelously regal bearing, Cates makes Princess Caraboo a truly charismatic figure, and a deft counterpoint to the smugly corrupt nobles around her.

The romantic subplot between Princess Caraboo and Gutch, who evolves from her chief skeptic to her chief supporter, adds the only false note to the story, and it's clear from their last scenes together that even Austin didn't buy it. But missteps made in such good will are easily forgiven.

NEWSWEEK, 10/3/94, p. 69, David Ansen

In 1817, on the English country estate of a nouveau riche coupled called the Worralls, an exotic young woman (Phoebe Cates) appears, speaking no recognizable language. Is she a gypsy? A vagrant looking to escape prison? Or is she, as all who fall under her spell are eager to believe, a shipwrecked Oriental princess? Princess Caraboo is based on a true story, but director Michael Austin, who wrote the script with John Wells, knows that the fun of it is as a fable of the prince/pauper/Pygmalion ilk. The tale is at times better than the telling, for Austin's cinematic style is more prosaic than magical. But there is both ample wit and charm here, and how many movies these days provide either? What Austin does have is a wonderful comic cast at his disposal: Jim Broadbent as the boorish, social-climbing Mr. Worrall and Wendy Hughes as his kindly, gullible wife; Kevin Kline evoking giggles as their snobbish Greek butler, and a hilarious John Lithgow as an Oxford don brought in to verify the mystery woman's authenticity. Romantic interest is supplied by Stephen Rea as a skeptical journalist determined to get to the bottom of Caraboo's story. Rea is hardly a conventional heartthrob: he has a face like an unmade bed. The diffident charm that was so effective in "The Crying Game" still works, but his self-effacement is approaching self-parody. Sooner or later, the princess captures everyone's heart; sooner or later, you, too, will succumb to "Caraboo's" modest, sweet enchantments.

NEW STATESMAN & SOCIETY, 12/16-30/94, p. 59, Jonathan Romney

It takes a lot of hindsight to say whether or not it's been a good year, so let's just say it's been a year. There's been a lot of good cinema and plenty of bad, but despite the diversity, it seems there's less to talk about, or less that people want to talk about. There seem to have been only three films this year that it's been mandatory to have opinions about—*Four Weddings and a Funeral, Pulp Fiction* and *Natural Born Killers*—and two of those are to do with Quentin Tarantino, and one hardly anyone's seen anyway. (To be honest, it shouldn't make too much difference to anyone if *NBK* never gets a British release; there are already plenty of Metallica videos in the shops). Upsettingly, academic friends tell me that their film classes now want to talk about Tarantino to the exclusion of all else; Jean-Luc Godard has become that guy that Quentin keeps referring to. Make a cultural difference now, engage a student in small talk about Chen Kaige instead.

It's a pretty ropey way to end the year, too: if you're in the doldrums between Christmas and New Year, get further into them with Louis Malle's *Vanya on 42nd Street*, his studiously informal theatrical version of Chekhov's *Uncle Vanya* as rewritten by David Mamet. It's a sober, well-meaning piece, full of lovingly crafted close-ups and characters calling each other "little father". The play-within-the-film stars Wallace Shawn and is directed by Andre Gregory, the stars of Malle's *My Dinner With Andre*, and the thesps you'd most like to slap. It's all so deadly serious; Malle seems to be doing penance for the idiocies of his *Milou* in *May* and *Damage*, but the idea of doing Chekhov at the pace of an underwater funeral went out with Stanislavsky. Some fine acting though, as if that was ever a reason for going to the cinema.

What's on offer before Christmas is hardly more inviting—martial arts in Rio (*Only the Strong*), Brian Blessed in a cut-price recreation of Culloden (*Chasing the Deer*), and not one but two Macaulay Culkin vehicles. Then there's Michael Austin's *Princess Caraboo*, which is of interest mainly because it's the sort of film that we can expect to see a lot of in the wake of *Four Weddings and a Funeral*—set in bucolic English locales, crammed with droll English insouciance and minor TV names, and likely to interest no one except American middle-brow audiences (it's actually a very transatlantic project, with US and UK producers).

Princess Caraboo is in some ways the ultimate English heritage film—a twee, decorative view of the past with plenty of familiar faces to guide us around the spacious lawns, but also going one better than Merchant-Ivory by taking its aesthetic of frocks and wigs from the honourable Gainsborough Films tradition of costume melodrama (veteran British cinematographer Freddie Francis photographs it in a style that can only be called "handsome").

Based on a true story, Princess Caraboo is set in England in 1817, where a mysterious young woman (Phoebe Cates) is discovered wandering around dressed like an extra in an Ingres painting and muttering a strange, mellifluous idiolect. She's taken in by a wealthy couple, and everyone is convinced that she's a princess from an island off the coast of Java. All walks of society salute her, only to end up with egg on their delicately powdered faces.

The film begins with a weary journalist, Gutch (Stephen Rea), telling the tale and mulling distractedly over a map of the "Spice Islands", which fairly spells out what English fantasies the film is to be about. In any other week, we'd have to roll up our sleeves and grapple with Questions Around Orientalism—but, please, it's been a long year. *Princess Caraboo* in any case manages to defuse those questions by not dealing with them terribly well, although it's not entirely the fault of the script (by director Austin and John Wells), which gets in a few sly jabs at Little Englishness. "A foreigner?" recoils a nob, presented with the mysterious waif. "Yes", replies the parson, played by Wells himself as a rat-wigged version of his Denis Thatcher, "but she's not French so you needn't be concerned."

Because it's a light comedy, there's no point expecting *Princess Caraboo* to be any pithier than it is—until you think back to Ealing and realise what Robert Hamer or Alexander Mackendrick would have done with it. It would have had bit parts for Alistair Sim or Miles Malleson, for a start. As it is, we get Jim Broadbent in uncharacteristically clumsy form as the Squire, a nicely abject John Lithgow, and John Sessions as the Prince Regent, done up in fancy dress as the Mikado (he actually looks like a panto dame with a head full of light fittings).

Kevin Kline is unwisely encouraged to air another one of his funny accents, as a moustache-curling Greek butler. Kline's act floats free of the film, and in a satire about English attitudes to those funny foreigners, can only be counted something of an own goal.

It's all terribly well done—the lovely houses, the way the aristos cock one snotty eyebrow, the curry-combing of the horses. But there's no bite to it, partly because Austin is so anxious to pay homage to a history of costume larks (not only Gainsborough, but the short-lived 1960s picaresque cycle of *Tom Jones* and its imitators); and partly because the film is so keen for us to fall in love with Phoebe Cates from the outset. She is, in fact, surprisingly charismatic, spinning a bewildering line in pert, bemused glossolalia, and seemingly sharing a joke with herself: as if anyone could *possibly* imagine her to be inscrutable!

But, perhaps for the sake of international sales, Austin can't resist over-explaining for us what a beastly place 1817 England was, with its hangings and snobbery and bad skin. He should either have down-played it in the interests of satire, or pushed it to the hilt; he does neither, leaving us instead with a lamentable feel-good ending that had me dashing my clay pipe to the ground in disbelief.

SIGHT AND SOUND, 1/95, p. 53, Philip Kemp

Devon, 1817. Two farm lads find a young woman wandering through the countryside wearing exotic clothes and speaking an unknown language. The local vicar takes her to Mrs Worrall at the manor house of Knole. Despite the hostility of the Greek butler, Frixos, Mrs Worrall is impressed with the stranger's bearing and lets her stay. But Mr Worrall, a banker, returns home next morning and packs her off to the Assizes as a vagrant.

In court, the woman conveys that she is Caraboo, a Javanese princess captured by pirates and enslaved, who jumped ship in the English Channel. Her story attracts the interest of John Gutch, a journalist. Mrs Worrall takes Caraboo back to Knole, where she is treated with honour. Her behaviour wins over Frixos and the other servants while Mr Worrall, whose bank is in trouble, sees the chance of lucrative trade with the Indies.

Gutch, though attracted to Caraboo, remains sceptical and consults Professor Wilkinson, an expert in exotic languages. At first dismissing Caraboo as a fraud, Wilkinson becomes besotted with her and is ignominiously ejected from Knole. Caraboo's fame spreads, attracting the interest of the Worralls' friends Lord and Lady Apthorpe. They abduct her for a grand ball at their house, where she dances with the Prince Regent.

Gutch has meanwhile traced Caraboo's real identity as a servant girl called Mary Baker. Gatecrashing the ball, he tries to warn her, but her ex-employer identifies her from a newspaper report. Furious, Worrall has Mary arrested and condemned to death. With Mrs Worrall's help, Gutch blackmails Worrall with evidence of his bank frauds; Mary is released and given passage to America. Gutch sadly sees her off, but at the last moment joins her on board. Back at Knole, Frixos brings Mrs Worrall a news item: the Princess Caraboo, her ship blown off course, has been entertained by the exiled Napoleon on St Helena.

At the climax of *Princess Caraboo* the heroine is feted at a costume ball of garish vulgarity, presided over by the Prince Regent (a rouged and prancing John Sessions) in a getup suggesting a ninth-rate touring production of *The Mikado*. Beside these grotesques, Caraboo's supposedly exotic garb appears the height of tasteful simplicity. Polite society, the film conveys, is all a masquerade, and a pretty inept one at that. The humble ex-servant, refugee from a home for reformed prostitutes, plays the game better and more convincingly than the sophisticates around her ever could. Which, of course, is precisely what they can't forgive her.

Michael Austin's film sketches in the background of a brutal and punitive age when begging meant flogging or jail, and capital crimes by the hundred clogged the statute book. (Parallels with present-day political tendencies aren't far to seek.) Bodies hang in the market square, a backdrop too common to excite much notice; armed dragoons clatter across country, striking terror into even the middle classes. These oppressive images underline Gutch's warnings to Caraboo of the danger she runs if she's found out. Yet a sense of danger is just what's lacking: the tone of the film remains light and playful, the threat to Mary/Caraboo stated but never felt. The reassuringly happy ending casts its glow well in advance.

This is partly because *Princess Caraboo* isn't simply about masquerade, but much of the time plays like one. Austin has encouraged (or allowed) most of his cast to adopt high-pantomime style, with Jim Broadbent's Mr Worrall setting the pace. His wife's sudden insight into his "true nature" might carry more weight if he weren't such a fatuous oaf from the word go. As the butler Frixos, Kevin Kline walks off with the Tom Conti Award for Duff Greek Accent of the Year, while various well-loved exponents of the British eccentric school (Murray Melvin, John Wells, Edward Tudor-Pole) turn in their zany cameos. Only John Lithgow, as the lovelorn professor, manages to infuse a nominally buffoonish role with real pain and desolation.

Against this tuppence-coloured setting, Phoebe Cates' portrayal of the bogus princess stands out with appealing seriousness. Resisting the temptation to tip us the wink, she maintains the enigma to the very moment of defeat—though once unmasked, her character carries less conviction. The working-class girl denied an outlet for her imagination and turning it to an elaborate scam on society needed more fury and resentment than the script gives her scope for; here too, the film's cheery tone lets her down. Given a darker vision, a closer engagement with its period and the courage to ditch the happy ending, Michael Austin's film could have tapped into something resonant and disturbing. As it is, *Princess Caraboo* is consistently good-looking (the cinematography is by the veteran Freddie Francis), amusing—and forgettable.

Also reviewed in:
NEW REPUBLIC, 10/10/94, p. 33, Stanley Kauffmann
NEW YORK TIMES, 9/16/94, p. C12, Caryn James
VARIETY, 8/29-9/4/94, p. 42, Daniel M. Kimmel
WASHINGTON POST, 9/16/94, p. F7, Hal Hinson

PRINCESS AND THE GOBLIN, THE

A Hemdale Communications release of a Siriol/Pannonia Film Company, co-production in association with S4C Wales/NHK Enterprises. *Executive Producer:* Steve Walsh and Marietta Dardai. *Producer:* Robin Lyons. *Director:* Jozsef Gemes. *Animation Director:* Les Orton. *Screenplay:* Robin Lyons. *Based on the novel by:* George MacDonald. *Editor:* Magda Hap. *Music:* Istvan Lerch. *Sound:* Clive Pendry. *Sound Editor:* Imre Andras. *Special Effects:* Zsuzsanna Bulyiki and Piroska Martsa. *Running time:* 82 minutes. *MPAA Rating:* G.

VOICES: Sally Ann Marsh (Princess Irene); Mollie Sugden (Lootie); Peter Murray (Curdie); Claire Bloom (Irene's Great Great Grandmother); Rik Mayall (Froglip); Robin Lyons (The Goblin King); Peggy Mount (Queen); Roy Kinnear (Mump); Victor Spinetti (Glump); Joss Ackland (King-Papa).

LOS ANGELES TIMES, 6/3/94, Calendar/p. 6, Charles Solomon

"The Princes and the Goblin," a new animated feature opening today, feels like 82 minutes of audio-visual junk food—cloying, devoid of significant content and ultimately unsatisfying.

Based on the 1872 novel by Scottish writer George MacDonald, this fairy tale focuses on Princess Irene (voice by Sally Ann Marsh), who leads a sheltered life in her father's castle with only her bumbling governess and her cat, Turnip, for company. On a walk, she meets Curdi (Peter Murray) a miner's son, who learns, that subterranean goblins are plotting to seize the kingdom. Curdi foils their plan with a little help from Irene and the royal guards because he knows the goblins' weaknesses: They hate singing and stepping on their feet is the only way to hurt them.

All ends happily, although the screenplay by producer Robin Lyons leaves many loose ends dangling. Why is Curdi the only person who knows how to defeat the goblins? While sneaking through the underground kingdom, he discovers the Queen Goblin (Peggy Mount) has six toes off each foot, while her subjects have only one: Why is this significant-sounding discovery never mentioned again? How do the goblins manage to flood a castle on a hill by unleashing one underground stream? (Can they teach my landlord how to generate that much water pressure?)

Parents who sit through the film will have ample time to devise answers, as the characters aren't interesting enough to hold thc viewer's attention. Irene and Curdi are perfect Victorian children who make waxworks figures seem lively. Curdi just wants to do good deeds; Irene will only go where the magic thread of her great-great-grandmother's ghost (Claire Bloom) leads—she takes no real risks and therefore doesn't really grow.

The animation, done by crews in Wales and Hungary, looks like Saturday morning kidvid. Director Jozsef Gemes, is widely respected for his epic paint-on-glass feature, "Heroic Times" (1982): He deserves better material—as do the children who'll be parked at a matinee of "Princess" while their parents shop in an adjacent mall.

NEW YORK POST, 6/3/94, p. 35, Michael Medved

What's a critic supposed to do when his 7-year-old daughter responds very differently from her father to a movie that's aimed squarely at her age group?

At the very least, I'm compelled to report her opinion and to note for the record that second-grader Sarah Medved unreservedly loves the new animated feature "The Princess and the Goblin." She's already watched it four times, and three of her classmates who have also seen the movie say that they share her enthusiasm.

I wish that I could wholeheartedly join this chorus of youthful praise, but to me "The Princess and the Goblin" seemed relentlessly adequate; a well-meaning fairy tale with animation that's capable rather than captivating.

The film is based on an 1872 novel by the beloved Scottish writer (and preacher) George MacDonald. The story centers on Princess Irene (the voice of Sally Ann Marsh), a spirited child she helps to defend her father's kingdom against a planned assault by amusingly grotesque goblins who live under the earth and want to overthrow the tyranny of the "sun people."

The goblin attack is led by the spoiled prince Froglip (voice of comedian Rik Mayall) who wants to kidnap and marry the human princess. Her defenders are a brave miner boy, Curdie (voice of Peter Murray) and the kindly ghost of her great-grandmother (voice of Claire Bloom).

Curdie understands that music is the best weapon against the goblins: Whenever he begins singing they cover their ears and run off in terror. Unfortunately most adult movie-goers will experience a similar reaction to his vocal stylings, especially when he repeatedly shrieks out the film's unbearable theme song, "The Spark Inside Us." Some sparks, it turns out are best kept inside.

Nevertheless, the animators in this Welsh-Hungarian co-production produce some genuinely exciting scenes, especially when the goblins unleash a huge flood that threatens the castle and all its inhabitants. The film also promotes values of duty, honor and family commitment that most parents want to convey to their kids.

The main reason the movie will play so much better to those kids than it does with adults might be described as the "Mr. Rogers" factor. It's a fact that many youngsters strongly prefer "Mr. Rogers" to "Sesame Street" even though few of their parents would endorse the choice.

It's a matter of pacing and tone: "Mr. Rogers" (as well as "The Princess and the Goblin") features a gentler, more easygoing aura that young kids find comfortable and reassuring.

Parents, meanwhile should feel reassured when their children remain sensitive and unspoiled enough to respond with wonder to a wholesome, likable piece of family entertainment like this one. No, it's hardly a classic like "Beauty and the Beast" but Sarah and her friends assure young moviegoers that they'll have a wonderful time.

NEWSDAY, 6/3/94, Part II/p. B11, Steve Parks

The princess, along with the rest of the Sun People, acts as though she hasn't been using enough sunscreen. She's been fried stiff. Her joints have atrophied. Her dollish face has hardened into a one-expression-fits-all countenance. And when she speaks, her lip-syncing will remind you of a bad kung-fu import.

The subterranean goblins, on the other hand, appear to have thrived in darkness. They're witty, colorful, acrobatic and, except for a mean streak and an intolerance for music, more fun than the boring Sun People who rule the above-ground kingdom.

This is hardly the first animated feature in which the bad guys have upstaged the good. But here, the animators seem to have been working on two different films. In fact, separate teams—one in Wales and another in Hungary—produced the animation for "The Princess and the Goblin."

The film is based on a 19th century Scottish children's fable. The goblins, banished long ago to the underground by the Sun People, are plotting a revolt. And since they live inside the very mountain on which the royal castle is perched, Princess Irene makes a convenient kidnap target. Her life in danger, the spirit of her great-great-grandmother appears to Irene, granting her the gift of an inexhaustible spool of magic thread. All she has to do is follow the thread in and out of danger with her new-found friend, Curdie, a miner's son. Curdie is the only Sun Person who knows how to fight the goblins—stomp on their sensitive, mono-toed feet, or sing to them.

For the most part, "The Princess and the Goblin" is charmingly innocent and old-fashioned, though a few scattered attempts have been made to de-sentimentalize it. A preschool- and grade-school-age audience attending a recent screening gave an in-unison endorsement—"G-R-R-R-oss!"—when one goblin picked his nose and another wolfed down a fistful of insects.

Especially appealing, in their comically repulsive way, are Prince Froglip, who intends to marry the kidnaped Princess Irene so he can rule the kingdom, and his mother, the Queen, who's the only goblin smart enough to protect her feet by wearing shoes.

The watercolor-style scenery, with its subtle use of mists and cobwebs, works handsomely with goblins in the foreground. But the lifelessly drawn Sun People look out of place against an alive, moving background. While kids who watch made-for-TV cartoons may excuse such technical lapses, they may not forgive the relative innocence. "The Princess and the Goblin" will appeal to younger children.

SIGHT AND SOUND, 1/93, p. 50, Leslie Felperin Sharman

In a mythical kingdom, King Papa lives in a castle with his daughter, Princess Irene. While the king is away on business, Irene gets lost in a nearby forest and encounters menacing creatures, the Cobs, who try to steal her cat, Turnip. They are saved by Curdie, a young miner's son, who reveals that both the Cobs and their owners, the Goblins, are repelled by singing. Later, back at the castle, Irene meets her great-great-grandmother, who has mystical powers and warns Irene not to be afraid of an imminent danger.

Curdie, meanwhile, gets lost underground while working in the mine, and discovers the Goblins' secret plot to flood the mine. Irene receives a magic ring and thread from her grandmother which will always lead her to safety. When Curdie returns to the mine a second time, he is captured after learning of the Goblins' plan to kidnap Princess Irene and marry her to the loathsome Prince Froglip so that he can usurp her father's power. Using the magic thread, Irene ventures into the underworld and rescues Curdie, and together they return to the castle to warn everyone.

Curdie is accidentally injured by two guards, and the warning is not conveyed until it is too late. The castle is besieged by Goblins, and Irene is captured. Curdie, magically healed by the grandmother, helps the guards to fight off the Goblins, who have also attempted unsuccessfully to flood the mine and the castle. In the midst of the deluge, Curdie rescues Irene from the clutches of Prince Froglip, and is rewarded with a kiss. Everyone lives happily ever after.

The Princess and the Goblin is a *My Little Pony* of a movie, and about as enjoyable as the film of that name which was released several years ago. The preponderance of background shots and static tableaux stalls the action, and suggests cost-cutting measures to save on cel animation. The movements of the characters are often jerky, while their sizes relative to each other change perceptibly without any *Alice in Wonderland*-type mushrooms or cakes in sight. The excellent draughtsmanship of the final flood sequence is lost in the welter of clumsy work that has preceded it.

The story itself is so predictable that one suspects its source is less "a novel by George MacDonald" than some generalised construct from Vladimir Propp's *Morphology of Folk Tales*. Even *Freddie as F.R.O.7.*, despite a similarly clumsy technical execution, had a certain charm and freshness. Despite having an accomplished Hungarian director, József Gémes, and an experienced team of European animators, *The Princess and the Goblin*, with its ersatz-Disney look, offers little hope to those who would like to see a distinctively European kind of animated feature. It will be even more unsatisfying for those looking for a good night out with the children this Christmas.

Also reviewed in:
CHICAGO TRIBUNE, 6/3/94, Friday/p. H, John Petrakis
NEW YORK TIMES, 6/3/94, p. C15, Stephen Holden
VARIETY, 1/11/93, p. 64, Derek Elley
WASHINGTON POST, 6/6/94, p. D7, Rita Kempley

PROFESSIONAL, THE

A Columbia Pictures release of a Gaumont/Les Films du Dauphin production. *Executive Producer:* Claude Besson. *Director:* Luc Besson. *Screenplay (French with English dialogue):* Luc Besson. *Director of Photography:* Thierry Arbogast. *Editor:* Sylvie Landra. *Music:* Eric Serra. *Sound:* Pierre Excoffier, Gérard Lamps, François Groult, Bruno Tarrière, and (music) William Flageolett. *Sound Editor:* Patrice Grisolet. *Casting:* Todd Thaler and Nathalie Cheron. *Production Designer:* Dan Weil. *Art Director:* Carol Nast and Gérard Drolon. *Set Decorator:* Carolyn Cartwright and François Benoît-Fresco. *Special Effects:* Al Griswold and Nicky Allder. *Costumes:* Magali Guidasci. *Make-up:* Geneviève Peyralade. *Running time:* 112 minutes. *MPAA Rating:* R.

CAST: Jean Reno (Leon); Gary Oldman (Stansfield); Natalie Portman (Mathilda); Danny Aiello (Tony); Peter Appel (Malky); Michael Badalucco (Mathilda's Father); Ellen Green (Mathilda's Mother); Elizabeth Regen (Mathilda's Sister); Carl J. Matusovich (Mathilda's Brother); randolph Scott and Keith A. Glascoe (Stansfield Men); Frank Senger (Fatman); Lucius Wyatt "Cherokee" (Tonto); Luc Bernard (Mickey); Jessie Keosian (Old Lady); Abdul Hassan Sharif (Mathilda's Taxi Driver); Stuart Rudlin (Leon's Taxi Driver); George Martin (Receptionist).

FILMS IN REVIEW, 1-2/95, p. 55, Andy Pawelczak

Nobody in *The Professional*, a violent thriller set in New York and written and directed by Luc Besson who made *La Femme Nikita*, looks, talks or behaves quite like the character he's supposed to be. Not quite French, certainly not American, they're like lost souls from some international casting agency in limbo brought to 15 minutes of imitation life by Besson's generous libations of blood. The stiff, unprofessional acting is about on a par with the acting in porn films. No doubt this was Besson's intention—the film has the feeling of high gloss porn with its rudimentary plot and pubescent heroine that the camera ogles incessantly. The only thing that distinguishes it from porn, besides the absence of hard core sex, is a viscous sentimentality that no self-respecting pornographer would ever stoop to.

The film's hero is Leon (Jean Reno), an idiot savant hit man with soul. (This is the season for soulful hit men, who are apotheosized in *Pulp Fiction* whose director, Quentin Tarantino, reportedly admires this film.) We know Leon has soul because he lavishes care on a houseplant, his only personal belonging in a shabby apartment, and has a fondness for Gene Kelly movies. (A clip of Kelly roller skating with his customary style on a New York street is the best bit of filmmaking in the movie.) Leon works for Tony (Danny Aiello), a mafia boss who treats his naive protege with condescending paternalism, withholding his salary on the grounds that banks can always be robbed. Though he's not very at home in the modern world, the taciturn, gentle Leon is a master hit man—in the film's opening scene, he wipes out an army of rival mobsters with the effortless panache of a Jean-Claude Van Damme.

Leon's life takes a fateful turn when he rescues Mathilda (Natalie Portman), a 14 year old neighbor who dresses like a hooker, from the rogue cops who have slaughtered her drug dealing family. He briefly considers killing her—after all, a young girl would be an encumbrance for a monastically disciplined, professionally devoted hit man like Leon—but humanity and affection win out and he agrees to teach her the tricks of his trade when she says she'd like to be a hit woman when she grows up. (I know, I know, this sounds very unlikely, but that's the kind of film it is—a fable for the terminally jaded.) The rest of the film titillates us with Leon and Mathilda's platonic relationship as she does housework in a skimpy tee shirt that emphasizes her budding breasts and plots revenge on her family's murderers.

Besson makes the requisite references to other movies to establish his credentials as a serious filmmaker, and at times he seems to be reaching, or overreaching, for a Sergio Leone-like flamboyance and wit. In one of the film's big, operatic set pieces, Gary Oldman, as a homicidal cop, bares his teeth, rants about Beethoven and waves his arms like a symphony conductor as he frantically rushes around an apartment killing its inhabitants. It's too bad—Oldman is far too good an actor to have his talents thrown away in a film like this.

LOS ANGELES TIMES, 11/18/94, Calendar/p. 10, Peter Rainer

"The Professional" is being touted as the Hollywood debut of "La Femme Nikita" director Luc Besson, but, of course, "Nikita" was pure Hollywood in every way except the subtitles. It was more Hollywood than its Hollywood remake, "Point of No Return."

Besson has a gift for amoral sleaziness that should serve him well over here. In his very first American film, he has gone straight for the smarm.

Consider this: It's about Leon (Jean Reno), a hit man who befriends Mathilda (Natalie Portman), a 12-year-old who has lost her family in a drug-deal rub-out. Seeking vengeance, Mathilda cajoles Leon into teaching her the tricks of the trade.

Besson makes sure his hit man—"cleaner"—is sympathetic, Leon may look like Sylvester Stallone after being run through a duck press, he may wear sunglasses indoors, but he knows where to draw the line in his job: "No women, no children." He drinks milk, tends to his best friend—a houseplant—and can't read. (Illiteracy, per Forrest Gump, seems to be a point of sympathy in the movies these days.) He allows a chummy Mafia capo (Danny Aiello) to bank his earnings. He loves Gene Kelly movies. (Kelly should sue.)

This sub-verbal lunk is a blood brother to Lennie in "Of Mice and Men"—in other words, Besson defuses the relationship with Mathilda by making Leon essentially sexless. We're supposed to regard his live-in relationship with the girl as a platonic, father-daughter thing, although she's a lot more wised-up than he is.

Does Besson recognize that he shows off Mathilda as a tart little Lolita? The first shot of her in the movie is a slow tilt up her stockinged legs, and in a couple of sequences he dresses her like Jodie Foster in "Taxi Driver." She does vampy impressions of Marilyn Monroe and Madonna, singing "Like a Virgin." (Madonna should sue.) If the point of all this is to show how an abused child becomes precociously sexual in order to find love, the intention is coated with gunk.

Natalie Portman isn't enough of an actress to unfold Mathilda's pain, and, in any event, Besson doesn't seem very interested in it. The girl's family—including her 7-year-old brother—has been wasted, but she's not terribly put out by it. (Her father was a sleazeball with a live-in lover, and her sister was "only" a half-sister.) Her vengeance on the Drug Enforcement Administration kingpin (an over-the-top Gary Oldman) who provoked the killings seems motivated more by pique than rage.

"The Professional" reaches its nadir—and that's saying something—when Leon teaches Mathilda the fine points of picking somebody off with a long-range rifle. From a tenement roof she plugs a Donald Trump-looking jogger in New York's Central Park. The bullet, of course, turns out to be a red-fluid-filled blank. Besson plays the scene for laughs. Hardy-har-har.

"The Professional" works in a sub-zone of Hollywood amoralism where violence is intended as turn-on and neglected children are displayed as moppets and killers are sweetened by their attentiveness to houseplants. It's a vile little exercise.

NEW YORK POST, 11/18/94, p. 48, Michael Medved

Just when you thought that the wildly overpraised "Pulp Fiction" offered the last word on eccentric and endearing hit men, along comes "The Professional" to present us with a paid assassin who's even more lovable.

In his first American film, French director Luc Bresson ("La Femme Nikita," "Subway") adds an uncomfortable element of sentimentality to his portrait of a ruthlessly efficient "cleaner": aside from his unusual livelihood, Leon (Jean Reno) is a pussycat who likes to drink milk, carries his beloved potted plant around with him everywhere, and adores old Gene Kelly movies.

His lonely Manhattan life is interrupted when the drug-dealing family in the apartment next door is wiped out by corrupt, vicious agents of the Drug Enforcement Administration, led by a psychotic coke-head and classical music buff, played with unforgettable ferocity and chilling dementia by Gary Oldman.

The only survivor of this massacre is a frightened 12-year-old girl (played by rising model Natalie Portman) who seeks refuge with the quiet, sad-eyed neighbor she hardly knows.

It's an odd, disturbing little tale, given more life than it deserves by strong acting and brilliant camera work.

The violence is horrifyingly graphic, but never particularly convincing; you're always conscious of watching sadistic mayhem that's artfully contrived rather than realistic.

The relationship between Reno's character and the girl who becomes his surrogate daughter is the center of the movie and veers unsteadily between soppy sweetness and approximations of incest—with the provocative child making sexual overtures to her middle-aged protector.

The connection between these two characters evokes moments of undeniable emotion, but never comes into clear focus.

The same could be said for the entire picture.

NEWSDAY, 11/18/94, Part II/p. B6, Jack Mathews

French director Luc Besson's first American film, "The Professional," a spinoff of his 1990 hit "La Femme Nikita," is as American as apple pie. It's about an illiterate mob assassin (Jean Reno), a sexy 12-year-old orphan (Natalie Portman) who wants him to teach her the trade, and the psychopathic New York cop (Gary Oldman) they both want to kill. Scores of people die, buildings are blown up, and no one is arrested.

"La Femme Nikita" was a lot like that, but it was in French and set in a foreign country, which meant art-house audiences here could ignore its silly plot and endless Peckinpah-lian shootouts, and probe its existentialism. The U.S. remake, an almost exact replica, fooled no one.

With "The Professional," Besson has more or less realigned characters from "La Femme Nikita." Its star, Leon (Reno), was a minor character in the first film, a coolly efficient hitman known as the "cleaner." Here, he has migrated to New York, where he works for a mob boss so mean he is played by Danny Aiello.

Leon is a perfect existential figure; he makes his living killing. But he is a moral killer ("no women or children" is his mantra) and from all the milk he guzzles, we know his work causes him pain. When Leon adopts the girl next door, after her abusive drug-dealing father and the rest of her family are murdered by bad cops, his empty life is suddenly given double-meaning—companionship and revenge.

"The Professional" may be the most stylish plumb-dumb movie of the year. It is beautifully photographed, and the violence, before it becomes numbingly monotonous, has an exaggerated balletic grace. And there is some perverse pleasure to be taken from the performances of Reno, playing the loner Leon like a lobotomized Travis Bickle, and Oldman, as a totally crazed cop who gets high on Beethoven before going on killing sprees, has some spectacular psychotic episodes.

Portman, with a face like Audrey Hepburn and a body like Anna Chlumsky, was a real find for Besson, who turns her into a precocious vamp who does Madonna and Marilyn Monroe impressions for her new roommate. The "La Femme Lolita" subplot, however, is mercifully unconsummated. It's hard enough accepting a fantasized relationship between an abused child and a lowlife killer without seeing where it might lead.

NEWSWEEK, 11/21/94, p. 96, Jack Kroll

The French establishment is always bellyaching about how their arts are being corrupted by American pop culture. They even pass laws against it. Well, it works both ways. With "The Professional," his first American movie, French director Luc Besson dishes out some corruption of his own. French filmmakers have always loved to make versions of American gangster flicks, their own *pâté de noir gras*, so to speak. But that symbiosis reaches decadence in "The Professional," with its flashy technique, emotional hollowness and intellectual pretentiousness. Besson, 35, got his Hollywood shot on the basis of his 1990 international hit, "La Femme Nikita" (remade by John Badham as "Point of No Return"). His antihero "professional" is Leon (Jean Reno), a hit man who becomes the reluctant custodian of a 12-year-old girl, Mathilda (Natalie Portman), when her family is massacred by a gang led by crooked DEA agent Stansfield (Gary Oldman).

"The Professional" is a mad Franco-American mélange. Leon is a recycling of the old French existential gangster, a morose killer who lives alone, sports shades and a stubble, drinks milk, can't read or write and loves only his houseplant. Oldman is a sadistic psycho who scarfs poppers before he kills (recalling Dennis Hopper in "Blue Velvet"). Guns bang symphonically, blood flows torrentially, Reno underacts Frenchily and Oldman overacts like James Woods afflicted by rabies. And Besson's manipulation of newcomer Portman approaches kiddie porn. See huge close-ups of her precociously beautiful face, esthetically bruised and bloodied. Glom her in a T shirt, provocatively poked by her budding breasts. Watch her shot from above on a bed, legs akimbo like a mini-Sharon Stone. Of course love (fatherly—uh, yeah) for little Natalie redeems the hit man. *Mais naturellement.* But Portman's real folks should be careful that their cameragenic daughter isn't turned into a new Linda Blair. "The Professional" is the pseudo-thinking man's "Pulp Fiction." Where Quentin Tarantino's movie is cool, complex, original, Besson's is vicious, sentimental, counterfeit.

SIGHT AND SOUND, 2/95, p. 47, Amanda Lipman

In New York, Leon a hitman, is given the job of scaring off a new gang leader. He executes his task, silently disposing of numerous sidekicks. Back at his dingy Little Italy apartment, Leon, meets a neighbour's 12-year-old daughter, Mathilda, on the stairs. Her father is being visited by Stansfield, a crooked police agent about some adulterated cocaine. The next morning, while Mathilda is at the shops, Stansfield and his men return and murder her father, stepmother, sister and little brother. They are still there when she comes back, so she walks straight up to Leon's apartment, begging him to let her in. He finally gives in, saying she can stay one night.

Discovering his profession, she persuades him to train her as a killer so she can avenge her brother's death. Leon collects some of his earnings from his mentor Tony, and he and Mathilda check into a hotel as father and daughter. But when Mathilda decides that she is falling in love with Leon she tells the hotel proprietor they are lovers, and they are thrown out.

Mathilda goes back to her family's apartment and finds a wad of cash her father has hidden. She hides as Stansfield enters and overhears his office address. She gets into the Department of Justice, and follows him into the men's room, but he traps her. Just as he is about to kill her, he is disturbed by a colleague, so holds her prisoner in his office instead. Leon, back from a job that involves killing one of Stansfield's bent cops, finds a note Mathilda has left and comes to her rescue. Stansfield, furious, demands that Tony tell him where Leon is. Leon's hotel is stormed by armed police but he fights them off. The couple manage to escape separately. Badly wounded,

Leon walks out of the front entrance where Stansfield shoots him. As he dies he hands Stansfield the pin from a grenade, which then explodes. Mathilda returns to school and explains her story.

Call him old-fashioned but Luc Besson seems to be devoted to the resolutely romantic action movie, as well as to a rather fixed narrative. After Christophe Lambert, Jean-Marc Barr and Anne Parillaud, Jean Reno takes on the mantle of the sullen, lonely but highly skilled anti-hero. Leon is also a sly tribute to Reno's role in *Nikita* as Victor the "cleaner", the man called in to mop up when an assassination goes wrong. As such it starts with an interesting enough premise: what does a hitman do when he goes home? So we see Leon, straight after a brilliant, emotionless display of professional violence, buy milk from his local store and engage in a po-faced spot of ironing and dusting.

But as soon as we watch him at home, it becomes obvious that this hitman has a weak spot—and is, therefore, about to meet his downfall. Although he sleeps sitting up, and with one eye open, cradling a pistol, he loves his houseplant. It does not take long for that needy, pretty little plant to take on a symbolic association with a needy, pretty little girl. Besson's self-referentiality is extended further through Mathilda herself—a kind of mini-Nikita with her dark bob, sultry sulkiness and sure aim with a gun. The difference is that Mathilda is only 12. It cannot be a complete coincidence that putting the names Leon and Nikita together almost gives us *Lolita*, for one theme of that novel is echoed strongly here. Mathilda effortlessly and manipulatively turns the surrogate father and daughter into a chaste pair of lovers, first with her admission of love for Leon, and then with her sly "confession" to the hotel proprietor. And naïf Leon takes her seriously. So socially removed is he from the world that he accepts the transition without question, while his physical attitude towards her remains almost devoutly pure. It is the camera's eye, not his, that lingers on Mathilda's pre-teen, skimpily clad body. Despite his considerable skills, Leon, according to the film, is emotionally too immature himself to know exactly what is going on.

The reason for this is that Leon is a figure seen through a child's eyes: those of Mathilda. It is her almost-adolescent wish-fulfilment that has created this strange deviant of the classic strong, silent male: part post-punk anti-hero, complete with unfathomable glasses and stubble; part classic hitman—he even has a violin case with a machine-gun inside it—and part quaint gentleman. Leon will not kill women or children.

This child's eye view paints the other characters in broad sweeps too: Gary Oldman's Stansfield is pure, crazy, corrupt cop, with extravagant mannerisms that range from an overwrought method of popping pills to an obsession with Beethoven and an ability to sniff the truth on people (a characterisation drawn from villains in comic books). Mathilda's father is a caricature of abusive vulgarity, with his stereotypically fat unkemptness and proclivity for slapping her whenever she gets in the way, while her step-mother is a walking Barbie doll, and her sister an aerobicised teenage nightmare.

Leon turns the stuff of conventional story books into a virtual reality fairytale for streetwise, techno-age children. In it are offbeat, modern versions of goodies and baddies, plenty of violence and even romance. Here, an ordinary hotel room can be transformed, in moments, into a blackened, gutted battlefield, swarming with armed police, still no match for superhero Leon, whose initial silent foray into a well-guarded hotel suite takes on the same intensity as getting through the levels of a computer game.

Mathilda's particular technological fantasy allows her to lose her nasty family, to learn to be a hitwoman, and to fall in love with her hero. When it is over, she shuts the book and goes back to school. She accepts Leon's death with as much worldly wisdom as she accepted that he was a killer. It is, she knows, a tough world. For these cynical and sophisticated children, movies have to better the crude computer-generated images of their toys, and Besson's visual style is a perfect amalgam of traditional and modern: looming, cartoon-style close-ups of faces; breath-taking frozen images such as a body hanging in a corridor, or a vertiginous view from the top of the stairs and big, immaculately orchestrated action sequences.

Besson likes to throw a rebellious woman into the works of his films. He obliges here by giving us a girl's eye view that goes defiantly against gender stereotype (though not without some leering on his part). But to look for further meaning in *Leon* will get the viewer nowhere. Like all his other films, it is, intellectually, gorgeously insubstantial. Meanwhile, the kids who would love it are officially barred by its 18 certificate.

TIME, 12/5/94, p. 93, Richard Schickel

Luc Besson is not an action director. He is a violence director, probably the best in the business right now. He discomfits a lot of people because he is always on the dangerous edge of aestheticizing psychopathically murderous behavior. It's a subject we prefer to see treated cartoonishly so that we can pretend our enjoyment of it is pure escapism.

Besson has a curious fondness for lost girls making their way in a brutal world. In *La Femme Nikita* his heroine was a drugged-out, teenage murderess-drifter rescued from the guillotine by an intelligence agency and given a new life as an assassin. In *The Professional*, set in New York City, his subject is a 12-year-old named Mathilda (Natalie Portman), the only member of her family to survive a criminal massacre. She turns to a neighbor for succor. Leon (Jean Reno) is an inarticulate fellow. He drinks milk by the gallon, tenderly cares for a plant that is his only friend and likes old Gene Kelly movies. He is devoted to his work as a "cleaner," a Mob hit man of rare talent.

The bonding of Mathilda and Leon may be among the strangest in the long, tiresome history of odd-couple movies. The sweetness that develops between them as they try to elude the rogue DEA agent who orchestrated her family's death (a divinely psychotic Gary Oldman) is crazily dislocating, the more so since Besson's French vision of the New York underworld is so eerily unreal. His final shootout is masterly cinema—this is a Cuisinart of a movie, mixing familiar yet disparate ingredients, making something odd, possibly distasteful, undeniably arresting out of them.

VILLAGE VOICE, 11/22/94, Film Special/p. 66, J. Hoberman

The season's number one box-office attraction in France (where, known as *Leon*, it opened with round-the-clock weekend screenings at Paris's largest theater), *The Professional* has also earned, so my sources tell me, the Quentin Tarantino seal of approval. No surprise, really; Luc Besson's latest may take *La Femme Nikita* down a notch as action-thriller but it sure does burnish the image of the soulful hit man.

As played by Besson axiom Jean Reno, *The Professional*'s lovable paid killer (or "cleaner" in the movie's parlance) is almost comically stylized—sad puppy-dog eyes, grizzled oval face, smoky French accent, an unquenchable desire to see Gene Kelly in *Singin' in the Rain*. He's also totally ascetic—a milk drinker who banks his money with an affably exploitive mafioso (Danny Aiello) and, between jobs, tenderly nurses a pet plant in the miserable East Harlem hovel that he seems to call home.

For its first 20 minutes—during which (1) Leon decimates the minions of a porcine drug kingpin and (2) Leon's next-door neighbors are wiped out by rogue cop Gary Oldman (as wired as Times Square) to punish the loser who double-crossed him—*The Professional* bids to be a repellent, amoral film. Fear not: Once morose Leon teams up with Mathilda, the family's 12-year-old daughter (she survived because she happened to be out shopping), *The Professional* becomes something weirder—something maybe like *Lethal Gigi*. As the Oldman character puts it: "Death is whimsical today." Or thank heaven for little girls and big guns.

Also reviewed in:
CHICAGO TRIBUNE, 11/18/94, Friday/p. F, Michael Wilmington
NEW YORK TIMES, 11/18/94, p. C18, Janet Maslin
VARIETY, 9/19-25/94, p. 77, Lisa Nesselson
WASHINGTON POST, 11/18/94, p. F7, Hal Hinson

PULP FICTION

A Miramax Films release of a Band Apart/Jersey Films production. *Executive Producer:* Danny DeVito, Michael Shamberg, and Stacey Sher. *Producer:* Lawrence Bender. *Director:* Quentin Tarantino. *Screenplay:* Quentin Tarantino. *Stories:* Quentin Tarantino and Robert Avary. *Director of Photography:* Andrzej Sekula. *Editor:* Sally Menke. *Music:* Karyn Rachtman and

Kathy Nelson. *Music Editor:* Rolf Johnson. *Sound:* Ken King. *Sound Editor:* Stephen H. Flick. *Casting:* Ronnie Yeskel and Gary M. Zuckerbrod. *Production Designer:* David Wasco. *Art Director:* Charles Collum. *Set Designer:* Daniel Bradford and Jacek Lisiewicz. *Set Decorator:* Sandy Reynolds-Wasco. *Set Dresser:* McPherson O. Downs, Joseph Grafmuller, and Daniel Rothenberg. *Special Effects:* Wesley Mattox, Stephen DeLollis, and Pat Domenico. *Costumes:* Betsy Heimann. *Make-up:* Michelle Buhler. *Stunt Coordinator:* Ken Lesco. *Running time:* 149 minutes. *MPAA Rating:* R.

CAST: John Travolta (Vincent Vega); Samuel L. Jackson (Jules Winnfield); Uma Thurman (Mia Wallace); Harvey Keitel (The Wolf); Tim Roth (Pumpkin); Amanda Plummer (Honey Bunny); Maria de Medeiros (Fabienne); Ving Rhames (Marsellus Wallace); Eric Stoltz (Lance); Christopher Walken (Koons); Bruce Willis (Butch Coolidge); Roseanna Arquette (Jody); Laura Lovelace (Waitress); Robert Ruth (Coffee Shop); Phil LaMarr (Marvin); Burr Steers (Roger); Frank Whaley (Brett); Alexis Arquette (Fourth Man); Paul Calderon (Paul); Bronagh Gallagher (Trudi); Steve Buscemi (Buddy Holly); Brenda Hillhouse (Butch's Mother); Sy Sher (Klondike); Angela Jones (Esmarelda Villalobos); Carl Allen (Dead Floyd Wilson); Don Blakely (Wilson's Trainer); Venessia Valentino (Pedestrian/Bonnie); Karen Maruyama (Gawker); Kathy Griffin (Herself); Duane Whitaker (Maynard); Peter Greene (Zed); Stephen Hibbert (The Gimp); Quentin Tarantino (Jimmie); Dick Miller (Monster Joe); Julia Sweeney (Raquel); Chandler Lindauer (Young Butch); Susan Griffiths (Marilyn Monroe); Lorelei Leslie (Mamie Van Doren); Brad Parker (Jerry Lewis); Josef Pilato (Dean Martin); Eric Clark (James Dean); Jerome Patrick Hoban (Ed Sullivan); Gary Shorelle (Ricky Nelson); Michael Gilden (Phillip Morris Page); Linda Kaye (Shot Woman); Lawrence Bender (Long Hair Yuppie Scum); Emil Sitka ("Hold Hands You Love Birds"); Robert Ruth and Rich Turner (Sportscasters).

FILMS IN REVIEW, 1-2/95, p. 56, Andy Pawelczak

Pulp Fiction is terminally hip. As the bodies pile up, so do attitude and inside jokes. A briefcase containing something—we don't know what—that emits a lambent glow can be traced back to Robert Aldrich's *Kiss Me Deadly*, a film based on a pulp novel by Mickey Spillane. A waiter in a cafe designed like a fifties movieland theme park looks like Buddy Holly, and a scene involving two noir tough guys takes place against Al Green singing "Let's Get Together" on the soundtrack. But director/writer Quentin Tarantino has more than pop cultural references in his bag of tricks. An important and appealing character gets bumped off in the film's second part, only to reappear in the third part thanks to the out-of-synch time frames of the movie's three interlocking episodes. When the character comes back into the picture, we heave a sigh of relief—it's as if the miracle of film has defeated death—but we watch his antics with a provisional feeling—we know something that he doesn't, that very shortly he's going to die. It's a weird, complex effect, and it makes the movie into something more than just a parody of pulp fiction.

Tarantino, of course, is the Hollywood wunderkind who worked as a video store clerk before writing and directing *Reservoir Dogs*, a low budget crime thriller that played like it was high on adrenaline, chutzpah and a steady diet of fast foods and old genre pictures. Tarantino is a pure product of America: if he were psychoanalyzed, he'd come up with old movie images rather than childhood memories. What his films lack in depth they make up for in surface dazzle and a powerful feeling for the contemporary. His characters speak a nervous, obscene, fluent vernacular that is as stylized and artful in its own way as David Mamet's but without Mamet's stilted cadences and self-conscious gutter poetry. D.H. Lawrence wrote about the existential bottom dog sensibility of Americans and Tarantino has it in spades. There's an end-of-the-line quality about his films, but he has a joking-on-the-edge-of-the-void insouciance and he's absolutely in love with the possibilities of narrative art. He's like his characters—he comes out of nowhere and perhaps he's going nowhere but in between he's going to get what he can out of living in the flattened out yet huge American present.

Pulp Fiction's structure of three shaggy dog stories gives Tarantino plenty of slack to practice his specialty, the loopy verbal riff that contrasts with the action on the screen. In the opening episode, Vincent Vega (John Travolta) reminisces about the hamburgers in Paris (Le Big Mac and the Royale Burger) as he and his partner Jules (Samuel L. Jackson) drive to an apartment where they are to kill several men. These are hit men who love to talk, who appreciate odd little conversational twists and grace notes, and their scenes together have an improvisational energy and back alley wit reminiscent of Scorsese's *Mean Streets*. The first episode focuses on Vincent and his unenviable task of entertaining his boss's wife, Mia (Uma Thurman), while her husband is out of town for a night. Her husband, Marsellus Wallace (Ving Rhames), is a mobster with a reputation for volatile jealousy, so Vincent is justifiably nervous as he resists Mia's allure during an evening that ends up in a grotesquely funny scene involving a drug overdose and a hypodermic syringe that is bigger than anything should be that goes into a human body. As Mia, Uma Thurman, in a black fright wig, is like a child's Halloween dress up version of a femme fatale. Part of the film's strategy is to make its hit men lovable, and Travolta, though he's put on some pounds since his *Saturday Night Fever* days, still has the right moves and enough charismatic charm to rivet your attention even when he's doing something as simple as wandering around an apartment in a drug-induced stupor.

The film's second section, about a boxer (Bruce Willis) who betrays Marsellus Wallace by winning a fight he was paid to throw, is the most parodistically noirish. Willis, in a very good, quiet performance, has the right battered look, but the episode goes over the top in a sado-masochistic scene involving a silent, leather-hooded character called the Gimp who steps out of pulp fiction's pulpiest menagerie. The scene is so stagy and excessive, even in this film which makes excess a sine qua non, that it momentarily throws you out of the movie, as does a too obvious joke in which Willis has to choose a weapon and escalates from a hammer to a power saw to a samurai sword. Tarantino regains control of the picture's tone in the third episode in which Jules and Vincent have to dispose of a bloody corpse. They call upon the help of a fixer, played by Harvey Keitel, whose calmly benign, business-like manner, in contrast to the outrageousness of the situation, makes the scene into a prolonged exercise in black humor with echoes of Abbott and Costello as Jules and Vincent bicker over the cleanup chores. Sam Jackson is very good in this episode as Jules, going from amoral ferocity to ardent conviction when his life takes an unexpected new turn.

As he did in *True Romance*, for which he wrote the screenplay, Tarantino studs the film with throw away routines and funny bits of business. Christopher Walken is very good in a brief role as a military officer who delivers a serious, emotion laden speech that gradually builds with frightening intensity to a weird scatological punch line. Tim Roth and Amanda Plummer are simultaneously scary and funny as two outlaws who exchange cuddly endearments before sticking up a diner in a scene reminiscent of the opening of *Natural Born Killers*, which was based on a story by Tarantino. Bruce Willis has an odd, inconsequential scene with an exotically sexy cabdriver named Esmeralda Villa Lobos. Tarantino doesn't suffer from any undue anxiety of influence—the cab scene could be an outtake from Jim Jarmusch's *Night on Earth*, or, if we cineanalytically dig deeper, perhaps it's a buried memory of a cab flirtation involving Bogart in *The Big Sleep*. The amazing thing is that underneath all the hip knowingness and rock 'n roll epiphanies you can sense an embryonic seriousness of purpose, even if you don't buy an important character's crazy religious conversion at the film's end. Unlike most movies today, *Pulp Fiction* yields its major meanings only after you've left the theater and given the picture some thought. Let's hope Tarantino's not a seven day wonder; meanwhile, he's our current Success Story, and young filmmakers all over America will be seeing this movie to get a rush of envy and ambition.

LOS ANGELES TIMES, 10/14/94, Calendar/p. 1, Kenneth Turan

The story is told of a crusty Midwestern newspaper editor who returned to work after a vacation and threw a fit. His prize headline type, enormous letters he'd been holding back for years for a truly big event, were used in his absence on a story detailing serious tornado damage. "You young fool," he snapped at the offending party, "I was saving that type for the Second Coming."

From the moment it hit the screen at Cannes, even before it was awarded that festival's celebrated Palme d'Or, "Pulp Fiction" and its writer-director Quentin Tarantino have been given the big-type, Second Coming treatment, drenching them in the kind of media awe and appreciation reserved for paradigms of cinematic accomplishment.

Of course, like that tornado, Tarantino is quite an event, a gifted writer and a man of filmmaking talent whose work both here and elsewhere can be impressive. But despite all the attention, this is not the resurrection of anything. "Pulp Fiction's" anthology of stories about gangster fun and games in Los Angeles doesn't merit sustained veneration.

Because "Pulp Fiction" is sporadically effective, the temptation to embrace the entire two hours and 29 minutes of Tarantiniana is strong. But in truth this is a noticeably uneven film, both too inward-looking and self-centered in its concerns and too outward-bound in the way it strains to outrage an audience, to be successful across the board.

The best thing about "Pulp Fiction," as with Tarantino's debut film, "Reservoir Dogs," are its words. They flow in hip torrents that are both idiosyncratic and familiar from lowlife characters who love to talk and can erupt in entertaining riffs on any subject on no notice at all.

The film's opening scene, for instance, shot in a simple two-shot that ensures the audience concentrate on the dialogue, has a pair of amateur heisters, Pumpkin (Tim Roth) and Honey Bunny (Amanda Plummer), talking with engaging bravado about the vagaries of small-time robbery.

In fact, "Pulp's" roster of criminals rarely talk shop; philosophical and even theological questions about loyalty, morality and the nature of miracles are their metier. This is more fun than it may sound because actors invariably spark to Tarantino's words, finding in them the kind of wicked twists that makes them a kick to speak.

This is especially true of the two actors who appear most in "Pulp's" series of independent but interrelated stories, John Travolta and Samuel L. Jackson. They play Vincent Vega and Jules Winnfield, respectively, hired muscle for Marcellus Wallace (Ving Rhames), local crime lord, who make small talk about the erotic nature of foot massage before "getting into character" and ruining several people's day.

Though Jackson gives a strong performance, Travolta ends up being more memorable only because his work is more of a surprise. His Vincent Vega is all sleepy boyishness and drug-mellowed bemusement, and seeing him so charming in the unexpected guise of a minor league thug is to remember why audiences fell in love with him in the first place.

But since Vincent and Jules are hit men, albeit romanticized ones, "Pulp Fiction's" stories have violence at their core (running the gamut from the threat of gunplay to assaultive, occasionally racist language and cascades of blood and brain matter), and this is where the film's problems begin.

Because Tarantino likes to tease audiences into somnolence before sneaking in an explosive jolt, the carnage is not as nonstop as in "Natural Born Killers," but there nevertheless is something wearing and repetitive about the film's reliance on shock value and bad-boy posturing to maintain our attention.

And while one of the attractions of "Reservoir Dogs" was that its disturbing scenes seemed to flow out of Tarantino's natural exuberance, in "Pulp Fiction" the writer-director appears to be straining for his effects. Some sequences, especially one involving bondage harnesses and homosexual rape, have the uncomfortable feeling of creative desperation, of someone who is afraid of losing his reputation scrambling for any way to offend sensibilities.

What makes this rather poignant is that what is felt most in "Pulp Fiction" is the hand of a filmmaker who loves movies past. Names like Douglas Sirk pop up in unlikely places, and the visual references or homages to a wide variety of films are to numerous to catalogue, even if one has seen enough celluloid to be sure of catching them all.

But while "Pulp Fiction's" best scenes, including Travolta and Uma Thurman as the boss's wife doing a languid twist, and a deadpan monologue from Christopher Walken about a prized gold watch, are informed with the director's personal sense of movie history, the personal has a tendency to turn uncomfortably solipsistic.

The result, especially in the scenes involving Bruce Willis as a nervy boxer, can be long patches of dialogue that must have tickled Tarantino but will not necessarily resonate for anyone else. The word *tedious* has not been much used in describing "Pulp Fiction," but there are extended moments when it fits rather too well.

So while seeing where "Pulp Fiction" is coming from is easy, guessing where Quentin Tarantino is headed is more difficult. A gifted mimic who knows how to make lively collages out of movie history, he seems unconcerned that his films feel more like heartless deadends than an opening to something new and involving.

And though in a rare plaintive moment in a recent interview Tarantino talked of his future and said, "I don't want to just be the gun guy," the evidence that he can live without the rush that violence or its threat brings is not convincing. If the kind of work Tarantino does best is where American filmmaking is heading, it will have to get there without me.

NEW YORK, 10/3/94, p. 96, David Denby

It's not hard to see why actors have been eager to work with the young writer-director Ouentin Tarantino. A bad-boy entertainer, "dark" but playful, Tarantino writes an American gutter rant—golden arias of vituperation interlaced with patches of odd, hilarious formality (the formality functions like an outbreak of classical movement in the middle of a modern-dance concert). His latest, *Pulp Fiction*, which won the Palme d'Or at Cannes last spring and just opened the New York Film Festival, is an ecstatically entertaining piece of suave mockery. Tarantino serves up low-life characters and situations from old novels and movies, and he revels in every manner of pulp flagrancy—murder and betrayal, drugs, sex, and episodes of sardonically distanced sadomasochism. But the language pours forth with a richness never heard in conventional pulp, and he plays havoc with our expectations. There are three overlapping stories in *Pulp Fiction*, and the structure is bound with words—anecdotes, debates, rococo profanities, biblical quotations. Amazingly, the complex of overturned expectations gets set right by the end.

Like Altman and Scorsese twenty years ago or Godard a decade before that, Tarantino, 31, has quickly become an international film-festival celebrity. At the moment, he's an avatar of American hip, perhaps the only one in the movie business. (Jim Jarmusch's stylized ennui has come to look like artistic and personal enervation.) Tarantino, commercial yet intransigent, is the hero of those who long to be produced, those who have daring ideas but no way of realizing them. Like the earlier movie men, Tarantino is immersed in cinema; he even comes garlanded with a myth comparable to Scorsese's asthmatic, movie-enriched childhood. A sort of Southern California swamp-mall creature, he rises, unschooled, from a clerk's position at a video store with thousands of films in his head and grand ambitions in his heart. Having seen and digested everything, he understands the logic and secrets of movie genres, the hidden strength of their conventions; therefore, he can play, he can mix cruelty and formal inventiveness (sometimes the formal play is itself cruel), teasing, undermining, subverting, while telling a story at the same time.

Pulp Fiction is about Los Angeles crumbums—gangsters, a boxer ordered to take a dive, molls, a pair of sadists. The movie is not meant to be sincere. In a Scorsese movie like *Mean Streets* or *GoodFellas*, the characters, as much as lovers in an opera by Verdi, suffer and die. But Tarantino's gangsters are not "real." *Pulp Fiction* is play, a commentary on old movies. Tarantino works with trash, and by analyzing, criticizing, and formalizing it, he emerges with something new, just as Godard made a lyrical work of art in *Breathless* out of his memories of casually crappy American B-movies. Of course Godard was, and is, a Swiss-Parisian intellectual, and the tonalities of his work are drier, more cerebral. *Pulp Fiction*, by contrast, displays an entertainer's talent for luridness. It's a very funky, American sort of pop masterpiece, improbable, uproarious, with bright colors and danger and blood right on the surface. And yet the movie is not heartless like *Natural Born Killers*; and for all its joking, *Pulp Fiction* is not a put-on. Tarantino gives us the great pulp theme without its attendant clichés. It's a movie about loyalty.

What a jump forward! I can't say I was a fan of Tarantino's 1992 debut film, *Reservoir Dogs*. The movie was like a nihilistic film-school exercise—a malignant gloss, perhaps, on Stanley Kubrick's early heist picture, *The Killing*. I enjoyed the virtuoso cursing, the grotesque ironies, but Tarantino depended on blood and sadism so thoroughly that the genre tease lost its wit. (Being bullied by hipness is the same as being bullied by anything else.) Apart from enjoying one baroquely nasty scene between Christopher Walken and Dennis Hopper, I also hated *True Romance*, a movie that Tarantino wrote but Tony Scott directed A commercial hack like Scott working on Tarantino's material revealed what trash unredeemed by irony might look like. *True Romance* was all processed, violent thrills, with cocaine dust for glamour.

Pulp Fiction isn't nihilistic, and it certainly isn't stupid. If the theme is loyalty, the basic dramatic unit is the couple—men and women and men and men. Two petty thieves sitting in a diner, played by Tim Roth and Amanda Plummer, skinny and intense, mated like rabbits, rise from their seats and announce a stickup. Light-weights, thrill-seeking amateurs, they pull out their guns—and the episode breaks off. That's the beginning of the movie, and we return to them at the end, though what appears in the interim isn't all flashback. Some of it takes place before that moment, some *after*. The chronology of the three stories is daringly skewed so we can see people in the midst of different yet connected actions. Call it *collateral* narration. What goes around comes around.

The two principal characters are hit men in black suits, white shirts, and black ties. John Travolta, overweight, puffy, with long hair falling from a knot in strands (at times, in his black suit, he looks like a Hasid), and Samuel L. Jackson, lean, curly-haired, with a mean tongue, work for a local crime boss (Ving Rhames). That morning, on the way to the job (killing yuppie punks who have taken something that belongs to their boss), the two hit men have a long conversation about a man who massaged the feet of the boss's wife and was tossed out the window. Is massaging a woman's feet an offense worthy of death, like adultery? The conversation goes on and on, with perfect seriousness—the two thugs could be disputatious monks in the late Middle Ages. The movie is less about crime than about what happens before and after crime—the shadows and echoes of an act rather than the act itself.

Tarantino has pushed to an extreme the pleasures of pulp, which are, of course, the pleasures of sensation and cheapness, and moods of shallow, voluptuous despair. Pulp fiction, especially in its aesthetically and intellectually respectable *noir* forms (the books of Dashiell Hammett and Raymond Chandler, the movies of John Huston, Howard Hawks, Robert Siodmak, Robert Aldrich, et al.), is a disillusioned, dark-shadowed urban poetry of losers, chippies, meatball thugs. But so much has been accomplished in the *noir* tradition, you can't do it straight anymore. So Tarantino works in banal daylight, on the L.A. streets, and we never do find out why the hit men kill the punks or what's in the stolen briefcase. And what had seemed incidental—the conversation about tending the boss's wife—turns out to be the essence of the first story.

Travolta is himself given the job of entertaining her for the evening. Witchy in dark hair, bangs, and matching ruby lips and nails, Uma Thurman's predatory moll has the lacquered beauty of those only-in-the-movies women (Veronica Lake, Jane Greer, Gene Tierney, et al.) from the forties. She takes Travolta to a glowing retro-fifties restaurant that features tables placed inside long-finned cars and a headwaiter imitating Ed Sullivan—the period references dance around deliriously. Afraid of his boss (if he sleeps with the wife, he'll die), Travolta walks on eggshells until the instant that Uma snorts heroin by mistake and the scene turns toward black comedy with moments so appalling you can't take your eyes off the screen even as you are close to nausea.

Most of the behavior onscreen is outrageous, yet each character feels justified in what he does and engages in long tirades of rational discourse when anyone disagrees. Samuel L. Jackson's blistering rant draws on the traditions of black street preachers and con artists; the rhetoric of insult and indignant, high-voiced hyperbole propels the language beyond Scorsese's tough-guy repetitions into a new movie poetry—Jackson dominates the screen. The movie is not so much a set of stories as a way of life and a habit of consciousness. Tarantino may be saying that Scorsese's kind of sincerity is no longer possible: These people know they are playing a role. Gangsters imitate movies and movies imitate gangsters in an endless chain. That situation could produce a stale, literary "postmodernist" cinema, but *Pulp Fiction* stays wild. The genre situations are invaded by weirdness, mess, coincidence. People talk much longer than you expect.

The second story begins with a stoic Hemingwayesque loser—a boxer, played by Bruce Willis, who has been paid by the crime boss to take a dive, and who refuses to go down. Holed up in a motel room with his kittenish French girlfriend (Maria de Medeiros, who could be Maria in the sleeping bag from *For Whom the Bell Tolls*), Willis realizes he has to return home to retrieve a family heirloom, a watch his father once stored up his ass in a Vietnamese prison camp. A sacred treasure! What follows, as Willis runs into the angry crime boss, and they both wind up as prisoners in an S&M dungeon, is so startlingly funny—so far out yet logical—that Tarantino seems to be goosing the entire solemn history of action cinema. And the last sequence, in which the two hit men, with a dead body on their hands, require the services of a gentleman hood, the Wolf (Harvey Keitel), also seems a kind of preposterous valedictory. The dead bodies must be disposed of. Farewell to pulp fiction! As we return to the diner, and the two rabbity amateurs from the opening scene, the executioner played by Samuel L. Jackson movingly resigns from crime.

Tarantino has himself expressed his desire to make other kinds of movies. In the roundelay of violence and comedy that is *Pulp Fiction*, he has hilariously summed up an immense genre and gloriously achieved his exit from it. Life beckons from beyond the video store.

NEW YORK POST, 9/23/94, p. 39, Thelma Adams

"Pulp Fiction"—which opens the 32nd New York Film Festival tonight—is eye candy.

Unlike Oliver Stone's "Natural Born Killers," which slings mud at Amerika while wallowing in the sensationalized violence it pretends to deplore, Quentin Tarantino's true crime adventure embraces an art form as stylized and American as jazz.

This eye-popping dark comedy has its roots in the well-crafted, hard-boiled fiction of Jim Thompson, Dashiell Hammett and Raymond Chandler, which in turn spawned Hollywood's film noir.

Unlike Stone-hearted killers Mickey (Woody Harrelson) and Mallory (Juliette Lewis), Tarantino thugs have warmth and dimension. They have soul. The writer/director's cultural touchstone is closer to Curtis Mayfield than Charles Manson.

Like pulp fiction itself, the violence is hyper-realistic: it's slowed-down, impeccably lit, detailed, heightened. It's truer than true. Tarrantino leaves the realism to his characters, who banter and argue, court and love, in real-time scenes longer than those usually found in American movies. Criminals spend more time chatting than shooting—and while they're jawing, they emerge as individuals.

My favorite scene in Tarrantino's sleeper debut, "Reservoir Dogs," was the lengthy luncheon discussion among six bandits prior to their failed heist—and their hilarious theories on tipping waitresses that almost split them apart.

In "Pulp Fiction," which scored the prestigious Palme D'Or at Cannes, the filmmaker repeats his knack for dialogue in the bickering between aging lounge lizard John Travolta (in his comeback role) and Geri-curled Samuel L Jackson.

As they head for an a.m. hit they argue about foot massage. The seemingly aimless debate not only defines the enforcers while touching on infidelity (is it kosher to massage the foot of another man's wife?) and homosexuality (would you massage the foot of another man?)—but introduces two characters, kingpin Marsellus Wallace (Ving Rhames) and his wife Mia (Uma Thurman), crucial to the plot.

These entertaining riffs cover the artful overlapping of three well-acted, well-told tales: a day-in-the-life of two hit men during which Jackson finds God and vows to lay down his gun: the fate of Honey Bunny (Tim Roth) and Pumpkin (Amanda Plummer), a nerdy Bonnie and Clyde whose decision to move up from knocking over liquor stores to coffee shops couldn't be more ill-timed; and the getaway of boxer Butch (Bruce Willis) who tries to put a fix on the fixer, Marsellus Wallace.

While there's splatter aplenty and a sensational shot of a hypodermic needle in use, "Pulp Fiction" deflates rather than romanticizes gunplay and drug use. After a gun misfires in their car, Travolta and Jackson (gore dripping off his Geri-curls) must scrub the brainy, bony mess off the upholstery. When party-girl Thurman snorts heroin, her glamorous facade falls as her mouth bubbles with saliva and her eyes glaze over in overdose. What could be more repulsive?

"Pulp Fiction" leaps off the screen like a punk diva into the mosh pit, a high-octane launch to the New York Film Festival.

NEWSDAY, 9/23/94, Part II/p. B4, John Anderson

"Burnt to a crisp, or bloody as hell?" waiter Steve Buscemmi asks hitman John Travolta, and unless one has wandered into "Pulp Fiction" by accident, this can't be a serious question. It's Quentin Tarantino's world, pal; everything on the menu, from screenplays to steaks, is served blood rare.

And yet ... and yet ... Having directed just one previous feature—the alarming and brilliant "Reservoir Dogs"—Tarantino has, through a combination of hype and screenplays ("True

Romance," "Natural Born Killers"), positioned himself as both art filmmaker and hyper-violent pop visionary, the mall rat's Godard, the cineophile's guilty pleasure.

So it's something of a tickle to find that "Pulp Fiction," which opens the New York Film Festival this evening and arrives with bellowingly positive word of mouth, turns out to be more tantalizing than terrifying, more mirth than mayhem, and with a level of self-awareness that's encouraging. Tarantino's going to be around for a while. And on only his second film, he's already using his own agitated image to move his audience where he wants them, and to deconstruct the very genre he's spearheading.

Take the first gunshot. Jules (Samuel L. Jackson) and his equally black-suited henchman Vincent (Travolta) have arrived at the apartment of some college-boy-wanna be bad guys, to retrieve a mysterious briefcase for their boss, Marcellus (Ving Rhames). En route, they've talked about television, and the fact that the Dutch eat french fries with mayonnaise. They've talked shop: Was Marcellus justified in tossing out a window a man who gave his wife Mia (Uma Thurman) a foot massage? When they get to the door, and you suspect all hell's finally going to break loose, it isn't quite time yet, so they take an extra little walk down the hall. And when they finally get around to killing the terrified double-crossers—an act prefaced by Jules' standard, pre-execution Old Testament invocation—there is no blood, not even a muzzle flash.

Not that there isn't violence, plenty of it, and buckets of blood in "Pulp Fiction," an anthology of sorts set in the '90s and based ostensibly on the lurid '30s-'40s crime magazines like Black Mask. But they come unexpectedly, inadvertently at times, sometimes as occupational hazards, sometimes as the unfortunate result of circumstance. "Pulp Fiction's" running gag is about violence as a job: Life's real concerns are always elsewhere—banal, perhaps, but never as banal as work.

The two lowlifes (Tim Roth and Amanda Plummer) who hold up a restaurant at the beginning of the film—and whose crime provides the movie's electrifying coda—are far more concerned with each other ("I love you, pumpkin" "I love you, honey bunny").

When Butch the boxer (Bruce Willis) who has double-crossed Marcellus after being paid to take a dive, and then winds up with him as prisoners of some southern sodomites—returns after a night of terror to his girlfriend Fabienne (Maria de Medeiros), his main concern is whether she's had her blueberry pancakes for breakfast. And when Vincent and Jules arrive at the home of Jules' friend Jimmie (Tarantino), with a brain-splattered car and a corpse, the crisis isn't criminal, it's domestic: They need to clean things up before Jimmie's wife gets home from the night shift, finds the house full of gangsters and divorces him.

Just as in "Reservoir Dogs" Tarantino gets uniformly fine performances out of his actors, but Jackson, who consistently delivers, and Travolta, who may have given his best performance here, are standouts. Also good are Plummer, Roth, Harvey Keitel (as the fixer who helps Jules and Vincent clean up) and Uma Thurman, whose calamitous night out with Vincent in a hallucinatory '50s theme restaurant ends with a particularly harrowing medical procedure.

All the characters in "Pulp Fiction" espouse a strong sense of ethics, and justice. "People like that should just be executed," says Lance (Eric Stoltz). "No trial, no jury ... " Who? Whoever keyed Vincent's vintage Malibu. This, from a dope dealer doling out $1,500 worth of heroin to a hitman. It's hilarious, of course, but the point is that personal morality is always subjective, that what people do with their workday has nothing to do with the morality they espouse. And that, in this, the criminal is no different from, say, the filmmaker. Or maybe even the audience.

NEWSWEEK, 10/10/94, p. 71, David Ansen

The miracle of Quentin Tarantino's "Pulp Fiction" is how, being composed of secondhand, debased parts, it succeeds in gleaming like something new. For a long time we've seen young, movie-mad American directors sink their teeth knowingly into old hollywood genres. When it works, we call it postmodernism; when it doesn't, it's vampirism. Tarantino, who educated himself working in a video store, is no exception. His movies—"Reservoir Dogs" and this Cannes grand-prize winner—are virtuosic reflections of reflections, B-movie archetypes respun with an art-house veneer by a guy equally conversant in Douglas Sirk, Sergio Leone and Jean-Luc Godard. But by the time this writer-director has finished twisting the clichés of the genre, he's turned Silly Putty into major architecture.

Set in today's L.A., but taking its spirit from '40s pulp magazines like Black Mask, this structurally audacious, 2½-hour movie unfolds separate but overlapping stories that start, stop and jump about in time. Yet by the end the jumbled chronology falls into perfect, startling place. The stories start from pulp ground zero. Two hit men, Jules (Samuel L. Jackson) and Vincent (John Travolta), are sent to retrieve a stolen briefcase by their boss (Ving Rhames) ... Vincent plays escort to the mobster's wife, Mia (Uma Thurman), knowing her husband once threw a man out a window for giving her a foot massage ... A boxer named Butch (Bruce Willis) is supposed to take a dive. He double-crosses the boss, takes the money and runs ...

We've seen these situations a thousand times—but not where this movie takes them. It's not just the plot twists that surprise, or the startling outbursts of violence, or the deft way that the most grisly scene can explode into black humor. This is one crime movie that revels in the quotidian details of character. "Pulp Fiction's" distinctive dialogue is a profane, hilarious amalgam of banality and formality. Tarantino relishes the small talk these pros exchange before they pull out their guns (Do you know what a Quarter Pounder is called in Amsterdam?" the dim charming Vincent asks his partner. "A Royale with cheese"). Tarantino shows us the before and after of violence: how to cope with the bloody mess of a man you have accidentally killed in the back seat of your car. The horrifically funny climax of Vincent's evening with Mia earns its power from the leisurely buildup of the date, which treats us to the memorable sight of Travolta and Thurman twisting on the dance floor of a '50s theme restaurant. Tarantino's unsentimental world has little use for conventional ideas of good guys and bad. No one is untarnished, but each of the main characters is granted a second chance—a shot at redemption. How they cope with that opportunity is what the movie is about.

Occasionally, Tarantino stumbles. There are smashing moments in the wild tale about Butch (Willis is very fine), but the domestic scenes between him and his girlfriend (Maria de Medeiros) are dull. And its gaudy climax—sadistic rednecks, S&M and male rape—traffics in Gothic clichés that the rest of the movie mocks. It's the only time Tarantino indulges in unadulterated villainy, and it's a failure of imagination, a movie kid's borrowed notion of evil.

The spectacular cast includes Tim Roth and Amanda Plummer as nervous stickup artists who call each other Pumpkin and Honey Bunny; Christopher Walken delivering an outrageous aria that explains how Butch came by his cherished gold watch, and Harvey Keitel as The Wolf, the meticulous mobster cleanup man. But the riveting Jackson, as the Bible-quoting Jules, and the beguiling Travolta, as heroin-shooting Vincent, must take pride of place. These guys pop off the screen into scumbag legend. Just when you thought the last thing the world needed was another violent, self-conscious, hipster hommage to film noir, along comes Tarantino to blow away your déjà vu.

NEW STATESMAN & SOCIETY, 10/28/94, p. 29, Jonathan Romney

I don't have that much to say about Quentin Tarantino's *Pulp Fiction*, but that's OK, because it has plenty to say for itself. Watching it is like sitting in a diner for hours on end while the guy opposite you simultaneously gabbles away, stuffing his face and juggles balls. Sort of how you'd imagine a dinner date with Tarantino to be.

I loved *Reservoir Dogs*. Loved the suits, loved the pace, loved the bloodshed, loved the shock of alarm when the film suddenly made you realise how much you loved the bloodshed ... Apart from the endless opening waffle about Madonna, which reminded me horribly of my days as a rock critic, *Reservoir Dogs* was cool. And since being *for* Tarantino or *against* him seemed overnight to become a yardstick of social hipness, I guess that made me cool too,

Pulp Fiction, though, leaves me cold. Even more than *Reservoir Dogs*, this is a film that you can't just like—you have to subscribe to it. It doesn't try to seduce or persuade you, nor does it clam up and cut to the chase, as *Reservoir Dogs* did. It just asks whether or not you can buy into a code of nerd-chic values largely determined by Tarantino's own obsessions. If you accept that B-movie in-jokes, veiled allusions to *Charlie's Angels*, knowing the difference between Jayne Mansfield and Mamie Van Doren, and caring about the international language of junk food is, like, as serious as your life, then this movie's for you. If you can't, then you're out of the game. *Pulp Fiction* bombards you with constant excess—of information, of narrative, of violence, of pop-culture trivia, of smart-ass high-banality backchat, flings it all in your lap like a warm ketchup-heavy cheeseburger, and demands that you either swallow it or sling it out.

On paper, *Pulp Fiction* offers plenty of incentive to join its club—a devious triple-layered, false-bottomed narrative structure, jolt after nerve-jangling jolt, and a brace of punchy, charismatic performances: John Travolta as flabby, slow-witted nice guy Vincent, who happens to be a ruthless hitman, Samuel Jackson as his fearsome Bible-spouting buddy Jules, who has "Bad Motherfucker" embroidered on his wallet, Harvey Keitel being the dapper elder statesman, and Bruce Willis finally putting his oxen lunkishness to good use as a boxer on the skids.

But before you can enjoy these pleasures, there are considerable obstacles to get past. *Pulp Fiction* opens with a diner conversation as rambling and one-note as the Madonna debate in *Dogs*—and if you don't buy the notion that Tim Roth and Amanda Plummer, as lovebird felons, are compelling company to hang out with, then you're going to be bored until the surf music kicks ln over the credits. Then, after a burst of Kook and the Gang, cut to Travolta and Jackson en route to a hit, lost in a colloquy on European burger bars and the erotics of foot massage. Again, if you couldn't care less that the French call a quarter-pounder with cheese a ***burger royal***, then you might already be wondering whether this film's for you. Every film entails a match or mis-match between its concerns and the viewer's, but few assert such a singular or fastidious set of obsessions.

The same applies to the Tarantino sense of humour and the way it works itself out in the violence. *Reservoir Dogs*' cruel ironies resolved themselves in the way that the violence came both randomly and inexorably. Here, though, the brutality is laid on as a succession of one-shot gags, *Road Runner* style. Mostly, these are at the expense of the little-league minor players who get blown away because they're not so cool—like the college boys who are the first to face Jules' Old Testament Vengeance.

Then there's the gruesome misogyny in the first story, in which Vincent goes out on the town with the boss's wife (Uma Thurman). Dressed up as a jokey dire warning about hard drugs, what happens to Thurman's Mia is no more than an excuse to see what a B-film vamp looks like when she gets real messed up. *Pulp Fiction* does indeed look like the director's book of imaginary dates—a whole succession of dream babes drop into the narrative almost at random, and only Thurman gets much to do. (Tarantino's beginning to look like the studio head's son in *The Player*, ordering starlets from the casting catalogue.)

Pulp Fiction isn't too choosy about who gets it in the neck—just about all our favourite characters suffer some humiliation along the way, sometimes ln outrageously cavalier fashion. But the narrative twists aren't as tight as you'd like. Tarantino's characters keep wilfully strolling into hell, but they nearly always stroll out again, mopping their brow with a whistle of relief. Pandora's box is opened only to be safely shut again. The film never puts us on the spot or makes us fear that we're going to find ourselves in a tight corner with its characters.

The blood-letting is pure joke-shop violence, designed to shake you out of your seat. But there's nothing behind the jokes, which are rather less funny and certainly less ironically biting, than the various Acme appliances that blow up in the Coyote's face in *Road Runner*. The murderous efficiency of *Dogs* has vanished. Here, Tarantino has the time and the budget to do what he likes, and he does every thing that comes into his head, But you miss that cold fast sleazy hit that the title promises. This isn't pulp fiction so much as a big flabby airport paperback with a flashy embossed cover.

SIGHT AND SOUND, 11/94, p. 50, Amanda Lipman

Honey Bunny and her boyfriend Pumpkin sit in a diner. Pumpkin persuades her that the only way for them to make a living is by holding up restaurants; they decide to start here and then. Two hitmen, Vincent, and Jules, drive to an assignment for their boss Marsellus; Vincent tells Jules that Marsellus has asked him to take his wife Mia out for the night. Jules and Vincent burst into an apartment where three boys are eating breakfast, take a briefcase, which apparently belongs to Marsellus, and kill two of the boys. In an empty bar, Marsellus pays a boxer, Butch, to lose an upcoming title fight. Vincent and Jules turn up, having swapped their suits for T-shirts and shorts. Vincent buys some heroin from his dealer. That evening, he takes Mia out to a gimmicky restaurant. When they return, Mia, who has been snorting cocaine all night, finds

Vincent's heroin. Thinking it is cocaine, she takes it and overdoses. Vincent takes her to his dealer's house and they manage to bring her back to life with an adrenaline injection. Mia and Vincent decide not to tell Marsellus what has happened.

The scene changes. A small boy is introduced to a Captain Koons, a Vietnam friend of his father's, who has come to give him his dead father's watch. The little boy is Butch, who, as an adult, wakes with a start just before his prize-fight, Butch wins the fight and escapes with his money to a motel where his girlfriend Fabienne is waiting for him. The next morning, Butch discovers that Fabienne has left his father's watch in his apartment, and decides to go back for it. Entering the apartment, he disturbs Vincent, who is sitting on the toilet. Butch kills him with his own gun, takes his watch and drives off. Seeing Marsellus in the road, he tries to run him down; both survive, and Marsellus chases Butch into a pawn shop. The owner points a gun at both of them, ties them up and, with a friend, Zed, rapes Marsellus.

Butch manages to escape but decides to go back and rescue Marsellus. Marsellus allows him to leave town with his money as long as he promises not to return. Butch drives off on Zed's motorbike to collect Fabienne.

The scene flashes back to Jules and Vincent in the apartment where they kill the two boys. There is another young man hiding in the bathroom; he bursts out firing at the two men, and misses. They shoot him, and Jules vows that after this job he will give up being a hit man. They take the remaining boy hostage but in the car Vincent accidentally kills him. Covered in blood, they drive to the house of a friend, Jimmy, and elicit the help of the 'Wolf'. He instructs them on how to clean up the mess, puts them in Jimmy's casual clothes and disposes of the car and the body. Jules and Vincent go for breakfast in the diner, just as Honey Bunny and Pumpkin announce their stickup. Jules talks them out of taking the mysterious briefcase he has for Marsellus, and persuades them to leave quietly.

It looks like a tribute to Quentin Tarantino's fast rise to fame that he has managed to draw quite such a varied crowd of names for *Pulp Fiction*. And yet when you examine those names, they are mostly those of actors in search of a hit. *Pulp Fiction* is full of five-minute culture jokes; could this be another one? Possibly; for several of the cast appear to be playing warped versions of characters for which they are known. Bruce Willis' tough guy Butch may be a *Die Hardsman*, but this time round, Butch is a little bit stupid and has a nasty temper. Rosanna Arquette's crazy lady from *After Hours* has turned into a junkie's housewife, utterly absorbed in the piercings on her body. Harvey Keitel reprises his role in the *Nikita* remake *The Assassin*, as the icy, mute killer, who cleans up after dead bodies and gets rid of the living ones. Only this time, the grim-faced Wolf has absurd touches of Regular Guy about him. He chats about coffee, and his clean-up operation does not involve acid baths but soapy sponges and hose-downs. Some of the actors are not even playing out their own former roles in this rag-bag of film references: to take just Tarantino's own work, Honey Bunny and Pumpkin, who open and close the film, are straight out of *True Romance*, while the hitmen Jules and Vincent could have been in *Reservoir Dogs*.

It is a remarkable achievement that the film manages to hold all these people together through four different storylines. Perhaps because we get to know him best, the link seems to be John Travolta's Vincent. Flashy Vincent is what the disco-loving street boy Tony Manero would have grown up to be after *Saturday Night Fever*. And he still needs to sort himself out. Vincent has enough sense not to let himself sleep with Marsellus's wife, Mia, when he gets the opportunity, but is stupid enough to leave his gun lying around while he goes to the bathroom. We see him shoot heroin, and we see him on the lavatory, and Vincent therefore becomes vulnerable. But like everyone else here, he has little regard for human life, and when he accidentally shoots his hostage's head off, he worries more about his suit than about what he has done.

Violence is still Tarantino's watchword, and *Pulp Fiction* abounds with other nasty, casual deaths. No one is immune: even Vincent, the hero of sorts, dies with an undignified snap of the fingers. Life in the 90s, Tarantino seems to be saying, is speedy and worthless. The people on the screen are, as the film's title makes plain, characters from trash novels. They are drug dealers, killers, crime lords, spoilt ladies, prize boxers, S&M rapists. Everyone is on the run, off their heads, or on the wrong side of the law. And yet in a way they could be us, too. If Tarantino has anything to say, it seems to be that there is no morality or justice in the patterns of life and death. Instead, the nihilist argument continues, there is trivia.

For if we are not supposed to empathise with the characters themselves, we cannot help recognising the junk culture world they inhabit: a world filled with ridiculous TV programmes, gimmicky restaurants where the waiters dress up as film stars and steaks are named after directors, and powerful drugs that demand their own place in a daily timetable. Trash is not just the written word, it is all around. And here it is endlessly recycled in the endless conversations of Tarantino's pulp protagonists.

In the car, Vincent and Jules are engrossed in the French names for hamburgers. As the camera follows them towards the apartment of boys they are about kill, they talk about foot massages. When Butch gets to the motel in which he is meeting Fabienne before they flee with his winnings, she starts chatting about the fatness of her stomach. This is the kind of stuff most of us actually do spend much of our time talking about, and it puts us on a level of understanding with the characters. The effect is strangely subtle in a film that is all about crude gestures. Mia, herself a bizarre mixture of spoilt child and wise woman, remarks that Marsellus' henchmen are worse than a sewing circle when it comes to gossip. And suddenly the killers have been emasculated.

True Romance seemed to become less Quentin Tarantino and more its director Tony Scott every time it lapsed into sentimentality, so it is hardly surprising that Tarantino imposes a sizeable emotional distance between the audience and the characters. When Butch dreams about Captain Koons (a hilarious cameo by Christopher Walken) giving him his father's watch, a sentimental episode from a thousand TV movies becomes more ludicrous and disgusting by the minute. And even though each section of the film ends with a moment of collaboration—between Vincent and Mia, Marsellus and Butch, and finally Jules, Pumpkin and Honey Bunny—the sense of shame that could bring about an attempt at a heartfelt moment is subsumed by the characters' self-interest. In the same way, it would be an effort to feel sentimental over the film's one big emotional transformation. Samuel L. Jackson's Jules is an extraordinary character, with touches of Robert Mitchum's preaching murderer in *The Night Of the Hunter*. He goes about his killing business with religious fervour, spouting Ezekiel at his terrified victims as if to justify his acts. And what changes his mind about his work? Not a crisis of conscience but a realisation of his own mortality. More self-reservation: the philosophical new Jules is as hard and cold as the old one. He resists the temptation to kill Pumpkin not because he has found mercy but because he has made a decision to stop killing.

Butch is the nearest we might get to a sentimentalist—he has a girl he loves and enough heart to go back and rescue his arch-enemy from the rapists. But Butch is not nice either. In Tarantino's movie reference library, Butch is more loudmouth Ralph Meeker in *Kiss Me Deadly* than sappy Fred MacMurray in *Double Indemnity*.

Tarantino sees such things and laughs, and makes us laugh, too. But it is not simply the nervous laughter of voyeurs relieved that these horrible things are happening to someone else and not to them. There are plenty of brilliantly funny moments, and it is to Tarantino's credit that he has managed to work modern, junk, and retro culture into his script with such ease. Some of the comedy is less engaging: there is occasionally too much slapstick screaming; the odd, knowing *Wayne's World*-style joke, in which the characters almost turn to the camera and start acting to us rather than to each other, seems out of place. We have to believe that they believe in what is happening, or everything falls apart.

Like *Reservoir Dogs*, this is stylishly shot in neo-cartoon style, with massive, distorting close-ups offset by attractively angled shots. The effect again, is of a hard, closed, rather linear world. But in some ways, there is more to *Pulp Fiction* than to the first film. For one thing, there are a few women in it, and a broader spectrum of characters. For another, by allowing just a few chinks in its dispassionate armour, mostly through Travolta's oddly affable Vincent Vega, it is easier to like rather than just admire.

VILLAGE VOICE, 10/11/94, p. 61, J. Hoberman

More than anything else, Quentin Tarantino is a spinner of tall tales—the superbly garrulous, living embodiment of the movie enthusiast's hey-wouldn't-it-be-great-if... aesthetic. *Pulp Fiction* trumps *Reservoir Dogs* to confirm the 31-year-old writer-director as current King of the Wild Frontier, but nearly as remarkable as *Pulp Fiction*'s loop-the-loop digressions, shock violence, and outrageous plot twists has been its capacity to mobilize media attention. There's a sense in which Tarantino's now legendary ascension from video store geek to Palme d'Or chic is his own greatest whopper.

A blood-soaked exercise in nihilo-Neanderthal absurdism, Tarantino's debut moved simultaneously backward and forward in cinema history. "The first coffee-house action movie," per *Vanity Fair* (forgetting *Breathless* and *Shoot the Piano Player*), *Reservoir Dogs* "spoke to Kurt Cobain" and attracted "people who thought they were too cool for *Lethal Weapon*" with, among other things, the ear slice *The New York Times Magazine* leapfrogged past psycho's shower sequence to term "the nastiest bit of screen violence" since Buñuel and Dali slashed an eyeball in *their* 1929 debut, *Un Chien Andalou*. The comparison is not entirely inapt. Just as *Un Chien Andalou* travestied the poetic avant-garde of the 1920s, so the independently produced *Reservoir Dogs* single-handedly shifted the Sundance Film Festival diet from granola and skim milk to french fries smothered in ketchup, after its world premiere there in 1992.

No less aggressive or stylized than its precursor, *Pulp Fiction* is a movie of interlocking stories set in an imaginary demimonde and held together by languorous fades, humorous ellipses, and nonstop conversation. The comic structure is largely based on a series of two-handers: Tim Roth playing verbal footsie with Amanda Plummer, a goofily stoned John Travolta escorting the haughty Uma Thurman, world-weary Bruce Willis coming home to kittenish (and ultimately tiresome) Maria de Medeiros, *Die Hard* Willis battling volcanic Ving Rhames, rattled Travolta debating the wired, superbad Samuel L. Jackson.

Tarantino has an unerring command of slang and, in lieu of visual ambience, invents an aural one. Every character has a rap or a riff, if not a full-fledged theory of life. (At times, *Pulp Fiction* suggests a two-fisted Jarmusch film.) No wonder actors love Tarantino. Not only does he write hilarious, convoluted dialogue but he permits them to posture through every scene as an extended one-on-one gabfest confrontation. Call the mode "Talk Talk Bang Bang." The language is as calculatedly brutal as the action—full of baroque racial, xenophobic invective as well as continual profanity.

Tarantino's America is a wondrously wild and crazy place. "They robbed a bank with a telephone," says one character in amazement—especially as he, and nearly everyone else in the cast, is packing heat. Violence erupts out of nowhere—or rather, it erupts out of some kind of "innocent" fun. A fetishistic close-up of fixing, shooting, and booting smack leads, by the by, to a bloody, drooling OD, hysterical panic, and finally, the most successfully horrific comedy sequence in the movie. Tarantino is too fascinated by the nuance of situation to be a master of suspense, but *Pulp Fiction* is predicated upon his gift for abruptly raising the stakes. A couple talk themselves into robbing the joint where they're having breakfast—chitchat giving way to lunatic frenzy. Two professional killers riff on European taste in American fast food en route to a wildly theatrical hit. Toying with one victim, the gunman offhandedly shoots a second, then apologizes to the survivor: "I'm sorry—did I break your concentration?"

Despite its title, *Pulp Fiction* has less to do with the hard-boiled detective stories published 60 years ago in *Black Mask* magazine than with the déclassé action movies of the early '70s. The movie resonates with echoes of biker and doper flicks, vigilante sagas like *Dirty Harry* and *Walking Tall*, the genres *Variety* dubbed spaghetti westerns, chopsocky, and, especially, blaxploitation, as well as the contemporary art-splatter of Hollywood auteurs Peckinpah, Scorsese, and De Palma—movies that were not only violent but steeped in moral confusion. More generally, the title suggests Tarantino's spongelike capacity to absorb whatever he sees. The '70s is always a touchstone, but *Pulp Fiction* lifts bits of business from *Kiss Me Deadly* and *Psycho* and Jean-Luc Godard, the inventor of movie postmodernism who has spawned yet another disciple.

In *Reservoir Dogs*, Tarantino's fanciful creatures asserted their reality by analyzing Madonna or musing upon the TV series *Get Christie Love*. *Pulp Fiction* is an even more naturalized hall of mirrors. Thurman wears Anna Karina's wig-hat; Willis does Ralph Meeker doing Brando. Jackson's Fu Manchu mustache, fierce mutton chops, and oiled 'fro make him pure essence of 1974. (All he lacks is the lime-green leisure suit.) Travolta's character is *Welcome Back, Kotter's* Vinnie Barbarino grown up into a hit man called Vincent Vega—as in star. "We're gonna be like three little Fonzies here," Jackson soothes the participants of one Mexican standoff by way of saying Be Cool.

Pulp Fiction's most elaborate set piece endearingly sends up Tarantino's own mind-set, inventing a made-for-57th Street theme-restaurant populated by '50s icons. "It's like a wax museum with a pulse," Travolta smirks—as if he weren't sitting in his own personal Hall of Fame, particularly once Thurman maneuvers him into a twist contest that quickly turns Bandstand extravaganza of tiptoe swiveling, lasso moves, and synchronized shoulder strokes.

Reservoir Dogs was so totally an exercise in style and attitude that one could rightly wonder if it had anything more on its mind. In fact, although populated almost exclusively by presumably straight male Caucasians, the movie was obsessed, in its own flavorsome terms, with niggers, bitches, and fags. (Tarantino's favorite compliment was L. M. Kit Carson's admiring observation that he had produced a real "white guy movie.") *Pulp Fiction* brings more to the surface. While a second viewing eliminates Tarantino's mainly excellent narrative surprises, it also reveals how cleverly he sets up his punch lines—the early reference to the gangster played by Rhames getting "fucked like a bitch," the instant hostility between the Travolta and Willis characters, the degree to which the elements in the latter's dream are reconfigured in a far more nightmarish reality.

Indeed, spinning variations on what Tarantino himself calls "the oldest chestnuts in the world" (the guy who takes out the mob boss's wife, the boxer who is supposed to throw the fight, and "the opening five minutes of every other Joel Silver movie"), *Pulp Fiction* manages to get more pathological than one could believe possible—whether transforming cold-blooded killers into philosopher dorks or seducing the opening night crowd at the New York Film Festival into laughing appreciatively when someone gets his head blown off and drenches a car's interior with blood. Tarantino, who associates a jocular attitude towards onscreen violence with the blaxploitation audience, demonstrates his own particular power by casting himself as the one character who can make the terrifying Jackson shuffle, even as he manages to enunciate the phrase "dead nigger" four times in as many minutes.

Whether or not *Pulp Fiction* is, as Janet Maslin enthused in the *Times*, "a stunning vision of destiny, choice and spiritual possibility," it amply demonstrates Tarantino's particular sense of movies as a medium that permits the quasi-divine manipulation of time and space, including the ability to resurrect the dead. *Pulp Fiction*'s narrative loops back on itself as elegantly as that of *Reservoir Dogs* but to far more self-consciously playful purpose. Butch not only escapes on a chopper emblazoned with the cockamamie "Grace," his getaway is accompanied by the theme from *The Twilight Zone*.

Never mind that Tarantino lifted "*Pulp Fiction*'s riff on Ezekiel 25:17 from an old kung fu movie or Jackson's redemption from *Kung Fu*, he is some kind of miracle worker. Reminiscing (with Dennis Hopper no less) in the current *Grand Street*, the filmmaker recalls, with some bemusement, the powers of persuasion he honed during his years behind a video store counter: "I remember—this is really weird—I created a following for Eric Rohmer in Manhattan Beach and the South Bay area." That was talk talk without the bang bang.

Also reviewed in:
CHICAGO TRIBUNE, 10/14/94, Friday/p. C, Michael Wilmington
NATION, 10/17/94, p. 434, Stuart Klawans
NEW REPUBLIC, 11/14/94, p. 26, Stanley Kauffmann
NEW YORK TIMES, 9/23/94, p. C1, Janet Maslin
NEW YORKER, 10/10/94, p. 95, Anthony Lane
VARIETY, 5/23-29/94, p. 52, Todd McCarthy
WASHINGTON POST, 10/14/94, p. F1, Rita Kempley
WASHINGTON POST, 10/14/94, Weekend/p. 48, Desson Howe

QUEEN MARGOT

A Miramax Films release of a Renn Productions/France 2 Cinema/D.A. Films/NEF Film produktion/Degeto/R.C.S. Films & TV with the participation of Centre National de la Cinématographie and Canal+. *Executive Producer:* Pierre Grunstein. *Director:* Patrice Chéreau. *Screenplay: (French with English subtitles)* Danièle Thompson and Patrice Chéreau. ***Based on the*** *novel by:* Alexandre Dumas. *Director of Photography:* Philippe Rousselot. *Editor:* François Gédigier and Hélène Viard. *Music:* Goran Bregovic. *Sound:* Joël Rangon. *Sound Editor:* Guillaume Sciama and Dominique Hennequin. *Casting:* Margot Capelier, Ann Dorthe Braker, and Mirta Guarnaschelli. *Production Designer:* Richard Peduzzi and Olivier Radot. *Set Decorator:* Sophie Martel. *Special Effects:* Georges Demetrau. *Costumes:* Moidele Bickel. *Make-up:* Thi-Loan Nguyen and Kuno Schlegelmilch. *Stunt Coordinator:* Philippe Guegan. *Running time:* 143 minutes. *MPAA Rating:* R.

CAST: Isabelle Adjani (Margot); Daniel Auteuil (Henri of Navarre); Jean-Hugues Anglade (Charles IX); Vincent Perez (La Môle); Virna Lisi (Catherine of Médici); Dominique Blanc (Henriette of Nevers); Pascal Greggory (Anjou); Claudio Amendola (Coconnas); Miguel Bosè (Guise); Asia Argento (Charlotte of Sauve); Julien Rassam (Alençon); Thomas Kretschmann (Nançay); Jean-Claude Brialy (Coligny); Jean-Philippe Ecoffey (Condé); Albano Guaetta (Orthon); Johan Leysen (Maurevel); Dörte Lyssewski (Marie Touchet); Michelle Marquais (The Nurse); Laure Marsac (Antoinette); Alexis Nitzer and Barbet Schroeder (Advisors); Emmanuel Salinger (Du Bartas); Jean-Marc Stehle (Innkeeper); Otto Tausig (Mendès); Bruno Todeschini (Armagnac); Tolsty (Hangman); Bernard Verley (The Cardinal); Ulrich Wildgruber (René).

FILMS IN REVIEW, 3-4/95, p. 60, Andy Pawelczak

At the beginning of *Queen Margot*, a historical romance based on a novel by Dumas and directed by Patrice Chereau, a written legend brings us up to speed on the movie's factual background. During the sixteenth century wars between the Catholics and Protestants in France, the Catholic Catherine de Medici has arranged a marriage between her daughter, Margot, and the Protestant Henri of Navarre in order to pacify France and wrest power away from Admiral Coligny, a Protestant who has gained an ascendancy over the mind of Catherine's son, King Charles IX. Your heart sinks—it's like reading a plot synopsis of an unfamiliar opera two minutes before the curtain rises. But the film is so compelling and vivid that 15 minutes into it you've more or less sorted out its characters and are caught up in its labyrinthine court intrigues.

The movie isn't like the old-fashioned Hollywood costume dramas in which the actors mouthed platitudinous speeches while striking dignified poses. The actor here have a contemporary look—scruffy beards, casual, loose-fitting clothes—and the action has a convincingly primitive tone. Princes and dukes brawl on the palace grounds, and Margot (Isabelle Adjani), disguised by a mask, slips out onto the streets to find a man, any man, to satisfy her sexually. When Margot hesitates during her marriage ceremony, her brother Charles (Jean-Hugues Anglade) creeps up behind her and in full view of the court literally shoves her into marriage. The film gives us a maggot's-eye view of history—it's Machiavelli with the rhetoric stripped away—and you can almost smell the sweat on its not-so-noble actors.

As Margot, Isabelle Adjani floats through the movie like a dream version of a romantic heroine. Margot, though she has the reputation of a sexually insatiable witch who surrounds her bed with her lovers' heads, is politically loyal to her husband Henri (Daniel Auteuil), whose life she helps to save, and romantically devoted to her lover, the Protestant La Mole (Vincent Perez). But the real stars of the movie are Virna Lisi and Jean-Hugues Anglade. As Catherine de Medici, Lisi, in white make-up and long stiff gowns, is like a sinister figure from Kabuki drama as she plots murders and carries on an almost incestuous relationship with her son. Anglade as King Charles, is a deeply ambivalent king who pulls at his shirt neurotically and rolls on the floor when his mother orders the death of his mentor, Admiral Coligny. He wants the death and he doesn't—Coligny rescued Charles from the malign influence of his mother but his death will free him from Coligny's equally oppressive domination.

The movie is filled with the staples of romantic costume drama—last minute escapes, dangerous assignations, poisoned lipstick—but Chereau directs with a darkly luminous intensity that lifts it all above cliche. The film's big set piece is the St. Bartholomew's Day Massacre which Chereau shoots with a majestically calm camera moving through the torch-lit scene of carnage. The scene reminds us of the horrors of fraternal bloodshed in the name of religion which we are still witnessing in Bosnia today.

LOS ANGELES TIMES, 12/14/94, Calendar/p. 2, Peter Rainer

Hollywood doesn't make many grand-scale costumey historical romances anymore—the kind of film that opens with a long crawl crammed with facts and dates and dynastical data. Movies are so good at taking us back in time that it's a shame so few do.

"Queen Margot," derived from an Alexander Dumas romance, is rich and full of verve. Director Patrice Chereau, an avant-garde theater and opera director best known for his massive modernization of Wagner's Ring cycle in Bayreuth in the late '70s, keeps the action buzzing and the faces looming. It's unusual to see a period film—it's set in 1572, at the time of the Saint Bartholomew's Day Massacre—that moves to a contemporary beat without sacrificing realism.

Chereau, with co-screenwriter Daniele Thompson, moves right into the torrid, horrific intrigue between the Catholics and the Protestants. He revels in the court intrigue, the scheming, the deviousness. You may not be able to sort out all the players and the plotting—at least not without an encyclopedia and penlight handy—but the broad historical outline survives.

And Chereau has cast actors with an operatic mien: Marguerite of Valois (Margot) is played by Isabelle Adjani, and her mother, Catherine of Medici, the Catholic Queen Mother of France, is played by Virna Lisi, who won the 1994 best actress award at Cannes for her performance. Their bond is obvious: Their faces are stamped with a larger-than-life furiousness.

The drama is propelled by the arranged (by Catherine) marriage of Margot to the Protestant Henri of Navarre (Daniel Auteuil). This union to reconcile the French turns out to be a ploy by Catherine to attract thousands of Protestants to Paris, where, six days after the wedding, they are destroyed en masse in the streets, in churches, in the Louvre.

The Saint Bartholomew Day's Massacre, which D. W. Griffith also dramatized in "Intolerance," is an orgy of bloodletting that threatens to flood both Catholics and Protestants in its wake. Margot, no friend of the Protestants, ends up their sympathizer. She forms an affection for Henri and a passion for the Protestant Lord of La Mole (Vincent Perez). She rebels against Catherine and her brother Charles IX (Jean-Hugues Anglade), and for a time becomes their captive.

It's difficult imagining Margot in captivity. In grand romantic tradition, her only captivator is La Mole. It's a passion that even survives his death. (Hint: She owes a lot to the court embalmer.)

Adjani, of course, is no stranger to grand passion in the movies. As Adele Hugo in Truffaut's "Story of Adele H," Adjani gave the definite crazed-by-love performance. Her Margot isn't in the same league with her Adele—and the movie isn't at all comparable to Truffaut's as a study in passion—but Adjani still burns a hole in the screen. Probably no major actress in movie history has managed to look as perpetually, ravishingly youthful as Adjani. She looks a couple of years older than she did in "Adele H," which came out almost 20 years ago.

Lisi, unrecognizable from her Hollywood days in '60s films like "How to Murder Your Wife" and "Assault on a Queen," gives a terrific dragon-lady performance. With her black veils and high domed forehead, she's a Medici right out of "Invaders From Mars." Lisi has a harsh raspy voice without a shade of lilt or sensuality. Her dark rage is almost comic in its magisterial meanness but Lisi doesn't camp it up. No one in the film does, with the possible exception of Anglade, who turns Charles IX into a reeling wreck—a bloodstained banshee of a king.

At a running time of 141 minutes—trimmed 23 minutes from the Cannes version—"Queen Margot" isn't always brisk. The intrigues get a bit thick, and after awhile, the costume design (by Moidele Bickel) and the cinematography (by the great Phillipe Rousselot) overwhelm the court shenanigans. "Queen Margot" is far from great but it doesn't make the standard mistake of most movie romances—it doesn't confuse authenticity with dullness. These days a period movie that brings you unabashedly into the period is rare.

NEW STATESMAN & SOCIETY, 1/13/95, p. 31, Jonathan Romney

It's the usual wedding reception—flirting, fist fights, bad dance music. The groom's getting roughed up by his in-laws, the bride's standing around with the girls eyeing up likely lads for the night, and the bride's mother has stepped out for a moment to confer with her poisoning consultant. The guests would do well not to stay overnight.

Historical distance gives you a different perspective on things. The subject of Patrice Chéreau's *La Reine Margot* is horrific beyond belief—the marriage in 1572 of the Catholic Marguerite of

Valois and the Protestant King Henri of Navarre, and the subsequent outbreak of the St Bartholomew's Day Massacre, in which thousands of Protestants were slaughtered in Paris. In its way the story is no less monstrous than the one told in *Schindler's List*, and yet our response is entirely different. We can't help but respond to Spielberg's film by acknowledging the rage and solemnity its theme elicits—that, rather than the sentimentality it also evokes. We wouldn't dream of smacking our lips over the sheer enormity of the scale of destruction, the intensity of the inhumanity—and that's partly to do with the Holocaust still being on our doorstep, a fact brought home in the final scene, where real life survivors from Schindler's factory are brought on to testify to the story's reality.

It may be historical distance alone that enables us to respond to *La Reine Margot* quite differently. There's a sense of horror, certainly—no film has quite evoked such a sense of the randomness and sheer entropic energy of mass bloodshed. But we also feel a peculiar relish, an ecstatic immersion in the lush materiality of it all. Chéreau starts us off swooning in the early scenes with fairly conventional pomp—the wedding in Notre Dame, with the courtiers stacked up in great vertical walls, and Isabelle Adjani's Margot looking perfectly angelic and artificial, like a Fabergé automaton. What has us swooning for much of the rest of the film is the sheer luxury of brutality—the bodies arrayed in piles in the streets in great Delacroix compositions of decomposition, and slabs of impenetrable dark.

Then it's the blood, which comes in more shades and textures than you'd think imaginable. If you're used to the e-zee-flow ketchup of *Pulp Fiction*, it comes as a shock to realise that the French do blood in as many different styles as their charcuterie. Dark and oily, as if congealing the minute it leaves the body; the rich ruby Bordeaux glistening on Adjani's radiant white gown; or the weedy liquid off-pink that seeps out of every pore of Jean-Hugues Anglade's Charles IX, after accidental contact with one of his mother's special poisons.

It's understandable that a film that discharges so many viscera goes to the viewer's gut too. Chéreau manages this because *La Reine Margot* is effectively conceived as grand opera for the screen. This is no loose comparison—Chéreau has directed *The Nibelungen* on stage, not to mention Shakespeare, Molière, Lope de Vega and Marlowe's own account of the slaughter, *The Massacre in Paris*. He's also directed Victor Hugo, and the film is closest to the spirit of Hugo—the excess of event, the Romantic sense of huge passions mobilised within an uncontainable mess of political chicanery, the private and the public reacting together like explosive gases in an unruly body. (The film's actually based on a Dumas novel; the writers also throw in some Heinrich Mann—all these sources surely adding to the chaotic dynamism.)

This excess makes *La Reine Margot* far more than just a walk-through diorama. Chéreau takes seriously the idea of an "historical tableau"; *La Reine Margot* really is like a huge canvas in which events are happening at once in every corner, so densely that you're only generally aware of swathes of form and movement; it verges on the abstract. Chéreau's great feat is to create that sense of enormity while for much of the tie concentrating on close-ups or small crowded compositions—zeroing in on little pockets of activity and picking up on corner's of darkness and decay.

La Reine Margot is anything but a history lesson. It's a costume drama for anyone who hated *A Man for all Seasons* or any of those films where you'd get 20 minutes of carousing fustian before being admitted to the private quarters of Cardinal Wolsey for a brief Jackdaw-pack résumé of the Reformation. *La Reine Margot* gabbles its way through the history, in a hurry to get to the next slaying; early on, Protestant Admiral Coligny (Jean-Claude Brialy, an armored side of beef urges the court to go to war against Holland, and the scene is broken up by Anglade's distracted bout of coughing and spluttering—the body politics disrupted by the body.

What's operatic above all is the way that the film paints history as made not by strategy but by odd physical outbursts—by fraternal passions (Margot's incestuous brothers crowding jealously around her), by dyspeptic madness (Anglade's volatile, decrepit Charles, suddenly, recklessly allying himself with his supposed enemy Henri), and above all by sex. *La Reine Margot* is the sexiest film I've seen in ages; amour here truly is *fou*—and a little unsavoury.

Margot goes out masked on her wedding night to pick up a bit of rough—or if you like, a bit of ruff—and anonymously tumbles the eventual love of her life, La Môle (Vincent Perez), again a gutterwall. The equation of love and death is embodied by her side-kick Henriette (Dominique Blanc), bosom relentlessly all aheave in a palpable tizz over the slaughter; when she helps Margot tend the bloodied La Môle, it's remarkably erotic, as they delicately manhandle a body that looks as if it's fished off the raft of Medusa.

The dark centre to it all is Virna Lisi's Catherine de Medici, a Mafia mamma who pulls all the strings, first seen in a extraordinary ruff that looks like a gilded spider web in advanced decay, later steeping her hands in blood while her henchman reads the future from a slice of freshly carved brain. She's the real focus of the film's energies, the counterpart to Adjani's luminous blankness.

Adjani is perfectly cast for her slightly inhuman mystique—at 40, she looks like a showroom ideal of an ageless 18 year old. In the wedding scene, puffed-up and powdered, her face too geometrically perfect, she embodies the myth of the perfect princess, the unreal prize that all these energies are circulating around. She does finally become some sort of tragic heroine, simply by virtue of having survived, and the film's closing shot practically consecrates Adjani's troubled blankness, as if that perfect white vacancy is all that's left. The idea of royalty as stardom has never been better explored. A pity no one though of it for a Royal Command Performance.

NEW YORK POST, 12/9/94, p. 50, Thelma Adams

Love and intrigue are the driving forces behind "Queen Margot," Patrice Chereau's rapturous historical epic based on a page-turner by Alexandre Dumas.

No one—not man or beast is safe in the court of the Catholic King Charles IX, an aerie of "silk-clad vultures." It's the 16th century, the height of the French Reformation, and Catholics and Protestants are feuding bitterly.

The movie opens on the wedding day of Charles' sister Margot, played by the ageless Isabelle Adjani, to Protestant King Henri de Navarre (Daniel Auteuil). Sumptuously shot by Philippe Rousselot (who also lensed "Interview With the Vampire"), the scene's gorgeousness is tempered by the royal family's actions.

When the proud beauty balks at the ceremony, a royal brother slams Margot's head forward and her gasp is read as a consent.

What begins as an arranged alliance for peace, changes irrevocably in the bloodbath of the St. Bartholomew's Day Massacre that followed.

The weakling Charles (Jean-Hugues Anglade)—goaded by his mother Catherine de Medici (Virna Lisi) and the Catholic nobles—seizes the opportunity to butcher the cream of the Protestant nobility while they remain in Paris celebrating the wedding. It is a filthy act of religious cleansing.

"What is betrayal but one's skill at following the flow of events?" Catherine, the black widow of Henri II, later explains to Henri de Navarre. The saturnine Lisi with her high forehead, bitterly clear eyes and lemon-twisted lips, plays one of the all-time horrific, controlling mothers. What can be expected from a woman whose hobby is poisoning?

Lisi, in an Oscar-worthy performance, dominates a number of emotionally charged scenes, the dark family drama at the heart of larger historic events. She bids goodbye to her second son, Anjou (the piercing Pascal Greggory), with passionate tears and a lover's kiss which he returns in full.

She weeps at the bedside of Charles, who she has inadvertently poisoned with an arsenic-laced book meant for Navarre; the king, cunningly played by Anglade, dismisses Catherine's grief, noting that when a mother takes the life she brought into the world she is no longer a mother.

Margot stings at Catherine's rejection when her mother refers to her three children (her three sons), omitting the fourth, her daughter.

Betrayed by her mother, shocked by the slaughter of the Protestants, Adjani ("The Story of Adele H.") evolves from a pampered, sexually predatory pawn in the family games, to a passionate woman capable of love and loyalty.

"Queen Margot" is frank in its treatment of sexuality—Margot is no virgin bride. From her incestuous relationships—with her brothers, her affair with the Catholic Duc de Guise, her flat refusal to share her bed with her husband, and her romance with the Protestant de la Mole (Vincent Perez) who she rescues on St. Bartholomew's Day, it's clear that sex, as much as blood or religion, determines the queen's destiny.

In debt to Dumas and history for a rip-roaring good story—and well-served by a universally seductive cast "Queen Margot" is richly entertaining. When the movie concluded after two-plus hours, I wanted it to continue for another.

NEWSDAY, 12/9/94, Part II/p. B9, Gene Seymour

Like its title character, Queen Margot" often gets outrageously carried away with itself but never looks anything less than grand. This adaptation of one of Alexandre Dumas' densely-plotted novels of high adventure and low intrigue may be weighed down at the beginning by its historical baggage. But once the sex, gore and dastardly deeds kick into gear, the movie holds your attention, even when it's being windy or silly.

The film begins in 1572 France, a time when that country's ruling Catholics engaged in vicious, on-and-off battle with Protestant insurgents. In an effort to rig some sort of peace between the warring parties, a marriage is arranged between Marguerite "Margot" de Valois (Isabelle Adjani), sister to King Charles IX (Jean-Hughes Anglade), to Henri de Navarre (Daniel Auteuil, a Protestant leader who someday will become King Henry IV.

Margot's mother is the brilliant, ruthless Catherine de Medici (Virna Lisi), who makes Dumas' Cardinal Richelieu seem like Adlai Stevenson. She masterminded the murder of Navarre's mother and sets in motion the chain of events leading to the infamous St. Barthlomew Massacre of thousands of Protestants in the streets of Paris.

Margot, who is, at first, less than thrilled about being forced to marry a man she compares to a wild boar, becomes incensed over her family's treatment of the Protestants. Partly it's her own compassion. Partly it's that she's fallen hard for Le Mole (Vincent Perez), a dashing young Protestant.

With its relentless accumulation of passionate trysts, brutal slashings, botched poisonings and shifting alliances, "Margot's" plot has as many hairpin twists as San Francisco's Lombard Street and almost as many jolts as Mexico's Baja. It also has a few potholes and even the occasional slow-to-a-crawl tie-up. It's not always a fun ride, but it's rarely boring.

One reason for this is the bewitching Adjani, who makes a luminously sensuous heroine—at least, when she's got something important to do. Towards the end, however, she fades into the background to allow other characters' craziness to surge forth.

Auteuil brings an affecting, odd-duck nobility to Navarre in contrast to the moody Perez, who's around to provide maximum hunk quotient. Lisi, a 1960's icon who, like Dumas' novel, hasn't been seen in America for quite sometime, is alluring and creepy as Catherine De Medici, who, by the way, was recently sighted inhabiting Amanda Plummer's body in the lesser "Nostradamus." (Coincidence? Or what?) The most intriguing performance is Anglade's as the mercurial, twitchy king, who's not quite as ridiculous as he often seems.

NEWSWEEK, 12/12/94, p. 72, David Ansen

Bloody, romantic, wildly operatic, "Queen Margot" is not for those w ho like their historical drams well mannered. French director Patrice Chéreau, *enfant terrible* of the theater and opera world, hurls us into the viper's nest of the 16th-century court of Charles IX (Jean-Hugues Anglade), the neurotic Catholic king whose sister, Margot (Isabelle Adjani), is forced to marry Protestant Henri of Navarre (Daniel Auteuil) in hope of ending the religious wars ripping France apart. The brief peace is destroyed when the king, the pawn of his bloodthirsty mother, Catherine de Médici (Virna Lisi), orders up the 1572 "ethnic cleansing" known as the St. Bartholomew's Day Massacre. Amid the terror, Margot saves the life of her hunky Protestant lover, La Môle (Vincent Perez)—and then must fight her family for her husband's and La Môle's survival. It's Romeo and Juliet knee-deep in carnage, staged with Jacobean fury, lurid sensuality and high style by the recklessly gifted Chéreau.

SIGHT AND SOUND, 1/95, p. 55, Chris Darke

Paris, August 18, 1572. Marguerite de Valois (Margot), sister of Charles IX, the Catholic King of France and daughter of Catherine de Medici, is to marry the Protestant Duke, Henri of Navarre, in a ceremony arranged to appease the two warring religious factions. Marguerite, forced to marry a man she does not love, acquiesces only under pressure but insists that she will not share the conjugal bed with her new husband, preferring the attentions of her lover, the ruthless, bloodthirsty Duc de Guise.

Catherine de Medici wishes to neutralise the perceived Protestant threat by killing their leaders. As King, Charles—though indecisive and half-mad—declares that the deaths of the leaders alone is insufficient; he wants all of them dead, so that not a single Protestant survives to blame him. Despite his words being uttered while in the throes of a fit, and under coercive pressure from the Dukes of Anjou, Guise and Tavannes, they are taken as the royal assent to what will become known as the Saint Bartholomew's Day Massacre.

On August 23 and 24 a militia of Catholic courtiers and the Parisian people indiscriminately slaughter over 6,000 Protestants, including many of the Huguenot guests at Margot's wedding. Navarre is saved from the bloodshed by the attentions of Margot and her courtiers. However, she also attends to a badly wounded young Protestant, La Môle, who she realises is the same man she picked up several days previously when scouring the streets for casual amorous encounters. They fall in love and she helps him escape to Holland.

During a hunting accident Navarre saves the life of Charles and earns the King's trust, friendship and protection. However, Catherine is plotting to have Navarre killed with a slow-acting poison secreted into the pages of a hunting book. She entrusts the task to her youngest son, the Duc d'Alençon. Unexpectedly, the King, rather than Navarre, handles the book. He dies a slow and agonising death, attended to by Margot. La Môle has returned from Holland to find Margot but is charged with regicide and is executed with his friend Coconnas. Margot visits the decapitated body, taking his head to have it embalmed. Reconciled with her husband, sickened by Catherine de Medici's savagery, Margot flees the court to join the Protestant camp.

Blood, poison and perfume: *La Reine Margot* is a suppurating broth of all three in which the idea of the 'body politic' receives a highly physical twist. Patrice Chéreau has chosen to film the close, hermetic and murderous life of the French court at the time of Catherine de Medici as a scrum of fluid alliances and shifting allegiances. These are negotiated against the backdrop of a coerced marriage of political convenience (Marguerite de Valois to Henri de Navarre), feral, in-bred desire (Catherine de Medici for her son Henri, Duc d'Anjou; the brothers for their sister Margot), merciless religious hatred (the court is Catholic, Navarre is Protestant), focused by the growing horror and despair of the young queen.

Despite having failed as the French entry to set this year's Cannes Festival alight—the Best Supporting Actress award to Virna Lisi being widely (and condescendingly) seen as a token bauble—*La Reine Margot* has gone on to reap both critical and commercial acclaim in France. As yet another in the seemingly interminable cycle of heritage films with which Claude Berri—here in the role of producer—has become synonymous, the film arrives here trailing the baggage of expectations associated with others of its genre, but succeeds in satisfyingly short-circuiting them.

Chéreau himself has stressed his desire to avoid reproducing in his own film what *Cahiers du cinéma* has referred to as "retro-nostalgia", and has spoken in interviews of using a "prophylactic measure" to circumvent it—"Every time an image from a TV film on Catherine de Medici came to mind I would think of the three *Godfather* films, of *Mean Streets* and *GoodFellas*." The Medicis as Mafia clan—it's a nice idea, and one that has clearly shaped the film's depiction of the family as the arena of morbid power-play, while also allowing it to pull clear of the dread gravitational pull of its generic satellites. The heritage film tends to rely on set-ups that maximise its qualities of spectacle—high angles, mid-long shots—to the end of privileging illustrative tableaux, while also placing the spectator in an Olympian and curiously touristic position. (It is no coincidence that the 'heritage film' coincides precisely with the trend for restaging national history and culture in theme parks.) Conversely, the Mafia film comes in close and claustrophobic, uses two-shots, close-ups and privileges interior spaces. That this strategy places the spectator in a more intimate relationship to the action is something that has not been lost on Chéreau, who brings his camera in among the bodies, knitting in and out of the bloodlines and circuits of power. *La Reine Margot*'s *mise en scène* is one in which the spectator experiences a physical disorientation to match that of the characters themselves and, interestingly, the few moments when the film does lapse into a kind of painterly academicism (Vermeer, Zurburan) are those when the action shifts beyond the walls of the Palais du Louvre to Holland.

The uncomfortable intimacy that the film encourages brings out some remarkable performances; Lisi, clad in black throughout, plays Catherine as a woman whose mourning is as constant as her venomous affections. When it becomes clear that the poison she intended for Navarre has mistakenly infected her eldest son, the vacillating, bloodthirsty Charles, a low-angle shot has her lurking in the gallery of the Cathedral casting a vampiric shadow—Queen Nosferatu, her hair scraped cruelly back to show a Max Schreck pate. Jean-Hugues Anglade's Charles is one of the film's real revelations; those with memories of his dream-wimp boyfriends in *Betty Blue* and *Nikita* will barely recognise him here. His is a performance of real range and authority, half slobbering dungeon freak barely ennobled by filthy lace and half strangely sympathetic victim of his mother's appalling plots. And at the centre of all the mayhem is Adjani's Margot, her face a set of nested ovals that coalesce to express muted horror, her white robes forever absorbing the blood of others including that of La Môle, her Protestant lover, whose severed head she cradles in her lap after his execution, just as she absorbs into her clothes the sweated blood of the slow-poisoned King.

Grand guignol, cloak and dagger, cruel Mafia claustrophobia: *La Reine Margot* is nothing if not explicit about power and religious hatred. Its currency is blood, its disguises perfume and lace; parricide, regicide and genocide its manifest destiny. Close to the bone, this is the shocking, slightly cold but undeniably powerful apotheosis of the French heritage film.

VILLAGE VOICE, 12/13/94, p. 72, Gary Dauphin

With sumptuous sets and costumes, characters lit as if by flickerless wood-burning fires, and sure direction from Patrice Chereau, you might be willing to forgive *Queen Margot* for its story line of a French court more centered on the boudoir than the throne room. Given that *Margot* is already laboring under two layers of interpretation (actual history and the Alexandre Dumas novel), Chereau must have figured this story would tell itself, which it does, throwing plot twist after passionately declared plot twist until the story threatens to become a dull drone of reversals, albeit beautifully rendered.

After flashing some dangerously solemn paragraphs outlining the machinations of Catherine de Médici during the wars between French Catholics and Protestants in the 16th century, *Queen Margot* sets the heavy stuff aside and unveils its *real* area of historical interest: namely what happens when the sworn enemies end up sharing the same bed. *Margot* begins on the eve of peacemaking nuptials between a Catholic princess (Marguerite/Margot de Valois, played by Isabelle Adjani) and a provincial Protestant prince (Henri de Navarre, played by a pudgy Daniel Auteuil). The story of how they go from antipathy to political accommodation is full of the usual rococo touches—sexual conquests, assassinations, poisoned lipsticks, and the graphic set piece of the Saint Bartholomew's Day Massacre (wherein 6000 of Henri and Margot's Protestant wedding guests are slaughtered for taking the trouble to attend.) Heck *Margot* even has an evil stepmother in the form of Catherine de Médici (a wonderfully curdled Virna Lisi), making everyone uneasy between her plotting and the slow revving of her post menopausal sexual engine for her sons: King Charles IX (Jean-Hugues Anglade) and the would-be kings, Anjou and Aleçon.

Adjani's Marguerite de Valois's is *Margot*'s center from beginning to end, though. Exuding the angelic one moment, she's rutting like a dog the next, glowing with an internal luminosity akin to that of Maria Falconetti in Dreyer's *The Passion of Joan of Arc*, only dark-haired and sluttier. Her virtue is tested not by the large number of lovers she takes but by the subsequent political fallout, as when she strikes out on her own to pick up the love of her life in an alleyway ("I need a man," reads the subtitle, but it sounds more romantic in French) Chosen at random is the sadly handsome Protestant La Môle (Vincent Perez), and Margot's subsequent interdenominational affair offers the film's only honest (although overwrought) liaison, counterpointing her best buddy Henriette (Dominique Blanc doing a wicked supporting turn), who picks her future lover during the massacre.

If the exact nature of male virtue seems a secondary issue to *Margot*, it's mostly because there are just too many males running around to take a careful accounting. they rage and plot, alternately wrestling and huddling together like rival gangs of early adolescents at a basement party, and only Anglade's Charles IX rises above them. Tortured and dominated in turn by his mother, his brothers, and various surrogate fathers, Charles's release through protracted-death-scene provides the only male counterpart to Margot's ongoing sexual simmer. Whether that lack of dramatic competition makes this truly Margot's movie or makes *Queen Margot* just truly empty, you'll have to decide for yourself, but like reactions to the similarly textured *Interview With the Vampire*, it'll probably depend on how you like your pretty French boys and girls consumed by the camera.

Also reviewed in:
CHICAGO TRIBUNE, 12/16/94, Friday/p. H, Michael Wilmington
NEW REPUBLIC, 12/19/94, p. 26, Stanley Kauffmann
NEW YORK TIMES, 12/9/94, p. C10, Janet Maslin
VARIETY, 5/23-29/94, p. 53, Todd McCarthy
WASHINGTON POST, 1/6/95, p. C7, Rita Kempley

QUIZ SHOW

A Hollywood Pictures release of a Wildwood Enterprises/Baltimore Pictures production. *Executive Producer:* Fred Zollo, Richard Dreyfuss, and Judith James. *Producer:* Michael Jacobs, Julian Krainin, Michael Nozik, and Robert Redford. *Director:* Robert Redford. *Screenplay:* Paul Attanasio. *Based on the book "Remembering American: A Voice From the Sixties" by*: Richard N. Goodwin. *Director of Photography:* Michael Ballhaus. *Editor:* Stu Linder. *Music:* Mark Isham. *Music Editor:* Craig Pettigrew. *Sound:* Gary Rydstrom, Tod A. Maitland, and (music) Stephen Krause. *Sound Editor:* Richard Hymns. *Casting:* Bonnie Timmermann. *Production Designer:* Jon Hutman. *Art Director:* Tim Galvin. *Set Decorator:* Samara Schaffer. *Set Dresser:* Joseph L. Bird, Gilbert H. Gertsen, John Oates, Matthew McCarthy, Conrad Brink, Troy R. Adee, Joseph F. Proscia, Gordon H. Gertsen, John Oates, Jr., Gary Levitsky and Jeffrey S. Brink. *Costumes:* Kathy O'Rear. *Make-up:* Sharon Ilson. *Running time:* 120 minutes. *MPAA Rating:* PG-13.

CAST: John Turturro (Herbie Stempel); Rob Morrow (Dick Goodwin); Ralph Fiennes (Charles Van Doren); Paul Scofield (Mark Van Doren); David Paymer (Dan Enright); Hank Azaria (Albert Freedman); Christopher McDonald (Jack Barry); Johann Carlo (Toby Stempel); Elizabeth Wilson (Dorothy Van Doren); Allan Rich (Robert Kintner); Mira Sorvino (Sandra Goodwin); George Martin (Chairman); Paul Guilfoyle (Lishman); Griffin Dunne (Account Guy); Michael Mantell (Pennebaker); Byron Jennings (Moomaw); Ben Shenkman (Childress); Timothy Busfield (Fred); Jack Gilpin (Jack); Bruce Altman (Gene); Martin Scorsese (Sponsor); Joda Hershman (Lester Stempel); Ernie Sabella (Car Salesman); Barry Levinson (Dave Garroway); Debra Monk (Kintner's Secretary); Mario Cantone (Passerby); Timothy Britten Parker (Researcher); Grace Phillips (Mrs. Nearing); Jerry Grayson (Limo Driver); Scott Lucy, Matt Keeslar, and Ron Scott Bertozzi (NBC Pages); Harriet Sansom Harris (Enright's Secretary); Mary Shultz (Freedman's Secretary); Dave Wilson (Director); Robert Caminiti (Associate Director); Eddie Korbich (Lighting Director); Le Clanche Du Rand (Cornwall Neighbor); Carole Shelley (Cornwall Aunt); Shaw Batten and Cornelia Ryan (Cornwall Cousins); Jeffrey Nordling (John Van Doren); Vince O'Brien (Bunny Wilson); Adam Kilgour (Thomas Merton, The Monk); Richard Seff (Congressman Devine); Bill Moor (Congressman Rogers); Nicholas Kepros (Congressman Flynt); Barry Snider (Congressman Spring); Chuck Adamson (Congressman Mack); Joseph Attanasio (Congressman Derounian); Dan Wakefield and Hamilton Fish (Professors at Book Party); Merwin Goldsmith (Writer at Book Party); Illeana Douglas (Woman at Book Party); Gretchen Egolf (Student at Book Party); Stephen Pearlman (Judge Schweitzer); Anthony Fusco (Librarian); Douglas McGrath (Snodgrass); Calista Flockhart and Alysa Shwedel (Barnard Girls); Steve Roland (Today Announcer); Bernie Sheredy, Joe Lisi, and Greg Martin (Reporters); Reno (Woman at Door); Neil Leifer (Psychoanalyst); Caryn Krooth (Blonde); Mario Contacessi (Waiter); Pat Russell (NBC Secretary); Bill Cwikowski (Challenger); William Fichtner (Stage Manager); Vincent J. Burns (Crew Member); Katherine Turturro (#1 Mom); Gina Rice (Mrs. John Van Doren).

CINEASTE, Vol. XXI, Nos. 1-2, 1995, p. 85, Thomas Doherty

With Robert Redford's *Quiz Show*, one of the most popular and ill-fated genres in television history has returned from kinescope oblivion for a second media life. Apparently, back when Eisenhower was in the White House and Elvis in the Army, the quiz show scandal rivaled Sputnik and fluoridated water as a threat to Cold War America. Drawing on a chapter in Richard N. Goodwin's *Remembering America*, director Redford and screenwriter Paul Attanasio depict this blip on the cultural radar as a low-definition metaphor for the loss of postwar innocence, the first slip in a long slide into credibility gaps and modified, limited hang-outs. First Geritol and NBC betray the nation on live TV, then Ike lies about the U2 spy plane, LBJ lies about Vietnam, and Nixon lies about everything.

So prominent a zeitgeist comeback suggests that the quiz show scandal has become emblematic of a set of issues that continue to bedevil television and American culture: the borders between reality and entertainment, the notion of the airwaves as a public trust, and the lengths to which ordinary Americans will go to gain fame, money, and—perhaps most of all—regular appearances on television. Yet the current fascination with the strange precable universe of the late 1950s may be more a wistful look back than an early warning signal. Despite appearances, *Quiz Show* commemorates the steady values and strict codes of a time when it was still possible to be shocked by improper behavior on television, when public disgrace exacted a high price instead of a rich payday.

The tarnished golden boy in the morality play is Charles Van Doren (Ralph Feinnes), once again a household name. A big-money winner on NBC's *Twenty-One*, scion of the prestigious literary family, and the kind of patrician marriage prospect white-gloved coeds swooned over, Van Doren was a face in the crowd who achieved a TV-fueled success undreamt of by Mujibur and Sirajul. Playing his nemesis and antithesis is Herbert Stempel (a twitchy John Turturro), the reigning champion on *Twenty-One* until Van Doren's natural telegeniety blows him off the screen. No wonder: even by the fashion-impaired standards of the 1950s, the rumpled and bespectacled Herbie is a dork for all seasons. Meanwhile, Congressional investigator Richard Goodwin (Rob Murrow) strides the Art Deco corridors of NBC Studios at 30 Rock determined to make television as honest and upright as the House Committee on Legislative Oversight.

Redford's eye for the discreet charm of stiff-necked WASP culture remains as clear as Waterford crystal. The most compelling sequences are not the deftly-edited and suspense-racked quiz show sessions on live TV, but the kabuki show reenactment of High Episcopalian manners in gentlemen's clubs and country houses. Visually and morally, the real contest is between the quick buck flash of video values and the steady satisfactions of a dutiful life by the book. Against the unctuously vapid accolades of the bitch goddess—*Twenty-One* producers Dan Enright (David Paymer) and Albert Freedman (Hank Azaria), a tagteam pair of oily tempters, and announcer Jack Berry (Christopher McDonald), a con artist as slick as his shellacked hair—stands the venerable poet Mark Van Doren (Paul Scofield), oozing patrician decency. At an open air birthday dinner at the Van Dorens's Connecticut home, father and son banter lines from Shakespeare while Thomas Merton and Edmund 'Bunny' Wilson trade bons mots. It is a serene, complacent, and very pleasant existence, watched with an admiring, ethnographic intensity by audience surrogate Goodwin. When the birthday presents are opened, fans of *All That Heaven Allows* will know what evil lurks uncoiled in the big oblong box, waiting to overturn the polite, print-oriented, Victorian world of the Van Dorens.

Not that every element in *Quiz Show* is a Fifties flashback. Though a scrupulously faithful period piece in set design and automobile interiors, the film's modern temper is reflected in its calibrated ethnic sensitivities. The Q&A sessions are a duel of biological opposites: Van Doren, the fair-haired Nordic aristocrat against Stempel, the swarthy workingstiff Jew, dulcet tenor against nasal whine, Columbia University lecturer against CCNY grad student. Goodwin, the Harvard-educated Brookline (not Brooklyn) Jew, functions as a bilingual chameleon able to converse with each species, albeit in a bizarrely slurred Boston accent. Projecting backwards, the film claims that *Twenty-One* practiced affirmative action for WASPs, rigging shows so Gentiles always followed Jews and always won more money. If that particular fix was in, the evidence is not put forward in Goodwin's *Remembering America*, in Martin R. Lawrence and Julian Krainin's PBS documentary *The Quiz Show Scandal* (1991), or in District Attorney Joseph Stone's *Prime*

Times and Misdemeanors, the most comprehensive account of the scandals. To see a morality play in terms of its ethnic, not ethical, dimension says a lot more about Hollywood in the 1990s than television in the 1950s.

(An interesting sidebar may shed light on the true nature of the Stempel-Van Doren axis. In Goodwin s account in *Remembering America*, Stempel tells the investigator that the main reason for his relentless antipathy to Van Doren is that Van Doren snubbed him after their final round on *Twenty-One*. Goodwin, however, reasonably discounts Stempel's version: "Whatever Van Doren's flaws, he was not a snob. He was much too well-bred to spurn a handshake. He just hadn't seen Stempel, and Stempel had interpreted the momentary inattention as confirmation of his most painful misconceptions." Which is precisely how Redford staged the scene in *Quiz Show*—a postvictory Van Doren, distracted and beset by well-wishers, fails to see Stempel attempt to congratulate him. Yet, when asked to review the film for *Entertainment Weekly*, Stempel still saw what he wanted to see—and praised Redford for accurately depicting how Van Doren had snubbed him!)

Since Goodwin is himself something of a political Sammy Glick, he seems as much Van Doren's fellow traveler as his nemesis. The film's introductory set piece finds him soaking in the celestial ambiance of an automobile showroom, bewitched by that year's model Cadillac, caressing the interior with the naked lust of unbridled consumerism, still fresh and freed of Depression-born guilt in the Fifties. While the rest of the committee staff toils like scriveners over small-time tax evaders, he's prescient enough to realize that in a videocentric culture anything to do with television offers a sputnik ride out of the trenches. Yet when Goodwin closes in on his prey, his killer instinct fails him. His explanation is plausible enough—that the recent memory of McCarthyite inquisitions makes him err on the side of caution—but his wife senses a less altruistic motive and barks that he's "the Uncle Tom of the Jews." It is not subservience, however, but identification. Goodwin is seduced by his goyisher doppelgänger because he too seeks a place in the kleig lights.

When the quiz show scandal becomes the subject of congressional hearings, when Charlie finally must face the music and fess up, the public humiliation before Congress and the nation is as nothing compared to the private disgrace in his father's eyes. In a lecture room at Columbia, father and son, old world and new, face off in a painful, generational culture clash that ends, of course, in forgiveness and reconciliation. Subpoenaed by a reluctant Goodwin, Charlie goes before Congress and the newsreel cameras for a ritual cleansing. After his testimony, the media rushes up for the postgame interviews. Mark Van Doren barely blinks when informed that Charlie's duplicity means his son's $50,000 a year job on *The Today Show* is kaput, but when he realizes the big lie will cost Charlie his post at Columbia, his vocation as a teacher, the old man winces as if hit by a riding crop. That look of stricken anguish says it all: video killed the genteel star. In an indictment that might have come from the lips of a Hollywood mogul, circa 1957, Goodwin underscores the moral. "We didn't get television," he intones. "Television got us."

The real Charles Van Doren, however, may have provided a more instructive epilogue to *Quiz Show*. After the trauma of public humiliation, Van Doren had the good grace to disappear and repent quietly, spending most of the last thirty years as an encyclopedia editor. Even now, when the financial stakes for cable-age exploitation are much higher than $64,000, he has spared America the spectacle of a *Hard Copy* interview or a reprise match-up with his old rival. Imagine a reunited Van Doren and Stempel, urged to dredge up their inner child by a solicitous Sally Jesse Raphael—Herbie expressing his anger at Charlie and Charlie blubbering about the pressure of living up to the family name. In the talk show Nineties, the quiz show Fifties seem the very model of decorum, not least in the person of Charles Van Doren, the last pure product of television to know shame.

FILMS IN REVIEW, 11-12/94, p. 56, Andy Pawelczak

In the pre-credit prologue to *Quiz Show*, an automobile salesman delivers a pitch about the virtues of an ermine white, Chrysler 300 convertible that sits in the center of a sleekly surreal showroom like the pigskin and steel embodiment of the American dream. As the salesman urges his customer to listen to the engine's power, the radio announces that the Russians have beaten us into space and all is not well with America. It's the perfect introduction to this movie about the quiz show scandals of the fifties, a tiny footnote to history that director Robert Redford and writer Paul Attanasio have made into a big, absorbing parable about hucksterism and the fetishism of the marketplace, manufactured euphoria and real malaise, power and corruption.

Charles Van Doren's fall from media grace is part of American folklore. A Columbia University instructor, son of a distinguished poet and scholar, Van Doren captured the television public with his low keyed, youthful charm and seeming erudition on the quiz show Twenty One. When we first see him, he's off by himself watching a quiz show on TV as his famous father, Mark, signs his latest book for an admiring, upscale public. It's a telling juxtaposition: classy high culture vs. vulgar popular culture, Shakespeare vs. the false immediacy of TV, father vs. son. Before long, Van Doren is applying for a spot on one of the low-end quiz shows, but when a *Twenty One* producer overhears his interview, he instantly knows he's found his next prime time star contestant. Van Doren is a quiz show producer's dream: he's smart, unpushy, hugely telegenic, and ostensibly uncontaminated by any sweaty, plebeian money lust. On the show, he gives the impression that he's in it purely for the challenge, like a gentleman amateur boxer who fights by Marquis of Queensbury rules, and the opportunity to demonstrate to the nation's youth, in the Sputnik era, the importance of education. Of course, he's a fraud—he's been given the answers or, at the very least, the questions in advance.

As Charles, Ralph Fiennes turns in a performance that is all nuance and shading: an inscrutable smile, a flicker of the eyes as he takes in the inner landscape and goes ahead and lies anyway. It's a subtle, accomplished performance that is even more impressive when you recall that Fiennes played the gross and monstrous Nazi commandant in *Schindler's List*. Though the film maintains a consistently sympathetic point of view on Charles, refusing to make him into either a dupe or a villain, he's hard to get a fix on; in a sense, there's no man in the man, which makes him a perfect subject for the hollowing out effect through which TV makes a flesh and blood person into a blank screen for the audience's fantasies.

The movie shows us Charles' pleasure in his newly minted wealth and celebrity—his classes fill up with adulatory students and young women mob his office—but ultimately it suggests that his deepest motivation is an oedipal rivalry with his father. As Mark Van Doren, Paul Scofield embodies a vanishing breed, the patrician intellectual who occupies the upper stories of culture and can afford to look down with benignly ironic detachment on the foibles of the ground floor tenants. In one of the films' best scenes, he trumps his son in a Shakespeare quoting game during a party attended by such literary luminaries as Edmund Wilson and Thomas Merton, only to be eclipsed himself when the guests show more interest in Charles' quiz show success than in Mark's birthday ode.

Redford and Attanasio structure the film around a Congressional investigation of quiz shows, conducted on the ground by a young lawyer, Dick Goodwin, a real life character who wrote the book on which the screenplay is based. Some critics have complained that the film exaggerates Goodwin's role and thus is as dishonest as the medium it indicts, but the investigatory structure adds dramatic momentum to the picture—in one scene, Goodwin watches *Twenty One* for clues as obsessively as assassination mavens watch the Zapruder footage—and ultimately Goodwin emerges as an interesting character in his own right. As played by Rob Morrow, of TV's *Northern Exposure*, he's a sincere Harvard graduate who tends to identify with the upper class Charles and finds it hard to believe he's in on the scam.

Charles' rival on the show is Herbert Stempel, a working class Jew from Queens, and the movie makes a lot out of the class and ethnic differences between the two men. Stempel is told to lose when the sponsor—chillingly played as a behind-the-scenes mogul by Martin Scorsese—decides he's too declasse to present his product. For Stemple, it's a disaster—he's hooked, not only on the money but on his 15 minutes of TV fame that he fully expected would last forever. In a hyperactive performance that doesn't meld with the rest of the movie, John Turturro makes Stempel into a bug-eyed grotesque, though at crucial moments he finds the role's underlying pathos. He has a wonderful moment at the end when reporters surround a crushed, humiliated Van Doren after his Congressional testimony. One reporter asks the forgotten Stempel what he thinks, and he says, "You guys never leave anyone alone, except when you're leaving him alone."

Robert Redford directs with an insider's eye for the business—the petty vanities of the quiz show host, the vulgarity of the producers, the casual exercise of power by the network president, the pretensions of the sponsor who's basically a snake oil salesman. The film's version of America reminded me of Robert Altman's *Nashville*—in both films, money, glitz and image emit a heady whiff of the void. But the movie itself is anything but empty: it's a witty, literate, grown up entertainment with more than just box office receipts on its mind.

Bravo Redford and Attanasio!

LOS ANGELES TIMES, 9/16/94, Calendar/p. 1, Kenneth Turan

As the subject for a major motion picture, the fuss surrounding the rigged TV quiz shows of the late 1950s does not seem particularly promising. Yes, people were shocked at the time, when it turned out that programs like "Twenty-One" and its most celebrated contestant, Charles Van Doren, were not dealing from a straight deck, but so many scandals have come and gone in the intervening years it's hard to work up much passion about that one.

So it is an especial triumph that "Quiz Show," directed by Robert Redford and written by Paul Attanasio, turns that footnote of television history into a thoughtful, absorbing drama about moral ambiguity and the affability of evil. Sticking moderately close to the facts and using real names whenever possible, it succeeds by pulling back and looking at the situation through an unexpectedly subtle and wide-ranging lens.

Of course, one of the focal points of any examination of the scandal has to be Van Doren, an intellectual golden boy whose downfall was classically tragic. And although he is beautifully played by Ralph Fiennes with a subtlety that is at least the equal of his Oscar-nominated performance in "Schindler's List," "Quiz Show" succeeds as well as it does because it is structured to make Van Doren's story only part of the whole.

Doing that structuring is screenwriter Attanasio, best known for having created the TV series "Homicide." Based loosely on a memoir by Richard Goodwin, a speech writer for President John F. Kennedy who began his Washington life as a congressional investigator looking into the scandal, Attanasio's script adroitly splits its focus three interconnected ways.

Instead of being the good versus evil faceoff that might be expected, "Quiz Show" has Van Doren, Goodwin (Rob Morrow) and Herbert Stempel (John Turturro), a disgruntled former contestant who blew the whistle on the show, warily dancing around one another. And, in what is partly a tribute to Redford's clout, this is one studio picture where even the heroes finally feel uncomfortable complicity.

Given the number of years he played the game in Hollywood, it shouldn't be surprising that director Redford is dead-on in depicting this atmosphere of variable morality, but it is satisfying nevertheless to see what an accomplished job of directing he does and how alive he is to the ambiguities in the situation. More than anything he's come up with since "Ordinary People," this picture fulfills the promise Redford owed in that debut film.

Perhaps because it doesn't play out in any explicit way, the scene "Quiz Show" opens with is especially telling. The year is 1957, the place a Chrysler showroom in Washington, where the cigar-smoking Richard Goodwin, first in his class at Harvard Law but mired in a low-level bureaucratic job, is getting an almost erotic charge out of examining a stunning new Chrysler 300D.

Later on, as the investigation of Van Doren proceeds, another film might have painted Goodwin as the unalloyed force for good, and this scene shrewdly checkmates that feeling. For, as Goodwin delicately runs his hands over the smooth leather and listens to the salesman's insinuating patter, the lust for conspicuous consumption is obvious in his eyes. None of us, "Quiz Show" takes care to point out, should think we are above temptation.

After this delicate opening, the film shifts to a brisk montage detailing the hoopla surrounding "Twenty-One," the program's showy obsession with security about its questions, and the fascination all America felt at contestants who were winning five-and six-figure amounts when that was real money.

But although awkward nerd Herbert Stempel seems secure as the show's reigning champion, behind the scenes a powerful cabal is not so sure. The program's sponsor (an icily modulated cameo by director Martin Scorsese) feels Herb's Everyman qualities have worn thin and wants him gone. Although the show trumpets its inviolability, co-producer Dan Enright (David Paymer at his best) gets the message. The end is near for "the freak with the sponge memory." What is wanted to take his place is someone polished enough to not only answer questions on the show but "get a table at '21' " as well.

Enter college English instructor Van Doren, spotted by co-producer Albert Freedman (Hank Azaria) trying out for a rival show. The son of one Pulitzer Prize winner, poet Mark (Paul Scofield), and the nephew of another, 33-year-old Charles has the diffident glow that comes with being a card-carrying member of America's intellectual aristocracy. A grown-up cherub, Van Doren is also naive enough to fall for Enright's rationalizations about why getting just the tiniest bit of help with the questions will turn him into a better role model for the youth of America.

Decent, affable, enormously likable, Van Doren is everything Stempel is not, and the first part of "Quiz Show" parallels the former's rise to national celebrity with the latter's fall to disgruntled oblivion. But once Goodwin enters the picture, motivated both by personal ambition (remember the Chrysler) and a public-spirited desire to "put television on trial," "Quiz Show's" themes deepen as the drama gains momentum.

A Jewish outsider whose Ivy League background allows him to pass in Van Doren's world of birthday lunches with Edmund Wilson and Thomas Merton, Goodwin feels especially torn as his investigations into Stempel's charges indicate that this charming man, with good reason America's sweetheart, had complicity. Should Goodwin (whose beefy role here was apparently the biggest departure from history) expose Van Doren, protect him or just throw up his hands and flee?

The uncertain interaction between Van Doren, Goodwin and Stempel, heightened by Attanasio's trenchant dialogue, is especially good at examining the peculiarly American quality the three men unknowingly share. Each in some way feels unappreciated, on the outside of the Big Dream, open to a quick way out of the slough of despond. And each ends up realizing that getting what they want is not what they want at all.

Cast partly against expectation, "Quiz Show" is compelling enough to survive an initial feeling that both Turturro as the needy Stempel and "Northern Exposure's" Morrow as the cocky Goodwin have a tendency to exaggerate their performances. Both roles, however, give less trouble as the film progresses, partly because the Brits they play against are so dazzling.

Paul Scofield, a celebrated stage actor, gives his best film performance since winning an Oscar for "A Man for All Seasons," as Charles' urbane, distant father. But it is Ralph Fiennes and his poignant and ravaged portrait of the son *in extremis* that provides "Quiz Show" with its center of gravity. Fiennes' ability to project the pain behind a well-mannered facade, to turn intellectual and emotional agony into a real and living thing, is devastating. Impressive as the film is in all respects, "Quiz Show" would have been a very different experience without him.

NEW YORK, 9/19/94, p. 72, David Denby

In *A River Runs Through It*, Robert Redford's previous movie as a director, there were moments when Redford seemed eager to make an Ektachrome ad. He set up shots in which the sun shimmered on the water and those two handsome guys holding bait and tackle grinned at each other ... and nothing happened. "Someone cue the fish!" I shouted to myself. Where was Redford's pulse? With *Ordinary People* and then *The Milagro Beanfield War*, Redford had settled into a groove of sensitive thoughtfulness, but he was spawning boredom. *Quiz Show*, however, is a very different story. I don't know whether it was Paul Attanasio's terrific screenplay that brought Redford to life, or the subject itself, or Redford's irritated memories of his early career in television, but whatever it was, he has triumphantly pulled together the elements of dramatic filmmaking. *Quiz Show* is remarkably entertaining, a movie that works as spectacle as tangled ethical drama, as an exposé of the fault lines of ethnicity and class in this country. Set in the late fifties, the movie is about people grabbing at something so hot it lights them up and turns them to ash a moment later. *Quiz Show* has the quickness of money.

The quiz-show scandals seem farcical now, but something important got lost back there. Eager to build ratings and knowing full well that a repeat winner and a growing pile of cash would create tremendous week-to-week suspense, the producers of *Twenty-One* fed the answers to some of the contestants. The great brains were selected for their appeal and variety, then coached in the arts of stammering, sweating, and pursing their lips. They became huge celebrities, fooling millions, and when the scandal broke, they shocked a nation that still believed what it heard from its leaders, its journalists and entertainers. In a mixed spirit of affection and scorn, Attanasio and Redford offer the comedy of fifties squareness. Jackpot quiz shows were an only-in-America phenomenon, the armchair sport of a country obsessed with facts—any facts—and indifferent to ideas. Selling the shows, the networks trumpeted the power of "education" as the answer to the Soviet challenge, but the true fascination was always money. In 1956, $100,000 was a staggering amount of cash for knowing the name of Paul Revere's horse.

There's no great visual invention here, no poetry or magic, but the movie is filled with good actors and juicy moments. Redford begins with a series of conventional but effective montages that capture the excitement around Rockefeller Center during the live-TV era. The shows featured ridiculous cornball tricks—drumrolls and loudly ticking clocks and contestants displayed like freaks in "isolation booths," all of it narrated by an emcee who seemed to come out of a radio-era echo chamber. "Are you ready, America?" asks the Jack Barry character in *Quiz Show*. God, were we ready. As Barry, the square-headed Christopher McDonald is engagingly slick, but he doesn't capture the full, heavy-browed ghastliness of Barry as I remember him. In general, Redford treats the villains lightly. David Paymer—tight-lipped, intelligent, remorselessly reasonable—is superb as producer Dan Enright, the blandly reassuring Mephistopheles who put the fix in motion, and Hank Azaria makes Enright's assistant, Albert Freedman, no worse than a show-biz vulgarian enjoying himself too much to go straight.

The movie has a hero of sorts—Richard Goodwin (Rob Morrow), an ambitious young congressional investigator who eagerly takes on TV. (This is the same Goodwin who later worked for the Kennedys and LBJ.) The stumpy but handsome Morrow, from the hit TV show *Northern Exposure*, is engagingly cocky, with a convincing intellectual vanity. Goodwin is our shrewd Woodward-and-Bernstein figure. But if you look closely, you will see that the movie is really about the defeat of Dick Goodwin. The theme of *Quiz Show* is the power of money—the way television became so successful that it rendered the emotion of shame, and a great many other ethical habits, simply irrelevant.

The man who appears to answer the horse question is Herbert Stempel (John Turturro), a 29-year-old graduate student from Queens with a photographic memory and not an ounce of judgment. Heavy around the gut, with a bad tooth and a desperate whine, the great Turturro plays him as a man without dignity—a lower-middle-class Jew who suffers viscerally from the sense of himself as an outsider, forcing his pain on anyone who will listen. Stempel becomes the patsy of Dan Enright, who sets him up as a popular, man-from-the neighborhood idiot savant and then forces him, when he becomes too much to bear to take a dive. The filmmakers could have sentimentalized Stempel, but they don't; they go all the way with his humiliation, his anguish and vengefulness. Carrying that extra weight, Turturro seems huge and cringing at the same time. Suffering humanity pours from his flesh, and he's so powerful he burns away any taint of ethnic stereotype. He makes Stempel a jerk on a Shakespearean scale.

The movie has surprising depth, and it stays free of priggishness and simple judgments. We're not invited to look down on the phosphorescent ecstasy of desperate strivers like Herbert Stempel. The brilliance of *Quiz Show* is that it places the quiz-show mess within the class and power structures of the time. Stempel the irritating Jew is killed off by his handlers while he's actually on the air. The head of the company that sponsors the show executes him with a telephone call. Martin Scorsese, playing this corporate cynic, the genius behind Geritol, is dry and clipped—a dandy little man who knows the score. Scorsese's tight smile says, "The future belongs to me."

Twenty-One finds its golden boy in Charles Van Doren (Ralph Fiennes), a popular English instructor at Columbia and son of the distinguished poet and teacher at the university Mark Van Doren (Paul Scofield). Having lost the tire he put around his middle to play the disintegrating Amon Goeth in *Schindler's List*, Fiennes stands revealed as a handsome young man with reddish hair, dark-blue eyes, a noble Roman profile, and an entirely engaging grin. Fiennes creates a fascinatingly ambivalent portrait of the charming and hapless Van Doren. A genuine intellectual, Charlie gets seduced by things (money, celebrity) and by something else as well, something mysterious that is at the dramatic heart of the movie. Anger, perhaps, and then guilt.

As we see, the young prince labors under the burden of his father's virtue. As Mark Van Doren, the renowned Scofield, 72 and largely absent from movies for years, suggests (even though he's English) a kind of oak-solid Yankee integrity. This nimble old poet-teacher, a true American aristocrat, could no more tell a lie—or do something just for money—than a cat could bark. White-haired and elegant like the real Mark Van Doren, Scofield is intellectually alive but puckishly academic and almost infuriatingly *good*. Attanasio plants a variety of hints, and Redford directs our attention to what's left unsaid between father and son. When Charlie becomes an instant celebrity, he roguishly enjoys it. He gets out from under his famous dad; he still wants to please him, but at some level, deep beneath the love, he wants to disgrace him and bring him down as well. The scenes between father and son reverberate with the stresses of love and rivalry and chagrin.

Redford and Attanasio deserve high praise for not taking the easy, populist way out and turning the Van Dorens into privileged phonies who deserve their troubles. On the contrary, the intellectual atmosphere of the Van Doren house is gracious and pleasantly combative. The ravenously ambitious Goodwin is so charmed by the Van Dorens' social and intellectual ease that he wants to be part of it; for a long time, he can't bring himself to go after Charlie. As a dramatic necessity, Redford and Attanasio have built up Goodwin's importance in the affair, but they've also made him into a terrific and finally self-deluded character, As much as Stempel, the Harvard-educated Goodwin is a Jewish outsider who wants to storm the gates of the citadel.

Quiz Show turns into a powerful series of confrontations—Arthur Miller without the pomposity. The ethical drama remains properly steeped in ambiguity. The key scene: At the Van Dorens' lovely house in the Connecticut countryside, Charlie gives his father, as a birthday present, a television set—the snake in the garden.

It's the late fifties, and the elder Van Dorens still don't have one. *Quiz Show*, it turns out, is about that moment in our history just before television began to devour everything. Television couldn't be stopped by scandal; people were enchanted by all that bold hucksterism. That's the painful truth that even the crusading Goodwin realizes by the end. In the years after the quiz-show flap, television would eat politics, journalism, and the very ethical standards by which television itself was once judged. The movie is a bitter reminder of the last instant when those things still had a proudly independent existence.

NEW YORK POST, 9/14/94, p. 35, Michael Medved

In 1956, a sweating, bespectacled, ex-GI from Queens used his sponge-like memory to establish himself as one of America's most unlikely TV stars.

Herbert Stempel reigned for several months as the seemingly unbeatable champ of the popular quiz show "Twenty-One" easily vanquishing all challengers until he faced Charles Van Doren an instructor at Columbia and product of one of the nation's most distinguished literary families.

The two unlikely rivals battled to several tie rounds before Stempel shocked the massive TV audience by blowing a simple question that millions of viewers could have easily answered.

Two years later, Stempel shocked the nation even more with his story that he'd been forced to take a dive. He charged that one of America's top-rated prime-time shows had been shamelessly rigged.

This fascinating story of the notorious network scandals of the late '50s comes roaring back to life in the new film "Quiz Show"—one of the best movies I've seen so far this year, and an unqualified triumph for director Robert Redford.

Redford draws uncannily effective performances from John Turturro as Stempel, Ralph Fiennes as Van Doren (as extraordinary here as he was in "Schindler's List", Paul Scofield as Van Doren's father (Pulitzer Prize-winning poet Mark Van Doren), and David Paymer as Dan Enright, the manipulative producer of "Twenty-One."

In addition, Rob Morrow (of TVs "Northern Exposure") holds his own in this elite company, gracefully handling the tricky, pivotal role of Richard Goodwin, the young congressional investigator who helped expose the fraud.

"Quiz Show" shows motivations and characterization with remarkable complexity, subtlety and balance. Thanks to the expertly crafted script by former film critic Paul Attanasio, the big scenes are deeply moving, but never stagy or contrived.

The screenplay also pays attention to touchy questions of Jewish insecurity—with the Jewish producers of "Twenty-One" deliberately dumping their grubby landsman Stempel for WASP golden boy Van Doren. Goodwin, with both Jewish roots and a Harvard degree, seems to fall somewhere between the two worlds; but when he visits the Van Dorens' Connecticut home, his outsider status is unequivocal.

Every detail in these encounters is rendered with the same glowing intensity that Redford brought to his previous films as director, especially "A River Runs Through It."

The story ultimate)y takes on dimensions of epic tragedy with its treatment of Charles Van Doren's disgrace and emerges as an early milestone in our society's media-driven loss of innocence.

NEWSDAY, 9/14/94, Part II/p. B2, Jack Mathews

The pre-release publicity done by director Robert Redford and screenwriter Paul Attanasio on behalf of "Quiz Show," their riveting re-enactment of the TV game show scandals of the 1950s, has been so thick with sanctimonious hypocrisies that they may have actually damaged the product.

Like it or not, movies based on real events, using real names, dates and places, have an implied truth for audiences, and the lies told by filmmakers working behind the shields of artistic and creative license are precisely the kinds of lies told by the producers who rigged the original shows.

"Hey, it's entertainment!," is how the TV executives defended their actions back then, and "Hey, it's entertainment!," is how Redford and Attanasio are defending the ways they have altered the very characters and events they are judging.

Still, if you set aside their egregious rationalizationsand accept the film purely as entertainment, it is a pretty sensational movie, the best in Redford's decorous directing career, and perhaps the most captivating non-action thriller since "All the President's Men."

"Quiz Show" is essentially a three-character drama, with villains and victims radiating away from the central premise, which is this: In the early flickering light of the television revolution, the networks have discovered the galvanizing power of intellectual combat. Two contestants in isolation booths several feet apart field impossibly difficult or obscure questions ("What was the color of Paul Revere's horse?"), with the big winners becoming immediate celebrities.

Faced with their own high-stakes competition against rival networks, the "Twenty One" producers heighten the show's entertainment value by making sure the contestants can answer the tough questions (by providing them the answers), by coaching their behavior, and by linking winning streaks to audience ratings.

When viewers get tired of one champ, another is crowned.

Charles Van Doren (Ralph Fiennes), a handsome Columbia University English teacher and scion of a famous New England literary clan, is "Twenty One's" great discovery. After knocking off Herb Stempel (John Turturro), a squirrelly grad student from Queens, Van Doren becomes an instant celebrity, makes the cover of Time magazine, and amasses winnings of $129,000 before "losing" his title and becoming a $50,000-a-year feature correspondent for Dave Garroway's "Today Show."

Enter Dick Goodwin (Rob Morrow), a scrappy young lawyer for a congressional committee supervising TV practices, whose tireless sleuthing leads him to a disenchanted and eager-to-sing Stempel, to the arrogant "Twenty One" producer Dan Enright (David Paymer), and to the celebrated Van Doren himself.

There is a miraculous amount of drama built into what was essentially a tedious investigatory process, and the filmmakers left no truth untwisted in making it so. Goodwin, who served as a consultant on the film, did not break the scandal—most of the work was done by the New York District Attorney's office—and didn't even get involved until Stempel and another contestant had blown the whistle.

Still, much as Alan Parker made a compelling story out of subverted facts in "Mississippi Burning," Redford has built a taut drama around his loosely reconstructed history, and gotten terrific performances from his three stars, particularly from Fiennes (the sadistic Nazi camp commander in "Schindler's List").

Morrow's Goodwin is the most factually false of the three principals, and it shows. He serves as Redford's moral alter ego, appalled by Van Doren's crime while being simultaneously seduced by his fame. Goodwin's ambivalence about Van Doren, whom he sees as a good man unwittingly drawn into a Faustian pact, is an empty and lazy script expedience.

"Quiz Show" is clearly intended to get at the root of America's moral dilemmas in the age of instant communications, celebrity and wealth, and its subtitles and realistic setting make it far more effective at that than Oliver Stone's in-your-face "Natural Born Killers." As entertainment, Redford has made his best movie, but its moral outrage is tempered by its own sin.

NEWSWEEK, 9/19/94, p. 62, David Ansen

The Fall season gets off to an auspicious, Oscar-contending start with *Quiz Show*, Robert Redford's savvy, snappy account of the TV quizshow scandals of the late '50s. Its arrival has already provoked a favorite American question: when did we as a nation lose our innocence? It's an absurd question, of course, that assumes a homogeneous "we." (Ask a Native American that, and you'll get a very early citing.) Absurd too because, since this is a nation with no historical memory, every generation has its own answer. But it's a vital question nonetheless, for no country has been so obsessed with the myth of its innocence as ours. It's the clean slate from which we are able continually to reinvent ourselves, the source of what has been best in our optimistic, idealistic culture and what has kept us childish, close-minded and brutally provincial.

No era was more invested in the myth than the boom years of the 1950s, when television arrived to beam back at us gift-wrapped images of our cheery, wide-eyed selves laugh track included. But it was through television and the print media that the cracks began to show . The demagoguery of Joe McCarthy was exposed on live TV. The U-2 spy-plane scandal: imagine, the United States spied on the Soviets, and had lied about it! Sherman Adams and his vicuña coat: we were shocked, shocked that a politician might take a gift!

Neck high in '90s cynicism, it's hard to believe the tremors these scandals provoked. What's a vicuña coat next to Iran-contra? Except by then the country was so blasé about governmental deception it could barely rouse itself to outrage. In the '50s, Ingrid Bergman was blacklisted from Hollywood for having a baby out of wedlock. Today, Oliver North makes hash of the Constitution and it jump-starts his political career. What used to ruin your life gets you invited on "Oprah" and a fat book deal. Shame is for losers; public confession and a 12-step program can turn you into a role model.

In 1959 Charles Van Doren, who had become a national hero as a contestant on the NBC quiz show "Twenty-One," fell from grace when he admitted before a congressional hearing that he'd been fed the answers. A patrician intellectual, the son of Pulitzer Prize-winning poet Mark Van Doren, this Columbia University instructor had been hailed as the exemplary American "egghead." He was the great white hope of higher education, the man who made the cerebral sexy. After the revelations—the American public's rude awakening to television's capacity for mendacity—he lost his teaching post, got dumped from the "Today" show and slid into self-imposed obscurity working for the Encyclopedia Britannica.

Why should we care about a man who sold his soul for $129,000 more than 35 years ago? Redford and screenwriter Paul Attanasio, who wasn't even born when Van Doren entered his soundproof booth to vanquish his competitor Herbert Stempel, must have worried that old Faustian bargains would seem small potatoes in an era when celebrity scandals involve charges of child molestation and murder. But "Quiz Show" is about more than a bygone media frenzy or some questionable notion of lost American innocence. Its true subjects owe little to nostalgia. It's about where the power and the profits lie, about institutions and their scapegoats, and about how class and ethnicity color our view of the world in our supposedly classless society.

Redford approaches the story from three angles. There's Van Doren (Ralph Fiennes), wearing his privilege diffidently, who strolls into the wolf s den of showbiz and allows himself to be convinced that his ethical lapse is justified by all the good will do the cause of education. Then there's Herbert Stempel (John Turturro). A Jew from Queens, seething with resentment that he had to take a fall for the glamour boy Van Doren, he's the first to spill the beans about the fraud, but he's so volatile, so transparently resentful—and so *unattractive* compared to Van Doren—that no one wants to believe him. The third figure is the movie's designated sleuth, Richard Goodwin (Rob Morrow), the hotshot Harvard law grad working for a congressional committee investigating game-show rigging. A Jew with a Harvard accent as thick as JFK's (for whom he would later write speeches), he wants to go after the networks themselves—not Van Doren, whose charm and lineage beguile him.

Attanasio's dense, smart screenplay takes some liberties with the facts: the chronology is toyed with, and Goodwin's role as a detective is fanciful—the grand-jury files that are denied him in the movie were in fact readily handed over, as he records in his book "Remembering America."

Fortunately, the point is not to portray Goodwin as some shining, crusading hero. What's intriguing is his divided loyalties—his eagerness to be part of the patrician world of the man he may destroy. Stempel, played with broad brilliance by Turturro as a near-stereotypical pushy, neurotic Jew, tells Goodwin that the show "always follows a Jew with a Gentile— and the Gentile wins more." Goodwin doesn't want to believe Van Doren's crooked any more than the TV audience wanted to; he goes out of his way to protect him, causing his wife to call him the "Uncle Tom of the Jews." "Quiz Show" reveals how the tyranny of image was already in place in the '50s. There's a wonderfully double-edged scene when Van Doren makes his eloquent *mea culpa* at the hearing, and the lawmakers, cowed by class, fall over themselves to praise the cheater's candor. These are social observations Hollywood movies rarely think to explore.

"Quiz Show" is superbly shot (by Michael Ballhaus), and the acting ensemble could hardly be better. Morrow, once you get over his Saul Rubinek eyebrows and ostentatious accent, gives a finely reactive performance. Fiennes is magnetic in just the right understated way, a portrait of easy charm with a guilty conscience. All down the line there are rich turns: David Paymer and Hank Azaria as the show's producer and his assistant, Paul Scofield as Mark Van Doren, Allan Rich as the tough NBC honcho Robert Kintner, Martin Scorsese wickedly sly as the head of Geritol, "Twenty-One's" sponsor. If there are villains in the piece, these last two men qualify—they're the ones who really called the shots. But we see how the power structure is rigged so that the truly guilty are untouchable. "Quiz Show" is witty enough never to need to get on a soapbox to make its points.

Robert Redford may have become a more complacent movie star in the last decade, but he has become a more daring and accomplished filmmaker. "Quiz Show is his best movie since "Ordinary People," and it confirms him as one of our most astute cinematic chroniclers and critics of WASP mores. He has kept his eye on the ball of power, and in this shrewd and highly entertaining look back, shows us some of the bounces that got us where we are today.

SIGHT AND SOUND, 3/95, p. 49, Philip Kemp

New York, 1958. The most popular quiz show on television is NBC's *Twenty One*, hosted by Jack Barry, and its current reigning champion is Herbie Stempel, a working-class Jew from Queens. Herbie's nervous mannerisms annoy Martin Rittenholm, owner of Geritol, the programme's sponsor, and he orders the producers Dan Enright and Al Freedman to find a more appealing challenger. The programme is watched by Charles Van Doren, a lecturer at Columbia and scion of a distinguished American literary family, who offers himself as a contestant. Dan and Al are delighted; by dangling the prospect of future television employment they persuade Herbie to "take a dive" and answer a question wrong. Charles becomes the new champion. The show's ratings soar; to preserve their asset the producers suggest they feed him pre-arranged questions. At first shocked, Charles lets the lure of further wealth and fame persuade him. Young, classy, good-looking, he wins week after week and attains the status of national hero.

Finding himself dropped by NBC, Herbie tries resentfully to expose the fix. He makes little headway, but his efforts attract the attention of Dick Goodwin, a bright young Federal lawyer working for a Congressional sub-committee. Coming to New York, Dick's initial inclination to believe Herbie is swayed by Charles's culture and charm—even more so when he is invited to the New England birthday party of his father, the eminent poet Mark Van Doren. However, he meets another ex-contestant, James Snodgrass, who gives him proof that questions were fixed. Meanwhile Charles, troubled by his conscience, persuades Dan to let him lose to a new challenger. Watched by Dick, he fails a question to which Dick knows Charles knew the answer. Charles gets a lucrative job on NBC's *Today* show.

Brushing off Dan's crude attempt at bribery, Dick arranges for Herbie to appear before the Committee. He privately confronts Charles with the truth but agrees not to involve him; his only concern is to nail NBC. But Herbie, giving testimony, gets overexcited and implicates Charles. Subpoenaed to appear, Charles confesses the fraud to his father, who agrees to accompany him to the hearings. In their testimony Rittenholm and NBC head Robert Kintner disclaim all knowledge of the fix, but Charles confesses. With one exception, the Committee commend him for his candour, although he loses his post at Columbia. Dan and Al admit the show was fixed, but deny that NBC or Geritol knew of it. Dick realises that the network has won.

Cheating on a quiz show—isn't that like plagiarizing a comic strip?" inquires Paul Scofield, elegantly rumpled as the patrician New England poet Mark Van Doren. The man, you can't help thinking, has a point. In retelling the famous *Twenty One* scandal of the late 50s, when it emerged that one of the top-rated television quiz shows was as fixed as an all-in wrestling match, Robert Redford's *Quiz Show* spends two hours working up a fine old head of moral indignation—as though this were another *JFK*, or at least *Eight Men Out*. The venality of the media, the complicity of the establishment, the racism and class snobbery pervading American society—each of these targets is hauled up and given a well-deserved wallop, and of course the *Twenty One* fraud was a symptom of a more widespread national corruption. But as symptoms go, it still looks like pretty small beer. "Who gets hurt?" protest the show's scuzzy producers when the truth comes out. "We give the public what they want." And what they expect, maybe. The film's production notes talk of "the facts that shocked a nation", but outside the synthetic outrage of the headlines was anybody really shocked—or even surprised?

To work on anything beyond an anecdotal level, a story like this needs to key into some definitive moment of lost national innocence—"They've shot the President!" or the agonised young fan's plea to disgraced White Sox fielder Shoeless Joe Jackson, "Say it ain't so, Joe!" Failing that, all we're left with is a well-staged drama-documentary with ideas above its station, and a display of hucksterism in the fine old American tradition of Barnum and Bailey or the travelling medicine show. A stronger sense of period might have helped. We get passing nods to McCarthyism, and there's a moment in a car showroom when news of the first sputnik comes over the radio—customer and salesman gazing nervously skyward as though Commie agents were about to drop through the ceiling. But what never quite comes over is the brittle, panicky tone of late-50s America, a society so desperate for heroes it could seek them in television quiz shows.

Shorn of its pretensions, though, *Quiz Show* serves up a diverting story and tells it well. Redford's direction is fluent and self-effacing, and he draws fine performances from his cast, not least a neat cameo from Martin Scorsese as the show's sponsor, purring with delight at his own impish cyncism. As the irritatingly geekish Herbie, John Turturro surpasses himself, lecturing his sullen wife on the virtues of education and eagerly pointing out to the Congressional Committee the finer points of his quiz show performance on tape ("Look! Look! There's the lip-biting!"). The least convincing character—strangely, since the script is based on his book—is the Federal sleuth, Dick Goodwin. He comes across as too schematic a figure, sharing an immigrant background with Herbie and an Ivy League education with Charles, socially suspended somewhere between them.

Class, in fact, is what the film is chiefly about. Repeatedly we see the American establishment closing ranks: the arty Van Doren clan, with their shared jokes and erudite Shakespeare quoting that keep Dick subtly excluded; the NBC chief and the Committee chairman chatting about next week's golf date before adopting their respective formal postures; the assembled Congressmen solemnly congratulating Charles on his sententious, high-flown confession. (The only Congressman to remain unimpressed bears an ethnic name, Derounian; significantly, he's played by Joseph Attanasio, father of the film's scriptwriter.) Yet *Quiz Show*, ironically, ends up endorsing the same snobbery that it berates, by making it seem that the scandal only mattered because it was a well-bred young academic who was caught cheating. If Herbie Stempel, the "annoying" Jewish guy with a side-walk haircut", as Scorsese's Mr Geritol describes him, had been the guilty party, would anyone today remember the affair—let alone make a movie about it?

TIME, 9/19/94, p. 77, Richard Schickel

It was one of those moments the moralist live for: nice young man—good family, college teacher, an earnest intellectual yet rather cuddlesome—is caught cheating not only in public but also on television. Fame and fortune were the prizes he very nearly got away with, but infamy was his final reward.

What instructive lessons could be derived from this outrage, this tragedy, this affront to the button-down proprieties of the 1950s? Surely something was revealed here about American materialism. Or the cynicism of its media masters. Or perhaps the gullible neediness of the public, yearning to identify with a guy who somehow managed to be smart, cute and lucky at once, just the way we all want to be.

In our tawdry age, one can almost wax nostalgic about a time when Charles Van Doren could cause nationwide outrage. For a few months in 1956 and 1957 he became a celebrity by remaining champion for weeks on a television quiz program called *Twenty-One*. In the process he won $129,000 and 500 marriage proposals. But two years later he admitted to a congressional committee that he had been fed the answers by the show's producers. Compared with the participants in today's scandals, Van Doren seems more pathetic than notorious; compared with contemporary affronts to our sensibilities, his misdeeds seem infinitely forgivable.

Indeed, watching the film *Quiz Show*, a compressed and therefore somewhat distorted version of his story, you can't help but think that these days Van Doren would have entered a 12-step program for liars, negotiated a million-dollar deal for a confessional book and eventually gone into politics. It is one of the several virtues of this thoughtful and hugely entertaining movie that it encourages such reflections. Written with clean-cut force by Paul Attanasio and directed with panache by Robert Redford—they know how to efficiently shape a character and point a scene—*Quiz Show* neither nostalgizes about nor inflates its drama. Rather it contextualizes it, makes us see it not merely as an antique controversy but as a symbolic turning point in recent cultural and social history.

This story actually begins with an edgy, brainy nerd named Herbert Stempel (wonderfully played by John Turturro), who was a steady winner on *Twenty-One*. The trouble was that white-bread America couldn't identify with him. Enter Van Doren (played a little too stiffly by Ralph Fiennes), trying to pick up a few dollars to supplement his instructor's pay at Columbia University. He was a godsend. Not just any old Wasp, but the scion of arguably the nation's most distinguished literary family. His father was Mark Van Doren, Pulitzer-prizewinning poet and scholar; his mother was a novelist; his uncle, a famous historian; his aunt, editor of a respected book-review journal.

What capital could be made of Van Doren on lowbrow TV. And what capital he could make of it. For Charlie Van Doren was overwhelmed by his bloodlines, needed to succeed somewhere on his own. And this new medium, despised by his family and their friends, seemed perfect. He could become a hero by co-opting it for truth and light. The producers persuaded him to accept answers in advance by telling him how much good he was doing the cause of education with his presence. And the schmuck (to borrow a word from Herbie Stempel's lexicon) believed them.

Between the Wasp damaged by privilege and the Jew damaged by underprivilege, the movie places a third figure, Richard Goodwin, a smart, completely unneurotic young man (played by Rob Morrow) working as a congressional-committee investigator. Historically, he does not deserve the central role the film gives him (Goodwin is the author of the book the script is based on and is one of the film's co-producers), but structurally this figure is a masterstroke. He's Jewish, but he's been to the right schools (as he never fails to mention, he graduated first in his class from Harvard Law School).

He understands where everybody's coming from. More important, he knows where TV is going—not just toward media dominance but toward cultural, social and political dominance as well. He wants to use the quiz-show scandal as a way—exactly how he doesn't really explain—to bring the entire medium to heel.

Was he really that prescient? Or as noble as he's portrayed here? Doubtful. But he was as ambitious. In a few years Goodwin would begin his long career as a Kennedy factotum-apologist. And seeing through his eyes, the movie gets one very big thing right. The genteel and patrician Wasps who still ruled the nation's cultural life lost their remaining power by their smug, simpering dismissal of TV and all the vulgar stirrings in postwar popular entertainment. Paul Scofeld's great performance as Mark Van Doren perfectly personifies their cluelessness. And impotence. This smart, sad movie is the epitaph of the tweedy elite. They should have taken more care to defend the values they appointed themselves to uphold, instead of twittering among their teacups. The film is set in a time when even game-show executives would recognize the name of a Pulitzer-prizewinning poet, but there's not much call these days for the collected works of Mark Van Doren.

VILLAGE VOICE, 9/20/94, p. 58, Georgia Brown

The momentous quiz show scandal of the late '50s marked my own first great disillusionment (outside my family, that is); I would have staked my so-called life that Mr. Van Doren, teacher of the great books, was no liar or cheat. So, as one who nearly bet her young life and lost, who saw no more than she was meant to see, I will say that Robert Redford's *Quiz Show* is a rich, tantalizing work—the best Hollywood movie of the year thus far—illuminating not just the peculiar culture of the '50s but much that is timeless in human affairs.

Although bracketed with Kurt Weill's "Mack the Knife," the film isn't Brechtian at all but a good old-fashioned entertainment somewhat in the mode of, but much more astute than, *All the President's Men*. Redford and screenwriter Paul Attanasio follow Richard Goodwin's chapter on the quiz shows in *Remembering America: A Voice From the Sixties*, taking Goodwin, the fledgling counsel for a congressional sub-committee, as their chief protagonist. Goodwin virtually assigned himself to look into charges that the quiz shows were rigged and in the course of his investigations struck up a heady friendship with the quiz shows' main celebrity, Charles Van Doren. Goodwin's attraction to glamour and power make him an astute choice for the movie's point of view, rather than, say, Joseph Stone, the Manhattan D.A. who conducted the initial investigation and did the real legwork.

In this version, Goodwin (Rob Morrow with thickened eyebrows) becomes something of a Nick Carroway to Van Doren's Gatsby. Except that, unlike Gatsby, Van Doren represents Americas patrician elite. (To convey Van Doren breeding, Redford calls on two Royal Shakespeare Company players: Ralph Fiennes for Charlie and Paul Scofield for poet patriarch Mark.) One *Quiz Show* subtlety has Goodwin simultaneously working to bring down his quarry while trying to spare him the punishment he sees due the producers and company men who rigged *Twenty-One* in the first place. Ultimately, nothing in Goodwin's scenario works: Van Doren is banished in disgrace while those behind the scenes are enriched and rewarded.

To Redford's credit, the movie boldly treats some very tricky human elements, namely class and ethnicity. Here is producer Dan Enright (David Paymer) and sidekick Albert Freedman (Hank Azaria) manipulating popular prejudice and seeking a "Great White Hope" for their show. It's a ploy quickly picked up by contestant Herb Stempel (John Turturro in another flamboyant performance), a Jewish hick from Queens who's beside himself at being forced to lose to the more refined Van Doren, Stempel's thesis: "They always follow a Jew with a Gentile, and the Gentile always wins more money." On the one hand, we have Jewish producers and network honchos crassly using non-Jews to bolster ratings; on the other, a young Jewish lawyer awed by the Van Doren gentry and repelled by Stempel.

Van Doren, as portrayed here, plays to Goodwin's parvenu longings, inviting him up to the family's Connecticut spread and seating him next to Bunny Wilson at the picnic table. In his memoir Goodwin prints an astonishing letter Van Doren wrote just after his public humiliation graciously absolving the investigator: "Hunters used to say that the stag loved the hunter who killed it ..."

A simpler movie would have taken the public's view and made this a morality play, focusing on the corruption of contestants. In Redford's version, Van Doren essentially takes the fall for all those who happily milked the fraud. Contestants only made a few thousand while networks and sponsors raked in millions. For refusing to testify against higher-ups, someone like Enright was rewarded handsomely in the long run. Redford's real villains are Enright and Freedman, NBC president Robert Kintner (Allan Rich), and a nameless Geritol sponsor played hilariously by Martin Scorsese. One of the movie's funniest lines is Stempel's: "They say Geritol cures tired blood and they call *me* a liar!"

Bathing Fiennes in that golden light reserved for Redford's own characters in films like *The Natural* and *The Great Gatsby*, Redford suggests, without pushing it, that certain aspects of myth and tragedy apply. (Compared to Fiennes, I'm here to tell you, the real life Charlie was a dork.) Van Doren is corrupt, yes, but like Gatsby he comes off as better than the operators surrounding him. Despite Richard Bernstein's claim in the Sunday *Times* that Redford exonerates Van Doren, the movie makes clear that he knowingly participated in the fix from the beginning. A charming liar, he seems motivated here both by greed and complicated rivalries with his famous dad. And yet, when the chips are down, he acts with dignity and some grace. (As to Bernstein's cranky thesis that by changing facts the movie is guilty of the quiz shows' crime—lying for entertainment's sake—I will only say that *Quiz Show*, in the way of good fictions, digs deeper than a comprehensive documentary, like the one that played on PBS some months ago.)

Goodwin's own seduction by Van Doren paralleled the American people's. His next infatuation would be ours as well, Hardly had he finished with one famous family, doomed as it was, than he was forging lasting links with another—one on the rise and far more potent. The Van Doren, ethic proved vulnerable to money and celebrity, but the Kennedy ethic—win at any cost, politics by image, incorporating and using greed—is still ascendant. Since Redford has given us this uncommonly thoughtful *Quiz Show*, he might even be the one to finally create a substantial *JFK*.

Also reviewed in:
NEW REPUBLIC, 10/10/94, p. 32, Stanley Kauffmann
NEW YORK TIMES, 9/14/94, p. C11, Janet Maslin
NEW YORKER, 9/19/94, p. 102, Terrence Rafferty
VARIETY, 9/12-18/94, p. 39, Todd McCarthy
WASHINGTON POST, 9/16/94, p. F1, Hal Hinson
WASHINGTON POST, 9/16/94, Weekend/p. 49, Desson Howe

RADIOLAND MURDERS

A Universal Pictures release of a Lucasfilm Ltd. production. *Executive Producer:* Geoge Lucas. *Producer:* Rick McCallum and Fred Roos. *Director:* Mel Smith. *Screenplay:* Willard Huyck, Gloria Katz, Jeff Reno, and Ron Osborn. *Story:* George Lucas. *Director of Photography:* David Tattersall. *Editor:* Paul Trejo. *Music:* Joel McNeely. *Music Editor:* Jamie Forester. *Choreographer:* Brad Moranz and Jennifer Moranz. *Sound:* Carl Rudisill. *Sound Editor:* Tom Bellfort. *Production Designer:* Gavin Bocquet. *Art Director:* Peter Russell. *Set Decorator:* Jim Ferrell. *Set Dresser:* Daniel Samppala, Leonard Smith, Carl Hector, Joe McGuire, Bruce S. Seymour, and Eric "Skip" Skipper. *Special Effects:* David Beavis. *Special Vocal Effects:* Frank Welker. *Visual Effects:* Thomas E. Kennedy. *Costumes:* Peggy Farrell. *Make-up:* Rudolph Eavey III. *Make-up (Mary Stuart Masterson):* Patty York. *Stunt Coordinator:* Leon Delaney. *Running time:* 112 minutes. *MPAA Rating:* PG.

CAST: Brian Benben (Roger); Mary Stuart Masterson (Penny); Ned Beatty (General Whalen); George Burns (Milt Lackey); Scott Michael Campbell (Billy); Brion James (Bernie King); Michael Lerner (Lieutenant Cross); Michael McKean (Rick Rochester); Jeffrey Tambor (Walt Whalen Junior); Stephen Tobolowsky (Max Applewhite); Chirstopher Lloyd (Zoltan); Larry Miller (Katzenback); Anita Morris (Claudette); Corbin Bernsen (Dexter Morris); Rosemary Clooney (Anna); Bobcat Goldthwait (Wild Writer); Robert Walden (Tommy); Dylan Baker (Jasper); Billy Barty (Himself); Tracy Byrd (Himself); Candy Clark (Billy's Mom); Anne De Salvo (Female Writer); Jennifer Dundas (Deirdre); Bo Hopkins (Billy's Father); Robert Klein (Father Writer); Harvey Korman (Jules Cogley); Joey Lawrence (Frankie Marshall); Peter MacNicol (Son Writer); Harold Bergman (Affiliate); Rita Butler (Affiliate's Wife); Dave Hager (Laughing Man); Kim Head (Waitress); Scott Hilley (Drunk Affiliate); Ed Lillard (Loud Affiliate); Leighann Lord (Morgana); Joann Luzzatto (P. A.); Eric Paisley (Enthusiastic Affiliate); Anthony Pender (Revolving Stage Operator); Jeffrey Pillars (Nerdy Stagehand); Steve Rassin (Page); Pam Stone (Dottie); Leslie Truman (Woman in Audience); Norm Woodel (Announcer); Bridget Newton, Amy Parrish and Nina Repeta (The Miller Sisters); Frank Trimble and Kevin Scott Warner (The Dead Tones); Frank J. Aard (Rollerskating Penguin); Ellen Albertini Dow (Organist); Mary Boucher (Soap Box Girl); Doug Chambers (Drummer); Ralph Corley (Milt Lackey Double); Tina Corsini (Betty Boop); Jim David (Biff Blaster); Deacon Dawson ("Peter Lorre" Willan/Happy); Hadley Eure ("Paprika" Actress); Don Ferguson (Johnny Ace); Wilbur Fitzgerald ("Tortured" Actor); Keith Flippen (Space Cadet Jimmy); Mousie Garner (Double Bass Performer); Randell Haynes (Difficult Actor/Interrogator); Mark Joy (Jack Granite); Rebecca Koon (Mildred's Mom/Ma);

Gary Kroeger (Gork, Son of Fire); Tammy Lauren ("In The Mood" Bandleader); Marguerite MacIntyre (Bubble Bath Announcer); Lori Mahl (Mildred/Johnny Ace Secretary); Charles Marsh (Upside Down Yodeller); Jim McKeny (Tom McCallum); Madison McKoy (Cab Calloway); Rod Mclachlan (Black Whip/Granite's Dog); Marc McPherson (Maynard); Pat Noday (Sherwood Smith); Richard K. Olsen ("Lt. Cross" Actor/Pa); Donna Peters ("Gork" Actress); Robert Raiford (Ben Butter); Robin Dale Robertson (Tempermental Actor); Jack Sheldon (Ruffles Reedy); Frank Terrio (Duck); Gary Anthony Williams (Dr. Ashton-Reeves).

LOS ANGELES TIMES, 10/21/94, Calendar/p. 14, Peter Rainer

"Radioland Murders" never let up and never shuts up. It's wearying—kind of like staring at a gasping hamster on an exercise wheel for two hours. The freneticism of this comedy-mystery is the work of highly talented people but there is a basic mistake at its core: The filmmakers think that a fast-paced movie must constantly be fast. They don't understand that a movie appears to move like a streak only when the pace is slowed from time to time. In "Radioland Murders," the *illusion* of nonstop speed is confused with its reality.

Reality in this movie is everywhere else in short supply. Set in 1939 in Chicago during the opening night of a new radio network, WBN, the film takes place almost entirely inside the studio as employees are lopped off one by one by a mysterious deep-voiced intruder who announces his murders over the air. The lead suspect is the show's head writer, Roger (Brian Benben), who is trying to win back his estranged wife, Penny (Mary Stuart Masterson), the station owner's secretary, while attempting to solve the crime.

Roger is far more interested in whodunit than we are. Since the clues are as scattershot as everything else in this film, the entire murder mystery plot resembles a "Hellzapoppin" for the short-attention-span generation. The only consolation is that, as the fun-less, knockabout subplots pile up, they just as quickly disappear. If you don't like the way the movie is going, don't worry—it will soon be going somewhere else.

In a larger sense, though, "Radioland Murders" is unvarying—not since "1941" has there been a movie that so throttled you with its hyperactivity. (And "1941) at least had a few visual splendors.) The film begins like a faster-than-a-speeding bullet trailer and after about a half hour, your worst fears begin to take hold—the whole *movie* is going to be this way.

The cast is so talented that you keep waiting for the talent to kick in. But the script by Willard Huyck, Gloria Katz, Jeff Reno and Ron Osborn doesn't allow for what the actors can do; the effect is like listening to a beautifully sung song played at chattering chipmunk speed. Besides Masterson and Benben (whose first and hopefully not last) starring movie role this is, Ned Beatty, Anita Morris, Michael Lerner and Stephen Tobolowsky, turn up. A few of them make tiny, tart impressions. George Burns has a cameo as a stand-up comic—he's still a gas—and Christopher Lloyd, as the sound effects man, is in his best wild-mad mode. Michael McKean, as the orchestra conductor, has a transported-by-his-own-ego grin that's a real goof.

The period re-creation is in the shiny-ersatz style, and the director Mel Smith (who made the great, underrated "Tall Guy" with Jeff Goldblum) reaches for a hefty nostalgia. But he doesn't have much of a feel for American pop Golden Age stuff. "Radioland Murders" isn't cynical—maybe it would be better if it was. Instead, it's just a squawking yesteryear contraption. It feels a lot longer than its 112 minutes.

NEW YORK POST, 10/21/94, p. 48, Michael Medved

"Radioland Murders" tries to combine elements of comedy and mystery, but the only real mystery surrounding this painfully unfunny project is how it ever got made in the first place.

George ("Star Wars") Lucas is probably the one to blame: As a fan of old-time radio, he dreamed up the original story about a series of grisly killings on the opening night of a new radio network back in 1939. Lucas (who's also credited as executive producer) then worked with Willard Huyck and Gloria Katz (among others) on the screenplay.

The press notes proudly remind us that Lucas, Huyck and Katz toiled together on "American Graffiti." Somehow the publicists neglected to mention that the same team also shared responsibility for "Howard the Duck." This new movie may become known as "Howard the Radio Station."

The inane plot centers on an overworked radio writer, played by Brian Benben (of HBO's "Dream On"), who's desperate to win back the affections of his estranged wife (Mary Stuart Masterson), who works as ultra-efficient Girl Friday to "The General" (Ned Beatty), gruff owner of the ambitious new network.

The couple's situation reaches its crisis on the station's glitzy night-of-nights, when it sends its signal across the country for the first time—and various members of the staff fall victim, one by one, to an ingenious and sadistic serial killer.

Accomplished performers such as Michael McKean, Corbin Bernsen, Stephen Tobolowsky, Robert Klein, Christopher Lloyd and the late Anita Morris play assorted casualties or suspects, while Michael Lerner is the cigar-chomping police lieutenant determined to crack the case.

All of these actors are embarrassingly bad, but it's hard to blame them for what goes wrong. They've obviously been asked to play every last scene at the level of wildly frenetic farce—mugging, shrieking, waving their arms and, on numerous occasions, literally crashing into walls. When the lines and gags are so insipid, delivering them with such manic energy only makes matters worse.

The attempts at evoking 1930s nostalgia are similarly feeble: despite lavish sets and costumes, displayed in campy musical numbers and silly commercials performed for a live audience in the radio studio, the atmosphere never feels for one moment authentic.

You don't have to know much about the glory days of radio (so lovingly recreated in Woody Allen's "Radio Days") to sense that the phony, frantic world of "Radioland" in no way does justice to the glamorous, imaginative medium that once transfixed America

The saddest part of all this stupidity is that it's directed by a talented British comedian named Mel Smith, whose one previous film was the delightful but under-appreciated romantic comedy "The Tall Guy" (with Jeff Goldblum and Emma Thompson).

If you want to do Smith a favor, skip his latest film and just rent "The Tall Guy" on video. As far as "Radioland Murders" is concerned, it's nothing but dead air.

NEWSDAY, 10/21/94, Part II/p. B7, John Anderson

What do "Radioland Murders" and the Depression-era feature "The Big Broadcast of 1937" have in common? George Burns, who blesses the new film with a bit of classic standup, and should have been allowed to sit down.

This radio, after all, no? Movies about radio—and there aren't that many—are never really about radio. "Radio Days," one of the better ones was a prompter for Woody Allen's tart memories; "WUSA," although prophetic, was about Paul Newman's politics. Inherently condescending—the dominant cultural medium lording it over one that currently survives on recycled music and reactionary politics—they're almost always about the movies.

How could it be otherwise? The makers of "Radioland Murders"—including executive producer George Lucas, who conceived the original story—set out to recapture the "magic" of early radio, and wound up stripping it away. The very act of looking makes it so. Radio is about personal, participatory imagination; movies, usually, are about passivity en masse. And there's so much going on in "Radioland Murders"—which seems afraid to take a breath, lest we look away—that we can do little but hang on for the ride, and hang our minds out to dry.

Set in 1939, on the night when Chicago's WBN is premiering as the nation's fourth broadcast network, "Radioland Murders" mixes the kind of hyper-nostalgic world of "My Favorite Year" ("Quiz Show" also comes to mind, although both are set much later) with the possessed-by-the-radio-gods rhetoric of Firesign Theater. The result is out-of-control alliteration, atrocious puns and structure balanced on pure artifice.

The story is pure, dial-spinning melodrama: Five minutes before the station—which is owned by the blustering General Whalen (Ned Beatty) and managed by the ultra-efficient Penny Henderson (Mary Stuart Masterson)—is about to hit the airwaves, the major sponsor (Brion James) rejects all the scripts.

As the writers scramble (they're an underutilized bunch that includes Harvey Korman, Robert Klein, Bobcat Goldthwait, Anne DeSalvo and Peter MacNicol) their most talented member, Roger Henderson (Brian Benben), is trying to convince Penny not to divorce him. Although she caught him *flagrante delicto* with the station's sultry singer, Claudette Katzenback (the late Anita Morris), he says he was framed. Adding to the mounting hysteria is a mysterious voice that causes frequent interruptions in the broadcast (among them, hacking during the cigarette commercial), each of which is followed by a gruesome murder.

The new-script dilemma provides plenty of opportunity for mix-ups—a soap opera, for instance, with dialogue from a space adventure. The pace is beyond frenetic, the pratfalls are abundant, the cast is OK, even if they aren't really acting. There are cameos by Billy Barty and Rosemary Clooney; Corbin Bernsen plays the station's host. The real nods to radio magic come from Burns—a true multimedia-ist—and Christopher Lloyd, as a manic sound-effects man armed with coconut shells and corrugated aluminum. His magic, too, is deflated, but at least there's a dividend of laughter. And Michael McKean provides some giddy moments as Rick Rochester, leader of the chameleonic Brass Rings Orchestra.

Lucas was 20 years in getting this project to the screen—it was originally intended as the followup to "American Graffiti," another movie with radio at its soul, but "Star Wars" got in the way. Two decades, it seems, were spent mortaring up every vacant space in the film. As a result, it can't so much breathe as gasp, while it careens.

TIME, 10/24/94, p. 78, Richard Schickel

Radioland Murders is many things: the multicorpse mystery story implied by its title; an old-fashioned romantic comedy in which a couple—nicely played by Mary Stuart Masterson and Brian Benben—are bickering their way toward divorce even though they're still in love; a satire of all the conventions of big-time radio, circa 1939; a group caricature of all the types—frantic sound-effects man, silky-voiced announcer—the medium once nurtured.

Yet none of this is really the film's subject. Its true topic is chaos. All the above and a lot more are crammed into a tight time frame—the prime-time hours during which a new network is presenting an extravagant premiere broadcast featuring all its stars and programs. The movie wants to show us the frenzy of such an enterprise, bring everyone involved as close as possible to panic but not in itself succumb to breakdown. This is a feat that has always interested George Lucas, who wrote the original story and is the executive producer. As we know from the *Star Wars* and *Indiana Jones* trilogies, he loves multilevel, multicharacter, broadly played popular fiction edited at a pace that flirts with incomprehensibility yet rigorously maintains narrative logic. *Radioland*, scripted by four writers and directed by Mel Smith, takes place under one roof on one night and puts this style under still greater pressure. Perhaps too much. The adventure form's spaciousness granted us breathing room, time to take things in. This comedy, dazzling as its rhythms often are, ought to give us the same kind of breaks.

VILLAGE VOICE, 11/1/94, p. 64, Laurie Stone

You can just imagine the brainstorm responsible for this wreck. George Lucas feels warm and fuzzy about the old days of radio. He wants to capture the cowboy crooners, the commercial jingles, the hard-boiled dicks, the sound effects that juiced the imagination of the country. Two teams of writers are credited with fleshing out Lucas's story, except there is no flesh and there isn't a story. Okay, then let's hire a bunch of talented comic actors: Brian Benben, Michael McKean, Jeffrey Tambor, Christopher Lloyd, Corbin Bernsen. We'll flash them on the screen or run them through clichéd slapstick routines until people laugh, goddammit.

Neither McKean, who plays a bandleader, nor Lloyd, as the sound effects guy, has a line of dialogue. Head writer Benben flashes his nitwit grace in a couple of isolated bits: an explanation of murders plaguing the radio station, using a shoe, a toupee, and a trumpet to represent the deceased, and a Harold Lloyd sequence, hanging from giant call letters outside the studio building. He does the lovelorn buffoon shtick he honed on *Dream On*, but here, without that show's context of rueful, self-knowing emotional arrest, a gargoylish, Jerry Lewis thing often overcomes him. Mary Stuart Masterson is fine as the unflappable secretary-turned-station head. But we don't care about any of the characters, because there is no satiric mooring for them, nor even a reference point for the nostalgia. This movie is one long prompt for a laugh track.

Also reviewed in:
CHICAGO TRIBUNE, 10/21/94, Friday/p. J, John Petrakis
NEW YORK TIMES, 10/21/94, p. C5, Caryn James

VARIETY, 10/17-23/94, p. 37, Brian Lowry
WASHINGTON POST, 10/21/94, p. C7, Hal Hinson
WASHINGTON POST, 10/21/94, Weekend/p. 48, Desson Howe

RAPA NUI

A Warner Bros. release of a TIG Productions/Majestic Films production in association with RCS. *Executive Producer:* Barrie M. Osborne and Guy East. *Producer:* Kevin Costner and Jim Wilson. *Director:* Kevin Reynolds. *Screenplay:* Tim Rose Price and Kevin Reynolds. *Story:* Kevin Reynolds. *Director of Photography:* Stephen F. Windon. *Editor:* Peter Boyle. *Music:* Stewart Copeland. *Music Editor:* Michael Dittrick. *Sound:* Gary Wilkins and (music) Jeff Seitz. *Sound Editor:* Karin Whittington. *Casting:* Elisabeth Leustig. *Production Designer:* George Liddle. *Art Director:* Ian Allan. *Set Decorator:* Brian Dusting. *Set Dresser:* Isidoro Tucki. *Special Effects:* Steven Richard Courtley. *Costumes:* John Bloomfield. *Make-up:* Peter Frampton. *Stunt Coordinator:* Glenn Boswell. *Running time:* 108 minutes. *MPAA Rating:* R.

CAST: Jason Scott Lee (Noro); Esai Morales (Make); Sandrine Holt (Ramana); Emilio Tuki Hito (Messenger); Gordon Hatfield (Riro); Faenza Reuben (Heke); Hori Ahipene (Overseer); Chiefy Elkington (Fisherman); Huihana Rewa (Old Woman); George Henare (Tupa); Eru Potaka-Dewes (Grandfather); Rawiri Paratene and Pete Smith (Priests); Mario Gaoa, Cliff Curtis, and Willie Davis (Short Ears); Lawrence Makoare (Atta); Te Whatanui Skipwith (Old Short Ear); Nathaniel Lees, Grant McFarland, and Wassie Shortland (Long Ear Chiefs); Tania Simon (Koreto); Rena Owen (Hitirenga); Zac Wallace (Haoa); Rakai Karaitiana (Pure White); Shane Dawson (Mud Color); Henry Vaeoso (Half & Half); Angela Gribben (Long Ear Girl); Karaitiana Beazley (Makita); Jenni Heka (Long Ear Girl); Pitake Tuke (Timid Short Ear); Liseli Mutti (Pua); Michael Yost (Young Long Ear Boy); Ross Clarke-Jones, Sasha Stocker, and Jake Spooner (Quicksilver Surfers); Jade Clayton (Ngaara).

LOS ANGELES TIMES, 9/9/94, Calendar/p. 4, Kenneth Turan

The pounding surf is loud, but the native drums are louder, more insistent. The perfumed air is thick with passion as two young lovers meet and embrace in the shadow of enormous stone monoliths. So what if their love is forbidden, their clothing minimal, their dialogue ridiculous? This is Hollywood and the show must go on.

Co-written (with Tim Rose Price) and directed by Kevin Reynolds, "Rapa Nui" is one of those giddy South Seas fantasies where haughty priests hiss about broken taboos and dialogue like "I don't need this, I've got chicken entrails to read" is thick upon the land. A heedless throwback to cinemascope epics of a simpler time, it is enjoyable in the way only inappropriately serious projects manage to be.

Mixing the earnestness of "The Ten Commandments" with genteel nudity, authentic locations brisk big-screen action, "Rapa Nui" is so wide-eyed and deferential about its clichéd situations that amusement is the only possible response. Adults will yearn to be teenagers again, the better to appreciate its guileless accomplishments.

More than being set on Easter Island, celebrated as the home of ancient stone idols weighing upward of 100 tons, "Rapa Nui" was actually shot there. Filming on one of the world's remotest inhabited locations was quite a feat, and it's unfortunate the same trouble wasn't taken with a story that plays like a rehash of themes worked to death for decades.

Anachronistically named (the title is the modern Polynesian designation for a locale its original inhabitants called Te Pito Te Henua), "Rapa Nui" takes place in the late 1600s, a generation before the arrival of Europeans doomed the island's traditional way of life.

Small though it is, Rapa Nui has a highly developed caste system revolving around the construction of those stone behemoths, known as *moais*. The effete, befeathered upper classes, named Long Ears because of the lobe extenders they prefer, do the supervising, while the sweaty, unadorned Short Ears do all the heavy lifting.

In rare moments of spare time, the Long Ears prepare for the sacred Birdman competition, a down-home version of the triathlon, where participants scale perilous cliffs and swim in shark-infested waters, all to bring back the first sooty tern egg of the season. The leader of the winner's clan gets to be the *Ariki-mau*, head man of the island.

The current *Ariki-mau* (New Zealand actor Eru Potaka-Dewes) has held the job so long he's fallen under the influence of Tupa (George Henare), a sinister priest, and no longer notices that the overworked and underfed Short Ears are on the verge of bringing the term *labor unrest* to the South Pacific.

Also oblivious is the *Ariki-mau*'s grandson Noro (Jason Scott Lee), so wrapped up in his forbidden love for Short Ear siren Ramana (Sandrine Holt) that he wouldn't notice if one of those enormous *moai* moved in next door.

Noro's mental fog is fated not to last, and soon he will have to grapple with some Big Questions. Where did his father disappear to and why won't anyone talk about it? Will Ramana have to spend time in the dread Cave of the White Virgins before they can marry? And how far will former friend and Short Ear spokesperson Make (Esai Morales) go to try to get Ramana for himself?

Not surprisingly, many of these questions get resolved during that climactic Birdman event, which is where Reynolds and company (especially cinematographer Stephen F. Windon and editor Peter Boyle) are at their best. Backed by a dashing percussive score by Stewart Copeland, the footage here is good fun in a Saturday-matinee way, and not the least of the reasons why it succeeds is that everyone is too busy rushing about to talk.

Though Lee and Holt are physically graceful performers—he is from Hawaii, she from Canada—Morales was raised in Brooklyn and the rest of the cast comes from New Zealand and other former outposts of the British Empire. This melange of accents gives "Rapa Nui's" already goofy "don't let them make fishhooks out of my thigh bones" dialogue a Tower of Babel quality it doesn't really need.

A director best known for "Robin Hood: Prince of Thieves," Reynolds has never brought anything close to emotional realism to a film, and "Rapa Nui" is no exception. And though the Birdman event apparently did exist, news reports indicate that much of the rest of the film's story line owes more to old movies than anthropological accuracy. But when those island drums are beating, audiences may be grinning too much to care.

NEW YORK POST, 9/9/94, p. 37, Michael Medved

Easter Island, a barren, windswept speck of land some 2,300 miles off the coast of Chile, is covered with several hundred huge stone heads soaring up to 50 feet in height. Since its discovery by Dutch sailors in 1722, no one—including the island's primitive inhabitants—has been able to satisfactorily explain how these awesome monuments got there.

Over the years, these mysterious "moai" (as the giant figures are known), have provoked all sorts of fanciful explanations, such as Erich ("Chariots of the Gods") von Daniken's insistence that they prove that extraterrestrials visited the Earth in prehistoric times.

Fortunately, the new film "Rapa Nui" bases its story line on far more persuasive theories.

Director/co-writer Kevin Reynolds ("Robin Hood: Prince of Thieves") has teamed with his old friend producer Kevin Costner, to create a spellbinding, provocative piece of work that combines authentic anthropological detail with old-fashioned Hollywood romance to transport you to a world more exotic (and absorbing) than any planet in science fiction.

Their adventure begins some years before first contact with the outside world with native society divided between "short ear" laborers and "long ear" rulers (complete with painfully elongated ear lobes). Naturally, one of the privileged long-ears (the superb Jason Scott Lee) loves a short-ear maiden (Sandrine Holt) who is cruelly confined for months in "the cave of the virgins" to qualify for marriage above her station.

Her isolation, however, can't end the attentions of a suitor (Esai Morales) from her own lowly tribe who's determined to compete in the potentially deadly Bird Man Race—an annual tradition that's an authentic piece of island lore.

Young champions representing every clan swim a mile through shark-infested surf to seize an egg from an offshore island then make a return trip without breaking the egg, clambering up sheer cliffs that rise more than 1,000 feet from the beach. The heart-stopping sequence that shows this competition, accompanied by Stewart Copeland's stunningly effective score, is one of the most bizarre and thrilling sporting events ever dramatized on film.

It's true that plot descriptions of "Rapa Nui" inevitably smack of "Monty Python"—an impression occasionally intensified by the jarringly proper New Zealand accents of some of the Maori actors employed to play their Polynesian cousins of Easter Island. Nevertheless, the visual splendor of the film, shot entirely on location, makes it easy to suspend disbelief.

Best of all, director Reynolds never condescends to his characters. In contrast to all other recent movie portrayals of primitive peoples, he makes no attempt to show the inhabitants of Easter Island as innocent, spiritually enlightened, harmonious or even environmentally responsible.

"Rapa Nui" offers an unblinking, uniquely honest view of a life that is indeed solitary, poor, nasty, brutish and short—but where isolated examples of human decency and courage still struggle against the odds. The title (which is the native name for Easter Island) may be difficult to remember, but the film itself is impossible to forget.

NEWSDAY, 9/9/94, Part II/p. B7, Gene Seymour

Couldn't you just imagine how the suits would reacts to a pitch like this:"Ever been to Easter Island in the South Pacific? Man, it's a wild place! Almost in the middle of nowhere with no trees. In fact, there's nothing except these big stone statues. And nobody really knows how they got there except there was once a real civilization there. Now there are only a few natives, who still call the place 'Rapa Nui.' Great title, huh?

"Anyway," the pitchman continues, "*how* did those statues get there? What happened to the trees? Where did that civilization go? Some story, huh?"

Who could possibly get a green light on something like "Rapa Nui"? The producers of "Dances With Wolves," Kevin Costner and Jim Wilson, that's who. They were even able to get Kevin Reynolds, director of the ponderous "Robin Hood: Prince of Thieves," the chance to co-write and direct the film.

One therefore had reservations going into this yarn about the island's Polynesian settlers who, almost three centuries ago, were divided in two classes: the Long Ear nobles and the Short Ear laborers. The Short Ears carve, carry and drag these heavy stone monoliths as religious icons for the nobles, and mess with the ecosystem in the process.

Is there a love story in all this? You bet there is. Long Ear Noro (Jason Scott Lee from "Dragon: The Bruce Lee Story") heir to the island's chieftainship, is in forbidden (natch) love with Ramana (Sandrine Holt), a Short Ear daughter of an island pariah. Make (Esai Morales from "La Bamba") is a Short Ear who not only is in unrequited (natch) love with Ramana, but also an estranged friend of Noro who feels, all too intensely, the unequal distribution of food and rights to his lower-caste fellows. The fates of these three are joined by an important island ritual: a grueling, perilous race to a giant rock a mile offshore. Whichever young Long Ear worthy returns first to the island's chief with an unbroken sunbird egg will become Birdman, the most powerful man on Rapa Nui.

The restive Short Ears, pressed hard by the sadistic Long Ear priests to build the biggest icon yet, say they will finish the statue only if Make is allowed to compete as their representative. If Noro wins, he also gets to marry Ramana. If Make wins, Ramana is his. If Make loses, he dies.

Got all that? Much to the credit of Reynolds and co-scripter Tim Rose Price, such details flow a lot easier in the movie than in printed summary. Still, I have a problem with Anglicized native dialogue, however stripped down and well-delivered by a decent, predominantly Polynesian cast.

Even with all these reservations, darned if the movie doesn't pull you in. The egg race is one of the most riveting athletic events ever used as a centerpiece for a feature film. Lee's athleticism is part of what makes it compelling. But Morales' burning-coal intensity is, over the long haul, more galvanizing. Whichever one wins, ultimately, it's the island that loses. The film's point is made—and resonates uncomfortably with our own time.

SIGHT AND SOUND, 1/95, p. 54, Joanna Berry

In 1722, the Dutch discovered a treeless island filled with giant statues, which they named Easter Island. The inhabitants, who called the island Rapa Nui, believed they were the only people on earth. Sixty-two years before, the inhabitants were divided into two classes—the Long

Ear nobility and the Short Ear labourers who made huge stone monoliths as a tribute to the island's first settler. Legend had it that he would return in a white canoe to lead his people to a new world.

Noro is a Long Ear chosen by Chief Ariki-Mau to take part in the annual 'Birdman race', in which a member of each Long Ear tribe races to bring back an egg laid by one of the island's sunbirds. Whoever wins becomes the powerful Birdman. Noro agrees to enter if he is allowed to marry Ramana, a Short Ear girl he has been seeing in secret. She is banished to the tiny dark Cave of the White Virgin for the six months before the race, and if she survives she can marry Noro.

Ariki-Mau and his high priest tell the Short Ears that they must build another, taller statue to please the gods. In the process, the island's remaining trees are sacrificed, and food becomes scarce. Forced to work day and night, they become rebellious, and to placate them Ariki Mau allows one Short Ear to enter the Birdman race. Make enters, as he also wants to win Ramana's hand, although he knows he will be put to death if he loses.

A weak and blind Ramana is released from the cave. The racers run down sheer cliffs and plunge into the surf below, swim to the rock for the eggs, then return to the island. Many don't make it and only Noro and Make are left at the end. Make wins, but as he walks to the high priest, he trips and his egg is smashed. Noro is declared the winner, and he spares Make's life. Ariki-Mau sees an iceberg has drifted near the island. Believing it is the legendary white canoe, he sails out to live there. The high priest goes to the Short Ear village to demand more work from them, but they capture and kill him, then go to the other villages and burn them. They smash the largest statues to show that the Long Ears no longer have control. Ramana and Noro escape from the destroyed island in a canoe to start a new life elsewhere.

Kevin Reynolds may have believed that teaming up with pal Kevin Costner again after their successful *Robin Hood: Prince of Thieves* was a good idea, but on the basis of *Rapa Nui*, it is probably better that the two Kevins go their separate ways. Of course, *Robin Hood* had Costner starring and Reynolds directing, whereas in this instance, Costner simply takes a back seat as producer, leaving Reynolds to direct lesser-known actors Jason Scott Lee and Esai Morales.

The tale of what could have happened on the island of Rapa Nui is not only hampered by its lack of a weighty lead, but also by its erratic cast choices. Morales and Lee handle themselves admirably as the two competing warriors, but (as happened in *Robin Hood*), they are surrounded by tribesmen speaking in Brooklyn, West Country and Australian accents. One can only surmise that the casting director's main specification was that the actors should look good in their very brief leather thongs.

In fact, both cast and production do look luscious, with bronzen figures toiling over the stone statues against the stark cliffs and beautiful waters of Easter Island. The prosthetic work used to create the unusually-shaped ears of the Long Ear tribe is flawless, while the tribes' painted faces add vibrant colour to the surroundings. All of this would be very well if this were a documentary or a travelogue, but it is not. Reynolds originally got the idea for the film from watching a TV documentary on the island, but he has constructed little story around that basic idea and instead has come up with a tale that could have taken place anywhere. Transfer *Rapa Nui* to New York and it could be the tale of a Shark and a Jet coming to blows.

Reynolds' forte is action rather than dialogue, judging from *Robin Hood* and the Birdman race sequences in *Rapa Nui*. Here, Reynolds manages to combine drama and tension, and the film only flags in one scene, when one of the competitors is chased and then chomped by a shark, in true *Jaws* fashion. The scenes showing the islanders making and transporting the statues are also magnificent, although somewhat marred now that it transpires Reynolds and his production team may be sued by the present-day residents of the island for destroying part of their land while making the movie.

Reynolds concentrates on the spectacle, at the expense of the more interesting parts of the storyline—the idea that the islanders were destroying their home by cutting down trees for logs to transport their worthless but beautiful monoliths, and the race and class antagonism between the two tribes. The script simply boils all of this down to the cliché of a love triangle between Noro, Make and Ramana. If Reynolds had intended to make a point about how easy it is to destroy the landscape by building and expanding, he could have found a better way of expressing it than Noro getting misty-eyed because the tree he carved his and his girlfriend's initials on is next for the chop.

Unfortunate moments like this pepper the movie, none of them are more ludicrous than when the chief of the village decides to leave and make his home on an iceberg that has appeared out of nowhere in warm waters. In fact, it is Eru Potaka-Dewes as chief Ariki-Mau who suffers most on Rapa Nui, as the unfortunate actor burdened with lines like, "Leave me alone, I'm going off to read my chicken entrails!"

Also reviewed in:
NEW YORK TIMES, 9/9/94, p. C3, Janet Maslin
VARIETY, 4/1 8-24/94, p. 61, David Stratton

READY TO WEAR

A Mirmax Film International release. *Executive Producer:* Bob Weinstein, Harvey Weinstein, and Ian Jessel. *Producer:* Robert Altman. *Director:* Robert Altman. *Screenplay:* Robert Altman and Barbara Shulgasser. *Director of Photography:* Pierre Mignot and Jean Lépine. *Editor:* Geraldine Peroni. *Music:* Michel Legrand. *Music Editor:* Suzanna Peric. *Sound:* Alain Curvelier. *Sound Editor:* Skip Lievsay. *Casting:* Guylene Pean. *Production Designer:* Stephen Altman. *Art Director:* William Amello. *Set Designer:* Jean Canovas. *Set Decorator:* Françoise Dupertuis. *Set Dresser:* David Ronan. *Costumes:* Catherine Leterrier. *Make-up:* Judith Gayo and Jacques Clemente. *Running time:* 132 minutes. *MPAA Rating:* R.

CAST: Danny Aiello (Major Hamilton); Anouk Aimée (Simone Lowenthal); Lauren Bacall (Slim Chrysler); Kim Basinger (Kitty Potter); Michel Blanc (Inspector Forget); Anne Canovas (Violetta Romney); Jean-Pierre Cassel (Olivier de la Fontaine); François Cluzet (Jean-Pierre); Rossy de Palma (Pilar); Rupert Everett (Jack Lowenthal); Kasia Figura (Vivienne); Teri Garr (Louise Hamilton); Richard E. Grant (Cort Romney); Linda Hunt (Regina Krumm); Sally Kellerman (Sissy Wanamaker); Ute Lemper (Albertine); Tara León (Kiki Simpson); Sophia Loren (Isabella de la Fontaine); Lyle Lovett (Clint Lammeraux); Chiara Mastroianni (Sophie); Marcello Mastroianni (Sergei/Sergio); Tom Novembre (Reggie); Stephen Rea (Milo O'Brannigan); Sam Robards (Craig); Tim Robbins (Joe Flynn); Georgianna Robertson (Dane Simpson); Julia Roberts (Anne Eisenhower); Jean Rochefort (Inspector Tantpis); Lili Taylor (Fiona Ulrich); Tracey Ullman (Nina Scant); Forest Whitaker (Cy Bianco); Tapa Sudana (Kerut); Laura Benson, Laurent Lederer, and Constant Anée (Milo's Entourage); Alexandra Vandernoot (Sky TV Reporter); Yann Collette (Coroner); Jocelyne Saint Denis (Hotel Manager); André Penvern (Hotel Clerk); Maurice Lamy (Bell Boy); Pascal Mourier (Fad TV Cameraman); Adrien Stahly and Denis Lepeut (Fad TV Sound Engineers); Harry Belafonte, Paolo Bulgari, Anello Capuano, Cher, Helena Christensen, Gamiliana, Elsa Klensch, Serge Molitor, Maude Montana, Thierry Mugler, Tatjana Patitz, Sonia Rykiel, Eve Salvail, and Nicola Trussardi (Themselves).

CHRISTIAN SCIENCE MONITOR, 12/23/94, p. 11, David Sterritt

Movies big and small are arriving side-by-side as Hollywood continues its blitz of late-year releases, hoping for holiday crowds at the box office plus eligibility for Oscars and other awards,

On the big-picture end of the spectrum, Robert Altman has concocted "Ready-to-Wear," a rambling visit with the international fashion industry. Taking a more modest approach, Robert Benton has made "Nobody's Fool," a return to the finely humanistic spirit that made his "Places in the Heart" and "Kramer vs. Kramer" so popular.

Among other interesting contrasts between these pictures, Altman's seems dedicated to squeezing as many stars as possible onto the screen, while Benton's strives for intimacy with a much smaller array of talent—most notably Paul Newman, who uses the occasion to offer his best performance in ages.

"Ready-to-Wear" is hitting the scene amid a massive publicity campaign by Miramax Films and more unfavorable press—from both fashion and movie observers—than any high-profile release in recent memory.

One problem seems to be that the picture is neither conventional enough to satisfy entertainment-seekers nor experimental enough to qualify as a full-fledged art film.

Another problem is that it's directed by Altman, who's been polarizing audiences for 25 years. Most agree that his major films of the 1970s, such as "MASH" and "Nashville," are innovative and stimulating, if not always as engaging as more mainstream fare. But his detractors have a long list of botched pictures—including a string of appalling '80s flops—to bolster their anti-Altman arguments. Recent successes like "The Player" and "Short Cuts" have failed to end this debate.

"Ready-to-Wear" finds Altman's mannerisms in full swing. Instead of a coherent plot, the film uses a large-scale event—a Paris fashion exhibition attracting designers, models, marketers, and journalists from around the world—as the focus for numerous shaggy-dog stories that intertwine with one another for well over two hours. Characters appear and disappear at the whim of a meandering screenplay and a restless pair of editing scissors. Sometimes they generate great amusement. Other times they make you wonder what in the world they're doing.

Altman has nothing substantial to say about the fashion world, or about the crowd of artisans, capitalists, curiosity seekers, and groupies who populate it. He's clearly more interested in the fun he can have fitting countless bits of behavioral detail into a single mercurial narrative.

He also remains fascinated by certain film techniques that have energized most of his best movie's—forming multiple layers of recorded sound into a sort of rolling acoustic wave for instance, and moving through wide-screen space with a zooming camera instead of relying mainly on shot-to-shot cuts.

What makes "Ready-to-Wear" a perversely compelling film is precisely the weirded-out cinematic artistry that lies behind its messy, often pointless mixture of plots, subplots, and digressions. There's no way of defending its many blunders, such as the idiotic frame story that has two French police officers solving a nonmurder that we spectators have known about from the beginning. But there's much to enjoy if you open your eyes and ears to Altman's amazing explorations of sound and image, and join him in savoring the improvisatory acting of the year's most eclectic cast.

While these virtues don't make "Ready-to-Wear" a great movie, the film has a wacky originality I find impossible to deny.

"Nobody's Fool" centers on a hard-luck guy named Sullivan played by Newman with a wisdom and panache that recall the best work of his career. Blessed with an optimism that's both illogical and unquenchable, Sully lurches from one construction job to another while trying to stay on reasonably good terms with friends and relatives—a former wife, an estranged son, an elderly neighbor, the tempting wife of his hard-boiled boss—who can't figure out why he's still drifting through life after passing his 60th birthday.

The movie's first few scenes are as self-indulgent as Sully himself, more concerned with exploiting small-town atmospherics than spinning an involving yarn. The filmmakers settle into their material soon, however, unfolding the story at a relaxed pace that never forces our involvement with the characters, Instead, it lets us discover their rich, perplexing depths through carefully wrought nuances of dialogue, gesture, and situation.

Newman's sensitive performance gets excellent support from a cast that includes Bruce Willis as Sully's on-and-off boss, Melanie Griffith as his maybe-someday girlfriend, Dylan Walsh as his long unseen son, Josef Sommer as an entrepreneur with a shady scheme, and the late Jessica Tandy as a landlady who refuses to give up hope in her seemingly incorrigible tenant.

Three cheers also go to cinematographer John Bailey, who gives the modest village of North Bath, N.Y., as magical a glow as you'll see onscreen this season.

FILM QUARTERLY, Summer 1995, p. 48, Robert Hilferty

First, the facts.

Robert Altman's new film is not a "behind-the-scenes" look at the fashion world. Nor is it a particularly *fashionable* treatment of that world. Nor is it a conventional narrative complete with audience-identification protagonist and tidy plot. Nor is it much like *Nashville*, despite its many characters and multiple vignettes.

That' s why it disappointed so many. The movie flew in the face of all expectation.

Altman's new cinematic panorama should be seen on its own terms first—then you can throw knives at the screen if you see fit. *Ready to Wear* is an idiosyncratic odyssey, an odd essay film with its own peculiar pattern and design. Far from being "unfocused," "flimsy," or "vapid" (recent critical put-downs), every element in the film—even down to the dogshit everyone's stepping in—has a rhyme and reason, and builds up carefully to the sublime finale: designer Simone Lo's naked *défilé*.

Although the movie juggles about three dozen characters and their overlapping situations, there emerges, amid the hustle and bustle of the splintered narrative, a dominant story line—that of Simone Lo (Anouk Aimée)—around which all others revolve like illuminating satellites.

What gets things rolling is Sergei Oblomov (Marcello Mastroianni), a 70-something master tailor who leaves Russia after the collapse of Soviet Communism and heads west in search of the love of his youth, his abandoned wife Isabella de la Fontaine (Sophia Loren). To get to her, he has secretly contacted her present husband, Olivier de la Fontaine, who is head of the French Fashion Council. Olivier meets Sergei at the airport and brings him back to Paris, but during a traffic jam on Pont Alexandre III, Olivier unexpectedly dies a déclassé death: he chokes on a piece of ham. Panicked, Sergei hops out of the limousine, and the chauffeur screams murder. Sergei jumps into the Seine. Although he's been falsely accused, he's safe: the authorities can't identify him because the only evidence they have are photos of what he was wearing.

Everyone in the fashion world seems more pleased than saddened by Olivier's sudden demise. Apparently he wasn't such a nice guy, and despite several claims by TV reporters that his death has eclipsed Paris's most important fashion week, *prêt-à-porter* proceeds as usual without a morsel of mourning—not even from his wife. Isabella thinks her husband is no more than the dog turd she steps in at the beginning of the film.

Simone Lo (changed from the original Lowenthal) acts more the widow, and everyone treats her as one—it's no secret she was Olivier's lover. Although she readily admits that she didn't like Olivier either, Simone seems to have some depth, unlike the other designers, who come off as frivolous, trendy, and self-important. Simone stands out as a genuine artist. Simone's son, Jack (Rupert Everett), makes a witty remark to characterize his mother: "You know, my mother makes dresses for herself. Dressing for men has never particularly interested her, although she's certainly undressed for a few of them. The main difference between men and women in fashion is this: women make dresses for themselves and for other women ... a man makes clothes for the woman he wants to be with, or in most cases, the woman he wants to be." This not-so-innocent comment, situating fashion on the gender battleground, inadvertently provides the key to the entire film.

These divergent—and possibly antagonistic—attitudes about fashion and its relation to women are played out on the body of supermodel Albertine (Ute Lemper). On the eve of the biggest show in Paris, she shows up pregnant. Albertine can't fit into the clothes earmarked for her, but on a deeper level, she now presents an image of womanhood totally unfit for the runway. Simone, however, is the only one who adjusts quickly and calls her pregnancy "wonderful"; someone like Cy Bianco (Forest Whitaker) thoughtlessly explodes at her because she's ruining his show. Albertine calls him "woman-hater."

Albertine's bursting belly raises two interesting questions which are at the crux of the movie: "What is the essence of womanhood?" and "Who's the father?" The first question is implicit in women's fashion. But clothing intended to enhance womanhood is usually in the service of some idea of "beauty," and the clothes may actually conceal, alter, or exaggerate the true woman underneath them. Women become fashion victims: they are trapped in an image of themselves that's not quite true, an image generated by male fantasy and anxiety over female sexuality. As Cher, who plays herself in the movie, says, "Fashion is about women trying to be beautiful, but none of us is going to look like Naomi Campbell ... so in a way I think it's kind of sad ... I'm a victim as well as a perpetrator." Albertine' s pregnancy brazenly confronts and complicates the issue, as framed by the high fashion industry, and will ultimately be taken up in the final *défilé*.

The second question is, of course, the fundamental issue of paternity. When Jack Lowenthal asks Albertine, "Who's the lucky man?" she blithely answers, "Well, maybe it's you, darling."

It sounds tongue-in-cheek, but the charge is a distinct possibility; Jack is a notorious philanderer (he's cheating with his own wife's sister). In fact, Altman creates an atmosphere of uncertain paternity: Jack doesn't even know who his own father is.

Altman's world is peopled with fatherless children and abandoned wives/mothers. The masculine penchant to flee the situation may be the basis of the warfare Altman sees being waged between the sexes not only in this film but in others as well (*Images, 3 Women, Short Cuts*). We eventually learn that Sergei abandoned Isabella on their wedding night to leave for Moscow.

"We were Communists," he says.

"*You* were a Communist," responds Isabella, "I was only fourteen."

Communism wasn't what it was cracked up to be, and Sergei ended up living in fear and poverty, making uniforms for Soviet officials. After Communism went out of fashion—Altman cleverly hints at the fad quality of political ideologies—Sergei tries to regain his lost youth. In trying to recapture their youthful passion, Isabella plays a sensuous Salome to Sergei's faltering Faust (in fact, "Salome" and "Faust" are the names of mirror hotel suites in the film). Isabella reveals a body that's scandalously well preserved—she's the spitting image of ageless Eternal Feminine—and does a tantalizing striptease only to discover that her first husband has fallen asleep. (This magnificent scene is ingeniously reproduced from a film Loren and Mastroianni made together over 30 years ago, *Yesterday Today and Tomorrow*.) She leaves a note on his chest: "Two husbands, two corpses."

Twice abandoned, twice betrayed.

Which brings us back again to the main story line. Simone Lowenthal, like Isabella, was probably abandoned in some way too—that's why her son has no father. Betrayal rears its ugly head again, in the form of another male close to home. Jack, without the approval of his mother, sells his mother's logo ("Lo") to a Texan manufacturer of cowboy boots, Clint Lammeraux (Lyle Lovett).

"You know, you're worse than your father," says Simone.

"Whoever that was," replies Jack.

"You sell and buy everything," Simone responds, "even your own mother."

In spite of Simone's protest, Jack sabotages his mother even further. Behind her back, he arranges a photo session featuring the boots. Imprinted prominently and gaudily with the "Lo" logo, these boots eclipse Simone's spring collection ("These Boots Are Made for Walkin'" plays on the sound track). Simone has been stepped on, not only as an artist but also as a woman (since her art celebrated the female body). She is powerless.

Or is she?

By sending her models down the runway totally nude, Simone is revolting. She is making an explosive statement, not only in defiance of her traitorous son, but also, symbolically, against the entire male order. To pull off such a coup, the solidarity of her models is necessary. Preceding Simone's final showdown, a confluence of new feminine alliances is forged in different corners of the movie but indirectly connected to Simone' s plight. For instance, the three fashion editors, who have been fierce competitors throughout the film, eventually join forces against star photographer Milo O'Brannigan (Stephen Rea). Throughout the film, he has humiliated these women by taking photos of them in compromising positions with a spy camera. They gain the upper hand after seizing his negatives, which include, not insignificantly, the treacherous boot shoot. At the same time, Jack's power starts to wane when his estranged wife and her sister, with whom he had been cheating, reunite against him. They call him a rat to his face.

Accompanied by the haunting song "You Are So Pretty the Way You Are," Simone's models take the runway: This defiant *défilé* doesn't end up defiling the female body with eroticization or desexualization. Rather, Simone presents Mother Nature's getup: the naked female body. This anticlimactic gesture might be considered ridiculous, even mildly pornographic, if it weren't for the presence of Simone's daring centerpiece, her pièce de resistance: Albertine's pregnant body, an impregnable fortress. Formerly banned from the runway, Albertine now rules it as a nude queen-bride, a fabulous figure right out of Botticelli's *Primavera*. Literally bursting with life, Albertine represents the feminine essence. With her, Simone unveils the primal beauty, power, and mystery of the female body: its ability to bear life—which all the (male-dominated) fashion in the world can't contain or control. Simone liberates the female body from fashion fascism, the mechanism which dictates, regulates, and disseminates images of women. (Altman laces his film with subtle and subliminal references to the Holocaust.)

The effect of Simone's *défilé* is not shocking. It's sublime.

Simone goes beyond making a feminist statement: the Eternal Feminine (think again of Sophia Loren's vibrant 60-year-old body), the origins of the species, the very beginnings of culture are put on display. As the new announcer of FAD-TV says, "Simone has spoken to women the world over, telling them not what to wear, but how to think about what they want and need from fashion."

(Altman creates an intriguing cross-reference by crosscutting a crossdressers' ball across town. As Simone's women undress, these men dress up. This juxtaposition visualizes metaphorically what Altman feels is really going on in fashion: men are not really making clothes for "real" women but for themselves. Or, to paraphrase Jack, they make clothes for the "ideal" woman they want to be with or the woman they want to be. A gigantic ice sea horse sits in the middle of the transvestites' banquet table. Why a sea horse? It's the only example in nature in which the *male* carries the fertilized eggs, a fact which underlines the central mystery of gender. In the case of men, no amount of dressing up as a woman makes a woman.

Ready to Wear is mythic narrative in the guise of satiric spoof. What Altman envisions here is women's revolt, a *Trojan Women* for postmodern times. Less interested in high fashion than in why humans, who are born naked, cover their bodies in the first place, Altman provides us with a menu of the uses of fashion—in concealing, revealing, or fabricating identity (ethnic, class, occupational, ideological, sexual, gender). And as one designer says, "Fashion is about looking good ... it's about getting a great fuck." Therein lies the paradox: we dress up in order to undress (for sex). Joe Flynn (Tim Robbins) and Anne Eisenhower (Julia Roberts) certainly have no use for fashion: they spend the entire time under bed sheets.

In revealing the ironies and absurdities that result from the age-old conflict between culture and nature, *Ready to Wear* resembles *A Wedding* more than *Nashville*. Here, the omnipotence of nature asserts itself in two areas: sex and death. In *A Wedding*, Altman shows how a socially constructed ritual comes apart at the seams when realities which run counter to the order-defining myths associated with marriage constantly intrude on the party (infidelity, homosexuality, interracial desire, etc.). In *Ready to Wear*, it's also the body's desires and function which are at odds with the aims of high fashion.

Death frames both films. In *A Wedding*, it's the controlling family matriarch played by Lillian Gish; in *Ready to Wear*, it's the head of the Fashion Council. In both cases, death is presented as an embarrassment, an inconvenience, an obscenity, a reality that's not dealt with, ignored. That's the way of human culture. But the show goes on.

In the face of chaotic Eros and dead-end Thanatos, what the hell does fashion amount to anyway? This is a question Altman keeps on posing as he exposes the color-blind phonies, the glamour hounds, and the trend-trotting ignoramuses who dominate that world. Everyone has a fake name, nobody wants to be who they are, nobody knows who they are. Altman's world of fashion is ultimately as drab and unfab as what Cher (of all people) says: "It' s not what you put on your body, but who you are inside."

In the last scene of *Ready to Wear*, Altman comes full circle and creates an ironic picture of the human life cycle. Seven naked newborns playing in the grass fill the screen. The camera pulls back to reveal that the toddlers are being photographed for a fashion ad. The campaign appears to be ripping off Simone Lo's "naked look." The slogan: "Get Real." As the fashion shoot takes place, Olivier de la Fontaine's funeral procession goes by. Isabella does not wear traditional black, but bright red. Perhaps this funeral is a cause for celebration: her liberation.

While Isabella may be making a fashion statement, Altman is not. Less about fab fabric than the tenuous fabric of society, *Ready to Wear* is an elaborate striptease of the human condition.

LOS ANGELES TIMES, 12/23/94, Calendar/p. 1, Kenneth Turan

The skill of the juggler often isn't apparent or appreciated until the moment when he can no longer keep the balls in the air. And the main distinction of "Ready to Wear (Pret-a-Porter)" is how accomplished it makes director Robert Altman's previous work appear.

Unable even to decide what its title is, "Ready to Wear" is a mass of confusion pretending to be a movie, a mess of characters in search of an author. Everyone is at cross-purposes with everyone else over everything from hotel rooms and lost luggage to sexual orientation and even apparently murder, but in a movic in which so much appears to be happening, very little is really going on.

With more than two dozen characters colliding like so many giddy bumper cars and actors relying on their skill at refurbishing dialogue, "Ready to Wear" sounds like Altman's most recent successes, "The Player" and "Short Cuts." But there is a diffcrence between creative improvisation and absolute chaos, and while those films were delicately balanced balls that magically stayed in the air, "Ready to Wear," with a script credited to Altman and Barbara Shulgasser, has a haphazard "Let's go to Paris and see what happens" feeling that wastes everyone's time and talent.

Paris is where the annual ready-to-wear shows take place, with the top fashion designers displaying their creations to an impatient public during an especially hectic week. Many of the industry's most celebrated designers, top names such as Issey Miyake, Jean-Paul Gaultier, Thierry Mugler and Sonia Rykiel, make obligatory cameo appearances, but despite fashion industry paranoia, any satirical intent on the film's part is stillborn.

Rather Altman and Shulgasser have grafted several increasing sour and feeble lines of farce action onto this setting. None of these is strong enough to be called a plot, but the centerpiece is an investigation into thc mysterious death of Olivier de la Fontaine (Jean-Pierre Cassel), head of the powerful Fashion Council, who leaves behind a wife (Sophia Loren), a mistress (Anouk Aimée) and a shadowy individual (Marcello Mastroianni) who has flown in from Moscow just to meet him.

Intercut with this is the rivalry between three fashion editors (Linda Hunt, Sally Kellerman, Tracey Ullman) for the services of a smug photographer (Stephen Rea), a rivalry for a single hotel room between journalists Tim Robbins and Julia Roberts and random bitchy behavior by clichéd gay designers Richard E. Grant and Forest Whitaker.

Other prominent figures, every one from Lauren Bacall and Lyle Lovett to Danny Aiello and Teri Garr, wander through little plotlets of their own, but the payoffs to their actions are so lacking that it's not worth the trouble to describe who they are or what they do.

Though actors invariably profess unceasing admiration for Altman, the director has cavalierly stranded most of them here with barely an interesting line or situation to their name. Lili Taylor as a New York Times reporter does emerge with her dignity intact, but only Kim Basinger, thoroughly amusing as an antic talking head for FAD-TV with more nerve than sense, gives a performance that truly entertains.

Balancing this is thc film's tendency to portray women in a mean-spirited light, forcing the actresses who play thc three fashion editors to participate in a sub-plot that is interested only in humiliating them. And Altman is the latest in a line of filmmakers who think making Julia Roberts look as plain as possible is a triumph of cleverness. Enough already.

Not clever or polished enough to be successful as farce, unwilling to supply any reason to care about any of its characters, unable to make the points about the role of fashion in society it thinks it is, "Ready to Wear" is madness without the usual Altman method. It's always been harder than it looks to make his kind of films, and this weak tea proves that point.

NEW STATESMAN & SOCIETY, 3/3/95, p. 34, Jonathan Romney

Robert Altman's *Pret-a-Porter* arrives in Britain having already been torn to shreds in the US, not least by fashion writers. They probably couldn't wait to get their claws into something, poor darlings, as a break from having to gush frantically the rest of the time. Mind you, it would have been interesting to see what country and western critics made of Altman's *Nashville* in 1975.

Fashion people complained that *Pret-a-Porter* was a flimsy, trivial caricature of a serious business. Film people felt it was a flimsy, trivial caricature of a flimsy, trivial business—and that, worse still, it wasn't *Nashville*. But why expect *Nashville*? The film is structured on a similar premise—a small, enclosed milieu (Paris in Fashion Week), with a mass of familiar faces shunted into assorted encounters. But that doesn't mean *Pret-a-Porter* claims to make any definitive statement about its milieu, nor that that milieu can be read as a microcosm of the world outside, in the way that *Nashville* seemed quite explicitly to be a state-of-the-nation report. *The Player* wasn't anything like that either—it was simply an intelligent psychological thriller that Altman turned on its head by roping in scores of famous faces.

He does the same here, to much lighter comic effect. Altman uses the recognition factor to excess, to remind us about the nature of celebrity—that the face of a star or a model is essentially no different from a brand name or a logo. What does it mean about fame when we know a supermodel's face but can't name her; or see Thierry Mugler interviewed when we have no idea what he looks like; or see a characteristic Vivienne Westwood collection presented under a fictional designer's name (Romney, as it happens); or see a mythical figure like Sophia Loren in a role that remains decorative at most? It's all surface, all illusion—who cares what is and isn't real here? What's admirable is the peevish flipness with which a notably unawed Altman throws all this stuff off.

This frenetically skittish film has so many famous names rushing around breathless that you imagine they all flew into Paris to fill their scenes in an afternoon. But there's no real linking thread, except for an opening plot that soon gets entangled with the rest. Marcello Mastroianni buys two identical Dior ties in Moscow, and sends one to Paris. Jean-Pierre Cassel receives it with disgust, then dies eating a ham sandwich. Models Tatjana Patitz and Helena Christiensen happen to witness his assumed murder.

As the entire fashion world arrives in town, Texan TV reporter Kitty Potter (an unexpectedly funny Kim Basinger) expounds her own breathless theories about what's going on and tries to make sense of it by interviewing the mandarins. "Terry Moogler" makes the most sense of it when he explains: "It's all about looking good—and getting a great fuck, honey."

That in any case is what most of the characters are trying to do. Mastroianni wants to be reunited with the love of his life—Sophia Loren, looming magnificently again, like a galleon raised from the deep. Tim Robbins and Julia Roberts give up and screw the week away. Designers Forest Whitaker and Richard E. Grant try to make out while their partners are doing the same.

Anyone seeking the embroiled complexity of *Short Cuts* seeks in vain. Everyone stays pretty much in their own world, the stories largely failing to connect. But that's the point-no one is aware of anyone else, except as mirrors for their own vanity. The film is a bedroom farce, in which no one's sure whether a bedroom is a place for love or just to hang your wardrobe.

The main premise may be obvious—we are what we wear—but what's exciting is the sheer energy and variety with which Altman gets it across. While models swank on and off the catwalk, Julia Roberts struggles with her dirty laundry. Mastroianni jumps from stolen suit to stolen suit and ends up in black leather, looking like a shrink-wrapped Ludovic Kennedy. Only Teri Garr makes it to the shops for a spree that culminates in the film's best punch-line.

Along with the clothes go the bodies, and not always the perfectly templated ones on the catwalk. The fashion kingpin who ends up autopsied by a croissant-chewing coroner reminds us of mortality. Faced with a heavily pregnant model, Grant swoons, "Pregnant is not my silhouette this season."

This world is a caricature, but then it's not meant to be remotely real. The cartoonishness makes for a startling clash when real figures like Sonia Rykiel appear, overperforming as much as the actors. It's beside the point to argue that parodying fashion is redundant because it parodies itself. The film is acutely aware that the fictional designers' conceits are both so wild and so plausible that you can't always tell what is real and what's laid on for our benefit.

If you are in the fashion world, you can probably see through all this—but how often do couturiers make it to the local multiplex anyway? Forget the real—Fashion Week's febrile, overpopulated promiscuity is simply a good excuse to make an Altman film, and that's all *Pret-a-Porter* sets out to be—a display of *Le style Altman* for spring 1995, There's no point complaining that things don't stay still long enough for us to appraise them—the catwalk's like that. The credit sequence announces the players on little scurrying swatches of fabric—and that's what the film is, a wilfully flimsy patchwork confection. Take it as that—a little something that Altman threw together—and you may find it's very you.

NEW YORK, 1/2/95, p. 67, David Denby

The only thing worse than a party at which nobody shows up is a party at which absolutely everybody shows up. What to do with them all? Robert Altman's fashion-world bash, *Ready to Wear* (formerly *Prêt-à-Porter*), has the feeling of an egregious social mistake. The sets are awash with familiar faces, and the host, however eager for everyone to enjoy himself, loses track of the ebb and flow of the event. Intrigues high and low spin off into different rooms without adequate resolution; the evening grows incoherent, tedious, and redundant. What is Lauren Bacall doing here? Why does Stephen Rea, as the world's hottest fashion photographer, humiliate the three fashion-mag editors played by Linda Hunt, Tracey Ullman, and Sally Kellerman, and then photograph them? Is he blackmailing them? Into *what*? Each woman already wants him to work for her. There are recurring motifs in the farcical atmosphere, but most of the movie's jokes function at so low a level that one hesitates to recount any of them. Actors come on in mid-anecdote and move off nattering about something we half understand. *Ready to Wear* is a mess—Altman's worst movie since those earlier overstuffed parties, *H.E.A.L.T.H.* and *A Wedding*.

The movie's failures wouldn't be so annoying if they were offered up in a better spirit. Altman treats the fashion world in Paris as something that needs to be exposed: He's *got* something on all these people, and he's shocked. The movie is a provincial piece of work: Kansas boy goes to the big city and discovers that some of the successful people are ... *insincere*. Would you believe it? *They say one thing and mean another*. Not only that—some of them are *gay*. I don't think anyone has found homosexuality so alien since Fellini put his last strutting queen in a movie.

What's also embarrassing is that while Altman is using low farce to expose the fashionable folk as phonies, he's ignoring everything that makes that world so fascinating—the hard work, the steel beneath the silk, the showmanship, the money-consciousness. He even misses the beauty. *Ready to Wear* is not particularly well photographed. The images are *filmy*—blurry and even ugly. Altman hates fashion so much he can only ridicule it. Anouk Aimée (who gives a mask-of-tragedy performance and doesn't seem to have been let in on the jokes) plays a designer whose company has been sold out from beneath by her no-good son. So Aimée decides to make a statement: She sends her models out there naked. Tall, high-breasted, long-limbed beauties, starkers on the runway. It's Altman's statement, too, and the worst thing is that he appears to think he's saying something devastating about beauty and naturalness and the obscenity of fashion. But Yves Saint Laurent did this 25 years ago with his "transparent" clothes, and it was considerably more interesting. Many of us were eager to see the fashion world satirized, but *Ready to Wear* falls so wide of the mark it just feels trivial.

NEW YORK POST, 12/23/94, p. 41, Michael Medved

The big running gag in "Ready to Wear (Pret-a-Porter)" has a selection of the film's glamorous characters stepping into piles of dog poop, then cursing and trying to scrape the mess off their shoes.

Somehow, this repeated bit of pathetic slapstick might stand as an appropriate summary for an ambitious project that stumbles at every turn and leaves behind a distinctly unpleasant aroma.

"Ready to Wear" (known by its original French title of "Pret-a-Porter" until just days before its release applies the same treatment to the crazy world of fashion that director Robert Altman used so successfully on the crazy world of country music in "Nashville," and the crazy world of Hollywood in "The Player."

He throws together real-life celebrities with a large cast of well-known actors, pursuing several simultaneous story lines that intersect in bizarre and unexpected ways, offering a panoramic view of the self-enclosed universe he's trying to expose. It doesn't matter if a few scenes or characters fall flat; the focus shifts so quickly that the audience is bound to encounter someone they like before too long.

Unfortunately that's not the case with "Ready to Wear," where each of the 30 characters is as starved of substance as the most anorexic supermodel. None of these sloppily sketched cartoon figures is in the least bit appealing or believable—and the emotional and humanizing scenes that turn up in all of the director's other films (especially last year's searing "Short Cuts") are nowhere to be found.

The main plot line begins with the death of the head of the Paris fashion council. who's apparently poisoned by a mysterious visitor from Russia (Marcello Mastroianni) who then begins stalking the victim's glamorous widow (Sophia Loren). Since the murder occurred on the very eve of the frantically hyped, semi-annual "Ready To Wear" show, two American reporters (Julia Roberts and Tim Robbins) are assigned to cover the case: Due to a hotel's incompetence, they end up for several days in the same room while awaiting the return of their lost luggage.

Three, highly competitive fashion editors (Tracey Ullman, Linda Hunt and Sally Kellerman) spend their time in Paris wooing the moody Irishman (Stephen Rea) who's the hot photographer of the moment. Forest Whitaker and Richard E. Grant play rival designers, while Kim Basinger (in what's easily the film's finest, funniest performance) portrays a ditzy TV reporter who aggressively interviews real and fictional celebrities. "Oh, Milo," she gushes in one typical approach, "you've had a lock on the look of the '90s for decades!"

With such wit in short supply, Altman fills his screen time with frantic couplings—including no less than 10 different (but similarly depressing) extra marital involvements. Instead of revealing character, the director reveals (female) bodies—not just prominent models in the pretentious "nude fashion show" finale, but Tracey Ullman and Sally Kellerman as well. The cumulative experience feels so shabby and debilitating that in the end it's not just the runway mannequins but the Emperor-director himself who's shown to be wearing no clothes.

NEWSDAY, 12/23/94, Part II/p. B7, Jack Mathews

The whimsical nature of Robert Altman has never been more evident, or more wasted, than in "Ready to Wear," the director's long-planned visit to the Paris fashion world and it's semiannual designer shows known as the *pret-a-porter*.

There is good reason Altman was unable to get this project off the ground until he'd had that amazing success with "The Player." Where, any reasonable studio executive or potential investor might ask, is the audience for a two-hour parade of inside jokes about the power, politics, pressures, sexual tension and chaos behind the scenes of a weeklong fashion show?

All of that might make a great backdrop for another story. Recall model Audrey Hepburn's wonderful costume changes in Stanley Donen's 1957 "Funny Face," which was a Fred Astaire musical! But in the inimitable Altman style, which takes us into the fashion milieu like a fiber optic probe wending its way through a human organ, you are asked to appreciate merely *being* there.

I'd rather spend my Paris vacation at the Louvre, and even though "Ready to Wear" includes one audacious parade of women in birthday suits (graphically answering the question, just how skinny are high-fashion models?), you'll see sexier shows and better clothes watching at home on VH1.

In what passes for a narrative idea, Marcello Mastroianni plays a mysterious Italian expatriate who comes to Paris from his adopted Moscow and, after being wrongly fingered as the killer of the head of the French fashion commission, insinuates himself in the midst of the spring *pret-a-porter*.

Mastroianni's presence there has a ripple effect on the participants, and though we keep coming back to him and eventually learn the nature of his quest (the still stunning Sophia Loren, playing an old girlfriend), we are really riding the ripple. And along the way, we see Altman's huge and recognizable cast mingling with such genuine fashion stars as Christian Lacroix, Issey Miyake, Jean Paul Gaultier and Sonia Rykiel.

Altman filmed in and around an actual week of the Paris ready-to-wear shows, and the verité feel he got from that is the movie's greatest strength. But none of the little episodes within the setting is particularly interesting, insightful or funny. There's a Designers in Heat subplot between bitchy Richard E. Grant and bearish Forest Whitaker. Danny Aiello is a cross-dressing American buyer and Teri Garr his shop-happy companion. Sally Kellerman, Linda Hunt and Tracey Ullman are giddy fashion magazine editors vying for the sexual and professional services of the sadistic high-fashion photographer Stephen Rea.

Back at the hotel, in scenes that could have been shot in a Hollywood studio, newspaper reporters Tim Robbins and Julia Roberts are making the most of a bad situation—hotel and luggage snafus have thrown the strangers together in the same suite—by mating like minks.

Oh, yes, and there's Kim Basinger, as the omnipresent TV fashion reporter, scrambling for interviews, fawning over the designers, and asking the kinds of airheaded questions that plague and demean celebrities in every field.

It's hard to know exactly what Altman, who co-wrote the script with Barbara Shulgasser, had in mind with "Ready to Wear', (the mundane title, a literal translation of *pret-a-porter*, is the film distributor's idea). He is a career curmudgeon, whose best ("Nashville," "The Player") and worst ("A Wedding," "H.E.A.L.T.H.") films have used his meandering, crosscutting style to point up the follies of ritualistic human behavior.

The target has to be worthy of scorn, and the director has to have his bile running, and neither is the case here. Altman has made the fashion world look pretty silly, but it is more of a nudge in the ribs than a stake through the heart. It's as if he admires the talent of these people too much to mock their garish lifestyles.

The result is a kind of genial, blunt-edged parody that's not apt to please or offend anyone.

NEWSWEEK, 1/9/95, p. 58, David Ansen

Robert Altman's comedy "Ready to Wear" ("Pret-a-Porter") has been torn limb from limb by most critics and roasted by the fashion industry. Now, it's true that Altman's take on the fashion world—that it's shallow, vain silly, pretentious—is lazy conventional wisdom. It's also true that if you're looking for a "good" story, you won't find it in this tangled web of improvisatory plot lines. Why are we following a murder investigation when there's no murder and no mystery? Why, having staged the humiliation of three high-and-mighty fashion editors (Linda Hunt, Sally Kellerman and Tracy Ullman) at the hands of a smugly sadistic photographer (Stephen Rea), does Altman prepare us for their revenge—and forget to show it? Of the 31 characters rushing about in the faux-documentary ambience Altman creates around the fever of a Paris fashion opening, only a few—like, Julia Roberts's wine-gulping Houston reporter, who spends the weekend shacked up in a hotel room with Tim Robbins's sportswriter—get to sink their teeth into a fully shaped scene. "Ready to Wear" is all appetizers: the main course never arrives.

Still, the critical savagery puzzles me. Altman's movie may be indefensible, but it's not unenjoyable. The fun of it is entirely superficial, like skimming a gossip column. Look—there's Cher! Isn't that Sonia Rykiel? Do you think Forest Whitaker is playing Patrick Kelly? There's amusement in Kim Basinger's dizzy impersonation of a haplessly gushing TV reporter; there's the chance to marvel at Anouk Aimee's grave elegance and Sophia Loren's time-defying beauty, and there's the simple pleasure of watching the 69-year-old Altman trying to keep several dozen balls simultaneously spinning in the air. All right, so he drops a lot of them this time. But when most every other filmmaker is tossing one ball at a time, why lynch the guy for trying?

SIGHT AND SOUND, 3/95, p. 47, Henry Sheehan

In Moscow, Sergei purchases two identical Dior neck ties. In Paris, the week of the *prêt à porter* fashion show, Olivier de la Fontaine, head of the french Fashion Council, receives one tie with a letter. After a bitter exchange with his wife Isabella, he puts on the tie, and leaves. He visits his lover, fashion designer Simone Lowenthal, also being visited by pregnant supermodel Albertine. At the airport, Kitty Potter, reporter for American fashion channel FAD, is interviewing celebrities, including Regina Krumm of *Elle*, Sissy Wanamaker of *Harper's Bazaar*, and Nina Scant of British *Vogue*. Fashion buyer Major Hamilton angles for an interview but is rejected. Louise Hamilton encounters a *Houston Chronicle* fashion reporter, Abbe Eisenhower, who has left her bags back in the US. De la Fontaine notes Sergei, just arrived, wearing the same tie. In the ride back to Paris, Olivier dies choking on a ham sandwich. Sergei panics and runs, jumping off the Pont Alexandre. Police Inspector Tantpis and newly widowed Isabella, participating in a dog show, are informed of the death (assumed to be murder) at the same time.

At the Grand Hotel, Eisenhower has to share a room with *Washington Post* sportswriter Joe Flynn, forced to stay in town and cover the 'murder'. Neither has any clothes but what they're wearing—Sergei having stolen Joe's suitcase— and their animosity turns into a hot sexual affair. English designer Cort Romney with his wife Violetta and 'street' designer Cy Bianco with his assistant/lover Reggie prepare for their shows, the House of Dior, Sonia Rykiel, Christian LaCroix, Issey Miyake, and Jean-Paul Gaultier have theirs; all and sundry are interviewed by

Kitty Potter. The three fashion editors pursue the services of sardonic, calculating fashion photographer Milo O'Brannigan. O'Brannigan—who tricks the women into posing for pictures in humiliating positions—is also working for Jack, Simone Lowenthal's son. Married to model Dane, Jack is having an affair with her sister Kiki. Isabella faints when she encounters Sergei at a fashion show, then keeps her cool when he turns up again at a Bulgari jewellery show; they had been married 42 years earlier in Italy. The Romney and Bianco shows are big successes, but each designer is cheating with the other's partner. The three editors have their revenge on O'Brannigan when Wanamaker steals his negatives. Tantpis learns from an autopsy that Olivier's death was an accident and the case is closed. Simone upsets the whole hypocritical applecart, staging her climactic show entirely with nude models, including Albertine.

For all the fuss it makes about going backstage at Parisian fashion shows, Robert Altman's *Pret-a-Porter* has remarkably little to show. Nowhere do we see anyone design anything, or figure out how to drape the models to best effect. A show is deemed a success solely on the buzz it sparks among the audience and the media; at no point do we see anyone buy or sell the fanciful togs on display, which would seem to be the point of the whole thing.

Despite Altman piling his trademark contempt onto television fashion reporter Kitty Potter (played with real comic charm by Kim Basinger), his whole approach merely mimics the shooting style of fashion shows on *MTV* and *CNN*: lots of handheld stuff, first closing up on the media lovelies in the audience, then watching the models strut their stuff with low-angle, idolatrous pans that self-consciously include the popping flashes of the photographers. From there it is backstage for the shoulder-to-shoulder post-show jam, a silkier version of the locker room interview. Altman had his cast mingle with the real life personages but all they do is duplicate the posturing of the media-savvy fashion crowd.

There are half-hearted attempts to comment on the whole idea of fashion or fads, but they don't amount to much. Julia Roberts and Tim Robbins play a pair of US journalists, forced to share a hotel room they cannot leave because each has lost baggage. Their forced intimacy soon contributes to some hot and heavy couplings, yet they cannot make any instant judgements on each other's amorous suitability because they're not wearing their usual sartorial signals. Amusing enough, except that even this simple encounter is blighted by Roberts' character becoming some sort of dipso/nympho, unable to resist sex after drinking. It is as if the director can't resist reducing the most innocent characterisation into a mechanism for contempt.

This sourness reaches its nadir with the three fashion editors pursuing fashion photographer Milo O'Brannigan. Although Linda Hunt tries to run a cool and collected variation on the career woman persona, Tracey Ullman and Sally Kellerman dive into stereotypical waters. O'Brannigan, played with condescension by Stephen Rea, tricks the women into humiliating intimacies and photographs them, thus cruelly turning the tables on these merchants of female imagery. Yet the point is utterly subsumed by the gusto with which Altman films their self-abasements; he even has Kellerman repeat her breast-flashing embarrassment from *MASH*. Whatever connivance the women may have in their own plight is swamped by the ferocity of the film's delight in it.

Sophia Loren and Marcello Mastroianni enact a travesty of some of their lesser vehicles, cooing and shouting at one another as they recall a past romance of comically impossible twists. As she is Olivier's widow and he a lowly communist tailor, one supposes there is a point being scored, but whatever it is dies aborning. Forest Whitaker and Richard E. Grant play over-the-top gay designers; the latter in particular confuses swish with character. Neither comes close to the kind of "what-of-it?" campness Kenneth Williams could toss off. Which is another way of saying the movie doesn't even live up to being *Carry On Couturier*.

What makes the movie reprehensible rather than merely miserable is how it marks the degeneration of the film technique associated with Jean Renoir's great middle period. In his hands, the unanchored camera could pick up and follow any character or story passing by. It joined peasant and noble, sinner and saint, in a narrative democracy that was ultimately one of the century's most sublime expressions of secular faith and hope. But in Altman's hands, the camera becomes an instrument for turning away, creating instead a democracy of contempt.

TIME, 12/19/94, p. 75, Richard Corliss

When you hear the word French, you may think of elegance, hauteur and haute couture. When Robert Altman hears the word, he thinks of farce, polluted rivers and dog doo under everyone's foot. *Prêt-à-Porter* (*Ready to Wear*) is the director's long-winded hate letter to the fashion industry and those who cover it. The film is a flaccid mess, missing its easy targets. It is also undiluted Altman—a movie that sums up his attitude toward actors, audiences, the press, humanity. When you hear the word contempt, you think of Robert Altman.

Fashion is in a particularly ugly, aimless, self-parodying phase at the moment, so perhaps it deserves a chronicler as cynical as this one. Anyway, a cynic is what it got during the industry's big *prêt-à-porter* shows in Paris last spring, when Altman mingled with the modish élite and found room in his film for many of them: designers Christian Lacroix, Jean Paul Gaultier and Issey Miyake, models Naomi Campbell and Christy Turlington and CNN fashion maven Elsa Klensch.

The movie weaves its little stories into this big scene. A designer (Anouk Aimée) fights a takeover by a Texan (Lyle Lovett). A photographer (Stephen Rea) toys with three magazine editors (Linda Hunt, Sally Kellerman, Tracey Ullman). Two reporters (Tim Robbins and Julia Roberts in a nice little sketch) cover the story from their hotel bedroom. Two handsome Italians (Sophia Loren, Marcello Mastroianni) replay an old love affair. And a FAD-TV reporter (Kim Basinger) chirpily reports every outrage on the runways and in the salons.

As *MASH* was to war movies, *Nashville* to country music, *A Wedding* to the middle-class family, *H.E.A.L.T.H.* to the organic-food business and *The Player* to Hollywood, so is *Ready to Wear* to fashion: a comic panorama of people pretending to get along under stress, creating a bogus community, playing games of power and privilege, establishing who's boss. The tone of an Altman film—the desperate milling, the sense of isolation within a crowd, the urgency to no clear end—is the reflection of life on any movie set and, indeed, in the working lives of most people. When the scheme works, as in *MASH* and *The Player*, it does so by giving people something fresh to do and witty to say. Then the bile has an urgent, instructive tang. It's called satire.

But *Ready to Wear*, which Altman wrote with Barbara Shulgasser, is a high concept poorly executed. Too often the characters are simply mannequins for nasty jokes. What, for example, is the essence of the fashion doyenne played by Lauren Bacall? That she is color-blind, and that her friends apparently don't tell her she's wearing shoes of different shades. Why is Danny Aiello, as a buyer for a Chicago store, in the film? So he can cross-dress in a Chanel suit. At 60, Loren looks great, in or out of her array of glorious millinery, but it's cruel to have her and Mastroianni reprise the strip-tease scene from *Yesterday, Today and Tomorrow* with a cheap new punch line. Kellerman must endure the same naked shame she did a quarter-century ago in *MASH*. The heart sighs for these game folks. So much effort expended to so little effect.

Never blame actors; their mission is to do whatever their director tells them. Blame Altman, whose mission here was to assemble some of the most glamorous performers in world cinema for a mass hazing, a humiliation on camera. He is like the scuzzy photographer played by Rea: he finds people eager to make unedifying fools of themselves, takes their picture, takes some money and calls it art. And he has done to his actresses what male fashion designers so often do to their models and customers: make beautiful women look ridiculous. Imitation is the sincerest form of parody.

Ready to Wear isn't about pricey clothes; Altman has no more interest or expertise in them than he did in country music when he made *Nashville*. Here he wanted only to find a new arena for his worst impulses. This strategy of derision exhausted itself ages ago. But for Altman, contempt never goes out of fashion.

VILLAGE VOICE, 12/27/94, p. 61, J. Hoberman

Fashion, it would appear, has never been more fashionable, but, if screening-room scuttlebutt offers any barometer, Robert Altman is once again passé.

Ready To Wear, Altman's ode to couture, seems poised to tank as it opens Christmas Day at 1000 theaters. It's not altogether true that the movie, known until recently as *Prêt-à-Porter*, puts the viewer on the rack; vicious word-of-mouth notwithstanding, *Ready to Wear* is less flaming disaster than lukewarm disappointment. *Short Cuts* provided something substantial to dislike; *Ready to Wear* looks as vapid as it feels. The texture is washed out, the fabric flimsy. The title's last-minute gringoization is symptomatic of an overall identity crisis. *Ready to Wear* is a mirthless romp. Unlike *The New Yorker*'s recent special issue, it's too tired to even make the case that fashion is "fun."

As if to emphasize the movie's status as gaseous blur, Altman uses his two best jokes to bracket the vagued-out proceedings. The title sequence has Marcello Mastroianni shopping for a designer tie in an emporium around the corner from...Moscow's Red Square! But, as *The Player* (re) established Altman as the maestro of cinematic name-dropping, the credits are rendered in Cyrillic characters only until the inevitable spin of fabulous monikers: Danny Aiello, Anouk Aimée Lauren Bacall, Kim Basinger...all the way through the alphabet to Forest Whitaker.

Something like 36 characters in search of an offer, *Ready To Wear*'s narrative plays like a bunch of pulverized one-act dramas in which everything more or less exists to serve as fodder for a misfired gag. Scene after scene of aimless milling around are interspersed with assorted bouts of spastic coupling and blasts of glitz and strobe runway glamour. Set during the week when Paris designers unveil their spring collections, the project reeks of bored self-contempt. (Cross-referenced events around town include a dog show and a cross-dresser's convention.) So many characters step in doggie doo on their way to do each other dirt, you have to wonder if Altman is proposing life as a Poodle Shit *La Ronde*.

Once fashion czar Jean-Pierre Cassell gags to death in his limo while stuck in a traffic jam on the Pont Alexandre III, Altman has his macguffin. Cassell was married to and cheating on a frighteningly well-preserved Sophia Loren who, at one point, recapitulates her striptease from *Yesterday, Today, and Tomorrow* for her former husband ... well, you'll see. Establishing a mystery insufficiently compelling to motivate a game of *Clue*, Altman whips a variety of schemes and subterfuges into a sub-soufflé froth of tepid intrigue. As rumpled Mastroianni capers about breaking into suites and stealing luggage, designer Anouk Aimée's pompously duplicitous son (Rupert Everett) sells her company to a vulgar Texas bootmaker (Lyle Lovett). Meanwhile, an unholy trio of fashion magazine editors, Linda Hunt, Sally Kellerman, and Tracey Ullman (enlivening this mediocrity as she did *Bullets Over Broadway*), vie for the services of a currently hot photographer, (Stephen Rea, playing an even more curdled version of the Keith Carradine character in *Nashville*).

The mystery, such as it is, disappears in a miasma of bedroom farce, Grand Guignol, and desultory quasidocumentary—in addition to the cameos by real models and designers, among other celebs, Altman filmed against the backdrop of the actual fashion shows from which, according to *Women's Wear Daily*, he was eventually banned. Increasingly grotesque, *Ready To Wear* is a gargoyle parade that suggests nothing so much as stupefied Fellini. Given the cast, the movie is haunted by the ghost of the European art film. Perhaps reflecting Altman's anxiety over shooting in Europe, two key American characters, Julia Roberts and Tim Robbins, spend virtually the entire movie in a hotel room.

"This could be absolutely brilliant or it could be absolute trash," *Premiere*'s reporter overheard Altman tell his cast, comforting them with the thought that, in any case, "it doesn't make any difference, because the audience has no taste." In that, I fear, we are not alone. Altman is the reigning master of actor humiliation. The players here are so bizarrely dressed (or undressed), so badly lit, and so uniformly buffaloed it seems cruel to single out any particular performance—although Kim Basinger works double time as the broadly parodic TV reporter who wanders tirelessly through the movie bugging the principals and butchering her high-school French.

Like, the obnoxious BBC correspondent Geraldine Chaplin played in *Nashville*, Basinger is the butt of Altman's jokes as well as the director's surrogate—never more so than in the final sequence when she finally drops her cast-iron poise and confesses that she doesn't know what this "bullshit" is all about. By then, of course, the movie has built up to a finale that effectively recasts the entire movie as an updated version of "The Emperor's New Clothes."

Also reviewed in:
CHICAGO TRIBUNE, 12/25/94, Tempo/p. 5, Michael Wilmington
NATION, 1/23/95, p. 106, Stuart Klawans
NEW REPUBLIC, 2/6/95, p. 24, Stanley Kauffmann
NEW YORK TIMES, 12/23/94, p. C1, Janet Maslin

VARIETY, 12/12-18/94, p. 75, Todd McCarthy
WASHINGTON POST, 12/23/94, Weekend/p. 36, Desson Howe

REALITY BITES

A Universal Pictures release of a Jersey Films production. *Executive Producer:* Stacey Sher and Wm. Barclay Malcolm. *Producer:* Danny DeVito and Michael Shamberg. *Director:* Ben Stiller. *Screenplay:* Helen Childress. *Director of Photography:* Emmanuel Lubezki. *Editor:* Lisa Churgin. *Music:* Karl Wallinger. *Music Editor:* Andrew Silver. *Sound:* Stephen Halbert. *Sound Editor:* Stephen H. Flick. *Casting:* Francine Maisler. *Production Designer:* Sharon Seymour. *Art Director:* Jeff Knipp. *Set Designer:* Michael Armani. *Set Decorator:* Maggie Martin. *Set Dresser:* Maike Both and James Malley. *Costumes:* Eugenie Bafaloukos. *Make-up:* Deborah Larsen. *Running time:* 99 minutes. *MPAA Rating:* PG-13.

CAST: Winona Ryder (Lelaina Pierce); Ethan Hawke (Troy Dyer); Janeane Garofalo (Vickie Miner); Steve Zahn (Sammy Gray); Ben Stiller (Michael Grates); Swoosie Kurtz (Charlane McGregor); Harry O'Reilly (Wes McGregor); Susan Norfleet (Helen Anne Pierce); Joe Don Baker (Tom Pierce); Renee Zellweger (Tami); James Rothenberg (Rick); John Mahoney (Grant Gubler); Eric Stuart (Damien); Barry Sherman (Grant's Producer); Chelsea Lagos (Troy Groupie); Bill Bolender (Truck Driver); Jubal Palmer (Player #1); Marti Greene (Player #2); John Walsh (Player #3); Helen Childress (Waitress); David Pirner (Phineas); Andy Dick (Rock); Keith David (Roger); Anne Meara (Louise); Kevin Pollack (Stand-Up Comic); Amy Stiller (Psychic Phone Partner); Afton Smith (Janine); Pat Crawford Brown (Cashier); Jeff Kahn (Stage Manager); Karen Duffy (Actress "Elaina"); Evan Dando (Actor "Roy").

CHRISTIAN SCIENCE MONITOR, 2/9/94, p. 16, Marilynne S. Mason

Director Ben Stiller's "Reality Bites" captures the disillusionment of baby-boomers' children as they graduate college. They speak in TV slogans and caustic pronouncements, are afraid of commitment and AIDS, and can't find meaningful work. These kids are also aware of the materialism of the age without the slightest idea of how to offset it. It's the '60s revisited without the concern for social justice. Nothing they do or think even smacks of genuine rebellion because rebellion has mutated into mere style. MTV is the status quo.

Stiller and screenwriter Helen Childress take up issues absolutely crucial to society. They get so much right in the film that the viewer feels betrayed by the ineffectual ending. When in doubt the story seems to say, let your lost protagonist find meaning in romantic love. The trouble is, the entire film has demonstrated how promiscuity makes love impossible—nobody trusts anybody else. The filmmakers grasp the horror of materialism, but in the end, they have nothing significant to say about it.

But "Reality Bites" was a masterpiece of social commentary compared to films like *River of Grass, Suture*, and *Blessing*. it was painfully clear that few of the American films did much more than whine about society's failure, indulging in angst-ridded dysfunction as if that were enough to make drama.

LOS ANGELES TIMES, 2/18/94, Calendar/p. 1, Kenneth Turan

We know them but we know them not, and the feeling is mutual. The children of television and divorce, they are cynical and suspicious beyond their years, especially of a certain earlier generation that "disemboweled the revolution for a pair of running shoes." But being smart and hip doesn't save them from being vulnerable, and that sense of characters at the mercy of life's mutability is what makes "Reality Bites" a romantic comedy that is cheerful, edgy and alive.

Starring Winona Ryder, Ethan Hawke and Ben Stiller, who also makes his directing debut, "Reality Bites" is not the first film to deal with the resentful members of Generation X, fed up with their label before it even caught on.

But, working from a clever and clear-eyed script by Helen Childress and with a graceful and talented cast, Stiller has seen to it that the protagonists of "Reality Bites" are individuals before they are archetypes. Their comic/romantic dilemmas may be venerable, but they do not feel arbitrarily imposed.

Writer Childress, herself only 23, has created characters with the distinctive sensibility of her mordant peers, just-out-of-college types who say things like "the Big Gulp is the most profound invention of my lifetime" and consider the Free Clinic AIDS test "the rite of passage for our generation."

It is a generation represented by four college friends, met in Houston on the day of their graduation through the video eye of Lelaina Pierce (Ryder), the class valedictorian. She is taping her pals for future use in a documentary about their search for identity that complements her day job as a production assistant for Grant Gubler (John Mahoney), the genial/sadistic host of local TV's "Good Morning, Grant!"

Having a job at all puts Lelaina one up on her trio of friends. Sammy Gray (Steve Zahn) is the most spaced-out, talking blankly bout liking "a career or something." Vickie Miner (Janeane Garofalo) is the most aggressive, especially where men are concerned, keeping a numbered list of conquests and embracing promiscuity because she never wants to lose the passion of that first night. And then there is Troy.

As played by Ethan Hawke, Troy Dyer, with his greasy hair, straggly goatee and a motley collection of pullover shirts, is in part the classic slacker, derided by Lelaina as "a master of time suckage" who does nothing but "eat and couch and fondle the remote."

On the other hand, Troy is probably the smartest of the group, a serious reader of philosophy who's had a half-buried romantic interest in Lelaina for years. But Troy, the James Dean hipster who waffles on commitment, is stuck in his romantic loner pose, refusing to acknowledge emotion and taking refuge in the kind of troubled sarcasm that make him his own worst enemy.

Troy and Lelaina might have remained in this extended limbo for a considerable time if it wasn't for her chance meeting with Michael Grates (Stiller): A college dropout turned vice president of In Your Face TV, described as "MTV with an edge," he is both squarer and more successful than all of Lelaina's friends put together. But, to their mutual surprise, these two have a real appeal for each other, which pushes the displaced Troy even further into an off-puttingly sardonic frame of mind.

In addition to pungent, gleefully funny dialogue, of which there is plenty, what makes a triangle this traditional feel fresh is the casting and performances, which, starting with Ryder as the cynosure of all eyes, couldn't be bettered across the board.

After such period films as "Bram Stoker's Dracula" and "The Age of Innocence," the actress returns here to the kind of talking-about-my-generation role she had in "Heathers," and it is a treat to see how much naturalness and assurance she brings to what could have been a predigested performance.

The same is even more true for the two men who are focused on her. Ethan Hawke allows himself to be much more disturbingly unpleasant and abrasive than usual as the agonized Troy, and director Stiller, understanding perfectly that the more honestly appealing Michael is, the more involving the joust with Troy becomes, does so well with his part that nothing about this rivalry seems at all predetermined.

Though Stiller and Childress have taken pains to be as specific to their generation as possible, they also understand that at their core these ideals versus the real world dilemmas are timeless. Stiller, whose dead-on comic touch is not surprising given the craftiness of his Fox network show, displays in addition an empathy for these characters that makes a nice fit with how smart their dialogue is. He believes their stories have value, and that makes all the difference.

NEW STATESMAN & SOCIETY, 6/24/94, p. 34, Jonathan Romney

This week's competition: what's the most embarrassing LP in your collection? Admit to something really naff and you could win first prize, a ticket to see *Reality Bites*. Second prize: two tickets to see *Shopping*. This is teen movies week, and both the above offerings recall that gruesome skit on youth TV in *The Young Ones*, in which grinning *Blue Peter* types hyperventilate furiously as they present "a show for the kids!" *by* the kids! *about* the kids!"

In *Reality Bites*, an engaging debut by sometime TV comic Ben Stiller, hip video-making kid Lelaina (Winona Ryder) is courted by a guy named Michael (Stiller himself, who's kind of cute and cool, except that he has no notion of what is and isn't hip. He wears a suit, he drives a car, he's an executive for "In Your Face TV", and the fond musical memory he tries to woo her with is Peter Frampton. Gross, right?

And in *Shopping*, two ram-raiding hipsters of an altogether tougher mettle (chisel-chopped hunk Jude Law, and Sadie Frost as Belfast's answer to Tank Girl) return to his den. There she sifts through his old records. "Duran ... Spandau ... *Twisted Sister* she sneers, in a crescendo of disbelief.

Now, I've never owned a record by *any* of the above artists—but watching these scenes, I felt an involuntary twinge of empathy for anyone who has, because the joke is entirely at their expense. The only possible response if you're one of the unfortunates squirming at these lines, is to stand up and testify that yes, you used to like *Frampton Comes Alive*—but you burnt your copy, along with everyone else, at the 1976 witch trials.

Of course, the question *Reality Bites* begs is: what can Peter Frampton possibly mean to the film's presumed target audience of mid-teens to mid-20s? To understand the excruciating tweeness of "Baby I Love Your Way", you would either need to be old enough to have owned it the first time round, or have been schooled in 1970s naffness by an older sibling anxious to stop you making the same aesthetic errors.

Either way, though, the rules of cool are hard and fast. The fact that Michael actually *likes* this stuff is enough to tell us that Lelaina cannot possibly end up with him. Instead, she'll bond with whining slacker Troy (Ethan Hawke)—for no other reason than that he has been bequeathed Kurt Cobain's cast-off shirts.

Here's the catch, though. Hot off the original soundtrack, a brand new version of Frampton's evergreen hit—twice as mawkish as the original—is causing a whole new generation of hearts to flutter. *Reality Bites* is up to its neck in this sort of knowing duplicity. It only serves to illustrate the impasse of today's media-literate postmodern youth culture, which is forever caught between deconstructing the object and buying it in a dance-remix CD version.

This otherwise amiable and witty film is fatally entangled in a hermetic set of style rules, which will make it completely unintelligible five years from now. To get the benefit, you have to subscribe to the notion that MTV itself is cool, but that anything vaguely *like* MTV is not; that Frampton sucks, but other pop acts of questionable vintage (like the Knack and Squeeze) are cool if treated with the right irreverent spirit—ie, if you and your pals sing their hits while drunk.

Reality Bites comes across as a punchier, more neurotic (but considerably less sexy) follow-up to Cameron Crowe's *Singles*. That wasn't so much the great grunge movie as a film about a bunch of people who happened to hang out in grunge clubs, even though they were demonstrably too old. What was good about *Singles* was that it was so non-judgmental—it was OK to be a nerd.

But the kids in *Reality Bites* seem to be setting each other little traps all the time, trying to out-cool each other by talking in lapidary zen *bons mots*. Of the slobbish Troy, Lelaina warns: "He will turn this place into a den of slack." Troy justifies his permanent pique with the observation: "I am not under any order to make the world a better place." He may walk it like James Dean, but he talks it like Rik Mayall.

Stiller's apparently well-meaning film may, of course, just be a blatantly creepy attempt to cash in on the current vogue for slacker cynicism. On the other hand, it may be that rare thing, a genuine teen movie—as snobbish, confused, half-likeable and self-deceiving as clever teenagers tend to be. At least it's smart enough to trip itself up.

Shopping is just a galumphing dullard of a film. Like so many of the current crop of half-baked Brit-brat movies (*The Young Americans, Beyond Bedlam*), Paul Anderson's film waves a vaguely jingoistic cultural flag, but can't help showing how desperately it wants to be a Hollywood product. The dollar sign for the "S" on the poster is presumably meant to be read as a jibe at the all-pervading power of mercantilism in Blighty.

The fact is, like *The Young Americans, Shopping* just thinks dollars are sexy, and would rather spend them on Melrose than at Brent Cross. It comes across as a feeble, would-be anarchic attack on materialism, but puts most of its energies into the fetishistic pleasure of watching Volvos burn, slowly. Hang on—isn't that what they do in the Volvo ads these days?

Shot in a limited palette of Beinix Blue and *Mad Max* Murk, *Shopping* is set in familiar terrain: a near-future post-apocalypse urban hell overrun by gangs of lawless ram-raiding teens. (Why mince words? I think they mean Manchester.) The force of authority is incarnated by dependable old Jonathan Pryce as Chief of Police. A jelly old beak in tweeds, with a bunch of Keystone plods at his command, he steps out from time to time like a disapproving headmaster to tut-tut at the young uns' high spirits.

When he looks our hero in the eye and asks him, "Why'd you do it, Billy?", the veneer of 1990s hipness drops away and suddenly *Shopping* is revealed as a cheap recladding of a London teen-gang exploitation flick of the 1950s. It's just a disappointment that Billy's next line isn't something like: "I knows a feller as wouldn't think twice about slicing you up, he wouldn't."

Still, they're dead'ard, these kids, with their street lingo, a strange mixture of rave-babble and *Sweeney*-speak ("Hear you had a run-in with the bizzies already." "Yeah, saw a bit of speed"). I bet *they* read *Loaded*. But either as style pundits or as your more traditional raging youth, they're pretty lame. When they rant their distaste for credit cards, Ferrero Kocher and Alessi kettles, they always look as if they've had to consult the *Class War* handbook out of the car they've stolen. Lelaina would have done the cooler thing, and improvised a college rock-rap version of "Money For Nothing".

NEW YORK, 2/28/94, p. 114, John Powers

It used to be that a generation wasn't a Generation unless it did something special—launch the Decadent Movement, say, or fight in the Spanish Civil War. Now, all it has to do is show up; ad agencies and trend-piece writers take care of the rest. This, of course, is exactly what has happened to members of "Generation X," whose defining characteristic may be their paralyzing realization that they've been turned into a marketing concept before they ever had the chance to accomplish anything. Precisely such an awareness permeates *Reality Bites*, a romantic comedy about a group of friends just out of college and living in Houston. Although Ben Stiller's directorial debut has the glibness of any movie descended from *The Big Chill* and *St. Elmo's Fire*, it's far more enjoyable and less pretentious than either. I haven't laughed so hard since *Groundhog Day*, which means I'll forgive this movie almost anything.

Lelaina Pierce (Winona Ryder) is working at a local TV station and making a video documentary "about people who are trying to find their identity without any role models or heroes." These people are, naturally, her friends: her sardonic roommate, Vickie (Janeane Garofalo), who works at the Gap; their gay pal Sammy (Steve Zahn), whose sexuality never affects the plot; and the rumpled, brilliant Troy (Ethan Hawke), with whom Lelaina swaps the sharp repartee that invariably spells love. A glamorously ineffectual dropout who reads Sartre and fancies himself Cool Hand Luke, Troy represents one direction that Lelaina's life might take. The other way is embodied by Michael Grates, played by Stiller himself, a video executive who not only falls for Lelaina but wants to show her documentary on the In Your Face music network. Although this opposition between the yuppie and the slacker appears up-to-date, there's something almost quaint about a set up in which the heroine's decision about how to live is reduced to a choice between two men. Ryder plays Lelaina as a spunky waif (her specialty), but I kept hoping the young Katharine Hepburn would show up to tell Ryder how movie stars played this role in the old days.

As a snapshot of a generation weaned on TV, *Reality Bites* may have more media references than any other movie in history. Normally this would be good reason to steer clear, as Hollywood's attempts to seem hip to pop culture are nearly always clueless, like the prefab rock and roll that plays under TV commercials. But for once, a movie gets things right, capturing its characters' bemused nostalgia for seventies trash culture and their nineties addiction to the clickity-click rhythms of the cable box—these kids are too smart for the bombastic self-pity of Pearl Jam. *Reality Bites* is never more delightful than when it is twitting MTV fashion shows and books about self-esteem, finding the fun in dredged-up hits by Peter Frampton and The Knack, spinning out hilarious riffs on 7-Eleven Big Gulps, "Alas, poor Yorick," and *I Know Why the Caged Bird Sings*. When a door swings shut, you can bet it will display a poster of Shaun Cassidy. Beautifully attuned to the pop demographic, the filmmakers know that a Milken-faced video executive like Michael would naturally listen to rap, whose patina of street rebellion often masks the materialism of a Tiffany display case.

The movie's so clever about media culture that at first I thought it was debunking the absurd idea that people in their twenties take their personal identities from TV shows and consumer items; later, I realized that the filmmakers actually think this cliché is true. In the film's most facile moment, the distraught Lelaina moans, "I don't understand why things can't go back to normal at the end of the half-hour like on *The Brady Bunch.*" Troy replies, "Because Mr. Brady died of AIDS"—the perfect clincher to a perfectly bogus exchange. (No doubt this line will be quoted everywhere as proof of the perceptiveness of *Reality Bites*.) While we're supposed to see the pain peeking out from behind Lelaina's allusion to the Bradys, we're actually struck by how half-witted this makes her seem.

One of the rare movies that so much as mentions work or unemployment, *Reality Bites* displays the confusions about social class produced by our shrinking economy. Lelaina and her friends have been raised to think they're too good to do the kind of jobs available to them—jobs still being done by the working class and immigrants. Helen Childress's script sometimes encourages this sense of innate superiority (there's a cruel scene at a fast-food restaurant), but it doesn't always let such snobbery pass. The movie's most emotionally charged moment comes when Lelaina wounds Vickie by turning up her nose at a job at the Gap. In her reflexive contempt for such work, we catch a glimpse of a larger social truth: *Reality Bites* is about young people's terror of falling out of the real middle class—not the middle class shown on television.

Promiscuous and self-hating, Vickie is the movie's most compelling character, not least because she does work at the Gap. She belongs to a group largely ignored by American movies, the legion of smart, attractive, independent women caught in work that underuses their talents: "I'm responsible for all these T-shirts," she quips. Vibrant in her wisecracks, Vickie is a good part made great by Janeane Garofalo, a spunky, wide-lipped, scene-stealing comedienne who delivers punch lines with the insolent ease of a kid popping bubble gum; her monologue about how *Melrose Place* would handle a character with AIDs may be the picture's high point. I hope someone will give Garofalo a starring role soon, lest she be sentenced to a lifetime of Carrie Fisher parts.

The story's turning point comes when Michael gets In Your Face TV to buy Lelaina's documentary, some of the scenes of which we've watched as she taped them. The network reedits her work into a show called "Reality Bites"—a music-laced, Cuisinarted version of her original tapes. She's aghast at how the program has trivialized her whole life. Yet the irony is that this program is only somewhat more superficial than *Reality Bites*. Stiller's movie spoofs MTV's style but relies on video tricks and its own rock montages. It puts down commercialism but keeps focusing our attention on diet Coke cans and Rolling Rock bottles. It derides the kids' parents for their empty marriages and middle-class compromises but winds up putting Troy in a suit and teaching him how to "commit." Put simply, the movie wants to have things both ways at once. This isn't necessarily a flaw. Part of what we love about Hollywood is the way it charms us into believing that we can have our cake and eat it too.

NEW YORK POST, 2/18/94, p. 49, Michael Medved

The billboards advertise "Reality Bites" as an epochal event—nothing less than a potentially definitive "Comedy About Love in the '90s."

While the actual film is hardly as grand and sweeping as all that, it commands attention as a slick, smart, likable little picture that follows a clutch of compelling characters through that awkward transition between free-wheeling college years and the dismal swamp known as The Real World.

Lelaina Pierce (Winona Ryder) may be the valedictorian of her class, but the best job she can get once she graduates condemns her to serving as production assistant for a smirking, tyrannical TV host (John Mahoney) of a local breakfast show.

Meanwhile, she shares a rented house in Houston with the cheerfully promiscuous Vickie (played by earthy, engaging newcomer Janeane Garofalo) who works as a clerk in a clothing store, and soon complicates their living arrangement by inviting another college pal to join them.

That new house mate is the brooding, brilliant Troy (Ethan Hawke, in his best performance to date) who is too proud (and pretentious) to toil at a regular job. He spends his days lounging on the couch reading Heidegger's "Being and Time" and devotes nights to rehearsals with an unpromising alternative band called "Hey, That's My Bike."

He and Lelaina repeatedly remind each other that they're not going to spoil their ideal friendship by getting sexually involved, but the equilibrium in their relationship begins to collapse when a stranger (described by Troy as a "Yuppie-head cheese-ball") enters their tight little circle and tries to sweep Lelaina off her feet.

Ben Stiller, who also did a superb job directing this picture, plays the outsider, a hard-driving, thirty-something TV executive who offers to find a place on his self-consciously hip cable network for the artsy videos Lelaina produces in her spare time.

Stiller brings depth and compassion to a role which, in lesser hands, might have emerged as obnoxious caricature. Ryder, meanwhile, makes a stunning leading lady—earnest and vulnerable, with each line of dialogue emerging with such effortless intensity that it reveals some new facet of her character's soul.

The script by 23-year-old Texan Helen Childress features so many juicy interchanges that it is a pleasure just to listen to these people talk. Vickie, for instance, declares of Troy: "He's weird. He's strange. He's a total nightmare for women. I can't believe I haven't slept with him yet."

On the other hand, when Lelaina asks Ben Stiller about his religious beliefs, he answers by saying. "I'm a non-practicing Jew," to which she responds, "I'm a non-practicing virgin."

The screenplay also includes shocking insights, such as the revelation that Evian is "naive" spelled backwards.

At times, the movie resembles an updated female version of "The Graduate"—with its plot focused on a confused, paralyzed one-time college hotshot, torn between a continuing affair with an older partner and a potentially deeper romance with someone of the same age.

Like "The Graduate," it makes brilliant use of music of the moment (in this case well-chosen numbers by the Knack, the Posies, Lenny Kravitz, Big Mountain and others) to try to capture the special generational zeitgeist, but the deeper anxiety it dramatizes is timeless.

The filmmakers may view the characters" self-pitying poses as the special province of the aggrieved members of Generation X, but even aging baby boomers who can remember what it felt like to be 21, with no plausible plans for the future, will instantly identify.

NEWSDAY, 2/18/94, Part II/p. 74, Jack Mathews

Beneath all the MTV and camcorder images, the pop references to 7-Eleven Big Gulps and Peter Frampton, the anxious dialogue about dead-end jobs and AIDS, and the obsession with '70s TV sitcoms, Ben Stiller's romantic comedy "Reality Rites" is a very old-fashioned and very predictable love story.

The first script by 24-year-old Helen Childress, "Reality Bites" takes the timeless dilemma of a young woman having to choose between two very different kind of men—one ambitious, trustworthy, committed and rather dull, the other aimless, brooding and sexually exciting—and sets it among members of what the media have labeled Generation X. They're the fruit of the baby boomers and the godchildren of the video revolution.

Lelaina Pierce (Winona Ryder), the valedictorian of her Houston college class, is almost literally tethered to the culture. She carries her camcorder like a third arm, intent on capturing the essence of her generation by doing a spontaneous documentary on the lives of her closest friends.

Her circle includes her spirited roommate, Vickie (Janeane Garofalo), a salesclerk at The Gap who, between one-night stands, frets over her latest AIDS test; their sexually inactive friend Sammy (Steve Zahn), who worries about breaking the news of his homosexuality to his mother; and Troy (Ethan Hawke), a high-IQ slacker and part time-rock musician who moves in with the two women after losing his job at a newsstand.

The romantic triangle that soon develops is between Lelaina, Troy and Lelaina's boyfriend, Michael (Stiller), a music-video executive who is determined to get her documentary (which looks like a very bad home movie to us) aired on his station's "In Your Face" TV show.

To their credit, Childress and Stiller, who is directing his first film, make Lelaina's choice less obvious than it would seem. Instead of being the kind of archetypal square who used to lose

Ginger Rogers to Fred Astaire, Stiller makes Michael a good-hearted, if over-anxious rival, and you won't be alone if you end up rooting for him to come out the winner.

Hawke's character, the sarcastic, condescending rebel, is the only pure stereotype in the movie, and though his cruel edges are smoothed over in time, he never quite seems like anybody's idea of the catch of the day.

"Reality Bites" is a great star vehicle for Ryder. She is in nearly every scene and is never uninteresting, even though the script often is. There is a long sequence of comic nonsense in which Lelaina, having lost her job as a gofer for an egomaniacal day-time TV personality (John Mahoney), gets addicted to a call-in psychic and runs up a $400 telephone bill.

The movie is laced with situations contrived to demonstrate the characters' pop sensibilities, and the strain is often apparent. Childress wrote some hilarious lines, using references to Big Gulps, "The Brady Bunch" and "Melrose Place," but it's a disposable kind of humor that, seen even five years from now, may make "Reality Bites" look as dated as "Beach Blanket Bingo."

NEWSWEEK, 2/21/94, p. 68, David Ansen

The danger of movies that try to define a generation is that they almost have to turn out ... *generic*. Baby boomers can remember with a shudder all those psychedelicized, lets-try-and-be-hip Hollywood "youthquake" movies in the late '60s. Now we're on the brink of a slew of Generation X movies. (You could hear the media's sigh of relief when they found this moniker: so *that's* who these kids are!) Xers have every right to be cynical about Hollywood's motives in merchandising their twentysomething angst for mainstream delectation.

All of which is to explain why one may approach the twentysomething comedy "Reality Bites" with some suspicion. All the X tropes are in place—broken families, the disillusioned world of one McJob after another, the slacker response, the fetishizing of '70s TV culture. But director Ben Stiller's confident first film, written by 23-year-old Helen Childress, never makes the mistake of taking itself too seriously. A witty and sweet-natured romantic comedy, it conjures up an amorous triangle whose appeal shouldn't be limited to fans of Pearl Jam. Irene Dunne faced the same dilemma back in the '30s that Winona Ryder does here: which guy deserves her heart?

Lelaina (Ryder), an ex-valedictorian, has the best job of her friends in her Houston circle—but not for long. An inspiring documentary filmmaker, she gets fired from a local morning TV show when she sabotages the show's unctuous host, then turns for help in her jobless depression to a telephone psychic, running up $400 in 1-900 calls. She's been making a documentary of her friends featuring her tart-tongued roommate Vickie (Janeane Garofalo), who works at The Gap and dumps man after man before they can dump her; the affably asexual Sammy (Steve Zahn), who's gay but celibate; and Troy (Ethan Hawke), a heady slacker heartthrob who won't hold a job.

Everybody can sense the sexual tension between Lelaina and Troy. "Would you two just do it and get it over with?" quips Vickie. But Lelaina doesn't want to ruin their friendship, and Troy, Mr. Cool, is too in love with his detachment to risk romance. Enter Michael (director Stiller), a young video executive who's instantly smitten with Lelaina—and wants to air her documentary on his MTV-style "In Your Face" show. Troy takes one look at his Italian suits and sneers, "He's the reason Cliff Notes were invented. " Refreshingly, the battle over Lelaina is not as cut and dried as one might fear. "Reality Bites" doesn't stack the deck to score easy points off the Yuppie. Michael's foolish and shallow, but he's a mensch. And Troy is much too aware he's the cutest dude around: his stoned arrogance has a cruel streak. Ryder, Hawke, Stiller and Garofalo turn these paradigms into wonderfully tasty characters. Written with verve and played with grace, "Reality Bites" is too smart to pass itself off as a definitive statement, but it gets the details delightfully right. Stiller, the 28-year-old son of actors Jerry Stiller and Anne Meara, showed his satirical skills on the Emmy-winning "The Ben Stiller Show." Now he demonstrates that he's a deft cinematic storyteller. He won't be worrying where his next job is coming from.

SIGHT AND SOUND, 7/94, p. 50, Mark Sinker

Four college friends are graduating, and one, Lelaina—who is making a video documenting their thoughts about their various futures—is giving the valedictorian speech. She invokes the ideals of the 60s, and wonders where this leaves Class of 94, facing a less secure world. The four, Lelaina, Vicky, Sammy and Troy, all live in the same house. Lelaina, whose father supports her, gets a job in TV, as assistant to chat-show host Grant Gubler, who ignores all her ideas. Vicky and Lelaina meet Mike, a young video executive for In Your Face TV, when their cars collide. Lelaina and Mike go on a date, where she mentions her video. Although Mike is far from hip to the household's lifestyle, he is fascinated by the project.

Back home, Troy goads Lelaina for dating Mike, and they fall out. After losing her job by making a fool of Gubler on air, she tries a string of no-hope alternatives, then gives up. Vicky and her father both tell her to shape up. Meanwhile Mike has screened her video for In Your Face TV, who love it.

Arriving to take Lelaina to a screening of the now-edited video, Mike gets into a sneering match with the far more articulate Troy. The video—titled *Reality Bites*—has been jazzed up beyond all recognition, with pop songs as flip commentary. Lelaina is outraged and storms out, arriving back at the house to pour her heart out to Troy. They make love. Next morning, he hurries off, upsetting her. That evening, Lelaina turns up to watch his band play. Mike arrives to apologise. She gets into an argument with Troy, and walks out again. Next day Troy flies home to Chicago, to his ill father. After weeks sadly thinking, Lelaina orders a cab to the airport; out of it steps Troy, whose father has died. They make up. As the credits roll, we see clips from the glib TV show Mike will make out of Lelaina's and Troy's story.

As a comedy of confusions, *Reality Bites* exhibits most of the confusions it wants to nail. Then it adds a few all its own—as if Mike, the likeable, uncomprehending character played by director Ben Stiller, were the real brains behind it. Mike can never quite get the argot or the references right—but in a film which devotes its first two thirds to a near impenetrable stream of pop and TV references, often improvised by the actors (as the film flicks expertly and seamlessly between film and video, steadicam and hand-held), the use of music always seems ever so slightly wrong. Vicky collects 70s memorabilia, but sings along impassioned to New Wave college bands like Squeeze and The Knack; Mike plays rap on his in-car stereo, but waxes nostalgic about Peter Frampton. Perhaps these are the perils of tie-in: better no music than the only music you can negotiate within the budget.

Pop reference demands absolute particularity to communicate; the tradeoff for apparent triviality of shared reference has to be its precision, in-depth knowledge of the superficial being the mark of true, disenchanted seriousness. In such all-important throw-aways, the film, a neatly layered construct of films within films, never quite gets its rhythm. In fact, Lelaina's slacker language is not much more convincing than Mike's. It comes close, but really this is another missed opportunity to cast Winona in the role she was born for—the face of her age.

Every now and then the film is genuinely smart and funny, mostly when Vicky is on screen. She briskly announces, "We're late for a jeans-folding seminar: let's locomote" (she works at The Gap), or, deadpanning, outside the clinic, into Lelaina's vid-cam, "Free Clinic Aids Test: the rite of passage for our generation. We're so lucky." Vicky's powerhouse character is a joy, a collage of never-before-matched stereotypes: she's happily promiscuous, she's good at her job, she's sensible, she's relentlessly smart-mouthed, even in the face of Aids. Mike, too, is simultaneously nerdy and professional successful, a solid, contradictory sitcom cartoon. But the movie makes Troy its moral centre, and Troy is a pain in the neck.

Teen emotions have rarely made it onto the screen. The problem lies in the immutability of on-screen personas, where the inner is all broadcast by the outer—and what the outer is wearing, or singing along to. If you're portraying something as-serious-as-your-life, you think in terms of inner fixity. When it's something confused and provisional, which the key stages of teen character often are, you end up with the depthless flibbertigibbet. On screen you only ever get one or the other. Ethan Hawke's Troy is all fixity, a 24-hour-a-day taste fascist, his self-absorbed no-compromise negativity intolerable, his creative intelligence dubious (he's a Greenwich Village folkie out of a 60s movie about beatniks). Lelaina, meanwhile, is all 80s mutability and surface: that is, until she chooses Troy over Mike. Truly, idealism is suffering—it must be. To catch the spirit of the 90s, Troy should have paired off with Mike; or else Mike, goaded once too often, should have lulled Troy. Perhaps, instead of the rather bogus true-love-triumphs plot-closure we get, there should have been a series of endings, *Wayne's World* style; as well as the *Graduate* ending, the *Easy Rider* ending, the *Something Wild* ending, the *Scooby Doo* ending...

The film does better when it comes to trash TV references—perhaps because these are the meat of the characters' comedy banter and peripheral to serious points being made, about idealism or about, as Lelaina puts it, "people trying to find out their identity without heroes or role models". Lelaina intends her documentary as Fred Wiseman for the 90s; In Your Face TV turns it into a cross between *The Living Soap* and *Get Stuffed!*, overdubbing Talking Heads ("The Road To Nowhere", naturally) to hammer home a comic point-missing cynicism. But it's a cynicism that the (real) movie can't muster the evidence to counteract, because—not understanding the dialectics of triviality and precision in pop culture reference—it doesn't know where to look. Most reviewers agree that it's the best bit of the film: perhaps because for all its parodic busyness, it seems less cluttered and anxious to please than the movie it appears in.

TIME, 2/21/94, p. 64, Richard Schickel

"I don't understand why things can't go back to normal at the end of the half-hour, like *The Brady Bunch*," one of the kids remarks as a new mini-crisis takes its place beside the last one nobody quite solved: "Because," someone replies, "Mr. Brady died of AIDs."

The idea that a 1970s sitcom could seem like paradise lost to a bunch of recent college grads looking (and not looking) for entry-level jobs while trying to find entry-level understanding of adulthood is a measure of something. The downsizing of American possibilities, maybe. Or the murkiness of American reality as it's refracted in sound-bite TV and a trashy commercial culture.

It may be, of course, that *Reality Bites* reflects no more than the latest styles in anomie among the young and the restive. But that in itself is a useful service when a lot of movies cater to this crowd but few attempt to understand them unsentimentally. Even fewer are lucky enough to have the wondrous Winona Ryder for the central role.

She's Lelaina, by day a production assistant on a fatuous morning TV show, by inclination a documentary filmmaker, trying to use her pals' lives and thoughts to make a statement about their generation. She's an up-and-doing spirit in a down-and-out milieu.

Ryder, in turn, is lucky with both script and direction. The former is by Helen Childress, 23, who not only has a good ear for the sound of her contemporaries but also knows how to shape it into dialogue that is pointed and full of unforced observations. Director Ben Stiller keeps things crisp, no small matter in a movie that features a fair amount of aimless activity and just plain lying around. The latter takes place in the "maxipad" Lelaina shares with Vickie (Janeane Garofalo), who sometimes imagines her own funeral as a scene from *Melrose Place* ("chokers and halter tops"), Sammy (Steve Zahn), who is gently receding into the wallpaper, and Troy (Ethan Hawke), who is a philosopher-couch potato, fired from his job as a newsstand clerk for eating a Snickers bar without authorization.

Troy is just the kind of broody lout a young woman like Lelaina goes for, despite the fact that junior TV-exec Michael (played by Stiller) is wooing her. Their triangle provides what passes for narrative structure, and its resolution is perhaps just a little too *Brady Bunch*—that is, too nice and neat. But that's a small price to pay for a movie in which Vickie, confronting a small, unexpected example of decency, finds it "screws up all my old ideas of good and evil." And in which a despondent Lelaina, seeking solace from an 900-number therapist, wails, "I can't evolve right now." The movie bobs along on this stream of funny offhandedness, never losing its balance. If it's 10 o'clock, and you want to know where your supposedly grownup children are, this is a good place to look for them.

VILLAGE VOICE, 2/22/94, p. 52, Georgia Brown

"How can we repair all the damage we inherited?" is the pertinent question asked by Lelaina Pierce (Winona Ryder), surely the most adorable valedictorian of the '90s. What's Lelaina's answer? Well, Lelaina doesn't know. It's just a question posed with all attendant irony at the opening of Ben Stiller's cute but toothless romantic comedy, *Reality Bites*. But at least someone is asking. Lelaina's best buddy, Troy Dyer (Ethan Hawke), wouldn't be caught dead speaking in earnest terms. "I would like to make a difference in people's lives," says Lelaina earnestly. "I'd like to buy them all coke," returns Troy.

Some may say that Lelaina can afford to be magnanimous. Her daddy (Joe Don Baker) has just given her a lightly used BMW and one year's use of a gas card. Lelaina even has a promising job as an assistant on Houston's popular TV show, *Good Morning, Grant*! (Grumpy old Grant is played by John Mahoney.) All around, girl graduates seem to be doing lots better than boy graduates. Even Lelaina's cynical roomie, Vickie (Janeane Garofalo in the Rosie O'Donnell role), is working her way up the ladder at the Gap. Stoned and confused, Troy and Sammy (Steve Zahn) lay about the house the women share.

Things change. Lelaina, in her BMW, runs into an ambitious video exec named Michael (Stiller) and releases his air bags.He admires her because she's unspoiled and "creative"; she likes his frank approval. Slovenly, sulky Troy is less than enchanted. Michael's arrival disturbs the group balance. Who will she choose, the yuppie or the youngblood? (For a long time we don't know what Troy's "thing" is: He turns out to be the leader of a band.) A friend wonders: Why do they always reject the nice Jewish guy for some dull and pretentious WASP?

Like *Dazed and Confused* (another Texas export), *Reality Bites* locates generation in shared media history. Linklater, however, creates determinedly eccentric narrative, whereas 23-year-old Helen Childress, writer of *Reality Bites*, is securely anchored in those sit-com conventions her characters want to reject. "I wish things did work out like on *The Brady Bunch*," Lelaina opines."Well, Mr. Brady died of AIDS," Troy reminds her. Of course, *Reality Bites* does work out like *The Brady Bunch*. And there's an audience for *that*.

Also reviewed in:
CHICAGO TRIBUNE, 2/18/94, Friday/p. A, Michael Wilmington
NATION, 3/21/94, p. 390, Stuart Klawans
NEW REPUBLIC, 3/28/94, p. 30, Stanley Kauffmann
NEW YORK TIMES, 2/18/94, p. C3, Caryn James
NEW YORKER, 3/7/94, p. 88, Terrence Rafferty
VARIETY, 1/31-2/6/94, p. 68, Leonard Klady
WASHINGTON POST, 2/18/94, p. G1, Rita Kempley
WASHINGTON POST, 2/18/94, Weekend/p. 55, Desson Howe

RECOLLECTIONS OF THE YELLOW HOUSE

An Invicta Filmes/GER coproduction with financial assistance from Instituto Portugués de Cinema/Radiotelevisão Portuguesa/EP Fundaçao Calouste Gulbenkian. *Executive Producer:* João Pedro Bénard. *Producer:* Joaquim Pinto and João Pedro Bénard. *Director:* João César Monteiro. *Screenplay (Portuguese with English subtitles):* João César Monteiro. *Director of Photography:* José António Loureiro. *Editor:* Helena Alves and Claudio Martinez. *Music:* Franz Shubert and Antonio Vivaldi. *Sound:* Rui Henriques and Francisco Veloso. *Sound Editor:* Vasco Pimentel. *Art Director:* Luis Monteiro. *Costumes:* Lucha Villas Boas. *Make-up:* Miguel Mendes. *Running time:* 120 minutes. *MPAA Rating:* Not Rated.

CAST: João César Monteiro (João de Deus); Manuela de Freitas (Dona Violeta); Sabina Sacchi (Mimi); Inêz de Medeiros (Mimi's Voice); Ruy Furtado (Señor Armando); Teresa Calado (Menina Julieta); Henrique Viana (Policeman); Duarte de Almeida (Ferdinando); Antonio Terrinha (Medic); Luis Miguel Cintra (Livio); Maria Angela de Oliveira (Deus' Mother); Violeta Sarzedas (Lonely Neighbour); Madalena Lua (Servant); João Pedro Bénard (Milkman's Employee); Manuel Gomez (Laurindo); Maria Da Luz Fernandez (Simple Neighbor); Vasco Sequeira (Tobernoiro); José Nunes (Official); João Santos (Beggar); Helena Ribas (Policewoman); Henrique Viana (Deputy Chief of Police); Adamastor Duarte (Policeman).

NEW YORK POST, 2/2/94, p. 31, Bill Hoffmann

Joao Cesar Monteiro's new Portuguese film, "Recollections of the Yellow House" bills itself as a "black comedy."

But forget about the comedy, the emphasis here is strictly bleak.

Monteiro directs himself as Joao de Deus, a middle-aged resident of a boarding house in a grimy Portuguese sea town.

Joao is a dyed-in-the-wool fatalist. He's so disheartened he even hesitates to buy a radio because the batteries, "like life," run out too fast.

His sole interests consist of complaining about pains in his stomach and groin and spying on Julieta—the beautiful, pouty-lipped daughter of his cranky landlady—as she bathes.

Joao is dying to carry her off to a new life of love. It's a dream he inevitably tries to realize with disastrous results.

The problem with Monteiro's character is that we rarely know what is going on inside his head. The reason for his cynical view of life remains unclear.

Oddly, Joao is the most sketchily drawn character. And since he's on screen constantly, it's impossible to be drawn in. We have to watch him like spectators up in the nosebleed section.

The most riveting performance comes from a fluffy white French poodle. The aging pooch has been soiling the carpet and the landlady orders the dog's owner to get rid of it.

Since the pet is too old for a new home, it's decided the dog should be put to sleep, and Joao agrees to deliver the beast to the doctor.

As a vet leads the doomed poodle by leash into the room where it'll be given a lethal injection, the dog suddenly stops, turns its head and gives one final, forlorn look to Joao as if to say, "Why?"

It's a glance that is completely heartbreaking and is the movie's most poignant moment."

If only Monteiro could have supplied more.

SIGHT AND SOUND, 8/91, p. 51, Jonathan Romney

Impoverished, middle-aged João de Deus lives in a Lisbon boarding-house, where he is plagued by bedbugs and his tyrannical landlady Dona Violeta. In love with her young daughter Julieta, a clarinet-playing police cadet, he spies on her and drinks her bathwater. João befriends Mimi, a young prostitute living in the house, and helps her to have her poodle put down. After Mimi's death, João finds her savings hidden in a doll. He asks Julieta to go away with him; when she refuses, he attempts to rape her, only to be interrupted by Dona Violeta. When João's mother dies, he is left destitute. After impersonating a military officer, he is committed to a lunatic asylum, but with the help of another inmate magically escapes, emerging finally from the Lisbon sewers.

Few directors can ever have cast themselves so unflatteringly as João César Monteiro. His João de Deu is an emaciated malingerer, self-centred, apparently heartless, fetishistic, an inept lover and attempted rapist, and narcissistic to an extreme, although his is a narcissism that verges on self-loathing. Monteiro originally offered the part to Roberto Benigni, but that would have made a very different film, and would certainly have made João a more likeable, more frivolous character. As it is, the director's presence here—he resembles a gangling, beaky Groucho Marx—dominates the tone of the film. Monteiro's jaundiced self-portraiture extends to Lisbon itself, whose touristic charms are effectively sabotaged during the opening shot—a long tracking view of the city, seen from a boat, accompanied by João's grumbling voice-over about bedbugs and his aching testicles.

Monteiro's shambling, poker-faced characterisation owes much to the anti-heroes of a literature of defiant introspection. There are echoes of Dostoevsky's *Underground Man* (the film's title, Monteiro has pointed out, also echoes his *House of the Dead*) and of Knut Hamsun's ascetic heroes, but more particularly of Beckett's early low-life novels, notably Murphy, and of Céline's amorally bitter incarnations of despair. What prevents the film from becoming the miserabilist testament it at first threatens to be is an extremely dry, poised sense of humour, much of it concentrated in Monteiro's performance which,
with painstakingly slow pacing, defuses the seriousness of anything else on screen.

The leisurely effect is furthered at times by a Tati-like attention to the arrangement of space within the frame—one scene has a group of neighbours scattered around a courtyard arguing, while João wanders curiously from one to another. Visually austere, and orchestrated in long slow takes, static framings and occasional languid tracking shots, the film lives up to its title with an all-pervading yellowness. 'Casa Amarela' is a Portuguese expression for the lunatic asylum, but

Dona Violeta's house is also yellow, as apparently is all of Lisbon, and as is João's own desiccated frame.

João's world might be read as a portrayal of Portugal as an effete, isolated society living on the 'recollections' of its former glories—Dona Violeta protests that her house is not old, but 'baroque'—in which the creative classes have degenerated into jaundiced, amoral *flâneurs* like João. When arrested and asked what he does, he peers through his stolen officer's monocle and replies, "I'm a left-wing intellectual", but the only evidence of intellectual activity is the fact that his pocket contains a copy of Hölderlin's Death of *Empedocles* (which the officer mistakes for a whodunit), and an early scene in which he undertakes to write to order a piece of sensationalistic news copy.

The mystery of João's identity, and how he came to be in Dona Violeta's house, extends into a wider sense of dislocated history that underlies the film's whole structure. Both in characterisation and in plot, the film is built on ellipses and inconsistencies. As well as being anti-narrative, it is resolutely anti-spectacle: Monteiro cuts away just as we think we are about to see a striptease act with a crocodile and a giant tube of toothpaste; and as Mimi begins to undress, the camera tracks slowly up to a poster on the wall, depicting Erich von Stroheim in full military regalia (a guise João later ineffectually apes).

It is by refusing to show anything remotely extraordinary that the film sustains a surreal tone even while eschewing surrealism. It is only at the end that events take a fantastic turn, with João's magical escape and final apotheosis, grandly emerging from the sewers in a posture echoing Max Schreck in Nosferatu, and finally dissolving before our eyes (a woman's cryptic voice-over, and the sound of bird song, vaguely suggest that he might have metamorphosed into a blackbird).

It is a fittingly inconsequential ending for a film that steadfastly refuses to resolve itself into any sort of traditional coherence, and a final prank by the driest of pranksters at the expense of Lisbon, and the viewer.

VILLAGE VOICE, 2/8/94, p. 64, Lawrence Chua

He is so skinny, he would almost have to tie knots in his legs to make knees. The scrawny but elegant protagonist of *Recollections of the Yellow House.* Senhor João (played by director and actor João César Monteiro) bears the burden of festering oral sores, ravenous lice, and pendulously swollen testicles. But watching João maneuver throughout this desolate and twisted burlesque is as much fun as knocking back a few Thorazine and watching, say, Almodóvar's *What Have I Done to Deserve This*?

Resident in a crumbling boarding house, Senhor João is so obsessed with his landlady's sullen daughter that he gulps down the soap froth she leaves behind in the bath, pausing only to pick a pubic hair from his teeth. Yet. João is only one among the host of freaks who live under the roof of the old yellow house. Fidgeting under the poverty of daily life, João shuffles deadpan into all of their lives: the anal landlady who continually reminds him that his barren room is "for one thing only," the senile black marketeer, the aging hustler who puts her poodle to sleep after it pees on the landlady's velvet drapes ... Somehow, João emerges from these encounters seemingly unscathed. "My age is greater than my feelings," he tells one of his neighbors over a nightcap. "It's my way of getting along." When the same neighbor dies of a botched abortion, João goes directly into her room and steals her savings.

But João is no simple emotional cripple. His most brutal actions belie the film's subversive intentions. When he is thrown out onto the street, the film's anarchistic humor sharpens into an eloquent demolition of the prisons of "normalcy" and "deviation." Eventually shut behind the walls of a mental institution, João waxes on the place of "proper" behavior in a society gone berserk. Monteiro the director navigates the brutally blurred lines between humor and horror with elan in this punishing comedy. Like his character João, he is constantly pushing at the frontiers of social etiquette.

Also reviewed in:
NEW YORK TIMES, 2/3/94, p. C18, Stephen Holden
VARIETY, 10/25-31/89, p. 34

RED

A Miramax Films release of an MK2 Productions/France 3 Cinema/CAB Productions/"Tor" Production film with the participation of Canal Plus. *Executive Producer:* Yvon Crenn. *Producer:* Marin Karmitz and Gérard Ruey. *Director:* Krzysztof Kieślowski. *Screenplay: (French with English subtitles):* Krzysztof Piesiewicz and Krzysztof Kieślowski. *Director of Photography:* Piotr Sobocinski. *Editor:* Jacques Witta. *Music:* Zbigniew Preisner and Van Den Budenmayer. *Choreographer:* Brigitte Matteuzzi. *Sound:* William Flageollet. *Sound Editor:* Piotr Zawadzki, Jean-Claude Laureux, Francine Lemaitre, and Nicolas Naegelen. *Casting:* Margot Capelier. *Production Designer:* Gérard Ruey. *Set Designer:* Claude Lenoir. *Costumes:* Corinne Jorry. *Make-up:* Nathalie Tanner and Catherine Zingg. *Stunt Coordinator:* Lucien Abbet, Phillippe Calame, and Silvio Stoppa. *Running time:* 96 minutes. *MPAA Rating:* Not Rated.

CAST: Irène Jacob (Valentine); Jean-Louis Trintignant (Judge Joseph Kern); Frédérique Feder (Karin); Jean-Pierre Lorit (Auguste); Samuel Lebihan (The Photographer); Marion Stalens (The Veterinarian); Teco Celio (The Barman); Bernard Escalon (The Record Salesman); Jean Schlegel (The Neighbor); Elzbieta Jasinska (The Girl); Paul Vermeulen (Karin's Friend); Jean-Marie Daunas (The Theater Guard); Roland Carey (The Smuggler).

FILMS IN REVIEW, 3-4/95, p. 60, Andy Pawelczak

Red is the third film in Krzysztof Kieslowski's *Tricolor* trilogy, named after the colors of the French flag. In *Blue*, emblematic of liberty, he told the cryptic tale of a woman's life after the death of her composer husband.

White, for equality, offered an absurdist view of contemporary Poland as it followed the hopelessly crossed love of its Chaplinesque hero. *Red*, representing fraternity, is the least elliptical and most emotionally direct of the three, an existential fairy tale set in a Geneva rendered magical by Kieslowski's color scheme and fluid camera work. It's an odd film, simultaneously hokey and haunting, ironic and deeply romantic, and how you respond to it depends, more than is usual I think, on your ability to suspend disbelief and go along with the film.

The movie is about a misanthropic recluse and a young woman who bring each other back to life. Valentine (Irene Jacob) is a beautiful model involved in a bad, hopeless love affair with a man we never see on the screen—we hear his voice on the telephone as he suspiciously asks if she's alone. Through an accident she meets the Judge (Jean-Louis Trintignant), an elderly man who spends his time eavesdropping on other people's telephone conversations. She's appalled and tells him so, and her denunciation lights a spark in his barren heart. This story is crosscut with the story of a young law student in love with a woman who betrays him. At first we're confused about how the two stories connect, but by the end Kieslowski builds in enough parallels that the denouement has the appearance of inevitability. The movie leaves it up to us to decide if we've been watching the mechanics of fate or pure, blind chance—or the flimflammery of the filmmaker.

The movie has an ambience that I can only describe as a kind of secular religiosity. When Valentine walks across the runway in a fashion show, Kieslowski shoots the scene from overhead and bathes it in a darkly glowing, sacerdotal light. He's not being sardonic, not making some obvious point about our fallen condition and the false gods we worship. In his complicated, Polish, half-ironic, half-ardent way, he means it—Valentine is a kind of Beatrice figure to both the Trintignant character and Kieslowski. At one point, Trintignant says that in order to help her troubled brother Valentine only has to *be*, and it's a clue to the film's deepest meaning. As played by the delicately beautiful Irene Jacob, Valentine is the embodiment of what the film is all about—the radiance of being.

As played by Trintignant, the retired Judge is initially a sinister, burnt out case. When we first see him, his face has an ashen pallor and his eyes are dead in their sockets. Like the jurist in Camus' novel *The Fall*, he has come to realize that judging other people is a futile exercise in vanity and he's finishing his days as an embittered, guilt ridden voyeur. Once he begins to awaken under the influence of Valentine's beauty and innocence, he becomes a quasi-mystical fairy godfather. The central scenes in the film involve the Judge's conversations with Valentine about guilt and innocence, truth and point of view. In addition to being a coded way of talking about the movies, about our desire to sit in the darkness and ferret out the secrets of the people on the screen, it's all a kind of high existential hokum. But Kieslowski films these scenes with such romantic exactitude and passion, capturing every nuance of expression in the two faces, that they become mysteriously genuine and moving.

Kieslowski recently announced his retirement from filmmaking, and *Red* has a summing-up, valedictory feeling with the Trintignant character as a stand-in for the director. In a certain sense, the real subject of the film is light—the way Trintignant's face is lit up from within, the luminosity of Irene Jacob's beauty as she's photographed against a billowing red curtain, the evanescent glow in the air as the sun dips below a mountain. It's an appropriate way to end a career in film—the celebration of light as metaphor and as the actual physical medium of cinema.

LOS ANGELES TIMES, 12/2/94, Calendar/p. 1, Kenneth Turan

Except for his imposing name, there is little about Polish filmmaker Krzysztof Kieslowski that fits the conventional American image of a great director. His public statements are spare, his subject matter intimate rather than epic, and his interest in anything as flamboyant as a cult of personality is nonexistent.

Yet, as "Red" underscores, Kieslowski is likely the world's most accomplished director, that rare artist with a virtuoso's exhilarating grasp of all aspects of filmmaking from editing and cinematography to music and acting.

More than that, Kieslowski is the type of master whose hallmark is unobtrusiveness, whose skill is the more impressive for its lack of self-important posturing, And his interest in narrative, emotion and the human condition make his films so accessible it is possible to underestimate how accomplished they are.

Coming after the invigorating "Blue" and the bitingly comic "White," "Red" is the final film in Kieslowski's "Three Colors" trilogy, inspired by the French flag and the motto of "Liberty, Equality, Fraternity." Co-written with longtime collaborator Krzysztof Piesiewicz, "Red" concentrates on fraternity, on the yearning for connection that even the most detached lives are prey to.

Simple on one level, profound on another, "Red" is also the best kind of adult fairy tale, a romance conceived and executed by a pessimist, For when a filmmaker as stern and uncompromising as the man who directed "Decalogue" decides to tell a story of love and hope, it is bound to be both different and convincing.

Kieslowski also believes in the importance of coincidence, and "Red" is rife with it. A tightly controlled film about the randomness of events, "Red" has as a major theme the pivotal role of chance and happenstance in shaping and defining its characters' lives.

At the center of things is Valentine (Irène Jacob), a young model living in a small apartment in Geneva. Though she is unaware of it, "Red's" elegant camera movements reveal that a handsome young man named Auguste (Jean-Pierre Lorit), busy with his preparation for exams to be a judge, lives in similar apartment just around the corner.

While Auguste has a beautiful blonde girlfriend named Karin (Frederique Feder), Valentine is involved in a ticklish phone relationship with a young man named Michel who is working outside the country. Fiddling with her car radio one night, Valentine hits a dog named Rita. The animal's collar lists an address, but returning the wounded Rita is not a simple affair.

For Rita's owner turns out to be an icily reserved man named Joseph Kern (Jean-Louis Trintignant), an unshaven former judge who is both reclusive and apparently contemptuous of all feeling. A "formidable individual, unapologetic about his misanthropy, he coldly tells Valentine he is indifferent to the dog's fate and would like nothing so much as for her to go away.

Leave she does, as disgusted at his attitude as he is at her evident concern and generosity. But circumstances bring her back to the judge's house, and though nothing conventional is to be expected, one of the accomplishments of "Red" is how convincingly it depicts the delicate and highly unlikely emotional connection that is forged between these two.

But there is more to Kieslowski's web than that. There is always Auguste, the young man who unknowingly lives in the periphery of Valentine's existence, and whose own life is gradually revealed to have curious parallels to that of the former judge. Kieslowski has dealt with this theme before, most notably in "The Double Life of Veronique," which also starred Jacob, but he handles it here with lovely delicacy.

Presented naked on a page "Red's" plot has the potential to sound contrived, but the skills of Kieslowski and his team, starting with Zbigniew Preisner's ethereal music and Piotr Sobocinski's gliding camera work (which looks effortless but at times required hours of work for the briefest shots), obviate that possibility.

Critical as well are the remarkable performances of the film's two leads. Jacob, a radiant actress with an open, wonderfully expressive face, must have served as much as a muse for Kieslowski during filming as she does for Joseph Kern in the finished product. And Trintignant, perhaps the preeminent French actor of his generation, is faultless opposite her, brittle anti-matter to her vibrant matter.

As with "Blue" and "White," Kieslowski uses this film's title color as a visual accent, forcing us to notice the bright red of a car, a Swiss Army knife, even a cigarette package. And though all three films stand alone, the director couldn't resist a finale that will be most fully understood by viewers who've seen the previous pair.

Kieslowski has also repeated a scene from both of the earlier files, showing an old woman vainly trying to stuff a wine bottle into a recycling bin, but with a difference. Here, for the first time, someone comes to the woman's aid. If "Red" does turn out to be, as Kieslowski claims, his final film as a director, there can be no doubt but that he's gone out in brilliant style.

NEW STATESMAN & SOCIETY, 11/11/94, p. 33, Jonathan Romney

It is often thought that the ultimate test of a film is whether it holds up on video. It is all very well, the theory goes, to sit cradled in the dark with several hundred other people engrossed in the quasi-religious glory of Panavision and Dolby stereo. But to be a real film, it must hold its own on the small screen.

This method quite often works; but sometimes it can reveal the absurdity of even thinking that film and video make in any way for related experiences. I have now seen Krzysztof Kieslowski's *Three Colours*: *Red* twice, the first time on screen, then on video. The first time I was quite awestruck; I felt not only that I had witnessed something genuinely magical, but also that all my misgivings about *Blue* and *White*, the preceding parts of Kieslowski's multinational trilogy, were misplaced. On the second viewing, though, I began to wonder whether I had simply let myself be conned by the film's considerable art, and that all its apparent depth was pure illusionist's sham.

I am still not entirely sure if *Red* is a profound achievement or a dour, tendentious piece of stuffed-shirt metaphysics. At a pinch, I might tend to the first opinion, if only because these days, the very fact of making a genuinely ambivalent film has to stand as some sort of profundity. *Red* is by far the warmest and the most satisfying of the trilogy, pointing in the direction of integration and reconciliation after the chilliness of *Blue* (about a woman cutting herself off from society) and the lugubrious cynicism of *White* (in which a hapless innocent learned to play society at all its own meanest tricks).

Set in Geneva, it's about chance and control: a young model, Valentine (Irène Jacob), by chance runs over a dog, which leads her to an encounter with its owner, embittered retired judge Kern (Jean-Louis Trintignant); he plays a god-like role, eavesdropping by radio people's telephone conversations and drawing a mental map of their lives and those lives' contingent causes. The story is rife with evident contrivance; for example, it is implied (only a second viewing makes this apparent) that Kern's radio-hamming is itself the direct cause of Valentine's running into the dog. The story abounds with the echoes and mirrors that underwrote Kieslowski's *The Double Life of Véronique*.

There may be a simple explanation of why I liked *Red* less the second time: it may be that, once you've pieced together its jigsaw narrative, there is simply no picture there the second time. It's almost a disappointment to find things falling into place. But part of the film's story is about the gradual discovery that finally there is no real story—not much happens on screen, the main events serving to bring people together so that they can tell each other about past events or make prognoses for the future.

But my main reason for liking *Red* less the second time, is that on video there really are dimensions lacking that narrative alone cannot account for. For a start, Kieslowski's films depend, more than most others, on the communal experience of being in a cinema, sitting silently for 96 minutes, prepared to take things seriously. (It is precisely Kieslowski's contract with the audience, this promise of serious content in exchange for serious attention, that lays him open to attacks as a retrograde high-art obscurantist). In films that largely concern society and individuals' ability or failure to interconnect, there's a very poignant sense that cinema is one of the few things that can, if only for 90 minutes at a time, mould us into micro-communities, congregations.

In addition, if there is a sense that there is less to Kieslowski's film than meets the eye—and what meets the eye is precisely the immediate impression that there is *more* than meets the eye—it is because Kieslowski is absolutely speaking the language of cinema. His films have arguments that solicit our intellectual responses, and *Red* at times expresses them more bluntly, if not crassly, than usual. What gives his films their genuine intellectual content is the way that they bypass the verbal and go for the emotive, the tactile, the visual—the way that they present *plastic* arguments.

Mystificatory though this may appear, it amounts only to this—Kieslowski might not be a great thinker, but when he is great it is because he is thinking in cinema. The moments in his films that strike chords are the moments that are most purely tactile, that cannot easily be spelled out. When Kieslowski gives us moments as moments, his films occasionally achieve the transcendent quality his adepts claim for them: these are the moments when he captures a hazy reflection in an amber paperweight or catches Irène Jacob's face in the rain (both in *The Double Life of Véronique*), or when he lets Zbigniew Preisner's music swell up in a particularly rapturous fashion.

All he is doing is giving us cinema to the hilt—and just as *Jurassic Park*'s dinosaurs don't carry their full weight when shrunk into 12 inches square, so you need the full cinema screen to catch properly the generosity and fine definitions of the music of Kieslowski's films. That Kieslowski aims for the abstract impact of music is signalled by the fact that the recurring artist figures in his films are musicians—notably, the apocryphal Dutch composer Van Den Budenmayer. (A tentative theory about the trilogy: it is structured around the sensations—*Blue*: sight, *White*: touch, ie ownership; *Red*: hearing).

Kieslowski is one of the few directors around who *scores* his films on every level. Piotr Sobocinski, his cinematographer on *Red*, has attested to the unusual closeness of his collaboration with Kieslowski, not just in the film's lighting, but in its whole conception; and it is clear from every shot just how much the look of the film is thought right through. It is fair to say that the colour red, with its various registers, is the film's true setting, rather than the city of Geneva.

Both *Blue* and *Red* suffer from an over-reliance on rhapsodic visual language which I find hard to trust. Kieslowski's poetry of the luminous may be more thoroughly integrated into the shape of his films than the superficial neon-ism of a Besson or a Beineix; but it may ultimately be of the same nature. Kieslowski relies massively on a certain glamour, most obviously in his use of the iconic beauty of Juliette Binoche in *Blue* and Irène Jacob here and in *Véronique*: and there is something calculating in the presentation of the numerous small ecstasies that Jacob seems infinitely susceptible to.

Watching her swoon in the rain in *Véronique*, or gulp joyously at a glass of water in *Red*, there's an uncomfortable sense that we're being persuaded to fall in love with her, in the most classic Hollywood fashion. *Red* ends with Jacob's face on a massive hoarding, an advert for chewing gum; this could be the most sophisticated film ever to use what are effectively the seductions of advertising. Then again, Kieslowski—who has announced *Red* as his farewell to cinema—could be one jump ahead of us: the brand of the gum is "Hollywood".

NEW YORK, 11/28/94, p. 85, David Denby

The Swiss actress Irène Jacob plays a model in Krzyztof Kieslowski's *Red*, but Jacob has softer and rounder features than most models—a warmth of flesh where angular severity would seem to be required. Not that anyone cares: Jacob seems approachable, open-eyed, womanish, beautiful but not chic. If only Kieslowski could figure out what to do with her! In both *The Double Life of Veronique* (1991) and this movie, the Polish director, current hero of the international cinema, draws on Irène Jacob's palpable readiness, her sensitivity and emotional transparency. Yet in neither movie has she possessed much specific character. For Kieslowski, I suspect, Jacob is not a dramatic actress, and not any woman in particular, but Woman herself, an everlasting possibility of radiant creatureliness. In *Veronique*, she played two women named Veronique, one in Poland, one in France, who saw each other only once but were connected by a filigree of coincidence and thematic cross-reference. Jacob appears to be the vessel of Kieslowski's central theme: the way modern people are utterly isolated in their material lives yet connected somehow by spirit. Irène Jacob is Kieslowski's metaphysical doll.

With *Red*, Kieslowski has completed the trilogy that began earlier with *Blue* and *White*, and it would be wonderful to announce that the three films amounted to a major work. (They've been hailed as such in Europe and in some quarters in America.) Unfortunately, it's not so; and, if I'm not mistaken, there's an element of dismay and put-on lurking in the praise. One senses an illusion close to cracking—the dissolution of a set of assumptions that animates a half-dozen film festivals a year. The truth is, the European cinema has lost its authority. It's not that there aren't good films every year. Of course there are (and there may be other good ones we don't see). But great films are not being made—not the way they were each year in the fifties and sixties—and much of what we see here of French, German, Italian, and Eastern European movies seems feeble or imitative or cultured in a trance-like way that means little to us. A nihilistic pop masterpiece like *Pulp Fiction* blows away European movies even faster than it does most American movies. For good or ill, American movies are eating the world market, and until new economic conditions emerge for the film business on the Continent, we may have to do without major European directors.

There are moments of great beauty in everything Kieslowski does, but he's essentially a constructor of intricate puzzles; an artificer, perhaps, but not an artist. He's a master of somber, disconsolate moods, of harmoniously depressed tonalities. The three films of the trilogy, whose colors refer to the French flag and to the French ideals, respectively, of liberty, equality, and fraternity, mark a passage from isolation to communion. In *Blue* (liberty), a composer dies, and his widow makes a separate life for herself; in *White* (equality), an impotent husband—a Pole—revenges himself against his dismissive French wife by becoming a rich man and trapping her in a murder charge. And now, in *Red*, Valentine (Jacob) and a young man, Auguste (Jean-Pierre Lorit), who is studying to be a judge, live around the corner from each other in Geneva, each impinging on the other's life, circulating in the other's aura, but they never quite meet—until a catastrophe brings them together at the end of the movie. Kieslowski gives his characters weight and presence just by observing them: The camera style isolates people on a city street and enfolds them in the rapture of silence and contemplation.

Valentine hits a dog with her car, and takes the animal to its owner, an embittered retired judge (Jean-Louis Trintignant) living alone in a dark-shadowed house. The judge spies on his neighbors, listening to their telephone calls, and he seems to know everything. Who is he? God, perhaps; God as a failure. Valentine begins to love the old man, whose life demonstrates amazing parallels with that of Auguste (whom she doesn't know). But in the long, groping scenes between Jacob and Trintignant, filled with tentative yet hollowly theatrical conversation, the movie falls into a swoon and dies. Kieslowski is trying to get at something mystical in these connections, but he's inept at staging conversation—he's no Ingmar Bergman—and inertia takes over. Indeed, the only narrative drive in all three of these movies is the story of the husband's revenge in life, and that was surprisingly nasty stuff. Woman as bitch, woman as redeemer! Kieslowski constructs his movies with ineffable moments and with tiny visual motifs touched by grace. Yet the avant-garde techniques cannot conceal an extraordinarily weak dramatic sense and some very hoary ideas about women. Irène Jacob is no more than an enigma in *Red*, a luminously beautiful eternal feminine. One waits for another director to notice that she's also a woman.

NEWSDAY, 11/23/94, Part II/p. B3, John Anderson

In the event that the term "Oscar-caliber" has any lingering meaning, it's time to reassess. In its infinite, intractable and byzantine wisdom, the Academy of Motion Picture Arts and Sciences last week disallowed Krzysztof Kieslowski's "Red" as Switzerland's entry for best foreign film, because the rules don't recognize it as Swiss. Never mind that, according those same rules, the film doesn't qualify as an entry from any country. Or that it is clearly the best foreign film of the year.

But let the Oscars render themselves artistically moot. "Red," the third and final movement in Kieslowski's "Three Colors"trilogy is a prickly, irritating, exhilarating, mordant, bittersweet film, a virtuoso technical performance—the Polish director's mastery of the medium seems absolute—and an archly constructed puzzle within a puzzle.

In "Blue," Kieslowski explored the loneliness of *liberte*; in "White" he examined the void of ultimate *egalite*. In "Red," where the color is a constant carmine filament, or, maybe a pulse, the cosmic joke is about the caprice of fate, the fallacy of human isolation, the existence of a supreme being—who in terms of the movie is Kieslowski—and, not coincidentally, the elusiveness of *fraternite*.

Like Kieslowski's "The Double Life of Veronique"—in which a woman and her double live parallel existences—"Red" is about luck and coincidence and whether that's all they are. Like "Veronique," "Red" stars Irene Jacob, the beautiful Swiss actress who plays Valentine—and who, like her name, is an emblem of romantic optimism.

A dancer and model, Valentine is oblivious to the idea that her vocations feed on youth, or that her heart could be broken, or that evil exists. When she injures a dog with her car one night, she naturally picks it up and finds its owner, a lonely ex-judge (Jean-Louis Trintignant), who appalls her with his callousness. Her emotional education has begun.

Valentine and the judge are both rising and converging: Her compassion is born of innocence, his of a knowledge of his own flawed nature. He's seen too much, she's seen nothing. And so, Valentine is lovely but blank (Jacob wears a look of perpetual hope), and the judge, who has led a loveless life and spends his days electronically monitoring his neighbors' phone calls (and is given a gristled portrayal by Trintignant), is inspired by innocence to love again.

From the beginning of the film, we have also watched the progress of Auguste (Jean-Pierre Lorit), a young lawyer whose girlfriend Karin (Frederique Feder) will betray him. The biographical similarities between Auguste and the judge are revealed gradually. Auguste and Valentine will cross paths constantly but obliviously, never meeting; she is busy conducting a telephone relationship with the unseen, unpleasant Michel. But we observe that Auguste's life is repeating Kern's, and, if not for kismet, Auguste and Valentine could be lovers. And if not for the tyranny of time, so could Valentine and the judge.

Part of the fun of "Red"—which is really more demanding than fun is watching Kieslowski impose his manipulating will with such whimsical abandon, producing an intricate choreography of missed connections; And part of the film's magic is how both life-affirming and melancholic this all turns out to be. The characters play a kind of blind man's bluff with each other, never aware of how interwoven their lives are; yet they are. and they suffer because of it. But the way Kieslowski "proves" the existence of a spiritual commonality is cause for celebration. Luck, in the cruel "Red" world, isn't just a fact. It can be a blessing.

NEWSWEEK, 11/28/94, p. 66, David Ansen

With "Red", the last and most stunning installment in Krzystof Kieslowski's "Three Colors" trilogy ("Blue" and "White" preceded it), the 53-year-old Polish director has announced his retirement. Even if he hadn't, this mysterious, fate-haunted film would still have the feeling of a summing up. Those who know this superb filmmaker's work ("The Double Life of Veronique," "The Decalogue") will recognize echoes and themes from all his movies in "Red." But no homework is required to appreciate the ravishing images of this fable on the theme of fraternity.

Kieslowski's heroine is a young student/model in Geneva, Valentine (Irene Jacob), whose accidental encounter with a reclusive ex-judge Jean-Louis Trintignant) changes the course of both their lives. She's run over his dog in the street; tracking him down to tell him, she discovers a bitterly indifferent, isolated man who secretly eavesdrops on his neighbors. "Red" is a love story, but in a mystical, almost metaphysical sense. Valentine's emotional generosity frees the misanthrope from his isolation. But too many years, and too much experience, separate them—they're not meant to be lovers. Their love for each other finds its form in her future relationship with a young Geneva law student, Auguste, whose life eerily parallels the judge's, a man Valentine will not meet until the film's final twist of destiny. The "story" of "Red" is, in realist terms, farfetched and schematic—sort of a high-toned version of a Claude Lelouch movie about predestined love. Its ideas, reduced to their kernels, flirt with banality. The real mystery of "Red" is how Kieslowski, through the magic of his exquisite eye and the conviction of his feelings, transforms such dicey material into an exhilarating experience. Is it profound or is it facile? When a movie gives you goose bumps, it may not matter.

SIGHT AND SOUND, 11/94, p. 54, Phillip Kemp

Valentine Dussaut, a model and Auguste Bruner, a law student, live near each other in Geneva and their paths frequently cross, though they don't know each other. Valentine's boyfriend Michel is a film-maker currently based in London, and the separation is straining their relationship. Auguste, who is preparing for his final exams, is having an affair with Karin, a slightly older woman who runs a telephone weather-forecast service.

One night Valentine accidentally runs over and injures a dog. Finding an address on its collar she takes the animal—an Alsatian bitch called Rita—back to its owner. He proves to be a retired judge, Joseph Kern, who tells her to do what she likes with the dog. Having had Rita's injuries attended to, Valentine learns the dog is pregnant and adopts her. One day Rita runs away. Valentine follows her back to Kern's house, where she discovers that the judge, an elderly and embittered man, spends his time tapping his neighbours' phones.

Initially disgusted, Valentine gradually becomes intrigued by Kern, realising that what motivates him is a desperate attempt to understand other people. For her part, she confides her own concerns: uneasiness about Michel, worry about her mother who is old and lonely, and her younger brother who is on drugs. Kern decides to denounce himself, and is prosecuted. Auguste, having passed his exams, is involved in the case. Karin goes to meet him at court, but encounters another man and starts an affair with him. Tormented with jealousy, Auguste spies on them making love.

Kern recognises in Auguste a counterpart of himself when young. When Valentine announces her intention of visiting Michel in London, Kern manoeuvres her into taking the same cross-Channel ferry on which Auguste is travelling. Although the forecast (according to Karin's weather service) is for fine weather, a tremendous storm blows up and the ferry capsizes. Only a handful of passengers survive: they include Julie and Olivier (from *Blue*), Karol and Dominique (*White*), and Valentine and Auguste. Kern, surrounded by Rita's puppies, sees on television an image of Valentine and Auguste standing side by side.

Connections, misconnections, coincidences and crossed lines: Kieslowski's films are full of them, and *Three Colours Red* even more than most. The film starts with a phone call whose electronic path (borrowing an idea from Truffaut's *Baisers volés*) the camera tracks along ducts and under the ocean—only for it to remain unanswered at the other end. All the film's main characters are phone freaks: Karin makes her living by phone, and Auguste has to dial her weather service to contact her; the judge taps into other people's calls; Valentine and Michel not only conduct their whole affair by phone, but constantly debate who called whom when and what they were doing at the time. In the background, meanwhile, anonymous extras dart in and out of phone booths, ceaselessly trying to get through. The impression is of a society desperate to make contact, but achieving it for the most part indirectly if at all.

"I feel there's something important happening around me," muses Valentine, "and it scares me." As before in *The Double Life of Véronique*, Irène Jacob conveys a sensibility operating at full stretch, picking up vibrations she's scarcely conscious of. (The huge advertising poster on which her face appears is not pasted up, but stretched taut on fabric over a frame.) But receptivity is a two-way process—it also transmits. Valentine's openness to life infects the judge (Trintignant's very skin seems dried out by self-loathing) and entices him out of his misanthropy—just as in *Blue*, Olivier and the stripper Lucille between them lured Julie from her numbed seclusion.

Liberty, equality and fraternity, as Kieslowski himself hinted, prove something of a red (white and blue) herring: the films' true theme emerges as social cohesion, the interdependence that links us to each other whether we like it or not. In each film someone tries to opt out. The widowed Julie (*Blue*) retreats into isolation; Karol (*White*) turns himself into a ruthless entrepreneur; in *Red* Kern sets up as God, spying on and controlling the lives of others. In the end each one is drawn back into the common flow, yielding to the pull of emotions and mutual ties. Common to all three films is the incident of a stooped old person struggling to push a bottle into a bottle bank, disregarded in *Blue* and *White* by Julie and Karol respectively. In *Red* the image is resolved as Valentine, the trilogy's warmest and most positive character, goes to help. The message adapts Auden: we must help one another or die.

But if *Red* works well enough on this redemptive level, it may be too superficial a reading; it's always risky to take Kieslowski ("Things are very rarely said straight out in my films") at face value. *Red* ostensibly rounds off the whole trilogy with a neat happy ending, but the closer one looks at it the more the ironies obtrude. For a start, just how "happy" is it for 1400 people to drown so that two strangers can meet? And can we assume from that final freeze-frame of Auguste and Valentine that they'll fall in love, or even notice each other? Kern may want to think so, and so may we, but there's precious little evidence for the idea. Kieslowski goes further, piling on the implausibilities: both couples from *Blue* and *White* turn up among the survivors—as if to mock our desire for a cosily romantic conclusion.

Viewed end-on from this sceptical angle, *Red* starts to unravel backwards—or rather to re-ravel into a different pattern. Maybe the whole ending is in the mind of the judge, still yearning to manipulate the lives of those around him? An outrageous series of coincidences links Kern with Auguste—both dropped a law-book that opened at the perfect exam question, both spied on their lover in bed with another man. Taken literally, this would be trickily over-contrived: but not if we accept that the two men, like Veronique and Veronika, are each other's doubles—only this time with a 40-year slippage. Kern and Valentine are soul-mates, and but for the age discrepancy they should have been lovers. With Auguste as the judge's surrogate (or his wish-fulfilment?), they can be.

Like all Kieslowski's films, *Red* is an elusive artefact, refracting different dramatic and emotional patterns according to viewpoint. As the third part of a trilogy it also casts new light on its predecessors, and anyone seeing it may well feel tempted to check out *Blue* and *White* again to see how they've changed. That would be worth doing, if only to enjoy the deftly contrasted visual games played with the three keynote colours. After the melancholy saturations of blue and the orgasmic flashes of white, red in the latest film serves as a focal point within each frame, picking out a jeep or a jacket, a girder or a flashing light. And if the technique occasionally recalls a Marlboro ad, Kieslowski is there before us: in one scene he has Auguste come home holding a carton of cigarettes. No prizes for guessing which brand.

TIME, 12/5/94, p. 93, Richard Corliss

Storytellers are tyrants, masters of sadistic caprice. They invent a character, put him through hell, maybe kill him off—ah, maybe not—to make a moral point, or just because they feel like it. They resemble hanging judges, and sometimes they must feel uneasy about their power over life and death, love and loneliness. Perhaps that is what prodded Polish director Krzysztof Kieslowski and his writing collaborator, Krzysztof Piesiewicz (himself a lawyer), to create *Three Colors: Red*, a movie about a judge racked by guilt, regret and his need to keep eavesdropping on other people's crimes and pain.

Decades ago, this Swiss judge (Jean-Louis Trintignant) was obliged to determine the case of a defendant with whom he had a personal score to settle—the accused had stolen the only woman the judge had ever loved. The judge passed sentence, then took to a life of electronic snooping on his neighbors. Into this lair of auditory voyeurism comes Valentine (Irene Jacob), a student and fashion model. Her passionate good nature stirs memories of that other young woman in the judge's life. He is touched, perhaps enough to end his sordid pastime.

Red is the final installment in the Kieslowski-Piesiewicz *Blue, White* and *Red* trilogy. The films treat the subjects of liberty, equality and fraternity in three different countries (France, Poland, Switzerland). *Red* was shot in Geneva, with a mostly Swiss cast, yet when the Swiss submitted the film for a foreign-language Oscar, the word came down that *Red* was ineligible—guilty, apparently, of insufficient Swissness. The decision was stupid. Someone should tell the Motion Picture Academy that films are made by individuals, not by nations.

Many critics place Kieslowski at the very apex of modern filmmakers. That's wrong, but he certainly forces audiences to do something they are rarely asked to: *look* at movies. To name your film *Red* guarantees that the viewer will be as alert as a traffic cop to the color scheme—to the red telephone, awning, sweater, and so on. Kieslowski has a fashion photographer's showy sense of pictorial alienation. He'll isolate Valentine (as in Valentine's Day, heart, red; get it?) in a corner of the film frame or pose her in an attitude of anxious ennui. It's the most literal-minded form of movie expressionism: meticulous, handsome, remote.

The style works nicely in *Red*. Visually and emotionally, this is the director's warmest film. At moments it glows, like the jacket of Valentine's absent lover; the garment's color is reflected in the young woman's face, suffusing her with long-distance affection. And as the friendship between her and the judge ripens into respect and something like love, the emotional crisis in the old man's life is replayed and miraculously resolved (we won't say how). Finally, the filmmakers concoct another miracle to unite the main characters from the trilogy's three episodes. That's the upside of narrative caprice: change your mind, wave a wand and everyone lives happily—or, in Kieslowski's films, thoughtfully—ever after.

VILLAGE VOICE, 11/29/94, p. 64, Georgia Brown

The film world, if we can still call it that, is split on Kieslowski. Some rave, some sneer, others fashionably waffle. Is this the tongue of an angel or a sounding brass and tinkling cymbal? Imagine that the director's decision to forsake moviemaking in favor of a bench somewhere in Poland has something to do with the lack of deference shown his four French films—*The Double Life of Veronique* and now the *tricouleur* triptych, *Blue, White* and *Red*. Judging by his tart, testy festival appearances, he has the artist's usual exacerbated capacity for hurt. Making Polish drama Western style—moisturized skin, perfect haircuts, and that vast consumer-driven backdrop—brought out a sumptuous polish that he may not have factored in. Some of what's said about Kieslowski reminds me of the abuse heaped on Ophüls's *The Earrings of Madame de* ...and *Lola Montes*: Too sentimental, too exquisite by half. Give us the old Polish frump.

Occasionally Kieslowski's French films make me wince; at the same time their radiance outshines everything. *The Decalogue*, based on the Ten Commandments and set in a Warsaw housing project, was always a soap opera, a vastly entertaining grammar of morals. And these are the same films; really—variations on a theme. In fact, never before and to such a degree has a narrative-based filmmaker *blended* his films, stitched them into a single overreaching quilt. Correspondence, contingency, and fearful symmetries are his subject. Now that the narratives of *Veronique* and *White* have connected France to Poland, all his characters inhabit one *Mitteleuropa* housing complex. With collaborator Krzysztof Piesiewicz, Kieslowski has invented a language—a "system of signs," Piesiewicz calls it—for interrogating lives and counterlives.

When *Blue*'s Julie (Juliette Binoche) wakes up black and very, very blue after a car wreck, she looks briefly into the face of Veronique's father (the same actor plays *Blue*'s hospital doctor) because *Blue* effectively is the Double Life of another woman torn between the underworld and the so-called real one. Likewise but in a less ponderous mode, *White* introduces the Double Life of Karol Karol, with his double moniker and his duplicitous shuffle between East and West, and now *Red* gives us the Double Life of Judge Joseph Kern (Jean-Louis Trintignant), a scruffy misanthrope at the end of his tether who lives simultaneously in past, present, and future.

In the beginning—of the universe, of *Red*—there is babble: phone cables carrying undifferentiated blah, blah, blah. (Later in *Red*, we listen in as several record-store customers in headsets provide a similar and not-unpleasant din.) Telephones are technological instruments for facilitating, or retarding, the old art of connection, or *fraternité* which is *Red*'s nominal theme. Here, two pairs of young lovers struggle to reach out and touch: Valentine (Veronique's Irene Jacob), a Geneva fashion model, and the peripatetic Michel, temporarily in England; Auguste (Jean-Pierre Lorit), a legal student studying for exams, and Karin (Frederique Feder), who dispenses phone-in weather forecasts. Weather, as you'll recall from *The Decalogue*'s first Commandment, is critical since it causes accidents (most of what we know of fate). Thus, prediction-playing God, of which there should be no other before Me—is a tricky business.

Kieslowski's narratives turn on accident—from dire car crash to chance meeting. In the early minutes of *Red*, we see many near misses but no collisions. Valentine and Auguste live kitty-corner from each other and cross paths several times a week but do not physically connect until *Red*'s final moments. (Much of this information becomes available only on second viewing, due to Kieslowski's elliptical editing.) When *Red*'s bump finally comes, it's from Valentine's car hitting a dog. Not Auguste's shaggy medium-sized dog, but a lanky German shepherd belonging, she finds out, to a cranky former judge who spend his retirement eavesdropping on his neighbors. That pesky telephone again.

Voyeurism, the moviemaker's and moviegoer's vice and virtue, has been used by Kieslowski before, most memorably in *A Short Film About Love*. Here our auditory spy resembles L. B. Jeffries in *Rear Window*, in that he too has a bad leg and snoops out of a great thwarted need to know, perhaps trap and punish, others. The judge, we find out, suffers the effects of an ancient betrayal that has all the marks of something primal. When his dog, Rita, brings the innocent Valentine to the house, the ice on his heart cracks a little. By the end, the windows in his house are shattering around him, crash, crash.

Glass—mirroring, containing, and, especially, breaking—may be Kieslowski's favorite sign. From that ominous cracked milk bottle at the opening of *The Decalogue*, through the various lenses, prisms, baubles, windows, and windshields of *Veronique* and *Blue*, he and his talented cinematographers have given us a lesson in the art and craft of reflection. In brief, glass is the translucent medium separating us from, but allowing us to glimpse, the other life: Call it sleep.

In *Blue*, the child seen through the back windshield just before dying recalls the final shot of Veronique communing with her dead singers' society behind her windshield (cars in Kieslowski roll around like little glass booths or coffins). All four French films end with faces looking through glass, the world overlaid in reflection. And each time this comes as a moment of rapturous repose after the hypnotic imagistic hubbub.

The brilliant saturated reds here were used before in *A Short Film About Love* to many of the same ends, but probably never before have three films been so strictly organized around color. But color in the series is inseparable from light, both from the sun and artificial sources, You can watch *Red* just by following the ebb and flow, the fascinating course of illumination, from the somber rhythm of taillights to the ecstatic pop, pop, pop of flashbulbs at a fashion show. It's still another thing when he puts you in the dark.

Twice in *Red* we're nearly sealed inside that other world. Once when a garage door closes and we—the viewers, not a character—are left in blackness. Another time, a ferry boat slowly raises its ramp and traps us in the hole. Except that each time there's a rent toward the bottom, a baby gap, a basement window onto the world outside. Many drown but a few slip through the tiny opening.

It's this sense of a tantalizing subliminal world just behind the "real" that we get from the great solemn filmmakers like Bresson, Tarkovsky, Ozu, and Hou Hsiao-Hsien. Theo Angelopoulos has his actors gazing intently off to the side into a captivating peripheral reality. In *Red*, when the judge tells Valentine he dreamed of her 20 or 30 years in the future—"You woke up and smiled at someone next to you"—he's describing the sublime, *moving* passage from Marker's *La Jetée* This is really another way of speaking about coming alive—waking. We see through a glass darkly; then face-to-face.

Meanwhile, back in the realm of narrative, we're still contemplating, *fraternité*, a dream of community and unsentimental love. The judge poses the issue of punishment for his neighbors' trespasses—not that he'll mete it out. Affected by these invisible sufferers and their fragmented stories, Valentine proposes to help, as she does with the dog and the old woman with the bottle. The judge dismisses the notion of altruism, saying she's projecting her own guilt for her mother and drug-addict brother. But later, literally under her influence, he makes a stunning confession of empathy: "Those people whose lives I judged ... in their place I'd lie, I'd steal, I'd kill." *He sees himself in the other*, which according to this daring, conscience-driven work, is love's [This review was printed incomplete.]

Also reviewed in:
CHICAGO TRIBUNE, 12/2/94, Friday/p. H, Michael Wilmington
NATION, 12/12/94, p. 738, Stuart Klawans
NEW REPUBLIC, 12/19/94, p. 26, Stanley Kauffmann
NEW YORK TIMES, 11/23/94, p. C18, Janet Maslin
NEW YORKER, 11/28/94, p. 155, Anthony Lane
VARIETY, 5/23-29/94, p. 52, LIsa Nesselson
WASHINGTON POST, 12/16/94, p. F1, Hal Hinson
WASHINGTON POST, 12/16/94, Weekend/p. 49, Desson Howe

RED BEADS

A Fortissimo Films release produced with the support of China Eastern Cultural Development Center. *Executive Producer:* Xiao Ming. *Producer:* Xiao Ming. *Director:* He Yi. *Screenplay (Mandarin with English subtitles):* Liu Xiaojing and You Ni. *Director of Photography:* Nie Tiejun and Yu Xiaoyang. *Editor:* Liu Xiaojing. *Music:* Guo Xiaohong. *Sound:* Guan Jian. *Art Director:* Wang Wangwang. *Costumes:* Yun Fang. *Running time:* 90 minutes. *MPAA Rating:* Not Rated.

CAST: Liu Jiang (Jingsheng); Shi Ke (Jiyun); Tian Guobin (Dr. Sha).

VILLAGE VOICE, 9/6/94, p. 55, Georgia Brown

Playing in the Public's "Thunder From the East: New Visions From China, Taiwan, and Hong Kong" series of Chinese films is He Yi's downright murky *Red Beads*. Shot in just 12 days and on a budget that would make *El Mariachi* look like an extravaganza, this cryptic first film smacks of political and social allegory.

Almost all of *Red Beads* takes place in an austere mental hospital where a young woman, Jiyun (played by Shi Ke, one of China's most popular actresses), has been committed by her mother. When asked by a shadowy staff psychiatrist, Dr. Sha (Tian Guobin), to recall her dreams ("When I know your dreams," he lies, "you can go home"), she says she dreams of corridors scattered with red beads: "I would pick them up and string them in a necklace." A concerned orderly, Jingsheng (Liu Jiang), assigned to look after Jiyun, begins reading her files and eventually falls in love with her. When the patient undergoes some form of lobotomy and becomes utterly docile, Jingsheng begins dreaming her infectious red beads dream.

This pessimistic story of confinement and mind control is shot in severe black and white with deep shadows slashing the frame. Faces are obscure, as if identity is lost or a secret. He Yi sometimes hides meaning so thoroughly, however, that the viewer may get lost too. You probably have to live in mainland China to get the message.

Also reviewed in:
NEW YORK TIMES, 9/2/94, p. C12, Caryn James
VARIETY, 12/13/93, p. 39, Derek Elley

RED LOTUS SOCIETY, THE

A Performance Workshop Films and Long Shong International Co. production. *Executive Producer:* Xie Mingchang and Chen Qiyuan. *Producer:* Wang Ying-hsiang and Nai-chu Ding. *Director:* Stan Lai. *Screenplay (Mandarin with English subtitles):* Stan Lai. *Director of Photography:* Christopher Doyle. *Editor:* Chen Bowen. *Music:* Fumio Itabashi. *Sound:* Du Duzhi. *Production Designer:* Samuel Wang. *Costumes:* Joann Li. *Running time:* 125 minutes. *MPAA Rating:* Not Rated.

CAST: Ying Zhaode (Ahda); Chen Wenming (Dan); Na Weixun (Kuei); Li Tongcun (Mao); Lee Lichun (Ahda's Father); Li Bojun (Old Master); Lu Yuzhou (Blind Man Lu); Lo Manfei (Miss Sung); Dai Liren (7th Brother); Shen Xixing (5th Sister); Feng Yigang (3rd Brother); Li Yuhang (Xiao Yu); Quan Guan (Zha); Quan Haochun (Ma).

NEW YORK POST, 10/5/94, p. 33, Thelma Adams

Ahda wants to vault—without a pole. The attractive Taiwanese youth (Ying Zhaode) craves the power to fly, and he's willing to give up all worldly things to learn the ancient art known as vaulting.

Beautifully shot and well acted, Stan Lai's "The Red Lotus Society" (at the New York Film Festival) weaves myth and magic into a tale about a young man on a mystical quest set against an urban contemporary background.

Lai shifts between past and present, using a story-telling old-timer (Li Tongcun) to recount past events about the mysterious secret Red Lotus Society, whose members mastered gravity-defying leaps.

Did the society ever exist? Are its members drifting through '90s Taiwan trying to make a buck? Is it possible to bridge traditional and contemporary culture? Can a modern man cultivate his soul through a belief in magic? Lai relates these issues with humor and warmth.

Unfortunately, the writer/director muddles the contemporary chronology and loses the audience with too many scenes fastened with inept transitions. "The Red Lotus Society" is cool—but confusing.

NEWSDAY, 10/5/94, Part II/p. B7, Jack Mathews

Taiwanese playwright and film director Stan Lai blends ancient Chinese martial arts philosophy with the hard realities of life in modern rat-race Taipei. The story, often as murky as it is mythical, tells of a Taiwanese youth whose obsession with the metaphysical art of "vaulting" (he wants to overcome gravity and fly) leads him to a series of strange mentors in the legendary Red Lotus society, whose seven members reportedly served as Nationalist spies against the Communists on mainland china. The question is not whether Ahda can get off the ground but whether he can handle the knowledge that comes with the ability.

Also reviewed in:
NEW YORK TIMES, 10/5/94, p. C18, Stephen Holden
VARIETY, 9/26-10/2/94, p. 62, Leonard Klady

RED ROCK WEST

A Roxie Releasing release of a Red Rock Films production. *Executive Producer:* Michael Kuhn and Jane McCann. *Producer:* Sigurjon Sighvatsson and Steve Golin. *Director:* John Dahl. *Screenplay:* John Dahl and Rick Dahl. *Director of Photography:* Mark Reshovsky. *Editor:* Scott Chestnut. *Music:* William Olvis. *Music Editor:* Alex Gibson and Sherry Whitfield. *Sound:* Jay Boekelheide and Mark Deren. *Sound Editor:* Patrick Dodd. *Casting:* Carol Lewis. *Production Designer:* Robert Pearson. *Art Director:* Don Diers. *Set Decorator:* Kate Sullivan. *Set Dresser:* Don G. Smith, Warren Sewell, and Dwain F. Wilson. *Special Effects:* Frank Ceglia. *Costumes:* Terry Dresbach. *Make-up:* Patty York. *Special Make-up Effects:* John Buechler. *Stunt Coordinator:* Dan Bradley. *Running time:* 98 minutes. *MPAA Rating:* Not Rated.

CAST: Nicolas Cage (Michael Williams); Lara Flynn Boyle (Suzanne Brown); Dennis Hopper (Lyle); J.T. Walsh (Wayne Brown); Craig Reay (Jim); Vance Johnson (Mr. Johnson); Robert Apel (Howard); Bobby Joe McFadden (Old Man); Dale Gibson (Kurt); Ted Parks (Cashier); Robert Guajardo (Doctor); Sarah Sullivan (Nurse); Timothy Carhart (Deputy Greytack); Dan Shor (Deputy Bowman); Michael Rudd (Red Rock Bartender); Dwight Yoakam (Truck Driver); Peter Kevin Quinn (Truck Driver's Buddy); Jeff Levine (Country Girl Bartender); Shawn Michael Ryan (Tai); Barbara Glover (Jane); Robert Beecher (Caretaker); Jody Carter (Caretaker's Wife); Babs Bram (Receptionist).

LOS ANGELES TIMES, 3/25/95, Calendar/p. 8, Kevin Thomas

John Dahl's terrific film noir "Red Rock West" brings to mind the Coen brothers"Blood Simple," Carl Colpaert's "Delusion" and his own "Kill Me Again" in its clever plotting and wide open spaces setting.

It's also got an admirable something more: a concern for decency, embodied by Nicolas Cage's entirely likable Michael. He's so honest that when a friend helps him line up,a job as an oil-rigger in Wyoming, he blow's the chance by admitting that he's got a game leg. When stopping for gas in his seedy old Cadillac, he resists reaching into an open till for some much-needed cash.

Temptation a third time around, however, is not exactly a charm. Landing in the tiny Wyoming burg "of Red Rock he heads for the local saloon whose proprietor (J.T. Walsh) promptly mistakes him for a Dallas hit man hired to rub out his pretty, much younger wife, Suzanne (Lara Flynn Boyle). While it's plain to see that Michael is not about to kill anybody, he's in such a moment of weakness he can no more resist taking the money and more than he can resist Suzanne's offer to double her husband's fee if he spares her.

Dahl and his co-writer brother, Rick, are endlessly imaginative in coming up with escalating plot twists and turns, but each convolution not only heightens suspense but also reveals character. The entire thrust of the film is concerned with how Michael, swiftly regretting his lapse and maintaining our sympathy, will manage—if ever—to work himself clear of spiraling entanglement, and escalating peril.

"Red Rock West," which was rescued from cable through the efforts of San Francisco exhibitor Bill Banning may be a classic B-picture, but it has an A-cast, which includes Dennis Hopper as a sly, witty Texan, a man in well-tailored all-black Western duds whose folksy drawl and friendly ways prove dangerously disarming.

There's a sense that Dahl and his actors are enjoying themselves, putting us into a sly dark joke, yet the film retains a serious dimension: It is not insignificant that Michael lost his oil-rigging job in Texas because the petroleum boom has gone dry or that he sustained the damage to his leg while serving in Lebanon.

Cage's naturalness as a nice guy in a big jam lends the film considerable substance while Hopper's wily foil, Boyle's tough dame and Walsh's minor-league baddie provide much amusement. With Mark Reshovsky's sleek camera work, authentic locales and William Olvis' mood-setting score, "Red Rock West" has style to burn.

NEW STATESMAN & SOCIETY, 7/2/93, p. 35, Jonathan Romney

[*Red Rock West* was reviewed jointly with *The Assassin*; see Romney's review in *Film Review Annual, 1994.*]

NEW YORK, 5/30/94, p. 59, David Denby

Red Rock West, a little B movie in the *noir* tradition, completed early in 1993, was rejected for theatrical exhibition in the U.S. by its original distributor and immediately put out to pasture in the cable and home-video markets. But then a theater owner in San Francisco named Bill Banning came to the rescue and decided to give the movie a shot, opening it at his own theater (the Roxie) and elsewhere (including the Lincoln Plaza Cinema); and so, thanks to Mr. Banning, I was recently able to see the best American movie released so far in the year of our Lord 1994.

A *film noir* needs a sap—an honest person who serves as a foil for the others—and it gets a beautiful one in the spaniel-eyed Nicolas Cage, who plays Michael, a Marine veteran who finds himself entirely broke in a small Wyoming town. Wandering into a bar, Michael is mistaken for a professional killer, and he falls in with some of the nastiest, most devious people to appear onscreen in years. There is the bar's owner, played by the impervious J. T. Walsh; his wife (Lara Flynn Boyle), a high-plains femme fatale; and the actual professional killer, who, in the convincingly psychopathic person of Dennis Hopper, turns out to be an affable fellow with veins that occasionally bulge threateningly in his forehead. In this corrupt world, Michael's honesty is a kind of curse—pitiable and finally hilarious.

Director John Dahl, who wrote the film with his brother Rick, offers the *noir* conventions of greed and lust without the overwrought, heavy-breathing self-consciousness of, say, *Body Heat*. These filmmakers are serious and witty. They transfer the *noir* locale from the usual dark city to the wide-open West, giving us the mean, laconic tongue of the plains rather than the nervous jabber of the streets. The speech seems stylized in a fresh way, and so is Dahl's economical direction, which is so formally rigorous that its regularities and variations (like Michael repeatedly passing a WELCOME TO RED ROCK sign) become a sly source of comedy. *Red Rock West* is lean and unpretentiously artful, like some of the classic little films of the forties. It puts all the slack, dull American movies of the season to shame.

NEW YORK POST, 4/8/94, p. 37, Larry Worth

When films intended for the local movie house instead premiere at the local video store, there's usually good reason. Like A) an incoherent story line, B) embarrassing performances or C) dreadful direction.

So how to explain the fate of "Red Rock West"? It's A) an intelligent, tightly written thriller with B) terrific turns from Nicolas Cage, Dennis Hopper, J.T. Walsh and Lara Flynn Boyle and C) showcases filmmaker John Dahl's diverse talents.

So go figure. Preferably at an area cinema where the 1992 film is getting a belated big-screen showing, having already hit HBO and the VCR market.

Dahl who co-wrote the screenplay with brother Rick creates instant intrigue with an anti-hero for the 90s: a down-on-his-luck drifter (Cage) who can't find a job while driving the winding back roads of Wyoming.

Dusty little Red Rock—complete with sleazy saloon—seems like every other town. Wrong. It also has a bartender (Walsh) who mistakes the stranger for a hired hit man, giving him $5,000 to knock off his wife.

Well, desperate men do desperate things. So this would-be-desperado pays a visit to his new employer's better half (Boyle). But she's no slouch. Quickly sizing up her executioner, the brunette beauty doubles the offer to have hubby axed.

That's when the real hit man (Hopper) pulls into Red Rock. And when the plot really takes off, giving rise to more razor-sharp twists than a barbed-wire fence.

A word to the wise: Take nothing—and no one—at face value. Whenever you think you've got the Dahl brothers' script figured out it produces yet another turn to send viewers reeling.

But John Dahl's best trick is adeptly blending suspense and comedy, all keyed to split-second timing. One minute, he's building tension you could slice with a cleaver; the next, he's juggling running jokes with deliciously dry wit.

In the latter department, Nicolas Cage proves a master of deadpan as a man caught in a physical and emotional quagmire. But whether doing one-armed push-ups on a highway in his underwear, staring into a speeding car's bumper or getting amorous with a pistol-packin' snake, he supplies the credibility and appeal to let the part fly.

And Dennis Hopper is a perfect nemesis. As viewers of "Blue Velvet" will recall, he makes a particularly memorable psycho. One need only watch him chow down on a big turkey sandwich after blowing a victim's head open to see that he's in peak nightmare form.

Lara Flynn Boyle and J.T. Walsh round out the winning troupe as the most duplicitous newlyweds since Jack Nicholson and Kathleen Turner played rival husband-and-wife hit men in "Prizzi's Honor."

Add in a wonderfully atmospheric setting and you've got a film that can match the Coen brothers' "Blood Simple" as the ultimate in neo-noir fun. As such, "Red Rock West" richly deserves viewing, on cable, video or—now—the silver screen.

NEWSDAY, 4/8/94, Part II/p. B7, Jack Mathews

When John Dahl's "Red Rock West" had its American premiere at the Hamptons International Film Festival last fall, it was a premiere with an asterisk. The movie, which is reminiscent of and compares well with the Coen brothers' "Blood Simple," had already been shown twice on HBO, and was scheduled for two more airings the following week.

"Red Rock West" is not a cable picture. It was made for $7.5 million, features big-screen stars Nicolas Cage and Dennis Hopper and is exactly the kind of movie, tongue-in-cheek film noir, that is best appreciated with the kind of responsive audience it had in the Hamptons.

But American distributors with an eye on the low grosses of Dahl's earlier thriller, "Kill Me Again," passed on it, and HBO had a bargain. Now, six months after it was shown on TV and weeks after its arrival in video stores, "Red Rock West" is being exhumed by tiny Roxie Releasing for a theatrical run, and considering the major studio dreck out there, it's worth a look.

"Red Rock" is a sly gem about an amiable, out-of-work drifter (Cage) who, while looking for an honest job in the Wyoming oil fields, is mistaken for a mail-order assassin, and though he wouldn't harm a fly, he is soon weighing counter offers from a husband (J.T. Walsh) and wife (Lara Flynn Boyle) who want each other dead.

When the real contract killer (Dennis Hopper) shows up, adding to the confusion, the whole thing turns into a delectable comic nightmare.

The movie, written by Dahl and his brother Rick doesn't end as well as it might. They suddenly abandon the restrained cleverness governing the rest of the movie and go for broad farce. But it's a great time getting there, especially when you have an audience to share it with.

SIGHT AND SOUND, 7/93, p. 49, Paul Tarrago

Penniless and 1200 miles from home after a job offer has fallen through, Michael pulls into Red Rock (pop. 874). Mistaken by the bartender for 'Lyle'— but playing along at the mention of paid employment—he's handed a $5,000 advance and details of the person he's meant to kill, the bartender's wife Suzanne. Michael immediately approaches his target and reveals her husband's intentions; she offers him twice the amount to kill her husband for her. Michael writes a note to the local sheriff detailing this family feud, then drives away, only to collide with a stranger whose truck has broken down. Taking the stranger to Red Rock's hospital, he fills out an accident report, looking for the first opportunity to get back on the road, but the sheriff arrives first, proving to be none other than Wayne the bartender; the doctor reveals that the run-over man had already been shot.

Wayne arrests Michael as the suspected killer, planning to dispose of him. Michael manages to evade him, but is almost run over by a fellow Texan, who offers him a ride; Michael is horrified to learn his name is Lyle. Coerced into joining him for a drink at Wayne's bar, Michael escapes through a window seconds before Wayne and Lyle come in search of him. Explaining the situation to Suzanne, Michael manages to knock Wayne out when he arrives at her house; Suzanne and Michael leave town, but stop off at a motel and toy with the idea of travelling to Mexico together. On Suzanne's suggestion, they return to town to pick up her money, which she claims is in Wayne's safe. In his office, they find the safe empty, but manage to hide just before Wayne returns; Wayne is then arrested by his own deputies, who have found a 'wanted' poster on the shot man's body, identifying Wayne and Suzanne as bank robbers. Lyle arrives to hear the story, and springs Wayne from jail. Wayne, Lyle, Michael and Suzanne drive to a cemetery where the bank loot is hidden. Tension between Lyle and Wayne over their 50/50 split of the money boils over, and both men are killed, leaving Michael and Suzanne to hop a passing freight train. When Michael tries to dump the money, Suzanne shoots at him with a now empty gun. He shoves her out of the train, and as police arrive, Michael—finding the last remaining wad of notes—continues on his way.

Two of the big commercial reasons for the current vogue for *film noir* are the scope the genre offers for cynical on-screen gesturing before the obligatory moral ending, and the carte blanche it provides for film-makers to assert style over theme. John Dahl's first feature *Kill Me Again* headed this way, but with Michael Madsen lending his best Mitchum-like menace, and a deceptively tricky plot, it still felt dangerous enough to be more than pastiche. His self-styled 'country *noir*' follow-up has bigger name actors and is much more convoluted; it's more of everything and in total quite a bit less. It's as if Dahl had looked back to his previous feature and, through a mist of praise, been influenced by his influences at second remove.

Michael, Suzanne and Wayne are archetypes grafted from the pages of James S. Cain—the innocent stranger and the corrupt couple, iconically signalled by Lara Flynn Boyle's 1940s stylings, from her brows to the cut of her jacket. But these allusions amount to mere translation of the films of the books, and the writing of Rick and John Dahl comes across like snippets of half-remembered plot lines, small parts of great wholes. This is collage culture, of a sort that Propaganda, the production company, knows very well from its output of videos, from Madonna to Coca-Cola.

The actors are relegated to the status of moving props, the honourable exception being J.T. Walsh, who manages to use Wayne's caginess as a space in which to hint; but read against Dennis Hopper's drawling killer or Nicolas Cage's born victim, his performance has little chance other than to glimmer in the background. A possible redemption—to let the audience in on its game of influences and appropriations, to be knowing but playful—is roundly avoided because Dahl seems to believe that *Red Rock West* genuinely is an up-front thriller, that the plethora of coincidences are readable as fate rather than script repair. *Kill Me Again*, though structured around a similar 'ingenu/psycho/femme fatale' triumvirate, kept its despairing inevitability as a final shock. Here, it's more like a drawn-out scramble in search of an unhappy ending.

Set in Arizona (here doubling as Wyoming), both of Dahl's films to date show a sense of landscape—of broken-down towns, communities based on oil that dried up with the wells—which he sets great store by, but rarely lingers on. There's a feeling that if Dahl jettisoned MTV *noir* and went for the stories of these decaying shacks, then the promising director of *Kill Me Again* might get a second breath. Until then it looks as if it's going to be hit-and-miss ersatz pulp all the way.

TIME, 5/9/94, p. 74, Richard Schickel

The job offer back up the road didn't pan out, and his last five bucks have disappeared into his gas tank. Looks like Red Rock, Wyoming is the end of the line for Michael (Nicolas Cage). And it's not exactly a job hunter's paradise. But when Michael stops in the local bar looking for a little vocational guidance, he is astonished to discover that he's just the man the proprietor is looking for. Wayne (J.T. Walsh) needs somebody to bump off his wife. As it turns out, Wayne is just a little too eager to fill this vacancy, for he violates the most basic rule of personnel placement: always check a prospective employee's references.

Had Wayne done so before handing over a $5,000 advance to Michael and telling him to get busy, Wayne would have learned that Michael was not Lyle from Dallas, the hit man he has been impatiently awaiting. And if Michael had been a little less desperate he might not have pocketed the cash. But then, if people were in general a little less stupid and a lot less greedy, there would have been no need to invent film noir in the first place.

Red Rock West belongs to that genre's low-budget country-and-western subspecies. Michael is a classic film noir protagonist, essentially a good, slightly dim sort who is drawn into evil's web because of a momentary weakness and whose struggles to escape serve only to entangle him more tightly. In film noir, the spider at the center of such a web is usually a woman, and in this case she is Suzanne (Lara Flynn Boyle), Michael's intended victim. After he spares her, she expresses her gratitude by luring him still nearer to destruction. Film noir also typically calls for a dash of psychopathy, and in *Red Rock West* that is provided by Dennis Hopper, who plays the professional killer and causes lightning flashes of madness to streak across the screen. *Red Rock West* has the customary film noir hint of civic corruption (barkeep Wayne is also the town sheriff) and reveals the equally conventional link between crimes present and a large crime past.

In film noir, evil is endemic in our history and our society, inescapably embracing both sexes and every social type. Putting it mildly, the genre is—or was—cynical and subversive. But given the power of humanistic piety in contemporary movies—it is virtually the only acceptable tone for American films seeking an adult audience—film noir, if it's done at all, is usually accompanied by nostalgic winks and genial, reassuring cues of self-consciousness. Just kidding, folks, say the filmmakers. *Red Rock West*, in contrast, is all furious conviction. Its humor is sardonic; its ironies are conveyed by violence; and its view of human nature is bleak.

Even more perverse, from the Hollywood packager's point of view, the film's stars do not have big-time chic and guaranteed box-office appeal, and, Hopper aside, they work in an intense but minimalist vein. Meanwhile, the director, John Dahl (who wrote the screenplay with his brother Rick) is young and virtually unknown.

As a result of all these commercial drawbacks, the original distributors sent *Red Rock West* straight to cable and video. Another outfit picked it up, however, and it is belatedly making its way into a few theaters. It's well worth tracking down, wherever you can find it. For it has the kind of tension and energy—maybe even a touch of delirium—that is only a memory in most of today's big studio movies. You just know that no one connected with *Red Rock West* owns a suit or a tie or knows how to write a self-protective memo.

VILLAGE VOICE, 4/12/94, p. 60, Julie Lang

Ladies and gents, welcome to Red Rock, Wyoming, population 874, where the oil wells run dry and the women wear K-Mart. Here, you got yer sheriff by the name of Wayne (J. T. Walsh), who incidently, might I add ominously, owns the Red Rock Bar; his pretty-as-peaches wife, Suzanne (Lara Flynn Boyle), whom Wayne wants shot cold, hard dead by Lyle (Dennis Hopper) from Dallas; and Michael (Nicolas Cage), a down-and-out Texan lookin' fer an honest home in which to hang his hat, who ends up being mistaken for Lyle.

It goes like this: Michael, dirt-poor and inquiring about a job—any job—at the local Red Rock Bar, is confused by Wayne for Lyle, who has set up a hit on his wife for 10 grand. Michael accepts the booty, and finds the little lady to explain Wayne's scheme. She in turn offers to double the cash if Michael will kill Wayne. "Why?" asks Michael, all moral and naive. "Have you ever been married before?" she purrs. He takes the cash and bails, but for the next 24 hours, he cannot escape this goddamn town for the life of him. He cannot escape being manhunted, shot at, tied up, handcuffed, beaten, literally and figuratively fucked, and basically brutalized in every possible way under the sun, barring annihilation.

The opening scene says it all: an old, rusty car parked alongside a barren highway, a terrain laden with gnarled, dirt-brown shrubs, and a windmill slowly creaking round and round. A bucket of dirty water rests beneath Michael as he shaves his stubble clean. A harmonica twangs, and if the sky were black, a coyote would howl. Then, the growl of an engine, and we're off, slicing across the arid earth. A job has fallen through for Michael, the gas runs low, the wallet's thin, and he must seek out any fortune at the Red Rock Bar. So, young man, welcome to *Red Rock West*, where John Wayne and Robert Mitchum do the do-si-do, but not without a whoop and a holler from Simone de Beauvoir.

As in *Raising Arizona*, Cage is at home where the deer and the antelope play, donning an "aww shucks golly gee" look, with a trick or two up his sleeve. Hopper is frighteningly (and predictably) brilliant as a hit man from Dallas, prancing around in the latest rhinestone-studded polyester suit, toting a gun with eyes of the insane. Boyle is conniving, demure on the outside, but black on the inside; she successfully rings a *Twin Peaks* bell. The film itself wallows seductively in the twisted, consumptive murk of America's small towns, which, for most of us, is best experienced on-screen.

Also reviewed in:
CHICAGO TRIBUNE, 5/6/94, Friday/p. F, Michael Wilmington
NEW YORK TIMES, 4/8/94, p. C12, Caryn James
VARIETY, 9/20/93, p. 28, Leonard Klady
WASHINGTON POST, 4/15/94, p. D1, Richard Harrington
WASHINGTON POST, 4/15/94, Weekend/p. 44, Joe Brown

REF, THE

A Buena Vista release of a Touchstone Pictures presentation. *Executive Producer:* Don Simpson and Jerry Bruckheimer. *Producer:* Ron Bozman, Richard LaGravenese, and Jeff Weiss. *Director:* Ted Demme. *Screenplay:* Richard LaGravenese and Marie Weiss. *Story:* Marie Weiss. *Director of Photography:* Adam Kimmel. *Editor:* Jeffrey Wolf. *Music:* David A. Stewart. *Music Editor:* Todd Kasow. *Sound:* Bruce Carwardine. *Sound Editor:* Stuart Levy. *Casting:* Howard Feuer. *Production Designer:* Dan Davis. *Art Director:* Dennis Davenport. *Set Decorator:* Jaro Dick. *Special Effects:* Bob Hall and Arthur Langevin. *Costumes:* Judianna Makovsky. *Make-up:* Irene Kent. *Make-up (Judy Davis):* Christine Hart. *Stunt Coordinator:* Branko Racki. *Running time:* 92 minutes. *MPAA Rating:* R.

CAST: Denis Leary (Gus); Judy Davis (Caroline Chasseur); Kevin Spacey (Lloyd Chasseur); Robert J. Steinmiller, Jr. (Jesse Chasseur); Glynis Johns (Rose); Raymond J. Barry (Huff); Richard Bright (Murray); Christine Baranski (Connie); Adam LeFevre (Gary); Phillip Nicoll (John); Ellie Raab (Mary); Bill Raymond (George); John Scurti (Steve); Jim Turner (Phil); Rutanya Alda (Linda); Herbie Ade (Bartender); Ron Gabriel (Limo Driver); Scott Walker (Prosecutor); Edward Saxon (Reporter); Donna Holgate (Newscaster); Kenneth Utt (Jeremiah Willard); Marilyn Stonehouse (Store Cashier); Victoria Mitchell (Store Customer); Cort Day

(Salvation Army Volunteer); Robert Ridgely (Bob Burley); Charles Ker, Derek Keurvorst, and Caroline Yeager (Town Citizens); J.K. Simmons (Siskel); Max Piersig and Victor Erdos (Cadets); John Benjamin Hickey, James Burke, Chris Phillips, and Stephen Hunter (Old Baybrook Policemen).

LOS ANGELES TIMES, 3/9/94, Calendar/p. 1, Kenneth Turan

"The Ref" puts the devil into business with Disney. An enthusiastically mean-spirited comedy about family problems and a rather extreme way to solve them, it has as much fun being malicious as Snow White did being squeaky clean.

Anchored by expert performances from Denis Leary, Judy Davis and Kevin Spacey and the appropriately biting script and direction, "The Ref" is one of those films in which everyone has a verbal stiletto out for everyone else. Though it doesn't manage to hold its edge all the way to the end—that darn Disney influence finally proves too strong—its comic venom is refreshing for as long as it lasts.

"The Ref's" setting couldn't be more mainstream: the Norman Rockwell town of Old Baybrook, Conn., on the night before Christmas. Several creatures are stirring, including a skilled cat burglar named Gus (Leary), hoping to make the proverbial last big score, and the Chasseurs, Lloyd (Spacey) and Caroline (Davis), a couple that after 15 years of marriage can't go 15 seconds without attempting to rip each other's throats out.

Squaring off before the blissful local marriage counselor (a just-so performance by an unbilled B. D. Wong) the Chasseurs engage in some dazzlingly hostile bickering, tossing knives at each other like an experienced circus act. First prize goes to Caroline for her vivid description of a dream in which various parts of her husband's anatomy are served up like a salad, but Lloyd is not without verbal resources of his own.

Meanwhile, Gus' robbery is going comically wrong, and he ends up needing a house to hide out in to avoid a police dragnet. Naturally he ends up with the Chasseurs, who are so bilious they keep on eviscerating each other even though their lives are in danger. "Oh my God," says Gus when he realizes what he's into. "I hijacked my parents."

The best part of "The Ref" involves this neat reversal of expectations, with the nominal hostage-taker ending up at the mercy of the out-of-control hostages, with Gus having no choice but to attempt to bring order out of the Chasseurs' chaos. "The only person who yells is me," he screams in exasperation, brandishing his weapon. "Only people with guns get to yell."

That line is typical of the dark spirit screenwriters Richard LaGravenese and Marie Weiss bring to "The Ref," a spirit that director Ted Demme, who recently did a Leary concert film, is not shy about conveying.

And aside from the forever out-of-sorts comic, well cast as the exasperated burglar, "The Ref" benefits from having actor's actors like Davis and Spacey in the leads. Both are impeccable, but not even Spacey can match the panache of Davis when she disdainfully calls sex with her husband "not really noteworthy."

Forcing Gus to referee the Chasseurs' marital battles is a clever conceit, and even though other elements of the film are amusing—like a Keystone Kops police force that would rather watch "It's a Wonderful Life" than solve crime—when the picture strays from that central premise it tends to lose comic focus.

"The Ref's" main subplots have to do with who is coming to the Chasseur's Christmas Eve dinner, everyone from bad-seed teen-age son Jesse (Robert J. Steinmiller Jr.) to the rest of Lloyd's family, especially his rich and grasping mother Rose (Glynis Johns) and Connie the relentless in-law (Christine Baranski).

Both Johns and Baranski are quite funny, but this flatter-the-rich-relative plot doesn't have the originality and bite of the rest of the picture and echoes the main outlines of the just-released and much less amusing "Greedy."

"The Ref" gets it into its head to actually solve all of the Chasseur family's multifarious problems—in a typical Touchstone/Disney sort of manner—which is a nice thought except that it forces several of the actors to make regrettably serious speeches. Still, it's not every movie that can create so much comedy out of misery, and it's "The Ref's" bad intentions that finally carry the day.

NEW YORK POST, 3/9/94, p. 30, Michael Medved

"The Ref" centers on a desperately dysfunctional suburban Connecticut couple (Judy Davis and Kevin Spacey) who suffer through a Christmas Eve experience that reaches record levels of unpleasantness.

They begin their holiday celebration by shouting obscenities at each other during a useless session with a marriage counselor. On the way home, they cross paths with a fugitive jewel thief (Denis Leary) who takes them hostage while trying to escape after a bungled heist.

The humor is supposed to emerge from the fact that even the presence of this menacing, gun-toting crook can't stop husband and wife from flailing at each other over their long history of betrayals and disappointments.

The unfortunate burglar, who initially tries to shut them up, begins to function as an unwitting referee in their marital warfare, at the same time that he must contend with their "demon seed" juvenile delinquent son (Robert J. Steinmiller Jr.), their insufferably annoying relatives who arrive for Christmas dinner, a drunk, abusive Santa and other hazards of the season.

As the bickering couple and their disagreeable family members snarl and scream through the long night's ordeal, all under the watchful gaze of their disgusted captor, the picture brings to mind other cinematic experiences: It's "Who's Afraid of Virginia Woolf?" meets "Ruthless People"—with a few hints of "The Desperate Hours" for good measure.

Comedy doesn't get much nastier than this, and while "The Ref" will never be cherished as a heartwarming yuletide classic, it just might earn a devoted cult audience.

Denis Leary, the slash-and-burn pacing-and-smoking comic from MTV, has already shown his star quality with scene-stealing performances as a murderous psychopath in a pair of mediocre action pictures ("Gunmen" and "Judgment Night.")

Here he projects the same corrosive wit and sense of danger, while generating surprising compassion for his hard-luck character who is (wouldn't you know it?) the product of an impoverished family and an unhappy childhood.

His co-stars are considerably less successful at engaging anyone's emotions: Judy Davis and Kevin Spacey are both skilled dutiful professionals who come across as believable but never sympathetic; outrageously obnoxious but hardly amusing.

Director Ted Demme (who previously created Leary's MTV specials plus the popular "Yo! MTV Raps") does a reasonably slick job using Toronto locations to create a storybook Connecticut Christmas—only to undermine the cozy images with his uncompromising hell-in-suburbia theme.

In place of "It's a Wonderful Life" (which the klutzy local policemen watch in the station house when they should be out pursuing escaped thief Leary) this movie offers an angry view of the holiday that suggests "It's a Horrible Life."

The entire exercise is unquestionably skillful, but despite a few fleeting, funny moments (like the "traditional" Swedish lit-candle crowns Davis forces her Christmas guest to wear), the project remains chilly, empty and mean-spirited that it will leave most audience members feeling frustrated.

NEWSDAY, 3/9/94, Part II/p. 61, John Anderson

We've probably all met people like Lloyd and Caroline Chasseur (Kevin Spacey and Judy Davis), a suburban couple so desperately unhappy their personalized welcome mat ought to feature twin chalk outlines. They're the type who display their domestic discontent anywhere. Who wouldn't stop fighting if you held them at gunpoint.

That they *are* held at gunpoint and never miss a venomous beat. is the big joke in "The Ref," a comedy with the worst name and some of the better dialogue of the year. It may have a misleading title, but it shows what can be done with a pretty basic comedic premise, once you attach a smart script and some first-class actors to it.

The hand holding the gun that's trained on Lloyd and Caroline belongs to Gus (Denis Leary), aka the most wanted man in Connecticut. He's blown a big-time burglary and in his flight has abducted the Chasseurs, who are so absorbed by their own acrimony it's as if Gus isn't even there. He has to keep showing them the gun, to remind them they're hostages. " I can't believe it," he says. "I hijacked my parents."

It'll get worse for Gus, who's been bitten by a dog and wet his pants (the source of a recurring gag) while fleeing his bungled heist. His henchman, Murray (Richard Bright), is drunk. Jesse (Robert J. Steinmiller Jr.), Lloyd and Caroline's malevolent son, is home from school, and the Chasseurs' other relations are also coming—reluctantly—for the holidays.

They include Lloyd's brother, Gary (Adam LeFevre), and his wife, Connie (Christine Baranski), a couple only slightly less disturbed than Lloyd and Caroline. And Lloyd's mother, Rose (Glynis Johns, in a flagrant display of yuletide bitchery), whose selfishness and domination of her sons turns out to be the root of all their happiness.

Director Ted Demme shows a deft, light touch, and the cast is uniformly solid: Davis and Spacey, two of the finer actors in film, are wonderfully nuanced as Lloyd and Caroline (what Alec Baldwin and Kim Basinger might have done with these roles!), who've pushed their bickering too far to retreat, until Gus shows up. Leary, whom I really didn't want to see playing another pragmatically vicious villain (as in "Judgment Night" and "Gunmen"), gets to show the flair for dark comedy that brought him to the fore in the first place. It's not an easy role; Gus has to maintain a hardness while slowly but surely getting sucked into the Chasseur *Weltschmerz*—where he eventually becomes a kind of pet. The only glaring misstep is the script's: Why would Gus, erudite enough to recognize a Chagall when he sees it, flounder so wildly trying to convince the rest of the family he's Lloyd and Caroline's therapist?

Otherwise, "The Ref ' is generally a no-lose situation, with a sympathetic/fatalistic take on domestic strife. When the incessantly bickering Lloyd and Caroline announce they're divorcing, and Gus cries out "But why ?" his myopia puts the whole miserable thing in a holiday nutshell.

NEWSWEEK, 3/14/94, p. 72, David Ansen

[*The Ref* was reviewed jointly with *Greedy*: see Ansen's review of that film.]

SIGHT AND SOUND, 7/94, p. 44, Woody Haut

Christmas Eve in the affluent Connecticut suburb of Old Baybrook. While Caroline and Lloyd Chasseur attend Doctor Wong's marriage counselling clinic, Gus, a working-class burglar, breaks into a safe at the Willard mansion. Filmed on video, sprayed with cat piss, attacked by a rotweiler, and left to his own devices by his low-life getaway man, Gus escapes arrest by kidnapping Caroline and Lloyd. Holding the still-bickering couple hostage in their luxurious home, Gus learns the Chasseurs are expecting Lloyd's relatives for Christmas Eve dinner. As the police search for the burglar, the Chasseurs' son, Jesse, reluctantly arrives from military school where he has been blackmailing his teacher over some compromising photographs.

Tied together, Caroline and Lloyd find the bounds of matrimony have not been altogether severed. While Jesse remains still tied by Gus in his room, Gus unties Caroline and Lloyd so that they can entertain Lloyd's miserly and domineering mother and his brother's family. After dinner, as useless presents are exchanged, Caroline gets drunk and various home truths are revealed. Naturally, it falls upon Gus, posing as Doctor Wong, to keep order. By the end of the evening, the family makes a stand against Lloyd's mother. As the police close in, the Chasseurs unite as a family to help Gus escape.

From the Capra-like opening—camera pans over shop-fronts, up to Doctor Wong's window—the film's warning seems obvious: commodity fetishism can cause discord and dysfunction. Yet *Hostile Hostages*, directed with conservative panache, is less about consumerism than contemporary family values in an era dominated by psycho-babble, greed and corruption. Though director Ted Demme, like Capra, exalts the individual, his drawing-room comedy scrapes the barrel for its final feel-good approach to deviancy and class.

With a script that alternates between witticism and cliché, *Hostile Hostages* has some humorous moments and caustic, though politically safe, dialogue—especially as delivered by Judy Davis, who upstages everyone as a sharp-tongued and neurotic yuppie. Gus, played by comedian Denis Leary—type-cast but uncomfortably required to stray from his usual caustic persona—listens to

Caroline and Lloyd's bickering and realises his worst nightmare has come true: "Great," he says, "I've kidnapped my fucking parents." When he orders Caroline to do what he says because "I have a gun," she replies, "But we have people coming for dinner." Meanwhile, a group of policemen gather round the television to watch Capra's *It's A Wonderful Life*. So involved are they in the film that when the video showing Gus robbing the Willard mansion arrives, they inadvertently tape Capra over the incriminating evidence.

Toying with deviancy, *Hostile Hostages* might sometimes be mistaken for a collaboration between Disney and Joe Orton. For Gus is too nice to be an authentic sociopath, while Jesse's blackmailing scheme is viewed as a mere peccadillo. In fact, Gus' smoking habits, and his corruption of Caroline who is driven back to the dreaded weed, constitute the film's only real deviant behaviour.

As a surrogate son, Gus may show more interest in smoking than in making sexual advances towards Caroline, but his private talks with Jesse possibly insinuate something more than brotherly love—perhaps caused by Leary's awkward transformation from tough guy to nice guy.

But in saving the marriage, Gus cramps everyone's style. Having described a dream to Doctor Wong in which Lloyd's head is on a platter, his penis protruding from his ear, Caroline is censoriously told by Gus that "dreams are private." Asked about his therapy technique, Gus, posing as Wong, says, "I just tell them they're wacko. They like to hear it." In a final therapeutic act, Lloyd's mother is also bound and gagged, and Gus escapes, presumably to another family needing rough trade and light bondage. Helping Gus get away, Lloyd says, "I can't spend my life sending everyone I care about to prison." Whether admitting he's entrapped his family, declaring his affection for Gus, or hinting that he planned to have his son arrested, Lloyd's born-again humanity is regarded with suspicion—at least by Jesse, who tells Gus, "Things will be different with Dad. If not, I can always blackmail him."

Originally titled *The Ref*, but renamed so that British viewers would not mistake it for a football film, *Hostile Hostages* is as much about cultural references as referees. Tightly edited, and shot for the most part within the Chasseur household, the film notes the family's paintings, CDs, knickknacks, and a copy of *A History of Western Philosophy* that sits on the bedside table. It's the film's sense of enclosure and concentration on objects that makes Gus' wide-angled moonlit escape through the snow appear so dreamlike and reminiscent of Adolfas Mekas' underground classic *Hallelujah the Hills*.

Lightweight and proscenium-oriented, *Hostile Hostages* might be worth seeing for its quirky and commodity-oriented view of suburban life, or for the way Davis fires off lines such as, "You think death scares me? You forget I've been married to *him* for 15 years." But the film fails to deliver what its opening scenes suggest. Homage it may be, but Demme's film is neither as innocent nor as democratic as Capra. And, other than Davis' and Leary's most dedicated fans, for whom is this film actually intended? Is it a feel-good film for deviant adolescents, or merely some kind of broken-family entertainment? After all, it will take more than an eventful Christmas Eve to rehabilitate the myth or remedy the dysfunctions of middle-class family life.

VILLAGE VOICE, 3/22/94, p. 54, Henry Cabot Beck

Cat burglar Gus (Denis Leary) cracks a safe and gets a face full of cat piss before dropping through a "fuckin' roadrunner booby trap" into the jaws of a rottweiler. On the run from the police, he kidnaps a couple so miserably unhappy that they never seem to let being held at gunpoint interfere with their incessant sniping. "I've hijacked my fucking parents," he says in disgust.

Leary takes on the part of a *Desperate Hours/Key Largo/Petrified Forest* crook, an underclass figure meant to point out the pretensions and illusions of the people he threatens, to facilitate the healing of old wounds and reawaken passion. The difference here is that Gus represents no real threat whatsoever; in spite of all his snarling and trademark tough-guy posturing, Leary is written as a pussycat with a pistol, squirting these battling Bickersons with water, not bullets, when he can no longer stand the din. Where he might have taken the story into some delicious dark areas, Leary instead comes across as a comedy-channel criminal Stanley to a movie full of bourgeois Blanches.

At first the film revels in its ripe vulgarity, all rapid-fire rejoinders with Leary as straight man. Judy Davis, in her second stint as the Neurotic American Wife, is never less than superb (sex with husband Kevin Spacey is "not particularly noteworthy," she tells her therapist, "a couple of nipple twists and it's over"), but midway through the film Gus loses control of his captives, the plot, and his character, leaving this slapstick farce grinding down into a sodden domestic drama. He becomes almost peripheral to the action, like a bad talk-show host. What starts out as a real Andrew Bergman sort of howler winds down into a John Hughes set piece where precocious teenagers blackmail teachers and funny hats are meant to substitute for comic invention

Also reviewed in:
CHICAGO TRIBUNE, 3/11/94, Friday/p. H, Michael Wilmington
NEW YORK TIMES, 3/9/94, p. C15, Caryn James
VARIETY, 3/7-13/94, p. 59, Steven Gaydos
WASHINGTON POST, 3/12/94, p. D3, Hal Hinson
WASHINGTON POST, 3/11/94, Weekend/p. 42, Desson Howe

RENAISSANCE MAN

An Andrew G. Vajna presentation in association with Touchstone Pictures of a Cinergi-Parkway production. *Executive Producer:* Penny Marshall and Buzz Feitshans. *Producer:* Sara Colleton, Elliot Abbott, and Robert Greenhut. *Director:* Penny Marshall. *Screenplay:* Jim Burnstein. *Director of Photography:* Adam Greenberg. *Editor:* George Bowers and Battle Davis. *Music:* Hans Zimmer. *Music Editor:* Laura Perlman. *Choreographer:* Donovan Henry. *Sound:* Les Lazarowitz and (music) Jay Rifkin and Alan Meyerson. *Sound Editor:* George Anderson. *Casting:* Paula Herold. *Production Designer:* Geoffrey Kirkland. *Art Director:* Richard Johnson. *Set Designer:* Robert Fechtman. *Set Decorator:* Jennifer Williams. *Set Dresser:* Mark Boucher, Mike Hanrahan, Lawrence Lira, Thom Magana, Philippe Rockholt, and Matthew Sullivan. *Special Effects:* Stan Parks. *Costumes:* Betsy Heimann. *Make-up:* Christina Smith. *Stunt Coordinator:* M. James Arnett. *Running time:* 124 minutes. *MPAA Rating:* PG-13.

CAST: Danny DeVito (Bill Rago); Gregory Hines (Sergeant Cass); Cliff Robertson (Colonel James); James Remar (Captain Murdoch); Lillo Brancato, Jr. (Donnie Benitez); Stacy Dash (Miranda Myers); Kadeem Hardison (Jamaal Montgomery); Richard T. Jones (Jackson Leroy); Khalil Kain (Roosevelt Hobbs); Peter Simmons (Brian Davis); Greg Sporleder (Mel Melvin); Mark Wahlberg (Tommy Lee Haywood); Ben Wright (Private Oswald); Ed Begley, Jr. (Jack Markin); Ann Cusack (Bill's Secretary); Jeb Brown (1st Young Executive); Paul Abbott (2nd Young Executive); Nat Mauldin (U Love To Rent Voice); Hakiem Greenhut (Paper Boy Voice); Roy K. Dennison (Bum); Alanna Ubach (Emily Rago); Jenifer Lewis (Mrs. Coleman); Matthew Keesler (Guard Gate MP); Gary Dewitt Marshall (Traffic MP); J. Leon Pridgen II (Captain Murdoch's Aide); J.J. Nettles (Bartender); Thomas D. Houck (Company Commander); Robert Head, Robert Steele, and Yolanda Tisdale (Male Platoon Drill Sergeants); Julio Dominguez, Ronald Elder, and Shelia Logan (Female Platoon Drill Sergeants); Kenneth McKee and José Ortez (MPs); Laurence Irby (Officer); Belinda Fairley (Female Private); Christopher Baker (Laundry 1st Private); Sal Rendino (Laundry 2nd Private); Gary T. McTague (Laundry Truck Driver); Alexander Zmijewski (Colonel James' Aide); Isabella Hofmann (Marie); Samaria Graham (Shana Leroy); R.M. Haley (Florist); Daniel Bateman (Graduation Drill Sergeant); Alphonsa Smith (Graduation Sergeant Major); Jim Ochs (Customs Officer); Don Reilly (Henry V); Randy Hall (Henry V Lead Archer).

LOS ANGELES TIMES, 6/3/94, Calendar/p. 4, Peter Rainer

"Renaissance Man" wants to own your tear ducts. It's got a sop for every audience and happy endings coming out of its ears. There's a fine line between delighting an audience and pandering to it. "Renaissance Man" leapfrogs across the line.

What complicates the issue is that, in snatches, the film does delight. Phony hokum becomes heartfelt hokum. Danny DeVito plays out-of-work ad exec Bill Rago, Princeton graduate, who grudgingly takes a job through the local welfare office teaching eight educationally disadvantaged Army recruits at a nearby post.

This "Dead Poets Society"/"Corn Is Green" setup always seems to work on some level—movies about the inspirations of education can be inspiring—and the liveliest moments in "Renaissance Man" involve Bill's classroom wheedlings and back talk. Initially marking time while hunting for a "real" job, he finds himself roused to help his troops. He discovers an improbable way to reach them—by teaching them "Hamlet."

Screenwriter Jim Burnstein reportedly worked a job very much like Bill's, but many of the incidents in the film seem trumped up. Bill's washout students are, of course, not really washouts; they just need to be cared for. They're like racially mixed Dead End Kids for the dysfunctional '90s. Most of them have sob stories: Miranda (Stacey Dash) was ditched by her mother; Brian (Peter Simmons) never knew his father who was killed in Vietnam; Jackson (Richard T. Jones) was a great pro football prospect before he became injured; Mel (Greg Sporleder) comes from an abusive family and dozes to blank out the pain.

Even the soldiers who don't seem touched by grief or anger—like country boy Tommy Lee (Mark Wahlberg, a.k.a. Marky Mark) or the well-read Roosevelt (Khalil Kain) or the jokester Jamaal (Kadeem Hardison)—seem stunted not by lack of aptitude but by lack of opportunity. Donnie (Lillo Brancato Jr.) starts out reading comic books and ends up reciting the "St. Crispin's Day" speech from "Henry V" to his flabbergasted drill sergeant (well played by Gregory Hines). It's an inspiring moment, but it would have been funnier—and probably truer to experience—if Donnie, an expert mimic, had recited the speech in his Al Pacino voice from "Scarface."

The soldiers get fired up about "Hamlet" by relating the play to their own lives—it's Shakespeare as therapist, as career adviser. The film's view of education is inspiring but also a bit bogus. It reduces great drama to a catalogue of shibboleths and life lessons. (This is also what the movie does to its own meanings.) And Bill's transformation is self-serving. He comes to recognize that his former advertising world lacks the "truth" of his new crusade but Burnstein and director Penny Marshall plug the Joy of Learning with slick commercial fervor, as if they were framing an ad campaign.

"Renaissance Man" never really shows us how Bill's brood might bring him into *their* culture. Through them he discovers his real calling, but the educational process is mostly one-way—*his* way. (The big dance number where the students do a rap version of "Hamlet" is the film's phoniest scene.) Bill is too busy getting his comeuppance in other ways: as a divorced father whose daughter wants his respect: as a former draft resister who learns, from the company colonel (Cliff Robertson), the true value of the military life.

DeVito is required to plod Bill through a lot of hare-brained paces, like the scene where he enters an endurance test to win the respect of his students. But DeVito is remarkably good in the role anyway; it seems to have touched something genuine in him. He's toned down his usual bug-eyed squalling, and the result is his best screen work since Barry Levinson's "Tin Men."

It is in Bill's early scenes, where he stands humiliated before his jobless life, that Penny Marshall's tact as a director comes through best. It doesn't come through often enough, though. She's a graceful, intelligent director who doesn't appear to have her heart in all the graceless grandstanding in "Renaissance Man." She doesn't have the gift for shamelessness, and that's why the film, with its pileup of sentimentalities, seems so processed. She's trying to engineer our emotions, but she's smart enough to know that an artist—not an engineer—is required for the job.

NEW YORK, 6/20/94, p. 79, David Denby

In Penny Marshall's *Renaissance Man*, Danny DeVito, a self-disgusted and unemployable ad executive, takes a job teaching "comprehension" to a bunch of basic-training losers whom the Army is about to give up on. DeVito teaches them *Hamlet*, which connects with their own experience in surprising ways, and in the process, he saves them and redeems himself. *Renaissance Man* is the kind of fable of rebirth that is very dear to my sentimental-liberal heart; such myths of regeneration through education are perhaps central to any society, especially this one, in which the inducements to stay dead are all but overpowering. But apart from DeVito's performance, which has interesting corners, what's on the screen is mainly an embarrassment.

Not to put too fine a point on it, Penny Marshall (*Big, Awakenings, A League of Their Own*) has become a hack: She works the audience over, producing easy emotion and easy laughter; her directing has a shrewd, can-do rhythm and pace, but you can't see anything of life peeking through the movieish tensions, climaxes, and resolutions. This might not be an issue if the movie were not insisting so loudly on the real-life troubles of all its characters. At the end of *Renaissance Man*, the recruits work up *Hamlet* into rap songs and drill chants. This is supposed to be a victory for them and for Shakespeare. It may suggest the limits of my charity if I point out that it isn't.

NEW YORK POST, 6/3/94, p. 41, Michael Medved

"Renaissance Man" represents an odd milestone in the career of director Penny Marshall.

With "Big," "Awakenings" and "A League of Their Own" she worked on tight well-constructed screenplays by superb writers, but here she performs minor miracles with this contrived material.

She even coaxes an unexpectedly adequate supporting performance from Calvin Klein poster boy Marky Mark in his movie debut—perhaps an even more formidable tribute to her talent.

The script, by first-timer Jim Burnstein, is reportedly inspired by his experiences teaching English at a National Guard base some 20 years ago. The movie's main character is a glib, cynical Detroit advertising executive (Danny DeVito) who loses his job and goes through a few weeks of desperation before he reluctantly accepts a temporary civilian position at a nearby Army post.

Officers Cliff Robertson and James Remar want him to teach a special remedial class for recruits who seem to be so slow-witted that they're in danger of flunking out of basic training.

In the course of helping these lost souls, DeVito naturally finds himself—inspiring his outcast students with the glories of "Hamlet" and discovering a new purpose in his lonely, previously pointless life.

This smug, hokey tale attempts to mix "Dead Poets Society" with elements of "An Officer and a Gentleman"—or a dozen other films that show the way that military training transforms insecure kids into proud, self-confident soldiers.

Unfortunately, "Renaissance Man" flagrantly falsifies the problems it poses, unrealistically suggesting that a sufficiently inspired teacher can magically turn even the most troubled, academically impaired students into Shakespeare enthusiasts. Wouldn't this picture have been more persuasive if at least one of DeVito's student's stubbornly failed to be transformed by his efforts?

DeVito handles his role like the old pro he is, milking the funny lines for all they're worth and delivering even his most embarrassing "inspirational" speeches ("I want you to know what it feels like to make the grade all on your own! I know you can do it!") without gagging.

Even more impressive are the heartfelt performances Marshall draws from each of the little-known young actors who play the lovable losers in DeVito's class; Khalil Kain, Richard T. Jones, Lillo Brancato Jr. (who played De Niro's son in "A Bronx Tale") and Stacey Dash are especially effective, and Mark Wahlberg (a.k.a. Marky Mark) does a fine job as a shy, soft-spoken redneck from Georgia. By the end of the picture we care about—and believe in—every one of these people.

In the end, no amount of fine acting or sensitive direction could make a cinematic silk purse out of this sentimental sow's ear of a screenplay, but the fact that Penny Marshall has come as close as she has says even more about her gifts than the big hits she's created in the past.

NEWSDAY, 6/3/94, Part II/p. B3, Jack Mathews

The boot camp comedy "Renaissance Man" written by a former English teacher and directed by gush maestro Penny Marshall, is built entirely around one dubious notion, that if you can overcome the language problem, you can make Shakespeare exciting, even to people too stupid to get through basic military training.

I don't know who should feel more insulted by the idea, the Army, Shakespeare or the audience. You decide.

"Renaissance Man" stars Danny DeVito as an out-of-work Madison Avenue ad executive who takes a temp job teaching language skills to a group of Army recruits so thick-headed they can't understand simple orders screamed into their faces by drill sergeants.

On the brink of being washed out of the service, the eight "Double-D" (dog-dumb) recruits, seven men and one woman, are given an opportunity to rescue themselves with a six-week course in remedial thinking, to be taught by reluctant unemployment-line draftee Bill Rago (DeVito).

Though Rago has no more interest in teaching the dummies than they have in learning, they are stuck with each other, so while they're together, Rago tries to pass along some of his love for Shakespeare by having them act out and analyze "Hamlet."

To paraphrase Polonius, there proves to be a method to his madness. The students love the story—sex! violence! incest!—and not only get past the Bard's Elizabethan English, but begin to overcome some of the fears of education that got them in trouble in the first place. It's "Dead Poets Society" for under-achievers.

First-time screenwriter Jim Burnstein was reportedly inspired to write this story by his own experiences teaching Shakespeare to soldiers at an Air National Guard base in Michigan, and his obvious passion for the subject is the best thing about his script. The movie lights up every time the students begin dissecting "Hamlet."

Even DeVito, whose screen persona has been evolving into something resembling a snapping turtle, seems moved by the connection Rago is able to make through Shakespeare. He is his old self when dealing with the military nonsense outside the classroom, but when Rago is with his students, DeVito becomes remarkably warm and sympathetic.

Every other element of the story—Rago's anti-authoritarian run-ins with the gung-ho drill sergeant (Gregory Hines), his insensitivity to his teenage daughter at home, his attempts to solve each of the student's life crises—is so contrived, the movie just creaks through all the exposition.

Burnstein lays on secondary issues about the failure of America's public school system, the shifting values of the new co-ed military and the regenerative powers of knowledge, but the only genuine question—can you make Shakespeare fun?—is pretty much answered when the guys in class stop complaining about having to play Gertrude and Ophelia.

Marshall, whose most recent movies ("Awakenings" and "A League of Their Own") have each given us two acts of story and one of shameless sentimentality, is given nine golden opportunities to wring us out again, and she doesn't waste any of them. If you're a sucker for her lingering close-ups of people bulging with restrained emotions, don't forget the Kleenex.

However, when they hear Rago's class perform "Hamlet Rap," co-written by Marky Mark (who plays one of the soldiers), Shakespeare scholars may be crying for a completely different reason.

SIGHT AND SOUND, 8/94, p. 50, Tom Tunney

Advertising executive Bill Rago loses his job after a traffic jam prevents him from landing a vital $6 million account. He then comes home to an answering machine full of irate messages from creditors plus a request from his daughter Emily to buy her a telescope and a plane ticket to Mexico so she can view a lunar eclipse.

Registering as unemployed, Rago is assigned a six-week job at the MacClane US Army Training Camp as teacher to eight recruits, whose lack of reading and writing skills mean that they are on the borderline of being rejected by the service. Nicknamed the 'Double Ds' ("Dumb as dogshit"), the class are a diverse ethnic and geographical mix: Hispanic Donnie Benitez, whites Brian Davis, Mel Melvin and Tommy Lee Haywood, and Afro-Americans Miranda Myers, Jackson Leroy, Roosevelt Hobbs and Jamaal Montgomery.

Rago has never taught before, but is touched by the bleak personal details revealed by his first class assignment. By chance having a copy of *Hamlet* with him, he decides to base future lessons on this text, getting his students to bang out a rhythm on their desks to accompany their recital of the blank verse. The class goes well, but Rago's relationship with Drill Sergeant Lou Cass—who thinks the lessons are a waste of time—becomes increasingly fractious. Benitez and Davis are late on parade and when Rago intervenes on their behalf, he and Cass almost come to blows.

Impressed by the incisive personality of Hobbs, Rago goes to commanding officer Colonel James to request that he be considered for officer training. Unfortunately, further research into Hobbs' background reveals him to be a fugitive crack dealer, and he is arrested and sent to jail.

Rago loses the confidence of the class when he is late for a lesson, but regains it when he successfully joins them on the Victory Tower assault course. The class then perform a 'Hamlet Rap' song for him.

Pawning an advertising award to pay for Emily's telescope and airline ticket, Rago then accompanies his class to Canada to see a stage performance of *Henry V*. Rago prepares his pupils for a final examination, which will decide whether they can stay in the Army. Seeking out the records on the military service of Melvin's father, who was killed in Vietnam, Rago receives unofficial help from a woman staff sergeant, with whom he becomes friends. During night. drill practice, Cass orders Benitez to recite some Shakespeare, hoping to humiliate him; Benitez responds impressively with the St Crispin's Day speech from *Henry V*.

Rago subjects his students to an oral exam, and deems them all to have passed. On graduation day, all eight recruits are part of the passing-out parade. Rago looks on proudly with his daughter, and Colonel James presents Melvin with the Silver Star medal his father won posthumously in the Vietnam War. James asks Rago if he is willing to take the next intake of recruits and the answer is a very cheerful yes.

One day, someone will make a movie about a nervous wreck of a teacher who finds his rebellious students impossible to handle and just gives up on them. *Renaissance Man*, though, follows the well-worn path of such classroom movies as *The Blackboard Jungle*, *To Sir With Love* and *Stand and Deliver*, in which a dedicated teacher inculcates a sense of self-esteem and achievement in his students and they go on to become useful members of society.

However, *Renaissance Man* is also an example of that well-populated sub-genre of the war film, the basic-training movie; it is also a Danny DeVito comedy vehicle; it has the discernible *auteur* dimension of a Penny Marshall film; and, more by default than design, it presents a fascinating picture of how far the exposed values of the American military have been rehabilitated by 90s Hollywood.

Basic training has been a natural subject for movie comedy from Chaplin onwards, and on that level, the film performs satisfactorily. DeVito's blustering style is well served, and many of his one-liners are excellent value, especially his succinct definition of stage drama—"You know, like TV without the box?"

As a Penny Marshall film, the movie can usefully be related to *A League of Their Own*. Similar values of team spirit, friendship and self-definition are celebrated, and DeVito's role here is similar to Tom Hanks' there: the initially reluctant instructor who comes both to admire and to be inspired by those he teaches. However, where that film had the benefit of a fresh subject and an immensely strong gallery of characters, *Renaissance Man* groans under its weight of clichés, character stereotypes and overall predictability—which brings us back to the film's status as a military movie made in the 90s.

The Pentagon applies very strict rules to those films it is prepared to support with hardware, personnel and base locations. Its regulations, which vitally include script approval, boil down to one demand: that the film present a positive image of the military. *Top Gun* was granted full support; *Apocalypse Now* was refused. Not surprisingly, *Renaissance Man* was afforded ample Pentagon help, for it whole-heartedly endorses a recruitment-advertisement view of military service.

Here, the US Army is one big happy family. Foul language, bullying, ritualised humiliation and violence of any sort are virtually non-existent here. The perfect demographic mix of white, Afro-American and Hispanic soldiers in Bill's class all have hard luck stories to tell about their experiences in civilian society, but once they have joined up and made the grade, those problems are solved. As Colonel James says in his Graduation Day speech, "the future's looking bright both for you and your country".

Looking at *Renaissance Man*, it is not difficult to believe that M*A*S*H was made almost a quarter of a century ago. Throughout, the values of Marshall's film and those of the Army are seen to be one and the same. Military posters are repeatedly in shot, proclaiming such messages as "Victory starts here" and "Pain is temporary: Pride is forever". Alongside that hackneyed optimism, however, is just a hint of the frighteningly fragmented society these young people have escaped from. They have been failed by the education system, the economy and a disintegrating social structure, but the Army gives them something to belong to. Rago himself is divorced and has difficulty in relating to his daughter, while one of his students, in a rare scene outside the classroom, gets a letter from home about his violent stepfather.

However, these tantalising undercurrents are almost instantaneously swept aside by the movie's insistently positive message about self-worth and service in the US military being indissolubly linked. Quoting some of the best-known passages in Shakespeare allows the film to present the identity crises of Rago and his students as a triumph for that "happy few", the US Army. Rago's quotation, "This above all: to thine own self be true," and the Army poster which proclaims, "Be all you can be" are here interchangeable.

This is a startling throwback to the Cold War pro-military values of such early 50s basic-training potboilers as *Take the High Ground* and *Battle Cry*. Then, however, the enemy was obviously external, whereas now it seems that the biggest enemy is American social reality itself—something so frightening to contemplate that it has to be both drowned in sentimentality and smothered by symmetrical plotting before it has a chance to draw breath.

The film also mawkishly sets about healing the wounds of Vietnam. Rago tells Colonel James that his only previous military experience was protesting against the War; by the film's conclusion, he has literally got with the programme and become a team player. Then there is that achingly contrived presentation of a father's medal to a son, who is seen to be following in the same great tradition.

Mel Gibson's recent *The Man Without a Face* had a child being taught Shakespeare so he could escape his dysfunctional family and go to military academy—and it was actually set at the height of the Vietnam War in 1968! *Renaissance Man* is even more mind-boggling in its use of the Bard. Hesitantly gesturing with one hand back to the searing Civvy Street despair of films such as *Boyz N the Hood*, it uses the other to hitch a ride on Shakespeare's silver wings to an idealised military community that is as far removed from that dangerous world as the Land of Oz is from Kansas.

TIME, 6/13/94, p. 74, Richard Schickel

Warm-hearted humanism is glopped all over *Renaissance Man* in the hopes that we won't notice that the story makes no sense. It proposes that the only job available to Bill Rago (Danny DeVito), a defrocked adman, is teaching an ill-defined lit course to a multicultural squad at an Army base. Why the commanding colonel thinks these studies are vitally necessary is not made clear. Especially since the kids turn out be quite sweet and bright and mostly doing fine in basic training. It's all really just a con on the part of the moviemakers, led by director Penny Marshall. The insensitive and materialistic teacher shall learn humility from his students, They shall in turn learn that underneath Shakespeare's big, arcane words and underneath Bill's hard shell, good hearts are athump. We shall all have a nice sniffle as we learn how easily class and racial distinctions can be dissolved by simple goodwill.

Here's an idea for *Speed II*: terrorist wires teacher's copy of *Hamlet*. If he gets to the "Oh what a rogue and peasant slave am I" soliloquy—*Ka-BOOM*!

VILLAGE VOICE, 6/7/94, p. 60, Beth Coleman

The army could have given us a more imaginative setup than this: middle-aged, out-of-steam advertising guy Bill Rago (Danny DeVito) gets canned. Unemployment, as the hand of fate, places him on a military base before a class of subremedial students. Drill Sergeant Cass (Gregory Hines) has nine weeks to make these ladies into men and Rago the same in which to school the Double D's—dumb as dogshit—on "basic comprehension." Above all to himself true, Rago ends up teaching *Hamlet*.

What saves *Renaissance* from falling on its own cliché is that this movie about good teachers in dark times stays mostly with the kids. By making a '90s *Breakfast Club* in combat boots, director Penny Marshall does for the dispossessed what John Hughes did for the mall rat. The eight retard recruits are a wonderful crew (an ensemble of relatively new faces, including the charismatic Khalil Kain as our young Dane, Lilio Brancato Jr. as a Bronx Shakespeare convert, and Marky Mark *not* as himself that divides into two basic categories—inner city trash and rural dirt.

Granted that "military intelligence" is the class's introduction to oxymoron, *Renaissance* hardly slams the army. If you treat drill camp like an especially tough prep school, then certainly the feud between target practice and humanities education disappears in the face of the greater good—an institution that curbs the chaos of these kids' lives. And anyway, it's either that or prison. In this man's army, the Bard's bottom line is the survival of the soldier and the student. Yo, lose the melancholic thinker.

Also reviewed in:
CHICAGO TRIBUNE, 6/3/94, Friday/p. C, Michael Wilmington
NEW YORK TIMES, 6/3/94, p. C6, Janet Maslin
VARIETY, 5/30-6/5/94, p. 51, Brian Lowry
WASHINGTON POST, 6/3/94, p. C1, Hal Hinson
WASHINGTON POST, 6/3/94, Weekend/p. 44, Desson Howe

RESISTANCE

An Angelika Films presentation of a Macau Light Film Corporation production with the participation of Australian Film Finance Corporation. *Producer:* Christina Ferguson, Pauline Rosenberg, and Jenny Day. *Director:* Paul Elliott and Hugh Keays-Byrne. *Screenplay*: The Macau Collective. *Director of Photography:* Sally Bongers. *Editor:* Stewart Young. *Music:* Davood A. Tabrizi. *Sound:* Peter Clancy. *Production Designer:* Macgregor Knox. *Costumes:* Sally Molineaux. *Stunt Coordinator:* Grant Page. *Running time:* 112 minutes. *MPAA Rating:* Not Rated.

CAST: Lorna Lesley (Jean Skilling); Helen Jones (Natalie); Robyn Nevin (Wiley); Bogdan Koca (Strickland); Stephen Leeder (Col. Webber); Harold Hopkins (Peach); Donal Gibson (Eric); Hugh Keays-Byrne (Peter); Kris McQuade (Ruth); Jennifer Claire (Ruby); Jack Thompson (Mr. Wilson); Maya Sheridan (sister).

NEW YORK POST, 11/23/94, p. 50, Bill Hoffmann

The scene is the Outback in present-day Australia. The economy is shot, the people live in stark poverty and martial law has been declared.

Gatherings of four or more are considered subversive. The only jobs are in government-run grain factories at harvest time.

Troops roam the countryside harassing the poor, enforcing their brutal laws with large tanks and machine guns.

That's the grim portrait of society directors Paul Elliott and Hugh Keays-Byrne paint in their ambitious, if wholly unsatisfying, new film "Resistance."

Set over a five-day period in a desert-like outpost called Ithaca Plains, "Resistance" zeroes in on a group of nomadic outcasts who live in small camps and eat hand to mouth.

We're treated to scene after scene of brutality and suffering as the military goes around squashing the little folk.

It's overkill. You want to say, "Enough already! We've got the point!"

Finally, amid the chaos, a mother of two (Lorna Lesley) and a native Outback girl (Helen Jones) band together to try to fight the sadistic soldiers.

That's all well and good but it takes three-quarters of the picture before they get their act together and make their strike.

When that happens the picture takes off and turns into riveting high-tension drama.

But, alas, it's too late, we've already lost interest and the fate of Australia doesn't matter anymore.

With some nice acting turns, superior photography and fine production values, "Resistance" looks spendid.

It's just a shame it couldn't have lived up to its title and showed a little more resistance.

NEWSDAY, 11/23/94, Part II/p. B12, Gene Seymour

Watching "Resistance," you're reminded of how fresh and exciting Australian cinema was about 15 years ago when movies like "Breaker Morant," "The Chant of Jimmie Blacksmith" and the "Mad Max" sagas made a beachhead on American shores. Though close to, but not quite part of such exalted company, "Resistance" is driven by the same momentum and urgency that powered those late-'70s breakthroughs to international glory.

Written and produced collaboratively by members of the Macau Light Corporation (and jointly directed by Paul Elliot and Hugh Keays-Byrne), "Resistance" is set in a time perilously close to our own when resources become scarce, money becomes tight and the powers-that-be protect their autonomy by declaring martial law nationwide.

This brutally enforced "state of emergency" reaches as far as Ithaca Plains, a tiny shantytown located in the middle of nowhere. It's a place where poor, itinerant workers live uneasily with the indigenous natives. They bicker over the few jobs available at a local wheat mill that's the only employer in the region.

Bad as things are, they start getting worse when a heavily armored anti-terrorist squad led by the drily menacing Col. Webber (Stephen Leeder) moves into the area to seize control of the town, the mill and the fates of those who live in Ithaca Plains' trailers and mud huts.

The army makes targets out of the few who are trying to keep peace among the locals. This turns an already bad situation worse. Neighbors inform on each other. Women and children become hunted down like helpless game. From such chaos, an unlikely alliance is forged between a fiery young native woman (Helen Jones) and a truck stop waitress (Lorna Lesley), who loses her convict husband to the state of emergency and may well lose her two children as well.

Though many hands went into its making, "Resistance" zooms along ahead with no seams or stretch marks. In both method and theme, the film makes a persuasive case for collective action as a means of confronting the public and private terrors swirling through a world undergoing the pre-millennial jitters.

VILLAGE VOICE, 12/6/94, p. 66, Jason Vincz

My sense of irony may be underdeveloped, but I'm fairly certain *Resistance* is not a parody. Unfortunately, it's hard to see the Fiendish Villains in this Australian smash-'em-up as anything else. Tuxedoed Aryans sing *lieder* after smoking locals with machine guns. Tattooed riot police beat old ladies while shotgunning caged pigeons at point-blank range. Sweaty leather fetishists do double takes before kicking over baby carriages. Evidently no one told the directors that such solemn absurdities are not shocking, or harrowing, or sad—they're funny.

Resistance lovingly portrays a group of Noble Workers who've gathered for the harvest at a Heartless Capitalist's wheat mill. Political riots convince the air-conditioned exploiter to bring in an army (the aforementioned Villains) to protect his mill from the masses. The plotless political muddle gives the relentlessly brutal bad guys free rein, leaving the Workers cowering and the audience napping.

Working mostly at the magic hour, Jane Campion's old cinematographer Sally Bongers stumbles across some nice visual nuggets, but somehow the outback's eerie emptiness never contributes any atmosphere. What nice performances there are get obliterated by clanking platitudes—"I think we all lost our innocence that day"—and after two meandering hours, you can't help snorting at the earnestly contrived sadism. Perhaps *Resistance* is the cinematic equivalent of Super Dave Osborne—that it's done with a straight face *is* the joke.

Also reviewed in:
NEW YORK TIMES, 11/23/94, p. C18, Stephen Holden
VARIETY, 11/23/92, p. 49, David Stratton

RICHIE RICH

A Warner Bros. release of a Silver Pictures production in association with Davis Entertainment Company. *Executive Producer:* Dan Kolsrud, Joe Bilella, and Jon Shapiro. *Producer:* Joel Silver and John Davis. *Director:* Donald Petrie. *Screenplay:* Tom S. Parket and Jim Jennewin. *Story (based on characters appearing in Harvey Comics):* Neil Tolkin. *Director of Photography:* Don Burgess. *Editor:* Malcolm Campbell. *Music:* Alan Silvestri. *Music Editor:* Kenneth Karman. *Sound:* Scott Smith and (music) Dennis Sands. *Sound Editor:* George Watters II. *Casting:* Margery Simkin. *Production Designer:* James Spencer. *Art Director:* William Matthews. *Set Designer:* Cydney Harris, Karen Fletcher Trujillo, and Susan Wexler. *Set Decorator:* John Anderson and Patricia Malone. *Special Effects:* Michael Wood. *Visual Effects:* Peter Donen. *Costumes:* Lisa Jensen. *Make-up:* Linda Melazzo. *Stunt Coordinator:* Jack Gill. *Running time:* 95 minutes. *MPAA Rating:* PG.

CAST: Macaulay Culkin (Richie Rich); John Larroquette (Lawrence Van Dough); Edward Herrmann (Richard Rich); Jonathan Hyde (Cadbury); Christine Ebersole (Regina); Chelcie Ross (Ferguson); Stephi Lineburg (Gloria); Mariangela Pino (Diane); Michael McShane (Professor Keenbean); Michael Maccarone (Tony); Joel Robinson (Omar); Jonathan Hilario (Pee Wee); Reggie Jackson (Baseball Coach); Claudia Schiffer (Aerobics Instructor); Wanda Christine (Newswoman at Factory); Stacy Logan (Nash); Eddie Bo Smith, Jr. (Ambler); Kent Logsdon (Zullo); Bob Riley (President); David A. Fawcett (Chauffeur); Dawn Maxey (Van Dough's Secretary); Ben Stein (Teacher); Sean A. Tate (Reynolds); Joel Ellegant (Ellsworth); Justin Zaremby (Reginald); John Drury and Diann Burns (Newscasters); Rush Pearson (Prison Lowlife); Rachel Stephens and Nydia Rodriguez (Richie's Secretaries); Sam Sanders (Detective); Mike Bacarella (Police Desk Sargeant); Marilyn Dodds Frank (Sculptress); Mindy Bell, James Deuter, and Rick Worthy (News Reporters); Michael Godleski (Foyer Guard); Matt DeCaro (Dave Walter); Rory Culkin (Young Richie); Peter Lampley (Baby Richie); Eddie Fernandez (Prison Assassin); Joanne Pankow (Maid); Jim Deeth (Helicopter Pilot); Lily Semel (Little Girl at Factory); Jim Blandford (Prison Guard); Dustin Drapkin (Boy on Baseball Field).

LOS ANGELES TIMES, 12/21/94, Calendar/p. 9, Kevin Thomas

"Richie Rich" presents an irresistible Macaulay Culkin in a wonderful part and bursts with the gadgetry that many adults thrill to as much as children do. At the same time, it never loses touch with its humanity, directed by Donald Petrie with humor and panache.

In the title role, based on the Harvey Comics character, Culkin is the richest 12-year-old in the world. Appropriately, Biltmore, the century-old Vanderbilt estate in Ashville, N.C., the largest mansion in America, serves as Richie's home, which for purposes of the story is somewhere outside Chicago. Richie is also a classic poor little rich boy, but not because he's unloved or neglected or even spoiled but because so much is expected of him, including the kind of public duties carried on by the more conscientious members of the House of Windsor.

Richie is a terrifically good kid, intelligent, polite, perfectly groomed, cheerful and rightly self-confident. He has everything the world has to offer but friends his own age. At a public ceremony, marking the renewal rather than the anticipated closure of a Rich-owned factory, Richie notices a bunch of neighborhood youngsters playing baseball nearby. The look of longing on Richie's face is the linchpin of the entire film, summing up what Richie doesn't have. Little do the other kids suspect that he's actually a crackerjack player—Reggie Jackson, after all, is his personal coach. Richie's butler (Jonathan Hyde, a delight) starts figuring a way to bring the kids and Richie together.

Meanwhile, Lawrence Van Dough (John Larroquette, a gleeful villain with a helmet of lacquered hair), a top executive at Rich Industries, is figuring out ways to get his hands on the Rich family fortune, which is in the neighborhood of $70 billion. Van Dough's machinations plunge Richie into high adventure, yet writers Tom S. Parker and Jim Jennewein, working from Neil Tolkin's story, never lose concern for their characters, who include Michael McShane as a colorful inventor, and Stephi Lineburg and Mariangela Pino as mother and daughter, hearty representatives of the normal world.

Instead of the usual self-absorbed parents poor little rich children are supposed to have, Richie's mother and father (Edward Herrmann and Christine Ebersole) are devoted to each other and to their only son. The refreshing point the picture makes is that vast wealth, in its insular qualities, has made them innocents. They're a silly and staggeringly naive couple, yet sincere do-gooders; they seem to have just stepped out of a Preston Sturges screwball comedy.

Production designer James Spencer and special effects coordinator Michael Wood have come up with much stylish wonderment for cinematographer Don Burgess to photograph gleamingly. There's even a hilariously cockamamie homage to "North by Northwest's" famous climactic sequence at Mount Rushmore. Yet "Richie Rich," a wide-appeal Christmas comedy-fantasy, steadfastly keeps its heart in the right place and even its values in proper perspective.

NEW YORK POST, 12/21/94, p. 40, Thelma Adams

A butler and single mom are thrown together in an unexpected embrace while discussing astrology. "Do I detect a rising fire sign, Herbert?" she asks.

Excuuuse me! If this is the kind of funny bone the makers of "Richie Rich" think they have to toss the parents in the audience. then they've misread the adults as much as the kids.

Salty seniors made director Donald Petrie's "Grumpy Old Men" a hit, but Mrs. Rich telling Mr. Rich that he has "a cute butt" does nothing for this wooden, overblown adaptation of the popular Harvey Comics about the world's richest—and loneliest—boy.

Macaulay Culkin, a real-life contender for world's richest kid, plays the title role without a shred of irony or insight. The boy with the bee-stung lips snags another multi-million-dollar paycheck, smugly sleepwalking through his work in a way that would have offended the hard-working good samaritan Richie—if there was more to the character than ink and paper.

Dead behind the eyes for most of the movie, Mac performs the usual tricks. He mugs for the camera a la "Home Alone" with the dubious novelty of a magnifying glass between his lips and the lens.

The adolescent Culkin began to grow out of the part as production neared and is surrounded by tall actors to compensate: Edward Herrmann and Christine Ebersole waddle along as his parents; the wickedly funny John Larroquette is surprisingly tepid as greedy villain Lawrence Van Dough.

Not every element is over-sized. The toys are big; the sets bigger. The finale on the face of Mount Richmore, ripped from the climax of "North by Northwest," is bloated in the extreme. But, deep within the episodic script by "The Flintstones" writers Tom S. Parker and Jim Jennewein, the heart is a tiny lump of coal.

The joyless "Richie Rich" is a spoiled child raised by wealthy parents who had other projects dearer to their hearts.

NEWSDAY, 12/21/94, Part II/p. B3, John Anderson

Despite 36 months of economic recovery, we must be in a Depression because Macaulay Culkin's "Richie Rich" is a Depression-era movie. It has a benevolent, if slightly dotty, financial despot in Edward Herrmann's Richard Rich Sr., a mob of unwashed, blue-collar paragons, and a moral that says friends are more valuable than money—all the while using money as a drug. It'll make the poor feel morally superior, the wealthy feel safe, and give both crowds the vicarious pleasures of unrestrained avarice. It's "My Man Godfrey" for the "Power Rangers" set.

But despite the intoxicating lushness of the Rich family fortune and the plot that revolves around it, "Richie Rich" also has a sense of humor, and a self-awareness about its own crass materialism that makes it more amusing than offensive. The supporting actors make the most of Tom S. Parker and Jim Jennewein's smart screenplay, resulting in a movie that wouldn't have been funny in the '80s but is very funny now.

Few of the chuckles in this Harvey comic come-to-life, however, are produced by its star, who is a cosmic black hole of personality. The "Home Alone" kid simply has no light in his eyes, his every smile seems forced, and few screen personalities, never mind real actors, have ever exuded a more innocuous presence.

But director Donald Petrie has a flair for comic timing and a supporting cast that shares it. They include the bounteous Herrmann as Richie's father, the gifted comedienne Christine Ebersole as Richie's mother, John Hyde as the trusted Gielgudian valet Cadbury (a plug?) and John Larroquette as the oleaginous Lawrence Van Dough, treacherous Rich family employee and arch-nemesis of the resourceful Richie.

Most of the plot is standard-issue good-vs.-evil and search-and-rescue—Van Dough puts a bomb on the Rich family plane in order to perpetrate a takeover, but Richie misses the plane, and his parents just miss being blown to bits. While the lifeboated Riches bob about the Caribbean like Mr. and Mrs. Thurston Howell III, Richie has to use his wits—and those of his new, ethnically-balanced group of working-class pals—to fend off Van Dough's attempts to appropriate the Riches' loot. Van Dough will fail, of course, but the end is immaterial. It's the means that justify the movie.

There are cute sight gags—baby Richie's crib with its mobile of ingots and currency; a schoolmate using a shredder to destroy a note passed in class; Reggie Jackson coaching Richie in baseball. There's also some blatant product placement, and outtakes from the Three Stooges and "North by Northwest"—the climactic episode on Mount Richmore is a wildly indulgent and illogical homage to Hitchcock. Macaulay of course, is no Cary Grant, nor even Larry, Curly or Moe. "Richie Rich," however, indicates he has some residual luck.

SIGHT AND SOUND, 6/95, p. 50, Tom Tunney

As the sole heir to a multi-billion dollar fortune, Richie Rich is the wealthiest child in the world. Living with his parents Mr and Mrs Rich and their butler Cadbury in a huge palatial mansion, he has his own McDonalds restaurant and his own amusement park, but the one thing lacking in his life is a group of friends his own age. After his father takes over the ailing United Tool Company, Richie, representing his dad, flies in by helicopter to the company town and makes a speech to the grateful workforce and their union representative Diane. Afterwards, he meets Diane's daughter Gloria and her friends, Tony, Omar and Pee Wee, all of whom regard his privileged background with a mixture of awe and disdain.

Having failed to interest his similarly rich classmates in having fun, Richie meets the street kids again for a game of baseball and then takes them back to his mansion to play. Meanwhile, Mr Rich's chief executive Van Dough schemes to take over the company, planting a bomb aboard the Richs' private airliner before they take off for to England to meet the Queen. The couple survive the explosion and take to their life raft in mid-ocean. Even with his parents missing believed killed, Richie is able to thwart Van Dough's plans because he still controls 51 per cent of the company stock, and his amazing financial acumen quickly makes him headline news.

Van Dough has Cadbury framed and arrested for the bombing and then, when Mr and Mrs Rich manage to reestablish contact with the outside world, gets to them first and holds them captive at the mansion. Richie, aided by eccentric inventor Professor Keenbean, springs Cadbury from jail and enlists the help of Gloria and the other kids in storming the mansion. Van Dough forces Mr and Mrs Rich to take him to their treasure vault inside a nearby hill which is carved, Mount Rushmore style, with huge effigies of their faces. Van Dough is disappointed to discover that the chamber contains only family trinkets and nothing of any financial value. After an involved struggle on the face of the mountain, Van Dough is subdued and then unceremoniously fired by Mr Rich. Richie entertains the other children at the mansion—at which Van Dough is now employed as a lowly gardener. His parents happily look on, pleased that their son now really is the richest boy in the world because he has friends.

Richie Rich is perversely reminiscent of the 1989 Michael Moore documentary *Roger and Me*. In *Roger and Me*, General Motors decided to close down their auto plant in Flint, Michigan and effectively destroyed the local economy. Here benevolent capitalist Mr Rich steps in to save the ailing United Tool Company and saves the local economy. If *Roger and Me* shows the ruthless reality of modern big business practice, then *Richie Rich* is its exact opposite, an unbearably coy fantasy of big business as it likes to think of itself in its advertising: as caring, responsible and people-oriented.

A film which wasn't so keen to peddle free enterprise propaganda might perhaps have had Mr Rich as an inventor whose patents had made him wealthy, or perhaps as a megarich movie or sports star. Presenting Rich instead as a successful business tycoon is a much more dubious proposition, particularly for any luckless adults in the audience who've had recent experience of redundancy or 'downsizing'. It seems as if Horatio Alger is alive and well and writing scripts in Hollywood.

The blandness and meretriciousness of the storyline also means that *Richie Rich* does nothing to extend Macaulay Culkin's range as an actor. As a Culkin star vehicle, the film has a fair selection of the expected nifty gadgets and slap-stick set pieces. The little 'robobee' flying robot and the *North by Northwest* inspired finale are presented with flair and the film's stock of witty one-liners is satisfyingly high. Unfortunately, the film-makers have shied away from any temptation to modify Culkin's pre-adolescent star persona even though he's now significantly taller and older-looking than he was in *My Girl* and *Home Alone 2*. Culkin is still playing a child rather than the young adolescent he obviously is. He remains stubbornly a figure teetering on the verge of responsibility; a character who defines himself principally in relation to his parents and to other grown-ups rather than in relation to his peers.

In the best of Culkin's earlier films, his trademark wide-eyed look served him well—because he so obviously was a talented child making comical headway in an adult's world. Here it seems unduly constricting, making him seem less of a star, more a passive spectator in his own story, a dull character whose unsubtle range of emotions only extends from a child's long face to a child's big smile. Increasingly, it's a persona which recalls the permanently bemused expression of Stan Laurel rather than a believable youngster. Macauley Culkin's next role will be vital. If it's a safe, committee-approved family film such as this one, then his career will have stalled completely in a mire of tired slapstick and cosy platitudes.

Also reviewed in:
NEW YORK TIMES, 12/21/94, p. C19, Stephen Holden
VARIETY, 1/2-8/95, p. 72, Joe Leydon
WASHINGTON POST, 12/21/94, p. C15, Rita Kempley
WASHINGTON POST, 12/23/94, Weekend/p. 37, Kevin McManus

RISK

A Seventh Art Releasing presentation of a Hank Blumenthal presentation in association with Naked Eye Productions. *Producer:* Gordon McLennan. *Director:* Deirdre Fishel. *Screenplay:* Deirdre Fishel. *Director of Photography:* Peter Pearce. *Editor:* Deirdre Fishel and Gordon McLennan. *Music:* John Paul Jones. *Sound:* Stuart Pearce. *Production Designer:* Flavia Galuppo. *Set Dresser:* Phillip Clarke. *Running time:* 85 minutes. *MPAA Rating:* Not Rated.

CAST: Karen Sillas (Maya); David Ilku (Joe); Molly Price (Nikki); Jack Gwaltney (Karl); Christie MacFayden (Alice).

LOS ANGELES TIMES, 12/16/94, Calendar/p. 8, Kevin Thomas

Deirdre Fishel's captivating debut feature, "Risk," a love story of exceptional insight t and reflection, reveals how a passionate affair can lead to a devastating confrontation with self. It's one of those mini-budget films with a raw, unpolished look and feel that complements rather than detracts from its material.

While her film has a steady, rhythmic flow, Fishel wisely focuses steadfastly. on her people, which results in an unfussy, natural style; there's no artiness here, no fancy camera angles. At the same time, "Risk" has a sense of nuance, of a comprehensive illumination of emotions, that seems distinctly feminine.

"Risk" really lives up to its title. Joe (David Ilku), a pleasant-looking, friendly young man zeros in on Maya (Karen Sillas), a striking young woman, while riding one evening on a New York bus. Although Maya, a struggling painter, backs off from his advances, she finds herself, a day or so later, letting him in her crummy apartment—and almost immediately joining him in her bathtub.

Maya and Joe, both so very attractive, are ripe for each other: she's finding it so hard to make it in her work that she's wondering what she should be doing with her life: for Joe reaching out to Maya is a way of breaking out of his self-described "anonymity"—living at a YMCA, apparently drifting from one minimum-wage job to another. They unleash a spirit of recklessness in each other to the extent that they're quickly off to rural Connecticut in a stolen car. (Not to worry, Fishel, though inspired by a news item, refuses steadfastly to turn her material into yet another "lovers-on-the-run" adventure.)

Fishel reveals what a fine writer she is in the deft way, in the course of the couple's journey, she shifts focus from Maya to Joe. Joe winds up on the doorstep of his pregnant older sister Nikki (Molly Price, in an admirably complex portrayal), with the hope of finding shelter for him and Maya and work from his builder brother-in-law Karl (Jack Gwaltney), who is leery of Joe.

But what has Maya gotten herself into? Why is Nikki's loving concern for her brother so intense? Why is Karl's resentment of Joe tinged with jealousy? Ultimately mature but made vulnerable through love, Maya becomes one of a zillion women who has let herself get carried away by an ardent lover she really doesn't know and may well be more deeply troubled than she could ever imagine.

Fishel is as skilled a director as she is a writer, and the portrayals of Sillas, seen recently—and impressively—in "What Happened Was ... " and Ilku have a completeness that's extraordinary. Ilku is as touching as he is unsettling as a young man for whom love releases at once terrible demons and a deep yearning to make something of his life. (In time we realize Joe's confident pursuit of Maya was in fact a remarkable act of courage.) Sillas' Maya, in turn, discovers her inherent resiliency and honesty tested as never before. "Risk" ends abruptly, leaving us confounded, which seems exactly as it should be.

NEW YORK POST, 10/5/94, p. 33, Larry Worth

Wanted: new agent for Karen Sillas. The up-and-coming, highly talented actress is continually getting cast in vehicles where she's the best thing around.

In that tradition comes "Risk," a story that huffs and puffs for an hour, then gets blown down in the final third.

The peripatetic script is about a woman's attempts to reach out to an emotionally disturbed sometime thief (occasionally effective David Ilku). But those holding their breath for a payoff had better look good in blue.

First-time writer/director Deirdre Fishel fails to carry through on the script's promise. Thankfully, Sillas' expressive face and commanding tones fill in a lot of the blanks.

So while Sillas' fans might want to check out her latest accomplishments, "Risk" remains too much of a gamble for most filmgoers.

NEWSDAY, 10/5/94, Part II/p. B7, Terry Kelleher

"I'm not even going to ask you how you know where I live," says a struggling painter named Maya (Karen Sillas), upon opening the door of her New York apartment to find a male stranger who came on to her aboard a city bus the night before.

Here in the crime-fearing, AIDS-fearing 1990s, you'd think most women *would* put the question, or even bolt the latch. But not this woman—she's the main character in a movie appropriately titled "Risk."

Frustrated by her stalled career, degraded by having to earn bread as a nude model and increasingly alienated from her art-crowd friends, Maya seems ready to roll the dice with someone completely different. So she scarcely thinks twice before inviting the quietly insistent Joe (David Ilku) into her home, her bathtub, her bed.

"Let me spend the night, or I'm going to have to kill myself," Joe says. A joke, maybe. But also a warning sign—a warning sign that Maya, despite her evident intelligence and savvy, chooses to ignore.

From the moment Joe steals a car, adding to his record of small-time crime, writer-director Deirdre Fishel keeps us guessing why Maya would accompany him on the road to self-destruction. Does she want to mold him? Mother him? Wallow with him?

Great sex might do as a motive, but Fishel doesn't make it look all that great. Unusual, yes. Not every guy enjoys wearing lipstick and women's underwear. But this quirk of Joe's appears to amuse Maya less as their relationship develops.

Joe and Maya hook up with his ambivalent sister, Nikki (Molly Price), and her abusive husband, Karl (Jack Gwaltney). "Why are you with Joe?" asks Nikki, whose attitude toward her brother alternates between tenderness and wariness. "None of your business," Maya replies. When Karl demands to know what's so "great" about Joe, Maya parries again: "If you had any of what Joe has, you wouldn't have to ask that question."

If we had any *idea* of what Joe has—besides increasingly obvious masochistic tendencies caused by severe childhood trauma—we wouldn't be in the dark, either.

The film does suggest, almost in passing, that mixed-up Joe may serve Maya as model and muse. But her artistic growth takes a backseat to his emotional disintegration. It's not a pretty sight; neither is it a particularly involving one.

Sillas, currently drawing favorable attention for her work in "What Happened Was ..." and the TV series "Under Suspicion," is the main attraction in Fishel's debut feature. The only problem with Sillas' performance in "Risk" is that she makes her character seem too smart not to walk away.

VILLAGE VOICE, 10/11/94, p. 74, Kathy Deacon

Maya (Karen Sillas) is an East Village artist, blond and angular. She smokes, swigs beer on a park bench, and paints with dogged persistence. She survives by modeling in the nude at City College and attending the art world's "dick-stroking events" for the free booze. No, the girls don't just watch, she asserts. "They strap them on at the door."

When a semiarticulate young man with a shy smile (Joe, played by David Ilku) tries to pick her up on the bus and later comes aknocking, Maya sizes him up for a second or two, then welcomes him into her shabby apartment, and dispensing with further formalities, they hop into the tub together. Her state of mind is something of a mystery, since nothing thus far has indicated she is particularly attracted to this man—and certainly she's no pushover.

Yet Joe (the "risk" of the film's title?), a good-looking drifter and petty thief who lives at the Y and hopes to "pull my ass up and do something with my life," turns out to be less a danger to Maya than to himself. Joe stands the traditional notion of male unresponsiveness and female victimization and dependency on its head. He feels insecure if Maya so much as leaves the room, or doesn't pay enough attention to him. "I'm trying to read your mind so I can touch you at the exact moment you want to be touched," he says. Maya does indeed appear to love him in return.

Events take an unpleasant turn as the roots of Joe's problems emerge, resonating at times in the monochromatic scenery and a pounding score by John Paul Jones. The fine acting of the nicely cast Ilku keeps *Risk* alive and mitigates some dislocating breaks in the rapidly developing plot. Sillas, as the stronger character, is affectless and inscrutable at times—yet entirely believable. Weak male characters in a relationship have usually been treated as comic—the classic wimp or Milquetoast types—but in her first feature film, Deirdre Fishel perceptively takes a wholly original tack.

Also reviewed in:
CHICAGO TRIBUNE, 4/21/94, Friday/p. L, Michael Wilmington
NEW YORK TIMES, 10/5/94, p. C18, Janet Maslin
VARIETY, 1/31-2/6/94, p. 68, Todd McCarthy

RIVER WILD, THE

A Universal Pictures release of a Turman-Foster Company production. *Executive Producer:* Ilona Herzberg and Ray Hartwick. *Producer:* David Foster and Lawrence Turman. *Director:* Curtis Hanson. *Screenplay:* Denis O'Neill. *Director of Photography:* Robert Elswit. *Editor:* Joe Hutshing and David Brenner. *Music:* Jerry Goldsmith. *Music Editor:* Ken Hall. *Sound:* Ivan Sharrock and Kirk Francis. *Sound Editor:* Charles L. Campbell and Louis L. Edemann. *Casting:* Nancy Klopper. *Production Designer:* Bill Kenney. *Art Director:* Mark Mansbridge. *Set Designer:* William Hiney. *Set Decorator:* Rick T. Gentz. *Set Dresser:* Ronald Sica and John Rozman. *Special Effects:* Roy Arbogast. *Costumes:* Marlene Stewart. *Make-up:* James R. Kail. *Make-up (Meryl Streep)*; J. Roy Helland. Stunt Coordinator: Max Kleven. *Running time:* 108 minutes. *MPAA Rating:* PG-13.

CAST: Meryl Streep (Gail); Joseph Mazzello (Roarke); Stephanie Sawyer (Willa); Buffy (Maggie); David Strathairn (Tom); Elizabeth Hoffman (Gail's Mother); Victor H. Galloway (Gail's Father); Diane Delano and Thomas F. Duffy (Rangers); Kevin Bacon (Wade); John C. Reilly (Terry); William Lucking (Frank); Benjamin Bratt (Ranger Johnny); Paul Cantelon (Violinist); Glenn Morshower (Policeman).

CHRISTIAN SCIENCE MONITOR, 9/30/94, p. 13, David Sterritt

The most interesting thing about "The River Wild" is Meryl Streep's performance. Or rather, it's the opportunity to see this highly skilled, notably cerebral actress in a movie that cares precious little about anything but hair-raising stunts, over-the-top suspense sequences, and the soggiest series of action scenes since Steven Spielberg made his first big splash in "Jaws."

Streep plays Gail, a 30-ish mother who lives in Boston with her architect husband and school-age children. While she's a regular city woman, she enjoys nothing more than an occasional sojourn in the Montana wilderness, where she grew up and had her first job as a river-rafting guide.

The story begins with a squabble between Gail and her spouse, a workaholic who regularly spoils vacation plans by getting stuck in the office with deadlines to meet. Sure enough, he's too busy for the family outing again this year, so Gail sets off for a small-scale rafting trip with only her young son Roarke for companionship.

Dad shows up for the adventure after all, landing in Montana just as the others are about to hop in their boat, but everyone groans when they see he's brought his sketchpads and preoccupations along with him.

Perhaps tensions will be eased by the new friendship Gail and Roarke have struck with three nice men headed for the same down-river journey.

But the further they go, the more those fellows seem a little—well, peculiar.

It doesn't take long to guess they're bad guys, who just robbed a cattle auction and committed a murder in the process. Soon they've killed one of their own, too, and the remaining villains have no idea how to handle their getaway boat. They decide to proceed with their escape as planned, using our heroine as their reluctant guide.

Having built her career on relatively dignified fare, from "Plenty" and "Ironweed" to "Sophie's Choice" and "The French Lieutenant's Woman," the talented Streep might be expected to row vigorously away from such obviously lowbrow material as "The River Wild" offers her.

True, the screenplay has an occasional clever line for her to say, and she gets to build a mildly interesting relationship with David Strathairn as her husband. But most of the time there's little for her to do but gaze at the scenery, smile at her son, scowl at the creeps on the other end of the boat, and wave her oars around during the action scenes.

What's a gifted artist like her doing in a place like this? One theory suggests that American actresses over 40 face such a dearth of decent opportunities that any potential hit—even a crassly calculated one like this—is too tempting to pass up.

A less gloomy hypothesis is that Streep enjoys being versatile as well as thoughtful in her work, and actually relished the challenge of casting off her high-art baggage and plunging into an entertaining no-brainer for a change.

Whatever the motivation, she does a credible job with the scanty material that floats her way, playing her meagerly written role so earnestly you'd almost think the project had some real meaning.

Unfortunately, her costars are less successful. As the architect, Strathairn gets to play a real intellectual, but wraps him in a stiff-bodied pretentiousness that conveys less mental energy than Streep's full-muscled approach. As the bad guys, Kevin Bacon and John C. Reilly look their parts but bring little imagination to them beyond some "Deliverance"-style nastiness.

"The River Wild" was directed by Curtis Hanson, who had a hit with "The Hand That Rocks the Cradle" two years ago. That picture brazenly recycled familiar thriller material, and since "The River Wild" is basically an outdoor variation on similar themes, it seems doubly derivative.

Its most effective scenes are spectacularly photographed, and the story springs a few surprises while keeping gratuitous violence to a comparatively low level.

But there's nothing to think about once the watery plot has run its course, and even Streep's plucky performance isn't enough to keep it steadily afloat.

LOS ANGELES TIMES, 9/30/94, Calendar/p. 1, Kenneth Turan

"The River Wild" takes your breath away two times over. And if the excitement of its climactic scenes of white water rafting on roller coaster waterways is not a surprise, the thrill of seeing Meryl Streep give a rip-roaring performance sort of is.

Sort of because over the last five years, starting with "She-Devil" and ending with "Death Becomes Her" and "The House of the Spirits," the nine-time Oscar-nominated actress has made such curious acting choices it has been possible to forget just how potent a talent she possesses.

"The River Wild," crisply directed by Curtis Hanson, wipes the slate clean. In her role as wife, mother and former white-water guide, Streep powerfully shows us what we've been missing, demonstrating such a radiant forcefulness, plus an easy facility with an impressive range of emotions, that she pretty much upstages even the on-rushing rapids.

Written by Denis O'Neill (with uncredited additions from a number of sources), "River Wild" does have occasional plot problems, but it is one of the few thrillers as concerned with character as with action. And it shows anyone still laboring under the delusion that Jamie Lee Curtis' role in "True Lies" was some kind of lofty role model of exactly what a heroic woman's part looks like.

The first time we see Streep's character, Gail, both she and the water she is moving over are noticeably tranquil. In smooth, easy strokes, Gail rows a scull along Boston's Charles River, her mastery of the boat obvious and impressive.

Back home, as the mother of a young son and daughter and the wife of a workaholic architect named Tom (David Strathairn) who habitually neglects his family, Gail is less in control and in fact worried that her marriage is in trouble.

On tap for everyone is a visit to a Gail's parents somewhere in the West, and, potentially a relationship enhancer, a chance for son Roarke (Joseph Mazzello) to travel with Gail and Tom down the very river his mother used to be a guide on.

Also rafting at the same time are a trio of tough-looking men, led by the handsome, muscular Wade (a buff Kevin Bacon). Wade acts awfully friendly, chatting with Roarke about Jane's Addiction and lightly flirting with Gail, but there is something vaguely disturbing about his demeanor.

This particular river turns out to have some unnerving characteristics. Bracketed by high cliffs on both sides, it is an almost impossible place to walk out of. And it ends in a horrific series of rapids, ominously known as the Gauntlet, that Gail ran when she was young and headstrong but are now illegal to cross because several people have died in the attempt.

Not surprisingly, circumstances lead the increasingly sinister Wade and company to attach themselves to Gail and her family, bringing on all manner of dramatic situations. Director Hanson, best known for "The Hand That Rocks the Cradle" does a skillful job of getting the most out of this material, helped by Bacon's striking ability to play both the attractive and the frightening aspects of his character.

This does not mean, however, that "River" is without its problematic aspects, starting with standard-issue touches like a loyal family dog named Maggie and an inability to find a satisfying, creditable role for Gail's superfluous husband, Tom. Similarly, though it is strong in basic outline, "River's" script has difficulty overall coming up with incidents that don't feel like filler intended to kill time until the climax.

Those scenes, set inevitably on that dread Gauntlet, are certainly rousing. Filmed by director of photography Robert Elswit on three different rivers (two in Montana and one in Oregon), the water shots are models of outdoor action footage, so vivid and realistic we just about feel the spray.

Streep apparently did almost all of her own work on the river, which was considerable, and she is as convincing in the heroic physical mode as she is in the film's more feeling scenes, where her face mirrors emotions from confused shyness to frightening rage.

Having abandoned for a while the portrayal of real people, Streep demonstrates here that what great actresses do is show us ordinary people in an extraordinary light. Though films like "The River Wild" are not usually the place to look for the best of female performances, Streep has taken this opportunity to once again rewrite the rules.

NEW YORK, 10/10/94, p. 72, David Denby

Who takes a dog—a *dog*—along on a dangerous rafting trip? And a kid? Who takes a dog and a little boy on a rubber raft that goes shooting down a treacherous river in the Northwest, past rocks and whirling pools? A family in the movies, that's who. Even though I've never before seen a family white-water thriller—a movie about parents and kids menaced by thugs as they go down the rapids—I felt as I watched *The River Wild* that I had been living with such movies my entire life. There are exciting moments in *The River Wild*, but most of the elements in it are as standardized and calculated as the shape of a new sports-utility vehicle. A family that is falling apart undergoes a terrible threat, and everyone ... *pulls together*. In a movie like this, each person is given exactly the trait he needs in order to fulfill his plot function. The child and the dog are there so they can be placed in jeopardy; the husband seems weak so he can demonstrate hidden strength. The picture is just full of surprises.

Yet there's one element in *The River Wild* that doesn't exactly fit—Meryl Streep, who plays Gail, the adventure-loving mother. Streep, as we've been told by the press, is unable to find a serious role; she's appearing in this obviously commercial instant-genre movie as a way of reestablishing her bankability. My feeling is that the movie is unworthy of her, yet there's no reason to grieve: Streep emerges with her honor intact. She gives her heart and soul and a good bit of her body to *The River Wild*, and her performance is fascinating. At the beginning of the movie, she pumps up a large rubber raft for the family adventure, and throughout *The River Wild*, she's the only thing keeping the picture afloat.

Gail is a former daredevil river guide—a rafter known, in her reckless youth, as "Whitewater." But years ago, she left the West, moved to Boston, and married an architect (David Strathairn), a rather sheepish man who feels he can't live up to her. There's a suggestion of sexual disappointment in the union, an absence: Nothing is going on in the marriage that's as exciting as those early churning rides over the rapids. Gail is hungry for the outdoors, for excitement and danger. Streep has developed some muscle in her upper arms, and she looks comfortable and even commanding as she stands in the raft, leaning back and pulling hard against the river. In the old days, of course, this sort of thing was faked in the studio—the star would have rowed in a water tank as the wind machine tousled her hair. But director Curtis Hanson (*The Bedroom Window, The Hand That Rocks the Cradle*) took his crew and actors to Montana and Oregon and worked the rivers wild. On the water, sweeping down the canyon-enclosed rapids, Streep looks robust, and she's convincing as an abrupt, competitive woman. Her eyes are alive, and she has a strong, contemptuous laugh. She shows more temperament in this role than in some of her more controlled outings (such as *The French Lieutenant's Woman*) in which she was witchy and distant—skilled and even haunting but not quite *there* in this vibrant way.

At the beginning of the movie, flirting with Kevin Bacon, a seemingly friendly traveler on the river, she appears to be ready for action. Gail loves her husband, but she's also exasperated with him, and Streep—eyes flickering, sudden smiles disappearing, sour and happy moods moving across her face like patches of cloud and blue—suggests an ambivalence in Gail only barely under control. Streep returns acting to its old (Garboesque) field of combat and desire: the face. She is always thinking, trying things out; she brings almost more consciousness to the role than it needs, and she's often working on a different level from the others. But that consciousness keeps you interested. A murdering robber (Bacon) and his mild accomplice (John C. Reilly) take over the raft, attempt to kill Gail's husband, and force Gail to take them through the notorious rapids known as the Gauntlet. Streep laughs uncontrollably at such an odd method of escape. They won't make it. But she's excited by the prospect of running the Gauntlet again. It might even be worth dying there.

During the white-water sequences, I could feel the audience press forward in their seats. The raft tumbles, spins, pitches, and the beauty of the tumultuous water is often stirring. The white-water episodes hold you, but when they end, the idiotic plot returns, with David Strathairn repeatedly getting beaten up, and the little kid always in the way, and the goddamned dog leaping from a ledge into the water like Robert Redford and Paul Newman in *Butch Cassidy and the Sundance Kid*. And when the movie is over, it's over. Nothing remains but the memory of Meryl Streep acting all the time and looking for a movie to fit herself into.

NEW YORK POST, 9/30/94, p. 37, Michael Medved

Move aside, Arnold, Sly and Bruce: Muscular Meryl has arrived and she's ready to show you a thing or two about how to star in a first-class action-adventure.

One of the many miracles of "The River Wild" is how well its unconventional casting works: Meryl Streep, Oscar-winning mistress of innumerable dialects, here puts the accent on physical strength and resolute courage.

After four months of workouts to prepare for the role, her body looks amazing: not over-developed in the superhuman Schwarzenegger (or Linda Hamilton) style, but strong and graceful, with plenty of power left in reserve.

She plays the part as a human being, rather than some implacable fighting machine, as her character displays many sorts of toughness. This heroine is a middle-aged mother who's deeply committed to keeping her marriage together, despite the fact that her architect husband (the grimacing, occasionally overacting David Strathairn) is destructively obsessed with his work.

In order to renew their relationship, and as a birthday gift to their 10-year-old son (the talented Joseph Mazzello of "Shadowlands" and "Jurassic Park"), Streep plans a rafting trip down an untamed river that she navigated frequently as a teen-ager.

Before long, this dream vacation becomes even more exciting than planned when the family encounters a pair of bad guys who want to use Streep's well-developed rafting skills for their own nefarious purposes.

To tell more than this about the plot would give away some of its surprises, and one of many advantages of this solid script (by debuting writer and amateur rafter Denis O'Neill) is the way it's impossible precisely to predict what's going to happen from scene to scene.

At the same time, the story never abandons its own internal logic and common sense—until the final sequence, when some convenient and necessary equipment implausibly turns up in the middle of the wilderness.

Director Curtis Hanson ("The Hand That Rocks the Cradle," "Bedroom Window") does an expert job of slowly building tension, and then releasing it in spectacular rapids-running scenes of unforgettable intensity.

Even though you defensively keep reminding yourself that this is just a movie, these beautifully edited sequences (shot on location in Oregon and Montana) may produce the sort of nervous stomach and elevated heart rate you associate with some monster roller coaster.

The movie's other big menace is Kevin Bacon, who offers the finest performance of his career as the chillingly convincing villain.

Unlike other action film heavies, he's not a sadistic psychopath: his viciousness is all the more frightening because it's the product of selfishness and amorality, rather than madness. It's easy to understand why the Joseph Mazzello character would initially find Bacon so appealing.

"I thought you were a nice guy!" the boy yells at him at one dangerous moment. "I am a nice guy," the thug insists. "Just a different kind of nice guy."

And the handsomely crafted "The River Wild" certainly qualifies as a different kind of thriller. Like it's altogether admirable heroine, it's not just strong; it's smart.

NEWSDAY, 9/30/94, Part II/p. B2, Jack Mathews

Where was "The River Wild" when we needed it, back in the early summer, when even the suggestion of a river ride in the Montana mountains would have been breezy relief to temperature and humidity readings of 100?

"The River Wild," despite the celebrated casting of Dame Meryl Streep, is a summer movie, pure and simple. It's an action thriller, a white knuckler on white water, with no greater ambition than to pin you to the back of your seat and make you beg for mercy. Acting here is less important than the rubber used to build the rafts, the wood for the oars and the water screaming south out of the Canadian Rockies.

I have no idea how much of her rafting Streep actually did, but her arduous physical conditioning for the role left her looking middle-age buff, and the film, directed by "The Hand That Rocks the Cradle's" Curtis Hanson, is so sensationally edited and paced that you'll have neither the time nor the inclination to look for doubles.

At its heart, "The River Wild" is a genre thriller, an almost dramatic replica of Martin Scorsese's "Cape Fear." A heartless killer enters the lives of a nuclear family, terrorizes the parents while charming their child, and ultimately forces the three of them into a life and death struggle over raging waters.

But where Scorsese concentrated on the psychological terror of his story, Hanson relies on physical action. The river, and its banks and bluffs, is the setting for the entire movie, and you're far too busy worrying about what's ahead to fret over plot contrivances.

The setup is this: Gail (Streep), a teacher of deaf children in Boston, her architect husband Tom (David Strathairn) and their son Roarke (Joseph Mazzello) have returned to the Montana high country of Gail's youth for a river outing to celebrate Roarke's l0th birthday. To Gail, the river, on which she'd worked as a guide, is like a wild lover she once had, and she and it are reunited in a moment of romantic nostalgia.

The outing is also something of a last-ditch effort to save the marriage, which has been put at risk by Tom's obsessive devotion to his work (he even brings the stuff with him). That the trip begins with all this family tension is nothing compared to what happens when they are joined by Wade (Kevin Bacon) and Terry (John C. Reilly), who identify themselves as novice rafters in need of a guide but in fact want Gail to help them make their getaway from a robbery that left a guard and an accomplice dead.

To succeed, the killers and the family have to run the Gauntlet, a section of river so dangerous it is off-limits to even the most skilled rafters.

Hanson and screenwriter Denis O'Neill have structured the film so the dramatic events of the story parallel the growing treachery of the river. In the early going as the deceptively agreeable Wade entertains Gail and Roarke and makes Tom jealous, the water is calm, playfully serene. As the killers begin to reveal themselves, the canyon fills with foreboding sounds, the river speeds up and the last exit before the Gauntlet is left behind. Finally, the story plunges headlong into the maelstrom, with Gail's skill and cunning matched against the madness of both nature and her psychotic passengers.

This kind of thriller seems to even things out among actors. Kevin Bacon isn't someone you'd normally compare to Robert De Niro, yet his nonchalance as the cold-blooded Wade makes him a far more effective villain than De Niro's overwrought Max Cady in "Cape Fear." At the same time, poor David Strathairn, an actor of great subtlety and internal dimension, looks as natural as a tap-dancing seal on this stage.

As for Streep, who continues her pursuit of commercial stardom ("She-Devil" and "Death Becomes Her" just didn't do it), she seems perfectly at ease and genuinely athletic. And if the film is successful, with Streep in a role that might as easily have been written for Bruce Willis or Sylvester Stallone, its impact on future roles for women may mark her greatest achievement yet.

NEWSWEEK, 10/3/94, p. 69, David Ansen

An unhappily married couple (Meryl Streep and David Strathairn) take their 10-year-old son (Joseph Mazello) on a white-water rafting trip in the Northwest, hoping it will patch up their family problems. Downriver they pick up two stranded, shady characters (Kevin Bacon and John C. Reilly) who—no surprise—turn out to be gun-toting desperadoes. But Mom has weapons of her own. She used to be a river guide, and thus is the only one who can get everyone down perilous rapids alive. She also knows sign language, being a teacher of the deaf. "The River Wild" is the sort of thriller in which every detail that gets planted gets used. In spite of the fact that everything turns out exactly as you think it will, director Curtis ("The Hand That Rocks the Cradle") Hanson's movie, written by Denis O'Neill, is a tense, satisfying entertainment. In an era of overproduced, hyperventilating action films, it has a becoming modesty; Hanson is wise enough to let the river, and the splendid scenery of Montana and Oregon, provide their own natural-born special effects.

"The River Wild" also demonstrates that the right actors can freshen up the oldest formulas (basically, it's a floating version of "The Desperate Hours," with a whiff of "Deliverance"). It takes a while to adjust to seeing Streep in an outdoorsy, can-do role. She invests so much emotion in the simplest expository scenes you think she's overqualified for the job. But once she hits the water, oars in hand, she takes command of the movie. We haven't seen this sturdy, physical, macho Streep before, yet she seems totally in her element. The fun, and the power, of the movie come from Streep's newly robust heart: she's a fiercely convincing matriarchal action hero. It was also clever to cast the boyish Bacon against type as the villain. He's a plausible, life-size nemesis. It makes sense that Streep's son would be drawn to his spontaneity, and Streep to his sexuality. Dad's a dour workaholic. But if the father is a Yuppie cliché, the formidable Strathairn plays him with poker-faced finesse, revealing subtle currents of pride and rage under Dad's pinched surface. All the actors stay within themselves, and the same could be said of the movie. It knows what it is, doesn't try to be more, and gets the job done. It must have been a fiendishly difficult movie to shoot, but the filmmakers make it look easy.

SIGHT AND SOUND, 1/95, p. 56, Olly Blackburn

Gail and Tom are a husband and wife undergoing a mid-marriage crisis because of the pressures of Tom's architectural job. For his birthday, they are due to take their son Roarke on a white-water rafting expedition in rural Colorado, where Gail grew up. At the last minute, work forces Tom to back out, leaving a disappointed Gail and Roarke to go it alone. The two arrive in Colorado and meet Gail's mother and deaf father, before setting off on their trip; at the last minute, Tom manages to join them.

Also journeying down the river are three ominous men—Wade, Terry and their guide Frank. Frank mysteriously disappears from the party and Wade, who has charmed Roarke into idolising him, manages to enlist Gail—who used to be a river guide herself—into helping him navigate the river. The more Roarke falls under Wade's spell, however, the more suspicious Tom and Gail become. They attempt, unsuccessfully, to shake off their travelling companions, who turn out to be armed robbers on the run with $250,000 of stolen money. Wade and Terry take the family hostage, forcing Gail to guide them down the river and through a pass of rapids so treacherous that they haven't been navigated for years. That night Tom manages to escape and together with Maggie, the family dog, he prepares an ambush to save his wife and son on the other end of the rapids.

Meanwhile, Wade, believing he has managed to kill Tom during his escape, shoots an over-eager Parks Ranger. He, Terry and their hostages make it through the rapids, but are ambushed by Tom at the other side. In the ensuing fight, Gail shoots Wade, and Terry is captured by the police. Tom, Gail and Roarke and reunited as a family by their experiences.

For years the conservative right has decried Hollywood for its degenerate reliance on sex and violence, the main genre culprit being the action flick. Watching *The River Wild*, however, one wonders what all the fuss is about: this is nakedly wholesome action, and it comes off as one part outward-bound promotional video, two parts Boys' Own adventure for the family: the Thrilling Three joined by Maggie the Wonderdog.

The River Wild is quite so transparent because, like most Hollywood cod allegories, it dutifully leaves behind a trail of cheap metaphors. Gail's mother counsels her on her failing marriage by declaring that feminine strength is the ability to stick by your man, no matter how big a shit he might be. All this is given the stamp of honest, rural wisdom by a background panorama of flowing corn and glacial blue skies. Roarke, on the other hand, is identified as the Achilles heel of the family because he wears a baseball cap for Ministry—an alternative/industrial band, emblematic of adolescent restlessness and contemporary decadence in general. Sure enough, Wade woos Roarke, and thus infiltrates the family, by giving him a Lollapalooza forage cap and playing nondescript grunge tunes. Modern music is an evil, hypnotic thing that suckers the young and pollutes the great outdoors.

The great outdoors is the thing here. It restores a marriage and heals a family. This is most apparent in Tom's Robert Bly transformation from non-communicative, spineless urban professional into a man of trekkin', fightin', cave-paintin' primal ingenuity. The plainest sign that he has become a better man is that Maggie, the family dog, no longer ignores her ineffectual master but faithfully follows him across mountains and through icy streams. Gail proves her conversion to a purer state in the most traditional Hollywood terms: she finally summons up the guts to gun Tom down. (*Die Hard, True Lies, Under Siege*—in action movies, killing people commonly signifies maturity).

During the body of the film, in which family and crooks accompany each other down the river, director Curtis Hanson tries his hand at tight-packed psychology. Wade's interest in Gail's navigational skills is fraught with sexual tension (namely a Timotei scene in which Wade ogles the naked Gail taking a dip in a rock pool) and, when Tom is believed dead, wife and son take on a vaguely existential do-or-die mentality while he shadows them downstream devising a rescue plan. But the film's mechanisms are so determinedly pat and its sympathies so blandly safe that the most obvious moral of the story seems to be: family members under threat must wear radio mikes at all times.

The River Wild is *Knife in the Water* for the family values set. The film's closing frame is of the family in a golden-silhouetted embrace against a backdrop of cresting torrents. But, for all its shampoo-commercial imagery of the torrential waves of reawakening, this is a positively unappealing experience.

TIME, 10/3/94, p. 74, Richard Schickel

It has taken a while to personify her perfectly on film, but here she is at last—the ideal woman of feminist song, story and legend. Her name is Gail, she is played—make that attractively humanized—by the admirable Meryl Streep in *The River Wild*, and if men have any sense left, they will add a few bass notes to the trilling chorus of approval that is soon likely to rise from the soprano section when this otherwise rather routine movie opens.

Gail teaches at a school for the deaf. She is a firm but good-humored mom. Her tolerance for the workaholic ways of her husband Tom (David Strathairn) is wearing thin, but she's laboring earnestly on the marriage. She is also an expert whitewater rafter, and has arranged a trip down a challenging, unnamed western river with Tom, their son Roarke (Joseph Mazzello) and the family dog (boy and dog are also estranged from Tom). The family that gets sprayed together stays together—or so Gail hopes.

Shoving off, they encounter a suspiciously charming fellow named Wade (Kevin Bacon) and his suspiciously charmless pal, Terry (John C. Reilly), also eager to shoot a few rapids. Wade is flirtatious with Gail, self-consciously chummy with Roarke.

You can guess the rest before it happens, since Denis O'Neill's script is rudimentary, Wade soon proves to be a great deal less than he seems (he and Terry are grand larcenists on the wilderness lam). They need Gail's skill and bravery to get them through the Gauntlet (hushed tones whenever it's mentioned)—a nasty set of falls, rapids and whirlpools. Tom takes a little more time to prove that he is a great deal more than he seems, a tenacious defender of (shall we say) family values,

The passage through the Gauntlet is a skillful blend of stunt and special-effects work, nicely orchestrated by the director, Curtis Hanson. He is less skillful at building suspense around the campsites, possibly because the screenplay is not very tightly or eccentrically wound, possibly because Bacon takes his best line too literally. "I am a nice guy," he says at one point. "I'm just a different kind of nice guy." As a result, Bacon doesn't hone Wade's menace as sharply as he might. He needs to become more erratic, more dangerous, as they paddle farther and farther from civilization, but he doesn't make it all the way to psychopathy.

It is Streep who rivets our attention and holds the picture together. Under Supermom's omnicompetence, there lurks the spirit of the larky girl who indeed ran the Gauntlet when she was old enough to know better and young enough not to give a damn. You can see that spunky, heedless young woman in her affectionate banter with her kids, in the sexiness of her response to Wade's come-ons, in the exultation with which she confronts the river's perils. This is smart and subtle acting and a gift that is above and beyond this movie's routine call to duty.

VILLAGE VOICE, 10/11/94, p. 66, Georgia Brown

It's tough keeping families together these days. I suppose this is the putative moral of *The River Wild*, a thoroughly ludicrous white-water thriller directed by Curtis Hanson and billed by the publicity machine as Meryl Muscles Back.

As our story opens, a well-to-do Boston family prepares for a rafting vacation out West. Quickly it's apparent that Mom (Streep) and son are allied in their contempt for Dad (David Strathairn), a timid bespectacled architect humiliated by a demanding job. Even the dog Maggie won't obey this sap. At base camp in Montana, while stocking her raft, Mom flirts brazenly with the smirking Wade (Kevin Bacon), who is stocking his own. The kid also thinks Wade is cool, showing that he too is no judge of character. Meanwhile, everyone in the audience can tell Wade and his two creepy mates are UP TO NO GOOD.

Sheepishly, Dad still tags along, and even saves the drowning Wade (bad move), but gets no credit. By now Bacon's usual cockiness has curdled into pure evil. Making a bid for family audiences, this PG-13 *Deliverance* (don't they wish) pulls back from rape of either Mom or Dad but doesn't flinch at child-slapping.

Everything about *The River Wild* is broad, hokey, and ham-fisted. All you can do is wait for wicked Wade to get his. Eventually, of course, the beleaguered family pulls together: Dad shows his balls, Mom her biceps, and the kid survives to be in awe of both. Oh, and the bitch finally comes when Dad calls.

Also reviewed in:
NEW REPUBLIC, 10/24/94, p. 30, Stanley Kauffmann
NEW YORK TIMES, 9/30/94, p. C8, Janet Maslin
VARIETY, 9/26-10/2/94, p. 60, Todd McCarthy
WASHINGTON POST, 9/30/94, p. F7, Rita Kempley
WASHINGTON POST, 9/30/94, Weekend/p. 45, Desson Howe

ROAD TO WELLVILLE, THE

A Columbia Pictures and Beacon release of a Dirty Hands production. *Executive Producer:* Tom Rosenberg and Marc Abraham. *Producer:* Alan Parker, Armyan Bernstein, and Robert F. Colesberry. *Director:* Alan Parker. *Screenplay:* Alan Parker. *Based on the novel by:* T. Coraghessan Boyle. *Director of Photography:* Peter Biziou. *Editor:* Gerry Hambling. *Music:* Rachel Portman. *Sound:* Nelson Stoll and (music) Dick Lewzey. *Sound Editor:* Alan Robert Murray and Terry Rodman. *Casting:* Howard Feuer and Juliet Taylor. *Production Designer:* Brian Morris. *Art Director:* John Willett and Richard Earl. *Set Decorator:* Claudette Didul. *Set Dresser:* John Ceniceros, John T. Bromell, Michael Shapiro, Larry Sauls, Bill Alford, Steve Peterman, Beth Christian, Hal Gardner, Larry Brew, Rick Gardner, Jennifer Debell, and Robert Schleinig. *Special Effects:* Alan E. Lorimer. *Costumes:* Penny Rose. *Make-up:* Peter Frampton. *Stunt Coordinator:* Gary Combs and John Robotham. *Running time:* 117 minutes. *MPAA Rating:* R.

CAST: Anthony Hopkins (Dr. John Harvey Kellogg); Bridget Fonda (Eleanor Lightbody); Matthew Broderick (Will Lightbody); John Cusack (Charles Ossining); Dana Carvey (George Kellogg); Michael Lerner (Goodloe Bender); Colm Meaney (Dr. Lionel Badger); John Neville (Endymion Hart-Jones); Lara Flynn Boyle (Ida Muntz); Traci Lind (Nurse Irene Graves); Camryn Manheim (Virginia Cranehill); Roy Brocksmith (Poultney Dab); Norbert Weisser (Dr. Spitzvogel); Monica Parker (Mrs. Tindermarsh); Michael Goodwin (Dr. Frank Linnman); Jacob Reynolds (Young George Kellogg); Marshall Efron (Bartholomew Bookbinder); Alexander Slanksnis (Mr. Unpronounceable); Carole Shelley (Mrs. Hookstratten); Gabriel Barre (Desk Clerk); Robert Tracey (Ernest O'Reilly); Ann Tucker (Hannah); Jemila Ericson (Mrs. Kellogg); Marianne Muellerleile (Nurse Bloethal); Jean Wenderlich (Ralph); Mark Jeffrey Miller (Woodbine); Joanne Pankow (Laughing Lady); Mary Jane Corry (Pianist); Richard Valliere (Reporter #1); George Nannarello (Reporter #2); James Bigwood (Reporter #3); David Kraus (Laughing Instructor); D. Anthony Pender (Waiter on Tain); Mary Lucy Bivins (Woman on Train); William Hempel (Bellman); Richard H. Thornton (Mr. Abernathy); Lisa Altomare (Mrs. Portois); Jim Bath (Bartender); Madeline Shaw (Waitress #1); Barbara Phillips (Waitress #2); Lindsay Hutchinson Berte (Breathing Instructor); Denise S. Bass (Nurse); Charlotte H. Ballinger (San Guest); John Henry Scott (Bath Attendant); Richard K. Olsen (Fox Fur Man); Ann Deagon (Fox Fur Woman); Thomas Myers, Jr. (Process Server); Beth Bostic (Miss Jarvis); Kerry Maher (Doorman); Sam Garner (Farrington).

FILMS IN REVIEW, 11-12/94, p. 60, Kenneth Geist

"Asshole" has become the common derogatory in our spoken language for the stupid or foolish. *The Road To Wellville* is the first American scatological film. It is financed and distributed by Columbia Pictures and represents the apotheosis of the Columbia regime of Guber & Peters, the charlatans who have bilked Sony of billions and given us *The Last Action Hero, Geronimo* and *I'll Do Anything* among their costly turkeys. That is, they have spearheaded the second crop of nuclear sized bombs to strike Japan.

The Road To Wellville was a well received, comic novel by the fine, eccentric writer T. Coraghessan Boyle, about the crackpot Dr. Kellogg who, at the turn of the century, gave America cornflakes and rich dupes a sanitorium featuring five-a-day enemas, abstinence, and other, sometimes lethal, treatments with electronic gizmos devised to cleanse the body of its wastes.

The cinematic *Wellville* is another film by the flashy, offbeat English director Alan Parker, who, in addition to his successful pictures like *Midnight Express* and *Birdy*, has made the bizarre and terrible *Bugsy Malone* and *Angel Heart*.

Parker and Columbia have packaged the project with names—Anthony Hopkins as the rabbit-toothed Dr. Kellogg; Dana Carvey as his filthy and rebellious son; Matthew Broderick and Bridget Fonda as a hypochondriacal, but secretly horny, rich couple come for the cure; and John Cusack as an indigent, would be cornflake tycoon who lacks capital and a product, much like Columbia's current personnel.

This exemplifies current Hollywood thinking: If we can stock the package with name players and a name director, then we should shoot it regardless of its content. That is, it's a "go," absent the reading and writing talents of a story executive who might have shot it down by a terse memo stating that Wellville was a truly shitty venture and that the English have a broader tolerance for toilet humor than we do. This supposedly uproarious comedy lacks a single chuckle because Parker is not a comic director.

Parker thought he was savaging American hucksterism, the country's credulous beliefs in the nostrums of persuasive fakers, and the indignities that acolytes will subject themselves to if the guru is highly regarded. But he doesn't come to grips with anything deeply satiric. The period look is so well captured by Peter Bizious' crisp photography and Brian Morris' production design that we only become irritated when the one set of muddy, downtown Battle Creek is used too often. Rachael Portman's jokey score is gratingly obvious.

But don't cry for Guber & Peters, who have now ejected on their golden parachutes from the former MGM lot they rebuilt at such astounding cost. According to James B. Stewart of *The New Yorker*, Guber and Peters siphoned off $200 million apiece from Sony.

Jon Peters, the former reform school hellion and Streisand's home hairdresser, has been rehired by Warners, who demanded hundreds of millions in compensation for Guber & Peters jumping ship without asking Warner's honcho Steve Ross for a release from their contracts. Can Peter Guber be far behind his sidekick? As the greatest Japan bashers on our side, who have almost singlehandedly redressed our trade deficit with the Nipponese, you have to give these extravagant, if wrong-headed guys more credit. Give them a billion or two and they may find another *Batman*.

LOS ANGELES TIMES, 10/28/94, Calendar/p. 1, Kenneth Turan

Has America been waiting for a broad farce about bodily functions? Is there a burgeoning market for jokes about colonics and stool samples, a hoard of viewers poised to laugh at belching, excrement tossing, spitting up, throwing up, flatulence and quick cuts from enemas to dark beer flowing from a tap? "The Road to Wellville" thinks so.

Adapted and directed by Alan Parker from T. Coraghessan Boyle's novel, "Wellville" plays like a foreign-language film without benefit of subtitles. Actors stride purposefully around a beautifully constructed environment, but the view from the seats is perplexing and disconnected.

Dr. John Harvey Kellogg, the real-life centerpiece of book and film, was a classic American eccentric, a health fanatic and corn flake inventor whose belief in what's been called "muscular vegetarianism" would fit right into today's California.

Instead, Kellogg turned the Michigan town of Battle Creek into a turn-of-the-century health mecca dominated by his sanitarium, an early version of the Canyon Ranch where celebrities like President Taft and J.C. Penney as well as ordinary folks subjected themselves to the man's vigorous regimen which included a not inconsiderable number of daily enemas.

For Kellogg believed that "universal constipation was the most destructive blockade that has ever opposed human progress." He declared himself an enemy of the civilized colon," and according to James C. Wharton's fascinating "Crusaders for Fitness," "personally inquired of the directors of the London and Bronx zoos how often their primates moved their bowels."

Kellogg (played by Anthony Hopkins with the kind of misguided energy that marks the entire enterprise) was a also a relentless enemy of sexuality. And "Wellville's opening scene shows the good doctor insisting to journalists from a Rube Goldberg exercise contraption that "sex is the sewer drain of a healthy body" and poetically denouncing masturbation as "the silent killer of the night."

Given how bizarre the real Kellogg was, it's unfortunate but not unexpected that writer-director Parker, never a noticeably subtle filmmaker ("Midnight Express," Mississippi Burning"), has chosen to overemphasize the grotesqueness, wasting no opportunity to feature close-ups of unusual-looking people doing strange and terrible things.

Parker's script has also given the entire story an overlay of stylized verbal artificiality that hamstrings stars Bridget Fonda and Matthew Broderick, both fine natural actors who are neither comfortable nor convincing in quasi-satirical roles.

She is Eleanor Lightbody, a self-described "Battle freak" headed for her third trip to "the San" with husband Will (Broderick), a weakened former substance abuser who can't digest anything stronger than tea and toast, in tow.

Since Kellogg preaches that sexual stimulation could be fatal the couple is separated after they check in. Will fantasizes over Nurse Graves (Traci Lind) and console the seriously ill Ida Muntz (Lara Flynn Boyle) while Eleanor hooks up with the free-spirited Virginia Cranehill (Camryn Manheim) and gets involved in some daring sexual experimentation.

"Wellville" has even more plot strands than these, including Kellogg's strained relationship with his degenerate adopted son George (Dana Carvey) and the attempt by businessman Charles Ossining (John Cusack) and con man Goodloe Bender (Michael Lerner) to cash in on the rage for breakfast cereal by starting a new brand called Per-Fo.

No flimsy production, the Peter Biziou-shot "Wellville" is vibrant and authentic on a physical level, helped by Penny Rose's detailed costumes and a convincing series of locales put together by production designer Brian Morris and art directors John Willett and Richard Earl.

But the fact that this part of "Wellville" seems to know what it's doing only adds to the overall confusion. Ham-fisted as satire, unfunny as slapstick farce and unconvincing as drama, this is one of those films that makes you wonder what the filmmakers thought they were doing. Or who they thought would enjoy whatever it was they did.

NEW YORK, 11/14/94, p. 78, David Denby

The Road to Wellville, a frantic comedy starring Anthony Hopkins and devoted to sex, feces, and enemas, is one of the most intricately tiresome movies ever made. Alan Parker's production is so elaborate—and at times so handsome—that one feels obliged to make at least a college try to sell the picture. All those actors in bowlers, all those women with leg-of-mutton sleeves ... no, I can't do it. The movie is an authentic dud.

Wellville is derived from T. Coraghessan Boyle's novel about the real-life health faddist John Harvey Kellogg—entrepreneur, surgeon, vegetarian, inventor, and one of the great American-Victorian fruitcakes. At Kellogg's spa, in Michigan, the wealthy neurotics (including Matthew Broderick and Bridget Fonda) arrive to be cleansed: Various instruments are introduced into their bodily orifices; they are slapped and massaged with belts, sprayed with freezing water, gently electrocuted, starved, and tormented in a variety of ways until they go bananas and fall into perverse sexual arrangements or spells of auto-stimulation. The movie is meant to be a period black comedy about people obsessed with shit and sex, but a period comedy with devastating contemporary overtones for our own health-obsessed, death-avoiding fitness culture.

The trouble is, no such connections are convincingly made. Kellogg had a colonic fixation and he hated sex, but the enema, apart from its necessary medical uses, is perhaps a perversion too specialized to make much connection with the general culture (though one hears odd things from relatives in California ...), and chastity is a vice hardly celebrated today outside the Vatican or the more radical wings of the feminist movement. Some of Kellogg's milder obsessions we do indeed honor, but they don't seem all that nutty: Vegetarianism and eating bran regularly are still in good repute; water treatments of one sort or another are practiced all over Europe, and on that enlightened continent suppositories are a common way to take medicine. So there! When push comes to shove, Parker would no doubt say I am as sick as Kellogg, but looking at his film, I'm not so sure he's in good shape himself. This is one of the most amorphously plotted movies I've ever seen. People natter on about their digestion, and run around the spa in their underwear doing stupid things or having stupid things done to them. Anthony Hopkins, acting high on the hog, plays the control freak Kellogg (rabbity front teeth, goatee, and gleaming rimless glasses) as a cross between Teddy Roosevelt at his most bombastic and George Bernard Shaw (a vegetarian). When Hopkins isn't shouting in a hilariously ugly midwestern accent and gleefully examining someone's privates, one withdraws a long, long way from the screen.

NEW YORK POST, 10/28/94, p. 48, Michael Medved

One of the surest signs of acting greatness is the ability to turn in a dazzling performance in an otherwise mediocre and misguided effort; in Alan Parker's thoroughly disappointing "The Road to Wellville," Sir Anthony Hopkins passes that test.

"Sir Tony" certainly makes the most of his role as Dr. John Harvey Kellogg, the eccentric turn-of-the-century health-and-fitness guru who invented the cornflake, peanut butter and the electric blanket.

Kellogg also established the world-famous Battle Creek Sanitarium, a grand spa where the rich-and-famous came to try out the mad doctor's spartan regimen of strict vegetarianism, total sexual abstinence and dozens of daily enemas.

Hopkins plays his part with so much infectious manic energy and such undeniable charisma that he makes it easy to see how Kellogg sold his oddball ideas to his followers.

With two uncannily enlarged front teeth and his impeccably accurate Middle American drawl, this flamboyant character is lightyears removed from Hopkins' repressed British butler of "The Remains of the Day."

Adapted from T. Coraghessan Boyle's earthy, outrageous novel, the film tells three different stories that only occasionally intersect.

Most prominently, it focuses on a well-to-do couple (Bridget Fonda and Matthew Broderick) who come to Battle Creek Sanitarium in 1907 in the hopes of reinvigorating their failing marriage.

The movie simultaneously follows the misadventures of an eager young entrepreneur (John Cusak) who's also headed to Battle Creek to cash in on the sudden boom in breakfast foods inspired by Dr. Kellogg's cornflake.

Meanwhile, Kellogg himself can't escape from his adopted son George (Dana Carvey)—a physically filthy, horrible vindictive lost soul who turns up periodically to demand money and embarrass his father.

Of the three stories, only the father-son conflict generates any emotional impact—largely because Carvey, as a dangerous but perpetually-grinning imp, nearly matches Hopkins in demented intensity.

The other characters are merely cartoons—so sketchily written and so feebly acted that it's hard to care much about them as they endure the sadistic torments of the Battle Creek "San."

When they attempt to escape Dr. Kellogg's reign of celibacy—in Broderick's case with a dying, green-faced fellow patient (Lara Flynn Boyle) and for Fonda through a quack German doctor who practices "womb manipulation"—their adventures come across as merely grotesque rather than bawdy or amusing.

The only hints of charm in the movie involve the handsome period costumes and the spectacular locations, shot at the magnificent Mohonk Mountain House near New Paltz, N.Y.

Writer-director Parker ("Fame," "Mississippi Burning," "The Commitments") obviously wants his movie to serve as withering commentary on the fanatic fadism of today's "health Puritans" but he undermines his own intentions by never acknowledging the valid insights that Kellogg achieved along with his idiosyncrasies, or showing the human needs addressed (then and now) by such radical notions.

His attempts at humor almost all involve malodorous bodily functions—with special emphasis on Matthew Broderick's vomiting on many of his fellow characters. To paraphrase the movie's single most memorable line: with friends like that who needs enemas?

NEWSDAY, 10/28/94, Part II/p. B2, Gene Seymour

Give Alan Parker credit, at least, for having fine taste in what he chooses to adapt for the screen. Both "Angel Heart" and "Birdy" were inventive, adventurous exemplars of contemporary American fiction. "The Road to Wellville," a novel published a year ago, must have been even more inviting to Parker's extravagant ambitions given the baroque imagination, epic reach and white-lightning prose of its author, T. Coraghessan Boyle.

Unfortunately, Parker ends up making as much of a botch of "Wellville" as he did of "Birdy" and "Angel Heart." It's a good-looking botch, to be sure. Parker and production designer Brian Morris did a first-rate job in simulating, both in detail and spirit, the candyland buoyancy of early 20th-Century middle America. But what inhabits such well-conceived space is a queasy, sprawling mess of a tale whose particulars are as unappetizing as the varied foodstuffs and gelatinous flesh sloshing their way throughout the movie.

Set in Battle Creek, Mich. ("cereal bowl of the nation"), in 1907, the movie weaves three interlocking stories around the San, a ritzy health spa overseen by Dr. John Harvey Kellogg (Anthony Hopkins), inventor of the corn flake, the electric blanket and various mechanical gizmos designed to clean vital organs of poisons induced by meat, alcohol and "sexual urges." The one shadow on Kellogg's peerless certainty is his adopted son, George (Dana Carvey), an embittered, disheveled ne'er-do-well, who harasses the spa's guests in revenge for childhood slights.

Among the prosperous Americans attracted to the San by Kellogg's gospel of high fiber and pure living is Elizabeth Lightbody (Bridget Fonda), a high-strung beauty who is taking along her skeptical husband, Will (Matthew Broderick), in hopes of curing his digestive "kink." At the sanitarium, Will finds constant humiliation and sexual temptation from a sultry nurse (Traci Lind) and a patient (Lara Flynn Boyle), who'd be just as pretty if it weren't for her pale green complexion.

The third narrative concerns Charlie Ossining (John Cusack), who arrives in Battle Creek with hopes of breaking into the emerging breakfast-food market with his own company. What breaks, however, are his dreams, subverted by his con-man partner (Michael Lerner.)

These storylines flow remarkably well for the first hour or so. But Parker's control over his epic slips so badly that the film ends up resembling one of Kellogg's dubious contraptions, sputtering all the way.

Speaking of sputtering, Hopkins plays Kellogg with the kind of peppy bombast and bullying bluster associated with Teddy Roosevelt. It's a vivid, but repellent caricature. Cusack has funny, slow-burning moments, but his whole role seems an afterthought.

Broderick and Fonda throw off so little electricity as a couple that one ends up agreeing with Kellogg they're better off separated from each other throughout their stay. Though a luminous presence, Fonda never quite convinces as a repressed, uptight woman. When she loosens up toward the end, one feels both she and the movie are breathing a sigh of relief. By then, however, it's too late.

Only Carvey, whose George is a mixture of winsome pugnaciousness, molten rage and ratty allure, can claim a triumph in what is, by far, his best film performance yet. Pity that Carvey's own sense of control over the complex elements of his role didn't rub off on the director.

NEWSWEEK, 10/31/94, p. 67, David Ansen

Set in 1907 at the Battle Creek, Mich., health spa run by Dr. John Harvey Kellogg, "The Road to Wellville" comes with an impressive pedigree. It is directed by Alan Parker, of "Mississippi Burning" and "Fame" fame. It's based on a satirical novel by critics' darling T. Coraghessan Boyle. Playing the vegetarian guru Kellogg, the inventor of the cornflake and a fanatic health zealot, is Oscar winner Anthony Hopkins, outfitted with Bugs Bunny teeth and a prairie-broad American accent. Anti-sex and anti-meat, this spartan loon is particularly obsessed with the alimentary canal; in his fervor to give his gullible patients "born again" bowels, he subjects them to a terrorizing regime of enemas, colonic washes, electrified-water therapy and unnecessary surgery.

Presumably Parker saw in Boyle's satire of turn-of-the-century faddism a distant mirror of our current neopuritanical fixation on fitness. What the movie reflects, however, is only the director's own desperately sour sense of humor and the curious judgment of a studio that thought anyone would be entertained by a two-hour movie about bowel movements. Watching this "satire" is akin to being trapped on a train next to a loud, obnoxious stranger nudging you in the ribs with his musty stockpile of sex and toilet jokes.

Bridget Fonda and Matthew Broderick play Eleanor and Will Lightbody, a pallid couple who come to Battle Creek for Kellogg's cure. Forbidden conjugal rights, they look elsewhere for erotic release while enduring the spa's anal humiliations. She falls under the influence of a quack German "womb manipulator," who gives her splendid orgasms. Poor Broderick, who must endure multiple enemas, mentally undresses his nubile nurse (Traci Lind) and hops into the sickly arms of fellow patient Lara Flynn Boyle, who is dying of something called green sickness. It's telling that when she expires, there's not a flicker of emotional resonance. Since Parker has no feeling for any of his cartoonish pawns, neither do we. Dana Carvey, as Kellogg's vengeful, dirt-smeared adopted son, gets to vent his Oedipal rage by hurling fecal matter at the spa's guests. All the actors, including John Cusack and Michael Lerner as unscrupulous capitalists attempting to start their own competing cornflake business, have been encouraged to mug broadly. This, and the relentlessly bouncy score, must be Parker's way of letting us know we're supposed to laugh. Deepest sympathies go out to the performers trapped in this mean and witless affair. In lieu of Oscars, send Purple Hearts.

SIGHT AND SOUND, 2/95, p. 50, Robert Yates

1907. Battle Creek, Michigan. Dr. John Harvey Kellogg's Sanitarium is dedicated to 'biological living' which proscribes meat, alcohol and sex. Eleanor Lightbody arrives with her husband Will who has, she fears, damaged his stomach through alcohol abuse and 'poisonous' food. While Kellogg is greeting them, his adopted adult son George starts kicking up a stir. He's come to the 'San', as usual, to demand money from his father. After a cursory examination, Will is thrust into a wheelchair and prescribed a rigorous round of enemas. Sexually frustrated, he fantasises about his allotted carer, Nurse Graves, and a fellow guest, Ida Muntz.

Charles Ossining, whom the Lightbodys met on the train to Battle Creek, joins the host of entrepreneurs in the burgeoning 'health food' business but finds that his partner, Goodloe Bender, has spent the start-up funds provided by Charles' aunt and has not secured a site for a factory. Later, Charles brightens when he meets George, making him a partner so that the projected product, Per-Fo, can carry the Kellogg name. The trio find a site, albeit an unhygienic one, and set about devising a recipe.

Will learns how to turn certain treatments to his advantage, enjoying the electric/sexual charge of the Sinusoidal Bath. Sex is banned in the 'San', but he manages to slip under Ida Muntz's sheets and to embrace Eleanor before she is chased away by Nurse Graves. Dr Lionel Badger, an 'expert on the clitoris' and no ally of Kellogg, arrives at the 'San', and his ideas begin to influence Eleanor. Meanwhile, George returns to throw boxes of excrement at the guests. We learn through a series of flashbacks that in childhood he constantly repulsed Kellogg's discipline through sheer obduracy.

Angered by a series of deaths (including that of Ida Muntz), Will visits the Red Onion Restaurant, where he drinks heavily and eats meat with Ossining, offering him $1,000 to help him with his business. Back at the 'San', Will disgraces himself, vomiting over Kellogg, who promptly decides to operate to remove a 'kink' from Will's intestines. Meanwhile, at Per-Fo, they decide to steal others' cornflakes and re-box them.

Increasingly influenced by Badger's rhetoric of sexual freedom and animal rights, Emily snatches a woman's fox collar and casts it into the lake. Baring her breasts, she invites the woman's protesting husband to flay her as he might a fox. While Will enjoys the pleasures of a penis-stimulating Dusselberg Belt, Eleanor visits a Dr Spitzvogel who performs 'womb manipulation', masturbation by another name.

At Bender's hotel, Charles discovers that his partner has checked out, leaving him to pick up the bill. Unable to pay, he flees, only to land in more trouble. His visiting aunt has inadvertently riled Kellogg by telling him of George's partnership with Charles. Kellogg exposes Charles' defrauding of his aunt, and the police, still chasing the unpaid bill, catch up with him.

Boating with Nurse Graves, Will resists making love to her. But, back on land, he discovers Eleanor being 'treated' by Spitzvogel. Will beats him; Eleanor protests that he was only making her feel happy, something Will wouldn't know about. Will replies that he has never felt better. They agree to return home. George sets fire to the 'San' and, in the confusion, falls into a vat of nut butter. Kellogg saves George and embraces him. A coda reveals that Will and Eleanor lived happily; Charles made his fortune from a cola drink; and Kellogg died at 70, while performing a stunt to demonstrate his health.

The film begins with a bout of laughter—forced laughter—the Sanitarium guests asked to guffaw repeatedly as part of a fitness regime. It's a novel strategy—open with an extended onscreen laugh, and hope the audience gets the idea. Add images of Kellogg spinning on one of his eccentric 'health machines' and the film offers not an introduction but an imperative: you will be amused.

Director Alan Parker's screenplay adapts T. Coraghessan Boyle's 1993 novel *The Road to Wellville*, a fictional recreation of Kellogg and his Sanitarium. At times Parker sticks very closely to the novel, lifting, for example, lines of dialogue from the text. However, he also makes major changes which tend to put a brighter spin on events. That's the least that can be said of Kellogg rescuing George from the vat. In the novel, Kellogg, in a feverish act of revenge, drowns George in the nut butter. So flagrant is this amendment that any send-up of syrupy Hollywood adaptations would have rejected it as over-the-top. Boyle's novel is hardly doom-laden. His prose revels in comic, grotesque characters, in the scabrous details of quackery. But there's a cutting edge of ambition, greed and mad conviction. After George's death, Kellogg the scientist dismisses his adopted son as an "experiment that hadn't worked". Parker's version allows for little but buffoonery.

Equipped with a set of false front teeth that his mouth can't contain, his face primed for disapproval, Anthony Hopkins gives Kellogg the look of a starched Bugs Bunny, and pitches his delivery somewhere between WC Fields and Billy Graham. It's a well conceived and executed turn, catching much of the spookiness that the script otherwise wants to forget. Battle Creek is a land of caricature, where the Lightbodys are dwarfed by outsize types such as Goodloe Bender (Michael Lerner reprising the bluster of his Jack Lipnick character from *Barton Fink*). As Ida Muntz, Lara Flynn Boyle wears a complexion so green she might have been dipped in pea juice.

However, in terms of excess, Hopkins' real competition comes from the pseudo-scientific devices littering the 'San'—Parker's design team partly working from the real Kellogg's documents.

Watching a screen filled with all this detail is akin to viewing a painstakingly realised comic illustration let down by a duff caption. There is so much going on—actors continually mugging, contraptions ceaselessly turning—that you feel beaten into submission. With *The Commitments*, Parker showed himself highly adept at directing comedy but this film sags because it persists in giving more of the same. Such unrelieved attention to sex and scatology is normally the preserve of the rag mag.

Any film adaptation of *The Road to Wellville* would face problems since much of the novel's vividness is carried in the narrative voice. The characters—more properly types—are supporting players. The film's visual clutter attempts to mirror Boyle's showy prose but completely misses his cool skewering of charlatans and fools. Instead, we get so many flabby capers.

VILLAGE VOICE, 11/8/94, p. 59, J. Hoberman

A materialist view of psychological malady, *The Road to Wellville* has been expensively adapted by Alan Parker from T. Coraghessan Boyle's 1993 historical novel of life among the health nuts and food faddists who flocked to fin-de-siècle Michigan.

"You are what you eat," the hippies used to say, and it's clear that, in the figure of Dr. John Harvey Kellogg, inventor of the Corn Flake and proprietor of the Battle Creek Sanatarium, Boyle discovered an American archetype—the crusading, puritanical cult leader, lining his pockets in the name of self-improvement even as he flushes out his gullible patients' alimentary canals. Unfortunate then that, however timely, *The Road to Wellville* (a title Boyle lifted from the pamphlet Kellogg's rival quack and cereal mogul C. W. Post distributed with each package of his Grape Nuts) reads as little more than an amiable jape.

If the novel is underplotted and overwritten, the movie is overdone and underwhelming. Attacking the material with his trademark heartiness, at one point cutting from the application of a colonic enema to a close-up of a bartender drawing beer from the tap, Parker is even more strenuously vacuous than Boyle. He compresses the narrative while adding an assortment of flashbacks and madcap chases, editing madly to avoid constructing a scene. As the mode is giddily robotic, so the movie is antic without being funny. (Perhaps only Michael Medved could be offended by the occasional anti-capitalist wisecracks.)

When in doubt, Parker wheels out Big Bertha to atomize his sitting ducks. Anthony Hopkins's Dr. Kellogg chomps and bellows through the proceedings—fitted out with prosthetic dentures to resemble a woodchuck who swallowed a cannon ball. Bridget Fonda and Matthew Broderick barely register as Eleanor and Will Lightbody, the dim young couple who wind up at the San, where he is more or less crucified in the name of health; everything is devoted to killing Will's desire. The novel, as much as it's anything, is the meandering account of how Will rehabilitates himself as a man. But as the neo-Victorian Boyle was provocatively chaste, vulgarian Parker tries to sex things up—literalizing Will's erotic daydreams and transforming imagined couplings into actual ones, giving Fonda a nude scene that allows her to be slobbered over by Dana Carvey, in the role of Kellogg's derelict son.

It's a curious movie and, perhaps because it feels even more pointless than the novel, Parker contrives to cancel everything out at the end. A tepidly feelgood father-son reconciliation is contrived as the world goes up in flames. It's a desperate attempt to convert toothless satire into an apocalyptic heartwarmer—the devil, definitely.

Also reviewed in:
CHICAGO TRIBUNE, 10/28/94, Friday/p. J, Michael Wilmington
NEW REPUBLIC, 11/28/94, p. 57, Stanley Kauffmann
NEW YORK TIMES,10/28/94, p. C13, Janet Maslin
VARIETY, 10/3-9/94, p. 62, Todd McCarthy
WASHINGTON POST, 10/28/94, p. F1, Hal Hinson

ROBERT A. HEINLEIN'S "THE PUPPET MASTERS"

A Hollywood Pictures release. *Executive Producer:* Michael Engelberg. *Producer:* Ralph Winter. *Director:* Stuart Orme. *Screenplay:* Ted Elliott, Terry Rossio, and David S. Goyer. *Based on the novel by:* Robert A. Heinlein. *Music Editor:* Ken Wannberg *Director of Photography:* Clive Tickner. *Editor:* William Goldenberg. *Music:* Colin Towns. *Sound:* Robert Anderson, Jr. and (music) David Hunt. *Sound Editor:* Curtis A. Schulkey and Mark Mangini. *Casting:* Sharon Howard-Field. *Production Designer:* Daniel A. Lomino. *Art Director:* James C. Hegedus. *Set Designer:* Alan Manzer. *Set Decorator:* Cloudia. *Special Effects:* Roy Arbogast. *Special Creature Effects:* David Sosalla. *Visual Effects:* Denise Davis. *Costumes:* Tom Bronson. *Make-up:* Ann Masterson. *Make-up (Donald Sutherland):* Ann Brodie. *Special Make-up Effects:* Greg Cannom. *Stunt Coordinator:* Chad Randall. *Running time:* 109 minutes. *MPAA Rating:* R.

CAST: Donald Sutherland (Andrew Nivens); Eric Thal (Sam Nivens); Julie Warner (Mary Sefton); Keith David (Holland); Will Patton (Graves); Richard Belzer (Jarvis); Tom Mason (President Douglas); Yaphet Kotto (Ressler); Gerry Bamman (Viscott); Sam Anderson (Culbertson); J. Patrick McCormack (Gidding); Marshall Bell (General Morgan); Nicholas Cascone (Greenberg); Bruce Jarchow (Barnes); Benjamin Mouton (Higgins); David Pasquesi (Vargas); Andrew Robinson (Hawthorne); Benj Thall (Jeff); Bo Sharon (Casey); Nick Browne (Mike); Donna Garrett (Miss Haines); William Wellman, Jr. (Doctor); Elizabeth Sung (Technician #1); Dinah Lenney (Technician #2); Tom Dugan (Operator #1); Dale Dye (Brande); John C. Cooke (Lt. Abbey); Fabio Urena (Infantryman); Michael Shamus Wiles (Captain Earley); Todd Bryant, Don James and J. Marvin Campbell (Soldiers); James Pearson (Merging Soldier); Evan C. Morris (Danny); K. T. Vogt (Slugged Woman); Dale Harimoto (Anchorwoman); Alexa Jago (Wendy Markham); Eric Briant Wells (Vince Hayward); Scott Armstron (Infected Boy); Marianne Curan (Newscaster); Katy Summerland (Graves Assistant).

FILMS IN REVIEW, 1-2/95, p. 59, Jim Welsh

Hollywood Pictures wants you to know that *Robert A. Heinlein's The Puppet Masters* is a science fiction classic, and that's why they put the author's name before the title. The film is a reworking of a familiar SF theme—the body-snatcher motif that was popularized in a B movie directed by Don Siegel in 1956 based on a *Collier's* magazine story by Jack Finney, *The Body Snatchers*. The film became a classic as an icon for Red scare paranoia during the McCarthy witch hunts of the 1950s. It was remade by Philip Kaufman during the 1970s as a film that starred Donald Sutherland, whose body was "snatched" at the end.

It is therefore amusing to see Sutherland as the CIA UFO investigator Andrew Nivens in *The Puppet Masters*, which concerns yet another attempted alien takeover. In the Finney version, the aliens sent absurd seed pods to earth. In Robert Heinlein's version, which seems to predate Finney, by the way, the aliens are rather like space glop jellyfish that attach themselves as parasites to the victim's back and neck, sending out nasty probes into the brain and spinal cord while taking over the body. These monsters recall the parasites of Ridley Scott's *Alien* and the parasites of the more campy *Invaders from Mars*.

The idea has been reworked in several films with varying degrees of absurdity, but it achieves a new scary dimension in *The Puppet Masters*, released in time for Halloween as a reasonably effective creature feature. Robert Heinlein's story first appeared in *Galaxy Science Fiction* in 1951. A UFO lands in Ambrose, Iowa, to threaten the American heartland. Representing the Office of Scientific Intelligence, a covert branch of the CIA, Andrew Nivens (Sutherland) and his son Sam (Eric Thal) are sent to Iowa to investigate, along with NASA exobiologist Mary Sefton (Julie Warner). By the time they arrive, the aliens have already taken over most of the town. Before long the parasites (which can reproduce in 12 hours, hatching grapefruit-sized eggs) have infiltrated the Iowa National Guard.

The investigators are spared at first and manage to escape the creepy population of zombies, but their driver is "snatched," taking the parasites with him to Washington, D.C. It begins to look

look as though the president of the United States may be taken over (and nearly is) before a solution can be found. The parasites consist mainly of brain tissue that is vulnerable to encephalitis; but the plot gets very complicated until this solution is discovered. The investigators have to "mind-meld" with the parasites in order to learn their secrets. One advantage for human types in this story is that the parasites can be removed, allowing the host to again become human. If the takeover were more permanent, the situation would be more frightening.

Science fiction is often obsessed with technology, and the trick of a good SF movie is to infuse it with human interest. *The Puppet Masters* works better in its special effects than in its characterization. There is a father-son conflict between Sam Nivens and his workaholic father; there is also a romantic link between Sam and his exobiologist sidekick Mary. Julie Warner is a game trooper, but the chemistry with Eric Thal could be more convincing. The fault would seem to be not in the stars nor in the screenplay, but in the directing by Stuart Orme, who comes to Hollywood Pictures from British television.

The Sutherland character is especially flat. Nivens is all business, which turns him into a sort of zombie even when he is not possessed by the aliens: He should be horrified by what he is witnessing, but he responds to the extraordinary as though it were all in a day's work. It's as though he has seen it all before in the last *Body Snatchers* movie that featured him. If he isn't frightened by these space-glop creatures, why should the viewer be? If Sutherland has seen it all before, so have we, in better movies than this one.

LOS ANGELES TIMES, 10/21/94, Calendar/p. 8, Chris Willman

You might be wondering what we need with another body snatchers movie when there's already been one *official* "Body Snatchers" remake released this year. But "Robert A. Heinlein's The Puppet Masters"—based on a 1951 story by guess-who that predates even Jack Finney's literary mother of all pods—is a kinder, gentler and more action-oriented sort of "B.S." It's *perky* paranoia.

Following a rumored alien infestation in a small Iowa town, a father-son team from a typical top-secret government organ—Donald Sutherland and Eric Thal—meet up with NASA exobiologist Julie Warner to go take a look-see.

There's a good joke early on, when Warner quickly determines the locals are no longer quite human by noticing that the menfolk don't try to look down her blouse. A shootout with the critter-controlled Iowans ensues—"It's the kid from the spaceship! Get him off the car!"—and these three high-tail it back to a state where the guys are more interested in drilling babes than drilling brains.

The army is sent in and, of course, legions of troops quickly fall to the shifty parasites, which attach themselves to human backs, send tentacles into the nervous system and instantly suck up the memory of their hosts. The alien advantage—and, in the inevitable twist, their downfall—is that they're 60% brain tissue.

This movie doesn't suffer the same problem of excess gray matter. In its favor, "Puppet Masters" has a strong sense of its own silliness and doesn't play around with superfluities like subtext. The movie isn't dumbing down science-fiction so much as being spiritually faithful to pre-Communist, old-school sci-fi—in which an invasion might not be such cause for political or spiritual *Angst* as for a team of brilliant scientists to exchange jocular banter or even smooches as they narrowly save the world via firearms and the best available medical research.

And so, after an agreeably hokey and halfway-fun first half, you keep waiting for the picture to take off into the goofy delirium it promises. That's about the mid-point where the unnecessarily long proceedings bog down in ill-edited shootouts and fisticuffs that take place largely in an underground "hive" set even Ed Wood might not have thought was great.

By this time, it's apparent that the best audience for "Puppet Masters" is an appreciative kid crowd (despite the R rating, which seems altogether too harsh for the relatively mild mayhem here), though boomers with inordinate fondness for Saturday matinees could find themselves fleetingly willing puppets of the nostalgia engendered in better moments.

NEW YORK POST, 10/21/94, p. 48, Michael Medved

Powerful pods from outer space arrive on Earth and begin taking over the bodies of unsuspecting humans, who begin to do their bidding like robots or zombies ...

If you haven't gotten enough of this plot with the three different versions of "Invasion of the Body Snatchers," then you might try "Robert A. Heinlein's The Puppet Masters," a surprisingly strong sci-fi thriller that introduces some of the most diabolically disturbing creatures ever to appear on film.

Actually, Heinlein wrote the story that inspired this movie way back in 1951, some five years before the first "Body Snatchers" movie. Like all of this distinguished author's work, the tale emphasized character development and relationships; through the movie version attempts to do the same, the human stars are definitively upstaged by the alien invaders.

They are truly breathtaking, these gut-churning creations that seem to combine the most disgusting elements of leeches and stingrays. The aliens like to fasten onto the backs of their victims, sucking their blood and then sending out a sharp tendril that pierces the brain of its host and takes over all mental and bodily functions.

After their landing in a small town in Iowa (don't all Hollywood aliens prefer small towns?), the invaders take possession of hundreds of men, women and children.

The only force capable of opposing them is the OSI (Office of Scientific Intelligence), a super secret federal agency created to cope with just such an emergency.

This organization is led by a ruthless martinet, nicely played by Donald Sutherland, who works alongside his sensitive son, Eric Thal (who played the Hasidic hunk in "A Stranger Among Us").

Inevitably, they're joined by a glamorous and brilliant scientist from NASA (Julie Warner), and if you don't think there's soon a budding romance between Thal and Warner, then you need a refresher course on sci-fi cliches.

The movie centers on the desperate efforts to contain the unstoppable invaders, and the taut, surprisingly logical screenplay (by two of the writers who worked on "Aladdin," of all things) combines with the riveting special effects to create two-thirds of an altogether superior product.

Unfortunately, the filmmakers (including British director Stuart Orme in his American feature-film debut) didn't know how to bring the story to a close. The climax goes on much too long, and sends our heroes implausibly into the very heart of the alien hive—that looks like the tacky "Great Pumpkin" decorations from some embarrassing Halloween party, or else one of those giant Swiss cheese effigies that you'll occasionally see along a roadside in Vermont.

There are also a lot of dumb macho heroics, involving grabbing hold of out-of-control helicopters, that may provide nice work for stuntmen but generates mostly weariness from the audience.

The botched conclusion doesn't altogether erase the tense, terrific material that proceeded it, but it makes you wonder how evil aliens managed to temporarily pierce the brains of the otherwise capable filmmakers.

NEWSDAY, 10/21/94, Part II/p. B7, Gene Seymour

As invaders-from-outer-space thrillers go, "Robert A. Heinlein's 'The Puppet Masters'" is so chipper and vivacious that it seems like a parody of such dark, paranoid classics of the genre from the '50s as "Invasion of the Body Snatchers" and "Invaders From Mars." "Who's Afraid of the Big, Bad Wolf?" (Well, it *is* a Disney-related production, after all.)

This isn't to say that there aren't grim moments, especially in the beginning when the invading entity from another world is first sighted in—where else?—Iowa. Some local boys are the first to become infected by these mondo-icky, glandular critters that attach themselves to the body, take over the nervous system and make each person do its bidding. Soon the whole town is transformed into bland "puppets," much like the pod people from "Body Snatchers."

But America's become much more hep to alien jive since the '50s. A federal strike force, led by an icy, silky bulldog named Andrew Nivins (Donald Sutherland), snatches a sample parasite and takes it back to Washington to see what makes it tick. Sutherland's "Well, well, well," muttered when he first sees the thing, is an especially delicious moment in a slyly imperious performance worthy of the late, great Claude Rains.

Needless to say, this thing multiplies like baby bunnies, infecting some of the feds, including Nivins' son (Eric Thal), who is working for dad as part of the strike force. No one seems immune as the plague infects all of Iowa and every soldier sent in to do battle. Nivins' team, composed of scientists that are standard-issue sultry (Julie Warner) and dotty (Will Patton), races against time to find the antidote.

Director Stuart Orme keeps the film moving along at a brisk pace, powered by a lot of hip, snappy patter from screenwriters David S. Goyer, Ted Elliott and Terry Rossio. (The latter two teamed up on Disney's "Aladdin.") The script tosses in an offhand, but intriguing analogy of drug addiction to the creature's effect and weaves in a lot of filial tension between father and son.

Still, for every ounce of intelligence tossed into "The Puppet Masters," there are a couple more ounces of the usual dopey plot contrivances. At one point, Thal and Warner sneak away from headquarters for a few minutes of intimacy. Run-amuck libido or not, you'd have to have the brains of a cantaloupe to leave a secure area during a national emergency. Also, why, when seeing something peculiar, do the people in these movies feel compelled to pick it up in their hands? In such company, no wonder Sutherland-Nivins feels like the smartest man in the world.

VILLAGE VOICE, 11/1/94, p. 64, Henry Cabot Beck

Raining down from the heavens outside a small Iowa town is a hail of pernicious manta-shaped alien slugs ("60 per cent brain") who attach themselves to the back of the locals and then invade their brains. When investigating scientist Mary Sefton (Julie Warner) opens her shirt exposing her Wonderbra to a couple of healthy males, the complete disinterest in peeking down her cleavage confirms the suspicions of mind-tampering for secret agent Sam Nivens (Eric Thal) and his father (Donald Sutherland), the crusty hard-assed chief of the top-secret "Office of Scientific Intelligence" (X Files-cum CIA). From here on it's spy versus slug in a race to keep the slippery devils from taking over the White House and the world, in that order.

What's gratifying about this adaptation of Robert Heinlein's 1951 novel is how closely it tries to follow Heinlein's themes and his Ayn Rand rocket-ship libertarianism. But this movie never stops to update his concerns or even to refer to the alienation that informed all three *Body Snatchers* films. What emerges as the true threat at the heart of *The Puppet Masters* is not the disaffection of family or community, but the compromising of our intelligence organizations by creatures who read spooks' minds and pass on information slug to slug. Heinlein created a world where all citizens were obliged to strip naked or be killed. A '90s version could go one step further by offering a slug-ridden president and a CIA that no longer has any need for secrets. In that movie we would be able to tell the politicians who only act like slugs from the real thing.

Also reviewed in:
NEW YORK TIMES, 10/22/94, p. 18, Stephen Holden
VARIETY, 10/24-30/94, p. 68, Steven Gaydos
WASHINGTON POST, 10/22/94, p. C2, Richard Harrington

ROMEO IS BLEEDING

A Gramercy Pictures release of a Polygram Filmed Entertainment presentation of a Working Title production. *Executive Producer:* Tim Bevan and Eric Fellner. *Producer:* Hilary Henkin and Paul Webster. *Director:* Peter Medak. *Screenplay:* Hilary Henkin. *Director of Photography:* Dariusz Wolski. *Editor:* Walter Murch. *Music:* Mark Isham. *Music Editor:* Tom Carlson. *Sound:* Gary Alper, Mark Harris, and (music) Stephen Krause. *Sound Editor:* Dane A. Davis. *Casting:* Bonnie Timmerman. *Production Designer:* Stuart Wurtzel. *Art Director:* W. Steven Graham. *Set Decorator:* Beth A. Rubino. *Set Dresser:* Michael Lee Benson, Jerry Kadar, and Michael Leather. *Special Effects:* Steve Kirshoff. *Costumes:* Aude Bronson-Howard. *Make-up:* Kathry Bihr, Ronnie Specter, Andrea Miller, and Bernadette Mazur. *Special Make-up Effects:* Neal Martz and Richard Alonzo. *Stunt Coordinator:* Jery Hewitt. *Running time:* 106 minutes. *MPAA Rating:* R.

CAST: Gary Oldman (Jack Grimaldi); Lena Olin (Mona Demarkov); Annabella Sciorra (Natalie Grimaldi); Juliette Lewis (Sheri); Roy Scheider (Don Falcone); Wallace Wood (Waiter); David Proval (Scully); Will Patton (Martie Cuchinski); Gene Canfield (Detective John Beechum); Larry Joshua (Detective Joey Tate); Michael Wincott (Sal); William Duff-Griffin (Paddy); James Cromwell (Cage); Paul Butler (Federal Agent Skouras); Tony Sirico (Malacci); Victoria Bastel and Katrina Rae (Girls); Joe Paparone (Ginny); Owen Hollander (Stan); Neal Jones (Clerk); James Murtaugh (Priest); Gary Hope (Driver); Americo Mongiello and James Mongiello (Men); Ron Perlman (Jack's Attorney).

LOS ANGELES TIMES, 2/4/94, Calendar/p. 4, Peter Rainer

"Romeo Is Bleeding" is choked with stylishness. It's a film noir for people who think the genre exists in order to overdose the audience on brittle-poetic dialogue. Edward Hopper-ish shadowscapes and artfully framed corpses. But it's not really a traditional noir in the manner of, say, "Double Indemnity" or "'Kiss Me Deadly." Its fanciness gives it away.

The disjointed, self-conscious, over-the-top stylistics are supposed to make it seem avant-garde but mostly it's just annoying. The artsy clutter gets in the way of the crime story, which is pretty flimsy to begin with.

Jack Grimaldi (Gary Oldman) is a cop on loan to a task force in charge of placing crooks in the witness relocation program. He's also working for the mob to finger the relocated stoolies. He stuffs the mob payoffs in a hole in his back yard; his wife (Annabella Sciorra) doesn't know about his criminal connections, and she doesn't know about his mistress (Juliette Lewis) either.

When Mona Demarkov (Lena Olin) enters his life, the film flips into one long tailspin. Jack is supposed to guard Mona for the witness protection program; he's also supposed to deliver her up to the mob's lizardly, philosophical chieftain (Roy Scheider).

Mona is a classic film noir *femme fatale* and the film's sole triumph. She's the only character whose over-the-top fury matches the film's hyperactive style. Mona seems to emanate from a roar of shadows and blood: She's a creature of doom with a bloodcurdling cackle.

Olin, who worked extensively with Ingmar Bergman, has been extraordinary in American movies before this—most notably in "Enemies, a Love Story"—but she's never been this rip-roaringly full of guile and bile. She's a great demented creation who uses her entire body as a sexual armament. She's so dangerous she's funny, with the sexiest low-slung voice since Bacall's heyday. But Olin manages to make her funniness scary too. (She's a real performer here, not just a parodist.)

With a character this vehement, you need an equally ferocious counterpart, but Gary Oldman staggers through his part looking wasted and anonymous. He doesn't give his deadbeat quality any edge, and his voice-overs on the soundtrack sound facetious. Director Peter Medak, working from a script by Hilary Henkin, never finds the right tone for the film's scattershot larcenousness, so he jumbles a whole party-platter of tones. The mixture of comic and crude and burlesque never gels.

NEW YORK, 2/14/94, p. 105, John Powers

As Jack Grimaldi, the doomstruck cop of *Romeo Is Bleeding*, Gary Oldman dives headlong into disaster and talks about it as he plummets: "Can I tell you what makes love so frightening?" he moans. "It's that you don't own it. It owns you." Such lines are the purest pulp, of course, and that's precisely the point. Jack has everything it takes to be a quintessential pulp loser: a nice wife, a nice house, a respectable job, and the burning certainty that he's not like the other schmucks. It's this certainty that prompts him to keep an adoring cocktail waitress on the side. It's this certainty that lands him on the payroll of a local Mafia chieftain. And it's this certainty that makes him a sitting duck for Mona Demarkov, a smirking gangland hit woman played by Lena Olin. From the moment he sees her, Jack's manageably corrupt routine drops open like a trapdoor, and he slides from one gaudy calamity to the next: bondage, dismemberment, premature burial. This is a movie that gets off on its own outrageousness.

Romeo Is Bleeding was written by the young screenwriter Hilary Henkin, who was obviously suckled on forties pictures like *Double Indemnity, The Woman in the Window*, and *Out of the Past*—*noir* classics in which duplicitous women lure ordinary Joes into a whirlpool of passion and murder. While these stories were often laughably formulaic, a generation of European expatriate directors handled them with an intelligence and conviction that reached the mass audience. Half a century later, we can still see why Robert Mitchum would fall for Jane Greer's sable seductiveness in *Out of the Past*, or why tawdry, shrewd Barbara Stanwyck would single out Fred MacMurray as her murder-mate in *Double Indemnity*. Caught in psychic darklands common to everyone, these actors make you feel their passions in your own body.

Like most of today's hip screenwriters, Henkin thinks *noir* is merely a style, not a sensibility. *Romeo Is Bleeding* has all the familiar trappings—inky photography, hard-boiled patois, ironies rolling toward the hero like cosmic bowling balls—yet even the film's rawest moments don't play the passion straight. It's *Noir* Lite. We know that what's drawing Jack to Mona isn't physical desire (Oldman and Olin have all the sexual chemistry of Siskel and Ebert) but merely the demands of the genre: In movies like this, guys like Jack always go crazy for babes like Mona. Henkin plays to this sense of knowingness, and we're supposed to laugh as she shuffles the clichés. Although I can't think of a movie with more failed pulp epigrams ("Whoever you shoot, you might as well marry 'em, for you're tied to 'em for life"), I can see how the script's loony twists might have looked great on paper. Onscreen, they just seem arbitrary, bloodless. Godard's *Band of Outsiders* and Altman's *The Long Goodbye* riffed on *noir*, too, but they grappled with what it meant to model yourself on old movies; they were bursting with ideas. *Romeo is Bleeding* serves up nothing but shtick. Roy Scheider, who's refined his acting to the point that he can play only reptiles, slithers through the old civilized-gangster bit, quoting Robert Lowell between threats. And Juliette Lewis turns up as Jack's bleached-blonde mistress who mimics Marilyn Monroe through a condescending Oueens accent.

The movie's so busy being a romp that everything stops dead whenever Jack speaks of his anguish or worries about losing his wife. This is no fault of Oldman's, whose rubbery mollusk's face is twisted by such overwhelming passions that he seems to be in a different universe from his winking co-stars'. It wasn't long ago that English actors were faulted for relying on well-oiled technique that couldn't match up to the physical audacity and brooding explosiveness of Brando or De Niro. Now Oldman, Daniel Day-Lewis, Tim Roth, *Naked's* David Thewlis, and *Schindler's List's* Ralph Fiennes are out-yanking the Yanks. They live inside their characters 24 hours a day—putting on weight, not removing filthy clothes, talking for months in a put-on brogue—while top Hollywood stars like Tom Hanks and Denzel Washington seem to glide through their roles without ever breaking a sweat. Oldman sweats buckets in *Romeo is Bleeding*. He also bleeds, sobs, pleads, leers, and, in the final scene, is devoured by a look of such piteous regret that I began wishing the movie had lived up to his belief in Jack's suffering.

It might have come closer with a better director. I hate to sound like a broken record, but last week, I asked how a studio could back a $40-million musical by a filmmaker with no visual style; this week, I find myself wondering why anyone would hire *Let Him Have It's* Peter Medak, whose knack is for sturdy realism, to make a black comedy demanding the anarchic glee of an Almodóvar or Joe Dante. Struggling against his instincts, Medak plays half the scenes turgidly straight and sends the other half capering over the moon. He could learn a lot from the scene-stealing panache of Lena Olin, who frolics down the mean streets like an S&M Barbarella, wiggling her tush, aiming her breasts like ball turrets, and flashing the avid grin of the biggest crocodile in the swamp. Mona's motivations range from the carnal to the venal—money is "better than sex," she says, making a beeline for Jack's zipper—and she has the one moment in the movie that people will be talking about. Clad in a black leather outfit that holds a prosthetic arm (don't ask), Mona leans over Jack, who's been handcuffed to the bed. "With or without?" she purrs. "Without," he croaks, and she flings the plastic limb onto the floor before jumping his bones. In such a wickedly funny moment, *Romeo is Bleeding* comes close to being the cult movie it so badly wants to be. Mona Demarkov isn't simply the reductio ad absurdum of the man-eater, she's a marvelous send-up of Olin, an unwaveringly sexual actress who could find the Joan Collins in Joan of Arc.

NEW YORK POST, 2/4/94, p. 36, Thelma Adams

Hard-boiled. Gruesome. Darkly comic.

"Romeo Is Bleeding" is a dizzy dance of death between the forces of good and evil and assorted double agents.

Warning: This is a movie for people who like to visit plush theaters and travel through the mind's dark alleys. It makes no pretenses about being uplifting, furthering family values or saving America from itself. Fierce, funny, biting and caustic, there's hardly a positive role model from opening credits to close.

This jazzy thriller is over-the-top, and I loved it.

Gary Oldman plays Jack, a corrupt Brooklyn sergeant who "fell in love with a hole in the ground." He's a deluded s.o.b. who listens to a voice in his head—a voice that invariably tumbles him into trouble. Jack's the classic unreliable narrator.

As the title character in "Dracula" and Sid Vicious in "Sid and Nancy," Oldman has played extremists before. In "Romeo Is Bleeding," he restrains himself until he explodes in shotgun bursts.

Oldman's a chameleon who seems to change his face to suit each new role. Jack's features are ordinary, shopworn devoid of character lines; he's an amiable boy in faded blue who's made sergeant but isn't rising any higher.

Hungry for money and sex, Jack plays both sides against the middle. He feeds mob boss Don Falcone (Roy Scheider) information about the whereabouts of protected witnesses and pockets envelopes of cash. A hapless Romeo, he bounces between his attractive wife (Annabella Sciorra) and devoted mistress (Juliette Lewis).

At home and work, Jack's out of his league— only he doesn't know it until Mona Demarkov (Lena Olin) shoots her way into his life. This seductive Russian assassin blows him sideways, forcing him to choose in a game where all the straws are short, all the cards marked.

As written by Hilary Henkin, Mona is the over-the-top role. Swedish actress Olin ("Enemies, A Love Story") grabs the screen and laughs in a way that would chill Jack Nicholson's Joker.

Mona's the slickest, sickest, sexiest villainess ever. "I guess you never forget the first time," she tells Jack in a quiet moment as they prepare to bury Don Falcone alive.

Is she discussing her lost virginity? No. She's reminiscing about her first kill—at 16.

Director Peter Medak ("The Krays," "The Ruling Class") delights in extremes—but never overwhelms his characters. They ripen in their florid circumstances.

Scheider excels as a thinking man's don, the pin-striped devil to whom Jack sells his soul. Down-to-earth Sciorra is not all that she seems as Jack's home-bound housewife. And, when it comes to sexual sizzle, for all Lewis' tarty platinum hair and lingerie-clad wiggles, she hasn't got anything on Olin sitting still.

Medak, working from Henkin's superb script, has pieced together a fractured narrative that is tense, twisted, gutsy, and as entertaining as any thriller in recent memory.

"Romeo Is Bleeding"—and there won't be any Juliet to mop up after him.

NEW STATESMAN & SOCIETY, 4/22/94, p. 34, Jonathan Romney

It's hard to imagine now that *film noir* could ever have been a genre, rather than just a parody of a genre—or that it could ever have been concerned with anything other than its own exhaustion. There may be plenty of knowingness in the films of Lang, Siodmak and Wilder, but you don't have to be a nostalgist to imagine them fuelled by something else. These days, though, the very intimation of *noir* flavouring in a movie means you're likely to wind up with nothing but a girl, a gun and a handful of crumbling tropes, with the whiff of irony hanging like cordite in the air.

It's hard to say when *noir* folded in on itself so definitively—arguably with Robert Aldrich's sardonic, stylised *Kiss Me Deadly* (1955), which started off slugging painfully up a hellish highway by night and ended up with the Big Bang, no less. The great stabs at *retro-noir* since then—*Chinatown, Night Moves*, Altman's *The Long Goodbye*—have all pursued that one way road to Nowheresville. But in the best of them there's at least a sense that they *start* somewhere, that their loser heroes set off equipped for the road.

Romeo is Bleeding, though, begins and ends nowhere. From the off, it's grounded in its own debilitating genre-consciousness. From the minute we see Gary Oldman slumped and wrecked in a desolate Arizona diner, and he starts telling us how he *lost it all*, we know we're in for pure genre retread and we're already geared up for the inevitable moral pay-off, We know too that the film is running on empty as far as imagery goes. The lonesome diner that sparked a thousand Levi's ads should have been demolished after Dennis Hopper's vacuous *The Hot Spot*.

Peter Medak's film started out as a Hilary Henkin script hailed as one of the ten best unproduced screenplays in Hollywood and it's possible to see from the film's baroque verbal overload that Henkin's conception might have had something going for it. But in the execution, the more overloaded it gets, the more vacuous it becomes. Everything's stylised—the self-conscious sense that we've heard this tale before; the good cop/bad cop dichotomy centered on Gary Oldman's venal dick; the moral structure encoded in the hair color of the three women (black, blonde, red; wife, mistress, she-devil; Annabella Sciorra, Juliette Lewis, Lena Olin).

These broad comic-book strokes might have served as a skeletal structure for us to fill out with our imagination. But there's no room to move; this film is too full. Too many characters, too many flashbacks *within* flashbacks, too many twists and ambiguities, too many embellishments. Roy Scheider has a walk-on part as a patrician mob don who quotes Robert Lowell. Cute, but where do we put it? There are strange dream sequences full of circus freaks and pervy overtones. Fine, but maybe they could actually fit somewhere. It looks as if some panicky recutting has gone on, which adds to the film's nightmare feel, but is ruinous to coherence.

In tone, it's just short of the rambling, dream-like mannerisms of Jerome Charyn's New York cop novels, but the febrile agitation somehow misses out on what could have been a good lurid focus—*amour fou* seasoned with a shot of death wish. It has a truly odd foil to Oldman's anti-hero in the shape of Mona Demarkov (Lena Olin), the ultimate castrating dame: a sexually lethal hit-woman with Madonna's wardrobe and Melina Mercouri's laugh. But apart from some demented fights, the relationship never catches fire: whenever they do meet, the pair get down to basics with a brio that's rather unimaginative. And by the end, you know Olin's thighs better than you know your own. It's all very fatiguing.

So we're on the highway to hell. Fine, but can we just get there please? It's very much redeemed by Mark Isham's soundtrack, which is equally self-parodic but dazzling—like everything he's ever done for Alan Rudolph put in a mixer, then *chilled*.

NEWSDAY, 2/4/94, Part II/p. 65, Jack Mathews

Lena Olin gives great underwear in Peter Medak's "Romeo Is Bleeding."

You can't help but notice. Olin, playing the most dangerous sex partner this side of Lorena Bobbitt, is showing off some item of lingerie in almost every scene she's in, even the violent ones, while having an arm blown off, say, or while trying to garrote a lover with a piano wire in the front seat of a car.

Her performance is a kind of a blur of silk and nylon and lace, of snaps and hinges, garter belts and leather vests, all worn under a smile and gaze that promise pain and pleasure in equal measure.

It is a weirdly fascinating performance in a weirdly bad move. Medak, the Hungarian director whose films have ranged from wicked social satire ("The Ruling Class") to camp comedy ("Zorro, the Gay Blade"), is attempting a dark parody of film noir in "Romeo," but it comes across more as a Quentin Tarantino fever dream, complete with torture and multiple amputations.

The dreamer is Sgt. Jack Grimaldi (Gary Oldman), a corrupt cop working for the federal government's Organized Crime Task Force, a weasely little gangster wannabe helping mob boss Don Falcone (Roy Scheider) bump off federal witnesses, and stashing his pay-offs in a hole in his backyard.

Oldman makes Jack one pathetic film noir hero. In his narration, which sounds like a coffeehouse reading of Raymond Chandler, Jack talks about the power of desire as if he were addicted to sex and danger, which the movie certainly serves up in gaudy, blood-spattering doses. But Jack, sallow and disheveled, appears to be in perpetual withdrawal.

Neither his sweet, unsuspecting wife (Annabella Sciorra) nor his eager mistress (Juliette Lewis) can pull him out of his emotional drift. Even when Olin's Mona Demarkov, a mob hitwoman and sexual terrorist, comes along to fill Jack's darkest fantasies, his highs look like lows.

Medak got lost in his own murky ambitions. "Romeo," with its smoke-and-shadows design and Mark Isham's wailing trumpet solos, is far too self-conscious to be taken seriously. And there is not much in Hilary Jenkin's script to make it worth the effort.

The saving grace, or perhaps its mitigating grace, is Olin's deliciously evil performance. Mona is a character out of a dominatrix thrill show, and Olin plays her with the relish of Anthony Hopkins under the skin of Hannibal Lecter.

It is a funny, bawdy performance, something in this otherwise empty experience for which she, and whoever half-dressed her, can be proud.

SIGHT AND SOUND, 5/94, p. 53, Geoffrey Macnab

Jack Grimaldi, sitting in a diner in the Arizona desert, reminisces about the events which led to his virtual disappearance from the face of the earth. His voice-over takes us back a few years to his time as a New York police officer, on loan to the Organized Crime Force, who spends his time in surveillance of mobsters. Happily married and seemingly dedicated to his job, he nonetheless has a sneaking suspicion that the mafia hoods he watches every day have a richer, more exciting time than he does. Deciding he wants a slice of the action, he ends up selling information to mob boss Don Falcone. This results in the assassination of a gangster on the witness protection programme, but also leads to the deaths of several of Jack's colleagues.

Jack collects his cash from a post box, hides it in a hole at the bottom of his garden, and doesn't mention it either to his wife Natalie or to his mistress Sheri. Don Falcone has a vicious new rival, his former lover, Mona Demarkov. The Feds capture her, and Jack is assigned to protect her. Falcone wants her dead, and offers him money to reveal her whereabouts. Jack takes her to a seedy, downtown motel, where she seduces him; the Feds burst into the room, and he is caught in flagrante delicto. He tells Falcone where she is being held, but before the mob can act, she manages to escape. Falcone tells Jack that unless he guarantees Mona's death, he will be killed himself. A few days later, at a mob funeral, Falcone has his henchmen chop off one of Jack's toes. Panicking, Jack returns home, confesses to Natalie, and tells her about the money he has stashed away. She agrees to disappear, and the couple arrange to meet in a few months' time in an Arizona diner. Meanwhile, Jack breaks off his affair with Sheri, whom he also persuades to leave town.

Mona offers Jack a small fortune to double-cross Falcone and fake the details of her death. She picks him up in her car, but, rather than give him the cash in exchange for fake ID papers, tries to strangle him. After a struggle, in which Jack shoots her and the car crashes, she manages to escape. Staking out the house where his mob contact Sal is hiding, Jack sees Mona and Sal in conversation; he rushes in and shoots a woman, whom he presumes to be Mona, only to discover he has killed Sheri.

Mona takes him prisoner. She has also captured Falcone, and forces Jack to dig a grave and bury Falcone alive. She allows Jack a chance to escape, but he fails to take it, and is arrested by his own former colleagues and charged with most of Mona's crimes. She plans to testify against him. Passing her in the court building, he grabs a gun and shoots her. Instead of being punished for the murder, he is acclaimed as hero and given a new identity. Back in the present day, he is still in the diner, endlessly waiting for Natalie to turn up.

Long before it was ever filmed, Hilary Henkin's screenplay for *Romeo is Bleeding* was being touted a "one of the ten best unproduced scripts in Hollywood." At least on paper, it had all the hallmarks of a contemporary *film noir* classic, with its labyrinthine plot, laconic dialogue powder-keg mix of obsession, lust and greed, not to mention its dark philosophising about human nature, its ever darker comedy, and its Gilda-like *femme fatale* heroine. It was just the kind of vehicle you could imagine Tourneur or Lang directing—the type of film which used to be shot in moody black and white, with chiaroscuro lighting, a craggy leading man and Barbara Stanwyck or Joan Crawford as the Circe luring him to his doom.

Unfortunately, the picture which has actually been made never really clicks, Neither the visual style nor the performances do justice to the material, and the whole affair seems horribly self-conscious, too aware of its own out-of-the-past cleverness to establish an identity of its own.

The story opens deep in the desert. Here, a grizzled Gary Oldman, in denims and white T-shirt, and looking like a refugee from a jeans commercial, recounts in flashback the whole sorry sequence of events which have led to his being stuck in the middle of nowhere. This is yet another tale of a corrupt cop, following in the patrol path of *Bad Lieutenant*, *Unlawful Entry* and a spate of movies stretching as far back as *Serpico*. Oldman is always watchable, but he is too febrile and expressive an actor for his role as Jack Grimaldi, and probably too young as well. The part demands a dour, phlegmatic sort, somebody like Robert Mitchum, who could sleepwalk his way through the action and throw away lines like "You walk around like you're somebody special. You're riding high in April ... Then life sends you Mona Demarkov" in best deadpan fashion. Instead, Oldman fidgets and frets, and when he has his toe lopped off, hobbles and hops. Opposite him, Lena Olin plays the ruthless Mona Demarkov as a high camp villainess, a sort of cross between Catwoman and Ma Baker. Often dressed more or less as she was in *The Unbearable Lightness of Being* (minus the bowler hat), she is much given to manic giggles as she commits each fresh atrocity, and is so cheerfully amoral that she ends up as an almost comic figure.

Director Peter Medak struggles to find a pitch for the film. On the one hand, he wants to make a hard-boiled urban cop thriller, where the violence is every bit as jolting as in *The Krays*, and where he can establish his credentials as a Scorsese imitator. On the other, he wants to keep matters lighthearted, and to extract the black comedy from the script. As a consequence, in the more bloody scenes, we don't know whether we're supposed to grimace or laugh. At one point, Jack shoots Mona after she tries to strangle him. She is lying prostrate in the back of the car, presumably bleeding to death, but suddenly develops some superhuman energy, grips Jack's head in a vice with her legs and, when the car crashes, clambers through the shattered windscreen, and limps off ridiculously into the distance.

This is real Jacobean revenge theatre stuff, lurid and extremely hammy, which typifies the film's wayward surrealism. The narrative is frequently interrupted by dream or fantasy sequences. Jack proves a less than reliable storyteller, sometimes skipping ahead of himself and then hastily backtracking. Such self-conscious stylisation works in itself, but can't help undermining scenes where Medak wants us to feel sympathy for the characters.

The movie shifts uneasily from low-key naturalism to comic fantasy, as if the director hasn't made up his mind which style he prefers. There is a fine gallery of character actors on display but Medak seems uncertain how to us them. Too often, he simply resorts to old clichés: the sturdy, reliable cops sit off-duty in the diner, swapping manly tales, as if to underline their camaraderie, while mafia hoodlums gobble down vast bowls of pasta or expound pretentious philosophies about the 'art' of crime. From subway to warehouse, from mob funeral to fairground, every backdrop is familiar. Without the aid of black and white photography, the film-makers struggle to create a menacing atmosphere. Mark Isham's laid-back score does nothing to crank up the tension. Juliette Lewis, as Grimaldi's mistress, is a mere cipher, and Roy Scheider, going through the motions as Don Falcone, seems relieved when Mona decides to bury him alive. Grimaldi's divided loyalties, his relationship with the wife he claims to love, and his efforts at preserving a cosy domesticity, even as he sinks further into a quagmire of corruption, provide some sort of dramatic tension. But it is not enough to sustain a film which often seems as aimless as the Marie Celeste.

TIME, 2/14/94, p. 69, Richard Schickel

Mona Demarkov (Lena Olin) displays a fetching array of frilly panties, garter belts, stocking tops and high heels in *Romeo Is Bleeding*. The sensible viewer may wonder if this is quite the right wardrobe for a woman in her line of work, which happens to be hit person for the Mob. Perhaps sturdy wool slacks and a pair of cross-trainers might be more appropriate.

But practical considerations are of no account in movies like this, which never bear the slightest resemblance to any known reality. Ostensibly this one is about Jack (Gary Oldman), a rogue cop with a nice wife (Annabella Sciorra), an eager mistress (Juliette Lewis) and a profitable sideline in helping the Mafia locate apostates who think they've found safety in the witness-protection program. But the Mafia don (a wildly miscast Roy Scheider) has given Jack a sort of promotion: he's entrusted with actually putting the hit on Mona, who, naturally, deploys all her sexual cunning to evade her fate.

This brings us to the movie's real business, which is to get Jack and Mona wrestling around together. Some blood is spilled on some of these occasions, so a sex-and-violence equivalency is established. There is also a bondage subtext that climaxes with Jack handcuffed to a bed and Mona in dominatrix black leather. Possibly writer Hilary Henkin sees Mona as a woman empowered by a brutal feminism. Possibly director Peter Medak, who specializes in Eurotrash artiness, sees the film as an upscale gloss on the gangster genre. Everyone else will observe that in structure and intent it is soft-core porn and, since it is written by a woman, something for Andrea Dworkin and Catherine MacKinnon to ponder.

VILLAGE VOICE, 2/8/94, p. 53, J. Hoberman

In *Romeo Is Bleeding*, the ensemble is a good deal flashier, and there's nothing that even begins to resemble "sincerity." [The reference is to *I'll Do Anything*.] Directed by Peter Medak from Hilary Henkin's script, this mordantly wacked-out, extremely funny noir stars Gary Oldman as an overextended rogue cop who "feeds the hole" in his Queens backyard by tipping the mob on the whereabouts of protected witnesses.

A quintessentially dumb smart guy, Oldman plays the angles and juggles two sensational women—Juliette Lewis in a blond Marilyn wig as his cartoon bimbo, and Annabella Sciorra as his dreamily laconic wife. Meanwhile, he himself is juggled by Lena Olin, dressed for success and verging on self-parody as a freelance Russian hit woman so come-hither hoarse and carnivorously sultry she might give jitters to the goddess Kali. Continuously onscreen, Oldman is alternately wired and incredulous, but Olin is the movie's prize conception. In *Romeo*'s acrobatic money scene, a spectacular stunt staged in a car careening along the Brooklyn waterfront, she emerges as pure life force—nerves of steel and thighs to match.

Romeo's cast—which also includes Roy Scheider as a mafia-don with the look and affect of a smoke whitefish, as well as cadaverous Michael Wincott as his gloomy henchman—is synonymous with its showboat attitude. The movie is a lovingly designed geek show. The emptier-out outer-borough locations, mainly Williamsburg and Long Island City, may be more effective than the various outer-borough New York accents. Still, this is a hard-edged, hip comedy that, while not particularly derivative, gives the impression of having swallowed the Coen Brothers whole. (An autopsy would also yield chunks of *GoodFellas, Thelma and Louise*, and *Basic Instinct*.)

Henkin's knowing, wise-girl script leaves little doubt that, as opposed to the same-sex approach-avoidance characteristic of much neo-noir, this scenario is the battle of the sexes. What's poignant is that Oldman seems so totally overmatched. Medak, whose gift for stylishly violent black comedy was most recently demonstrated in *The Krays*, treats the script's assortment of amputations and female gunslingers as the stuff of comic nightmare. The baroque narrative is given an additional fillip by Mark Isham's faux jazz score—in fact, it's faux faux jazz, riffing on the idea of cool.

Also reviewed in:
CHICAGO TRIBUNE, 2/4/94, Friday/p. C, Mark Caro
NEW REPUBLIC, 3/7/94, p. 30, Stanley Kauffmann
NEW YORK TIMES, 2/4/94, p. C15, Janet Maslin
VARIETY, 9/27/93, p. 36, Todd McCarthy
WASHINGTON POST, 2/4/94, p. C1, Rita Kempley
WASHINGTON POST, 2/4/94, Weekend/p. 43, Joe Brown

RUDYARD KIPLING'S "THE JUNGLE BOOK"

A Walt Disney Pictures release of a Sharad Patel production in association with Edward S. Feldman. *Executive Producer:* Sharad Patel, Mark Damon, and Lawrence Mortorff. *Producer:* Edward S. Feldman and Raju Patel. *Director:* Stephen Sommers. *Screenplay:* Stephen Sommers, Ronald Yanover, and Mark D. Geldman. *Story:* Ronald Yanover and Mark D. Geldman. *Based on characters from "The Jungle Book" by:* Rudyard Kipling. *Director of Photography:* Juan Ruiz-Anchia. *Editor:* Bob Ducsay. *Music:* Basil Poledouris. *Music Editor:* Tom Villano. *Sound:* Joseph Geisinger, Paul Bacca and (music) Tim Boyle. *Sound Editor:* Leslie Shatz and Teresa Eckton. *Casting:* Celestia Fox. *Production Designer:* Allan Cameron. *Art Director:* Steve Spence, Nitin Desai, Ram Yedekar, and James Feng. *Set Decorator:* Crispian Sallis. *Set Dresser:* Nandita Roy and Sharifa Malik. *Special Effects:* Eddie Surkin. *Visual Effects:* Denise Davis. *Costumes:* John Mollo. *Make-up:* Cindy Williams, Mustaque Ashrafi, and Noriko Watanabe. *Stunt Coordinator:* Gerry Crampton, David Ellis, and Tim Davison. *Running time:* 108 minutes. *MPAA Rating:* PG.

CAST: Jason Scott Lee (Mowgli); Cary Elwes (Boone); Lena Headey (Kitty Brydon); Sam Neill (Major Brydon); John Cleese (Dr. Plumford); Jason Flemyng (Wilkins); Stefan Kalipha (Buldeo); Ron Donachie (Harley); Anirudh Agrawal (Tabaqui); Faran Tahir (Nathoo); Sean Naegeli (Mowgli, age 5); Joanna Wolff (Kitty, age 5); Liza Walker (Alice); Rachel Robertson (Rose); Natalie Morse (Margaret); Gerry Crampton (Sgt. Major); Amrik Gill (Butler); Rick Glassey (Sgt. Claibourne); Casey (Baloo); Shadow (Bagheera); Shannon (Grey Brother); Lowell (King Louis); Bombay (Shere Khan).

LOS ANGELES TIMES, 10/23/94, Calendar/p. 8, David Kronke

Though aimed at younger audiences, "Rudyard Kipling's The Jungle Book" makes its case for the nobility of the "wild child" in a manner more entertaining and far less condescending than the recent Jodie Foster vehicle, "Nell."

This is Hollywood's third pass on Kipling's adventures of Mowgli, the young Indian raised by wild animals. In Zoltan Korda's 1942 adaptation, Mowgli simply wandered from his family before encountering his bestial tutors. This being 1994, however, gunshots and fireballs and vehicular peril must accompany his disappearance from civilization (some of this film's mayhem, in fact, may be too extreme for younger moviegoers).

Virtually the whole of Disney's 1967 animated "Jungle Book"—paid homage to here in a throw-away line about "bare necessities"—took place in the middle of a trick shot here, where the tyke Mowgli steps behind some brush and emerges as the fully grown, fully buff Jason Scott Lee.

Returning to civilization, Mowgli is smitten with Kitty (Lena Headey) a young woman he knew as a child. Kitty and the jolly Dr. Plumford (John Cleese) take to this placid savage, while Kitty's boyfriend, the yuppie-prototype Boone (Cary Elwes), clearly does not; her father, Major Brydon (Sam Neill), is likewise less than sanguine about his daughter making time with such a raw specimen.

Ever the colonialist, Boone decides to exploit the locals, bullying Mowgli into showing him an enormous hidden treasure trove. Mowgli must dispatch Boone and his cackling cronies and rescue Kitty, Brydon and Plumford.

Director/co-writer Stephen Sommers earlier scripted the banal "Gunmen" and wrote and directed "The Adventures of Huck Finn." In a strange way, he's melding those two pictures into one, and in a stranger way, he succeeds, for his "'Jungle Book" provides both rowdy thrills and old-fashioned family entertainment.

Sommers achieves some neat effects here, particularly in scenes in which scores of animals react to Mowgli's misadventures in an amusingly anthropomorphic fashion (29 trainers are credited). His location crew—the film was shot in England, India and the United States—found expansive panoramas and gorgeous scenery. Yet there's the occasional cheesy process shot or unconvincing matte painting, suggesting Sommers overreachcd a bit on his limited budget.

Still, not many live-action Disney films in the past few years have been accused of being too ambitious, and Sommers offers enough wit to engage the adults while kids can enjoy the evergreen premise of Kipling's yarn.

Lee plays an innocent credibly and expressively in an almost mute performance. Elwes' character revels in evil with absolutely brittle wit. One wishes that more use could have been found for Neill and Cleese, who seem more than willing to play along.

But even at its most workman-like, "Jungle Book" entertains in a way both contemporary and traditional. And how long has it been since you've seen a movie where someone drowns in quicksand?

NEW YORK POST, 12/23/94, p. 53, Michael Medved

The Walt Disney company has a sacred, inalienable right to make stupid movies—including this silly romance about the love between an Indian jungle boy and an English Colonel's daughter during the colorful period of the British Raj.

It's outrageous, however, for the studio to attempt to mislead the public by labeling this original story "The Jungle Book." Even worse, they add insult to injury by advertising it as "Rudyard Kipling's The Jungle Book."

That makes as much sense as Quentin Tarrantino retitling "Pulp Fiction" as "Irving Stone's Lust for Life"—since both Stone's novel and Tarrantino's film feature one major character named "Vincent." Virtually the only point that this Jungle Junk shares with Kipling's beloved tales is the name of the main character.

The original Mowgli is a small Indian boy who lives as a wild child raised by wolves, learning the language of the forest and studying the wisdom of all its inhabitants.

In 1967, Disney released a comical animated version that trivialized Kipling's noble animal characters, but still followed the basic outline of his stories. This time, however, Mowgli isn't even a boy—he's a full-grown (and well-muscled) man played by Jason Scott Lee.

The animals don't really talk to him anymore, but merely serve as the hero's cleverly trained assistants—much the way that Tarzan used his faithful chimp, Cheetah.

And like Tarzan himself, Mowgli gets a Jane—a Brit beauty named Kitty (Lena Headey) who's the daughter of a starchy colonial Colonel (Sam Neill).

It turns out that Mowgli and Kitty were childhood friends before he disappeared into the jungle, and he's always cherished the bracelet she gave him long ago.

Director/co-writer Stephen Sommers, who made a similar hash of last year's "Huck Finn," at least provides some handsome, elaborate sets and locations (with Tennessee and South Carolina standing in for India) and both the human and animal stunt work is impressive.

Unfortunately, Sommers also offers up some dozen gratuitously gruesome deaths, shown in such unnecessary detail that the film becomes questionable fare even for the kiddie audience for which it's intended.

Hawaiian-born Jason Scott Lee is an undeniably magnetic screen presence whose acting seems more mannered and one-dimensional with each major outing. In this film, his performance features precisely the same glowering intensity he brought to "Dragon" or "Rapa Nui," but no actor could successfully convey some of the lines he's required to deliver.

He tells his pleading lover, for instance: "I am not a man. And I am not an animal. Why should I stay? I run with the wolf pack. You run with the man pack." It's enough to make you wish that Mowgli had stuck with jungle languages, and to send the man pack running from the theaters.

NEWSDAY, 12/23/94, Part II/p. B19, John Anderson

You have to give Disney credit for something. The undisputed king of animation remakes its own 1968 cartoon classic (Kipling? What's a Kipling?) into live action, which is not its area of most notable achievement, and does so for no discernible purpose other than to assert its position as box-office pasha and mogul of the medium. What's next? Don't ask. At this point, if Disney wanted to remake "Triumph of the Will" as a cartoon, parents and their walking snowsuits would be lined up around the block.

If there's a real reason for "The Jungle Book," though, it would be Jason Scott Lee, who helped make "Dragon," the somewhat fanciful Bruce Lee bio, such a memorable film and who invests

Mowgli, the wild child of the Kipling fables, with unmistakable cunning: No Sabu stare of wide-eyed wonder, no innocent awe, but the look of a character who might well have been raised by wolves. And who might be willing to make you his next meal.

This feral quality gives an adult texture to an otherwise fine family film, which is full of breath-taking and irrelevant landscapes, animal sequences painfully free of peril, and such a gleeful willingness to vilify the British that one almost roots for them (almost). But while Lee props up the cast, the story, or stories, stand on their own.

Four-year-old Mowgli is the son of a guide who's leading a troop of British soldiers deep into the Indian forests, when Shere Khan, the near-mythic tiger, launches an attack, provoked by the soldiers' violation of the jungle code (one only kills what one can eat). Mowgli is last seen heading into the woods on a flaming wagon full of kerosene and is presumed dead. But he survives, and grows up under the watchful eyes of Baloo the bear, Bagheera the panther and Grey Brother the wolf.

Jungle life must be good, because Mowgli grows up to look like Jason Scott Lee and his childhood sweetheart Kitty grows up to be Lena Headey and they're reunited, although Kitty is engaged to the arrogant and contemptible Capt. Boone (Cary Elwes), who is under the command of her father, Maj. Brydon (Sam Neill), and who takes an immediate dislike to Mowgli, who's much better looking and wears a loincloth.

The culture clash and Mowgli's reintroduction to British Raj culture is painful and humiliating, and takes up too much of the movie, but provides the emotional context for Boone's comeuppance and Mowgli and Kitty's psychic-sexual clinch at movie's end. Oh yes, and there's a treasure hunt that offers some hair-raising moments, though most of the hair seems to be borrowed from "Raiders of the Lost Ark."

But tut, tut, enough quibbling. Suffice to say that "The Jungle Book" is entertaining and politically correct, no animals were harmed and the Third World is avenged, at least temporarily, and that Lee is fun to watch and what more do you want from a remake of a cartoon that's an adaptation of a largely unread work from a guy who coined the term "white man's burden"?

SIGHT AND SOUND, 3/95, p. 50, Jonathan Romney

India, the days of the Raj. British army office major Brydon arrives to take up his new post, together with his five-year-old daughter Kitty and his friend Dr Julius Plumford. They are accompanied by an Indian guide and his son Mowgli, also five. Their journey is interrupted by the tiger, Shere Khan, who, Mowgli's father explains, has come to remind them of the jungle law. In camp, Mowgli, entranced by Kitty, presents her with a flower. When he demands a kiss, she runs off but then gives him her bracelet. That night, Mowgli's father is killed by Shere Khan, and the boy is carried off on a flaming cart into the jungle, together with his pet wolf cub, Grey Brother. There they encounter the black panther, Bagheera, who leads them to the safety of a wolf pack. Mowgli later frees the bear cub Baloo from being trapped by a log.

Years later, Mowgli, Grey Brother and Baloo, all adult, are still inseparable. A monkey steals Kitty's bracelet from Mowgli, who pursues it to Hanuman, an ancient city inhabited by apes. Their orang-utan king leads him to a vault filled with treasures, including a jewelled dagger. Mowgli defeats the giant snake Kaa, and wins back the bracelet.

Kitty ventures into the jungle and encounters Mowgli. He is challenged by her suitor, Captain William Boone, but fends off the officer and his men. Mowgli sneaks into town to visit Kitty; she realises who he is, but he is apprehended by Boone's soldiers and imprisoned by the brutal Sergeant Harley. Kitty tells her father of Mowgli's identity, and proposes to "civilise" him; Mowgli is freed and Kitty and Plumford teach him English and the ways of British life. He in turn introduces her to the secrets of the jungle. Brydon, anxious about their friendship, proposes that she return to England.

Buldeo, an Indian guide, tells Boone about Hanuman, and Boone determines to find its treasure. He proposes marriage to Kitty, who reluctantly accepts. At a grand reception, the engagement is announced, and Mowgli, insulted by Boone's officers, returns to the jungle. Kitty breaks off the engagement and prepares to return to England. As she leaves, Boone and his men set off for Hanuman; Mowgli, attacked, manages to escape them, but Baloo is shot. Kitty's party is ambushed by Buldeo and his bandits, who shoot Brydon. Mowgli intervenes, but Kitty is abducted. Mowgli leads Boone and his men towards the city, but then escapes, and sends the wounded Brydon home by elephant. Boone's men die one by one: Harley in quicksand, a bandit falling from a rock, and the officer Wilkins attacked by Shere Khan.

In the lost city, the party are greeted by the orang-utan—dubbed "King Louis"—and Buldeo drowns in a chamber of sand. Boone and Mowgli do battle in the treasure chamber. Boone, attempting to escape with his loot, is killed by the great snake. Outside the city, Mowgli finally encounters Shere Khan, who greets him peacefully, recognising him "not as a man but as a creature of the jungle". Mowgli and Kitty return to be reunited with Brydon, Plumford, and a healed Baloo.

Director Stephen Sommers seems to have become Disney's resident *retour aux sources* specialist, with this convincingly Kipling-esque *Jungle Book* following his respectful return to Mark Twain in *The Adventures of Huck Finn*. The real source here, however, is the 1942 *The Jungle Book*, made under the aegis of Alexander Korda. There are several moments of pure Korda here— notably Mowgli's chase through a teeming market, reminiscent of *The Thief of Baghdad* as well as its most recent descendant, Disney's *Aladdin*, and the extraordinary matte shots of the monkey city of Hanuman, in which the films slips into an effective but incongruous pastiche of 40s Technicolor.

Most Korda-esque, however, is the reference in Jason Scott Lee's performance to that vintage icon of kitsch exoticism, Sabu. Languorously snoozing loin-clothed on a branch, or resplendent in turbaned chic, Lee knowingly plays up the camp aspects of his forbear as a sexy pose, but rather plays down the androgyny—nothing too louche for the underage Saturday matinee crowd, even if they have been raised on Brad Pitt and Take That.

Lee's casting is the film's most troubling aspect. He has Sabu's repertoire of attitudes to a tee—skittishly cheeky, lovelorn, or crouching defensively in time-honoured wild-child fashion—but never for a second do we believe he's Indian. Having starred in *Dragon: The Bruce Lee Story*, *Rapa Nui* and *A Map of the Human Heart*, Lee seems to have become Hollywood's all-purpose ethnic—Chinese, Inuit, Easter Islander, any nationality considered. This lapse seems all the more sloppy in view of the fact that the film, despite the presence of the father and son Patel team and the veteran Shri Rajendra Kumar in the production credits, has no real Asian characters to speak of. Apart from a caravan of non-speaking parts, there is only Mowgli's father, present simply to represent a sly *joie de vivre* principle, and Buldeo, whose evil nature is signalled from the outset by black robes and bristling moustache, making him a dead ringer for the wicked Jafar in *Aladdin*—nothing like a little helpful sign posting for the under-fives.

This apart, the film pays efficient lip service to Disney's current mood of political correctness. It is quite clear who the villains are here—not the denizens of the jungle (Shere Khan is less a ravening monster than a righteous, if wilful, deity), but rather the venal colonialists under the command of caddish Cary Elwes (looking more than ever like a corrupt Macauley Culkin). The film plays effectively on the reversal of 'jungle' and 'civilisation', with King Louis and his apes embodying a more engaging aristocratic ideal than Boone and his posh but brutal retinue. It's hard to see, though, quite what the film imagines the Raj itself to be about, and what Brydon's role as commanding officer is meant to be, other than to exemplify the good man among bounders and fulminate jovially against elephants.

The film's trump card, however, and its drawback for younger audiences, is the fact that it is relatively free of animals. Sommers avoids the anthropomorphism of Disney tradition; the beasts don't talk or indeed do much at all, other than act as a correlative to Mowgli himself. He's said to be obscurely akin to the tiger, and it is Shere Khan who finally endorses his status as an authentic jungle dweller. We never learn anything about Mowgli's youth among the wolves, and cuteness is definitely out—apart from the uncomfortable sight of the cub Baloo with his head jammed in a log. The hordes of monkeys come off best, in effectively creepy sequences that owe a lot to *Indiana Jones and the Temple of Doom*. But on the whole, the animal kingdom is marked as more definitively 'other' than it has ever been before in a Disney film. The human/animal distinction is paradoxically marked by the use of digitals to bring Mowgli and the wild cats together face to snout in seamlessly composed shots that actually signal their irreducible separation.

Still we know what we're getting from the start. As Sam Neill announces in his opening voice-over, "this is a story about fangs and claws and talons but mostly it is about love." In other words, we get a good barnstormer, more Rider Haggard than Kipling, and a love intrigue between

Mowgli and a brisk Lena Headey that is unusually sexually charged for Disney (although the question of racial difference is neatly elided in the chaste final kiss). The film slyly acknowledges the fact that younger viewers may feel short-changed by the absence of a recognisable cartoon Baloo and co; John Cleese—a bluff, jolly uncle throughout—gestures at the food and other splendours of a Raj ball and invites Mowgli to partake of "the bare necessities of life".

VILLAGE VOICE, 1/3/95, p. 74, Devon Jackson

So how does this *Jungle Book* rate against the Sabu and Louis Prima versions of '42 and '67? Let's just say that's it's so godawful predictable that even I—a *Voice* writer—can hardly raise a hackle. Sure, it'll bunch up your panties, but nothin' to roar about. Here Disney exploits itself and Kipling (again) for reasons that can only be guessed at: To cash in on the *Gump* zeitgeist for simplistic heroes? To cash in on the sex appeal of Jason Scott Lee as "Mowgli (something for moms and dads to drool over—and little boys and girls too)? To complement the rererelease of their animated *Book*? To remind grownups (Disney suits) of our need, in this crazy technocratic world of today, to reconnect with nature and regain an unsullied sense of ourselves?

Way static, way unlyrical, was too long, and way too violent (Mowgli's underwater battle with an oversize snake is as disturbingly edited as *Psycho*'s shower scene), today's *Jungle* piles on the moribund clichés and worse, abuses Lee, a talented stud, who looks here more like Extreme's Nuno Bettencourt with the extremely bad hair of Raffi. Go rent *Rapa Nui* instead, the totally unappreciated Easter Island allegory—and in which Lee wears even less clothing.

Also reviewed in:
CHICAGO TRIBUNE, 12/25/95, Tempo/p. 5, John Petrakis
NEW YORK TIMES, 12/23/94, p. C5, Stephen Holden
VARIETY, 12/19/94-1/1/95, p. 72, Brian Lowry
WASHINGTON POST, 12/23/94, Weekend/p. p. 36, Desson Howe

SAFE PASSAGE

A New Line Cinema release of a Pacific Western production. *Executive Producer:* David Gale, Betsy Beers, and Ruth Vitale. *Producer:* Gale Anne Hurd. *Director:* Robert Allan Ackerman. *Screenplay:* Deena Goldstone. *Based on the novel by:* Ellyn Bache. *Director of Photography:* Ralf Bode. *Editor:* Rick Shaine. *Music:* Mark Isham. *Music Editor:* Tom Carlson. *Sound:* Tod Maitland and (music) Stephen Krause. *Sound Editor:* Richard King. *Casting:* Pam Dixon Mickelson. *Production Designer:* Dan Bishop. *Art Director:* Jefferson Sage. *Set Decorator:* Dianna Freas. *Set Dresser:* Anthony Baldasare, Peter J. Von Bartheld, Dan Kenney, Robin Koenig, and Jerry Kadar. *Special Effects:* Steve Kirshoff. *Costumes:* Renee Ehrlich Kalfus. *Make-up:* Marilyn Carbone and Michal Bigger. *Stunt Coordinator:* Glory Fioramonti, Jery Hewitt, and Bill Anagnos. *Running time:* 97 minutes. *MPAA Rating:* PG-13.

CAST: Susan Sarandon (Mag Singer); Nick Stahl (Simon); Sam Shepard (Patrick); Marcia Gay Harden (Cynthia); Robert Sean Leonard (Alfred); Sean Astin (Izzy); Priscilla Reeves (Mrs. Silverman); Joe Lisi (Dog Owner); Matt Keeslar (Percival); Marvin Scott (Newsperson #1): Bill Boggs (Newsperson #2); Kathryn Kinley (Newsperson #3); Cindy Horn (Newsperson #4); Christopher Wynkoop (Evangelist); Philip Arthur Ross (Merle); Steven Robert Ross (Darren); Jesse Lee (Percival, age 9 and 10); Jordan Clarke (Coach); Jeffrey DeMunn (Doctor); Philip Bosco (Mort); Jason London (Gideon); Rutanya Alda (Beth); Kazuya Takahashi (TV News Cameraman); Lisa Castleman and Sally Nacker (TV Reporters); Ralph Howard (Radio Reporter); David Leary (Voice of Marine Spokesman); Ralph Byers (Voice of Sinai Reporter).

LOS ANGELES TIMES, 12/23/94, Calendar/p. 6, Peter Rainer

There are so many family crises in "Safe Passage" that it seizes up right in front of our eyes. Did even Eugene O'Neill cram as much mother-father-son misery into one evening?

It's about Mag Singer (Susan Sarandon), her seven sons and her estranged husband, Patrick (Sam Shepard). The subplots and crossplots total about 14—any of them would be enough to fill out a movie. And yet, all together, they form a big glob of undifferentiated upset. The film wears you out without bringing you deep down into the Singers' predicament.

The crux of the film is that one of the Singer boys, Percival (Matt Keeslar), is a Marine stationed in a barracks in the Sinai that has been bombed by terrorists. It's not clear whether he has survived. As the family assembles in Mag's house to await the news—all but her youngest, Simon (Nick Stahl), have moved out—they rehash their connection to Percival and to each other.

It doesn't take long to sort out the players since everybody seems to be tagged with just one distinct personality trait apiece. Izzy (Sean Astin) is the brainy scientist who figures why his father keeps going periodically blind; Alfred (Robert Sean Leonard) is the control freak who is paired with an "older" woman (Marcia Gay Harden): Simon puts Jell-O in his hair so he can have dreadlocks; Gideon (Jason London) is the star athlete who feels guilty that he outran Percival in high school; the college-age twins Merle and Darren (Philip and Steve Ross) are, well, twins. Their dad is an inventor—a tinkerer, really.

Percival we see entirely in flashbacks—both the childhood and the adult variety. We also see him in the home movies and videos from Sinai that punctuate the family wailing and cheering. This business of watching home movies of a loved one has become such a movie cliché that you'd think the screenwriter, Deena Goldstone, and the director, Robert Allan Ackerman, would cook up something else. But "Safe Passage" is unafraid of the unadorned cliché. It tries to raise cliché to the level of art by sheer voluminous effort.

With the exception of Sarandon, and possibly Shepard and Astin, none of the performers have much authenticity. Sarandon is excellent—she takes her wiggy Mother Courage role about as far as it can go. Her Mag has a well-worn look; you can believe that this woman spent all those years mothering and mediating her brood. And she has a look in her eye for her husband that's a woozy combination of lust and stupefaction. Sarandon makes the movie worth seeing—barely.

NEW YORK POST, 1/6/95, p. 42, Michael Medved

The unexplained title "Safe Passage" makes no sense for this flawed but flamboyantly well-acted movie. A more suitable designation might have been "All My Sons"—which would have also conveyed the soap-opera atmosphere that prevails with this picture.

Susan Sarandon plays the lavishly long-suffering mother of seven (count 'em, seven!) strapping boys, portrayed by an impressive assortment of Hollywood hunks.

Each of these lads boasts some identifying dilemma: Izzy (sean Astin) is a lonely intellectual, Gideon (Jason London) is a brooding athlete, the twins (Philip and Steven Ross) are twins.

The oldest boy, Alfred (Robert Sean Leonard), is a tightly wound freak with a much older single-mother girlfriend (Marcia Gay Harden).

It's troubled child Percival, however, who trumps the rest of them with the biggest bummer of the bunch: The others may be depressed, but Percy might just be dead. As played by magnetic newcomer Matt Keeslar, this surly kid went off and joined the Marines; as the movie opens, the TV reports a terrorist bombing of his Middle Eastern barracks. For several days, the family huddles together in their New Jersey home to await word on whether he's alive or dead.

The boys also want to see if their cranky, cantankerous, impossibly protective mom will make good on her threat to go to work for the first time and to abandon her marriage of 25 years. If she passes a civil service exam and gets a job as a social worker, she's prepared to leave behind husband Sam Shepard, an eccentric inventor who's already been thrown out of the house and suffers from baffling attacks of blindness.

For all its melodramatic story elements and a colorful cast of characters, "Safe Passage" offers almost nothing in the way of plot. The movie's only tension involves the question of whether poor Percival survived, and it's hardly satisfying to watch characters awaiting an outcome which their own actions can do nothing to determine.

You know the filmmakers are desperate to kill time when they offer several sessions with family members nostalgically viewing hokey home movies and videos. Like the recently released Paul Newman vehicle "Nobody's Fool," this picture is a maddeningly static adaption of an atmospheric novel (this one by Ellyn Bache) that relies on rich characterizations to make up for the absence of an absorbing story.

And certainly Sarandon's characterization is ferociously fine: She's never seemed so entirely at home, so much her own natural self—which is the best indication of a superb performance.

She also generates sparks with the perfectly cast Sam Shepard, making it easy to accept the idea that they've lived through a quarter century of a difficult marriage without ever losing the irrational passion for each other that made her a teen-aged mother in the first place.

This problematic picture opened two weeks ago in Los Angeles to qualify for Oscar consideration, and it's entirely possible that Sarandon will get another nomination for best actress.

If so, she'll end up competing with other worthy actresses—including Jessica Lange, Jodie Foster, Jennifer Jason Leigh and Miranda Richardson—who turned in great performances in fundamentally mediocre movies.

NEWSDAY, 1/6/95, Part II/p. B2, John Anderson

From the moment Mag Singer sits up in bed—anxious, sweat-soaked, hair in a pre-Raphaelite halo and sheets in a knot—you know it's gonna be a long night.

Susan Sarandon is Singer, and Singer is Sarandon—earthy, sexy, noble, of a certain age and proud of it. It's all too-obvious coalescence of art and life. If ever there was an actress who needed this role less, it's Sarandon.

The nightmare from which Mag has awakened—ours will continue till the closing credits—has been preceded by the kind of scene that usually ends a movie: Singer's seven sons, in sepia tones and slo-mo, trotting together over a hill, waving as if to say goodbye to all that. We feel we should know who they are. Singer does, of course, and knows, too, that something horrible has happened.

But despite what we're supposed to accept as her epic intuition, she doesn't know to whom. Which provides the opportunity for us to meet each son, as Mag goes through the catalog convinced that one of her progeny has been the victim of a terrific disaster.

Was it Alfred, who's a stiff, has always been a stiff and as such is a natural role for Robert Sean Leonard? no. Is it Izzy (Sean Astin), the brains of the group and the non-athlete, who's always craved the attention of his aging jock father, Patrick (Sam Shepard)? Is it Percival (Matt Keeslar), the problem child (relatively, given that this brood makes the Bradys look like the Mansons), who's joined the Marines and may have been asleep in the barracks that were just bombed by Mideast terrorists?

Bingo. The only question at this point is where Mag got these names ("Le Morte d'Arthur"?). Everything else is settled: She's thrown Patrick out and wants to pursue her own career dreams—as a social worker, naturally—now that her absurd number of sons is almost grown. Patrick, in turn, is going blind from some mysterious malady and keeps gravitating back to the house. Alfred is involved romantically with—can you believe it, Sigmund?—a slightly older woman named Cynthia (Marcia Gay Harden), who has two kids and hits if off immediately with Mom. Izzy the doctor is going to cure Dad's blindness. And all we have to do is sit and wait and find out if it's seven sons or six.

"Safe Passage" has all the riveting dramatics of a made-for-TV movie, a script with more new-age pronouncements than anyone really needs and scenes of such forced conviviality and familial warmth that your appetite will be whetted for a good old-fashioned Menendez movie. For her part, Sarandon is one of our faves, but after "The Client" and her performance as Marmee in the otherwise perfect "Little Women," she needs to give self-righteousness a break. When, in a flashback, you see her carry the unconscious, 10-year-old Percival (Jesse Lee) off the football field, in front of all his friends, you'll be wondering whether he bombed the barracks himself.

SIGHT AND SOUND, 9/95, p. 60, Geoffrey Macnab

Mag Singer, a middle-aged wife and mother with seven sons (six full-grown) rings her estranged husband, Patrick, to warn him that she's had a premonition something terrible is going to happen to one of the children. Although sceptical, he drops by the house to see that she is alright. They argue. He is struck down by a mysterious old allergy which causes him temporary loss of sight.

While he is convalescing, they hear an important newsflash. There has been an explosion in an American army base in the Sinai desert. One of their children, Percival, is a Marine and may be among the dead. Bodies are still being recovered, and it will be some time before they know for sure whether or not he survived.

The rest of the family return home to join their parents as they await further news. But, as they mount a vigil, old tensions soon bubble to the surface. Izzy, a bumbling, scientific type, irritates his father with his determination to work out the cause of the allergy. Gideon, a gifted athlete, is racked with guilt, convinced he is somehow responsible for his brother's decision to join the Marines in the first place. Alfred, the most level-headed member of the family, turns up with his older girlfriend in tow, and straightaway tries to take control of the household.

Mag struggles to cope with the unexpected reunion. She is due to take a civil service exam, and had been looking forward to getting herself a job and starting a new life independent of the family. After three days, there is still no news from Sinai. However, family harmony is gradually restored. Mag and Patrick patch up their differences. Izzy helps cure Patrick's allergy. The telephone rings. Sure enough, Percival is alive and well.

Safe Passage is set deep in the heart of the suburbs, in one of those big detached houses, identical to every other alongside it. At first, this seems more mausoleum than happy home. Everything is packed away in boxes. "I had too many children, I was asking for trouble," Susan Sarandon's character, Mag Singer, complains, and it's hard not to agree: outside 50's Hollywood musicals, seven sons is a little on the excessive side. Six of them are fully grown and have fled the roost. She is estranged from her husband. She's entering late middle age without a job or a qualification. Now, she wants her independence.

In other words, we're presented with a perfect picture of domestic dysfunction. The fact that Mag's husband is played by Sam Shepard, that great chronicler of unhappy American families, reinforces the sense that this is going to be a film about the transience of relationships and the monotony of married life. Unfortunately, it's nothing of the sort. A contrived plot twist or two later, and most of her family are back in harness. The seventh son, played by Matt Keeslar, is missing, possibly dead, after an explosion in the Middle East, and the family are mounting a vigil until they hear what has happened to him.

Confining your characters to a single location may work in a play or sitcom, but it makes for claustrophobic viewing in a movie. Director Robert Allan Ackerman is a veteran of the stage. He clearly loves his actors and seems determined to shoot them all in big close-ups as often as possible. Deena Goldstone's script, adapted from a novel by Ellyn Bache, is top heavy with dialogue but decidedly short on action. Mag ventures out into the snow to help her youngest son with his paper round and protect him from their neighbours' fearsome dog. In one scene, she gets as far as the local school, where she is taking her Civil Service exam. On the whole, though, events unfold inside the house. It used to be a common complaint against British movies that they featured too much tea drinking. Sam Shepard goes through gallons here. Tea even turns out to be crucial to the plot, a sure sign that entropy is setting in somewhere.

With this particular family, and with dreary production design which foregrounds greys and browns, it's hard not to yearn for the brashness and brio of America's best television family comedies such as *Roseanne*. The kind of upper middle-class America that *Safe Passage* evokes is more like that portrayed in Robert Redford's equally earnest *Ordinary People*. The outside world hardly seems to intrude. There's no sex, no violence, nothing to shake the audience. The Middle East is referred to vaguely, because that is where the missing son is posted. But the film-makers never stop to ask what he, or the American army, is doing there. It's somewhere away from home, and hence somewhere bad.

This son, Percival, is defined as the problem child by a glib flashback which shows him smoking a joint with his mother and talking about how he doesn't want to go to college. The rest of the family are allowed a few minor foibles, but they're otherwise presented as ordinary, well-adjusted all-American boys. What is extraordinary is the way that none of them show the slightest interest in popular culture: there's no room for computers or *Beavis and Butthead* or music of any sort.

Given the material, it's scarcely surprising that the acting is on the earnest, self-conscious side. Shepard spends much of the film lying on his back with his eyes covered (his character has an allergy which causes temporary bouts of blindness) while Sarandon oscillates between strained eccentricity (she wrestles with dogs, throws crockery and has 'premonition dreams') and Mother Courage-like stoicism. Certain scenes are neatly observed: for instance, Sarandon's frustration at the way her husband dunks his teabag seven times in the mug and then lobs it into the sink for somebody else to dispose of, or the moment when she launches into a diatribe about their faltering relationship without realising he's already fast asleep. Overall, though, this is a depressingly conservative vision of present-day family life. It hints at all sorts of tensions simmering away between husbands, wives and children, but then simply sweeps them under the carpet in the name of domestic harmony.

VILLAGE VOICE, 1/10/95, p. 54, Alex Patterson

Under the opening credits, earth-mom Mag (Susan Sarandon) has what she calls a premonition dream: her seven twentyish sons jogging through the browns and greens of some New Jersey nowhere in soft-focus and slow-mo. One of them seems distressed, ergo, something awful must have happened in the waking world. Perhaps it has. A bomb has gone off in a part of the Middle East where one of her boys is stationed in the marines. Our one-woman fertility clinic again puts her planned career as a social worker on hold till she finishes fretting about her children (including immature, estranged husband Sam Shepard).

With its wintry homestead, its emphasis on household chores (no one will be admitted during the gripping garage cleaning sequence), and its testosterone-heavy cast waiting on a endangered loved one, *Safe Passage*'s drab dramatics smell of a made-for-TV movie. In fact, this may be indie film's answer to the Waltons' Christmas special.

Playing the parent of a teenager has traditionally ended an actress's chances for romantic roles, so I suppose appearing as matriarch to an entire tribe of fur-faced yups qualifies the under-the-hill Sarandon as Mother Courage. But debuting director Robert Allan Ackerman and screenwriter Deena Goldstone (adapting Ellyn Bache's novel) are against her: when Mag makes such pop-psych pronouncements as "You're absent from your own life and it's breaking my heart," it sounds like she's already passed that social work test. As for gender politics, Mag's request that her husband stop tossing tea bags into the sink will have to suffice. Relentlessly small-scale and low-key, *Safe Passage* is an "admirable" little picture, it's just not a very good one.

Also reviewed in:
CHICAGO TRIBUNE, 1/6/94, Friday/p. H, Johanna Steinmetz
NEW YORK TIMES, 1/6/95, p. C3, Caryn James
VARIETY, 12/19/94-1/1/95, p. 73, Leonard Klady
WASHINGTON POST, 1/6/95, p. C7, Rita Kempley

SALMONBERRIES

A Roxie Releasing release of a PeleMele Film production supported by Filmfürderungsanstalt Bundesministerium des Innern Bayerischer Rundfunk/Redaktion Dietrich v. Watzdorf. *Producer:* Eleonore Adlon. *Screenplay (English and German with English subtitles):* Percy Adlon and Felix O. Adlon. *Director of Photography:* Tom Sigel. *Editor:* Conrad Gonzalez. *Music:* Bob Telson. *Sound:* Pat Liberson and (music) John Richards. *Sound Editor:* Jose Arajuo. *Casting:* Alison Roth, Annette Benson, and Carol Carlson. *Production Designer:* Amadeus Capra. *Art Director:* John Myhre. *Set Decorator*: Gary B. Matteson and Wolfgang Kallnischkies. *Set Dresser:* Casey Reid and Tom Waisanen. *Costumes:* Cynthia Flynt. *Make-up:* Pamela Peitzman. *Stunt Coordinator:* Jeff Janson. *Running time:* 94 minutes. *MPAA Rating:* Not Rated.

CAST: k.d. Lang (Kotzebue); Rosel Zech (Roswitha); Chuck Connors (Bingo Chuck); Jane Lind (Noayak); Oscar Kawagley (Butch); Wolfgang Steinberg (Albert); Christel Merian (Albert's Wife); Eugene Omiak (Ovy); Wayne Waterman (Ronnie); Alvira H. Downey (Izzy); George Barril (Bingo Attendant); Gary Albers (Tightrope Walker).

LOS ANGELES TIMES, 4/7/94, Calendar/p. 7, Kevin Thomas

Bavarian-born filmmaker Percy Adlon has a special knack for making believable and engaging the seemingly most unlikely friendships and romances.

In "Celeste" he explored a loving bond between the ailing Marcel Proust and his sturdy, unsophisticated but unswervingly devoted housekeeper. In "Sugarbaby" he delved into a romance between a zaftig and confident mortuary worker and a handsome subway train driver, and in "Bagdad Cafe" he established a devoted, mutually supportive tie between an unresourceful stranded German woman and the overworked African American proprietor of a ramshackle motel and restaurant.

Now in the endearing, remarkably assured and stunning-looking "Salmonberries," a kind of serious—yet humor-spiked—counterpart of "Bagdad Cafe," Adlon takes on his greatest challenge yet, letting us wonder whether a friendship forged against all odds can turn into a romance. To tell his offbeat story—and just as unexpectedly evoke the need for reconciliation between the reunited Germanys—Adlon has selected a locale even more remote than the desert roadside compound of "Bagdad Cafe." It's the actual northwestern Alaskan outpost of Kotzebue, a tiny community of utilitarian tar paper houses, converted barracks and house trailers.

For 21 years it has been home to the local librarian, Roswitha (Rosel Zech), now 45, an elegant, formal East German emigre who has suddenly become the object of the attentions of a youth inarticulate to the point of rage. Not until the youth stops knocking books off shelves and instead abruptly disrobes does Roswitha realize that her suitor is a woman played by k.d lang (whose haunting song "Barefoot" is heard on the soundtrack). Abandoned in Kotzebue as a baby, she bears the name of the town itself.

Craving friendship, love and a sense of identity, Kotzebue is so doggedly persistent that she breaks down the severe Roswitha's resistance to the extent that she actually enables this remote woman to confront a tragic past that has had her in its thrall the entire time she's been in Alaska. Roswitha's only joy has come in gathering salmonberries, but her increasing reclusiveness means that her shelf-lined bedroom is now crowded with jars of the preserved berries that she had intended to give away. With the utmost sensitivity, Adlon raises crucial questions of cultural and sexual identity.

There are a couple of deft moments from the late Chuck Connors as Kotzebue's seedy foster father and a wrenching scene played almost wordlessly by German actor Wolfgang Steinberg, but "Salmonberries," gorgeously photographed by Tom Sigel, is by and large a two-character story, and novice actress lang is as impressive as the veteran Zech. After lang asked Adlon to direct a music video for her, he wrote the script of "Salmonberries" especially for her. Unaccountably, this prize-winning film has had to wait for more than two years for a theatrical release.

NEW YORK POST, 9/2/94, p. 45, Larry Worth

Earlier this year, "Red Rock West" hit video stores, was resurrected for movie theaters, then became an art-house hit.

Producers of 1991's "Salmonberries"—which suffered a similar circuitous journey to the big screen—are hoping for a similar triumph.

They shouldn't hold their breath.

The production's chief lure: Canadian country crooner k.d. lang's acting debut. But even the singer's die-hard fans will be hard-pressed to cheer her efforts.

Actually, the problem has less to do with lang than writer-director Percy Adlon. Although he proved a master at lensing offbeat relationships in "Bagdad Cafe" and "Sugarbaby," he's now running on empty.

Set in a snow-battered Alaskan outpost, the meandering plot concerns the growing bond between two lonely women.

Kotzebue (lang) is an inarticulate drifter who lets her masculine looks convince people she's a man. In between random acts of violence, she's on a quest for her roots.

As Adlon wrote the screenplay specifically for lang, he made Kotzebue a lesbian, here trying to bed the pretty, frustratingly heterosexual Roswitha (Rosel Zech).

But Roswitha, the town librarian with a passion for the titular salmonberries, has her own problems. Namely, she's haunted by nightmares about her escape from East Germany.

The women's muddled pasts serve as launching pads for various subplots, one of which features the late Chuck Connors in an embarrassing turn. But when interest occasionally sparks, Adlon's distracting camera tricks kill any momentum.

The director succeeds only in capturing the Arctic's frightening desolation and chilling beauty. The biting winds, crusty snow and gun-metal skies create a properly ominous landscape.

It also emerges as a perfect canvas for Rosel Zech, best known for the title role in Fassbinder's "Veronica Voss." She delivers a bitingly effective performance as the reclusive librarian.

But each time Zech and lang share the screen. Zech inadvertently stresses the dramatic drawbacks of the androgynous lang. As a result, lang's plaintive rendering of the theme song is her best contribution.

Long before the disappointing finale, "Salmonberries" points out exactly what "Red Rock West" didn't: Some films deserve a video burial.

NEWSDAY, 9/2/94, Part II/p. B8, John Anderson

Set in northwestern Alaska and just as remote, Percy Adlon's "Salmonberries" arrives like the reception on some Yukoner's shortwave radio, dial spinning through intermittent snatches of coherence, and delivering mostly static.

Largely unseen since winning the best film award at the 1991 Montreal Film Festival, Adlon's story—of a young Eskimo woman seeking her genealogy, and the East German expatriate with whom she forms a romantic bond—is visually disarming, sexually frank and dramatically inept. Much of this can be blamed on k.d. lang, whose fleeting nude scene has provided much of the film's notoriety (although not, until now, distribution) and who contributes a wonderful vocal performance to the sound track ("Barefoot"). As an actress, however, she's better off singing.

Most of the problem, though, belongs to Adlon ("Bagdad Cafe," "Sugarbaby") who might have made this film for the people who are in it. What, for instance, is at the root of the fixation that Kotzebue (lang)—the inarticulate and volatile Eskimo named for the town in which she was abandoned—develops for Roswitha (Rosel Zech), the town librarian, who has lived in Alaska since her husband was killed during their escape from East Germany? Kotzebue develops an unrequited sexual attraction for Roswitha, sure. And they both come to recognize that they share an outcast status: The butch-looking Kotzebue, who passes for male and works the Alaskan pipeline; the elegant, European Roswitha, self-exiled to the frozen north. But Adlon works backwards, establishing relationships and situations without justification, throwing plausibility into the snowy wind.

Add to this some excruciatingly precious dialogue and some hackneyed plot twists—the main one involving the gnarled and crusty Chuck Connors as Bingo Chuck, a different kind of "Rifleman"—and what you have is mostly a painful experience. Adlon makes lovely images, such as the windowed room in which Roswitha keeps hundreds of jars of preserved berries, or Kotzebue howling with the wolves from the center of a satellite dish. But he's been sabotaged to a large degree by lang's success: she's far too recognizable at this point for audiences to think she's a man, and the film depends too much on Kotzebue's sexual surprise to work otherwise.

SIGHT AND SOUND, 4/92, p. 59, Philip Strick

Roswitha, a German émigré in her forties, is a librarian at the Alaskan settlement of Kotzebue. One day, a young worker from the nearby lead mine demands information about the region but angrily rejects the books available. Claiming to be a descendant of the founders of Kotzebue, the youth reveals with a dramatic gesture that 'he' is a woman. Angry but intrigued, Roswitha lectures the intruder about the settlement's Russo-German origins and discovers that the young woman's only clue to her own identity is the name Kotzebue, scrawled on the cardboard box in which she was abandoned as a baby.

"Kotz" brings Roswitha a fresh-caught fish as a conciliatory gift; in return, Roswitha opens one of her innumerable jars of salmonberries, which have fomented to the strength of a liqueur. Slightly tipsy, Kotz wanders into the night, howling like a dog. Assisting the reluctant Roswitha with her shopping next day, Kotz takes her for a ride behind a motorised sleigh. Roswitha warms to her strange companion and talks of her own background. Twenty years ago, her husband was killed as they made their escape from East Berlin; since then, she has endured long years of loneliness at Kotzebue, cut off from her homeland and her past. Unable to restart the snowmobile, Kotz drags Roswitha on the sleigh back to the settlement; cold and furious, Roswitha demands that the girl leave her alone.

But Kotz sees on television the celebration at the destruction of the Berlin Wall, and thinks of a way to help Roswitha. She robs the office of the local bingo operator, Chuck, who catches her in the act but, on seeing the Eskimo ornaments she wears, lets her go. She buys two round-trip plane tickets to Berlin and presents them to Roswitha. They fly to Berlin, and check in at a hotel. Roswitha believes that her brother, Albert, must have alerted the authorities to the escape attempt, and now she confronts him with the betrayal; shamefacedly, he gives her the directions to her husband's grave so that, finally, she is able to pay her last respects to her lost love.

Back at the hotel, she embraces Kotz in gratitude but recoils in alarm at the latter's ardent response; an entire night passes as she tries to explain that their friendship requires no physical passion. They return gloomily to Alaska where Roswitha, having recognised that Kotz's Eskimo ornaments are identical to those worn by Chuck's woman, Noayak, her assistant at the library, draws them to Noayak's attention. Confronted, Chuck admits it was his habit to give such ornaments to his many Eskimo girlfriends, and concedes that he may well be Kotz's father. Less than happy at this idea, Kotz returns to Roswitha's door, and knocks hopefully.

Forced to move on from the 'Marianne Trilogy' following the amiable refusal of his chunky heroine to risk self-parody in further adventures, Percy Adlon still maintains an interest in what he has suggested as an underlying theme—the interaction between the German woman and the American continent. In *Salmonberries*, his new slenderised version of Teutonic maternalism is a castaway, like her two immediate predecessors, in a remote community which tolerantly reads from her presence whatever it needs. Displaced from desert sands to Alaskan snows, such figures as the Eskimo bookworm obsessed with *Madame Bovary*, and the craggy bingo hall proprietor with a colourful past (Chuck Connors in the Jack Palance role), provide an almost transparent paraphrase of the Bagdad Café environment, amply continuing its haunting sense of hunger, inertia and timelessness.

The catalytic intruder in this instance is not in fact the German, whose spirit has become as bottled up over the years as her vast collection of salmonberries, but the unclassifiable 'American' youth (part-Eskimo, part-Canadian, and part-k.d. lang, which is to say wholly unlike anyone else) who appears to have sprung from some obscure pupation. The resulting interplay is accordingly not so much between nationalities but—in a return to the partnership of *Sugarbaby*—a collusion between opposites who discover unexpectedly that they have something in common. That 'something' is not altogether clear, although it could be no more elaborate than the desire for companionship.

All they really share is their foreignness, an attribute from which Adlon has extracted much humour in the past, but here, unfortunately, treats with an excess of respect and sympathy. Having written his film specifically for the ultra-foreign k.d. lang, whose inscrutably androgynous features conceal a miraculous vocal turbulence, he has landed himself with a defiant enigma, indeterminate of age, origin and purpose. Such presence requires a more exotic fable that this mundane account of adolescent fixation, despite its tentative and implausible links with the reunification of Germany (an uneasy courtship between East and West?)

Where part of the charm of Adlon's earlier films, with their odd angles and unexpected rhythms, was the impression they gave of a hearty disregard for the rules of cinema, the disingenuous expressionism of *Salmonberries* wears that charm perilously thin. Four lightning flashes, for example, illuminate the librarian and her visitor as they stand face-to-face at an early meeting. Stoically ignored by the cast, these burn-outs clearly indicate a moment of electric recognition, but by whom, and of what, the script neither clarifies nor develops.

In isolation, though, there are sequences containing much to admire, like Roswitha's bathroom collapse amid an elaborate light-fitting and a slowly dripping tap, a splendidly disconcerting montage. There is, for the sake of droll incongruity, a nicely framed scene of a tightrope-walker balancing outside the Berlin hotel at night. And there are magnificent views of the Alaskan setting at Kotzebue itself, heavy in greys and browns, the snowmobiles buzzing through the mists, the tired houses wreathed in storms. It is ironic that in sending his two women on a seductive journey through this spectacular wilderness, accompanied by one of lang's yearning refrains, Adlon placidly incorporates shots that link his lonely dreamers first with two crosses and then with a couple of elk. It's difficult to take them seriously after that.

VILLAGE VOICE, 9/6/94, p. 62, Randy Gener

If you chart Percy Adlon's edge-of-the-earth love stories, you'll find two eccentric, isolated lines converging in carefully calibrated fashion. Against a seemingly intractable landscape, he maps *Harold and Maude*-ish tales in which dislocation and friendship fuse into mutual devotion. *Salmonberries*, Adlon's 1991 k.d. lang debut vehicle, given second life by Roxie Releasing after three years in distribution limbo, reconnoiters similar turf. Set in northwest Alaska, it's a dyke *My Own Private Idaho*—an angsty, gorgeous torch and tundra courtship dance between a 45-year-old East German librarian, Roswitha (Rosel Zech, Fassbinder's unforgettable Veronika Voss), and a 19-year-old Eskimo wild child, Kotzebue (fearless and willful lang). Like the salmon-colored arctic berries Roswitha preserves in jelly jars and leaves to ripen on shelves for several years, its dyke horniness is strange, rich, intoxicating.

Roswitha is as formal, reclusive, and girlish as Kotzebue is angry, inchoate, and androgynous. As Adlon tracks their quests, Roswitha's emotional reserve cracks and Kotzebue's butchness melts. She helps her émigré friend grapple with a violent past: in the late '60s, her husband was shot as they tried to cross the Wall. This sends the two women to Berlin, where Adlon parallels the cultural gulf between East and West Germany and the sexual one between straights and gays, both initially awkward and hostile, but resolved with painful, loving sensitivity. In an emotionally fraught series of 10 fade-outs, Roswitha retreats from Kotzebue's sexual advances and tries to explain that "this is not me." This is where Adlon's symbolism (jars breaking, drips of water, lang tumbling to the floor) has been pointing throughout, but its heavy-handedness can't trivalize the movie's tough-minded, melancholic view of life's basic ineffableness. Pop Arty colors keep shifting, the background darkens, the camera angles go off-kilter. Something about the bleak moodiness of Alaska mutes and disjoints Adlon's leavening quirkiness. He doesn't connect the dots, and neither does he hand you emotions neatly tagged—they're naked, as confident and enigmatic as lang standing nude before Zech. The two women sustain each other emotionally, but also pull back. Should they have had hot sex in Berlin? Years of moviegoing have conditioned us to such fantast. Yet as lang sings "Barefoot," orgasm seems an easy release. Wrapped in lang's languorously sexy voice, the movie has been making restless, ardent love to us all along.

Also reviewed in:
NEW YORK TIMES, 9/2/94, p. C12, Janet Maslin
VARIETY, 9/9/91, p. 66, Suzan Ayscough
WASHINGTON POST, 8/26/94, p. D7, Hal Hinson

SANKOFA

A Mypheduh Films release of a Negod-Gwad production in co-production with the Ghana National Commission on Culture, DiProCi of Burkina Faso, NDR/WDR Television in association with Channel Four Television. *Producer:* Haile Gerima. *Director:* Haile Gerima. *Screenplay:* Haile Gerima. *Director of Photography:* Augustín Cubano. *Editor:* Haile Gerima. *Music:* David J. White. *Sound:* Charles Dixon and Yassala B. Sessouma. *Production Designer:* Kerry Marshall. *Set Dresser:* Michael N.O. Amon-Kwafo. *Costumes:* Tracey White. *Make-up:* Henry Brown and Vincentia Akwetey. *Running time:* 125 minutes. *MPAA Rating:* Not Rated.

CAST: Kofi Ghanaba (Sankofa, the Divine Drummer); Oyafunmike Ogunlano (Mona/Shola); Alexandra Duah (Nunu); Nick Medley (Joe); Mutabaruka (Shango); Ofemo Omilami (Noble Ali); Reginald Carter (Father Raphael); Mzuri (Lucy); Jimmy Lee Savage (Mussa); Hasinatu Camara (Jumma); Jim Faircloth (James); Stanley Michelson (Mr. Lafayette); John A. Mason (Big Boy); Loise Reid (Esther); Roger Doctor (Nathan); Alditz McKenzie (Kuta); Chrispan Rigby (Photographer); Maxwell Parris (Baby Ngozi); Hosanna Ghanaba (Linguist for Divine Drummer).

NEW YORK POST, 4/8/94, p. 36, Thelma Adams

Branded. White slavers rip the clothes off the shoulders of a terrified, dark-skinned woman. As a hot poker sears her from behind, she arches her back and thrusts her rounded breasts toward the sweet spot of the frame.

The powerful image, appearing early in "Sankofa" which opens today, is part bodice-ripper, part poetry. The victim's pain bonds us to the woman—and yet her torture is eroticized, her sacrifice to white oppression unequivocal.

The director, Ethiopian-born, American-educated Haile Gerima ("Ashes and Embers," "Harvest: 3,000 Years"), obsesses on women-in-peril. A pregnant woman is strung up by the hands and whipped until her baby must be cut from her dead corpse; the heroine is viciously raped from behind by her white master and strung up, naked, breasts to the camera, and severely whipped.

These images are powerful, highly charged, and very selective. Gerima is a visual poet of oppression. With "Sankofa," the Howard University professor throws his hat into the great American victim sweepstakes and sacrifices an important work of art.

Gerima, who also wrote and edited "Sankofa," has been developing the script for 20 years, ever since he studied film at UCLA. The story line intrigues: Mona (Oyafunmike Ogunlano), an African American model on a photo shoot in Ghana, adjacent to the ruins of a slave market, time-travels to the era of slavery.

Captured and branded, Mona finds herself as a house slave named Shola on a sugar plantation in the Americas. She loves a rebellious field slave named Shango (Mutabaruka), is nurtured by the maternal Nunu (Alexandra Duah), and is radicalized.

Gerima uses Mona's pilgrimage through time to illustrate his theme of Sankofa, an Akan word which means "one must return to the past in order to move to the future."

This emphasis on understanding the past—and slavery in particular—to clarify the present and transform the future is strong. But the heavy-handed Gerima pushes it further. A voice-over intones: "It is from here [Africa] that we were snatched and taken away by the white man." The narrative goes so far as to equate slavery with genocide.

This slant is repeated in the treatment of the white characters. This is cracker country. The plantation owner and his crew are cardboard cutouts of cruelty. If the master had a long mustache, he would twirl it. There are no white women.

Mona's flaccid cameraman is also pure cliche, saying "let the camera get you hot" to the writhing, fright-wigged model. Even his camera becomes a weapon of oppression. (And if the truth is in the details, there are no makeup artists, wardrobe people, lighting experts, production assistants in this alleged photo shoot).

The imbalance is even more clear given the piercing performances of Mutabaruka and Alexandra Duah, portrayals that are sacrificed to Gerima's agenda-machine.

There is a need for black filmmakers to accurately address their own history, to place black characters at the center of the frame and outside the 'hood. But, the fact that a vacuum exists does not erase "Sankofa's" flaws.

French director Eric Rohmer has said, "The role of cinema is to be above politics. Films are a bad arena for political struggle."

Political art is boring; political statements that emerge out of a well-constructed drama and complex characters carry more weight. "Sankofa," despite its strengths, is a wasted opportunity.

NEWSDAY, 6/10/94, Part II/p. B7, Terry Kelleher

Commitment is stamped all over "Sankofa."

Producer-director-writer Haile Gerima and co-producer Shirikiana Aina struggled nine years to complete their movie for less than $1 million. When they couldn't find a distributor venturesome enough to release such an unconventional, uncompromising work, they formed their own company to do the job. Now the picture is finding an audience in several major cities.

Not everyone who applauds the phenomenon of "Sankofa" will receive the film itself with equal enthusiasm. The coherence of Gerima's storytelling fails to match the passion of his pan-Africanist preaching. But in the end, this drama of slavery and redemption summons the power to transcend its flaws.

According to Gerima, an Ethiopian-born American, "Sankofa" means "returning to your roots" in the Akan language. His central character returns against her will. Mona (Oyafunmike Ogunlano) is a black fashion model posing saucily outside a castle in Ghana, heedless of the site's significance in the history of the slave trade. Suddenly, in the film's most frightening scene, she is thrown into the dungeon and hurled back in time. Stripped, manhandled and shackled, the American beauty becomes just another piece of African cargo.

"Sankofa" could have been more fascinating if Gerima had chosen to explore the logic of his fantasy premise. How would this woman adjust her 1990s perspective to fit a 19th Century situation? But Mona is abruptly transformed into Shola—"house slave on the Lafayette plantation," as she announces in voiceover—and we must infer that her memory is erased in the process.

Shola loves the rebellious Shango (Mutabaruka, whose Jamaican-accented dialogue is subtitled to unintentionally humorous effect) and draws strength and wisdom from Nunu (beautifully played by Alexandra Duah), who embodies the spirit of Mother Africa. Ofemo Omilani earns sympathy for the conscience-stricken character of Noble Ali, a "headman" ordered to flog fellow slaves caught running away.

The movie grows lurid in depicting the emotional torture of Nunu's light-skinned son, Joe (Nick Medley), the "rotten fruit" of her rape aboard the slave ship. Some may commend Gerima for having the courage to condemn Christianity unequivocally as an instrument of white oppression, but a few are sure to cry foul when Joe—mentored by a pompous priest who seems to regard sadism as a sacrament—sinks to madness and murder out of twisted devotion to the Virgin Mary.

"Sankofa" closes with Shola/Mona's re-emergence in the present, a development that raises all sorts of questions. Gerima answers not with words, but with arresting images that speak of unity, continuity and the indomitability of a race.

SIGHT AND SOUND, 7/94, p. 53, Ben Thompson

Mona, a black American model, is posing for a white photographer on the ramparts of Ghana's infamous Cape Coast castle, where slaves used to be imprisoned before being shipped across the Atlantic. An old African man in traditional robes shouts at her, "Back to your past! Return to your source!" She is shaken, as are a passing group of white tourists, whom the man also attempts to intimidate. Their guide explains that he is Sankofa, who claims to be the guardian of the slaves' spirits and who beats his drums every day to keep in contact with them.

Mona follows the sightseers down into the castle dungeon, hearing the guide explain how the captive Africans were treated. The door slams behind her, and she finds herself transported back in time to the slave era, surrounded by silent, manacled men and women, and branded with a red-hot iron. As Shola, a house slave on an American sugar plantation, she is repeatedly raped by her master, but finds solace in the company of field-slaves, especially her beloved, the rebellious Shango, and the wise, powerful Nunu, who is said to have killed an overseer with her magical powers.

The slaves are treated very cruelly, not only by their white masters but also by the head slaves, among them Nunu's mulatto son Joe, who is set apart by his embrace of the white man's Christianity. A group of slaves, among them the pregnant Kuta, run away, trying to get to the hills where escapees live freely; they are recaptured and fatally flogged. Taking hold of Kuta's dying body, Nunu delivers her child. Called Kwame, 'the witness', the infant is raised by the other slaves. Noble Ali, one of the head slaves, is conscience-stricken by his part in the death of the baby's mother, and joins the 'clandestine rebels'.

After an unsuccessful rebellion, slaves are suspended in cages to be eaten by vultures. Nunu is sent away to be sold, but is happy to be rejected and sent back as too old. Shola runs away but is recaptured and tortured by the master and the priest Father Raphael. Her friend Juma wants to sleep with Joe, but he rejects her. Shola persuades Shango to give him a love potion, but it is poisonous and Joe goes mad. Nunu chases him to the river and saves his life by purging him, but he responds by drowning her. In an agony of remorse, he takes her body to the church and lays it on the altar. When Father Raphael accuses Nunu as a heathen, Joe kills him and locks himself in the church, which is eventually burnt down with him inside. No sign of Nunu's body is found.

There is another, larger rebellion. Shola kills her master as he threatens to rape her again. The escaping slaves are hunted down, but Shola runs on until in death her soul flies back to Africa.

Mona emerges naked from the dungeon. A woman clothes her in traditional dress. She spurns the photographer and joins a group of black people sitting in contemplation at the ocean's edge. A woman who looks like Nunu smiles at her.

'Sankofa' means "returning to your roots, recuperating what you've lost and moving forward". That sounds like a straight-forward process, but in deciding to confront the issue of slavery, *Sankofa*'s Ethiopian-born producer-writer-director Haile Gerima was setting out on a rocky path.

From its impressive opening sequence onwards, *Sankofa* strives for, and by and large achieves, a cinematic language worthy of the importance of its subject matter. The mesmeric drumming and hollering of Kofi Ghanaba underpins our introduction to powerful visual images of birds and the African coast line that will recur throughout the film (Ghanaba's past as respected American jazz musician Guy Warren, and adviser to Ghana's President Nkrumah renders him doubly qualified for the role). An urgent voice sounds a lengthy clarion call: "Stolen Africans ... from Nabama to Surinam ... step out and claim your story". The film's titles also benefit from a snappy ripple effect.

The dice seem to be loaded from the off against Mona. With her tacky swimsuit and dyed orange hair, she is meant to be a grotesque figure, and there is a hint of spite in the way the camera first lingers over her branding, then celebrates the unsmiling humility with which she finally takes her place among the Africans at the water's edge. This slant is hardly surprising, as Gerima's intentions are avowedly didactic—to address "the continuing problem of those persons in the Africa diaspora who neglect their own history".

Once the action has switched to the plantation, this didacticism is never awkward. *Sankofa*'s treatment of its painful subject matter is commendably unexploitative. It is not by any means unrelentingly grim, resisting the temptation to wallow in the horrors it depicts. The white people in the film—photographer, tourists and slave-masters alike—are not exactly sympathetic, but then why should they be?

Most of *Sankofa*'s occasional lighter moments are supplied by the Ghanaian actress Alexandra Duah, who is superb in the potentially irritating fount-of-all-wisdom role of Nunu. But all the performances are good. Oyafunmike Ogunlano succeeds in carrying the part of Mona/Shola through what might have been an "it was only a dream" ending. The Jamaican dub poet Mutabaruka makes a persuasive screen debut as the rebellious Shango, and Nick Medley is effectively tormented as the benighted Joe.

The real star of the film, though, is the man behind the camera. The cinematography is outstanding: from the peaceful bustle of the Ghanaian coast to the swishing canes of the American plantation, Gerima creates an extraordinary sense of motion. David White's score, blending chants and jazz, drums and blues, makes a vital contribution to this, and the dual symbolism of the vulture, as harbinger of both death and escape, is more powerful than anyone raised on Bird's Eye being the bird of freedom has any right to expect. But it is the stately progress of the camera across a living landscape that leaves *Sankofa*'s most abiding impression. Other film-makers have struggled to make such a grand and historical impact on 30 times this budget.

VILLAGE VOICE, 11/30/93, Film Special/p. 32, Gary Dauphin

The most accomplished of the new films being screened here, *Sankofa*, by veteran Ethiopian-born director Hailie Gerima, takes that collision of contexts as its explicit subject [The reference is to the Contemporary Films of the African Diaspora festival.] *Sankofa* is the Akan word for "recuperating what you've lost," and this tale of finders keepers unites two black women in one body: Shola, a 19th-century house slave, and Mona, a contemporary fashion model who's somehow misplaced her black identity. The film opens with Mona cavorting rather indecently on the site of a onetime West African slave market, only to have her shoot interrupted by an attack of spirit possession and time travel. Mona finds herself back in slave days, reliving Shola's brutal passage from passive survivor to active, albeit quixotic, rebel.

The film climaxes with a single shot taken from a vulture's-eye view: airborne and triumphant, while an otherworldly African coastal vista fills the screen, Mona/Shola complete the circle, returning to their common point of origin after a stopover of centuries. It's a bit of virtuosic film-making, and if you look very carefully at that shot you'll notice the shadow cast by the helicopter doing the filming glide serenely across the screen. Gerima is too accomplished a craftsman to have made such an error, but even if it is just an accident, it leads into the film's homecoming coda, Mona, emerging from her own shadows reintegrated into the Extended African Family. It's a stirring, visually arresting sequence and all the while the memory of the play of shadows (of the camera, of the apparatus, of a lost history) hangs over it, reminding the viewer that a lyrical moment of filmic closure is one thing, but healing the wounds of great bloody crimes in real life is something else altogether, no matter how beautiful the image of clean, unscarred skin.

VILLAGE VOICE, 4/12/94, p. 56, Georgia Brown

When Julie Dash's *Daughters of the Dust* opened at Film Forum two years ago, white reviewers (like me) had no inkling it would begin packing in sellout crowds. This was a "difficult" art film; it seemed a specialized text of interest mainly to film study programs. But busloads pulled in from points north, west, and south. These predominately female spectators (at least in the downtown run) savored the film's leisurely pace and clearly weren't put off by what I saw as maddeningly cryptic exposition. They came back again and again. *Daughters* proved that non-narrative cinema can be read by anyone with a will, or a need. People are famished and the movie fed them.

Closer in style to *Daughters* than to any of the Hollywood 'hood filmz, Haile Gerima's *Sankofa*—which already has had limited openings in Baltimore and Boston—looks poised to pull in the same parched, hollow-eyed audiences. Even more so than *Daughters*, the film is didactic and digressive—its present posited as simultaneous with its past. Characters are mouthpieces, action is strictly stylized, and violence—which there is plenty of—takes place offscreen. The film is deliberately broken by lyric passages and appeals to subliminal sensory experience. What it has, however, is urgency.

Sankofa begins on the Ghanaian shore, at Cape Coast Castle, one of the original 360 fortresses where slaves were held before the perilous crossing. Currently the castle is a tourist attraction. On the beach facing the fort, an American model, Mona (Oyafunmike Ogunlano), writhes on the sand, commanded by a young blond photographer: "Let the camera do it to you, Mona." " Show what you're made of." Mona is wearing a Tarzan-Jane-style leopard skin and a straight-hair, Tina Turner wig. Suddenly, the shoot is interrupted by a tall, robed figure. "Back to your past!" the specter thunders. "Return to your source!" Mona giggles and ducks behind the camera guy who looks more bemused than protective.

These events are repeated the next day. This time the specter also shoos away some white tourists: "Go! This is sacred ground ... Blood spilled here." He in turn is chased off by a government soldier. But when the figure reappears, Mona follows him into the fort where suddenly, inexplicably, she's captured, bound, and (protesting, "I'm not an African!") branded. All around captives in irons look on silently.

Gerima collapses time more successfully with music—a brilliant score by David White takes off with the thrilling drumming of Kofi Ghanaba—than with imagery. But the image is here. The film's title, *Sankofa*, refers to an Akan figure—a bird with its head facing backward—literally meaning to go back and retrieve what was lost. In this case, Gerima makes the backward-facing bird (past and present in one figure) a pale-eyed vulture that slaves believed would take their remains back to Africa. The sight of any bird flying reminded them of escape and freedom.

For Mona this passage back is also a water crossing. Now we are somewhere in the Americas, on the Lafayette sugar plantation, and Mona has been preincarnated as Shola, a house slave. Born into captivity she accepts its brutal premises—for instance, the right of the master to rape her when he's inclined. Having fallen in love with a field slave, though, she finds out that those who've come directly from Africa retain memories of freedom and a far different life.

One of Sankofa's most forceful points is how quickly memory can be lost—how the first diaspora-born generation, isolated from land, language, lore, sheds centuries of cultural identity. When Shola says, "If you was born a slave like me, it was easier to accept things," she speaks for generations to come, even those born after so-called emancipation.

So this is Mona/Shola's coming-of-age story, Reeducating Shola to her African roots are her lover, the untamable Shongo (Mutabaruka, the Jamaican dub poet), a leader in a secret society of rebels, and the older Nunu (Ghanaian actress Alexandra Duah), another rebel but also mother figure. Raped on the slave ship, Nunu has a grown, blue-eyed son, Joe (Nick Medley), now a plantation headman (kapo) as well as a devout Catholic convinced his real mother is the Virgin

Mary. His cry, "I'm different!" contains an extraordinary confusion of pride and shame. This who-is-my-real-family? conflict initially drives him mad and eventually, though too late, drives him sane. (For me, the Mona/Shola figure is much less compelling than the mixed-up Joe.)

Currently a film professor at Howard, the Ethiopian-born Gerima, along with Charles Burnett, Billy Woodberry, and Larry Clark, was a member of the L.A. black filmmaking collective of the late '60s and the '70s. Rejecting the Hollywood model, the school's main priority was to create a socially responsible cinema. I suppose its key phrase could be one from Gerima's 1982 *Ashes and Embers*: "Pass it on. Pass it on." It's fitting that *Sankofa*, with its homemade, in-the-family distribution system, will take life essentially by word of mouth.

Also reviewed in:
NEW YORK TIMES, 4/8/94, p. C8, Caryn James
VARIETY, 3/15/93, p. 64, David Stratton

SANTA CLAUSE, THE

A Walt Disney Pictures release in association with Hollywood Pictures. *Executive Producer:* Richard Baker, Rick Messina, and James Miller. *Producer:* Brian Reilly, Jeffrey Silver, and Robert Newmyer. *Director:* John Pasquin. *Screenplay:* Leo Benvenuti and Steve Rudnick. *Director of Photography:* Walt Lloyd. *Editor:* Larry Bock. *Music:* Michael Convertino. *Music Editor:* Ken Wannberg. *Sound:* David Lee and (music) Dennis Sands. *Sound Editor:* Bruce Stubblefield and Hari Ryatt. *Casting:* Renée Rousselot. *Production Designer:* Carol Spier. *Art Director:* James McAteer. *Set Decorator:* Elinor Galbraith. *Set Dresser:* Carlos Caneca and David Evans. *Special Effects:* Bob Hall. *Costumes:* Carol Ramsey. *Make-up:* Barry R. Koper. *Special Make-up and Animatronic Effects:* Alec Gillis and Tom Woodruff, Jr. *Stunt Coordinator:* Shane Cardwell. *Running time:* 95 minutes. *MPAA Rating:* PG.

CAST: Tim Allen (Scott Calvin); Judge Reinhold (Neal); Wendy Crewson (Laura); Eric Lloyd (Charlie); David Krumholtz (Bernard); Larry Brandenburg (Detective Nunzio); Mary Gross (Ms. Daniels); Paige Tamada (Elf Judy); Peter Boyle (Mr. Whittle); Judith Scott (Susan); Jayne Eastwood (Waitress); Melissa King (Little Girl); Bradley Wentworth (Elf at North Pole); Azura Bates (Elf in Hangar); Joshua Satok (Elf Larry); Zach McLemore (Bobby); Joyce Guy (Principal Compton); Lindsay Lupien (Kid Two); Alexandra Petrocci (Kid Three); Jesse Collins (Ad Executive); David Paul Grove (Waiter); Steve Vinovich (Dr. Novos); Aimee McIntyre (Ruth); Tabitha Lupien (Ballet Girl); Lachlan Murdoch (Fax Kid); Dennis O'Connor (Mailman); David Sparrow (Bobby's Dad); Ron Hartmann (Judge); Nic Knight (Quintin); Scott Wickware (Malone); Gene Mack (Newman); Brett Moon (Elf One); Ryan Moon (Elf Two); Jack Newman (Santa in Street); Michael Caruana (Officer #1); Cody Jones (Child Two); Micha Jackson (Child One); Kenny Vadas (E.L.F.S Leader); Brian Reilly (Tinsel Man); Gordon Masten (Desk Sergeant); Philip Williams (Sharpshooter); Chris Benson (Fireman); Laura Catalano (Veronica); Peter Kosaka (Japanese Businessman); Ivanka Kotalto (E.L.F.S. #2); Todd Davis (E.L.F.S. #3); Marc Pichette (E.L.F.S. #4); John Pasquin (Santa #6); Tony Krolo (Coffee Cop); Alec Bachlow (Neighbor); Jimmy Labriola (Truck Driver); Steve Kosaka, Lawrence Nakamura, Hun Sun Tran, and Steve Tsukamoto (Japanese Businessmen); Frank Welker and Kerrigan Mahan (Reindeer Voices), Nina Keogh (Puppet Judy); Bob Dermer (Puppet Punch).

LOS ANGELES TIMES, 11/11/94, Calendar/p. 10, Kevin Thomas

Few TV stars have made the move to the big screen with such stellar panache as "Home Improvement's" Tim Allen in Disney's lavish yet venturesome, sweet-and-sour holiday fantasy "The Santa Clause," a film that dreams of childhood.

Although the spirit of Christmas surely prevails, there's a real edge to this picture, yet it doesn't cut out the youngsters who will find so much to embrace in this genuinely imaginative work with its amazing special effects and an enchantingly realized—and immense—Santa's workshop kingdom at the North Pole. "The Santa Clause" is a Christmas picture for the frequently splintered families of the hard-driving '90s.

Eight-year-old Charlie (Eric Lloyd) is not looking forward to spending Christmas Eve with his father, Scott (Allen), with good reason. Scott may be a marketing whiz with a toy company, but that doesn't mean he's attuned to kids. He's a divorced workaholic who's never made time for his son and his ex-wife, Laura (Wendy Crewson), now married to Neal (Judge Reinhold), a decent but slightly sanctimonious psychiatrist who is the principal target of Scott's incessant sarcasm. What's more, Charlie has just begun doubting the existence of Santa Claus. He's really depressed after his father burns the turkey, and they have Christmas dinner at the only restaurant in their picture-book suburb still open: Denny's.

Suddenly, after father and son have gone to bed, they hear a clatter on Scott's roof: It's Santa and his reindeer! But Santa slips, falling to the snow-covered ground and telling Scott, before he evaporates, that he must don Santa's suit, and that the reindeer will guide him on completing the delivery of his Christmas packages.

What Scott doesn't realize is that the clothes make the man: Put on Santa's outfit—even reluctantly—and you become Santa. Although aided by Hollywood wizardry, Allen makes that transformation come from within; his is a fine, wide-ranging portrayal of a man awakening to his emotions. There's real poignancy and irony in Scott's ultimate fate that will be appreciated by grown-ups without being a downer for kids.

Writers Steve Rudnick and Leo Benvenuti, former stand-up comics both, reportedly originally came up with a far darker story, but enough serious shading remains to set off the sentimental aspects of "The Santa Clause" to just the right degree. The sense of reality they bring to Charlie's life makes it all the more possible for youngsters of his age to go along with the movie's infinite capacity for magic in making Santa and his annual rounds plausible.

At the same time the writers, as they evoke the spirit of Christmas (the key purpose of all such holiday tales), have created grownups with whom adults can identify only too easily. In short, "The Santa Clause" proceeds from an exceedingly well-thought-out script, which in turn has been brought to life by "Home Improvement's" original producer and director, John Pasquin, in a notably demanding feature debut that has required him to keep in balance: human feelings and values and large-scale fantasy razzle-dazzle.

All of the film's technical and creative contributions are top-notch, but as it should be, it's the people who win us over. Lloyd matches Allen's impact with a portrayal of an intelligent boy caught up in incredible events. Adding crucial normalcy to the picture are Crewson and Reinhold's perfectly decent couple. David Krumholtz brings an earthy, matter-of-fact quality to the North Pole's head elf, Bernard. You don't have to be a big fan of holiday fare to come away impressed—and, most important, moved—by "The Santa Clause."

NEW YORK POST, 11/11/94, p. 49, Larry Worth

Long before hearing "and to all a good night," "The Santa Clause" proves a surprisingly pleasant present for moviegoers.

For that matter, it's the best yuletide treat since "How the Grinch Stole Christmas," maybe because both share a refreshing irreverence for the jolly old elf and joy to the world.

In Leo Benvenuti and Steve Rudnick's sharp, funny script, Santa doesn't drink milk (he's lactose intolerant), checks out beautiful babes (preferring the naughty to the nice) and delivers unique ho-ho-ho's (deliciously mean-spirited one-liners).

Essentially, Benvenuti and Rudnick take the old Santa story and give it a thorough dusting off, updating it for '90s sensibilities. That's true from the getgo as St. Nick falls from the roof of Scott Calvin's suburban home and goes to that great elf-land in the sky, leaving behind eight restless reindeer, a sleighful of toy's and an oversized red suit.

Divorced dad Scott is awoken by the clatter. But he soon regrets rising to see what's the matter.

Egged on by his young son, Scott slips into the big guy's jacket and trousers and completes the night's work, meanwhile discovering how Santa enters houses without chimneys and one bagful of goodies accommodates the world's children.

Everything's merry until Scott reads the fine print, i.e. the titular Santa clause: that whomever inherits the suit has till next Thanksgiving to tie up his personal life before *becoming* the new Kris Kringle.

Therein lies the bulk of the plot, as Scott, a high-powered ad exec with a decidedly cynical bent, finds himself gaining weight uncontrollably, sporting a full beard by noon— and preparing to bid loved ones goodbye.

Under John Pasquin's brisk direction, the results offer a generous serving of belly laughs, tinged with a bit of sadness. And while paying homage to the is-he-or-isn't-he theme of "Miracle on 34th Street," Pasquin avoids the requisite sentimental goo.

The results are skillfully packaged, especially since it marks Pasquin's big-screen debut. That also explains some of the problems: abandoned subplots, an uneven blend of special effects (ranging from the phenomenal to the cheesy) and glossing over a troubling end twist.

But even when the eggnog starts to curdle, Tim Allen's wit and timing make for a wonderfully charismatic presence. Best known as the star of TV's "Home Improvement," he taps into all-new appeal as the cocky hero with boots of clay .

The fine supporting cast includes Wendy Crewson as Scott's level-headed ex-wife, a hilarious Judge Reinhold as her psycho-babble-spouting lover and Peter Boyle's Scrooge-like boss. Young Eric Lloyd also earns praise by sidestepping the precocious child cliches.

Yes Virginia, there is a "Santa Clause." And it's destined to become a holiday classic.

NEWSDAY, 11/11/94, Part II/p. B2, John Anderson

If there had been one person at Jonestown screaming "Don't drink the Kool-Aid!" would it have made any difference? No, and all the words in the world won't keep the family entertainment-starved hordes from "The Santa Clause" this holiday season.

"The Santa Clause" won't kill you, of course, but it will leave an artificially sweetened taste in the mouth. And the sense that you're being steered down the same old ski trail of man-made powder and prepackaged sentiment. And, just to complete the holiday gift pack of mixed emotions, a guilty feeling, too: Disney has given us a gift, after all. Should we be disappointed just because some assembly is required, and batteries aren't included?

This is a film of parts. Old movie bits—from "Miracle on 34th Street" to "It's a Wonderful Life" to "Santa Claus Conquers the Martians"—are strung together like popcorn, along with one novel premise: Santa Claus has been many, many people over the centuries. When one Santa becomes unable to perform his duties—nobody ever says drop dead—the next person to put on the suit becomes Santa Claus.

So the moral is, don't put on the suit.

No one in the film complains about the commercialization of Christmas, which is a good thing: This *is* the commercialization of Christmas. The star is television's biggest attraction—Tim Allen, of the No. 1-rated "Home Improvement"—in a movie guaranteed to be resurrected seasonally. There's plenty of product placement (including a sly but obvious plug for Allen's own TV show), enough high-tech recreational equipment to keep Christmas lists filled in perpetuity and a plot that's sure to warm the hearts of dysfunctional families everywhere, while irritating psychiatrists, stepparents and police officers.

Allen is Scott Calvin (notice the initials), a highly compensated executive at a toy company who's just had a very good year professionally, and he has other Scrooge-like characteristics, too. He's a sour fellow, divorced from Laura (Wendy Crewson), who's remarried to Neal (Judge Reinhold), a psychiatrist Scott can't help but insult at every opportunity. He's also father to Charlie (Eric Lloyd), who, not surprisingly, is reluctant to spend Christmas Eve with Dad. His case is strengthened when the perpetually distracted Scott has to baste the Christmas turkey with a fire extinguisher. (To avoid plugging anything, let's just say they go out to eat at a certain restaurant chain that's been accused of racial discrimination.)

That night they hear a noise, and watch as Santa Claus falls off their roof and dissolves. Is this a metaphor for the modern yule-tide spirit? No, this is just how the line of succession works. "The reindeer will know what to do," says a card in the pocket of the bright red suit, but Scott doesn't read the fine print, and of course puts on the suit. From here, it's a combination of toy workshop and therapist's couch. After making the holiday rounds, Scott and Charlie wind up at the North Pole, where the elves look like children, and Bernard (David Krumholtz), a mensch on ice, gets a little testy with Scott when he balks at becoming the Big Guy. Charlie, naturally, is all for it, and his certainty that Dad is Santa over the next 12 months prompts Neal and Laura to cut off Scott's visitation.

Scott, meanwhile, becomes Santa Claus, and his enormous weight gain is easily the film's best special effect: With a series of "fat suits," Scott blossoms into Coca-Cola's vision of Père Noël. The reindeer, on the other hand, look like antlered dogs, and most of the other effects are simply cheesy: Six carolers on the street sound like the Mormon Tabernacle Choir; animation provides the cop-out explanation for how Santa gets down the chimney when all a kid has is central heating.

There are some amusing moments, sure, and Allen can deliver a joke. Unfortunately, most of the jokes are at the expense of Charlie's stepfather. Or an over-weight, doughnut-eating cop who gets humiliated by elves. Or psychiatrists in general. Or authority figures in general. Or anyone who goes to a holiday movie this year expecting anything like Christmas spirit.

NEWSWEEK, 11/21/94, p. 96, Jeff Giles

[*The Santa Clause* was reviewed jointly with *Miracle on 34th Street*; see Giles' review of that film.]

SIGHT AND SOUND, 12/95, p. 50, Tom Tunney

Taking his own Charlie home on Christmas Eve, divorced toy company executive Scott Calvin sees a sleigh and reindeer floating over his house. When the exhausted Santa Claus falls off the roof, Scott dons his red outfit only to discover that by wearing it and boarding the sleigh he's now a party to the "Santa Clause". This holds that, "the wearer waives any rights to previous identity, real or implied, and fully accepts the duties and responsibilities of Santa Claus until such time that the wearer becomes unable to do so either by accident or design."

Skeptical at first, Scott becomes convinced of his new status when the reindeer drag him and Charlie around the globe so that he can deliver the world's children their Christmas toys from a magical self-refilling bag. Then the duo are taken to the North Pole where they meet the elves in charge of the toy factory. Scott has a tough job explaining away his son's story of their adventures to his ex-wife and her new partner Neal. Over the next year and as Christmas approaches, Scott finds himself putting on huge amounts of weight and growing a large white beard, despite his best efforts at diet, shaving and exercise.

Due to his apparently bizarre behaviour, Scott loses custody of his son and all visiting rights. Ignoring this judgement, he and Charlie go back to the North Pole and set about tackling the delivery of the year's Christmas's toys. Arrested by the police after being mistaken for a burglar in one house, Scott is sprung from the police station by a group of elves. Back home he convinces Charlie that he, Laura and even Neal are all family. Laura and Neal are now finally convinced that he really is Santa and Laura throws the papers awarding her custody into the fire. Scott gives the two adults the toys they had most wanted but never received as children, a whistle and a *Mystery Date* Game. Then, wishing a "Merry Christmas to all," he takes Charlie up for one final spin in his sleigh.

One of the defining conventions of contemporary Hollywood children's films is that the key adult characters are almost always divorced, widowed or remarried. This accurately reflects the state of family life in the modern USA, but it also gives the scriptwriters the difficult task of matching the regulation optimistic contours of a children's movie with the direct experiences of its potential audience, many of whom will come from 'broken homes'. Thus, the most recent big screen *Lassie* movie is less about the dog than about a little girl who has a new stepmother and calls the dog she finds "Lassie" because *Lassie* is her favourite television show.

Complete with a passing reference to the original *Miracle on 34th Street*, this amusing saga of a divorcé-turned-Santa *The Santa Clause* falls into a similar pattern of self-consciousness both about its own status as a children's movie and about the fragility of the family values it celebrates. However, unlike the 1994 *Lassie*, the film manages its difficult balancing act exceptionally well, mainly because here the focus is much more on the non-conforming adult character rather than the restless child.

Tim Allen's self-deprecating performance is one of the main reasons for the film's success. Supplied with a steady stream of sarcastic one-liners, his permanently bemused attitude keeps cuteness at bay while at the same time he does reluctantly get into the merry spirit of things—memorably telling one child to fax in her list of toy requests and refusing another's offering of milk with the excuse that he's "lactose intolerant". Adults will appreciate this sustained line in humour, while younger children will simply enjoy the film's rich diet of glitzy special effects and busy knock-about comedy.

Of course, two prime requirements of a film about Santa are, firstly, to reassure young audiences he really does exist, and secondly, to explain how does he get in through the chimney when many homes nowadays don't have one.

Explaining the first issue, the binding 'Santa Clause' decisively disapproves that old Chico Marx quip that "there ain't no Sanity Clause," though quizzical grown-ups may still be left wondering what happened to the poor exhausted chap who fell off Scott's roof: did he die or was he magically spirited off to some Arctic nursing home for worn out ex-Santas? However, it's the issue of Santa's chimney delivery system which, while doing a great service to previously lost-for-words parents, also tells us most about the movie's wish-fulfilment agenda. When Scott arrives to deliver his toys, even the most modern home is magically accorded a grand fireplace for him to drop in through. State-of-the-art special effects and the old-fashioned images of Christmas are thus united. Santa is firmly squeezed into the sooty past of the traditionally idealised Victorian Christmas.

But what Scott's Santa also has to face up to is a son he doesn't get on with and an ex-wife who increasingly wishes to deny him visiting rights. The contradiction that the film must resolve is the depiction of an apparent cosmic order in which every child can be happy and every home can have a magic fireplace, against the contrary facts that most American marriages end in divorce and that computer games have replaced traditional toys in many children's Christmas stockings.

In many recent Hollywood films aimed at children, addressing this kind of contradiction results in tacked-on optimism. Here, through a good script and a strong central performance, it becomes a positive strength. Instead of replacing Laura's new humourless partner Neal in the family circle, Scott eventually accepts Neal into it and also accepts his own lonely fate literally to work as Santa until the next upholder of the "Clause" comes along.

Far superior to the 1985 British disaster *Santa Claus*, this is a polished example of festive film-making, but there are enough comical cracks in its facade to ensure that it should appeal to die-hard cynics too. Here is a divorced Santa who really only takes on the job because there's simply nowhere else for a creative nice guy like him to go.

Also reviewed in:
CHICAGO TRIBUNE, 11/11/94, Friday/p. H, Michael Wilmington
NEW YORK TIMES, 11/11/94, p. C24, Janet Maslin
VARIETY, 11/14-20/94, p. 47, Leonard Klady
WASHINGTON POST, 11/11/94, p. D1, Rita Kempley
WASHINGTON POST, 11/11/94, Weekend/p. 48, Desson Howe

SARRAOUNIA

A Soleil O production with the participation of the Ministères Français de la Culture et des Relations Extérieures, Ministères de l'Information et de la Culture du Burkina Faso. *Producer:* Med Hondo. *Director:* Med Hondo. *Screenplay (French with English subtitles):* Med Hondo and Abdul War. *Based on the novel by:* Abdoulaye Mamani. *Director of Photography:* Guy Famechon. *Editor:* Marie-Thérèse Boiché. *Music:* Pierre Akendengue, Abdoulaye Cissé, and Issouf Compaore. *Sound:* Varetan Karakeusian and Patrick Mare. *Production Designer:* Jacques d'Ovidio. *Special Effects:* Jean-Louis Trinquier. *Costumes:* Julie Lherm. *Make-up:* Gill Robillard, Jocelyne Lemery, and Aminata Zoure. *Running time:* 120 minutes. *MPAA Rating:* Not Rated.

CAST: Aï Keïta (Sarraounia); Jean-Roger Milo (Captain Voulet); Féodor Atkine (Captain Chanoine); Didier Sauvegrain (Doctor Henric); Roger Mirmont (Lieutenant Joalland); Luc-Antoine Diquero (Lieutenant Pallier); Jean-Pierre Castaldi (Sergeant Boutel); Tidjani Ouedraogo (Coulibaly); Wladimir Ivanosky (Sergeant-Major Laury); Didier Agostini (Marshal Tourot); Jean Edmond (Colonel Klobb); Philippe Bellay (Lieutenant Meynier); Tagara Yacouba Traore (Dawa); Aboubacar Traore (Baka); Abdoulaye Cissé (Gogue); Jean-François Ouedraogo (Dan Zaki); Florence Bewendé (Amina); Hama Gourounga (Emir's Envoy); Baba Traore (Serkin Gobir); Djibril Sidibe (Serkin Arewa); Sekou Tall (Emir of Sokoto); Rajoun Tapsirou (Amenokal); Jacob Sou (Makoni); Temeddit Ag Hoye (Targuia); Ben Idriss Traore (Warrior Baka).

MONTHLY FILM BULLETIN, 1/88, p. 8, James Leahy

Sarraounia, Queen of the Aznas, trained since childhood in the arts of herbalism and war, leads her people to victory over the Fulanis of Sokoto when they attack Lugu. After the victory celebrations, her general and former lover, Baka quits her service, jealous of the *griot* (a poet/musician) who now loves her. A map of Africa is shown with the green areas being submerged under the colonialists' blood red. An army led by a Frenchman, Captain Voulet, approaches Lugu, burning villages, killing, raping and torturing. Sarraounia's Islamic neighbours debate whether to ally themselves with her, a 'witch' and an 'unbeliever', or to collaborate with the French. The Emir of Sokoto, in British territory, plots against the 'infidel' Sarraounia. Determined to attack Sarraounia for reasons of prestige, Voulet ignores a letter from his superiors (executing the corporal who bears it as a spy), and severs his ties with the high command of Niger. Another army column, led by Colonel Klobb, is meanwhile attempting to overtake him. Preparations are made for the defence of Lugu, and for sacrifices to avert the spilling of the defenders' blood. The French officers enjoy a formal dinner, bragging about the bestial fascinations of oriental brothels and their dislike of the roughness of 'nigger women'. A thunderstorm throws the camp into chaos; some of the black porters and women escape. Voulet's men are forced to whip each other for trying to desert, whereas new forces rally to Sarraounia: Baka, and the Prince of Matankari, a neighbouring Islamic city. Voulet's forces breach the walls of Lugu, but Sarraounia's strategic withdrawal to the forest leaves them bewildered. During the ensuing skirmishes, Sarraounia appears an elusive vision, tormenting her enemies. The column withdraws from Lugu and burns the village. When Klobb at last catches up, Voulet fires on his fellow Frenchman and kills him. The blacks in Voulet's command mutiny: Voulet's black aide, Coulibaly, is shot and his second-in-command, Captain Chanoine, is stabbed by the women. Lieutenant Joalland, the most soldierly of the officers, ineffectually attempts to take command. Sarraounia makes a speech about religious and personal tolerance, and the need to fight to preserve freedom. As her army returns to Lugu, the *griot* sings of his own role, keeping alive the names of great heroes and glorious deeds.

Perhaps no scene better exemplifies Med Hondo's methods and ambitions in this magnificent film than that in which a Tuareg caravan transporting grain and slaves to the North, encamps for the night. It is peripheral to the narrative, as the Tuareg are to the geographical area and to the opposing forces the film depicts. The chiefs regret the coming of the white men, who will create a new order. They are resigned ("May God's will be done") whereas the women are singing of Sarraounia and Tafinat (their own heroine): "Time flows on forever/Men are born and die/But fame defies time". Resignation and resistance are juxtaposed in the same shot. The spectator knows that colonialism did create a new order, but is reminded that resistance is both possible and powerful, and of the conflicts and contradictions within Africa (internal slavery, plunder and exploitation, for example).

Ideas which are explored throughout the film are here evoked: the role of women in society (amongst the Tuareg, they are honoured and respected; in Voulet's army they are mere chattels, sexual slaves); the role of the *griot* (poet-musician, and now, by extension, film-maker) who transmits history in "vivid songs". In scale, it is an epic scene, in the sense in which that term was used in relation to 60s film-making and, at the same time, it is reminiscent of earlier epics (*The Iliad, The Aeneid*). More importantly, it is epic in the Brechtian sense; the scene is a *gestus*, a formal unit that generates precise social and historical meaning. Such a scene is inconceivable in a modern Western movie, if not for reasons of budgetary constraint, then on account of an ideological conception of narrative and thematic coherence: what are the Tuareg doing in the story of Sarraounia and the Aznas against Voulet and the French. It does demonstrate the remarkable ease and fluidity with which Med Hondo is able to combine the differing, and often conflicting notions and traditions of the epic.

Perhaps only an African (and quite possibly only this individual) film-maker could have achieved this synthesis, for it draws as much on deep, traditional cultural roots as on Western intellectualism. Apart from the pan-African awareness of colonialism, there is, for example, the African tradition for formal yet democratic public debate, which exists even in conservative and hierarchial societies. Moreover, just as such political debate can often spontaneously emerge out of a ritual performance—a ceremonial song or dance, for example—so it finds its place easily in the dramatic representations of the cinema. It is stylised, a ritual, yet observed in naturalistic detail , for details of gesture may convey a precise political meaning. Realistically it is part of a long-established system of cultural discourse. The closest aesthetic parallel is with classic Japanese cinema, and the latter's evocations of a radically more conservative society, traditions and custom—surely no admirer of Mizoguchi or even Kurosawa can fail to be spellbound by *Sarraounia*?

An equally extraordinary synthesis is achieved in the acting: the Europeans are individualised in the classic French manner, which contrasts with the lower-key, ensemble acting of the unconquered Africans. Though perhaps alien to European audiences (but no more so than Japanese acting) this is not difficult to read for those prepared to relax and *watch*. Thus, though the Africans are prepared to sink their individuality in the collective, be it the hierarchical society of the collaborators, or the looser brotherhood of the cause of resistance and liberty, the spectator remains subtly aware of them as individuals. A third acting style, more impulsive and violent, articulates the selfishness and rootlessness of the black 'Frenchmen': chaos and anarchy prevail; they have no true discipline; they have abandoned that of their own cultures, while the French discipline them by bribery and fear.

Sarraounia's resistance generates conflicts in them which are articulated in politically meaningful but disorderly debate. Simultaneously, the resistance she leads penetrates Voulet's veneer of civilisation, revealing him as paranoid and hysterical, deluded by his greed for power and grandeur. *Sarrounia* is probably the most violent film to come out of Africa, but nowhere is violence indulged for its own sake. Colonial conquest was violent and cruel, and if the British are let off lightly, we must remember that the events depicted here occurred only two years after Rhodes' suppression of the uprising in Matabeleland. Theories of race and empire were endemic in this era, the credo not only of buccaneers like Rhodes and Voulet but also of most political leaders and thinkers in the metropolitan countries.

Sarrounia is a landmark in the history of African cinema, for its range and complexity, and because it goes beyond resistance to articulate a notion of "a very beautiful civilisation" of tolerance and fraternity which conjures up the generous spirit of Jean Renoir. It would be nice to think it might become a landmark in world cinema.

NEW YORK POST, 12/16/94, p. 68, Bill Hoffmann

"Sarraounia" is the rousing, true story of a spirited African warrior queen who leads her forces to a brief but glorious victory over the French Colonialists at the turn of the century.

Charged with a commanding cast, fine cinematography and compelling story, "Sarraounia" stands out as one of truly great "mainstream" efforts to come out of African cinema today.

The scene is Niger, Africa, in the 1890s. As part of colonial expansion into Africa, a French military force is plundering its way through the country, pillaging and burning villages and killing or making slaves of the natives.

The squad's two captains are merciless swine who do their murderous job with such gusto they have excommunicated themselves from their more compassionate French commanders.

Thousands are dying and word spreads through the surrounding kingdoms that a destructive death machine of "evil white men" will soon obliterate them.

But one kingdom without the intense fear of the others is the Azans, led by a tireless, outspoken leader named Queen Sarraounia.

Sarraounia is believed to have magic powers and is referred to as a "witch." Whether she's possessed or not is moot; what the queen does have is the power of mobilizing her troops and getting them psyched up for battle.

The two evil captains start hearing of Sarraounia's magic long before they get to her kingdom and they are determined to quash her.

To give away more would spoil the many cinematic flourishes director Med Hondo has in store. This is straightforward storytelling at its best.

I would like to have known a little more of Sarraounia's upbringing to learn how she became so cool, so confident in a male-dominated society but that's a small complaint.

"Sarraounia" is a whopper of a movie. It takes you places other movies about Africa have never gone. And it does so in a smart, very entertaining way.

The vibrant music performed by Akendengue adds force to the story.

African cinema has steadily grown over the years, polishing and remaking itself with each new production. With "Sarraounia," it reaches new heights.

NEWSDAY, 12/16/94, Part II/p. B15, Gene Seymour

"Sarraounia" represents something of a landmark in the presentation of African films in this country. For once American audiences get to see a historical movie about African colonization told by direct descendants of the colonized instead of the colonizers.

Filmed eight years ago in Burkina Faso by Mauritanian director Med Hondo, "Sarraounia" has as its title character a wise, charismatic tribal queen (Aï Keïta), whose skills in martial arts and primitive medicines are formidable enough to protect her people from invading tribes, thus making her a legend far beyond her kingdom's borders. She senses correctly that the most dangerous invaders of all are coming: the French, who, along with the rest of Europe, have decided at the 19th Century's nadir to carve up the African continent as if it were a holiday turkey. She doesn't know the half of it. The battalion that's headed in her direction, led by a preening, bespectacled sociopath captain named Voulet (Jean-Roger Milo), is an especially brutal bunch of oafish Caucasian officers and mercenary African infantrymen, raping, burning and killing everything in their path.

As Sarraounia prepares her tribe for war, Voulet and his motley officers become more addled and crazed by their confusion over the culture they're trying to dominate. They can't understand why their African charges, though easily manipulated by the spoils of conquest (and the ever-present possibility of execution), are so intimidated by the prospect of doing battle with the "witch queen."

Rich, dense layers of character development and sweeping visual passages help give "Sarraounia" a legitimate claim to join the ranks of great historical epics. If anything hobbles this claim, it's that Sarraounia, after a while, seems more like a mere concept of great heroine while those around her, even her craven rivals, acquire relatively greater definition. But her purely iconic trappings may have been exactly what Hondo was after in fashioning what amounts to a sustained praise song in tribute to an ideal of justice and freedom.

Also reviewed in:
VARIETY, 9/10/86, p. 19

SATIN SLIPPER, THE

An M-G-M release of a Films du Passage (Paris)/Metro E Tal (Lisbon) coproduction in association with I.N.A. (Paris), WDR (Cologne), SSR (Geneva), with the participation of the French and Portuguese Ministries of Culture and the Portugese Film Institute. *Producer:* Paolo Branco and Arthur Castro Neves. *Director:* Manoel de Oliveira. *Screenplay (French and Portugese with English subtitles):* Manoel de Oliveira. *From the play by:* Paul Claudel. *Director of Photography:* Elso Roque. *Music:* João Paes. *Set Designer:* Antonio Casimiro. *Costumes:* Jasmine. *Make-up:* Dominique De Vorges. *Running time:* 428 minutes. *MPAA Rating:* Not Rated.

CAST: Luis Miguel Cintra (Don Rodigue); Anne Consigny (Dona Prouhèze); Patricia Barzyk (Dona Sept-Epées); Jean-Yves Bertheloot (The King); Takashi Kawahara (Daibutsu); Catherine Jarret (Actress 1); Anny Romand (Actress 2).

NEW YORK POST, 9/15/94, p. 36, Larry Worth

The costumes are lovely, the sets are arresting and the performers are stunning. But those exiting "The Satin Slipper" will be more aware of its drawback: a seven-hour running time.

That's like sitting through a double feature of "Gone With the Wind" and "War and Peace." Granted Paul Claudel's 16th-century tale of star-crossed romance between a Spanish knight and his lady fair is intriguing. But the principals are a far cry from Scarlett and Rhett, and the author is certainly no Tolstoy.

As with many crucial scenes, the lovers' meeting takes place off-camera So, viewers are told that the dashing Don Rodrigue was washed ashore from an African shipwreck and saved by the gorgeous—and married—Dona Prouheze. They fell instantly in lust, and were quickly separated.

Despite Rodrigue's orders from the King of Spain and Prouheze's from her husband, the two then try their darnedest to reunite—as continents, decades and the very forces of heaven and earth prove their enemies.

So far, so good. But Claudel's epic play suffers under director Manoel de Oliveira's treatment. Clearly, any work of such daunting duration needs severe editing. But de Oliveira was less than discriminating.

Endless speeches on the art, politics and philosophies of the day sometimes take 30 minutes before the central story reclaims the limelight. In addition the script has so many subplots that it's hard to keep track of the peripherals, and how their histories interrelate.

But all is hardly lost, as de Oliveira cleverly lenses the production like a play within a play, using stage artifices and one-dimensional scrims to accompany the action. His long, lingering camerawork and penchant for painting-like tableaus are consistently alluring.

Ditto for the performers. In particular, the beautiful Patricia Barzyk is quietly moving as the strong, desperately unhappy heroine. Luis Miguel Cintra is a perfect match as her would-be paramour, a brave soldier who weathers more tragedies than Job.

But while "The Satin Slipper" often shines, it still asks a great deal from viewers. And for some, the payoffs might not justify the seven-hour sacrifice.

VILLAGE VOICE, 9/20/94, p. 53, J. Hoberman

A more epic "new age" opens this week when the full seven-hour version of Portuguese director Manoel de Oliveira's *The Satin Slipper* has its local premiere at the Public Theater. [The reference is to *The New Age*.] De Oliveira has argued that cinema is a technology for preserving theater; with *The Satin Slipper*, he's used cinema to midwife as well as embalm, filming Catholic symbolist Paul Claudel's vast, enigmatic, all but unstageable drama of imperial ambition and impossible love.

The Satin Slipper begins with the suitably grandiose declaration that "the scene of this play is the world" and then sets about making it literal. Set in the 16th century and concerning, usually tangentially, the multidecade affair between conquistador Don Rodrigue and the aristocratic Doña Prouheze, the action hops from Spain to North Africa to Japan to Sicily to the Rousseau-like American jungle (as well as all seas in between), events spiraling out from the tale of unconsummated—ultimately religious—passion like the stars of a distant galaxy.

Highly stylized, populated by an assortment of celestial creatures as well as swashbuckling Spaniards, *The Satin Slipper* was written between 1919 and 1924, overlapping the period during which Claudel served as French ambassador to Japan (and studied Noh drama). De Oliveira effectively puts this theatricality in italics. A series of stagy two-shots or posed tableaux, with actors typically declaiming toward the camera, his version of *The Satin Slipper* never pretends to be anything other than a filmed play. The effect not so much theater canned as theater twice removed. De Oliveira documents stage artifice as though it were nature. (One crucial scene is dominated by the motorized blades of a painted windmill on the flat set.) The deadpan performances, long takes, and absence of cross-cutting accentuate the atmosphere of frozen pomp.

An initially light and fanciful medieval flavor gives way to a baroque, self-conscious narrativity. Crucial events are represented only through language. The presence of invisible forces and the sense of an implacable destiny are embodied by both the Catholic dream "to unite all humanity" and the letter from Prouheze to Rodrigue that travels, unopened, around the world. De Oliveira's images grow increasingly beautiful and the narrative more compelling as *The Satin Slipper* spins into its final movement (shown as an autonomous film during the 1985 New York Film Festival), which is played out entirely at sea. Free-floating theatricality is raised to the level of mass delusion: As the Spanish armada sails toward England, its success a given, the king of Spain commissions an actress to play Mary Stuart and tempt the arrogant Rodrigue with the promise of the English throne.

De Oliveira remains astonishingly active at age 86, but *The Satin Slipper* represents the summit of his art, ranking with such earlier, hyperliterary evocations of frustrated passion as *Doomed Love* (1978) and *Francisca* (1981). It seems perverse for the Public to have scheduled this presentation at the hectic start of the fall season, but the movie, like the play is intended to upstage your life—it's the aesthete's nightmare, an inconvenient masterpiece.

Also reviewed in:
NEW YORK TIMES, 9/14/94, p. C16, Stephen Holden
VARIETY, 5/15/85, p. 22

SAVAGE NIGHTS

A Gramercy Pictures release of Banfilm Ter/La Sept Cinéma/Erre Produzioni/SNC with Sofinergie II, and CNC Procirep and Canal+. *Executive Producer:* Jean-Frédéric Samie. *Producer:* Nella Banfi. *Director:* Cyril Collard. *Screenplay (French with English subtitles):* Cyril Collard and Jacques Fieschi. *Based on the novel by:*: Cyril Collard. *Director of Photography:* Manuel Teran. *Editor:* Lise Beaulieu. *Sound:* Dominique Hennequin and Michel Brethez. *Sound Editor:* Patrice Grisolet and Frédéric Attal. *Art Director:* Jacky Macchi and Katja Kosenina. *Costumes:* Régine Arniaud. *Make-up:* Hertz Nativ. *Running time:* 126 minutes. *MPAA Rating:* Not Rated.

CAST: Cyril Collard (Jean); Romane Bohringer (Laura); Carlos Lopez (Samy); Corine Blue (Laura's Mother); René-Marc Bini (Marc); Maria Schneider (Noria); Clméntine Célarié (Marianne); Laura Favali (Karine); Denis D'Archangelo (Singer); Jean-Jacques Jauffret (Pierre Ollivier); Aissa Jabri (Kader); Francisco Gimenez (Paco); Marine Delterme (Sylvie); Yannick Tolila (Nurse); Olivier Pajot (Lempereur); Diego Porres (Jaime); Stephan Lakatos (Jipe); Christophe Chantre (Martial); Michel Voletti (Mr. André); Régine Arniaud (Véro); Anna Lopez Villanua (Samy's Mother); Olivier Chavarot (Olivier); Samir Guesmi (Jamel); Claudio Zaccai (Doctor); Dominique Figaro (Camillle); Rosa Castro (Housekeeper); Nella Banfi (Manager); Olivia Reynaud (Laura's Friend); Claude Winter (Jean's Mother).

CINEASTE, Vol. XX, no. 4, 1994, p. 50, Howard Feinstein

Director Roger Spottiswoode's much-maligned HBO film version of Randy Shilts's *And the Band Played On* points out that public and private institutions in France and the U. S. were equally lax in recognizing the severity of the AIDS epidemic in its early stages. Powerful medical administrators and researchers in both countries placed professional recognition over social obligation. Our own Dr. Robert Gallo of the National Cancer Institute is alleged to have stolen a sample of the HIV virus and the credit for discovering it from his colleagues at Paris's Pasteur Institute, and a threatened French lawsuit over his fraudulent patent nearly delayed the development of a reliable AIDS test for years.

The cult of personality in the Age of AIDS once again rears its ugly head in the French film *Savage Nights*, written and directed by Cyril Collard, who also stars. The picture—a slick if incoherent assortment of tracking shots, jump cuts, oblique angles, and other self-conscious formal footwork—charts the romantic and carnal escapades of the bisexual, HIV-positive Jean, a director of TV commercials in Paris in 1986. Already seriopositive himself when he wrote an autobiographical novel, then adapted it to film, the bisexual Collard, like Gallo, ultimately lifts his personal concerns above responsible representation, ethical issues, and political ramifications.

Compare a couple of graphically-similar scenes from the self-effacing Spottiswoode's *And the Band Played On* and *Savage Nights*. In the first sequence of *And the Band Played On*, Dr. Don Francis (Matthew Modine), of the Central Africa-based National Health Organization, stumbles upon an outbreak of Ebola Fever, something of a precursor to AIDS, back in 1976. With her last breath, a weak woman clenches his hand and screams something in a language we and he don't understand. After she expires, the horrified Francis stares phobically at his blood-drenched hand.

Toward the end of the film, after he has worked tirelessly to probe the mystery of AIDS and to educate an ignorant public about its prevention, Francis visits dying AIDS activist Bill Kraus (Ian McKellen). Racked with dementia and speaking gibberish, Kraus grasps Francis's hand, an act that triggers flashbacks of the African woman. Francis reciprocates, grabbing Kraus's hand with his free one. These scenes from *And the Band Played On* are as life-affirming as they are appropriate to the narrative. Francis's loving gesture reinforces the rage that has been his modus operandi throughout the film, while suggesting that he will continue to funnel his anger into constructive action.

In *Savage Nights* Jean stops a group of skinheads from attacking a young Arab by slicing his own fist, then threatening their National Front leader—a fat pimp—with his infected blood. Scared shitless by the tainted bodily fluid, the trembling fascist orders the youths to disperse. The scene is not the expression of an AIDS sufferer's passivity transformed into active anger, even if Collard tries to justify the act by a quote from Genet earlier in the film ("Only violence can put an end to man's evil ways"). It is, rather, a cheap dramatic device, irresponsible and unimaginative. The choice is particularly noxious, given public hysteria about potential contamination by AIDS patients. It perpetuates the fear that *And the Band Played On*'s Francis had shown in the face of an unknown disease in the mid-Seventies. This and other scenes make *Savage Nights* the first AIDS vanity production, a self-serving testament that, like the camera itself, focuses almost entirely on Collard.

Savage Nights is especially reckless in a French context. With one of the highest AIDS rates in the world, France has been notoriously slow in raising public consciousness of the epidemic (PSAs for safe sex began only last year). Defenders of the film claim that just by putting AIDS on the screen, it succeeds in provoking debate on a repressed issue. (The guilt-ridden French awarded *Savage Nights* the César for Best Film of 1992. Collard had died only three days before the ceremony.) But at what cost! And a host of additional stereotypes and irresponsible choices adds to its shame.

Dr. Gallo's Achilles heel was that his taste for personal glory far outweighed his unquestionable scientific expertise. Collard also celebrates himself to excess—often a weakness in filmmakers who direct themselves (he just can't resist close-ups of his character). At the same time, he manages to put down his homosexual side. Sure, Jean is amused by a couple of cute little gay eccentrics—a pearl-laden, Piaf-belting transvestite, for example—but he seems to despise his sexual gay self. Judging by the evidence on the screen, he resents the indiscriminate homosexual activity that drove him and gave him AIDS.

All of Jean's male sexual activity—save his bizarre affair with Samy, a street-tough hustler who becomes a neofascist—is impersonal, performed in dark, secluded places. This happens. What is egregious is not just that Jean is almost always the pawed object of desire—virtually a nonparticipant—but that he formally and thematically contrasts these unfulfilling (and deadly) encounters with one of his rare heterosexual relationships.

Almost always shown in bright light, cameras sometimes circling vertiginously around them, Jean and the seventeen-year-old Laura (Romane Bohringer) forge a bond. He calls her his salvation. This Angel of Mercy is meant to save him from the Sodom and Gomorrah of queerdom. (Pat Robertson might approve.) It is unpardonable to dismiss same-sex desire, as Collard does, particularly now. Compounding Collard's insensitivity to gays is his classist decision to make Jean and Laura the children of the *haute bourgeoisie*, and Samy the mutant son of an idealized lumpenproletariat. (One gets the impression that Collard uses the lovely music and camaraderie in Samy's Spanish family to set the stage for his own Iberian catharsis at film's end.)

Even in a straight relationship, however, Collard's narcissism rules. He has unsafe sex with Laura without informing her of his condition. "Like I'd forgotten the virus was part of me," he confesses later (and only upon a friend's urging), and "that our love would save us." At first, she screams and yells, but later asks him to make love *again* without a condom—as will the macho Samy. (Collard's idea of a structuring device is the sudden, unmotivated cut from a loud argument to an affectionate rapprochement.)

In late April of this year, *The New York Times* reported that the French did not question Collard's choices for Jean's careless sexual behavior until earlier that month. Word leaked out that noted novelist Suzanne Prou's twenty-six-year-old granddaughter, Erica Prou, who had died last November of AIDS, had been Collard's lover in 1984 and was infected by him. In the ensuing backlash, writers and activists began rethinking the film and novel, and Collard's romantic linking of love and death.

Collard is contemptuous of women, whether he considers them his salvation or just plain in his way. Laura is a hysteric, as is Marianne, Samy's inconvenient live-in. Jean picks up a young woman for a *ménage-à-trois* with Samy, fully expecting to leave her out of the tryst. For good measure, Laura's mother is a meddlesome harpie. No late-in-life attraction to a young girl can mask Collard/Jean's misogyny. Jean asks a doctor to test Laura for AIDS without her knowledge. Didn't Collard know about the debates on the role of men in decisions concerning a woman's right to her own body?

Self-indulgence is often the handmaiden of art, but in the time of a devastating plague, it becomes insidious. Collard's hubris is boundless—"I want your cock inside me," Laura tells Jean in front of her mother, "nobody's made me come like that before"—and he insufferably struts around shirtless or in tanktops, ogling the camera from below like a lost puppy. (Collard told an interviewer that he had not planned to be in the film, but actors either were afraid to take the role of an HIV-positive man or interpreted the part too earnestly.)

The zoned-out New Age ending—prefigured by *Last Tango*'s Maria Schneider as a Moroccan seer who urges him to "learn from your disease"—is not as far removed from the overall plotline as some reviewers have remarked. The whole Parisian dynamic has been out of touch with the facts of the Eighties—and with the realities of Collard's own life. When the film opened in France, he insisted that he had not made an AIDS film. ("Jean doesn't let himself get locked into the status of being HIV-positive, like some people for whom the illness becomes a sort of identity card.") What he did make was a hurtful treatise on self-love and social irresponsibility—an anti-AIDS film.

FILMS IN REVIEW, 5-6/94, p. 55, Eva H. Kissin

Savage Nights is a kind of brilliant nightmare, a desperate tale of a young bisexual with AIDS living out his final months in profound personal agony. Caught between his male lover and a young woman's overly possessive feelings—and his disease—Jean, played by writer-director, Cyril Collard, acts out his desperation in wild sexual forays and frantic accidents. A good deal of the action takes place at night under dark concrete pillars on the Left Bank suggesting the urban landscape of a Zola novel.

A particularly poignant scene occurs during a visit to his bourgeois parents when Jean suggests he will probably die before his father. After a miserable family dinner, he drives off wildly, using his red sports car as an unconscious and unsuccessful suicide weapon.

The images in the film are as disconnected as any nightmare, but the protagonist's personality and his doomed situation hold it all together. Nevertheless, it is far too long and could stand some disciplined pruning.

Romane Bohring (*The Accompanist*) is especially ardent as the eighteen-year-old lover, and Collard himself can be both charming and selfish as he desperately searches for the strength to face his approaching death.

The terrible irony of the film is that the material is truly autobiographical—written, directed and acted by Collard who died four days before it was released, slated to win four Cesars.

LOS ANGELES TIMES, 3/4/94, Calendar/p. 18, Kenneth Turan

"Savage Nights," the born-to-be-controversial French film, teaches several lessons, most of them unintentional.

It shows how a sensation in one culture can turn wearing in another, that a story nominally about AIDS may be about something else entirely and, contrary to what so many movies have indicated, that having a fatal illness does not necessarily ennoble the person involved.

Written, directed by and starring Cyril Collard, "Savage Nights" was, if press reports are to be believed, the biggest phenomenon in France since EuroDisney. Collard, at the time an AIDS patient, based the film on his autobiographical novel, which follows the life of a bisexual Parisian filmmaker after he's been diagnosed as HIV positive.

"Savage Nights" was a major *succes d'estime* in France, where public discussion of AIDS was previously limited. It was nominated for numerous Cesars, the French Oscars, and won four, including best picture and best new actress for co-star Romane Bohringer. Bohringer's tearful, nationally televised acceptance speech, dedicating her award to Collard, who had died just 72 hours before, was an electric moment for French cinema.

Perhaps no film could stand up to such an advance billing, but "Savage Nights" seems particularly disappointing. Though he clearly touched the nerve of a nation, Collard was not a particularly adept filmmaker. "Savage Nights" is more irritating than insightful and more interesting as a study of what the French go wild about than for anything it has to say about AIDS or the people who have it.

A free spirit introduced shooting film in Morocco in 1986, Jean (Collard) is no sooner back in Paris than he notices a spot on his arm. He is tested for AIDS by a nurse who says, "Nobody lives forever," and when the results come back positive, he has a dream in which a mysterious Arab woman advises him to "let go of your illusion. Learn from your disease."

One of the points of "Savage Nights" seems to be that past this juncture disease is mentioned almost not at all. Rarely does Jean seem to focus on what is happening to him, and though near the finale he has a fit and screams, "I want to live," by that late date the audience is ready to do some screaming of its own.

The adulation of the French nation notwithstanding, Jean is not a very likable human being. A handsome hothead who drives a red Fiat sports car way too fast, Jean is one of those romanticized "live fast, die young, I don't give a damn" kinds of guys rarely glimpsed outside of commercials for up-market cars and fancy perfume.

More than that, Jean is selfish, self-absorbed and self-indulgent, not always in that order, and leads a frantic sex life. "Sometimes I'll do anything just to keep from thinking I'm wasting away," he says in a rare reference to illness, and anything comes to include an affair with the surly Samy (Carlos Lopez), evenings of anonymous group passion under bridges by the Seine, and a heated liaison with Laura (Bohringer).

All of 17 years old though hardly inexperienced, Laura falls in love with Jean with the intensity of a youthful dreamer. In the film's most controversial scene, he agrees to have unprotected sex with her because they both somehow believe that the intensity of their love will ward off the disease.

But as much as Jean cares about Laura, he cares about himself more, and it isn't in him to offer anything resembling commitment. This drives Laura more than a little crazy, and the increasing volatility of their relationship is one of "Savage Night's" more tedious elements.

In theory, it could be argued that Jean's refusal to compromise his hedonistic lifestyle in the face of AIDS is a courageous decision and a welcome relief from the usual portrayals of the helpless victims of disease. But to believe that is to ignore the thrust of Jean's behavior. If he was callously self-involved before he was infected, just being able to maintain that same high level of boorish behavior despite being ill hardly seems worth standing up and applauding.

In fact, more than a study of illness "Savage Nights" feels like a loving portrait of a narcissist by a narcissist, focusing on the way everyone within sight struggles for Jean's favors. Women fight with women, men fight with men, and both sexes fight with each other, all for the dubious joy of possession. Finally, even the dour Samy has had enough. "You're a bunch of masochists. I'm going to bed," he grumbles at one point, which might be the most sensible thing anyone says all night.

All its difficulties aside, "Savage Nights" does feature the vital and accomplished debut performance of Romane Bohringer, who went on to emphasize her startling versatility with the quite different title role in "The Accompanist." And the picture does teach one final lesson: the French idea of what constitutes an enviable romantic relationship has undergone quite a change. If you're expecting Renoir, Cocteau, Truffaut or even Godard or Bertrand Blier, you're going to be in for something of a surprise.

NEW STATESMAN & SOCIETY, 6/25/93, p. 35, Jonathan Romney

The English print of *Les Nuits Fauves (Savage Nights)* is prefaced with a sombre announcement that makes you sit up and pay serious attention. It tells you that the director and star, Cyril Collard, died of Aids-related illness this year, aged 35 just three days before the film was awarded four of France's prestigious Cesar awards.

Collard was quickly canonised as "France's own James Dean", becoming not only a tragic hero but an icon of "revolt": a word with peculiarly literary and philosophical overtones in French pop culture. It evokes Genet and Rimbaud, rather than Axl Rose. There can't be a French culture magazine that hasn't featured Collard on a cover this year. He's no longer just a film director and actor, but a pop star and a saint as well.

All of which makes *Les Nuits Fauves* remarkably difficult to read. It presents all the teasing paradoxes of a film that is quite clearly autobiographical but which, because it's a fiction, can't be read strictly as such. Based on Collard's autobiographical novel, it features the director himself as Jean. Having discovered he is HIV positive, Jean embarks on an unsafe-sex relationship with a young woman, Laura, while at the same time getting involved with a sexy, semi-Fascist boy, Samy.

Jean also indulges other appetites to the full: making films, taking crazed high-speed drives through Paris by night, nocturnal orgies with male lovers by the Seine. Jean lives life like there's no tomorrow, which indeed there isn't. He's immune even to car crashes—immune to everything except his physical lack of immunity. But it's as if his life force is all the greater because he has passed his mortality on to others—as he does in a symbolic, and possibly a literal way, to Laura.

The film is hard to watch now because all the time the protagonist is proclaiming his own unquenchable life-force, we know he's already doomed. Or at least we know Collard is. Can we say the same about Jean, and assume that Jean and Collard are one and the same? The film plays quite calculatedly on these paradoxes of identity and impending mortality—as if in the full knowledge that Jean's *cri de coeur* from *within* life (he declares "Je suis *dans* la vie") would soon be read as Collard's cry from *outside* it.

What has made Collard an icon is not simply the fact of his death, but the sheer appetite that he exudes. There's an immense energy in the acting, particularly in the febrile scenes between Jean and Laura—unbridled psycho-dramas in the style of Collard's one-time employer, director Maurice Pialat, with Romane Bohringer displaying a rare ferocity. There's a similar verve to the wheeling camera work, the nervy editing, the soundtrack (from flamenco to the Pogues to Collard's own rather ropey pop songs), and the very shape of the narrative, which skips drunkenly between scenes, sub-plots, sexual encounters.

Collard described both himself and his film as "bulimic", and it's this restless omnivorousness that makes the film so gripping throughout. The whole thing is in the image of Jean's own polysexuality.

This is not a film about Aids, but about Collard. He put's himself at the centre of the drama: not only the raging desire around which everything revolves, but also the object of desire that everyone tussles over. There's one scene in which Jean is racked by panic at the thought of dying. But otherwise he remains flirtatiously impassive throughout, wearing a smile of wolfish amusement.

And the film's not about sex, but about desire—specifically, about Collard's desire to be seen and desired. He is interested not in any specific sexuality, hetero-, homo-, or bi-, but in polysexuality in an almost abstract form, as pure hunger. Inevitable, then, that *Les Nuits Fauves* should have been accused of failing to project any sense of a gay identity. Most of its images of gay sex—the tusslings in the Seine catacombs, a bit of fascistic SM—are presented under the sign of darkness, clearly labelled "wild side". Gay sex is presented as a side order, a dangerous nocturnal flirtation—but not as dangerous as the transcendental peril of boy-girl love.

There's no doubt that the film privileges heterosexual love, even treating Aids as an outcrop of a straight tradition of discourse on *amour fou*. The film begins with Jean being told—apparently in a dream—that the virus can teach him how to love. The rest traces his sentimental education. But if he learns to love, it's at the expense of others, notably Laura. Once he's told her he's seropositive, she chooses to risk exposure to the virus, to seal their pact; but once he's gone off with Samy and she becomes jealous, it seems to be love itself, rather than the virus, that's destroying her. She goes literally mad with love.

Laura is victimised by the narrative in other ways. She's identified from the beginning as a child, rather than a woman. Jean gives her puppies and soft toys, she tells him about sex at 13 with an older man, and at 17 she still snuggles up in Mummy's bed in her pajamas. She represents the part of Jean that's all childlike appetite, but it's the part he rejects.

What she has picked up from him is not the virus itself, but love *as* a virus—a contagion that she, as a child, as a woman, can't quite handle. It's simply too strong for a little girl. This is French cinema's favourite story: a woman paying for her man's sentimental education.

The problem with *Les Nuits Fauves* is not so much that it's narcissistic but that it's narcissistic in this macho way. Of course Collard is expressly fashioning a shiny memorial to his self. It's no accident that Collard quotes Jean Genet early on. Genet's myth of self is one that depends on consuming others to live; a process that may not be cynical but is certainly merciless.

Part of the film's reception in France has been to do with sentimental reverence—as if Collard's death made his work beyond reproach. And the film goes out of its way to defuse accusations that it's glorifying such sentimental woolliness. The person who talks in grandiose terms about rebel destiny is an old hippie. You feel the film wants you to subscribe to the notion. Jean is quite clearly presented as irresponsible, yet what you take away from the film is the sense of the absolute imperative of *amour fou* over workaday contingencies such as safe sex.

The trouble is not that *Les Nuits Fauves* refuses to wave a sensibly admonishing finger. But its depoliticises Aids in a more insidious way. What the film is about, finally, is inverting the old metaphor that sees love as a malady. It takes a specific malady and presents it *as* love. That's nothing new: the inversion goes back at least as far as *La Dame aux Camélias*. But times are too tough to indulge in the old Romantic fantasies, and it seems trivial to use such a hugely charged issue as a vehicle for such banal mythifying. We're beyond love's sweet sickness now.

NEW YORK, 3/7/94, p. 64, John Powers

Messy and disturbing, *Savage Nights* comes to America wrapped in a golden shroud. Its writer, director, and star, Cyril Collard, died of AIDS at the age of 35, three days before the picture was named Best Film at the 1993 French academy awards. Although premature death is no proof of artistic merit, Collard deserved the prize, for his portrait of an HIV-positive man goes far beyond the soppy clichés that turn most AIDs movies into glorified civics lessons. *Savage Nights* is a picture about living, not dying. Its hero, Jean, is not a saintly victim, or even a nice guy. And the virus is not the prism through which we view his life: While Jean's disease gives each moment the sting of mortality, the movie isn't about AIDs. It's about modern "savages" who prowl the neon wilderness of Paris seeking incandescent intensities of experience.

Collard plays Jean, the reckless, bisexual filmmaker/musician who claims he never learned how to say no and spends most of the movie proving it. When not having it off with anonymous men on the banks of the Seine, he's busy wooing or battling his two lovers. Samy (Carlos Lopez) is a chiseled slab of riffraff who shares Jean's bottomless appetite for physical sensation—rugby, S&M, or neo-Fascist thuggery, it's all the same to him. In contrast, Jean "feels clean" when he's with Laura (Romane Bohringer), a 17-year-old middle-class girl whom he meets at an audition for a commercial. Not that their relationship is healthy: The more Jean runs away from her passion, the more self-destructively she worships him. Infatuation seizes Laura like a disease, and Collard admires the audacity of her lovestruck extravagance. Like Jean and Samy, she risks everything in the riptides of romanticism.

It's precisely this headlong passion that made *Savage Nights* a cult movie among young French viewers, who rightly perceived that it assailed conventional ideas of morality and liberal good sense. Nowhere is this assault more flagrant than in the shocking sequence during which Jean has unprotected sex with Laura without telling her he's HIV-positive. This is obviously a terrible thing to do, but Collard is no safe-sex moralist. He wants to make us see what's human in an act that at first looks monstrous: Jean isn't merely selfish and irresponsible; he's a shaken man who hasn't yet fully grasped what it means to have HIV. "It's as if it isn't part of me," he says of the virus, sounding eerily like Jeff Goldblum in *The Fly*.

Jean's disease becomes one measure of Laura's adoration—a wild, pure, adolescent yearning that leads her to remove his condom the next time they have sex. "Ever since you told me you're HIV-positive," she cries, "I no longer care about myself." She's convinced that her love's magic touch can save him or at least let them share in the same eternal doom. Such rabid ardor is not easy to put across, but as Laura, the young actress Romane Bohringer shows here (as she did in *The Accompanist*) a genius for portraying devotion. Shuttling between abject submission and obscenity-spewing hysteria, she burrows so far inside her role that we start reading Laura's character traits in Bohringer's physiognomy—the scarred chin, the womanly body still plump with baby fat, the dark, strangely intent eyes that are like tokens of addiction. Her dazzling performance is perfectly attuned to the movie's inner rhymes: Just as Laura's searing love finds a cruel riposte in Jean's cool narcissism, so does Bohringer's breathless immersion in her part make the perfect emotional counterpoint to Collard's cocksure detachment.

With his tank tops, jaunty earring, and complacent, slightly shopworn smile, Collard is no great actor, but he has the killer charisma of the born sexual fascist; his Jean is a Gallic cousin to the remote charmers that used to be played by Robert Redford and Warren Beatty. Jean 's whole existence is encapsulated in the recurring image of him hot-rodding through Paris in his snazzy red convertible, the symbol of both his pedal-to-the-metal quest for freedom and, paradoxically, the solipsism that imprisons him. Even when Jean is being a coldhearted jerk, we can't forget that he's staring into an abyss that haunts our entire culture. Jean never stops raging against the dying of the light, and we can sense a kind of heroism in his refusal to abandon his earlier way of living. "Once you stop searching," he says, "you die."

Jean's ferocious desire for life is mirrored in the film's torqued-up style, with its circling hand-held camera, its car-crash editing rhythms—scads of scenes piling up against one another—and its explosions of primary color, an homage to the Fauve artists alluded to in the film's French title, *Les Nuits Fauves*. Like the sixties New Wave directors, Collard has a tactile sense of the medium—you can almost feel the grain of the film.

Sometimes, though, all this relentless energy becomes overbearing. There are too many sequences, too many crescendos, and too many flattering shots of Jean, as if Collard were creating a mash note to himself.

Still, it's easy to forgive self-indulgence in a movie about emotional excess, especially when its best scenes have the tough-minded honesty you might expect from one who worked as an assistant to director Maurice Pialat. Some of these scenes are quietly devastating, as when Jean meets with Laura and her mother (the lovely Corine Blue) at a fast-food restaurant. Although the other is a likable woman who tries to be open-minded about her daughter's lover, Jean snickers in her face as if she belonged to an inferior species, and she walks out in a huff. Small but emotionally resonant, this is the kind of precisely observed moment that is one of the glories of French filmmaking. We're left marveling at the chasm between the characters and wondering where our own allegiances should lie.

Collard has said that *Savage Nights* is ultimately about Jean's escape from the prison house of self. Perhaps because this idea is so very conventional, the movie rushes through the personal-transformation stuff: Jean's making his peace with the shattered Laura, using his virus-infected blood to stop neo-Fascists from beating an Arab, jetting off to "authentic" locales like the desert and Rio de Janeiro. (There are shots of sand and clouds, boats chuffing away from port, blood-orange suns setting in fast motion over the sea.) Collard asks us to believe that these experiences induce a radiant epiphany. "The world isn't something that goes on around me," Jean announces. "I'm part of it." In the abstract, such words bespeak a spiritual breakthrough, but *Savage Nights* doesn't put his redemption across cinematically. I found myself wondering whether Collard was trying to give his film a life-affirming resolution that he couldn't achieve in his own life, or whether he really had reached inner peace but couldn't figure out how to put it up on the screen. For his sake, I hope it was the latter.

NEW YORK POST, 2/25/94, p. 42, Thelma Adams

Jean (Cyril Collard) swings both ways.

It is Paris, 1986, and Jean is HIV-positive. Days intensified by death's shadow flow into "Savage Nights," a risky French film about high-risk behavior.

"Savage Nights" marks the feature directorial debut of Cyril Collard, who wrote the script based on his autobiographical novel, "Les Nuits Fauves."

In contrast to Hollywood's first AIDS movie, "Philadelphia," Collard takes an unflinching look at homosexual lust. He documents the anonymous group gropes occurring nightly by the banks of the Seine, providing a gritty view of gay lives and double lives.

Jean is no saint. He's the opposite of Andrew Beckett (Tom Hanks) in "Philadelphia," a too-good-to-be-true gay character designed to charm American audiences all the way to Wichita .

Jean's a thirtysomething photographer prowling Paris for his pleasure. Blue-eyed and charming, he's sexy but callow and not particularly likable.

Romane Bohringer, who plays Laura, the 18-year-old Jean seduces and deserts, is the movie's greatest asset. Notable in "The Accompanist" for an intensely passive, tightly coiled role, here Bohringer gives a passionate, loose-limbed, explosive performance as a young woman whose body has ripened but who is emotionally ill-equipped to deal with adult responsibilities.

Jean and Laura make love without protection—both before and after Jean admits he is HIV-positive. Collard is playing with fire, controversially presenting unsafe sex as Laura's ultimate testament of love and her belief that as true lovers, she and Jean are invulnerable.

"Savage Nights" weakens considerably when it saddles its fresh, contradictory look at eros and AIDS with a shopworn love triangle. It's a hobby horse that is as typically French as "Philadelphia" (with Hanks wearing a gleaming halo) is American.

Jean falls for Samy (the non-actor Carlos Lopez), an athletic young stud. As a trio, Jean, Samy, and Laura are trite and uninteresting, "Jules and Jim" without mystery or chemistry.

The plot derails. Laura cracks up. Samy becomes a violent skinhead. Jean takes a good look in the mirror, but by that point he seems too shallow, too willing to put others at risk. Collard has done his job of humanizing Jean too well: he is so unsympathetic that the audience doesn't share in his catharsis.

Well-received in France, "Savage Nights: won four Cesar Awards (the French Oscars)—for picture, debut film, female newcomer, (Romane Bohringer) and editing. Cyril Collard died from AIDS in March 1993, just three days before the awards ceremony.

Collard's first feature film, passionate and flawed, was also his last.

NEWSDAY, 2/25/94, Part II/p. 67, Jack Mathews

Whatever people think of the content or quality of Cyril Collard's "Savage Nights," an "AIDS movie" that makes "Philadelphia seem about as provocative as "Guess Who's Coming to Dinner," it is an astonishing personal achievement, and the dramatic last act in Collard's own life.

The French musician and filmmaker, who adapted the script from his own novel, then directed and starred in the movie, died from complications of AIDS last March, three days before "Savage Nights" won the Cesar award as the best film of 1992. He was 35.

"Savage Nights" (in French, with English sub-titles) tells the loosely autobiographical story of Jean (Collard), a bisexual Paris film technician who, shortly after AIDS testing became widely available in 1986, learns he is HIV-positive and, like hundreds of others in the early days of AIDS awareness, does nothing about it. He begins exercising strenuously, as if to sweat the invaders out of his system, but otherwise goes recklessly about his life, driving too fast, drinking too much, spending too many nights groping with strangers under a bridge along the Seine.

Most particularly, he does nothing when his relationship with an 18-year-old model named Laura (Romane Bohringer) reaches the moment of truth in bed, and he doesn't face it. Doesn't tell her, doesn't wear a condom. Before his death, Collard said Jean's indiscretion with Laura would mark him a criminal in many people's minds today, and he doesn't come off much better even in the film's time frame, when the behavioral code for HIV bearers was still being written.

Jean means no harm. Earlier, while having his blood drawn for a test, he goes out of his way to warn the bare-handed nurse to be careful. But irresponsibility is a natural by-product of the sort of narcissistic pleasure-seeking that motivates Jean, his homosexual lover Samy (Carlos Lopez) and the hungry crowd cruising the banks of the Seine.

What makes Jean so interesting a fictional character is that he is as much bisocial as bisexual. He drifts with ease over the line separating traditional middle-class lifestyles from the dark, often dangerous sexual underworld where he apparently contracted the virus now eliminating his choices.

Collard wrote what in many ways is a conventional romantic melodrama, a love triangle with Jean in the middle of his two jealous lovers, the aggressively self-destructive Samy and the impressionable Laura. It's about a man with two lovers who don't want to be protected from him, and given the stakes, it is like no love story you've ever seen.

Laura's recklessness (after getting over her initial shock, she refuses to let him use a condom) is naively transcendant. She thinks their love will keep her and Jean safe. Samy, a hooligan who leaves his girlfriend to move in with Jean, is simply turned on by all things dangerous.

"Savage Nights" is a very uneven film. It is beautifully shot and edited, and Collard, who had directed several short films and many rock videos before, got a remarkable performance from Bohringer. Laura is the tragic figure of the story, a young woman driven to a nervous breakdown by her obsession with man who won't—can't—commit to her, and Bohringer plays her with a fragile innocence that is painful to see betrayed.

Collard, who decided to play Jean after being turned down by several image-conscious French stars, gives Jean an emotional honesty that wouldn't be there with anybody else. You cannot forget you're watching a dying man playing a dying man, and his gradual revelations about the true values of life, at least as he narrates them, don't have a whiff of fictional conceit.

But Jean is a very complex character, and Collard, though he may have lived the life, wasn't enough of an actor to delineate the dimensions of his own personality. Jean seems less reckless than merely passive, and the other actors, Bohringer in particular, are reacting to dynamics that aren't apparent to us.

The movie also gets bogged down in a murky sub-plot about skinheads, a gang of life-size viruses infesting the neighborhood where Samy does his most adventuresome cruising. It all seems devised for one overplayed scene where Jean comes to Samy's rescue by threatening to spill his infected blood on the thugs.

The episode lends an air of exploitation to an already difficult subject, and whatever its point, it is an unnecessary and awkward distraction.

SIGHT AND SOUND, 6/93, p. 62, Amanda Lipman

In 1986, Jean, a photographer, goes on a working trip to Morocco. Back in Paris, he discovers that he has contracted the HIV virus. While making a commercial, he meets Laura, an 18-year-old who has come to audition. They are attracted to each other, but Jean is also involved with a wild young man, Samy. Having seduced Samy, Jean finds himself torn between Laura, Samy and covert gay cruising episodes. After Jean and Laura have sex without using any protection, Jean is too ashamed to confess to her. When he finally admits his HIV status, she is angry that he did not tell her the truth. She is also jealous of his relationship with Samy. When Laura decides to go away for a while, Samy moves in with Jean. Although he comes from a Spanish immigrant family, he is increasingly drawn to a group of fascist thugs, as well as ritualised S/M.

Jean starts AZT treatment. When Laura returns, she is angry that Samy is living with Jean. Jean visits his parents and confides in his mother, who tells him that the virus may teach him how to love. On his way home, speeding in his car, he is involved in a crash but is unhurt. He decides to stop seeing Laura but she telephones him constantly, hurling abuse at him. When she claims that she has caught the HIV virus, he goes to see her. After a struggle, she is taken to a residential clinic, where a test reveals that she does not have the virus. When Jean next sees her, she has a new boyfriend and does not wish to go back to him. Jean discovers that Samy has become involved with a fascist gang and one night finds him beating up an Arab. Jean holds the gang to ransom by threatening them with his infected blood. He writes to Laura, saying that he is not ready to settle down, then journeys to the desert where he seems to find peace.

There was a personal project for Cyril Collard, who not only directed and starred in the film but also wrote the original novel. And although neither are autobiographical, they are based in certain realities, not least Collard's seropositivity—he was apparently one of the first well-known people in France to talk openly about his HIV status. Collard did his film apprenticeship with director Maurice Pialat, and it shows in his loud, jagged, often quasi-documentary style. In keeping with the speedy frenzy that guides Jean, *Les Nuits Fauves* appears to be shot largely with hand-held cameras that fuzz and blur urgently between images and jerkily rhythmic cuts. Jean's world is defined either by the deep, bright colours of his apartment, which overlooks a glowing Paris, or by the dark cruising alleys by the Seine, where only his face is visible as he enfolds himself in masculine bodies.

Much of the dialogue has an emotional, improvised feel, which works brilliantly in scenes such as Jean's hesitating confession to Laura that he is HIV positive, or the couple's first kiss. The *vérité* effect is alternated with high drama—Laura's descent into hysteria; Samy's grimacing preoccupations with self-mutilation; the attack on the Arab boy. And the whole is polished off with tangential, semi-documentary forays: a drunken, singing drag queen in a bar, who takes on the role of Greek chorus; or the touchingly innocent Spanish song and dance evenings with Samy's family.

The clashing styles fit together with extraordinary ease, only adding to the sense of frenzy that drives the three mixed-up characters. Of these, Laura is probably the least prepossessing because she falls so squarely into the cliché of the coltish, spoiled and sadly mad French heroine. As soon as she starts shrieking, irritating echoes of Betty Blue or Nikita sound. But at least this gamine manages to redeem herself; and at least her anger in her *amour fou* is seen as in some way justified. Samy, too, is drawn in broad strokes as the naive, but crudely ambitious boy toy. But if the film draws a curious blank over his response to the homosexual implications of his relationship with Jean, he is given moments of emotion and bewilderment that make him painfully real.

What is remarkable about Collard's performance is the way he transforms a number of male clichés into a credible, even sympathetic character. Jean's penchant for speeding cars, his fast and loose life, professional success, constant hunger for new sensations, sexiness and huge charm are all treated with a hint of irony. When Jean leaps into his car, the deftly edited driving scenes have a studio-bound hyper-reality that seems to mock a little. The differences between his two relationships also serve to put him into context: if Laura adores him, Samy is using him. And his own relationship with his changing body makes him increasingly complex. His final discovery that he is 'in life' may seem twee but it is, in its way, surprisingly potent. What makes it so is the element that changes the nature of the changes Jean desires—the HIV virus.

Although it is hard to write about the film without emphasising the importance of the virus to it, *Savage Nights* does just that, without diminishing its importance—and certainly without the usual heavy-handed symbolism. Instead of trying to make meaning of the virus, the film looks sideways at its connection with Jean's own sense of denial and acceptance; the move from his initial impulse, even once he has the virus, that nothing will happen to him. What is important about the final scene is that it links HIV with life rather than death. Unlike Laura's tantrums or Samy's grim self-destruction, it touches on how something positive can come from suffering, while refraining from the idea that sick people have recourse only to spiritualism.

The intentional rough edges, speedy camera and quick-fire editing give *Les Nuits Fauves* a lightness of touch that allows it to slip deftly over its 'big' themes, and even to push through heavy-handed moments like Jean's infected-blood ransom. The film's style also gives the impression that it's catching the characters off-guard, fleshing them out to hint at the gap between how the threesome see themselves and how others see them. If it opts for a moral mode, making them all learn something, it does so with stunning visual flair that translates itself easily into emotional sympathy.

TIME, 3/14/94, p. 105, Richard Corliss

Paris and Philadelphia were never exactly sister cities, except maybe to Benjamin Franklin. In current movie terms, and when the incendiary issue of AIDS is raised, the towns couldn't be further apart. The hit film *Philadelphia* treats its subject gingerly, making its hero a saint and a near monogamist. Cyril Collard's French film *Savage Nights* is defiantly incorrect, even reckless, in its political agenda. Its hero is a fellow who is HIV positive but continues to have unprotected sex. *C'est la vie. C'est la mort.* No big difference.

Writer-director Collard plays Jean, a bisexual filmmaker determined to keep searching for truth—and partying hard—in the face of death. He vacillates between Samy (Carlos Lopez), a rough-trade Spaniard, and Laura (Romane Bohringer, recently seen illuminating *The Accompanist*), a would-be actress. Jean wants to have safe sex with Laura, but she will let no condom come between them. Ever the gent, Jean obliges.

One would like to embrace *Savage Nights*. Its dour attitude and grungy visual style are an antidote to Hollywood's reductive take on AIDS stories. Collard, who died of AIDs last year, a few days before his film was awarded a César (France's Oscar) for Best Picture, comes across as a director showing real skill with his young cast, and as a skulkily seductive actor.

But the movie finally confounds everyone's best intentions, including the audience's. It is both sensational and sentimentalized. It ricochets from one lurid fresco to another. O.K., these days narrative coherence is for wimps. But since *Savage Nights* staggers along at two hours plus, it is less an inside tour of the lower depths than a life sentence down there. Even art-house moviegoers sympathetic to Collard's aims may decide they'd rather be in Philadelphia.

VILLAGE VOICE, 3/1/94, p. 45, J. Hoberman

What can you say about a 33-year-old neophyte filmmaker who died—of AIDS—after completing and starring in a quasi-autobiographical movie about a filmmaker who is dying of AIDS? "If the plastic arts were put under psychoanalysis, the practice of embalming the dead might turn out to be a fundamental factor in their creation," is how André Bazin began his 1945 essay "The Ontology of the Photographic Image."

Cyril Collard's *Savage Nights*, included in last year's "New Directors" series, begins with the director/star piloting his red convertible straight at the camera and ends with his character Jean hanging out in a harbor at "the edge of Europe." In the frantic interim, the hero pursues—and is pursued by—the Spanish immigrant Samy (Carlos Lopez) and the 18-year-old would-be actress Laura (this year's gamine, Romane Bohringer). In between, he cruises the sleaze zone and dreams of Morocco, where a wan-looking Maria Schneider (1973's gamine in *Last Tango in Paris*) materializes like the patron saint of Mad Love.

Considering that *Savage Nights* is his psychodrama, Collard is content to underplay amid the hysteria he churns up. With his puppy-dog good looks and wistful *Mona Lisa* smile, his Jean is the film's universal object of desire, complete with apartment perfectly positioned to catch the last rays of spectacular Parisian sunsets. Jean has been largely making it with boys, but he embraces Laura as his lost innocence.

It's at this point that the movie becomes provocatively skittish. Jean is ashamed to inform Laura about his past or his HIV status; they have sex sans condom and he gives her the best orgasm she's ever had. Later, when Jean finally tells her that he has the virus, he won't apologize for having put her at risk. It's a bravura scene, one long take with both of them in the frame. Although Bohringer has a peasant stolidness, she's nothing if not a physical actress—after a suitable double take, her Laura ricochets off the ceiling. Still, when they fuck again, she won't let him use a condom—that's how strong her love is.

As should be clear, *Savage Nights* is not exactly *La Decisión*, the comic-strip AIDS melodrama that's been running in the subway. The beauty of self-destruction is projected onto the teenage bad girl. Breaking with her overprotective mother, spitting in her employer's face, Laura simulates her own trip to the edge. Her first meeting with rival Samy is a suitably extravagant psychic fender bender, filled with wanton smashing and fighting in the street, but you know she's really spinning out of control when she tells Jean that she thinks she'll go to film school.

Like the novel that preceded it, *Savage Nights* is an assemblage of jagged vignettes—some quasi-documentary in the manner of Maurice Pialat, for whom Collard worked as an assistant director. Sexual politics aside, the movie displays a panoply of Gallic tics, including a song about Gaulois and a derelict gay bar where a bucktoothed transvestite with a modified crew cut sings "Mon Homme." Rarely less than overwrought—a movie of sun-dappled, tousled glamour with many potential video interludes of fast driving, lovemaking, and trips to the mall—*Savage Nights* suffers for being both Collard's first and last feature. (Much of the time he seems to be directing the action even as it happens.)

Although Collard flirts with a Genet-like descent into criminality and degradation, his movie's true desire is to maintain forward momentum. Once Jean cracks up his Fiat, Laura begins leaving messages on his answering machine, and Samy starts hanging with the neighborhood skinheads, *Savage Nights* lurches into its downward spiral. But the frenzy is largely spent and, at 126 minutes, the movie meanders on too long. Given the circumstances of its making, however, why should it ever wish to end?

Collard's tract has none of the careful modulation of *Philadelphia*. It's a balancing act without a net—a work of raging narcissism and manic despair, a melodramatic star vehicle that dares the viewer to find it self-indulgent, crying, like the image of Susan Hayward in the old movie poster, "I Want To Live!"

Also reviewed in:
NATION, 3/21/94, p. 390, Stuart Klawans
NEW YORK TIMES, 2/25/94, p. C16, Janet Maslin
VARIETY, 12/7/92, p. 73, David Rooney
WASHINGTON POST, 3/11/94, p. G6, Richard Harrington

SCENT OF GREEN PAPAYA, THE

A First Look Pictures release of Les Productions Lazennec in co-production with LA SFP Cinéma with the participation of Canal Plus/the Centre National de la Cinématographie with financial support from the Fondation Gan pour le Cinéma and assistance from Procirep. *Executive Producer:* Christophe Rossignon. *Director:* Tran Anh Hung. *Screenplay (Vietnamese with English subtitles):* Tran Anh Hung. *Director of Photography:* Benoît Delhomme. *Editor:* Nicole Dedieu and Jean-Pierre Roques. *Music:* Tiêt Ton-That. *Sound:* Michael Guiffan. *Casting:* Nicolas Cambois. *Set Designer:* Alain Nègre. *Costumes:* Jean-Phillippe Abril. *Make-up:* Amélie Rouffio. *Running time:* 100 minutes. *MPAA Rating:* Not Rated.

CAST: Tran Nu Yên-Khê (Mùi, age 20); Lu Man San (Mùi, age 10); Truong Thi Lôc (Mother); Nguyen Anh Hoa (Old Thi); Vuong Hoa Hôi (Khuyen); Trung Tran Ngoc (Father); Talisman Vantha (Thu); Souvannavong Kéo (Trung); Nguyen Van Oanh (Mr. Thuan); Neth Gérard (Tin); Do Nhat (Lam); Vo Thi Hai (Grandmother); Nguyen Thi Thanh Tra (Maï); Bui Lam Huy (Doctor); Nguyen Xuan Thu (Antique Dealer).

CHRISTIAN SCIENCE MONITOR, 1/26/94, p. 10, David Sterritt

Vietnam has an unusually high profile on American movie screens just now.

Oliver Stone's third film on the Vietnam war, "Heaven and Earth," has garnered much attention and publicity despite its regrettably shallow approach to complex issues. A series of six films called "Love and War: Cinema of Vietnam," presented by Asian CineVision, is being theatrically released. And the Museum of Modern Art in New York is about to launch "Vietnamese Cinema," a series comprising seven films produced in Vietnam and selected in cooperation with a Vietnamese curator.

Rounding out this activity, a prize-winning film by a Vietnamese director is now having its American theatrical première. "The Scent of Green Papaya" is the first movie ever submitted by Vietnam for consideration as a possible Academy Award nominee for best foreign-language film, and it has already won the Camera d'Or for best film by a first-time director at the Cannes film festival.

The popularity of "The Scent of Green Papaya" within the film community may well be repeated among general audiences. It is a gorgeously filmed movie, with likable performances and long stretches of lucid visual storytelling.

Its effectiveness is hampered by its limited emotional range, though, and by its determination to remain entrancingly beautiful no matter what happens in the lives of its characters. It also raises important historical questions about the long history of French colonialism in Vietnam. But despite its status as a French-Vietnamese coproduction, the film fails to explore those questions.

The story centers on a character named Mui, first seen as a 10-year-old peasant girl in the early 1950s.

Engaged as a servant by a merchant-class family in Saigon, she learns the rituals of her new vocation—particularly those connected with preparing and serving food—from an old woman who works alongside her. She also learns important lessons about life by observing the household that surrounds her, including an abandoned wife and two children whose mischievous behavior may mask deeper disturbances.

The film's second part takes place in 1962, when Mui has been ousted from her longtime relationship with the merchant family and has gone to work for a successful musician. She has admired him since childhood, and falls goofily in love with him now that he's her boss—notwithstanding his elegant, French-style habits and his attachment to a girlfriend who's as Eurocentric as he is.

The film's most compelling scenes show Mui setting her hopes on romance with him, half yearning and half fearing that he might return her affection.

Tran Anh Hung, who directed "The Scent of Green Papaya," was born in Vietnam and moved to Paris with his family when he was about the age of Mui in the movie. In film school he studied cinematography rather than directing, and this has affected his work. Every composition, color, and camera movement in "The Scent of Green Papaya" is carefully and lovingly arranged—which makes for a great deal of visual beauty, but hampers the story's dramatic power with a sense of self-consciousness and artificiality. No event or feeling is strong enough to muss up the picture's impeccable good looks, or take on a life of its own beyond the gate of Tran's controlling camera.

Adding to this problem is the fact that Tran and his collaborators chose to film the movie in France, after deciding that Vietnam couldn't provide the settings and backgrounds necessary for a tale of the 1950s and '60s. Their studio sets are as painstakingly crafted as their cinematography, but seem less real and vital than the characters who inhabit them.

It's to the credit of the performers—especially Tran Nu Yen-Khe and Lu Man San, who play Mui at two different ages—that they remain engaging and alive under these circumstances. Too often, the movie that encloses them is more photographic than cinematic, and this condition can be a hindrance to emotionally vigorous acting.

The irony of "The Scent of Green Papaya" is that it looks and sounds more like a French art movie—reflecting the cautious "tradition of quality" in French filmmaking—than a product of Vietnam's own national cinema, which barely exists as an industry, but has produced a considerable body of work despite chronically low budgets and shortages of equipment and technicians.

Vietnam is free of French rule in political affairs, but French influence clearly lingers in the style and substance of some Vietnamese cultural products—including this movie, which depicts the strong French influence on Vietnam in aesthetic terms that seem equally French in their own right.

Tran's film would be stronger if it didn't just reproduce this influence, but examined it with a curious and critical eye. Perhaps this will happen in the next movie he has planned—the story of a contemporary bicycle-taxi driver, to be filmed on location in Ho Chi Minh City, with a technical crew trained in advance by Christophe Rossignon, the producer of Tran's movies.

If that film supplements the niceties of European art cinema with a sense of living Vietnamese authenticity, it could be a work of real importance.

CHRISTIAN SCIENCE MONITOR, 2/9/94, p. 17, Marilynne S. Mason

Vietnamese director Tran Anh hung's elegant *The Scent of Green Papaya*, winner of the Camera d'Or at Cannes, follows the live of a servant girl to young adulthood and a happy ending. The Cinderella fable moves slowly and gracefully, revealing layers of cultural detail in stately cinematic poetry—a tale so subtle , so quietly told, the viewer has to see the end before the whole meaning of the film breaks through.

FILMS IN REVIEW, 3-4/94, p. 57, Eva H. Kissin

This film is most striking for its time and place—Saigon in 1951—a Vietnamese experience, if you will. The plot is extremely simple; too simple, in fact. It follows the career of a ten-year-old country girl, Mui, who has walked all day from her village to arrive at her new job in a comfortable upper middle-class household in Saigon.

Extreme modesty characterizes Mui's behavior with her downcast eyes, humble posture and almost silent manner. She cooks and cleans endlessly in her new master's compound. Her amusements are limited to her acute observations of the growing things around her in the master's garden. When she is not constantly scrubbing the red tile floors or accepting the teasing of the master's small son, she studies the local beetles or appreciates the sweet smell of papaya and its perfect egg-like white seeds as she cuts it up for one of the elegant dishes she prepares for dinner.

Mui's progress in her work and her removal to another job 10 years later is the slender thread that holds the film together. The real emphasis is on mood. The photographer, Tran Anh Hung who won a Camera d'Or at Cannes, moves the camera actively around the compound concentrating on the hot, moist sleeping bodies, the slight lift of the gauze curtains by a passing breeze, and the rich black hair of the young girl. He doesn't neglect the elegantly prepared Vietnamese dishes that cause late afternoon moviegoers secret hunger pangs.

Sounds are also significant in this sensual film where the twang of oriental instruments or the romantic urgings of "Clair de Lune" accompany the camera on its journey. A small touch like Mui's slipping her bare feet into her master's shoes after she has cleaned them, provides a moment of reality that is generally missing.

While the aesthetic and sensual pleasures of this film are undeniable, it is notably lacking in substance. Lu Man San does fine as the little maiden, and Tran Nu Yen Khe as her mature version, but the viewer leaves the theatre essentially unfulfilled -searching for dinner in a local Asian restaurant.

LOS ANGELES TIMES, 2/2/94, Calendar/p. 1, Kenneth Turan

"The Scent of Green Papaya," a film as delicate and evocative as its name, recognizes that out of illusion can come reality.

Though its re-creation of the streets and houses of prewar Vietnam is ravishing, "Papaya" was shot exclusively on a sound stage outside of Paris. And though its actors are all Vietnamese, almost every one had been tainted by French culture and had to be freshly tutored in the graceful gestures and body language of their homeland.

Yet so well did all of this artifice succeed that "Papaya" managed a number of remarkable firsts. It won the prestigious Camera d'Or at Cannes as best first feature for its writer-director Tran Anh Hung, is Vietnam's first official submission for the best foreign language Oscar and is the first film to present a look from the inside at a culture and a sensibility we think we know but don't, that of the once-divided country that was simultaneously our enemy and our friend.

And though there is no lack of incident or emotion in "Papaya," it is primarily a fable—like memory film, an idealized tribute to the spirit of Vietnam's beautiful prewar days and the concern with textures, colors, tastes and smells that made the simple acts of everyday life into a complete aesthetic experience.

Symbolizing the tranquil, unhurried pace of Vietnam past is Mui, first glimpsed as a 10-year-old girl (Lu Man San) arriving in Saigon in 1951 to become a servant for a well-to-do family. Innocent but curious and hard-working, with a surprisingly broad and cheery smile, Mui stands for the grace and beauty invested in ordinary things by a culture where women did the meaningful work but were constrained to remain in the shadows.

Two kinds of knowledge come to Mui as she quietly works, and what turns out to have lasting value are not the behind-closed-doors secrets of her employers but an understanding of what it means to perform ordinary tasks (like the preparing of unripe papaya as a breakfast vegetable) with delicacy and grace.

Mui's mistress (Truong Thi Loc) not only runs the house but also the family cloth business, while her husband (Tran Ngoc Trung), distraught over the death of their daughter, rarely leaves the house and mostly ignores his two youngest sons. His own mother, a premature widow, rarely even leaves the second floor, much to the concern of Mr. Thuan (Nguyen Van Oanh), a discreet elderly admirer.

One of the points of Tran Anh Hung's film is to underline this discretion, the decorum and restraint that was the rule in most strata of Vietnamese society, qualities that have become natural to Mui by the time the film jumps forward 10 years and becomes something of a Cinderella story.

Now a beautiful young woman (played by Tran Nu Yên-Khê), Mui finds herself working for Khuyen (Vuong Hoa Hoi), a wealthy classical composer and friend of her original family, a young man she has felt an attraction toward from the beginning. Still, she goes on as before, smiling and preparing savory Vietnamese dishes that cinematographer Benoit Delhomme photographs as if they were clusters of diamonds.

It really can't be overemphasized how exquisite everything is in "The Scent of Green Papaya," not only the food, but also the vases and screens that decorate the houses, even a drop of sap dripping onto a thick green leaf. Just as the film's story is a series of small incidents that build almost imperceptibly to a dramatic climax, so it is visually, as all the careful, unhurried shots of domestic rituals and objects end up supplying an unexpected quiet sensuality to Mui's story.

Filmmaker Tran Anh Hung, who was 12 when his family moved to France in 1975, attempted to shoot in Saigon, but logistical difficulties made Paris inevitable. Even though Nguyen Anh Hoa, who plays the old servant woman, had to be brought over from Vietnam to tutor the mostly amateur cast in correct behavior, the director's sureness of vision and remarkable control of the medium ensured that his native country's singular way of seeing the world would be done justice.

Which makes it all the more unsettling, as the roar of a presumably military jet reminds us near the end, that the time was not far off when this most delicate civilization would be crushed to dust in a ruinous war. In addition to everything else it does, "The Scent of Green Papaya" is intended as a cultural memorial, and a fine and poignant one it turns out to be.

NEW STATESMAN & SOCIETY, 3/25/94, p. 41, Jonathan Romney

Given that *The Scent of Green Papaya* can't actually give you what its title announces, it still comes up remarkably close. This is a sensuous, evocative film on every level, plying you subtly with sounds, sights and textures, and the overall effect is something akin to an olfactory sense of place and things.

It's every bit as fragrant as *The Age of Innocence*, in which Scorsese conjectured a sort of *fin-de-siècle* Smell-O-Vision. But where that film got to the mind's nostril by bombarding you with the sight of fine lace and roses, Tran Anh Hung's film, it's truer to say, *suffuses* its impressions.

This Vietnamese director's remarkable debut feature appears to be simplicity itself, but in a very complex, artificial form. Told in a skeletal narrative, it's the story of a ten-year-old country girl, Mui, who comes to a quiet district of Saigon in the 1950s to live as a servant in a family house.

She gets to know the family, the courtyard and its cooking rituals; she develops a wonder-struck, almost microscopic view of its objects, flora and fauna—crickets, lizards, frogs, the papayas she peels and chops. And, except for the father's decamping and the family's descent on hard times, it seems a remarkably easy flow.

Events occur, but somehow their impact is never as cataclysmic as the hermetically sealed environment would lead you to expect. Time passes and, in a startling dissolve, we jump ten years into Mui's adulthood and her transfer to the house of a young musician—an effortless, absolutely satisfying change of key.

There's a conventional response, with firms that deal with sensuous minutiae, to assume that they're simple and have it at that—all the more so when dealing with third-world cinema. But the simplicity of Tran's film is the result of elaborate artifice. It was filmed not in Vietnam, but in a French studio set. All bar one of its amateur cast were recruited in France, which meant that even gestures had to be learned. The younger cast members had never known the traditional posture of crouching on their heels.

This unfamiliarity gives the film its peculiar alertness. Like Mui, we have to be inducted step by step into this world. The process begins with a long tracking shot that brings us and her down a street and into the courtyard where she's to spend the next ten years. The feeling of enclosure never lets up; we never see a sky. Effectively, the whole film dwells behind the fence and the outside world is excluded except for the sounds it transmits.

Set-bound films often have a mood of claustrophobia about them, but it's rarely used so artfully. The sets themselves, as cluttered and segmented with frames, foliage, gauzes and screens as in a Von Sternberg film, hem in our senses even further. They evoke a small world that's at once an airy oasis and a complex, involuted labyrinth. The labyrinthine feel comes to the fore in the second half, when Mui plays a tentative sexual game of tag around the house with her musician, the camera weaving sinuously in between the walls.

Rather than inducing claustrophobia, the set-bound direction allows the inner world to open up and reveal small, isolated marvels. Our gaze and Mui's become one: seeing the white bead-like papaya seeds for the first time, or the glistening skin of a frog in closeup, we feel we're being shown something new and miraculous. The sense of revelation extends even to what might otherwise be cliches of sensuality: Mui's delight in pouring water over herself might seem all too familiar, if not for the way that Tran jump-cuts, creating a completely novel, energised image.

Like Victor Erice's *The Quince Tree Sun*, Tran's film is a rare example of cinematic still life—a rebuttal of the assumption that cinema has to be about motion, when in fact it can be purely about time and its malleability. Allowing a space for stillness, these films restore cinema's contemplative possibilities. They give it something of the empty time we experience in life, and encourage us not to escape from the immediate confines of our senses but to burrow further into them.

But it would be wrong to suggest that the film is some wispy gossamer thing, a fragile vase (one of its few incidents, pointedly, involves a vase being *smashed*). It's also about shocks, small horrors, but they become strangely pleasurable marvels in Mui's eyes. The house's younger son wages war on her, farting defiantly, dangling a dead lizard in her face. But things we might conventionally expect to be horrific in this kind of domestic drama (imagine Mui's situation retold by a Dickens) are transmuted into little comic thrills. In this light, Mui's viewpoint seems not so much passive, more a wry mechanism for making the world more than bearable.

What is perplexing, though, is the way the film develops its apparent elegy to the virtues of female servitude. Mui's life may appear infinitely rich to us, but that's much to do with the way the film builds a mystique of everyday objects. We see the glistening papaya seeds only two or three times; Mui sees them every day. Tran impresses on us the ritualistic nature of her life, and the repetition of objects reinforces a sense of their unfamiliarity (to us) and familiarity (to her).

But is Mui's apparent passivity, as a receiver of impressions, presented as a privileged way of seeing the world or simply a survival tactic? Mui, by force of circumstance, rejects the external world, which after all seems to bring the family only grief. Or could we read the film as a sort of psychopathological case study, along the lines of *The Remains of the Day*? In James Ivory's film, though, the butler's taut English self-denial was seen as an unequivocal ill and the film's major flaw was the relentlessness with which it made its point. But Tran allows us no easy purchase on Mui, who as played first by Lu Man San, then Tran Nu Yen-Khe, seems reduced to a sensuous recording skin of pure consciousness.

Mui seems to be a consciousness entirely adequate to the world she inhabits, and she achieves a final, mysterious apotheosis under the eye of a benevolently looming Buddha. Tran provides the most traditional of happy endings for a female servant's story, so much so that it fairly defeats interpretation. Can Mui really be the beatific soul she appears, a distilled ideal of female consciousness, attaining nirvana through her finely tuned senses, immersing herself in seeing and serving, getting her reward in the end?

Possibly—but then again, Mui's final golden moment arrives just as her world is passing, its disappearance heralded by the soundtrack bursts of jets and distant gunfire, and the increasing presence of western culture. (Khuyen, the adored musician she goes to work for, is a thoroughgoing Francophile and Chopin obsessive). Her story ends just as she breaks her silence, when she first presents herself expressly as a woman by putting on lipstick in emulation of Khuyen's skittish westernised fiancee.

This myth of grace-in-servitude is so hard to take as such that the film finally seems to be deploying an irony so oblique as to be barely readable. What's most impressive about it is that it allows these meanings to float suspended, only partly perceived, in a liquid of pure *impression*. It ends with an accurate, if hubristic, touch of self-reference, with one of the passages Mui is practising to read: "If there's a verb meaning 'to move harmoniously', it must be used here." The face of the smiling Buddha that follows might be assent or irony or gnomic blankness. How we're to read this harmony, it doesn't let on.

NEW YORK POST, 1/28/94, p. 44, Michael Medved

"The Scent of Green Papaya" represents a worthy new addition to the ranks of memorable fruit-or-vegetable movies, joining such distinguished predecessors as "Attack of the Mushroom People," Woody Allen's "Bananas," and, of course, "Attack of the Killer Tomatoes."

As a matter of fact, "Papaya" may appeal to an even more specialized audience than these prior vegetarian titles, since a poetic little picture that devotes much of its attention to lyrical loving evocations of various household chores will hardly excite a mass audience accustomed to sweaty sex and car crashes.

Nevertheless, this fine film (which represents Vietnam's first-ever submission for Oscar consideration as best foreign language picture) is so original and so powerfully peculiar that it seems certain to attract a cult following.

The story begins in 1951 when a 10-year-old peasant girl, Mui, arrives from the provinces to work as a servant for a wealthy merchant family in Saigon. The shy and sweet-tempered child soon learns to stir-fry vegetables, arrange trays to bring to the dining room table, scrub tile floors, dust elegant vases and furniture, and prepare the papayas that grow on a tree outside her window.

Presented in painstaking detail, accompanied by exotic, evocative music by Ton-That Tiet these tasks take on qualities of cherished ritual following the example of "Like Water for Chocolate," "The Scent of Green Papayas" infuses traditional women's work with dignity, meaning and magic.

The 10-year-old Mui (played by a bewitchingly. beautiful young actress named Lu Man San) also finds time to watch the sad collapse of the proud family she serves, with the grandmother obsessed by mourning for dead relatives and the mother abandoned with her three sons by a chronically straying husband.

The second section of the movie skips 10 years with Mui now working for a wealthy friend of the eldest son of her previous household. The only conventional plot in the picturesque atmospheric movie involves the complications that inevitably develop in the relationship between Mui and her new master, an unmarried composer deeply immersed in the world of Western music, dreaming endlessly at the piano over the works of Chopin and Debussy.

The actress who plays Mui as a 20-year-old (Tran Nu Yen-Khe) seems self-conscious and artificial when compared to her younger counterpart, and the film's ultimate resolution comes across as totally inconsistent—in both tone and substance—with everything we've seen before.

Still and all, the picture provides moments of astonishing tranquility and crystalline clarity, marking the first movie view of Vietnamese culture in which war or colonialism are never a major focus.

Writer-director Tran Anh Hung, 31, has lived in France since 1975, but based this film on nostalgic recollections of his childhood home in Saigon.

It is no small tribute to his formidable gifts that he filmed this gorgeously detailed re-creation of vanished Vietnam—so vivid that you can feel the tropical heat and, yes, smell the papayas—entirely on a sound stage in a Parisian suburb.

NEWSDAY, 1/28/94, Part II/p. 63, John Anderson

The roar of a fighter jet, splitting the serene peace of a Saigon morning in '61, is the only intimation of grim history in "The Scent of Green Papaya," Tran Anh Hung's remembrance of Vietnam past. Otherwise the film dwells in memory with such Proustian persuasiveness you can almost imagine a world without that war.

"Papaya's," Vietnam is at once a green-gladed fiction and a self-contained eulogy for the world of Tran's birth (which he left with his family for Paris in 1975). It's a world that has, literally, disappeared: The director reportedly searched Vietnam for the proper locations, but it had all been erased. So he recreated it all on a French sound stage. And while this may add a bittersweet footnote to Vietnamese cinema, it in no way distorts the portrait he wanted to paint. Even if "Papaya" is as sensuous as all outdoors, the atmosphere that the main character, tiny Mui (Lu Man San) finds when she gets to Saigon in 1951 is as insular, artificial and claustrophobic as any stage set in the world.

We first see the 10-year-old girl searching the 1951 Saigon streets—a tiny embodiment of the director—and finally finding the door of the merchant family she'll serve for the next decade. It's a troubled world she enters, as troubled as it is precise. The men of the house live idle lives, while the women, even the mother (Truong Thi Loc), are devoted to servitude. It's the women who are the family's, and country's, strength; their ritualized routine is the film's center and its celebration.

Around this circulates the family's woes. The father (Tran Ngoc Trung), who, while life goes on around him, sits on his bed playing a blues-hued lute in front of the family's electric fan, has made periodic disappearances with his wife's money. He always came back, but once his timing was tragic: Their youngest child, a girl, had died the day before. His melancholy is palpable, but whether it's because of the girl's death or the fact that he's a colonial is unclear. He's doomed in any event, because he's a man without purpose.

The children are disturbed, too; the eldest is mostly absent, but Lam (Do Nhat), the middle child, tortures insects and broods; the youngest boy, Tin (Neth Gerard) is obnoxious and flatulent, and delights in making work for Mui—muddying clean laundry, for instance, or peeing in a just-washed vase.

Mui, for her part, is sweetness and patience personified; Tran loves her face, and so do we. She is the agent of his own lost innocence. After the old servant woman Thi (Nguyen Anh Hoa) cuts the green papaya from the tree, Mui watches the milky sap drip onto a broad green leaf; she smiles, not knowing why. Tran does, and it's a moment of projected joy.

Father will leave, only to return home and die; sons will marry, mother will be disappointed. Mui grows up and leaves to join the household of Khuyen, who had been a guest in the old house and is now a composer, living well in Saigon, where we hear the jets fly overhead. This last third, with the birdlike older Mui (Tran Nu Yen-Khe) in love, is essentially an epilogue, but it's too long for that. And too involved in Mui and Khuyen's dance of seduction. It makes us long for the little girl, just as Tran longs for his lost country.

NEWSWEEK, 3/7/94, p. 66, David Ansen

Tran Anh Hung, the gifted director of *The Scent of Green Papaya*, left his native Vietnam for France in 1975 when he was 12. Re-creating the Saigon of his childhood on sound stages near Paris, he produced this exquisitely sensuous memory film—nominated for the foreign-film Oscar—about a servant girl's transformation. It begins in 1951, when the 10-year-old Mui (Lu Man San) comes to work in a large household, then jumps to 1961, when the beautiful young woman (Tran Nu Yen-Khe) falls in love with her second master, a young composer. Tran's meditative film raptly celebrates a vanished civilization by evoking in luminous detail the everyday rituals of domestic life. Two off-screen sounds of passing planes are the only hints of the wars that will tear this world apart, but so evocative is Tran's minimalism—which puts the viewer in an altered, contemplative state—that no more is needed.

SIGHT AND SOUND, 4/94, p. 49, Tony Rayns

Saigon, 1951. Ten-year-old Mùi arrives from her village home to work as the junior maid in a middle-class household; her father has died and her mother has been forced to send her to work. The elderly servant The trains Mùi in her duties and explains the family situation. The household's only income is from the mother's small cloth and yarn shop; the father is an idler who has three times vanished for long periods, taking all the family savings with him. His mother, a pious Buddhist, has not left her upstairs room for seven years, since the death from illness of her granddaughter To. The grandmother is also in permanent mourning for her own husband, who died young, and has rejected overtures from the kindly Mr Thuan, who adores her from afar. The three surviving children are all sons: the teenaged Trung and the two young boys Lam and Tin.

Mùi has hardly got the measure of her work before the father vanishes again, leaving his wife to sell heirlooms to buy rice. Mùi gets her first (unvoiced) crush on Khuyen, Trung's classmate and a frequent visitor to the house. The youngest son Tin takes delight in tormenting Mùi and one day causes her to break an antique vase; but the mother, who treats Mùi more and more like her own late daughter, is indulgent and forgiving. Mùi befriends Mr Thuan and helps him sneak upstairs for a glimpse of Grandma. While her son is still away, Grandma falls nervously ill and the mother collapses under the strain.

Ten years later. Trung is married, and his mercenary wife Thu pressures her mother-in-law to economise by dismissing Mùi. Mùi moves to work instead for Khuyen, who has become an accomplished pianist and has a boisterous fiancee. Mùi is a calm and silent presence in the new house. But Khuyen's fiancee discovers that Mùi dotes on her employer and flounces out. Khuyen starts to reciprocate Mùi's quiet affection and decides to teach her to read. Some time later, Mùi has become his wife.

Tran Anh Hung, born in Vietnam and educated in Paris, was inspired to become a film-maker by the example of Lam Lê, the pioneer French-Vietnamese director, and he worked on Lê's seminal *Dust of Empire*. Tran's two short films, *La Femme mariée de Nam* (1987) and *La Pierre de l'attente* (1991)—are both close in spirit to Lê's film, but *The Scent of Green Papaya* picks up their elliptical narrative structures and their accumulation-of-details style and turns them into something distinct and underivative. This is a remarkably confident and achieved debut feature.

In part, the confidence must be related to the conditions of production. Tran was obliged to abandon his original plan to shoot in Vietnam and made the entire film instead in a studio at Bry-sur-Marne, a limitation that clearly meshed with the aesthetic decision to build the film from rigorously controlled patterns of salient detail. *Green Papaya* is analytic (and defiantly idiosyncratic) in structure, in ways that allow Tran to prevent the film from falling into the James Ivory trap of wallowing in nostalgia for more elegant times, but also allow him to stress the metaphorical dimension of Mùi's growth to maturity. He has described his film as an attempt to deal with "the problem of servitude", especially as it affects Vietnamese women. Mùi's trajectory from naivety and wonderment through the inculcated routines of domestic labour to the subtler servitude of devotion to a man works as a doubled-edged metaphor.

In one way, this is an account of a Vietnamese woman achieving a kind of fulfilment: realising her own potential without remotely transcending her allotted social role. In another, Mùi's case is a cypher for a much larger social process: the shift from the countryside to cities, the developing sophistication and education, and then, inevitably, the 'westernisation', rendered here through the decor of Khuyen's house and the young musician's absorption in Debussy and Chopin. Both stages of the process find Mùi learning by example. First she learns the preparation of food (notably the chopping of papaya for salad) from Thi; then she learns to read from Khuyen. Tran uses images rather than words to underline his theme: both periods in Mùi's education are presented as patterns of gestures copied from the educator until perfected.

Metaphor apart, the film is overwhelmingly sensual in its depiction of its milieu. In part, this is a triumph for the cinematographer and art directors, who have recreated the light, the colours and the timbre of two Vietnamese houses in the studio with almost hallucinatory intensity. But it is also a triumph of Tran's own visual sensibility. The film alternates between huge close-up details (the middle son Lam tormenting ants on a window ledge, Mùi's finger probing the seed-pulp inside an unripe papaya) and extended wide-angle tracking shots through the houses, following the to-ings and fro-ings of the various characters and thus stressing the interconnectedness of the household routines. Both types of shot are used to focus on Mùi herself for much of the time, but both are also sometimes used to broaden the focus, acknowledging Mùi's place in a larger domestic and social fabric. The general sense of off-screen realities is amplified by the soundtrack, which contains occasional hints of the anti-colonial war then being fought in the faraway North.

There is sadly no real Vietnamese tradition for Tran to draw on in constructing his images and metaphors. Vietnamese film production dates back to the 1930s (when it was largely in the hands of Vietnamese-Chinese), but most production since the 1930s—including the communist government's propaganda output—has been locked into stale conventions of theatricality and melodrama. Implicitly acknowledging his own cultural identity as a westernised émigré artist, Tran has combined ideas and influences from both oriental and occidental sources to underpin his vision. The use of the studio and the *mise en scène* of tracking shots is indebted to western tradition, from von Sternberg to Bresson. The use of a small boy given to domestic mischief and provocative farting is a respectful nod to Ozu.

Tran insists that his future projects will be shot in Vietnam, and that they will deal with the country's present-day realities and problems; *Green Papaya* will be his only period movie, and it expresses things that he needed to get out of his system. It's hard to imagine what the film might mean to a Vietnamese audience, either in Vietnam or in the global diaspora, but its established success suggests that its central conundrum—the tangled lines between servitude and love—achieves a universality. Not bad for a first-time director far from home.

TIME, 3/7/94, p. 75, Richard Corliss

In most moviegoers' minds, Vietnam is Oliver Stone territory—the metaphorical battleground on which he has played out his burly war games of the conflicted American spirit. French filmmakers have also taken bittersweet tours of Vietnam; in movies like *The Lover* and *Indochine*, Saigon has the poignant glamour of a beautiful woman's photo in an old man's memory book.

Finally, the task of remembering Vietnam has fallen to a Vietnamese writer-director. The Saigon on view in Tran Anh Hung's *The Scent of Green Papaya*, recently nominated for a foreign-language-film Oscar, is serene, shimmering and stripped of melodrama. Set in two ominously tranquil periods—1951, a few years before the French collapse at Dien Bien Phu, and 1961, just before the U.S. buildup—*Green Payaya* is seemingly apolitical. Yet in Tran's family drama one can see a society torn between East and West, passivity and passion, duty and will, ancient rites and modern desires.

Mui (Lu Man San) is 10 when, after leaving her family and her village, she arrives in Saigon to be the servant girl in a middle-class home. Here the mother still mourns the death of her daughter, who would have been Mui's age. The father luxuriates in a torpid guilt. Upstairs Grandma intones prayers for the family dead. Downstairs the couple's three boys make mischief. The youngest taunts Mui with merciless glee; he is just about the only sign of wayward life in this house-and-garden mausoleum.

Mui is a welcome sign of nature. She is radiant in her servitude; her toil gives her joy because it allows her to see in closeup how the world grows. She is enthralled to slice open a papaya, or watch an ant carry its backpack of crumbs. And with the same fascination, but etched in loss for her own child, the mother watches Mui. At night as a breeze whispers through the sheer canopy on Mui's bed, the girl says the word mother in her sleep. The mother of the house, eavesdropping on this intimacy dries her own tears on the canopy.

Ten years pass. Mui (now played by Tran Nu Yen-Khe) a beautiful young woman, is sold to a handsome pianist (Vuong Hoa Hoi). Cinderella finds her Prince Charming, and an aristocrat is ennobled when he falls in love with a pretty peasant. Every fable deserves a happy ending.

In this haunted fairyland, the director creates images of exquisite rightness from a pristine, pastel palette, lifting the viewers senses into a delicate rapture. The mood, the pacing, the search for beauty in a harsh society are ever so—how shall we say?—Vietnamese. Yet the film was not made in Vietnam. It could not have been: the country has hardly any film industry. So Tran, whose family immigrated to France in 1975, when he was 12, and who describes his film as a tribute to "the freshness and beauty of my mother's gestures," shot the film on a sound stage outside Paris. Meticulously, lovingly, he re-created a world that ceased to exist before he was born.

And then, in an act of both appropriation and reconciliation, the authorities of Tran's homeland adopted his movie: they made *The Scent of Green Papaya* the official Oscar entry from the Socialist Republic of Vietnam. Perhaps, for a nation emerging from centuries of war, the movie is the best kind of foreign aid—the kind that comes, express mail, from an émigré's wise and tender heart.

VILLAGE VOICE, 2/1/94, p. 56, Georgia Brown

Movies with good food (*Like Water for Chocolate* and *Babette's Feast*) tend to be movies about women's lot. (The emphasis in *Tampopo* was more on the truck-driving cowboy who saved the widow's ramen shop.) Tran Anh Hung's gentle, if slightly precious, *The Scent of Green Papaya* (from last year's New York Film Festival) centers on a pint-size peasant girl, Mui, her culinary training, and her acclimation to a mildly eccentric Saigon family. Shots of yummy stir-fries should guarantee an art-house hit. (If some movies function as foreplay, others serve as *hors d'oeuvre)*

In that the film is a tribute to perfect, saintly service it could also be viewed as a Vietnamese *Remains of the Day*—except that Mui doesn't construe her calling as a life sentence to chastity.

Tran divides his film into two sections. The first, dated 1951, records the arrival from the countryside of 10-year-old Mui (Lu Man San) into an urban, upper middle-class household. In the second, 10 years later, she's grown (and played by Tran Nu Yen-Khe), not nearly so adorable, and sets her sights for her new master.

Part One is more satisfying in its modesty, and because the child playing Mui is perfectly at ease in front of the camera and a joy to watch. Part Two, which develops into a soap opera, I find a bit creepy. A hypothetical Part Three has been omitted entirely, although the opening legend on Two, "1961, Saigon" will have many viewers tensing for the blow that never comes. Presumably, the date summons nostalgia for pre-war intactness.

Filmed on a set near Paris (Tran's family moved to France when he was 12), *Green Papaya* takes place almost entirely inside the two homes where Mui works. These city houses open onto gardens and a front compound and seem to teem with natural life. Outside Mui's window grows the title's papaya tree. On her first morning, one of these long green vegetables is cut by the old cook (Nguyen Anh Hoa), leaving the stem to bleed a milky liquid.

Tree's milk/breast milk. Coming to Saigon, Mui wins two new protective mothers: the kindly old housekeeper as well as her long-suffering mistress who misses a dead daughter. Her three sons presumably haven't filled the gap. The one who most wants to comfort her takes his rage out on ants. (Microscopic close-ups.) The master of the house is a distant, idle music lover, noted for periodically absconding with all the funds and leaving the family destitute. His mother blames her daughter-in-law: "You don't know how to make him happy." Whether her remarks represent casual stupidity or casual cruelty is never clarified since the film's sole focus is the unfailingly cheerful, grateful-to-be-there Mui.

What bugs me about the second, "grown-up" half? Besides the fact that little Mui is gone, suddenly something delicate and quiet turns into a slightly hysterical Cinderella story. The setting shifts to the arty, Eurocentric decor of the new master's house. And Mui's new master, a composer and insistent pianist, is only slightly less self-absorbed than the old one. Good thing that Mui has turned into the perfect servant. She'll make him a perfect wife.

Also reviewed in:
CHICAGO TRIBUNE, 3/11/94, Friday/p. D, Michael Wilmington
NEW YORK TIMES, 1/28/94, p. C5, Janet Maslin
NEW REPUBLIC, 2/28/94, p. 30, Stanley Kauffmann
VARIETY, 6/7/93, p. 42, Derek Elley
WASHINGTON POST, 2/18/94, p. G7, Hal Hinson
WASHINGTON POST, 2/18/94, Weekend/p. 56, Desson Howe

SCOUT, THE

A Twentieth Century Fox release of a Ruddy Morgan production. *Executive Producer:* Jack Cummins and Herbert S. Nanas. *Producer:* Albert S. Ruddy and Andre E. Morgan. *Director:* Michael Ritchie. *Screenplay:* Andrew Bergman, Albert Brooks, and Monica Johnson. *Based upon "The New Yorker" article by:* Roger Angell. *Director of Photography:* Laszlo Kovacs. *Editor:* Don Zimmerman and Pembroke Herring. *Music:* Bill Conti. *Music Editor:* Jeff Carson. *Sound:* Kim Ornitz and (music) Lee DeCarlo. *Sound Editor:* Don Hall. *Casting:* Richard Pagano, Sharon Bialy, and Debi Manwiller. *Production Designer:* Stephen Hendrickson. *Art Director:* Okowita. *Set Designer:* Thomas Betts and Gina B. Cranham. *Set Decorator:* Merideth Boswell. *Set Dresser:* Bruce Bellamy, Edward McCarthy, Mark Weissenfluh, Alice Baker, and John H. Maxwell. *Special Effects:* Carrol Lynn. *Costumes:* Luke Reichle. *Make-up:* Robert Ryan. *Stunt Coordinator:* Juan Manuel Vilchis, Glenn Randall, Jr. and Mike Russo. *Running time:* 101 minutes. *MPAA Rating:* PG-13.

CAST: Albert Brooks (Al Percolo); Brendan Fraser (Steve Nebraska); Dianne Wiest (Doctor Aaron); Anne Twomey (Jennifer); Lane Smith (Ron Wilson); Michael Rapaport (Tommy Lacy); Barry Shabaka Henley (McDermott); John Capodice (Caruso); Louis Giovannetti (World Series Catcher); Stephen Demek (Yankee Catcher); Ralph Drischell (Charlie); Brett Rickaby (George's Assistant); Jack Rader (Mr. Lacy); Marcia Rodd (Mrs. Lacy); Steve Eastin (Clubhouse Manager); Lee Weaver (Ben); John LaMotta (Elevator Guard); Luis

Cortes (Mexican Desk Clerk); Chuck Waters (Photographer); Antonio Lewis Todd (Yankee Player); Abel Woolridge (Nachito Fan); Gabriel Pingarron (Mexican Umpire); Lolo Navarro (Widow in Stands); Frank Slaten (College Umpire); Charlie Stavola (Doorman); Jimmy Raitt (World Series Umpire); Larry Loonin (Radar Gun Man); Harsh Nayyar (Cab Driver); J.K. Simmons (Assistant Coach); Bob Costas (Himself); John Roland (Himself); George M. Steinbrenner, III (Himself); Rosanna Scotto (Herself); Tony Bennett (Himself); Carl White (Himself); Bobby Murcer (Himself); Steve Garvey (Himself); Tim McCarver (Himself); Tom Kelly (Himself); John Sterling (Himself); Ken Brett (Himself); Bret Saberhagen (Himself); Reggie Smith (Himself); Keith Hernandez (Himself); Roy Firestone (Himself); Bob Sheppard (Himself); Phil Pote (Himself); Bob Tewksbury (Himself); Ozzie Smith (Himself).

LOS ANGELES TIMES, 9/30/94, Calendar/p. 6, Peter Rainer

For those of us who fervently believe Albert Brooks is the funniest man in American and can do no wrong, "The Scout" offers up a dilemma. As New York Yankee baseball scout Al Percolo, Brooks is hilariously "right," but, boy did he pick the wrong vehicle.

Not that you can blame him exactly. There's a lot of talent in this baseball comedy, which was directed by Michael Ritchie and co-written by Brooks and Andrew Bergman and Monica Johnson, and co-stars Brendan Fraser and Dianne Wiest. That's exactly why its creeping mediocrity seems like a perverse joke.

The creep doesn't really start until the film enters its second half-hour or so. Until then, it's a knock-about showcase for Brooks, and it's a stitch—pure Brooksian riff. Wearing a straw hat and a paunch, Al weasels his way in the good graces of a God-fearing pitching phenom (Michael Rapaport) only to have the boy throw up and punk out just before his Yankee Stadium debut.

Demoted by the Yankees general manager (Lane Smith) to scouting the Mexican backwaters, Al bounces from town to town until he accidentally happens upon a local sensation unknown to any previous scout—Steve Nebraska (Fraser), a gangly, dippy American mysteriously ensconced without family in Mexico. Brought into the makeshift Mexican stadium on a cheap-jack throne, looking like a bargain-bin Cleopatra entering Rome, he proceeds to whiff batters with his m 100-plus-m.p.h. fastball and then, taking the plate, slams the ball out of the park.

Al is flabbergasted at his fortune—he feels like he's bringing King Kong to New York in glory. (Early on, we see Al watching "Kong," his favorite movie, on TV—the "original" version! he exults) But, when the Yankees drop him before his arrival, he cooks up a personal contract with Steve and negotiates a $55-million salary—with the caveat that Steve wait out the rest of Yankees' dismal season unless they win the pennant. (Guess what happens.) The only hitch: The Yankees require a psychiatric bill of health before they sign. And Steve, who seems to be humming to his own off-key melody, is no shoo-in for sanity.

As long as "The Scout" is sending up baseball escapades, it's on sure footing. Yankees owner George Steinbrenner, playing himself, is unexpectedly hilarious: He has a great moment when he rolls his eyes at a reporter's crack that his team has no chance at a pennant. There's been so much folkloric blather about baseball lately—including the 18-hour PBS "Baseball" series—that the livid silliness of the best parts of "The Scout" are tonic.

But the filmmakers don't seem to know what's good about their subject and what should be ejected from the game. Once Steve makes it to New York and moves in with Al—who takes a fatherly responsibility for his prize—the film quickly devolves into a series of vaguely serious and unfunny set pieces backed by an infernally "Rocky"-esque Bill Conti score.

Cutting shears seem to have excised vast swatches of continuity. Steve, for example, inexplicably loses his love for the sport. We never find out what he was doing in Mexico or anything about the whereabouts of his family. He's billed as a stud, but the film allows him no dalliances (unless one counts a cryptic suggestion of one with a Yankee assistant played by Anne Twomey in what must be the tiniest cameo ever recorded by a celebrated, Tony-nominated Broadway actress).

When he enters therapy with—har-har—Dr. H. Aaron (Wiest) we don't find out much more about their sessions than the obvious—he's looking for a father-figure. We don't know just how nut-brained Steve really is.

Fraser is enjoyable in a bland callow way that doesn't really give the film much of a center. He doesn't spark Brooks, who works best when he's acting one-on-one, and that's unfortunate since the entire cramped, skimpy production is practically a duet for two actors. (It might have been developed from a two-character play, although, in fact, the script, in various stages of development, has been around since 1982.) The film edges toward sappiness instead of nuttiness. It turns into just what you don't want it to become: a buddy-buddy bond-a-thon.

Ritchie is sometimes a whiz at comedy. Couldn't he see the potential in pairing Brooks with Wiest? In their one real scene together, when Al is trying to cajole the doctor into signing a clean bill of health sight unseen, the air is frisky with comic possibilities. (It's reminiscent of that great scene in Vegas in Brooks' "Lost in America," where he tries to talk Garry Marshall into giving back the money.) These two work so well together that you expect some kind of romance to develop, or perhaps a group therapy situation. Instead, you're left with a hunk of heartfelt whimsy.

You can tolerate "The Scout" for Brooks' bull-necked exasperation and fixated double takes. Against all odds he creates a lived-in character beneath that straw hat. But, as you leave the theater, the heavy musk of wasted opportunity crowds the air.

NEW YORK POST, 9/30/94, p. 47, Michael Medved

In the middle of this miserable strike, baseball fans may be desperate for even a vague taste of our favorite game, but that's still no excuse to waste time on an annoying, underachieving comedy like "The Scout."

The tremendously talented Albert Brooks (who also co-wrote the screenplay) plays a fast-talking scout for the Yankees who's obsessed with the movie "King Kong." He dreams of venturing into the jungle of amateur ball and bringing back some amazing specimen who, like Kong, will proceed to dazzle New York.

He thinks he's finally found his wonder of nature in the Mexican boondocks when he sees a goofy, gangly American kid playing ball for a village team. Steve Nebraska (Brendan Fraser) throws a fast ball that burns into the strike zone at 110 miles per hour, and bashes 600-foot home runs every time he swings a bat. Brooks brings the phenom back to New York, where the Yanks sign the untried kid for $55 million. The only problem is that they insist that a psychiatrist (Dianne Wiest) must certify that he's sane enough to play big league ball before they'll begin paying what they've promised.

It hardly seems credible that sanity would be treated as a prerequisite for todays big leaguers (especially in view of the strike) and the film fails to explore the specific nature of its characters' nuttiness. We learn next to nothing about the bizarre creature played by Fraser (who seems to be doing a variation of his Neathanderthal antics in "Encino Man"). How did he end up in Mexico in the first place? When did he develop—or discover—his superhuman athletic abilities? Why hasn't he tried playing professional ball before Brooks discovers him? None of this is answered (other than a brief, trendy invocation of an "abusive father") so his character remains far less nuanced or convincing than the original King Kong.

The film's intended humor consists of interminable sequences of Brooks snarling at his head-case discovery to prevent the kid from doing something dumb or destructive. Some of this is genuinely funny, but all such scenes go on much too long, until we're as frustrated as the characters themselves. Ozzie Smith, George Steinbrenner and Tony Bennett all make amusing cameo appearances, but it's a measure of the film's failure that it seems to immediately lose energy whenever the real celebrities walk away and leave us alone with the fictional characters.

Director Michael Ritchie has done some entertaining sports films in the past ("Downhill Racer," "The Bad News Bears," "Semi-Tough") but here he can't seem to decide whether to go for realism or supernatural fantasy, and settles for a slap-dash style that makes an anemic effort to have it both ways.

Like one of baseball's weakest hitting relief pitchers (remember bespectacled Ryne Duren with his .061 lifetime batting average?) "The Scout" steps up to the plate, makes a few feeble, formulaic waves at the ball, then shrugs its cinematic shoulders and quickly gives up.

NEWSDAY, 9/30/94, Part II/p. B3, John Anderson

We can't watch baseball this fall, but thanks to Rupert Murdoch's 20th Century Fox, we can watch George Steinbrenner. It's comforting in a way, this solidarity among union men. Teamwork. That's what the game is all about.

Steinbrenner is one of a number of baseball figures—most of whom should have known better—who pop up in "The Scout," an Albert Brooks-driven comedy that rubs salt in the wound of a dead season. The film was made long before the strike, of course, and any baseball movie opening during a baseball strike is going to inherit a subtext. But you can't watch "The Scout" in a vacuum, or without a creeping sense of class consciousness.

Brooks, wearing a perpetual squint (or is it a wince?), plays Al Percolo, a hard-luck Yankees scout who's been banished by his Steinbrenner-like general manager, Ron Wilson (Lane Smith), to the Mexican outback. There, goats roam the playing fields; games are interrupted if the pitcher gets a phone call. And there, living like some ash-swinging, horsehide-heaving Aztec deity, is Steve Nebraska (Brendan Fraser), the game's greatest prodigy and a local demigod. Al, taking a cue from Robert Armstrong (whom we see in some footage from "King Kong"), brings his savage prize back to the big city.

The fictional Nebraska personifies how the real-life owners—and many fans—view their striking employees: a souffle-head with a gift, an athletic idiot savant, a *baseball player*. And a kid who, it becomes immediately clear, is deeply disturbed. His press-conference outburst worries the Yankees, who've just paid him $55 million ("Whatever it takes," says No-Salary Cap Steinbrenner, when Wilson asks him how much they should spend). "How can you justify that kind of money?" a reporter asks Wilson, and the movie's answer is, you can't. Nebraska is an intemperate animal, and money will only make him dangerous.

The setup is a send-up of baseball business, and the movie's best sequence: Al and other scouts watching a high school star (Michael Rapaport), bemoaning the fact that he's off limits to them, and then Al meeting, wooing and signing the kid to pitch in Yankee Stadium, where he promptly loses his lunch and flees.

That's when Al's stock drops and he goes south—as does "The Scout" once Al finds Steve. Fraser is neither a comic nor a physical actor, and his attempts to make Steve deliriously goofy are just uncomfortable. Dianne Wiest's role as Dr. H. Aaron (ho ho), the psychiatrist who helps Steve "reconnect his life." is ungratifying. Brooks is good, but again, we never really see his eyes. He may be hiding.

At a screening this week, one scene indicated that the public is as divided as the principals over the baseball strike: Al, having arranged to use Yankee Stadium for a demonstration of Steve's talent, brings on Keith Hernandez and Bret Saberhagen to hit and pitch. "I "haven't gotten paid yet," Saberhagen whispers to Al, who mumbles, "He's making millions, and he needs my money?" Half the audience applauded. Which is about twice as much as "The Scout" has a right to expect.

TIME, 10/10/94, p. 82, Richard Schickel

"Why don't you just fire me?" asks Al Percolo (Albert Brooks), the down-trodden but game talent hunter in *The Scout*. "I thought of that," snaps the meanest general manager in baseball history (Lane Smith), "but I like this better." Al is talking about his scouting assignment so deep in the Mexican bush leagues that they play in the rain because it makes sliding easier. There he discovers Steve Nebraska (Brendan Fraser), a phenom with a fast ball so potent it knocks over the catcher and the umpire. Steve is in dire need of an understanding father figure—especially after he gets a $55 million contract with the Yanks.

What Steve has instead is awful, desperate Al (Brooks is, of course, a peerless portrayer of all the great American falsities—piety, humility and the good cheer with which we habitually mask desperation). Steve also has his own violent innocence, which tests the limits of Al's smarminess hilariously. The script, by Brooks, Andrew Bergman and Monica Johnson, draws a specific parallel between Steve and another primitive creature imported to amuse jaded New Yorkers—King Kong—and it is a measure of director Michael Ritchie's deftness that he gets the right kind of laughs from the device. Ritchie avoids the kind of sentiment that so often encrusts tall sporting tales, and even gets a funny performance out of baseball's very own Kong, Yankee boss George Steinbrenner. *The Scout* is the best comedy-fantasy about baseball ever made, which goes to show that if Hollywood keeps trying, eventually someone will get it right.

VILLAGE VOICE, 10/11/94, p. 75, J. Hoberman

Based on a *New Yorker* piece by a surely mortified Roger Angell, *The Scout* transposes King Kong to the American League. Albert Brooks, who starred and cowrote, plays a baseball scout exiled to the Mexican outback where he discovers the "primitive" talent Steve Nebraska (Brendan "Encino Man" Fraser) and brings him back to Yankee Stadium to start the first game of the World Series.

Brooks may be a champion nudge but even he can't kick this sodden fantasy into gear. The movie is amazingly unfunny. Amid plugs aplenty and ponderous cameos from Tony Bennett, George Steinbrenner, and half the Fox 5 news team, one glimpses a bizarre father-son story complete with recovered memories of childhood abuse and Dianne Wiest as a shrink. I don't know if Brooks is responsible for the over-the-top smarminess of the line, "This is what George Steinbrenner brings to the Yankees—a real sense of excitement," but in some ways the movie is prophetic. It ends with the possibility that no one will ever get another hit.

Also reviewed in:
NEW YORK TIMES, 9/30/94, p. C23, Caryn James
VARIETY, 9/26-10/2/94, p. 61, Brian Lowry
WASHINGTON POST, 9/30/94, p. F1, Hal Hinson

SECOND BEST

A Warner Bros. release of a Regency Enterprises and Alcor Films presentation of a Sarah Radclyffe/Fron Film production. *Executive Producer:* Arnon Milchan. *Producer:* Sarah Radclyffe. *Director:* Chris Menges. *Screenplay (based on his novel):* David Cook. *Director of Photography:* Ashley Rowe. *Editor:* George Akers. *Music:* Simon Boswell. *Music Editor:* Jupiter Sen. *Sound:* Peter Glossop. *Sound Editor:* Peter Best. *Casting:* Susie Figgis. *Production Designer:* Michael Howells. *Art Director:* Roger Thomas. *Set Decorator:* Sam Riley. *Costumes:* Nic Ede. *Make-up:* Jenny Shircore. *Running time:* 105 minutes. *MPAA Rating:* PG-13.

CAST: William Hurt (Graham Holt); John Hurt (Uncle Turpin); Chris Cleary Miles (James); Nathan Yapp (Jimmy); Keith Allen (John); Doris Irving (Adoption Shop Volunteer); Alfred Lynch (Edward); Rachel Freeman (Elsie); Gus Troakes (Jeffo); Mossie Smith (Lynn); Martin Troakes (Colin); James Warrior (Senior Social Worker); Jane Horrocks (Debbie); Shaun Dingwall (Graham, age 20); Paul Wilson (Colin, age 20); Alan Cumming (Bernard); Jake Owen (Jimmy, age 3); Sophie Dix (Mary); Prunella Scales (Margery); Jennifer Whitefoot (Tine); Jubal Bright (Leggo); Colin Bufton (Rusty); Richard Storr (Jed); Owen Shepherd (Fang); Richard Murray (Vernon); Ross Edwards (Pimple); Bryn Askham (Chris); Geoffrey Leesley (Eric); Doris Hard (Mrs. Hawkins); Shirley King (Enid); Adam Wills (Graham, age 12); Giles Emmerson (Vicar); Mrs. George (Herself); Nerys Hughes (Maureen); Philip Swancote (Policeman); Anne Morrish (Lizzie); Peter Copley (Percy); Esther Coles (Staff Nurse); Jodhi May (Alice); Tessa Gearing (Mrs. Hilliard).

LOS ANGELES TIMES, 9/30/94, Calendar/p. 8, Kevin Thomas

"Second Best" is such a splendid, intimate film you worry that it's going to get lost in the thicket of much bigger, far more highly publicized fall releases. The irony is that for all its modesty of scale it has the universal appeal of a richly realized father-and-son relationship, portrayed by William Hurt, in one of the finest performances of his career, and by a remarkable newcomer, neophyte actor Chris Cleary Miles.

The crux of the matter is that Hurt and Miles are not in fact father and son. Hurt, accent-perfect plays Graham Holt, a 42- year-old bachelor, the grocer/postmaster of a small picture postcard

Welsh town. He has lived his entire life in the drab but cozy house attached to the store, but his mother has now been dead for 18 months and his father is bedridden and speechless from a stroke. But as Graham later on tells Miles' troubled 10-year-old James: "To be nothing, to feel nothing, doesn't work."

Director Chris Menges and writer David Cook, in adapting Cook's novel, crosscut between the past histories of Graham and James until they cross paths. James is haunted by a traumatic event he witnessed as a toddler, the meaning of his fragmented memories of it are fully revealed only at the film's climax. Motherless and his father imprisoned, James grows up in an orphanage. The devotion of Graham's parents, on the other hand, was so complete as to shut him out of their love. As a result, Graham has developed a diffidence so inhibiting that we can actually believe that, as physically attractive as he is, he could put off women. In his need for love and to ease his loneliness, however, he has no real idea of what he'll be getting into in trying to adopt a child.

Jane Horrocks' tart social worker makes it clear to Graham that as a single, middle-aged male he's going to have to settle for an older, difficult child. The film's crucial underlying strength now emerges, which is in its determinedly unsentimental, unhurried (yet not slow-paced) depiction of the prickly development of a relationship between man and boy that is at all times fraught with uncertainty because of the boy's giving in swiftly to terrible rages. The question is whether Graham will be able to assert himself strongly and wisely enough to hold on to James.

In any event, the film proceeds flawlessly under the controlled yet unobtrusive direction of Menges, the gifted cameraman who turned equally gifted director with the memorable "A World Apart" with Barbara Hershey. There are other sterling performances from, among others, another notable Hurt—John Hurt—as Graham's raffish uncle and from Keith Allen as James' loving but feckless actual father. "Second Best" is so wrenchingly effective you hope fervently that Menges will freeze his final frame at precisely the perfect moment—and he does.

NEW YORK POST, 9/30/94, p. 46, Michael Medved

The trouble with movies about claustrophobic, emotionally crippled lives is that they often turn out to be claustrophobic, emotionally crippled movies.

That is certainly the case with "Second Best," where the meticulous performance by William Hurt isn't nearly enough to give the listless material the energy it needs. Hurt plays Graham Holt, the lonely, middle-aged postmaster in a tiny village in Wales.

In this decidedly unglamorous role, our fearless star bears no resemblance whatever to the brooding romantic lead fondly remembered by many of his American fans; here, his squinty eyes, thick horn-rims and wavy, fly-away hair make him look like a member of the British road company of "Revenge of the Nerds."

While nursing his invalid father through a terminal illness, Hurt's character realizes that he's never made a significant connection with another human being. He therefore applies to adopt a child, despite the fact that he's not married and has no prospects for matrimony in his future.

The wary officials at a local orphanage assign him a deeply troubled boy on a trial basis and the movie focuses on Hurt's relentless efforts to build their relationship. "I wont be second best" he ultimately tells the child. "If it's going to work it has be as father and son."

The problem is that the boy (effectively played by an 11- year-old first-time actor named Chris Cleary Miles) already has a father to whom he feels ferociously loyal: a charismatic career criminal (Keith Allen) who's serving time in prison. Will Hurt be able to supersede this destructive relationship and connect with the emotionally wounded boy? And will the child's worthless father turn up at precisely the wrong moment forcing a crisis?

All of this plays out so predictably that director Chris Menges ("A World Apart" and Goldie Hawn's ill-fated "Criss-Cross") seems to realize that he has to try to nourish his audience by throwing in some additional elements. He therefore comes up with a series of distracting flashbacks that show the boy's traumatic history, along with additional snippets highlighting painful moments from Hurt's own desolate childhood.

These scenes pop up at random, illogical intervals, floating past us like chunks of undercooked meat in a thin, luke-warm gruel.

Menges who did the stunning camera work on both "The Mission" and "The Killing Fields" before turning to direction, always brings a rich, evocative look to his films and "Second Best," with its poetic views of Welsh villages and countryside, is no exception.

Hurt, despite a few problems with the difficult accent and a tendency to overdo the geeky, lonely guy number, creates a memorable character and generates authentic emotion in some of his interaction with his young co-star.

Unfortunately, these isolated instances can't provide the film with the sense of shape or momentum it lacks. This remains, at best, a vivid sketch, rather than a satisfying motion picture—a movie which, despite its obvious virtues, is decidedly second best.

NEWSDAY, 9/30/94, Part II/p. B9, Jack Mathews

Emotional pain, deep and enduring, is the subject of Chris Menges' "Second Best," and emotional pain, deep and enduring, is what it is to sit through it.

The movie, an overly earnest melodrama about a Welsh postmaster's relationship with the troubled 10-year-old boy he hopes to adopt, is a fastidiously symmetrical script. Everything in balance, everything done for a purpose, every trait of one character playing as counterpoint to that in another. It has the spontaneity of a map of the tiny village where it is set, and despite its implied human complexities, the simplicity as well.

Loss, loneliness and the need for love are the common denominators between the man and the boy whose lives first intersect in the bureaucratic tangle of the British adoption system, then in a sort of courtship ritual of supervised visits and meetings.

Graham (William Hurt, under a shock of curly hair) is a passive, virginal 42-year-old bachelor who, after the loss of his mother and a stroke that left his father vegetating upstairs, decides to attempt to adopt a son. It is a daring act for a man who's lived his entire life in the same house, which is adjacent to the post office where he's worked his entire career. But Graham is desperate for love, family love, and sees adoption as his only chance at having it.

The system, Graham is told, allots only the hardest-to-place kids to single applicants, and James (Chris Cleary Miles), who harbors a mysterious hatred for his dead mother and an obsessive passion for his imprisoned father, is about the toughest case available. He agrees to see Graham only because his home is in the village where he last saw his real father.

In short order, David Cook's script, adapted from his own novel, diagrams the contrasting personalities of Graham and James, and they look like a pair of giant gears ready to mesh. Graham is unfulfilled because his father never returned his love, and James is panicked by the fear he will never again have the love his father heaped upon him.

The question is not whether they are a match, but how long it will take for them to acknowledge it, and whether their bond will then be strong enough to survive the sudden, disruptive entry into their lives of James' father (Keith Allen).

"Second Best" feels like a movie that couldn't crack the novel. It is a story that is almost entirely internal, about the healing of two wounded spirits, and Menges' attempts to dramatize emotions with flashbacks to significant crises merely underscores how plodding the whole thing is.

I wanted to care for Graham and James, to work up some enthusiasm for their mutual rescue operation, and the actors—particularly Miles, in his first role—create sympathetic characters. But in their haste to reveal every emotional dynamic at play, the filmmakers removed any role the viewer might have in the equation. To become emotionally involved in this kind of relationship, you have to have some doubts about it. Whether Graham will end up ranked No. 1 in the boy's heart, or have to be content as second best, is not enough.

SIGHT AND SOUND, 1/95, p. 56, Geoffrey Macnab

James, a young boy, is whisked away from the school playground by his runaway father, John. Together, they hide out in the woods. Eventually, John decides to give himself up to the police. James is taken into care. Graham Holt, a shy, middle-aged postmaster living in a small Welsh village, wants to adopt a child and applies to become a father to James. Initially, the social workers are sceptical about Holt's qualifications, but he manages to convince them he deserves at least a trial.

On his first, visits to Holt's home, James is well-behaved. Holt has been warned that he is a "problem child"—the boy is still obsessed with his real father and haunted by his mother's suicide. Nevertheless, the two establish a rapport, going camping together and tracking down each other's relatives. James realises that Holt also had an unhappy childhood and treats him with a measure of sympathy.

After the so-called "honeymoon period", James's behaviour deteriorates. He is prone to violent outbursts and makes it very clear to Holt that his loyalties lie first and foremost with his real father. James receives a letter from his father consenting to the adoption; he allows Holt to read it. Not long afterwards, he comes to live with Holt permanently and starts at the local school.

One day, James's father arrives in the post office, haggard and ill. He explains to Holt that he has been in and out of prison several times, but thought it best to conceal the fact from his son. He now has Aids and simply wants to see James again before he dies. Holt allows him to stay. However, when James comes back from school and is re-introduced to the father he idolised, he is shocked and disgusted by his illness. In the middle of the night, he runs off and hides in a hole in the woods. Holt eventually finds him, curled up and half frozen. The two sleep in the woods. The next morning, as they head back to Holt's home, Holt makes it clear to James that the adoption can only work if the boy treats him as a real father.

William Hurt knows how to play in minor key, as he showed in *The Accidental Tourist*. Nevertheless, it comes as a slight surprise to see the former Oscar winner transformed into a tousle-haired, anorak-wearing Welsh postmaster. Not that Hurt gives a bad or showy performance—although his accent wavers at times, he approaches his role in quiet, understated fashion, moving slowly and enunciating his words in a laborious monotone. He captures perfectly his character's anguish and disappointment in himself: his sense that he was always destined to be "second best".

But stars have baggage attached. Each new part they play is refracted, at least in fans' eyes, through its predecessors. In a downbeat, naturalistic drama such as *Second Best*, this is a distraction. Hurt's self-restraint risks seeming mannered, a star's conceit as he is cast against type. The problem is heightened by his lack of rapport with his would-be foster son in the film. As James, the "problem child", Chris Cleary Miles is good at tantrums, but less effective when it comes to suggesting the character's vulnerability. It is perhaps an unfair comparison to make, but the performance that director Chris Menges elicits from him is nowhere near as convincing as the one Ken Loach managed to coax out of David Bradley in a similar part in *Kes*.

The parallels with Loach's picture, which Menges photographed, are apparent. As in *Kes*, landscape is used in symbolic fashion. The woods and hills are depicted as untrammelled, edenic territory where the boy can escape the strictures of adults. Perhaps, though, *Second Best* is a little too picturesque. Compared with Menges' directorial debut, the Shawn Slovo story *A World Apart*, in which the child's experiences growing up during apartheid are put in context by the political struggle going on around her, the drama here seems confined, even claustrophobic. David Cook's adaptation of his own novel is short on incident. The often inscrutable emotions of the characters are what matters. Elliptical flashback sequences, poetic motifs (for instance, time-lapse images of clouds racing across the sky) and various mementos—shells, torn photographs, old army emblems—are used to hint at the sense of loss Holt and James both feel. Throwaway details—the food Holt eats, his oppressive daily routine—take on weighty significance.

"Right now, you're not even a candidate to adopt my stick insect," Debbie, the social worker, barks out at a bewildered-looking Holt when he first tries to foster the boy. On one level, *Second Best* is yet another saga about a repressed, middle-aged man learning to confront his feelings and thereby redeeming his life. A curious aspect to the story is the way women are excluded. James is depicted as a budding little misogynist. He has nothing but hostility for his mother and for anybody who reminds him of her. In flashbacks to her suicide, we're not even shown her face. This particular psycho-drama is about fathers and sons. The boys don't seem to be able to work out their problems when there are women around.

It is hard not to admire the skill with which the film is crafted. Menges eschews the easy options of melodrama, but still manages to tell his story in pictures: the opening sequence, in which James's father plucks him away from school and hides out with him in the woods, features virtually no dialogue. The Welsh landscapes are lovingly photographed. It is also intriguing to see William Hurt act alongside the likes of Nerys Hughes, Jane Horrocks and Keith Allen.

However, just as Hurt's performance seems too studied in its modesty, there is something contrived about *Second Best* as a whole that stops it from tugging at the emotions in the way that might have been expected.

VILLAGE VOICE, 10/11/94, p. 66, Georgia Brown

More maddening because it's more emotionally grueling [the reference is to *The River Wild*] is Chris Menges's *Second Best*, recommended only to masochists. Menges (*A World Apart*) and writer David Cook, adapting his novel, put you through a wringer and then slap you with an ending so wrong it makes you retch.

It's a pity the movie misfires, since William Hurt does a fine job disguising himself as Graham Holt, a lonesome, frizzy-headed bachelor, postmaster in a picturesque Welsh village tentatively tending his aged dad. Chris Cleary Miles also is winning as James, the orphanage kid Graham decides to adopt. The boy's not so devious design is to get back together with his errant Dad, a sentimental con man who's been stringing the kid along for years. Quite improbably, the fussy old Graham loosens up the kid and gets loosened up himself.

The film abounds with flashbacks; it's a wonder there's any time for forward motion. Some of this is, as they say over there, treacle, though toward the end glimpses into James's past grow truly grim, even horrid. Since the filmmakers decide to explore psychologically loaded material, one, expects them to handle it with care. Expect in vain.

Also reviewed in:
CHICAGO TRIBUNE, 10/14/94, Friday/p. P, Mark Caro
NEW YORK TIMES, 9/30/94, p. C10, Janet Maslin
VARIETY, 9/19-25/94, p. 79, Todd McCarthy

SECRET ADVENTURES OF TOM THUMB, THE

A Zeitgeist Films release of a bolex brothers production for BBC Bristol/La Sept/Manga Entertainment Limited in association with Lumen Films. *Executive Producer:* Colin Rose and Thierry Garrel. *Producer:* Richard "Hutch" Hutchison. *Director:* Dave Borthwick. *Screenplay:* Dave Borthwick. *Editor:* Dave Borthwick. *Music:* Startled Insects. *Sound:* Andy Kennedy. *Sound Editor:* Chris Dickens. *Production Designer:* Dave Borthwick. *Set Dresser:* Cathy Price and Beverly Knowlden. *Costumes:* Jane Adams. *Make-up:* Jean Thurlow. *Animation:* Dave Borthwick, Frank Passingham, and Lee Wilton. *Running time:* 60 minutes. *MPAA Rating:* Not Rated.

WITH: Nick Upton; Deborah Collard; Frank Passingham; John Schofield; Mike Gifford; Robert Heath; George Brandt; Andy Davis; Dave Alex Riddett; Andy Joyce; Richard Goleszowski; Tim Norfolk; John Beedel; Andy McCormack; Brett Lane.

VOICES: Heln Veysey; Paul Veysey; Peter Townsend; Marie Clifford; Tim Hands; Andrew Bailey; Nick Upton; John Schofield.

LOS ANGELES TIMES, 1/13/95, Calendar/p. 4, Kevin Thomas

Once upon a time, in Dave Borthwick's dazzling "The Secret Adventures of Tom Thumb," a poor couple (Nick Upton, Deborah Collard) living in a single drab room off a dark alley are overjoyed when the wife gives birth to a baby boy so tiny he can be held in his father's hand.

The couple's happiness, however, is short-lived, for two sinister men, possibly government agents, snatch the tiny being, named Tom Thumb by his father, and take him to a laboratory, where the most bizarre experiments in mutation are taking place.

A masterwork of dark imagination two years in the making, the 61-minute, near-wordless English production combines live action and animation in such a way that the humans move jerkily like figures in the early "flickers" while its tiny people, creations of latex and foam over replicas of the human skeletons, move easily and seem completely alive. Tom Thumb, as he grows (a little) could indeed be E. T.'s brother and is just as endearing.

What Borthwick seems to have in mind is an allegory on the evil, corrupt human race, which has despoiled the planet to the extent that the insect kingdom is taking over the rule of the universe.

For all the bleakness of its concerns, it has a take-your-breath-away beauty and is a touching, though cautionary, work of consistently stunning imagination. Although all of a piece and truly original, the film echoes many others.

Its design and fatalistic vision suggests the influence of German Expressionism, Fritz Lang's "Metropolis" in particular, and Tom's new pal, Jack the Giant Killer, a sworn enemy of wicked "big people," wears a medieval uniform much like that of the title figure in "The Golem." The lab, which Tom and Jack vow to destroy, is an ultra-realistic metallic maze. Too intense for small children, "The Secret Adventures of Tom Thumb" is an unexpected pleasure for sophisticated adults.

It has been aptly paired with Peter Capaldi's 24-minute "Franz Kafka's "It's a Wonderful Life," which Capaldi has said was inspired by his slip of the tongue: however, Frank Capra and Franz Kafka have more in common than perhaps even Capaldi realizes.

Anyway, it's Christmas Eve and Kafka (Richard E. Grant) is working away in his garret experiencing a fearsome case of writer's block over the beginning sentence of his "Metamorphosis." His quandary is exacerbated by the sounds of Yuletide revelry and various interruptions. The way in which Capaldi resolves Kafka's crisis is clever and amusing.

NEW YORK POST, 4/13/94, p. 39, Thelma Adams

"The Secret Adventures of Tom Thumb" makes "Tim Burton's The Nightmare Before Christmas" look like "Thumbelina."

Opening today at the Film Forum with the Czech animated short "Food," Dave Borthwick's animated hour-long adventure is a grimmer than Grimm rendering of the tale of a thumb-sized boy born to full-sized parents.

Wee Tom is a freak of genetic engineering, delivered into a toxic, kill-first, ask-questions-later world. He is swiftly separated from his slovenly but devoted parents by wicked state agents.

The innocent imp lands in a lab where severed hands and mouths are kept alive in glass jars, crying and knocking to be set free. Rescued by a lizard-like mutant, Tom escapes.

Borthwick creates a grotesquely inspired landscape. It swarms with bugs. It bubbles with green chemical pools along filth-strewn banks.

A fierce forefinger-sized warrior adopts Tom. They struggle in the shadow of the valley of clumsy giants (Tom's father among them).

Using a 3-D technique known as pixilation, Borthwick animates live actors a frame at a time. Their actions seem more jerky and coarse than the fantastic clay models like Tom or his reptile pal. They use mumblespeak, a vaguely recognizable tongue that also serves to distance us from the "human" figures.

The result is a bleak yet passionate fable about being born different in an alien and squalid world, and the redemptive power of family love.

Skip lunch before you see Jan Svankmajer's "Food." It also uses pixilation, this time to achieve a gross and hilarious critique of human appetite and state suppression.

Breakfast, lunch and dinner are the three ravenous and frustrated segments of this Kafkaesque tour de farce.

If there's such an expression as "I'm so hungry, I could eat my own arm," here we see two starved diners who fail, to get their waiter's attention. The pair chow down on everything in sight from plates to shoe leather and, ultimately, each other.

Both movies share a sharp ugliness and are dazzlingly twisted. They're on the frontier of a brave new world of animation.

NEWSDAY, 4/13/94, Part II/p. B7, Joseph Gelmis

This is a truly weird animation program, in both style and content. The feature and short are horrific critiques of society that transform live actors into grotesque cartoon figures through a stop-action animation process called "pixilation."

With stop-motion filming of puppets, as in Tim Burton's "The Nightmare Before Christmas," the usual object is to create fluid lifelike movements by painstakingly filming slight changes in the puppet's limbs one frame at a time.

But in both "The Secret Adventures of Tom Thumb" and "Food," the stop process deliberately makes the live actors look like automatons. Their movements are jerky, their faces and bodies manipulated in some scenes to make them behave or look like puppets.

The technique is disturbing, because the actors appear repulsive, yet perversely fascinating and perfectly suited to the jaundiced view of human nature expressed by the two films.

Think of "Tom Thumb" as "Eraserhead Meets Jack the Giant-Killer." It's a dark mix of early David Lynch, the brothers Quay and the brothers Grimm. Made in Bristol, England, a burgeoning area for independent animation, the film pits giants (human actors) against little people (puppets and claymation creatures) in a squalid industrial wasteland. A pathetic mutant freak baby and a vengeful little hunter (Jack, who kills humans with poisoned darts) invade a laboratory where gruesome experiments are performed and Jack unleashes the world-destroying power of a genie imprisoned there.

Writer-editor-director Dave Borthwick fills the screen with appalling lower depths images of godforsaken ruins, piles of junk and garbage, and legions of vermin. The human actors obscenely grunt gibberish instead of words. If you enjoy allegorical subtexts and metaphorical images, you'll be kept busy decoding esoteric references. What's the meaning of the crucifix with a Santa Claus on the cross? And why that final ominous shot of flies forming a halo around the shadow of Tom Thumb's head in heaven, where he is reunited with his murdered parents?

"Food," by influential Czechoslovakian animator Jan Svankmajer, is an outrageous comic take on human hunger and gluttony. Of the three meals in the film, the most memorable occurs at a restaurant where two ravenous guys, unable to get a passing waiter to take their order, start eating their clothes, the dishes, cutlery, glasses, the table, and then each other.

Like most of Svankmajer's work, inspired by years of living in a police state, run first by the Nazis and then by the Communists, this strange black comedy resonates in the mind, as food for thought.

SIGHT AND SOUND, 1/94, p. 52, Leslie Felperin Sharman

An accident in an artificial sperm bank leads to a woman giving birth to a tiny mutant boy whom she and her husband name Tom. Masked men steal Tom, take him to a laboratory for tests, and kill his mother. With the help of a mutant creature, Tom escapes and meets a community of people his own size, apparently also victims of the laboratory. The leader of the little people, Jack, fancies himself a 'giant' slayer. He and Tom Thumb meet up with Tom's father, but the father is killed in a brawl. Using another full-sized man to gain access to the laboratory, Tom and Jack destroy the central power source, blowing up both themselves and the lab. In Heaven, Tom is reunited with his parents. The final image is of flies forming a halo around his shadow on the wall.

With the London-based live-action film industry suffering from a permanent state of anaemia, patriotic cinephiles can at least be proud of the robust health of the Bristol and South Wales animation scene. The output of Aardman Animations, Fairweather Films et al has mainly consisted of excellent shorts and television work. However, with the exception of the execrable British-Hungarian co-production *The Princess and the Goblin*, financing for full length features has been scarce. After making a ten-minute version, which caused an outrage when shown on BBC2 in 1988, small independent production company the bolexbrothers (founded by Dave Borthwick and Dave Riddett) managed to garner enough capital to make this striking film against the odds.

The dark revisionist retelling of a classic fairy tale is now a standard trope of independent animation story-telling, one that has received very different treatment by such diverse artists as Vera Neubauer (*Princesses*), Phil Mulloy (*Red Riding Hood*), and Paul Berry (*The Sandman*). The bolexbrothers project the story of Tom Thumb through the prism of science-fiction dystopia, enabling them to make sly digs at genetic engineering and animal testing, but it's more a mutation of the story than a wholesale destruction. Despite the emphasis on monstrosity, flecks of pathos shine through that may in particular move younger viewers (if they're not cowering under the seats in fear).

The animation itself is technically faultless. To combine 'pixilated' actors who move jerkily in tandem with animated models is no mean feat. Resisting the temptation to cheat with straight filming when no models are involved, the film makers have crafted a superbly integrated product, a coherent vision of a chaotic and disharmonious world, full of filth, detritus and lurid decay. It's so successful that one feels churlish in pointing out that, aesthetically, the film is a wee bit derivative.

The look of the seedy sets and mutant creatures owes much to the inevitable influences of Svankmajer and the Brothers Quay, the story is more accessible than the work of either. Tom himself bears a resemblance to the baby in *Eraserhead* while the laboratory and the sequences both recall *Brazil*. Also, the menagerie of twitching animated insects works as an affectionate homage to the early work of Wladislaw Starewicz, whose late work *Tale of the Fox* will be re-released just before this film's distribution. Nonetheless, the whole is greater than its slightly ragged parts, adding up to a mesmerising debut feature that bodes well for future work.

Also reviewed in:
CHICAGO TRIBUNE, 1/13/95, Tempo/p. 5, John Petrakis
NEW YORK TIMES, 4/13/94, p. C19, Caryn James
VARIETY, 1/10-16/94, p. 59, Derek Elley
WASHINGTON POST, 11/5/94, p. D6, Rita Kempley

SECRET RAPTURE, THE

A Castle Hill Productions release of a Greepoint Films production for the National Film Trustee Company in association with Channel Four Film/British Screen. *Producer:* Simon Relph. *Director:* Howard Davies. *Screenplay:* David Hare. *Director of Photography:* Ian Wilson. *Editor:* George Akers. *Music:* Richard Hartley. *Sound:* Danny Hambrook. *Sound Editor:* Peter Best. *Casting:* Jane Fothergill. *Production Designer:* Barbara Gosnold. *Art Director:* Fiona McNeil. *Costumes:* Consolata Boyle. *Make-up:* Jenny Shircore, Robert McCann and Ann McEwan. *Running time:* 96 minutes. *MPAA Rating:* R.

CAST: Juliet Stevenson (Isobel Coleridge); Joanne Whalley-Kilmer (Katherine Coleridge); Penelope Wilton (Marion French); Neil Pearson (Patrick Steadman); Alan Howard (Tom French); Robert Stephens (Max Lopert); Hilton McRae (Norman); Robert Glenister (Jeremy); Richard Long (3rd Businessman); Finty Williams (Greta); Saira Todd (Kiki); Julia Lane (June Allardyce); Philip Voss (Civil Servant); Diane Fletcher (Day Nurse); Janet Steel (Night Nurse); Christopher Hadfield (Young Robert); Peter Whitaker (Old Robert); Miranda Burton (Young Marion); Florence Hoath (Young Isobel); David Houri (Peter French); Jocelyn Barker (Sarah French).

LOS ANGELES TIMES, 6/10/94, Calendar/p. 4, Kevin Thomas

Over the years British playwright-screenwriter David Hare has taken grand passions with increasing seriousness, a dangerous development when his plots have come to resemble nothing so much as '40s melodramas. Under Howard Davies' ham-fisted direction, "The Secret Rapture," Hare's adaptation of his own play, swiftly descends to the level of lurid soap opera.

Before you think you've had a bad day, consider the plight of Juliet Stevenson's Isobel Coleridge. First, she's informed that her wanton, manipulative, alcoholic, recently widowed young stepmother Katherine (Joanna Whalley-Kilmer), who sits on the board of her London graphic design firm, has gone spectacularly off the wagon in public and has stabbed a potential client when he tells her he has passed on her company.

Isobel then catches Patrick (Neil Pearson), her live-in lover and business partner, cheating on her, then she's told off by her rich, cold, bitchy, jealous, obtuse older sister Marion (Penelope Wilton) for failing to control Katherine.

Never mind that it was Marion, in order to escape any responsibility for Katherine, who enlisted Patrick to help her pressure Isobel into accepting the idea that her—Marion's—husband (Alan Howard) should buy Isobel and Patrick's small but successful business and expand it greatly so as to give Katherine something to do—she's supposed to drum up business. All this and much, much more is every bit as ludicrous as it sounds.

It would seem that Hare wants to show us how a seemingly solid romantic and professional partnership such as Isobel and Patrick's can be undone by her blinding sense of duty to the reckless Katherine and by his vulnerability to the temptation of potential riches offered by Marion's buyout plan.

The big trouble is that all the constant shifting in allegiance and attitudes is breathtakingly abrupt and seems imposed from without by Hare rather than coming from within his characters. For example, we can conceive how Patrick could be enthusiastic about Marion's infusion of capital, but not when it includes Katherine's sure-to-be-disastrous involvement.

To pull off "The Secret Rapture's" escalating *Sturm und Drang* would require the mastery of an R. W. Fassbinder or an Andre Techiné, expert in playing against the old women's picture melodramatics with an affectionate bemusement while taking their heroines seriously and finding meaning in their plights. But this requires a sense of humor, something that in this instance neither Hare nor Davies possesses.

NEW YORK POST, 4/29/94, p. 41, Bill Hoffmann

"The Secret Rapture" is one of those gloomy "We're so Repressed" British soap operas that is so busy and top heavy with tragedy and angst that it never gets off the ground.

From the opening strains of a mournful trumpet to the startlingly dark photography (even during sunny scenes), you can sense this is one drama that won't lighten up, even for a second.

That's too bad, because "The Secret Rapture" has an intelligent premise and a top-flight cast, headed by stage actress Juliet Stevenson. It might have soared, if it wasn't so uncompromisingly bleak.

Stevenson plays Isobel, who along with her older sister, Marion (Penelope Wilton), are mourning the death of their father.

Dear old dad has left behind a beautiful alcoholic wife, Katherine (Joanne Whalley-Kilmer), who is younger than both his daughters and the black sheep of this proper British family.

Dad's dying wish was that the family take care of his wife. Isobel instinctively assumes that burden, allowing Katherine—after much verbal pushing and shoving to work at her graphic design business.

Instantly, Katherine is taking over, wheeling and dealing behind Isobel's back and even convincing older sister Marion to buy out the company so it can expand.

Predictably, this move spells disaster for the firm, as well as for the family's already strained relationships.

All of the performances are solid, but screenwriter David Hare ("Damage") is so busy moving the plot forward, he barely spends time establishing his characters.

The result: We really don't care. Add to this a relentless barrage of depressing dialogue and we *really* don't care.

Topping it all off is a violent, inappropriate ending with a fancy-schmancy touch.

You can't beat Britain for searing drawing room drama played by a smart set of Shakespearean-trained pros.

"Howard's End," "Enchanted April" and "The Remains of the Day" are perfect examples.

"Secret Rapture" is the exception that proves the rule.

NEWSDAY, 4/29/94, Part II/p. B9, Jack Mathews

The opening scene of "The Secret Rapture," adapted by David Hare from his play and directed by his British countryman Howard Davies, shows a grieving woman holding and kissing the face of a corpse. Her anguish appears to be that of a widow, trying desperately to lure her mate's spirit back into his body.

But, like most that follows in this dense and grotesquely bleak psychological journey, things aren't quite what they seem. The woman, we soon learn, is the dead man's daughter, and her troubles have just begun.

When "The Secret Rapture" was produced on stage in the late '80s, it was largely seen as a repudiation of the mood of greed spawned by the leadership of Margaret Thatcher. What the central character, Isobel Coleridge, grieved most for in her late father was the simple purity, the goodness, that seemed to have died with him.

That theme has been relegated to a barely perceptible subplot in the film, though Isobel's insecure older sister Marion (Penelope Wilton) and her wealthy husband Tom French (Alan Howard) again dictate the action with their money. But they're just catalysts in a story focusing on the disillusionment and emotional isolation forcing a seemingly assured woman to re-evaluate her life.

When her father's death calls her back to the stone farmhouse in which she and Marion grew up, Isobel (Juliet Stevenson, in a tour de force performance) is living a life of blissful routine, She and her lover Patrick (Neil Pearson) are partners in a small, successful graphic arts business, and enjoying a sexual relationship that threatens to crack the plaster in their London flat.

All that changes after Isobel returns from her father's funeral with her young stepmother in tow. Katherine (Joanne Whalley-Kilmer), an alcoholic and ex-prostitute who had married the old man for his kindness, is a piece of work. She insinuates herself in Isobel and Patrick's business, and persuades them to expand their operation with capital from Tom and Marion, and install Katherine as their sales manager.

The decision to sell out and lose their independence, made with Patrick's cooperation over Isobel's objections, is the beginning of the end of the couple's relationship, and eventually turns the story from a character study into a shockingly mundane melodrama, the last act dissolving into chaos, madness and murder.

If the business decision makes no sense for Isobel, it makes even less sense for the audience, who may find it impossible to believe she would allow Katherine and Marion to take over her life in the first place. The subtext of Hare's script makes the case that Isobel isn't the pillar of strength she, seems, that being spiritually cut off from her father has merely brought out the self-doubts that were always in her.

But Hare and Davies, a veteran theater director making his first foray into film, draws the other characters' weaknesses in such broad strokes, they seem to be inhabiting a different story from Isobel's.

"The Secret Rapture," like all of Hare's work, is thick with ambitious notions about family conflict, dependence and the thin line separating self-assurance from self-doubt, especially as they affect the lives of women in today's society. But the ambitions remain trapped in a story that seems to have lost its way from the stage to the screen.

SIGHT AND SOUND, 6/94, p. 60, Philip Kemp

Robert Coleridge dies at his Somerset home in the arms of his daughter Isobel. Her sister Marion, a junior Tory minister, arrives from London with her businessman husband Tom. After the funeral, the sisters discuss the problem of their stepmother—Robert's alcoholic, unstable young widow, Katherine. Against her better judgement, Isobel is persuaded to take Katherine back to London and give her a job in the small graphic design company she runs with her lover, Patrick. Patrick resents Katherine's disruptive, manipulative behaviour, but Isobel feels unable to get rid of her.

At Katherine's suggestion, Tom's company puts up expansion capital for the design business. Since this will mean losing control, Isobel objects but is outvoted when Patrick, enticed by the hope of big profits, agrees to the deal. The enlarged company moves into smart new offices, but Isobel is now too busy to have much time for Patrick, who starts an affair with his assistant, Greta. Katherine takes over the sales side, but when a record company fails to come through with an expected contract she goes berserk and stabs one of the executives. Isobel catches Patrick with Greta, and they have a violent row. After committing Katherine to hospital, she vanishes.

In Isobel's absence the firm collapses, and is sold off. When Isobel reappears, she smuggles Katherine out of the hospital and together they take refuge in Robert's old house, now deserted. Patrick shows up, obsessively seeking Isobel, and is let in by Katherine. He begs Isobel to take him back; when she refuses, he threatens her with a gun. As she walks out of the house, he shoots her dead. Marion and Tom come down for the funeral, but Marion finds herself unable to attend it. Left alone in front of the house, she calls out desolately for Isobel.

At the end of *The Secret Rapture* Marion French, rising junior Tory minister, realises that her sister's death has undermined her whole rationale for existence: "I can't remember why I was so angry. I was angry with Isobel the whole of my life. It marked me. I was angry with everyone. I don't know why ... Isobel, where are you? Why don't you come home?"

It's a speech that typifies the strengths and weaknesses of this adaptation of David Hare's 1988 play. As delivered by Penelope Wilton (recreating her stage role), it's powerful and moving. Yet at the same time it's a touch too stagey, too explicit in its spelling out of emotional patterns for the show-don't-tell medium of cinema. A film, of course, deserves to be judged in its own right; but when it sticks so closely to its source, it's hard not to keep recalling how much better this scene or that worked on stage.

The original production was directed by Howard Davies, here tackling his first film. To debut with material he was thoroughly familiar with was an understandable move, but maybe an ill-advised one; a better choice might have been something he could come to fresh. Though the action has been intelligently and unfussily opened up, a sense of the proscenium arch lingers over several scenes—and over some of the performances. Alan Howard betrays a tendency to orate, and there's a hammy (though mercifully brief) cameo from Robert Stephens.

But where the film gains, rather unexpectedly, is in playing down the affinity between personal and political that's central to all Hare's work. On stage *The Secret Rapture* evoked the exploitation by Thatcherite forces of the selfless and unmercenary impulses of those who still believed in society. By laying less stress on Marion's membership of the Thatcher government (a regime that spent most of its time being "angry with everyone"), and Tom's oily brand of God-endorsed profiteering, the film loses this allegorical dimension. Instead what emerges—thanks especially to the passionate complexity of Juliet Stevenson's performance—is a study of goodness as selfishness in its most lethal guise.

"There are people who wish me ill!" exclaims Isobel, as the revelation sinks in of what's being done to her. Stevenson delivers the line with not a hint of reproach or self-pity, but with a fierce joy; this at last is her justification for being. The title, Hare has explained, refers to the moment when a nun looks to be reunited with Christ in death, and Isobel wills her own destruction like a martyr. Goodness needs, and if necessary will create, its opposite. "All my life, people have said, 'Isobel's the nice one'," Marion complains, with the bitterness of one forced into a role she never chose. Filmed plays often try to expand the scope of the original; *The Secret Rapture* narrows it down to the moral killing-ground between the characters, and is all the better for it.

VILLAGE VOICE, 5/10/94, p. 62, Eileen D. Callinan

I remember hearing the bells tolling for my grandmother outside the church where they recited the eulogy for her final mass. Later, while we struggled to cope with the business of dissolving her estate, all hell broke loose between my mother and her sister, as if my grandmother's presence had maintained an unspoken law and order, keeping old grievances in check until her passing.

The Secret Rapture speaks to these crises, which death inevitably leaves for the living. Two English sisters' volatile relationship becomes a living hell after their father dies, leaving them to deal with an alcoholic stepmother (Joanne Whalley-Kilmer) who's younger than both sisters. Isobel (Juliet Stevenson) is a lot like her father and was his favorite child. Marion (Penelope Wilton), her older sister, always hated her for that. Isobel has come to a turning point in her relationship with her sister. Their kinship wasn't woven from the thread of love and mutual respect, as she had always thought; now it has faded and is falling apart.

Isobel's relationship with her boyfriend, Patrick (Neil Pearson), also begins to unravel when stepmom Katherine comes to live and work with them. Tension starts to fray all their lives. Until this point, Patrick and Isobel's relationship was hot. Cinematographer Ian Wilson casts a dangerously dark light through the horizontal slats of Isobel's blinds, zebra-striping their bodies, illuminating their steamy sexual chemistry. Isobel eventually leaves the family, then reemerges like a phoenix reborn from her own emotional ashes. She begins to take her life into her own hands; at one point, in her childhood home, she lights dozens of candles, suggesting an escape from the darkness of her past.

The film's final moments move from the slow spiral of a love affair toward the dismal abyss of rejection, betrayal, and the ultimate violence. Marvelously acted, directed, and filmed, *The Secret Rapture*'s multilayering of relationships delves into the lives of a British family at a thrilling emotional pace, creating a mood that resonates long beyond the final dissolve.

Also reviewed in:
CHICAGO TRIBUNE, 2/2/94, Friday/p. L, Michael Wilmington
NEW YORK TIMES, 4/29/94, p. C15, Stephen Holden
VARIETY, 9/20/93, p. 29, Leonard Klady

SECUESTRO: A STORY OF A KIDNAPPING

An E.M. Films release. *Producer:* Camilla Motta. *Director (Spanish with English subtitles):* Camila Motta. *Director of Photography:* Barry Ellsworth. *Editor:* Holly Fisher. *Music:* German Arreta and Nicholas Uribe. *Running time:* 92 minutes. *MPAA Rating:* Not Rated.

NEW YORK POST, 1/19/94, p. 30, Thelma Adams

In Colombia, a kidnapping occurs every seven hours.

In many documentaries, attention lapses after seven minutes.

Not so "Secuestro: A Story of Kidnapping," which starts a two-week run today at the Film Forum. First-timer Camila Motta tears off a challenging subject: the kidnapping of her sister, Sylvia, from the streets of Bogota by 10 armed men and the subsequent negotiations to win her freedom.

Motta's tense docu-thriller is part anatomy of a kidnapping, part dissection of a society ripped between the haves and have-nots.

On one side is Camila's father, Arturo, a wealthy businessman with the looks of a chinless Jean-Paul Belmondo. On the other, the faceless kidnappers, known only as "Frank," who are heard in a series of 20 taped conversations—crime sound-bites—that make up the telephone negotiations for Sylvia's life.

The kidnappers are professionals. They have a goal, says Arturo, "and it's entirely financial."

Motta exploits this tension: Arturo and "Frank" share a common ground as they dicker, trying to cut the best possible deal. As in "New Jack City," which set up a parallel between urban drug lords and Wall Street raiders, Motta presents her father and the kidnappers as mirror images in a shared drive for profit.

As the camera flows seamlessly from the gorgeous neighborhood where Camila was raised to the rutted, dirt roads of the barrio where Sylvia was held captive for three months, Motta suggests that the criminals are part of a political redistribution of wealth in divided Colombia.

There are shades of Patty Hearst, the kidnapped San Francisco heiress turned radical guerrilla, on the streets of Bogota. Camila—a Colombia-born, New York-educated daughter of privilege—might not agree with the kidnappers' methods, but she makes their motives understandable.

Similarly, Sylvia, interviewed after her release, describes her affectionate parting from a female captor. "I gave her some of my gold chains so she'd remember me," says the victim.

The kidnappers bank on this identification. By assigning a "good" guard, the abductors hope to ensure the victim won't crack.

Surprisingly cool in her approach, Camila Motta makes an arresting debut. Bolstered by an excellent team—including cinematographer Barry Ellsworth, editor Holly Fisher, and composers German Arrieta and Nicolas Uribe—this is among the most creatively complex and insightful documentaries in recent years.

"Secuestro: A Story of a Kidnapping" is gripping from start to finish.

NEWSDAY, 1/19/94, Part II/p. 59, John Anderson

Writer, director and producer Camila Motta proves in "Secuestro: The Story of Kidnapping," that she has talent for arresting visuals and narrative tension. That she was willing to take considerable chances in telling her story, which concerns a three-month-long Colombian abduction. And that she had the good sense to ignore the idea that a filmmaker can be too close to his or her subject to render it clearly.

How close? The abductee was her sister, Sylvia who was 20 and on her way to school when 10 armed men snatched her off a small road outside Bogota. She spent the next three months (March-June, 1985) chained to a bed in a 9-by-12-foot room, while her father negotiated her freedom. "I felt death," Arturo Motta says, recalling the phone call telling him his daughter had been seized But then, businessman that he is, he proceeded to execute the art of the deal, with. Sylvia's life hanging in the balance.

As the film informs us, a kidnaping takes place in Colombia every seven hours, so it really is big business. And that's how Arturo plays it.

Camila Motta doesn't argue against this, as her father explains, coming to an agreement too soon with such an unknown and perhaps inexperienced criminal element might have endangered his daughter as much as playing hard ball.

But as Sylvia's price drops from 30 million pesos ($450,000) to 15, to 10, we also hear the voice of the victim—who suffered a kind of sensory deprivation during her captivity—wondering if enough was being done to rescue her, wondering whether her family would get used to her absence. Wondering whether she'd ever get out at all.

We don't see Sylvia until the story reaches the point where she's free. And the director, by constantly moving her camera around Bogota in a kind of directionless search, evokes the feeling of utter futility that affected the Motta family.

We're shown the day-to-day life of Bogota's streets, but except for interviews with one of kidnapers' confederates, the perpetrators are a faceless bunch, whom we are exposed to only in the taped conversations with Arturo Motta and in mug shots shown late int he film.

By overlapping the voices of the principals and some supposed experts—one of whom waxes inane about Colombia's heritage of violence being a result of the Spanish Conquest—Camila Motta creates palpable tension, confusion and considerable drama.

Cinematographer Barry Ellsworth, who contributed the stunning black-and-white photography in Todd Haynes' "Poison" a few years ago (and is Motta's co-producer) creates impressionistic re-enactments of Sylvia's captivity—the Parchesi game she plays with her captors is rendered ominous—and re-enactments of the abduction. This is heretical documentary technique, perhaps, but in terms of making Sylvia's story as effective and moving as possible, it's brilliant.

She has, through talent and tenacity, re-created a crime and a moment whose emotional impact otherwise would have been lost.

VILLAGE VOICE, 1/25/94, p. 62, Amy Taubin

An unlikely mix of *Hard Copy* and avant-garde signature effects, *Secuestro: A Story of a Kidnapping* is a seriously intended but superficial documentary about a recent form of entrepreneurial activity in Colombia. In 1985, Sylvia Motta, the 20-year-old daughter of an upper-middle-class industrialist, was kidnapped and held for three months while the kidnappers and her father negotiated the conditions of her release. The negotiations followed a predictable pattern—in Colombia, a kidnapping occurs once every seven hours. Claiming redistribution of wealth as a justification, professional kidnappers set a high price on the abducted, knowing that they will eventually settle for roughly 12 per cent of their original demand.

Using tape recordings of telephone conversations between pater Motta and the kidnappers as a basis for her narrative, filmmaker Camila Motta (sister of the victim) reconstructs the ritualized business dealings that led to Sylvia's release. The conversations— Brecht couldn't have written them better—are played back over disjunctive, cleanly photographed images of urban decay; to avoid being traced the kidnappers apparently used every public phone booth in Bogotá.

Motta fleshes out the film with talking heads: the father, the police chief, one of the kidnappers, Sylvia herself, and an unidentified political theorist. Because of the hyperactive editing, none of them gets a chance to speak more than two consecutive sentences. Sylvia mentions that she got pretty angry with her father for taking so long to make a deal, but this admission passes like an aside. Every now and then, a bit optically printed, semi-abstract, slo-mo imagery is introjected to indicate Sylvia's anxiety in captivity. An avant-garde filmmaking cliché, it's far less expressive of Sylvia's subjectivity than would have been her answers to a few thoughtfully formulated questions.

Also reviewed in:
NEW YORK TIMES, 1/19/94, p. C20, Stephen Holden

SERIAL MOM

A Savoy Pictures release of a Polar Entertainment production. *Executive Producer:* Joseph Caracciolo, Jr. *Producer:* John Fielder and Mark Tarlov. *Director:* John Waters. *Screenplay:* John Waters. *Director of Photography:* Robert M. Stevens. *Editor:* Janice Hampton and Erica Huggins. *Music:* Basil Poledouris. *Music Editor:* Tom Villano. *Sound:* Rick Angelella and (music) Rick Riccio. *Sound Editor:* John Nutt. *Casting:* Paula Herold and Pat Moran. *Production Designer:* Vincent Peranio. *Art Director:* David J. Bomba. *Set Dresser:* Michael Sabo and Lianne Williamson. *Special Effects:* Joey DiGaetano. *Costumes:* Van Smith. *Costumes (Kathleen Turner):* Cindy Flowers. *Make-up:* Betty Beebe. *Make-up (Kathleen Turner):* Tom Case. *Stunt Coordinator:* Steve M. Davison. *Running time:* 93 minutes. *MPAA Rating:* R.

CAST: Kathleen Turner (Mom/Beverly Sutphin); Sam Waterston (Dad/Eugene Sutphin); Ricki Lake (Misty Sutphin); Matthew Lillard (Chip Sutphin); Scott Wesley Morgan (Detective Pike); Walt MacPherson (Detective Gracey); Justin Whalin (Scotty); Patricia Dunnock (Birdie); Lonnie Horsey (Carl); Mink Stole (Dottie Hinkle); Mary Jo Catlett (Rosemary Ackerman); John Badila (Mr. Stubbins); Kathy Fannon (Mrs. Sterner); Doug Roberts (Mr. Sterner); Traci Lords (Carl's Date); Tim Caggiano (Marvin Pickles); Jeff Mandon (Howell Hawkins); Colgate Salsbury (Father Boyce); Patsy Grady Abrams (Mrs. Jenson); Richard Pilcher (Herbie Hebden); Beau James (Timothy Nazlerod); Stan Brandorff (Judge); Kim Swann (Lu-Ann Hodges); Suzanne Somers (Herself); Bus Howard (Gus); Alan J. Wendl (Sloppy); Patricia Hearst (Juror #8); Nancy Robinette (Jury Forewoman); Peter Bucossi (Rookie Cop); Loretto McNally (Policewoman); Wilfred E. Williams (Press A); Joshua L. Shoemaker (Court TV Reporter); Rosemary Knower (Court Groupie A); Susan Lowe (Court Groupie B); John Calvin Doyle (Carl's Brother); Mary Vivian Pearce (Book Buyer); Brigid Berlin (Mean Lady); Jordan Brown (Police Officer); Anthony "Chip" Brienza (Vendor); Jeffrey Pratt Gordon (Flea Market Boy); Shelbi Clarke (Flea Market Girl); Nat Benchley (Macho Man); Kyf Brewer (Dealer); Teresa R. Pete (Baby's Mother); Zachary S. Pete (Church Baby); Richard Pelzman (Doorman); Chad Bankerd (Kid A); Johnny Alonso (Kid B); Robert Roser (Kid C); Mike Offenheiser (Joe Flowers); Lee Hunsaker (Girl); Michael S. Walter (Burglar A); Mojo Gentry (Burglar B); Gwendolyn Briley-Strand (Mrs. Taplotter); Jennifer Mendenhall (Reporter); Joan Rivers (Herself); Catherine Anne Hayes (TV Serial Hag); Susan Duvall (Lady C); Valerie Yarborough (Press); Jordan Young (Kid); John A. Schneider (Husband A); Lyrica Montague (Court Clerk).

LOS ANGELES TIMES, 4/13/94, Calendar/p. 1, Peter Rainer

It's official: Mainstream John Waters is weirder than underground John Waters. "Serial Mom," his latest and one of his best, is like an early '60s TV sitcom that keeps lunging into profane naughtiness. Waters builds our disbelief of shows like "Leave It to Beaver" and "Ozzie and Harriet" right into the movie; he animates our fantasies of what these spic-and-span people might *really* be like.

He also builds into "Serial Mom" the no-brained affection we have for those shows. Waters, like David Lynch, can't truly be called a subversive filmmaker or a satirist because he shares most of the middle-class values he pokes. That's why he's a naughty black comic and not an enraged one. Deep down he wishes life were like "Leave It to Beaver."

But in the meantime there's the real world of serial murders and mania to contend with. Waters' conceit in "Serial Mom" is to give us a June Cleaver type—Kathleen Turner's Beverly Sutphin—who is also a serial murderer on the sly.

She's not the usual predator, though. Even though she cherishes her shoe box filled with tapes from Ted Bundy and letters from Richard Speck, her rampages are almost always in defense of her family—her meek dentist husband Eugene (Sam Waterston) and daughter Misty (Ricki Lake), who is having boyfriend trouble, and son Chip (Matthew Lillard), who works in a video store and has a yen for ultra-gore films. She's a valiant fantasy Mom—the kind of Mother Courage who will impale her daughter's no-good boyfriend with a lance and leave his liver flapping; or run down the high school math teacher who foolishly suggests her son's gore fixation could do with a bit of therapy. Make no mistake: This is a pro-family values film.

Part of the fun in "Serial Mom" is seeing what sets Beverly off. It's usually not what you expect. (After the law catches up with her, at her trial, a juror played by Patty Hearst is seen wearing white shoes *after* Labor Day—a fashion no-no for Beverly of homicide-inducing proportions.)

Those '60s sitcom mothers were all-of-a-piece with the TV commercial housewives who were (and still are) forever fretting over household odors and spots. Beverly carries that fretting to its nut-brain conclusion: She's so hemmed in by her chirpy PTA-and-cornflakes life that even the slightest deviations drive her wild. (She's like a campier female version of Terry O'Quinn's serial murderer husband in "The Stepfather" who couldn't abide any cracks in his sitcom comfiness.) Waters gets at the freakiness inside all that peachy-keen rigor.

"Serial Mom" is also a jab at the supposed uplift provided by "wholesome" TV shows and movies. With all the ruckus raised in the media about the harmful effects of on-screen violence and sex, "Serial Mom" weighs in for the other side: It implies that it's the antiseptic family entertainments that may have done us the real harm. The *real* nut cases in the movie aren't the hormonally inflamed teen-agers and avenging matriarchs. It's the suburban Baltimore do-gooders, the upright judges and deacons—you know, the pillars of society.

Kathleen Turner jump-started her stardom as a film noir femme fatale in "Body Heat" but her Garbo-esque smokiness and throaty come-hithers always camouflaged a wicked comic gift. As the hit woman in "Prizzi's Honor," her infatuated deadpan was hilariously apt; in her funniest role, in the neglected "The Man With Two Brains," she zigged to Steve Martin's every zag. (Quite a feat.)

Turner is one of those actresses who always seems partially zonked—fogged in by her own self-absorption. But she's smart enough to play around with her zonkiness. In "Serial Mom," Beverly's avidity for wasting the opposition is so furiously funny that you can see why she can't stop herself—she's having way too much fun. It's the joy that comes from clearing the air and clobbering complacencies.

Waters indulges in a few too many cute tricks, such as periodically flashing the date and time of the action on the screen, "Law & Order"-style, and sometimes his mimicking of straight-arrow TV shows is too close for comfort to the shows themselves. But this double-image effect is part of what makes "Serial Mom" distinctive. It's not just Waters' riff on old TV sitcoms. It's also his *ode* to those shows.

The movie also probably comes closer to how we actually relate to the current wave of serial carnage than a lot of the more "serious" fare. Waters plays it as giddy black comic vaudeville, and that connects up with our helplessness. The joke in this movie is that killers attract stardom and groupies and have TV movies made about them. (Beverly's life will be re-enacted by Suzanne Somers.) It is, of course, a real-life joke.

It's not that Waters set out to make a social statement here. It's just that the landscape and his mindscape turn out to be a perfect fit.

God help us all.

NEW YORK POST, 4/13/94, p. 35, Thelma Adams

Imagine Mrs. Cleaver wielding a cleaver and you've got "Serial Mom."

Wearing white shoes after Labor Day? Not buckled up? Refuse to recycle? Forget to floss? You might have made Mom's day.

Meet Beverly Sutphin (Kathleen Turner). She's so cheerful, she's scary. But even the Beaver's mother must have had a dark side—and if anyone could mine it for its black comic potential, it's writer/director John Waters.

Kathleen Turner steps into a role tailor-made for Waters' muse, the late Divine. The cross-dressing diva achieved cult status performing trampy, unthinkable acts in the midnight movie classic "Pink Flamingos."

Just before his untimely death, Divine played supermom to Ricki Lake's teen sweetheart in the irrepressible "Hairspray," Waters' most mainstream, commercially successful comedy.

Turner's almost enough woman to follow in Divine's size 14, triple-Es. In fact, with her over-the-top female energy, Turner's almost too much woman for conventional leads.

Turner turned up the "Body Heat," and saved "Prizzi's Honor." Now, her Beverly Sutphin bursts the seams of her Land's End khaki skirt.

Whether serving the perfect meat loaf, recycling to Barry Manilow's "Daybreak," or removing wiggling entrails from the tip of a fire poker, Beverly bristles with good health and well-being.

As Beverly's dentist husband, sober Sam Waterston ("I'll Fly Away") provides Turner with the perfect foil. His mild-mannered Eugene Sutphin is delightfully ineffective. Weak about the mouth, baby browns slightly watery, Waterston takes the understanding papa to the outer limits without being campy.

"Your mother may have some problems, that's all, son," Waterston reassures his son—even after dad has found letters from Richard Speck addressed to Beverly and a tape from Ted Bundy tucked under his mattress.

Rounding out the suburban Baltimore family are Waters' discovery Ricky Lake as Misty, a boy-crazed flea market entrepreneur, and Matthew Lillard as Chip, a horror enthusiast whose favorite movie is "Blood Feast."

The director takes advantage of his blue-chip cast and piles on strong support from Waters' regular, Mink Stole, as a terrorized neighbor and cameos by Suzanne Somers, convicted felon/heiress Patty Hearst, and former porn pinup Traci Lords.

Waters has toned down his taste for the grotesque but, given his extreme beginnings, there's enough blood on the windshield of the family station wagon to gross out those unfamiliar with Baltimore's most infamous son.

The setup of "Serial Mom" is deliriously funny. When Waters cuts to the chase, the plot bogs down. A final courtroom scene with Beverly defending herself revives the pace. Turner's manic energy is contagious. '

Even when the pacing sags, there's always something deliciously quirky happening on screen. Who can resist such inspired throwaways as Joan Rivers hosting a show on "serial hags: women who love men who mutilate"?

NEWSDAY, 4/13/94, Part II/p. B7, Jack Mathews

Though she started her movie career as a sultry femme fate in Lawrence Kasdan's "Body Heat," Kathleen Turner never seemed more comfortable on screen than when she is doing comedy. Broad slut comedy, as in "The Man With Two Brains"; romantic adventure comedy, as in the two "Romancing the Stone" movies, and cynical black comedy, as in "Prizzi's Honor" and "The War of the Roses."

But never has she relished a role with the abandon she brings to Beverly Sutphin, the mad-as-a-hatter, buoyantly homicidal suburban housewife in John Waters' hysterical "Serial Mom."

Beverly Sutphin is June Cleaver with the soul of Charles Manson. She's a woman with a Pinesol twinkle who sends her family off with a good breakfast, separates her recyclables from her disposables, then spends her day making obscene phone calls and bumping off offensive neighbors.

Although Beverly collects books and memorabilia on serial killers, and has tucked away an autographed photo of Richard Speck and a personal audio letter from Ted Bundy, she is more of a matriarchal mass murderer, targeting anyone who shows bad manners—a person who would pull into her parking space at a supermarket, say, or make the mistake of being rude to her dentist husband, Eugene (Sam Waterston); their lovesick daughter, Misty (Ricki Lake), or their gore-film worshipping son, Chip (Matthew Lillard).

Waters, who's made a career parodying the feel-good American middle-class myth, missed a good opportunity by ending his story in a courthouse instead of on a TV talk show (or maybe he decided that would have been too tacky even for him). And those who've been waiting for him to return to the scatological sexual perversity of his early cult films will again be disappointed.

"Serial Mom" is a lot raunchier than either of his previous attempts at a mainstream hit, the PG-rated "Hairspray" and the PG-13 "Cry-Baby," but there are none of the dung, bug or dogfood-eating scenes for which he's famous, no 300-pound transvestites wrestling with a girdle. With the exception of one scene, in which Beverly removes a fire poker from the back of a victim and finds a chunk of kidney clinging to it, this is an amazingly restrained piece of sick filmmaking.

Sick and slick. Though it has a contemporary setting, with corner video stores, flea markets and the metal funk music of a group called L7, the Sutphins' neighborhood is center-cut '50s television suburbia. The sets are designed and lighted like "Father Knows Best," and the tone is as persistently cheerful as a Doris Day medley.

Turner has taken on this role at exactly the right moment in her career, when her own outsized image is in need of some self-parody, and she is clearly having the time of her life. When she turns that husky voice into a telephone weapon, screaming creative obscenities at poor Dottie Hinkle (Waters regular Mink Stole), both she and the audience may be doubled-over with laughter.

Waters' movies have always been too silly to have any real satiric punch, and in his attempts to gross out audiences in his early underground films, he was merely tossing them crumbs. The more he gave them, the more they wanted, and the farther he got from the mainstream audience he now covets.

All that is irrelevant to the new generation of moviegoers likely to make "Serial Mom" his most commercial movie. John Waters, and perhaps Kathleen Turner, begin new careers today.

SIGHT AND SOUND, 6/94, p. 60, Kim Newman

Baltimore. Outwardly an ideal homemaker, Beverly Sutphin is the devoted wife of dentist Eugene and the caring mother of college student daughter Misty and high school kid son Chip. However, ever since neighbour Dottie Hinkle stole her parking place at the market, Beverly has been harassing the woman with obscene phone calls. Summoned to Chip's school by a teacher concerned with the boy's addiction to gory horror movies, Beverly runs the offending man down and kills him. Then, when Misty's boyfriend Carl two-times her, Beverly murders him with a poker.

The police suspect Beverly but can prove nothing. When Eugene has to work over a weekend, Beverly reacts by murdering a patient who has taken insufficient care of his teeth and also dispatches his snoopy wife. As evidence piles up against Beverly, the police try to arrest her at church; she escapes with the help of Chip and his girlfriend Birdie, who give her a place to hide at the video store where Chip has a job.

Learning that a patron consistently refuses to rewind tapes she rents, Beverly tracks the woman down and bludgeons her to death with a leg of lamb, then takes off in pursuit of Scott, one of Chip's friends, who has witnessed the crime. Beverly corners Scott at a rock concert and sets fire to him as a punishment for refusing to wear a seatbelt and is cheered by the crowd as she is arrested.

Acting in her own defence at the trial, Beverly convinces the jury that she is a victim of circumstantial evidence. Acquitted, she immediately murders a juror who has been wearing white shoes after Labor Day. Suzanne Somers, cast in a TV movie based on the case, arrives to pose with Beverly for publicity photographs and angers the Serial Mom by forcing her to be photographed from her bad side ...

Though it seems like band-wagon-jumping to add another film to the already groaning serial killer shelf, John Waters has been interested in the inter-relationship of homicidal depravity and celebrity since his early, underground efforts. After his ventures into almost moral musical matters (*Hairspray, Cry-Baby*), *Serial Mom* finds 'the Pope of Trash' returning to the themes and approaches of such efforts as *Pink Flamingos, Female Trouble* and *Polyester*, with Kathleen Turner effectively replacing the late Divine in the role of the gleefully moralist murderess. As in *Pink Flamingos*, the plot is merely an excuse for the heroine to perpetrate a series of atrocities against good taste by doing horrendous things to cartoonishly hateful secondary characters, while as in *Female Trouble*, the protagonist's crimes win her a position as a pop culture heroine.

Asides of Joan Rivers doing a show on Serial Hags (women who love mass murderers); Beverly treasuring an autographed photograph of Richard Speck; a personal taped message from Ted Bundy; and the Sutphin family selling off 'Serial Mom' memorabilia outside Beverly's trial—all these are amusing but obvious skits on the whole phenomenon of the media canonisation of mass murder. But they are also merely afterthoughts to the nightclub execution finale of *Female Trouble*, which nearly twenty years ago anticipated both the social trend and Waters' satire of it.

Though Turner delivers a perfectly modulated performance that shows just how limited Divine was as a performer, the professional qualities of *Serial Mom* serve to distance it from the home movie look and village panto acting of Waters' earliest efforts. Waters has reached a level of technical competence but little else: though nicely shot and helped by a good score by Basil Poledouris and fine acting, this still lurches from joke to joke, just like *Pink Flamingos*.

Waters seems to be stranded between defiant amateurism and simple middle-of-the-road ineptitude. Laughs keep coming, whether from Turner's eerie simper or at stray lines (like Chip's reference to the video patron's rudeness: "Must be from watching all those family films"), but there is something insubstantial about Waters' satire of sit-com suburbia, coming after the funnier or more disturbing likes of *Parents, The Stepfather, Society* or *Blue Velvet*.

Waters remains an innovator with an identity crisis: his concerns have been influential and his films are impressive if taken one by one, but his range is too narrow to sustain a satisfying body of work. That said, it's hard to dislike a movie which includes Kathleen Turner singing along to "(The Sun'll Come Up) Tomorrow" from *Annie* as she takes a leg of lamb to the head of the woman who won't rewind her video tapes.

VILLAGE VOICE, 4/19/94, p. 49, J. Hoberman

Is there any space left for John Waters—I mean, after Howard Stern? An aesthete as well as a moralist, a Manson fan long before it became chic, the baddest bad boy of '70s indies has had his work cut out reinventing himself as a middle-aged punk.

With *Serial Mom*, Waters concludes the nostalgic digression of period pieces *Hairspray* and *CryBaby*, returning to the critique of the American family he last articulated in *Polyester*. Statistics suggest that serial murder is overwhelmingly the province of white males between the ages of 20 and 40, many of them traumatized by childhood abuse. Waters's premise short-circuits this domestic drama to make the real killer ... Mom, played with her customary ferocity by the game Kathleen Turner.

Like *Psycho*, the standard Hollywood take on the subject before *The Silence of the Lambs* reconfigured the victim and set one serial killer to catch another, Waters's film is an example of neo-Momism. In the midst of World War II, Philip Wylie's best-selling *Generation of Vipers* had presented the American mother as a domineering, hypocritical monster of repression; the heroine of *Serial Mom* is all that and more.

Married to a suburban dentist (Sam Waterston), Turner bans chewing gum in the house but makes hilariously obscene calls to her anxious, geeky neighbor (Waters regular Mink Stole), soothes her soul with the sounds of Barry Manilow yet treasures a tabloid atrocity scrapbook complete with autographed picture of mass-murderer Richard Speck. Does Turner embody the schizoid nature of the American media? Is she a secret surrealist? Or just a sitcom *baleboosteh* so well organized that she can excuse herself from dinner, commit a gruesome double murder, and still get home in time to serve her family dessert?

Serial Mom occasionally hints at some more systemic form of repression, as when Waters contrives to have the police burst in on a teenage onanist in flagrante. (There's also the submerged gag that, addicted to celluloid gore, disgusted by the idea of adult sexuality, and saddled with an insane mother, Turner's son is himself a nascent killer.) But, despite some zesty gross-outs or a shock close-up of a tooth being drilled, *Serial Mom* is essentially a one-joke movie. A zillion squad cars trail Turner and her family as they drive to church as though waiting for the star's latest outrage. The ensuing sequence, complete with organist playing "There's a Place for Us" and sermon on capital punishment, is the most suggestively tasteless in the movie, but it's capped by a rote bit where Turner hawks a loogie on a crying baby and escapes in the confusion.

"Do you think I need a lawyer?" Turner wonders once she has been apprehended. "You need an agent!" her media-wise children advise her. (Not for nothing is their house a treasure trove of Pee-wee Herman collectibles.) Celebrated by Baltimore punks, she becomes a T-shirt madonna, "a new face in the deck of serial-killer trading cards." As a meditation on crime and celebrity, *Serial Mom* remakes *Female Trouble*—the 1974 masterpiece that Waters made with his profits from *Pink Flamingos*. (Touted for Turner's role in the made-for-TV movie, Suzanne Somers disrupts the trial and battles the defendant for camera angles.) But, unlike *Female Trouble*, which ends with Divine in the electric chair, the film's equivalent to winning an Academy Award, *Serial Mom* feels thin and inconsistent.

Although illustrating Waters's epigram that "all people look better under arrest," *Serial Mom* is what film critic Robin Wood would call an "incoherent text." Turner alone encompasses Waters's characteristic narrative structure—pitting one repressed and judgmental clan against a trashier but more free-spirited group. Her character is not quite p.c. and not entirely bourgeois conformist. Certain killings are a function of motherhood (she punishes her son's math teacher and daughter's errant boyfriend) while some imply a more socially conscious sense of order. Failure to floss (altruistic in a dentist's wife), indifference to recycling are capital offenses. Still other murders are punishment for style crimes.

If little more than a riff on the fascination of serial murder, *Serial Mom* is nothing if not topical. The Voice runs a cover story on the subculture of serial-killer fans. *The New York Review of Books* publishes Joyce Carol Oates on Jeffrey Dahmer et al. "Somehow it has happened that the 'serial killer' has become our debased, condemned, yet eerily glorified Noble Savage, the vestiges of the frontier spirit ..." *Multiple Maniacs* has never seemed more prophetic. (If *The New York Review* had an ounce of wit, they'd have assigned Waters rather than Elizabeth Hardwick to critique the Menendez case.)

Just as Nick Broomfield's documentary *Aileen Wuornos: The Selling of a Serial Killer* is like a nightmare remake of *Pink Flamingos* in which Wuornos (a natural role for Divine) and the lover who sold her out compete against her fat hippie lawyer (also Divine), her mercenary "born again" adoptive mother, and the Florida State police for the title of "the filthiest people alive," so Joey Buttafuoco and Tonya Harding, Lorena and John Wayne Bobbitt (whose joint accomplishment was anticipated by a single throwaway gag in *Desperate Living*) are Waters characters.

Serial Mom is only intermittently amusing and scarcely ever shocking, but John Waters doesn't have to run for governor. Thanks to Oprah, Geraldo, and Court TV, American social reality has already become one of his films.

Also reviewed in:
CHICAGO TRIBUNE, 4/15/94, Friday/p. C, Michael Wilmington
NEW YORK TIMES, 4/13/94, p. C15, Caryn James
NEW YORKER, 5/2/94, p. 108, Anthony Lane
VARIETY, 4/4-10/94, p. 35, Todd McCarthy
WASHINGTON POST, 4/15/94, p. D1, Rita Kempley
WASHINGTON POST, 4/15/94, Weekend/p. 44, Joe Brown

SEX OF THE STARS, THE

A First Run Features release of a Les Productions du Regard & Bloom Films production with the participation of Telefilm Canada/SOGIC/ONFC/Les Productions Constellation Inc. *Producer:* Pierre Gendron and Jean-Roch Marcotte. *Director:* Paule Baillargeon. *Screenplay (French with English subtitles):* Monique Proulx. *Director of Photography:* Eric Cayla. *Editor:* Hélène Girard. *Music:* Yves Laferrire. *Sound:* Richard Besse and Viateur Paiement. *Production*

Designer: Real Ouellette. *Costumes:* Gaudeline Sauriol and Christiane Tessier. *Running time:* 104 minutes. *MPAA Rating:* Not Rated.

CAST: Denis Mercier (Marie-Pierre); Marianne-Coquelicot Mercier (Camille); Tobie Pelletier (Lucky); Sylvie Drapeau (Michèle); Luc Picard (J. Boulet); Giles Renaud (Jacob); Jean-René Ouellet (The Cruiser); Danielle Proulx (The Singer); Paul Dion (Man in the Bar); Kim Yaroshevskaya (Building Caretaker); Gisèle Trépanier (Carmen); Frédéric Pierre (Bouclouche); Violaine Gélinas (Lucky's Girlfriend); Izabel Rousseau (Stand-in for Marie-Pierre).

NEW YORK POST, 10/28/94, p. 46, V. A. Musetto

Camille is a studious, androgynous schoolgirl living with her mother in a comfortable Montreal townhouse. She's "12-and-three-quarters" (her words) and has two obsessions: astronomy and her father, who years before abandoned his daughter and cold-fish wife for New York.

Now he's back—with a shocking difference. Surgery and hormones have changed the man known as Henri-Pierre into a matronly woman who goes by the name Marie-Pierre. ("I've become what I am," he/she confides.)

Sounds like the plot for a "high-concept" tearjerker, doesn't it? Fear not. All concerned with the French-Canadian "The Sex of the Stars," have avoided the temptation in favor of a sensitive, delicately told story of a girl coming to grips with stark reality.

"Is that padding? Are your nails real?" Camille anxiously asks. "Everything's real" Marie-Pierre replies gently.

"I like stars because they don't have a sex," the troubled Camille confesses at another point.

Marianne-Coquelicot Mercier, who had never acted before, is truly marvelous as Camille (she reminded me of the young French actress Charlotte Gainsbourg). Also turning in poignant performances are Denis Mercier (no relation) as Marie-Pierre and Tobie Pelletier as Lucky, a schoolmate of Camille's who sells his body to older men on the streets of Montreal.

The director is Paule Baillargeon, whom you might remember as the curator in Patricia Rozema's delightful "I've Heard the Mermaids Singing" (1987). In an interview, Baillargeon has said that male producers and crew members, who felt uncomfortable with the subject matter, resisted the making of "The Sex of the Stars."

Fortunately, she prevailed.

NEWSDAY, 10/28/94, Part II/p. B7, Jack Mathews

What 12-year-old Montreal astronomy buff Camile likes most about the heavens she studies every night through her telescope in "Le Sexe des Etoiles" ("The Sex of the Stars") is that the stars seem to run in pairs, yet have no gender. No males, no females. Just couples.

At first, that observation seems to grow naturally out of the anxieties of a shy, intellectually curious girl facing adolescence and the hormonal aggression of boys. And to some extent, it does. But very soon in this fine French-Canadian film, directed by the actress Paule Baillargeon, it reveals two other meanings, one of which is a bomb.

Camille's obsession with astronomy is, in fact, an emotional stand-in for her relationship with her father, who'd introduced her to the stars before disappearing seven years earlier. And (here's the bomb) dad has suddenly reappeared, post-transexual surgery, every inch a lady.

It is a testament to Baillargeon's passion for the material, adapted from the novel by Monique Proulx, that there isn't a moment of sensationalism to this revelation. Camille's bitter mother, Michele (Sylvie Drapeau), was obviously aware of her husband's femaleness, and Camille (Marianne-Coquelicot Mercier, a non-actress, perfectly cast) is so determined to have her father (Denis Mercier) back, she simply looks past the physical changes—at least, for a while—and sees only him, Pierre, not Marie-Pierre.

Denis Mercier is a tall, athletic-looking Quebec actor, and that actually adds to the struggle of his character. Just as Marie-Pierre has escaped the man's body she was born into, and is ready to begin a new life, she has to confront the fact that she has a daughter desperately in need of a father.

What Baillargeon and Proulx have done is cut past not only the physical veneer we wear, but past our very identities, to deal with the issues of parental love and responsibility. Marie-Pierre knows he can never be a man again, but that no surgery can remove the instincts of a parent.

VILLAGE VOICE, 11/1/94, p. 64, James Hannaham

According to Shaw, "youth is wasted on the young." But in childhood, you don't appreciate your naïveté because your parents raise you with the impression that tangled questions can be answered simply. They lie to you about death and sex to make things easier for themselves and to make you feel comfortable. However, you can only wish you didn't know things you already know, and as you grow older, the more hurt you feel when life's complexities reveal themselves to you like successive sucker punches, the more likely you are to wear black nail polish and/or make beautiful, touching-yet-unsentimental films about outcast kids like *The Sex of the Stars*.

In the right corner, weighing in at 90 pounds, we have Camille (Marianne Mercier), a 12¾-year-old androgynous girl with a love of astronomy surpassed only by her love for her estranged father Pierre, to whom she has written unanswered letters for many years, begging him to bring her to live with him in New York. She cloaks her brilliance in melancholy, doing poorly in school and spending hours stargazing and moping instead of studying. Michèle (Sylvie Drapeau), her overprotective mother, dates the school psychologist to whom Camille can disclose nothing as a result. Her prodigal father, whom Michèle abhors, shows up soon enough, but with a sex change.

At this point, *The Sex of the Stars* could address the audience's burning curiosity about transsexuals with broad strokes and blatant tearjerking. Instead, this amazingly well-lit, meditative film offers no pat answers for either its characters or viewers, while we watch Camille's disappointments accrue: the school bell cuts short her presentation on the birth of stars, her father refuses to save her from the life she despises, and she gets mixed signals from Lucky, the tough and similarly androgynous boy who walks with a cane and takes her to a transvestite bar to show her "people like your Dad." It hurts her badly, like all first encounters with reality. Like Lasse Hallström, director Paule Baillargeon makes such emotional material look mundane and therefore squeezes out your tear ducts without a saccharine sting. "People are fucked up, it's not your fault," Lucky philosophizes after confessing his own secret to Camille, and they cling together, two parts per million in a community of children who were never innocent, just betrayed.

Also reviewed in:
NEW YORK TIMES, 10/28/94, p. C6, Stephen Holden
VARIETY, 9/13/93, p. 33, David Stratton

SHADOW, THE

A Universal Pictures release of a Bregman/Baer production. *Executive Producer:* Louis A. Stroller and Rolf Deyhle. *Producer:* Martin Bregman, Willi Baer, and Michael S. Bregman. *Director:* Russell Mulcahy. *Screenplay (based on Advance Magazine Publishers, Inc.'s character "The Shadow":* David Koepp. *Director of Photography:* Stephen H. Burum. *Editor:* Peter Honess. *Music:* Jerry Goldsmith. *Music Editor:* Kenneth Hall and Darrell Hall. *Sound:* Keith Wester and (music) Bruce Botnick. *Sound Editor:* Martin Maryska. *Casting:* Mary Colquhoun. *Production Designer:* Joseph Nemec III. *Art Director:* Dan Olexiewicz, Steve Wolff, and Jack Johnson. *Set Designer:* William Law III, Carl J. Stensel, and James Tocci. *Set Decorator:* Garrett Lewis. *Set Dresser:* Michael R. Driscoll, Michael Schmidt, Jack Forwalter, Mark Woods, and Don Chafey. *Special Effects:* Kenneth D, Pepiot. *Costumes:* Bob Ringwood. *Make-up:* Ronnie Specter, Jo-Anne Smith-Ojeil, and Jane Fielder. *Make-up (Alec Baldwin):* Carl Fullerton. *Special Make-up Effects:* Greg Cannon. *Visual Effects:* Alison Savitch. *Stunt Coordinator:* Dick Ziker. *Running time:* 112 minutes. *MPAA Rating:* PG-13.

CAST: Alec Baldwin (Lamont Cranston/The Shadow); John Lone (Shiwan Khan); Penelope Ann Miller (Margo Lane); Peter Boyle (Moe Shrevnitz); Ian McKellen (Reinhardt Lane); Tim

Curry (Farley Claymore); Jonathan Winters (Wainwright Barth); Sab Shimono (Dr. Tam); Andre Gregory (Burbank); Brady Tsurutani (Tulku); James Hong (Li Peng); Arsenio "Sonny" Trinidad (Wu); Joseph Maher (Isaac Newboldt); John Kapelos (Duke Rollins); Max Wright (Berger); Aaron Lustig (Doctor); Ethan Phillips (Nelson); Sinoa (Singer); Rudolph Willrich and Verlon Edwards (Waiters); Wesley Mann (Bellboy); Joe d'Angerio (English Johnny); Larry Joshua (Maxie); Larry Hankin (Taxi Driver); Woon Park, Brian Khaw, and Nathan Jung (Tibetan Kidnapers); Al Leong (Tibetan Driver); Gerald Okamura (Tibetan Passenger); Fred Sanders (Cop); Alix Elias (Woman in Taxi); Abraham Benrubi and Steve Hytner (Marine Guards); Lily Mariye (Mrs. Tam); Patrick Fischler, Jeff Cahill, and John L. Weaver (Sailors); Kate McGregor-Stewart (Mrs. Shrevnitz); Michael Hadge and Roland Brown (Inmates).

CHRISTIAN SCIENCE MONITOR, 7/1/94, p. 13, David Sterritt

"The Shadow," one of this season's more than rambunctious action-adventure epics, comes to the screen with a long pedigree. In fact, the main character's history is considerably more interesting than the shenanigans he goes through in his new movie.

Unlike later superheroes from Superman to Spiderman, the Shadow did not spring full-blown from the imagination of an enterprising artist. He began as a mere disembodied voice, according to an essay distributed to the press by Universal Pictures, proprietor of the new "Shadow" film.

This voice belonged to the host of an early 1930s radio series called "Detective Story Hour," and listeners found his mysterious tones more tantalizing than the whodunit yarns he introduced. Responding to this unexpected interest, one of the show's writers decided to juice up the announcer's presence by giving him a name to suit his enigmatic image: the Shadow.

Since the program was sponsored by a pulp-fiction magazine, fans started asking for Shadow material at their local newsstands, not realizing that no such material existed. Quick to seize on a potential market the magazine's publisher hired a prolific pulp author to crank out a series of Shadow adventures The first appeared in 1931 and became an immediate hit. Staff artists provided appropriately cryptic illustrations showing little more than a pair of penetrating eyes veiled by a swirling cloak and a rakishly angled hat.

Armed only with superior brains and heroic morals in his early crime-fighting career, the Shadow evolved over the years into a partly supernatural figure with the power to "cloud men's minds" and put the most dastardly villain at his mercy.

Quite a guy. And quite a moneymaker for the media wizards who nurtured his career in magazine stories and radio episodes for the next 25 years. Even the great Orson Welles had a hand in his success, portraying him on radio in the late '30s; by that time the Shadow—or Lamont Cranston, his secret identity—had acquired a love interest named Margo Lane, a history of yoga training, and a talent for telepathy. No less a pop-culture connoisseur than author Jack Kerouac numbered himself among the character's admirers, patterning the phantasmagoric hero of his novel "Doctor Sax: Faust Part Three" after the Shadow's spooky appearance, outlandish abilities, and triumphant "mwee-hee-hee-ha-ha" laugh.

It's a pity the Shadow's latest incarnation doesn't live up to his illustrious past. Set during his original heyday in the 1930s, the new movie is a hodgepodge of violent action, ostentatious effects, and lunkheaded jokes, stitched together by a hackneyed plot wherein he woos Margo Lane, fights a would-be world conqueror, and saves New York from a cataclysmic bomb blast.

The picture's only real value lies in the questions it raises about Hollywood's current priorities.

Watching the action race foolishly across the screen, I found myself pondering the fact that the producers have taken a cluster of fictional elements rooted in the '30s—complete with period costumes, settings, and story ingredients—and treated them in a wholly contemporary way, with dialogue and special effects positively drenched in stylistic mannerisms of the '90s.

Why have they taken this approach? It isn't hard to figure out the answer. The current crop of Hollywood filmmakers is long on technological resources but sadly short on original ideas—which explains the endless stream of sequels, remakes, and otherwise recycled projects that try to pass as fresh entertainment nowadays. Resuscitating a superhero like the Shadow provides yet another opportunity to unleash the special-effects gang on an action-filled story, without going through the bother of dreaming that story up.

Dredging up a pulp-fiction character from 60 years ago also provides another opportunity that's more pernicious than the opportunism just described. In the '30s as today, sensitivity to ethnic bias was not particularly acute in some media circles, and it wasn't uncommon to find non-white characters used in flagrantly unflattering ways. Accordingly, the Shadow's archenemy during the late '30s and early '40s was Shiwan Khan, heir to all the evil ambitions that his Asian ancestor Genghis Khan had unloosed upon the world.

While one might excuse the appearance of this "yellow peril" villain in a pulp-fiction commodity half-a-century old, it seems odd that a present day Hollywood studio would produce a racially charged story that pits its handsome white hero against a horde of monstrous "Mongol warriors." There's nothing subtle about this attempt to exploit racial stereotypes in the guise of old-fashioned fun.

"The Shadow" was directed by Russell Mulcahy, who counts several action films and hundreds of rock videos among his credits. Alec Baldwin and John Lone play the American hero and Mongolian villain, respectively, and Penelope Ann Miller wrestles with the thankless love-interest role. David Koepp wrote the scruffy screenplay, and Stephen H. Burum did the flashy camera work.

FILMS IN REVIEW, 7-8/94, p. 58, Jeff Laffel

When I was a young boy, the days of pulp fiction were already over, but every now and again I would get my hands on an old copy of *Amazing Action*, or some such magazine, and spend a day lost in a world of tough detectives who drank scotch neat as they smoked Camel after Camel, and stared after some lost love in an office with cracked, peeling walls. They would invariably be in shirtsleeves, wearing a snap brimmed hat, as they sat almost buried in a Morris chair waiting for their next client, who was usually a tall, willowy blond who always entered from a rain slicked pavement. And then, on Sundays, at five in the afternoon, the world of pulp fiction came to life on the radio when an eerie, disembodied voice would intone, "The weed of crime bears bitter fruit. Crime does not pay. The Shadow knows, " and then there would come a maniacal laugh, a piece of music (which I found later was written by Camille Saint Saëns) and a half hour filled with mystery and terror. All this was very dear to me growing up, and it was with a great deal of trepidation that I awaited Universal's film version of *The Shadow*. I didn't have to worry; *The Shadow* is terrific.

Director Russell Mulcahy and writer David Koepp have joined forces to bring *The Shadow* to blazing life on the big screen. There are a number of problems that prevent the film's being a classic, but there is enough good in it to make it terrific summer fun as well as a great future video.

The story begins in Tibet, where Lamont Cranston, a wealthy socialite has "gone native" and has become the scourge of the Himalayas. He is kidnapped and given a chance to have the good in him restored, and, later, is sent as a form of penance to New York City as *The Shadow*, to fight the forces of crime and corruption. Shortly after Lamont arrives back in the Apple, another visitor from Tibet, Shiwan Khan, the last descendant of Genghis, arrives as well. He, too, has gone through the redemption course, but has failed it miserably, killing the good teacher in the process, and now has decided to take over the world. At first, Khan recruits Lamont Cranston to join his nefarious band and, when Cranston refuses, he adds The Shadow's name to his enemies list. Cranston meets the beautiful Margo Lane, and together they battle Khan. That's the plot, and at first it seems as though it will sustain the film, but it doesn't, and we find ourselves with redundant scenes that slow the momentum in a number of places. What is lacking here is a second villain, à la the *Batman* films, to pick up the slack when Khan begins to wear out his welcome. Another structural mistake is the Tibetan opening followed by written words telling us what transpired from the time Cranston left Tibet and came to New York. The problem here is that Cranston is such a bad guy that he loses our sympathy, though he tells us later that he constantly regrets his past. A flashback after Khan arrives or when Margo guesses the identity of The Shadow would have worked better.

But I said *The Shadow* is terrific, and it is, for it is true to the feel of both written pulp fiction and the old radio show.There is an art deco feel to the film as there was in *Indiana Jones and The Temple of Doom*, that makes all the make believe great fun. From skyscrapers to martini glasses, from old Pepsi bottles to pneumatic tubes used to send secret messages, to an incredible Busby Berkeley overhead shot of Khan rising from the floor in his robes, all is Deco and all is well. A big hand to production designer Joseph Nemec III and director of photography Stephen Burum for creating and sustaining the "feel" of the film. (I think it is important here to note that the production design is not cartoon like, as was Warren Beatty's *Dick Tracy*. Reality mixes with fantasy here and the combination works beautifully).

Though set in the past, *The Shadow*'s special effects are right up to the minute. I particularly liked a pesky, demonic dagger that causes Cranston a great deal of trouble as well as a nightmare in which Cranston literally tears his face off in front of our eyes.

The cast is delightful. Alec Baldwin gives his best performance in years as the tormented Shadow. His vulnerability is covered by a tough, brittle exterior. When the surface is taken away, we see a man in pain, afraid of what he used to be and afraid of entering into a relationship with Margo, beautifully played by Penelope Ann Miller. Both Baldwin and Miller find as much depth as can be found in the characters of an action film, and their sexual attraction for each other is believable, funny and erotic, all at the same time. John Lone doesn't have much more to do than play Yul Brynner as Khan, but he does it well. Tim Curry starts off weakly and ends by giving a terrific imitation of Charles Laughton at his most flamboyant. Jonathan Winters has a ball playing Cranston's police commissioner uncle and Peter Boyle is fun as the cab driver Moe. The only mystery regarding the casting is that of Sir Ian McKellen as Margo's father, Reinhardt Lane. Why an actor of Sir Ian's majesty would first take a part like this and then, once accepting it, sleep walk through it, is enough to make one wonder.

There are bits and pieces about the film that endeared it to me. The brilliant composer Jerry Goldsmith has composed a beautiful score for *The Shadow* based, if I am not mistaken, on the original Saint Saëns radio show signature music, "Le Rouet de Omphale." There were many nods to other films and film personalities of the past, including an atom bomb rolling after Margo and her father à la *Raiders Of The Lost Ark* and the transformed face of the Shadow himself, based on the drawing used as a cover for the old Street and Smith pulps of The Shadow but looking too much like the wonderful Charles Middleton, the Ming of the Flash Gordon serials.

And speaking of serials, I left the theater after seeing *The Shadow* hoping that the film would do well enough to spawn a number of sequels with better and a lot more villains, faster moving plots and the lead actors intact. For *The Shadow* is a lot less pretentious than *Batman* and a whole lot of fun, like the *Indiana Jones* films.

"What movie knows how to provide a bang up, entertaining, fun-filled time in the theater? *The Shadow* knows." And it delivers!

LOS ANGELES TIMES, 7/1/94, Calendar/p. 1, Kenneth Turan

In his six decades as a bulwark against evil, a certain high-profile crime fighter has survived confrontations with the Red Blot and the Gray Fist, the Condor and the Cobra, the Vindicator, the Voodoo Master and the Silent Seven. After all that, surviving "The Shadow," the film that carries his name, shouldn't be too difficult.

Actually, there are times when this action-adventure starring Alec Baldwin as the man with the all-knowing laugh seems on its way to not only surviving but also prospering. Set largely in a mythical, dreamlike New York between the wars, it has the benefit of a combination of gorgeous production design (by Joseph Nemec III) and eye-catching visual effects (supervised by Alison Savitch). If ever a film looked exactly the way you hoped and imagined it would, "The Shadow" is it.

But if ever a film made you wince whenever its actors opened their mouths, "The Shadow" is that as well. Determined to follow the treacherous tongue in cheek path of the glib "Batman" movies, "The Shadow" winks strenuously and continuously at the audience, forcing its cast to struggle with the flat witticisms that litter David Koepp's script like so many expired balloons.

Between the early 1930s and the mid-1950s, the Shadow was a respected fixture on the American popular culture scene. A pulp magazine detailed his exploits for 18 years, a radio program (that briefly starred Orson Welles) did the same for more than 20, and there was exposure in feature films, comic books and even board games.

The key figure in all of this was the hard-working Walter Gibson, who under the pen name Maxwell Grant wrote 283 Shadow novels totaling something like 15 million words. Although he is mentioned only at the tail end of an extended credits crawl, it was Gibson who thought up the film's villain, Shiwan Khan, "the Master of Oriental Nemesis," several of its key characters, as well as the broad outlines of a plot about a madman using a stolen scientific device to threaten world dominion.

What the movie does come up with on its own is a back story detailing how Lamont Cranston became the Shadow. Baldwin's character is introduced as Ying Ko, the Butcher of Lhasa, a ruthless drug lord with long fingernails and a yen to control the entire opium output of Tibet.

But Ying Ko is abducted by a powerful and altruistic holy man known as the Tulku, who teaches the secret of clouding men's minds and helps him to struggle against the darkness in his own spirit. Thus equipped, Ying Ko heads back home to New York and a double life as the wealthy socialite Cranston and the relentless Shadow.

It is in New York that the film's ravishing look really kicks in. Working with cinematographer Stephen H. Burum, costume designer Bob Ringwood and three art directors, production designer Nemec dazzles in every single scene, creating atmospheric city streets, elegant nightclubs and knockout interiors that are characterized by a carefully though-out use of detail. Not even the original "Batman" or the gaudy "Dick Tracy" managed to look this breathtaking this consistently.

Once Shiwan Khan (John Lone), a rogue pupil of the Tulku's and the last living descendant of the great Genghis, shows up in Manhattan, "The Shadow's" extensive use of special effects comes into greater play. Ten separate companies contributed their skills, coming up with such nifty tricks as forms materializing out of fire, a wonderfully elaborate Shadow message service and a knife with an evil mind of its own.

Keeping all of this moving is director Russell Mulcahy, himself a visual technician known for his music videos and the loud and tedious "Highlander." Although he is still uncertain in handling actors, Mulcahy, a lifetime Shadow fan, overall does the best job of his career, orchestrating explosions and broken glass so that they meld with the rest of the picture instead of overwhelming it.

But just as Cranston has to fight against the crasser side of his nature, so "The Shadow" must contend with the unfortunate way the film has been dramatically imagined. Not surprisingly, it is a losing battle.

From "Star Wars" through "Batman," the camping up of pulp material has become a genre in itself, and giving the script assignment to the derivative Koepp, who has made a nice career ("Jurassic Park," "Carlito's Way," "The Paper") out of crafting reasonable facsimiles of previously successful material, probably seemed like the smart money decision.

But writing truly wised-up repartee is harder than it looks, and, like a small boy scrawling graffiti on a monument, the dialogue in "The Shadow" consistently undercuts the wonderful mood the visuals have worked so hard to create.

Except for Jonathan Winters as police commissioner Wainwright Barth, the actors are understandably flummoxed by the script's self-conscious cutesiness. Baldwin, Lone and Penelope Ann Miller as the glamorous Margo Lane continually struggle for the right tone, while Tim Curry as a mad scientist gives up the fight and goes totally over the top. And what could have been a classic ends up yet another story of what might have been.

NEW YORK, 7/25/94, p. 47, David Denby

The director of *The Shadow*, Russell Mulcahy, is another of the music-video people who are destroying American movies. Scenes begin boldly and then peter out; the characters and their dilemmas don't mean a thing. Mulcahy fills the sets with thirties Deco but then lights everything so dimly that *The Shadow* might have been called *The Shroud*. Who is the movie *for*? This murkily lit, rhythmless, unfunny fantasy is too boring to keep children away from the video games in the theater lobbies. The only person I've heard of who enjoyed it is Caryn James of the New York *Times*, who must have run out of quarters.

NEW YORK POST, 7/1/94, p. 42, Michael Medved

Who knows what stupidity lurks in the hearts of Hollywood?

"The Shadow" knows—since this lavish and ludicrous loser now takes its place as the most embarrassing big studio bomb of the summer.

Universal Pictures will try to promote the central figure in this misguided mess as a grim, dark, stylish super hero in the tradition of Batman; actually, this guy would fit more comfortably alongside Hudson Hawk and Howard the Duck.

As the on-screen idiocy unfolds, it looks like the producers spend $50 million for showy sets, costumes and special effects, but invested only about 50 cents on a script.

Actually, we know they must have spent more than that since they hired one of the hottest scribes in Hollywood—David Koepp, whose other recent credits include "The Paper," "Carlito's Way" and a modest little picture called "Jurassic Park."

Here, he has reportedly attempted to "put a contemporary spin" on the classic radio show (which aired from 1931 to 1954) and the result feels like an uncomfortable cross between "Little Buddha" and "Dick Tracy."

The action (if that's the right word) begins in Tibet, where our hero (Alec Baldwin) has established himself as a vicious drug lord known as "Ying Ko, the Butcher of Lhasa."

Is he supposed to be Chinese, Tibetan, American or Slobovian? Who knows and who cares, since all we want is to see Baldwin get that awful, greasy shoulder-length fright wig off his head.

He finally does so under the tutelage of the Tulku (Brady Tsurutani), a sort of Himalayan Yoda who transforms the bad guy into a crime-fighting good guy and endows him with all sorts of mystical and telepathic powers.

Later, Baldwin goes to New York (re-created in its glitzy 1930s splendor), where he lives the life of millionaire playboy Lamont Cranston, while assuming the secret identity of The Shadow to battle evil-doers at night.

In other aspects of the role Baldwin turns in the sort of sedated, frightfully unfocused performance that will appeal to people who feel that Arnold Schwarzenegger emotes too much in his movies.

Similarly sleepwalking through the picture is John Lone (of "Last Emperor" fame) who plays the chief villain of the piece—a descendant of Genghis Khan who arrives in town enclosed as a museum-bound Mongolian mummy, determined to rebuild his family's franchise by conquering the world.

His battle against The Shadow takes place almost entirely through their marshaling of various "mystical" powers: watching endless scenes of the two of them causing daggers to fly through the air or attempting to "cloud" one another's minds is like viewing some intense, elaborate sporting event where you have no idea of the rules.

One rule that contemporary filmmakers ought to follow in the future is to avoid casting the incomparably bland and boring Penelope Ann Miller as a romantic lead. She plays the hero's love interest, Margo Lane (yet another possessor of paranormal telepathic powers!) with so little flair that one is left to wonder, along with the hero's Uncle Wainwright (Jonathan Winters), "What the hell do you see in her?"

The great Ian McKellan plays Miller's father, a brilliant scientist who's been hypnotized by the evil Khan into passing on the secrets of a doomsday bomb.

And bomb is most certainly the operative word, as Australian director and rock video specialist Russell Mulcahy ("Highlander") occasionally dazzles the eye but consistently numbs the mind. Though the picture's running time is only normal length (112 minutes), it feels even longer than the interminable "Wyatt Earp."

Early in the film, as The Shadow prepares to ambush a group of swaggering gangsters, one of the thugs delivers prophetic words that eloquently summarize the public's inevitable reaction to the entire movie. "I don't like this," he declares. "This stinks. Let's get the hell out of here!"

NEWSDAY, 7/1/94, Part II/p. B2, Jack Mathews

"Who knows what evil lurks in the hearts of men?"

In light of recent news events, that slogan from the old radio show, "The Shadow," seems more relevant than ever, and though The Shadow is one of the least known comic superheroes to today's audiences, a crimefighter with the inside dope on man's dark side holds a lot of promise.

But in adapting "The Shadow" for the screen, writer David Koepp ("Jurassic Park") and director Russell Mulcahy have stuck too much to the times in which the character evolved, and to a tone only those with a proven passion and developed imagination for comic book adventure could love.

"The Shadow" is certainly a visual feast, with sets, costumes and effects as good, and, in their variety, even better than those of the two "Batman" movies. Production designer Joe Nemec III has created an ingenious Manhattan fantasyland that, like The Shadow himself, is simultaneously dark and light. It's as if the vibrant colors from "Dick Tracy" had bled into the blue-black world of "Batman" and brought some hope to the city.

But the illusion remains on the surface. The characters—Alec Baldwin's Shadow most especially—never come alive as breathing figures, their lines are as flat as if they were still sitting on the page, and when audiences get their first look at The Shadow, emerging from the darkness of playboy Lamont Cranston's soul, they're liable to erupt in laughter.

The filmmakers have honorably attempted to make their Shadow in the image of his original creator, Walter Gibson, with a hawk-like nose and deep, piercing eyes. But with his black fedora and cape, and a red bandanna covering all of his face except the black eyes and massive schnozz, the battle-ready Shadow looks more like Jimmy Durante out trick-or-treating.

Fortunately, he fights dirty, making himself invisible and hitting his opponents when they aren't looking.

The story, based loosely on the running radio show battles between The Shadow and his arch-nemesis Shiwan Khan (John Lone), opens high in the Tibetan Himalayas, where a murderous druglord known as the Butcher of Lhasa is transformed by a spiritual guru, given lessons in the art of clouding men's minds and slipping around in the dark, then, like so many people who have screwed up, is transferred to New York to seek redemption.

There, with the help of an assistant (Peter Boyle) who doubles as a reckless cab driver, he emerges from Lamont Cranston's inner sanctum to seek out and thwart evil. But when Shiwan Khan, last descendant of Genghis, arrives with plans to build a bomb and take over the world, The Shadow doesn't know if he can stop him or not.

Nothing that happens between The Shadow and Khan is particularly interesting, or new. In fact, as Khan uses his superior skills (they both had the same teacher back in Tibet) to neutralize The Shadow's power, the story feels like a replay of "Superman II," where a trio of banished Kryptonites showed up in Metropolis and turned the Man of Steel into Play-Doh.

What's missing here is the sense of humor and playfulness that enlivened the "Superman" movies. The Shadow is a serious guy. That lump of evil is working inside him like a spicy burrito, and nothing, not even Penelope Ann Miller's Margo Lane, the golden-haired socialite who sashays through this like Jessica Rabbit, can lighten him up.

You can admire "The Shadow" for its look and visual effects (there is a flying knife, with its own sick soul, that does some amazing stunts), but in the end, that is all there is. We still don't know what evil lurks in the hearts of men.

NEWSWEEK, 7/11/94, p. 50, Jack Kroll

Before Superman, before Batman, before anythingman, there was The Shadow. In this $45 million epic, Alec Baldwin is Lamont Cranston, a zillionaire who swaps his tux for the black cloak of the crimefighter who "clouds men's minds." The script by David Koepp ("Jurassic Park") pits Shadski against Shiwan Khan (John Lone), a Genghis Khan wanna-be who's also an ace mind-clouder. So is Cranston's squeeze, Margo Lane (Penelope Ann Miller), so there's a lot of cumulus in everyone's cranium. The movie, half camp, half straight, has its moments, but Australian director Russell Mulcahy lacks the loopy flair of "Batman's" Tim Burton. Still, the art deco—1930s New York, Miller's silvery dresses—is gorgeous.

SIGHT AND SOUND, 11/94, p. 52, Kim Newman

Tibet, the 1930s. Under the name Ying Ko, American Lamont Cranston has become a criminal warlord. Abducted by the Tulku, a holy man, Cranston is taught to renounce evil and use latent psychic powers. Seven years later, Cranston returns to New York and becomes The Shadow, a vigilante who uses a network of agents and his ability to make himself invisible to fight crime. The last descendant of Genghis Khan, Shiwan Khan—who has also studied under the Tulku—comes to New York, vowing to use his powers to become ruler of the world. Cranston meets Margo Lane, a socialite with whom he has a telepathic bond. Khan offers Cranston a partnership, claiming that he has killed their teacher and reasserted his own evil inclinations, but Cranston resists temptation.

When Margo's scientist father is enslaved by Khan, she comes to Cranston for help, realising he is The Shadow. Cranston deduces that Dr Lane's work, combined with an unstable element in Khan's possession and a device invented by Farley Claymore, can be used to create an atomic bomb. Cranston visits Claymore, who has willingly joined Khan, and is left to drown in a sealed chamber. Cranston uses his mental link with Margo to summon her to his rescue. Khan threatens to destroy New York unless a huge ransom is paid, and Cranston realises his enemy has managed to hypnotise the city into not seeing the Hotel Monolith, his headquarters. Cranston enters the hotel just as the device is being triggered and, summoning all his powers, defeats Khan. Dr Lane, freed of the spell, defuses the bomb. Khan, stabbed in the hand, loses his powers. Khan is confined in an asylum and Cranston turns his powers of fascination on Margo.

In the cycle of super-hero movies, *The Shadow*, which opts for faithful reconstruction of period and milieu rather than adapting its characters to the demands of contemporary audiences, seems likely to join the ranks of also-rans such as *The Rocketeer* and *Dick Tracy*. Originally a radio character who narrated crime stories, The Shadow was transformed in 1931 by author Walter Gibson (writing as Maxwell Grant) into a crime fighter with the ability to "cloud men's minds". The Shadow returned to radio (voiced by a young Orson Welles) in this form, also turning up in a few minor films and a 1940 serial featuring the hawk-nosed Victor Jory as Cranston.

Though clumsily plotted, *The Shadow* displays considerable bravura as it trots out the hero's best-known exploits. He is glimpsed first in eerie outline tormenting gangsters, a great tracking shot revealing Alec Baldwin as the slouch-hatted and scarved figure of the pulp covers, reaching for his gleaming twin automatic pistols. Due attention is also paid to trademarks such as The Shadow's chilling laugh and catch phrases ("The weed of crime bears bitter fruit" and "Who knows what evil lurks in the hearts of men?").

At the time the original stories were written, Hollywood was loath to make pulp super-productions and Irving Thalberg was unlikely to have predicted that it would be *The Shadow* rather than *Anthony Adverse* that would be remade in the 90s (though it was apparently MGM's 1932 *Mask of Fu Manchu* that inspired Gibson to create the character of Shiwan Khan). Nicely over-acted all round (even if Baldwin's black-fingernails turn as Ying Ko doesn't quite come off), with a pleasing period look and suitably outrageous perils, this Shadow movie, displaying the big special effects the original serials could never manage, would have delighted fans in 1937.

Nevertheless, this remake never really rises above mere pastiche. While the *Batman* films (live and animated), television's *Lois and Clark: The New Adventures of Superman*, and the shape-shifting *The Mask* demonstrate that the comic-book formula can still be reinvented in interesting ways, *The Shadow* remains slick second-hand pulp.

VILLAGE VOICE, 7/12/94, p. 44, Georgia Brown

Now, I happen to have grown up on the Shadow. The Shadow was a very scary guy. And let me tell you, *this* is not the Shadow.

This *Shadow*, more *Flash Gordon* even than *Batman*, is yet another pastiche assembled by production designers and producers who, in their mania to recycle pop culture material and previous movies, pay scant attention to basics. In this case, for instance, they fail to define just what the Shadow's powers are: One minute he's dodging a magic knife with head and teeth or bending minds to his bidding; another, he's bleeding and drowning in a flooding chamber. (Why didn't he will the bad guy to turn the water off?) And instead of battling local crooks, here he's up against mythical evil: the "last descendent of Ghengis Khan."

The radio program, where most of us who know the Shadow made his acquaintance, was profoundly eerie. As a kid I could hardly bear to listen when that preternatural voice suddenly emanated from the room where he couldn't be seen. (With my own reality problems, I couldn't be sure such power didn't exist.) Critic Elliot Stein tells me Orson Welles played the Shadow for a time, and it figures.

But enough of the real Shadow. *The Shadow* as directed by Russell Mulcahy starts off in the poppy fields of Tibet where stoned drug lord Lamont Cranston (Alec Baldwin) is tamed by a powerful *Tulku* and sent back to NYC to atone for his sins. "Six years later," in the hub of the deco renaissance, the crime-fighting Cranston masquerades as suave playboy, commuting by taxi between up-town mansion and his "inner sanctum" headquarters. (A sop to those with memories, Jonathan Winters plays his dotty Police Commissioner uncle.)

So here comes Khan—via the Museum of Natural History and *Ghostbusters*—with powers to hypnotize *la toute* New York so they cannot see the building he's erected on the corner of Second and Houston. On the other hand, Khan is determined to get his hands on—for back up?—an atom bomb.

Since you can tell this is too dumb for words, I won't waste any more.

Also reviewed in:
CHICAGO TRIBUNE, 7/1/94, Friday/p. H, Michael Wilmington
NATION, 7/25-8/1/94, p. 138, Stuart Klawans
NEW YORK TIMES, 7/1/94, p. C1, Caryn James
NEW YORKER, 7/18/94, p. 74, Terrence Rafferty
VARIETY, 7/11-17/94, p. 42, Brian Lowry
WASHINGTON POST, 7/1/94, p. D1, Rita Kempley
WASHINGTON POST, 7/1/94, Weekend/p. 34, Desson Howe

SHAWSHANK REDEMPTION, THE

A Columbia Pictures release of a Castle Rock Entertainment presentation. *Executive Producer:* Liz Glotzer and David Lester. *Producer:* Niki Marvin. *Director:* Frank Darabont. *Screenplay:* Frank Darabont. *Based on the short novel "Rita Hayworth and Shawshank Redemption" by:* Stephen King. *Director of Photography:* Roger Deakins. *Editor:* Richard Francis-Bruce. *Music:* Thomas Newman. *Music Editor:* Bill Bernstein. *Sound:* Willie Burton and (music) Dennis Sands. *Sound Editor:* John M. Stacy. *Casting:* Deborah Aquila. *Production Designer:* Terence Marsh. *Art Director:* Peter Smith. *Set Designer:* Antoinette Gordon and Joe Hodges. *Set Decorator:* Michael Seirton. *Set Dresser:* Lee Baird, Christopher Neely, John M. Heuberger, and Jack Hering. *Special Effects:* Bob Williams. *Costumes:* Elizabeth McBride. *Make-up:* Kevin Haney. *Stunt Coordinator:* Jerry Gatlin. *Running time:* 142 minutes. *MPAA Rating:* R.

CAST: Tim Robbins (Andy Dufresne); Morgan Freeman (Ellis Boyd "Red" Redding); Bob Gunton (Warden Norton); William Sadler (Heywood); Clancy Brown (Captain Hadley); Gil Bellows (Tommy); Mark Rolston (Bogs Diamond); James Whitmore (Brooks Hatlen); Jeffrey DeMunn (1946 D.A.); Larry Brandenburg (Skeet); Neil Giuntoli (Jigger); Brian Libby (Floyd); David Proval (Snooze); Joseph Ragno (Ernie); Jude Ciccolella (Guard Mert); Paul McCrane (Guard Trout); Renee Blaine (Andy Dufresne's Wife); Scott Mann (Glenn Quentin); John Horton (1946 Judge); Gordon C. Greene (1947 Parole Hearings Man); Alfonso Freeman (Fresh Fish Con); V.J. Foster (Hungry Fish Con); John E. Summers (New Fish Guard); Frank Medrano (Fat Ass); Mack Miles (Tyrell); Alan R. Kessler (Laundry Bob); Morgan Lund (Laundry Truck Driver); Cornell Wallace (Laundry Leonard); Gary Lee Davis (Rooster); Neil Summers (Pete); Ned Bellamy (Guard Youngblood); Joseph Pecoraro (Projectionist); Harold E. Cope, Jr. (Hole Guard); Brian Delate (Guard Dekins); Don R. McManus (Guard Wiley); Donald E. Zinn (Moresby Batter); Dorothy Silver (1954 Landlady); Robert Haley (1954 Food-Way Manager); Dana Snyder (1954 Food-Way Woman); John D. Craig (1957 Parole Hearings Man); Ken Magee (Ned Grimes); Eugene C. De Pasquale (Mail Caller); Bill Bolender (Elmo Blatch); Ron Newell (Elderly Hole Guard); John R. Woodward (Bullhorn Tower Guard); Chuck Brauchler (Man Missing Guard); Dion Anderson (Head Bull Haig); Claire Slemmer (Bank Teller); James Kisicki (Bank Manager); Rohn Thomas (Bugle Editor); Charlie Kearns (1966 D.A.); Rob Reider (Duty Guard); Brian Brophy (1967 Parole Hearings Man); Paul Kennedy (1967 Food-Way Manager).

CHRISTIAN SCIENCE MONITOR, 9/27/94, p. 14, David Sterritt

Prison movies come in many shapes and sizes. At one end of the spectrum are Hollywood potboilers ranging from the classic "20,000 Years in Sing Sing" to the trashy "Tango & Cash" and the witty "Escape From Alcatraz." At the opposite end are metaphorical films using imprisonment to explore issues of guilt, salvation and freedom.

"The Shawshank Redemption," starring Tim Robbins and Morgan Freeman, leans toward the second group—which is surprising, since it's a high-profile Hollywood release with a story based on a Stephen King novella.

The picture has moments of King-style sensationalism, to be sure, and one subplot (about a gang of homosexual predators) seems gratuitous. Much of the time, though, the filmmakers find more interesting things to focus on than the claustrophobic brutality of most prison movies; and there's no quarreling with their message that hope, trust, and friendship are among the most powerful of human values.

The film takes its title from Shawshank State Prison, a maximum-security jail run by a Bible-quoting warden who's as corrupt as he is sanctimonious. The story begins when a banker named Andy arrives after being convicted of a double murder.

He maintains his innocence, but nobody cares about him or his protestations. Slowly accepting the prison and its routines, he finds consolation in small pleasures—an interest in geology, a good memory for music—and starts to make friends.

Chief among his new acquaintances is Red, a longtime con with a capitalistic flair for providing items his fellow prisoners want. Drawn together by their nose for business, their ironic outlook on life, and their basic sense of decency, Andy and Red become close companions, wending their way together toward the story's surprising and upbeat climax.

Written and directed by Frank Darabont, whose previous credits lie mostly in TV and horror movies, "The Shawshank Redemption" has a clever plot, conveyed through a well-crafted screenplay that loses momentum only when twists and turns stretch it about 30 minutes too long. What gives the picture most of its zest and poignancy, however, is the excellence of its lead performances.

As the uptight banker, Robbins does some of his subtlest acting to date. As his hardened but resilient friend, Freeman is simply miraculous, giving the role so much depth, dignity, and good humor that you feel you've known this man forever. It's the kind of deeply felt performance that Freeman does better than anyone else, and if reward matches achievement, he should win about a dozen Oscars for it.

Also central to the movie's success is superb camera work by Roger Deakins. His eye for color, composition, and movement has never been sharper, and his use of aerial photography is breathtaking. Other contributors include production designer Terence Marsh, costume designer Elizabeth McBride, film editor Richard Francis-Bruce, and composer Thomas Newman. The solid supporting cast includes Bob Gunton, Clancy Brown, William Sadler, and the marvelous James Whitmore in a brief but memorable appearance as the oldest con in the joint.

FILMS IN REVIEW, 11-12/94, p. 55, Andy Pawelczak

Stephen King gives his tales of horror and the supernatural a literal veneer by infusing them with hints of myth and archetypes. The hero of *The Shawshank Redemption*, a prison movie based on a non-generic novella by King, is a version of the hero with a thousand faces who descends into hell in order to be born again. The movie is full of carefully orchestrated archetypal symbols: rites of renewal, cloacal integuments to be cast off, cleansing baptismal rain, a journey from darkness to light. Unfortunately, it's also full of predictable character types, and its realistic surface text isn't strong enough to carry the heavy symbolism and give it new life.

Andy Dufresne (Tim Robbins) is a middle class banker falsely accused of killing his wife and her lover and sentenced to life imprisonment. The movie follows Andy's 20 years behind the walls (the passage of time is registered by changing pinups, from Rita Hayworth to Marilyn Monroe to Raquel Welch) and has its quota of sadistic guards, even more sadistic homosexuals, and quasi-saintly long term prisoners. The film differs from most prison dramas by not focusing on an escape plan, and that's part of its problem: it just episodically meanders along for most of its length, and though it pulls all its pieces together by the end, by then it's too late.

Though not quite Billy Budd, Andy is the film's representative of innocence traduced. At first the other prisoners are put off by his cool detachment, but this wouldn't be a prison movie if he didn't turn out to be a stand-up guy, and Andy ultimately wins over his fellow cons by his stoicism and his adroit manipulation of the prison administrators, through which he secures a new library for the men. As Andy, Tim Robbins turns in a characteristically low keyed, anti-charismatic performance. Though Andy spends a lot of time in the hole for defying the guards, Robbins is not as strenuously heroic as Paul Newman in *Cool Hand Luke*, nor as endowed with quiet machismo as Clint Eastwood in *Escape From Alcatraz*.

What focus the movie has is on Andy's relationship with the other prisoners and particularly with his closest friend Red (Morgan Freeman), a smart jail house entrepreneur who traffics in contraband goods. Freeman is a very good actor with a face that looks as if it has been eroded and pitted by the Congo, Nile, and Mississippi rivers, not to mention several hundred years of American history. Unfortunately, he doesn't have much to do here except add gravitas and dignity to the movie—like Dilsey, the black servant in Faulkner's *The Sound And The Fury* he endures. It's too bad that Hollywood, in this film and in *Driving Miss Daisy*, has seen fit to turn him into an icon of black patience and forgiveness—for an idea of his range, watch *Street Smart*, a 1980s movie in which he plays a ferocious pimp. In *Shawshank*'s supporting cast, Bob Gunton is appropriately gimlet eyed as a bible thumping, Fascistic warden, and Clancy Brown is convincing as a brutal guard. James Whitmore appears in a sentimental role as an elderly con who can't stand life on the outside once he's released.

Frank Darabont, a first time director who also wrote the screenplay, is given to panoptical overhead shots of the prison yard. The prison itself is convincingly scary, a Kafkaesque enclosure with stone walls thick enough to crush an angel's courage and hope, but the drama inside never gets off the ground. At one point, Red says that Andy, who's an amateur geologist, is a product of pressure and time, like geological strata. It's a good image, but unfortunately we rarely feel either the pressure or the time, and as a result the big, quasi-spiritual epiphany at the end left me unmoved and dissatisfied.

LOS ANGELES TIMES, 9/23/94, Calendar/p. 1, Kenneth Turan

Awash in a bad news culture where horrors compete for media attention, America's appetite for feel-good movies is all but insatiable. How else to explain "The Shawshank Redemption," a film that hides a warm and cuddly fantasy about prison life behind sleek brutality, so much the better to convince us that even inside those walls life can be grand.

Starring Tim Robbins and Morgan Freeman as two lifers who demonstrate the great things prison can do for you, "Shawshank's" sentimentality is of a New Hollywood variety. Its message of hope and friendship comes premixed with a sizable dollop of unappetizing violence, intended to convince audiences that what they're watching isn't a big glob of cotton candy after all.

Adapted from a Stephen King novella, "Shawshank" also labors under its literary origins, with many of its situations feeling like thin doodles blown up to big-screen size. And its entire last section has the kind of serious plausibility problems that are only apparent when the written word takes physical form.

The film gets its name from a fictional prison that is supposedly Maine's toughest. It is to Shawshank sometime in 1947 that bank vice president Andy Dufresne (Robbins) is sent to serve a double life sentence for the murders of his wife and her boyfriend.

In a brief prologue, we've seen Andy looking potentially murderous with a bottle and a gun in his hand, but he claims to be guilty only of confusion, not homicide. This strategy convinces no one, and Andy, a loner who strikes the judge as icy and remorseless, is convicted without a second thought.

Andy's arrival at Shawshank is observed by Red Redding (Freeman), an impassive 20-year veteran of the place who lets on that "there must be a con like me in every prison in America. I'm the guy who can get it for you."

The story of Andy's time at the Big House is related by Red in an extensive voice-over that is one of the film's strongest points. In fact anything Freeman touches is the better for it; his effortless screen presence lends "Shawshank" the closest thing to credibility it can manage.

The film's periodic bouts of violence are probably also intended as a reality booster. For Shawshank is run by a harsh warden (Bob Gunton) who believes in discipline and a sadistic guard captain (Clancy Brown) who knows how to enforce it.

What this leads to is a series of off-putting violent episodes—one man beaten to death, Andy regularly pulverized by a psychotic homosexual (Mark Rolston) and his pals—that are unpleasant to endure while adding nothing to the film's sense of truth.

That's because writer-director Frank Darabont, in his theatrical feature debut, has envisioned the rest of the cons as a bunch of swell and softhearted guys who were probably put away for overzealous toenail clipping.

This blubbery Boys Club atmosphere is underlined by the nicknames of Red's crew, guys like Skeet, Jigger and Snooze, who the audience is invited to view as harmless as Snow White's dwarfs. The inappropriateness of having them in the same film with vicious attempted gang rapes seems not to have occurred to anyone with any influence.

Instead, "Shawshank" concentrates on an overly long, two-hour-and-22-minute parade of prison vignettes that show, among other things, how Andy uses his financial expertise to make himself indispensable to the warden and his lackeys. Some of these moments are effective, but even nice performances like James Whitmore's as a veteran con lose something by being overly familiar.

Though Tim Robbins always seems to be playing a part, he is good at it, and it is nice to see the chaste though loving relationship between Andy and Red develop over 20 years. Paradoxically, it is "Shawshank's" zealousness in trying to cast a rosy glow over the prison experience that makes us feel we're doing harder time than the folks inside.

NEW YORK, 9/26/94, p. 96, David Denby

The Shawshank Redemption, two hours and 22 minutes long and set in a maximum-security prison, is a very solemn affair indeed. It's a gray, gray movie, dour and unconvincing, and despite several moments of rhetoric that are meant to lift your spirits, sitting through it is like doing hard time—you learn the virtues of patience and endurance. I thought the movie was awful, yet I'm afraid that some people will be impressed. At the moment, our culture is so slaphappy and derisive that a touch of virtue can seem like the Sermon on the Mount. The impossible-to-remember title alone serves as a guarantee of seriousness.

The filmmakers offer a gratifying idea: Convicts who spend 20 or even 40 years in prison can hold on to their humanity; they can even discover hope. Despite the most degrading and sadistic confinement, the soul can survive. This is good news, but the issue of rehabilitation, at the moment, lies far from our preoccupations, which are more likely to focus on preventing people from becoming criminals in the first place and putting them away if they do fall. *The Shawshank Redemption* seems to have been made in another era—the fifties, perhaps, when rehabilitation was a fond idea and prisons could still seem like a monstrous mistake. The movie burns with dubious ardor. No one could disagree with its point of view. No one is likely to be much interested, either.

But even to speak of *The Shawshank Redemption* in such terms is already to take it far more seriously than it deserves. Despite the movie's grim and grimy aspect, it is not a serious expose of prison conditions. The movie is based on a gimmicky Stephen King story; the writer-director, Frank Darabont, has a horror-film background (Darabont's screenplay credits include *A Nightmare on Elm Street 3, The Blob, The Fly II*, and *Frankenstein*). Early in the movie, the camera rises over the prison's Gothic towers, and for a moment we think we're looking at a stage set, but then we see men in uniform running in the prison's central yard. It's the most impressive shot in the movie: Welcome to the house of horrors. Perhaps, I thought, just perhaps, Darabont will strike gold by using what he learned from shiver movies. But once he gets down to the ground, Darabont proves to be literal-minded and plodding. Is he doing penance for his sinful past? Men sit, and they talk, and they sit some more and talk some more, and occasionally someone gets beaten up. As a viewing experience, it's very much like prison.

In 1946, a successful young banker, Andy Dufresne (Tim Robbins), convicted of murdering his wife and her lover, enters Shawshank for life. Mild-mannered and reserved, he's nothing like the other prisoners, and he attracts the attention of the prison "fixer," Red (Morgan Freeman), a lifer who has seen everything. Red, narrating the movie in tones of ripest wisdom, doesn't expect

Andy to survive. The prison is run by a corrupt, Bible-thumping warden (Bob Gunton) who looks the other way as the sadistic head guard (Clancy Brown) beats people to a pulp. Men crumble and die all the time.

Andy proves to be tough, shrewd, and resourceful. But his endurance is meaningless since he's not a character, he's just a writer's willed invention, a man of intellect and class who resists the low scum all around him. Tim Robbins, looking grave, holds everything inside and achieves an almost complete opacity. With his serious brow and big, pursed lips, he has a comical air of preoccupation. He can't often use his charming, sudden smile here, and he's just wooden a lot of the time, a man in a deep trance. When Andy survives beating after beating from primeval homosexual toughs, we have no idea what's supposed to be going on in his mind (or his body). Andy is an abstraction—someone for Red to appreciate and to interpret for us. Morgan Freeman, a great actor, is given almost nothing to do but look at Robbins fondly and speak wisdom in his beautiful, layered voice.

The movie has no life. And by asking for life, I don't mean freak-outs and riots or Oliver Stone's kind of frenzy; nor do I mean the routine yet effective genre excitement of a movie like *Escape from Alcatraz* (we've all seen enough of that kind of film). I mean that there's nothing going on in *The Shawshank Redemption* from shot to shot—no expressive life, no spontaneity or feeling. It's a stunted movie. The characters repeat their traits over and over and wear out our interest. The sadism is unconvincing and finally numbing; the warden seems hardly possible as a functioning man, and Clancy Brown, as the guard, conveys his distaste for what he's doing by closing his face to the camera. Unrelenting, Darabont lays on the gray skies and somber compositions as if a sunny day or a few jokes would destroy the theme of man's unconquerable spirit.

Set far from our own period, perhaps as a way of making the story seem more "universal" or "timeless," *The Shawshank Redemption* collapses into symbolic gestures. Andy plays some Mozart over the prison loudspeakers, and the convicts—every last one of them—stand stock still in the yard, as if pierced through the bowels by angels' arrows. Paroled, the ancient prison librarian lets his pet crow go free from the window but can't handle freedom himself once he gets to the outside. The warden's biblical imprecations, woven into a framed needlepoint in his office, come back to haunt him. And so on. One glum cliché follows another, and then the ending, when it finally arrives, violates the movie's theme of redemption. In the end, *The Shawshank Redemption* is less about redemption than about revenge. That's a mood the audience will understand.

NEW YORK POST, 9/23/94, p. 46, Michael Medved

"The Shawshank Redemption" is a hackneyed prison movie with acting so strong that it often seems more substantive thán it is.

Tim Robbins plays a soft-spoken Maine banker who's convicted of murdering his cheating wife in 1946. Despite protesting his innocence, he draws a life sentence at the tough Shawshank State Prison where a wily long-term inmate who knows all the ropes (Morgan Freeman) teaches him the art of survival.

Eventually, Robbins becomes popular with the guards and with the corrupt warden (Bob Gunton) by giving them personal finance advice, and he uses this privileged position to win concessions for himself and the other prisoners.

When a new inmate shows up after 20 years with crucial evidence that Robbins might be innocent after all, the warden has other plans for his favorite inmate—who knows too many of the prison's secrets.

The story is based on a little-known Stephen King novella ("Rita Hayworth and the Shawshank Redemption") and feels like a recycling of dozens of old prison movies rather than an authentic, freshly imagined view of life behind bars; you keep expecting to see Jimmy Cagney banging his tin plate in the dining hall.

All your favorite cliches make their expected appearance, as the prisoners eat worm-ridden gruel, or display their unbreakable spirit through long weeks in solitary confinement (known, naturally, as "the hole"). The picture offers many unmistakable echoes of "Cool Hand Luke," but no hint of the subversive sense of humor that represented that film's saving grace.

In contrast, "Shawshank Redemption" revels in its graphic scenes of cruelty while taking all of its "triumph of the human spirit" blather much too seriously for its own good. "Some birds aren't meant to be caged." Morgan Freeman solemnly intones about Tim Robbins. "Their feathers are just too bright."

Freeman, one of the most masterful performers in movies today, is certainly too bright for this predictable pap—and his heartfelt performance almost single-handedly moves the film to a higher level: you can see his character (a red-haired Irishman in the original novella) gather wisdom and grace along with his gray hairs. Robbins is also better than his role deserves. conveying a quirky, hidden quality that keeps the audience guessing along with his fellow prisoners.

The warden, on the other hand, comes across as a vicious, one-dimensional caricature of an Evangelical Christian. Debuting writer/director Frank Darabont (who previously wrote "The Blob" remake and "The Fly II") goes out of his way to highlight the gold cross on the warden's lapel, and his constant references to the Bible while he's engaged in torture, thievery and even murder. It's a particularly blatant example of the sort of anti-religious stereotype that's gratuitous)y insulting at the same time it's dramatically unconvincing.

The impressive location (a 100-year-old abandoned gothic penitentiary in Ohio) gives the movie an impressive look, but long before the "Shawshank Redemption" wheezes to its conclusion, many moviegoers will join the prisoners in an overwhelming desire to escape.

NEWSDAY, 9/23/94, Part II/p. B2, Jack Mathews

It is becoming a year of spiritual reflection in Hollywood. First, Robert Zemeckis takes us on a tour of the bright side of contemporary America's troubled past on the wings of the angelically innocent Forrest Gump. Now, first-time director Frank Darabont's "The Shawshank Redemption" finds something hopeful, indeed soulful, about life behind bars.

Darabont, a writer mostly of horror movies, here making his debut as a director, has drawn his story out too long and lays too much sentiment over its final minutes. But you've never seen a prison movie quite like it, and I found its eccentric rhythms and the performances of co-stars Tim Robbins and Morgan Freeman nearly irresistible.

Adapted from a novella by Stephen King, from the same collection of pieces that inspired Rob Reiner's "Stand By Me," "The Shawshank Redemption" is a love story, at its heart, about two inmates who become soulmates at Maine's toughest maximum security prison, and keep each other's spirits propped up with hope as they march through a time tunnel with no light at the other end. Robbins is Andy Dufresne, an emotionally reserved Maine banker sent to Shawshank in 1947, having been convicted—perhaps wrongly—for the double murder of his wife and her lover. Freeman is Red, the sanguine lifer who runs the prison population's flourishing black market, a guy who can smuggle in a Rita Hayworth poster, which Andy wants for his wall, or a tool for carving chess pieces out of rocks, which is his new hobby.

The two men bond almost immediately, and over the next two decades—a period ended by a spectacularly satisfying plot twist—see each other through some of the most brutal and, alternately, exhilarating times.

It is hard to know exactly what Darabont, who wrote the screenplay, hoped to achieve with "Shawshank." The movie has such dramatic shifts of mood, from brutal realism to zenlike calm, you don't know whether to be repulsed by prison life or envy it.

The corrupt warden (Bob Gunton) and his sadistic head guard (Clancy Brown) are meaner than the Haitian military, and there are roving gangs of "bull queens" ready to corner any stragglers. But once Andy figures out how to use his accounting skills to turn the prison authorities into his protectors (he does their taxes, launders their kickback money), Shawshank begins to resemble a clubhouse for his and Red's gang. It's "Hogan's Heroes" on Devil's Island.

It's probably best to think of the movie as a parable, an attempted reminder that there are lives being lived in the waste bins of American justice, and that not a few of them are worthwhile.

Darabont is aiming for something fantastic, almost surreal, but couldn't bring himself to go all the way. In an opening aerial view, Shawshank is like a castle with a huge central courtyard, but from then on, it is used like a set for a claustrophobic one-act play. We have moved inside this shrunken world with Andy, to know how he feels. Yet, we never really get to know *him*. To protect the surprise ending of Stephen King's shaggy dog story, Darabont also had to protect the thoughts inside Andy's head.

It is easier to talk about the problems of "Shawshank" than its pleasures, because the latter have to do mostly with the film's odd pace and emotional tones. You admire Red and Andy for their resilience, their patience and—stacked as the deck may be—for their humanity. Two hours and 22 minutes may be too long, but you could do worse time.

SIGHT AND SOUND, 2/95, p. 52, Lizzie Francke

1946. On trial for murdering his wife and her lover, Andy Dufresne, a mild-mannered New England banker who claims he is innocent, is given a double life sentence and sent to Shawshank State Prison. He strikes up a friendship with Red, a fellow prisoner who has already served 20 years of his life sentence, and who does a flourishing trade smuggling goods into the penitentiary. Andy is sent to work in the laundry, where one day he is attacked by some fellow inmates led by the mean Bogs. The beatings become a regular occurrence. One day, Andy overhears one of the guards talking about his finances and offers him advice; soon he is acting as broker for all the guards. After a particularly savage attack by Bogs, Andy spends a month in the infirmary. Red procures various gifts for Andy including a Rita Hayworth poster, which takes pride of place in Andy's cell. The warden sends Andy to work in the library, where he runs his financial advice shop. Andy starts writing to the State to request better library facilities. Meanwhile Brooks, a veteran prisoner, finds that his parole has come through; once outside, he commits suicide. This news upsets Andy and Red. After years of writing to the State, funds come through to improve the library.

The Rita pin-up is replaced by one of Marilyn Monroe. The warden decides to set up a 'inside out' programme with the prisoners working in the community; this transpires to be a scam for the warden to make money. Andy is requested to cook the books, and invents a silent partner, 'Randall Stevens', in whose account the money is stored. Meanwhile Raquel Welch replaces Monroe. A new young inmate, Tommy, tells Andy that on a previous sentence, he shared a cell with a man who confessed to murdering a young banker's wife and her lover—the crime Andy was wrongly convicted of. Andy goes to the warden, who is un-cooperative; Andy refers to the warden's scam, and is sent to solitary. Meanwhile the warden has Tommy shot. Andy confides to Red about his dreams of living in Mexico, and tells his friend that if he should ever get out, he should go and dig up a box that he once hid while courting with his wife. That night Andy disappears. Over the years he has been digging a tunnel, with his posters hiding the hole. Writing to the police, he informs them about the warden's corruption. At the same time he is able to assume the identity of Randall Stevens and reap the rewards. Months later Red is granted parole and ends up in the same halfway house that Brooks stayed in. Contemplating suicide, Red decides to look for Andy's box. Finding it, he discovers a wad of money and directions to Mexico. Red jumps bail and meets up with Andy in his dream location.

With its unlikely coincidences and upbeat denouement, this is the prison movie as male melodrama par excellence. In a film where the only women are either feckless and dead (the prologue contains a brief peek of Dufresne's wife) or pin-ups, it is also very much a nostalgic, 'platonic' man romance that yearns for an uncomplicated time when men could be men in the movies. Spanning the years 1945 to 1967, it could conceivably have been made during that period. Its liberal intentions and strong sense of performance also hanker for an era of quality cinema when actors could be giants. The towering Tim Robbins has a solidity and gentle interiority that occasionally reminds one here of Burt Lancaster. Of equal excellence is Morgan Freeman as Red, who holds the film together with his poetic, often quipping narration. These are two good, highly likeable men whose moral worth is never in question. Their different social backgrounds are levelled by this, as much as by the fact that they have been brought together to be part of a very particular community. (Though they are both inside, there is still some sense of differentiation: the working-class Red helps his fellow inmates by procuring cigarettes and whisky, while the Ivy League-educated Andy aspires to build up the library.

In opposition to Red, Andy and a small band of friends—including Brooks, an insular veteran con whose interests are an obvious nod to *The Birdman of Alcatraz*—are the corrupt officials who perpetuate a regime of hardship. Like many a Warner Bros film before it, *The Shawshank Redemption* is keen to reveal how damaging prison life can be. In the opening scene, a new recruit is beaten senseless by the guards because he cries in the night. Equally brutal is the inmate Bogs, whose gang attempts to rape Andy. Red refers to them as 'queers'. In the context of this film, it acts like a disclaimer. 'Queer' means over there, different and dangerous in its violent manifestation of masculinity, and nothing to do with the admiration that Red has for Andy. (He says of him "some birds ought not to be caged, their feathers are too bright".) Andy is intimately related to all that is beautiful in Red's world, as in one scene when Andy hijacks the prison intercom system and broadcasts an aria from *The Marriage of Figaro*. The music gives Red a "heartache". Such lyricism seeks to be a cover for any desire that there may be between the two.

Likewise, the presence of the ultimate cover girl Rita Hayworth speak volumes. She is after all the great disclaimer in *Gilda*, a film bubbling with repressed male desire, which the Shawshank boys watch several times over. Her presence in that film too might be described as being paper thin. In *The Shawshank Redemption*, she is the first in a succession of women whose function is deceptive. The posters serve to hide Andy's secret (and the tunnel, which connects up with the sewage drains, seems to be a very specific sort of back passage). It provides a means for the great escape to a utopic future. Sun, sea and freedom in Mexico—the euphoric ending to many a story of love on the run.

TIME, 9/26/94, p. 78, Richard Schickel

Revenge is a dish best served cold. And as coolers go, it's hard to think of anyplace more chilling than Shawshank, the fictional state reformatory to which Andy Dufresne (Tim Robbins) is sentenced to serve two consecutive life terms for murdering his wife and her lover.

Its architectural style is Victorian Gothic, its penology just plain gothic. Or maybe Visigothic. It is a place designed not to reform but to drive you crazy. Cool is what you need to survive here, and supercool is what you need to maintain a semblance of humanity. Andy, who insists he has been wrongly convicted, looks fragile. But he has a lot of tensile strength, as the joint's brutal homosexual ring ultimately finds out. He has even more mental strength, patiently working up—for 19 years—an escape attempt that will not only bring down the insufferably pious and hypocritical warden Norton (Bob Gunton, an oil slick in shoes) but also turn a tidy profit for him and his best friend, Red Redding (Morgan Freeman).

Andy was a banker on the outside, trained to take the long, interest-bearing view, and he's well played by Robbins, an actor who once made an agreeable specialty of nutsiness but is even better at bland scheming. He makes his way in prison society by doing tax work for the screws, ultimately making himself invaluable to the crooked warden and a source of solid ironic humor to the audience. Even so, his character could not survive without Red's example. Red is the guy who can get you anything, from a pack of butts to a movie-star poster. He's all self-containment, never raising his voice or anyone's suspicions about his activities. And Freeman, who is simply a neat actor, a man who has never struck a false note in his career, both narrates this tale and anchors it with his authoritative playing.

The movie needs the kind of authenticity that Freeman brings to it. *The Shawshank Redemption* is based on a Stephen King novella that is just a little too smooth for its own good. It's satisfying to watch all the book's moving parts mesh, but a certain lifelike uncertainty is sacrificed to the neatness. Happily, writer-director Frank Darabont understands this. He makes you feel the maddening pace of prison time without letting his picture succumb to it. He is also efficient and clever with secondary characters like James Whitmore's con librarian, who's been in so long he can't survive on the outside.

There may be something redemptive in this story—a triumph of the tormented human spirit and all that—but neither Darabont nor the actors overplay the point. They are content to update the old prison genre deftly and unpretentiously. It always did work when it was done well, and it still does; and if using *Redemption* in the title instead of the more accurate *Revenge* helps to bring in the upwardly mobile, who cares? James Cagney would have felt right at home in Shawshank.

VILLAGE VOICE, 9/27/94, p. 66, Leslie Camhi

Bad timing may be coloring my response to *The Shawshank Redemption*, which is based on a Stephen King story about a likeable, alleged life murderer. In director Frank Darabont's debut, Tim Robbins plays Andy Dufresne, a Maine banker whose wife is found dead with her lover, a local golf pro. Dufresne's "icy" attitude (is WASP culture itself on trial?) combines with circumstantial evidence to convict him.

Well, nice white men do sometimes get sent to prison, but as fellow inmate Red (Morgan Freeman) tells it, Andy is the closest thing to Christ ever interned at Shawshank penitentiary. The place does need redeeming. It's full of stereotypes: Hadley, the sadistic "screw"; Norton, the unscrupulous Bible-thumping warden; and the nastiest gay social club I've ever seen. The "Sisters" take an unfortunate liking to Andy, but they soon receive their savage due. Other relationships in this all-male society, even Andy's fondness for a fledgling convict, proceed without a hint of sexual suspicion. Rectal obscenities, however, are spouted by almost all the major characters, and the film's climax is astoundingly anal.

Shawshank seems shot by a cinematographer who's read Foucault, with spectacular sequences of synchronized prisoners filing into their cells; the Victorian Ohio state prison where it was filmed looks great. Freeman has some fine meditations on confinement, James Whitmore is touching as an aging prison librarian, and the script is literary in a way that's hard to believe but uplifting. For a homophobic buddy movie about guys in the pen, it's pretty moving.

Also reviewed in:
CHICAGO TRIBUNE, 9/23/94, Friday/p. D, Michael Wilmington
NEW YORK TIMES, 9/23/94, p. C3, Janet Maslin
NEW YORKER, 9/26/94, p. 108, Anthony Lane
VARIETY, 9/12-18/94, p. 42, Leonard Klady
WASHINGTON POST, 9/23/94, p. F1, Rita Kempley
WASHINGTON POST, 9/23/94, Weekend/p. 48, Desson Howe

SILENT FALL

A Warner Bros. release of a Morgan Creek production. *Executive Producer:* Gary Barber. *Producer:* James A. Robinson. *Director:* Bruce Beresford. *Screenplay:* Akiva Goldsman. *Director of Photography:* Peter James. *Editor:* Ian Crafford. *Music:* Stewart Copeland. *Music Editor:* Michael Dittrick. *Sound:* Chris Newman. *Sound Editor:* Donald J. Malouf. *Casting:* Shari Rhodes and Joseph Middleton. *Production Designer:* John Stoddart. *Art Director:* David Bomba. *Set Decorator:* Patty Malone. *Set Dresser:* Liz Weber, Tom Scruggs, Dale Davis, and Elizabeth Bell. *Costumes:* Colleen Kelsall. *Make-up:* Kathryn Bihr and Cheryl Kinion. *Stunt Coordinator:* Randy Fife. *Running time:* 104 minutes. *MPAA Rating:* R.

CAST: Richard Dreyfuss (Jake Rainer); Linda Hamilton (Karen Rainer); John Lithgow (Dr. Harlinger); J.T. Walsh (Sheriff Mitch Rivers); Ben Faulkner (Tim Warden); Liv Tyler (Sylvie Warden); Zahn McClarnon (Deputy Bear); Brandon Stouffer and Treva Moniik King (Halloween Kids); John McGee, Jr. (Deputy); Ron Tucker (Forensic Detective); Catherine Shaffner (Martha); Heather M. Bomba and Marianne M. Bomba (Twins); Jane Beard (Carol Simmons); Mary Kate Law (Hostess); Helen Hedman (Mitch Rivers' Wife); Steven Burnette (Mitch Rivers' Son); Sean Baldwin (Halloween Monster).

LOS ANGELES TIMES, 10/28/94, Calendar/p. 2, Peter Rainer

In "Silent Fall," the only apparent eyewitness to a double homicides is the wealthy victims' 9-year-old autistic son, Tim (Ben Faulkner). The boy is traumatized twice over—his closed-off condition prevents him from even expressing his grief.

What lifts the movie above its standard murder mystery trappings is the way it attempts to get inside the boy's misery anyway. Psychiatrist Jake Rainer (Richard Dreyfuss), a specialist in autism, takes Tim on as a patient in an attempt to ward off a more severe drug therapy administered at the behest of the Baltimore police force. He's gentle with the boy, but he also knows he's on a deadline: If he can't force out the identity of the killer, then Tim may as well be dead too.

It's a so-so thriller with a first-rate atmosphere. Director Bruce Beresford is working from a by-the-book script by Akiva Goldsman that piles up the preposterousness. As a murder mystery it's schematic and too easy to figure out—the pool of potential murderers is too small and the clues are as heavy as anvils. As a psychological study it's uneven: Jake feels he was once responsible for the death of an autistic boy in his practice and so his relationship with Tim is supposed to be mutually healing.

It's a touchy-feely premise that only works because of Dreyfuss' performance, and even Dreyfuss can't do much with the scenes between Jake and his scowling, suffering wife (Linda Hamilton), who gets to show her displeasure by gutting chickens for dinner. She urges him so many times to "push" his emotions that we begin to wonder: Could Jake be pregnant? Is this some sort of new Lamaze procedure for uncommunicative hubbies?

Tim's older sister, Sylvie (Liv Tyler), claims to have witnessed the aftermath of the murder, though not the killer's face, and her reasoned calm with Tim rings true. She has the practiced ease of someone who is prepared for all the boy's fearful contingencies. (That's what links her with Jake.) When she's with Tim, his fear subsides, and yet there's something creepy in the way they shield each other from abuse. When they fall asleep together on the floor of the murder site, it's a horrific frieze—babes in arms in hell.

Beresford overrides the script's overemphatic clunkiness by drawing out the story's more ambiguous meanings. Tim doesn't speak in his own voice, when he speaks at all. Instead, he mimics exactly, the voices of TV pitchmen, family—anybody. Jake tries to get him to re-create the voices during the murder, and the scenes in which the boy calmly and emphatically spews out the victims' cries is genuinely upsetting. Beresford avoids turning Tim into a demon seed; little Ben Faulkner has a plangent, innocent quality that makes his agonies palpable (even though the boy has blocked his own pain). Tim isn't Rainboy—he's never perceived as any kind of savant.

It's rare for a thriller to be as evocative as "Silent Fall" without delivering the goods. Perhaps the reason the film is more of a letdown than the average misfired mystery is because, in places, the psychological details in the scenes between Jake and Tim are so good. Dreyfuss shows us the little boy Jake still has tucked inside himself. But he doesn't go elfin on us. He's a *man* grappling with inchoate feelings. Beresford would have done better to jettison the thriller stuff and hunker down with the doctor-child relationship.

The film's unevenness suggests Beresford probably felt the same way.

NEW YORK POST, 10/28/94, p. 48, Michael Medved

The big claim to authenticity for "Silent Fall," the turgid melodrama about an autistic boy who's the only witness to the brutal slaying of his mother and father, is the fact that the parents of screenwriter Akiva Goldsman are prominent child psychologists who work with autistic children.

Apparently such expertise is not hereditary, since nothing in Goldsman's film feels convincing and his script includes an abundance of painfully clunky lines like, "I think autism is just great, overwhelming fear of the world ... There's a boy in here. He's just trapped behind a wall."

These priceless insights are delivered by Richard Dreyfuss, who plays an unconventional psychologist who's at first reluctant to get involved in the murder case.

His character is still recovering from a career-shattering experience with one of his former patients, but J.T. Walsh, sheriff of their picturesque town on Maryland's Eastern Shore, needs the good doctor's help to break through to the troubled 9-year-old (newcomer Ben Faulkner) who could identify the killers.

In the process, Dreyfuss duels a rival psychologist (John Lithgow, in the sort of sneering, officious role he seems to own) who wants to medicate the child, as well as handling the complicated emotions of the boy's passionately protective 18- year-old sister (Liv Tyler).

Linda Hamilton plays Dreyfuss' wife in a relationship so perfunctory and perplexing that you can only guess that her key scenes have been cut from the final version of the movie.

Dreyfuss handles his wretchedly written role with his usual dignity and professionalism, but with none of the perfectly observed nuances he brought to his previous part as a shrink in "What About Bob?"

Director Bruce Beresford bears the lustrous reputation associated with "Breaker Morant," "Tender Mercies" and "Driving Miss Daisy," so it's hard to understand why he's squandered his talents on any of his last three projects—"Rich in Love," "A Good Man in Africa" and now this one.

Liv Tyler, just 16 when shooting this movie, offers the only sparks of genuine energy in the murky muddle, handling the role of grieving big sister with sweetness, precocious sexiness and an off-center air of potential menace that makes her scenes intensely watchable.

Tyler's the current cover girl for Rolling Stone magazine (where she's posed beside her father, lead singer Steven Tyler of Aerosmith) and it's safe to assume her career will soar despite this film's silent (but inevitable) fall.

NEWSDAY, 10/28/94, Part II/p. B7, Jack Mathews

Akiva Goldsman's script for the thriller "Silent Fall" is the reason every cabdriver, bookie and waiter in L.A. is writing a screenplay. They see something this badly written attracting a major director ("Driving Miss Daisy's" Bruce Beresford), a major star (Richard Dreyfuss), and a major studio (Warner Bros.), and figure their own phones will ring any minute.

"Silent Fall," as the pitch must have gone, is the story of an autistic 9-year-old boy who witnessed the double murder of his parents, and the child psychiatrist brought in to attempt to open the door to the boy's closed-off mind and let the secrets to the mystery spill out.

For a while, this set-up contains the seeds of both good intentions and a decent drama. Goldsman, whose parents worked with autistic children, makes a passing effort to explain the neurological disorder, and the conflicting clinical approaches— analysis vs. drug therapy—of dealing with it.

The information, delivered by Dreyfuss' Dr. Jack Rainer, is a little speechy, more like a health report on a TV news program than backdrop for a murder mystery, but nonetheless fascinating. Some autistics, the so-called idiot savants, are [this review was printed incomplete].

SIGHT AND SOUND, 6/95, p. 53, John Wrathall

Jake Rainer, a psychiatrist who gave up working with children after the drowning of an autistic boy in his care, is called in by Sheriff Rivers to calm Tim Warden, an autistic nine-year-old found wielding a kitchen knife at the scene of the murder of his parents. Rainer is reluctant to get involved, but Tim's 18-year-old sister Sylvie, who also witnessed the murder but claims to remember nothing, persuades him to help Tim in order to prevent the boy falling into the hands of a less sensitive psychiatrist, Dr Harlinger, who wants to pump him full of drugs. Tim refuses to speak, but he responds to the card games with which Rainer tries to break through to him. And after Sylvie reveals Tim's talent for mimicry, Rainer induces the boy to repeat the words he overheard during the murder. Tim becomes a suspect himself, however, when Dr Harlinger shows that, under hypnosis, the boy would be capable of the strength necessary to inflict the knife wounds found on his parents' bodies, while Rivers discovers pornographic photos of Tim taken by his father, supplying a motive. Rivers gives Rainer one more day to unravel the mystery before he arrests Tim.

Sylvie, after failing to seduce Rainer, invites him to dinner at her parents' house, drugs him and dumps him in a frozen lake. Looking on, Tim rings Sylvie and imitates Sheriff Rivers, asking her to come to the police station; when she has gone, he saves Rainer before he drowns. Using a jack, two queens and a king from a pack of cards to represent the members of his family, Tim reenacts the murder for Rainer, showing that Sylvie is the killer. Returning from the police station, where she steals Sheriff Rivers' gun, Sylvie confesses to Rainer that she murdered her parents when she caught her father abusing Tim, the same way he had abused her. She is about to shoot Rainer when Tim stops her, speaking for the first time in his own voice. "One year later", Tim is living happily with Rainer and his wife, while Sylvie is being treated in hospital.

In what must be a deliberate nod to John Carpenter's *Halloween*, the opening scenes of *Silent Fall* take place at Halloween, with a little boy suspected of butchering members of his own family after catching them *in flagrante*. Tim, the film seems to be suggesting, could have grown up to be Michael Myers (the *Halloween* killer) if he hadn't had the good fortune to fall into the hands of a sympathetic child psychiatrist like Dr Rainer. In the hands of Donald Pleasence's Dr Loomis, who in Halloween refers to his patient simply as "The Evil", or here John Lithgow's Dr Harlinger, who hopes to unlock the boy's secret with the malevolent movie shrink's favourite devices (a truth serum and hypnosis), it could have been otherwise.

Halloween isn't the only point of reference here. In fact, the pitch is rather easy to reconstruct: *Rain Man* meets *Witness*, with a hint of child abuse thrown in for topicality. That doesn't mean the script is entirely by numbers. To his credit, writer Akiva Goldsman (the son, the press notes inform us, of "two prominent child psychiatrists who ran a centre for autistic children") makes Tim's autism fundamental to the solution of the mystery. The idea that Rainer can discover, via Tim's talent for mimicry, what was said at the time of the murder, without being sure which character spoke which line, is a fascinating screenwriter's conceit. Equally Rainer's assertion that autistics respond to anything that's in sequence, like playing cards, and his use of card tricks to break through Tim's barrier of silence, pay off ingeniously when Tim acts out the murder using the Jack, Queen, King of Hearts (for himself and his parents) and the Queen of Diamonds (for Sylvie). That said, the way we learn the relevant psychological background information, through a convenient discussion about the nature of autism between Rainer and Sylvie, is ham fisted. Furthermore, a major implausibility breaks the logic when, having established that Tim can only repeat phrases he has overheard, the plot requires him to improvise in the voice of Sheriff Rivers in order to lure Sylvie away from the house.

Given the script's rich possibilities, *Silent Fall* could clearly have been a much better film; that it turned out quite so bland can only be blamed on the director, Bruce Beresford. After his last four films, all upmarket literary adaptations, conspicuously failed to match the success of *Driving Miss Daisy*, Beresford was perhaps looking for a safe commercial bet. But that doesn't explain why such a versatile director should have made something so utterly lacking in character, atmosphere or suspense. Of Beresford's 19 films to date, perhaps only *Her Alibi*, his previous shot at a crowd-pleasing Hollywood thriller, is weaker, which suggests that he's simply not cut out for the genre. Another former Oscar-winner badly in need of a hit, Richard Dreyfuss seems similarly uninspired here. In fact the most convincing performance comes from nine-year-old Ben Faulkner—although even a vastly more experienced actor would have had trouble making Tim's climactic plea for Rainer's life anything but ludicrous. As for Linda Hamilton, the fact that the thankless Mrs Rainer is her first film role since *Terminator 2* is yet another indictment of Hollywood's continuing failure to find a use for women actors over the age of 35.

VILLAGE VOICE, 11/8/94, p. 70, Kathy Deacon

On a beautiful waterfront estate in a posh town where the sheriff's everyone's friend and drinking companion, a CEO and his wife have been brutally knifed to death in their bedroom. The only apparent witnesses are the couple's 18-year-old daughter Sylvie (Liv Tyler), who claims she didn't see the murderer, and their nine-year-old autistic son Tim (Ben Faulkner), who is found at the crime scene hysterically clutching the murder weapon. The sheriff calls upon Jake Rainer (Richard Dreyfuss), a prominent psychiatrist and authority on autistic children.

Many years ago, in guilt and remorse after one of his charges committed suicide, Jake gave up working with autistic children and now confines his practice to adults. (One of them, a caricature of a desperate middle-aged woman, is made into a foil for Tim, merely to show that Jake has fallen away from his true calling.) Jake agrees to take on the case to prevent a rival therapist from administering drugs to elicit clues.

"Get me a murderer, Jake or I'm going to have to use Harlinger's medication on that boy," the sheriff warns. Jake, of course, ultimately does just that, thanks in no small part to Tim's uncanny ability to mimic voices that he's heard. We don't learn a lot about autism here, despite the convincing quality of Faulkner's Tim—whose progress nevertheless seems ordained by the script rather than by Jake's work.

The film strains credibility in other ways (e.g., why is sister Sylvie just given a tranquilizer and sent back to live alone in the house where her parents have just been murdered?). Nevertheless the film is suspenseful and nicely paced the first three-quarters of the way through. Then suspense gives way to melodrama as the plot starts racing toward its tidy resolution—it all ties up oh-so-nicely, A la *Murder She Wrote*, and the total effect is no less contrived.

Also reviewed in:
CHICAGO TRIBUNE, 10/28/94, Friday/p. L, Michael Wilmington
NEW YORK TIMES, 10/28/94, p. C10, Caryn James
VARIETY, 10/31-11/6/94, p. 90, Emanuel Levy
WASHINGTON POST, 10/28/94, p. F7, Hal Hinson
WASHINGTON POST, 10/28/94, Weekend/p. 44, Desson Howe

SILENT TONGUE

A Trimark Pictures release of a Le Studio Canal + presentation of a Belbo/Alive production. *Executive Producer:* Jacques Fansten, Gene Rosow, Bill Yahraus, and Shep Gordon. *Producer:* Carolyn Pfeiffer and Ludi Boeken. *Director:* Sam Shepard. *Screenplay:* Sam Shepard. *Director of Photography:* Jack Conroy. *Editor:* Bill Yahraus. *Music:* Patrick O'Hearn. *Sound:* Susumu Tokunow and (music) Patrick O'Hearn. *Sound Editor:* John A. Larsen. *Casting:* Elizabeth Shull. *Production Designer:* Cary White. *Art Director:* John Frick and Michael Sullivan. *Set Decorator:* Barbara Haberecht. *Set Dresser:* Shane C. Patrick. *Special Effects:* John K. Stirber. *Costumes:* Van Broughton Ramsey. *Make-up:* David Atherton. *Stunt Coordinator:* Dutch Lunak. *Running time:* 98 minutes. *MPAA Rating:* PG-13.

CAST: Richard Harris (Prescott Roe); Sheila Tousey (Awbonnie/Ghost); Alan Bates (Eamon McCree); River Phoenix (Talbot Roe); Dermot Mulroney (Reeves McCree); Jeri Arredondo (Velada McCree); Tantoo Cardinal (Silent Tongue); Bill Irwin (Comic); David Shiner (Straight Man); Arturo Gil (Little Person Acrobat #1); Joseph Griffo (Little Person Acrobat #2); Billy Beck (Petrified Man); Phillip Attmore (Boy Tap Dancer); Al Lujan (Kiowa Drummer); Devino Tricoche (Fire-Eater); April Tatro (Contortionist); Tim Carroll (Stage Coach Driver); Nicholas Ortiz Y Pino (Young Reeves); Robert Harnsberger (Buffalo Hunter); Fred Maio (Owner); David E. Wynne, Sky Fabin, and Leslie Flemming (Easterners); Jill Momaday (Prostitute); Lynn Davis (Prarie Girl); Tim Scott (The Lone Man).

LOS ANGELES TIMES, 2/25/94, Calendar/p. 10, Kevin Thomas

"Silent Tongue" directed by actor-playwright Sam Shepard is an alternately infuriating and exhilarating example of the Western as an art film. A stylized allegory of the white man's brutalization of Native Americans, it's the kind of picture easily dismissed as pretentious. Richard Harris and Alan Bates, however, are absolutely splendid, indeed possessed of Shakespearean grandeur, as two seemingly very different Irishmen who have sought their fortunes on the American frontier. But their considerable impact is fatally undermined by Shepard's altogether too theatrical and literal treatment of the supernatural.

A grief-stricken Harris travels over vast expanses in tracking down Bates, the boozy but surprisingly sharp proprietor of a traveling medicine show who's become hooked on his own product. In the past Harris had purchased from Bates one of his two daughters by the long-departed Kiowa (Tantoo Cardinal) known as Silent Tongue, who had been rendered speechless when her tongue was cut out—a victim of Bates' rape.

This daughter, Awbonnie (Sheila Tousey), had brought happiness and calm to Harris' highly—but mysteriously—disturbed son (River Phoenix, in his small next-to-last screen role that asks only that he seem profoundly agitated), but she has died in childbirth, leaving the son so distraught that he cannot bear to bury her corpse, despite the imprecations of her ghost to do so. Harris, beside himself with worry, will pay Bates any amount to sell him his other daughter (Jeri Arredondo), although her older half-brother (Dermot Mulroney) is none too happy about seeing yet another half-sister sold off. Gradually, a drama of revenge against Harris and Bates is set in motion.

As long as Shepard sticks with the tragic Harris and the oily Bates, contrasting examples of the kind of men who exploited Native Americans, "Silent Tongue" is fairly engrossing, although scarcely fresh or original in its anti-white man, pro-Native American stance. The trouble is a great deal of the movie is taken up with the nonstop harangues of Awbonnie's ghost, who for some reason has had one side of her face disfigured by paralysis and whose deep-voice rage recalls Judith Anderson's Medea.

Tousey might possibly be fine if this were a play instead of a film, but she's way over the top for the screen. Shepard might better have either presented Awbonnie's ghost as a silent, accusing figure or let us hear her voice without showing her beyond a wispy, fleeting apparition. In any case, the combination of Awbonnie's bizarre physical presence and her ceaseless declaiming is too much not to stop the movie dead in its tracks.

This is unfortunate for Shepard, who seems closer in spirit to Leone and Jodorowsky than to Ford. The contributions of cinematographer Jack Conroy, production designer Cary White, costume designer Van Ramsey and composer Patrick O'Hearn couldn't be more appropriately moody and atmospheric.

"Silent Tongue" has a sophisticated concern for textures and authentic details; this is one Western set in 1873 that doesn't have 1910 props. In its best moments Bates' seedy caravan recalls in its mix of period quaintness and frank sensuality Ingmar Bergman's tin traveling circus in "Sawdust and Tinsel." Ultimately, however, the title of "Silent Tongue" becomes ironic for a movie that talks too much.

NEW YORK POST, 2/25/94, p. 43, Bill Hoffmann

It's a pity about "Silent Tongue."

This atmospheric great-looking western sets up a thoughtful, absorbing plot, then drops the ball midway by turning into a hackneyed horror picture.

That's a damn shame for writer/director Sam Shepard, who has assembled a great cast of veteran players and newcomers and makes wonderful use of the stark New Mexico desert.

It's the mid-19th century and Alan Bates plays Eamon McCree, a boozing Irishman who runs a down-and-out traveling medicine show. McCree is a tortured soul, having fathered two daughters by raping a Kiowa Indian woman 20 years earlier, then selling one of them to frontiersman Prescott Roe (Richard Harris) as a bride for his son Talbot (River Phoenix).

Roe resurfaces to tell McCree that his daughter has died in childbirth and Talbot is going mad over her passing.

Roe begs McCree to sell him his other daughter, saying it's the only chance to save Talbot.

When McCree refuses, Roe kidnaps the girl and the chase is on through an inhospitable desert full of vengeful Indians and poisonous snakes.

At this point, we're totally hooked and Shepard seems to have the makings of a western classic,

Then, inexplicably, he makes a fatal error by introducing the ghost of Talbot's late wife to haunt everybody.

Harris and Bates, as great as they are—and they're fine here—can't compete with Freddy Krueger.

It's also a sad farewell performance for Phoenix, who does little more than brood, talk in tongues and act crazy with an unflattering, over-the-top gusto.

I couldn't help wondering if Phoenix was zoned out on drugs. Let's just say he's done better work.

So has Shepard. That's why watching "Silent Tongue" is so ultimately depressing.

NEWSDAY, 2/25/94, Part II/p. 67, John Anderson

Sam Shepard's place in the American theater seems secure and for that you can credit "Buried Child," "True West," and "Fool for Love." His place in American cinema seems secure, too, and for that you can blame "Silent Tongue."

This has been a troubled project from the start; it was shown at the 1993 Sundance Festival, got a largely negative response, and Shepard set about reworking it. His recutting, however, has done nothing to make the experience any more pleasant, or thought-provoking, although it has given much more prominence to the performance of River Phoenix. Which is kind, in a way. The late actor is no better or worse than any of the others in this impossibly inane movie, but at least he doesn't have to read the reviews.

A more relentlessly deluded film is hard to imagine, unless they'd cast Madonna in it. "Silent Tongue" has to make do with Richard Harris and Alan Bates, who looks like a leprechaun with a liver condition. The script defies belief, and is delivered with all the appropriate Shakespearean pretensions. The perspective of the film is suffocating, even though it was shot on wide-open expanses of New Mexico. If Shepard wanted to make a statement about the claustrophobic spiritual circumstances of his characters, so be it, but the effect is like watching a football game through a keyhole. In fact, just to think about it makes me queasy.

So does the story: Eamon McCree (Bates), proprietor of the Kickapoo Traveling Medicine Show, is a slave to his own elixir, and a generally vile character. He raped Silent Tongue (Tantoo

Cardinal), a mute Kiowa woman, then married her and raised their daughters, Awbonnie (Sheila Tousey) and Velada (Jeri Arredondo). After Silent Tongue went back to the Kiowas—whom she preferred to McCree even though they had cut out her tongue—Eamon sold Awbonnie to Prescott Roe (Harris) as a wife for his son.

After Awbonnie dies in childbirth, along with the baby, Prescott decides the only thing that will save his son Talbot (Phoenix) from losing his mind (it's futile, belive me) is Valada whom he tries to buy from Eamon, and then kidnaps. This really ticks off Reeves McCree (Dermot Mulroney) the girls' half brother, who wasn't that wild about having his other sister sold in the first place. So he and Dad take off after Prescott. Awbonnie, meanwhile, can't rest, presumably because of the injustice to her mother. Or the fact that her body is up in a tree. Or because white men are evil. Or whatever.

You have to presume a lot because, postmodernist that he is, Shepard wants us to bring our own interpretations to this pretentious claptrap, which isn't worth the effort. Add a star if you need a nap.

SIGHT AND SOUND, 3/95, p. 54, Geoffrey Macnab

The American prairies sometime in the 1870s. Horse dealer Prescott Roe comes looking for Eamon McCree, a drunken mountebank who runs a bizarre travelling medicine show. The previous year Prescott swapped three horses for McCree's half-Indian daughter, Awbonnie. She married Prescott's son, Talbot, but died in childbirth. Now, Prescott wants to barter for her twin sister, Velada, in the hope she'll be able to assuage Talbot's all-consuming grief. Upbraided by his son Reeves, McCree refuses to make an immediate sale. In desperation, Prescott kidnaps Velada and rides off with her towards the wilderness where Talbot is mounting 24 hour vigil over Awbonnie's corpse. In a nightmare, McCree remembers how he once raped an outcast Kiowa Indian, Silent Tongue, (so called because the Indians ripped out her tongue for lying). He married her, and she gave birth to Velada and Awbonnie, but then fled back to her tribe. He is woken by his son, Reeves, who insists they go in pursuit of the kidnapper.

Velada manages to escape from Prescott. Rather than desert him, she strikes a deal. In exchange for horses and money she will try to ease Talbot out of his grief. Awbonnie's furious spirit is tormenting Talbot. She wants her corpse to be buried or burned so she will be free to leave for the spirit land, but he can't bring himself to let her go. Spotting Indians on the horizon and convinced they've been sent by Silent Tongue to punish him, McCree shoots his mules, hides behind them and lets rip with his rifle. They ride off. He follows Reeves on foot, but is later abandoned by him.

Prescott hides as Velada approaches Talbot. She manages to make him eat. Awbonnie's ghost lets loose the horses and sets a hawk on Prescott. He is possessed by her spirit and eventually hurls her corpse on the fire, freeing her to fly off to the spirit world. The Indians capture McCree and march through the desert, torturing him with their lances. Prescott and Talbot are last seen hobbling wearily together into the distance.

Sam Shepard's second film as director is a bleak, ritualistic western which owes as much to Aeschylus as to John Ford. Nemesis comes not in the shape of a gun-toting cowboy, but as a force of nature, the equivalent of the 'fury' in Greek Tragedy whose inexorable hounding of the protagonist is set in motion by his guilt and grief. Right from the opening scene, as River Phoenix mounts a vigil over the corpse of his dead Indian wife, the story is given a supernatural dimension. The earth is parched. Bones and feathers litter the ground. Ominous birds of prey hover in an all-too-blue sky. With this kind of landscape, it's scarcely a surprise that formal realism is often abandoned and that a vengeful ghost is at the core of the narrative.

Despite its sometimes ponderous mysticism, *Silent Tongue* also has a clear political agenda. If not exactly a revisionist western, the film records at least obliquely how Native Americans in general, and their women in particular, were persecuted by the terrified white man. The title refers to the story of a Kiowa Indian who has her tongue ripped out for lying, but her brutal punishment at the hands of her own people is nothing to the way she and her daughters are treated by the new settlers. Their bodies are bartered for horses, their myths plundered to provide the travelling medicine show with comic sketches. ("It's the primitive that feeds my livelihood," explains McCree, the Irish mountebank who rapes Silent Tongue and sells her children for livestock.)

Shepard is not given to grand statements. His primary focus is on traumatised individuals within a broken family. As the wrinkled, weather-bitten horse trader, Prescott Roe, who emerges like some latterday prophet out of the dusty prairies, Richard Harris isn't so far removed from Travis in *Paris, Texas*. His son's wake by his dead wife's corpse recalls Jake's tormented obsession with Beth in *A Lie Of the Mind*. As a piece of writing, though, *Silent Tongue* is a notch or two beneath the standard of Shepard's best work. It is short on the memorable monologues that are his trademark. Some of the characters, notably Alan Bates' drunken Irish medicine peddler and Tantoo Cardinal's Silent Tongue, are more exaggerated archetypes than fully hewn individuals. The story sometimes seems as strained and as one-dimensional as the eerie little comic masques the medicine show presents. Shepard seems to be trying to express in images what he would normally be able to convey through dialogue alone. In the case of most directors, this would hardly warrant as a criticism. With Shepard, however, the strain of reaching for a visual language drags the picture under the weight of heavy-handed symbolism. *Mise en scène* is often cluttered: the travelling medicine show comes complete with camels, horses, dwarves, clowns, skulls and living Christ-like statues, none of which serve any narrative function whatsoever. The black and white flashback sequence in which McCree chases Silent Tongue over a skeleton-littered desert ends with an all too predictable silent scream. Amid this welter of overblown imagery, it is little wonder that Shepard's cast are in hyperbolic mode. As the grief-stricken husband, River Phoenix comes on like Simon of the Desert, rolling his eyeballs. Alan Bates is all drunken blarney. Dermot Mulroney, his hot-tempered son, merely sneers like a disaffected adolescent.

One of Shepard's most celebrated roles as a screen actor was in *Days Of Heaven*, and the experience of working with Terrence Malick and Nestor Almendros has obviously affected his own approach to film-making. The way he shoots the denuded landscapes in natural light, his enthusiasm for roseate dawns and dusks, even the circus troupe itself might have been borrowed from Malick's film.

Even as classical revenge drama, *Silent Tongue* falls slightly short. The bloody finale described in the production notes doesn't actually occur, and the story whimpers out with Harris and Phoenix cast adrift in the wilderness. Although his work has been filmed successfully by Antonioni, Altman and Wenders, Shepard is still feeling his way as a filmmaker. Here, his attempt at meshing western myth, Greek tragedy and family psychodrama together ends up an unwieldy mess. Shepard will surely one day make a movie which does him justice as both writer and director, but this isn't it.

VILLAGE VOICE, 3/1/94, p. 57, Ann Powers

Nearing the millennium, America looks with trepidation at its founding myths. As the rock era's Euripides, Sam Shepard has specialized in myths gone mad, bubbling up like vomit on the tongues of his tortured, drifting citizens. *Silent Tongue* places Shepard's obsessions within the milieu of the Old West, which has been subject to filmmakers' kangaroo courts ever since the '60s made imperialism gauche. The film takes on two of the West's daunting, intertwined political sins: the traffic in women and the abuse of Native Americans. But since it's Shepard, revenge for these wrongs comes supernaturally and resonates classically. Prescott Roe (an ochre-faced Richard Harris) seeks to purchase the second child of the union between the medicine show con man Eamon McCree (a florid Alan Bates) and the mutilated Kiowa Indian Silent Tongue (a mostly absent Tantoo Cardinal) to appease the grief of his son, Talbot (an unfortunately overheated River Phoenix), who's gone mad since the death of his wife, McCree's elder daughter, Awbonnie (a charismatic Sheila Tousey). Awbonnie's fierce ghost haunts Talbot with lines like, "I am not your life!" ' She also torments her pragmatic sister, Velada (Jeri Arredondo), the misguided Prescott, and the decadent Eamon, whose Indian-hating is the source of all the trouble in the first place.

Shepard convincingly presents the culture of Indian-hating as a blurring of the lines between guilt and fear within white men's psyches. Bates's Eamon—who's given to proclamations like, "She's an Indian! She was born to suffer!"—is the film's Agamemnon; having sacrificed everything decent about himself, he dooms everyone he meets. His son Reeves (Dermot Mulroney, in a disappointingly Keanu-like performance) abandons him, and Eamon eventually gets his due. But his probably fine monologues are lost on the prairie winds, and Shepard's climaxes carry neither the strength nor the intricacy film demands; it's all too operatic for the medium. Besides, Shepard's karmically honorable desire to allow the Kiowa women their revenge on the men who brutalized them falls short, because his heart remains with the pathetic fathers and their failing sons. The film tries hard, it has texture and a fabulous ghost. But for real postmodern mythmaking, I'll stick with Hong Kong action flicks.

Also reviewed in:
NEW YORK TIMES, 2/25/94, p. C3, Caryn James
VARIETY, 2/8/93, p. 75, Todd McCarthy
WASHINGTON POST, 4/15/94, p. D6, Rita Kempley

SIMPLE TWIST OF FATE, A

A Touchstone Pictures release. *Executive Producer:* Steve Martin. *Producer:* Ric Kidney. *Director:* Gillies MacKinnon. *Screenplay:* Steve Martin. *Suggested by the novel "Silas Marner" by:* George Eliot. *Director of Photography:* Andrew Dunn. *Editor:* Humphrey Dixon. *Music:* Cliff Eidelman. *Music Editor:* Scott Stambler. *Sound:* Mary H. Ellis and (music) Armin Steiner. *Sound Editor:* Fred Judkins. *Casting:* Dianne Crittenden. *Production Designer:* Andy Harris. *Art Director:* Tim Galvin. *Set Designer:* Julie Sanford and Jonathan Short. *Set Decorator:* Maria Nay. *Special Effects:* Thomas R. Ward. *Costumes:* Hope Hanafin. *Costumes (Steve Martin):* Dennis Schoonderwoerd. *Make-up:* Judy Ponder-Patton. *Make-up (Steve Martin):* Frank Griffin. *Stunt Coordinator:* Webster Whinery. *Running time:* 106 minutes. *MPAA Rating:* PG-13.

CAST: Steve Martin (Michael McCann); Gabriel Byrne (John Newland); Laura Linney (Nancy Newland); Catherine O'Hara (Mrs. Simon); Alana Austin (Mathilda McCann, age 10); Alyssa Austin (Mathilda McCann, age 5); Alaina Moble and Callie Mobley (Mathilda McCann, age 3); Victoria Evans and Elizabeth Evans (Mathilda McCann, age 1-1½); Stephen Baldwin (Tanny Newland); Byron Jennings (Keating); Michael des Barres (Bryce); Tim Ware (Rob); David Dwyer (Joe the Bartender); Tom Even (Dad the Cop); Ed Grady (Judge Marcus); Amelia Campbell (Marsha Swanson); Danny Nelson (Dr. Roberts); Kellen Crosby (Lawrence, age 11); Adam Crosby (Lawrence, age 8); Chase Conner (Lawrence, age 5); Carolyn McCormick (Elaine McCann); Terry Loughlin (Cal); Eric Brooks (Butler); Leon Lamar (Stablehand); Shauna Leigh Austin (D.C. Teacher); Suzanne Stewart (Judge's Wife); Dan Chandler (Cop); Deborah Duke (Esther); Michelle Benjamin-Cooper (Teacher); Muriel Moore (Mrs. Latham); Boyce Holleman (Politician #1); Judson Vaughn (Politican #2); Afemo Omilami (Bailiff); Janell McLeod (Court Stenographer); Mary Ann Hagan (Girl at Polo Game); Kathrin Nicholson (T.V. Reporter); D. Henderson Baker (T.V. Cameraman); Mary Nell Santacroce (Female Social Worker); Ric Reitz (Male Social Worker); Libby Whittemore (Playground Mom); Scott Higgs (Summons Server); Pamela Fitch (Mathilda's Pal); Stephanie Astalos-Jones (Parent); Don Young (Graveyard Worker); Jon Kohler (Janitor).

CHRISTIAN SCIENCE MONITOR, 9/6/94, p. 13, David Sterritt

Star and screenwriter Steve Martin introduced his new picture, "A Simple Twist of Fate," by describing it as a dramatic comedy. It turned out to be a straight-on drama, however, with occasional jokes to lighten the atmosphere—which needs plenty of lightening, since the story is based on George Eliot's novel "Silas Marner," a book that's about as frolicsome as the miserly old man it's named after.

Departing liberally from its source, the movie transforms Marner into Michael McCann, a likable teacher who becomes an embittered recluse after learning that his wife is pregnant by another man. Living in the same rural community, meanwhile, is a wealthy politician who protects his public image by hiding the existence of his drug-addicted lover and their illegitimate little girl.

When the unfortunate lover abruptly dies, the child wanders into Michael's home. He adopts her, and regains the joy of living by seeing the world through her fresh eyes. Then the politician decides to acknowledge her and take her into his household, leading to a custody battle between the biological and adoptive fathers.

Directed by Gillies MacKinnon from Martin's screenplay, the movie is occasionally confusing, frequently contrived, and always as corny as can be. Surprisingly, though, a couple of things make it enjoyable despite all this. One is the quality of its acting, especially by Martin and Gabriel Byrne, who gives a nicely understated performance as the politician.

The other big asset is the almost magical beauty of Andrew Dunn's camera work, charged with a dreamlike delicacy from beginning to end. If you *look* at "A Simple Twist of Fate," instead of just listening to the dialogue and following the plot, it takes on a haunting loveliness that almost compensates for its shortcomings in other areas.

LOS ANGELES TIMES, 9/2/94, Calendar/p. 1, Kevin Thomas

Nobody ever accused Steve Martin of not taking chances, and with the captivating heart-tugger "A Simple Twist of Fate" he took the all-out plunge of basing this film on no less than George Eliot's 1861 novel, "Silas Marner"—that grim morality play most of us did not escape having to read in high school.

What Martin, as star as well as writer, and director Gillies MacKinnon have created in their very free adaptation is a family film that might be best described as a serious comedy, not unlike "Roxanne," Martin's spin on "Cyrano de Bergerac." Not all the risks they take with shifting tones, in setting the near-incredible against the painfully real, pay off, but on the whole they've come through with an involving entertainment suffused with genuine emotion.

It's not hard to understand why Martin was attracted to a warhorse of Victorian literature, for in the 19th Century, writers confidently took on grand themes, drew rich characters and made bold use of coincidence to evoke a sense of the workings of fate. Those novels still live, but as the 20th Century draws to a close, they're almost impossible to write in such a fragmented society with so little faith in God and in an uncertain universe.

Within a few minutes of the film's start, Martin's Michael McCann, a happy, dedicated schoolteacher in a Southern small town, finds himself utterly devastated when his wife finally confesses that the baby she is expecting isn't his. The next thing we know is that he has become a solitary, reclusive cabinetmaker who, like Silas Marner, devotes his evenings to surveying his ever-expanding collection of gold coins. Whoosh!—the coins disappear; whoosh! a golden-haired toddler wanders into McCann's home one wintry night.

It in fact took lots more than one twist of fate to bring together the lonely man and the seemingly abandoned child, involving intricate plotting that pays off later on. The heart of the film is in its father-and-daughter relationship. It is a pleasure to watch McCann come alive, thanks to the little girl whom he adopts and who grows into a bright, pretty and independent-thinking 10-year-old, Mathilda (Alana Austin, whose younger sister Alyssa plays Mathilda at 5). It is in amusing Mathilda that Martin is able to play the comedian, but the film celebrates above all the joy that loving a child can bring.

No idyll lasts forever, and Mathilda now finds herself responding to a nearby rich senator (Gabriel Byrne) and his wife (Laura Linney), who are childless and begin showering the child with attention and even the gift of a horse. You don't want to give too much away, but the day looms when the senator feels he can actually take Mathilda from McCann in a custody battle.

It's in the courtroom scenes that Martin and MacKinnon hit a snag. Up until then they've been successful in playing a contemporary sensibility against solid Victorian values, but in deflecting the clichés inherent in courtroom drama they become facetious. The result is the emergence of an artificial, contrived quality epitomized by Catherine O'Hara, heretofore seen as a sensible local antiques dealer who secretly adores McCann, making a total fool of herself on the witness stand. As talented as O'Hara is, she's hard put to make credible a smart woman suddenly turned into an idiot. Luckily, yet another not-so-simple twist of fate saves the scene and the film just in the nick of time.

"A Simple Twist of Fate" is a handsome production with a soaring score that has a substance that can be derived only from an array of exceptionally well-written, well-played individuals. Byrne and Linney could so easily have been painted as villains of the deepest dye but instead have been given human dimension; you're not asked to like them but you are able to understand them. Aside from the courtroom scene, O'Hara shines, and Stephen Baldwin is wonderfully sleazy as

Byrne's no-good younger brother. But it's Martin and the little girls who play Mathilda who win your heart.

NEW YORK POST, 9/2/94, p. 45, Larry Worth

Steve Martin rode to fame in the '70s as the ultimate "wild and crazy guy." Two decades later, Martin has come up with his wildest—and definitely craziest—project: writing, executive producing and starring in a modern-day update of "Silas Marner."

The classic tale is now called "A Simple Twist of Fate." But as in George Eliot's 1861 novel, hard luck turns a nice man into a skinflint; good luck—in the form of a little girl left on his doorstep—turns him human again. At least until he engages in a custody fight 10 years later with her biological father.

But as played by Martin, the self-employed, woodcutter hero comes off less like Marner than kindly Gepetto, right down to the child who subs nicely for Pinocchio. Is it just a coincidence that the film is a product of Walt Disney's Touchstone Pictures?

Actually, it isn't all Mickey Mouse. Within the first half, a heroin addict kills herself, a car accident results in a bloody death, a thief plunders an innocent's riches and a married man learns that his wife's baby was fathered by another.

Then, the toddler joins the scene and director Gillies MacKinnon switches from sex to saccharine. The mix doesn't gel, which becomes immediately obvious. After just watching a poor, drug-addled mother collapse and die in the snow, her child wanders into the protagonist's house, grabs his leg and says "Mama." He simply responds: "Boy, are you confused."

Are viewers supposed to chuckle, with the mother's corpse growing icicles a few feet away? Well, the child hasn't got an exclusive on confusion. Martin's script is "Mildred Pierce" played for yuks, worsened as it shoots from one issue to another like an out-of-control pinball.

Further, the dialogue is a consistent test of credibility, compounding developments that might have been OK in Eliot's time, but now seem plain silly.

Martin is no better in front of the camera, juggling his "Pennies from Heaven" dramatics and recycled antics from "Parenthood." Ultimately, he shortchanges the character by making him neither moving nor funny. Simply irritating.

Director MacKinnon of "The Playboys" fame is the perfect complement, manipulating viewers with sledgehammer theatrics and a score that tells you when to laugh and cry.

Saving graces aren't found among the supporting players. The usually-reliable Gabriel Byrne ODs on menacing tones and wrinkled brows as the girl's natural dad. If the character had a moustache, he'd be twirling it.

Meanwhile, Catherine O'Hara tries to keep a straight face while spouting silly lines as Martin's sweet-as-pie sounding board; Stephen Baldwin is all smirk as an evil sibling.

The sole redeeming feature is 11-year-old Alana Austin, who plays the girl everyone wants to adopt. She sidesteps the script's cloying sentimentality, even injecting a trace of tenderness into what could have been precious.

But even if Austin was the next Shirley Temple, Martin's shortcomings would still dominate. Here's hoping he has no plans for "Mill on the Floss."

NEWSDAY, 9/2/94, Part II/p. B2, John Anderson

Besides being yet another movie that shares its title with a rock song (one by Bob Dylan, which isn't in the film), "A Simple Twist of Fate" makes use of several very *au courant* references: The raging debate over biological vs. adoptive parentage, for instance. And heroin. And George Eliot.

Despite this, it wants to be a timeless story, an archetypal one. We can tell by the music—which tells us far too often how we're supposed to be feeling—and by its simple truths: That the concept of family goes beyond chromosomes. That money can't buy everything.

By the time this Steve Martin-powered vehicle—in which he is producer, writer and star—finally runs out of gas, which is none too soon, money actually *has* bought everything. But even that is beside the point.

Like its inspiration—Eliot's "Silas Marner"—"A Simple Twist of Fate" concerns a reclusive, gold-hoarding miser whose life is redeemed when he adopts an orphaned baby girl. Years later, when her wealthy biological father claims her, she chooses to remain with her adoptive parent.

It's a classic story, one that touches the love nerve—as did the recent Kimberly Mays-Regina Twigg case in Florida that this tale recalls. The problem with Martin 's adaptation is that he and director Gillies MacKinnon ("The Playboys") are treading far too delicately and respectfully for their film to have much human drama, or human warmth. With a story like this—the ending may not be a foregone conclusion, but the rest of the plotline certainly is—you need to leaven your dough with a little humor. What we have here is very little humor. And stale matzoh.

Unlike the original Silas, who was cast out of his religious community after a false charge of theft, Michael McCann (Martin) is more of a sexual exile: His very pregnant wife has informed him that no, the child isn't his. And so, the cuckolded choir instructor flees to smalltown Virginia.

There, he becomes the subject of local gossip, buys gold from his one friend, Mrs. Simon (Catherine O'Hara), an antiques dealer, and makes furniture for people like unscrupulous politician John Newland (Gabriel Byrne) and his wife, Nancy (Laura Linney, of "Tales of the City").

Nancy can't have children, but Newland can—and has, with his junkie mistress Marsha (Amelia Campbell). On her way to confront him one snowy night, Marsha runs out of gas and freezes to death. The baby, who will be named Mathilda, wanders into Michael's funky cabin.

Michael, whose gold has been stolen in the night by Newland's drunken brother Tanny (Stephen Baldwin), has become even more bitter, but the baby—played at various ages by Victoria and Elizabeth Evans, Alana and Callie Mobley and Alyssa Austin—brings him around.

There are warm and wonderful moments of bonding; of Michael alone, on a stool, being interrogated by local adoption officials (whose decision is influenced by Newland). Of Michael pushing Mathilda through town in an antique pram. Of Mathilda calling Michael "Daddy." And of Michael saving Mathilda's life by scooping her off the edge of a nearby cliff while hooked to their recreational weather balloon. All of this advances the story in some way, but it's photo-album stuff, heartstring-tugging pap that relies on Martin for juice. And he's seldom been more seriously unfunny.

Mathilda, well-played as an older child by Alana Austin, becomes the object of a court fight that is too predictable to summarize. Newland is morally outgunned from the beginning. The laughs, when they do come, are inappropriate.

"When you turn a gift away from your door," Michael tells him, "it goes to whoever takes it in." It's a line that sounds profound, but means nothing. Except that perhaps Martin should stop mucking around in English Lit 101 and get back to the French classics. "Roxanne" anyone?

SIGHT AND SOUND, 7/95, p. 52, Nick James

Divorced after learning that the child he was to have with his former wife was another man's, cabinet maker Michael McCann has moved to dark house near a small Virginian town, withdrawn into himself and become a miser hoarding gold coins. Local politician John Newland has a troublesome brother, Tanny, given to public carousing, and a secret illegitimate daughter whose mother is a drug addict. Tanny is John's go-between with the mother, but on the eve of election night, he has an accident in John's car and a girl he picked up is drowned. Needing to make a quick getaway, he sneaks into McCann's house and steals the gold coins.

On election night, the strung out junkie mother, having waited in vain for Tanny to arrive with her money, tries to drive to John's palatial home, but runs out of petrol in a snowstorm. She staggers with the toddler to within a few feet of Michael McCann's place before collapsing. The toddler finds her own way to a seat in front of Michael's fire but he finds the mother frozen to death. Michael sees the child's coming as a sign and decides to adopt her. John Newland uses his influence to see that he succeeds. Michael names the child Mathilda and the responsibility brings him out of himself.

When Mathilda is 10, Michael takes her with him to the Newland house to deliver a cabinet. John has the career he wanted but he and his wife Nancy have failed to produce a child and seeing Mathilda causes him increasing heartache. He invites her up to ride his horses and confesses to Nancy that Mathilda is his natural child. They decide to try and gain custody of her through the courts. The combination of political influence and expensive advocacy looks certain to win for the Newlands, despite Mathilda's brilliant staging of a fake breakdown to sway Judge Marcus' sympathy Michael's way. Marcus says that it is only the opportunities offered by the Newland's wealth which make the difference but his decision is interrupted by a discovery that changes everything. In having the quarry pumped dry to form a lake for their new home elsewhere, The Newlands have uncovered Tanny's corpse with all of Michael's gold coins on him, therefore Judge Marcus decides against the Newlands. John and Mathilda, however, remain on good terms.

A better name for this film might be *Several Complicated Twists of Fate* as the chances of having a complete collection of gold coins stolen on the same night that a girl is nearly drowned nearby in a politician's car are remote enough—without having an infant appear out of a snowstorm at your fireside on the following night leading you to find her junkie mother frozen to death. This is the fairytale-like premise, borrowed from George Eliot's *Silas Mariner*, for a film that remains semi-realist throughout. Yet Steve Martin's script seems to acknowledge that an excess of Victorian melodramatic event has occurred in its first phase, and is resolutely determined from that point onwards to be as character-driven and action-free as a script performed by an actor chiefly known for his talent in slapstick can possibly be.

This it does with intermittent success. As in most films that have to show several stages in a child's life, scenes describing the intervening years of Mathilda's growth between her mother's death and her crucial tenth year have a water-treading feel about them, as if their only true function is to show that Michael McCann is a wonderful dad and Mathilda a well brought-up girl. They do allow, however, for many of the film's more quirky moments, shot with a child's sense of wonderment; in particular, the scenes of Steve Martin dangling from an old weather balloon and his later use of it to save Mathilda from falling into the local quarry, which turns into an epiphanic moment.

It is in these more offbeat and incidental scenes that Gillies MacKinnon's touch becomes recognisably that of the director of *The Grass Arena* and *Playboys*. Behind an often sentimental surface, MacKinnon sets a sombre and gritty undertone of mood that suggests the force of Michael McCann's hurt, to which Steve Martin can only hold a tight mask and which grants Gabriel Byrne's more relaxed performance an extra poignancy. When elements of Martin's comedy persona leak through in playing with Mathilda, a lack of control becomes more apparent—sometimes its appropriate and in character, other times it would be possible to insert the entire scene into *Parenthood*. Such disjunctures would appear to be inherent in Martin's attempt at creating a serious role for himself. His script wants to redeem a self-pitying miser and a forlorn political opportunist without recourse to sentiment and still contain such snappy wisecracks as computer hacker Mrs Simons' remark: "I can flush the Vatican toilet if I want to", into the bargain.

A Simple Twist of Fate's barrier to success may be its ambitiousness. A fairy tale cannot easily contain a modern debate about paternal rights any more than a biblical parable can afford to hedge its bets. *Simple Twist* has attributes of both forms but it never satisfactorily resolves them into a coherent whole. Characterisation is also perhaps too subtle. Each time we learn to like one incarnation of Mathilda, she puts on a few years and we have to start again. Since Michael remains a reticent figure throughout, despite his apparent reflowering under the influence of raising Mathilda, the only constantly compelling character is Newland, a fact which puts a spin of divided loyalties into the climactic court case, but which also undermines the idea that Michael is over his trauma. Michael's tragedy from the beginning is that he's been outdone by a more handsome man, and the suspicion remains that the court's decision may yet be reversed in a putative future by his own self-pity.

VILLAGE VOICE, 9/13/94, p. 66, Georgia Brown

I hate to say anything Steve Martin does isn't brilliant, perfectly poised, suffused with the lightness of being. So I hate to say *A Simple Twist of Fate* is as clunky as its title. I especially hate having to admit that even that is an understatement.

While I know nothing of Martin's personal life, this wistful tale's very strangeness suggests that he was compelled to write it out of some profound hurt. It's as if every single scene—and most, for one reason or another, come off as bizarre—exists merely to convince us of the critical issue: The damaged man deserves love.

Not surprisingly, Martin's character, Michael McCann, is another lonely guy. In the first scene (Washington, D.C., 1979, though it feels like Hicksville, 1947), he's a school music teacher suddenly informed by his very pregnant wife that she's had a genetic test and the baby isn't his. "Five years later," Michael is a self-employed carpenter working out of a run-down farmhouse somewhere in the South. He seems to have stepped back even further in time—like a century or two (Martin says the inspiration for the script came from *Silas Marner*). A miserly recluse mocked by the locals, his whole fortune is in gold coins hidden in the false bottom of a drawer.

Characters pop out of this picture as fast as they emerge. (The film is directed, clumsily, by British TV's Gillies MacKinnon, who made *The Playboys* with Albert Finney.) In the first few minutes—after that cheating wife and her fetus drop from sight—one woman dies in a car crash, another freezes to death in a snowstorm, and a glinty-eyed young man (Stephen Baldwin) absconds with Michael's gold. By no means the simplest twist of fate: One cold night when the door is open, a toddler toddles into Michael's living room. (Her mother froze but she wore her snowsuit.) After a hearing in which Michael compares himself to a bowl of Jell-O "quivering before you," child-welfare agents award this one-year-old to the town weirdo. Sure they would.

Sticklers for verisimilitude should stay home. Is it plausible that the child's natural father, a polo-playing pol (Gabriel Byrne speaking with a Southern accent), would sue for custody when the child was 12 or so, that the child's wishes in the matter would be ignored, and that the judge would plan to award her to the absentee father *because he has enough money to send her to Harvard*?

Yes, there are a *few* laughs, usually when Martin's character interacts with his sane friend Mrs. Simon (Catherine O'Hara), a single mother running an antique shop. But as therapy, let's hope this works for Martin because it won't do much for his fans.

Also reviewed in:
CHICAGO TRIBUNE, 2/2/94, Friday/p. C, Michael Wilmington
NEW YORK TIMES, 9/2/94, p. C3, Janet Maslin
VARIETY, 9/5-11/94, p. 53, Leonard Klady
WASHINGTON POST, 9/2/94, p. D6, Hal Hinson

SIRENS

A Miramax Films release of an Australia/United Kingdom coproduction with the assistance of The New South Wales Film & Television Office and the participation of Australian Film Finance Corporation Pty Limited. *Executive Producer:* Justin Ackerman, Hans Brockmann, and Robert Jones. *Producer:* Sue Milliken. *Director:* John Duigan. *Screenplay:* John Dugan. *Director of Photography:* Geoff Burton. *Editor:* Humphrey Dixon. *Music:* Rachel Portman. *Sound:* David Lee. *Sound Editor:* Susan Midgley and Alan Bell. *Casting:* Liz Mullinar. *Production Designer:* Roger Ford. *Art Director:* Laurie Faen. *Set Decorator:* Kerrie Brown. *Costumes:* Terry Ryan. *Make-up:* Noriko Watanabe. *Running time:* 96 minutes. *MPAA Rating:* R.

CAST: Hugh Grant (Anthony Campion); Tara Fitzgerald (Estella Campion); Sam Neill (Norman Lindsay); Elle MacPherson (Sheela); Portia De Rossi (Giddy); Kate Fischer (Pru); Pamela Rabe (Rose Lindsay); Ben Mendelsohn (Lewis); John Polson (Tom); Mark Gerber (Devlin); Julia Stone (Jane); Ellie MacCarthy (Honey); Vincent Ball (Bishop of Sydney); John Duigan (Earnest Minister); Lexy Murphy (British Bulldog Girl); Scott Lowe (Station Master); Bryan Davies (Barman); Lynne Emanuel (Barmaid); Kitty Silver (Pub Woman 1); Carolyn Devlin (Pub Woman 2); Peter Campbell (Pub Drunk).

FILMS IN REVIEW, 5-6/94, p. 54, Barbara Cramer

From Australia: a feast of Eden before Eve ate the apple, and larger than life erotic fantasy you might wish never ended. Based on the fancied mid-lifestyle of an actual person, 1930's bohemian Aussie artist Norman Lindsay (played by Sam Neill), it's more of a *what if* rather than a *what really was*.

Whatever, *Sirens* is lusciously mounted, effervescent enchantment. Written and directed with style and substance by John Duigan, it juxtaposes the ages old clash between religion and art—but don't for a minute think this is a weighty treatise on, say, church caveats vs. human desire. There's also a lot of non-ecumenical buoyant behavior (fun, sex and games) thrown in for ballast.

En route to a new parish near Sydney, Anthony Campion (Hugh Grant), an upright, uptight London cleric, makes a brief pit stop at Lindsay's secluded idyll on a church mission. He hopes to persuade the famed artist to replace his satirical painting "The Crucified Venus," depicting lecherous priests ogling a voluptuous nude, with one less controversial for an upcoming international exhibition.

But there's trouble in Paradise, and the priggish parson, with wife Estella (Tara Fitzgerald) in tow, finds things they never taught at seminary. The Anglican pair (he's ultra-conventional, she's a bored-in-bed, sexually-repressed newlywed) is nonplussed by Lindsay's lush, beguiling realm of the senses. They find him at work on a new canvas "The Sirens" (the mythic nymphs who lured sailors to their doom). What's more, he's surrounded by a trio of buxom, bare breasted beauties clad only in insouciance who, when not posing in the buff, happily cavort in various stages of undress without tinge of inhibition. There's also a handsome, blind groom on site (Mark Gerber), an enigmatic Pan-like creature (with a Braille technique straight out of Esalen encounters) with a sublime body that the ladies covet. And that includes the minister's wife.

Lindsay's character, the director notes, "is basically a catalyst for change and an observer;" as such, though his (Neill's) is an important presence, he does little more than stand by with an air of omniscience and detached amusement, paternally surveying his seraglio. In essence, the film's focus is on Estella's sexual awakening (and female sensuality in general). Tentatively, she muddles through a personal dialectic of her own—first as a voyeur, then as an active participant. Her reflections on what seems an alien culture, coupled with her unrequited yearnings, osmose into liberating non-conformist, non-Anglo-Saxon attitudes. In just a few days, she becomes, as it were, a cultural anthropologist who beds down with the natives. Her life will never be the same,

Not quite Hugh Grant's smug pastor, who's divinely assured of his moral certitudes and fails to join into the spirit of the sport. In a published interview, the young actor (currently ubiquitous in three other high profile films: Merchant Ivory's period piece *Remains Of The Day*; Mike Newell's screwball romance *Three Weddings and A Funeral*; Roman Polanski's kinky *Bitter Moon*) described his character as "a bit of a twit ... but instead of playing him that way, what if he thinks he's groovy and trendy? Then when he's finally confronted with the real stuff, he's deeply shaken, and his true conservatism comes out. That's much more interesting."

As for the women, in breadth and depth, the four other females filling the pastoral landscape are in startling physical counterpoint to Fitzgerald's diminutive manse mouse. They're Amazons by comparison: Pamela Rabe as Lindsay's wife and personal muse, and sirens Kate Fischer, Portia De Rossi, and 6-foot supermodel Elle MacPherson (cover girl for the *Sports Illustrated* swimsuit issue), who gained 20 lbs. for her debut role as one of the beauteous Botticellis. Cinematographer Geoff Burton said "Our aim was to make [them] absolutely ravishing—not that they need much help." (They don't.)

Sirens was filmed in rugged bush country at Lindsay's actual estate, the vast, edenic Springwood, now owned by Australia's National Trust. The house, studio and grounds, including his sculptures, are just as he left it upon his death at 90 in 1969. Director Duigan (*The Year My Voice Broke, Flirting*) picked both his cast and content wisely, with an artist's eye for aesthetics, and a storyteller's for unmitigated amusement and audacity.

LOS ANGELES TIMES, 3/9/94, Calendar/p. 7, Peter Rainer

"Sirens," set in the 1930s, is a high-class exploitation film about letting yourself go in the lush Australian Blue Mountains. The Rev. Anthony Campion (Hugh Grant) and his wife Estella (Tara Fitzgerald) are visiting the mountain retreat of artist Norman Lindsay (Sam Neill) at the behest of the Archbishop of Sydney to convince him to withdraw his scandalous painting "The Crucified Venus" from an international exhibition. It's not long before the couple become transfixed by pagan revelry and prancing nude models.

This is one of those films that's usually described in deep tones as a "sensual awakening," but, to its credit, the cast seems to be having a high old time acting flouncy and coy. They don't make too much of the "awakening" stuff because they're too busy trying to put the audience into a dreamy, woozy snooze, filled with images of naked Amazonian maidens paddling delicately through lily ponds or wafting through the air in their see-through chiffon nighties. Writer-director John Duigan doesn't have a perfervid imagination, and it's probably just as well. Given the flimsiness of the material, why settle for D. H. Lawrence when you can have the Playboy Channel instead?

There's more than a little of the Playboy philosophy in Lindsay's spoutings about free love and Bohemia. (Lindsay, a real painter, died in 1969 at the age of 90; so much for clean living.) But he spends most of his time painting while everyone else is panting. His three muse voluptuaries—Sheela (Elle MacPherson), Pru (Kate Fischer) and Giddy (Portia De Rossi)—can't seem to touch anything without fondling it. The prim Estella can't keep her eyes off them and their dalliances with the odd-job man (Mark Gerber) and other assorted locals. She's being "sensually awakened," remember?

Grant is doing his fuddy-dud gent number but he's aware of how silly the reverend must seem in this roundelay. His Anthony pretends to be a kind of swinger himself, trying to match wits with Lindsay by shocking him with quotes from James Joyce. But he's no match for the lushness or the ladies, and, at least intellectually, he gives in to his frailty, and his wife's, with aplomb. He's a sport.

And it's Elle MacPherson's screen debut, which ought to be worth a footnote in the film history books (and a photo spread in Playboy's "Sex in the Cinema 1994"). According to the press kit, Macpherson gained 20 pounds for the film, "lending her body a Botticelli contour." It then goes to reassure us that "she resumed her typical diet midway through production to prepare for her next assignment, a cover shoot for the Sports Illustrated swimsuit issue."

Whew!

NEW YORK POST, 3/4/94, p. 35, Thelma Adams

"Sirens" seduces from beginning to end.

Written and directed by Australian John ("Flirting") Duigan this beautifully shot, beautifully played movie about love and lust, art and religion, refuses to take itself too seriously.

The story is loosely based on the life of Norman Lindsay (Sam Neill), a bohemian artist who created a utopia in the Australian Blue Mountains with his wife Rose (Pamela Rabe). Adding modest Sheela (Elle MacPherson), Prue (Kate Fischer) and Giddy (Portia De Rossi), Duigan focuses on a single imagined event.

An Anglican clergyman, Anthony Campion (Hugh Grant) travels through the Australian wilderness—a landscape as seductive, playful and dangerous as a beautiful woman—to persuade Lindsay to pull a "blasphemous" painting titled "The Crucified Venus" from an international exhibition.

Anthony and his wife, Estella (Tara Fitzgerald), arrive at Lindsay's compound like Adam and Eve awaking in Eden. The young marrieds love each other—they affectionately refer to each other as Pooh (he's a heavy sleeper) and Piglet—but emotionally and sexually, they are proper strangers. From the first, there are snakes in the garden and Estella, like Eve, is tempted.

"Sirens" celebrates sexuality and the female form without exploiting it. The actresses display more nudity than in such recent movies as "The Getaway" where the Amazonian Kim Basinger bares all with a bored Playboy centerfold's drop of the robe. And yet, there is nothing smirky when Lindsay says, "The female body is the most beautiful thing in the world."

Duigan playfully unwraps the variety of the female form from supermodel MacPherson's finger-sucking earth-mother abandon to Fitzgerald's scrubbed British modesty. The nudity has a golden-tinged idealized quality that recalls the Pre-Raphaelites and such paintings ad John William Waterhouse's "Ophelia."

Duigan deftly raises the issue of artistic censorship. A similar debate heated up domestically when the National Endowment for the Arts funded Andres Serrano and his "Piss Christ" and the religious right cried out.

While Lindsay worked without government subsidy (a key point in the N.E.A. debates), his discussions with Campion thoughtfully lay out the rationale behind artistic freedom while still allowing the young clergyman his due— that a painting of a nude, voluptuous woman nailed to a cross offends some citizens' deeply-held religious beliefs.

Sam ("The Piano") Neill fans will hunger for more from his portrait of a scandalous artist. But, while the plot revolves around Lindsay and his activities, it's the transformation of the repressed Estella that dominates—and rightly so. Relative newcomer Fitzgerald (who bears a resemblance to Isabella Rossellini) gives a finely wrought performance that opens out to a final scene of frisky marital eroticism.

Hugh Grant, who has had little rest since "The Remains of the Day," displays a British upper-crust attractiveness, a combination of intellectual awareness and sexual naivete. He is the month's romantic lead, with two other pictures opening in New York in March: "Bitter Moon" Roman Polanski's cynical exploration of marital lust and repression; and "Four Weddings and a Funeral," a romantic romp with Andie MacDowell.

Taken together, the ensemble is delightful, Duigan's touch light and sure. "Sirens" seduces—and it also satisfies.

NEWSDAY, 3/4/94, Part II/p. 80, John Anderson

Please turn to Page 22 in the Gospel According to Hef for a discussion of "Sirens," the new work by the entertaining, if not always cogent John Duigan. Here we will learn that this film is not, as it may seem, an attempt to film a Sports Illustrated swimsuit issue without the swimsuits. No, no, no. Rather, it is an illuminating treatise on Bohemian vs. Victorian mores, the role of the human body in religious art, the role of trade unionism in British colonial history and the role of the shark attack in Australian population planning.

From the opening black-and-white sequence at sea, and what looks a lot like the Titanic in "A Night to Remember," we know we're in serious territory, because only serious filmmakers use black and white. And because Estella Campion (Tara Fitzgerald) is heading for a collision with her own personal iceberg.

It comes via Norman Lindsay (Sam Neill), a defiantly unorthodox Australian painter whose nude oil, entitled "The Crucified Venus," has outraged the constipated curators of an international art show in 1930s Sydney. And Mr. Anthony Campion (Hugh Grant), Anglican minister and recent arrival from England, is sent to Lindsay's estate to see if the artist might be convinced to change his art.

Campion fancies that he was quite a progressive back at Oxford, but he's no match for Lindsayland, which he sees as Sodom and Gomorrah, but which is actually a combination Garden of Eden and Estella's sexual Waterloo.

Lindsay's live-in-models—the Estella-baiting Sheela (Elle MacPherson), the doctrinaire mock-Marxist Pru (Kate Fischer) and the sweetly silly Giddy (Portia De Rossi)—present a formidable trinity of temptation for Anthony, but he's too repressed to be aroused. Which is one reason Estella responds, first to the antics of the three "sirens"—the subject of Lindsay's latest painting—then to the virtues of Devlin (Mark Gerber), a hunky local handyman who was blinded in a prizefight and wanders about the grounds, a combination Ulysses/Caliban ready to turn certain ladies into libertines.

Duigan intimates mortality constantly—the Titanic, a mosquito, a recurring joke about people lost to sharks. And he adorns his film with biblical and mythological allusions—including a rather obvious serpent who keeps crawling about. But it's all an attempt to put a high gloss on a trite film.

If he wanted to make the point that it is civilization that's prurient, rather than the naked human form, that's fine; if you find yourself distracted by the women as Lindsay and Campion conduct their pseudo-serious art debates, then he's made his point—to a point. But the women doff their clothes with such frequency that by repetition they become ludicrous, as does Estella's erotic dreaming, from which we're never quite sure she's awakened.

Of "The Crucified Venus," Anthony tells Estella he finds the painting "downright arrogant." Which is how one would describe a writer/director like Duigan using what is virtually a 19th-Century scenario to make a case against censorship in the 20th, with its multi-media complexity and amorphous rules. By the final and quite astounding closing scene, "Sirens" has not only exploited what it purports to defend, it's made the sight of beautiful nudes boring. Which is quite an accomplishment.

SIGHT AND SOUND, 8/94, p. 53, Amanda Lipman

Anthony Campion, a young vicar newly arrived from England, and his wife Estella are taken by the Bishop of Sydney around an exhibition of Australian artists. Included is Norman Lindsay's painting of a naked woman on a cross, which has offended the church. The Bishop asks Campion to visit Lindsay on his distant estate and persuade him to substitute another picture for the exhibition.

Lindsay's bohemian household is inhabited by his wife Rose, his two daughters and his three models, Pru, Sheela and Giddy. After a boisterous dinner, during which Lindsay refuses to change his paintings, the models dress up as fairies for the little girls. The next morning, Sheela invites Estella for a swim. Shocked by Pru and Sheela's nudity and by the appearance of the odd-job man, Devlin—almost blind as the result of a boxing match—Estella runs back to the house. Because of a derailed train, Estella and Anthony have to stay longer. That night Estella—unaware that Lindsay is watching her—spies on Pru and Sheela playing strip poker with two men. At a picnic, Pru and Sheela tease Giddy because she fancies Devlin. Out walking, Estella sees Devlin, naked and about to masturbate. His dog barks and she runs off, terrified. She is rescued, by the three models, who dress her up and take her to town for a drunken afternoon where they encounter the disapproval of the local people. A flustered Anthony sees them all tickling and stroking Giddy. Estella is tied to a tree by the others, and has to call Devlin to untie her. Back at the house, Anthony is angry with her, and they row.

In church, Estella imagines herself naked in front of everyone. Giddy has decided to sleep with Devlin that night. But she is so drunk that she falls asleep. After sex with Anthony, Estella creeps into Lindsay's studio where Devlin is waiting, and they make love. At dinner the next day, Devlin takes her hand under the table. When Giddy starts accusing Pru and Sheela of having slept with her man, Estella runs from the table. Anthony follows her and his kindness wins her over. She goes to Giddy that night, gives her her wedding ring "for luck", and tells her to go to Devlin. In a dream-like state she wanders down to the lake and lies in it, caressed by the hands of the three women. Giddy wakes her up in bed, delighted. Anthony is outraged because Lindsay has painted Estella's dream into a picture. But Estella is complimentary. Anthony tells her that the church has given in over the paintings. On the train home, Estella coyly starts tickling Anthony with her foot. On a ridge on the Blue Mountains, Pru, Sheela, Giddy, Rose and Estella, naked, sway mystically.

Anyone expecting the sharply observational adolescent comedy of John Duigan's *The Year My Voice Broke* and *Flirting* is in for a surprise. For though sex is again pretty much the main preoccupation of the characters, there is little of the wry, sympathetic humour of Duigan's earlier films. Instead, he has decided to celebrate the liberation of mind and body, as uptight, English Estella gives in to her passions in a sunny, bohemian Australian household.

The Piano has shown how sexy a film about repression and seduction can be; in *Sirens*, the theme is faintly ludicrous. This would be fine if the subject were treated in a matchingly ludicrous spirit, but Duigan appears to have taken it completely seriously. So when we want to laugh at the tinkly, almost soft-focus scenes of the women tickling and stroking each other, or the final image of them standing on the rocks and 'becoming one' with nature, or even the Lady Chatterley-style seduction of Estella by the extra-virile, blind odd-job man Devlin—all clenched hands and heaving passion—it is for the wrong reasons.

Not that there is no potential here—particularly when the film concentrates on Estella's repressed sexuality rather than on her liberation. Her dreams of nakedness in holy places and nude female statues coming to life have an engaging hyper-reality. A true spy in the house of love, she is endlessly peeping at sexual activity from a distance before running away from it. And looking (or not looking) provides quite a powerful central motif. Lindsay sees Estella spying, Giddy spies on Devlin and Estella making love (although she does not recognise Estella), while Anthony can only bear to spy briefly on his wife frolicking with the models, or to catch a glimpse of Giddy (to whom he is secretly attracted) modelling naked for Lindsay. Devlin's blindness means that he cannot look at Estella (and, by implication, her guilt) as she betrays her husband with him.

There is also something imposingly larger than life about the film. The world outside the house is made up of some crudely engaging caricatures. Inside it, the statuesque Sheela emanates a lazy, flirting sensuality that thrusts itself perceptibly into Estella's consciousness. And the Lindsay household reverberates with the noise of endless arguments about philosophy, religion, socialism, women's rights and art—so much so, in fact, that when distinctly anachronistic phrases such as "negative images" creep into the conversation, the impression is that Duigan is really taking time off to explore a few more of his own preoccupations in a rambling, European film style.

The film is laden with symbols and visual metaphors—snakes slithering about; rose petals dropping in slow motion on the sleeping Estella's face; the endless Australian disasters that she reads about in the newspapers; the wild animals that seem quite at home in this house of animal passions. These could help to work this either into a lavish fantasy, or into a camply outrageous romp. But the film does not quite have the courage to go for one or the other and tends, instead, to fall limply between the two.

It is only Hugh Grant who gives *Sirens* a dose of what it needs. Taking his cue from his role in Roman Polanski's recent *Bitter Moon*—a potentially pretentious drama that opted instead for entertainingly bizarre humour—Grant plays another ridiculous Englishman abroad. This time, he is a naif who thinks himself 'progressive', but the impact is much the same. Ever apologising, or bashfully averting his gaze from the naked women draped around the place, trying to make cheerful conversation, or clumsily attempting to make love to his wife, the Pooh half of the Campions' self-styled 'Pooh and Piglet' duo is a riot. It's just a shame that no-one else rises to it—and that, rather like Lindsay's paintings, the film is never more than boisterously and earnestly twee.

VILLAGE VOICE, 3/15/94, p. 53, Laurie Stone

Snakes slithering through lush gardens. Apples munched noisily. Temptation, anyone? Happily, here sexual awakening is a fall forward rather than a terrifying plunge, like the one portrayed in writer-director John Duigan's last film, his stunning adaptation of Jean Rhys's *Wide Sargasso Sea*. Overripeness rules in both movies, not only in the effulgent nature and human beasties shown, but in dense art sources—*Sea* reconfiguring Charlotte Bronte, *Sirens* drawing on *A Midsummer Night's Dream*, Pre-Raphaelite painting, D. H. Lawrence, E. M. Forster, and John Fowles. A real anecdote sparked the screenplay: the Australian artist Norman Lindsay, who delighted in goosing the church, penetrated zestfully with his etching, *The Crucified Venus*, which depicted a juicy female nude nailed to a cross by jeering clergymen. Duigan sets his movie in the 1930s and invents two sexual naifs: a British minister (Hugh Grant), who tries to persuade Lindsay (Sam Neill) to withdraw his work from an exhibition and the minister's wife (Tara Fitzgerald).

On the compound, which includes Lindsay's wife, two children, three lusty female models, and a blind Mellors type, sex isn't merely sport and drive but the key to social transformation. *Fuck Repression* is tattooed, figuratively, on the foreheads of the bohemians. *Well, yeah,* say the Brits in about one minute, for they aren't prudes, just asleep. There's no conflict, no danger, but who cares? *Sirens* is alluring softcore, with alas, a ratio of five naked women (including Elle MacPherson, whose acting relies heavily on finger-licking) to one lone man. He's choice, though, played by Mark Gerber, who has genial genitals and a taut tush. Everything in the movie—including the majestic Blue Mountains, outside Sydney, where the film was shot—quakes, heaves, then lies back and smiles. So will you.

Also reviewed in:
CHICAGO TRIBUNE, 3/11/94, Friday/p. C, Michael Wilmington
NEW REPUBLIC, 4/4/94, p. 25, Stanley Kauffmann
NEW YORK TIMES, 3/4/94, p. C16, Janet Maslin
VARIETY, 1/24-30/94, p. 64, David Stratton
WASHINGTON POST, 3/11/94, p. G1, Hal Hinson

SLEEP WITH ME

A United Artists release of an August Entertainment presentation in association with Paribas Film Corporation and Revolution Films. *Executive Producer:* Joel Castleberg. *Producer:* Michael Steinberg, Roger Hedden, and Eric Stoltz. *Director:* Rory Kelly. *Screenplay:* Duane

Dell'Amico, Roger Hedden, Neal Jimenez, Joe Keenan, Rory Kelly, and Michael Steinberg. *Director of Photography:* Andrzej Sekula. *Editor:* David Moritz. *Music:* David Lawrence. *Sound:* Giovanni Di Simone. *Casting:* Ellie Kanner. *Production Designer:* Randy Eriksen. *Art Director:* J. Michael Gorman. *Set Decorator:* Adam Mead Faletti. *Costumes:* Isis Mussenden. *Make-up:* Kathleen Karridene. *Running time:* 86 minutes. *MPAA Rating:* R.

CAST: Eric Stoltz (Joseph); Meg Tilly (Sarah); Craig Sheffer (Frank); Todd Field (Duane); Susan Traylor (Deborah); Dean Cameron (Leo); Thomas Gibson (Nigel); Tegan West (Rory); Amaryllis Borrego (Amy); Parker Posey (Athena); Joey Lauren Adams (Lauren); Vanessa Angel (Marianne); Adrienne Shelly (Pamela); Quentin Tarantino (Sid); June Lockhart (Caroline); David Kriegel (Josh); Lewis Arquette (Minister); Adelaide Miller (Blonde Actress); Alexandra Hedison (Brunette Actress); David Kirsch (Agent Trainee); Phil Brock (Agent).

LOS ANGELES TIMES, 9/23/94, Calendar/p. 2, Peter Rainer

For most of its length "Sleep With Me," directed by first-timer Rory Kelly, offers up maundering set pieces involving its young actors carousing, yelling, arguing. Talking nonstop is a tic they can't shake.

Is the talk worth listening to? That depends on who is talking and when. The film's gimmick is that six screenwriters—all friends, each contributing a separate segment—worked on it independently. The result is no more or less of a patchwork than most bigger-budgeted Hollywood films—many of which also have six writers, or more, if you include all the uncredited hands. In fact, the near-seamlessness of the script—credited to Kelly, Duane Dell'Amico, Roger Hedden, Neal Jimenez, Joe Keenan and Michael Steinberg—is somewhat off-putting. With all these supposedly different sensibilities at work, why concoct something that rolls along without a bump?

Fashioned as a new-style love triangle movie, "Sleep With Me" ends up, despite its free-form acting and "modern" attitudes, being rather conventional. It mints the same old familiar romantic clichés for the late-20s, early 30s generation.

Joseph (Eric Stoltz) and his best friend, Frank (Craig Sheffer), have a problem: Joseph's wife, Sarah (Meg Tilly). Beginning with a casual flirtation on the day before her wedding, Sarah comes on to Frank and drives him to distraction. It turns out he always loved her; she's flattered, wary, seductive, standoffish. When Frank declares his love for her at a gathering of friends, Joseph turns against both his wife and his friend. Frank spends most of the rest of the movie crashing various parties in order to importune Sarah; most of his circle of friends, who also include a snooty Brit (Thomas Gibson) and a struggling screenwriter (Todd Field), keep their distance too, or else try to foment the fighting. The guys' weekly poker game degenerates.

The actors are talented and loose-limbed enough to keep the wayward sequences watchable. but there's precious little character development. Once you get their drift, the scenes begin to pile up rather than develop. There may be a certain dramatic logic to this: We're probably meant to register how these layabouts fritter away their time and recycle the same peeves. But the effect is like a great big actors' studio exercise—lots of gnashing and carrying on. And Kelly tries to give it all a forlorn friskiness.

There are some terrific moments, like the funny-hostile scene where a sometime girlfriend of Frank's played very well by Vanessa Angel, talks about rebirthing and her love for men: or a party scene where a nonstop gabber played by Quentin Tarantino goes on about the homoerotic subtext of "Top Gun." (The funniest thing is , he's right.) "Sleep With Me" keeps you in a whirl while its's spinning, but there's not much to savor when it comes to a stop.

NEW YORK POST, 9/23/94, p. 49, Michael Medved

"Sleep With Me" is one of those experimental, conversation piece projects where the behind-the-scenes story of how the film was made is far more interesting than anything that appears on screen.

Six young writers toiled together on this screenplay, but rather than collaborating in the normal style, they each took responsibility for writing a separate segment of the story, then stitching together their independent products.

It may have been fun to work that way, but the movie that emerges from the process isn't much fun to watch.

As with most other projects about "Generation X-ers" ("Reality Bites," "Bodies, Rest and Motion." "Threesome") we get lots of cigarette smoke, earrings, pseudo-hip dialogue, and, for some odd reason, a romantic triangle.

It's as if the smug, shallow characters who regularly turn up in such fare are so bored with their own listless lives that sexual competition among best friends is the only activity that can engage their attention.

Here the best friends and rivals are a pair of sulky, self-indulgent stiffs played by Eric Stoltz and Craig Sheffer. They're both deeply in love with Meg Tilly, though Sheffer tries to hide his feelings until after his two pals get married in a beach-front ceremony.

At that point he begins pursuing the confused but flattered woman through a series of increasingly outrageous public humiliations.

The three stars are all appealing and accomplished performers, but there's nothing they can do with the underwritten characters. Despite the combined efforts of the six screenwriters, we know nothing at all about the people on screen—with few clues as to where they come from, how they know each other, or even what they do for a living.

The Sheffer character remains the biggest mystery: the only explanation for his obsession with his best friend's introverted, enigmatic wife remains a brief reference to once seeing her on a cloudy day looking beautiful with a green umbrella.

In place of characterization, "Sleep With Me" offers knowing references to other films. Sheffer likes to attend parties with a camcorder in hand, taping attractive women in the style of James Spader in "sex, lies and videotape."

In this case, we get so many pointless minutes of his black-and-white video-view of the world that you want to smash his camera once and for all.

There's also a superficial similarity to "Four Weddings and a Funeral," with a group of bickering buddies who function as a makeshift family getting together in a series of significant social occasions.

The key difference is that the people in the British film proved profoundly likable, while this crowd, despite the talented young cast (especially director Quentin Tarantino in a truly amusing cameo) features the sort of one-dimensional jerks you wish you'd never met.

"Who are these people? They're making me sick!" one of the characters perceptively declares—a statement which, together with the movie's concluding musical selection "Throwin' Time Away," might serve as an apt summary for the entire project.

NEWSDAY, 9/23/94, Part II/p. B7, Gene Seymour

The chief impression one gets from watching "Sleep With Me" is that it must have been fun to hang out with the cast and crew when the cameras weren't rolling. Everybody seems to be having a good time acting out what could be pitched to a producer as "Jules and Jim" coming to blows in southern California.

The three sides of this particular love triangle are Joseph (Eric Stoltz), Frank (Craig Sheffer) and Sarah (Meg Tilly), who have known each other since college. Their easy camaraderie reaches a crossroads when Joseph asks Sarah to marry him. Just before the wedding, Frank suddenly realizes he's in love with Sarah.

Frank keeps his feelings to himself well after the knot is tied. But tension between Joseph and Frank leaks out at poker games and parties attended by other varied single and married friends in their social circle, who become by-standers to the inevitable meltdown of Frank and Joseph's friendship and Sarah's own tangled feelings.

It's hard to believe a film that boasts three producers, including co-star Stoltz, and five scriptwriters, including, director Rory Kelly, co-producer Michael Steinberg and Neal Jimenez ("The Waterdance"), could seem so bouncy and weightless.

Then again, that may be part of the problem. It's so bouncy and weightless it doesn't seem to amount to much. The three principals try hard to make you care what happens. As the triangle's hypotenuse, Tilly is especially effective. She shows, at times, the kind of vitality and spark that director Ernst Lubitsch would have loved to exploit in his more elegant romantic comedies. Her lively, self-possessed Sarah doesn't deserve either of these sullen schmoes.

The collective input from different writers (and probably from a few of the actors) is one of those utopian ideas that works only in fits and starts, hampering the film's rhythm.

Many of the lines are funny, especially those belonging to Todd Field as a married and harried screenwriter who strikes gold toward the end. But the dialogue, like the film as a whole, isn't quite as fresh as it tries to be. Some scenes go on too long. Some, like the sequence of an afternoon tea that boils over into chaos, are disorienting and embarrassing in ways that may not have been intended.

The movie self-consciously aims for a hip apotheosis, which it achieves only toward the end with a hilarious cameo by filmmaker Quentin Tarantino giving a manic—and logical—homoerotic exegesis of "Top Gun." The rest, despite Tilly's energy and the random, dead-on observations on love and marriage, is just the same old soap suds.

SIGHT AND SOUND, 11/94, p. 53, Geoffrey Macnab

Joseph, Frank and Sarah, three young friends, are driving back to Los Angeles after a road trip. They pull in to a garage, where Joseph proposes to Sarah and she accepts. The day before the wedding, Frank accompanies Sarah on a walk along the beach. They mull over the past and Sarah reveals that there was a time when she had hoped they would become a couple. She kisses Frank under the pier. A few weeks later, Joseph, Frank and their friends are playing their regular game of poker. There is tension between Joseph and Frank. When Frank ups the ante, Joseph, a struggling garden designer, can't afford to stay in the hand. He throws down his cards in disgust and walks off.

At a barbecue, Frank has borrowed a video camera and is wandering around, filming guests and asking them searching questions. He eventually corners Sarah and reveals that he is obsessed by her. Soon afterwards, Frank throws a dinner party. After the meal, the guests, including Joseph and Sarah, are sitting around making small talk, when Frank blurts out that he loves Sarah and kisses her. The party breaks up in disarray.

Joseph and Sarah's English friend Nigel has invited them round to meet his formidable mother-in-law. Frank has turned up uninvited with his new girlfriend Pamela in tow. As Frank and Sarah remonstrate about the dinner party, Joseph strikes up a conversation with a woman he meets in the kitchen. He leaves with her. Frank offers to drive Sarah home. They drop off a confused Pamela on the way, and end up making love. Joseph, meanwhile, stops himself at the last minute from committing adultery with the beautiful stranger.

The final party of the year is thrown by Duane, who has just sold a film script. Frank, in disgrace with his friends, has not been invited. He tries to gatecrash so he can see Sarah, but is turned away at the door. He creeps round the house, climbs in through a window, and eventually corners Sarah in the bathroom. He asks her to come outside to his car to talk to him. As he waits for her, Joseph confronts him. A slanging match breaks out between the three friends. It ends with Sarah jumping in the car and driving off. However, she stops at the lights. Joseph runs after her.

"A movie about a group of friends written by a group of friends," as Rory Kelly has described his debut movie, *Sleep With Me* is more than a little self-regarding. The script was fashioned by six writers—among them Kelly and Michael Steinberg, who made *Bodies, Rest & Motion*—and involves its lead characters wandering between various social gatherings, working through their emotional problems en route. Those concerned are slightly older versions of *Beverly Hills 90201* types—pampered, good-looking, with a veneer of cynicism and preoccupied with nothing so much as themselves. They're all aware of how clever and photogenic they are, seem intent on capturing as much of their lives on videotape as possible. It's little wonder the film has the feel of a glorified home movie—there is an improvised quality to much of the acting, and the narrative does not so much flow as jolt along, with inter-titles to bridge awkward gaps. There is no real sense of milieu: characters converge on each other's houses and backyards, but the outside world rarely intrudes. Kids, the old and the ugly are kept out of frame.

In a perverse way, this narrowness is part of the film's strength. By setting the action in a hermetically sealed community, Kelly creates a suitably oppressive backcloth for the main drama—the tortuous love triangle between Frank, Joseph and Sarah. Relationships in this community are conducted in a rigorously superficial way, and emotions are only ever expressed ironically or flippantly. The freewheeling, seemingly relaxed Californians turn out to have their own norms of behaviour. In their way, they're as censorious as the priggish, uptight New Englanders of *The Age of Innocence*. When Frank threatens the harmony of the group, they all close ranks against him.

Inevitably, the six discrete segments vary in tone and quality. Comedy and mawkish drama do not always gel and there are moments, notably when video cameras are around, at which characters plumb the depths of pretentiousness. It, is not always clear whether Kelly wants to celebrate or satirise the attitudes and antics of the group. But there is some blisteringly funny dialogue along the way; Meg Tilly, Craig Sheffer and Eric Stoltz manage to look suitably anguished without becoming too earnest, and Kelly isn't afraid to crank up the dramatic tension by registering pauses and embarrassed silences. There are also some nicely judged character turns from the likes of Thomas Gibson and Hal Hartley regular Adrienne Shelley.

It was a mistake, though, to allow Quentin Tarantino his cameo. The machine-gun way he rattles off his monologue about *Top Gun*—"the story of a man's struggle with his homosexuality"—leaves the rest of the cast looking lumbering. His reading of Tony Scott's film could apply to this movie too: if *Top Gun* is a love story between Tom Cruise and Val Kilmer, it could just as well be argued that the relationship that really matters in *Sleep With Me* is the one between Eric Stoltz and Craig Sheffer, and that this is nothing but an old-fashioned buddy story at heart.

VILLAGE VOICE, 9/27/94, p. 66, Beth Coleman

Created by six writers as a series of public gatherings, *Sleep With Me* shows us that three adults can behave with the restraint of fevered five-year-olds, yet still nothing really gets broken, or fixed. Joseph (Eric Stoltz) marries Sarah (Meg Tilly); Frank (Craig Sheffer), the couple's best friend, loves Sarah; and Joe loves ... social sanctity. It remains a mystery what Sarah loves, other than high-school revenge games, in this three of hearts.

The boys chat endlessly about homoerotic bonding (Quentin Tarantino makes his cameo as the party sleaze, checking the chicks as he gives his gay allegory of *Top Gun*), but the ostensible subject is marriage—Can't live with it, can't live without it. (Someone with a black marker needs to add "Don't" to the movie poster.)

Avoiding the difficulties of emotions, *Sleep* reveals the effects of smog inhalation: there're a lot of screaming fights in convertibles and front yards, much group brouhaha, and a little sex. It's not that the performances are bad (particularly Sheffer's young Byron in Calvin menswear), but the endless styling, nastiness, and smugness—rendered boringly—leaves the thin script in shreds. As their friend, the endearingly disaffected Duane (Todd Field), points out, "Maybe you guys have too much time on your hands."

Also reviewed in:
NEW YORK TIMES, 9/23/94, p. C10, Caryn James
VARIETY, 5/30-6/5/94, p. 44, Todd McCarthy

SLINGSHOT, THE

A Sony Pictures Classics release of an AB Svensk, Filmindustri/SVT Kanal 1 Drama/Nordisk Film A/S/Svenska Film Institute production. *Producer:* Waldemar Bergendahl. *Director:* Ake Sandgren. *Screenplay (Swedish with English subtitles):* Ake Sandgren. *Based on the novel by:* Roland Schütt. *Director of Photography:* Göran Nilsson. *Editor:* Grete Moldrup. *Music:* Böjrn Isfält. *Sound:* Michael Dela and Nalle. *Sound Editor:* Willie Peterson-Berger and Jean-Frédéric Axelsson. *Casting:* Catti Edfeldt, Anette Mandoki, Lars Lindström, and Jana Pospisilov. *Production Designer:* Lasse Westfelt. *Art Director:* Lasse Westfelt and Tomás Moravec. *Set Decorator:* Kristoffer Sjöstörm, Per Johannson, and Lisbet Janson. *Costumes:*

Inger Pehrsson. *Make-up:* Helena Carmback. *Running time:* 102 minutes. *MPAA Rating:* R.

CAST: Jesper Salén (Roland Schütt); Stellan Skarsgård (Fritiof Schütt); Basia Frydman (Zipa Schütt); Niclas Olund (Bertil Schütt); Ernst-Hugo Järegård (Lundin); Reine Brynolfsson (Hinge Bergegren); Jacob Leygraf (Stickan); Frida Hallgren (Margit); Axel Düberg (Inspector Gissle); Ing-Marie Carlsson (Karin Adamsson); Ernst Günther (Principal); Tomas Norström (Boxing Trainer); Rolf Lassgård (Prisoner); Jurek Sawka (Kopowski, the Orthopedist); Par Ericsson (Perling, Director of the Boys' Home).

LOS ANGELES TIMES, 7/8/94, Calendar/p. 18, Kevin Thomas

"The Slingshot," a bitter-sweet but warm account of growing up in Sweden in the 20s, takes its title from the devices fashioned by its ingenious 10-year-old hero Roland Schütt (Jesper Salén) from condoms his mother sells to her friends. Roland's enterprise is doubly significant: As the film is based on an autobiographical novel, it foreshadows Roland's adult career as an inventor (the real Schütt is now in his 80s), and it reveals that Sweden was once far from the progressive nation it is today. No wonder Roland's mother, Zipa (Basia Frydman), is mightily upset with him: Between 1910 and 1937 the dissemination of birth control information was illegal in Sweden.

Zipa's family-planning advocacy, however, is but part of the larger commitment to socialism. She's a diminutive, fiery woman, a Russian Jew, whereas her husband, Fritiof (Stellan Skarsgard), is a tall, strapping fellow, expansive, a bit pompous but an even more fervent socialist than his wife. He runs a Stockholm tobacco shop, and his family—which includes an older son Bertil (Niclas Olund) an aspiring boxer—lives behind it in small but well-appointed quarters, Although there's not much money left over to buy the things boys crave, like a bicycle, the Schütts, for all the radical pronouncements made in their parlor, are definitely members of the middle class, albeit in the lower rungs.

"A revolutionary never closes his eyes," preaches Fritiof to Roland, who is in the process of establishing his own sense of identity amid considerable conflict and adversity. That he is an uncircumsized, baptized Christian—as presumably is his father—does not prevent him from being subjected to a chronic, crude and sometimes physically brutal anti-Semitism (whose worse practitioners are in fact his repellent teacher and principal; these two old men are virtual Nazis). Roland is not really interested in his father's politics, but he does develop the courage to look his adversaries straight in the eye.

The key significance of Roland's story, told by writer-director Ake Sandgren in leisurely, anecdotal fashion with both humor and poignancy amid impeccable period settings, is that it reveals the bedrock importance of strong family life. That Roland learns, quite literally, to roll with the punches, is because he's been blessed with loving parents. That Fritiof is clearly not very ambitious and that he's full of hot air doesn't much matter when you think of the love he's capable of expressing for his sons and the large amount of time he spends with them. Sandgren is a fine director of actors, his way with young Salén is a wonder, but it's Skarsgard's Fritiof that fills the screen with a rounded portrait of a voluble, grandiose dreamer who also happens to be a very good father.

NEW YORK POST, 6/3/94, p. 41, Thelma Adams

Oh, No! Another Swedish coming-of-age film.

Just as the four-star "Sunday's Children" ends an extended Film Forum run "The Slingshot" arrives. The Swedish entry to the Academy for Best Foreign-language film ("Belle Epoque" won) received five nominations for the Swedish Oscar.

Based on inventor Roland Schütt's novel, this song of wee Roland (Jesper Salen) chronicles the terrors of youth—and then some—in '20s Stockholm.

There's the stock bullying brother, Bertil (Niclas Olund). He boxes to please father Fritiof (Stellan Skarsgard), a blustery socalist and practices on Roland's nose.

Jewish mama Zipa (Basia Frydman) pauses from selling condoms (then illegal in Sweden) to bandage Roland's "nozzle." When dared the boy sticks his tongue on a frozen metal pole and Zipa rescues him with a blowtorch. Ouch!

If this isn't enough of a masochistic tango (the movie could be subtitled "A Boy and His Bandages"), the pre-teen also gets whipped bloody by his teacher, impaled on a sewing-machine needle, and tossed into jail.

There's the obligatory bitter-sweet sexual awakening. Roland encounters a teen prostitute who for a crown lets the boy tie her shoes and peek up her dress. I found this to be a rude, rather than a poignant, awakening—but then again I didn't come of age as a Swedish boy. Lucky for me since sex and death are linked together shortly thereafter.

Roland is pummeled so mercilessly because he is both Jew and Socialist, conditions that allow him to be bombarded by countless anti-Semitic and anti-Socalist comments by the fascists at school and the thugs on the block.

What joy there is to be found in this coming-of-age comedy lies in the lively performance of Jesper Salen. Roland is bratty, sensitive, and ingenious—a character surrounded by caricatures as false as his father's mustache.

Roland uses his mother's stock of condoms to create a mighty slingshot—and he is as resilient and impudent as the invention that gives the movie its title.

If only Ake Sandgren, the writer/director, had been as inventive as his hero, he might have shunned the yellow light he uses to halo the past and resisted trampling on ground so well traveled in "My Life as a Dog."

NEWSDAY, 6/3/94, Part II/p. B11, John Anderson

Given our general view of Sweden as politically liberal and sexually enlightened (or libertine), Ake Sandgren's "The Slingshot," set in '20s Stockholm, requires some adjustment. Anti-Semitism is not just rampant but flagrant. The monarchy is staunchly, and righteously, repressive. Condoms are illegal.

As a result, Roland (Jesper Salen), the idealistic-pragmatic 10-year-old at the center of Sandgren's bittersweet comedy, is under a double yoke: Besides having a brother (Niclas Olund) who wants to be a boxer and uses Roland's face as a speed-bag, their crippled, domineering father, Fritof (Stellan Skarsgard), is a fervid socialist; their mother, Zipa (Basia Frydman), is a Jew and shopkeeper who covertly dispenses contraceptive advice and prophylactics. They attend party meetings and battle the raiding police—Dad with his fists, Mom with her hat pin. And they're oblivious to the abuse heaped on their younger son.

"You can be exactly what you want to be," Zipa tells him, despite overwhelming evidence to the contrary.

Roland's circumstances make him immediately sympathetic, but his character makes him heroic. Inhabiting his own cool universe, he observes the antics of his doctrinaire parents, his cruel teachers and his duplicitous contemporaries at an existential distance. He's ingenious—instantly repairing a bike chain with his belt buckle, or using his mother's condoms for several lucrative inventions, including the weapon of the title. And he's courageously, if unwisely, defiant—answering a dare, he gets his tongue stuck to a frozen lamppost. When his contemptible teacher (Ernst-Hugo Jaregard) excuses him from singing Christian songs in class, Roland sings louder and faster than anyone else.

Despite his age, Roland is also the one fully defined character in Sangdren's film (the Swedish Academy Award winner for best picture). Clearly, his father is as bitter about his hobbling sciatica as he is about socialism's plight; his mother deludes herself that what she's found in Sweden, including bigotry and general ignorance, isn't exactly what she fled in Russia. Bertil, Roland's boxing brother, turns out to possess a streak of cowardice that's fatal in the ring.

Roland, on the other hand, has reachable dreams: a bicycle, or perhaps Margit (Frida Hallgren), the teenage prostitute with whom he forms a bond born of both lust and independence.

"The Slingshot," based on Roland Shutte's autobiography, may not equal Truffaut's "400 Blows" or any one of several recent Bergman films as definitive statements about wayward childhood. But Roland, whom fate often treats with disdain, has potential: Sandgren presents his flat face as a unformed map, but one with the intelligence to avoid the shoals and reefs and wreckage of blinkered adults. At least we hope he will. And something to hope for seems enough to ask of a film, in an age when childhood seems to equal yabba dabba.

SIGHT AND SOUND, 11/94, p. 48, Philip Kemp

1920s Stockholm. 12-year-old Roland Schütt lives with his father Fritiof, an ardent socialist, his Russian Jewish mother Zipa, and his older brother Bertil, a would-be boxing champion. Fritiof, crippled with sciatica and needing regular morphine injections for the pain, is none the less chosen to model for a portrait of the King, much to his sardonic amusement. The family attend a political meeting to promote the use of condoms (illegal in Sweden) which is raided by police, but the audience, including Fritiof and Zipa, furiously resist. Roland, who has a mechanical bent, repairs a bicycle for an older boy, Stickan, who offers to sell it to him. Having no money, Roland promises to pay for it later and meantime to repair and paint bikes for Stickan's friends. His financial situation worsens when, in a fight, he destroys Bertil's boxing gloves and must reimburse his father for a new pair. At school he incurs the enmity of his teacher, Lundin, who hates him as a Jew and a socialist.

Once Roland has painted the bike, Stickan, not having been paid, takes it back. Zipa is secretly instructing women in the use of condoms; to raise money, Roland steals some to sell as balloons, but the outraged Zipa bursts them. Undaunted, he devises catapults from scrap metal and condom rubber. They sell fast, but when the school authorities find out Lundin sadistically beats Roland. A Russian orthopaedist, Kopowski, cures Fritiof's sciatica by the traction method. The police arrive at the Schütts' house, since the bikes Stickan brought for repair were stolen. Roland protests his innocence, but after a night in the cells signs a confession, and is sentenced to reform school. Before leaving he takes revenge on Lundin by putting lice on the staff toilet—a trick learned from a cellmate. The reform school, out in the country, proves to be not such a bad place, and Roland dives happily into the lake with a new friend.

The Swedish period childhood film has almost become a small sub-genre in itself, with its characteristic bitter-sweet flavour, scrupulous recreation of evocative detail and (as the production notes for *The Slingshot* usefully summarise) its "mixture of tragedy, farce, heartbreak and exhilaration". *My Life As a Dog* is widely seen as having set the pattern, but Lasse Hallström's film also had its predecessors—among them Allan Edwall's gentle *Ake and His World*, Jan Troell's grittier *Here Is Your Life*, and even Bergman's masterly valediction *Fanny and Alexander*. Though from time to time risking a sense of déjà vu, *The Slingshot* more than earns its place in the tradition.

Ake Sandgren's film, which he scripted from an autobiographical novel by the real Roland Schütt, revolves—as any good rites-of-passage movie must—around the hero's struggle to establish a sense of identity. "How do I know whether I was meant to be Swedish?" Roland muses, faced with his double outsider status as a Jew and a socialist. "Was I meant to be who I am?" Everyone seems determined to foist an identity on him; at one point his mother, sensitive to her own alien origins, sends him off to school in full Swedish national costume, complete with ludicrous red bobbles on his hat. His Jewishness is literally knocked into him by almost everyone he meets—not since *Chinatown* can a nose have come under such sustained assault—and his teacher, with unconcealed pleasure, beats him as "a Jew—a socialist—and a criminal."

But though beleaguered and accident prone, Roland never comes across as the passive victim. There's an engaging doggedness about him (Jesper Salén's performance tempers wide-eyed innocence with a hint of truculence) anchored in the one aspect of his identity he never doubts—his chosen vocation as an inventor. "The Underwater Sock, by Roland Schütt," he remarks proudly, experimenting with a condom as footwear, and names his pet toad Ericsson after the great Swedish-American marine inventor. Even though his dexterity usually gets him into trouble, it's through his increasingly ingenious devices that he gains in confidence until he can at last welcome the reform school as a liberation, free from the constrictions of his emotionally rapacious family.

Around him Sandgren creates a busy, pungent townscape of foundries, cart horses and cobbled alleys (Prague, accommodating as ever, standing in for 20s Stockholm), vividly evoked but never made to seem cosy. The film's strength is in not going for easy nostalgia, making it clear that, for all its picturesque period charm, this was in many ways a harsh, callous world where only Roland's own resilience will keep him from a lifetime of petty crime. (It's intriguing too, as spike-helmeted police brutally suppress a family planning lecture, to realise how recent is Sweden's reputation for social enlightenment.) And now and then Sandgren jolts us with an outlandish image, as when Roland and his father, mistrustfully entering Kapowski's surgery, are confronted by a row of bodies crucified in mid-air, hanging alive but unblinking with arms outstretched in literally suspended animation. It's unexpectedly gothic moments such as this that sum up *The Slingshot*'s subtly off-centre appeal.

VILLAGE VOICE, 6/7/94 p. 49, J. Hoberman

There's another form of child abuse on display Ake Sandgren's *The Slingshot*—set in an unfamiliar, pre-World War II, working-class Sweden of brutes, blood, and anti-Semitism. [The reference is to *The Boys of St. Vincent*; see Hoberman's review.] His innocence continually betrayed, 10-year-old Roland is the metaphoric child of Karl Marx and Margaret Sanger: His father is a self-righteously two-fisted socialist with aristo pretensions; his Russian-Jewish mother is a crusader for birth control. Not only is this congenital nonconformist beaten by his sadistic teachers, his older brother is a boxing fool—by the end of the movie, Roland's perpetually bandaged nose has been spread out all over his face.

This course of study at the school of hard knocks notwithstanding, Roland is an impressively willful, single-minded, and ingenious boy. (The film's title comes from one of the more inventive uses he makes of his mother's condom supply.) The production may be a bit chintzy around the edges, but the period details are skillfully handled—*The Slingshot* doesn't feel like an empty world stocked with antiques. The movie is funnier than it might have been, but also less anarchic. In the over-long spectacle of a rough childhood sentimentalized, the production evinces the cautious good taste one has come to associate with Sony Classics.

Also reviewed in:
CHICAGO TRIBUNE, 7/22/94, Friday/p. J, Michael Wilmington
NEW YORK TIMES, 6/3/94, p. C19, Caryn James
VARIETY, 9/13/93, p. 34, Gunnar Rehlin
WASHINGTON POST, 7/15/94, p. B6, Rita Kempley

SOME FOLKS CALL IT A SLING BLADE

A 1994 New Directors film. *Producer:* Adam Lindemann, George Hickenlooper, and Kevin Hudnell. *Director:* George Hickenlooper. *Screenplay:* Billy Bob Thornton. *Director of Photography:* Kent Wakeford. *Editor:* Henni Boumeester and George Hickenlooper. *Music:* Bill Boll. *Art Director:* Deborah Smith. *Running time:* 25 minutes. *MPAA Rating:* Not Rated.

CAST: Billy Bob Thornton (Karl); J.T. Walsh (Charles); Molly Ringwald (Teresa Tatum); Jefferson Mays (Gerry Woolridge); Suzanne Cryer (Frances).

NEW YORK POST, 6/10/94, p. 42, Bill Hoffmann

[*Some Folks Call It a Sling Blade* was reviewed jointly with *Minotaur*; see Hoffmann's review of that film.]

NEWSDAY, 6/10/94, Part II/p. B15, Gene Seymour

[*Some Folks Call It a Sling Blade* was reviewed jointly with *Minotaur*; see Seymour's review of that film.]

Also reviewed in:
NEW YORK TIMES, 6/10/94, p. C12, Stephen Holden

SPANKING THE MONKEY

A Fine Line Features release of a Buckeye Communications production. *Executive Producer:* Stanley F. Buchthal, David O. Russell, and Janet Grillo. *Producer:* Dean Silvers. *Director:* David O. Russell. *Screenplay:* David O. Russell. *Director of Photography:* Michael Mayers. *Editor:* Pamela Martin. *Music:* Mark Sandman. *Sound:* William Tzouris. *Sound Editor:* Steven Visscher. *Casting:* Ellen Parks. *Production Designer:* Susan Block. *Set Dresser:* Todd Nicky, Lars Bjornlund, Sarah Bernoy, Michael DeCola, Russell Glober, Lucio Seixas, and Chantal Toub. *Costumes:* Carolyn Greco. *Make-up*: Evelyn Ortman. *Running time:* 98 minutes. *MPAA Rating:* Not Rated.

CAST: Jeremy Davies (Raymond Aibelli); Alberta Watson (Susan Aibelli); Benjamin Hendrickson (Tom Aibelli); Carla Gallo (Toni Peck); Matthew Puckett (Nicky); Judette Jones (Aunt Helen); Elizabeth Newitt (Bus Woman); Liberty Jean and Archer Martin (Motel Women); Zak Orth (Curtis); Josh Weinstein (Joel); Judah Domke (Don); Nancy Fields (Dr. Wilson); Carmine Paolini (Mailman); Neil Connie Wallace (Walter Hooten); Lleana Stratton (Fran Gibson); Jed Resnick (Fran's Son); Angela Grillo (Nurse); Jim Marcus (Dr. Marcus); Richard Husson (Dr. Peck); Ty-Ranne Grimstad (Secretary); William Keeler (Dean); Dean Silvers (Boss); John Schmerling (Trucker).

LOS ANGELES TIMES, 7/28/94, Calendar/p. 2, Peter Rainer

"Spanking the Monkey," the first feature by writer-director David O. Russell, is an odd choice for a debut film—even by the odd standards of American independent cinema. It's a whimsical black comedy about incest, and it never lets up. The matter-of-factness of Russell's approach is harrowing and also—this is the odd, daring part—funny. He keeps his camera on an even keel as he dispassionately records the wayward passions of his people.

Ray Aibelli (Jeremy Davies) is an MIT freshman who is called home from a summer internship with the Surgeon General to care for his bedridden mother (Alberta Watson) while his errant traveling salesman father (Benjamin Hendrickson) conveniently hits the road. Ray is miserable about the change in his summer plans; he doesn't want to be back in the suburbs, which he's been trying to escape.

He's trying to escape his parents, too. His father, who gives the boy boot-camplike instructions about taking care of the dog, his mother and the car, has no feeling for Ray's ambitions to become a doctor. His mother, Susan, her leg in a cast, lolls about her bedroom like a blitzed empress. As if for sport—to relieve the boredom—she moves closer and closer to Ray's privacies. She asks him to scrub her back, to prop her up while she takes a shower.

Ray seems alternately blank-faced and razor-sharp. He's the kind of very bright science maven who doesn't comprehend his own emotional circuitry. Russell makes us recognize the boy's conflicts even as Ray doesn't; we watch as he moves imperceptibly, inevitably toward his mother's clutches.

What Ray and his mother do, along with its repercussions, is presented as all-of-a-piece with the Aibelli's larger human comedy. It's the logical extension of the sultry love-hate horror at the heart of the family's functional dysfunctionalism.

Ray is sexually unawakened prior to his woozy, boozy encounter with his mother. He masturbates in the bathroom—*spanking the monkey* is slang for masturbation—while the family dog scratches at the door. He has a tingly tussle with a local high school girl (Carla Gallo) that leads to something a bit more ferocious than either of them bargained for. But his mother—she's such a *casual* monster—wades right into the boy's Oedipal entanglements. She gives him her version of a college tutorial. He gets his summer internship.

Russell has an adept visual sense but what really distinguishes "Spanking the Monkey" is the acting. Russell is unusual among first-time directors in his ability to mold and shape performance. Ray isn't some goggle-eyed twerp; he's a quirky, funny boy in pain. His mother is in pain too, which she inflicts with abandon—with innocence, almost—on her son. Davies and Watson are both extraordinary. They're like a creepy Jean Cocteau couple in home-grown suburbia U.S.A.

The ending of "Spanking the Monkey" is a large letdown, and the film could be even wiggier and more disturbing, but it's much more than a promising first feature. Russell bears watching.

NEW YORK, 7/25/94, p. 47, David Denby

The young writer-director David O. Russell, in his lovely first feature film, the erotic comedy *Spanking the Monkey*, obviously has his heart in the right place. Russell makes the villain of his film a dog. Every time the hero, Ray (Jeremy Davies), an MIT sophomore, goes to the bathroom to masturbate, the family's German shepherd whines piteously at the door. The dog, however, is not the only creature who ruins Ray's summer at home and brings him to the point of madness. There is also his unhelpful dad, a philandering salesman always on the road, and his mom, Susan, who is recovering in bed from a multiple fracture of the leg. Depressive, malicious, and extremely needy, Susan is not behaving well. In the darkly beautiful person of Canadian actress Alberta Watson, she can't stop herself from making trouble for the son who takes care of her. Russell handles the subject of mother-son incest as part of the normal painful comedy of a young man's sexual coming-of-age, and he gets away with it because he's such a cool, funny observer. He gets things subtly right—the peculiar antagonism of friends who are jealous of the hero's seriousness; the sultry teenage girl who wants him yet runs to her father every time something goes wrong. A brilliant debut film ...

NEW YORK POST, 7/15/94, p. 38, Bill Hoffmann

As anyone who's made it through the eighth grade knows, "Spanking the Monkey" is a smirky, infantile term for masturbation.

So it's logical that a movie bearing this title would be the worst kind of exploitive claptrap for morons.

Luckily, David Russell's provocative new entry is quite the opposite; it's a disturbing yet highly entertaining look at the perverse circumstances surrounding a young man's coming of age.

Raymond Aibelli is a responsible college freshman all set to to take a prestigious summer job in Washington when his mother fractures her leg and his always-on-the-go salesman dad orders him stay home and take care of her.

That means the uncomfortable but necessary tasks of emptying her bedpan, massaging her legs and assisting her in the shower fall squarely on Ray's shoulders.

It gets a little claustrophobic, but Ray has an outlet; he likes to lock himself in the bathroom and do what comes naturally.

Unfortunately, each time he's heading for ecstasy, the mood is spoiled by his pesky dog, Frank, who scratches and barks at the door.

Ray's also being pursued by an adorable nymphette neighbor who seems to want to go all the way but gets her shrink dad involved when the apple of her eye gets too frisky.

These frustrations, and the all-too-intimate grooming sessions with mom take their toll on Ray, whose ideas of love and family begin to cross the line. Is lack of masturbation the cause of the world's ills?

Will Ray end up sleeping with his mother or will he prevail and get the dreamy girl next door?

I won't spoil the suspense here, but it doesn't really matter anyway.

More powerful are the compelling, believable characters and crisp dialogue that first-time director Russell treats us to in this tension-charged black comedy.

Ray's problems seem terrifyingly real, from his overbearing dad to his confused, spaced-out mother to his jailbait girlfriend. Russell makes the most of his talented cast in building the drama.

It's an astonishing debut for a novice filmmaker, and a real find for moviegoers.

NEWSDAY, 7/15/94, Part II/p. B10, John Anderson

Suburbia's psychodrama has been played out by everyone from Billy Joel to Bart Simpson, but first-time director David O. Russell is after something more Cheeveresque in "Spanking the Monkey," where the family unit is populated by total strangers, all primed to implode.

Chief among the unstable devices is Ray Aibelli (Jeremy Davies), a premed student making a quick visit home before heading to Washington and a summer job in the surgeon general's office.

But his video-salesman father (Benjamin Hendrickson) puts Ray's life on rewind: His mother, Susan (Alberta Watson), has broken her leg, is bedridden and depressed and Tom, with expert timing, has to leave on a business trip. Further establishing Ray as the sacrificial lamb, he says the boy can't leave his mother alone, can't use the car, and leaves him with a toothbrush, so Ray can brush the dog's teeth.

Self-absorption is the strongest Aibelli family trait: Susan, played expertly by Watson, was a medical student herself until Ray came along. Bitter and frustrated over both her noncareer and nonmarriage, she lies in bed watching medical tapes and editing Ray's thesis. She calls him *Raymond.* Politeness in her mouth turns to poison. Ray, in turn, grows more resentful, and develops a warped relationship with Toni, the girl next door (a winning Carla Gallo). "I know your type," he tells her, but we know his: A priggish self-promoter who's really only out for No. 1. "I wrote about children with AIDS," he says of his paper. Why? "Because that's where people say the future is."

A great line, and like more than a few debut films, "Spanking the Monkey" (whose onanistic title seems like a bit of commercial suicide) is better on the page than on the screen—writers being limited only by mind, directors by money. But Russell has also made a good-looking movie, with a subtly ironic story that finds much of its humor in the utter humorlessness of its characters.

Critics have been asked to be discreet about "Spanking the Monkey," but this isn't a gimmick film. On the contrary, how it deals with what turns out to be its climax—the sexual collision of mother and son—is one of its strongest points. You believe it thoroughly, because nothing in the characters' makeup would prevent it.

NEWSWEEK, 7/18/94, p. 58, David Ansen

Smart, skinny, sexually frustrated Ray Aibellie is about to have a suburban summer in hell. He's just finished his freshman year at MIT when he's summoned home to play nursemaid to his convalescent mom, bedridden with a broken leg. His salesman dad, a philandering petty tyrant, is out on the road. So it's just Ray (Jeremy Davies) and his overprotective, sharp and seductive mother (Alberta Watson) cooped up in the house. He makes her drinks, carries her to the shower and, in his spare moments, wages a dismally inept seduction of a local teenage girl. Slowly, with outrageous matter-of-factness, David O. Russell's black comedy *Spanking the Monkey* edges toward its taboo subject—incest. Russell's accomplishment is to mesmerize us and make us laugh (nervously) without trivializing the psychological havoc being wreaked. Avoiding both flippancy and melodrama, this first-time writer/director and his sensitive cast navigate the tricky terrain with startling assurance. This discomfiting comedy of dysfunction is no joke.

SIGHT AND SOUND, 8/95, p. 55, Ben Thompson

Medical student Raymond Aibelli goes home to upstate New York after his freshman year at MIT, expecting to stay just a few days before taking up a prestigious internship. Ray's tyrannical commercial traveller father gives him a list of instructions: he is off on a sales trip, and Ray must stay and look after his attractive but deeply unhappy mother, Susan, who has fractured her leg in the course of a bungled suicide attempt.

Ray tends to his mother's every need; preparing meals, pouring vodka tonics, carrying her back and forth to the bathroom. She is miserable and manipulative, revealing that she was forced to agree to give up her own medical career in order to have a child. Family dog Lucky's rabid interest in Ray's trips to the bathroom prevents him from masturbating. He goes out with some old schoolmates to a dangerous clifftop above a tiny pool, but he gets in a fight with one of them who draws attention to the sexiness of his mother.

Out walking Lucky, Ray meets Toni, a high school student who seems to be attracted to him. Their brief courtship is unsatisfactory—as they kiss she keeps asking him what is wrong and even suggests he might be gay. Ray gets rough with her, and is horrified when her psychiatrist father phones Susan to complain. His mother now has him washing her back and applying lotion to her thighs. Hope of escape flickers as Ray talks her into summoning an irritating aunt to take over his nurturing duties, but the night before he is due to leave for his internship mother and son get drunk and end up spending the night together.

Woken by the aunt, they evade discovery, but Ray has missed his train, and he explodes at the aunt, who promptly storms off. Forced to take his mother to the doctor's, he finds out that she should have been mobile some time before. His philandering father then drops by and tells him that, since business has been so bad, he can no longer pay Ray's college tuition. Ray finds solace with Toni, but Susan discovers them together and hits her. As she runs off to tell her dad, a furious and frustrated Ray almost rapes his mother. He tells his father on the phone that he has slept with her, and after Toni's dad has come round and Susan has flirted with him as if nothing had happened, Ray tries to kill first himself and then his mother. He goes off with the gang of schoolfriends to the clifftop, stunning them all by jumping into the ravine. Unbeknownst to anyone, he survives the fall and hitches a lift into the dawn onboard a giant truck.

Spanking the Monkey might be a sly Beavisite euphemism for masturbation, but there is no trace of either fevered self-indulgence or an adolescent smirk in this bold and beguilingly subtle Oedipal drama. The humour which is a constant factor in writer/director/executive producer David O. Russell's startlingly accomplished and vivid feature debut never diminishes the psychological impact of a compelling storyline. In fact it heightens it so that the taboo subject matter appears not as a potentially exploitative novelty but as the organic and inexorable outcome of an entirely convincing situation.

Russell, a New Yorker with a video project about housing conditions and two shorts, *Bingo Inferno* (1987) and *Hairway to the Stars* to his credit, has an impressive eye for detail. The domestic rituals of food-making, ablution and brushing the family dog's infected gums are used to heighten Ray's feelings of frustration and claustrophobia. As the story takes ever more dangerous and sensual turns, clever physical observations—from the sublimely off-putting brace-like contraption Toni removes from her mouth in mid-kiss, to the fascinating texture of the denim covering on Susan's plaster cast—are the signposts pointing the way. The dialogue glistens too, full of little mirror fragments reflecting back and forth, like the argument Ray has with his mother over whether the correct word for him to use in his college project on HW positive children is "stigmatise" or "ostracise".

The hero—and for all his sweatiness and his hysteria, such a mighty weight of psychosexual forces are arrayed against Ray that he *is* a hero—seems to have some subconscious idea of what is happening to him but does not, at least until the very end, have the ability to do anything about it. Similarly, the audience are so effectively sucked into his story that they are unable to pull themselves back from it enough to judge him until Ray starts to do so himself (at one point, harrowingly scraping his skin to a red ruin with a metal brush). That this should be the case is a tribute to two impeccable central performances from Jeremy Davies and Alberta Watson: he nervy, she needy, their characters entwine with suitably epoch-making consequences.

Spanking the Monkey's great virtue is the complexity of its power relations. Feeling her life slipping out of control, Susan uses the power that she has to profoundly destructive effect. Elsewhere it is equally hard to separate weakness from strength. The apparently vulnerable Toni has a clear idea of what she wants, and is quite ready to blow the whistle the minute she's not getting it. Even the despotic, bullying father figure is shown—amid the relentless powerplay of someone else's office—as a figure of some pathos. In fact, the family dog in this film has more depth to its character than the lead role in many a less adventurous production. David O. Russell is to be roundly congratulated: however many awkward silences this film causes at future Russell family gatherings, the pleasure will have been worth the pain.

TIME, 9/12/94, p. 86, Richard Corliss

[*Spanking the Monkey* was reviewed jointly with *Clerks*; see Corliss' review of that film.]

VILLAGE VOICE, 7/19/94, p. 54, Gary Indiana

These days, there are fewer and fewer really worthwhile movies about middle-class, white, male, "alienated," heterosexual premed students with a poorly repressed desire to fuck their mothers, and from this perspective alone *Spanking the Monkey* is a considerable achievement. Indeed, the audacity of this first film by David Russell resides largely in making the audience forget how much its story reeks of adolescent solipsism and the histrionic self-pity of those with the least to complain about.

I mention this mainly because the film's production notes include several pages of the director's "thoughts on making his first movie and the process of filmmaking itself" that would be more than ample in a press kit for Kurosawa; Russell has the uninhibited ability to talk and think about himself endlessly, with real fascination, a trait that bodes well for his career if not for his future audiences.

That said, *Spanking the Monkey* really is wonderful, a sort of Hal Hartley movie for the happy few who can't stomach Hal Hartley, with an excellent cast and script, vivacious photography, and enough sense to reel itself in from its ever-incipient tendency toward self-congratulation. Ray, the protagonist, comes home for a weekend at the beginning of summer and is trapped by his father into looking after his mother, who's in bed with a broken leg, while Dad, a nattering, pushy salesman, jets around the country, banging call girls and peddling videos, checking in by phone with control-freak regularity.

The situation is quite brutal, since it forces Ray to give up a valuable summer internship in the Surgeon General's office. The parents act as if snuffing this opportunity were their due, and Ray a sort of intermediary target in their own ongoing war. Russell develops all this with a nervous comedic tone that never gets too broad nor too rapid, nor, best of all, too cheap. Ray's parents are selfish and proprietary, but they're also entirely credible, complex adults, frustrated by money worries and the knowledge that they're too smart and too sensitive for the suburban banality they're stuck in.

Alberta Watson, who plays Ray's mother, gives one of the most finely calibrated performances I've seen in years, reminiscent in quality if not scale of those of Gena Rowlands in John Cassavetes's films. Her character develops from petulant grump to high-spirited, immobilized farceur, weighted if not embittered by her own loss of possibilities, envious of Ray's, witty enough to keep him around by deploying as much charisma as guilt. Benjamin Hendrickson, as Ray's father, though seen less, is equally surprising, a bluff, hysteria-prone bully whose fears make him oddly sympathetic if not likeable. In fact, all of Russell's characters emit the existential possibility of acting differently than we expect them to: their mood swings, which are frequent, reveal more rather than fewer qualities.

Jeremy Davies, who plays Ray, is the same young actor recently seen grunging around in a Subaru commercial, comparing the Subaru to punk rock. He is a charmed presence in the same way that Matthew Modine is, blandly gorgeous and artlessly narcissistic, conveying openness and inaccessibility at the same time. Like Modine, he doesn't have to do much with his face or his body to reduce the viewer to abject sympathy: which makes it hard to tell whether he's supremely talented or just unbelievably cute. *Spanking the Monkey* calls for him to be, much of the time, mildly resentful, restrained, thoughtful, conciliatory, and horny, all of which he does extremely well.

One of the best things about *Spanking the Monkey* is the way it pictures the physical repulsion and attraction between young adults and their parents, especially sons and mothers. It's also note-perfect in the small details of suburban upper-middle-class life. Russell's take on well-mined material is so fresh and cleverly understated that we really do forget that we've seen this movie before, which is why I'm going to just skip the plot. The only really negative thing to be said is that this film seems ready to end a good 20 minutes before it does. It doesn't, but one doesn't mind this, or even that the real ending is its one banal moment.

Also reviewed in:
CHICAGO TRIBUNE, 7/22/94, Friday/p. H, Johanna Steinmetz
NEW REPUBLIC, 8/1/94, p. 28, Stanley Kauffmann
NEW YORK TIMES, 7/15/94, p. C5, Caryn James
VARIETY, 2/7-13/94, p. 39, Todd McCarthy
WASHINGTON POST, 7/22/94, p. C1, Hal Hinson
WASHINGTON POST, 7/22/94, Weekend/p. 42, Joe Brown

SPECIALIST, THE

A Warner Bros. release. *Executive Producer:* Steve Barron, Jeff Most, and Chuck Binder. *Producer:* Jerry Weintraub. *Director:* Luis Llosa. *Screenplay:* Alexandra Seros. *Suggested by the "Specialist" novels by:* John Shirley. *Director of Photography:* Jeffrey L. Kimball. *Editor*: Jack Hofstra. *Music:* John Barry. *Music Editor:* Clif Kohlweck. *Choreographer*: Pedro Pablo Pena. *Sound:* Andy Wiskes and (music) Shawn Murphy. *Sound Editor*: Mark Stoeckinger. *Casting:* Jackie Burch. *Production Designer:* Walter P. Martishius. *Art Director:* Alan Muraoka. *Set Decorator:* Scott Jacobson. *Special Effects:* Clay Pinney. *Costumes:* Judianna Makovsky. *Make-up:* Steve LaPorte. *Stunt Coordinator:* Alan Graf. *Running time:* 110 minutes. *MPAA Rating:* R.

CAST: Sylvester Stallone (Ray Quick); Sharon Stone (May Munro); James Woods (Ned Trent); Rod Steiger (Joe Leon); Eric Roberts (Tomas Leon); Mario Ernesto Sanchez (Charlie); Sergio Dore, Jr. (Strongarm); Chase Randolph (May's Dad); Jeana Bell (May's Mom); Britanny Paige Bouck (Young May); Emilio Estefan, Jr. (Piano Player); LaGaylia Frazier (Singer); Ramon Gonzales-Cuevas (Priest at Cemetery); Tony Munafo (Tony); Cheito Quinonez (Singer at Party); Tony Tatis (Backup Singer); Mercedes Enriquez (Pregnant Woman on Bus); Yeniffer Behrens (Schoolgirl on Bus); Alan Graf (Bus Driver); Juan Cejus (Latin Thug); Marcela Cardona (Tina); Brent Sexton (Manny); Yami Hildalgo (Hooker); Alfredo Alvarez-Calderon (Bomb Expert); Steve Raulerson (Chief of Police); Dave Caprita (OPS Buddy); Mayte Vilan (Ordinance Expert); Bud Ekins (Veteran Cop); John Archie and Carmen More (Cops); Frank A. DeVito III (Young Squad Expert); Bobbi Evors (Woman at Poker Game); Jon Brent Curry (Parking Attendant); Chris Conrad (Officer); Anabel Gracia (Young Girl at Funeral); Guillermo Gentille (Priest); Ashley Winston Nolan (Hotel Clerk); Victoria Bass (Socialite); Antoni Corone (Marksman); Steve Gladstone (Teckie); Jackie Davis (Grocery Store Owner).

LOS ANGELES TIMES, 10/8/94, Calendar/p. 1, Peter Rainer

"The Specialist" could have used one. Slovenly, incoherent, hootable, this Sylvester Stallone action thriller is definitely a no yo.

Stallone plays explosives expert Ray Quick, a former CIA operative who is enticed out of his shadowy confines by May Munro (Sharon Stone), a woman he has met only by telephone. As a young girl in Miami, May witnessed the murder of her parents at the hands of the criminal Leon family. Now she seeks pay-back. Insinuating herself into the Leon compound, and into the bed of the family's half-crazed heir apparent Tomas (Eric Roberts), May works with Ray to blow the perpetrators sky high.

If this were all there was to "The Specialist," which was directed by Luis Llosa and scripted by Alexandra Seros, it would be sub-routine—at best. Its only redemption is the world-class scenery chewing of James Woods as Ned Trent, Ray's ex-CIA bomb buddy and now his mortal enemy, and Rod Steiger, playing the Leon of all Leons. These actors know instinctively how to play up cornball villainy. They put on a hell of a show—it's the only way they can keep their self-respect amid all the explosions. (Everything else but the bombs in this movie fails to detonate.)

Stallone is also trying to "deepen" his role. He attempts this by looking sodden and slugged for most of the film. Ray Quick seems eerily out of it for someone who is supposedly a micro-electronic explosives specialist. Is it possible all those booms have knocked out his hearing? If so, he's lucky—he doesn't have to hear all the bad dialogue. (During foreplay—this is after they finally meet face to face—May tells Ray, "I always know you focus your detonator.")

Stallone in his recent films seems to have regressed to the Paleolithic Era—but he's a *sensitive* caveman. He's also buffed, and, in case we didn't notice, he displays his pecs at every opportunity. In his love scenes with Stone, the emphasis is all on him: It's like watching a Soloflex commercial with little bits of Stone—or, more likely, her body double—pecking through the musculature.

Stone once again misjudges her talents. Cast as a predator in "Basic Instinct," she was deliciously tart. But as "Sliver" so amply demonstrated, Stone loses her edge when cast as a victim, and essentially that's what she's playing here too. She's not even allowed a chance to explore May's victimization. What does May think about sleeping with the man who murdered her parents? Apparently, it's not so hot but, hey, sometimes you gotta do these things, no?

In contrast to Stallone's lunkiness and Stone's glaceed blankness, Woods seems to be having a high old time acting vehement. Nobody can do ferrety sleazoids better than Woods. He's perfectly cast as a demolition expert because, in general, he always acts like there's a bomb about to go off underneath him. He's turned the hotfoot into an acting style, and his line deliveries are as charged as a string of firecrackers.

As for Steiger, he appears to be delighting himself with his ornate Cuban accent. His crime lord is a courtly asp who can turn murderous in a blink. By contrast, Eric Roberts seems to be taking the whole thing much too seriously. He's made the mistake of trying to preserve his actor's integrity by reaching for depth. In "The Specialist," that's tantamount to high-platform diving into an empty pool.

Come to think of it, that describes the entire movie.

NEW YORK POST, 10/7/94, p. 47, Thelma Adams

"The Specialist" is so bad it's good.

Sharon Stone, Sylvester Stallone and James Woods—glamour, Goliath, and gonzo—compete for closeups in Luis Llosa's irresistibly ridiculous revenge fantasy.

So why does Stone have that pained look throughout "The Specialist?" It's not just that her cheeks look good sucked in or that she's perfecting her Kim Novak ice queen routine. It's that at a tender age, her character, May, was the sole witness to her parents' brutal murder by Cuban-American mobsters.

Now, May's grown up—one sign is that she doesn't have to wear underwear anymore—and she wants revenge. She calls Ray (Stallone), a former CIA bomb specialist turned free agent to get him to off triggerman Tomas (Eric Roberts) and his band of Miami weasels.

But first May sleeps with Tomas to get close enough to her parents' killer so that she's the last person he sees before he dies. Twisted?

May isn't the only one with a history, In 1984, Ray and Ned Trent (James Woods) were on a covert mission to kill a drug dealer. When an innocent victim got in the way, Ray wanted to stop the hit; Ned didn't. Ray made sure Ned lost his job and now, a decade later, Ned is playing out his own revenge fantasy, using May as bait.

The resulting cat-and-rat chase through Miami Vice territory is just a vehicle for the three stars to vogue for the camera. Ego-driven Stallone and Stone self-consciously stroke the lens. Woods, with his usual intensity and biting humor, acts from his gut like a man possessed.

It's no wonder Stallone called for a reshoot in his fight scene with Woods, because it didn't look like Sly kicked butt enough; Woods, with his snarly swagger, steals every scene he's in.

In case it's not absolutely clear who's the hero here Stallone stops for kittens. Woods kills kids. Stallone offers up his bus seat to a pregnant lady. Wood gives the leading lady a split lip.

And where does Stone fit in all of this? She makes a stunning knitwear model and is the sole recipient of a navel close-up.

For all of Stone's blond beauty, her cold-heart-melting-into-cheerleader-exuberance routine doesn't do much for me, but then again she's the perfect foil for her co-star Stallone. They have the same plasticity and limited sense of humor.

The movie's climax—a scene that is both silly and enormously entertaining—pairs Stone and Stallone in some aggressive lovemaking. Stone towers over Stallone until they step into the shower for some slippery fun. The two naked superstars groping each other is more athletic than erotic—but they certainly are game for anything.

In this threesome, it's Woods who wins out—and he didn't even have to take his clothes off!

Rod Steiger earns unintentional laughter as an aging Cuban-American kingpin who's a cross between Brando in "The Godfather" and Ricky Ricardo.

"The Specialist" didn't blow me away but, whether you laugh at it or with it, it's such a hoot that it makes for good slush.

NEWSDAY, 10/8/94, Part II/p. B5, Jack Mathews

All that weight room work Sylvester Stallone has put in over the last few years has really paid off. Here he is 48 years old, doing a nude scene in "The Specialist" with Hollywood's reigning sex goddess, Sharon Stone, and he looks better than she does!

Let me put that another way. When the two of them are buck naked in the soft-porn-shower scene that is the only reason anyone might want to see this colossally silly action picture, his body is such a tangle of knobs and bulges and striated wiring, you can't take your eyes off of it. He's even got muscles on his keister. Now, which Nautilus machine does that?

That scene, by the way, occurs exactly one hour and 15 minutes into the movie, three minutes after Stallone and Stone meet, in church. Don't ask. They just happen to end up there after Stallone, an ex-CIA explosives expert now free-lancing as an assassin, has blown up a good portion of Miami Beach trying to wipe out the mobsters who murdered Stone's parents.

In flashbacks, we learn that Stone's May Munro was a kid hiding in the closet when Tomas Leon (Eric Roberts) ordered the executions of her mother and father. We're never quite sure why that hit was made, but May is so determined to avenge the deaths she seeks out Ray Quick (Stallone), apparently through E-mail, and gets him to take on the job.

"The Specialist," directed by Luis Llosa ("Sniper"), is such a daffy story, it seems picky to wonder why May didn't hire herself an old-fashioned marksman. Ray's bomb work is amazingly efficient, but really messy and out of character.

In the opening scene, set in Colombia in 1984, Ray has a falling out with his cold-blooded CIA teammate Ned Trent (James Woods), precisely because Ned doesn't mind killing an innocent child along with their real target. Ten years later, here's Ray—Mr. Conscience—blowing up restaurants and parking garages to take out one or two guys. No wonder the CIA wants to keep its budgets secret.

Stallone doesn't seem to have much interest in any of this himself. Except for the shower scene, where he behaves like a guy coming off a fast, he sleepwalks his way through the role. Stone is much more animated, and actually affecting in moments.

But the best scenes all feature Ned, back as both a mob crony and special Miaml Beach task force chief (again, don't ask), and Woods' over-the-top tough guy mannerisms and temper tantrums provide comic relief where it is sorely needed.

SIGHT AND SOUND, 1/95, p. 58, Michael Atkinson

Ray Quick and Ned Trent are US demolition experts assigned to assassinate a South American drugs bigwig by blowing up a bridge as he drives over it. When the approaching vehicle is acknowledged to contain children, Quick tries to stop the explosion. Trent prevents him. After the explosion, they are permanently estranged.

Years later, Quick is repeatedly asked by May Munro over the phone to help her kill a Cuban drug lord who murdered her father. Living in seclusion, in a waterfront compound rigged to explode if it is penetrated, Quick vacillates. He finally agrees to help only after Munro—who's positioned herself as girlfriend of the drug lord's son—vows to do it herself. Soon we realise that Trent, who is now in the pay of the drug lord, has set Munro to ferret out Quick. Trent can use his employer's resources to eliminate Quick, as soon as he begins offing the drug lord's men.

Munro and Quick make love, and this apparently muddies Munro's resolve. She then seems to have been caught in one of Quick's explosions—she wasn't, and she uses her apparent death to break her connection to both Trent and the drug lord's son. Quick meets her surreptitiously, but the two are cornered in a hotel room by Trent and his men. Quick escapes (he rigs a series of explosions that dumps the whole hotel suite into the ocean), and Munro is used by Trent as bait to get Quick out into the open again. They escape yet again, leading Trent to Quick's dockyard compound, where everything explodes. Eventually, Quick offs Trent and the two lovers drive off together.

Quentin Tarantino is right—we love pulp, the crustier and sillier the better. Pulp is by definition yesterday's trash, garnished with nostalgic kitsch. Contemporary B-movies and fiction won't be real pulp until decades hence, and Tarantino's *Pulp Fiction* is too knowing to be mistaken for the real thing. True pulp is most often badly conceived, crudely executed and has little to recommend it beyond the allure of juvenile lust and the smell of ripe cheese. It brings us down a peg or two, it throws raw porterhouse into our inner psychopath's rusty cage, and best of all, it never minds if we don't think very highly of it. Like a cheap whore, it prefers that we simply do our dirty business and be on our way.

More than any other recent film *The Specialist* deserves the title *Pulp Fiction*. Sloppy, adolescent and proud of it, the movie rarely tries to be witty, and never important. It seems allergic to narrative logic as we've come to know it in Hollywood films. Based on John Shirley's series of paperback thrillers—which are pulp by now—*The Specialist* is all attitude, nudity and pyrotechnics, with acting that stretches from somnambulism to eye-popping *grand mal*. But the film's connection with its source material is vital. It places what might otherwise be yet another action film in a context that glories in its own triviality. Like many films based on comics, *The Specialist* is borne from the baby-boomer childhood of the 70s—it's a movie for the kids we were when there seemed to be nothing but time to ponder the equities of superheroes, breakfast cereal, Bugs Bunny quips, old horror movies and board games. Like most Hollywood movies, it's of a specific time and place, and if you cannot connect with the cultural circuits it pulses along—if you've never read a *Specialist* or *Executioner* or *Doc Savage* paperback—then you're unlikely to recognise the film's Ghost of Trash Culture Past.

All the same, perhaps the more enlightened reading of director Llosa's first shot at the big time (he'd previously directed *Sniper*) would be as blinkered, time-wasting idiocy. It is poorly-judged, thoughtless and often boring. Even the languorous sex scenes garner unintentional laughs. The average audience's primary concern will be for Sly's ageing physique; the veins bulge so alarmingly on his shoulders and neck we begin to imagine eventual Cronenbergian implosions. At the very least, a loved one should tell him to ease off with the free weights.

But there's a great deal of pulpy pleasure to be had. There's oodles of 70s Latin disco offsetting the laconic 90s baloney. In one scene in the back of a hushed church, Stallone hikes up Stone's skirt and discovers a gun in her garter. In another, a waterfront explosion results in a rain of flaming crabs. As sweaty drug lord Joe Leon, Rod Steiger uses a preposterous Cuban accent like a small gauge shotgun, while Eric Roberts seethes lispily as his son. Still, the real star of the movie is Woods, who has returned to portraying weasels after an inexplicable day-trip as leading man. Nobody can exude wormy, dead-eyed rage like Woods, and in scene after scene he takes wolf-sized bites out of an otherwise mundane action scenario.

The Specialist is indeed a movie of junky incidental treats. The bulk of it is enervating—Stallone has become an anti-actor, while Stone fleshes out a role that is tellingly reminiscent of the vapid blonde sluts she played before *Basic Instinct*. As Hollywood product, Llosa's movie is a botch, but as an artefact of our pulpiest urges, a high-rent condo bursting with cheap cultural effluvia, it is sometimes sublime.

VILLAGE VOICE, 10/18/94, p. 61, Georgia Brown

Sharon Stone brought this on herself. I mean, she read the script, didn't she? All of *Basic Instinct*'s pussy power goes down the drain with this sensationally sleazy action pic directed by Peruvian Luis Llosa with consummate vulgarity. Virtually the film's only woman, the sultry Stone gets yanked, pawed, told off, and slapped silly, only to slink back for more. One contemptuous codger (played by Rod Steiger) simply swipes her face with his spittle.

She's supposed to be out for revenge, As a child she cowered in a closet watching a sadistic Miami trio murder her parents. Now, while submitting to further abuse by the same bunch, she tempts the soulful, reclusive Sylvester Stallone into settling her scores. On the side of the meanies is Stallone's old nemesis from his days in an elite CIA bomb squad, a vicious chap played by sultan of sneer James Woods. "You were the rigger and I was the trigger," boasts the slimeball. This movie's principle: Why use a clean, little bullet when you can create mushroom orange fireballs, mucho property damage, and flying, singed bodies. You know the impulse.

Having shirked their workouts, Woods and Steiger are reduced to chewing the scenery while others model their bods. A couple of bronze posing-torso sequences between Stone and Stallone had the screening audience hooting. The year of *Speed, True Lies, and Blown Away* finally leads to the big bomb.

Also reviewed in:
NEW YORK TIMES, 10/8/94, p. 11, Caryn James
VARIETY, 10/10-16/94, p. 84, Godfrey Cheshire
WASHINGTON POST, 10/8/94, p. C1, Hal Hinson

SPEECHLESS

A Metro-Goldwyn-Mayer Pictures release of a Forge production. *Executive Producer:* Harry Colomby. *Producer:* Renny Harlin and Geena Davis. *Director:* Ron Underwood. *Screenplay:* Robert King. *Director of Photography:* Don Peterman. *Editor:* Richard Francis-Bruce. *Music:* Marc Shaiman. *Music Editor:* Scott Stambler. *Sound:* Richard Bryce Goodman and (music) Shawn Murphy. *Sound Editor:* Wylie Stateman and Gregg Baxter. *Casting:* Howard Feuer. *Production Designer:* Dennis Washington. *Art Director:* Tom Targownik. *Set Designer:* Richard McKenzie and Eric Orbom. *Set Decorator:* Marvin March. *Set Dresser:* Carrie Perzan, Sara Gardner Gail, and James Buckley. *Special Effects:* Frank L. Toro. *Costumes:* Jane Robinson. *Make-up:* Bonita DeHaven. *Make-up (Michael Keaton):* Bob Mills. *Stunt Coordinator:* Mike Cassidy. *Running time:* 98 minutes. *MPAA Rating:* PG-13.

CAST: Michael Keaton (Kevin); Geena Davis (Julia); Christoopher Reeve (Freed); Bonnie Bedelia (Annette); Ernie Hudson (Ventura); Charles Martin Smith (Kratz); Gailard Sartain (Cutler); Ray Baker (Garvin); Mitchell Ryan (Wannamaker); Willie Garson (Dick); Paul Lazar (Harry); Richard Poe (Tom); Harry Shearer (Chuck); Steven Wright (Eddie); Jodi Carlisle (Doris Wind); Cynthia Mace (Michelle Hortz); Steve Gonzalez (Jim Rodriguez); Robin Pearson Rose (Teacher); John Link Graney (Fresh Faced Kid); Yasmine Abdul-Wahid (Female Student); Mickey Cottrell (Debate Moderator); David Cromwell (Pete); Cris Franco (Messenger); Brad Blaisdell (Bartender); Steven Hartman (Stevie); Richard McGonagle (Dignitary); Heather Medway (Make-up Girl); Robert Figueroa (Cab Driver); Marques Johnson (Hartford); Frank DiElsi (Rip); Peter MacKenzie (Andy); Tim Perez (Robert Gonzalez); Michelle Holden (Beth Yeats); Tony Genaro (Truck Driver); Michael McCarty (Veterinarian); Loyda Ramos (Maid); Brendon Chad (Truck Driver's Son); Joan Stuart Morris (Waitress); Brian John McMillan (Bear Man); Mary Pat Gleason (Desk Clerk); Will Nye and Rob LaBelle (Security Guards).

CHRISTIAN SCIENCE MONITOR, 12/16/94, p. 11, David Sterritt

[*Speechless* was reviewed jointly with *Nell*; see Sterritt's review of that film.]

LOS ANGELES TIMES, 12/16/94, Calendar/p. 1, Kenneth Turan

Machines don't make movies In Hollywood just yet, but when they do "Speechless" is what they'll be like.

A mild romantic comedy so full of familiar feints and dodges it plays like a rerun the first time you see it, "Speechless" contains very little that hasn't been on view elsewhere in a better light. And the few clever bits it does contain tend to feel out of place, nervy escapees from a funnier piece of work.

Although real life has caught up with the film's premise with the marriage of Clinton campaigner James Carville to Mary Matalin, his opposite number in the Bush camp, screenwriter Robert King's notion of constructing a romance between warring speech writers in a contentious political campaign is a clever one.

Kevin Vallick (Michael Keaton) and Julia Mann (Geena Davis) meet high-concept cute, both reaching for the last container of Nytol at an all-night emporium in a New Mexico town. The stuff must not be too effective, because the two of them meet again a few hours later at a we-never-close diner where they trade insomnia cures and wide grins.

Although the plot initially keeps the pair in the dark about it, Kevin and Julia have something big in common. He is a speech writer for the Republican candidate for U.S. Senate, a politician she considers "a simpleton." She, meanwhile, does the same thing for the Democratic candidate, someone he considers "a tax-and-spend, knee-jerk liberal."

And although Kevin is a wacky TV-sitcom writer who was once voted most likely to embarrass his family while Julia is a former class valedictorian who believes politics is about changing the world more than merely winning, the film heavily hints that they are Hollywood's latest candidates for the perfect couple.

Once the pair's initial connection is made, "Speechless" has a tendency to go on autopilot. None of the succeeding events—from a late-night drive where the car (surprise) runs out of gas, to the couple playfully splashing water on each other in a public fountain, to the inevitable rifts, misunderstandings and huffy glances they share—offers enough of a spin on standard situations to be of much interest.

Quirkier and more engaging are the fleeting glimpses into the vicissitudes of political campaigns "Speechless" provides, such as the way candidates mangle their carefully crafted speeches and how a fuzzy, heart-tugging story about a bear down a well can keep nominally more serious political news off all the channels.

The best performance in the film, in fact, comes not from the leads but Christopher Reeve as smug network TV reporter "Baghdad Bob" Freed, the kind of self-satisfied operative who lives in his flak jacket and tells everyone to just "call me Baggy."

Although cast as Julia's former fiance and a romantic rival to Kevin, Reeve is best as a comic stiff, and his brisk series of tongue-limbering exercises before going on air may be the funniest moment in the film.

By contrast, Keaton and Davis, who also co-produced the film with husband Renny Harlin give uninspired performances. Although both began their movie careers in off-beat roles and in fact shared screen credit in the decidedly nutty "Beetlejuice," they are intent here on recasting themselves as conventional matinee idols, complete with high-gloss grins and perky twinkles in their eyes. The result is certainly mainstream, but it is also less involving than what either of them has done in the past.

Pushing everybody the wrong way is the film's loopy music (by Marc Shaiman) and glib direction (by Ron Underwood). Underwood, whose major credit is "City Slickers," has produced a series of overly ingratiating set pieces from which recognizable humanity has been surgically removed. Causing neither noticeable pain nor pleasure, "Speechless" just sits there with its mouth open, catching flies.

NEW YORK POST, 12/16/94, p. 64, Michael Medved

Contemporary politics has gotten so bizarre that it's become a tricky subject for movie comedy. Since it's almost impossible to top real-life absurdities, the best cinematic approach may be the dead-pan, documentary style of the often hilarious 1972 Robert Redford film "The Candidate," which presented the pressures of a Senate campaign without sentimentality or exaggeration.

"Speechless" also focuses on a Senate race, but it does so in a silly sitcom style that makes even the old "Benson" TV show look like an example of hard-hitting political commentary. Here, the campaign is just window dressing for the central love story, but that romance is so feeble that it definitely could have used a more potent distraction.

Geena Davis plays a speech writer for a liberal Senate candidate in New Mexico. She leaves her hotel room one night to search for some sleeping pills and gets into a fight with stranger Michael Keaton over the one remaining box of Nytol on the shelf of a convenience store.

Instead of sleeping, they go out for a romantic ride through the desert and promise to meet again the next night. But in the interim they discover the awful truth: He's a one-time TV comedy writer who's crafting speeches for the Republican nominee, while she holds the corresponding post for the Democratic arch-enemy.

For the rest of the movie, their unstoppable attraction struggles to overcome their political rivalry, as well as competing claims by Keaton's ex-wife and campaign associate Bonnie Bedelia, and by Davis' one-time fiance Christopher Reeve, who does a nice job as a laughably conceited (is there any other kind?) network reporter.

Of course, the basic setup is uncomfortably close to the well-publicized passion between Clinton strategist James Carville and Bush aide Mary Matalin during the 1992 presidential campaign, but this screenplay originated two years earlier so the producers need not worry about lawsuits.

Moreover, Carville and Matalin both cared deeply about issues, while the characters in this movie see politics as simply an amusing way to make a living; had the picture treated their ideological orientation more seriously, their relationship might have generated more sizzle.

Toward the end of the movie, the comedy takes a disastrous turn toward third-rate slapstick that undermines even its value as amiable diversion. During the climactic candidate's debate, the lovebirds sneak off to a TV control room and make out, where they inadvertently push buttons that disrupt the broadcast.

The election-night sequence is even worse: The movie's not even clear on the outcome of the campaign, but it clearly makes a fool of poor Michael Keaton, who's asked to make a hugely overdone, painfully unfunny, public declaration of love.

Both he and Davis are superb actors (as viewers of under-appreciated gems like "My Life" and "Angie" can attest), And they manage to create appealing characters even here, though they generate no real chemistry with one another. As a result, "Speechless" seems pointless and many moviegoers will be able to catch a few z's, even without a box of Nytol.

NEWSDAY, 12/16/94, Part II/p. B2, Jack Mathews

The producers of Ron Underwood's "Speechless," a comedy about a romance between members of opposing staffs in a U.S. Senate campaign, are going out of their way to disclaim any connection between their movie and the James Carville-Mary Matalin romance that provided comic relief during the 1992 presidential race.

There are crucial differences. Michael Keaton is not as funny as Carville, Geena Davis is not as mean as Matalin and their party affiliations are reversed. Davis is the spin doctor for the feed-the-poor liberal running for the vacant Senate seat in New Mexico, and Keaton works for the let-them-eat-cake conservative.

But the questions of trust, philosophical compatibility and discretion that Carville and Matalin have discussed in their post-election best-seller provide the foundation for the movie, too, and it doesn't matter which affair came first, or that Underwood and screenwriter Robert King couldn't come up with much in the way of an actual story. The circumstances are irresistible.

And so, for the most part, are the fiancé Bob Freed (a perfect Christopher Reeve), a TV newsman-celebrity whose self-affixed nickname of "Baghdad" Bob proclaims his journalistic heroism during the Persian Gulf War.

"Speechless" takes a little time setting itself up, having Kevin and Julia meet during a mutually sleepless night on the campaign trail. A little flirtatious banter, some coffee and pie, a moonlight ride in his sports car, a quick game of tongue tag, and there they are, in love, before even realizing they're natural enemies.

Once they become rivals, and the film focuses on the tension between principal characters—Kevin (Keaton), a former TV sitcom writer brought in to add humor and humanity to the Republican candidate's campaign; Julia (Davis), the Democrat's idealistic head speechwriter, and her trailing them and the two campaigns, "Speechless" gets into a rhythm that is both very funny and often very telling, at least about the emotional swings for political staffs.

The running joke is that just as the campaign enters its final month, neither candidate can get a break on the local TV news because of the continuing story about attempts to rescue a bear cub that has fallen into a well. How that bear's fate becomes a factor in both the Senate race and the romance between Kevin and Julia is the clear highlight of the movie.

Underwood, whose brief directing career includes the sharp-witted "City Slickers" and the treacly "Heart and Souls," is somewhere in the middle of his game with "Speechless." He infuses the film with the same frenetic pace and energy of the political campaign, and he overcomes the weak romantic chemistry between his stars by concentrating on their humor, which is considerable.

But Underwood is, at heart, a sentimentalist, and he could not resist going for a bell-ringing, knockout last scene, nearly squandering the film's goodwill in the process. There are three candidates for 1994's most overdone Big Kiss ending—the other two featured Andy Garcia and Meg Ryan, kissing to applause in the middle of an AA meeting in "When a Man Loves a

Woman," and Robert Downey Jr. and Marisa Tomei, cheered on by fellow airline passengers in "Only You"—and the winner is: "Speechless."
I'm afraid that's the only award it has in store.

VILLAGE VOICE, 12/27/94, p. 61, J. Hoberman

The romantic comedy *Speechless* is set on prime Altman territory, amid the star-spangled hoopla of a political campaign. But here, unlike the TV miniseries *Tanner '88*, which Altman used to comment on and even intervene in an ongoing presidential election, excitement is largely overdetermined.

Geena Davis, who coproduced, and Michael Keaton play speechwriters attached to rival candidates in a New Mexico senatorial race. Although Robert King's script evidently predates the analogous James Carville-Mary Matalin story recently packaged under the tele-friendly rubric *All's Fair*, it does assimilate the basic Carville-Matalin aesthetic. Keaton's character not only writes for TV situation comedies, he lives in one and even educates Davis to a sitcom way of knowledge.

Directed by Ron Underwood, whose greatest previous success has been *City Slickers*, *Speechless* tries to hit the ground running, but trips over the sanctimonious track of patriotic music that's been laid down to suggest decency, democracy, and *Dave*, and only intermittently thereafter regains its step. Davis and Keaton meet cute—two wired insomniacs, sleepless in Albuquerque, grabbing for the last box of Nytol in the hotel drugstore—and, unaware of their professional identities, fall for each other blind. With Davis playing an idealist and Keaton pretending to be impressed, the two carry on behind the backs of their respective campaigns, the better to act out an ambivalence complicated by the return of her fiancé (Christopher Reeve).

Designed as a nouveau Katharine Hepburn-Spencer Tracy comedy, the camera doting on Davis's dynamic flouncing from scene to scene, the movie includes a fair amount of face-to-face counter-spinning. The funniest scene has the now-rival couple unexpectedly thrown together on a platform before an audience of schoolchildren, venting their sexualized hostility in a manner suggesting the mumbled subliminal commentary on *Saturday Night Live*'s "Weekend Update." Exploiting Keaton's mischievous timing and Davis's regal geekiness, *Speechless* enlivens moments of sodden snap with interludes of rote physical comedy—like the stars trying to make out in a tiny car. (Their contortions hardly compensate for an absence of chemistry.)

Although the xenophobic campaign issue has something to do with digging a big ditch between the U.S. and Mexico, *Speechless* is topical mainly for its feel-good cynicism. Both candidates are maladroit, interchangeably corrupt glad-handers. The election-night flurry of red, white, and blue balloons that cascades around the victorious lovers serves to ratify the only possible happy ending for a movie about the political process.

Also reviewed in:
CHICAGO TRIBUNE, 12/16/94, Friday/p. C, Michael Wilmington
NATION, 1/23/95, p. 108, Stuart Klawans
NEW REPUBLIC, 1/23/95, p. 30, Stanley Kauffmann
NEW YORK TIMES, 12/16/94, p. C10, Janet Maslin
VARIETY, 12/12-18/94, p. 76, Brian Lowry
WASHINGTON POST, 12/16/94, p. F1, Rita Kempley
WASHINGTON POST, 12/16/94, Weekend/p. 49, Desson Howe

SPEED

A Twentieth Century Fox release. *Executive Producer:* Ian Bryce. *Producer:* Mark Gordon. *Director:* Jan De Bont. *Screenplay:* Graham Yost. *Director of Photography:* Andrzej Bartkowiak. *Editor:* John Wright. *Music:* Mark Mancina. *Sound:* David R.B. MacMillan and (music) Jay Rifkin and Alan Meyerson. *Sound Editor:* Stephen Hunter Flick. *Casting:* Risa Bramon Garcia and Billy Hopkins. *Production Designer:* Jackson DeGovia. *Art Director:* John

R. Jensen. *Set Designer:* Louis Mann, Peter Romero, and Stan Tropp. *Set Decorator:* K.C. Fox. *Set Dresser:* Douglas James McKay, Joseph L. Byrne, Mark Davidson, Jim Scolari, and Gaylene West. *Special Effects:* John Frazier. *Visual Effects:* Boyd Shermis. *Costumes:* Ellen Mirojnick. *Make-up:* Norman Leavitt and Pete Altobelli. *Stunt Coordinator:* Gary M. Hymes. *Running time:* 120 minutes. *MPAA Rating:* R.

CAST: Keanu Reeves (Jack Traven); Dennis Hopper (Howard Payne); Sandra Bullock (Annie); Joe Morton (Capt. McMahon); Jeff Daniels (Harry); Alan Ruck (Stephens); Glenn Plummer (Jaguar Owner); Richard Lineback (Norwood); Beth Grant (Helen); Hawthorne James (Sam); Carlos Carrasco (Ortiz); David Kriegel (Terry); Natsuko Ohama (Mrs. Kamino); Daniel Villarreal (Ray). Simone Gad (Bus Passenger #1); Loretta Jean Crudup (Bus Passenger #2); Sherri Villanueva (Bus Passenger #3); Margaret Medina (Robin); Robert Mailhouse (Young Executive); Jordan Lund (Bagwell); Patrick Fischler (Friend of Executive); Patrick John Hurley (CEO); Susan Barnes (Female Executive); Richard Dano (Swat Driver); Michael Sottile (Swat Cop); Jane Crawley and Anne O'Sullivan (Baby Carriage Women); Beau Starr (Commissioner); John Capodice (Bob); Tommy Rosales, Jr. (Vince); James DuMont (Workman); Antonio Mora (News Anchor #1); Patty Toy (News Anchor #2); Todd Gordon (News Cameraman); Bruce Wright (Reporter #1); Mark Kriski (Reporter #2); Dagny Hultgreen (Reporter #3); Richard Schiff (Train Driver); Joseph Carberry (Cop); Sandy Martin (Bartender); Neisha Folkes-LéMelle (Mrs. McMahon).

FILMS IN REVIEW, 7-8/94, p. 54, Jeff Laffel

It's always hard to review a genre film. One assumes that the reader of the piece knows the review is based on its own merits as well as comparisons with other films of its type, but often all films become lumped together and we find a *Fright Night* being reviewed using the same criteria as one would use in reviewing a *Howards End.* Richard Corliss summed it up very well when he wrote, in his review of *Indiana Jones And The Temple Of Doom* that, "One can't fault a theme park for not being a cathedral." That being said, we turn to Twentieth Century Fox's new action/adventure film, *Speed.*

The premise is simple. A disgruntled middle-aged former policeman, Howard Payne (Dennis Hopper), looking for compensation for being unceremoniously forced to leave his job after an accident, sets up a hostage situation and is foiled by one of the LAPD's finest, Jack Traven (Keanu Reeves) and his buddy Harry (Jeff Daniels). Wanting vengeance on the two (not to mention 3.7 million dollars), Payne rigs a bomb on a Los Angeles bus. The bomb becomes armed as soon as the bus goes over 50 mph and is set to detonate if, once armed, the speed of the bus drops to below 50. Traven gets on the bus, and there's the plot.

From its stylishly Deco 3-D credits, to its over-the-top, totally outrageous ending, *Speed* is a goofy, silly, pulse-pounding, knuckle-biting, unpretentious whirlwind of comic book fun. Here is a film that sets out to entertain and succeeds on almost every level. The dizzying, whirling (sometimes DePalmaesque) camera of Andrzej Bartkowiak spins us into the action, and that, mixed with the superb editing of John Wright and the no nonsense "take no prisoners"-style direction of Jan De Bont has the audience squealing in delight as if sitting in the first car of a hurtling roller coaster. The surround sound comes from everywhere at once, and if there should be a momentary lull in the sound department, the stirring musical score of Mark Mancina fills the temporary void. (What a laser disc this is going to make!)

I said that this was a comic book of a film, and I mean that in the nicest possible way. This film harkens back to the days when comics cost a dime and weren't mean spirited, with their protagonists suffering angst and living in *Blade Runner*-type surrounds. The action in *Speed* is bright and "in your face," and there are good guys and there are bad guys and they are, amazing as it may seem, quite distinguishable from one another. Keanu Reeves, who has pumped up for this role and flexes as often as possible, is delightful as the single-minded, square-jawed good guy of old, tossing off "Arnold-like" one-liners with aplomb. For the first time in a number of films, Reeves looks like he is having a great time, and it is infectious. Jeff Daniels is stolid as Reeve's hapless partner., Dennis Hopper chews the scenery with Alan Rickman-like glee and Sandra Bullock is delightful as the ordinary woman thrown into an extraordinary situation.

Problems? Okay, there are a few. There is one tourist on the speeding bus whose character gets tiresome very quickly. A minor glitch. A more serious problem, though by no means terminal, is the fact that the film goes too far with the premise and arrives at overkill about fifteen minutes before the final credits roll. I think, here, writer Graham Yost, who up to this point wrote a fast, funny screenplay, winds up giving us too much of a good thing.

But those are minor quibbles in what is, all in all, a terrifically entertaining movie. Explosions by the score, last minute rescues the like of which haven't been seen since "Indy" went on his last adventure and a baby carriage that takes its place next to the ones in *Potemkin, The Untouchables* and *Rosemary's Baby*. On this ride there are few speed bumps to stop the action, but lots of green lights to speed us along in one of the most delightful films of the year. Subtle it's not ... fun it is. *Speed* is one hell of a ride.

LOS ANGELES TIMES, 6/10/94, Calendar/p. 1, Kenneth Turan

Action directing is a put-up-or-shut-up game, a skill that can't be faked or finessed; even a 10-year-old can tell if you've got it or not. And on the evidence of the invigorating "Speed," Jan De Bont has definitely got it.

Though this story of a mad bomber versus the LAPD's stalwart SWAT team is De Bont's first film as a director, he has not exactly come out of nowhere. A cinematographer for more than 30 years, De Bont has worked frequently with fellow Dutchman Paul Verhoeven and has been behind the camera on such big-time action pictures as "Die Hard," "The Hunt for Red October," "Black Rain" and "Lethal Weapon 3."

De Bont's newness does show in the pro forma nature of some of the characterizations as well as the film's uninspired dialogue and overall derivativeness. But "Speed" moves too fast for any of that to matter much, and where pure action is concerned, De Bont and his team have turned in a visually sophisticated piece of mayhem that makes the implausible plausible and keeps the thrills coming.

Making "Speed" involving is the premise of Graham Yost's script, which does a neat twist off the traditional action premise of coping with machines that are going too fast. Here the problem is not, as might be expected, restraining a runaway bus on a crowded freeway, but just the opposite: making sure it doesn't even come close to slowing down.

For the diabolical madman (a smooth Dennis Hopper) that no action film can exist without has rigged up a deadly explosive device that will detonate if the bus is allowed to go under 50 m.p.h. Quite a dilemma for leap-before-you-look hero Jack Traven (Keanu Reeves) and his SWAT team pals.

Centering action on familiar items like one of Santa Monica's friendly Big Blue Buses and its load of drab citizens (plus Sandra Bullock as the inevitable attractive and available woman) is a proven way to make tension personal to an audience. And screenwriter Yost has helped things out by coming up with a surprising variety of problems that can bedevil an ungainly vehicle attempting to keep up speed.

Working with director of photography Andrzej Bartkowiak, editor John Wright and veteran stunt coordinator Gary Hymes, De Bont has taken great pains to make these crises exciting on screen. For the bus sequences, for instance, he had 10 identical vehicles on call and routinely used four to six cameras to film them, moving up to as many as a dozen when recording the most challenging stunts.

None of this work would have mattered, of course, if De Bont didn't also have an understanding of the mechanics of on-screen movement and a fine sense of the visual possibilities action presents. Nothing "Speed puts on screen, from fiery explosions to mayhem on the freeway, hasn't been done many times before but De Bont and company manage to make it feel fresh and exciting.

De Bont's talent is visible not only in the bus sequences but also in "Speed's" nervy opening sequences involving a bomb in an elevator, shot in a specially constructed fully operational five-story shaft. It's here that we first meet the forceful Jack Traven, his slightly saner partner Harry Temple (Jeff Daniels) and Capt. McMahon (Joe Morton), their no-nonsense superior.

With a brush-cut hairdo and an intense game face that is anything but Buddha-like, Reeves not only give "Speed's" strongest performance, his unexpected intensity is crucial in giving the film its drive. Playing Traven with an appropriate edge of take-charge surliness Reeves is surprisingly believable as a barely human law enforcement machine that even his pals view as "deeply nuts."

Reeves' co-stars, however, haven't been given very much to work with in the way of dialogue or directorial help in building character. As a result, "Speed" has a ways to go before it can equal what "The Fugitive" and "In the Line of Fire" accomplished in matching drama to action.

But if no one is going to leave theaters raving about acting and characterization, it will probably matter little. Tension and release is the name of "Speed's" particular game, and so far this summer no film has played it so well.

NEW LEADER, 7/4-18/94, p. 18, David Bromwich

"This movie makes me want to go out and ..." With most films, the sentence is easy to complete. *Speed*, a light-weight thriller of urban terrorism directed by Jan De Bont, short-circuits every question more abstract than "Where will this end?" How it will end is clear all along, from the tone of distinctly circumscribed mayhem. The plot has the sort of excess one associates with farce, three hijackings laid end-to-end: an elevator, a bus, and a subway train. Audiences have talked about the second because it lasts longest, and because a subway in L.A. does not compute. After the elevator blows up, and before the train charges through a street-level barrier, a bomb is rigged to go off when the bus does less than 50 miles per hour. The city's odd and galvanizing rhythms—of avenue crossed by street and park, and freeway passing into freeway—give the film its natural pace. The rest is editing, done with conspicuous virtuosity and no cheating.

Keanu Reeves, as the bomb squad cop who saves the bus, is not yet an actor, but in *Speed* his upper arms and generous smile are exactly what is wanted, and he will surely be the successor to Harrison Ford in action pictures of the coming years. The grownup note in Ford—the suggestion of someone smart enough to be crooked if he wanted to—isn't available from Reeves. But he is convincing at the outer edge of the required somatic exertions: a scene in which he cracks with frustration, then pulls himself together as he sees the faces of the people who depend on him. "Real cute and watchable," the person beside me murmured. *Speed*, which skims vulgarity but never sinks, has something of the same quality.

The maniac is typecast as Dennis Hopper. He has played versions of the same part memorably, from *Blue Velvet* to *Red Rock West*, and now stands every moment at the brink of nonstop mugging. Here, he curbs the sadistic overtones, which could only weight the story with an unmeant earnestness. This terrorist is simply a man with a grievance who knows how to make bombs and wants some money fast. Yet *Speed* is not about the man who commits atrocious deeds. It is about the threat of atrocity and the pressure to respond to it, almost impersonally. That pressure—a potent element in a normal fantasy of the way modern life could go wrong—the film renders very effectively; some of the means employed are: (1) an early, apparently pointless, smooth and disorienting 360-degree shot, circling around two cops as they get out of their car; (2) plenty of low-angle shots from the rear of the bus forward, or from wheel-level forward as the bus plows ahead; (3) music that presses, but not too hard; (4) rapid cuts between the problem-solving at headquarters and on-the-scene maneuvers by Reeves on the bus; (5) attention to the uncanny properties of public places, e.g. cargo elevators that operate (for whom?) alongside the regular elevators in large buildings, or the puzzle of mapped but unbuilt stretches of freeway; (6) a dramatic focus that keeps the maniac far from the center of action and never flirts with his point of view.

The last omission lends the film an unexpected civility—the quality partly squandered by *In the Line of Fire*, a comparable thriller with more human depth, which took on a nasty edge from John Malkovich's seductive portrait of the assassin. It is a curious development, and symptomatic of the climate in movie-making today, that both films show the crime being solved and the killer traced by brainwork, yet both close out as shoot-'em-ups. The brainwork doesn't matter. These day-at-the-office narratives of urban terror, meanwhile, are adapting us to something well worth not getting adapted to. They accept as a fact of experience the presence in our society of a high proportion of maniacs. The predictable reaction of the police becomes: "Oh, another; where this time?"; and of the victims: "Well, our turn was bound to come."

Quite as matter-of-fact is the assumption that the proper temper for meeting disaster is extreme passiveness. Not only does nothing else succeed, nothing else is possible. The social contract of cooperative suffering requires that we appear as spectators of the very horrors we are casualties of. *Speed* catches this habit of mind in an audience-pleasing moment when the bus leaps across a 50-foot gap in a freeway overpass and a passenger shouts, in the true manic spirit of the disaster binge, "Yes! We're way out of control!" I preferred a quieter moment, when the woman driving the bus weeps with shame at her own gladness in being still alive, after a passenger has been killed trying to get off, and Reeves comforts her: "We all feel that way." The emotion is well known to everyone, yet I can't recall ever seeing it in a movie.

Modest and suggestive as it is, *Speed* sent me back to William James' essay on "Some Mental Effects of the Earthquake" of San Francisco. From his home in Palo Alto, James' response to the first distant shake took him by surprise. "'Go it,' I almost cried aloud, 'and go it *stronger*!'" The sense of exhilarated welcome—"Yes! We're way out of control!—yielded later to a pleasure in the way a human society improvised itself out of the chaos. People cared for each other spontaneously, but they also took charge as specialists, without having to be appointed. "Much of this readiness was American, much of it Californian," says James. "The terms 'awful,' 'dreadful,' fell often enough from people's lips, but always with a sort of abstract meaning, and with a face that seemed to admire the vastness of the catastrophe as much as it bewailed its cuttingness."

What will strike anyone who watches *Speed* is how reduced our admirable "readiness" has become. Or rather, how cramped are its few heroic occasions. So many disasters must be dealt with instantly, and so many have, somewhere behind them now, technology whose workings ordinary people can never hope to penetrate. The solution is to become very small and hope the inevitable explosion will somehow spare oneself. This movie makes me want to go out and ... With *Speed*, I suspect the hidden answer is *never think, ever again*.

NEW YORK, 6/13/94, p. 82, David Denby

The ideal of velocity that the great silent-film comics aimed at—continuous and lethal motion, an accelerating frenzy of danger, hilarity, madness—has been fulfilled and redefined in *Speed*, a movie that hits the summer-season jackpot. This nonsensical but deeply satisfying action movie is based on a premise so fiendishly logical that it's almost witty. In Los Angeles, a techno-madman (Dennis Hopper) rigs a city bus in such a way that a bomb in the bus's undercarriage becomes armed when the vehicle goes over 50 miles per hour; but if the bus then falls below 50, the bomb goes off. The madman will disarm the bus by remote control and spare the passengers in exchange for a great deal of money. What to do? The bomb is like some monstrous torture apparatus that chokes you when you try to escape from it.

The Fugitive, from last summer, was essentially a nonstop chase. *Speed* is not a chase but a ceaseless hurtling projectile, a virtuoso machine-poem of force. The nicest thing about it is that it offers thrills without sadism. The screenwriter, Graham Yost, and the director, Jan De Bont—both working in their current capacities for the first time—want only to entertain us. The basic situation may be preposterous, but the filmmakers stage the action realistically from moment to moment as a series of insanely complicated and dangerous puzzles. How to keep the bus going? How to remove the passengers at high speed? Yost and De Bont have nothing to say, no social point to make, and, for once, this action-film blankness is a boon. Any burden of "meaning" would be foreign to the athletic soul of *Speed*.

Right at the beginning, De Bont, the Dutch-born former cameraman who shot *Die Hard* and *Lethal Weapon 3*, works at a high level of tension. We're plunged into an ongoing crisis. Inside a downtown office building, the camera travels up and down the shafts of an elevator bank. We can see the five or six sets of doors at each floor from inside the shaft, and we get a palpable sense of dismay, a premonition of the frightening vulnerability of Americans in public places. Some passengers enter an elevator; a small bomb blows, snapping one of the cables, and the elevator, still booby-trapped, hangs there, in danger of falling to the basement. The bomber makes a demand for money.

The L.A.P.D. swat team shows up, and two longtime partners, Harry (Jeff Daniels) and Jack (Keanu Reeves), climb onto the top of the elevator, trying to free the passengers. Yost's script is unusually terse: The two men communicate almost in code. What happens then—cables snapping, winches falling into shafts or getting jammed against steel partitions only to tear loose again—might be a dynamized lesson in gravity and Newton's laws of motion. We're off to the races. The bus comes next.

The movie bears some resemblance to *In the Line of Fire*. Once again, the bad guy is an articulate and malevolent sport (as usual in American movies, intelligence and wit are associated with evil) who enjoys tormenting doggedly honest public servants. Eyes burning in his bulky forehead, Dennis Hopper has become our No. 1 movie crazy, a gleeful, ranting psychocomic at home in nihilistic states of contempt. Hopper can do this stuff over and over because he brings a sense of play to the roles. And Jeff Daniels, so boring as a leading man, appears to have found a new way of amusing himself, too, in the role of an aging police hero who's become disgruntled and fatalistic; Daniels's look of agonized comprehension when he realizes the jig is up may be his finest moment as an actor.

As for Keanu Reeves: After seeing *Speed* and the current *Little Buddha*, his friends, I trust, will advise him never again to sit under a tree in golden body paint, looking like a broiled Peking duck. Reeves gives a smashing physical performance as an action hero. Short-haired and bullet-headed, he offers a little personality—but not too much. There's a fascination in such minimal, hardball acting: What will the hero respond to? Reeves, warming up here and there, convinces us that his Jack, trying to save passengers held hostage by the bomber, is not only a selfless cop with fabulous physical instincts but a good man.

The bus driver is injured, so a young woman (Sandra Bullock) takes the wheel, her foot on the pedal and all of Los Angeles in the way. With Jack coaching her (he has boarded the bus in mid-trip), she bashes cars out of the bus's path, shears off a series of roadway signs and heads for the freeway. For decades the movies have been looking for a way of making action go faster and faster and never stop, and now they've found one. The only immediate solution to the rigged-bus problem is to keep on going. And going. The bus jumps over gaps in an unfinished freeway, circles, leans like a Harley-Davidson, and finally finds the airport runways. De Bont's visual-mechanical inventiveness never fails; he even throws in a possible satirical reference to that textbook film classic the "Odessa Steps" sequence from *Potemkin*.

Apart from general good humor, *Speed* has no extra dimensions. It's a loony American artifact: No other culture could conceivably make a movie so single-minded in its pursuit of excitement. That it's virtually the only kind of great film that Hollywood now turns out with regularity shouldn't blind us to its kinetic virtues. *Speed* is a summer-season masterpiece—brainless, relentless, and almost always overwhelming.

NEW YORK POST, 6/10/94, p. 43, Michael Medved

A collection of frightened hostages ... a psychotic terrorist mastermind ... a maverick cop in a lonely battle to foil the bad guy's diabolical plans ...

Sure enough, it's "Die Hard" time again in Hollywood, where, after applying this familiar formula to an office building (the original "Die Hard"), an airport ("Die Hard II"), a boat ("Under Siege"), an airplane ("Passenger 57"), and a mountain ("Cliffhanger"), imaginative minds have now taken the show on the road with "Speed"—which has been aptly described as "Die Hard on a Bus."

The vehicle in question is making a routine run from Venice beach to downtown Los Angeles when mad bomber Dennis Hopper gleefully informs intrepid cop Keanu Reeves that he's loaded the bus with high explosives, which will only be disarmed if he gets millions in ransom.

The detonating mechanism is activated as soon as the driver hits the freeway and reaches 50 miles per hour. At that point, he must keep the bus going at that speed or above; as soon as he falls below 50, the bombs will go off—blowing both vehicle and passengers to kingdom come.

Anyone who's ever tried driving in L.A. at rush hour knows how hard it is to keep going at a reasonable speed, and this beleaguered bus also faces unfinished freeways, punctured tires, depleted fuel, and a trigger-happy gang member among the passengers.

Also along for the ride is Sandra Bullock ("Demolition Man"), as a feisty student with a suspended license who takes the wheel when the driver's incapacitated.

These far-fetched elements come together more effectively than expected thanks to the talented Jan De Bont, who previously worked as cinematographer on "Lethal Weapon 3" "Basic Instinct" and (you guessed it) "Die Hard." Here, he makes a smashing directorial debut.

His jaw-dropping special effects, stunningly staged chase scenes and impeccable pacing instantly establishes him as one of today's top action amateurs, along side John McTiernan and Jim Cameron.

De Bont is helped considerably by his capable cast, particularly the pumped-up and self-assured Keanu Reeves, who unmistakably performed many of his own death-defying stunts. Reeves projects a stolid intensity and self-effacing heroism that make him much better suited to this sort of role than macho show-offs like Stallone and Willis.

In Dennis Hopper, Reeves enjoys an ideal foil: an utterly engaging maniac who milks big laughs out of a series of sardonic lines ("No, it's poor people who are crazy, Jack. I'm eccentric.") but whose pitch-perfect performance never goes over the top.

In addition to all the bus business, De Bont throws in spectacular bonus sequences on an elevator and a subway, giving action fans more than their money's worth. If you're looking for logic and credibility in your entertainment, you've boarded the wrong bus. But when it comes to visceral thrills, this vehicle stays up to speed.

NEWSDAY, 6/10/94, Part II/p. B3, Jack Mathews

The first rule of action filmmaking is to never have an early scene that is so big it cannot be topped later, the idea being that if the climax isn't more exciting than everything that's gone before, audiences will feel cheated and let down.

Veteran cinematographer Jan De Bont noted exceptions to the rule while working the camera for such maverick directors as John McTiernan ("Die Hard") and Paul Verhoeven ("Basic Instinct"), and he throws the book away for his own directing debut on "Speed," a full-throttle action thriller that may leave audiences worn down, but hardly cheated.

For most of the film, the pace is literally full-throttle, aboard a bus careering wildly down the streets and freeways of Los Angeles, then on one of the city's spanking new underground trains, as cool SWAT team daredevil Jack Traven (Keanu Reeves) tries to thwart a mad bomber (we know he's mad because he's played by Dennis Hopper).

Hopper's Howard Payne, a bitter ex-cop extorting a few million from his old employer, has rigged the bus with a bomb that will be activated when the vehicle reaches 50 mph, and detonated when it dips back below that speed.

For about an hour—with a cool woman passenger (Sandra Bullock) behind the wheel, Traven trying to defuse the bomb, and all the same news helicopters that brought us the L. A. riots hovering above—the bus lumbers on. Down busy streets, past panicked pedestrians, and leaping across missing spans of concrete on an unfinished freeway.

As vigorous as all this action is, nothing in it tops the harrowing opening sequence, in an elevator shaft of a downtown high-rise. There, Traven and his bomb expert partner Harry (Jeff Daniels) rappel from the roof to try to rescue office workers trapped inside an elevator rigged with explosives.

Dramatically, this 20-minute first act matches exactly the arc of the bus sequence, which, in turn, matches the arc of the climactic run in the Metro. In fact, each of three action sequences plays like a condensed version of the overall story.

Not that there is much of a story to condense, or characters to distill. We have an extortionist with bombs, a cop with cojones, a passenger with looks, and a ticking clock. You'll be home counting the plot holes before you know it.

First-time screenwriter Graham Yost is a genuine pack rat. He lifted the best notions from most of the top-grossing action films of the last decade, fashioning Jack Traven mostly from Mel Gibson's suicidally brave cop in the "Lethal Weapon" movies, and Hopper's psychopath from Alan Rickman's sadistic terrorist in the first "Die Hard."

These characters exist only on the surface, and because we've seen Hopper play evil so often, it's hard to work up much of a hate for him here. Reeves, on the other hand, strikes a refreshingly different note with Traven. Using none of the pun-filled wit that has become the common denominator of the modern action hero, and with an intensity that may be a meditative hangover from "Little Buddha," Reeves goes about his business with the concentration of someone actually trying to stop a killer.

The flirtation between Traven and the bus' reluctant driver is too silly to even acknowledge, but plausibility was never an issue with "Speed." Having spent much of my life in L. A. rush hour traffic, the idea of a bus reaching 50 mph, let alone maintaining it, is science-fiction.

NEWSWEEK, 6/13/94, p. 53, David Ansen

It's not easy producing mindless fun. Look at "The Flintstones." Thirty-three writers slaved to get the mindless part right, but where was the fun? (Yes, I know how big it opened; for that it deserves a place in the documentary "That's Marketing, Part I.") For truly *ingenious* mindless fun, a summer popcorn movie deluxe, take "Speed." This is real escapism; a preposterously exciting thriller that takes itself seriously enough to produce gasps of tension and lightly enough so you giggle while grabbing the armrest.

Here's the deal: a ransom-demanding psycho (Dennis Hopper) has planted a bomb on an L.A. bus. The bomb will explode if the bus falls below 50 mph. Can LAPD cop Jack Traven (buffed-up Keanu Reeves) save the day? A simple premise, but first-time director Jan De Bont and screenwriter Graham Yost pile on the complications with relish. Of course, the bus driver has to get shot by a paranoid passenger ... Of course, a plucky woman (Sandra Bullock) must take the wheel, heading straight for a baby carriage ... and wouldn't you know, when the bus finds its way to a safe, unopened freeway, there'll be an unfinished gap in the overpass lurking just ahead ...

Nor is the bus the whole story. First we're treated to a bombing attempt in a crowded, high-rise elevator, and for a grand finale we get a life-and-death struggle aboard a speeding Metro Rail train. Though it's not as glossily imposing as "Die Hard" (photographed by De Bont), it shares that same giddy, can-you-top-this spirit. It's not a movie about star turns: Reeves, Bullock and Hopper are team players here, and they get the job done with an admirable lack of histrionic fuss (OK maybe not Hopper: he wouldn't be Hopper if he didn't get to rant a bit). Relentless without being overbearing, this is one likely blockbuster that doesn't feel too big for its britches. It's a friendly juggernaut.

SIGHT AND SOUND, 10/94, p. 51, Ben Thompson

Demented ex-cop Howard Payne kills a security guard and booby-traps a lift in an LA skyscraper, demanding a huge ransom. SWAT team members Jack Traven and his partner Harry arrive and pull off a daring rescue. Realising that Payne is still in the building, they track him down, but he captures Harry, and Jack can only save his partner by shooting him in the leg. The bomb goes off and Payne is assumed to have been killed.

Jack is in a cafe with a bus-driver friend when his bus outside blows up. Jack receives a telephone warning from Payne about a bomb on another bus, which will be armed when the bus goes over 50mph and will detonate if its speed drops below that level. Jack rushes across town, boards the bus and explains the situation. The passengers panic. One, a criminal, waves a gun to force the bus to stop. In the struggle to disarm him, the driver is shot. Annie, a young passenger, takes the wheel and the police navigate a safe route through traffic while Payne watches the drama on television.

He gives his permission by phone for the injured man to leave the bus. An elderly woman tries to leap off after him but falls to her death. The bus approaches an unfinished section of the highway, but Annie manages to leap the gap and reach the airport, where they circle the runway while Jack struggles to disarm the bomb. Harry finds Payne's home, but it is booby-trapped and he and several other policemen are killed. Eventually, Jack realises that Payne has a camera on board the bus. He gets a TV technician to make a video loop of the passengers sitting in their seats which is replayed to Payne while the passengers are lifted off. Jack and Annie escape seconds before the bus hits an empty airplane and explodes.

The police deliver the ransom, planning to trap Payne, but he outsmarts them, kidnapping Annie and escaping on the subway with Jack in hot pursuit. The train driver is killed, Annie is chained to a post and Jack and Payne fight it out on the roof until Payne is decapitated by a signal light. The train crashes through into the street, and Jack and Annie survive.

Speed's uninspiring title sequence gives little clue to the thrills that are to follow. In this film the cavalry arrives in the first three minutes when Keanu Reeves' cop car comes flying over the hill. His partner Jeff Daniels may not be an obvious choice to save a lift-load of passengers from death at the hands of crazed explosives expert Dennis Hopper, but with Reeves' help save them he does, with as much wear and tear on the audience's nerves as on the buckling lift cables. "

For all its breathless rush from one action set-piece to another, and its determination not to insult the intelligence with disaster-movie-style character development, *Speed* is strangely humanistic. The rescuees—hapless passengers who only want to get from one place to another—are treated with indulgence. Reeves' calm, gum-chewing response to the feckless stupidity of the imperilled public is to see them as innocent bystanders who have every right to be saved by him.

First time director Jan De Bont, who cut his cinematic teeth as Paul Verhoeven's cameraman, has the latter's eye for kinetic excitement without his sadism. *Speed*'s biggest shock, when the hurtling bus bears down on a pram and hits it, has a benign twist. And the climax is downright euphoric. Admittedly, there is nothing benign about Dennis Hopper, who does his psycho turn on auto-pilot. Reeves on the other hand, with *Little Buddha* just a bad memory, is a revelation, expanding on the action hero potential he demonstrated in *Point Break*. Speed's single Arnie-ism—reporting Hopper's final decapitation as "He lost his head"—is unworthy of Reeves, but by that time the audience is too busy picking pieces of its spine out of the cinema upholstery to notice.

TIME, 6/13/94, p. 74, Richard Schickel

Making movies, as people in Hollywood are fond of saying on those rare occasions when false modesty strikes them, is not exactly brain surgery. This is especially true if you're aiming for a summer release, when the ruling assumption is that the entire population is brain dead, incapable of responding to anything but high action, low comedy or soft sentiment. The question is, if the expectations are so low, how come most summer movies fail so dismally to make even a few cerebral ganglia twitch?

When a summer film goes right, it all seems so easy. Take *Speed.* You've probably heard that this is the one where a terrorist wires a bus with a bomb that becomes armed when the vehicle reaches 50 m.p.h.; if the bus subsequently slows down below that speed, the bomb will detonate. Talk about simple. But the film's sheer cut-to-the-chase straight-frowardness is part of its appeal.

Speed has terrified (and nicely particularized) passengers, a resourceful hero (Keanu Reeves), a gutsy heroine (the always appealing Sandra Bullock) and a terrific villain (Dennis Hopper, doing what he does best—rationalism gone gaga). The can't-slow-down bus ride is bookended with a pair of thrill sequences, either one of which would provide enough of a plot for most movies. *Speed* begins with a crowded elevator that is sometimes in free fall and is rigged to explode at a certain floor, and it ends with a driverless subway running out of control, the heroine helpless inside.

The movie has two virtues essential to good pop thrillers. First, it plugs uncomplicatedly into lurking anxieties—in this case the ones we brush aside when we daily surrender ourselves to mass transit in a world where the loonies are everywhere. Second, it is executed with panache and utter conviction. Possibly this is because *Speed* is the first feature for director Jan De Bont and writer Graham Yost, and they haven't yet learned all the bad things that can happen to good (and not so good) moviemakers in Hollywood. They can get all the instruction they need about such failings at the mall over the next couple of weeks. For example: [See Schickel's reviews of *City Slickers II, The Cowboy Way*, and *Renaissance Man.*]

VILLAGE VOICE, 6/14/94, p. 47, J. Hoberman

Back in the celluloid Stone Age, an attraction known as Hale's Tours seated viewers inside a mock train and projected moving landscapes on a screen outside. Hale's Tours only briefly challenged the nickelodeon as a cinematic delivery system but its successors live on. The ace pulse-pounder *Speed* is a trip that bids to storm box-office heaven by putting its audience in a city bus forced to keep moving above 50 miles per hour lest it detonate the bomb that master extortionist Dennis Hopper has wired to the chassis.

Directed with workmanlike concentration by Dutch-born cinematographer Jan De Bont (*Die Hard, Lethal Weapon 3, Basic Instinct*), from Graham Yost's script, *Speed* is an expert and often exhilarating exercise in industrial choreography and bonehead repartee. The basic ride is roller-coaster bumper cars with a few added fillips. Although the action is mainly set where the tire meets the road, the opening sequence plays a passenger elevator like a yo-yo while a subway set piece runs a series of late variations on the theme of mass transit gone berserk, depositing the shell-shocked principles—Keanu Reeves and Sandra Bullock—on Hollywood Boulevard, embracing in the wreckage under a gentle rain of falling glass.

That this last scene has *2001* emblazoned on the marquee of Mann's Chinese Theater may be De Bont's acknowledgment that *Speed* is a kind of sci-fi, namely hot-rod *ballet mécanique*. An LAPD SWAT-team squad car is virtually launched to the rescue, the camera swooning around it—one machine nosing another like an eager dog. Work is libidinal play for bomb defusers Reeves and Jeff Daniels and, as in Kubrick, machines can be the objects of desire. "The man sure has a hard-on for this bus," a passenger notes as the gesticulating Reeves, having failed to catch it on foot, hijacks a fancy sports car and prepares to jump from one moving vehicle to another.

One product of the hyperindividualist '80s was the Ramboticized disaster film—the one-man, one-catastrophe thriller exemplified by *Die Hard*. *Speed* is more streamlined and less overweening than its immediate precursors, jettisoning the masculinist ideological baggage and keeping only a small valise of Hawksian professionalism. As the ads promise, the movie is a rush. It's as visceral and (relatively) content free as air-conditioning, albeit not without a certain class consciousness: The luckless bus is stocked with an assortment of poor, old, and lumpen Angelenos, as well as one obnoxious tourist ("the Hugh Grant part," my editor noted).

There are plenty of riffs on the local traffic but, as a foreigner himself, De Bont realizes that L.A. bus patrons are the least powerful, most expendable people in town and the utter unfairness of their situation lends the doings an additional cosmic flavor. Indeed, the whole spectacle is set in motion by a sort of mad deity: Hopper, like the John Malkovich loony in *In the Line of Fire*, is a disgruntled, philosophical terror-*artiste*. He not only rants throughout but, thanks to the magic of remote control and video surveillance technology, treats the action as a form of interactive TV—cackling like the Wicked Witch of the West as he monitors everything that happens on the bus, particularly once passenger Bullock replaces the driver.

As an action-disaster heroine, Bullock (last seen as Sylvester Stallone's futuristic, malaprop-prone dream-girl in *Demolition Man*) improves upon the stewardess played by Karen Black in *Airport 1975*. Whereas a late-in-the-film pilot injury compelled Black to land the 747, loudmouthed Bullock is early on drafted to take the wheel of the craft she calls an "oversized Pinto" and is soon careening up on the freeway shoulder, winging, nudging, smashing, and otherwise plowing her way through traffic.

Everyone is something of a wiseacre here, but *Speed*'s humor is more visual than verbal—Bullock flashing her directional before executing an outrageous hairpin turn, doors sheared off expensive convertibles, cop cars brutally swatted away. (By focusing so strenuously on the logistics of the ride, *Speed* becomes a movie about its own making.) When Bullock beggars Evel Knievel by propelling the bus over a 50-foot gap in the freeway, you can sense the Hong Kong influence on the Hollywood action movie. The bus seems to spring across the chasm the way a kung fu master bounds over his opponents in an HK martial arts flick. Speed might have been a classic vehicle for the comic daredevil Jackie Chan.

As it is, Reeves makes a particularly lovable dummy cum savior. Hair cropped close, he acts tough by packing his mouth full of chewing gum and dropping his voice a full octave: "*Stawp* the bus!" (Reeves must have been forbidden by his agent to use the word *excellent* despite the ample opportunities the script affords.) After playing bodhisattva, Reeves's career will never be the same. The joke of having a bus blow up in the background just over his shoulder is like a meditation gag out of *Little Buddha*. Reeves might be pumped up but he's too enlightened to swagger.

Also reviewed in:
CHICAGO TRIBUNE, 6/10/94, Friday/p. H, Michael Wilmington
NATION, 7/25-8/1/94, p. 137, Stuart Klawans
NEW REPUBLIC, 7/4/94, p. 26, Stanley Kauffmann
NEW YORK TIMES, 6/10/94, p. C12, Janet Maslin
NEW YORKER, 6/13/94, p. 101, Anthony Lane

VARIETY, 6/6-12/94, p. 33, Todd McCarthy
WASHINGTON POST, 6/10/94, p. D6, Hal Hinson
WASHINGTON POST, 6/10/94, Weekend/p. 42, Desson Howe

SPIKE & MIKE'S SICK AND TWISTED FESTIVAL OF ANIMATION '94

28 animated featurettes from 28 artists. *Running time:* 88 minutes. *MPAA Rating:* Not Rated.

NEW YORK POST, 9/5/94, p. 16, Larry Worth

Those seeking a humorous walk on the wild side won't get much satisfaction from "Spike & Mike's Sick and Twisted Festival of Animation '94."

Boring, yes. Unimaginative, yes. And definitely sophomoric.

But funny? Let's just say it puts Beavis and Butt-head (who were spawned by an earlier entry in the Spike & Mike series) on a level with "Fantasia."

Ironically, fans of the MTV icons—who might be the only ones to snicker at the juvenile humor here—are denied admittance due to a no-one-under-18 policy. (The ads proclaim: "Bring ID for a mind-blowing plethora of sick and twisted.")

But it's no great loss since the 28 featurettes (20 premieres and eight "favorites") comprising this year's S&M installment are pretty dull going. Indeed, their biggest asset is brevity.

More often then not, the animators simply have their creations voice four-letter words, as if it's a novelty to see animals say—or act out—the "F" word. Maybe they've forgotten, but "Fritz the Cat" and Ralph Bakshi covered that ground two decades ago.

Also on the subject of sex, at least three vignettes titter a about the use of condoms, making one wonder if Spike & Mike are trying to put a message in their madness.

But that notion is dispelled later on, as a recurring theme of mutilation and bloodshed dominates. There's "Performance Art," featuring the antics of Chainsaw Bob, never mind sci-fi entries like "Mutilator II" and "Slaughter Day." Still, the titles prove more interesting than their subjects.

Only "Lloyd's Lunch Box" will give gore-fans something to really lick their chops over, with a young man dismembering himself in truly horrific fashion over a seven-day period.

Other entries try to get timely, with references to Bill and Hillary Clinton's carnal relations, or having a bulimic Arnold Schwarzenegger surface as "The Bulimiator." Predictably, the addition of famous faces does nothing for the non-existent level of wit.

One might assume Weird Al Yankovic would be a highlight as his claymation facsimile cavorts with Barney in a spoof of "Jurassic Park," to the tune of "MacArthur Park." But under the guidance of Scott Nordlund and Mark Osborne, it makes as much sense as a cake left in the rain.

Clearly, if this is the best that Spike & Mike can come up with, the time has come to rest on their laurels. What started out as a deliciously perverse antidote to Disney and company now brings new meaning to drawn-out.

Also reviewed in:
WASHINGTON POST, 5/10/94, p. B2, Richard Harrington

STAR TREK GENERATIONS

A Paramount Pictures release. *Executive Producer:* Bernie Williams. *Producer:* Rick Berman. *Director:* David Carson. *Screenplay:* Ronald D. Moore and Brannon Braga. *Story:* Rick Berman, Ronald D. Moore, and Brannon Braga. *Based upon "Star Trek" created by:* Gene Roddenberry. *Director of Photography:* John A. Alonzo. *Editor:* Peter E. Berger. *Music:*

Dennis McCarthy. *Music Editor:* Stephen M. Rowe. *Sound:* Bob Baron and (music) Robert Fernandez. *Sound Editor:* James W. Livingston. *Casting*: Junie Lowry-Johnson and Ron Surma. *Production Designer:* Herman Zimmerman. *Art Director:* Sandy Veneziano. *Set Designer:* Robert Fechtman, Ron Wilkinson, and Dianne Wager. *Set Decorator:* John M. Dwyer. *Special Effects:* Terry D. Frazee. *Visual Effects:* Ronald B. Moore. *Computer Imaging*: Joni Jacobson. *Animation*: Eric Guaglione. *Costumes:* Robert Blackman. *Special Make-up Effects:* Michael Westmore. *Make-up:* June Haymore, Gil Mosko, and Debbie Zoller. *Stunt Coordinator:* Bud Davis. *Running time:* 110 minutes. *MPAA Rating:* PG.

CAST: Patrick Stewart (Captain Jean-Luc Picard); William Shatner (Captain James T. Kirk); Jonathan Frakes (Commander William Riker); Brent Spiner (Lieutenant Commander Data); LeVar Burton (Lieutenant Commander La Forge); Michael Dorn (Lieutenant Commander Worf); Gates McFadden (Dr. Beverly Crusher); Marina Sirtis (Counselor Deanna Troy); Malcolm McDowell (Dr. Soran); Walter Koenig (Commander Pavel Andreivich Chekov); Barbara March (Lursa); Gwynyth Walsh (B'Etor); Alan Ruck (Captain Harriman); James Doohan (Scotty); Whoopi Goldberg (Guinan); Jacqueline Kim (Demora); Jeanette Goldstein (Science Officer); Thomas Kopache (Com Officer); Glenn Morshower (Navigator); Tim Russ (Lieutenant); Tommy Hinkley, John Putch, and Christine Jansen (Journalists); Michael Mack (Ensign Hayes); Dendrie Taylor (Lieutenant Farrell); Patti Yasutake (Nurse Ogawa); Grtanville Ames (Transporter Chief); Henry Marshall (Security Officer); Brittany Parkyn (Girl with Teddy Bear); Majel Barrett (Computer Voice); Rif Hutton (Klingon Guard); Brian Thompson (Klingon Helm); Kim Braden (Picard's Wife); Christopher James Miller (Picard's Nephew).

LOS ANGELES TIMES, 11/17/94, Calendar/p. 1, Kenneth Turan

Going boldly where no one has gone before is not what it used to be. Contentedly settled into a prosperous middle age, the "Star Trek" series now seems more comfortable retracing its own footsteps, carefully offering its horde of fans interludes that aspire to do no more than fit snugly into the patterns of the past.

As a result, seeing "Star Trek: Generations," the seventh and latest Trekker theatrical feature, feels more like engaging in some kind of recurring religious ritual than taking part in the conventional moviegoing experience.

Once again we are back on the deck of the Starship Enterprise, a notoriously unstable place where losing one's footing is an occupational hazard and life lessons are not hard to come by. "You better take a look at this," someone is likely to say, and within moments terms like "drive plasma," "temporal flux" and "low-level ionic pulse" are being tossed around as if they actually meant something.

Not only are the actors soothingly familiar from their previous television appearances, but—except for cinematographer John Alonzo—all the key creative personnel (from director David Carson to writers Ronald D. Moore & Brannon Braga to the producer, production designer, editor, makeup artist, costume designer, hair stylist and composer) also cut their teeth on the small screen versions.

"Generations" seems even more familiar than most because its plot involves two separate starship lineages. Together again for the first time are James T. Kirk (William Shatner), the original series' 23rd-Century captain, and, fresh from its successor, "Star Trek: The Next Generation," 24th-Century Capt. Jean-Luc Picard (Patrick Stewart).

Yet a third captain, a wimpy sort named Harriman (Alan Ruck), starts things off in a prologue where he welcomes now-retired old-timers Kirk, Scotty (James Doohan) and Chekov (Walter Koenig) back as celebrity guests on the first Starship Enterprise in 30 years not to have the Big K in charge.

This premiere voyage for the new ship is supposed to be a quiet one, but, wouldn't you know it, a distress call is picked up from a transport ship caught in a mysterious ribbon of energy. When the dithery Harriman starts to fret and whine, Kirk, noticeably paunchy but still patriarchal, hits him hard but fair with a vintage Trek homily: "Risk is part of the game if you want to sit in that chair."

That pesky ribbon of energy also comes to engage the "Next Generation" folks, whose antics occupy most of the movie. Aside from Picard, the big screen welcomes both Lt. Cmdr. Geordi La Forge (LeVar Burton), he of the all-seeing visor, and the android Data (Brent Spiner), an artificial life form whose lack of *joie de vivre* makes him the New Age counterpart of Spock.

In fact, the main subplot of "Generations" concerns what transpires when Data, tired of never getting the joke, inserts an emotion chip into his cranium and discovers humor, sadness and all the other feelings that humans are prey to.

The main story, when it finally reveals itself after a considerable amount of dithering, concerns the machinations of the villainous Dr. Soran (Malcolm McDowell), a 300-year-old El Aurian who likes to say things such as: "Time is the fire in which we burn"—and will do whatever it takes to get back to that ribbon of energy.

The doctor turns out to be so devious that one Enterprise captain is not enough to deal with him. Both Kirk and Picard are mobilized for the task, and it won't surprise anyone familiar with his Royal Shakespeare Company background that the commanding Stewart makes Shatner look like a graduate of the Klingon Academy of Dramatic Arts.

Still, fans of the series will no doubt be happy to see Kirk again under any circumstances, and if you hunger for the "Star Trek" experience, this will keep you nicely occupied. As for moviegoers not washed in the blood, either a video trip back in time or a look forward to the next installment will be necessary to figure out what the fuss is about. For when someone in "Generations" says, "Somehow I doubt that this will be the last ship to carry the name Enterprise," you can take it to the bank. Literally.

NEW YORK POST, 11/18/94, p. 39, Michael Medved

Why don't they wear seat belts on the Enterprise?

This question arises with unprecedented force after watching "Star Trek Generations," which features literally dozens of shots of crew members tossed out of their chairs and bouncing around the ship's interior during a crash landing, a battle with Klingons, or just, it would seem, during mid-space turbulence.

Even today's Hyundai comes equipped with shoulder harnesses, so why not include at least this much protection on an intergalactic cruiser that travels at warp speed?

It makes no sense, but then neither does anything else about this bloated bomb that turns "Star Trek" into "Star Drek." It's the seventh motion picture in this profitable series and by far the worst—even less satisfying than "Star Trek V: The Final Frontier," the previous runt of the litter.

Part of the problem involves the inane plot contortions necessitated by the movies "high concept": getting Enterprise captains James Tiberius Kirk (William Shatner) and Jean-Luc Picard (Patrick Stewart) together for the first time. The difficulty is that the two heroes live in different centuries, so the writers and producers (from the "Next Generation" TV show) had to cook up an especially elaborate "cute meet."

After a prologue in which Captain Kirk comes out of retirement for an ill-fated test run on a newly souped-up version of the Enterprise, the action shifts forward some hundred years to the "Next Generation" crew, who are busy battling a marauding band of buxom female Klingons, who look more like refugees from a wretched caveman movie, or a women-in-prison flick, than the formidable mistresses of futuristic technology.

There's also a confusing challenge from a mad alien scientist (played by a sneering Malcolm McDowell) who's trying to blast his way into "the Nexus" (a time warp, not a computer network) by blowing up a planet inhabited by 200 million innocent critters.

Needless to say, Picard must stop this nefarious scheme, and since reliable help is hard to find in the 24th century, he must travel back to the past to bring Kirk out of retirement for the second time in the movie—which is a particularly nifty feat, since this latest retirement was necessitated by his heroic death earlier in the film.

In the midst of this incoherent idiocy, the producers at least provide some impressive special effects including an Enterprise crash landing in extreme slow motion, with hundreds of edits of terrified crew members and loads of ear-splitting screeching on the sound track.

Unfortunately, the lavish sets and dazzling explosions only provide distractions in the midst of the plodding plot, which culminates in an old-fashioned fistfight involving three superannuated actors (Shatner, Stewart, and McDowell) whose stodgily choreographed fisticuffs resemble the bare-knuckle brawls in Grade B westerns of 60 years ago.

On the matter of seat belts, the theaters showing this stupidity might be well advised to have them installed. At least that way, moviegoers might remain in their places, facing the screen, and conquering the natural impulse to escape.

NEWSDAY, 11/18/94, Part II/p. B2, John Anderson

An object is hurtling through star-dappled space, end over end at a speed that can only be measured in light years. Is it a Federation starship: A Klingon bird-of-prey? A piece of intergalactic jetsam from some Romulan garbage barge? No, it's ... it's ... it's a bottle of Dom Perignon.

The champagne smashes into the side of a ship, and we realize that we're at a double christening: of the Enterprise B, newest pride of the United Federation of Planets, and of the latest installment in the series that's going where no series has gone before. It's whimsical. It's arch. It's self-congratulatory. It is, of course, "Star Trek."

Having spawned four television series, six movies and a kind of hot-house subculture—all of which can make the uninitiated feel like an alien—"Star Trek"turns out to have some spark left in its old dilithium crystals."Star Trek Generations" employs a can't-lose-at-the-box-office premise, of course: Joining the characters from the two separate "ST" eras—the original from 1966-69, and the relatively recent "Next Generation" and "Deep Space Nine" and the upcoming "Voyager" series. But it does so without resting on its laurels. Or whatever they grow on space stations.

Full-bore Trekkies will reach nirvana in the teaming of Capt James T. Kirk (William Shatner, "legendary" commander of the Enterprise, with his austere, iron-spined, bald-as-a-nose-cone successor, Capt. Jean-Luc Picard (Patrick Stewart). Through a warpage of time and space—and the nefarious antics of the El Aurian physicist Dr. Soran (Malcolm McDowell), who's trying to claw his way back to a cosmic Shangri-La called the Nexus—they bridge their respective epochs and together save countless lives and planets.

It's a battle of the space hams: McDowell, wearing the mad-eyed stare he's had since "Caligula," is no match for the scenery chewing of Shatner; as a pure actor, Shatner is light years behind Stewart. A celestial collision would seem inevitable, but these three heavenly bodies manage to strike sparks, without smashing each other to bits.

The "Star Trek" movies, and the TV shows to some degree, have forged an idiosyncratic charm by combining cut-and-dried villainy with amorphous moral questions—about time, space, fate, saving the whales, saving Ricardo Montalban—that then render Kirk and crew (James Doohan's Scotty and Walter Koenig's Chekov resurface here) temporarily impotent. As is customary, the "serious" story is then adorned with a human(oid)-interest subplot. So while Riker (Jonathan Frakes), Geordi (LeVar Burton), Troy (Marina Sirtis) and Worf (Michael Dorn) tumble about the bridge, Data (Brent Spiner), the lovable android and surrogate Spock, finally gets up the nerve to have the "emotion chip" implanted in his circuitry, and has to contend with unfamiliar feelings. And he's not the only one.

The Nexus, where Soran is so desperate to return, is a dimension of utter contentment and timelessness; one may visit any stage of his or her life, change history, correct mistakes, resurrect love. Soran is willing to destroy everything to find such peace, making him a rather timeless symbol of aggression. Kirk, when he gets there, is willing to go with the flow. It's up to Picard to maintain his focus, fight the good fight and drag the reluctant and corpulent Kirk back into the fray. And it's up to Stewart to maintain some level of dramatic integrity, when all those around him are losing theirs.

The special effects—and the crash of the Enterprise (it's hard to remember which version it is at this point) is a thrilling example—are not just spectacular, but beautiful. Director David Carson, a veteran of '"Next Generation" and "Deep Space Nine," is not content with eliciting the "ooohs," he wants to get, the "aaahhhs" as well. And he will, along with other unsolicited remarks.

"Somehow," someone says, looking over the wreckage, "I don't think this will be the last ship to carry the name Enterprise." "Neither do I," quipped someone in the audience, an echo of wisecracks to come.

SIGHT AND SOUND, 3/95, p. 55, Philip Strick

For the first time in 30 years, a new starship Enterprise is launched without Captain James T. Kirk at the helm. He is aboard merely as a guest, along with Scotty and Chekov. The *Enterprise* receives a distress call from two cargo ships menaced by an inexplicable electrical force. She arrives in time to rescue some of the passengers: among them is Guinan, a wise and centuries-old alien, and the sinister Dr Soran, an El Aurian furious at having to leave what he calls a vital experiment. Under threat herself, the partially equipped *Enterprise* is only saved by Kirk's ingenuity; part of the starship is shorn away in the process, and Kirk is lost.

A ceremony 78 years later on the Holodeck of the *Enterprise* celebrates the promotion of Security Officer Worf to Lieutenant Commander. News arrives of an attack on the Amagosa Observatory, and Captain Jean-Luc Picard orders an immediate investigation, confiding to the Ship's Counsellor, Deanna Troy, that his nephew has been killed. At the Observatory they find Dr Soran, who sifts through the wreckage, escorted by Chief Engineer Geordi LaForge and Second Officer Data, an android who has attempted to fathom human humour by installing an 'emotion chip'. Confused by feelings of fear, Data fails to intervene when Soran suddenly kidnaps Geordi onto a Klingon ship piloted by renegade Klingons Lursa and B'Etor.

Guinan, now a member of the *Enterprise* team, recognises Soran. Like her, he was once trapped in the Nexus, the mysterious electrical vortex roaming the galaxies, within which one enters a time-suspended state of pure joy. Soran will do anything to return there. Data and Picard work out that he plans to intercept the Nexus by destroying the Veridian star-system with Klingon-supplied technology. Recovering Geordi and shooting down the Klingons, but not before the *Enterprise* has been severely damaged, Picard pursues Soran to the surface of Veridian 3 while the salvaged top section of the *Enterprise* is crashlanded by First Officer Riker. Picard is swept away by the Nexus as the star-system is devastated.

Picard finds himself at a magical Christmas party with the family he always longed for but never had. Painfully turning away, with Guinan's help he traces a placid Captain Kirk enjoying his own rustic paradise and at last persuades him to return through time to protect the Veridian system against Soran's missile attack. They battle together against Soran until he is killed by a reprogrammed missile. Crushed by girders, Kirk also dies, but the Veridian system is saved, and Picard rejoins the crew of the crashed *Enterprise*, confident that a new starship will soon be under his command.

With the creation of the Nexus, the first Star Trek feature of the post-Roddenberry generation has opened an all too convenient Pandora's Box. Unlike the innumerable other malignancies that have menaced the universe since the series was precariously launched in 1964—such as 'V'ger' in *Star Trek: the Motion Picture* faithfully transferred to the cinema screen and others continuing as reliable plot devices in *The Next Generation*—the Nexus confers all the random blessings and risks of a whole range of National Lotteries. A ribbon of time-warping energy adrift in the spaceways, it offers both the *Solaris* effect which brings dreams to life, and the infinite opportunity to reshape history. In other words, it's the ultimate solution to all screenwriting problems. Potentially a haven for the weak and the infirm, as well as for retired Starfleet personnel, the Nexus must surely represent the Grail for all future Star Trek quests, a transcendent objective for life-forms throughout the galaxies. It is also the simplest possible means of endlessly reviving Kirk, Spock, Tasha Yar, or any other lost colleagues for further profitable adventures.

Since Superman resuscitated Lois Lane, the 'laws' of time-reversal, never too easy to grasp, seem to have gone haywire. In *Star Trek: Generations*, the peculiar logic of the Nexus collapses under the slightest probe, taking much of the story with it. Granted that wild-eyed Dr Soran, driven to desperation after being plucked from Nirvana by a succession of well-meaning rescuers, is prepared to destroy a star-system in order to gratify his addiction, and must be prevented from doing so, it is nevertheless curiously short-sighted of Picard to resort to ungainly fisticuffs as the sole deterrent. All that is required is to return, via the Nexus, to the first meeting with Soran and drop him off in one of those convenient little spaceshuttles in the path of the vortex for reunion with his own brand of ecstasy.

The usual objection to time-tinkering of this sort is the supposed paradox of running into oneself (the worst possible disaster, according to the *Back to the Future* trilogy), but since Picard does not meet himself grappling with Soran this rule appears either to have been disregarded or explained away somewhere in the small print. The Nexus, in fact, offers an enviable flexibility: you can do anything, meet anyone, go anywhere. The 78 years between Kirk's first 'death' and Picard's catching up with him seem to have gone by in as long as it takes to fry an egg, while Guinan can apparently shift in and out of the Nexus as she pleases, despite her professed terror of its attractions.

Since these delights involve much the same finely-detailed charades as feature on the Holodeck of the *Enterprise*, where the Starship's entire crew, dressed up in silly costumes like a Monty Python sketch, while away the hours at play ("This," exults Picard, "is real freedom!"). it is difficult to interpret them as any kind of menace—particularly as the problems of the galaxies, one long round of warfare and planetary disintegration, evidently can be put on hold until one is ready to go and deal with them. A reversal might even be implicit whereby the Nexus, with its Christmas parties and its exuberant bouts of equestrianism, is the only true reality while the Klingons, or a berserk Malcolm McDowell, or all the capricious Starfleet executives put together, are mere figments of the fevered imagination, on no account to be taken seriously.

The durability of *Star Trek*, as Roddenberry always maintained, is a matter not so much of the ingenuity with which emergencies of an incalculable scale are coolly solved on a weekly basis, but of an underlying odyssey, complete with sirens, whirlpools, and dragon's teeth, in which the officers of the *Enterprise* wrestle with themselves, duty and mortality at constant odds. In *Star Trek: Generations* the issues are achingly of human-ness: sacrifice, joy, humour, belong and the cruel penalties for self-indulgence. From Kirk's bemused recognition that he is only again on the starship's bridge as a PR exercise, to Picard's imagined and heartrendingly unreachable family, the two Captains live an inner life which, to an audience that has known them for years, is uniquely accessible from the slightest of hints. Family, in fact, is the essence of the attraction: the dedicated Trekkie occupies a dimension of Generations unknown to the casual observer in which the whereabouts of family members Sulu or Uhura or Wesley are matters of inescapable parallel conjecture.

What the Nexus is sadly unlikely to achieve is the return of a less mature Enterprise contingent from the early years. already multi-wrinkled in *The Undiscovered Country*, what is left of the original unit is now creaking somewhat; in this sense, the death of Kirk marks an inevitable valediction. Nicely judged by Shatner, the final improvisation is both characteristically fey and affectingly memorable, despite the tawdry surroundings (the first version took him out by laser-blast but the fans complained). It marks the end of the Roddenberry era with at least an adequate dignity, while the exchanges between Shatner and the ageless Patrick Stewart, a fascinating duel between levity and authority, produce admirable performances at both extremes. And if the 'humanisation' of Data, a well-worn theme of the *Next Generation* episodes, is given excessive screen time while Beverly and a fetchingly revamped Deanna get rather too little, the spectacular aspects of the screenplay are handled with daunting skill by newcomer David Carson, clearly well prepared by his television apprenticeship. The sequence of the *Enterprise* top section saucering into a crash-landing on an alien planet is as glorious as anyone, Trekkie or not, could wish for.

VILLAGE VOICE, 11/29/94, p. 73, Henry Cabot Beck

First off, yes, Captain James Tiberius Kirk does shuffle off to ham actor's heaven, wisely chewing only a modest portion of galactic scenery on his way out. Surrounded as he is by Patrick Stewart as ur-control freak Picard and a brilliantly low-keyed Malcolm McDowell as an alien villain less predatory than preoccupied, Shatner takes his moment with unaccustomed dignity. His final words: "Oh my!"

Picard and Kirk meet in a kind of fantasy dimension, a cosmic never-land called The Nexus where time and space have no meaning. The Nexus acts like a drug, addicting those who enter it by making it possible to sort through the past and correct personal choices and bad career moves. When Kirk is found chopping wood by a picturesque cabin, you realize that the Captain's secret fantasy isn't about going back to the first season to rub elbows with Spock and Doc, but rather to give up space hopping and become William Shatner, enjoying a rustic, self-satisfied life like some pudgy, priapic Peter Pan.

Picard's vision of paradise turns out to be a reverse version of *It's a Wonderful Life* when he finds himself surrounded by children on Christmas morning, his wife beckoning him to a turkey dinner. But the Federation Starship Enterprise, regardless of era, is a boys-only club, and captain bonding must occur if the universe is to be saved.

In any case, *Generations* has some of the best special effects of any of the films, some terrific action sequences, and some first-rate acting. And in spite of the hokum that drives the plot, the film is unlikely to disappoint fans, although it is equally unlikely to win over any anti-Trekkers. *Star Trek Generations* is a dish best served to those who care the most or not at all.

Also reviewed in:
CHICAGO TRIBUNE, 11/18/94, Friday/p. C, Michael Wilmington
NEW YORK TIMES, 11/18/94, p. C3, Janet Maslin
VARIETY, 11/14-20/94, p. 47, Leonard Klady
WASHINGTON POST, 11/18/94, p. F7, Rita Kempley
WASHINGTON POST, 11/18/94, Weekend/p. 50, Desson Howe

STARGATE

A Metro-Goldwyn-Mayer release of a Le Studio Canal+/Centropolis Film production in association with Carolco Pictures Inc. *Executive Producer:* Mario Kassar. *Producer:* Joel B. Michaels, Oliver Eberle, and Dean Devlin. *Director:* Roland Emmerich. *Screenplay:* Dean Devlin and Roland Emmerich. *Director of Photography:* Karl Walter Lindenlaub. *Editor:* Michael J. Duthie and Derek Brechin. *Music:* David Arnold. *Music Editor:* Laurie Higgins Tobias. *Sound:* David Ronne and (music) Jeff Foster. *Sound Editor:* Sandy Gendler and Val Kuklowsky. *Casting:* April Webster. *Production Designer:* Holger Gross. *Art Director:* Peter Murton, Frank Bollinger, and Mark Zuelzke. *Set Designer:* Steven Alesch, Mick Cukurs, Luis Hoyos, Barbara Ann Jaeckel, Patrick Janicke, Patricia Klawonn, and Clare Scarpulla. *Set Decorator:* Jim Erickson. *Set Dresser:* Jeff Debell, J. Gregory Evans, Chris Fielding, James Malley, Herb Morris, Mark Sakamoto, and Josh Warner. *Special Effects:* Trevor Wood and John Cazin. *Special Creature Effects:* Patrick Tatopoulos. *Digital and Visual Effects:* Jeffrey A. Okun. *Costumes:* Joseph Porro. *Make-up:* Greg Nelson. *Make-up (Kurt Russell):* Dennis Liddiard. *Stunt Coordinator:* Andy Armstrong. *Running time:* 125 minutes. *MPAA Rating:* PG-13.

CAST: Kurt Russell (Colonel Jonathan "Jack" O'Neil); James Spader (Dr. Daniel Jackson); Jaye Davidson (Ra); Viveca Lindfors (Catherine); Alexis Cruz (Skaara); Mili Avital (Sha'uri); Leon Rippy (General W.O. West); John Diehl (Lieutenant Kawalsky); Carlos Lauchu (Anubis); Djimon (Horus); Erick Avari (Kasuf); French Stewart (Lieutenant Feretti); Gianin Loffler (Nabeh); Christopher John Fields (Lieutenant Freeman); Derek Webster (Lieutenant Brown); Jack Moore (Lieutenant Reilly); Steve Giannelli (Lieutenant Porro); David Pressman (Assistant Lieutenant); Scott Smith (Officer); Cecil Hoffman (Sarah O'Neil); Rae Allen (Barbara Shore); Richard Kind (Gary Meyers); John Storey (Mitch); Lee Taylor-Allan (Jenny); George Gray (Technician); Kelly Vint (Young Catherine); Erik Holland (Professor Langford); Nick Wilder (Foreman Taylor); Sayed Badreya (Arabic Interpreter); Michael Concepcion (Horus #1); Jerry Gilmore (Horus #2); Michel Jean-Phillipe (Horus #3); Dialy N'Daiye (Horus #4); Gladys Holland, Roger Til, Kenneth Danziger, and Christopher West (Professors); Robert Ackerman (Companion); Kieron Lee (Masked Ra); Frank Welker (Voice of the Mastadge).

LOS ANGELES TIMES, 10/28/94, Calendar/p. 15, Peter Rainer

According to "Stargate," the great ancient Egyptian civilization that gave us the pyramids actually began on another planet—the planet Abydos, millions of light-years from Earth. The film mainlines our fascination with that ancient culture by making its achievements—quite literally—otherworldly.

Now if only the rest of the film weren't so earthbound.

Dr. Daniel Jackson (James Spader) is a brainy, controversial Egyptologist hired for a top-secret military project translating the hieroglyphics on a giant, mysterious stone uncovered in 1928 in Giza, Egypt. This he does lickety-split. His conclusion: The stone is a giant ring—a portal—into another dimension. So, of course, when a time-traveling team headed up by the ramrod, disconsolate Col. Jack O'Neil (Kurt Russell) decides to pass through that portal, Daniel is on board.

The planet Abydos, with its desert-scapes and pachyderm-like creatures and fur-cloaked denizens, seems to have been colonized by aliens from—Hollywood. There's a lot of "Star Wars" on this orb, as well as portals to everything from "Lawrence of Arabia" to "The Man Who Would be King." (Of course, "Star Wars" wasn't exactly created from whole loincloth either.) Pretty soon we're mired in the usual science versus military squabbles, with Daniel doing his decoding thing in order to get the militia returned to Earth before the malevolent, godlike Ra, played by Jaye Davidson, incinerates them all.

All this nonsense is made intermittently enjoyable because of the Saturday-afternoon serial quality of the storytelling (which is full of holes). Director Roland Emmerich, who also co-wrote the script with Dean Devlin, doesn't take the mumbo-jumbo terribly seriously, although he doesn't pull the film through the portals of camp either. He respects the pop junkiness of the project. Even the tackiness of the sets and effects—despite a budget upward of $60 million—seems partly intentional. It's "Flash Gordon" with computerized whammies.

Spader is surprisingly funny and resilient as the Egyptologist who feels more at home on Abydos than he ever did on Earth. He fits into the planet's slave-like culture and becomes its crusader. He finds himself by losing himself in the solar system—not a bad way to go these days. O'Neil, who is recovering from the accidental death of his son, has a buzz-cut and a cold stare; Russell is such a muscle-man tough-guy that he practically effaces himself.

The real hoot here is Jaye Davidson's Ra, with his hermaphrodite airs and flouncy Space-Age get-ups. Davidson's voice was apparently electronically altered to sound lower and boomier: He's like a fey Darth Vader, and he seems entranced by the Garbo-esque rapture of it all.

Without Davidson "Stargate" might seem clunky and routine, but he gives it a weirdo charge. It may be a lousy movie, but it's a more *enjoyably* lousy movie than most.

NEW YORK POST, 10/28/94, p. 49, Thelma Adams

"Stargate," like "Heaven's Gate" and Watergate, is an unnatural disaster.

German director Roland ("Universal Soldier") Emmerich's science fiction adventure pastiche—Indiana Jones and the Temple of Dune—finds failed Egyptologist Dr. Daniel Jackson (James Spader) hopping in bed with the U.S. military.

In an underground bunker, the most somber, dehumanized soldiers since the "question authority" '60s guard an ancient Egyptian portal to the stars. Jackson unlocks the "Stargate" and spins into space with no more preparation than a 5th Avenue candy bar tucked into his kit. Boyishly charming, Spader has the hardest working bangs in show business.

Colonel Jack O'Neil (Kurt Russell) joins Jackson on the interstellar superhighway. A grim, tooth-grinding Russell harbors not one but two dark secrets. The colonel's son has just killed himself in a gun mishap—and the soldier's mission is to blow the gate and everything he finds on the other side of the universe to oblivion with a big, shiny bomb.

Russell doesn't have much to laugh about in an embarrassingly humorless role—but things could have been worse. He could have been cast as Ra, the Egyptian god credited with building the stargate.

In a planet far, far away that looks surprisingly like Arabia, the uptight captain and the floppy academic encounter a campy incarnation of Ra (Jaye Davidson). For a reason as mysterious as time itself the all-powerful being has adopted the simpering, corsetted, slim-hipped body of a young waif and surrounded himself with loin-clothed young boys.

Davidson, who became an instant star after "The Crying Game," is astonishingly bad, an acting black hole. One can only hope that Spader, Russell and Davidson took a flat fee on this fiasco.

By the time the special effects gear up, the human effects have flatlined. "I am no longer amused," Davidson tells Spader as he puts an electric whammy between the doctor's eyes. I knew how he felt.

NEWSDAY, 10/18/94, Part II/p. B2, John Anderson

Totally preposterous and hence a lot of fun, "Stargate" is not just your average reality-warping, eye-popping, faux-historic science-fiction extravaganza. It's also subversive. How else would you describe a film in which an oppressed people throw off the yoke of tyranny by nuking God?

That God turns out to be Ra, the erstwhile Egyptian sun deity, and Ra turns out to be Jaye Davidson, who brought a little something extra to "The Crying Game" a couple of years back, only makes the scenario more giddy. "Stargate," obviously, is not averse to mischief, especially concerning the always prickly question of divine gender (Davidson's vogueing recalls the queen in Disney's "Sleeping Beauty") and it's a good thing. Following the lead of Erich Von Daniken's best seller "Chariots of the Gods?," which hypothesized that aliens built the pyramids, "Stargate" opens with a scene as dusty as Tut. A desert landscape, an archeological dig—a subtitle reading "Giza, Egypt, 1928"—and a mysterious, ominous find: a huge metallic wheel that could have been the Pharaohs' Goodyear ad, and a gold locket, which goes into a little girl's pocket.

Flashing to the present, that girl is now Catherine (Viveca Lindfors), who is part of a top-secret project to discover the meaning of that wheel, known as the Stargate. Enlisting the aid of a brilliant and sweetly flaky young Egyptologist named Daniel Jackson (James Spader), they learn in days what the military has failed to deduce for years: That the Stargate is a kind of celestial sextant, that its symbols denote constellations and correspond to symbols on a wheel somewhere on the dark side of the universe. By lining up those symbols intergalactically, they can travel to that world.

Jackson eagerly joins the intergalactic expeditionary force, led by Jack O'Neil (Kurt Russell), a Special Forces colonel mourning his young son, who accidentally shot himself to death. Not enough is made of this, especially since Colonel ("I've got nothing to live for") Jack clearly has not mended his weapons-happy ways. He travels to the unnamed planet with a secret agenda that will imperil everyone on both worlds.

It's there we find Ra, and his story: A member of a dying alien race, he found the human body adaptable, inhabited one, and created the basis for civilization on both planets. In addition to his funky Mesopotamian roots, he has a vengeful Old Testament disposition, a voice like Howard Stern impersonating Bob Guccione, a Keanu Reeves haircut and Tammy Wynette's wardrobe.

Odd as it may seem, "Stargate" remains fairly convincing, if nutty, thanks largely to Spader, who plays the gifted Jackson like a kid in a cosmic candy store. Russell, in tight T and buzz cut, might have been portraying Young Ollie North, although North is a better actor. But it's Spader's movie—he even meets a beautiful female humanoid named Sha'uri (Mila Avital), who teaches him ze vays of interplanetary luff—and this keeps "Stargate" from becoming the usual celebration of technosterone.

In addition to the tongue-in-cheek approach of director Roland Emmerich, the film is aided by some exciting special effects—if you're going to see "Stargate," see it in a theater with digital sound—and a premise with enough historical bones to make it interesting, if not entirely plausible. "Stargate" clearly doesn't take itself more seriously than it has to, of course, and this is a virtue.

SIGHT AND SOUND, 2/95, p. 53, Kim Newman

1928. Giza, Egypt. A large circular artefact is discovered near the great pyramid. Catherine, daughter of one of the archaeologists, is given an amulet found with the artefact. The present day: Dr Daniel Jackson, ridiculed for a theory that the pyramid was not built by ancient Egyptians, is approached by Catherine and invited to join a US government project examining the Giza artefact, a teleportation gate linked to another situated elsewhere in the universe. The military side of the project is commanded by Colonel Jack O'Neil, an officer traumatised by the recent accidental death of his son. Jackson deciphers the instructions of the stargate and a team commanded by O'Neil ventures through, emerging into a desert world.

Jackson needs to find a key to the other stargate before the team can return. The amulet, which Catherine has given Jackson, convinces a local human chieftain that the Americans have come from the Gods, and Jackson learns from hieroglyphs that the inhabitants of the planet are descended from kidnapped ancient Egyptians. The absolute ruler of the world is Ra, an alien intelligence who lives on in the eternally renewed body of one of the Egyptians. Having been thrown off Earth by a slave revolt, Ra oppresses his people. O'Neil has brought an atom bomb to close the gate if he perceives a threat to Earth, but Ra gets hold of the device.

Jackson falls in love with Sha'uri, daughter of the chieftain, while O'Neil finds a substitute son in Sha'uri's brother Skaara. Jackson is killed and then revived by Ra, who tells him he plans to avenge himself on Earth by transmitting O'Neil's bomb back there along with a mineral which will boost its destructive power a hundredfold. The Americans lead a revolt against Ra, and the slaves rally to overthrow Ra's goons. Ra's pyramid spaceship takes off but O'Neil and Jackson teleport the bomb into it, destroying the tyrant. Jackson opts to stay with Sha'uri, while the surviving soldiers return to Earth.

Enormous production values, seamless special effects and an old-fashioned deployment of huge sets and armies of extras are harnessed in the service of an amazingly ramshackle script that recycles pulpy chunks of the lesser science fiction stories of the 30s and the 'lost world' romances of Rider Haggard and his imitators. While a very few elements, such as the growling GI who has the archetypal grunt name of 'Kawalsky', suggest nostalgic knowingness of cliché, this is mainly played remarkably straight. Director Emmerich hammers home every point with undue emphasis: Kurt Russell is first seen contemplating his gun and his son's photograph as he sits gloomily in the kid's abandoned room, but a couple of lesser characters then have to discuss the boy's death to make sure that those at the back of the class who haven't been paying attention get the point.

As the plot zooms to the other side of the universe, things get even sillier: Jackson only admits he can't make the stargate work both ways once they've arrived, then spends odd moments contemplating hieroglyphs to work out how it works, though the evil Ra seems quite willing to set the co-ordinates when it comes to sending back Earth's bomb. That Americans—who have somehow gained possession of an historical artefact unearthed in Egypt and feel empowered to act on behalf of all humanity—send Ra the bomb that threatens the home planet is less an irony than lazy plotting. This lack of focus becomes disastrous in the finale as three climaxes—the slave revolt, Jackson trying to revive his temporarily dead love interest, a fistfight between O'Neil and the head goon—are cut against each other, with the bomb ticking away in the background.

The 'heart-warming' business of O'Neil's relationship with a desert urchin is extremely tiresome, but the equally clichéd relationship of the eager Jackson and the winning Sha'uri is a more acceptable evocation of the native romances of Hollywood sarong epics. Jaye Davidson, a limited performer who has miraculously found another part only he could play, swans about in Egyptian frocks and a computer-generated shape-shifting headdress as the evil Ra, merging from a Dr Phibes-style hi-tech sarcophagus to add a welcome note of Edgar Rice Burroughs-ish camp to the surprisingly stolid desert rebellion plot. There is a smug element of unattractive patronising as slaves whipped up against their masters act like every American administration's fantasy of a grateful Third World populace begging for military aid. They are presumably capable of abandoning the Ancient Egyptian system, all they've known, for a simulation of parliamentary democracy. The triteness is such that Jackson's decision to stay behind with his native girl prompts less romantic admiration than wonderment that anyone would volunteer to spend the rest of his life on a planet without dentists.

TIME, 11/21/94, p. 116, Richard Schickel

The makers of the upcoming *Star Trek* picture, *Generations* can find either comfort or anxiety in the success of *Stargate*. It has spent two weeks at the top of box-office charts, surprising even its distributors and proving there's still a general audience for sci-fi. But if *Stargate* has already sated that crowd, then *Generations* might end up as leftovers.

One thing *Stargate* definitely proves, though, is the old adage, If you're going to steal, steal big. If you're caught, you can always claim you were doing an homage. Director Roland Emmerich's chief honorees are the *Indiana Jones* and *Star Wars* sagas. In a prologue set in 1928, archaeologists in Egypt uncover a large metallic ring. Fifty years later, Daniel Jackson (James Spader), a nerdy but stalwart linguist, deciphers the ring's hieroglyphics. They suggest it was left behind centuries ago by supersmart aliens (oh, hi there, *2001*). By twiddling a few dials, scientists set the ring humming, and Jackson and a quarrelsome combat team led by Colonel Jack O'Neil (a glum Kurt Russell) are transported to a galaxy far, far away.

The movie, which does have a sort of cheeky energy, goes into narrative and cliché overload once the spacemen start exploring the unnamed planet—Shall we call it Lucasland?—where they set down. There's a slave population to be freed, a tyrant to be deposed, some cheapish special effects to put on display, and a lot of problems about getting safely back to Earth to solve. Tying all this together, *Stargate* stumbles to a hasty, muddled ending instead of soaring to a conclusion worthy of the only thing that's first rate about it—its sources.

VILLAGE VOICE, 11/15/94, p. 67, Jeff Salamon

Jaye Davidson's famous member isn't the only thing absent from this misbegotten outer space extravaganza. Logic, exposition, and character development never rear their heads either. Too bad; the notion the film exploits—that the wonders of ancient Egypt were the product of extraterrestrial contact—is resonant enough to have spawned a genre of channelling books and one gonzo "nonfiction" classic, Robert K. G. Temple's *The Sirius Mystery*. Unfortunately, the trippiest *Stargate* gets are brief scenes of hyperspeed space travel that approach *2001* on the DMT-simulation scale. The rest is on the level of unsuccessful attempts to feed Kurt Russell Schwarzeneggerian kiss-off lines like "Say hello to King Tut, asshole." (Or something like that; I'm not sure of the exact wording—which is precisely my point, right?) James Spader, as a hapless linguist, is relatively amusing for 45 minutes, but then he falls in love with The Beautiful Alien girl and spends the last hour of the film looking forlorn and pretty. The best thing in *Stargate*—which was, inexplicably, the highest grossing film in America last week—is Davidson, who has real presence as the evil sun god Ra. Presiding over a rainbow tribe of young servants and sycophants, he exudes high concept: Josephine Baker as Darth Vader.

Also reviewed in:
CHICAGO TRIBUNE, 10/28/94, Friday/p. D, Johanna Steinmetz
NEW YORK TIMES, 10/28/94, p. C6, Caryn James
VARIETY, 10/24-30/94, p. 67, Leonard Klady
WASHINGTON POST, 10/28/94, p. F7, Hal Hinson

STEFANO QUANTESTORIE

An Italtoons release of a Penta Film/Bambu coproduction. *Producer:* Ernesto di Sarro. *Director:* Maurizio Nichetti. *Screenplay (Italian with English subtitles):* Maurizio Nichetti and Laura Fischetto. *Director of Photography:* Maurrio Battistoni. *Editor:* Rita Rossi. *Music:* Sergio Conforti and Paolo Panigada. *Art Director:* Maria Pia Angelini. *Costumes:* Maria Pia Angelini. *Running time:* 90 minutes. *MPAA Rating:* Not Rated.

CAST: Maurizio Nichetti (Stefano); James Spencer Thiérrée (Young Stefano); Amanda Sandrelli (Toy Seller); Elena Sofia Ricci (Hostess); Caterina Sylos Labini (Wife); Renato Scarpa (Father); Milena Vukotic (Mother).

NEW YORK POST, 11/23/94, p. 51, Larry Worth

When one actor plays multiple roles in the same film, the result is hit or miss.

In 1949's "Kind Hearts and Coronets," Alec Guinness did it to perfection. In 1965's "The Family Jewels," Jerry Lewis did it to death.

So what about Maurizio Nichetti's decision to play six parts in "Stefano Quantestorie"? Well, let's just say that if a substitute host is needed for the Labor Day telethon ... Clearly, performer/director/writer Nichetti is a man of considerable wit, comic timing and great imagination, as he so effectively demonstrated in "The Icicle Thief" and "Volere/Volare." But in an unfortunate change of pace, his third effort's a bona fide horror.

Co-written with Laura Fischetto, Nichetti's script is almost impossible to follow, with countless scenes featuring flashbacks within flashbacks and fantasy segments segueing into yet more fantasies.

Nichetti begins by playing Stefano, a policeman who's smitten by the picture of a comely robbery suspect. He's even more intrigued when he finds she's really a toy maker who thrives on reading fairy tales to children.

But before they can live happily ever after, Stefano's parents grow concerned about his bachelor status, leading to a sequence wherein he's married his childhood sweetheart-turned-shrew. And that's a launching pad for a handful of subplots in which Nichetti pops up as a womanizing airline pilot, a saxophone player, a math teacher and a bank robber—all named Stefano.

Making matters more confusing, supporting characters also adopt new identities from vignette to vignette. Ultimately all of Nichetti's various selves crisscross into one stream of consciousness free-for-all.

What initially seems an ode to "It's a Wonderful Life"—seeing how one's existence would be different if other choices had been made—quickly degenerates into a pointlessly surreal "Sybil." Specifically, Nichetti replaces the most crucial ingredient—whimsy—with speeded-up action, bad slapstick and endless cliches.

Judging from the weak finale, Nichetti never figured out how to end it. Too bad he ever figured out how to start it.

VILLAGE VOICE, 12/5/94, p. 66, Lawrence O'Toole

Stefano Quantestorie is a testosterone fantasy of what one man might have amounted to had his life swerved in other directions—an amorous airline pilot, a cuckolded teacher, a henpecked husband, and so on—with Nichetti (*The Icicle Thief*) taking on all the roles. Each of the characters' stories dovetails neatly in a cops-and-robbers tale meant to build as blithely as a Rossini overture, but Nichetti's filmic talent is a tiny one—precise and strained. Both this film and *Icicle Thief* are the equivalent of watching faeries build pyramids. Every joke is like watching a huge slab hauled across the quarry by those poor little people.

To be fair. I laughed out loud once and smiled several times. For the role of Stefano's younger self Nichetti has employed a genial young actor named James Spencer Thiérrée, grandson of Charlie Chaplin, who also happens to resemble his granddad. Inviting comparison, Nichetti certainly courts catastrophe.

Now for the bad news: Nichetti's view of women. They are either shrewish wives, whining and demanding mothers, empty-headed sweet young things, or bored adulteresses. (One of the latter gets bumped off for her straying.) These women have *nothing* interesting to say—they're props—and the director seems to like it that way. When they are objects of desire, he films them as if they spend every waking hour using fabric softener. Beneath Nichetti's sweetness, which he works at hard, there beats the heart of a penis.

Also reviewed in:
NEW YORK TIMES, 11/23/94, p. C18, Caryn James
VARIETY, 3/1/93, p. 57, Deborah Young

STRAWBERRY AND CHOCOLATE

A Miramax Films release of a Robert Redford presentation of an IMCINE/Telemadrid/SGAE/Tabasco Films coproduction. *Executive Producer:* Camilo Vives, Frank Cabrera, and Georgina Balzaretti. *Director:* Tomás Gutiérrez Alea and Juan Carlos Tabio. *Screenplay (Spanish with English subtitles based on his story "El Lobo, El Bosque y el Hombre Nuevo"):* Senel Paz. *Director of Photography:* Mario García Joya. *Editor:* Rolando Martínez, Miriam Talavera, and Osvaldo Donatien. *Music:* José María Vitier. *Sound*: Silvia Rodriguez. *Sound Editor:* Germinal Hernández. *Production Designer:* Fernando O'Reilly. *Set Decorator:*

Orlando González. *Costumes:* Miriam Dueñas. *Make-up:* María Elena del Toro and Graciela Grossas. *Running time:* 110 minutes. *MPAA Rating:* Not Rated.

CAST: Jorge Perugorría (Diego); Vladimir Cruz (David); Mirta Ibarra (Nancy); Francisco Gattorno (Miguel); Jorge Angelino (Germán); Marilyn Solaya (Vivian); Andrés Cortina (Santeria Priest); Antonio Carmona (Boyfriend); Ricardo Avila (Taxi Driver); María Elena del Toro and Zolanda Ovia (Passengers); Diana Iris del Puerto (Neighbor).

LOS ANGELES TIMES, 1/27/95, Calendar/p. 1, Kevin Thomas

On a sunny day in 1979 a young gay man, Diego, zeros in on David, a university student, sitting alone in a Havana outdoor cafe, eating chocolate ice cream. Diego, who orders strawberry, flirts shamelessly, even managing to get the increasingly uneasy David, a political science major, to go to his apartment.

Despite all his brazen determination and shameless ploys, Diego succeeds only in driving David away, but this is just the beginning of "Strawberry and Chocolate," Tomás Gutiérrez Alea's triumphant seriocomic tale of sex and politics, a candid and critical view of Cuban society with implications timeless and universal. On another level, the film, which is Cuba's official Oscar entry, is a warm, funny and wise heart-tugger with the wide appeal of "The Adventures of Priscilla, Queen of the Desert" or even "La Cage aux Folles."

Alea, Cuba's major veteran director, is best known for his landmark "Memories of Underdevelopment" (1968), in which an upper-middle-class man in his 30s, on the eve of his departure in flight of Castro's triumph, decides to stay and cast his lot with the new order. But Alea's view has evolved revealingly in the decades since and the irresistible "Strawberry and Chocolate" is an uncommonly shrewd blend of seriousness and schmaltz.

In all likelihood Vladimir Cruz's David and Jorge Perugorría's Diego would never have had further contact had David not mentioned the incident to his roommate Miguel (Francisco Gattorno). David remarks that Diego, a Ministry of Culture employee, is helping his sculptor friend Germán (Jorge Angelino), also gay, plan an exhibition of his work in collaboration with a foreign embassy. Miguel, a stereotypical macho Latino homophobe, smells subversive activity instantly and insists that David spend enough time with Diego to get him and Germán into trouble.

At the heart of "Strawberry and Chocolate" is the friendship that develops between a gay man and a straight man, which is almost never depicted on the screen and surely never with such depth and insight. Alea and writer Senel Paz, working from Paz's short story "The Wolf, the Forest and the New Man," have really got it right.

(Because of Alea's ongoing struggle with lung cancer, he has a co-director, Juan Carlos Tabío, who shot some scenes while Alea was hospitalized. Alea is back at work on a new film, "Guantanamera.")

A proud member of the Communist League, David discovers his world opening up, for Diego is a witty, challenging, formidably well-read and cultured intellectual, a blunt but constructive critic of David's writing. Meanwhile, Diego quietly downplays the truth that he has fallen in love with his new friend. Thankfully, he's no martyr and is simply too gutsy and tough not to be able to handle his emotions for the sake of a relationship that has real meaning for him. On the other hand, it has clearly never occurred to David that a gay man could possess strength of character or even that gays have to be resilient and must have the capacity to create their own universes simply if they are to survive in a largely hostile world.

Perugorría and Cruz are wonderful actors and have been intriguingly cast. Although unapologetically effeminate and sometimes flamboyant, Diego is handsome, hairy-chested and husky, whereas the straight David is slight and doe-eyed, almost delicate. Rounding out a key trio of terrific portrayals is that of Mirta Ibarra as Nancy, David's neighbor, an immensely likable and vital but highly vulnerable former prostitute in her 40s.

As graceful as the antique wrought-iron railings glimpsed throughout, "Strawberry and Chocolate" looks gorgeous but evokes a sense of sadness, for it is set in the heart of old Havana with its avenues of magnificent 19th-Century buildings threatening to crumble into dust. Diego's charming, artifact-cluttered apartment, the film's main setting, is composed of a couple of small rooms in a large structure of decayed grandeur.

The constant paranoia, the homophobia that signifies a much wider oppression and the lack of freedom of expression that was true of Cuba in 1979 may have diminished, even dramatically in some instances. However, the country is still far from a paradise for gays, and the Havana that we see on the screen is inescapably—and significantly—the seedy, impoverished city of today.

NEW YORK, 2/6/95, p. 59, David Denby

Tomás Gutiérrez Alea's *Strawberry and Chocolate* is mainly set in an old Havana apartment building whose chipped and gnarled walls offer a nostalgic reminder of the old Spanish Baroque colonial city—sinfully decadent glories, out of place in the austerely functional Communist state. In this peculiar ruin, three characters who seem stranded from a Tennessee Williams play—a flamboyant and intelligent gay artist (Jorge Perrugoría), a retired prostitute (Mirta Ibarra), and a handsome young (male) virgin (Vladimir Cruz)—fall in and out of love and long for greater freedom. The movie doesn't have much of a story, but it's a touching plea for friendship, sex, and art. If the revolution isn't going to succeed, the movie seems to be saying, couldn't we at least have a little more of the old Cuban spirit of live and let live?

NEW YORK POST, 1/20/95, p. 42, Thelma Adams

"Art is to feel, not to transmit things. Let government radio do that." says Diego. the Cuban intellectual in Tomas Gutierrez Alea's wise and witty social comedy.

Diego (Jorge Perrugoria) and David (Vladimir Cruz) are as different as "Strawberry and Chocolate."

Diego is gay; David is straight. Diego doesn't endorse any revolution that rejects him as a dance partner; David is a Young Communist. Diego lives in the moment; David pins his hopes on the future, come the completion of the revolution.

As a junior government spy, David sets out to destroy Diego, the deviant. Instead, David learns tolerance from Diego, the man.

From the perspective of screenwriter Senel Paz, to be gay in Cuba is to be invisible or imprisoned. As the platonic friendship between the two men deepens behind closed doors. the flamboyant Diego assures David: "If I see you on the street, I don't know you."

As a gay film, "Strawberry and Chocolate" is on a par with "Philadelphia." It's tame compared to what New York audiences have become accustomed to—from Stephen Frears' "My Beautiful Laundrette" to the out-and-over-the-top films of Gregg Araki ("Totally F--ked Up").

"Strawberry and Chocolate" is much more radical in the context of Cuba's restrictions on freedom of expression—but gay rights aren't Alea's sole concern.

The director of the Cuban classic, "Memories of Underdevelopment," stalks human intolerance. "Strawberry and Chocolate" laments the twisting of revolutionary ideals into tools of repression.

The movie is a pointed and outspoken critique of the aftermath of the Cuban revolution enriched by a bittersweet passion for Cuba and its pock-marked, crumbling capital.

The filmmakers' strongest weapon is the character of Diego, the flirtatious, intelligent, imperfect life force of "Strawberry and Chocolate."

The characterization starts off excessively mannered, with the sunflower-carryingDiego mincing and coy.

These affectations soon melt away, as Perrugoria reveals layer after layer of passion, hope, religious zeal, despair and compassion.

Diego emerges as a man who loves—and is betrayed by—Cuba.

NEWSDAY, 9/23/94, Part II/p. B5, John Anderson

Robert Redford joined with Miramax in presenting this controversial Cuban film by Tomas Gutierrez Alea, which is set in Havana and concerns the growing friendship between cultured, openly gay Diego (Jorge Perugorria) and straight, but far less sophisticated David (Vladimir Cruz). Communist dogma, immigration, intellectual freedom and love between a gay and straight man are the issues in what was undoubtedly a brave project for a Cuban to undertake. New York audiences, however, may find the story naive and the portrayal of the gay Diego more than a little stereotypical.

NEWSDAY, 1/20/95, Part II/p. B7, Gene Seymour

It's always nice to see the cultural blockade between Cuba and the United States busted open by films like "Strawberry and Chocolate."

The film's glimpses of Havana's streets and architecture, its backdrops of Cuban people of different colors making their way through life are, in some ways, more enlightening than its cute, cunning story.

The title comes from the ice cream eaten at the film's start by the two protagonists: a callow college student named David (Vladimir Cruz), who just got dumped by his girlfriend, and a preening gay esthete named Diego (Jorge Perrugoria), who's vainly trying to pick David up at the ice cream stand. David, by the way, prefers chocolate while Diego is ecstatic over strawberry.

Though David, a grimly dedicated Marxist, refuses to so much as embrace Diego, he is fascinated by the older man's highly informed passion for art, opera and literature. Diego, simmering with unrequited love for David, nonetheless respects his friend's personal space. But David's motives in maintaining contact with Diego aren't entirely benign.

A fellow student (Francisco Gattorno) encourages David to spy on this suspiciously heretical "Marielito" who so flagrantly keeps copies of Time magazine, bottles of Johnny Walker Red and other "poisonous" playthings of the United States. Even Diego's close friend and neighbor, sexy, suicidal Nancy (Mirta Ibarra), warns David that hanging out with Diego could be hazardous to his political health.

The film, adapted from Senel Paz' short story, "The Wolf, the Forest and the New Man," is set in the late 1970s, probably not long before the 1979 "Marielito" exodus that was one of many manifestations of the Cuban government's hostility toward homosexuals. The earlier time frame may explain the film's somewhat quaint depiction of Diego's personality, which seems more "Boys in the Band" than "Angels in America."

Still, though Tomas Gutierrez Alea's film often seems like a serio-comic Cuban version of "The Odd Couple," its sweetness is offset a little by its rueful reflections on the fragile emotions trampled by a society's stringent demands.

SIGHT AND SOUND, 12/94, p. 48, Philip Kemp

David, a student at Havana University, takes his girlfriend Vivian to a cheap motel, but seeing her tears declares he won't sleep with her until they are married. He is devastated when she marries someone else. At a cafe he meets a gay artist, Diego, who takes him back to his apartment on a pretext of showing David some photographs. At the flat David sees religious statues made by Diego's friend Germán; Diego explains he plans to mount an exhibition of them with the help of a foreign embassy. At once intrigued and repelled by Diego's conversation, David recounts the experience to his fellow student Miguel, who tells him to keep up his contacts with this potential subversive.

Discontented in her marriage, Vivian invites David to become her lover, but he refuses. Visiting Diego again, he is introduced to Cuban culture and Scotch whisky, and also meets his neighbour Nancy, the Neighbourhood Vigilance officer for Diego's apartment block. When she attempts suicide, David helps Diego get her to hospital and donates blood for her. Though still wary of Diego's homosexuality, David is increasingly drawn to his cultured lifestyle, and his own suppressed ambition to write is rekindled.

Germán's exhibition is banned; furious, he smashes his own work. Despite David's warnings, Diego sends a letter of protest to the Cuban authorities. Nancy, attracted to David and learning he is a virgin, resolves to initiate him. After lunch at the apartment, Diego leaves David and Nancy alone together and they make love. Miguel, believing David has been corrupted, visits Diego and attacks him, but David intervenes. Under pressure to leave Cuba, Diego decides to give in. After a return visit to the cafe where they met, Diego and David say farewell—and embrace for the first time.

Tomás Gutiérrez Alea has always presented the Cuban authorities with something of a problem. The country's most prominent film-maker and a committed supporter of Castro's revolution, he has nonetheless repeatedly used his films to show up the flaws and idiocies of the regime: pig-headed bureaucracy in the black comedy of *Death of a Bureaucrat*, macho sexism in *Up to a Point*. Equally worrying to officialdom is his sympathetic treatment of those who find themselves marginalised by Castroism, like the vacillating bourgeois hero of his *Memories of Underdevelopment.*

Both these elements—the satire, and the sympathy for outsiders— come together in *Strawberry and Chocolate*, the first Cuban film to dare suggest it's OK, and maybe even more than OK, to be gay. Castro's regime has long been notorious for a rampant homophobia that has driven a lot of people into exile—not least Gutiérrez Alea's one-time colleague, the great cinematographer Nestor Almendros. This self-inflicted wound by a society that already has all the enemies it needs is what the film passionately deplores; as Diego asserts, "I'm a part of this country. And without me you'd be missing a part." Through Diego, David comes to discover a whole submerged heritage of Cuban culture, rejected by this regime or that—from the gay novelist José Lezama Lima, his books suppressed under Communism, to the composer Ignacio Cervantes, driven out by the Spanish. Cervantes' rueful "Farewell to Cuba" recurs through the film as a leitmotif; José Maria Vitier's score recalls it again as Diego himself prepares for exile.

In some quarters—and not only gay activist ones—*Strawberry and Chocolate* has apparently given offence. There are certainly more compelling reasons for deploring institutionalised homophobia than that it impoverishes cultural life, and the overall tenor of the film's argument—that just being gay doesn't mean you're not a nice person—may well appear culpably naive. Stereotypes aren't absent, either; our first view of Jorge Perugorría's Diego, primping and fluttering and striking queenly poses, arouses all the most dismal expectations. But Diego gains steadily in dignity as the film progresses, and in those early scenes we're after all seeing him through the eyes of David, a Party stalwart with all his prejudices bristlingly erect. (He had instantly figured Diego for a *maricón*, he tells Miguel, because he ordered strawberry ice cream when there was chocolate on offer.)

In any case, Gutiérrez Alea isn't concerned only with Cuban homophobia—an attitude openly sanctioned by Castro himself—but uses it to symbolise a geriatric revolution seizing up in every joint. In the entrance to Diego's apartment block, a crumbling baroque *palacio* from colonial days, a huge mural of Fidel is flaking off the wall—one disintegrating regime superimposed on another. At one point Diego plays David some Callas, commenting, "Why can't we produce voices like that? We can't always listen to Maria Remola." For Remola, a superannuated Cuban singer who refuses to retire, read Fidel, still heard blaring out daily on public loudspeakers. The revolution badly needs a new voice—and its condition at the grassroots is embodied in Diego's friend Nancy, the Neighbourhood Vigilance officer. Supposedly local guardian of revolutionary fervour, Nancy operates a thriving black market service for neighbours, prays to an image of St Barbara and repeatedly attempts suicide. It's a measure of the undoctrinaire warmth of Gutiérrez Alea's film that she also relieves David of his virginity, in a scene of genuine erotic tenderness.

About to depart, Diego takes David on a farewell tour of Havana, "one of the world's most beautiful cities. You just have time to see it before it collapses in shit." The scene gains added poignancy from Gutiérrez Alea's own condition: now seriously ill with cancer, he had to call in Juan Carlos Tabio to help him complete the film. Behind the film's wit and playfulness can be sensed a note of desperation, the urgency of a man who sees his native city and his native country collapsing in shit, and fears that their time, like his, is running short.

VILLAGE VOICE, 1/24/95, p. 54, Georgia Brown

In Tomas Gutierrez Alea's cloying *Strawberry and Chocolate*, all messages are spelled out in bold. Situated in contemporary Havana, this coy comedy begins, more or less, when David (Vladimir Cruz), a straight, none-too-bright university student, is picked up in a café by Diego (Jorge Perrugoria), a doting queen with a civilizing mission. Diego wants David, but David—despite the movie's prolonged tease—remains firmly hetero. Since Diego can't have him, he supplies a surrogate—his flaky fortysomething neighbor, Nancy (Mirta Ibarra), who, when she's not attempting suicide, is happy to accept a young man's virginity. The cluck's so dumb, he's ready to marry her.

If you saw Nestor Almendros and Orlando Jimenez Leal's damning 1983 documentary, *Improper Conduct* (attacked and condescended to by the American left), or simply read the papers, you may think gays in Cuba are routinely persecuted. No, according to *S&C*, they get along just swell—notwithstanding a few macho party members—and, despite a few quibbles, are loyal patriots. Because he's steeped in the glories of Cuban history and culture, Diego isn't ashamed to promote a few foreign products: Indian teas, Maria Callas, *Time* magazine, Johnny Walker Red, John Donne. One of the first sentences from his mouth: "Where's my *Cahiers du Cinéma*?" Swishy, perennially in heat, and preternaturally moist-eyed, Diego is a bundle of gay clichés.

At one point he invites his protégé for an architectural tour, à la *Hannah and her Sisters*, of glorious Old Havana. Oddly, this tour is very short—a couple of facades, a couple stained-glass windows. I would have loved to see more. It makes you wonder if anything's left.

Although ostensibly the film dares question the State—"When will they learn that art is one thing and propaganda another?"—*Strawberry and Chocolate* is more propaganda than art. (This ingratiating film seems to have been designed with film festivals in mind; it certainly scored with the NYFF.) The title, I neglected to tell you, has to do with Diego's preference for strawberry ice cream. David likes chocolate, but Havana proves a place where the two tastes can meet. It's just too, too sweet.

Also reviewed in:
CHICAGO TRIBUNE, 2/10/95, Friday/p. F, Michael Wilmington
NEW REPUBLIC, 2/6/95, p. 24, Stanley Kauffmann
NEW YORK TIMES, 1/20/95, p. C14, Caryn James
VARIETY, 2/21-27/94, p. 48, David Stratton
WASHINGTON POST, 2/10/95, p. B7, Rita Kempley
WASHINGTON POST, 2/10/95, Weekend/p. 37, Desson Howe

STREET FIGHTER

A Universal Pictures release of an Edward R. Pressman and Capcom Co. Ltd. production based on the Capcom video game "Street Fighter II." *Executive Producer:* Tim Zinnemann, Jun Aida, and Sasha Harari. *Producer:* Edward R. Pressman and Kenson Tsujimoto. *Director:* Steven E. de Souza. *Screenplay:* Steven E. de Souza. *Director of Photography:* William A. Fraker. *Editor:* Dov Hoenig. *Music:* Graeme Revell. *Music Editor:* Josh Winget. *Sound:* Gary Wilkins and (music) Dan Wallin. *Sound Editor:* Richard L. Anderson and John Dunn. *Casting:* Mary Jo Slater and Steven Brooksbank. *Production Designer:* William Creber. *Art Director:* Ian Gracie. *Set Designer:* Michael Chorney. *Set Decorator:* Lesley Crawford. *Set Dresser:* Nic Brunner, Michael Iacono, and Jo-Ann Beikoff. *Special Effects:* Jenny O'Connell. *Costumes:* Deborah La Gorce Kramer. *"Bison" Costume*: Marilyn Vance. *Make-up:* Zoltan. *Stunt Coordinator:* Charles Picerni. *Running time:* 101 minutes. *MPAA Rating:* PG-13.

CAST: Jean-Claude Van Damme (Colonel Guile); Raul Julia (Bison); Ming-Na Wen (Chun-Li); Damian Chapa (Ken); Kylie Minogue (Cammy); Simon Callow (A.N. Official); Roshan Seth (Dhalsim); Wes Studi (Sagat); Byron Mann (Ryu); Grand L. Bush (Balrog); Peter Tuiasosopo (Honda); Jay Tavare (Vega); Andrew Bryniarski (Zangief); Gregg Rainwater (T. Hawk); Miguel A. Nunez, Jr. (Dee Jay); Robert Mammone (Carlos Blanka); Kenya Sawada (Captain Sawada); Gerry Day (Lab Guard); Sander Vanocur (GNT News Anchor); Adrian Cronauer (A.N. Forces D.J.); David Green (MP Guard); Kenzo Tsujimoto (A.N. Commander); Ed Pressman (Lonely Cook); Ray Swenson (Bison's Architect); Joe Bugner (Bison's Torturor); Brian Moll, Maria Dickson, and Norman Steiner (Bison's Scientists); Andrew Cottgrove (Bison Trooper); Seng Kawee (Waiter); Kamilyn Kaneko, David de Souza, and Scott Rosen (A.N. Soldiers); Christine M. Walton (Bison Computer Voice); Darcy LaPier and Jeri Barchilon (Guile's and Blanka's Dates).

LOS ANGELES TIMES, 12/24/94, Calendar/p. 1, David Kronke

Movies inspired by video games are a tacit admission that the filmmakers couldn't come up with any idea better than replicating two-dimensional characters that exist only as fuzzy images battering one another senseless in mall arcades.

Talk of whether the movie "Street Fighter" is "faithful" to its video-game inspiration is pointless—video games cost a quarter and last a few minutes: seeing the film costs much more and goes on interminably.

Jean-Claude Van Damme stars as Col. Guile, who leads an insurrection against the "power-mad dictator" Gen. Bison (Raul Julia) in a piece of real estate called Shadaloo.

A rainbow coalition of ethnicities and accents battle on both fronts, the film's one and only progressive aspect. After 95 minutes of random explosions, jaw-dropping plot holes, wooden acting and special effects that would have made Ed Wood Jr. proud, the good guys claim victory, pick up their toys and go home.

Screenwriter Steven de Souza, who has written such hits as "48 HRS." and the "Die Hard" films, writes and makes his directorial debut here; clearly, his action sensibility (diluted for younger audiences) has hit autopilot. If the story isn't quite incoherent, then de Souza's klutzy direction renders it so.

This is a movie where a character must pause in the middle of the action to remind the audience, "Those guys are good guys, like us."

"Street Fighter" features some of the worst editing to grace a studio film in a while—nearly every stunt is interrupted mid-cut in an effort to conceal the fact that a piece of action really didn't take place, there are major continuity errors and a number of scenes that are glaringly missing. Apparently, de Souza failed to cover himself on many shots, so this Cuisinart-style editing was as good as any.

A few examples of the narrative and technical ineptitude at work here: Everyone falls for it when Guile fakes, badly, his own death; after the opening sequence, all journalists covering the Shadaloovian conflagration disappear save one; a speedboat is hidden by a "cloaking device," but the wake it cuts in the water remains completely visible; one character, who has had hair throughout the movie, shows up bald in his last scene.

Performances scarcely seem a consideration: de Souza didn't even bother to get takes where his actors deliver lines without awkward pauses. Van Damme remains a glorified stunt man: agile as all get-out, but no thespian.

Julia, appearing in the last theatrical release before his death, does little more than shout histrionically and try to pop his eyes from their sockets—a depressing way to remember him.

De Souza's wit, which gave his earlier action scripts a tart edge, has failed him here. He pitches this entire movie at the sub-literate set that, with glassy eyes, unthinkingly pumps quarter after quarter into video games.

The film's best gag is a visual one, so twisted and arcane it clearly must have eluded the Studio Taste Police: Bison has a painting of himself rendered in the same style that mass murderer John Wayne Gacy used for his creepy clown self-portraits.

NEW YORK POST, 12/23/94, p. 48, Larry Worth

Director Steven E. de Souza concludes his first film, "Street Fighter," with a dedication to its late co-star, the great Raul Julia. But if he really treasured Julia's memory, he'd have burned the master print.

It's downright painful to watch the cadaverous Julia's actions as arch villain General Bison, with his eyeballs practically popping out over sunken cheeks and chin.

Equally shocking: Julia's the best thing about this horrifyingly inept cash-in on Capcom's popular video game. The spin Julia puts on his putrid dialogue proves him a master craftsman to the end.

That's what separates him from Jean-Claude Van Damme as the titular hero, officially dubbed Colonel Guile (rhymes with bile).

Recently, Van Damme's been bumming a ride on Schwarzenegger's band wagon as a straight-faced purveyor of snappy dialogue and crackling punches. Sometimes it works, as in this year's "Time Cop," and sometimes not. Count this as a major-league not.

Guile is supposed to be saving the Southeast Asian port of Shadaloo and ultimately the world from power-mad (is there any other kind?) dictator Bison. At stake are relief workers being ransomed for $20 billion to finance an army of super-warriors.

One hint that something's amiss: Audiences will find themselves rooting for the super-warriors. And why not? Van Damme produces zero charisma and barely showcases his trademark kicks. He may have dyed his hair red but his face should be even redder.

Ditto for director/writer de Souza. He's produced an action film that unreels in slow motion, wasted his Thailand locales and shown himself to be devoid of comic flair.

De Souza doesn't even know enough to keep his stars front and center. Instead, they compete with subplots about an incredible hulk, Australian pop singer Kylie Minogue's catfights with "Joy Luck Club" alumna Ming-Na Wen, and a sumo wrestler's quest to let his mind be one place while his body is somewhere else. Viewers are guaranteed to be trying that concept out for themselves.

It seems video amusements just weren't meant to be turned into movies as clearly demonstrated a year ago with "Mario Bros." Hopefully, "Street Fighter" will bring new meaning to "game over."

NEWSDAY, 12/26/94, Part II/p. B2, Gene Seymour

There's probably no point in assessing "Street Fighter" as a movie because it's really a toy. More to the point, it's the cinematic equivalent of one of those big, shiny, unwieldy contraptions your parents used to spend hours putting together only to shatter within seconds of your first touch.

If you don't mind disposables, then dig in. A lot of people—little ones, especially—are satisfied with simply letting their brains gobble up the clattering din and flashy effects of a movie like this. And there's just enough amiable, low-brow humor strewn through the mix to keep it from total flimsiness.

Still, it's hard to get too involved in the fate of characters that, after all, were inspired by a video game. The main antagonists are Jean-Claude Van Damme, as good-guy-super-soldier William Guile, and the late Raul Julia, as bad-guy-crazed-warlord Bison.

If you know the game (and I don't), then you may already know how this works: Power-mad Bison is holding several hostages for ransom in his mountain stronghold. He wants the money to continue his ruthless drive to take over the world with genetically-engineered super soldiers. Guile, leading a multi-national strike force, is the only dude with the smarts, the moves and the muscle to stop him.

Bison has other antagonists to worry about, including an intrepid TV reporter (Ming-Na Wen), a one-eyed, short-fused arms dealer (Wes Studi) and a pair of supercool hustlers (Damian Chapa, Byron Mann), whom Guile presses into service as undercover moles boring into Bison's compound. All of them know how to kick, poke and punch with as much lethal power as Guile himself.

This plot has so little connection with anything resembling reality that the actors seem content to let their inner cartoon characters do the talking. Van Damme looks so relaxed and in command of the situation you'll wait in vain for a tense facial tic. Chapa and Mann's chemistry is so good, you wonder when they'll get their own Saturday afternoon action series.

Others are wasted, notably the fine Roshan Seth as a scientist forced to create Bison's monster war machines. In fact, this whole subplot seem's to have been squeezed into insignificance by writer-director Steven de Souza, who, as the writer of "Die Hard" (yaay!) and "Beverly Hills Cop III" (booo!), knows how to keep a junk-food plot moving along so quickly that no one has time to think about what they're watching.

And Julia? Sigh. What can you say? The man puts everything he has into playing the pop-eyed, sputtering Bison. He's as adroit at adding shadows and soul to this vapid caricature as he was at playing Macheath in "Threepenny Opera." Still, you can't help feeling that an actor as gifted and important as Julia deserved a better epitaph than playing a third-rate dictator.

SIGHT AND SOUND, 5/95, p. 54, Leslie Felperin

The Allied Nations (AN) peacekeeping team, led by Colonel Guile comes to Shadaloo to rescue 50-odd relief workers who have been kidnapped by a power mad dictator, General Bison. He threatens to kill them if the AN fails to pay him a ransom within three days. He is also forcing Dr Dhalsim to turn Guile's friend Carlos into a brainwashed, genetically mutated killing machine. Ace reporter Chun-Li and her crew are covering events for television. Two gun-runners, Ryu and

Ken, are about to be killed by Sagat, an underworld crime boss, when Guile invades Sagat's fighting arena and arrests everyone. He forces Ryu and Ken to act as spies for him, and arranges for them to feign killing him during an escape. Chun-Li discovers the hoax, but escapes arrest and steals a device to help her track the escapees bound for Bison's headquarters.

At the headquarters, Dr Dhalsim partially reprogrammes Carlos with wholesome images to counteract the effects of the previous aggression-inducing programming. Chun-Li and her crew sneak into the hideout, but they are captured. When Bison tries to seduce her with a power-share in his projected New World Order, she attempts to kill him, revealing that she is seeking revenge for Bison's murder of her father. Meanwhile, the AN decides to submit to Bison's demands, but Guile and his loyal forces refuse to call off their planned invasion. Guile and his two lieutenants, Cammy and Hawk, infiltrate the hideout. Ryu and Ken fight Sagat and his henchmen. Chun-Li, Cammy and Hawk fight assorted members of Bison's army. Carlos, having escaped, fights with everyone. Guile manages to electrocute Bison, but Bison's special outfit regenerates him, so they fight again. Guile eventually kills him. Guile and his friends free the hostages and escape before the hideout blows up.

After the fiasco that was *Super Mario Brothers*, the film industry has been hesitant about translating computer games into film. *Street Fighter* (based on the game *Street Fighter II*) turns out to be much more user-friendly than might have been expected. This is not so surprising, given that the line-'em-up, rip-their-spines-out format of fight games is already premised on the filmic, having borrowed most of its imagery from Kung Fu movies. Such platform games classics as *Super Mario Brothers* and *Sonic the Hedgehog*, with their fluffy animals and basically toothless villains, have too wide a whimsical streak to succeed.

Yet *Street Fighter* has great in-built playability, and the cast and film-makers play it for all its worth, keeping the tone right on the cusp between straight-faced shoot-'em-up and self-parodying kitsch. The dialectic is best personified by its two leads. Jean-Claude Van Damme juts his jaw manfully and looks lovely in uniform—street fighting and sleepwalking are interchangeable for him. The late Raul Julia, on the other hand, is magisterially hysterical. Lit from below to accentuate his cheekbones, eyes wide with maniacal glee, he camps his socks off. His absence from the inevitable sequel is to be mourned.

Having little to do apart from fight and prepare to fight, the rest of the cast acquit themselves adequately. Kylie Minogue as Cammy perhaps deserves a footnote for her hilarious miscasting as a military wench with Heidi plaits. The merest glimpse of her holding a bazooka and looking mean is enough to induce giggles in the most dour of viewers. Simon Callow and Roshan Seth take the money and run as an AN bureaucrat and Dr Dhalsim respectively. Blink, and you could easily miss them, as no single shot in the entire film lasts more than a minute. Veteran screenwriter on such action flicks as *48 Hrs.*, the *Die Hard* films, and the forth-coming *Judge Dredd*, Steven E. de Souza makes his debut here as director. He maintains the action at maximum speed, like a virtuoso 11-year-old who has mastered all the cheats on the original game. The gore rating in the film, adjustable in the game, is kept low in the interests of the target audience of pre-pubescents. They, and many more, are likely to find *Street Fighter* mind-numbingly addictive.

Also reviewed in:
CHICAGO TRIBUNE, 12/25/94, Tempo/p. 4, John Petrakis
NEW YORK TIMES, 12/24/94, p. 11, Stephen Holden
VARIETY, 1/2-8/95, p. 72, Emanuel Levy
WASHINGTON POST, 12/23/94, Weekend/p. 38, Desson Howe
WASHINGTON POST, 12/24/94, p. B3, Richard Harrington

SUGAR HILL

A Twentieth Century Fox Film release of a Beacon presentation of a South Street Entertainment Group production. *Executive Producer:* Armyan Bernstein, Tom Rosenberg, and Marc Abraham. *Producer:* Rudy Langlais and Gregory Brown. *Director:* Leon Ichaso. *Screenplay:* Barry Michael Cooper. *Director of Photography:* Bojan Bazelli. *Editor:* Gary Karr. *Music:* Terence

Blanchard. *Music Editor:* Michael Linn, Marty Wereski and Alex Steyermark. *Choreographer:* Ertha Robinson. *Sound:* Malcolm Morris. *Sound Editor:* Steve Williams. *Casting:* Mary Gail Artz and Barbara Cohen. *Production Designer:* Michael Helmy. *Art Director:* J. Jergensen. *Set Decorator:* Kathryn Peters. *Special Effects*: John Alexander, Dick Albain, Ed Albain, Duncan Puett, and Jerry Winchell. *Costumes:* Eduardo Castro. *Make-up:* Laini Thompson. *Stunt Coordinator:* Tony Brubaker, Jeff Haberstad, and Mike Russo. *Running time:* 125 minutes. *MPAA Rating:* R.

CAST: Wesley Snipes (Roemello Skuggs); Khandi Alexander (Ella Skuggs); Devaughn Nixon (Raynathan, age 11); Marquise Wilson (Roemello, age 10); O.L Duke (Tutty); Clarence Williams III (A.R. Skuggs); Abe Vigoda (Gus Molino); Anthony Thomas (Worker); Michael Wright (Raynathan Skuggs); John Pittman (Lucky); Steve J. Harris (Ricky Goggles); Michael Guess (Y.G. "Young Gun"); Kimberly Russel (Chantal); Theresa Randle (Melissa); Abdul Mutakabbir, Yusaf Ramadan and Karl Johnson (Bouncers); Andre Lamal (Martin David); Dulé Hill (Roemello Skuggs, age 17); Sam Gordon (Raynathan Skuggs, age 18); Larry Joshua (Harry Molino); Raymond Serra (Sal Marconi); Frank Ferrara (Sal's Bodyguard); Donald Adeosun Faison (Kymie Daniels); Bryan Clark (Dean); Lord Michael Banks (Nigerian); Alex Brown (Nigerian #2); Joe Dallesandro (Tony Adamo); Ernie Hudson (Lolly Jonas); Nicki Corello (Cuco); Leslie Uggams (Doris Holly); Natalie Belcon (Lynette); Brendan Jefferson (Kid); Denetria Champ (Diva); Phyromn Taylor (Preacher); Sam Bottoms (Oliver Thompson); Maria Kelley (Cuco's Girlfriend); Vondie Curtis-Hall (Mark Doby).

LOS ANGELES TIMES, 2/25/94, Calendar/p. 1, Kenneth Turan

Though Roemello Skuggs (Wesley Snipes) "serves up more heroin in Harlem than McDonald's does hamburgers," don't think he's a typical urban drug dealer.

Smart enough to have been offered a full academic scholarship to Georgetown (he didn't go, but that's another story), Roemello is an introspective kind of guy who reads the New York Times, plays a fine game of chess and has an eye for art and design. A drug lord who wants out and the hero of "Sugar Hill", he is presented as the exemplar of a lost generation, an individual who could have made something of his life if he hadn't been trapped by the familiar socio-economic dynamics of the drug trade.

Yet watching "Sugar Hill" does not particularly arouse concern for Roemello, whose weary desire to quit his infernal business parallels the action in "Carlito's Way" and innumerable other genre vehicles. Rather it is the gifted personnel who made this film who seem more trapped than anyone they portray on screen.

For until it sinks under the weight of excessive violence and a welter of overwrought plot contrivances, "Sugar Hill," named for a once-vibrant Harlem neighborhood, has much going for it. Writer Barry Michael Cooper ("New Jack City") and Cuban-born director Leon Ichaso ("Crossover Dreams") know how to make this kind of material watchable and they've also managed to sprinkle thoughtful moments amid the general bloodshed.

These scenes showcase the acting styles of a cast that is deep in ability. Snipes' authoritative performance is no surprise; his status as a preeminent screen actor grows with every picture. But at various moments "Sugar Hill" also gets fine work from Michael Wright as Raynathan, the hot-headed brother; from Theresa Randle as Melissa, the straight girlfriend; from Clarence Williams III, ex of "The Mod Squad," as the addicted father, and a number of other performers.

But if African American actors can claim a talent pool that is as impressive in its own way as Britain's, why do they invariably have to perform in a repetitive cycle of exploitative dramas about drugs in the cities and crime in the streets? It's as pointless and exasperating as if Daniel Day-Lewis, Anthony Hopkins, Emma Thompson and all the lesser Brits had to make film after film about Robin Hood and his Merry Men in order to get any time on screen.

And whenever the "Sugar Hill" filmmakers do manage to shoehorn in a sensitive, affecting scene, like Roemello feeding noodles to his ailing father, it is doubly frustrating to find it in a film whose off-putting violence will place it out of bounds to many serious filmgoers. What a waste.

With its jazzy score and discreetly muted color cinematography (by Bojan Bazelli, who did fine work on Abel Ferrara's "Body Snatchers"), "Sugar Hill" certainly makes an attempt to be taken seriously. But the careful line it walks between the epic-heroic and the pretentious blurs as its story unfolds, and finally its flimsy narrative can't support the serious notions everyone wants to hang on it.

It is typical of "Sugar Hill's" style that it opens with Roemello enmeshed in one of his bouts of high-flown introspection while simultaneously reliving, in wrenching flashback, the scene of his mother dying of an overdose. "Dear mother, it seems like an eternity since you've been gone, so much has happened, so many dreams have turned into nightmares," he muses in voice-over. "The boy you love has become the man you feared."

In plainer English, that means that Roemello and his brother now traffic in the substances that ruined both his parents' lives, even working with Gus (Abe Vigoda), the very mob figure who destroyed his family. No wonder he's having second thoughts about his career choice.

More than psychological factors, however, cause Roemello to wonder if he's doing the right thing. The mob is bringing in Lolly ("The Hand That Rocked the Cradle's" Ernie Hudson), a dealer from Brooklyn who specializes in crack cocaine, to share the neighborhood trade, and Roemello has met Melissa, an aspiring actress who might be the best reason of all to pack up and get away.

This story line is terribly familiar, but that doesn't mean it can't be energized, and for a while director Ichaso and company do an effective job of alternating flash with the film's more deliberate moments.

But finally Roemello talks once too often of being "consumed by chaos, guilt, grief," and the intensity of the violence becomes such that anyone intrigued by the film's softer moments will tune out. Wading through blood is too much of a price to pay for "Sugar Hill's" pluses, and it's a shame the movie business has made it difficult for them to be experienced any other way.

NEW YORK POST, 2/25/94, p. 43, Michael Medved

"Sugar Hill" is a profound tragedy, but not at all in the way the filmmakers intended.

What inspires pity and fear about this project is the fact that a cast full of magnificent actors and a prodigiously gifted director came together to waste their efforts on an empty, cliche-ridden screenplay that is in every way unworthy of their talents.

This sorry script is the work of Barry Michael Cooper, respected journalist with the Village Voice and Spin magazine, and one of three credited screenwriters on the surprise hit "New Jack City."

Once again, Wesley Snipes plays a charismatic drug lord who rules the streets of Harlem, but in contrast to the flamboyant, hyper-kinetic Nino Brown of "New Jack City," Roemello Skuggs is brooding, introspective, and plagued with doubts over the source of his fabulous wealth—and of all those absolutely stunning Gianni Versace suits.

As his character intones in some of the self-pitying and pretentiously poetic narration that periodically afflicts the sound track, "I am consumed by chaos, consumed by guilt, consumed by grief."

The grief concerns his mother, who dies of a drug overdose in front of her two boys in a shocking flashback near the beginning of the movie. But much of the chaos revolves around his dangerous, psychotic but endearing older brother and partner-in-crime, played by the always excellent Michael Wright ("The Five Heartbeats").

Wright will do anything to stop his brother from getting out of the drug trade and leaving their uptown empire in his unsteady hands. Meanwhile, they face potentially deadly challenges from a ruthless former boxing star (Ernie Hudson) and his mob-connected ally (Abe Vigoda), who pretends to be nothing more thana a humble Harlem grocer.

When Snipes falls in love with a sweet, hauntingly lovely middle-class woman (Theresa Randle) who disapproves of his criminal enterprises, he faces a major crossroads in his life.

Cuban-born director Leon Ichaso ("Crossover Dreams," El Super") draws heartfelt performances from every single member of his diverse cast. He also infuses scene after scene with unexpected visual splendor.

His preference for hazy Rembrandt lighting and his painterly composition of so many shots work especially well with the elegant, elegiac jazz score by trumpeter Terence Blanchard.

Unfortunately, all this artistry adds up to an artificial and static quality: the interiors, including a corner grocery store and a run-down apartment, are much too striking and over designed. More seriously, Ichaso inserts pregnant pauses between almost all lines of dialogue, killing forward momentum and making the characters sound as if they're declaiming rather than speaking to one another.

There are also sever gratuitously grotesque scenes—including that savage beating and degradation of an innocent woman and the outrageously extended torture killing of a rival gangster.

Despite these shocking elements, "Sugar Hill" (named for the Harlem neighborhood the two protagonists admired as boys) amounts to a shameless glamorization of big-time drug dealers.

Unlike "New Jack City, this picture never confronts the unspeakably ugly impact of the highly profitable trade they ply. Instead, it concentrates on Snipes' terrific clothes and sensitive face, as he repeatedly insists, "I'm gonna go away" or "I'm done. I'm finished."

The problem is that the audience is also quickly done and finished with this nonsense, and begins wishing that Snipes would indeed go away before he actually gets around to it.

NEWSDAY, 2/25/94, Part II/p. 62, Jack Mathews

Cuban-born director Leon Ichaso and former Village Voice writer Barry Michael Cooper pose a formidable tag team when it comes to exploiting the drug underworld and its accompanying violence in the inner city.

Cooper, whose debut screenplay was for the hit "New Jack City," does his work first, using contemporary characters, issues, settings and language in a story written in the melodramatic style of a '30s Warner Bros. gangster movie; then Ichaso ("Crossover Dreams"), who has made some very striking films on low budgets, puts a gloss on it so smooth you can see your own reflection.

The result of their collaboration, "Sugar Hill," is almost hateable for its numbing brutality and cynical slickness. It lures you in with its tragic tale of two generations of a Harlem family torn apart by drugs, promises some "Godfather"-like ruminations on honor among thieves, then gets down to its real business—graphic, crowd-pleasing, gang-war mayhem.

You can hear the squeals of delight (I've already heard them, at the preview) when two members of the good drug gang beat a member of the bad drug gang senseless, shoot him in the legs, then urinate in his face. What a hoot!

And the crowds will turn out. Wesley Snipes, a terrific actor in danger of becoming a black Charles Bronson, is a bona-fide movie star, and his Roemello Skuggs is as coolly tough a character as any he's played.

Roemello is a drug lord with style and a conscience. He doesn't use the stuff himself, having watched his mother die from an overdose and his drug-dealing dad maimed by the mob for pumping some of the supplies up his own arm. And after meeting Melissa (Theresa Randle), the sort of wholesome beauty George Bailey found in "It's a Wonderful Life," he's ready to turn the whole business over to his flakey brother Raynathan (Michael Wright) and head for his own Bedford Falls somewhere in the South.

But first, he has to deal with Lolly (Ernie Hudson), a crack dealer moving in on the Skuggs brothers' Harlem market, and since the only lawman in the entire war zone is on the other side's payroll, it's going to be rough.

The most maddening thing about "Sugar Hill" is not so much its exploitation of violence as its attempts to fob itself off as *anti*-violence, as some sort of earnest cautionary tale about where it all leads. With no good guys to point out these sociological truths, we're stuck listening to regional Mafia boss Gus Molino (Abe Vigoda) whine about the glory of Harlem before the mob and drugs took over, and Roemello, who owes his wealth to the customers he's destroying, lecture neighborhood children on the stupidity of admiring gangsters.

Hello?

An enormous amount of talent went into this ugly enterprise. Ichaso is a stylish director, and the early minutes of the film, when we meet the grown Skuggs brothers and visit their tragic childhood in black-and-white flashbacks, promises a much better movie than we get, And before the story and its characters disintegrate in an explosion of gangland clichés, Snipes and Clarence Williams III, as Roemello's junkie father, play some honestly emotional scenes together.

I would have admired "Sugar Hill" a lot more if it had made no attempt at all to legitimize itself, or its characters. The movie, with not one but two bad endings, ends up being as wrong-headed as Roemello himself, peddling violence to those addicted to it while lecturing them on how awful the stuff is.

SIGHT AND SOUND, 10/94, p. 52, Nick Hasted

Sugar Hill, Harlem. Lying in bed, Roemello Skuggs remembers his childhood ... His mother, a heroin addict, asks his older brother Raynathan to help her jack up. As they both watch, she spasms and dies ... Now both brothers, grown up, are major drug dealers in their old neighbourhood, working for an ageing Italian gangster, Gus. At a club, Roemello meets a girl, Melissa, whom he wants to see again. Driving, he thinks back once more ... He watches as his father, a drug dealer for the Mob, is shot, but not killed. Later he shoots the gunman. Then he goes to meet Gus, the gunman's relative, who ordered his father shot ... Walking with Raynathan, Roemello meets a young boy from the suburbs, who shows off his gun; Roemello warns him off the streets. At a drug sales meeting with Gus, the brothers are told a new dealer, Lolly, needs a piece of their market. Afterwards, Roemello tells his brother he wants to quit the business. He tells his father, A.R., now an addict who he looks after, that he's quitting; A.R. tells him to take care of Lolly first. Later, Lolly burns his best friend Ricky to death. Melissa sees Ricky's body in the street just after Roemello, and runs away.

Roemello meets Gus, who tells him not to get worked up. Visiting Lolly, Roemello arranges a truce, then regains Melissa's trust. He makes Raynathan have dinner with their father for the first time in years, but Raynathan tells his father he should die. Then Raynathan kidnaps, shoots and tortures an Italian ally of Lolly's; coming across them. Roemello finishes the man off. Raynathan admits he has started a gang war because he is scared of his brother leaving. As they walk, an attempted drive-by is interrupted by the suburban kid, who is shot dead.

Melissa hears about it, and tells Raynathan she can no longer see him.

Roemello asks Raynathan to quit the streets, but Raynathan says it is too late. Meanwhile, Melissa is almost raped by a date. Roemello asks A.R. to quit Harlem, but he won't. Melissa and Roemello decide to leave for North Carolina that night. Roemello tells Gus, then his brother. Raynathan goes to their father and kills him with an overdose. Then he meets Gus, Gus's son and Lolly, and shoots them. Roemello and Melissa see A.R.'s body, then meet Raynathan in the street. Seeing Roemello is really leaving, Raynathan goes for his gun. In a struggle, Roemello is shot, then Raynathan shoots himself. Later, Roemello is seen in North Carolina in a wheelchair, happy, with Melissa and their son.

It is appropriate that the only sustained calm in this slice of ghetto life is the credits sequence, trad jazz playing over sepia photos of Harlem's 20s heyday. It is clearly where director Ichaso would be happiest. His film is a mess of styles because his idea of Harlem is a mess. Beginning in the 60s, shot in an unnatural MTV-style black-and-white, *Sugar Hill* switches to a present-day panorama, with a sun-streaked New York overlooked by the stylish 90s silhouette of gangster Roemello (Wesley Snipes). Around this, the camera hovers and twitches. But despite the presence of Bojan Bazelli, cinematographer of *King of New York* and *Deep Cover*, the two films which defined the cinematic ghetto of the 90s, Ichaso can't settle.

It's a fault compounded by the film's uneven tone. Making a first scene the screaming entreaty of a mother to her son to jack her up is arresting, but the scene is performed and scored so melodramatically that true sympathy is not reached. The bloody struggle between brothers near the end similarly seems strained. Even the music seems compromised. While Ichaso and his characters wallow in jazz, the hip-hop reluctantly allowed in beside it is treated with distrust. At every level, this is a film falling short of conviction.

It's as if Ichaso would prefer modern Harlem not to exist. Unlike John Singleton, whose *Boyz N the Hood* entered ghetto life with sadness, then—like its character Furious—resolutely stayed there, Ichaso wants to get out. His viewpoint is that of Melissa's mother and of Martin Luther King, who stare down together at Melissa as she disowns Roemello. Like the jazz CDs hoarded by A.R., they suggest a 60s generation's dismay at a situation which has somehow escaped it.

This sense of alienation—the exact opposite of what is intended—is confirmed by A.R. himself. A jazz musician sunk to dealer and addict, still fumbling at a piano at Roemello's insistence, he is a dribbling relic of something good. When he intones "I am Harlem!", shortly before a patricidal overdose, the washing of hands is deafening.

If *Sugar Hill* has a healing figure, it should be Roemello, who tells us that he knows what he is—one of Harlem's devastators. And yet, as he warns kids off the streets and spoon-feeds his father, we see only decency. Incapable of portraying the tortured complexity of a bad man turning good, Barry Michael Cooper's script simply elides the bad. So, despite a performance by Snipes of pressurised grace, Roemello is left as a saint—a man so disconnected from the ghetto pain he in fact helped cause that his salvation is just a plane ride away.

Amidst such sappiness, Ichaso shows evidence of talent. *Sugar Hill* shares the trend—which began with *Boyz*—away from generic thrillers towards more encompassing tales of crime; and moments like Raynathan's repulsion at his father's table ring quietly true. By contrast, the giggling excitement of the hardcore thrillers which the film nods at too briefly is seized on with relief, momentarily freeing Ichaso from his story's weight. A drive-by interrupted by a furiously pedalling kid on a bike, pistol raised like a cowboy, even welds thrills and tragedy with broad strokes otherwise absent. But finally the film lacks the stomach to see things through. "No son, this will not happen again," Roemello soothes from his Carolina bolthole. Of course it will. *Sugar Hill* doesn't solve the crime, it just leaves the scene.

VILLAGE VOICE, 3/8/94, p. 60, Selwyn Seyfu Hinds

At the nexus of art, commercialism, and everyday life where black culture defines itself, an identity war is being waged—a war in which complexity has lost much ground to the forces of reductionism and nifty catchall terms. What are you? *Gangsta. Hardrock. Boho. Beaaach! A real mu'fucking g*, maybe? If you have yet to categorize yourself, don't fret, those of us who construct the critical rhetoric of black art will certainly do it for you.

Sugar Hill is one of those narrative crossroads. It's ostensibly about a Harlem drug kingpin struggling to break out of the vicious cycle of drugs, dough, and death. But much as you may be tempted to point and scream, "Look! It's Carlito meets Nino meets the Godfather meets Superfly!" chances are you probably won't. *Sugar Hill* is less about a gangster getting out the game than it is an examination of the tortured relationship between Roemello Skuggs (Wesley Snipes), his brother Raynathan (Michael Wright), and their broken, drug-addicted father (Clarence Williams III). The film also stars Theresa Randle as Melissa, Roemello's supposedly inspirational (but actually stereotypical) love interest.

Now, I do love Wesley Snipes. But I've had just about enough of the cartoonish roles he's been playing of late. It's a relief to see him as Roemello, a character with an emotional breadth that renders him more genuine, more accessible, and ultimately more frightening than platinum hair and a million Uzis ever could. Black figures in pop culture don't get much of a chance to be vulnerable. When they do, such moments have no more resonance than Nino's crocodile tears in *New Jack City*. It's not that surprising that, in *Sugar Hill*, Roemello cries; the curious thing is, he's believable. And Michael Wright is excellent as Roemello's older brother, Raynathan. Wright projects an instability of self that emphatically says *I will soon blow the fuck up*. You wonder who else he will take with him.

The pairing of the unsettling Raynathan with the disturbingly cool Roemello is only one of the film's complex juxtapositions. This urban crime tale is rife with bohemian markers. Between the brilliant colors, panoramic city sunsets, the freaking Terence Blanchard Orchestra, and *extremely* dope clothing (that I, for one, have never seen Uptown drug dealers wearing), *Sugar Hill* pummels the viewer into granting it sophistication. Couple the film's overwhelmingly classy sensibilities with its heavy emotional content, and it becomes a bit much. Yet perhaps it's this very characteristic that makes the film work. *Sugar Hill*'s drug dealers may not sport Timberlands and wool hats, or shoot people to the tune of Cypress Hill. But the sight of a young Roemello, resplendent in prep school uniform, having just won a scholarship to Georgetown, emptying a .38 into a man, represents the kind of uneasy meshing of images and narratives that makes *Sugar Hill* successful.

Also reviewed in:
CHICAGO TRIBUNE, 2/25/94, Friday/p. A, Clifford Terry
NEW YORK TIMES, 2/25/94, p. C10, Janet Maslin
VARIETY, 9/13/93, p. 33, Todd McCarthy
WASHINGTON POST, 2/25/94, p. D6, Richard Harrington
WASHINGTON POST, 2/25/94, Weekend/p. 38, Joe Brown

SUNDAY'S CHILDREN

A Sandrew Film and Theater AB production in cooperation with Svenska Filminstitutet, Sweetland Films, Sveriges Television Kanal 1, Metrononome Prods, Finlands Filmstiftelse, Islands Film Fond & Norsk Film with support of Nordic Film & TV Fund & Eurimages/Europarådet. *Executive Producer:* Klas Olofsson. *Producer:* Katinka Faragó. *Director:* Daniel Bergman. *Screenplay (Swedish with English subtitles):* Ingmar Bergman. *Director of Photography:* Tony Forsberg. *Editor:* Darek Hodor. *Music:* Rune Gustafsson. *Sound:* Klas Engström and Patrik Grede. *Production Designer:* Sven Wichmann. *Costumes:* Mona Theresia Forsén. *Running time:* 118 minutes. *MPAA Rating:* Not Rated.

WITH: Thommy Berggren (Father); Lena Endre (Mother); Henrik Linnros (Pu); Jakob Leygraf (Dag); Malin Ek (Märta); Marie Richardson (Marianne); Irma Christensson (Aunt Emma); Birgitta Valberg (Grandmother); Börje Ahlstedt (Uncle Carl); Maria Bolme (Maj); Majilis Granlund/Birgitta Ulfsson (Lalla); Carl Magnus Dellow (The Watchmaker); Per Myrberg (Ingmar).

CHRISTIAN SCIENCE MONITOR, 4/20/94, p. 15, David Sterritt

Just over 10 years ago, Ingmar Bergman announced that the widely acclaimed "Fanny and Alexander" would mark his last hurrah as a filmmaker. Although some critics had written him off as earnest but ponderous, others were saddened by the departure of an artist who had explored cinematic moods—from high tragedy to low comedy—during his four-decade career.

What nobody foresaw was that Bergman would find a variety of ways to circumvent his own retirement—directing television movies, staging theater productions, and writing screenplays for other filmmakers to direct. His latest enterprise as a screenwriter, "Sunday's Children," completes a trilogy of family-oriented movies that began with "Fanny and Alexander" and continued with "The Best Intentions," written by Bergman and directed by Danish filmmaker Bille August.

Besides dealing with members of Bergman's family in bygone times—it begins a few years after "The Best Intentions" leaves off—the new picture was directed by Daniel Bergman, his youngest son. Although it lacks the urgency and originality of the elder Bergman's greatest achievements, such as "The Silence" and "Persona," it has enough visual and emotional interest to make a worthy addition to his body of work.

Set in rural Sweden during the late 1920s, the story centers on a young boy named Pu, clearly modeled on Ingmar Bergman himself. Pu's father is a country clergyman whose duties include traveling to the capital and ministering to the royal family. While this is an enviable position, it doesn't assuage problems in the pastor's marriage. Pu is young enough to be fairly oblivious to such difficulties, but his awareness grows with the passage of time. So do the subtle tensions that mar Pu's own relationship with his father, whose desire to show affection and compassion is hampered by a certain stiffness in his demeanor and chilliness in his emotions.

The film's most resonant passages take place when Pu learns to see his father with new clarity while accompanying him on a cross-country trip to another parish. In a remarkable change of tone, this portion of the story is punctuated with flash-forwards to a time 40 years in the future, showing the relationship between parent and child to be dramatically reversed: The father is now cared for by the son, and desires a forgiveness for past shortcomings that the younger man resolutely refuses to grant.

Brief and abrupt though they are, these scenes make a pungent contrast with the sunny landscapes and comic interludes in the early part of the movie.

"Sunday's Children" is a film of many levels, and all are skillfully handled by Daniel Bergman in his directorial debut. Gentle scenes of domestic contentment are sensitively interwoven with intimations of underlying malaise. While the more nostalgic sequences are photographed with an eye-dazzling beauty that occasionally threatens to become cloying, any such result is foreclosed by the jagged interruptions of the flash-forward sequences—an intrusive device that few filmmakers are agile enough to handle successfully, but that is put to impressive use by the Bergman team.

Henrik Linnros gives a smartly turned performance as young Pu, and Thommy Berggren—who starred in the popular "Elvira Madigan" years ago—is steadily convincing as his father. Top honors go to the screenplay, though, which carries the crowded canvas of "Fanny and Alexander" and the emotional ambiguity of "The Best Intentions" into fresh and sometimes fascinating territory.

FILMS IN REVIEW, 7-8/94, p. 56, Eva H. Kissin

In the later years of his life, Ingmar Bergman's art has become increasingly personal. A recent film, *Best Intentions*, describes his father's courtship of his mother, Karin, the daughter of a wealthy family. Her people's attempt to separate the inseparables, the poor minister and the affluent young woman, fails, and their marriage seen in a second film, *Sunday's Children*, fulfills their prophecy of doom.

Sunday's Children (those born on Sunday with special vision) is the tale of two days in the life of Pu, Sunday-born, eight-year-old Ingmar. Brilliantly played by Henrik Linnros with both the fragility and distance of childhood, the small boy observes the world and attempts to make sense of it. When we first see him waiting for his father's train, he is already an outsider, an artist-observer, who stands apart from the rest of his waiting family.

The little station of Dufnas, a country town where the family spends its summers, is a marvelous bit of early twentieth century Swedish bourgeois life. It appears so orderly. The stationmaster stamps the tickets with orderly aplomb, and wears his operetta uniform like an officer in a select corps of the Swedish army.

The same orderliness appears later at the family dinner table until it is displaced by father's resentment when Karin announces the imminent arrival of her mother. In this orderly dining room where prayers begin and end every meal, and each child appears to carry out his appointed task cleaning up in an efficient manner, the order is merely superficial. All sorts of emotions are boiling just below the surface.

Later in the evening, when the family must sit together at the dining room table as the only source of light, there is the same trapped orderliness of family life, where people stay together only because they must.

Little Pu, whose mouth is always open with awe as well as with adenoids, has begun to sense this ugly, barely suppressed bubbling. Curious about a local suicide, he is both intrigued and frightened by the Scandinavian world of spirits and haunts behind the suicide. The mysteries of the female body also draw him, but he must pay his big brother for a peep at his pornographic pictures before the two boys go to sleep.

In the middle of the long Swedish night, he awakens to hear his mother argue with his father about leaving with the children to go and live near Grandma. By morning, Pu's bullying older brother has persuaded him to eat a worm to show his bravery.

This is all a good deal for a small boy to swallow along with the worm, and the next day, when his generally kind father slaps him, he is thoroughly confused. It would seem that little Pu had eaten his worm and lost his faith simultaneously, at an early age.

Fifty years later, visiting his dying father, Pu, now Ingmar, recalls their day together with mixed feelings. It is difficult for him to reconcile the humiliating slap and the kindly father who gave the shivering child his coat during a rainstorm on their way home.

His aged father, reading his wife's diary of fifty years, is equally troubled to learn that she considered her life a fiasco, and that they had indeed led disparate lives.

Family memories fuse and separate, comfort and destroy—but in the hands of Ingmar Bergman, who wrote the script, and his son, Daniel, who made the film, memories become art. It may have been a bad marriage, but it produced two generations of artists who ordered their memories into great cinema.

All of the acting—Lena Endre as Karin, Thommy Berggren as the father and Per Myrberg as Ingmar—is compelling in its repressed northern style.

LOS ANGELES TIMES, 8/26/94, Calendar/p. 8, Kenneth Turan

As hard as it is to be a father, being a son can be more difficult still. Well into his 70s, master Swedish filmmaker Ingmar Bergman is still struggling with his personal history, trying to come to terms with the painful, conflicted relationship he had with his father, and exceptional films continue to result.

Though he no longer directs, Bergman has not stopped writing scripts about his family and passing them on to deserving pinch-hitters. He gave the Palme d'Or-winning "Best Intentions" to Bille August, and the director of "Sunday's Children" is Bergman's own son Daniel, which makes its father-son theme more poignant. The younger Bergman's feature debut, it is a remarkable beginning, simple, unhurried, yet deeply emotional.

This is more than a matter having the best of scripts to work with, which Daniel Bergman does. Only in his early 30s, the younger man avoids missteps and displays the kind of ease with intense material that argues for the inheriting of directorial talent.

Where "Best Intentions" dealt with the courtship and early married years of Bergman's mismatched parents, "Sunday's Children" picks the story up in 1926, with 8-year-old Ingmar, nicknamed Pu, occupying an uneasy spot as the middle child of the stern preacher Henrik (Thommy Berggren, the star of "Elvira Madigan") and his more worldly wife, Karin (Lena Endre).

Set during a summer vacation in rural Sweden, "Sunday's Children' establishes its theme immediately with the Bergmans gathering at the train station to welcome the head of the family home after a day spent preaching to the king and queen in Stockholm.

Initially distant, refusing to stand near anyone, young Pu suddenly breaks into a mad run and leaps passionately into his father's arms. It's all there in that brief sequence, the separation and mistrust he feels toward his family and the parallel, almost painful need to be loved without reservation.

The only person who can manage that, however, is the family's unaffected young servant Maj (Maria Bolme). Pu's mother is a distant figure, his older brother Dag (Jakob Leygraf) is a pitiless tease, and his father, though loving in his own way, is also rigid, unyielding and at the mercy of a hateful temper that is terrifying when unleashed.

Making things more difficult for Pu is that, like his father, he is a Sunday's child, gifted by tradition with special sight. Young as he is, he sees what others do not, what he is not meant to, picking up emotional currents to which his elders seem oblivious.

That kind of characterization is only as believable as the actor who plays it, and young Henrik Linnros is marvelous at projecting an air of melancholy unexpected in one so small. With sadness and hurt visible in his eyes, Linnros possesses a naturalness that makes you believe he is being, not acting.

"Sunday's Children" is an episodic, memory-driven film, with the Bergmans presenting a series of vignettes of incidents remembered and influences never forgotten. Many of these, not surprisingly, were troubling to young Pu, including a servant's reciting of a dark tale of violence, sexuality and suicide. Pu then visits the spot where the story's subject hanged himself and, in a vision, asks the corpse, "When will I die?" The answer, "Always," is especially haunting given what we know about who the lad grew up to be.

The most daring aspect of "Sunday's Children" is its periodic flash-forwards to 1968, some 40 years later, when a glum 50-year-old Ingmar pays back these old scores by pitilessly lecturing his lonely and dying father. It is only now, a quarter of a century later, that the elder Bergman is able to take the tentative steps toward forgiveness that this film represents.

For though it can't shake its air of sadness, "Sunday's Children" by no means ends up a dour picture. Director Daniel Bergman has the gift of being able to recapture lost time, especially time as it is viewed through the special lens of childhood, and there are elegiac moments in this film that will stay with you forever. For all its melancholy, this is a world we do no want to leave.

NEW YORK POST, 4/20/94, p. 46, Thelma Adams

Fathers and sons make a fitting theme for "Sunday's Children," which was written by Ingmar Bergman and directed by his son, Daniel.

The movie has a surface stillness upon which the filmmakers skip stones until the cumulative ripples of emotion are overpowering.

The main story passes in a weekend spent in the Swedish countryside circa 1920. Young Pu (Henrik Linnros) must decide if he will accompany his father (Thommy Berggren) to a distant town to preach on Sunday.

With this dilemma, the Bergmans capture the conflicts of an entire family at a critical point where the parents contemplate separation.

Will Pu side with his stern father or not? The golden-haired Pu, the title's Sunday's child, represents Ingmar as a boy in this autobiographical outing.

According to legend, a child born on Sunday will be a seer—what greater gift to a filmmaker?

Ingmar Bergman has the ability to define critical emotional relationships as easily as another writer dashes off a comma.

When the film opens, Pu meets his father's train. Seeing the black-clad preacher, Pu runs full-tilt towards him, leaping into his father's embrace for a two-legged, two-armed hug. The son's love is ecstatic, unself-conscious.

Just when the movie seems to be floating along on the scrim of memory, Bergman father and son rip into the nostalgia and deepen the wounds by leaping to 1968.

A gray-haired character named Ingmar (Per Myrberg) visits his ailing father. The love between them has toughened and eroded. The strict preacher is child-like and needy; the golden-haired youth has become stern and withdrawn. The father seeks forgiveness; the character Ingmar, pulling his father's bony hand from his lapels, refuses.

The deft insertion of these later scenes makes the return to the past all the more poignant. The Sunday that father and son spend together is frozen in time.

The preacher sours the day when he slaps Pu for disobedience; a rainy bike ride where the father shares his coat—and a moment of uncritical love—with his son redeems the outing.

While the movie's last image is of father and son side-by-side on a country road, the sickroom scenes, from 1968 lend a melancholy aftertaste.

"Sunday's Children" is the emotional reckoning of a mature man trying to understand and reconcile his conflicting feelings for his dead father.

The triumph is in the present, where father and son, Ingmar and Daniel work together to create an artful and moving portrait of an eternally sticky relationship.

NEWSDAY, 4/20/94, Part II/p. B9, John Anderson

Like the wild strawberries that appear so mischievously in "Sunday's Children," simple truth is a rare and delicious thing, as elusive on film as it is to the memory. Ingmar Bergman knows this, and in his screenplay for this fantastic and somewhat tragic cine-memoir, he has some sport pointing out that perception and reality are often like apples and oranges. Or strawberries.

Directed by his son, Daniel, this is the third and perhaps darkest in the elder Bergman's family chronicle: "Fanny and Alexander" (1983), which he wrote and directed, concerned his maternal grandparents; "The Best Intentions" (1992), directed by Bille August, was about his parents' courtship and early marriage. In "Sunday's Children," he grapples with himself, as a child and an older man, and with his father, Henrik (Thommy Berggren), who is either a loving man or a martinet, depending on which Ingmar is on screen. What's missing, and profoundly sad, is how they got from there to here.

The 8-year-old Ingmar, called Pu (Henrik Linnros) worships his father, a Lutheran minister who is returning from having preached for the King and Queen of Sweden. It's the early '20s, and the family, which is spending the summer in the countryside, has come to meet his train. Pu however, has walked alone, because their relationship is special; that there is water under the bridge he crosses is just the first hint of the recriminations to follow.

Pu also loves his mother, Karin (Lena Endre), and his nanny, Maj (Maria Bolme), and the rest of their large extended family. They are a source of joy for him, just as his brother, Dag (Jacob

Leygraf) is a source of humiliation. But generally, Pu's world is a burnished world full of wonder, steam trains and fairy tales.

He's a hot-tempered lad and a "Sunday's child," whose birthday is supposed to signify an affinity for the supernatural. Pu is also a kid who finds himself in the wrong place at the wrong time: watching Maj necking with the blacksmith, or watching his mother tell his father she's taking the children and leaving.

This sets Pu's world off-kilter, although it's not a total surprise to us. As "The Best Intentions" showed, there exists a history of loathing between Henrik and his mother-in-law (Birgitta Valberg). She believes Karin has married below her station. Henrik resents her intrusions, her money, his wife's discontent and his own poverty. The film-making Bergmans exercise a gentle hand in peeling away their characters' civil facade, lacing an ordinary dinner conversation with bile, and generally imbuing Pu's golden world with enough shadows to eventually crowd out the light.

And it's a dark scene we get when the film shifts seamlessly to 1968, where the aging Ingmar (Per Myrberg) is visiting his now-enfeebled father. Henrik has found diaries written by his wife, whose version of history troubles him. "I never knew the woman I lived with for more than 50 years," he says. It's apparent, however, he never knew himself. His son is brutally frank. "We were unspeakably scared of you," he says. The viewer has seen Henrik's temper only once, when he slapped the young Pu repeatedly for disobeying him, but we must accept the unforgiving Ingmar's account—that the violence escalated, that life with Henrik was a trial—even as the entire film urges us to throw hindsight to the wind.

In the end, the ineluctable distortion of personal reality is the film's unavoidable point, and the genius of Ingmar Bergman, who's supposed to be retired, the unavoidable conclusion. And while his father's hand is all over this film Daniel Bergman has executed his family obligations, with great heart.

VILLAGE VOICE, 4/26/94, p. 56, Georgia Brown

What Ingmar Bergman has done after retiring from film directing—i.e., revisit and revise his life—may be every bit as interesting as what he did before. In a way, I value it more. (I'm speaking as one who was never hooked on Bergman.) Who would have thought that the tormented genius had the resources to look back with so much empathy and generosity? These qualities didn't seem part of his makeup. Artists, like the rest of us, typically stay with the myths they have created for themselves. Nerve endings atrophy and insulation against insight thickens.

The first stage of the revision began in the candid autobiography, *The Magic Lantern* (1987). Then came *The Best Intentions* (1992), the story of Bergman's parents' messy courtship and early marriage. At the end of the film—written by Bergman but directed by Bille August—the infant Ingmar looms in the womb. The miracle of the movie lay in its loving understanding of Bergman's father, a figure loathed by his sons.

Sunday's Children, written by Ingmar and directed by his son Daniel Bergman, picks up more or less where *The Best Intentions* left off—the seeds of discord germinating. The new film explores the effects of the strain on the children. But mainly it's a father-son story. Told from the perspective of eight-year-old Ingmar, nicknamed Pu (Henrik Linnros), the film takes place during a summer holiday in the Swedish countryside and culminates in a day trip taken by Pu and his father.

In the beginning, the boy arrives at the station to greet his father's train. His mother (Lena Endre) and brother Dag come too, but separately, and when Pu spies their party through the station house window, they could well be strangers. His mother mouths something and beckons; he ignores her. Little Pu is locked into some private drama with his tall clergyman father (Thommy Berggren). "Father's been advising the King and Queen," he informs the doddering stationmaster. "I think the Queen's in love with Father."

Better, we suppose, the Queen should be in love with the King. But like most analysts of the nuclear family, Pu already knows that determining who loves who, or who hates what, is tricky business. The child's taste for genre is formed early: Mystery? Horror? Romance?

Family tensions buzz like mosquitoes around Pu's head. Father and Mother are arguing over an impending visit by Mother's mother (Birgitta Valberg) and brother Carl (Borje Ahlstedt). The sprawling but distinctly flimsy yellow summerhouse stands for economic strains: Grandmother disapproves of the house; Father feels humiliated. Pu's primary worries blend with, are confused with, other wonders of the daily round: a kid his age sucks at his mother's tit; a calf is slaughtered; Uncle Carl betrays matricidal impulses; flies worry a young woman's laid-out corpse. The cook relates the grisly story of a local watchmaker's suicide. On Dag's dare, Pu eats a worm, and instead of being credited for bravery, is mocked for stupidity.

Then the worst. Pu witnesses a late-night quarrel: His mother announces she wants to separate; his father reacts with fury and helplessness. Trying to save his father's feelings, Pu agrees to accompany him to a neighboring parish where he's delivering a sermon for the Feast of the Transfiguration. ("Behold, this is my beloved son in whom I am well pleased. Hear ye him." Ah, just the words any child is dying to hear:) On the journey there, Pu falls victim to one of his father's sudden rages; violence reinforces a prior position, "that God is a lot of piss and shit." A display of thunder and lightning on the way back makes him revise this opinion.

The legend holds that a child born on Sunday sees visions and ghosts. (The Bible, by the way, is filled with visions the child is supposed to accept literally while visions of his own are discouraged.) It's the artist's burden. Bergman has always lamented his inability to separate fantasy from reality. "Close your mouth," everyone says to Pu. "It makes you look stupid." The revelation is that Father is a Sunday's child too, that he and Ingmar have much in common.

Four times Pu sees into the future—reaching toward the wished-for death of the father. In these flashes-forward, a cold 50-year-old Ingmar (Per Myrberg) visits his aged father and, whenever required, withholds his blessing. It's only now that Ingmar, in his mid seventies, feels ready to forgive—although who can say what motivates Daniel Bergman, age 31, to direct his father's belated apology. (Three years after Daniel was born to Bergman and pianist Käbi Laretei, his father took up with Liv Ullmann.) The direction here, like August's of *The Best Intentions*, is distinguished for its simplicity and clarity.

Matching the screenplay almost scene by scene is Bergman's recently published short novel, *Sunday's Children*. Reading the book provokes reflections on what cinema does that writing can't, and vice versa. Once attractive actors are picked—and it's clear they aren't villains—our sympathies are with them always. In novels, p.o.v. can shift more readily. So the film is inevitably somewhat more affectionate, less qualified. Also, it's hard to show the extreme spite and violence of a child's imagination, especially with a young actor who looks like an angel.

Also reviewed in:
CHICAGO TRIBUNE, 10/7/94, Friday/p. M., Michael Wilmington
NEW REPUBLIC, 5/16/94, p. 32, Stanley Kauffmann
NEW YORK TIMES, 4/20/94, p. C20, Vincent Canby
VARIETY, 8/31/92, p. 61, Gunnar Rehlin
WASHINGTON POST, 12/24/93, Weekend/p. 36, Desson Howe
WASHINGTON POST, 12/25/93, p. B10, Rita Kempley

SURE FIRE

A Strand Releasing release of a Complex Productions film . *Producer:* Henry S. Rosenthal. *Director:* Jon Jost. *Director of Photography:* Jon Jost. *Editor:* Jon Jost. *Music:* Erling Wold. *Sound:* Alenka Sunday Pavlin. *Running time:* 86 minutes. *MPAA Rating:* Not Rated.

CAST: Tom Blair (Wes); Kristi Hager (Bobbi); Robert Ernst (Larry); Kate Dezina (Ellen); Phillip R. Brown (Phillip); Dennis R. Brown (Dennis); Rick Blackwell (Dick); Robert Nalwalker (Sheriff); Haley Westwood (Haley); Kaye Evans (Kaye); Henry M. Blackwell, J.T. Reynolds, Thomas D.A. Smith, and John Betenson (Cowboys).

LOS ANGELES TIMES, 9/30/93, Calendar/p. 3, Kevin Thomas

For 30 years independent filmmaker Jon Jost toiled in obscurity, his films never receiving regular theatrical releases. That changed in 1992 when his last film, "All the Vermeers in New

York," a poignant, romantic fable about the eternal and painful discrepancy between life and art—and of the values and instabilities of the 1980s—was released.

Now his "Sure Fire," shot in 1988 and completed two years later, surfaces for a one-week run at the Sunset 5, where this weekend the first complete local retrospective of Jost's films will commence.

Jost may have a firmer grasp of the American character than any other contemporary filmmaker. He goes beyond careful observation of behavior to understanding what drives people from within. He often deals with the travails of rural or small-town men and women, but he is equally knowledgeable about the more sophisticated yet often equally troubled denizens of Manhattan, San Francisco and Los Angeles.

His style is fluid and unpretentious, not imposed from without but expressive of what's going on inside individuals at a particular moment. To that end, however, he is not afraid to draw upon techniques of the experimental cinema in which he began, just as he allows his actors moments that can be described only as theatrical. His films seem so natural as to make you feel as if you're eavesdropping on life as you watch them.

"Sure Fire" has a wonderfully deceptive simplicity yet evokes the dark underside of American life with the resonance of a Eugene O'Neill play. It is set in the tiny town of Circleville, Utah, where we see two 40ish men chatting over coffee at the local diner. Soon we discover how very different they are: Tom Blair's Wes is a wiry, intense realtor, who's convinced himself that he can turn his economically depressed town into a magnet for prosperous California retirees. By "thinkin' all the time," he believes he can make himself rich. By contrast, Robert Ernst's Larry is a weary, edgy third-generation rancher on the verge of losing everything.

Wes is willing to rescue Larry but at the price of literally owning him. What makes these two men friends at all is simply that they've known each other all their lives in a very small community. Wes' wife (Kristi Hager) and Larry's wife (Kate Dezina), realists both but filled with longing, have about had it with their respective spouses.

Tension builds for certain, but there's absolutely nothing predictable about "Sure Fire," which packs a jolt that's totally unexpected and allows Jost to work out, in devastating metaphor, his freely admitted unhappy relationship with his own father.

Jost incorporates three Mormon texts in his film, all emphasizing the need to stick to "the straight and narrow" in God's example yet suggesting that even then his realms may always be beyond mere mortals. Jost inspires his actors, all of whom contributed to the dialogue, to reach into themselves deeply.

While all four of his principals arc impeccable, Blair is downright amazing in the way he sustains and illuminates Wes' maddeningly manic personality. (If he weren't so naive he'd fit right in with the equally desperate guys of "Glenngarry Glenn Ross.") Jost throughout contrasts the uptightness of Wes and the quieter anxiety of Larry against vast landscapes, and Erling Wold's elegiac score, performed with Peter Siegel at the pedal steel guitar, complements its every haunting moment.

NEW YORK POST, 1/12/94, p. 30, Bill Hoffmann

Jon Jost sure knows how to set a mood.

And in his new drama, "Sure Fire," the mood is ominous and blankets the screen like a fog.

The scene is Circleville, Utah, a down-and-out farm town where sipping coffee and chewing the fat at the local diner is a daily ritual for the local townsfolk.

Enter Wes, an ambitious real estate dealer, who has dreams of turning his depressed community into a vacation getaway for stressed-out Californians.

Wes' sales pitch is as high-pitched as an infomercial—and about as sincere as a carnival barker.

Unfortunately, his take-no-prisoners approach also extends into his family life, where he's a control freak in every aspect of his wife's and son's lives. Even his lifelong bosom-buddy from high school gets the Wes treatment.

That's where the dark soul of "Sure Fire" lies. Everybody secretly hates Wes. Instead of confronting him, however, they let him rattle on in a series of terribly demeaning, fascinating-to-watch monologues about how to be successful in life, the Wes way.

Ultimately, Wes' son will talk back to his insufferable father, an act that will have tremendous consequences.

As Jost is an experimental filmmaker, "Sure Fire" steers clear of a traditional narrative form, something that can be disconcerting at times. But there is a wonderful richness here that transcends the quirky style.

Long (and I mean long), mournful shots of the Utah desert are heavily filtered, making its harsh, haunting beauty even more startling.

These shots bring a stark, sinister air to the movie. Impending violence seems to lurk behind every corner.

Tom Blair as Wes is a marvel to watch, hypnotizing in his portrayal of a man who wants to be on the cutting edge of life, but is simply on the edge.

Kristi Hager and Phillip R. Brown as Wes' wife and son are wonderful in their understated anger.

If there's any problem with the film, it's that it ends abruptly. Jost builds up a fine cast of characters we care about and want to see more of.

The director—whose last effort, "All the Vermeers in New York" became a quirky cult favorite—is a true actor's filmmaker, letting his players bare their souls in long, often painful takes.

But their efforts are sometimes clipped short by his unconventional pacing and sense of space and time.

Jost has his own way of doing things and "Sure Fire" does require patient viewing at times.

He might want to hit me for saying this, but I believe there might be a great Hollywood director hiding in Jost.

Given a name cast, a bigger budget and a structured script, I believe Jost could explode into the mainstream in a big way (and mainstream cinema could certainly use a shot in the arm these days).

That said, there is wonderfully original filmmaking at work in "Sure Fire." It's a must-see for those interested in the very latest in truly independent American cinema.

NEWSDAY, 1/12/94, Part II/p. 53, John Anderson

Somewhere during the course of Jon Jost's "Sure Fire," you'll begin to find something horribly familiar about Wes (Tom Blair), the real-estate developer with the heart of aluminum.

It's not his looks. It's the awkward cadence of his voice that starts to wheedle its way under your skin. The irritating lack of sincerity. That rare combination of the avuncular and the unctuous.

Yes, folks, it's George Bush, back and more symbolic than ever. And while it might have been fun to figure this out for yourself, it's probably a better idea to get it out of the way: Because Blair's semi-impersonation, as fun as it is, is something of a distraction. And it's also the only overt political reference in a film that's vehemently political.

Overall, Jost isn't interested so much in the causes of spiritual atrophy as its effects. His films—"All the Vermeers in New York," "Rembrandt Laughing," "Last Chants for a Slow Dance"—have proved him to be a post-nuclear Thornton Wilder with a conspiracy theory. He burrows into the zeitgeist, rather than blowing it open, and elevates the mundane. And, especially in "Sure Fire," he creates potent if amorphous emotion.

Begun in 1988, during the Bush-Mondale campaign, and filmed entirely in Utah, "Sure Fire" is perversely pastoral in its use of landscape—the camera seeks relief from its characters in the sky, or even in the stultified ranchland around them—and savvy in its use of Erling Wold's ethereal music, and Peter Siegel's Nashville-by-way-ofTransylvania pedal steel guitar. The result is pure, fractured Americana.

Jost's films are found art in a way, picking up ethos and atmosphere wherever they're shot. Here, true West is true angst, with the Mormon texts ("*The works, and the designs, and the purposes of God, cannot be frustrated* ...") that cross the screen taking on a gothic flavor. It's not that Jost is religious or anti-religious. What his film and Mormon elders share is an appreciation for, and expectation of, human failure.

The film is elegiac for a West that never existed, and despairing for the one that does: Wes, whose plan to sell unsullied, crime-free Utah to smog-sickened Californians, is a Manifest Destineer, a doggedly self-absorbed and self-deluded hustler whose pursuit of success alienates everyone around him.

He's both frightening and vulnerable in his megalomania, but evokes more aggravation than pathos. The embodiment of economic imperialism, conservative hubris and domestic unrest, he's too far gone to realize his life is not what he thinks it is. When he finally realizes the truth, the ensuing, startling denouement takes on an odd inevitability.

The crisis point in "Sure Fire," though, is less important than the lines that intersect it. Wes' wife, Bobbi (Kristi Hager) is beyond rescue, repelled by his personality and resigned to leaving.

His friend Larry (Robert Ernst) hates himself for being in financial trouble, but hates Wes more for his unwanted, ungracious help. Larry's wife, Ellen (Kate Dezina), is dissatisfied, although the couple still harbors some passion.

But Wes has too much on his mind to notice anything. "You gotta have an edge," he tells Larry. "I'm always thinking, thinking, thinking." He punctuates his sentences with "Golly." He tells Bobbi he wants something done on Thursday. "Thursday. Thursday. *Thuuuuursday*. Got it ...?"

You're surprised she doesn't kill him on the spot. But then, Wes is basically dead already. And so, you can hear Jost hoping, is his era.

SIGHT AND SOUND, 7/93, p. 51, Philip Kemp

Circleville, Utah. In a café, Wes and his friend Larry talk about a local woman, Sandra Jean, who has disappeared. Wes asks Larry to pick up a rifle for him in the neighbouring town. As Wes is about to leave, the sheriff takes a phone call: Sandra Jean's body has been found. Wes calls on Dick Blackwell, a banker, to get backing for a property scheme, and tells him to transfer funds from Wes's own account to cover interest payments due on Larry's overdraft.

Wes's wife Bobbi visits Larry's wife Ellen, who is missing her daughter, away at college. Bobbi relates a distressing dream about a bird caught on barbed wire. When Larry gets home, the news that Wes has paid the interest causes a row between Larry and Ellen. Wes arrives home, shows his son Phillip how to trampoline, and gives Bobbi elaborate instructions on various tasks. She reacts coldly.

On the way to a deer hunt, Wes patronisingly offers Larry a job, which he turns down. At the camp, in front of Larry and another friend, Dennis, Wes presents Phillip with his first rifle and delivers a long lecture on how to use it. Later, alone with Phillip, Wes attempts a man-to-man talk about sex. Phillip reveals Bobbi is planning to leave for California, adding that if she does he will go with her. Wes is furious.

The hunting party splits into pairs, and Wes accompanies Phillip. In the woods, Larry and Dennis hear two distant shots, and come upon Wes and Phillip dead, apparently both shot by Wes. With Larry and Ellen, the sheriff goes to break the news to Bobbi.

It is 14 years since the last UK release of Jon Jost fiction feature. That film, *Last Chance for a Slow Dance*, also had Tom Blair playing a rampant egomaniac who ends up committing an act of senseless violence. But where Tom Bates in the earlier film was aggressively nihilistic, an unrepentent destroyer, the Wes of *Sure Fire* is a more ambivalent, even pitiable, figure. Far better integrated into his community than Bates, from one angle he could even be seen as an ideal citizen—supportive husband, solicitous father, generous friend and keen entrepreneur. Which is clearly how he wants to see himself.

It's his desperate need to have everyone else go along with this self-image that turns Wes into a monster of control, unable to relax his grip on those around him. At one point we see him pumping bullets into a target, each time hitting closer to the centre, exercising over his gun the kind of mastery he longs to exercise over people. Soon afterwards, telling his wife Bobbi how to handle a young man working for them, he lays down a long, manically detailed scenario of what she should say and do, right down to the exact words, gestures and tone of voice. Conventional film grammar would punctuate such a monologue with occasional cutaway shots of Bobbi; Jost instead holds steadily on Wes, tracking slowly in, giving us no clue how his wife's reacting or even if she's still in the room. Only at the very end of the spiel do we see her exasperated glare, as her "Are you done, Wes?" comes with the force of a slap.

Here as elsewhere the film's pared-down economy (not just financial, though that too) serves to clinch the impact of the scene. Jost can do more with less than almost any other filmmaker around, and there are passages in *Sure Fire* whose austerity would make Bresson look fidgety.

The camera moves very little, often not at all, yet there's no feeling of stasis—rather of poised stillness, an unwavering gaze that takes in, and enhances, the emotional intensity of the action.

Naturalism has never been Jost's aim, but his stylised, even minimalist technique can create an exceptionally rich sense of place. *Sure Fire* was shot entirely on location, using only four professional players (the rest of the cast were local people) and allowing the story to develop out of "the opportunities at hand". The stern, beautiful landscape of Utah becomes as much a character as any of the actors, and Jost uses it to enlarge and comment on what happens. In the final scene, rather than follow the sheriff into Bobbi's house—since we can predict just what he's likely to say—the camera leaves him on the porch and rises to execute a slow 360° pan around the treetops and the distant mountains. As it circles, blood-red letters appear along the bottom of the screen: the last of three quotes from the Book of Mormon that punctuate the film.

Jost has long since sloughed off the Godardian didacticism that encumbered early works like *Angel City*, and these Mormon texts hardly feel like the film's "message". Instead the effect of their lapidary certainties ("The works, and the designs, and the purposes of God cannot be frustrated"), set against the stark outlines of trees and mountains, is of a meditation on the landscape and all the national myths tied up with it—Manifest Destiny, the frontier, go-getting, men in a man's world, and so on—that could give rise to someone like Wes.

Sure Fire is dedicated to Jost's father, a professional soldier, and the film is partly "a kind of self-therapeutic, highly metaphoric working out of a bad relationship with my father" which no doubt accounts for its insight into the pathos in Wes, the loneliness behind his non-stop bluster. But Wes also stands for something Jost hates and vehemently opposes in his film-making career: "the American Way [that] has no place or time for smallness, because it is all too desperately busy trying to mask its emptiness with bombast." In a *Film Comment* article last year, Jost likened Hollywood movies to the fleshy magnitudes of Rubens, and his own determinedly small-scale work to the quiet subtlety of Vermeer. The comparison might sound pretentious; but it's one that the richness and poetic complexity of *Sure Fire* go a long way towards justifying.

VILLAGE VOICE, 1/18/94, p. 50, Georgia Brown

Jon Jost's singeing *Sure Fire* makes me think about how far Hollywood is from America. The men who decide what movies will be made—at least those profiled in *The New York Times Magazine*—all seem to have grown up on Long Island. Maybe this is why you never see films today with a clear idea of Ohio or the problems people wrestle with in Winnemucca. (No wonder the vast heartland's resentment at being left out.) The gulf between Altman's *Short Cuts* and Carver's stories starts here: Whereas Carver always stayed with inarticulate heartland loners, Altman relocates to smooth-talking, heartless urbanites. A true-blue American realist, Jost has affinities with Carver and Richard Ford. At the same time, like Errol Morris, he may hardly look like a realist at all. Beginning with its title, Jost's film pays homage to the American vernacular, to the crisp punch of cliché. "It's a surefire winner!" crows Wes (Tom Blair), a small-town real estate mogul, about a scheme for luring disaffected Californians to Utah. (Wes is also a sure shot, as we see from watching backyard target practice.) Another Fire referred to, however, is the Lord's: It blazes yellow from the trees; it lights up the mountains; the late afternoon sky ignites in a blue flame. This is God's country in more ways than one, and the ending, with a 360-degree pan, paraphrases the Almighty's course: "one eternal round."

The insufferably pompous Wes probably believes his voice and the Almighty's are more or less in sync. To those around him, he lays down the law. He patronizingly instructs his wife, Bobbi (Kristi Hager), how to complete a simple task; he lectures his teen-age son, Phillip (Phillip R. Brown), on the ways to hold a gun and a girl; he approaches his old friend Larry (Robert Ernst) like a heaven-sent benefactor—buying him coffee, paying off the interest on his loan—while his real opinion of Larry is that the guy's a dumb loser, good only to serve Wes's greater good.

Blair's Wes is scary. He speaks in a menacing, flat monotone—at times sounding eerily like George Bush. His house is ominously neat, its owner's character hidden under stark suburban surfaces. Those who know Wes well know of his righteous wrath and straight and narrow path. His wife and children are contemplating a dash for freedom.

What saves the film from sheer pain are Jost's fantastically elegant lyric passages—and, over these, the sweet music composed and performed by Erling Wold. A one-man band, Jost shoots his films himself, and he's a wonderful cameraman. Between stylized dramatic monologues and dialogues, he edits in gorgeous landscape footage, punctuating human bewilderment with glorious clarity. He puts sacred words, in the form of Mormon texts, directly on screen in glowing red: "And I beheld a rod of iron ..."

And the iron rod was up my father's arse. In notes and interviews Jost has said that this tragedy of paternalism and fanaticism—dedicated to his army officer father—is semi-autobiographical. (In the mid '60s, Jost served two years in jail for defying his father's military and refusing to serve in Vietnam; he later went on to work against the war.) As critic Jonathan Rosenbaum has pointed out, the film also serves as a self-portrait. Somewhat like Wes, Jost is an obsessed entrepreneur, a fanatic peddler of personal dreams who's famous for tirades, instructive lectures, that can alienate even his natural allies.

I first saw *Sure Fire* at the 1990 Toronto Film Festival (it's sure been a longtime a-coming to New York) where it struck me as an American masterpiece, a searing rendering of the ongoing parent-child, Abraham/Isaac story. The unexpected force comes from material deeply felt and urgently communicated. *Sure Fire* burns slowly, then explodes.

Also reviewed in:
NEW YORK TIMES, 1/12/94, p. C13, Stephen Holden
Variety, 12/31/90, p. 34

SURVIVING THE GAME

A New Line Cinema release of a New Line production in association with David Permut Productions. *Executive Producer:* Kevin J. Messick. *Producer:* David Permut. *Director:* Ernest Dickerson. *Screenplay:* Eric Bernt. *Editor:* Sam Pollard. *Music:* Stewart Copeland. *Music Editor:* Michael Dittrick. *Sound:* Felipe Borrero and (music) Jeff Seitz. *Sound Editor:* Steven D. Williams. *Production Designer:* Christiaan Wagener. *Art Director:* Madelyne Marcom. *Set Decorator:* George Toomer, Jr. *Set Dresser:* John Reneau, Chris Karges, David Bowen, Michael Moran, and Matt Skerritt. *Special Effects:* Joseph Mercurio. *Costumes:* Ruth Carter. *Make-up:* Vonda K. Morris. *Stunt Coordinator:* Bob Minor. *Running time:* 94 minutes. *MPAA Rating:* R.

CAST: Ice-T (Mason); Rutger Hauer (Burns); Charles S. Dutton (Cole); Gary Busey (Hawkins); F. Murray Abraham (Wolfe, Sr.); John C. McGinley (Griffin); William McNamara (Wolfe, Jr.); Jeff Corey (Hank); Bob Minor (Security Guard); Lawrence C. McCoy (Hotel Clerk); George Fisher (Taxi Driver); Jacqui Dickerson (Taxi Passenger); Victor Morris (Homeless Father); Frederick Collins, Jr. (Homeless Child); Steven King (Mercedes Driver); Sheila Scott (Bag Lady); Steven Lambert (1st Trophy Hunted); Kevin Harris (Homeless Man).

LOS ANGELES TIMES, 4/14/94, Calendar/p. 3, Kevin Thomas

If you have the feeling you've already seen "Surviving the Game" you may very well have, for it's basically the same story as "Hard Target." That film may not have been top-drawer John Woo, but alongside "Surviving the Game," it's a masterpiece.

Eric Bernt's hopeless script spends an incredible 37 minutes to set up an action picture that runs only 96 minutes. Worse yet, we can see what the film's hero, a Seattle homeless man played by Ice-T, is getting into long before he can. Apparently having lost his wife and child in some kind of fire for which he somehow holds himself responsible and now having just had his boozy sidekick Jeff Corey and his dog die on him, he throws himself in front of a truck but is saved by Charles S. Dutton's forceful homeless shelter volunteer.

Dutton is no ordinary do-gooder. He's in a partnership with a steely Rutger Hauer in Hell's Canyon Outfitters, which charges its clients a whopping $50,000 each to join its very special hunting expeditions in the Northwestern wilderness. (At least the film has gorgeous scenery.)

You'd think a guy as wary as Ice-T's Jack Mason has been established to be would be a tad suspicious when, despite having no experience whatsoever, he's offered the job of hunting guide. It cannot come as a shock to you when eventually Hauer, pointing a gun at him, tells him, "We're the hunters, you're the hunted."

The film's remaining 59 minutes are ultra-violent and entirely predictable as Mason is given a sportsmanly head start in his run for life by a bunch of sickos, which include Gary Busey, F. Murray Abraham and John McGinley. There's more than a hint that if Hauer and company are successful in capturing Ice-T, they'll roast him for dinner.

It is exceedingly hard to understand why Spike Lee's great cameraman Ernest Dickerson, in his second outing as a director—his first was the uneven but promising "Juice"—was attracted to such trite material, which his direction frankly makes all the more obvious. Ironically, Ice-T, in only his fourth feature, holds on to his cool and carries the picture while most everyone else hams it up. If you're in the mood for a good running-the-gauntlet movie, you're better off renting Cornel Wilde's classic "The Naked Prey" (1966).

NEW YORK POST, 4/16/94, p. 17, Bill Hoffmann

You'd think that any 1990s remake of the often-copies '30s classic "The Most Dangerous Game"—in which humans hunt humans—would be a sadistic, ultra-violent piece of trash with no redeeming value.

Then along comes director Ernest Dickerson with "Surviving the Game," breathing new life into a well-worn genre and pulling a fine, dramatic performance out of controversial rapper Ice-T.

Yes, Dickerson has to conform to all the usual trappings of action movies: grisly violence, rampant cursing and extreme machismo.

But he goes out of his way to introduce another element that most action flicks have long missed; he spends time developing his characters!

For Mason (Ice-T), a wornout homeless man in Seattle, life seems more unfair by the moment.

He decides to end it all after his dog gets hit by a cab (and in a truly demented twist, the cabbie demands a $16.50 fare after his passenger flees).

Fortunately (or so it seems for a while), mission worker Cole (Charles S. Dutton) pushes him out of the path of a speeding truck and then offers him a job as a guide with his company, Hell's Canyon, which brings, yuppie hunters to the Washington State wilderness to hunt big game.

"This is going to be quite a learning experience for you," says Cole's partner, Burns (Rutger Hauer) with an evil smirk.

Soon, Mason finds he's the big game and is forced to defend himself against six bloodthirsty hunters dying to slaughter him (and place his head in the group's infamous "trophy room.")

Each hunter has his own reason for wanting human blood, except for young Wolf (William McNamara) whose dad (F. Murray Abraham) drags him along without divulging what's really going to happen.

Brilliantly, Dickerson dispels any hint of racism in this hunt by casting Dutton as the man who has betrayed Mason.

Before any blood is spilled, each character gets ample screen time to spout on about his phobias. That makes for more audience involvement than the standard blow-'em-away fare.

"Surviving the Game" still can't hold a candle to the 1932 original with Joel McCrea, but in its own pumped-up, up-to-the-second way, it scores a bull's-eye.

NEWSDAY, 4/16/94, Part II/p. B5, Terry Kelleher

Oh, it's all right for F. Murray Abraham. He's sinking his teeth into the juicy role of Roy Cohn in Broadway's "Angels in America." But how are the rest of us supposed to get rid of the bad taste left by the bloody, nasty "Surviving the Game"?

Abraham is just one of the overacting villains in the second directorial outing by Ernest Dickerson, still most conveniently identified as "Spike Lee's cinematographer." From the violent urban realism of "Juice" to the violent wilderness fantasy of "Surviving the Game," Dickerson is covering ground but not making progress.

This is the latest in a line of movies with a debt to Richard Connell's short story "The Most Dangerous Game," whose central element is the hunting of humans for sport. The '90s angle in

Eric Bernt's script is that the quarry has become a homeless Seattle man called Mason (Ice-T), lured into the mountains with the promise of employment.

Turns out Mason's job is to be sacrificed for the fun of an affluent weekend-warrior party: haughty leader Burns (Rutger Hauer), oddly amiable Cole (Charles S. Dutton), crazed psychiatrist Hawkins (another fang-baring display by Gary Busey), high-strung Griffin (John C. McGinley), Wall Street big shot Wolfe (Abraham) and his sensitive son Derek (William McNamara, looking like a queasy Ricky Nelson).

The publicity promises that Mason will use "street smarts" to thwart his pursuers. Luckily, his inner-city survival skills include jumping off a cliff into rushing rapids and hanging upside down from a tree limb while dodging a hail of bullets. But his favorite weapon is street *language*. Who needs a high-powered rifle and an Eddie Bauer outfit when you can snarl obscenities?

"You worm, you're nothing!" Wolfe cries as he tightens his grip on Mason 's throat. "Die! Die!" "___ you!" Mason replies, and suddenly Wolfe's stock takes a fatal plunge.

VILLAGE VOICE, 5/3/94, p. 49, J. Hoberman

Not just another American tale of wilderness pluck, *Surviving the Game* is the second recent action flick to reconfigure the sadistic premise of *The Most Dangerous Game*. In the 1932 prototype of this oft-remade thriller, a crypto-Nazi count hunts innocent Americans for sport. Perhaps such behavior no longer seems exotic—in *Surviving the Game*, as last summer's *Hard Target*, the hunters are heartless capitalists who prey upon the homeless.

Surviving the Game lacks *Hard Target*'s stylistic panache, but it's more sincerely agonized. John Woo's vehicle for Jean-Claude Van Damme, *Hard Target* implied a parallel tale of successful immigration. *Surviving the Game*, directed by Ernest Dickerson and starring Ice-T, is something else again. Lured by the promise of a job from the prisonlike security of Seattle's skidrow, the bruised and brooding antihero is flown to a remote wilderness cabin, along with that evening's dinner, a wild pig. Feasting with the white hunters he's supposed to help guide, Ice-T is the only one not in on the joke.

"Each man out here will experience the animal within himself—the purity of the primal essence," predicts group theoretician Gary Busey, a CIA shrink whose formative childhood experience was going mano-a-mano with the family dog. Hunting Ice-T, an arch-trickster with a full head of dread, will be an exercise in male bonding. There are no bad girls in *Surviving the Game*. Indeed, there are virtually no females of any kind—although the worst insult is "bitch': and when a tiger of Wall Street, unconvincingly played by F. Murray Abraham, wants to incite his son's bloodlust, he warns the lad that he's too much like mother. Casting sullen Ice-T amid these raving hot dogs—including a nearly unrecognizable Rutger Hauer, who extends his journey into hyperreality by acting more American than the Americans—is a master stroke.

As did *Juice*, Dickerson's more obviously naturalistic debut, *Surviving the Game* frames credible ensemble work in a mildly arty mise-en-scène. The most compelling thing is the image of a lone Rasta running for his life in the Pacific Northwest. Charged with intimations of Bob Marley and Harriet Beecher Stowe, it's not the same thing as being naked in New York—which may be why *The New York Times* dissed the movie with the ultimate pull quote, "racially inflammatory."

Also reviewed in:
NEW YORK TIMES, 4/16/94, p. 11, Janet Maslin
VARIETY, 4/25-5/1/94, p. 30, Brian Lowry
WASHINGTON POST, 4/16/94, p. C2, Richard Harrington

SUTURE

A Samuel Goldwyn Company release of a Kino-Korsakoff production. *Executve Producer:* Steven Soderbergh and Michael Halberstadt. *Producer:* Scott McGehee and David Siegel. *Director:* Scott McGehee and David Siegel. *Screenplay:* Scott McGehee and David Siegel. *Director of Photography:* Greg Gardiner. *Editor:* Lauren Zuckerman. *Music:* Cary Berger.

Sound: Doc Kane. *Sound Editor:* Dave Whittaker, Geoffrey Rubay, and Rick Freeman. *Casting:* Sally Dennison and Patrick Rush. *Production Designer:* Kelly McGehee. *Set Decorator:* Nanci Wenz and Steven James Rice. *Costumes:* Mette Hansen. *Make-up:* Katherine James and Lynn E. Champagne. *Special Make-up Effects:* David Ayres. *Running time:* 96 minutes. *MPAA Rating:* Not Rated.

CAST: Dennis Haysbert (Clay Arlington); Mel Harris (Dr. Renee Descartes); Sab Shimono (Dr. Max Shinoda); Dina Merrill (Alice Jameson); Michael Harris (Vincent Towers); David Graf (Lt. Weismann); Fran Ryan (Mrs. Lucerne); John Ingle (Sidney Callahan); Sandy Gibbons (Dr. Fuller); Mark Demichele (Detective Joe); Sandra Lafferty (Nurse Stevens); Capri Darling (Soprano); Carol Kiernan (Ticket Agent); Laura Groppe (Sportswoman); Lon Carli (Man with Camera); Ann Van Wey (Mrs. Lucerne's Nurse); Sam Smiley and Seth Siegel (Doctors); Jack Rubens (Arthur Towers); Mark Siegel (Emergency Room Doctor); Jack Rubens (Voice of Captain Sparks).

CHRISTIAN SCIENCE MONITOR, 2/9/94, p. 17, Marilynne S. Mason

Perhaps destined to be a cult classic, the popular melodramatic thriller "Suture" has one central joke (a black actor plays a dead ringer for a white character) and excellent photography, but it remains a triumph of style over substance.

LOS ANGELES TIMES, 3/25/94, Calendar/p. 14, Peter Rainer

The black-and-white low-budget "Suture" is the first feature from San Francisco filmmakers Scott McGehee and David Siegel, who have won numerous prizes for several of their short films. It's a strange debut: technically assured and arty. The assurance is rare for a first feature, the artiness isn't.

It's a psychological thriller without psychological depth. Clay Arlington (Dennis Haysbert) meets with his half-brother Vincent (Arthur Towers) at the funeral of their wealthy father in Phoenix. The brothers are supposed to share an amazing resemblance although—and here's where the artiness comes in—Haysbert is black and Towers is white.

The "resemblance" is a joke played straight: it's also meant to clue us to the nature of identity, the mysteries of blood ties and all that jazz. When Vincent cooks up a scheme to frame his brother for a murder he himself is suspected of, the result is something right out of Hitchcock by way of Wim Wenders: Clay, who survives an explosion and suffers amnesia, is mistaken for Vincent and surgically reconstructed to his brother's likeness. (His post-surgical look is the same as his pre-surgical look. Go figure.) Clay, with the help of a psychiatrist (Sab Shimono), recreates a new past for himself—his brother's.

McGehee and Siegel draw on many visual and thematic sources besides Hitchcock and Wenders—particularly the John Frankenheimer film "Seconds," which was also about a man with post-surgical identity crisis. And yet their style is distinctive. They bring a saving humor to this deadpan art piece; they seem tickled by the idea of casting a black actor and a white actor as near-identical siblings.

Yet they don't really explore the emotional suggestiveness in that casting, and so it ends up as a kind of fancy in-joke for aesthetes. McGehee and Siegel are filmmakers from the eyes out: they are drawn to the doubling imagery because of its emblematic rather than its psychological possibilities. (In a film like Ingmar Bergman's "Persona, we got both.)

They have such a strong and unsettling graphic sense that without any psychological force, the film turns into a kind of abstraction. It could stand to be a bit pulpier. Perhaps they were afraid that pulp would turn the movie into an extended "Outer Limits" episode?

The acting is mostly overemphatic and stiff, in the manner of grade D '50s sci-fi films, but with an ironic overlay. Example: The plastic surgeon who falls in love with Clay, played by "thirtysomething's" Mel Harris, is named Renee Descartes. That's the kind of joke that plays, maybe, once. Not five times.

Still, McGehee and Siegel have the flair to bring something distinctively new to black comedy once they shake out their art-film kinks. "Suture" is the archetypal "promising" first feature. '

NEW YORK POST, 3/18/94, p. 33, Larry Worth

Is it a thriller? A commentary on race relations? A meditation on identity? Well, like the Rorschach prints that keep showing up behind the characters, "Suture" is open to interpretation.

But no matter how audiences read it, the film is daringly original.

And as with any true original, it challenges the audience with a mind-blowing journey to the outer limits. All you have to do is accept a devilishly wild premise: that a white man and a black man could be mistaken as twins.

The narrative is an extended flashback to the meeting of two estranged half-brothers at an airport. Sleek, WASPish Vincent (Michael Harris) comments to his sibling, Clay (Dennis Haysbert, who heated up an interracial romance with Michelle Pfeiffer in "Love Field") on "how much we look alike. Our physical similarity is disarming."

The reasons for Vincent's enthusiasm soon become apparent, Widely believed to have just killed his father, Vincent is planning to fake his death, using Clay as his stooge. Vincent has just outfitted Clay from his wardrobe, then switched driver's licenses before rigging his own car to explode, And sure enough, Clay is behind the wheel when it bursts into flames.

Then the unthinkable happens. Clay survives. Horribly scarred, missing an eye and with a face wrapped in bandages, he looks like the hockey-masked Jason Voorhees. Worse, he's got amnesia. So, as the police close in on their "suspect," it's up to the doctors to make Clay remember a life he never led—Vincent's.

That's the launching pad for a fascinating look at transplanted personalities, a theme which hasn't been tapped since Nicolas Roeg's "Performance" and Robert Altman's "Three Women."

Advertised as "a thriller where nothing is black and white," the interplay of Haysbert and Harris later evokes a meditation on racial boundaries. And lensing the production in—you guessed it—crisp black and white was clearly no accident. But it's stunningly effective.

On a more basic level, writer/producer/directors Scott McGehee and David Siegel create a tightly knit psycho-drama perhaps inspired by the talents of executive producer Steven "sex, lies and videotape" Soderbergh.

The actors also hit the mark, particularly Dennis Haysbert. With his whispery voice and tentative ways, he's hauntingly effective at feeling his way through a maze of deceit and betrayal.

And while Michael Harris is appropriately sleazy as Vincent another Harris—Mel of TV's "Thirtysomething"—stands out as Clay's vulnerable doctor. Equally noteworthy is Dina Merrill's turn as a family friend who may know more than she lets on.

So does it all finally jell? Not exactly. But in its refusal to sew dangling threads into a neat little package, "Suture" holds attention from first frame to last, and your thoughts for considerably longer.

NEWSDAY, 3/18/94, Part II/p. 69, John Anderson

Steven Soderbergh says that when he saw a rough cut of "Suture," the remarkable debut by writer-directors scott McGehee and David Siegel, he immediately signed on as an executive producer. "I couldn't believe people wouldn't want to see this movie," he said.

It's easy to see why he was excited. McGehee and Siegel have created a film that operates on several very precarious levels, and fairly dances. Like Soderbergh's own "sex, lies, and videotape," it, questions the meaning of identity, and the fate of the ego vs. modern technology. Like his "Kafka," it explores variations on totalitarianism—in this case, the tyranny of anonymity and of modern medicine—and almost as an afterthought debunks racism and ageism. But first and foremost, it's a thriller of the first rank.

From the nerve-racking opening sequence to the, gunshot that sends us flashing back, McGehee and Siegel evoke dread, often through a Hitchcockian use of the mundane. Clay Arlington (Dennis Haysbert), after all, is a pretty basic guy: A heavy-equipment operator from Needles, Calif., he arrives in Phoenix assuming he'll spend the weekend getting to know his half-brother, who has invited him to visit after the funeral of their father.

The brother, Vincent Towers (Michael Harris), has other plans. A well-to-do socialite of uncertain occupation, he is the prime suspect in their father's death, and he's brought Clay to Phoenix for a specific reason: To kill him with a car bomb, assuming that the police will think the remains belong to Vincent. And why shouldn't they? As everyone points out, Clay and Vincent are the spitting image of each other.

The film's "gimmick," which turns out to be no gimmick at all, is that Dennis Haysbert is a large black man, Michael Harris a lanky white, and the action proceeds as if their characters were twins. When Clay arrives at the hospital after the explosion, he has a ruined face, amnesia, and is carrying Vincent's identification. The assumption, naturally, is that he's Vincent.

The plastic surgeon, Dr. Renee Descartes (Mel Harris), with whom Clay will fall in love, works from a picture of Vincent in restoring Clay's face. His psychiatrist, Dr. Max Shinoda (Sab Shimono) suspects that all is not right with "Vincent," amnesia notwithstanding, but never questions *who* he is, because the assumption of identity is too great. When Alice Jameson (Dina Merrill), the real Vincent's lover, spots a scar on Clay's back that she's never seen before, we can see her mind explain it away.

Clay doesn't know who Clay is either, but we're not sure anyone else does, or whether we're seeing what we think we're seeing: Dr. Shinoda is an Asian who quotes from Shakespeare and Auden as if to buoy his own identity. Renee is a plastic surgeon because plastic surgery runs in her family. Alice, who is much older than Vincent (we think), defines herself through him. Vincent, meanwhile, needs to kill his brother again.

All this involution gives "Suture" a certain smugness. But considering how smartly executed and beautifully shot it is—Greg Gardiner's black-and-white cinematography is gorgeous—a little self-indulgence is understandable.

SIGHT AND SOUND, 2/95, p. 54, Chris Darke

Clay Arlington arrives in Phoenix to meet his half-brother Vincent Towers, whom he encountered at the funeral of their wealthy and powerful father Arthur, who was murdered. Vincent is suspected of the crime. Inviting Clay to stay at his home, Vincent informs him that he has to leave overnight on business and asks him to drive him to the airport. The car is rigged to explode and, before departing, Vincent triggers the car bomb. Dressed in Vincent's clothes and carrying identification Vincent has planted on him, Clay survives the explosion, but suffers from complete amnesia. Requiring extensive plastic surgery, Clay is remade as Vincent. Two specialists treat him; plastic surgeon Dr Renee Descartes and psychoanalyst Dr Max Shinoda. Shinoda begins to discover elements of a personality that do not tally with Vincent's cold and anti-social reputation.

The Phoenix police continue their murder investigation, questioning a witness who claims to remember clearly the killer's face. The opportunity to identify Vincent must wait for his plastic surgery to be completed. Meanwhile, Clay begins to recall details of his past in dreams and flashbacks which confirm Shinoda's suspicions that Vincent Towers is someone completely different. On leaving hospital, Clay moves into Vincent's house and remains haunted by dreams in which he remembers himself as an impoverished crane operator and visualises a dusty, rundown town. Under analysis, it transpires that the place he remembers is called Needles. Accompanied by Descartes, who is in no doubt that he is Vincent Towers, Clay visits Needles but finds it ugly, depressing and without memories. The two of them spend the night together in a motel.

The police call in Clay for the line-up, but the witness cannot identify Vincent and the investigation is terminated. Clay is suspicious that he is still being tailed, but on telephoning the police, is assured that they no longer suspect him. The phone call triggers his memory of the call that Vincent made to him in the car before the explosion. It is Vincent who has returned to kill Clay, who stands to inherit their father's wealth. Vincent breaks into the house but is shot by Clay.

In their final session Dr Shinoda attempts to persuade his patient to acknowledge his true identity as Clay Arlington: "I am Vincent Tower", is his obstinate response.

Suture, the noun, comes with three definitions: one each from medicine, Lacanian psychoanalysis and 70s French film theory. *Suture* the film deploys all three in a generic cocktail of paranoid thriller, *film noir* and American avant-garde. The first definition simply means the stitching together of a wound. The second concerns the relationship between the individual subject and its place within language and derives from Lacan's celebrated dictum that "the unconscious is structured like a language".

The psychoanalytical idea of "suture" refers to processes by which the subject is "stitched into" language or a chain of discourse which both defines and is defined by the work of the unconscious. In the late 60s, theorist Jean-Pierre Oudart applied this idea of suture to cinema contending that the psychic processes which constitute subjectivity are reiterated in film by operations such as shot/reverse-shot which bind the spectator into the coherence of the filmic system. If the unconscious is structured like a language, then one such language that discloses this structuring is cinema.

While it is perfectly possible to appreciate McGehee and Siegel's film knowing nothing of psychoanalytic film theory, the film-makers have clearly constructed their film to accommodate several layers of pleasure and interpretation. One such level is that of *Suture*'s genre and tone. Generically the film sits somewhere between Hitchcock's *Spellbound*, which the film-makers acknowledge as the source of the basic story of an amnesiac suspected of murder, and John Frankenheimer's *Seconds*, in its concern with an identity transformed by plastic surgery.

In tone, however, *Suture* veers dangerously close at times to *Twilight Zone* parody spookiness. This impression is reinforced by voice-over interjections at the film's beginning and end by Freudian analyst Dr Shinoda—whose office is emblazoned with two huge Rorschach ink-blots. Presenting the psychoanalyst's attempt to delve into Vincent/Clay's authentic personality in semi-parodic terms makes it as doubtful a method of evaluating the truth as those represented by police Lt. Weismann and plastic surgeon Dr Renee Descartes. The police case against Vincent/Clay rests on the testimony of a partially blinded eye witness who must identify someone who has undergone extensive plastic surgery. The futility of such an investigation is ironically juxtaposed with the plastic surgeon's devotion to the pseudo-science of physiognomy which, resting on Italian Renaissance ideals of beauty, declares that personality is legible through physical features. That the plastic surgeon should be named Descartes screams out that *Suture* has intentions beyond the capable remodelling of genre premises, it wants also to deconstruct their underlying philosophical presuppositions.

Conceptual ambition is matched by formal audacity—Clay, Vincent's half-brother is played by Dennis Haysbert, a black actor whose blackness is never acknowledged. It acts as a distanciation effect: while the characters don't see Clay as a black man, we do. It's a nice idea but, in execution, a host of implied ideological problems remain unaddressed. It also returns us to the notion of suture because, as spectators, we are constantly aware of the illusory, incomplete nature of identification with screen characters. In this sense, it is a winning strategy, working with the film's conclusion that Clay, by denying his real identity, is living a lie with potentially disastrous psychological repercussions.

Suture also brings this formally disorientating approach to bear on the editing, where an apparently normal continuity cut within a scene will jarringly displace us from one space to another, and, in the use of overlapping sound where one scene intrudes aurally into another, each technique serving to disallow the easy "suturing" of the spectator into the film.

Vincent's pad, a plush modernist rotunda, is as half-unpacked and as yet unlived-in as the shifting personality of Clay/Vincent. Clay's memory returns in flashes and dreams, triggered by everyday events, such as a phone call to the police after they have concluded their investigation. Vincent returns like a repressed memory, but armed with a gun and he has to be denied by Clay, who kills him by shooting off his face. The call to the police that Clay makes revives his memory of the call that Vincent made to him on the car phone just before the explosion. Crucially, this moment has the cumulative effect of Clay's total remembrance of his past—from hereon in, the implication is that Clay is fully conscious of his imposture.

In the light of this, the film's closing images—a series of still photos of Clay and Renee holidaying socialising and playing the beautiful couple—take on the pathos of a life lived purely as social performance and surface appearance, but whose reality speaks of entrapment, imprisonment and psychic entropy.

VILLAGE VOICE, 3/22/94, p. 54, Lawrence Chua

He can walk the walk and talk the talk, but even in that fine linen suit he'll still be sent to the messenger room when he shows up for his meeting. More than an exercise in clever casting, Scott McGehee and David Siegel's ambitious feature debut, *Suture*, is a hard-boiled thriller with a subversive heart. Shot in glorious wide-screen black-and-white Panavision, *Suture* exudes a smart-assed style that beckons closer inspection of its already riveting pulp narrative.

Clay Arlington (*Love Fields*'s Dennis Haysbert) is the estranged, working-class half-brother of moneyed and mysterious Vincent Towers (Michael Harris), who is under investigation for the murder of his father. Clay and Vincent bear an uncanny resemblance to one another. Planting his driver's license and credit cards on Clay, Vincent plots to kill his brother, but Clay survives the bombing, disfigured and amnesiac. Everyone assumes he's Vincent. "You lack memories," his psychoanalyst, Dr. Shinoda (Sab Shimono), tells him. "Try and view this as an opportunity to explore your past." In the process, Clay falls in love with the brilliant, beautiful blond plastic surgeon, Renée Descartes (Mel Harris). The police, meanwhile, still want to "put a noose around [Clay's] neck."

All of this would be enough to propel any well-made film through its paces, but McGehee and Siegel sift even more layers of intrigue and meaning on top of *Suture*. Clay, for example, really doesn't look anything like Vincent. For starters, he's black. His presence disrupts the conventions of the thriller, at the same time unseating the audience's position as passive spectator to the events unfolding onscreen. As Descartes snips and removes the stitches from Clay's face, she waxes that his nonexistent Greco-Roman nose proves he "isn't inclined to deviant behavior, like killing people." Within the film's leisurely pace and broad, inviting spaces, the audience has a little moment to take a reality check.

Suture takes place in a social vacuum, an airless landscape where markings like class and race are exchanged as easily as plaid for silk. Personal memory and official history, glimpsed within videotapes and still photographs, intersect and collide as Clay maneuvers the terrifying elegance of inside (the hospital and Vincent's tastefully furnished home) and out (the wide-open Arizona desert). Clay sets about trying to reconstruct his own history, but in the end convinces himself that it's enough to merely slip into a preexisting identity, unnoticed by everyone around him. Well, almost everyone.

Also reviewed in:
CHICAGO TRIBUNE, 7/8/94, Friday/p. H, Michael Wilmington
NEW YORK TIMES, 3/18/94, p. C15, Caryn James
VARIETY, 9/27/93, p. 37, Todd McCarthy
WASHINGTON POST, 4/29/94, p. C6, Desson Howe

SWAN PRINCESS, THE

A Columbia TriStar Films International/Nest Entertainment release of a Rich Animal Studios production. *Executive Producer:* Jared F. Brown and Sheldon Young. *Producer:* Richard Rich and Jared F. Brown. *Director:* Richard Rich. *Screenplay:* Brian Nissen. *Story (based on "Swan Lake"):* Richard Rich and Brian Nissen. *Director of Photography:* Steven Wilzbach. *Character Animator:* Steven E. Gordon. *Effects Animator:* Michel Gagne. *Editor:* James Koford and Armetta Jackson-Hamlett. *Music:* Lex de Azevedo. *Lyrics*: David Zippel. *Music Editor:* Douglas Lackey. *Choreographer:* Lisa Clyde. *Casting:* Geoffrey Johnson, Vincent G. Liff, and Tara Jayne Rubin. *Art Director:* Mike Hodgson and James Coleman. *Running time:* 90 minutes. *MPAA Rating:* G.

VOICES: Jack Palance (Rothbart); Howard McGillin (Prince Derek); Michelle Nicastro (Princess Odette); John Cleese (Jean-Bob); Steven Wright (Speed); Steve Vinovich (Puffin); Mark Harelik (Lord Rogers); James Arrington (Chamberlain); Joel McKinnon Miller (Bromley); Dakin Matthews (King William); Sandy Duncan (Queen Uberta); Brian Nissen (Narrator); Adam Wylie (Derek); Adrian Zahiri (Odette); Tom Alan Robbins (Musician); Bess Hopper (Hag): Cate Coplin, Tom Slater and Jim Pearce (Dancers).

LOS ANGELES TIMES, 11/18/94, Calendar/p. 4, Kevin Thomas

"The Swan Princess," the German fairy tale that is the basis for the beloved "Swan Lake" ballet, now emerges as a lavish animated musical fantasy to enchant children, especially little girls, during the holiday season. Sprightly and engaging, it unfolds with clarity and makes excellent use of its voice talents, most notably that of Jack Palance as the villainous Rothbart; the colorful witty, familiar menace of his voice allows him to all but steal the show.

Prince Derek (Howard McGillin) and Princess Odette (Michelle Nicastro) grow up in adjoining kingdoms, and from childhood Derek's mother, Queen Uberta (Sandy Duncan), and Odette's father, King William (Dakin Matthews), are determined matchmakers to the extent that the kids can't stand each other until they grow up and realize how attractive, each other is. But just as they're falling in love, Odette is kidnaped by Rothbart, who kills her father and who has the power to turn himself into a dragon at will.

Since Odette, not surprisingly, refuses to marry him so that he can assume the throne of her country, he casts a spell on her, turning her into a swan who can resume her human form only when moonlight shines upon her wings. She now lives in a lake in an enchanted forest. She can regain her freedom only through the love of a prince who can prove his devotion before the whole world.

Before it's happily-ever-after time, director Richard Rich and writer Brian Nissen come up with considerable diversion and adventure. Some of the film's most charming moments occur in byplay between the captive Princess and her new friends, a dapper French frog (John Cleese), a lethargic turtle (Steven Wright) and a sturdy puffin (Steve Vinovich).

Rich has done a terrific job of directing his cast: Their voices convey character and personality. Along with Palance, Duncan is a special delight: Her Queen Uberta speaks in the fluttery manner of Billie Burke, It's worth noting that McGillin is starring on Broadway in "Kiss of the Spider Woman" and that Liz Callaway, who provides the singing voice of Odette, is now in "Cats," also on Broadway.

Although it's possible for am adult to be caught up in "The Swan Princess," it would be more enjoyable for many of us if visually the film weren't so determinedly old-fashioned. Traditional to a "T," it features the usual painterly storybook backdrops, some as kitschy as old calendar landscapes, with the equally typical simply drawn humans and anthropomorphized animals.

Although Rich, a major Walt Disney alumnus, had an army of skilled artists and technicians at his command for more than four years, he seems to have no innovative impulse in him. His is a sentimental vision, painstakingly and successfully realized, but "The Swan Princess" could have just as easily been made 40 years ago, or even earlier—it is almost devoid of contemporary sensibility to an extent that's a little creepy. Fittingly, it may well be one of the last animated features to employ the time-consuming techniques of hand-drawing and coloring of nearly every single image rather than using computer-generated graphics.

Lyricist David Zippel and composer Lex de Azevedo have come up with six new songs, which are fun and serve the story effectively. Rothbart has a robust anthem, "No More Mr. Nice Guy" (sung by de Azevedo); there's the Busby Berkeley-esque "Princesses on Parade," those young women vying for Derek's hand once Odette has vanished; and a stirring love son, "Far Longer Than Forever," a sure-fire bet for Your Hit Parade—if this were 1952.

NEW YORK POST, 11/18/94, p. 49, Michael Medved

In a year when Hollywood seems to have rediscovered family films, "The Swan Princess" stands out as one of the very best of them—enchanting, witty, infused with love in every frame. It's the work of Richard Rich, a veteran of the Walt Disney company (where he directed "The Fox and the Hounds") who's been laboring for the last eight years to establish his own animation studio to rival his former employers. The lush, lovely quality of this film shows how well he's succeeded; it's one of the first non-Disney animated features that deserves comparison with the contemporary classics "Beauty and the Beast" and "The Lion King."

The story is based on the same fairy tale that inspired the "Swan Lake" ballet, and while the music isn't exactly Tchaikovsky, it's nonetheless richly entertaining. Six cleverly worded songs by Tony Award-winning lyricist David ("City of Angels") Zippel and composer Lex de Azevedo help tell the story of Princess Odette, who's pledged to Prince Derek in an effort to unite two neighboring kingdoms. At the big moment of proposing marriage, however, Derek declares that the only basis for his affection is Odette's beauty—a pre-feminist faux pas that leads the strong-willed young woman to storm off in anger.

Unfortunately, she's intercepted on the way back to Papa's castle by the evil sorcerer Rothbart (the voice of Jack Palance) who casts a spell on her. Unless she agrees to marry him, she will remain a graceful swan, who can only briefly assume human form when moonlight shines upon her wings. confined to a shadowy lake in an enchanted forest, she waits for the spell to be broken by the pure love of a human prince, while she keeps company with a lethargic turtle named Speed (comedian Steven Wright), and a talkative frog (Monty Python's John Cleese) who believes that one kiss from Odette will turn him into a prince.

The idea of equipping the frog with an exaggerated French accent may be stretching the humor just a bit; more successful are references to the off-screen personality of Jack Palance in the scene where his evil enchanter demonstrates his strength by doing a series one-handed push-ups.

A sense of fun never leaves the proceedings, and while the animation may not be as lifelike or richly dimensional as Disney's state-of-the-art, it has its own brightly colored charms. The signature romantic tune, "Far Longer Than Forever" is a winner that will probably nab an Oscar nomination, despite the fact that it, like much else in the movie, unmistakable echoes "Beauty and the beast." If you're going to borrow, the filmmakers seem to have reasoned, why not borrow from the best?

Meanwhile, "The Swan Princess" arrives in theaters just as "The Lion King" is re-released for its special holiday run. This Swan may not be the king of beasts but if, like most American parents, you've already seen "Lion King" at least once with your kids, then pass it up this time around and give the bird a chance.

NEWSDAY, 11/18/94, Part II/p. B6, Jack Mathews

A young boy walking out of the theater after a preview screening of the new animated feature "The Swan Princess" was asked by a radio reporter what he thought of it.

"It was kind of beautiful," the boy said.

Well, it is. It is also kind of like "Beauty and the Beast" and "The Little Mermaid." It is a fairy tale done in the modern Disney style, with lots of Broadway songs and production numbers, and a supporting cast made up of adorable anthropomorphic creatures with B movie accents and tons of wisecracks.

It is not a Disney movie, of course. Made by former Disney studio director Richard Rich, "Swan Princess" is more of a commercial "appreciation," like Tony Bennett cutting an album of songs associated with Frank Sinatra. But it is still quality work.

"The Swan Princess" is not quite in a class with the movies it emulates. Its song team, Tony-award winning lyricist David Zippel ("City of Angels") and veteran TV series composer Lex de Azevedo, aren't Alan Menken and Howard Ashman. And though it cost an estimated $40 million, its animation style is already dated by the standards set in Disney's "The Lion King."

None of that is apt to matter to children, however, and adults tagging along will find it a perfectly pleasant experience.

Based loosely on "Swan Lake," "Swan Princess" is the story of a princess (voice of Michelle Nicastro) who is kidnaped and turned into a swan by a sorcerer (Jack Palance) determined to take over her father's kingdom, and of the attempts by her prince (Howard McGillin) to rescue her. On the way to the climactic battle between Prince Derek and the evil Rothbart, you'll hear show tunes eerily reminiscent of those in "Beauty and the Beast," and some magic seemingly stolen from octowitch Ursula's bag of tricks in "The Little Mermaid."

You'll also get "Beauty-Mermaid" déjà vu from the forest menagerie who protect the princess. There is a blow-hard French frog named Jean-Bob (John Cleese), an ironic turtle named Speed (Steven Wright), and a colorful, highly protective bird named Puffin (Steve Vinovich).

Prince Derek and Princess Odette could have been drawn more interestingly, and Rothbart, with Jack Palance hamming it up, could have been given more to do. But "The Swan Princess" is a very satisfying children's fantasy, and if it is largely a work of imitation, it chose the best models.

SIGHT AND SOUND, 2/96, p. 54, Leslie Felperin

The infant daughter of King William, Odette, is to marry Derek, the son of Queen Uberta. Each summer the two children are forced to spend the summer together, but they squabble and fight. When they come of age, Derek suddenly perceives Odette's beauty and announces his love. Odette is offended that Derek is only taken with her looks and she leaves with her father. On the way home they are set upon by the wizard Rothbart, disguised as a monstrous animal, who captures Odette and kills everyone else. Derek is distraught.

Rothbart turns Odette into a swan, but each night, provided that the moon shines on the lake, she turns back into her true form. She befriends a frog named Jean-Bob, a turtle named Speed and a Puffin named Puffin. Rothbart insists he wants to marry her so that they may rule her kingdom together but she rebuffs him. Derek, meanwhile, hones his archery and hunting skills, determined to track down a great animal who abducted Odette. His mother Uberta tries to fix him up with other princesses but he refuses. Odette and her friends lure Derek to her lake so that he can see what she has become. She explains the nature of her curse and that it can only be broken by his kissing her and announcing his undying love in public. Derek promises to do what Odette asks at the ball his mother is throwing the next night.

Unfortunately, Rothbart overhears their plans and resolves to thwart them. He imprisons Odette and disguises his hag housekeeper as Odette to send her to the ball, so that when Derek makes his announcement to another, the real Odette will die. Odette manages to escape but she is too late to stop Derek. She flies back to the lake to die, with Derek in pursuit. Rothbart explains that only by killing him can Derek break the spell. Derek manages to defeat him and, by kissing Odette and declaring his love—for her courage and strength as well as her beauty—she is literally disenchanted. The two lovers are married at last.

Appearing in Greek and Irish mythology, a story by Hans Christian Andersen, W.B. Yeats' poetry and a ballet by Tchaikovsky, the swan is one of the most evocative of animal symbols in the arts. Graceful in the water, endowed with a wonderfully phallic neck, a curvaceous, uterine body and, in some species, a black mask around its eyes, it's a bird puffed up with connotations. However, swans everywhere will probably want to distance themselves from *The Swan Princess*. It's an ugly duckling of a film, which does not do the species much credit.

Plainly derivative of standard fairy tales, the story is not all that bad. Its plot components (enchanted princess, evil wizard, misunderstanding parents) have to be predictable to be intelligible for the child audience and to have the archetypal spin needed to sell it to literary-minded parents. The film even jokingly plays with genre expectations by including a frog (played by John Cleese) who believes himself to be 'really' an enchanted prince. Less forgivable is the film's slavish aping of Disney conventions such as the inclusion of a triumvirate of animal helpers, the soppy Tim Rice-esque songs, and the spelt-out 'prosocial' morality (suggesting this time that we love people for who they are, not what they look like).

But *The Swan Princess* hasn't got the state-of-the-art techniques of a Disney film at its disposal. Granted, director Richard Rich (who also made *The Rescuers, Black Cauldron* and *The Fox and the Hound*) wouldn't have the massive budget of a Disney film, but even so, many have proved before him that good animation need not cost a fortune. Here the quality of draughtsmanship is particularly bad. Prince Derek's hands look like shrivelled bunches of bananas. Odette's eyes have so much white in them (a conventional animation signifier of innocence) that she looks permanently surprised, and overall she is an unattractively petulant figure. One almost wishes that she could stay a swan, except that she's not even a very convincing one. The movements are all wrong: she flies with her neck locked in place like a goose, instead of the characteristic undulating motion of a swan.

Would it have really cost that much to have got such details right? The elaborate ballroom scene, seems to have swallowed much of the budget, but again the choreography and feel is derivative—a pastiche of songs in Disney's *Beauty and the Beast* and *Aladdin* which were themselves pastiches of old Busby Berkeley routines. I ask not for a revolutionary departure from form or precedent just as no-one should criticise Yeats for going back to old myths such as Leda and the Swan). Just for a little more thought and style.

Also reviewed in:
CHICAGO TRIBUNE, 11/18/94, Friday/p. I, Johanna Steinmetz
NEW YORK TIMES, 11/18/94, p. C20, Caryn James
VARIETY, 11/21-27/94, p. 37, Brian Lowry

TEMPTATION OF A MONK

A Northern Arts Entertainment Ltd. release of a Tedpoly Films production. *Executive Producer:* Kay Wong. *Producer:* Teddy Robin. *Director:* Clara Law. *Screenplay (Mandarin with English subtitles):* Eddie Fong and Lillian Lee. *Director of Photography:* Andrew Lesnie. *Editor:* Jill Bilcock. *Music:* Tats Lau. *Sound:* Gary Wilkins and Ross Linton. *Production Designer:* Timmy Yip, Yang Zhanjia, and William Lygratte. *Running time:* 118 minutes. *MPAA Rating:* Not Rated.

CAST: Joan Chen (Princess Scarlet/Violet); Wu Hsin-kuo (General Shi); Zhang Fengyi (General Huo); Michael Lee (Old Abbott); Lisa Lu (Shi's Mother).

NEW YORK POST, 12/16/94, p. 64, Thelma Adams

I confess I didn't get Clara Law's swooningly operatic "Temptation of a Monk" until I saw it twice.

The first time I watched this feudal saga of seventh-century China, I wrestled with the plot. I confused General Shi (Wu Hsin-kuo) with his rival, General Huo (Zhang Fengyi). Joan ("Twin Peaks") Chen playing both Princess Scarlet, Shi's love, and the black widow Violet, a Huo assassin, added to the chaos.

As it turns out, the plot is no more complicated than "Hamlet," only less familiar. Shi defends the Crown Prince, the heir to the Tang Dynasty. Huo protects a rival prince who wants to jump the line of succession.

Huo convinces Shi that the younger prince would make the better emperor and enlists Shi's aid in what he promises will be a bloodless coup. So, Huo lied; the Crown Prince and his family are beheaded.

Riddled with remorse, Shi rejects the spoils of his betrayal. When he abandons his life of privilege (and Scarlet's love) and enters a monastery. Shi becomes a threat to the new regime and a wanted man. So much for the plot, which, like "Farewell My Concubine," was adapted by popular novelist Lillian Lee from her own fiction.

On a second viewing, I could relax and enjoy Zhang's athletic grace and the regal glow of Chen's princess along with the sinewy seductive cunning of her assassin.

Visually luscious scene follows luscious scene. The costumes and choreography of the opening deer hunt between the two generals is reminiscent of Kurosawa's "Ran." Colors are daringly used: The peacock tones of a delirious whore-house scene contrast with the drab greens and dead-leaf browns of the preceding monastery scenes. Four concubines in mint green preparing tea in a dark room form a haiku.

The 27-year-old Law engages in battle scenes with gusto. Filmed in slow motion and artfully choreographed, they occasionally border on Monty Python with severed limbs, decapitated heads and spurting blood. At one point, Shi snatches an arrow in mid-air between his teeth. As a monk breaking his vows, Shi's lovemaking is as ferocious as his swordplay.

The intimate encounter between the general and his mother is no less bold. On the night of the coup, Shi returns home with a scorched heart. The dowager puts an end to any temptation he might have to accept the spoils of his duplicity. She imperiously beats the great warrior with a rod, gives him his marching orders (he is to wander until he can restore the family honor), and plunges a dagger into her chest.

"The Temptation of a Monk" is ultimately about a warrior's fall in the material world and his rise in the spiritual one. Plagued by the enormity of his betrayal, Shi's donning of monk's robes begins as a refuge from foes and then opens up a rocky path toward bliss. Law's ambitious epic is also a twisted route to ecstasy.

NEWSDAY, 12/16/94, Part II/p. B15, John Anderson

Hong Kong filmmaker Clara Law juggles time and sensibility like ceremonial swords. Earlier this year, "Autumn Moon" wove a modern parable out of urban sex and cynicism. And now, in "Temptation of a Monk," she's invested a 7th-Century Chinese knight with what seems to be a 20th-Century sense of alienation, angst and spiritual yearning.

Political appeasement, sexual sabotage and an appetite for instant gratification also are among the modern problems that afflict General Shi (Wu Hsin-kuo), an armored imperial warrior who forges a fatally pragmatic pact with a rival general, Huo (Zhang Fengyi of "Farewell My Concubine").

The result of Shi's betrayal by Huo is a fratricidal coup against the rightful Crown Prince and his brother, setting up a third as emperor-to-be and triggering a bloodbath among the military.

Implicated in the murders and racked with guilt, the fugitive Shi flees the Forbidden City to become a Buddhist monk. And along the way he persuades a band of his surviving former soldiers—who intended to kill him—to join him in his spiritual quest.

As monks, they're not much. Their devotion to the 12 Prohibitions of Buddhism is diluted by the gnawing in their bellies; their visit to a brothel is a hallucinatory revel in things carnal. Shi's encounter with Scarlet (Joan Chen), sister of the murdered princes, finds him abandoning his vow of celibacy. Her murder at the hands of Huo's men prompts him to abandon his vows of mercy and forgiveness.

In telling Shi's tale of revenge and self-realization, Law makes wonderful use of the forbidding Chinese frontier as a canvas for elaborate battle scenes, or a mute universe of spiritual need. And she well serves the venerable tradition of Hong Kong cinema with her stylized, slow-motion martial-arts ballets, which are deliriously brutal and poetic.

Joan Chen, in her first Chinese-language film since crossing over to the West with "The Last Emperor" and "Twin Peaks," does double duty as both the doomed Scarlet and a seductive assassin sent to pleasure and then murder Shi.

And Wu, as the doubting, anxious Shi, is a modern man stuck in a feudal world. Or a feudal man stuck in an anxious world.

VILLAGE VOICE, 12/20/94, p. 60, Georgia Brown

With *Temptation of a Monk*, Hong Kong's Clara Law—mostly known for intimate and topical contemporary dramas—leaps lance-first into the costume epic. Based like *Farewell My Concubine* on a Lillian Lee novel, *Temptation* is a bloody treatise on loyalty, honor, and the difficulty of spiritual purification. Opening in 626 A.D., during China's Tang dynasty, the film begins with a stately, stylized ceremony that may remind Westerners of Kurosawa's *Ran* and *Kagemusha*. Although Law hasn't comparable resources at her command (or the same mastery of crowd scenes), she seems to share a taste for colorful spectacle and magnificent scenery.

Two generals face off, each the chief protector of one of the Emperor's sons. Playing some ceremonial games, General Shi (Wu Hsin-kuo) demonstrates superior skills, but his counterpart General Huo Da (Zhang Fengyi) has a darker purpose: to make his own prince the ascendant heir. Because he knows *his* prince is unfit to rule, Shi joins the plot, treachery commences, and his prince is beheaded. Rather than enlist in the new regime, the guilt-ridden Shi, encouraged by his mother, goes into hiding. The following years constitute a bumpy journey to enlightenment—the condition he'll need for his final confrontation with Huo. A couple of times Shi faces steamy erotic temptations—both in the form of Joan Chen.

Although the movie is packed with incident, much of it grisly, *Temptation* also gives the impression of moving mighty slowly, like the glacial progress of enlightenment itself. Law uses distancing devices—slow motion, heavy masklike makeup and creates characters that are difficult to penetrate or even to fix in mind. Though we follow Shi closely over the course of his adventure, he never becomes more than a type. Judging by the director's comments, she intends *Temptation* in some way to imitate Buddhist principles. Relinquishment of the movies' usual pleasures, however, doesn't necessarily yield enlightenment.

Also reviewed in:
NEW YORK TIMES, 12/16/94, Stephen Holden
VARIETY, 9/27/93, p. 41, David Stratton

TERMINAL VELOCITY

A Hollywood Pictures release of an Interscope Communications/Polygram Filmed Entertainment production in association with Nomura Babcock & Brown. *Executive Producer:* Ted Field, David Twohy, and Robert W. Cort. *Producer:* Scott Kroopf and Tom Engelman. *Director:* Deran Sarafian. *Screenplay:* David Twohy. *Director of Photography:* Oliver Wood. *Editor:* Frank J. Urioste and Peck Prior. *Music:* Joel McNeely. *Music Editor:* Curtis Roush. *Sound:* Stephen Von Hase Mihalik and (music): Shawn Murphy. *Sound Editor:* David Kneupper and Kelly Oxford. *Casting:* Terry Liebling. *Production Designer:* David L. Snyder. *Art Director:* Sarah Knowles. *Set Designer:* John O. Warnke. *Set Decorator:* Beth A. Rubino. *Set Dresser:* Howard R. Cole and Loy Hopkins. *Special Effects:* Lawrence J. Cavanaugh. *Costumes:* Poppy Cannon-Reese. *Make-up:* Jeanne Van Phue. *Make-up (Charlie Sheen):* David L. Anderson. *Stunt Coordinator:* Buddy Joe Hooker. *Aerial Stunt Coordinator:* Buddy Joe Hooker and Jerry Myers. *Running time:* 102 minutes. *MPAA Rating:* PG-13.

CAST: Charlie Sheen (Ditch Brodie); Nastassja Kinski (Chris Morrow); James Gandolfini (Ben Pinkwater); Christopher McDonald (Kerr); Gary Bullock (Lex); Hans R. Howes (Sam); Melvin Van Peebles (Noble); Suli McCullough (Robocam); Cathryn de Prume (Jareb); Richard Sarafian, Jr. (Dominic); Lori Lynn Dickerson (Helicopter Newscaster); Terry Finn (Birthday Mom); Martha Vazquez (Newscaster); Tim Kelleher (Jump Junkie #1); Brooke Langton (Jump Junkie #2); Tim Lounibos (Jump Junkie #3); Sofia Shinas (Broken Legs); Matthew Mazuroski (Jump Instructor "Tom"); Cindi Shope (Babe); Chester Bennett (Blad); Billy Hank Hooker (Gunman #1); John C. Meier (Gunman #2); Mr. Shutov (Foreign Minister); Terey Summers (Cashier); Sandy Gibbons (Greyhound Clerk); Sam Smiley (Corvette Owner); Kurek Ashley (Cargo Pilot); Rance Howard (Stunt Pilot/Chuck); Paul Guyot (Car Wash Attendant); Robert L. Lee (FAA Inspector #1); Michael Gaughan (FAA Inspector #2); James R. Wilson (Bartender); Michelle Crisa (Stewardess).

LOS ANGELES TIMES, 9/23/94, Calendar/p. 4, Kevin Thomas

"Terminal Velocity," a rousing, good-looking action-adventure with romance and comedy, couldn't be more up to the minute, yet its pleasure hark back to movies' earliest days of exuberant, lightning-fast, cliff-hanging serials of the silent era and the aerial exploits of such classics as "Wings" and "Hell's Angels."

The special effects are state of the art—how could they dare be otherwise nowadays?—but they don't overwhelm the people. There's a consistent sense of humor and lightness of touch that's often lacking in such hard-driving pictures. "Terminal Velocity" succeeds because it's without pretense, unashamedly offering pure entertainment. There's an appealing throwaway quality to the entire undertaking that attests to the consistent sound judgment of director Deran Sarafian and writer David Twohy, who co-wrote "The Fugitive," in not taking themselves too seriously.

The film is chock full of mind-boggling incidents, with twists and turns at every instant. At heart its premise is simple and timely, shrewdly not revealed to us and our equally bewildered hero, Charlie Sheen's daredevil sky diver Ditch Brodie, until more than an hour into the story. Against mounting yet mysterious danger the filmmakers created imaginative and amusing characters for Sheen and leading lady Nastassja Kinski to play to the hilt.

Brodie is a warm and funny guy, a reckless grandstander and an uninhibited pursuer of beautiful women. When Kinski's beguiling Chris Morrow turns up at an Arizona parachuting center, Brodie figures he can give her a lesson and wine her and dine her into a quick seduction, getting to sleep early. No sooner are they up in the air, however, than Brodie is hurtled into danger and excitement that it looks like he'll never be able to stop running, let alone get some rest. He's hard put to keep up with the tenacious, no-nonsense Morrow, who's as formidable as Jackie Chan in outwitting ferocious bad guys James Gandolfini and Christopher McDonald. (Brodie's crusty pilot is played by Melvin Van Peebles, a groundbreaking black actor/filmmaker of the late '60s and early '70s).

There's no point in revealing what Morrow is up to, but, as the film approaches its climactic sequence, it pauses to allow Kinski a big scene in which her selfless heroine confronts Brodie with his immature All-American self-absorption and ignorance. Even the blithest of escapist entertainment needs a serious moment to give its people a crucial measure of reality.

NEW YORK POST, 9/23/94, p. 47, Thelma Adams

Remember "Death Warrant" or "Back in the U.S.S.R."? I didn't think so. Today, director Deran Sarafian adds another forgettable actioner to his resume: "Terminal Velocity."

Charlie Sheen plays a swaggering skydiving instructor. Nastasja Kinski, his perky pupil has a few tricks up her parachute She's an ex-KGB agent racing around Arizona to retrieve stolen Russian gold.

The twist here is that Kinski is the lethal action heroine; she tosses her bangs aside just in time to point and shoot with deadly accuracy. Sheen, the smart-ass screw-up with Elvis-impersonator looks, tumbles along for comic relief.

This post-Cold War adventure flies and falls on the premise that evil Russians are so out they might just be in again. If the bad Rooskies, played by James Gandolfini and Christopher McDonald, were more threatening than laughable or the plot was remotely plausible, the producers might have had a chance at good slush.

No speech is more ridiculous than the pretty spook's impassioned plea about her foes: "Once they're in power, it'll be the Cold War all over again."

While many thriller writers might welcome the Cold War's return as a chance to dust off all those scripts rotting away in Hollywood footlockers, we just can't believe Kinski and Sheen are in a position to save the free world or that any of this matters enough to suspend disbelief at the obvious howlers.

The pace of David Twohy's script is all velocity but no "Speed." Can this be the same guy who wrote "The Fugitive"? Twohy's also responsible for the coming Kevin Costner money pit, "Waterworld," currently being positioned in the trades as the next "Heaven's Gate."

"Terminal Velocity" is made less painful by Sheen's delivery of one-liners. When Kinski appeals to Sheen's patriotic duty, he snaps "Pack the bags we're going on a guilt trip." Outrageous aeronautical stunts provide the main thrill. A car plummets off a moving plane while Sheen scrambles to unlock the trunk; his KGB sweetheart is trapped inside. Skydivers plunge into factory towers, through deadly windmill clusters, and land between the cacti on the desert floor.

In the end, the sound of a body hitting the dust after a 120 mph fall without a parachute and the sound this amiable dud will make when it strikes the box office are the same. Thump.

NEWSDAY, 9/23/94, Part II/p. B7, Terry Kelleher

"Terminal Velocity"? *Au contraire.* A fast pace is the main thing keeping this picture alive.

Now, we're not suggesting for one second that Charlie Sheen with a parachute is as breathtaking as Keanu Reeves on a bus. But "Terminal Velocity" shares with "Speed" a commendable instinct to keep moving lest logic catch up to the plot.

Sheen plays "Ditch" Brodie, a cocky (it goes without saying) skydiving instructor with a reputation for stupid publicity stunts—the type who descends unannounced on ball fields and boxing rings. Giddy with excitement, an attractive customer calling herself Chris Morrow (Nastassja Kinski) tells Ditch she's dying for an introductory lesson. So he promptly takes her up, with the eventual goal of bedding her down. Unfortunately, the moment he turns his back on her, she tumbles from the plane and fails to open the chute en route to the hard ground. R.I.P., right?

Of course not. An unscathed Chris soon re-enters Ditch's life and reveals herself as a good ex-KGB agent trying to prevent bad ex-KGB agents from getting their bloody Stalinist hands on $600 million in bullion. Though he's no internationalist, this particular cause has a certain appeal for Ditch, who happens to be a former world-class gymnast still frustrated over being denied a chance to strike "Russian gold" at the boycotted 1980 Olympics.

You probably don't believe any of this, and writer David Twohy (co-scripter of "The Fugitive") probably doesn't care. One sign Twohy isn't taking his own story seriously: Chris gives Ditch an impassioned political pitch at the counter of a sleepy Arizona diner, while the other patrons listen with bored incomprehension. The plot of "Terminal Velocity" is merely a pretext for director Deran Sarafian and his crew to put on a display of aerial stunts and special effects so over-the-top that you have to appreciate the sense of fun they bring to their craft. For a climax, Ditch drives a car off a plane at X-thousand feet, wins a fight with a hammy villain (Christopher McDonald) hanging from the hood, then parachutes into a field of windmills.

Ditch wisecracks all the way, as per action-comedy custom, but Twohy has a special surprise for the audience: A number of the jokes are actually funny. The down side to this air show is that Sarafian, who overdid the violence in "Death Warrant,' and "Gunmen," tends to misgauge the balance between action and comedy. "Terminal Velocity" comes close to slowing down not when the principals pause to banter, but when the director indulges his weakness for protracted gun battles and fisticuffs.

SIGHT AND SOUND, 5/95, p. 56, Trevor Johnston

Having witnessed a jumbo jet landing at night in the middle of Arizona's Sonoran desert, a female Russian agent in the area is murdered just after reporting it to her superiors. Meanwhile, Phoenix-based daredevil skydiver Ditch Brodie has his parachuting school shut down by the Federal Aviation Authority when he takes apparent aerial neophyte Chris Morrow for her first lesson, only to have her jump out of the plane without him and plummet to her death. Further investigation on Brodie's part leads him to the same apartment where the Russian agent was killed, a tussle with the same blonde-haired assailant and the discovery of a Russian identity card revealing Morrow as an experienced skydiver. Under threat of a manslaughter charge from DA Ben Pinkwater, Brodie seeks the help of a colleague's video evidence and identifies another plane in the air at the time of the 'accident'. Giving chase to the same aircraft leads him to an abandoned building in the desert and the revelation that Chris is alive, having faked her own demise by means of a body double thrown from the second plane.

Without further adieu the pair retrieve a computer mini-disc from a nearby industrial installation, narrowly escaping the attentions of peroxided Russian mafia assassin Kerr and his henchmen. Taking shelter in a deserted shack, Morrow explains that she's a KGB agent tracking down a planeload of gold originally destined for humanitarian aid in Moscow but which has been hijacked by a renegade band of her ex-colleagues in cahoots with the Russian mafia. At the next town, Brodie's resentment at feeling used prompts the two to part despite the romantic attraction flickering between them, but his change of heart sees him commandeering a small plane to rescue Morrow from airborne kidnappers Kerr and Pinkwater (the latter a KGB man all along). A daring struggle in mid-air leaves Kerr dead and Brodie and Morrow parachuting to safety, while a further tussle on the ground dispatches Pinkwater too. Damage from the fight has forced the Russian plane to land and be surrounded by police. As a reward for their bravery, Morrow and Brodie receive gold medals from the Russian president in Moscow.

That James Cameron's *Terminator 2* and *True Lies* have upped the stakes on the thrills Hollywood action pics are routinely required to deliver is clearly evident from this counterpart to John Badham's *Drop Zone* in a mini-cycle of skydiving stunt spectaculars. *Terminal Velocity* marks the big time calling card of up-and-coming mayhem specialist Deran Sarafian after a number of noteworthy video rental titles (*Gun Men* and *Road Flower* among them). While the most recent benchmark in aerial sequences has obviously been Kathryn Bigelow's *Point Break*, what Sarafian achieves here in the film's major setpiece goes further than the mid-air tussle between Reeves and Swayze, but it also reinforces the tension that exists in Cameron's recent work between digital imaging technology and the no-frills, no-effects footage that confirms that, yes, the stuntmen are actually there risking their lives.

The sequence in question involves a red convertible thrown out the back of a cargo plane with stunt doubles for daredevil skydiver Charlie Sheen in the driving seat, for Russian mafia heavy Christopher McDonald hanging on to the windshield, and for Nastassja Kinski locked in the boot. In the course of the next few minutes, 'Sheen' punches out the villain who falls to his death, then clambers along to the trunk to extricate 'Kinski' and usher her to safety as she holds on to him while he opens his parachute. Intercutting the usual wind-swept close-ups of the major players plus computer manufactured low-angle shots of the vehicle hurtling to the ground and narrowly passing the camera on its way, Sarafian knows that the money shot here isn't the extremely expensive morphed inserts but the long-shot showing the real stunt people perilously going about their business in mid-air, and the whole segment carries a very definite visceral thrill because so much of his coverage is gathered in this way. Ironically, despite the vast bounds in film-making technology, the way to thrill an audience still lies in depicting unadorned physical danger that has its celluloid antecedents as far back as Mack Sennett, Buster Keaton and Harold Lloyd.

Although it might seem unbalanced to concentrate so much on a single sequence, it is the only point at which the film transcends routine. Marshalling the various players into position for it does seem the entire narrative's *raîson d'être*. The sub-*Vertigo* revelation about Kinski's death in the first reel, for instance, isn't especially surprising in itself but it does allow the film-makers to pulp one body ('Terminal Velocity' is a technical term from coroners' reports on such incidents) to show the fatal risks inherent in jumping out of planes from a great height. Charlie Sheen doesn't have the physical command to put over iron man heroics in the Schwarzenegger or Stallone mould so he partly plays it for laughs, while Kinski, cast perhaps for her 'foreignness', seems slightly too mature to be doing all this running and jumping around.

Add the perfunctory deployment of cartoon-strip villains embodying the twin menace of both KGB and mafia, the lack of any psychological motivation for Sheen's death-defying antics and the machine-tooled suggestion of attraction between male and female leads and you have a dispiritingly formulaic context for the showmanship of the major stunt sequence already described. Sadly, without the pull of genuine audience involvement, the moviemakers virtually throw it away.

Also reviewed in:
NEW YORK TIMES, 9/23/94, p. C20, Stephen Holden
VARIETY, 9/26-10/2/94, p. 60, Steven Gaydos
WASHINGTON POST, 9/23/94, p. F1, Hal Hinson
WASHINGTON POST, 9/23/94, Weekend/p. 48, Joe Brown

TERROR 2000

A Leisure Time Features release of a DEM FILM production in association with Norddeutscher Rundfunk/Westdeutscher Rundfunk. *Executive Producer:* Renee Gundelach. *Producer:* Christian Fürst. *Director:* Christoph Schlingensief. *Screenplay (German with English subtitles):* Oskar Roehler, Uli Hanisch, and Christoph Schlingensief. *Director of Photography:* Reinhard Köcher. *Editor:* Bettina Boehler. *Music:* Jaques Arr. *Sound:* Eki Kuchenbecker. *Production Designer:* Uli Hanisch. *Costumes:* Tabea Braun and Julia Koep. *Make-up:* Heide Hass. *Running time:* 79 minutes. *MPAA Rating:* Not Rated.

CAST: Margit Carstensen (Margret); Peter Kern (Peter Körn); Alfred Edel (Bössler); Udo Kier (Jablo).

NEW YORK POST, 11/18/94, p. 48, Larry Worth

If there's anything worse than mindless splatterfests, it's mindless splatterfests masquerading as social commentary.

The most recent example: "Terror 2000," director Christoph Schlingensief's bid for a cult classic on the midnight movie circuit. But no matter what time of day it's seen, the production is a complete waste of time and celluloid.

Before the opening credits, a social worker escorting a group of Polish refugees from Warsaw to Dresden by train is savagely beaten and mutilated by four psychotics. And that's just the warmup.

What follows is an unremitting parade of carnage. The recurring motif is of someone getting their brains shot across a bystander's face.

Schlingensief's justification is that he's parodying the recent German violence against immigrants and the country's rising neo-Nazi movement. So, in between beheadings, characters ask questions like "Where does all this hatred come from?" as the camera pans to a burning swastika.

In reality, the non-stop mayhem is simply gore for gore's sake—an excuse to link a combination of rape scenes (two of which are intercut to let viewers compare degrees of bestiality), dismemberment tableaus and shots of people urinating.

As a co-writer of the script, Schlingensief proves an equal opportunity offender, targeting blacks, women, gays, the handicapped, Jews and especially Poles in his camera's cross hairs.

An attempt to blur the line between civilization's heroes and villains is equally off-putting.

The cast, which includes German film veterans Udo Kier, Margit Carstensen and Peter Kern yells 99 percent of the dialogue, leaving the ugly goings-on with no redeeming value.

Germany's return to xenophobia and fascism is indeed a horrible problem. But "Terror 2000" seems all the more hideous for exploiting them in the name of the almighty buck.

NEWSDAY, 11/18/94, Part II/p. B9, Gene Seymour

The blood spilled in "Terror 2000" is more bogus than anything the World Wrestling Federation's yet concocted. But there are plenty of other effects in this frenzied fever dream about neo-Nazism in post-Cold War Germany to jolt, disorient and (for sure!) gross out even the most broad-minded sensibilities.

Though German in subject, "Terror 2000's" style owes more to the back-alley sleaze of Russ Meyer, the high-camp histrionics of John Waters and the extravagant scatology of William S. Burroughs. Director Christoph Schlingensief also shows affection for the gaudy, low-budget horror shlock that used to have trailers warning the audience, "Just keep telling yourself, 'It's only a movie, It's only a movie ...'" Perhaps the director had to keep telling himself the same thing in order to confront his film's grim theme.

The plot, such as it is, concerns the kidnapping of a Polish refugee family and a goony social worker (writer Gary Indiana doing a goonybird Jerry Lewis cameo) by a motley gang of backwater neo-Nazis led by a slovenly shopping center magnate (Alfred Edel).

The government assigns a celebrated husband-and-wife detective team (Peter Kern and Margrit Carstensen) to the case. Despite their reputation, the pair seem every bit as clueless and grotesque as the goons they're tracking down.

In fact, just about everyone in the film—bigots, racial minorities, police, refugees, liberals—gets the coyote-ugly treatment from Schlingensief. His over-the-top misanthropy would be exhilarating if one didn't wonder whether such unrelenting grotesqueness ends up pounding the audience into a state of indifference over what's being depicted.

VILLAGE VOICE, 11/22/94, Film Special/p. 66, Richard Gehr

As though his subject were just too tawdry to face head on, Christoph Schlingensief borrows generously from American exploitation cinema's sleazier moves to make a few depressing points about postunification Germany's intolerant tendencies in this hectic political cartoon. Equally beholden to Russ Meyer and Rainer Fassbinder, though lacking the former's passion and the latter's political acumen, this brief yet tiring film begins with glum black-and-white shots of immigrant hostels as its Criswell-esque narrator intones, "Enjoy the world we're living in. Enjoy yourselves," then proceeds to ensure you do nothing of the sort.

Performed with campy gusto by a dream team of New German Cinema regulars (who include Peter Kern, Margit Carstensen, Alfred Edel, and Udo Kier), *Terror 2000* concerns the bungling attempts of a pair of detectives to locate a fatuous social worker (played by *Voice* writer Gary Indiana) and a Polish family abducted by neo-Nazis en route to the "United Colours" refugee camp in Rassau. Amid flashbacks to an earlier, more romantic kidnapping, the detectives enlist a psychic and pose as neo-Nazis in their quest. Although it all makes little sense, the point being that contemporary Germany is out of control, the action restarts every couple of minutes with a pumping musical riff that conflates the James Bond and Batman themes. If postunification Germany is hell, *Terror 2000* could well be its handbasket.

Also reviewed in:
NEW YORK TIMES, 11/18/94, p. C20, Stephen Holden
VARIETY, 12/21/92, p. 63, Eric Hansen

THAT'S ENTERTAINMENT! III

A Metro-Goldwyn-Mayer release in association with Turner Entertainment Company. *Executive Producer:* Peter Fitzgerald. *Producer:* Bud Friedgen and Michael J. Sheridan. *Director:* Bud Friedgen and Michael J. Sheridan. *Screenplay:* Bud Friedgen and Michael J. Sheridan. *Editor:* Bud Friedgen and Michael J. Sheridan. *Film Restoration:* Richard P. May. *Additonal Photography*: Howard A. Anderson III. *Music Supervisor:* Marilee Bradford. *Additional Music*: Marc Shaiman. *Sound:* Dave Kelson, Bill Teague, and (music) Hummie Mann. *Sound Editor*: Bill Bell. Running time: 113 minutes. *MPAA Rating:* G.

CAST: June Allyson; Cyd Charisse; Lena Horne; Howard Keel; Gene Kelly; Ann Miller; Debbie Reynolds; Mickey Rooney; Esther Williams.

LOS ANGELES TIMES, 5/6/94, Calendar/p. 1, Kenneth Turan

"That's Entertainment! III" is the sunniest of *memento mori*, a showy tribute to the flabbergasting musicals of Metro-Goldwyn-Mayer that emphasizes both how delightful the genre was and how inescapably extinct it's become.

Though the visibility of Westerns and science-fiction movies fluctuates according to popular taste, it's doubtful we'll ever see anything like the flood of musicals that characterized MGM in its grandest days. It's not only the money they cost, it's how time-intensive these films were to make, and how much they depended on the army of support personnel only a literal principality like Metro could afford to keep on call.

As the Roman numerals conveniently indicate, this is the third "That's Entertainment!" musical compilation, and though it contains some familiar chestnuts like Mickey Rooney and Judy Garland blasting a peppy "Good Morning" from "Babes in Arms," it benefits from the extra work Bud Friedgen and Michael J. Sheridan had to do in order to avoid the usual suspects.

Editors on the first two films and producer-writer-directors and editors here, Friedgen and Sheridan have spent at least part of the 18 years since Part Two was released methodically investigating the considerable material in the MGM vaults, and what they have unearthed is dazzling.

Most obvious are the obscure musical items that fans know well but that most audiences may not because the films they come from are less familiar. Energetic, enthusiastic numbers such as Cyd Charisse's boxing-oriented "Baby, You Knock Me Out" from "It's Always Fair Weather" or Ricardo Montalban, Ann Miller and Charisse throwing themselves into "Dance of Fury" from "The Kissing Bandit."

Also utilized is irresistible behind-the-scenes material, for instance an in-house film that shows just how complex the logistics were when Eleanor Powell danced from stage to stage in the celebrated "Fascinatin' Rhythm" number from "Lady Be Good." New technology has also been put to use, with Fred Astaire and Ginger Rogers dancing the swing trot from their last film together, "The Barkleys of Broadway," now visible without the opening credits that previously obscured their footwork.

Best of all, however, are the outtakes, numbers completely filmed but cut from the final version, often shown here in split screen with unexpected results. On view, for instance, are the India Adams-dubbed Joan Crawford and Cyd Charisse each doing "Two Faced Woman," the former used in "Torch Song," the latter cut from "The Band Wagon," decisions unfortunate on both counts.

Judy Garland, the icon of the MGM musical, gets special attention here. Friedgen and Sheridan have discovered not only "March of the Doagies," an elaborate sequence cut from "The Harvey Girls," but also "Mr. Monotony," Garland's first use of her trademark half-tuxedo and cut from "Easter Parade," and, strangest of all, "I'm an Indian Too," a politically incorrect number

Garland filmed for "Annie Get Your Gun" before temperament problems led her to be dropped in favor of Betty Hutton.

Though these clips can't and don't miss, another aspect of "That's Entertainment! III" is more problematical, and that, paralleling the first two films, is its use of nine different MGM stars to introduce the individual segments.

Some of these situations are unobjectionable, for instance, having a relaxed Esther Williams revisit her trademark saucer pool and talk us through a selection of clips from her surreal water ballets. And having Lena Horne speak frankly about the frustration of being a showstopping African American performer the studio didn't know what to do with is a welcome dose of levelheadedness. Most of the talk from most of the performers, however, is laden with "I loved every minute of it" banalities that do nothing but detract from the magic on screen.

Also, to put it gently, no amount of magic, both movie and otherwise, can make these stars look as youthful as they did 18 and 20 years ago, let alone in their primes, and to compare a weakened Gene Kelly with the lithe athlete who danced with a newspaper and a squeaky floor in "Summer Stock" is a melancholy task.

On the other hand, seeing visible signs of aging does add a kind of unforeseen poignancy to "That's Entertainment! III," a reminder of how completely these performers have moved off screen and what an irreplaceable vacuum their absence has left in our moviegoing lives. The tagline for the original "That's Entertainment!" turns out to be even more sadly apropos today: "Boy, Do We Need It Now!"

NEW YORK POST, 5/6/94, p. 37, Michael Medved

Both the best and the worst features of "That's Entertainment! III" stem from the filmmakers' attempts to alter and enhance the formula that made the first two films so successful in the mid-1970s.

First the good news. In addition to more than 50 rousing dance numbers culled from vintage MGM musicals this new film includes priceless outtakes and behind-the-scenes footage retrieved from studio vaults and never before seen by the public.

For instance, producers/directors Bud Friedgen and Peter Fitzgerald (who worked as editors on the first two films) found amazing footage showing Metro technicians in the act of shooting Eleanor Powell's breathtaking "Fascinatin' Rhythm" number from "Lady Be Good" (1941).

You see the technical crew moving cameras, parting curtains and breaking away sets so the incomparably lovely and athletic star can dance seamlessly (in a single continuous take!) between stages.

The movie also highlights Judy Garland performances that ended up on the cutting-room floor, ranging from the spectacularly seductive ("Mr. Monotony" from 1948's "Easter Parade"—in which she wore her trademark half-tuxedo for the first time) to the downright embarrassing ("I'm an Indian Too" from 1949's "Annie Get Your Gun").

This off-key and uncomfortable performance helps to explain the studio's move (citing "emotional problems") to drop Garland from the starring role and to replace her with Betty Hutton.

A much less defensible decision involved Lena Horne's bewitching rendition of "Ain't It the Truth," cut from "Cabin in the Sky" in 1943. As Horne comments ruefully in her voice-over narration, the song never made it into the movie "because the studio bosses thought it too risque to show a black girl in a bubble bath."

Horne's bittersweet recollections of the racism that crippled her career certainly enrich this movie. But the insipid scripted reminiscences by other MGM legends (Gene Kelly, Esther Williams, Mickey Rooney, and many more) definitely do not. And that's the bad news.

These now superannuated stars pose at various sites in the historic Metro lot (today Sony Columbia Studios) reading stilted comments like "Oh, what times we had!" that don't for one moment sound sincere, personal or revealing.

The filmmakers might have made better use of these great stars by presenting them in unguarded, interview settings—or altogether avoiding their pointless interruptions of this otherwise impressive picture.

As it stands, these "host" segments introduce a pompous, self-congratulatory tone that slows down the furious energy of the old production number and makes this latest offering—welcome though it is—somewhat less joyous and intoxicating than its two terrific predecessors.

NEWSDAY, 5/6/94, Part II/p. B7, Jack Mathews

How much meat can there be left on old Leo the Lion's carcass?

"That's Entertainment!," released 20 years ago, was (is!) a breathtaking compilation of the very best moments from the studio that defined the Hollywood musical. "That's Entertainment! Part 2," came along two years later, blending leftovers from the musicals with the best clips from MGM's comedies and dramas.

Since then, the studio that once boasted having "more stars than there are in the heavens," has been through hell. It has been bought, disassembled and sold, then bought, disassembled and sold again, and the hallowed grounds once tread by Andy Hardy, Dorothy and the Munchkins, is now owned by Japanese electronics giant, Sony Corp.

Nevertheless, producers Bud Friedgen and Michael J. Sheridan, with financing from the bank-owned remnants of MGM, and with access to a library now owned by Ted Turner, decided to stretch for one more "That's Entertainment!" And though they had to go into the film vault and dust off unused outtakes from such classics as "Easter Parade" and "Show Boat" to pull it off, they have done it in surprisingly grand style.

The clips in "That's Entertainment! III" can't be compared with those gems used in the original, but they add up to a far better entertainment than "Part 2." In fact, some of the outtakes included here are so good, it's a wonder director Jack Haley Jr., whose father played the Tin Man in "Wizard of Oz," didn't think to include some of them in "That's Entertainment."

For the first time, you will see Judy Garland singing "Mr. Monotony," a fabulous number cut from "Easter Parade," and "March of the Doagies," shot for but left out of "The Harvey Girls." There's Debbie Reynolds doing a cut number from "Singin' in the Rain," and beautiful Lena Horne, in a bubble bath, singing "Ain't It the Truth," eliminated from "Cabin in the Sky."

Horne, one of the film's nine hosts, tells us she wasn't made to feel too much a part of old Hollywood, then gamely narrates a sequence from the 1951 "Show Boat," in which Ava Gardner played the part of Julie Laverne that Horne created on Broadway.

The sequence includes the number "Can't Help Lovin' Dat Man" as it appeared in the movie, with Gardner's voice dubbed by studio soprano Annette Warren. Then it is replayed, with the track of Gardner's own voice, which is surprisingly warm and markedly more suited to the mood than Warren's, and finally, we get the rendition by Horne that might have been.

Friedgen and Sheridan, editors on the earlier compilations, used their skills to great effect, splitting the screen periodically to show us two related images. In one sequence, we see the finished cut of a sprawling Eleanor Powell dance number, choreographed by Busby Berkeley for the 1941 "Lady Be Good," and simultaneously watch workmen frantically moving props out of the way so Berkeley's camera crew could keep up with her.

Some of the outtakes included in "III" went unused for good reason. Judy Garland's awkward rendition of "I'm an Indian, Too" for the 1950 "Annie Get Your Gun" was scuttled when she was replaced on the film by Betty Hutton. And though it is great comic relief, the image of the three contortionist Ross Sisters tying themselves into fleshy knots for "Broadway Rhythm," is nearly obscene on the big screen.

Keep in mind that this review is picking highlights from a highlights film. The bulk of "III" is made up of scenes that were rejected twice before, which means you'll be seeing a lot more of Esther Williams than you might like, and not enough of Fred Astaire, Gene Kelly and Busby Berkeley.

Still, in the long drought that has followed the end of the era of the Hollywood musical, even picked-over scenes from MGM help quench the thirst.

SIGHT AND SOUND, 1/95, p. 64, Andy Medhurst

An anthology drawn from classic MGM musicals, including not only familiar numbers but also out-takes, behind-the-scenes footage and other previously unseen material, linked by reminiscences from Gene Kelly, Cyd Charisse, Lena Horne, Howard Keel, June Allyson, Mickey Rooney, Debbie Reynolds, Esther Williams and Ann Miller.

By the third episode of any series of films, an audience is entitled to feel wary, fearful of the law of diminishing returns, and it's undeniable that *That's Entertainment! III* is a weaker offering than its predecessors (released in 1974 and 1976), acknowledging this by reprising their finest moments in its closing montage. Given the fact, however, that third-string MGM product was still better than most studios' first-rate output, this is still an irresistible goodie bag of a film, joyously overflowing with showbiz excess and ridiculous, life-enhancing virtuosity. You leave it feeling sandbagged by glamour.

The early *That's Entertainment!* films may have cherry-picked all the paradigmatic numbers, but *III* still delights with 'lesser' routines from *On the Town* and *Singin' in the Rain*, clips from films just outside the pantheon (there are two particularly terrific numbers from *It's Always Fair Weather*), and glimpses of once-popular stars who haven't managed to secure the long-term reputation they deserved—the leather lungs of Betty Hutton all but steal the show.

In a new and politically-conscious departure for the series, the tone is not entirely celebratory. Lena Horne's contribution cuts through the sugar to point out how the MGM musical played its part in the history of Hollywood racism, confining her to minor roles and denying her the part in *Showboat* that eventually went to Ava Gardner. Salutary as this is, it's also a little evasive, inasmuch as Horne is allowed to speak only in terms of personal disappointments, leaving broader questions of ethnic representation unexplored. The sequencing of the film further defuses her critique by following it with 'I'm an Indian Too' from *Annie Get Your Gun*, a howling example of racial insensitivity. Horne aside, the surviving stars are content to wander, slightly dazed, through the backlots of their own nostalgia, and the primary pleasure to be gleaned from seeing them do this is to marvel at the artistry of California's cosmetic surgeons, June Allyson's improbably taut visage being especially compelling.

Another innovation in this third film is the inclusion of unseen footage. We're shown numbers filmed for but then trimmed from (among others) *The Harvey Girls*, *Easter Parade* and *Cabin in the Sky*, a treat for genre completists, even if, in truth, none of them were greatly missed in the finished pictures. Demystifying clips show how dance routines were put together in the studio (though personally I prefer my musicals still mystifying), while split-screen comparisons present different versions of the same song. Elsewhere there are snippets of the novelty acts MGM occasionally employed in search of a gimmick. The Ross Sisters, close-harmony contortionists who resemble The Andrews Sisters auditioning for Tod Browning's *Freaks*, here receive their overdue footnote in film history.

It's a film destined for video, where it can be productively raided for the treats it contains—Mickey Rooney in drag as Carmen Miranda, the rationality-defying Miranda herself, the spellbinding speed of Ann Miller's tap dancing, and enough Judy to send my Garland-queen subsiding into sighs of bliss. There are educational moments too—Esther Williams' ability to grin radiantly underwater is clearly the inspiration for the entire sport of synchronised swimming, and Joan Crawford in blackface in *Torch Song* (made, for heaven's sake, in 1953) is the most politically incorrect slice of kitsch ever committed to celluloid. The final impressions left by a film like this are a kind of awe, that so much sweat should be expended on so much gossamer, and a deep gratitude, that such all-singing all-dancing feasts are still there for the relishing whenever the end of the century wears us down.

VILLAGE VOICE, 5/10/94, p. 53, J. Hoberman

That's Entertainment! III may be as strenuously feel-good as any sequel in town but it exudes a melancholy that's even more profound than the sight of Gene Kelly as codger. MGM's third trip to the vault has the feel of living hieroglyphics. Shown to best advantage on the big Ziegfeld screen, the fantasies here are doubly vicarious. The audiences that originally feasted on them are a fading presence. When the movie burns, it's with the fire of someone else's youth.

Following the pattern of its now ancient predecessors—*That's Entertainment!* (1974) and *That's Entertainment! Part 2* (1976), both released when the World War II generation still ruled the earth—*TE! III* begins by cannibalizing early talkies for maximum delirium. These used to represent antiquity but now the end is present at the beginning: A long-forgotten prison extravaganza from *The March of Time* (1930)—a score of comely, bare-midriffed inmates executing something called the Lock Step—prepares us for *TE! III*'s penultimate number, Elvis's startlingly comparable "Jailhouse Rock." The footage incarcerated between these two sequences represents the full flowering of socially sanctioned, organized libido.

As in *That's Entertainment! Part 2*, Kelly is the star: His athletic cavorting with Vera-Ellen in *On the Town* (1949) and *Words and Music* (1948), even his mannered prancing in An *American in Paris* (1951), epitomizes the energy and optimism of postwar America. But however enamored of the past, *TE! III* is blithely ahistorical. The movie offers no explanation for Hollywood's wartime interest in Latin America (or rather its market), for example. Segueing from one reverie to the next, *TE! III*'simply presents a pair of late examples of expedient Good Neighborism as pure surreality—Cyd Charisse and Ann Miller competing for Ricardo Montalban's attentions in *The Kissing Bandit* (1948), and Carmen Miranda flanked by two clowns as she hisses "Cha Boom Pa Pa" in *Nancy Goes to Rio* (1949).

Given this vanished, inexplicable world, *TE! III* seems continually amazed at its own existence. What created the golden age? The filmmakers use a split screen to compare the precision of two Fred Astaire takes or match Eleanor Powell tapping with documentary footage revealing the crew's split-second timing in dismantling the sets to allow the camera more intimate access. By celebrating the regimentation inherent in mass entertainment, *TE! III* endorses the notion of Hollywood as glamour factory—although, maximally star-oriented, the movie never mentions a director or even a producer. (The only nonperformer to get a spoken credit is the studio clothier Adrian.)

With their deracinated diesel-powered vaudeville aesthetic, the MGM musicals of the late '30s through early '50s gave the sense of (mainly) white, Protestant America carefully cutting loose. No one doubts that Powell and Astaire could truly tap; bad faith erupts with a number taken from the 1953 *Torch Song*. The grotesque image of middle-aged Joan Crawford swathed in blue glitter lamé and wearing what's euphemistically termed "tropical make-up," backed by similarly sepia-tinted chorus line, and lipsynching a number called "Two Faced Woman," is like a glimpse into a secret life. In this sense, Lena Horne—the black superstar who might have been—functions as the movie's cautious self-reproach. Introduced singing "Where or When," she speaks the unspeakable: "I never felt like I really belonged in Hollywood."

Further analysis of this apartheid would surely detract from our entertainment. *ET! III*, as if to compensate, however, samples a number cut from *Cabin in the Sky* (1943) as too risqué—Horne celebrating various Biblical bad girls while immersed in her bubble bath. Evidently conscious of itself as a repository of American culture, MGM was the only studio to save its outtakes. Thus, on the far side of political correctness, we also have Judy Garland's stridently affectless, near psychotic rendition of "I'm an Indian Too," demonstrating why she was replaced with Betty Hutton on *Annie Get Your Gun* (1949). (Garland appears to better advantage wearing her trademark half tux and singing "Mr. Monotony," a song dropped from the preceding year's *Easter Parade*.)

What was entertainment? An extraterrestrial archeologist might conclude that it has something to do, not only with singing and dancing, but with aqua swimming pools and blood red lipstick, with men and women in uniform, with curvilinear staircases and polished floors, with repetitive forms and undulating hips—not to mention boilerplate cliché. "I loved every minute of it," says Esther Williams of her underwater ballets. "What a time it was, life was simpler then," are Kelly's eerily dissociated parting words. You can believe that or believe your eyes.

Also reviewed in:
CHICAGO TRIBUNE, 7/22/94, Friday/p. C, Michael Wilmington
NEW YORK TIMES, 5/6/94, p. C17, Caryn James
NEW YORKER, 5/16/94, p. 108, Anthony Lane
VARIETY, 4/25-5/1/94, p. 29, Todd McCarthy

THIEVES QUARTET

A Headliner Entertainment Group release of a Mooncoin film. *Executive Producer:* Michael Legamaro. *Producer:* Colleen Griffen. *Director:* Joe Chappelle. *Screenplay:* Joe Chappelle. *Director of Photography:* Greg Littlewood. *Editor:* Randy Bricker and Scott Taradash. *Music:* John Zorn. *Sound:* Byron Smith. *Casting:* Cherie Mann. *Make-up:* Linda Samordral-Smith. *Running time:* 90 minutes. *MPAA Rating:* Not Rated.

CAST: Phillip Van Lear (Jimmy Fuqua); Joe Guastaferro (Art Bledsoe); Michele Cole (Jessica Sutter); James "Ike" Eichling (Mike Quinn); Richard Henzel (Morgan Luce); Jamie Denton (Ray Higgs); Dawn Maxie (Jill Luce).

NEW YORK POST, 6/24/94, p. 38, Larry Worth

Quentin Tarantino catapulted to fame and fortune with his debut feature about criminals falling out after a heist gone bad.

Don't expect the same for writer/director Joe Chappelle: His "Thieves Quartet" is closer to "The Gang That Couldn't Shoot Straight" than to "Reservoir Dogs."

Lensed on a small budget around Chicago and Lake Michigan, it tells of a plan by four small-time crooks to kidnap a wealthy heiress and exact a multimillion-dollar ransom from her powerful father.

But while the abduction goes off smoothly, the scheme begins unraveling when murder enters the picture. Like rats on a sinking ship, it's only a matter of time before the culprits turn on each other.

A growing sense of despair accompanies the goings-on. But it has less to do with Chappelle's mood-creating skills than viewers' realization that the elements aren't clicking.

The neo-film noir's first half hour is painfully slow. And by the time a few twists are revealed, the audience is past caring.

Further hampered by an obtrusive jazz score, Chappelle's plot is too dependent on wild coincidences, a sure sign of either lazy screenwriting or a paucity of credible ideas. And while his refusal to make characters into clear-cut villains or heroes is laudable, they're still of only marginal interest.

Chappelle's strength is in utilizing locales. One can almost feel the wintry gusts whipping off Lake Michigan, and the seamier side of the Windy City comes through loud and clear. In addition, Chappelle uses moderation in making an intrinsically violent story devoid of gratuitous carnage.

Among the cast, Phillip Van Lear commands the most attention as an ex-con wrestling with his conscience. Michele Cole's confused moll and James Eichling's trigger-happy thug also prove arresting. Yet, the gang's fourth member, Joe Guastaferro—in the crucial role of mastermind—is embarrassingly bad.

Unfortunately, such a mix typifies the production. The M.O. for these "Thieves" is a giant step back for every step forward.

NEWSDAY, 6/24/94, Part II/p. B7, Jack Mathews

The best thing that can be said for first-time writer-director Joe Chappelle's "Thieves Quartet" is that it occasionally triggers memories of Carl Franklin's "One False Move," a low budget thriller that knocked the socks off a few critics before heading to the video shelves a couple of years ago.

Why "Thieves Quartet," which takes us along on the kidnap-for-ransom of a Chicago heiress, is pausing at theaters at all is an even greater mystery than it tells.

What made the killers in "One False Move" tolerable was the contrast and inevitable confrontation with the small-town sheriff who brought them down. In "Thieves Quartet," the only cop with dialogue is an amoral hick who seems to drop in from another movie.

The rest of the time we spend with Art (Joe Guastaferro), a bartender and former '60s radical, and the three losers he recruits to help him kidnap a young woman, score a $2 million ransom, then flee to South America. But the best laid plans of lowlifes often go astray, especially when they mostly hate each other from the beginning, and how the stitching comes out of Art's intricate scheme is what "Thieves Quartet" is all about.

Chappelle is not a bad writer, and the setup and execution of the kidnaping and ransom are handled pretty well. The problem is that before, between and after those events, we're stuck with a quartet of unappealing characters and four immensely uninteresting actors.

Besides Art, the combo includes his girlfriend, Jessica (Michele Cole,), whose crude flirtations add sexual tension to the fragile alliance; Mike (James Eichling), a bitter and quick-triggered ex-cop; and Jimmy (Phillip Van Lear), a onetime college basketball star who was caught shaving points in the Game of the Year.

We know Mike and Jimmy are headed for trouble the moment we learn that Mike lost money on the game Jimmy dumped. As far as crooked cops are concerned, there is no statute of limitation for cheaters.

"Thieves Quartet" apparently gets its name from Art's love of jazz, which, judging by the nicely moody score by post-modernist composer-musician John Zorn, is really Chappelle's love of jazz. Spend your money on the sound track.

VILLAGE VOICE, 7/5/94, p. 56, Lawrence Chua

Pulp is a dish best served chilled. But in *Thieves Quartet*, it's so cold it's flavorless. This arduous first film unfolds during wintertime somewhere along the Chicago waterfront. Jimmy (Phillip Van Lear), an African American ex-con and athlete who now washes cars for a living, joins a motley foursome in a mad bid for upward mobility. Masterminding the team is a moody hippie named Art, who, along with his girlfriend Jessica—a surly blond who doesn't cross her legs when she sits down-and nasty, trigger-happy ex-cop Mike, kidnap the mousy daughter of a millionaire. It looks easy enough, but Jessica's pesky hormones, Mike's itchy machismo, Jimmy's sterling conscience, and Art's thinly disguised greed keep on getting in the way.

So too does the film's tepid plot. I'd tell you more about it, but there isn't any. The problem with *Thieves Quartet*, like Art's scheme, is that it isn't complex, just meandering. For veteran con artists and murderers, the players in this ensemble are outrageously predictable. For criminals inspired by poverty, they're inert and colorless. If someone had bothered to flesh them out, they might be characters. Rife with musical allegories (Miles quotes, rare jazz albums used as lures, John Zorn's generic soundtrack), *Thieves Quartet* constantly references jazz's interplay of composition and improvisation. Unfortunately, nothing in this film is elaborate enough to sustain that premise.

The dialogue, though, is not without occasional lapses into charm. Lying in a puddle of blood, one rival bubbles to another, "It should've been you." After another shoot-out, busty Jessica surveys the carnage and screams, "Can you believe this shit?" Now that you mention it, no.

Also reviewed in:
NEW YORK TIMES, 6/24/94, p. C10, Stephen Holden
VARIETY, 6/27-7/3/94, p. 86, Steven Gaydos

THIRTY TWO SHORT FILMS ABOUT GLENN GOULD

A Samuel Goldwyn Company release of a Rhombus Media Inc production with the participation of Telefilm Canada/Ontario Film Development Corporation in association with Canadian Broadcasting Corporation/Société Radio-Canada/NOS-Television/RTP-Portugal/OY Yielsradio AB (YLE)/The National Film Board of Canada/Glenn Gould Limited. *Executive Producer:* Dennis Murphy. *Producer:* Niv Fichman, Larry Weinstein, Barbara Willis Sweete, and Michael Allder. *Director:* François Girard. *Screenplay:* François Girard, Don McKellar and Nick McKinney. *Director of Photography:* Alain Dostie. *Editor:* Gaétan Huot. *Sound:* Stuart French, Daniel Masse, and Gérard Dacquay. *Sound Editor:* Jane Tattersall and John D. Smith. *Casting:* Deirdre Bowen. *Set Decorator:* Alexa Anthony. *Set Dresser:* Ian Nothnagel.

Costumes: Linda Muir. *Make-up:* Kathryn Casault. *Running time:* 94 minutes. *MPAA Rating:* Not Rated.

CAST: Colm Feore (Glenn Gould); Derek Keurvorst (Gould's Father); Katya Ladan (Gould's Mother); Devon Anderson (Glenn, age 3); Joshua Greenblatt (Glenn, age 8); Sean Ryan (Glenn, age 12); Kate Hennig (Chambermaid); Sean Doyle (Porter); Sharon Bernbaum (Female Guide); Don McKellar (Concert Promoter); David Hughes (Stagehand); Carlo D. Rota (CBS Producer); Peter Millard (CBS Engineer); John Dolan (CBS Assistant Engineer); Allegra Fulton (Waitress); Gerry Quigley (Music Critic); Gale Garnett (Journalist); David Young (Writer); James Kidnie (Photographer); Maia Filar (Girl); Marina Anderson (Mother); Marie Josée Gauthier (Professor); Nick McKinney (Interpreter); Moynan King (Questioning Woman); Knowlton Nash (V.O. Announcer); Michael Kopsa and Len Doncheff (Brokers); Ian D. Clark (Phillip Brennan); David Clement (Desmond); Jimmy Loftus and Frank Canino (Waiters).

CHRISTIAN SCIENCE MONITOR, 4/14/94, p. 14, David Sterritt

The title of "Thirty-Two Short Films About Glenn Gould" is a little misleading since this is actually a single movie divided into 32 parts.

It's an uneven picture, and at times an eccentric one. But these qualities are fully in keeping with Gould himself, whose life and work oscillated between the brilliant and the ornery, often combining the two in ways that puzzled even his most steadfast admirers.

Not quite fiction and not quite documentary, the movie is as unpredictable as its subject: the most fascinating pianist—and perhaps the most fascinating musician of any kind—to achieve prominence during the past several decades. In all, it's the most engrossing arts-related film in a very long time.

"Thirty-Two Short Films About Glenn Gould" was directed by Canadian filmmaker François Girard, and stars actor Colm Feore as the great pianist. The movie's design is borrowed from J.S. Bach's magnificent Goldberg Variations, in which 30 interrelated episodes are juxtaposed with an aria that introduces and concludes the work.

This aria is echoed in the movie by two leisurely scenes of Gould visiting the snow-covered reaches of the Canadian Arctic, which exercised a strong hold on his imagination.

Between these vignettes are 30 separate scenes covering many key issues in Gould's career, from his unconventional living habits to his still-debated decision to leave the concert stage at the peak of his career.

While many of the episodes are engaging and even amusing, others touch on the pianist's dark side, including the overuse of prescription drugs that may have contributed to his untimely death in 1982.

One section of the movie is labeled "Questions With No Answers," raising such unresolved matters as Gould's failure to write much music of his own, despite his stated wish to become an active composer, and his seemingly inconsistent views on technical perfection in the recording studio—where he labored to create ideal performances through editing techniques, yet put up with imperfect pianos and his own irksome tendency to hum along as he played.

An additional "question with no answer" that occurs to me is whether Gould would have liked this movie. I suspect the answer is both yes and no.

On the positive side, Gould would surely have applauded the film's multifaceted structure, which resembles the segmentation of a musical suite (a form he greatly loved) rather than the welded-together unity of a sonata movement. He would also have liked the movie's way of combining words, images, and music, weaving them together while allowing each a full measure of individual dignity and importance.

What might have bothered Gould about the movie is its continual focus on him as a musical superstar. One of his chief reasons for abandoning the recital stage was a conviction that artists can labor more effectively in private, away from a public that often cares less about musical exaltation than bout spotting flaws in performances.

On the other hand, Gould wasn't exactly camera shy, and he participated in many public activities—including a long list of recording sessions—while continuing to make his voice heard through writing and radio broadcasting. While he might have found this film too revealing for comfort, it's possible that he would have secretly enjoyed all the attention.

Written by director Girard and Don McKellar, the movie takes many of its verbal ingredients from Gould's own articles and statements, Also included are spontaneous interviews with people who knew the pianists well as staged "interviews" with Gould associates played by actors. A good deal of Gould's recorded music graces the sound track, and one of his spoken-word recordings (a portion of "The Idea of North," made for Canadian radio) superbly illustrates his theories about counterpoint and the speaking voice.

"Thirty-Two Short Films About Glenn Gould" has some serious shortcomings. For one thing, it's often hard to distinguish the performances by actors and actresses from appearances by "real people" sharing first-hard experiences about the pianist's life.

It's also unfortunate that the real Gould makes no appearance beyond a still photo at the very end—although this is an understandable decision, since such an appearance might have interfered with the credibility of Feore's acting in the title role.

These problems aside, "Thirty-Two Short Films About Glenn Gould" is a treat for music-lovers and a wonderful introduction to Gould for those who haven't yet encountered his remarkable career.

LOS ANGELES TIMES, 4/14/94, Calendar/p. 4, Kenneth Turan

Everything that is distinctive and irresistible about "Thirty Two Short Films About Glenn Gould"—its audacity, its nervy playfulness, how smart and confident a motion picture it is—comes through from its first scene.

It's a deceptive episode, simple yet exhilarating. The camera is motionless, fixed on a frozen landscape, dazzling and empty. Then a figure appears at the far distance, walking toward us but taking his own time about it. The closer he gets, and it takes nearly two minutes (an eternity in film terms) for him to arrive, the more aware we become of the rising music in the background, the liquid, intoxicating piano playing of the man himself, Glenn Gould.

A consummate musician who shocked the concert world by abandoning live performance for recordings when he was only 32 and who'd given layers of new meanings to the concept of the eccentric virtuoso by the time he died from a stroke at age 50 in 1982, Gould was too original a figure to fit into a conventional filmed bio, and Canadian director François Girard, who co-wrote the screenplay with Don McKellar, has not even attempted to give him one.

Instead, Girard has orchestrated (and that really does seem to be the best word) a film infused with its subject's singular spirit. A window into what it might be like to be a genius that is as off-center and uncompromising as the man himself, this is that rare piece of work that not only knows exactly what it wants to do but also just how to go about doing it.

The concept is to assemble a portrait of Gould as if it were a mosaic, combining unrelated facets of his life, personality and career. That there are 32 of these is a nod to Bach's Goldberg Variations, Gould's debut recording and the music behind that opening scene. The episodes range in length from less than a minute to more than 10, each one self-contained and carefully set off from the others with its own on-screen title.

If this sounds schematic, the reality is the opposite. For after "Lake Simcoe," which straightforwardly deals with Gould's sheltered youth as a prodigy sure of his future by age 5, the filmmakers have been quite thoughtful about the points they want to make about Gould and lively and inventive in how they've illustrated them.

To indicate his interests outside of music, for instance, there is a sly comic sequence called "The Tip" showing Gould manipulating the stock market, plus an excerpt from "The Idea of North," a dizzying sound collage documentary made for radio. To show how others felt about him and his numerous peculiarities, real-life friends are interviewed, while actors playing journalists demonstrate the kind of inanities the man who treasured solitude had to put up with.

First and finally, though, there is always the music, the center of Gould's life. His hypnotic playing of everything from Bach to Schoenberg hovers in the background of about three-quarters of the sequences, and the film casually utilizes an impressive variety of ways to convey the music in visual terms, most memorably in "CD 318," where we are taken inside Gould's favorite instrument to see exactly how its sounds are made.

It is in the showcasing of the passion with which Gould approached music that "Thirty Two Short Films" surpasses itself. In sequences like "Hamburg," where the pianist, loping around a hotel room like Groucho Marx, insists that a chamber maid share his pleasure in his latest recording, to "Passion According to Gould," where he goes into a pure trance at the caress of his own music, the often-cliched joy of creation has rarely been so well and beautifully put on screen.

For a film this ambitious to be successful, the execution must match the ideas, and it does. Alain Dostie's measured, eloquent camera work provides crystalline images that are often hypnotic, and the Girard-McKellar script, which makes extensive use of ironic voice-over adapted from Gould's own words, conveys the wry and acerbic sensibility of a man who felt "the ideal audience-to-artist relationship is a one-to-zero relationship,"

Not every actor can pull off a character like Gould, simultaneously self-assured and erratic, and "Thirty Two Short Films" would be difficult to imagine without Colm Feore, a mainstay of Canada's Stratford Shakespeare Festival, in the title role. In addition to a confident and insinuating voice, Feore has the passionate spirit essential to playing Gould, a spectral wraith as transfixed by the sounds he created as the actor is by the opportunity to convey that obsession.

In the end, the great thing about "Thirty Two Short Films About Glenn Gould" is that rather than creating a desire to meet this formidable individual, it makes you feel as if in some way you actually had. "Gould was inexplicably gifted," biographer Otto Friedrich wrote, "with a phenomenal natural talent for playing the piano." Exactly what that means is what this film is so marvelous at conveying.

NEW STATESMAN & SOCIETY, 6/17/94, p. 33, Jonathan Romney

François Girard's film *Thirty Two Short Films About Glenn Gould* has a more challenging project—to *de*-represent the great Canadian pianist, to skirt around him altogether.

Girard's film often appears unashamedly awestruck about its subject, dizzy about the idea of enigma. But then part of its insight is to accept cliché as part of myth. When the young Gould's parents hush respectively as the little maestro listens to Wagner; or Gould reveals his departure from the concert stage in an autograph to a retiring stagehand, the effect could make us cringe, if they weren't simply individual scenes from a set of representations of Gould's life.

Basing his structure on Bach's *Goldberg Variations*, Girard gives us 32 pictures of his subject from different angles. They are cigarette cards to Keiller's postcards. Some depict clichés, some theorise, some are all but blank, but, around the central absence of the "real" Gould, a composite adds up.

Just as the idea of London is bigger than the city limits, the idea of Gould takes in the notions of "myth", "enigma", "genius", along with more basic facts—such as the fact that he also played the piano. The film's brilliant stroke is never to show Gould playing the piano at all, although we hear his recordings throughout. His life at the keyboard becomes the film's centre by virtue of not being there.

Girard at once pays homage to and deconstructs the myth of the holy body and soul of the artist by making Gould disappear. With an impersonation of wonderful cerebral archness by Colm Feore, Gould's *real* body can be represented *in absentia* only through X-ray footage of a pianist at work, and beautiful, luminous close-ups of the millions of pills he used to take.

Not being there was the great controversial property of Gould's life. He revolutionized the idea of classical recording by withdrawing from the concert stage and devoting himself to the studio as a medium for the pursuit of some morally charged notion of truth—not just in music but in understanding of the world and himself. His radio documentaries, such as the tissue of voices, *The Idea of North*, and a mannered, ironic interview with himself, deal with an idea of voices in a void, talking without the certainty of being heard. Gould asks himself why he gave up concerts. The reason: rather than the one-to-one relationship that's supposed to underlie performance (and all discourse, for that matter). Gould is after a one-to-zero relationship. "The artist," he says, "should operate in secret."

Hence the idea of Gould as a living radio, a remarkably sensitive machine for transmitting and receiving messages in the dark. He would phone his friends with marathon talking jags regardless of whether or not they stayed awake. Conversely, another section of the film comprises a set of questions posed by interviewers, but no replies—just a Bach prelude playing on.

A man whom Gould once interviewed talks about Gould "conducting" him as he spoke; a scene in a diner shows Gould, all ears, composing a fugue out of the voices around him. After Gould's death, the Voyager space probe shot his recording of a Bach prelude into space—the ultimate example of technology supporting his voice's transmission to distant unknown ears, or to none at all.

The film's iconic image has Feore as Gould huddled up against the wind in a vast, empty icefield, talking to a disembodied voice about his radio work on the notion of isolation. He walks out of the void at the beginning of the film, and back into it at the end. It's the one touch where Girard whole-heartedly embraces romantic metaphor.

At the start, it's as if the film is undertaking to thaw the Glenn Gould myth out of cold storage. At the end, after the Voyager footage, we see Gould walking out to the edge of his own galaxy, to the chilly deep space of his own posterity. It's a powerful image but there's nothing sentimental about it; the picture simply recedes, that's all. It reminds us that after all, we don't know, can't know Glenn Gould, any more than we can know any celebrity; but we *do* know 32 things about him, to add up as best we can.

NEW YORK, 4/25/94, p. 89, David Denby

During a New York Philharmonic concert in the early sixties, I watched the great Canadian pianist Glenn Gould fiddle with his seat endlessly and lean back and wave his arms in the air in gestures that probably sent the orchestra into silent convulsions. Gould, the great eccentric among modern virtuosos, disliked the heroic arc of the romantic piano concertos and quickly gave up playing the big works. He preferred short solo pieces, or collections of pieces (like Bach's *Goldberg Variations*). By 1964, he had given up playing in public altogether, even in solo recitals, retiring to the studio, where the microphone perfectly captured his strengths—the extraordinary rhythmic control, the articulation and weighting of every note, even at breakneck speeds.

In the opening sequence of *Thirty Two Short Films About Glenn Gould*, a Canadian *hommage* to the great genius/crank, we see an actor (Colm Feore) walking across an empty ice field. Photographed from a great distance, the figure appears to be moving both toward and away from the camera at the same time. An appropriately ambiguous evocation of Gould: After retiring, he became one of the most publicly communicative recluses in the history of art. He was there; he wasn't there. Always shy and haughty, a neurotic who wrapped himself in layers of clothing and hated being touched, Gould would not venture into any situation where the public could approach him. At the same time, he made dozens of records, conducted radio interviews, wrote copiously, and spoke to many persons at length on the telephone.

Who knows what drove him out of the concert hall? Gould had grand theories about destroying the romantic ego of the virtuoso and so on, but the reasons for his exit could have been entirely banal—he hated the pressure and social demands. François Girard, who directed the film (and wrote it with Don McKellar), takes an open-ended, even quizzical, attitude toward Gould. In tune with its subject, the movie is also shy, nervous, and haughty, a kaleidoscopic, mildly avant-gardist enterprise that mixes styles and points of view. There are acted-out sections featuring Feore in solipsistic glory; a variety of divertissements; some actual, newly filmed interviews with Gould's acquaintances or fellow musicians. There is much Bach, Beethoven, and Schoenberg on the soundtrack in dazzling performance.

Does the movie add up? No, it doesn't, but then Gould didn't either. As an aesthetic temperament, he was strikingly incoherent—a self-absorbed individualist who wanted to end egotism in music. The movie is faithful to Gould's contradictions without risking the indiscretion of an interpretation.

NEW YORK POST, 4/14/94, p. 40, Shirley Fleming

The Canadian pianist Glenn Gould, one of the most remarkable keyboard artists of our time, was famous not only for his illuminating and idiosyncratic performances of Bach (among much else) but for his glaring eccentricities.

They included a phobia about cold (he wore scarfs and gloves in the summertime); a yearning for solitude, offset by compulsive telephoning to friends at all hours of the night; intense hypochondria supported by mountainous quantities of pills; and the decision in his early 30s to retire from the concert stage and play only for recordings.

He ate quantities of ketchup, and drove his Lincoln Continental at perilous speeds. He could talk incessantly, in convoluted and edgy fashion, about everything from the stock market to immortality. He died in 1982 at the age of 50.

It is all captured vividly in "Thirty-two Short Films About Glenn Gould," a prize-winning semi-documentary from Canada that uses actors as well as interviews with those who knew him well, the violinist Yehudi Menuhin among them.

The film's segments, paralleling the 32 sections of Bach's "Goldberg Variations" with which Gould was closely identified, each focus on a single facet of an extremely complex man. Most of the sound track is drawn from recordings by Gould himself.

The role of the pianist is taken by Colm Feore, who does not really look like Gould but does seem to capture the loose-limbed movement, the intensity, and the interior quality of the man.

The photography, directed by Alain Dostie, is compellingly beautiful, capturing the snowy sweep of Northern Canada that so fascinated Gould as well as the dark-night qualities that seemed to possess him.

The tension of the film builds as it moves from one apparently isolated instance to the next, finally involving us deeply in the pianist's odd life.

An associate once said of Gould, "This wasn't ever a person who was at peace, even troubled peace." This beautiful and imaginative portrait makes that very clear.

NEWSWEEK, 4/25/94, p. 62, David Ansen

How does one make a movie about the life of someone as brilliant, solitary and *inward* as the great Canadian pianist Glenn Gould? It's not the easiest task to dramatize a man whose most sustained human contacts, as he grew ever more reclusive, were over the telephone. For this singular man, Québécois director François Girard has fashioned a singular solution called, quite accurately, "Thirty Two Short Films About Glenn Gould." With his co-writer Don McKellar, he has structured his film after Bach's "Goldberg Variations" (the piece that brought Gould his first fame), inventing 32 brief, often playful and sometimes abstract variations on Gould's life, accompanied by Gould performances of Bach, Beethoven, Hindemith, Sibelius and a blast of Wagner's "Liebestod."

Freed from conventional biographical narrative, Girard's elegant, coolly funny movie employs myriad techniques: animation by Norman McLaren; documentary interviews with colleagues, family and acquaintances; X-ray photography (in a segment describing the massive amounts of pills the hypochondriacal Gould would consume in a day); a fanciful enactment of Gould interviewing himself. Colm Feore, the Canadian stage actor who plays the intensely self-involved Gould, mesmerizes without ever raising his voice. Gould, who gave up concert appearances at the age of 31, withdrawing into the heady solitude of the recording studio, believed in the anonymity of the artist. Like other famous recluses (Salinger comes to mind), his withdrawal only fed the cult of his personality. By the time of his death, in 1982 at the age of 50, he had become an international legend; a Gould performance of Bach was sent into space on both the Voyager satellites.

The movie, and Feore's quietly obsessive performance, is a demonstration of the social power of the man who walks away from the world (Gould, who produced a radio documentary on "The Idea of North," longed to live a winter above the Arctic Circle). He lived his life in an aural universe, and in one fine vignette in a truck-stop café, we hear the world through Gould's ears as he tunes in and out of conversations, background noises, Petula Clark's "Downtown" on the radio. His was a busy solitude, teeming with intellect; Girard refuses the easy pathos of equating isolation with loneliness. Feore's wry Gould wears a half smile of self-amusement. This crisply captivating portrait of the artist finds an unconventional style to match Gould's own: ascetic, speculative, passionately detached. Only a very unusual film about a famous pianist would refuse to show even one scene where Feore sits at a piano and plays.

SIGHT AND SOUND, 7/94, p. 55, Mark Sinker

The film is based on the life of Canadian concert pianist, writer and enigma Glenn Gould, who died in 1982. It is programmed as 32 brief sections, to mirror the structure of Bach's *Goldberg Variations*, the CBS recording that made Gould famous in the mid-50s: each section is accompanied by a passage or movement from one of the many recordings he made. These include dramatised scenes from Gould's life—his childhood; his key concerts, including the dramatic and controversial retirement from concert-playing in the early 60s, startling the classical music industry; his pioneering documentary work for Canadian radio; his obsessive need to live his life over the telephone, rather than face to face; the way he dressed; his alarming prescription-drug regimen; his intimations of his early death at 50; his worries that he would not be remembered; and, in the closing scene, the fact that the Voyager probe, launched into space to greet other civilisations that might be there, carried among other artefacts Gould's recording of Bach's *Prelude in D Minor*. The film includes excerpts from some of Gould's near-avant-garde radio documentary work, particularly the legendary *The Idea Of North*, and recreates excerpts from several of the face-to-face and phone interviews he gave; it also includes interviews with friends, relatives, colleagues and acquaintances from Yehudi Menuhin to Megan Smith, a chambermaid.

From the Canada of the 50s arrived a young pianist of startling talent, who was also that rarest of monsters in music performance, classical or otherwise—the unsentimental intellectual. His portrait, in François Girard's hands, is elegaic, austere and amused: Canadian, you might almost say, in its cool, intelligent, elegant nonconformity. It fits the memory peoplt seem to have of Gould, and the fascination with his unselfish self-absorption, his wayward intellectual clarity, his easy, slightly fussy open-mindedness.

The intention is not to provide a linear narrative, nor to act out Gould's performances—he never touches a piano on-screen—but rather to portray facets of the character and inner life of this intensely private performer, to draw out the philosophical and personal reasons which shaped his life-choices. Girard's film catches Gould's love of solitude—there are images of a thickly-wrapped distant figure, a lost dot on a wide icefield, or alone before a show, warming his forearms in a basin of water, next to a shelf-full of bottles of coloured pills. It catches the *physics* of piano-playing—striking X-ray motion footage of a pianist playing, or just the symmetrical patterns of the hammers falling, as they play Bach. It also catches a flavour of the naive and parochial isolation of the high-culture industry of the 50s and early 60s, the anachronistic pre-Beatles stolidity of a world which is, without realising it, wearing itself to nothing, running ever more frantically on the spot. Gould, highly intelligent, almost insanely self-protective, got out before he was harmed, mentally or physically, by the touring schedules the industry was beginning to demand in order to satisfy audiences swelled ever larger by records and radio; he retired to a twilight world where he could pursue the perfection of studio performance.

What the film can't catch, however, is the symbolic explosiveness of this career decision, and the degree to which he hoped his retirement would stand as a bloody indictment of the classical music industry. This is perhaps inevitable: film operates so entirely in the realm of mechanical reproduction that it can hardly make sense of the belief that live performance is intrinsically better, however botched, than a studio-edited collage of inspired fragments. It was this belief that Gould refused to accept, and that galvanised him into his unprecedented decision. He took it for moral rather than musical reasons, as he put it in his famous interview—erudite, witty, and ever so faintly pompous—with himself, here recreated. In Britain, Gould's cachet has never been that great (nor was that of his countryman and fellow media-visionary Marshall McLuhan): he rocks the boat too much, reveals the workings too openly. His eccentricities—the way he hummed while playing, the way he dressed—were always carefully pulled out of context by critics, in order to amuse and thus to discredit. The mind behind them—to a British 'serious' music public profoundly suspicious of mind—was not to be engaged with.

This was a man—Malcolm McLaren and John Lydon in one well-spoken virtuoso body—with outrageously aggressive attitudes, theoretically backed up, towards the canon, He hated Mozart, for example, while some of his interpretations of standard repertoire drew furious criticism. He took the line that with ever more conventional versions available, it was his duty to find other ways to express a composer's ideas; to challenge casual routine.

The film also omits portrayal of Gould's polite but firm tantrums over bad pianos, bad acoustics, bad audiences. His obsession with Petula Clark was wide-eyed fan-boy stuff, but bolstered by his fascination by the tricks of studio technology, which were only permitted on the other side of the tracks. This obsession is coded in the film's truck-stop scene as background music, and calmly over-ridden when the idea for one of his polyphonic radio compositions for voice comes to him: the important edges out the trivial, but such judgements are the film-maker's, not Gould's. The saintly Yehudi Menuhin is interviewed, rebutting the Gould thesis, questioning the idea that 'morality' came into it. He all but calls it a big fuss over nothing; "things aren't perfect—but that's life," is his mild, wounding reproof.

Gould's point was that classicism's conventions are defended in the name of a Platonic perfection that they have usually been instrumental in bartering away; he countered them by ferocious application to the Platonic. He refused to put up with boredoms and discomforts to mollify a genteel know-nothingism he thought barbaric. *Thirty Two Short Films* flourishes its episodic nature, and makes it work, charmingly enough. But out of respect for the music—rare enough, to be sure—Girard has picked a form which sells Gould's deepest philosophies short. The irony is that to pass on the true, paradoxical force of Gould's ideas, a film with more single-minded narrative flow is probably needed. That might be a better way to encapsulate the iconoclast who can say, so guilelessly, halfway through this film, "I just don't like the sound of pianos that much."

TIME, 4/18/94, p. 73, Richard Schickel

If celebrity—its getting, having and spending—is the great theme of late 20th century life, then reclusivity is surely its most haunting variation. To be known for your unknowability, or anyway your elusiveness, is a possibly unintentional yet perversely elegant strategy for drawing attention to yourself, as Garbo and J.D. Salinger have demonstrated.

But they had to stop performing and publishing to pull it off, Glenn Gould, the genius-struck Canadian concert pianist, could have his cake and eat it too. He quit making public appearances in 1964, but he never stopped recording—and obsessively re-recording to achieve the perfect performance—and reports of his increasingly curious ways continued to flourish until his death in 1982. And beyond. The latest account of the pianist's eccentricities is *Thirty Two Short Films about Glenn Gould.* A quasi-documentary, it alternates sympathetic eyewitness accounts of his behavior with fact-based, fictionalized fragments of his life, in which actor Colm Feore displays a fine touch of madness.

Director and co-screenwriter François Girard's allusive approach suits a subject who loathed grandiosity. A portrait emerges of one of those functioning paranoids—such disparate figures as Bobby Fischer and John McEnroe come to mind—who see all around them a conspiracy to rob their art of its purity. The sounds of sucking, the grindings of the publicity machine—they drown out the high, clear notes such figures strive so hard to strike and, in Gould's case, the genius of the composers he was serving. Doubtless we now have a chemical to treat what ailed him. But there is something exemplary in his withdrawal, something touching about this man who eventually haunted truck stops trying to understand the rhythms of ordinary life, and placed all-night phone calls to friends trying to make them understand his extraordinary one.

VILLAGE VOICE, 4/19/94, p. 54, Georgia Brown

Glenn Gould's attitude toward the Beatles is refreshing. He once wrote an article comparing them unfavorably with Petula Clark. But then Gould admitted that his relation to the pop scene was rather distant, [see Brown's review of *Backbeat*].

Some there are who might not think Gould a natural subject for a film, but they wouldn't be Canadians. In Canada, the pianist came as close as one could come to being the national saint. François Girard told *Filmmaker* magazine that it was only because he was from Montreal that he had the "distance" to jump right in; filmmakers from Toronto, Gould's hometown, were paralyzed by reverence. Not surprisingly, Girard's *Thirty Two Short Films About Glenn Gould* won four Canadian Genies (Oscars), including Best Picture and Best Director.

Girard structures his biographical fantasy after Bach's *Goldberg Variations,* which Gould first recorded at 22—a recording that reputedly changed people's lives and created a fervent, unceasingly loyal cult. (Others, generations later, began to soak up Gould after reading *The Silence of the Lambs* and wondering why Hannibal Lecter elects to skin two jailers while listening to the recording. Had he lived so long, Gould—a vegetarian who called himself the Last Puritan and left half his estate to the ASPCA—would probably have been repelled.)

Anyway, following *The Goldberg Variations*, Girard divides the film into 32 sections, or "short films," each cleverly timed to a single Gould piano piece—or, in one instance, to Petula's "Downtown." Chronological episodes with actors, interviews with close acquaintances, and other, more abstract tableaux take us through the pianist's life, beginning with the prodigy child on his mother's lap, to his death, a few days after his 50th birthday, in 1982.

Framing the film are visions of Gould (played by the rakish Colm Feore) as a lone figure walking across a snow-covered beach toward the camera, and at the end, walking out into the white void. The expanse of snow looks for a moment like an Arctic tundra, an image that connects with *The Idea of North*, Gould's creative radio documentary examining the effects of living cut off in the arctic. This man who lived conspicuously alone and, even in summer, bundled up in multiple coats, gloves, and scarves had a lifelong fascination with both the cold and the solitude of the far north.

Thirty Two Short Films may look unorthodox to some but it's fairly predictable within documentary traditions (recent bio-pics such as Errol Morris's *A Brief History of Time*, about Stephen Hawking, or Derek Jarman's *Wittgenstein* have much more personality). Here the content of the fictional segments is taken from various biographical sources, and although the treatment is sometimes coy, sometimes fey, the material itself is usually interesting.

Since Gould literally had no private life to speak of, the drama here is almost entirely interior. The one notable event in his life was his sudden retirement from the concert stage at age 31. Beyond this, film episodes revolve around Gould's hypochondria and pill popping, his stock speculating, long late-night phone calls, and compulsive driving (though the film doesn't mention that he named two cars Lance and Longfellow). There're also allusions to Gould's exquisite physical sensitivity, his extraordinary hearing, as well as his startling dishevelment (though Feore, I'm afraid, always manages to look dashing). The greatest pleasure, of course, comes from the soundtrack, Gould's splendid, often ecstatic interpretations of Schoenberg, Sibelius, Hindemith, and especially Bach.

By the way, the half of Gould's estate not left to the Toronto Humane Society went to the Salvation Army, another haven in a heartless world. The act of a haunted, humble man.

Also reviewed in:
CHICAGO TRIBUNE, 4/29/94, Friday/p. C, Johanna Steinmetz
NATION, 5/2/94, p. 606, Stuart Klawans
NEW REPUBLIC, 4/25/94, p. 26, Stanley Kauffmann
NEW YORK TIMES, 4/14/94, p. C15, Janet Maslin
NEW YORKER, 4/18/94, p. 104, Anthony Lane
VARIETY, 9/27/93, p. 39, Leonard Klady
WASHINGTON POST, 5/13/94, p. D6, Desson Howe

3 NINJAS KICK BACK

A TriStar Pictures release of a Sheen production in association with Ben-Ami/Leeds Productions. *Executive Producer:* Simon Sheen and Yoram Ben-Ami. *Producer:* James Kang, Martha Chang, and Arthur Leeds. *Director:* Charles T. Kanganis. *Screenplay:* Mark Saltzman. *Based on a Screenplay by:*: Simon Sheen. *Director of Photography:* Christopher Faloona. *Editor:* Jeffrey Reiner. *Music:* Richard Marvin. *Sound:* Clifford Gynn and (music) Joel Iwataki. *Sound Editor:* Edward Carr. *Casting:* Yoshiyuki Maejima, Waya Yokoe, and Kazumi Isao. *Production Designer:* Hiroyuki Takatsu and Gregory Martin. *Art Director:* Scott Meehan. *Set Dresser:* Karin McGaughey. *Special Effects:* Larry Roberts and Richard Albain. *Costumes:* Takeshi Yamazaki and Miye Matsumoto. *Make-up:* Kiyomi Hirose. *Stunt Coordinator:* Al Jones. *Running time:* 99 minutes. *MPAA Rating:* PG.

CAST: Victor Wong (Grandpa); Max Elliott Slade (Colt); Sean Fox (Rocky); Evan Bonifant (Tum Tum); Caroline Junko King (Miyo); Dustin Nguyen (Glam); Alan McRae (Sam); Margarita Franco (Jessica); Jason Schombing (Vinnie); Angeloi Tiffe (Slam); Sab Shimono (Koga); Don Stark (Umpire); Kellye Nakahara-Wallett (Nurse Hino); Scott Caudill (Darren); Tommy Clark (Keith); Jeremy Linson (Evan); Brian Wagner (Gerald); Maital Sabban (Lisa DiMarino); Gino Dentie (Night Club Manager); Marcus Gaimatti (Announcer); Jill Ito (Ticket Clerk); Michael Paciorek (First Base Umpire); Donna-Marie Recco (Hot Dog Vendor); Joey Travolta (Mustangs Coach); Robert Miano (Shuttle Driver); Glen Chin (Nurse Shibuya); Killer Khan (Ishikawa); Shiao-Hu Tso (Young Mori); Kazuaki Naruse (Young Koga); Syunichiro Yunoki (Young Grand Master); Hachiro Yamauchi (Ninja Master); Toshiyo Matsunaga (Miyo's Mother); Yoshiko Kamiya (Lady in Limousine); Katsumi Honda (Chauffeur); Syogo Nakajima (Jail Guard); Kyoji Kamui and Seigen Nakayama (Koga's Henchmen); Naoki Fujii (Mugger); Takao Ito and Kensuke Goto (Ninja Masters); Yousyu Kondo and Takeshi Yamamoto (Yakusas); Masaki Kiryu, Hideki Chiba, Morihito Yagami, and Kazuya Matsui (Ninjas).

LOS ANGELES TIMES, 5/6/94, Calendar/p. 18, Kevin Thomas

"3 Ninjas Kick Back" is just as lively and engaging as the 1992 original. Writer Mark Saltzman and director Charles T. Kanganis, neither of which were involved in the earlier film, do a fine job of keeping things happening and moving in an easy yet highly kinetic fashion. Although aimed at children, this smart-looking TriStar release is actually more inventive and better-paced than many a comedy for adults.

The sly and ingratiating Victor Wong is back as the Japanese American martial arts whiz who coaches his three grandsons, Rocky (Sean Fox), Colt (Max Elliott Slade, the only actor to reprise his role as one of the brothers) and Tum Tum (Evan Bonifant) in the art and philosophy of self-defense: When we catch up with them, however, they find their passion for baseball vying with their love of martial arts to the extent that they would rather remain home for the upcoming big game when their grandfather goes off to Japan to present a ceremonial dagger he himself had won 50 years earlier to the winner of a ninja tournament.

The dagger is no ordinary weapon, and the man (Sab Shimono), now a shady business tycoon, defeated by Wong half a century ago, covets it mightily because legend has it that the dagger can open the door to a cave of gold hidden beneath an ancient castle. Lending comic relief are Shimono's wanna-be heavy-metal rocker nephew (Dustin Nguyen) and his equally inept cohorts (Jason Schombing, Angelo Tiffe) struggling to get their hands on the dagger.

Like its predecessor, this film shows a genuine concern for values as well as action with its emphasis on discipline, integrity and fair play, and it even dares to suggest that it's possible for a girl (Caroline Junko King) to be better at martial arts than a boy. And when the boys' busy father (Alan McRae), an FBI agent, wonders why his sons respond to their grandfather more than they do to him, his wife (Margarita Franco) gently points out that her father listens to what they have to say.

NEW YORK POST, 5/6/94, p. 39, Larry Worth

At one point in "Three Ninjas Kick Back," of the titular imps looks into the camera and asks: "Don't you just hate us?"

In a word, yes.

"Three Ninjas," the 1992 comedy about a trio of youngsters tutored by their grandfather in the martial arts, was bad enough. Now along comes a sequel which is 25 percent "Ninja" retread, 25 percent "Home Alone," 25 percent "Sandlot" and 25 percent "Goonies." In other words, 100 percent fiasco.

The boys—teen-aged Rocky and Colt and supposedly precious Tum Tum, 8—still get a kick out of twisting limbs the Eastern way. But they're equally caught up, respectively, by females, fights and food.

Priorities are put in order during a visit to Grampa's, when he shows them a dagger which doubles as the key to a legendary cave of gold. Faster than you can swing a nunchuk, three heavy-metal stooges are attacking the house to return the prize to Grampa's rival in Japan.

Naturally, the boys' jury-rigged contraptions—straight from the Macaulay Culkin school of sadism—have the creeps fleeing for their lives. But not for long.

They pursue Gramps and the kids until everybody ends up in the labyrinthian tunnels leading to the treasure trove. But the yawns don't stop there.

Sundry sub-plots concern a ninja championship, the introduction of a young female fighter and a baseball tourney in which the competitors sport—gasp—rat tails and earrings (clearly identifying them as villains).

Thanks to screenwriter Mark Saltzman, the scenes boil down to two unappetizing flavors: kids outsmarting adults or battling anything with a raised arm that shouts "aiiiieeee."

Director Charles T. Kanganis occasionally uses fast-action photography for comic effect. Too bad he didn't employ it during his bathroom humor and groin jokes. Ironically, the film's only real laugh is courtesy of an "earthquake," created by jiggling the camera.

Little wonder that only one of the original teen-age mutant wannabes—Max Elliott Slade as Colt—returned for the saga's continuation. But new cohorts Sean Fox and Evan Bonifant are interchangeable with the roles' former no-talents. Sadly, veteran trouper Victor Wong's work as Grampa slides into the same black hole.

Worst of all, yet another sequel is clearly threatened. One can only hope it's about a psychotic sumo wrestler intent on squashing "Three Ninjas."

NEWSDAY, 5/6/94, Part II/p. B9, Steve Parks

"3 Ninjas Kick Back" has nothing to do with bribery—though some parents regard kid-movie sequels as a form of extortion. But if your kids demand to see this one, bribe a sitter to take them in your place.

Although my 8-year-old was mostly off the edge of his seat—bouncing on his toes and squealing over each whirling-dervish fight scene—there's little entertainment here for anyone over age 11. Tops.

To get an idea of the comic sophistication in this sequel to "3 Ninjas," imagine a beefy kid in a Little League uniform who announces—nonverbally—ashe steps into the batter's box that he's had too many beans with his burritos. Never mind that no one in this film could pronounce the word flatulence. That doesn't stop them from carrying the joke even further—and to much less effect—than did Mel Brooks in "Blazing Saddles." But it's the karate role models, not the comedians, who drive the implausible action of "3 Ninjas Kick Back," shot on location in Japan. This time, girls have their own champion to root for. The oldest of the "3 Ninjas," handsome Rocky (Sean Fox) falls in puppy love with his demur Japanese friend and martial artist, Miyo (Caroline Junko King). The youngest of the child-ninja brothers, adorably played by Evan Bonifant, lives up to his nickname, Tum-Tum, by eating his way through each adventure, The middle brother, Colt (Max Elliott Slade) mostly delivers straight lines whenever the trio isn't "kicking butt." Slade is the only original "ninja" returning for the sequel, along with Victor Wong as the boys' Grandpa and karate mentor. Wong is so stiff that his character's nimble karate moves become an unintended sight gag.

The plot of "Kick Back" involves a ceremonial dagger Grandpa won in a tournament 50 years ago. But the loser of that tournament has a long memory. He dispatches his nephew to retrieve the dagger, which according to legend, is the key to a cave of gold. The nephew and his heavy-metal sidekicks turn out to be the "Three Stooges" of villainy. Each of their pratfalling, pie-throwing, cross-dressing scenes is so telegraphed that they lose whatever slim laugh potential they may have had. None of this will matter to young "3 Ninjas" fans. And none will fail to grasp the promise of more to come implicit in the final line: "Hope there's more to eat in our next adventure," says Tum-Tum threateningly. Steel yourself for "3 Ninjas 3."

Also reviewed in:
NEW YORK TIMES, 5/7/94, p. 18, Stephen Holden
VARIETY, 5/9-15/94, p. 72, Emanuel Levy
WASHINGTON POST, 5/6/94, p. 37, Desson Howe

THREESOME

A TriStar Pictures release of a Motion Picture Corporation of America production. *Executive Producer:* Cary Woods. *Producer:* Brad Krevoy and Steve Stabler. *Director:* Andrew Fleming. *Screenplay:* Andrew Fleming. *Director of Photography:* Alexander Gruszynski. *Editor:* William C. Carruth. *Music:* Thomas Newman. *Music Editor:* Bill Bernstein. *Sound:* Giovanni Di Simone and (music) Dennis Sands. *Sound Editor:* William Carruth. *Casting:* Ed Mitchell and Robyn Ray. *Production Designer:* Ivo Cristante. *Art Director:* Ken Larson. *Set Decorator:* Tim Colohan. *Set Dresser:* Eric London. *Costumes:* Deborah Everton. *Make-up:* Patty York. *Stunt Coordinator:* B.J. Davis. *Running time:* 93 minutes. *MPAA Rating:* R.

CAST: Lara Flynn Boyle (Alex); Stephen Baldwin (Stuart); Josh Charles (Eddy); Alexis Arquette (Dick); Martha Gehman (Renay); Mark Arnold (Larry); Michele Matheson (Kristen); Joanne Baron (Curt Woman); Jennifer Lawler (Neighbor); Jack Breschard (Priest); Jillian Johns and Amy Ferioli (Partygoer); Jason Workman (Medical Student); Katherine Kousi (Laundry Girl); Anna Marie O'Donnell (Lady at Library); Kathleen Beaton (Girl at Registration).

LOS ANGELES TIMES, 4/8/94, Calendar/p. 1, Peter Rainer

The strange thing about "Threesome" is that it looks like a TV sitcom but it walks and talks like a soft-porn roundelay. It's as if "Three's Company" suddenly got a case of hot monkey love.

The threesome in question involves Stuart (Stephen Baldwin) and Eddy (Josh Charles), college roommates who couldn't be further apart in temperament, and Alex (Lara Flynn Boyle), who, through a computer mix-up, ends up sharing a dorm suite with them. They hit it off—sometimes literally—in that seriously rowdy way that filmmakers always imagine college students behave.

Stuart is a business major but most of his business seems hormonally inspired: he's a jock rake with an itch for Alex. (He thinks everything she does is sexy, even throwing food at him.) Eddy is a more languid and "sensitive" type, which, in movie-ese, means he's sexually confused. Alex's high-powered attempts to seduce him are rebuffed because, although he doesn't let his dorm mates know it for a while, he's attracted to Stuart.

Writer-director Andrew Fleming invests a lot of faith in these three: They're featured in practically every scene, with occasional drop-ins by other students. It's a strategy that only works if the characters are fascinating enough to sustain an entire movie and the hi-jinks in "Threesome" don't sustain. It becomes "Tiresome."

Despite the likability of the three actors, Stuart, Eddy and Alex never achieve fully human status. Fleming zeros in on the sex and the romance but keeps out just about everything else that might allow us to connect with them. ("Carnal Knowledge" had the same problem.) We don't get any sense of what it really means for these three to go to college—as if it would be too "square" to actually deal with how they were affected by their studies. It's all on a paper-thin "personal" level. That's what's sit-com-ish about it.

A movie about sexual confusion and role-playing shouldn't be quite so grinningly content with itself. There's no particular terror or upset in the lives of these three. Alex's rejection, Eddy's wavering, Stuart's rollickings are all experienced on the same level as a fatuous coming-of-age scenario. The sex scenes—such as Alex writhing on Eddy's library desk or talking to him on the phone while being made love to by Stuart—seem shoe-horned into the movie in order to make it sparkle for the youth market, "Threesome" gives raciness a bad name. It's almost enough to bring out the prude in you.

Besides "Carnal Knowledge," Threesome" has its other influences and, in one of its more shameless scenes, we see one of them. Eddy is shown watching a movie—described only as "an old French film about two men who loved the same woman." That Truffaut's "Jules and Jim" should be tossed off in this way is a measure of this movie's Liteness. Should we be thankful Eddy wasn't watching "Citizen Kane," a classic "about a newspaper big-shot"? Or "Psycho"—a movie "about a guy and a shower"?

NEW YORK POST, 4/8/94, p. 29, Michael Medved

Because Alex (Lara Flynn Boyle) happens to bear a boy's first name, some bone-headed bureaucrat at her California university has mistakenly assigned her to share a dorm suite with two male roommates.

One of them, Stuart (Stephen Baldwin) is a cheerfully obtuse party-animal with tattoos on both biceps and an insatiable appetite for babes and brewskis. He instantly develops the hots for Alex, but she has focused her lustful attentions on their other roommate, the bookish and sensitive Eddy (Josh Charles).

He won't respond to her advances, however, because he's a shy virgin who strongly suspects that he might be gay—and who begins to feel a vague longing for the macho Stuart.

This is the sitcom setup for "Threesome," which goes on to work endless and exhausting variations on its three characters' attractions and anxieties. Solid acting and snappy dialogue keep the proceedings reasonably intriguing. But after a while, the movie begins to feel like the world's longest tease—an artificially extended buildup before the characters stumble into the inevitable "solution" to their situation promised by the title.

When that climax finally arrives, it isn't nearly as shocking—or as satisfying—as all the heavy-breathing anticipation would have led us to expect.

But that, to be fair, is part of the picture's point; the unconventional arrangement among these roommates is never treated as a subject for cheap titillation, or even rhapsodic romanticism, but simply as a necessary rite of passage for three likable but unremarkable college kids trying to come to terms with sex.

Writer/director Andrew Fleming (who previously created music videos and the little-seen thriller "Bad Dreams") is a skillful storyteller who does a good job making us care about each of these people—particularly Eddy, who may be the first-ever character in a big studio film to be shown struggling with deep-seated ambivalence about his own sexual orientation.

In the process, the movie flirts with the politically incorrect notion that Eddy isn't genetically predestined to become either straight or gay, and that his painful navigation among various alternatives involves a strong element of choice.

This process might have been more compelling to watch if the film (shot largely on location at UCLA) had portrayed contemporary campus life in more complex and convincing terms. Sex may indeed be an all-consuming obsession for many undergraduates, but real-life students must occasionally put up with classes, extracurricular activities, and other distractions.

The movie also reduces all characters beyond its central "Threesome" to two-dimensional jokes. Every time the principals try to venture beyond their charmed circle to date some "outsider," that candidate turns out to be a lunk-headed loser.

One of these bubble-brains is a buxom blonde (Michele Matheson) who babbles embarrassingly about the Catholic school she once attended—thereby highlighting another curious tendency in this picture.

Filmmaker Fleming fires five different cheap shots, in the form of quick gags or contemptuous references, at organized religion. Since none of the main characters ever mentions anything about coming from a religious background, these passing insults seem particularly pointless—a gratuitous, mean-spirited intrusion in a film that otherwise brings a surprisingly serious and sensitive tone to its subject matter.

NEWSDAY, 4/8/94, Part II/p. B3, John Anderson

It's a dumbing-down world, where ratings dictate content and polls dictate politics. So why not film romance by sexual demographic? You can cover—or uncover—all the bases. Skew young. Add a few pretty bodies, a few hip cultural references. Stir well.

The result would be "Threesome," a coming-of-age-on-campus movie about a trio of college friends who constitute a three-ring congress of sexual equality, and a triumvirate of, well, not stereotypes, exactly. Each character is more an amalgamation of traits that don't necessarily make sense when added together, but individually should touch just about every member of the under-20 audience for whom this film is tailored. They're not offensive people, exactly, just patronizingly obvious.

There's Eddy (Josh Charles), the sensitive transfer student and "sexually ambivalent" intellectual. And there's Stuart (Stephen Baldwin), the iron-pumping, Bud-sucking party monster with the heart of gold. Eddy, who refers to Freud as "the Big Dude," and Stuart, who lives to dance the horizontal mambo, are mismatched roommates, but they eventually get comfortable with each other—even on film, their dorm suite emits the piquant bouquet of stale beer, old pizza and older underwear. But just as they do, Alex (Lara Flynn Boyle), whose male-ish name has prompted the school's computer to glitch, becomes the third member of their untidy group.

There's a campus housing shortage, there's no easy way out, so the three commence their not-so-delicate dance around each other. Alex is attracted to Eddy; Eddy is attracted to Stuart, and Stuart, who's attracted to knotholes in trees, wants Alex. All three are smart, even if they never go to class (except Eddy, who gets to watch "Jules and Jim;" "Threesome's" most obvious antecedent). But their shared-sexual confusion gives way to an intimacy, both physical and spiritual, that causes them to tighten their circle to the point of obliviousness, and viciousness, toward anyone outside it. "It got to the point where we were the only ones who got the joke," says Eddy, in one of the film's few moments of honest introspection.

The jokes, as it were, are parachuted in to douse whatever flame "Threesome" might spark, as are the extended sequences of the three gamboling about in a desperate kind of glee, spraying each other with shaving cream, and having pillow fights. Writer-director Andrew Fleming, who proved in his first feature, "Bad Dreams," to be a natural scavenger of style, has rendered something like Truffaut-meets-"Animal House," with a dash of "Four Friends" and "Tell Me That You Love Me, Junie Moon." But his characters are too smoothly charming, talented and attractive to justify the clinging quality of their relationship. What need—social, sexual or otherwise—would they have that would require such an obsessively aberrant solution? "I'm so sick of this," Alex cries. "It's not normal." No, nor even believable.

"Threesome" may be well received by audiences unfamiliar with any of this film's predecessors, who are seeing "people" like Alex, Eddy and Stuart on screen for the first time. But movies like this have a basic flaw: In taking pains to extol the virtues of free thinking and free love, they operate on the assumption such behavior is shocking. Otherwise, where's the tension? The heroic music that throbs and swells as the three principals get down to doing what comes "naturally," is barely enough to drown out the snicker.

NEWSWEEK, 4/18/94, p. 60, David Ansen

Alex and Eddy and Stuart are thrown together as college roommates. There's one embarrassing glitch: Alex (Lara Flynn Boyle) is a girl.

Nor does the pairing of party-animal Stuart (Stephen Baldwin) and introspective Eddy (Josh Charles) seem auspicious: one decorates his wall with bare-bottomed cheerleaders, the other hangs his poster of Munch's "The Scream." Unlikely as it may seem, these three form—for a time—an inseparable bond, glued together by raging hormones. Stuart lusts after Alex; Alex lusts after Eddy; and Eddy, our "sexually ambivalent" narrator, lusts after Stuart.

"Threesome," a merrily libidinous comedy, has sex on the brain. The only time the jock hedonist Stuart ever cracks a book (Dostoevsky no less) it's just a ploy to seduce Alex—and it backfires. But to criticize "Threesome" for its narrow focus on college life misses the point. This isn't an angst-filled recollection but a guilt-free fantasy. Thirty-one-year-old writer/ director Andrew Fleming, working in swift, bold, audience-friendly strokes, captures the giddy anticipation of sexual possibilities that every undergraduate, first freed from the constraints of family, ever dreamed of. Alex and Stuart and Eddy, vowing a solemn and soon-to-be-broken oath to refrain from sleeping with each other, form their own self-absorbed family, arrogant in its cliquishness but, for all its kinkiness, essentially innocent.

Fleming's funny, deceptively smart screenplay manages to mate Noel Coward and "Animal House." (Talk about strange bedfellows!) Both gross and sophisticated, this twentysomething cartoon couldn't fly unless the chemistry among the three actors were right. And it is. Boyle (from "Twin Peaks") seems freer, earthier, than she has before: she lets rip her wonderfully throaty Irish laugh. Stressed out with the frustration of this lopsided *ménage à trois*, she regresses hilariously into an exasperated child: "I need new shoes!" Baldwin—the youngest of the four acting Baldwin brothers—has the funniest part; under his Neanderthal façade, he reveals a sweet, endearing clownishness. Charles, the sober one, anchors the story in real feeling. Usually, in such a mainstream kind of movie, the gay character is relegated to the sidelines; a token outsider. "Threesome," refreshingly, makes him the audience's surrogate, the voice of something like reason.

There are many ways Fleming's movie could have cut deeper. Some scenes, like Lara's Harry and Sallyish pantomime of an orgasm on a library table, exist only for easy yucks. Fleming keeps things on the surface, but it's a bright, generous surface. Like the current Spanish-art-house hit and Oscar-winner "Belle Epoque" (in which a young Spanish soldier sleeps with the four obliging daughters of his host), "Threesome" uses knockabout sexual fantasy to offer up a pipe dream of Eden—albeit a pop, pizza-strewn, polymorphously perverse Eden. Fleming's vision may be less tony than the overrated Best Foreign Film, but it's truer. And a lot more fun.

SIGHT AND SOUND, 10/94, p. 54, Stella Bruzzi

At the start of the college year two students—Eddy and Stuart—find themselves reluctantly sharing a dorm. Stuart hangs soft porn posters on his walls while Eddy puts up Munch's *The Scream*; Eddy studies while Stuart pulls the girls. Their uneasy equilibrium is disrupted by the arrival of Alex, a woman who has mistakenly been designated a bed in their male dorm. Before long Alex attempts to seduce Eddy while Stuart makes advances to Alex. Alex cannot understand why Eddy is not interested in her; he explains that he is a "sexually ambivalent" virgin and fancies Stuart.

Rumours start to fly about the threesome, who become even closer sexually and socially, gradually losing interest in other people. Alex continues to pursue Eddy, while Eddy chases Stuart and Stuart goes after Alex—meanwhile both men sleep independently with Alex. Their final sexual encounter involves all three.

The bubble bursts when Alex wrongly suspects that she's pregnant. The year ends and the three go their separate ways. Despite meeting up at graduation and doing lunch roughly once a year, they virtually lose touch. Stuart settles down in a monogamous heterosexual relationship, Alex remains single and Eddy refers obliquely in voice-over to a "boyfriend".

From Eddy's opening voice-over offering an expansive, pedantic account of the Latin roots of the word "deviant" there's the unmistakable odour of loucheness mingled with pseudo-intellectuality hanging over *Threesome*, as if the film were trying to be risqué and earnest at the same time. Hence, perhaps, the enigmatic references by Eddy to his French cinema course, a certain tendency in French cinema having been to make art house films out of the parochial and insignificant world of human emotions. Late in the film Eddy makes just such an oblique allusion to that classic threesome movie, *Jules et Jim*. This is a mistake, because in comparison *Threesome* palls, replacing Truffaut's tongue-in-cheek detachment with coyness.

Threesome is in too many ways an extended game of dare—a lesson in how to avoid being boring by carving out a place in the memories of boring contemporaries. Alex (that prevalent college-movie anomaly, the haute coutured student) breaks free of her chains of dullness after an initial phase which involves clutching a teddy and acting in a lesbian version of *Oedipus Rex*. Stuart on the other hand, is the prime instigator of the film's naughtiness. He licks the thighs of the models in his soft porn poster, masks his face with a pair of Alex's panties and advises the reluctant Eddy to "at least get a blowjob" out of Alex's infatuation with him. Stephen Baldwin's sniggering, grinning, oafish Stuart is Butt-Head on steroids. To be a cool dude entails frequent sex, and a necessary achievement is having a threesome. So these three are the coolest on the block.

Or rather they would be if they were attractive and their *ménage à trois* credible. Instead of unleashing a truly daring fantasy, *Threesome*, simply a traditional coming-of-age movie with twist, sticks to its coy, preppy pen, promising but never delivering the much-vaunted "deviancy". There are scenes which are plain embarrassing, like Alex's writhing on the library table as Eddy reads Hawthorne to her (a nod in the direction of *A Fish Called Wanda*), or Eddy's subsequent attempt at seducing the defiantly heterosexual Stuart. The sincerely dull Eddy is the linchpin here, the 'gay' who runs a mile when the one other gay character, Dick, makes advances to him.

Director Andrew Fleming presents a limited picture of student life (sex and pizza) and an even narrower vision of sexuality. There's none of the power play found in the triangle operating in *Cabaret*, for instance, where each party is made vulnerable by their unconventional situation. In *Threesome* the danger is imagined or promised, as when Dick and his sidekick, spying through binoculars, assume that Eddy and Stuart are having sex when Eddy is merely helping a drunk Stuart to his feet. Similarly the threesome scenes are titillating but sanitised, as the physical object of desire for both men remains Alex, despite the final bed scene during which Stuart allows Eddy to rest a hand on his buttock. Having already been told in Eddy's voice-over that his ideal partner would be a combination of his two roommates, it is hardly surprising that he finally decides to sleep with Alex, and it's difficult to entirely dispel the notion that she could guide him back to heterosexuality.

The message is deeply reactionary: threesomes are dandy as long as the piggy in the middle is female. Because this is ultimately as outrageous as *Threesome* gets, the film sidesteps any more complex or problematic questions about desire and sexuality, opting instead to ease its characters into monogamy. For such a would-be racy film, *Threesome* offers an oppressive and unflinching idea of "normality", its weirdest moment being, absurdly enough, when both Eddy and Stuart jump naked into the lake with only their shoes and socks on. Is this the 90s version of keeping one foot on the ground during a bed scene?

VILLAGE VOICE, 4/12/94, p. 60, Amy Taubin

Alex is infatuated with Eddy who yearns after Stuart who has the hots for Alex. Nothing if not high concept, *Threesome* is *Jules and Jim* at UCLA, but since these are twentysomething Californians in the laissez-faire '90s, everyone lives to laugh-it-over after graduation. Instead of choking back tears over Jeanne Moreau singing "la femme fatale qui fume fatale," you can dance up the aisle to General Public's "I'll Take You There."

Thanks to a stubborn computer, Alex (Lara Flynn Boyle) is assigned to a dorm suite already occupied by odd-couple Eddy (Josh Charles) and Stuart (Stephen Baldwin). Immune to the appeal of party-animal Stuart, Alex makes a play for the introspective Eddy. Alex's attentions have a catalytic effect on Eddy. He's forced to admit to himself and his roommates that he's interested in guys, not girls, and that the bods' in his dreams is Stuart's. Stuart's response is stunningly benign for a straight dude. "I'm secure enough in my sexuality not to feel threatened ... Ever butt-fuck anyone? Ever been butt-fucked?" It's just healthy curiosity. *Threesome*'s message is that homosexuality is not contagious.

The three make a pact not to let sex get in the way of camaraderie and enter an environment of delusional desire where no one is getting what he/she wants but all live in hope. Director-writer Andrew Fleming is pretty good at evoking the hysteria imminent in such sexual sublimation. Boyle and Charles, although a bit poised for undergrads, deliver an attractive mix of energy and angst. It's Baldwin, however, a boy bimbo with well-tended pecs and baby blues to die for, who steals the show. *Threesome* is tenderer and more ambitious than *Reality Bites*, but it trips over its determination to be both cool and liberal with puppy-dog naïveté. Is that Keith Haring mural on the dorm wall an original or a copy, and either way, what's it doing there? When Eddie, Alex, and Stuart, against their better judgment, finally hit the sack together, the film can't help but congratulate itself on its transgression, even though Alex is placed safely in the middle and the guys never so much as touch toes.

Also reviewed in:
CHICAGO TRIBUNE, 4/8/94, Friday/p. C, Michael Wilmington
NEW YORK TIMES, 4/8/94, p. C12, Janet Maslin
VARIETY, 2/7-13/94, p. 38, Todd McCarthy
WASHINGTON POST, 4/8/94, p. C7, Desson Howe
WASHINGTON POST, 4/8/94, Weekend/p. 45, Joe Brown

TIGRERO: A FILM THAT WAS NEVER MADE

An Arrow Releasing release of a Marianna Films production in co-production with Premiere/Sky Light Cinema-Mira Set. *Producer:* Mika Kaurismaki. *Director:* Mika Kaurismaki. *Screenplay:* Mika Kaurismaki. *Director of Photography:* Jacques Cheuiche. *Editor:* Mika Kaurismaki. *Music:* Nana Vasconcelos, Chuck Jonkey, and The Karaja Indians. *Running time:* 75 minutes. *MPAA Rating:* Not Rated.

WITH: Samuel Fuller; Jim Jarmusch; The Karaja Indians.

NEW YORK POST, 12/21/94, p. 41, Thelma Adams

In 1954, producer Daryl Zanuck sent Sam Fuller to Brazil to scout locations for an action adventure movie. The "Pickup on South Street" director settled beside crocodile-infested waters among the Karaja Indians. He returned to Hollywood with raw footage—and a story idea about a jaguar hunter or tigrero, a desperate wife and her weak husband.

But "Tigrero"—a hard-bitten adventure starring John Wayne, Ava Gardner and Tyrone Power on location in the croc-eat-croc jungle setting—never got the green light. Insurers halted the project: Wayne was too valuable to risk as croc fodder.

Opening today at Film Forum, "Tigrero—A Film That Was Never Made," trails Fuller's failed film. Director Mika Kaurismaki ("Zombie and the Ghost Train") followed iguana-faced octogenarian Fuller and downtown director Jim Jarmusch ("Mystery Train") to Brazil.

The funny, funky odd couple travel south to relive Fuller's memories and scratch at the raw materials of filmmaking. Fuller and Jarmusch's most interesting chats center on the preparation for "Tigrero"—how Fuller's search for settings evolved into the making of an original Hollywood script.

Fuller's Brazilian adventure wasn't a total loss; he recycled color footage of Karaja tribal rites as a dream sequence in his 1963 black-and-white melodrama, "Shock Corridor."

The cinematic archaeology is more effective than the amateur ethnographic filmmaking Kaurismaki practices among the natives. The Westerners can't escape their preconceptions of the noble savage ("They're way ahead of us," says Fuller) and the oppressiveness of progress despite their mutual dependence for expression on a very modern tool lacked by the Indians—the camera. While Jarmusch remains with the Karaja, Fuller offers the jaunty exit line, "I have to go back to the uncivilized world. I'll see you at M-G-M."

NEWSDAY, 12/21/94, Part II/p. B11, John Anderson

Sam Fuller should have his own talk show, and does, in a way, in Mika Kaurismaki's "Tigrero: A Film That Was Never Made," which is about a never-realized Fuller project, and about Fuller himself.

In 1954, at Darryl Zanuck's behest, the director of "I Shot Jesse James," "The Steel Helmet" and "Pickup on South Street" set out for the Amazon Rain Forest with a 16mm camera, 75 boxes of cigars and two cases of vodka to scout locations for a jungle adventure called "Tigrero." It was to star John Wayne, Ava Gardner and Tyrone Power. And it was never made.

Like "It's All True," which through recovered and restructured film footage recounted the unhappy fate of Orson Welles' Brazilian film projects, "Tigrero" is about political sabotage, lack of vision and what might have been. In "Tigrero's" case, it's also about the 82-year-old Fuller's vision, and through his conversations with the younger and aesthetically sympathetic director Jim Jarmusch, about the directorial process, the filmmaker's vision and a remarkable people.

What Fuller goes back to Brazil in search of, besides his own history, is the Karaja, an aboriginal tribe that has remained spiritually untouched by encroaching civilization, but has suffered nonetheless. "Tigrero" celebrates both their strength and that of the medium of film itself: The documentary's most remarkable moment is when Fuller shows the Karaja the footage he shot of them 40 years earlier. They see their loved ones come back to life, and their own younger selves. It's a quasi-religious experience for them, and reminds the more jaded viewer just what film can mean.

Both Fuller and Jarmusch are raconteurs, and their conversation—for Jarmusch, it's sort of "My Dinner With Sam"—is entertaining, although too purposely full of background information to seem informal. But Mika Kaurismaki (Aki's brother) may simply be emulating the rigorous economy of Fuller, who, as we're shown, managed to work some of his unused color Brazilian footage into his black-and-white 1963 psychodrama "Shock Corridor."

VILLAGE VOICE, 12/27/94, p. 76, Luis H. Francia

Forty years after he first shot some footage in Brazil's Amazon wilderness for a film that would have starred John Wayne but was ultimately shelved, Samuel Fuller returns with Jim Jarmusch as interviewer-narrator and Mika Kaurismäki as the director. A whole lot has changed since, of course; now the Karajá Indians, whom Fuller met in 1954, have succumbed to the signifiers of a pervasive, corrupting modernity: T-shirts, *telenovelas*, and textbooks.

Part Margaret Mead documentary, part diary cum fiction, *Tigrero* alternates between Fuller's naive if enthusiastic reminiscences, and the Karajá's attempts at preserving their mores. The 82-year-old Fuller's stories of Hollywood and the Amazon (it's clear which is the jungle), and the contrast between then and now constitute the film's modest virtues. Viewing the Karajá view ghosts past via Fuller's old footage, one can almost feel their melancholy. A woman recalls the kindness of her late husband while a son tells of his father being attacked by a crocodile.

While it's fun watching the deadpan Jarmusch and Fuller bond, I found the film oddly empty. No interaction beyond interviews seems to have taken place between the outsiders and the Indians. At the end, when Jarmusch asks Fuller, who's leaving to "go back to the uncivilized world," to pick him up in 40 years, it's meant as a joke. Benign, yes, but reflective of countless white males who came and overstayed their welcome—a Conradian irony Kaurismäki or, for that matter, the other principals sadly miss.

Also reviewed in:
CHICAGO TRIBUNE, 3/31/95, Friday/p. K, Michael Wilmington
NEW YORK TIMES, 12/21/94, p. C18, Caryn James
VARIETY, 2/28-3/6/94, p. 70, David Stratton

TIMECOP

A Universal Pictures release of a Largo Entertainment presentation in association with JVC Entertainment of a Signature/Renaissance/Dark Horse production. *Executive Producer:* Mike Richardson. *Producer:* Moshe Diamant, Sam Raimi, and Robert Tapert. *Director:* Peter Hyams. *Screenplay:* Mark Verheiden. *Story:* Mike Richardson and Mark Verheiden. *Based on the comic series created by:* Mike Richardson and Mark Verheiden. *Director of Photography:* Peter Hyams. *Editor:* Steven Kemper. *Music:* Mark Isham. *Music Editor:* Tom Carlson. *Sound:* Eric Batur. *Sound Editor:* Bruce Richardson. *Casting:* Penny Perry. *Production Designer:* Philip Harrison. *Art Director:* Richard Hudolin. *Set Designer:* Bjorn Ollner. *Set Decorator:* Rose Marie McSherry and Ann Marie Corbett. *Set Dresser:* Brent Bennett, Gordon Clapp, Glenn MacDonald, and Peter Stoffels. *Special Effects:* John Thomas. *Costumes:* Dan Lester. *Make-up:* Zoltan Elek and Margaret Solomon. *Stunt Coordinator:* Glenn Randall. *Running time:* 95 minutes. *MPAA Rating:* R.

CAST: Jean-Claude Van Damme (Max Walker); Mia Sara (Melissa Walker); Ron Silver (McComb); Bruce McGill (Matuzak); Gloria Reuben (Fielding); Scott Bellis (Ricky); Jason Schombing (Atwood); Scott Lawrence (Spota); Kenneth Welsh (Utley); Brent Woolsey (Shotgun); Brad Loree (Reyes); Shane Kelly (Rollerblades); Richard Faraci (Cole); Steve Lambert (Lansing); Kevin McNulty (Parker); J.J. Makaro and Yves Cameron (McComb Guards); David Jacox, Jr. and Mike Mitchell (McComb Men); Jacob Rupp (Palmer); Sean O'Byrne (Aide Lawrence); Gabrielle Rose (Judge Marshall); Malcolm Stewart (Nelson); Alfonso Quijada (Photographer); Yvette Ferguson (Atwood Secretary); Glen Roald (Doorman);

Theodore Thomas (Pete); Lon Katzmann (Handlebar); Duncan Fraser (Irish Cop); Tony Morelli (Tweed); Nick Hyams (Newsboy); Kelli Fox (Aide); Pamela Martin (TV Commentor); Tom McBeath (T.E.C. Technician); Frank Cassini (T.E.C. Agent); Veena Sood (Nurse); Cole Bradsen (Boy); James Lew and Charles Andre (Knives); Scott Nicholson, Ernie Jackson, and Tom Erikson (Guards); Laura Murdoch (Virtual Reality Woman); Dalton Fisher (Washington Cop); Doris Blomgren (Old Woman); Ian Tracey (Soldier); Caallum Keith Rennie (Stranger); Tom Glass (Wagon Driver).

LOS ANGELES TIMES, 9/16/94, Calendar/p. 10, Kenneth Turan

Heads are often spinning in Jean-Claude Van Damme's movies, usually because the erstwhile Muscles From Brussels has sent them into orbit with one of his well-placed martial arts kicks. In "Timecop," however, the spinning has a different cause: the dizzying premise behind the inevitable action.

Adapted, like so many recent movies seem to be, from a comic-book series, "Timecop" is based on a venerable science-fiction riff: going back in time, even if it were possible, would be terrifically risky, because anything you did in the past would have incalculable effects on the present. And if you happened to run into yourself back then, so much the worse.

With side trips to the Civil War South and Wall Street during the great stock market crash, "Timecop" is serious about this travel business to the point of dividing moments spent in its Washington, D.C., setting between a pair of different decades.

One part of the film is set in 1994, the year in which a time travel device has just been invented. An up-and-coming young senator named Aaron McComb (Ron Silver) is placed in charge of congressional oversight for the machine, and a D.C. cop named Max Walker (Van Damme) with a loving wife (Mia Sara) is transferred to the Time Enforcement Commission to help police the new technology.

By 2004, things are different. McComb has become an unruly presidential candidate desperate for money to finance a losing campaign, and Walker, his life marred by tragedy, is kept awfully busy going back to the past to corral larcenous types who think it would be nice to buy up Beverly Hills before the celebrities got there.

The Mark Verheiden script has both Walker and McComb making more trips between 1994 and 2004 than an airport shuttle. And given that everything has changed in 2004 every time one or the other comes back from 1994, things get awfully confusing awfully fast.

Though his directing style (witness previous science-fiction films like "Outland" and "2010") is all crude energy, Peter Hyams does keep things moving fast enough to make figuring out how internally coherent all these plot complications are just about impossible.

Never the most expressive of actors, "Timecop" marks Van Damme's attempt to expand his range, to turn himself into something of a romantic hero. His battered Hamlet look is suitably brooding, and as a concession to this new image, he probably beats the tar out of fewer people than he has in the past.

But even though this is supposed to be a kindlier Van Damme vehicle, his movies couldn't exist without his trademark ability to deliver the kind of accurate, powerful kicks any World Cup team would envy. All his soulful glances notwithstanding, "Timecop" still depends too much on violence to make it appealing to the uninitiated or the unwary.

NEW YORK POST, 9/16/94, p. 45, Michael Medved

Nobody goes back.

That's the motto of "Time Enforcement Commission" —a super-secret federal agency designed to prevent abuse of new time travel technology. If someone goes back to the past and makes even the most minor alteration in historical events, it can have a devastating impact on the present. Therefore. TEC cops must occasionally hurtle through time themselves in order to catch unscrupulous operators before they can do lasting damage.

For Jean-Claude Van Damme's grim, sulky character, it's all in a day's (or decade's) work—until he draws an assignment that brings him into an uncomfortable confrontation with his own past.

It's the year 2004, and this kick-boxing, dialogue-chomping tough guy is asked to go back 10 years, where he comes face to face with his own adored wife (Mia Sara)—just before she's sadistically murdered by mysterious thugs. Van Damme knows that he can prevent the tragedy, change the past and bring his sweetie back to life, but to do so would violate the fundamental principle of his job.

That's the intriguing premise behind "Timecop," the big new sci-fi, foot-in-your-eye thriller that features the most adequate performance of Van Damme's entire career. While his development as an actor still lags well behind Schwarzenegger's (or even Steven Seagal's), the "Muscles from Brussels" is no longer just an embarrassing behemoth: he now shows real emotion in a few scenes and actually makes you care about his character.

The same can't be said about the film's arch-villain—a ruthless presidential candidate played by Ron Silver. When it comes to raw acting ability, Silver can kick Van Damme (and most everyone else) around the block, but his part's been written as such a two-dimensional cipher that there's not much to do with the character.

The only motivation for the man's monstrous evil is that he's supposed to be a Republican—of course, a grievous sin in the eyes of most Hollywood producers. "When I'm in office," the candidate snarls, "it'll be the '80's all over again! The top 10 percent will get richer and the other 90 percent can move to Mexico!"

The movie also falls short in precisely those areas that Van Damme's devoted fans care about most: fights and special effects. There's nothing particularly imaginative about thc martial arts battles, and they seem so clumsily snipped together that you notice the chops by the film editor more than those by the characters.

As to time-machine razzle-dazzle, the special effects look expensive but never convincing—with lots of cheesy electrical flashes when all else fails.

Veteran director Peter Hyams ("Outland," "2010") wastes a special opportunity in scenes where major characters confront past versions of their own personalities—the physical differences between the 1994 and 2004 models are so subtle that the encounters become confusing rather than intriguing.

When word gets out about the many shortcomings in this mediocre project, you can count on the fact that despite Van Damme's demonstrated box office appeal, nobody goes back.

NEWSDAY, 9/16/94, Part II/p. B3, Gene Seymour

So, let's see if I've got this straight: If I go back in time, it's all right to meet my past self, even talk to it. But I can't shake hands with it because matter can't occupy the exact same space. If I do ... what? I cancel myself out of existence? That's wack! But at least, I can be in the same room with myself, right? Cool.

I've a weakness for time travel stories and I've read enough of them to lose track of what is or isn't permitted on excursions to the past. Heck, some stories say if you so much as nudge a pebble, the universe is a done deal.

One of the many charms of "Timecop" is that the rules here aren't nearly as rigid. To say the least.

This is time travel as blood sport. Under the conditions laid down here, it's possible to go back to the Civil War and mow down a battalion of Confederate soldiers with automatic weapons, steal their gold and use it to finance present-day terrorism.

It's to stop such abuses that a top-secret force of time-patrolling cops is set up. One of them is a Washington, D. C., patrolman named Max Walker (Jean-Claude Van Damme), whose wife is murdered in a horrific explosion just before he joins the unit.

Ten years later, Walker still broods over his loss while becoming a temporal manhunter of terrifying facility. Meanwhile, a ruthless, right-wing senator (Ron Silver) is lobbying hard to have the time enforcers mothballed. Walker finds out that the senator, backed by an army of goons, is hopping around the epochs himself, looting and speculating his way to a mighty war chest that will finance a run for the presidency.

All of this plays a lot less tortuously than it sounds. Director Peter Hyams, one of Hollywood's more underappreciated craftsmen, moves the story along with blithe efficiency and energetic humor. Silver proves again that he's so much more beguiling on film when he's being really bad.

"It's gonna be like the Eighties," his senator snarls at one point when discussing his presidential agenda. "The top 10 percent will have it all and everyone else will move to Mexico for a better life." Trenchant, nasty little lines like this add zesty seasoning to this convoluted plot, which reaches such a satisfying end one dreads that an all-but inevitable sequel will muck it up all over again.

As for Van Damme, his growth as the compleat action-hero-who-can-act continues apace. The acrobatic kicks and splits are as eye-catching as ever. The stunts are orchestrated with panache and restraint. (At no time do your senses feel pounded into submission.) But what's even more gratifying is that Van Damme no longer seems to feel obliged to lay on the pathos to prove his depth. He's wearing his laconic, good-guy persona with infectious ease, though you wish he'd lay off some of the more gratuitous wisecracks.

SIGHT AND SOUND, 1/95, p. 59, Kim Newman

Washington, 1994. Following the invention of a time travel process, the American government establishes the Time Enforcement Commission, a police force which will prevent miscreants from tampering with the past. The ambitious Senator McComb volunteers to head the committee on financing TEC, and police chief Matuzak is appointed its head. Max Walker, a Washington policeman, is attacked by mysterious hit-men who murder his wife, Melissa.

In 2004, the embittered Walker is a timecop and McComb has been subverting the past to finance a presidential campaign. Walker hauls Atwood, a former partner, out of 1929 where he has been profiting from the Wall Street Crash, and learns that McComb is behind the manipulations. Learning of a major anomaly in 1994, Walker goes back, along with Internal Affairs cop Sara Fielding, and discovers that McComb is advising his younger self not to give up ownership of a company which will have a monopoly on time travel technologies. Fielding, who has been bought off by McComb, prevents Walker from foiling the Senator, but McComb shoots her and strands her in the past. Walker returns to 2004 and finds McComb's position improved by his tampering, and the TEC on the point of being disbanded.

Matuzak is killed helping Walker take one last trip to 1994 to find the wounded Fielding, who can testify against McComb. Walker finds Fielding but McComb's henchmen kill her; at the hospital Walker discovers that Melissa was on the point of telling him she was pregnant when she was murdered. Walker makes contact with Melissa and intervenes, helping his younger self see off McComb's hit team. McComb is on the point of killing Melissa when his younger self, called by Walker, arrives. Walker pushes the two McCombs together and a time paradox kills the Senator. Returning to 2004, Walker finds Matuzak still running the TEC and discovers that, in this time line, Melissa has survived and they have a son.

Peter Hyams, whose science fiction-fantasy-action career ranges from the amiably professional (*Capricorn One, Running Scared*) to the frankly mediocre (*Stay Tuned, 2001*), handles *Timecop* with exactly the expected ordinary skill. He never treats star Jean-Claude Van Damme to the kind of semi-mythic treatment given him by John Woo in *Hard Target* though he does allow for specifically Jean-Claude bits of business, such as doing a mid-air splits in the kitchen to avoid being electrocuted. With a blithely paradox-heavy time travel scenario, nipping at the heels of the *Terminators* and the *Back to the Futures*, this is exactly the sort of film you would expect to be cooked up by a comic book company eager to expand into features.

Once the premise is established, it is assumed the US government can be trusted—leaving aside the power-crazy interventions of a rogue senator—to preserve the integrity of history, which is to say that their policing of the past serves to uphold America's global preeminence. It is wrong for McComb to give his younger self stock market tips, but the prohibition on tampering with the past only notionally extends to preventing Walker from saving his murdered wife.

In a typical bit of have-it-all plotting, the finale has the hero returned to his present to find all the likeable characters who have been killed returned to life with no memory of the threat posed by the vanished McComb. Completely unstressed is the fact that Walker returns to a son whose name he doesn't know, presumably cancelling out an unseen incarnation of himself who has lived through ten happy years with Melissa.

While its time-twisting is on a superficial, though highly engaging, TV movie level (it's a lot less satisfying than the made-for-cable *Timescape*), is a worthy entry in the post-modern action movie mode lately typified by *Demolition Man*. It is so confident of its conventions that it can spring surprises: Fielding, a young black woman with attitude, is so clearly in the spirit of the feisty ethnic partners Arnie is often given that it is a genuine shock that she turns out, albeit shakily, to be a wrong 'un. And there is a 'Scenes We'd Like to See' moment, when Walker thinks of the appropriate witticism ("Freeze") a scene after he has despatched a vile baddie by icing his arm and breaking him apart, with a far less satisfying one-liner. Effects-wise, the movie is nothing new, though the paradox-driven disposal of the villain is suitably gruesome in a fairly fresh manner.

VILLAGE VOICE, 9/27/94, p. 66, Lisa Kennedy

Part *Crow* part *T2*, *Timecop* begins not so much with a bang as an accelerated snicksnicksnicksnick. In a PSA for space-time gun control, six Confederate soldiers carrying a load of gold are held up by one cocksure marauder with two nothing-semi-about-'em automatics from the 21st century. The world has become a place where men travel back in time only for monetary gain, never to exact social change, not even to save their wives' lives.

In the first minutes of *Timecop*, as the plot is being slapped down in a hurry, a flack makes a pitch before a Senate subcommittee to fund yet another federal police force—the Time Enforcement Commission. He tells the good senators—and one really bad one played by Ron Silver—that first, this won't entail future travel, because the future doesn't exist yet (so much for wrestling with the complexities of space time physics); and second, that TEC cops cannot go back and kill, say, Hitler, but they can go back and make sure the U.S. economy's protected from the getgo.

When Jean-Claude Van Damme's Walker joins the newly formed unit, his wife has just found out she's pregnant. Before she can tell him, they're attacked and she's killed for no apparent reason by a gang out of *Die Hard*'s Eurothug catalogue. This trauma provides Walker a motivation beyond protecting property, and his vigilance with time bandits is in direct proportion to his constant, suppressed desire to go back and save his wife. It also sets up the only interesting relationship in the flick, that of time to melancholy.

While *Timecop*'s is a promising premise—shades of the temporal convolutions brought to us by star Van Damme's ur-nemesis and his *Terminator* flicks—its pay off is slight. With nothing really at stake but a dirty presidential campaign and a suburban relationship, Van Damme's ambitions remain bland.

Also reviewed in:
NEW YORK TIMES, 9/16/94, p. C1, Janet Maslin
VARIETY, 9/12-18/94, p. 41, Brian Lowry
WASHINGTON POST, 9/16/94, p. F7, Richard Harrington
WASHINGTON POST, 9/16/94, Weekend/p. 49, Joe Brown

TO LIVE

A Samuel Goldwyn Company release of an ERA International (HK) Ltd. production in association with Shanghai Film Studios. *Executive Producer:* Christophe Tseng and Kow Fuhong. *Producer:* Chiu Fusheng. *Director:* Zhang Yimou. *Screenplay (Mandarin with English subtitles):* Yu Hua and Lu Wei. *Based on the novel "Lifetimes" by:* Yu Hua. *Director of Photography:* Lu Yue. *Editor:* Du Yuan. *Music:* Zhao Jiping. *Sound:* Tao Jian. *Art Director:* Cao Jiuping. *Costumes:* Dong Huamiao. *Make-up:* Sun Wei. *Running time:* 129 minutes. *MPAA Rating:* Not Rated.

CAST: Ge You (Fugui); Gong Li (Jiazhen); Niu Ben (Townchief Niu); Guo Tao (Chunsheng); Jiang Wu (Erxi); Ni Dahong (Long Er); Liu Tianchi (Fengxia as adult); Zhang Lu (Fengxia as teen); Xiao Cong (Fengxia as child); Dong Fei (Youqing); Huang Zhongle (Fugui's Father); Liu Yanjing (Fugui's Mother); Li Lianyi (Lao Quan); Zhao Yuxiu (Dr. Wang); Zhang Kang (Mantou).

FILMS IN REVIEW, 11-12/94, p. 58, Kevin Lewis

Though it is purely accidental, *To Live* can be viewed as a sequel to *The Good Earth*. The mood and the themes of that epic are similar to this superb new movie which captured the Grand Jury Prize at the Cannes Film Festival.

To Live traces the fortunes and tragedies of an aristocratic couple in old China from the 1940s through the 1970s. Fugui's gambling caused him to lose his ancestral home and his wife and child. He regains his family and becomes a traveling puppetmaster, entertaining the troops in the civil war of the late 1940s. Because Fugui sees the gambler who bested him and who now lives in his ancestral home, shot when Mao becomes ruler of China, he determines that he will be a loyal follower just "to live." His wife, the stronger character of the two, is an outspoken critic of the new China and chastises her husband for his fear. That fear causes the death of their young son and ultimately their daughter over the succeeding decades.

Director Zhang Yimou, whose previous successes have included *Red Sorghum* and *Story Of Qui Ju*, succinctly dissects the corruption and incompetence of the Maoist society. No matter how faithfully Fugui hews to the Party line, he suffers humiliation and tragedy. Maoist China is depicted as a state that turns on its people and destroys itself at every turn. The last third of the movie, showing that the Chinese health system is incompetent and cruel because most of the doctors have been executed in the latest purge, and are replaced by students in the operating room, is shocking. The folly of shoe-horning a society to fit a political dogma has never been better shown.

Ge You, as Fugui, won the Best Actor award at the Cannes Film Festival; he is magnificent and subtly delineates every phase of a once-arrogant playboy brought down step-by-step by a relentless society. As his wife Jiazhen, Gong Li is unforgettable. Much of her performance depends on subtext and subliminal thoughts. Though she is outwardly proud and outspoken, she suggests the need to comply with what she knows is wrong, "to live," and save her anguished husband additional hardship.

This Samuel Goldwyn release deserves wide distribution for it is one of the great films of our times, a film which succeeds on emotional, political and intellectual levels.

LOS ANGELES TIMES, 12/14/94, Calendar/p. 1, Kevin Thomas

Zhang Yimou's masterful, stirring "To Live" takes us from the turbulent, treacherous China of the '40s civil war to the brutal Cultural Revolution and beyond through the lives of one couple, who in the course of hardship and tragedy emerge as symbolic of the ordinary Chinese and their capacity to endure and to hope for a better future.

Based on Yu Hua's "Lifetimes," the superb "To Live" is fortunately more absorbing than grueling—and it is indeed the latter. It possesses both vast scope and intimacy, humor and sorrow, complex characterizations, richness of incident and an awareness of the quixotic role fate plays in all our destinies.

It is the latest triumph of China's most renowned filmmaker, whose 1988 debut feature, "Red Sorghum," won international acclaim and whose "Ju Dou" (1990) and "Raise the Red Lantern" (1992) received Oscar nominations for best foreign film. In adapting his own novel to the screen, Yu Hua's co-writer was Lu Wei, who also wrote the screenplay for Chen Kaige's towering "Farewell My Concubine."

In a small village in Northern China an indolent young man, Xu Fugui (Ge You), gambles away his family's fortune to the extent that he loses his family's ancient, magnificent townhouse. The man (Ni Dahong) to whom Fugui lost his ancestral home refuses to lend him money but lends him something that proves to be of far greater value: an old chest filled with his shadow puppets—the one thing that diverted Fugui during his gambling days.

He has a real aptitude for putting on puppet shows with these lacy figures; more than once the puppets, so suggestive of the human predicament, will prove to be his salvation and that of his family.

Fugui's beautiful wife, Jiazhen (Gong Li), dreams modestly of living a quiet life with her family but almost immediately the Communists win control of the country. From here on the couple's life will be hard, blighted by terrible tragedy yet also sustained by their steadfast mutual love and devotion, and by warm camaraderie of friends and neighbors.

By now what many mainstream Chinese have had to endure under Communism is common knowledge around the world, yet "To Live's" forthright depictions of the hardships and sacrifices incurred by the revolution itself, the Great Leap Forward in industrial production in the '50s and the horrors of the Cultural Revolution of the mid-60's to the mid-'70s, have brought down the wrath of the Chinese government upon Zhang and his film.

As punishment for Zhang illegally distributing his picture, he has been forbidden to make films in China with foreign financing for the next two years, and he and Gong Li, the radiant star of all his films, may not present or discuss in any context their film, which earlier this year won the grand jury prize at Cannes and a best actor award for Ge You.

The cruel irony of this banishment is that the epic vision of "To Live" moves beyond the critical to the historical; it celebrates all people at anytime, anyplace, who persist in the face of cataclysmic social, political and economic upheaval.

It is also notably fair-minded; you could easily make a case that the advent of communism was the instrument of Fugui's salvation, turning him from a totally irresponsible archetypal representative of the decadent ruling class into a proletarian hero, a strong and responsible husband and father in the face of grim adversity and loss. Similarly, the man (Niu Ben) who becomes the leader of the new Communist system in Fugui's village is a wise, kind individual, a practical man and not a knee-jerk political ideologue.

However, Zhang does not shy away from the horrors of the crazed Cultural Revolution with its cadres of hysterical young people raging through the streets, pursuing their savage inquisition. Yet in the film's most stunning sequence, Zhang expresses the absurdity of this long ordeal by injecting dark humor in a tragic situation.

When a young woman in childbirth starts hemorrhaging, student nurses do not know what to do because the hospital's professional staff has been carted off to a concentration camp. A frail doctor (Zhao Yuxiu) is in the last moment sprung from captivity, but he's so weak from beatings and starvation that his oddly comical nonstop gorging on dumplings makes him too sick to attend to the woman.

"To Live," which has been gloriously photographed by Lu Yue, is a remarkable accomplishment, spanning many years with both vibrant passion and absolute conviction. It is the most straightforward of all of Zhang's films, and its simplicity of style serves perfectly its great themes, which are timeless and universal.

NEW YORK, 11/21/94, p. 76, David Denby

"What class are we?" asks a panicked husband, formerly a rich man. "We're not landlords, are we?" The handsome, patrician Xu Fugui (Ge You), a gambler, has lost everything. Tossed about in the maelstrom of the Chinese civil war and Communist revolution, he rejoins his beautiful wife, Jiazhen (Gong Li), and anxiously tries to adjust his identity. The new state is sternly virtuous, and for these two, rebellion is not even remotely possible. They've come down in the world; they're *poor* now—that's all right, isn't it? Xu Fugui's panic is one of many harrowing and comic moments in *To Live*, the spellbinding new film by the great Chinese director Zhang Yimou (*Raise the Red Lantern*). A fully felt masterpiece, the anger of *To Live* lies concealed beneath reserves of patience and irony. When that anger explodes, it does so not overtly, on the screen, but inside the viewer, as an outraged, expanding awareness of violation. The movie begins, and one sinks into the narrative with deep satisfaction, held by the unobtrusive yet always supple technique, the "invisible" camera movement and editing. I can think of few other films whose emotional effect is so out of proportion to the means required to produce it.

To Live, largely set in a small city in the north, begins in the forties when Chiang Kai-shek is still in power, and takes the couple and then their children and friends through the civil war, the Great Leap Forward, the Cultural Revolution, and into the seventies. Except for a couple of war scenes, the movie stays small in scale; it's a neighborly epic befitting a tightly wound society. The vast social changes stay out of sight yet impinge on everything. Yimou, taking a rounded view, is willing to admit that Communist idealism really meant something once, that the state forged a new kind of cooperative personality capable of kindness and generosity. But the revolution betrayed everyone, broke everyone's heart. When the children die because of insanities perpetrated by the state, Fugui and Jiazhen feel guilty, as if the deaths were their own fault. They have been separated from their grasp of truth without losing anything else in their humanity, which makes them infinitely touching. At the burial, well out in the country, you can still hear, faintly, the sound of loudspeakers in the city exhorting people to greater effort. That scene of distant intrusion on grief may be one of the most devastating critiques of totalitarianism ever made.

NEW YORK POST, 11/18/94 p. 48, Thelma Adams

Fate and history whittle down a fallen aristocrat's philosophy to a single, simple mantra: "To Live."

In the 129 minutes I spent in the thrall of Zhang Yimou's sweeping humanist epic, I experienced an entire lifetime with all its joys and sorrows and emerged wiser and exhilarated.

A key member of China's Fifth Generation of filmmakers, the director of "Red Sorghum" casts his muse Gong Li as the wife of the aristocrat, Ge You. The pair weathers personal tragedies and political movements—civil war, the Great Leap Forward, the Cultural Revolution—but their endurance in the face of incredible odds is life-affirming.

Awarded best actor at this year's Cannes Film Festival, Ge begins as a swaggering irresponsible gambler and matures into a modest elder living in poverty. It is a performance of astonishing depth, made stronger because it is tempered by wit.

Some critics have knocked "To Live" (which also screened at the New York Film Festival) as yet another Chinese historical epic in the wake of "Farewell My Concubine" and "The Blue Kite." That's parochial thinking—how many times have we seen the West won and returned for more?

NEWSDAY, 11/18/94, Part II/p. B6, John Anderson

Banned in its homeland, where filmmaking has become as much an act of political defiance as art, "To Live" is both Zhang Yimou's most emotionally draining and rewarding movie and one that might have been made by a different filmmaker entirely. The emphasis has shifted from the classical mise-en-scène of "Raise the Red Lantern," the obscure symbolism of "Ju Dou," the stiffly obvious comedy of "The Story of Qiu Ju." In their place are slow dissolves, naked emotion and gentle humor. Anger and bitterness about the legacy of Mao Zedong has turned to shame—the shame of the living. It's a film in which life is cheap and fleeting, and all the more precious.

Zhang is a director going for broke, and it's paid off—onscreen, at least. At home, where Beijing has been busy blackballing "uncooperative" filmmakers for several months, the director has been banned for two years from making any more films with foreign money (most of his movies have been co-productions) and is forbidden, along with his star and now wife, Gong Li, from promoting or discussing this film in any way. "To Live," which was a prize winner at Cannes this year, won't get an Oscar nomination, because it has no country to represent it. It is a free-floating thing, as are its characters.

Fugui (Ge You) is a dissolute child of property and inveterate gambler; Jiazhen (Gong) is his unhappy and pregnant wife, who leaves with their daughter, Fengxia (played as a child and teen by Xiao Cong and Zhang Lu), on the very night he loses the family home to the scheming Long Er (Ni Dahong). Agonized and reeling in the street, Fugui cries, "I've got nothing left." It is a plaintive, ironic understatement and one of the movie's many moments of foreboding. Because even though a penitent Fugui will reunite with Jiazhen, and their love will burn hot, and they'll survive the rigors of Mao's revolution, and they'll suffer the cruelest of calamities, they've always got something else to lose.

As played by the elastic Ge You and the heartbreaking Gong Li, Fugui and his conscience, Jiazhen, are the most memorable of Zhang's characters, perhaps because they represent nothing but humanity. Beijing and the Great Leap Forward/Cultural Revolution may be hazards in their lives, but fate is the engine propelling them, usually toward death. Zhang seems to have resigned himself to this; we can no more control what happens than we can dictate when we are born, he says. Good intentions carry no weight, and in Fugui's case can consistently backfire.

Like the traditional puppets with which Fugui makes his living—and which make mute commentary on Fugui's existence—he is controlled by unseen hands: Dragooned by the Nationalist army during the civil war, he becomes a POW, entertains the Reds and becomes a part of the revolution. He conforms to the party's policies du jour, is a good communist, good father, good husband. He and Jiazhen simply want to live. What they have to do to accomplish that, however, is haunting and melancholy, less a testament to human tenacity than to the amount of grief one soul can harbor.

NEWSWEEK, 12/12/94, p. 72, David Ansen

In the 1940s, at the start of Zhang Yimou's wrenching Chinese epic "To Live," the dissolute hero, Fugui (Ge You), loses everything—his home, his family, his wife, Jiazhen (Gong Li)—at the gambling tables. It's one of the film's bitter ironies that this cataclysm may be Fugui's luckiest moment, for after the civil war brings Mao to power, the penniless Fugui can pass as a proletarian and stave off the axe of political retribution. But as the film progresses from the Great Leap Forward in the '50s through the madness of the Cultural Revolution—captured with a whiplash mix of black comedy and tragedy—the man who's lost everything discovers there's far more to lose. Superbly shot, this angry, tear-drenched saga is Zhang's ("Raise the Red Lantern") most openly emotional film. If it's better at charting the tidal waves of misfortune that break upon Fugui and his family than at exploring nuances of character, maybe that's Zhang's point: in Mao's China, individualism was the most dangerous luxury.

SIGHT AND SOUND, 10/94, p. 45, Tony Rayns

North China, circa 1946. In a series of dice games, gambler Xu Fugui loses his family mansion and entire inheritance to Long Er, the boss of a shadow-puppet troupe. Fugui's pregnant wife Jiazhen has despaired of reforming him and returned to her parents with their deaf-mute daughter Fengxia. The shock of losing house and home gives Fugui's father a fatal heart attack. Fugui sets up as a market vendor to care for his ailing mother. Seeing his new humility, Jiazhen returns to him with Fengxia and their newborn son Youqing.

A year later. Long Er refuses Fugui a loan to open a shop but gives him his old puppets and suggests that he starts up a troupe of his. Fugui performs all over the region, narrating the stories while his best friend Chunsheng works the puppets. During one show, however, they are press-ganged as labourers by soldiers of the KMT (Nationalist) army. The kindly officer Lao Quan befriends them and tells them a Communist victory in the civil war is imminent. As the Communist People's Liberation Army approaches, there is mass desertion and Lao Quan is killed by a sniper. Fugui and Chunsheng surrender to the PLA and are soon putting on a makeshift puppet show to entertain the troops.

By the time Fugui returns home (without Chunsheng, who has joined the PLA as a driver), China has a Communist government. Fugui's mother has died, and Jiazhen and Fengxia have been given work delivering water in the town. New town leader Niu welcomes back Fugui as a hero of the revolution and invites him to watch the prosecution of Long Er, on trial for counter-revolutionary sabotage. The execution of Long Er teaches Fugui to maintain his own political credentials. In 1958, as Mao Zedong calls for the 'Great Leap Forward' into Communism, Fugui saves his puppets from the drive to smelt all household metal by offering to put on a morale boosting show for the metal workers. During the show, Youqing (exhausted from long hours with his metal-smelting team) is killed while sleeping by a wall that is accidentally demolished by the district chief's car. The culprit turns out to be Chunsheng. Jiazhen angrily refuses his offer of compensation and tells him he owes them a life.

By June 1966, in the wake of the Cultural Revolution few figures of authority are left unscathed. Niu tells Fugui to burn his shadow puppets and proposes a husband for Fengxia: Wan Erxi, lame in one leg, leader of his factory's Red Guards. The match is a success and the couple marry. Chunsheng is meanwhile denounced as a "capitalist roader"; intending suicide, he secretly visits Fugui to beg forgiveness for killing his son. Jiazhen forgives him and urges him to fight on: the life he owes them should be his son. When Fengxia goes into labour with her first child, her husband and parents are shocked to find the hospital staffed by junior nurses, all the qualified personnel having been denounced. Wan Erxi invents a political pretext for fetching Dr Wang Bin; the old man is weak and starving, so Fugui buys him steamed bread buns. Fengxia gives birth to a healthy son (nicknamed Mantou—"Little Bun"), but then haemorrhages. Dr Wang is unable to help, having cboked on the buns and passed out.

Years later life has returned to normal. Erxi and Mantou are living with the now elderly Fugui and Jiazhen. Mantou buys some chicks while on a family visit to the graves of Fengxia and Youqing. Back home, Fugui pulls out the chest that used to house his puppets as a home for the chickens.

Two years ago, Zhang Yimou seemed to have redeemed himself in the eyes of the Chinese Communist Party. The authorities showered *The Story of Qiu Ju* with awards, and at the same time 'un-banned' his earlier *Ju Dou* and *Raise the Red Lantern*. But *To Live* has got him into trouble again. The film is in limbo at home, and its Hong Kong based production company Era International has been criticised for allowing its sale and distribution everywhere else without Beijing's seal of approval. Zhang's immediate future as a director is again uncertain.

The film itself does little to court controversy. Taken alongside *The Blue Kite* and *Farewell My Concubine*, the two other recent Chinese movies to tackle aspects of China's modern history across the lives of individuals, *To Live* seems cautious, if not timid. The only way that it challenges current Party orthodoxy is by gently mocking the naivety of the Mao personality cult in the 50s and 60s and by presenting the excesses of the Cultural Revolution in black-comedy terms. Its only tendentious comment springs from the repetition of a fable of progress that Fugui uses to teach his son and later his grandson—the second time, conspicuously omitting 'Communism' from the evolutionary scheme of things. Compared with Chen Kaige's wholesale revisionism and flirtation with deviant sexuality or Tian Zhuangzhuang's implication that all the foundations for the collective madness of the Cultural Revolution were laid in the 50s, these transgressions are at best minor. Had the film been made by someone less high profile than Zhang Yimou, or had not been completed so soon after *The Blue Kite*, it would probably have incurred no disapproval.

Zhang has given relatively few interviews about the film, but in all those that have reached print insists that his aim was to make a genuinely populist film: an account of four turbulent decades from a grass-roots perspective, emphasising not the tragedies and sufferings that Chinese people have learned to regard as endemic, but rather the fortitude and general good humour that sustain them. In Zhang's view, this distances *To Live* from films like *The Blue Kite* and *Farewell My Concubine*, which he criticises for adopting an 'elitist' stance and for dwelling excessively on victim figures. It's not hard to guess why Zhang feels the need to open up a space between his film and those others, but his analysis seems oddly awry. *To Live* actually fits neatly between the low-key naturalism of *The Blue Kite* and the high-powered histrionics of *Farewell My Concubine* and its script is closer to conventional melodrama than either of them.

But Zhang, of course, is after something more than melodrama, even if he uses some of the tenets of melodrama to broaden the film's appeal. What he picked up on in Yu Hua's lengthy (and considerably more melodramatic) novel was the underlying sense of resilience in ordinary lives, and he has clearly realised that the best way to express this on screen is through his cast. *To Live* is the first Zhang Yimou film in which the cinematography and editing are more at the service of the actors than of the director's vision, and in which the design and colour schemes are relegated to supporting roles. (It's also the first since *Red Sorghum* in which Gong Li's role is less important than her male co-star's.) Zhang's formalist proclivities are more or less limited to the *leitmotiv* shot of the stone-flagged street that prefaces each 'chapter', the minor changes in its appearance reflecting the passing years and the changing political climate. He even succeeds in resisting the temptation to turn the shadow-puppet sequences into anything more than channels for Fugui's unsophisticated wit and exuberance.

The simultaneous reliance on melodrama and determination to transcend its potential excesses results in some fancy directorial footwork. Zhang softens (but in no way subverts) most of the emotional climaxes by cutting from close-ups to long shots or letting Zhao Jiping's plaintive score rather than the actors' performances carry the weight of the scene; the only exceptions are the deaths of the children Youqing and Fengxia, which are registered mainly through the traumatised reactions of Fugui and Jiazhen respectively. More impressively, Zhang minimises the feeling of melodrama by foregrounding domestic matters of little narrative consequence wherever he can get away with it. This strategy is nowhere clearer than in the final shot, an extended take of the surviving members of the family eating together happily—not Zhang Yimou's first 'open' ending, but by far his least portentous.

It's crucial to the film's effect that much of it seems more comic than tragic. In this respect, the choice of Ge You to play Fugui was inspired. Ge (best known in China for irreverent satirical comedy and best known here as the gay aesthete in *Farewell My Concubine*) is cast against type as a simple man with little capacity for anger. Ge You, whose poker-thin face is inherently comic, gives a masterfully underplayed performance. *To Live* is at its best when Zhang trusts his lead actor's face to carry the weight of the film's argument that ordinariness and optimistic resilience are essentially the same thing.

TIME, 12/5/94, p. 90, Richard Corliss

How severe may the punishment be for the crime of being a rich wastrel in a poor land? If the land is China in the first three decades of Mao's reign, the sentence is severe. *To Live*, the new film from Zhang Yimou, China's top director, is a visually ravishing, emotionally relentless catalog of the indignations visited on a family that had the bad luck to have it good before the revolution.

It is 1947. A rich merchant's son named Fugui (played by Ge You, who won the best-actor prize at the Cannes festival this year) waters the local casino tables with his father's fortune. Fugui is a cool dude in line for comeuppance, and he soon learns humility the hard way; it arrives like a 30-year plague. He and his wife (Gong Li) are bankrupted, then branded as decadent curs. But the pestilence is not localized; every family suffers. In the '60s, doctors are locked up, leaving the hospitals in the control of those bullying incompetents, the Red Guards. All that keeps the country together is the stalwart heroism of millions of families like Fugui's.

This trials-of-Job saga has been told more powerfully in other brave Chinese films (*Farewell My Concubine* and *The Blue Kite*), and *To Live* lacks the surprise and sumptuousness of Zhang's *The Story of Qui Ju* and *Raise the Red Lantern*. But the Chinese censors can still be shocked—and vindictive. Zhang was recently forced, under the threat of never making another film in his homeland, to write an apology for wanting to promote *To Live* at Cannes. So one has to ask, How severe is the punishment for the crime of being an honest artist in a corrupt land?

VILLAGE VOICE, 11/22/94, Film Special/p. 64, Georgia Brown

A movie made to finesse Chinese censors can easily slip through the grasp of Western audiences. Zhang Yimou's *To Live* seems a perfect example since it has lost thus far on both counts: The censors weren't fooled—the picture has yet to open in China—and Western critics generally have been underwhelmed. In Cannes, the film's string-bean star, Ge You, won Best Actor, but *To Live* itself picked up a kind of blasé festival buzz. It was variously dismissed as "surprisingly conventional" (*Variety*), a step backward from the refreshing spontaneity of *The Story of Qui Ju*, or as a misguided attempt to rival *Farewell My Concubine* in its sweeping overview of China's past 50 years.

Maybe it takes two viewings. I now see this as Zhang's most powerful film yet—a fierce condemnation of Mao's Revolution and a far more moving historical melodrama than either *Concubine* or *The Blue Kite*. Tone is Zhang's obsessive art-house aestheticism—those cool, hard symmetries raised to the max in *Raise the Red Lantern*. But what makes this film hard to assimilate immediately is its necessary disguise—a light, hustling surface and masking deeper strains of terror and woe.

To Live opens in the '40's, in the provinces, where the heedless Fugui (Ge) is gambling away the family fortune. Pregnant with her second child, his distressed wife Jiazhen (Gong Li) threatens to leave—an ultimatum that he instantly dismisses. So, in more or less one blow, he loses home and possessions, wife and child, as well as his aged father who suffers a heart attack in an apoplectic fit. About six months later, Jiazhen, with two children now, returns, but the high life—comfort and ease—is gone forever.

It's an irony that Fugui's quick descent saves his life; as a *wuchanzhe* or "man with no property," a sort of bumbling everyman, he's better positioned to survive the vast changes to come. To support his family, Fugui takes to the countryside with a trunk of shadow puppets, and in 1949 his troupe is caught up in the civil war—first, by Chiang Kai-shek's army, then by the Revolutionary forces. When Fugui finally returns home he finds his mother, dead, his daughter deaf from a fever, and his wife struggling to feed the children. He's just in time to see his double—the man now living in his family's former luxury—executed as a decadent counterrevolutionary. To live is to in the right place, to die in the wrong place.

On to the late '50s and the mass hysteria of The Great Leap Forward (i.e., the great flip backward). Zhang's outrage emerges obliquely, with moments of great pathos usually inserted at the tail end of comic high jinks. In this case, the village's donation to the Communist Party of precious household utensils—melted into enough so-called steel for "three cannonballs aimed at Taiwan"—suddenly translates into Fugui and Jiazhen's "donation" of their beloved son. A decade later the grotesque anti-intellectualism of the cultural Revolution costs the couple their other child.

In the novel by Yu Hua, only Fugui survives. Zhang has said that in a film such a bleak ending would be "unbearable." What he also may be saying is that in China, movies are subject to more rigorous censorship than novels. As it is, *To Live* approaches the unendurable once events sink in. Those giant Mao posters make good jokes, but they're also oversized reminders of a nation's (continuing) madness.

Just before his son Youqing is killed, Fugui tells the boy a kind of parable in which a little family starts out as a chicken, grows into a goose, a sheep, and finally an ox. "After the ox, Daddy?" asks Youqing. "After the ox, communism," Daddy replies confidently. At the end, this tale is repeated with the couple's grandson, Little Bun. But now when the child asks what comes after the ox, ideology is the unspoken negative. "Little Bun will grow up," Jiazhen states simply.

To live is to hope for change; if you live long enough it might come about. But the implication of Zhang's devastating history play is that natural law has been subverted and a generation skipped. *To Live* sings not only the survivors' sad song but a requiem for the Revolution's casualties.

Also reviewed in:
CHICAGO TRIBUNE, 12/23/94, Friday/p. L, Michael Wilmington
NEW YORK TIMES, 11/28/94, p. C12, Caryn James
NEW YORKER, 11/28/94, p. 159, Anthony Lane
VARIETY, 5/23-29/94, p.53, Derek Elley
WASHINGTON POST, 12/23/94, p. D6, Hal Hinson
WASHINGTON POST, 12/23/94, Weekend/p. 36, Eve Zibart

TOM & VIV

A Miramax Films release of a Samuelson Productions/Harvey Kass/IRS Media Inc. production with the participation of British Screen. *Executive Producer:* Paul Colichman and Miles A. Copeland III. *Producer:* Marc Samuelson, Harvey Kass, and Peter Samuelson. *Director:* Brian Gilbert. *Screenplay:* Michael Hastings and Adrian Hodges. *Based on the play by:* Michael Hastings. *Director of Photography:* Martin Fuhrer. *Editor:* Tony Lawson. *Music:* Debbie Wiseman. *Choreographer:* Carol Fletcher. *Sound:* Peter Glossop. *Sound Editor:* Rodney Glenn and Bill Trent. *Casting:* Michelle Guish and Donald Paul Pemrick. *Production Designer:* Jamie Leonard. *Art Director:* Mark Raggett. *Set Decorator:* Jill Quertier. *Special Effects:* Derek Langley. *Costumes:* Phoebe De Gaye. *Make-up:* Morag Ross. *Running time:* 125 minutes. *MPAA Rating:* R.

CAST: Willem Dafoe (Tom Eliot); Miranda Richardson (Vivienne Haigh-Wood); Rosemary Harris (Rose Haigh-Wood); Tim Dutton (Maurice Haigh-Wood); Nickolas Grace (Bertrand Russell); Geoffrey Bayldon (Harwent); Clare Holman (Louise Purdon); Phillip Locke (Charles Haigh-Wood); Joanna McCallum (Virginia Woolf); Joseph O'Connor (Bishop of Oxford); John Savident (Sir Frederick Lamb); Michael Attwell (W.L. Janes); Sharon Bower (Secretary); Linda Spurrier (Edith Sitwell); Roberta Taylor (Ottoline Morrell); Christopher Baines (Verger); Anna Chancellor (Woman); John Clegg and Simon Robson (Men); James Greene (Dr. Cyriax); Lou Hirsch (Captain Todd); Edward Holmes (Telegraph Boy); Simon McBurney (Dr. Reginald Miller); William Osborne (Curate); Hugh Simon (Concierge);

Derek Smee (Mr. Davis); Peter Stockbridge (Porter); Judith Sweeney (Nurse); Giles Taylor (Young Man).

CINEASTE, Vol. XXI, No. 3, 1995, p. 40, Ed Kelleher and Cynthia Lucia

"At some point in their marriage, Tom went mad and promptly certified his wife. " That was Edith Sitwell's appraisal of the relationship between T.S. Eliot and Vivienne Haigh-Wood. Viv was the woman who offered Eliot entree into the British upper class, apparently inspired "The Waste Land," and wound up abandoned in a Finsbury Park asylum, where she died in 1947, a year before her ex-husband was awarded the Nobel Prize for Literature. Brian Gilbert's *Tom & Viv* would like to arrive at a conclusion approaching Sitwell's but not before positioning itself as both a literary biopic and a revisionist melodrama/woman's film. Exploring the troubled marriage between Eliot (Willem Dafoe) and the often erratic Vivienne (Miranda Richardson), the film attempts to reposition the poet by offering some insight into his aristocratic pretensions and his embrace of the Church of England, while he proclaims that "poetry is not an expression of emotion but an escape from emotion." *Tom & Viv* traces the marriage, which began in 1915, when Eliot studied and taught at Oxford, and ended two decades later. Having achieved stunning literary success, he left London for a Harvard professorship, separating from Viv and committing her.

Extricating Viv from the occasional footnote or passing reference in the pages of many an Eliot biography (with the exception of Peter Ackroyd's 1984 biography), *Tom & Viv* also aspires to a feminist reading of traditional suppositions, whether cultural or medical, regarding female creativity, stability, and sexuality. Unlike the play by Michael Hastings on which it is based, however, Gilbert's film (which credits Hastings and Adrian Hodges as screenwriters) ultimately dares not 'disturb the universe,' that male-dominated enclave which venerates T.S. Eliot and has long dispatched women to a Finsbury Park outpost all their own.

Instead of letting the viewer discover Tom's and Viv's objectives in good time, the film explicates them in the first ten minutes, Tom loves Viv, but he also loves her family's long-established position within the British upper class. Viv loves Tom, but she also delights in shocking her reserved family by choosing a penniless poet from St. Louis who rooms with his mentor Bertrand Russell (Nickolas Grace), often described as "the most hated man in London." By anointing Viv's brother Maurice (Tim Dutton) as the film's narrator, Gilbert shortchanges Viv just as decisively as the post-Victorian British culture which silenced her. Viv "suffered from what we used to call women's troubles," as the slow-witted Maurice notes, and what might have been treated medically as a hormonal imbalance was diagnosed as "moral insanity." As positioned within the film's conventional narrative structure, Viv cannot assume the authority she deserves and which she was given in Hastings's theatrical script. On stage, the interplay of several narrative voices explored her complexity, rescuing her from the margins of her own life.

One voice that is barely audible in the movie is that of Louise Purdon. Originally a night nurse at Viv's chemist, Allen & Hanbury, Louise, in real life, became a social activist via the National Society for Lunacy Law Reform. Through Louise's activism, as presented in the play, Viv was emboldened to escape from the asylum, if only for one night. But the film is happy to present Louise merely as a loyal friend who excels at needlepoint, clearly passing up the opportunity to give her political voice. In doing so, it also passes up the opportunity to present Viv as anything more than the melodramatic cliché—the woman at the window forever looking out at a landscape she cannot inhabit.

The film similarly adopts a timeworn Hollywood approach in excluding the viewer deliberately from the intimacy of Tom and Viv's honeymoon, not out of prudishness but a squeamish avoidance of an aspect of female sexuality that it assumes the viewer, like Tom, will find revolting. Viv's hormonal imbalance is discovered by the viewer after the fact—we see her huddled in an Eastbourne hotel suite with bloodstained sheets signifying a 'shameful' breach in their new marriage. Tom stands at the window looking puzzled, betrayed, even trapped. The sheets become a recurring symbol of Viv s 'imperfections' which are perceived as 'staining' not only her marriage but also Tom's artistic and careerist ambitions. Seconds later, Tom has disappeared from the window of the hotel room while Viv remains inside gulping medication and scrubbing away, Lady Macbeth-like, at the sheets. Juxtaposed with scenes of her increasing anxiety are images of Tom walking alone on the beach. This crosscutting of images imposes a view of their relationship in which Viv is consigned to the role of hysterical female trapped by her own biology, and Tom is permitted the role of suffering poet cleansed, even transformed, by nature. Sustained throughout the film, which offers no revisionist alternative, this melodramatic view recalls the Hollywood woman's film which pathologizes female sexuality as destructive to the social order.

By not showing us how Viv's blood got on the sheets, director Gilbert sidesteps an opportunity to enter into a critical dialog with the conventional melodrama. (When Viv's mother Rose [Rosemary Harris] asks, "How often is Granny visiting you!," and then rephrases the question with yet another euphemism, "the curse," the film presents this exchange without irony, thereby offering the cinematic equivalent of the very reliance on euphemism it ought to be questioning.) In choosing to concentrate on Tom's reaction, the film endorses his need to be part of a patriarchal social order from which an unstable presence like Viv must be exiled. *Tom & Viv*, for all its revisionist posturing, has stacked its deck against Viv. Initially presented as a free spirit in the cinematic tradition of such characters, Viv disregards staid Oxford rules, blithely dances on the lawn in front of the sign that reads, 'Keep Off the Grass,' and, in an image that the film will exploit in its final moments, tosses a bouquet of flowers in the air. But the free spirit soon gives way to a darker figure who becomes an obstacle to T.S. Eliot's ambition.

The patriarchal order of *Tom & Viv* is defined by the aristocratic Haigh-Wood household. Tom believes that "family unity is the root of all culture," but he is talking about upper class family unity. One suspects that had Viv been a member of the lower class, Tom might not have married her at all, or would certainly have divorced her after the unfortunate honeymoon. When Tom comes to the Haigh-Wood family, he can boast of little more than a one-hundred-dollar-a-year stipend from Harvard. Twelve years later, when Vivienne's father Charles dies, Tom becomes the de facto head of the family, with Viv, a woman of considerable intelligence, relegated to the role of irresponsible financial dependent. While Viv has every reason to question her exclusion from Charles's will, the film plays down her objections in order to cast her as a hysterical intruder on a family inheritance meeting. Why, for example, should Viv's reasonable concerns about family finances be challenged as disruptive, when Maurice's desire to "try [his] luck in Africa" is seen as perfectly rational and appropriate, however disastrous the result! "Darling, leave it to the boys; they know best," is the admonition Viv receives from her mother, who believes that Tom and Maurice are more capable than the women of the family. Clearly, for Tom, family unity has paid off.

On a wider cultural level the patriarchal order is embodied by the institutions of medicine, religion, and law, presided over by powerful male figures. The implicit trust Rose Haigh-Wood places in "the boys" is extended to the doctors who variously characterize her daughter's ailment as "intestinal catarrh," "a febrile disease of the mind," and, finally, "moral insanity." But Rose's trust (and Tom's) is misplaced; the medical discourse here defines Viv as the Other in that her biological condition is read as outside the realm of her own comprehension. In two separate scenes, Tom and Rose visit doctors who insist upon discussing Viv when she is not in the room. Through cross-cutting between the consultation room and a room next door where Viv must wait, the film enlists the viewer's complicity in the diagnosis. With red lipstick, Viv scrawls her defiance on a medical mannequin, a stand-in for all female patients. To the doctors, Viv is the Other; to Viv, the mannequin is an absurd reminder of her own exiled position. The film recognizes that exile but, at the same time, through editing, legitimizes the diagnosis, leaving the viewer with a final close-up of Tom as he repeats the word, "insanity." Dafoe invests this moment with a powerful clash of emotions: disbelief and compassion, recognition and horror that Viv's behavior could undermine the position Eliot worked so hard to reach among the literary elite of London.

Even before this dramatic moment, Tom has reached out to another wing of the patriarchal order. Through its structure, the film implies that as Tom loses faith in medical remedies, he increasingly places faith in religion. Just as he married into the aristocratic Haigh-Wood family, Tom now 'marries' into the Church of England via religious conversion, perhaps hoping to find the stability missing in his relationship with Viv. Juxtaposed with scenes in which the medical prognoses become increasingly grim are those in which Tom seeks spiritual guidance. In one such scene, immediately following the verdict of Viv's moral insanity, Tom ushers a Church of England bishop into his home, only to find Viv unconscious on the floor. "What has she done!," the bishop asks, incredibly enough. Moments later, the bishop comforts a sobbing Tom, who confesses, "I crave companionship, yet I am completely alone." In the next scene, Tom is baptized and becomes further assimilated into the aristocratic 'Englishness' he craves. In this somewhat reductionist view, the film implies that Tom will have the structured companionship of organized religion while, in effect, dismissing a skeptical Viv to a future in which she will have no such solace—in fact, she will be completely alone.

Tom will find further consolation, even justification, in the arms of the Law. Not only does the law exclude Viv from her rightful share of the Haigh-Wood estate, but it becomes the arbiter of her fate. The Lunacy Act condemned thousands of women to live out their lives in asylums, not necessarily because they were insane, but in some cases, like Viv's, as a means of containing unconventional, potentially embarrassing behavior. As a doctor in the film points out, "[the disease] is notorious in attacking young women of exceptional gifts. The patient fails to understand her social position and her duty to society. She becomes vulgar, impulsive, and frequently shows a rebellious disregard for propriety."

The language of law and medicine converge in a crucial scene in which Viv must solve what amounts to a parlor game puzzle in order to prove her sanity. Before a group of tuxedo-clad doctors and legal officers, probably fresh from their private men's club, she must answer correctly or be shipped off to a lunatic asylum. (In one of the film s ironic touches, this scene echoes an earlier one in which Viv assures that Tom's youthful 'brilliance' will be recognized at an elite garden party by signaling him the correct parlor game answer.) Although Viv knows the answer when she is 'tested,' she looks in vain to Tom for a more significant signal—that he still loves her, that he won't abandon her.

More than a decade after Viv's incarceration, a U.S. Army medical officer visits her at Northumberland House. In contrast to their convergence, deemed necessary for Viv's committal, law and medicine now diverge in this somewhat ambiguous scene. Now past menopause, Viv learns that her original gynecological condition was, in fact, a hormonal imbalance now easily treatable. She also learns that, despite their divorce, Tom controls her money and, since no one has made application for her release, she is, in fact, paying for her own confinement. For Viv, Tom is now only a voice on the radio. Yet she refuses to hold her long-absent ex-husband accountable for her present position, telling the officer, "T.S. Eliot is the greatest living poet in the English language ... he has my undying love. He will have it until the last breath leaves my body, and he knows it. And nobody can ever take that away." Viv is in a no-win situation: neglected and abandoned but resigned to the knowledge that her lasting link to the world is through her former life with Eliot.

Tom & Viv is even more ambiguous in its final sequence, an elaborate set-piece which attempts to bring about what apparently did not happen in real life—a satisfying closure in the relationship between Tom and Viv. Eliot, having just read his poetry at a BBC broadcast, coincidentally runs into a now remote Bertrand Russell. Meanwhile, Maurice visits his sister for the first time in eleven years. Through intercutting, the film struggles to create a critical cinematic dialog which will acknowledge Eliot's negligence as husband, but instead recuperates his image as poet. As Eliot and Russell descend in the BBC elevator, Richard Strauss's "Biem Schlafengehen," from *Vier Letzte Lieder*, ironically celebrates Tom's soul as, in Hermann Hesse's phrase, it "soars in free flight." But the irony lacks conviction. "Don't think it doesn't hurt," Tom tells Russell, "she's with me all the time, every minute of the day." Tom's declaration rings hollow but is meant to be rescued by his recital of a confessional passage from *Four Quartets*. Coupled with the majestic music of Strauss, that passage endorses Tom's intentions which stand in contrast to his behavior. Viv tells Maurice that she hasn't heard from Tom in ten years, yet she presents her brother with a gift of chocolate fudge which he is to deliver to Tom. "I've learned to cook," Viv says casually, and as Maurice leaves with the fudge she, just as casually, takes up a position at the window. Tom's poetry (which Viv helped to write) elevates him to the ranks of the immortal, while Viv assumes her 'proper' place—the place of all women in melodrama. The iron gates of the asylum and the elevator release Maurice and Tom, respectively; doors open for these men, yet Viv must surrender to the social order. Viv's mortality as woman is made literal when she disappears from the window entirely, accepting footnote status, as Maurice, the narrator, is granted the final word, patronizing and strangely accurate at the same time: "Vivie was, of course, the strong one. She made cowards of us all." Tom, the artist as immortal, is granted the film's final image. In close-up, Tom cinematically displaces Viv, mediating her suffering.

Tom & Viv has the trappings of a literary biopic, but the way it departs from the norms, even the clichés, of that subgenre are significant. Perhaps because the act of writing itself is not especially cinematic, literary figures in movies are usually shown staring pensively at a blank sheet of paper, or, when sufficiently provoked, as in Fred Zinnemann's *Julia*, throwing a typewriter out the window. Eliot, in *Tom & Viv*, is rarely shown actually writing anything. Indeed, Tom's evolution as a writer is measured almost exclusively by his ascent up the social and monetary ladder, surely an unusual yardstick for someone who has chosen the generally unrewarding path of poetry. On those occasions when he is shown writing, Viv is right there with him; in fact, she is doing most of the work. It is Viv who furnishes inspiration and clarity, in spite of, or perhaps as a result of, her odd behavior.

When Tom is unable to write because he suffers from a migraine, Viv is a supportive, commonsense presence—more stable and solid than Tom, Viv's family, or the film, for that matter, has led us to suspect. Viv points out a certain self-destructive undercurrent in Tom's neurotic belief that he must be sick in order to write but can't write when he's sick. (Perhaps this neurosis formed the very crux of the marriage—Viv was the 'sickness' he needed in order to create, but once his position as a major poet was assured, the 'sickness' got in his way.) In another commonsense moment, Viv bristles at Tom's decision to take a position at Lloyds bank—a job secured by her father. Viv sees his decision as impossible when he announces that he can work during the day and write at night; more poignantly, she understands that in taking the job, he is abandoning their artistic collaboration. Viv promptly repays Tom by spending a rather disastrous week at the seaside with Bertie Russell.

Nowhere is Tom's betrayal of his wife as artistic collaborator more painful, however, than in a scene where the two are editing his work, and a Church of England bishop appears for a visit, clearly prearranged by Tom. As Eliot dispatches Viv to Selfridges to 'do a little shopping,' we share in her assessment of Tom as an "egotistical shit." While the film allows us to see the truth of her words in this scene, it suggests we adopt another response in a pivotal scene when, denied access to Tom's office at Faber & Faber, Viv pours boiled chocolate through the publisher's front-door mail slot. Here, Viv is reduced to little more than a cartoon figure, comically funneling her hot preparation (with all its female kitchen-role implications) into the vestibule of this male-dominated intellectual concern. Moments earlier, the film had prepared the audience by offering a close-up of Viv peering wide-eyed through the slot. The depiction of this unfortunate incident seems designed to produce audience laughter at the cost of empathy for Viv.

An important Eliot subject which *Tom & Viv* avoids completely is the poet's occasional flirtation with fascism. In his introduction to the text of the play, Michael Hastings refers to Eliot's "preference for fascism" and notes that in 1933 he "lectured at the University of Virginia about the undesirability of having large numbers of free-thinking Jews." In Hastings's play, Viv tells Louise, "Tom adores the fascists," and calls her Northumberland House black shirt and grey skirt "the fascist uniform." While Hastings may be excessive in reading Eliot's anti-Semitic attitudes as his embracing fascism, the film's reluctance to address Eliot's rather 'slippery' politics cannot be ignored. The implications of such a husband committing his wife to an asylum with a fascistic dress code remain unexplored in the movie. This raises a question about the target audience for the film. Is it likely to be those disposed to venerate Eliot or those more likely to feel sympathy for his unfortunate wife, whose offense was that she "failed to understand her social position"? "Are we going to be more ladylike now, Vivienne?," asks one of the officers as Viv is hauled out of a cafe prior to confinement. Perhaps Tom didn't 'go mad' before certifying his wife, but as the film shows, he didn't exactly protest. It remains for the Bertrand Russell character to offer *Tom & Viv*'s final assessment: "She always was unstable."

CHRISTIAN SCIENCE MONITOR, 12/2/94, p. 14, David Sterritt

[*Tom & Viv* was reviewed jointly with *Cobb*; see Sterritt's review of that film.]

FILMS IN REVIEW, 1-2/95, p. 55, Andy Pawelczak

My favorite movie about a writer is *The Shining*, and my favorite moment in the movie occurs when Shelley Duvall peeks at the opus Jack Nicholson has been writing and it turns out to be 500 pages of "All work and no play makes Jack a dull boy" in different typographical arrangements, There's nothing as uncanny and dramatic
in *Tom And Viv*, the tale of the poet T.S. Eliot's relationship with his wife Vivian. We see Eliot suffering over his typewriter once, but otherwise there's not much sense of what a writer's life is like, and Eliot wasn't just a writer—he was *the* writer of his time and place. Instead, the film offers a very familiar version of post-Victorian repression as Eliot puts on the armor of a business suit and labors in a bank while his wife rants and raves and longs for the liberated life of poetry.

The film, based on a play by Michael Hastings, seems to have taken its idea of Eliot from a footnote to *The Wasteland* in which Eliot quotes the philosopher F.H. Bradley: "In brief, regarded as an existence which appears in a soul, the whole world for each is peculiar and private to that soul." The film's Eliot is so private that he's a vacuum at the center of the movie. Willem Dafoe does the best he can with the role, but it's so poorly written that there's not much he can do except look tortured. With the sharp planes of his face heightened by the lighting, he looks like a cubist Christ in an incongruous bowler hat. Though the film tells us that Eliot was determined to disguise his poetic vocation from the eyes of the world, surely Eliot was as hopeful of writing a bon mot as any other wordsmith, but you'd never know it from this film, where Tom never utters a word that isn't commonplace.

Lacking a coherent personality at its center, the film displaces its interests onto Vivian, and here a new set of problems emerges. We're told that Vivian, an antic free spirit, wants to escape tight, little England, but then what does she see in Tom, who is practically a paradigm of Victorian uptightness, more British than the British, as someone says. Viv, it turns out, suffers from a hormonal imbalance that precipitates wild mood swings and erratic menstrual bleeding. On their honeymoon, Eliot is filled with disgust at her menstruation—we see her obsessively washing the bloody sheets—and walks out alone on the beach, a scene that is meant to evoke a line from Eliot's *The Love Song of J. Alfred Prufrock*, a poem that on one level is about sexual anxiety: "I shall wear white flannel trousers, and walk upon the beach." As Tom retreats more and more behind an imperturbable social mask, a face prepared "to meet the faces that you meet," Viv becomes more manic until finally Tom has her committed to an asylum where she spends the next 13 years without a single visit from her husband.

No doubt there's an idea in this film, but between the inspiration and its execution falls the shadow. Viv is Eliot's alter ego, the incarnation of his repressed crazy side, and ultimately an important source of his poetry in that period of his life. Miranda Richardson occasionally gets the sense of uncanniness we feel around the mad, as Viv says all the things that respectable, socialized people never say. She's Tom's oracle, his pipeline to the unconscious. After all, "The Wasteland" is more than just an epic of repression or a melancholy meditation on the decline of civilization. Eliot is the canonical poet of what Harold Bloom calls the Chaotic Age, and "The Wasteland," in giving form to that chaos, rises to extraordinary shamanistic intensities. The film has some sense of Viv's oracular role in Tom's poetry, but ultimately caricatures it in a heavy handed scene in which Viv recites part of "The Wasteland": "My nerves are bad tonight. Yes, bad. Stay with me./Speak, to me. Why do you never speak? Speak./What are you thinking of? What thinking? What?/I never know what you are thinking. Think:" Granted, there's something in these lines about Tom and Viv—we never know what Tom is thinking either—but as Viv keens the lines, Tom and Viv's mother (intelligently played by Rosemary Harris) exchange a knowing look, and the poem is reduced to a commentary on Viv's illness and the Eliot marriage.

But everything about this movie is reductive. Bertrand Russell (Nickolas Grace), Tom's mentor and friend, is a frivolous roue, and Virginia Woolf, Edith Sitwell and Ottoline Morrell are wonderful examples of the taxidermist's art—they're a trio of stuffed birds. Eliot, a man possessed of a delicate and intricate psychic equilibrium, is reduced to a repressive, opportunistic heavy with poetically haunted eyes, a more talented version of George Eliot's Mr. Casaubon in *Middlemarch*. Viv becomes the archetypal victim of both Tom and a medical establishment that diagnoses her as morally insane because her behavior is inappropriate to her social station.

The movie's direction, by Brian Gilbert, is so somnolent that I felt like a patient etherised upon a table and found myself thinking "Hurry up please, it's time." I don't think *Tom And Viv* will cause a rush on bookstores for Eliot's poetry, which is too bad—I reread some of it for this review and it's still powerful and incantatory.

LOS ANGELES TIMES, 12/2/94, Calendar/p. 4, Peter Rainer

"Tom & Viv" is a respectable attempt at a difficult subject. It's about the troubled marriage of T.S. Eliot (Willem Dafoe) and his first wife, Vivienne Haigh-Wood (Miranda Richardson), and the ways in which the trouble inspired the artist.

Based on the Michael Hastings stage play and directed by Brian Gilbert, "Tom & Viv" creaks. It's in the "Masterpiece Theatre" mode, except it's no masterpiece. But once you get past the rather uninspired treatment—the way each scene appears to be hermetically sealed—the film begins to work anyway. Gilbert and Hastings, along with co-screenwriter Adrian Hodges, don't set up Tom and Viv as icons. Most Hollywood movies about famous artists show us people who knew they were living great and famous lives that one day would be made into movies.

"Tom & Viv" takes almost the opposite approach: The sorrowing lives that we see are so miserably confused and painful that the characters seem in danger of going up in smoke before our eyes. Vivienne, the free spirit with her battery of psychological and physical problems, has lows that cancel out her highs; Tom plods through most of the movie like an undertaker at his own funeral. We're not exactly in Scott and Zelda country.

Tom is first introduced to Vivienne at Oxford in 1914, and their courtship is freewheeling and a little dizzying for both of them. Clearly Tom is enraptured by her manic gambols, and it's pretty funny watching this musty man attempting to keep up with her. but when he leaves Oxford to elope with her, their honeymoon turns into a nightmarish episode that set the tone for a marriage that lasted more than 20 years.

Vivienne's long-term suffering with an out-of-control menstrual cycle, coupled with the toxicity of her prescribed medications, keep her spinning more and more into mania as the years progress. Along with her brother, Maurice (Tim Hutton), who narrates the film, Tom finally commits her to an asylum in 1936. (She died in 1947.)

The pathos of the marriage is counterbalanced by the ardor that fired it. The filmmakers' approach is evenhanded: They don't assign blame to either Tom or Vivienne for what happened. (If anything, the blame the medical authorities who failed to diagnose the bio-physical nature of Viv's mental imbalance.) Even when we observe Vivienne puttering in placid comfort in the asylum, still adoring the husband who hasn't communicated with her in 10 years, it's impossible to affix blame. Perhaps that's because in Tom's deep-set eyes we can see the weight of remorse and sadness—and the love—that Vivienne still inspires in him.

The filmmakers want to present Vivienne as Tom's angel—his muse. And here the movie begins to stretch its good will. Much is made of how she "understood" his poetry, how she came up with the title for "The Wasteland." The pathos of their marriage is translated into Tom's inspiration—and that's a pretty shaky formulation. It's also offensively reductive: The correspondence between an artist's inner life and his outer one is far too complicated and discontinuous for such a treatment.

And it's particularly dubious in the case of T.S. Eliot because he was a sufferer from way back—his first poem, written when he was 9, was about the sadness of returning each Monday to school. The greatness of a poem like "The Wasteland" takes in so much of the modern condition (even now) that the film's attempt to scrunch its meanings into the framework of a bad marriage seems foolish. Sometimes the high brow on this film is set awfully low.

With the exception of Bertrand (Bertie) Russell and a few cameos from Bloomsbury types like Virginia Woolf, "Tom & Viv" seems distinctly underpopulatedwith great and famous names. The filmmakers want to focus on the marriage, but the narrowness doesn't do justice to the other influences in Eliot's life—Ezra Pound, for example, who rescued the poet and his art many times, is nowhere to be found.

Dafoe does surprisingly well as Eliot, though it's such a reactive role that most of the time he's virtually immobile. Dafoe actually resembles—or is made to resemble—Eliot in all his whorled, fluted handsomeness. He has a shadowed gravity that goes well with the poetry. But the stand-out performances belong to Richardson and to Rosemary Harris as Vivienne's mother.

Harris gives such delicacy and understanding to her role that it transforms the movie's meanings. At first, the character she is playing seems stuffy and over-refined but then we see that the stuffiness is a camouflage for her caring. Her lifelong concern for Vivienne is in her every gesture; she's infinitely tolerant of her daughter's upsets and yet they drag her way down. It's a great, valiant small performance.

And Richardson, who played the role in a BBC radio dramatization, is superb. She doesn't go hog-wild in her ups and downs— even at her giddiest we can spot Vivienne's suffering, and her despair carries a trace of jest. Vivienne's unquenchable love for Tom seems, finally, heroic. Richardson shows us the sane, composed, ardent woman that was nestling inside Vivienne all along.

NEW YORK POST, 12/2/94, p. 49, Michael Medved

Great poetry is like sausage: You'll enjoy it more if you don't know too much about what went into it. The major poets of this century all seem to have been difficult, deeply troubled individuals, from Ezra Pound to Robert Lowell to T.S. Eliot, who was arguably the most influential of them all.

The impressive new movie "Tom & Viv," based on a successful London stage play of 10 years ago, focuses on the most controversial aspect of the great poet's life: his tragic first marriage to Vivienne Haigh-Wood.

We first meet the future Nobel Prize-winner (the "Tom" of the title, played by Willem Dafoe) as a young American Midwesterner, studying at Oxford in 1914. He's infatuated with "Viv" (Miranda Richardson), a manic, high-strung non-conformist from a well-to-do, aristocratic British family. The young lovers elope, but during their brief honeymoon at a coastal resort, Viv reacts to Tom's brief walk along the beach by throwing a fit and trashing their hotel room.

As his literary career progresses, she becomes more and more erratic and unmanageable. Eventually, a medical specialist diagnoses Mrs. Eliot as suffering from "moral insanity."

With her own inheritance signed over to her husband's exclusive control, she is powerless to resist the now-famous poet's determination to rid himself of her embarrassing presence.

Miranda Richardson merits an Oscar nomination for her passionate yet perfectly balanced performance: She projects so much raw vitality, and such strange internal logic to her character's outrageous behavior, that she never entirely sacrifices the sympathy of the audience, even while causing endless pain to the people around her.

Eliot's character, meanwhile, emerges with less force and clarity. Dafoe does a solid job of communicating the poet's chilly, forbidding personality, though he never manages to suggest the emotional depths behind his poems.

Another difficulty involves Dafoe's accent: From the time we first meet his character, he speaks with the plummy tones of the British upper crust which undermines the notion that he's actually a social-climbing kid from St. Louis who's attracted to Viv in part because of her family's connections.

As in so many other recent British films, the costumes and locations are stunningly evocative, and the supporting cast (particularly a newcomer named Tim Dutton as Viv's well-meaning, ineffectual brother) is consistently superb. While "Tom and Viv" never quite achieves the moments of high tragedy it seems to be reaching for, it certainly inspires pity and ends memorably—and most appropriately—not with a bang, but with a whimper.

"Tom & Viv" opens today for one week in order to qualify for Oscars. It will reopen in January.

NEWSDAY, 12/2/94, Part II/p. B7, Gene Seymour

You've heard this story a million times. Many of you have lived it:

She loves him. He loves her. They marry. They find out they want different things. Things from dicey to irreconcilable. Either they muddle through as best they can or go their separate ways with varying degrees of respective pain.

A chilling third option is carried out in "Tom and Viv," Brian Gilbert's sometimes languid, but fascinating film, in which poet T.S. Eliot (Willem Dafoe), commits his volatile, passionate wife,

Vivienne Haigh-Wood (Miranda Richardson), to an asylum. And leaves her there till the day she dies.

Eliot's desperate, dubious and queasy act was the climax of a tumultuous relationship between two people who had little in common from the beginning except a furious passion for each other.

When they meet in 1914, Eliot is a star American student at Oxford University who's drawn to the aristocratic restraint that Vivienne, a smart, spirited, fun-loving daughter of the upper classes, wants badly to escape. She believes Tom's American background provides such freedom. She couldn't be more wrong. As Viv's younger brother, Maurice (Tim Dutton), observes, Eliot wanted more than anything to be a "perfect Englishman."

Worse, Vivienne is afflicted by a hormonal imbalance that gives her, in Maurice's words, "what used to be called women's problems." Eliot's emotionally remote reaction to her ailments—combined with ill-prescribed medication and know-nothing diagnoses from what are, allegedly, England's best doctors—cause her moods to swing in perilously wild directions.

The script by Michael Hastings and Adrian Hodges (adapted from Hastings' stage play) makes it clear that Eliot prospered artistically from the tension, especially in the beginning. "You're in every line," Tom assures Viv soothingly. Anyone who's read "The Waste Land" knows this to be the case.

The more famous Eliot becomes, the stiffer his upper lip gets. Both of which provoke Vivienne to spectacularly predictable displays of temperament that seem uproarious and harrowing. Unamused and increasingly desperate, Eliot convinces Vivienne's brother and mother (Rosemary Harris) that her committal is the only solution.

Ten years later Viv's told by an American doctor that such drastic action was unnecessary. Yet, she's incensed at any suggestion that "the greatest living poet" is anything other than a decent, noble gentleman. The rest of us have our doubts. But Dafoe's mix of eerie intensity and airy sensitivity almost succeed in explaining, without excusing, his actions.

Richardson, meanwhile, ends up owning the movie by doing what she's always done best: being high-strung. In films like "The Crying Game" and "Damage," Richardson's broad-brush approach to a characters' moods has seemed a tad overcooked. Here it's just right. Her long goodbye look to Dafoe toward the end justifies every high expectation critics have had for her film career.

NEW STATESMAN & SOCIETY, 3/18/94, p. 50, Jonathan Romney

Here's a basic law of cinema. Painters stand on storm-lashed promontories or lurk in quaint dank garrets, squinting into the middle distance, flailing arms as they sweep their brush across the canvas or leaning forward intently as they dab away with the microscopic tip of a sable brush. You might even get the odd yelp of ecstatic insight, in Spanish if you're lucky. Whereas writers ... well, they may take a drag at that Woodbine or the odd swig of Jack Daniels. But mostly they just sit tight at their desk and purse their lips. And the quality of a life of letters as captured on film tends to be proportionate to the quality of the literary lip.

The notion of showing the scribbler's art on film very nearly suffered a mortal blow in the Coen Brothers' *Barton Fink*. While John Turturro strained and kvetched away at his Remington in pursuit of his social-realist ideals, John Goodman was belting up the hotel corridor with a flame thrower roaring, "I'll show you the life of the mind!"

Cinema is usually ill-equipped to show the life of the mind at all. There have been brave attempts to get around this problem, notably an odd mini-genre of surreal adventure yarns about male writers in which desk jockeys find themselves becoming intrepid explorers of Nighttown: a sort of Spillane-goes-to-Hades school.

The hero of Wim Wenders' *Hammett* barely touched his keyboard, but got embroiled instead in a labyrinthine farrago that would have made his Nick and Nora Charles characters reach for the nearest cocktail. Steven Soderbergh's recently released *Kafka* used much the same narrative ploy to catch a suitably Kafka-ish tone, but presented its hero as an insurance man first, a skullduggery merchant second and a writer on the side.

The most extreme version, David Cronenberg's *Naked Lunch*,just about got it right. As delirious and shapeless as William Burroughs' books, its parodic fantasy variation on the theme of literary aspiration zoomed right in on writers' fetishism about their tools. Its focus was a struggle over their favourite typewriters between Peter Weller's Burroughs figure and a Paul Bowles surrogate. It played an agreeably nasty turn on the notion of literary inspiration, too—Burroughs' trusty Smith-Corona would turn into a hideous hybrid bug and start spitting out demands for "reports". For all its flaws, *Naked Lunch* is one of the few films to have captured the absurdity of the notion of the Great Work—either as serious as your life or an evasive pastime for drug-addled boys.

In all these films, though, the possibility of the male hack having a real life rather than a dream one seemed slim indeed. Hence the power of the literary lip as filmic icon, zipped tight, still or trembling, a fearsome signifier of sublimated libido. Weller's Burroughs and Jeremy Irons' Kafka were champion stiffs, but Willem Dafoe's turn as T S Eliot in the forthcoming *Tom and Viv* is surpassing in this respect, and the film ends up with an image of him that's quite blatantly intended to be iconic: behind bars (in a lift), sucking in lips and cheeks, with dead eyes to match an accent painstakingly learned from Eliot's radio readings.

The film isn't the slightest bit ironic about the Role of the Author, and in fact presents Eliot as a dull over-worker who's somewhat inconvenienced by the hormonal agonies of his wife, Vivienne Haigh-Wood (Miranda Richardson). But there's one light touch, which treats the difficult trope of the literary greatest hit with droll subtlety. The Eliots sit at the Haigh-Wood house giving her bemused folks a special sneak preview of *The Waste Land* and announcing it under its original title of "He do the Police in Different Voices". "Think of it as a shattered vase," Viv advises with relishable apprehension.

Tom and Viv is horribly weighed down by the requirements of the heritage movie—all those vintage cars and famous people. No one actually says, "My dear, you must meet Virginia Woolf", but it's a close thing. It is, though, desperately uneasy with its attempts to struggle out of the confines of its genre, which is the male artist-female muse film. It can handle the fact that Haigh-Wood was written out of Eliot's career, having provided the title of *The Wasteland* and some of his best-known riffs. But it can't quite deal with her as a writer, rather than as the impassioned Repressed of her husband's grim-lipped stuffiness. She's simply his avenging angel, the throbbing, bloody Problematic Feminine.

SIGHT AND SOUND, 5/94, p. 57, Claire Monk

Summer 1914. Vivienne Haigh-Wood, daughter of an English propertied family, visits T. S. (Tom) Eliot, a young American postgraduate fellow at Merton College, Oxford, and modernist poet; she is accompanied by her younger brother Maurice, a junior army officer. Tom and Viv instantly fall in love. Knowing that Viv suffers from mood swings and almost constant menstrual bleeding caused by hormonal problems, Maurice is disturbed to learn that the pair plan to marry rapidly without permission from Viv's parents, but merely warns him always to be kind to Viv. The drugs prescribed by Viv's physician offer no relief but cause (undiagnosed) side-effects for which further drugs are prescribed. Desperate for relief, Viv frequently binges on a mixture of medication, despite warnings from her pharmacist Louise.

On her wedding night, Viv bleeds heavily. Next morning, Tom walks alone on the beach, while she takes a cocktail of medicines and trashes the hotel room. Viv's father Charles is initially hostile to Tom, but her mother Rose approves of him. Tom and Viv live frugally in London, and she supports his writing critically, secretarially and emotionally. Ill from overwork, he often finds her unconscious from a drug overdose. They have moments of happiness, and in public, Tom pays tribute to their love. But as his fame and status among the Bloomsbury set increase, Viv becomes more confrontational. She is furious when he 'compromises' his poetry by taking a job in a City bank, and is increasingly excluded as he turns towards Anglo-Catholicism.

In 1922 Tom publishes *The Waste Land*. At a dinner party, Virginia Woolf suggests in Viv's presence that Tom would benefit from his wife's removal. Viv's father dies, and she learns that her mother has helped Maurice and Eliot make themselves sole trustees of his estate. In 1925 Tom becomes a director of the publisher Faber & Gwyer (later Faber & Faber) and, encouraged by his entourage, increasingly makes himself inaccessible to Viv. A medical specialist tells Tom and Rose she has a disorder called 'moral insanity'. Maurice and Tom claim to Rose that Viv is now a serious threat to Tom's career, and propose to have her committed. In 1937, Rose and Maurice bring in doctors to 'test' Viv's sanity, and she is committed, losing her financial and voting rights. Louise vows to fight for a change in the law.

After nearly a decade in a private asylum, the menopause has brought an end to Viv's symptoms. Charles Todd, a US research fellow, visits her with news of a treatment break-through for her former condition, and questions the legality of Tom's control of her estate; she declares she still loves him. Tom has not contacted Viv for ten years, yet tells his friend and former tutor Bertrand Russell that she is still "with him every minute of the day". After several years in Africa, Maurice visits Viv, who tells him she is as sane as he is, and hands him a chocolate cake to give to Tom. A caption tells us she died in the asylum on 22 June 1947.

"How often is Granny visiting you?" the quintessentially proper Rose Haigh-Wood suddenly asks Viv, after removing her daughter from the dining room when Viv's insistence on discussing pacifism threatens the peace of the 1914 English family dinner. "I thought Granny was dead," retorts Viv, before replying that she is menstruating three times a week. The presence of such startling moments—at once shrouded in euphemism and uncomfortably explicit—marks *Tom & Viv* as a welcome departure from the pretence of some recent revisionist costume dramas (Coppola's *Dracula* and Poliakoff's *Century* spring to mind) that taboos and mores were the same 'then' as they are now. While it inevitably allots us the pleasures of superior knowledge, director Brian Gilbert makes a real effort to position us to understand the specific fears and ignorances of another time.

Tom & Viv creates a significant genre disturbance by its insertion of gynaecology—the female body as messy, uncontrollable organism—into a past which a spate of recent films have unerringly imagined as a place of controlled emotions and sexual restraint. All the more disappointing, then, that this disturbance is diluted by heritage aspirations of the dullest kind. While the film's sharp scripting is directly traceable to co-screenwriter Michael Hastings' subtle, impressionistic play of the same name, the aesthetic imposed by Gilbert is a slick, self-conscious exercise in period-by-numbers. Gleaming vintage cars, wildflower-rich cornfields, Oxford architecture, gawping undergraduates and punts clog the screen in the first few minutes alone. The mismatch between these nostalgic signifiers and the modernism of *Tom & Viv's* protagonists betrays not only a deeply impoverished conception of the genre but something calculated in the whole project. Inoffensively beautiful and flawlessly acted, *Tom & Viv* often feels more like a PR event than a movie which might spontaneously move or amuse.

At the same time, *Tom & Viv* is all the more problematic to criticise, in view of its status as part of a real-life struggle to remind the world that Vivienne Eliot existed at all. Just as Eliot eradicated Viv from his life, so his publisher Faber & Faber and his widow (the secretary who blocked Viv's access to Tom later became his wife) have continued the process since his death actively obstructing the work of anyone likely to challenge their version of the Eliot myth. To comment on Eliot's radical denial of his 17 years with Viv, or to suggest (as Hastings did) that their life together lay at the heart of Eliot's poetry and that Viv was almost certainly his writing partner on *The Waste Land*—all this is asking for trouble, and indeed the second Mrs Eliot did her utmost to prevent the recent reprint of Hastings' play.

Perhaps Willem Dafoe's peculiar, monotone performance as Eliot—his automaton delivery lifted from the poet's wartime BBC broadcasts but his accent strangely Germanic—is an ironic response to this enforced caution; but it serves equally well as a commentary on Eliot's perverse belief that a poet should reject emotion and the 'vulgarity' of personality. The portrayal is surprisingly free of the classic problems of literary biopic representation: Eliot seems the opposite of a 'Great Man', and spends pleasingly little time hunched over a typewriter struggling to represent unrepresentable creative processes. The problem with Dafoe's inexpressiveness is that it leaves Eliot's psyche uninterrogated. By failing to show us that he was sick as chronically as Viv and broke down from overwork as frequently as she overdosed, or to articulate the misogynist body-loathing behind his conversion to Anglo-Catholicism, or to mention his fascism, the film privileges Eliot with a false 'normality'. The effect is to leave the pathologisation of Viv's instabilities unchallenged.

Thus Richardson's sympathetic, surprisingly humorous performance can't quite rescue Viv from the tension of simultaneously embodying two contradictory discourses: the feminist reclamation of the woman artist written out of male history, and the misogynist conception of female creativity as intrinsically rooted in hysteria. Her very casting—in a role which extends rather than transcends her familiar range of gong-winning histrionics—at first seems unwise, as she cavorts Isadora Duncan-style across Merton College quad and slings Eliot's banking clothes out of their flat window; but as society and family close in on Viv, Richardson brings a wry self-awareness and subversive inner logic to her acts of revenge. Pulling a toy knife on Virginia Woolf while out shopping, and pouring melted chocolate through Faber & Gwyer's letterbox—acts like these come to seem expressions of supreme sanity. Perhaps Viv's ghost might like to try the latter trick on *Tom & Viv*'s makers. In this lavish reclamation of her reputation, the fact that she was a talented, and much admired writer independently of Eliot is never mentioned.

Also reviewed in:
NEW REPUBLIC, 1/23/94, p. 30, Stanley Kauffmann
NEW YORK TIMES, 12/2/94, p. C3, Caryn James
NEW YORKER, 12/12/94, p. 125, Anthony Lane
VARIETY, 4/18-24/94, p. 61, Derek Elley
WASHINGTON POST, 2/17/95, p. F1, Hal Hinson

TOTALLY F***ED UP

A Strand Releasing presentation of a Desperate Pictures production in association with Blurco/Muscle & Hate Studios. *Producer:* Andrea Sperling and Gregg Araki. *Director:* Gregg Araki. *Screenplay:* Gregg Araki. *Editor:* Gregg Araki. *Sound:* Marianne Dissard. *Make-up:* Victoria Levy. *Running time:* 79 minutes. *MPAA Rating:* Not Rated.

CAST: James Duval (Andy); Roko Belic (Tommy); Susan Behshid (Michele); Jenee Gill (Patricia); Gilbert Luna (Steven); Lance May (Deric); Alan Boyce (Ian); Craig Gilmore (Brendan); Nicole Dilenberg (Dominatrix); Johanna Went (Excalibur Lady); Robert McHenry (Andy's Trick); Brad Minnich ("Don't Touch Mine" Guy); Michael Costanza (Everett); Joyce Brouwers (Deric's Mom); Clay Walker (Homeless AIDS Guy); Aymee Valdes (Hysterical Bloody Lady); Jon Gerrans (Trashbag Slave); David Finkelstein (Woof Woof Doggie); Pryor Praczukowski (BVD Corpse).

LOS ANGELES TIMES, 11/2/94, Calendar/p. 4, Kevin Thomas

In his fourth and best feature "Totally F***ed Up," provocative and talented independent filmmaker Gregg Araki delves into the troubled world of gay teenagers.

As in his first two films, the "no-budget" "Three Bewildered People in the Night" (1987) and "The Long Weekend (O'Despair)" (1989), he evokes desolate images of L.A, especially at night, which makes our town, in the words of one of this film's young men, "the alienation capital of the world."

As an angry gay man, Araki here addresses the disproportionately high suicide rate among gay teens. Although more serious than he has ever been, Araki speaks his mind without being preachy and, what's more, as in "The Living End" (1992), which told of two very different HIV-positive young men on the run, uses color and direct sound without losing the grit of his earliest pictures.

Principal among six friends, two of them a solid, good-humored lesbian couple (Susan Behshid, Jenee Gill), is the lonely Andy (James Duval), an appealing youth with a James Dean look and vulnerability, who doesn't believe love exists—until he's swept off his feet by the handsome, slightly older but vastly more experienced Ian (Alan Boyce).

Meanwhile, Andy's pals Steven (Gilbert Luna), an aspiring filmmaker, and his lover Deric (Lance May) soon experience a crisis in their relationship when Steven strays, trying to blame it on the fact that the new guy in his life just happened to have a bootleg Nine Inch Nails tape to tempt him with. Rounding out the group is the more easygoing skater dude Tommy (Roko Belic).

Araki effectively punctuates his story with quotes in the manner of one of his acknowledged idols, Jean-Luc Godard, and probing interviews by Steven, who's always poking a camcorder in his friends' faces. Indeed, the film is tautly, faultlessly structured, and once again Araki manages to create a spontaneous, off-the-cuff quality while actually maintaining tight control of his material.

Once again we're in the world of looming billboards, deserted parking structures and all-night coffee shops in which his disaffected young people do an awful lot of hanging out. Whereas in his first two films Araki brought out the humor in his people's self-absorption, here he's lashing out at the gay-bashing and what he aptly sums up as "institutionalized homophobia" that makes the teen years so tough on so many kids.

Araki presents none of his young people, all of whom are played so expertly by his cast, as gay stereotypes but rather as indistinguishable in dress and mannerisms from other L.A. teen-agers. (Only one of the actors is actually gay.) The irony is that if any of these young men had been even slightly obviously homosexual, they might have developed lots more resiliency.

NEW YORK POST, 10/7/94, p. 47, Thelma Adams

Teen angst isn't my favorite subject. In "Totally F***ed Up," writer/director Gregg Araki argues that homosexual teen-age angst is even angstier.

Araki kicks off his ensemble descent into acne hell with a grim statistic: 30 percent of all teen suicides are gay. (Tear my hair and beat my chest, Gregg!)

Then the director of the cult road movie "The Living End" sets up his own video-obsessed "The Real World," where all the characters are homosexual and under 20. Raw and gritty and riding on grant money (the National Endowment for the Arts and the J. Paul Getty Foundation coughed up), Araki eschews MTV's slickness but retains its smugness.

Of course, we must be interested in this dirty half-dozen. They include a philandering videomaker, his doe-eyed boyfriend, two hip and jolly lesbians, a beautiful boy trapped beside his family's beautiful pool, and a skateboarder.

The gang hangs out on the street and in apartments without furniture, living—as one character puts it—[the] lifestyles of the bored and disenfranchised."

We are voyaging beyond the valley of the Twinkies, where the dazed and confused speak directly to the camera calling AIDS "government-sponsored genocide" and whining about safe sex.

Saucily played by Jenee Gill and Susan Behshid, the lesbian couple in particular have their appealing moments. Araki has a talent for vernacular dialogue and for guiding non-actors into fresh performances.

But Araki's take on his characters is too external, too sketchy. I found the alienation of the characters alienating. I didn't care what happened to them, and couldn't take them as seriously as they took themselves. They bored me.

When the plot started nosing back toward suicide and the inevitable climax, rather than feeling the shared pain of the sextet of outsiders, I began to handicap who was going to drink the dran-O.

NEWSDAY, 10/7/94, Part II/p. B7, John Anderson

Clear-eyed, angry and anxious to offend, Gregg Araki's "Totally F***ed Up: is both a lament and a screed, a mixed-media Molotov thrown at hetero'merica, an emancipation proclamation for a lost generation of gay youth.

Does it succeed? That depends. Araki, whose "The Living End" was a downbeat breakthrough in maverick gay cinema, has acknowledged Jean-Luc Godard as the primary inspiration for "TFU" particularly the 1966 "Masculin/Feminin." And among the Godardian influences is a disinterest, even a hostility, toward the goals of traditional cinema.

What he wants to do, and does, is evoke a sense of resigned fatalism among his characters that's both inevitable and self-protective. His six young, gay, post-plague principals. Andy (James Duval), Tommy (Roko Belic), Michele (Susan Behshid), Patricia (Jenee Gill), Steven (Gilbert Luna) and Deric (Lance May)—experience love, sexual awakening, venal betrayals and fag-bashing. But the awkwardness is more painful, the betrayals more grievous and the assaults more terrifying because of the siege mentality inflicted by a nation's homophobia. It's justified, it's sad, and it's shared by characters and director alike.

Subtle? Not Araki. Opening up with a news clipping about the disproportionate rate of suicide among gay teenagers—lest one mistake where this is going—he interpolates crackling, computer-dating-style profiles of the kids with facetious, in-your-face titles ("Another homo movie by Gregg Araki" is one) before moving into its earnest filmed narrative. He bounces back and forth, breaking into the action with various venomous observations on titlecards ("Tom Cruise: Rock Hudson for the '90s"), interpolating whimsical bits of footage and digressions, and making himself one more character in his film.

The actors—only one of whom, Araki has said, is actually gay— are uniformly affecting, although James Duval's Andy, who strongly suggests the late River Phoenix, is the centerpiece. While the happy lesbians Patricia and Michele react to certain sex talk with "Gross-o-rama!!" and "Barf me out to the extreme!" Andy's revulsion is more deep-seated and self-directed. "All the stuff fags are supposed to like, I hate," he says, rationalizing away love, to say nothing of unsafe sex. "I'm glad things have changed," he says, meaning AIDS. When he falls, he falls hard.

Tommy is a rowdy boy, who's homophobe father beats him up and throws him out. Steven cheats on Deric, who can't forgive him. The two women, turkey baster in hand, host an artificial insemination party. Someone winds up face down in a pool. Amid the chaos we get incidental hetero sight gags—a hooker dragging an inert man down a flight of stairs, a woman walking a man on a leash, another woman chained to a wall, yet another, apparently battered and screaming, at a hospital emergency room, where the group has gathered for one of their own—a gang of one's own, one might say. One might also call Araki a segregationist, a condition that carries its own kind of fatalism. But anger can mean power, and it does in "TFU."

SIGHT AND SOUND, 2/95, p. 55, Tony Rayns

The film opens with a newspaper clipping, reporting that gay kids form a disproportionately high percentage of teenage suicides. In 15 numbered chapters, the film presents a group portrait of six gay/lesbian teenagers in present-day Los Angeles.

1: Film school student Steven is making a video documentary about the lives of his friends: Andy, who describes himself as "totally fucked up" and thinks he may be bisexual; Tommy, a boyish skateboarder; Deric (Steven's steady boyfriend), who paints and plans to start college soon; and the lesbian couple Michele and Patricia.

All of them find life boring. 2: The six talk about their experiences of sex in the age of Aids. Tommy is the only one relaxed about casual sex. 3: Everyone in the group enjoys getting high. 4: While Michele shops for Patricia's birthday, Steven confides his fear of settling down with Deric. Patricia longs to have a fatherless child.

5: Most of the six want to believe in love; Andy is adamant that it is a non-existent fantasy. After another dull evening, the boys head home discussing the sexuality of well-known movie and rock stars. For his video, Steven asks them about masturbation. 6: The girls ask the boys to pool specimens of their sperm, in an attempt to artificially inseminate Patricia. 7: The six feel alienated from both society and mainstream gay culture. One night Andy is cruised by Ian, who aspires to write like novelist Dennis Cooper. They agree to meet for a date.

8: Tommy has one-off sex in a car with Everett. Steven comes home from casual sex with Brendan to find a note from his mother that Deric called twice. At the end of a relaxed evening together, Andy allows Ian to seduce him. 9: Andy asks Tommy about submitting to sodomy. Steven confides to Michele that he was unfaithful to Deric, but starts lying to Deric to fob him off. 10: Andy feels a growing attachment to Ian, unaware that Ian has other boyfriends. Deric watches Steven's unedited tapes and comes across his confession of infidelity; enraged and deeply hurt, Deric storms out. Tommy's parents discover that he is gay and throw him out of the house; he moves in to stay with Deric.

11: Steven sends Deric a videotaped apology, but Deric can't forgive him. Andy is stood up by Ian, and gets his answerphone when he calls. 12: Deric, thinking of cruising the night streets, is beaten up by queer-bashers. He calls Steven, who rushes him to hospital and fetches the others. Andy visits Ian's apartment in the small hours and finds that he has company already. 13: Andy feels mentally broken. 14: Deric convalesces at home, but still refuses to take calls from Steven. Andy visits him, reporting that his "love affair" is over. At night, Andy cruises and has casual sex with a stranger. 15: Steven picks a fight with Tommy. Andy totters home and tries to phone his friends, getting either no answer or busy tones. He downs a tumbler of liquor, and then brews himself a cocktail of household chemicals and swallows that. He is found floating face down in his family's pool.

As many critics have discovered, it's often hard to keep the solipsistic airhead act that Gregg Araki puts on when he presents his films in public separate from rational appraisal of the films themselves. But the effort has to be made, not least because the films are in some ways getting better. *Totally F***ed Up* (the title is not written but spoken by Andy in the opening moments) announces itself as "another homo movie by Gregg Araki", but it's actually quite different in stance, style and structure from *The Living End*, Araki's first agit-queer movie. In some ways it revisits the manic, depressed LA soulscapes of his first two features, *Three Bewildered People in the Night* (1987) and *The Long Weekend (o'Despair)* (1989); however the protagonists this time are not failed performance and video artists but relatively cheerful and resilient kids in their late teens. And this time the film is framed as an explicit homage to Godard.

For *Masculin Féminin*'s "15 Precise Acts", Araki substitutes "15 random celluloid fragments". Each chapter is a mini collage: Araki's observational and storytelling footage is intercut with video material supposedly from Steven's documentary, and the whole is interspersed with Araki's attempts at sardonic, Godardian captions. The first 6½ chapters are organised around themes such as sex and dope, and designed to establish the characters, their preoccupations and problems; the caption "START NARRATIVE HERE " midway through chapter 7 heralds the somewhat half-hearted shift to story-telling mode and the subsequent chronicling of Andy's heartbreak, Deric's split from Steven and Tommy's expulsion from his family home. Very little of this is authentically "random" except for the Godardian composition of shots (there's a lot of tight framing that makes very inexpert reference to offscreen space) and the role of the lesbian couple Michele and Patricia. The girls are all too clearly present for PC reasons of balance and solidarity, but the only problems Araki can think of giving them are those of shopping and prospective lesbian parenting; most of the time they are there only as confidantes for the screwed-up boys.

As the film goes on, its purported randomness looks more and more like a cop-out, a mask for an underlying (and decidedly un-Godardian) sentimentality. Aside from a couple of anecdotal references to homophobia on TV and in the press, nothing here addresses the sociological questions raised by the newspaper clipping on which the film opens. Showing Tommy (apparently the only working-class kid in the group) being thrown out by his parents and having Deric being beaten up (off screen) by queer-bashers does not amount to an analysis of society's homophobia. Leaving all the parents off screen is not an adequate answer to the obvious questions about the presence or absence of parental support. And showing Andy's suicide does nothing to explain why more gay kids than straight kids kill themselves. Andy drinks Drano on impulse and drowns in the family swimming pool because he gave his anal virginity to a guy who subsequently two-timed him and because he couldn't get any of his friends on the phone when he needed to; sad, but not much sadder than spending a late adolescence holed up in your room with your Jesus and Mary Chain records, a habit by no means exclusive to gay teenagers. Araki, himself no spring chicken himself at the age of 35, may pride himself on getting so close to emotionally inarticulate teenagers, but he ought to be experienced enough to know that empathy alone gets you nowhere.

And yet the film has cherishable qualities. Its observation of the gay, teen and gay-teen subcultures in LA is spot on: a bootleg tape of Nine Inch Nails in concert used as an aid to seduction, an Aids patient begging on the sidewalk, a relationship forged in the toilet of a theatre screening *My Beautiful Laundrette*, lousy re-run tapes on the phone-sex lines. It's both admirable and believable that no-one inside or outside the core group ever draws attention to the group's variegated racial mix.. The sex scenes involving Andy—particularly his seduction by Ian in chapter 8, but also his failure to agree on a mutually pleasurable act with a casual pick-up in chapter 2—are models of 1990s safe-sex realism. Best of all is the casting: all six principals are new to movies, but Araki makes up for the shortcomings of his scripting by guiding them into performances of great naturalness and charm. All of which suggests that Araki may yet make a terrific film. Maybe next time.

VILLAGE VOICE, 10/11/94, p. 74, Randy Gener

A newspaper item forebodingly tells of troubled gay boys committing suicide. A title flashes: "More Teen Angst," Four totally f***ed up fags and a coupla lovey-dovey dykes are semiseriously interviewed via a home video camera. Another title: "To Live and Fry in L.A." Marx is dead. Coca-Cola is a cliché. These are the postpunk children of MTV and HIV. Are we paying homage to *Masculin-Féminin* yet?

An arrow points: "Start narrative here." Hunky Tommy says, "Everything that homos are supposed to like—disco music, drag shows, Joan Crawford—I hate." He likes to suck d*** but hasn't told mom and pop about it yet. Tired of poking his thing into Deric, Steven obsessively pokes a camera at friends. He surveys fresh meat, then hides his guilt-ridden face behind a pink copy of Andre Bazin's *What is Cinema*? Mopey, affectless Andy talks tough, poses a lot, and loathes buttf***ing. Until he gets cruised by a UCLA stud who loosens his tight rump. An old-fashioned romantic, he. Falls in love. Gets burned.

Ah, to be young, cynical, and hopeless! Start review here: In Gregg Araki's *Totally F***ed Up*, queer boys who go fish get f***ed over. Gargling life-is-shit alienation and lick-my-butt nihilism, it coughs and spits, rebels and rages. At Jesse Helms. At government conspiracy. At urban loneliness. At Tom Cruise. At A-to-Z narrativity. At sex. At lies. At videotape. Spiked with harsh wit and slap-dash genius, this devilish Godardian cocktail dares to be elatingly rude; it's ecstatically free-associative, secure in its own cool impudence.

The theme—the risks and pain of young love—frankly, connects with John Hughes's flicks and harks back to Araki's past no-budget self-absorptions, *The Long Weekend (O'Despair)* and *Three Bewildered People in the Night*. The quasi-documentary style irreverently subverts *The Real World* and musters enough irreverent sting to expose and mock its own self-indulgence and attitudinizing. As if by way of atonement, instead of the killer lesbians of *The Living End*, Araki shows happy dykes hosting an artificial insemination party (his male gaze narrows when it comes to showing why suicide occurs less frequently among lesbians). What's disarming is how much ardor, longing, and pure feeling he's able to stuff into a self-consciously disjointed movie that scrambles genres and lays on brazen ideology. *Totally F***ed Up* is a spunky collage that, for all its cocksure defiance, sure knows how to have fun with cocks.

Also reviewed in:
NATION, 10/17/94, p. 435, Stuart Klawans
NEW YORK TIMES, 10/7/94, p. C8, Janet Maslin
VARIETY, 10/4/93, p. 40, Todd McCarthy

TRADING MOM

A Trimark Pictures release. *Executive Producer:* Robert Little. *Producer:* Raffaella De Laurentiis. *Directed:* Tia Brelis. *Screenplay:* Tia Brelis. *Based on the novel "The Mommy Market" by:* Nancy Brelis. *Director of Photography:* Buzz Feitshans IV. *Editor:* Isaac Sehayek. *Music:* David Kitay. *Production Designer:* Cynthia Charette. *Set Decorator:* Lisa Caperton. *Make-up:* Jennifer Bell. *Running time:* 82 minutes. *MPAA Rating:* PG.

CAST: Sissy Spacek (Mommy, Mama, Mom, Natasha); Anna Chlumsky (Elizabeth); Aaron Michael Metchik (Jeremy); Asher Metchik (Harry); Maureen Stapleton (Mrs. Cavour).

LOS ANGELES TIMES, 5/13/94, Calendar/p. 4, Kevin Thomas

When writer-director Tia Brelis was growing up she was beguiled by a story her mother Nancy told her over and over called "The Mommy Market." Subsequently, her mother published it as a novel; no wonder Brelis chose to adapt it as her debut feature under the title "Trading Mom."

It's a charmer, about three children (Anna Chlumsky, Aaron Michael Metchik and Asher Metchik), fed up with their harried single mother (Sissy Spacek) and dreaming of trading her in for a more amenable model. When they confide their feelings to a neighbor lady (Maureen Stapleton), devoted to caring for her vast and beautiful untrammeled garden, she astounds them by revealing that via some hocus-pocus they can make their mother disappear but at the cost of erasing all memories of her. She then tells them of a bazaar, the Mommy Market, where they can pick out a new mother. The droll, captivating Stapleton is of course actually giving them a chance to learn to appreciate their mother as they never have before.

Filmed in and around Richmond, Va., "Trading Mom" has a lovely, shimmering look to it, and it affords Spacek a comical tour de force as all three mothers the kids try out. They are a rich, glamorous Frenchwoman who is interested only in the children's appearances; a hearty, outdoorsy Britisher who can cook the pancakes the kids crave as daily fare but who takes their sports activities so seriously she's only interested in their winning; and finally the deceptively sweet Russian circus juggler who takes her show-must-go-on belief all too literally.

Brelis brings to her film an appropriately lyrical quality to the telling of her mother's fairy tale, and elicits enchanting portrayals from her cast. "Trading Mom" is largely given over to fantasy, but the magic spell it casts is real.

NEW YORK POST, 5/13/94, p. 38, Michael Medved

Some 30 years ago, children's author Nancy Brelis published a charming book called "The Mommy Market" and now her daughter Tia Brelis, a recent graduate of NYU film school, has written and directed the screen version of her mother's tale.

It's a touching act of devotion (emphasized by the film's dedication "to our mothers"), but good intentions can't overcome the amateurish direction and awful acting that make this picture an unwatchable dud.

Sissy Spacek plays an overburdened single mom in Virginia whose three kids (led by 12-year-old Anna Chlumsky of both "My Girl" movies) resent her efforts to keep a clean house and enforce some modicum of discipline. "You know what would be really cool?" asks the ear-ring-wearing older boy (Aaron Michael Metchik). "Presto, you zap mom, and then she's history!"

Thanks to an incantation they learn from a mystical neighbor (Maureen Stapleton), the kids get their wish. One stormy night, they make their mother disappear and then get the chance to go to "The Mommy Market," where they can select up to three different candidates for the inestimable privilege of serving as their mother.

They choose a wealthy French glamour-puss, then a remorselessly demanding outdoors woman who does a bad Kate Hepburn imitation, and finally a flaky Russian circus performer.

Using silly makeup and abysmally exaggerated accents, Spacek plays all three of the potential replacement moms. In view of her dreadful performances, who can blame the kids for reaching the conclusion that their own mother was the best. But is it too late to get her back?

The plot might have worked with a touch of magical whimsy and outrageous humor, but director Brelis fails on both counts.

The amazing Mommy Market looks like nothing more than a tacky crafts-fair and attempts at slapstick are so embarrassingly inept they're painful to watch. In one scene, Spacek falls into a horse stall, while the animal lifts his tail and deposits great blobs of brown goo all over her heavily rouged face.

This act might represent an appropriate reaction to one of the unquestioned low-points of Spacek's great career.

NEWSDAY, 5/13/94, Part II/p. B7, John Anderson

"Don't you wish we had one of those mothers who did everything for you?" asks young Harry Martin (Asher Metchik), referring perhaps to some extinct creature he saw on "Nick-at-Nite." What he and the other young Martins have instead is a conscientious single mom (Sissy Spacek) with a demanding job, a dirty house and three kids who don't appreciate her.

They will, though. "Trading Mom," a sensitive comedy starring Spacek as Mommy *and* her three disastrous replacements, may be the mother of all mother movies. Sure, most kids (except mine) have wished for different parents at one time or another—they can be so irritating about civility and clean ears—but the idea of actually losing one is terrifying. And to lose your mother in a fit of pique? A nightmare.

The realization of such a primal fear will guarantee an emotional response in audiences, despite a setup that's a bit hard to swallow: The Martin kids—Harry, Elizabeth (Anna Chlumsky) and Jeremy (Aaron Michael Metchik, Asher's brother)—are unhappy with their mother, but for what seems like very little reason (some kids have real problems). "No wonder Dad left her," they say (Ouch!). Employing an ancient chant taught them by the magical Mrs. Cavour (Maureen

Stapleton), the brats not only make Mommy disappear, they can't remember her. And so, they go to the Mommy Market ("New shipments of Mommies daily!") to get a new model.

From here, the bittersweetness and silliness are distributed in equal doses, and—with the exception of one foul scene involving a horse—the formula works wonderfully.

The trio's first pick—they're given only three chances to choose—is Mama (pronounced *à la Francais*), a wealthy, well-dressed and oppressively mannered matron who gives Elizabeth a bouffant and the boys Little Lord Fauntleroy suits.

The second, Mom, is an outdoorsy type and devoted taxidermist who's so competitive she ruins the neighborhood kickball game.

The third, Natasha, a circus juggler (little Harry's choice) brings the whole troupe to live with the kids, including Andre the Giant. (The film was made a few months before the actor-wrestler's death in January, 1993.)

Spacek, who gets to really ham it up, is virtually unrecognizable as Mama, whose accent resembles Bronson Pinchot's in "Beverly Hills Cop." As Mom, her teeth are bucked and she wears Boy Scout gear. Natasha looks like Coal Miner's Carnie. And during the dream sequence in which the kids try to remember their mother, and thus retrieve her, she's appropriately ethereal.

The market itself has moms who bake, sing, play piano, play Nintendo, practice martial arts and rappel down mountains.

And what about dads? Well, as a Mommy Market manager explains, kids can't go to the Mommy Market and Daddy Market at the same time. "It's always disastrous," he says. "Trading Mom" is often wiser than it looks.

Also reviewed in:
NEW YORK TIMES, 5/13/94, p. C10, Caryn James
VARIETY, 3/21-27/94, p. 58, Emanuel Levy

TRAPPED IN PARADISE

A Twentieth Century Fox release. *Executive Producer:* David Permut. *Producer:* Jon Davison and George Gallo. *Director:* George Gallo. *Screenplay:* George Gallo. *Director of Photography:* Jack N. Green. *Editor:* Terry Rawlings. *Music:* Robert Folk. *Music Editor:* J. J. George. *Sound:* Bruce Carwardine and (music) Armin Steiner. *Sound Editor:* Gary S. Gerlich. *Casting:* Donna Isaacson. *Production Designer:* Bob Ziembicki. *Art Director:* Gregory P. Keen. *Set Decorator:* Gord Sim. *Set Dresser:* Richard Ferbrache and Gord Deyell. *Special Effects:* Martin Malivoire. *Costumes:* Mary E. McLeod. *Make-up:* Peter Montagna, Donald Mowat, and Allen Weisinger. *Stunt Coordinator:* Branko Racki. *Running time:* 111 minutes. *MPAA Rating:* PG-13.

CAST: Nicolas Cage (Bill Firpo); Richard B. Shull (Father Ritter); Jon Lovitz (Dave Firpo); Dana Carvey (Alvin Firpo); Jack Heller (Chief Parole Officer); Mike Steiner (Monty Dealer); Greg Ellwand (Cop #1); Kirk Dunn (Cop #2); Blanca Jansuzian (Shopkeeper); Florence Stanley (Ma Firpo); Cherie Ewing (Woman in Restaurant); Jeff Levine (Man in Restuarant); Sandra Myers (Diner #1); Frank Berardino (Diner #2); Mabel & Sarge (Merlin); Paul Lazar (Deputy Timmy Burnell); Andrew Miller (Deputy Myers); Sean McCann (Chief Burnell); Gerard Parkes (Father Gorenzel); Mädchen Amick (Sarah Collins); Donald Moffat (Clifford Anderson); Frank Blanch (Rutag Guard); John Ashton (Ed Dawson); John Bergantine (Clovis Minor); Angela Paton (Hattie Anderson); Vivian Reis (Lila); Bernard Behrens (Doc Milgrom); Bunty Webb (Hertha Weyerhauser); Kay Hawtrey (Rose Weyerhauser); Vic Manni (Vic Mazzucci); Frank Pesce (Caesar Spinoza); Vic Noto (Inmate #1); Nicky Pops Anest (Inmate #2); Rocco Savastano (Inmate #3); George Aggie Anest (Inmate #4); George Gallo Sr. (Don Vito); Al Cerullo (Helicopter Pilot); James W. Evangelatos (Agent #2); Richard Jenkins (Shaddus Peyser); Jonathan Allore (Agent Boyle); Mark Melymick (Agent Cooper); Scott Wickware (Agent Giardello); Sean O'Bryan (Dick Anderson); Zoe Erwin

(Marla Anderson); Tripod (Himself); John Dawe (Newscaster); Marcia Bennett (Bus Station Clerk); Brett Miller (State Trooper); Richard McMillan (Agent #1); Robert Thomas (Agent #2); Pierre Larocque (Trucker #1); Tom McCleary (Trucker #2); Bill Currie (Bus Driver).

LOS ANGELES TIMES, 12/2/94, Calendar/p. 6, Kevin Thomas

"Trapped in Paradise" may well be the worst Christmas movie since 1964's "Santa Claus Conquers the Martians"—that's the one in which Pia Zadora played a Martian child. It holds its audience hostage for an unconscionable 111 minutes with a rambling, unfunny, thickly sentimental comedy that plays like third-rate Frank Capra.

As bad as it is, it's understandable that players of the caliber of Nicolas Cage, Jon Lovitz, and Dana Carvey become involved because by and large their parts are well-written and because at the film's core is a viable idea: a trio of inept bank robbers find themselves stuck on a snowy Christmas Eve in a Norman Rockwell/Grandma Moses village called Paradise, Pa., where most everybody is so darn nice that these bad guys find themselves swamped by sheer goodness.

Unfortunately, writer-director George Gallo allows his essentially simple story to wander quite literally all over the countryside, piling it on with needless digressions and failing to make any of them more than faintly amusing. As it is, it takes him an interminable 45 minutes for his premise to kick in, and that's when the three brothers Firpo find themselves inadvertently sitting down to Christmas dinner with the family of the saintly president (Donald Moffat) of the local bank they've just knocked over.

Typically, just as this sequence starts building amusingly, Gallo yanks the Firpos away from the table and sends them on their wanderings.

The taut structure and crisp writing and direction needed to get away with such old-fashioned holiday uplift is precisely what's lacking. Robert Folk's heart-tugging score also detracts, giving the film the glazed quality of a candied apple.

The stars themselves are fine—Cage as the smartest, most-conflicted of the brothers, a classic good-bad guy; Lovitz as a crass, cynical compulsive liar, and Carvey as a goofy, high-voiced kleptomaniac—but the movie is too much a mess for their considerable presence to redeem it.

NEW YORK POST, 12/2/94, p. 51, Michael Medved

Christmas time is Capra-time for Hollywood, not only because of "It's a Wonderful Life," but because this is the season when one contemporary director or another will inevitably try to recapture the spirit of the master.

Writer-director George Gallo harvested a previous crop of "Capra-corn" three years ago with "29th Street," a funny, touching father-and-son saga about one of the first winners of the New York state lottery.

"Trapped in Paradise" is an even more obvious effort to appeal to those who love the redemptive messages in Frank Capra's work, but it goes too far in idealizing the small town at the center of the story. Gallo's vision of Paradise, Pa., is so pure that it makes Capra's Bedford Falls look as decadent as Las Vegas; so idyllic that it makes Norman Rockwell look like a hard-hitting urban realist of the Ashcan School.

This story begins in the big bad city, where restaurant manager Nicolas Cage welcomes back his two goofball brothers who've just been paroled from prison. These no-goodniks—the scheming, devious Jon Lovitz and sweet-tempered kleptomaniac Dana Carvey—are determined to manipulate their straight-arrow brother into joining them in their continuing life of crime.

A sentimental errand for a convict acquaintance leads to snowy Paradise on Christmas Eve, where the lightly guarded local bank presents a tempting target that the brothers can't resist.

They pull off their heist, despite hilarious incompetence, but when they try to escape in a blizzard they must rely on the incomparable kindness of the townspeople—especially the local bank president, Donald Moffat, and his warm-hearted family. Inevitably, the display of down-to-earth goodness, and the presence of a lovely, idealistic bank clerk played by Madchen Amick, inspires Nicolas Cage to go straight and to make up for his crime. But how can he change course with the FBI hot on their trail?

From beginning to end, this plot is formulaic fun, and the spicy, colorful performances help you to overcome its idiotically implausible elements—especially Dana Carvey's entertaining overacting as a light-fingered space-case with the endearing loopiness of a larcenous Harpo Marx.

Gallo also makes the most of his scenic locations (actually shot in Orlando), reflecting his other career as an award-winning painter of rural landscapes. His delicious Christmas-spirit atmosphere is hard to resist, though the picture postcard perfection would have worked better if he'd allowed his townspeople a few more foibles and failings.

"Groundhog Day" and "Grumpy Old Men" also conveyed deep affection for picturesque snowbound villages, without reducing their inhabitants to smiling plastic figures in an electric train holiday window display.

Gallo also reappears a distressing tendency from "29th Street"—trying to show his criminal characters' earthiness with an abundance of earthy language. Here, these altogether unnecessary obscenities make the film a questionable choice for the children who would otherwise provide an ideal audience for this warm-hearted blend of sentiment and silliness.

NEWSDAY, 12/2/94, Part II/p. B7, Jack Mathews

George Gallo makes a lot of jokes at the expense of the mentally deficient in "Trapped in Paradise," and given the quality of those jokes, it took a lot of nerve. Stupid is as stupid does.

"Trapped in Paradise," which is no such thing for those sitting through it, is a disaster with sleigh bells, a comedy intended to bring holiday cheer through the redemption of a trio of sibling thieves who, on Christmas Eve, rob the bank of a Hallmark village in Pennsylvania, and are then shamed by the sweet-natured generosity of the locals into giving the money back.

The story continues the themes of greed, easy money and redemption begun by Gallo in his screenplays for Martin Brest's fine road comedy "Midnight Run," and his own so-so "29th Street." In both of those films, the comedy grew naturally from realistic situations; in "Trapped in Paradise," Gallo is reaching for the kind of madcap tone in Stanley Kramer's "It's a Mad, Mad, Mad, Mad World," and falls instead into the irritating realm of Jerry Lewis.

Falling in with him are Nicolas Cage, Jon Lovitz and Dana Carvey, playing the brothers Firpo, of Queens. Bill (Cage) is the semi-bright, quasi-honest one, who is deceived by his recently paroled brothers Dave (Lovitz), a pathological liar, and Alvin (Carvey), a kleptomaniac, into driving to Paradise, Pa., on a bogus mission of mercy whose real purpose is to knock over the local bank.

Getting the money proves easier than getting out of town, however, and through a series of spectacularly silly events—involving FBI agents, the local sheriff and his retarded son, a pair of bumbling cops, and a couple of escaped killers—the Firpo brothers end up spending Christmas Eve with the Norman Rockwell family of the bank president (Donald Moffat).

Cage is a far funnier actor than either of his co-stars and actually develops something approaching a real character. Lovitz and Carvey are merely doing "Saturday Night Live" shtick, and they become tiresome (particularly Carvey, who seems to be doing an impression of Mickey Rourke before his voice changed) five minutes after they appear on screen.

"Trapped in Paradise" is not meant to be mean-spirited, and it all ends in a blizzard of Christmas day sentimentality. But using idiots and innocents as comic foils isn't my idea of getting into the holiday spirit.

SIGHT AND SOUND, 4/95, p. 52, Nick Hasted

New York City. Restaurateur Bill Firpo finds a wallet stuffed with money, and pockets it. At confession, he says that he returned it. The Priest tells him that his two crooked brothers, Dave and Alvin, are about to be released from jail. Warily, Bill picks them up and on the way home, the kleptomaniac Alvin begs to be let out at a candy store, where he tries to rob the till. Having tried to stuff the money back, the horrified Bill is forced to join his brothers in a getaway from the police. Back home, the acerbic Ma Firpo is reduced to tears by a letter that Dave and Alvin have brought from prison, begging them to visit an inmate's daughter named Sarah in the small town of Paradise. Initially, Bill is dismissive, but when he hears that the wallet has been found at the candy store, he agrees to drive to Paradise.

They arrive on Christmas Eve finding Sarah at the poorly guarded local bank in Paradise. When a huge supply of money is brought in, Bill is tempted, especially when his brothers reveal that they have guns in the car. Donning masks, they rob the bank, and make their inept escape. Back at the jail, feared criminal Vic Mazzucci is bragging of his perfect plan to rob the Paradise bank when news of the robbery interrupts him. While trying to leave Paradise, the brothers crash their car into an icy river, and are brought back to the home of the bank president Mr Anderson. Without guessing their identity, he tells them that the money was the town's Christmas Club savings, and that the robbery will cause the bank to close. Anderson's family, and Sarah, who is their lodger, treat the brothers with kindness. They are driven to the bus station, but when recognised, flee again. Bill stops off at a church, and suggests to Sarah, who suspects him of the robbery, that he wants to change. The brothers try a third getaway on a sled, but stop to rescue its horse. Bill convinces his brothers to give the money back.

While thumbing a ride back to Paradise, Bill is almost caught by Vic, who has escaped, kidnapping Ma Firpo *en route*. The brothers return the money, but the police follow them to Anderson's house. Inside, they find Vic, armed and holding Ma and the household captive. Sarah reveals she is Vic's daughter, and Dave admits that he had planned the robbery from the beginning. In a shootout with the police, Vic is captured. The townspeople provide the brothers with an alibi, and Sarah forgives Bill. As Dave, Alvin and Ma return to New York City, Bill and Sarah stay behind in Paradise.

Noted for his script for *Midnight Run*, George Gallo's second writing-directing effort after the barely seen *29th Street* is, according to its producer "in the tradition of Frank Capra".

But for most of its length, *Trapped in Paradise* is as far from Capra's harsh sentiment as it is from Gallo's previously droll humour. We first see Paradise as a model enclosed in a paperweight, and this image of suspension proves apt. The real Paradise is picture-postcard perfect, its niceness unrelenting, badness beyond its ken. There's a Stephen King story in which a couple, happening upon a similar wonderful town, freeze in horror at its unnaturalness. Such a suspicion has become deep-rooted in cinema ever since David Lynch's small town exposé, *Blue Velvet*. But Gallo intends no such subversion. Refuting these fashionable archetypes, *Trapped in Paradise* has a different sort of oddness. Partly based on Gallo's own birthplace, Paradise is a distillation of genuine small town goodness. The wasted presence of Lynch veterans Nicolas Cage and Mädchen Amick only emphasises this perverse return to wholesomeness. Remarkable as it sounds, this is a comic confection built on faith in human nature alone.

Sadly, its just this earnest quality which causes the film often to be very bad indeed. Comparison with Gallo's earlier work suggests that faith has undermined his comic talent. *Midnight Run* had old-fashioned screwball comic discipline, its sentimentality rigorously tempered by wit and tension. *Trapped·in Paradise* by contrast, sides so unquestioningly with small town values that the possibility of tension never arises. The communal innocence which allows the Firpo brothers to rob Paradise blind is never contrasted with the virtues of intelligence or imagination. The Firpos themselves are merely childish, never cynical enough to test Paradise's mettle, fitting easily into a town which appears to be a haven for the mentally subnormal. The soft-headedness of the whole project is summed up by Donald Moffat's straight-faced revelation that the stolen bank money is the town's Christmas savings. This rivals *Gremlins*' infamous monologue on the death of Santa Claus for sentimental dementia.

Indulging his own screenplay to an untenable extent, Gallo abandons any sense of perspective. Given the slightness of the plot, the two-and-a-half hour running time is clearly ill-considered. There are some very funny lines ("You're dumber than a boxful of hair"), but these are never far from stretches of utter mediocrity. *Trouble in Paradise* veers widely in pitch and quality, stumbling between the blandness of its subject and the occasional wit of its writer. Cage sums up this uncertainty best, mugging, muttering and shouting a performance of almost wasted effort. It's left to Dana Carvey to add a little grace. His one-note, sweet impressions of imbecility has the simple confidence of Hollywood comedy at its most innocent and effective. It' exactly the old-fashioned tone which Gallo must have wished for, but misses by a country mile.

Also reviewed in:
CHICAGO TRIBUNE, 12/2/94, Friday/p. J, John Petrakis
NEW YORK TIMES, 12/2/94, p. C16, Janet Maslin

VARIETY, 12/5-11/94, p. 74, Todd McCarthy
WASHINGTON POST, 12/2/94, p. F7, Hal Hinson
WASHINGTON POST, 12/2/94, Weekend/p. 54, Desson Howe

TRIAL BY JURY

A Warner Bros. release of a Morgan Creek production. *Executive Producer:* Gary Barber. *Producer:* James G. Robinson, Chris Meledandri, and Mark Gordon. *Director:* Heywood Gould. *Screenplay:* Jordan Katz and Heywood Gould. *Director of Photography:* Frederick Elmes. *Editor:* Joel Goodman. *Music:* Terence Blanchard. *Music Editor:* Thomas Milano. *Sound:* Bill Daly. *Sound Editor:* Michael Hilkene. *Casting:* Heidi Levitt. *Production Designer:* David Chapman. *Art Director:* Barbra Matis. *Set Decorator:* Steve Shewchuk. *Set Dresser:* Bill Johnson and Ken Clark. *Special Effects:* Laird McMurray. *Costumes:* Mary Malin. *Make-up:* Katherine James and Patricia Green. *Stunt Coordinator:* Branko Racki and Peter Bucossi. *Running time:* 108 minutes. *MPAA Rating:* R.

CAST: Joanne Whalley-Kilmer (Valerie Alston); Armand Assante (Rusty Pirone); Gabriel Byrne (Daniel Graham); William Hurt (Tommy Vesey); Kathleen Quinlan (Wanda); Margaret Whitton (Jane Lyle); Ed Lauter (John Boyle); Richard Portnow (Leo Greco); Lisa Arrindell Anderson (Eleanor Lyons); Jack Gwaltney (Teddy); Graham Jarvis (Mr. Duffy); William R. Moses (Paul Baker); Joe Santos (Johnny Verona); Beau Starr (Phillie); Bryan Shilowich (Robbie); Stuart Whitman (Emmett); Kevin Ramsey (Edmund); Fiona Gallagher (Camille); Kay Hawtrey (Clara); Ardon Bess (Albert); Karina Arroyave (Mercedes); Andrew Sabiston (Elliot); Paul Soles (Mr. Kriegsberg); Jovanni Sy (Louis); Damon d'Oliveira (Rafael); Andrew Miller (Krasny); Richard Fitzpatrick (Balsam); Robert Breuler (Judge Feld); Ron Hale (Bailiff); Sandi Ross (Court Officer); William Duell (Jimmy); John Capodice (Limpy Demarco); Andrew Lewarne (Petrie); David Eisner (Melman); Tanja Jacobs (Susan Fine); Diego Fuentes (Cop #1); Tony Meyler (Cop #2); Scott Wickware (Cop #3); Johnie Chase (Cop #4); Gene Mack (House Detective); Susan Jay (Sookie); Elena Kudaba (Elena); Gord Welke (Hansen); Stan Coles (Detective Gray); Mike Starr (Hughie Bonner); William Corno (Associate); David Cronenberg (Director); Fleure Presner (Supermodel); Junior Williams (Waiter); Chris Gibson (Hang Out Waiter); Rick Meilleur (Reporter); Wray Downs (Pianist #1); Gene Dinovi (Pianist #2).

LOS ANGELES TIMES, 9/10/94, Calendar/p. 2, Kevin Thomas

"Trial by Jury," an absorbing and ingenious courtroom drama/lady-in-distress thriller, is all the more entertaining for having successfully made consistently plausible the increasingly improbable. It's the kind of film that requires star authority to bring it off, and it receives it in abundance from Joanne Whalley-Kilmer, in perhaps her best big-screen role since playing Christine Keeler in "Scandal," the 1989 retelling of Britain's Profumo affair.

Whalley-Kilmer is Valerie Alston, a beautiful Manhattan divorcée with a 7-year-old son (Bryan Shilowich) and a SoHo antique clothing boutique. When she's selected to serve as a juror on the trial of a notorious gangster, Rusty Pirone (Armand Assante), charged with a raft of crimes, including 11 murders, she sees it as simply doing her duty as a good citizen. Yet almost immediately she is plunged into a nightmare, blackmailed by Pirone's henchman, led by cynical ex-cop Tommy Vesey (William Hurt), who threaten to harm her son if she not only doesn't find Pirone innocent but also if she fails to persuade enough of her colleagues to go along with her in order to create a hung jury.

Of course, Valerie should turn instantly to U.S. Atty. Daniel Graham (Gabriel Byrne) for protection, but Pirone's strategies are so diabolically terrifying, her decision not to is wholly and unsettlingly credible.

Written by Jordan Katz and Heywood Gould and directed by Gould, whose first film was "One Good Cop" with Michael Keaton, "Trial by Jury" starts out as a solid, conventional genre piece only to turn unpredictable. Whereas Valerie's complex and seemingly endless ordeal could bring about a nervous breakdown or worse, it instead toughens her, her loss of innocence confronting her not only with some especially sordid and scary realities of life but also allowing her to discover capabilities within herself she initially would rather have never uncovered.

It is entirely appropriate that Valerie deals in the glamorous gowns of the '40s and '50s, because when Whalley-Kilmer wears them she recalls the movie heroines of that era. You can easily imagine Barbara Stanwyck tearing into the role of Valerie under the direction of Douglas Sirk.

What cinches the film's success is the exceptional support Whalley-Kilmer receives from her three leading men: Assante as the once icily repellent yet undeniably sexy Pirone (who must surely use John Gotti's tailor), Byrne as the fiery, determinedly idealistic Graham and Hurt as the coolly ambiguous Vesey, whose fall into Pirone's clutches is never properly explained but which is effectively papered over by Hurt's sheer presence. Also contributing strongly in smaller roles, among many others are Kathleen Quinlan as a lethally tough villain and Stuart Whitman as Whalley-Kilmer's warm, loving father.

NEW YORK POST, 9/9/94, p. 44, Michael Medved

The dreary thriller "Trial by Jury" accomplishes only one thing—persuading the members of its audience to avoid jury duty at all costs.

Joanne Whalley-Kilmer stars as a heroic, hard-working single mother (Is there any other kind in contemporary movies?) who decides to do her civic duty and serve on the jury in a high-profile murder case.

The defendant is a suave mobster (Armand Assante) in expensive suits, who knows that the only way to avoid conviction is to intimidate one of the jurors so he'll get off with a hung jury.

The job of finding and frightening an appropriately vulnerable victim falls to a corrupt, world-weary ex-cop (William Hurt). He's utterly vicious when he approaches Whalley-Kilmer to threaten the life of her young son, but growing feelings for the lovely lady ultimately interfere with his work.

Meanwhile, crusading prosecutor Gabriel Byrne will stop at nothing to get a guilty verdict on the biggest case of his career.

These actors are all solid, watchable pros, but they're too caught up in the hammy excesses of their roles to pay much attention to one another. In some of the scenes they share, the performances come across as so self-absorbed that you can imagine they were filmed on separate sound stages, on different days, and only came together in the editing room.

With her fascinating face and huge, expressive eyes, Joanne Whalley-Kilmer can certainly hold the screen, but here, as in all her performances ("Scandal," "Kill Me Again"), she seems to be keeping something back—as if saving emotional resources for big pay-off scenes that never arrive.

The preposterous plot is meant to convey the deepest cynicism about our criminal justice system, which is allegedly incapable of protecting even a public-spirited juror from the bloody reach of organized crime. The message appears to be that trusty Hollywood cliche about meeting criminals on their own vicious terms in order to survive.

As Whalley-Kilmer declares: "You do what you have to do ... You don't think about right and wrong."

But you do think about plausible and silly, and the situations in which she finds herself seem more contrived than chilling. For example, there's a scene in which the defendant in a major murder trial take advantage of his bail to force his way into a juror's apartment to rape her that is so laughably far-fetched it's impossible to feel the terror the filmmakers intend.

Director-writer Heywood Gould made his debut with a little-seen Michael Keaton gem called "One Good Cop" three years ago, which displayed an abundance of the warmth, conviction and richness of characterization that this project so conspicuously lacks.

"Trial by Jury" offers none of the wit of the sparkling Gilbert and Sullivan operetta whose title it unapologetically borrows, but its story line is very nearly as silly.

NEWSDAY, 9/12/94, Part II/p. B10, John Anderson

When Valerie Alston (Joanne Whalley-Kilmer), who has every excuse to go home, is asked why she's willing to serve as a juror, she utters the D word (duty). Smirks break out all over the courtroom; heads will be shaking in movie theaters. Valerie, poor, smugly idealistic Valerie, is a sitting duck. And when she's subsequently terrorized, raped, abducted, almost murdered and has to change from a nice, motherly boutique owner into something like Catwoman, you're almost expected to blame the victim.

You have only yourself to blame, however, if you attend "Trial by Jury," which might have been called "Trial by Movie," and is one of the nastier films to come along this year. Certainly, it will do nothing for the cause of getting people to serve on juries. But there's also a callousness toward its characters—and, as a result, toward its audience—that's insulting.

Valerie, a divorced mother of one who runs an antique clothing shop—a good device for getting the wan-looking Whalley-Kilmer into some great outfits—is put on the panel hearing the murder case against mobster, killer and hormonal nightmare Rusty Perone (Armand Assante). Abetted by ex-cop and general low-life Tommy Vesey (William Hurt, who sounds like he's in the throes of some Sam Fuller hallucination) they choose Valerie as a way of deadlocking the jury by threatening to kill her son and generally terrorizing her. Meanwhile, prosecutor Graham (Gabriel Byrne) thinks the conviction is in the bag.

Besides being implausible and rich in laughable dialogue, director Heywood Gould uses various kinds of outrages for brief, sordid titillation then ignores the obvious ramifications, to move on to the next sordid outrage. Valerie's rape by Perone, for instance, which takes place in her apartment, during the trial, while police are guarding her building, is not just manipulative, it's ludicrous. Why would Perone be walking around while he's the defendant in a capital case? Why would he risk going to a juror's apartment? And while I'm no expert in rape psychology, why does Valerie seem less terrified after the rape than she did before?

And why, after Valerie does deadlock the jury, is Perone scott free? In such cases, it's up to the prosecutor whether to retry the case—and given Graham's pathological hatred of Perone, he certainly would.

Ah, the bliss of ignorance—something "Trial by Jury" has in abundance.

SIGHT AND SOUND, 1/95, p. 60, Woody Haut

Valerie, a young divorcee, runs and antique clothing shop in New York. An idealist, she believes in truth, justice and doing her civic duty, and attempts to convey this to her seven-year-old son. Valerie is called for jury service on the trial of mob boss Rusty Pirone, who is accused of the brutal murder of 11 people. As the case goes to trial, the prosecution's star witness is murdered. US attorney Daniel Graham knows he must go to trial with little more than circumstantial evidence against the mobster, yet he is certain the jury believes Pirone to be guilty.

Valerie soon finds herself manipulated by ex-cop Tommy Vesey, who is on Pirone's payroll. Threatening to harm Valerie's son, he coerces her into voting for Pirone's acquittal. Then Pirone visits Valerie's bedroom, where he terrorises her. With her idealism stripped from her, Valerie only wants to survive, and so convinces enough jury members to vote for Pirone's acquittal. Pirone is set free. Believing Valerie will eventually turn him in, he orders her death. After being abducted, Valerie is rescued by Vesey, who is killed in the process. Before he dies, Vesey tells Valerie to settle with Pirone. She visits Pirone and kills him with an ice pick.

Juggling its themes of crime, corruption and identity. *Trial By Jury* is uncertain whether it wants to be a courtroom drama, social commentary or *film noir*. In the opening scene, a prostitute kills a star witness by sticking an ice pick in his neck, and quips, "Who says acupuncture doesn't work?" Meanwhile, Valerie, about to report for jury service, accompanies her son to school. "But why do we have juries?" he asks. "In case the police make mistakes," she answers, not yet realising that juries need policing as much as the police need juries. In court, neither the prosecution nor the defence can believe their luck: the former have found an idealist in a world of cynics, while the latter believe she will succumb through sheer innocence to Pirone's old-fashioned Mafia charisma.

Corruption in *Trial By Jury* has become a national disease, already affecting both ex-cop Vesey and state prosecutor Graham. Valerie soon joins their ranks. Doing Pirone's bidding among her fellow jurors, she flirts, cajoles and cites the constitution in his defence. The jurors later attest to her powers of persuasion. Some regard Valerie as an arch-manipulator; others see her simply as an independent woman with strong opinions. Only the prosecutor, Graham, noting various changes in her character, suspects Pirone's intervention.

Technically, *Trial By Jury* seldom exceeds the ordinary, moving between Valerie's apartment with its 50s vintage decor; a well-lit courtroom; the dingy bar inhabited by Pirone's friends; and daylight shots in Central Park, and in rural New York, where Valerie's father innocently resides. Reining in on the barflies, the camera reserves its wider angles for the courtroom. As in De Palma's *The Bonfire of the Vanities*, there is a feeling of courtroom spaciousness as the camera shifts its point of view and settles on specific characters and objects: a spectator sleeps while Valerie is interviewed as a prospective juror; while, as though emphasising Pirone's out-of-date criminality, a court reporter types on a laptop computer.

Although the film falls back on a number of courtroom clichés, *Trial By Jury*'s failure cannot be attributed to its actors. Joanne Whalley-Kilmer, wide-eyed and class-ridden, Gabriel Byrne with his mercenary charm, and William Hurt, his feeble working-class accent overshadowed by a convincing sense of despair, perform competently; while Armand Assante, in *Mambo Kings* mode, is typecast with minimal damage. But the film lacks the camera work and directorial panache to negotiate the claustrophobic space it inhabits. Had it remained in the courtroom, it might have been able to concentrate on the legal system as a metaphor for the disintegration of American values. But director Heywood Gould, also a writer of crime fiction, is lured into the subtleties of Valerie's guilt, for she as much on trial as Pirone.

Once the verdict is delivered, *Trial By Jury* ceases to be an examination of American values, to become a *film noir* in search of an ending. This is inevitable, for had the film concluded after the trial, or with Vesey's death, Valerie's situation would have remained unresolved. The film effectively ends after Valerie, dressed as a 40s femme fatale, murders Pirone; but still Gould prolongs the agony. Visiting a less naive Valerie, Graham asks if Pirone really had put pressure on her. Admitting to corruption, but not to murder, Valerie says, "It's not about right or wrong. It's about doing what you have to do." In view of Hollywood's obsession with false resolutions and demoralised identities, *Trial By Jury* gives new meaning to "innocent until proven guilty", and issues a dubious warning: corrupt an idealistic middle-class woman and a femme fatale vigilante will eventually emerge.

Also reviewed in:
NEW YORK TIMES, 9/10/94, p. 14, Caryn James
VARIETY, 9/12-18/94, p. 42, Steven Gaydos
WASHINGTON POST, 9/10/94, p. C3, Richard Harrington

TRUE LIES

A Twentieth Century Fox release of a Lightstorm Entertainment production. *Executive Producer:* Robert Shriver, Rae Sanchini, and Lawrence Kasanoff. *Producer:* James Cameron and Stephanie Austin. *Director:* James Cameron. *Screenplay:* James Cameron. *Based upon a screenplay by:* Claude Zidi, Simon Michael, and Didier Kaminka. *Director of Photography:* Russell Carpenter. *Editor:* Conrad Buff, Mark Goldblatt, and Richard A. Harris. *Music:* Brad Fiedel. *Music Editor:* Allan Rosen. *Choreographer:* Lynn Hockney. *Sound:* Lee Orloff and (music) Tim Boyle. *Sound Editor:* Wylie Stateman and Gregg Baxter. *Casting:* Mali Finn. *Production Designer:* Peter Lamont. *Art Director:* Robert Laing and Michael Novotny. *Set Designer:* Joseph Hodges. *Set Decorator:* Cindy Carr. *Set Dresser:* Glen Kennedy. *Special Effects:* Thomas L. Fisher. *Costumes:* Marlene Stewart. *Make-up:* Jeff Dawn, Tania McComas, and Richard Snell. *Stunt Coordinator:* Joel Kramer. *Running time:* 135 minutes. *MPAA Rating:* R.

CAST: Arnold Schwarzenegger (Harry Tasker); Jamie Lee Curtis (Helen Tasker); Tom Arnold (Gib); Bill Paxton (Simon); Tia Carrere (Juno); Art Malik (Aziz); Eliza Dushku (Dana); Grant Heslov (Faisil); Marshall Manesh (Khaled); James Allen (Colonel); Dieter

Rauter (Boathouse Guard); Jane Morris (Janice); Katsy Chappell (Allison); Crystina Wyler (Charlene); Ofer Samra (Yusif); Paul Barselou (Old Guy in Bathroom); Chuck Tamburro (Helicopter Pilot); Jean-Claude Parachini (Jean-Claude); Uzi Gal (Lead Terrorist); Majed Ibrahim (High-Rise Terrorist); Armen Ksajikian (Juno's Chauffeur); Mike Cameron (Citation Pilot); Charles Cragin (Samir); Louai Mardini (Breadvan Terrorist #1); Gino Salvano (Breadvan Terrorist #2); Scott Dotson, Sgt. (Harrier Pilot); Tom Isbell (Reporter at Hi-Rise); John Bruno (Custodian); Emily Schweber (Casting Associate).

LOS ANGELES TIMES, 7/14/94, Calendar/p. 1, Kenneth Turan

James Cameron has a most active imagination. Not for him the mere copying of what has gone before, even if his past does include "Aliens," "The Terminator" and "Terminator 2." Compelled to come up with sequences that other manipulators of mayhem have yet to imagine, he pushes the envelope further and further into the unknown with each film he makes.

So "True Lies," Cameron's latest $100-million-plus effort as a writer-director, considerably ups the ante for action films with snazzy sequences like a horse and motorcycle chase through a hotel and the inventive use of Harrier jets (capable of both flying horizontally and hovering like helicopters). As the perfectionist creator of bravura set pieces, Cameron is still the leader of the pack.

Unlike the director's past films, "True Lies" is not nonstop action. Based on a French film called "La Totale!," it is partly a romantic spoof of action films in general and James Bond-type spy thrillers in particular. Even though this halfway house approach means less time for explosions, both Cameron and star Arnold Schwarzenegger prove pleasantly adept at kidding the superhuman image they've worked so hard to build up elsewhere.

And yet, and yet ... Despite all this success, all is not well with "True Lies." A strain of crudeness and mean-spirited humiliation, especially toward women, runs through the film like a nasty virus, vitiating all it touches. Most audiences, understandably diverted, will either not notice or perhaps not even mind, but it is disturbing and it shouldn't be ignored.

The crux of that original French film is a twist on a Scarlet Pimpernel theme about a secret agent whose life is a secret to those closest to him. While timid Helen Tasker (Jamie Lee Curtis) thinks her husband of 15 years is a plodding computer salesman, in reality he's an ace operative for Omega Sector, "The Last Line of Defense," one of those clandestine government bureaus that filmmakers hold dear.

Speaker of six languages (all, apparently, with an Austrian accent) and a whiz with weapons and gadgetry, Harry Tasker (Schwarzenegger) is introduced in a Bond-like scene crashing a heavily guarded party hosted by a wealthy Arab banker and his *femme fatale* girlfriend Juno (Tia Carrere).

Both in that sequence and the ones that follow, "True Lies" is able to effectively kid itself, to playfully mock the conventions of espionage thrillers. Casting the breezy Tom Arnold as Harry's partner Gib helps, but more important is Cameron's unerring ability to find the humor in Schwarzenegger, something the people at "Last Action Hero," for instance, were unable to manage.

But, while Harry's been busy defending the free world, his marriage has been disintegrating faster than a U.N. cease-fire, and "True Lies'" plot revolves around his attempts to hold it together while duking it out with Juno, her cohorts at the terrorist Crimson Jihad and their stock of stolen nuclear arms.

Being the kind of exceptional action director it takes to bring all this off demands, in part, a willingness never to grow up, to retain a young person's enthusiasm for violence and things that explode. And it's that streak of juvenilia, unfortunately, that has come out in "True Lies" in other ways as well.

Taken individually, the cruder and childish things about this film, its determination to use caricatured unshaven Arabs as terrorists, the pleasure it takes in continually mortifying a weasely used-car salesman (Bill Paxton) in the most personal ways, might be overlooked, but added together they leave a sour taste.

Even more off-putting is "True Lies' " treatment of women, specifically Curtis' character. Although having Helen play most of the film as plain and mousy is perfectly OK, an extended sequence where she awkwardly prances around a hotel suite in skimpy underwear, although obviously meant to be funny, comes across as an exercise in painful humiliation. Perhaps Cameron, whose earlier films were rooted for their strong women, simply lost his bearings in this new genre and miscalculated his effects, but the results are not pleasant to watch.

Perhaps, it could be argued, all this is taking a bit of diversionary fluff far too seriously. Oh the other hand, when a staggering sum of money is spent on a film that will get the widest possible exposure worldwide, a society ignores the regrettable parts of its message (which includes a casual approach to wholesale slaughter) only at its own risk. Good as he is in so many areas, even a celebrated perfectionist like Cameron can't perfect what he doesn't know how to do.

NEW STATESMAN & SOCIETY, 8/12/94, p. 33, Jonathan Romney

[*True Lies* was reviewed jointly with *Forrest Gump*; see Romney's review of that film.]

NEW YORK, 7/25/94, p. 46, David Denby

In *True Lies*—the $120-million action spoof directed by James Cameron, and very possibly the most expensive movie ever made—a nuclear explosion is used as the background of a kiss between the two stars. It's a joke, but what can you say about such a moment—that the joke is in bad taste? It is in bad taste, but the scale of the shot, and of other special effects in the movie, tends to reduce questions of taste to petty haggling. Can you complain when one of the Florida Keys gets nuked and no one says anything about it? You can, but in a movie like this one, so many people die that worrying about corpses you can't even see is almost an indulgence. We're talking about size and spectacle here. The director gathers the metal, then he moves it, throws it away, burns it, blows it, bakes it. Perhaps nihilism comes naturally to a director with $120 million to spend. Nuke the sets, nuke the actors, nuke the audience if need be.

Every summer season, critics and movies find themselves at odds. Looking for entertainment, and even art, critics wind up passing judgment on what can only be called industrial products. *The Flintstones* is what—a movie? It's more like a theme park, a trade show ... a multifunctional marketing vehicle. It sells itself, it sells toys, it sells food, it sells books and music. You can say it's zero as art, but you haven't said much of anything, since art was far from the minds of the people making it.

In my new role as trade-show journalist, I can report that *True Lies* is not one of James Cameron's more imaginative thrillers, that much of the movie is derived from other products. But I can also say that Cameron is a man who puts the metal on the screen. Guns, cars, men, helicopters, a horse—a terrific horse—39 stuntmen and stuntwomen, four stand-ins (including a person known as a "utility stand-in"), a Harrier jet hovering outside an office building like a gigantic fly.... Watching *True Lies*, I felt the power of money, the power of the technology that money can buy, and the hopelessness of such notions as originality, modesty, wit. In the corrupt, insane game of making action films with bigger and bigger budgets, Cameron is now the king. It's a stupid place to set up a throne, but if the movie is a huge hit, no one will care.

Yet the problem of reviewing it remains. *True Lies* is better than the last *Indiana Jones* movie but not as good as Cameron's two *Terminator* movies, which offer a richer fantasy life; nor is it as good as *The Fugitive* and *Speed*, which are both far more disciplined and compact and therefore exciting. Cameron is moderately inventive in a gross, big-movie way. He stages a preposterous but entertaining chase in Washington, D.C., with a horse following a motorcycle through *luxe* hotel lobbies. He does good work with a helicopter and a limo moving below it on the narrow causeway through the Florida Keys. There's a funny shot of huge Arnold Schwarzenegger jerking the tiny family dog across the street. At times, the very giganticism of the movie appears to be mocking itself. Perhaps you can't spend this much money without tickling your own toes. But when Cameron just blows things up or torches people by the dozen, he's only a hack director with a fatter wallet than the other hacks. What was distinctive about him—the goofy humor and techno-lyricism of his violent science-fiction fantasies—has been lost in more familiar kinds of action-movie and pulp-fiction tropes. He steals from Spielberg and from the many fellows who directed the James Bond series over the years. Structurally, the movie is a mess—lumpy, often stupid, even crass. Yet it puts the power on the screen, starting with that prime piece of Hapsburg-American machinery Arnold Schwarzenegger.

This is Schwarzenegger's most ironic performance (his work in *Last Action Hero* was more desperate than ironic). Well sheathed in a tux, he speaks many languages fluently ("perfect Arabic," a subtitle informs us) and devastates the ladies. Audiences enjoy knowing how much violence lies below the debonair-Arnold stuff; they wait for the violence to explode in weird, nifty ways. From Clint Eastwood, Schwarzenegger has learned about the comic effect of a slow burn; he does a wonderful scowl, narrowing his eyes to a slit, high in the concave bunker of his face. He has too much bulk to move gracefully, but you feel the power of those limbs, even in this joshing action extravaganza, in which nothing is meant to be taken straight. He's developed a taste for mockery and a parodistic way with such emotions as jealousy and rage.

He's easy enough to take, but Cameron, who wrote the movie, should have found him a distinctive character to play. Schwarzenegger's Harry Tasker, a suave intelligence agent who travels to glamorous altitudes and battles international terrorism, resembles James Bond in almost every respect. The movie begins with Arnold below water outside a Swiss chateau at which some sort of fabulous international-arms-dealer party is going on. He gets out of the lake, removes his goggles and wet suit, and enters the party in a tuxedo. Has Cameron no shame? We've seen that opening before. At the end of the party, Arnold is pursued by men on skis, a tipoff of *On Her Majesty's Secret Service*. The party itself could have come from any one of a dozen other Bond movies. In the middle of it, Tia Carrere turns up as an exotic shady lady in a slit dress, recapping the performances of the semi-anonymous actresses (Honor Blackman, Barbara Bach, etc.) who played the many varieties of Pussy Galore. Carrere pulls a business card out of her decolletage, and when Arnold, holding her in his heavy paws, swings her into a tango, her eyes flash at him darkly.

Harry Tasker lives in Washington, D.C., and is married to Helen (Jamie Lee Curtis), a bored legal secretary who thinks her husband is a traveling computer salesman. In effect, Harry has abandoned her. He's always away, and his true wife is his sidekick, Gib, played by Tom (give this man a job) Arnold. Tom Arnold is heavy, but he moves well, and in this James Belushi role, he's very entertaining—verbally surefooted and quick. He jabbers, and Schwarzenegger glowers. The two men are part of a government anti-terrorist unit, and the plot, which disappears every now and then like a heavy suitcase lost in the middle of a journey, has something to do with a band of Middle Eastern terrorists trying to blow up American cities (oh, *that* funny plot).

The terrorists have to be foiled. But first, the filmmakers need to pull Jamie Lee Curtis into the movie. Amazingly, *True Lies* stops dead for something like 40 minutes to accomplish this. There is some dreadful stuff, too weak even to summarize, about a horny used-car salesman who poses as a spy in order to get Jamie Lee into bed. As Arnold traps and unmasks this impostor, the movie goes sour. A very good actor, Bill Paxton, plays the salesman, and we don't enjoy seeing Paxton humiliated (he pees on himself). Trying to find out if Jamie Lee slept with the bum, Arnold humiliates her too. At one point, she does a fabulous strip for him. Jamie Lee Curtis is in great shape, and as she gets into the dance and tries to find some use for her hands, she's very funny. She has slit eyes, too—she matches up with Schwarzenegger better than most actresses. But once Cameron establishes that she's dynamite, he doesn't use her desire for excitement or her awakened sensuality. Part of the action now, she's just another hapless, helpless female, and Schwarzenegger has to rescue her.

True Lies turns into the continuation of the Gulf War by other means. The terrorists are treated contemptuously as a bunch of losers—as fuzz-faced buffoons, shouting gibberish at one another. Shot, stabbed, torched, blown up, the Arabs, or whatever they are, drop like flies (like *Iraquis*, Cameron is saying to the audience). Cameron sits at the apex of the American power machine, yet he works in the derisive spirit of a lousy Third World director, treating enemies as both menacing and completely ridiculous. At times, the fun gets a little heavy. Perhaps there's something not entirely hip about a $120-million joke. I enjoyed parts of *True Lies*, but I was left with few emotions apart from the desire to give up trade-show movies altogether.

NEW YORK POST, 7/15/94, p. 33, Michael Medved

Helen Tasker (Jamie Lee Curtis) is more than a bit bored with her husband, Harry, an introverted workaholic who seldom makes it home in time for dinner.

"It's not like he's saving the world," she complains to a friend. "He's just a computer salesman."

But since Harry is played by Arnold Schwarzenegger, he is, of course, no ordinary technonerd and *is* saving the world—as ace agent for a highly classified federal operation devoted to fighting international terrorism.

Writer-director James Cameron's "True Lies" asks us to believe that this agency is so super-secret that for more than 15 years Harry's been forced to deceive his wife about his job—living the life of a Walter-Mitty-in-reverse, pretending to an existence of middle-class tedium when his actual work is full of globe-trotting thrills.

When he returns home, understandably exhausted from slaughtering scores of skiing goons on a daring raid on a tightly-guarded Swiss chateau, she thinks he's been at a convention, selling business machines.

No wonder she takes this dull, preoccupied guy for granted and begins to develop a guilty fascination with a mysterious and seductive stranger (Bill Paxton).

As comedy of marital misunderstanding, "True Lies" is only so-so. Curtis plays a character who is so relentlessly stupid, so pathetically gullible to both her husband and the stranger, that it's hard to feel much sympathy for her situation.

This entire middle section of the movie begins to sag (unlike Curtis's well-toned body), but it is bracketed by extended action sequences so brilliantly and breathlessly staged that most moviegoers will happily forgive and forget this film's slower moments.

James Cameron has established a well-deserved reputation as a master of elaborately choreographed movie mayhem, but here all the chases and bloody confrontations recall the playful spirit of James Bond films rather than the darker atmosphere of Cameron's work on "Aliens" and the "Terminator" movies.

Here, Schwarzenegger uses a helicopter, a Harrier jet fighter, and even a horse to pursue the drooling, stereotyped terrorists of "Crimson Jihad" who plan to blow up U.S. cities with their stolen nuclear weapons.

The special effects are predictably spectacular, but Cameron's witty, resourceful writing in planning these inventive sequences adds even more to the satisfaction of the audience.

He's also helped by two unexpectedly accomplished comedic performances. Tom Arnold (of all people) nearly steals the movie as Schwarzenegger's wise-cracking sidekick on the Omega Force, delivering his dialogue with the fresh, spontaneous feel of edgy ad-libs.

And then there's the other Arnold, (Schwarzenegger, that is), who displays such a convincing range of emotions, with reactions to his co-stars that are both richly communicative and flawlessly well-timed, that you begin to wonder if it's another special effect.

As an actor, this hardworking superstar seems to get better every time; he's come an incredibly long way since the stolid grunts of "Conan the Barbarian."

Not that his performance here is ready for Oscar consideration, or will make moviegoers forget about Anthony Hopkins (or Tom Hanks); but it should enable Arnold himself to forget the disappointments of "The Last Action Hero" and to start counting the money from this undeniably effective commercial concoction.

NEWSDAY, 7/15/94, Part II/p. B2, Jack Mathews

It is not hard to understand how the budget for James Cameron's "True Lies" grew to an estimated $120 million. It costs almost as much to blow things up as it does to build them, and in creating this noisy spectacle, his film company pretty much had to do both.

Then there is Arnold Schwarzenegger, who, despite the humiliation of "Last Action Hero," is still a $15 million man.

What is harder to understand is how a movie could end up with some of the greatest stunts in film history without having a moment—not a single nanosecond!—of suspense. From the opening scene, an elaborate parody of the prologue to the first James Bond movie, "Dr. No," "True Lies" is such a colossal lark it could almost be taken as a sequel to "Last Action Hero."

"True Lies" won't be the flop that "Last Action Hero" was. Though it is just as silly, the jokes and the performances operate at a much higher level, and it doesn't wink at us every two seconds to let us know it knows what it is. But people reasonably expecting another nail-biter from the maker and star of "Terminator" and "T2" may feel the joke is on them.

The screenplay, by Cameron with inspiration from three other writers, is the best high-concept gimmick for Schwarzenegger since he played Danny De Vito's identical twin. Arnold is Harry Tasker, a super-spy whose wife Helen (Jamie Lee Curtis) accepts him for the dull computer sales rep she thinks she married, even though he has spent the last 17 years keeping the world safe for democracy.)

She's Lois Lane to his Clark Kent, never wondering why such a seeming wimp has biceps on his fingertips.

Schwarzenegger and Curtis actually make a terrific team. Ah-nuld has always had the innate good sense to know that self-parody is the best form of self-promotion, and though I will probably be laughing at his accent into the next century, he is simply the most engaging action star of his generation. And as she has often shown, most notably in "A Fish Called Wanda," there isn't a better light comedienne around than Curtis.

But I wish Cameron had been a little less enchanted by his casting genius. The movie is much too long for something so devoid of context, yet he devotes almost an hour to a slapstick subplot about Harry's paranoid attempt to find out if Helen is cheating on him. It's like a separate movie, a domestic farce within an action comedy, the first having nothing to do with the second, except to create an excuse for Helen to tag along on Harry's next adventure.

There are some funny moments in the domestic story, most of them supplied by Bill Paxton, as a smarmy used car salesman pretending to be a spy in order to lure bored housewives like Helen into bed. That irony, however, and Harry's frantic attempts to pry a confession of infidelity from her, grow old long before the truth is out.

In fact, a couple of these scenes would be abusively sexist if the movie had an ounce of reality to it. It's hard to get worked up about questions of faith in a marriage where the wife doesn't even know who the husband is.

The story preceding and following the one-hour marital subplot pits Harry and his fast-talking sidekick Gib (Tom Arnold, in a scene-stealing supporting performance) against a group of caricatured Arab terrorists who have invaded the United States, armed with nuclear warheads. Cameron takes this cliché and flaunts it, adds more to it, and sends it all up with a climactic chase that cuts across the Florida Keys to a mid-air shootout with Harrier jets, helicopters and missiles over downtown Miami.

There is no overstating the spectacular nature of the film's stunts. But for all the effort and money that went into them, they have no visceral impact. You watch them in detached awe, like a good fourth of July fireworks display, knowing that for all the noise and spectacle, nobody is going to get hurt.

NEWSWEEK, 7/18/94, p. 58, David Ansen

Nobody does it bigger—or better—than James Cameron. Three years after "Terminator 2" blew away the summer competition, he weighs in with the $100 million-plus "True Lies," one of the most expensive movies ever. It stars Arnold Schwarzenegger as a computer sales rep with a teenage daughter and a bored wife (Jamie Lee Curtis) he suspects is cheating on him. It's a remake of a French comedy called "La Totale." That's not a misprint, and no one will ever mistake this gargantuan thrill machine for *une petite farce française*. In fact, unbeknownst to his wife, Helen, Arnold's Harry Tasker is a spy for the ultrasecret Omega agency, currently occupied with trying to stop fanatical Arab terrorists from setting off A-bombs in the U. S. of A. In his spare time, he wreaks humiliating revenge on a sleazeball used-car salesman (Bill Paxton) who's trying to seduce his wife by pretending to be a spy; in the process, Harry enmeshes her in his "real life" adventures. Transformed from a prim Mrs. Clark Kent into a sexy adventuress, Helen joins Harry in saving the nation.

It sounds silly. It *is* silly—spectacularly and knowingly so. "True Lies" is the sort of movie where lovers kiss against the billowing mushroom cloud of an atomic bomb and no one worries about fallout. It's the sort of movie in which the hero, on a hijacked horse, chases a villain on a motor scooter through a hotel lobby and into a glass elevator, the horse's tail flicking the faces of the black-tie passengers. It has a half dozen heart-stopping action sequences so outlandishly elaborate they'll probably add millions of dollars to all future cliffhangers that try to keep up with Cameron's state-of-the-art effects. And it has Arnold, in a tux, dancing a tango. For the first time

Cameron turns away from his gritty, techno-future milieu and enters the luxe pipe-dream world of James Bond, a world "True Lies" both parodies and effectively trumps.

This preposterous commingling of domestic comedy, genre sendup and explosive violence shouldn't work. Amazingly, it does. For no matter how cartoonishly over-the--top "True Lies" becomes, we actually care about Harry and Helen. Cameron's storytelling has a loopy conviction that keeps us hooked. Unlike Schwarzenegger's leadenly self-reflexive "Last Action Hero," "True Lies" is able to have its cake, eat it and smash it in its own face.

Schwarzenegger seems especially comfy in "True Lies"; Cameron gets the best out of him by never pushing him beyond his limits. The star's got an easy tenderness with Curtis, who handles both the comedy and the mayhem with snappy, no-nonsense finesse. Tom Arnold provides unexpectedly delightful comic support as Harry's faithful sidekick; Art Malik has just the right degree of fun with the nutty Crimson Jihad head terrorist, and the oft-humiliated Paxton makes a colorful scumbag foil. "True Lies" may come via France, but it provides the kind of insanely extravagant film only Hollywood would be crazy enough to bankroll. Crazy like a Twentieth Century Fox.

SIGHT AND SOUND, 9/94, p. 49, Leslie Felperin Sharman

Harry Tasker is a top operative for a secret paramilitary agency called Omega Sector. He is investigating a group of Arab terrorists engaged in smuggling nuclear weapons out of the former Soviet Union. His wife Helen, a legal secretary, thinks he is a humble computer sales representative. While Harry chases terrorists around Washington DC and dances the tango with Juno, an art dealer involved with the terrorists, Helen feels neglected and begins a flirtation with a used car salesman named Simon, who pretends that he is a spy to seduce her. After discovering Simon and Helen's relationship, Harry, with the help of his partner Gib, uses all the resources available to him to spy on his wife and eventually humiliate Simon. By blackmailing Helen, he lures her to a hotel room and, posing as a mysterious Frenchman, coerces her into dancing seductively while he sits hidden by shadows in a corner. This romantic scene is interrupted by the invasion of the terrorists who kidnap them both and whisk them off to a tropical island in the Caribbean.

At the terrorists' base, Harry is forced to reveal his true profession to Helen. The terrorists attempt to torture him, but he manages to free both himself and Helen. A shootout ensues, and in the melee, Helen is captured and Harry escapes, though Helen thinks he has been killed. Gib rescues Harry from the island and they go in pursuit of Helen and the terrorists. They succeed in saving Helen only to learn that Helen and Harry's teenage daughter, Dana, has been kidnapped by the terrorists, who are threatening to detonate a nuclear warhead in Miami. Harry hijacks a Harrier Jumpjet, rushes to Miami, saves Dana (who has managed to disarm the nuclear warhead), and wipes out the terrorists with one fortuitously aimed missile. One year later, Harry and Helen are working together for Omega Sector.

The central conceit of *True Lies* is its conflation of two antipathetic genres—the action-adventure film and the screwball marriage farce. The first is easily enough accomplished, given a mass of heavy plant, explosions and special effects. The second requires a lighter touch, a witty script and actors with sure comic timing. Each kind of film has a different narrative density, and sadly for the makers of *True Lies*, no one figured out how to emulsify the constituent elements. Instead, despite the efforts of its contrived script, the film keeps separating out like a salad dressing without any mustard.

The far more effective part is the adventure scenario, in which Arnie leaps into heroic action with his usual Teutonic panache. Rumour had it that he would be doing more 'serious acting' in this film, but he hardly seems to be stretching himself: For the most part, his role consists of providing close-ups and dialogue shots to cut in between footage of his stunt doubles. Squiring them around the sets and ladling in the effects that are his trademark, director James Cameron is in his element engineering this sort of stuff.

He's far less assured when dealing with 'feminine' story elements, despite the fact that the *Terminator* films, along with the *Alien* films, are often cited by feminists as positive landmarks in the development of modern womanhood's image in film. Jamie Lee Curtis' role as Helen is disappointingly thin and facile—though Curtis has enough nuance to maintain a presence, she has little to do apart from undergoing the standard transformation from dowdy wimp to feisty heroine.

She only kills people by accidentally dropping her gun, though she does throw a few convincing punches at Bond-girl bomb-hell-esque Tia Carrere.

Helen's ineptitude is consistent with the demands of the action genre, just as the crudely drawn Arab characters must be shown to be too stupid to remember the batteries for the video camera recording their list of demands. In order for *True Lies* to succeed as romance, there would have to be more parity between the sexes and more humanism than is on display here. Instead, the script is lethally ironic about its one-dimensionality. For example, when a character asks why someone is called 'the sand spider', the self-referential reply is "Because it sounds really scary."

In the end, *True Lies* is neither as good as expected nor as bad as reported. Given its confusion as to whether it is *The Thin Man* revisited or James Bond updated, it muddles through well enough. Most of the $120 million it apparently cost seems to be up on the screen, but it is too routine to fire the imagination beyond the usual pyromaniacal impulses.

TIME, 7/18/94, p. 55, Richard Corliss

Hidden behind a two-way mirror, U.S. secret agent Harry Tasker is grilling a suspect. His voice electronically disguised, Harry pries and threatens until the suspect turns hysterical and throws a chair against the mirror. The interrogation victim is Harry's loving wife Helen. The spy has been having a little wicked fun.

What an odd action film *True Lies* is.

So far, 1994 has been a rough year for some acclaimed writer-directors. They spend all their ingenuity and a good deal of money putting a personal twist on an old genre—Lawrence Kasdan with his *Wyatt Earp* western, James L. Brooks with the would-be musical *I'll do Anything*, Barry Levinson with his behind-the-screen *Jimmy Hollywood*—and what happens? A big nothing. The critics cluck; the public stay home in droves. One hates to see ambiguous artists fail, even if their fizzles can be more provocative than the minor films that become major hits. But somehow these men became estranged from their audiences.

Could this fate befall James Cameron, Hollywood's most daring and extravagant auteur? Not bloody likely. An '80s-style artist-brigand, Cameron makes ripe allegories, often about the search for a redeemer, that are both personal and popular. *The Terminator, Aliens, The Abyss* and *Terminator 2: Judgment Day* all took big risks, with film form and finance, that paid off. Cameron is a daredevil director: he goes skydiving without a chute and lands in clover.

Now he has produced an abrasive essay in gung-ho gigantism. *True Lies* is a remake of Claude Zidi's 1992 French film *La Totale!*, a teeny domestic farce about a spy (Thierry Lhermitte) whose neglected wife (Miou-Miou) thinks he works for the phone company. In Cameron's version, Schwarzenegger is the secret agent, Jamie Lee Curtis is his wife—and the sky is the limit. Cameron has taken another out-of-favor genre (the James Bond thriller), welded it to romantic comedy and upped the ante until the fates of a marriage, the world and a few A-list reputations dangle in the balance.

If *True Lies* cost more than $100 million, so what? Hollywood frets when a huge-budget film is a flop (like Schwarzenegger's *Last Action Hero*) and purrs when one is a hit (like *T2*). As Schwarzenegger notes, "The press thinks movie studios should be reviewed like the government—as if public money were spent and a crime committed. Well, it's not their money, it's the studios' money. Sometimes money is spent wisely, sometimes not. But it's like that in every business."

To Cameron, moviemaking isn't just a business, it's an adventure. "I like to keep challenging myself," he says, "so I try different things. And a lot of the things I like to try are expensive. I will say what I say about every budget: the price of a ticket is $7.50, and you're getting a lot of movie for it. End of story."

End of the budget story, anyway. The box-office story unfolds this weekend. *True Lies* will probably connect with the movie public; it delivers lots of ballistics for the buck. *T2* dazzled with the computer magic of morphing, but the software used in *True Lies* is less noticeable than the hardware. Says Cameron: "There's nothing that gets the back of your mind screaming, 'That's impossible!' It's revolutionary technology in the service of a photorealistic end product." That translates into seamless digital imagery and nifty stunts. When a Harrier jet isn't flying around Miami, a villain is negotiating a breathless motorcycle leap from a hotel rooftop into an elevated swimming pool across the street. Things go boom in the night. Jamie Lee performs a striptease. Arnold hurts people. There's something for everybody.

Well, not quite everybody. For a viewer sympathetic to Schwarzenegger's and Cameron's best selves—the ironist with muscles and the mordant fabulist—*True Lies* is a loud misfire. It rarely brings its potent themes to life. And it seems not to realize that Harry is less a hero than a wife-abusing goon.

Fade in on one of those elegant parties that James Bond used to attend, then leave in rubble. Harry prowls about in a tuxedo; he speaks French, Arabic and a Little English. He even tangos. Then he is pursued by the usual inept Middle East terrorists—the ones with a quillion rounds of ammunition and lousy aim. He escapes with the help of spy's-best-friend Tom Arnold and arrives home, where Helen awaits him in sweet ignorance; she thinks Harry is a workaholic salesman for a computer company. Helen always waits; she is Penelope, unaware that she's married to Ulysses.

There ought to be a double resonance in this tale, for the story is about two kinds of mystery, two kinds of lies: domestic and cinematic. Married people may become so involved in their careers that they sink into a genial ignorance of each other's emotional lives. Moviegoers may become so seduced by the image on the screen that they forget their sainted star is likely to be an ordinary troubled oaf like themselves.

Cameron was eager to plumb these dark waters. "I liked the comedy potential of the lies, the facades, the allegory of relationships," he says. "For me, this movie is about the unknowability of people. And I loved the potential of Arnold playing the spy role. Arnold lives in a strange, dialectic world. On one hand, he's a family man; on the other, he's a superstar, which means that so much is expected of him." The role is oddly similar to Schwarzenegger's persona in *Last Action Hero*: someone who plays a superman at work but in the real world is stranded without a script. Harry is, after all, just a performer. Other agents are his directors; they tell him what to say, how to act, who to be.

At least, when Harry is playing the spy, he knows his part. But he doesn't know how to act like a good husband, or even a jealous one. When a sleazy salesman (Bill Paxton) brags that Helen is his mistress, Harry uses all his spy tricks to catch her in the act—or lure her into it. The man who has no time to be with his wife does have time to prey on her, especially in the two-way mirror scene.

Schwarzenegger sees this stark encounter as Helen's chance for liberation: "During the interrogation, she says her life is boring. She needs excitement, to be at risk. My character realizes he hasn't given her the life she wanted, so he starts giving her the excitement right there. She was begging for it." To Cameron, the scene is open to several interpretations. "I want couples to argue about it afterward," he insists. "That's part of the fun."

Will audiences have fun at *True Lies*? Count on it. They will giggle at the embarrassment of Paxton's character, who is punished by having to pee in his pants—twice. They will savor the spectacle of the delightful Curtis screaming in inane fear more often than any other actress since Fay Wray in *King Kong*. They will enjoy the lavishing and squandering of talent by Hollywood's shrewdest showman.

No question, you get a lot of movie for your $7.50. It's just not the right movie.

VILLAGE VOICE, 7/19/94, p. 50, Georgia Brown

Well, what did I expect from the most expensive movie ever made ... a reason to live? No, what I expected from James Cameron's reputedly $120 million *True Lies* was about what I got: mind-boggling firepower and cartoony over-the-top action—a horse on a skyscraper roof is fun! Following *Speed* and *The Lion King*, Cameron's rocketing, red-glaring, bomb-bursting comic action pic unaccountably missed the Fourth, but it will certainly give the summer box office something to sing about.

Thinking about it later, however, you could get queasy. Here's a PG-13 family entertainment with a running joke about a poor bloke's "minuscule dick" (this dangling particle seems to be the raison d'être for the film's epilogue). Even spookier, here's yet another reminder of the lengths "loving" partners will go to control their mates.

Although adapted from a French movie called *La Totale!*, *True Lies* seems primarily dedicated to polishing the tarnished reputation of the white, married-American male. The demigod hero must prove himself on the domestic front—where wife and daughter consider him a wimp and a bore— while also serving notice to upstart nations and rabid sects that *we* are still number one. And who better to represent the home team than an emigrant made good? Like Kissinger, Schwarzenegger—who here gets to show a tender, lovesick side—is now so familiar that the accent needn't be justified by the plot.

When we first meet Harry (Schwarzenegger), he's a sleek James Bond type wearing a wet suit over his tux while breaching state-of-the-art security at a fabulous Swiss chateau. I should say *schloss*. The estate's guards are echt *deutsch*—white-helmeted storm troopers with snarling Dobermans. Inside, however, where a dress ball is in full swing, the hosts appear to be Saudi or Kuwaiti royals. Luckily, Harry commands several languages (one subtitle reads "Perfect Arabic"). But after he tangos with an Asian goddess called Juno (Tia Carrere), the guards get wind of the penetration; and he must flee the area in a *Star Wars/Raiders/*Bond chase through snowy woods.

All the above action, as I recall, takes place over the film's credits. Cut to the Washington Monument—longest, hardest, whitest of them all: Brave Harry is home.

For a long time Cameron has suffered an acute case of Lucas/Spielberg envy. According to the usual awestruck *Premiere* story, he was driving a truck for a living when *Star Wars* came out ("I was pissed off ... I wanted to *make* that movie") and more or less "projected himself into the business. *The Abyss*, as many noted, was his *Close Encounters of the Damp Kind*. But unlike Spielberg, Cameron has always flaunted a crude, unsuburban tastelessness that can, in the right setting, come off as wholly refreshing (*The Terminator*).

Maybe it takes true life to throw a harsh glare on a line like, "Women: You can't live with 'em, and you can't kill 'em," here delivered by Tom Arnold and perhaps originally meant to make us think of the woman *he* can't kill. But then, as Arnold S. has already shown in *Terminator* and *Total Recall*, you can kill 'em. In Cameron's films, marriages tend to be battlegrounds, with the little woman giving as good as she gets. (In true life, some of us may not thank Cameron for neutralizing his third wife, Kathryn Bigelow, by writing *Point Break* for her to direct.)

When we meet Harry's wife, Helen (Jamie Lee Curtis), she looks like a tightly wound Marian Librarian. A lowly legal secretary, she complains wistfully to coworkers that Harry the traveling computer salesman isn't exactly exciting. He isn't even home most of the time. When he is, the couple's disdainful 14-year-old, Dana (Eliza Dushku), uses the occasion to lift some cash. "You're not her parent, anyway," offers Harry's buddy Gib (Arnold) in consolation. "Her parents are Axl Rose and Madonna." When Harry later comes to Dana's rescue in a hovering Harrier jet, the bewildered child, hanging by her fingertips, can only gasp out, "*Dad*?"

I'm not saying it isn't fun to watch Harry prove his secret prowess and mastery of sundry weaponry. (Maybe this is how the child of presumed Milquetoast Aldrich Ames felt.) Simultaneously, it's pleasant seeing Helen metamorphose into a capable warrior—despite a tacky fistfight with Juno in a limo. Even more fun are Curtis's fumblings toward grace and seductiveness in her awkward in-between phase. But then there's the creepy stuff—like Harry's out-sized revenge on Helen's pathetic suitor (Bill Paxton), or a disturbing spousal interrogation with Harry generously sharing his wife's humiliation with buddy Gib.

Moreover—though maybe it's just imitating *Indiana Jones and the Temple of Doom*—*True Lies* is casually racist. Arabs divide into corrupt sheiks amassing Swiss bank accounts and a bunch of loony fanatics calling themselves the Crimson Jihad. The latter's wild-eyed leader, Aziz (Art Malik), is introduced smacking Juno—the film's mercenary Dragon Lady—so hard you hope Carrere has dental insurance.

Of these two overcompensating males, Aziz is obsessed by cone-shaped warheads, while Harry finally is phallically defined by the ample nose of the jet plane. In a penultimate apocalyptic clinch, Harry and Helen kiss while a thermonuclear device detonates in the background—the image mimicking in color and composition a vintage *Life* magazine ad. What's the product? The lost dream, of course.

Far and away the best things in this campy, big-dick action pic are several small, wonderful slapstick moments—none of which costs more than Jamie Lee Curtis's salary. That mushroom cloud and all are just to show the world Cameron sits in the cockpit.

Also reviewed in:
CHICAGO TRIBUNE, 7/15/94, Friday/p. C, Michael Wilmington
NATION, 9/5-12/94, p. 250, Stuart Klawans
NEW REPUBLIC, 9/5/94, p. 34, Stanley Kauffmann
NEW YORK TIMES, 7/15/94, p. C1, Janet Maslin
NEW YORKER, 7/25/94, p. 77, Anthony Lane
VARIETY, 7/11-17/94, p. 41, Brian Lowry
WASHINGTON POST, 7/15/94, p. B1, Rita Kempley
WASHINGTON POST, 7/15/94, Weekend/p. 38, Desson Howe

24TH INTERNATIONAL TOURNEE OF ANIMATION, THE

A Samuel Goldwyn Company release of 14 animated film shorts. *Producer:* Terry Thoren. *Running time:* 90 minutes. *MPAA Rating:* Not Rated.

CHRISTIAN SCIENCE MONITOR, 1/21/94, p. 14, David Sterritt

"The 24th International Tournee of Animation" is the latest edition of what may be the best-known annual cartoonfest in the world. It began as a touring exhibition in the mid-1960s and changed in 1986 from a museum-oriented show to a compilation program shown in regular movie theaters.

Operating as a cooperative venture that returns half of its profits to the filmmakers who create its offerings, it has become a must-see event for the legion of cartoon fans who don't think a movie needs live action—or a running time of more than a few minutes—to be as worthwhile as a Hollywood blockbuster.

This year's Tournee in New York has some impressive names in its credits. One is magazine cartoonist Gahan Wilson, whose "Diner" tells the darkly comic tale of a macabre eatery with monsters for employees and victims for customers.

Another is Paul Tippett, who worked on the special effects for "Jurassic Park" with Steven Spielberg and company. He delves into similar territory in his "Prehistoric Beast," shown here in excerpted form.

There's also Paul Berry, a lead animator for "The Nightmare Before Christmas" and maker of "The Sandman," which has been nominated for an Academy Award notwithstanding its gruesome horror-film elements. And don't overlook the California Raisins, the brainchild of animator Will Vinton's studio, who get a mini-tribute at the end of the Tournee.

Interestingly, these major cartoon-world figures don't contribute the most interesting work to the Tournee lineup.

Wilson's grim comedy gets repetitious after the first few gags, while Tippett's dinosaur extravaganza is more showy than stirring. Ditto for "The Sandman" until its hair-raising climax, and even Vinton's virtuosic Claymation images—molded from clay, an excellent medium for cartoon artistry—look sadly flat in the video-transfer form used by the Tournee. But the madly inventive item called "Mr. Resistor" makes a potent impression despite everything.

Happily, some unexpected winners compensate for the disappointments. "The Man Who Yelled," by Mo Willems, is a funny vignette about the filmmaker's own eagerness to tell us a story about—well, a man who yelled. "The Billy Nayer Show," made in the lifelike "rotoscope" technique by performance artists Cory McAbee and Bobby Lurie, presents a lounge-singing routine that manages to be amusing and inexplicable at the same time. "Get a Haircut" is Mike Smith's lively cartoon-accompaniment to a recent George Thorogood song.

And the provocative "I Think I Was an Alcoholic" is John Cahallan's unexpectedly hilarious look at the deadly serious subject of overcoming alcohol abuse.

Inventive and outrageous in almost every frame, it's a strong reminder that the Tournee is a cartoon show for grown-ups, not children.

Also on the program is the exuberant "We Love It," by Vincent Cafarelli and Candy Kugel, an on-target satire of Hollywood hypocrisy.

"The Stain" is a surrealistic fable of family life by Marjut Rimminen and Christine Roche, while "Little Wolf" gives An Vrombaut's view of animals and the world of nature. "The Square of Light" is Claude Luyet's arty look at prize-fighting. "Words, Words, Words" is Michaela Pavlatova's parody of pointless social chatter. "The Ride to the Abyss" is Georges Schwizgebel's ambitious but ultimate4y aimless meditation on Berlioz's musical classic, "The Damnation of Faust.

Entries in this Tournee come from Britain, Switzerland, and former Czechoslovakia, as well as the United States, which contributed more than half the program.

It's an uneven show, but some of its components are splendid on their own ornery terms—and there's always the chance that some offering will take on a life of its own in the future, considering that filmmaker Tim Burton and "Beavis and Butt-Head" creator Mike Judge had early work in previous Tournee editions.

In any event, spectators have the comforting thought that if an offering lets them down, another one will push it off the screen in just a few minutes.

LOS ANGELES TIMES, 1/21/94, Calendar/p. 4, Charles Solomon

"The 24th International Tournee of Animation" an uneven program of 14 short films from Europe and the United States opening today confirms that stop-motion animation, a technique once relegated to Speedy Alka-Seltzer commercials and low-budget movie monsters, is enjoying a comeback.

"Prehistoric Beast" (U.S.), by Oscar-winning special-effects artist Phil Tippett, which depicts two dinosaurs stalking each other in a Mesozoic forest, eclipses the other films. This superbly animated short was a test For "Jurassic Park," and it looks. like a sequence from a big-budget feature.

Paul Berry's previously reviewed "The Sandman" (U.K.) is also technically polished, if grisly.

Twenty-one minutes of the 90-minute program are devoted to "A Salute to the Dimensional Artistry of Will Vinton Studios" (U.S.), a collage of shorts and commercials that showcases the studio's recent forays into conventional stop-motion and computer animation, instead of their popular clay films. (Vinton coined the term claymation.)

It's an odd time to be saluting Vinton, as his studio recently lost the leadership of clay animation to London's Aardman Animations ("Creature Comforts"). The characters made from old trophies and scraps of electrical junk in Vinton's "Mr. Resistor" ape the nightmarish work of the brothers Quay, but lacks their eerie surrealism.

The "Tournee" is weakest in the field of drawn animation. "The Billy Nayer Show" by Cory McAbee and Bobby Lurie and "Le Carre de Lumiere" ("The Square of Light," Switzerland) by Claude Luyet rely too heavily on traced live-action footage.

Viewers will quickly weary of the crude drawings and rudimentary movements in "We Love It" (U.S.) by Vincent Cafarelli and Candy Kugel and "The Man Who Yelled" (U.S.) by Mo Willems.

Many of the films in"The 24th International Tournee of Animation simply don't represent the best work being done in world animation. But stop-motion fans will enjoy some of them.

NEW YORK POST, 1/21/94, p. 38, Thelma Adams

Toons have escaped the Saturday morning ghetto. From "The Simpsons" and "Beavis and Butt-head," to "Aladdin" and "Tim Burton's Nightmare Before Christmas," animation isn't just kids' stuff—it's big money.

"The 24th International Tournee of Animation" and its predecessors can take partial credit for this renaissance. For years, the feature-length program of animated shorts has served as animation's "farm team," broadening the audience for such talents as Matt Groening, Tim Burton, and Mike Judge, the creator of "Beavis and Butt-head."

Designed to have something for everyone, the Tournee yielded 30 four-star minutes in an otherwise painless 90-minute program.

"The Stain" is a tour de force of black humor and visual energy. This fractured fairy tale about a "delicious cozy little family"—with incestuous and suicidal tendencies—makes "Twin Peaks" look like "Father Knows Best."

Animators Marjut Rimminen and Christine Roche rocket the story between them, and their two contrasting styles, to create a pocket-sized Greek tragedy with a mighty kick.

Paul Berry's "The Sandman" is another dark fairy tale. Berry, lead animator on "Tim Burton's Nightmare Before Christmas," works in a Grimm vein in this Academy Award-nominated short.

Stop-motion puppets participate in a dark and fearsome nightmare about the Sandman, who steals the eyes from sleeping boys and feeds them to his chicks. Brrr! This is chilly stuff served up with an icy precision.

Popular print cartoonists John Callahan and Gahan Wilson make their animation debuts. No Smurfs here as Callahan draws a sobering confessional, "I Think I Was an Alcoholic," culled from his book "Digesting the Child Within."

In "Diner," Wilson goes for the macabre and serves up a satisfying portion of his dark humor.

Also notable are New Yorker Mo Willems' hip "The Man Who Yelled," and Daniel Suter's swirling "The Square of Light," which puts the viewer behind the eyes of a boxer. For those who aren't sick of Dinomation, an excerpt from Phil Tippett's "Prehistoric Beast" chews its way across the screen.

A 22-minute salute to the Will Vinton Studios—the pioneers of Claymation—dragged on. The dimensional animation techniques get better, but the recycled ideas offer nothing newer than Roadrunner chases and rap rip-offs.

Vinton the father of the California Raisins, the Michael (Jackson) Raisin, and the Domino's Pizza Noid, exploits his vast talent for schlock—and it pays off. His two dinosaur critics Herb and Rex—Siskel and Ebert clones—critique the omnibus selection and nail the problem between animated commercials: "cinematic sellout."

I like the Raisins, but my heart belongs to Gumby.

NEWSDAY, 1/21/94, Part II/p. 75, Gene Seymour

If there is a spirit presiding over this most recent of producer Terry Thoren's "Tournees," it belongs to the late cartoonist Charles Addams, master of the ghoulish goose. Most of the 14 animated shorts served on this platter twitch and throb like the menacing critters that sprouted from Addams' warped mind.

Indeed, one of the high points of this "24th International Tournee of Animation" comes from Gahan Wilson, who, along with the elegantly perverse Edward Gorey, is Addams' most noteworthy descendant. Wilson's "Diner" is, as you'd suspect, a roadside eatery serving up severed human body parts. Imagine how Tex Avery would ape "Texas Chainsaw Massacre" with Wilson's unbaked-cookie characters at each other's throats. And heads. And guts. Great fun.

Wilson's giddy, ornate mutation is cotton candy compared with John Callahan's spare, haunting "I Think I Was an Alcoholic." This autobiographical black-and-white short by the syndicated newspaper cartoonist is a rueful, darkly funny account of his long drinking life from childhood through the drunk-driving accident that left him a quadraplegic. As a convincing testament of art's triumph over personal pain, Callahan's film is easily the triumph of the festival.

Other unsettling concoctions include British animator Paul Berry's "The Sandman," which takes the childhood myth of what happens during sleepy-time to horrific extremes. Creepiest of all is "The Stain," by Marjut Rimminen and Christine Roche. It's a combination of "Rashomon" and fairy tale with sinister and dreadful portent seeping all over a house occupied by a handicapped girl, her abusive sister and her tormented twin brothers.

Not even the program's centerpiece, "A Salute to the Dimensional Artistry of the Will Vinton Studios," dispels this exotic and macabre atmosphere. Yes, the California Raisins make a couple of brief appearances here. There's a guest shot by Michael Jackson as a moon-walking raisin, which, given present circumstances, is bizarre enough.

But the Vinton Claymators also serve up a small-scale cybernetic fantasy starring the intrepid "Mr. Resistor," who looks a lot like the little electronic guy that hung around Gyro Gearloose's shoulders in those old Donald Duck comic books. He is besieged, at one point, by an angry mob of trophy figurines who are out to mutilate his (literally) wiry limbs. It's not as surreal as the animation of the Brothers Quay. But it's close.

Other highlights: Michaela Pavlatova's "Words, Words, Words" in which barroom conversation is cleverly conceptualized into pure color and shape; Mike Smith's "Get a Haircut," a raucous, head-banging (pun intended) rock video; Claude Luyet's "The Square of Light," which should convince even the hardest skeptics that boxing is an art form.

And there's an excerpt from "Prehistoric Beast," Phil Tippett's stunning reenactment of dinosaur turf-mongering that led to his being tapped to work on "Jurassic Park." The rest is film history—as is much else in this bizarre bazaar of toons.

Also reviewed in:
CHICAGO TRIBUNE, 9/17/93, Friday/p. L, John Petrakis
NEW YORK TIMES, 1/21/94, p. C6, Stephen Holden
WASHINGTON POST, 9/17/93, p. D8, Richard Harrington

TWO SMALL BODIES

A Castle Hill Productions release of a Daniel Zuta Filmproduktion film for ZDF television (Germany). *Producer:* Daniel Zuta and Beth B. *Director:* Beth B. *Screenplay:* Neal Bell and Beth B. *Based on the play by:* Neal Bell. *Director of Photography:* Phil Parmet. *Editor:* Melody London and Andrea Feige. *Music:* Swans. *Casting:* Jeffrey Passero. *Art Director:* Agnette Schlosser. *Costumes:* Bea Gossman. *Running time:* 85 minutes. *MPAA Rating:* Not Rated.

CAST: Fred Ward (Lt. Brann); Suzy Amis (Eileen Maloney).

LOS ANGELES TIMES, 5/27/94, Calendar/p. 11, Kevin Thomas

"Two Small Bodies," a thoroughly captivating film adaptation of Neal Bell's play, seemingly is simplicity itself.

A trench-coated police detective (Fred Ward) comes to a suburban house to interrogate a single mother (Suzy Amis) on the disappearance of her two young children. Very early on it's clear that Ward's Lt. Brann believes that Amis' Eileen Maloney, estranged from her husband, has murdered her kids—and that Brann, who speaks only with love of his own two children, will quickly become obsessed with the case.

"Two Small Bodies" allows its stars to shine in far-ranging, deeply probing characterizations of the kind that actors all too rarely get to play on the screen, even those as talented as Ward and Amis.

Brann and Maloney's ensuing battle of wits yields an amazing thicket of thoughts, emotions and evolving perceptions, and they have been elucidated with an unsettling thoroughness by the veteran independent filmmaker known as Beth B. Indeed, Beth B., who collaborated on the screenplay with Bell as well as directed the film, is ideal for this assignment. Such earlier films as "Vortex" (1983) and "Black Box" (1978), made with her husband, Scott B., have been concerned with the abuse of power, both political and sexual.

Worn and pale when we first meet her, Eileen, a strip joint hostess, reminds us of Meryl Streep's mother of a missing child in Fred Schepisi's "A Cry in the Dark" in that she seems simply weary; rather than heartbroken or distraught, which is how mothers are supposed to act in such circumstances. (It is possible, after all, for a mother to be a grudging, reluctant parent without being a child killer.)

Right off her aura of cool resignation throws Brann, a sexy ultra-macho type with a traditional view of women's roles as a wife and mother. His relationship with Eileen teeters like a seesaw, as the impact of his menace wavers as Eileen appears to gather strength, acquiring an increasingly blunt, hard edge, seeming to agree with much of what he has to say about her.

Through this endless parrying much emerges. First, we find ourselves not quite so quick to believe that Eileen may in fact be guilty of infanticide, and then we start wondering about Lt.

Brann. How do we know he really is a cop? Could he be the killer of the children himself?—if they are in fact dead.

Suspense, in turn triggers paradox: Could a man as sexually dominant as Brann, a man who sees himself as a good guy, be finding himself tantalized by the prospect of yielding to what he sees as the embodiment of evil? And then there is the role of illusion, seemingly so much more crucial to men than to women, who constantly find themselves in situations where they feel that they must pretend to be other than what they are to men, many of whom even today still see women as either madonnas or whores. Illusion, in fact, battles with truth throughout "Two Small Bodies," which is so compelling that it never once seems a filmed play.

NEW YORK POST, 4/15/94, p. 38, Thelma Adams

"Two Small Bodies," Beth B's latest film, refers to the corpses of Eileen Maloney's children.

The title also alludes to Eileen (Suzy Amis) and Lt. Brann (Fred Ward). These two bruised characters—a stripper and a cop—circle each other in a fierce dance of suspicion, accusation, violence and lust.

If this two-person tarantella sounds cliched, you haven't missed the point. Downtown artist and filmmaker Bet B ("Vortex") intends to reinvent the B-movie form—the rundown detective interrogates the fallen mother—and shed light on the shifting balance of power between men and women, the law and lawlessness.

At first, it's annoying. the actors struggle to find their legs within their roles; Ward's too intense, Amis has the tentativeness of an honor student playing a floozy in a high school play.

But each actor reclaims their character. Ward (the villain in "Naked Gun 33⅓") plays the detective with a Charles Bronson, Cro-Magnon, short-foreheaded, thick-skinned relentlessness. If there's pain here, it's buried under rock.

Bell and B toss in an unexpected scene. One morning, Lt. Brann arrives at Eileen's house. He changes his clothes in front of her.

As Brann struts around Eileen's kitchen in his BVDs, rubbing his crotch, he's threatening and unpredictable. Brann's machismo is as clear as the tattoo on his biceps.

Does Brann know what he's doing? Is his near-nakedness a ploy to get Eileen to admit she killed her kids and where their bodies are stashed? Or is Brann unstable himself?

Amis ("Ballad of Little Jo") steps into the groove set by Ward. Their tug-of-war achieves the tension required to carry a movie that has no other actors, only two small bodies.

Fine-boned and raw, Eileen carries a wiry strength in her skinny frame. Beneath her translucent skin and behind her pale, worried eyes, she's a match for Brann.

Under Brann's constant interrogation, Eileen finally admits her guilt: "I smothered them to death with motherly love ... I told them that TV was good for their minds ... I told them to play in traffic."

Did Eileen kill her kids? The battle of wits rages on while the writing careens from razor-sharp repartee to stilted artiness. "Two Small Bodies" is stagy, uneven and, at times, unintentionally funny. But it will doubtless be a while before Ward and Amis get such strong leads in a mainstream movie. Watching two brave actors butt heads in this stark adult drama about mothers and other strangers is worth a look.

NEWSDAY, 4/15/94, Part II/p. B9, John Anderson

Director Beth B asks a bit too much of us in "Two Small Bodies," a title that refers both to a pair of murdered children, and the two adults who play a macabre game of sexual politics over their unseen corpses.

Are the characters performing an interpretive dance about gender dynamics? Is it all just a sendup of film noir? Did I leave the coffeepot on?

Watching Lt. Brann (Fred Ward) interrogate his suspect—Eileen Maloney (Suzy Amis), a hostess in a topless bar and the mother of the missing kids—what's impressive is the awkward and artificial content of their exchanges. Maloney exhibits an almost total lack of grief, Brann a total lack of professionalism. "Mind if ask you a few questions?" he asks each time—and there are many—that he arrives at Maloney's house to question her.

His questions become increasingly personal and suggestive; at one point, after a long night, he brings his clothes and changes in Eileen's kitchen. He's a too-obvious mix of male impotence and power, but the lack of urgency, the stiff, rehearsed quality of the characters' dialogue and the sense one has that they know the outcome before-hand, led me to believe that Maloney was a a prostitute and Brann had paid her to enact some elaborate sexual fantasy about being a cop on a murder case.

But no, hunting for alternate plotlines would be futile her; the screenplay, by B and playwright Neal Bell, which was adapted from his play, is to be taken at face value. B does have a rather arresting visual style; her use of moonlight and claustrophobic spaces is evocative, and she uses her set to tell her story. The initial scenes—a rain-beaded car window moving under gnarled tree limbs, Eileen kicking a child's toy, and gazing at a crayon drawing—set the narrative up immediately. What follows, however, is a film that tries much too hard to be profoundly symbolic without providing dramatic ballast.

Ward and Amis work hard with what they've been given, although there's no spontaneity, and hence no tension. The effect is a weariness that infects this movie right to its bones.

VILLAGE VOICE, 4/19/94, p. 58, Amy Taubin

The name of the game is guilt—and its pleasures. Beth B's *Two Small Bodies* lays bare the sado-masochistic fantasy that launched 10,000 movies (conservative estimate): the fantasy of the investigation and punishment of the bad girl. It's a scenario as provocative to some women as it is to most men.

In patriarchy, women are, by definition, bad—potential or actual rebels against an order they didn't create and which operates to their disadvantage. Embraced by the radical feminists of the '60s, the bad girl was mainstreamed in the '80s as Madonna. Currently, as slug-of-the-year (a label affixed to art shows, female westerns, Versace rags, Tonya Harding), the bad girl has been all but robbed of threat, allure, power—and meaning.

Two Small Bodies, however, is a throwback to the feminist bad girl as she was embodied in New York punk, where Beth B came of age as a filmmaker and artist. A two-character chamber piece, the film reveals itself immediately as the ritual enactment of a reverse fantasy. Eileen Maloney (Suzy Amis) is suspected by police lieutenant Brann (Fred Ward) of having murdered her children. Brann turns up at Eileen's suburban two-story at any hour of the day or night to inspect the scene of the alleged crime and interrogate Eileen, who defiantly cops to all manner of bad behavior—short of killing her children. His "belief" that she is guilty of the worst possible crime (infanticide) justifies his brutality toward her. Her knowledge that he is sexually aroused by her criminality (sucked into her story, he becomes complicitous in her guilt) gives her power over him.

B's direction is a major tour de force. Confining the film to three rooms and a backyard, she finds infinite variety in a ritual defined by its repetition. She is well served by Phil Parmet's moody-blue cinematography, Melody London and Andrea Feige's punchy editing, and the Swans' coolly ominous score. Exceedingly well matched, Ward and Amis are both at the top of their game, bringing fluidity and nuance to a clunkily obvious script (adapted by Neal Bell and B from a play by Bell). But if Ward is only compelling as a catalyst, the delicate, slightly shopworn Amis evokes the guilt and loss that inspires Eileen's masquerade. In that sense, *Two Small Bodies* is a mystery from beginning to end, provoking our desire to investigate the woman.

Also reviewed in:
CHICAGO TRIBUNE, 7/15/94, Friday/p. J, Michael Wilmington
NEW YORK TIMES, 4/15/94, p. C10, Caryn James
VARIETY, 9/20/93, p. 30, Deborah Young

UNDER ONE ROOF

A Castle Hill Productions release. *Producer:* Glaucia Camargos. *Director:* Paulo Thiago. *Screenplay (Portuguese with English subtitles):* Alcione Araujo. *Director of Photography:* Antonio Penido. *Editor:* Marco Antonio Cury. *Music:* Tulio Mourao. *Sound:* Tulio Mourao. *Sound Editor:* Jorge Salhanha. *Art Director:* Clovis Bueno. *Costumes:* Kalma Murtinho. *Running time:* 95 minutes. *MPAA Rating:* Not Rated.

CAST: Norma Bengell (Gertrudes); Maria Zilda Bethlem (Madalena); Lucelia Santos (Lucia); Paulo Cesar Pereio (Astronaut); Marco Frota (Plumber/Alfredo); Paulo Gorgulho (Gentlemen/Fisherman); Luis Tadeu Teixeira (Violent Man).

NEW YORK POST, 3/25/94, p. 37, Bill Hoffmann

One's hopeless. one's hopelessly horny and another one's half crazy.

Each of these distinctly offbeat women has a personality quirky enough to fill a movie on their own.

But director Paulo Thiago has them all loving and warring together in "Under One Roof"—an odd little psycho-drama that tries to be a thoughtful study of women on the edge.

But it plays more like a three-ring circus: confusion rules. Sometimes it works, sometimes it doesn't.

Gertrudes—a plumpish, worrisome piano teacher owns a boarding house in Brazil and plays mother hen to two oddball tenants.

There's 35-year-old Madelena, a sassy, irreverent bachelorette who works in an insane asylum by day and dresses like a hooker and tirelessly chases men by night.

Madelena loves to shock the ultra-conservative Gertrudes, by running around the house naked and bragging about her sexual conquests.

Why must she shamelessly flit into the night looking for sex? Gertrudes asks, "I look for a little pleasure. None here. I look for happiness. None here either," Madelena snaps.

Then there's Lucia, a stunningly beautiful teen who's mentally unstable, cannot work and walks around in the dark with a flashlight as her guide.

Some moments, she's perfectly lucid. In others she turns into a babbling paranoiac in need of constant supervision.

Gertrudes is forever frustrated by the two young women—but she desperately needs them to help fill the terrible void left by her husband's death.

She looks forward to her daily outrage with Madelena and she lovingly comforts Lucia during her worst fits.

Madalena's choice in men is horrendous. She sleeps with gangsters, sadists and other sleaze. One of her pickups gives her a gun to protect her from "people like me."

Lucia is also highly sex-charged—seducing the plumber's son (a Roger Daltrey lookalike) as he fixes the pipes, then straddling her motorcycle topless as he gives it a tune-up.

Gertrudes is not without her own demons. The apparition of her late spouse visits when she is alone. In one chilling scene, she dances with the ghost (actually a pillow) and then hacks at it with a carving knife.

All of this mayhem provides many spurts of pure cinematic pleasure.

But it never adds up as a whole and the dreamlike ending showing the supposed liberation of our heroines is unsatisfying. Like any good three-ring circus, it should have had a climax.

Director Thiago has the potential of becoming Brazil's version of Pedro Almodovar. If he can juggle his narrative and his quirkiness with just a bit more control he'll be a major force in Brazilian cinema.

NEWSDAY, 3/25/94, Part II/p. B2, Jack Mathews

The elements of a decent play percolate under the surface of director Paulo Thiago's "Under One Roof," the story of three women of three generations sharing an apartment in modern-day Brazil. A movie, however, it isn't.

Thiago makes efforts to take his characters outdoors, for a walk or a motorcycle ride or, in the case of the insatiable Madalena (Maria Zelda Bethlem), on sexual forays. But the real action is in their apartment, where they fire psychological volleys at each other and attempt to hide the despair that links them.

Quite a threesome. Gertrudes (Norma Bengell), both roommate and landlady, is a 60-year-old widow haunted by the memory (and the occasional apparition) of her dead husband, taking cover from her pain by doting on 20-year-old Lucia (Lucelia Santos), a malingerer feigning madness and malnutrition.

The 35-year-old Madalena serves as both the fulcrum and a source of friction between the others. She spends her days working as a nurse at a mental hospital and the rest of her time either taunting old-fashioned Gertrudes with her liberated ideas, or acting them out with a variety of men she picks up in bars. Thiago frequently crosses the line between reality and fantasy—the magic realism so popular in Latin America—but the results are more confusing than enlightening. There's no question Gertrudes is conjuring up her husband, a silent stiff in a naval uniform, but is Lucia really having sex with the plumber (Marco Frota) who comes to fix the toilet, or are we just getting a cheap thrill?

Madalena is definitely going to bed with some unsavory fellows, one of whom who peddles pistols to hit men, but how about the handsome fisherman (Paulo Gorgulho) with the Lancelot smile? A dream, or another cheap thrill?

Sorting through the imagery isn't the fun it ought to be, because the characters themselves aren't much fun. Though the performances of the three actresses are very good, Madalena and Lucia are ultimately too cruel and self-absorbed to be sympathetic figures, and Gertrudes is too willing a victim.

For all its suggested internal conflicts and excursions into fantasy, "Under One Roof" plays out entirely on the emotional surface. What we have here is a mock family, a mother and her rebellious daughters, but the dynamics just sit there, announced and undeveloped.

A good writer, a good playwright, could ponder the meaning of life with that set-up, and whether the women were shown to resolve their conflicts or not, we would come to understand the common bonds between them.

"Under One Roof" leaves you feeling you've wandered into a room full of bickering neighbors—and wishing you hadn't.

VILLAGE VOICE, 4/5/94, p. 68, Ellen Cohn

I am shy. I don't shout "steeeerotypes" in a crowded theater even when it's painfully true. Besides, when a film is about contemporary women, I hold out hope. Deceived again.

Set in a Brazilian coastal town, *Under One Roof* focuses on three women who share an apartment. Gertrudes, a sixtyish piano teacher who may have once had a concert career, rents two spare bedrooms to "well-bred ladies"—for companionship as much as for income, She's not having luck with her boarders. The 20-year-old Lucia is an agitated depressive who in her maddest moments shrieks that she's pursued by demons. Surreptitiously hoarding food in her room while she pretends not to eat, Lucia encourages the older woman to pamper and protect her. Madalena, the liveliest of the trio, is a flamboyant thirysomething nurse who works in a mental hospital by day and bed-hops by night. Lucia has a crush on her and her hot-to-trot wardrobe. Under one roof, the women also live under a cloud—each fantasizing about Mr. Right and the day all her dreams come true.

Thiago finds no way to enliven the proceedings (repeated shots of the sea from the apartment window don't do it) or to elevate the women's lives into even second-rate soap. Next time, I'll scream.

Also reviewed in:
NEW YORK TIMES, 3/25/94, p. C18, Stephen Holden

UNFORGETTABLE SUMMER, AN

An MK2 Productions USA release of an MK2 Productions/La Sept Cinema/Le Studio de Creation Cinematographique de Roumanie production with the participation of Canal Plus, CNC, and Filmex. *Producer:* Marin Karmitz and Constantin Popescu. *Director:* Lucian Pintilie. *Screenplay (French, Romanian and English with English subtitles):* Lucian Pintilie. *Based on the novella "The Salad" by:* Petru Dumitrius. *Director of Photography:* Calin Ghibu. *Editor:* Victorita Nae. *Music:* Anton Suteu. *Sound:* Andrei Papp. *Production Designer:* Paul Bortnovschi. *Costumes:* Miruna Boruzescu. *Running time:* 82 minutes. *MPAA Rating:* Not Rated.

CAST: Kristin Scott-Thomas (Marie-Thérèse Von Debretsy); Claudiu Bleont (Capt. Petre Dumitriu); Olga Tudorache (Mme. Vorvoreanu); George Constantin (Gen. Tchilibia); Ion Pavlescu (Serban Lascari); Marcel Iures (Gen. Ipsilanti); Razvan Vasilescu (Lt. Turtureanu); Cornel Scripcaru; Tamara Cretulescu; Mihai Constantin.

NEW YORK POST, 11/11/94, p. 49, Bill Hoffmann

"An Unforgettable Summer" is a haunting beauty of a movie about the cruelty and utter pointlessness of war.

It stands out as one of the truer filmgoing experiences of the year with a brutal honesty, touching poignancy and an ultimately shattering conclusion that will take your breath away.

The scene is a desolate, dry-as-dust Romanian border province called Dobroudja, which uneasily co-exists with Bulgaria in 1925, as the two countries struggle for control of the territory.

A young Romanian captain (Claudiu Bleont) has been sent there after his wife, Marie-Therese (Kristin Scott-Thomas) spurns the advances of a superior officer, General Ipsilanti (Marcel Iures).

Marie-Therese is a hopelessly optimistic woman who despite her aristocratic upbringing, embraces the spartan outpost and its helpless peasant residents as her own.

But her world is shattered when eight Romanian frontier guards are massacred by bandits and Ipsilanti orders the random roundup of innocent Bulgarian villagers for execution.

Marie-Therese showers these hapless men with kindness as they faithfully work on her vegetable garden, play with her children and await their fate.

She begs her husband to save them, leading to a final, blistering confrontation between her spouse and the general.

Scott-Thomas is wonderful as a woman who is stunned by the inanity of her husband's profession, yet can't stop being a good wife.

Writer-director Lucian Pintilie has given us a brief but unforgettable portrait of lives bound by rules so rigid the only outcome can be more human suffering.

In showing us this, Pintilie gives a new, harrowing interpretation of the phrase "man is his own worst enemy."

It's a point that will linger with you long after this must-see movie is over.

NEWSDAY, 11/11/94, Part II/p. B7, Jack Mathews

As we have learned during the breakup of the former Yugoslavia, the collapse of Eastern European communism has been a mixed blessing to many of the liberated. One of the privileges of freedom is the right to exercise prejudice, and the ancient hatreds that have surfaced in the absence of a totalitarian government, and under the genocidal euphemism of "ethnic cleansing," have been hideous.

But they are ancient, and deep-rooted, as Romanian director Lucian Pintilie ("The Oak") demonstrates in his illuminating "An Unforgettable Summer," the story of a family caught in a political vise along the 1925 Romanian-Bulgarian border.

The setting is a dusty military outpost in an area called Dobruja on the shore of the Black Sea, where an ambitious Romanian officer (Claudiu Bleont) has exiled himself and his family in order to escape a superior's persistent advances toward his beautiful, aristocratic Hungarian wife (Kristin Scott-Thomas) back in Bucharest.

For a while, life on the border is bliss for the Dumitriu family, because Marie-Therese (Scott-Thomas, the ardent Fiona in "Four Weddings and a Funeral") is a passionate optimist, seeing only the beauty in the parched land, and only goodness in the local villagers. There are ominous signs—children throw mud at the house, a bullet is fired through their open door—but it isn't until Capt. Dumitriu is ordered to execute a band of innocent Bulgarian farmers in retaliation for a raid on his own men that their lives begin to unravel.

Pintilie has painted a picture of a society so ethnically obsessed it can barely communicate in any other terms. Through Marie-Therese, the only major character who does not view people as breeds, he is suggesting both the frustration of the past and present, and the hope of the future.

If you think of people as optimists, pessimists and pragmatists, positive change seems likeliest through the influence of optimists, like Marie-Therese, or pragmatists, like her stern, Prussian-trained husband. Early during their life in Dobruja, an officer, begins a savage beating of a peasant soldier right in front of Dumitriu and the horrified Marie-Therese, and she has to beg her husband to intercede.

When told not to beat the men anymore, the officer tells Capt. Dumitriu, "But soldiers are beaten in every unit."

"Not mine," says Dumitriu, with his consciousness raised a notch.

It's a long way from there to the end of ethnic cleansing, but it's a start.

VILLAGE VOICE, 11/15/94, p. 55, J. Hoberman

Despite a deceptively bland and pastoral title, Lucian Pintilie's *An Unforgettable Summer* is as savage in its way as the manic farce of the veteran Romanian director's 1992 *The Oak*. All nostalgia for the Good Old Days must be seen in the context of the newly rebalkanized Balkans.

An Unforgettable Summer is set in the relative calm of 1925 (eight years before Pintilie's birth), evoking the lost Kingdom of Romania as a diminished successor to the vanished Austro-Hungarian Empire. By joining World War I late and on the winning side, Romania had greatly enhanced its territories in the postwar settlement—as well as becoming a truly multinational state. The brittle facade of what the movie's press release is pleased to term Romania's "fairy tale monarchy" is suggested by the revelries with which *An Unforgettable Summer* opens.

Pintilie contrives a parody of sentimental *Mittleuropa* cineglitz in which, the night of a grand ball, the army temporarily shuts down the satiny bordello patronized by its officers; led by their resident Hungarian firebrand, the whores run amok. The sequence initially seems to be suffering a surfeit of schlag—it's an exercise in controlled vulgarity that, not untypical for Pintilie, climaxes in a staccato display of ugly force, segueing into the ball itself.

Having demolished his post-Hapsburg setting, Pintilie moves on to the human drama. *An Unforgettable Summer* is basically the tragedy of a brilliant young couple, Captain Dumitriu and his wife Marie-Thérèse. The diminutive captain, trained in Prussia, is a monocled popinjay. (Claudiu Bleont's herky-jerky body language and quizzically magnified right eye suggest a performance manufactured in the Factory of the Eccentric Actor.) The vivacious Marie-Thérèse, daughter of a Romanian diplomat and raised in England (and hence played, with aplomb, by Kristin Scott-Thomas), attracts the unwelcome attentions of her husband's foppish commanding officer.

The captain asks to be reassigned and winds up in charge of a godforsaken garrison on the Bulgarian border—an inhospitable, recently acquired tract of land inhabited not only by Romanians and Bulgarians but an assortment of Turks, Greeks, and Macedonians. (It has since reverted to Bulgaria.) The genre-literate might imagine *An Unforgettable Summer* as a sort of sardonic East European *Fort Apache*, with the "civilized" military family set down on hostile terrain populated by primitive natives given to wild "Asiatic" music and enigmatic revels, and policed by a degenerate battalion of absurd but brutal operetta soldiers.

Ethnic contempt is a given. While the movie isn't glazed over with period detail, Pintilie handles its international bias—a French-Romanian coproduction with an English star—by going totally polyglot. As befits a woman named for a Hapsburg empress, the Scott-Thomas character speaks three languages (there are passages in Hungarian as well); played by the lone non-Romanian performer, she's a natural magnet for hostility. Well before her tolerance for the locals is established, the soldiers instinctively loathe their captain's wife, taking potshots at her dressing room mirror and referring to her as a "Magyarish bitch."

The free-spirited Marie-Thérèse responds to her situation by bathing with her three young children in the dusty, open courtyard of their new quarters. Despite these intimations of paradise, and her somewhat overwrought tendency to put the brightest shine on the grimmest reality, the posting grows increasingly nightmarish. After a group of Romanian soldiers are ambushed, massacred, and mutilated by obscurely nationalist "bandits," Captain Dumitriu is instructed to round up a random group of Bulgarian peasants and, after a time during which they are put to work tending his garden, execute them.

Like *The Oak*, *An Unforgettable Summer* is set in the Romanian outback and focuses on the antiauthoritarian misadventures of a splendidly eccentric woman with an insanely honest consort. The difference is that here, the system isn't crumbling; however decadent, it's still capable of exerting its will. Indeed, given the power of protocol, *An Unforgettable Summer* is a far more understated movie than the wild and crazy *Oak*, albeit subtly spiced with grotesque types and lethal slapstick. The compositions are effectively spared the sharpness and clarity of the mise-en-scène evoke the "empty world" existentialism of East European classics like Jancsó's *The Round-Up*; the theater of cruelty is complicated by a chorus of three heedless children.

Pintilie's intelligence is everywhere apparent. It's a pleasure to watch a movie in which every shot has been designed to frame several things at once. A minuet on the subject of authority and responsibility, *An Unforgettable Summer* is scaled down but it's hardly inconsequential. Because to live in this particular world is to be made horribly complicit in stupid atrocity, the viewer too has to endure the pathetic whimpering of doomed innocents and the agonized indecision of a would-be suicide. Because Pintilie is a poet, however, death is most concretely visualized in a close-up of a bug drowning in a sea of salad dressing.

The meaning of the opening shot, in which a barren hill is compared in its monumental majesty to Fujiyama, is only apparent in the movie's final minute—when the narrator, with an absence of irony that, naturally, provides the most distancing wrench in perspective, refers to everything that has transpired as "the most beautiful summer of my childhood."

Also reviewed in:
CHICAGO TRIBUNE, 2/10/95, Friday/p. H, Michael Wilmington
NEW YORK TIMES, 2/11/94, p. C12, Caryn James
NEW YORKER, 11/14/94, p. 143, Anthony Lane
VARIETY, 5/30-6/5/94, p. 46, Lisa Nesselson
WASHINGTON POST, 1/20/95, p. D1, Hal Hinson

VANYA ON 42ND STREET

A Sony Pictures Classics release of a Laura Pels Productions and Mayfair Entertainment production. *Producer:* Fred Berner. *Director:* Louis Malle. *Screenplay:* David Mamet. *Adapted from "Uncle Vanya" by:* Anton Chekhov. *Director of Photography:* Declan Quinn. *Editor:* Nancy Baker. *Music:* Joshua Redman. *Sound:* Tod A. Maitland. *Sound Editor:* Ron Bochar. *Production Designer:* Eugene Lee. *Set Decorator:* Randi Savoy. *Costumes:* Gary Jones. *Make-up:* Sharon Ilson. *Running time:* 119 minutes. *MPAA Rating:* PG.

CAST: Wallace Shawn (Vanya); Julianne Moore (Yelena); Brooke Smith (Sonya); Larry Pine (Dr. Astrov); George Gaynes (Serybryakov); Lynn Cohen (Maman); Phoebe Brand (Marina); Jerry Mayer (Waffles); Madhur Jaffrey (Mrs. Chao); Andre Gregory (Himself).

FILMS IN REVIEW, 1-2/95, p. 59, Andy Pawelczak

Chekhov has never played very well in America. The most astonishing thing about *Vanya on 42nd St.* is that it is as full a realization of Chekhov as any I've ever seen and is fully situated on 42nd St., the broken down but somehow still vital crossroads of America. All hands, from Louis Malle, the film's director, to Andre Gregory who initiated and developed the stage production to the superb actors, contributed to this achievement but David Mamet deserves special attention for his adaptation of the text from a literal translation. I'm not a Mamet fan—his writing is too stylized and attenuated for me—but here he's found a way to give Chekhov's lines an authentic American music without losing the Chekhovian essence.

The production dates back to 1989 when Andre Gregory, an avant garde stage director who also starred, together with Wallace Shawn, in Malle's *My Dinner With Andre*, gathered a group of actors to work on *Uncle Vanya*. The work-in-progress was performed for small audiences of invited guests until Malle stepped in to film the production in an abandoned theater on 42nd St. What at first blush might seem to be a gimmick turns out to be a coup. The crumbling nineteenth century theater with its peeling walls and remnants of baroque splendor is the perfect setting for this play whose themes are decay and the passage of time.

The film opens with the actors and their guests arriving in the theater and politely chatting. Without any transition and before we quite know what's happening, the play has begun with the actors performing in street clothes in an off-stage area of the theater. Astrov (Larry Pine), a doctor from a remote province, is visiting the estate of Alexander Serebryakov (George Gaynes), a retired professor from Moscow who has moved to his country estate for pecuniary reasons. As Astrov talks with Marina (Phoebe Brand), the family's old servant, the play's main themes are introduced: she tells him he's gotten older and is losing his looks, he complains about the sterility of life in the provinces and says he doesn't feel things anymore. Enter Vanya (Wallace Shawn), the brother of the old professor's dead first wife, who has devoted his life to running the estate so his revered brother-in-law can live well in Moscow. Vanya is one of the great theatrical figurations of the unlived life—he's filled with rage at how he's wasted his life in the service of the professor who is an idol with feet of clay, a pompous old windbag without talent or real accomplishments.

As Vanya, Wallace Shawn brings a neurotic edge to the role that is very different from the drunk befuddlement of other productions. His Vanya is like a cornered rat in the ruined theater—he's a Vanya who bites. At the beginning of the film, Shawn shows his guests some old busts of Shakespearean characters, and his Vanya is as haunted by Shakespeare as he is by his own personal ghosts. With his gallows humor and impotent tirades against his mother and the old professor, he's a kind of sadly diminished Hamlet, even down to his dream that he could have been a Schopenhauer, the gloomy German philosopher who was himself a lesser Hamlet. And like Hamlet, he's an actor, spitting out his vituperations with grand theatrical energy.

Yelena (Julianne Moore), the professor's young and beautiful second wife who is loved by both Vanya and Astrov, reaches for a Shakespearean largeness also—at one point, she tells Astrov that she's nobler than he thinks she is. Julianne Moore takes real risks in her performance, abandoning the usual hauteur that actresses bring to the role and letting us see Yelena's vulnerability and terrible sexual disappointment along with her great capacity for life. Brooke Smith as Sonya, the professor's daughter who unrequitedly loves Astrov, is the production's center of radiance, an incarnation of youth and fragile, impossible hope. Larry Pine's Astrov is reminiscent of O'Neill's drunken, poetic failures and reminds us that O'Neill is a drop in the Chekhovian ocean.

Louis Malle's tight compositions take us into the inner workings of this family of co-dependents who helplessly grind against each other in claustrophobic intimacy. Malle and Gregory's great accomplishment is getting the play's emotion up on the screen without losing its delicacy and poetry—at times, the actors are like naked flames of feeling in the darkness. Through it all there's the sense that this is a *Vanya* for America which is subtly present in Mamet's cadences and in the way the actors tentatively occupy space in the dark, cavernous theater. And it's there in the play's themes, too—paralysis, fantasies of renewal, the preoccupation with last things, the good-byes that are permanent and heartbreaking. Finally, *Vanya on 42nd St.* demonstrates that we still have something to learn from Chekhov about spiritual grace and tenderness and what it means to be human in an age of diminishing expectations.

LOS ANGELES TIMES, 11/4/94, Calendar/p. 10, Kenneth Turan

"Vanya on 42nd Street" is an afterthought to be thankful for. A movie version of an exploration of Anton Chekhov's ""Uncle Vanya" that was not originally intended for an audience, let alone film, it is that rare melding of cinema and drama that does honor to both disciplines.

If movie stars fantasize about Oscars, theatrical actors dream of playing Chekhov and inhabiting his sensitive and complex characters. The Russian dramatist, who died in 1904 at age 44, wrote four remarkable plays in the last decade of his life: "The Sea Gull," "The Three Sisters," "The Cherry Orchard" and "Uncle Vanya."

Theatrical director Andre Gregory (known to film audiences as the title character in "My Dinner With Andre") decided in 1989 that he wanted to work on a production of the play using a contemporary adaptation by David Mamet.

After gathering his cast, which included "Dinner" co-star Wallace Shawn as Vanya, Gregory and company worked on and off on the piece for four years, first in a New York loft space and then, in 1991, before small invited audiences of 20 or 30 in a decaying movie theater near Times Square.

In 1992, the company's oldest actress, 89-year-old Ruth Nelson, died, and the performances stopped. Then, a year later, there was an urge to begin again, and, with Nelson's Group Theater colleague Phoebe Brand joining the cast, Louis Malle, the director of "Dinner," agreed to film it.

In keeping with the spirit of the original workshops, Malle and Gregory made a number of smart choices. They reproduced the atmosphere of the invited performances by filming in front of a small audience in the crumbling interior of Times Square's once-glamorous New Amsterdam Theater.

Everyone ambles into the theater, director Gregory and the audience exchange greetings, the actors chat as they gather on the stage and, unless you've read the text the night before, the opening lines of the play blend so seamlessly with the conversation that it takes a minute or two to realize the action has started.

As with many of Chekhov's plays, "Vanya" concerns an extended family, and is set on the estate of Serybryakov (George Gaynes), a retired professor who gained control of the land when his first wife died.

In the past Serybryakov has been an absentee landlord, content to live off the revenues and allowing his daughter, Sonya (Brooke Smith), and his brother-in-law, Vanya (Shawn), to run the place for him. But now, at the play's opening, financial difficulties have forced him to return to the estate, bringing with him his young and alluring second wife Yelena (Julianne Moore).

The presence of this couple stirs up a lifetime's worth of resentments not only for Vanya, who is in love with Yelena and has begun to fear his years of toil have been for nothing, but also for the local doctor Astrov (Larry Pine), whom young Sonya has innocently had her eye on.

To watch this "Vanya" is to marvel, as always with Chekhov, at his insights, at how rigorously and effortlessly non-judgmental he is, at how much empathy he has for all his characters, for the resentments they feel at being trapped by the frustrations of their idle, often squandered lives.

Under Gregory's and Malle's direction, the actors captivate. Shawn is strong as the prickly, ironically self-deprecating Vanya, but the surprise of the production is Julianne Moore's Yelena.

Moore, who got her role in Robert Altman's "Short Cuts" after the director saw her in one of the "Vanya" run-throughs, shows us that the Raymond Carver adaptation used only a thimbleful of her abilities. Here the actress utilizes all the opportunities this role provides, and her Yelena understandably intoxicates and frustrates every male she encounters.

Malle has used his documentary background to unobtrusively serve and enhance the production. "We all want to talk," Vanya says at one point, and this version of the play underscores once again how sublime it is when Chekhov's characters unburden their souls and do just that.

NEW YORK POST, 10/19/94 p. 36, Thelma adams

Call it "My Dinner With Uncle Vanya." Louis Malle, Andre Gregory and Wallace Shawn are reunited with "Vanya on 42nd Street," an updated production of Anton Chekhov's classic about provincial life. It's the best filmed play in recent memory.

Gregory directs the play within the Malle-directed film. Shawn plays Vanya. David Mamet wrote the lucid adaptation which cuts to the chase without sacrificing the heart and soul of this drama about family and friends, haves and have-nots.

Vanya is a play with very long legs, a comic tragedy whose themes continue to strike chords with modern audiences. It is set in a crumbling country estate maintained by Vanya and his plain niece, Sonya (Brooke Smith).

Vanya and Sonya's routine is disturbed when Sonya's father, a self-centered academic, visits the estate with his beautiful second wife, Yelena (Julianne Moore); Vanya falls for Yelena and into a deep depression.

The presence of the professor and his wife throw the provincials' lives into glaring relief, and then they depart. Externally nothing changes, but there's been a glacial shift in the interior lives of Vanya, Sonya, and Yelena.

Touching on environmentalism, the aridity of "political correctness" and the cost of sacrifices made to false principles, and the way in which inertia seals the fates of those who think too much and act too little too late, the play resonates for modern audiences.

Shawn, with his kissable bald spot, shows an agility in shifting from comedic whining to expressing emotional depths. His Vanya is a desperate delight.

The ensemble of actors practiced the piece together for more then four years before they turned to the camera, and theirs is a universally engaging and intimate performance. Julianne Moore, the true redhead of "Short Cuts," stands out with a Diane Keatonish Yelena, but there isn't a slacker in the bunch.

The usually voluble Gregory shows an admirable restraint as he appears before the rehearsal and between acts, coaxing the actors into their roles. The pleasure of watching the sleepy, overwrought New York actors stepping from the frenzy of 42nd Street into the lanes of the past is fittingly brief but sweet. A perfect frame, the dramatic devices that weld the film to the play enhance but don't overwhelm Chekhov's drama.

NEWSDAY, 10/19/94, Part II/p. B9, Jan Stuart

How do you make a movie of "Uncle Vanya"? A camera is not an X-ray machine. How does it get inside all those bottled family resentments and heartaches welling up like a constipated samovar? If you are Louis Malle and Andre Gregory, you don't worry too much about opening it up. You resist the researched period frou-frou that wins all the Best Achievement in Pretty awards at the Oscars. Rather, you close down on it: strip decor to a few suggestive essentials, then rub our noses in the play's theatrical lineage by plunking the actors in the middle of an abandoned vaudeville palace almost as old as the play.

Voila, "Vanya on 42nd Street," an exquisite alchemy of stage and celluloid so artless in its approach to both we feel as if we're bearing witness to the invention of drama. It's the love child of a once-renegade film auteur hopping into bed with a once-renegade theater director: as unobtrusively as possible, Malle is attempting to re-create the living-room intimacy of Gregory's 1991 staging of "Uncle Vanya" at the old Victory Theater, here moved across the street to the bombed-out New Amsterdam.

First, though, we've got to slog through a phony pre-performance sequence that stirs unfortunate memories of the prologues to the movie "Chorus Line" and "Godspell," wherein the performers tear through the bustling streets of Manhattan on their way to greasepaint heaven. Gregory runs into his Vanya and dinner-with-Andre companion, Wallace Shawn, munching on a knish on 42nd Street. He asks him what it is. It's a silly, insidey joke and a false move. Really, do we want to see Chekhov directed by someone who doesn't know a knish when he sees it?

After much stilted chitchat about the crumbling glory of the New Amsterdam Theater, Malle slips into the play on cat's paws. An informal conversation between actors Phoebe Brand and Larry Pine (a fine performer with a deep, serrated-knife voice that cuts like Jason Robard's) segues subtly into small talk between a matronly nursemaid named Marina and a tippling physician named Dr. Astrov.

The transition is so liquid it's almost startling. The artificiality of the theater troupe's "offstage" exchanges has the odd effect of bolstering Chekhov's stage reality, as Malle slides us into the unhappy country household of a fusty retired academic (George Gaynes, formidably surviving six "Police Academy" pictures) and his elegant wife Yelena (Julianne Moore). Through David Mamet's vivid and respectful translation, the starchy cadences of fin de siecle Russia strike the contemporary moviegoer's ear with far greater finesse than, say, Mamet's own films "Homicide" or "House of Games."

The lure, ultimately, is in watching a bunch of smart, unfussy actors wrap their craft around bourgeois angst in the provinces. Shawn, the embodiment of brainy mid-life disarray, fits Vanya like a moth-eaten glove, sputtering with unrequited desire for Yelena and clenched-teeth jealousy of her craggy husband. If Moore suffers at first from a case of the Diane Keaton giggles, she is a sensuous and commanding Yelena, a perfect balance of spoiled, suffocated and humane. The real news is Brooke Smith, incandescent as Vanya's plain-Jane sister Sonya. The genuine, washed-away sincerity with which Smith utters her fadeout words of consolation to a despairing brother is almost unbearably moving.

As readings of "Uncle Vanya" go, Gregory's approach is surprisingly austere. Vanya's gun-toting outburst, often pumped up for laughs, plays here as the soberest of family melodramas; you can feel Shawn working throughout to diffuse his naturally dishevelled comic edge. But Malle respects the stage director's designs; he refrains from camera histrionics, using closeups judiciously to attain a claustrophic intensity that recalls the best of Ingmar Bergman. His restraint is so consistent that when he interpolates a cinematic device (a voiceover interior monolog for Yelena), it strikes us as a jarring violation.

Perhaps there is a pretentiousness to the assertive air of anti-pretension (all those humble Greek-diner coffee cups on the tables). We certainly could have lived without Gregory's periodic appearances, making patronizing scene-change introductions. When "Vanya on 42nd Street" hums, though, it's like riding a great, sorrowful wave.

NEWSWEEK, 10/31/94, p. 67, Jack Kroll

The movie's first shot is of New York's Times Square: in-line skaters weaving through crowds, hookers in hotpants, peep shows. The camera picks out a group of people including a moon-faced little guy munching a gyro and a lean, intense guy fingering Hindu beads. They all enter a disused theater. The lean guy is stage director Andre Gregory, the little guy is playwright-actor Wallace Shawn. The title appears: "Vanya on 42nd Street." Shawn looks beat; he lies down on a bench. You didn't realize it but the play has begun. It's Chekhov's "Uncle Vanya" (adapted by David Mamet), being run through by a group of actors under Gregory before a handful of invited viewers in the decaying old New Amsterdam Theatre.

These actors had been workshopping the play on and off for four years. Now Louis Malle has filmed their work. It's not a formal production of the play, it's actors getting into it, sliding their end-of-century New York lives into Chekhov's end-of-century Russian lives. Shawn is Vanya, managing a declining estate for Alexandr, an elderly retired professor (George Gaynes), and his young wife, Yelena (Julianne Moore). A pall of frustration hangs over everyone: Vanya hopelessly loves Yelena; so does Dr. Astrov (Larry Pine), who's hopelessly loved by Sonya (Brooke Smith), Vanya's niece—all under the implacable eye of Vanya's mother (Lynn Cohen).

Chekhov is the stage's great poet of hopelessness; he makes it dynamic, turning the decay of people's hopes, of their land, of their society, into a dramatic sonata of missed connections. The play is perfect for the camera; this is a "Vanya" of faces, each face a stage on which a life is being enacted. Shawn is hardly classic casting, but his natural style, a fusion of farce and pathos, is perfect for the anguished clown that is Vanya. George Gaynes, who was the inane commandant in the "Police Academy" movies, captures the higher inanity with Alexandr, a phony unaware that his selfishness has wrecked nearly everyone's life.

Cinematographer Declan Quinn's lens catches every nuance in Julianne Moore's beautiful face: chagrin at her own seductiveness, disgust at the weakness of Vanya, pain at the failed idealism of Astrov, compassion for the yearnings of Sonya. but the most Chekhovian actors are the oldest, 86-year-old Phoebe Brand as the nanny, Marina, and the youngest, Brooke Smith (she was the girl in the pit in "The Silence of the Lambs"). Sonya's lament, "Lord, how could you make me so plain?" is doubly affecting because Smith has her own beauty, with her strong, heart-shaped face, tumble of dark-blond hair and avid eyes, "Uncle Vanya" comes to life on crummy old 42nd Street, another place of battered dreams.

SIGHT AND SOUND, 1/95, p. 61, Philip Strick

Between 1969 and 1992, André Gregory directed rehearsals of Chekhov's *Uncle Vanya* at the disused Victory Theatre in New York, with audiences of not more than 30 sharing the stage with the actors. In April 1994, rehearsals resumed at the derelict New Amsterdam on 42nd Street in order for the production to be filmed by Louis Malle within a two-week schedule.

Converging from the 42nd Street crowds, actors and guests greet each other in the theatre's ruined auditorium. The opening lines of the play form a casual part of the conversation. Dr Astrov, on one of his visits to the neighbouring estate of Professor Serebryakov, chats with the family's old nursemaid Marina and with Vanya, the Professor's former brother-in-law, who has managed the estate for 25 years. Vanya reports that the Professor, now at retirement age, has returned to the estate to write an intended masterpiece that will crown his career as an academic. He is accompanied by his strikingly beautiful second wife, Yelena, loyal but increasingly listless and bored, with whom Vanya has fallen hopelessly in love. More interested in Astrov, whose main pursuits appear to be vodka and forestry, Yelena irritably brushes off Vanya's approaches.

Marking the end of the first act, Gregory moves his guests to another stage area where the play resumes. During a night heavy with an approaching storm, the members of Serebryakov's household discuss their lives. The Professor is petulant with gout and Yelena tries to comfort him; Astrov has been summoned, but the Professor refuses to see him, much to the indignation of Sonya, the young daughter by his first marriage. Vanya and Astrov drink copiously, and Sonya encourages the doctor to talk about himself until the storm has passed and he departs. Sonya and Yelena, previously uncomfortable with each other, clear the air in reconciliation; Yelena admits to profound unhappiness, while Sonya confides she is in love with Astrov. Actors and audience then mingle for a buffet lunch.

The next act, Gregory explains, takes place three months later. Doggedly maintaining his infatuation with Yelena, Vanya goes to pick some autumn roses for her. When Sonya sadly remarks that Astrov doesn't seem to notice her, Yelena agrees to find out just how he feels about her step-daughter. It is quickly evident, however, that Astrov is fascinated not by Sonya but by Yelena, and he is eagerly kissing her despite her protests, just as Vanya returns with the roses. Oblivious to the resulting tensions, the Professor announces to the entire family his intention to sell the estate.

When the mood is calmer, the Professor and his wife prepare to leave. Astrov and Sonya persuade Vanya to give up a bottle of morphine he has hidden away. Yelena admits to Astrov that he interested her and permits a farewell embrace. Amid mutual apologies with Vanya, who promises to manage the estate exactly as before, Serebryakov grandly sweeps Yelena away, and Vanya and Sonya settle down to some overdue paperwork. Accepting a final vodka from Marina, Astrov also departs. Sonya consoles Vanya with her faith that eternal rest awaits them, and Gregory joins the cast around the worktable.

The phenomenon captured by *Vanya on 42nd Street*, thanks to the brooding environment of the New Amsterdam, once-glorious home to the Ziegfeld Follies, is one of transition. Monitored by André Gregory, smiling inscrutably over his worry-beads like a tribal guru, the uncostumed players emerge and vanish among the theatre's ruined decor to share the exploration of a hypothetical present of no particular period or nationality. Their rehearsal is simply one of many, part of an unfinished history with—like the building that contains it—no final objective. Gregory's directorial function in this seems confined to marking out the acts, as if protecting his cast and their handful of spectators from total absorption.

If the production reflects any of his remaining influence on what the players have, over many months, developed from Chekhov for themselves, it is in his choice of background. Befitting its surroundings, this *Uncle Vanya* is a study of decay, the inevitability of which is recognised, briefly resisted, but finally accepted with stoical grace by a small band of penitents.

Since what we know of Gregory on film, given his career as an American theatre director, comes chiefly from *My Dinner with André*, it is tempting to link his version of Chekhov with the adventures he described in his earlier encounter with both Wallace Shawn and Louis Malle. Benignly whimsical, these journeys of self-discovery suggested a Gregory for whom communal activity is its own reward or punishment—for whom, in other words, the sociable process of rehearsal would always be preferable to a final performance. This argument aside. With its rather tenuous evidence (although one might note with interest that *Uncle Vanya* was first planned by Chekhov with a co-writer, a team effort that quickly collapsed, and that he married one of the first actresses to play Yelena), there is no doubt that Malle has filmed Gregory's work with a clear respect for the original text.

The text is not, of course, what it was, given the many amendments undergone since the play's first short-lived appearance as *The Wood Demon*. David Mamet's translation, a force to be reckoned with like Michael Frayn's before him, disposes of the troublesomely knocking Watchman and leaves Telegin to run all the errands as well as playing an essential (if muted) guitar, although the contentious 'Waffles' nickname has been reinstated. Where Frayn was unhappy about Serebryakov's plan to retire to Finland (actually within 20 miles of St. Petersburg, but how would a Western audience know?), Mamet retains the location without comment. Cutting around residual pomposity, he provides a flowing colloquialism, echoing the appealing rhythms and enhanced accuracy of his own plays. Among many enjoyable touches, Vanya describes Yelena as "a panorama of inaction", Yelena refers to Astrov as "an original", Marina observes, "We are all freeloaders under God", and Vanya mutters like a defeated salesman, "You don't know how hard this is for me". In its desperation, its subterfuges and its frailty, this is recognisably a Mamet *Vanya*.

As did Frayn, Mamet translates Sonya's concluding promise as "We will rest", confirming a reading of Chekhov as the champion not of lethargy but of hard work. Filming Sonya's outburst as the surprise it is, an unforeseen epilogue protesting a previously unremarked faith, Malle is consistent to what he has been able to bring to the play as film-maker: following several cues from Chekhov, it is a drama in which the characters learn to *look* at each other. Closely watched in turn by an unfidgeting camera, they gaze among themselves with a remarkable hunger, justifying the calculated pauses between Chekhov's speeches with an intensity that would surely be lost in conventional theatre. To this extent, the skill of Gregory's cast, with all its silences, has resulted in a triumph, dominated by the scrutiny, part-seductive, part-fearful, of Julianne Moore as the haunted Yelena. Although, in his one error, Malle allows her an unspoken soliloquy at odds with the rest of the piece, her function at the centre of his film transcends similar encounters with foolish old men in the likes of *Pretty Baby, Milou in May* and (as strikingly close precedents) *Atlantic City* and *Damage*. And if Shawn, spluttering on the edge of over-acting, is probably a touch too comical for Vanya's good, his predicament is at least no longer locked away on a remote Russian estate.

VILLAGE VOICE, 10/25/94, p. 69, Luis H. Francia

Chekhov would have loved the crumbling magnificence of Times Square's New Amsterdam Theatre. In Louis Malle's assured, absorbing *Vanya on 42nd Street*, the theater's faded opulence and rat-infested cavernous hall become the perfect setting for the ruined moral architecture of Chekhov's play, here filmed as a cast rehearsal of the David Mamet adaptation directed by Andre Gregory. The "rehearsal" label allows a fascinating interplay between the viewers' present and the play's verities—and resists any attempt to construe the performances as definitive. For the ambiguities in Chekhov's universe are much too subtle for such certainties.

Veering between happiness and duty, the characters lead frayed lives, especially Vanya himself, a 47-year-old who has devoted his life to running the family estate so his brother-in-law, the scholarly but utterly sterile Serybryakov, can devote himself to his books. Wallace Shawn's Vanya bumbles about, a near-comic embittered failure, his ungraceful physique embodying the frustrations of a spirit wanting to soar but realizing, too late, he can't.

What frustrates him even more is his infatuation with the beautiful Yelena, the widowed Serybryakov's second, much younger wife. The latter (played with precise, tremulous bravery by Julianne Moore) unwittingly assumes twin roles of temptress and savior, not just for Vanya but for Dr. Astrov, a man whose lofty ideals are less so when it comes to her. Most of the rest are dogged by their failures: Serybryakov's daughter Sonya, unable to make the doctor love her; Yelena, who views her marriage as a prison; and even Vanya's mother, who takes refuge in incessant pamphleteering.

That the cast had been rehearsing for four years, off and on, is apparent in the ease and love they bring to their parts, in the way that they interact with one another. As with *My Dinner With Andre*, Malle lets the language and the actors' skills flourish. Theater of the cinema or cinema of the theater? Impossible to distinguish, and I for one don't intend to spoil my remembered pleasures by trying.

Also reviewed in:
CHICAGO TRIBUNE, 12/23/94, Friday/p. J, Michael Wilmington
NEW REPUBLIC, 11/7/94, p. 37, Stanley Kauffmann
NEW YORK TIMES, 10/19/94, p. C13, Janet Maslin
NEW YORKER, 10/31/94, p. 105, Terrence Rafferty
VARIETY, 9/12-18/94, p. 40, Todd McCarthy
WASHINGTON POST, 12/21/94, p. C15, Hal Hinson
WASHINGTON POST, 12/23/94, Weekend/p. 38, Desson Howe

WAGONS EAST!

A TriStar release of a Carolco/Outlaw production in association with Goodman-Rosen productions. *Executive Producer:* Lynwood Spinks. *Producer:* Gary Goodman, Barry Rosen, Robert Newmyer, and Jeffrey Silver. *Director:* Peter Markle. *Screenplay:* Matthew Carlson. *Story:* Jerry Abrahamson. *Director of Photography:* Frank Tidy. *Editor:* Scott Conrad. *Music:* Michael Small. *Music Editor:* Bunny Andrews. *Sound:* Pud Cusak and (music) Andrew Boland. *Sound Editor:* Emile Razpopov and Dessie Markovsky. *Casting:* Richard Pagano, Sharon Bialy, Debi Manwiller, and Tory Herald. *Production Designer:* Vince J. Cresciman. *Art Director:* Hector Romero C. *Set Designer:* Miguel Angel Gonzalez B. *Set Decorator:* Enrique Estevez L. *Special Effects:* Jesus "Chu Chu" Duran G. *Costumes:* Adolfo "Fito" Ramirez. *Make-up:* Jack Petty and Humberto Escamilla Z. *Stunt Coordinator:* Bud Davis. *Running time:* 100 minutes. *MPAA Rating:* PG-13.

CAST: Joe Bays (River Townsman); Abe Benrubi (Abe Ferguson); Jill Boyd (Prudence Taylor); John Candy (James Harlow); Douglas Carlson (Bar Patron); Melinda Culea (Constance Taylor); Ryan Cutrona (Tom); Ricky Damazio (Smith); Bud Davis (Desperado Leader); Bill Day Dodge (Elder); Thomas F. Duffy (Clayton Ferguson); David Dunard (Harry Bob Ferguson); Steve Eastin (Bartender); Roger Eschbacher (Reporter); Rodney A. Grant (Little Feather); Stuart Grant (White Cloud); Ellen Greene (Belle); Randy Hall (Pony Express Rider); Chad Hamilton (Ricky Jones); Don Lake (Lt. Bailey); Ed Lauter (John Slade); Richard Lewis (Phil Taylor); John C. McGinley (Julian); Marvin McIntyre (Irving Ferguson); Robin McKee (Lindsey); Joel McKinnon Miller (Zack Ferguson); Mauricio Martinez (Card Player); Denver Mattson (Card Player); Russell Means (Chief); Lochlyn Munro (Billy); Ingrid Nuernberg (Henrietta Wheeler); Patrick Thomas O'Brien (Stranger); Ethan Phillips (Smedly); Robert Picardo (Ben Wheeler); Jimmy Ray Pickens (Scout); Tony Pierce (Junior Ferguson); Charles Rocket (Larchmont); William Sanderson (Zeke); Derek Senft (Jeremiah Taylor); Marci Smolin (Woman on Trail); William Tucker (Reporter); Martin Wells (Taylor); Gaillard Sartain (J.P. Moreland).

LOS ANGELES TIMES, 8/26/94, Calendar/p. 6, Chris Willman

John Candy has one truly funny moment in "Wagons East!" the Western comedy that had nearly finished shooting when he died suddenly early this year. As the reluctant wagonmaster James Harlow, he turns back to the barful of eager-for-exodus townsfolk who're counting on him and proclaims, "We leave at dawn." The cloud of a second thought passes over his face, then a shrug: "... Noonish," he wavers.

That perfect kicker was improvised by Candy on the set, so clearly the great comic had some of his best instincts intact to the end. But these instincts obviously rarely extended to picking projects, and "Wagons East! " is a typically rickety vehicle, just dumb enough that it actually submerges Candy's sweet, perky persona in what's basically a sullen, grizzled straight-man role. He'd made worse, but fans hoping against hope for a worthy career kicker might want to get their horses turned around now.

The script takes off from an all-too-promisingly rich premise: The pioneers of a Western town—fed up with bank robberies, a lack of culture and dust in general—become the first Americans to turn tail and head back east en masse. "This country was *founded* by quitters," co-star Richard Lewis explains to his kids. "English quitters, French quitters ... " A tribe of initially warlike Native Americans even opts to help with the settlers' reverse wagon drive. "I just like seeing them go in that direction," the chief explains to *his* confused son, in subtitles.

Quickly, though, the picture slips out of satire into listless, sub-Brooksian spoofery and scatology—it's "Snoozing Saddles," all the way down to a shameless re-creation of its obvious antecedent's campfire-fart scene. There are anachro-Western types aplenty: a gold-hearted hooker (Ellen Greene, sounding as if she might any moment break into "Suddenly Seymour"); an effete, terribly tasteful gay settler (John C. McGinley, saying "super!" a lot and wearing lavender); a Wile E. Coyote-like villain sent by the railroad barons to stop the settlers' return (Ed Lauter) and so on.

Director Peter Markle is a little too busy balancing this scattershot ensemble to devote quality time to leads Lewis and Candy, who both seem unnaturally tamed. The movie could have used more of Lewis' neurotic shtick ("I'm anti-handgun," he explains, challenged to a duel) to get across just how much these bi-continental wannabes really belong back Manhattan way. And Candy's countenance is curiously buried beneath a frontiersman's beard and long, floppy bangs; without much to do but look haggard and withdrawn, he seems vaguely ghostly before his time.

After some of the summer's bigger-budget comedy busts, "Wagons East!" feels fairly painless, at least, though Matthew Carlson's script ought to have screamed "small screen" to the green-lighters who let this convoy pass. As for last chances for fearless Candy fans, there's always the (long-delayed) "Canadian Bacon" still on the burner.

NEW YORK POST, 8/26/94, p. 44, Michael Medved

For devoted fans of the late John Candy, the only good news about "Wagons East!" is that their favorite star won't have to attend the opening.

Candy died of a heart attack during the last week of filming on this wretched comedy; among the 40 films of his too-brief career, this one is not only the last, it's the least. ("Canadian Bacon," a Michael Moore comedy which also stars Candy, was made before "Wagons East!" and is yet to be released.)

Candy seems to hide behind the beard he grew for the part, playing the ill-fated wagon master who once guided the Donner Party to mass starvation and cannibalism in the snows of the Sierra Nevada; he gets another job 20 years later, leading a group of disillusioned settlers who've given up on the Wild West and want to return to the comforts of civilization.

Trying to mine laughs out of references to the Donner Party makes as much sense as gleaning yucks from the situation in "Alive!" "Wagons East!" is indeed a chuckle-free disaster, as starved for funny gags as the doomed settlers were for nourishment.

The cast of characters includes Richard Lewis as a failed rancher who's lost his herd to rustlers; Ellen Greene as the standard-issue hooker with the heart of gold; and John C. McGinley as a swishy stereotype who spends his time on the trail sipping chablis or braiding the hair of Indian braves.

Rodney A. Grant (of "Dances With Wolves") plays one of those braves, who accompanies the wagon train and wants to change his name from "Little Feather" to "Big Snake that Makes Women Faint."

This reference highlights one of the most peculiar aspects of this movie's attempts at humor: a relentless emphasis on the male organ that includes some dozen lines of dialogue and many additional scenes of cast members who are poked, punched or kicked in the groin. There's also a sequence in which a boy urinates into a canteen and a cowpoke then comes up and eagerly drains the contents, emitting a satisfied belch.

Actually, belches, snores and other rude noises will emerge from all audiences subjected to this idiocy. Though "Wagons East!" runs only 100 minutes, you get the sense you've endured an epic ordeal; it feels even longer, in fact, than "Wyatt Earp."

The movie's single funniest line comes near the conclusion of the journey when Ellen Greene looks up at the stars and tells John Candy: "This trip has been so wonderful ... Don't you wish it would never end?"

In a sorry season for westerns, from Costner's bloated "Earp," to bum steers like "Bad Girls" and "The Cowboy Way," this latest offering rides low in the saddle as worst of the herd. Like the settlers in the film who are ready to give up on the frontier, the movie itself makes you wonder whether Hollywood's renewed fascination with the western is such a good idea after all.

NEWSDAY, 8/26/94, Part II/p. B2, Jack Mathews

The end credits on Peter Markle's "Wagon East!" begin with a dedication to the memory of its star, John Candy, who died of a heart attack in the last days of the film's production in Mexico earlier this year. Fans of the amiable giant would do well to settle for the memories they already have.

Candy, like most comedy actors trying to keep busy, has been in a lot of second-rate films, but nothing quite as listless, badly written or wasteful of his talent as this bloated Western send-up about a drunken wagon master conducting a reverse migration of disenchanted easterners from the frontier.

The story, reportedly suggested to producer Barry Rosen by an L.A. cab driver longing to return to the East Coast, has a promising comedic idea in it. In the rundown town of Prosperity, a handful of settlers from the East decides to call it quits on the West, and organize a wagon train pointed in the opposite direction of the Great Migration.

As the wagons poke across the plains, they pick up a few more unhappy settlers, some friendly Indians anxious to encourage their evacuation and a saboteur hired by a railroad baron concerned that they could be starting a bad trend.

Among the tenderfoots are: Phil (Richard Lewis), an ex-surgeon whose cattle-ranching dreams are thwarted by pesky rustlers; Ben (Robert Picardo), a banker fed up with holdups; Belle (Ellen Greene), a saloon hooker whose clients seldom pay their tabs, and Julian (John C. McGinley), a lavender-clad bookshop keeper tired of seeing Jane Austen first editions used as toilet paper.

And at the front of the wagons, Candy's James Harlow, a Cat Ballou-like cowboy so bleary-eyed he can barely tell whether the sun is rising or setting.

That virtually nothing about this set-up pays off is attributable to a ceaselessly vapid script by former "Wonder Years" writer-producer Matthew Carlson and to the flat-footed direction of Peter Markle ("Youngblood"). "Wagons East!" is a string of gags intended as send-ups of Western clichés, but they are executed as if the actors themselves didn't find them funny.

Richard Lewis is at a loss to even conjure up a consistent personality. He starts off doing a bad imitation of Gene Wilder in "Blazing Saddles," seems to think better of it and then spends the rest of the movie blending into the sagebrush.

McGinley's portrayal of the swishy Julian, who can't abide the crudity of the cowboys for whom he had left the East, is a milestone in gay ridicule. He lusts after the naïve young cowboy in the wagon train, makes bitchy comments about the dress and intellectual gaucheness of the louts among them and effects every mannerism of a preening queen.

Candy seems oblivious to all of this. Harlow is a man with a past—he was one of the human flesh-eating survivors of the Donner Party—and is either sleeping or sulking throughout the trip. Candy had completed most of his scenes before his death, but he is conspicuously absent from the big showdown between the wagon train and Lauter's gunslinger, and was at least spared that embarrassment.

"Wagons East!" isn't a dedication to Candy's memory; it's a smudge on it.

SIGHT AND SOUND, 4/95, p. 53, Tom Tunney

Several disgruntled citizens in the Western town of Prosperity ban together and decide to head back East. Farmer Phil Taylor is tired of having his cattle rustled; banker Ben Wheeler is sick of his bank being robbed: saloon girl Belle is annoyed at getting IOUs instead of cash; newly arrived mail order bride Lindsey is dismayed to discover that she's been bought jointly by the oafish Ferguson brothers to share between them; and the final straw for bookseller Julian is when one would-be customer wants to buy a book to use as toilet paper. The party hire the disgraced, permanently drunken wagon master James Harlow to lead them. Joined by the Fergusons, failed prospector Zeke and young cowboy Billy, the group soon attract several other wagons and this growth into a popular movement attracts the attention of greedy railroad tycoon J. P. Moreland (Gaillard Sartain) who fears that a mass exodus back East will depress land values. Moreland hires ruthless gunslinger John Slade to stop them.

Harlow accidentally leads the group into an Indian camp; the chief agrees to assign some braves as escorts. Slade's attempts to disrupt the migrants' journey, first by breaking their water barrels and then by causing a landslide, aren't successful. When he threatens the group face to face, he's beaten to the draw and shot dead by Julian. Moreland now turns to General Larchmont and his Cavalry to attack the party. 20 years previously Larchmont had requisitioned the supplies of an earlier Harlow wagon train and was thus directly responsible for the cannibalism and subsequent disgrace which ruined the latter's career. Larchmont is sent packing by Harlow and Moreland is killed under a wagon when the group happen upon the land rush he's organised. Julian decides to head back West to San Francisco with an Indian friend and Clayton Ferguson is killed by a meteorite—thus freeing Lindsey for Billy. They and the remainder of the group, still following Harlow, resume their journey East.

Wagons East! is a series of discrete comedy sketches masquerading as a whole film. Just how much of its inadequacy can be ascribed to the death of John Candy in mid-production is a difficult question, although the result suggests much hasty re-jigging to cover for Candy's absence and some manipulation of footage already in the can. The bizarre result is that in an ostensible John Candy comedy vehicle he has only a supporting role. He rides his horse, falls asleep in the saddle and leads the wagon train, but the majority of the physical and verbal comedy is handled by other actors.

In his place the film offers a disjointed series of gags, most of which are reminiscent of earlier and better films. The cartoon-like antics of the villain Jack Slade are an obvious throwback to the Kirk Douglas character in *The Villain*. The inevitable saloon scene in which assorted genteel characters try to order drinks other than whiskey is almost as old as the Western itself. Also in a dishevelled tradition mined to exhaustion by movie and television comedy sketch writers are the uncouth antics of the Ferguson brothers, while the Cavalry attack to the strains of Wagner suggests less a knowing nod to *Apocalypse Now* than a failure to think up something more appropriate to a Western spoof.

That said, there is a germ of a funny film here. The inverted logic of the story is deliciously pessimistic. Here the West isn't a focus for hopes, ambitions and aspirations: instead, it's a place where dreams resolutely don't come true. This is a fertile premise and the story is lightly peppered with effective gags along those lines. Yet the individual pieces fail to add up because the gags are spread too sparingly between the supporting players. Meanwhile the direction and editing trundle along at the same slow pace as the wagons themselves and the film's flat, televisual style makes its budget limitations all too apparent. John C. McGinley (*On Deadly Ground, Watch It, A Midnight Clear*) performs a scene stealing charismatic rescue job as the effete Julian, which almost comes off. However, like Candy's, his character is never on screen for long enough and the other leads, stand-up comedian Richard Lewis as Phil and Robert Picardo as the banker Ben, fail to register effectively, defeated by the woefully variable nature of their material.

The reason why the comedy Western is a notoriously difficult form to pull off is mainly because the mainstream Western includes a strong vein of self-parody. Nevertheless, the revisionist premise of *Wagons East!* hits the occasional comic bullseye, when the script wittily foregrounds its modern PC sensibility. Taunted by Jack Slade as a "cissy boy", Julina's rejoinder is "Cissy boy! That's so Dodge City!" Phil's cows have 'Phil's Cows' branded on them and faced with further theft he announces "I'm anti-hand gun". The group are quite happy to call themselves quitters ("This country was founded by quitters, English quitters, German quitters..."); and when attacked by the Cavalry put their wagons in a square rather than the traditional circle. Unfortunately, the conventionality of Candy's character works against this more promising style of comedy. Harlow, the slobbish loser who becomes a winner once he's recognised and overcome his inadequacies, is recognisably similar to earlier Candy characters in *Uncle Buck, Planes, Trains and Automobiles* and *Cool Runnings* but nothing at all like the comprehensively idiotic hero which the story really requires.

Also reviewed in:
CHICAGO TRIBUNE, Friday/p. B, Michael Wilmington
NEW YORK TIMES, 8/26/94, p. C16, Stephen Holden
VARIETY, 8/29-9/4/94, p. 43, Todd McCarthy
WASHINGTON POST, 8/26/94, p. D7, Rita Kempley

WAR, THE

A Universal Pictures release of an Island World picture. *Executive Producer:* Eric Eisner and Todd Baker. *Producer:* Jon Avnet and Jordan Kerner. *Director:* Jon Avnet. *Screenplay:* Kathy McWorter. *Director of Photography:* Geoffrey Simpson. *Editor:* Debra Neil. *Music:* Thomas Newman. *Music Editor:* Bill Bernstein. *Choreographer:* Jamale Graves. *Sound:* Mary H. Ellis and (music) Dennis Sands. *Sound Editor:* George Watters II. *Casting:* David Rubin and Debra Zane. *Production Designer:* Kristi Zea. *Art Director:* Jeremy Conway. *Set Designer:* Julie S. Sanford. *Set Decorator:* Karen O'Hara. *Set Dresser:* Karen Young, Jennifer Annette Johnston, Eddie Lee Mayner, Scott Stader, Tommy Lee Watson, Jr. and Sharon Joan Braunstein. *Special Effects:* Paul Lombardi. *Special Mechanical Effects:* Chuck Stewart. *Costumes:* Molly Maginnis. *Make-up:* Fern Buchner and Rosemarie Zurlo. *Make-up (Kevin Costner):* Frank Perez. *Stunt Coordinator:* Jery Hewitt. *Running time:* 127 minutes. *MPAA Rating:* PG-13.

CAST: Elijah Wood (Stu); Kevin Costner (Stephen); Mare Winningham (Lois); Lexi Randall (Lidia); LaToya Chisholm (Elvadine); Christopher Fennell (Billy); Donald Sellers (Arliss); Leon Sills (Leo); Will West (Lester Lucket); Brennan Gallagher (Marsh); Adam Henderson (Chet); Charlette Julius (Amber); Jennifer Tyler (Ula); Lucas Black (Ebb); Justine Lucas (Willard): Raynor Scheine (Mr. Lipnicki); Christine Baranski (Miss Strapford); Bruce A. Young (Moe); Mary Nell Santacroce (Mrs. Higgins); Nick Searcy (John Ray Wilkins); Gary Basaraba (Dodge); Judson Vaughn (Soldier); Jay Brooks (Old Man); Afemo Omilami (Quarry Man); Tim Ware (Fat Man at Auction); J. Don Ferguson (Mine Foreman); Ron Clinton Smith (Ambulance Attendant); Tom Even (Doctor); Dorothy Davis (Nurse); Bill Coates (Catfish Man); Wilson L. Middlebrooks (Field Foreman).

LOS ANGELES TIMES, 11/4/93, Calendar/p. 1, Peter Rainer

Goodness in "The War" positively plops off the screen. It's a movie about how love is all there is. As Vietnam vet Stephen Simmons (Kevin Costner) says to his son Stu (Elijah Wood), "In the absence of love, there's nothing in this world worth fightin' for."

Nothing????

Set in Mississippi in 1970, "The War," directed by Jon ("Fried Green Tomatoes") Avnet and scripted by Kathy McWorter, dawdles on for more than two hours dispensing life lessons. It's an entire compendium of family values civics lessons—it's like "Forrest Gump" if Forrest had directed. The warm nostalgic glow of goodness turns everything to pablum.

Stephen, suffering from post-traumatic stress, has trouble landing a job in his hometown. But he's an angelically decent man; the war has taught him that violence doesn't solve anything. He passes his wisdom on to his son and his daughter Lidia (Lexi Randall), who are caught up in a feud with a family, the Lipnickis, even more dirt-poor than they are.

For a movie that's supposed to be so all-embracingly "understanding," it's odd how many arrant caricatures abound. The Lipnicki kids, for example, make their entrances like the zombies from "Night of the Living Dead," though they move considerably faster. Scowling, hard-muscled and perpetually muddy, they seem to be in the movie for the sole purpose of testing the Simmons family creed of nonviolence. Why, Stephen gives two of the younger Lipnicki whippersnappers a cotton-candy stick each and they *still* try to knock down Stu and Lidia's tree fort.

The tree supporting that fort—a great, curlicued 800-year-old oak—is easily the most interesting and venerable thing in the movie. And it's a tribute to this movie's wet-noodled whimsy that one cares more about the survival that oak than about most of the characters. Avnet and McWorter work in at least half-a-dozen children-in-peril or adults-in-peril or adults-and-children-in-peril subplots to no avail. They also work in a lot of vintage hits on the soundtrack, such as Cat Stevens' "Peace Train." They introduce a cliffhanger about a house up for auction that one can see coming a mile (maybe two miles) away.

The centerpiece sequence is a particularly bad idea. The Vietnam War is somehow likened to the final, epic battle for the tree fort that matches the Lipnickis against Stu and Lidia and Lidia's friends Elvadine (the live-wired LaToya Chisholm) and Amber (Charlette Julius).

The crosscuts between Vietnam flashbacks and kid wars are supposed to point up the futility of violence. What it really points up is the stupidity of misplace symbolism. Cross a hawk and a dove and you get a turkey.

Costner coasts on his low-key moodiness. He's self-effacing in a movie-starrish way—lots of closeups of his placid pain and furrowed brow. Costner looked as if he might be getting back the edge to his acting in "A Perfect World"—it was his best performance since "Bull Durham"—but he's blandly noble here. So is just about everybody else in "The War"—deep down that is. Even a racist school teacher, played by Christine Baranski as if she was Madame DuFarge at the guillotine, turns nice.

Elijah Wood—that terrific little actor—has the spunk and fury to make Stu into more than just a peacenik. But he's weighted down by homilies. (His performance resembles a champion swimmer paddling through heavy molasses.)

As his mother, Mare Winningham is effective, as usual, but her role is equally weighted. By the time "The War" is over, you may think it's real connection to Vietnam is symbolism of a quite different sort: It's endless, costly and misbegotten.

NEW YORK POST, 11/4/94, p. 53, Michael Medved

Kevin Costner's new movie wages a "War" of attrition against our better judgment, eventually wearing down all resistance with its relentless sincerity and superior acting.

It's one of those heartfelt, overly earnest message movies that transcends its own preachiness to make an undeniable emotional connection with its audience.

Costner plays a decent, soft-spoken Mississippian who leaves his family behind when he goes off to fight in Vietnam. By the time of his return in 1970, their home's been repossessed, the wife (Mare Winningham) and two kids are stuck in a welfare shack, and dad is suffering (like all other Vietnam vets in Hollywood movies) from horrifying flashbacks and severe psychological disorientation.

He nonetheless struggles to get a job and teach his children the pacifist philosophy he's brought home from the war: "In the absence of love, there's nothin' in this world worth fightin' for."

Unfortunately, the kids don't listen and plunge headlong into an escalating series of their own fights. Stuart (Elijah Wood) and his twin sister Lidia (Lexi Randall) mobilize their friends to build an elaborate fort in a huge tree.

They then defend this project against the attacks of the Lipnicki clan—a bunch of junkyard rednecks so mean, lowdown and filthy that they make Faulkner's Snopes family look like refined aristocrats. There's also a subplot in which Lidia's racist teacher (Christine Baranski) tries to separate her from the black best friends with whom she regularly does an amusing, lip-synching imitation of the Supremes.

Director Jon Avnet ("Fried Green Tomatoes") does a remarkable job coaxing natural, endearing performances out of all his actors—especially the kids, 11 of whom make their debuts in the movie.

As for Elijah Wood, who's done such mannered self-conscious work in disappointing films like last year's "Huck Finn" and this year's "North," he delivers a surprisingly mature and moving performance. His relationship with his father provides the emotional center of the picture and Costner offers impeccable support, creating far deeper identification with his hard-luck character than he does with any of his far showier hero roles.

As with "Tomatoes," some of Avnet's biggest scenes are more than a bit over-cooked; the Southern-fried nostalgia feels glossy rather than gritty. Director and script (by first-timer Kathy McWorter) also strain much too hard to establish a connection between Costner's hackneyed wartime experience and the disorganized violence his kids experience: There is a huge difference between a soldier who agrees to serve his country to the best of his ability and a vicious, sadistic boyhood bully.

Nevertheless, there's an aura of spirituality and of unabashedly Christian faith that provides this implausible tale with unexpected depth.

"The War" stands as eloquent rebuttal to anyone who believes that the sympathetic invocation of religion in movies will always serve some right-wing purpose: This movie, with its prayer, Bible references and uncompromising pacifist message, should become a special favorite of the religious left.

In any event, the unmistakable love lavished on every scene and every minor character can make a believer of even the most skeptical critic.

NEWSDAY, 11/4/94, Part II/p. B2, Jack Mathews

Deep in the woods of Mississippi is an ancient oak tree, its spidery, moss-covered limbs cradling the tree house of every child's dream. Nearby, a decaying water tower stands guard over a rock quarry and a gleaming pond. Somewhere else is an abandoned house, about to be auctioned, its beauty in the eye of the first dreamy-eyed beholder who can come up with the winning bid.

If these sound like the flourishes of an overwrought southern novel, flourishes is all they are. Jon Avnet's "The War," from a first screenplay by Kathy McWorter, is an overstuffed shell of a movie novel, laced with evocative images, criss-crossing metaphors and sentimental impressions, even a couple of warmly moving performances from its stars, Kevin Costner and the gifted 13-year-old Elijah Wood. What it is not is a very cohesive or believable story.

Avnet, eager to duplicate the success he had with "Fried Green Tomatoes," adapted from Fannie Flagg's novel about the friendship between two Alabama women during the Depression, has moved over one state and forward nearly 40 years to chart one summer in the life of the struggling Simmons family.

It's 1970, and Stephen (Costner), a post-traumatic-stressed Vietnam vet, has just returned from a long stay in a mental hospital. His wife, Lois (Mare Winningham), has been working two jobs and waiting patiently, while the pubescent twins—Stu (Wood) and Lidia (Lexi Randall)—have been trying to stay clear of the vicious Lipnicki kids, a band of roving rednecks who are meaner than the junkyard dogs they resemble.

The story, told in flashback by Lidia, is all about wars and battles—some physical, some mental—and the lessons to be learned from them. Lidia, perhaps the most precocious white liberal living below the poverty line in the entire South, is helping her black friends battle a racist teacher. Stu and his buddies are trying to maintain a measure of dignity while being taunted and beaten by the Lipnickis. And Stephen, guilt-wracked over events in Vietnam, is fighting just to keep his emotions in check.

The chief symbol of "The War," however, is not a battlefield, but a pair of houses—the tree house Stu built in that crab-legged oak and the fixer-upper Stephen hopes to move the family into.

"The War" works best during the ceasefires in quiet moments between Stephen and the son who idolizes him. Costner is very good playing characters whose emotions have to be tugged out of him, and Wood is simply the most convincing child actor around.

But every time there is a confrontation between the Simmons and the Lipnickis, whether a cute trick to lure the bullies into a cesspool, a battle royale (and rank Vietnam metaphor) to defend the tree house or a death-defying stunt and rescue in the water town, the movie feels as make-believe and emotionally false as a game of hide and seek.

NEWSWEEK, 11/7/94, p. 74, David Ansen

Jon Avnet's "The War" has a lot on its big, soft mind. War, for one. It's bad. Racism, for another. It's bad, too. Love? It makes the world go round. You might also like to know that "with God's help, human beings can do anything." Kathy McWorter, the writer of this high-minded family drama, populates her saga with dirt-poor Mississippi characters, all of whom are solemnly able to dispense homilies at the drop of a hat. The year is 1970. Kevin Costner stars as a Vietnam vet suffering from posttraumatic stress and struggling to support his wife (Mare Winningham) and two kids (Elijah Wood and Lexi Randall). Though broke, tormented and unable to hold a job, he's as warm and wise as any junior senator from Mississippi campaigning for re-election. The kids have built a treehouse, which is under siege by a nasty gaggle of unwashed redneck kids. This will escalate into a highly symbolic children's war, from which many lessons will be learned. Avnet, who made Fried Green Tomatoes," serves up these refried banalities with a serene disregard for the way people actually behave. It's impossible to tell whom this movie was made for. Even William Bennett would have trouble staying awake.

SIGHT AND SOUND, 2/96, p. 57, Tom Tunney

Summer 1970: Vietnam veteran Marine Stephen Simmons drifts in and out of unemployment in the small town of Juliette, Mississippi. Stephen lives in a dilapidated shack with his wife, Lois, young son Stu and daughter Lidia. Stephen confides to Stu that the reason for his restless behaviour is that he had to abandon his best friend, Dodge, during a battle. Stu, Lidia and friends decide to build a treehouse. Though the Simmons kids have been involved in a long-running feud with the violent Mr Lipnicki's brood, Lidia bribes young Billy Lipnicki to let them into his father's scrapyard to take materials for the tree house.

Meanwhile, Stephen secures a job in a mine and puts in a sealed bid for an old house. On his way to put in the bid, Mr Lipnicki deliberately crashes his car into the back of Stephen's. After Lipnicki threatens Stu, Stephen overpowers Lipnicki, and gets him to apologise. He then tells Stu to apologise to Lipnicki. At school Lidia's new teacher, Miss Strapford, attempts to racially segregate the class. Lidia's best friend Elvadine gives her a piece of her mind and Lidia backs her up, Miss Strapford is forced to reverse her decision.

Stephen is badly injured during a roof collapse at the mine, but he also saves his friend Moe from certain death. Stephen subsequently dies in hospital. The tree house is now completed, but the other Lipnicki kids force the truth from Billy and take it over. Stu, Lidia and their friends force them out by throwing in a bag containing a hornet's nest, but the Lipnickis come back with a tractor and petrol bombs and a full scale battle ensues in which the tree house is destroyed. Billy climbs a derelict water tower to retrieve a key from its roof and falls through into the water. Stu pulls Billy out. Lidia revives him with the kiss of life and Billy tells them that while he wasn't breathing he saw an angel which looked like a bigger version of Stu. An official from the auction house tells Lois that her husband's bid for the house has been successful. The overjoyed family prepare to move in.

Forrest Gump presented post-war US history as a tale told by a jovial idiot and, on those deeply ironic terms, it did capture the sense of a nation's history running tragically out of control. *The War* is *Forrest Gump* without the jokes, without the irony and without any of its historical context. Though ostensibly set in 1970, this mess of mawkishness, trite moralising and inept plot contrivance inhabits an historical vacuum of truly staggering proportions. The framing device for the story is Lidia's reading aloud of her school assignment of "What I learned this summer." And, the key idea she learns from her deep-thinking dad is that "the only thing that truly keeps people safe and happy is love." However, think what America as a whole learned that summer and Stephen's cloying words of wisdom become laughably inadequate. The deadly watershed for 1970 was the shooting of four Kent State University students during an anti-Vietnam War protest.

That event crystallised the murderous divisions which the Vietnam War forced onto US society. Given that its central character is a Vietnam veteran and that its very title is *The War*, one would think that the script might address this sense of division. Not so, apart from one brief radio snippet of President Nixon, the 1970 setting is no more than an excuse to bathe the drama in a warm glow of nostalgia. Producer-director Jon Avnet was also responsible for *Fried Green Tomatoes at the Whistle Stop Cafe*, so it's not surprising that what's on offer here is another quaintly dilapidated Deep South. This a world where children dance to Supremes songs in the street, where Costner drawls "Y'all" at the end of every other sentence and where dignity, kindness and hard work finally triumph. On its own flowery wallpaper terms, that's fair enough, but what's unforgivable is the way in which the screenplay relentlessly suppresses anything that might interfere with this cosy vision.

Here, Stephen's experiences in Vietnam become not a question of their futility: instead they are transformed into an issue of personal redemption. As with *The Deer Hunter* and *Jackknife*, it's not enough for Stephen to fight a few inconclusive battles and then come home disillusioned,

Stephen must also bear the guilty burden of not rescuing his best buddy. This allows the war to be presented as a specifically personal test of character rather than a collision of impersonal ideologies which chewed up and destroyed individual lives by the million.

With a few notable exceptions (*Apocalypse Now, Forrest Gump*) such a vision of the Vietnam War as something completely beyond the individual's control has proved unpalatable. Instead, Hollywood film-makers have characteristically displayed a hunger to redeem the conflict. Hence that much-overused plot device of rescuing (or failing to rescue) the buddy which crops up in almost every film in the sub-genre. *The War* follows this strategy in such a clumsy way that it becomes ludicrous, proffering two redemptive rescue scenes. Stephen saves Moe's life in the mining disaster; Stu follows in the same heroic tradition when he rescues Billy from drowning. Hence the war of the title is awkwardly transmuted into a facile symbol of Mankind's "war" to improve itself.

Stephen himself has learnt from the war: he now doesn't believe in violence. But the screenplay refuses to let him take the next two logical steps, to recognise himself as a victim and then to protest. Instead he maintains an unshakeable optimism in the power of the individual ("Our children should believe anything is possible."). The most likely thing "possible" for Stu would be the draft—hence the huge success with the 1970 US cinema audience of Robert Altman's corrosively cynical *MASH.* Here, however, the war in Vietnam and the burgeoning civil strife in America are replaced by the easily resolvable struggle between the kids for the tree house. The script brims with faith in God, guardian angels and the power of love, but the real powers which inform it are of contrivance .

Avnet presents the rural Deep South as an idealised controlled environment. Here there are no hippies or yuppies, skyscrapers, traffic jams or drugs. The odd hint of racism is there only to be tidily rebuked and, if people don't have much money, at least they have each other. It's the South as a communal theme park. It is deeply depressing that such a lacklustre scenario should be graced with an impressive cast and production design. Most of the young cast are new to movies and their faces and performances are refreshingly free of cuteness. Unfortunately, Costner lumbers though reams of homespun wisdom like an out-of-work preacher in search of a ministry. His performance contains not the smallest hint that he recognises the script for the pompous drivel it so obviously is. It's a critical cliché now to say that Costner and Tom Hanks are the 90s heirs to the All-American integrity once proffered by Henry Fonda and James Stewart. However, any more such unctuous roles as this and a more accurate comparison for Saint Kevin would be with Pat O'Brien or Bing Crosby.

TIME, 11/7/94, p. 73, Richard Corliss

The voice, with its deep drawl and homespun poetry, sounds familiar. "Mah names Lidia Simmons, an' Ah'm 12 yeahs ol'. An' these here're mah memoirs." Jeez Louise—it's Forrest Gump as a girl! With scenes of slow-talking good guys in the U.S. South and dead buddies on Vietnam battlefields, *The War* might seem the first in a bunch of Gumpthings hoping to replicate that film's $285 million success story. But on a smaller scale, *The War* is a bigger movie and, for all its weepy trappings, a more adventurous one. It hints that it will be a familiar, *Stand By Me*-ish rite-of-passage picture; then it explodes into a kid's version of *Apocalypse Now.*

Lidia (Lexi Randall) and her younger brother Stu (Elijah Wood) have it rough. Mom (Mare Winningham) has to be the family glue, because Dad (Kevin Costner) has returned from Vietnam damaged and crushed. By most standards, he is a failure, so he pours his ambitions into his kids, who think he's a saint. "Maybe he died in that war," one of them says, "and God sent him back to us for one last visit." If so, it is to supervise, by remote control, a replay of his and America's Vietnam trauma.

Writer Kathy McWorter and director Jon Avnet alternate these moral mud baths with warm soaks in sentimentality. Sometimes *The War* is so noble you want to spank it. But as it spins fascinatingly out of control, the film is nevertheless secured by the four splendid actors who play the Simmons family. Costner, a daring actor in his narrow range, lets his voice and heart break subtly on every line. And the two kids are fine—full of sense, discretion and what we used to call gumption.

VILLAGE VOICE, 11/15/94, p. 67, Alex Patterson

The kind of uplifting, liberal-humanist domestic drama that makes you wish Hollywood would stick to lowbrow mayhem, *The War* takes on big issues—Vietnam fallout, racial conflict, loving your neighbor—only to pound them to pulp.

In the Mississippi of the early '70s, Kevin Costner is a working-class dad whose post-Nam nightmares lose him job after job. Mare Winningham (who apparently didn't get enough of her costar in the disastrous *Wyatt Earp*) is long-suffering Momma, who stands by her man even when he's no longer standing. Elijah Wood (*The Good Son*) and newcomer Lexi Randall are Stu and Lidia, their tough-but-vulnerable offspring who escape their depressing home life in their elaborate tree house—a hideaway so impressive it provokes a takeover bid from the local junkman's cretinous clan. Git the shootin' iron, pa, them hillbillies is a-feudin' *agin*!

Amidst melodrama, strained comic relief and jungle flashbacks, director Jon Avnet (*Fried Green Tomatoes*) and screenwriter Kathy McWorter have important lessons to impart, i.e., wars are not good for children and other living things. But the script is clumsy, sentimental, and littered with anachronistic Valspeak ("awesome, ""humongous," "wussy," "I don't *think* so"). *The War* has also been retrofitted with a sub-*Gump* soundtrack of classic rock; this allows Avnet to score a scrap between 10-year-olds with "Gimme Shelter" and "Who'll Stop the Rain"—choices as pompous "as the slo-mo photography that attempts to transform a treefort tussle into the Tet offensive.

This *War*, like many a war before it, does spring from noble intentions: the makers seem sincere in their attempt to put a human face on rural poverty. But they're more concerned with making an "epic," bloating to 127 minutes what might have been a modestly entertaining afterschool special.

Also reviewed in:
CHICAGO TRIBUNE, 11/4/94, Friday/p. I, Johanna Steinmetz
NEW YORK TIMES, 11/4/94, p. C10, Janet Maslin
VARIETY, 10/31-11/6/94, p. 88, Brian Lowry
WASHINGTON POST, 11/4/94, p. F7, Rita Kempley

WEDDING GIFT, THE

A Miramax Films release of a BBC Films production in association with Island World. *Executive Producer:* Richard Broke and Margaret Matheson. *Producer:* David Lascelles. *Director:* Richard Loncraine. *Screenplay:* Jack Rosenthal. *Director of Photography:* Remi Adefarasin. *Editor:* Ken Pearce. *Music:* Colin Towns. *Production Designer:* Tony Burrough. *Running time:* 87 minutes. *MPAA Rating:* PG-13.

CAST: Julie Walters (Diana Longden); Jim Broadbent (Deric Longden); Thora Hird (Deric's Mother); Sian Thomas (Aileen Armitage); Andrew Lancel (Nick Longden); Anastasia Mulroney (Sally Longden); Joanna McCallum (Doctor Roper); Dinah Handley (Hospital Receptionist); Peter Whitfield (Fred); Candida Rundle (Young Nurse); Andrew Nicholson (Gerald); Martin Wenner (Young Doctor); Graham Turner (Postman); Ann Rye (Joan); Moya Brady (Sheila); Angela Walsh (Karen); Andy Rashleigh (Chemist); Frances Cox (Minnie Bonsall); Diane Parish (Waitress); Adrian Schiller (London Doctor); Malcolm Raeburn (VAT Man).

LOS ANGELES TIMES, 7/15/94, Calendar/p. 7, Kevin Thomas

"The Wedding Gift" is a well-made, heartwarming love story involving a devoted couple in their 40s confronting the wife's mysterious debilitating illness, which is marked by blackouts and has left her disabled to the extent that she must wear braces on her hands to keep them from curling inward and use a wheelchair much of the time. Since the couple is played by two of the most skillful actors in British films, Julie Walters and Jim Broadbent, "The Wedding Gift" exudes vitality and good humor. You may be moved to tears, but the vivacious Walters, who first made her mark with "Educating Rita," and Broadbent, a sort of English Randy Quaid, make the film, which is based on a true story, uplifting rather than depressing.

The film opens in a charming small city in the English county of Derbyshire, where Broadbent's Deric Longden owns and operates a lingerie factory. He and his wife, Diana (Walters), live in a large, comfortable home and have two adult children (Andrew Lancel, Anastasia Mulroney). Deric's forgetful but actually quite sharp and doughty mother (Thora Hird) lives nearby. Clearly, Diana and Deric have had an exceptionally solid marriage; they're both blessed with humor, and they're fast friends as well as lovers. They unhesitatingly, indeed reflexively, put each other first.

The Longdens are too intelligent not to be grateful that they've been lucky, but now Diana's illness is putting a rapidly escalating strain on them. Nobody has ever made Deric feel so alive as Diana has, and his response to her deteriorating condition has been selfless and heroic.

In the course of Diana's increasing incapacitation, Deric has seen his business lose as much as 10,000 pounds a year and has become so weary caring for her that he tends to fall asleep at the wheel of his car. So intense is his devotion to Diana, however, that it threatens to suffocate her; he would even deny her the pills that would allow her to end her life at the point at which she decides her helplessness has become intolerable to her and too crushing a burden upon him. What makes the film so touching and endearing lies in the strategy that Diana chooses to return Deric's love.

There's no small dose of sitcom shtick in Jack Rosenthal's script, based on the real-life Deric Longden's books, "Diana's Story" and "Lost for Words." But it both undercuts the sadness of the Longdens' plight and highlights the serious right-to-die issue, plus some sharp commentary on the inefficiency and inadequacy of Britain's socialized medicine system.

Rosenthal also has the knack of deftly characterizing even the film's bit parts, This has allowed director Richard Loncraine, best known for two delightfully outrageous comedies, "Brimstone and Treacle" and "The Missionary," to make everyone seem individual and very much alive.

Sharing the stellar acting honors with Walters and Broadbent is the lovely Sian Thomas as a near-sightless novelist whose work is much admired by Deric, a fledgling writer himself. By the time it ends, "The Wedding Gift" has both illuminated and celebrated love in its purest, deepest form.

NEW YORK POST, 7/20/94, p. 31, Thelma Adams

"The Wedding Gift" goes from sad to worse, which is not a bad thing if you're prepared with a wad of Kleenex.

Based on a true story, Richard ("Bellman and True") Loncraine's British weepy stars Julie Walters as Diana Longden, a wife with a debilitating, mysterious disease.

Writer Jack Rosenthal allows Diana and husband Deric (Jim Broadbent) no honeymoon period. Scene one: They're driving on a wintry day. Hearing her favorite song, Diana says, "I'd like you to play this at my funeral." Hanky alert.

The Longdens form an irresistible 40ish couple. The parents of two nearly grown kids, they're a companionable pair linked by a ripened love and a tart sense of humor.

We might be clutching our hankies, but we're having a jolly time touring England with them. Diana is approaching the end of her tether. Her hands curl back on themselves. She can no longer walk unaided. She blacks out. The pain is nearly unendurable.

Diana's doctors don't know what she has, although they venture a guess—hysteria. She might be funny, but she's not hysterical. ("The Wedding Gift," is not an advertisement for national health.)

The title signals the one possible plot twist, apart from miraculous recovery. When Deric meets beautiful, blind novelist Aileen Armitage (Sian Thomas), Diana is jealous, but she's not threatened. Through Aileen Diana gives Deric one last wedding gift.

The Longdens and their repartee are the movie's chief delight. They're that rare thing, in movies: a middle-aged couple who have built an oasis in each other's love.

Walters, who opens in "Just Like a Woman" on Friday, radiates intelligence. The "Educating Rita" star is a warm presence who projects beauty even in the most unglamorous situations.

Broadbent is a good match for Walters: less animated, less physically attractive. but equally warm. Thomas' novelist is a wry addition as self-reliant as Diana but a little more Laura Ashley. Given Diana's condition much of the joshing between her and Deric is strained. There are times where the script seems to strain as well, telegraphing each action before it arrives, going for the easy laugh when another layer of insight would be welcome.

Even Diana's stern doctor is a quipmeister. After an unsuccessful evaluation she taps Diana's medical file and says: "[She's] the most written about woman in history—apart from Joan Collins."

The delights of "The Wedding Gift" outweigh its limitations. Sometimes you need a good laugh—and a good cry.

NEWSDAY, 7/20/94, Part II/p. B9, John Anderson

Thanks to the filtration system known as "Masterpiece Theater," American audiences are under the misapprehension that the English can turn out nothing but sterling cinema. What "The Wedding Gift" proves, happily, is that they're as adept at mawkish sentiment as we are.

Of course, had CBS, NBC or ABC produced it, "The Wedding Gift" would have starred Valerie Bertinelli and Patrick Duffy, instead of Julie Walters and Jim Broadbent, who are among the world's brighter comic actors. Walters, of whom little has been seen here since her Oscar-nominated "Educating Rita," is Diana Longden, long-suffering practitioner of gallows humor whose mysterious disease has left her all but crippled; Broadbent, who was the co-medic fulcrum of "The Crying Game," "Enchanted April" and "Widows Peak," is her husband, Derek, who sacrifices himself and his business to care for, and fight for, his wife.

Considering how much there is to cover here—not only the story of the progressively crippling illness, but Diana's cagey attempt to steer Derek toward a blind writer played by Sian Thomas, so he'll have someone to look after when she's gone—director Richard Loncraine is wise to bring us in where he does. Diana, has already been afflicted three years when we meet her, in yet another hospital with yet another callous doctor reading her file—something she's forbidden to read herself. The problem is not just the over-crowded, impersonal medical system (Bob Dole, take note), but the fact that Diana is an embarrassment to every doctor she meets: They simply can't figure out what's wrong with her, and so dismiss her complaints as hysteria.

In addition to some very predictable dramatic devices—including Diana's agonized walk down the aisle at her son's wedding—there are some wonderfully daffy fringe characters in this BBC production, of the sort that would never see the light of American network television. Chiefly, Thora Hird, who as Derek's nutty mother lightens up Loncraine's decidedly gray film with riotous non sequiturs. Graham Turner's brief scene as a nasty postman is good, too, as are the women who work at Derek's failing lingerie factory.

The point on which the entire film turns—Diana's enlisting Aileen, whom Derek has met at a literary lunch, to fall in love with her husband—is handled sensitively, if not convincingly. Could it happen? Possibly, although it illustrates the other problem with "The Wedding Gift": A glaring lack of anger and resentment between a couple who are fighting a daily, losing battle against a disease no one wants to help them cure. For all of Broadbent and Walters' charm and art, their characters are simply too good, too selfless, too movie-of-the-week.

VILLAGE VOICE, 8/2/94, p. 50, Laurie Stone

Diana Longden awakes each day to discover she is Gregor Samsa—in the grip of horrifying transformations. Her fingers are turning into claws, her bones snapping like twigs, her legs becoming Silly Putty. For years she suffers from a type of chronic fatigue syndrome, but doctors don't diagnose her until after she dies, and during her ordeals brand her "hysterical." Her husband, Deric, nurses her devotedly, and his business goes to hell. These people are Brits, so of course we're talking comedy—*No tears, what, what, can't let a little agony and paralysis dampen our spirits.*

Such overkill gallantry could easily have swamped the story, have drifted into unintentional, Pythonesque satire—of bleeding stumps and stiff upper lips. But owing to calibrated performances by Julie Walters as Diana and Jim Broadbent as Deric, *The Wedding Gift* doesn't serve up illness du jour but something far rarer in art and life: profound married love. We feel this couple's physical tie as central, so when sickness strikes, they emit no squeamishness but switch gears, continuing to inhale each other through afflicted flesh. Instead of an invalid married to a saint, we get the Wife of Bath in league with Tom Jones—a Jones whose face is perpetually squinched into a wince.

Their absorption floats the movie, a margin of grace amid nightmare. Diana suffers the pain of having Deric, in dressing her, inch panty hose up her frozen thighs; it's their way of seizing sex, whose limitation they tease with black comic, Orton-esque jeers. Sexiness attaches Diana to life, and humor plants her in the driver's seat. "How you keeping?" a hospital clerk asks, as she sits contorted in a wheelchair. Walters smiles and sasses, "As long as you got your health." Knowing that sex and humor can't triumph over death but must keep bubbling anyway, Diana matches Deric's generosity. Before checking out, she blesses her husband's relationship with a blind novelist he has met. "You sure know how to pick 'em," is her parting shot.

Also reviewed in:
CHICAGO TRIBUNE, 7/22/94, Friday/p. F, Michael Wilmington
NEW REPUBLIC, 8/22 & 29/94, p. 34, Stanley Kauffmann
NEW YORK TIMES, 7/20/94, p. C18, Caryn James
VARIETY, 6/27-7/3/94, p. 87, Brian Lowry
WASHINGTON POST, 8/5/94, p. C2, Rita Kempley
WASHINGTON POST, 8/5/94, Weekend/p. 38, Desson Howe

WES CRAVEN'S NEW NIGHTMARE

A New Line Cinema release. *Executive Producer:* Robert Shaye and Wes Craven. *Producer:* Marianne Maddalena. *Director:* Wes Craven. *Screenplay (based on characters created by):* Wes Craven. *Director of Photography:* Mark Irwin. *Editor:* Patrick Lussier. *Music:* J. Peter Robinson. *Music Editor:* Lise Richardson. *Sound:* Jim Steube and (music) Robert Fernandez. *Casting:* Gary Zuckerbrod. *Production Designer:* Cynthia Charette. *Art Director:* Troy Sizemore and Diane McKinnon. *Set Designer:* Stephen Alesch. *Set Decorator:* Ruby Guidara. *Set Dresser:* Grant Scharbo and Catherine Ernst. *Special Visual Effects:* William Mesa. *Special Mechanical Effects:* Lou Carlucci. *Costumes:* Mary Jane Fort. *Make-up:* Ashlee Petersen. *Stunt Coordinator:* Tony Cecere. *Running time:* 112 minutes. *MPAA Rating:* R.

CAST: Jeffrey John Davis (Freddy's Hand Double); Heather Langenkamp (Herself); Miko Hughes (Dylan); Matt Winston (Chuck); Rob LaBelle (Terry); David Newsom (Chase Porter); Wes Craven (Himself); Marianne Maddalena (Herself); Gretchen Oehler (Script Supervisor); Tracy Middendorf (Julie); Cully Fredricksen (Limo Driver); Bodhi Elfman (TV Studio P.A.); Sam Rubin (Himself); Robert Englund (Himself); Claudia Haro (New Line Receptionist); Sara Risher (Herself); Robert Shaye (Himself); Cindy Guidry (Kim at New Line); Ray Glanzmann (Highway Patrolman); Yonda Davis (Highway Patrolwoman); Michael Hagiwara (Coroner); W. Earl Brown (Morgue Attendant); Kenneth Zanchi (Minister); Nick Corri (Himself); Tuesday Knight (Herself); Beans Morocco (Graveyard Worker); John Saxon (Himself); Freddy Krueger (Himself); Tamara Mark (Patrice Englund); Fran Bennett (Dr. Heffner); Lin Shaye (Nurse with Pills); Deborah Zara Kobylt (Newscater); Diane Nadeau (Counter Nurse); Star-Shemah (ICU Nurse #1); Lou Thornton (ICU Nurse #2); Cynthia Savage (ICU Nurse #3); Jessica Craven (Junior Nurse with Needle); Sandra Ellis Lafferty (Senior Nurse with Needle); Thomas G. Burt (Security Officer); Tina Vail (Nurse Abbott).

LOS ANGELES TIMES, 10/14/94, Calendar/p. 4, Peter Rainer

Freddy Krueger fans will exult and horror movie mavens will not be surprised: "Wes Craven's New Nightmare" is much better than the usual run of scare pictures.

Craven directed the original "Nightmare on Elm Street" movie, still by far the best, but had no real involvement in any of the five sequels. His "New Nightmare" draws on some Old

Nightmares from the series but also gets at something new to the genre. It's a complicated, tricky attempt to bring out the elements of horror movie-making in a way that's deliberately self-conscious. It's post-modernism for the mall crowd—a movie-within-a-movie.

The premise is that Freddy is not a movie monster but an archetypal demon who, now that the "Nightmare" series has ended, has become unleashed into the real world via Craven's new script. He infects the dreams of the family of the actress—Heather Langenkamp—in the original "Nightmare." (She was also in "Part 3" but who besides Freddy, is counting?) He wreaks all kinds of razor-fingered havoc until Heather pursues him through her dreams into a kind of boiler-room perdition in order to save her child (Miko Hughes). As if this weren't enough, Craven also works in the Northridge earthquake, just in case his meta-mystical heebie-jeebies weren't to your taste. One way or the other, "Nightmare" has moments that will probably scare the bejabbers out of just about anybody.

Besides Langenkamp, Robert Englund also turns up, of course, playing the actor who plays Freddy (as well as Freddy himself). Craven play himself; so do John Saxon, and the chairman of the "Nightmare" releasing company, New Line's Robert Shaye. It's a gimmick, an in-joke, and yet there's something inherently creepy about all this self-referencing. It punctures our it's-only-a-movie reassurances. After all these people know it's only a movie too, and yet dreadful things keep happening to them.

There's another novel twist to this "Nightmare." It works in the filmmakers' attitudes toward the horror genre by imagining what it might be like for an actress like Langenkamp to confront her own child watching her in "Nightmare"—and being terrorized by her. Craven, in effect, does the same thing to himself; he's spooked by what he first unleashed. His "New Nightmare" isn't the Pirandellian masterpiece that his enthusiasts are calling it, but it's more than diverting. It's compelling—it challenges you to keep up with it.

NEW STATESMAN & SOCIETY, 1/6/94, p. 33, Jonathan Romney

People tend to get mistrustful when a genre gets too self-conscious; sometimes for good reason—a genre that can't play itself straight knows it's on the verge of collapse. Greeting the Schwarzenegger meta-vehicle *Last Action Hero* with a frosty reception, critics and punters alike seemed to sense that it would be impossible to take Arnie seriously ever again. His next "real" action film, the risible *True Lies* followed; QED.

Self-reflexivity in fiction films is usually held to be permissible either in high art or in comedy. The one place you'd expect such trickery not to work is in horror. You'd imagine that, to be effective, horror has to be taken on some level as being "for real". *Wes Craven's New Nightmare* refutes that fairly thoroughly. It works brilliantly both as a horror film (it's not that scary, but it is ingenious and startling) and as a meditation on genre conventions. Strictly, it isn't another in the *Nightmare on Elm Street* series, but a commentary on Craven's original *Nightmare* and its five inferior sequels. In fact, it's probably the first film to examine explicitly the sequel as a genre ln itself.

In the original *Nightmare*, nocturnal revenant Freddy Krueger had the power to haunt people's dreams, and only by staying awake could they elude his fatal turbo-powered manicure. The trick of the film was to con us that we were in the dreamland where we were in the waking world, and vice versa; the whole thing was a sly manipulation of that wary fictional let-out, "only a dream after all". But the *Nightmare*, once out of Craven's hands, got tamer and tamer, and Freddy turned into a comic-cuts bogeyman, no more threatening than Count Duckula.

Back at the helm, Craven recharged Freddy's shock potential by revealing him to be a paper ghoul, and defying us to find him scary—and despite the odds, he is. Ten years after the original *Nightmare*, the heroine of the new film is Heather Langenkamp—played by Heather Langenkamp, who played the heroine in the first film. Langenkamp is still haunted by Freddy—in her nightmares, on TV (*Nightmare* seems to be showing every night, at all hours), and in real life. She can't get away from Freddy, even on a chatshow where all thc audience members are dressed as him and where she's joined by the actor who played him, Robert Englund—played by Robert Englund. It's a wonderfully telling scene; Langenkamp shoots him an equivocal look, not only because he's her nightmare incarnate, but also because he's getting more applause—the king of the night lording it over a minor daytime soap star.

Langenkamp is summoned to the (real-life) New Line Productions, where its (real-life) president Robert Shaye wants her to be reunited with Englund in "the definitive Nightmare". Wes Craven (Wes Craven) is working on a new script: its gist is that a timeless spirit of evil has been released by the termination of the *Nightmare* series. Fade to black, on a cut to Craven's word processor, on which we see the script of the film we're watching...

To a student of Gide, Robbe-Grillet and co, all of this is fairly routine stuff—you just don't expect to find it in a horror film. Craven uses it to make a serious (not just formal) point about the repetitive, addictive nature of the genre. Horror, we tend to assume, is about the unexpected—but Craven shows how much it's about the expected by overtly repeating shocks from the earlier films, giving us Freddy's greatest hits one more time—the tongue in the telephone, the dragging-the-victims-up-the-wall trick. They're the same but, because of the singularly odd context, crucially different.

On an explicit level, the aim is indeed to give the punters more of the same—but Craven is also asking, *why* always the same? The film is about its own bad faith, about the repetition compulsion that motivates Freddy's fans and creators alike—and at least the fans can't be accused of being in it for the money. Ten years on, *Nightmare* is still Langenkamp's biggest success; Craven hasn't come up with anything as good since; and Englund, who plays himself as a ham buffoon going through the motions, can't get himself taken seriously in any other role. If Craven must give in to make forces and the death of inspiration, then he intends to take everyone with him, not least of all New Line, who squarely take the rap for bowdlerising Craven's initially potent concept. There's certainly something strange about a hideously scarred child-killer becoming a kiddies' favourite, "like Santa Claus or King Kong".

Craven asks timely questions about children and horror, in view of the panic that surrounded *Child's Play 3*, cited as a possible bad influence on the killers of Jamie Bulger. Are horror videos bad for children? Perhaps, and perhaps literally so—Freddy seems to be getting at Langenkamp's son Dylan through *Nightmare* revivals on TV. Or is it more a case of adults projecting their own fears onto children? While Langenkamp is apprehensive about reading Dylan *Hansel and Gretel* it's through repeated readings of that supremely horrific yarn that he's able to acquire a necessary understanding of evil and defeat the monster. The child's ambivalent role in horror cinema—a prey, hero or monster, the focus of family terrors, fuelling adults' own infantile imagination—is brought to the fore in a series of allusions to *Poltergeist, The Exorcist* and other canonic demon-child scarers. Hell here, for once, really is a-poppin'.

NEW YORK POST, 10/14/94, p. 37, Thelma Adams

"Just when you thought it was safe to get back in bed ..." horror star Robert Englund (playing himself) teases a studio audience in "Wes Craven's New Nightmare."

This rippingly good movie-within-a-movie—a pop "Day for Nightmare"—revives the razor-fingered, dream-haunting Freddy Krueger.

Supposedly dispatched in "Freddy's Dead: The Final Nightmare," the scarfaced demon now haunts the creators of "A Nightmare on Elm Street" and its five profitable sequels.

Set in contemporary Hollywood, the movie imagines that Englund (who has paved his swimming pool with Freddy money) has started to paint eerie portraits of his alter-ego. Nightmares plague Nancy Kerrigan lookalike Heather Langenkamp. The actress played a teen dynamo in the first "Nightmare" and returned as an older, wiser shrink in the third.

Langenkamp's son Dylan (Miko Hughes) has started to have close encounters with Krueger and has learned the simple lesson: Don't sleep.

Meanwhile, the special-effects men on a secret new "Nightmare" are meeting untimely ends. Appearing in a cameo, New Line Cinema president Robert Shaye, who built a movie empire on Krueger's back, has been getting troubling phone calls.

Is it a coincidence? Mass hysteria? A payback for releasing excessive visual violence into the cultural mainstream? Or is Freddy back in town?

Craven, who created Krueger but had little to do with the sequels to date, plays himself as a coda to the "Nightmare" saga. It seems that the writer/director has been having dreams which have inspired him to start work on a new script.

"I sort of think of it as a nightmare in progress," Craven tells Heather.

The trouble is that Heather's life is following Craven's script and her son's sanity is at risk. What's an actress/mother to do?

If you're Heather, you pursue Freddy yourself, after failing to enlist the aid of frustratingly useless adults—in this case Craven, Englund, and John Saxon, who played Langenkamp's screen father.

In addition to Craven's technical virtuosity, what places him in the pantheon of great contemporary horrormeisters—David Cronenberg, John Carpenter, and George Romero—is his ability to hook into our fears.

Earthquakes add to Heather's jitters, but it's the fact that this teen raised on horror flicks now has a son to protect that plugs into the anxieties of a generation that grew up on "Nightmare" and now has a brood of their own.

When Dylan freaks out and is hospitalized, Dr. Heffner (Fran Bennett) and her nurses (played by relatives of Shaye and Craven) disapprove of Heather, Heffner criticizes Heather for the part she played in so many children's nightmares and asserts that Dylan may be traumatized by watching his mom's movies.

Without losing narrative momentum, Craven counters that the nightmares are there already—and kids are more in touch with them than adults. Horror movies are a vehicle for expressing and dealing with fears that already exist.

It's no coincidence that Dylan's favorite bedtime story is Grimms' cannibalistic horror, "Hansel and Gretel." Freddy Krueger is no more than a wicked witch who wily children can outsmart and kill and kill again.

NEWSDAY, 10/14/94, Part II/p. B2, Jack Mathews

Throughout the first six installments of "A Nightmare on Elm Street" horror movie series, scar-faced Freddy Krueger has behaved more like a high school bully than a formidable monster. He's been an underachiever, content to terrorize the teenagers of tiny Springwood, Ohio (pop: 15,265), by invading their dreams and impaling them on his knife-like fingers, never dreaming himself of becoming a worldwide menace.

With "Wes Craven's New Nightmare," we find out why. Freddy, who we thought was merely the angry spirit of the murdered son of a nun who'd been raped in an insane asylum, is actually an ancient demon trapped in a role in a hit series. Sort of like David Caruso.

As long as the series is alive, director Wes Craven himself explains to one of his stars midway through this inventively campy new episode, Freddy is a harmless movie villain, able to kill a career maybe, but nothing more. If the series ends, which is what we and Freddy (who apparently gets Daily Variety delivered to him in hell) were assured at the end of the 1991 "Freddy's Dead: The Final Nightmare," he's free to "cross over" and attack real people.

"New Nightmare" is a spectacular achievement, not as a film, necessarily, but as an act of commercial revivification. Craven, who has now directed Nos. 1 and 7, has figured out how to both renege on New Line's promise to kill the series, and make it seem like a public service. If they don't make these movies, you see, we all may die in our sleep!

Do I scoff? Oh, sure. The "Nightmare" series epitomizes the lowered standards of modern horror movies. In the original 1984 "A Nightmare on Elm Street," Craven introduced a novel monster, but it was essentially just another slasher film, cut from the same cloth as "Halloween" and "Friday the 13th." Though subsequent episodes were well-directed ("The Mask's" Chuck Russell did No.3 and Renny Harlin, who would later do "Die Hard 2" and "Cliffhanger," directed no. 4), they were all more inspired by stunts, special effects, makeup, and precious puns than good story sense.

"New Nightmare" is loaded with those things, too, and the ending is as mundane and unconvincing as any that have gone before. But the idea of a movie monster crashing through the "fourth wall" of the filmmaking process to move among the people who invented him is irresistible, particularly in a series about the blending of reality and fantasy, and Craven plays it with such deadpan earnestness, you hang on every page.

Literally, in some cases. The actors happen onto copies of the script for the movie they're in, and invariably open to the page they're on.

Most of these moments belong to Heather Langenkamp, the actress who, as Nancy Thompson in the original "Nightmare," conjured up Freddy in her sleep, then reappeared in "Nightmare 3" as a dream therapist trying to help the next wave of haunted Springwood youth beat the devil. Now a mother, wife and sometime actress living in suburban L. A., Langenkamp finds herself dreaming of Freddy, and waking up to discover he'd actually been there.

"New Nightmare" is a movie within a movie, in progress. Langenkamp isn't offered the role by New Line Cinema chief Robert Shaye (playing himself) until the movie is well under way. She's still saying no well after Freddy's channeled through her to kill off some of "Nightmare's" veteran special effects crew, including her husband (David Newsom), and threatening her, her son (Miko Hughes), and former "Nightmare" cast members John Saxon, Nick Corri, Tuesday Knight, and Robert Englund, who, in the identity crisis of the year, plays both Freddy and himself.

The movie is terrific fun as long as it's playing with itself, but every time it veers off into one of the series' patented nightmares, you can feel just how tired and badly in need of a rest the concept is. "New Nightmare" is still the smartest and best of the seven, the first one aimed at adults, and let's just hope Craven will allow Freddy and the series to end on a happy note.

SIGHT AND SOUND, 1/95, p. 62, Kim Newman

Ten years after starring in Wes Craven's *A Nightmare on Elm Street* actress Heather Langenkamp is married to effects technician Chase and has a small son, Dylan. Troubled by bad dreams and a phone caller who sounds like Freddy Krueger of the *Elm Street* films, Heather is reunited on a talk show with Robert Englund, who played Freddy, then summoned to the offices of New Line Cinema. The company's chairman Robert Shaye offers her the lead role in a new film being written by Craven, which will bring back Freddy even though the monster was definitively killed in *Freddy's Dead, The Final Nightmare*. Craven explains that in this new script, he will reveal that Freddy is the manifestation of an ancient evil which has appeared throughout history and can only be bound when confined within a successful story, and that the cessation of the *Elm Street* series has loosed it on the real world.

Heather dreams that Chase is killed by Freddy and learns that her husband has been killed in an apparent car accident. At the funeral she is knocked out by a slight earth tremor and dreams that Freddy tries to drag Dylan into his underworld. Heather comes to believe that Freddy is trying to make his way into the real world through Dylan, who sometimes acts as if possessed. Dylan is taken into hospital for tests, and a doctor, suspicious of Heather because she disapproves of horror films, guesses the child is suffering from sleep deprivation, having been kept awake by his irrational mother. While Heather protests, Dylan is sedated and falls under Freddy's power. Freddy kills Dylan's babysitter, and the boy escapes from the hospital. Heather appeals to actor friend John Saxon for help, but Saxon acts as if he were her father, the role he played in A Nightmare on Elm Street, and Heather finds herself on Elm Street. Venturing into the underworld, Heather faces Freddy and, with Dylan's help, defeats him. Craven's completed screenplay dispels Freddy from reality.

This is a rare film, coming honestly by its possessive credit—even though its title sounds more like an ad line than something anyone would actually want to title a movie, *Wes Craven's New Nightmare* wins points for the most unique sequel premise in horror movie history. It opens with a reprise of the first sequence of *A Nightmare on Elm Street*, as a clawed Freddy glove is meticulously assembled, then pulls a (not entirely unexpected) double reverse as the scene is revealed to be a) taking place on a film set, where effects men are labouring to create a remote-controlled killer glove; and b) a bad dream where that glove runs wild and kills a couple of minor characters. Later, of course, it is revealed that the people who die in Heather Langenkamp's dream have really been killed.

Playing at once to series fans and to the post-modern ironist in every multiplex, this *Nightmare* squirms remarkably around the supposedly definitive wrap-up of *Freddy's Dead*, pulling back into another plane of reality, where actors, directors and New Line execs play themselves. For those aware of the history between creator Wes Craven and New Line chairman Robert Shaye, there's another level of irony in Shaye's claim (scripted by Craven) that "Wes says he hasn't called me for ten years because he hasn't had any new nightmares". Craven, in a creditable performance, perceptibly chokes back glee when he suggests that Freddy has only been allowed to escape from the cage of *A Nightmare on Elm Street* because the increasingly shoddy and jokey sequels have allowed him to manifest himself in a more streamlined and nasty form in the real world. There is a certain fudging in the exact status of Freddy, who is subtly and interestingly linked with such figures as the Witch in 'Hansel and Gretel' (Dylan insists on the importance of his mother reading all of the fairy tale's ending to restore the balance). It seems odd that Freddy should have more power to do evil if his popularity *decreases*, especially since Craven admits that the formless demon likes taking the Freddy shape, so it's hard to judge whether or not the Freddy of this film *wants* Craven to shoot his new script.

Also slightly limiting Craven's ambitions is the need to bring back the cast of the first film. While Langenkamp improves on her terrible performance in *A Nightmare on Elm Street, Part 3: Dream Warriors*, she still hasn't quite got the range to carry a whole movie. The always-welcome Saxon doesn't really differentiate between himself and his screen character, playing a scene as a concerned friend with just the measure of intensity he always brings. Robert Englund, slyly sending himself up as the ham actor, has to moderate his Freddy performance, but comes across as merely different rather than more scary. This Freddy, who memorably expands his mouth to fit Dylan's entire head into it, is certainly stronger stuff than anything seen in the franchise films, but doesn't come up to the benchmark figure of the first *Nightmare*. Though it taps into fascinating material (the Freddy back-story is potentially far more rewarding than the one in *Freddy's Dead*), this *Nightmare* could do with a longer view applied to the script, which might have explored the successive manifestations of the pre-Freddy monster.

The major achievement of the film, given the complicated mix of in-jokery and philosophy and the by-now familiar nature of Freddy's schtick, is that Craven manages to make things scary again. Reprising some of the business from *A Nightmare on Elm Street* (the phone sprouting a tongue, the teenager gutted in mid-air, the stairs that become a mire), Craven generally does it more creepily this time round, and, drawing a remarkable performance from child actor Miko Hughes, makes genuinely upsetting Freddy's attempts to destroy Dylan's mind. From unnerving touches like the earthquake which cracks the wall of Heather's house, mimicking the scratches of a Freddy glove, to major sequences like the sleepwalking child wandering into heavy freeway traffic, Craven is still one of the horror cinema's most imaginative creators of purely frightening moments. Dispensing with the adolescent concerns of the sequels, and ditching embarrassing frills like heavy metal music, feeble teen performances and bad one-liners, this is a worthy follow-up to the first film and a sly critique of all the watering-down that has happened since.

VILLAGE VOICE, 10/18/94, p. 61, Gary Dauphin

Horror flicks being an ill-acquired and often unjustifiable taste, you'll forgive me for liking the idea of *Wes Craven's New Nightmare* long before I'd actually seen it. Craven's original *Nightmare on Elm Street* was one of a handful of genuinely chilling movies made during the '80s, and by chilling I'm referring to the sustained buzz of unease that marks, say, anything by Cronenberg, the first *Halloween, Alien*, and maybe *The Shining* (this hinges on how much Jack Nicholson's grin freaks me out at any given moment). Withholding on the masturbatory pacing of BOO!-gotcha slasher fare and too subtle for the visual ataxia splattered across the screen in *Evil Dead-Hellraiser* flicks, Craven and that first *Elm Street* movie not only delivered goose bumps, but also gave the world Freddy Krueger, a foulmouthed riff on the horror antihero.

As lucrative as even the bad *Elm Street* sequels were for Craven, they were apparently a heavy load for his mental résumé. Surviving the success of a great/terrible character like Freddy called for either a string of non-*Elm Street* hits (which Craven hasn't had) or a return to the scene of the last successful caper. This is where *New Nightmare* comes in. For the seventh in the series, Craven reunites the principals from the first movie (John Saxon, Robert Englund, and Heather Langenkamp) and casts them as, well, their own B-movie selves. It seems that Langenkamp is getting scary phone calls from a crazed fan imitating Freddy Krueger, but to make matters worse, her son starts speaking in tongues, namely Freddy's. Things progress rather bloodlessly from there until Heather seeks advice from Wes Craven (played by Wes Craven). In a line as lecherously terrifying as any of Freddy's rantings, the director looks into his own camera and announces, "The only way to stop Freddy is to make another *Nightmare* movie, Heather." *New Nightmare* saves the really spooky slice-and-dice for the last reel, which reaches back to the series' beginnings in childhood myths, leaving the audience with the strangely plausible moral that "only a really good story can contain evil like Freddy." Too bad the good stories come only every six installments.

Also reviewed in:
NEW YORK TIMES, 10/14/94, p. C8, Janet Maslin
VARIETY, 9/19/-25/94, p. 76, Joe Leydon
WASHINGTON POST, 10/14/94, p. F9, Richard Harrington
WASHINGTON POST, 10/14/94, Weekend/p. 48, Desson Howe

WHAT HAPPENED WAS ...

A Samuel Goldwyn Company release of a Good Machine production of a Genre film. *Executive Producer:* Ted Hope and James Schamus. *Producer:* Robin O'Hara and Scot Macaulay. *Director:* Tom Noonan. *Screenplay:* Tom Noonan. *Director of Photography:* Joe DeSalvo. *Editor:* Richard Arrley. *Music:* Ludovico Sorret. *Sound:* Rick Stevenson. *Production Designer:* Dan Ouellette. *Set Decorator:* Andra Kanegson. *Set Dresser:* Constance LeMasson. *Costumes:* Kathy Nixon. *Make-up:* Kathryn Nixon and Nina Port. *Running time:* 92 minutes. *MPAA Rating:* Not Rated.

CAST: Karen Sillas (Jackie); Tom Noonan (Michael).

CHRISTIAN SCIENCE MONITOR, 9/8/94, p. 14, David Sterritt

A small but absorbing American picture called "What Happened Was..." has gathered as much praise as anything I've seen here [Montreal World film Festival], and deservedly so. It originated as a stage play written by and starring Tom Noonan, whose performances in movies ranging from "Mystery Train" to "Last Action Hero" have established him as a versatile character actor.

Noonan's film version of "What Happened Was..." retains the look and feel of a theatrical production, focusing on only two characters—a secretary and a paralegal who work for a Manhattan law firm—as they eat a modest dinner, have a friendly but awkward conversation, and work their way up to a little flirting that neither seems comfortable with.

On paper, this sounds like a sure-fire candidate for most tedious movie of the season: a full-length drama about two small-timers whose biggest achievement is thinking up some limp remark to keep the conversation from falling totally apart before it's time to say goodbye. What makes it a riveting experience is its combination of sensitive screenwriting—charged with clear understanding of the characters and strong compassion for their lonely lives—and stunningly good performances by Karen Sillas as the hostess and Noonan as her gentleman caller.

Also striking is the film's use of expressive camera work to bring out subtle dynamics of the ever-shifting relationship it portrays. Noonan is equally inventive as an actor, screenwriter, and director.

LOS ANGELES TIMES, 10/6/94, Calendar/p. 10, Peter Rainer

First-time couples looking for a good date movie may want to shy away from "What Happened Was ..." On the other hand, the first date on display in this film is so inexorably weird that it might actually make you appreciate your partner. So it could turn out to be a good date movie about a bad date.

Got that?

Jackie (Karen Sillas) is a secretary in a prestigious law firm. She's been eyeing Michael (Tom Noonan), a bookish type who works there as a paralegal. She invites him to her Manhattan loft apartment for dinner, dresses alluringly, and attempts to draw him out over drinks. Sirens wail faintly in the background. The urban grunge outside seems to have crept indoors, into Jackie's low-lit apartment. This isn't just a bad date movie, it's a bad date movie *New York style*.

"What Happened Was ...," directed by Noonan and scripted by him based on theatrical improvisations, transforms the steady-state anxiety of a first date into a horror scenario. What's shocking—and gruesomely funny—about the film is that it's a familiar horror. Noonan and Sillas capture the feints and pauses and little seductions and infelicities that punctuate The Date. But the movie isn't some '90s-era dating dos-and-don'ts manual for aging singles. It's not likely to provoke gleeful howls of recognition from its audience—it's too strange for that, and too tough-minded.

Just when you think the movie is turning into one of those reveal-your-vulnerability love-fests, it turns a corner on you. The more these people "open up" to each other, the creepier it all seems. Emotional openness in "What Happened Was ...," isn't a latchkey to love, it's a red flag.

Jackie and Michael's predicament may be generic but they certainly aren't. Their characters have been worked up in highly specific ways—we don't always know where we're going with them. When Jackie reveals that she's been writing a children's book, and Michael agrees to listen to it, what transpires is a real lulu of a monologue. Jackie's story, which careens from fairytale innocence into Gothic horror, is probably meant to be taken symbolically but it's too clotted with psychodrama to really function for audiences. Like Michael, you tune out, but what,s important here is that Jackie has suddenly flipped our expectations. Michael has his turn later. His light voice and almost spectral, weightless presence suddenly seem brackish. Noonan is perhaps best known to filmgoers for the creepola he played in "Manhunter" and he can't—may not want to shake those associations in this film. Michael is a sensitive, broken-down, somewhat delusionary man with a dogged sense of justice: a phantasmal wimp steeled by a need for payback. He claims he's working at the law firm because he's working on a book exposing the legal profession.

As a piece of drama, "What Happened Was ..." isn't any great shakes; it's essentially an actors' workshop exercise that exists primarily as a showcase for its cast. And because Noonan and, especially, Sillas are so good, it triumphs. (It won the 1994 Sundance Film Festival Grand Jury Prize.)

Sillas has appeared in two films by the fluky minimalist Hal Hartley, and she can currently be seen to not particularly good advantage as a police detective on CBS' "Under Suspicion." She's a rare sort of actress: forbidding and yet emotionally naked. Sillas doesn't sentimentalize Jackie's desperation in "What Happened Was ...": Jackie is an innocent with a hard edge. She's looking to be brought out—redeemed—by love. But she is also smart enough to recognize that only minor victories may be possible in her life anymore: She idealizes Michael but she's also a rock-bottom realist when the chips are down. "What Happened Was ..."isn't much more than a splendid acting exercise but, with all the phony-baloney movies out there about romance, it seems the most honest of the bunch.

NEW YORK POST, 9/9/94, p. 45, Thelma Adams

"Dates are weird sometimes," says Jackie (Karen Sillas). "This is a date?" asks Michael (Tom Noonan). In his stagy directorial debut, "What Happened Was ...," actor Noonan heightens the awkward humor and seat-squirming embarrassment as Jackie and Michael lurch through first-date hell towards intimacy. It's "No Exit" with a bottle of wine and a microwaved meal.

The two leads couldn't be more different. The stoop-shouldered, gawky, skeletal Michael—a paralegal—clutches his worn briefcase like a life raft. He shields himself with sarcastic humor which often passes over Jackie's head. When threatened, a vein rises like a wiggly road on his large forehead.

His co-worker Jackie—a fleshy, attractive colleen in her mid-30s senses her prime is past and responds with wine-gulping nervousness. Her hands are never still: clearing the table can become an act of aggression; illustrating an anecdote, an obvious seduction. Jackie still has her looks, but she's sending out "vibes," as she says, which chase men away.

Both Michael and Jackie are uncomfortable in their own skins. They are two people who live lives of quiet desperation, whose lives have taken dangerous twists from which recovery is uncertain.

What earned "What Happened Was ..." both the Grand Jury prize and the Waldo Salt Screenwriter's Awards at the 1994 Sundance Film Festival is the scalpel-driven skill with which Noonan carves his characters.

Each actor receives his dramatic moment—a predictable device played out unpredictably and a point of grace. This allows both Noonan, who has played bad guys and character roles from "Manhunter" to "F/X," and Hal Hartley muse Sillas, to stretch and convey a range of emotions from palm-sweating fear to giddy laughter.

Noonan's talky comic-drama is a study in social vertigo. Michael and Jackie are not two people falling in love; but two people who are simply falling. Will they be able to catch each other? Only a hopeless romantic would have faith in that.

NEWSDAY, 9/9/94, Part II/p. B2, John Anderson

A woman stares apprehensively from the window of her dimly lit Manhattan apartment. Vulnerable, singular, she watches as lurid videos flash out of the darkened building across the street. The night is inky. The air seems oppressive. And as a subtle sense of terror rises, the camera rushes into her face, now rigid with fear.

Is death lurking?

No. A date.

Tom Noonan's painfully funny and painfully painful "What Happened Was ..."is the dark side of the Dewars' ad: "Now that he's finally agreed to come over for dinner, what are you going to serve?" Wine, as it happens, and Jackie (Karen Sillas) is already imbibing liberally. The gentleman caller, so to speak, is Michael (Noonan), a co-worker at the law firm where they work, he as a paralegal, she as an "executive assistant." ("Is that what they call secretaries these days?" he asks, gallingly. "That's what it says on the paycheck," she mutters, coldly.) She's had her eye on him for some time, and he on her, but their respective intentions, as usual, are like points on a compass. Jackie and Michael could be the cover people for a Deborah Tannen book on gender linguistics. They simply don't speak the same language. Noonan, who wrote, directed and stars in this spare but subtly detailed drama, has captured more than the clumsy, humiliating anxiety and doomed expectations of a first date—which is shown mostly in real time, with all its inescapable humiliation intact. He's also tapped into the solitary confinement of modern urban life, the era of diminished expectations, feminist backlash, male hubris, and the byzantine nature of simple human interaction, boiled them down to their bones, and arrived at fractured humanity.

"What Happened Was ..." was the last film chosen for Sundance Film Festival this year, and wound up winning the best picture prize and screenwriting award. It's that kind of movie: Easily dismissable as nothing more than a filmed play—which Noonan developed in workshops at his Paradise Theater in the East Village—it is deceptively visual, rich in detail and possessed of a subtle, decadent iconography. Jackie's ceramic cat, for example, which she clutches in her sleep int he film's opening scene, and later breaks. A sex toy, or part of her own desperately innocent glass menagerie?

Neither Michael, who's too smart for his job, nor Jackie, who's not, is an innocent, of course. They're adults-at-large, a little lost and certainly not what they advertise themselves to be. Michael is a writer, he says, working on a book about the "lonely, damaged, crippled people," victimized by the legal profession; the irony escapes him completely. Jackie is a writer, too, she says, and proceeds to read him her "children's story"—a tale of rape, incest, cannibalism and ritual murder that aptly captures the film's mix of mock horror and embarrassed laughs. Both Noonan and Sillas are first rate, and Jackie the more empathetic character. Earthy, concerned with looming middle-age , she's as honest, even with herself, as she can be ("They call you Mr. Strange around the office," she tells Michael. "I just tell them you're insecure."). Michael, for his part, is pedantic and smug, although as the layers of artifice peel away he becomes, if not likable, then at least pitiable. Together they're like most people, a point Noonan drives home soundly.

VILLAGE VOICE, 9/13/94, p. 64, Georgia Brown

Until the very end of Tom Noonan's cunning *What Happened Was ...*, you never know whether Jackie or Michael—one or the other or both—will turn out to be natural born killers. One of the virtues of this $300,000 picture is how it intimates violence, conjures violence, dances with violence, and yet remains fixed on the way *we* live now. Of course, it's this uncommon resistance to flamboyant behavior that makes this Sundance Grand Jury Prize winner something other than your ordinary movie-movie.

The turf in Noonan's one-set, two-character, real-time, layers-of-the-onion psychological drama is Jackie's (Karen Sillas) midnight-blue studio, a cubbyhole apartment that could be located almost anywhere in Manhattan. The slap-dash decor—a wrinkled photo-poster of Martin Luther King, a *Cats* poster, a discarded store mannequin to fling scarves and such on—gives nothing away. The film's only glimpse of an outside world comes courtesy of Jackie's precious but pathetic, blocked "view"—looking out onto a dingy stepped-back neo-Gothic tower. There are few alternate signs of life in this closed universe, though we do see into some of her neighbors' living rooms. One shadowy guy in particular seems to give himself over to crypto-porn.

Tonight Jackie breezes in from work—in her suit jacket and Reeboks—and races around preparing for a gentleman caller. She tries on, then rejects, an unflattering purplish lace top, nukes something white in the microwave, removes a dowdy cake from a bakery box, gulps white wine, and lights a slew of candles. A secretary (or "executive assistant") in a law office, Jackie has mustered the courage to invite over a paralegal she's had her eye on. Clearly, the two have been inching toward some outside-the-workplace encounter. At least she has. If it were left to the tall, bald, slightly ghoulish Michael (played by writer-director Noonan), a first date might have been a couple years away. Michael's charming defense is to act as if he's just dropping by. He keeps briefcase in hand.

But I'm already giving away "plot." Noonan's strategy is *very* controlled revelation. Moreover, facts put on the table are liable to be deceptive. While the couple eat their homely little meal, for example, Michael drops that he went to Harvard. (Jackie went to a technical college in the Bronx.) This Harvard info instantly alters our vision of Michael, who has heretofore come across as geek, shlump, and perennial loser. Now he can be seen as either an intellectual guerrilla or rebel with a grudge—against Harvard ("totally racist, sexist, and corrupt"), law school, and now the legal establishment. He says he's writing an exposé of "the system." He works, he says, on behalf of all the "lonely, damaged," defenseless souls who are seen only as prey.

But we have much more to learn about this self-employed spy in the world of others. Here is a man who reveals that as a kid he was obsessed by *The Iliad*: "I have," he adds, "a very high tolerance for pain." When the extent of his despair is revealed, that zigzag vein in his temple begins to look like Frankensteinian scar tissue, as if he's been sewn up after something crucial was either inserted or removed.

But Jackie's revelation of self is more stunning. Just as this is her place, the movie is closer to being her story. Her disclosures come late, after we've written her off as too limited to keep up with Michael's grand critique. (As this metropolitan Eleanor Rigby, Sillas does a wonderful job both with her hair up and then letting it down.) The woman has gone through a great deal (we never learn actual details) and survived. As she reads aloud from her macabre "children's story"—it's titled "What Happened Was"—we read both the essence of her history and the stages of Michael's fear. Still reflexively deploying his wide-open smile, Michael realizes he's strayed into the deep end of the pool. The man can't swim.

In real life, the multifaceted Noonan runs the Paradise Theater on East Fourth, where this script was developed in workshop. Although he sometimes acts in movies—he played creepy villains in films like *Manhunter* and *Last Action Hero*—Noonan's heart obviously belongs to the stage. And watching *What Happened Was*, it's hard not to be ever conscious that the piece is more play than film; in this whole process of character revelation, it certainly follows the logic of plays. What it gains by being filmed—besides a larger audience—is proximity to movie genres. Movie viewers are programmed to look for dead bodies and Noonan wisely plays on these expectations. Will this film be a thriller or a horror pic? Which of the pair will crack first? Once, I literally lurched in my seat, thinking she'd slashed him with the cake knife.

The tease is instructive. What doesn't happen in *What Happened* illuminates the desperation, the grief, behind movie-movie violence. Early in the film, Jackie says she feels like she's in a movie, like her life isn't real: "Sometimes it's hard to believe I have a life." While they know what she means, viewers will find her far more real than most screen characters. If Jackie and Michael were really in the movies, you might say, they'd be killers.

Also reviewed in:
CHICAGO TRIBUNE, 12/9/94, Friday/p. H, Michael Wilmington
NEW YORK TIMES, 9/9/94, p. C16, Janet Maslin
VARIETY, 2/7-13/94, p. 37, Emanuel Levy
WASHINGTON POST, 9/30/94, p. F7, Rita Kempley
WASHINGTON POST, 9/30/94, Weekend/p. 45, Desson Howe

WHEN A MAN LOVES A WOMAN

A Touchstone Pictures release. *Executive Producer:* Simon Maslow, Ronald Bass, and Al Franken. *Producer:* Jordan Kerner and Jon Avnet. *Director:* Luis Mandoki. *Screenplay:* Ronald Bass and Al Franken. *Director of Photography:* Lajos Koltai. *Editor:* Garth Craven. *Music:* Zbigniew Preisner. *Music Editor:* Roy Prendergast. *Choreographer:* Miranda Garrison. *Sound:* Thomas D. Causey and (music) Rafal Paczkowksi. *Sound Editor:* George Watters II. *Casting:* Amanda MacKey and Cathy Sandrich. *Production Designer:* Stuart Wurtzel. *Art Director:* Steven A. Saklad. *Set Designer:* Stan Tropp. *Set Decorator:* Kara Lindstrom. *Set Dresser:* Michael P. Sweeney. *Special Effects:* Thomas R. Ward. *Costumes:* Linda Bass. *Make-up (Meg Ryan):* Leonard Engelman. *Make-up (Andy Garcia):* Rick Sharp. *Stunt Coordinator:* Mickey Gilbert. *Running time:* 126 minutes. *MPAA Rating:* R.

CAST: Andy Garcia (Michael Green); Meg Ryan (Alice Green); Ellen Burstyn (Emily); Tina Majorino (Jess Green); Mae Whitman (Casey Green); Lauren Tom (Amy); Philip Seymour Hoffman (Gary); Eugene Roche (Walter); Gail Strickland (Pam); Steven Brill (Madras Tie Guy); Susanna Thompson (Janet); Erinn Canavan (Shannon); Latanya Richardson (Dr. Gina Mendez); Bari K. Willerford (Malcolm); James Jude Courtney (Earl); Jacques de Groot (Guy in the Back); Anne Ohliger (Jess, 4 years old); Tony Montero (Bartender); Cynthia Mace (De-tox Nurse); Jennie Yee (Vu); William Frankfather (Al-Anon Leader); Ellen Geer (Woman at Al-Anon); Liz Lang (AA Woman); Syd Field (Patient #1); Peer Ebbighausen (Patient #2); Ronald Bass (AA Man #1); Joe Drago (AA Man #2); Amy Treese (AA Man #3); Brandis Kemp (AA Woman #2); Judith Friend (AA Woman #4); Deana Kobrynski (AA Woman #5).

FILMS IN REVIEW, 7-8/94, p. 52, Andy Pawelczak

At the beginning of *When A Man Loves A Woman*, we hear a few bars of the title song by Percy Sledge, and then we don't hear it again for the rest of the movie. It's too bad—a little infusion of rhythm'n blues might have enlivened this earnest, formulaic paean to A.A.'s twelve step program. The director, Luis Mandoki, and writers, Ron Bass and Al Franken, have put in all the right, pretested ingredients but neglected to add a soul.

We know what's coming right at the beginning when Alice (Meg Ryan) drunkenly comes home late and her airline pilot husband, Michael (Andy Garcia), tells her that if she has pressures she should confide in him. He's making excuses for her malfeasance, and very soon the picture turns into a textbook illustration of the fashionable concept of co-dependence. Michael's idea of helping her out is to take her on a weekend jaunt to Mexico, where, of course, she gets drunk and the filmmaker has the chance to shoot a long close up as husband and wife rotate in a turquoise blue pool and discuss her problem. Back in San Francisco, she gets drunk some more, hits her child, passes out in the shower and ends up in a detox center where Michael introduces her to the attendant by saying, "We're Alice Green." By this time it's pretty clear, to even the teetotalling Anabaptists in the audience, that the real source of Alice's problem is Michael's refusal to let her have her own identity—as the picture tells us over and over again, he likes picking up the pieces when she falls apart.

The movie completely misses the fun of drinking: the relaxation after the first drink, the Christmas lights going on in your head after the second, the bonhommie with strangers and the sense of restraints being lifted after the third, the gratifying sense of your own brilliant wit after the fourth, the sheer unmatched excitement of saying the hell with it as you order the drink that you know will take you over the line into Dionysus' own sacred drunkenness. It doesn't get much of the degradation and horror either: the morose doldrums of solitary drinking in the horse latitudes of three o'clock in the morning, the unbottling of primitive, mind destroying rage, the unforgivable insults and harangues that no amount of morning after pain and regret will ever expiate. Instead, we get some pop psychological pieties about cutting the co-dependency knot and facing up to reality, salutary things that we could all use more of, I'm sure, but platitudinous nonetheless. It's just such banalities that drive many people to drink.

As Michael, Andy Garcia makes a classically romantic entrance as he steps off a trolley car in a long shot encompassing a busy San Francisco street scene. Garcia has the drop dead male gorgeousness and the air of effortless non-acting that characterized some of the big stars of the forties, but Mandoki, the director, doesn't quite know what to do with that slightly anachronistic charisma. Garcia has a few good scenes in the detox center when Michael feels excluded from his wife's new circle of friends and confused by her embryonic independence and assertiveness; you can feel his anxiety in his careful, guarded watchfulness. Ultimately, though, it's hard to buy that this romantic hero manqué is the oblivious enabler of his wife's alcoholism. As Alice, Meg Ryan goes through her paces, but it's all pretty predictable—includingthe obligatory withdrawal symptoms scene—and we never really get inside the character.

Luis Mandoki's direction doesn't leave much to the imagination. His camera moves in relentlessly for every big emotional moment, and he shamelessly milks those scenes involving Michael and Alice's confused, frightened children. In the big scene in which Alice gives her A.A. qualifying speech, he gets all the details wrong. The room looks like a ballroom for the young ladies cotillion—a far cry from the shabby church basements of most A.A. meetings—and the alcoholics have the polished, optimistic faces of Sunday school teachers. As I write this, I'm looking at a photograph of James Agee, novelist, poet, film critic and drunk par excellence; now there's a face that could serve as a canonical text for a sermon on the self-destructive rigors and self-indulgent epiphanies of drinking, everything that this movie so carefully airbrushes away.

LOS ANGELES TIMES, 4/29/94, Calendar/p. 1, Kenneth Turan

What does happen when a man loves a woman? Is it really necessary, as the Percy Sledge song mournfully insisted, to spend your last dime and sleep out in the rain? Or is a middle ground possible, one with perhaps a bit less suffering and a bit more dry land? Hollywood wants to know.

With Sledge on the soundtrack and Meg Ryan and Andy Garcia in starring roles as a couple as much in trouble as they are in love, "When a Man Loves a Woman," directed by Luis Mandoki from a script by Ronald Bass and Al Franken, demonstrates why emotional turmoil is always a tricky subject for studio films to deal with effectively.

For though everyone yearns for the impact only the realistic treatment of problems delivers, there is inevitably a timid reluctance to renounce the slickness of Hollywood that serves as a convenient safety net. And seriousness of purpose does not mix well with excessive contrivance, not well at all.

All of this is more unfortunate than usual with "When a Man Loves a Woman," because Garcia and especially Ryan have worked extremely hard on their performances, with excellent results. But the honesty of their work only serves to point up the surrounding artificiality, which displays their accomplishments in a shallow light.

Pleasantly settled in San Francisco, Michael and Alice Green are introduced joking around at the Buena Vista, a celebrated local cafe. He is a dark and killer-handsome pilot, she a lively mother of two young girls (only one of whom is Michael's) who works at a local school. The fun all four have together, complete with cloying remarks like "God, woman, just look at her" from one of those precocious tykes to the other about their mom, s treacly enough to make one yearn for the trouble to come.

But though it may set your teeth on edge, this fantasy setup is simply the opening thrust of a classic Hollywood one-two situation. The idea is to first envy the Greens their seemingly ideal life and their glamorous external trappings, only to pity them and feel superior later on when it turns out that they've a worse set of crises than most people in the audience. Which they do.

It doesn't take too long for the first sign of trouble to appear. One sad look from older daughter Jess (Tina Majorino) at her mother as she lies in bed hung over from an anniversary celebration is the key: Alice turns out to be a Problem Drinker with a quart of vodka a day habit and a genius for denial.

While a difficulty like that might be enough for most movies, "When a Man Loves a Woman" isn't about to take any chances. Among the many other things that go wrong in the Greens' lives is a threat to his job, a major child-care blowup, painful conflicts about Jess' absent father and overbearing grandmother, even child abuse and several near-death experiences. It gets so that when anyone sets foot in the street you fear at the very least they'll be struck by a passing bus.

And that doesn't even count the way the situations are milked on screen, often by having 9-year-old Majorino, a charming actress, pull some of the longest faces ever recorded as she responds to loaded "What's an alcoholic?"-type questions from her perky younger sister.

This consistent artificiality is not at all in keeping with the strength of the performances, especially Ryan's. Always an audience favorite, the actress uses that sympathy to her advantage here, strongly and graphically portraying a woman who not only acts badly in the grip of alcoholism but continues to be mired in pain and confusion both in treatment and afterward. And though Garcia has to spend most of the movie saying supportive things like "You're not alone, honey, never," he, too, has his impressive moments, when this habit of insisting everything will be OK is called into question. When the movie allows itself to focus on Alice and Michael dealing one-on-one with these core difficulties, it is at its most persuasive.

Overall, however, the Greens' predicament doesn't move you as much as the quality of the acting makes you think it would. As crisis mounts on crisis, the wires of manipulation become too visible and you start to feel uncomfortably like an emotional dartboard.

It is a measure of "When a Man Loves a Woman's" lack of restraint that when Michael and Alice take a vacation in Mexico, prominently visible on her beach blankets is a copy of Amy Tan's "The Kitchen God's Wife," which just happens to be executive producer and co-screenwriter Bass' next project. Filmmakers who wouldn't hesitate at the thought of such a shameless plug can't be trusted to deal with the issues this film raises with the straightforwardness they deserve.

NEW YORK, 5/9/94, p. 66, David Denby

Meg Ryan doesn't crack up as often as the young, easily tickled Goldie Hawn, who seemed to giggle more than she breathed, but she has those high, rounded cheeks and the baby-doll smile of a woman who is still (in spirit) partly a teenager. The shrewdest thing about *When a Man Loves a Woman* is that it allows us to think at first that Meg Ryan is just being giddy. As Alice Green, a San Francisco school administrator, wife, and mother, Ryan is pitched a little higher than usual, but only a little. Horsing around with her handsome and ardent husband, Michael (Andy Garcia), she climbs atop a Porsche whose alarm won't shut off and smashes a few eggs on its sloping roof. She can't stop, and Garcia, looking troubled, finally tosses a few eggs himself. She's drunk, but then Meg Ryan has often seemed a little soused (even when she wasn't), and we don't make much of it. The movie cruelly and intelligently presents drunkenness as indistinguishable at first sight from high spirits and mischief and self-abandon—good things that seem like nothing more than an enlarged capacity for pleasure.

Only after a while do we realize that Alice is always drunk, that she has stashed bottles everywhere in her lovely house, and that Michael, who is still aloft from the romance of their marriage and enjoys taking care of Alice when she crashes, hasn't yet understood what a lush she is. The details of Alice 's collapse, when it comes, are intimate and scandalous. Sloshed, she slaps her little daughter and then passes out and falls, stiff as a board, through a shower door. By this time, we have noticed that Meg Ryan's face is longer and thinner than we had thought, that the rubber-cheeked adorableness has practically disappeared.

When a Man Loves a Woman gets high marks for intelligence and candor. This movie, written by Ronald Bass (*Rain Man*) and Al Franken (of *Saturday Night Live*) and directed by Luis Mandoki (*White Palace*), has a measured step-by-step meticulousness. There's nothing obviously wrong in Alice's life that would account for her condition—the movie avoids easy explanations and also many of the obvious scenes of its genre while offering its star a chance for sustained characterization. Of its kind, the picture is first-rate. But it suffers terribly from the limits that American culture now places on the treatment of such subjects. "Hopefully, after seeing this film, audiences will want to work harder on their marriage and their parenting," says Ronald Bass. The painful illiteracy and glum presumption of that sentence give the show away. In brief, after a striking beginning, *When a Man Loves a Woman* turns into a pushy therapeutic exercise. It features endless talk, a stunted *mise en scène*, a moral atmosphere of dogged and literal-minded persistence. It overvalues its own sobriety.

Almost 50 years ago, Billy Wilder and Charles Brackett made a rather lurid and harrowing movie about an alcoholic, *The Lost Weekend*, in which a failed artist (Ray Milland) suffers a personal catastrophe for which he is entirely responsible. *In When a Man Loves a Woman*, alcoholism appears, on the contrary, as a social catastrophe for which *everyone* is responsible. Despite its intelligence, the movie is fogged with a clammy I'm dysfunctional/You're dysfunctional knowingness (the very thing Al Franken's *SNL* character Stuart Smalley has long parodied). We're all sick, we all need help. But this is a therapeutic rather than a dramatic solution to the problem of making a movie about an alcoholic.

Meg Ryan suggests something of the mixture of pride and deceit that allows the drunkard to fool others and herself for months, sometimes years. Once sober, Alice discovers she has no self to fall back on. She has to invent a self, which is hard work, and Ryan gives a fine, desperate performance. Garcia might have been excellent, too, but the movie both hounds him and reins him in. His Michael, a terrific husband—smart, sensitive, loving—is made to appear guilty of the unspeakable sin of trying to protect and help his wife. He has to accept that as the husband of an alcoholic, he *can't*. (Half the women in the audience, I would bet, wouldn't mind being insulted in the same way.) A great deal is made of this, as if his competence as a husband, and his pleasure in his competence, were a serious moral failing—and a serious dramatic issue, too. Garcia, brimming eyes filled with rage, is thoroughly curbed; then his Michael is dragged shamefaced into Al-Anon, a group for people close to alcoholics. The movie's drabness becomes almost punitive.

When a Man Loves a Woman turns into an earnest and highly prolonged counseling appointment. Since it's a detailed piece of work, it will doubtless enjoy a long run at training sessions for psychiatric social workers. But it collapses as art. *The Lost Weekend*, not a nice movie, suggested something of the moral and emotional landscape of the drunkard. But this movie could have been made by the managerially ambitious people who run dry-out clinics. The filmmakers have got us where they want us—in therapy, "hopefully" learning about partnering and parenting.

NEW YORK POST, 4/29/94, p. 43, Michael Medved

In movies, as in life, it's far easier to set up problems than to solve them.

"When a Man Loves a Woman," for example, does a good job getting its two main characters into trouble—showing a romantic San Francisco couple (Meg Ryan and Andy Garcia) whose picture-perfect yuppie marriage is tragically shattered by her chronic alcoholism.

When they finally confront the crisis, however, the movie falters badly, degenerating into a soporific second half full of painfully unpersuasive California psycho-babble. ("Now, thanks to this program, I not only have my own feelings, but I have feelings about my feelings," one recovering alcoholic typically announces at an Al Anon meeting.)

By the end of the picture, both Ryan and Garcia seem far less sympathetic than they did during earlier stages; they not only wear out one another with their self-pitying, accusatory talk, but also exhaust the patience of the moviegoer.

The actors do their best with this difficult material. Ryan in contrast to all her pleasant, endearing romantic-comedy roles, lends a suitably desperate, dangerous edge to her part as a high school guidance counselor and loving mother who is secretly guzzling a quart of vodka each day—though no one ever explains how she remains so consistently glamorous and athletically slim in spite of this prodigious consumption.

Garcia always seems to bring an obtuse, inscrutable quality to characters, but here it fits his part precisely: he's supposed to be a self-assured airline pilot who's so determined to play the perfect, all-forgiving husband that he inadvertently adds to his wife's problems.

The kids who play their adorable daughters (Mae Whitman and Tina Majorino) are both deeply affecting, and their reactions to their mother's horrifying behavior provide the movie with its most wrenching moments.

Despite the silly, irrelevant title and an even sillier, more irrelevant tacked-on ending, "When a Man Loves a Woman" does little to soften its grim messages with sentiment.

The problem is that all the well-intentioned seriousness becomes monochromatically somber, thanks in part to the moody, autumnal Rembrandt lighting that director Luis Mandoki ("Gaby—A True Story," "White Palace") uses for nearly all his big scenes.

For a script co-written by the hilarious Al Franken of "Saturday Night Live" (who also plays a small part in the film) "When a Man Loves a Woman" is shockingly devoid of even the smallest touches of passing humor.

The screenplay, which also enlisted the formidable talents of Ron ("Rain Man" "Joy Luck Club") Bass concentrates on the insights of the celebrated "12-Step Program," but altogether ignores one of that program's most essential elements: the belief in a higher power that can help us regain control of our lives.

Some reference to the redemptive impact of faith would have been realistic in the situation the movie describes, providing some badly needed hope or solace amid all the bleak, unfocused chatter that makes this picture feel like an especially exhausting and unproductive group therapy session.

NEWSDAY, 4/29/94, Part II/p. B3, Jack Mathews

The key to succeeding with any drama about alcoholism is making audiences empathize enough with the characters involved to have a stake in the outcome of their struggle. Otherwise, you'd stand to gain as much from an hour listening to reformed alcoholics tour their private hells on "Oprah."

Luis Mandoki's "When a Man Loves a Woman" does draw us in, but just barely, and thanks more to the superb chemistry between stars Andy Garcia and Meg Ryan than the very ordinary script by Oscar winner Ron Bass ("Rain Man") and "Saturday Night Live" veteran Al Franken.

On the surface, "When a Man Loves a Woman" looks like a partial replay of Blake Edwards' "Days of Wine and Roses" which along with Billy Wilder's "The Lost Weekend," are the defining movie dramas on alcohol abuse. It's the story of a yuppie couple—Michael is an airline pilot, Alice is a school counselor—whose social drinking ends in an alcoholic nightmare.

Where "Days of Wine and Roses" led to both partners' dependence, it is only Ryan's Alice Green left holding the bottle in "When a Man Loves a Woman." Holding bottles, stashing them, emptying them with ferocious regularity, and damning the missed appointments, hangovers and other consequences that follow.

Vodka is Alice's poison of choice, but a few beers will tide her over, and not until she nearly drowns in a drunken stupor, then terrifies her young daughter by passing out and falling through a glass shower door, does she begin to try to reclaim her life.

The details of Alice's alcoholism and attempted recovery seem very knowing, but there is nothing particularly new or unusual about her experience. She goes through detox, joins Alcoholics Anonymous, and, in looking for the emotional causes beneath her addiction, discovers feelings of anger and bitterness far more threatening to her marriage than her previous drinking.

In the cold light of her sobriety, she realizes that behavior Michael regarded as devotion, she experienced as condescending and controlling. To his dismay, he learns that his idea of support was no support at all.

Bass and Franken don't make a very good case against Michael, but the burden of recovery shifts to him anyway. Before he can win back Alice, he must go through his own form of detox, and rid himself of those debilitating attitudes.

"When a Man Loves a Woman" begins and ends in rank movie clichés, and peppers the midsection with a bunch more. But the performances of Ryan and Garcia, and of the amazing 9-year-old Tina Majorino, as Alice's daughter from an earlier marriage, keep the story grounded in some semblance of reality. While delivering Alice's six-months-of-sobriety speech at an AA meeting, Ryan does what may be the best five minutes of acting in her career.

The film's real strength, however, is that intangible quality we call screen chemistry. When Garcia and Ryan were cast as lovers, it felt right, even before we knew the subject, and it feels right watching. There is a spark between the stars that ignites their scenes together, and though

Mandoki ("Born Yesterday") waits until the worst possible moment to show them in a lip-smashing close-up, they're a movie match we'd like to see made again soon.

Perhaps in something non-alcoholic.

SIGHT AND SOUND, 9/94, p. 50, Woody Haut

Michael and Alice Green are a happily married middle-class couple with two young children and a spacious house in San Francisco. But Alice's drinking problem, hitherto a secret, reaches critical proportions when, while Michael is away, she arrives home drunk, hits her daughter and passes out. In a clinic to dry out, Alice must reassess her life. Meanwhile, at home, Michael copes as best he can.

Visiting her at the clinic, Michael feels excluded when he sees Alice with her new friends. When she returns home, she is a different person—sober, critical and irritable. Finding Alice and Gary—a friend from the clinic—talking in the sitting room, Michael storms upstairs. Alice insists there is nothing romantic going on, and asks Michael to see a counsellor with her. The counsellor recommends he attend A.A. meetings for partners of alcoholics. Unable to cope with Alice, he moves out. When their paths cross, Alice tells Michael she would like him to attend her speech at A.A. celebrating six months of sobriety. He says he has been forced to take a job in Denver. They part amicably. After Alice gives her speech, accepting responsibility for her drinking, an apologetic Michael appears.

With sledgehammer subtlety, Luis Mandoki's film explores the effect of alcoholism on the family, and is noteworthy for casting Meg Ryan as an alcoholic—an interesting deviation from her usual flighty wholesomeness. Andy Garcia too is convincing as her manipulative and personable husband. Together, though, Alice and Michael, with no friends, have some questionable tendencies regarding public display. This is apparent from the film's first scene, in which a stranger chats up Alice in a crowded bar, only to be interrupted by Michael, who pretends to make a play for her. Soon Alice, with everyone watching, is straddling and passionately kissing her husband. In the final scene, the couple, speaking in the third person, parody themselves as observed phenomena. Says Michael to Alice, and to anyone else in earshot, "He tried everything except really listening." This time they kiss in a more wholesome setting.

It is not the acting that makes this film so abysmal, nor the script, which manages to avoid embarrassment at its own pretensions. This is probably due to the expertise of Ronald Bass (*The Joy Luck Club, Black Widow, Rain Man*) or perhaps the contribution of *Saturday Night Live* satirist Al Franken. The problem lies, rather, with the direction, with its lugubrious atmospherics. Aided by cinematographer Lajos Koltai, director Luis Mandoki, previously responsible for *White Palace* and *Born Yesterday*, has made something that—apart from some unnecessary jump-cuts denoting life-fissures rather than shifts in time or space—is barely distinguishable from an episode of *Thirtysomething*. That series, however, would never have wasted the talents of Ellen Burstyn who, as Alice's mother, is on screen for all of two minutes.

Ever since *Ordinary People*, exploiting the dysfunctions of modern middle-class family life has been a lucrative subject, its popularity corresponding to the rise of Reaganism, now repackaged as Clinton-style family values and 'tough love'. With its theme of alcoholism, *When a Man Loves a Woman* also belongs to a genre that includes *Lost Weekend, Under the Volcano, Barfly* and the work of John Cassavetes, but strives unconvincingly for realism. Nevertheless, the film has some nice touches, the most memorable of them occurring when, early in the morning, the alarm on the neighbour's Porsche goes off: Alice, in her nightgown, grabs some eggs, runs out and throws them at the car. It's a therapeutic moment, a yuppie equivalent of Charles Bronson's crusade against inner-city muggers.

Exploiting its audience and subject matter, Mandoki's film, in an era of homelessness and Aids, amounts to little more than emotional pornography. Yet the production team insists on selling the film with the usual psycho-babble. Says producer Jordan Kerner, "Family in the 90s is really about the taking of responsibility for each other." Bass is more propagandistic, claiming, "After seeing this film, audiences will want to work harder on their marriage and their parenting." So much for those not conforming to type. With family values the last refuge of scoundrels, and the line between nuclear-family love and oppression looking exceedingly thin, Michael tells Alice, "I won't let you leave me, I won't let you leave this family, I won't let you destroy yourself."

The film's free-market morality rankles, and it's too bad that Alice doesn't run off with her A.A. friends, particularly the ex-armed robber who Michael assumed to be a child molester. It's yet another film that exploits symptoms rather than causes.

TIME, 5/16/94, p. 81, Richard Schickel

Take your choice—tragedy or a 12-step program. The path to either of the only two possible endings for a story about alcoholism is, dramatically, entirely predictable. So when Alice Green's social drinking starts turning into antisocial behavior in *When a Man Loves a Woman*, you have an awful feeling that you've been down this slippery slope before.

The skid marks left by dozens of previous books, movies and teleplays show the terrain: innocent children imperiled by drunken carelessness; a steadfast spouse trying to understand and cope; an alarming incident that brings the victim to the edge of self-destruction—and self-awareness; the decision to seek professional help; the terrors of detox; the fragile return to sobriety and the recriminatory rebalancing of power in a damaged family; and finally the tearful public confession, carrying with it an implicit promise of a responsible future, which offers audiences a reassuring sense that they have once again witnessed a triumph of the human spirit.

When a Man Loves a Woman doesn't miss any of these beats, yet director Luis Mandoki fails to make them resonate. Perhaps the title, which could as easily identify a romantic comedy, tells us something: this movie, written by Ronald Bass and Al Franken, doesn't want to harrow; it wants to ingratiate. As Alice, Meg Ryan never lets drink ravage her; even her hangovers are perky. As her husband, Andy Garcia is unfailingly, rather boringly, stalwart, Well, this is the '90s, when weekends aren't allowed to be lost, only politely postponed.

Also reviewed in:
CHICAGO TRIBUNE, 5/6/94, Friday/p. C, Michael Wilmington
NEW YORK TIMES, 4/29/94, p. C1, Janet Maslin
VARIETY, 4/25-5/1/94, p. 29, Leonard Klady
WASHINGTON POST, 5/13/94, p. D6, Rita Kempley
WASHINGTON POST, 5/13/94, Weekend/p. 48, Joe Brown

WHERE THE RIVERS FLOW NORTH

A Caledonia Pictures release. *Producer:* Bess O'Brien and Jay Craven. *Director:* Jay Craven. *Screenplay:* Don Bredes and Jay Craven. *Based on a novel by:* Howard Frank Mosher. *Director of Photography:* Paul Ryan. *Editor:* Barbara Tulliver. *Music:* The Horse Flies. *Production Designer:* David Wasco. *Set Decorator:* Sandy Wasco. *Costumes:* Stephanie Kerley. *Running time:* 104 minutes. *MPAA Rating:* Not Rated.

CAST: Rip Torn (Noel Lord); Tantoo Cardinal (Bangor); Bill Raymond (Wayne Quinn); Michael J. Fox (Clayton Farnsworth); John Griesemer (Henry Coville); Mark Margolis (New York Money); Dennis Mientka (Sheriff); Sam Lloyd (Judge); Rusty Dewies (The Champ); Treat Williams (Champ's Manager).

LOS ANGELES TIMES, 12/7/94, Calendar/p. 4, Kevin Thomas

"Where the Rivers Flow North" affords Rip Torn with one of the best roles of his screen career and Native Canadian actress Tantoo Cardinal an equally fine opportunity to shine in this modest, beautiful, deeply felt film about a strong man who finally cannot bring himself to accept the inevitability of change.

In director Jay Craven and his co-writer Don Bredes' skillful adaptation of Howard Frank Mosher's novel, Torn plays Noel Lord, a long-haired, aging logger living with a hearty, middle-aged Native American called Bangor (Cardinal) in the gorgeous Vermont wilderness. Lord has a lifetime lease on this land, where his ancestors are buried.

That's not about to stop a company (headed by a forceful Michael J. Fox) already well under way in constructing a $30-million dam that will leave Lord's property under 50 feet of water. True to its period, the film wisely steers clear of highly contemporary environmental issues.

The dam builders may be tough, but they're not presented as truly evil; the dam will contribute enormously to the regional economy as a source of hydroelectric power. Although Lord is mule-stubborn, "Where the Rivers Flow North," which is set in 1927, refreshingly does not evolve into a predictable David vs. Goliath struggle. The conflict is instead really within Lord himself.

More sensible and realistic than Lord, Bangor argues for accepting a buyout, for she acknowledges that even without the prospect of the dam, their way of life is becoming increasingly less tenable. But Lord is caught up totally in trying to outfox his adversaries.

This film may well represent Torn's best work since the similarly rural "Heartland" and "Payday," in which he so unforgettably played a doomed country star based on Hank Williams. Torn's specialty is playing colorful, sometimes backwoodsy eccentrics, and at times he tends to go over the top. (One wag said that the best thing about "The Beans of Egypt, Maine" was that Torn wasn't in it!)

That's what makes his rigorously understated playing of the taciturn Lord all the more impressive and gratifying; clearly, Torn respected his role, and it shows Cardinal more than holds her own with Torn, and has such a vibrant presence that she easily offsets the tendency toward quaintness in her Pidgin English dialogue.

"Where the Rivers Flow North," which in its concluding sequence could wind up a bit faster, is primarily but not exclusively a, two-character drama (set off with earthy humor). Treat Williams cameos deftly as a carnival fight promoter, and Bill Raymond elicits sympathy as the dam company representative who has the thankless task of trying to negotiate with Lord.

The film is an evocative, painstaking period piece enhanced stunningly by a spare, pulsating score by the Horse Flies with Ben Wittman. Since "Where the Rivers Flow North" so successfully transports us to the past, it is truly lamentable that three sequences are marred by the presence of an illusion-destroying overhead mike dangling over the actors' heads. To offset this, projectionists would have to keep a constant eye on the screen and try to adjust the image accordingly.

NEW YORK POST, 3/4/94, p. 34, Larry Worth

Rip torn is a fine character actor who remains underrated. so it's unfortunate that his best vehicle in years—"Where the Rivers Flow North"—could get hyped as the new Michael J. Fox movie.

Granted, Fox's participation in a supporting role may lend a commercial draw to this small, art-house production. But the former sitcom star surfaces as a weak link in an otherwise compelling drama.

The story line is a variation on the old chestnut about big business squeezing the last drop of blood from the little guy. Not that Noel Lord (Torn) seems like a little guy with his hulking frame, shoulder-length hair and metal claw cutting a mean figure along the untamed frontiers of Vermont's timberland in 1927.

Lord and his Native American housekeeper, Bangor, dig in their boots as plans for the region's first hydro-electric dam threaten their rustic existence. Equally obstinate, the ruthless Power Company head (Fox) won't abide two rebels impeding the steamroller of progress.

However, director/co-writer Jay Craven wisely emphasizes the plot's other battle: verbal fireworks between Lord and Bangor. The golden agers' unusual intimacy may be peppered with insults, but their gazes speak volumes on a deep-seated love. It's a union equally colored by poignance and humor.

Craven and cohort Don Bredes' script showcases a knack for unpredictable dialogue, with much of Bangor's penned in third person. But Torn and Cardinal's oil-and-vinegar chemistry is what makes the coupling so memorable. His stubborn ways are perfectly offset by her childlike manners.

Cameos from Treat Williams and Amy Wright prove unexpected highlights. Ditto for an offbeat score, sun-filtered camerawork and the Green Mountain State's untapped beauty.

Sadly, Craven's leisurely paced narrative boomerangs in the final 15 minutes. Edited after its inclusion in 1993's Boston Film Festival, the cuts lead to a needlessly choppy finale.

But that's a small drawback. More than enough assets remain to warrant an immediate excursion to "Where the Rivers Flow North."

NEWSDAY, 3/4/94, Part II/p. 80, John Anderson

A Western set in northern Vermont, "Where the Rivers Flow North" moves confidently and slowly, like water rising, until you're up to you chin and don't want to escape.

In this debut feature by documentary-maker Jay Craven—a small film that managed to attract sizable names like Michael J. Fox and Treat Williams—Noel Lord (Rip Torn) is a logger who works an already marshy Vermont tract destined for total submersion. When the nearby hydroelectric dam is complete, the land that Lord and his family have lived on for generations will be under 50 feet of water. Lord, of course, resists both the entreaties and cash of power-company flunky Wayne Quinn (Bill Raymond), and Craven seems to be setting us up for a classic enemy-of-the-people scenario.

But Lord isn't that simple, nor is this film, which was shot in the Northeast Kingdom region of Vermont and uses its harsh, cold terrain to great effect, Lord has a plan; that he doesn't quite confide it to his woman companion Bangor (Tantoo Cardinal) says much about their relationship, which is somewhere between marriage and an employment opportunity. Lord knows he's got to go, that he can't stop the dam, but he's going to get as much as he can out of Quinn, and his boss Clayton Farnsworth (Fox), who are desperate to keep to their construction schedule.

"Where the Rivers Flow North" flows at its own pace, and with great confidence. Like Lord, Craven feels no compunction to follow any beat but his own, even if the story seems to take a bit of time to find its rhythm. It does, though, during a carnival sequence where the hook-handed Lord challenges and defeats the carnie fighter who takes on all comers. Bolstered by the infectious old-timey, Celtic-inflected music of the Horseflies, both the movie and Lord's plan crystallize, even if the odds of the gray-maned, cruel Lord defeating The Champ (Rusty Dewees) seem rather preposterous.

Torn is at his best, imbuing Lord with a wry fatalism that preshadows his doomed efforts to escape the modern world. Cardinal, who had pivotal roles in "Dances With Wolves" and "Black Robe" (and a mercifully small one as the title character in Sam Shepard's "Silent Tongue") is the perfect condiment to Torn's sinewy old logger. A bit touched by the sun, her Bangor is a gap-toothed eccentric who believes Lord when he tells her Quinn is Calvin Coolidge, and who is occasionally incomprehensible: Her speech, a combination of Irish, Native American and Down East inflections, is the most peculiar amalgamation since Robert Shaw in "The Sting." But Bangor is as moving as progress.

VILLAGE VOICE, 3/8/94, p. 60, Devon Jackson

Well, since so many critics (the men especially) have been prodding people to go see a misogynistic piece of crap like *Blink*—"See it for Madeleine Stowe!" they slather—I say, instead, go support a flawed but treasurable little first-time indie that features an equally spirited performance of a far more complex female character—courtesy of the transcendent Tantoo Cardinal.

Set in the backwoods of Vermont in 1927, *Rivers* has the atmosphere and sumptuous look of John Sayles's *Matewan* and a plot that plays like a classic '60s western: as Bangor, Cardinal invigorates the seemingly subordinate role of Native American helpmate and companion to Rip Torn's Noel Lord, a crotchety old log driver intent on not having his way of life decimated by the encroaching Power Company with their plans to despoil the region with its first hydroelectric dam. It's a gentle movie about rough-hewn characters (Bangor lost a tooth somewhere in life, and Lord, a hand) who aren't entirely out of sync with the philosophies of multi-culturalism and Iron John.

Yeah, it's sorta predictable (Lord gives in to the Company but before you expect him to), and yes, it's a bit improbable (Lord wins a fistfight while chained to his opponent), but Cardinal and Torn bring so much to their roles (unlike the miscast Michael J. Fox and Treat Williams, part-time Vermonters who were doing the director a favor) and have such good chemistry that they give the film the momentum it needs. And if director Jay Craven had spent less money on the too-perfect costumes and paid a bit more attention to storytelling (the montage of Lord and Bangor cutting down 100 pines doesn't quite work), it might've been tighter, more effective. But he did bring in a great cinematographer (Paul Ryan), and he had the wisdom to end the film on a beautiful shot of Cardinal all alone at the picture show, munching on a candy cane, crying. See this film for Tantoo Cardinal!

Also reviewed in:
NEW YORK TIMES, 3/4/94, p. C15, Caryn James
VARIETY, 6/14/93, p. 57, Leonard Klady
WASHINGTON POST, 5/6/94, p. B7, Desson Howe
WASHINGTON POST, 5/6/94, Weekend/p. 47, Joe Brown

WHITE

A Miramax Films release of a MK2 Productions SA (Paris)/France 3 Cinema (Paris)/Cab Productions SA (Lausanne)/TOR Production (Warsaw) with the participation of Canal+. *Executive Producer:* Yvon Crenn. *Producer:* Marin Karmitz. *Director:* Krzysztof Kieslowski. *Screenplay (Polish and French with English subtitles):* Krzysztof Piesiewicz and Krzysztof Kieslowski. *Director of Photography:* Edward Klosinski. *Editor:* Urszula Lesiak. *Music:* Zbigniew Preisner. *Sound:* Jean-Claude Laureux and (music) William Flageollet. *Sound Editor:* Piotr Zawadzki, Jean-Claude Laureux and Francine Lemaître. *Casting:* Margot Capelier and Teresa Violetta Buhl. *Set Designer:* Halina Dobrawolska and Claude Lenoir. *Set Decorator:* Magdalena Dipont. *Set Dresser:* Tomasz Kowalski, Dariusz Lipiński, Henryk Puchalski, Michel Charvaz, Julien Poitou-Weber, Jean-Pierre Delettre, Christian Aubenque, and Lionel Acat. *Costumes:* Elzbieta Radke, Teresa Wardzała, Jolanta Łuczak, and Virginie Viard. *Make-up:* Jolanta Pruszynska, Jadwiga Cichocka, and Jean-Pierre Caminade. *Running time:* 92 minutes. *MPAA Rating:* R.

CAST: Zbigniew Zamachowski (Karol Karol); Julie Delpy (Dominique); Janusz Gajos (Mikolaj); Jerzy Stuhr (Jurek); Grzegorz Warchol (Elegant Man); Jerzy Nowak (Peasant); Aleksander Bardini (Notary); Cezary Harasimowicz (Inspector); Jerzy Trela (Monsieur Bronek); Cezary Pazura (Owner of the Exchange Office); Michel Lisowski (Interpreter); Piotr Machalica (Tall Man); Barbara Dziekan (Cashier); Marzena Trybala (Mariott's Employee); Philippe Morier Genoud (Judge); Francis Coffinet (Bank's Employee); Yannick Evely (Subway's Employee); Jacques Disses (Dominique's Lawyer); Teresa Budzisz-Krzyzanowska (Madame Jadwiga).

FILMS IN REVIEW, 7-8/94, p. 54, Andy Pawelczak

Karol, the hairdresser hero of *White*, smuggles himself from Paris to Poland in a suitcase which is stolen by a gang of airport thieves before he can disembark. When the thieves discover the suitcase contains a man instead of booty, they beat him up and throw him on a garbage dump. Karol looks around the dump and sighs, "Jesus, home at last."

Cut to a bloodied Karol staggering down the street to the hairdressing salon which he owns with his brother. When Karol comments on the woebegone salon's incongruous new neon sign, his brother says, "This is Europe now."

As part of an outlandish plot, Karol needs a dead body. An employee says, "We'll buy one, You can buy anything today. Would you mind a Russian import, boss?"

This is contemporary, neo-capitalist Poland through the wry, off-center lens of Krzyztof Kieslowski, who both wrote and directed *White*. By now, every critic from Hong Kong to Los Angeles, the long way around, has said that *White* is a black comedy. And indeed it is, in addition to being a ninety minute long Polish joke and the work of an authentically individual filmmaker smitten by Chaplin and the French New Wave. *White* is the second part of a trilogy that began with *Blue* and ends with *Red*, a film that received great acclaim at Cannes this year. (I'll abstain from writing about the connections between the films until *Red* opens here later this year.) The films are named after the colors of the French flag, with blue representing liberty, white equality and red fraternity. In a recent interview in *Sight And Sound* Kieslowski, in characteristically laconic fashion, said that in the case of *White* the thematic connection is extremely loose—its hero wants to be better than everyone else rather than equal.

When we first see Karol (Zbigniew Zamachowski)—Kieslowski named him after Charlie Chaplin—he's on his way into an august French courthouse for his divorce hearing, when a pigeon defecates on him. Such is Karol's life—in his down-at-the-heels shoes and shabby East European coat, he's one of the put upon little guys of the earth, lurching from one misadventure to another. He doesn't want a divorce from his beautiful French wife, but she's implacable as she tells the court the marriage was never consummated. Karol objects that when they first met in Poland he gave his wife pleasure, but since their marriage and residence in Paris he has been unable to perform his conjugal duties. Of course, he loses, and before he's even outside the precincts of the courthouse his now ex-wife unceremoniously dumps his suitcase and waves goodbye.

That battered suitcase is destined to become a symbol of all the woes of East European life as the homeless Karol drags it around the streets of Paris, and eventually stations himself in the Metro to beg by playing a lugubrious Polish song on a comb wrapped in tissue paper. Here he meets a fellow Pole, Mikolaj (Janusz Gajos), a melancholy tournament bridge player who offers to help Karol get back to Poland if he agrees to murder a man who wants to die. The Metro scenes are among the best in the picture with their deadpan, Beckett-like sense of comic dereliction as the two men get drunk together and Karol does Mikolaj's hair. When a pigeon lands on them, it's simultaneously the most ordinary of events and a mysterious harbinger of perhaps better things to come.

Once Karol is back in Poland, things do get better. He gets a job as bodyguard to a black marketeer and soon, through some adroit double dealing, becomes a wealthy entrepreneur himself, complete with a chauffeured burgundy Volvo and an office equipped with two fax machines. None of these improbable events seriously stretches credibility—in the film's anarchic, greed intoxicated Poland, everything seems possible. The rest of the film is about Karol's bizarre plot to entice his ex-wife to Poland and includes a reprise of that symbolic suitcase, this time in the form of a coffin that plays an important part in Karol's plan and in the film's death/rebirth thematic design.

Despite Kieslowski's bracingly sardonic, bummed out view of things, his mise-en-scène is exuberantly colorful and alive. And in Zbigniew Zamachowski he has the perfect match for his absurdist sensibility. In the course of the film, Karol goes from soulful Chaplinesque tramp to East European parvenu with slicked back hair and faintly predatory eyes. Part of the magic of Zamachowski's performance is in the way he physically inhabits each successive persona; in one particularly nice scene, we watch as Karol subtly adjusts his posture to fit his idea of a gun toting tough guy.

White's major flaw is an enigmatic ending that detracts from the emotional resonance of the film's closing moments. The great filmmakers have always known that the mystery of the human face is the most moving and profound cinematic spectacle, and Kieslowski knows this too; but his final shots feel like willful mystification rather than a summoning of genuine mystery. But that's a small reservation about a smart, witty, consistently engrossing film. Kieslowski might not be the Great White Hope of cinema—particularly since he just announced his retirement from filmmaking—but he's certainly one of the most interesting directors on the current scene.

LOS ANGELES TIMES, 6/17/94, Calendar/p. 15, Kevin Thomas

As in the monumental "The Decalogue," in which Polish director Krzysztof Kieslowski probed the relevance of the Ten Commandments in modern life, Kieslowski has been considering the contemporary meaning of the French Revolution slogan "Liberty, Equality and Fraternity" in his provocative ongoing "Three Colors" trilogy, which began with "Blue."

His second installment, "White," a darkly whimsical cautionary take on the dangerous distortions of the notion of equality, begins in Paris but is set primarily in Warsaw, which allows Kieslowski to revel in warm, wry Eastern European absurdist humor while considering the moral chaos of his post-communist country.

The film opens with a wistful, unprepossessing-looking young man named Karol Karol (Zbigniew Zamachowski) apprehensively approaching one of Paris' grand and imposing government buildings. Trying for an optimistic attitude, the poor guy is dumped on by a pigeon, a harbinger of far worse to come.

In a dizzyingly swift sequence, his beautiful but awesomely cruel French wife Dominique (Julie Delpy) of six months divorces him, closes their joint account and even devises a way of making him wanted by the police. Although they had been lovers prior to tying the knot, Karol has been unable to consummate the marriage. (Delpy can be glimpsed in "Blue," "Blue's" Juliette Binoche in "White.")

Karol is reduced to playing his comb as a harmonica, hoping that passersby in a Metro station will toss him coins. He encounters Mikolaj (Janusz Gajos), a fellow countryman, who offers to get him back to his native Warsaw—with strings attached. This journey, too inspired and funny to reveal here, further brutalizes and humiliates Karol to the extent that he is ripe for exploiting ruthlessly the new anything-goes Polish society and economy.

Not content to resume working at the beauty salon his sweetly solicitous brother (Jerzy Stuhr) has been running single-handedly in his absence, he soon becomes a tycoon. But when he at last risks a call to Dominique, her response inspires in him a course of action at once drastic and stunningly ironic.

The tribulations of Karol allow Kieslowski not only to comment on the current state of Poland but also on the exceedingly perverse twists and turns that love can take, especially when couples get carried away in playing games with consequences that spin out of their control. There's lots of plot in "White," but it is the work of a master of the visual; here Kieslowski has a strong assist from the precise yet buoyant camerawork of Edward Klosinski, who shot his monumental "Decalogue."

Kieslowski is generous in his praise of his longtime colleagues who serve him so well, co-writer Krzysztof Piesiewicz and composer Zbigniew Preisner, who this time has come up with a mournful yet jaunty tango to accompany Karol on his destiny. There's lightness in the performances of the film's principals despite the convolutions of their roles, and a lightness in this most rueful of comedies.

NEW YORK POST, 6/10/94, p. 42, Thelma Adams

Things that are "White": A bridal veil.

Winter.

An alabaster-skinned blonde.

Like a poet, Krzysztof Kieslowski works these images into his latest film, a charming, highly original variation on the theme of equality.

"White" follows "Blue" in the Polish director's groundbreaking tri-color trilogy, in which he uses the French motto "Liberty, Equality, Fraternity" as a jumping-off point for a meditation on the new Europe that is more personal than political.

While "Blue" told the somber story of a young widow (Juliette Binoche) who liberated herself from grief, irony dominates "White." "Blue" was rooted in tragedy; "White" is a black comedy.

(Fraternity is left to the coming "Red," shown to critical acclaim at the Cannes Film Festival last month and expected to open here this fall.)

The movies overlap, but you don't need to have seen "Blue" to enjoy "White."

French model Dominique (Julie Delpy) is about to clean out her husband, a successful Polish hairdresser, Karol Karol (Zbigniew Zamachowski).

The love between Karol and Dominique is defined by inequality. They divorce because Karol loves Dominique, but she doesn't reciprocate. Karol's attempt to redress that imbalance fuels the plot.

Karol—penniless, single, robbed of business, home, car, and dignity—returns to Warsaw, literally and ironically, in a box. When the box reaches Poland, it is hijacked to a dump. The thieves, disappointed to find a bum rather than booty, thrash Karol. "Home at last," he says, hitting rock bottom.

Before long, Karol has shown a shrewdness not initially apparent. The hairdresser builds himself back up, only to set an elaborate trap for Dominique. He settles the score, but equality remains elusive.

Karol Karol (literally Charlie Charlie) is an homage to Charlie Chaplin but not an impersonation. A pale-faced, gentle, shoulder shrug of a man Zamachowski creates an inconspicuous hero. The Polish actor delivers a refreshingly comic performance of great warmth and hidden strength.

The ethereal beauty Julie ("Europa Europa") Delpy plays Karol's wife as a fierce little minx. She might look like a marble angel, but she has used her beauty to tip the scales of love in her favor—without experiencing the feeling of love herself.

In the script, there's an inequality of character development. While Zamachowski steals scene after scene, more could have been made of the seductive Delpy, whose incendiary power is shown in a short scene when she commits arson. Credit Kieslowski: He has a great eye for actors and coaxes unexpected performances from his cast.

NEWSDAY, 6/10/94, Part II/p. B7, John Anderson

White as a void—a colorless field of infinite possibility and ultimate *égalité*—is the significant and dominant hue of Krzysztof Kieslowski's "White," which follows "Blue" (*liberté*) and precedes "Red" (*fraternité*) in the Polish director's "Three Colors" trilogy.

That Kieslowski's series will become one of the landmark film events of the '90s seems likely. Although "White" betrays a workmanlike quality in its construction that was missing from "Blue," which was released in New York last December, Kieslowski's films (which include the ambitious and largely unseen "Decalogue") marry politics, religion, art and commerce with such balance, control and sense of the absurd that he's not just among Europe's most important filmmakers, but its artistic conscience as well.

His perversity, too, seems custom cut for the era. In "Blue" he used a woman who'd lost her husband and child to test the limits of personal liberty; in "White," he makes equality as crippling as totalitarianism.

But if "Blue" was a dirge, "White" is Fellini music played on a cello; bittersweet, low-slung, with Zbigniew Zamachowski as an eastern bloc Chaplin named Karol Karol (Charlie Charlie in Polish), a bemused expatriated hairdresser in Paris whose French wife is suing him for divorce. It's just the beginning of Karol's misfortunes; that he's caught unaware by each one means only that he has—through either wisdom or stupidity—failed to resign himself to misfortune.

And beginning with the large French bird dropping that anoints him en route to divorce court—a white drip augured by the sound of pigeons—Karol is a compost heap of post-Wall anxiety. His wife, the beautiful Dominique (Julie Delpy), claims their marriage was never consummated. But when they first met back in Poland, Karol says, he functioned perfectly normally. Was it marriage or France that rendered him nonfunctional? Kieslowski winks.

Delpy, who has said that Kieslowski referred to her character as a "crazy cat," has Dominique wave goodbye to Karol with clawlike fingers, dropping his trunk in the court parking lot. Wounded and angry, she's frozen his bank accounts; the bank manager, a good capitalist, unceremoniously cuts his ATM card in two. Karol ends up on the street, where he watches an old man struggle to put a bottle in the trash—a reprise of an identical scene in "Blue" that featured an old woman and Juliet Binoche (who makes a fleeting appearance in Karol's courtroom). Finally, a victim of freedom, he takes to playing a comb and toilet paper in a station of the Metro.

It's here he meets the melancholy Mikolaj (Janusz Gajos), who recognizes the Polish song Karol plays and offers to help him go back to Poland, which he eventually does, hidden inside his trunk. It's one of Kieslowski's big jokes smuggling oneself back into Poland. The other's include Karol's success as an entrepreneur once he gets there—unscrupulous land speculation makes him rich—and the idea that you can buy *anything* today in Warsaw. Karol does: land, a gun, a corpse with which to feign his own death, and, oddly enough, love.

Kieslowski erects unifying, circular mechanisms for his characters and his themes: We hear the sound of pigeons, for instance, with all it implies, each time Karol is tortured by memories of Dominique—whom Kieslowski never forgets, even when Karol seems to. Only after she realizes she still loves Karol does the sound of the pigeons haunt her. Which doesn't mean he's won, or lost, or can escape himself, as evidenced by Kieslowski's ending, straight out of "City Lights," with a tearful Karol gazing at his now-untouchable love.

SIGHT AND SOUND, 6/94, p. 63, Philip Strick

Karol, a Polish hairdresser in Paris, is rendered impotent by the stresses of working in a foreign country where the language and the people are a mystery to him. His petulant French wife Dominique, exasperated at the non-consummation of their marriage after six months, obtains a divorce and burns down their hair-dressing salon. His credit cards invalidated, Karol resorts to begging on the Metro, where he is befriended by another Pole, Mikolaj, who is willing to help him get back to Poland. Karol hides in a trunk, which Mikolaj checks in as his luggage on a flight to Warsaw. On arrival, however, the trunk is stolen by airport thieves, and Karol finds himself beaten up on a rubbish dump.

Rebuilding his life, and determined to win back Dominique, Karol works at the salon of his brother Jurek and also lands a job as security guard at a Bureau de Change. Overhearing his employer's plans to buy a tract of real estate for guaranteed resale at enormous profit, Karol invests his own savings in the farmlands involved. He is also reunited with Mikolaj, whose story about a man willing to pay someone to assist at his suicide turns out to refer to himself. Karol stages an execution with blank ammunition: the scare brings Mikolaj to his senses but gratefully he pays up anyway. Karol accepts this as a loan and pronounces them partners. Achieving a ten-fold profit on the resale of the farmlands to his disgruntled employer, Karol is suddenly a wealthy man.

His fortunes improve rapidly and he is soon the head of an international trading company. He tries to get in touch with Dominique; she refuses to talk to him, but in a country where anything can be bought Karol is determined to rescue their relationship. Forewarning Mikolaj of his scheme, he buys a corpse and has it buried under his name; his entire wealth is bequeathed to Dominique.

She arrives from France for the funeral and to claim her inheritance, later finding Karol in her hotel room. She is overjoyed and he is no longer impotent. The morning after a night of ecstasy, Karol has disappeared and the police arrive. Unable to prove that he is still alive, Dominique is arrested on suspicion of collusion in her husband's murder. Destitute once more, Karol waves to her in her cell at police headquarters.

On the evidence so far, Kieslowski's meditations on tri-color have little to do with France. Nor does his colour-coding appear much more than arbitrary: in disappointing contrast to the first part of his current trilogy, where the use of blue provided a striking coherence, the glimpses of white in the second are linked only to a few blazes of marital bliss.

Of the conventional symbolism of whiteness—representing, among other things, innocence, fear, cowardice, impartiality or death—there is little trace. If *Three Colours: Blue* was full of elegant contrivance, *White* announces itself as broad comedy with a more raucous imagery, a different cameraman, and a cast that operates at a frantic volume. Pelted by a pigeon within moments of reaching the screen, its hero is clearly of the little-man-makes-good mould, favoured as much by Polish audiences over the years as by admirers of Norman Wisdom or Jerry Lewis.

That Kieslowski and comedy form an uncomfortable partnership, however, is quickly apparent. Among the many frustrations of *Three Colours: White* is the director's customary reluctance to explain his images. Increasingly fascinated by the effect that a special lens or a fragment of music can have on the simplest narrative, he has acquired a style of dramatic ambiguity, the reticence of the script offset by eloquent visuals.

At its most inventive, as with the mid-conversation blackouts in *Blue*, this tongue-tied expressionism can work formidably well. Elsewhere, it is damagingly trivial: the glimpse of Juliette Binoche wandering into the courtroom in *White* is a light-hearted nudge to those familiar with *Blue* (who will also, presumably, be expected to respond to the reappearance of a bottle bank) but has no relevance to Karol's predicament. Like the coincidences and asides in The *Decalogue*, extended into a fine art for *The Double Life of Véronique*, it is mere game-playing by Kieslowski and his co-writer Piesiewicz, who render each scene a puzzle by the wilful displacement of supporting information.

So much mystery is generated in this manner that *White* unfolds in a fog of imprecision. It's an excusable way to introduce us to characters with little confidence in themselves, and Kieslowski would surely argue that only in hindsight can events be given an accurate focus. But the main disadvantage of his method is exposed by the film's final sequence: we are given no guidance as to how long Dominique will be imprisoned, or how Karol is able to signal to her, or what they convey to each other. And while these details may be unimportant to the emotional limbo in which the couple now find themselves, we are at least entitled to know why Karol is weeping. Is it at the price he has paid for a masterstroke of revenge, or is he grief-stricken that wife and wealth continue to elude him, or is he just happy?

Clarification would be helpful in order to reinforce whatever it is that the director wants to tell us, either about the new Polish capitalism or as part of his proclaimed assessment of 'quality'. As a satire on today's Poland, *White* reveals opportunists at every turn, but fudges the issue when it comes to Karol's meteoric rise to riches, shown merely as a brisk montage of affluence so that the central plot can then resume.

As for egalitarianism, Kieslowski has disarmingly asserted that entrepreneurs in a free society seek to achieve better than the average; their objective is not equality but superiority, which Karol, once he has accomplished it, proceeds to throw away. Recalling that Kieslowski's analysis of 'liberty' in *Blue* similarly concluded with freedom being relinquished, his trilogy seemingly aims to prove that human nature habitually prefers the opposite to the values claimed by the French Revolution. In a relationship which—like Karol's odd obsession with the alabaster bust of a girl—is far too complex for words, the only final equality between the French girl and her Polish lover is that, in a sense, they both end up behind bars. Whether this far-from-comic predicament is really what Kieslowski intends us to accept, echoing the anguish but sadly nothing like the intensity of *Three Colours: Blue*, only the concluding colours of his study of 'fraternity' will confirm.

TIME, 6/27/94, p. 71, Richard Corliss

Love, the movies tell us, is a grand spur to achievement. But so is hatred. Give a fellow a good grudge and a thirst for revenge, and he will find his wits sharpened, his energy focused, his ambition liberated from the timid bonds of morality. On this kind of obsession, companies have been built and countries destroyed. It's surely a strong enough motivation for one devilishly clever Polish movie: Krzysztof Kieslowski's *Three Colors: White*.

Karol Karol (Zbigniew Zamachowski) and Dominique (Julie Delpy) are hairdressers. She's French and gorgeous; he's Polish and not. They marry; he moves to Paris to be with her; they open a salon. But suddenly he is impotent, and Dominique sues for divorce. When Karol tries to reconcile, she sets their salon on fire and tells the police he did it. He is reduced to begging in the Metro. Could life get worse? Oh, yes. As Karol watches her bedroom from the street, Dominique makes adulterous love and, when he calls, moans her infidelity into the phone. Before he can hang up, the phone company steals his last two francs. Karol tucks himself into his only suitcase and escapes France as airplane luggage. On arrival in Warsaw, his case is swiped by thieves who beat Karol when they find him inside. "Home at last;' he murmurs.

Home is a former Soviet satellite in its convulsive lurch toward capitalism. Anything is possible for a man with a dream and no scruples about realizing it. Karol plunges into the black market, into real estate and international finance; he comes this close to murder. And all in an elaborate scheme to lure Dominique to Poland for some sweet, fatal revenge.

White is the second episode in Kieslowski's *Blue-White-Red* trilogy analyzing liberty, equality and fraternity in modern Europe—but never mind, the film works fine on its own. The director, who earned world-class status in the mid-'80s with *The Decalogue* (a 10-part Polish TV series of modern fables, each illustrating one of the Commandments), is in an impish mood here. He finds hairpin turns and deadpan delight in the sexual and political intrigue devised by screenwriter Krzysztof Piesiewicz. And Zamachowski, who has some of Dustin Hoffman's molelike ingenuity, plays Karol Karol (Charlie Charlie in Polish) as a Chaplin figure hatching a Kafka plot.

At its heart, *White* is a Polish joke played on the French. For Kieslowski it can be seen as a declaration of both love and disdain for a foreign country and a language in which he works but which he does not quite understand. In *White* Karol could be Kieslowski: resourceful, isolated, powerless, homesick. And Dominique could be France:beautiful, haughty, unforgiving, irresistible. "After all she did," Karol says, " I still love her."

At the end, Karol still feels that way. Despite the betrayals it depicts, *White* is no essay in misogyny. It ends on a note of profound poignancy: two people gazing at each other through the prison bars of their impossible, inescapable love.

VILLAGE VOICE, 6/14/94, p. 52, Georgia Brown

The hard news in Cannes was Krzysztof Kieslowski's announcement that he was retiring from filmmaking. It lent urgency to the screening of *Red*, or *Rouge*, as I keep thinking of this final film in the *Trois Couleurs* trilogy. Naturally everyone asked why he was quitting and what he would do. He was tired, he said, "fed up with filmmaking" after shooting three features back-to-back—a *trois*-country marathon starting in September '92, ending just eight months later in May '93—and he just wanted to sit on a bench in the country. Which country, France or Poland? Poland, he snapped, as if to say, Why ask such a stupid question?

"To make film is not really a serious business" is another thing Kieslowski likes to throw out at those who obviously take cinema to heart. Tall, bent, almost gaunt, usually grim and glowering, this is not a charming public man. He specializes in squashing tender fans. And as I've noticed with other famously difficult "artistes," he occasionally opens up for some first-class assholes. But Kieslowski considers himself merely a practitioner, not an artist. "In filmmaking," he says, "we get maybe 35 per cent of what we want."

Sorry, but he is an artist, and whatever his temperament, Kieslowski has made a mark. Whereas his Polish masterpiece, *The Decalogue*, a 10-part series based on the Commandments, has never been released here (the woman who owns the rights is holding out for an exorbitant sum), his European co-pros—*The Double Life of Veronique* and now *Blue, White*, and *Red*—are, visually, aurally, and in terms of scope and" intent, superior to anything around.

White differs from the solemn *Blue* and the exquisite *Red* (due later this year) in being a black comedy and in taking place not in the bourgeois West but mostly in a freewheeling, broken-down Poland. My colleague J. Hoberman calls *White* a Polish joke.

One more timorous provincial come to Paris, Karol Karol (Zbigniew Zamachowski), a hairstylist from Warsaw, definitely seems out of his element. The first things Kieslowski shows us are Karol's bulky suitcase and his cheap, scuffed East bloc shoes. A few minutes into the film, the diminutive Karol (named after Charlie Chaplin, Kieslowski says) gets shat on by a passing Parisian pigeon. The milky liquid on his shoulder is a double insult since Karol is just on his way into divorce court, where his coolly beautiful French wife, Dominique (Julie Delphy), accuses him of not being able to consummate their marriage.

What worked fine in the East is kaput in the West. Could impotence be a sign of Polish rage at French affluence and hauteur? In no mood to analyze or commiserate, Dominique responds with a scorned woman's fury, confiscating the (white) car, the fancy shop, and all the money. Karol's bank and credit cards are duly shredded, and when he catches a night's sleep in what was "their" shop, Dominique sets fire to the curtains and sics the police on him. Another nasty divorce story.

His anatomical doodad may not function, but Karol has a trustier phallus—his little comb. Initially, he'd wooed Dominique with it—he met her while winning a hairdressing contest in Budapest—and now, down-and-out, he wraps the comb in toilet paper and serenades passersby in the Metro. "This is our last Sunday/Today we are leaving each other ... " go the Polish lyrics. He's kept company by a creamy alabaster bust of a milkmaid, a docile stand-in for Dominique.

"Your fly is open," remarks a fellow Pole who recognizes the song. A good angel, the melancholy, wise-eyed Mikolaj (Janusz Gajos), a tournament bridge player, invites Karol to drink with him on the platform. Come morning, Mikolaj agrees to smuggle the passportless Karol back into Poland inside the huge suitcase. Now, the rest of the movie begins.

Kieslowski and longtime co-writer, Krzysztof Piesiewicz, like to use visual signs—symbols, in the old New Critical sense—to make their points. Broken glass is one of their most resonant images, standing for shattered illusions, visitations from some ineffable power. In *White*, there's the comb and the box. The comb, having teeth, is the sign of Karol's dogged personality. The box (suitcase, coffin, jail cell) stands for confinement, and, paradoxically, liberation or rebirth. (There's also a tricky Warsaw telephone booth that Karol nearly gets stuck in.)

In the tricolor scheme, white corresponds to equality (blue to liberty and red to fraternity) and Karol is bent on getting even with Dominique. Getting even is not what the French—or October—revolutionaries may've had in mind when they set up the political ideal of equality, but it seemed uppermost in the minds that threw up the forest of guillotines. (Balancing equations seems to be what Kieslowski and Piesiewicz mean by doubling elements like funerals and false murders.)

Once *White* moves to Poland Karol runs the risk of losing his soul, but Kieslowski gains the services of great actors with distinctive, inhabited faces—many of them familiar from *The Decalogue* or the works of Wadja and Zanussi. The remarkable Jerzy Stuhr has a small part as Karol's meek brother.

As I remember, all 10 episodes of *The Decalogue* turn on the experience of loss—number nine dealing specifically with a husband's lost potency. In the tricolor films, loss sets off the story. The impassive heroine in *Blue* loses husband and child, and then loses the husband's love a second time to a mistress she didn't know he had—a pregnant mistress at that. She elects to break free (the subject is liberty) of her former life, but at the end discovers she has unfinished business to take care of. Set in motion by a lost dog, *Red* is about a man who nurses a loss over decades, until he learns, in another generation, to love again (fraternity). In *White*, faced with divorce and his wife's contempt (her apartment is situated next to an ad for Godard's *Le Mépris*), Karol conducts his lover's revenge.

About *White*'s cryptic final minutes—having to do with love and confinement and the terrible chasm between lovers—I sometimes think Kieslowski edits his material so stringently he loses his audience. This said, what is clear is that the final, glowing close-up of Karol's teary, melting grin is meant to recall the last frame of Chaplin's *City Lights*, when two imprisoned souls; their former fortunes reversed, have just found and lost each other once again.

Also reviewed in:
CHICAGO TRIBUNE, 6/17/94, Friday/p L, John Petrakis
NATION, 7/25-8/1/94, p. 137, Stuart Klawans
NEW REPUBLIC, 6/13/94, p. 32, Stanley Kauffmann
NEW YORK TIMES, 6/10/94, p. C23, Caryn James
NEW YORKER, 6/20/94, p. 88, Terrence Rafferty
VARIETY, 1/31-2/6/94, p. 68, Lisa Nesselson
WASHINGTON POST, 6/24/94, p. B7, Hal Hinson
WASHINGTON POST, 6/24/94, Weekend/p. 42, Desson Howe

WHITE FANG 2: MYTH OF THE WHITE WOLF

A Walt Disney Pictures release. *Producer:* Preston Fischer. *Director:* Ken Olin. *Screenplay:* David Fallon. *Director of Photography:* Hiro Narita. *Editor:* Elba Sanchez-Short. *Music:* John Debney. *Music Editor:* Tom Carlson and Jeff Charbonneau. *Sound:* Rob Young and (music) John Richards. *Sound Editor:* G. Michael Graham. *Casting:* Gail Levin. *Production Designer:* Cary White. *Art Director:* Glen W. Pearson. *Set Decorator:* Tedd Kuchera. *Set Dresser:* Macleod Sinclaire. *Special Effects:* William Orr. *Visual Effects:* Peter Montgomery. *Costumes:* Trish Keating. *Make-up:* Rosalina Da Silva. *Stunt Coordinator:* Betty Thomas, J.J. Makaro, and Danny Virtue. *Running time:* 105 minutes. *MPAA Rating:* PG.

CAST: Scott Bairstow (Henry Casey); Charmaine Craig (Lily Joseph); Al Harrington (Moses Joseph); Anthony Michael Ruivivar (Peter); Victoria Racimo (Katrin); Alfred Molina (Reverend Leland Drury); Paul Coeur (Adam John Hale); Geoffrey Lewis (Heath); Matthew Cowles (Halverson); Woodrow W. Morrison (Bad Dog); Reynold Russ (Leon); Nathan Young (One Ear); Charles Natkong Sr. (Sshaga-Holy Man); Edward Davis (Sshaga-Apprentice); Byron Chief Moon (Matthew); Tom Heaton (Miner #1); Trace Yeomans (Chief's Mother); Thomas Kitchkeesic (Native Boy).

LOS ANGELES TIMES, 4/15/94, Calendar/p. 6, Kevin Thomas

Although it is difficult to imagine anyone over the age of 10 getting caught up in "White Fang 2: Myth of the White Wolf," it just might connect with fifth and sixth graders. Parents would do well to consider dropping off their children at the theater and picking them up later rather than submit themselves to this less-than-riveting sequel of the 1991 success.

Ethan Hawke, star of the first film, appears at the beginning to sign off, writing to his pal Henry (Scott Bairstow) that he's going to stay in San Francisco to help rebuild the city after the 1906 earthquake. Thus Henry, up in the Alaskan wilderness, has become master to the noble White Fang, the half-dog, half-wolf super-canine. In no time the young man and the animal are caught up in their own adventure.

Native Americans of the Haida Tribe are facing starvation because inexplicably the caribou have vanished for two years. A Haida prophecy says that a wolf will lead them to the caribou, and when Henry miraculously survives a near-drowning, the Haida insist that the spirit of White Fang, whom they presume to have drowned, lives on in Henry. By the time White Fang pops up, no worse for wear, Henry, although understandably perplexed and decidedly uncertain how he can help the Haida, throws in his lot with them.

"White Fang 2" is politically correct with a vengeance that's stultifying. Director Ken Olin and writer David Fallon and their crew admirably go all out to re-create a Haida village authentically. But the actors playing the principal Haida—Charmaine Craig as a beautiful, demure Native American princess and Al Harrington as her wise chieftain uncle—are burdened with cliched characters.

With the exception of Henry, soon an adopted Haida, all the other whites are villains of the deepest dye, led by Alfred Molina's fake preacher and his sidekick Geoffrey Lewis.

Righting ancient wrongs against Native Americans on the screen has solid educational value for youngsters, but here it's been done too obviously and too heavy-handedly to engage adults. On the plus side Olin makes the most of the film's numerous action sequences. The scenery, photographed gleamingly by Hiro Narita, is gorgeous, and Henry, Craig's Lily and White Fang himself are appealing. "White Fang 2," however, really does need John Debney's thundering score, to keep its exceedingly simple story pumped up.

NEW YORK POST, 4/15/94, p. 39, Michael Medved

The main problem with "White Fang 2" isn't the silly plot, it's the sluggish pace. Debuting director Ken Olin (best known for playing the part of Michael on the TV series "Thirtysomething," may it rest in peace) ignores the most fundamental rule of Disney outdoor adventure movies: you can get away with even the most preposterous story lines if you can just keep the action moving along.

At the center of this film, however, Olin gets bogged down in a swamp of New Age/Native American mumbo-jumbo ("There is nothing else in the world but you, this arrow and the tree. And you are all one") so that parents as well as children will be squirming in their seats and checking out the refreshment stand.

The tall tale that Olin tells so tediously bears only the most casual connection to the "White Fang" of 1991, or to the stirring Jack London novel that inspired it. The original story portrayed a powerful creature, half-dog, half-wolf, who's badly abused by callous prospectors during the Klondike gold rush, until a young idealist gradually wins the animal's undying devotion.

This previous hero, played by Ethan Hawke, appears in the new film for only a minute—just long enough to explain in a letter from San Francisco that he's left his cabin in the gold country, along with his beloved White Fang, to the care of a young friend, Henry (played by sturdy but unremarkable newcomer Scott Bairstow).

The new boy on the block and his furry friend eventually cross paths with a drop-dead gorgeous Indian princess (Charmaine Craig) who wants them to fulfill her uncles' prophetic dream of a white wolf who will come to the rescue of their starving tribe.

"Without the caribou, the balance in our lives is gone," the old man explains. "My dream told of the wolf that would lead us to the caribou."

After a good deal of tiresome indecision, Henry decides to go off in search of the missing herd, thereby defying an evil preacher, Reverend Leland Drury (Alfred Molina) whose nefarious plans include genocide for the noble natives.

When all else fails, the scenery (shot in Colorado and British Columbia) is reliably lovely and some of the performances are better than this material deserves.

Charmaine Craig is a Harvard senior making her movie debut: she projects high-voltage star power and even looks sensitive and self-assured when delivering the lines, "In my clan there have been many chiefs and warrior women. And I carry them all inside me. Even those yet to be born." Al Harrington (who played Ben Kokua on "Hawaii Five-O") portrays the tribe's chief with surprising warmth and dignity.

White Fang himself emerges less successfully, partially because he's portrayed by five different dogs. No wonder the poor creature displays a schizophrenic on-screen personality, and seems to change shape from shot to shot.

Kids, of course, won't notice such details and will probably enjoy the action sequences and the animals, including WF's new love interest, a wolf named Cinnamon. There's no reason, however, they had to be subjected to the movie's long slow spots, a gratuitous crooked clergyman stereotype, and a pompous script that is so ruthlessly politically correct that when the caribou finally do turn up you half expect the hungry tribe to turn vegetarian.

NEWSDAY, 4/15/94, Part II/p. B7, Jack Mathews

The subtitle of "White Fang 2," the sequel to Disney's 1992 adaptation of the famous Jack London novel, is "Myth of the White Wolf," but given its dependence on the clichés of old Hollywood dog movies, it's more like "Myth of Rin Tin Tin."

In the first movie, as in the book, White Fang used his hybrid skills as a half-wolf, half-dog both to survive the harshness of nature and to enjoy the benefits of being a domestic pet. He was a natural wonder, all cunning and instincts, and after being rescued from an evil dogfight manager by young gold miner Jack Conroy (Ethan Hawke), he became the best friend a man in the wilds could have.

But he was still an animal. In "White Fang 2," he's Arnold Schwarzenegger! He can not only track his master halfway across the wilds, he can spot a villain from 400 yards away, sneak up on him from behind (so as not to get shot), and drop-kick his butt off a butte.

In this episode, White Fang also falls in love, with a full-blooded wolf, a crosscultural romance mirroring the one blooming between his master Henry Casey (Scott Bairstow) and a Haida tribal princess (Charmaine Craig). This is cute stuff, especially the nose-nuzzling between the canines, and we can't rule out the possibility of this movie ending with a double wedding.

"White Fang 2," directed by "thirtysomething" cast alumnus Ken Olin, picks up where the first ended, sort of. Ethan Hawke appears briefly in a prologue, writing a letter to his pal Henry Casey explaining why he had to return to San Francisco and entrust White Fang to Henry's care. Then we cut back to the Yukon, where life has become as much a cartoon as an adventure.

Separated briefly by a boating accident, Henry and White Fang team up with the son (Anthony Michael Ruivivar) and niece (Craig) of a spiritual Haida tribal chief (Al Harrington) to solve the mystery of the missing caribou. Seems the herd hasn't returned this year, threatening the Haida with starvation, and there is a sinister-looking minister (Alfred Molina) suspiciously anxious to help them relocate.

Gold fever is the source of conflict in both "White Fang" stories, but the sequel abandons any sense of reality. Molina's phony pastor is a villain out of "Perils of Pauline," all but strumming his mustache as he plots his evil deeds, and the heroic feats of Henry and White Fang are as conveniently choreographed as an episode of "Lassie."

For parents looking for a joyful experience for their young grade-schoolers, that's not all bad. The first film, with its dogfights and its authentic brushes with death, was pretty intense. "White Fang 2" has some mildly depicted violence, and a key character is lost in the final battle, but it is all wrapped in a spiritual security blanket and leavened by the tenderness of the two love stories. Whether the picture calls for another sequel, Disney had enough cunning of its own to leave its options open. In the last scene of the movie, we meet ... White Fang's kids!

Also reviewed in:
CHICAGO TRIBUNE, 4/15/94, Friday/p. L, Michael Wilmington
NEW YORK TIMES, 4/15/93, p. C23, Stephen Holden
VARIETY, 4/18-24/94, p. 62, Joe Leydon
WASHINGTON POST, 4/15/94, p. D6, Rita Kempley

WIDOWS' PEAK

A Fine Line Features and Rank Film Distributors release of a Jo Manuel Productions film with the participation of British Screen. *Executive Producer:* Michael White. *Producer:* Jo Manuel. *Director:* John Irvin. *Screenplay (based on a story by):* Hugh Leonard. *Director of Photography:* Ashley Rowe. *Editor:* Peter Tanner. *Music:* Carl Davis. *Music Editor:* Andrew Glen. *Sound:* Peter Lindsay and (music) Mike Ross Turner. *Sound Editor:* Les Wiggins. *Casting:* Nuala Moiselle. *Production Designer:* Leo Austin. *Art Director:* David Wilson and Richard Elton. *Special Effects:* Gerry Johnston. *Costumes:* Consolata Boyle. *Make-up:* Lois Burwell and Morna Ferguson. *Stunt Coordinator:* Marc Boyle. *Running time:* 101 minutes. *MPAA Rating:* PG.

CAST: Mia Farrow (Miss O'Hare); Joan Plowright (Mrs. Doyle Counihan); Natasha Richardson (Edwina Broome); Adrian Dunbar (Godfrey); Jim Broadbent (Clancy); Anne Kent (Miss Grubb); John Kavanagh (Canon); Ryhagh O'Grady (Maddie); Gerard McSorley (Gaffney); Michael James Ford (Rokesby); Garrett Keogh (Grogan); Britta Smith (Mrs. Colgan); Sheila Flitton (Mrs. Mulrooney); Marie Conmee (Mrs. Lawless); Ingrid Craigie (Mrs. Purdieu); Doreen Keogh (Mrs. Buckley); Eileen Colgan (Mrs. Fogarty); Oliver Maguire (Kilkelly); Felim Drew (FX); Jasmine Russell (Bridgie); Tina Kellegher (Dolores); David Ganly (Liam); Nick Grennell (Compere); Don Wycherley (Rural Lout); Malcolm Douglas (Townie); Clive Geraghty (Garda Super); Pauline Cadell (Sister Teresa); Rachel Dowling (Tall Thin Girl); Aisling Flitton (Mary Lucy); Marie McDermottroe (Penitent); Donal Byrne (Singer); Kevin O'Farrell (O'Farrell).

FILMS IN REVIEW, 7-8/94, p. 53, Andy Pawelczak

Widows' Peak has three generations of formidable actresses, 1920s' costumes and manners, rolling Irish countryside and lilting brogues, and enough genteel charm for a month's *Masterpiece Theaters*. But, as written by Hugh Leonard and directed by John Irvin, it's such a slight confection that it disappears without a trace before you even leave the theater.

Widows' Peak is a section of the town of Kilshannon that is populated exclusively by well off widows. The film tries to get some amiable comic mileage out of this, but none of it is much funnier than a scene in which the widows traipse through a cemetery until their doyenne, Mrs. Doyle Counihan (Joan Plowright), instructs them not to spoil their deceased husbands by visiting their graves too long. The one exception to the widows-only rule is Catherine O'Hare (Mia Farrow), a poor woman who is patronized by her affluent neighbors. The reason for her residence in Widows' Peak is one of the film's secrets that isn't revealed until the end, though there's a clue early on that detection minded viewers will quickly register.

This hermetic, matriarchal paradise is disrupted by the arrival of Edwina Broome (Natasha Richardson), the American-raised widow of a British army officer. In her elegant, sexy evening gowns and big touring car, Edwina is a refugee from the Jazz Age, and she quickly attracts the romantic attention of Godfrey (Adrian Dunbar), Mrs. Doyle Counihan's oppressed, mama's-boy son. Miss O'Hare's reaction is even stronger yet: She objects to the presence of a British army officer's widow in Widows' Peak and soon becomes convinced that Edwina, for unexplained reasons, is plotting to kill her. Once the murder mystery plot kicks in, the film picks up a little speed, though never much more than an old fashioned touring car that ambles along as its passengers take in the Irish sights.

Mia Farrow is as agelessly beautiful as ever, but her acting here has regressed to the period of *Rosemary's Baby*. As Catherine O'Hare she wears a haunted, slightly dishevelled look, and at one point she's even referred to as a witch. Joan Plowright delivers a one note performance as the snobbish, intrusive Mrs. Doyle Counihan, the tyrannical final arbiter of right and wrong in Widows' Peak. Natasha Richardson, speaking in a flat, nasal American accent, never rises above a cartoon of flirtatious sexuality. The men in *Widows' Peak* don't have much to do. Adrian Dunbar is appropriately pallid as Mrs. Doyle Counihan's ineffectual son, and Jim Broadbent has a few comic moments as a whiskey imbibing dentist who announces that the women of Widows' Peak were born for widowhood.

As written by Hugh Leonard (author of *Da*), *Widows' Peak* has its share of arch Irishisms ("It's as dull as a wet Good Friday," etc.) and ethnic detail, including a traditional dance presided over by an alertly puritanical priest, but they don't compensate for the absence of a compelling story line and characters. Inexplicably, Leonard, or perhaps the film's director, John Irvin, throws in a reference to *Casablanca* when Edwina says she came to Kilshannon for the climate. Godfrey says, "What climate? We're in Ireland," and she responds, "Was I misinformed?" (Bogart: "I came to Casablanca for the waters." Claude Rains: "There are no waters in Casablanca." Bogart: "I was misinformed.") A sop to the cineastes in the audience? It's one mystery that remains unexplained by film's end.

LOS ANGELES TIMES, 5/13/94, Calendar/p. 8, Peter Rainer

"Widows' Peak" is a lilting little whodunit trussed up as a domestic comedy. Set in the village of Kilshannon, Ireland, in the early 1920s, it's an actors' holiday of a movie. The lead female performers—Mia Farrow, Joan Plowright, Natasha Richardson—make it something of a holiday for us, too.

The Widows' Peak of the title is a high bluff overlooking Kilshannon that is home to a community of well-to-do widows who spend much of their time gossiping and snooping into one another's business. Mrs. Doyle-Counihan (Plowright), who wields a mean telescope for her spy-mastering, is the peak's unofficial matriarch. Twice-widowed, she has a prim imperiousness; the peak is her eminent domain.

Her son Godfrey (Adrian Dunbar) is a gangly twit who attempts to lead a double life. Around his mother he's a lap dog but in the presence of the village's mysterious new war widow, Edwina Broome (Natasha Richardson), he tries to be a smoothie. (She sees right through him—no great achievement.) Then there's Miss O'Hare (Mia Farrow), also something of a mystery, who is the only non-widow allowed to live on Widow's Peak. (Godfrey is the only man allowed.) She's a fragile waif with a not-so-fragile disposition. Her instant dislike of Edwina becomes a free-for-all spat that turns the village inside out.

Irish playwright Hugh Leonard ("Da") and director John Irvin let these actors exult in their roles without allowing the film to devolve into broad blarneyisms. It's all a bit too composed and patterned, and the plot twists aren't particularly twisty. But the scenery and costumes have been chosen with great care and intelligence; it may be a "Masterpiece Theatre" piffle but it's a well-done piffle. It doesn't overvalue its literacy or good cheer.

It would have been easy for Plowright to play Mrs. Doyle-Counihan as a ramrod but there are many more shadings in the performance. Doyle-Counihan is careful to sit apart from the villagers at public gatherings, but she's not a snob exactly—she's just devoted to protocol. There's a wonderful moment when she's watching a Cecil B. DeMille biblical movie and whispers excitedly to Miss O'Hare that she's heard that "we see God in the second half." This no-nonsense woman who has outlasted two husbands still has the capacity for wonder, at least when the lights are down.

Farrow is remarkably good in a difficult role. In her own way, Miss O'Hare is as tough as Doyle-Counihan but she always looks like she's about to fade away. Farrow shows a mettle here that she didn't always have an opportunity to demonstrate in her many Woody Allen movies, where she was often cast as a simpering rag doll. Richardson brings her out—she's not just a co-performer, she's an opponent. Richardson is such a different kind of performer—savvy and sharp where Farrow is nervy and neurasthenic—that their battles resemble a competition between performing styles.

NEW YORK, 5/23/94, p. 73, David Denby

Most people in the audience for *Widows' Peak* will have figured out the movie's mild little mystery well before they were supposed to. So *Widows' Peak* becomes one of those affairs that cause one to marvel at the British capacity for innocence: Do they really think that those hackneyed plots will fool anyone? Playwright Hugh Leonard, a piker in the Agatha Christie trade, supplies some Irish color (the movie is set in a small Irish village in the late twenties) and some good anti-English jokes. Leonard's conceit: In the small town, a bunch of man-hating, happy rich widows rule the roost. Director John Irvin hits a note of black comedy when the widows scurry wildly, like ants attacking a cheesecake, over a hilltop cemetery, laying wreaths at their husbands' graves. But most of Irvin's direction is clumsy, and one's interest shifts to the three stars.

Joan Plowright, playing another tyrant and hypocrite, has inherited the Edith Evans, or eccentric-dowager, position in British movies; this is perhaps her most acid performance yet. And Natasha Richardson amuses herself playing a shallow, manipulative woman—an American widow with a dazzling smile, a flat, nasty voice, and an ambiguous past. The script calls for Mia Farrow to be distant and slightly goony, and it calls for her to be warm and luminous. The trouble is, Farrow doesn't pull the two halves together into a believable person. Unchained from Woody, Farrow could be a fascinating performer, but what she does here is so odd, it's not quite acting.

NEW YORK POST, 5/13/94, p. 39, Michael Medved

"In Kilshannon, widows are as plentiful as freckles on a redhead," says Clancy the dentist (Jim Broadbent), a perceptive observer of local manners and morals in the delightfully devious new mystery/comedy "Widows' Peak."

Set in Ireland in 1926, the action takes place largely on the hill where most of these well-to-do dowagers make their gracious homes (hence the designation "Widows' Peak") and gossip endlessly about less fortunate mortals.

The acknowledged leader of this tight little group is the imperious Mrs. Doyle-Counihan (Joan Plowright) who tolerates only one non-widow in their midst: the poor spinster Miss O'Hare (Mia Farrow) who exerts a surprising hold on the ladies of the town, based on mysterious events of the distant past.

The arrival of a spectacularly glamorous outsider (Natasha Richardson who, with long blonde hair, bears a surprising resemblance to Sharon Stone) shatters the peaceful equilibrium of this pleasant, proper world.

Richardson plays an Americanized Englishwoman and the widow of a British war hero, and she immediately captures the fancy of Mrs. Doyle-Counihan's bored, lay-about son (Adrian Dunbar, who was so good in the fondly remembered "Hear My Song").

At the same time that she provokes romantic attentions, the new widow on the peak inspires a fanatical and unreasoning hatred from Miss O'Hare, who warns the townspeople that Richardson is planning a dastardly murder. As the story unfolds, some of them begin to suspect that these dire warnings might be justified.

What makes all of this so absorbing to watch is not only the ingenious plot twists (with an even bigger, better surprise than "The Crying Game") but the rich and beautifully detailed characterizations. All of the performances are impeccable, as the superb ensemble cast keeps audience sympathies continually shifting from one to another of its members.

Irish playwright Hugh Leonard ("Da") wrote the sparkling screenplay and originally intended Mia Farrow's part for her mother, Maureen O'Sullivan. Though strictly speaking Miss Farrow may be old enough to play the role, she looks so much younger than her 49 years that her casting at times seems questionable.

Nevertheless, director John Irvin makes the most of her haunting beauty—as he does of the stunning costumes and ravishing Irish locations, which never detract attention from the line but merely add to the sense of sumptuous entertainment.

Irvin's career has heretofore featured under-appreciated action films ("Hamburger Hill", "Raw Deal") and the sensitive romance "Turtle Diary." But "Widows' Peak"—which deserves to become a sleeper hit like "Enchanted April" and "Four Weddings and a Funeral"—will place him in the first rank of contemporary directors where he belongs.

NEWSDAY, 5/13/94, Part II/p. B3, John Anderson

Mrs. Doyle Counihan (Joan Plowright), the picture of self-satisfaction, motors through the rustic Irish village of Kilshannon, oblivious—or indifferent—to the several local men she leaves scattered in her wake. It's just her worldview, really: Having buried both her husbands, Mrs. Doyle Counihan believes men to be of very little consequence, and most useful when they're being mourned.

Twice bereaved and twice as rich as any other woman living on what the "townies" call Widows' Peak, Mrs, Doyle Counihan reigns supreme in her town of women. She leads outings to the local cemetery ("Back *that* at a hundred to eight, ya bollocks," one woman mutters, after smashing a ceramic horse on her husband's headstone). And she keeps an eye on local goings on through the telescope perched at her living room window. Basically, she's insufferable.

"Widows' Peak" is no "Enchanted April," which also featured Plowright, revolved around female relationships and was set in a picturesque landscape. "Widows' Peak" director John Irvin, working from a sharply funny Hugh ("Da") Leonard script, dismisses the pastoral Ireland with a few postcard shots; then he gets down to laying out the considerably more intriguing, and far less bucolic, social landscape of '30s Kilshannon. It's clear that the quaint and the cruel will mix here, but not in equal measure, and that Doyle Counihan's kingdom is ripe for a fall.

How? Well, "Widows' Peak" has as many twists as it does widows, but it begins with the arrival of Edwina Broome (Natasha Richardson), the wealthy widow of an English war hero. Beautiful, flirtatious and not-quite-candid, she's fled the Riviera to escape "men" (cut to her pinched-faced welcoming committee, nodding appreciatively), dreads "fortune-hunters" and seems to set her cap for young Godfrey Doyle Counihan (Adrian Dunbar), heir to the money, if not the throne, of Widows' Peak.

And while "the Mommy," as he calls her, doesn't think of her son as a man, Godfrey is the only one living on Widows' Peak (his grandmother's will forbade leasing any property on the hill to couples, people with children, or single men). The only other non-widow is Miss Catherine O'Hare (Mia Farrow), an "old maid" who grows roses and is presumed to be slightly mad. Miss O'Hare, who's being courted by the local dentist Clancy (a deliriously funny Jim Broadbent), takes an immediate dislike to Edwina, partly because Edwina is English, and partly because ... well, the makers of "Widows' Peak" take a perverse pleasure in taking us down seemingly familiar paths that lead to surprising destinations. At no time is anything misleading actually committed; in retrospect, you should have seen it all coming, but don't.

Of course, by saying this, I'm letting the cat halfway out of the bag, but even on second viewing "Widows' Peak" was full of charm. The British Richardson, speaking with an American accent, is sexy and mysterious; the American Farrow, speaking with an Irish accent, is a delightful surprise, given her fairly one-dimensional tenure in Woody Allen's movies. The British Broadbent, playing a slightly tipsy Irishman, is as funny as ever, and Plowright defines imperious. And while some might view "Widows' Peak" as rooted in a fear of matriarchy, the dynamic of its cast of characters is simply that of a lot of Hollywood films, in reverse: Women are the heroes and the villains, and the men are merely decoration.

SIGHT AND SOUND, 5/94, p. 61, Amanda Lipman

Ireland, the 20s. Kilshannon is a small town inhabited largely by widows and led by Mrs Doyle Counihan (known as Mrs DC). Her son Godfrey is being treated by the local dentist Clancy, who professes to be in love with Catherine O'Hare, a poor spinster. Mrs DC takes Catherine for a ride and tells her to be careful about marrying. They visit the local solicitor where they learn that an Englishwoman will be taking up residence in the town; Catherine has a violent outburst against the English. Edwina Broome, the new arrival, who is in fact American, drives into town but is forced to stop just outside by a puncture. Godfrey meets her and warns her about his mother's insatiable need to control. Edwina has tea with Mrs DC and the widows. Catherine is venomously unfriendly. Edwina tells them about her marriage to an deceased English soldier in the south of France. Mrs DC is keen for Godfrey to court her.

Edwina, who purposely seems to have recruited the town snoop as her maid, receives Godfrey's attentions. They go to a local dance, where Edwina and Catherine cause a fight over which of them is a prize winner. War breaks out between the two women. At the local regatta, where Edwina accepts Godfrey's marriage proposal and sinks Catherine's boat, a drunken English soldier turns up and professes to know Edwina. Catherine marches him home to find out more.

That night, Edwina finds her maid going through her letters and locks her in a room until she tells her the truth about Catherine. Shortly after, Edwina and Godfrey's engagement is announced. Catherine meets Clancy, who makes her admit to having an illegitimate child, then leaves her. Catherine bursts in on the DCs at lunch. She tells her story—that she had an illegitimate child by an English soldier and that the women of the town took her baby away and in return let her live free in the part of town known as Widows Peak. She says that she traced the baby and found out that it had died; she then denounces Edwina as a fortune-hunting prostitute. Edwina walks out.

The next day, Edwina is seen getting onto Catherine's boat. The morning after, she is rescued from the boat but there is no sign of Catherine. Mrs DC leads a campaign branding her as a murderess. Catherine turns up, claiming that she went ashore to see her sister. She says she will be going to live with her. Mrs DC is visited by her solicitor, now representing Edwina, who is suing her for defamation. She collapses in horror. That night, Godfrey tries to run away in a boat, but the boat is leaking and sinks.

On a luxurious liner, Edwina, the drunken soldier, Catherine and Clancy discuss the whole affair. It transpires that Edwina is Catherine's daughter, and that the plot was cooked up by them to take revenge. Carl Davis' opening score swirls over an undulating Irish view suggesting that *Widows Peak* will be a melancholy mood piece. But that's probably just the first of the several of the film's so-called jokes. Here's another: Joan Plowright, Mia Farrow and Jim Broadbent rolling out their best Irish accents, and Natasha Richardson going American again. As it happens, most of them pull it off. It is only Plowright, in scenery-chewing, vowel-rolling, pantomime dame style, who is prone to forget the necessary intonations.

Although this is a film of mainly broad comic strokes, it does reveal a certain delicacy of touch in John Irvin, the director who brought us *Hamburger Hill*. The wooing of Farrow's spinsterish Catherine by Broadbent's bluff dentist Clancy is shown in one tea-time scene, in which, aping her every move, Clancy ends up making a shy, smiling fool of himself. Many of the broad strokes work well enough too: Richardson's vampish Edwina—a mix of strong-willed *femme fatale* and outsider aiming to please—is interesting enough to keep us wondering what she is really up to. Farrow, who looks as if she has stepped out of *The Purple Rose of Cairo* complete with subdued print dresses and quiet persona, suddenly turns out to have a lacerating tongue and an extraordinary amount of obstinacy. Even Adrian Dunbar's Godfrey remains engaging—the 'mammy's boy' endlessly trying to convince Edwina of his manliness, while being treated by his mother like a small child.

Less fortunately, the film cannot resist the occasional compulsion to do what it obviously considers the really Irish thing, and go into frenetic, farcical overdrive. Hence its ludicrously snoopy maid—who, if she really were that bad at being nosy, would not get away with anything; a prurient priest flanked by fatuously ingenuous nuns; and whooping, dancing rustics. At least the inevitable dancing scene has a point—it sets up the apparent rift between Catherine and Edwina.

Like better comedy, *Widows Peak* has a darker side to its humour. Its observations may be simplified, but they point to a closed, suspicious community that Plowright's Mrs Doyle Counihan rules from her house on top of the hill, literally watching over her neighbours (or rather subjects) through her telescope. She has the power to take a woman's illegitimate daughter away from her, and to keep her adult son as an emasculated child.

It may be for those reasons that as the film moves from comedy to drama, and a more sinister side of the charming little village emerges, we are still prepared to be more or less convinced by it. But all that disappears with the final joke. Such a ludicrous denouement not only makes little logical sense but also undermines every scrap of sympathy or understanding the characters and their situations may have managed to evoke.

Writer Hugh Leonard is better known for his heartfelt dramas such as *Da*, and his literary TV adaptations, than for his comedy. Here it seems as if, unsure that the comedy will stand up on its own, he is covering his back with a top layer of shock tactics. But if the film-makers don't have enough confidence in the film, why should an audience bother?

VILLAGE VOICE, 5/31/94, p. 60, Beth Coleman

The best property in this idyllic country town in 1920s Ireland is on the hill—overseeing all, yet inaccessible to the dross that might wash up from the bay shores below. Widows' Peak is the pet name given to the promontory, for the women, and it is only women, who live up there all happily wear black as they make their graveside pilgrimages early enough to get back for tea. The head gentlewoman Mrs. Doyle Counihan (Joan Plowright), herself only ever referred to by full title, runs the town like an empress dowager. "These are women born for widowhood," our erstwhile narrator, the local dentist-surgeon (Jim Broadbent) tells us. They fairly glow in the unfettered power of gossip, propriety, and black brocade.

Dressed in threadbare browns and whites, Miss O'Hare (a delightful Mia Farrow) is the exception to the rule of black. She tends her prize roses and secrets as we wait for a plot to arrive. And it does, roaring up the hill in the shape of a modern widow—lots of red lipstick, cigarettes, and a big motor car. Natasha Richardson's gamine matron spells trouble something like S-E-X. What starts out as catfighting in the henhouse between the Miss and the young Mrs. blossoms into a murder mystery that brings the industrial age to this town. A fate the old widows, like inhabitants of a girl's Brigadoon, had worked to avoid.

By way of pamphlets printed on home presses and the lawyer lurking around the police house, the men's world of war, politics, and general nastiness capsizes the matriarch's ship. Is this good or bad? We will never know. *Peak* can't decide itself whether to mourn the passing of a gentler time before sensational boat tours of the murder site or to nail the crew of old biddies for the oppressive snobs they are.

Also reviewed in:
NEW REPUBLIC, 6/20/94, p. 26, Stanley Kauffmann
NEW YORK TIMES, 5/13/94, p. C16, Caryn James
VARIETY, 4/18-24/94, p. 62, Derek Elley
WASHINGTON POST, 5/25/94, p. C10, Rita Kempley
WASHINGTON POST, 5/27/94, Weekend/p. 44, Joe Brown

WITH HONORS

A Warner Bros. release of a Spring Creek production. *Executive Producer:* Jon Peters and Peter Guber. *Producer:* Paula Weinstein and Amy Robinson. *Director:* Alek Keshishian. *Screenplay:* William Mastrosimone. *Director of Photography:* Sven Nykvist. *Editor:* Michael R. Miller. *Music:* Patrick Leonard. *Music Editor:* Danny Garde and Alex Gibson. *Sound:* Curt Frisk. *Sound Editor:* Scott Hecker. *Casting:* Marion Dougherty and Ness Hyams. *Production Designer:* Barbara Ling. *Art Director:* Bill Arnold. *Set Designer:* Suzan Wexler. *Set Decorator:* Cricket Rowland. *Special Effects:* John Milinac. *Costumes:* Renee Ehrlich Kalfus. *Make-up:* Marilyn Carbone. *Make-up (Joe Pesci):* James Sarzotti. *Stunt Coordinator:* Rick LeFevour. *Running time:* 103 minutes. *MPAA Rating:* PG-13.

CAST: Joe Pesci (Simon Wilder); Brendan Fraser (Monty Kessler); Moira Kelly (Courtney Blumenthal); Patrick Dempsey (Everett Calloway); Josh Hamilton (Jeff Hawkes); Gore Vidal (Professor Philip Hayes Pitkannan); Deborah Lake Fortson (Homeless Woman); Marshall Hambro (Security Guard); Melinda Chilton (Helga); Harve Kolzow (Harvard Cop); James Deuter (Judge); Caroline Gibson (Donation Student); M. Lynda Robinson (Newspaper Purchaser #1). Richard Auguste (Newspaper Purchaser #2); Patricia B. Butcher (Librarian); Mary Seibel (Social Security Clerk); Mara Brock (Ms. Moore); Clebert Ford (Homeless Man); Wiliam Ashby King (Church Custodian); Frank J. Tieri (Homeless Man #2); Shanesia Davis (Doctor Kay); Rick LeFevour (Mailman); Sunshine H. Hernandez (Marilyn Monroe); Monica Rochman (Sophomore); Kurt Clauss (The Face); Claudia Haro (Marty); Daniel Blinkoff (Frank); Holly Wenz-Nolan (Frank's Daughter); Richard Bednar (Dean).

FILMS IN REVIEW, 7-8/94, p. 57, Andy Pawelczak

It's a depressing truism about contemporary culture that it recycles the past endlessly. Not even Marx, who once remarked that history repeats itself, the first time as tragedy, the second time as farce, could have anticipated the pervasive déjà vu of the waning years of the century.

Today, we even hear talk of the need for a revival of benign colonialism. On a more mundane, less world-historical level, the hero of *With Honors* has the looks and style of Rock Hudson, and the villain, played by the writer Gore Vidal, is the kind of browbeating Ivy League professor that used to be played by John Houseman. This is even more of a downer in a movie that enjoins us, via a quote from Walt Whitman, not to take the world at second or third hand, or look at it through the eyes of the dead. Did the filmmakers know what they were doing? Did they care?

The movie's plot is your basic serviceable rich-kids-take-in-wise-homeless-man fable à la *Down and Out in Beverly Hills*. Monty (Brendan Fraser), a smart, serious Harvard student, drops the only copy of his senior thesis down a grating in front of the Harvard Library, where it comes into the possession of Simon (Joe Pesci), a shaggy homeless man who likes to read. Simon agrees to give it back to the desperate Monty one page at a time in return for such amenities as food and shelter. It isn't long before Simon has moved in with Monty and his roommates—the pretty Courtney (Moira Kelly) with whom Monty is secretly in love; Everett (Patrick Dempsey), the college radio announcer who affects a dandyish counter-culture style; and Jeff (Josh Hamilton), the only roommate who resists Simon's raffish charm. And charming he is, of course, as he must be if he is to teach the bookish Monty how to be human in the movie's hour and forty minutes running time.

As Simon, Joe Pesci has a high, squeaky voice, an antic manner and a perky, jerky walk that began to grate on my nerves very quickly. Ultimately, Simon isn't really all that different from the Harvard kids. When we meet the son that he abandoned thirty years before, he turns out to be a rich, buttoned-down preppie type, proving that Simon himself has the right genetic material and just made a few wrong choices in life. With this narrative sleight of hand, the hidden and not-so-hidden injuries of class do a neat disappearing act.

And that's what the whole movie is like—designed not to offend or challenge anyone. Even the big classroom confrontation scene between Simon and Monty's mentor, Prof. Pitkannan (Gore Vidal in a nice bit of casting—he's a genuine American aristocrat), manages to fudge the real political issues. Pitkannan isn't a Reaganite conservative but simply an upper class elitist who distrusts the great unwashed. And Simon, of course, is a populist democrat in the tradition of Walt Whitman, not to mention an expert on the Constitution. Is there any doubt about who will win this battle of the father figures for the soul of Monty?

As directed by Alek Keshishian (whose previous movie was the Madonna documentary *Truth or Dare*), the film lavishes attention on the details of Harvard life—polished oak tables, church like anterooms burnished by diffused light—at the expense of character development. But then what can you expect of a movie that tells us there's nothing very wrong with an America in which spoiled kids can make a mascot of a homeless man?

LOS ANGELES TIMES, 4/29/94, Calendar/p. 6, Peter Rainer

Harvard and the homeless—what a concept! "With Honors" gives us Monty (Brendan Fraser), an industrious political science student who reluctantly befriends Simon (Joe Pesci), a ragamuffin misfit who lives in the boiler room of Harvard's Widener Library. This is a life-lesson movie where most of the lessons run one-way. Simon's got all the answers. Monty at first doesn't even know the questions. By the end he learns to shed his snobbishness and see Simon as a person, not a thing.

This journey-to-wisdom, scripted by playwright William Mastrosimone, is preordained from the first contrivance. Monty loses his entire senior thesis on his computer during a power outage and then loses his one printed copy by accidentally dropping it down a grate and into Simon's hideaway. Simon, sensing an angle, makes the sputtering student a deal: He will return one page of his 100-page thesis at a time for an equal number of favors.

At first the favors are tiny—like a supply of glazed doughnuts with no cracks in the glaze. Then Monty, exasperated, puts Simon up in the abandoned VW van in the front yard of the house he shares with three other students. Simon gets blankets, food and wine but no entry into the house—at least not until another series of contrivances kicks in.

"With Honors" works best when it's not trying to clobber us with socially conscious parables about how we should respect our fellow man. We should, of course, but shouldn't an audience's intelligence also be respected? There's a scene where Monty is chewed out by his arch Nobel laureate professor, played by Gore Vidal no less, that really takes the "Paper Chase" cake. Vidal, trying for John Housemam's plump smoothness, tears into the boy's notions of democracy until the Harvard-T-shirted Simon, who has accompanied Monty to class, quashes the snob with a ringing endorsement of we-the-people. The theater owners playing this film should hand out copies of the Constitution to patrons as they exit the multiplex.

The college roommate atmosphere, which seemed so phony in the recent "Threesome," actually seems almost believable in "With Honors," perhaps because the director Alek Keshishian is a Harvard '86 grad, He quickly establishes the other roomies: Courtney (Moira Kelley) as a tart, Winona Ryder look and a furtive crush on Monty; Jeff (Josh Hamilton) is a premed student who takes one look at Simon and puts a bolt on his door. Everett (Patrick Dempsey) is a college radio DJ with a pet rooster and a love of vino—he's the kind of gentle eccentric who blooms on every campus. Their glancing, cantankerous interactions are familiar and funny. They turn to cardboard only when Simon is required to set each one of them on the road to self-betterment.

Brendan Fraser has a strong brooding presence, a hurt quality that at least makes Monty's attachment to Simon believable. Simon fills in for Monty's errant father, and Monty takes the place of the son Simon walked out on years before. It's all terribly schematic, but Fraser and Pesci work well together. Fraser takes some of the nattering edge off of Pesci's performance. (In "Jimmy Hollywood" there was no such buffer, and Pesci's performance felt like an assault.) Pesci enjoys playing this ragamuffin sage and some of his enjoyment cuts through the corn.

Not all of it, though. In the end there's still a large portion of the cornfield left unharvested and flapping in the wind.

NEW YORK POST, 4/29/94, p. 42, Michael Medved

If hard-driving scholarship student Monty Kessler (Brendan Fraser) manages to finish his senior thesis on time, then he'll achieve his cherished goal of graduating from Harvard "with honors."

Unfortunately, some freakish mishaps seem to stand in his way: when an intense winter storm causes his computer drive to crash, he rushes out to make a copy of the existing pages of his draft, but trips in the snow and drops the precious manuscript through a sidewalk grate.

The only copy of the thesis thereby falls into the grubby hands of Simon Wilder (Joe Pesci), a bearded free spirit who's set up cozy quarters in a boiler room in the library.

The university authorities promptly evict him when Monty alerts them to the existence of the hideaway.

Simon agrees to return the thesis page by page, but only in exchange for food and shelter—an arrangement that causes considerable dismay to Monty's three housemates (Patrick Dempsey, Moira Kelly and Josh Hamilton).

Gradually, however, all four Harvard seniors come to acknowledge the individualistic virtues of the homeless Simon.

All of this is just as contrived and smug and preachy as it sounds, but it's made surprisingly watchable by an altogether superior cast.

Pesci turns in his most memorable performance since "GoodFellas," generating a warmth and sweetness that he's never before displayed on screen.

Until the story goes sappy and sentimental in its final minutes, "With Honors" marks an auspicious feature film debut for director Alek Keshishian (Harvard, '86) , who previously created the Madonna documentary "Truth or Dare."

Even the screenplay's corniest scene—a classroom confrontation between the homeless savant and a pompous professor played by Gore Vidal—is handled with a nice sense of balance and restraint.

Keshishian's cause is helped immeasurably by the glorious cinematography by the great Sven Nykvist, of Bergman fame.

NEWSDAY, 4/29/94, Part II/p. B7, Jack Mathews

Joe Pesci has been wearing more bad toupees lately than Michael Milken and Phyllis Diller together.

First, the balding star dons a Day-Glo orange tuft to play freakish David Ferrie in Oliver Stone's "JFK," then a shoulder-length blond cascade for Barry Levinson's "Jimmy Hollywood," and now, for Alek Keshishian's "With Honors," something resembling a mop used to clean up after the Exxon Valdez.

These rugs would turn anybody into a comic figure, but they make the pint-sized Pesci stand out like Cousin It at a party at the Addams mansion, an insurmountable distraction in a drama about a philosophical homeless person with a fatal lung disease.

In a story that begs comparison to "Down and Out in Beverly Hills," Pesci plays Simon Wilder, an ex-merchant marine and society dropout wintering in the warm clime of Harvard University's library basement. There, curled up between the groaning boilers, he reads Emile Zola, sips rotgut and waits for the asbestos fibers he'd inhaled decades earlier to finish him off.

Through a series of improbable events, Simon comes into possession of a student's unfinished honors thesis, and after being evicted from the library and threatened with a jail sentence, he uses that thesis to get himself through the winter. He agrees to return the 88 pages, one at a time, in exchange for favors from Monty Kessler ("Encino Man's" Brendan Fraser), the panicked student who lost them.

Soon, Simon is living with Monty and his three roommates in Cambridge, determinedly winning each of them over with his goofy manner, sharp wit and world-wise musings. Simon may not remember to flush, but he has a degree from the School of Hard Knocks, and before this semester's over, his four hosts—so bright, so earnest, sooooo inexperienced—will have PhD's in humility and humanity.

The script, by playwright William Mastrosimone ("Extremities"), is a study in cliched sentimentality—its political issues, class themes and emotional conflicts so transparently developed, you can stay a step ahead of them all the way to the excruciatingly maudlin end.

Keshishian, whose fine work on the Madonna documentary "Truth or Dare" earned him his first feature assignment, treats the most mundane revelations here as epiphanies, as if it will come as shock that (a) college students don't know as much as they think they do, (b) the homeless are people, too, and (c) graduating with honors is not as important as graduating with wisdom.

Pesci has a high time hamming it up as Simon, whose behavior ranges from mad babbling to manic speeches to anguished self-loathing. Mastrosimone tailored a lot of cheap jokes for him, and many of them work. The character, however, does not. He's like a pencil sketch of the traumatized history professor played by Robin Williams in "The Fisher King," his complexities implied but rarely demonstrated.

Pesci is a fascinating actor to watch, and that may be enough to get his most ardent fans through this career lapse. For others, it's just another bad hair day.

VILLAGE VOICE, 5/10/94, p. 62, Evette Porter

If there's anything really surprising about *With Honors*, Alek Keshishian's feature, it's that it's so damned predictable. You'd think after Madonna (*Truth or Dare*), he'd have more of an edge. In contrast, *With Honors* is *The Fisher King* entwined in ivy. It's the story of a homeless man, Simon Wilder (Joe Pesci), who teaches a bunch of smugly cynical Harvard students a few lessons about life. Monty (Brendan Fraser), an aspiring neocon political wonk, loses his honor's thesis when it falls through a grate in front of Widener Library, only to be found by Simon. The two strike a bargain: a page at a time in return for some meager act of kindness. But instead of returning the favor, Monty has Simon arrested.

In a scene out of *My Cousin Vinny*, Simon talks his way out of a legal bind and into a living arrangement with Monty and his three roommates. Over time, Monty and his friends—Everett (Patrick Dempsey), a trust-fund boho and Keshishian stand-in, Courtney Blumenthal (Moira Kelly), an Upper East Side wannabe WASP, and the film's least sympathetic character, Jeff (Josh Hamilton), a premed closet case—grow fond of Pesci and his boorish ways. In Capra-esque style, the story of Simon's life propels their own character reversals. "I'm not a loser. I'm a fighter,"

Simon says after another courtroomlike debate with Monty's professor (Gore Vidal), thus revealing the wisdom and scholarship of simple men.

Pulling all the usual heartstrings, *With Honors* recalls *The Paper Chase*, this time relying on the mystique of Harvard undergrad to create its sense of irony. Bathing the screen in Crimson, Keshishian (a Harvard alum) shamelessly exploits every toadyism from crew jocks to trust funds, but all he manages to do is bury his story in Ivy League mush.

Also reviewed in:
CHICAGO TRIBUNE, 4/29/94, Friday/p. A, Michael Wilmington
NEW YORK TIMES, 4/29/94, p. C12, Caryn James
VARIETY, 4/18-24/94, p. 62, Brian Lowry
WASHINGTON POST, 4/29/94, p. C6, Desson Howe
WASHINGTON POST, 4/29/94, Weekend/p. 46, Jeanne Cooper

WOLF

A Columbia Pictures Release. *Executive Producer:* Neil Machlis and Robert Greenhut. *Producer:* Douglas Wick. *Director:* Mike Nichols. *Screenplay:* Jim Harrison and Wesley Strict. *Director of Photography:* Giuseppe Rotunno. *Editor:* Sam O'Steen. *Music:* Ennio Morricone. *Music Editor:* Suzana Peric. *Sound:* Arthur Rochester and Danny Michael. *Sound Editor:* Stan Bochner. *Casting:* Juliet Taylor. *Production Designer:* Bo Welch. *Art Director:* Tom Duffield. *Set Designer:* Jacques Valin and Sean Haworth. *Set Decorator:* Linda DeScenna. *Special Effects:* Stan Parks and Daniel A. Sudick. *Costumes:* Ann Roth. *Costumes (Jack Nicholson):* Lori Stilson. *Costumes (Michelle Pfeiffer):* Jennifer Morrison. *Make-up (Jack Nicholson):* Stephen Abrums. *Make-up (Michelle Pfeiffer):* Ronnie Specter. *Special Make-up Effects:* Rick Baker. *Stunt Coordinator:* M. James Arnett. *Running time:* 121 minutes. *MPAA Rating:* R.

CAST: Jack Nicholson (Will Randall); Michelle Pfeiffer (Laura Alden); James Spader (Stewart Swinton); Kate Nelligan (Charlotte Randall); Richard Jenkins (Detective Bridger); Christopher Plummer (Raymond Alden); Eileen Atkins (Mary); David Hyde Pierce (Roy); Om Puri (Dr. Vijay Alezias); Ron Rifkin (Doctor); Prunella Scales (Maude); Brian Markinson (Detective Wade); Shirin Devrim (Older Woman); Peter Gerety (George); Bradford English (Keyes); Kirby Mitchell (Younger Man); Madhur Jaffrey (Editress); William Hill (Preppie); Cynthia O'Neal (The Dance Woman); Eva Rodriguez (Maid); Allison Janney (Young Business Person); Tom Oppenheim (Young Butler); Starletta Dupois (Victim's Mother); Thomas F. Duffy (Tom); Star Jasper, Erik Anderson, and Michelle Hurd (Hookers); John Hackett (Cop in Central Park); Stewart J. Zully (Gary); Marvin Chatinover, Howard Erskine, and Garrison Lane (Tycoons); Irene Forrest (Gloria); Timothy Thomas (Intellectual Man); Joanna Sanchez (Receptionist); Kaity Tong (TV Newscaster); Jose Soto and Van Baily (Boys); Lisa Emery (Intellectual Woman); Lia Chang (Desk Clerk); James Saito (Servant); Osgood Perkins (Cop); Leigh Carlson, Alice Liu, and Max Weitzenhoffer (Party Guests); Dwayne McClary (Gang Member); Michael Raynor (Pigeon Man); Jennifer Nicholson (Young Publishing Executive); Arthur Rochester (Man by Elevator); Jack Nesbit (Man in Conference Room); Dale Kasman and Jeffrey Allen O'Den (Office Workers); Neil Machlis (Sleazy Lawyer); Kenneth Ebling (Ticket Taker).

CHRISTIAN SCIENCE MONITOR, 6/17/94, p. 12, David Sterritt

Once upon a time, the dark-toned fantasies called horror movies were aimed more at grownups than at youngsters. Starting with early classics such as "Dracula" and "Frankenstein" and continuing with pictures ranging from "Cat People" and "Dead of Night" to "The Birds" and "Rosemary's Baby," serious moviegoers would approach their works with at least a little thought, pondering the themes and suspending disbelief long enough for the stories to cast a reasonable scary spell.

The horror game has shifted to a younger arena in recent decades, however with endless "Halloween" and "Friday the 13th" sequels aiming their gory outbursts primarily at the under 30 crowd. When a more mature picture does come along—the flamboyant "Bram Stoker's Dracula" is a good example—it's likely to be a postmodern pastiche, embedding its story in an ironic style full of knowing winks to fans who know this territory all too well.

In this atmosphere, Mike Nichols's ambitious "Wolf comes as a surprise. While it contains enough gore and sexuality to mark it as a contemporary film, in many ways it's a throwback to the largely vanished period when a supernatural subject didn't automatically disqualify a movie from retaining a fair share of dignity and sobriety. "Wolf" builds its story with a care and deliberation rarely associated with the horror genre nowadays.

It even has enough sensitivity to resurrect what might be the most poignant of the classical horror-film conventions: the notion that the monster of the tale may not *like* being a monster, but hates his evil impulses as much as anyone. Not since Lon Chaney Jr. starred in "The Wolf Man" more than 50 years ago—in an era when fantasies like "King Kong" and "The Bride of Frankenstein" showed a measure of real sympathy for the unhappy lives of their bizarre creatures—has a monster been as self-critical as Jack Nicholson's character often is.

Nicholson plays the top editor of a respected publishing company about to be engulfed by a big-money takeover. His troubles begin with a venerable horror-movie flourish—a painful bite from a mysterious wolf that improbably crosses his path on a wintry New England night.

In an interesting twist on the old horror-film formulas, his transformation into a werewolf starts psychologically rather than physically. Too hesitant and submissive for his own good in the early scenes, he soon begins asserting himself with wolfish abandon—standing up to his new boss, maneuvering himself back into his right job, taking gleeful revenge on an upstart who's been doing him wrong.

The story turns more ordinary when tangible werewolf traits—the traditional hairy face, pointy fangs, and so forth—become the movie's main interest, along with a predictable escalation in carnage and killing. These ingredients carry the yarn to a violent yet oddly romantic finale that ties up all the plot's loose ends while leaving plenty of opportunity for a Hollywood-style sequel.

Although the comparative seriousness of "Wolf" is one of its most appealing characteristics, the film errs in a couple of important respects. Its attention to credible plot development and fully rounded characterization is careful to the point of fussiness, paying dividends at first but weighting down the action during the picture's second hour. Then the filmmakers swing to the other extreme, flinging so much mayhem that you think you've strayed into another movie.

This notwithstanding, "Wolf" has many more assets than the average modern-day horror yarn, Nicholson gives one of his most ingenious performances in a long while, finding complexities in his troubled character that lend the picture much of its emotional authenticity. Fantasy fans will surely measure his acting here against his work in "The Shining," and there's little doubt that the new picture wins.

The strong cast of "Wolf" also includes Michelle Pfeiffer as the wolfman's girlfriend, Christopher Plummer as his steely-eyed employer, James Spader as his professional rival, and Kate Nelligan as his less-than-faithful wife.

Just as important to the evocative cinematography by Giuseppe Rotunno, whose handling of expressive colors and tonalities of light and shadow is as deft as one has come to expect from this fine artist. Also worth a special nod is Ennio Morricone's atmospheric music. Jim Harrison and Wesley Strick wrote the screenplay, and Sam O'Steen did the editing.

These and other contributions have been orchestrated into an effective whole by director Nichols, a veteran filmmaker whose work attains this level of expertise all too rarely.

FILMS IN REVIEW, 9-10/94, p. 57, Andy Pawelczak

At one point in *Wolf*, the new anti-generic werewolf movie directed by Mike Nichols, Jack Nicholson says to Michelle Pfeiffer, "If civilization fails, if the world ends, I'll still understand what God meant, if I'm with you." It's an amazing line, too literary and pretentious by far, but somehow it works, and the movie backs up its sense of both the forces that imperil civilization and the glories of God's intentions—by which I mean civility, art, compassion, tenderness. Not that the movie is a theological tract or yet another doomsday diatribe about the decline and fall of practically everything, though it is that, too. *Wolf* is a rarer phenomenon, a witty, literate, entertaining, deeply romantic Hollywood film that takes real risks, some of which pay off handsomely.

Will Randall (Jack Nicholson) is editor-in-chief of a prestigious Manhattan publishing house. In an industry more concerned with the bottom line than with quality, Will's taste and originality are liabilities, and he's being forced out by the company's new owner, a Rupert Murdoch-like mogul named Raymond Alden (Christopher Plummer). "You're a nice person," Alden says. "Thank God I'm replacing you." Will doesn't have the killer instinct necessary for survival in the Darwinian world of corporate take-overs and empire building. Explaining how he signed an author, he says, "I did it the old fashioned way. I begged."

At the beginning of the movie, Will gets bitten by a wolf while on a business trip to Vermont. Once the wolf bite begins to take effect and the well-known atavism sets in, he undergoes an at-first subtle transformation. His posture gets straighter, his stomach flatter, his hair fuller, and the look of gleeful intransigence returns to his eye. Nicholson is wonderful in these early scenes as the tired, defeated Will secures a new lease on life and enters into office warfare with Alden and with Stewart Swinton (James Spader), Will's young protege who has been conspiring to replace him.

All of this is a mid-life fantasy of rejuvenation with more than a dash of Robert Bly-like male revivalism and faux totemism thrown in, but, in the first half at least, the script is so smart and accurate about the New York publishing world and Nichols' direction so crisp that the movie escapes puerility. Rumor has it that the script, credited to the novelist Jim Harrison and Wesley Strick (*True Believer, Cape Fear*), underwent five rewrites and a final touch-up by Elaine May. There's a question of who's the real auteur here, but all the signs point to an authentic collaboration. The exploration of the wolf within has always been Nicholson's territory, and he recently went through a mid-life crisis of his own about which he said, "I don't really have the time but I have to do the time." Harrison, who looks like a truck driver and writes like the poet laureate of a vanishing pristine America, writes novels about poetic lone wolves out on an angst ridden quest for freedom and truth. When Pfeiffer says to Nicholson, "Why does it always have to be the worst pain, the worst defeat, the worst news," you can hear the genuine Harrison note as he deflates his own macho romanticism. Nichols' career has been in a slump since before *Regarding Henry* so *Wolf*'s theme of mid-life rebirth must have appealed to him.

A lot of critics have complained that Michelle Pfeiffer, as the millionaire Alden's daughter with whom Nicholson gets involved, just serves as wolf bait, but in fact she turns in a subtly modulated and moving performance. Pfeiffer projects a neurasthenic, wounded glamor that reminded me of Faye Dunaway in *Chinatown*, and her Beauty-and-the-Beast love scenes with Nicholson are more complexly adult and tender than anything in recent movies. James Spader is terrific as a yuppie from hell who turns smarminess into an art form, and Christopher Plummer's tycoon is a smooth faced viper.

The movie falls apart in the last third when Nicholson becomes a full fledged werewolf and genre mechanics take over. The special effects are feeble compared to a real genre movie like *An American Werewolf in London*, and the finale is a long, boring fight. But the first two-thirds are very good indeed, and the final shots of Pfeiffer—moonstruck and mysterious—are worth the wait.

LOS ANGELES TIMES, 6/17/94, Calendar/p. 1, Kenneth Turan

Michelle Pfeiffer, Jack Nicholson and the passionate animal inside him, hellbent on getting out. "Wolf" sounds so simple, so effective, so foolproof. Would that it were.

Directed by Mike Nichols and written by novelist Jim Harrison and Wesley Strick (with an uncredited assist from Elaine May), "Wolf's" problem, as those very different sensibilities indicate, is that it can't seem to decide what kind of a movie it wants to be.

Rather than the straight-ahead endeavor the premise promises, "Wolf" meanders down several paths. At varying times it is a satirical look at New York publishing, a star vehicle, a meditation on the nature of disease and immortality and even, in its spare time, a standard-issue werewolf horror thriller.

Some of these sections are effective, some less so, but they pull in so many different directions that finally all they have in common is how awkwardly they mix with one another. And without coherence, a movie that is only sporadically involving is the inevitable result.

Part of the difficulty with "Wolf" is that whatever its aspirations are, it must be firmly grounded in the horror genre to have any effectiveness at all. But neither the screenwriters nor Nichols, who considers the movie "a poetic expression of an inner state," possess the requisite touch, dooming sections of the picture to be flat or silly rather than gripping.

"Wolf" begins traditionally enough, with a man driving alone through a cold and snowy Vermont night. He is New York publishing executive Will Randall (Nicholson), who has so much trouble coping with the elements that his car hits what looks to be a wolf. And when Randall gets out to investigate, the beast retaliates by taking a bite out of his hand.

Back in Manhattan, no one believes the animal really was a wolf and Randall is too busy with his own crises at the publishing firm MacLeish House, where he is editor in chief and his friend and protege Stewart Swinton (James Spader) is head of marketing, to think about it much.

Newly acquired by pompous billionaire Raymond Alden (Christopher Plummer), one of those who believes that taste and individuality are literary handicaps, MacLeish is in the throes of an amusingly portrayed shake-up that threatens to affect everyone's future.

But while Randall tries to cope with interoffice politics, he starts to notice changes in his life, changes, the film interestingly claims, that may not be all bad. His eyesight and hearing get more acute, his sense of smell heightens, he even edits copy at a greatly increased rate and finds a way to open wife Charlotte's (Kate Nelligan) robe with his teeth.

"The wolf passed something along to me," he tells new friend Laura Alden (Pfeiffer), the billionaire's bored and sarcastic daughter, in one of the film's sporadic philosophical moments. "But I'm afraid it will have a price."

Even with a prop pipe and an exhausted voice, Nicholson is problematic at best in the film's initial stages, when the script insists he is the kindest, most decent and civilized literary editor in all of Manhattan, which is casting against type with a vengeance.

Invariably an involving actor to watch, Nicholson is adept and surprisingly low-key and subtle in many of the scenes that require him to increasingly feel the presence of the wolf within. The joke of the transformation, however, is that as Will Randall becomes less like himself, he becomes more like Jack Nicholson, albeit a Nicholson who is thankfully resistant to the fearful extremes of mugging.

And, in the star vehicle, "Jack's back and Michelle's got him" part of the movie, Nicholson and Pfeiffer play nicely together, though the part of Laura is uninvolving enough to make it uncertain why Pfeiffer took it on in the first place.

Also uncertain is "Wolf's" treatment of the conventional horror moments that any film of this type must have. Despite Rick Baker's restrained makeup, seeing Nicholson's Randall sniff the air, curl his lip and engage in some of the bloodier aspects of werewolf behavior is much more unconvincing than it needs to be.

Perhaps, the odd affecting moment like Randall's dialogue with werewolf expert Dr. Vijay Alezias (Om Puri) aside, it is not really possible to make a genteel werewolf movie. In any event with its final third focused firmly on disturbing physical violence, "Wolf" resists carrying even that notion all the way to the end. Though its premise must have had intellectual appeal to all involved, "Wolf" doesn't feel like anyone believed its story could really happen, and that is a tough barrier to overcome.

NEW STATESMAN & SOCIETY, 8/19/94, p. 33, Jonathan Romney

The trouble with reviewing a film called *Wolf* is that, even before you've seen it, you find yourself reaching for that mental file card marked "Lycanthropy, cinema images of". You're halfway to writing that think-piece that has already been written into the film. Then you yearn for some lost age in which Hollywood's unconscious really was unconscious—a time when monster movies were just monster movies, and it was left to the critics to unpick the thorny undergrowth in which stirred the murky, unspeakable Repressed.

Now it's all done for you. There seems little mileage in explicating what films are "really" about because that is invariably clear on the surface. Hollywood movies are made by people who have been through film school, boned up on their Bettelheim, and come to a subject fully armed with subtext. What was once cinema's unconscious has simply risen to the top.

Coppola's *Bram Stoker's Dracula*, for example, was such a knowing exercise in meta-Gothic that you could just sit there ticking off the up-to-date Repressed Top Ten. Castration anxiety, yup; Aids, OK; homophobia, present and correct ...

So you pretty much know what you'll get with Mike Nichols' *Wolf* and what will be done to give it that 1990s twist. The werewolf myth is about letting the beast break through the veneer of civilisation: we're talking hairy chests, howling at the moon. Ergo we're talking a project pitched at the people who put Robert Bly's Iron John at the top of the bestseller lists. The one daring thing about *Wolf* is that it turns its back on the dominant audience of teen-twenties multiplex goers to court a generation that wants to be reassured that you can grow older and still feel tough, sexy, sophisticated.

Its hero is Will Randall (Jack Nicholson), a weary, middle-aged book editor who gets bitten by a wolf. He feels those old lycanthropic twinges, and then starts living a little. Rejuvenated overnight, he gets mad and gets even with his nasty new boss, his creepy work rival and his unfaithful wife, then makes out with Michelle Pfeiffer as the boss's daughter. He acquires vastly improved repartee, terrific business acumen, and gets to outleap and gore deer in the woods. It's not so much a wish-fulfilment fantasy as a Five-Point Self-Realisation Package. Feel that bite! Howl that howl! You'll shed unsightly pounds as well!

But there's no resonance in the myth once it's stripped of all the disturbing things that traditionally come along with the fangs and side-whiskers: the self-fear, the sense of punishment, of possession as curse. An expert in matters lupine tells Will, "The demon wolf is not evil," and spins a lovely Bly line about "power without guilt". But what a weedy fantasy it is—how blandly therapeutic. It's so *efficient*, with every wish realised, every score settled and the slate left perfectly clean.

Indeed, Will even gets to clean up the city, in one scene that gives away the film's true allegiances. He metes fang-and-claw justice to a gang of black muggers in Central Park. Here are the forces of darkness in service to white middle-class paranoia; the children of the night signed up with Neighbourhood Watch.

Initially, *Wolf* promises something quite engaging. Apart from the pleasure of seeing Jack Nicholson exude unusually warm gravitas in an elder-statesman role (his most subdued and *human* performance since *The King of Marvin Gardens* in 1972), there's considerable relief when what looks set to be a boogly-eyed horror film takes a rather elegant detour into the *real*. We find ourselves immersed in the tawdry politics of the publishing company where Randall is the last old-school Man of Taste (he told Judith Krantz no semi-literate 14 year old would read her books). For a while, it looks as if an injection of moon madness into this urbane milieu will have a nice satirical pay-off.

At the party held by the new boss (Christopher Plummer), things get interesting. Just when Will has lost his job, he finds the horses shying away, as if he'd become *persona non grata* even in the stables. Later, fully wolfed up, he vengefully pisses on his rival James Spader's shoes and sweetly announces, "Just marking my territory."

The film is best at moments like this, when the hoary apparatus of horror supplies a novel take on the professional jungle. But then the banal old fantasies come to the fore as Will starts sprouting John McCririck whiskers and makes for the woods. He simply does what every middle-aged guy caught in the rat-race dreams of doing. It's hardly the rampaging Id set free; more like desire whitewashed as some sort of manageable will-to-fun.

We find the same thing in the current release *The Mask*. Its hero turns into a cartoon monster when he dons an ancient mask whose property, as a psychiatrist tells him, is to make repressed desires real. But where the original comic let rip the nihilistic spirit of massacre, the film version turns a psychotic ghoul into a Bugs Bunny fit for family viewing.

The same goes for *Wolf*. Nothing Will does horrifies us; we only want to root for this regular guy coming into his own. The only twist is that he isn't turning into a wolf at all; he's turning into Jack Nicholson. We're treated to the strange, frustrating sight of an actor playing interestingly against type, but then becoming predictably like himself.

This self-referential appeal to a star persona is the film's only interesting twist. Where most Wolf Men and Mr Hydes have morphed away from the norm, the character of Will is simply a delaying tactic before good old Jack, bustling and sniggering, jumps out of the mild-man skin.

How much more interesting it would have been to see him in *Curse of the Mummy*, as a rampant extrovert who gets unnaturally wrapped up in himself.

Wolf prefers to give vent to the unconscious of the traditional horror film, in order to repress current anxieties that it can't quite manage. It's the conservative man's riposte to the uncontainable anti-social drives of modern American culture, which emerge in movies by Quentin Tarantino or in gangsta rap records. The film attempts to tame the wild imagination by domesticating it as healthy therapy—by legalising it.

What shows through this emollient fantasy is a new Repressed. There is one thing that *Wolf* can't handle. It lies in that complex negotiation of mood and style in the film's first half hour; in some of the barbed amorous dialogue between Nicholson and Pfeiffer; and in those scenes where the film actually bothers with language. For *Wolf* only breathes when it's a comedy of manners that works around the werewolf theme, instead of gasping under its dead weight. Take away the banal high-concept and you get that risky excess that only one in a hundred Hollywood films (such as the recent, underrated *Fearless*) even tries to deal with. For want of a better word, you could call it the real.

NEW YORK, 6/20/94, p. 77, David Denby

Horror-film buffs will be disappointed with Mike Nichols's *Wolf.* So will moviegoers hoping for a delirious visual experience. *Wolf,* an urbane wolfsbane movie, doesn't give us much of a jolt, and although its dark-blue moonlight colors look great, Nichols and cinematographer Giuseppe Rotunno don't liberate the visual scheme for the movie. Nichols is a director who mocks a horror picture even as he's making one. Set in the wolf-eat-wolf world of New York publishing, the movie has a slightly uneasy tone, the tone of smart people doing something not quite natural to them. Yet a lot of it is witty and rather touching, and until the cruddy final scenes, I enjoyed it a great deal. Nichols and writers Jim Harrison and Wesley Strick have jettisoned the silver bullets, the Carpathian claptrap of the old Lon Chaney Jr. cornball scare movies. Instead, the filmmakers have seized hold of the liberationist undertones. Becoming a wolf is not just suffering; it's also an escape into freedom.

Movie-world buzz has it that Jack Nicholson is too old for his part, but having seen him, I can't imagine anyone else doing it. As Will Randall, the editorial director of a small, quality-lit publishing house, Nicholson, keeping his voice low, has somehow captured the weariness, the modulated irony and deep-down integrity of the aging New York literary man. Nicholson doesn't glower and pose; he sticks to his business of playing a highly controlled and self-conscious intellectual. He has the strong forehead of a man of character. Driving through the Vermont mountains, Will hits a wolf, and then, when he gets out of his Volvo to check the animal's condition, he gets bitten. Right away Mike Nichols tips us off that the movie is not quite meant to be taken straight. The seemingly dead animal cocks a yellow eye at Nicholson before chomping on his wrist.

When Will returns to town, he discovers, as he expected, that the billionaire publisher (Christopher Plummer) who has purchased the publishing house wants to replace him. The surprise is that the replacement is his friend and protege (James Spader), a young marketing genius who thinks books should "sizzle." Betrayed on all sides, Will begins sprouting tufts on his hands, and he wakes to the pleasure of strength and potency. His senses are sharpened: He smells more, sees more; he even reads better. (I know a few editors who could use a bite.) Becoming a wolf is not just a metaphor for sexual arousal: Will's desire for everything in life has been aroused. The wolf bite is his Faustian bargain. The price is that he turns savage under the moon. Miraculously, Nicholson does most of his work without special makeup; his teeth grow a little longer, but the wolfishness is mainly physical and spiritual. Invigorated, Will takes on the publishing magnate and the slimy protege. In part the movie is about fear of old age, and a last leap at youth.

The satirical point in all this, of course, is that wolves are all around us and sometimes inside us. Christopher Plummer is a terrifyingly sophisticated magnate, a man amused by the knowledge that decency and taste are a drag on profits, and James Spader outdoes himself playing James Spader. Surely this is the culminating performance of his yuppie-creep phase. The baby-faced Spader, literally dripping with sincerity (he's moist), looks most vulnerable as he's being most vicious. And Spader pulls off a comic tour de force: In the movie's most audacious scene, Spader, bitten and himself metamorphosing, kneels and sniffs at Michelle Pfeiffer in ecstasies of obsequious lust.

Mike Nichols, that compound of talent and cynicism, has never been sharper at getting the undertones of hostility in ordinary speech. For once, a sophisticated New York milieu that doesn't seem fake or strained! And yet, in many ways, *Wolf* is Nichols's gentlest movie. When Will meets Laura (Pfeiffer), the billionaire's beautiful, hard-living, and miserable daughter, Nichols establishes a lovely rueful tone—and he sustains it. Pfeiffer's Laura falls in love with the much older man because he has an aura of defeated integrity, and she feels defeated herself. A few flashes of literate and tender banter between these two struck me as almost a revelation. The sound of grownups talking! Who cares if it's in a werewolf picture? The trouble is, the tenderness is finally too tame. The relationship doesn't go wild when it should. What's the point of making a modern wolfman movie if you aren't going to have a great, snarling sex scene?

Will pursues deer through the woods and chews up muggers in Central Park. He doesn't suffer as Lon Chaney Jr. did. He's almost enthralled by the wolf within. I only wish Mike Nichols had liberated the wolf inside himself as well. If he had, he might have freed the camera and made us crazy with pleasure. Nichols uses New York poorly (most of *Wolf* was shot on sets), and the movie ends flatly. The pleasures of *Wolf* are minor—but they're distinct and memorable.

NEW YORK POST, 6/17/94, p. 39, Thelma Adams

Women who run with wolves—and the men who love them.

Next on "Geraldo"? Not this week. It's "Wolf," the latest movie from Mike Nichols, the Oscar-winning director of "The Graduate," "Silkwood" and "Working Girl."

This lavishly silly, downright entertaining werewolf (literally man-wolf) pic stars Jack Nicholson as Will Randall, a toothless, has-been editor. Bitten by a Vermont wolf, Randall becomes bloody thirsty and virile—just what's needed to revive his career in the wolf-eat-wolf world of modern publishing.

Like previous movies about the curse of lycanthropy, from 1935's "Werewolf of London" to "I Was a Teen-age Werewolf," the movie plays on the tension between society's restrictions and the animal locked within each man. (For the female version, nothing beats Jacques Tourneur's classic 1942 B-movie "Cat People.")

"Wolf" features the first werewolf to drive a Volvo! Nicholson, with his joyless smile, accordion brow and rounded shoulders is roused out of a midlife funk by his transformation. So, he eats human flesh. At least no one pushes him around anymore.

For Nicholson it's old-home week. He got his start in Roger Corman horror cheapies like "The Cry Baby Killer" and "The Raven."

Nicholson's joined by terror-titan Christopher Plummer as Randall's cutthroat employer, the terrifying yuppie James Spader as his smarmy protege, the wonderful Kate Nelligan as his wife, and Michelle Pfeiffer, who makes the most of the thankless girlfriend role.

The dynamite cast and a screenplay (by Jim Harrison and Wesley Strict) that crackles with one-liners raises "Wolf" to pleasing entertainment.

Nichols, as always, is an apt director of actors with a keen social awareness and comic timing. But, dear director, where are your fangs?

Waffling between camp and social commentary, "Wolf" fails to stir much tension or terror. It's slightly scarier than Barney, and less tense than a Mets game.

The special effects rely on a scare-stopping, slow-motion technique. When Nicholson leaps like a wolf, scaling trees and walls he bears an uncanny resemblance to Mary Martin in "Peter Pan."

Still, as he ages, Nicholson has become an actor hardly able to conceal the wolf within. With fur and fangs and a delightful snarl, Nicholson's midlife werewolf is laughable but irresistible.

NEWSDAY, 6/17/94, Part II/p. B2, Jack Mathews

Lycanthropy, a serious-sounding word from the Greek words for "wolf" and "man." is a bona fide psychiatric condition describing people who believe they are wolves, even if they are really only lawyers, agents and film producers trying to get ahead in a dog-eat-dog world.

The term also refers, of course, to werewolves, people who in folklore actually turn into beasts, with fangs, pointy ears, furry faces and clawed paws, feeding at night, usually under full moons, and bearing strong resemblance to Lon Chaney Jr.

I would like to tell you that Mike Nichols' "Wolf" is about clinical lycanthropy, that Jack Nicholson's Will Randall, a low-keyed, urbane Manhattan book editor, is merely driven wild by his job-stealing protégé and an unfaithful wife. That his suddenly acute senses and renewed vitality are caused by some internal chemistry, and not by the wolf spit injected in the opening scene.

But, no, after a sharply sophisticated and compelling first hour or so, "Wolf ' merely veers off in the direction where more than two dozen werewolf films have gone before, and despite its A-list look and estimated $70-million budget, it ends up as much a B movie as any of them.

"Wolf" was conceived as a star vehicle for Nicholson, whose feral brow has been put to use in such previous supernatural thrillers as "The Shining" and "The Witches of Eastwick," and until Will Randall starts spending his nights baying at the moon and pigging out on Central Park muggers, he gives a solid, surprisingly restrained performance.

In the early segments, when Randall is simultaneously trying to calm the beast within and plotting to get even with the boss (Christopher Plummer) and colleague (James Spader) who drove him out of his job, there is a measured coolness about Nicholson that makes us almost giddy with anticipation. We know there's a current of rage just beneath the surface of his characters, and keep waiting for the real Jack to emerge and really scare somebody.

Instead, a damn wolf pops out.

And that's not the movie's biggest problem! The script, by novelist Jim Harrison ("Warlock") and hot screenwriter Wesley Strick ("Cape Fear"), is essentially a love story, between a genteel man turning into an animal and a hellcat society babe (Michelle Pfeiffer) who needs taming, and it doesn't work for a minute.

Laura Alden, the rebellious daughter of Randall's billionaire boss, is a paper-thin cliché, even when written as a woman in her late teens or early 20s, and she collapses under Pfeiffer's earnest attempts to give her weight. There is no chemistry between the high-powered stars, because there is no credibility to their characters' relationship.

The film's best conceit, almost its saving grace, is the parallel drawn between the savage nature of man in mythology and in the modern book world. Production designer Bo Welch and cinematographer Giuseppe Rotunno have turned that world into an architectural zoo, a latticework of bars, grids, tiles, windows and shadows, caging its characters and their high ambitions.

With the wolf instincts growing stronger in him, Randall begins to pace behind those bars, and—at about the moment the movie self-destructs—to leap over them.

What Nichols and the writers seem to have intended was for the two worlds to merge, for the savage battle for control of the book company to simply give way to a life-and-death struggle between real animals. That would indeed be a neat trick, but the shift from Manhattan to the pastoral grounds of a Long Island mansion where the finale occurs, is done with a teeth-rattling jolt.

Nichols was the wrong gun-for-hire on this project. An actor's director, he gets the most he can from the cast but has no feel whatsoever for the horror elements and relies on quick cuts, slow motion and other cheesy editing effects to get through the action sequences.

The producers have asked critics not to reveal details of that last act, and their secrets are safe with me. I'd be embarrassed to repeat them.

NEWSWEEK, 6/20/94, p. 59, David Ansen

Werewolf movies, even the tackiest ones, ripple with primal resonance. Give us a full moon, feral fangs and a furry guy howling in the dark, and you've got a perfect snapshot of a *homo sapiens* in the grip of his darkest atavistic suspicion: *underneath this thin windbreaker of civilization, I'm a raging beast!*

From "The Werewolf" in 1913 through "I Was a Teenage Werewolf" (1957) to "An American Werewolf in London" (1981), this turf has been endlessly plowed. The dark beauty of Mike Nichols's *Wolf* is that it manages to seduce us afresh, taking dreamlike advantage of our *déjà vu*. Spiked with social satire, strategic jolts of horror and a "Beauty and the Beast" romanticism that owes more to Cocteau than Disney, it recasts a too-familiar story in a literate, contemporary idiom. This is a werewolf movie for adults: it's got sophisticated teeth.

It's also got Jack Nicholson, who was born with a beastly glint in his eye. Playing a civilized, mild-mannered book editor, Will Randall, he's a man of "taste and individuality"—two distinct liabilities in the mid-'90s world of corporate publishing. His company has been swallowed by a voracious conglomerate headed by Christopher Plummer, and he's about to be replaced as editor in chief by his young ruthless protégé (the hilariously smarmy James Spader).

But suddenly this diffident fellow feels invigorated, impassioned, vengeful. Horses freak when he approaches. Can it be the result of the wolf bite on the wrist he got on a dark Vermont country road? How else to explain his inhumanly acute sense of smell, of hearing—and the feral brilliance of his scheme to get his old job back? It is one of the droller conceits of the script-written by Jim Harrison, Wesley Strick and an uncredited Elaine May—that to succeed in the new corporate New York world it can only help to be an animal.

Nichols and an impeccable cast bring this treacherously urbane milieu to life in swift, sure strokes, blanketed in cinematographer Giuseppe Rottuno's inky chiaroscuro. And when Michelle Pfeiffer's Laura Alden enters the tale—she's the moody, neurotic daughter of Plummer's magnate—the writing loses none of its edge. As Will's newfound libido gets unleashed—not to mention his nocturnal forays in pursuit of raw meat—"Wolf" smoothly shifts into high romantic gear. This is dangerous dramatic stuff—the slightest inappropriate titter and the whole house of cards collapses—but Nicholson and Pfeiffer navigate with hushed conviction. When we laugh—and we do—it's only when they want us to. Will's lycanthropic metamorphosis—and his own torn response to it—has a resonant ambiguity. He's both terrified of his own savagery and liberated by it. He's like a junkie in the grip of a passionate high, knowing he's destroying himself and unable to stop.

"Wolf" only loses its eerie sure-footedness at the end, when it gives in to the genre and settles for chases, leaps and fights. This isn't Nichols's strength, and it's the only part of the movie that feels mundane. There's a final twist that doesn't quite deliver all it should. But such is the spell that "Wolf" has cast—like being draped in a voluptuous, smartly tailored cloak—that you don't want it to end. From such a seductive nightmare, who'd want to wake?

SIGHT AND SOUND, 9/94, p. 52, Philip Kemp

Driving at night through Vermont, Will Randall hits a wolf and apparently kills it. But when he approaches the animal, it revives and bites him before vanishing into the woods. The next day, at the MacLeish publishing house in New York, where Will works as editor-in-chief, the talk is of the party being given that evening by Raymond Alden, a tycoon who recently acquired MacLeish. Will fears he's about to be sacked; his assistant Roy, his secretary Mary and his protege, head of marketing Stewart Swinton, assure him of their loyalty.

With his wife Charlotte, Will attends the party on Alden's estate. Alden offers him a demeaning post with less money, adding that Stewart has been pushing for Will's job. Shaken and feeling suddenly ill, Will is helped by Alden's daughter Laura. The next day he sleeps round the clock and when Charlotte comes home makes passionate love to her. At work he finds his senses intensely heightened, and after Charlotte leaves—supposedly—for a seminar, detects a strange smell on her clothes. Going to Stewart's apartment, he confronts her there, and bites Stewart's hand.

Will moves into a hotel. With Roy and Mary's help he plans to go independent and entice MacLeish's top authors away. Visiting Alden's estate to turn down his offer he meets Laura again, and they spend the afternoon together. At sundown he feels strange, and Laura gives him a bed in her summer-house. That night he hunts and kills a deer in the woods, waking covered in blood but with no memory of what happened. After giving Alden his ultimatum, Will consults an expert on animal possession, Dr Alezias, who tells him he may be turning into a wolf and gives him an amulet to prevent the process. At night Will roams through Central Park Zoo, savaging three muggers who attack him.

Reinstated in his job, with increased power and salary, Will humiliates and fires Stewart. Charlotte comes to his hotel, but he rejects her and spends the night with Laura. In the morning the police arrive: Charlotte is dead, her throat torn out. Laura gives him an alibi but conceals him on the Alden estate, locking him in the stables before returning to make a statement. At the precinct she meets Stewart and realises he too is becoming a wolf. She flees back to the estate where Will, thanks to the amulet, has subdued his wolfish tendencies. Stewart pursues her, kills two guards and attacks her. Will hurls away the amulet and bounds to the rescue; after a violent fight Laura shoots Stewart dead. Will escapes into the woods, and all the killings are ascribed to Stewart. Laura, a lupine gleam in her eyes, lopes off to meet the wolf Will has become.

Of all the screen monsters, the werewolf has always had the strongest claim on our sympathy. Few movie lycanthropes get that way because they deserve to, let alone want to, and the very first *Wolf Man* film (1940) roped in mystic old Maria Ouspenskaya to warn Lon Chaney Jr that virtue was no protection: "Even the man who is pure of heart/And says his prayers by night/May become a wolf when the wolfbane bloom ...". Nearly always the victims are racked with remorse over their nocturnal carnage; more recently, thanks to advances in special effects. moral anguish has manifested itself in transformation scenes of sinew-wrenching physical agony (*The Company of Wolves, An American Werewolf in London*). At the same time, though, a more subversive theme has been emerging: that the feral state might have a lot going for it. Despite all that distressing bloodshed, the werewolf—animal id rampant—is clearly in touch with healthy natural instincts repressed beneath our over-civilised veneers. Maybe werewolves, like blondes, have more fun.

Any day now, someone is going to come up with a film that explores the tension between these rival myths of screen lycanthropy (*The Howling* sniffed round the idea but backed off, being a bit ahead of its time). Mike Nichols' *Wolf* could have been that film, but finally isn't. After a few ritual nods to the agony-and-remorse school, it decisively comes down on the fun side. The pre-wolf Will Randall is a stooped, put-upon figure, sneered at by the predatory new boss for his wimpish virtues of "taste and individuality" and wretchedly confessing to Laura that he doesn't "have the courage to be jobless at my age." One good shot of wolfblood and he sheds 15 years along with his glasses and his moral scruples; he acquires hyper-acute senses, high-octane sexual allure and new-found skills in corporate in-fighting. All this, along with superhuman strength and a knack for 20-foot kung-fu leaps. The trappings may be more sophisticated, but the angle isn't so far from that of the anodyne *Teen Wolf* movies: werewolves are simply cool dudes who can pull the chicks.

Essentially, *Wolf* is a slick variant on the old wish-fulfilment formula of the worm that turns. and not least of its pleasures is Nicholson playing the worm. True, his meek act doesn't convince for a second—the Nicholson screen persona has expanded quite some way since *The King of Marvin Gardens*—but then it's not meant to. The fun is waiting for the moment when the eyes glint, the teeth are bared, and Wolfman Jack makes his welcome entrance. Almost more enjoyable, because less predictable, is watching smooth arch-yuppie James Spader go wolf. (Not that anybody does go wolf in full-splatter *American Werewolf* style, since Wolf isn't that visceral a film. Metamorphosis is achieved by extra facial hair, plus a lot of snarling, nose-wrinkling and jaw-jutting.) At one point the two dominant males clash in—where else?—the executive toilet, with Will not only sacking Stewart but literally pissing on him ("Just marking my territory").

Never quite getting its conventions in focus, *Wolf* plays mix-and-match with werewolf lore from a dozen sources. Gazing at night from his hotel window, supersenses alert, Will picks up a whole alternative frequency of jungle cries that evoke Michael Wadleigh's under-rated *Wolfen*: the idea of a prowling feral subculture infesting the New York streets. At other times the film resorts to some hoary old routines from way back: the zoo creatures gibbering and howling as the wolfman prowls among them, the ill starred muggers picking what looks like an easy hit. The ending is a mess, gabbled through at speed in the hope we won't notice: the police, it seems, happily believe that a man with six bullets in him tore someone's throat out (or maybe that a man with his throat torn out fired off six bullets). But *Wolf*'s chief failing is the complacent, accept-your-true-nature attitude it shares with Nichols' last film, *Regarding Henry*. Indeed the two films are mirror images: Henry is a ruthless hot shot until an accident turns him gentle and caring, Will takes the opposite journey. In both cases the final message is one of reassurance. And reassurance isn't what any worthwhile werewolf movie should be about.

TIME, 6/20/94, p. 62, Richard Schickel

The sudden appearance of unsightly body hair aside, there are, it turns out, certain advantages to lycanthropy, especially in its early stages. Unnoticed by previous wolfman epics, they prove useful to Will Randall (Jack Nicholson), an editor fighting for his professional life, and equally beneficial to *Wolf* in establishing a tone—half social satire, half dark romance—that is unique in the annals of horror movies.

What hard-pressed executive would not covet the boons conferred on the depressed and integrity-ridden Will after he's nipped on the wrist by a rough beast slouching along a Vermont roadway? All his senses are suddenly sharpened: he can smell liquor on a colleague's breath at a dozen paces, overhear plotting phone calls far down the corridor, even—literally—sniff out his wife's affair with his chief rival (James Spader). He becomes, you might say, an animal in bed. And he, naturally, develops a taste for the jugular in matters of business.

Still, wolfmen need sympathy. They are, after all, profoundly victims, since they are usually nice guys who didn't ask for supernatural powers and take no pleasure in possessing or being possessed by them. It's Michelle Pfeiffer's task to provide Will with TLC, and as Laura Alden, his super-rich boss's daughter, she is tough, patient and fearless when at the end she must become an especially passionate animal-rights activist.

But it's Nicholson's transformations that lie at the heart of the movie's success. This may be slam-dunk casting, demonic being the thing we most happily pay our money to see him do. But he calibrates his shifts to the lupine—a cock of the head, a twitch of the nostril, a panicky glint in the eye—with delicious subtlety. Mike Nichols, the director, finds all the right angles to enhance Nicholson's effects, which are wholly a product of the actor's technique, not a makeup artist's.

Nichols and the writers (novelist Jim Harrison and Wesley Strick) are treading a fine high wire; one misstep and off you tumble into self-satire, the modern horror film's omnipresent danger. But by provoking authentic laughter with their satirical thrusts at current corporate styles (Spader is a hilarious model of yuppie unctuousness), they make sure we are amused often and always at the right moments. If Nichols had less skill, we would crack up when the moon is full and Nicholson's stunt double starts leaping around the countryside, but using low light and slow motion, the director displays great tact in those passages.

There is probably not enough terror in *Wolf* to satisfy today's hard-core horror fan—no chain saws or razor-sharp fingernails—but there is a well-measured sense of pity for Will. You could, if you wish, find in him a symbol for all kinds of human bedevilment. Mix that with humor, intelligence and high-style filmmaking and you have a true summer rarity—a genre movie for grownups.

VILLAGE VOICE, 6/21/94, p. 50, Georgia Brown

If on a winter's night a traveler hits a black wolf with his car, he shouldn't get out and poke the body with a stick. Then again, if he's Will Randall (Jack Nicholson) and nothing short of a complete personality change will suffice, maybe he should. The wolf's bite, occurring at the beginning of Mike Nichols's *Wolf*, transmits some primal feral spark that Will, editor in chief of a prestigious New York publishing house, sorely needs. Last of the serious book people, Randall stands for civilization as we know it.

The product of numerous rewrites—beginning with five drafts by Michigan wild man Jim Harrison—*Wolf* owes something to the Grimm brothers, Ovid (*Metamorphoses*), Kafka (*Metamorphosis*), Jung, Robert Bly, and perhaps even Maurice Sendak. It's about getting in touch with your inner wild thing, "welcoming the Hairy Man," as *Iron John* puts it, "reviving the inner warrior." Nichols, who apparently underwent a personal crisis a few years ago, seems obsessed with tales of midlife transformation, wounds and their repercussions. In some ways, *Wolf* resembles the much maligned *Regarding Henry* (maligned by me, I'm afraid), in which a weaselly corporate lawyer gets in touch with the inner child after being shot in the temple by a mugger.

Will's puncture wound is in the hand not the head, and whereas the venal, driven Henry required slowing down, the passive, defeated Will needs to be revved up. A man of taste and sensibility, Will survives by a thread into the era of communications mergers and media empires.

(In an early exchange, his wife, played by Kate Nelligan, asks about a contract signing. "I did it the old-fashioned way," says Will bitterly. "I begged for it.") Now his company is being absorbed into a conglomerate, and he faces a humiliating demotion. The new boss, a ruthless media tycoon named Alden (Christopher Plummer), is far more impressed by the unctuous, young, hand-kissing Yalie, Stewart Swinton (James Spader). Alden's daughter Laura (Michelle Pfeiffer), the story's princess (later revealed as one of those women who run with the wolves), initially gravitates to Will merely because she senses Daddy's contempt.

Fortunately for Will, that wolf serum begins to kick in. His hand grows hair. His head grows hair. His eyesight is suddenly so keen he can shuck his tortoiseshells. His ears swivel and quiver as he picks up inane chatter in distant offices. His nose twitches as he sniffs the tequila a coworker had for breakfast or a rival's odor on his wife's clothing. He's a superhero coming into his superpowers.

What isn't comic book is Nicholson's electric, extremely sexy transformation. Although a good deal of publicity has been given to Rick Baker's painstaking werewolf makeup, the real story here is Jack's astounding craft. In the beginning we see a dyspeptic, kind of owlish guy, bitter from the long effort of repressing his distaste for shallow hype and successful toadies. Definitely unappealing. Then a physical sea change begins taking place. Will's eyes glitter, his muscles go on alert. Standing poised for action, he exudes virility. Instantly, he's in perfect shape. Running down the street in his leather jacket, pacing himself for the distance but really flying, he's like a cross between James Mason and Eamonn Coghlan.

Nicholson may be in terrific form, but Nichols is not. From the very first scene with the wolf in the road, something basic is awry. When the beast's yellow eye snaps open while Will isn't looking, the screening audience (not known for tact) burst out laughing. Then the wolf dashes back into the woods and every tree seems to harbor its own wolf. ("Wolves in Vermont, Will? I don't think so," says the doctor treating the bite.) The problem here and later in the movie is that myth and metaphor are hung out like flags for the salute. In any proper thriller, interpretation or zeitgeist-consciousness ought to come later—only on reflection.

Another problem: the film doesn't develop a credible grammar for its werewolf passages. Basically, these movies can go two ways: either leave the horror to the imagination, the way Tourneur did in *Cat People*—you never see but you sense—or do as Cronenberg does in the painfully visceral *The Fly*: show every grotesque permutation. Taking the mushy middle way, Nichols shows and he doesn't. We see Will's face turning and the man-beast leaping, but the movie avoids the descriptive gore—never gives us the means to feel fear, or even anxiety. (Here, when Will comes near horses and they whinny and rear, it plays like the joke in *Young Frankenstein*.) While Will is growing more terrified at his own violence, we look on with detachment. Finally, in what production notes call *Wolf*'s "third act"—asking reviewers not to give it away—violence suddenly becomes graphic, but also ludicrous. Sadly, the ending is a mess.

Still, I admit a soft spot for this loupy fable. Certain moments in Nicholson's performance (like the gentle, confused look he gives the dying Indian sage when asked to bite his hand) felt like strange, luminous celluloid flashpoints, not quite like anything seen before. Unlike Coppola's slick and garish *Dracula*—all style and no convictions—*Wolf* in its clumsy way exudes some of its hero's torn earnestness, the beast's desperation to find a humane way.

Also reviewed in:

CHICAGO TRIBUNE, 6/17/94, Friday/p. C, Michael Wilmington
NATION, 7/25-8/1/94, p. 139, Stuart Klawans
NEW REPUBLIC, 7/11/94, p. 26, Stanley Kauffmann
NEW YORK TIMES, 6/17/94, p. C4, Janet Maslin
NEW YORKER, 7/11/94, p. 83, Anthony Lane
VARIETY, 6/13-19/94, p. 52, Todd McCarthy
WASHINGTON POST, 6/17/94, p. B1, Hal Hinson
WASHINGTON POST, 6/17/94, Weekend/p. 38, Desson Howe

WOMEN FROM THE LAKE OF SCENTED SOULS

A Yellow Line International release of a Tianjin Film Studio/Changchun Film Studio production. *Director:* Xie Fei. *Screenplay (Mandarin with English subtitles):* Xie Fei. *From the short story "Xianghuntagnpande xiangyou fang" by:* Zhou Daxin. *Director of Photography:* Bao Xiaoran. *Music:* Wang Liping. *Sound:* Liu Xiaochuan. *Art Director:* Ma Huiwu and Wang Jie. *Costumes:* Zhang Qing. *Running time:* 105 minutes. *MPAA Rating:* Not Rated.

CAST: Siqin Gaowa (Xiang); Wu Yujuan (Huanhuan); Lei Luosheng (Que); Chen Baoguo (Ren); Jing Lei (Zhier).

CHRISTIAN SCIENCE MONITOR, 10/13/93, p. 12, David Sterritt

[*Women From the Lake of Scented Souls* was reviewed jointly with *Farewell My Concubine*, see *FILM REVIEW ANNUAL, 1994*]

NEW YORK, 2/28/94, p. 115, John Powers

Xiang, the tough-cookie heroine of *Women From the Lake of Scented Souls*, runs a sesame-oil business, carries on a love affair behind her husband's back, and connives to marry off her epileptic son to a girl who loves someone else. She thinks she has it made, but as any fan of Joan Crawford or Bette Davis could have warned her, women like this never get away scot-free. Xie Fei's nicely turned melodrama may lack the exquisite intensity of the best new Chinese films, but it still makes you envy Asian cinema's joy in telling the grown-up stories of passion and greed that once came out of Hollywood. It will be decades before the Chinese feel the need to make a movie of *The Flintstones*.

NEW YORK POST, 2/16/94, p. 32, Thelma Adams

Where are the great roles for women? China provides one answer with "Women From the Lake of Scented Souls."

The movie, which shared top prize at last year's Berlin Film Festival, begins as a melodrama: A capable woman sacrifices all for her family; her husband drinks, loafs, and abuses her; her feckless lover dumps her as she enters middle age; her grown son, retarded and epileptic, requires constant care.

Billed as a Chinese "Mildred Pierce," the Joan Crawford classic about a tough mother who forfeits everything (lover included) for her ungrateful daughter, the reference is a good hook for U.S. audiences hesitant to embrace Chinese movies.

Like the pie-baking Crawford, who succeeds in business but fails at home, Xiang prospers overseeing the family sesame oil business but her domestic life leaves her lonely and dissatisfied.

When a female Japanese entrepreneur invests in the oil business, she alters the course of Xiang's rural North China village. The encounter brings change but doesn't secure happiness.

Writer/director Xie Fei masterfully builds emotional power from an essentially soapy story. The movie stands out in its subtle treatment of an important theme: the subjugation of women, and the ways in which women assist their own suppression.

Xiang, in a strong, earthy performance from the Mongolian Chinese actress Siqin Gaowa, confesses her sorrow's source. At 7, she was sold by her father to her husband's family. At 13, she married a man she would never like, much less love. Her mother-in-law instructed her to be patient; 20 years later, Xiang still tolerates her husband's brutal assaults.

What transforms melodrama into tragedy are Xiang's actions once she prospers. Intent on buying a wife for her retarded son, she chooses Huanhuan (Wu Yujuan), the eldest daughter of a destitute family. In Mildred Pierce fashion, Xiang ruthlessly eliminates all opposition and buys the reed-like beauty for her son, despite the fact that Huanhuan loves another.

Xiang revisits the sins of the father (and the mother!) as she pursues her plans regardless of the girl's happiness. In this painterly, gracefully balanced movie, Xie Fei gradually pulls the two women together, showing how their fates are mirrored.

Xie seems to say that the traditional Chinese vision of women, marriage, and childbearing could not survive without the complicity of women. Abuse of power, lack of compassion, and the willingness to sacrifice another soul to a lifetime of domestic dissatisfaction are not the domain of either sex. It's a pact that both share in equally in a larger system that continues to barter brides and value sons over daughters.

"Human life is a long way to go," Xiang laments on the shores of the local lake when she reslizes she has gone from being victim to victimizer, that her decision to purchase a wife for her son has condemned another woman to a lifetime of sorrow.

The director brooks no happy endings. Xiang's realization has come too late; the cycle has begun again. Will Huanhuan have the strength—or the economic freedom—to break the pattern?

NEWSDAY, 2/16/94 Part II/p. 57, John Anderson

Combine a Dickensian sense of cosmic justice with "Lear's" sense of cosmic rage, set it all amid a Faulknerian landscape of noise and idiots and you have "Women from the Lake of Scented Souls," a Mongolian "Mildred Pierce."

Why the strictly western references to a film about a merchant woman in the north of China? Because the West doesn't want to do it anymore. When it comes to basic human tragedy and impulse, our literature and cinema have turned archetype into parody; cynicism rules, and disenchantment holds its coat.

The Chinese seem to have no such problem, which may account for the burgeoning popularity of their sweeping cinema. The big story, the unabashed classicism mixed with modern problems you find in the films of directors Chen Kaige, Zhang Yimou and Tian Zhuangzhuan, would probably either embarrass or befuddle their western colleagues. It's the kind of thing, however, to which audiences respond lustily.

As they will to "Women from the Lake of Scented Souls." Is it coincidence that the two most ardently feminine films now in theaters were made by men? That they're both from Asia? That they both have "scent" in the title? Probably. Despite their one obvious similarity—a fascination and reverence about women in their respective cultures—the Vietnam of "Scent of Green Papaya," and the China of "Lake of Scented Souls" are like different planets, one a fragrant garden, the other a muusty tract of unresolved conflict.

Xiang (Siqin Gaowa) is a driven, hardworking woman who was sold to her husband Que (Lei Luosheng) at age 7, and came to his bed at age 13. Her life is one of labor and brutish sex. Her grown son is an imbecile, considered unmarriagable because of his epilepsy. Her younger daughter, Zhier (Jing Lei) is the product of her longtime liaison with Ren (Chen Baoguo), who delivers merchandise to her little lakeside shop. Xiang is at once the model of industry, and the result of China's festering sexism and failed attempts at equality.

It is Xiang's sesame oil that lubricates the mills of the gods. Its quality has attracted the attention of a Japanese investor, and Xiang's expectations of wealth prompt her to try and marry off her troubled son Dunzi to Huanhuan (Wu Yujuan), an industrious local girl who reminds Xiang of herself.

What Xiang fails to see, with the lack of foresight that tickled the Greeks, is that she's creating for Huanhuan the same kind of domestic imprisonment in which she's dwelt; Dunzi is all inept sex drive and no brain. The marriage does take place, with inevitable results, and all of Xiang's subsequent remorse and attempts to atone will be for naught.

Although his film is a simple village parable (unlike the gritty urban landscape of his previous film, "Black Snow") Xie lacks the paternalistic pride in the peasantry of Zhang. Or the visual poetry of Chen. "Scented Souls," previously burdened with the graceless title "Woman Sesame Oil Maker" is not a lyrical movie. Its perspective is flat, and basic. But its story is transcendently universal, and irresistible.

VILLAGE VOICE, 2/22/94, p. 52, Georgia Brown

Exercising a healthy respect for melodrama, Chinese filmmakers are demonstrating how politically powerful the genre can be. No wonder their movies make the regime so jittery. In dramas about women who violate parameters of traditional place, Zhang Yimou celebrates female resilience and the subversive will. A woman's picture like Chen Kaige's *Farewell, My Concubine* or a family chronicle like Tian Zhuangzhuang's *The Blue Kite*, gives priority to individual destinies. Last year in Berlin, two Chinese melodramas shared the Golden Bear: Ang Lee's *Wedding Banquet*—the genial comedy that introduced bourgeois Taiwan to gay marriage—and Xie Fei's *Women From The Lake of Scented Souls*, dealing eloquently with woman's desire.

One of China's Fourth Generation directors—a teacher of Chen, Zhang, and Tian-Xie (now in his mid fifties) made *Girl From Hunan*, which played here a few years ago. In that film a young girl is married off to a toddler, becoming in one fell swoop both wife and babysitter. (How many Western women with adult spouses have shared her fate?) Eventually she falls in love with someone her age and passion turns into tragic conflagration. Xie's *Black Snow* won Berlin's Silver Bear in 1990 but never gained a distributor here. For his new film, he's adapted a novel by Zhou Daxin, *The Sesame Oil Mill by the Pool of Scented Souls*.

Xiang (Siqin Gaowa) is a kind of Mildred Pierce of Hebei Province—ruthless, you bet, but immensely sympathetic. An entrepreneur and mother of two, Xiang has made a local sesame oil workshop pay off, turning out a superior product. No thanks to her shiftless husband, Que (Lei Luosheng), who only wants to drink up the profits. One day a Japanese businesswoman (a spiritual cousin from overseas) arrives in town with a bottle of Xiang's oil and proposes subsidizing the enterprise—automating the shop to increase production and marketing the product abroad.

But prospects of success don't relieve Xiang of domestic burdens. Immediately pressing is the need to marry off her son, Dunzi, an epileptic and something of a village idiot. Dunzi has his sights on the lovely Huanhuan (Wu Yujuan). But Huanhuan loves the gentle, good-looking Jinhai. Xiang's first machination is to offer Jinhai a job in the city selling her oil, tacking on stipulations about his eventual marriage. Using her new influence with local authorities, she also succeeds in threatening Huanhuan's parents with financial ruin. Presto, we attend the wedding of the hapless Huanhuan and the childlike Dunzi.

On a visit to the city, Xiang confesses to her chic new Japanese partner that she herself was sold at seven, then married off at 13. Earlier weave learned of her longterm affair with a married man, Ren (Chen Baoguo), who works out of the city handling marketing and delivering supplies. Her teenaged daughter, in fact, is his. (When her drunken husband forces sex, Xiang gulps birth control pills hidden under the mattress. Pity her when he discovers her secret! She may bring home his bacon but he has the right to use his fists when he chooses.) The implication is that Huanhuan is being initiated into the same life—married to a dolt, perhaps becoming the concubine of Jinhai on his visits home.

"What's a concubine?" Xiang asks Ren, when he uses the word in connection with the Japanese woman. The realization that there is a word, a definition, applying to herself has a profound affect. A word takes her actions out of the personal, the willed, and into the socially determined. Suddenly she's humiliated: What once was liberating becomes confining.

Around the idealized figure of Huanhuan, Xie weaves lyrical passages, putting human suffering into the perspective of heaven and earth: splendid sunsets, placid lakes, plaintive song. But these expressions of pathos are for Xiang as well—for her lost childhood, silent endurance, the sings she's committed against her better nature. Nearby by Soul Lake, Xiang tells her Japanese guest, is named for two legendary lovers, suicides who perished there; her oil, she explains, is distinguished because of the water's purity. Oil making itself seems a metaphor for life; the grinding down and distillation of favor according to age-old methods.

For all its richness, Xie's work is tactful—instructive without being didactic. Similarly, Siqin's very moving performance is muted rather than flamboyant and the ending eschews both tragedy and false (temporary) happy ending. Most poignant are small, nuanced details of character—expressions of desire, jealousy, the ever present fear of a desolate old age. The film is at once a cry for social change and a lament for all those souls, over centuries, who drowned.

Also reviewed in:
CHICAGO TRIBUNE, 2/9/94, Friday/p. H, Michael Wilmington
NEW YORK TIMES, 2/16/94, p. C20, Janet Maslin
VARIETY, 3/1/93, p. 57, Derek Elley
WASHINGTON POST, 12/17/94, p. C1, Hal Hinson

WONDERFUL, HORRIBLE LIFE OF LENI RIEFENSTAHL, THE

A Kino International release of an Omega Films Gmbh/Nomad Films/ZDF/Channel Four Television/Arte production. *Producer:* Hans-Jürgen Panitz, Jacques De Clercq, and Dimitri De Clercq. *Director:* Ray Müller. *Screenplay (German with English subtitles):* Ray Müller. *Director of Photography:* Walter A. Franke, Michel Baudour, Jürgen Martin, Ulrich Jaenchen, and (underwater camera) Horst Kettner. *Editor:* Beate Köster, Stefan Mothes, and Vera Dubsikova. *Music:* Ulrich Bassenge and Wolfgang Neumann. *Sound:* Thomas Bastian and Haimo Sahliger. *Production Designer:* Michael Graser: *Running time:* 180 minutes. *MPAA Rating:* Not Rated.

LOS ANGELES TIMES, 4/14/94, Calendar/p. 6, Kenneth Turan

What did she know and when did she know it? That this question, with its overtones of criminal suspicion, turns out to be a central concern of "The Wonderful, Horrible Life of Leni Riefenstahl" is an indication of why the career of this most controversial of film directors makes such a potent and engrossing documentary.

Riefenstahl was a documentary filmmaker herself, as artistic and creative a figure as ever worked in the medium. But her truncated career will always have an asterisk next to it, because her two greatest films were made under the generous patronage of the Nazi Party and her personal friend Hitler.

Both "Triumph of the Will," a celebration of the 1934 Nazi Party Congress in Nuremberg, and "Olympia," a epochal look at the 1936 Berlin Olympic Games, are indisputably masterpieces, evidence of extraordinary visual and organizational gifts. Yet, also indisputably, they happened to be made to trumpet the virtues of an unspeakable regime.

Making the obvious questions about artistic responsibility in a totalitarian society that much more complex is the strong personality of the director herself. Still a pariah in Germany, Riefenstahl remains remarkably vibrant in her 90s, improbably going from friendship with Hitler to membership in Greenpeace. Assertive and persuasive, Riefenstahl is, paradoxically, a life force who ended up on the side of death.

German writer-director Ray Muller's aim with "The Wonderful, Horrible Life" was to view Riefenstahl, "a legend with many faces, loathed and admired," as much as possible without preconceptions, to make a film that would continue the debate, not end it. The result, three hours long and filled to capacity with extensive clips, newsreel footage and both staged and candid interviews, is prodigiously researched, always fascinating, and completely successful.

It is a life with a reverse fairy tale quality to it, starting out with success and luck and ending with the opposite. A dancer who worked for famed producer Max Reinhardt, Riefenstahl had her life changed in 1924 when she was literally transfixed by a poster for a silent film she saw by chance in a subway station.

The film "Mountain of Destiny," directed by Dr. Arnold Fanck, was the first of a genre that came to be known as Bergfilms, tales of Alpine derring-do that featured actual locations and real-life climbing. Riefenstahl talked her way into Fanck's next film, became a star, and eventually directed herself in 1932's eerie "The Blue Light."

Her association with Hitler began equally accidentally after a friend dragged her to a rally. She was intrigued, wrote him a letter, and found that he was a fan. As a real-life heroic superwoman who had become an expert mountaineer, Riefenstahl embodied the ideology Hitler was exploiting.

Learning from her largely unseen first attempt, "Victory of the Faith," a record of the 1933 party congress of which only a fragment remains, Riefenstahl in "Triumph of the Will" pumped up the dramatic intensity to make what is generally considered the most riveting propaganda film ever. Though she says today she's not proud of it, her eyes do gleam as she screens key segments.

Riefenstahl next embarked on a filmed record of the Olympics. Using 30 cameramen, the director shot 250 miles of film, so much it took 10 weeks just to watch and two full years to edit.

The result not only pioneered almost all the techniques used in current sports filming, but in a way that has never been bettered.

Persuasiveness itself, Riefenstahl is not at a loss for explanations for almost everything thrown at her. Art and politics don't mix, she insists, she never thought about ideology, never knew about any of the regime's numerous atrocities until after the war.

Even more intriguing than these formal interviews, where Riefenstahl is on her best behavior, are candid glimpses when she seems to be unaware of being filmed. Here we see Riefenstahl's indomitable will, insisting where the camera must go. And, chatting with some former cameramen, we see what appears to be genuine puzzlement about Hitler.

Even her legendary determination, however, couldn't help her after the war, when she was detained by the Allies for pro-Nazi activities, charges later reduced to being "a sympathizer." She had something of a public renaissance in the 1970s with still photographs of the Nuba tribe in southern Sudan, and then moved on to her current underwater work.

True to his word, Muller doesn't take sides, but the feeling is inescapable that Riefenstahl's blindness was self-inflicted, the willful looking the other way of someone who had powerful reasons to wish all the bad things would simply disappear. By the time she insists to Muller, "What do I have to regret, where does my guilt lie?" the answer is more obvious than she wants to admit.

NEW YORK, 3/28/94, p. 97, John Powers

No documentary could have a more riveting anti-hero than *The Wonderful, Horrible Life of Leni Riefenstahl*. When Riefenstahl was 23, she became transfixed by a movie poster and looked up its lead actor, Luis Trenker, boldly saying that she wanted to be his co-star in his next picture. And she was. One of her great fans was Adolf Hitler, who asked her to direct *Triumph of the Will*, a myth-drenched propaganda film set at the annual Nazi Party Congress in 1934, and *Olympia*, a dazzling documentary about the 1936 Berlin Olympics. Invariably termed the two greatest films ever made by a woman (they are certainly the most monumental), these pictures established her unsurpassed eye for iconic imagery and cinematic rhythm but also her larger blindness. Riefenstahl always had the moral horizon of a mole, and she was shaken but not shattered by her postwar notoriety, which was all the greater because she was a beautiful woman. At 60, she went to live with the Nuba tribe in Africa, taking a series of famous and quite lovely photos. Now 91 and an avid scuba diver, she's at work on an underwater film that includes footage of her petting a deadly stingray—an image so plump with metaphor it needs no commentary.

Wonderful, Horrible's true drama lies in this lucid, amazingly well preserved woman's trying to carve herself a positive niche in history even as filmmaker Ray Müller seeks to make her confront her past as a Nazi pom-pom girl. Despite her best efforts she keeps giving herself away—her eyes light up when she talks about *der Führer*. Confronted with an accusation, she invariably protests too much. Riefenstahl is hell-bent on proving she's a major artist, but the more she talks about her obsessive attention to detail, the more we scoff at her claims that she never had a clue what deifying images of Hitler might mean. Whenever she's unhappy with Müller, she pitches a fit or threatens to withdraw from the film. But she always comes back, yearning for vindication. Stunningly unrepentant—she insists she's an apolitical artist and guilty of nothing—Riefenstahl dominates the screen with her spooky charisma. Narcissistic and triumphantly willful, she could have sprung from the head of Ayn Rand.

NEWSDAY, 3/16/94, Part II/p. 65, John Anderson

Displaying one of the more selective memories of the 20th Century, the 91-year-old Leni Riefenstahl recalls being compared by Josef von Sternberg to his most famous star, Marlene Dietrich.

"He told me I was the exact opposite of Dietrich," she says, time having diminished neither her envy, nor her joy: Dietrich, after all, was so obvious, so coarse; Riefenstahl, herself a major star of the German cinema, so much more refined.

Their respective qualities as sex objects may indeed have been what von Sternberg was referring to, but we'll never know, certainly not by listening to Leni Riefenstahl. In the end, it never occurs to her that the fabled director might have been talking, not about their bodies, but their souls—the differences that led Dietrich to defy Hitler and see her life's work banned in her homeland, while Riefenstahl became Hitler's greatest promoter, and the world's most notorious filmmaker.

Unfiltered by introspection, the Riefenstahl we meet in Ray Muller's "The Wonderful, Horrible Life of Leni Riefenstahl," is an enigma, an infuriation, the personification of German culpability and of art without conscience. Through film clips, home movies, interviews and newsreel footage, as well as Riefenstahl's own brief but potent filmography—including "Triumph of the Will," the Rosetta Stone of propaganda films, and the stunning "Olympia," her two-part chronicle of the 1936 Berlin Olympics—we see that as a filmmaker she was, quite simply, a genius. Her innovations and uncompromising standards made her an artist of the first rank; that she was a woman in her time makes these accomplishments even more extraordinary.

She was, and is, the control freak's control freak, something we watch Muller learn during the making of the film: Physically active and intellectually astute, the movie's imperious subject tries to direct the director. But she needs to control history, too. Her indignant denials that she mixed socially with Nazi leaders—despite quotations to the contrary from Goebbels' diaries, or informal photographs of her and the Führer—or that she actually helped orchestrate the '34 Nuremberg rally chronicled in "Triumph of the Will," abrade her dignified veneer. And it's a veneer that barely masks a strength of personality, and will, that made her a world-class director when most movie women were decorative.

Trained as a dancer, she made it to the screen in the conventional way: via her face. Fascinated by her picture, director Arnold Fanck, whose "mountain films" had so intrigued Riefenstahl, wrote one for her, and "The Sacred Mountain" became her screen debut.

Her first film as director was "The Blue Light," which prompted Adolph Hitler to ask her to make a film about the 1933 Nazi rally. Riefenstahl's angry reaction to Müller's question about this film, "Victory of Faith," are revealing: Underfinanced and a logistical nightmare, the film is a failure, presumably because Riefenstahl had to shoot where and when she could.

Not so its sequel. "Triumph of the Will" is one of the great films of the century, whether or not one dismisses subsequent history. What one cannot dismiss, despite Riefenstahl's protestations, is the incriminating passion with which the film was made. Certainly, there are aspects to "Triumph" that are astounding simply on a technical basis—the way Hitler is isolated throughout the piece, for instance, and contrasted with the swelling, throbbing Nazi mass before him. But the way Riefenstahl's eye lingers on that mass, watching it swim and pulse and jackboot its way across the parade grounds, is admiring, and sexual, even if to the contemporary eye it might resemble a piece of diseased tissue writhing under a microscope.

"The Horrible, Wonderful Life of Leni Riefenstahl," which follows her through her postwar trials, her extensive filming of the Nuba people in Africa and her recent underwater photography, is irony-rich. "If it had been harmful," she says of "Triumph of the Will," "the French wouldn't have given it a gold medal." She compares herself to Soviet filmmakers under Stalin, which is contemptible. She recalls nothing about book burnings or racial theories, although she can give a detailed recital of how G.W. Pabst constructed a scene years before the war. In her alpine chateau at war's end, she never even heard the Allied bombers overhead on their way to Berlin. When she asks a prosecutorial Müller, "what am I guilty of" you can only shake your head.

VILLAGE VOICE, 3/22/94, p. 48, Georgia Brown

Here's Leni Riefenstahl, "Hitler's favorite filmmaker," on the Nazi era: "I don't think about it anymore ... It's like another world." Ha. The woman has just produced a 669-page autobiography—a 90th birthday present to herself—and subsequently, self-promotional genius that she is, approached producers about a documentary on her life. The result, *The Wonderful, Horrible Life of Leni Riefenstahl*, is directed by the not exactly penetrating Ray Müller. Despite him, the film is absolutely mesmerizing.

Originally Müller's title was *Leni Riefenstahl: The Power of Images*, but Britain's Channel 4 wanted something jazzier. "I hate the English title," snapped one otherwise proud producer at the New York Film Festival. No wonder. It sounds so ... well, deflationary. "The Power of Images" may be what Müller thought he was directing, but fortunately his own images are quite banal, making it far easier to see his subject rather than her idealized portrait.

Spanning the century, Riefenstahl's life (she was born in 1902) certainly has been eventful. Her breezy, entirely self-justifying autobiography (reviewed glowingly by John Simon on page one of the *Times* book review a couple of months ago) reads like Scarlett O'Hara's diaries and has the flavor and nutritional value of M&Ms. (To tell the truth, I elected to spare the *Voice* $35 and myself the exertion of lugging this tome home and merely read chunks sitting on the floor of Barnes & Noble.) The film, I note, avoids mentioning the author's sex drive or the myriad affairs she had on the way to the top. The movie avoids many things—like interviews with counterwitnesses or critics (no doubt Leni exacted many concessions for her cooperation)—but its very sloppiness encourages reading between the images.

Skipping any childhood his subject may have had, Müller begins with Leni full-blown, executing her first major hustle. Having started as a modern dancer ("I only went on as an experiment, but was such a wild success ..." she reports with her usual candor), she turned to film after injuring her leg. On the way to the doctor, she was so smitten by a poster for Arnold Fanck's *Peaks of Destiny*, she forgot the leg and went to the movies. Of course, she approached Fanck directly. Seduced, he immediately went home and wrote a new script expressly for her. Thus began an impressive career as a fearless mountain-scaling movie star in a peculiarly Germanic genre, *das Bergfilm*—idylls of the peaks, melodramas of moral purity and athleticism.

What a life! Leni's story hurtles from one exotic episode and setting to the next. Although she only directed two narrative films, *The Blue Light* and *Tiefland*, clearly the woman has a highly developed sense of drama. Both films, which Leni also starred in, should be seen to appreciate the author's lifelong persecution complex. (In conjunction with the bio-doc, Film Forum will show Riefenstahl's four feature films.)

Just as she excitedly sought out Fanck, so she approached Hitler, sending him a fan letter after an early party rally. Adolf, it turned out, admired Leni's work, too, so much that he asked her to document the 1933 Nazi Party rally. Today, the one-hour *Victory of the Faith* mortifies the director. "It's got nothing to do with my technique," she shrieks when Müller insists on bringing it up. It's instructive to see some portions of *Victory* included here. Forget *technique*: The rally itself is a ragged, after-you-Gaston affair. When she accepts Hitler's invitation to record next year's rally, you can bet it's with the stipulation that the Nazis get their act together.

And so they do. (Not with Leni's help, she claims, though the evidence is otherwise.) The meticulously manipulated result, the deco dreampiece *Triumph of the Will*, has one purpose: to glorify the might, the machinelike precision, the wholesome virility of the Party, the Reich, and the Führer. "Do you notice," points out Leni today, "there's no commentary?" (Unlike *The Wonderful, Horrible Life*, which uses a lame, intermittent voiceover.) This alone, she claims, is evidence that the film is not propaganda. It's mere coincidence that the subject was Nazis, Leni maintains. "Whether it was about politics or vegetables or fruit, I didn't give a damn." As always, *perfection* was her only goal.

According to Leni, *Triumph* isn't about war (much less ethnic cleansing) but the "creation of jobs." "Work and peace" are its subjects. If the movie had been about war—get this—"the French would never have given it a gold medal in 1937." Also, there's "nothing here about anti-Semitism." You see, Leni didn't approve of Hitler's fixation on Jews. Friends who emigrated, she recalls, urged her to stay and "be a bulwark against anti-Semitism." The gal couldn't wait to comply.

Her next project (funded by the Propaganda Ministry), *Olympia*, the two-part, nearly four-hour epic of the '36 Olympics, is usually cited as her great achievement. Today, Riefenstahl describes the lengths she and her crew went to obtain the shots they wanted. (What she doesn't say is that when they couldn't get the best light during competition, they staged events later.) Finished, this symphony to world harmony—and ode to the body athletic—opened at a gala celebration for Hitler's 49th birthday. The year was 1938. Another blow for peace.

Triumph of the Will and *Olympia* are usually called masterpieces. Well, to each her own. If you like your masterpieces grandiose, seamless, tightly controlled. If you favor idealized versions of events stage-managed to order. Obviously, techniques Riefenstahl developed have helped skew visual reality ever since.

Leni says she began to suspect Hitler's judgment when she attended a Nazi art exhibition. "Kitsch!" she spits scornfully. She forgets that Hitler admired her art. (Would it be sacrilegious to call *Triumph of the Will* and *Olympia* high kitsch?)

Leni has a comeback for every quibble. When, in the '60s (and her sixties), she went to the Sudan to photograph the big, handsome, naked Nuba, some critics scolded her for neglecting the aged and ugly. Nonsense, she says. The old "sit inside or in shadows where there's not enough light to photograph."

No sitting in the shade for Leni. In her nineties, she can be forgiven for looking a trifle kitschy. A few years ago, Leni took up scuba diving so she could make an underwater film with bright fish—fish wearing the flashy neon colors and natty patterns Leni herself likes to wear. Only when padding around in a sky-blue wet suit can she be said to look almost vulnerable. Watching her pat a stingray's head, you might revise that notion.

Today, a poster-size photo of her young, beautiful, mountain-conquering self hangs on her studio wall. Within hailing distance is the desk of her tall, handsome, much younger, seemingly submissive helper. Hörst is his name. In his *Premiere* column, my colleague J. Hoberman called *Wonderful, Horrible* "the *Sunset Boulevard* of the Third Reich."

Once, fed up with Herr Müller's flawed taste—or was it one of his pathetic shows of will?—Leni takes him by the jacket and gives him a good shake. How it must gall her to have to put up with someone so ungifted, so visually obtuse. Think what she herself could have done. But then we wouldn't have such a riveting, wonderful-horrible, seams-showing portrait of a 20th-century life.

Also reviewed in:
CHICAGO TRIBUNE, 6/24/94, Friday/p. J, John Petrakis
NEW REPUBLIC, 3/14/94, p. 30, Stanley Kauffmann
NEW YORK TIMES, 3/16/94, p. C20, Vincent Canby
VARIETY, 9/13/93, p. 34, Deborah Young
WASHINGTON POST, 4/29/94, p. C1, Desson Howe

WOODSTOCK: THE DIRECTOR'S CUT

A Warner Bros. release of a Wadleigh-Maurice, Ltd. production. *Producer:* Bob Maurice. *Director:* Michael Wadleigh. *Screenplay:* Michael Wadleigh. *Editor:* Martin Scorsese and Thelma Schoonmacher. *Music Adviser:* Eric Blackstead. *Sound:* Larry Johnson and (music) Dan Wallin. Running time: 240 minutes. MPAA Rating: Not Rated.

WITH: Joan Baez; Joe Cocker; Arlo Guthrie; Richie Havens; Jimi Hendrix; Janis Joplin; John Sebastian; Canned Heat; Country Joe and The Fish; Creddence Clearwater Revival; Crosby, Stills, Nash, and Young; Jefferson Airplane; Mountain; Santana; Sha-Na-Na; Sly and the Family Stone; Ten Years After; The Who.

NEW YORK POST, 6/29/94, p. 34, Thelma Adams

"You leave the theater feeling that 'Woodstock' is not only a great movie but, somehow, also a great rip-off," wrote New York Post columnist Alfred G. Aronowitz in 1970.

This week, Warner Bros., capitalizing on Woodstock's 25th anniversary, is releasing a so-called director's cut of the highest-grossing documentary of all time.

A director's cut implies that Michael Wadleigh was dissatisfied with the first version, which won the young director an Oscar for best documentary. Not true. "The first version of this film was truly a director's cut," Wadleigh, who controlled the final cut of the original, says in the press notes for the new version.

The new-and-improved four-hour "marketing opportunity," like its 184-minute forerunner, is entertaining. If it's less remarkable than the three-day music festival, at least it's a good-natured documentary that captures an event that named a generation.

The film has been digitally remixed—and additional concert footage includes Jimi Hendrix and Janis Joplin.

The range of the musical acts remains astonishing—along with the fact that here was a young audience ready for anything musically (and sexually, if you check out the action in the bushes).

From the purity of Joan Baez's scrubbed "Joe Hill" through Joe cocker's blistering "With a Little Help From My Friends," the hard-driving Who, steaming Santana, Sly and the Family Stone, Richie Havens, and the relative newcomers Crosby, Stills and Nash, the music hold up surprisingly well.

It's poignant to see rock dinosaurs CSN shyly announce, "This is the second time we've ever played in front of people. We're scared s---less."

It takes over three hours to get to him, but it's Hendrix's show. If you haven't seen the electric guitar player do the national anthem, making his instrument shoot musical rockets, it's worth the wait.

The scene itself is a "trip" back to the "groovy" era when beer cans still had pull tabs and braless, horseback-riding hippies went around barefoot, intent on getting back to the earth. When the rains came, turning the site into Mudstock, they had their opportunity.

Wadleigh interviews a wrinkled local tavern owner who says of the hippie invasion, "This thing was too big, too big for the world."

The Greatful Dead's Jerry Garcia calls it a "biblical, epical, unbelievable scene."

Who can resist the sight of a naked man dancing with a sheep to the beat of Carlos Santana?

Among the biggest treats of the expanded "Woodstock" is the inclusion of Janis Joplin, who performed for the cutting-room floor in 1970. Barefoot, rings on her fingers, scraggly-haired, she reaches into her gut and rips out the blues.

Viewed in 1994, Joplin's performance is achingly ironic in a 1970 film almost completely irony-free. Wadleigh mirrors the self-congratulatory tone of the concert billed as three days of peace and music on Yasgur's farm in remote Bethel, N.Y.

But, after 25 years, the "Purple Haze" has cleared. The party was short-lived, the peace just a cease-fire. Within a few years, Joplin and Hendrix were both dead, overdosed.

NEWSDAY, 6/29/94, Part II/p. B3, Jack Mathews

The utopian world of peace and love envisioned by the hundreds of thousands who gathered in rural New York for the Woodstock Music and Art Fair in August, 1969, began to unravel almost before the marijuana smoke had cleared.

Within months, we would learn about the arrests of a band of communal "hippies" charged in the Tate-Labianca killings in Los Angeles, the murder of an 18-year-old spectator by Hell's Angels cynically hired as security for a Rolling Stones concert in Altamont, Calif., and of four Kent State students shot to death while protesting U.S. expansion of the Vietnam War.

Fourteen months after Woodstock, two of its star attractions—Jimi Hendrix and Janis Joplin, both 27—would be dead from drug overdoses.

But to those attending the three-day concert in New York, and the millions of others who joined them when Michael Wadleigh's three-hour documentary arrived in theaters the following spring, Woodstock symbolized the solidarity of a generation rejecting the values of its elders, and the wretched condition of life it blamed them for.

It was idealism entertaining itself.

Seen now, Wadleigh's "Woodstock," lengthened to nearly four hours with additional concert footage, plays as cultural kitsch, and those who've regretted all these years having missed it, may finally be glad they did. You could have been one of those stoned bubbleheads interviewed on camera, or among those in that yoga class learning how to get high through hyperventilation, and your descendants would be snickering at you for generations to come.

When "Woodstock" was first released, its humor came out of its interviews with the bewildered townspeople. Today, the biggest laughs are generated by the kids trying to put a philosophical spin on the excesses of sex, drugs and rock and roll, and being unable to say much more than that the whole scene is just such a groove.

Whatever else it has become, "Woodstock," an Oscar winner for documentary feature, stands up as a great piece of filmmaking. Using double and triple split-screen images, the 28-year-old Wadleigh and his young editors, Thelma Schoonmaker (24) and Martin Scorsese (27), found a way to draw movie audiences into the intoxicating midst of the festival while documenting its immensity and its impact on the community surrounding it.

Wadleigh's camera crews were everywhere, roaming the vast crowd, checking out the nude bathers in the bordering lakes and ponds, following a pair of lovers into the high grass for an indiscreet nooner, visiting with every reveler, farmer, promoter and worker who would pause to look into their lenses. The musicians were shot from so many angles, and often in such tight close-up, you wonder how anybody else could have seen them.

And what a lineup! The Beatles and Rolling Stones weren't there (thank God, they'd still be moving people out), but Woodstock was otherwise a who's-who of the late '60s folk and rock scene. Janis Joplin, a cutting-room floor casualty of the original film, now joins Hendrix, The Who, Joe Cocker, Sly and the Family Stone, Joan Baez and Country Joe and the Fish for the country's greatest celebration of good intentions.

The documentary isn't totally clear-headed journalism. It stresses the shared goodwill, the absence of violence, the stoicism with which a half-million people endured bad weather, bad drugs, and concession and toilet facilities set up for a crowd anticipated at less than half its size. We see one person being hauled off on a stretcher, an apparent overdose, and a teenage girl having a spectacular anxiety attack. And over the PA system, we hear about a broken leg, lost friends and the birth of a baby. But through most of it, the filmmakers seem as high as everyone else.

The stated goal of Woodstock, its plea for universal peace and brotherhood, was a dream wrapped in a fantasy, a sweet illusion, as some have called it. But if, in the end, it really was nothing more than a hell of a party, it and the film that followed were pleasant lulls in the revolution.

SIGHT AND SOUND, 9/95, p. 55, Mark Sinker

In promo literature, Michael Wadleigh has been claiming that present-generation pop—he cites Nirvana—has at last swung back to the unvarnished realism of the Woodstock moment. The original movie came out in 1970: Jimi Hendrix and Janis Joplin and 'the 60s' all died that year. When Kurt Cobain of Nirvana committed suicide earlier this year, his mother, as everyone now knows, lambasted him for ignoring her and joining them in what she had called "that stupid club". One thing the Unrepentant Hippie's Cut of *Woodstock* can do is retrospectively sanctify. Jimi and Janis are now recast, as the twin spirits of the event, the movie and the age.

In the midst of Hendrix's closing set, mostly shot in tight focus on his guitar fingers, the camera sneaks a look back from the stage to the audience (as has also happened during other performances). This reverse shot breaks with narrative continuity. We see not the massed mudstruck gazing back at us, but a suddenly bare, torn hillside: aftermath of Pop Festival as Civil War battle; Jimi's intimation of all mortality. "The show is over," as Vassily Rozanov put it long ago. "The audience get up to leave their seats. Time to collect their coats and go home. They turn around... no more coats and no more home." This jump-cut alone accords with Nirvana's staggeringly bleak nihilism.

But the brutalised rage of today's pop culture is quite out of sympathy with everything else. This is a film in which every song, every interview, every shot, is still a beatification of impracticality; it is a film unable, though visibly haunted by Vietnam (alien insect-copters permanently a-hover), to face up to its subject's necessary impermanence. It is, as it always was, a triumph of editing (by Thelma Schoonmaker and Martin Scorsese) and of after-the-fact 'scripting'. The fact that—like the Festival itself—the movie scrambled together something memorable out of disaster, was extrapolated into visions of a brave, reshaped future for society.

It is memorable, and it is moving. It's more gripping than you expect: it doesn't feel nearly four hours long. Even when it's boring—Alvin Lee's Ten Years After, come on home—it's not boring (the triple-screen visuals are searingly exciting). Brilliant framing stylisation of certain performances enable three and a half days of footage to be concentrated, so that particular performers star in a mini-drama of the counterculture's chance to change things. Joan Baez, alone in a pool of blackness, rain puddling on the stage near her, sings 'Swing Low Sweet Chariot' and 'Joe Hill' ("*an organising* song," she calls it—this a dig?): it becomes the political-moral centre of the film. The Who, just tipping off into the rise and rise of *Tommy*, stand for rock's aesthetic possibility, its chaotic power, its pretentious overreach.

There's more footage of Jimi, consolidating him as the languid, blazing seer who sees through mere spectacle to the death's-head that mocks all. There's all-new footage of Janis, desperate, confused, unprotected, of all the performers the one most 'of' the audience, with most to gain from freedoms that seem to have been won, and haven't.

Not all the recut footage is to the point. Some acts are included for fact's sake only. Jefferson Airplane, their time done, the movement grown beyond them, could have stayed omitted without loss. A little Canned Heat goes a long way. The footage of Crosby, Stills, Nash and Young still lacks any image of Neil Young. John Fogerty has refused the director and the public any hint of Creedence Clearwater Revival's attendance. We still have to make do with Sha-Na-Na's ever-awful 'doo-wop' revival. The camera lingers too long now on skinny-dipping kids, marvelling that such things could come to pass, and misreading them.

If Richard Nixon can be rehabilitated, why not Woodstock? The Director's Cut—remixed! remastered! restored!—has not excised the original's complacency: belief that this festival changed things (John Sebastian blathering about raising his kids right) feels edged out by belief that things never change. The recut movie closes, post-credits, with a scrolling digital list of those now dead, from John Lennon down to a Grateful Dead keyboard player, not lost but gone before: never-ending roll-call of the 60s departed, self-righteous, self-assured, still claiming all attention, still suffocating all futures.

But the festival's 'real stars' have been allowed back in. Folks from the crowd explain themselves incoherently: multi-racial, happily bedraggled, less hairy than you recall, they remind you that this was a Children's Crusade, no more. Queuing, calling home, patiently waiting, their innocent yattering is as quaint with age as a sepia photo; all that's disagreeable about it is our knowledge of the violence that will in the years to come be mobilised against it.

VILLAGE VOICE, 7/12/94, p. 41, J. Hoberman

Rand's diatribe, which might be titled "The Sky Above, the Mud Below," juxtaposes the Summer of '69's two most awesome media events—the Moon Flight and Woodstock. Forrest watches the former, but how is it that he missed what *Time* hailed as "one of the significant political and sociological events of the age"? Would he have been upstaged by the prattling of John Sebastian?

Michael Wadleigh's *Woodstock*, rereleased in a remixed and expanded "director's cut" to commemorate the silver anniversary of the ultimate hippie arcadia, repackaged Woodstock as self-conscious, self-congratulatory spectacle in which love children play at being love children, more than once remarking that the whole world was watching. Just as TV coverage of O. J. Simpson inevitably became TV coverage of the TV coverage, so Woodstock only achieved Woodstock in the glare of its own hype: The concert's promoters soon realized that all profit from an event so heavily publicized that tickets became superfluous would ultimately derive from promoting this unintentional free concert as a celebration of freedom.

If you build it, they will come. "Warners is treating the film as a psychological, spiritual and emotional event," *Variety* reported in March 1970. With masterful publicity, the studio contrived a perhaps spurious hullabaloo over a potential X-rating and the possibility of cutting the official three-hour version. Heralded by a four-page ad in the *Voice*, *Woodstock* opened with tickets an unprecedented five bucks. Still, a feast of mainly mediocre music and rampant rhetoric, whose dramatic highpoints are changes in the weather and Jimi Hendrix's god-like arrival, *Woodstock* is an over-rated concert film (*Monterey Pop* and even *Gimme Shelter* are each superior) and an underrated technical accomplishment. An anarchic youth cult equivalent to *Triumph of the Will*, it generates considerable visual interest through incoherent split screen, reckless camera smears, and the placement of the lens two inches from Joe Cocker's knee.

Is there anything to the director's cut? The latrine-cleaner who sued to have his interview removed is still present although the Credence Clearwater Revival footage promised in Warners's initial press missives is nowhere apparent. This new version seems to have beefed up several sets but the added Joplin and Hendrix footage is less than epochal: Janis is heard wailing over some step-printed glamour close-ups and "Voodoo Chile" becomes the basis for a new downbeat closer showing the abandoned, post-festival mud and litter of the now-sacred terrain.

NO ONE WHO WAS THERE WILL EVER BE THE SAME was the movie's original sell line. (The expanded *Woodstock* may not expand anyone's consciousness but the movie still has a residual power to put you through changes: Clocking in at nearly four hours, this is the air-conditioning bargain of the summer.) The invitation now is to EXPERIENCE THE EVENT THAT NAMED A GENERATION, although as a generational portrait *Woodstock* is a telling embarrassment. (The high-concept synopsis is basically Benares in the Catskills or white kids sing the blues.)

There's undeniable poignance to the singalongs orchestrated by Country Joe and, to different effect, Sly Stone—and that geezer interviewed to open the film is no longer Dad. "I took a trip to our future," Abbie Hoffman would write. These days, after all, Richie Havens is the voice of the Red Cross, *Tommy* plays Broadway, and the mysteries of kundalini yoga may be studied in malls across America. Given the intensity of the culture klatch that took place, Woodstock was the original Renaissance Weekend.

Also reviewed in:
CHICAGO TRIBUNE, 8/12/94, Friday/p. J, Michael Wilmington

WORK ON THE GRASS

A Film Forum presentation. *Producer:* Tetsuo Shinohara, Akemi Sugawara, and Shogo Ueno. *Director:* Tetsuo Shinohara. *Screenplay (Japanese with English subtitles):* Tetsuo Shinohara. *Director of Photography:* Shogo Ueno. *Editor:* Yoko Nishioka. *Music:* Hiroyuki Murakami. *Running time:* 42 minutes. *MPAA Rating:* Not Rated.

CAST: Naoki Goto (Gardener); Hikari Ota (Writer).

NEW YORK POST, 8/17/94, p. 36, Larry Worth

[*Work on the Grass* was reviewed jointly with *Dream Girls*; see Worth's review of that film.]

VILLAGE VOICE, 8/23/94, p. 58, Amy Taubin

[*Work on the Grass* was reviewed jointly with *Dream Girls*; see Taubin's review of that film.]

Also reviewed in:
NEW YORK TIMES, 8/17/94, p. C12, Stephen Holden

WYATT EARP

A Warner Bros. release of a TIG Productions/Kasdan Pictures production. *Executive Producer:* Jon Slan, Dan Gordon, Charles Okun, and Michael Grillo. *Producer:* Jim Wilson, Kevin Costner, and Lawrence Kasdan. *Director:* Lawrence Kasdan. *Screenplay:* Dan Gordon and Lawrence Kasdan. *Director of Photography:* Owen Roizman. *Editor:* Carol Littleton. *Music:* James Newton Howard. *Music Editor:* Jim Weidman. *Sound:* John Pritchett and (music) Shawn Murphy. *Sound Editor:* Robert Grieve, Stu Bernstein, and Bobby Mackston. *Casting:* Jennifer Shull. *Production Designer:* Ida Random. *Art Director:* Gary Wissner. *Set Designer:* Charles Daboub, Jr., Tom Reta, and Barry Chusid. *Set Decorator:* Cheryl Carasik. *Special Effects:* Burt Dalton, Joe Heffernan, Dick Hogle, and Sol Rivera. *Costumes:* Colleen Atwoood. *Make-up:* Michael Mills, F. X. Perez, Gerry Quist, and Bonita DeHaven. *Stunt Coordinator:* Norman Howell. *Running time:* 190 minutes. *MPAA Rating:* PG-13.

CAST: Kevin Costner (Wyatt Earp); Dennis Quaid (Doc Holliday); Gene Hackman (Nicholas Earp); David Andrews (James Earp); Linden Ashby (Morgan Earp); Jeff Fahey (Ike Clanton); Joannna Going (Josie Marcus); Mark Harmon (Johnny Behan); Michael Madsen (Virgil Earp); Catherine O'Hara (Allie Earp); Bill Pullman (Ed Masterson); Isabella Rossellini (Big Nose Kate); Tom Sizemore (Bat Masterson); JoBeth Williams (Bessie Earp); Mare Winningham

(Mattie Blaylock); James Gammon (Mr. Sutherland); Rex Linn (Frank McLaury); Randle Mell (John Clum); Adam Baldwin (Tom McLaury); Annabeth Gish (Urilla Sutherland); Lewis Smith (Curly Bill Brocius); Ian Bohen (Young Wyatt); Betty Buckley (Virginia Earp); Alison Elliott (Lou Earp); Todd Allen (Sherm McMasters); Mackenzie Astin (Young Man on Boat); James Caviezel (Warren Earp); Karen Grassle (Mrs. Sutherland); John Denis Johnston (Frank Stillwell); Tea Leoni (Sally); Martin Kove (Ed Ross); Jack Kehler (Bob Hatch); Kirk Fox (Pete Spence); Norman Howell (Johnny Ringo); Boots Sutherland (Marshall White); Scott Augare (Indian Charlie); Gabriel Folse (Billy Clanton); Kris Kamm (Billy Claiborne); John Lawlor (Judge Spicer); Monty Stuart (Dutch Wiley); Hugh Ross (Erwin Sutherland); Gregory Avellone (Traveler); Michael McGrady (John Shanssey); Mary Jo Niedzielski (Martha Earp); Scott Paul (Young Morgan); Oliver Hendrickson (Young Warren); Darwin Mitchell (Tom Chapman); Steve Kniesel (Bullwacker); Larry Sims (Dirty Sodbuster); Greg Goossen (Bullwacker's Friend); Heath Kizzier (Red); Clark Sanchez (Mike Donovan); Ed Beimfohr (Farro Dealer); Giorgio E. Tripoli (Judge Earp); Ben Zeller (Dr. Seger); Rockne Tarkington (Stable Hand); Scott Rasmussen (Minister); Ellen Blake (Paris); Steph Benseman (Pine Bluff Sheriff); Bob "Dutch" Holland (Tubercular Inmate); Steve Cormier (Tent Saloon Bartender); Matt Langseth (Link Borland); David Doty (Mayor Wilson); Steven G. Tyler (Deputy Ford); Billy Streater (Marshall Meagher); David L. Stone (Larry Deger); Jake Walker (Mannen Clements); Matt O'Toole (Gyp Clements); Geo Cook (Big Cowboy); Dillinger Steele and Steve Lindsay (Drunk Cowboys); Dick Beach (Wagner); Benny Manning (Walker); Kathleen O'Hara (Hotel Resident); Nicholas Benseman (Delivery Boy); Sarge McGraw (Deputy Black); Steven Hartley (Spangenberg); Brett Cullen (Saddle Tramp); Marlene Williams (Saloon Dealer); Paul Ukena (Bar Regular); Owen Roizman (Danny); Karen Schwartz (Marshall White's Wife); Glen Burns (Bar Patron); John Furlong (Clem Hafford); Zack McGillis (Rancher); Adam Taylor (Texas Jack); Rusty Hendrickson (Turkey Creek Jack); Hanley Smith (Billiard Parlor Patron); John Kasdan (Bar Boy); Dale West (Station Master); Michael Huddleston (Albert); Al Trujillo (Camp Foreman); John Doe (Tommy Behind-the-Deuce); Matt Beck (McGee); Gary Dueer (Dick Gird).

CHRISTIAN SCIENCE MONITOR, 6/24/94, p. 12, David Sterritt

When the old "Wyatt Earp" television series made its debut in the 1950s, it was greeted as an example of the "adult western," a new breed of horse operas more serious than the Roy Rogers and Hopalong Cassidy romps that had dominated the tube.

Grown-up westerns were already established in movie theaters, where filmmakers like John Ford and Howard Hawks had charged them with surprising sophistication. Treatments of the Earp saga in the 1940s and '50s, like Ford's classic "My Darling Clementine" and John Sturges's more flamboyant "Gunfight at the O.K. Corral," were enjoyed by moviegoers of nearly all ages.

The genre underwent big changes in the 1960s and '70s, when a wave of revisionist pictures challenged many aspects of the frontier myth; these films showed a social responsibility ("Cheyenne Autumn," "Little Big Man") and an unromantic grittiness ("McCabe and Mrs. Miller," "The Wild Bunch") that westerns had never known before. More conservative attitudes returned in the more conservative '80s, and remain in the '90s with all-in-fun epics like "Maverick" and old-guy-strapping-on-his-gun adventures like "Unforgiven."

The new "Wyatt Earp" movie stars Kevin Costner in the title role. Since he rehabilitated the screen image of native Americans in "Dances With Wolves," a rare, '90s western concerned with social issues, one might have expected a similarly progressive agenda this time around.

The auteur of "Wyatt Earp" is not Costner but director Lawrence Kasdan, however. His idea of a good western is a straightforward clean-up-the-town story—like "Silverado," which he made with Costner nine years ago—sporting a maximum of nostalgic images and a minimum of thoughtful themes.

Kasdan is capable of insightful filmmaking, as he proved in "Grand Canyon." But he puts his imaginative notions back into the holster when he gallops into Old West territory, preferring largeness of scale to boldness of conception. "Wyatt Earp" runs well over three hours, and while it's full of action-packed twists, it has only about three ideas to propel it.

The tale begins just after the Civil War, when Wyatt is a boy and the Earp clan goes West in search of new opportunities. Wyatt's dad states the major motifs of the movie in a couple of speeches about family values and self-protection. Blood is thicker than water, so treat everyone outside your family as a stranger. And if you get in a fight with a bad guy, be sure to kill him before he kills you.

Wyatt tries to live peaceably as a young man, but the frontier is short on law and order, and he soon starts obeying his father's lessons, His derring-do lands him a job as deputy marshal, and he keeps Dodge City reasonably quiet until the tragic death of his wife transformed him into a trouble-making drunk.

Later he reforms and gets back into the peace-officer business, dispensing justice with help from his brothers and the notorious Doc Holliday, who has given up dentistry for various forms of hustling. Wyatt also finds time to fall in love with one woman, take another as his common-law wife, and feud with a couple of violent gangs, before the O.K. Corral shootout changes his life forever.

This is standard plot material in most respects, and Kasdan has done little to make it seem new. Fans of time-tested formulas may applaud his fidelity to the genre, but others will wish he'd come up with a few original notions to energize this *very* long picture.

The movie's old-fashioned approach brings liabilities of its own, moreover. In resurrecting the most conservative form of the western, Kasdan has also resurrected some of its more regrettable conventions, such as its glorification of gunplay and vigilante justice. Also unfortunate is its treatment of female characters, who—with the partial exception of Josie, the hero's third wife—either remain ciphers, with tiny roles in the story, or serve as stumbling blocks to Wyatt's career, by dying young or retreating into pathetic helplessness.

On the plus side, "Wyatt Earp" is smartly acted by Costner along with Gene Hackman as Wyatt's dad, Dennis Quaid as Doc Holliday, and Bill Pullman as Bat Masterson's nicer brother. Joanna Going does well as the feisty Josie, and while the screenplay gives the other actresses little to work with, some manage to make their talents visible—notably Annabeth Gish as Wyatt's first love, Mare Winningham as the prostitute he lives with, and Isabella Rossellini in the improbable role of Doc Holliday's wife.

The film is handsomely photographed by Owen Roizman, who knows how to fill the screen with a magnificent vista. Ida Random designed the production and James Newton Howard composed the syrupy score. Kasdan wrote the screenplay with Dan Gordon.

FILMS IN REVIEW, 9-10/94, p. 58, Harry Pearson, Jr.

Two words kept running through my mind as I first squirmed, then yawned my way through the 189 minutes of Lawrence Kasdan's *Wyatt Earp*, and those two words were *Heaven's Gate*. As this folly of a film unfolded before my eyes, in all of its unbelievable inauthenticities—from the feelings to the historical facts—I wondered whether Kasdan's reputation as a serious artist could survive a disaster of this magnitude, Certainly, Michael Cimino, an outsider who was not at all liked in Hollywood (and not just because of his arrogance) was ruined by *Heaven's Gate*, which cost less than this exercise in intellectual self-indulgence. But then, Kasdan is well liked and well connected in Filmland and his past sins (the scripts for *My Bodyguard* which he now, of course, disclaims, sort of, and *Continental Divide* and, lest we forget, *Return Of The Jedi* and his direction of *I Love You To Death*) have been placed in the background in face of his artistic pretensions (*The Big Chill*, yawn) and, more significantly, his commercial successes (like the script for *Raiders Of The Lost Ark*, a sort of nasty thing saved by Steven Spielberg's whiplash direction). Already folks are saying, putting the spin on an unrotatable truth, that it failed because Disney and presumably competitive *Tombstone* got to market first. Or, failing that, that *Earp*'s length (the movie, the movie) didn't allow enough turnover for theaters to chalk up the kind of grosses they normally would have with a two-hour "epic." Have they forgotten, so soon, Kevin Costner's *Dances With Wolves*, where the same argument did not seem to deter the public from attending in lemming-like fashion?

Well, say what you will, *Tombstone* was as historically authentic a telling of the main chapter in the Earp legend as we've had on the screen, and a hugely entertaining movie at that. (About the only relief we're treated to in *Earp* is Dennis Quaid's performance as Doc Holliday, where the actor squeezes the maximum out of every line allotted him in a script that reduces Holliday from Earp's significant male other into little more than an extra with some good dialogue.

Another distortion of the historical truth and a perversion of the film's most likely entertainment value—we all recall how well Val Kilmer stole each and every scene he happened to have in *Tombstone*.) And *Heaven's Gate*, like *Earp* in its leftist sensibility and moralizing—hey, I'm a liberal, but I never sermonize when I entertain—is at least as wildly unfaithful to the facts, but it had gumption, get up and go, if no great sense.

Here, we have every scene with any potential for suspense cut away from, mostly so that the director can show us the Earp men's carping women, who are as misogynistically depicted as any within recent screen memory (so much for liberalism); and a stellar cast of the ladies (JoBeth Williams, Catherine O'Hara, and Isabella Rossellini) find themselves, like Jodi in *Maverick*, with no roles to play, only attitudes. The buildup to the gunfight is undercut by this, and it appears that Kasdan, who is wonderful at directing the sudden, impulsive action (Costner and the billiard ball) doesn't seem to know his left from his right when it comes to staging a gunfight or confrontation. Even small details are so wrong as to be inexplicable. When the script takes note of its own discrepancies the effect is ludicrous. Holliday's mistress, for instance, had the nickname Big Nose Kate (à la Kathy Baker; they gave nicknames in those days for the most concrete reasons) and so, who shows up to play her: right, Isabella Rossellini, of fabulously refined nasal appendage. Earp, I think it is, notes that her nose doesn't look so big to him. True, says she (lamely), but there are other reasons for the nickname. What other reasons? Another delicious inauthenticity concerns Earp's first mistress (that we historically know of) and her use of laudanum (opium) to the point of addiction. Someone asks where she got it, when laudanum was commonly available in patent medicines of the time, The explanation is, in Chinatown.

Kasdan's take on *Earp* is that the man went too far in enforcing the law, or trying to enforce the law. He's like Darryl Gates transposed back to then. To explain why, we have to go back in time—and this means suffering for 90 minutes or so before Earp ever gets to Tombstone—to his teenage days, and his respect for his father, a cameo played with no great conviction by Gene Hackman, who really has absolutely nothing to do here, a lawyer who believes in the law and the sanctity of blood "kin." Next thing we know, the family is headed out West, where young Earp gets his first taste of violence—and, in a screen first, we see someone who, shot, fouls himself in death both coming and going. So far as violence goes, we know Kasdan isn't going to top that. Later, Earp goes back East, and in the most ludicrous of all of the movie's many, many moments, falls in love, gets married, and loses his wife to typhus or typhoid (the movie never says which; she just sort of sweats a lot and fades away; doesn't even turn yellow and start to smell). All we get to see of the relationship is her gardening, and him looking at her with Oatmeal in his eyes. On their wedding night there is no shivaree, and there are no friends in attendance when she dies (so unlike life in rural and smalltown America, then and now); they seem to live in total isolation from any existing society. You sit there thinking: These people have no life of their own; i.e., you can't imagine them having an existence beyond what you see on the screen—and in great films, you automatically assume this. We have no idea what makes the relationship tick. So when she dies, Wyatt goes crazy, burns down the house, and turns into all alcoholic (thus, suggests Kasdan, Earp's lifelong aversion to alcohol). He finally winds up a horse thief in an Arkansas jail, and ready to hang, when Dad shows up to rescue him. Therefore, we are to believe, we know the basis of his character. Except that it never happened. He stayed on for at least six months in the town where his wife died, and having proved an indifferent student of the law, struck out for St. Louis and the beginning of his Western adventures. If you think this is a distortion, just wait till you get to Dodge City, where, the movie would have it, he is run out of town for being too vigorous an enforcer of the law. When he finally gets to Tombstone, Kasdan's sequencing is so addled that we never quite understand what's going on, nor exactly what prompted the fight, which Kasdan has taking place in an alley outside the corral. And so on. Here, too, he is accused by his political sympathizers as being too harsh in enforcing the law, whereas the historical record amply demonstrates he had the town's unwavering support—the Clanton gang was really and truly bad news.

There is a TV-music style score by James Newton Howard which is the most obnoxiously intrusive I remember from any film in years. We have clumsy use of the Panavision framing—and did Owen Roizman have to photograph a sometimes dumpy, overweight-looking Costner so often from the side, where his lack of a chin makes him resemble an earnest chipmunk?

At the end of this thing, Earp, now aged and on a boat to the Alaska goldfields, encounters a kid, whose father was a character back in Tombstone times (about whom the most interesting story remains untold herein), who recollects how Earp saved his father from a mob—historic truth, but told so flatly here there is no shred of suspense, thus we don't understand the courage. This is called having it both ways, for the kid is grateful Earp enforced the law, and so we are supposed to he grateful for fascist policemen? He says to his wife that nobody would believe his story was the truth. And she replies that it is nothing but. Well, it ain't. Even though the appended biographical notes at the end try to lend a documentary flavor to what was clearly intended as an "epic," The stuff of Earp's life, if told truly (as in *Tombstone*), does make for epic drama and adventure. It's too bad Kasdan didn't stick to the facts since they make the better story, instead of his mumbo-jumbo interpretation of them.

LOS ANGELES TIMES, 6/24/94, Calendar/p. 1, Kenneth Turan

Impressive but uninviting, "Wyatt Earp" is easier to admire from a distance than pull up a chair and enjoy close-up. A self-conscious attempt at epic filmmaking that feels orchestrated as much as directed, it has noticeable virtues but chooses not to wear them lightly. And at three hours plus, it finally encourages audiences to feel as trail weary and exhausted as any of its characters.

Directed by Lawrence Kasdan (who co-wrote the script with Dan Gordon), "Wyatt Earp" uses the tale of that straight-shooting frontier marshal, the prime mover of the celebrated gunfight at the O.K. Corral, as a way to examine the panorama of the American West from the Civil War years to the turn of the century. And with Kevin Costner in the sturdy title role, Kasdan has the right man to help him do it.

Costner, whose own mammoth "Dances With Wolves" started the most recent trend in elephantine Westerns, is doing what most modern actors avoid, and that is growing, and improving within a fairly narrow range. By doing a variation of the kind of innate heroism that characterized John Wayne, he carries "Wyatt Earp" on his shoulders, and if that finally proves too much of a burden, the blame is not his.

Director Kasdan, whose best remembered films remain his first two, "Body Heat" and "The Big Chill," has ventured into the West before; his 1985 "Silverado" almost killed the genre's revival before it began."Wyatt Earp" is more satisfying, partly because its reported $60-million budget allowed for something like a hundred speaking parts and 92 different sets, including 10 distinctive saloons.

Though it is always diverting to see loving re-creations of everything from the laying of railroad track to the skinning of buffalo, all carefully photographed by Owen Roizman, in some ways this overly schematic pictorialism is evidence of where "Wyatt Earp" goes wrong.

For while it is hard to deny a film its ambition, "Wyatt Earp" is forever trying too hard; its excessive determination to be seen as a classic is too earnest and obvious to be successful. Especially since Kasdan, though clearly a student of the genre in general and the films of John Ford in particular, has to make do without the innate feeling for the iconography and emotional potency of the West that made both "Dances With Wolves" and Clint Eastwood's "Unforgiven" so successful.

Since that Tombstone, Ariz., gunfight (which historians pinpoint as having really taken place at a less euphonious location at the other end of the block) is what most people associate with Earp, Kasdan opens his picture with a brief pre-corral sequence. It is the morning of the battle and the marshal is drinking coffee in one of those saloons, waiting to be joined by brothers Virgil (Michael Madsen) and Morgan (Linden Ashby) and best friend Doc Holliday (Dennis Quaid).

For the idea of family, the notion, repeatedly articulated by Earp patriarch Nicholas (Gene Hackman) that "nothing counts so much as blood; the rest are just strangers," is taken totally to heart by the five Earp brothers. They may form romantic liaisons or even marry, but it is the brothers who come first, and Wyatt who is first among equals.

Introduced as an Iowa teen-ager attempting to flee the cornfields and enlist on the Union side in the Civil War, Wyatt is next tracked a rough frontier town in Wyoming, where the duality of his nature is exposed. As played by Costner, Wyatt in his early 20s is half-boy, half-killer, someone shyly awkward who can turn hard and relentless when he has to.

According to the Gordon-Kasdan script, what tipped the balance in Wyatt's personality was the outcome of his romance with hometown sweetheart Urilla Sutherland (Annabeth Gish). Post-

Urilla, he was different, "a cold man, God forgive you," as an acquaintance puts it, whose implacable, unbending approach to law enforcement accompanied him and his brothers from Wichita to Dodge City to Tombstone.

To his credit, Costner can convincingly play both sides of the equation, the sheepish, grinning suitor as well as the careworn, emotionally blocked marshal who dresses all in black and barks at miscreants, "I'm Wyatt Earp—it all ends now." Also worth seeing are Dennis Quaid, who lost 43 pounds to amusingly portray the tubercular gambler Doc Holliday, and Joanna Going, of TV's "Going to Extremes," who plays Josie Marcus, a later love of the marshal's.

That "Wyatt Earp" takes pains to accurately identify Marcus as Jewish, or to cast European-born Isabella Rossellini as Holliday's Hungarian paramour, Big Nose Kate, is an indication of the film's interest in historical accuracy. In fact, of the almost numberless pictures made about Earp and Tombstone (of which John Ford's "My Darling Clementine" remains the best), this is probably the most true to life.

But despite all these things to admire, "Wyatt Earp" offers little to get excited about. Partly it is the film's habit of pushing too hard, of forcing its emotional moments, and partly it is the glum, morose way Kasdan has envisioned Wyatt's story as a kind of Greek tragedy with boots on. Though superior to the recent Kurt Russell/Val Kilmer "Tombstone," it could do with some of that movie's sense of fun. Not exactly a failure, "Wyatt Earp" is more accurately described as simply not the picture it wants so hard to be.

NEW YORK, 7/11/94, p. 46, David Denby

It's probably a lost cause, but I would like to convince you nonetheless that Lawrence Kasdan's three-hour-and-ten-minute *Wyatt Earp* is worth seeing for a single supporting performance—that of Dennis Quaid, who plays the hero's friend, the consumptive gunfighter Doc Holliday. Quaid lost 43 pounds for the role, and what's left of him has the bitter purity of spider's blood. Small and febrile now, Quaid wears black clothes and gloves and carries a cane; his dark eyes glitter in a hollowed bone-china face. There's a dandified touch of beard under his mouth, and he speaks with the courtliness of a southern gent who cares for nothing so much as the perfect phrasing of insults. Quaid delivers his killer lines with a weighted, burnished power—he's mesmerizing. Everything he does is pointed and precise, yet the performance has a grand-style theatricality at the same time. He *is* the nineteenth century.

The question is, Why is the brilliant Doc Holliday drawn into close friendship with Kevin Costner's dense Wyatt Earp? My God, what a strange, sad movie. *Wyatt Earp* is a talent-laden bore—an epic with a malevolent cipher at its center, an immense historical re-creation devoted to a profoundly uninteresting man.

As everyone knows, there always was a large element of ambiguity in the Western movie hero. Whether operating on the right or wrong side of the law, he is a man who kills. Simple-minded filmmakers merely try to glorify him; he represents honor or civilization or lonely integrity. The more thoughtful stretch the ambiguities to the breaking point—Anthony Mann, for instance, who in the early fifties made a beautiful (and underrated) series of films with James Stewart (*Winchester 73, The Far Country*, etc.) in which the hero was an egotistical and self-serving loner, a man just barely acknowledging the claims of society. By the time John Ford made *The Man Who Shot Liberty Valance*, in 1962, the hero had become a fake. Someone else did his dirty work for him. But since the country needed heroes, Ford reasoned, he was a necessary fake. In the movie's most famous line, "When the legend becomes fact, print the legend."

Clint Eastwood, who made the best recent Western, *Unforgiven*, gave us a deeply flawed man who comes to realize the inadequacy, even absurdity, of the killer's code he has lived by. But if you make the Western hero a real man, how do you sustain him as a hero? At the end, Eastwood mythicized his hero once again, sending him back into the fray to avenge a friend's death. Eastwood found a solution to the problem; Kasdan, in his would-be epic, gores himself on the horns of the dilemma.

Kasdan begins stolidly with midwestern cornfields, the setting of primal American myth. As a neo-Copland musical score (by James Newton Howard) sounds hollowly on the track, young Wyatt, growing up during the Civil War, tries to run away to join his brothers in the Army. He's stopped by his gruff father (Gene Hackman), and later the tough old guy lays down some principles: Strike first and strike to kill; stick with your own family, with blood. In the scenes of Wyatt's early manhood, Kasdan sustains the square, heartfelt approach, and there's one great moment: When Wyatt is challenged by a thug, he picks up a pool ball and, following the old man's advice, plunks the guy right in the esophagus. *Wham*! Costner, with long wavy hair and a shy smile, makes Wyatt almost startled by the speed of his victory; you can see his amazed enjoyment of the adulation of the people watching. Kasdan and Costner recapture something of the soft romantic appeal of the young Gary Cooper or Henry Fonda, the self-confidence so quietly expressed that it comes out as bashfulness.

Lawrence Kasdan was criticized (by me, among others) for the insubstantial jokiness of his earlier Western, *Silverado*, but now he's aiming for weight and simplicity. Except for a few outdoor scenes, the picture has the severe look of nineteenth-century tinted photographs: The brownish western towns yield dark, dowdy interiors, the rented rooms are cramped and charmless, the saloons raw-looking, some of them mere tents in the open. Kasdan and production designer Ida Random have captured the harsh yet flimsy appearance of the impromptu mining and cow towns, the oddity of the American Victorian newness.

Up through the first hour or so, I was willing to give this ambitious movie a break. But as Wyatt Earp matures and turns into the iron-willed marshal of Dodge City, a hard and vengeful man, the movie becomes opaque. Costner's performance shrivels—it gets lost and dies somewhere in the dark suits, the large, soft hat, the thick mustache. Earp, in this telling, is remote, cold, and not particularly intelligent. He sticks to his father's principles: Shoot first. Of course, Kasdan is trying to be honest about the Western hero. But how are we supposed to take him? What does he represent? Right? Justice? Sheer aggression? He's certainly ambiguous—and entirely unsatisfying. The famous shootout with the Clanton and McLaury gangs is more like a slaughter than a duel, and when one of Wyatt's brothers is assassinated in return, and the movie collapses into revenge drama, we lose all interest. Why should we care? None of his brothers is interesting; they're all dominated by Wyatt, and he's an inarticulate cold cod. Kasdan is trying to make a family epic—*The Godfather* out West. But he made it without passion or vividness.

Edging into the movie, such actresses as Isabella Rossellini, Mare Winningham, and Joanna Going, who plays Wyatt's third wife, a young Jewish beauty from San Francisco, are quickly pushed out again. The women knock themselves silly against the wall of Wyatt's solemn bravery. In response, Costner is astoundingly ungenerous; he doesn't give the passionate ladies more than a flicker of his attention, and all around me in the audience women were laughing derisively. Kasdan, in his confusion, appears at first to take the female characters' point of view. But finally, and rather pathetically, he rejects it for without the male mystique of violence, he must have reasoned, there is no Western movie. Kasdan can't resolve the ambiguities of a modern view of the Old West, and in the end, his dour, recessive, unromantic hero is hopelessly inadequate as the protagonist of epic themes.

NEW YORK POST, 6/24/94, p. 39, Michael Medved

Somewhere, buried deep inside the bloated, overweight, carcass of Lawrence Kasdan's "Wyatt Earp" there's a taut, terrific little movie struggling to get out.

Unfortunately, stirring moments and a few fine performances are ultimately crushed under an avalanche of loose ends and irrelevant indulgence.

The movie covers 40 years in the life of the famous lawman, but it creeps along at such a glacial pace that by the end of its three hours and one minute you feel as if you've aged even more than the characters.

It's actually the young Wyatt who fares worst since Kevin Costner is hardly a credible choice to play a fresh-faced 19-year-old.

Trying to convey Earp's innocent idealism as a law student and adoring husband to his first wife (Annabeth Gish), Costner offers so many goofy, open-mouthed, gee-whiz expressions that he begins to resemble Jethro of "Beverly Hillbillies" fame.

As the character gets older and grows a moustache, becoming a cynical peace officer "as tarnished as his badge," Costner finally settles into his role and the quality of the entire enterprise notably improves.

Part of that improvement stems from the arrival of Dennis Quaid as Doc Holliday, the doomed, tubercular Georgia gentleman turned gambler and gunfighter.

It's a dependable pattern in Wyatt Earp movies (there've been nearly a dozen of them) that the actor playing this part always steals the film and Quaid is no exception.

He lost 43 pounds in order to look appropriately and (horrifyingly) frail, but the riveting intensity of his portrayal is even more impressive than the physical transformation.

This movie's other most committed performance also turns up during its second half, as soap star Joanna Going makes a stunning, passionate big screen debut playing Josie Marcus—the 19-year-old Jewish runaway who became Wyatt's third wife.

The sets, locations and camera work are consistently superior, but director Kasdan ("The Big Chill," "Grand Canyon") displays an unfortunate tendency to gild the lily—overloading many scenes with lightning flashes, swelling music and other hokey contrivances to unnecessarily underscore already dramatic material.

Such melodramatic excess works against the aura of authenticity that Kasdan works so hard to project, including gory images of gunshot wounds that are utterly realistic and uniquely chilling.

This movie also remains more faithful to the known facts of Earp's life than any previous movies about the legendary lawman emphasizing the moral ambiguities in his troubled personality.

But in courageously cutting its protagonist down to size, "Wyatt Earp" faces a fatal dilemma: If this guy is no hero, then why does he merit a three-hour movie with such reverent attention to every detail of his life?

In recent years, ambitious epics like this one have often been reissued in special editions on laser disc or video that restored missing footage that had been cut from the original theatrical release.

One can only hope that with "Wyatt Earp" we will one day see such an improved version, but one that features less—not more—material than we get in this formless and frustrating movie.

NEWSDAY, 6/24/94, Part II/p. B2, Jack Mathews

In their attempt to create a full psychological portrait of the legendary frontier lawman Wyatt Earp, writer-director-producer Lawrence Kasdan and star-producer Kevin Costner have managed something I would have thought impossible. They've made him boring.

Boring, mean, pig-headed, even a little pathetic. You don't want to spend a lot of time with a guy like this, and Kasdan's "Wyatt Earp" runs on for three hours and 10 minutes, just a half-hour shy of the original version of Michael Cimino's 1980 "Heaven's Gate," which, in ways, it resembles.

Both Westerns use real-life events to tell sweeping sagas of the settling of the Old West, both feature stunning landscapes and meticulously authentic sets, both go to great pains to re-create the socio-political context of the time, and—despite or because of their length—both lack pace and dramatic focus.

To his credit, Kasdan built his story around known facts, while Cimino blew the relatively bloodless Johnson County Wars into a Western Gettysburg. Nor is the style of "Wyatt Earp" remotely as self-indulgent as "Heaven's Gate." But with its needlessly dramatized biographical detail, it is nearly as plodding and aimless.

Everything we would like to know about Wyatt Earp could be told within the context of the story of the Gunfight at the O. K. Corral, the infamous 1881 shootout that has been the focus of several previous movies, including the John Ford classic "My Darling Clementine." That event, and the bloody vendetta that followed, are here, but the feud between the Earp brothers, with their friend Doc Holliday, and a gang of rancher/rustlers led by Ike Clanton isn't even introduced until more than halfway through the movie.

Kasdan starts his story on the morning of the Gunfight at the O. K. Corral, as a clearly hardened Wyatt sits in a Tombstone, Ariz., saloon, calmly drinking a cup of coffee. Then, we are off on a long flashback sojourn through the events that got him there and made him the tough nut he was.

Earp's pre-Tombstone résumé is that of an Illinois farm boy who became a drunk, horse thief and drifter after his young wife died of typhoid, and though he was always planning to strike it rich in some boomtown, he found his niche cracking skulls as a lawman in Wichita and Dodge City, Kan. From all this anecdotal back story, we learn how the Earp brothers had the importance of family loyalty drilled into them by their lawyer dad (a wasted Gene Hackman), and how Wyatt developed his dangerous ambivalence about the law.

There are nice moments in the early going, particularly between the young Earp and Urilla (Annabeth Gish), his ill-fated wife. There is also some dreadful melodrama, as Wyatt hits the skids and has to be rescued from the bottle and an Arkansas gallows by his father. And the scenery is spectacular, as Earp and the Masterson brothers, Bat (Tom Sizemore) and Ed (Bill Pullman), roam the range hunting buffalo.

The movie doesn't settle into anything resembling a story, however, until Wyatt and his brothers Virgil (Michael Madsen), James (David Andrews) and Morgan (Linden Ashby) begin divvying out their special brand of law-and-order in Dodge City. It is there that Wyatt meets and befriends the tubercular killer, gambler and former dentist Doc Holliday, whose portrayal by an emaciated and growling Dennis Quaid gives "Wyatt Earp"' its only true source of energy.

Quaid, who dropped 43 pounds preparing for the role, takes the film's flashiest role and hams it almost to the point of parody. But after the aimlessness and listless characters preceding him, Doc definitely spells relief, and the film—already one hour and 20 minutes along—finally begins to take root.

The second half moves quicker, if only because we're familiar with the Tombstone part of the Earp story, and know where it's headed. But even on that level, the film is a disappointment. For all the attention to detail and motivation, Costner's Earp isn't a very interesting person, and his feud with the Clantons lacks real conviction.

Ultimately, "Wyatt Earp" tries to cover too much, and depends too heavily on its star. Costner can be very engaging in tightly drawn, intimate roles, but he simply does not have the forcefulness to fit the steely, outsized personality of this version of Wyatt. He talks mean, acts mean and does mean things, but he just looks like a guy in need of a good hug. Because Costner makes Earp such a weak magnet, the characters both drawn to and repelled by him seem even weaker. The Clanton gang has inspired some of the Western genre's greatest villains, but here, Ike (Jeff Fahey) and the others are mostly faceless thugs, and the satisfaction Wyatt gets from gunning them down is lost on us. In fact, if any actor other than Quaid made an impression during the production, the performance hit the cutting room floor. Isabella Rossellini has one big scene as Doc Holliday's tempestuous lover, then vanishes without a trace, and without providing a clue how a woman of such elegant beauty got saddled with the nickname of Big Nose Kate.

After "Tombstone," a recent hit that simply used the Earps and Clantons for a frontier version of an inner-city gang war, you have to applaud the purity of Kasdan's intentions. As a time, dates, names and places biography, he has given us the most honest look at Wyatt yet.

But in the end, he has merely proven the wisdom of John Ford, whose winning philosophy about Westerns was summed up by a reporter at the end of "The Man Who Shot Liberty Valance":

"When the legend becomes the fact, print the legend."

NEWSWEEK, 7/4/94, p. 71, David Ansen

"This is the West, Sir. When the legend becomes fact, print the legend." That often-quoted line from John Ford's "The Man Who Shot Liberty Valance" defines the tug of war between the classical and revisionist Western. Go for the myth or deconstruct it?

Lawrence Kasdan's three-hour-plus epic "Wyatt Earp" aims to be the last word on the legendary lawman, an ambiguous figure filmmakers have been mythologizing ever since his death in 1929. The legendary Earp, embodied by the serenely laconic Henry Fonda, was apotheosized in John Ford's spare and beautiful "My Darling Clementine" (1946), a movie blissfully unconcerned with the facts. The legend also prevailed in the now-dated "Gunfight at the O.K. Corral" (1957), with Burt Lancaster's stolid Wyatt playing off Kirk Douglas's bitter, tubercular Doc Holliday.

Now, within months, we have two Earp sagas that move closer to the facts—"Tombstone," in which Kurt Russell's Wyatt turned into a bloodthirsty avenging angel (and Val Kilmer stole the film as a suavely dissolute Doc), and Kasdan's research-heavy opus. It's perhaps no coincidence that these law-and-order Westerns have come out of Hollywood now: the anarchic Old West may seem disturbingly New to filmmakers in post-riot Los Angeles. Was Wyatt the Daryl Gates of his day—a hero to some, a loose cannon to others?

Kasdan's "Wyatt Earp," starring Kevin Costner, is the first to give us Earp from childhood to middle age. The defining moment for this Wyatt, who starts life as an innocent aspiring lawyer, is the death of his young wife, Urilla (Annabeth Gish). In despair, he descends into darkness and horse thievery, but even after he pulls himself together and goes on to his famous exploits as a deputy, he's become a hardened, near-heartless man. The filmmakers want us to feel he's a tragic hero, living—and killing—for his brothers, unable to trust anyone who isn't "blood."

Gorgeously shot by Owen Roizman, designed with all the detail a $60 million budget can buy and pumped up with an overbearing James Newton Howard score, "Wyatt Earp" is big, solemn—and barely alive. Kasdan's trouble is that he seems to want to print the legend *and* the facts. What results is a stately, curiously remote muddle, with all the structural problems that come with the biopic form. Kasdan and Dan Gordon's screenplay shows us the gritty violent reality of the West, where cowboys vomit at the sight of a bloody skinned buffalo. Yet when it comes to Wyatt's love life—first with his wife, then with Josie Marcus (Joanna Going)—its mushy romanticism is as phony as old Hollywood ever got. For a movie so sure of its importance, it seems oddly uncertain of what it wants to say.

In its second hour, when the Earp brothers clean up Dodge City and move on to Tombstone, the movie finds its rhythm. Dennis Quaid's ravaged, growly-voiced, volatile Doc Holliday sashays onto the scene and provides some dramatic sting. Costner seems more interested in being an icon than an actor. "Wyatt Earp" demands a performance that risks all; Costner would rather coast on his soft-spoken charisma.

It's in the interminable aftermath of the O.K. Corral shoot-out that "Wyatt Earp" completely wears out its welcome. Wyatt sets off to avenge the killing of his brother Morgan, picking off his enemies one by one. We feel nothing but impatience, because in three hours, Kasdan hasn't found the time to individualize the villains. What kind of a Western has anonymous bad guys? This is neither classic nor revisionist. It's just bad storytelling.

SIGHT AND SOUND, 9/94, p. 53, Philip Kemp

Lamarr, Missouri. During the Civil War, young Wyatt Earp tries to run away and join his elder brothers James and Virgil in the Union army, but is stopped by his father Nicholas. After Virgil and James return, the restless Nicholas decides the family should move west to California. A few years later, Wyatt returns to Lamarr to study law with his grandfather, Judge Earp, and marry his sweetheart, Urilla Sutherland. During pregnancy Urilla contracts typhoid and dies. Desolated, Wyatt takes to drink and burns down their house. Nine months later he fetches up in Arkansas begging and stealing, and is jailed for horse-theft. His father bails him out and tells him to leave Arkansas for good. Heading west Wyatt becomes a buffalo-hunter, taking on as skinners the brothers Ed and Bat Masterson, but tires of the job and leaves for Wichita, where James Earp runs a saloon and his wife Bessie works as a hooker.

When Wyatt disarms a drunken gunman the town marshall recruits him as deputy. Wyatt enlists James to help him and summons his brothers Virgil and Morgan, who arrive with their wives Allie and Lou. The Earps' cleaning up of Wichita brings an invitation from Dodge City, where they're joined by the Masterson brothers. But Wyatt's enthusiasm for violent arrests is criticised and he's sacked. In Texas, bounty-hunting for a railroad, he meets the tubercular gambler Doc Holliday. But when news comes that Ed Masterson has been killed in Dodge, Wyatt returns and reimposes order. Doc, who has taken a liking to him, arrives with his mistress, Big Nose Kate.

Wyatt persuades his brothers to move to Tombstone, Arizona, to mine silver. But mining proves unprofitable and the Earps revert to law enforcement, backing Marshall Fred White. By jailing gunmen Frank Stillwell and Pete Spence they earn the enmity of the Clanton-McLaury gang and the resentment of Sheriff Johnny Behan. When Behan's mistress, the Jewish actress Josie Marcus, arrives in town, Wyatt is strongly attracted to her. Mortified, his mistress Mattie Blaylock attempts suicide with laudanum.

The Clantons plan to ambush Wyatt, but the plan misfires and Marshall White is killed instead. As tension rises Doc Holliday offers his support, and he and the Earps meet the Clantons in a showdown near the OK Corral. Several of the gang are killed. Behan arrests Holliday and the Earps, but they are cleared in court. Soon afterwards Frank Stillwell shoots Morgan dead, and Virgil is ambushed and badly wounded. The youngest Earp, Warren, arrives to help escort Morgan's body back to California by train. The Clantons are waiting at Tucson but are outgunned, and Wyatt kills Stillwell. Returning to Tombstone, he hunts down the last members of the gang before leaving with Josie. Seventeen years later, on a boat heading for Alaska, Wyatt is recognised by a young man who thanks him for having once saved his uncle, Tommy O'Rourke, from a lynch mob.

It's one of the great ironies of the Western myth that Wyatt Earp, a small-time gambler whose law enforcement activities were minimal and ethically suspect, should have become its most enduringly heroic figure—mainly thanks to his luck in surviving long enough (he died in 1929) to manipulate his own image for posterity. Even posthumously his luck has held. Films such as John Sturges' *Hour of the Gun* and Frank Perry's *Doc* that set out to question the legend have suffered neglect, while the celebratory treatments—Ford's *My Darling Clementine*, Sturges' *Gunfight at the OK Corral*—are remembered. Kasdan, well aware of these contradictory readings, offers an account that veers between celebration and scepticism before settling for moral ambiguity only to tip over, in an awkwardly tacked-on coda, into something dangerously close to acclamation.

At three and a quarter hours, Wyatt Earp is nearly as long as *Clementine* and *Gunfight* together, allowing Kasdan to cover far more territory than either Ford or Sturges dreamed of: nearly 40 years of Earp's life and a swathe of frontier America from Missouri to California. Yet though Owen Roizman's photography gives us all the sweeping landscapes and visual splendour we expect from the genre, the final effect is oddly claustrophobic. The key conflicts take place within Earp's psyche, and within the close-knit circle of his family. The group loyalty of kinship is what motivates him, rather than abstract notions of civilisation (as with Ford) or justice (Sturges). "Nothing counts so much as blood," Gene Hackman's patriarch instructs his sons. "The rest are just strangers."

The scene suffers from being pointedly intended to "explain" Earp, and the same goes for several other episodes: the death of his wife, and the moment when, having disarmed his first gunfighter, he stands raptly holding the gun at arm's length, while James Howard's score soars lyrically and the sky explodes in fireworks. The fireworks, way over the top, are a giveaway; this is a would-be epiphany that's far too self-conscious to carry weight. In a looser-limbed, more self-mocking western (Kasdan's own *Silverado*, for one) the scene could play as parody, but Wyatt Earp is too mindful of its own epic pretensions to send itself up.

Humour, even of the traditional laconic kind, is in short supply. Barring some heavy-handed joshing over Bat Masterson's name, the only light note is struck by Dennis Quaid's goateed Doc Holliday—in any case a relatively subdued figure by comparison with Victor Mature or Kirk Douglas. And if the omission isn't necessarily crippling in a Western (after all, there aren't too many laughs in *High Noon*) Kasdan's film does seem increasingly weighed down by its own seriousness. In this it takes its cue from Costner, who most of the time plays Earp with an impassivity that suggests he might be auditioning for Mount Rushmore.

Big set-piece action sequences don't figure much, either. The climactic gunfight, far from the choreographed elegance of Sturges' version, is reduced to a squalid little close-quarters shootout in a side-street (which, to be fair, is probably about how it was). The rationale for this massive movie can only be the elucidation of Earp himself, since in character terms no-one else really features; yet even after three hours, he remains a curiously unfocused figure. There's little sense in Costner's stolid performance of the charisma that could impel his brothers, older and younger alike, to follow him blindly into one half-baked scheme after another.

Pro or con, all Wyatt Earp movies treat him as a figure of legendary stature, whether for good or evil. (A truly revisionist film would present him as a shabby, mercenary grifter of no importance, and would probably never get made.) Kasdan, clearly uneasy with the legend, can't bring himself to destroy it and ends up endorsing it. In the final showdown Earp walks into point-blank gunfire, unscathed and invulnerable. And at the end of the coda, a cliché flashback (Earp facing down a lynch mob) dragged in for no good dramatic reason, he muses, "Some people say it didn't happen that way." "Never mind them, Wyatt," responds Josie, "it happened that way," The echo of Ford's *Liberty Valance*—"When the legend becomes fact, print the legend"—is unmistakable. But the flatness of the exchange only underlines how far Kasdan has fallen short of his models.

TIME, 7/4/94, p. 73, Richard Schickel

You can play Wyatt Earp heroically, as a mythipoeic legend of the Old West, riding out of some misty nowhere to bring peace justice and other good values to the American frontier. You can play him antiheroically (which is probably closer to the historical truth), as a wandering thug who, when he isn't dealing faro or looking for a gold strike, occasionally makes a living as a peace officer not entirely immune to corruption. What you shouldn't do—especially at 3 hours and 15 minutes, a length that implicitly promises epic grandeur—is turn his story into a solemn biopic, grinding relentlessly, without selectivity or point of view, through a rootless and episodic life from adolescence to old age.

The director of *Wyatt Earp*, Lawrence Kasdan (he also wrote the screenplay with Dan Gordon), is obviously of the school that believes all inclusiveness is a reasonable trade-off for insight. Or maybe, like a lot of literary biographers these days, he can't bear to omit any of his research. But his approach prevents *Wyatt Earp* from developing a compelling dramatic arc, and it doesn't help a rather glum and withdrawn Kevin Costner make the eponymous protagonist into a dynamic or even very attractive figure. Mostly he is fate's pawn, grimly enduring one damn thing after another.

Poor chap. He doesn't have much in the way of inner resources. Aside from the good reflexes that make him handy with a revolver, all he has to go on is some dubious advice from his moralizing father (Gene Hackman): put your trust in blood kin and in the law. What Earp sees in his brothers is impossible to say, since they are so poorly particularized—and encumbered with unpleasantly fractious wives to boot. Wyatt himself tolerates a thoroughly depressing relationship with a common-law wife (Mare Winningham), as they all lurch querulously toward the legendary gunfight with another extended family at the O.K. Corral. The exact nature of the quarrel between the Earps and Ike Clanton's crowd is never satisfactorily explained. Like almost everything else in this fragmented and ambiguous movie, it just sort of happens.

It's the more conventional movie figures who fare best in this lugubrious context. Dennis Quaid is Doc Holliday, the tubercular gunman-gambler, who gallantly and sardonically confronts his mortality, and Joanna Going plays Josie, the smart, spunky romantic who is Earp's last great passion. These are familiar, forthright characters, and the actors energize the film by playing them with headlong confidence.

It's too little and too late. And oddly enough, too soon as well. Wyatt Earp drones past its logical conclusion, which is, of course, the great shoot-out. Since Earp's life uninstructively limped along after that event, so must the movie, further abusing our overtaxed patience and undertaxed intelligence.

VILLAGE VOICE, 7/5/94, p. 49, J. Hoberman

Wyatt Earp has the self-regarding solemnity one associates with Kevin Costner vehicles—and then some. If the movie were a fan (its own), it would insist on singing every verse of "The Star Spangled Banner." This flick can't help pondering its spiritual aura.

Filled with cosmic significance, *Wyatt Earp* isn't exactly Bresson. If anything, it projects the same anxious megalomania as *Silverado*, writer-director Lawrence Kasdan's 1985 attempt to jump-start the western. Every scene is overwrought, then further inflated with the gaseous fanfares of James Newton Howard's grandiose score. Call it *Dances With Bankers*. A saga of epic cornfields, rude cow towns, thunderous buffalo herds, this $65 million account of America's archetypal frontier lawman is the most lavishly produced western since *Heaven's Gate* plunged UA into financial purgatory.

Wyatt Earp looks pretty good—scenes lit by kerosene lantern alternate with searing yellow buttes under baby blue skies—and, at 189 minutes, it feels mighty long. Unlike all previous Earpiads, including last December's *Tombstone*, this one means to chart the full trajectory of its subject's life. The real Earp worked as a teamster, a buffalo hunter, and a card-sharp before finding steady employment policing a succession of wide-open boomtowns; after six years as a lawman, he returned to gambling, drifting from one mining camp to another to wind up in Hollywood as a living fossil of Western lore.

Earp's mythic stature was in part a function of his longevity. The Gunfight at the OK Corral only became famous once he began palling around with movie cowboys like William S. Hart and

Tom Mix; it was two fanciful biographies, *Tombstone* and *Wyatt Earp: Frontier Marshall* (published in 1931, soon after Earp's death) that created the image of the legendary town-tamer. Essentially picaresque, the true story of Wyatt Earp might have made an ironic epic not unlike *Little Big Man*, but Kasdan and Costner have something more elevating in mind.

Their young Earp is a corn-fed farmboy in an orange toupee who falls apart after the death of his wife (Annabeth Gish), riding down to sinful Arkansas to become a drunken horse thief. After an extralegal rehab stage-managed by the Earp family patriarch (Gene Hackman), Wyatt learns to sublimate his dark side by dealing faro in Wichita. When he's first made deputy, the music swells and the camera drifts up to heaven: Kasdan's Earp is supposed to be tragically flawed, but Costner plays to the crowd as a natural-born enforcer, secure of his entitlements even when threatened by a local civilian review board for his "hardass" technique. This no-prisoners attitude extends to Costner's costars. Dennis Quaid gives a credibly cadaverous performance as frontier existential Doc Holliday. (Unlike Val Kilmer in *Tombstone*, he's not permitted to come anywhere close to stealing the picture.)

Wyatt Earp includes more about its subject than you might ever want to know. Even after big brother Virgil begs Wyatt to "finish it," the movie has 30 minutes left to run. (During the final few reels, the comings and goings in the audience at the Warners screening suggested a rehearsal for rush hour in Grand Central Station.) A coda has the retired lawman looking like a monument and recognized by a young fan. There's a flashback to an episode of Dodge City heroism in which a solitary Earp stands up to a crazed lynch mob. "Some people say it didn't happen that way," he muses, as if a member of his own audience. "Never mind, Wyatt," his wife (Joanna Going) replies, "It happened that way." If you say so.

In the classic Earp westerns, *Dodge City* (1939) and *My Darling Clementine* (1946), and even the tepid Ronald Reagan vehicle *Law and Order* (1953), Earp is shown as a progressive lawman who destroys the criminal forces of social injustice in the name of decency. (It's the same role Costner played in *The Untouchables*.) *My Darling Clementine* elevated the showdown between the Earps and the Clantons to nothing less than the battle of civilization against barbarism—this signaled early on when private citizen Earp is hailed as a public hero for running a drunken Indian out of town. Although the lavishly definitive *Gunfight at the O.K. Corral* (1957) put additional emphasis on family honor, the image of the socially responsible town marshal was reiterated on TV's *The Life and Legend of Wyatt Earp* (ABC, 1955-61).

Thereafter, revisionism set in. James Stewart provided a scurrilously comic Earp cameo in *Cheyenne Autumn* (1964), James Garner appeared as a ruthless avenger Earp in *Hour of the Gun* (1967), a movie that ceded moral authority to Jason Robard's Doc Holliday. As embodied by Harris Yulin in the 1971 *Doc* (a counterculture western directed by Frank Perry from Pete Hamill's script), Earp was the actual villain—an opportunistic monster of middle-class hypocrisy laying his bourgeois deathtrip on Holliday, a moody hophead and righteous dropout played by Stacy Keach.

Tombstone, which opens with shots culled from early westerns and ends with narrator Robert Mitchum describing Earp's Hollywood funeral, unabashedly positions its subject as a seminal figure in western movies. *Wyatt Earp* has more to do with canonizing Kevin Costner as the player of players on *Entertainment Tonight*. (The requisite *Premiere* puff admiringly calls him *Wyatt Earp*'s "dead center.") Costner bogarts the movie even as he withholds motivation. In *Tombstone*, Virgil is the gung ho law-and-order type and Wyatt the vacillating square. Here, Costner is the absence that all women love and all men must obey. It's a tautological performance: I must be a star to generate a film so long, so expensive, so empty, and so abstract.

For all the evident production design, *Wyatt Earp* shows scant interest in historical context. Even more than *Silverado*'s, this is a homogenous West: there are almost no Asians, Latinos, blacks, or Native Americans (The "hebe whore" who becomes the third Mrs. Earp carries the burden of universal Otherness.) As recent neowesterns have pretty much telegraphed their target audiences, *Wyatt Earp* must be for white guys. Indeed, the founding father of the Earp clan talks like a children's primer found in Nazi Germany: "Nothing counts so much as blood—the rest are just strangers" Pa Earp believes in the sanctity of the Law except, of course, as it applies to kin. Wyatt inherits this mystical father right—commanding his brothers and dissing their wives. (In this, the character stands in for the producer-actor.) The male Earps are mainly pimps and gamblers, most of their women are whores, and nobody has any kids. What's wild, however, isn't the movie's insistence on family values so much as its dogged celebrity worship. Whatever the star does must be cool.

Tombstone proposes the Clanton gang as the "earliest example of organized crime in America" and dramatizes a shift from town taming to summary justice. *Wyatt Earp* is even less concerned with legal niceties in celebrating the hero's smug vigilante vengeance. Clan warfare has an additional edge of justified sadism, with Wyatt emptying out his revolver into enemy corpses (something even the bad guys never have the time for) and ultimately being admired for it.

Trying to make his version of *Unforgiven*, Costner seems not to have grasped the sociopathic subtleties of his own performance in *A Perfect World*. His narcissism renders *Wyatt Earp* bleak in a way clearly not intended. The movie posits its lawman as a sullen, would-be führer in a sagebrush Bosnia, suggesting—hot damn!— that that's how we liked it.

Also reviewed in:
CHICAGO TRIBUNE, 6/24/94, Friday/p. F, Michael Wilmington
NATION, 7/25-8/1/94, p. 139, Stuart Klawans
NEW YORK TIMES, 6/24/94, p. C1, Caryn James
NEW YORKER, 7/18/94, p. 72, Terrence Rafferty
VARIETY, 6/20-26/94, p. 41, Todd McCarthy
WASHINGTON POST, 6/24/94, p. B1, Rita Kempley
WASHINGTON POST, 6/24/94, Weekend/p. 42, Desson Howe

YOU SO CRAZY

A Samuel Goldwyn Company release of an HBO Independent Productions. presenation in association with You So Crazy Productions. *Executive Producer:* Martin Lawrence. *Producer:* Timothy Marx and David Knoller. *Director:* Thomas Schlamme. *Director of Photography:* Arthur Albert. *Editor:* John Neal and Stephen Semel. *Production Designer:* Richard Hoover. *Art Director:* John Gisondi. *Running time:* 85 minutes. *MPAA Rating:* Not Rated.

WITH: Martin Lawrence.

LOS ANGELES TIMES, 4/27/94, Calendar/p. 1, Kenneth Turan

No need to worry about thoughtless critics giving away all the best jokes in "You So Crazy," the new Martin Lawrence performance film. If they work for mainstream publications, they won't be able to.

For Lawrence is almost always in-your-face raunchy and scatological, an enthusiastic dispenser of profanity whose explicit detailing of all kinds of sexual situations led to "Crazy" getting an NC-17 rating and undergoing a change in distribution. The same tendencies got Lawrence uninvited from "The Tonight Show" after his use on "Saturday Night Live" of what Daily Variety described as "coarse material" elicited hundreds of complaining phone calls.

But Lawrence, the star of Fox network's "Martin" and the former host of HBO's "Def Comedy Jam," is more than someone who talks dirty. As this film of a Brooklyn Academy of Music concert shows, he is an alive comic presence, an adept social commentator, and, most surprising, a promoter of values that can only be called mainstream.

Wearing a leather outfit with a large peace sign on the front and something unprintable on the back, Lawrence can't stand still. He prowls back and forth like a fighter, an impish performer who knows how clever and sassy he is and relishes the knowledge.

Like Richard Pryor, not surprisingly one of his models, Lawrence really doesn't deliver jokes. He tells stories, dispenses advice, describes outrageous situations. A vivid mimic, Lawrence just doesn't talk the talk, he grandly pantomimes every last sexual detail he can think of.

Again like Pryor in his early days, sex and race are Lawrence's two main subjects. He cheerfully skewers white people for being "too chipper: they know it's their country." His more outrageous routines deal with masturbation, oral sex, what goes on in prisons and what mealtime was like for Jeffrey Dahmer. All are offshoots of the kind of no-holds-barred frankness that always characterizes street humor, displaying an absence of shame that places them several steps past what anyone is used to hearing on the big screen.

Yet for all the delight he takes in being unvarnished and verbally beyond the pale, the thrust of Lawrence's performance supports quite solid values. He encourages fathers to take care of their children, men and women to love each other and communicate better, and everyone to use condoms and stay away from crack. Though he may not talk like a conventional role model, beliefs like this make him sound like a candidate for the position.

Very fluidly directed by Thomas Schlamme, who used eight cameras and director of photography Arthur Albert to make sure every thing went smoothly, this is a model performance film from a visual point of view. Startling and funny, today's version of comedy that goes beyond the socially acceptable, "You So Crazy's" lack of boundaries will unnerve people who think they're beyond all of that. Which is no doubt part of the point.

NEW YORK POST, 4/27/94, p. 41, Thelma Adams

In the feature-length one-man-show "You So Crazy," Martin Lawrence commits the stand-up comedian's ultimate crime.

No, it's not that Lawrence uses obscene language—although he proudly offers obscenities like a toddler uttering his first "doody."

Dismiss Lawrence's prejudices against Mexicans and whites—although he confesses to the audience that what bothers him about white people is that they're too chipper.

Forget about the comic's rude references to women and their anatomy. He offers tips on feminine hygiene ("This would be a good place for a Stick-Up [room deodorizer]") and, while he doesn't suggest keeping women barefoot and pregnant, Martin's ideal woman would "f--- him wild and cook."

So, where does the star of Fox TV's sitcom "Martin" cross the line? What's his crime?

Martin's not funny. Raunchy, raw, rude, crude offensive—yes to all of the above. But he couldn't squeeze a laugh from a hyena.

It's a shame, too, because Martin is a talented performer. Director Thomas Schlamme ("So I Married an Axe Murderer") captures his subject on a stage set like a schoolyard at night before a predominantly black audience. Wearing a loose, black leather baseball uniform, Martin has presence and poise.

He's a physical and surprisingly graceful comic. During his routine, he impersonates an uptight white, a drunk, a woman on crack, and a jealous lover stumbling into a club in pajamas and footsies looking for his girlfriend.

But rather than working from his strengths—his likability and physical humor—Lawrence mines material that is shopworn and shocking. He's like a boy begging the nuns to scrub his mouth with Comet.

Lawrence fails not because he's sexist and offends my sensibilities, or homophobic (in an extended riff on rape in prison that verges on sadomasochistic fantasy) and offends some other segment of the population—the comic fails because he's doing the nasty and no one cares.

Lawrence's material ("I'd have f---ed Dorothy right on the Yellow Brick Road") is beneath him and the audience.

And what about that irritating title? "You So Crazy" is street shorthand for "You're so crazy," what girlfriends have apparently been telling Lawrence for a long time.

I wouldn't mind if Lawrence was crazy. I could handle borderline obscene. Just make me laugh.

NEWSDAY, 4/27/94, Part II/p. B3, Gene Seymour

The cuddly-huggy sitcom days seem numbered for Martin Lawrence. And just as well, too. Even with its naughtiness airbrushed for TV family-hour consumption, Lawrence's comic persona could never be mistaken for Sinbad's. The strain of containing both Lawrence's bristling talent and restless ambition within the confines of his weekly "Martin" series became apparent with each season. One always knew it wouldn't be long before he was ready to raise the stakes.

Consider those stakes raised—and how! Let us count the ways: The brouhaha over his scatological "Saturday Night Live" hosting stint and his subsequent suspension from NBC appearances, his pugnacious battle to overturn the original NC-17 rating of this now-unrated live-concert film, whose release has been delayed by the controversy.

People who know and love Lawrence only from "Martin" will no doubt be thrown by "You So Crazy," filmed last year at the Brooklyn Academy of Music. There isn't a whole lot here that's cuddly-huggy here and a bit more that's icky-sticky. Still, Lawrence surprises you in ways that may not be obvious to those scanning this film for cuteness *or* grossness.

True, there's an obligatory spiel about racism in which Lawrence recalls how, before fame and glory came his way, whites looked at him with as much casual disdain as they did most young black men; Now, he says, they call out, "Yew *go*, Martin!" (Lawrence's catch-phrase, filtered here through a hayseed accent.)

But even the cheapest observations Lawrence shares on this subject are irradiated by a genuine sense of wonder that people can't be more tolerant, more considerate toward each other. Priests, school principals and even other comedians say such things all the time. But the force of Lawrence's empathy—one area in which he beats his role model, Eddie Murphy, by a mile—gives conviction to sentiments that lesser talents would simply toss in to balance more corrosive patter.

Other unexpected qualities, like tenderness and a sweet sense of detail, emerge from his reminiscences of growing up poor, black, in a large family. When talking of his mother's efforts to keep her kids warm and fed, Lawrence mentions the many things he could do with a slice of white bread. ("Remember syrup sandwiches?" he says.)

But by far, the funniest, most surprising displays of Lawrence's empathy come when he steps into the dicey realm of relations between the sexes. Male hubris is a target, rather than a manifestation, of his routines. The feelings of women, meanwhile, are evoked with shrewdness and empathy. He gets the decline of a romance nailed right down to the copy of "Waiting to Exhale" the woman is reading when she breaks it off.

Such barbed, keenly wrought bits compete for attention with the extended riffs on masturbation and female genitalia that got him in trouble with NBC. Ironically, it's the nastier routines that make Lawrence look more standard-issue than the longer, richer material where his capacity for truth-telling thrives.

As character-comedy-performance films go, "You So Crazy" doesn't belong in the exalted company of "Richard Pryor: Live in Concert" or Eric Bogosian's "Sex, Drugs and Rock and Roll." But whether the pop mainstream likes it or not, Lawrence seems headed toward the tricky, perilous high wire where only the bravest (Pryor, Lenny Bruce) and the richest (Murphy, Robin Williams, Whoopi Goldberg) comedians have dared to walk.

NEWSWEEK, 5/9/94, p. 69, David Ansen

Because Martin Lawrence's mouth is what gets him in trouble, it's easy to overlook the fact that this stand-up comic throws his entire body into his work, prowling the stage in constant, restless motion, stirring up laughs in his audience like a cook stirring a big pot of very funky stew. The star of the sitcom "Martin" and the man who was banned by NBC for transgressing network standards on "Saturday Night Live" now offers up his undiluted stage show in the unrated concert film "You So Crazy." Lawrence's raunchiness has not been exaggerated: no sexual or scatological detail (and they usually go together) is beyond the pale of his comic investigation, whether he is offering tips to the brothers on how to avoid unwanted intimacies behind bars or investigating the most private bedroom details. His view of the world is that of a gynecologist on laughing gas.

Lawrence is a storyteller, not a jokester, with a mimic's gift for playing both sides of a relationship. Though he sees both men and women as walking sex organs, his humor lacks the misogynistic and gay-bashing edge of his idol, Eddie Murphy. There's a sweetness behind the strut that tempers the relentless lowness of the material. Compared with his other role model, Richard Pryor, he's earthbound: Lawrence's mind never startles you with the uniqueness of its perceptions. At heart, he's a traditional moralist, exhorting couples to communicate, kids to keep off crack and use condoms. Though he touches on some topical items such as Rodney King, Jeffrey Dahmer and "Driving Miss Daisy" he's at his best exploring the down-and-dirty revelations of sexual relationships. It's when he's closest to disgusting his audience, funnily enough, that he touches the deepest chords. It's crude and sometimes exhausting, but when "You So Crazy" is cooking, it takes you to the other, liberating side of embarrassment.

VILLAGE VOICE, 3/1/94, p. 57, Gary Dauphin

Poor Martin Lawrence. He's as funny as he wants to be, the black male comic of the moment, the lead in a hit TV show, even the star of *You So Crazy*, his own very funny concert film, but he'll never be Richard Pryor. Black people like their geniuses fucked up and tragic; Martin, with his homey odes to Mom and a drooly excuse for a mouth, is just too well adjusted to ever be Richard.

Don't let the NC-17 rating fool you: frequent use of the words *dick* and *pussy* aside, Martin isn't really into the raw shit. His thing is that he's bugged out at regular intervals, much like an amusement park ride that hides its last, big dip behind what looks and feels like a homestretch roll. Martin will tell you in a minute that he loves his mom and go on like that for a dopey while, and then before you know it he's up there explaining that his dick isn't really that big, but yeah, he'd let his boy suck it if the brother really wanted and no one was watching. Among fellas this kind of up and down (usually on our own cocks) is what passes for vulnerability, and when Martin's routines push that envelope it's by avoiding the sexual-politics-as-drive-by style that seems so popular with his peers and competitors. Martin's jokes will jab and prick at his sexual anxieties, but he always tries to mitigate the danger by using his own body as a distraction, reassuring the audience via "I'm so stupid" faces, mock tears, or sheepish looks of injury that *he's* the one who's the most mortified.

In *You So Crazy*, this all holds true until the end of the performance, when Martin, figuring he's done his good deed for the day, starts riffing out of nowhere about stuff like eating some pussy gone a little gamy: "Why don't you put a Tic-Tac up in that shit?" he asks, cracking himself up before leaving the stage. Standard black-boy comedic stuff, but Martin is so, well, funny-looking, that his looks just might compete with his misogyny for your attention. Martin's ears project out to here, and under that leather outfit his body seems to carry baby fat in places that can't help but evoke certain qualities of cuddly safety and good-naturedness. Which, all in all, gets back to why Martin will never be Richard "That Nigger's Crazy" Pryor. Safety should be among the last things a black audience wants from a stand-up comic and besides: we all know the props go to the brothers who look like they've really lost their minds.

Also reviewed in:
NEW YORK TIMES, 4/27/94, p. C18, Caryn James
VARIETY, 2/14-20/94, p. 38, Brian Lowry
WASHINGTON POST, 4/27/94, p. B1, Desson Howe

YOUNG BLACK CINEMA II

A series of nine shorts by various directors. *Running time:* 120 minutes. *MPAA Rating:* Not Rated.

NEWSDAY, 9/9/94, Part II/p. B9, Gene Seymour

It's been two years—and too long—since the Public Theater last hosted an anthology of short films by African-American filmmakers. It's true that much of the hype over the emergence of black film directors has cooled since then. But the value of such a showcase extends beyond revealing the next Julie Dash or John Singleton. It gives room for African-American imagination to display its diversity and energy.

The first short is probably the most imaginative and certainly the most acerbic. Lewis Payton Jr.'s "Slowest Car in Town" follows the descent of an elevator carrying a well-dressed bespectacled buppie. As it stops on each floor, beautiful white women flinch, wither, react in horror to what they imagine this mild-mannered fellow to be. (One sees him as a slathering crack addict, another a convict, still another a homeless bum.) Before long, their hysteria becomes his nightmare as he is actually reduced to subhuman status by their racism. Clever, corrosive work.

Robert Patton-Spruill's "The Gaming Table" is gaudier and noisier with the same issues as it moves the locale of Amiri Baraka's classic one-act play, "Dutchman," from a subway car to an extravagantly decadent dance club. The content is essentially the same: supercool young black man sexually and racially harassed by a white woman in a queasy, insinuating dance of death.

Still, the balance of these films is less concerned with what white people think than with what's going on within "the community." Austin Phillips' "Familiar Differences" is a bittersweet story of a former drug dealer who is trying, after a year's absence, to reconnect with his wife and young daughter. The characters and story are well-conceived enough to make you wonder what happens after its somewhat inconclusive ending. Technically, however, it's a little ragged around the edges.

So is Anaye Milligan's "Downtown With the Cat," in which a young hoodlum is recruited for a mob hit that goes haywire. A better script, however, may provide a good home for Milligan's well-honed instincts for tension.

Amateurism, meanwhile, works to Dwight Smith's advantage in "Samson and Delilah," the biblical tale recast as an off-the-rack hip-hop video. Smith's strictly-from-high-school dynamics are also in evidence in Michael Dennis' whimsical "The Hardest Part," in which a student awaits a long-sought date while his skeptical, motor-mouth buddy tags along. Kimson Albert's "How Can I Be Down" is a trenchant, all-too-real animated film tracking the roots of a school shooting incident. All of which would seem to indicate "the hood" remains the main point of origin for much of black cinema.

Still, there are welcome signs in this anthology that other territory is being explored. "Notes on a Minor Key," directed by music video maker Adisa and written by Avery O. Williams, is a haunting recollection by Grandpa Kansas (Keith David from "Platoon") about the bright and terrible day in the late 1940s when his red-hot swing combo was ripped apart by jealousy and selfishness. Pat Hartley's "Hung Up" is an amusing, technically adroit ditty about missed connections at the twilight of a love affair. The protagonists, by the way, are white. But they could just as easily be black. What a concept!

VILLAGE VOICE, 9/13/94, p. 70, Jame Hannaham

In the dark, an official, velvety voice counts down from 18. Footsteps click across a marble floor. A figure stands in an elevator, seen only from the neck down. A very uptight, supergroomed white woman gets on. We now see her fellow passenger, the buppie protagonist of Lewis Payton Jr.'s hilarious *Slowest Car in Town*, decked out in suit and nerd specs. The elevator descends one floor, and the terrified ofayette flees. A series of similar incidents in this cramped space forces our assimilated brother to confront his negritude in uproarious ways, slyly implying that the opinions of these Elite models mean much to him. The minimal dialogue and tight structure of this movie, the best of the Public Theater's "Young Black Cinema II," heighten its claustrophobic negrophobia until its Truffaut-ish final moment.

The films that take themselves more seriously, though competent and promising, have the kind of disparity between form and context that one expects of young filmmakers. Austin Phillips's *Familiar Differences*, a sensitive "hood for the '90s" tale told from the perspective of a prodigal father who barges in on his daughter and her mother after a year's absence, is shot and written with a mostly steady hand but is really poorly lit. Robert Patton-Spruill's *The Gaming Table* transforms the subterranean locale of Amiri Baraka's *Dutchman* to a Limelight-like dance club, with ridiculously extravagant production values (crazed lighting, bizarrely colored drinks, dancers surrounded by roses) and self-important acting that overpower what's left of the play, transforming it into a pretentious MTV spot.

However, amateurism can be an end in itself, and Dwight Smith's Lustracurl advertisement come to life, *Samson and Delilah*, is so incredibly goofy that it's smart. "High school students" dressed in cheap-assed gold-lamé outfits and ratty, nappy wigs, looking like Robert Townsend making fun of Rick James, reenact the biblical tale in rap to the mechanical clapping of a low-budget beatbox, Kimson Albert (no relation to Fat) also makes the best of what's available with *How Can I Be Down*?, an animated anecdote from the life of the Fever, a gang of three infiltrated by a doofus who ends up showing them a thing or two when some ninjahead toughs start playing keep-away with his skullcap. Even brothers who ain't down, these films mostly say, still got the power.

Also reviewed in:
NEW YORK TIMES, 9/9/94, p. C17, Stephen Holden

ZERO PATIENCE

A Cinevista release of a Zero Patience Productions, Ltd. film with the participation of Telefilm Canada/The Ontario Film Development Corporation in association with Channel Four TV with assistance from Cineplex Odeon Films Canada/Ontario Arts Council/Canada Council/Canadian Film Centre/CRB Foundation. *Executive Producer:* Alexandra Raffé. *Producer:* Louise Garfield and Anna Stratton. *Director:* John Greyson. *Screenplay:* John Greyson. *Director of Photography:* Miroslaw Baszak. *Editor:* Miume Jan. *Music:* Glenn Schellenberg. *Choreographer:* Susan McKenzie. *Sound:* Urmas John Rosin. *Sound Editor:* Jane Tattersall. *Casting:* Dorothy Gardner. *Production Designer:* Sandra Kybartas. *Set Decorator:* Armando Sgrignuoli. *Special Effects:* Sean Kelly. *Costumes:* Joyce Schure. *Make-up:* Sylvain Cournoyer. *Running time:* minutes. *MPAA Rating:* Not Rated.

CAST: John Robinson (Sir Richard Francis Burton); Normand Fauteux (Zero); Dianne Heatherington (Mary); Ricardo Keens-Douglas (George); Bernard Behrens (Doctor Placebo); Charlotte Boisjoli (Zero's Mum); Marla Lukofsky (African Green Monkey); Michael Callen (Miss HIV); Brenda Kamino (Dr. Chen); Scott Hurst (Michael); Von Flores (Ray); Duncan McIntosh (Ross); Cassel Miles (Barry); Benjamin Plener (Ted); David Gale, Charles Azulay, and Howard Rosenstein (Shower Guys); Peggy Baker (Snake); Bill Coleman (Fox); David Gonzales (Mouse); Yvonne Ng (Parrot); Janice Hladkl (Syphylis); Johann Hladkl (Mycoplasma); Louise Garfield (CMV); David Roche, Marni Jackson, and Andrew Paterson (Reporters); Jeffrey Akomah, Rae Ellen Hutley, and Kate Rodrigues (School Kids); Glen Hanson and Marty Rotman (Museum Guards); Ann Medina (Narrator); Benedict Campbell (Newscaster's Voice); Richard Fung and Edward Sheng (Bathhouse Patrons); Glenn Schellenberg (Bathhouse Attendant); Anna Stratton (Ms Strutting); Mark Rourke (Diver).

NEW YORK POST, 3/30/94, p. 33, Thelma Adams

Is it in bad taste to say that "Zero Patience," the first AIDS musical, is filled with catchy tunes?

It's probably more sacrilegious to admit that the songs, despite titles like "Contagious," aren't infectious enough to justify this well-intentioned activist flop.

There's a place in the small but growing cluster of AIDS movies ("Savage Nights," "Philadelphia") for a cheeky musical that draws on the camp extravaganzas pioneered by Bette Midler and others on New York's bath house circuit. Who worried about taste when the Divine Miss M. donned a mermaid costume and climbed into a wheelchair for a paraplegic musical number on wheels?

If only John Greyson's "Zero Patience" had been as inspired as it is outrageous. But Greyson and composer Glenn Schellenberg have an agenda—to debunk myths about the genesis of AIDS that most people in his audience (this movie will preach to the converted) no longer hold.

Is AIDS a mutated green monkey virus? Is HIV the sole cause of the disease? Is the promiscuous Patient Zero, a Canadian flight attendant, responsible for bringing AIDS to North America?

Is this the subject for a musical or the text for a biology film strip?

Greyson and Schellenberg shoehorn their politics into a far-fetched plot. They resurrect the infamous Patient Zero (Normand Fauteaux) to haunt Sir Richard Francis Burton (John Robinson)—The Victorian explorer, after dipping into the fountain of youth, is practicing taxidermy at 170 and designing a diorama about the origins of AIDS for a natural history museum.

In this warped "West Side Story," Patient Zero sings Tony to Burton's Maria. All this could have been freaky, frothy fun if only the songs had been as memorable as "America" and Burton and Zero had emerged as 3-D lovers rather than competing agendas.

Such musical high points as exist are hard to get through the censors at a family paper, But three nude men singing about bathhouse etiquette approaches Gilbert and Sullivan's three little maids.

Zero's former lover, George (Ricardo Keens-Douglas), delivers the most poignant song. "I'm positive I'm alive," he sings as his health deteriorates, "I'm positive that I'm going to die ... sometime."

I'm positive that an AIDS musical could work—think what "La Traviata" did for tuberculosis. But I have zero patience for uneven agit-pop.

NEWSDAY, 3/30/94, Part II/p. B9, John Anderson

If audacity is a virtue, "Zero Patience," John Greyson's melange of AIDS activism, HIV-positivism and MGM-meets-MTV esthetics, is a paragon. At the very least its marriage of medical skepticism, 19th-Century orientalism, "Rocky Horror"-style camp and synchronized swimming make for a musical manifesto that's irresistibly in-your-face.

The title is a twofold reference. The first is to the time's-run-out attitude of gay AIDS activists towards opportunistic researchers, indifferent politicians, mutton-headed media and a terrorized straight world. The second is to one of two main characters, Patient Zero (Normand Fauteux), the French Canadian air steward alleged by Randy Shilts to have brought AIDS to North America. Zero's real name is never used in the film, but "Zero Patience" is more about the dangers of myth and myth-making than it is about hard facts, even if it uses facts to puncture every AIDS theory extant.

Just consider Zero's counterpart: Sir Richard Francis Burton (John Robinson), English explorer, translator, "sexologist" and, currently, chief taxidermist of Canada's Natural History Museum (blame the Fountain of Youth). The museum's director, Dr. Placebo (Bernard Behrens), has bad news: Burton's Hall of Contagion project has had its funds cut, there will be no "plague rat" display. The desperate Burton, in need of a "prima mobila," settles on Zero. Zero, languishing in an aquatic limbo populated by synchronized swimmers—who represent cultural vacuity, limber viruses, or both—performs the first of the film's half dozen or so songs, and its best. "Tell a story/clear my name," he sings, invoking the cult of blame that's grown up around him. He also invokes Scheherazade, a unifying legend in an atmosphere of fabrication: Her 1,001 tales were translated by Burton, and like the PWA's, she lived a night by night existence. The difference between them, of course, is that for her, reprieve was possible.

Zero is sprung from limbo as Burton sets out to demonize him: Interviews with Zero's friends and family—his still-grieving mother (Charlotte Boisjoli), his HIV-positive ACT-UP friend Mary (the abrasive Dianne Heatherington)—are manipulated, their words turned against him. Of course, Burton's project wins the sponsorship of Gilbert and Sullivan Pharmaceuticals, for obvious reasons: Keep AIDS a gay disease, keep the general population polarized, and no one will care that the cost of your drugs constitutes extortion.

Burton is educated and seduced by Zero, the narrative propelled by over-the-top musical sequences; one features their rectums, singing to each other. With the exception of the first song—reprised in a hilariously moving Barbra Streisand send-up by the late singer/activist Michael Callen, as Miss HIV—the Glenn Schellenberg music is lyric-driven and forgettable. And the staging of the dance numbers is generally claustrophobic. And no one among a cast of characters that's almost entirely HIV-positive looks remotely sick: A guy with Kaposi's sarcoma wears paste-on moles. But what's meant to be poignant gives you pause, as when the stricken George (Ricardo Keens-Douglas) recalls not visiting Zero on his deathbed—"If the prettiest party boy could get sick, we all could get sick." Bringing you up short is generally the idea. "Zero Patience" is pure propaganda, meant to disabuse a 20th-Century world of its 19th-Century presumptions. It does so with bravado.

SIGHT AND SOUND, 9/94, p. 54, Paul Julian Smith

Richard Burton, the Victorian sexologist and traveller, has miraculously survived into the twentieth century, where he has become a taxidermist in a Natural History Museum. He plans an exhibit on Aids for the museum's Hall of Contagion. Meanwhile Patient Zero, the French Canadian flight attendant and supposed origin of the HIV infection in North America, is brought back from limbo to tell his tale. When Burton decides to make Zero (whom he has not met) the centre piece of his exhibition, twin quests begin. Zero pays invisible visits to his ex-lover George, his physician Dr Cheng, his mother, and Aids activist and former co-worker Mary; while Burton visits the same people and uses his interviews with them to edit a hostile and prejudiced account of Zero's life and death. He also carries out 'research' with a camcorder in a gay bath house.

Finally, Zero and Burton meet for a first time. While Burton can see Zero, his camera cannot pick him up. Musical numbers treat the varied questions of anal sex, mortality, and the African Green Monkey, another spurious origin of Aids. Stripped naked by the monkey in the museum display, the two men finally make love. Analysing Zero's blood the next day, Burton is turned on to Aids activism by Miss HIV and vows to combat myths about the disease. Unfortunately, he is unable to change the exhibit as he would wish. However, Mary and other ACT UP activists invade the museum and transform it. Finally, Zero decides it is time for him to abandon his ghostly existence on earth and he is taken up away from Burton on to the video screen.

John Greyson's affecting Aids musical begins with a class reciting the story of Scheherazade. Like *The Arabian Nights, Zero Patience* will be a story of a narrative and survival (of narrative as survival), in which the ghostly revenant Zero will be granted a temporary reprieve from death just so long as he has a story to tell. That story will bring scintillating visual pleasure with it, from the first number in which some nifty synchronized swimming is combined with sexy callisthenics by Zero, toying with a glitter ball in a fetching one-piece suit. But the question of visibility is typically ironised from the beginning: the wraithlike Zero complains, "How can I get laid if nobody can see me?"; and the equally supernatural Richard Burton aims to put Zero in an HIV multimedia horror show modelled (like *Zero Patience* itself) on a music video aesthetic.

As in Greyson's earlier *Urinal*, then, *Zero Patience* confronts the problem of representing a culture of surveillance without reproducing that culture's coercive and dehumanizing effects; and like *Urinal* once more, it appeals to history (the portraiture of figures such as Burton) and to a shift of emphasis from private, sexual experience to that public policing of images which (in Foucaldian style) sets up dissenting desire as perversion. Much of *Zero Patience* has Burton reiterate the tired clichés and hectoring prejudices of a straight male order: that the historical Zero (a French Canadian gay flight attendant with an enviable sex life) was promiscuous, irresponsible, even a serial killer. Such earnestness, combined with John Robinson's sometimes over-emphatic performance, can prove tiresome. But there are fine moments when surveillance is subverted by sly humour. For example, Burton's attempt to document the sex action in a gay bath house with a camcorder hidden under his towel (Toronto independent film-maker Richard Fung makes a fleeting appearance here) gives rise to a musical lesson on erection etiquette from a male trio in the showers. Greyson's mimetic strategy of parodying oppression works best, as here, when swiftly diverted into humour.

Indeed, the best musical numbers subvert not only Burton's prurient positivism, but also some theoretical sacred cows closer to home for film and queer theorists. Thus a duet of talking arseholes *à la* Cronenberg contend that "the Law of the Father doesn't recognize the hole" and "your rectum ain't a grave"—surely the first time Lacan and Leo Bersani have been set to such a jaunty beat—and a "cofactorial conga" set in an animated dayglo bloodstream offers a user-friendly version of competing theories of infection. And it is to *Zero Patience*'s credit that it sets out to question not only the 'culture of certainty' of homophobes and pharmaceutical companies, but also what Greyson sees as the inflexibility of some Aids activists themselves.

Moreover there is a serious, contextualising argument here about the history of epidemiology. Burton's waxwork 'Hall of Contagion' memorialises (or fetishises) Zero's legendary predecessors as founts of contagion, such as Typhoid Mary. And the film achieves a rare resonance when the love scene between Zero and Burton is cross-cut with an animated, elegiac diorama from the same display, in which Dutch sailors, held to be plague bearers, were thrown naked into the sea.

In *Urinal* a tea room queen vindicates his own image captured on a police camera, "reclaiming [in Greyson's words] surveillance in a graceful and surprising way". In the final scene of *Zero Patience*, Zero, now reclaimed himself for queer history as the "slut who inspired safer sex", disappears into a video screen, defiantly smoking a cigarette, laughing and smiling to the lover he is leaving for ever. It is a suitably inspiring image for a film which attempts to combine memory of those we have lost with pride in those we are, a graceful and surprising moment indeed.

VILLAGE VOICE, 3/29/94, p. 51, Georgia Brown

John Greyson's glossy, free-wheeling AIDS musical, *Zero Patience* owes something to Jarman, at least on the level of its unapologetic, celebratory queerness. It has a wonderful opening: a child in a classroom recites, ever so haltingly, a passage about Scheherazade and the dire necessity of her 1001 stories. The suggestion is that Greyson's own urgent tale, like so many others in the age of AIDS, is an effort to ward off the storyteller's death, for one more night anyway.

The classroom text is Sir Richard Burton's *Arabian Nights*. Free associating, Greyson's text has the same Burton (John Robinson)—famous in his day for exhaustive studies on penis size—currently working as a taxidermist designing dioramas for Toronto's Natural History Museum. Together with the museum's prissy director, Dr. Placebo (Bernard Behrens), Burton is planning a new exhibit on plagues—a Hall of Contagious Diseases. For an AIDS tableau, he wants to feature the French Canadian flight attendant who supposedly introduced the virus to North America. Called Patient Zero, he'll be set up next to Typhoid Mary. As if in response to the interest, Zero's ghost (Normand Fauteux) returns to defend his reputation. As the only one who can see him, Burton turns out to be his only hope.

Zero Patience lies somewhere between cabaret and one of those naive junior high teaching films with dancing chromosomes and singing nuclei. As a didactic entertainment, the movie's simplest lesson is tolerance. Another lesson, somewhat more complex, is the futility and destructiveness of scapegoating. Is Zero a villain, a victim, or maybe even a hero in that, by volunteering for the study, he pioneered the safer sex crusade? The bottom line is that Zero was a person. At the end, gaining Burton's love and trust, his ghost can rest. Burton, for his part, after more than a century of trial and error, can finally become human.

But I'm making it sound far too solemn. After all, a song is sung by buttholes. Greyson is a spoofer, an angry but essentially light-hearted parodist. (Todd Haynes he isn't.) He also keeps within the bounds of what I would call tolerant liberal taste. Too bad Cortines can't be persuaded to introduce the musical muckraker to city schools.

Also reviewed in:
NEW YORK TIMES, 3/26/94, p. 14, Stephen Holden
VARIETY, 7/19/93, p. 72, Dennis Harvey
WASHINGTON POST, 6/10/94, p. D6, Rita Kempley

ADDENDUM

The following reviews arrived too late to be included in previous issues of FILM REVIEW ANNUAL. The issues of FILM REVIEW ANNUAL in which the credits and film reviews appear are given in parenthesis after the names of the film.

FROM HOLLYWOOD TO HANOI (*Film Review Annual, 1994*)

LOS ANGELES TIMES, 4/28/95, Calendar/p. 8, Kevin Thomas

"From Hollywood to Hanoi," an extraordinarily moving and engrossing documentary, covers lots of terrain, emotional as well as cultural and geographical, as a beautiful young actress who calls herself Tiana returns to her native country for the first time in more than 20 years. (Sunday makes the 20th anniversary of the fall of Saigon.)

For Tiana, an Anglicization of Thi Thanh Nga, the daughter of a former minister of information for the South Vietnamese government, the return is a journey of self-discovery, an attempt to reconcile her American identity with her cultural roots. Yet from the moment of her arrival in Ho Chi Minh City, her own odyssey takes on an epic dimension as she seizes her unique opportunity to use her film as an instrument of reconciliation between Vietnam and the United States.

Thanks to the passion, dedication and determination of Tiana and her skilled and selfless crew, "From Hollywood to Hanoi" accomplishes its goals. One of its strengths and charms is that it never loses its highly personal quality—the sense that it starts out like a home movie/travelogue for the folks back home, complete with delightfully corny asides aimed at her relatives she encounters immediately the enormous toll exacted by the war. She has a joyous "hen party" reunion with her pretty actress cousins, one of whom is considered "the Elizabeth Taylor of Vietnam." But there are also meetings with an elderly aunt—so impoverished she couldn't even afford to buy stamps to try to write for help from her relatives in America—and an elderly uncle—minister of defense for South Vietnam and also a former senator whom Tiana believed to be dead but who survived 13 years in North Vietnamese "re-education" camps. Understandably, he is as bitter about the communist North Vietnamese victors as is Tiana's own father.

Moving beyond family reunions, Tiana visits a hospital where victims of Agent Orange are treated; talks to a group of Vietnamese fathered by American soldiers, whose mixed ancestry has made life hard for them in Vietnamese society and who dream of being reclaimed and taken to America by the fathers they never knew, and listens to the haunted survivors of the My Lai Massacre.

As an indomitable charmer and the member of a large, once-prominent family, Tiana proceeds to Hanoi, arriving in the midst of the immense, emotion-charged celebration of the centennial of the birth of Ho Chi Minh. She manages to meet with Gen. Vo Nguyen Giap, former commander of the victorious North Vietnamese army, premiere Pham Van Dong and senior Politburo advisor Le Duc Tho, who explains why he refused to accept the Nobel Prize in 1975 with Henry Kissinger—and expresses sorrow upon learning that Humphrey Bogart is no longer alive. Giap's wife addresses American mothers, speaks of a common bond of loss and grief.

Le Duc Tho's juxtaposed comment on peace and an American movie icon cut right to the heart of, "From Hollywood to Hanoi," while for all its spirit of reconciliation is also a sharp commentary on the potency of American pop culture. Tiana is highly critical of the way, particularly through movies, the Vietnamese people have been depicted before and after the war in Southeast Asia. Indeed, Tiana's clips from her own roles in cheap American action movies could alone explain her need to return to Vietnam to try to forge a new identity.

HOLD ME, THRILL ME, KISS ME (*Film Review Annual, 1994)*

SIGHT AND SOUND, 9/95, p. 52, Kim Newman

Burglar Eli Morrow meets a rich neurotic, Twinkle, while robbing her parents' house. After helping him take a large amount of cash, she bullies him into marrying her. At the altar, Eli refuses to go through with it even though Twinkle pulls a gun on him. They squabble and the gun goes off, apparently killing Twinkle.

While waiting in the small town of El Monte to meet Mr Jones, a fixer who can get him a fake passport, a drunken Eli is picked up by Sabra, a stripper, who takes him back to her trailer and leaves him handcuffed to her bed. In the morning, he is released by Dannie, Sabra's animal-loving sister. Mr Jones tells Eli his passport will be ready within six weeks. Returning to the trailer park, Eli befriends Dannie, who is a virgin because she doesn't want to do anything her sister does. When the jealous Sabra has Dannie's dog Gus put down, Dannie doses her chocolate milk with household solvents but has a change of heart. Sabra interrupts Dannie pouring the milk away and knocks her out with a frying pan. Sabra then chokes to death on the poisoned milk.

Dannie and Eli exchange confessions of accidental murders. They bury Sabra in Gus's grave at a pet cemetary and commence an affair. Eli's stash of money is discovered by Olga, an old Hungarian woman, and her grasping son Laszlo runs off with most of it. When he goes to pay off Mr Jones with the last of the money, Eli finds him dead and Twinkle, Jones' murderess, alive. Twinkle tries to kill Dannie but Eli shoots her again. Dannie then finishes Twinkle off and the lovers take a plane to Rio.

"I guess killing your sister and burying your dog and losing your virginity all in one day is a lot for a girl," says Dannie. Although *Hold Me Thrill Me Kiss Me* is mainly smart and funny, it's hard not to feel, from its gunplay-at-the-altar outset, that we've been here before.

This is one more in a parade of indie films (Barry Shils' *Motorama*, Abbe Wool's *Roadside Prophets*, Daniel Appleby's *Bound and Gagged: A Love Story*, John Dahl's *Red Rock West*) that can no longer be seem as simple rip-offs of obvious predecessors (David Lynch, John Waters, George Kuchar) but have to be considered as a genre of their own, one that is becoming almost as overpopulated as the Western was in the 50s and that endlessly recycles the same basic ingredients. This film displays many here, including a cool, but decent, rebel hero, colourful credits, alternative celebrity cameos (including Timothy Leary amongst others), a trailer trash backdrop, dayglo costumes and decors, small town weirdness, a stolen cash macguffin, well-chosen rock soundtrack, kinky sex and cosy callousness.

Max Parrish's Eli, a nice guy criminal with a decent streak belied by his feckless crookedness, and Adrienne Shelly's Dannie, an innocent waif who transforms amusingly but without much justification into a cold killer, are the supposed heart of the film. However, their love, first expressed when Eli buys her a baby seal tattoo (which Sabra sneers at as the wimpiest body adornment on record), hardly ignites the screen. Refraining mostly from *Wild at Heart*-cum-*Natural Born Killers* sex ("I don't want to be handcuffed for my first time"), the couple don't have that outlaws-on-the-run desperation and have to fall back on swapping stories about lost pets. Both players seem to be coasting on their hangdog looks, although Shelly gets to glam up after she becomes a murderess.

El Monte, California, is populated by the usual indie movie crowd of eccentric loungers and deadbeats, but only Olga and her whining son intersect with the plot. Diane Ladd's irrelevant trailer queen is left with nothing much to do, and suggests some scenes trimmed along the way. Until her death, the film is stolen by Andrea Naschak's amazingly crass, vulgar and ghastly Sabra, a silicone slut seen gleefully dragging a dog off to the pound to die. Naschak's performance is so loathsome, indeed, that even Sean Young's rich bitch maniac is upstaged.

HYENAS (*Film Review Annual, 1993)*

NEW YORK POST, 8/18/95, p. 46, Larry Worth

Taking a well-established story and transporting it to a different time and place can go either way. Who'd have believed "Romeo and Juliet" could assume new life as "West Side Story"? Or that "The Wizard of Oz" would crumble when reincarnated as "The Wiz"?

The latest metamorphosis moves celebrated Swiss playwright Friedrich Durrenmatt's "The Visit" from its Central European setting (immortalized in the Anthony Quinn-Ingrid Bergman 1964 film version) to a desolate African village. And the result?

"Hyenas," is the most exhilarating mix of exotica, comedy and tragedy since 1959's "Black Orpheus" (itself transporting the Orpheus-Eurydice legend to Brazil's Carnival time).

Once again, the plot takes off when an older woman returns to her roots, a down-and-out town that's on the verge of financial collapse. As she's now "richer than the World Bank," the lady agrees to pour millions into the economy.

But there's a catch: Locals must agree to kill off the town's most popular man, who not so coincidentally is her former lover. Naturally, the proposal horrifies everyone—at least initially.

And just as "The Visit" served as an allegory about greed, manipulation and corruption, the Senegalese setting gives new dimension to each plot twist. One need only recall real-life African tragedies in Rwanda and Ethiopia to understand how the lure of salvation could produce dispensable morals and forgotten principles.

Director Djibril Diop Mambety then goes a giant step further; he interjects a "Twilight Zone-like" humor as clergy, police and spousal loyalties come face to face with sinfully pleasurable temptation.

At some points, as in depicting a rope-raised toll gate surrounded by arid countryside, matters verge on parody. But without exception, Mambety fine-tunes the moment into brilliant social satire.

Along the way, he also captures the rich ambience of local customs, chants and eccentricities that allows the characters to thrive. Even better, he never resorts to cliches.

So instead of having a Lena Horne-a-like descend on the unfortunates, Mambety cast the superb Ami Diakhate as a one-legged, one-armed harpy with whining voice and disturbingly Machiavellian demeanor. Similarly, Mansour Diouf's hero is an amalgam of average looks, dubious motives and cowardly actions.

The director errs only in his penchant for symbolism. With his all-too-frequent shots of descending vultures and prowling hyenas, viewers will quickly O.D. on his message about mankind as the ultimate predator.

But that's a small price to pay for the film's thought-provoking message, never mind the searing visuals. Amazingly, the bark of "Hyenas" is as powerful as its bite.

Also reviewed in:
NEW YORK TIMES, 8/18/95, p. C6, Stephen Holden

OAK, THE (*Film Review Annual, 1994*)

LOS ANGELES TIMES, 3/27/95, Calendar/p. 13, Kevin Thomas

Lucian Pintile's post-Ceaucescu saga "The Oak" (1991) is deliberately brutal, nasty, shocking and profane: a picaresque journey into chaos, a portrait of a nation on the brink. The central characters, a teacher (Maia Morgenstern) and a doctor (Razvan Vasilescu) in love, act like a criminal couple on the run. The film starts when the heroine's father dies under a toppled projector and she sets fire to his room—and this is just the beginning.

PEKING OPERA BLUES (*Film Review Annual, 1990*)

FILM QUARTERLY, Spring 1995, p. 34, Julian Stringer

Tsui Hark is one of the most famous prolific of Hong Kong's post-1979 generation of New Wave film-makers. On the basis of the very successful domestic release of titles he has directed for his own Film Workshop production company in Kowloon—including *All the Wrong Clues for the Right Solution* (1981), *Zu: Warriors from the Magic Mountain* (1983), *Aces Go Places III* (1984), *Shanghai Blues* (1984), and *Once upon a Time in China* (1991)—as well as production credits for well-known movies by John Woo and Ching Siu Tung,[1] Tsui's work has made the transition to the large Chinese communities of the United States and also to a small section of the white North American and European markets. His Cantonese cinema, are regularly shown at international film festivals, and are written about by Western journalists and scholars. Of all his films, it is perhaps the 1986 action-comedy *Peking Opera Blues* that is most often singled out for attention.

Peking Opera Blues is set in China in 1913, two years after the Republican revolution that toppled the Last Emperor, and a time when the country was being fought over by competing warlords. The film opens with General Tsao taking charge of the city palace after the ignoble departure of General Tun. The general's daughter, Tsao Wan (played by Brigitte Lin), has returned from studying overseas to be with her father. Because of her pro-democracy sympathies, she immediately embarks upon a plan to steal, with the help of the young guerrilla Ling Pak Hoi (Mark Cheng), some incriminating documents hidden in the general's safe. The plan fails, but in the process the two revolutionaries meet up with Sheung Hung (Cherie Chung), a gold-digging musician, Pat Neil (Sally Yeh), daughter of the owner of the Peking Opera House, and a young Chinese soldier, Tung Man (Cheung Kwok Keung). The five form an unlikely alliance. Another plan to steal the documents during a Peking Opera performance is foiled by Commander Liu and his men from the "Ticketing Office" (a bunch of extremely violent tax collectors). After this, thc plot revolves around a series of disguises, separations, betrayals, rescues, violent confrontations, and narrow escapes. The five friends finally achieve their revolutionary goal, but nothing much happens as a result. An end title tells us that the generals are at it once more; war has broken out, the country has split in two; thus, "the Chinese Democratic Revolution began all over again."

Despite the fact that *Peking Opera Blues* was not picked up by a major American distributor after its initial New York release ln 1987, many of thc critics who saw the film predicted that—despite its atrociously inadequate and confused subtitles—its accelerated narrative pace, brilliantly choreographed fight scenes, and irresistible star performances could make it a box-office success in thc West.

As *Peking Opera Blues* is a cornerstone of the Hong Kong New Wave cinema, and as Hong Kong is likely to elicit more international attention over the next few years because of the extraordinary nature of its current political situation, thc film may yet provide a key reference point for Western audiences trying to understand what cinema and life in Hong Kong are all about. Most obviously, the film can take its place among those titles that invite interpretation as allegories about 1997, the year when Hong Kong will revert back to Chinese sovereignty after 99 years of British colonial rule. Thc arbitrary, short-sighted nature of the original 1898 hand-over treaty between the two countries (with Britain fearing at the time that a more permanent settlement might encourage its international rivals to seek similar economic footholds in the South China Seas region) is clearly alluded to in the film. Early on, a Chinese warlord meets with representatives from the five foreign banks he is clandestinely doing business with. They tell him how much the dividend on his investment will be after so many years, whereupon the general happily puts his name to the document that will then become the object of a frantic, pro-democracy search. "What will the world look like 47 years later?," he laughs. "Who knows? Give me a pen."

The political implications of such autonomy from, and imminent return to, the mainland provide the point of departure for *Peking Opera Blues*'s narrative. The use of a theatrical setting—most of thc action is set in the distinctive Chun Wo Ban, the Peking Opera House of the film's title—is a means to establish one distinct, bordered space within a larger, encroaching space. Furthermore, theatrical disguises, role-playing, and mistaken identities are all used to highlight some very real questions about cultural affiliation. This is a film that explores the ambivalence of Hong Kong's national identity.

In its concern with the attempt of a group of young guerrilla fighters to overthrow the generals and establish democratic rule, the film constructs two kinds of Chinese. The mainland Chinese are the villains; they comprise the national army, the Ticketing Officers and the warlords. The overseas Chinese are the heroes; they include the five revolutionaries, and the denizens of the Opera House. This Good Chinese/Bad Chinese dichotomy is posited as a political confrontation. The generals in Peking cannot comprehend the coexistence of social power, while the guerilla fighters are concerned with overthrowing monarchism and restoring democracy.

As Tsui Hark himself has put it: "I don't know how the messages come across outside the country, but the film clearly takes a poke at the audience, saying that Chinese people do not know what democracy is. The first democratic revolution collapsed because of a power struggle ... the film also takes a sly poke at the current Government."[2] According to *Peking Opera Blues*, democracy can only be achieved through violent means as all other avenues of approach have already been foreclosed. In common with many recent films from Hong Kong (such as *A Better Tomorrow, The Killer, The Wicked City*, and *The Heroic Trio*), this one also indulges in the fantasy of a small group of Good Chinese overcoming all odds to "magically" kill off the Bad Chinese.

Tsui's film style expresses this at every turn. His work has a restless, knife-edge quality that insists on moving a narrative along at breakneck speed—in other words, there is no time left to play with, the present is forever slipping through your fingers, whatever has to be said must be said very quickly. J. Hoberman once described the director as a "comic Eisenstein ... [I]t's not just his machine gun editing, but his use of typage, his analysis of circus attractions, his fascination with signs, and his interest in political upheaval that link him to the Soviet master."[3] It might be suggested, in support of such a contention, that in *Peking Opera Blues* montage is used for the purposes of (Marxist?) political analysis. Although Hoberman doesn't provide textual evidence for his argument, a brief analysis of a short moment from a single scene is enough to bear it out.

As almost every critic who has written about the film has observed, *Peking Opera Blues* is built around three charismatic women who want different things from Chinese society (social change; access to culture and/or men; money in order to be able to escape to another country). When Pat Neil first meets the other two major female characters as they inadvertently enter the grounds of her father's house while trying to hide from the men from the Ticketing Office, their initial interaction establishes, with great economy, just what it is that the women are after. (The shots also confirm the film's interest in establishing female agency as a main narrative drive; the two male characters with them are denied the kind of point-of-view shots granted to their female counterparts.)

The six shot units I want to concentrate on are examples of both Hollywood-style shot/reverse shot; configurations, and Soviet-style dialectical montage. An image of each female character looking offscreen is followed, in quick succession, by a shot of what she is looking at. Pat Neil looks first; she sees a handsome guerrilla fighter. Sheung Hung looks next and sees the box that contains the valuable pearls she has been trying to retrieve. The last look is reserved for Tsao Wan; she looks over her shoulder and what she sees is the blood dripping from the wound in the arm of the Chinese soldier she had earlier helped to save. Sexmoneyrevolution. These two final shots are the most telling. The suggestion of violent social conflict is set up dialectically, with a thesis (Tsao Wan's look) and its antithesis (the blood of the soldier) producing a synthesis related to political struggle. Here, as in the numerous famous examples from Eisenstein's *Strike* and *Battleship Potemkin*, it is up to the viewer to make the revolutionary connection.

It is also possible to find, in the director's style, a parallel to Eisenstein's desire to achieve synthesis within each individual shot. A recurrent trait of *Peking Opera Blues* is its use of rack focus within single frames to reveal two simultaneous levels of action—more often than not, these levels consist of a Chinese authority figure overseeing a guerrilla fighter, thus linking the Good/Bad Chinese characters in a perpetual power conflict.

At first glance (given the Western tendency to follow narratives through a single protagonist), it might seem as if it is one person, Tsao Wan, who is the character most likely to see the "heroic" project through. Certainly she is an extraordinary woman: she studied gynecology overseas; sports short hair and dons mannish suits; she rescues her male and female comrades and is rescued by them; she can come across as a loving, vulnerable daughter or an ambitious, zealous revolutionary; she cherishes genuine female friendship but also connives to get what she wants even from the people closest to her. Above all, and this occurs in a scene that has no equivalent in any Western film I can think of, she is capable of withstanding ruthless torture by the authorities.

Tsao Wan's position is established by the first scene in which she appears. She is initially introduced in relation to her father. At the beginning of the film, he is the most powerful warlord in China—more than that, since he is fighting with other warlords for absolute rule of the country, there is a sense in which Tsao Wan's father is "China." This early scene also introduces most of the narrative themes, and I read it as being constructed so as to have a great symbolic importance for the domestic Hong Kong audience. After a suspected guerrilla attack on his trigger-happy army has been thwarted, the general turns in the carriage he is sharing with his daughter in order to reassure her of their safety. He takes her hand: "Wan, are you scared?" "I'm alright, Papa." "You've been away and living in comfort for years. Now you have to get used to the way of living of your native land." "I'll certainly make it."

That last line, which I've quoted directly from the film's English subtitles, constitutes Tsao Wan's crucial response to her return to the mainland, her subordination once again to the authority of Chinese leaders. It is not hard to see how her words are related very precisely to the social problem that provides the main contextual discourse surrounding the production of *Peking Opera Blues*.

In 1984, after two years of formal negotiations, British Prime Minister Margaret Thatcher flew to Beijing for the official signing of the Sino-British Joint Declaration on the Future of Hong Kong, the treaty that would lay out the terms for the handover 13 years later. The details of this arrangement provokes mixed reactions. While the optimists in Hong Kong looked forward to reunification with the "Motherland," the pessimists felt that Britain had not established sufficient grounds for the maintenance of democratic rights once China reannexed their country. They felt that the old European masters wanted to take what they could before the new masters arrived, and had therefore betrayed Hong Kong by not looking out for its interests. Tsui Hark must be counted as one of these pessimists—as he often taken to be the great cynic of modern Hong Kong cinema.

"Hong Kong people find themselves in a helpless situation" he once explained. "They keep on thinking it's going to get better and better, and suddenly it's a nightmare. They have no petition in deciding their future, they have no voice, no rights. Nothing."[4] In *Shanghai Blues*, where a once bustling, cosmopolitan trading city is sucked dry by a Japanese takeover, Tsui used the historical tragedy of Shanghai as an analogy to the potential disaster represented by 1997, while for the third installment of the "Better Tomorrow" series (*Love and Death in Saigon*, 1989), he implied the same thing through a story about the problems of getting in and out of war-torn Vietnam.

With hindsight, it might be suggested that Tsui Hark's cynicism was proven to be justified in that it foreshadowed the events that occurred in China on June 4, 1989. The massacre of student protesters by Chinese Government troops in and around Beijing's Tiananmen Square shocked the people of Hong Kong and threw the two countries into a diplomatic crisis. Amid unprecedented scenes of public mourning and grief (the center of Hong Kong was occupied on June 5 by nearly one million people), pessimism was proved prescient. Now, the settlement began to perceive 1997 as a threat that had suddenly become all too real. At the same time, the language coming out of China changed. Up until this point, diplomatic relations between Beijing and London had been concerned with protecting the joint aspiration for Hong Kong of "one country, two systems," but that was now transformed into the language of subversion. China proclaimed that it would not allow itself to be undermined by Hong Kong "guerrillas," and reiterated that Hong Kong was Chinese, and would be expected to follow the rule of Chinese law."[5]

In June, 1989, then, people from Hong Kong were viewed by the mainland Chinese leaders in the same way that they are viewed by the generals and warlords of *Peking Opera Blues*, namely as guerrilla fighters, terrorists, and ordinary people seeking to undermine official Chinese authority. The Hong Kong Alliance in Support of the Patriotic Movement in China, formed in the optimism of May, became a troublesome organization that had to be eliminated. *Peking Opera*

Blues can be seen to be politically prescient in that it is using this language of subversion three years before Tiananmen Square.

In the West, too, it might now be easier to perceive how the film's seductive, fantasy-like qualities are put into the service of a very real political despair. Consider the movement of the narrative in relation to the British Government's reaction to Tiananmen Square. On June 6, the then Foreign Secretary, Sir Geoffrey Howe, stood up in the Houses of Parliament in London to make the speech that would constitute the official British response to the massacre and would explain the implications of the Chinese Army's actions to the inhabitants of the British Empire's last major colony. He said that although Her Majesty's Government was most concerned about what China had just done, the 3.25 million British Dependent Territory citizens ln Hong Kong would not be given the right of abode in the United Kingdom because "they will appreciate the reasons why we could not easily contemplate a massive new immigration commitment which would more than double the ethnic minority population of the United Kingdom—a possibility that cannot be disregarded." Such a treacherous about-turn in immigration policy adds bitter irony to the explanation of how it is possible to read *Peking Opera Blues* as a film in which the much-noted energy of popular Hong Kong cinema is channeled into a clear social dynamic—here, the characters are not just breathlessly running around, they are *running away*.

The movie opens on this note. One warlord has lost money to another in a few games of mah jongg. As he cannot now afford to pay his army, the soldiers are about to riot. In a scene of panic and impending (comic) violence, he decides to flee, taking all his remaining wealth with him. This first warlord later returns to Peking after the second has himself been forced to depart. After this, the theme of running away is habitually returned to. For example, after refusing to become a "husband" to the Head of" the Ticketing Office, Fa, the Opera House star singer, exits through one of its windows, heading for another province.

One scene is of particular importance in relation to the theme of running away: the three heroines, all from different social classes and so representative of a certain political unity, are relaxing and drinking together in Tsao Wan's home—in other words, in the domain of her father, the most powerful warlord in Peking, the epitome of China itself. They gather around a globe and Sheung Hung frantically searches its surface with a magnifying glass. As the conversation continues, the scene switches from light-hearted comedy to melancholic sadness.

Sheung Hung:	The world is so big. Where can I go?
Tsao Wan:	Are you planning to go somewhere?
Sheung Hung:	Everyone is running away. Running for life.
Pat Neil:	But this is a nice place why do we have to run away?
Tsao Wan:	We're running around, and finally we go back the same route.

This obvious reference to 1997 exhibits an unmistakable concern with the idea of migrating in order to find a better future. But it is not clear exactly what kind of future it will be.

Audiences who are not too concerned about the 1997 factor as it manifests itself in recent Hong Kong movies have seen the film as explicitly political, but they tend to focus on different issues. Most have remarked on the highly suggestive gender politics of *Peking Opera Blues*, and in particular on its confusion of sex roles brought about by the use of a theatrical setting and the presence of three strong female leads. Specifically, these female protagonists initiate much of thc action with their flamboyant energy. It is also worth pointing out in this regard not just the democratic spread of the group of five guerrilla fighters as a *whole*, all exhibiting equal bravery, equal beauty, equal comic skills, and taking up relatively equal amounts of screen time, but also the way in which the film organizes and presents their interrelationship. I am thinking here of how, when the film starts, we are with a dashing, fantastically athletic young male hero, Ling Pak Hoi. After a while, however, he tends to slip into the background as the ingenuity and bravery of each individual woman is stressed. When the young hero finally does save Tsao Wan, right at the end of the film, by pulling her to safety on the roof tops, it is not that much of a heroic gesture—he just happens to be in the right place at the right time.

When *Peking Opera Blues* was shown at the London Lesbian and Gay Film Festival in October, 1989, it was presented as a film about cross-dressing. According to thc Festival's publicity brochure, "It's against the context of how women usually behave in films that the adventurous heroine of *Peking Opera Blues* [i.e. Tsao Wan] becomes so appealing (well OK, she also looks pretty cute in a suit). Her role defies categorizing, upending all the usual expectations with no explanation. *Peking Opera Blues* also compounds its status by refusing to patronize its other female characters."

In recognizing that Tsui Hark's movie is not an "explicitly lesbian film," the festival organizers were picking up on a possibility and then framing that possibility within the concerns of a British subcultural audience, regardless of what the film's sexual dynamics might actually suggest to (gay? straight?) viewers from Hong Kong. The 1989 London Lesbian and Gay Film Festival, by this time thc largest such event in the world, was openly opposed to the Conservative British Government's notorious Section 28 bill, then passing into law, which prohibits the "promotion" of homosexuality by local government authorities and educational establishments. In mobilizing a dazzling array of films from around the world, the festival's organizers could defy the Tory element by willfully "promoting" the commonality and universality of gay identity.

It might still be argued, however, that a European or North American reading of *Peking Opera Blues* as primarily concerned with gender confusion and sexual role playing is politically partial, not to mention textually blind. The London brochure admits that the film is not explicitly lesbian, but "forgets" that the film could be seen as offensive in its use of stereotyped, effeminate male "actresses." The Peking Opera House itself could also be seen as a symbol of officially sanctioned gender confusion in that it only allows men on stage. Although scenes like the ones in which Sheung Hung is regularly thrown out of the theater's doors and onto the street or Pat Neil is told that in order to play a woman on stage she will have to reincarnate as a man are a literal illustration of gender confusion, such inequality in itself creates transgressive sex roles.

On top of this, there is the much larger question of priorities. Could it be the case that any claims we might want to make as "competent" Western readers when it comes to gender and representation allow us to ignore the larger but perhaps less accessible political crises? However, the political takes many different forms, and since the film was used positively by the London audience in 1989 (and could be used in such ways again), it is necessary to hold on to the freedom represented by such committed acts of resistance. Moreover, in the context of a broader general interest Chinese cinema, *Peking Opera Blues* can be said to raise a number of questions about the nature of spectatorial pleasure as currently understood by Western film theorists.

Peking Opera Blues is characteristic of much of Hong Kong cinema in that it approximates the conventions of classic Hollywood cinema, but takes those conventions a step further by its heightened use of invisible editing, crosscutting, points of visual and aural identification, and so on. If the film sometimes seems strange to Western viewers because of its language and iconography, it also looks very familiar in that it plays by the rules of continuity established by the American cinema. In this way, it might have something to say to a Western feminist film practice and criticism that does not reject the pleasures offered by popular cinema, but wishes to see them reorganized. Throughout the 1970s, feminist theorists argued for a negation of easy cinematic pleasure, and it might be that it is only now possible to begin to imagine new, non-oppressive, popular-action narrative cinema. Here, women can do what men can do, but they can also be enjoyed as love and erotic interests without inevitably being submitted to the sadistic scopophilia of the male gaze. In lieu of a more thorough examination of the textual strategies of recent Hong Kong movies, then, it might be suggested that *Peking Opera Blues* represents one example of what such a form of cinema might look like to Western audiences.

Whether *Peking Opera Blues* is understood as a 1997 allegory, a popular text that allows the people of Hong Kong to talk to each other about their unknown tomorrow, or whether its reception in the West merely allows Western critics to bring into their analyses of Chinese cinema the ideological tenets of their own cultural position, it is hard not to be touched by the concerns that energize its narrative. To me, those concerns hide behind a painted smile. Like foundation on an opera singer's cheek, like Hong Kong itself, Tsui Hark's film resembles nothing so much as a holding operation. Reading it in light of the 1997 metadiscourse, it is worth stressing that when Hong Kong's future is different than it is today, *Peking Opera Blues* will have crossed over to mean something else again.

NOTES

1. Films with John Woo include *A Better Tomorrow* (1986) and *The Killer* (1989); films with Ching Siu Tung include *A Chinese Ghost Story* (1987) and *Swordsman II* (1991).
2. Quoted by Pat Aufderheide, "Dynamic duo", *Film Comment* 24, no. 3 (May-June 1988), p. 44.
3. J. Hoberman, *Village Voice*, January 31, 1989, p. 59.
4. Quoted by Lawrence Chua, "Separation anxiety, " *Village Voice*, October 4, 1990. p. 74.
5. See Michael C. Davis, "Tiananmen in Hogh Kong," in Bih jaw Lin (ed.), *The Aftermath of the 1989 Tiananmen Crisis in Mainland China* (Boulder, CO: Westview Press, 1992), pp. 364-85.

POETIC JUSTICE (*Film Review Annual*, 1994)

SIGHT AND SOUND, 5/95, p. 53, Kim Newman

South Central Los Angeles. Traumatised by her boyfriend's murder, beautician and private poet Justice turns down the blatant advances of Lucky, a mailman. Lucky, discovering that the mother of his daughter is still on drugs, takes the child home to his mother. When Justice's car fails, she is unable to drive to Oakland for a 'Hair Fair' and is forced to take a pre-existing offer to ride with her heavy-drinking friend Lesha, who is going out with Lucky's co-worker Chicago.

Despite qualms, Justice, Lesha, Lucky and Chicago make the trip. During stop-overs at a huge family reunion where the quartet scam free food at an African fair, Justice and Lucky argue but become friends, while Lesha and Chicago break up. In Oakland, Lucky and Justice have sex, but the relationship wavers when Lucky admits that he needs a woman to take care of his daughter.

Lucky's cousin, a rap musician, is killed in a shooting and he is upset, rejecting Justice and begging the dead man's family to give him sound equipment so he can carry on where his cousin left off. Back in Los Angeles, Lucky visits the salon where Justice works and the couple are reconciled.

George Lucas stepped into fantasy for his subsequent films. In a strange way, John Singleton (whose *Graffiti*-styled *Boyz 'N' the Hood* was made in his early twenties) has also made that leap, although he tends towards a ramshackle indulgence of approach rather than subject. There is a real attempt to expand the wounded black macho of *Boyz* by focusing on a woman, but Justice's habit of spouting Maya Angelou's poetry is just as conventional and far less convincing than the resorting to guns of the earlier film's young men.

Jackson, who inflated her bottom De Niro-style to play the dumpy but cute Justice, may have been cast for commercial reasons, but does as well as anyone could with a role conceived in terms of soap opera. Typically laughable is the moment when Justice criticises Lesha's drunkenness by sobbing that her mother was an alcoholic, whereupon the two women hug and bond, stomping on the priceless dialogue exchange "you alcoholic bitch"—"don't you be calling me no bitch".

The bittiness might have seemed less irksome had the film played entirely as a road movie, but the quartet's trip to Oakland only starts a half hour into the action and ends a good three plot twists before the film. The opening scenes are particularly clumsy with a minutes of Gershwin-scored white Hollywood fantasy starring Billy Zane and Lori Petty scoring cheap laughs before we pull back to see this is merely *Deadly Diva*, an Allan Smithee film playing at the drive-in where Justice's boyfriend gets shot. Scenes at the salon, mail office and in the street introduce the characters but never make clear how well they know each other.

This basic messiness is compounded by Singleton's uncaring use of contrivance to bring his characters together. Off the road, the plot details become fuzzy: nod off for a moment and you'll miss the identity of the rap artist whose death so upsets Lucky, Justice and Lucky's partial estrangement over his daughter and even the couple's coy sex scene (which begins with a manicure). Nevertheless, there are things to admire, with stretches of vigorously profane dialogue between the mushy poetry and an interesting mix of road movie incident and allegory. Lucky has a good-humoured but uneasy encounter with a white trucker at a gas station, getting to the pump before his rival by deception, whereupon the trucker stands back silently while Lucky makes fun

on consumerism to segments of the population that have little access to commodities, and considering the drastic social and economic differences present within the narrow urban map, it is easy to grasp why this younger stratum of society has opted instead for fast alternatives.

The social class that produced Rodrigo stems from the conflict between traditional *paisa* (native) culture, embodying the values of hard work, religion, and family, and the disruption instigated by the spirit of modernity, bringing with it the codes of punk and the rules of mass consumption. While the older generation still supports and enforces the virtues of old-fashioned economic success, the dissonance rooted in easy access to money foments the crisis of the social model for the younger generation. Religion, a legacy of the conservative *paisa* culture, has also played a major role in the enactment of the social order. Official Catholicism, transmitted by a repressive power that well into the twentieth century kept the custom of hourly tolling bells, nevertheless failed to consolidate a position as moral arbiter in Medellín. Amazingly, most *traquetos* uphold a firm faith in the Virgin Mary, even beyond their concern for Christ. A scene in the film shows a teen holding a wallet stuffer of María Auxiliadora to the beat of "No te desanimes, mátate" ("Cheer up, kill yourself").[1]

In 1984, the M-19 (a revolutionary group renowned for its failed attack on the Colombian Palace of Justice) was not yet politically viable (in spite of the ceasefire decreed by then President Betancur), and resorted to the formation of recruitment camps in the steep hills of the Medellín slums. Much of the instruction, aside from routine ideological indoctrination, was of a military nature. In mid-1985, when this was declared illegal by the government, the sprouting of a literal army of the unemployed, trained but untested in the ways of war, was an obvious byproduct of the ironically named "peace" camps. Here lay the breeding ground for many of the leaders of the 120 gangs that later ran uncontrolled in Medellín. By August 1989, 70 per cent of violent deaths in that city occurred among those aged between 14 and 20, and such a trend began to leave an impact in the national political arena. The figure of a teenager from the *comunas*, barely an adolescent, responsible for the assassination of high political figures and openly exhibiting a kamikaze élan in his criminal techniques, became a commonplace in Colombian eyes.

But as Medellín's well-being plummeted (it used to be known as *la ciudad de la eterna primavera*—the city of eternal spring), the youth of the slums developed a nurturing, if paradoxical, relationship with British punk rock. In a region with an underdeveloped taste for musical gaiety and rhythm, salsa and its variations encountered a sterile turf, while the strident message of punk readily advanced and allowed young men the possibility of identification and expression.[2] In the punk cult of nonconformity, the *pistolocos*, as punk's followers came to be known, found an echo and a response, a voice for their predicament."[3]

The sudden popularity of the punk creed was viewed as paradoxical by local sociologists, for its agenda preached broad contempt for the bourgeoisie and notions like brand loyalty, fashion, and consumerism were strictly frowned upon. The *pistolocos* on the other hand, absorbed typically bourgeois concepts and professed high regard for trendy sneakers and powerful motorbikes. Perhaps because they based their mores on a highly visual culture, optical cues in their behavior and attire prevailed. Chuck Norris and Sylvester Stallone films were overt sources for independent training: "One has to know how to hold the gun, shoot and retreat. With movies we also learn a lot. We see action films, Chuck Norris, Black Cobra, Commando, Stallone, and check out how to hold guns, how to cover someone, how to retreat. That's all we talk about when we see films."[4]

Such quotes could lead to perhaps precipitous conclusions about the role of action cinematography. But images have succeeded in conquering the language. Among the most popular expressions one might cite a euphemism for the act of killing: *tomarle la foto*, literally, to take someone's picture. It is interesting to note that much of the coquettish ambivalence of these youths' relationship with death has modified their vocabulary, which is extensively used in the film. Upon a gang member's demise, the common thing is to hear farewells that more closely resemble congratulations. Such is the message uttered by a friend of Johncito, a youngster whose wake we witness near the end of the story. The friend proceeds to open the coffin, lament the bad luck of "those poor suckers that are still here," and congratulate the corpse. In the background we recognize the opening lyrics for the title song of Pink Floyd's album *Wish You Were Here*: "So you wish you could tell heaven from hell, blue skies from pain ... " These lyrics are key to understanding the technique, Gaviria chose in the elaboration of a game between celestial open spaces and dark, gritty vignettes of the city.

In the cinematic language of neorealism and in punk, Gaviria found a mode of representation well suited to the issues. *Rodrigo D.* forced the country to face the extremes that resulted from widespread economic injustice. In that sense, the film was clearly a success. (Because of its low production costs, it was a financial breakthrough for FOCINE, struggling after a series of financial flops. The film's nationwide audience of 300,000 is considered high by Colombian standards.) Shortly after assuming office in 1990, President César Gaviria Trujillo created a special program for youth counseling in the slums of Medellín. The program, supported with money donated by the European community, has proved mildly successful.

NOTES

1. A theme of Mutantes, the local punk band for which Ramiro Meneses, the actor in the role of Rodrigo, plays in real life.
2. Only in recent years have Caribbean melodies achieved solid ground in Medellin, mostly as the result of heavy FM airplay and more contact with other provinces.
3. Parodying a national campaign against violence, "*La Paz, un compromiso de todos*," the album *La muerte, un compromiso de todos (Death, a commitment by everyone)*, by La Pestilencia, a punk band from Bogotá became the bestselling Colombian rock album of the 1980s.
4. Salazar, Alonso J. "La resurreción de Desquite." *No nacimos pa' semilla—La cultura de las bandas juveniles de Medellín*, 7th ed. (Santa Fe de Bogotá: CINEP, 1990).

SIX DEGREES OF SEPARATION (*Film Review Annual, 1994*)

SIGHT AND SOUND, 7/95, p. 53, Geoffrey Macnab

Early morning. Flan and Ouisa Kittredge scurry around their New York apartment, as if they have just been burgled. Later that day, at a wedding out of town, the Kittredges tell some fellow guests an amazing story. We flash back to the previous evening. They are entertaining their wealthy South African friend, Geoffrey. They're making small talk when Paul, a smartly dressed young black man who claims to know their children, stumbles into the apartment, saying he has just been mugged in Central Park.

They patch up Paul's stab wound and invite him to stay for dinner. He proves delightful company. First, he cooks them a delicious meal and then he spins a yarn about being Sidney Poitier's son. They believe his every word. Before heading off to his hotel, Geoffrey makes arrangements to give Flan the loan he needs. Flan is so pleased he insists Paul spend the night. But when the Kittredges wake up the next morning, they hear noises from his room. Paul is in bed with a male prostitute. Outraged, they evict both men from the apartment.

A few days later, the Kittredges meet their old friends, Kitty and Larkin, and discover they too were conned by Paul. So was Dr Fine, an obstetrician. All Paul's victims have one thing in common—their children are at college together. The police can do nothing: Paul has committed no crime. The children learn that Paul is a hustler who was picked up off the street by their friend, Trad Conway. In return for sexual favours, Conway taught Paul all about his wealthy friends.

A distraught young woman appears at the apartment block. A few days previously, she and her boyfriend met Paul in Central Park. He told them a story about being Flan's illegitimate son. They believed him and gave him a place to stay. He stole their savings and seduced the boyfriend, who later committed suicide. When the woman learns the truth, she wants to press charges against him. The police now have a case.

Paul is still at large. One evening, he telephones just as Ouisa is changing for dinner. She encourages him to give himself up to the police. He agrees on condition she delivers him into their hands. But she and Flan are caught up in the traffic. By the time they reach the meeting place, the cops, tipped off, have already made the arrest. Not long afterwards. The Kittredges are at a smart lunch. Ouisa, realising she doesn't even know Paul's real name, tells the rest of the guests that she read of a prison suicide that morning, and is sure it was him. They scoff at her. She leaves the meal in disgust.

Six Degrees of Separation invites two, very different responses. On the one hand, it is a brilliantly observed, precious little comedy about a clique of wealthy New Yorkers who are only too pleased to have been duped by a young black man claiming to be Sidney Poitier's son. (Outside fine art and money, it is implied, they have nothing much to talk about anyway.) On the other, it is an allegory excoriating race, class and everything else which divides contemporary America. Its strength is it weakness: it is nothing if not smart. John Guare's screen adaptation of his own Broadway hit play crackles with ideas and witty dialogue. Arguably, though, it is too brittle to do justice to the weighty themes it broaches.

"This paltry thing—our life—he wanted it," Ouisa Kittredge observes to her husband when he complains about her fascination with the imposter. But there is very little paltry about the Kittredges. They're glamorous, middle-aged urbanity personified. If Guare is implying that there's a certain, gaping superficiality about their lifestyle, it is portrayed as highly desirable for all that. They're society aesthetes who spend their days chattering with one another and with friends at a series of swank functions. Gossip is at the heart of their existence: the way the narrative unfolds, with flashbacks and jumps forward as the Kittredges recount events to various different audiences, reinforces the sense that we're in the realm of anecdote and makes the implicitly tragic ending all the more jarring. Even the title, with its insistence that "everybody on this planet is separated by only six other people," sounds like a conversational gambit at a dinner party. And there's always an element of contrivance about what are supposed to be the film's most seismic moments.

The film's central metaphor is also a little clumsy. The Kittredges' favourite possession is a double-sided Kandinsky painting which depicts "chaos and control". Paul, the con artist, represents the former while the couple embody the latter, but the deck is stacked against him. Events are seen almost entirely from the Kittredges' perspective. Gay, black, from the underclass, Paul is regarded less as a character than as an 'exotic other,' a catalyst to stimulate their imaginations and consciences. "Everybody's a phoney," he tells them as he launches on his brilliant, plagiarised monologue linking Salinger's *A Catcher In The Rye* to Mark Chapman, John Hinckley and the corruption of American life. The Kittredges briefly recognise that they and their society pals are as fraudulent as he is, but this isn't a revelation they or the movie take much interest in.

Just occasionally, the satire hits home. John Guare and director Fred Schepisi set out to show how the lives of seemingly unrelated characters briefly intersect. There's a scene in which the Kittredges' friends, Larkin and Kitty, spot the body of a suicide on the street on their way out of a roller skating disco. They react complacently—death is something they see every day—unaware that the boy has killed himself because of Paul, and indirectly, because of them. It is all too apparent how cosseted these wealthy New Yorkers are. Their apartments are virtual fortresses. Their class system, with its rigid code of behaviour, is impenetrable to outsiders, and their consciences are closed to everything that happens beyond their orbit.

Perhaps *Six Degrees Of Separation* isn't the most trenchant allegory ever made but it's a wonderful piece of story-telling. With unlikely incident layered upon unlikely incident, it achieves a bizarre, dreamlike quality reminiscent of one of those Buñuel satires in which the dinner party never ends and the bourgeois idyll turns into a nightmare. It's a talkative affair—all the dialogue from Guare's original play seems to survive intact—but its sudden shifts in time and location, and its determinedly elliptical structure, are probably more suited to cinema than stage. Stockard Channing, everybody's favourite character turn from *Grease*, and Donald Sutherland make a fine comic double-act as the archetypal smart New Yorkers while Will Smith, television's *Fresh Prince Of Bel Air*, shows just the right measure of charisma and vulnerability as the con artist. Given Fred Schepisi's track record—*The Chant of Jimmy Blacksmith, A Cry in the Dark*—the director might have been expected to strike a more sombre note. Instead, he foregrounds the comedy. As a result, the film is a dazzling but determinedly superficial affair.

WHO'S THE MAN? (*Film Review Annual, 1994*)

SIGHT AND SOUND, 7/95, p. 57, Mark Sinker

Ed Lover and Doctor Dré are the worst barbers in Harlem. Their boss Nick threatens them with the sack, unless they take the test to join the police. They tell him they're going into rap promotion. Their show is successful, but then they're robbed by a gang. The smooth Lionel is trying to persuade Nick to sell his barbershop—all that's left in an otherwise vacant lot—to property developer Demetrius. But Nick is committed to the neighbourhood. Lover and Dré take the test, which they try to fail. But they get accepted.

In a Harlem church, Nick preaches a sermon against gentrification and corruption. Demetrius watches the ensuing demonstrations on television, and afterwards speaks with two sinister men. Newly graduated as cops, Lover and Dré get a broken-down squad car, but their pals revamp it into a hip-hop blasting monster. They discover the surveyors at the building site taking suspicious soil samples for Demetrius, and confiscate one for analysis.

That night, we see Nick lying dead in a pool of blood at the shop, which then explodes. After the memorial service, Lionel and his cute niece Teesha tell Lover and Dré that they have inherited the shop. They find a gun in the burnt-out ruins, but are removed from the case when a suspect is murdered. Sergeant Griles, who taught them at the Academy, takes over.

The soil sample suggests there's oil in Harlem, and they stake out Demetrius. Up before the captain, the pair tell him of their suspicions, but he kicks them out of the force. They go to Teesha's show, where she tells them the fabric she uses is stored in a warehouse in Brooklyn. They discover more guns there, but are surprised by Demetrius' hitmen. They are rescued by Griles, who would have been there earlier but was held up by "proper police procedure". Demetrius is arrested, but hints at another's involvement. Lover confronts Lionel, who lets slip that he murdered Nick. He now draws a gun on Lover, but Dré rescues him. The two turn down the chance of being the youngest detectives on the force, and reopen the barber's shop. Dré shoots at a rat and hits oil. They become popular barbers, though they're still the worst in Harlem.

When comedy duos like Abbott and Costello play cops, no one cares about improbabilities or nonsensical plot: that's the point of the humour (such as it is). Dré's and Lover's police training seems to take about ten minutes *in toto*, and they're exactly the same idiotic slobs at the end of it: this is just part of the fun, so far so classic. However, classic comedy duos rarely have pretensions to sober social message-bearing. To its increasing detriment hip-hop culture does. Dré and Lover—in real life a popular video-jock team on *Yo! MTV Raps!*, which director Demme (Jonathan Demme's nephew) created—are thus caught between cartoon goofiness, which they have a desultory gift for, and political truth-telling. Perhaps the anger is honestly felt, but it's hardly coherently addressed. 'Serious' black pop, it seems, aspires mainly to the condition of Cheech and Chong.

Though not a mere jukebox of a movie, the film is fully *MTV*-oriented, which means that beside the obligatory music-only passages (one at the fashion show, where the camera lingers on the slinky babes, the other an irrelevant chase scene, set to Eric B and Rakim's 'Follow The Leader'), the action is studded with cameos of rap stars: Ice-T as (surprise surprise) a drug-dealing gangster, and Monie Love as a girl who laughs when his dorky real name is revealed; the Geto Boys' Bushwick Bill as a drunk vagrant dwarf who falls over, Kriss Kross, a pair of 12-year-old rappers, as two annoying kids, Pepa and YoYo as girls who slap Lover's face for impugning their honour, and so on.

Of course corrupt landlords do menace inner-city areas, and perhaps do more harm than drug gangs, a line this film implicitly takes. However, a plot which lurches from mildly pointed clowning (the police rookies at the firing range hitting the cardboard baby) to the violent death of the neighbourhood's father figure and beloved conscience, the only "serious" good character, to the totally cartoonish crime-motive (bad white guy prospecting for oil in Harlem) is a plot that makes formal demands on performers, writers and director that nothing in their résumés has prepared them for. Both communitarian-conservative and libertarian-criminal tendencies in black culture—and in the duo's own responses—are left unexamined, though manifestly at odds. (The film was made two years ago, and is only belatedly released here: this conflict has since sharpened hugely in the States.) Stand-up comic Denis Leary, the one performer whose established political intelligence might have been up to the challenge, is content with a deranged parody of that comedy staple the shrieking sergeant: an overdetermined assault on a feeble target.

The film is a morass of wasted opportunities and overlooked ironies. Nothing connects. Yes, Black America is eternally and justifiably suspicious of the police, so that the duo prefer to be down with their old street buddies than upholding the law. But as they never actually seem to arrest anyone, there's no tension in the role they're playing, just the daftness of the randomly inappropriate: such as the spherical Dré looking entertainingly silly in uniform.

There *are* intriguing moments, events and scenery caught on camera that tell truths no one involved could have quite known. One of the duo's wastrel street-buddies stands up and sings a gospel lament at Nick's memorial, all movingly fussy virtuosity. The encounters between the duo and the eccentric Japanese forensic scientist Fuji are percussive dialogues of mutual incomprehension. The sheer gift of many of the participants for self-mockery and off-the-cuff entertainment makes up (to a degree) for the lack of overall relevant professionalism or structure. But in the end, the two stars simply aren't funny enough often enough to stop the story's buried implications rising like bile to ruin the aftertaste. And no one else gets a look in.

AWARDS

ACADEMY OF MOTION PICTURE ARTS AND SCIENCES
67th Annual Academy Awards — March 27, 1995

BEST PICTURE — *Forrest Gump*
Other Nominees: *Four Weddings and a Funeral; Pulp Fiction: Quiz Show; The Shawshank Redemption*

BEST ACTOR — Tom Hanks in *Forrest Gump*
Other Nominees: Morgan Freeman in *The Shawshank Redemption*; Nigel Hawthorne in *The Madness of King George*; Paul Newman in *Nobody's Fool*; John Travolta in *Pulp Fiction*

BEST ACTRESS — Jessica Lange in *Blue Sky*
Other Nominees: Jodie Foster in *Nell;* Miranda Richardson in *Tom & Viv*; Winona Ryder in *Little Women*; Susan Sarandon in *The Client*

BEST SUPPORTING ACTOR — Martin Landau in *Ed Wood*
Other Nominees: Samuel L. Jackson in *Pulp Fiction*; Chazz Palminteri in *Bullets Over Broadway*; Paul Scofield in *Quiz Show*; Gary Sinise in *Forrest Gump*

BEST SUPPORTING ACTRESS — Dianne Wiest in *Bullets Over Broadway*
Other Nominees: Rosemary Harris in *Tom & Viv*; Helen Mirrin in *The Madness of King George*; Uma Thurman in *Pulp Fiction*; Jennifer Tilly in *Bullets Over Broadway*

BEST DIRECTOR — Robert Zemeckis for *Forrest Gump*
Other Nominees: Woody Allen for *Bullets Over Broadway*; Quentin Tarantino for *Pulp Fiction*; Robert Redford for *Quiz Show*; Krzysztof Kieslowski for *Red*

BEST FOREIGN-LANGUAGE FILM — *Burnt by the Sun* (Russia)
Other Nominees: *Before the Rain* (Madedonia); *Eat Drink Man Woman* (Taiwan)); *Farinelli: Il Castrato* (Belgium); *Strawberry and Chocolate* (Cuba)

BEST ORIGINAL SCREENPLAY — Quentin Tarantino and Roger Avary for *Pulp Fiction*

Other Nominees: Woody Allen and Douglas McGrath for *Bullets Over Broadway*; Richard Curtis for *Four Weddings and a Funeral*; Frances Walsh and Peter Jackson for *Heavenly Creatures*; Krzysztof Piesiewicz and Krzysztof Kieslowski for *Red*

BEST ADAPTED SCREENPLAY — Eric Roth for *Forrest Gump*
Other Nominees: Alan Bennett for *The Madness of King George*; Robert Benton for *Nobody's Fool*; Paul Attanasio for *Quiz Show*; Frank Darabont for *The Shawshank Redemption*

BEST CINEMATOGRAPHY — John Toll for *Legends of the Fall*
Other Nominees: Don Burgess for *Forrest Gump*; Piotr Sobocinski for *Red*; Roger Deakins for *The Shawshank Redemption*; Owen Roizman for *Wyatt Earp*

BEST FILM EDITING — Arthur Schmidt for *Forrest Gump*
Other Nominees: Frederick Marx, Steve James, and Bill Haugse for *Hoop Dreams*; Sally Menke for *Pulp Fiction*; Richard Francis-Bruce for *The Shawshank Redemption*; John Wright for *Speed*

BEST ART DIRECTION — Ken Adam with set decoation by Carolyn Scott for *The Madness of King George*
Other Nominees: Santo Loquasto with set decoration by Susan Bode for *Bullets Over Broadway*; Rick Carter with set decoration by Nancy Haigh for *Forrest Gump*; Dante Ferretti with set decoration by Francesca Lo Schiavo for *Interview With The Vamapire*; Lilly Kilvert with set decoration by Dorree Cooper for *Legends of the Fall*

BEST COSTUME DESIGN — Lizzy Gardiner and Tim Chappel for *The Adventures of Priscilla, Queen of the Desert*
Other Nominees: Jeffrey Kurland for *Bullets Over Broadway*; Colleen Atwood for *Little Women*; April Ferry for *Maverick*; Moidele Bickel for *Queen Margot*

BEST MAKE-UP — Rick Baker, Ve Neill, and Yolanda Toussieng for *Ed Wood*
Other Nominees: Daniel C. Striepeke, Hallie D'Amore, and Judith A. Cory for *Forrest Gump*; Daniel Parker, Paul Engelen, and Carol Hemming for *Mary Shelley's Frankenstein*

BEST ORIGINAL SCORE — Hans Zimmer for *The Lion King*
Other Nominees: Alan Silvestri for *Forrest Gump*; Elliot Goldenthal for *Interview With the Vampire*; Thomas Newman for *Little Women*; Thomas Newman for *The Shawshank Redemption*

BEST ORIGINAL SONG — "Can You Feel the Love Tonight" from *The Lion King*, music by Elton John and lyrics by Tim Rice
Other Nominees: "Circle of Life" from *The Lion King*, music by Elton John and lyrics by Tim Rice; "Hakuna Matata" from *The Lion King*, music by Elton John and lyrics by Tim Rice; "Look What Love Has Done" from *Junior*, music and lyrics by Carole Bayer Sager, James Newton Howard, James Ingram, and Patty Smyth; "Make Up Your Mind" from *The Paper*, music and lyrics by Randy Newman

BEST SOUND — Gregg Landaker, Steve Maslow, Bob Beemer, and David R.B. MacMillan for *Speed*
Other Nominees: Donald O. Mitchell, Michael Herbick, Frank A. Montano, and Arthur Rochester for *Clear and Present Danger*; Randy Thom, Tom Johnson, Dennis Sands, and William B. Kaplan for *Forrest Gump*; Paul Massey, David Campbell, Christopher David, and Douglas Ganton for *Legends of the Fall*; Robert J. Litt, Elliot Tyson, Michael Herbick, and Willie Burton for *The Shawshank Redemption*

BEST SOUND EDITING — Stephen Hunter Flick for *Speed*
Other Nominees: Bruce Stambler and John Leveque for *Clear and Present Danger*; Gloria S. Borders and Randy Thom for *Forrest Gump*

BEST VISUAL EFFECTS — Ken Ralston, George Murphy, Stephen Rosenbaum, and Allen Hall for *Forrest Gump*
Other Nominees: Scott Squires, Steve Williams, Tom Bertino and John Farhat for *The Mask*; John Bruno, Thomas L. Fisher, Jacques Stroweis, and Patrick McClung for *True Lies*

BEST DOCUMENTARY FEATURE — *Maya Lin: A Strong Clear Vision*
Other Nominees: *Complaints of a Dutiful Daughter; D-Day Remembered; Freedom on My Mind; A Great Day in Harlem*

BEST DOCUMENTARY SHORT — *A Time for Justice*
Other Nominees: *Blues Highway; 89MM OD Europy (89MM From Europe)*; *School of the Americas Asssassins; Straight From the Heart*

BEST ANIMATED SHORT — *Bob's Birthday*
Other Nominees: *The Big Story; The Janitor; The Monk and the Fish; Triangle*

BEST LIVE-ACTION SHORT — (tie) *Franz Kafka's It's a Wonderful Life* and *Trevor*
Other Nominees: *Kangaroo Court; On Hope; Syrup*

HONORARY AND SPECIAL AWARDS

Honorary Oscar to Michelangelo Antonioni "for lifetime achievement."

Irving G. Thalberg Memorial Award to Clint Eastwood "for a consistently high quality of motion picture production."

Jean Hersholt Humanitarian Award to Quincy Jones.

SCIENTIFIC AND TECHNICAL AWARDS

Technical Awards of Merit (Oscar Statuette):

Petro and Paul Vlahos for "the conception and development of an electronic Blue Screen Compositing process for films."

Eastman Kodak Co. for "the EXR Color Intermediate Film 5244, a film with improved color reproduction, tone reproduction and overall image structure.

Scientific and Engineering Awards (Plaque) to:

George Sauve, Bill Bishop, Arpag Dadourian, Ray Feeney and Richard Patterson for "the Cinefusion software implementation of the Ultimatte Blue Screen compositing technology."

Lincoln Hu and Michael MacKenzie of Industrial Light & Magic, and Glenn Kennel and Mike Davis of Eastman Kodak, for "joint development work on a linear array CCD (Charge Couples Device) film input scanning system.

Ray Feeney, Will McCown and Bill Bishop of RFX Inc. and Les Dittert of Pacific Data Images for "their development work with area array CCD film input scanning systems."

Gary Demos and Dan Cameron of Information Intl., David DiFrancesco and Gary Starkweather of Pixar and Scott Squires of ILM for "their pioneering work in the field of film input scanning used extensively in special and visual effects."

Iain Neil, for "the optical design," and Al Saiki, for "the mechanical design, of the Panavision 11:1 Primo Zoom lens."

William A. Warner, "for the concept," and the technical staff of Avid Technology for "the development, of the digital Avid Film Composer for motion picture editing."

Paul Bamborough for "the concept," Nick Pollack and Arthur Wright for "the hardware devolopment," and Neil Harris and Duncan MacLean for "the software development, of the digital Lightworks Editor for motion pictures."

James Ketcham of JSK Engineering for "the concept and design of the MC211 microprocessor-based motion controller for synchronizing sprocketed film with time-code-based machines.

Technical Achievement Awards (Certificate) to:

Audio Tracks Inc. for "the design and development of the ADE (Advanced Data Encoding) System.

Colin Broad, of CB Electronics, for the design and development of the EDL (Edit Decision List) Lister.

B. Russell Hessey, of Special Effects Spectacular Inc., and Vincent T. Kelton, for "the hardware design," and George Jackman of De La Mare Engineering Inc. for "the pyrotechnic development, in the non-gun safety blank firing system."

Emanuel Previnaire of Flying-Cam, for "his pioneering concept and for the development of mounting a motion picture camera on a remote-controlled miniature helicopter."

Jacques Sax, of Sonosax, for "the design and development of the Sonosax SX-S portable audio mixer."

Dieter Sturm, of Sturm's Special Effects Intl., for "the creation and development of the Bio-Snow 2 Flake."

David A. Addleman and Lloyd A. Addleman for "the development of Cyberware 3030 3-D Digitizer.

Mark R. Schneider, Herbert R. Jones, Christopher D. Conover and John R.B. Brown, for "the development of the Polhemus 3 Space Digitizing System.

Jack Smith, Michael Crichton and Emil Safier, for "pioneering computerized motion picture budgeting and scheduling."

Stephen Greenfield and Chris Huntley, of Screenplay Systems, for "development of the Scriptor software, which assists writers by automatically formatting their work into screeplay page layouts."

Frieder Hochheim, Gary Swink, Dr. Joe Zhou and Don Northrop, for "the develoment of the Kino Flo Portable, Flicker Free, High Output fluorescent lighting system."

Clay Davis and John Carter, of Todd AO, for "the pioneering effort of computer-controlled list management style ADR (Automated Dialogue Replacement)."

Stephen W. Potter, John B. Asman, Charles Pell and Richard Larson, of LarTec Systems, for "the advancement and refinement of the computer-controlled list management style ADR system via the LarTech ADR System."

Art Fritzen, of the California Fritzen Propeller company, "as designer and sole manufacturer of the eight-bladed ritter fan propeller, creating a quiet wind machine for use in motion pictures."

NATIONAL SOCIETY OF FILM CRITICS
January 3, 1995

BEST PICTURE — *Pulp Fiction*

BEST ACTOR — Paul Newman in *Nobody's Fool*

BEST ACTRESS — Jennifer Jason Leigh in *Mrs. Parker and the Vicious Circle*

BEST SUPPORTING ACTOR — Martin Landau in *Ed Wood*

BEST SUPPORTING ACTRESS — Dianne Wiest in *Bullets Over Broadway*

BEST DIRECTOR — Quentin Tarantino for *Pulp Fiction*

BEST SCREENPLAY — Quentin Tarantino and Roger Avary for *Pulp Fiction*

BEST FOREIGN FILM — *Red* (Switzerland, France and Poland)

BEST DOCUMENTARY — *Hoop Dreams*

BEST CINEMATOGRAPHY — Stefan Czapsky for *Ed Wood*

SPECIAL CITATIONS — Bela Tarr's *Satantango*, a seven-hour Hungarian film, for experimental work and *The Pharoah's Belt*, an animated film by Lewis Klahr

NEW YORK FILM CRITICS CIRCLE
January 22, 1995

BEST PICTURE — *Quiz Show*

BEST ACTOR — Paul Newman in *Nobody's Fool*

BEST ACTRESS — Linda Fiorentino in *The Last Seduction*

BEST SUPPORTING ACTOR — Martin Landau in *Ed Wood*

BEST SUPPORTING ACTRESS — Dianne Wiest in *Bullets Over Broadway*

BEST DIRECTOR — Quentin Tarantino for *Pulp Fiction*

BEST SCREENPLAY — Quentin Tarantino and Roger Avary for *Pulp Fiction*

BEST CINEMATOGRAPHER — Stefan Czapsky for *Ed Wood*

BEST FOREIGN-LANGUAGE FILM — *Red* (Switzerland, France and Poland)

BEST DOCUMENTARY — *Hoop Dreams*

BEST NEW DIRECTOR — Darnell Martin for *I Like It Like That*

SPECIAL AWARD — Jean-Luc Godard for his "influence on world cinema"

GOLDEN GLOBE
52nd Annual Awards—January 21, 1995

BEST PICTURE (drama) — *Forrest Gump*

BEST PICTURE (comedy or musical) — *The Lion King*

BEST ACTOR (drama) — Tom Hanks in *Forrest Gump*

BEST ACTOR (comedy or musical) — Hugh Grant in *Four Weddings and a Funeral*

BEST ACTRESS (drama) — Jessica Lange in *Blue Sky*

BEST ACTRESS (comedy or musical) — Jamie Lee Curtis in *True Lies*

BEST SUPPORTING ACTOR — Martin Landau in *Ed Wood*

BEST SUPPORTING ACTRESS — Diane Wiest in *Bullets Over Broadway*

BEST DIRECTOR — Robert Zemeckis for *Forrest Gump*

BEST SCREENPLAY — Quentin Tarantino and Roger Avary for *Pulp Fiction*

BEST ORIGINAL SCORE — Hans Zimmer for *The Lion King*

BEST ORIGINAL SONG — "Can You Feel the Love Tonight" from *The Lion King*, music by Elton John and lyrics by Tim Rice

BEST FOREIGN-LANGUAGE FILM — *Farinelli: Il Castrato* (Belgium)

LOS ANGELES FILM CRITICS ASSOCIATION
December 10, 1994

BEST PICTURE — *Pulp Fiction*

BEST ANIMATED FILM — *The Lion King*

BEST ACTOR — John Travolta in *Pulp Fiction*

BEST ACTRESS — Jessica Lange in *Blue Sky*

BEST SUPPORTING ACTOR — Martin Landau in *Ed Wood*

BEST SUPPORTING ACTRESS — Diane Wiest in *Bullets Over Broadway*

BEST DIRECTOR — Quentin Tarantino for *Pulp Fiction*

BEST SCREENPLAY — Quentin Tarantino and Roger Avary for *Pulp Fiction*

BEST CINEMATOGRAPHY — Stefan Czapsky for *Ed Wood*

BEST SCORE — Howard Shore for *Ed Wood*

BEST FOREIGN-LANGUAGE FILM — *Red* (Switzerland, France and Poland)

BEST DOCUMENTARY FILM — *Hoop Dreams*

CAREER ACHIEVEMENT AWARD — (tie) Billy Wilder and Pauline Kael

NEW GENERATION AWARD — John Dahl

NATIONAL BOARD OF REVIEW

1994 NBR Awards — February 27, 1995

BEST PICTURE — (tie) *Forrest Gump* and *Pulp Fiction*

BEST ACTOR — Tom Hanks in *Forrest Gump*

BEST ACTRESS — Miranda Richardson in *Tom & Viv*

BEST SUPPORTING ACTOR — Gary Sinise in *Forrest Gump*

BEST SUPPORTING ACTRESS — Rosemary Harris in *Tom & Viv Wives*

BEST DIRECTOR — Quentin Tarantino for *Pulp Fiction*

BEST FOREIGN-LANGUAGE FILM — *Eat Drink Man Woman* (Taiwan)

BEST DOCUMENTARY — *Hoop Dreams*

CANNES FILM FESTIVAL

47th Annual Awards — May 23, 1994

BEST PICTURE (Golden Palm Award) — *Pulp Fiction*

BEST DIRECTOR — Nanni Moretti for *Cara Diario*

BEST ACTOR — Ge You in *To Live*

BEST ACTRESS — Verni Lisi in *Queen Margot*

BEST SCREENPLAY — Michel Blanc for *Grosse Fatique (Dead Tired)*

GRAND JURY PRIZE — (shared) *Burnt by the Sun* and *To Live*

JURY PRIZE — *Queen Margot*

CAMERA D'OR — *Coming to Terms With the Dead*; (special mention) *The Silence of the Palace*

PALME D'OR (short film) — *El Heroe*

JURY PRIZE (short film) — *Lemming Aid* and *Syrup*

INDEX

CAST

PRODUCERS

DIRECTORS

SCREENWRITERS

CINEMATOGRAPHERS

EDITORS

MUSIC

PRODUCTION CREW